Features

Visit us on the Web at
http://www.census.gov/compendia/statab

ACKNOWLEDGMENTS

Ian R. O'Brien, Chief, Statistical Compendia Branch, was responsible for the technical supervision and coordination of this volume. Assisting in the research and analytical phases of assigned sections and in the development aspects of new tables were **Richard P. Kersey**, **Jean F. Mullin**, **Michael Sellner**, and **Sean R. Wilburn**. **Catherine Lavender** provided primary editorial assistance. Other editorial assistance was rendered by **Stacey Barber**, **Alethea S. Carter**, **Brian Clark**, **Jennifer Grimes**, **April C. Harris**, **Connie Nadzadi**, **Alexandra Nguyen**, **Christine Nguyen**, **Juan Rodriquez**, and **Kevin Younes**.

Maps were designed and produced by **Connie Beard**, **Jessica Dobrowski**, and **Rachael Linonis** of the Cartographic Products Branch within the Geography Division.

Monique D. Lindsay, **Christine E. Geter**, **Theodora Forgione**, **Linda Chen**, and **Donald Meyd** of the Administrative and Customer Services Division, **Francis Grailand Hall**, Chief, provided publications and printing management, graphics design and composition, and editorial review for print and electronic media. General direction and production management were provided by **Claudette E. Bennett**, Assistant Division Chief.

The cooperation of many contributors to this volume is gratefully acknowledged. The source note below each table credits the various government and private sector agencies that have collaborated in furnishing the information for the *Statistical Abstract*.

Statistical Abstract
of the United States: 2011

Issued October 2010

U.S. Department of Commerce
Gary Locke,
Secretary

Vacant,
Deputy Secretary

Economics and Statistics
Administration
Rebecca M. Blank,
Under Secretary for Economic Affairs

U.S. CENSUS BUREAU
Robert M. Groves,
Director

SUGGESTED CITATION

U.S. Census Bureau,
*Statistical Abstract
of the United States:
2011*
(130th Edition)
Washington, DC,
2010

ECONOMICS
AND STATISTICS
ADMINISTRATION

**Economics
and Statistics
Administration**

Rebecca M. Blank,
Under Secretary for
Economic Affairs

U.S. CENSUS BUREAU

Robert M. Groves,
Director

Thomas L. Mesenbourg,
Deputy Director and
Chief Operating Officer

Ted A. Johnson,
Associate Director for
Administration and
Chief Financial Officer

Francis Grailand Hall,
Chief, Administrative and
Customer Services Division

Published in the United States of America
by Bernan Press, a wholly owned subsidary of
The Rowman & Littlefield Publishing Group, Inc.
4501 Forbes Boulevard, Suite 200
Lanham, Maryland 20706

Bernan Press
800-865-3457
info@bernan.com
www.bernan.com

Library of Congress Control Number: 2010916880
ISBN 13: 978-1-59888-493-7

Preface

The *Statistical Abstract of the United States,* published since 1878, is a comprehensive collection of statistics on the social, political, and economic organization of the United States. It is designed to serve as a convenient volume for statistical reference and as a guide to other statistical publications and sources. The latter function is served by the introductory text to each section, the source note appearing below each table, and Appendix I, which is comprised of the *Guide to Sources of Statistics,* the *Guide to State Statistical Abstracts,* and the *Guide to Foreign Statistical Abstracts.*

This volume includes a selection of data from many statistical sources, both government and private. Publications cited as sources usually contain additional statistical detail and more comprehensive discussions of definitions and concepts. Data not available in publications issued by the contributing agency, but obtained from the Internet or unpublished records are identified in the source notes. More information on the subjects covered in the tables may generally be obtained from the source.

Except as indicated, figures are for the United States as presently constituted. Although emphasis in the *Statistical Abstract* is primarily given to national data, many tables present data for regions and individual states and a smaller number for metropolitan areas and cities. Appendix II, Metropolitan and Micropolitan Statistical Areas: Concepts, Components, and Population, presents explanatory text, a complete current listing, and population data for metropolitan and micropolitan areas defined as of November 2008. Statistics for the Commonwealth of Puerto Rico and for island areas of the United States are included in many state tables and are supplemented by information in Section 29. Additional information for states, cities, counties, metropolitan areas, and other small units, as well as more historical data, are available in various supplements to the *Statistical Abstract* (see inside back cover).

Statistics in this edition are generally for the most recent year or period available by summer 2010. Each year over 1,400 tables and charts are reviewed and evaluated; new tables and charts of current interest are added, continuing series are updated, and less timely data are condensed or eliminated. Text notes and appendices are revised as appropriate. In addition two special features USA Statistics in Brief, and State Rankings can be found on our Web site: <http://www.census.gov/compendia/statab/>.

Changes in this edition—This year we have introduced 65 new tables covering a wide range of subject areas. These include a presentation of new data from the 2007 Economic Census, a comprehensive revision to the Bureau of Economic Analysis's (BEA) National Income and Product Accounts (NIPA), as well as new data from the American Housing Survey and new data from the National Center for Health Statistics' National Survey of Family Growth. In addition, we have introduced new material on a wide variety of topics, such as, sleep deprivation, cyber-bullying, financial crimes, earthquakes, and hours spent doing unpaid housework. For a complete list of new tables, see "New Tables," p. xi.

Statistical Abstract on other media—The *Abstract* is available on the Internet and on CD-ROM. Both versions contain the same material as the book, except for a few copyrighted tables for which we did not receive permission to release in these formats. Our Internet site <http://www.census.gov/compendia/statab> contains this 2011 edition plus selected earlier editions in Adobe Acrobat .pdf format. The CD-ROM version and internet site also include spreadsheet files for each table in the book.

Statistics for states and metropolitan areas—Extensive data for the states and metropolitan areas of the United States can be found in the *State and Metropolitan Area Data Book: 2010.* This publication, as well as, selected rankings of the states and metropolitan areas, is also available on our Internet site at <http://www.census.gov/compendia /smadb>.

Statistics for counties and cities—Extensive data for counties can be found in the *County and City Data Book: 2007.* It features 175 data items covering everything from age and agriculture to water use and retail trade for all states and counties with U.S. totals for comparison. Also included are 80 data items for cities with population of 25,000 or more. Six tables present nearly 80 additional data items from the 2005 American Community Survey for 242 incorporated places with populations of 100,000 or more. This publication is available on our Internet site at <http://www.census.gov /statab/www/ccdb.html>. For a database with over 6,800 county items, check out USA Counties at <http://censtats.census .gov/usa/usa.shtml>.

Limitations of the data—The contents of this volume were taken from many sources. All data from censuses, surveys, and from administrative records are subject to error arising from a number of factors: Sampling variability (for statistics based on samples), reporting errors in the data for individual units, incomplete coverage, nonresponse, imputations, and processing error. (See also Appendix III, p. 921). The Census Bureau cannot accept responsibility for the accuracy or limitations of the data presented here, other than for those for which it collects. The responsibility for selection of the material and for proper presentation, however, rests with the Census Bureau.

For additional information on data presented—Please consult the source publications available in local libraries, on the Internet, or contact the agency indicated in the source notes. Contact the Census Bureau only if it is cited as the source.

Suggestions and comments—Users of the Statistical Abstract and its supplements (see inside back cover) are urged to make their data needs known for consideration in planning future editions. Suggestions and comments for improving coverage and presentation of data should be sent to the Director, U.S. Census Bureau, Washington, DC 20233; or e-mail us at <ACSD.US.Data@census.gov> or visit <ask.census.gov> for further information on the Abstract.

Contents

[Numbers following subjects are page numbers]

New Tables

Guide to Tabular Presentation

Example of Table Structure

Table 535. Seizure Statistics for Intellectual Property Rights (IPR) by Commodity and Trading Partner: 2008 and 2009

[In thousands of dollars (272,729 represents $272,729,000, except as indicated). Customs and Border Protection (CBP) is dedicated to protecting against the importation of goods which infringe/violate Intellectual Property Rights (IPR) by devoting substantial resources toward identifying and seizing shipments of infringing articles]

Commodity	2008	2009	Trading partner	2008	2009
Number of IPR Seizures	14,992	14,841	China	221,662	204,656
Total domestic value of IPR seizures [1]	272,729	260,698	Hong Kong	13,434	26,887
Footwear	102,317	99,779	India	16,258	3,047
Consumer electronics [2]	22,998	31,774	Taiwan	2,632	2,454
Handbags/wallets/backpacks	29,609	21,502	Korea, South	1,028	1,510
Wearing apparel	25,120	21,462	Paraguay	(NA)	1,496
Watches /parts	(NA)	15,534	Philippines	(NA)	1,480
Computers/Technology Components	7,590	12,546	Switzerland	(NA)	1,278
Media [3]	5,967	11,100	Pakistan	780	711
Pharmaceuticals	28,107	11,058	Vietnam	748	604
All other commodities	29,942	35,943	All other countries	13,938	16,575

NA Not available. [1] Domestic value is the cost of the seized goods, plus the costs of shipping and importing the goods into the U.S. and an amount for profit. [2] Consumer electronics includes cell phones and accessories, radios, power strips, electrical tools and appliances. [3] Includes motion pictures on tape, laser disc, and DVD; interactive and computer software on CD-ROM and floppy discs; and music on CD or tape.

Source: U.S. Department of Homeland Security, Customs and Border Protection, "Import, Commercial Enforcement, Intellectual Property Rights, Seizure Statistics," <http://www.cbp.gov/xp/cgov/trade/priority_trade/ipr/seizure/>.

Headnotes immediately below table titles provide information important for correct interpretation or evaluation of the table as a whole or for a major segment of it.

Footnotes below the bottom rule of tables give information relating to specific items or figures within the table.

Unit indicators show the *specified quantities* in which data items are presented. They are used for two primary reasons. Sometimes data are not available in absolute form and are estimates (as in the case of many surveys). In other cases we round the numbers in order to save space to show more data, as in the case above.

EXAMPLES OF UNIT INDICATOR INTERPRETATION FROM TABLE

Year	Item	Unit Indicator	Number shown	Multiplier
2008	Total domestic value of IPR seizures	$ Thousands	272,729	1,000

To Determine the Figure it is Necessary to Multiply the Number Shown by the Unit Indicator:

Value of seizures by Customs and Border Protection – 272,729 x $1,000 = $272,729,000 ($273 million)

When a table presents data with more than one unit indicator, they are found in the headnotes and column headings (Tables 2 and 26), spanner (Table 37), stub (Table 25), or unit column (Table 155). When the data in a table are shown in the same unit indicator, it is shown as the first part of the headnote (Table 2). If no unit indicator is shown, data presented are in absolute form (Table 1).

Vertical rules are used to separate independent sections of a table (Table 1), or in tables where the stub is continued into one or more additional columns (Table 2).

Averages—An average is a single number or value that is often used to represent the "typical value" of a group of numbers. It is regarded as a measure of "location" or "central tendency" of a group of numbers.

The *arithmetic mean* is the type of average used most frequently. It is derived by summing the individual item values of a particular group and dividing the total by the number of items. The arithmetic mean is often referred to as simply the "mean" or "average."

The *median* of a group of numbers is the middle number or value when each item in the group is arranged according to size (lowest to highest or visa versa); it generally has the same number of items above it as well as below it. If there is an even number of items in the group, the median is taken to be the average of the two middle numbers.

Per capita (or per person) quantities—a per capita figure represents an average computed for every person in a specified group (or population). It is derived by taking the total for an item (such as income, taxes, or retail sales) and dividing it by the number of persons in the specified population.

Index numbers—An index number is the measure of difference or change, usually expressed as a percent, relating one quantity (the variable) of a specified kind to another quantity of the same kind. Index numbers are widely used to express changes in prices over periods of time, but may also be used to express differences between related subjects for a single point in time.

To compute a price index, a base year or period is selected. The base year price (of the commodity or service) is then designated as the base or reference price to which the prices for other years or periods are related. Many price indexes use the year 1982 as the base year; in tables this is shown as "1982 = 100." A method of expressing the price relationship is: The price of a set of one or more items for a related year (e.g. 1990) **divided by** the price of the same set of items for the base year (e.g. 1982). The result multiplied by 100 provides the index number. When 100 is subtracted from the index number, the result equals the percent change in price from the base year.

Average annual percent change— Unless otherwise stated in the *Abstract* (as in Section 1, Population), average annual percent change is computed by use of a *compound interest formula.* This formula assumes that the rate of change is constant throughout a specified compounding period (1 year for average annual rates of change). The formula is similar to that used to compute the balance of a savings account that receives compound interest. According to this formula, at the end of a compounding period the amount of accrued change (e.g., school enrollment or bank interest) is added to the amount that existed at the beginning of the period. As a result, over time (e.g., with each year or quarter), the same rate of change is applied to a larger and larger figure.

The *exponential formula,* which is based on continuous compounding, is often used to measure population change. It is preferred by population experts, because they view population and population-related subjects as changing without interruption, ever ongoing. Both exponential and compound interest formulas assume a constant rate of change. The former, however, applies the amount of change continuously to the base rather than at the end of each compounding period. When the average annual rates are small (e.g., less than 5 percent) both formulas give virtually the same results. For an explanation of these two formulas as they relate to population, see U.S. Census Bureau, *The Methods and Materials of Demography,* Vol. 2, 3d printing (rev.), 1975, pp. 372–381.

Current and constant dollars— Statistics in some tables in a number of sections are expressed in both current and constant dollars (see, e.g., Table 659 in Section 13, Income, Expenditures, Poverty, and Wealth). Current dollar figures reflect actual prices or costs prevailing during the specified year(s). Constant dollar figures are estimates representing an effort to remove the effects of price changes from statistical series reported in dollar terms. In general, constant dollar series are derived by dividing current dollar estimates by the appropriate price index for the appropriate period (e.g., the Consumer Price Index). The result is a series as it would presumably exist if prices were the same throughout, as in the base year—in other words, as if the dollar had constant purchasing power. Any changes in this constant dollar series would reflect only changes in real volume of output, income, expenditures, or other measure.

Explanation of Symbols

The following symbols, used in the tables throughout this book, are explained in condensed form in footnotes to the tables where they appear:

– Represents zero or rounds to less than half the unit of measurement shown.

B Base figure too small to meet statistical standards for reliability of a derived figure.

D Figure withheld to avoid disclosure pertaining to a specific organization or individual.

NA Data not enumerated, tabulated, or otherwise available separately.

S Figure does not meet publication standards for reasons other than that covered by symbol B, above.

X Figure not applicable because column heading and stub line make entry impossible, absurd, or meaningless.

Z Entry would amount to less than half the unit of measurement shown.

In many tables, details will not add to the totals shown because of rounding.

Telephone & Internet Contacts

To help Abstract users find more data and information about statistical publications, we are issuing this list of contacts for federal agencies with major statistical programs. The intent is to give a single, first-contact point-of-entry for users of statistics. These agencies will provide general information on their statistical programs and publications, as well as specific information on how to order their publications. We are also including the Internet (World Wide Web) addresses for many of these agencies. These URLs were current in July 2010.

Executive Office of the President

Office of Management and Budget
Administrator
Office of Information and Regulatory Affairs
Office of Management and Budget
725 17th Street, NW
Washington, DC 20503
Information: 202-395-3080
Internet address:
http://www.whitehouse.gov/omb

Department of Agriculture

Economic Research Service
Information Center
U.S. Department of Agriculture
1800 M Street, NW
Washington, DC 20036-5831
Information and Publications:
202-694-5050
Internet address:
http://www.ers.usda.gov/

National Agricultural Statistics Service
National Agricultural Statistics Service
USDA-NASS
1400 Independence Ave., SW
Washington, DC 20250
Information hotline: 1-800-727-9540
Internet address:
http://www.nass.usda.gov/

Department of Commerce

U.S. Census Bureau
Customer Services Branch
4600 Silver Hill Road
Washington, DC 20233
Information and Publications:
1-800-923-8282
Internet address:
http://www.census.gov/

Bureau of Economic Analysis
Bureau of Economic Analysis
1441 L Street, NW
Washington, DC 20230
Information and Publications:
202-606-9900
Internet address: http://www.bea.gov/

International Trade Administration
International Trade Administration
1401 Constitution Ave., NW
Washington, DC 20230
Information: 1-800-872-8723
Internet address: http://trade.gov/

National Oceanic and Atmospheric Administration
National Oceanic and Atmospheric Administration Central Library
U.S. Department of Commerce
1315 East-West Highway
SSMC3, 2nd Floor
Silver Spring, MD 20910
Library: 301-713-2600 x.124
Internet address:
http://www.lib.noaa.gov/

Department of Defense

Department of Defense
Office of Public Communication
1400 Defense Pentagon
Washington, DC 20301-1400
Information: 703-571-3343
Internet address:
http://www.defenselink.mil

Department of Education

National Library of Education
U.S. Department of Education
400 Maryland Avenue, SW
Washington, DC 20202
Education Information and Statistics:
1-800-872-5327
Education Publications: 1-877-433-7827
Internet address: http://www.ed.gov/

Department of Energy

Energy Information Administration
National Energy Information Center
Energy Information Administration
1000 Independence Ave., SW
Washington, DC 20585
Information and Publications:
202-586-8800
Internet address:
http://www.eia.doe.gov/

Department of Health and Human Services

Health Resources and Services Administration
HRSA Information Center
P.O. Box 2910
Merrifield, VA 22116
Information Center: 1-888-275-4772
Internet address: http://www.hrsa.gov/

Substance Abuse and Mental Health Services Administration
Substance Abuse and Mental Health Services Administration
1 Choke Cherry Road
Rockville, MD 20857
Information: 240-276-2130
Publications: 1-877-726-4727
Internet address:
http://www.samhsa.gov/

Centers for Disease Control and Prevention
Public Inquiries/MASO
1600 Clifton Road
Atlanta, GA 30333
Public Inquiries: 1-800-311-3435
Internet address: http://www.cdc.gov/

Centers for Medicare and Medicaid Services (CMS)
U.S. Department of Health and Human Services
7500 Security Boulevard
Baltimore, MD 21244
Information: 1-877-267-2323
Internet address:
http://www.cms.hhs.gov/

National Center for Health Statistics
National Center for Health Statistics
3311 Toledo Road
Hyattsville, MD 20782
Information: 1-800-232-4636
Internet address:
http://www.cdc.gov/nchs

Department of Homeland Security

Office of Public Affairs
245 Murray Lane, SW
Washington, DC 20528
Information and Publications:
202-282-8010
Internet address: http://www.dhs.gov

Department of Housing and Urban Development

Office of the Assistant Secretary for Community Planning and Development
4517th St., SW
Washington, DC 20410
Information: 202-708-1112
Publications: 1-800-767-7468
Internet address: http://www.hud.gov/

Department of the Interior

U.S. Geological Survey
USGS National Center
12201 Sunrise Valley Drive
Reston, VA 20192
Information and Publications:
1-888-275-8747
Internet address for minerals:
http://minerals.usgs.gov/
Internet address for other materials:
http://ask.usgs.gov/

Department of Justice

Bureau of Justice Statistics
Statistics Division
810 7th Street, NW
Washington, DC 20531
Information and Publications:
1-800-851-3420
Internet address:
http://www.ojp.usdoj.gov/bjs/

National Criminal Justice Reference Service
P.O. Box 6000
Rockville, MD 20849-6000
Publications: 1-800-851-3420
Internet address: http://www.ncjrs.gov/

Federal Bureau of Investigation
Federal Bureau of Investigations
J. Edgar Hoover Building
935 Pennsylvania Avenue, NW
Washington, DC 20535-0001
Information: 202-324-3000
Internet address: http://www.fbi.gov/

Department of Labor

Bureau of Labor Statistics
Office of Publications and Special Studies Services
Bureau of Labor Statistics
Postal Square Building
2 Mass. Ave., NE
Washington, DC 20212-0001
Information and Publications:
202-691-5200
Internet address: http://www.bls.gov/

Employment and Training Administration
U.S. Department of Labor
Francis Perkins Building
200 Constitution Ave., NW
Washington, DC 20210
Information and Publications:
1-877-872-5627
Internet address: http://www.doleta.gov/

Department of Transportation

Federal Aviation Administration
800 Independence Ave., SW
Washington, DC 20591
Information and Publications:
1-866-835-5322
Internet address: http://www.faa.gov/

U.S. Census Bureau, Statistical Abstract of the United States: 2011

Bureau of Transportation Statistics
1200 New Jersey Avenue, SE
Washington, DC 20590
Products and Statistical Information:
1-800-853-1351
Internet address: http://www.bts.gov/

Federal Highway Administration
Office of Public Affairs
U.S. Department of Transportation
1200 New Jersey Avenue, SE
Washington, DC 20590
Information: 202-366-0660
Internet address:
http://www.fhwa.dot.gov/

National Highway Traffic Safety
Administration
Office of Public & Consumer Affairs
1200 New Jersey Avenue, SE - West
Building
Washington, DC 20590
Information and Publications:
1-888-327-4236
Internet address:
http://www.nhtsa.dot.gov/

Department of the Treasury
Internal Revenue Service
Statistics of Income Division
Internal Revenue Service
P. O. Box 2608
Washington, DC 20013-2608
Information and Publications:
202-874-0410
Internet address:
http://www.irs.gov/taxstats/

Department of Veterans Affairs
Department of Veterans Affairs
Office of Public Affairs
810 Vermont Ave., NW
Washington, DC 20420
Information: 202-273-6000
Internet address: http://www.va.gov/

Independent Agencies
Administrative Office of the U.S. Courts
Office of Public Affairs
1 Columbus Circle, NE
Washington, DC 20544
Information: 202-502-2600
Internet address:
http://www.uscourts.gov/

Board of Governors of the Federal Reserve
System
Division of Research and Statistics
Federal Reserve System
20th & Constitution Avenue, NW
Washington, DC 20551
Information: 202-452-3000
Publications: 202-452-3245
Internet address:
http://www.federalreserve.gov/

Environmental Protection Agency
Environmental Protection Agency
Ariel Rios Building
1200 Pennsylvania Ave., NW
Washington, DC 20460
Publications: 1-800-490-9198
Internet address: http://www.epa.gov/

National Science Foundation
Office of Legislation and Public Affairs
National Science Foundation
4201 Wilson Boulevard
Arlington, Virginia 22230
Information: 703-292-5111
Publications: 703-292-7827
Internet address: http://www.nsf.gov/

Securities and Exchange Commission
Office of Public Affairs
Securities and Exchange Commission
100 F Street, NE
Washington, DC 20549
Information: 202-942-8088
Publications: 202-551-4040
Internet address: http://www.sec.gov/

Social Security Administration
Social Security Administration
Office of Public Inquiries
6401 Security Boulevard
Baltimore, MD 21235
Information and Publications:
1-800-772-1213
Internet Address:
http://www.socialsecurity.gov/

Section 1
Population

This section presents statistics on the growth, distribution, and characteristics of the U.S. population. The principal source of these data is the U.S. Census Bureau, which conducts a decennial census of population, a monthly population survey, a program of population estimates and projections, and a number of other periodic surveys.

Decennial censuses—
The U.S. Constitution provides for a census of the population every 10 years, primarily to establish a basis for apportionment of members of the House of Representatives among the states. For over a century after the first census in 1790, the census organization was a temporary one, created only for each decennial census. In 1902, the Census Bureau was established as a permanent federal agency, responsible for enumerating the population and also for compiling statistics on other population and housing characteristics.

Historically, the enumeration of the population has been a complete (100 percent) count. That is, an attempt is made to account for every person, for each person's residence, and for other characteristics (sex, age, family relationships, etc.). Since the 1940 census, in addition to the complete count information, some data have been obtained from representative samples of the population. In the 1990 and 2000 censuses, variable sampling rates were employed. For most of the country, 1 in every 6 households (about 17 percent) received the long form or sample questionnaire; in governmental units estimated to have fewer than 2,500 inhabitants, every other household (50 percent) received the sample questionnaire to enhance the reliability of sample data for small areas. Exact agreement is not to be expected between sample data and the 100-percent count. Sample data may be used with confidence where large numbers are involved and assumed to indicate trends and relationships where small numbers are involved.

Current Population Survey (CPS)—This is a monthly nationwide survey of a scientifically selected sample representing the noninstitutionalized civilian population. The sample is located in 824 areas with coverage in every state and the District of Columbia and is subject to sampling error. At the present time, about 60,000 occupied households are eligible for interview every month; of these, about 8 percent are, for various reasons, unavailable for interview.

While the primary purpose of the CPS is to obtain monthly statistics on the labor force, it also serves as a vehicle for inquiries on other subjects. Using CPS data, the Census Bureau issues a series of publications under the general title of *Current Population Reports*.

Estimates of population characteristics based on the CPS will not agree with the counts from the census because the CPS and the census use different procedures for collecting and processing the data for racial groups, the Hispanic population, and other topics. Caution should also be used when comparing estimates for various years because of the periodic introduction of changes into the CPS. Beginning in January 1994, a number of changes were introduced into the CPS that affect all data comparisons with prior years. These changes included the results of a major redesign of the survey questionnaire and collection methodology and the introduction of 1990 census population controls, adjusted for the estimated undercount. Beginning with the 2001 CPS Annual Demographic Supplement, the independent estimates used as control totals for the CPS are based on civilian population benchmarks consistent with Census 2000. In March 2002, the sample size of the Annual Demographic Supplement was increased to approximately 78,000. In 2003 the name of the March supplement was changed to Annual Social and Economic Supplement. These changes in population controls had relatively little impact on derived measures such as means, medians, and percent distribution, but did have a significant impact on levels.

American Community Survey (ACS)— This is a nationwide survey to obtain data about demographic, social, economic, and housing information of people, households, and housing units. The survey collects the same type of information that has been collected every 10 years from the long-form questionnaire of the census, which the American Community Survey will replace. Beginning 2006, the estimates include the household population and the population living in institutions, college dormitories, and other group quarters.

Population estimates and projections— Estimates of the United States population are derived by updating the resident population enumerated in Census 2000 with information on the components of population change: births, deaths, and net international migration. The April 1, 2000, population used in these estimates reflects modifications to the Census 2000 population as documented in the Count Question Resolution program.

Registered births and deaths are estimated from data supplied by the National Center for Health Statistics. The net international migration component consists of four parts: (1) the net international migration of the foreign born, (2) the net migration of natives to and from the United States, (3) the net migration between the United States and Puerto Rico, and (4) the net overseas movement of the Armed Forces population. Data from the ACS are used to estimate the annual net migration of the foreign-born population. Estimates of the net migration of natives and net migration between Puerto Rico and the United States prior to 2005 are derived from the Demographic Analysis and Population Estimates (DAPE) project (see Population Division Working Paper Series, No. 63 and No. 64). Estimates for net migration between Puerto Rico and the U.S. for 2005 and later years are derived from the ACS and the Puerto Rico Community Survey. Estimates of the net overseas movement of the Armed Forces are derived from data collected by the Defense Manpower Data Center.

Estimates for state and county areas are based on the same components of change data and sources as the national estimates with the addition of net internal migration. Estimates of net internal migration are derived from federal income tax returns from the Internal Revenue Service, group quarters data from the Federal-State Cooperative Program, and Medicare data from the Centers for Medicare and Medicaid Services.

The population by age for April 1, 1990, reflects modifications to the 1990 census data counts. The review of detailed 1990 information indicated that respondents tended to report age as of the date of completion of the questionnaire, not as of April 1, 1990. In addition, there may have been a tendency for respondents to round up their age if they were close to having a birthday. A detailed explanation of the age modification procedure appears in 1990 Census of Population and Housing, Data Paper Listing CPH-L74.

Population estimates and projections are available on the Census Bureau Web site, see <http://www.census.gov>. These estimates and projections are consistent with official decennial census figures with no adjustment for estimated net census coverage. However, the categories for these estimates and projections by race have been modified and are not comparable to the census race categories (see section below under "Race"). For details on methodology, see the sources cited below the individual tables.

Immigration— Immigration (migration to a country) is one component of international migration; the other component is emigration (migration *from* a country). In its simplest form, international migration is defined as any movement across a national border. In the United States, federal statistics on international migration are produced primarily by the U.S. Census Bureau and the Office of Immigration Statistics of the U.S. Department of Homeland Security (DHS).

The Census Bureau collects data used to estimate international migration through its decennial censuses and numerous surveys of the U.S. population.

The Office of Immigration Statistics publishes immigration data in annual flow reports and the *Yearbook of Immigration Statistics*. Data for these publications are collected from several administrative data sources including the DS-230 Application for Immigrant Visa and Alien Registration (U.S. Department of State) for new arrivals, and the I-485 Application to Register Permanent Residence or Adjust Status (U.S. Citizenship and Immigration Services—USCIS) for persons adjusting immigrant status.

An immigrant, or legal permanent resident, is a foreign national who has been granted lawful permanent residence in the United States. New arrivals are foreign nationals living abroad who apply for an immigrant visa at a consular office of the Department of State, while individuals adjusting status are already living in the United States and file an application for adjustment of status to lawful permanent residence with USCIS. Individuals adjusting status include refugees, asylees, and various classes of nonimmigrants. A refugee is an alien outside the United States who is unable or unwilling to return to his or her country of origin because of persecution or a well-founded fear of persecution. Asylees must meet the same criteria as refugees, but are located in the United States or at a port of entry. After 1 year of residence, refugees and asylees are eligible to adjust to legal permanent resident status. Nonimmigrants are foreign nationals granted temporary entry into the United States. The major activities for which nonimmigrant admission is authorized include temporary visits for business or pleasure, academic or vocational study, temporary employment, and to act as a representative of a foreign government or international organization. DHS collects information on the characteristics of a proportion of nonimmigrant admissions, those recorded on the I-94 Arrival/Departure Record.

U.S. immigration law gives preferential immigration status to persons with a close family relationship with a U.S. citizen or legal permanent resident, persons with needed job skills, persons who qualify as refugees or asylees, and persons who are from countries with relatively low levels of immigration to the United States. Immigration to the United States can be divided into two general categories: (1) classes of admission subject to the annual worldwide limitation and (2) classes of admission exempt from worldwide limitations. Numerical limits are imposed on visas issued and not on admissions. In 2008, the annual limit for preference visas subject to limitation was 388,704, which included a family-sponsored preference limit of 226,000 and an employment-based preference limit of 162,704. Classes of admission exempt from the worldwide limitation include immediate relatives of U.S. citizens, refugees and asylees adjusting to permanent residence, and other various classes of special immigrants.

Metropolitan and micropolitan areas— The U.S. Office of Management and Budget (OMB) defines metropolitan and micropolitan statistical areas according to published standards that are applied to Census Bureau data. The general concept of a metropolitan or micropolitan statistical area is that of a core area containing a substantial population nucleus, together with adjacent communities having a high degree of economic and social integration with that core. Currently defined metropolitan and micropolitan statistical areas are based on application of 2000 standards to 2000 decennial census data as updated by application of those standards to more recent Census Bureau population estimates. The term "metropolitan area" (MA) was adopted in 1990 and referred collectively to metropolitan statistical areas (MSAs), consolidated metropolitan statistical areas (CMSAs), and primary metropolitan statistical areas (PMSAs). The term "core-based statistical area" (CBSA) became effective in 2003 and refers collectively to metropolitan and micropolitan statistical areas. For descriptive details and a list of titles and components of metropolitan and micropolitan statistical areas, see Appendix II.

Urban and rural— For Census 2000, the Census Bureau classified as urban all territory, population, and housing units located within urbanized areas (UAs) and urban clusters (UCs). A UA consists of densely settled territory that contains 50,000 or more people, while a UC consists of densely settled territory with at least 2,500 people but fewer than 50,000

Population 3

people. From the 1950 census through the 1990 census, the urban population consisted of all people living in UAs and most places outside of UAs with a census population of 2,500 or more.

UAs and UCs encompass territory that generally consists of:

- A cluster of one or more block groups or census blocks each of which has a population density of at least 1,000 people per square mile at the time.

- Surrounding block groups and census blocks each of which has a population density of at least 500 people per square mile at the time.

- Less densely settled blocks that form enclaves or indentations, or are used to connect discontiguous areas with qualifying densities.

They also may include an airport located adjacent to qualifying densely settled area if it has an annual enplanement (aircraft boarding) of at least 10,000 people.

"Rural" for Census 2000 consists of all territory, population, and housing units located outside of UAs and UCs. Prior to Census 2000, rural consisted of all territory, population, and housing outside of UAs and outside of other places designated as "urban." For Census 2000, many more geographic entities, including metropolitan areas, counties, and places, contain both urban and rural territory, population, and housing units.

Residence—In determining residence, the Census Bureau counts each person as an inhabitant of a usual place of residence (i.e., the place where one lives and sleeps most of the time). While this place is not necessarily a person's legal residence or voting residence, the use of these different bases of classification would produce the same results in the vast majority of cases.

Race—For the 1990 census, the Census Bureau collected and published racial statistics as outlined in Statistical Policy Directive No. 15 issued by the OMB. This directive provided standards on ethnic and racial categories for statistical reporting to be used by all federal agencies. According to the directive, the basic racial categories were American Indian or Alaska Native, Asian or Pacific Islander, Black, and White. (The directive identified Hispanic origin as an ethnicity.) The question on race for Census 2000 was different from the one for the 1990 census in several ways. Most significantly, respondents were given the option of selecting one or more race categories to indicate their racial identities. Because of these changes, the Census 2000 data on race are not directly comparable with data from the 1990 census or earlier censuses. Caution must be used when interpreting changes in the racial composition of the United States population over time. Census 2000 adheres to the federal standards for collecting and presenting data on race and ethnicity as established by the OMB in October 1997. Starting with Census 2000, the OMB requires federal agencies to use a minimum of five race categories: White, Black or African American, American Indian or Alaska Native, Asian, and Native Hawaiian or Other Pacific Islander. Additionally, to collect data on individuals of mixed race parentage, respondents were allowed to select one or more races. For respondents unable to identify with any of these five race categories, the OMB approved and included a sixth category— "Some other race" on the Census 2000 questionnaire. The Census 2000 question on race included 15 separate response categories and three areas where respondents could write in a more specific race group. The response categories and write-in answers can be combined to create the five minimum OMB race categories plus "Some other race." People who responded to the question on race by indicating only one race are referred to as the *race alone* population, or the group that reported only one race category. Six categories make up this population: White alone, Black or African American alone, American Indian and Alaska Native alone, Asian alone, Native Hawaiian and Other Pacific Islander alone, and Some other race alone. Individuals who chose more than one of the six race categories are referred to as the *Two or More Races* population, or as the group that reported more than one race. Additionally, respondents who reported one race together with those who reported the same race plus one or more other races are combined to create the race alone or in *combination* categories. For example, the *White alone or* *in combination group* consists of those respondents who reported only White or who reported White combined with one or more other race groups, such as "White and Black or African American," or "White and Asian and American Indian and Alaska Native." Another way to think of the group who reported White alone or in combination is as the total number of people who identified entirely or partially as White. This group is also described as people who reported White, whether or not they reported any other race.

The *alone or in combination* categories are tallies of *responses* rather than *respondents*. That is, the alone or in combination categories are not mutually exclusive. Individuals who reported two races were counted in two separate and distinct alone or in combination race categories, while those who reported three races were counted in three categories, and so on. Consequently, the sum of all alone or in combination categories equals the number of races reported, which exceeds the total population.

The concept of race, as used by the Census Bureau, reflects self-identification by people according to the race or races with which they most closely identify. These categories are sociopolitical constructs and should not be interpreted as being scientific or anthropological in nature. Furthermore, the race categories include both racial and national-origin groups. Additionally, data are available for the American Indian and Alaska Native tribes. A detailed explanation of race can be found at <http://www.census.gov /prod/cen2000/doc/sf1.pdf>.

Data for the population by race for April 1, 2000, (shown in Tables 6, 9, and 10) are modified counts and are not comparable to Census 2000 race categories. These numbers were computed using Census 2000 data by race and had been modified to be consistent with the 1997 OMB's "Revisions to the Standards for the Classification of Federal Data on Race and Ethnicity," (Federal Register Notice, Vol. 62, No 210, October 1997). A detailed explanation of the race modification procedure appears at <http://www.census .gov/popest/archives/files/MRSF-01-US1 .html>.

In the CPS and other household sample surveys in which data are obtained through personal interview, respondents are asked to classify their race as: (1) White; (2) Black, African American, or Negro; (3) American Indian or Alaska Native; (4) Asian; or (5) Native Hawaiian or Other Pacific Islander. Beginning January 2003, respondents were allowed to report more than one race to indicate their mixed racial heritage.

Hispanic population—The Census Bureau collected data on the Hispanic-origin population in the 2000 census by using a self-identification question. Persons of Spanish/Hispanic/Latino origin are those who classified themselves in one of the specific Hispanic origin categories listed on the questionnaire—Mexican, Puerto Rican, Cuban, as well as those who indicated that they were of Other Spanish/ Hispanic/Latino origin (persons whose origins are from Spain, the Spanish-speaking countries of Central or South America, or the Dominican Republic).

In the CPS, information on Hispanic persons is gathered by using a self-identification question. The respondents are first asked whether or not they are of Hispanic, Spanish, or Latino origin and based on their response are further classified into the following categories: Mexican or Mexican American or Chicano; Puerto Rican; Cuban; Central or South American; or Other Hispanic, Spanish, or Latino origin group.

Traditional and current data collection and classification treat race and Hispanic origin as two separate and distinct concepts in accordance with guidelines from the OMB. Race and Hispanic origin are two separate concepts in the federal statistical system. People who are Hispanic may be any race and people in each race group may be either Hispanic or Not Hispanic. Also, each person has two attributes, their race (or races) and whether or not they are Hispanic. The overlap of race and Hispanic origin is the main comparability issue. For example, Black Hispanics (Hispanic Blacks) are included in both the number of Blacks and in the number of Hispanics. For further information, see <http://www.census.gov/population /www/socdemo/compraceho.html>.

Foreign-born and native populations—The Census Bureau separates the U.S. resident population into two groups based on whether or not a person was a U.S. citizen or U.S. national at the time of birth. Anyone born in the United States, Puerto Rico, or a U.S. Island Area (such as Guam), or born abroad to a U.S. citizen parent is a U.S. citizen at the time of birth and consequently included in the *native population*. The term *foreign-born population* refers to anyone who is not a U.S. citizen or a U.S. national at birth. This includes naturalized U.S. citizens, legal permanent resident aliens (immigrants), temporary migrants (such as foreign students), humanitarian migrants (such as refugees), and people illegally present in the United States. The Census Bureau provides a variety of demographic, social, economic, geographic, and housing information on the foreign-born population in the United States at <http://www.census.gov/population/www/socdemo/foreign/>.

Mobility status—The U.S. population is classified according to mobility status on the basis of a comparison between the place of residence of each individual at the time of the survey or census and the place of residence at a specified earlier date. Nonmovers are all persons who were living in the same house or apartment at the end of the period as at the beginning of the period. Movers are all persons who were living in a different house or apartment at the end of the period than at the beginning of the period. Movers are further classified as to whether they were living in the same or different county, state, region, or were movers from abroad. Movers from abroad include all persons whose place of residence was outside the United States (including Puerto Rico, other U.S. Island Area, or a foreign country) at the beginning of the period.

Living arrangements—Living arrangements refer to residency in households or in group quarters. A "household" comprises all persons who occupy a "housing unit," that is, a house, an apartment or other group of rooms, or a single room that constitutes "separate living quarters." A household includes the related family members and all the unrelated persons, if any, such as lodgers, foster children, or employees who share the housing unit. A person living alone or a group of unrelated persons sharing the same housing unit is also counted as a household. See text, Section 20, Construction and Housing, for definition of housing unit.

All persons not living in housing units are classified as living in group quarters. These individuals may be institutionalized, e.g., under care or custody in juvenile facilities, jails, correctional centers, hospitals, or nursing homes; or they may be residents in noninstitutional group quarters such as college dormitories, group homes, or military barracks.

Householder—The householder is the person in whose name the home is owned or rented. If a home is owned or rented jointly by a married couple, either the husband or the wife may be listed first.

Family—The term family refers to a group of two or more persons related by birth, marriage, or adoption and residing together in a household. A family includes among its members the householder.

Subfamily—A subfamily consists of a married couple and their children, if any, or one parent with one or more never-married children under 18 years old living in a household. Subfamilies are divided into "related" and "unrelated" subfamilies. A related subfamily is related to, but does not include, the householder or the spouse of the householder. Members of a related subfamily are also members of the family with whom they live. The number of related subfamilies, therefore, is not included in the count of families. An unrelated subfamily may include persons such as guests, lodgers, or resident employees and their spouses and/or children; none of whom is related to the householder.

Married couple—A married couple is defined as a husband and wife living together in the same household, with or without children and other relatives.

Statistical reliability—For a discussion of statistical collection and estimation, sampling procedures, and measures of statistical reliability applicable to Census Bureau data, see Appendix III.

Figure 1.1
Percent Change in Population for States: April 1, 2000 to July 1, 2009

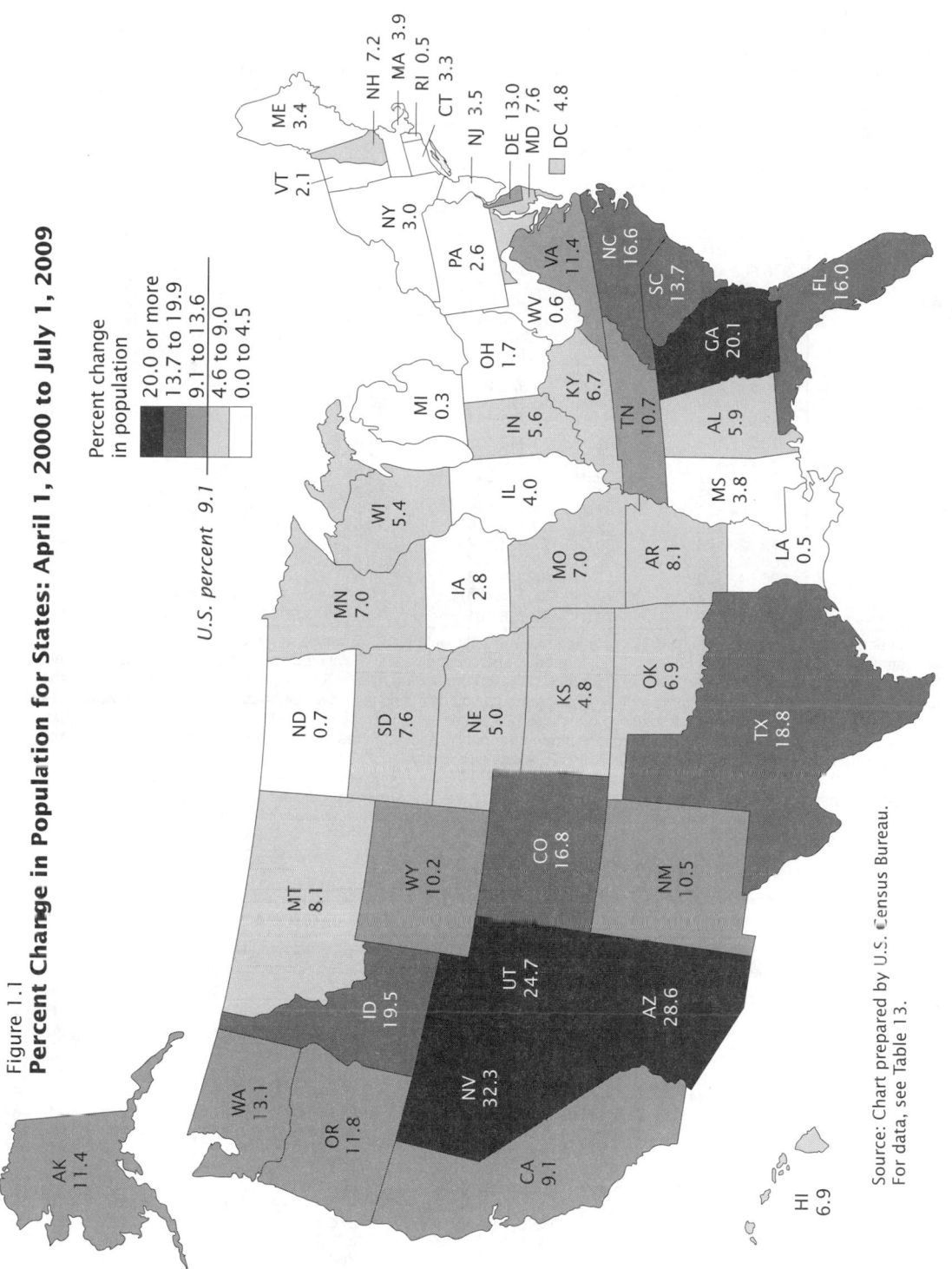

Percent change
in population

	20.0 or more
	13.7 to 19.9
	9.1 to 13.6
	4.6 to 9.0
	0.0 to 4.5

U.S. percent 9.1

AK 11.4

WA 13.1
OR 11.8
CA 9.1
NV 32.3
ID 19.5
UT 24.7
AZ 28.6
MT 8.1
WY 10.2
CO 16.8
NM 10.5
ND 0.7
SD 7.6
NE 5.0
KS 4.8
OK 6.9
TX 18.8
MN 7.0
IA 2.8
MO 7.0
AR 8.1
LA 0.5
WI 5.4
IL 4.0
MI 0.3
IN 5.6
KY 6.7
TN 10.7
MS 3.8
AL 5.9
OH 1.7
WV 0.6
VA 11.4
NC 16.6
SC 13.7
GA 20.1
FL 16.0
PA 2.6
NY 3.0
VT 2.1
ME 3.4
NH 7.2
MA 3.9
RI 0.5
CT 3.3
NJ 3.5
DE 13.0
MD 7.6
DC 4.8

HI 6.9

Source: Chart prepared by U.S. Census Bureau.
For data, see Table 13.

Table 1. Population and Area: 1790 to 2000

[Area figures represent area on indicated date including in some cases considerable areas not then organized or settled, and not covered by the census. Area data include Alaska beginning in 1870 and Hawaii beginning in 1900. Total area figures for 1790 to 1970 have been recalculated on the basis of the remeasurement of states and counties for the 1980 census, but not on the basis of subsequent censuses. The land and water area figures for past censuses have not been adjusted and are not strictly comparable with the total area data for comparable dates because the land areas were derived from different base data, and these values are known to have changed with the construction of reservoirs, draining of lakes, etc. Density figures are based on land area measurements as reported in earlier censuses]

Census date	Resident population				Area (square miles)		
	Number	Per square mile of land area	Increase over preceding census		Total	Land	Water [1]
			Number	Percent			
1790 (Aug. 2)	3,929,214	4.5	(X)	(X)	891,364	864,746	24,065
1800 (Aug. 4)	5,308,483	6.1	1,379,269	35.1	891,364	864,746	24,065
1810 (Aug. 6)	7,239,881	4.3	1,931,398	36.4	1,722,685	1,681,828	34,175
1820 (Aug. 7)	9,638,453	5.5	2,398,572	33.1	1,792,552	1,749,462	38,544
1830 (June 1)	12,866,020	7.4	3,227,567	33.5	1,792,552	1,749,462	38,544
1840 (June 1)	17,069,453	9.8	4,203,433	32.7	1,792,552	1,749,462	38,544
1850 (June 1)	23,191,876	7.9	6,122,423	35.9	2,991,655	2,940,042	52,705
1860 (June 1)	31,443,321	10.6	8,251,445	35.6	3,021,295	2,969,640	52,747
1870 (June 1)	[2] 39,818,449	[2] 11.2	8,375,128	26.6	3,612,299	3,540,705	68,082
1880 (June 1)	50,189,209	14.2	10,370,760	26.0	3,612,299	3,540,705	68,082
1890 (June 1)	62,979,766	17.8	12,790,557	25.5	3,612,299	3,540,705	68,082
1900 (June 1)	76,212,168	21.5	13,232,402	21.0	3,618,770	3,547,314	67,901
1910 (Apr. 15)	92,228,496	26.0	16,016,328	21.0	3,618,770	3,547,045	68,170
1920 (Jan. 1)	106,021,537	29.9	13,793,041	15.0	3,618,770	3,546,931	68,284
1930 (Apr. 1)	123,202,624	34.7	17,181,087	16.2	3,618,770	3,554,608	60,607
1940 (Apr. 1)	132,164,569	37.2	8,961,945	7.3	3,618,770	3,554,608	60,607
1950 (Apr. 1)	151,325,798	42.6	19,161,229	14.5	3,618,770	3,552,206	63,005
1960 (Apr. 1)	179,323,175	50.6	27,997,377	18.5	3,618,770	3,540,911	74,212
1970 (Apr. 1)	203,302,031	57.5	23,978,856	13.4	3,618,770	3,536,855	78,444
1980 (Apr. 1)	[3] 226,542,199	64.0	23,240,168	11.4	3,618,770	3,539,289	79,481
1990 (Apr. 1)	[4] 248,718,302	70.3	22,176,103	9.8	[5] 3,717,796	3,536,278	[5] 181,518
2000 (Apr. 1)	[6] 281,424,603	79.6	32,706,301	13.1	3,794,083	3,537,438	256,645

X Not applicable. [1] Data for 1790 to 1980 cover inland water only. Data for 1990 comprise Great Lakes, inland, and coastal water. Data for 2000 comprise Great Lakes, inland, territorial, and coastal water. [2] Revised to include adjustments for underenumeration in southern states; unrevised number is 38,558,371 (10.9 per square mile). [3] Total population count has been revised since the 1980 census publications. Numbers by age, race, Hispanic origin, and sex have not been corrected. [4] The April 1, 1990, census count includes count question resolution corrections processed through December 1997, and does not include adjustments for census coverage errors. [5] Data reflect corrections made after publication of the results. [6] Reflects modifications to the Census 2000 population as documented in the Count Question Resolution program.

Source: U.S. Census Bureau, 2000 Census of Population and Housing, *Population and Housing Counts*, Series PHC-3-1, United States Summary; *Notes and Errata, 2000* SF/01-ER, <http://www.census.gov/prod/cen2000/notes/errata.pdf>; *Areas of the United States: 1940*; Area data for 1990: unpublished data from TIGER ®; and Davis, Warren, personal correspondence, U.S. Census Bureau, June 23, 2006.

Table 2. Population: 1960 to 2009

[In thousands, except percent (180,671 represents 180,671,000). As of July 1. Civilian population excludes Armed Forces. For basis of estimates, see text of this section]

Year	Resident population, including Armed Forces overseas		Resident population	Civilian population	Year	Resident population, including Armed Forces overseas		Resident population	Civilian population
	Population	Percent change [1]				Population	Percent change [1]		
1960	180,671	1.60	179,979	178,140	1989	247,342	0.95	246,819	245,131
1965	194,303	1.26	193,526	191,605	1990	250,132	1.13	249,623	247,983
1970	205,052	1.17	203,984	201,895	1991	253,493	1.34	252,981	251,370
1971	207,661	1.27	206,827	204,866	1992	256,894	1.34	256,514	254,929
1972	209,896	1.08	209,284	207,511	1993	260,255	1.31	259,919	258,446
1973	211,909	0.96	211,357	209,600	1994	263,436	1.22	263,126	261,714
1974	213,854	0.92	213,342	211,636	1995	266,557	1.18	266,278	264,927
1975	215,973	0.99	215,465	213,789	1996	269,667	1.17	269,394	268,108
1976	218,035	0.95	217,563	215,894	1997	272,912	1.20	272,647	271,394
1977	220,239	1.01	219,760	218,106	1998	276,115	1.17	275,854	274,633
1978	222,585	1.06	222,095	220,467	1999	279,295	1.15	279,040	277,841
1979	225,055	1.11	224,567	222,969	2000	282,385	1.11	282,172	280,927
1980	227,726	1.19	227,225	225,621	2001	285,309	1.04	285,082	283,845
1981	229,966	0.98	229,466	227,818	2002	288,105	0.98	287,804	286,537
1982	232,188	0.97	231,664	229,995	2003	290,820	0.94	290,326	289,107
1983	234,307	0.91	233,792	232,097	2004	293,463	0.91	293,046	291,785
1984	236,348	0.87	235,825	234,110	2005	296,186	0.93	295,753	294,562
1985	238,466	0.90	237,924	236,219	2006	298,996	0.95	298,593	297,413
1986	240,651	0.92	240,133	238,412	2007	302,004	1.01	301,580	300,425
1987	242,804	0.89	242,289	240,550	2008	304,798	0.93	304,375	303,202
1988	245,021	0.91	244,499	242,817	2009	307,439	0.87	307,007	305,782

[1] Percent change from immediate preceding year.

Source: U.S. Census Bureau, 1960 to 1979: Current Population Reports P25-802 and P25-917; 1980 to 1989: "Monthly Estimates of the United States Population: April 1, 1980 to July 1, 1999, with Short-Term Projections to November 1, 2000," released January 2001; <http://www.census.gov/popest/archives/1990s/nat-total.txt>; 1990 to 1999: "National Intercensal Estimates (1990-2000)," August 2004; <http://www.census.gov/popest/archives/EST90INTERCENSAL/US-EST90INT-datasets.html>; 2000 to 2009: "Monthly Population Estimates for the United States: April 1, 2000 to December 1, 2009 (NA-EST2009-01)," December 2009, <http://www.census.gov/popest/national/tables/NA-EST2009-01.xls>.

Table 3. Resident Population Projections: 2010 to 2050

[In thousands, except percent (310,233 represents 310,233,000). As of July 1. Projections are based on assumptions about future births, deaths, and net international migration. More information on methodology and assumptions is available at <http://www.census.gov/population/www/projections/methodstatement.html>]

Year	Population	Percent change [1]	Year	Population	Percent change [1]	Year	Population	Percent change [1]
2010......	310,233	1.0	2024......	354,235	0.9	2038......	399,184	0.8
2011......	313,232	1.0	2025......	357,452	0.9	2039......	402,415	0.8
2012......	316,266	1.0	2026......	360,667	0.9	2040......	405,655	0.8
2013......	319,330	1.0	2027......	363,880	0.9	2041......	408,906	0.8
2014......	322,423	1.0	2028......	367,090	0.9	2042......	412,170	0.8
2015......	325,540	1.0	2029......	370,298	0.9	2043......	415,448	0.8
2016......	328,678	1.0	2030......	373,504	0.9	2044......	418,743	0.8
2017......	331,833	1.0	2031......	376,708	0.9	2045......	422,059	0.8
2018......	335,005	1.0	2032......	379,912	0.9	2046......	425,395	0.8
2019......	338,190	1.0	2033......	383,117	0.8	2047......	428,756	0.8
2020......	341,387	0.9	2034......	386,323	0.8	2048......	432,143	0.8
2021......	344,592	0.9	2035......	389,531	0.8	2049......	435,560	0.8
2022......	347,803	0.9	2036......	392,743	0.8	2050......	439,010	0.8
2023......	351,018	0.9	2037......	395,961	0.8			

[1] Percent change from immediate preceding year. 2010, change from 2009.

Source: U.S. Census Bureau, "2008 National Population Projections," August 2008, <http://www.census.gov/population/www/projections/2008projections.html>.

Table 4. Components of Population Change: 2000 to 2009

[In thousands, except percent (281,425 represents 281,425,000). Resident population]

Period	Population as of beginning of period	Net increase [1] Total	Net increase [1] Percent [2]	Births	Deaths	Net international migration [3]	Population as of end of period
April 1, 2000 to July 1, 2000 [4]	281,425	747	0.3	989	561	319	282,172
July 1, 2001 to July 1, 2002......	285,082	2,722	1.0	4,007	2,430	1,078	287,804
July 1, 2002 to July 1, 2003......	287,804	2,523	0.9	4,053	2,423	822	290,326
July 1, 2003 to July 1, 2004......	290,326	2,719	0.9	4,113	2,450	986	293,046
July 1, 2004 to July 1, 2005......	293,046	2,707	0.9	4,121	2,433	948	295,753
July 1, 2005 to July 1, 2006......	295,753	2,840	1.0	4,178	2,418	1,006	298,593
July 1, 2006 to July 1, 2007......	298,593	2,987	1.0	4,305	2,425	866	301,580
July 1, 2007 to July 1, 2008......	301,580	2,795	0.9	4,283	2,439	863	304,375
July 1, 2008 to July 1, 2009......	304,375	2,632	0.9	4,263	2,486	855	307,007

[1] Net increase includes a residual. This residual represents the change in population that cannot be attributed to any specific demographic component. [2] Percent of population at beginning of period. [3] Net international migration includes the international migration of both native and foreign-born populations. Specifically, it includes: (a) the net international migration of the foreign born, (b) the net migration between the United States and Puerto Rico, (c) the net migration of natives to and from the United States, and (d) the net movement of the Armed Forces population between the United States and overseas. [4] The April 1, 2000, population estimates base reflects changes to the Census 2000 population from the Count Question Resolution program and geographic program revisions.

Source: U.S. Census Bureau, "Population, Population change and estimated components of population change: April 1, 2000 to July 1, 2009," December 2009, <http://www.census.gov/popest/national/files/NST-EST2009-alldata.txt>

Table 5. Components of Population Change by Race and Hispanic Origin: 2000 to 2009

[In thousands (25,582 represents 25,582,000). Resident population. Covers period April 1, 2000, to July 1, 2009. The April 1, 2000, Population Estimates base reflects changes to the Census 2000 population from the Count Question Resolution program]

Race and Hispanic origin	April 1, 2000 to July 1, 2009				
	Net increase [1]	Natural increase	Births	Deaths	Net international migration [2]
Total.............................	**25,582**	**15,876**	**38,359**	**22,483**	**8,944**
One race................................	24,156	14,557	36,894	22,337	8,850
White................................	16,192	9,744	28,859	19,115	5,840
Black or African American................	3,936	3,062	5,783	2,720	777
American Indian and Alaska Native...........	487	403	513	110	77
Asian................................	3,425	1,270	1,650	379	2,119
Native Hawaiian and Other Pacific Islander......	116	78	90	12	36
Two or more races........................	1,426	1,318	1,464	146	95
Race alone or in combination: [3]					
White................................	17,483	10,949	30,186	19,237	5,914
Black or African American................	4,699	3,779	6,539	2,760	818
American Indian and Alaska Native...........	736	625	816	192	99
Asian................................	3,983	1,779	2,204	425	2,164
Native Hawaiian and Other Pacific Islander......	231	180	210	30	48
Hispanic [4]............................	13,113	8,216	9,261	1,045	4,776
White alone, not Hispanic..................	4,274	2,435	20,573	18,138	1,343

[1] See footnote 1, Table 4. [2] See footnote 3, Table 4. [3] In combination with one or more other races. The sum of the five race groups adds to more than the total population because individuals may report more than one race. [4] Persons of Hispanic origin may be any race.

Source: U.S. Census Bureau, "Cumulative Estimates of the Components of Resident Population Change by Race and Hispanic Origin for the United States: April 1, 2000 to July 1, 2009 (NC-EST2009-05)," June 2010, <http://www.census.gov/popest/national/asrh/NC-EST2009/NC-EST2009-05.xls>.

Population 9

Table 6. Resident Population by Sex, Race, and Hispanic-Origin Status: 2000 to 2009

[281,425 represents 281,425,000. As of July, except as noted. Data shown are modified race counts; see text, this section]

Characteristic	Number (1,000)					Percent change, 2000 to 2009
	2000 [1] (April)	2005	2007	2008	2009	
BOTH SEXES						
Total	**281,425**	**295,753**	**301,580**	**304,375**	**307,007**	**9.1**
One race	277,527	291,087	296,587	299,216	301,683	8.7
White	228,107	237,251	240,947	242,685	244,298	7.1
Black or African American	35,705	37,813	38,742	39,205	39,641	11.0
American Indian and Alaska Native	2,664	2,924	3,038	3,095	3,151	18.3
Asian	10,589	12,571	13,307	13,665	14,014	32.3
Native Hawaiian and Other Pacific Islander	463	527	553	566	578	25.0
Two or more races	3,898	4,666	4,993	5,159	5,324	36.6
Race alone or in combination: [2]						
White	231,436	241,276	245,268	247,156	248,919	7.6
Black or African American	37,105	39,618	40,723	41,277	41,804	12.7
American Indian and Alaska Native	4,225	4,620	4,791	4,877	4,961	17.4
Asian	12,007	14,294	15,156	15,578	15,990	33.2
Native Hawaiian and Other Pacific Islander	907	1,035	1,086	1,112	1,137	25.4
Not Hispanic	246,118	253,201	256,071	257,396	258,587	5.1
One race	242,712	249,167	251,776	252,969	254,028	4.7
White	195,577	198,074	199,109	199,529	199,851	2.2
Black or African American	34,314	36,150	36,931	37,319	37,682	9.8
American Indian and Alaska Native	2,097	2,242	2,302	2,332	2,361	12.6
Asian	10,357	12,289	13,003	13,349	13,686	32.1
Native Hawaiian and Other Pacific Islander	367	413	431	440	449	22.2
Two or more races	3,406	4,034	4,295	4,428	4,559	33.8
Race alone or in combination: [2]						
White	198,477	201,543	202,817	203,357	203,800	2.7
Black or African American	35,499	37,670	38,596	39,058	39,495	11.3
American Indian and Alaska Native	3,456	3,687	3,782	3,829	3,874	12.1
Asian	11,632	13,828	14,647	15,047	15,437	32.7
Native Hawaiian and Other Pacific Islander	752	845	882	900	918	22.1
Hispanic [3]	35,306	42,552	45,508	46,979	48,419	37.1
One race	34,815	41,920	44,811	46,247	47,655	36.9
White	32,530	39,177	41,838	43,156	44,447	36.6
Black or African American	1,391	1,663	1,811	1,886	1,960	40.9
American Indian and Alaska Native	566	682	735	763	790	39.6
Asian	232	282	305	316	328	41.0
Native Hawaiian and Other Pacific Islander	95	115	122	126	130	36.1
Two or more races	491	632	698	731	764	55.6
Race alone or in combination: [2]						
White	32,959	39,732	42,451	43,799	45,119	36.9
Black or African American	1,606	1,947	2,128	2,219	2,309	43.8
American Indian and Alaska Native	770	934	1,009	1,048	1,087	41.2
Asian	375	467	509	531	553	47.4
Native Hawaiian and Other Pacific Islander	155	190	205	212	220	41.8
MALE						
Total	**138,056**	**145,561**	**148,612**	**150,074**	**151,449**	**9.7**
One race	136,146	143,262	146,147	147,525	148,817	9.3
White	112,478	117,433	119,428	120,366	121,236	7.8
Black or African American	16,972	18,017	18,484	18,716	18,936	11.6
American Indian and Alaska Native	1,333	1,465	1,524	1,553	1,581	18.6
Asian	5,128	6,079	6,431	6,603	6,769	32.0
Native Hawaiian and Other Pacific Islander	235	268	281	288	294	25.0
Two or more races	1,910	2,299	2,465	2,549	2,633	37.8
Race alone or in combination: [2]						
White	114,116	119,423	121,568	122,582	123,528	8.2
Black or African American	17,644	18,894	19,452	19,730	19,996	13.3
American Indian and Alaska Native	2,088	2,288	2,375	2,419	2,462	17.9
Asian	5,834	6,939	7,355	7,559	7,758	33.0
Native Hawaiian and Other Pacific Islander	456	521	547	560	573	25.6
Not Hispanic	119,894	123,579	125,080	125,773	126,393	5.4
Hispanic [3]	18,162	21,981	23,532	24,302	25,057	38.0
FEMALE						
Total	**143,368**	**150,192**	**152,968**	**154,301**	**155,557**	**8.5**
One race	141,381	147,825	150,440	151,691	152,866	8.1
White	115,628	119,818	121,519	122,319	123,063	6.4
Black or African American	18,733	19,796	20,258	20,488	20,705	10.5
American Indian and Alaska Native	1,331	1,459	1,514	1,542	1,570	18.0
Asian	5,461	6,493	6,877	7,063	7,244	32.6
Native Hawaiian and Other Pacific Islander	227	259	272	278	284	25.1
Two or more races	1,987	2,367	2,528	2,610	2,691	35.4
Race alone or in combination: [2]						
White	117,321	121,853	123,700	124,574	125,391	6.9
Black or African American	19,461	20,723	21,272	21,546	21,808	12.1
American Indian and Alaska Native	2,137	2,332	2,415	2,458	2,499	16.9
Asian	6,173	7,355	7,802	8,019	8,232	33.4
Native Hawaiian and Other Pacific Islander	451	514	539	552	565	25.3
Not Hispanic	126,224	129,622	130,991	131,624	132,195	4.7
Hispanic [3]	17,144	20,571	21,977	22,677	23,362	36.3

[1] See footnote 4, Table 4. [2] In combination with one or more other races. The sum of the five race groups adds to more than the total population because individuals may report more than one race. [3] Persons of Hispanic origin may be any race.

Source: U.S. Census Bureau, "Annual Estimates of the Resident Population by Sex, Race, and Hispanic Origin for the United States: April 1, 2000 to July 1, 2009 (NC-EST2009-03)," June 2010, <http://www.census.gov/popest/national/asrh/NC-EST2009/NC-EST2009-03.xls>.

10 Population

Table 7. Resident Population by Sex and Age: 1980 to 2009

[In thousands, except as indicated (226,546 represents 226,546,000). 1980, 1990, and 2000 data are enumerated population as of April 1; data for other years are estimated population as of July 1. Excludes Armed Forces overseas. For definition of median, see Guide to Tabular Presentation]

Age	1980 [1] Total	Male	Female	1990 [2] Total	Male	Female	2000 [3] Total	Male	Female	2003	2004	2005	2006	2007	2008	2009 Total	Male	Female
Total	226,546	110,053	116,493	248,791	121,284	127,507	281,425	138,056	143,368	290,326	293,046	295,753	298,593	301,580	304,375	307,007	151,449	155,557
Under 5 years	16,348	8,362	7,986	18,765	9,603	9,162	19,176	9,811	9,365	19,940	20,243	20,484	20,613	20,921	21,153	21,300	10,887	10,413
5 to 9 years	16,700	8,539	8,161	18,042	9,236	8,306	20,550	10,523	10,026	19,778	19,655	19,632	19,831	20,054	20,313	20,610	10,536	10,074
10 to 14 years	18,242	9,316	8,926	17,067	8,742	8,325	20,528	10,520	10,008	21,193	21,113	20,837	20,579	20,319	20,104	19,974	10,223	9,751
15 to 19 years	21,168	10,755	10,413	17,893	9,178	8,714	20,219	10,391	9,828	20,574	20,808	21,120	21,367	21,562	21,628	21,538	11,051	10,487
20 to 24 years	21,319	10,663	10,655	19,143	9,749	9,394	18,963	9,688	9,275	20,685	20,959	21,081	21,161	21,217	21,322	21,540	11,094	10,446
25 to 29 years	19,521	9,705	9,816	21,336	10,708	10,629	19,382	9,799	9,583	18,971	19,372	19,866	20,511	21,018	21,442	21,678	11,116	10,562
30 to 34 years	17,561	8,677	8,884	21,838	10,866	10,973	20,511	10,322	10,189	20,551	20,260	19,846	19,433	19,353	19,516	19,889	10,108	9,781
35 to 39 years	13,965	6,862	7,104	19,851	9,837	10,014	22,707	11,319	11,388	21,284	20,896	20,818	20,959	20,993	20,847	20,538	10,353	10,185
40 to 44 years	11,669	5,708	5,961	17,593	8,679	8,914	22,442	11,130	11,313	22,903	22,943	22,726	22,320	21,858	21,394	20,992	10,504	10,487
45 to 49 years	11,090	5,388	5,702	13,747	6,741	7,006	20,093	9,890	10,203	21,714	22,053	22,402	22,696	22,787	22,802	22,831	11,296	11,536
50 to 54 years	11,710	5,621	6,089	11,315	5,494	5,821	17,586	8,608	8,978	19,004	19,447	19,940	20,407	20,962	21,432	21,761	10,678	11,084
55 to 59 years	11,615	5,482	6,133	10,489	5,009	5,480	13,469	6,509	6,961	15,706	16,460	17,315	18,170	18,209	18,541	18,975	9,205	9,770
60 to 64 years	10,088	4,670	5,418	10,627	4,947	5,679	10,806	5,137	5,669	12,100	12,573	12,981	13,340	14,459	15,082	15,812	7,577	8,235
65 to 74 years	15,581	6,757	8,824	18,048	7,908	10,140	18,391	8,303	10,088	18,381	18,502	18,666	18,936	19,389	20,139	20,792	9,593	11,199
75 to 84 years	7,729	2,867	4,862	10,014	3,745	6,268	12,361	4,879	7,482	12,968	13,077	13,176	13,207	13,213	13,211	13,148	5,447	7,700
85 years and over	2,240	682	1,559	3,022	841	2,181	4,240	1,227	3,013	4,574	4,684	4,862	5,063	5,264	5,450	5,631	1,783	3,848
5 to 13 years	31,159	15,923	15,237	31,839	16,301	15,538	37,026	18,964	18,062	36,774	36,396	36,162	36,159	36,180	36,297	36,487	18,660	17,827
14 to 17 years	16,247	8,298	7,950	13,345	6,860	6,485	16,093	8,285	7,808	16,544	16,854	17,104	17,239	17,239	16,980	16,761	8,592	8,170
18 to 24 years	30,022	15,054	14,969	26,961	13,744	13,217	27,141	13,873	13,268	28,912	29,286	29,405	29,541	29,734	30,090	30,412	15,652	14,760
18 years and over	162,791	77,473	85,321	184,841	88,519	96,322	209,130	100,996	108,133	217,068	219,553	222,004	224,583	227,240	229,945	232,458	113,311	119,147
55 years and over	47,253	20,458	26,796	52,200	22,450	29,748	59,267	26,055	33,212	63,729	65,296	67,000	68,715	70,535	72,423	74,358	33,605	40,752
65 years and over	25,550	10,306	15,245	31,084	12,494	18,589	34,992	14,410	20,582	35,923	36,263	36,704	37,206	37,867	38,800	39,571	16,824	22,747
75 years and over	9,969	3,549	6,421	13,036	4,586	8,449	16,601	6,106	10,495	17,542	17,762	18,038	18,270	18,478	18,661	18,779	7,230	11,548
Median age (years)	30.0	28.8	31.3	32.8	31.6	34.0	35.3	34.0	36.5	35.9	36.0	36.2	36.3	36.5	36.7	36.8	35.4	38.2

[1] Total population count has been revised since the 1980 census publications. Numbers by age and sex have not been corrected. [2] The data shown have been modified from the official 1990 census counts. See text of this section for explanation. The April 1, 1990, estimates base (248,790,925) includes count question resolution corrections processed through August 1997. It generally does not include adjustments for census coverage errors. However, it includes adjustments estimated for the 1995 Test Census in various localities in California, New Jersey, and Louisiana; and the 1998 census dress rehearsals in localities in California and Wisconsin. These adjustments amounted to a total of 81,052 persons. [3] The April 1, 2000 population estimates base reflects changes to the Census 2000 population from the Count Question Resolution program.

Source: U.S. Census Bureau, Current Population Reports, P25-1095; "Table US-EST90INT-04—Intercensal Estimates of the United States Resident Population by Age Groups and Sex, 1990–2000: Selected Months," September 2002, <http://www.census.gov/popest/archives/EST90INTERCENSAL/US-EST90INT-04.html>; and "Annual Estimates of the Resident Population by Sex and Five-Year Age Groups for the United States: April 1, 2000 to July 1, 2009 (NC-EST2009-01)," June 2010, <http://www.census.gov/popest/national/asrh/NC-EST2009/NC-EST2009-01.xls>.

Table 8. Resident Population Projections by Sex and Age: 2010 to 2050

[In thousands, except as indicated (310,233 represents 310,233,000). As of July 1. Projections are based on assumptions about future births, deaths, and net international migration. More information on methodology and assumptions is available at <http://www.census.gov/population/www/projections/methodstatement.html>. For definition of median, see Guide to Tabular Presentation]

Age	2010 Total	2010 Male	2010 Female	2015 Total	2015 Male	2015 Female	2020	2025	2030	2035	2040	2045	2050	Percent distribution 2010	2015	2020	2025	2050
Total	310,233	152,753	157,479	325,540	160,424	165,116	341,387	357,452	373,504	389,531	405,655	422,059	439,010	100.0	100.0	100.0	100.0	100.0
Under 5 years	21,100	10,779	10,320	22,076	11,278	10,798	22,846	23,484	24,161	25,056	26,117	27,171	28,148	6.8	6.8	6.7	6.6	6.4
5 to 9 years	20,886	10,654	10,232	21,707	11,074	10,633	22,732	23,548	24,232	24,953	25,893	26,998	28,096	6.7	6.7	6.7	6.6	6.4
10 to 14 years	20,395	10,421	9,975	21,658	11,049	10,609	22,571	23,677	24,567	25,319	26,105	27,108	28,274	6.6	6.7	6.6	6.6	6.4
15 to 19 years	21,770	11,159	10,611	21,209	10,844	10,365	22,554	23,545	24,723	25,682	26,501	27,354	28,422	7.0	6.5	6.6	6.6	6.5
20 to 24 years	21,779	11,100	10,680	22,342	11,378	10,963	21,799	23,168	24,191	25,408	26,408	27,272	28,171	7.0	6.9	6.4	6.5	6.4
25 to 29 years	21,418	10,873	10,545	22,400	11,353	11,048	22,949	22,417	23,804	24,855	26,102	27,138	28,039	6.9	6.9	6.7	6.6	6.4
30 to 34 years	20,400	10,308	10,092	22,099	11,182	10,917	23,112	23,699	23,216	24,647	25,745	27,040	28,126	6.6	6.8	6.8	6.6	6.4
35 to 39 years	20,267	10,191	10,076	20,841	10,506	10,335	22,586	23,645	24,279	23,848	25,321	26,462	27,799	6.5	6.4	6.6	6.6	6.3
40 to 44 years	21,010	10,509	10,500	20,460	10,247	10,214	21,078	22,851	23,944	24,612	24,224	25,726	26,897	6.8	6.3	6.2	6.4	6.1
45 to 49 years	22,596	11,165	11,430	21,001	10,447	10,553	20,502	21,154	22,943	24,061	24,759	24,411	25,933	7.3	6.5	6.0	5.9	5.9
50 to 54 years	22,109	10,827	11,282	22,367	10,977	11,390	20,852	20,404	21,087	22,884	24,025	24,750	24,445	7.1	6.9	6.1	5.7	5.6
55 to 59 years	19,517	9,450	10,067	21,682	10,524	11,158	21,994	20,575	20,186	20,903	22,703	23,867	24,621	6.3	6.7	6.4	5.8	5.6
60 to 64 years	16,758	8,024	8,733	18,861	9,023	9,838	21,009	21,377	20,080	19,760	20,513	22,305	23,490	5.4	5.8	6.2	6.0	5.4
65 to 69 years	12,261	5,747	6,514	15,812	7,449	8,364	17,861	19,957	20,381	19,230	18,989	19,776	21,543	4.0	4.9	5.2	5.6	4.9
70 to 74 years	9,202	4,191	5,011	11,155	5,109	6,046	14,452	16,399	18,404	18,879	17,906	17,754	18,570	3.0	3.4	4.2	4.6	4.2
75 to 79 years	7,282	3,159	4,123	7,901	3,480	4,421	9,656	12,598	14,390	16,249	16,771	16,016	15,964	2.3	2.4	2.8	3.5	3.6
80 to 84 years	5,733	2,302	3,431	5,676	2,342	3,334	6,239	7,715	10,173	11,735	13,375	13,925	13,429	1.8	1.7	1.8	2.2	3.1
85 to 89 years	3,650	1,297	2,353	3,786	1,409	2,376	3,817	4,278	5,383	7,215	8,450	9,767	10,303	1.2	1.2	1.1	1.2	2.3
90 to 94 years	1,570	473	1,097	1,856	591	1,265	1,976	2,047	2,360	3,044	4,180	5,007	5,909	0.5	0.6	0.6	0.6	1.3
95 to 99 years	452	108	344	546	142	404	669	739	795	952	1,270	1,803	2,229	0.1	0.2	0.2	0.2	0.5
100 years and over	79	15	65	105	21	84	135	175	208	239	298	409	601	(Z)	(Z)	(Z)	(Z)	0.1
5 to 13 years	37,123	18,945	18,178	39,011	19,900	19,111	40,792	42,490	43,858	45,170	46,743	48,664	50,697	12.0	12.0	11.9	11.9	11.5
14 to 17 years	16,994	8,713	8,281	17,019	8,699	8,320	18,048	18,892	19,796	20,496	21,126	21,834	22,728	5.5	5.2	5.3	5.3	5.2
18 to 24 years	30,713	15,675	15,037	30,885	15,746	15,139	30,817	32,555	34,059	35,695	37,038	38,234	39,538	9.9	9.5	9.0	9.1	9.0
16 years and over	243,639	118,739	124,900	255,864	124,858	131,006	268,722	282,014	295,595	309,084	322,265	335,328	348,811	78.5	78.6	78.7	78.9	79.5
18 years and over	235,016	114,316	120,700	247,434	120,547	126,887	259,702	272,585	285,688	298,809	311,669	324,389	337,437	75.8	76.0	76.1	76.3	76.9
16 to 64 years	203,410	101,447	101,963	209,027	104,316	104,711	213,917	218,107	223,503	231,540	241,027	250,872	260,264	65.6	64.2	62.7	61.0	59.3
55 years and over	76,504	34,766	41,737	87,381	40,090	47,291	97,807	105,860	112,358	118,206	124,455	130,628	136,658	24.7	26.8	28.6	29.6	31.1
65 years and over	40,229	17,292	22,937	46,837	20,542	26,295	54,804	63,907	72,092	77,543	81,238	84,456	88,547	13.0	14.4	16.1	17.9	20.2
75 years and over	18,766	7,354	11,412	19,870	7,985	11,885	22,492	27,551	33,308	39,435	44,343	46,926	48,434	6.0	6.1	6.6	7.7	11.0
85 years and over	5,751	1,893	3,859	6,292	2,163	4,130	6,597	7,239	8,745	11,450	14,198	16,985	19,041	1.9	1.9	1.9	2.0	4.3
Median age (years)	36.9	35.5	38.2	37.1	35.9	38.4	37.7	38.2	38.7	39.0	38.9	38.9	39.0	(X)	(X)	(X)	(X)	(X)

X Not applicable. Z Less than 0.05 percent.
Source: U.S. Census Bureau, "2008 National Population Projections," August 2008, <http://www.census.gov/population/www/projections/2008projections.html>.

Table 9. Resident Population by Race, Hispanic Origin, and Age: 2000 and 2009

[In thousands, except as indicated (281,425 represents 281,425,000). 2000, as of April and 2009, as of July. For definition of median, see Guide to Tabular Presentation]

Age	Total 2000[1]	Total 2009	White alone 2000[1]	White alone 2009	Black or African American alone 2000[1]	Black or African American alone 2009	American Indian, Alaska Native alone 2000[1]	American Indian, Alaska Native alone 2009	Asian alone 2000[1]	Asian alone 2009	Native Hawaiian, Other Pacific Islander alone 2000[1]	Native Hawaiian, Other Pacific Islander alone 2009	Two or more races 2000[1]	Two or more races 2009	Hispanic origin[2] 2000[1]	Hispanic origin[2] 2009	Not Hispanic White alone 2000[1]	Not Hispanic White alone 2009
Total	281,425	307,007	228,107	244,298	35,705	39,641	2,664	3,151	10,589	14,014	463	578	3,898	5,324	35,306	48,419	195,577	199,851
Under 5 years	19,176	21,300	14,657	15,875	2,925	3,230	233	298	708	1,006	41	53	613	838	3,718	5,485	11,288	11,016
5 to 9 years	20,550	20,610	15,638	15,640	3,320	2,987	258	255	716	949	44	48	524	729	3,624	4,792	12,392	11,275
10 to 14 years	20,528	19,974	15,843	15,210	3,221	3,030	264	240	715	844	42	44	443	605	3,163	4,060	12,961	11,516
15 to 19 years	20,219	21,538	15,745	16,386	3,024	3,457	251	272	776	853	44	47	380	522	3,172	4,032	12,836	12,707
20 to 24 years	18,963	21,540	14,826	16,610	2,729	3,253	218	274	848	915	46	47	297	440	3,409	3,884	11,681	13,046
25 to 29 years	19,382	21,678	15,217	16,761	2,645	3,098	204	260	1,019	1,125	42	50	254	383	3,385	4,150	12,077	12,927
30 to 34 years	20,511	19,889	16,349	15,381	2,710	2,715	202	221	980	1,229	39	49	231	295	3,125	4,030	13,451	11,646
35 to 39 years	22,707	20,538	18,372	16,025	2,910	2,723	217	210	937	1,276	38	44	233	260	2,825	3,758	15,753	12,535
40 to 44 years	22,442	20,992	18,346	16,684	2,772	2,715	202	205	870	1,117	33	40	219	230	2,304	3,306	16,213	13,616
45 to 49 years	20,093	22,831	16,615	18,478	2,330	2,834	169	215	770	1,032	27	39	183	232	1,775	2,894	14,973	15,794
50 to 54 years	17,586	21,761	14,794	17,833	1,846	2,573	135	192	641	921	21	32	149	210	1,361	2,274	13,530	15,727
55 to 59 years	13,469	18,975	11,479	15,738	1,332	2,094	95	157	443	789	15	26	106	170	960	1,720	10,582	14,145
60 to 64 years	10,806	15,812	9,214	13,382	1,082	1,541	70	120	350	616	11	19	78	133	750	1,274	8,511	12,198
65 to 69 years	9,534	11,784	8,238	10,068	895	1,092	52	82	279	437	8	13	61	92	599	891	7,675	9,235
70 to 74 years	8,858	9,008	7,799	7,699	742	843	38	58	224	332	6	10	49	65	477	676	7,348	7,066
75 to 79 years	7,416	7,326	6,634	6,339	557	644	27	41	159	246	4	7	36	49	327	509	6,325	5,860
80 to 84 years	4,945	5,822	4,466	5,133	350	451	15	27	90	172	2	4	22	35	180	362	4,296	4,792
85 to 89 years	2,790	3,662	2,525	3,277	200	247	8	15	43	100	1	2	12	21	98	207	2,432	3,081
90 to 94 years	1,113	1,502	1,007	1,357	82	89	3	6	15	40	1	1	4	9	39	82	970	1,280
95 to 99 years	287	402	254	363	27	22	1	2	4	12	–	–	1	3	11	28	243	336
100 years and over	50	64	41	57	7	3	–	–	1	3	–	–	–	1	3	7	39	51
5 to 13 years	37,026	36,487	28,381	27,732	5,923	5,380	471	446	1,288	1,625	78	83	885	1,221	6,186	8,045	22,754	20,408
14 to 17 years	16,093	16,761	12,523	12,738	2,426	2,671	205	207	590	676	33	37	315	433	2,438	3,220	10,290	9,802
18 to 24 years	27,141	30,412	21,197	23,377	3,944	4,676	315	387	1,178	1,261	64	67	444	643	4,744	5,503	16,827	18,335
16 years and over	217,151	240,990	178,790	194,435	25,633	29,735	1,857	2,308	8,304	11,046	328	424	2,237	3,042	24,204	33,282	156,352	163,637
18 years and over	209,130	232,458	172,546	187,954	24,431	28,361	1,755	2,200	8,003	10,707	311	405	2,084	2,832	22,964	31,669	151,245	158,626
16 to 64 years	182,159	201,419	147,826	160,141	22,773	26,345	1,713	2,076	7,489	9,705	305	386	2,051	2,767	22,471	30,521	127,023	131,935
55 years and over	59,267	74,358	51,656	63,415	5,274	7,026	310	509	1,508	2,745	48	84	371	578	3,444	5,755	48,422	58,044
65 years and over	34,992	39,571	30,964	34,294	2,860	3,391	144	232	815	1,340	23	38	186	275	1,734	2,761	29,329	31,702
75 years and over	16,601	18,779	14,927	16,527	1,223	1,456	55	92	312	572	8	15	77	117	657	1,194	14,306	15,400
85 years and over	4,240	5,631	3,827	5,054	316	361	13	24	63	154	2	4	18	34	151	324	3,685	4,748
Median age (years)	35.3	36.8	36.6	38.3	30.0	31.3	27.7	29.5	32.5	35.3	26.8	29.9	19.8	19.7	25.8	27.4	38.6	41.2

– Represents or rounds to zero. [1] April 1, 2000, population estimates base reflects changes to the Census 2000 population from the Count Question Resolution program. [2] Persons of Hispanic origin may be any race.

Source: U.S. Census Bureau, "Annual Estimates of the Resident Population by Race, Hispanic Origin, Sex and Age for the United States: April 1, 2000 to July 1, 2009 (NC-EST2009-04)," June 2010, <http://www.census.gov/popest/national/asrh/NC-EST2009-asrh.html>.

Table 10. Resident Population by Race, Hispanic Origin, and Single Years of Age: 2009

[In thousands, except as indicated (307,007 represents 307,007,000). As of July 1. For derivation of estimates, see text, this section]

Age	Total	Race						Hispanic origin [1]	Non-Hispanic White alone
		White alone	Black or African American alone	American Indian, Alaska Native alone	Asian alone	Native Hawaiian and Other Pacific Islander alone	Two or more races		
Total.............	307,007	244,298	39,641	3,151	14,014	578	5,324	48,419	199,851
Under 5 years old	21,300	15,875	3,230	298	1,006	53	838	5,485	11,016
Under 1 year old	4,261	3,163	656	62	198	11	173	1,105	2,187
1 year old.........	4,298	3,183	664	62	206	11	172	1,124	2,190
2 years old.........	4,336	3,226	662	62	204	11	171	1,126	2,228
3 years old.........	4,224	3,163	631	57	198	10	164	1,082	2,202
4 years old.........	4,181	3,140	616	56	200	10	158	1,048	2,208
5 to 9 years old	20,610	15,640	2,987	255	949	48	729	4,792	11,275
5 years old.........	4,186	3,169	599	53	199	10	155	1,015	2,251
6 years old.........	4,139	3,143	588	52	196	10	149	987	2,243
7 years old.........	4,108	3,120	595	51	188	9	145	963	2,238
8 years old.........	4,167	3,160	612	51	191	10	144	949	2,293
9 years old.........	4,010	3,048	593	48	174	9	136	878	2,250
10 to 14 years old	19,974	15,210	3,030	240	844	44	605	4,060	11,516
10 years old.........	3,946	3,004	588	48	167	9	130	827	2,254
11 years old.........	3,941	2,997	596	47	168	9	125	813	2,258
12 years old.........	3,957	3,013	598	47	169	9	119	805	2,281
13 years old.........	4,033	3,077	611	48	172	9	117	808	2,341
14 years old.........	4,096	3,119	637	49	169	9	113	807	2,383
15 to 19 years old	21,538	16,386	3,457	272	853	47	522	4,032	12,707
15 years old.........	4,134	3,138	658	51	168	9	109	801	2,407
16 years old.........	4,225	3,205	683	53	169	9	106	804	2,472
17 years old.........	4,307	3,276	692	55	170	9	104	808	2,539
18 years old.........	4,389	3,345	705	56	171	10	102	808	2,608
19 years old.........	4,484	3,422	719	57	175	10	101	811	2,681
20 to 24 years old	21,540	16,610	3,253	274	915	47	440	3,884	13,046
20 years old.........	4,340	3,322	682	56	177	10	94	775	2,613
21 years old.........	4,291	3,301	659	55	177	9	90	774	2,591
22 years old.........	4,266	3,295	642	54	178	9	87	771	2,588
23 years old.........	4,306	3,332	638	55	187	10	85	777	2,618
24 years old.........	4,336	3,361	633	54	195	10	83	787	2,636
25 to 29 years old	21,678	16,761	3,098	260	1,125	50	383	4,150	12,927
25 years old.........	4,264	3,299	617	53	204	10	80	793	2,568
26 years old.........	4,330	3,353	620	54	214	10	79	821	2,594
27 years old.........	4,350	3,364	620	52	227	10	77	840	2,587
28 years old.........	4,380	3,386	620	51	238	10	75	843	2,608
29 years old.........	4,353	3,359	621	50	242	11	71	853	2,570
30 to 34 years old	19,889	15,381	2,715	221	1,229	49	295	4,030	11,646
30 years old.........	4,136	3,191	581	47	241	10	66	817	2,436
31 years old.........	4,013	3,107	551	45	239	10	61	812	2,356
32 years old.........	3,950	3,056	539	45	243	10	58	807	2,309
33 years old.........	3,844	2,971	517	43	248	9	55	798	2,231
34 years old.........	3,945	3,055	527	42	258	9	54	796	2,315
35 to 39 years old	20,538	16,025	2,723	210	1,276	44	260	3,758	12,535
35 years old.........	3,824	2,960	509	41	254	9	52	764	2,249
36 years old.........	3,909	3,021	529	41	258	9	51	759	2,316
37 years old.........	4,093	3,186	546	42	258	9	52	750	2,490
38 years old.........	4,316	3,391	568	43	252	9	53	742	2,703
39 years old.........	4,396	3,467	571	43	255	9	52	743	2,778
40 to 44 years old	20,992	16,684	2,715	205	1,117	40	230	3,306	13,616
40 years old.........	4,156	3,293	526	41	239	8	48	689	2,654
41 years old.........	4,077	3,226	528	40	230	8	45	674	2,601
42 years old.........	4,084	3,254	525	40	213	8	44	647	2,654
43 years old.........	4,196	3,336	551	41	215	8	45	646	2,737
44 years old.........	4,479	3,575	585	44	220	8	47	651	2,971
45 to 49 years old	22,831	18,478	2,834	215	1,032	39	232	2,894	15,794
45 years old.........	4,543	3,650	576	44	218	8	47	626	3,070
46 years old.........	4,524	3,647	565	43	215	8	47	594	3,097
47 years old.........	4,535	3,680	558	43	200	8	46	573	3,148
48 years old.........	4,576	3,728	557	42	195	8	46	548	3,220
49 years old.........	4,653	3,772	579	43	204	8	47	552	3,260

See footnote at end of table.

U.S. Census Bureau, Statistical Abstract of the United States: 2011

Table 10. Resident Population by Race, Hispanic Origin, and Single Years of Age: 2009—Con.

[In thousands, except as indicated (307,007 represents 307,007,000). As of July 1. For derivation of estimates, see text, this section]

| Age | Total | Race | | | | | | Hispanic origin [1] | Non-Hispanic White alone |
		White alone	Black or African American alone	American Indian, Alaska Native alone	Asian alone	Native Hawaiian and Other Pacific Islander alone	Two or more races		
50 to 54 years old	21,761	17,833	2,573	192	921	32	210	2,274	15,727
50 years old...........	4,460	3,638	541	40	189	7	44	498	3,177
51 years old...........	4,456	3,647	529	40	189	7	44	473	3,210
52 years old...........	4,397	3,607	520	39	182	6	42	454	3,187
53 years old...........	4,218	3,462	493	37	180	6	41	429	3,065
54 years old...........	4,230	3,477	490	37	180	6	40	420	3,088
55 to 59 years old	18,975	15,738	2,094	157	789	26	170	1,720	14,145
55 years old...........	4,040	3,339	456	35	168	6	37	383	2,985
56 years old...........	3,898	3,235	428	33	162	5	36	359	2,903
57 years old...........	3,759	3,128	407	31	154	5	33	335	2,818
58 years old...........	3,652	3,034	402	30	148	5	32	323	2,735
59 years old...........	3,626	3,002	401	30	158	5	32	321	2,704
60 to 64 years old	15,812	13,382	1,541	120	616	19	133	1,274	12,198
60 years old...........	3,479	2,910	364	27	143	5	30	289	2,642
61 years old...........	3,438	2,903	341	26	135	4	29	275	2,647
62 years old...........	3,587	3,081	321	26	126	4	30	262	2,838
63 years old...........	2,666	2,252	259	20	108	4	23	230	2,039
64 years old...........	2,642	2,236	257	20	104	3	22	218	2,032
65 to 69 years old	11,784	10,068	1,092	82	437	13	92	891	9,235
65 years old...........	2,588	2,209	240	18	97	3	21	202	2,020
66 years old...........	2,656	2,288	236	18	90	3	21	191	2,110
67 years old...........	2,329	1,992	213	16	87	3	18	174	1,830
68 years old...........	2,145	1,828	202	15	82	2	17	163	1,675
69 years old...........	2,067	1,752	201	14	81	2	16	161	1,601
70 to 74 years old	9,008	7,699	843	58	332	10	65	676	7,066
70 years old...........	1,949	1,666	180	13	73	2	14	148	1,527
71 years old...........	1,893	1,617	176	12	70	2	14	142	1,485
72 years old...........	1,765	1,508	165	11	66	2	13	133	1,384
73 years old...........	1,712	1,462	162	11	62	2	12	127	1,343
74 years old...........	1,689	1,446	160	11	60	2	12	126	1,328
75 to 79 years old	7,326	6,339	644	41	246	7	49	509	5,860
75 years old...........	1,529	1,310	143	9	54	2	11	111	1,206
76 years old...........	1,506	1,295	138	9	53	1	10	105	1,197
77 years old...........	1,463	1,268	127	8	48	1	10	101	1,173
78 years old...........	1,422	1,241	117	7	46	1	9	97	1,150
79 years old...........	1,406	1,225	119	7	45	1	9	96	1,135
80 to 84 years old	5,822	5,133	451	27	172	4	35	362	4,792
80 years old...........	1,295	1,135	104	6	40	1	8	85	1,055
81 years old...........	1,249	1,099	98	6	37	1	8	79	1,025
82 years old...........	1,173	1,035	90	5	34	1	7	71	968
83 years old...........	1,083	957	83	5	31	1	6	66	895
84 years old...........	1,023	907	76	5	29	1	6	60	850
85 to 89 years old	3,662	3,277	247	15	100	2	21	207	3,081
90 to 94 years old	1,502	1,357	89	6	40	1	9	82	1,280
95 to 99 years old	402	363	22	2	12	–	3	28	336
100 years old and over ...	64	57	3	–	3	–	1	7	51
Median age (years)	36.8	38.3	31.3	29.5	35.3	29.9	19.7	27.4	41.2

– Represents or rounds to zero. [1] Persons of Hispanic origin may be any race.

Source: U.S. Census Bureau, "Monthly Resident Population Estimates by Age, Sex, Race and Hispanic Origin for the United States: April 1, 2000 to July 1, 2009," June 2010, <http://www.census.gov/popest/national/asrh/2009-nat-res.html>.

Population 15

Table 11. Resident Population Projections by Race, Hispanic-Origin Status, and Age: 2010 and 2015

[In thousands, except as indicated (310,233 represents 310,233,000). As of July 1. Projections are based on assumptions about future births, deaths, and net international migration. More information on methodology and assumptions is available at <http://www.census.gov/population/www/projections/methodstatement.html>. For definition of median, see Guide to Tabular Presentation]

Age group	Total 2010	Total 2015	White alone 2010	White alone 2015	Black or African American alone 2010	Black or African American alone 2015	American Indian and Alaska Native alone 2010	American Indian and Alaska Native alone 2015	Asian alone 2010	Asian alone 2015	Native Hawaiian and Other Pacific Islander alone 2010	Native Hawaiian and Other Pacific Islander alone 2015	Two or more races 2010	Two or more races 2015	Hispanic origin [1] 2010	Hispanic origin [1] 2015	Not Hispanic White alone 2010	Not Hispanic White alone 2015
Total	310,233	325,540	246,630	256,306	39,909	42,137	3,188	3,472	14,415	16,527	592	662	5,499	6,435	49,726	57,711	200,853	203,208
Under 5 years	21,100	22,076	15,944	16,563	3,034	3,191	286	311	943	1,004	53	56	840	951	5,053	5,622	11,375	11,487
5 to 9 years	20,886	21,707	15,888	16,412	3,011	3,084	264	292	927	1,018	49	55	746	845	4,888	5,452	11,448	11,465
10 to 14 years	20,395	21,658	15,560	16,467	3,021	3,080	244	271	894	1,034	45	52	631	754	4,513	5,401	11,440	11,540
15 to 19 years	21,770	21,209	16,570	16,143	3,410	3,096	268	252	932	1,030	48	48	541	639	4,473	5,040	12,472	11,524
20 to 24 years	21,779	22,342	16,731	16,976	3,330	3,449	275	273	938	1,047	47	50	459	546	4,010	4,873	13,049	12,499
25 to 29 years	21,418	22,400	16,544	17,125	3,107	3,374	261	279	1,063	1,106	48	49	395	467	3,887	4,311	12,959	13,160
30 to 34 years	20,400	22,099	15,711	16,915	2,845	3,158	228	264	1,245	1,305	52	52	319	405	4,039	4,166	11,974	13,068
35 to 39 years	20,267	20,841	15,674	15,946	2,691	2,872	210	230	1,376	1,413	47	54	269	325	3,868	4,236	12,078	12,023
40 to 44 years	21,010	20,460	16,610	15,763	2,713	2,690	205	211	1,199	1,476	42	48	241	272	3,431	3,979	13,423	12,062
45 to 49 years	22,596	21,001	18,202	16,561	2,838	2,679	216	204	1,064	1,272	40	43	236	242	3,002	3,491	15,415	13,316
50 to 54 years	22,109	22,367	18,049	17,998	2,650	2,765	200	214	957	1,115	34	40	219	234	2,425	3,036	15,800	15,177
55 to 59 years	19,517	21,682	16,134	17,691	2,170	2,545	165	196	840	1,001	27	34	181	216	1,862	2,450	14,409	15,417
60 to 64 years	16,758	18,861	14,087	15,582	1,671	2,042	130	160	704	875	21	27	145	176	1,417	1,867	12,769	13,849
65 to 69 years	12,261	15,812	10,446	13,285	1,130	1,528	87	123	483	717	15	21	99	138	974	1,387	9,534	11,994
70 to 74 years	9,202	11,155	7,867	9,511	845	990	61	80	350	469	10	14	69	91	710	920	7,201	8,650
75 to 79 years	7,282	7,901	6,331	6,780	619	690	41	53	236	310	7	9	48	60	514	637	5,848	6,183
80 to 84 years	5,733	5,676	5,093	4,957	427	458	26	32	151	186	4	5	33	38	354	424	4,759	4,558
85 to 89 years	3,650	3,786	3,290	3,374	247	271	14	17	78	99	2	3	19	22	195	257	3,106	3,131
90 to 94 years	1,570	1,856	1,423	1,674	106	125	5	7	27	39	1	1	8	10	78	117	1,350	1,564
95 to 99 years	452	546	407	492	35	40	1	2	7	9	–	–	2	3	26	35	383	459
100 years and over	79	105	69	92	8	10	–	–	1	1	–	–	1	1	6	9	63	83
5 to 13 years	37,123	39,011	28,273	29,577	5,412	5,529	459	511	1,636	1,844	85	97	1,259	1,454	8,501	9,786	20,536	20,678
14 to 17 years	16,994	17,019	12,941	12,937	2,619	2,478	205	204	741	818	38	39	450	543	3,595	4,112	9,648	9,175
18 to 24 years	30,713	30,885	23,536	23,483	4,741	4,703	387	374	1,315	1,468	66	70	668	787	5,788	6,869	18,225	17,173
16 years and over	243,639	255,864	196,026	203,643	30,201	32,171	2,343	2,547	11,466	13,267	435	489	3,168	3,747	34,372	40,202	164,202	166,441
18 years and over	235,016	247,434	189,473	197,229	28,844	30,940	2,237	2,446	11,095	12,861	416	470	2,950	3,487	32,576	38,192	159,295	161,868
16 to 64 years	203,410	209,027	161,100	163,478	26,783	28,059	2,108	2,232	10,132	11,437	397	436	2,890	3,384	31,515	36,416	131,959	129,819
55 years and over	76,504	87,381	65,147	73,437	7,258	8,698	531	671	2,877	3,706	87	114	604	755	6,136	8,104	59,421	65,888
65 years and over	40,229	46,837	34,926	40,164	3,418	4,111	235	314	1,333	1,831	39	53	278	363	2,858	3,786	32,243	36,623
75 years and over	18,766	19,870	16,613	17,368	1,442	1,594	87	111	500	645	14	18	110	133	1,173	1,479	15,509	15,978
85 years and over	5,751	6,292	5,189	5,632	397	445	20	26	113	149	3	4	29	36	305	418	4,902	5,238
Median age (years)	36.9	37.1	38.4	38.6	31.7	32.8	29.9	31.1	36.0	37.5	30.5	32.0	19.9	20.2	27.5	27.8	41.3	42.1

– Represents or rounds to zero. [1] Persons of Hispanic origin may be any race.

Source: U.S. Census Bureau, "2008 National Population Projections," August 2008, <http://www.census.gov/population/www/projections/2008projections.html>.

Figure 1.2
Center of Population: 1790 to 2000

[Prior to 1960, excludes Alaska and Hawaii. The median center is located at the intersection of two median lines, a north-south line constructed so that half of the nation's population lives east and half lives west of it, and an east-west line selected so that half of the nation's population lives north and half lives south of it. The mean center of population is that point at which an imaginary, flat, weightless, and rigid map of the United States would balance if weights of identical value were placed on it so that each weight represented the location of one person on the date of the census]

Year	Median center		Mean center		
	Latitude-N	Longitude	Latitude-N	Longitude-W	Approximate location
1790 (August 2)	(NA)	(NA)	39 16 30	76 11 12	In Kent County, MD, 23 miles E of Baltimore MD
1850 (June 1)..	(NA)	(NA)	38 59 00	81 19 00	In Wirt County, WV, 23 miles SE of Parkersburg, WV[1]
1900 (June 1)..	40 03 32	84 49 01	39 09 36	85 48 54	In Bartholomew County, IN, 6 miles SE of Columbus, IN
1950 (April 1)..	40 00 12	84 56 51	38 50 21	88 09 33	In Richland County, IL, 8 miles NNW of Olney, IL
1960 (April 1)..	39 56 25	85 16 60	38 35 58	89 12 35	In Clinton County, IL, 6.5 miles NW of Centralia, IL
1970 (April 1) .	39 47 43	85 31 43	38 27 47	89 42 22	In St. Clair County, IL, 5.3 miles ESE of Mascoutah, IL
1980 (April 1)..	39 18 60	86 08 15	38 08 13	90 34 26	In Jefferson County, MO, .25 mile W of DeSoto, MO
1990 (April 1)..	38 57 55	86 31 53	37 52 20	91 12 55	In Crawford County, MO, 10 miles SE of Steelville, MO
2000 (April 1)..	38 45 23	86 55 51	37 41 49	91 48 34	In Phelps County, MO, 3 miles E of Edgar Springs, MO

NA Not available.   [1]West Virginia was set off from Virginia, Dec. 31, 1862, and admitted as a state, June 19, 1863.

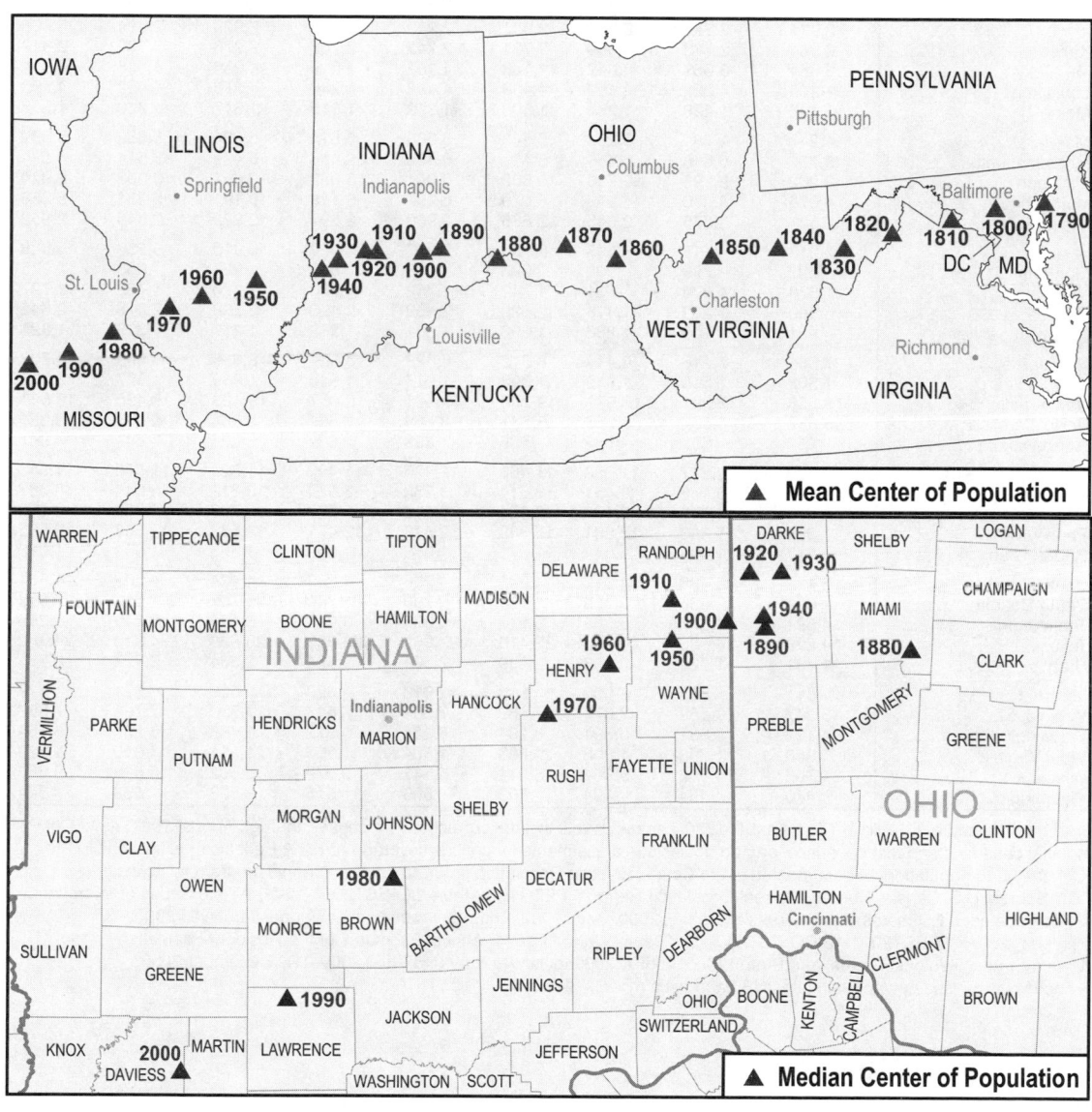

U.S. Census Bureau, Statistical Abstract of the United States: 2011

Table 12. Resident Population—States: 1980 to 2009

[In thousands (226,546 represents 226,546,000). 1980, 1990, and 2000 data as of April 1, data for other years as of July 1. Insofar as possible, population shown for all years is that of present area of state. See Appendix III]

State	1980 [1]	1990, estimates base [2]	2000, estimates base [3]	2004	2005	2006	2007	2008	2009
United States	226,546	248,791	281,425	293,046	295,753	298,593	301,580	304,375	307,007
Alabama	3,894	4,040	4,447	4,512	4,545	4,598	4,638	4,677	4,709
Alaska	402	550	627	662	669	677	682	688	698
Arizona	2,718	3,665	5,131	5,759	5,975	6,192	6,362	6,499	6,596
Arkansas	2,286	2,351	2,673	2,746	2,776	2,815	2,842	2,868	2,889
California	23,668	29,811	33,872	35,558	35,795	35,979	36,226	36,580	36,962
Colorado	2,890	3,294	4,302	4,600	4,661	4,753	4,842	4,935	5,025
Connecticut	3,108	3,287	3,406	3,475	3,477	3,485	3,489	3,503	3,518
Delaware	594	666	784	827	840	853	865	876	885
District of Columbia	638	607	572	580	582	584	586	590	600
Florida	9,746	12,938	15,983	17,375	17,784	18,089	18,278	18,424	18,538
Georgia	5,463	6,478	8,187	8,914	9,097	9,330	9,534	9,698	9,829
Hawaii	965	1,108	1,212	1,253	1,266	1,276	1,277	1,287	1,295
Idaho	944	1,007	1,294	1,392	1,426	1,464	1,499	1,528	1,546
Illinois.	11,427	11,431	12,420	12,645	12,674	12,718	12,779	12,843	12,910
Indiana.	5,490	5,544	6,081	6,214	6,253	6,302	6,346	6,388	6,423
Iowa	2,914	2,777	2,926	2,941	2,949	2,964	2,979	2,994	3,008
Kansas.	2,364	2,478	2,689	2,731	2,742	2,756	2,776	2,797	2,819
Kentucky	3,661	3,687	4,042	4,148	4,182	4,219	4,256	4,288	4,314
Louisiana	4,206	4,222	4,469	4,489	4,498	4,240	4,376	4,452	4,492
Maine.	1,125	1,228	1,275	1,308	1,312	1,315	1,317	1,320	1,318
Maryland	4,217	4,781	5,297	5,543	5,583	5,612	5,634	5,659	5,699
Massachusetts.	5,737	6,016	6,349	6,451	6,453	6,466	6,499	6,544	6,594
Michigan	9,262	9,295	9,938	10,089	10,091	10,082	10,051	10,002	9,970
Minnesota	4,076	4,376	4,919	5,079	5,107	5,148	5,191	5,231	5,266
Mississippi	2,521	2,575	2,845	2,886	2,900	2,897	2,922	2,940	2,952
Missouri.	4,917	5,117	5,597	5,758	5,807	5,862	5,910	5,956	5,988
Montana.	787	799	902	926	935	946	957	968	975
Nebraska	1,570	1,578	1,711	1,742	1,752	1,760	1,770	1,782	1,797
Nevada	800	1,202	1,998	2,329	2,409	2,493	2,568	2,616	2,643
New Hampshire.	921	1,109	1,236	1,293	1,301	1,312	1,317	1,322	1,325
New Jersey	7,365	7,748	8,414	8,612	8,622	8,624	8,636	8,663	8,708
New Mexico	1,303	1,515	1,819	1,892	1,917	1,943	1,969	1,987	2,010
New York	17,558	17,991	18,977	19,298	19,331	19,357	19,423	19,468	19,541
North Carolina	5,882	6,632	8,046	8,531	8,669	8,867	9,064	9,247	9,381
North Dakota	653	639	642	636	635	637	638	641	647
Ohio.	10,798	10,847	11,353	11,465	11,475	11,492	11,521	11,528	11,543
Oklahoma	3,025	3,146	3,451	3,514	3,533	3,574	3,612	3,644	3,687
Oregon.	2,633	2,842	3,421	3,574	3,618	3,678	3,733	3,783	3,826
Pennsylvania	11,864	11,883	12,281	12,388	12,418	12,471	12,523	12,566	12,605
Rhode Island	947	1,003	1,048	1,071	1,065	1,060	1,055	1,054	1,053
South Carolina.	3,122	3,486	4,012	4,201	4,256	4,339	4,424	4,503	4,561
South Dakota.	691	696	755	774	780	789	797	805	812
Tennessee	4,591	4,877	5,689	5,917	5,996	6,089	6,173	6,240	6,296
Texas	14,229	16,986	20,852	22,418	22,802	23,369	23,838	24,304	24,782
Utah.	1,461	1,723	2,233	2,439	2,500	2,584	2,664	2,727	2,785
Vermont.	511	563	609	618	619	620	620	621	622
Virginia.	5,347	6,189	7,079	7,469	7,564	7,647	7,720	7,795	7,883
Washington	4,132	4,867	5,894	6,184	6,261	6,372	6,465	6,566	6,664
West Virginia	1,950	1,793	1,808	1,803	1,804	1,807	1,811	1,815	1,820
Wisconsin	4,706	4,892	5,364	5,511	5,541	5,572	5,602	5,628	5,655
Wyoming	470	454	494	503	506	513	523	533	544

[1] See footnote 3, Table 1. [2] The April 1, 1990, census counts include corrections processed through August 1997, results of special censuses and test censuses, and do not include adjustments for census coverage errors. [3] Reflects modifications to the Census 2000 population as documented in the Count Question Resolution program and geographic program revisions.

Source: U.S. Census Bureau, Current Population Reports, P25-1106; "Table CO-EST2001-12-00—Time Series of Intercensal State Population Estimates: April 1, 1990 to April 1, 2000," April 2002, <http://www.census.gov/popest/archives/2000s /vintage_2001/CO-EST2001-12/CO-EST2001-12-00.html>; and "Table 1: Annual Estimates of the Resident Population for the United States, Regions, States, and Puerto Rico: April 1, 2000 to July 1, 2009 (NST-EST2009-01)," December 2009, <http://www.census.gov/popest/states/NST-ann-est.html>.

Table 13. State Population—Rank, Percent Change, and Population Density: 1980 to 2009

[As of April 1, except 2009, as of July 1. Insofar as possible, population shown for all years is that of present area of state. Minus sign (–) indicates decrease. See Appendix III]

State	Rank 1980	Rank 1990	Rank 2000	Rank 2009	Percent change 1980–1990	Percent change 1990–2000	Percent change 2000–2009	Population per square mile of land area [1] 1990	Population per square mile of land area [1] 2000	Population per square mile of land area [1] 2009
United States	(X)	(X)	(X)	(X)	**9.8**	**13.1**	**9.1**	**70.3**	**79.6**	**86.8**
Alabama	22	22	23	23	3.8	10.1	5.9	79.6	87.6	92.8
Alaska	50	49	48	47	36.9	14.0	11.4	1.0	1.1	1.2
Arizona	29	24	20	14	34.8	40.0	28.6	32.3	45.2	58.0
Arkansas	33	33	33	32	2.8	13.7	8.1	45.1	51.3	55.5
California	1	1	1	1	26.0	13.6	9.1	191.1	217.2	237.0
Colorado	28	26	24	22	14.0	30.6	16.8	31.8	41.5	48.4
Connecticut	25	27	29	29	5.8	3.6	3.3	678.5	702.9	726.2
Delaware	47	46	45	45	12.1	17.6	13.0	341.0	401.1	453.1
District of Columbia	(X)	(X)	(X)	(X)	–4.9	–5.7	4.8	9,884.4	9,316.4	9,766.4
Florida	7	4	4	4	32.7	23.5	16.0	239.9	296.4	343.8
Georgia	13	11	10	9	18.6	26.4	20.1	111.9	141.4	169.7
Hawaii	39	41	42	42	14.9	9.3	6.9	172.6	188.6	201.7
Idaho	41	42	39	39	6.7	28.5	19.5	12.2	15.6	18.7
Illinois	5	6	5	5	(Z)	8.6	4.0	205.6	223.4	232.3
Indiana	12	14	14	16	1.0	9.7	5.6	154.6	169.5	179.1
Iowa	27	30	30	30	–4.7	5.4	2.8	49.7	52.4	53.8
Kansas	32	32	32	33	4.8	8.5	4.8	30.3	32.9	34.5
Kentucky	23	23	25	26	0.7	9.6	6.7	92.8	101.7	108.6
Louisiana	19	21	22	25	0.4	5.9	0.5	96.9	102.6	103.1
Maine	38	38	40	41	9.2	3.8	3.4	39.8	41.3	42.7
Maryland	18	19	19	19	13.4	10.8	7.6	489.1	541.9	583.1
Massachusetts	11	13	13	15	4.9	5.5	3.9	767.4	809.8	841.0
Michigan	8	8	8	8	0.4	6.9	0.3	163.6	175.0	175.5
Minnesota	21	20	21	21	7.4	12.4	7.0	55.0	61.8	66.2
Mississippi	31	31	31	31	2.2	10.5	3.8	54.9	60.6	62.9
Missouri	15	15	17	18	4.1	9.3	7.0	74.3	81.2	86.9
Montana	44	44	44	44	1.6	12.9	8.1	5.5	6.2	6.7
Nebraska	35	36	38	38	0.5	8.4	5.0	20.5	22.3	23.4
Nevada	43	39	35	35	50.1	66.3	32.3	10.9	18.2	24.1
New Hampshire	42	40	41	40	20.5	11.4	7.2	123.7	137.8	147.7
New Jersey	9	9	9	11	5.2	8.6	3.5	1,044.5	1,134.4	1,174.0
New Mexico	37	37	36	36	16.3	20.1	10.5	12.5	15.0	16.6
New York	2	2	3	3	2.5	5.5	3.0	381.0	401.9	413.9
North Carolina	10	10	11	10	12.8	21.4	16.6	136.2	165.2	192.6
North Dakota	46	47	47	48	–2.1	0.5	0.7	9.3	9.3	9.4
Ohio	6	7	7	7	0.5	4.7	1.7	264.9	277.3	281.9
Oklahoma	26	28	27	28	4.0	9.7	6.9	45.8	50.3	53.7
Oregon	30	29	28	27	7.9	20.4	11.8	29.6	35.6	39.9
Pennsylvania	4	5	6	6	0.0	0.4	1.0	265.1	274.0	281.3
Rhode Island	40	43	43	43	5.9	4.5	0.5	960.3	1,003.2	1,007.9
South Carolina	24	25	26	24	11.7	15.1	13.7	115.8	133.2	151.5
South Dakota	45	45	46	46	0.8	8.5	7.6	9.2	9.9	10.7
Tennessee	17	17	16	17	6.2	16.7	10.7	118.3	138.0	152.8
Texas	3	3	2	2	19.4	22.8	18.8	64.9	79.6	94.7
Utah	36	35	34	34	17.9	29.6	24.7	21.0	27.2	33.9
Vermont	48	48	49	49	10.0	8.2	2.1	60.8	65.8	67.2
Virginia	14	12	12	12	15.8	14.4	11.4	156.3	178.8	199.1
Washington	20	18	15	13	17.8	21.1	13.1	73.1	88.6	100.1
West Virginia	34	34	37	37	–8.0	0.8	0.6	74.5	75.1	75.6
Wisconsin	16	16	18	20	4.0	9.6	5.4	90.1	98.8	104.1
Wyoming	49	50	50	50	–3.4	8.9	10.2	4.7	5.1	5.6

X Not applicable. Z Less than 0.05 percent. [1] Persons per square mile were calculated on the basis of land area data from the 2000 census.

Source: U.S. Census Bureau, Current Population Reports, P25-1106; "ST-99-3 State Population Estimates: Annual Time Series, July 1, 1990 to July 1, 1999," December 1999, <http://www.census.gov/population/estimates/state/st-99-3.txt>; "Table CO-EST2001-12-00—Time Series of Intercensal State Population Estimates: April 1, 1990 to April 1, 2000," April 2002, <http://www.census.gov/popest/archives/2000s/vintage_2001/CO-EST2001-12/CO-EST2001-12-00.html>; and "Table 2: Cumulative Estimates of Resident Population Change for the United States, Regions, States, and Puerto Rico and Region and State Rankings: April 1, 2000 to July 1, 2009 (NST-EST2009-02)," December 2009, <http://www.census.gov/popest/states/NST-pop-chg.html>.

Table 14. State Resident Population—Projections: 2010 to 2030

[In thousands (4,596 represents 4,596,000) As of July 1. These state projections were produced in correspondence with the U.S. interim projections released in March 2004. Projections in this table were developed for each of the 50 states and the District of Columbia by age and sex for the years 2000 to 2030, based on Census 2000 results. These projections differ from forecasts in that they represent the results of the mathematical projection model given that current state-specific trends in fertility, mortality, domestic migration, and net international migration continue. The projections to 2009 have been superseded by population estimates which are shown in Table 12. Minus sign (–) indicates decrease]

State	Number (1,000)					Change, 2000 to 2030		Rank	
	2010	2015	2020	2025	2030	Number (1,000)	Percent	Total popula-tion, 2030	Percent change, 2000 to 2030
Alabama	4,596	4,663	4,729	4,800	4,874	427	9.6	24	35
Alaska	694	733	774	821	868	241	38.4	46	12
Arizona	6,637	7,495	8,456	9,532	10,712	5,582	108.8	10	2
Arkansas	2,875	2,969	3,060	3,151	3,240	567	21.2	32	21
California	38,067	40,123	42,207	44,305	46,445	12,573	37.1	1	13
Colorado	4,832	5,049	5,279	5,523	5,792	1,491	34.7	22	14
Connecticut	3,577	3,635	3,676	3,691	3,689	283	8.3	30	38
Delaware	884	927	963	991	1,013	229	29.2	45	18
District of Columbia	530	508	481	455	433	–139	–24.2	(X)	(X)
Florida	19,252	21,204	23,407	25,912	28,686	12,703	79.5	3	3
Georgia	9,589	10,231	10,844	11,439	12,018	3,831	46.8	8	8
Hawaii	1,341	1,386	1,412	1,439	1,466	255	21.0	41	22
Idaho	1,517	1,630	1,741	1,853	1,970	676	52.2	37	6
Illinois	12,917	13,097	13,237	13,341	13,433	1,014	8.2	5	39
Indiana	6,392	6,518	6,627	6,721	6,810	730	12.0	18	31
Iowa	3,010	3,026	3,020	2,993	2,955	29	1.0	34	48
Kansas	2,805	2,853	2,891	2,919	2,940	252	9.4	35	36
Kentucky	4,265	4,351	4,424	4,490	4,555	513	12.7	27	30
Louisiana	4,613	4,674	4,719	4,762	4,803	334	7.5	26	41
Maine	1,357	1,389	1,409	1,414	1,411	136	10.7	42	32
Maryland	5,905	6,208	6,498	6,763	7,022	1,726	32.6	16	16
Massachusetts	6,649	6,759	6,856	6,939	7,012	663	10.4	17	33
Michigan	10,429	10,599	10,696	10,714	10,694	756	7.6	11	40
Minnesota	5,421	5,668	5,901	6,109	6,306	1,387	28.2	20	20
Mississippi	2,971	3,014	3,045	3,069	3,092	248	8.7	33	37
Missouri	5,922	6,070	6,200	6,315	6,430	835	14.9	19	27
Montana	969	999	1,023	1,037	1,045	143	15.8	44	25
Nebraska	1,769	1,789	1,803	1,813	1,820	109	6.4	38	42
Nevada	2,691	3,058	3,452	3,863	4,282	2,284	114.3	28	1
New Hampshire	1,386	1,457	1,525	1,586	1,646	411	33.2	40	15
New Jersey	9,018	9,256	9,462	9,637	9,802	1,388	16.5	13	24
New Mexico	1,980	2,042	2,084	2,107	2,100	281	15.4	36	26
New York	19,444	19,547	19,577	19,540	19,477	501	2.6	4	46
North Carolina	9,346	10,011	10,709	11,449	12,228	4,178	51.9	7	7
North Dakota	637	635	630	621	607	–36	–5.5	49	50
Ohio	11,576	11,635	11,644	11,606	11,551	197	1.7	9	47
Oklahoma	3,592	3,662	3,736	3,821	3,913	463	13.4	29	29
Oregon	3,791	4,013	4,260	4,536	4,834	1,413	41.3	25	10
Pennsylvania	12,584	12,711	12,787	12,802	12,768	487	4.0	6	45
Rhode Island	1,117	1,140	1,154	1,158	1,153	105	10.0	43	34
South Carolina	4,447	4,642	4,823	4,990	5,149	1,137	28.3	23	19
South Dakota	786	797	802	802	800	46	6.0	47	43
Tennessee	6,231	6,502	6,781	7,073	7,381	1,691	29.7	15	17
Texas	24,649	26,586	28,635	30,865	33,318	12,466	59.8	2	4
Utah	2,595	2,783	2,990	3,226	3,485	1,252	56.1	31	5
Vermont	653	673	691	703	712	103	16.9	48	23
Virginia	8,010	8,467	8,917	9,364	9,825	2,747	38.8	12	11
Washington	6,542	6,951	7,432	7,996	8,625	2,731	46.3	14	9
West Virginia	1,829	1,823	1,801	1,766	1,720	–88	–4.9	39	49
Wisconsin	5,727	5,883	6,005	6,088	6,151	787	14.7	21	28
Wyoming	520	528	531	529	523	29	5.9	50	44

X Not applicable.

Source: U.S. Census Bureau, "Table A1: Interim Projections of the Total Population for the United States and States: April 1, 2000 to July 1, 2030," April 2005, <http://www.census.gov/population/www/projections/projectionsagesex.html>.

Table 15. State Resident Population—Components of Change: 2000 to 2009

[Covers period April 1, 2000, to July 1, 2009. Minus sign (–) indicates net decrease or net outflow]

State	Numeric population change [1]	Births	Deaths	Natural increase (births minus deaths)	Net migration Total	Net migration Inter-national [2]	Net migration Domestic
United States	25,581,948	38,358,804	22,483,225	15,875,579	8,944,170	8,944,170	(X)
Alabama	261,326	566,363	427,844	138,519	136,452	50,742	85,710
Alaska	71,542	97,287	28,894	68,393	–724	8,308	–9,032
Arizona	1,465,171	875,726	411,488	464,238	986,764	272,410	714,354
Arkansas	216,064	361,135	258,324	102,811	112,923	36,478	76,445
California	3,090,016	5,058,440	2,179,958	2,878,482	306,925	1,816,633	–1,509,708
Colorado	722,733	641,107	272,191	368,916	357,683	144,861	212,822
Connecticut	112,681	388,331	271,426	116,905	16,608	112,936	–96,328
Delaware	101,565	106,409	66,314	40,095	66,047	19,523	46,524
District of Columbia	27,602	73,986	50,911	23,075	–17,427	24,179	–41,606
Florida	2,555,130	2,046,244	1,566,658	479,586	2,034,234	851,260	1,182,974
Georgia	1,642,430	1,301,426	616,981	684,445	849,133	281,998	567,135
Hawaii	83,640	168,965	83,575	85,390	5,843	38,951	–33,108
Idaho	251,846	211,735	95,443	116,292	134,462	22,121	112,341
Illinois.	490,751	1,681,839	960,627	721,212	–228,888	403,978	–632,866
Indiana.	342,593	810,225	512,148	298,077	71,633	93,367	–21,734
Iowa.	81,476	361,766	255,370	106,396	–15,876	36,329	–52,205
Kansas.	129,936	370,672	225,837	144,835	–17,574	52,388	–69,962
Kentucky	271,825	519,005	370,888	148,117	126,831	44,314	82,517
Louisiana.	23,104	595,844	382,645	213,199	–285,765	33,046	–318,811
Maine.	43,386	128,319	116,170	12,149	38,804	8,079	30,725
Maryland	402,934	698,269	405,035	293,234	95,290	191,262	–95,972
Massachusetts.	244,468	729,448	508,747	220,701	–31,623	245,145	–276,768
Michigan	31,235	1,196,297	802,544	393,753	–372,082	168,668	–540,750
Minnesota	346,722	654,294	348,464	305,830	62,426	106,388	–43,962
Mississippi	107,330	403,008	263,192	139,816	–18,973	17,572	–36,545
Missouri.	390,896	726,153	507,227	218,926	105,461	63,420	42,041
Montana.	72,799	108,579	77,395	31,184	42,980	3,042	39,938
Nebraska.	85,354	241,832	139,626	102,206	–9,156	31,988	–41,144
Nevada	644,825	333,232	165,152	168,080	485,443	110,681	374,762
New Hampshire.	88,784	135,471	92,897	42,574	53,460	18,373	35,087
New Jersey	293,361	1,038,937	664,523	374,414	–60,000	399,803	–459,803
New Mexico.	190,630	265,766	136,175	129,591	70,558	47,343	23,215
New York	564,642	2,323,103	1,417,221	905,882	–846,993	839,590	–1,686,583
North Carolina	1,334,478	1,143,251	685,324	457,927	889,589	214,573	675,016
North Dakota	4,649	76,697	53,637	23,060	–15,217	4,568	–19,785
Ohio.	189,495	1,389,016	999,895	389,121	–247,751	120,452	–368,203
Oklahoma	236,412	481,766	325,299	156,467	92,977	53,514	39,463
Oregon.	404,220	433,972	284,372	149,600	274,031	95,484	178,547
Pennsylvania	323,696	1,350,244	1,183,448	166,796	136,359	176,498	–40,139
Rhode Island	4,894	115,762	89,989	25,773	–14,632	30,017	–41,610
South Carolina.	549,410	537,443	355,877	181,566	376,441	65,869	310,572
South Dakota.	57,548	105,163	64,270	40,893	13,367	6,545	6,822
Tennessee	606,978	754,589	525,554	229,035	356,078	91,508	264,570
Texas	3,930,484	3,568,617	1,444,493	2,124,124	1,781,785	933,083	848,702
Utah.	551,368	479,519	124,262	355,257	118,543	65,961	52,582
Vermont.	12,939	59,886	47,266	12,620	3,877	5,001	–1,124
Virginia.	803,542	957,904	532,166	425,738	375,639	204,219	171,420
Washington	770,052	772,324	424,029	348,295	440,958	202,442	238,546
West Virginia	11,433	192,926	193,308	–382	21,653	5,635	16,018
Wisconsin	291,066	654,879	429,869	225,010	59,904	70,347	–10,443
Wyoming	50,487	65,633	38,277	27,356	25,660	3,278	22,382

X Not applicable. [1] Total population change includes a residual. This residual represents the change in population that cannot be attributed to any specific demographic component. [2] Net international migration includes the international migration of both native and foreign-born populations. Specifically, it includes: (a) the net international migration of the foreign born, (b) the net migration between the United States and Puerto Rico, (c) the net migration of natives to and from the United States, and (d) the net movement of the Armed Forces population between the United States and overseas.

Source: U.S. Census Bureau, "Cumulative Estimates of the Components of Resident Population Change for the United States, Regions, States, and Puerto Rico: April 1, 2000 to July 1, 2009 (NST-EST2009-04)," December 2009, <http://www.census.gov/popest/states/tables/NST-EST2009-04.xls>.

Table 16. Resident Population by Age and State: 2009

[In thousands, except percent (307,007 represents 307,007,000). As of July. Includes Armed Forces stationed in area]

State	Total	Under 5 years	5 to 17 years	18 to 24 years	25 to 34 years	35 to 44 years	45 to 54 years	55 to 64 years	65 to 74 years	75 to 84 years	85 years and over	Percent 65 years old and over
U.S.	307,007	21,300	53,249	30,412	41,566	41,530	44,592	34,787	20,792	13,148	5,631	12.9
AL	4,709	315	814	465	619	616	675	553	353	216	82	13.8
AK	698	54	129	80	106	91	106	79	33	15	5	7.6
AZ	6,596	518	1,214	611	957	870	858	701	454	293	120	13.1
AR	2,889	205	505	273	389	367	399	337	221	136	57	14.3
CA	36,962	2,754	6,682	3,746	5,385	5,219	5,200	3,828	2,179	1,366	603	11.2
CO.....	5,025	364	863	501	734	711	745	573	296	170	67	10.6
CT	3,518	210	598	341	411	488	562	420	248	163	77	13.9
DE	885	60	147	84	115	117	130	105	68	42	16	14.3
DC	600	37	77	72	113	85	78	67	38	23	10	11.7
FL	18,538	1,166	2,892	1,667	2,357	2,432	2,643	2,185	1,561	1,120	515	17.2
GA	9,829	751	1,833	980	1,393	1,438	1,386	1,034	579	317	120	10.3
HI......	1,295	89	201	125	191	169	176	155	90	66	32	14.5
ID......	1,546	125	294	161	210	190	206	172	102	60	25	12.1
IL	12,910	894	2,283	1,299	1,783	1,762	1,878	1,417	836	525	234	12.4
IN......	6,423	446	1,144	644	839	850	939	733	437	274	118	12.9
IA......	3,008	204	509	321	367	368	440	355	217	151	76	14.8
KS	2,819	205	500	307	369	349	404	317	183	124	60	13.0
KY	4,314	288	726	416	579	583	635	515	312	185	73	13.2
LA	4,492	319	804	478	625	562	643	508	300	184	70	12.3
ME	1,318	71	200	118	150	173	217	184	108	69	28	15.6
MD.....	5,699	381	971	548	757	800	887	662	380	226	89	12.2
MA.....	6,594	386	1,047	668	856	932	1,028	783	451	302	142	13.6
MI......	9,970	616	1,734	995	1,203	1,334	1,538	1,210	712	444	183	13.4
MN.....	5,266	364	897	526	700	695	811	603	346	219	106	12.7
MS	2,952	223	545	314	393	369	406	325	203	124	50	12.8
MO.....	5,988	404	1,028	592	786	769	890	697	431	272	119	13.7
MT.....	975	62	157	104	120	112	148	129	75	46	20	14.6
NE	1,797	135	317	197	232	219	254	202	119	82	40	13.4
NV	2,643	204	477	229	394	376	362	295	178	96	32	11.6
NH	1,325	75	214	130	150	184	223	169	95	59	25	13.5
NJ	8,708	555	1,491	756	1,110	1,253	1,367	1,002	607	395	172	13.5
NM.....	2,010	152	358	202	278	245	279	234	140	87	35	13.0
NY	19,541	1,223	3,201	1,924	2,649	2,703	2,943	2,279	1,358	875	387	13.4
NC	9,381	665	1,613	942	1,235	1,318	1,334	1,080	654	389	149	12.7
ND	647	43	101	89	82	72	92	74	44	33	17	14.7
OH	11,543	740	1,975	1,084	1,478	1,520	1,754	1,386	836	542	227	13.9
OK	3,687	272	647	387	505	452	512	416	264	163	69	13.5
OR	3,826	248	625	364	525	503	550	493	275	167	74	13.5
PA	12,605	747	2,028	1,220	1,538	1,649	1,933	1,543	954	683	309	15.4
RI......	1,053	60	167	112	132	143	163	126	73	52	25	14.3
SC	4,561	311	770	453	599	601	647	557	344	202	77	13.7
SD	812	60	140	88	103	93	116	96	58	40	20	14.5
TN	6,296	426	1,068	585	849	862	915	752	465	271	105	13.4
TX	24,782	2,074	4,822	2,523	3,648	3,417	3,327	2,432	1,383	825	331	10.3
UT	2,785	274	595	342	442	334	313	234	136	83	32	9.0
VT	622	32	94	69	69	79	102	86	48	29	12	14.5
VA	7,883	533	1,314	815	1,085	1,110	1,165	901	531	310	119	12.2
WA.....	6,664	451	1,119	645	949	906	987	802	437	256	113	12.1
WV.....	1,820	106	280	170	225	234	270	246	153	97	38	15.8
WI	5,655	364	946	591	707	742	874	669	390	256	115	13.5
WY	544	40	92	60	75	64	80	67	37	22	9	12.3

Source: U.S. Census Bureau, "Annual Estimates of the Resident Population by Sex and Age for States and for Puerto Rico: April 1, 2000 to July 1, 2009," June 2010, <http://www.census.gov/popest/states/asrh/SC-EST2009-02.html>.

Table 17. Age Dependency Ratios by State: 2000 and 2009

[2000, as of April; 2009, as of July]

State	Age dependency ratio [1]		Child dependency ratio [2]		Old-age dependency ratio [3]	
	2000	2009	2000	2009	2000	2009
United States	61.6	59.2	41.5	38.6	20.1	20.5
Alabama	62.1	60.8	40.9	38.5	21.1	22.2
Alaska	56.5	51.2	47.6	39.7	8.9	11.4
Arizona	65.7	65.0	44.2	43.3	21.6	21.7
Arkansas	65.1	63.6	42.0	40.2	23.1	23.4
California	61.1	58.1	44.0	40.4	17.1	17.7
Colorado	54.5	54.0	39.5	37.6	14.9	16.4
Connecticut	62.7	58.3	40.2	36.4	22.5	22.0
Delaware	60.8	60.5	39.9	37.5	20.9	23.0
District of Columbia	47.8	44.3	29.7	27.5	18.1	16.9
Florida	67.7	64.3	38.3	36.0	29.5	28.3
Georgia	56.5	57.8	41.5	41.5	15.0	16.3
Hawaii	60.4	58.6	39.2	35.6	21.3	23.0
Idaho	66.1	64.6	47.4	44.6	18.7	20.0
Illinois.	61.8	58.6	42.3	39.0	19.5	19.6
Indiana.	62.0	60.4	41.9	39.7	20.1	20.7
Iowa.	66.6	62.6	41.8	38.5	24.8	24.0
Kansas.	66.0	61.4	44.0	40.4	22.0	21.0
Kentucky	59.0	58.1	39.1	37.2	19.9	20.9
Louisiana	63.6	59.6	44.6	39.9	18.9	19.7
Maine.	61.3	56.7	38.1	32.2	23.2	24.4
Maryland	58.5	56.0	40.6	37.0	17.9	19.0
Massachusetts.	59.2	54.6	37.6	33.6	21.6	21.0
Michigan	62.3	58.8	42.4	37.4	19.9	21.3
Minnesota	61.9	57.9	42.4	37.8	19.6	20.1
Mississippi	64.8	63.3	44.9	42.5	19.9	20.9
Missouri.	64.0	60.4	41.8	38.3	22.1	22.0
Montana.	63.7	59.0	41.7	35.8	21.9	23.1
Nebraska.	66.3	62.7	43.8	40.9	22.6	21.8
Nevada	57.7	59.7	40.4	41.1	17.3	18.5
New Hampshire.	58.8	54.7	39.8	33.8	19.0	20.9
New Jersey	61.4	58.6	40.0	37.3	21.4	21.4
New Mexico.	65.6	62.3	46.3	41.2	19.3	21.1
New York	60.3	56.4	39.6	35.4	20.7	21.0
North Carolina	57.4	58.7	38.4	38.5	19.0	20.2
North Dakota	66.0	58.5	41.6	35.3	24.4	23.3
Ohio.	63.2	59.8	41.5	37.6	21.7	22.2
Oklahoma	64.1	62.3	42.4	40.4	21.7	21.8
Oregon.	60.1	57.0	39.6	35.8	20.5	21.2
Pennsylvania	65.1	59.9	39.3	35.2	25.8	24.7
Rhode Island	61.8	55.8	38.2	33.6	23.5	22.3
South Carolina.	59.4	59.6	40.1	37.8	19.3	21.8
South Dakota.	70.0	64.1	45.6	40.3	24.4	23.8
Tennessee	58.6	58.9	39.0	37.7	19.6	21.2
Texas	61.7	61.5	45.7	44.9	16.1	16.5
Utah.	68.6	67.3	54.3	52.2	14.4	15.1
Vermont.	58.6	53.3	38.4	31.1	20.2	22.2
Virginia.	55.6	55.3	38.2	36.4	17.4	18.9
Washington	58.5	55.4	40.7	36.6	17.8	18.8
West Virginia	60.2	58.8	35.6	33.7	24.5	25.1
Wisconsin	62.9	57.8	41.6	36.6	21.3	21.2
Wyoming	60.7	57.6	41.9	38.2	18.8	19.4

[1] The age dependency ratio is derived by dividing the combined under 18 and 65-and-over populations by the 18-to-64 population and multiplying by 100. [2] The child dependency ratio is derived by dividing the population under 18 by the 18-to-64 population and multiplying by 100. [3] The old-age dependency ratio is derived by dividing the population 65 and over by the 18-to-64 population and multiplying by 100.

Source: U.S. Census Bureau, Table GCT-T6-R "Age Dependency Ratio of the Total Population"; Table GCT-T7-R "Child Dependency Ratio of the Total Population"; and Table GCT-T8-R "Old-Age Dependency Ratio of the Total Population," <http://factfinder.census.gov/>, accessed July 2010.

Population 23

Table 18. Resident Population by Age and State—Projections: 2010 and 2015

[In thousands (1,092 represents 1,092,000). As of July 1. These projections were produced in correspondence with the U.S. interim projections released in March 2004. Projections in this table were developed for each of the 50 states and the District of Columbia by age and sex for the years 2000 to 2030, based on Census 2000 results. These projections differ from forecasts in that they represent the results of the mathematical projection model given that current state-specific trends in fertility, mortality, domestic migration and net international migration continue. The projections to 2009 have been superseded by population estimates which are shown in Table 16]

| State | Population (1,000) | | | | | | | | | | Percent of population, 2015 | |
| | Under 18 years old | | 18 to 44 years old | | 45 to 64 years old | | 65 to 74 years old | | 75 years old and over | | Under 18 years old | 65 years old and over |
	2010	2015	2010	2015	2010	2015	2010	2015	2010	2015		
AL	1,092	1,089	1,605	1,575	1,251	1,259	354	427	295	312	23.4	15.9
AK	184	199	270	280	184	178	35	49	21	26	27.2	10.2
AZ	1,688	1,892	2,349	2,529	1,678	1,892	516	711	406	470	25.2	15.8
AR	703	721	996	998	765	782	227	274	185	194	24.3	15.8
CA	9,497	9,820	14,787	15,240	9,391	9,835	2,333	2,972	2,060	2,256	24.5	13.0
CO	1,189	1,256	1,863	1,886	1,263	1,280	282	369	235	258	24.9	12.4
CT	814	807	1,257	1,251	990	1,001	253	308	262	270	22.2	15.9
DE	202	210	309	305	249	264	68	87	57	61	22.6	16.0
DC	114	112	237	225	118	108	32	34	29	27	22.1	12.2
FL	4,086	4,455	6,315	6,614	5,431	6,002	1,773	2,345	1,646	1,789	21.0	19.5
GA	2,502	2,679	3,724	3,822	2,382	2,543	564	723	417	464	26.2	11.6
HI	316	330	477	479	357	350	101	131	90	96	23.8	16.3
ID	400	427	554	583	381	400	99	129	82	91	26.2	13.5
IL	3,197	3,215	4,842	4,798	3,277	3,307	826	979	774	799	24.5	13.6
IN	1,596	1,614	2,328	2,333	1,656	1,664	425	508	386	398	24.8	13.9
IA	711	707	1,049	1,031	800	794	217	259	233	236	23.4	16.3
KS	699	708	1,004	1,001	727	724	185	225	190	194	24.8	14.7
KY	1,002	1,007	1,540	1,526	1,165	1,181	309	376	249	262	23.1	14.6
LA	1,172	1,176	1,665	1,642	1,194	1,192	313	379	270	285	25.2	14.2
ME	269	269	462	455	413	415	110	142	102	108	19.3	18.0
MD	1,406	1,487	2,212	2,283	1,568	1,601	386	478	332	359	23.9	13.5
MA	1,484	1,474	2,440	2,402	1,817	1,857	454	567	454	458	21.8	15.2
MI	2,487	2,479	3,822	3,799	2,785	2,814	699	852	635	654	23.4	14.2
MN	1,290	1,349	2,027	2,069	1,433	1,475	343	429	327	346	23.8	13.7
MS	759	753	1,052	1,028	781	801	209	254	170	179	25.0	14.4
MO	1,411	1,436	2,111	2,123	1,578	1,589	432	518	390	404	23.7	15.2
MT	212	216	324	326	287	284	77	100	68	74	21.6	17.4
NE	446	454	619	608	460	455	119	145	125	126	25.4	15.2
NV	665	752	961	1,033	735	851	199	264	131	158	24.6	13.8
NH	304	313	494	508	408	418	97	129	82	88	21.5	14.9
NJ	2,088	2,104	3,252	3,239	2,446	2,528	632	760	600	625	22.7	15.0
NM	479	485	669	654	553	560	153	201	126	142	23.7	16.8
NY	4,421	4,353	7,227	7,077	5,144	5,173	1,346	1,589	1,306	1,354	22.3	15.1
NC	2,269	2,438	3,471	3,586	2,445	2,611	641	810	520	565	24.4	13.7
ND	142	139	223	219	174	169	46	56	51	51	21.8	17.0
OH	2,744	2,723	4,123	4,054	3,121	3,093	816	980	771	786	23.4	15.2
OK	895	915	1,264	1,260	938	933	266	316	229	238	25.0	15.1
OR	863	916	1,412	1,470	1,022	1,036	263	348	231	242	22.8	14.7
PA	2,748	2,741	4,385	4,334	3,496	3,487	960	1,159	997	990	21.6	16.9
RI	249	248	410	412	300	304	76	94	82	81	21.8	15.4
SC	1,036	1,061	1,579	1,581	1,226	1,271	343	439	263	290	22.9	15.7
SD	194	196	269	264	209	209	55	67	60	61	24.6	16.1
TN	1,479	1,539	2,249	2,275	1,673	1,720	461	570	368	399	23.7	14.9
TX	6,785	7,376	9,417	9,848	5,859	6,248	1,426	1,826	1,162	1,287	27.7	11.7
UT	819	872	1,021	1,073	520	556	127	162	108	119	31.3	10.1
VT	132	132	232	235	195	193	50	67	43	46	19.6	16.9
VA	1,880	1,982	2,997	3,085	2,139	2,207	554	703	441	490	23.4	14.1
WA	1,488	1,561	2,481	2,591	1,777	1,833	429	567	367	399	22.5	13.9
WV	382	373	618	595	536	525	156	190	136	140	20.4	18.1
WI	1,319	1,343	2,076	2,067	1,561	1,591	392	487	380	395	22.8	15.0
WY	116	115	177	174	154	150	40	52	33	37	21.9	16.8

Source: U.S. Census Bureau, "File 2. Annual projections by 5-year and selected age groups by sex," April 2005, <http://www.census.gov/population/www/projections/projectionsagesex.html>.

U.S. Census Bureau, Statistical Abstract of the United States: 2011

Table 19. Resident Population by Race, Hispanic Origin, and State: 2009

[In thousands (307,007 represents 307,007,000). As of July. Hispanic origin is considered an ethnicity, not a race. Hispanics may be of any race]

State	Total population	One race — White alone	One race — Black or African American alone	One race — American Indian/ Alaska Native alone	One race — Asian alone	One race — Native Hawaiian and Other Pacific Islander alone	Two or more races	Hispanic origin	Non-Hispanic White alone
U.S.	307,007	244,298	39,641	3,151	14,014	578	5,324	48,419	199,851
AL	4,709	3,340	1,241	25	49	2	52	153	3,203
AK	698	491	29	106	35	5	33	44	455
AZ	6,596	5,677	290	321	173	14	121	2,032	3,780
AR	2,889	2,328	455	25	34	3	43	173	2,170
CA	36,962	28,245	2,454	447	4,690	159	966	13,681	15,413
CO	5,025	4,496	222	62	137	8	100	1,018	3,553
CT	3,518	2,956	366	14	127	3	52	434	2,575
DE	885	655	187	3	27	1	13	64	598
DC	600	244	324	2	19	1	10	53	201
FL	18,538	14,726	2,983	94	445	19	271	3,992	11,028
GA	9,829	6,392	2,971	37	290	9	130	820	5,649
HI	1,295	391	42	8	502	119	233	116	324
ID	1,546	1,459	16	24	18	2	26	165	1,306
IL	12,910	10,196	1,927	46	568	9	165	1,969	8,338
IN	6,423	5,638	588	21	94	3	79	351	5,315
IA	3,008	2,825	84	13	50	2	34	134	2,701
KS	2,819	2,495	175	29	65	2	52	263	2,253
KY	4,314	3,866	339	12	46	2	49	115	3,763
LA	4,492	2,903	1,443	29	66	2	49	163	2,760
ME	1,318	1,267	15	8	13	(Z)	14	18	1,251
MD	5,699	3,589	1,691	21	298	5	96	411	3,239
MA	6,594	5,665	469	21	335	6	99	583	5,188
MI	9,970	8,092	1,414	62	242	4	156	421	7,715
MN	5,266	4,665	250	67	199	4	83	226	4,468
MS	2,952	1,785	1,097	16	26	1	28	74	1,720
MO	5,988	5,084	688	31	91	5	88	204	4,901
MT	975	880	7	63	7	1	17	30	854
NE	1,797	1,637	83	20	31	2	24	150	1,499
NV	2,643	2,123	218	40	174	14	74	700	1,476
NH	1,325	1,262	18	4	26	1	14	37	1,229
NJ	8,708	6,599	1,260	32	683	8	126	1,453	5,323
NM	2,010	1,680	63	195	30	3	38	916	822
NY	19,541	14,351	3,352	110	1,388	21	320	3,274	11,710
NC	9,381	6,917	2,028	117	192	7	119	718	6,267
ND	647	589	8	36	5	(Z)	8	15	576
OH	11,543	9,772	1,395	30	185	5	156	326	9,489
OK	3,687	2,876	297	296	60	4	151	302	2,612
OR	3,826	3,436	78	60	143	11	98	428	3,047
PA	12,605	10,742	1,371	29	318	6	140	647	10,196
RI	1,053	930	68	7	29	1	18	128	824
SC	4,561	3,140	1,287	20	60	3	51	207	2,960
SD	812	714	10	69	7	(Z)	12	23	694
TN	6,296	5,049	1,060	22	88	4	74	262	4,817
TX	24,782	20,352	2,977	193	884	32	344	9,148	11,583
UT	2,785	2,580	38	39	57	22	48	343	2,261
VT	622	598	6	2	7	(Z)	7	9	590
VA	7,883	5,735	1,574	30	397	7	140	570	5,228
WA	6,664	5,584	259	117	464	33	207	687	4,973
WV	1,820	1,718	66	4	12	1	18	23	1,697
WI	5,655	5,056	348	57	122	3	69	299	4,785
WY	544	509	8	14	5	1	8	44	469

Z Less than 500.

Source: U.S. Census Bureau, "Annual State Resident Population Estimates for 6 Race Groups (5 Race Alone Groups and One Group with Two or more Race Groups) by Age, Sex, and Hispanic Origin: April 1, 2000 to July 1, 2009," June 2010, <http://www.census.gov/popest/states/asrh/files/SC-EST2009-alldata6-ALL.csv>.

Population   25

Table 20. Large Metropolitan Statistical Areas—Population: 2000 to 2009

[As of April 1; beginning 2005 as of July 1 (695 represents 695,000). Covers metropolitan statistical areas with 250,000 and over population in 2009, as defined by the U.S. Office of Management and Budget as of November 2008. All geographic boundaries for 2000 to 2009 population estimates are defined as of January 1, 2009. For definitions and components of all metropolitan and micropolitan areas, see Appendix II. Minus sign (–) indicates decrease]

| Metropolitan statistical area | Number (1,000) | | | | | | Percent change | Rank, 2009 |
	2000, estimates base [1]	2005	2006	2007	2008	2009	2000 to 2009 [1]	
Akron, OH	695	701	700	701	700	700	0.7	72
Albany–Schenectady–Troy, NY	826	846	851	852	854	858	3.8	58
Albuquerque, NM	730	799	818	835	847	858	17.6	57
Allentown–Bethlehem–Easton, PA–NJ	740	786	796	805	812	816	10.2	62
Anchorage, AK	320	352	359	361	366	375	17.2	135
Ann Arbor, MI	323	344	346	348	345	348	7.7	145
Asheville, NC	369	391	398	404	409	413	11.8	118
Atlanta–Sandy Springs–Marietta, GA	4,248	4,947	5,120	5,268	5,386	5,475	28.9	9
Atlantic City–Hammonton, NJ	253	268	269	270	271	272	7.6	166
Augusta–Richmond County, GA–SC	500	517	523	529	535	539	7.9	95
Austin–Round Rock, TX	1,250	1,464	1,529	1,595	1,654	1,705	36.4	35
Bakersfield, CA	662	747	768	785	797	807	22.0	63
Baltimore–Towson, MD	2,553	2,650	2,662	2,670	2,678	2,691	5.4	20
Baton Rouge, LA	706	730	765	772	779	787	11.5	66
Beaumont–Port Arthur, TX	385	380	373	376	377	378	–1.7	133
Birmingham–Hoover, AL	1,051	1,090	1,104	1,113	1,123	1,131	7.6	47
Boise City–Nampa, ID	465	544	567	586	599	606	30.4	85
Boston–Cambridge–Quincy, MA–NH	4,392	4,459	4,473	4,504	4,545	4,589	4.5	10
Boulder, CO [2]	270	287	291	296	300	303	12.5	154
Bradenton–Sarasota–Venice, FL	590	668	677	683	686	688	16.6	75
Bridgeport–Stamford–Norwalk, CT	883	891	889	889	894	901	2.1	56
Brownsville–Harlingen, TX	335	371	377	383	389	396	18.2	128
Buffalo–Niagara Falls, NY	1,170	1,139	1,131	1,126	1,124	1,124	–4.0	50
Canton–Massillon, OH	407	408	408	409	409	408	0.3	121
Cape Coral–Fort Myers, FL	441	542	566	585	589	587	33.1	86
Cedar Rapids, IA	237	247	249	252	255	256	8.0	175
Charleston, WV	310	304	304	303	303	304	–1.8	153
Charleston–North Charleston–Summerville, SC	549	601	618	632	647	659	20.1	80
Charlotte–Gastonia–Concord, NC–SC	1,331	1,519	1,584	1,651	1,706	1,746	31.2	33
Chattanooga, TN–GA	477	503	511	516	520	524	10.0	98
Chicago–Naperville–Joliet, IL–IN–WI	9,099	9,362	9,399	9,452	9,516	9,581	5.3	3
Cincinnati–Middletown, OH–KY–IN	2,010	2,102	2,123	2,148	2,159	2,172	8.1	24
Clarksville, TN–KY	232	252	253	262	262	269	15.7	167
Cleveland–Elyria–Mentor, OH	2,148	2,118	2,106	2,099	2,094	2,091	–2.6	26
Colorado Springs, CO	537	588	601	607	617	626	16.5	83
Columbia, SC	647	692	705	720	733	745	15.1	69
Columbus, GA–AL	282	288	290	287	287	293	3.9	160
Columbus, OH	1,613	1,714	1,737	1,759	1,780	1,802	11.7	32
Corpus Christi, TX	403	410	412	412	413	416	3.2	116
Dallas–Fort Worth–Arlington, TX	5,162	5,816	5,999	6,157	6,301	6,448	24.9	4
Davenport–Moline–Rock Island, IA–IL	376	373	374	375	377	379	0.8	132
Dayton, OH	848	844	842	840	837	835	–1.5	61
Deltona–Daytona Beach–Ormond Beach, FL	443	486	494	499	497	496	11.9	103
Denver–Aurora–Broomfield, CO [2]	2,179	2,354	2,400	2,449	2,500	2,552	17.1	21
Des Moines–West Des Moines, IA	481	523	534	544	554	563	16.9	90
Detroit–Warren–Livonia, MI	4,453	4,494	4,485	4,457	4,424	4,403	–1.1	11
Duluth, MN–WI	275	274	274	274	275	276	0.3	165
Durham–Chapel Hill, NC	424	458	468	479	491	501	18.3	102
El Paso, TX	680	709	721	728	738	751	10.5	68
Erie, PA	281	279	280	280	280	280	–0.2	163
Eugene–Springfield, OR	323	335	339	345	348	351	8.7	144
Evansville, IN–KY	343	348	349	350	351	352	2.7	143
Fayetteville, NC	337	345	348	351	354	360	7.1	139
Fayetteville–Springdale–Rogers, AR–MO	347	414	430	444	455	465	33.9	108
Flint, MI	436	439	437	434	429	424	–2.8	114
Fort Collins–Loveland, CO	251	275	281	287	293	298	18.6	156
Fort Smith, AR–OK	273	282	286	289	291	293	7.3	159
Fort Wayne, IN	390	403	406	410	412	414	6.2	117
Fresno, CA	799	867	878	890	903	915	14.6	54

See footnotes at end of table.

U.S. Census Bureau, Statistical Abstract of the United States: 2011

Table 20. Large Metropolitan Statistical Areas—Population: 2000 to 2009—Con.

[As of April 1; beginning 2005 as of July 1 (695 represents 695,000). Covers metropolitan statistical areas with 250,000 and over population in 2009, as defined by the U.S. Office of Management and Budget as of November 2008. All geographic boundaries for 2000 to 2009 population estimates are defined as of January 1, 2009. For definitions and components of all metropolitan and micropolitan areas, see Appendix II. Minus sign (–) indicates decrease]

Metropolitan statistical area	Number (1,000)						Percent change	
	2000, estimates base [1]	2005	2006	2007	2008	2009	2000 to 2009 [1]	Rank, 2009
Gainesville, FL	232	248	254	257	259	261	12.2	174
Grand Rapids–Wyoming, MI	740	767	771	775	777	778	5.1	67
Greeley, CO [2]	181	226	234	242	249	255	40.9	177
Green Bay, WI	282	296	298	301	302	305	7.9	152
Greensboro–High Point, NC	643	674	686	696	707	715	11.1	71
Greenville–Mauldin–Easley, SC	560	591	603	617	630	640	14.2	82
Hagerstown–Martinsburg, MD–WV	223	250	256	261	264	266	19.5	170
Harrisburg–Carlisle, PA	509	520	526	530	534	537	5.5	96
Hartford–West Hartford–East Hartford, CT	1,149	1,179	1,183	1,186	1,191	1,196	4.1	45
Hickory–Lenoir–Morganton, NC	342	354	357	360	363	365	6.9	138
Holland–Grand Haven, MI	238	254	257	259	261	262	9.9	173
Honolulu, HI	876	900	903	899	903	908	3.6	55
Houston–Sugar Land–Baytown, TX	4,715	5,300	5,485	5,598	5,727	5,867	24.4	6
Huntington–Ashland, WV–KY–OH	289	285	285	285	285	286	–1.0	162
Huntsville, AL	343	370	379	388	397	406	18.6	125
Indianapolis–Carmel, IN	1,525	1,645	1,672	1,698	1,721	1,744	14.3	34
Jackson, MS	497	521	531	534	537	541	8.8	94
Jacksonville, FL	1,123	1,249	1,279	1,301	1,317	1,328	18.3	40
Kalamazoo–Portage, MI	315	321	322	323	324	327	3.7	148
Kansas City, MO–KS	1,836	1,959	1,985	2,012	2,046	2,068	12.6	29
Killeen–Temple–Fort Hood, TX	331	354	359	372	380	379	14.7	131
Kingsport–Bristol–Bristol, TN–VA	298	300	302	304	305	306	2.4	151
Knoxville, TN	616	658	671	682	692	699	13.5	73
Lafayette, LA	239	247	255	257	260	263	10.2	172
Lakeland–Winter Haven, FL	484	539	557	573	580	583	20.6	87
Lancaster, PA	471	489	494	499	504	508	7.9	101
Lansing–East Lansing, MI	448	456	456	456	455	454	1.3	110
Las Vegas–Paradise, NV	1,376	1,709	1,778	1,839	1,879	1,903	38.3	30
Lexington–Fayette, KY	408	439	448	455	464	471	15.3	106
Lincoln, NE	267	284	287	291	295	298	11.7	157
Little Rock–North Little Rock–Conway, AR	611	646	658	666	676	685	12.3	76
Los Angeles–Long Beach–Santa Ana, CA	12,366	12,761	12,714	12,693	12,768	12,875	4.1	2
Louisville/Jefferson County, KY–IN	1,162	1,209	1,223	1,237	1,250	1,259	8.3	42
Lubbock, TX	250	263	266	269	272	277	10.8	164
Madison, WI	502	540	547	555	562	570	13.6	88
Manchester–Nashua, NH	381	399	401	403	404	406	6.6	127
McAllen–Edinburg–Mission, TX	569	665	684	702	721	741	30.1	70
Memphis, TN–MS–AR	1,205	1,261	1,281	1,291	1,299	1,305	8.3	41
Miami–Fort Lauderdale–Pompano Beach, FL	5,008	5,443	5,467	5,465	5,502	5,547	10.8	7
Milwaukee–Waukesha–West Allis, WI	1,501	1,536	1,540	1,545	1,550	1,560	3.9	39
Minneapolis–St. Paul–Bloomington, MN–WI	2,969	3,133	3,168	3,204	3,238	3,270	10.1	16
Mobile, AL	400	398	402	405	409	412	3.0	119
Modesto, CA	447	499	503	506	507	510	14.2	100
Montgomery, AL	347	356	363	366	366	366	5.7	136
Myrtle Beach–North Myrtle Beach–Conway, SC	197	229	241	251	259	264	34.2	171
Naples–Marco Island, FL	251	307	312	313	316	319	26.7	149
Nashville–Davidson—Murfreesboro—Franklin, TN	1,312	1,451	1,489	1,525	1,556	1,582	20.6	38
New Haven–Milford, CT	824	839	841	844	846	848	2.9	60
New Orleans–Metairie–Kenner, LA	1,317	1,313	988	1,109	1,169	1,190	–9.6	46
New York–Northern New Jersey–Long Island, NY–NJ–PA	18,323	18,798	18,826	18,901	18,969	19,070	4.1	1
Norwich–New London, CT	259	265	268	264	266	267	3.0	169
Ocala, FL	259	302	314	323	327	329	26.9	147
Ogden–Clearfield, UT	443	491	503	517	531	542	22.3	93
Oklahoma City, OK	1,095	1,155	1,175	1,191	1,208	1,227	12.0	44
Olympia, WA	207	228	233	239	246	251	21.0	178
Omaha–Council Bluffs, NE–IA	767	810	820	829	839	850	10.7	59
Orlando–Kissimmee, FL	1,645	1,940	2,000	2,035	2,061	2,082	26.6	27
Oxnard–Thousand Oaks–Ventura, CA	753	786	788	790	795	803	6.6	65
Palm Bay–Melbourne–Titusville, FL	476	526	530	534	536	536	12.6	97
Pensacola–Ferry Pass–Brent, FL	412	445	450	450	453	455	10.4	109
Peoria, IL	367	367	369	371	373	376	2.5	134
Philadelphia–Camden–Wilmington, PA–NJ–DE–MD	5,687	5,851	5,881	5,913	5,940	5,968	4.9	5
Phoenix–Mesa–Scottsdale, AZ	3,252	3,885	4,047	4,176	4,287	4,364	34.2	12
Pittsburgh, PA	2,431	2,372	2,361	2,357	2,355	2,355	–3.1	22

See footnotes at end of table.

Table 20. Large Metropolitan Statistical Areas—Population: 2000 to 2009—Con.

[As of April 1; beginning 2005 as of July 1 (695 represents 695,000). Covers metropolitan statistical areas with 250,000 and over population in 2009, as defined by the U.S. Office of Management and Budget as of November 2008. All geographic boundaries for 2000 to 2009 population estimates are defined as of January 1, 2009. For definitions and components of all metropolitan and micropolitan areas, see Appendix II. Minus sign (−) indicates decrease]

| Metropolitan statistical area | Number (1,000) | | | | | | Percent change | |
	2000, estimates base [1]	2005	2006	2007	2008	2009	2000 to 2009 [1]	Rank, 2009
Portland–South Portland–Biddeford, ME............	488	511	512	514	516	517	6.0	99
Portland–Vancouver–Beaverton, OR–WA...........	1,928	2,084	2,124	2,164	2,204	2,242	16.3	23
Port St. Lucie, FL..................................	319	376	387	399	405	406	27.2	126
Poughkeepsie–Newburgh–Middletown, NY..........	622	662	665	668	672	677	8.9	77
Providence–New Bedford–Fall River, RI–MA	1,583	1,610	1,604	1,599	1,599	1,601	1.1	37
Provo–Orem, UT....................................	377	464	491	522	540	556	47.4	91
Raleigh–Cary, NC	797	953	999	1,046	1,090	1,126	41.2	49
Reading, PA..	374	394	399	402	405	407	9.0	123
Reno–Sparks, NV	343	395	402	411	417	419	22.3	115
Richmond, VA......................................	1,097	1,174	1,196	1,212	1,227	1,238	12.9	43
Riverside–San Bernardino–Ontario, CA	3,255	3,861	3,969	4,049	4,093	4,143	27.3	14
Roanoke, VA.......................................	288	292	295	297	299	300	4.2	155
Rochester, NY.....................................	1,038	1,033	1,031	1,031	1,033	1,036	−0.2	51
Rockford, IL.......................................	320	339	344	351	353	354	10.5	142
Sacramento—Arden–Arcade—Roseville, CA........	1,797	2,029	2,051	2,075	2,101	2,127	18.4	25
St. Louis, MO–IL [3]	2,699	2,773	2,792	2,806	2,819	2,829	4.8	18
Salem, OR...	347	371	379	385	391	396	14.1	129
Salinas, CA	402	405	401	402	406	410	2.1	120
Salt Lake City, UT	969	1,045	1,073	1,093	1,112	1,130	16.7	48
San Antonio, TX...................................	1,712	1,878	1,933	1,985	2,031	2,072	21.1	28
San Diego–Carlsbad–San Marcos, CA..............	2,814	2,942	2,947	2,976	3,019	3,054	8.5	17
San Francisco–Oakland–Fremont, CA	4,124	4,150	4,163	4,202	4,260	4,318	4.7	13
San Jose–Sunnyvale–Santa Clara, CA..............	1,736	1,737	1,755	1,778	1,811	1,840	6.0	31
San Luis Obispo–Paso Robles, CA.................	247	258	259	262	265	267	8.2	168
Santa Barbara–Santa Maria–Goleta, CA	399	400	399	400	404	407	1.9	124
Santa Cruz–Watsonville, CA.......................	256	249	249	250	253	256	0.2	176
Santa Rosa–Petaluma, CA.........................	459	461	460	461	466	472	2.9	105
Savannah, GA.....................................	293	314	321	330	335	343	17.0	146
Scranton—Wilkes–Barre, PA.......................	561	549	548	549	549	549	−2.0	92
Seattle–Tacoma–Bellevue, WA	3,044	3,202	3,260	3,307	3,357	3,408	12.0	15
Shreveport–Bossier City, LA.......................	376	381	387	388	389	392	4.1	130
South Bend–Mishawaka, IN–MI	317	316	316	317	318	318	0.3	150
Spartanburg, SC	254	266	271	277	283	287	13.0	161
Spokane, WA......................................	418	440	447	456	462	469	12.1	107
Springfield, MA....................................	680	692	693	695	697	699	2.8	74
Springfield, MO	368	400	411	420	426	431	17.0	111
Stockton, CA......................................	564	654	660	665	669	675	19.7	78
Syracuse, NY......................................	650	646	645	644	645	646	−0.6	81
Tallahassee, FL....................................	320	341	347	354	357	360	12.4	140
Tampa–St. Petersburg–Clearwater, FL	2,396	2,639	2,685	2,711	2,730	2,747	14.7	19
Toledo, OH..	659	673	674	675	673	672	2.0	79
Trenton–Ewing, NJ	351	362	363	363	365	366	4.4	137
Tucson, AZ..	844	949	975	997	1,010	1,020	20.9	52
Tulsa, OK...	860	882	893	906	916	929	8.1	53
Utica–Rome, NY	300	294	293	293	293	293	−2.2	158
Vallejo–Fairfield, CA	395	407	406	406	406	407	3.2	122
Virginia Beach–Norfolk–Newport News, VA–NC......	1,577	1,659	1,672	1,672	1,670	1,674	6.2	36
Visalia–Porterville, CA.............................	368	404	410	416	422	430	16.8	112
Washington–Arlington–Alexandria, DC–VA–MD–WV ..	4,796	5,229	5,265	5,313	5,378	5,476	14.2	8
Wichita, KS	571	584	588	595	603	613	7.3	84
Wilmington, NC....................................	274	316	329	340	348	355	29.2	141
Winston–Salem, NC	422	453	463	472	480	485	14.9	104
Worcester, MA....................................	750	787	792	796	799	804	7.2	64
York–Hanover, PA	382	407	415	422	426	429	12.4	113
Youngstown–Warren–Boardman, OH–PA	603	581	576	571	566	563	−6.6	89

[1] The April 1, 2000, estimates base reflects changes to the Census 2000 population resulting from legal boundary updates as of January 1 of the estimates year, other geographic program changes, and Count Question Resolution actions. [2] Broomfield County, CO, was formed from parts of Adams, Boulder, Jefferson, and Weld Counties, CO, on November 15, 2001, and is coextensive with Broomfield city. For purposes of defining and presenting data for metropolitan statistical areas, Broomfield city is treated as if it were a county at the time of the 2000 census. [3] The portion of Sullivan city in Crawford County, Missouri, is legally part of the St. Louis, MO–IL MSA. Data shown here do not include this area.

Source: U.S. Census Bureau, "Table 1—Annual Estimates of the Population of Metropolitan and Micropolitan Statistical Areas: April 1, 2000 to July 1, 2009 (CBSA–EST2009–01)," <http://www.census.gov/popest/metro/CBSA-est2009-annual.html>.

Table 21. 50 Largest Metropolitan Statistical Areas in 2009—Components of Population Change: 2000 to 2009

[Covers period April 1, 2000 to July 1, 2009 (1,227 represents 1,227,000). Covers metropolitan statistical areas as defined by the U.S. Office of Management and Budget as of November 2008. All geographic boundaries for 2000 to 2009 population estimates are defined as of January 1, 2009. For definitions and components of all metropolitan and micropolitan areas, see Appendix II. Minus sign (–) indicates decrease or outmigration]

Metropolitan statistical area	Number (1,000)							Percent change
	Total change [1]	Natural increase			Net migration			
		Total	Births	Deaths	Total	Interna- tional	Domes- tic migra- tion	
Atlanta-Sandy Springs-Marietta, GA	1,227	458	724	265	643	215	429	28.9
Austin-Round Rock, TX	455	158	223	65	303	68	234	36.4
Baltimore-Towson, MD	138	106	322	216	9	46	–36	5.4
Birmingham-Hoover, AL	80	38	140	102	42	15	27	7.6
Boston-Cambridge-Quincy, MA-NH.	196	190	516	326	–38	197	–236	4.5
Buffalo-Niagara Falls, NY	–46	6	118	112	–45	10	–55	–4.0
Charlotte-Gastonia-Concord, NC-SC	415	123	222	99	298	50	248	31.2
Chicago-Naperville-Joliet, IL-IN-WI.	482	662	1,300	638	–184	378	–562	5.3
Cincinnati-Middletown, OH-KY-IN	162	109	274	165	5	23	–18	8.1
Cleveland-Elyria-Mentor, OH.	–57	49	244	195	–108	29	–137	–2.6
Columbus, OH	189	120	239	119	75	41	34	11.7
Dallas-Fort Worth-Arlington, TX.	1,286	611	921	310	652	335	317	24.9
Denver-Aurora-Broomfield, CO [2]	373	215	345	131	164	98	66	17.1
Detroit-Warren-Livonia, MI.	–49	180	539	359	–270	97	–367	–1.1
Hartford-West Hartford-East Hartford, CT.	47	33	126	93	22	31	–9	4.1
Houston-Sugar Land-Baytown, TX	1,152	552	836	284	543	300	244	24.4
Indianapolis-Carmel, IN.	219	118	235	117	101	29	73	14.3
Jacksonville, FL.	205	68	164	96	143	16	127	18.3
Kansas City, MO-KS	231	127	270	143	67	36	32	12.6
Las Vegas-Paradise, NV	527	135	247	112	400	88	311	38.3
Los Angeles-Long Beach-Santa Ana, CA	509	1,104	1,815	711	–532	833	–1,365	4.1
Louisville/Jefferson County, KY-IN.	96	49	151	102	51	17	34	8.3
Memphis, TN-MS-AR.	100	86	184	98	12	20	–9	8.3
Miami-Fort Lauderdale-Pompano Beach, FL.	539	211	650	438	235	522	–287	10.8
Milwaukee-Waukesha-West Allis, WI.	59	80	199	119	–47	28	–74	3.9
Minneapolis-St. Paul-Bloomington, MN-WI	301	248	424	176	68	87	–20	10.1
Nashville-Davidson-Murfreesboro-Franklin, TN.	270	93	196	103	161	38	123	20.6
New Orleans-Metairie-Kenner, LA.	–127	51	156	106	–287	15	–302	–9.6
New York-Northern New Jersey-Long Island, NY-NJ-PA.	746	1,067	2,371	1,304	–846	1,116	–1,962	1.1
Oklahoma City, OK	132	73	164	91	66	25	41	12.0
Orlando-Kissimmee, FL.	438	119	248	129	323	98	225	26.6
Philadelphia-Camden-Wilmington, PA-NJ-DE-MD . . .	281	208	702	494	11	127	–116	4.9
Phoenix-Mesa-Scottsdale, AZ.	1,112	356	600	243	764	220	543	34.2
Pittsburgh, PA	–76	–29	230	259	–32	20	–52	–3.1
Portland-Vancouver-Beaverton, OR-WA	314	129	267	138	196	74	122	16.3
Providence-New Bedford-Fall River, RI-MA.	18	40	177	137	–13	36	–49	1.1
Raleigh-Cary, NC.	329	92	139	48	233	38	194	41.2
Richmond, VA	141	54	144	90	94	18	76	12.9
Riverside-San Bernardino-Ontario, CA	888	341	577	237	563	94	469	27.3
Sacramento-Arden-Arcade-Roseville, CA.	331	132	266	134	208	67	141	18.4
St. Louis, MO-IL [3].	130	106	339	234	–13	31	–44	4.8
Salt Lake City, UT	161	137	189	52	8	43	–34	16.7
San Antonio, TX.	360	159	283	124	211	33	177	21.1
San Diego-Carlsbad-San Marcos, CA.	240	242	423	182	–23	103	–127	8.5
San Francisco-Oakland-Fremont, CA	194	251	520	269	–81	267	–347	4.7
San Jose-Sunnyvale-Santa Clara, CA.	104	174	258	84	–64	176	–240	6.0
Seattle-Tacoma-Bellevue, WA	364	197	393	196	172	131	41	12.0
Tampa-St. Petersburg-Clearwater, FL	351	28	292	265	337	77	260	14.7
Virginia Beach-Norfolk-Newport News, VA-NC	98	107	220	113	–18	2	–20	6.2
Washington-Arlington-Alexandria, DC-VA-MD-WV . . .	680	441	721	280	213	320	–107	14.2

[1] Total population change includes residual. This residual represents the change in population that cannot be attributed to any specific demographic component of change. See "State & County terms & definitions" at <http://www.census.gov/popest/topics /terms/states.html>. [2] Broomfield County, CO, was formed from parts of Adams, Boulder, Jefferson, and Weld Counties, CO on November 15, 2001, and is coextensive with Broomfield city. For purposes of defining and presenting data for metropolitan statistical areas, Broomfield city is treated as if it were a county at the time of the 2000 census. [3] The portion of Sullivan city in Crawford County, Missouri, is legally part of the St. Louis, MO-IL MSA. Data shown here do not include this area.

Source: U.S. Census Bureau, "Table 10—Cumulative Estimates of the Components of Population Change for Metropolitan and Micropolitan Statistical Areas: April 1, 2000 to July 1, 2009 (CBSA-EST2009-10)," <http://www.census.gov/popest/metro /CBSA-est2009-comp-chg.html>.

Table 22. Metropolitan Statistical Areas With More Than 750,000 Persons in 2009—Population by Age: 2009

[In thousands (858 represents 858,000). As of July 1. Covers metropolitan statistical areas as defined by the U.S. Office of Management and Budget as of November 2008. All geographic boundaries are defined as of January 1, 2009. For definitions and components of all metropolitan and micropolitan areas, see Appendix II]

Metropolitan statistical area	Number (1,000)						Percent under 18 years	Percent 65 years and over
	Total	Under 18 years	18 to 44 years	45 to 64 years	65 to 74 years	75 years and over		
Albany-Schenectady-Troy, NY	858	183	313	242	60	59	21.3	13.9
Albuquerque, NM	858	212	324	219	55	49	24.7	12.1
Allentown-Bethlehem-Easton, PA-NJ	816	185	279	228	60	64	22.7	15.2
Atlanta-Sandy Springs-Marietta, GA	5,475	1,477	2,186	1,342	275	196	27.0	8.6
Austin-Round Rock, TX	1,705	430	764	377	76	58	25.2	7.9
Bakersfield, CA	807	251	310	174	41	31	31.0	9.0
Baltimore-Towson, MD	2,691	623	1,001	730	181	156	23.1	12.5
Baton Rouge, LA	787	196	315	192	47	37	25.0	10.7
Birmingham-Hoover, AL	1,131	273	414	297	78	70	24.1	13.0
Boston-Cambridge-Quincy, MA-NH	4,589	994	1,758	1,246	301	290	21.7	12.9
Bridgeport-Stamford-Norwalk, CT	901	224	310	248	61	59	24.8	13.2
Buffalo-Niagara Falls, NY	1,124	242	387	318	87	91	21.5	15.8
Charlotte-Gastonia-Concord, NC-SC	1,746	459	689	424	96	77	26.3	9.9
Chicago-Naperville-Joliet, IL-IN-WI	9,581	2,437	3,654	2,416	573	501	25.4	11.2
Cincinnati-Middletown, OH-KY-IN	2,172	533	798	576	139	125	24.6	12.2
Cleveland-Elyria-Mentor, OH	2,091	487	700	593	157	155	23.3	14.9
Columbus, OH	1,802	443	725	445	105	86	24.6	10.6
Dallas-Fort Worth-Arlington, TX	6,448	1,806	2,598	1,490	312	241	28.0	8.6
Dayton, OH	835	190	295	227	65	59	22.7	14.8
Denver-Aurora-Broomfield, CO	2,552	641	1,002	653	140	116	25.1	10.0
Detroit-Warren-Livonia, MI	4,403	1,067	1,546	1,228	292	271	24.2	12.8
El Paso, TX	751	236	276	160	41	39	31.4	10.6
Fresno, CA	915	276	353	197	47	43	30.1	9.8
Grand Rapids-Wyoming, MI	778	199	292	199	46	42	25.6	11.4
Hartford-West Hartford-East Hartford, CT	1,196	267	425	335	85	84	22.3	14.1
Honolulu, HI	908	201	350	220	63	73	22.2	14.9
Houston-Sugar Land-Baytown, TX	5,867	1,673	2,297	1,401	285	211	28.5	8.5
Indianapolis-Carmel, IN	1,744	453	659	441	102	88	26.0	10.9
Jacksonville, FL	1,328	323	495	352	84	74	24.4	11.9
Kansas City, MO-KS	2,068	522	761	542	127	115	25.3	11.7
Las Vegas-Paradise, NV	1,903	501	745	453	120	84	26.3	10.7
Los Angeles-Long Beach-Santa Ana, CA	12,875	3,256	5,163	3,065	726	664	25.3	10.8
Louisville/Jefferson County, KY-IN	1,259	300	454	344	85	75	23.9	12.7
Memphis, TN-MS-AR	1,305	355	482	331	75	61	27.2	10.5
Miami-Fort Lauderdale-Pompano Beach, FL	5,547	1,252	1,991	1,421	405	479	22.6	15.9
Milwaukee-Waukesha-West Allis, WI	1,560	382	569	414	96	99	24.5	12.5
Minneapolis-St. Paul-Bloomington, MN-WI	3,270	806	1,258	864	181	161	24.7	10.5
Nashville-Davidson—Murfreesboro—Franklin, TN	1,582	387	622	404	94	76	24.4	10.7
New Haven-Milford, CT	848	192	309	228	59	60	22.6	14.0
New Orleans-Metairie-Kenner, LA	1,190	282	432	330	79	68	23.7	12.3
New York-Northern New Jersey-Long Island, NY-NJ-PA	19,070	4,424	7,136	5,023	1,294	1,194	23.2	13.0
Oklahoma City, OK	1,227	306	473	302	78	68	24.9	11.9
Omaha-Council Bluffs, NE-IA	850	222	322	211	50	45	26.2	11.1
Orlando-Kissimmee, FL	2,082	496	802	505	142	138	23.8	13.4
Oxnard-Thousand Oaks-Ventura, CA	803	209	286	213	50	45	26.1	11.8
Philadelphia-Camden-Wilmington, PA-NJ-DE-MD	5,968	1,399	2,183	1,594	396	395	23.4	13.3
Phoenix-Mesa-Scottsdale, AZ	4,364	1,187	1,699	981	259	238	27.2	11.4
Pittsburgh, PA	2,355	476	790	683	191	215	20.2	17.2
Portland-Vancouver-Beaverton, OR-WA	2,242	534	872	592	131	113	23.8	10.9
Providence-New Bedford-Fall River, RI-MA	1,601	349	584	441	111	115	21.8	14.2
Raleigh-Cary, NC	1,126	299	457	273	56	41	26.5	8.6
Richmond, VA	1,238	292	464	333	80	69	23.6	12.0
Riverside-San Bernardino-Ontario, CA	4,143	1,217	1,571	937	230	189	29.4	10.1
Rochester, NY	1,036	232	366	293	74	71	22.4	14.0
Sacramento—Arden-Arcade—Roseville, CA	2,127	533	795	545	135	118	25.1	11.9
St. Louis, MO-IL [1]	2,829	676	1,010	771	190	181	23.9	13.1
Salt Lake City, UT	1,130	332	463	239	52	45	29.3	8.6
San Antonio, TX	2,072	571	784	489	122	106	27.5	11.0
San Diego-Carlsbad-San Marcos, CA	3,054	740	1,218	748	177	171	24.2	11.4
San Francisco-Oakland-Fremont, CA	4,318	933	1,686	1,160	275	264	21.6	12.5
San Jose-Sunnyvale-Santa Clara, CA	1,840	452	738	449	104	96	24.6	10.9
Seattle-Tacoma-Bellevue, WA	3,408	776	1,362	910	191	169	22.8	10.6
Tampa-St. Petersburg-Clearwater, FL	2,747	593	949	732	223	251	21.6	17.2
Tucson, AZ	1,020	239	368	260	77	76	23.4	15.1
Tulsa, OK	929	239	335	240	62	54	25.7	12.5
Virginia Beach-Norfolk-Newport News, VA-NC	1,674	405	658	418	107	87	24.2	11.5
Washington-Arlington-Alexandria, DC-VA-MD-WV	5,476	1,338	2,152	1,436	311	239	24.4	10.0
Worcester, MA	804	189	287	226	51	50	23.6	12.6

[1] The portion of Sullivan city in Crawford County, Missouri, is legally part of the St. Louis, MO-IL MSA. Data shown here do not include this area.

Source: U.S. Census Bureau, USA Counties, <http://censtats.census.gov/usa/usa.shtml>, accessed August 2010.

Table 23. Metropolitan Statistical Areas With More Than 750,000 Persons in 2009—Population by Race and Hispanic Origin: 2009

[In thousands (854 represents 854,000). As of July 1. Covers metropolitan statistical areas as defined by the U.S. Office of Management and Budget as of November 2008. All geographic boundaries are defined as of January 1, 2009. For definitions and components of all metropolitan and micropolitan areas, see Appendix II]

Metropolitan statistical area	Total	White alone	Black or African American alone	American Indian and Alaska Native alone	Asian alone	Native Hawaiian and Other Pacific Islander alone	Two or more races	Hispanic origin [1]
Albany-Schenectady-Troy, NY	858	750	66	2	26	(Z)	13	30
Albuquerque, NM	858	732	33	54	18	2	19	389
Allentown-Bethlehem-Easton, PA-NJ	816	744	39	2	21	1	10	97
Atlanta-Sandy Springs-Marietta, GA	5,475	3,391	1,742	22	236	5	80	548
Austin-Round Rock, TX	1,705	1,451	134	13	77	2	28	521
Bakersfield, CA	807	688	53	15	33	2	18	387
Baltimore-Towson, MD	2,691	1,752	779	9	107	2	42	98
Baton Rouge, LA	787	488	277	2	12	(Z)	7	23
Birmingham-Hoover, AL	1,131	787	316	4	13	1	10	42
Boston-Cambridge-Quincy, MA-NH	4,589	3,860	362	13	282	4	68	382
Bridgeport-Stamford-Norwalk, CT	901	748	97	3	41	1	12	143
Buffalo-Niagara Falls, NY	1,124	944	137	9	19	(Z)	14	40
Charlotte-Gastonia-Concord, NC-SC	1,746	1,253	410	9	50	1	22	160
Chicago-Naperville-Joliet, IL-IN-WI	9,581	7,177	1,716	38	520	8	122	1,904
Cincinnati-Middletown, OH-KY-IN	2,172	1,838	265	5	38	1	26	47
Cleveland-Elyria-Mentor, OH	2,091	1,607	412	5	39	1	27	95
Columbus, OH	1,802	1,454	257	5	55	1	29	61
Dallas-Fort Worth-Arlington, TX	6,448	5,032	938	50	317	10	101	1,802
Dayton, OH	835	684	122	2	13	(Z)	13	16
Denver-Aurora-Broomfield, CO	2,552	2,228	151	27	91	4	51	570
Detroit-Warren-Livonia, MI	4,403	3,171	1,007	15	146	2	62	168
El Paso, TX	751	693	28	9	9	1	10	614
Fresno, CA	915	740	53	18	83	2	19	451
Grand Rapids-Wyoming, MI	778	687	60	4	14	1	13	64
Hartford-West Hartford-East Hartford, CT	1,196	997	135	4	42	1	18	139
Honolulu, HI	908	242	38	6	398	77	147	73
Houston-Sugar Land-Baytown, TX	5,867	4,379	1,010	38	353	8	80	2,016
Indianapolis-Carmel, IN	1,744	1,423	257	5	34	1	23	90
Jacksonville, FL	1,328	959	298	5	41	1	23	82
Kansas City, MO-KS	2,068	1,721	253	12	45	3	34	154
Las Vegas-Paradise, NV	1,903	1,467	201	20	146	12	57	557
Los Angeles-Long Beach-Santa Ana, CA	12,875	9,652	979	123	1,821	45	254	5,763
Louisville/Jefferson County, KY-IN	1,259	1,048	171	4	18	1	16	41
Memphis, TN-MS-AR	1,305	666	595	5	24	1	14	59
Miami-Fort Lauderdale-Pompano Beach, FL	5,547	4,149	1,163	27	130	7	70	2,234
Milwaukee-Waukesha-West Allis, WI	1,560	1,227	255	10	44	1	22	136
Minneapolis-St. Paul-Bloomington, MN-WI	3,270	2,783	224	28	173	3	60	160
Nashville-Davidson—Murfreesboro—Franklin, TN	1,582	1,274	246	6	34	1	21	97
New Haven-Milford, CT	848	690	111	3	30	1	13	117
New Orleans-Metairie-Kenner, LA	1,190	721	416	6	32	1	15	78
New York-Northern New Jersey-Long Island, NY-NJ-PA	19,070	13,139	3,676	96	1,829	24	306	4,151
Oklahoma City, OK	1,227	970	135	49	36	1	37	126
Omaha-Council Bluffs, NE-IA	850	745	68	6	17	1	14	67
Orlando-Kissimmee, FL	2,082	1,613	338	11	80	3	38	495
Oxnard-Thousand Oaks-Ventura, CA	803	699	17	11	54	2	19	309
Philadelphia-Camden-Wilmington, PA-NJ-DE-MD	5,968	4,337	1,256	17	272	4	82	426
Phoenix-Mesa-Scottsdale, AZ	4,364	3,805	225	110	133	10	81	1,382
Pittsburgh, PA	2,355	2,095	192	4	37	1	26	29
Portland-Vancouver-Beaverton, OR-WA	2,242	1,953	70	25	125	8	61	239
Providence-New Bedford-Fall River, RI-MA	1,601	1,436	88	9	40	2	26	158
Raleigh-Cary, NC	1,126	831	227	6	45	1	16	105
Richmond, VA	1,238	808	372	6	34	1	17	53
Riverside-San Bernardino-Ontario, CA	4,143	3,388	336	60	240	16	104	1,920
Rochester, NY	1,036	873	119	3	23	(Z)	17	55
Sacramento—Arden-Arcade—Roseville, CA	2,127	1,602	162	26	240	14	83	410
St. Louis, MO-IL	2,829	2,212	515	9	55	1	36	66
Salt Lake City, UT	1,130	1,025	22	12	34	15	21	183
San Antonio, TX	2,072	1,829	144	22	41	4	33	1,109
San Diego-Carlsbad-San Marcos, CA	3,054	2,424	170	32	317	17	94	957
San Francisco-Oakland-Fremont, CA	4,318	2,749	383	29	976	32	149	894
San Jose-Sunnyvale-Santa Clara, CA	1,840	1,149	52	15	567	8	49	499
Seattle-Tacoma-Bellevue, WA	3,408	2,641	202	42	374	23	125	274
Tampa-St. Petersburg-Clearwater, FL	2,747	2,280	329	13	79	3	43	415
Tucson, AZ	1,020	894	40	37	27	2	20	344
Tulsa, OK	929	720	86	68	15	1	40	75
Virginia Beach-Norfolk-Newport News, VA-NC	1,674	1,039	534	8	53	2	37	75
Washington-Arlington-Alexandria, DC-VA-MD-WV	5,476	3,394	1,457	23	482	7	113	713
Worcester, MA	804	728	31	2	30	1	11	69

Z Less than 500. [1] Persons of Hispanic origin may be any race. [2] The portion of Sullivan city in Crawford County, Missouri, is legally part of the St. Louis, MO-IL MSA. Data shown here do not include this area.

Source: U.S. Census Bureau, USA Counties, <http://censtats.census.gov/usa/usa.shtml>, accessed August 2010.

U.S. Census Bureau, Statistical Abstract of the United States: 2011

Table 24. Population by Core Based Statistical Area (CBSA) Status and State: 2009

[2000, as of April 1; 2009 as of July 1 (307,007 represents 307,007,000). Covers core-based statistical areas (metropolitan and microplitan statistical areas) as defined by the U.S. Office of Management and Budget as of November 2008. All geographic boundaries for 2000 to 2009 population estimates are defined as of January 1, 2009. For definitions and components of all metropolitan and micropolitan areas, see Appendix II. Minus sign (–) indicates decrease]

State	Total population, 2009 (1,000)	Inside Core-Based Statistical Area (metropolitan or micropolitan statistical area), 2009				Outside CBSA, 2009		Percent change, 2000–2009 [1]		
		Total		Metro-politan (1,000)	Micro-politan (1,000)	Number (1,000)	Percent	Metro-politan	Micro-politan	Outside CBSAs
		Number (1,000)	Percent							
U.S.	**307,007**	**287,806**	**93.7**	**257,355**	**30,450**	**19,201**	**6.3**	**10.4**	**4.4**	**–**
AL	4,709	4,230	89.8	3,369	861	478	10.2	7.5	6.2	–4.8
AK	698	530	75.9	473	57	168	24.1	17.6	–2.6	1.4
AZ	6,596	6,505	98.6	6,122	384	91	1.4	30.4	10.5	1.6
AR	2,889	2,314	80.1	1,745	569	576	19.9	15.0	0.5	–2.6
CA	36,962	36,704	99.3	36,129	576	257	0.7	9.2	4.1	5.7
CO	5,025	4,617	91.9	4,338	278	408	8.1	18.0	13.9	7.3
CT	3,518	3,518	100.0	3,212	306	–	–	3.1	5.1	–
DE	885	885	100.0	692	193	–	–	10.4	23.1	–
DC	600	600	100.0	600	–	–	–	4.8	–	–
FL	18,538	18,128	97.8	17,452	677	410	2.2	16.2	13.4	12.9
GA	9,829	8,984	91.4	8,020	964	845	8.6	22.9	9.0	9.0
HI	1,295	1,295	100.0	908	388	–	–	3.6	15.6	–43.5
ID	1,546	1,347	87.1	1,014	333	199	12.9	25.7	12.4	4.3
IL	12,910	12,311	95.4	11,259	1,052	599	4.6	5.0	–1.9	–4.0
IN	6,423	6,063	94.4	5,035	1,027	360	5.6	7.4	–0.1	–1.5
IA	3,008	2,220	73.8	1,707	514	788	26.2	9.1	–2.4	–5.8
KS	2,819	2,418	85.8	1,930	488	400	14.2	10.1	–1.4	–9.1
KY	4,314	3,296	76.4	2,492	805	1,018	23.6	9.6	5.4	1.1
LA	4,492	4,188	93.2	3,357	832	304	6.8	0.5	1.9	–2.9
ME	1,318	935	70.9	773	162	384	29.1	5.0	3.3	0.5
MD	5,699	5,616	98.5	5,396	220	83	1.5	7.5	11.7	5.5
MA	6,594	6,566	99.6	6,566	–	27	0.4	3.8	–	11.4
MI	9,970	9,206	92.3	8,135	1,071	764	7.7	0.4	1.6	–2.8
MN	5,266	4,622	87.8	3,953	668	645	12.2	9.2	3.5	–1.4
MS	2,952	2,311	78.3	1,312	999	641	21.7	9.8	–0.3	–1.1
MO	5,988	5,203	86.9	4,508	694	785	13.1	8.6	5.5	–0.2
MT	975	648	66.5	345	303	327	33.5	9.6	16.8	–0.3
NE	1,797	1,457	81.1	1,054	404	339	18.9	11.8	1.9	–9.0
NV	2,643	2,594	98.1	2,377	217	49	1.9	34.2	21.0	2.1
NH	1,325	1,277	96.4	829	448	48	3.6	7.6	6.2	9.6
NJ	8,708	8,708	100.0	8,708	–	–	–	3.5	–	–
NM	2,010	1,933	96.2	1,336	597	77	3.8	16.4	1.3	–6.9
NY	19,541	19,118	97.8	18,002	1,116	423	2.2	3.4	–1.3	–1.5
NC	9,381	8,655	92.3	6,626	2,029	726	7.7	20.9	8.6	4.5
ND	647	461	71.3	316	145	186	28.7	11.3	–3.7	–10.5
OH	11,543	11,037	95.6	9,330	1,707	506	4.4	2.1	–0.1	0.3
OK	3,687	3,128	84.8	2,361	767	559	15.2	9.4	4.5	–0.1
OR	3,826	3,686	96.4	2,989	698	139	3.6	14.2	5.1	–0.4
PA	12,605	12,226	97.0	10,625	1,602	379	3.0	3.0	1.4	–1.0
RI	1,053	1,053	100.0	1,053	–	–	–	0.5	–	–
SC	4,561	4,293	94.1	3,493	800	268	5.9	16.4	9.2	–3.3
SD	812	596	73.4	377	219	216	26.6	20.8	1.8	–5.0
TN	6,296	5,667	90.0	4,628	1,039	629	10.0	12.3	8.6	3.2
TX	24,782	23,405	94.4	21,791	1,614	1,378	5.6	21.4	4.7	0.9
UT	2,785	2,648	95.1	2,480	168	136	4.9	25.9	22.5	8.2
VT	622	458	73.7	208	250	164	26.3	4.6	–	2.7
VA	7,883	7,051	89.4	6,772	279	832	10.6	12.7	6.8	2.7
WA	6,664	6,436	96.6	5,849	586	229	3.4	13.5	11.7	5.8
WV	1,820	1,375	75.6	1,013	362	444	24.4	3.1	–0.7	–3.5
WI	5,655	4,889	86.5	4,134	755	766	13.5	6.8	2.7	0.9
WY	544	392	72.0	163	229	152	28.0	10.3	12.3	7.2

– Represents or rounds to zero. [1] The April 1, 2000 estimates base reflects changes to the Census 2000 population resulting from legal boundary updates as of January 1 of the estimates year, other geographic program changes, and the Count Question Resolution program.

Source: U.S. Census Bureau, "Metropolitan and Micropolitan Statistical Area Estimates Population and Population Change by CBSA Status," <http://www.census.gov/popest/metro/CBSA–est2009–CBSAstatus.html> and unpublished data.

Table 25. Population in Coastal Counties: 1980 to 2009

[Population as of April 1, except as indicated (3,537 represents 3,537,000). Areas as defined by U.S. National Oceanic and Atmospheric Administration, 1992. Covers 675 counties and equivalent areas with at least 15 percent of their land area either in a coastal watershed (drainage area) or in a coastal cataloging unit (a coastal area between watersheds). See Appendix III]

Year	Total	Counties in coastal regions Total	Atlantic	Gulf of Mexico	Great Lakes	Pacific	Balance of United States
Land area, 2000 (1,000 sq. mi.)....	3,537	889	148	115	115	511	2,649
POPULATION							
1980 (mil.)...................	226.5	119.8	53.7	13.1	26.0	27.0	106.7
1990 (mil.)...................	248.7	133.4	59.0	15.2	25.9	33.2	115.3
2000 (mil.)...................	281.4	148.3	65.2	18.0	27.3	37.8	133.1
2009 (July 1) (mil.)...........	307.0	158.8	69.9	20.4	27.4	41.1	148.2
1980 (percent)...............	100	53	24	6	11	12	47
1990 (percent)...............	100	54	24	6	10	13	46
2000 (percent)...............	100	53	23	6	10	13	47
2009 (July 1) (percent).........	100	52	23	7	9	13	48

Source: U.S. Census Bureau, U.S. Summary, 1980 Census of Population, Vol. 1, Chapter A (PC80-1-A-1); 1990 Census of Population and Housing (CPH1); and unpublished data.

Table 26. States With Coastal Counties—Population, Housing Units, Establishments, and Employees by Coastal Region and State: 2000 to 2009

[281,425 represents 281,425,000. Population and housing as of July 1, except 2000 as of April 1. See headnote, Table 25. Minus sign (–) indicates decrease]

Coastal region and state	Population 2000 [1] (1,000)	Population 2009 Number (1,000)	Percent of state, total	Percent change, 2000–2009	Per square mile, 2009 [2]	Housing units Number 2000 [1] (1,000)	Housing units Number 2009 (1,000)	Percent change, 2000–2009	Private nonfarm [3] Establishments, 2008 (1,000)	Private nonfarm [3] Employees, 2008 (1,000)
United States, total	281,425	307,007	(X)	9.1	87	115,904	129,970	12.1	7,601	120,904
Interior U.S.	133,103	148,162	(X)	11.3	56	55,918	63,882	14.2	3,565	58,425
Coastal counties, total ..	148,322	158,845	(X)	7.1	179	59,986	66,000	10.2	4,036	62,478
Atlantic.................	65,198	69,949	(X)	7.3	473	26,821	29,412	9.7	1,874	28,339
Maine.................	1,184	1,230	93.3	3.9	61	599	651	8.6	39	480
New Hampshire.......	1,007	1,087	82.1	8.0	258	432	476	10.3	32	467
Massachusetts..........	6,125	6,366	96.5	3.9	963	2,531	2,653	4.8	169	2,972
Rhode Island............	1,048	1,053	100.0	0.5	1,008	440	452	2.8	30	430
Connecticut.............	3,406	3,518	100.0	3.3	726	1,386	1,446	4.3	92	1,538
New York	13,573	14,198	72.7	4.6	1,832	5,285	5,540	4.8	396	5,587
New Jersey	8,312	8,598	98.7	3.4	1,218	3,269	3,481	6.5	236	3,552
Pennsylvania...........	5,750	6,080	48.2	5.7	883	2,334	2,465	5.6	146	2,609
Delaware	784	885	100.0	13.0	453	343	396	15.5	25	389
Maryland	4,865	5,224	91.6	7.4	689	1,970	2,140	8.6	126	2,034
District of Columbia	572	600	100.0	4.8	9,766	275	285	3.7	21	466
Virginia................	4,794	5,359	68.0	11.8	385	1,912	2,192	14.6	135	2,242
North Carolina..........	1,985	2,157	23.0	8.7	110	905	1,055	16.6	48	651
South Carolina..........	1,653	1,899	41.6	14.9	125	750	919	22.5	47	641
Georgia	822	920	9.4	12.0	76	346	402	16.3	20	283
Florida	9,320	10,776	58.1	15.6	576	4,043	4,858	20.2	311	4,000
Gulf of Mexico	18,003	20,421	(X)	13.4	178	7,718	9,144	18.5	463	7,028
Florida	6,249	7,292	39.3	16.7	232	3,074	3,782	23.0	185	2,321
Georgia	95	100	1.0	5.9	63	40	46	13.2	2	30
Alabama	712	757	16.1	6.3	87	319	371	16.3	18	261
Mississippi.............	588	606	20.5	3.1	89	246	267	8.4	12	187
Louisiana..............	3,510	3,529	78.6	0.5	137	1,439	1,520	5.6	83	1,309
Texas	6,850	8,136	32.8	18.8	202	2,599	3,158	21.5	163	2,921
Great Lakes.............	27,325	27,371	(X)	0.2	237	11,405	12,099	6.1	654	11,151
New York	3,650	3,581	18.3	−1.9	167	1,586	1,635	3.1	83	1,376
Pennsylvania...........	281	280	2.2	−0.2	350	114	119	3.9	7	119
Ohio..................	4,418	4,356	37.7	−1.4	413	1,869	1,959	4.8	106	1,846
Michigan	8,859	8,899	89.3	0.5	174	3,782	4,055	7.2	207	3,256
Indiana................	1,378	1,432	22.3	3.9	352	556	610	9.8	33	587
Illinois................	6,021	6,000	46.5	−0.4	4,306	2,322	2,444	5.3	150	2,715
Wisconsin	2,469	2,575	45.5	4.3	167	1,055	1,147	8.7	61	1,151
Minnesota	248	248	4.7	−0.1	23	121	130	7.2	7	101
Pacific	37,796	41,104	(X)	8.8	80	14,042	15,433	9.9	1,044	15,960
Washington	4,587	5,192	77.9	13.2	210	1,919	2,213	15.3	146	2,072
Oregon................	1,808	1,973	51.6	9.1	94	794	873	10.0	61	822
California..............	29,660	32,058	86.7	8.1	412	10,650	11,593	8.9	787	12,347
Alaska	530	585	83.8	10.6	2	219	237	8.2	17	214
Hawaii	1,212	1,295	100.0	6.9	202	461	516	12.0	33	504

X Not applicable. [1] Reflects modifications to the Census 2000 population as documented in the Count Question Resolution program and geographic program revisions. [2] Calculated on the basis of land area data from the 2000 census. [3] Covers establishments with payroll. Excludes most government employees, railroad employees, self-employed persons. Employees are for the week including March 12.

Source: U.S. Census Bureau, USA Counties, <http://censtats.census.gov/usa/usa.shtml>, accessed August 2010, and "County Business Patterns," <http://www.census.gov/econ/cbp/index.html>.

Table 27. Incorporated Places With 175,000 or More Inhabitants in 2009— Population: 1990 to 2009

[In thousands, except as indicated (223 represents 223,000). As of April 1, except beginning 2005 as of July 1. Beginning with 2000 estimates base, data refer to boundaries in effect on January 1, 2009; 1990 and 2000 census data, boundaries in effect on January 1, 2000. Minus sign (−) indicates decrease. See Appendix III]

Incorporated place	Number (1,000)					Percent change		Rank, 2009
	1990	2000, estimates base [1]	2005	2008	2009	1990 to 2000 [2]	2000 to 2009 [1]	
Akron, OH	223	217	211	208	207	−2.7	−4.6	99
Albuquerque, NM	387	450	498	523	529	15.9	17.7	34
Amarillo, TX	158	174	182	187	189	10.0	9.1	122
Anaheim, CA	267	329	329	333	338	23.0	2.8	56
Anchorage, AK	226	260	277	280	286	15.0	9.9	66
Arlington, TX	262	333	361	375	380	27.1	14.1	49
Arlington, VA [3]	171	189	200	210	217	10.9	14.8	95
Atlanta, GA	394	419	483	537	541	5.8	29.2	33
Augusta-Richmond County, GA [4]	186	195	192	194	194	4.8	−0.4	114
Aurora, CO	222	276	296	317	323	24.6	17.0	58
Austin, TX	497	668	708	767	786	32.1	17.7	15
Bakersfield, CA	188	244	292	319	324	31.4	33.2	59
Baltimore, MD	736	651	640	638	637	−11.5	−2.1	21
Baton Rouge, LA	223	229	222	225	225	2.2	−1.4	88
Birmingham, AL	266	242	232	230	230	−8.7	−5.1	83
Boise City, ID	142	195	200	205	206	30.8	5.4	100
Boston, MA	575	589	610	637	645	2.5	9.5	20
Brownsville, TX	114	143	164	174	177	22.6	24.1	130
Buffalo, NY	328	293	278	271	270	−10.8	−7.7	70
Chandler, AZ	91	177	232	247	250	94.7	41.0	73
Charlotte, NC	428	568	631	688	704	26.4	24.0	18
Chesapeake, VA	152	199	217	220	222	31.1	11.7	91
Chicago, IL	2,783	2,896	2,825	2,830	2,851	4.1	−1.5	3
Chula Vista, CA	135	174	209	219	224	28.3	28.9	90
Cincinnati, OH	365	331	331	333	333	−9.1	0.5	57
Cleveland, OH	506	477	449	434	431	−5.5	−9.7	43
Colorado Springs, CO	282	361	394	397	400	28.0	10.7	46
Columbus, GA	[4] 179	186	188	187	190	[4] 4.0	2.2	121
Columbus, OH	639	713	739	759	769	11.3	7.8	16
Corpus Christi, TX	258	277	281	285	287	7.4	3.6	65
Dallas, TX	1,007	1,189	1,246	1,280	1,300	18.1	9.3	9
Denver, CO	468	554	561	593	610	18.6	10.2	24
Des Moines, IA	193	199	194	198	201	2.8	0.8	110
Detroit, MI	1,028	951	921	913	911	−7.5	−4.2	11
Durham, NC	149	188	206	223	229	25.5	22.0	85
El Paso, TX	516	564	587	609	620	9.3	10.0	22
Fontana, CA	88	145	178	187	188	46.7	29.6	123
Fort Lauderdale, FL	150	171	183	183	185	1.6	8.3	126
Fort Wayne, IN	206	254	250	254	256	−0.1	0.8	72
Fort Worth, TX	449	543	622	704	728	19.1	33.9	17
Fremont, CA	173	203	199	202	206	17.3	1.0	102
Fresno, CA	355	430	457	473	480	20.3	11.7	36
Garland, TX	181	216	213	219	222	19.3	2.9	92
Gilbert, AZ	30	115	183	217	222	265.6	93.6	96
Glendale, AZ	151	220	244	252	253	45.0	15.2	76
Glendale, CA	180	195	197	195	197	8.3	1.0	113
Grand Rapids, MI	189	198	193	193	194	4.7	−2.1	115
Greensboro, NC	192	228	236	251	255	16.9	12.1	74
Henderson, NV	65	175	232	254	256	169.4	46.1	71
Hialeah, FL	188	226	223	217	219	20.5	−3.3	94
Honolulu, HI [3]	376	372	375	373	375	−1.2	0.8	50
Houston, TX	1,697	1,974	2,076	2,238	2,258	15.1	14.4	4
Huntington Beach, CA	181	190	192	191	193	4.7	2.0	116
Huntsville, AL	161	160	166	177	180	−1.7	12.3	129
Indianapolis, IN [4]	732	782	789	801	808	6.9	3.3	14
Irvine, CA	111	144	185	205	210	28.4	45.5	97
Irving, TX	155	192	190	201	206	23.5	7.3	101
Jacksonville, FL	635	736	787	810	814	15.8	10.6	13
Jersey City, NJ	229	240	237	240	243	4.8	1.0	78
Kansas City, MO	435	442	464	480	482	1.5	9.2	35
Knoxville, TN	174	176	180	185	185	−0.1	5.1	125
Laredo, TX	126	178	206	221	226	40.1	27.0	86
Las Vegas, NV	259	480	545	563	568	84.7	18.2	28
Lexington-Fayette, KY	225	261	278	292	297	15.6	13.8	63
Lincoln, NE	193	227	242	251	254	17.0	12.1	75
Little Rock, AR	177	183	186	190	192	3.4	4.7	119
Long Beach, CA	430	462	468	460	463	7.4	0.2	38
Los Angeles, CA	3,486	3,695	3,795	3,802	3,832	6.0	3.7	2
Louisville/Jefferson County, KY [4]	[5] 269	554	560	563	567	[5] −4.7	2.3	29
Lubbock, TX	187	200	213	221	226	6.9	13.0	87
Madison, WI	191	209	223	232	235	9.0	12.4	81

See footnotes at end of table.

U.S. Census Bureau, Statistical Abstract of the United States: 2011

Table 27. Incorporated Places With 175,000 or More Inhabitants in 2009—Population: 1990 to 2009—Con.

[In thousands, except as indicated (223 represents 223,000). As of April 1, except beginning 2005 as of July 1. Beginning with 2000 estimates base, data refer to boundaries in effect on January 1, 2009; 1990 and 2000 census data, boundaries in effect on January 1, 2000. Minus sign (–) indicates decrease. See Appendix III]

Incorporated place	Number (1,000)					Percent change		Rank, 2009
	1990	2000, estimates base [1]	2005	2008	2009	1990 to 2000 [2]	2000 to 2009 [1]	
Memphis, TN	664	691	681	677	677	–2.1	–2.0	19
Mesa, AZ	291	398	451	464	467	36.2	17.4	39
Miami, FL	359	362	391	431	433	0.8	19.5	42
Milwaukee, WI	629	597	602	604	605	–5.1	1.3	26
Minneapolis, MN	368	383	376	382	385	3.9	0.7	48
Mobile, AL	198	204	190	193	193	0.3	–5.4	118
Modesto, CA	166	189	204	202	203	13.5	7.3	105
Montgomery, AL	191	202	201	203	202	5.6	0.2	106
Moreno Valley, CA	119	143	175	189	192	19.9	34.5	120
Nashville-Davidson, TN [4]	488	546	580	598	605	11.7	11.0	25
New Orleans, LA	497	485	455	337	355	–2.5	–26.8	53
New York, NY	7,323	8,009	8,214	8,347	8,392	9.4	4.8	1
Newark, NJ	275	272	276	277	278	–0.6	2.1	68
Newport News, VA	171	180	191	193	193	5.1	7.1	117
Norfolk, VA	261	234	237	235	233	–10.3	–0.5	82
North Las Vegas, NV	48	116	176	218	224	140.8	94.2	89
Oakland, CA	372	399	392	403	409	7.4	2.4	44
Oklahoma City, OK	445	506	532	552	560	13.8	10.7	31
Omaha, NE	373	409	432	448	455	4.6	11.3	40
Orlando, FL	166	194	217	232	236	12.0	21.5	80
Oxnard, CA	142	171	181	185	188	19.6	9.9	124
Philadelphia, PA	1,586	1,518	1,518	1,540	1,547	–4.3	2.0	6
Phoenix, AZ	989	1,322	1,470	1,570	1,594	33.6	20.5	5
Pittsburgh, PA	370	334	316	312	312	–9.6	–6.8	61
Plano, TX	128	222	250	269	274	73.5	23.2	69
Portland, OR	486	529	534	556	566	8.9	7.0	30
Raleigh, NC	221	288	348	394	406	24.9	40.6	45
Reno, NV	139	183	206	218	220	29.8	20.0	93
Richmond, VA	203	198	198	203	204	–2.4	3.3	103
Riverside, CA	227	256	286	293	298	12.6	16.2	62
Rochester, NY	230	220	210	207	207	–4.4	–5.7	98
Sacramento, CA	370	407	449	461	467	10.0	14.6	37
Salt Lake City, UT	160	182	177	181	183	13.6	0.7	127
San Antonio, TX	998	1,160	1,259	1,349	1,374	14.7	18.4	7
San Bernardino, CA	171	188	199	198	198	8.3	5.3	111
San Diego, CA	1,111	1,223	1,284	1,306	1,306	10.1	6.8	8
San Francisco, CA	724	777	778	808	815	7.3	5.0	12
San Jose, CA	783	901	909	949	965	14.2	7.1	10
Santa Ana, CA	294	338	337	337	340	14.8	0.7	55
Scottsdale, AZ	130	203	228	236	238	55.8	17.4	79
Seattle, WA	516	563	575	603	617	9.1	9.5	23
Shreveport, LA	199	201	198	199	199	0.6	–0.7	109
Spokane, WA	178	197	198	202	203	9.8	3.1	104
St. Louis, MO	397	348	353	357	357	–12.2	2.4	52
St. Paul, MN	272	287	277	279	281	5.5	–1.9	67
St. Petersburg, FL	240	249	248	245	244	3.3	–1.8	77
Stockton, CA	212	243	282	285	288	15.0	18.3	64
Tacoma, WA	177	194	194	197	200	9.1	3.1	108
Tampa, FL	280	303	326	340	344	8.4	13.3	54
Tempe, AZ	142	159	167	176	179	11.7	12.5	133
Toledo, OH	333	314	317	317	316	–5.8	0.8	60
Tucson, AZ	418	487	525	541	544	16.4	11.6	32
Tulsa, OK	367	393	381	386	390	7.0	–0.9	47
Virginia Beach, VA	393	425	437	432	434	8.2	2.0	41
Washington, DC	607	572	582	590	600	–5.7	4.8	27
Wichita, KS	311	352	355	366	372	10.7	5.7	51
Winston-Salem, NC	168	201	217	228	230	10.6	14.1	84
Worcester, MA	170	173	175	183	183	1.8	6.0	128
Yonkers, NY	188	196	198	200	201	4.2	2.6	107

– Represents or rounds to zero. [1] Based on the April 1, 2000, population estimates base which reflects changes to the Census 2000 population from the Count Question Resolution program and geographic program revisions. [2] Based on 2000 Census numbers as tabulated. [3] The population shown is for the census designated place (CDP). [4] Represents the portion of a consolidated city that is not within one or more separately incorporated places. [5] Data are for the incorporated place of Louisville city before consolidation of the city and county governments.

Source: U.S. Census Bureau, 2000 Census of Population and Housing, *Population and Housing Unit Counts PHC-3*, and "Annual Estimates of the Resident Population for Incorporated Places Over 100,000, Ranked by July 1, 2009 Population: April 1, 2000 to July 1, 2009 (SUB-EST2009-01)," June 2010, <http://www.census.gov/popest/cities/tables/SUB-EST2009-01.xls>.

U.S. Census Bureau, Statistical Abstract of the United States: 2011

Table 28. Incorporated Places by Population Size: 1990 to 2009

[153.1 represents 153,100,000. See Appendix III]

Population size	Number of incorporated places				Population (mil.)				Percent of total			
	1990	2000	2005	2009	1990	2000 [1]	2005	2009	1990	2000 [1]	2005	2009
Total.............	19,262	19,510	19,510	19,510	153.1	177.5	185.1	192.2	100.0	100.0	100.0	100.0
1,000,000 or more.....	8	9	9	9	20.0	23.0	23.7	24.5	13.1	12.9	12.8	12.7
500,000 to 999,999	15	21	23	25	10.1	13.6	15.0	16.8	6.6	7.6	8.1	8.7
250,000 to 499,999	41	38	38	41	14.2	13.7	13.8	14.4	9.3	7.7	7.5	7.5
100,000 to 249,999	131	176	183	201	19.1	26.2	27.8	30.0	12.5	14.7	15.0	15.6
50,000 to 99,999	309	375	415	434	21.2	25.8	28.8	29.8	13.8	14.5	15.5	15.5
25,000 to 49,999	567	659	680	684	20.0	23.1	23.7	23.8	13.1	13.0	12.8	12.4
10,000 to 24,999	1,290	1,470	1,504	1,536	20.3	23.1	23.6	24.3	13.3	13.0	12.8	12.6
Under 10,000.........	16,901	16,762	16,658	16,580	28.2	29.0	28.7	28.7	18.4	16.3	15.5	14.9

[1] The April 1, 2000 population estimates base reflects changes to the Census 2000 population from the Count Question Resolution program and geographic program revisions.

Source: U.S. Census Bureau, *1990 Census of Population and Housing, Population and Housing Unit Counts (CPH-2-1)*; and "Annual Estimates of the Resident Population for Incorporated Places: April 1, 2000 to July 1, 2009 (SUB-EST2009-04-XX)" (released June 2010), <http://www.census.gov/popest/cities/SUB-EST2009-4.html>.

Table 29. Urban and Rural Population by State: 1990 and 2000

[222,361 represents 222,361,000. As of April 1. Resident population. For urban definitions, see text, this section]

State	Urban population				Rural population, 2000 (1,000)	State	Urban population				Rural population, 2000 (1,000)
	1990		2000, current definition				1990		2000, current definition		
	Former definition (percent)	Current definition (percent)	Number (1,000)	Percent			Former definition (percent)	Current definition (percent)	Number (1,000)	Percent	
U.S., total...	75.2	78.0	222,361	79.0	59,061						
						MO.....	68.7	69.6	3,883	69.4	1,712
AL	60.4	56.8	2,466	55.4	1,981	MT	52.5	56.4	488	54.1	414
AK	67.5	61.0	411	65.6	216	NE	66.1	67.2	1,194	69.8	518
AZ	87.5	86.5	4,524	88.2	607	NV	88.3	87.4	1,829	91.5	170
AR	53.5	52.0	1,404	52.5	1,269	NH	51.0	57.2	732	59.3	503
CA	92.6	93.7	31,990	94.4	1,882	NJ	89.4	93.5	7,939	94.4	475
CO......	82.4	83.8	3,633	84.5	668	NM.....	73.0	75.0	1,364	75.0	456
CT	79.1	87.0	2,988	87.7	418	NY	84.3	87.4	16,603	87.5	2,374
DE	73.0	79.2	628	80.1	156	NC	50.4	57.8	4,849	60.2	3,200
DC	100.0	100.0	572	100.0	–	ND	53.3	53.4	359	55.9	283
FL	84.8	88.0	14,270	89.3	1,712						
						OH.....	74.1	77.5	8,782	77.4	2,571
GA	63.2	68.7	5,864	71.6	2,322	OK.....	67.7	65.2	2,255	65.3	1,196
HI.......	89.0	90.5	1,108	91.5	103	OR.....	70.5	74.9	2,694	78.7	727
ID.......	57.4	62.2	859	66.4	434	PA	68.9	76.8	9,464	77.1	2,817
IL.......	84.6	86.4	10,910	87.8	1,510	RI......	86.0	89.9	953	90.9	95
IN.......	64.9	69.1	4,304	70.8	1,776	SC	54.6	61.5	2,427	60.5	1,585
IA.......	60.6	59.4	1,787	61.1	1,139	SD	50.0	50.3	391	51.9	363
KS	69.1	69.5	1,921	71.4	768	TN	60.9	62.7	3,620	63.6	2,069
KY	51.8	55.9	2,254	55.8	1,788	TX	80.3	81.2	17,204	82.5	3,648
LA	68.1	72.9	3,246	72.6	1,223	UT	87.0	86.8	1,970	88.2	263
ME......	44.6	42.6	513	40.2	762						
						VT	32.2	40.2	232	38.2	376
MD......	81.3	85.0	4,559	86.1	738	VA	69.4	71.5	5,170	73.0	1,909
MA......	84.3	90.5	5,801	91.4	548	WA.....	76.4	79.9	4,831	82.0	1,063
MI.......	70.5	75.2	7,419	74.7	2,519	WV.....	36.1	46.9	833	46.1	976
MN......	69.9	69.0	3,490	70.9	1,429	WI	65.7	67.3	3,664	68.3	1,700
MS......	47.1	49.1	1,387	48.8	1,457	WY.....	65.0	67.1	321	65.1	172

– Represents zero.

Source: U.S. Census Bureau, 2000 Census of Population and Housing, *Population and Housing Unit Counts PHC-3*. See also <http://www.census.gov/prod/cen2000/index.html>.

U.S. Census Bureau, Statistical Abstract of the United States: 2011

Table 30. Mobility Status of the Population by Selected Characteristics: 1981 to 2009

[As of March (221,641 represents 221,641,000). For persons 1 year old and over. Based on comparison of place of residence in immediate prior year and year shown. Excludes members of the Armed Forces except those living off post or with their families on post. Based on Current Population Survey, Annual Social and Economic Supplement. See text, this section and Appendix III. For composition of regions, see map, inside front cover]

| Mobility period and characteristic | Total (1,000) | Non–movers | Movers (different house in United States) | | Different county | | | Movers from abroad |
			Total	Same county	Total	Same state	Different state	
1981	221,641	83	17	10	6	3	3	1
1991	244,884	83	16	10	6	3	3	1
2001	275,611	86	14	8	6	3	3	1
2009, total	**297,182**	**88**	**12**	**8**	**4**	**2**	**2**	**–**
1 to 4 years old	16,886	81	19	14	5	3	2	–
5 to 9 years old	20,245	86	14	10	4	2	2	–
10 to 14 years old	19,907	89	11	8	3	2	1	–
15 to 19 years old	21,227	87	12	9	3	2	1	–
20 to 24 years old	20,632	73	27	18	8	6	3	1
25 to 29 years old	21,256	74	25	16	8	5	4	1
30 to 44 years old	60,586	86	14	9	4	2	2	–
45 to 64 years old	78,655	93	6	4	2	1	1	–
65 to 74 years old	20,404	97	3	2	1	1	1	–
75 to 84 years old	13,005	97	3	2	1	1	–	–
85 years old and over	4,378	96	4	2	2	1	–	–
Northeast	53,537	92	8	5	2	1	1	–
Midwest	64,719	88	11	8	4	2	2	–
South	109,236	86	13	9	4	2	2	–
West	69,689	85	14	10	4	2	2	–
Persons 16 years old and over	236,024	88	12	8	4	2	2	–
Civilian labor force	153,129	87	13	9	4	2	2	–
Employed	138,959	87	12	9	4	2	1	–
Unemployed	14,170	79	20	13	7	4	3	1
Armed Forces	939	66	31	14	16	4	12	4
Not in labor force	81,957	91	9	6	3	2	1	–
Employed civilians, 16 years old and over	138,959	87	12	9	4	2	1	–
Management, business, and financial	21,651	90	10	6	4	2	2	–
Professional	30,566	88	11	7	4	2	2	–
Service	23,989	84	15	11	4	3	1	–
Sales	15,384	87	13	9	4	2	2	–
Office and administrative support	18,176	88	12	9	3	2	1	–
Farming, fishing, and forestry	899	87	12	10	2	1	–	1
Construction and extraction	7,123	86	14	10	4	3	1	1
Installation, maintenance, and repair	5,055	87	13	9	4	2	1	–
Production	7,702	89	11	8	3	2	1	–
Transportation and material moving	8,413	86	13	10	3	2	1	–
Tenure:								
Owner occupied units	206,924	95	5	3	2	1	1	–
Renter occupied units	90,258	71	28	20	8	5	3	1

– Represents or rounds to zero.

Source: U.S. Census Bureau, Current Population Survey, 2009 Annual Social and Economic Supplement, "Geographical Mobility: 2008 to 2009, Detailed Tables," <http://www.census.gov/population/www/socdemo/migrate.html>.

Table 31. Movers by Type of Move and Reason for Moving: 2009

[As of March (37,105 represents 37,105,000). For persons 1 year old and over. Based on comparison of place of residence in 2008 and 2009. Excludes members of the Armed Forces except those living off post or with their families on post. Based on Current Population Survey, Annual Social and Economic Supplement. See text, this section and Appendix III]

Reason for move	All movers	Intra-county	Inter-county	From abroad	Reason for move	All movers	Intra-county	Inter-county	From abroad
Total (1,000)	**37,105**	**24,984**	**11,034**	**1,087**	Housing-related reasons	45.9	57.2	24.3	5.7
					Wanted to own home/not rent	5.5	6.6	3.6	0.2
PERCENT DISTRIBUTION					New/better house/apartment	14.5	18.6	6.5	2.5
Total	100.0	100.0	100.0	100.0	Better neighborhood/less crime	5.0	6.2	2.9	0.7
					Cheaper housing	11.1	13.9	5.8	0.4
Family-related reasons	26.3	26.5	26.6	19.9	Other housing	9.7	11.9	5.5	1.9
Change in marital status	5.4	5.5	5.4	2.9					
To establish own household	9.5	11.6	5.4	2.6	Other reasons	9.8	7.5	13.6	25.9
Other family reasons	11.5	9.5	15.8	14.4	Attend/leave college	2.6	1.5	4.5	8.6
Work-related reasons	17.9	8.9	35.5	48.5	Change of climate	0.5	0.1	1.5	–
New job/job transfer	8.7	2.1	22.0	28.1	Health reasons	1.6	1.4	2.0	3.1
To look for work/lost job	2.7	1.0	5.4	15.8	Natural disaster	0.4	0.5	0.2	–
Closer to work/easier commute	5.0	5.0	5.6	1.0	Other reason	4.8	4.1	5.4	14.3
Retired	0.4	0.2	0.8	0.9					
Other job-related reason	1.0	0.6	1.8	2.7					

– Represents or rounds to zero.

Source: U.S. Census Bureau, Current Population Survey, 2009 Annual Social and Economic Supplement, "Geographical Mobility: 2008 to 2009, Detailed Tables," <http://www.census.gov/population/www/socdemo/migrate.html>.

Population 37

Table 32. Mobility Status of Households by Household Income: 2009

[As of March (117,205 represents 117,205,000). Covers householders 15 years old and over. Based on comparison of place of residence in 2008 and 2009. Excludes members of the Armed Forces except those living off post or with their families on post. Based on Current Population Survey, Annual Social and Economic Supplement. See text, this section and Appendix III]

Household income in 2008	Total (1,000)	Non-movers	Movers (different house in United States) Total	Same county	Different county Total	Same state	Different state	Movers from abroad
Householders, 15 years and over.......	117,205	88	12	8	4	2	1	–
Less than $5,000......................	3,559	79	20	13	7	4	3	2
$5,000 to $9,999.....................	4,819	83	17	12	5	3	2	–
$10,000 to $14,999..................	6,847	86	14	10	4	3	1	–
$15,000 to $24,999..................	13,803	85	15	11	4	3	1	–
$25,000 to $34,999..................	12,734	85	14	11	4	3	1	–
$35,000 to $49,999..................	16,432	86	13	10	4	2	2	–
$50,000 to $69,999..................	17,290	89	10	7	3	2	2	–
$70,000 to $99,999..................	17,703	91	9	6	3	2	1	–
$100,000 and over...................	24,018	93	7	4	3	1	1	–

– Represents or rounds to zero.
Source: U.S. Census Bureau, Current Population Survey, 2009 Annual Social and Economic Supplement, "Geographical Mobility: 2008 to 2009, Detailed Tables," <http://www.census.gov/population/www/socdemo/migrate.html>.

Table 33. Mobility Status of Resident Population by State: 2008

[In percent, except as indicated (299,926 represents 299,926,000). Based on comparison of place of residence in 2007 and 2008. The American Community Survey universe includes the household population and the population living in institutions, college dormitories, and other group quarters. Based on a sample and subject to sampling variability. See text, this section and Appendix III]

State	Population 1 year old and over [1] (1,000)	Same house in 2007	Different house in United States in 2007 Same county	Different county	State	Population 1 year old and over [1] (1,000)	Same house in 2007	Different house in United States in 2007 Same county	Different county
U.S.....	299,926	84.4	9.2	5.7					
					MO.......	5,835	83.0	9.6	7.0
AL	4,601	84.6	9.1	6.0	MT	954	82.6	9.0	8.1
AK	675	76.9	13.3	9.0	NE	1,758	83.1	9.8	6.7
AZ	6,396	80.8	12.9	5.7	NV	2,560	79.0	14.7	5.6
AR	2,818	81.8	10.8	7.0	NH	1,302	86.9	6.9	5.8
CA	36,216	84.5	10.4	4.2					
					NJ	8,572	89.4	5.8	4.0
CO	4,865	80.2	9.9	9.2	NM	1,957	83.3	10.0	6.2
CT	3,461	87.5	7.5	4.3	NY	19,249	88.7	6.7	3.8
DE	862	85.3	8.5	5.7	NC	9,098	82.7	9.3	7.3
DC	584	80.1	10.8	7.6	ND	634	83.0	9.1	7.2
FL	18,108	83.6	9.8	5.8					
					OH.......	11,341	84.9	9.8	5.0
GA	9,548	82.6	8.7	8.2	OK.......	3,591	80.5	11.0	8.1
HI........	1,271	84.0	9.6	4.9	OR.......	3,739	82.1	10.4	7.0
ID........	1,499	80.2	11.2	7.9	PA	12,301	87.4	7.5	4.7
IL........	12,726	86.4	8.6	4.5	RI........	1,039	87.5	7.8	4.1
IN........	6,289	83.8	9.7	6.1					
					SC	4,420	84.9	8.3	6.4
IA........	2,960	83.3	9.8	6.5	SD	793	84.8	8.1	6.8
KS	2,761	82.1	10.3	7.0	TN	6,134	83.5	9.8	6.3
KY	4,210	84.5	8.6	6.4	TX	23,922	81.7	10.8	6.7
LA	4,350	84.6	9.1	6.0	UT	2,683	81.6	10.5	6.9
ME.......	1,303	85.4	8.6	5.7					
					VT	615	86.6	7.6	5.5
MD......	5,563	86.6	6.7	5.9	VA	7,670	83.7	7.0	8.5
MA......	6,424	86.2	7.8	5.0	WA......	6,457	82.0	10.8	6.2
MI.......	9,884	85.1	9.4	5.0	WV......	1,795	87.2	7.1	5.4
MN......	5,149	85.9	7.6	6.1	WI	5,558	85.5	8.9	5.3
MS.......	2,898	84.7	8.8	6.3	WY.......	526	82.1	9.6	8.0

[1] Includes persons moving from abroad, not shown separately.
Source: U.S. Census Bureau, 2008 American Community Survey, B07003, "Residence 1 Year Ago by Sex," <http://factfinder.census.gov/>, accessed September 2009.

Table 34. Persons 65 Years Old and Over—Characteristics by Sex: 1990 to 2009

[As of March, except as noted (29.6 represents 29,600,000). Covers civilian noninstitutional population. Excludes members of Armed Forces except those living off post or with their families on post. Data for 1990 are based on 1980 census population controls; 2000 data based on 1990 census population controls; beginning 2005, data based on 2000 census population controls and an expanded sample of households. Based on Current Population Survey. See text, this section and Appendix III]

Characteristic	Total				Male				Female			
	1990	2000	2005	2009	1990	2000	2005	2009	1990	2000	2005	2009
Total (million)	**29.6**	**32.6**	**35.2**	**37.8**	**12.3**	**13.9**	**15.1**	**16.3**	**17.2**	**18.7**	**20.0**	**21.5**
PERCENT DISTRIBUTION												
Marital status:												
Never married	4.6	3.9	4.1	4.2	4.2	4.2	4.4	4.4	4.9	3.6	3.9	4.0
Married	56.1	57.2	57.7	57.2	76.5	75.2	74.9	74.4	41.4	43.8	44.7	44.1
Spouse present.............	54.1	54.6	54.8	54.8	74.2	72.6	71.7	72.0	39.7	41.3	42.0	41.8
Spouse absent.............	2.0	2.6	2.9	2.3	2.3	2.6	3.2	2.4	1.7	2.5	2.7	2.3
Widowed	34.2	32.1	30.3	29.0	14.2	14.4	13.7	12.9	48.6	45.3	42.9	41.3
Divorced	5.0	6.7	7.9	9.6	5.0	6.1	7.0	8.3	5.1	7.2	8.5	10.7
Educational attainment:												
Less than ninth grade	28.5	16.7	13.4	10.7	30.0	17.8	13.2	10.4	27.5	15.9	13.5	10.9
Completed 9th to 12th grade, but no high school diploma	[1] 16.1	13.8	12.7	11.0	[1] 15.7	12.7	11.9	10.0	[1] 16.4	14.7	13.3	11.7
High school graduate.........	[2] 32.9	35.9	36.3	36.5	[2] 29.0	30.4	31.6	32.0	[2] 35.6	39.9	39.9	39.9
Some college or associate's degree	[3] 10.9	18.0	18.7	20.2	[3] 10.8	17.8	18.4	19.4	[3] 11.0	18.2	19.0	20.8
Bachelor's or advanced degree	[4] 11.6	15.6	18.9	21.7	[4] 14.5	21.4	24.9	28.2	[4] 9.5	11.4	14.3	16.8
Labor force participation: [5]												
Employed...................	11.5	12.4	14.5	16.1	15.9	16.9	19.1	20.5	8.4	9.1	11.1	12.8
Unemployed...............	0.4	0.4	0.5	1.1	0.5	0.6	0.7	1.5	0.3	0.3	0.4	0.8
Not in labor force	88.1	87.2	84.9	82.8	83.6	82.5	80.2	78.1	91.3	90.6	88.5	86.4
Percent below poverty level [6]	11.4	9.7	9.8	(NA)	7.8	6.9	7.0	(NA)	13.9	11.8	11.9	(NA)

[1] Represents those who completed 1 to 3 years of high school. [2] Represents those who completed 4 years of high school. [3] Represents those who completed 1 to 3 years of college. [4] Represents those who completed 4 years of college or more. [5] Annual averages of monthly figures. Source: U.S. Bureau of Labor Statistics, *Employment and Earnings*, January issues. See footnote 2, Table 584. [6] Poverty status based on income in preceding year.

Source: Except as noted, U.S. Census Bureau, Current Population Reports, *The Older Population in the United States: March 2002*, P20-546, 2003, and earlier reports; "Educational Attainment," <http://www.census.gov/population/www/socdemo/educ attn html>; "Families and Living Arrangements," <http://www.census.gov/population/www/socdemo/hh-fam.html>; and "Detailed Poverty Tabulations from the CPS," <http://www.census.gov/hhes/www/cpstables/032009/pov/toc.htm>.

Table 35. Persons 65 Years and Over—Living Arrangements and Disability Status: 2008

[In thousands (38,812 represents 38,812,000), except as indicated. The American Community Survey universe includes the household population and the population living in institutions, college dormitories, and other group quarters. Based on a sample and subject to sampling variability; see text, this section and Appendix III]

Relationship by household type	Number	Percent distribu- tion	Type of disability	Total	65 to 74 years old	75 years old and over
Total.....................	**38,812**	**100.0**	**Persons with any disability**.........	**14,180**	**5,278**	**8,902**
In households	36,899	95.1				
In family households	25,260	65.1	With a hearing disability.............	5,854	1,867	3,987
Householder	12,523	32.3	With a vision disability	2,847	919	1,928
Spouse	8,962	23.1	With a cognitive disability	3,661	1,116	2,545
Parent	2,193	5.7	With a ambulatory disability...........	9,196	3,324	5,871
Other relatives................	1,424	3.7	With a self-care disability.............	3,419	969	2,450
Nonrelatives.................	158	0.4	With an independent living disability	6,384	1,722	4,662
In nonfamily households	11,639	30.0				
Householder	11,144	28.7				
Living alone	10,632	27.4				
Not living alone	513	1.3				
Nonrelatives.................	495	1.3				
In group quarters	1,913	4.9				

Source: U.S. Census Bureau, 2008 American Community Survey, B09017, "Relationship by Household Type (Including Living Alone) for the Population 65 Years and Over;" B18101, "Sex by Age by Disability Status;" B18102, "Sex by Age by Hearing Difficulty;" B18103, "Sex by Age by Vision Difficulty;" B18104, "Sex by Age by Cognitive Difficulty;" B18105, "Sex by Age by Ambulatory Difficulty;" B18106, "Sex by Age by Self-Care Difficulty;" B18107, "Sex by Age by Independent Living Difficulty," <http://factfinder.census.gov/>, accessed October 2009.

Table 36. Selected Characteristics of Racial Groups and Hispanic Population: 2008

[In thousands (200,030 represents 200,030,000), except as indicated. The American Community Survey universe includes the household population and the population living in institutions, college dormitories, and other group quarters. Based on a sample and subject to sampling variability; see text, this section and Appendix III. For definition of median, see Guide to Tabular Presentation]

Characteristic	Total population	White alone	Black or African American alone	American Indian, Alaska Native alone	Asian alone
EDUCATIONAL ATTAINMENT					
Persons 25 years old and over, total	**200,030**	**155,486**	**22,611**	**1,455**	**9,189**
Less than 9th grade.	12,740	8,075	1,321	141	809
9th to 12th grade, no diploma	17,329	11,822	3,053	214	560
High school graduate (includes equivalency)	57,032	45,080	7,110	442	1,468
Some college, no degree.	42,565	33,453	5,484	363	1,178
Associate's degree	15,006	11,959	1,677	111	610
Bachelor's degree	35,003	28,477	2,604	127	2,734
Graduate degree	20,354	16,621	1,362	57	1,830
Percent high school graduate or higher.	85.0	87.2	80.7	75.6	85.1
Percent bachelor's degree or higher	27.7	29.0	17.5	12.7	49.7
OCCUPATION					
Employed civilian population, 16 years old and over, total . . .	**146,266**	**113,032**	**15,931**	**998**	**6,892**
Management, professional, and related occupations	51,064	41,370	4,369	241	3,275
Management, business and financial operations occupations	20,538	17,041	1,585	99	1,084
Professional and related occupations	30,526	24,329	2,784	142	2,191
Service occupations	25,084	17,523	3,913	231	1,116
Sales and office occupations.	37,253	29,126	4,229	239	1,517
Farming, fishing, and forestry occupations	998	740	51	16	12
Construction, extraction, and maintenance occupations	13,613	10,975	915	129	244
Construction and extraction occupations.	8,632	6,907	513	95	104
Installation, maintenance, and repair occupations	4,981	4,067	403	34	140
Production, transportation, and material moving occupations.	18,254	13,297	2,453	142	728
Production occupations	9,314	6,834	1,056	73	504
Transportation and material moving occupations	8,940	6,464	1,397	69	224
FAMILY INCOME IN THE PAST 12 MONTHS					
Total families	**75,031**	**58,602**	**8,454**	**545**	**3,156**
Less than $10,000.	3,211	1,883	874	48	106
$10,000 to $19,999	5,264	3,401	1,096	68	182
$20,000 to $29,999	6,575	4,641	1,089	70	205
$30,000 to $39,999	6,973	5,162	986	67	222
$40,000 to $49,999	6,809	5,247	822	54	221
$50,000 to $59,999	6,441	5,111	694	48	218
$60,000 to $74,999	8,704	7,037	838	54	327
$75,000 to $99,999	11,048	9,132	915	65	454
$100,000 to $124,999	7,353	6,149	524	35	379
$125,000 to $149,999	4,215	3,550	269	15	251
$150,000 to $199,999	4,252	3,616	221	12	296
$200,000 or more	4,185	3,674	127	11	295
Median family income in the past 12 months (dol.)	63,366	67,785	41,874	43,190	80,101
POVERTY STATUS IN THE PAST 12 MONTHS [2]					
Persons below poverty level	39,108	23,935	8,662	571	1,384
Percent below poverty level.	13.2	10.7	24.1	24.2	10.5
Families below poverty level	7,252	4,319	1,757	109	252
Percent below poverty level.	9.7	7.4	20.8	19.9	8.0
HOUSING TENURE					
Total householders	**113,101**	**89,002**	**13,368**	**796**	**4,242**
Owner-occupied	75,373	63,692	6,094	438	2,521
Renter-occupied	37,728	25,310	7,274	357	1,721

See footnotes at end of table.

U.S. Census Bureau, Statistical Abstract of the United States: 2011

Table 36. Selected Characteristics of Racial Groups and Hispanic Population: 2008—Con.

[See headnote, page 40]

Characteristic	Native Hawaiian and Other Pacific Islander alone	Some other race alone	Two or more races	Hispanic origin [1]	White alone, not Hispanic
EDUCATIONAL ATTAINMENT					
Persons 25 years old and over, total	**247**	**8,232**	**2,811**	**25,558**	**139,290**
Less than 9th grade	12	2,202	180	6,031	4,440
9th to 12th grade, no diploma	22	1,405	254	3,997	9,393
High school graduate (includes equivalency)	84	2,146	703	6,641	40,877
Some college, no degree	69	1,266	753	4,235	30,745
Associate's degree	25	388	238	1,353	11,072
Bachelor's degree	26	593	442	2,267	26,908
Graduate degree	11	232	241	1,033	15,855
Percent high school graduate or higher	86.6	56.2	84.6	60.8	90.1
Percent bachelor's degree or higher	14.9	10.0	24.3	12.9	30.7
OCCUPATION					
Employed civilian population, 16 years old and over, total	**205**	**6,870**	**2,339**	**20,663**	**100,157**
Management, professional, and related occupations	49	1,033	727	3,794	38,799
Management, business and financial operations occupations	20	433	275	1,616	15,935
Professional and related occupations	29	600	452	2,178	22,864
Service occupations	50	1,760	491	5,049	14,465
Sales and office occupations	57	1,441	643	4,593	26,216
Farming, fishing, and forestry occupations	1	166	12	469	454
Construction, extraction, and maintenance occupations	21	1,130	200	3,138	9,072
Construction and extraction occupations	13	877	124	2,390	5,465
Installation, maintenance, and repair occupations	8	253	76	747	3,608
Production, transportation, and material moving occupations	28	1,339	267	3,621	11,151
Production occupations	11	715	123	1,894	5,716
Transportation and material moving occupations	17	624	144	1,727	5,435
FAMILY INCOME IN THE PAST 12 MONTHS					
Total families	**87**	**3,142**	**1,044**	**9,678**	**52,483**
Less than $10,000	5	231	66	633	1,517
$10,000 to $19,999	7	413	98	1,202	2,662
$20,000 to $29,999	7	460	104	1,354	3,797
$30,000 to $39,999	8	417	111	1,245	4,392
$40,000 to $49,999	6	361	98	1,055	4,596
$50,000 to $59,999	8	278	84	860	4,566
$60,000 to $74,999	11	318	119	993	6,406
$75,000 to $99,999	15	325	142	1,038	8,462
$100,000 to $124,999	10	168	89	575	5,768
$125,000 to $149,999	5	76	48	292	3,348
$150,000 to $199,999	3	61	44	256	3,432
$200,000 or more	2	36	41	177	3,538
Median family income in the past 12 months (dol.)	63,448	41,153	54,882	43,437	70,835
POVERTY STATUS IN THE PAST 12 MONTHS [2]					
Persons below poverty level	68	3,349	1,140	9,795	18,028
Percent below poverty level	16.3	22.8	16.8	21.3	9.3
Families below poverty level	11	658	145	1,838	3,222
Percent below poverty level	13.1	21.0	13.9	19.0	6.1
HOUSING TENURE					
Total householders	**117**	**3,976**	**1,600**	**12,627**	**80,953**
Owner-occupied	56	1,703	870	6,198	59,446
Renter-occupied	61	2,274	731	6,429	21,507

[1] Persons of Hispanic origin may be of any race. [2] For explanation of poverty level, see text, Section 13.

Source: U.S. Census Bureau, 2008 American Community Survey, B15002, "Sex by Educational Attainment for the Population 25 Years and Over"; B24010, "Sex by Occupation for the Employed Civilian Population 16 Years and Over"; B19101, "Family Income in the Past 12 Months (In 2008 Inflation-Adjusted Dollars)"; B19113, "Median Family Income in the Past 12 Months (In 2008 Inflation-Adjusted Dollars)"; B17001, "Poverty Status in the Past 12 Months by Sex by Age"; B17010, "Poverty Status in the Past 12 Months of Families by Family Type by Presence of Related Children Under 18 Years by Age of Related Children"; B25003, "Tenure," <http://factfinder.census.gov/>.

Table 37. Social and Economic Characteristics of the Hispanic Population: 2009

[As of March, except labor force status, annual average (47,485 represents 47,485,000). Excludes members of the Armed Forces except those living off post or with their families on post. Based on Current Population Survey; see text, this section and Appendix III]

Characteristic	Number (1,000)					Percent distribution				
	His-panic, total [1]	Mexi-can	Puerto Rican	Cuban	Central, South Ameri-can	His-panic, total [1]	Mexi-can	Puerto Rican	Cuban	Central, South Ameri-can
Total persons	**47,485**	**31,550**	**4,224**	**1,647**	**7,583**	**100.0**	**100.0**	**100.0**	**100.0**	**100.0**
Under 5 years old	5,396	3,919	462	85	673	11.4	12.4	10.9	5.1	8.9
5 to 14 years old	8,640	6,072	800	192	1,115	18.2	19.2	19.0	11.7	14.7
15 to 44 years old	22,648	15,174	1,907	659	3,871	47.7	48.0	45.2	40.0	51.1
45 to 64 years old	8,084	4,879	794	385	1,528	17.0	15.5	18.8	23.4	20.1
65 years old and over	2,717	1,505	262	326	396	5.7	4.8	6.2	19.8	5.2
EDUCATIONAL ATTAINMENT										
Persons 25 years old and over	**25,956**	**16,461**	**2,244**	**1,164**	**4,696**	**100.0**	**100.0**	**100.0**	**100.0**	**100.0**
High school graduate or more	16,066	9,168	1,718	914	3,160	61.9	55.7	76.6	78.5	67.3
Bachelor's degree or more	3,428	1,566	370	325	920	13.2	9.5	16.5	27.9	19.6
LABOR FORCE STATUS [2]										
Civilians 16 years old and over	**32,585**	**20,984**	**2,867**	**1,349**	**(NA)**	**100.0**	**100.0**	**100.0**	**100.0**	**100.0**
Civilian labor force	21,971	14,082	1,772	802	(NA)	67.4	67.1	61.8	59.5	(NA)
Employed	19,285	12,313	1,525	734	(NA)	59.2	58.7	53.2	54.4	(NA)
Unemployed	2,686	1,769	246	68	(NA)	8.2	8.4	8.6	5.0	(NA)
Unemployment rate [3]	12.2	12.6	13.9	8.5	(NA)	(X)	(X)	(X)	(X)	(X)
Male	13.1	13.1	16.9	8.9	(NA)	(X)	(X)	(X)	(X)	(X)
Female	11.0	11.6	10.8	7.8	(NA)	(X)	(X)	(X)	(X)	(X)
Not in labor force	10,614	6,902	1,095	547	(NA)	32.6	32.9	38.2	40.5	(NA)
HOUSEHOLDS										
Total	**13,425**	**8,335**	**1,369**	**630**	**2,362**	**100.0**	**100.0**	**100.0**	**100.0**	**100.0**
Family households	10,503	6,731	985	440	1,839	78.2	80.8	72.0	69.8	77.9
Married-couple families [4]	6,911	4,613	518	313	1,144	51.5	55.3	37.8	49.7	48.4
Male householder, no spouse present	1,021	652	89	32	208	7.6	7.8	6.5	5.1	8.8
Female householder, no spouse present	2,571	1,466	378	95	487	19.2	17.6	27.6	15.1	20.6
Nonfamily households	2,923	1,604	384	190	523	21.8	19.2	28.0	30.2	22.1
Male householder	1,578	917	186	79	293	11.8	11.0	13.6	12.5	12.4
Female householder	1,345	687	199	111	230	10.0	8.2	14.5	17.6	9.7
Size:										
One person	2,195	1,175	326	151	363	16.4	14.1	23.8	24.0	15.4
Two people	3,067	1,733	361	211	558	22.8	20.8	26.4	33.5	23.6
Three people	2,613	1,522	277	124	536	19.5	18.3	20.2	19.7	22.7
Four people	2,597	1,717	221	90	480	19.3	20.6	16.1	14.3	20.3
Five people	1,705	1,221	120	36	265	12.7	14.6	8.8	5.7	11.2
Six people	754	567	40	15	106	5.6	6.8	2.9	2.4	4.5
Seven people or more	494	400	24	4	53	3.7	4.8	1.8	0.6	2.2
FAMILY INCOME IN 2008										
Total families [5]	**10,503**	**6,731**	**985**	**440**	**1,778**	**100.0**	**100.0**	**100.0**	**100.0**	**100.0**
Less than $5,000	436	281	56	7	65	4.1	4.2	5.6	1.8	3.6
$5,000 to $14,999	1,092	741	123	40	154	10.4	11.0	12.5	9.1	8.6
$15,000 to $24,999	1,504	1,021	132	56	231	14.3	15.2	13.4	12.8	13.0
$25,000 to $34,999	1,496	1,009	131	47	238	14.2	15.0	13.3	10.6	13.4
$35,000 to $49,999	1,761	1,169	131	74	313	16.8	17.4	13.3	16.9	17.6
$50,000 to $74,999	1,867	1,143	176	70	359	17.8	17.0	17.9	15.9	20.2
$75,000 and over	2,346	1,369	236	145	418	22.3	20.3	23.9	32.9	23.5
POVERTY STATUS IN 2008										
Families below poverty level [6]	2,239	1,565	224	55	314	21.3	23.2	22.7	12.6	17.6
Persons below poverty level [6]	10,987	7,821	1,065	277	1,431	23.2	24.8	25.2	16.8	18.9
HOUSEHOLD TENURE										
Total occupied units	**13,425**	**8,335**	**1,369**	**630**	**2,280**	**100.0**	**100.0**	**100.0**	**100.0**	**100.0**
Owner occupied	6,418	4,109	515	367	920	47.8	49.3	37.6	58.2	40.3
Renter occupied [7]	7,007	4,226	854	263	1,360	52.2	50.7	62.4	41.8	59.7

NA Not available. X Not applicable. [1] Includes other Hispanic groups not shown separately. [2] Source: U.S. Bureau of Labor Statistics, "Employment and Earnings Online," January 2010, <http://stats.bls.gov/opub/ee/home.htm>. [3] Total unemployment as percent of civilian labor force. [4] In married-couple families, Hispanic origin refers to the householder. [5] Includes families in group quarters. [6] For explanation of poverty level; see text, Section 13. [7] Includes no cash rent.

Source: Except as noted, U.S. Census Bureau, "Educational Attainment," <http://www.census.gov/population/www/socdemo/educ-attn.html>; "Families and Living Arrangements," <http://www.census.gov/population/www/socdemo/hh-fam.html>; "Detailed Income Tabulations from the CPS," <http://www.census.gov/hhes/www/income/dinctabs.html>; "Detailed Poverty Tabulations from the CPS," <http://www.census.gov/hhes/www/cpstables/032009/pov/toc.htm> ; and unpublished data.

Table 38. Native and Foreign-Born Population by State: 2008

[266,099 represents 266,099,000. The American Community Survey universe includes the household population and the population living in institutions, college dormitories, and other group quarters. Based on a sample and subject to sampling variability; see text, this section and Appendix III. See headnote, Table 42]

State	Native population (1,000)	Foreign-born population			State	Native population (1,000)	Foreign-born population		
		Number (1,000)	Percent of total population	Percent entered 2000 or later			Number (1,000)	Percent of total population	Percent entered 2000 or later
U.S.	266,099	37,961	12.5	29.5	MO.	5,696	215	3.6	39.7
AL	4,530	132	2.8	46.8	MT.	946	21	2.2	28.5
AK	642	44	6.5	29.1	NE.	1,686	98	5.5	38.1
AZ	5,568	933	14.3	33.2	NV	2,109	491	18.9	30.9
AR	2,746	109	3.8	36.6	NH	1,250	66	5.0	27.5
CA	26,898	9,859	26.8	24.0	NJ	6,965	1,718	19.8	29.6
CO	4,440	499	10.1	34.3	NM.	1,793	191	9.6	29.6
CT	3,047	454	13.0	29.9	NY	15,254	4,237	21.7	25.5
DE	806	67	7.7	36.9	NC	8,581	641	7.0	42.5
DC	514	78	13.2	40.5	ND	626	15	2.3	40.3
FL	14,937	3,392	18.5	29.2	OH	11,059	427	3.7	36.0
GA	8,775	910	9.4	39.2	OK	3,459	183	5.0	34.4
HI	1,059	229	17.8	28.5	OR	3,424	366	9.7	32.9
ID.	1,434	89	5.9	35.6	PA	11,788	660	5.3	32.6
IL	11,119	1,782	13.8	27.0	RI.	922	128	12.2	24.2
IN.	6,121	256	4.0	41.2	SC	4,285	195	4.4	41.4
IA.	2,890	112	3.7	40.7	SD	789	15	1.9	28.9
KS	2,638	164	5.9	36.5	TN	5,966	248	4.0	43.8
KY	4,150	120	2.8	49.2	TX	20,440	3,887	16.0	31.1
LA	4,276	135	3.1	29.6	UT	2,510	226	8.3	35.8
ME	1,277	39	3.0	20.6	VT	597	25	3.9	30.6
MD.	4,936	698	12.4	35.7	VA.	6,973	796	10.2	34.7
MA.	5,561	937	14.4	32.1	WA.	5,745	804	12.3	31.2
MI.	9,421	583	5.8	31.9	WV.	1,791	23	1.3	38.9
MN.	4,880	341	6.5	38.4	WI	5,380	248	4.4	34.0
MS.	2,878	61	2.1	51.3	WY.	520	12	2.3	37.9

Source: U.S. Census Bureau, 2008 American Community Survey, C05002, "Place of Birth by Citizenship Status" and C05005, "Year of Entry by Citizenship Status," <http://factfinder.census.gov/>, accessed October 2009.

Table 39. Nativity and Place of Birth of Resident Population— 25 Largest Cities: 2008

[778 represents 778,000. The American Community Survey universe includes the household population and the population living in institutions, college dormitories, and other group quarters. Based on a sample and subject to sampling variability; see text, this section and Appendix III. See headnote, Table 42]

City	Total population (1,000)	Native population			Foreign born			
		Total (1,000)	Born in United States (1,000)	Born outside United States (1,000)	Total		Entered 2000 or later	
					Number (1,000)	Percent of total population	Number (1,000)	Percent of foreign-born population
Austin, TX	778	622	611	11	156	20.0	73	46.6
Baltimore, MD	637	600	595	5	37	5.9	17	45.4
Boston, MA	613	448	431	17	165	26.9	56	34.1
Charlotte, NC	685	586	580	6	99	14.5	48	48.2
Chicago, IL.	2,741	2,155	2,103	52	587	21.4	161	27.4
Columbus, OH.	740	669	663	6	71	9.6	35	49.2
Dallas, TX	1,227	901	891	9	326	26.6	120	36.9
Denver, CO	599	491	483	8	108	18.1	38	35.6
Detroit, MI	777	740	736	4	38	4.9	12	32.7
El Paso, TX	602	442	430	12	161	26.6	33	20.8
Fort Worth, TX	678	550	542	9	128	18.8	44	34.5
Houston, TX.	2,024	1,450	1,430	20	574	28.4	204	35.6
Indianapolis, IN [1]	799	745	739	5	54	6.7	27	49.3
Jacksonville, FL	812	746	727	19	66	8.1	22	33.7
Los Angeles, CA	3,803	2,305	2,266	39	1,498	39.4	382	25.5
Memphis, TN	636	603	599	4	33	5.2	17	51.6
Nashville-Davidson, TN [1]	601	533	529	5	68	11.3	34	50.0
New York, NY.	8,364	5,323	4,999	324	3,041	36.4	784	25.8
Philadelphia, PA.	1,447	1,296	1,243	53	151	10.5	51	33.9
Phoenix, AZ.	1,525	1,170	1,155	15	355	23.3	134	37.7
San Antonio, TX.	1,293	1,128	1,102	26	165	12.7	39	24.0
San Diego, CA.	1,267	948	927	21	319	25.2	83	26.1
San Francisco, CA.	809	526	515	11	283	35.0	67	23.5
San Jose, CA.	917	568	557	11	349	38.1	92	26.2
Washington, DC.	592	514	506	8	78	13.2	32	40.5

[1] Represents the portion of a consolidated city that is not within one or more separately incorporated places.
Source: U.S. Census Bureau, 2008 American Community Survey, C05002, "Place of Birth by Citizenship Status" and C05005, "Year of Entry by Citizenship Status," <http://factfinder.census.gov/>, accessed October 2009.

Population 43

Table 40. Native and Foreign-Born Populations by Selected Characteristics: 2009

[In thousands (301,483 represents 301,483,000). As of March. The foreign-born population includes anyone who is not a U.S. citizen at birth. This includes legal permanent residents (immigrants), temporary migrants (such as students), humanitarian migrants (such as refugees), and persons illegally present in the United States. Based on Current Population Survey, Annual Social and Economic Supplement which includes the civilian noninstitutional population plus Armed Forces living off post or with their families on post; see text, this section, and Appendix III]

Characteristic	Total population	Native population	Foreign-born population			
			Total	Natural-ized citizen	Not U.S. citizen	Year of entry: 2000 to March 2009
Total.	**301,483**	**264,733**	**36,750**	**15,475**	**21,274**	**11,549**
Under 5 years old	21,187	20,924	263	57	206	263
5 to 14 years old	40,152	38,550	1,602	291	1,311	1,279
15 to 24 years old	41,859	38,126	3,734	845	2,889	2,097
25 to 34 years old	40,520	32,921	7,600	1,851	5,749	3,767
35 to 44 years old	41,322	33,063	8,259	3,128	5,131	2,188
45 to 54 years old	44,366	37,707	6,659	3,525	3,134	1,085
55 to 64 years old	34,289	30,092	4,196	2,600	1,596	496
65 to 74 years old	20,404	17,900	2,504	1,719	785	254
75 to 84 years old	13,005	11,548	1,458	1,080	378	96
85 years old and over	4,378	3,903	475	377	98	24
Median age (years)	36.7	35.6	41.0	49.3	35.8	30.2
Male.	148,094	129,810	18,285	7,176	11,109	5,970
Female.	153,388	134,924	18,465	8,299	10,166	5,579
MARITAL STATUS						
Persons 15 years old and over.	**240,144**	**205,259**	**34,885**	**15,126**	**19,759**	**10,007**
Married	125,076	103,356	21,720	10,096	11,624	5,650
Widowed	14,261	12,559	1,701	1,120	581	181
Divorced	23,277	21,143	2,134	1,182	952	318
Separated	5,412	4,278	1,134	400	734	291
Never married	72,118	63,923	8,196	2,328	5,868	3,567
EDUCATIONAL ATTAINMENT						
Persons 25 years old and over.	**198,285**	**167,133**	**31,152**	**14,282**	**16,870**	**7,911**
Not high school graduate.	26,415	16,820	9,594	2,749	6,845	2,503
High school graduate/some college	113,296	100,650	12,646	6,606	6,041	2,743
Bachelor's degree	37,636	32,107	5,529	3,129	2,399	1,639
Advanced degree	20,938	17,556	3,382	1,797	1,585	1,025
EARNINGS IN 2008 [1]						
Persons 15 years old and over with earnings...	**104,017**	**87,690**	**16,327**	**7,473**	**8,854**	**4,363**
Under $15,000.	6,369	4,766	1,603	427	1,176	622
$15,000 to $24,999	15,928	12,093	3,835	1,224	2,611	1,338
$25,000 to $34,999	18,660	15,620	3,040	1,292	1,748	765
$35,000 to $49,999	22,392	19,551	2,841	1,537	1,303	593
$50,000 to $74,999	21,793	19,334	2,459	1,448	1,011	541
$75,000 and over.	18,875	16,325	2,550	1,545	1,005	505
Median earnings (dollars) [2]	41,030	41,818	32,631	41,399	27,532	26,931
HOUSEHOLD SIZE [3]						
Total households.	**117,181**	**101,586**	**15,595**	**7,667**	**7,928**	**3,672**
One person	31,657	28,734	2,923	1,607	1,316	629
Two persons	39,242	35,395	3,847	2,172	1,675	859
Three persons	18,606	15,647	2,960	1,352	1,607	852
Four persons	16,099	13,227	2,873	1,278	1,594	699
Five persons	7,406	5,680	1,726	730	996	361
Six persons	2,640	1,879	762	325	437	173
Seven persons or more	1,529	1,024	505	203	302	99
INCOME IN 2008 [3]						
Total family households	**78,850**	**66,883**	**11,967**	**5,830**	**6,137**	**2,733**
Under $15,000.	5,685	4,470	1,215	370	845	367
$15,000 to $24,999	6,900	5,429	1,470	512	958	432
$25,000 to $34,999	7,544	6,114	1,430	605	825	346
$35,000 to $49,999	10,765	8,898	1,867	842	1,025	440
$50,000 to $74,999	15,459	13,326	2,133	1,100	1,033	430
$75,000 and over.	32,496	28,646	3,850	2,400	1,450	717
Median income (dollars) [2]	62,621	65,319	50,002	61,705	40,406	41,054
POVERTY STATUS IN 2008 [4]						
Persons below poverty level	39,829	33,293	6,536	1,577	4,959	2,757
Persons at or above poverty level	261,212	231,021	30,191	13,894	16,297	8,772
HOUSEHOLD TENURE [3]						
Total households.	**117,181**	**101,585**	**15,596**	**7,668**	**7,928**	**3,671**
Owner occupied unit	78,825	70,757	8,068	5,159	2,909	943
Renter occupied unit [5]	38,356	30,828	7,528	2,509	5,019	2,728

[1] Covers only year-round, full-time workers. [2] For definition of median, see Guide to Tabular Presentation. [3] Based on citizenship of householder. [4] Persons for whom poverty status is determined. Excludes unrelated individuals under 15 years old. [5] Includes occupiers who paid no cash rent.

Source: U.S. Census Bureau, Current Population Survey, "Annual Social and Economic Supplement," <http://www.census.gov/population/www/socdemo/foreign/datatbls.html>.

Table 41. Foreign-Born Population—Selected Characteristic by Region of Origin: 2009

[In thousands (36,750 represents 36,750,000). As of March. The term foreign-born refers to anyone who is not a U.S. citizen at birth. This includes naturalized U.S. citizens, legal permanent residents (immigrants), temporary migrants (such as foreign students), humanitarian migrants (such as refugees), and persons illegally present in the United States. Based on Current Population Survey, Annual Social and Economic Supplement; see text, this section and Appendix III]

Characteristic	Total foreign-born	Europe	Asia	Latin America Total	Caribbean	Central America [1]	South America	Other areas
Total	**36,750**	**4,571**	**9,924**	**19,883**	**3,335**	**14,209**	**2,338**	**2,372**
Under 5 years old	263	27	100	110	7	92	10	26
5 to 14 years old	1,602	167	433	884	103	707	75	118
15 to 24 years old	3,734	298	804	2,341	305	1,817	219	291
25 to 34 years old	7,600	574	1,825	4,733	520	3,744	469	468
35 to 44 years old	8,259	746	2,229	4,763	629	3,582	553	521
45 to 54 years old	6,659	779	1,926	3,488	697	2,262	528	466
55 to 64 years old	4,196	746	1,323	1,916	479	1,170	267	211
65 to 74 years old	2,504	571	779	1,010	324	554	131	144
75 to 84 years old	1,458	461	416	509	213	233	63	72
85 years old and over	475	202	89	129	58	48	23	55
EDUCATIONAL ATTAINMENT								
Persons 25 years old and over	**31,152**	**4,080**	**8,588**	**16,547**	**2,919**	**11,593**	**2,034**	**1,937**
Less than ninth grade	6,128	358	640	4,997	369	4,449	179	133
9th to 12th grade (no diploma)	3,466	174	446	2,783	300	2,354	129	63
High school graduate	7,682	1,082	1,692	4,424	900	2,838	687	484
Some college or associate's degree	4,965	881	1,249	2,353	728	1,180	444	482
Bachelor's degree	5,529	919	2,719	1,436	449	599	389	455
Advanced degree	3,382	666	1,842	554	174	174	206	320
High school graduate or more	21,557	3,548	7,502	8,767	2,251	4,790	1,726	1,740
Bachelor's degree or more	8,911	1,585	4,561	1,990	623	772	595	775
INCOME IN 2008								
Total family households	**11,965**	**1,508**	**3,293**	**6,436**	**1,179**	**4,531**	**726**	**729**
Under $15,000	1,215	66	251	827	130	640	56	71
$15,000 to $24,999	1,470	178	256	974	162	758	54	62
$25,000 to $34,999	1,430	112	226	1,003	155	759	89	89
$35,000 to $49,999	1,867	197	406	1,174	188	845	141	91
$50,000 to $74,999	2,133	263	579	1,180	228	806	146	111
$75,000 and over	3,850	691	1,575	1,279	315	724	240	305
Median income (dol.) [2]	50,002	65,434	71,597	39,432	45,211	36,374	52,074	60,711
POVERTY STATUS IN 2008 [3]								
Persons below poverty level	6,536	412	1,206	4,546	614	3,701	233	372
Persons at or above poverty level	30,191	4,157	8,713	15,323	2,719	10,502	2,105	1,998

[1] Includes Mexico. [2] For definition of median, see Guide to Tabular Presentation. [3] Persons for whom poverty status is determined. Excludes unrelated individuals under 15 years old.

Source: U.S. Census Bureau, Current Population Survey, "Annual Social and Economic Supplement," <http://www.census.gov/population/www/socdemo/foreign/datatbls.html>.

Table 42. Foreign-Born Population by Citizenship Status and Place of Birth: 2008

[In thousands, except percent. (37,961 represents 37,961,000). The term foreign-born refers to anyone who is not a U.S. citizen at birth. This includes naturalized U.S. citizens, legal permanent residents (immigrants), temporary migrants (such as foreign students), humanitarian migrants (such as refugees), and persons illegally present in the United States. The American Community Survey universe includes the household population and the population living in institutions, college dormitories, and other group quarters. Based on a sample and subject to sampling variability; see text, this section and Appendix III]

Region	Foreign-born population, total	Naturalized citizen	Not U.S. citizen Number	Not U.S. citizen Percent of foreign-born
Total [1]	**37,961**	**16,330**	**21,631**	**57**
Latin America	20,150	6,318	13,832	69
Caribbean	3,408	1,853	1,555	46
Central America	14,175	3,357	10,818	76
Mexico	11,413	2,523	8,889	78
Other Central America	2,763	834	1,929	70
South America	2,567	1,107	1,460	57
Asia	10,356	5,953	4,403	43
Europe	4,969	2,998	1,971	40
Africa	1,436	(NA)	(NA)	(NA)
Northern America	827	(NA)	(NA)	(NA)
Oceania	223	(NA)	(NA)	(NA)

NA Not available. [1] Includes persons born at sea.

Source: U.S. Census Bureau, 2008 American Community Survey, B05002, "Place of Birth by Citizenship Status"; C05006, "Place of Birth for the Foreign-Born Population"; and B05007, "Place of Birth by Year of Entry by Citizenship Status for the Foreign-Born Population," <http://factfinder.census.gov>, accessed September 2009.

Table 43. Persons Obtaining Legal Permanent Resident Status: 1901 to 2009

[8,795 represents 8,795,000. For fiscal years ending in year shown; see text, Section 8. Rates based on Census Bureau estimates as of July 1 for resident population through 1929 and for total population thereafter (excluding Alaska and Hawaii prior to 1959)]

Period	Number (1,000)	Rate [1]	Year	Number (1,000)	Rate [1]
1901 to 1910	8,795	10.4	1990	1,536	6.1
1911 to 1920	5,736	5.7	1995	720	2.7
1921 to 1930	4,107	3.5	2000	841	3.0
1931 to 1940	528	0.4	2002	1,059	3.7
1941 to 1950	1,035	0.7	2003	704	2.4
1951 to 1960	2,515	1.5	2004	958	3.3
1961 to 1970	3,322	1.7	2005	1,122	3.8
1971 to 1980	4,399	2.0	2006	1,266	4.2
1981 to 1990	7,256	3.0	2007	1,052	3.5
1991 to 2000	9,081	3.4	2008	1,107	3.6
2001 to 2009	9,458	3.5	2009	1,131	3.7

[1] Annual rate per 1,000 U.S. population. Rate computed by dividing sum of annual immigration totals by sum of annual U.S. population totals for same number of years.

Source: U.S. Department of Homeland Security, Office of Immigration Statistics, *2009 Yearbook of Immigration Statistics*. See also <http://www.dhs.gov/ximgtn/statistics/publications/yearbook.shtm>.

Table 44. Refugee Arrivals and Individuals Granted Asylum by Country of Nationality: 2005 to 2009

[For year ending September 30. Data shown provide information on the number of persons admitted to the United States as refugees or granted asylum in the United States in the year shown. In cases with no country of nationality refers to country of last residence. For definitions of refugee and asylee, see text, this section. Based on data from the Bureau of Population, Refugees, and Migration of the U.S. Department of State and the Executive Office for Immigration Review of the U.S. Department of Justice]

Country of nationality	Refugee arrivals			Country of nationality	Asylees		
	2005	2008	2009		2005	2008	2009
Total	53,738	60,107	74,602	Total	25,221	22,838	22,119
Iraq	198	13,822	18,838	China	5,251	5,459	6,109
Burma	1,447	18,139	18,202	Ethiopia	730	897	1,113
Bhutan	–	5,320	13,452	Haiti	2,935	1,236	998
Iran	1,856	5,270	5,381	Colombia	3,363	1,644	993
Cuba	6,360	4,177	4,800	Iraq	286	996	908
Somalia	10,405	2,523	4,189	Nepal	313	496	671
Vietnam	327	251	1,571	Venezuela	1,104	1,052	583
Burundi	2,009	1,112	1,486	Guatemala	388	541	513
Ukraine	424	727	1,135	Russia	487	571	494
Liberia	214	2,889	762	Egypt	336	416	481
Other countries [1]	30,498	5,877	4,786	Other countries [1]	10,028	9,530	9,256

– Represents zero. [1] Includes unknown.

Source: U.S. Department of Homeland Security, Office of Immigration Statistics, Annual Flow Report, *Refugees and Asylees: 2009*. See also <http://www.dhs.gov/xlibrary/assets/statistics/publications/ois_rfa_fr_2009.pdf>.

Table 45. Estimated Unauthorized Immigrants by Selected States and Countries of Birth: 2000 and 2009

[In thousands (8,460 represents 8,460,000). As of January. Unauthorized immigrants refers to foreign-born persons who entered the United States without inspection or who were admitted temporarily and stayed past the date they were required to leave. Unauthorized aliens who have applied for but have not yet received approval to lawfully remain in the United States are considered to be unauthorized. These estimates were calculated using a "residual method," whereby estimates of the legally resident foreign-born population were subtracted from the total foreign-born population in order to derive the unauthorized immigrant population. All of these component populations were resident in the United States on January 1, 2009, and entered during the 1980–2008 period. Persons who entered the United States prior to 1980 were assumed to be legally resident. Estimates of the legally resident foreign-born were based primarily on administrative data of the Department of Homeland Security, while estimates of the total foreign-born population were obtained from the American Community Survey of the U.S. Census Bureau. Estimates for 2000 are based on the same methodology, assumptions, and definitions with the exception that data from Census 2000 were used to estimate the foreign-born population in 2000 that entered the United States from January 1, 1980 through December 31, 1999]

State of residence	2000	2009	Country of birth	2000	2009
United States, total . . .	**8,460**	**10,750**	**Total**	**8,460**	**10,750**
California	2,510	2,600	Mexico	4,680	6,650
Texas	1,090	1,680	El Salvador	430	530
Florida	800	720	Guatemala	290	480
New York	540	550	Honduras	160	320
Illinois	440	540	Philippines	200	270
Georgia	220	480	Korea	180	200
Arizona	330	460	India	120	200
North Carolina	260	370	Ecuador	110	170
New Jersey	350	360	Brazil	100	150
Nevada	170	260	China	190	120
Other states	1,760	2,730	Other countries	2,000	1,650

Source: U.S. Department of Homeland Security, Office of Immigration Statistics, "Estimates of the Unauthorized Immigrant Population Residing in the United States: January 2009." See also <www.dhs.gov/xlibrary/assets/statistics/publications/ois_ill_pe_2009.pdf>.

Table 46. Immigrant Orphans Adopted by U.S. Citizens by Sex, Age, Region, and Country of Birth: 2009

[For years ending September 30]

Region and country of birth	Total	Male	Female	Under 1 year old	1 to 4 years old	5 years old and over
REGION						
Total	**12,782**	**5,561**	**7,221**	**3,208**	**6,580**	**2,994**
Africa	2,722	1,342	1,380	892	1,074	756
Asia	5,991	2,232	3,759	2,079	3,127	785
Europe	2,343	1,260	1,083	91	1,432	820
North America	1,325	552	773	59	846	420
Oceania	33	18	15	21	6	6
South America	354	154	200	66	86	202
Unknown	14	3	11	–	9	5
COUNTRY						
Total [1]	**12,782**	**5,561**	**7,221**	**3,208**	**6,580**	**2,994**
Armenia	20	11	9	12	(D)	(D)
Brazil	33	14	19	(D)	(D)	24
China	2,990	682	2,308	475	2,148	367
Colombia	237	112	125	62	55	120
Ethiopia	2,221	1,097	1,124	835	850	536
Ghana	104	40	64	8	41	55
Guatemala	773	306	467	46	650	77
Guyana	36	10	26	(D)	(D)	29
Haiti	336	151	185	–	147	189
India	298	84	214	34	189	75
Jamaica	52	22	30	3	5	44
Japan	43	21	22	30	8	5
Kazakhstan	298	163	135	126	137	35
Kenya	20	9	11	–	11	9
Korea, South	1,106	674	432	947	142	17
Kyrgyzstan	18	4	14	9	4	5
Latvia	27	11	16	–	5	22
Liberia	37	18	19	(D)	(D)	24
Lithuania	22	11	11	–	10	12
Marshall Islands	21	11	10	18	(D)	(D)
Mexico	76	39	37	8	23	45
Morocco	19	12	7	11	(D)	(D)
Nicaragua	25	5	20	–	8	17
Nigeria	122	61	61	14	70	38
Pakistan	34	14	20	21	6	7
Peru	29	15	14	(D)	(D)	21
Philippines	292	147	145	(D)	(D)	172
Poland	52	24	28	(D)	(D)	26
Russia	1,580	899	681	86	1,220	274
Rwanda	20	12	8	7	10	3
Taiwan	254	134	120	133	86	35
Thailand	59	33	26	(D)	34	(D)
Uganda	67	39	28	7	34	26
Ukraine	605	290	315	(D)	(D)	457
Vietnam	490	222	268	262	203	25
All other countries	206	90	116	22	82	102

– Represents zero. D Data withheld to limit disclosure. [1] Includes unknown and countries not shown separately.
Source: U.S. Department of Homeland Security, Office of Immigration Statistics, *2009 Yearbook of Immigration Statistics.* See also <http://www.dhs.gov/ximgtn/statistics/publications/yearbook.shtm>.

Table 47. Petitions for Naturalization Filed, Persons Naturalized, and Petitions Denied: 2009

[For fiscal years ending in year shown; see text, Section 8. Naturalizations refer to persons 18 and over who become citizens of the United States]

Year	Petitions filed	Persons naturalized				Petitions denied
		Total	Civilian	Military	Not reported	
1985	305,981	242,451	236,202	3,237	3,012	3,610
1990	233,843	267,586	245,410	1,618	20,558	6,516
1995	959,963	485,720	472,518	3,855	9,347	46,067
1996	1,277,403	1,040,991	924,368	1,214	115,409	229,842
1997	1,412,712	596,010	532,871	531	62,608	130,676
1998	932,957	461,169	437,689	961	22,519	137,395
1999	765,346	837,418	740,718	711	95,989	379,993
2000	460,916	886,026	812,579	836	72,611	399,670
2001	501,643	606,259	575,030	758	30,471	218,326
2002	700,649	572,646	550,835	1,053	20,758	139,779
2003	523,370	462,435	449,123	3,865	9,447	91,599
2004	662,796	537,151	520,771	4,668	11,712	103,339
2005	602,972	604,280	589,269	4,614	10,397	108,247
2006	730,642	702,589	684,484	6,259	11,846	120,722
2007	1,382,993	660,477	648,005	3,808	8,664	89,683
2008	525,786	1,046,539	1,032,281	4,342	9,916	121,283
2009	570,442	743,715	726,043	7,100	10,572	109,813

Source: U.S. Department of Homeland Security, Office of Immigration Statistics, *2009 Yearbook of Immigration Statistics.* See also <http://www.dhs.gov/ximgtn/statistics/publications/yearbook.shtm>.

Table 48. Persons Obtaining Legal Permanent Resident Status by Class of Admission: 2000 to 2009

[For years ending September 30. For definition of immigrants, see text, this section]

Class of admission	2000	2005	2006	2007	2008	2009
Total	**841,002**	**1,122,257**	**1,266,129**	**1,052,415**	**1,107,126**	**1,130,818**
New arrivals	407,279	383,955	446,881	431,368	466,558	463,042
Adjustments	433,723	738,302	819,248	621,047	640,568	667,776
Family-sponsored preferences	235,092	212,970	222,229	194,900	227,761	211,859
Unmarried sons/daughters of U.S. citizens and their children	27,635	24,729	25,432	22,858	26,173	23,965
Spouses, unmarried sons/daughters of alien residents and their children	124,540	100,139	112,051	86,151	103,456	98,567
Married sons/daughters of U.S. citizens [1]	22,804	22,953	21,491	20,611	29,273	25,930
Brothers or sisters of U.S. citizens [1]	60,113	65,149	63,255	65,280	68,859	63,397
Employment-based preferences	106,642	246,877	159,081	162,176	166,511	144,034
Priority workers [1]	27,566	64,731	36,960	26,697	36,678	40,924
Professionals with advanced degrees or aliens of exceptional ability [1]	20,255	42,597	21,911	44,162	70,046	45,552
Skilled workers, professionals, unskilled workers [1]	49,589	129,070	89,922	85,030	48,903	40,398
Special immigrants [1]	9,014	10,133	9,539	5,481	9,524	13,472
Employment creation (investors) [1]	218	346	749	806	1,360	3,688
Immediate relatives of U.S. citizens	346,350	436,115	580,340	494,920	488,483	535,554
Spouses	196,405	259,144	339,843	274,358	265,671	317,129
Children [2]	82,638	94,858	120,064	103,828	101,342	98,270
Parents	67,307	82,113	120,441	116,734	121,470	120,155
Refugees	56,091	112,676	99,609	54,942	90,030	118,836
Asylees	6,837	30,286	116,845	81,183	76,362	58,532
Diversity [3]	50,920	46,234	44,471	42,127	41,761	47,879
Cancellation of removal	12,154	20,785	29,516	14,927	11,128	8,156
Parolees	3,162	7,715	4,569	1,999	1,172	2,385
Nicaraguan Adjustment and Central American Relief Act (NACARA)	20,364	1,155	661	340	296	296
Haitian Refugee Immigration Fairness Act (HRIFA)	435	2,820	3,375	2,448	1,580	552
Other	2,955	4,624	5,425	2,453	2,042	2,735

[1] Includes spouses and children. [2] Includes orphans. [3] Includes categories of immigrants admitted under three laws intended to diversify immigration: P.L. 99-603, P.L. 100-658, and P.L. 101-649.

Source: U.S. Department of Homeland Security, Office of Immigration Statistics, *2009 Yearbook of Immigration Statistics*. See also <http://www.dhs.gov/ximgtn/statistics/publications/yearbook.shtm>.

Table 49. Persons Obtaining Legal Permanent Resident Status by Selected Country of Birth and Selected Characteristics: 2009

[For year ending September 30]

Age, marital status, class of admission	Total [1]	Mexico	China	Philippines	India	Dominican Republic	Cuba	Vietnam	Colombia
Total	**1,130,818**	**164,920**	**64,238**	**60,029**	**57,304**	**49,414**	**38,954**	**29,234**	**27,849**
Under 18 years old	223,117	34,137	9,662	11,934	7,258	15,278	5,578	6,186	4,743
18 to 24 years old	155,443	27,691	6,604	6,535	5,011	7,855	4,916	4,575	3,634
25 to 34 years old	277,867	36,736	13,046	11,566	18,331	8,293	8,434	5,565	6,300
35 to 44 years old	210,901	29,239	15,786	10,057	11,100	7,544	9,538	5,033	5,515
45 to 54 years old	124,621	15,563	9,432	7,348	5,991	4,659	4,919	4,236	4,558
55 to 64 years old	80,208	11,573	4,672	7,399	5,311	3,283	3,117	2,479	2,097
65 years old and over	58,659	9,981	5,036	5,190	4,301	2,502	2,452	1,159	1,002
Unknown	2	–	–	–	1	–	–	1	–
Single	417,232	58,269	17,945	21,304	11,937	27,942	17,107	10,503	8,696
Married	654,674	99,665	43,206	35,124	42,545	19,343	15,659	17,165	17,485
Other	54,454	6,409	2,956	3,504	2,691	2,044	5,954	1,513	1,567
Unknown	4,458	577	131	97	131	85	234	53	101
Family-sponsored preferences	211,859	57,177	11,013	14,286	12,911	20,611	1,022	12,748	3,127
Employment-based preferences	144,034	8,660	11,295	8,516	20,264	408	13	(D)	2,850
Immediate relatives of U.S. citizens	535,554	96,187	23,244	37,037	21,532	28,212	3,385	13,038	17,551
Diversity programs	47,879	12	28	4	63	16	183	(D)	10
Refugee and asylee adjustments	177,368	466	18,486	108	2,228	135	34,301	2,535	4,227
Other	14,124	2,418	172	78	306	32	50	498	84

– Represents zero. D Data withheld to avoid disclosure. [1] Includes other countries not shown separately.

Source: U.S. Department of Homeland Security, Office of Immigration Statistics, unpublished data.

Table 50. Persons Obtaining Legal Permanent Resident Status by Country of Birth: 1981 to 2009

[In thousands (7,256.0 represents 7,256,000). For years ending Sept. 30. Persons by country prior to 1996 are unrevised]

Country of birth	1981–1990, total	1991–2000, total	2001–2008, total	2009	Country of birth	1981–1990, total	1991–2000, total	2001–2008, total	2009
All countries [1]	**7,256.0**	**9,080.5**	**8,327.6**	**1,130.8**	Syria	20.6	26.1	20.9	2.4
Europe [1]	**705.6**	**1,226.0**	**1,069.8**	**105.4**	Taiwan [5]	([6])	106.3	73.2	8.0
Albania	(NA)	26.2	40.7	5.1	Thailand	64.4	48.4	48.5	10.4
Belarus	(X)	[2] 28.9	21.2	2.4	Turkey	20.9	26.3	31.6	5.0
Bosnia and Herzegovina	(X)	[2] 38.8	86.6	1.5	Uzbekistan	(X)	[2] 22.9	25.7	5.5
Bulgaria	(NA)	23.1	33.5	3.1	Vietnam	401.4	420.8	246.3	29.2
France	23.1	27.4	31.3	4.5	**Africa** [1]	**192.3**	**382.5**	**632.0**	**127.1**
Germany	70.1	67.6	63.2	7.6	Egypt	31.4	46.7	55.3	8.8
Ireland	32.8	58.9	12.4	1.6	Ethiopia	27.2	49.3	80.0	15.5
Italy	32.9	22.5	21.0	2.9	Ghana	14.9	35.6	49.7	8.4
Poland	97.4	169.5	100.4	8.8	Nigeria	35.3	67.2	82.6	15.3
Portugal	40.0	22.7	9.1	0.9	Somalia	(NA)	20.1	46.2	13.4
Romania	38.9	57.5	44.7	4.9	**Oceania**	**(NA)**	**47.9**	**47.2**	**5.6**
Russia	(X)	[2] 127.8	124.8	8.2	**North America** [1]	**3,125.0**	**3,910.1**	**2,893.3**	**375.2**
Serbia and Montenegro [3, 4]	19.2	25.8	40.8	3.2	Canada	119.2	137.2	138.7	16.1
Soviet Union [3]	84.0	103.8	26.6	5.9	Mexico	1,653.3	2,250.5	1,389.2	164.9
Ukraine	(X)	[2] 141.0	129.6	11.2	Cuba	159.2	178.7	245.9	39.0
United Kingdom	142.1	135.6	124.9	15.7	Dominican Republic	251.8	340.8	225.8	49.4
Asia [1]	**2,817.4**	**2,973.2**	**2,949.2**	**413.3**	Haiti	140.2	181.7	166.9	24.3
Armenia	(X)	[2] 26.6	23.5	3.4	Jamaica	213.8	173.4	139.1	21.8
Bangladesh	15.2	66.0	75.3	16.7	Trinidad and Tobago	39.5	63.2	50.1	6.3
Cambodia	116.6	18.5	28.8	3.8	El Salvador	214.6	217.3	214.1	19.9
China [5]	[6] 388.8	424.4	527.6	64.2	Guatemala	87.9	103.0	138.0	12.2
Hong Kong	63.0	74.0	35.8	2.7	Honduras	49.5	66.7	52.5	6.4
India	261.9	383.0	536.0	57.3	Nicaragua	44.1	94.6	53.2	4.1
Iran	154.8	112.5	93.2	18.6	Panama	29.0	24.0	14.0	1.8
Iraq	19.6	40.7	33.1	12.1	**South America** [1]	**455.9**	**539.3**	**715.9**	**102.9**
Israel	36.3	31.9	36.5	5.6	Argentina	25.7	24.3	40.3	5.8
Japan	43.2	61.4	62.1	7.7	Brazil	23.7	52.2	96.8	14.7
Jordan [7]	32.6	39.7	30.5	4.3	Colombia	124.4	130.8	201.1	27.8
Korea [8]	338.8	171.1	173.4	25.9	Ecuador	56.0	76.3	88.9	12.1
Laos	145.6	43.5	13.6	1.7	Guyana	95.4	73.8	62.8	6.7
Lebanon	41.6	43.4	32.2	3.8	Peru	64.4	105.6	114.5	17.0
Pakistan	61.3	124.5	117.1	21.6	Venezuela	17.9	29.9	63.8	11.2
Philippines	495.3	505.3	469.0	60.0					

NA Not available. X Not applicable. [1] Includes countries not shown separately. [2] Covers years 1992–2000. [3] Prior to 1992, data include independent republics; beginning in 1992, data are for unknown republic only. [4] Yugoslavia (unknown republic) prior to February 7, 2003. [5] See footnote 4, Table 1331. [6] Data for Taiwan included with China. [7] Prior to 2003, includes Palestine; beginning in 2003, Palestine included in Unknown. [8] Prior to 2009, includes a small number of cases from North Korea.

Source: U.S. Department of Homeland Security, Office of Immigration Statistics, *2009 Yearbook of Immigration Statistics*. See also <http://www.dhs.gov/ximgtn/statistics/publications/yearbook.shtm>.

Table 51. Refugees and Asylees Obtaining Legal Permanent Resident Status by Country of Birth: 1991 to 2009

[For years ending September 30]

Country of birth	1991–2000, total	2001–2008, total	2009	Country of birth	1991–2000, total	2001–2008, total	2009
Total [1]	**1,016,820**	**1,011,706**	**177,368**	Iraq	22,488	16,986	7,948
Europe [1]	**425,047**	**281,571**	**10,453**	Laos	37,203	5,939	427
Albania	3,250	9,310	966	Pakistan	1,649	7,024	808
Armenia	1,794	10,654	1,100	Thailand	22,716	13,302	4,827
Azerbaijan	[2] 10,566	5,611	299	Vietnam	206,530	33,423	2,535
Belarus	[2] 21,592	8,396	623	**Africa** [1]	**51,469**	**174,890**	**45,315**
Bosnia and Herzegovina	[2] 37,251	81,662	596	Ethiopia [6]	17,829	24,854	4,382
Croatia	1,786	9,398	81	Kenya	1,438	10,258	3,677
Moldova	[2] 10,150	9,333	969	Liberia	3,836	20,626	5,524
Poland	7,451	361	30	Sierra Leone	272	8,738	1,147
Romania	15,682	1,223	126	Somalia	16,737	42,726	12,628
Russia	[2] 54,488	29,792	2,214	Sudan	5,174	20,151	2,380
Serbia and Montenegro [3, 4]	6,242	24,289	684	**Oceania**	**291**	**1,262**	**139**
Soviet Union [3]	117,783	6,042	413	**North America** [1]	**183,251**	**249,489**	**42,700**
Ukraine	[2] 96,974	53,372	2,964	Cuba	142,571	212,226	34,301
Uzbekistan	[2] 17,991	11,678	1,951	Guatemala	2,029	5,753	1,002
Asia [1]	**350,702**	**251,321**	**69,561**	Haiti	9,354	21,605	5,402
Afghanistan	9,711	12,064	950	Nicaragua	22,468	1,747	192
Burma	721	9,238	12,221	**South America** [1]	**5,840**	**51,624**	**8,926**
Cambodia	6,358	1,469	166	Colombia	1,129	33,578	4,227
China [5]	7,577	78,203	18,486	Peru	2,500	5,848	887
India	2,538	20,458	2,228	Venezuela	1,390	7,260	2,152
Iran	24,251	30,976	9,804				

[1] Includes other countries and unknown not shown separately. [2] Covers years 1992–2000. [3] Prior to 1992, data include independent republics; beginning in 1992, data are for unknown republic only. [4] Yugoslavia (unknown republic) prior to February 7, 2003. [5] See footnote 4, Table 1331. [6] Prior to 1993, data include Eritrea.

Source: U.S. Department of Homeland Security, Office of Immigration Statistics, *2009 Yearbook of Immigration Statistics*. See also <http://www.dhs.gov/ximgtn/statistics/publications/yearbook.shtm\>.

Table 52. Population by Selected Ancestry Group and Region: 2008

[In thousands (304,060 represents 304,060,000). Covers single and multiple ancestries. Ancestry refers to a person's ethnic origin or descent, roots, or heritage; or the place of birth of the person, the person's parents, or ancestors before their arrival in the United States. The American Community Survey universe includes the household population and the population living in institutions, college dormitories, and other group quarters. Based on a sample and subject to sampling variability; see text, this section and Appendix III. For composition of regions, see map, inside front cover]

Ancestry group	Total, (1,000)	North-east	Mid-west	South	West	Ancestry group	Total, (1,000)	North-east	Mid-west	South	West
		Percent distribution by region						Percent distribution by region			
Total population [1]	**304,060**	**18**	**22**	**37**	**23**	Iranian	440	11	7	25	57
						Irish	36,278	26	24	32	18
Afghan	88	19	7	28	46	Israeli	147	42	7	22	30
Albanian	201	54	25	15	7	Italian	17,749	45	17	22	17
American	17,927	10	20	56	13	Latvian	93	27	27	21	25
Arab	1,550	25	24	28	23	Lithuanian	712	38	28	19	14
Egyptian	180	36	11	25	27	Northern European	227	12	21	20	47
Iraqi	69	6	37	27	30	Norwegian	4,643	5	49	12	33
Jordanian	59	24	24	32	20	Pennsylvania German	339	58	24	12	7
Lebanese	502	24	27	29	20	Polish	9,887	33	37	18	12
Moroccan	77	39	13	34	15	Portuguese	1,419	44	3	13	39
Palestinian	86	18	27	27	28	Romanian	469	24	26	22	28
Syrian	150	39	19	24	18	Russian	3,130	36	17	21	26
Arab	260	19	29	28	24	Scandinavian	563	8	32	16	43
Armenian	464	23	9	9	60	Scotch-Irish	3,538	12	17	51	20
Assyrian/ Chaldean/Syriac	90	4	60	2	33	Scottish	5,827	16	20	37	27
Australian	99	18	18	26	39	Serbian	180	21	45	17	17
Austrian	772	31	23	23	23	Slavic	138	27	27	21	25
Basque	58	6	5	10	79	Slovak	808	44	33	14	9
Belgian	395	11	56	17	17	Slovene	178	15	57	13	15
Brazilian	352	45	6	35	14	Sub-Saharan African [1]	2,891	21	19	44	16
British	1,114	16	17	38	29	Cape Verdean	99	89	1	6	3
Bulgarian	94	20	28	25	27	Ethiopian	165	8	20	40	33
Cajun	106	3	5	84	8	Ghanian	88	49	10	38	4
Canadian	716	28	17	26	29	Nigerian	266	27	16	47	10
Croatian	427	22	41	15	21	Somalian	83	8	46	19	27
Czech	1,594	11	45	27	17	African	1,858	15	20	48	17
Czechoslovakian	320	22	33	26	20	Swedish	4,390	13	38	16	32
Danish	1,459	8	32	15	45	Swiss	997	16	34	19	30
Dutch	4,929	15	35	27	23	Turkish	190	39	13	29	20
Eastern European	409	44	14	21	21	Ukrainian	998	40	20	18	22
English	27,516	17	21	37	25	Welsh	1,980	20	22	31	27
European	3,006	13	20	32	35	West Indian [1,2]	2,532	48	4	44	5
Finnish	688	13	46	13	28	British West Indian	85	70	4	23	3
French (except Basque)	9,447	25	23	33	20	Haitian	806	43	2	53	2
French Canadian	2,079	41	20	23	16	Jamaican	950	50	5	41	5
German	50,272	16	39	26	20	Trinidadian and Tobagonian	198	60	2	34	4
Greek	1,351	34	22	24	20	West Indian	273	58	4	32	5
Guyanese	215	79	2	17	2	Yugoslavian	343	19	31	22	28
Hungarian	1,539	32	31	20	18						

[1] Includes other groups not shown separately. [2] Excludes Hispanic-origin groups.

Source: U.S. Census Bureau, 2008 American Community Survey, B04006, "People Reporting Ancestry," <http://factfinder.census.gov/>, accessed November 2009.

Table 53. Languages Spoken at Home by Language: 2008

[283,150 represents 283,150,000. The American Community Survey universe includes the household population and the population living in institutions, college dormitories, and other group quarters. Based on a sample and subject to sampling variability; see text, this section and Appendix III]

Language	Number (1,000)	Language	Number (1,000)
Total population 5 years old and over	**283,150**		
Speak only English	227,366	Other Indic languages	653
Spanish or Spanish Creole	34,560	Other Indo-European languages	447
French (including Patois, Cajun)	1,333	Chinese	2,466
French Creole	646	Japanese	440
Italian	782	Korean	1,052
Portuguese or Portuguese Creole	661	Mon-Khmer, Cambodian	183
German	1,122	Hmong	190
Yiddish	169	Thai	141
Other West Germanic languages	277	Laotian	147
Scandinavian languages	134	Vietnamese	1,225
Greek	337	Other Asian languages	705
Russian	864	Tagalog	1,488
Polish	620	Other Pacific Island languages	355
Serbo-Croatian	274	Navajo	171
Other Slavic languages	332	Other Native North American languages	193
Armenian	231	Hungarian	94
Persian	379	Arabic	786
Gujarathi	333	Hebrew	213
Hindi	560	African languages	742
Urdu	353	Other and unspecified languages	126

Source: U.S. Census Bureau, 2008 American Community Survey, B16001, "Language Spoken at Home by Ability to Speak English for the Population 5 Years and Over," <http://factfinder.census.gov/>, accessed November 2009.

Table 54. Language Spoken at Home by State: 2008

[283,150 represents 283,150,000. The American Community Survey universe includes the household population and the population living in institutions, college dormitories, and other group quarters. Based on a sample and subject to sampling variability; see text, this section and Appendix III]

State	Population 5 years and over (1,000)	English only (1,000)	Language other than English — Number (1,000)	Language other than English — Percent of population 5 years and over	State	Population 5 years and over (1,000)	English only (1,000)	Language other than English — Number (1,000)	Language other than English — Percent of population 5 years and over
U.S.	283,150	227,366	55,784	19.7	MO	5,513	5,207	306	5.6
AL	4,355	4,177	178	4.1	MT	906	864	42	4.7
AK	635	541	94	14.8	NE	1,653	1,502	151	9.1
AZ	5,985	4,338	1,647	27.5	NV	2,402	1,731	671	27.9
AR	2,656	2,493	163	6.1	NH	1,241	1,143	98	7.9
CA	34,064	19,646	14,417	42.3	NJ	8,125	5,857	2,268	27.9
CO	4,583	3,806	777	17.0	NM	1,837	1,187	650	35.4
CT	3,291	2,638	653	19.8	NY	18,285	12,978	5,308	29.0
DE	813	727	86	10.6	NC	8,576	7,737	839	9.8
DC	555	475	80	14.4	ND	601	568	33	5.5
FL	17,188	12,741	4,447	25.9	OH	10,739	10,096	643	6.0
GA	8,954	7,839	1,115	12.5	OK	3,380	3,095	285	8.4
HI	1,202	897	306	25.4	OR	3,548	3,051	498	14.0
ID	1,403	1,261	142	10.1	PA	11,710	10,607	1,102	9.4
IL	12,007	9,383	2,624	21.9	RI	990	792	198	20.0
IN	5,933	5,506	427	7.2	SC	4,180	3,927	253	6.1
IA	2,804	2,623	180	6.4	SD	746	702	45	6.0
KS	2,600	2,343	257	9.9	TN	5,800	5,468	333	5.7
KY	3,987	3,818	169	4.2	TX	22,314	14,767	7,547	33.8
LA	4,102	3,769	333	8.1	UT	2,468	2,122	346	14.0
ME	1,245	1,156	89	7.1	VT	588	557	31	5.3
MD	5,262	4,467	794	15.1	VA	7,251	6,284	967	13.3
MA	6,117	4,832	1,284	21.0	WA	6,116	5,096	1,020	16.7
MI	9,379	8,551	828	8.8	WV	1,711	1,674	37	2.1
MN	4,865	4,395	470	9.7	WI	5,267	4,841	426	8.1
MS	2,723	2,625	97	3.6	WY	495	466	29	5.9

Source: U.S. Census Bureau, 2008 American Community Survey, C16005, "Nativity by Language Spoken at Home by Ability to Speak English for the Population 5 Years and Over," <http://factfinder.census.gov/>, accessed November 2009.

Table 55. Language Spoken at Home—25 Largest Cities: 2008

[714 represents 714,000. The American Community Survey universe includes the household population and the population living in institutions, college dormitories, and other group quarters. Based on a sample and subject to sampling variability; see text, this section and Appendix III]

City	Population 5 years and over (1,000)	English only (1,000)	Language other than English, total [1] — Number (1,000)	Language other than English, total [1] — Percent of population 5 years and over	Speak English less than "very well" (1,000)	Spanish (1,000)	Other Indo European languages (1,000)	Asian and Pacific Island languages (1,000)
Austin, TX	714	460	254	35.6	114	197	23	28
Baltimore, MD	591	547	44	7.5	18	16	16	8
Boston, MA	574	369	206	35.8	95	86	71	37
Charlotte, NC	628	514	114	18.1	59	67	24	15
Chicago, IL	2,535	1,619	916	36.1	434	628	176	81
Columbus, OH	679	600	78	11.5	37	25	19	19
Dallas, TX	1,108	615	493	44.5	282	441	18	24
Denver, CO	547	386	161	29.4	81	125	16	12
Detroit, MI	722	655	67	9.3	35	45	8	3
Fort Worth, TX	610	404	206	33.8	107	177	12	15
Houston, TX	1,849	1,011	838	45.3	476	690	54	75
Indianapolis, IN [2]	734	663	71	9.7	39	48	11	8
Jacksonville, FL	750	661	90	11.9	36	39	24	20
Los Angeles, CA	3,515	1,397	2,118	60.3	1,083	1,541	255	280
Memphis, TN	583	539	44	7.5	22	27	7	6
Nashville-Davidson, TN [2]	555	472	84	15.1	46	41	15	14
New York, NY	7,788	4,053	3,735	48.0	1,838	1,891	1,055	610
Philadelphia, PA	1,340	1,071	269	20.1	121	123	79	53
Phoenix, AZ	1,385	846	539	38.9	277	467	33	22
San Antonio, TX	1,185	643	542	45.7	169	504	15	18
San Diego, CA	1,183	731	452	38.2	190	255	52	132
San Francisco, CA	767	427	339	44.3	189	86	51	197
San Jose, CA	843	390	453	53.7	215	195	56	193
Seattle, WA	552	448	105	18.9	48	20	22	49
Washington, DC	555	475	80	14.4	25	38	22	10

[1] Includes other language groups not shown separately. [2] Represents the portion of a consolidated city that is not within one or more separately incorporated places.

Source: U.S. Census Bureau, 2008 American Community Survey, C16005, "Nativity by Language Spoken at Home by Ability to Speak English for the Population 5 Years and Over," <http://factfinder.census.gov/>, accessed November 2009.

Table 56. Marital Status of the Population by Sex, Race, and Hispanic Origin: 1990 to 2009

[In millions, except percent (181.8 represents 181,800,000). As of March. Persons 18 years old and over. Excludes members of Armed Forces except those living off post or with their families on post. Beginning 2005, population controls based on Census 2000 and an expanded sample of households. Based on Current Population Survey, see text, this section and Appendix III]

Marital status, race and Hispanic origin	Total				Male				Female			
	1990	2000	2005	2009	1990	2000	2005	2009	1990	2000	2005	2009
Total [1]	**181.8**	**201.8**	**217.2**	**226.9**	**86.9**	**96.9**	**104.8**	**110.0**	**95.0**	**104.9**	**112.3**	**116.9**
Never married	40.4	48.2	53.9	59.1	22.4	26.1	29.6	32.4	17.9	22.1	24.3	26.7
Married [2]	112.6	120.1	127.4	130.3	55.8	59.6	63.3	64.8	56.7	60.4	64.0	65.5
Widowed	13.8	13.7	13.8	14.2	2.3	2.6	2.7	2.8	11.5	11.1	11.1	11.4
Divorced	15.1	19.8	22.1	23.2	6.3	8.5	9.2	9.9	8.8	11.3	12.9	13.3
Percent of total	100.0	100.0	100.0	100.0	100.0	100.0	100.0	100.0	100.0	100.0	100.0	100.0
Never married	22.2	23.9	24.8	26.1	25.8	27.0	28.2	29.5	18.9	21.1	21.6	22.8
Married [2]	61.9	59.5	58.6	57.4	64.3	61.5	60.4	58.9	59.7	57.6	56.9	56.0
Widowed	7.6	6.8	6.4	6.3	2.7	2.7	2.6	2.6	12.1	10.5	9.9	9.8
Divorced	8.3	9.8	10.2	10.2	7.2	8.8	8.8	9.0	9.3	10.8	11.5	11.4
White, total [3]	**155.5**	**168.1**	**177.5**	**184.3**	**74.8**	**81.6**	**86.6**	**90.4**	**80.6**	**86.6**	**90.9**	**93.9**
Never married	31.6	36.0	39.7	43.5	18.0	20.3	22.6	24.8	13.6	15.7	17.0	18.7
Married [2]	99.5	104.1	108.3	110.0	49.5	51.8	54.0	55.0	49.9	52.2	54.2	55.0
Widowed	11.7	11.5	11.5	11.8	1.9	2.2	2.3	2.4	9.8	9.3	9.2	9.4
Divorced	12.6	16.5	18.1	19.1	5.4	7.2	7.6	8.3	7.3	9.3	10.4	10.7
Percent of total	100.0	100.0	100.0	100.0	100.0	100.0	100.0	100.0	100.0	100.0	100.0	100.0
Never married	20.3	21.4	22.3	23.6	24.1	24.9	26.1	27.4	16.9	18.1	18.7	19.9
Married [2]	64.0	62.0	61.0	59.7	66.2	63.5	62.4	60.8	61.9	60.3	59.7	58.6
Widowed	7.5	6.8	6.5	6.4	2.6	2.7	2.6	2.6	12.2	10.8	10.2	10.0
Divorced	8.1	9.8	10.2	10.3	7.2	8.8	8.8	9.2	9.0	10.7	11.5	11.4
Black, total [3]	**20.3**	**24.0**	**25.2**	**26.8**	**9.1**	**10.7**	**11.2**	**12.0**	**11.2**	**13.3**	**13.9**	**14.7**
Never married	7.1	9.5	10.2	11.2	3.5	4.3	4.7	5.2	3.6	5.1	5.5	6.0
Married [2]	9.3	10.1	10.3	10.8	4.5	5.0	5.0	5.3	4.8	5.1	5.2	5.5
Widowed	1.7	1.7	1.7	1.7	0.3	0.3	0.3	0.3	1.4	1.4	1.4	1.4
Divorced	2.1	2.8	2.9	3.1	0.8	1.1	1.1	1.2	1.3	1.7	1.8	1.9
Percent of total	100.0	100.0	100.0	100.0	100.0	100.0	100.0	100.0	100.0	100.0	100.0	100.0
Never married	35.1	39.4	40.6	41.9	38.4	40.2	42.0	43.3	32.5	38.3	39.5	40.7
Married [2]	45.8	42.1	41.0	40.2	49.2	46.7	45.5	44.0	43.0	38.3	37.4	37.2
Widowed	8.5	7.0	6.6	6.5	3.7	2.8	2.7	2.7	12.4	10.5	10.0	9.5
Divorced	10.6	11.5	11.7	11.4	8.8	10.3	9.8	10.0	12.0	12.8	13.3	12.6
Asian, total [3]	**(NA)**	**(NA)**	**9.4**	**10.2**	**(NA)**	**(NA)**	**4.5**	**4.8**	**(NA)**	**(NA)**	**4.9**	**5.4**
Never married	(NA)	(NA)	2.3	2.4	(NA)	(NA)	1.3	1.4	(NA)	(NA)	1.0	1.1
Married [2]	(NA)	(NA)	6.2	6.9	(NA)	(NA)	2.9	3.2	(NA)	(NA)	3.3	3.7
Widowed	(NA)	(NA)	0.4	0.5	(NA)	(NA)	0.1	0.1	(NA)	(NA)	0.3	0.4
Divorced	(NA)	(NA)	0.5	0.5	(NA)	(NA)	0.2	0.2	(NA)	(NA)	0.3	0.3
Percent of total	100.0	100.0	100.0	100.0	100.0	100.0	100.0	100.0	100.0	100.0	100.0	100.0
Never married	(NA)	(NA)	24.8	23.7	(NA)	(NA)	29.7	28.4	(NA)	(NA)	20.3	19.4
Married [2]	(NA)	(NA)	65.6	67.1	(NA)	(NA)	64.7	66.6	(NA)	(NA)	66.5	67.6
Widowed	(NA)	(NA)	4.3	4.8	(NA)	(NA)	1.3	1.6	(NA)	(NA)	6.7	7.6
Divorced	(NA)	(NA)	5.3	4.4	(NA)	(NA)	4.1	3.4	(NA)	(NA)	6.4	5.4
Hispanic, total [4]	**13.6**	**21.1**	**27.5**	**31.0**	**6.7**	**10.4**	**14.1**	**16.0**	**6.8**	**10.7**	**13.4**	**15.0**
Never married	3.7	5.9	8.6	10.1	2.2	3.4	5.2	6.0	1.5	2.5	3.4	4.1
Married [2]	8.4	12.7	15.6	17.4	4.1	6.2	7.8	8.7	4.3	6.5	7.8	8.7
Widowed	0.5	0.9	1.0	1.1	0.1	0.2	0.2	0.2	0.4	0.7	0.8	0.9
Divorced	1.0	1.6	2.2	2.5	0.4	0.7	0.9	1.1	0.6	1.0	1.3	1.4
Percent of total	100.0	100.0	100.0	100.0	100.0	100.0	100.0	100.0	100.0	100.0	100.0	100.0
Never married	27.2	28.0	31.3	32.4	32.1	32.3	36.7	37.5	22.5	23.4	25.6	27.1
Married [2]	61.7	60.2	57.0	56.1	60.9	59.7	55.6	54.5	62.4	60.7	58.7	57.9
Widowed	4.0	4.2	3.7	3.4	1.5	1.6	1.5	1.3	6.5	6.5	6.1	5.7
Divorced	7.0	7.6	7.9	8.0	5.5	6.4	6.3	6.8	8.5	9.3	9.7	9.4
Non-Hispanic White, total [3,4]	**(NA)**	**(NA)**	**151.9**	**155.6**	**(NA)**	**(NA)**	**73.4**	**75.5**	**(NA)**	**(NA)**	**78.5**	**80.0**
Never married	(NA)	(NA)	31.8	34.3	(NA)	(NA)	17.8	19.3	(NA)	(NA)	13.9	15.0
Married [2]	(NA)	(NA)	93.5	93.7	(NA)	(NA)	46.6	46.8	(NA)	(NA)	47.0	46.9
Widowed	(NA)	(NA)	10.6	10.8	(NA)	(NA)	2.1	2.2	(NA)	(NA)	8.5	8.6
Divorced	(NA)	(NA)	16.0	16.8	(NA)	(NA)	6.8	7.3	(NA)	(NA)	9.2	9.5
Percent of total	100.0	100.0	100.0	100.0	100.0	100.0	100.0	100.0	100.0	100.0	100.0	100.0
Never married	(NA)	(NA)	20.9	22.1	(NA)	(NA)	24.3	25.5	(NA)	(NA)	17.7	18.8
Married [2]	(NA)	(NA)	61.5	60.2	(NA)	(NA)	63.5	62.0	(NA)	(NA)	59.7	58.6
Widowed	(NA)	(NA)	6.9	6.9	(NA)	(NA)	2.8	2.9	(NA)	(NA)	10.8	10.8
Divorced	(NA)	(NA)	10.6	10.8	(NA)	(NA)	9.3	9.7	(NA)	(NA)	11.7	11.8

NA Not available. [1] Includes persons of other races not shown separately. [2] Includes persons who are married with spouse present, married with spouse absent, and separated. [3] Beginning 2005, data represent persons who selected this race group only and exclude persons reporting more than one race. The CPS in 1990 and 2000 only allowed respondents to report one race group. See also comments on race in the text for this section. [4] Hispanic persons may be any race.

Source: U.S. Census Bureau, *America's Families and Living Arrangements*, Current Population Reports, P20-537, 2001 and earlier reports. See also <http://www.census.gov/population/www/socdemo/hh-fam.html>.

Table 57. Marital Status of the Population by Sex and Age: 2009

[As of March (109,973 represents 109,973,000). Excludes members of Armed Forces except those living off post or with their families on post. Population controls based on Census 2000 and an expanded sample of households. Based on Current Population Survey; see text, this section and Appendix III]

Sex and age	Number of persons (1,000)					Percent distribution				
	Total	Never married	Married [1]	Widowed	Divorced	Total	Never married	Married [1]	Widowed	Divorced
Male.................	**109,973**	**32,444**	**64,772**	**2,808**	**9,949**	**100.0**	**29.5**	**58.9**	**2.6**	**9.0**
18 to 19 years old	4,084	4,006	72	1	5	100.0	98.1	1.8	–	0.1
20 to 24 years old	10,414	9,055	1,269	5	84	100.0	87.0	12.2	–	0.8
25 to 29 years old	10,849	6,626	3,885	3	335	100.0	61.1	35.8	–	3.1
30 to 34 years old	9,570	3,345	5,640	3	582	100.0	34.9	58.9	–	6.1
35 to 39 years old	10,164	2,288	6,916	24	935	100.0	22.5	68.0	0.2	9.2
40 to 44 years old	10,314	1,894	7,092	48	1,280	100.0	18.4	68.8	0.5	12.4
45 to 54 years old	21,772	3,224	15,206	236	3,107	100.0	14.8	69.8	1.1	14.3
55 to 64 years old	16,501	1,297	12,555	384	2,265	100.0	7.9	76.1	2.3	13.7
65 to 74 years old	9,400	448	7,445	549	958	100.0	4.8	79.2	5.8	10.2
75 years old and over	6,906	262	4,690	1,555	400	100.0	3.8	67.9	22.5	5.8
Female	**116,889**	**26,655**	**65,499**	**11,437**	**13,298**	**100.0**	**22.8**	**56.0**	**9.8**	**11.4**
18 to 19 years old	3,965	3,793	157	2	14	100.0	95.7	4.0	0.1	0.3
20 to 24 years old	10,196	7,893	2,126	26	151	100.0	77.4	20.9	0.3	1.5
25 to 29 years old	10,383	4,803	5,021	30	530	100.0	46.3	48.4	0.3	5.1
30 to 34 years old	9,686	2,543	6,311	60	772	100.0	26.3	65.2	0.6	8.0
35 to 39 years old	10,270	1,681	7,311	113	1,166	100.0	16.4	71.2	1.1	11.3
40 to 44 years old	10,553	1,384	7,571	150	1,447	100.0	13.1	71.7	1.4	13.7
45 to 54 years old	22,590	2,436	15,583	735	3,837	100.0	10.8	69.0	3.3	17.0
55 to 64 years old	17,777	1,260	11,962	1,459	3,096	100.0	7.1	67.3	8.2	17.4
65 to 74 years old	11,003	458	6,227	2,689	1,628	100.0	4.2	56.6	24.4	14.8
75 years old and over	10,466	403	3,231	6,173	659	100.0	3.9	30.9	59.0	6.3

– Represents or rounds to zero. [1] Includes persons who are married with spouse present, married with spouse absent, and separated.

Source: U.S. Census Bureau, "America's Families and Living Arrangements: 2009, Table 1A. Marital Status of People 15 Years and Over, by Age, Sex, Personal Earnings, Race, and Hispanic Origin: 2009," <http://www.census.gov/population/www /socdemo/hh–fam/cps2009.html>.

Table 58. Living Arrangements of Persons 15 Years Old and Over by Selected Characteristics: 2009

[In thousands (240,032 represents 240,032,000). As of March. See headnote, Table 57]

Living arrangement	Total	15 to 19 years old	20 to 24 years old	25 to 34 years old	35 to 44 years old	45 to 54 years old	55 to 64 years old	65 to 74 years old	75 years old and over
Total [1]	**240,032**	**21,219**	**20,610**	**40,487**	**41,301**	**44,361**	**34,278**	**20,403**	**17,372**
Alone	31,657	144	1,395	3,795	3,698	5,499	5,750	4,657	6,721
With spouse	121,689	153	2,851	19,189	26,672	28,766	23,349	13,162	7,547
With other persons	86,686	20,922	10,304	17,503	10,931	10,096	5,179	2,584	3,104
White [2]	194,288	16,218	16,053	31,684	32,755	36,154	28,721	17,419	15,283
Alone	25,462	98	1,069	2,825	2,673	4,320	4,591	3,839	6,046
With spouse	104,036	129	2,450	16,079	22,226	24,334	20,304	11,663	6,853
With other persons	64,791	15,994	12,534	12,780	7,856	7,500	3,826	1,917	2,384
Black [2]	28,906	3,349	2,971	5,375	5,168	5,284	3,530	1,854	1,375
Alone	4,645	29	224	652	745	913	904	642	535
With spouse	8,979	11	211	1,450	2,130	2,385	1,629	780	381
With other persons	15,282	3,309	2,536	3,273	2,293	1,986	997	432	459
Asian [2]	10,773	806	852	2,155	2,327	1,962	1,373	753	544
Alone	854	8	59	196	175	131	107	92	88
With spouse	6,353	7	108	1,169	1,730	1,529	1,042	516	253
With other persons	3,566	791	685	790	422	302	224	145	203
Hispanic origin [3]	33,440	3,878	3,610	8,126	7,028	5,121	2,961	1,627	1,090
Alone	2,195	24	120	348	359	411	369	301	263
With spouse	15,055	62	700	3,764	4,263	3,072	1,824	918	453
With other persons	16,190	3,792	2,790	4,014	2,406	1,638	768	408	374
Non-Hispanic White [2, 3]	163,299	12,671	12,773	24,171	26,196	31,383	25,968	15,884	14,253
Alone	23,443	79	972	2,502	2,345	3,946	4,246	3,557	5,795
With spouse	89,879	73	1,794	12,524	18,227	21,460	18,595	10,788	6,418
With other persons	49,977	12,519	10,007	9,145	5,624	5,977	3,127	1,539	2,040

[1] Includes other races and non-Hispanic groups, not shown separately. [2] See footnote 3, Table 56. [3] Persons of Hispanic origin may be any race.

Source: U.S. Census Bureau, "America's Families and Living Arrangements: 2009, Table A2. Family Status and Household Relationship of People 15 Years and Over, by Marital Status, Age, Sex, Race, and Hispanic Origin: 2009" and unpublished data. See also <http://www.census.gov/population/www/socdemo/hh–fam/cps2009.html>.

U.S. Census Bureau, Statistical Abstract of the United States: 2011

Table 59. Households, Families, Subfamilies, and Married Couples: 1980 to 2009

[In thousands, except as indicated (80,776 represents 80,776,000). As of March. Excludes members of Armed Forces except those living off post or with their families on post. Beginning 2005, population controls based on Census 2000 and an expanded sample of households. Based on Current Population Survey, see text, this section and Appendix III. Minus sign (–) indicates decrease]

Type of unit	1980	1990	2000	2005	2007	2008	2009	Percent change 1980–1990	1990–2000	2000–2009
Households	**80,776**	**93,347**	**104,705**	**113,343**	**116,011**	**116,783**	**117,181**	**16**	**12**	**12**
Persons per household	2.76	2.63	2.62	2.57	2.56	2.56	2.57	(X)	(X)	(X)
White [1]	70,766	80,163	87,671	92,880	94,705	95,112	95,297	13	9	9
Black [1]	8,586	10,486	12,849	13,809	14,354	14,551	14,595	22	23	14
Hispanic [2]	3,684	5,933	9,319	12,178	12,973	13,339	13,425	61	57	44
Family households.	59,550	66,090	72,025	76,858	78,425	77,873	78,850	11	9	9
Married couple.	49,112	52,317	55,311	57,975	58,945	58,370	59,118	7	6	7
Male householder [3]	1,733	2,884	4,028	4,901	5,063	5,100	5,252	66	40	30
Female householder [3]	8,705	10,890	12,687	13,981	14,416	14,404	14,480	25	17	14
Nonfamily households.	21,226	27,257	32,680	36,485	37,587	38,910	38,331	28	20	17
Male householder	8,807	11,606	14,641	16,543	17,338	17,872	17,694	32	26	21
Female householder	12,419	15,651	18,039	19,942	20,249	21,038	20,637	26	15	14
One person	18,296	22,999	26,724	30,137	31,132	32,167	31,657	26	16	18
Families	**59,550**	**66,090**	**72,025**	**76,858**	**78,425**	**77,873**	**78,850**	**11**	**9**	**9**
Persons per family	3.29	3.17	3.17	3.13	3.13	3.15	3.15	(X)	(X)	(X)
With own children [4]	31,022	32,289	34,605	36,211	36,757	35,709	35,635	4	7	3
Without own children [4]	28,528	33,801	37,420	40,647	41,668	42,164	43,215	18	11	15
Married couple.	49,112	52,317	55,311	57,975	58,945	58,370	59,118	7	6	7
With own children [4]	24,961	24,537	25,248	25,919	26,158	25,173	25,129	–2	3	(Z)
Without own children [4]	24,151	27,780	30,062	32,056	32,787	33,197	33,989	15	8	13
Male householder [3]	1,733	2,884	4,028	4,901	5,063	5,100	5,252	66	40	30
With own children [4]	616	1,153	1,786	2,021	2,015	2,162	2,111	87	55	18
Without own children [4]	1,117	1,731	2,242	2,880	3,049	2,937	3,141	55	30	40
Female householder [3]	8,705	10,890	12,687	13,981	14,416	14,404	14,480	25	17	14
With own children [4]	5,445	6,599	7,571	8,270	8,585	8,374	8,394	21	15	11
Without own children [4]	3,261	4,290	5,116	5,711	5,832	6,030	6,086	32	19	19
Unrelated subfamilies	360	534	571	515	567	526	397	48	7	–30
Married couple.	20	68	37	62	89	95	46	(B)	(B)	(B)
Male reference persons [3].	36	45	57	61	52	63	41	(B)	(B)	(B)
Female reference persons [3]. . . .	304	421	477	392	429	368	311	39	13	–35
Related subfamilies	1,150	2,403	2,984	3,427	3,829	3,855	3,971	109	24	33
Married couple.	582	871	1,149	1,336	1,645	1,664	1,681	50	32	46
Father-child [3]	54	153	201	387	331	335	306	(B)	31	52
Mother-child [3].	512	1,378	1,634	1,704	1,852	1,855	1,985	169	19	21
Married couples.	**49,714**	**53,256**	**56,497**	**59,373**	**60,676**	**60,129**	**60,844**	**7**	**6**	**8**
With own household	49,112	52,317	55,311	57,975	58,945	58,370	59,118	7	6	7
Without own household	602	939	1,186	1,398	1,731	1,759	1,726	56	26	46
Percent without	1.2	1.8	2.1	2.4	2.9	2.9	2.8	(X)	(X)	(X)

B Not shown; base less than 75,000. X Not applicable. Z Less than 0.5 percent. [1] Beginning with the 2003 Current Population Survey (CPS), respondents could choose more than one race. Beginning 2005, data shown represent persons who selected this race group only and exclude persons reporting more than one race. The CPS prior to 2003 only allowed respondents to report one race group. See also comments on race in the text for this section. [2] Persons of Hispanic origin may be any race. [3] No spouse present. [4] Under 18 years old.

Source: U.S. Census Bureau, "Families and Living Arrangements," <http://www.census.gov/population/www/socdemo/hh-fam.html>.

Table 60. Married Couples by Race and Hispanic Origin of Spouses: 1980 to 2009

[In thousands (49,714 represents 49,714,000). As of March. Persons 15 years old and over. Persons of Hispanic origin may be of any race. Based on Current Population Survey; see headnote, Table 59 and Appendix III]

Race and origin of spouses	1980	1990	2000	2008	2009
Married couples, total [1]	**49,714**	**53,256**	**56,497**	**60,129**	**60,844**
Interracial married couples, total	651	964	1,464	2,340	2,437
White [2]/Black [2]	167	211	363	481	550
Black husband/White wife	122	150	268	317	354
White husband/Black wife	45	61	95	164	196
White [2]/other race [3]	450	720	1,051	1,737	1,759
Black [2]/other race [3]	34	33	50	122	128
HISPANIC ORIGIN					
Hispanic/Hispanic	1,906	3,085	4,739	6,390	6,317
Hispanic/other origin (not Hispanic).	891	1,193	1,743	2,222	2,421
All other couples (not of Hispanic origin).	46,917	48,979	50,015	51,517	52,107

[1] Includes other married couples not shown separately. [2] See footnote 1, Table 59. [3] "Other race," is any race other than White or Black, such as American Indian, Japanese, Chinese, etc. This total excludes combinations of other races by other races.

Source: U.S. Census Bureau, "Families and Living Arrangements, Table MS-3. Interracial Married Couples: 1980 to 2002," and unpublished data, <http://www.census.gov/population/www/socdemo/hh-fam.html>.

Table 61. Households and Persons Per Household by Type of Household: 1990 to 2009

[As of March (93,347 represents 93,347,000). See headnote, Table 59]

Type of household	Households						Persons per household		
	Number (1,000)			Percent distribution					
	1990	2000	2009	1990	2000	2009	1990	2000	2009
Total households	93,347	104,705	117,181	100	100	100	2.63	2.62	2.57
Family households.	66,090	72,025	78,850	71	69	67	3.22	3.24	3.22
Married couple family	52,317	55,311	59,118	56	53	50	3.25	3.26	3.22
Male householder, no spouse present.	2,884	4,028	5,252	3	4	4	3.04	3.16	3.23
Female householder, no spouse present	10,890	12,687	14,480	12	12	12	3.10	3.17	3.21
Nonfamily households	27,257	32,680	38,331	29	31	33	1.22	1.25	1.25
Living alone	22,999	26,724	31,657	25	26	27	1.00	1.00	1.00
Male householder	11,606	14,641	17,694	12	14	15	1.33	1.34	1.34
Living alone	9,049	11,181	13,758	10	11	12	1.00	1.00	1.00
Female householder	15,651	18,039	20,637	17	17	18	1.14	1.17	1.17
Living alone	13,950	15,543	17,899	15	15	15	1.00	1.00	1.00

Source: U.S. Census Bureau, *America's Families and Living Arrangements*, Current Population Reports, P20-537, 2001, and earlier reports. See also <http://www.census.gov/population/www/socdemo/hh-fam.html>.

Table 62. Households by Age of Householder and Size of Household: 1990 to 2009

[In millions (93.3 represents 93,300,000). As of March. Based on Current Population Survey; see headnote, Table 59]

Age of householder and size of household	1990	2000	2005	2009					
				Total [1]	White [2]	Black [2]	Asian [2]	Hispanic [3]	Non-Hispanic White [3]
Total.	93.3	104.7	113.3	117.2	95.3	14.6	4.6	13.4	82.9
Age of householder:									
15 to 24 years old	5.1	5.9	6.7	6.4	4.9	1.0	0.3	1.2	3.9
25 to 29 years old	9.4	8.5	9.2	9.5	7.4	1.3	0.4	1.6	6.0
30 to 34 years old	11.0	10.1	10.1	9.8	7.6	1.4	0.6	1.7	6.0
35 to 44 years old	20.6	24.0	23.2	22.2	17.3	3.1	1.1	3.4	14.2
45 to 54 years old	14.5	20.9	23.4	24.6	20.0	3.1	1.0	2.5	17.6
55 to 64 years old	12.5	13.6	17.5	19.9	16.5	2.3	0.7	1.6	15.0
65 to 74 years old	11.7	11.3	11.5	12.8	10.9	1.3	0.4	0.9	10.1
75 years old and over	8.4	10.4	11.6	12.0	10.7	1.0	0.2	0.6	10.1
One person	23.0	26.7	30.1	31.7	25.5	4.6	0.9	2.2	23.4
Male.	9.0	11.2	12.8	13.8	(NA)	(NA)	(NA)	(NA)	(NA)
Female.	14.0	15.5	17.3	17.9	(NA)	(NA)	(NA)	(NA)	(NA)
Two persons	30.1	34.7	37.4	39.2	33.3	4.0	1.3	3.1	30.4
Three persons	16.1	17.2	18.3	18.6	14.6	2.5	1.0	2.6	12.2
Four persons	14.5	15.3	16.4	16.1	12.9	1.9	0.9	2.6	10.5
Five persons	6.2	7.0	7.2	7.1	5.9	1.0	0.3	1.7	4.3
Six persons	2.1	2.4	2.5	2.6	2.0	0.4	0.1	0.6	1.3
Seven persons or more	1.3	1.4	1.4	1.5	1.1	0.2	0.1	0.5	0.7

[1] Includes other races, not shown separately. [2] Beginning with the 2003 Current Population Survey (CPS), respondents could choose more than one race. 2005 and 2009 data represent persons who selected this race group only and exclude persons reporting more than one race. The CPS in prior years only allowed respondents to report one race group. See also comments on race in the text for this section. [3] Hispanic persons may be any race.

Source: U.S. Census Bureau, *America's Families and Living Arrangements*, Current Population Reports, P20-537, 2001, and earlier reports; "Families and Living Arrangements." See also <http://www.census.gov/population/www/socdemo/hh-fam.html>.

Table 63. Unmarried-Partner Households by Region and Sex of Partners: 2008

[The American Community Survey universe includes the household population and the population living in institutions, college dormitories, and other group quarters. For composition of regions, see inside front cover. Based on a sample and subject to sampling variability; see text, this section and Appendix III]

Item	Total	Northeast	Midwest	South	West
Total households	113,101	20,689	25,861	41,807	24,744
Unmarried-partner households	6,214	1,181	1,457	2,033	1,543
Male householder and male partner	271	54	46	93	78
Male householder and female partner.	2,903	536	688	960	719
Female householder and female partner. . .	294	65	57	93	80
Female householder and male partner	2,746	527	665	887	666
All other households	106,888	19,508	24,404	39,774	23,202

Source: U.S. Census Bureau, 2008 American Community Survey, B11009, "Unmarried-Partner Households and Household Type by Sex of Partner," <http://factfinder.census.gov/>, accessed November 2009.

U.S. Census Bureau, Statistical Abstract of the United States: 2011

Table 64. Families by Number of Own Children Under 18 Years Old: 2000 to 2009

[As of March (72,025 represents 72,025,000). Based on Current Population Survey; see headnote, Table 67]

Race, Hispanic origin, and year	Number of families (1,000) Total	No children	One child	Two children	Three or more children	Percent distribution Total	No children	One child	Two children	Three or more children
ALL FAMILIES [1]										
2000.	72,025	37,420	14,311	13,215	7,080	100	52	20	18	10
2005.	76,858	40,647	15,069	13,741	7,400	100	53	20	18	10
2009, total	**78,850**	**43,215**	**15,217**	**13,139**	**7,279**	**100**	**55**	**19**	**17**	**9**
Married couple.	59,118	33,989	9,732	9,861	5,536	100	57	16	17	9
Male householder [2]	5,252	3,141	1,300	583	229	100	60	25	11	4
Female householder [2]	14,480	6,086	4,185	2,696	1,514	100	42	29	19	11
WHITE FAMILIES [3]										
2000.	60,251	32,144	11,496	10,918	5,693	100	53	19	18	9
2005.	63,079	34,255	11,872	11,127	5,825	100	54	19	18	9
2009, total	**64,163**	**36,192**	**11,886**	**10,503**	**5,583**	**100**	**56**	**19**	**16**	**9**
Married couple.	50,762	29,712	8,122	8,318	4,609	100	58	16	16	9
Male householder [2]	3,996	2,360	1,016	458	163	100	59	25	11	4
Female householder [2]	9,405	4,119	2,748	1,726	811	100	44	29	18	9
BLACK FAMILIES [3]										
2000.	8,664	3,882	2,101	1,624	1,058	100	45	24	19	12
2005.	8,902	4,077	2,059	1,641	1,125	100	46	23	18	13
2009, total	**9,357**	**4,377**	**2,176**	**1,615**	**1,190**	**100**	**47**	**23**	**17**	**13**
Married couple.	4,386	2,387	759	706	533	100	54	17	16	12
Male householder [2]	812	477	206	84	46	100	59	25	10	6
Female householder [2]	4,159	1,513	1,210	824	611	100	36	29	20	15
ASIAN FAMILIES [3]										
2005.	3,142	1,535	730	646	230	100	49	23	21	7
2009, total	**3,492**	**1,793**	**744**	**690**	**265**	**100**	**51**	**21**	**20**	**8**
Married couple.	2,827	1,350	621	622	234	100	48	22	22	8
Male householder [2]	233	185	23	18	6	100	79	10	8	3
Female householder [2]	432	257	100	50	25	100	59	23	12	6
HISPANIC FAMILIES [4]										
2000.	7,561	2,747	1,791	1,693	1,330	100	36	24	22	18
2005.	9,521	3,528	2,130	2,163	1,699	100	37	22	23	18
2009, total	**10,503**	**4,123**	**2,398**	**2,315**	**1,667**	**100**	**39**	**23**	**22**	**16**
Married couple.	6,911	2,582	1,445	1,652	1,231	100	37	21	24	18
Male householder [2]	1,021	647	216	103	55	100	63	21	10	5
Female householder [2]	2,571	894	737	560	381	100	35	29	22	15
NON-HISPANIC WHITE FAMILIES [3,4]										
2005.	54,257	30,965	9,924	9,151	4,217	100	57	18	17	8
2009, total	**54,429**	**32,356**	**9,671**	**8,354**	**4,050**	**100**	**59**	**18**	**15**	**7**
Married couple.	44,264	27,292	6,755	6,751	3,466	100	62	15	15	8
Male householder [2]	3,066	1,765	823	366	112	100	58	27	12	4
Female householder [2]	7,100	3,298	2,094	1,237	472	100	46	29	17	7

[1] Includes other races and non-Hispanic groups, not shown separately. [2] No spouse present. [3] Beginning with the 2003 Current Population Survey (CPS), respondents could choose more than one race. 2009 data represent persons who selected this race group only and exclude persons reporting more than one race. The CPS prior to 2003 only allowed respondents to report one race group. See also comments on race in the text for this section. [4] Hispanic persons may be any race.

Source: U.S. Census Bureau, *America's Families and Living Arrangements*, Current Population Reports, P20-553 and earlier reports; "Families and Living Arrangements," and unpublished data. See also <http://www.census.gov/population/www/socdemo/hh-fam.html>.

Table 65. Family Households With Own Children Under Age 18 by Type of Family, 2000 and 2009, and by Age of Householder, 2009

[As of March (34,605 represents 34,605,000). See headnote, Table 67]

Age of Householder	Family households with children Number (1,000)	Percent of all family households	Married couple households with children Number (1,000)	Percent of all married couple households	Male householder with children [1] Number (1,000)	Percent of all male householder families [1]	Female householder with children [1] Number (1,000)	Percent of all female householder families [1]
2000, total	34,605	48	25,248	46	1,786	44	7,571	60
2009, total	**35,635**	**45**	**25,129**	**43**	**2,111**	**40**	**8,394**	**57**
15 to 24 years old	1,717	51	649	54	151	18	916	68
25 to 34 years old	9,965	75	6,498	72	618	52	2,849	91
35 to 44 years old	14,162	81	10,501	81	765	67	2,897	83
45 to 54 years old	8,254	46	6,305	45	468	43	1,480	46
55 to 64 years old	1,282	10	997	9	92	17	193	13
65 years old and over	254	2	178	2	18	4	59	3

[1] No spouse present.

Source: U.S. Census Bureau, *America's Families and Living Arrangements*, Current Population Reports, P20-537, 2001; "America's Families and Living Arrangements: 2009," <http://www.census.gov/population/www/socdemo/hh-fam/cps2009.html>.

Table 66. Families by Type, Race, and Hispanic Origin: 2009

[In thousands (78,850 represents 78,850,000). As of March. Excludes members of Armed Forces except those living off post or with their families on post. Population controls based on Census 2000 and an expanded sample of households. Based on Current Population Survey, see text of this section and Appendix III]

Characteristic	All families	Married couple families						Female family householder [4]						Male family householder, [4] all races
		All races [1]	White [2]	Black [2]	Asian [2]	Hispanic [3]	Non-Hispanic White [2,3]	All races [1]	White [2]	Black [2]	Asian [2]	Hispanic [3]	Non-Hispanic White [2,3]	
All families	78,850	59,118	50,762	4,386	2,827	6,911	44,264	14,480	9,405	4,159	432	2,571	7,100	5,252
Age of householder:														
Under 25 years old	3,395	1,203	1,054	74	39	315	758	1,356	834	416	47	310	560	836
25 to 34 years old	13,347	9,021	7,576	688	527	1,668	6,007	3,138	1,863	1,082	71	687	1,253	1,188
35 to 44 years old	17,547	12,915	10,797	1,049	783	1,999	8,916	3,484	2,198	1,061	98	691	1,591	1,149
45 to 54 years old	18,119	13,981	11,872	1,176	371	1,443	10,525	3,063	2,101	778	94	455	1,689	1,076
55 to 64 years old	13,462	11,417	9,926	805	490	838	9,144	1,493	981	415	58	232	756	552
65 to 74 years old	7,903	6,716	6,000	397	221	442	5,575	984	704	210	32	129	584	204
75 years old and over	5,075	3,864	3,536	199	96	206	3,338	963	723	196	33	66	657	248
Without own children under 18	43,215	33,989	29,712	2,387	1,350	2,582	27,292	6,086	4,119	1,513	257	894	3,298	3,141
With own children under 18	35,635	25,129	21,049	1,999	1,477	4,329	16,971	8,394	5,286	2,645	175	1,677	3,802	2,111
One own child under 18	15,217	9,732	8,122	759	621	1,445	6,755	4,185	2,748	1,210	100	737	2,094	1,300
Two own children under 18	13,139	9,861	8,318	706	622	1,652	6,751	2,696	1,726	824	50	560	1,237	583
Three or more own children under 18	7,279	5,536	4,609	533	234	1,231	3,466	1,514	811	611	25	381	472	229
Average per family with own children under 18	1.86	1.93	1.93	2.02	1.71	2.13	1.88	1.74	1.68	1.85	1.61	1.94	1.58	1.55
Age of own children:														
Of any age	47,112	31,742	26,547	2,592	1,850	5,171	22,578	12,277	7,987	3,599	303	2,216	6,009	3,093
Under 25 years old	41,772	29,285	24,537	2,350	1,710	4,858	19,967	9,910	6,309	3,046	222	1,929	4,600	2,576
Under 12 years old	26,077	18,644	15,538	1,475	1,161	3,450	12,293	5,979	3,729	1,922	114	1,278	2,611	1,454
Under 6 years old	15,629	11,368	9,510	844	730	2,187	7,450	3,378	2,041	1,132	64	799	1,352	883
Under 3 years old	9,191	6,814	5,688	491	455	1,271	4,501	1,828	1,098	630	20	436	720	549
Under 1 year old	3,397	2,535	2,139	187	133	441	1,733	645	405	200	8	178	256	217
Members 65 and older:														
Without members 65 and older	62,297	46,116	39,273	3,595	2,296	5,959	33,677	11,857	7,523	3,606	312	2,246	5,520	4,325
With members 65 and older	16,552	13,002	11,489	792	531	952	10,586	2,623	1,882	553	120	325	1,579	927
Marital status of householder:														
Married, spouse present	59,118	59,118	50,762	4,386	2,827	6,911	44,264	(X)	(X)	(X)	(X)	(X)	(X)	(X)
Married, spouse absent	2,743	(X)	(X)	(X)	(X)	(X)	(X)	2,172	1,382	616	104	569	865	571
Separated	1,946	(X)	(X)	(X)	(X)	(X)	(X)	1,599	1,028	488	28	430	634	347
Other	797	(X)	(X)	(X)	(X)	(X)	(X)	573	354	128	76	139	231	224
Widowed	2,709	(X)	(X)	(X)	(X)	(X)	(X)	2,247	1,646	460	81	248	1,412	462
Divorced	6,461	(X)	(X)	(X)	(X)	(X)	(X)	4,794	3,630	883	112	648	3,052	1,667
Never married	7,819	(X)	(X)	(X)	(X)	(X)	(X)	5,267	2,746	2,199	135	1,106	1,770	2,551

X Not applicable. [1] Includes other races and non-Hispanic groups, not shown separately. [2] Beginning with the 2003 Current Population Survey (CPS), respondents could choose more than one race. Data represent persons who selected this race group only and exclude persons reporting more than one race. See also comments on race in the text for this section. [3] Persons of Hispanic origin may be any race. [4] No spouse present.

Source: U.S. Census Bureau, "America's Families and Living Arrangements: 2009" and unpublished data, <http://www.census.gov/population/www/socdemo/hh-fam/cps2009.html>.

Table 67. Family Groups With Children Under 18 Years Old by Race and Hispanic Origin: 1990 to 2009

[In thousands. As of March (34,670 represents 34,670,000). Family groups comprise family households, related subfamilies, and unrelated subfamilies. Excludes members of Armed Forces except those living off post or with their families on post. Beginning 2005, population controls based on Census 2000 and an expanded sample of households. Based on Current Population Survey, see text, this section and Appendix III]

Race and Hispanic origin of householder or reference person	Number (1,000)					Percent distribution		
	1990	2000	2005	2008	2009	1990	2000	2009
All races, total [1]	**34,670**	**37,496**	**39,317**	**38,938**	**38,943**	**100**	**100**	**100**
Two-parent family groups [2]	24,921	25,771	26,482	27,344	27,321	72	69	70
One-parent family groups	9,749	11,725	12,835	11,594	11,622	28	31	30
Maintained by mother	8,398	9,681	10,366	9,753	9,880	24	26	25
Maintained by father	1,351	2,044	2,469	1,841	1,742	4	5	4
White, total [3]	**28,294**	**30,079**	**30,960**	**30,451**	**30,292**	**100**	**100**	**100**
Two-parent family groups [2]	21,905	22,241	22,319	22,857	22,735	77	74	75
One-parent family groups	6,389	7,838	8,641	7,594	7,557	23	26	25
Maintained by mother	5,310	6,216	6,747	6,138	6,232	19	21	21
Maintained by father	1,079	1,622	1,894	1,456	1,325	4	5	4
Black, total [3]	**5,087**	**5,530**	**5,495**	**5,603**	**5,683**	**100**	**100**	**100**
Two-parent family groups [2]	2,006	2,135	2,065	2,256	2,296	39	39	40
One-parent family groups	3,081	3,396	3,430	3,347	3,387	61	61	60
Maintained by mother	2,860	3,060	3,037	3,080	3,093	56	55	54
Maintained by father	221	335	393	267	294	4	6	5
Asian, total [3]	**(NA)**	**1,469**	**1,757**	**1,789**	**1,829**	**100**	**100**	**100**
Two-parent family groups [2]	(NA)	1,184	1,472	1,513	1,572	(NA)	81	86
One-parent family groups	(NA)	285	285	276	257	(NA)	19	14
Maintained by mother	(NA)	236	222	225	201	(NA)	16	11
Maintained by father	(NA)	49	63	51	56	(NA)	3	3
Hispanic, total [4]	**3,429**	**5,503**	**6,752**	**7,213**	**7,337**	**100**	**100**	**100**
Two-parent family groups [2]	2,289	3,625	4,346	5,072	5,013	67	66	68
One-parent family groups	1,140	1,877	2,406	2,141	2,324	33	34	32
Maintained by mother	1,003	1,565	1,964	1,903	2,041	29	28	28
Maintained by father	138	313	442	238	283	4	6	4
Non-Hispanic White, total [3, 4]	**(NA)**	**24,847**	**24,730**	**23,765**	**23,512**	**100**	**100**	**100**
Two-parent family groups [2]	(NA)	18,750	18,253	18,099	18,035	(NA)	75	77
One-parent family groups	(NA)	6,096	6,476	5,666	5,477	(NA)	25	23
Maintained by mother	(NA)	4,766	4,984	4,423	4,405	(NA)	19	19
Maintained by father	(NA)	1,331	1,492	1,243	1,072	(NA)	5	5

NA Not available. [1] Includes other races and non-Hispanic groups, not shown separately. [2] Beginning 2007, includes children living both with married and unmarried parents. [3] Beginning with the 2003 Current Population Survey (CPS), respondents could choose more than one race. Beginning 2005, data represent persons who selected this race group only and exclude persons reporting more than one race. The CPS prior to 2003 allowed respondents to report only one race group. See also comments on race in the text for this section. [4] Hispanic persons may be any race.

Source: U.S. Census Bureau, *Families and Living Arrangements*, Current Population Reports, P20-537, 2001 and earlier reports; and "Families and Living Arrangements," <http://www.census.gov/population/www/socdemo/hh-fam.html>.

Table 68. Parents and Children in Stay-At-Home Parent Family Groups: 1995 to 2009

[In thousands (22,973 represents 22,973,000). Family groups with children include those families that maintain their own household (family households with own children); those that live in the home of a relative (related subfamilies); and those that live in the home of a nonrelative (unrelated subfamilies). Stay-at-home family groups are married-couple family groups with children under 15 where one parent is in the labor force all of the previous year and their spouse is out of the labor force for the entire year with the reason 'taking care of home and family.' Only married couples with children under 15 are included. Based on Current Population Survey; see Appendix III]

Year	Married-couple family groups with children under 15 years old			Children under 15 years old in married-couple family groups		
	Total	With stay-at-home mothers	With stay-at-home fathers	Total	With stay-at-home mothers	With stay-at-home fathers
1995	22,973	4,440	64	41,008	9,106	125
1997	22,779	4,617	71	40,798	9,788	140
1996	22,808	4,633	49	40,739	9,693	115
1998	22,881	4,555	90	41,038	9,432	196
1999	22,754	4,731	71	41,003	9,796	143
2000	22,953	4,785	93	41,860	10,087	180
2001	22,922	4,934	81	41,862	10,194	148
2002	23,339	5,206	106	41,802	10,573	189
2003	23,209	5,388	98	41,654	11,028	175
2004	23,160	5,571	147	41,409	11,205	268
2005	23,305	5,584	142	41,111	11,224	247
2006	23,232	5,646	159	41,259	11,372	283
2007	23,507	5,563	165	41,559	11,193	303
2008	22,445	5,327	140	41,037	11,132	234
2009	22,523	5,095	158	41,208	10,934	290

Source: U.S. Census Bureau, "Families and Living Arrangements, Table SHP-1. Parents and Children in Stay-At-Home Parent Family Groups: 1994 to Present," <http://www.census.gov/population/www/socdemo/hh-fam.html>.

Table 69. Children Under 18 Years Old by Presence of Parents: 2000 to 2009

[As of March (72,012 represents 72,012,000). Excludes persons under 18 years old who maintained households or family groups. Based on Current Population Survey; see headnote, Table 67]

Race, Hispanic origin, and year	Number (1,000)	Both parents [1]	Percent living with— Mother only Total	Divorced	Married, spouse absent	Never married	Widowed	Father only	Neither parent
ALL RACES [2]									
2000.	72,012	69.1	22.4	7.9	4.5	9.2	1.0	4.2	4.2
2005.	73,494	67.3	23.4	7.9	4.6	10.1	0.8	4.8	4.5
2008.	74,107	69.9	22.8	7.5	4.6	9.8	0.9	3.5	3.8
2009.	74,230	69.8	22.8	7.0	4.9	10.0	0.8	3.4	4.0
WHITE [3]									
2000.	56,455	75.3	17.3	(NA)	(NA)	(NA)	(NA)	4.3	3.1
2005.	56,234	73.5	18.4	7.9	4.0	5.8	0.7	4.7	3.4
2008.	56,482	76.0	17.5	7.5	3.9	5.3	0.7	3.6	2.9
2009.	56,254	75.8	17.7	7.0	4.2	5.8	0.7	3.4	3.1
BLACK [3]									
2000.	11,412	37.6	49.0	(NA)	(NA)	(NA)	(NA)	4.2	9.2
2005.	11,293	35.0	50.2	8.7	8.1	32.0	1.3	5.0	9.8
2008.	11,342	37.5	51.1	8.6	8.2	32.7	1.6	3.3	8.1
2009.	11,235	38.1	50.2	7.9	8.7	32.4	1.3	3.5	8.3
ASIAN [3]									
2005.	2,843	83.6	10.2	4.0	2.3	2.7	1.3	3.6	2.5
2008.	2,980	85.1	10.2	2.7	3.5	3.2	0.9	2.3	2.4
2009.	3,035	85.2	10.2	2.8	4.5	2.0	1.0	2.5	2.0
HISPANIC [4]									
2000.	11,613	65.1	25.1	(NA)	(NA)	(NA)	(NA)	4.4	5.4
2005.	14,241	64.7	25.4	6.1	7.1	11.4	0.8	4.8	5.2
2008.	15,642	69.7	24.1	5.8	7.0	10.5	0.7	2.3	3.9
2009.	16,360	68.7	24.9	5.2	7.2	11.7	0.8	2.5	3.9
NON-HISPANIC WHITE [3, 4]									
2005.	43,106	75.9	16.4	8.5	3.1	4.2	0.7	4.8	2.9
2008.	42,052	77.8	15.5	8.1	3.0	3.7	0.7	4.1	2.6
2009.	41,418	78.1	15.3	7.6	3.1	3.9	0.7	3.8	2.8

NA Not available. [1] Beginning in 2007, includes children living both with married and unmarried parents. [2] Includes other races and non-Hispanic groups, not shown separately. [3] Beginning with the 2003 Current Population Survey (CPS), respondents could choose more than one race. Beginning 2005, data represent persons who selected this race group only and exclude persons reporting more than one race. The CPS prior to 2003 allowed respondents to report only one race group. See also comments on race in the text for this section. [4] Hispanic persons may be any race.

Source: U.S. Census Bureau, "Families and Living Arrangements," <http://www.census.gov/population/www/socdemo/hh-fam.html>.

Table 70. Grandparents Living With Grandchildren by Race and Sex: 2008

[6,432 represents 6,432,000. Covers both grandparents living in own home with grandchildren present and grandparents living in grandchildren's home. The American Community Survey universe includes the household population and the population living in institutions, college dormitories, and other group quarters. Based on a sample and subject to sampling variability; see text, this section and Appendix III]

Race, Hispanic origin, and sex	Grandparents living with own grandchildren, total	Grandparents responsible for grandchildren Total	30 to 59 years old	60 years old and over
Grandparents living with own grandchildren under 18 years old (1,000)	**6,432**	**2,618**	**1,754**	**864**
PERCENT DISTRIBUTION				
Total.	100.0	100.0	100.0	100.0
White alone.	62.1	63.6	63.4	64.2
Black or African American alone.	19.1	23.7	23.9	23.3
American Indian and Alaska Native alone.	1.4	1.9	1.9	1.8
Asian alone.	7.5	3.1	2.1	5.1
Native Hawaiian and Other Pacific Islander alone.	0.3	0.2	0.2	0.3
Some other race alone.	7.9	5.6	6.5	3.8
Two or more races.	1.7	1.8	2.0	1.5
Hispanic origin [1].	23.5	18.6	20.4	14.8
White alone, not Hispanic.	47.5	51.6	50.5	54.0
Male.	35.6	37.5	35.4	41.9
Female.	64.4	62.5	64.6	58.1

[1] Persons of Hispanic origin may be any race.

Source: U.S. Census Bureau, American Community Survey 2008, Subject Table S1002, "Grandparents," <http://factfinder.census.gov/>, accessed November 2009.

Table 71. Nonfamily Households by Sex and Age of Householder: 2009

[In thousands (17,694 represents 17,694,000). As of March. See headnote, Table 72]

Item	Male householder					Female householder				
	Total	15 to 24 yrs. old	25 to 44 yrs. old	45 to 64 yrs. old	65 yrs. old and over	Total	15 to 24 yrs. old	25 to 44 yrs. old	45 to 64 yrs. old	65 yrs. old and over
Total.................	**17,694**	**1,596**	**6,561**	**6,248**	**3,289**	**20,637**	**1,366**	**4,017**	**6,687**	**8,566**
One person (living alone) ...	13,758	870	4,569	5,272	3,048	17,899	667	2,925	5,976	8,331
Nonrelatives present	3,936	726	1,994	975	242	2,738	699	1,092	711	235
Never married	9,052	1,513	4,796	2,239	504	6,573	1,310	2,929	1,766	568
Married [1]	1,596	46	555	727	270	1,187	32	292	564	298
Widowed	1,822	6	26	313	1,477	7,324	13	75	1,140	6,095
Divorced	5,225	33	1,185	2,967	1,041	5,554	11	722	3,216	1,606

[1] No spouse present, includes separated.

Source: U.S. Census Bureau, "America's Families and Living Arrangements: 2009, Table A2. Family Status and Household Relationship of People 15 Years and Over, by Marital Status, Age, and Sex: 2009," <http://www.census.gov/population/www/socdemo/hh-fam/cps2009.html>.

Table 72. Persons Living Alone by Sex and Age: 1990 to 2009

[As of March (22,999 represents 22,999,000). Excludes members of Armed Forces except those living off post or with their families on post. Beginning 2005, population controls based on Census 2000 and an expanded sample of households. Based on Current Population Survey, see text, this section and Appendix III]

Sex and age	Number of persons (1,000)						Percent distribution				
				2009					2009		
	1990	2000	2005	Total	Male	Female	1990	2000	Total	Male	Female
Total.................	**22,999**	**26,724**	**30,137**	**31,657**	**13,758**	**17,899**	**100**	**100**	**100**	**100**	**100**
15 to 24 years old	1,210	1,144	1,521	1,539	870	667	5	4	5	6	4
25 to 34 years old	3,972	3,848	3,836	3,795	2,310	1,486	17	14	12	17	8
35 to 44 years old	3,138	4,109	3,988	3,698	2,259	1,439	14	15	12	16	8
45 to 64 years old	5,502	7,842	10,180	11,249	5,272	5,976	24	29	36	38	33
65 to 74 years old	4,350	4,091	4,222	4,657	1,454	3,203	19	15	15	11	18
75 years old and over	4,825	5,692	6,391	6,721	1,594	5,128	21	21	21	12	29

Source: U.S. Census Bureau, *America's Families and Living Arrangements*, Current Population Reports, P20-537, 2001, and earlier reports. See also <http://www.census.gov/population/www/socdemo/hh-fam.html>.

Table 73. Group Quarters Population by Type of Group Quarter and Selected Characteristics: 2008

[In percent, except as indicated (8,247 represents 8,247,000). The American Community Survey universe includes the household population and the population living in institutions, college dormitories, and other group quarters. Based on a sample and subject to sampling variability; see text, this section and Appendix III]

Characteristic	Total group quarters population [1]	Adult correctional facilities	Nursing facilities/ skilled nursing facilities	College/ university housing	Characteristic	Total group quarters population [1]	Adult correctional facilities	Nursing facilities/ skilled nursing facilities	College/ university housing
Total population (1,000)...	**8,247**	**2,140**	**1,846**	**2,381**	One race (1,000)	8,037	2,069	1,831	2,313
PERCENT DISTRIBUTION					PERCENT DISTRIBUTION				
Male...................	58.5	90.6	31.7	46.6	White	69.5	48.2	84.5	76.6
Female.................	41.5	9.4	68.3	53.4	Black or African American....	22.0	41.0	12.2	12.8
					American Indian and				
Under 15 years old	0.9	(X)	(X)	(X)	Alaska Native............	1.1	1.9	0.5	0.7
15 to 17 years old	1.9	0.5	(X)	1.5	Asian	3.3	0.9	1.4	7.7
18 to 24 years old	37.8	18.3	0.2	95.7	Native Hawaiian and				
25 to 34 years old	12.1	32.6	0.9	2.2	Other Pacific Islander	0.2	0.2	0.1	0.1
35 to 44 years old	10.3	26.7	1.6	0.3	Some other race	3.8	7.8	1.3	2.0
45 to 54 years old	8.7	16.3	4.6	0.2					
55 to 64 years old	5.2	4.6	7.7	0.1	Two or more races (1,000)....	210	71	14	68
65 to 74 years old	4.2	0.9	12.9	–					
75 to 84 years old	7.7	0.2	28.8	(X)	Hispanic origin [2]............	10.8	19.7	4.3	6.4
85 years old and over	11.2	–	43.3	(X)	Not Hispanic	89.2	80.3	95.7	93.6
					White alone, Not Hispanic ...	61.8	36.4	81.0	70.7

– Represents zero. X Not applicable. [1] Includes other types of group quarters, not shown separately. [2] Persons of Hispanic origin may be any race.

Source: U.S. Census Bureau, 2008 American Community Survey, S2601A, "Characteristics of the Group Quarters Population"; and S2601B, "Characteristics of the Group Quarters Population by Group Quarters Type," <http://factfinder.census.gov/>, accessed November 2009.

Table 74. Population in Group Quarters by State: 2000 to 2009

[In thousands (7,780 represents 7,780,000). 2000, as of April; beginning 2005, as of July. For definition of group quarters, see text, this section]

State	2000 [1]	2005	2009	State	2000 [1]	2005	2009	State	2000 [1]	2005	2009
U.S. ...	**7,780**	**8,103**	**8,277**								
AL	115	118	123	KY	115	122	124	ND	24	26	27
AK	19	23	21	LA	136	132	124	OH	299	305	316
AZ	110	113	119	ME	35	38	38	OK	112	112	118
AR	74	78	83	MD	134	139	144	OR	77	82	84
CA	820	833	844	MA	221	237	248	PA	433	455	470
CO	103	109	113	MI	250	258	257	RI	39	38	38
CT	108	113	115	MN	136	142	144	SC	135	140	146
DE	25	24	24	MS	95	97	100	SD	28	31	31
DC	36	35	35	MO	164	169	169	TN	148	152	151
FL	389	411	432	MT	25	26	27	TX	561	594	592
GA	234	265	277	NE	51	52	54	UT	40	44	45
HI	36	38	35	NV	34	33	33	VT	21	21	22
ID	31	34	34	NH	36	38	39	VA	231	244	255
IL	322	337	345	NJ	195	195	195	WA	136	139	145
IN	178	183	189	NM	36	42	42	WV	43	46	46
IA	104	104	105	NY	581	602	608	WI	156	164	166
KS	82	82	82	NC	254	273	289	WY	14	14	15

[1] The April 1, 2000, Population Estimates base reflects changes to the Census 2000 population from the Count Question Resolution program and geographic program revisions.

Source: U.S. Census Bureau, "Annual Resident Population Estimates, Estimated Components of Resident Population Change, and Rates of the Components of Resident Population Change for States and Counties: April 1, 2000 to July 1, 2009," March 2010, <http://www.census.gov/popest/counties/files/CO-EST2009-ALLDATA.csv>.

Table 75. Self-Described Religious Identification of Adult Population: 1990 to 2008

[In thousands (175,440 represents 175,440,000). The methodology of the American Religious Identification Survey (ARIS) 2008 replicated that used in previous surveys. The three surveys are based on random-digit-dialing telephone surveys of residential households in the continental U.S.A. (48 states): 54,461 interviews in 2008, 50,281 in 2001, and 113,723 in 1990. Respondents were asked to describe themselves in terms of religion with an open-ended question. Interviewers did not prompt or offer a suggested list of potential answers. Moreover, the self-description of respondents was not based on whether established religious bodies, institutions, churches, mosques or synagogues considered them to be members. Quite the contrary, the surveys sought to determine whether the respondents themselves regarded themselves as adherents of a religious community. Subjective rather than objective standards of religious identification were tapped by the surveys]

Religious group	1990	2001	2008	Religious group	1990	2001	2008
Adult population, total [1]	**175,440**	**207,983**	**228,182**	Church of the Brethren	206	358	231
Total Christian [2]	151,225	159,514	173,402	Nondenominational [3]	194	2,489	8,032
Catholic	46,004	50,873	57,199	Disciples of Christ	144	492	263
Baptist	33,964	33,820	36,148	Reformed/Dutch Reform	161	289	206
Protestant-no denomination supplied	17,214	4,647	5,187	Apostolic/New Apostolic	117	254	970
Methodist/Wesleyan	14,174	14,039	11,366	Quaker	67	217	130
Lutheran	9,110	9,580	8,674	Christian Reform	40	79	381
Christian-no denomination supplied	8,073	14,190	16,834	Foursquare Gospel	28	70	116
Presbyterian	4,985	5,596	4,723	Total other religions [2]	5,853	7,740	8,796
Pentecostal/Charismatic	3,116	4,407	5,416	Jewish	3,137	2,837	2,680
Episcopalian/Anglican	3,043	3,451	2,405	Muslim	527	1,104	1,349
Mormon/Latter-Day Saints	2,487	2,697	3,158	Buddhist	404	1,082	1,189
Churches of Christ	1,769	2,593	1,921	Unitarian/Universalist	502	629	586
Jehovah's Witness	1,381	1,331	1,914	Hindu	227	766	582
Seventh-Day Adventist	668	724	938	Native American	47	103	186
Assemblies of God	617	1,105	810	Wiccan	8	134	342
Holiness/Holy	610	569	352	Pagan	(NA)	140	340
Congregational/United Church of Christ	438	1,378	736	Spiritualist	(NA)	116	426
Church of the Nazarene	549	544	358	Other unclassified	837	386	735
Church of God	590	943	663	No religion specified, total [2]	14,331	29,481	34,169
Orthodox (Eastern)	502	645	824	Atheist	(4)	902	1,621
Evangelical/Born Again [3]	546	1,088	2,154	Agnostic	4 1,186	991	1,985
Mennonite	235	346	438	No religion	13,116	27,486	30,427
Christian Science	214	194	339	Refused to reply to question	4,031	11,246	11,815

NA Not available. [1] Refers to the total number of adults in all fifty states. All other figures are based on projections from surveys conducted in the continental United States (48 states). [2] Includes other groups, not shown separately. [3] Because of the subjective nature of replies to open-ended questions, these categories are the most unstable as they do not refer to clearly identifiable denominations as much as underlying feelings about religion. Thus they may be the most subject to fluctuation over time. [4] Atheist included in Agnostic.

Source: 1990 data, Barry A. Kosmin and Seymour P. Lachman, "One Nation Under God: Religion in Contemporary American Society, 1993"; 2001 data, Barry A. Kosmin and Ariela Keysar, Religion in A Free Market: Religious and Non-Religious Americans, Who, What, Why, Where; 2008 data, Institute for the Study of Secularism in Society and Culture, Trinity College, Hartford, CT. See also <http://www.trincoll.edu/Academics/AcademicResources/values/ISSSC/archive.htm> and <www.AmericanReligionSurvey-ARIS.org> (copyright).

Table 76. Religious Bodies—Selected Data

[Membership data: 2,500 represents 2,500,000. Includes the self-reported membership of religious bodies with 750,000 or more as reported to the Yearbook of American and Canadian Churches. Groups may be excluded if they do not supply information. The data are not standardized so comparisons between groups are difficult. The definition of "church member" is determined by the religious body]

Religious body	Year reported	Churches reported	Membership (1,000)
African Methodist Episcopal Church	1999	4,174	2,500
African Methodist Episcopal Zion Church	2008	3,393	1,400
American Baptist Churches in the USA	2008	5,469	1,331
Assemblies of God	2008	12,377	2,900
Baptist Bible Fellowship International	1997	4,500	1,200
Catholic Church	2008	18,674	68,115
Christian Churches and Churches of Christ	1988	5,579	1,072
Christian Methodist Episcopal Church	2006	3,500	850
Church of God in Christ	1991	15,300	5,500
Church of God (Cleveland, Tennessee)	2008	6,677	1,072
Church of Jesus Christ of Latter-day Saints	2008	13,363	5,974
Churches of Christ	2006	13,000	1,639
Episcopal Church	2008	6,964	2,057
Evangelical Lutheran Church in America	2008	10,396	4,634
Greek Orthodox Archdiocese of America	2006	560	1,500
Jehovah's Witnesses	2008	12,728	1,114
Lutheran Church—Missouri Synod	2008	6,123	2,337
National Baptist Convention of America Inc.	2000	(NA)	3,500
National Baptist Convention, U.S.A., Inc.	2004	9,000	5,000
National Missionary Baptist Convention of America	1992	(NA)	2,500
Orthodox Church in America	2004	737	1,064
Pentecostal Assemblies of the World, Inc.	2006	1,750	1,500
Presbyterian Church (U.S.A.)	2008	10,751	2,845
Progressive National Baptist Convention, Inc.	1995	2,000	2,500
Seventh Day Adventist Church	2008	4,870	1,022
Southern Baptist Convention	2008	44,848	16,228
United Church of Christ	2008	5,320	1,112
United Methodist Church	2007	34,136	7,854

NA Not available.

Source: National Council of Churches USA, New York, NY, *2010 Yearbook of American & Canadian Churches*, annual (copyright). See also <http://www.ncccusa.org>, or call 888-870-3325.

Table 77. Christian Church Adherents, 2000, and Jewish Population, 2009— States

[133,377 represents 133,377,000. Christian church adherents were defined as "all members, including full members, their children and the estimated number of other regular participants who are not considered as communicant, confirmed or full members." The Jewish population includes Jews who define themselves as Jewish by religion as well as those who define themselves as Jewish in cultural or ethnic terms. Data on Jewish population are based on scientific studies and informant estimates provided by local Jewish communities]

State	Christian adherents 2000		Jewish population 2009		State	Christian adherents 2000		Jewish population 2009	
	Number (1,000)	Percent of population [1]	Number (1,000)	Percent of population [1]		Number (1,000) [2]	Percent of population [1]	Number (1,000) [2]	Percent of population [1]
U.S.	**133,377**	**47.4**	**6,544**	**2.1**	MO	2,813	50.3	59	1.0
AL	2,418	54.4	9	0.2	MT	401	44.4	1	0.1
AK	210	33.6	6	0.9	NE	995	58.2	7	0.4
AZ	1,946	37.9	106	1.6	NV	604	30.2	74	2.8
AR	1,516	56.7	2	0.1	NH	571	46.2	10	0.8
CA	14,328	42.3	1,220	3.3	NJ	4,262	50.7	505	5.8
CO	1,604	37.3	90	1.8	NM	1,041	57.2	11	0.6
CT	1,828	53.7	119	3.4	NY	9,569	50.4	1,625	8.3
DE	299	38.2	15	1.7	NC	3,598	44.7	30	0.3
DC	331	57.8	28	4.7	ND	468	72.9	(Z)	(Z)
FL [3]	5,904	36.9	614	3.3	OH	4,912	43.3	148	1.3
GA	3,528	43.1	128	1.3	OK	2,079	60.3	5	0.1
HI	431	35.6	8	0.6	OR	1,029	30.1	48	1.3
ID	624	48.3	2	0.1	PA	6,751	55.0	295	2.3
IL	6,457	52.0	278	2.2	RI	646	61.7	19	1.8
IN	2,578	42.4	17	0.3	SC	1,874	46.7	11	0.2
IA	1,698	58.0	6	0.2	SD	510	67.6	(Z)	(Z)
KS	1,307	48.6	18	0.6	TN	2,867	50.4	19	0.3
KY	2,141	53.0	11	0.3	TX	11,316	54.3	130	0.5
LA	2,599	58.2	11	0.2	UT	1,659	74.3	5	0.2
ME	450	35.3	14	1.1	VT	230	37.8	5	0.9
MD	2,012	38.0	241	4.2	VA	2,807	39.7	98	1.2
MA	3,725	58.7	282	4.3	WA	1,872	31.8	44	0.7
MI	3,970	39.9	87	0.9	WV	646	35.7	2	0.1
MN	2,974	60.5	47	0.9	WI	3,198	59.6	28	0.5
MS	1,549	54.5	2	0.1	WY	229	46.4	1	0.2

Z Fewer than 500 or .05 percent. [1] Based on U.S. Census Bureau data for resident population enumerated as of April 1, 2000, and estimated as of July 1, 2009. [2] Jewish population of the United States is believed to be between 6.0 and 6.4 million. Over count is mostly due to a significant number of Jews who live in more than one State. [3] An additional 79,000 Jews live in Florida less than 8 months out of the year and are not counted here.

Source: Christian church adherents—Dale E. Jones, Sherri Doty, Clifford Grammich, James E. Horsch, Richard Houseal, John P. Marcum, Kenneth M. Sanchagrin, and Richard H. Taylor, *Religious Congregations and Membership in the United States: 2000* (copyright, 2002); Glenmary Research Center, Nashville, TN, <www.glenmary.org/grc>. Jewish population—Ira M. Sheskin (University of Miami) and Arnold Dashefsky (University of Connecticut), "Jewish Population of the United States, 2009," published by the Mandell L. Berman North American Jewish Data Bank in cooperation with the Association for the Social Scientific Study of Jewry and the Jewish Federations of North America. See also <www.jewishdatabank.org>.

62 Population

Section 2
Births, Deaths, Marriages, and Divorces

This section presents vital statistics data on births, deaths, abortions, fetal deaths, fertility, life expectancy, marriages, and divorces. Vital statistics are compiled for the country as a whole by the National Center for Health Statistics (NCHS) and published in its annual report, *Vital Statistics of the United States,* in certain reports of the *Vital and Health Statistics* series, *National Vital Statistics Reports and Health, United States.* Reports in this field are also issued by the various state bureaus of vital statistics. Data on fertility and selected characteristics of women who had a child in the last year, and on marital status and marital history are compiled by the U.S. Census Bureau from its Current Population Survey (CPS; see text, Section 1) and published in *Current Population Reports*, P20 Series. Data on abortions are published by the Alan Guttmacher Institute, New York, NY, in selected issues of *Perspectives on Sexual and Reproductive Health* online at <www.guttmacher.org/sections/abortion.php>.

Registration of vital events—The registration of births, deaths, fetal deaths, and other vital events in the United States is primarily a state and local function. There are 57 vital registration jurisdictions in the United States: the 50 states, five territories (Puerto Rico, etc.) District of Columbia, and New York City. Each of the 57 jurisdictions has a direct statistical reporting relationship with NCHS. Vital events occurring to U.S. residents outside the United States are not included in the data.

Births and deaths—The live-birth, death, and fetal-death statistics prepared by NCHS are based on vital records filed in the registration offices of all states, New York City, and the District of Columbia. The annual collection of death statistics on a national basis began in 1900 with a national death-registration area of ten states and the District of Columbia; a similar annual collection of birth statistics for a national birth-registration area began in 1915, also with ten reporting

states and the District of Columbia. Since 1933, the birth- and death-registration areas have comprised the entire United States, including Alaska (beginning 1959) and Hawaii (beginning 1960). National statistics on fetal deaths were first compiled for 1918 and annually since 1922. Prior to 1951, birth statistics came from a complete count of records received in the Public Health Service (now received in NCHS). From 1951 through 1971, they were based on a 50-percent sample of all registered births (except for a complete count in 1955 and a 20- to 50-percent sample in 1967). Beginning in 1972, they have been based on a complete count for states participating in the Vital Statistics Cooperative Program (VSCP) (for details, see the technical appendix in *Vital Statistics of the United States*) and on a 50- percent sample of all other areas. Beginning in 1986, all reporting areas participated in the VSCP. Mortality data have been based on a complete count of records for each area (except for a 50-percent sample in 1972). Beginning in 1970, births to and deaths of nonresident aliens of the United States and U.S. citizens outside the United States have been excluded from the data. Fetal deaths and deaths among Armed Forces abroad are excluded. Data based on samples are subject to sampling error; for details, see annual issues of *Vital Statistics of the United States.*

Mortality statistics by cause of death are compiled in accordance with World Health Organization regulations according to the *International Classification of Diseases* (ICD). The ICD is revised approximately every 10 years. The tenth revision of the ICD was employed beginning in 1999. Deaths for prior years were classified according to the revision of the ICD in use at the time. Each revision of the ICD introduces a number of discontinuities in mortality statistics; for a discussion of those between the ninth and tenth revisions of the ICD, see *National Vital Statistics Reports*, Vol. 56, Nos. 2 and 10. Preliminary mortality data are

U.S. Census Bureau, Statistical Abstract of the United States: 2011

based on a percentage of death records weighted up to the total number of deaths reported for the given year; for a discussion of preliminary data, see *National Vital Statistics Reports*, Vol. 56, No. 16. Information on tests of statistical significance, differences between death rates, and standard errors can also be found in the reports mentioned above. Some of the tables present age-adjusted death rates in addition to crude death rates. Age-adjusted death rates shown in this section were prepared using the direct method, in which age-specific death rates for a population of interest are applied to a standard population distributed by age. Age adjustment eliminates the differences in observed rates between points in time or among compared population groups that result from age differences in population composition.

Fertility and life expectancy—The total fertility rate, defined as the number of births that 1,000 women would have in their lifetime if, at each year of age, they experienced the birth rates occurring in the specified year, is compiled and published by NCHS. Other data relating to social and medical factors that affect fertility rates, such as contraceptive use and birth expectations, are collected and made available by both NCHS and the Census Bureau. NCHS figures are based on information in birth and fetal death certificates and on the periodic National Surveys of Family Growth; Census Bureau data are based on decennial censuses and the CPS.   Data on life expectancy, the average remaining lifetime in years for persons who attain a given age, are computed and published by NCHS. For details, see *National Vital Statistics Reports*, Vol. 57, No. 14 and <http://www.cdc.gov /nchs/fastats/lifexpec.htm>.

Marriage and divorce—In 1957 and 1958 respectively, the National Office of Vital Statistics established marriage- and divorce-registration areas. Beginning in 1957, the marriage-registration area comprised 30 states, plus Alaska, Hawaii, Puerto Rico, and the Virgin Islands; it currently includes 42 states and the District of Columbia. The divorce-registration area, starting in 1958 with 14 states, Alaska, Hawaii, and the Virgin Islands, currently includes a total of 31 states and

the Virgin Islands. Procedures for estimating the number of marriages and divorces in the registration states are discussed in *Vital Statistics of the United States, Vol. III—Marriage and Divorce*. Total counts of events for registration and nonregistration states are gathered by collecting already summarized data on marriages and divorces reported by state offices of vital statistics and by county offices of registration. The collection and publication of detailed marriage and divorce statistics was suspended beginning in January 1996. For additional information, contact the National Center for Health Statistics online at <http://www.cdc.gov/nchs/datawh /datasite/frnotice.htm>.

Vital statistics rates—Except as noted, vital statistics rates computed by NCHS are based on decennial census population figures as of April 1 for 1960, 1970, 1980, 1990, and 2000; and on midyear population figures for other years, as estimated by the Census Bureau (see text, Section 1).

Race—Data by race for births, deaths, marriages, and divorces from NCHS are based on information contained in the certificates of registration. The Census Bureau's Current Population Survey obtains information on race by asking respondents to classify their race as (1) White, (2) Black, (3) American Indian or Alaska Native, (4) Native Hawaiian or Other Pacific Islander, and (5) Asian. Beginning with the 1989 data year, NCHS is tabulating its birth data primarily by race of the mother. In 1988 and prior years, births were tabulated by race of the child, which was determined from the race of the parents as entered on the birth certificate. Trend data by race shown in this section are by race of mother beginning with the 1980 data. Hispanic origin of the mother is reported and tabulated independently of race. Thus, persons of Hispanic origin may be any race. The majority of women of Hispanic origin are reported as White.

Statistical reliability—For a discussion of statistical collection, estimation, and sampling procedures and measures of reliability applicable to data from NCHS and the Census Bureau, see Appendix III.

64 Births, Deaths, Marriages, and Divorces

Table 78. Live Births, Deaths, Marriages, and Divorces: 1960 to 2007

[4,258 represents 4,258,000. Beginning 1970, excludes births to, and deaths of nonresidents of the United States. See Appendix III]

Year	Number					Rate per 1,000 population				
		Deaths					Deaths			
	Births (1,000)	Total (1,000)	Infant [1] (1,000)	Marriages [2] (1,000)	Divorces [3] (1,000)	Births	Total	Infant [1]	Marriages [2]	Divorces [3]
1960........	4,258	1,712	111	1,523	393	23.7	9.5	26.0	8.5	2.2
1970........	3,731	1,921	75	2,159	708	18.4	9.5	20.0	10.6	3.5
1971........	3,556	1,928	68	2,190	773	17.2	9.3	19.1	10.6	3.7
1972........	3,258	1,964	60	2,282	845	15.6	9.4	18.5	10.9	4.0
1973........	3,137	1,973	56	2,284	915	14.8	9.3	17.7	10.8	4.3
1974........	3,160	1,934	53	2,230	977	14.8	9.1	16.7	10.5	4.6
1975........	3,144	1,893	51	2,153	1,036	14.6	8.8	16.1	10.0	4.8
1976........	3,168	1,909	48	2,155	1,083	14.6	8.8	15.2	9.9	5.0
1977........	3,327	1,900	47	2,178	1,091	15.1	8.6	14.1	9.9	5.0
1978........	3,333	1,928	46	2,282	1,130	15.0	8.7	13.8	10.3	5.1
1979........	3,494	1,914	46	2,331	1,181	15.6	8.5	13.1	10.4	5.3
1980........	3,612	1,990	46	2,390	1,189	15.9	8.8	12.6	10.6	5.2
1981........	3,629	1,978	43	2,422	1,213	15.8	8.6	11.9	10.6	5.3
1982........	3,681	1,975	42	2,456	1,170	15.9	8.5	11.5	10.6	5.1
1983........	3,639	2,019	41	2,446	1,158	15.6	8.6	11.2	10.5	5.0
1984	3,669	2,039	40	2,477	1,169	15.6	8.6	10.8	10.5	5.0
1985........	3,761	2,086	40	2,413	1,190	15.8	8.8	10.6	10.1	5.0
1986........	3,757	2,105	39	2,407	1,178	15.6	8.8	10.4	10.0	4.9
1987	3,809	2,123	38	2,403	1,166	15.7	8.8	10.1	9.9	4.8
1988........	3,910	2,168	39	2,396	1,167	16.0	8.9	10.0	9.8	4.8
1989	4,041	2,150	40	2,403	1,157	16.4	8.7	9.8	9.7	4.7
1990........	4,158	2,148	38	2,443	1,182	16.7	8.6	9.2	9.8	4.7
1991........	4,111	2,170	37	2,371	1,187	16.2	8.6	8.9	9.4	4.7
1992........	4,065	2,176	35	2,362	1,215	15.8	8.5	8.5	9.3	4.8
1993........	4,000	2,269	33	2,334	1,187	15.4	8.8	8.4	9.0	4.6
1994	3,953	2,279	31	2,362	1,191	15.0	8.8	8.0	9.1	4.6
1995........	3,900	2,312	30	2,336	1,169	14.6	8.7	7.6	8.9	4.4
1996........	3,891	2,315	28	2,344	1,150	14.4	8.6	7.3	8.8	4.3
1997........	3,881	2,314	28	2,384	1,163	14.2	8.5	7.2	8.9	4.3
1998 [4]	3,942	2,337	28	2,244	1,135	14.3	8.5	7.2	8.4	4.2
1999 [4]	3,959	2,391	28	2,358	(NA)	14.2	8.6	7.1	8.6	4.1
2000 [4]	4,059	2,403	28	2,329	(NA)	14.4	8.5	6.9	8.3	4.1
2001 [4]	4,026	2,416	28	2,345	(NA)	14.1	8.5	6.8	8.2	4.0
2002 [5]	4,022	2,443	28	2,254	(NA)	13.9	8.5	7.0	7.8	3.9
2003 [5]	4,090	2,448	28	2,245	(NA)	14.1	8.4	6.9	7.7	3.8
2004 [5]	4,112	2,398	28	2,279	(NA)	14.0	8.2	6.8	7.8	3.7
2005 [5]	4,138	2,448	28	[6] 2,249	(NA)	14.0	8.3	6.9	[6] 7.6	[6] 3.6
2006 [5]	4,266	2,426	29	[6,7] 2,160	(NA)	14.2	8.1	6.7	[6,7] 7.4	[6] 3.7
2007 [5]	4,316	2,424	29	[6] 2,205	(NA)	14.3	8.0	6.8	[6] 7.3	[6] 3.6

NA Not available. [1] Infant mortality rate; infants under 1 year, excluding fetal deaths. [2] Includes estimates for some states through 1965 and also for 1976 and 1977 and marriage licenses for some states for all years except 1973 and 1975. Beginning 1978, includes nonlicensed marriages in California. [3] Includes reported annulments and some estimated state figures for all years. [4] Divorce rate excludes data for California, Colorado, Indiana, and Louisiana; population for this rate also excludes those states. [5] Divorce rates exclude data for California, Georgia, Hawaii, Indiana, Louisiana and Minnesota, in 2005 and 2006; California, Georgia, Hawaii, Indiana, and Louisiana, in 2004; California, Hawaii, Indiana, Louisiana, and Oklahoma in 2003; and California, Indiana, and Oklahoma in 2002. Populations for these rates also exclude these states. [6] Provisional data. Includes nonresidents of the United States. [7] Excludes Louisiana.

Source: U.S. National Center for Health Statistics, Vital Statistics of the United States, and National Vital Statistics Reports (NVSR), <http://www.cdc.gov/nchs/nvss.htm>.

Table 79. Live Births, Birth Rates, and Fertility Rates by Hispanic Origin: 2000 to 2007

[4,059 represents 4,059,000. Represents registered births. Excludes births to nonresidents of the United States. Data are based on Hispanic origin and race of mother. Persons of Hispanic origin may be of any race. See Appendix III]

Hispanic-origin status and race of mother	Number of births (1,000)				Birth rate per 1,000 population				Fertility rate [1]			
	2000	2005	2006	2007	2000	2005	2006	2007	2000	2005	2006	2007
Total [2]	4,059	4,138	4,266	4,316	14.4	14.0	14.2	14.3	65.9	66.7	68.5	69.5
Hispanic	816	986	1,039	1,062	23.1	23.1	23.4	23.4	95.9	99.4	101.5	102.3
Mexican	582	693	718	723	25.0	24.7	24.8	24.4	105.1	107.7	109.0	108.0
Puerto Rico	58	63	67	68	18.1	17.2	17.6	17.4	73.5	72.1	74.0	73.6
Cuban	13	16	17	17	9.7	10.2	10.4	10.2	49.3	50.4	49.3	49.7
Central and South American [3] ...	113	151	165	170	21.8	22.8	23.9	25.0	85.1	93.2	98.6	104.9
Other and unknown Hispanic ...	49	62	72	85	(3)	(3)	(3)	(3)	(3)	(3)	(3)	(3)
Non-Hispanic [4]	3,200	3,123	3,196	3,222	13.2	12.4	12.6	12.7	61.1	60.4	62.0	62.9
White	2,363	2,280	2,309	2,310	12.2	11.5	11.6	11.6	58.5	58.3	59.5	60.1
Black	604	584	617	627	17.3	15.7	16.5	16.6	71.4	67.2	70.6	71.6

[1] Live births per 1,000 women aged 15 to 44 years in specified group. [2] Includes all races and Hispanic origin status not stated. [3] Rates for the Central and South American population include other and unknown Hispanic. [4] Includes other races not shown separately.

Source: U.S. National Center for Health Statistics, National Vital Statistics Reports (NVSR), Births: Final Data for 2007, Vol. 58, No. 24, August 2010.

Table 80. Births, Birth Rates, and Fertility Rates by Race, Sex, and Age: 1980 to 2007

[Births in thousands (3,612 represents 3,612,000). Except as indicated, births by race of mother. Excludes births to nonresidents of the United States. For population bases used to derive these data; see text, this section and Appendix III]

Item	1980	1990	1995	2000	2001	2002	2003	2004	2005	2006	2007
Live births [1]	**3,612**	**4,158**	**3,900**	**4,059**	**4,026**	**4,022**	**4,090**	**4,112**	**4,138**	**4,266**	**4,316**
White	2,936	3,290	3,099	3,194	3,178	3,175	3,226	3,223	3,229	3,310	3,337
Black	568	684	603	623	606	594	600	616	633	666	676
American Indian, Eskimo, Aleut	29	39	37	42	42	42	43	44	45	47	49
Asian or Pacific Islander	74	142	160	201	200	211	221	229	231	241	254
Male	1,853	2,129	1,996	2,077	2,058	2,058	2,094	2,105	2,119	2,184	2,209
Female	1,760	2,029	1,903	1,982	1,968	1,964	1,996	2,007	2,019	2,081	2,108
Males per 100 females (sex ratio)	105	105	105	105	105	105	105	105	105	105	105
Age of mother:											
Under 20 years	562	533	512	478	454	433	421	422	421	442	445
20 to 24 years	1,226	1,094	966	1,018	1,022	1,022	1,032	1,034	1,040	1,081	1,082
25 to 29 years	1,108	1,277	1,064	1,088	1,058	1,060	1,086	1,104	1,132	1,182	1,208
30 to 34 years	550	886	905	929	943	951	976	966	951	950	962
35 to 39 years	141	318	384	452	452	454	468	476	483	499	500
40 to 44 years	(NA)	(NA)	(NA)	90	93	96	101	104	105	106	105
45 to 54 years	(NA)	(NA)	(NA)	4	5	5	6	6	6	7	7
Mean age of mother at first birth (years)	22.7	24.2	24.5	24.9	25.0	25.1	25.2	25.2	25.2	25.0	25.0
Birth rate per 1,000 population	**15.9**	**16.7**	**14.6**	**14.4**	**14.1**	**13.9**	**14.1**	**14.0**	**14.0**	**14.2**	**14.3**
White	15.1	15.8	14.1	13.9	13.7	13.5	13.6	13.5	13.4	13.7	13.7
Black	21.3	22.4	17.8	17.0	16.3	15.7	15.7	16.0	16.2	16.8	16.9
American Indian, Eskimo, Aleut	20.7	18.9	15.3	14.0	13.7	13.8	13.8	14.0	14.2	14.9	15.3
Asian or Pacific Islander	19.9	19.0	16.7	17.1	16.4	16.5	16.8	16.8	16.5	16.6	17.2
Age of mother:											
10 to 14 years	1.1	1.4	1.3	0.9	0.8	0.7	0.6	0.7	0.7	0.6	0.6
15 to 19 years	53.0	59.9	56.0	47.7	45.3	43.0	41.6	41.1	40.4	41.9	42.5
20 to 24 years	115.1	116.5	107.5	109.7	106.2	103.6	102.6	101.7	102.2	105.9	106.4
25 to 29 years	112.9	120.2	108.8	113.5	113.4	113.6	115.6	115.5	115.5	116.7	117.6
30 to 34 years	61.9	80.8	81.1	91.2	91.9	91.5	95.1	95.3	95.8	97.7	99.9
35 to 39 years	19.8	31.7	34.0	39.7	40.6	41.4	43.8	45.4	46.3	47.3	47.5
40 to 44 years	3.9	5.5	6.6	8.0	8.1	8.3	8.7	8.9	9.1	9.4	9.5
45 to 54 years [2]	0.2	0.2	0.3	0.5	0.5	0.5	0.5	0.5	0.6	0.6	0.6
Fertility rate per 1,000 women [3]	**68.4**	**70.9**	**64.6**	**65.9**	**65.3**	**64.8**	**66.1**	**66.3**	**66.7**	**68.5**	**69.5**
White [3]	65.6	68.3	63.6	65.3	65.0	64.8	66.1	66.1	66.3	68.0	68.8
Black [3]	84.9	84.8	71.0	70.0	67.6	65.8	66.3	67.6	69.0	72.1	72.7
American Indian, Eskimo, Aleut [3]	82.7	76.2	63.0	58.7	58.1	58.0	58.4	58.9	59.9	63.1	64.9
Asian or Pacific Islander [3]	73.2	69.6	62.6	65.8	64.2	64.1	66.3	67.1	66.6	67.5	71.3

NA Not available. [1] Includes other races not shown separately. [2] The number of births shown is the total for women aged 45–54 years. The rate is computed by relating the births to women aged 45–54 years to women aged 45–49 years. [3] Number of live births per 1,000 women, 15 to 44 years old in specified group.

Source: U.S. National Center for Health Statistics, National Vital Statistics Reports (NVSR), *Births: Final Data for 2007*, Vol. 58, No. 24, August 2010.

Table 81. Births and Multiple Births by Race and Hispanic Origin of Mother: 1990 to 2007

[Represents registered births. Excludes births to nonresidents of the United States. Data are based on Hispanic origin and race of mother. Persons of Hispanic origin may be of any race. See Appendix III]

Birth order	1990 [1]	2000	2004	2005	2006	2007
All births, total number [2]	**4,158,212**	**4,058,814**	**4,112,052**	**4,138,349**	**4,265,555**	**4,316,233**
Twin births	93,865	118,916	132,219	133,122	137,085	138,961
Triplet and higher order multiple births	3,028	7,325	7,275	6,694	6,540	6,427
Multiple birth rate [3]	23.3	31.1	33.9	33.8	33.7	33.7
Twin birth rate [4]	22.6	29.3	32.2	32.2	32.1	32.2
Triplet and higher order multiple birth rate [5]	72.8	180.5	176.9	161.8	153.3	148.9
Non-Hispanic White births, total number	**2,626,500**	**2,362,968**	**2,296,683**	**2,279,768**	**2,308,640**	**2,310,333**
Twin births	60,210	76,018	83,346	82,223	83,108	83,632
Triplet and higher order multiple births	2,358	5,821	5,590	4,966	4,805	4,559
Multiple birth rate [3]	23.8	34.6	38.7	38.2	38.1	38.2
Twin birth rate [4]	22.9	32.2	36.3	36.1	36.0	36.2
Non-Hispanic Black births, total number	**661,701**	**604,346**	**578,772**	**583,759**	**617,247**	**627,191**
Twin births	17,646	20,173	20,605	21,254	22,702	23,101
Triplet and higher order multiple births	306	506	577	616	580	612
Multiple birth rate [3]	27.1	34.2	36.6	33.8	37.7	37.8
Twin birth rate [4]	26.7	33.4	35.6	32.2	36.8	36.8
Hispanic births, total number	**595,073**	**815,868**	**946,349**	**985,505**	**1,039,077**	**1,062,779**
Twin births	10,713	16,470	20,351	21,723	22,698	23,405
Triplet and higher order multiple births	235	659	723	761	787	857
Multiple birth rate [3]	18.4	21.0	22.3	22.8	22.6	22.8
Twin birth rate [4]	18.0	20.2	21.5	22.0	21.8	22.0

[1] Data by Hispanic-origin status exclude data for New Hampshire and Oklahoma, which did not report Hispanic origin. [2] Includes other races not shown separately. [3] Number of live births in all multiple deliveries per 1,000 live births. [4] Number of live births in twin deliveries per 1,000 live births. [5] Births in greater than twin deliveries per 100,000 live births.

Source: U.S. National Center for Health Statistics, National Vital Statistics Report (NVSR), Births: Final Data for 2007, Vol. 58, No. 24, August 2010.

Table 82. Births—Number and Rate by State and Island Areas: 2007

[Number of births, except rate. By place of residence. Registered births. Excludes births to nonresidents of the United States. By race and Hispanic origin of mother. See Appendix III]

State	All races [1]	Non-Hispanic White	Non-Hispanic Black	Asian or Pacific Islander	American Indian, Eskimo, Aleut	Hispanic [2]	Birth rate [3]	Fertility rate [4]
United States	**4,316,233**	**2,310,333**	**627,191**	**254,488**	**49,443**	**1,062,779**	**14.3**	**69.5**
Alabama	64,804	38,508	19,734	942	189	5,406	14.0	68.7
Alaska	11,052	6,293	417	860	2,791	694	16.2	77.2
Arizona	102,981	42,518	3,913	3,482	6,666	46,369	16.2	81.1
Arkansas	41,378	27,736	8,064	709	250	4,517	14.6	73.1
California	566,414	155,912	31,783	74,305	3,627	297,092	15.5	72.5
Colorado	70,809	41,843	3,121	2,511	758	22,249	14.6	69.8
Connecticut	41,660	24,915	5,171	2,422	235	8,830	11.9	59.5
Delaware	12,170	6,496	3,214	530	16	1,912	14.1	68.4
District of Columbia	8,864	2,257	4,910	219	2	1,451	15.1	60.0
Florida	239,165	107,816	51,799	8,201	801	70,839	13.1	68.4
Georgia	151,137	68,659	49,620	5,941	410	24,763	15.8	73.3
Hawaii	19,134	4,494	425	12,971	79	3,007	14.9	76.0
Idaho	25,019	20,187	139	422	452	3,872	16.7	83.4
Illinois	180,836	95,135	31,558	9,644	281	44,146	14.1	67.3
Indiana	89,864	68,916	10,224	1,705	119	8,807	14.2	69.7
Iowa	40,886	34,516	1,802	1,047	319	3,356	13.7	70.1
Kansas	42,004	30,512	3,054	1,385	376	6,690	15.1	75.6
Kentucky	59,368	49,831	5,415	1,038	112	3,093	14.0	68.6
Louisiana	66,301	35,824	25,709	1,165	484	3,186	15.4	73.4
Maine	14,120	13,185	326	223	125	209	10.7	55.6
Maryland	78,095	36,177	26,156	5,025	152	10,606	13.9	65.6
Massachusetts	77,967	53,287	7,260	5,943	186	10,900	12.1	57.4
Michigan	125,261	85,989	22,130	4,481	756	8,712	12.4	61.4
Minnesota	73,735	53,850	6,569	5,226	1,769	5,938	14.2	69.7
Mississippi	46,491	23,065	20,887	477	309	1,709	15.9	76.9
Missouri	81,930	62,222	12,598	1,972	433	4,668	13.9	68.8
Montana	12,439	9,618	62	144	1,602	371	13.0	68.6
Nebraska	26,934	20,007	1,795	785	623	4,068	15.2	76.2
Nevada	41,181	16,987	3,604	3,459	572	16,132	10.1	79.5
New Hampshire	14,168	12,618	204	547	54	593	10.8	53.8
New Jersey	116,063	56,243	17,816	11,756	189	30,034	13.4	66.1
New Mexico	30,616	8,765	526	524	3,923	17,019	15.5	76.6
New York	253,451	125,674	42,729	24,054	637	60,134	13.1	62.1
North Carolina	131,037	72,453	30,618	3,987	1,772	22,113	14.5	69.6
North Dakota	8,840	7,239	139	137	1,028	278	13.8	69.8
Ohio	150,879	115,272	24,174	3,680	325	6,628	13.2	65.5
Oklahoma	55,065	35,331	4,912	1,254	6,495	7,173	15.2	76.0
Oregon	49,378	34,265	1,144	2,684	951	10,133	13.2	66.1
Pennsylvania	150,713	107,779	21,281	6,286	424	13,813	12.1	61.9
Rhode Island	12,376	6,000	1,044	531	158	2,589	11.7	55.8
South Carolina	62,875	34,640	20,506	1,175	276	6,211	14.3	69.9
South Dakota	12,261	9,347	212	149	2,163	471	15.4	80.0
Tennessee	86,711	58,577	17,763	2,179	397	8,389	14.1	68.8
Texas	407,625	140,199	46,356	16,144	1,086	204,505	17.1	80.1
Utah	55,130	42,839	540	1,748	765	9,044	20.8	94.4
Vermont	6,513	6,178	95	91	14	80	10.5	53.2
Virginia	108,884	62,264	23,763	7,871	174	14,967	14.1	67.0
Washington	88,978	56,310	3,816	9,294	2,505	16,857	13.8	67.0
West Virginia	21,994	20,682	778	181	24	253	12.1	63.1
Wisconsin	72,784	54,542	7,237	2,895	1,256	6,933	13.0	65.0
Wyoming	7,893	6,361	79	87	333	970	15.1	77.7
Puerto Rico	46,642	1,389	128	(NA)	(NA)	45,106	11.8	55.2
Virgin Islands	1,697	122	1,087	26	5	384	15.5	75.0
Guam	3,483	210	31	3,173	7	67	20.1	91.2
American Samoa	1,288	(NA)	(NA)	1,288	–	(NA)	20.1	90.5
Northern Marianas	1,387	(NA)	(NA)	1,367	–	(NA)	16.4	40.0

– Represents or rounds to zero. NA Not available. [1] Includes persons of other groups, not shown separately. [2] Persons of Hispanic origin may be any race. [3] Per 1,000 estimated population. [4] Number of births per 1,000 women aged 15 to 44 years.

Source: U.S. National Center for Health Statistics, National Vital Statistics Reports (NVSR), *Births: Final Data for 2007*, Vol. 58, No. 24, August 2010.

Table 83. Total Fertility Rate by Race and Hispanic Origin: 1980 to 2007

[Based on race of mother. Excludes births to nonresidents of United States. The *total fertility rate* is the number of births that 1,000 women would have in their lifetime if, at each year of age, they experienced the birth rates occurring in the specified year. A total fertility rate of 2,110 represents "replacement level" fertility for the total population under current mortality conditions (assuming no net immigration). See Appendix III]

Race and Hispanic origin	1980	1990	2000	2003	2004	2005	2006	2007
Total [1]	**1,840**	**2,081**	**2,056**	**2,043**	**2,046**	**2,054**	**2,101**	**2,122**
White	1,773	2,003	2,051	2,061	2,055	2,056	2,096	2,112
Black	2,177	2,480	2,129	1,999	2,033	2,071	2,155	2,168
American Indian, Eskimo, Aleut.	2,165	2,185	1,773	1,732	1,735	1,750	1,829	1,867
Asian or Pacific Islander	1,954	2,003	1,892	1,873	1,898	1,889	1,919	2,039
Hispanic [2]	(NA)	2,960	2,730	2,786	2,825	2,885	2,960	2,995

NA Not available. [1] For 1970 to 1991 includes births to races not shown separately. Beginning 1992 unknown race of mother is imputed. [2] Persons of Hispanic origin may be any race.

Source: U.S. National Center for Health Statistics, National Vital Statistics Report (NVSR), *Births: Final Data for 2007*, Vol. 58, No. 24, August 2010,

Table 84. Teenagers—Births and Birth Rates by Age, Race, and Hispanic Origin: 1990 to 2007

[Birth rates per 1,000 women in specified group. Based on race and Hispanic origin of mother. See text this section]

Item	Number of births					Birth rate				
	1990	2000	2005	2006	2007	1990	2000	2005	2006	2007
All races, 15 to 19 years	[2] **521,826**	**468,990**	**414,593**	**435,436**	**444,899**	**59.9**	**47.7**	**40.5**	**41.9**	**42.5**
15 to 17 years	183,327	157,209	133,191	138,943	140,566	37.5	26.9	21.4	22.0	22.2
18 to 19 years	338,499	311,781	281,402	296,493	304,333	88.6	78.1	69.9	73.0	73.9
White	354,482	333,013	295,265	308,344	314,560	50.8	43.2	37.0	38.2	38.8
Black	151,613	118,954	103,905	111,019	113,561	112.8	77.4	61.9	64.6	64.9
American Indian, Eskimo, Aleut. . . .	(NA)	8,055	7,807	8,261	8,956	81.1	58.3	52.7	55.0	59.3
Asian or Pacific Islander	(NA)	8,968	7,616	7,812	7,822	26.4	20.5	17.0	17.0	16.9
Hispanic [1]	(NA)	129,469	136,906	145,669	148,563	100.3	87.3	81.7	83.0	81.8
Non-Hispanic White	(NA)	204,056	165,005	169,729	172,941	42.5	32.6	25.9	26.6	27.2
Non-Hispanic Black	(NA)	116,019	96,813	103,725	106,143	116.2	79.2	60.9	63.7	64.2

NA Not available. [1] Persons of Hispanic origin may be any race. [2] Includes races other than White and Black not shown separately.

Source: U.S. National Center for Health Statistics, National Vital Statistics Reports (NVSR), *Births: Final Data for 2007*, Vol. 58, No. 24, August 2010.

Table 85. Births to Unmarried Women by Race, Hispanic Origin, and Age of Mother: 1990 to 2007

[1,165 represents 1,165,000. Excludes births to nonresidents of the United States. Persons of Hispanic origin may be of any race. Marital status is inferred from a comparison of the child's and parents' surnames on the birth certificate for those states that do not report on marital status. No estimates included for misstatements on birth records or failure to register births. Based on race and Hispanic origin of mother. See also Appendix III]

Race and age of mother	Number (1,000)				Percent distribution				Birth rate [1]			
	1990	1995	2000	2007	1990	1995	2000	2007	1990	1995	2000	2007
Total live births [2]	**1,165**	**1,254**	**1,347**	**1,715**	**100.0**	**100.0**	**100.0**	**100.0**	**43.8**	**44.3**	**44.1**	**52.3**
White	670	785	866	1,160	57.5	62.6	64.3	67.6	32.9	37.0	38.2	48.1
Black	455	421	427	481	39.1	33.6	31.7	28.0	90.5	74.5	70.5	72.6
American Indian, Eskimo, Aleut	(NA)	(NA)	(NA)	32	(NA)	(NA)	(NA)	1.9	(NA)	(NA)	(NA)	(NA)
Asian or Pacific Islander . . .	(NA)	(NA)	(NA)	42	(NA)	(NA)	(NA)	2.4	(NA)	(NA)	20.9	27.3
Hispanic	[3] 219	278	348	546	[3] 18.8	22.1	25.8	31.8	[3] 89.6	88.8	87.2	108.4
Non-Hispanic White	[3] 443	504	522	643	[3] 38.0	40.2	38.7	37.5	[3] 24.4	28.1	28.0	33.3
Non-Hispanic Black	(NA)	(NA)	415	449	(NA)	(NA)	30.8	26.2	(NA)	(NA)	(NA)	(NA)
Under 15 years	11	11	8	6	0.9	0.9	0.6	0.3	(NA)	(NA)	(NA)	(NA)
15 to 19 years	350	376	369	380	30.0	30.0	27.4	22.2	42.5	43.8	39.0	37.4
20 to 24 years	404	432	504	645	34.7	34.5	37.4	37.6	65.1	68.7	72.2	80.6
25 to 29 years	230	229	255	389	19.7	18.2	18.9	22.7	56.0	54.3	58.5	76.9
30 to 34 years	118	133	130	186	10.1	10.6	9.7	10.8	37.6	38.9	39.3	57.9
35 to 39 years	44	60	65	86	3.8	4.8	4.8	5.0	17.3	19.3	19.7	28.7
40 years and over	9	13	16	22	0.7	1.0	1.2	1.3	3.6	4.7	5.0	[4] 6.8

NA Not available. [1] Rate per 1,000 unmarried women (never-married, widowed, and divorced) estimated as of July 1. Total rate and rates by race cover women 15 to 44 years old. [2] Includes races other than White and Black, not shown separately. [3] Excludes data for New Hampshire and Oklahoma, which did not report Hispanic origin. [4] Birth rates computed by relating births to unmarried mothers aged 40 years and over to unmarried women aged 40–44 years.

Source: U.S. National Center for Health Statistics, National Vital Statistics Reports (NVSR), *Births: Final Data for 2007*, Vol. 58, No. 24, August 2010.

Table 86. Percentage of Births to Teens, Unmarried Mothers, and Births With Low Birth Weight by Race and Hispanic Origin: 1990 to 2007

[Represents registered births. Excludes births to nonresidents of the United States. Data are based on race and Hispanic origin of mother. See Appendix III]

Characteristics	1990	1995	2000	2004	2005	2006	2007
Percent of births to teenage mothers	**12.8**	**13.1**	**11.8**	**10.3**	**10.2**	**10.4**	**10.5**
White...................	10.9	11.5	10.6	9.3	9.3	9.4	9.5
Black...................	23.1	23.1	19.7	17.1	16.9	17.0	17.2
American Indian, Eskimo, Aleut..............	19.5	21.4	19.7	17.9	17.7	17.6	18.4
Asian or Pacific Islander	5.7	5.6	4.5	3.4	3.3	3.3	3.1
Hispanic origin [1]...................	16.8	17.9	16.2	14.3	14.1	14.3	14.2
Non-Hispanic........................	(NA)	(NA)	10.7	9.1	8.9	9.1	9.2
White	(NA)	(NA)	8.7	7.4	7.3	7.4	7.5
Black	(NA)	(NA)	19.8	17.3	17.0	17.2	17.3
Percent of births to unmarried mothers	**26.6**	**32.2**	**33.2**	**35.8**	**36.9**	**38.5**	**39.7**
White...................	16.9	25.3	27.1	30.5	31.7	33.3	34.8
Black...................	66.7	69.9	68.5	68.8	69.3	70.2	71.2
American Indian, Eskimo, Aleut..............	53.6	57.2	58.4	62.3	63.5	64.6	65.3
Asian or Pacific Islander	13.2	16.3	14.8	15.5	16.2	16.5	16.6
Hispanic origin [1]...................	36.7	40.8	42.7	46.4	48.0	49.9	51.3
Non-Hispanic........................	(NA)	(NA)	30.8	32.5	33.4	34.8	35.9
White	(NA)	(NA)	22.1	24.5	25.3	26.6	27.8
Black	(NA)	(NA)	68.7	69.3	69.9	70.7	71.6
Percent of births with low birth weight [2]	**7.0**	**7.3**	**7.6**	**8.1**	**8.2**	**8.3**	**8.2**
White...................	5.7	6.2	6.5	7.1	7.2	7.2	7.2
Black...................	13.3	13.1	13.0	13.4	13.6	13.6	13.6
American Indian, Eskimo, Aleut..............	6.1	6.6	6.8	7.5	7.4	7.5	7.5
Asian or Pacific Islander	(NA)	6.9	7.3	7.9	8.0	8.1	8.1
Hispanic origin [1]...................	6.1	6.3	6.4	6.8	6.9	7.0	6.9
Non-Hispanic........................	(NA)	(NA)	7.9	8.5	8.6	8.7	8.6
White	(NA)	(NA)	6.6	7.2	7.3	7.3	7.3
Black	(NA)	(NA)	13.1	13.7	14.0	14.0	13.9

NA Not available. [1] Hispanic persons may be any race. Includes other types, not shown separately. [2] Births less than 2,500 grams (5 pounds–8 ounces).

Source: U.S. National Center for Health Statistics, National Vital Statistics Reports (NVSR), *Births: Final Data for 2007*, Vol. 58, No. 24, August 2010.

Table 87. Births by Race, Hispanic Origin, and Method of Delivery: 1990 to 2007

[In thousands (4,111 represents 4,111,000), except rate. 1990 excludes data for Oklahoma, which did not report method of delivery on the birth certificate. Persons of Hispanic origin may be any race. See Appendix III]

Method of delivery	1990	2000	2005	2007 Total [1]	2007 Hispanic	2007 Non-Hispanic White	2007 Non-Hispanic Black
Births, total.............	**4,111**	**4,059**	**4,138**	**4,316**	**1,063**	**2,310**	**627**
Vaginal....................	3,111	3,108	2,874	2,933	737	1,566	413
Cesarean deliveries..........	914	924	1,249	1,367	323	736	212
Not stated	85	27	16	16	3	9	2
Cesarean delivery rate [2]	22.7	22.9	30.3	31.8	30.4	32.0	33.9

[1] Includes other races, not shown separately. [2] Cesarean rates are the number of cesarean deliveries per 100 total deliveries for specified category.

Source: U.S. National Center for Health Statistics, National Vital Statistics Reports (NVSR), *Births: Final Data for 2007*, Vol. 58, No. 24, August 2010, and earlier reports.

Table 88. Induction of Labor by Gestational Age: 1990 to 2007

[In percent. Data are for singleton births]

Gestational age	1990 [1]	1995	2000	2001	2002	2003	2004	2005	2006	2007
All gestations...........	**9.6**	**16.1**	**20.1**	**20.7**	**20.9**	**20.9**	**21.6**	**22.7**	**23.0**	**23.2**
Under 37 weeks (preterm)....	6.9	11.6	14.8	14.7	14.7	14.5	15.1	15.6	15.6	15.6
Under 32 weeks...........	5.0	7.8	9.2	8.9	8.8	8.6	8.7	8.9	8.9	9.0
32–33 weeks.............	6.4	10.6	13.3	12.8	12.8	12.8	13.0	13.4	13.5	13.5
34–36 weeks.............	7.5	12.6	16.2	16.2	16.2	16.0	16.7	17.3	17.3	17.2
37 weeks and over (term)	9.9	16.7	20.8	21.6	21.8	21.9	22.5	23.7	23.9	24.2
37–39 weeks.............	7.9	14.3	18.9	19.6	19.8	19.8	20.6	21.7	22.0	22.1
40–41 weeks.............	10.7	18.5	22.9	24.1	24.6	24.8	25.3	26.8	27.4	27.9
42 weeks and over.........	14.9	21.3	24.4	24.4	24.3	24.3	25.4	26.2	26.8	26.9

[1] Oklahoma did not report induction of labor.

Source: U.S. National Center for Health Statistics, "VitalStats," August 2010, <http://www.cdc.gov/nchs/vitalstats.htm>.

Births, Deaths, Marriages, and Divorces **69**

Table 89. Births to Teenage Mothers and Unmarried Women and Births With Low Birth Weight—States and Island Areas: 2000 to 2007

[Represents registered births. Excludes births to nonresidents of the United States. Based on 100 percent of births in all states and the District of Columbia]

State and Island Area	Births to teenage mothers, percent of total [1]		Births to unmarried women, percent of total		Percent of births with low birth weight [2]		State and Island Area	Births to teenage mothers, percent of total [1]		Births to unmarried women, percent of total		Percent of births with low birth weight [2]	
	2000	2007 [3]	2000	2007	2000	2007		2000	2007 [3]	2000	2007	2000	2007
U.S.	**11.8**	**10.5**	**33.2**	**39.7**	**7.6**	**8.2**	NV	12.7	10.8	36.4	42.0	7.2	8.2
AL	15.7	13.6	34.3	38.3	9.7	10.4	NH	6.8	6.6	24.7	31.4	6.3	6.3
AK	11.8	10.1	33.0	37.3	5.6	5.7	NJ	7.1	6.4	28.9	34.4	7.7	8.5
AZ	14.3	12.7	39.3	45.2	7.0	7.1	NM	17.4	15.7	45.6	51.8	8.0	8.7
AR	17.3	14.6	35.7	43.4	8.6	9.1	NY	8.2	7.0	36.6	40.7	7.7	8.1
CA	10.6	9.5	32.7	38.9	6.2	6.9	NC	13.0	11.7	33.3	41.2	8.8	9.2
CO	11.7	9.7	25.0	25.4	8.4	9.0	ND	9.2	8.0	28.3	32.6	6.4	6.3
CT	7.8	6.9	29.3	35.1	7.4	8.1	OH	12.1	11.0	34.6	42.2	7.9	8.8
DE	12.3	10.4	37.9	46.8	8.6	9.3	OK	15.9	13.9	34.3	41.3	7.5	8.2
DC	14.2	12.1	60.3	58.5	11.9	11.1	OR	11.3	8.9	30.1	35.1	5.6	6.1
FL	12.6	10.9	38.2	46.1	8.0	8.7	PA	9.9	9.3	32.7	39.7	7.7	8.4
GA	13.9	12.2	37.0	43.6	8.6	9.5	RI	10.2	9.7	35.5	44.0	7.2	8.0
HI	10.3	8.5	32.2	36.9	7.5	8.0	SC	15.3	13.4	39.8	46.6	9.7	10.1
ID	11.6	9.1	21.6	25.5	6.7	6.5	SD	11.6	9.8	33.5	38.4	6.2	7.0
IL	11.4	10.1	34.5	40.1	7.9	8.5	TN	14.7	13.2	34.5	42.8	9.2	9.4
IN	12.5	11.2	34.7	42.4	7.4	8.5	TX	15.3	13.5	30.5	40.7	7.4	8.4
IA	10.0	8.7	28.0	34.3	6.1	6.8	UT	8.9	6.9	17.3	19.7	6.6	6.7
KS	12.0	10.3	29.0	36.5	6.9	7.1	VT	8.0	7.6	28.1	36.6	6.1	6.2
KY	14.1	12.9	31.0	39.3	8.2	9.3	VA	9.9	8.6	29.9	35.2	7.9	8.6
LA	17.0	13.7	45.6	51.4	10.3	11.2	WA	10.2	8.4	28.2	33.2	5.6	6.3
ME	9.4	8.4	31.0	39.1	6.0	6.3	WV	15.9	12.5	31.7	40.3	8.3	9.5
MD	9.9	8.9	34.6	40.9	8.6	9.1	WI	10.2	8.7	29.3	35.4	6.5	7.0
MA	6.6	6.4	26.5	33.4	7.1	7.9	WY	13.5	11.8	28.8	34.7	8.3	9.1
MI	10.5	10.1	33.3	39.4	7.9	8.4							
MN	8.3	7.1	25.8	32.7	6.1	6.7	PR	(NA)	18.3	49.7	59.3	10.8	12.4
MS	18.8	17.1	46.0	53.7	10.7	12.3	VI	(NA)	12.8	66.7	71.5	9.1	11.7
MO	13.1	11.4	34.6	40.5	7.6	7.9	GU	(NA)	(NA)	54.8	59.9	7.6	8.90
MT	11.6	9.7	30.8	35.9	6.2	7.2	AS	(NA)	7.4	35.5	33.0	2.7	3.3
NE	10.2	8.6	27.2	33.4	6.8	7.0	MP	(NA)	8.5	(NA)	46.7	8.9	6.3

NA Not available. [1] Defined as mothers who are 19 years of age or younger. [2] Less than 2,500 grams (5 pounds–8 ounces).
[3] 2007 data are preliminary and based on a substantial proportion of vital records for that year.

Source: U.S. National Center for Health Statistics, National Vital Statistics Reports (NVSR), *Births: Final Data for 2007*, Vol. 58, No. 24, August 2010.

Table 90. Infants Who Were Ever Breastfed by Maternal Age and Race-Ethnicity: 1999 to 2006

[In percent. Covers period from 1999 through 2006. Breastfeeding was defined as ever having been breastfed or received breast milk. Based on data from National Health and Nutrition Examination Surveys (NHANES)]

Race and ethnicity	Under 20 years old	20 to 29 years old	30 years old and older
Total	**43**	**65**	**75**
Non-Hispanic White	40	65	77
Non-Hispanic Black	30	44	56
Mexican American	66	75	76

Source: U.S. National Center for Health Statistics, Breastfeeding in the United States Findings from the National Health and Nutrition Examination Surveys: 1999–2006, NCHS Data Brief, No. 5, April 2008. See <http://www.cdc.gov/nchs/data/databriefs/db05.htm\>

Table 91. Women Who Had a Child in the Last Year by Age: 1990 to 2008

[3,913 represents 3,913,000. As of June. See headnote Table 92]

Age of mother	Women who had a child in last year (1,000)			Total births per 1,000 women			First births per 1,000 women		
	1990	2000	2008	1990	2000	2008	1990	2000	2008
Total	**3,913**	**3,934**	**3,960**	**67.0**	**64.6**	**64.2**	**26.4**	**26.7**	**25.3**
15 to 29 years old	2,568	2,432	2,372	90.8	85.9	76.7	43.2	43.1	37.4
15 to 19 years old	338	586	371	39.8	59.7	35.6	30.1	38.7	23.1
20 to 24 years old	1,038	850	864	113.4	91.8	85.1	51.8	47.1	46.8
25 to 29 years old	1,192	996	1,138	112.1	107.9	109.8	46.2	43.7	42.7
30 to 44 years old	1,346	1,502	1,587	44.7	46.1	51.6	10.6	12.5	13.1
30 to 34 years old	892	871	874	80.4	87.9	90.9	21.9	27.5	27.6
35 to 39 years old	377	506	550	37.3	45.1	52.9	6.5	9.6	9.5
40 to 44 years old	77	125	163	8.6	10.9	15.2	1.2	2.3	3.5

Source: U.S. Census Bureau, Current Population Reports, P20-555 and earlier reports, and unpublished data.

Table 92. Women Who Had a Child in the Last Year by Selected Characteristics: 1990 to 2008

[58,381 represents 58,381,000. As of June. Covers civilian noninstitutional population. Since the number of women who had a birth during the 12-month period was tabulated and not the actual numbers of births, some small underestimation of fertility for this period may exist due to the omission of: (1) Multiple births, (2) Two or more live births spaced within the 12-month period (the woman is counted only once), (3) Women who had births in the period and who did not survive to the survey date,(4) Women who were in institutions and therefore not in the survey universe. These losses may be somewhat offset by the inclusion in the Current Population Survey (CPS) of births to immigrants who did not have their children born in the United States and births to nonresident women. These births would not have been recorded in the vital registration system. Based on June supplement, Current Population Survey. The 2003 Current Population Survey allowed respondents to choose more than one race. Beginning 2003 data represent persons who selected this race group only and exclude persons reporting more than one race. The Current Population Survey in prior years allowed respondents to report only one race group. See also comments on race in Section 1]

| Characteristic | Total women (1,000) | Percent childless | Women who had a child in the last year | | | |
| | | | Total births | | First births | |
			Number (1,000)	Per 1,000 women	Number (1,000)	Per 1,000 women
1990.	58,381	41.6	3,913	67.0	1,540	26.4
2000.	60,873	42.8	3,934	64.6	1,626	26.7
2008, total [1]	**61,692**	**45.7**	**3,960**	**64.2**	**1,560**	**25.3**
Age:						
15 to 19 years old	10,405	93.7	371	35.6	240	23.1
20 to 24 years old	10,156	70.6	864	85.1	475	46.8
25 to 29 years old	10,362	46.2	1,138	109.8	443	42.7
30 to 34 years old	9,618	26.8	874	90.9	265	27.6
35 to 39 years old	10,403	19.4	550	52.9	99	9.5
40 to 44 years old	10,748	17.8	163	15.2	37	3.5
Race and Hispanic origin:						
White alone	47,616	46.4	3,034	63.7	1,183	24.8
White alone, non-Hispanic.	37,846	48.5	2,276	60.1	925	24.4
Black alone	8,940	41.4	613	68.5	258	28.9
Asian alone	3,276	46.1	188	57.4	80	24.5
Hispanic [2]	10,586	38.1	819	77.4	277	26.1
Marital status:						
Married, husband present	26,271	18.1	2,445	93.1	895	34.1
Married, husband absent [3]	2,515	22.7	189	75.0	53	21.1
Widowed or divorced	4,480	21.0	147	32.9	44	9.9
Never married	28,426	77.2	1,179	41.5	568	20.0
Educational attainment:						
Not a high school graduate	12,882	62.5	703	54.6	248	19.2
High school, 4 years	15,010	33.5	1,067	71.1	427	28.4
Some college, no degree.	12,953	48.7	789	60.9	309	23.8
Associate's degree	5,115	31.7	306	59.9	89	17.5
Bachelor's degree	11,094	47.8	694	62.6	287	25.9
Graduate or professional degree.	4,638	40.6	400	86.3	200	43.2
Labor force status:						
In labor force	42,809	44.6	2,261	52.8	1,015	23.7
Employed.	39,641	44.0	2,051	51.7	910	23.0
Unemployed.	3,168	52.0	210	66.2	104	33.0
Not in labor force	18,883	48.3	1,699	90.0	545	28.9
Family Income:						
Under $10,000.	3,422	41.2	298	87.2	122	35.5
$10,000 to $19,999	4,500	39.4	356	79.1	140	31.2
$20,000 to $24,999	2,586	44.3	190	73.3	70	27.1
$25,000 to $29,999	2,927	43.0	230	78.6	93	31.7
$30,000 to $34,999	2,966	42.9	228	76.7	57	19.1
$35,000 to $49,999	7,473	46.8	454	60.8	195	26.0
$50,000 to $74,999	10,134	47.0	594	58.6	229	22.6
$75,000 and over.	17,203	47.9	1,020	59.3	404	23.5

[1] Includes women of other races and women with family income not reported, not shown separately [2] Persons of Hispanic origin may be any race. [3] Includes separated women.

Source: U.S. Census Bureau, Current Population Reports, P20-555 and unpublished data.

Table 93. Women Who Had a Child in the Last Year by Age and Labor Force Status: 1980 to 2008

[3,913 represents 3,913,000. As of June. See headnote, Table 92]

| Year | Total, 15 to 44 years old | | | 15 to 29 years old | | | 30 to 44 years old | | |
| | Number (1,000) | In the labor force | | Number (1,000) | In the labor force | | Number (1,000) | In the labor force | |
		Number (1,000)	Percent		Number (1,000)	Percent		Number (1,000)	Percent
1990.	3,913	2,068	53	2,568	1,275	50	1,346	793	59
1995.	3,696	2,034	55	2,252	1,150	51	1,444	884	61
2000.	3,934	2,170	55	2,432	1,304	54	1,502	866	58
2004.	3,746	2,045	55	2,205	(NA)	(NA)	1,542	(NA)	59
2006.	3,974	2,221	56	2,399	1,273	53	1,576	948	60
2008.	3,960	2,261	57	2,372	1,299	55	1,587	962	61

NA Not available.

Source: U.S. Bureau of the Census, Current Population Reports, P20-555 and earlier reports, and unpublished data.

U.S. Census Bureau, Statistical Abstract of the United States: 2011

Table 94. Persons Who Have Ever Had Sexual Contact by Selected Characteristics: 2002

[In percent except as indicated (61,147 represents 61,147,000). Based on the National Survey of Family Growth, see Appendix III]

Characteristic	Number (1,000)	Any	One	Two	3 to 6	7 to 14	15 or more	Median number [1]	Any same-sex sexual contact [2]
Males, 15 to 44 years old [3]	**61,147**	**90.3**	**12.8**	**8.1**	**27.5**	**19.3**	**22.6**	**5.4**	**6.0**
15 to 19 years old	10,208	61.6	23.0	9.2	20.7	6.2	2.5	1.9	4.5
20 to 24 years old	9,883	91.1	15.9	11.7	33.5	14.1	15.9	3.8	5.5
25 to 44 years old	41,056	97.3	9.6	7.0	27.8	23.7	29.2	6.7	6.5
25 to 29 years old	9,226	95.2	10.0	8.8	29.4	23.2	23.8	5.9	5.7
30 to 34 years old	10,138	97.2	10.7	6.9	28.5	21.9	29.2	6.4	(NA)
35 to 39 years old	10,557	98.2	8.9	7.0	28.0	25.5	28.8	6.9	(NA)
40 to 44 years old	11,135	98.2	8.8	5.4	25.6	24.2	34.2	8.2	(NA)
White only, non-Hispanic	38,738	90.3	13.4	8.3	27.1	19.2	22.3	5.3	(NA)
Black only, non-Hispanic	6,940	91.8	5.8	5.9	24.1	22.2	33.8	8.3	(NA)
Hispanic or Latino origin	10,188	91.8	13.7	8.6	32.8	18.6	18.1	4.5	(NA)
Currently married	25,808	100.0	15.4	8.5	30.5	22.3	23.3	5.2	3.4
Currently cohabiting	5,653	100.0	4.7	6.4	34.1	26.6	28.3	6.6	5.3
Never married, not cohabiting	25,412	76.8	13.9	8.7	24.0	13.8	16.4	4.3	8.6
Formerly married, not cohabiting	4,274	100.0	0.7	3.6	22.5	24.6	48.6	11.9	7.1
Females, 15 to 44 years old [3]	**61,561**	**91.4**	**22.5**	**10.8**	**32.6**	**16.3**	**9.2**	**3.3**	**11.2**
15 to 19 years old	9,834	62.2	27.2	9.0	19.1	5.0	1.9	1.4	10.6
20 to 24 years old	9,840	91.1	24.6	13.0	32.2	14.4	6.9	2.8	14.2
25 to 44 years old	41,887	98.4	20.9	10.7	36.0	19.4	11.4	3.8	10.7
25 to 29 years old	9,249	97.5	22.5	11.7	31.3	20.1	11.9	3.5	14.1
30 to 34 years old	10,272	98.0	20.5	9.4	38.8	18.0	11.3	3.8	(NA)
35 to 39 years old	10,853	98.9	20.2	11.2	35.8	20.5	11.2	3.9	(NA)
40 to 44 years old	11,512	98.6	20.4	10.5	37.4	19.1	11.2	3.8	(NA)
White only, non-Hispanic	39,498	92.1	21.0	10.6	32.1	18.2	10.2	3.6	(NA)
Black only, non-Hispanic	8,250	92.4	12.4	8.4	44.8	18.0	8.8	4.1	(NA)
Hispanic or Latino origin	9,107	89.5	34.6	14.9	27.2	8.2	4.6	1.7	(NA)
Currently married	28,327	100.0	30.8	12.2	34.0	15.6	7.4	2.7	7.2
Currently cohabiting	5,570	100.0	13.7	12.2	39.2	20.4	14.5	4.3	17.6
Never married, not cohabiting	21,568	75.4	18.3	9.4	27.7	12.8	7.2	3.1	13.5
Formerly married, not cohabiting	6,096	100.0	6.5	8.1	37.8	28.5	19.1	5.6	16.3

NA Not available. [1] Excludes those who have never had sexual intercourse with a person of the opposite sex. For definition of median, see Guide to Tabular Presentation. [2] Same-sex sexual contact was measured using significantly different questions for males and females. [3] Includes person of other or multiple races and origin groups, not shown separately.

Source: U.S. National Center for Health Statistics, *Advance Data*, No. 362; "Sexual Behavior and Selected Health Measures: Men and Women 15–44 Years of Age, United States, 2002," September 2005, and unpublished data.

Table 95. Males and Females Who Have Had Sexual Contact in Last 12 Months by Number and Sex of Partners: 2002

[In percent except as indicated (61,147 represents 61,147,000). Based on the National Survey of Family Growth, see Appendix III]

Sex and age	Number (1,000)	Total	No partners in last 12 months	One partner — Same sex [1]	One partner — Opposite sex	Two or more partners — Same sex only [1]	Two or more partners — Opposite sex only	Two or more partners — Both same and opposite sex [1]	Number of partners not ascertained
Males 15 to 44 years old	**61,147**	**100.0**	**14.8**	**0.7**	**62.2**	**0.9**	**17.6**	**1.0**	**2.6**
15 to 19 years old	10,208	100.0	45.1	0.8	29.7	(S)	21.8	0.9	1.4
20 to 24 years old	9,883	100.0	14.2	0.4	48.8	0.9	30.9	1.5	3.2
25 to 44 years old	41,056	100.0	7.4	0.7	73.6	1.1	13.4	1.0	2.8
25 to 29 years old	9,226	100.0	10.0	0.5	66.6	0.9	18.4	1.1	2.5
30 to 34 years old	10,138	100.0	5.6	0.9	74.3	1.0	14.5	1.3	2.4
35 to 39 years old	10,557	100.0	7.1	0.9	76.5	1.2	11.4	0.5	2.5
40 to 44 years old	11,135	100.0	7.0	0.7	75.9	1.3	10.1	1.0	3.8
Females 15 to 44 years old	**61,561**	**100.0**	**13.9**	**1.1**	**66.8**	**0.2**	**12.7**	**3.1**	**2.2**
15 to 19 years old	9,834	100.0	42.9	1.7	30.5	(S)	16.8	5.8	2.1
20 to 24 years old	9,840	100.0	12.5	0.4	58.9	(S)	21.1	4.8	1.9
25 to 44 years old	41,887	100.0	7.4	1.1	77.2	0.2	9.8	2.0	2.2
25 to 29 years old	9,249	100.0	6.1	0.5	74.1	0.4	14.1	2.8	2.0
30 to 34 years old	10,272	100.0	7.1	0.5	78.5	(S)	9.7	2.1	1.9
35 to 39 years old	10,853	100.0	7.3	1.8	76.8	(S)	9.4	2.5	2.0
40 to 44 years old	11,512	100.0	9.0	1.4	78.8	(S)	6.7	0.9	3.0

S Does not meet standards for reliability or precision. [1] Same-sex sexual contact was measured using significantly different questions for males and females.

Source: U.S. National Center for Health Statistics, *Advance Data*, No. 362; "Sexual Behavior and Selected Health Measures: Men and Women 15–44 Years of Age, United States, 2002," September 2005, and unpublished data.

Table 96. Select Family Planning and Medical Service Use by Women, 15 to 44 Years of Age: 2002

[61,561 represents 61,561,000. Based on the National Survey of Family Growth, see Appendix III]

Characteristic	Number (1,000)	Percent using—							
		Family planning services			Medical services				
		At least one family planning service	Birth control method	Birth control checkup or test	At least one medical service	Preg-nancy test	Pap smear	Pelvic exam	Counsel-ing/test/treat-ment for sexually trans-mitted diseases
All women [1]	**61,561**	**41.7**	**33.9**	**23.6**	**69.1**	**19.7**	**64.4**	**59.7**	**12.6**
15 to 19 years old	9,834	39.9	31.1	22.0	40.6	18.3	34.6	27.0	15.2
15 to 17 years old	5,819	31.8	22.2	15.8	28.0	11.4	23.2	17.9	11.1
18 to 19 years old	4,016	51.6	43.9	31.0	58.9	28.2	51.2	40.2	21.1
20 to 24 years old	9,840	63.3	54.0	35.7	75.7	31.5	69.7	60.6	22.3
25 to 29 years old	9,249	55.4	46.3	30.2	75.9	30.2	70.7	66.0	16.6
30 to 34 years old	10,272	47.0	39.1	27.2	78.1	22.2	72.7	69.7	12.2
35 to 39 years old	10,853	30.5	23.9	18.6	71.5	13.6	68.3	65.9	6.9
40 to 44 years old	11,512	19.5	14.0	10.8	71.8	5.9	69.4	67.0	4.4
Currently married	28,327	39.5	31.5	21.3	77.2	21.1	73.1	69.8	8.1
Currently cohabiting	5,570	50.4	43.2	30.2	77.2	31.0	72.2	64.7	20.3
Never married, not cohabiting	21,568	44.4	36.4	25.4	55.8	16.5	50.7	43.9	15.9
Formerly married, not cohabiting	6,096	34.5	28.0	22.0	71.0	14.1	66.0	64.0	14.4
White only, Non-Hispanic	39,498	43.1	36.4	25.4	70.1	17.3	66.1	63.2	11.8
Black only, Non-Hispanic	8,250	39.4	30.6	21.8	74.4	23.7	69.1	58.1	15.7
Hispanic [2]	9,107	39.7	28.9	20.6	63.4	24.3	57.1	48.5	12.5

[1] Includes other races not shown separately. [2] Persons of Hispanic origin may be of any race.

Source: U.S. National Center for Health Statistics, special tabulations from the *Advance Data*, Number 350, "Use of Contraception and Use of Family Planning Services in the United States: 1982–2002," December 2004.

Table 97. Current Contraceptive Use by Women by Age, Race, Hispanic Origin, Marital, and Cohabitation Status: 2006 to 2008

[61,864 represents 61,864,000. Based on the Continuous National Survey of Family Growth conducted from July 2006 through December 2008. Contraceptive use reported by women 15–44 years of age during heterosexual vaginal intercourse. Women using more than one method of contraception are classified by most effective method reported]

Contraceptive status and method	Unit	2006–2008							
			Race/ethnicity			Marital and cohabitation status			
		All wo-men [1]	White only, Non-His-panic	Black only, Non-His-panic	His-panic [2]	Never mar-ried, not cohab-iting	Cur-rently mar-ried	For-merly mar-ried, not cohab-iting	Cur-rently cohab-iting
All women	(1,000)	**61,864**	**37,660**	**8,452**	**10,377**	**22,847**	**27,006**	**5,190**	**6,821**
PERCENT DISTRIBUTION									
Using contraception (contraceptors) [3]	Percent	61.8	64.7	54.5	58.5	39.3	78.6	60.6	71.2
Female sterilization	Percent	16.7	14.9	21.8	19.6	4.5	23.6	35.3	16.3
Male sterilization	Percent	6.1	8.3	1.1	3.4	0.3	12.7	2.3	2.2
Pill	Percent	17.3	21.2	11.4	11.4	18.1	16.3	11.4	23.2
Implant, Lunelle™	Percent	0.7	0.5	0.6	1.5	0.6	0.7	(S)	1.0
3-month injectable (Depo-Provera™)	Percent	2.0	1.4	4.1	2.6	2.2	1.4	2.6	3.1
Intrauterine device (IUD)	Percent	1.5	1.6	1.7	1.2	1.5	1.0	0.8	3.7
Diaphragm	Percent	3.4	3.3	2.8	4.8	1.1	5.3	2.1	4.7
Condom	Percent	10.0	9.5	8.8	9.4	9.1	11.7	4.1	10.2
Periodic abstinence-calendar rhythm	Percent	0.5	0.5	(S)	0.6	0.2	1.0	(S)	0.4
Periodic abstinence-natural family planning	Percent	0.1	(S)	(S)	(S)	(S)	0.2	(S)	(S)
Withdrawal	Percent	3.2	3.3	2.1	3.0	1.5	4.5	1.4	5.3
Other methods [3]	Percent	0.3	0.3	(S)	0.5	0.2	0.3	(S)	(S)
Not using contraception	Percent	38.2	35.3	45.5	41.5	60.7	21.4	39.4	28.8
Surgically sterile-female (noncontraceptive)	Percent	0.4	0.2	0.4	0.7	0.4	0.3	1.0	(S)
Nonsurgically sterile-female or male [4]	Percent	1.7	1.6	1.8	1.8	2.1	1.0	2.7	2.2
Pregnant or postpartum	Percent	5.4	4.9	5.7	8.3	2.6	7.2	2.6	10.5
Seeking pregnancy	Percent	4.1	3.5	4.4	6.2	1.3	6.4	0.8	7.1
Other nonuse:									
Never had intercourse or no intercourse in 3 months before interview	Percent	19.2	18.3	22.6	18.8	45.6	0.9	21.1	1.8
Had intercourse in 3 months before interview	Percent	7.3	6.7	10.6	5.8	8.7	5.5	11.3	6.9

S Figure does not meet publication standards. [1] Includes other races not shown separately. [2] Persons of Hispanic origin may be any race. [3] Includes diaphragm, emergency contraception, female condom or vaginal pouch, foam, cervical cap, Today™ sponge, suppository or insert, jelly or cream, and other methods. [4] Persons sterile from illness, accident, or congenital conditions.

Source: U.S. National Center for Health Statistics, *National Survey of Family Growth*, "Use of Contraception in the United States: 1982–2008," Series 23, No. 29, May 2010. See also <http://cdc.gov/nchs/nsfg/>.

Table 98. Outcomes of Assisted Reproductive Technology (ART) by Procedures: 2000 to 2006

[In 1996, Centers for Disease Control (CDC) initiated data collection regarding Assisted Reproductive Technology (ART) procedures performed in the United States, as mandated by the Fertility Clinic Success Rate and Certification Act. ARTs include those infertility treatments in which both eggs and sperm are handled in the laboratory for the purpose of establishing a pregnancy (i.e., in vitro fertilization and related procedures)]

Year	Procedures started [1]	Number of pregnancies	Live birth deliveries [2]	Live born infants
2000.	99,629	30,557	25,228	35,025
2001.	107,587	35,726	29,344	40,687
2002.	115,392	40,046	33,141	45,751
2003.	122,872	43,503	35,785	48,756
2004.	127,977	44,774	36,760	49,458
2005.	134,260	47,651	38,910	52,041
2006.	138,198	50,571	41,343	54,656

[1] Excludes procedures for which new treatments were being evaluated [2] A live-birth delivery is defined as the delivery of one or more live born infants.

Source: U.S. Centers for Disease Control and Prevention, Morbidity and Mortality Weekly Report (MMWR) Surveillance Summary Reports, *Assisted Reproductive Technology Surveillance—United States, 2006,* Vol. 58, No. SS-5, June 2009. See also <http://www.cdc.gov/mmwr/preview/mmwrhtml/ss5805a1.htm\>.

Table 99. Abortions—Number and Rate by Race: 1990 to 2006

[58,700 represents 58,700,000]

	All races			White			Black			Other		
	Women 15 to 44	Abortions		Women 15 to 44	Abortions		Women 15 to 44	Abortions		Women 15 to 44	Abortions	
Year	years old (1,000)	Number (1,000)	Rate per 1,000 women [1]	years old (1,000)	Number (1,000)	Rate per 1,000 women [1]	years old (1,000)	Number (1,000)	Rate per 1,000 women [1]	years old (1,000)	Number (1,000)	Rate per 1,000 women [1]
1990 [2]	58,700	1,609	27.4	48,224	1,039	21.5	7,905	505	63.9	2,571	65	25.1
1991.	59,305	1,557	26.2	48,560	982	20.2	8,053	507	62.9	2,692	68	26.2
1992.	59,417	1,529	25.7	48,435	943	19.5	8,170	517	63.3	2,812	69	24.4
1993 [2]	59,712	1,495	25.0	48,497	908	18.7	8,282	517	62.4	2,933	70	23.9
1994 [2]	60,020	1,423	23.7	48,592	856	17.6	8,390	492	58.6	3,039	76	23.7
1995.	60,368	1,359	22.5	48,719	817	16.8	8,496	462	54.4	3,153	80	25.3
1996.	60,704	1,360	22.4	48,837	797	16.3	8,592	483	56.2	3,275	81	24.6
1997 [2]	61,041	1,335	21.9	48,942	777	15.9	8,694	479	55.1	3,405	79	23.1
1998 [2]	61,326	1,319	21.5	49,012	762	15.5	8,785	476	54.2	3,528	81	23.1
1999.	61,475	1,315	21.4	48,974	743	15.2	8,851	485	54.8	3,650	87	24.0
2000.	61,631	1,313	21.3	48,936	733	15.0	8,907	488	54.8	3,788	92	24.4
2001 [2]	61,673	1,291	20.9	48,868	717	14.7	8,962	476	53.1	3,843	99	25.7
2002 [2]	62,044	1,269	20.5	48,998	706	14.4	9,026	468	51.8	4,020	96	23.8
2003 [2]	61,911	1,250	20.2	48,782	695	14.2	9,054	458	50.6	4,075	97	23.8
2004.	62,033	1,222	19.7	48,758	674	13.8	9,116	453	49.7	4,160	95	22.9
2005.	62,074	1,206	19.4	48,678	662	13.6	9,177	452	49.3	4,219	92	21.9
2006 [2]	62,258	1,242	19.9	48,686	681	14.0	9,248	464	50.2	4,325	97	22.3

[1] Aged 15–44. [2] Total numbers of abortions have been estimated by interpolation.

Source: R.K. Jones, M.R.S. Zolna, S.K. Henshaw, and L.B. Finer, *Abortion in the United States: Incidence and Access to Services, 2005*, Perspectives on Sexual and Reproductive Health, 2008, 40(1):6-16, and unpublished data from Guttmacher Institute.

Table 100. Abortions by Selected Characteristics: 1990 to 2006

[1,609 represents 1,609,000. Number of abortions from surveys conducted by source; characteristics from the U.S. Centers for Disease Control's (CDC) annual abortion surveillance summaries, with adjustments for changes in states reporting data to the Centers for Disease Control each year]

Characteristic	Number (1,000)			Percent distribution			Abortion rate per 1,000 women [1]		
	1990	2000	2006	1990	2000	2006	1990	2000	2006
Total abortions	**1,609**	**1,313**	**1,242**	**100.0**	**100.0**	**100.0**	**27.4**	**21.3**	**19.9**
Age of woman:									
Less than 15 years [1]	13	9	6	0.8	0.7	0.5	7.9	4.4	3.1
15 to 19 years	351	235	200	21.8	17.9	16.1	40.6	24.0	19.3
20 to 24 years	532	430	407	33.1	32.7	32.8	56.7	45.9	39.9
25 to 29 years	360	303	301	22.4	23.0	24.2	34.0	31.8	29.7
30 to 34 years	216	190	180	13.4	14.5	14.5	19.7	18.6	18.5
35 to 39 years	108	110	109	6.7	8.4	8.8	10.7	9.7	10.3
40 years and over [2]	29	37	38	1.8	2.8	3.1	3.2	3.2	3.4
Race and ethnicity of woman:									
White	1,039	733	681	64.6	55.8	54.9	21.5	15.0	14.0
Black	505	488	464	31.4	37.2	37.3	63.9	54.8	50.2
Other	65	92	97	4.0	7.0	7.8	25.1	24.4	22.3
Hispanic	195	261	277	12.1	19.8	22.3	35.1	30.3	27.1
Non-Hispanic White	852	479	420	52.9	36.5	33.8	19.7	11.7	10.7
Marital status of woman: [3]									
Married	341	246	212	21.0	19.0	17.0	10.6	7.9	7.2
Unmarried	1,268	1,067	1,030	79.0	81.0	83.0	47.7	34.9	31.5
Number of prior live births:									
None	780	533	508	49.0	41.0	40.9	32.0	20.2	(NA)
One	396	361	336	25.0	28.0	27.1	36.9	32.5	(NA)
Two	280	260	238	17.0	20.0	19.1	20.5	18.9	(NA)
Three	102	104	104	6.0	8.0	8.4	15.6	14.8	(NA)
Four or more	50	56	56	3.0	4.0	4.5	14.7	16.5	(NA)
Number of prior induced abortions:									
None	891	699	672	55.0	53.0	54.1	(NA)	(NA)	(NA)
One	443	355	327	28.0	27.0	26.4	(NA)	(NA)	(NA)
Two or more	275	259	243	17.0	20.0	19.5	(NA)	(NA)	(NA)
Weeks of gestation:									
Less than 9 weeks	825	749	755	51.3	57.1	60.8	(NA)	(NA)	(NA)
9 to 10 weeks	416	269	222	25.8	20.5	17.9	(NA)	(NA)	(NA)
11 to 12 weeks	195	138	123	12.1	10.5	9.9	(NA)	(NA)	(NA)
13 weeks or more	173	156	142	10.8	11.9	11.4	(NA)	(NA)	(NA)

NA Not available. [1] Denominator of rate is women aged 14. [2] Denominator of rate is women aged 40–44. [3] Separated women are included with married.

Source: R. K. Jones, M.R.S. Zolna, S. K. Henshaw, and L. B. Finer, *Abortion in the United States: Incidence and Access to Services, 2005,* Perspectives on Sexual and Reproductive Health, 2008, 40(1):6-16; S.K. Henshaw and K. Kost, *Trends in the Characteristics of Women Obtaining Abortions, 1974–2004,* New York: Guttmacher Institute, 2008; and unpublished data from the Guttmacher Institute.

Table 101. Abortions—Number and Rate by State of Occurrence: 2000 and 2005, and by Residence: 2005

[Number of abortions by state of occurrence from surveys of hospitals, clinics, and physicians identified as providers of abortion services conducted by the Guttmacher Institute. The Guttmacher Institute reallocates abortions to the woman's state of residence for survey years. Abortion rates are computed per 1,000 women 15 to 44 years of age on July 1 of specified year]

State	Occurrence				Residence, 2005		State	Occurrence				Residence, 2005	
	Number (1,000)		Rate [1]					Number (1,000)		Rate [1]			
	2000	2005	2000	2005	Number	Rate [1]		2000	2005	2000	2005	Number	Rate [1]
U.S.	**1,312,990**	**1,206,200**	**21.3**	**19.4**	**1,198,960**	**19.3**	MO	7,920	8,400	6.6	7.0	14,900	12.5
AL	13,830	11,340	14.2	12.1	10,840	11.5	MT	2,510	2,150	13.5	11.9	2,020	11.2
AK	1,660	1,880	11.7	13.2	2,130	14.9	NE	4,250	3,220	11.6	9.1	2,990	8.4
AZ	17,940	19,480	16.5	16.1	19,710	16.3	NV	13,740	13,530	32.4	27.7	12,990	26.6
AR	5,540	4,710	9.8	8.4	5,200	9.3	NH	3,010	3,170	11.2	11.8	3,060	11.4
CA	236,060	208,430	31.2	26.9	206,260	26.6	NJ	65,780	61,150	36.3	34.5	60,330	34.0
CO	15,530	16,120	16.0	16.2	14,720	14.8	NM	5,760	6,220	14.7	15.7	6,690	16.9
CT	15,240	16,780	21.1	23.8	17,340	24.6	NY	164,630	155,960	39.1	37.7	152,340	36.9
DE	5,440	5,150	31.3	29.2	4,140	23.5	NC	37,610	34,500	21.1	18.9	29,730	16.3
DC	9,800	7,230	68.2	50.0	6,390	44.2	ND	1,340	1,230	9.9	9.6	890	7.0
FL	103,050	92,300	32.0	26.7	85,360	24.7	OH	40,230	35,060	16.5	14.9	33,140	14.1
GA	32,140	33,180	16.9	16.6	32,040	16.0	OK	7,390	6,950	10.1	9.7	7,420	10.3
HI	5,630	5,350	22.2	21.3	5,330	21.2	OR	17,010	13,200	23.6	18.1	11,900	16.3
ID	1,950	1,810	7.0	6.2	2,540	8.7	PA	36,570	34,150	14.3	13.9	38,110	15.5
IL	63,690	50,970	23.2	18.9	48,420	18.0	RI	5,600	5,290	24.1	23.3	4,680	20.6
IN	12,490	11,150	9.4	8.6	13,180	10.2	SC	8,210	7,080	9.3	8.0	13,320	15.0
IA	5,970	6,370	9.8	10.9	6,130	10.5	SD	870	790	5.5	5.1	980	6.4
KS	12,270	10,410	21.4	18.6	5,620	10.0	TN	19,010	18,140	15.2	14.5	15,520	12.4
KY	4,700	3,870	5.3	4.5	6,060	7.0	TX	89,160	85,760	18.8	17.4	84,560	17.1
LA	13,100	11,400	13.0	11.8	10,330	10.7	UT	3,510	3,630	6.7	6.4	3,610	6.4
ME	2,650	2,770	9.9	10.7	2,840	10.9	VT	1,660	1,490	12.7	11.9	1,810	14.5
MD	34,560	37,590	29.0	31.3	35,250	29.3	VA	28,780	26,520	18.1	16.4	30,590	18.9
MA	30,410	27,270	21.4	19.8	27,800	20.2	WA	26,200	23,260	20.3	17.8	23,680	18.1
MI	46,470	40,600	21.6	19.5	39,930	19.2	WV	2,540	2,360	6.8	6.7	2,700	7.7
MN	14,610	13,910	13.5	13.1	13,370	12.6	WI	11,130	9,800	9.6	8.6	10,920	9.6
MS	3,780	3,090	6.0	5.0	7,930	12.9	WY	100	70	1.0	0.7	1,220	12.2

[1] Rate per 1,000 women, 15 to 44 years old.

Source: R. K. Jones, et al., *Abortion in the United States: Incidence and Access to Services, 2005,* Perspectives on Sexual and Reproductive Health 40:6, 2008, and unpublished data. See also <http://www.guttmacher.org/>.

Births, Deaths, Marriages, and Divorces 75

Table 102. Expectation of Life at Birth, 1970 to 2007, and Projections, 2010 to 2020

[In years. Excludes deaths of nonresidents of the United States. See Appendix III]

Year	Total — Total	Total — Male	Total — Female	White — Total	White — Male	White — Female	Black — Total	Black — Male	Black — Female
1970.........	70.8	67.1	74.7	71.7	68.0	75.6	64.1	60.0	68.3
1980.........	73.7	70.0	77.4	74.4	70.7	78.1	68.1	63.8	72.5
1981.........	74.1	70.4	77.8	74.8	71.1	78.4	68.9	64.5	73.2
1982.........	74.5	70.8	78.1	75.1	71.5	78.7	69.4	65.1	73.6
1983.........	74.6	71.0	78.1	75.2	71.6	78.7	69.4	65.2	73.5
1984.........	74.7	71.1	78.2	75.3	71.8	78.7	69.5	65.3	73.6
1985.........	74.7	71.1	78.2	75.3	71.8	78.7	69.3	65.0	73.4
1986.........	74.7	71.2	78.2	75.4	71.9	78.8	69.1	64.8	73.4
1987.........	74.9	71.4	78.3	75.6	72.1	78.9	69.1	64.7	73.4
1988.........	74.9	71.4	78.3	75.6	72.2	78.9	68.9	64.4	73.2
1989.........	75.1	71.7	78.5	75.9	72.5	79.2	68.8	64.3	73.3
1990.........	75.4	71.8	78.8	76.1	72.7	79.4	69.1	64.5	73.6
1991.........	75.5	72.0	78.9	76.3	72.9	79.6	69.3	64.6	73.8
1992.........	75.8	72.3	79.1	76.5	73.2	79.8	69.6	65.0	73.9
1993.........	75.5	72.2	78.8	76.3	73.1	79.5	69.2	64.6	73.7
1994.........	75.7	72.4	79.0	76.5	73.3	79.6	69.5	64.9	73.9
1995.........	75.8	72.5	78.9	76.5	73.4	79.6	69.6	65.2	73.9
1996.........	76.1	73.1	79.1	76.8	73.9	79.7	70.2	66.1	74.2
1997.........	76.5	73.6	79.4	77.2	74.3	79.9	71.1	67.2	74.7
1998.........	76.7	73.8	79.5	77.3	74.5	80.0	71.3	67.6	74.8
1999.........	76.7	73.9	79.4	77.3	74.6	79.9	71.4	67.8	74.7
2000 [1].........	76.8	74.1	79.3	77.3	74.7	79.9	71.8	68.2	75.1
2001 [1].........	76.9	74.2	79.4	77.4	74.8	79.9	72.0	68.4	75.2
2002 [1].........	76.9	74.3	79.5	77.4	74.9	79.9	72.1	68.6	75.4
2003 [1,2].........	77.1	74.5	79.6	77.6	75.0	80.0	72.3	68.8	75.6
2004 [1,2].........	77.5	74.9	79.9	77.9	75.4	80.4	72.8	69.3	76.0
2005 [1,2].........	77.4	74.9	79.9	77.9	75.4	80.4	72.8	69.3	76.1
2006 [1,2].........	77.7	75.1	80.2	78.2	75.7	80.6	73.2	69.7	76.5
2007 [1,2].........	77.9	75.4	80.4	78.4	75.9	80.8	73.6	70.0	76.8
Projections: [3]									
2010.........	78.3	75.7	80.8	78.9	76.5	81.3	73.8	70.2	77.2
2015.........	78.9	76.4	81.4	79.5	77.1	81.8	75.0	71.4	78.2
2020.........	79.5	77.1	81.9	80.0	77.7	82.4	76.1	72.6	79.2

[1] Life expectancies for 2000–2007 were calculated using a revised methodology and may differ from those previously published. [2] Multiple-race data were reported by 25 states and the District of Columbia in 2006, by 21 states and the District of Columbia in 2005, by 15 states in 2004, and by 7 states in 2003. The multiple-race data for these reporting areas were bridged to the single-race categories of the 1977 OMB standards for comparability with other reporting areas. [3] Based on middle mortality assumptions; for details, see source U.S. Census Bureau, 2008 National Population Projections (released August, 2008), <http://www.census.gov/population/www/projections/2008projections.html>.

Source: Except as noted, U.S. National Center for Health Statistics, National Vital Statistics Reports (NVSR), *Deaths: Final Data for 2007*, Vol. 58, No. 19, May 2010.

Table 103. Life Expectancy by Sex, Age, and Race: 2007

[Average number of years of life remaining. Excludes deaths of nonresidents of the United States]

Age	Total [1] — Total	Total [1] — Male	Total [1] — Female	White — Total	White — Male	White — Female	Black — Total	Black — Male	Black — Female
0.............	77.9	75.4	80.4	78.4	75.9	80.8	73.6	70.0	76.8
1.............	77.5	74.9	79.9	77.8	75.4	80.2	73.6	70.1	76.8
5.............	73.6	71.0	76.0	73.9	71.4	76.3	69.7	66.2	72.9
10.............	68.6	66.1	71.0	68.9	66.5	71.3	64.7	61.3	67.9
15.............	63.7	61.1	66.1	64.0	61.6	66.3	59.8	56.3	63.0
20.............	58.8	56.4	61.2	59.2	56.8	61.5	55.1	51.7	58.1
25.............	54.1	51.8	56.3	54.4	52.2	56.6	50.4	47.2	53.3
30.............	49.4	47.1	51.5	49.7	47.5	51.7	45.8	42.7	48.5
35.............	44.6	42.5	46.7	44.9	42.8	46.9	41.2	38.2	43.8
40.............	39.9	37.8	41.9	40.2	38.1	42.1	36.7	33.8	39.1
45.............	35.4	33.3	37.2	35.6	33.6	37.4	32.3	29.5	34.7
50.............	30.9	29.0	32.7	31.1	29.2	32.8	28.1	25.4	30.4
55.............	26.7	24.9	28.2	26.8	25.1	28.4	24.2	21.7	26.3
60.............	22.5	20.9	23.9	22.6	21.0	24.0	20.6	18.3	22.4
65.............	18.6	17.2	19.9	18.7	17.3	19.9	17.2	15.2	18.7
70.............	15.0	13.7	16.0	15.0	13.8	16.0	14.1	12.4	15.2
75.............	11.7	10.6	12.5	11.7	10.6	12.4	11.2	9.9	12.1
80.............	8.8	7.9	9.4	8.8	7.9	9.3	8.7	7.7	9.4
85.............	6.5	5.8	6.8	6.4	5.7	6.8	6.7	6.0	7.1
90.............	4.6	4.1	4.8	4.6	4.1	4.8	5.1	4.6	5.3
95.............	3.2	2.9	3.3	3.2	2.9	3.3	3.8	3.5	3.9
100.............	2.3	2.1	2.3	2.2	2.0	2.2	2.8	2.6	2.8

[1] Includes races other than White and Black.

Source: U.S. National Center for Health Statistics, National Vital Statistics Reports (NVSR), *Deaths: Final Data for 2007*, Vol. 58, No. 19, May 2010.

Table 104. Selected Life Table Values: 1959 to 2007

[Decennial life tables are based on population data from a decennial census and reported deaths of the 3-year period surrounding the census year; the census year is the middle year. The annual tables are based on deaths in a single year, and except for census years, on postcensal population estimates. Beginning in 1970, data excludes deaths of nonresidents of the United States. See Appendix III]

Age and sex	All races						White						Black[1]					
	1959–1961	1969–1971	1979–1981	1989–1991	1999–2001	2007	1959–1961	1969–1971	1979–1981	1989–1991	1999–2001	2007	1959–1961	1969–1971	1979–1981	1989–1991	1999–2001	2007
EXPECTATION OF LIFE IN YEARS																		
At birth: Male	66.8	67.0	70.1	71.8	74.1	75.4	67.6	67.9	70.8	72.7	74.7	75.9	61.5	60.0	64.1	64.5	68.1	70.0
Female	73.2	74.6	77.6	78.8	79.5	80.4	74.2	75.5	78.2	79.5	80.0	80.8	66.5	68.3	72.9	73.7	75.1	76.8
Age 20: Male	49.8	49.5	51.9	53.3	55.2	56.4	50.3	50.2	52.5	54.0	55.7	56.8	45.8	43.5	46.5	46.7	49.8	51.7
Female	55.6	56.6	59.0	59.9	60.3	61.2	56.3	57.2	59.4	60.4	60.7	61.5	50.8	51.2	54.9	55.5	56.5	58.1
Age 40: Male	31.4	31.5	33.6	35.1	36.6	37.8	31.7	31.9	34.0	35.6	37.0	38.1	28.7	27.6	29.5	30.1	32.1	33.8
Female	36.6	37.6	39.8	40.7	41.0	41.9	37.1	38.1	40.2	41.0	41.3	42.1	32.2	33.3	36.3	37.0	37.7	39.1
Age 50: Male	23.0	23.1	25.0	26.4	27.8	29.0	23.2	23.3	25.3	26.7	28.1	29.2	21.3	20.7	22.0	22.5	24.1	25.4
Female	27.7	28.8	30.7	31.4	31.7	32.7	28.1	29.1	31.0	31.7	32.0	32.8	24.3	25.5	27.8	28.4	29.0	30.4
Age 65: Male	13.0	13.0	14.2	15.1	16.1	17.2	13.0	13.0	14.3	15.2	16.2	17.3	12.8	12.5	13.3	13.3	14.1	15.2
Female	15.8	16.8	18.4	19.0	19.1	19.9	15.9	16.9	18.6	19.1	19.2	19.9	15.1	15.7	17.1	17.4	17.7	18.7
NUMBER OF SURVIVORS OUT OF 1,000 BORN ALIVE[2]																		
At birth: Male	1,000	1,000	1,000	1,000	1,000	1,000	1,000	1,000	1,000	1,000	1,000	1,000	1,000	1,000	1,000	1,000	1,000	1,000
Female	1,000	1,000	1,000	1,000	1,000	1,000	1,000	1,000	1,000	1,000	1,000	1,000	1,000	1,000	1,000	1,000	1,000	1,000
Age 20: Male	955	961	973	979	984	985	959	965	975	981	986	987	931	941	961	963	973	975
Female	968	973	982	986	989	990	971	976	984	988	990	991	947	957	972	976	981	983
Age 40: Male	916	915	933	938	954	955	924	926	940	946	959	959	857	834	885	879	919	927
Female	946	951	965	970	975	979	953	958	969	975	978	978	897	908	941	944	956	961
Age 65: Male	642	643	706	740	781	810	658	663	724	760	795	809	514	475	551	568	646	682
Female	785	797	835	851	864	875	807	816	848	863	874	883	608	647	733	750	778	805
PERCENT SURVIVING OUT OF 1,000 BORN ALIVE																		
At birth: Male	100.0	100.0	100.0	100.0	100.0	100.0	100.0	100.0	100.0	100.0	100.0	100.0	100.0	100.0	100.0	100.0	100.0	100.0
Female	100.0	100.0	100.0	100.0	100.0	100.0	100.0	100.0	100.0	100.0	100.0	100.0	100.0	100.0	100.0	100.0	100.0	100.0
Age 20: Male	95.5	96.1	97.3	97.9	98.4	98.5	95.9	96.5	97.5	98.1	98.6	98.7	93.1	94.1	96.1	96.3	97.3	97.5
Female	96.8	97.3	98.2	98.6	98.9	99.0	97.1	97.6	98.4	98.8	99.0	99.1	94.7	95.7	97.2	97.6	98.1	98.3
Age 40: Male	91.6	91.5	93.3	93.8	95.4	95.5	92.4	92.6	94.0	94.6	95.9	95.9	85.7	83.4	88.5	87.9	91.9	92.7
Female	94.6	95.1	96.5	97.0	97.5	97.6	95.3	95.8	96.9	97.5	97.8	97.8	89.7	90.8	94.1	94.4	95.6	96.1
Age 65: Male	64.2	64.3	70.6	74.0	78.1	79.7	65.8	66.3	72.4	76.0	79.5	80.9	51.4	47.5	55.1	56.8	64.6	68.2
Female	78.5	79.7	83.5	85.1	86.4	87.5	80.7	81.6	84.8	86.3	87.4	88.3	60.8	64.7	73.3	75.0	77.8	80.5

[1] Prior to 1970, data for the Black population are not available. Data shown for 1959–1970 are for the Non-White population. [2] The number of persons from the original synthetic cohort of 1,000 live births, who survive the beginning of each age interval.

Source: U.S. National Center for Health Statistics, National Vital Statistics Reports (NVSR), "U.S. Decennial Life Tables for 1999–2001," United States Life Tables, Vol. 57, No. 1, August 2008; United States Life Tables, 2006, Vol. 58, No.21, June 2010; and Deaths: Final Data for 2007, Vol. 58, No.19, May 2010.

Births, Deaths, Marriages, and Divorces 77

Table 105. Expectation of Life and Expected Deaths by Race, Sex, and Age: 2007

[Life expectancies were calculated using a revised methodology and may differ from those previously published. The methodology uses vital statistics death rates for ages under 66 and modeled probabilities of death for ages 66 to 100 based on blended vital statistics and Medicare probabilities of dying]

Age (years)	Expectation of life in years					Expected deaths per 1,000 alive at specified age [2]				
	Total [1]	White		Black		Total [1]	White		Black	
		Male	Female	Male	Female		Male	Female	Male	Female
At birth...	77.9	75.9	80.8	70.0	76.8	6.76	6.18	5.09	14.43	11.89
1........	77.5	75.4	80.2	70.1	76.8	0.46	0.44	0.40	0.69	0.62
2........	76.5	74.4	79.2	69.1	75.8	0.28	0.28	0.22	0.46	0.40
3........	75.5	73.4	78.2	68.1	74.8	0.22	0.22	0.17	0.35	0.58
4........	74.5	72.4	77.2	67.2	73.9	0.17	0.18	0.12	0.28	0.24
5........	73.6	71.4	76.3	66.2	72.9	0.16	0.17	0.13	0.25	0.20
6........	72.6	70.5	75.3	65.2	71.9	0.15	0.16	0.13	0.23	0.17
7........	71.6	69.5	74.3	54.2	70.9	0.14	0.15	0.12	0.21	0.14
8........	70.6	68.5	73.3	63.2	69.9	0.12	0.13	0.11	0.18	0.13
9........	69.6	67.5	72.3	62.2	68.9	0.10	0.10	0.10	0.14	0.13
10.......	68.6	66.5	71.3	61.3	67.9	0.09	0.08	0.09	0.11	0.13
11.......	67.6	65.5	70.3	60.3	66.9	0.09	0.08	0.09	0.11	0.15
12.......	66.6	64.5	69.3	59.3	66.0	0.13	0.13	0.11	0.20	0.17
13......	65.6	63.5	68.3	58.3	65.0	0.21	0.23	0.15	0.37	0.20
14......	64.6	62.5	67.3	57.3	64.0	0.31	0.37	0.21	0.60	0.24
15......	63.7	61.6	66.3	56.3	63.0	0.42	0.52	0.27	0.85	0.28
16......	62.7	60.6	65.4	55.4	62.0	0.52	0.66	0.33	1.07	0.33
17......	61.7	59.6	64.4	54.4	61.0	0.62	0.79	0.37	1.27	0.37
18......	60.8	58.7	63.4	53.5	60.1	0.71	0.93	0.40	1.46	0.41
19......	59.8	57.7	62.4	52.6	59.1	0.79	1.06	0.42	1.63	0.45
20......	58.8	56.8	61.5	51.7	58.1	0.87	1.19	0.43	1.81	0.50
21......	57.9	55.9	60.5	50.8	57.1	0.95	1.32	0.45	2.00	0.56
22......	56.9	54.9	59.5	49.9	56.2	1.00	1.40	0.46	2.13	0.61
23......	56.0	54.0	58.5	49.0	55.2	1.02	1.41	0.48	2.19	0.66
24	55.1	53.1	57.6	48.1	54.2	1.01	1.38	0.49	2.19	0.70
25......	54.1	52.2	56.6	47.2	53.3	0.99	1.33	0.50	2.17	0.75
26......	53.2	51.2	55.6	46.3	52.3	0.97	1.29	0.51	2.16	0.80
27......	52.2	50.3	54.6	45.4	51.4	0.96	1.26	0.52	2.16	0.85
28......	51.3	49.4	53.7	44.5	50.4	0.97	1.25	0.53	2.18	0.89
29......	50.3	48.4	52.7	43.6	49.4	0.98	1.26	0.55	2.23	0.94
30......	49.4	47.5	51.7	42.7	48.5	1.01	1.28	0.58	2.29	1.00
31......	48.4	46.5	50.8	41.8	47.5	1.04	1.30	0.61	2.35	1.06
32......	47.5	45.6	49.8	40.9	46.6	1.07	1.33	0.65	2.46	1.15
33......	46.5	44.7	48.8	40.0	45.7	1.12	1.37	0.70	2.50	1.25
34......	45.6	43.7	47.9	39.1	44.7	1.17	1.42	0.75	2.57	1.36
35......	44.6	42.8	46.9	38.2	43.8	1.23	1.47	0.80	2.66	1.48
36......	43.7	41.9	45.9	37.3	42.8	1.30	1.55	0.86	2.77	1.61
37......	42.8	40.9	45.0	36.4	41.9	1.39	1.64	0.93	2.90	1.74
38......	41.8	40.0	44.0	35.6	41.0	1.50	1.76	1.02	3.06	1.88
39......	40.9	39.1	43.1	34.7	40.1	1.63	1.91	1.12	3.26	2.03
40......	39.9	38.1	42.1	33.8	39.1	1.77	2.08	1.23	3.49	2.19
41......	39.0	37.2	41.2	32.9	38.2	1.93	2.26	1.35	3.73	2.36
42......	38.1	36.3	40.2	32.1	37.3	2.10	2.46	1.48	4.02	2.58
43......	37.2	35.4	39.3	31.2	36.4	2.30	2.69	1.63	4.35	2.84
44......	36.3	34.5	38.3	30.3	35.5	2.52	2.94	1.78	4.72	3.15
45......	35.4	33.6	37.4	29.5	34.7	2.73	3.19	1.95	5.09	3.46
46......	34.5	32.7	36.5	28.7	33.8	2.96	3.44	2.11	5.49	3.76
47......	33.6	31.8	35.6	27.8	32.9	3.20	3.72	2.28	5.97	4.09
48......	32.7	31.0	34.7	27.0	32.0	3.46	4.04	2.46	6.56	4.43
49......	31.8	30.1	33.7	26.2	31.2	3.75	4.39	2.64	7.26	4.80
50......	30.9	29.2	32.8	25.4	30.4	4.07	4.76	2.85	8.02	5.20
51......	30.1	28.4	31.9	24.7	29.5	4.40	5.16	3.07	8.79	5.60
52......	29.2	27.5	31.0	23.9	28.7	4.74	5.55	3.31	9.56	6.00
53......	28.3	26.7	30.1	23.2	27.9	5.07	5.94	3.54	10.27	6.36
54......	27.5	25.9	29.2	22.4	27.1	5.40	6.32	3.79	10.93	6.70
55......	26.7	25.1	28.4	21.7	26.3	5.74	6.71	4.06	11.60	7.05
56......	25.8	24.2	27.5	21.0	25.5	6.12	7.14	4.35	12.31	7.43
57......	25.0	23.4	26.6	20.3	24.7	6.52	7.60	4.69	12.98	7.82
58......	24.2	22.6	25.7	19.7	23.9	6.97	8.11	5.10	13.61	8.26
59......	23.4	21.8	24.9	19.0	23.1	7.46	8.67	5.56	14.24	8.76
60......	22.5	21.0	24.0	18.3	22.4	8.01	9.29	6.08	14.93	9.33
61......	21.7	20.3	23.2	17.7	21.6	8.60	9.94	6.63	15.70	9.97
62......	21.0	19.5	22.3	17.1	20.9	9.22	10.63	7.21	16.49	10.67
63......	20.2	18.7	21.5	16.5	20.1	9.88	11.35	7.80	17.23	11.37
64......	19.4	18.0	20.7	15.8	19.4	10.57	12.14	8.43	17.90	12.06
65......	18.6	17.3	19.9	15.2	18.7	11.37	13.04	9.17	18.53	12.76
70......	15.0	13.8	16.0	12.4	15.2	15.74	18.00	13.37	21.82	16.61
75......	11.7	10.6	12.4	9.9	12.1	22.84	25.46	20.70	25.61	22.53
80......	8.8	7.9	9.3	7.7	9.4	30.49	32.34	29.91	26.44	28.09
85......	6.5	5.7	6.8	6.0	7.1	34.84	34.14	37.36	23.26	30.71
90......	4.6	4.1	4.8	4.6	5.3	30.92	26.79	36.48	16.31	27.45
95......	3.2	2.9	3.3	3.5	3.9	18.42	13.23	23.72	8.34	18.14
100.....	2.3	2.0	2.2	2.6	2.8	18.46	8.98	24.93	9.63	29.19

[1] Includes other races, not shown separately. [2] Based on the proportion of the cohort who are alive at the beginning of the indicated age who will die before reaching the age shown plus 1. For example, out of every 1,000 people alive and exactly 50 years old at the beginning of the period, 4.07 people will die before reaching their 51st birthdays.

Source: U.S. National Center for Health Statistics, unpublished data.

78 Births, Deaths, Marriages, and Divorces

Table 106. Life Expectancy by Sex, Race, and State: 1979 to 1991

[Average number of years of life remaining. Excludes deaths of nonresidents of the United States. Decennial life tables are based on population data from a decennial census and reported deaths of the 3-year period surrounding the census year; the census year is the middle year. The annual tables are based on deaths in a single year, and except for census years, on postcensal population estimates]

State	Total, 1979–1981	1989–1991						
		Total	Male			Female		
			Total	White	Black	Total	White	Black
United States	**73.88**	**75.37**	**71.83**	**72.72**	**64.47**	**78.81**	**79.45**	**73.73**
Alabama	72.53	73.64	69.59	71.12	64.37	77.61	78.85	73.76
Alaska	72.24	74.83	71.60	72.82	(B)	78.60	79.40	(B)
Arizona	74.30	76.10	72.66	73.04	67.20	79.58	79.84	74.90
Arkansas	73.72	74.33	70.54	71.54	64.03	78.13	78.89	73.58
California	74.57	75.86	72.53	72.61	65.43	79.19	79.26	74.07
Colorado	75.30	76.96	73.79	73.88	68.96	80.01	80.13	75.89
Connecticut	75.12	76.91	73.62	74.25	66.04	79.97	80.37	75.44
Delaware	73.21	74.76	71.63	72.75	65.51	77.74	78.62	72.91
District of Columbia	69.20	67.99	61.97	71.36	57.53	74.23	81.06	71.61
Florida	74.00	75.84	72.10	73.19	64.26	79.60	80.46	73.28
Georgia	72.22	73.61	69.65	71.46	63.98	77.46	78.94	73.34
Hawaii	77.02	78.21	75.37	75.12	(B)	81.26	81.09	(B)
Idaho	75.19	76.88	73.88	73.90	(B)	79.93	79.93	(B)
Illinois	73.37	74.90	71.34	72.83	62.41	78.31	79.33	72.39
Indiana	73.84	75.39	71.99	72.44	65.87	78.62	79.03	73.56
Iowa	75.81	77.29	73.89	73.98	(B)	80.54	80.62	(B)
Kansas	75.31	76.76	73.40	73.72	67.48	79.99	80.25	75.04
Kentucky	73.06	74.37	70.72	71.01	66.06	77.97	78.24	74.13
Louisiana	71.74	73.05	69.10	71.15	63.84	76.93	78.54	73.16
Maine	74.59	76.35	72.98	72.98	(B)	79.61	79.61	(B)
Maryland	73.32	74.79	71.31	73.20	64.99	78.13	79.23	74.31
Massachusetts	75.01	76.72	73.32	73.54	68.17	79.80	79.95	76.50
Michigan	73.67	75.04	71.71	73.06	63.68	78.24	79.14	73.18
Minnesota	76.15	77.76	74.53	74.78	(B)	80.85	81.02	(B)
Mississippi	71.98	73.03	68.90	70.74	64.66	77.10	78.82	73.82
Missouri	73.84	75.25	71.54	72.43	63.87	78.82	79.48	73.52
Montana	73.93	76.23	73.05	73.59	(B)	79.49	79.92	(B)
Nebraska	75.49	76.92	73.57	73.87	(B)	80.17	80.44	(B)
Nevada	72.64	74.18	70.96	71.26	(B)	77.76	77.99	(B)
New Hampshire	74.98	76.72	73.52	73.48	(B)	79.77	79.74	(B)
New Jersey	74.00	75.42	72.16	73.37	63.87	78.49	79.34	72.88
New Mexico	74.01	75.74	72.20	72.66	(B)	79.33	79.53	(B)
New York	73.70	74.68	70.86	72.01	63.86	78.32	79.03	74.35
North Carolina	72.96	74.48	70.58	72.21	64.38	78.27	79.44	74.24
North Dakota	75.71	77.62	74.35	74.74	(B)	80.99	81.32	(B)
Ohio	73.49	75.32	71.99	72.70	65.80	78.45	78.95	74.29
Oklahoma	73.67	75.10	71.63	71.76	67.10	78.49	78.59	74.48
Oregon	74.99	76.44	73.21	73.28	(B)	79.67	79.73	(B)
Pennsylvania	73.58	75.38	71.91	72.81	63.33	78.66	79.28	73.02
Rhode Island	74.76	76.54	73.00	73.31	(B)	79.77	79.97	(B)
South Carolina	71.85	73.51	69.59	71.62	64.07	77.34	78.97	73.35
South Dakota	74.97	76.91	73.17	74.30	(B)	80.77	81.59	(B)
Tennessee	73.30	74.32	70.38	71.38	64.41	78.18	79.10	73.24
Texas	73.64	75.14	71.41	72.08	65.36	78.87	79.42	74.23
Utah	75.76	77.70	74.93	75.00	(B)	80.38	80.44	(B)
Vermont	74.79	76.54	73.29	73.25	(B)	79.68	79.65	(B)
Virginia	73.43	75.22	71.77	73.04	65.75	78.56	79.48	74.37
Washington	75.13	76.82	73.84	73.97	67.91	79.74	79.81	75.58
West Virginia	72.84	74.26	70.53	70.66	65.00	77.93	78.02	74.36
Wisconsin	75.35	76.87	73.61	73.99	66.42	80.03	80.27	75.27
Wyoming	73.85	76.21	73.16	73.27	(B)	79.29	79.46	(B)

B Base figure too small to meet statistical standards for reliability.

Source: U.S. National Center for Health Statistics, National Vital Statistics Reports (NVSR), *U.S. Decennial Life Tables for 1989–91*, Vol. 1, No. 3., and *Trends and Comparisons of United States Life Table Data: 1900–1991*. See also <http://cdc.gov/nchs /products/life_tables.htm#life>.

Table 107. Deaths and Death Rates by Sex, Race, and Hispanic Origin: 1970 to 2007

[1,921 represents 1,921,000. Rates are per 1,000 population for specified groups. Excludes deaths of nonresidents of the United States and fetal deaths. For explanation of age adjustment, see text, this section. The standard population for age adjustment is the projected year 2000 population of the United States. See Appendix III. Data for Hispanic origin and specified races other than White and Black should be interpreted with caution because of inconsistencies between reporting Hispanic origin and race on death certificates and censuses and surveys]

Sex and race	1970	1980	1990	2000	2001	2002	2003	2004	2005	2006	2007
Deaths [1] (1,000)	**1,921**	**1,990**	**2,148**	**2,403**	**2,416**	**2,443**	**2,448**	**2,398**	**2,448**	**2,426**	**2,424**
Male [1] (1,000)	1,078	1,075	1,113	1,178	1,183	1,199	1,202	1,182	1,208	1,202	1,204
Female [1] (1,000)	843	915	1,035	1,226	1,233	1,244	1,246	1,216	1,240	1,224	1,220
White (1,000)	1,682	1,739	1,853	2,071	2,080	2,103	2,104	2,057	2,098	2,078	2,074
Male (1,000)	942	934	951	1,007	1,011	1,025	1,026	1,007	1,028	1,022	1,024
Female (1,000)	740	805	902	1,064	1,068	1,077	1,078	1,049	1,070	1,055	1,050
Black (1,000)	226	233	265	286	288	290	291	287	293	290	290
Male (1,000)	128	130	145	145	146	147	148	146	149	149	148
Female (1,000)	98	103	120	141	142	143	143	141	144	141	141
Asian or Pacific Islander (1,000)	(NA)	11	21	35	37	38	40	41	43	45	46
Male (1,000)	(NA)	7	12	19	20	20	21	21	23	23	24
Female (1,000)	(NA)	4	9	16	17	18	19	19	20	21	22
American Indian, Eskimo, Aleut (1,000)	6	7	8	11	12	12	13	13	14	14	14
Male (1,000)	3	4	5	6	6	7	7	7	8	8	8
Female (1,000)	2	3	3	5	6	6	6	6	6	6	6
Hispanic origin [2]	(NA)	(NA)	(NA)	107	113	117	122	122	131	133	136
Male (1,000)	(NA)	(NA)	(NA)	60	63	66	68	69	74	74	76
Female (1,000)	(NA)	(NA)	(NA)	47	50	51	54	54	57	59	60
Non-Hispanic, White (1,000)	(NA)	(NA)	(NA)	1,960	1,963	1,982	1,979	1,933	1,967	1,945	1,940
Male (1,000)	(NA)	(NA)	(NA)	945	946	958	956	938	954	948	949
Female (1,000)	(NA)	(NA)	(NA)	1,015	1,017	1,024	1,023	995	1,013	997	991
Death rates [1]	**9.5**	**8.8**	**8.6**	**8.5**	**8.5**	**8.5**	**8.4**	**8.2**	**8.3**	**8.1**	**8.0**
Male [1]	10.9	9.8	9.2	8.5	8.5	8.5	8.4	8.2	8.3	8.1	8.1
Female [1]	8.1	7.9	8.1	8.6	8.5	8.5	8.4	8.2	8.2	8.1	8.0
White	9.5	8.9	8.9	9.0	9.0	9.0	8.9	8.6	8.7	8.6	8.5
Male	10.9	9.8	9.3	8.9	8.8	8.8	8.8	8.5	8.6	8.5	8.5
Female	8.1	8.1	8.5	9.1	9.1	9.1	9.0	8.7	8.8	8.6	8.5
Black	10.0	8.8	8.7	7.8	7.7	7.7	7.6	7.4	7.5	7.3	7.2
Male	11.9	10.3	10.1	8.3	8.2	8.2	8.1	7.9	8.0	7.9	7.8
Female	8.3	7.3	7.5	7.3	7.3	7.2	7.2	7.0	7.0	6.8	6.8
Asian or Pacific Islander	(NA)	3.0	2.8	3.0	3.0	3.0	3.0	3.0	3.1	3.1	3.1
Male	(NA)	3.8	3.3	3.3	3.4	3.3	3.3	3.2	3.3	3.3	3.3
Female	(NA)	2.2	2.3	2.6	2.7	2.7	2.8	2.7	2.8	2.9	2.9
American Indian, Eskimo, Aleut	(NA)	4.9	4.0	3.8	3.9	4.0	4.2	4.2	4.4	4.4	4.4
Male	(NA)	6.0	4.8	4.2	4.2	4.4	4.6	4.5	4.8	4.8	4.9
Female	(NA)	3.8	3.3	3.5	3.6	3.7	3.9	3.8	4.0	4.0	4.0
Hispanic origin [2]	(NA)	(NA)	(NA)	3.0	3.1	3.0	3.1	3.0	3.1	3.0	3.0
Male	(NA)	(NA)	4.1	3.3	3.3	3.3	3.3	3.2	3.3	3.2	3.2
Female	(NA)	(NA)	2.9	2.7	2.8	2.7	2.8	2.7	2.8	2.7	2.7
Non-Hispanic, White	(NA)	(NA)	(NA)	9.9	9.9	10.0	9.9	9.7	9.8	9.7	9.6
Male	(NA)	(NA)	9.9	9.8	9.8	9.8	9.8	9.6	9.7	9.6	9.6
Female	(NA)	(NA)	9.0	10.1	10.1	10.1	10.1	9.8	9.9	9.7	9.7
Age-adjusted death rates [1,3]	**12.2**	**10.4**	**9.4**	**8.7**	**8.5**	**8.5**	**8.3**	**8.0**	**8.0**	**7.8**	**7.6**
Male [1]	15.4	13.5	12.0	10.5	10.3	10.1	9.9	9.6	9.5	9.2	9.1
Female [1]	9.7	8.2	7.5	7.3	7.2	7.2	7.1	6.8	6.8	6.6	6.4
White	11.9	10.1	9.1	8.5	8.4	8.3	8.2	7.9	7.9	7.6	7.5
Male	15.1	13.2	11.7	10.3	10.1	9.9	9.7	9.4	9.3	9.1	8.9
Female	9.4	8.0	7.3	7.2	7.1	7.0	6.9	6.7	6.7	6.5	6.3
Black	15.2	13.1	12.5	11.2	11.0	10.8	10.7	10.3	10.2	9.8	9.6
Male	18.7	17.0	16.4	14.0	13.8	13.4	13.2	12.7	12.5	12.2	11.8
Female	12.3	10.3	9.8	9.3	9.1	9.0	8.9	8.6	8.5	8.1	7.9
Asian or Pacific Islander	(NA)	5.9	5.8	5.1	4.9	4.7	4.7	4.4	4.4	4.3	4.2
Male	(NA)	7.9	7.2	6.2	6.0	5.8	5.6	5.3	5.3	5.2	5.0
Female	(NA)	4.3	4.7	4.2	4.1	4.0	3.9	3.8	3.7	3.6	3.5
American Indian, Eskimo, Aleut	(NA)	8.7	7.2	7.1	6.9	6.8	6.9	6.5	6.6	6.4	6.3
Male	(NA)	11.1	9.2	8.4	8.0	7.9	8.0	7.6	7.8	7.4	7.4
Female	(NA)	6.6	5.6	6.0	5.9	5.8	5.9	5.6	5.7	5.6	5.3
Hispanic origin [2]	(NA)	(NA)	(NA)	6.7	6.6	6.3	6.2	5.9	5.9	5.6	5.5
Male	(NA)	(NA)	8.9	8.2	8.0	7.7	7.5	7.1	7.2	6.8	6.5
Female	(NA)	(NA)	5.4	5.5	5.4	5.2	5.2	4.9	4.9	4.7	4.5
Non-Hispanic, White	(NA)	(NA)	(NA)	8.6	8.4	8.4	8.3	8.0	8.0	7.8	7.6
Male	(NA)	(NA)	11.7	10.4	10.1	10.0	9.8	9.5	9.5	9.2	9.1
Female	(NA)	(NA)	7.3	7.2	7.1	7.1	7.0	6.8	6.8	6.6	6.5

NA Not available. [1] Includes other races not shown separately. [2] Persons of Hispanic origin may be any race. [3] See text, this section.

Source: U.S. National Center for Health Statistics, National Vital Statistics Reports (NVSR), *Deaths: Final Data for 2007*, Vol. 58, No. 19, May 2010.

Table 108. Death Rates by Age, Sex, and Race: 1950 to 2007

[Rates per 100,000 population]

Characteristic	All ages[1]	Under 1 year	1 to 4 years	5 to 14 years	15 to 24 years	25 to 34 years	35 to 44 years	45 to 54 years	55 to 64 years	65 to 74 years	75 to 84 years	85 years and over
MALE												
1950	1,106	3,728	152	71	168	217	429	1,067	2,395	4,931	10,426	21,636
1960	1,105	3,059	120	56	152	188	373	992	2,310	4,914	10,178	21,186
1970	1,090	2,410	93	51	189	215	403	959	2,283	4,874	10,010	17,822
1980	977	1,429	73	37	172	196	299	767	1,815	4,105	8,817	18,801
1990	918	1,083	52	29	147	204	310	610	1,553	3,492	7,889	18,057
2000	853	807	36	21	115	139	255	543	1,231	2,980	6,973	17,501
2004	818	754	32	19	115	140	244	544	1,129	2,645	6,394	15,031
2005	827	762	33	19	118	143	243	548	1,131	2,612	6,350	14,889
2006	815	756	31	18	119	147	239	541	1,110	2,516	6,178	14,309
2007	810	748	31	17	116	144	232	530	1,101	2,457	6,038	14,006
White:												
1990	931	896	46	26	131	176	268	549	1,467	3,398	7,845	18,268
2000	888	668	33	20	106	124	234	497	1,163	2,906	6,933	17,716
2004	854	632	29	18	108	127	229	504	1,066	2,584	6,385	15,251
2005	865	640	31	17	110	131	229	509	1,068	2,553	6,343	15,157
2006	852	633	28	16	112	135	224	505	1,051	2,456	6,182	14,577
2007	848	628	28	16	108	134	218	498	1,043	2,397	6,049	14,286
Black:												
1990	1,008	2,112	86	41	252	431	700	1,261	2,618	4,946	9,130	16,955
2000	834	1,568	55	28	181	261	453	1,018	2,080	4,254	8,486	16,791
2004	793	1,414	49	26	164	252	397	955	1,961	3,818	7,710	14,453
2005	799	1,437	47	27	172	254	396	949	1,954	3,747	7,667	13,810
2006	787	1,407	47	25	171	254	392	922	1,892	3,669	7,393	13,206
2007	776	1,363	45	25	168	240	379	877	1,871	3,605	7,169	12,965
Asian or Pacific Islander:[2]												
1990	334	605	45	21	76	80	131	287	789	2,041	5,009	12,446
2000	333	529	23	13	55	55	105	250	642	1,661	4,328	12,125
2004	321	443	21	15	54	51	91	242	545	1,363	3,766	10,118
2005	334	465	21	14	57	56	94	242	545	1,404	3,759	9,839
2006	331	470	18	11	62	54	89	233	551	1,329	3,606	9,525
2007	331	484	25	12	61	50	89	229	523	1,305	3,538	8,918
American Indian, Eskimo, Aleut:[2]												
1990	476	1,057	77	33	220	256	365	620	1,211	2,462	5,389	11,244
2000	416	700	45	20	136	179	295	520	1,090	2,478	5,351	10,726
2004	454	1,076	55	24	137	189	321	544	1,067	2,197	4,584	7,924
2005	482	882	72	23	145	206	337	589	1,124	2,254	4,373	8,419
2006	477	1,058	58	17	156	194	309	592	1,030	2,147	4,198	7,540
2007	488	1,010	64	23	144	198	333	573	1,037	2,132	4,193	7,639
FEMALE												
1950	824	2,855	127	49	89	143	290	642	1,405	3,333	8,400	19,195
1960	809	2,321	98	37	61	107	229	527	1,196	2,872	7,633	19,008
1970	808	1,864	75	32	68	102	231	517	1,099	2,580	6,678	15,518
1980	785	1,142	55	24	58	76	159	413	934	2,145	5,440	14,747
1990	812	856	41	19	49	74	138	343	879	1,991	4,883	14,274
2000	855	663	29	15	43	64	143	313	772	1,921	4,815	14,719
2004	815	613	27	14	44	64	144	314	707	1,761	4,522	13,280
2005	825	619	25	14	43	64	144	320	699	1,736	4,520	13,298
2006	806	622	26	13	43	64	142	318	687	1,678	4,388	12,759
2007	797	618	26	13	42	64	137	315	670	1,633	4,304	12,442
White:												
1990	847	690	36	18	46	62	117	309	823	1,924	4,839	14,401
2000	912	551	26	14	41	55	126	281	731	1,868	4,785	14,891
2004	872	514	24	13	42	57	130	285	672	1,724	4,514	13,451
2005	883	515	23	13	42	58	130	291	664	1,700	4,519	13,498
2006	864	517	24	12	42	59	129	292	655	1,646	4,395	12,966
2007	855	517	23	12	41	60	126	291	638	1,600	4,318	12,647
Black:												
1990	748	1,736	68	28	69	160	299	639	1,453	2,866	5,688	13,310
2000	733	1,280	45	20	58	122	272	588	1,227	2,690	5,697	13,941
2004	700	1,150	41	21	54	112	256	564	1,129	2,386	5,300	12,897
2005	704	1,180	37	19	51	110	250	568	1,104	2,342	5,264	12,790
2006	684	1,195	39	17	51	107	245	548	1,076	2,240	5,029	12,197
2007	676	1,132	39	17	49	102	229	537	1,047	2,210	4,903	11,997
Asian or Pacific Islander:[2]												
1990	234	518	32	13	29	38	70	183	483	1,089	3,128	10,254
2000	262	434	20	12	22	28	66	156	391	996	2,882	9,052
2004	275	392	22	10	24	27	54	146	340	933	2,558	8,126
2005	283	395	18	12	26	29	58	143	353	906	2,530	7,793
2006	286	357	21	10	25	29	57	145	333	898	2,526	7,560
2007	287	398	18	10	24	28	55	136	329	833	2,471	7,334
American Indian, Eskimo, Aleut:[2]												
1990	330	689	38	26	69	102	156	381	806	1,679	3,073	8,201
2000	346	492	40	18	59	85	172	285	772	1,900	3,850	9,118
2004	380	715	53	20	65	103	192	340	704	1,701	3,533	7,094
2005	399	753	46	17	68	91	194	366	699	1,781	3,603	7,065
2006	400	690	51	17	64	92	205	342	687	1,657	3,746	6,634
2007	400	830	46	13	61	91	196	346	694	1,612	3,437	6,248

[1] Figures for age not stated are included in "All ages" but not distributed among age groups. [2] The death rates for specified races other than White and Black should be interpreted with caution because of inconsistencies between reporting race on death certificates and censuses and surveys.

Source: U.S. National Center for Health Statistics, *Health, United States, 2009.* See also <http://cdc.gov/nchs/hus.htm>.

Table 109. Age-Adjusted Death Rates by Sex, Race, and Hispanic Origin: 1970 to 2007

[Age-adjusted rates per 100,000 population; see headnote, Table 107. Populations enumerated as of April 1 for census years and estimated as of July 1 for all other years. Beginning 1970, excludes deaths of nonresidents of the United States. Data for Hispanic origin and specified races other than White and Black should be interpreted with caution because of inconsistencies reporting race on death certificates and on censuses and surveys. See Appendix III]

Sex, race, and Hispanic origin	1970	1980	1990	2000	2002	2003	2004	2005	2006	2007
ALL RACES [1]										
Total.	1,223	1,039	939	869	845	833	801	799	777	760
Male.	1,542	1,348	1,203	1,054	1,014	994	956	951	925	906
Female.	971	818	751	731	715	706	679	678	658	643
WHITE										
Total.	1,193	1,013	910	850	829	817	786	785	764	749
Male.	1,514	1,318	1,166	1,029	993	974	937	933	908	891
Female.	944	796	729	715	701	693	667	667	648	635
BLACK										
Total.	1,518	1,315	1,250	1,121	1,083	1,066	1,027	1,017	982	958
Male.	1,874	1,698	1,645	1,404	1,341	1,319	1,269	1,253	1,216	1,184
Female.	1,229	1,033	975	920	902	886	855	846	813	794
ASIAN OR PACIFIC ISLANDER										
Total.	(NA)	590	582	506	474	466	444	440	429	415
Male.	(NA)	787	716	624	578	563	535	534	516	499
Female.	(NA)	426	469	417	396	393	376	369	363	351
AMERICAN INDIAN, ESKIMO, ALEUT										
Total.	(NA)	867	716	709	677	685	650	663	642	627
Male.	(NA)	1,112	916	842	794	797	758	775	740	737
Female.	(NA)	662	562	605	581	592	558	568	556	533
HISPANIC ORIGIN [2]										
Total.	(NA)	(NA)	(NA)	666	629	621	587	591	564	546
Male.	(NA)	(NA)	886	818	767	748	707	717	676	655
Female.	(NA)	(NA)	537	546	518	516	486	485	469	453
NON-HISPANIC, WHITE										
Total.	(NA)	(NA)	(NA)	856	838	826	797	797	777	763
Male.	(NA)	(NA)	1,171	1,035	1,002	984	949	945	923	907
Female.	(NA)	(NA)	735	722	710	702	678	678	660	648

NA Not available. [1] For 1970 to 1990 includes deaths among races, not shown separately. [2] Persons of Hispanic origin may be any race.

Source: U.S. National Center for Health Statistics, National Vital Statistics Reports (NVSR), *Deaths: Final Data for 2007*, Vol. 58, No. 19, May 2010.

Table 110. Death Rates by Hispanic-Origin Status, Sex, and Age: 2000 to 2007

[Rates per 100,000 U.S. standard population. Rates are based on populations enumerated as of April 1 for census years and estimated as of July 1 for all other years. Excludes deaths of nonresidents of the United States. Data for Hispanic-origin should be interpreted with caution because of inconsistencies between reporting Hispanic origin and race on death certificates and censuses and surveys]

Age	Hispanic male			Hispanic female			Non-Hispanic White male			Non-Hispanic White female		
	2000	2005	2007	2000	2005	2007	2000	2005	2007	2000	2005	2007
Age adjusted [1]	818	717	655	546	485	453	1,035	945	907	722	678	648
Crude [2]	331	334	322	275	278	272	979	971	960	1,007	993	968
Under 1 year	637	670	633	554	555	540	659	626	617	531	497	500
1 to 4 years	32	33	28	28	25	24	32	30	28	24	22	23
5 to 14 years	18	15	16	13	12	12	20	17	16	14	13	12
15 to 24 years	108	120	115	32	37	34	104	106	105	43	42	43
25 to 34 years	120	116	110	43	41	43	123	134	141	57	62	63
35 to 44 years	211	182	166	101	91	83	234	236	228	128	137	134
45 to 54 years	439	417	399	224	216	204	498	517	509	285	299	301
55 to 64 years	966	876	831	548	494	477	1,171	1,080	1,058	742	677	651
65 to 74 years	2,288	2,029	1,863	1,423	1,292	1,162	2,931	2,585	2,433	1,891	1,730	1,635
75 to 84 years	5,395	4,857	4,365	3,625	3,366	3,196	6,978	6,420	6,153	4,819	4,580	4,385
85 years and over . . .	13,086	10,141	8,954	11,203	9,068	8,319	17,853	15,401	14,588	14,972	13,683	12,857

[1] See headnote, Table 107. [2] The total number of deaths in a given time period divided by the total resident population as of July 1.

Source: U.S. National Center for Health Statistics, National Vital Statistics Reports (NVSR), *Deaths: Final Data for 2007*, Vol. 58, No. 19, May 2010.

Table 111. Deaths and Death Rates by State and Island Areas: 1990 to 2007

[2,148 represents 2,148,000. By state of residence. Except as noted, excludes deaths of nonresidents of the United States. Caution should be used in comparing death rates by state; rates are affected by the population composition of the area. See also Appendix III]

State	Number of deaths (1,000)						Death rate per 1,000 population [1]						Age-adjusted rate 2007 [2]
	1990	1995	2000	2005	2006	2007	1990	1995	2000	2005	2006	2007	
United States	2,148	2,312	2,403	2,448	2,426	2,424	8.6	8.7	8.5	8.3	8.1	8.0	7.6
Alabama	39	42	45	47	47	47	9.7	10.0	10.1	10.3	10.2	10.1	9.3
Alaska	2	3	3	3	3	3	4.0	4.2	4.6	4.8	5.0	5.1	7.6
Arizona	29	35	41	46	46	46	7.9	8.4	7.9	7.7	7.5	7.2	6.8
Arkansas	25	27	28	28	28	28	10.5	10.8	10.6	10.1	9.9	9.9	8.8
California	214	224	230	237	237	234	7.2	7.1	6.8	6.6	6.5	6.4	6.7
Colorado	22	25	27	30	30	30	6.6	6.7	6.3	6.4	6.2	6.2	7.0
Connecticut	28	29	30	29	29	29	8.4	9.0	8.8	8.4	8.3	8.2	6.9
Delaware	6	6	7	7	7	7	8.7	8.8	8.8	8.9	8.4	8.5	7.7
District of Columbia	7	7	6	5	5	5	12.0	12.4	10.5	10.0	9.2	8.8	8.7
Florida	134	153	164	171	170	168	10.4	10.8	10.3	9.6	9.4	9.2	6.9
Georgia	52	58	64	67	68	68	8.0	8.1	7.8	7.4	7.2	7.2	8.4
Hawaii	7	8	8	9	9	9	6.1	6.4	6.8	7.2	7.3	7.4	6.1
Idaho	7	9	10	11	11	11	7.4	7.3	7.4	7.4	7.2	7.2	7.3
Illinois	103	108	107	104	102	101	9.0	9.2	8.6	8.1	8.0	7.8	7.6
Indiana	50	53	55	56	56	54	8.9	9.2	9.1	8.9	8.8	8.5	8.1
Iowa	27	28	28	28	27	27	9.7	9.9	9.6	9.4	9.2	9.1	7.2
Kansas	22	24	25	25	25	24	9.0	9.3	9.2	9.0	8.9	8.8	7.8
Kentucky	35	37	40	40	40	40	9.5	9.6	9.8	9.6	9.5	9.5	9.0
Louisiana	38	40	41	44	40	40	8.9	9.1	9.2	9.8	9.3	9.3	9.3
Maine	11	12	12	13	12	12	9.0	9.5	9.7	9.7	9.3	9.5	7.7
Maryland	38	42	44	44	44	44	8.0	8.3	8.3	7.8	7.8	7.8	7.8
Massachusetts	53	55	57	54	53	53	8.8	9.1	8.9	8.4	8.3	8.2	7.1
Michigan	79	84	87	87	86	87	8.5	8.8	8.7	8.6	8.5	8.6	8.1
Minnesota	35	38	38	38	37	37	7.9	8.1	7.7	7.3	7.2	7.1	6.6
Mississippi	25	27	29	29	29	28	9.8	10.0	10.1	10.0	9.8	9.7	9.4
Missouri	50	54	55	55	55	54	9.8	10.2	9.8	9.4	9.4	9.2	8.3
Montana	7	8	8	9	8	9	8.6	8.8	9.0	9.1	9.0	9.0	7.7
Nebraska	15	15	15	15	15	15	9.4	9.3	8.8	8.5	8.4	8.6	7.4
Nevada	9	13	15	19	19	19	7.8	8.2	7.6	7.9	7.6	7.3	8.0
New Hampshire	8	9	10	10	10	10	7.7	8.0	7.8	7.8	7.7	7.8	7.3
New Jersey	70	74	75	72	70	70	9.1	9.3	8.0	8.3	8.1	8.0	7.2
New Mexico	11	13	13	15	15	15	7.0	7.4	7.4	7.8	7.8	7.9	7.6
New York	169	168	158	152	149	148	9.4	9.3	8.3	7.9	7.7	7.7	6.9
North Carolina	57	65	72	75	75	76	8.6	9.0	8.9	8.6	8.4	8.4	8.3
North Dakota	6	6	6	6	6	6	8.9	9.3	9.1	9.0	9.2	8.7	6.8
Ohio	99	106	108	109	107	107	9.1	9.5	9.5	9.5	9.3	9.3	8.3
Oklahoma	30	33	35	36	35	36	9.7	10.0	10.2	10.2	9.9	10.0	9.2
Oregon	25	28	30	31	31	31	8.8	9.0	8.6	8.5	8.5	8.4	7.5
Pennsylvania	122	128	131	130	126	125	10.3	10.6	10.7	10.4	10.1	10.1	7.9
Rhode Island	10	10	10	10	10	10	9.5	9.8	9.6	9.3	9.1	9.2	7.5
South Carolina	30	34	37	39	39	39	8.5	9.1	9.2	9.1	9.0	8.9	8.5
South Dakota	6	7	7	7	7	7	9.1	9.5	9.3	9.1	9.1	8.6	6.9
Tennessee	46	51	55	57	57	57	9.5	9.8	9.7	9.6	9.4	9.3	8.9
Texas	125	138	150	156	157	161	7.4	7.4	7.2	6.8	6.7	6.7	7.8
Utah	9	11	12	13	14	14	5.3	5.6	5.5	5.4	5.4	5.3	6.9
Vermont	5	5	5	5	5	5	8.2	8.5	8.4	8.1	8.1	8.3	7.3
Virginia	48	53	56	58	58	58	7.8	8.0	8.0	7.6	7.5	7.6	7.7
Washington	37	41	44	46	46	47	7.6	7.5	7.5	7.3	7.2	7.3	7.2
West Virginia	19	20	21	21	21	21	10.8	11.1	11.7	11.4	11.4	11.6	9.5
Wisconsin	43	45	46	47	46	46	8.7	8.8	8.7	8.4	8.3	8.3	7.3
Wyoming	3	4	4	4	4	4	7.1	7.7	7.9	8.0	8.4	8.2	8.0
Puerto Rico	26	30	28	30	28	28	7.3	8.1	7.2	7.5	7.2	7.4	7.3
Virgin Islands	(Z)	1	1	1	1	1	4.6	5.8	5.3	6.1	5.7	6.4	7.0
Guam	1	1	1	1	1	1	3.9	4.1	4.2	4.0	4.0	4.5	7.3
American Samoa	(NA)	(NA)	(Z)	(Z)	(Z)	(Z)	(NA)	(NA)	3.3	4.4	4.6	3.9	10.5
Northern Marianas	(NA)	(NA)	(Z)	(Z)	(Z)	(Z)	(NA)	(NA)	1.9	2.3	2.1	1.6	9.1

NA Not available. Z Less than 500. [1] Rates based on enumerated resident population as of April 1 for 1990 and 2000; estimated resident population as of July 1 for all other years. [2] See text, this section.

Source: U.S. National Center for Health Statistics, National Vital Statistics Reports (NVSR), *Deaths: Final Data for 2007*, Vol. 58, No. 19, May 2010.

U.S. Census Bureau, Statistical Abstract of the United States: 2011

Table 112. Fetal and Infant Deaths: 1990 to 2005

[The term "fetal death" defined on an all inclusive basis to end confusion arising from the use of such terms as stillbirth, spontaneous abortion, and miscarriage have been adopted by the National Center for Health Statistics (NCHS) as the nationally recommended standard. Fetal deaths do not include induced terminations of pregnancy. See also Appendix III]

Year	Fetal deaths [1]			Infant deaths		Fetal mortality rate [2]			Perinatal mortality rate	
	Total [1]	20 to 27 weeks [3]	28 weeks or more [3]	Less than 7 days	Less than 28 days	Total [1]	20–27 weeks [3]	28 weeks or more [3]	Defi-nition I [4]	Defi-nition II [5]
1990......	31,386	13,427	17,959	19,439	23,591	7.49	3.22	4.30	8.95	13.12
1995......	27,294	13,043	14,251	15,483	19,186	6.95	3.33	3.64	7.60	11.84
1996......	27,069	12,990	14,079	14,947	18,556	6.91	3.33	3.60	7.43	11.64
1997......	26,486	12,800	13,686	14,827	18,507	6.78	3.29	3.51	7.32	11.51
1998......	26,702	13,229	13,473	15,061	18,915	6.73	3.35	3.41	7.21	11.50
1999......	26,884	13,457	13,427	14,874	18,700	6.74	3.39	3.38	7.12	11.44
2000......	27,003	13,497	13,506	14,893	18,733	6.61	3.31	3.32	6.97	11.19
2001......	26,373	13,122	13,251	14,622	18,275	6.51	3.25	3.28	6.90	11.02
2002......	25,943	13,072	12,871	15,020	18,791	6.41	3.24	3.19	6.91	11.05
2003......	25,653	13,168	12,485	15,152	18,935	6.23	3.21	3.04	6.74	10.83
2004......	25,655	12,894	12,761	14,836	18,602	6.20	3.13	3.09	6.69	10.70
2005......	25,894	13,327	12,567	15,013	18,782	6.22	3.21	3.03	6.64	10.73

[1] Fetal deaths with stated or presumed gestation of 20 weeks or more. [2] Rate per 1,000 live births and fetal deaths in specified group. [3] Not stated gestational age proportionally distributed. [4] Infant deaths of less than 7 days and fetal deaths with stated or presumed period of gestation of 28 weeks or more, per 1,000 live births and fetal deaths. [5] Infant deaths of less than 28 days and fetal deaths with stated or presumed period of gestation of 20 weeks or more per 1,000 live births and fetal deaths.

Source: U.S. National Center for Health Statistics, National Vital Statistics Reports (NVSR), *Fetal and Perinatal Mortality, U.S., 2005*, Vol. 57. No. 8, January 2009.

Table 113. Infant, Neonatal, and Maternal Mortality Rates by Race: 1980 to 2006

[Deaths per 1,000 live births, except as noted. Data based on death certificates, fetal death records, and birth certificates. Excludes deaths of nonresidents of the United States. See also Appendix III]

Race and year	Infant [1]	Neonatal [1]		Post-neonatal [1]	Fetal mortality rate [2]	Late fetal mortality rate [3]	Perinatal mortality rate [4]	Maternal mortality rate [5]
		Under 28 days	Under 7 days					
ALL RACES								
1980.........	12.6	8.5	7.1	4.1	9.1	6.2	13.2	9.2
1990.........	9.2	5.8	4.8	3.4	7.5	4.3	9.1	8.2
1995.........	7.6	4.9	4.0	2.7	7.0	3.6	7.6	7.1
2000.........	6.9	4.6	3.7	2.3	6.6	3.3	7.0	9.8
2001.........	6.8	4.5	3.6	2.3	6.5	3.3	6.9	9.9
2002.........	7.0	4.7	3.7	2.3	6.4	3.2	6.9	8.9
2003.........	6.9	4.6	3.7	2.2	6.2	3.0	6.7	[6] 12.1
2004.........	6.8	4.5	3.6	2.3	6.2	3.1	6.7	[6] 13.1
2005.........	6.9	4.5	3.6	2.3	6.2	3.0	6.6	[6] 15.1
2006.........	6.7	4.5	(NA)	2.3	(NA)	(NA)	(NA)	13.3
WHITE [7]								
1980.........	10.9	7.4	6.1	3.5	8.1	5.7	11.8	6.7
1990.........	7.6	4.8	3.9	2.8	6.4	3.8	7.7	5.4
1995.........	6.3	4.1	3.3	2.2	5.9	3.3	6.5	4.2
2000.........	5.7	3.8	3.0	1.9	5.6	2.9	5.9	7.5
2001.........	5.7	3.8	3.0	1.9	5.5	2.9	5.9	7.2
2002.........	5.8	3.9	3.1	1.9	5.5	2.8	5.9	6.0
2003.........	5.7	3.9	3.1	1.8	5.2	2.7	5.8	[6] 8.7
2004.........	5.7	3.8	3.0	1.9	5.3	(NA)	(NA)	[6] 9.3
2005.........	5.7	3.8	3.0	1.9	5.3	(NA)	(NA)	[6] 11.1
2006.........	5.6	3.7	(NA)	1.8	(NA)	(NA)	(NA)	9.5
BLACK [7]								
1980.........	22.2	14.6	12.3	7.6	14.7	9.1	21.3	21.5
1990.........	18.0	11.6	9.7	6.4	13.3	6.7	16.4	22.4
1995.........	15.1	9.8	8.2	5.3	12.7	5.7	13.8	22.1
2000.........	14.1	9.4	7.6	4.7	12.4	5.4	13.0	22.0
2001.........	14.0	9.2	7.6	4.8	12.1	5.3	12.8	24.7
2002.........	14.4	9.5	7.8	4.8	11.9	5.2	12.8	24.9
2003.........	14.0	9.4	7.5	4.6	12.0	5.1	12.4	[6] 30.5
2004.........	13.8	9.1	7.3	4.7	11.5	(NA)	(NA)	[6] 34.7
2005.........	13.7	9.1	7.3	4.7	11.4	(NA)	(NA)	[6] 36.5
2006.........	13.3	8.8	(NA)	4.5	(NA)	(NA)	(NA)	32.7

NA Not available. [1] Infant (under 1 year of age), neonatal (under 28 days), early neonatal (under 7 days), and postneonatal (28 days–11 months). [2] Number of fetal deaths of 20 weeks or more gestation per 1,000 live births plus fetal deaths. [3] Number of fetal deaths of 28 weeks or more gestation (late fetal deaths) per 1,000 live births plus late fetal deaths. [4] Number of late fetal deaths plus infant deaths within 7 days of birth per 1,000 live births plus late fetal deaths. [5] Per 100,000 live births from deliveries and complications of pregnancy, childbirth, and the puerperium. Beginning 2000, deaths are classified according to the tenth revision of the International Classification of Diseases; earlier years classified according to the revision in use at the time; see text, this section. [6] Increase partially reflects the use of a separate item on the death certificate on pregnancy status by an increasing number of states. [7] Infant deaths are tabulated by race of decedent; fetal deaths and live births are tabulated by race of mother.

Source: U.S. National Center for Health Statistics, *Health, United States, 2009*. See also <http://cdc.gov/nchs/hus.htm>.

Table 114. Infant Mortality Rates by Race, States, and Island Areas: 1980 to 2007

[Deaths per 1,000 live births, by place of residence. Represents deaths of infants under 1 year old, exclusive of fetal deaths. Excludes deaths of nonresidents of the United States. See headnote 112 and Appendix III]

State	Total [1]				White				Black			
	1980	1990	2000	2007	1980	1990	2000	2007	1980	1990	2000	2007
United States	**12.6**	**9.2**	**6.9**	**6.8**	**10.9**	**7.6**	**5.7**	**5.6**	**22.2**	**18.0**	**14.1**	**13.2**
Alabama	15.1	10.8	9.4	9.9	11.6	8.1	6.6	8.0	21.6	16.0	15.4	14.4
Alaska	12.3	10.5	6.8	6.5	9.4	7.6	5.8	5.2	19.5	(B)	(B)	(B)
Arizona	12.4	8.8	6.7	6.8	11.8	7.8	6.2	6.5	18.4	20.6	17.6	15.0
Arkansas	12.7	9.2	8.4	7.7	10.3	8.4	7.0	6.5	20.0	13.9	13.7	13.2
California	11.1	7.9	5.4	5.2	10.6	7.0	5.1	4.9	18.0	16.8	12.9	12.4
Colorado	10.1	8.8	6.2	6.1	9.8	7.8	5.6	5.9	19.1	19.4	19.5	13.2
Connecticut	11.2	7.9	6.6	6.6	10.2	6.3	5.6	5.9	19.1	17.6	14.4	12.1
Delaware	13.9	10.1	9.2	7.5	9.8	9.7	7.9	6.1	27.9	20.1	14.8	11.8
District of Columbia	25.0	20.7	12.0	13.1	17.8	(B)	(B)	8.5	26.7	24.6	16.1	16.6
Florida	14.6	9.6	7.0	7.1	11.8	6.7	5.4	5.5	22.8	16.8	12.6	12.2
Georgia	14.5	12.4	8.5	8.0	10.8	7.4	5.9	5.6	21.0	18.3	13.9	12.8
Hawaii	10.3	6.7	8.1	6.5	11.6	6.1	6.5	6.1	(B)	(B)	(B)	(B)
Idaho	10.7	8.7	7.5	6.8	10.7	8.6	7.5	6.6	(NA)	(B)	(B)	(B)
Illinois.	14.8	10.7	8.5	6.7	11.7	7.9	6.6	5.2	26.3	22.4	17.1	14.2
Indiana.	11.9	9.6	7.8	7.6	10.5	7.9	6.9	6.6	23.4	17.4	15.8	16.0
Iowa.	11.8	8.1	6.5	5.5	11.5	7.9	6.0	5.3	27.2	21.9	21.1	11.6
Kansas.	10.4	8.4	6.8	7.9	9.5	8.0	6.4	7.0	20.6	17.7	12.2	19.0
Kentucky	12.9	8.5	7.2	6.7	12.0	8.2	6.7	6.0	22.0	14.3	12.7	12.7
Louisiana	14.3	11.1	9.0	9.2	10.5	8.1	5.9	6.1	20.6	16.7	13.3	14.1
Maine.	9.2	6.2	4.9	6.3	9.4	6.7	4.8	6.3	(B)	(B)	(B)	(B)
Maryland	14.0	9.5	7.6	8.0	11.6	6.8	4.8	4.8	20.4	17.1	13.2	13.6
Massachusetts.	10.5	7.0	4.6	4.9	10.1	6.1	4.0	4.5	16.8	11.9	9.9	8.8
Michigan	12.8	10.7	8.2	7.9	10.6	7.4	6.0	6.1	24.2	21.6	18.2	16.4
Minnesota	10.0	7.3	5.6	5.6	9.6	6.7	4.8	4.7	20.0	23.7	14.6	11.7
Mississippi	17.0	12.1	10.7	10.0	11.1	7.4	6.8	6.7	23.7	16.2	15.3	13.9
Missouri.	12.4	9.4	7.2	7.5	11.1	7.9	5.9	5.9	20.7	18.2	14.7	16.5
Montana.	12.4	9.0	6.1	6.4	11.8	6.0	5.5	5.9	(NA)	(B)	(B)	(B)
Nebraska.	11.5	8.3	7.3	6.8	10.7	6.9	6.4	6.1	25.2	18.9	20.3	14.0
Nevada	10.7	8.4	6.5	6.4	10.0	8.2	6.0	6.0	20.6	14.2	12.7	12.4
New Hampshire	9.9	7.1	5.7	5.4	9.9	6.0	5.5	5.3	22.5	(B)	(B)	(B)
New Jersey	12.5	9.0	6.3	5.2	10.3	6.4	5.0	4.1	21.9	18.4	13.6	11.0
New Mexico	11.5	9.0	6.6	6.3	11.3	7.6	6.3	6.0	23.1	(B)	(B)	(B)
New York	12.5	9.6	6.4	5.6	10.8	7.4	5.4	5.0	20.0	10.1	10.9	8.8
North Carolina	14.5	10.6	8.6	8.5	12.1	8.0	6.3	6.4	20.0	16.5	15.7	15.1
North Dakota	12.1	8.0	8.1	7.5	11.7	7.2	7.5	6.8	27.5	(B)	(B)	(B)
Ohio.	12.8	9.8	7.6	7.7	11.2	7.8	6.3	6.3	23.0	19.5	15.4	14.8
Oklahoma	12.7	9.2	8.5	8.5	12.1	9.1	7.9	7.3	21.8	14.3	16.9	18.0
Oregon.	12.2	8.3	5.6	5.8	12.2	7.0	5.5	5.7	15.9	(B)	(B)	(B)
Pennsylvania	13.2	9.6	7.1	7.6	11.9	7.4	5.8	6.1	23.1	20.5	15.7	15.1
Rhode Island	11.0	8.1	6.3	7.4	10.9	7.0	5.9	6.5	(B)	(B)	(B)	16.0
South Carolina	15.6	11.7	8.7	8.6	10.8	8.1	5.4	6.0	22.9	17.3	14.8	13.7
South Dakota	10.9	10.1	5.5	6.4	9.0	8.0	4.3	5.6	(NA)	(B)	(B)	(B)
Tennessee	13.5	10.3	9.1	8.3	11.9	7.3	6.8	6.4	19.3	17.9	18.0	15.7
Texas	12.2	8.1	5.7	6.3	11.2	6.7	5.1	5.7	18.8	14.7	11.4	11.5
Utah.	10.4	7.5	5.2	5.1	10.5	6.0	5.1	5.0	27.3	(B)	(B)	(B)
Vermont.	10.7	6.4	6.0	5.1	10.7	5.9	6.1	4.8	(B)	(B)	(B)	(B)
Virginia.	13.6	10.2	6.9	7.8	11.9	7.4	5.4	5.8	19.8	19.5	12.4	15.4
Washington	11.8	7.8	5.2	4.8	11.5	7.3	4.9	4.3	16.4	20.6	9.4	10.3
West Virginia	11.8	9.9	7.6	7.5	11.4	8.1	7.4	7.0	21.5	(B)	(B)	(B)
Wisconsin	10.3	8.2	6.6	6.5	9.7	7.7	5.5	5.4	18.5	19.0	17.2	15.2
Wyoming	9.8	8.6	6.7	7.4	9.3	7.5	6.5	6.7	25.9	(B)	(B)	(B)
Puerto Rico	(NA)	(NA)	9.7	8.5	(NA)	(NA)	10.2	9.1	(NA)	(NA)	(B)	(B)
Virgin Islands	(NA)	(NA)	13.4	(B)	(NA)	(NA)	(B)	(B)	(B)	(B)	(B)	(B)
Guam.	(NA)	(NA)	5.8	10.3	(NA)	(NA)	(B)	(B)	(B)	(B)	(B)	(B)
American Samoa.	(NA)	(NA)	(B)	(B)	(B)	(B)	(B)	(B)	(B)	(B)	(B)	(B)
Northern Marianas . . .	(NA)	(NA)	(B)	(B)	(B)	(B)	(B)	(B)	(B)	(B)	(B)	(B)

B Base figure too small to meet statistical standards for reliability. NA Not available. [1] Includes other races, not shown separately.

Source: U.S. National Center for Health Statistics, National Vital Statistics Reports (NVSR), *Deaths: Final Data for 2007*, Vol. 58, No. 19, May 2010, and earlier reports.

Table 115. Age-Adjusted Death Rates by Major Causes: 1960 to 2007

[Rates per 100,000 population; see headnote, Table 107. Beginning 1999, deaths classified according to tenth revision of International Classification of Diseases (ICD); for earlier years, causes of death were classified according to the revisions then in use. Changes in classification of causes of death due to these revisions may result in discontinuities in cause-of-death trends. See Appendix III]

Year	Diseases of the heart	Malignant neoplasms (cancer)	Cerebrovascular diseases	Chronic lower respiratory diseases	Accidents [1]	Alzheimer's disease	Diabetes mellitus	Influenza and pneumonia	Nephritis, nephrotic syndrome and nephrosis	Intentional self-harm (suicide)
1960.	559.0	193.9	177.9	12.5	63.1	(NA)	22.5	53.7	10.6	12.5
1961.	545.3	193.4	173.1	12.6	60.6	(NA)	22.1	43.4	10.0	12.2
1962.	556.9	193.3	174.0	14.2	62.9	(NA)	22.6	47.1	9.6	12.8
1963.	563.4	194.7	173.9	16.5	64.0	(NA)	23.1	55.6	9.2	13.0
1964.	543.3	193.6	167.0	16.3	64.1	(NA)	22.5	45.4	8.9	12.7
1965.	542.5	195.6	166.4	18.3	65.8	(NA)	22.9	46.8	8.3	13.0
1966.	541.2	196.5	165.8	19.2	67.6	(NA)	23.6	47.9	7.9	12.7
1967.	524.7	197.3	159.3	19.2	66.2	(NA)	23.4	42.2	7.3	12.5
1968.	531.0	198.8	162.5	20.7	65.5	(NA)	25.3	52.8	6.1	12.4
1969.	516.8	198.5	155.4	20.9	64.9	(NA)	25.1	47.9	6.0	12.7
1970.	492.7	198.6	147.7	21.3	62.2	(NA)	24.3	41.7	5.5	13.1
1971.	492.9	199.3	147.6	21.8	60.3	(NA)	23.9	38.4	5.2	13.1
1972.	490.2	200.3	147.3	22.8	60.2	(NA)	23.7	41.3	5.2	13.3
1973.	482.0	200.0	145.2	23.6	59.3	(NA)	23.0	41.2	5.0	13.1
1974.	458.8	201.5	136.8	23.2	52.7	(NA)	22.1	35.5	4.7	13.2
1975.	431.2	200.1	123.5	23.7	50.8	(NA)	20.3	34.9	4.7	13.6
1976.	426.9	202.5	117.4	24.9	48.7	(NA)	19.5	38.8	4.9	13.2
1977.	413.7	203.5	110.4	24.7	48.8	(NA)	18.2	31.0	4.8	13.7
1978.	409.9	204.9	103.7	26.3	48.9	(NA)	18.3	34.5	4.8	12.9
1979.	401.6	204.0	97.1	25.5	46.5	(NA)	17.5	26.1	8.6	12.6
1980.	412.1	207.9	96.4	28.3	46.4	(NA)	18.1	31.4	9.1	12.2
1981.	397.0	206.4	89.5	29.0	43.4	0.9	17.6	30.0	9.1	12.3
1982.	389.0	208.3	84.2	29.1	40.1	1.3	17.2	26.5	9.4	12.5
1983.	388.9	209.1	81.2	31.6	39.1	2.2	17.6	29.8	9.6	12.4
1984.	378.8	210.8	78.7	32.4	38.8	3.1	17.2	30.6	10.0	12.6
1985.	375.0	211.3	76.6	34.5	38.5	4.1	17.4	34.5	10.4	12.5
1986.	365.1	211.5	73.1	34.8	38.6	4.6	17.2	34.8	10.4	13.0
1987.	355.9	211.7	71.6	35.0	38.2	5.5	17.4	33.8	10.4	12.8
1988.	352.5	212.5	70.6	36.5	38.9	5.8	18.0	37.3	10.4	12.5
1989.	332.0	214.2	66.9	36.6	37.7	6.1	20.5	35.9	9.6	12.3
1990.	321.8	216.0	65.3	37.2	36.3	6.3	20.7	36.8	9.3	12.5
1991.	312.5	215.2	62.9	37.9	34.7	6.3	20.7	34.7	9.3	12.3
1992.	304.0	213.5	61.5	37.7	33.2	6.3	20.7	32.8	9.4	12.0
1993.	308.1	213.5	62.7	40.7	34.2	7.1	21.9	35.0	9.7	12.1
1994.	297.5	211.7	62.6	40.3	34.2	7.7	22.6	33.6	9.4	11.9
1995.	293.4	209.9	63.1	40.1	34.4	8.4	23.2	33.4	9.5	11.8
1996.	285.7	206.7	62.5	40.6	34.5	8.5	23.8	32.9	9.6	11.5
1997.	277.7	203.4	61.1	41.1	34.2	8.7	23.7	33.3	9.8	11.2
1998.	267.4	202.1	62.8	43.8	35.6	8.6	24.2	24.2	9.8	11.1
1999.	266.5	200.8	61.6	45.4	35.3	16.5	25.0	23.5	13.0	10.5
2000.	257.6	199.6	60.9	44.2	34.9	18.1	25.0	23.7	13.5	10.4
2001.	247.8	196.0	57.9	43.7	35.7	19.1	25.3	22.0	14.0	10.7
2002.	240.8	193.5	56.2	43.5	36.9	20.2	25.4	22.6	14.2	10.9
2003.	232.3	190.1	53.5	43.3	37.3	21.4	25.3	22.0	14.4	10.8
2004.	217.0	185.8	50.0	41.1	37.7	21.8	24.5	19.8	14.2	10.9
2005.	211.1	183.8	46.6	43.2	39.1	22.9	24.6	20.3	14.3	10.9
2006.	200.2	180.7	43.6	40.5	39.8	22.6	23.3	17.8	14.5	10.9
2007.	190.9	178.4	42.2	40.8	40.0	22.7	22.5	16.2	14.5	11.3

NA Not available. [1] Unintentional injuries.

Source: U.S. National Center for Health Statistics, *Health, United States, 2009*. See also <http://www.cdc.gov/nchs/hus.htm> and National Vital Statistics Reports (NVSR), *Deaths: Final Data for 2007*, Vol. 58, No. 19, May 2010; and unpublished data.

Table 116. Leading Causes of Deaths by Race: 2006

[Cause of death based on International Classification of Diseases (ICD), tenth edition)]

Cause of death	White Deaths	White Percentage of total deaths	Black Deaths	Black Percentage of total deaths	American Indian/ Alaskan Native Deaths	American Indian/ Alaskan Native Percentage of total deaths	Asian/ Pacific Islander Deaths	Asian/ Pacific Islander Percentage of total deaths
All causes	2,077,549	100.0	289,971	100.0	14,037	100.0	44,707	100.0
Diseases of heart	545,974	26.3	72,253	24.9	2,736	19.5	10,673	23.9
Malignant neoplasms	482,575	23.2	63,082	21.8	2,447	17.4	11,784	26.4
Cerebrovascular diseases	115,864	5.6	17,045	5.9	548	3.9	3,662	8.2
Chronic lower respiratory diseases	114,993	5.5	7,730	2.7	508	3.6	1,352	3.0
Accidents (unintentional injuries)	103,853	5.0	13,917	4.8	1,704	12.1	2,125	4.8
Alzheimer's disease	67,088	3.2	4,455	1.5	169	1.2	720	1.6
Diabetes mellitus	57,204	2.8	12,813	4.4	811	5.8	1,621	3.6
Influenza and pneumonia	49,401	2.4	5,311	1.8	267	1.9	1,347	3.0
Nephritis, nephrotic syndrome and nephrosis	35,793	1.7	8,397	2.9	288	2.1	866	1.9
Intentional self harm (suicide)	30,138	1.5	1,954	0.7	395	2.8	813	1.8
Septicemia	27,373	1.3	6,108	2.1	207	1.5	546	1.2
Chronic liver disease and cirrhosis	24,191	1.2	2,349	0.8	596	4.2	419	0.9
Assault (homicide)	8,860	0.4	9,032	3.1	254	1.8	427	1.0
Human immunodeficiency virus (HIV)	5,103	0.2	6,854	2.4	69	0.5	87	0.2

Source: U.S. National Center for Health Statistics, National Vital Statistics Reports (NVSR), *Deaths: Leading Causes for 2006*, Vol. 58, No.14, March 2010.

Table 117. Leading Causes of Deaths by Hispanic Origin: 2006

[Race and Hispanic origin are reported separately on death certificate. Persons of Hispanic origin may be any race. Cause of death based on International Classification of Diseases (ICD), tenth edition]

Cause of death	Hispanic Deaths	Hispanic Percentage of total deaths	Non-Hispanic Deaths	Non-Hispanic Percentage of total deaths	Non-Hispanic White Deaths	Non-Hispanic White Percentage of total deaths	Non-Hispanic Black Deaths	Non-Hispanic Black Percentage of total deaths
All causes	133,004	100.0	2,288,424	100.0	1,944,617	100.0	286,581	100.0
Diseases of heart	28,921	21.7	601,431	26.3	516,883	26.6	71,461	24.9
Malignant neoplasms	26,633	20.0	532,404	23.3	455,978	23.4	62,475	21.8
Accidents (unintentional injuries)	12,052	9.1	109,172	4.8	91,830	4.7	13,684	4.8
Cerebrovascular diseases	7,005	5.3	129,892	5.7	108,886	5.6	16,882	5.9
Diabetes mellitus	6,287	4.7	66,008	2.9	50,950	2.6	12,671	4.4
Chronic liver disease and cirrhosis	3,592	2.7	23,892	1.0	20,605	1.1	2,310	0.8
Assault (homicide)	3,524	2.6	14,959	0.7	5,408	0.3	8,902	3.1
Chronic lower respiratory diseases	3,310	2.5	121,035	5.3	111,559	5.7	7,657	2.7
Influenza and pneumonia	2,966	2.2	53,249	2.3	46,419	2.4	5,242	1.8
Certain conditions originating in the perinatal period	2,804	2.1	11,494	0.5	6,042	0.3	4,906	1.7
Nephritis, nephrotic syndrome and nephrosis	2,592	1.9	42,668	1.9	33,208	1.7	8,334	2.9
Alzheimer's disease	2,399	1.8	69,948	3.1	64,660	3.3	4,422	1.5
Intentional self harm (suicide)	2,177	1.6	31,035	1.4	27,952	1.4	1,909	0.7
Septicemia	1,829	1.4	32,331	1.4	25,556	1.3	6,045	2.1
Human immunodeficiency virus (HIV)	1,617	1.2	10,427	0.5	3,519	0.2	6,767	2.4

Source: U.S. National Center for Health Statistics, National Vital Statistics Reports (NVSR), *Deaths: Leading Causes for 2006*, Vol. 58, Number 14, March 2010.

Table 118. Deaths and Death Rates by Selected Causes: 2006 and 2007

[Rates per 100,000 population. Figures are weighted data rounded to the nearest individual, so categories may not add to total or subtotal. Excludes deaths of nonresidents of the United States. Deaths classified according to tenth revision of International Classification of Diseases (ICD). See also Appendix III]

Cause of death	2006			2007		
	Number	Rate	Age-adjusted rate [1]	Number	Rate	Age-adjusted rate [1]
All causes [2]	**2,426,264**	**810.4**	**776.5**	**2,423,712**	**803.6**	**760.2**
Major cardiovascular diseases [2]	823,746	275.1	261.2	806,156	267.3	249.9
Diseases of heart	631,636	211.0	200.2	616,067	204.3	190.9
Acute rheumatic fever and chronic rheumatic heart disease	3,257	1.1	1.1	3,201	1.1	1.0
Hypertensive heart disease	29,788	9.9	9.4	30,780	10.2	9.5
Hypertensive heart and renal disease	2,918	1.0	0.9	2,987	1.0	0.9
Ischemic heart disease	425,425	142.1	134.9	406,351	134.7	126.0
Acute myocardial infarction	141,462	47.2	45.0	132,968	44.1	41.4
Other heart diseases	170,248	56.9	53.9	172,748	57.3	53.4
Heart failure	60,337	20.2	18.9	56,565	18.8	17.3
Essential (primary) hypertension and hypertensive renal disease	23,855	8.0	7.5	23,965	7.9	7.4
Cerebrovascular diseases	137,119	45.8	43.6	135,952	45.1	42.2
Atherosclerosis	8,652	2.9	2.7	8,232	2.7	2.5
Malignant neoplasms [2]	559,888	187.0	180.7	562,875	186.6	178.4
Malignant neoplasms of lip, oral cavity, and pharynx	7,720	2.6	2.5	8,067	2.7	2.5
Malignant neoplasms of esophagus	13,686	4.6	4.4	13,592	4.5	4.3
Malignant neoplasms of stomach	11,345	3.8	3.7	11,388	3.8	36.0
Malignant neoplasms of colon, rectum and anus	53,549	17.9	17.2	53,586	17.8	16.9
Malignant neoplasms of liver and intrahepatic bile ducts	16,525	5.5	5.3	17,146	5.7	5.4
Malignant neoplasms of pancreas	33,454	11.2	10.8	34,117	11.3	10.8
Malignant neoplasms of trachea, bronchus and lung	158,664	53.0	51.5	158,760	52.6	50.6
Malignant melanoma of skin	8,441	2.8	2.7	8,461	2.8	2.7
Malignant neoplasm of breast	41,210	13.8	13.2	40,970	13.6	12.9
Malignant neoplasm of ovary	14,857	5.0	4.8	14,621	4.8	4.6
Malignant neoplasm of prostate	28,372	9.5	9.2	29,093	9.6	9.2
Malignant neoplasms of kidney and renal pelvis	12,379	4.1	4.0	12,703	4.2	4.0
Malignant neoplasms of bladder	13,474	4.5	4.3	13,843	4.6	4.4
Malignant neoplasms of meninges, brain and other parts of central nervous system	12,886	4.3	4.2	13,234	4.4	4.2
Malignant neoplasms of lymphoid, hematopoietic and related tissue [2]	55,045	18.4	17.9	54,991	18.2	17.6
Non-Hodgkins' lymphoma	20,594	6.9	6.7	20,528	6.8	6.5
Leukemia	21,944	7.3	7.1	21,825	7.2	7.0
Accidents (unintentional injuries)	121,599	40.6	39.8	123,706	41.0	40.0
Transport accidents [2]	48,412	16.2	16.0	46,844	15.5	15.3
Motor vehicle accidents	45,316	15.1	15.0	43,945	14.6	14.4
Nontransport accidents [2]	73,187	24.4	23.8	76,862	25.5	24.6
Falls	20,823	7.0	6.6	22,631	7.5	7.0
Accidental drowning and submersion	3,579	1.2	1.2	3,443	1.1	1.1
Accidental exposure to smoke, fire and flames	3,109	1.0	1.0	3,286	1.1	1.1
Accidental poisoning and exposure to noxious substances	27,531	9.2	9.1	29,846	9.9	9.8
Chronic lower respiratory diseases [2]	124,583	41.6	40.5	127,924	42.4	40.8
Emphysema	12,551	4.2	4.1	12,790	4.2	4.1
Asthma	3,613	1.2	1.2	3,447	1.1	1.1
Influenza and pneumonia [2]	56,326	18.8	17.8	52,717	17.5	16.2
Pneumonia	55,477	18.5	17.5	52,306	17.3	16.1
Septicemia (blood poisoning)	34,234	11.4	11.0	34,828	11.5	11.0
Viral hepatitis	7,250	2.4	2.3	7,407	2.5	2.3
Human immunodeficiency virus (HIV) disease	12,113	4.0	4.0	11,295	3.7	3.7
Anemias	3,996	1.3	1.3	4,829	1.6	1.5
Diabetes mellitus	72,449	24.2	23.3	71,382	23.7	22.5
Nutritional deficiencies	2,556	0.9	0.8	2,852	0.9	0.9
Malnutrition	2,377	0.8	0.7	2,644	0.9	0.8
Parkinson's disease	19,566	6.5	6.3	20,058	6.7	6.4
Alzheimer's disease	72,432	24.2	22.6	74,632	24.7	22.7
Chronic liver disease and cirrhosis	27,555	9.2	8.8	29,165	9.7	9.1
Alcoholic liver disease	13,050	4.4	4.1	14,406	4.8	4.5
Nephritis, nephrotic syndrome, and nephrosis [2]	45,344	15.1	14.5	46,448	15.4	14.5
Renal failure	43,344	14.5	13.9	43,263	14.3	13.6
Intentional self-harm (suicide)	33,300	11.1	10.9	34,598	11.5	11.3
Intentional self-harm (suicide) by discharge of firearms	16,883	5.6	5.5	17,352	5.8	5.6
Assault (homicide)	18,573	6.2	6.2	18,361	6.1	6.1
Assault (homicide) by discharge of firearms	12,791	4.3	4.3	12,632	4.2	4.2
Events of undetermined intent	5,131	1.7	1.7	5,381	1.8	1.8
Drug-induced deaths [3]	38,396	12.8	12.7	38,371	12.7	12.6
Alcohol-induced deaths [3]	22,073	7.4	7.0	23,199	7.7	7.3

[1] See text, this section. [2] Includes other causes, not shown separately. [3] Included in selected categories.

Source: U.S. National Center for Health Statistics, National Vital Statistics Reports (NVSR), *Deaths: Final Data for 2007*, Vol. 58, No. 19, May 2010.

Table 119. Deaths by Age and Selected Causes: 2007

[Deaths are classified according to the tenth revision of the International Classification of Diseases. See Appendix III]

Cause of death	All ages¹	Under 1 year	1 to 4 years	5 to 14 years	15 to 24 years	25 to 34 years	35 to 44 years	45 to 54 years	55 to 64 years	65 to 74 years	75 to 84 years	85 years and over
All causes²	2,423,712	29,138	4,703	6,147	33,982	42,572	79,606	184,686	287,110	389,238	652,682	713,647
Septicemia	34,828	283	78	74	160	297	910	2,431	4,231	6,345	10,403	9,614
Human immunodeficiency virus (HIV) disease	11,295	5	4	10	160	1,091	3,572	4,156	1,721	448	109	16
Malignant neoplasms²	562,875	72	364	959	1,653	3,463	13,288	50,167	103,171	138,466	163,608	87,656
Malignant neoplasm of esophagus	13,592	–	–	–	5	28	246	1,452	3,379	3,726	3,376	1,380
Malignant neoplasms of colon, rectum, and anus	53,586	–	1	1	35	275	1,302	4,793	9,058	11,634	15,417	11,069
Malignant neoplasms of liver and intrahepatic bile ducts	17,146	6	19	25	38	90	368	2,503	4,181	3,884	4,266	1,766
Malignant neoplasm of pancreas	34,117	–	1	2	5	52	538	2,808	6,507	8,671	10,317	5,217
Malignant neoplasms of trachea, bronchus, and lung	158,760	1	1	4	25	135	1,852	12,480	31,216	48,157	48,358	16,528
Malignant neoplasm of breast	40,970	–	–	–	15	344	2,184	5,990	8,756	8,179	9,075	6,426
Malignant neoplasm of ovary	14,621	–	1	–	28	79	352	1,532	2,997	3,616	3,946	2,071
Malignant neoplasm of prostate	29,093	–	–	–	1	–	21	428	2,271	5,716	11,257	9,397
Malignant neoplasm of bladder	13,883	1	–	–	–	7	93	570	1,564	2,817	5,009	3,782
Malignant neoplasms of lymphoid, hematopoietic and related tissue²	54,991	26	111	352	630	771	1,464	3,606	7,694	12,223	17,884	10,228
Non-Hodgkins lymphoma	20,528	2	5	33	133	206	516	1,392	2,922	4,476	6,868	3,975
Leukemia	21,825	21	106	314	428	438	657	1,362	2,801	4,611	6,858	4,228
Diabetes mellitus	71,382	7	5	21	168	610	1,984	5,753	11,304	15,112	21,189	15,227
Parkinson's disease	20,058	–	–	–	2	–	12	60	396	2,310	9,363	7,911
Alzheimer's disease	74,632	–	–	–	–	1	8	95	728	3,984	23,309	46,804
Major cardiovascular diseases²	806,156	571	230	338	1,369	3,950	14,867	46,280	80,797	115,623	229,350	313,044
Diseases of heart²	616,067	424	173	241	1,084	3,223	11,839	37,434	65,527	89,589	171,257	235,249
Hypertensive heart disease	30,760	1	1	–	44	338	1,372	3,604	4,487	4,009	6,324	10,598
Ischemic heart diseases	406,351	24	8	21	151	1,048	6,219	24,390	46,164	63,027	116,152	149,126
Acute myocardial infarction	132,968	10	4	11	54	400	2,402	9,467	17,835	23,441	37,629	41,711
Heart failure	56,565	21	11	12	43	87	317	1,073	2,758	5,749	15,935	30,558
Essential (primary) hypertension and hypertensive renal disease	23,965	1	1	–	23	85	384	1,235	2,124	3,133	6,442	10,536
Cerebrovascular diseases	135,952	132	52	83	195	505	2,133	6,385	10,500	18,007	41,979	55,975
Influenza and pneumonia	52,717	222	109	103	163	331	784	1,909	3,152	5,547	14,859	25,535
Pneumonia	52,306	209	90	68	153	322	771	1,890	3,115	5,509	14,780	25,396
Chronic lower respiratory diseases²	127,924	43	57	118	149	263	796	4,153	12,777	28,664	48,041	32,857
Emphysema	12,790	3	–	1	1	10	60	486	1,590	3,294	4,835	2,509
Pneumonitis due to solids and liquids	16,988	10	8	16	47	70	154	436	884	1,724	5,187	8,451
Chronic liver disease and cirrhosis	29,165	4	4	–	30	384	2,570	8,212	8,004	5,167	3,694	1,093
Nephritis, nephrotic syndrome, and nephrosis²	46,448	144	22	24	86	261	754	2,233	4,440	7,752	14,711	16,021
Renal failure	43,263	138	16	18	77	237	696	2,091	4,205	7,330	13,718	14,737
Accidents (unintentional injuries)²	123,705	1,285	1,588	2,194	15,897	14,977	16,931	20,315	12,193	8,753	13,736	15,803
Transport accidents	46,844	127	581	1,374	10,928	7,452	6,829	7,199	4,838	3,194	2,983	1,326
Motor vehicle accidents	43,945	124	551	1,285	10,568	7,087	6,370	6,530	4,359	2,940	2,845	1,277
Nontransport accidents	76,862	1,158	1,007	820	4,969	7,525	10,102	13,116	7,355	5,559	10,753	14,477
Falls	22,631	24	36	32	233	334	593	1,304	1,739	2,594	6,552	9,188
Accidental poisoning and exposure to noxious substances	29,846	19	34	81	3,159	5,700	7,575	9,006	3,120	602	355	192
Intentional self-harm (suicide)	34,598	(NA)	(NA)	184	4,140	5,278	6,722	7,778	5,069	2,444	2,119	858
Assault (homicide)	18,361	352	398	346	5,551	4,758	3,052	2,140	980	411	268	80
Assault (homicide) by discharge of firearms	12,632	15	48	201	4,669	3,751	2,038	1,159	446	185	88	23
Enterocolitis due to clostridium difficile	6,372	4	1	1	4	14	31	107	313	876	2,538	2,647

– Represents zero. NA Not available. ¹ Includes persons with age not stated, not shown separately. ² Includes other causes, not shown separately.

Source: U.S. National Center for Health Statistics, National Vital Statistics Reports, *Deaths: Final Data for 2007*, Vol. 58, No. 19, May 2010.

Table 120. Deaths and Death Rates by Leading Causes of Death and Age: 2007

[Rates per 100,000 population in specified group. Data are based on the tenth revision of the International Classification of Diseases (ICD). See Appendix III]

Age and cause of death	Number	Rate	Age and cause of death	Number	Rate
ALL AGES [1]			Accidents	16,931	39.2
All causes	**2,423,712**	**803.6**	Malignant neoplasms	13,288	30.8
Diseases of heart	616,067	204.3	Diseases of heart	11,839	27.4
Malignant neoplasms	562,875	186.6	Intentional self-harm (suicide)	6,722	15.6
Cerebrovascular diseases	135,952	45.1	Human immunodeficiency virus (HIV)		
Chronic lower respiratory diseases	127,924	42.4	disease	3,572	8.3
Accidents (unintentional injuries)	123,706	41.0	Assault (homicide)	3,052	7.1
Alzheimer's disease	74,632	24.7	Chronic liver disease and cirrhosis	2,570	6.0
Diabetes mellitus	71,382	23.7	Cerebrovascular diseases	2,133	4.9
Influenza and pneumonia	52,717	17.5	Diabetes mellitus	1,984	4.6
Nephritis, nephrotic syndrome and			Septicemia	910	2.1
nephrosis	46,448	15.4	**45 TO 54 YEARS**		
Septicemia	34,828	11.5	**All causes**	**184,686**	**420.9**
			Malignant neoplasms	50,167	114.3
1 TO 4 YEARS			Diseases of heart	37,434	85.3
All causes	**4,703**	**28.6**	Accidents	20,315	46.3
Accidents (unintentional injuries)	1,588	9.6	Chronic liver disease and cirrhosis	8,212	18.7
Congenital malformations, deformations			Intentional self-harm (suicide)	7,778	17.7
and chromosomal abnormalities	546	3.3	Cerebrovascular diseases	6,385	14.6
Malignant neoplasms	364	2.2	Diabetes mellitus	5,753	13.1
Assault (homicide)	398	2.4	Human immunodeficiency virus (HIV)		
Diseases of heart	173	1.1	disease	4,156	9.5
Influenza and pneumonia	109	0.7	Chronic lower respiratory diseases	4,153	9.5
Septicemia	78	0.5	Viral hepatitis	2,815	6.4
Certain conditions originating in the			Assault (homicide)	2,140	4.9
perinatal period	70	0.4	Septicemia	2,431	5.5
In situ neoplasms, benign neoplasms					
and neoplasms of uncertain or			**55 TO 64 YEARS**		
unknown behavior	59	0.4	**All causes**	**287,110**	**877.7**
Cerebrovascular diseases	52	0.3	Malignant neoplasms	103,171	315.4
			Diseases of heart	65,527	200.3
5 TO 14 YEARS			Chronic lower respiratory diseases	12,777	39.1
All causes	**6,147**	**15.3**	Accidents (unintentional injuries)	12,193	37.3
Accidents (unintentional injuries)	2,194	5.5	Diabetes mellitus	11,304	34.6
Malignant neoplasms	959	2.4	Cerebrovascular diseases	10,500	32.1
Assault (homicide)	346	0.9	Chronic liver disease and cirrhosis	8,004	24.5
Congenital malformations, deformations			Intentional self-harm (suicide)	5,069	15.5
and chromosomal abnormalities	374	0.9	Nephritis, nephrotic syndrome and		
Diseases of heart	241	0.6	nephrosis	4,440	13.6
Intentional self-harm (suicide)	184	0.5	Septicemia	4,231	12.9
Chronic lower respiratory diseases	118	0.3			
In situ neoplasms, benign neoplasms			**65 TO 74 YEARS**		
and neoplasms of uncertain or			**All causes**	**389,238**	**2,011.3**
unknown behavior	84	0.2	Malignant neoplasms	138,466	715.5
Cerebrovascular diseases	83	0.2	Diseases of heart	89,589	462.9
Septicemia	74	0.2	Chronic lower respiratory diseases	28,664	148.1
			Cerebrovascular diseases	18,007	93.0
15 TO 24 YEARS			Diabetes mellitus	15,112	78.1
All causes	**33,982**	**79.9**	Accidents (unintentional injuries)	8,753	45.2
Accidents (unintentional injuries)	15,897	37.4	Nephritis, nephrotic syndrome and		
Assault (homicide)	5,551	13.1	nephrosis	7,752	40.1
Intentional self-harm (suicide)	4,140	9.7	Septicemia	6,345	32.8
Malignant neoplasms	1,653	3.9	Influenza and pneumonia	5,547	28.7
Diseases of heart	1,084	2.6	Chronic liver disease and cirrhosis	5,167	26.7
Congenital malformations, deformations					
and chromosomal abnormalities	402	0.9	**75 TO 84 YEARS**		
Cerebrovascular diseases	195	0.5	**All causes**	**652,682**	**5,011.6**
Human immunodeficiency virus (HIV)			Diseases of heart	171,257	1,315.0
disease (B20-B24)	160	0.4	Malignant neoplasms	163,608	1,256.3
Influenza and pneumonia	163	0.4	Chronic lower respiratory diseases	48,041	368.9
Pregnancy, childbirth and the puerperium	160	0.4	Cerebrovascular diseases	41,979	322.3
Diabetes mellitus	168	0.4	Alzheimer's disease	23,009	176.7
Septicemia	160	0.4	Diabetes mellitus	21,189	162.7
			Influenza and pneumonia	14,859	114.1
25 TO 34 YEARS			Nephritis, nephrotic syndrome and		
All causes	**42,572**	**104.9**	nephrosis	14,711	113.0
Accidents (unintentional injuries)	14,977	36.9	Accidents (unintentional injuries)	13,736	105.5
Intentional self-harm (suicide)	5,278	13.0	Septicemia	10,403	79.9
Assault (homicide)	4,758	11.7			
Malignant neoplasms	3,463	8.5	**85 YEARS AND OVER**		
Diseases of heart	3,223	7.9	**All causes**	**713,647**	**12,946.5**
Human immunodeficiency virus (HIV)			Diseases of heart	235,249	4,267.7
disease	1,091	2.7	Malignant neoplasms	87,656	1,590.2
Diabetes mellitus	610	1.5	Cerebrovascular diseases	55,975	1,015.5
Cerebrovascular diseases	505	1.2	Alzheimer's disease	46,804	849.1
Congenital malformations, deformations			Chronic lower respiratory diseases	32,857	596.1
and chromosomal abnormalities	417	1.0	Influenza and pneumonia	25,535	463.2
Influenza and pneumonia	331	0.8	Nephritis, nephrotic syndrome and		
Septicemia	297	0.7	nephrosis	16,021	290.6
			Diabetes mellitus	15,227	276.2
35 TO 44 YEARS			Accidents (unintentional injuries)	15,803	286.7
All causes	**79,606**	**184.4**	Septicemia	9,614	174.4

[1] Includes deaths under 1 year of age.

Source: U.S. National Center for Health Statistics, National Vital Statistics Reports (NVSR) *Deaths: Final Data for 2007*, Vol. 58, No. 19, May 2010.

Table 121. Age Adjusted Death Rates for Major Causes of Death—States and Island Areas: 2007

[Age adjusted rates per 100,000 resident population estimated as of July 1. By place of residence. Excludes nonresidents of the United States. Causes of death classified according to tenth revisions of International Classification of Diseases. See text, this section and Appendix III]

State and Island Areas	All causes of death	Diseases of heart	Malig- nant neo- plasms	Cerebro- vascular diseases	Chronic lower respira- tory disease	Accidents Total	Motor vehicle acci- dents	Alz- heimer's disease	Diabetes mellitus	Influ- enza and pneu- monia	Inten- tional self- harm (suicide)
U.S.	**760.2**	**190.9**	**178.4**	**42.2**	**40.8**	**40.0**	**14.4**	**22.7**	**22.5**	**16.2**	**11.3**
AL	930.7	235.5	197.3	54.5	50.2	53.9	25.9	30.1	26.0	17.8	12.5
AK	755.1	147.9	179.9	44.3	44.4	55.3	15.2	20.8	23.4	12.9	22.1
AZ	682.1	152.5	152.8	32.7	40.2	49.4	17.6	29.6	17.4	13.5	16.1
AR	882.8	221.8	200.4	57.4	51.7	47.6	23.7	24.6	26.5	22.3	14.3
CA	674.2	177.9	161.7	42.2	37.4	31.9	11.7	24.3	21.8	18.9	9.8
CO	700.8	145.3	153.7	39.0	49.1	44.2	12.3	27.8	16.7	14.3	16.4
CT	694.1	171.0	170.7	34.2	33.1	35.8	8.7	16.9	15.8	17.6	7.4
DE	773.6	200.2	193.9	39.4	40.1	34.8	13.6	20.9	23.4	12.2	10.7
DC	866.9	239.4	199.1	36.9	22.4	32.4	8.9	21.8	25.2	13.2	5.8
FL	685.9	162.4	166.6	33.6	36.7	46.5	18.1	16.2	21.1	8.6	13.3
GA	839.8	203.0	181.8	49.7	43.8	44.2	18.5	25.3	19.5	18.3	10.7
HI	607.4	140.2	146.2	39.6	19.3	33.3	10.3	14.1	18.5	11.6	9.7
ID	734.6	164.1	165.6	43.2	46.6	43.1	18.5	28.2	22.7	15.1	15.1
IL	759.8	192.8	185.9	43.9	36.7	33.4	10.6	19.9	21.8	18.8	8.5
IN	809.9	203.0	193.2	45.7	49.2	38.7	14.8	24.2	23.4	16.1	12.4
IA	718.6	174.8	177.7	42.1	44.7	37.3	15.0	27.9	20.5	18.0	10.6
KS	783.0	178.7	180.0	46.0	48.8	41.2	15.9	25.2	22.8	19.9	13.7
KY	896.9	220.9	213.5	48.1	59.0	55.1	20.0	27.1	24.1	20.1	15.1
LA	926.4	230.0	200.3	50.1	39.7	57.6	24.0	31.3	33.3	20.3	12.2
ME	773.6	172.9	191.9	40.3	44.8	41.5	14.7	27.9	21.9	14.1	13.7
MD	782.7	202.4	180.7	42.7	35.1	26.2	12.0	16.0	23.4	17.9	9.0
MA	707.5	165.5	179.8	36.5	31.6	30.8	6.7	20.9	16.6	19.5	7.6
MI	806.1	221.5	187.3	44.3	43.6	36.1	12.0	22.1	26.3	15.0	11.0
MN	661.5	129.8	169.7	38.1	32.8	37.4	11.7	19.6	19.6	10.2	10.8
MS	943.0	266.5	200.4	53.0	47.5	61.9	31.6	26.5	21.8	18.3	13.8
MO	826.7	214.4	191.6	40.2	47.4	48.4	17.6	24.3	22.3	18.9	13.5
MT	772.7	163.1	172.1	38.5	55.0	60.2	27.6	22.1	23.1	15.8	19.4
NE	743.7	165.3	177.3	43.1	45.8	35.7	15.7	22.9	23.3	15.1	10.2
NV	803.5	200.0	180.2	38.3	47.5	48.4	16.0	12.3	12.9	18.4	18.3
NH	727.0	174.9	184.5	34.3	44.0	38.5	10.3	28.9	20.1	14.5	11.1
NJ	724.2	191.9	180.4	35.8	31.3	26.8	8.2	18.0	24.4	13.7	6.7
NM	755.9	159.2	157.3	39.2	43.6	66.7	19.2	15.5	32.7	14.6	20.4
NY	686.4	225.1	168.0	28.2	30.8	25.3	7.4	8.8	17.5	20.0	7.0
NC	834.4	191.0	189.0	50.3	47.1	48.3	20.0	27.7	23.4	18.4	11.7
ND	679.5	164.1	165.3	37.3	32.9	39.3	17.5	40.4	28.3	14.6	14.4
OH	830.8	204.8	197.9	45.3	50.7	41.1	12.1	27.4	29.1	13.3	11.0
OK	920.4	241.6	198.2	53.8	61.2	58.4	20.4	23.0	29.3	20.1	14.7
OR	753.9	156.9	179.3	43.6	46.3	41.5	13.0	27.6	27.0	11.1	15.2
PA	790.1	199.4	188.2	42.9	38.1	40.9	12.5	19.8	22.0	15.2	11.2
RI	750.0	203.6	179.6	33.5	32.7	34.6	7.6	22.2	19.2	16.1	8.7
SC	849.7	192.9	186.7	53.4	44.0	53.0	24.2	30.9	26.2	15.8	11.7
SD	693.5	159.1	171.3	38.7	47.0	41.8	18.3	30.2	25.6	17.9	12.5
TN	885.2	220.6	200.3	53.9	49.2	52.1	21.0	35.9	26.2	22.5	13.3
TX	777.7	191.9	170.3	49.0	41.2	41.4	16.2	24.7	24.9	16.1	10.4
UT	694.2	152.1	128.8	38.9	31.9	34.4	12.4	20.5	27.6	16.0	15.4
VT	729.3	161.2	188.5	37.6	44.9	44.7	10.9	28.4	24.4	9.8	13.8
VA	770.6	182.7	182.7	44.5	37.7	38.1	13.9	23.4	19.7	16.6	11.2
WA	722.2	167.3	177.7	41.4	42.4	39.8	9.9	40.7	23.2	11.1	13.0
WV	951.7	229.4	207.6	48.9	58.6	65.9	23.6	23.1	35.5	17.8	15.9
WI	732.3	171.9	177.9	42.3	38.7	43.8	14.2	24.3	18.3	15.5	12.7
WY	802.0	178.3	174.4	39.5	56.5	57.0	25.3	21.0	26.2	20.9	19.7
PR [1]	726.7	138.4	121.3	41.3	27.9	29.9	11.0	40.7	66.5	25.6	6.9
VI [1]	700.2	234.7	109.2	36.8	(S)	30.7	(S)	(S)	45.4	(S)	(S)
GU [1]	694.9	228.4	122.3	50.1	23.2	26.2	16.0	(S)	44.0	(S)	16.0
AS [1]	1,054.4	278.0	150.1	94.2	(S)	(S)	(S)	(S)	126.1	(S)	(S)
MP [1]	913.0	167.0	239.5	(S)	(S)	(S)	(S)	(S)	(S)	(S)	(S)

S Figure does not meet standards of reliability or precision. [1] Age-adjusted death rates for Puerto Rico, Virgin Islands, American Samoa, and Northern Marianas are calculated using different age groups in the weighting procedure. See source "Technical Notes."

Source: U.S. National Center for Health Statistics, National Vital Statistics Reports, (NVSR), *Deaths: Final Data for 2007*, Vol. 58, No. 19, May 2010.

U.S. Census Bureau, Statistical Abstract of the United States: 2011

Table 122. Death Rates From Heart Disease by Selected Characteristics: 1980 to 2007

[Rates per 100,000 population. See headnote Tables 107 and 115. See Appendix III]

Characteristics	1980	1990	2000	2002	2003	2004	2005	2006	2007
All ages, age adjusted [1]	**412.1**	**321.8**	**257.6**	**240.8**	**232.3**	**217.0**	**211.1**	**200.2**	**190.9**
All ages, crude rate [2]	**336.0**	**289.5**	**252.6**	**241.7**	**235.6**	**222.2**	**220.0**	**211.0**	**204.3**
Under 1 year	22.8	20.1	13.0	12.4	11.0	10.3	8.7	8.4	10.0
1 to 4 years	2.6	1.9	1.2	1.1	1.2	1.2	0.9	1.0	1.1
5 to 14 years	0.9	0.9	0.7	0.6	0.6	0.6	0.6	0.6	0.6
15 to 24 years	2.9	2.5	2.6	2.5	2.7	2.5	2.7	2.5	2.6
25 to 34 years	8.3	7.6	7.4	7.9	8.2	7.9	8.1	8.2	7.9
35 to 44 years	44.6	31.4	29.2	30.5	30.7	29.3	28.9	28.3	27.4
45 to 54 years	180.2	120.5	94.2	93.7	92.5	90.2	89.7	88.0	85.3
55 to 64 years	494.1	367.3	261.2	241.5	233.2	218.8	214.8	207.3	200.3
65 to 74 years	1,218.6	894.3	665.6	615.9	585.0	541.6	518.9	490.3	462.9
75 to 84 years	2,993.1	2,295.7	1,780.3	1,677.2	1,611.1	1,506.3	1,460.8	1,383.1	1,315.0
85 years and over	7,777.1	6,739.9	5,926.1	5,446.8	5,278.4	4,895.9	4,778.4	4,480.8	4,267.1
Male, age adjusted [1]	**538.9**	**412.4**	**320.0**	**297.4**	**286.6**	**267.9**	**260.9**	**248.5**	**237.7**
White	539.6	409.2	316.7	294.1	282.9	264.6	258.0	245.2	234.8
Black	561.4	485.4	392.5	371.0	364.3	342.1	329.8	320.6	305.9
American Indian, Alaska Native	320.5	264.1	222.2	201.2	203.2	182.7	173.2	170.2	159.8
Asian, Pacific Islander	286.9	220.7	185.5	169.8	158.3	146.5	141.1	136.3	126.0
Hispanic origin [3]	(NA)	270.0	238.2	219.8	206.8	193.9	192.4	175.2	165.0
Non-Hispanic, White [3]	(NA)	413.6	319.9	297.7	286.9	268.7	262.2	250.0	239.8
Male, crude rate [2]	**368.6**	**297.6**	**249.8**	**240.7**	**235.0**	**222.8**	**221.1**	**214.0**	**208.4**
Under 1 year	25.5	21.9	13.3	12.9	12.1	10.9	9.4	8.8	10.9
1 to 14 years	2.8	1.9	1.4	1.1	1.1	1.1	1.0	1.1	1.0
5 to 14 years	1.0	0.9	0.8	0.7	0.7	0.6	0.6	0.7	0.6
15 to 24 years	3.7	3.1	3.2	3.3	3.4	3.2	3.6	3.3	3.2
25 to 34 years	11.4	10.3	9.6	10.5	10.5	10.5	10.8	11.2	10.5
35 to 44 years	68.7	48.1	41.4	43.1	42.8	40.9	40.7	39.5	38.6
45 to 54 years	282.6	183.0	140.2	138.4	136.2	132.3	131.5	128.9	124.6
55 to 64 years	746.8	537.3	371.7	343.4	331.7	312.8	306.9	296.8	288.8
65 to 74 years	1,728.0	1,250.0	898.3	827.1	785.3	723.8	692.3	660.5	624.9
75 to 84 years	3,834.3	2,968.2	2,248.1	2,110.1	2,030.3	1,893.6	1,829.4	1,743.5	1,656.5
85 years and over	8,752.7	7,418.4	6,430.0	5,823.5	5,621.5	5,239.3	5,143.4	4,819.9	4,621.8
Female, age adjusted [1]	**320.8**	**257.0**	**210.9**	**197.2**	**190.3**	**177.3**	**172.3**	**162.2**	**154.0**
White	315.9	250.9	205.6	192.1	185.4	172.9	168.2	158.6	150.5
Black	378.6	327.5	277.6	263.2	253.8	236.5	228.3	212.5	204.5
American Indian, Alaska Native	175.4	153.1	143.6	123.6	127.5	119.9	115.9	113.2	99.8
Asian, Pacific Islander	132.3	149.2	115.7	108.1	104.2	96.1	91.9	87.3	82.0
Hispanic origin [3]	(NA)	177.2	163.7	149.7	145.8	130.0	129.1	118.9	111.8
Non-Hispanic, White [3]	(NA)	252.6	206.8	193.7	187.1	175.1	170.3	160.9	153.0
Female, crude rate [2]	**305.1**	**281.8**	**255.3**	**242.7**	**236.2**	**221.6**	**218.9**	**208.0**	**200.2**
Under 1 year	20.0	18.3	12.5	11.8	9.8	9.7	8.0	7.9	9.0
1 to 14 years	2.5	1.9	1.0	1.0	1.3	1.2	0.9	0.9	1.1
5 to 14 years	0.9	0.8	0.5	0.6	0.5	0.6	0.6	0.6	0.6
15 to 24 years	2.1	1.8	2.1	1.7	2.1	1.7	1.7	1.8	1.9
25 to 34 years	5.3	5.0	5.2	5.2	5.7	5.2	5.3	5.1	5.3
35 to 44 years	21.4	15.1	17.2	18.0	18.6	17.7	17.1	17.0	16.2
45 to 54 years	84.5	61.0	49.8	50.6	50.2	49.6	49.2	48.5	47.2
55 to 64 years	272.1	215.7	159.3	147.2	141.9	131.5	129.1	124.1	117.9
65 to 74 years	828.6	616.8	474.0	440.1	417.5	388.6	372.7	346.3	325.4
75 to 84 years	2,497.0	1,893.8	1,475.1	1,389.7	1,331.1	1,245.6	1,210.5	1,136.7	1,079.7
85 years and over	7,350.5	6,478.1	5,720.9	5,283.3	5,126.7	4,741.5	4,610.8	4,322.1	4,099.3

NA Not available. [1] Age-adjusted death rates were prepared using the direct method, in which age-specific death rates for a population of interest are applied to a standard population distributed by age. Age adjustment eliminates the differences in observed rates between points in time or among compared population groups that result from age differences in population composition. [2] The total number of deaths in a given time period divided by the total resident population as of July 1. [3] Persons of Hispanic origin may be any race. Prior to 1997 excludes data from states lacking an Hispanic-origin item on their death certificates. See text, this section.

Source: U.S. National Center for Health Statistics, *Health, United States, 2009.* See also <http://cdc.gov/nchs/hus.htm>.

Table 123. Death Rates From Cerebrovascular Diseases by Sex and Age: 1990 to 2007

[Rates per 100,000 population. See headnote, Tables 107 and 115. See Appendix III]

Characteristics	Total				Male				Female			
	1990	2000	2005	2007	1990	2000	2005	2007	1990	2000	2005	2007
All ages, age adjusted [1]	**65.3**	**60.9**	**46.6**	**42.2**	**68.5**	**62.4**	**46.9**	**42.5**	**62.6**	**59.1**	**45.6**	**41.3**
All ages, crude rate [2]	**57.8**	**59.6**	**48.4**	**45.1**	**46.7**	**46.9**	**38.8**	**36.4**	**68.4**	**71.8**	**57.8**	**53.5**
Under 1 year	3.8	3.3	3.1	3.1	4.4	3.8	3.5	3.5	3.1	2.7	2.6	2.6
1 to 4 years	0.3	0.3	0.4	0.3	0.3	(B)	0.5	0.2	0.3	0.4	0.3	0.4
5 to 14 years	0.2	0.2	0.2	0.2	0.2	0.2	0.3	0.2	0.2	0.2	0.2	0.2
15 to 24 years	0.6	0.5	0.5	0.5	0.7	0.5	0.4	0.5	0.6	0.5	0.5	0.4
25 to 34 years	2.2	1.5	1.4	1.2	2.1	1.5	1.5	1.2	2.2	1.5	1.2	1.3
35 to 44 years	6.4	5.8	5.2	4.9	6.8	5.8	5.2	5.3	6.1	5.7	5.1	4.6
45 to 54 years	18.7	16.0	15.0	14.6	20.5	17.5	16.5	16.2	17.0	14.5	13.6	12.9
55 to 64 years	47.9	41.0	33.0	32.1	54.3	47.2	38.5	38.0	42.2	35.3	27.9	26.6
65 to 74 years	144.2	128.6	101.1	93.0	166.6	145.0	113.6	105.2	126.7	115.1	90.5	82.7
75 to 84 years	498.0	461.3	359.0	322.3	551.1	490.8	372.9	333.2	466.2	442.1	349.5	314.9
85 years and over	1,628.9	1,589.2	1,141.8	1,015.5	1,528.5	1,484.3	1,023.3	895.7	1,667.6	1,632.0	1,196.1	1,072.4

B Figure too small to meet statistical standards for reliability. [1] See footnote 1, Table 122. [2] The total number of deaths in a given time period divided by the total resident population as of July 1.

Source: U.S. National Center for Health Statistics, *Health, United States, 2009.* See also <http://cdc.gov/nchs/hus.htm>.

Table 124. Death Rates From Malignant Neoplasms by Selected Characteristics: 1990 to 2007

[Rates per 100,000 population. Excludes deaths of nonresidents of the United States. Beginning 1999, deaths classified according to tenth revision of International Classification of Diseases (ICD); for earlier years, causes of death were classified according to the revisions then in use. Changes in classification of causes of death due to these revisions may result in discontinuities in cause-of-death trends. For explanation of age adjustment, see text, this section. See Appendix III]

Characteristic	1990	2000	2003	2004	2005	2006	2007
All ages, age adjusted [1]	**216.0**	**199.6**	**190.1**	**185.8**	**183.8**	**180.7**	**178.4**
All ages, crude [2]	**203.2**	**196.5**	**191.5**	**188.6**	**188.7**	**187.0**	**186.6**
Under 1 year	2.3	2.4	1.9	1.8	1.8	1.8	1.7
1 to 4 years	3.5	2.7	2.5	2.5	2.3	2.3	2.2
5 to 14 years	3.1	2.5	2.6	2.5	2.5	2.2	2.4
15 to 24 years	4.9	4.4	4.0	4.1	4.1	3.9	3.9
25 to 34 years	12.6	9.8	9.4	9.1	9.0	9.0	8.5
35 to 44 years	43.3	36.6	35.0	33.4	33.2	31.9	30.8
45 to 54 years	158.9	127.5	122.2	119.0	118.6	116.3	114.3
55 to 64 years	449.6	366.7	343.0	333.4	326.9	321.1	315.4
65 to 74 years	872.3	816.3	770.3	755.1	742.7	727.2	715.5
75 to 84 years	1,348.5	1,335.6	1,302.5	1,280.4	1,274.8	1,263.8	1,256.3
85 years old and over	1,752.9	1,819.4	1,698.2	1,653.3	1,637.7	1,606.1	1,590.2
AGE-ADJUSTED RATES							
Male.	280.4	248.9	233.3	227.7	225.1	220.1	217.5
Female.	175.7	167.6	160.9	157.4	155.6	153.6	151.3
White male.	272.2	243.9	230.1	224.4	222.3	217.9	215.1
Black male.	397.9	340.3	308.8	301.2	293.7	284.9	282.3
American Indian, Alaska Native male	145.8	155.8	139.9	147.1	147.6	135.5	139.4
Asian, Pacific Islander male	172.5	150.8	137.2	136.3	133.0	126.7	130.2
Hispanic male [3]	174.7	171.7	156.5	151.2	152.7	143.4	141.4
Non-Hispanic, White male [3]	276.7	247.7	234.6	229.2	227.3	223.4	(NA)
White female	174.0	166.9	160.2	157.0	155.2	153.6	151.2
Black female	205.9	193.8	187.7	182.5	179.6	176.1	174.9
American Indian, Alaska Native female	106.9	108.3	105.6	108.6	105.9	108.3	102.1
Asian, Pacific Islander female	103.0	100.7	96.7	92.0	94.5	92.2	90.0
Hispanic female [3]	111.9	110.8	105.9	101.4	101.9	100.4	98.6
Non-Hispanic, White female [3]	177.5	170.0	163.8	160.9	159.1	157.6	(NA)
DEATH RATES FOR MALIGNANT NEOPLASM OF BREASTS FOR FEMALES							
All ages, age adjusted [1]	33.3	29.4	26.6	24.4	24.1	23.5	22.9
All ages, crude [2]	34.0	31.3	28.9	27.5	27.3	26.9	26.5
Under 25 years	(B)	(B)	(B)	(B)	(B)	(B)	(B)
25 to 34 years	2.9	2.6	2.2	2.0	1.8	1.8	1.7
35 to 44 years	17.8	14.1	12.0	11.3	11.3	10.8	10.1
45 to 54 years	45.4	38.3	32.9	29.3	28.7	27.6	26.7
55 to 64 years	78.6	66.8	59.2	55.8	54.5	53.7	51.3
65 to 74 years	111.7	98.3	88.9	81.6	79.2	76.9	77.3
75 to 84 years	146.3	137.6	128.9	119.5	119.2	119.2	116.3
85 years old and over	196.8	201.7	200.8	178.6	177.9	169.9	170.4
DEATH RATES FOR MALIGNANT NEOPLASM OF TRACHEA, BRONCHUS, AND LUNG							
All ages, age adjusted [1]	37.1	41.3	41.3	40.9	40.5	40.0	50.6
All ages, crude [2]	39.4	45.4	46.1	45.9	45.9	45.7	52.6
Under 25 years	(Z)	(Z)	(Z)	(Z)	(Z)	(Z)	0.1
25 to 34 years	0.5	0.5	0.4	0.3	0.3	0.4	0.3
35 to 44 years	5.2	5.3	5.1	5.2	5.1	4.5	4.3
45 to 54 years	34.5	25.0	24.4	24.2	24.5	24.6	28.4
55 to 64 years	105.0	93.3	87.1	83.9	80.7	78.2	95.4
65 to 74 years	177.6	206.9	204.8	205.0	199.6	197.0	248.8
75 to 84 years	190.1	265.6	279.4	277.0	280.9	280.3	371.3
85 years old and over	138.1	212.8	221.0	221.3	226.2	226.9	299.8

B Base figure too small to meet statistical standards for reliability of a derived figure. NA Not available. Z Less than 0.05. [1] See footnote 1, Table 122. [2] The total number of deaths in a given time period divided by the total population as of July 1. [3] Excludes data from states lacking an Hispanic-origin item on their death certificates. See text, this section.

Source: U.S. National Center for Health Statistics, *Health, United States, 2009.* See also <http://www.cdc.gov/nchs/hus.htm>.

Table 125. Death Rates From Suicide by Selected Characteristics: 1990 to 2007

[Rates per 100,000 population. Excludes deaths of nonresidents of the United States. Beginning 2000, deaths classified according to tenth revision of International Classification of Diseases. See Appendix III]

Characteristic	1990	2000	2003	2004	2005	2006	2007
All ages, age adjusted [1]	**12.5**	**10.4**	**10.8**	**10.9**	**10.9**	**10.9**	**11.3**
All ages, crude rate [2]	**12.4**	**10.4**	**10.8**	**11.0**	**11.0**	**11.1**	**11.5**
Under 1 year	(X)	(X)	(X)	(X)	(X)	(X)	(X)
1 to 4 years	(X)	(X)	(X)	(X)	(X)	(X)	(X)
5 to 14 years	0.8	0.7	0.6	0.7	0.7	0.5	0.5
15 to 24 years	13.2	10.2	9.7	10.3	10.0	9.9	9.7
25 to 44 years	15.2	13.4	13.8	13.9	13.7	13.8	14.3
45 to 64 years	15.3	13.5	15.0	15.4	15.4	16.0	16.8
65 to 74 years	17.9	12.5	12.7	12.3	12.6	12.6	12.6
75 to 84 years	24.9	17.6	16.4	16.3	16.9	15.9	16.3
85 years and over	22.2	19.6	16.9	16.4	16.9	15.9	15.6
AGE-ADJUSTED RATES							
Male	21.5	17.7	18.0	18.0	18.0	18.0	18.4
Female	4.8	4.0	4.2	4.5	4.4	4.5	4.7
White male	22.8	19.1	19.6	19.6	19.6	19.6	20.2
Black male	12.8	10.0	9.2	9.6	9.2	9.4	8.8
American Indian, Alaska Native male	20.1	16.0	16.6	18.7	18.9	18.3	18.1
Asian, Pacific Islander male	9.6	8.6	8.5	8.4	7.3	7.9	9.0
Hispanic male [3]	13.7	10.3	9.7	9.8	9.4	8.8	10.1
Non-Hispanic, White male [3]	23.5	20.2	21.0	21.0	21.2	21.4	21.9
White female	5.2	4.3	4.6	5.0	4.9	5.1	5.2
Black female	2.4	1.8	1.9	1.8	1.9	1.4	1.7
American Indian, Alaska Native female	3.6	3.8	3.5	5.9	4.6	5.1	4.9
Asian, Pacific Islander female	4.1	2.8	3.1	3.5	3.3	3.4	3.5
Hispanic female [3]	2.3	1.7	1.7	2.0	1.8	1.8	1.9
Non-Hispanic, White female [3]	5.4	4.7	5.0	5.4	5.3	5.6	5.7

X Not applicable. [1] Age-adjusted death rates were prepared using the direct method, in which age-specific death rates for a population of interest are applied to a standard population distributed by age. Age adjustment eliminates the differences in observed rates between points in time or among compared population groups that result from age differences in population composition. [2] The total number of deaths in a given time period divided by the total resident population as of July 1.
[3] Persons of Hispanic origin may be any race. Excludes data from states lacking an Hispanic-origin item on their death certificates.
Source: U.S. National Center for Health Statistics, *Health, United States, 2009*. See also <http://www.cdc.gov/nchs/hus.htm>.

Table 126. Death Rates From Human Immunodeficiency Virus (HIV) disease by Selected Characteristics

[Rates per 100,000 population. Excludes deaths of nonresidents of the United States. Beginning 2000, deaths classified according to tenth revision of International Classification of Diseases. See Appendix III]

Characteristic	1990	2000	2003	2004	2005	2006	2007
All ages, age adjusted [1]	**10.2**	**5.2**	**4.7**	**4.5**	**4.2**	**4.0**	**3.7**
All ages, crude [2]	**10.1**	**5.1**	**4.7**	**4.4**	**4.2**	**4.0**	**3.7**
Under 1 year	2.7	(B)	(B)	(B)	(B)	(B)	(B)
1 to 4 years	0.8	(B)	(B)	(B)	(B)	(B)	(B)
5 to 14 years	0.2	0.1	0.1	0.1	(B)	(B)	(B)
15 to 24 years	1.5	0.5	0.4	0.5	0.4	0.5	0.4
25 to 34 years	19.7	6.1	4.0	3.7	3.3	2.9	2.7
35 to 44 years	27.4	13.1	12.0	10.9	9.9	9.2	8.3
45 to 54 years	15.2	11.0	10.9	10.6	10.6	10.1	9.5
55 to 64 years	6.2	5.1	5.4	5.4	5.3	5.5	5.3
65 to 74 years	2.0	2.2	2.4	2.4	2.3	2.5	2.3
75 to 84 years	0.7	0.7	0.7	0.8	0.8	0.8	0.8
85 years and over	(B)	(B)	(B)	(B)	(B)	(B)	(B)
AGE-ADJUSTED RATES							
Male	18.5	7.9	7.1	6.6	6.2	5.9	5.4
Female	2.2	2.5	2.4	2.4	2.3	2.2	2.1
White male	15.7	4.6	4.2	3.8	3.6	3.4	3.1
Black male	46.3	35.1	31.3	29.2	28.2	26.3	24.5
American Indian, Alaska Native male	3.3	3.5	3.5	4.3	4.0	3.3	3.6
Asian, Pacific Islander male	4.3	1.2	1.1	1.2	1.0	1.1	0.8
Hispanic male [3]	28.8	10.6	9.2	8.2	7.5	7.0	6.3
Non-Hispanic, White male [3]	14.1	3.8	3.4	3.1	3.0	2.8	2.5
White female	1.1	1.0	0.9	0.9	0.8	0.7	0.7
Black female	10.1	13.2	12.8	13.0	12.0	12.2	11.3
American Indian, Alaska Native female	(B)	1.0	1.5	1.5	1.5	1.5	1.7
Asian, Pacific Islander female	(B)	0.2	(B)	(B)	(B)	(B)	(B)
Hispanic female [3]	3.8	2.9	2.7	2.4	1.9	1.9	1.8
Non-Hispanic, White female [3]	0.7	0.7	0.6	0.6	0.6	0.6	0.5

B Base figure too small to meet statistical standards. [1] Age-adjusted death rates were prepared using the direct method, in which age-specific death rates for a population of interest are applied to a standard population distributed by age. Age adjustment eliminates the differences in observed rates between points in time or among compared population groups that result from age differences in population composition. [2] The total number of deaths in a given time period divided by the total resident population as of July 1. [3] Persons of Hispanic origin may be any race. Excludes data from states lacking an Hispanic-origin item on their death certificates.
Source: U.S. National Center for Health Statistics, *Health, United States, 2009*. See also <http://www.cdc.gov/nchs/hus.htm>.

Table 127. Deaths—Life Years Lost and Mortality Costs by Age, Sex, and Cause: 2007

[2,424 represents 2,424,000. Life years lost: Number of years person would have lived in absence of death. Mortality cost: value of lifetime earnings lost by persons who die prematurely]

Characteristics	Number of deaths (1,000)	Life years lost [1]		Mortality cost [2]	
		Total (1,000)	Per death	Total (mil. dol.)	Per death (dol.)
2007, total [3]	**2,424**	**40,818**	**16.8**	**583,618**	**240,815**
Under 5 years	34	2,624	77.5	38,535	1,138,699
5 to 14 years	6	432	70.3	8,496	1,382,118
15 to 24 years	34	2,021	59.5	57,179	1,682,634
25 to 44 years	122	5,437	44.5	169,893	1,390,540
45 to 64 years	409	12,842	31.4	260,417	636,449
65 years and over	1,818	17,462	9.6	49,098	27,004
Heart disease	616	8,163	13.3	92,451	150,073
Cancer	563	10,573	18.8	146,054	259,482
Cerebrovascular diseases	136	1,598	11.8	14,866	109,352
Accidents and adverse effects	124	4,112	33.3	104,100	841,739
Other	985	16,372	16.6	226,147	229,594
Male	**1,204**	**21,809**	**18.1**	**414,563**	**344,375**
Under 5 years	19	1,426	75.3	23,427	1,237,768
5 to 14 years	4	244	68.2	5,370	1,497,810
15 to 24 years	25	1,473	58.2	44,863	1,772,114
25 to 44 years	80	3,461	43.3	122,768	1,536,573
45 to 64 years	288	7,480	26.0	183,288	636,255
65 years and over	788	7,725	9.8	34,847	44,221
Heart disease	310	4,500	14.5	71,307	230,172
Cancer	293	5,709	19.5	100,577	343,440
Cerebrovascular diseases	54	629	11.6	9,374	173,243
Accidents and adverse effects	80	2,780	34.8	80,665	1,010,899
Other	467	8,191	17.5	152,640	326,672
Female	**1,220**	**19,009**	**15.6**	**169,055**	**138,604**
Under 5 years	15	1,198	80.3	15,107	1,012,972
5 to 14 years	3	188	73.3	3,126	1,220,231
15 to 24 years	9	549	63.3	12,316	1,421,237
25 to 44 years	42	1,976	46.7	47,126	1,114,587
45 to 64 years	121	5,362	44.3	77,129	636,911
65 years and over	1,030	9,737	9.5	14,251	13,833
Heart disease	306	3,663	12.0	21,144	69,044
Cancer	270	4,864	18.0	45,477	168,423
Cerebrovascular diseases	82	969	11.8	5,492	67,111
Accidents and adverse effects	44	1,332	30.4	23,435	534,105
Other	518	8,181	15.8	73,507	141,980

[1] Based on life expectancy at year of death. [2] Cost estimates based on the person's age, sex, life expectancy at the time of death, labor force participation rates, annual earnings, value of homemaking services, and a 3 percent discount rate by which to convert to present worth the potential aggregate earnings lost over the years. [3] Total excludes 201 deaths for which age is unknown.

Source: Wendy Max and Yanling Shi, Institute for Health & Aging, University of California San Francisco, CA., unpublished data.

Table 128. Percent Reaching Stated Anniversary, by Sex and Year of Marriage, for First and Second Marriages: 2004

[In percent except number of marriages. Data are for first marriages only]

Sex and year of marriage	Number of marriages (1,000)	Anniversary [1]							
		5th	10th	15th	20th	25th	30th	35th	40th
FIRST MARRIAGES									
Men									
1955 to 1959	**3,884**	**96.4**	**88.3**	**80.3**	**73.8**	**70.4**	**67.3**	**64.7**	**61.4**
1960 to 1964 [2]	4,602	95.1	85.0	75.2	69.7	65.0	62.4	59.7	52.5
1965 to 1969 [2]	6,161	90.5	76.9	67.4	62.3	58.6	55.5	48.2	(X)
1970 to 1974 [2]	7,075	88.5	74.4	64.6	58.1	53.8	46.2	(X)	(X)
1975 to 1979 [2]	7,001	88.1	73.0	65.2	59.6	49.5	(X)	(X)	(X)
1980 to 1984 [2]	7,625	88.7	73.7	65.3	53.8	(X)	(X)	(X)	(X)
1985 to 1989 [2]	7,838	89.3	76.4	60.6	(X)	(X)	(X)	(X)	(X)
1990 to 1994 [2]	8,070	89.4	70.0	(X)	(X)	(X)	(X)	(X)	(X)
Women									
1955 to 1959	**4,890**	**94.0**	**86.8**	**79.4**	**72.4**	**67.2**	**63.5**	**58.9**	**54.7**
1960 to 1964 [2]	5,548	92.8	82.3	72.7	66.5	60.4	56.1	52.7	44.9
1965 to 1969 [2]	7,023	89.5	74.9	65.7	60.0	55.1	51.3	43.8	(X)
1970 to 1974 [2]	8,139	87.1	71.6	61.4	55.4	50.6	42.1	(X)	(X)
1975 to 1979 [2]	7,714	85.3	70.0	61.4	55.7	46.4	(X)	(X)	(X)
1980 to 1984 [2]	8,058	86.5	70.7	63.1	52.4	(X)	(X)	(X)	(X)
1985 to 1989 [2]	8,064	85.7	73.0	56.9	(X)	(X)	(X)	(X)	(X)
1990 to 1994 [2]	8,546	87.2	69.2	(X)	(X)	(X)	(X)	(X)	(X)

X Not applicable. [1] People reaching stated anniversary for specified marital order. [2] Approximately 10 percent of the cohort has not reached the stated age by the end of the latest specified time period. Because of this, estimates for this group for the highest anniversary are low.

Source: U.S. Census Bureau, Survey of Income and Program Participation (SIPP) Reports, "Number, Timing and Duration of Marriages and Divorces: 2004," <http://www.census.gov/population/www/soodemo/marr-div/2004detailed_tables.html>.

Births, Deaths, Marriages, and Divorces 95

Table 129. Marriages and Divorces—Number and Rate by State: 1990 to 2008

[2,443.5 represets 2,443,500. By place of occurrence. See Appendix III]

State	Marriages [1]						Divorces [3]					
	Number (1,000)			Rate per 1,000 population [2]			Number (1,000)			Rate per 1,000 population [2]		
	1990	2000	2008	1990	2000	2008	1990	2000	2008	1990	2000	2008
United States [4]	**2,443.5**	**2,329.0**	**2,157.0**	**9.8**	**8.3**	**5.4**	**1,182**	**(NA)**	**(NA)**	**4.7**	**4.1**	**(NA)**
Alabama	43.1	45.0	40.6	10.6	10.3	(NA)	25.3	23.5	20.3	6.1	5.4	(NA)
Alaska	5.7	5.6	5.8	10.2	8.9	(NA)	2.9	2.7	3.0	5.5	4.4	(NA)
Arizona [5]	36.8	38.7	37.8	10.0	7.9	(NA)	25.1	21.6	24.0	6.9	4.4	(NA)
Arkansas	36.0	41.1	30.5	15.3	16.0	(NA)	16.8	17.9	15.8	6.9	6.9	(NA)
California	237.1	196.9	247.0	7.9	5.9	(NA)	128.0	(NA)	(NA)	4.3	(NA)	(NA)
Colorado	32.4	35.6	36.0	9.8	8.6	(NA)	18.4	(NA)	21.0	5.5	(NA)	(NA)
Connecticut	26.0	19.4	19.1	7.9	5.9	(NA)	10.3	6.5	12.0	3.2	2.0	(NA)
Delaware	5.6	5.1	4.8	8.4	6.7	(NA)	3.0	3.2	3.1	4.4	4.2	(NA)
District of Columbia	5.0	2.8	2.4	8.2	5.4	(NA)	2.7	1.5	1.6	4.5	3.0	(NA)
Florida	141.8	141.9	147.9	10.9	9.3	(NA)	81.7	81.9	79.9	6.3	5.3	(NA)
Georgia	66.8	56.0	57.4	10.3	7.1	(NA)	35.7	30.7	(NA)	5.5	3.9	(NA)
Hawaii	18.3	25.0	25.5	16.1	21.2	(NA)	5.2	4.6	(NA)	4.6	3.9	(NA)
Idaho	14.1	14.0	14.6	13.9	11.0	(NA)	6.6	6.9	7.4	6.5	5.4	(NA)
Illinois	100.6	85.5	74.9	8.8	7.0	(NA)	44.3	39.1	32.5	3.8	3.2	(NA)
Indiana	53.2	34.5	51.7	9.6	5.8	(NA)	(NA)	(NA)	(NA)	(NA)	(NA)	(NA)
Iowa	24.9	20.3	19.6	9.0	7.0	(NA)	11.1	9.4	7.8	3.9	3.3	(NA)
Kansas	22.7	22.2	18.8	9.2	8.3	(NA)	12.6	10.6	10.0	5.0	4.0	(NA)
Kentucky	49.8	39.7	33.9	13.5	10.0	(NA)	21.8	21.6	19.7	5.8	5.4	(NA)
Louisiana	40.4	40.5	30.0	9.6	9.3	(NA)	(NA)	(NA)	(NA)	(NA)	(NA)	(NA)
Maine	11.9	10.5	9.8	9.7	8.3	(NA)	5.3	5.8	5.6	4.3	4.6	(NA)
Maryland	46.3	40.0	33.6	9.7	7.7	(NA)	16.1	17.0	16.2	3.4	3.3	(NA)
Massachusetts	47.7	37.0	36.9	7.9	6.0	(NA)	16.8	18.6	12.9	2.8	3.0	(NA)
Michigan	76.1	37.0	55.5	8.2	6.7	(NA)	40.2	39.4	33.5	4.3	4.0	(NA)
Minnesota	33.7	66.4	28.6	7.7	6.9	(NA)	15.4	14.8	(NA)	3.5	3.1	(NA)
Mississippi	24.3	33.4	15.2	9.4	7.1	(NA)	14.4	14.4	12.7	5.5	5.2	(NA)
Missouri	49.1	19.7	40.1	9.6	7.9	(NA)	26.4	26.5	22.1	5.1	4.8	(NA)
Montana	6.9	43.7	7.5	8.6	7.4	(NA)	4.1	2.1	4.0	5.1	2.4	(NA)
Nebraska	12.6	6.6	12.4	8.0	7.8	(NA)	6.5	6.4	5.9	4.0	3.8	(NA)
Nevada	120.6	13.0	112.2	99.0	76.7	(NA)	13.3	18.1	16.9	11.4	9.6	(NA)
New Hampshire	10.5	144.3	9.0	9.5	9.5	(NA)	5.3	7.1	5.1	4.7	5.8	(NA)
New Jersey	58.7	11.6	46.7	7.6	6.1	(NA)	23.6	25.6	25.8	3.0	3.1	(NA)
New Mexico [5]	13.3	50.4	8.0	8.8	8.3	(NA)	7.7	9.2	8.1	4.9	5.3	(NA)
New York [5]	154.8	14.5	126.9	8.6	8.9	(NA)	57.9	62.8	53.2	3.2	3.4	(NA)
North Carolina	51.9	162.0	64.3	7.8	8.5	(NA)	34.0	36.9	35.6	5.1	4.8	(NA)
North Dakota	4.8	65.6	4.3	7.5	7.3	(NA)	2.3	2.0	1.9	3.6	3.2	(NA)
Ohio	98.1	4.6	68.9	9.0	7.9	(NA)	51.0	49.3	38.1	4.7	4.4	(NA)
Oklahoma	33.2	88.5	26.0	10.6	4.6	(NA)	24.9	12.4	19.4	7.7	3.7	(NA)
Oregon	25.3	15.6	26.1	8.9	7.8	(NA)	15.9	16.7	14.8	5.5	5.0	(NA)
Pennsylvania	84.9	26.0	70.0	7.1	6.1	(NA)	40.1	37.9	34.4	3.3	3.2	(NA)
Rhode Island	8.1	73.2	6.5	8.1	8.0	(NA)	3.8	3.1	2.8	3.7	3.1	(NA)
South Carolina	55.8	8.0	33.3	15.9	10.9	(NA)	16.1	14.4	12.8	4.5	3.7	(NA)
South Dakota	7.7	7.1	6.2	11.1	9.6	(NA)	2.6	2.7	2.4	3.7	3.6	(NA)
Tennessee	68.0	88.2	58.5	13.9	15.9	(NA)	32.3	33.8	25.5	6.5	6.1	(NA)
Texas	178.6	196.4	177.0	10.5	9.6	(NA)	94.0	85.2	79.8	5.5	4.2	(NA)
Utah	19.4	24.1	23.9	11.2	11.1	(NA)	8.8	9.7	10.0	5.1	4.5	(NA)
Vermont	6.1	6.1	4.9	10.9	10.2	(NA)	2.6	5.1	2.3	4.5	8.6	(NA)
Virginia	71.0	62.4	56.3	11.4	9.0	(NA)	27.3	30.2	29.5	4.4	4.3	(NA)
Washington	46.6	40.9	41.6	9.5	7.0	(NA)	28.8	27.2	25.7	5.9	4.7	(NA)
West Virginia	13.0	15.7	13.0	7.2	8.7	(NA)	9.7	9.3	8.9	5.3	5.2	(NA)
Wisconsin	38.9	36.1	31.4	7.9	6.8	(NA)	17.8	17.6	16.9	3.6	3.3	(NA)
Wyoming	4.9	4.9	4.7	10.7	10.3	(NA)	3.1	2.8	2.7	6.6	5.9	(NA)

NA Not available. [1] Data are counts of marriages performed, except as noted. [2] Based on total population residing in area; population enumerated as of April 1 for 1990 and 2000; estimated as of July 1 for all other years. [3] Includes annulments. Includes divorce petitions filed or legal separations for some counties or states. [4] U.S. total for the number of divorces is an estimate which includes states not reporting. Beginning 2000, divorce rates based solely on the combined counts and populations for reporting states and the District of Columbia. [5] Some figures for marriages are marriage licenses issued.

Source: U.S. National Center for Health Statistics, National Vital Statistics Reports (NVSR), *Births, Marriages, Divorces, and Deaths: Provisional Data for 2009*, Vol. 58, No. 25, August 2010, and prior reports.

This section presents statistics on health expenditures and insurance coverage, including Medicare and Medicaid, medical personnel, hospitals, nursing homes and other care facilities, injuries, diseases, disability status, nutritional intake of the population, and food consumption. Summary statistics showing recent trends on health care and discussions of selected health issues are published annually by the U.S. National Center for Health Statistics (NCHS) in *Health, United States*. Data on national health expenditures, medical costs, and insurance coverage are compiled by the U.S. Centers for Medicare & Medicaid Services (CMS) and appear on the CMS Web site at <http://www.cms.gov /NationalHealthExpendData/> and in the annual *Medicare and Medicaid Statistical Supplement* to the *Health Care Financing Review*. Statistics on health insurance are also collected by NCHS and are published in Series 10 of *Vital and Health Statistics*. NCHS also conducts periodic surveys of nutrient levels in the population, including estimates of food and nutrient intake, overweight and obesity, hypercholesterolemia, hypertension, and clinical signs of malnutrition. Data are published in Series 10 and 11 of *Vital and Health Statistics*. Statistics on hospitals are published annually by the Health Forum, L.L.C.; an American Hospital Association (AHA) company, in AHA Hospital Statistics. The primary source for data on nutrition and on annual per capita consumption of food is *Diet Quality and Food Consumption*, issued by the U.S. Department of Agriculture. Data are available on the Web site at <http://www.ers.usda.gov/Briefing /DietQuality>.

National health expenditures— CMS compiles estimates of national health expenditures (NHE) to measure spending for health care in the United States. The NHE accounts are structured to show spending by type of expenditure (i.e., hospital care, physician and clinical care, dental care, and other professional care; home health care; retail sales of prescription drugs; other medical nondurables; vision products and other medical durables; nursing home care and other personal health expenditures; plus other health expenditures such as public health activities, administration, and the net cost of private health insurance; plus medical sector investment, the sum of noncommercial medical research and capital formation in medical sector structures and equipment; and by source of funding (e.g., private health insurance, out-of-pocket payments, and a range of public programs including Medicare, Medicaid, and those operated by the U.S. Department of Veterans Affairs (VA)).

Data used to estimate health expenditures come from existing sources, which are tabulated for other purposes. The type of expenditure estimates rely upon statistics produced by such groups as the AHA, the Census Bureau, and the U.S. Department of Health and Human Services (HHS). Source of funding estimates are constructed using administrative and statistical records from the Medicare and Medicaid programs, the U.S. Department of Defense and VA medical programs, the Social Security Administration, Census Bureau's *Governmental Finances*, state and local governments, other HHS agencies, and other nongovernment sources.

Medicare, Medicaid, and CHIP— Since July 1966, the federal Medicare program has provided two coordinated plans for nearly all people aged 65 and over: (1) a hospital insurance plan, which covers hospital and related services and (2) a voluntary supplementary medical insurance plan, financed partially by monthly premiums paid by participants, which partly covers physicians' and related medical services. Such insurance also applies, since July 1973, to disabled beneficiaries of any age after 24 months of entitlement to cash benefits under the social security or railroad retirement programs and to persons with end stage renal disease. On January 1, 2006,

Medicare began to provide coverage for prescription drugs as mandated by the Medicare Prescription Drug, Improvement, and Modernization Act of 2003 (MMA). This benefit is available on a voluntary basis to everyone with Medicare, and beneficiaries pay a monthly premium to enroll in one of Medicare's prescription drug plans.

Medicaid is a health insurance program for certain low-income people. These include: certain low-income families with children; people on supplemental security income; certain low-income pregnant women and children; and people who have very high medical bills. There are special rules for those who live in nursing homes and for disabled children living at home. Medicaid is funded and administered through a state/federal partnership. Although there are broad federal requirements for Medicaid, states have a wide degree of flexibility to design their program. The Children's Health Insurance Program Reauthorization Act of 2009 (CHIPRA or Public Law 111-3) reauthorized the Children's Health Insurance Program (CHIP). The program went into effect on April 1, 2009. CHIP replaces the State Children's Health Insurance Program (SCHIP). It will preserve coverage for the millions of children who rely on CHIP today and provides the resources for states to reach millions of additional uninsured children. CHIP was designed as a federal/state partnership, similar to Medicaid, with the goal of expanding health insurance to children whose families earn too much money to be eligible for Medicaid, but not enough money to purchase private insurance.

Health resources—Hospital statistics based on data from AHA's yearly survey are published annually in *AHA Hospital Statistics* and cover all hospitals accepted for registration by the Association. To be accepted for registration, a hospital must meet certain requirements relating to number of beds, construction, equipment, medical and nursing staff, patient care, clinical records, surgical and obstetrical facilities, diagnostic and treatment facilities, laboratory services, etc. Data obtained from NCHS cover all

U.S. hospitals that meet certain criteria for inclusion. The criteria are published in *Vital and Health Statistics* reports, Series 13. Statistics on the demographic characteristics of persons employed in the health occupations are compiled by the U.S. Bureau of Labor Statistics and reported in *Employment and Earnings* (monthly) (see Table 615, Section 12, Labor Force, Employment, and Earnings). Data based on surveys of health personnel and utilization of health facilities providing long-term care, ambulatory care, emergency room care, and hospital care are presented in NCHS Series 13, data from the National Health Interview Survey. Statistics on patient visits to health care providers, as reported in health interviews, appear in NCHS Series 10, data from the National Health Care Survey.

The CMS's *Health Care Financing Review* and its annual *Medicare and Medicaid Statistical Supplement* present data for hospitals and nursing homes as well as extended care facilities and home health agencies. These data are based on records of the Medicare program and differ from those of other sources because they are limited to facilities meeting federal eligibility standards for participation in Medicare.

Disability and illness—General health statistics, including morbidity, disability, injuries, preventive care, and findings from physiological testing are collected by NCHS in its National Health Interview Survey and its National Health and Nutrition Examination Surveys and appear in *Vital and Health Statistics*, Series 10 and 11, respectively. Annual incidence data on notifiable diseases are compiled by the Public Health Service (PHS) at its Centers for Disease Control and Prevention in Atlanta, Georgia, and are published as a supplement to its *Morbidity and Mortality Weekly Report* (MMWR). The list of diseases is revised annually and includes those which, by mutual agreement of the states and PHS, are communicable diseases of national importance.

Statistical reliability—For discussion of statistical collection, estimation, and sampling procedures and measures of reliability applicable to data from NCHS and CMS, see Appendix III.

Table 130. National Health Expenditures—Summary, 1960 to 2008, and Projections, 2009 to 2019

[In billions of dollars (27 represents $27,000,000,000). Excludes Puerto Rico and Island Areas]

Year	Total expenditures [1]	Private expenditures Total [2]	Private expenditures Out-of-pocket	Private expenditures Insurance	Public expenditures Total	Public expenditures Federal	Public expenditures State and local	Health services and supplies Total [3]	Hospital care	Physician and clinical services	Prescription drugs	Nursing home care
1960	27	21	13	6	7	3	4	25	9	5	3	1
1961	29	22	13	6	7	3	4	26	10	6	3	1
1962	32	24	14	7	8	4	4	29	11	6	3	1
1963	35	26	15	8	9	4	5	31	12	7	3	1
1964	39	29	17	9	10	4	5	34	13	8	3	1
1965	42	32	18	10	10	5	6	37	14	8	4	1
1966	46	32	18	10	14	8	6	41	16	9	4	2
1967	52	33	18	10	19	12	7	47	18	10	4	2
1968	59	37	21	12	22	14	8	53	21	11	5	3
1969	66	41	23	13	25	16	9	59	24	12	5	3
1970	75	47	25	15	28	18	10	67	28	14	5	4
1971	83	51	26	18	32	21	12	74	31	16	6	5
1972	93	57	29	21	36	23	13	83	34	17	6	5
1973	103	63	32	23	40	25	15	93	38	19	7	6
1974	117	69	34	26	47	30	17	106	45	22	7	7
1975	133	77	37	30	56	36	19	121	52	25	8	8
1976	152	89	41	37	63	43	20	139	60	28	9	10
1977	173	102	45	45	71	47	23	159	67	33	9	12
1978	194	114	48	52	80	54	26	179	76	35	10	14
1979	220	128	52	60	91	61	30	203	87	41	11	16
1980	253	147	58	69	106	72	35	233	101	47	12	18
1981	294	171	65	81	123	83	39	271	118	55	13	21
1982	331	195	72	94	136	92	44	305	134	61	15	23
1983	365	215	78	105	150	103	47	336	145	68	17	26
1984	402	238	86	119	163	113	50	371	155	77	20	28
1985	439	262	95	131	177	123	54	409	165	90	22	31
1986	471	277	103	136	194	133	61	439	177	100	24	34
1987	513	301	109	149	212	144	68	478	190	112	27	36
1988	574	344	119	176	230	155	75	535	207	127	31	40
1989	639	383	125	205	256	174	82	596	227	142	35	46
1990	714	427	136	234	287	194	93	667	252	158	40	53
1991	782	456	140	255	326	223	102	731	277	175	44	58
1992	849	485	143	275	364	253	111	794	300	190	48	62
1993	912	512	145	295	400	279	121	853	317	201	51	65
1994	962	526	143	308	436	304	132	900	330	211	54	68
1995	1,017	551	146	325	465	328	138	953	341	221	61	74
1996	1,068	580	152	343	489	348	140	1,002	352	229	68	80
1997	1,125	614	162	359	512	365	146	1,054	365	241	78	84
1998	1,190	662	175	385	528	372	156	1,111	376	256	89	90
1999	1,265	709	184	417	556	390	166	1,180	395	270	105	91
2000	1,353	756	193	455	596	418	179	1,264	417	289	121	95
2001	1,469	807	200	498	662	465	197	1,376	451	313	138	102
2002	1,602	881	211	551	722	509	213	1,498	488	338	158	106
2003	1,735	957	225	605	779	552	227	1,623	527	367	174	110
2004	1,855	1,015	235	646	840	600	240	1,734	566	394	189	115
2005	1,983	1,083	248	691	900	641	258	1,852	608	422	200	121
2006	2,113	1,137	255	728	976	710	266	1,975	649	447	217	125
2007	2,240	1,201	270	760	1,039	755	283	2,090	688	473	227	132
2008	2,339	1,232	278	783	1,107	817	290	2,181	718	496	234	138
2009, proj	2,472	1,269	284	809	1,203	919	285	2,306	761	528	246	144
2010, proj	2,570	1,304	292	829	1,266	966	300	2,395	789	536	260	149
2011, proj	2,703	1,353	300	862	1,350	985	365	2,519	827	556	275	156
2012, proj	2,850	1,407	311	894	1,444	1,057	386	2,655	876	582	288	164
2013, proj	3,025	1,484	327	942	1,541	1,131	410	2,817	932	612	303	173
2014, proj	3,225	1,584	348	1,005	1,642	1,207	435	3,003	996	647	322	183
2015, proj	3,442	1,697	372	1,076	1,744	1,282	462	3,202	1,063	684	344	194
2016, proj	3,684	1,814	395	1,149	1,870	1,376	493	3,426	1,138	728	368	205
2017, proj	3,936	1,926	417	1,220	2,010	1,483	527	3,660	1,213	777	395	218
2018, proj	4,204	2,040	441	1,291	2,164	1,601	563	3,909	1,292	828	425	231
2019, proj	4,483	2,154	466	1,361	2,328	1,728	600	4,170	1,374	882	458	246

[1] Includes medical research and medical facilities construction, not shown separately. [2] Includes other private expenditures, not shown separately. [3] Includes other objects of expenditure, not shown separately.

Source: U.S. Centers for Medicare & Medicaid Services, Office of the Actuary, "National Health Statistics Group," <http://www.cms.hhs.gov/NationalHealthExpendData/>.

Table 131. National Health Expenditures by Type: 1990 to 2008

[In billions of dollars (714.2 represents $714,200,000,000), except percent. Excludes Puerto Rico and Island Areas]

Type of expenditure	1990	2000	2003	2004	2005	2006	2007	2008
Total	**714.2**	**1,352.9**	**1,735.2**	**1,855.4**	**1,982.5**	**2,112.5**	**2,239.7**	**2,338.7**
Annual percent change [1]	11.8	6.9	8.3	6.9	6.9	6.6	6.0	4.4
Percent of gross domestic product	12.3	13.6	15.6	15.6	15.7	15.8	15.9	16.2
Private expenditures	**427.4**	**756.5**	**956.6**	**1,015.5**	**1,082.8**	**1,136.8**	**1,201.0**	**1,232.0**
Health services and supplies	401.0	705.5	894.0	947.6	1,008.5	1,058.7	1,112.6	1,138.1
Out-of-pocket payments	136.1	192.6	224.7	234.8	247.5	254.9	270.3	277.8
Insurance premiums [2]	233.7	454.8	604.6	646.1	691.0	727.6	759.7	783.2
Other	31.1	58.0	64.7	66.6	70.0	76.1	82.6	77.2
Medical research	1.0	2.5	3.3	3.4	3.7	4.0	4.3	4.7
Medical structures and equipment [3]	25.4	48.5	59.3	64.5	70.5	74.2	84.1	89.2
Public expenditures	**286.8**	**596.4**	**778.6**	**839.9**	**899.8**	**975.7**	**1,038.7**	**1,106.7**
Percent federal of public	67.6	70.0	70.9	71.4	71.3	72.7	72.7	73.8
Health services and supplies	265.8	558.6	729.5	786.0	843.4	916.8	977.1	1,043.1
Medicare [4]	109.5	224.4	282.4	311.3	339.8	403.4	432.2	469.2
Public assistance medical payments [5]	78.7	207.4	282.3	303.4	325.3	325.1	345.0	362.0
Temporary disability insurance [6]	0.1	0.1	0.1	0.1	0.1	0.1	0.1	0.1
Workers' compensation, medical [6]	17.4	25.3	31.8	32.4	32.2	32.2	33.0	33.1
Defense Dept. hospital, medical	10.4	13.7	21.8	24.5	26.2	29.1	31.7	33.1
Maternal, child health programs	1.7	2.7	2.7	2.6	2.6	2.7	2.7	2.7
Public health activities	20.0	43.0	53.6	53.8	56.4	60.6	64.8	69.4
Veterans' hospital, medical care	10.8	18.9	26.3	27.7	29.6	31.7	33.8	38.1
Medical vocational rehabilitation	0.3	0.4	0.5	0.5	0.5	0.5	0.5	0.5
State and local hospitals [7]	13.2	13.7	16.8	17.9	18.8	19.4	20.7	22.1
Other [8]	3.8	9.0	11.3	11.8	11.8	12.0	12.6	12.8
Medical research	11.7	23.0	32.1	35.5	37.0	37.8	38.2	38.9
Medical structures and equipment [3]	9.2	14.7	17.0	18.4	19.4	21.1	23.5	24.7

[1] Change from immediate prior year. [2] Covers insurance benefits and amount retained by insurance companies for expenses, additions to reserves, and profits (net cost of insurance). [3] Represents expenditures for total medical sector acquisitions of structures and equipment including structures that house medical professionals' offices. [4] Represents expenditures for benefits and administrative cost from federal hospital and medical insurance trust funds under Old Age, Survivors, Disability and Health Insurance (OASDHI) programs; see text, this section. [5] Payments made directly to suppliers of medical care (primarily Medicaid). [6] Includes medical benefits paid under public law by private insurance carriers, state governments, and self-insurers. [7] Expenditures not offset by other revenues. [8] Covers expenditures for Substance Abuse and Mental Health Services Administration, Indian Health Service; school health and other programs.

Source: U. S. Centers for Medicare & Medicaid Services, Office of the Actuary, "National Health Expenditure Group," <http://www.cms.hhs.gov/NationalHealthExpendData/>.

Table 132. National Health Expenditures by Object, 1990 to 2008, and Projections, 2009

[In billions of dollars (714.2 represents $714,200,000,000). Excludes Puerto Rico and Island Areas]

Object of expenditure	1990	2000	2003	2004	2005	2006	2007	2008	2009 proj.
Total	**714.2**	**1,352.9**	**1,735.2**	**1,855.4**	**1,982.5**	**2,112.5**	**2,239.7**	**2,338.7**	**2,472.2**
Spent by—									
Consumers	369.9	647.4	829.3	881.0	938.5	982.5	1,030.0	1,060.9	1,092.3
Out-of-pocket	136.1	192.6	224.7	234.8	247.5	254.9	270.3	277.8	283.5
Private insurance	233.7	454.8	604.6	646.1	691.0	727.6	759.7	783.2	808.7
Public	286.8	596.4	778.6	839.9	899.8	975.7	1,038.7	1,106.7	1,203.4
Other [1]	57.5	109.0	127.3	134.5	144.3	154.3	171.0	171.1	176.5
Spent for—									
Health services and supplies	666.8	1,264.1	1,623.5	1,733.6	1,851.9	1,975.4	2,089.7	2,181.3	2,306.2
Personal health care expenses	607.6	1,139.2	1,447.5	1,549.9	1,655.2	1,762.9	1,866.4	1,952.3	2,068.3
Hospital care	251.6	416.9	527.4	566.5	607.5	649.4	687.6	718.4	760.6
Physician and clinical services	157.5	288.6	366.7	393.6	422.4	446.5	472.6	496.2	527.6
Dental services	31.5	62.0	76.9	81.5	86.3	90.7	96.4	101.2	104.4
Other professional services [2]	18.2	39.1	49.0	52.9	55.9	58.4	62.2	65.7	69.6
Home health care	12.6	30.5	38.0	42.7	48.1	53.0	59.3	64.7	72.2
Prescription drugs	40.3	120.6	174.2	188.8	199.7	217.0	226.8	234.1	246.3
Other nondurable medical products	22.5	29.8	32.1	32.7	34.0	35.3	37.4	39.0	40.8
Durable medical equipment [3]	11.3	19.4	22.4	22.8	23.8	24.7	25.5	26.6	27.0
Nursing home care	52.6	95.3	110.5	115.2	120.7	125.1	132.4	138.4	144.1
Other personal health care	9.6	37.1	50.4	53.3	56.9	62.7	66.3	68.1	75.7
Public administration and net cost of private health insurance [4]	39.3	81.8	122.3	129.8	140.3	152.0	158.4	159.6	162.8
Public health activities	20.0	43.0	53.6	53.8	56.4	60.6	64.8	69.4	75.2
Medical research [5]	12.7	25.6	35.5	38.9	40.7	41.8	42.5	43.6	48.0
Medical structures and equipment [6]	34.7	63.2	76.3	83.0	90.0	95.3	107.5	113.9	117.9

[1] Includes nonpatient revenues, privately funded construction, and industrial inplant. [2] Includes services of registered and practical nurses in private duty, podiatrists, optometrists, physical therapists, clinical psychologists, chiropractors, naturopaths, and Christian Science practitioners. [3] Includes expenditures for eyeglasses, hearing aids, orthopedic appliances, artificial limbs, crutches, wheelchairs, etc. [4] Includes administrative expenses of federally financed health programs. [5] Research and development expenditures of drug companies and other manufacturers and providers of medical equipment and supplies are excluded from research expenditures, but are included in the expenditure class in which the product falls. [6] Represents expenditures for total medical sector acquisitions of structures and equipment including structures that house medical professionals' offices.

Source: U.S. Centers for Medicare & Medicaid Services, Office of the Actuary, "National Health Statistics Group," <http://www.cms.hhs.gov/NationalHealthExpendData/>.

Table 133. Health Services and Supplies—Per Capita Consumer Expenditures by Object: 1990 to 2008

[In dollars, except percent. Based on U.S. Census Bureau estimates of total U.S. population as of July 1, excluding Armed Forces and federal employees abroad and civilian population of outlying areas. Excludes research, structures, and equipment]

Object of expenditure	1990	1995	2000	2003	2004	2005	2006	2007	2008
Total, national [1]	**2,627**	**3,545**	**4,474**	**5,588**	**5,912**	**6,260**	**6,612**	**6,926**	**7,164**
Annual percent change [2]	10.6	4.7	6.1	7.4	5.8	5.9	5.6	4.7	3.4
Hospital care	991	1,268	1,476	1,815	1,932	2,053	2,174	2,279	2,359
Physician and clinical services	621	821	1,022	1,262	1,342	1,428	1,495	1,566	1,629
Dental services	124	166	219	265	278	292	304	319	332
Other professional services [3]	72	106	138	169	180	189	195	206	216
Home health care	50	114	108	131	146	163	178	197	212
Prescription drugs	159	227	427	600	644	675	726	752	769
Other nondurable medical products	88	95	106	110	112	115	118	124	128
Durable medical equipment [3]	44	57	69	77	78	80	83	85	87
Nursing home care	207	276	337	380	393	408	419	439	455
Other personal health care	38	86	131	173	182	192	210	220	224
Public administration and net cost of private health insurance	155	216	290	421	443	474	509	525	524
Public health activities	79	115	152	185	184	191	203	215	228
Total, private consumer [4]	**1,457**	**1,753**	**2,292**	**2,855**	**3,004**	**3,172**	**3,289**	**3,414**	**3,484**
Hospital care	430	443	558	706	753	796	856	890	927
Physician and clinical services	384	491	597	742	789	851	891	934	959
Dental services	120	158	209	248	261	274	285	299	308
Other professional services [3]	49	68	88	106	113	116	120	126	131
Home health care	20	39	44	36	37	38	38	39	41
Prescription drugs	130	178	329	439	465	489	479	486	483
Other nondurable medical products	86	90	100	104	105	108	111	116	120
Durable medical equipment [3]	36	44	53	54	55	57	58	60	60
Nursing home care	87	99	130	135	135	137	140	150	155
Net cost of private health insurance	115	144	184	284	293	308	311	314	302

[1] Includes private and public health expenditures. [2] Change from immediate prior year. [3] See footnotes for corresponding objects in Table 132. [4] Represents out-of-pocket payments and private health insurance.

Source: U. S. Centers for Medicare and Medicaid Services, Office of the Actuary, "National Health Statistics Group," <http://www.cms.hhs.gov/NationalHealthExpendData/>.

Table 134. Public Expenditures for Health Services and Supplies: 2008

[In millions of dollars (1,043,129 represents $1,043,129,000,000). Excludes Puerto Rico and Island Areas. Excludes research, structures, and equipment]

Type of selected service	Total	Federal	State and local	Medicare [2] (OASDHI)	Workers' compensation [3]	Public assistance [4]	Defense Dept. [5]	Veterans
Total [1]	**1,043,129**	**773,984**	**269,145**	**469,209**	**33,107**	**361,962**	**33,064**	**38,077**
Hospital care	409,050	330,701	78,349	211,326	6,989	128,148	16,062	26,518
Physician and clinical services	172,296	144,634	27,662	102,722	11,982	39,569	6,888	4,345
Prescription drugs	87,031	72,505	14,526	52,081	3,233	23,914	5,179	2,429
Nursing home care	86,170	62,110	24,061	25,731		56,782	–	3,650
Public administration and net cost of private health insurance	65,933	45,538	20,396	24,897	8,016	29,062	3,385	209
Public health activities	69,431	10,464	58,967	–	–	–	–	–

– Represents zero. [1] Includes other items not shown separately. [2] Covers hospital and medical insurance payments and administrative costs under Old-Age, Survivors, Disability and Health Insurance (OASDHI) program. [3] Medical benefits. [4] Covers Medicaid and other medical public assistance. Excludes funds paid into Medicare trust fund by states to cover premiums for public assistance recipients and medically indigent persons. [5] Includes care for retirees and military dependents.

Source: U. S. Centers for Medicare and Medicaid Services, Office of the Actuary, "National Health Statistics Group," <http://www.cms.hhs.gov/NationalHealthExpendData/>.

Table 135. Personal Health Care—Third–Party Payments and Private Consumer Expenditures, 1990 to 2008, and Projections, 2009

[In billions of dollars (607.6 represents $607,600,000,000), except percent. See headnote, Table 136]

Item	1990	2000	2003	2004	2005	2006	2007	2008	2009, proj.
Personal health care expenditures	607.6	1,139.2	1,447.5	1,549.9	1,655.2	1,762.9	1,866.4	1,952.3	2,068.3
Third–party payments, total	**471.4**	**946.6**	**1,222.8**	**1,315.1**	**1,407.7**	**1,508.0**	**1,596.1**	**1,674.5**	**1,784.8**
Percent of personal health care	77.6	83.1	84.5	84.8	85.0	85.5	85.5	85.8	86.3
Private insurance payments	204.7	402.8	522.0	560.3	599.8	634.6	665.1	691.2	718.5
Public expenditures	236.2	486.8	637.3	689.4	739.3	798.8	850.1	907.8	989.2
Other [1]	30.5	57.0	63.5	65.3	68.7	74.6	81.0	75.5	77.1
Private consumer expenditures [2]	**340.8**	**595.4**	**746.7**	**795.1**	**847.3**	**889.5**	**935.4**	**969.0**	**1,002.1**
Percent met by private insurance	60.1	67.6	69.9	70.5	70.8	71.3	71.1	71.3	71.7
Hospital care	109.2	157.8	205.0	220.7	235.5	255.7	268.4	282.2	291.6
Percent met by private insurance	89.6	91.3	91.6	91.6	91.6	91.8	91.7	91.8	92.0
Physician and clinical services	97.4	168.8	215.7	231.4	251.6	266.3	282.0	291.9	306.3
Percent met by private insurance	69.0	80.9	82.6	82.7	82.6	82.6	82.5	82.8	83.1
Prescription drugs	33.0	92.9	127.5	136.2	144.6	143.1	146.7	147.0	149.8
Percent met by private insurance	32.2	64.0	65.4	66.1	66.3	67.2	66.7	67.0	67.3

[1] Includes nonpatient revenues and industrial inplant health services. [2] Includes expenditures, not shown separately. Represents out-of-pocket payments and private health insurance benefits. Excludes net cost of insurance.

Source: U. S. Centers for Medicare and Medicaid Services, Office of the Actuary, "National Health Statistics Group," <http://www.cms.hhs.gov/NationalHealthExpendData/>.

U.S. Census Bureau, Statistical Abstract of the United States: 2011

Table 136. Personal Health Care Expenditures by Object and Source of Payment: 2008

[In millions of dollars (1,952,255 represents $1,952,255,000,000). Excludes Puerto Rico and Island Areas. Covers all expenditures for health services and supplies, except net cost of insurance and administration, public health activities, and administration for government and philanthropic agencies for fund-raising activities]

Object of expenditure	Total	Private Payments					Public	Third party pay- ments [2]
		Total	Consumer			Other [1]		
			Total	Out-of- pocket payments	Private health insurance			
Total....................	1,952,255	1,044,490	968,957	277,778	691,179	75,533	907,765	1,674,477
Hospital care...............	718,360	309,310	282,209	23,197	259,013	27,101	409,050	695,164
Physician and clinical services ..	496,165	323,869	291,919	50,117	241,802	31,950	172,296	446,048
Dental services	101,230	93,907	93,773	44,606	49,167	134	7,323	56,624
Other professional services [3]....	65,700	43,336	39,797	16,419	23,378	3,539	22,364	49,281
Home health care	64,666	13,535	12,368	6,555	5,813	1,167	51,131	58,111
Prescription drugs	234,073	147,042	147,042	48,528	98,513	–	87,031	185,544
Other nondurable medical products..................	38,976	36,502	36,502	36,502	–	–	2,473	2,473
Durable medical equipment [3]....	26,556	18,141	18,141	14,947	3,194	–	8,415	11,609
Nursing home care	138,447	52,277	47,206	36,908	10,299	5,071	86,170	101,540
Other personal health care	68,083	6,571	–	–	–	6,571	61,511	68,082

– Represents zero. [1] Includes nonpatient revenues and industrial inplant. [2] Covers private health insurance, other private payments (excluding out-of-pocket payments) and government. [3] See footnotes for corresponding objects on Table 132.

Source: U.S. Centers for Medicare and Medicaid Services, Office of the Actuary, "National Health Statistics Group," <http://www.cms.hhs.gov/NationalHealthExpendData/>.

Table 137. Hospital Care, Physician and Clinical Service, Nursing Home Care, and Prescription Drug Expenditures by Source of Payment: 1990 to 2008

[In billions of dollars (251.6 represents $251,600,000,000). Personal health care expenditures, excludes Puerto Rico and Island Areas]

Source of payment	1990	2000	2003	2004	2005	2006	2007	2008
Hospital care, total	**251.6**	**416.9**	**527.4**	**566.5**	**607.5**	**649.4**	**687.6**	**718.4**
Out-of-pocket payments	11.3	13.7	17.2	18.6	19.8	21.1	22.3	23.2
Third-party payments..................	240.3	403.2	510.2	547.8	587.8	628.3	665.3	695.2
Private health insurance	97.9	144.1	187.7	202.1	215.7	234.6	246.1	259.0
Other private funds	10.4	21.9	24.7	25.3	26.9	30.6	34.0	27.1
Public.............................	132.0	237.2	297.7	320.5	345.1	363.1	385.1	409.1
Federal..........................	101.7	191.9	241.0	259.7	277.5	291.1	307.6	330.7
State and local....................	30.3	45.3	56.7	60.7	67.6	72.0	77.5	78.3
Medicare [1]	67.8	124.4	152.9	165.3	179.1	187.4	196.2	211.3
Medicaid [2]	26.7	71.1	90.3	96.8	105.1	110.8	119.5	122.7
Physician and clinical services, total ...	**157.5**	**288.6**	**366.7**	**393.6**	**422.4**	**446.5**	**472.6**	**496.2**
Out-of-pocket payments	30.2	32.2	37.6	40.1	43.8	46.3	49.2	50.1
Third-party payments..................	127.4	256.5	329.1	353.6	378.6	400.2	423.4	446.0
Private health insurance	67.2	136.6	178.1	191.4	207.8	220.0	232.7	241.8
Other private funds	11.3	22.2	26.0	26.5	27.4	29.0	30.7	32.0
Public.............................	48.8	97.6	125.1	135.7	143.4	151.2	160.0	172.3
Federal..........................	38.0	78.9	102.6	112.0	118.3	125.5	132.7	144.6
State and local....................	10.8	18.7	22.5	23.7	25.1	25.7	27.2	27.7
Medicare [1]	29.4	58.2	73.5	80.8	86.0	91.3	95.3	102.7
Medicaid [2]	7.0	19.1	25.4	27.8	29.7	31.0	33.2	36.2
Nursing home care, total.............	**52.6**	**95.3**	**110.5**	**115.2**	**120.7**	**125.1**	**132.4**	**138.4**
Out-of-pocket payments	19.0	28.7	30.5	30.9	31.6	32.6	35.4	36.9
Third-party payments..................	33.6	66.6	79.9	84.2	89.1	92.5	96.9	101.5
Private health insurance	2.9	7.9	8.7	8.7	8.9	9.2	9.8	10.3
Other private funds	3.8	4.5	4.2	4.3	4.4	4.5	5.2	5.1
Public.............................	26.9	54.1	67.1	71.3	75.8	78.8	81.9	86.2
Federal..........................	16.3	36.4	46.0	49.1	51.9	54.3	57.2	62.1
State and local....................	10.6	17.8	21.1	22.2	24.0	24.5	24.7	24.1
Medicare [1]	1.7	10.1	14.7	16.9	19.0	21.0	23.4	25.7
Medicaid [2]	24.1	42.0	49.7	51.5	53.7	54.5	54.9	56.3
Prescription drugs, total.............	**40.3**	**120.6**	**174.2**	**188.8**	**199.7**	**217.0**	**226.8**	**234.1**
Out-of-pocket payments	22.4	33.4	44.1	46.2	48.8	46.9	48.9	48.5
Third-party payments..................	17.9	87.2	130.1	142.6	150.9	170.1	177.8	185.5
Private health insurance	10.6	59.5	83.4	90.0	95.8	96.2	97.8	98.5
Other private funds	–	–	–	–	–	–	–	–
Public.............................	7.3	27.7	46.6	52.5	55.1	73.9	80.0	87.0
Federal..........................	3.2	15.9	27.8	31.4	32.6	58.7	65.4	72.5
State and local....................	4.0	11.8	18.9	21.1	22.5	15.2	14.7	14.5
Medicare [1]	0.2	2.1	2.5	3.4	3.9	39.6	46.0	52.1
Medicaid [2]	5.1	20.2	32.5	36.3	37.2	19.1	18.8	19.4

– Represents zero. [1] Medicare expenditures come from federal funds. [2] Medicaid expenditures come from federal, state, and local funds.

Source: U.S. Centers for Medicare and Medicaid Services, Office of the Actuary, "National Health Statistics Group," <http://www.cms.hhs.gov/NationalHealthExpendData/>.

Table 138. Consumer Price Indexes of Medical Care Prices: 1980 to 2009

[1982–1984 = 100. Indexes are annual averages of monthly data based on components of consumer price index for all urban consumers; for explanation, see text, Section 14 and Appendix III]

Year	Medical care, total	Medical care services					Medical care commodities		Annual percent change [3]		
		Total [1]	Professional services			Hospital and related services	Total [2]	Prescription tion drugs and medical supplies	Medical care, total	Medical care services	Medical care commodities
			Total [1]	Physicians	Dental						
1980....	74.9	74.8	77.9	76.5	78.9	69.2	75.4	72.5	11.0	11.3	9.3
1985....	113.5	113.2	113.5	113.3	114.2	116.1	115.2	120.1	6.3	6.1	7.2
1990....	162.8	162.7	156.1	160.8	155.8	178.0	163.4	181.7	9.0	9.3	8.4
1995....	220.5	224.2	201.0	208.8	206.8	257.8	204.5	235.0	4.5	5.1	1.9
2000....	260.8	266.0	237.7	244.7	258.5	317.3	238.1	285.4	4.1	4.3	3.2
2003....	297.1	306.0	261.2	267.7	292.5	394.8	262.8	326.3	4.0	4.5	2.5
2004....	310.1	321.3	271.5	278.3	306.9	417.9	269.3	337.1	4.4	5.0	2.5
2005....	323.2	336.7	281.7	287.5	324.0	439.9	276.0	349.0	4.2	4.8	2.5
2006....	336.2	350.6	289.3	291.9	340.9	468.1	285.9	363.9	4.0	4.1	3.6
2007....	351.1	369.3	300.8	303.2	358.4	498.9	290.0	369.2	4.4	5.3	1.4
2008....	364.1	384.9	311.0	311.3	376.9	534.0	296.0	378.3	3.7	4.2	2.1
2009....	375.6	397.3	319.4	320.8	388.1	567.9	305.1	391.1	3.2	3.2	3.1

[1] Includes other services not shown separately. [2] Includes other commodities not shown separately. [3] Percent change from the immediate prior year.

Source: Bureau of Labor Statistics, "CPI Detailed Report, Data for January 2010," <http://www.bls.gov/cpi/cpi_dr.htm>. See also "Monthly Labor Review Online," <http://www.bls.gov/opub/mlr/>.

Table 139. Average Annual Expenditures Per Consumer Unit for Health Care: 2006 to 2008

[In dollars, except percent. See text, Section 13 and headnote, Table 679. For composition of regions, see map, inside front cover]

Item	Health care, total		Health insurance	Medical services	Drugs and medical supplies [1]	Percent distribution		
	Amount	Percent of total expenditures				Health insurance	Medical services	Drugs and medical supplies [1]
2006...................................	2,766	5.7	1,465	670	631	53.0	24.2	22.8
2007...................................	2,853	5.7	1,545	709	599	54.2	24.9	21.0
2008...................................	2,976	5.9	1,653	727	596	55.5	24.4	20.0
Age of reference person:								
Under 25 years old	682	2.3	389	143	150	57.0	21.0	22.0
25 to 34 years old	1,737	3.6	983	472	282	56.6	27.2	16.2
35 to 44 years old	2,499	4.2	1,341	711	447	53.7	28.5	17.9
45 to 54 years old	2,930	4.8	1,523	838	570	52.0	28.6	19.5
55 to 64 years old	3,825	7.0	1,945	1,022	858	50.8	26.7	22.4
65 to 74 years old	4,770	11.5	2,001	853	1,026	60.7	17.8	21.1
75 years old and over	4,413	13.9	2,783	728	902	63.1	16.5	20.4
Race of reference person:								
White and other........................	3,169	6.0	1,743	787	638	55.0	24.8	20.1
Black	1,595	4.3	1,015	292	288	63.6	18.3	18.1
Origin of reference person:								
Hispanic...............................	1,571	3.6	816	407	349	51.9	25.9	22.2
Non-Hispanic...........................	3,160	6.1	1,763	768	628	55.8	24.3	19.9
Region of residence:								
Northeast..............................	3,035	5.5	1,758	693	584	57.9	22.8	19.2
Midwest...............................	3,049	6.4	1,729	717	602	56.7	23.5	19.7
South.................................	2,849	6.1	1,592	655	603	55.9	23.0	21.2
West..................................	3,057	5.5	1,588	881	588	51.9	28.8	19.2
Size of consumer unit:								
One person	1,821	6.0	1,070	387	363	58.8	21.3	19.9
Two or more persons	3,448	5.9	1,892	865	691	54.9	25.1	20.0
Two persons	3,972	7.4	2,204	937	830	55.5	23.6	20.9
Three persons	2,944	4.9	1,615	716	613	54.9	24.3	20.8
Four persons	3,039	4.6	1,700	798	540	55.9	26.3	17.8
Five persons or more.................	3,022	4.6	1,527	946	548	50.5	31.3	18.1
Income before taxes:								
Quintiles of income:								
Lowest 20 percent.....................	1,624	7.3	985	296	342	60.7	18.2	21.1
Second 20 percent	2,457	7.7	1,438	476	543	58.5	19.4	22.1
Third 20 percent......................	2,886	6.8	1,667	625	593	57.8	21.7	20.5
Fourth 20 percent	3,518	6.0	1,869	980	669	53.1	27.9	19.0
Highest 20 percent	4,391	4.5	2,306	1,255	830	52.5	28.6	18.9
Education:								
Less than a high school graduate	2,008	6.7	1,204	359	444	60.0	17.9	22.1
High school graduate.....................	2,733	6.7	1,576	576	580	57.7	21.1	21.2
High school graduate with some college.....	2,788	5.9	1,490	721	578	53.4	25.9	20.7
Associate's degree	3,158	5.9	1,770	796	592	56.0	25.2	18.7
Bachelor's degree	3,477	5.3	1,893	933	651	54.4	26.8	18.7
Master's, professional, doctoral degree......	4,270	5.4	2,286	1,193	791	53.5	27.9	18.5

[1] Includes prescription and nonprescription drugs.

Source: U.S. Bureau of Labor Statistics, *Consumer Expenditure Survey*, annual, <http://www.bls.gov/cex/>.

Health and Nutrition 103

Table 140. Medicare Disbursements by Type of Beneficiary: 1990 to 2009

[In millions of dollars (109,709 represents $109,709,000,000). For years ending Sept. 30. Distribution of benefits by type is estimated and subject to change. See headnote, Table 145]

Selected type of beneficiary	1990	1995	2000	2005	2006	2007	2008 [1]	2009
Total disbursements	**109,709**	**180,096**	**219,276**	**336,876**	**380,457**	**434,829**	**455,076**	**499,837**
HI, Part A disbursements [2]	**66,687**	**114,883**	**130,284**	**184,142**	**184,901**	**202,827**	**230,240**	**241,618**
Benefits	65,722	113,394	125,992	181,934	185,100	203,990	226,275	237,946
Aged	58,503	100,107	110,261	155,925	157,273	172,748	184,267	201,135
Disabled.	7,218	13,288	15,731	26,009	27,827	31,242	33,524	36,811
SMI, Part B disbursements [2]	**43,022**	**65,213**	**88,992**	**151,537**	**161,647**	**179,651**	**177,709**	**200,931**
Benefits	41,498	63,490	88,875	147,449	154,381	172,698	183,289	197,263
Aged	36,837	54,830	76,340	122,905	127,848	142,839	151,298	162,403
Disabled.	4,661	8,660	12,535	24,544	26,534	29,859	31,991	34,860
SMI, Part D disbursements [2]	(X)	(X)	(X)	1,198	33,909	52,351	47,126	57,288
Benefits	(X)	(X)	(X)	73	33,506	51,336	46,734	56,889
Transitional assistance benefit payments	(X)	(X)	(X)	1,125	229	10	–	–

– Represents or rounds to zero. X Not applicable. [1] A transfer of expenditures between Parts A and B took place during 2008 that corrected for accounting errors that happened during FY 2005–2007. The transfer is reflected in the "Benefits" data and is the sum of "Aged, Disabled, and Transfer." The Part A "Benefits" total increased by $8,484,000,000 while Part B "Benefits" total decreased by the same amount. [2] Other types, not shown separately.

Source: U.S. Centers for Medicare and Medicaid Services, Trustees Report and Trust Funds, and unpublished data. See also <http://www.cms.hhs.gov/ReportsTrustFunds/>.

Table 141. Children's Health Insurance Program (CHIP)—Enrollment and Expenditures by State: 2000 and 2009

[(3,357.4 represents 3,357,400) For year ending September 30. This program provides health benefits coverage to children living in families whose incomes exceed the eligibility limits for Medicaid. Although it is generally targeted to families with incomes at or below 200 percent of the federal poverty level, each state may set its own income eligibility limits, within certain guidelines. States have three options: they may expand their Medicaid programs, develop a separate child health program that functions independently of Medicaid, or do a combination of both. See text, this section, regarding the change from SCHIP to CHIP]

State	Enrollment [1] (1,000)		Expenditures [2] (mil. dol.)		State	Enrollment [1] (1,000)		Expenditures [2] (mil. dol.)	
	2000	2009	2000	2009		2000	2009	2000	2009
U.S.	**3,357.4**	**7,717.3**	**1,928.8**	**7,319.0**	MO	72.8	103.7	41.2	100.9
AL	37.6	110.2	31.9	116.4	MT	8.3	25.7	4.3	31.4
AK	13.4	11.7	18.1	16.2	NE	11.4	48.1	6.1	36.7
AZ	59.6	105.1	29.4	194.3	NV	15.9	34.0	9.0	22.7
AR	1.9	101.3	1.5	79.5	NH	4.3	13.2	1.6	13.3
CA	484.4	1,748.1	187.3	1,139.2	NJ	89.0	167.0	46.9	442.5
CO	34.9	102.4	13.9	102.3	NM	8.0	16.1	3.4	283.0
CT	19.9	21.8	12.8	34.5	NY	769.5	532.6	401.0	345.3
DE	4.5	12.6	1.5	11.4	NC	103.6	252.6	65.5	220.0
DC	2.3	9.3	5.8	11.2	ND	2.6	7.0	1.8	13.1
FL	227.5	417.4	125.7	286.4	OH	118.3	265.7	53.1	252.0
GA	120.6	254.4	48.7	225.6	OK	57.7	123.7	51.3	116.0
HI	(Z)	24.7	0.4	20.1	OR	37.1	62.1	12.5	74.4
ID	12.4	44.3	7.5	39.6	PA	119.7	264.8	70.7	246.3
IL	62.5	376.6	32.7	247.6	RI	11.5	19.6	10.4	19.5
IN	44.4	138.6	53.7	81.0	SC	60.4	85.0	46.6	84.2
IA	20.0	52.6	15.5	59.2	SD	5.9	15.3	3.1	16.7
KS	26.3	48.1	12.8	50.9	TN	14.9	83.3	41.7	113.7
KY	55.6	73.1	60.0	110.4	TX	131.1	869.9	41.4	702.2
LA	50.0	170.1	25.3	189.7	UT	25.3	59.8	12.8	55.6
ME	22.7	31.3	11.4	34.8	VT	4.1	7.1	1.4	6.0
MD	93.1	124.6	92.2	154.9	VA	37.7	167.6	18.6	148.4
MA	113.0	143.0	44.2	227.4	WA	2.6	27.4	0.6	33.5
MI	55.4	72.0	36.2	186.9	WV	21.7	38.2	9.7	38.2
MN	(Z)	5.5	(Z)	34.6	WI	47.1	132.9	21.4	91.0
MS	12.2	86.8	21.1	148.6	WY	2.5	8.9	1.0	9.1

Z Less than 50 or $50,000. [1] Number of children ever enrolled during the year in Children's Health Insurance Program. [2] Expenditures for which states are entitled to federal reimbursement under Title XXI and which reconciles any advance of Title XXI federal funds made on the basis of estimates.

Source: U.S. Centers for Medicare & Medicaid Services, *The Children's Health Insurance Program (CHIP), Annual Enrollment Report* and the Statement of Expenditures for the CHIP Program (CMS-21). See also <http://www.cms.gov/NationalCHIPPolicy> and <http://www.cms.hhs.gov/medicaid/mbes/default.asp>.

Table 142. Medicare Enrollees: 1990 to 2009

[In millions (34.3 represents 34,300,000). As of July 1. Includes Puerto Rico and Island Areas and enrollees in foreign countries and unknown place of residence. SMI is Supplemental Medical Insurance. See headnote, Table 145]

Item	1990	1995	2000	2005	2006	2007	2008	2009
Total.	**34.3**	**37.6**	**39.7**	**42.6**	**43.4**	**44.3**	**45.2**	**45.9**
Aged	31.0	33.2	34.3	35.8	36.3	37.0	37.8	38.3
Disabled	3.3	4.4	5.4	6.8	7.1	7.3	7.4	7.6
Hospital insurance, Part A	**33.7**	**37.2**	**39.3**	**42.2**	**43.1**	**43.9**	**44.9**	**45.6**
Aged	30.5	32.7	33.8	35.4	36.0	36.6	37.5	38.0
Disabled	3.3	4.4	5.4	6.8	7.1	7.3	7.4	7.6
SMI, Part B	**32.6**	**35.6**	**37.3**	**39.8**	**40.4**	**41.1**	**41.7**	**42.4**
Aged	29.6	31.7	32.6	33.8	34.1	34.6	35.2	35.7
Disabled	2.9	3.9	4.8	6.0	6.2	6.4	6.6	6.7
SMI, Part D	(X)	(X)	(X)	1.8	30.5	31.2	32.3	33.2
Medicare Advantage [1]	1.3	2.7	6.2	5.8	7.3	8.7	10.0	10.9

X Not applicable. [1] Prior to 2004, Medicare Advantage was referred to as Medicare + Choice.

Source: U.S. Centers for Medicare and Medicaid Services, Office of the Actuary, CMS Statistics Medicare Enrollment, "National Trends," <http://www.cms.hhs.gov/MedicareEnrpts/>.

Table 143. Medicare—Enrollment by State and Other Areas: 2000 to 2008

[In thousands (39,620 represents 39,620,000). Hospital (HI) and/or supplementary medical insurance (SMI) enrollment as of July 1]

State and area	2000	2005	2007	2008	State and area	2000	2005	2007	2008
All areas [1]	**39,620**	**42,395**	**44,263**	**45,412**	MT	137	146	156	160
U.S.	**38,762**	**41,003**	**43,259**	**44,385**	NE	254	259	268	271
AL	685	740	789	809	NV	240	294	318	330
AK	42	51	57	60	NH	170	185	204	212
AZ	675	777	841	870	NJ	1,203	1,215	1,257	1,283
AR	439	464	496	509	NM	234	261	285	294
CA	3,901	4,158	4,369	4,492	NY	2,715	2,758	2,841	2,891
CO	467	513	558	579	NC	1,133	1,255	1,359	1,405
CT	515	520	537	549	ND	103	103	105	107
DE	112	125	136	141	OH	1,701	1,731	1,805	1,841
DC	75	72	74	75	OK	508	531	565	578
FL	2,804	3,008	3,133	3,212	OR	489	532	567	584
GA	916	1,016	1,111	1,153	PA	2,095	2,108	2,184	2,221
HI	165	180	189	194	RI	172	171	175	178
ID	165	188	207	214	SC	568	637	697	724
IL	1,635	1,674	1,741	1,775	SD	119	123	129	132
IN	852	893	941	964	TN	829	903	975	1,004
IA	477	484	500	506	TX	2,265	2,491	2,708	2,802
KS	390	397	412	418	UT	206	231	254	264
KY	623	668	711	728	VT	89	95	102	105
LA	602	630	639	656	VA	893	981	1,045	1,079
ME	216	233	247	253	WA	736	807	873	903
MD	645	687	723	745	WV	338	351	367	373
MA	961	961	997	1,019	WI	783	818	854	874
MI	1,403	1,460	1,541	1,580	WY	65	70	74	76
MN	654	691	729	749	Outlying areas [2]	537	622	(NA)	(NA)
MS	419	449	469	479	Pending state				
MO	861	901	946	966	designations [3]	321	769	(NA)	(NA)

NA Not available. [1] Includes outlying areas and pending state designation. [2] Includes American Samoa, Federated States of Micronesia, Guam Marshall Islands, Northern Marianas, Puerto Rico, Virgin Islands, and Wake Island. [3] Include foreign countries and unknown places of residence.

Source: U.S. Centers for Medicare and Medicaid Services, "Data Compendium," <http://www.cms.gov/DataCompendium/>.

Table 144. Medicaid—Selected Characteristics of Persons Covered: 2008

[In thousands, except percent (42,411 represents 42,411,000). Represents number of persons as of March of following year who were enrolled at any time in year shown. Excludes unrelated individuals under age 15. Persons did not have to receive medical care paid for by Medicaid in order to be counted. See headnote, Table 565]

Poverty status	Total [1]	White alone [2]	Black alone [3]	Asian alone [4]	His-panic [5]	Under 18 years	18–44 years	45–64 years	65 years and over
Persons covered, total	**42,411**	**29,082**	**9,613**	**1,538**	**11,517**	**22,324**	**10,701**	**5,957**	**3,428**
Below poverty level	17,716	10,979	5,141	585	5,274	9,810	4,609	2,331	965
Above poverty level	24,695	18,103	4,472	953	6,243	12,514	6,092	3,626	2,463
Percent of population covered	14.1	12.1	25.3	11.6	24.3	30.1	9.7	7.6	9.1
Below poverty level	44.5	40.7	54.8	37.1	48.0	69.7	30.9	32.4	26.4
Above poverty level	9.5	8.5	15.6	8.1	17.1	20.9	6.4	5.1	7.2

[1] Includes other races, not shown separately. [2] White alone refers to people who reported White and did not report any other race category. [3] Black alone refers to people who reported Black and did not report any other race category. [4] Asian alone refers to people who reported Asian and did not report any other race category. [5] Persons of Hispanic origin may be of any race.

Source: U.S. Census Bureau, Income, Poverty, and Health Insurance Coverage in the United States: 2008, Current Population Reports, P60-236, 2009; Table HI02, "Health Insurance Coverage Status and Type of Coverage by Selected Characteristics for People in the Poverty Universe: 2008" and Table HI03, "Health Insurance Coverage Status and Type of Coverage by Selected Characteristics for Poor People in the Poverty Universe: 2008." See also <http://www.census.gov/hhes/www/cpstables/032010/health/toc.htm>.

Table 145. Medicare Benefits by Type of Provider: 1990 to 2009

[In millions of dollars (65,721 represents $65,721,000,000). For years ending Sept. 30. Distribution of benefits by type is estimated and subject to change. The Medicare program has two components: Hospital Insurance (HI) or Medicare Part A and Supplementary Medical Insurance (SMI) consisting of Medicare Part B and Part D. See text in this section for details. See footnote 1, Table 140, for 2008 data changes]

Type of provider	1990	1995	2000	2005	2006	2007	2008	2009
Hospital insurance benefits (Part A), total	**65,721**	**113,395**	**125,992**	**181,934**	**185,100**	**203,990**	**226,275**	**237,946**
Inpatient hospital	57,012	81,095	86,561	122,656	122,101	125,918	128,754	137,477
Skilled nursing facility	2,761	8,684	10,269	18,712	19,658	22,161	23,919	25,494
Home health agency	3,295	15,715	4,880	5,885	5,864	6,233	6,570	6,844
Hospice	318	1,854	2,818	7,679	8,811	10,448	11,399	12,514
Managed care	2,335	6,047	21,463	27,001	28,667	39,230	47,150	55,617
Supplementary medical insurance benefits (Part B), total	**41,498**	**63,490**	**88,876**	**147,449**	**154,381**	**172,698**	**174,805**	**197,263**
Physician fee schedule	(NA)	31,110	35,958	57,211	57,923	58,832	59,762	61,665
Durable medical equipment	(NA)	3,576	4,577	7,894	8,266	8,138	8,534	9,056
Carrier lab [1]	(NA)	2,819	2,194	3,521	3,678	4,049	4,172	4,654
Other carrier [2]	(NA)	4,513	7,154	15,195	15,253	15,695	16,395	17,029
Hospital [3]	(NA)	8,448	8,516	18,970	20,042	22,725	23,054	24,971
Home health	(NA)	223	4,281	6,750	7,442	9,056	9,956	10,456
Intermediary lab [4]	(NA)	1,437	1,748	2,821	2,813	3,048	2,976	3,199
Other intermediary [5]	(NA)	5,110	6,099	11,353	11,751	13,430	13,236	14,498
Managed care	(NA)	6,253	18,348	23,735	27,213	37,724	45,203	51,735
Supplementary medical insurance benefits (Part D), total [6]	**(X)**	**(X)**	**(X)**	**1,198**	**33,735**	**51,346**	**46,734**	**56,889**

NA Not available. X Not applicable. [1] Lab services paid under the lab fee schedule performed in a physician's office lab or an independent lab. [2] Includes free-standing ambulatory surgical centers facility costs, ambulance, and supplies. [3] Includes the hospital facility costs for Medicare Part B services which are predominantly in the outpatient department. The physician reimbursement associated with these services is included on the "Physician Fee Schedule" line. [4] Lab fee services paid under the lab fee schedule performed in a hospital outpatient department. [5] Includes ESRD free-standing dialysis facility payments and payments to rural health federally qualified health centers. [6] Starting with 2006, Part D provides subsidized access to drug insurance coverage on a voluntary basis for all beneficiaries and premium and cost-sharing subsidies for low-income enrollees. Benefits prior to 2006 were for transitional assistance to beneficiaries with low income.

Source: U.S. Centers for Medicare and Medicaid Services, unpublished data. See also <http://www.cms.hhs.gov/ReportsTrustFunds/>.

Table 146. Medicare Insurance Trust Funds: 1990 to 2008

[In billions of dollars (126.3 represents $126,300,000,000). SMI is Supplemental Medical Insurance. See headnote, Table 145]

Type of trust fund	1990	1995	2000	2004	2005	2006	2007	2008	2009
TOTAL MEDICARE									
Total income	126.3	175.3	257.1	317.7	357.5	437.0	462.1	480.8	511.4
Total expenditures	111.0	184.2	221.8	308.9	336.4	408.3	431.7	468.1	511.1
Assets, end of year	114.4	143.4	221.5	288.8	309.8	338.5	368.9	381.6	381.8
HOSPITAL INSURANCE (Part A)									
Net contribution income [1]	72.1	103.3	154.5	167.2	182.6	194.3	205.4	213.5	206.3
Interest received [2]	8.5	10.8	11.7	16.0	16.1	16.4	17.4	16.3	17.0
Benefit payments [3]	66.2	116.4	126.8	167.6	180.0	189.0	200.2	232.3	242.3
Assets, end of year	98.9	130.3	177.5	269.3	285.8	305.4	326.0	321.3	300.8
SMI (Part B)									
Net premium income	11.3	19.7	20.6	31.4	37.5	42.9	46.8	50.2	56.7
Transfers from general revenue	33.0	39.0	65.9	100.4	118.1	132.7	139.6	146.8	163.8
Interest received [2]	1.6	1.6	3.5	1.5	1.4	1.8	2.2	3.6	3.1
Benefit payments [3]	42.5	65.0	88.9	135.0	149.2	165.9	176.4	180.3	199.6
Assets, end of year	15.5	13.1	44.0	19.4	24.0	32.3	42.1	59.4	80.3
SMI (Part D)									
Net premium income	(X)	(X)	(X)	–	–	3.5	4.0	5.0	6.3
Transfers from general revenue [4]	(X)	(X)	(X)	0.4	1.1	39.1	38.7	37.3	48.5
Interest received	(X)	(X)	(X)	–	–	–	–	–	–
Benefit payments [4]	(X)	(X)	(X)	0.4	1.1	47.0	48.8	49.0	62.6
Assets, end of year	(X)	(X)	(X)	–	–	0.8	0.8	0.9	0.7

– Represents zero. X Not applicable. [1] Includes income from taxation of benefits beginning in 1994. Includes premiums from aged ineligibles enrolled in Hospital Insurance (HI). [2] Includes recoveries of amounts reimbursed from the trust fund. [3] Beginning 1998, monies transferred to the SMI trust fund for home health agency costs, as provided for by P.L. 105-33, are included in HI benefit payments but excluded from SMI benefit payments. [4] These amounts for 2004 and 2005 include amounts transferred for transitional assistance for Part D of Medicare.

Source: U.S. Centers for Medicare and Medicaid Services, Annual Report of the Board of Trustees of the Federal Hospital Insurance Trust Fund and Annual Report of the Board of Trustees of the Federal Supplementary Medical Insurance Trust Fund. See also <http://www.cms.hhs.gov/ReportsTrustFunds/>.

Table 147. Medicaid—Beneficiaries and Payments: 2000 to 2008

[For year ending September 30 (42,887 represents 42,887,000)]

Basis of eligibility and type of service	Beneficiaries (1,000) [1]				Payments (mil. dol.)			
	2000	2005	2007	2008 [2]	2000	2005	2007	2008 [2]
Total	42,887	57,650	56,821	58,133	168,443	274,851	276,246	296,284
Age 65 and over	3,730	4,395	4,044	4,143	44,560	63,415	57,179	60,908
Blind/Disabled	6,890	8,211	8,427	8,697	72,772	119,305	119,617	129,207
Children	19,018	341	26,585	27,068	23,490	41,863	47,731	51,152
Adults	8,671	532	12,365	12,859	17,671	32,165	33,697	37,099
Foster care children	761	875	942	959	3,309	5,286	5,985	5,927
Unknown	3,817	5,268	4,418	4,362	6,639	12,539	11,581	11,480
BCCA WOMEN [3]	(NA)	29	41	44	(NA)	281	456	510
Capitated care [4]	21,292	33,496	36,627	37,865	25,026	46,421	58,536	68,015
Clinic services	7,678	11,918	11,698	11,834	6,138	8,921	8,668	9,107
Dental services	5,922	9,317	9,533	9,788	1,413	3,040	3,244	3,803
Home health services	1,007	1,195	1,190	1,143	3,133	5,362	6,348	6,602
ICF/MR services [5]	119	1,098	104	102	9,376	11,709	11,778	12,568
Inpatient hospital services	4,913	5,480	5,134	5,244	24,131	35,131	36,919	37,162
Lab and X-ray services	11,439	15,959	15,788	15,590	1,292	2,917	2,928	2,919
Mental health facility services [6]	100	120	112	108	1,769	2,301	2,397	2,374
Nursing facility services	1,706	1,711	1,645	1,617	34,528	44,790	46,523	47,711
Other care [7]	9,022	12,346	12,001	12,242	14,755	26,421	31,281	34,172
Outpatient hospital services	13,170	16,234	14,896	14,766	7,082	10,011	10,358	10,875
Other practitioner services	4,758	5,893	5,426	5,147	664	1,180	921	889
PCCM services [8]	5,649	8,723	7,090	8,718	177	232	235	276
Prescribed drugs	20,325	28,390	23,923	24,003	19,898	42,849	22,160	23,384
Physician services	18,965	2,438	22,047	21,650	6,809	11,269	10,075	10,489
Personal support services [9]	4,559	6,807	6,563	6,365	11,629	20,657	23,197	24,521
Sterilizations	137	176	147	138	128	211	163	143
Unknown	74	73	91	87	496	1,428	516	1,274

NA Not available. [1] Beneficiaries data do not add due to number of beneficiaries that are reported in more than one category. [2] 2008 data not available for Hawaii, North Dakota, Utah, Vermont, and Wisconsin; 2007 data is reported. [3] Women-Breast and Cervical Cancer Assistance. [4] HMO payments and prepaid health plans. [5] Intermediate care facilities and or for mentally retarded. [6] Inpatient mental health-aged and inpatient mental health-under 21. [7] Includes beneficiaries of, and payments for, other care not shown separately. [8] Primary Care Case Management Services. [9] Includes personal care services, rehabilitative services, physical occupational targeted case management services, speech therapies, hospice services, nurse midwife services, nurse practitioner services, private duty nursing services, and religious nonmedical health care institutions.

Source: U.S. Centers for Medicare and Medicaid Services, "Medicaid Program Statistics, Medicaid Statistical Information System," <http://www.cms.gov/MedicaidDataSourcesGenInfo/02_MSISData.asp>.

Table 148. Medicaid—Summary by State: 2000 and 2008

[(42,887 represents 42,887,000). For year ending September 30]

State	Beneficiaries [1] (1,000)		Payments [2] (mil. dol.)		State	Beneficiaries [1] (1,000)		Payments [2] (mil. dol.)	
	2000	2008 [3]	2000	2008 [3]		2000	2008 [3]	2000	2008 [3]
U.S.	42,887	58,133	168,443	296,284	MO	890	1,054	3,274	5,226
AL	619	830	2,393	3,508	MT	104	113	422	655
AK	96	119	473	974	NE	229	249	960	1,536
AZ	681	1,399	2,112	6,584	NV	138	249	516	1,130
AR	489	827	1,543	3,251	NH	97	131	651	935
CA	7,918	10,515	17,105	32,245	NJ	822	1,065	4,714	7,713
CO	381	626	1,809	2,985	NM	376	507	1,249	3,058
CT	420	524	2,839	4,144	NY	3,420	4,869	26,148	43,041
DE	115	181	529	1,137	NC	1,214	1,785	4,834	8,925
DC	139	168	793	1,739	ND	63	71	358	493
FL	2,373	2,871	7,433	13,224	OH	1,305	2,062	7,115	12,062
GA	1,369	1,712	3,624	6,863	OK	507	765	1,604	3,350
HI	194	224	600	993	OR	558	487	1,714	2,460
ID	131	233	594	1,263	PA	1,492	2,134	6,366	12,501
IL	1,519	2,317	7,807	10,235	RI	179	204	1,070	1,648
IN	706	1,126	2,977	4,941	SC	689	871	2,765	4,347
IA	314	498	1,477	2,691	SD	102	137	402	673
KS	263	351	1,227	2,296	TN	1,568	1,471	3,491	6,362
KY	764	893	2,921	4,475	TX	2,633	3,993	9,277	16,657
LA	761	1,157	2,632	4,991	UT	225	243	960	1,395
ME	194	306	1,310	1,355	VT	139	157	480	812
MD	626	757	3,003	5,578	VA	627	839	2,479	4,661
MA	1,060	1,230	5,413	8,991	WA	896	1,188	2,435	5,834
MI	1,352	1,790	4,881	9,231	WV	342	378	1,394	2,402
MN	558	763	3,280	6,646	WI	577	967	2,968	4,441
MS	605	657	1,808	3,124	WY	46	69	215	503

[1] Persons who had payments made on their behalf at any time during the fiscal year. [2] Payments are for fiscal year and reflect federal and state contribution payments. Data exclude disproportionate share hospital payments. Disproportionate share hospitals receive higher medicaid reimbursement than other hospitals because they treat a disproportionate share of medicaid patients. [3] 2008 data not available for Hawaii, North Dakota, Utah, Vermont, and Wisconsin; 2007 data are reported.

Source: U.S. Centers for Medicare and Medicaid Services, "Medicaid, Program Statistics, Medicaid Statistical Information System," <http://www.cms.gov/MedicaidDataSourcesGenInfo/02_MSISData.asp>

U.S. Census Bureau, Statistical Abstract of the United States: 2011

Table 149. Medicaid Managed Care Enrollment by State and Other Areas: 1995 to 2009

[For year ending June 30. (33,373 represents 33,373,000)]

State and other areas	Total enroll-ment [1] (1,000)	Managed care enrollment [2]		State and other areas	Total enroll-ment [1] (1,000)	Managed care enrollment [2]		State and other areas	Total enroll-ment [1] (1,000)	Managed care enrollment [2]	
		Number (1,000)	Percent of total			Number (1,000)	Percent of total			Number (1,000)	Percent of total
1995.....	33,373	9,800	29.4	HI......	235	228	97.0	NY	4,422	2,927	66.2
2000.....	33,690	18,786	55.8	ID......	198	167	84.1	NC	1,442	1,012	70.2
2004.....	44,356	26,914	60.7	IL	2,321	1,278	55.1	ND	60	41	67.6
2005.....	45,392	28,576	63.0	IN......	962	712	74.0	OH.....	1,952	1,375	70.4
2006.....	45,653	29,830	65.3	IA......	398	330	82.9	OK	626	553	88.5
2007.....	45,962	29,463	64.1	KS	297	257	86.6	OR	475	418	88.1
2008.....	47,143	33,428	70.1	KY	769	638	83.0	PA	1,920	1,577	82.1
2009,				LA	1,007	692	68.7	RI......	178	111	62.1
total...	50,472	36,202	71.7	ME.....	280	178	63.7	SC	763	763	100.0
U.S.....	49,451	35,225	71.2	MD.....	787	620	78.7	SD	107	85	79.7
AL	812	540	66.5	MA.....	1,227	731	59.6	TN	1,231	1,231	100.0
AK	102	–	–	MI......	1,630	1,447	88.8	TX	3,343	2,161	64.6
AZ	1,223	1,096	89.6	MN.....	675	426	63.1	UT	238	205	85.9
AR	645	511	79.2	MS.....	674	513	76.1	VT	157	137	87.8
CA.....	6,956	3,633	52.2	MO.....	895	883	98.7	VA	815	521	63.9
CO.....	468	445	95.1	MT	85	56	66.6	WA.....	1,103	949	86.0
CT	456	343	75.2	NE	215	180	83.6	WV.....	326	150	46.0
DE	171	126	73.9	NV	213	179	83.7	WI	1,005	607	60.4
DC.....	154	150	66.0	NH	124	97	77.6	WY.....	64	–	–
FL	2,426	1,601	92.0	NJ	969	726	74.9	PR	1,013	978	96.5
GA.....	1,386	1,275	92.0	NM.....	465	345	74.2	VI.....	8	–	–

– Represents zero. [1] The unduplicated Medicaid enrollment figures include individuals in state health care reform programs that expand eligibility beyond traditional Medicaid eligibility standards. [2] The unduplicated managed care enrollment figures include enrollees receiving comprehensive and limited benefits.

Source: U.S. Centers for Medicare and Medicaid Services, "2009 Medicaid Managed Care Enrollment Report," <http://www.cms.hhs.gov/MedicaidDataSourcesGenInfo/04_MdManCrEnrllRep.asp>.

Table 150. Persons Enrolled in Health Maintenance Organizations (HMOs) by State: 2007 and 2008

[As of January 1 (74,698 represents 74,698,000). Data are based on a census of health maintenance organizations]

State	Number 2008 (1,000)	Percent of population		State	Number 2008 (1,000)	Percent of population		State	Number 2008 (1,000)	Percent of population	
		2007	2008			2007	2008			2007	2008
U.S.	74,698	24.7	24.8								
AL	201	3.6	4.3	KY	408	8.1	9.6	ND	10	0.2	1.5
AK	7	1.0	1.1	LA	352	8.6	8.2	OH.....	2,466	20.3	21.5
AZ	1,942	29.2	30.6	ME.....	152	29.4	11.5	OK	263	7.2	7.3
AR	106	3.4	3.7	MD.....	1,701	29.3	30.3	OR	1,007	25.3	26.9
CA.....	16,415	44.6	44.9	MA.....	2,964	48.1	46.0	PA	3,744	30.6	30.1
CO.....	1,053	23.8	21.7	MI......	2,841	28.1	28.2	RI......	223	22.6	21.0
CT	1,349	41.2	38.5	MN.....	939	14.1	18.1	SC	417	7.8	9.5
DE	201	26.0	23.3	MS.....	54	0.9	1.8	SD	148	17.7	18.5
DC.....	377	64.0	64.1	MO.....	1,164	23.0	19.8	TN	1,897	31.1	30.8
FL	4,400	24.1	24.1	MT	62	5.1	6.5	TX	3,702	12.8	15.5
GA.....	2,099	26.5	22.0	NE	135	6.9	7.6	UT	970	35.1	36.7
HI......	650	46.7	50.6	NV	608	23.0	23.7	VT	86	19.9	13.8
ID......	86	4.6	5.7	NH	219	23.2	16.7	VA	1,665	21.5	21.6
IL	1,762	13.9	13.7	NJ	2,284	26.5	26.3	WA.....	1,423	20.0	22.0
IN......	1,098	24.1	17.3	NM.....	591	23.3	30.0	WV.....	277	11.3	15.3
IA......	327	9.7	11.0	NY	6,500	32.3	33.7	WI	1,507	23.8	26.9
KS	471	14.9	17.0	NC	838	8.3	9.2	WY.....	21	2.6	4.1

Source: HealthLeaders-InterStudy, Nashville, TN, *The Competitive Edge* (copyright). See also <http://www.interstudypublications.com/>.

U.S. Census Bureau, Statistical Abstract of the United States: 2011

Table 151. Health Insurance Coverage Status by Selected Characteristics: 2007 and 2008

[(299,106 represents 299,106,000). Persons as of following year for coverage in the year shown. Government health insurance includes Medicare, Medicaid, and military plans. Based on Current Population Survey, Annual Social and Economic Supplement (ASEC); see text, Section 1 and Appendix III]

Characteristic	Number (1,000)							Percent			
		Covered by private or government health insurance					Not covered by health insur- ance	Covered by private or government health insurance			Not covered by health insur- ance
			Private		Government						
	Total persons	Total [1]	Total	Group health [2]	Medi- care	Medic- aid		Total [1]	Private	Medic- aid	
2007 [3]	299,106	253,449	201,991	177,446	41,375	39,554	45,657	84.7	67.5	13.2	15.3
2008	301,483	255,143	200,992	176,332	43,029	42,641	46,340	84.6	66.7	14.1	15.4
Age:											
Under 18 years	74,510	67,161	47,282	43,874	623	22,555	7,348	90.1	63.5	30.3	9.9
Under 6 years	25,273	23,064	14,828	13,989	252	9,178	2,209	91.3	58.7	36.3	8.7
6 to 11 years	24,001	21,791	15,456	14,503	179	7,250	2,211	90.8	64.4	30.2	9.2
12 to 17 years	25,236	22,307	16,998	15,382	192	6,127	2,929	88.4	67.4	24.3	11.6
18 to 24 years	28,688	20,488	16,947	13,450	254	3,798	8,200	71.4	59.1	13.2	28.6
25 to 34 years	40,520	29,766	25,879	24,130	546	3,748	10,754	73.5	63.9	9.2	26.5
35 to 44 years	41,322	33,287	29,780	27,899	970	3,155	8,035	80.6	72.1	7.6	19.4
45 to 54 years	44,366	37,312	33,234	30,861	1,967	3,313	7,054	84.1	74.9	7.5	15.9
55 to 64 years	34,289	29,989	25,584	22,906	3,365	2,644	4,301	87.5	74.6	7.7	12.5
65 years and over	37,788	37,142	22,287	13,212	35,304	3,428	646	98.3	59.0	9.1	1.7
Sex:											
Male	148,094	122,886	98,346	87,414	18,860	19,421	25,208	83.0	66.4	13.1	17.0
Female	153,388	132,257	102,647	88,917	24,169	23,220	21,131	86.2	66.9	15.1	13.8
Race: White alone [4]	240,852	205,962	166,916	145,183	36,469	29,224	34,890	85.5	69.3	12.1	14.5
Black alone [4]	38,076	30,792	19,894	18,371	4,539	9,686	7,284	80.9	52.2	25.4	19.1
Asian alone [4]	13,315	10,971	9,081	8,094	1,258	1,540	2,344	82.4	68.2	11.6	17.6
Hispanic origin [5]	47,485	32,928	20,779	19,094	3,218	11,559	14,558	69.3	43.8	24.3	30.7
Household income:											
Less than $25,000	55,814	42,142	16,567	10,152	15,732	19,889	13,673	75.5	29.7	35.6	24.5
$25,000–$49,999	69,621	54,712	38,734	31,899	13,211	12,736	14,908	78.6	55.6	18.3	21.4
$50,000–$74,999	57,525	49,491	43,134	38,848	6,093	5,164	8,034	86.0	75.0	9.0	14.0
$75,000 or more	118,523	108,798	102,558	95,433	7,993	4,852	9,725	91.8	86.5	4.1	8.2
Persons below poverty	39,829	27,707	8,540	5,477	5,355	17,716	12,122	69.6	21.4	44.5	30.4

[1] Includes other government insurance not shown separately. Persons with coverage counted only once in total, even though they may have been covered by more than one type of policy. [2] Related to employment of self or other family members. [3] The estimates are revised from the originally published data. [4] Refers to people who reported specified race and did not report any other race category. [5] Persons of Hispanic origin may be any race.

Source: U.S. Census Bureau, *Income, Poverty, and Health Insurance Coverage in the United States: 2008*, Current Population Reports, P60-236, 2009, Table HI01, "Health Insurance Data, Health Insurance Coverage Status and Type of Coverage by Selected Characteristics: 2008" and Table HI03, "Health Insurance Coverage Status and Type of Coverage by Selected Characteristics for Poor People in the Poverty Universe: 2008." See also <http://www.census.gov/hhes/www/cpstables/032010/health/toc.htm>.

Table 152. Persons With and Without Health Insurance Coverage by State: 2008

[255,143 represents 255,143,000. Based on the Current Population Survey, Annual Social and Economic Supplement (ASEC), see text, Section 1 and Appendix III]

State	Total persons covered (1,000)	Total persons not covered		Children not covered		State	Total persons covered (1,000)	Total persons not covered		Children not covered	
		Number (1,000)	Percent of total	Number (1,000)	Percent of total			Number (1,000)	Percent of total	Number (1,000)	Percent of total
U.S. [1]	255,143	46,340	15.4	7,348	9.9	MO	5,132	739	12.6	96	6.8
AL	4,159	561	11.9	41	3.6	MT	819	158	16.1	23	10.5
AK	539	133	19.8	26	14.5	NE	1,565	211	11.9	46	10.1
AZ	5,264	1,273	19.5	278	16.0	NV	2,097	487	18.8	129	19.1
AR	2,322	505	17.8	65	9.2	NH	1,168	133	10.2	11	3.6
CA	29,868	6,822	18.6	998	10.5	NJ	7,323	1,201	14.1	231	11.3
CO	4,136	780	15.9	150	12.3	NM	1,510	468	23.7	82	16.1
CT	3,094	343	10.0	44	5.4	NY	16,617	2,720	14.1	310	7.1
DE	769	94	10.8	19	9.1	NC	7,832	1,421	15.4	216	9.3
DC	533	59	10.0	7	6.3	ND	552	74	11.8	12	7.9
FL	14,430	3,619	20.0	676	16.7	OH	10,088	1,309	11.5	161	5.8
GA	7,850	1,703	17.8	266	10.5	OK	3,060	498	14.0	65	7.2
HI	1,159	98	7.8	15	5.4	OR	3,194	621	16.3	102	11.6
ID	1,282	236	15.6	37	8.9	PA	10,984	1,211	9.9	185	6.7
IL	11,065	1,638	12.9	205	6.4	RI	921	123	11.8	19	7.9
IN	5,522	772	12.3	96	6.0	SC	3,762	707	15.8	137	12.8
IA	2,707	283	9.5	38	6.0	SD	698	100	12.5	20	9.9
KS	2,394	330	12.1	78	11.0	TN	5,252	931	15.1	139	9.4
KY	3,574	682	16.0	102	10.0	TX	18,110	6,084	25.1	1,217	17.9
LA	3,465	869	20.1	127	11.3	UT	2,396	364	13.2	83	9.5
ME	1,182	137	10.4	16	5.7	VT	555	57	9.2	5	3.8
MD	4,870	669	12.1	81	6.0	VA	6,786	962	12.4	129	6.9
MA	6,069	352	5.5	49	3.4	WA	5,732	808	12.4	107	6.8
MI	8,665	1,151	11.7	113	4.7	WV	1,528	271	15.0	24	6.3
MN	4,676	444	8.7	81	6.6	WI	5,020	535	9.6	77	5.8
MS	2,388	519	17.9	105	13.4	WY	458	72	13.6	12	8.8

[1] The estimates are revised from the originally published data.

Source: U.S. Census Bureau, *Income, Poverty, and Health Insurance Coverage in the United States: 2008*, Current Population Reports, P60-236, 2009, Table HI05, "Health Insurance Coverage Status and Type of Coverage by State for All People: 2008." See also <http://www.census.gov/hhes/www/cpstables/032010/health/toc.htm>.

Health and Nutrition 109

Table 153. People Without Health Insurance for the Entire Year by Selected Characteristics: 2007 and 2008

[In thousands, except as noted (299,106 represents 299,106,000). Based on the Current Population Survey; Annual Social and Economic Supplement (ASEC); see text, Section 1 and Appendix III]

Characteristic	2007			2008		
		Uninsured Persons			Uninsured Persons	
	Total persons	Number	Percent distribution	Total persons	Number	Percent distribution
Total [1, 2]	299,106	45,657	100.0	301,483	46,340	100.0
Under 18 years	74,403	8,149	17.8	74,510	7,348	15.9
18 to 24 years	28,398	7,991	17.5	28,688	8,200	17.7
25 to 34 years	40,146	10,329	22.6	40,520	10,754	23.2
35 to 44 years	42,132	7,717	16.9	41,322	8,035	17.3
45 to 64 years	77,237	10,785	23.6	78,655	11,355	24.5
65 years and over	36,790	686	1.5	37,788	646	1.4
Male........................	146,855	24,546	53.8	148,094	25,208	54.4
Female......................	152,250	21,111	46.2	153,388	21,131	45.6
White alone [3]	239,399	34,300	75.1	240,852	34,890	75.3
White alone or in combination.....	244,145	34,977	76.6	245,920	35,680	77.0
Black alone [3]	37,775	7,372	16.1	38,076	7,284	15.7
Black alone or in combination.....	39,683	7,624	16./	40,216	7,602	16.4
Asian alone [3]	13,268	2,234	4.9	13,315	2,344	5.1
Asian alone or in combination.....	14,444	2,321	5.1	14,548	2,484	5.4
Hispanic [4].................	46,026	14,770	32.3	47,485	14,558	31.4
White alone, not Hispanic	196,768	20,548	45.0	197,159	21,322	46.0

[1] Includes other races, not shown separately. [2] The estimates are revised from the originally published data. [3] Refers to people who reported specified race and did not report any other race category. [4] Persons of Hispanic origin may be of any race.

Source: U.S. Census Bureau, *Income, Poverty, and Health Insurance Coverage in the United States: 2008*, Current Population Reports, P60-236, 2009, and "Health Insurance Coverage Status and Type of Coverage by Selected Characteristics: 2008." See also <http://www.census.gov/prod/www/abs/p60.html> and <http://www.census.gov/hhes/www/cpstables/032010/health/toc.htm>.

Table 154. Percent of Workers Participating in Health Care Benefit Programs and Percent of Participants Required to Contribute: 2009

[Based on National Compensation Survey, a sample survey of 8,782 private industry establishments of all sizes, representing about 108 million workers; see Appendix III. See also Table 655. For more information, see <www.bls.gov/ncs/ebs/benefits/2009/home.htm>]

Characteristic	Percent of workers participating—				Single coverage medical plans		Family coverage medical plans	
	Medical care	Dental care	Vision care	Out-patient prescrip-tion drug coverage	Employee contri-butions required (percent)	Average monthly contri-bution [1] (dol.)	Employee contri-butions required (percent)	Average monthly contri-bution [1] (dol.)
Total.........................	52	36	21	51	78	92.43	88	349.36
Worker characteristics:								
Management, professional, and related ...	67	50	28	65	80	90.42	91	346.44
Management, business, and financial	76	57	30	74	81	87.12	91	329.63
Professional and related	63	46	27	61	80	92.29	91	355.93
Service	29	20	12	28	82	96.88	90	380.16
Sales and office.....................	51	35	18	49	82	95.55	92	366.58
Sales and related....................	41	27	14	39	85	102.00	93	372.96
Office and administrative support	57	40	20	55	80	92.23	92	363.41
Natural resources, construction, and maintenance	61	38	25	58	64	98.20	76	359.12
Production, transportation, and material moving.....................	58	39	24	56	76	85.24	84	301.94
Production	66	44	25	63	78	84.55	85	293.99
Transportation, and material moving ...	51	33	22	49	73	86.23	83	313.06
Full-time [2].........................	65	45	25	62	78	91.42	88	345.79
Part-time [2]	13	10	6	13	78	108.02	88	406.86
Union [3]	79	61	46	74	51	79.29	58	262.30
Nonunion...........................	49	33	18	48	83	93.86	94	358.77
Average hourly wage [4]								
Less than $7.85.....................	13	8	(NA)	12	85	94.25	91	366.64
$8.00 to under $10.50................	22	14	8	21	84	99.92	92	382.35
$10.50 to under $15.50...............	54	36	19	52	82	94.51	92	364.75
$15.50 to under $24.22...............	67	44	26	65	76	91.31	88	345.20
$24.22 to under $36.43...............	72	55	33	70	74	88.61	84	327.24
$36.43 or greater....................	73	58	33	71	78	87.61	87	321.30

NA Not available. [1] The average is presented for all covered workers and excludes workers without the plan provision. Averages are for plans stating a flat monthly cost. [2] Employees are classified as working either a full-time or part-time schedule based on the definition used by each establishment. [3] Union workers are those whose wages are determined through collective bargaining. [4] The National Compensation Survey—Benefits program presents wage data in percentiles rather than dollar amounts; see "Technical Note" in source.

Source: U.S. Bureau of Labor Statistics, *National Compensation Survey: Employee Benefits in Private Industry in the United States, March 2009*, September 2009. See also <http://www.bls.gov/ncs/ebs/publications.htm>.

110 Health and Nutrition

Table 155. Retail Prescription Drug Sales: 1995 to 2009

[2,125 represents 2,125,000,000]

Sales outlet	Unit	1995	2000	2003	2004	2005	2006	2007	2008	2009
Number of prescriptions	Mil.	2,125	2,865	3,215	3,274	3,279	3,419	3,510	3,535	3,606
Traditional chain.	Mil.	908	1,335	1,483	1,500	1,518	1,605	1,660	1,682	1,727
Independent.	Mil.	672	698	736	738	714	732	744	732	732
Mass merchant	Mil.	238	293	345	353	359	375	390	400	423
Supermarkets	Mil.	221	394	462	470	465	476	478	480	487
Mail order.	Mil.	86	146	189	214	223	232	238	241	238
Percent distribution of brand/generic mix:										
Brand drugs.	Percent	59.8	57.6	55.0	54.1	50.6	44.8	40.5	35.1	32.2
Generic drugs	Percent	40.2	42.4	45.0	45.9	49.4	55.2	59.5	64.9	67.8
Retail sales	Bil. dol.	72.2	145.6	204.2	216.7	226.1	243.2	249.2	254.1	259.6
Traditional chain.	Bil. dol.	27.8	59.1	86.6	86.7	90.7	96.0	101.2	104.2	104.1
Independent.	Bil. dol.	22.0	33.4	41.2	44.2	45.4	46.7	44.6	44.0	43.5
Mass merchant	Bil. dol.	7.7	13.5	16.1	16.8	17.5	21.6	23.6	24.8	25.0
Supermarkets	Bil. dol.	7.4	17.4	25.2	26.4	26.9	28.1	27.3	25.8	25.6
Mail order.	Bil. dol.	7.4	22.1	35.0	42.7	45.5	50.9	52.5	55.4	61.3
Average prices [1]										
All prescriptions.	Dollars	30.01	45.79	59.52	62.64	63.87	66.97	69.91	72.87	76.94
Brand drugs.	Dollars	40.22	65.29	85.57	91.80	97.65	112.24	124.16	141.80	155.45
Generic drugs	Dollars	14.84	19.33	27.69	28.23	29.21	30.17	33.02	35.62	39.73

[1] Excludes mail order.

Source: National Association of Chain Drug Stores, Alexandria, VA, *NACDS Foundation Chain Pharmacy Industry Profile, 2009*, (copyright). See also <http://www.nacds.org>.

Table 156. Annual Revenue for Health Care Industries: 2006 to 2008

[In millions of dollars (1,566,423 represents $1,566,423,000,000). For taxable and tax-exempt employer firms. Estimates have been adjusted to the results of the 2002 Economic Census. Based on the Service Annual Survey and administrative data; see Appendix III. All firms in NAICS 6211, 6212, 6213, and 6215 are defined as taxable]

Kind of business	2002 NAICS code [1]	Total, all firms [2]			Taxable employer firms		
		2006	2007	2008	2006	2007	2008
Health care and social assistance	**62**	**1,556,423**	**1,656,825**	**1,751,366**	**775,463**	**831,302**	**889,548**
Ambulatory health care services [3]	621	645,308	687,640	730,300	582,292	621,010	659,933
Offices of physicians	6211	327,588	346,778	363,860	327,500	345,770	303,800
Offices of dentists	6212	87,861	93,434	98,051	87,861	93,434	98,051
Offices of other health practitioners.	6213	46,971	50,419	53,941	46,971	50,419	53,941
Offices of chiropractors	62131	10,232	10,839	10,968	10,232	10,839	10,968
Offices of optometrists	62132	10,214	11,032	11,768	10,214	11,032	11,768
Offices of mental health practitioners	62133	4,291	4,555	4,885	4,291	4,555	4,885
Offices of PT/OT/speech therapy & audiology [4]	62134	14,817	16,081	17,894	14,817	16,081	17,894
Outpatient care centers.	6214	73,731	79,300	86,443	35,392	39,189	44,062
Medical & diagnostic laboratories	6215	37,224	38,574	42,139	37,224	38,574	42,139
Home health care services	6216	46,931	52,179	55,760	31,988	36,229	38,981
Other ambulatory health care services	6219	25,002	27,956	30,106	15,268	17,387	18,899
Hospitals [3]	622	644,592	685,424	721,046	76,864	83,628	93,234
General medical & surgical hospitals	6221	603,488	641,040	673,356	62,967	68,110	75,292
Psychiatric & substance abuse hospitals	6222	14,848	15,792	16,643	2,646	3,029	3,393
Other specialty hospitals	6223	26,256	28,592	31,049	11,251	12,489	14,549
Nursing and residential care facilities [3]	623	150,398	159,987	168,106	89,069	95,251	101,558
Nursing care facilities	6231	85,707	90,934	95,822	63,494	68,138	72,319
Residential mental retardation/health facilities	6232	23,910	25,546	27,527	7,115	7,699	8,582
Residential mental retardation facilities	62321	16,416	17,701	19,210	4,981	5,337	5,830
Community care facilities for the elderly	6233	32,084	34,382	35,506	17,174	17,930	19,017
Continuing care retirement communities.	623311	18,138	19,920	20,535	5,895	6,461	6,985
Homes for the elderly	623312	13,946	14,462	14,971	11,279	11,469	12,032
Other residential care facilities	6239	8,697	9,125	9,251	1,286	1,484	1,640
Social assistance [3].	624	116,125	123,774	131,912	27,238	31,413	34,823
Individual and family services	6241	56,972	61,325	64,843	8,758	10,166	11,330
Community food and housing, and emergency and other relief services	6242	18,881	18,537	20,354	(S)	172	220
Vocational rehabilitation services.	6243	13,550	13,452	14,037	2,754	2,727	2,958
Child day care services	6244	26,722	30,460	32,678	15,580	18,348	20,315

S Figure does not meet publication standards. [1] North American Industry Classification System (NAICS), 2002; see text, Section 15. [2] Includes taxable nonemployer firms, not shown separately. [3] Includes other kinds of business, not shown separately. [4] Offices of physical, occupational, and speech therapists, and audiologists.

Source: U.S. Census Bureau, *Service Annual Survey 2008: Health Care and Social Assistance Sector Services*, January 2010, <http://www.census.gov/services/index.html>.

Table 157. Revenue for Selected Health Care Industries by Source of Revenue: 2003 and 2008

[In millions of dollars (270,326 represents $270,326,000,000). For taxable and tax-exempt employer firms. Estimates have been adjusted to the results of the 2002 Economic Census. Based on Service Annual Survey and administrative data; see Appendix III]

Source of revenue	Offices of physicians (NAICS 6211)[1]		Offices of dentists (NAICS 6212)[1]		Hospitals (NAICS 622)[1]		Nursing and residential care facilities (NAICS 623)[1]	
	2003	2008	2003	2008	2003	2008	2003	2008
Total..................	270,326	363,860	73,372	98,051	529,202	721,048	132,994	168,106
Medicare	66,396	74,821	(S)	809	165,078	184,708	17,741	28,704
Medicaid	19,181	18,306	2,565	4,055	63,589	70,192	54,407	61,455
Other government [2]........	2,908	5,316	(S)	611	27,898	36,894	10,377	12,160
Worker's compensation.....	8,659	7,389	(S)	96	5,799	7,169	(S)	(S)
Private insurance..........	130,920	185,656	37,450	44,149	201,605	307,576	6,453	8,437
Patient (out-of-pocket)......	27,432	36,905	32,050	43,873	28,741	32,554	[3] 32,656	[3] 39,169
Other patient care sources, n.e.c [4]................	9,672	19,400	(S)	3,751	10,406	23,845	3,696	7,110
Nonpatient care revenue....	5,158	16,068	(S)	707	26,086	58,108	7,620	10,638

S Figure does not meet publication standards. [1] North American Industry Classification System (NAICS), 2002; see text Section 15. [2] Veterans, National Institute of Health, Indian Affairs, etc. [3] Represents payment from patients and their families plus patients' assigned social security benefits. [4] n.e.c. represents not elsewhere classified.

Source: U.S. Census Bureau, "Service Annual Survey 2008: Health Care and Social Assistance Sector Services," January 2010, <http://www.census.gov/services/index.html>.

Table 158. Employment in the Health Service Industries: 1990 to 2009

[In thousands (9,296 represents 9,296,000). See headnote, Table 631. Based on the 2007 North American Industry Classification System (NAICS); see text, Section 15. For more information on the NAICS changes, please see <http://stats.bls.gov/ces/cesnaics07.htm>]

Industry	2007 NAICS code	1990	2000	2004	2005	2006	2007	2008	2009
Health care and social assistance [1]...	62	9,296	12,718	14,190	14,536	14,925	15,380	15,798	16,101
Ambulatory health care services [1]........	621	2,842	4,320	4,952	5,114	5,286	5,474	5,647	5,777
Offices of physicians	6211	1,278	1,840	2,048	2,094	2,148	2,202	2,253	2,280
Offices of dentists	6212	513	688	760	774	786	808	818	818
Offices of other health practitioners......	6213	276	438	527	549	573	600	627	651
Medical and diagnostic laboratories	6215	129	162	190	198	204	211	217	216
Home health care services	6216	288	633	777	821	866	914	961	1,024
Hospitals [1].........................	622	3,513	3,954	4,285	4,345	4,423	4,515	4,627	4,677
General medical and surgical hospitals...	6221	3,305	3,745	4,042	4,096	4,163	4,242	4,337	4,378
Psychiatric and substance abuse hospitals	6222	113	86	92	93	98	99	102	105
Other hospitals	6223	95	123	151	156	163	174	188	195
Nursing and residential care facilities [1]	623	1,856	2,583	2,818	2,855	2,893	2,958	3,016	3,081
Nursing care facilities	6231	1,170	1,514	1,577	1,577	1,581	1,603	1,619	1,644

[1] Includes other industries, not shown separately.

Source: U.S. Bureau of Labor Statistics, Current Employment Statistics, "Employment, Hours, and Earnings—National," <http://www.bls.gov/ces/data.htm>, accessed May 2010.

Table 159. Osteopathic Physicians: 2001 to 2010

[As of May 31. Osteopathic physicians are fully qualified physicians licensed to practice medicine and to perform surgery. Osteopathic medicine has a strong emphasis on the interrelationship of the body's nerves, muscles, bones and organs. Doctors of osteopathic medicine, or D.O.s, apply the philosophy of treating the whole person to the prevention, diagnosis and treatment of illness, disease, and injury]

Characteristics	2001	2005	2010	Characteristics	2001	2005	2010
Total number of DOs	46,990	56,512	70,480	Unknown..........................	28	318	412
Female................	10,875	15,147	22,537	Self-identified practice specialty [1]	31,996	38,442	50,355
Male..................	36,115	41,365	47,942	Family and general practice..............	14,102	17,800	19,720
				General internal Medicine	2,592	3,107	5,641
Age				General pediatrics/adolescent medicine ...	958	1,176	2,211
Less than 35 years old ...	9,866	12,983	16,277	Obstetrics and gynecology	1,219	1,465	2,165
35 to 44 years old	14,798	16,179	20,118	Pediatric specialties...................	320	348	380
45 to 54 years old	12,754	13,845	15,950	Osteopathic specialties [2]	414	464	902
55 to 64 years old	4,706	7,998	11,195	Other specialties	12,001	13,431	18,984
65 years old and over	4,838	5,189	6,528	Unknown	390	651	352

[1] DOs are assumed to be in active practice if they are under age 65 and have not informed the AOA that they have retired or are inactive. DOs are assumed to be in postdoctoral training (internship, residency or fellowship) if they graduated within the last 3 years or if the AOA has received information that they are in a postdoctoral program. [2] Osteopathic self-identified practice specialties include FOM (Family Practice/OMT), FPO (Family Practice/OMM), NMO (Neuromusculoskeletal Med/OMM), NMS (Neuromusculoskeletal Med/OMT), OM1 (Osteopathic Manipulative Med +1), OMM (Spec Prof in Osteo Manip Med), OMS (Sports Medicine-OMM), and OMT (Osteo Manipulative Medicine). OMT is the therapeutic application of manually guided forces by an osteopathic physician to improve physiologic function and/or support homeostasis that has been altered by somatic dysfunction. OMM is the application of osteopathic philosophy, structural diagnosis, and use of OMT in the patient's diagnosis and management.

Source: American Osteopathic Association, Chicago, IL, AOA Annual Statistics, annual. See also <http://www.osteopathic.org/index.cfm?PageID=aoa_annualrprt>.

Table 160. Physicians by Sex and Specialty: 1980 to 2008

[In thousands (467.7 represents 467,700). As of Dec. 31, except 1990 as of Jan. 1, and as noted. Includes Puerto Rico and Island Areas]

Activity	1980 Total	1980 Office-based	1990 Total	1990 Office-based	2000 Total	2000 Office-based	2008 Total	2008 Office-based
Doctors of medicine, total [1]	**467.7**	**272.0**	**615.4**	**361.0**	813.8	490.4	954.2	556.8
Place of medical education:								
U.S. medical graduates	370.0	226.2	483.7	286.2	616.8	376.5	697.1	419.9
International medical graduates [2]	97.7	45.8	131.8	74.8	197.0	113.9	245.0	137.0
Sex:								
Male	413.4	251.4	511.2	311.7	618.2	382.3	677.8	399.7
Female	54.3	20.6	104.2	49.2	195.5	108.1	276.4	157.1
Allergy/immunology	1.5	1.4	3.4	2.5	4.0	3.1	4.3	3.3
Anesthesiology	16.0	11.3	26.0	17.8	35.7	27.6	42.2	31.4
Cardiovascular diseases	9.8	6.7	15.9	10.7	21.0	16.3	22.7	17.4
Child psychiatry	3.3	2.0	4.3	2.6	6.2	4.3	7.4	5.3
Dermatology	5.7	4.4	7.6	6.0	9.7	8.0	11.0	9.1
Diagnostic radiology	7.0	4.2	15.4	9.8	21.1	14.6	25.4	17.2
Emergency medicine	5.7	3.4	14.2	8.4	23.1	14.5	31.7	20.0
Family practice	27.5	18.4	47.6	37.5	71.6	54.2	85.4	67.4
Gastroenterology	4.0	2.7	7.5	5.2	10.6	8.5	12.7	10.1
General practice	32.5	29.6	22.8	20.5	15.2	13.0	9.6	8.0
General surgery	34.0	22.4	38.4	24.5	36.7	24.5	38.0	24.8
Internal medicine	71.5	40.6	98.3	58.0	134.5	89.7	160.1	107.9
Neurological surgery	3.3	2.5	4.4	3.1	5.0	3.7	5.5	4.0
Neurology	5.7	3.3	9.2	5.6	12.3	8.6	15.2	10.4
Obstetrics and gynecology	26.3	19.5	33.7	25.5	40.2	31.7	42.6	34.0
Ophthalmology	13.0	10.6	16.1	13.1	18.1	15.6	18.2	15.7
Orthopedic surgery	14.0	10.7	19.1	14.2	22.3	17.4	24.8	19.1
Otolaryngology	6.6	5.3	8.1	6.4	9.4	7.6	10.2	8.0
Pathology	13.6	6.1	16.6	7.5	18.8	10.6	19.8	11.1
Pediatrics	29.5	18.2	41.9	27.1	63.9	43.2	77.1	52.9
Physical med./rehab	2.1	1.0	4.1	2.2	6.5	4.3	8.5	6.1
Plastic surgery	3.0	2.4	4.6	3.8	6.2	5.3	7.2	6.1
Psychiatry	27.5	16.0	35.2	20.1	39.5	25.0	40.9	26.5
Pulmonary diseases	3.7	2.0	6.1	3.7	8.7	5.9	10.7	7.5
Radiology	11.7	7.8	8.5	6.1	8.7	6.7	9.1	6.8
Urological surgery	7.7	6.2	9.4	7.4	10.3	8.5	10.5	8.7
Unspecified	12.3	5.0	8.1	1.6	8.3	3.8	8.7	3.7
Not classified	20.6	(X)	12.7	(X)	45.1	(X)	50.3	(X)
Other categories [3]	32.1	(X)	55.4	(X)	75.2	(X)	119.7	(X)

X Not applicable. [1] Includes other categories not shown. [2] International medical graduates received their medical education in schools outside the United States and Canada. [3] Includes inactive and address unknown.

Source: Except as noted, American Medical Association, *Physician Characteristics and Distribution in the U.S.*, Chicago, IL, annual (copyright).

Table 161. Active Physicians and Nurses by State: 2008

[As of December 31. Excludes doctors of osteopathy, physicians with addresses unknown, and inactive status. Includes all physicians not classified according to activity status. As of May. Nurses data comes from the Bureau of Labor Statistics]

State	Physicians Total	Physicians Rate [1]	Nurses Total	Nurses Rate [1]	State	Physicians Total	Physicians Rate [1]	Nurses Total	Nurses Rate [1]
United States	**822,016**	**270**	**2,542,760**	**835**	Missouri	14,476	243	60,100	1,009
Alabama	10,151	217	41,560	889	Montana	2,120	219	7,480	773
Alaska	1,546	225	5,350	777	Nebraska	4,410	247	18,930	1,062
Arizona	13,586	209	37,780	581	Nevada	4,849	185	15,950	610
Arkansas	5,799	202	23,000	802	New Hampshire	3,703	280	13,110	992
California	98,457	269	240,470	657	New Jersey	27,196	314	75,590	873
Colorado	12,768	259	39,440	799	New Mexico	4,799	242	11,900	599
Connecticut	13,195	377	35,370	1,010	New York	76,022	391	168,850	867
Delaware	2,167	247	9,060	1,034	North Carolina	23,506	254	84,230	911
District of Columbia	4,799	813	9,240	1,566	North Dakota	1,573	245	6,340	988
Florida	45,707	248	146,040	793	Ohio	30,647	266	114,930	997
Georgia	20,979	216	64,920	669	Oklahoma	6,304	173	26,760	734
Hawaii	4,035	313	8,760	680	Oregon	10,513	278	29,980	792
Idaho	2,557	167	10,850	710	Pennsylvania	38,103	303	129,060	1,027
Illinois	35,964	280	108,820	847	Rhode Island	3,942	374	11,360	1,078
Indiana	13,810	216	56,500	884	South Carolina	10,225	227	36,880	819
Iowa	5,651	189	30,170	1,008	South Dakota	1,767	220	10,010	1,244
Kansas	6,298	225	25,020	894	Tennessee	16,356	262	61,570	987
Kentucky	9,859	230	41,080	958	Texas	52,070	214	164,400	676
Louisiana	11,682	262	39,610	890	Utah	5,694	209	17,230	632
Maine	3,608	273	14,050	1,065	Vermont	2,317	373	5,900	950
Maryland	23,657	418	50,780	897	Virginia	21,339	274	60,040	770
Massachusetts	30,598	468	79,670	1,218	Washington	17,711	270	52,020	792
Michigan	25,161	252	86,580	866	West Virginia	4,209	232	16,910	932
Minnesota	15,366	294	55,730	1,065	Wisconsin	14,549	259	51,700	919
Mississippi	5,221	178	27,350	930	Wyoming	995	187	4,300	807

[1] Per 100,000 resident population. Based on U.S. Census Bureau estimates as of July 1.

Source: Physicians: American Medical Association, *Physician Characteristics and Distribution in the U.S.*, Chicago, IL, annual (copyright); Nurses: Bureau of Labor Statistics, Occupational Employment Statistics, Occupational Employment and Wages," May 2008 Wage and Employment Statistics," <http://www.bls.gov/oes/home.htm#data>.

Table 162. Percent Distribution of Number of Visits to Health Care Professionals by Selected Characteristics: 2000 and 2008

[Covers ambulatory visits to doctor's offices and emergency departments, and home health care visits during a 12-month period. Based on the redesigned National Health Interview Survey, a sample survey of the civilian noninstitutionalized population]

Characteristic	None 2000	None 2008	1–3 visits 2000	1–3 visits 2008	4–9 visits 2000	4–9 visits 2008	10 or more visits 2000	10 or more visits 2008
All persons [1,2]	**16.7**	**15.5**	**45.4**	**46.8**	**24.6**	**24.8**	**13.3**	**12.9**
SEX [2]								
Male	21.7	20.3	45.9	47.5	22.3	22.2	10.1	10.0
Female	11.9	10.8	44.8	46.2	27.0	27.3	16.3	15.8
AGE								
Under 18 years old	12.3	10.1	53.8	56.6	26.2	26.1	7.6	7.3
18 to 44 years old	23.5	22.7	45.2	46.3	19.1	19.4	12.2	11.7
45 to 64 years old	15.0	14.4	43.4	44.5	25.7	25.7	15.9	15.5
65 to 74 years old	9.0	7.0	34.5	35.7	34.5	36.4	22.1	20.9
75 years old and over	5.8	3.9	29.3	29.4	39.3	39.1	25.6	27.6
RACE [2,3]								
Race alone:								
White	16.1	15.4	45.1	46.2	25.2	25.1	13.6	13.3
Black or African American	17.2	15.4	46.7	48.3	23.4	24.2	12.6	12.2
American Indian or Alaska Native	21.3	15.4	43.0	42.8	20.0	29.1	15.7	12.7
Asian	20.3	18.2	49.2	53.7	20.8	20.9	9.7	7.2
Two or more races	12.1	11.9	41.7	44.9	28.2	25.2	18.0	18.0
HISPANIC ORIGIN AND RACE [2,3,4]								
Hispanic or Latino	26.8	24.3	41.8	44.0	19.8	20.6	11.6	11.1
Mexican	31.0	26.6	40.8	43.4	17.8	19.1	10.3	11.0
Not Hispanic or Latino	15.2	13.7	45.9	47.3	25.3	25.6	13.6	13.4
White, non-Hispanic	14.5	13.1	45.4	46.7	25.9	26.2	14.1	14.0
Black, non-Hispanic	17.1	15.2	46.8	48.7	23.5	23.9	12.6	12.1

[1] Includes other categories not shown separately. [2] Estimates are age adjusted to the year 2000 standard using six age groups: Under 18 years, 18–44 years, 45–54 years, 55–64 years, 65–74 years, and 75 years and over. [3] Estimates by race and Hispanic origin are tabulated using the 1997 standards for federal data on race and ethnicity. Estimates for specific race groups are shown when they meet requirements for statistical reliability and confidentiality. The categories "White only," "Black or African American only," "American Indian and Alaska Native (AI/AN) only," and "Asian only" include persons who reported only one racial group; and the category "2 or more races" includes persons who reported more than one of the five racial groups in the 1997 standards or one of the five racial groups and "Some other race." [4] Persons of Hispanic or Latino origin may be any race or combination of races.

Source: U.S. National Center for Health Statistics, *Health, United States, 2010.* See also <www.cdc.gov/nchs/hus.htm>.

Table 163. Adults 18 Years and Over Who Used Complementary and Alternative Medicine (CAM) in the Past Twelve Months by Type of Therapy: 2002 and 2007

[The denominators for statistics shown exclude persons with unknown CAM information. Estimates were age adjusted to the year 2000 U.S. standard population using four age groups: 18 to 24 years, 25 to 44 years, 45 to 64 years, and 65 years and over]

Therapy	2002 Number (1,000)	2002 Percent	2007 Number (1,000)	2007 Percent
Alternative medical systems:				
Acupuncture	2,136	1.1	3,141	1.4
Homeopathic treatment	3,433	1.7	3,909	1.8
Biologically based therapies:				
Nonvitamin, nonmineral, natural products [1]	38,183	18.9	38,797	17.7
Diet-based therapies [2,3]	7,099	3.5	7,893	3.6
Vegetarian diet	3,184	1.6	3,351	1.5
Atkins diet	3,417	1.7	2,673	1.2
South Beach	(X)	(X)	2,334	1.1
Megavitamin therapy	5,739	2.8	(X)	(X)
Manipulative and body-based therapies:				
Chiropractic care [4]	15,226	7.5	(X)	(X)
Chiropractic or osteopathic manipulation [4]	(X)	(X)	18,740	8.6
Massage	10,052	5.0	18,068	8.3
Movement therapies	(X)	(X)	3,146	1.5
Pilates	(X)	(X)	3,015	1.4
Mind-body therapies:				
Meditation	15,336	7.6	20,541	9.4
Guided imagery	4,194	2.1	4,866	2.2
Progressive relaxation	6,185	3.0	6,454	2.9
Deep breathing exercises	23,457	11.6	27,794	12.7
Yoga	10,386	5.1	13,172	6.1
Tai chi	2,565	1.3	2,267	1.0
Energy healing therapy/Reiki	1,080	0.5	1,216	0.5

X Not applicable. [1] While questions were asked about nonvitamin, nonmineral, natural products in both 2002 and 2007, the data are not comparable due primarily to question order and the specific nonvitamin, nonmineral, natural product covered. [2] The totals of the numbers and percents of the categories listed under "Diet-based therapies" are greater than the number and percent of their respective category heading because respondents could choose more than one of the categories. [3] While questions were asked about Diet-based therapies in both 2002 and 2007, the data are not comparable because respondents were asked about the South Beach Diet in 2007, but not in 2002. [4] While questions were asked about chiropractic therapy in both 2002 and 2007, the data are not comparable because respondents were asked about chiropractic care in 2002 and chiropractic or osteopathic manipulation in 2007.

Source: U.S. National Center for Health Statistics, *Complementary and Alternative Medicine Use Among Adults and Children: United States, 2007*, National Health Statistics Reports, Number 12, 2008. See also <http://www.cdc.gov/nchs/data/nhsr/nhsr012.pdf>.

Table 164. Ambulatory Care Visits to Physicians' Offices and Hospital Outpatient and Emergency Departments: 2008

[(1,189.6 represents 1,189,600,000). Based on the annual National Ambulatory Medical Care Survey and National Hospital Ambulatory Medical Care Survey and subject to sampling error; see source for details]

Characteristic	Number of visits (mil.)				Visits per 100 persons			
	Total	Physician offices	Out-patient dept.	Emer-gency dept.	Total	Physician offices	Out-patient dept.	Emer-gency dept.
Total..............................	1,189.6	956.0	109.9	123.8	398.3	320.1	36.8	41.4
Age:								
Under 15 years old	192.7	147.2	22.3	23.2	315.5	241.0	36.6	37.9
15 to 24 years old	105.3	73.9	11.6	19.8	253.3	177.8	27.8	47.7
25 to 44 years old	256.0	194.6	26.2	35.2	314.8	239.4	32.2	43.3
45 to 64 years old	341.6	284.1	31.1	26.3	440.7	366.5	40.2	34.0
65 to 74 years old	144.9	127.1	10.3	7.5	728.8	639.5	51.7	37.6
75 years old and over	149.2	129.0	8.4	11.8	859.7	743.5	48.3	67.9
Sex:								
Male................................	482.5	383.3	42.5	56.7	329.9	262.1	29.1	38.8
Female..............................	707.1	572.7	67.4	67.0	463.9	375.7	44.2	44.0
Race: [2]								
White	970.9	802.4	79.2	89.4	406.5	335.9	33.1	37.4
Black/African American...............	158.4	104.0	25.4	29.0	420.9	276.4	67.5	77.0
Asian	43.9	38.4	2.9	2.6	325.7	285.1	21.6	19.0
Native Hawaiian/Other Pacific Islander ...	[1] 5.6	[1] 4.5	0.3	[1] 0.8	[1] 1,019.4	[1] 820.7	[1] 60.3	[1] 138.4
American Indian/Alaska Native	4.4	3.0	[1] 0.4	[1] 1.1	145.1	98.9	[1] 13.3	[1] 32.9
More than one race reported..........	6.4	3.6	[1] 1.7	[1] 1.1	124.3	71.1	[1] 32.5	[1] 20.6
Expected sources of payment: [3]								
Private insurance....................	729.3	631.6	45.8	51.9	(X)	(X)	(X)	(X)
Medicare	275.1	231.4	20.9	22.8	(X)	(X)	(X)	(X)
Medicaid/SCHIP [4]	175.9	111.6	34.6	29.7	(X)	(X)	(X)	(X)
Worker's compensation	13.1	10.5	1.0	1.6	(X)	(X)	(X)	(X)
No insurance: [5]	71.3	43.5	8.7	19.1	(X)	(X)	(X)	(X)
Self pay	64.0	40.1	6.1	17.9	(X)	(X)	(X)	(X)
No charge	7.7	3.6	[1] 2.4	1.5	(X)	(X)	(X)	(X)
Other...............................	39.7	27.5	6.5	5.7	(X)	(X)	(X)	(X)
Unknown	39.1	28.7	2.9	7.5	(X)	(X)	(X)	(X)

X Not applicable. [1] Figure does not meet standards of reliability or precision. [2] Race data were missing for 30.2 percent of ambulatory care visits, including 33.0 percent of visits to physician offices, 21.1 percent of visits to hospital outpatient departments, and 16.0 percent of visits to emergency departments. Missing data were imputed, and readers are advised to treat the resulting estimates with caution. More information is available at the Web site below. [3] Estimates include all expected sources of payment reported at the visit. [4] SCHIP is State Children's Health Insurance Program. [5] "No insurance" is defined as having only "self-pay" or "no charge/charity" as payment sources.

Source: U.S. National Center for Health Statistics, *National Health Statistics Reports*, <http://www.cdc.gov/nchs/ahcd.htm>.

Table 165. Visits to Office-Based Physicians and Hospital Outpatient Departments by Diagnosis: 2003 and 2008

[405.5 represents 405,500,000). Based on the International Classification of Diseases, 9th Revision, Clinical Modification, (ICD-9-CM). See headnote, Table 164]

Leading diagnosis	Number (mil.)		Rate per 1,000 persons [1]		Leading diagnosis	Number (mil.)		Rate per 1,000 persons [1]	
	2003	2008	2003	2008		2003	2008	2003	2008
Male, all ages	405.5	425.8	2,908	2,911	Female, all ages.............	595.1	640.1	4,074	4,199
Under 15 years old [2]	89.1	89.6	2,870	2,869	Under 15 years old [2]	78.0	79.9	2,630	2,679
Routine infant or child health check	16.8	23.1	541	740	Routine infant or child health check	14.0	21.9	472	733
Acute upper respiratory infections [3]................	7.8	8.1	250	259	Acute upper respiratory infections [3].................	7.8	7.1	262	239
Otitis media and Eustachian tube disorders	8.4	7.4	269	236	Otitis media and Eustachian tube disorders	6.4	6.2	217	209
Acute pharyngitis.............	2.1	3.4	66	107	Acute pharyngitis.............	3.3	3.1	110	105
15 to 44 years old [2]	104.0	93.4	1,710	1,524	15 to 44 years old [2]	208.3	212.8	3,386	3,458
General medical examination ..	4.4	4.8	72	78	Normal pregnancy.............	25.6	24.7	415	401
Acute upper respiratory infections [3]................	4.0	3.2	65	53	Gynecological examination	9.8	10.1	160	165
Spinal disorders.............	3.4	3.2	56	52	Complications of pregnancy, childbirth, and the puerperium. .	7.4	7.7	121	124
Essential hypertension	2.1	2.8	35	46					
45 to 64 years old [2]	112.6	127.2	3,404	3,376	45 to 64 years old [2]	167.9	188.1	4,781	4,720
Essential hypertension	7.6	8.6	231	227	Essential hypertension	8.2	12.0	234	302
Diabetes mellitus.............	5.2	6.4	156	171	Arthropathies and related disorders	8.1	7.9	231	198
Spinal disorders.............	4.7	5.4	143	144	Rheumatism, excluding back....	6.0	6.4	170	161
Arthropathies and related disorders	4.5	4.1	135	110					
65 years old and over [2]	99.8	115.5	6,881	7,211	65 years old and over [2]	140.9	159.3	7,123	7,509
Essential hypertension	7.2	8.8	496	546	Essential hypertension	11.1	15.4	563	728
Heart disease [4]	3.7	6.7	256	416	Arthropathies and related disorders	8.1	7.7	408	364
Malignant neoplasms.........	6.3	6.3	434	392	Heart disease [4]	4.3	6.9	218	328
Ischemic heart disease	3.6	6.0	250	376					

[1] Based on U.S. Census Bureau estimated civilian population as of July 1. [2] Includes other first-listed diagnoses, not shown separately. [3] Excluding pharyngitis. [4] Excluding ischemic.

Source: U.S. National Center for Health Statistics, *National Health Statistics Reports*, <http://www.cdc.gov/nchs/ahcd.htm>.

Health and Nutrition 115

Table 166. Visits to Hospital Emergency Departments by Diagnosis: 2008

[56,742 represents 56,742,000. See headnote, Tables 164 and 165]

Leading diagnosis	Number (1,000)	Rate per 1,000 persons [1]	Leading diagnosis	Number (1,000)	Rate per 1,000 persons [1]
MALE			**FEMALE**		
All ages.	**56,742**	**388**	**All ages.**	**67,020**	**440**
Under 15 years old [2]	**12,762**	**409**	**Under 15 years old [2]**	**10,395**	**348**
Acute upper respiratory infections [3]	1,129	36	Acute respiratory infections [3]	916	31
Otitis media and eustachian tube disorders	826	26	Otitis media and Eustachian tube disorders	696	23
Open wound of head	742	24	Pyrexia of unknown origin	650	22
Pyrexia of unknown origin	718	23	Contusion with intact skin surface	363	12
Contusion with intact skin surface	577	18	Acute pharyngitis	308	10
15 to 44 years old [2]	**23,246**	**379**	**15 to 44 years old [2]**	**31,763**	**516**
Open wound, excluding head	1,264	21	Abdominal pain	2,103	34
Contusion with intact skin surfaces	1,186	19	Complications of pregnancy, childbirth and the puerperium	1,394	23
Cellulitis and abscess	921	15	Contusion with intact skin surface	1,121	18
Chest pain	869	14	Chest pain	1,121	18
Sprains and strains, excluding ankle and back	765	12	Spinal disorders	1,048	17
45 to 64 years old [2]	**12,542**	**333**	**45 to 64 years old [2]**	**13,793**	**346**
Chest pain	786	21	Chest pain	850	21
Open wound, excluding head	565	15	Abdominal pain	701	18
Spinal disorders	512	14	Spinal disorders	512	13
Abdominal pain	452	12	Contusion with intact skin surface	433	11
Cellulitis and abscess	373	10	Cellulitis and abscess	389	10
65 years old and over [2]	**8,192**	**511**	**65 years old and over [2]**	**11,069**	**522**
Chest pain	456	28	Chest pain	628	30
Heart disease, excluding ischemic	442	28	Contusion with intact skin surface	541	25
Pneumonia	356	22	Heart disease, excluding ischemic	537	25
Contusion with intact skin surface	254	16	Abdominal pain	459	22
Chronic and unspecified bronchitis	241	15	Urinary tract infection site not specified.	316	15

[1] Based on U.S. Census Bureau estimated civilian noninstitutional population as of July 1. [2] Includes other first-listed diagnosis, not shown separately. [3] Excluding pharyngitis.

Source: U.S. National Center for Health Statistics, *National Health Statistics Reports*, <http://www.cdc.gov/nchs/ahcd.htm>.

Table 167. Procedures for Inpatients Discharged From Short-Stay Hospitals: 1990 to 2007

[(23,051 represents 23,051,000). Procedure categories are based on the International Classification of Diseases, 9th Revision, Clinical Modification. See headnote, Table 172]

Sex and type of procedure	Number of procedures (1,000)				Rate per 1,000 population [1]			
	1990	1995	2000	2007	1990	1995	2000	2007
Surgical procedures, total [2]	**23,051**	**22,530**	**23,244**	**27,111**	**92.4**	**86.2**	**83.6**	**90.2**
Cesarean section	945	785	855	1,339	3.8	3.0	3.1	4.5
Repair of current obstetric laceration	795	964	1,136	1,261	3.2	3.7	4.1	4.2
Cardiac catheterization	995	1,068	1,221	1,061	4.0	4.1	4.4	3.5
Reduction of fracture [3]	609	577	628	677	2.4	2.2	2.3	2.3
Male, total [2]	**8,538**	**8,388**	**8,689**	**10,679**	**70.6**	**65.9**	**63.9**	**72.3**
Cardiac catheterization	620	660	732	639	5.1	5.2	5.4	4.3
Coronary artery bypass graft [4]	286	423	371	291	2.4	3.3	2.7	2.0
Reduction of fracture [3]	300	251	285	325	2.5	2.0	2.1	2.2
Female, total [2]	**14,513**	**14,142**	**14,556**	**16,432**	**113.0**	**105.3**	**102.4**	**107.5**
Cesarean section	945	785	855	1,339	7.4	5.8	6.0	8.8
Repair of current obstetric laceration	795	964	1,136	1,261	6.2	7.2	8.0	8.3
Hysterectomy	591	583	633	517	4.6	4.3	4.5	3.4
Diagnostic and other nonsurgical procedures [5]	**17,455**	**17,278**	**16,737**	**17,882**	**70.0**	**66.1**	**60.2**	**59.5**
Angiocardiography and arteriography [6]	1,735	1,834	2,005	1,861	7.0	7.0	7.2	6.2
Respiratory therapy	1,164	1,127	991	1,093	4.7	4.3	3.6	3.6
Manual assisted delivery	750	866	898	1,224	3.0	3.3	3.2	4.1
Diagnostic ultrasound	1,608	1,181	886	866	6.4	4.5	3.2	2.9
Fetal electrocardiogram and fetal monitoring	1,377	935	750	765	5.6	3.6	2.7	2.5
Male, total [5]	**7,378**	**7,261**	**6,965**	**7,284**	**61.0**	**57.1**	**51.2**	**49.3**
Angiocardiography and arteriography [6]	1,051	1,076	1,157	1,034	8.7	8.5	8.5	7.0
Respiratory therapy	586	572	507	553	4.9	4.5	3.7	3.7
Computerized Axial Tomographic scan [7]	736	473	345	297	6.1	3.7	2.5	2.0
Female, total [5]	**10,077**	**10,016**	**9,772**	**10,598**	**78.5**	**74.6**	**68.8**	**69.4**
Manual assisted delivery	750	866	898	1,224	5.9	6.5	6.3	8.0
Fetal EKG and fetal monitoring	1,377	935	750	765	10.8	7.0	5.5	5.0
Respiratory therapy	578	555	484	540	4.5	4.1	3.4	3.5
Diagnostic ultrasound	941	682	501	482	7.3	5.1	3.5	3.2

[1] Based on Census Bureau estimated civilian population as of July 1. Population estimates based on the 1990 census were used to calculate rates for 1990 through 2000. Population estimates based on the 2000 census were used to calculate rates for 2001 through 2007. [2] Includes other types of surgical procedures, not shown separately. [3] Excluding skull, nose, and jaw. [4] It is possible for a discharge to have more than one of these recorded. [5] Includes other nonsurgical procedures, not shown separately. [6] Using contrast material. [7] Also known as CAT scan.

Source: U.S. National Center for Health Statistics, *Vital and Health Statistics*, Series 13, and unpublished data, <http://www.cdc.gov/nchs/products/series.htm>.

Table 168. Hospitals—Summary Characteristics: 1990 to 2008

[For beds, (1,213 represents 1,213,000). Covers hospitals accepted for registration by the American Hospital Association; see text, this section. Short–term hospitals have an average patient stay of less than 30 days; long–term, an average stay of longer duration. Special hospitals include obstetrics and gynecology; eye, ear, nose, and throat; rehabilitation; orthopedic; and chronic and other special hospitals except psychiatric, tuberculosis, alcoholism, and chemical dependency hospitals]

Item	1990	1995	2000	2003	2004	2005	2006	2007	2008
Number:									
All hospitals	6,649	6,291	5,810	5,764	5,759	5,756	5,747	5,708	5,815
With 100 beds or more	3,620	3,376	3,102	3,007	2,972	2,942	2,928	2,901	2,884
Nonfederal [1]	6,312	5,992	5,565	5,525	5,520	5,530	5,526	5,495	5,602
Community hospitals [2]	5,384	5,194	4,915	4,895	4,919	4,936	4,927	4,897	5,010
Nongovernmental nonprofit	3,191	3,092	3,003	2,984	2,967	2,958	2,919	2,913	2,923
For profit	749	752	749	790	835	868	889	873	982
State and local government	1,444	1,350	1,163	1,121	1,117	1,110	1,119	1,111	1,105
Long term general and special . . .	131	112	131	126	108	115	127	135	128
Psychiatric	757	657	496	477	466	456	462	444	447
Tuberculosis	4	3	4	4	4	3	2	1	1
Federal	337	299	245	239	239	226	221	213	213
Beds (1,000): [3]									
All hospitals	1,213	1,081	984	965	956	947	947	945	951
Rate per 1,000 population [4]	4.9	4.1	3.5	3.3	3.3	3.2	3.2	3.1	3.1
Beds per hospital	182	172	169	167	166	165	165	166	164
Nonfederal [1]	1,113	1,004	931	917	908	901	901	899	905
Community hospitals [2]	927	873	824	813	808	802	802	801	808
Rate per 1,000 population [4]	3.7	3.3	2.9	2.8	2.8	2.7	2.7	2.7	2.7
Nongovernmental nonprofit	657	610	583	575	567	561	559	554	557
For profit	102	106	110	110	112	114	115	116	121
State and local government	169	157	131	120	127	128	128	131	131
Long term general and special . . .	25	19	18	18	15	15	16	17	16
Psychiatric	158	110	87	85	86	82	84	79	79
Tuberculosis	(Z)	(Z)	(Z)	(Z)	(Z)	(Z)	(Z)	(Z)	(Z)
Federal	98	78	53	47	47	46	46	46	46
Average daily census (1,000): [5]									
All hospitals	844	710	650	657	658	656	653	645	649
Community hospitals [2]	619	548	526	539	541	540	538	533	536
Nongovernmental nonprofit	455	393	382	389	388	388	384	380	380
For profit	54	55	61	65	68	68	67	66	70
State and local government	111	100	83	84	84	85	86	87	86
Expenses (bil. dol.): [6]									
All hospitals	234.9	320.3	395.4	498.1	533.8	570.5	607.3	638.5	690.0
Nonfederal [1]	219.6	300.0	371.5	467.2	499.0	533.7	569.8	599.7	646.1
Community hospitals [2]	203.7	285.6	356.6	450.1	481.2	515.7	551.8	581.0	626.6
Nongovernmental nonprofit	150.7	209.6	267.1	337.7	359.4	386.0	412.8	435.5	468.1
For profit	18.8	26.7	35.0	44.0	48.9	51.8	54.9	55.8	61.8
State and local government	34.2	49.3	54.5	68.4	72.8	77.9	83.9	89.8	96.7
Long term general and special . . .	2.7	2.2	2.8	3.6	3.6	3.6	4.0	3.9	4.5
Psychiatric	12.9	11.7	11.9	13.1	13.8	13.9	15.0	14.5	14.7
Tuberculosis	0.1	0.4	(Z)	(Z)	(Z)	(Z)	(Z)	(Z)	(Z)
Federal	15.2	20.2	23.9	30.9	34.8	36.8	37.5	38.8	44.0
Personnel (1,000): [7]									
All hospitals	4,063	4,273	4,454	4,650	4,695	4,790	4,907	5,024	5,116
Nonfederal [1]	3,760	3,971	4,157	4,350	4,379	4,479	4,569	4,699	4,775
Community hospitals [2]	3,420	3,714	3,911	4,108	4,147	4,260	4,343	4,465	4,550
Nongovernmental nonprofit	2,533	2,702	2,919	3,058	3,076	3,154	3,207	3,286	3,340
For profit	273	343	378	391	405	421	423	432	450
State and local government	614	670	614	658	665	681	713	747	760
Long term general and special . . .	55	38	41	45	42	38	43	44	41
Psychiatric	280	215	200	194	185	182	180	187	182
Tuberculosis	1	1	1	1	1	1	1	1	(Z)
Federal	303	301	297	300	315	311	339	325	341
Outpatient visits (mil.)	368.2	483.2	592.7	648.6	662.1	673.7	690.4	693.5	710
Emergency	92.8	99.9	106.9	115.1	116.9	118.9	122.6	124.7	126.7

Z Less than 500 or $50 million. [1] Includes hospital units of institutions. [2] Short-term (average length of stay less than 30 days) general and special (e.g., obstetrics and gynecology; eye, ear, nose and throat; rehabilitation, etc. except psychiatric, tuberculosis, alcoholism, and chemical dependency). Excludes hospital units of institutions. [3] Number of beds at end of reporting period. [4] Based on Census Bureau estimated resident population as of July 1. 1990, and 2000 based on enumerated resident population as of April 1. Estimates reflect revisions based on the 2000 Census of Population. Estimates reflect revisions based on the 2000 Census of Population. [5] The average number of people served on an inpatient basis on a single day during the reporting period. [6] Excludes new construction. [7] Includes full-time equivalents of part-time personnel.

Source: Health Forum, An American Hospital Association Company, Chicago, IL, *AHA Hospital Statistics 2010 Edition*, and prior years (copyright). See also <www.ahadata.com>.

Table 169. Average Cost to Community Hospitals Per Patient: 1990 to 2008

[In dollars, except percent. Covers non-federal short-term general or special hospitals (excluding psychiatric or tuberculosis hospitals and hospital units of institutions). Total cost per patient based on total hospital expenses (payroll, employee benefits, professional fees, supplies, etc.). Data have been adjusted for outpatient visits]

Type of expense and hospital	1990	1995	2000	2002	2003	2004	2005	2006	2007	2008
Average cost per day, total	**687**	**968**	**1,149**	**1,290**	**1,379**	**1,450**	**1,522**	**1,612**	**1,690**	**1,782**
Annual percent change [1]	7.8	4.0	4.2	6.0	6.9	5.1	5.0	5.9	4.8	5.4
Nongovernmental nonprofit	692	994	1,182	1,329	1,429	1,501	1,585	1,686	1,772	1,876
For profit	752	947	1,057	1,181	1,264	1,362	1,412	1,472	1,519	1,556
State and local government.	635	878	1,064	1,188	1,238	1,291	1,329	1,400	1,460	1,552
Average cost per stay, total	**4,947**	**6,216**	**6,649**	**7,346**	**7,796**	**8,166**	**8,793**	**8,970**	**9,342**	**9,788**
Nongovernmental nonprofit	5,001	6,279	6,717	7,458	7,905	8,266	8,670	9,190	9,574	10,081
For profit	4,727	5,425	5,642	6,161	6,590	7,139	7,351	7,422	7,740	7,985
State and local government.	4,838	6,445	7,106	7,773	8,205	8,473	8,793	9,147	9,446	9,827

[1] Change from immediate prior year.

Source: Health Forum, An American Hospital Association Company, Chicago, IL, *AHA Hospital Statistics 2010 Edition*, and prior years (copyright). See also <www.ahadata.com>.

Table 170. Community Hospitals—States: 2000 and 2008

[In thousands, (823.6 represents 823,600). For definition of community hospitals see footnote 2, Table 168]

State	Number of hospitals		Beds (1,000)		Patients admitted (1,000)		Average daily census [1] (1,000)		Outpatient visits (mil.)		Average cost per day (dol.)	
	2000	2008	2000	2008	2000	2008	2000	2008	2000	2008	2000	2008
United States	**4,915**	**5,010**	**823.6**	**808.1**	**33,089**	**35,761**	**525.7**	**536.2**	**521.4**	**624.1**	**1,149**	**1,782**
Alabama	108	109	16.4	15.3	680	687	9.8	9.6	8.0	9.0	980	1,352
Alaska	18	22	1.4	1.6	47	58	0.8	0.9	1.3	1.7	1,495	2,231
Arizona	61	71	10.9	13.1	539	716	6.8	8.8	5.3	7.7	1,311	2,082
Arkansas	83	86	9.8	9.7	368	376	5.7	5.4	4.4	5.0	908	1,381
California	389	352	72.7	69.6	3,315	3,461	47.8	49.2	44.9	48.9	1,438	2,279
Colorado	69	78	9.4	10.1	397	442	5.4	6.0	6.7	8.4	1,280	2,143
Connecticut	35	35	7.7	7.9	349	401	5.8	6.3	6.7	8.1	1,373	2,026
Delaware	5	7	1.8	2.1	83	104	1.4	1.7	1.5	1.7	1,311	2,043
District of Columbia	11	10	3.3	3.4	129	137	2.5	2.6	1.3	2.4	1,512	2,352
Florida	202	211	51.2	52.8	2,119	2,397	31.0	33.6	21.8	24.4	1,161	1,722
Georgia	151	153	23.9	25.6	863	959	15.0	16.9	11.2	14.2	978	1,313
Hawaii	21	25	3.1	3.1	100	111	2.3	2.3	2.5	2.0	1,088	1,510
Idaho	42	39	3.5	3.3	123	136	1.8	1.8	2.2	2.9	1,003	1,757
Illinois.	196	191	37.3	34.5	1,531	1,611	22.4	22.1	25.1	31.0	1,278	1,856
Indiana.	109	123	19.2	17.6	700	733	10.8	10.5	14.1	17.0	1,132	1,950
Iowa.	115	118	11.8	10.5	360	373	6.8	6.1	9.2	10.4	740	1,190
Kansas.	129	132	10.8	10.3	310	328	5.7	5.7	5.3	6.5	837	1,234
Kentucky	105	105	14.8	14.2	582	610	9.1	8.8	8.7	9.7	929	1,427
Louisiana	123	130	17.5	16.0	654	637	9.8	9.2	10.0	11.2	1,075	1,484
Maine.	37	37	3.7	3.5	147	149	2.4	2.3	3.2	5.1	1,148	1,828
Maryland	49	50	11.2	12.0	587	711	8.2	9.0	6.0	8.1	1,315	2,183
Massachusetts.	80	75	16.6	15.7	740	808	11.7	11.4	16.7	20.5	1,467	2,293
Michigan	146	153	26.1	25.3	1,106	1,222	16.9	17.4	24.9	28.0	1,211	1,841
Minnesota	135	130	16.7	15.6	571	641	11.2	10.6	7.3	10.0	932	1,601
Mississippi	95	98	13.6	13.1	425	431	8.0	7.7	3.7	5.0	719	1,148
Missouri	119	123	20.1	19.0	773	841	11.7	12.0	14.8	18.8	1,185	1,887
Montana.	52	48	4.3	3.8	99	104	2.9	2.5	2.6	3.2	579	1,078
Nebraska	85	86	8.2	7.3	209	215	4.8	4.3	3.4	4.6	743	1,398
Nevada	22	35	3.8	5.1	199	247	2.7	3.6	2.2	2.9	1,285	1,990
New Hampshire	28	28	2.9	2.9	111	124	1.7	1.8	2.8	4.5	1,201	1,923
New Jersey	80	73	25.3	20.9	1,074	1,086	17.3	15.3	16.3	18.1	1,299	2,150
New Mexico	35	36	3.5	3.9	174	174	2.0	2.2	3.1	4.3	1,388	1,932
New York	215	194	66.4	61.2	2,416	2,528	52.1	49.1	46.4	52.6	1,118	1,770
North Carolina	113	116	23.1	23.1	971	1,042	16.0	16.4	12.4	17.7	1,061	1,515
North Dakota	42	41	3.9	3.4	89	89	2.3	2.0	1.7	1.7	747	1,038
Ohio.	163	181	33.8	33.9	1,404	1,548	20.6	21.4	26.9	32.9	1,198	1,942
Oklahoma	108	115	11.1	11.0	429	463	6.2	6.7	4.7	5.4	1,031	1,491
Oregon.	59	58	6.6	6.8	330	349	3.9	4.2	7.3	8.6	1,461	2,512
Pennsylvania	207	201	42.3	40.4	1,796	1,901	28.8	28.3	31.8	38.5	1,080	1,714
Rhode Island	11	11	2.4	2.5	119	127	1.7	1.8	2.1	2.6	1,313	2,061
South Carolina.	63	69	11.5	12.5	495	529	8.0	8.1	7.8	5.9	1,101	1,764
South Dakota.	48	53	4.3	4.1	99	102	2.8	2.7	1.7	1.9	476	929
Tennessee.	121	137	20.6	21.1	737	859	11.5	13.4	10.3	11.2	1,078	1,359
Texas	403	426	55.9	61.0	2,367	2,586	33.1	36.7	29.4	34.8	1,274	1,859
Utah.	42	43	4.3	4.9	194	226	2.4	2.8	4.5	5.3	1,375	2,031
Vermont.	14	14	1.7	1.3	52	51	1.1	0.9	1.2	3.3	888	1,453
Virginia.	88	90	16.9	17.6	727	796	11.4	12.2	9.5	13.3	1,057	1,698
Washington	84	86	11.1	11.3	505	579	6.6	7.3	9.6	11.4	1,511	2,490
West Virginia	57	56	8.0	7.5	288	284	4.8	4.5	5.2	6.6	844	1,235
Wisconsin	118	126	15.3	13.7	558	617	9.1	8.7	10.9	14.2	1,055	1,754
Wyoming	24	24	1.9	2.1	48	53	1.1	1.1	0.9	1.0	677	1,047

[1] The average number of people served on an inpatient basis on a single day during the reporting period.

Source: Health Forum, An American Hospital Association Company, Chicago, IL, *AHA Hospital Statistics 2010 Edition*, and prior years (copyright). See also <www.ahadata.com>.

Table 171. Hospital Use Rates by Type of Hospital: 1990 to 2008

Type of Hospital	1990	1995	2000	2004	2005	2006	2007	2008
Community hospitals: [1]								
Admissions per 1,000 population [2]	125	116	117	119	119	118	117	118
Admissions per bed	34	35	40	43	44	44	43	44
Average length of stay (days) [3]	7.2	6.5	5.8	5.6	5.6	5.5	5.5	5.5
Outpatient visits per admission	9.7	13.4	15.8	16.3	16.5	16.9	17.1	17.5
Outpatient visits per 1,000 population [2]	1,207	1,556	1,852	1,946	1,976	2,002	2,000	2,053
Surgical operations (million [4])	21.9	23.2	26.1	27.4	27.5	28.1	28.1	27.5
Number per admission	0.7	0.7	0.8	0.8	0.8	0.7	0.8	0.8
Nonfederal psychiatric:								
Admissions per 1,000 population [2]	2.9	2.7	2.4	2.7	2.5	2.3	2.3	2.4
Days in hospital per 1,000 population [2]	190	122	93	88	89	83	82	80

[1] Short term (average length of stay less than 30 days) general and special (e.g., obstetrics and gynecology; eye, ear, nose and throat; rehabilitation, etc. except psychiatric, tuberculosis, alcoholism and chemical dependency). Excludes hospital units of institutions. [2] Based on U.S. Census Bureau estimated resident population as of July 1. Estimates reflect revisions based on the 2000 census of population. 1990 and 2000 based on enumerated resident population as of April 1. [3] Number of inpatient days divided by number of admissions. [4] 21.9 represents 21,900,000.

Source: Health Forum, An American Hospital Association Company, *AHA Hospital Statistics 2010 Edition*, Chicago, IL, and prior years (copyright). See also <www.ahadata.com>.

Table 172. Hospital Utilization Rates by Sex: 1990 to 2007

[(30,788 represents 30,788,000). Represents estimates of inpatients discharged from noninstitutional, short-stay hospitals, exclusive of federal hospitals. Excludes newborn infants. Based on sample data collected from the National Hospital Discharge Survey, a sample survey of hospital records of patients discharged in year shown; subject to sampling variability]

Item and sex	1990	1995	2000	2002	2003	2004	2005	2006	2007
Patients discharged (1,000)	30,788	30,722	31,706	33,727	34,738	34,864	34,667	34,854	34,369
Patients discharged per 1,000 persons, total [1]	122	116	113	118	120	119	117	117	114
Male	100	94	91	95	98	97	96	95	94
Female	143	136	134	139	141	141	138	138	134
Days of care per 1,000 persons, total [1]	784	620	555	572	578	574	562	558	554
Male	694	551	486	506	507	505	498	495	494
Female	869	686	620	635	646	641	624	619	612
Average stay (days)	6.4	5.4	4.9	4.9	4.8	4.8	4.8	4.8	4.8
Male	6.9	5.8	5.3	5.3	5.2	5.2	5.2	5.2	5.3
Female	6.1	5.0	4.6	4.6	4.6	4.5	4.5	4.5	4.6

[1] Rates are computed using Census Bureau estimates of the civilian population as of July 1. Rates for 1990 and 1995 were based on population estimates adjusted for the net underenumeration in the 1990 census. Rates for 2000 and later were calculated using 2000-based postcensal estimates.

Source: U.S. National Center for Health Statistics, *Vital and Health Statistics*, Series 13 and unpublished data. See also <http://www.cdc.gov/nchs/products/series.htm#sr13>.

Table 173. Hospital Utilization Measures for HIV Patients: 1990 to 2007

[HIV represents human immunodeficiency virus. See headnote, Table 172]

Measure of utilization	Unit	1990	1995	2000	2004	2005	2006	2007
Number of patients discharged	1,000	146	249	173	204	185	223	221
Male	1,000	114	183	115	132	113	145	146
Female	1,000	32	66	58	73	72	78	75
Rate of patient discharges [1]	Rate	5.8	9.4	6.2	7.0	6.3	7.5	7.4
Number of days of care	1,000	2,188	2,326	1,257	1,477	1,244	1,418	1,483
Male	1,000	1,777	1,649	895	876	751	907	1,009
Female	1,000	411	677	362	601	493	511	474
Rate of days of care [1]	Rate	86.9	87.6	45.2	50.5	42.2	47.6	49.3
Average length of stay	Days	14.9	9.3	7.3	7.2	6.7	6.3	6.7
Male	Days	15.5	9.0	7.8	6.7	6.7	6.2	6.9
Female	Days	12.9	10.3	6.3	8.3	6.8	6.5	6.3

[1] Per 10,000 population. Based on Census Bureau estimated civilian population as of July 1. Populations for 1990 and 1995 were adjusted for the net undernumeration in the 1990 census. Populations for 2000 and later were 2000-based postcensal estimates.

Source: U.S. National Center for Health Statistics, *Vital and Health Statistics*, Series 13 and unpublished data. See also <http://www.cdc.gov/nchs/products/series.htm#sr13>.

Health and Nutrition 119

Table 174. Hospital Discharges and Days of Care: 2002 and 2007

[(33,727 represents 33,727,000). See headnote, Table 172. For composition of regions, see map, inside front cover]

Age, race, and region	Discharges Number (1,000) 2002	Discharges Number (1,000) 2007	Discharges Per 1,000 persons [1] 2002	Discharges Per 1,000 persons [1] 2007	Days of care per 1,000 persons [1] 2002	Days of care per 1,000 persons [1] 2007	Average stay (days) 2002	Average stay (days) 2007
Total [2]	33,727	34,369	118	114	572	554	4.9	4.8
Age:								
Under 1 year old	810	698	201	164	1,134	847	5.6	5.2
1 to 4 years old	713	642	46	39	159	128	3.5	3.3
5 to 14 years old	1,016	841	25	21	109	114	4.4	5.4
15 to 24 years old	3,083	3,062	77	73	266	258	3.5	3.5
25 to 34 years old	3,897	4,032	99	100	328	342	3.3	3.4
35 to 44 years old	3,757	3,477	84	81	368	346	4.4	4.3
45 to 64 years old	7,723	8,753	116	114	575	587	5.0	5.1
65 to 74 years old	4,642	4,722	254	244	1,412	1,328	5.6	5.4
75 years old and over	8,085	8,142	467	439	2,795	2,488	6.0	5.7
Race:								
White	20,806	20,483	90	85	436	415	4.9	4.9
Black	3,995	4,321	109	112	584	608	5.3	5.4
Asian/Pacific Islander	538	497	45	36	243	165	5.4	4.6
American Indian/Eskimo/Aleut	173	[3] 113	63	[3] 39	330	[3] 185	5.2	4.8
Region:								
Northeast	6,990	7,361	129	135	727	779	5.6	5.8
Midwest	7,503	7,706	115	116	512	499	4.4	4.3
South	12,994	12,689	127	116	618	567	4.9	4.9
West	6,239	6,612	96	95	430	409	4.5	4.3

[1] Rates were calculated using U.S. Census Bureau 2000-based postcensal estimates of the civilian population as of July 1.
[2] Includes other races not shown separately. [3] Figure does not meet standard of reliability or precision.

Source: U.S. National Center for Health Statistics, Vital and Health Statistics, Series 13 and unpublished data. See also <http://www.cdc.gov/nchs/products/series.htm#sr13>.

Table 175. Hospital Discharges and Days of Care by Selected Diagnosis: 2007

[(13,834 represents 13,834,000). Represents estimates of inpatients discharged from noninstitutional, short-stay hospitals, exclusive of federal hospitals. Excludes newborn infants. Diagnostic categories are based on the International Classification of Diseases, Ninth Revision, Clinical Modification. See headnote, Table 172]

Sex, age, and selected first-listed diagnosis [1]	Discharges Number (1,000) [2]	Discharges Per 1,000 persons [2]	Average stay (days)[2]	Sex, age, and selected first-listed diagnosis [1]	Discharges Number (1,000) [2]	Discharges Per 1,000 persons [2]	Average stay (days)[2]
Male				**Female**			
All ages [3]	13,834	93.7	5.2	All ages [3]	20,535	134.4	4.5
Under 18 years [3]	1,458	38.6	4.8	Under 18 years [3]	1,325	36.7	4.6
Injury	145	3.8	3.1	Injury	80	2.2	[4] 3.9
Asthma	[4] 94	[4] 2.5	[4] 2.3	Acute bronchitis and			
18–44 years [3]	2,607	46.1	4.8	bronchiolitis	58	1.6	2.8
Injury	370	6.5	4.4	18–44 years [3]	7,362	132.4	3.2
				Childbirth	3,986	71.4	2.6
Schizophrenia, mood disorders, delusional disorders, nonorganic				Schizophrenia, mood disorders, delusional disorders, nonorganic			
psychoses [5]	325	5.8	7.2	psychoses [5]	325	5.9	6.4
Alcohol and drug [6]	183	3.2	4.4	Injury	162	2.9	3.6
Heart disease	144	2.5	(NA)	Uterine fibroids	85	1.5	2.4
45–64 years [3]	4,316	115.7	5.3	45–64 years [3]	4,437	113.2	4.9
Heart disease	753	20.2	3.8	Heart disease	452	11.5	4.0
Injury	239	6.4	5.4	Cancer, all	252	6.4	5.8
Cancer, all	231	6.2	6.6	Osteoarthritis	179	4.6	3.5
65–74 years [3]	2,274	255.9	5.3	65–74 years [3]	2,447	233.8	5.5
Heart disease	513	57.8	4.4	Heart disease	367	35.1	4.8
Cancer, all	149	16.8	7.2	Osteoarthritis	149	14.3	3.6
Stroke	100	11.2	5.2	Cancer, all	144	13.8	6.2
Pneumonia	82	9.2	5.0	Pneumonia	87	8.3	5.3
75–84 years [3]	2,211	416.3	5.7	75–84 years [3]	2,976	386.0	5.6
Heart disease	502	94.5	4.7	Heart disease	550	71.3	4.7
Pneumonia	123	23.1	5.3	Injury	195	25.3	5.5
Cancer, all	102	19.2	7.1	Pneumonia	125	16.2	5.4
Stroke	95	17.8	4.8	Stroke	132	17.2	4.8
85 years and over [3]	967	544.1	5.8	85 years and over [3]	1,987	532.0	5.5
Heart disease	194	109.3	5.0	Heart disease	367	98.2	4.7
Pneumonia	70	39.4	5.6	Injury	209	56.0	5.3
Injury	64	36.1	6.1	Pneumonia	129	34.5	5.9

[1] The first-listed diagnosis is the one specified as the principal diagnosis or the first diagnosis listed on the face sheet or discharge summary of the medical record. It is usually the main cause of the hospitalization. The number of first-listed diagnoses is the same as the number of discharges. [2] Crude estimates. [3] Includes discharges with first-listed diagnoses not shown in table. [4] Estimates are considered unreliable. [5] These estimates are for nonfederal short-stay hospitals only and do not include mental illness discharges from other types of facilities such as Veterans Affairs hospitals. [6] Includes abuse, dependence, and withdrawal. These estimates are for non-federal short-stay hospitals only and do not include alcohol and drug discharges from other types of facilities or programs such as the Department of Veterans Affairs or day treatment programs.

Source: U.S. National Center for Health Statistics, National Hospital Discharge Survey, <http://www.cdc.gov/nchs/nhds.htm>.

Table 176. Selected Cosmetic Plastic Surgical and Nonsurgical Procedures: 2003 to 2009

[In thousands (8,252.0 represents 8,252,000). As of December 31. The final data are projected to reflect nationwide statistics and are based on a survey of doctors who have been certified by the American Board of Medical Specialties recognized boards, including but not limited to the American Board of Plastic Surgery. Data for the procedures include but are not limited to those performed by American Society for Aesthetic Plastic Surgery (ASAPS) members. ASAPS members are plastic surgeons certified by the American Board of Plastic Surgery who specialize in cosmetic surgery of the face and the entire body. Procedures are ranked by total number in the most current year]

Procedure	2003	2004	2005	2006	2007	2008	2009
Total all procedures..................	8,252.0	11,855.0	11,428.8	11,456.8	11,701.0	10,258.6	9,993.7
Total surgical procedures.............	1,819.5	2,120.0	2,131.0	1,922.8	2,079.0	1,766.7	1,471.6
Breast augmentation...................	280.4	334.1	364.6	383.9	399.4	355.7	312.0
Lipoplasty (Liposuction)...............	384.6	478.3	455.5	403.7	456.8	341.1	283.7
Blepharoplasty (eyelid surgery)..........	267.6	290.3	231.5	210.0	240.8	195.1	149.9
Rhinoplasty (nose reshaping)...........	172.4	166.2	200.9	141.9	151.8	152.4	138.3
Abdominoplasty (tummy tuck)...........	117.7	151.0	169.3	172.5	185.3	147.4	127.9
Total nonsurgical procedures.........	6,432.5	9,735.0	9,297.7	9,534.0	9,622.0	8,491.9	8,522.1
Botox injection [1].....................	2,272.1	2,837.3	3,294.8	3,181.6	2,775.2	2,464.1	2,557.1
Hyaluronic acid [2]	116.2	882.5	1,194.2	1,593.6	1,448.7	1,262.8	1,313.0
Laser hair removal....................	923.2	1,411.9	1,566.9	1,475.3	1,412.7	1,281.0	1,280.0
Microdermabrasion [3]	858.3	1,098.3	1,023.9	993.1	829.7	557.1	621.9
Chemical peel	722.2	1110.4	556.2	558.4	575.1	591.8	529.3
Total female procedures.............	7,177.9	10,681.4	10,443.8	10,516.7	10,602.5	9,394.8	9,058.5
Total surgical procedures.............	1,559.4	1,887.3	1,918.1	1,730.5	1,877.1	1,600.7	1,310.7
Breast augmentation...................	280.4	334.1	364.6	383.9	399.4	355.7	312.0
Lipoplasty (Liposuction)...............	323.0	416.6	402.9	350.4	398.8	309.7	243.2
Blepharoplasty (eyelid surgery)..........	216.8	249.3	198.1	182.4	208.2	166.4	124.9
Abdominoplasty (tummy tuck)...........	112.7	145.3	164.1	164.8	180.5	143.0	123.0
Breast reduction	147.2	144.4	160.5	145.8	153.1	139.9	113.5
Total nonsurgical procedures.........	5,618.6	8,794.1	8,525.7	8,786.2	8,725.4	7,794.1	7,747.8
Botox injection [1].....................	1,963.0	2,525.4	2,990.7	2,881.1	2,445.7	2,239.0	2,299.3
Hyaluronic acid [2]	104.7	838.9	1,149.2	1,519.9	1,364.5	1,200.4	1,221.8
Laser hair removal....................	695.2	1,215.1	1,334.7	1,308.7	1,227.0	1,101.3	1,114.0
Microdermabrasion [3]	774.3	999.1	939.5	922.0	743.7	517.3	565.0
Chemical peel	640.1	977.3	533.0	530.1	536.0	554.5	492.3
Laser skin resurfacing	116.5	520.3	432.6	528.1	479.8	532.0	463.3
Sclerotherapy (Spider veins)...........	431.3	479.2	548.0	541.3	467.8	417.5	442.0
IPL laser treatment [4]	(X)	(X)	(X)	(X)	584.5	479.9	404.5
Total male procedures...............	1,074.1	1,173.6	984.9	940.0	1,098.6	863.7	935.2
Total surgical procedures.............	260.1	232.7	212.9	192.3	202.0	166.0	160.9
Lipoplasty (Liposuction)...............	61.6	61.6	52.5	53.3	58.0	31.5	40.5
Rhinoplasty (nose reshaping)	53.4	39.0	45.9	33.1	31.7	30.2	32.7
Blepharoplasty (eyelid surgery)..........	50.8	41.1	33.4	27.0	32.6	28.7	25.0
Gynecomastia (male breast reduction)	22.0	19.6	17.7	23.7	20.3	19.1	16.8
Hair transplantation...................	14.9	19.5	11.2	11.2	16.5	18.1	13.1
Facelift............................	13.6	11.8	13.0	14.1	12.4	13.4	10.5
Total nonsurgical procedures.........	814.0	932.6	772.0	747.7	896.6	697.8	774.4
Botox injection [1].....................	309.1	311.9	304.1	300.5	329.5	225.1	257.8
Laser hair removal....................	228.0	196.8	232.2	166.6	185.7	179.7	166.0
Hyaluronic acid [2]	11.5	43.6	45.0	73.6	84.2	62.4	91.2
Microdermabrasion [3]	84.0	99.2	84.4	71.1	85.9	39.8	56.9
Laser skin resurfacing	11.0	69.4	43.1	48.5	30.1	38.9	49.0
IPL laser treatment [4]	(X)	(X)	(X)	(X)	63.2	46.9	47.7

X Not applicable. [1] As of 2009, includes Dysport. [2] In 2003, the FDA has approved hyaluronan injections for filling soft tissue defects such as facial wrinkles. [3] Procedure for reducing fine lines, "crow's feet," age spots, and acne scars. [4] IPL is intense pulse light. One of the procedures available for facial rejuvenation.

Source: The American Society for Aesthetic Plastic Surgery, *Statistics*, annual (copyright), <http://www.surgery.org/media/statistics>.

Table 177. Organ Transplants: 1990 to 2009

[As of end of year. Based on reports of procurement programs and transplant centers in the United States, except as noted]

Procedure	Number of procedures						Number of centers		Number of people waiting, 2009	1-year patient survival rates, 2008 (percent)
	1990	1995	2000	2005	2008	2009	1990	2009		
Transplant: [1]										
Heart..............	2,095	2,342	2,172	2,125	2,163	2,212	148	126	3,149	88.4
Heart-lung	52	69	47	35	27	29	79	50	76	66.2
Lung..............	203	869	955	1,406	1,478	1,661	70	67	1,771	83.5
Liver..............	2,631	3,818	4,816	6,443	6,318	6,320	85	132	16,106	87.7
Kidney	9,358	10,957	13,258	16,481	16,517	16,829	232	240	85,668	98.4
Kidney-pancreas	459	915	910	903	837	854	(NA)	(NA)	2,187	94.7
Pancreas	60	103	420	541	436	379	84	144	1,453	90.5
Intestine............	1	21	29	178	185	180	(NA)	44	255	79.1
Multi-organ..........	71	124	213	518	(NA)	(NA)	(NA)	(NA)	(NA)	(NA)

NA Not available. [1] Kidney-pancreas and heart-lung transplants are each counted as one procedure. All other multiorgan transplants, excluding kidney-pancreas and heart-lung, are included in the multiorgan row. Based on the Organ Procurement and Transplant Network (OPTN) as of July 2, 2010. The data have been supplied by United Network for Organ Sharing (UNOS) under contract with Health and Human Services (HHS). This work was supported in part by Health Resources and Services Administration, contract 231-00-0015. The authors alone are responsible for the reporting and interpretation of these data. Data subject to change based on future data submission or correction.

Source: U.S. Department of Health and Human Services, Health Resources and Services Administration, Office of Special Programs, Division of Transplantation, Rockville, MD; United Network for Organ Sharing, Richmond, VA; University Renal Research and Education Association, Ann Arbor, MI; and unpublished data. See also <http://optn.transplant.hrsa.gov/>.

Table 178. Cancer—Estimated New Cases, 2010, and Survival Rates: 1990–1992 to 1999–2006

[1,530 represents 1,530,000. The 5-year relative survival rate, which is derived by adjusting the observed survival rate for expected mortality, represents the likelihood that a person will not die from causes directly related to their cancer within 5 years. Survival data shown are based on those patients diagnosed while residents of an area listed below during the time periods shown. Data are based on information collected as part of the National Cancer Institute's Surveillance, Epidemiology and End Results (SEER) program, a collection of 9 population-based registries in five states (Connecticut, Hawaii, Iowa, New Mexico, Utah) and four metropolitan areas (Atlanta, Detroit, San Francisco-Oakland, and Seattle-Puget Sound)]

| Site | Estimated new cases,[1] 2010 (1,000) | | | 5-year relative survival rates (percent) | | | | | | | |
| | | | | White | | | | Black | | | |
	Total	Male	Female	1990–1992	1993–1995	1996–1998	1999–2006	1990–1992	1993–1995	1996–1998	1999–2006
All sites [2]	1,530	790	740	62.4	63.5	65.6	69.5	48.3	53.0	55.6	59.8
Lung	223	117	106	14.5	15.1	15.4	17.0	10.8	13.1	12.7	13.3
Breast [3]	209	2	207	86.7	88.0	89.6	91.5	71.8	72.9	76.5	79.0
Colon and rectum	143	72	70	63.2	61.5	64.1	68.3	53.8	52.9	55.1	57.4
Colon	103	49	53	64.0	61.4	63.8	67.6	54.3	52.4	54.7	56.1
Rectum	40	23	17	61.3	61.7	64.7	69.9	52.2	54.5	56.3	61.0
Prostate	218	218	(X)	95.3	96.2	98.1	99.9	85.5	91.6	94.3	98.1
Bladder	71	53	18	81.9	82.3	80.8	82.7	64.8	61.8	62.6	66.9
Corpus uteri	43	(X)	43	87.3	86.6	86.9	87.3	57.0	61.7	64.2	63.5
Non-Hodgkin's lymphoma [4]	66	35	30	53.0	54.5	61.0	70.8	42.1	42.1	54.4	60.5
Oral cavity and pharynx	37	25	11	58.7	60.9	61.0	65.1	33.4	38.4	36.6	45.7
Leukemia [4]	43	25	18	48.2	49.9	51.1	56.5	37.3	42.3	39.3	47.6
Melanoma of skin	68	39	29	89.7	89.7	91.1	93.3	60.3	67.4	74.9	74.7
Pancreas	43	21	22	4.7	4.2	4.4	5.9	3.8	3.7	3.6	5.0
Kidney	58	35	23	62.1	63.2	63.4	70.3	57.8	58.6	67.5	67.6
Stomach	21	13	8	19.4	20.6	21.0	25.8	23.8	20.3	23.6	26.5
Ovary	22	(X)	22	42.5	42.7	45.1	45.2	38.1	43.3	41.2	37.1
Cervix uteri [5]	12	(X)	12	72.0	74.8	74.6	72.6	58.9	64.2	65.3	63.8

X Not applicable. [1] Estimates provided by American Cancer Society, <www.cancer.org>, are based on rates from the National Cancer Institute's SEER program. [2] Includes other sites, not shown separately. [3] Survival rates for female only. [4] All types combined. [5] Invasive cancer only.

Source: U.S. National Institutes of Health, National Cancer Institute, <http://seer.cancer.gov/csr/1975_2006/>.

Table 179. Cancer—Estimated New Cases and Deaths by State: 2010

[In thousands (1,529.6 represents 1,529,600). Excludes basal and squamous cell skin cancers and in situ carcinomas except urinary bladder]

| State | New cases [1] | | | Deaths | | | State | New cases [1] | | | Deaths | | |
	Total [2]	Female breast	Lung & bron- chus	Total [2]	Female breast	Lung & bron- chus		Total [2]	Female breast	Lung & bron- chus	Total [2]	Female breast	Lung & bron- chus
U.S.	1,529.6	207.1	222.5	569.5	39.8	157.3	MO	31.2	3.9	5.4	12.6	0.9	4.0
AL	23.6	3.5	4.2	10.2	0.7	3.2	MT	5.6	0.7	0.7	2.0	0.1	0.6
AK	2.9	0.4	0.4	0.9	0.1	0.3	NE	9.2	1.2	1.2	3.5	0.2	0.9
AZ	29.8	4.0	4.0	10.6	0.7	2.7	NV	12.2	1.4	1.9	4.6	0.3	1.3
AR	15.3	1.8	2.6	6.5	0.4	1.9	NH	7.8	1.0	1.1	2.7	0.2	0.8
CA	157.3	21.1	18.5	55.7	4.2		NJ	48.1	6.8	6.3	16.5	1.4	4.2
CO	21.3	3.1	2.3	6.9	0.5	1.7	NM	9.2	1.2	0.9	3.4	0.2	0.8
CT	20.8	3.0	2.6	6.9	0.5	1.8	NY	103.3	14.6	13.7	34.5	2.5	8.7
DE	4.9	0.7	0.8	1.9	0.1	0.6	NC	45.1	6.5	7.5	19.1	1.3	5.7
DC	2.8	0.4	0.4	1.0	0.1	0.2	ND	3.3	0.4	0.4	1.3	0.1	0.3
FL	107.0	14.1	18.4	40.9	2.7	11.6	OH	64.5	8.3	10.7	25.0	1.7	7.3
GA	40.5	6.1	6.3	15.6	1.1	4.6	OK	18.7	2.3	3.3	7.7	0.5	2.4
HI	6.7	0.9	0.8	2.3	0.1	0.6	OR	20.8	2.9	2.8	7.5	0.5	2.1
ID	7.2	0.9	0.9	2.5	0.2	0.6	PA	75.3	10.0	10.5	28.7	2.0	8.0
IL	63.9	8.8	9.2	23.4	1.8	6.5	RI	6.0	0.8	0.8	2.2	0.1	0.6
IN	33.0	4.4	5.4	12.9	0.9	4.0	SC	23.2	3.3	4.0	9.2	0.6	2.9
IA	17.3	2.0	2.5	6.4	0.4	1.8	SD	4.2	0.5	0.5	1.7	0.1	0.5
KS	13.6	1.8	2.0	5.4	0.4	1.6	TN	33.1	4.7	6.0	13.6	0.9	4.5
KY	24.2	3.3	4.8	9.7	0.6	3.4	TX	101.1	12.9	14.0	36.5	2.8	9.6
LA	21.0	2.5	3.3	8.5	0.6	2.6	UT	10.0	1.3	0.6	2.8	0.3	0.5
ME	8.7	1.2	1.4	3.2	0.2	1.0	VT	3.7	0.5	0.5	1.3	0.1	0.4
MD	27.7	4.2	4.2	10.3	0.8	2.8	VA	36.4	5.5	5.5	14.2	1.1	4.1
MA	36.0	5.3	5.0	13.0	0.8	3.5	WA	34.5	4.9	4.3	11.6	0.8	3.1
MI	55.7	7.3	8.2	20.7	1.3	5.8	WV	10.6	1.3	2.1	4.7	0.3	1.5
MN	25.1	3.3	3.2	9.2	0.6	2.5	WI	29.6	4.1	4.0	11.3	0.7	2.9
MS	14.3	2.0	2.4	6.1	0.4	2.0	WY	2.5	0.3	0.3	1.0	0.1	0.3

[1] Estimates are offered as a rough guide and should be interpreted with caution. [2] Includes other types of cancer, not shown separately.

Source: American Cancer Society, Inc., *Cancer Facts and Figures—2010*, Atlanta, GA, (copyright). See also <http://www.cancer.org/docroot/STT/stt_0.asp>.

122 Health and Nutrition

Table 180. Selected Notifiable Diseases—Cases Reported: 1980 to 2008

[190.9 represents 190,900. As of June 30, 2009. Figures should be interpreted with caution. Although reporting of some of these diseases is incomplete, the figures are of value in indicating trends of disease incidence. Includes cases imported from outside the United States]

Disease	1980	1990	1995	2000	2004	2005	2006	2007	2008
AIDS [1]	(2)	41,595	71,547	40,758	44,108	41,120	38,423	37,503	39,202
Botulism [3]	89	92	97	138	133	135	165	144	145
Brucellosis (undulant fever)	183	85	98	87	114	120	121	131	80
Chickenpox (Varicella) [4] (1,000)	190.9	173.1	120.6	27.4	32.9	32.2	48.4	40.1	30.4
Coccidoidomycosis	(2)	(2)	(2)	2,867	6,449	6,542	8,917	8,121	7,523
Cryptosporidiosis	(2)	(2)	(2)	3,128	3,577	5,659	6,071	11,170	9,113
Domestic arboviral diseases: [5]									
West Nile: neuroinvasive	(2)	(2)	(2)	(2)	(2)	1,309	1,495	1,227	689
nonneuroinvasive	(2)	(2)	(2)	(2)	(2)	1,691	2,774	2,403	667
Enterohemorrhagic Escherichia coli 0157:H7	(2)	(2)	2,139	4,528	2,544	2,621	(2)	(2)	(2)
Giardiasis	(2)	(2)	(2)	(2)	20,636	19,733	18,953	19,417	18,908
Haemophilus influenza	(2)	(2)	1,180	1,398	2,085	2,304	2,436	2,541	2,886
Hansen disease (Leprosy)	223	198	144	91	105	87	66	101	80
Hepatitis: A (infectious) (1,000) [6]	29.1	31.4	31.6	13.4	5.7	4.5	3.6	3.0	2.6
B (serum) (1,000)	19.0	21.1	10.8	8.0	6.2	5.1	4.7	4.5	4.0
C/Non-A, non-B	(2)	2,600	4,576	3,197	720	652	766	845	877
Legionellosis	(2)	1,370	1,241	1,127	2,093	2,301	2,834	2,716	3,181
Lyme disease	(2)	(2)	11,700	17,730	19,804	23,305	19,931	27,444	35,198
Malaria	2,062	1,292	1,419	1,560	1,458	1,494	1,474	1,408	1,255
Meningococcal infections	2,840	2,451	3,243	2,256	1,361	1,245	1,194	1,077	1,172
Mumps (1,000)	8.6	5.3	0.9	0.3	0.3	0.3	6.6	0.8	0.5
Pertussis [7] (1,000)	1.7	4.6	5.1	7.9	25.8	25.6	15.6	10.5	13.3
Psittacosis	124	113	64	17	12	16	21	12	8
Rabies, animal	6,421	4,826	7,811	6,934	6,345	5,915	5,534	5,862	4,196
Rocky Mountain spotted fever	1,163	651	590	495	1,713	1,936	2,288	2,221	2,563
Rubella [8]	3,904	1,125	128	176	10	11	11	12	16
Salmonellosis [9] (1,000)	33.7	48.6	46.0	39.6	42.2	45.3	45.8	48.0	51.0
Shigellosis [10] (1,000)	19.0	27.1	32.1	22.9	14.6	16.2	15.5	19.8	22.6
Streptococcal disease, invasive, Group A	(2)	(2)	(2)	3,144	4,395	4,715	5,407	5,294	5,674
Streptococcus pneumoniae, invasive:									
Drug-resistant	(2)	(2)	(2)	4,533	2,590	2,996	3,308	3,329	3,448
Age less than 5 years	(2)	(2)	(2)	(2)	1,162	1,495	1,861	563	532
Tetanus	95	64	41	35	34	27	41	28	19
Toxic-shock syndrome	(2)	322	191	135	95	90	101	92	71
Trichinosis	131	129	29	16	5	16	15	5	39
Tuberculosis [11] (1,000)	27.7	25.7	22.9	16.4	14.5	14.1	13.8	13.3	12.9
Typhoid fever	510	552	369	377	322	324	353	434	449
Sexually transmitted diseases:									
Chlamydia (1,000)	(2)	(2)	478	702	929	976	1,031	1,108	1,211
Gonorrhea (1,000)	1,004	690	393	359	330	340	358	356	337
Syphilis (1,000)	69	134	69	32	33	33	37	41	46

[1] Acquired immunodeficiency syndrome was not a notifiable disease until 1984. Includes all cases reported to the Division of HIV/AIDS Prevention, National Center for HIV/AIDS, Viral Hepatitis, STD, and TB Prevention. [2] Disease was not notifiable. [3] Includes foodborne, infant, wound, and unspecified cases. [4] Chickenpox was taken off the nationally notifiable list in 1991 but many states continue to report. [5] The national surveillance case definitions for the arboviral diseases was revised in 2005, and nonneuroinvasive arboviral diseases were added to the list of nationally notifiable infectious diseases. [6] Data on chronic hepatitis B and hepatitis C virus infection (past or present) are not included because they are undergoing data quality review. [7] Whooping cough. [8] German measles. Excludes congenital syndrome. [9] Excludes typhoid fever. [10] Bacillary dysentery. [11] Newly reported active cases.

Source: Centers for Disease Control and Prevention, *Summary of Notifiable Diseases, United States, 2008, Morbidity and Mortality Weekly Report*, Vol. 57, No. 54, 2010. See also <http://www.cdc.gov/mmwr/mmwr_nd/index.html>.

Table 181. AIDS, Chlamydia, and Lyme Disease, 2008, Cases Reported by State

State	AIDS [1]	Chla-mydia	Lyme disease	State	AIDS [1]	Chla-mydia	Lyme disease	State	AIDS [1]	Chla-mydia	Lyme disease
U.S.	39,202	1,210,523	28,921								
AL	402	24,760	6	KY	293	12,163	5	ND	12	1,921	8
AK	27	4,861	6	LA	903	22,659	3	OH	701	47,117	40
AZ	570	24,769	2	ME	30	2,608	780	OK	137	14,803	1
AR	100	14,136	–	MD	2,389	24,669	1,746	OR	207	10,744	18
CA	4,818	148,798	74	MA	622	17,503	3,960	PA	1,244	42,233	3,818
CO	343	19,180	2	MI	651	44,923	76	RI	88	3,317	186
CT	408	12,519	2,738	MN	207	14,351	1,046	SC	723	26,323	14
DE	166	3,868	772	MS	356	21,253	1	SD	11	2,956	3
DC	767	6,924	71	MO	417	24,817	6	TN	589	28,038	7
FL	5,064	71,017	72	MT	48	3,101	6	TX	2,861	100,870	105
GA	2,153	42,629	35	NE	73	5,573	8	UT	65	6,021	3
HI	97	5,982	–	NV	307	9,670	9	VT	10	1,190	330
ID	31	4,194	5	NH	30	2,109	1,211	VA	698	31,218	886
IL	1,360	59,169	108	NJ	1,627	22,405	3,214	WA	390	21,402	22
IN	424	22,154	42	NM	109	9,262	4	WV	67	3,316	120
IA	71	9,372	85	NY	4,171	88,359	5,741	WI	174	20,996	1,493
KS	122	9,208	16	NC	1,384	37,516	16	WY	13	1,577	1

– Represents zero. [1] Includes 072 cases of AIDS in persons with unknown state or area of residence that were reported in 2008.

Source: Centers for Disease Control and Prevention, *Summary of Notifiable Diseases, United States, 2008, Morbidity and Mortality Weekly Report*, Vol. 57, No. 54, 2010. See also <http://www.cdc.gov/mmwr/mmwr_nd/index.html>.

U.S. Census Bureau, Statistical Abstract of the United States: 2011

Table 182. Reported AIDS Cases for Adults and Adolescents by Transmission Category and Sex: 2007

[Provisional. For cases reported in the year shown. Includes Puerto Rico, Virgin Islands, Guam, and U.S. Pacific Islands. Acquired immunodeficiency syndrome (AIDS) is a specific group of diseases or conditions which are indicative of severe immunosuppression related to infection with the human immunodeficiency virus (HIV). Data are subject to retrospective changes and may differ from those data in Table 180. For information on HIV death rates, go to Table 126]

Transmission category	2007			Cumulative through 2007 [1]		
	Total	Male	Female	Total	Male	Female
Persons 13 years old and over, total	**38,297**	**28,320**	**9,977**	**1,021,242**	**820,037**	**201,205**
Male-to-male sexual contact	14,383	14,383	(X)	445,645	445,645	(X)
Injection drug use	4,736	3,103	1,633	235,842	166,251	69,591
Male-to-male sexual contact and injection drug use	1,514	1,514	(X)	67,797	67,797	(X)
Hemophilia/coagulation disorder	46	37	9	5,567	5,212	355
High-risk heterosexual contact	7,504	2,791	4,713	142,852	52,623	90,229
Sex with injection drug user	985	281	704	38,766	11,941	26,825
Sex with bisexual male	233	(X)	233	5,415	(X)	5,415
Sex with person with hemophilia	14	4	10	603	90	513
Sex with HIV-infected person, transfusion recipient	56	31	25	1,403	584	819
Sex with HIV-infected person, risk factor not specified	6,216	2,475	3,741	96,665	40,008	56,657
Receipt of blood transfusion, blood components, or tissue	109	50	59	9,315	5,181	4,134
Other/risk not reported or identified	10,005	6,442	3,563	114,224	77,328	36,896

X Not applicable. [1] Includes persons with a diagnosis of AIDS, reported from the beginning of the epidemic through 2007. Cumulative total includes persons with characteristics unknown. The first AIDS cases were reported in the United States in June 1981.

Source: U.S. Centers for Disease Control and Prevention, Atlanta, GA, *HIV/AIDS Surveillance Report, 2007*, Volume 19, <http://www.cdc.gov/hiv/surveillance/resources/reports/2007report/> (revised February 2009).

Table 183. Estimated Numbers of Persons Living With Acquired Immunodeficiency Syndrome (AIDS) by Year, Age, and Selected Characteristics: 2000 to 2007

[Includes Puerto Rico, Virgin Islands, Guam, and U.S. Pacific Islands. These numbers do not represent reported case counts. Rather, these numbers are point estimates, which result from adjustments of reported case counts. The reported case counts are adjusted for reporting delays and for redistribution of cases in persons initially reported without an identified risk factor. The estimates do not include adjustment for incomplete reporting. See the Commentary section in the report]

Age and characteristic	2000	2004	2005	2006	2007
Total [1, 2]	**322,242**	**411,089**	**432,029**	**451,837**	**470,902**
AGE AS OF END OF YEAR					
Less than 13 years old	2,916	1,797	1,485	1,193	929
13 and 14 years old	518	802	801	757	680
15 to 24 years old	5,086	7,013	7,700	8,184	8,821
25 to 34 years old	55,678	47,368	45,623	44,829	44,729
35 to 44 years old	145,524	164,185	163,885	161,009	155,702
45 to 54 years old	85,268	136,084	149,317	162,562	175,604
55 to 64 years old	21,701	42,954	50,485	58,464	67,101
65 years old and over	5,550	10,886	12,733	14,839	17,336
RACE/ETHNICITY					
White, not Hispanic	119,172	143,338	149,107	154,770	160,010
Black, not Hispanic	132,104	174,479	183,930	192,793	201,404
Asian/Pacific Islander	2,498	3,834	4,191	4,564	5,011
American Indian/Alaska Native	1,073	1,462	1,563	1,632	1,698
Hispanic [3]	64,833	84,427	89,415	94,100	98,726
TRANSMISSION CATEGORY MALE ADULT/ADOLESCENT					
Males 13 years old and over, total	250,315	314,618	329,884	344,370	358,332
Male-to-male sexual contact	143,390	186,036	196,868	207,551	218,136
Injection drug use	58,238	64,651	65,716	66,509	67,121
Male-to-male sexual contact and injection drug use	24,968	28,510	29,248	29,771	30,196
High-risk heterosexual contact [4]	20,839	32,153	34,671	37,065	39,353
Other [5]	2,880	3,267	3,381	3,474	3,527
FEMALE ADULT/ADOLESCENT					
Females 13 years old and over, total	68,015	92,443	98,101	103,447	108,576
Injection drug use	28,212	32,824	33,684	34,314	34,845
Heterosexual contact [4]	38,131	57,368	62,037	66,626	71,088
Other [5]	1,671	2,250	2,380	2,506	2,643
CHILD (LESS THAN 13 YEARS OLD AT DIAGNOSIS)					
Total	3,912	4,028	4,044	4,021	3,992
Perinatal	3,709	3,828	3,841	3,822	3,800
Other [6]	202	201	203	198	192

[1] Includes persons of unknown or multiple race and of unknown sex. Because column totals were calculated independently of the values for the subpopulations, the values in each column may not sum to the column total. [2] Persons who reported multiple racial categories or whose race was unknown are included in the total numbers. [3] Hispanics can be of any race. [4] Heterosexual contact with a person known to have, or to be at high risk for, HIV infection. [5] Includes hemophilia, blood transfusion, perinatal and risk not reported or not identified. [6] Includes hemophilia, blood transfusion, and risk not reported or not identified.

Source: U.S. Centers for Disease Control and Prevention, Atlanta, GA, *HIV/AIDS Surveillance Report, 2008*, Volume 20, <http://www.cdc.gov/hiv/surveillance/resources/reports/2008report/>.

Table 184. Learning Disability or Attention Deficit Hyperactivity Disorder for Children 3 to 17 Years of Age by Selected Characteristics: 2008

[In thousands, except percent (61,907 represents 61,907,000). Learning disability is based on the question, "Has a representative from a school or a health professional ever told you that (child's name) has a learning disability?" Attention Deficit Hyperactivity Disorder is based on the question, "Has a doctor or health professional ever told you that (child's name) had Attention Hyperactivity Disorder or Attention Deficit Disorder?"]

| Selected characteristic | Total | Ever told had— | | | |
| | | Learning disability | | Attention deficit hyperactivity disorder | |
		Number [1]	Percent [2]	Number [1]	Percent [2]
Total [3]	**61,907**	**5,012**	**8.2**	**4,968**	**8.1**
SEX [4]					
Male	31,724	3,174	10.1	3,508	11.2
Female	30,183	1,839	6.2	1,459	4.9
AGE					
3 to 4 years old	8,848	206	2.3	171	1.9
5 to 11 years old	28,250	2,485	8.8	2,059	7.3
12 to 17 years old	24,809	2,321	9.4	2,738	11.1
RACE					
Race Alone [4, 5]	59,721	4,841	8.2	4,807	8.1
White	46,514	3,853	8.3	3,922	8.5
Black or African American	9,596	860	9.2	792	8.3
American Indian or Alaska Native	983	[6] 91	[6] 9.1	(B)	(B)
Asian	2,491	[6] 30	[6] 1.2	(B)	(B)
Native Hawaiian or Other Pacific Islander	137	(B)	(B)	(B)	(B)
Two or more races [4, 7]	2,186	171	[6] 8.7	161	8.1
Black or African American and White	777	[6] 61	[6] 8.7	[6] 75	[6] 11.0
American Indian or Alaska Native and White	475	(B)	(B)	(B)	(B)
HISPANIC ORIGIN AND RACE: [4, 8]					
Hispanic or Latino	12,922	750	5.9	535	4.2
Mexican or Mexican American	8,729	482	5.6	276	3.3
Not Hispanic or Latino	48,985	4,262	8.8	4,433	9.1
White, single race	34,836	3,158	9.1	3,425	9.8
Black or African American, single race	9,209	844	9.4	774	8.5

B Base figure too small to meet statistical standards for reliability of a derived figure. [1] Unknowns for the columns are not included in the frequencies, but they are included in the "Total" column. [2] Unknowns for the column variables are not included in the denominators when calculating percentages. [3] Includes other races not shown separately. [4] Percents are age-adjusted to the 2000 projected U.S. standard population using age groups 3–4 years, 5–11 years, and 12–17 years. [5] Refers to persons who indicated only a single race group. [6] Figures do not meet standard of reliability or precision. [7] Refers to all persons who indicated more than one race group. [8] Persons of Hispanic or Latino origin may be any race or combination of races.

Source: National Center for Health Statistics, *Summary Health Statistics for U.S. Children: National Health Interview Survey, 2008*, Vital and Health Statistics, Series 10, Number 244, 2009. See also <http://www.cdc.gov/nchs/data/series/sr_10/sr10_244 .pdf>.

Table 185. Children and Youth With Disabilities Served by Selected Programs: 1995 to 2008

[In thousands (5,078.8 represents 5,078,800). As of fall. For children and youth aged 6 to 21 served under the Individuals with Disabilities Education Act (IDEA) Part B. Includes outlying areas]

Disability	1995	2000	2003	2004	2005	2006	2007	2008
Total	**5,078.8**	**5,773.9**	**6,045.4**	**6,116.4**	**6,113.5**	**6,085.6**	**5,999.2**	**5,889.8**
Specific learning disabilities	2,601.8	2,881.6	2,867.1	2,839.3	2,782.8	2,711.8	2,616.3	2,525.9
Speech or language impairments	1,026.9	1,093.4	1,128.1	1,149.6	1,156.9	1,162.1	1,151.9	1,122.0
Mental retardation	585.6	613.4	582.6	567.6	546.0	523.5	497.5	476.1
Emotional disturbance	439.2	474.3	484.5	484.5	472.5	458.8	439.7	418.1
Multiple disabilities	94.5	122.9	132.7	133.4	134.0	133.8	132.5	124.1
Hearing impairments	68.0	70.8	72.0	72.6	72.4	72.8	72.0	70.8
Orthopedic impairments	63.2	73.0	68.2	65.4	63.1	62.0	60.5	62.4
Other health impairments	134.2	294.0	452.7	512.2	561.6	600.4	630.7	648.4
Visual impairments	25.5	26.0	25.9	26.1	26.0	26.5	26.4	25.8
Autism	29.1	79.6	141.1	166.5	193.8	224.6	258.0	292.8
Deaf-blind	1.4	1.3	1.7	1.7	1.6	1.4	1.4	1.7
Traumatic brain injury	9.6	14.9	22.5	23.3	23.5	23.8	23.9	24.9
Developmental delay [1]	(X)	28.6	66.3	74.4	79.1	84.0	88.6	96.9

X Not applicable. [1] States had the option of reporting children aged 3 to 9 under developmental delay beginning 1997.
Source: U.S. Department of Education, Office of Special Education, <http://www.ideadata.org/index.html>.

Table 186. Children Under 18 Years of Age Receiving Special Education or Early Intervention Services: 2008

[In thousands, except percent (73,858 represents 73,858,000). Receiving special education or early intervention services is based on the question, "Do any of the following (family members under 18 years of age) receive special education or early intervention services?"]

Selected Characteristic	Total	Persons under 18 years who were receiving special education early intervention services	
		Number [1]	Percent [2]
Total [3]	**73,858**	**4,672**	**6.3**
SEX [4]			
Male..	37,749	3,133	8.3
Female......................................	36,108	1,539	4.3
AGE			
Under 12 years	49,087	2,810	5.7
12 to 17 years	24,771	1,863	7.5
RACE			
Race Alone [4, 5]	71,310	4,498	6.3
White	55,603	3,634	6.5
Black or African American....................	11,415	707	6.2
American Indian or Alaska Native	1,154	96	8.1
Asian	2,979	58	1.9
Native Hawaiian or Other Pacific Islander	159	(B)	(B)
Two or more races [4, 6].......................	2,547	174	6.9
HISPANIC ORIGIN AND RACE: [4, 7]			
Hispanic or Latino	15,802	669	4.3
Mexican or Mexican American..................	10,765	396	3.7
Not Hispanic or Latino.......................	58,055	4,004	6.9
White, single race	41,323	3,029	7.3
Black or African American, single race	10,929	682	6.3

B Base figure too small to meet statistical standards for reliability of a derived figure. [1] Unknowns for the columns are not included in the frequencies, but they are included in the "Total" column. [2] Unknowns for the column variables are not included in the denominators when calculating percentages. [3] Includes other races not shown separately. [4] Percents are age-adjusted to the 2000 projected U.S. standard population using two age groups 0–11 years, and 12–17 years. [5] Refers to persons who indicated only a single race group. [6] Refers to all persons who indicated more than one race group. [7] Persons of Hispanic or Latino origin may be any race or combination of races.

Source: National Center for Health Statistics, *Summary Health Statistics for the U.S. Population: National Health Interview Survey, 2008*, Vital and Health Statistics, Series 10, Number 243, 2009. See also <http://www.cdc.gov/nchs/data/series /sr_10/sr10_243.pdf>.

Table 187. Disabilities Tallied by Age Group and by State: 2008

[In thousands (35,916 represents 35,916,000). Based on data from the American Community Survey (ACS). People aged 5 to 14 were classified as having a disability if they were reported to have any one of the five limitations: hearing difficulty, vision difficulty, cognitive difficulty, ambulatory difficulty, or self-care difficulty. People aged 15 and over were classified as having a disability if they reported any one of the five limitations listed above or independent living difficulty. See text, Section 1 and Appendix III]

State	Total	5 to 17 years	18 to 64 years	65 years and over	State	Total	5 to 17 years	18 to 64 years	65 years and over
U.S.	35,916	2,741	18,995	14,180	MO.......	804	64	441	299
AL	742	50	416	276	MT	128	8	69	51
AK	78	7	53	19	NE	189	14	94	81
AZ	769	58	402	309	NV	257	19	135	103
AR	485	41	272	172	NH	141	14	75	52
CA	3,677	259	1,873	1,545	NJ	838	62	405	370
CO........	456	28	256	173	NM.......	268	17	144	107
CT	356	28	180	149	NY	2,150	155	1,085	910
DE	112	10	58	44	NC	1,169	88	648	433
DC........	64	5	36	23	ND	68	3	33	31
FL	2,315	146	1,061	1,108	OH	1,479	125	798	556
GA	1,106	95	618	393	OK	580	46	326	209
HI	131	7	56	67	OR	495	36	264	194
ID........	177	14	93	71	PA	1,612	122	827	663
IL	1,303	95	661	547	RI	132	11	69	51
IN	787	66	431	291	SC	609	39	336	234
IA	345	30	170	145	SD	84	5	42	37
KS	334	29	175	131	TN	903	67	506	330
KY	710	54	418	238	TX	2,755	248	1,506	1,000
LA	639	50	356	233	UT	239	24	127	88
ME........	206	16	113	77	VT	84	7	45	31
MD........	557	44	294	219	VA	812	64	428	320
MA........	728	63	383	282	WA.......	779	57	430	292
MI........	1,299	110	711	478	WV.......	338	17	201	119
MN........	494	42	254	198	WI	591	48	307	236
MS........	483	34	280	169	WY.......	62	4	34	24

Source: U.S. Census Bureau, 2008 American Community Survey, B18101, "Sex by Age by Disability Status," <http://www.factfinder.census.gov/>, accessed February 2010.

Table 188. Children Immunized Against Specified Diseases: 1995 to 2008

[In percent. Covers civilian noninstitutionalized population aged 19 months to 35 months. Based on estimates from the National Immunization Survey. The health care providers of the children are contacted to verify and/or complete vaccination information. Results are based on race/ethnic status of the child]

Vaccination	1995, total	2000, total	2008 [1] Total	2008 [1] White [2]	2008 [1] Black [2]	2008 [1] Hispanic [3]	2008 [1] American Indian/ Alaska Native only [2]	2008 [1] Asian [2]
Diphtheria-tetanus-pertussis (DTP) diphtheria-tetanus:								
3+ doses	95.0	94.0	96.2	96.2	94.6	96.6	93.0	98.6
4+ doses	79.0	82.0	84.6	85.0	80.1	84.9	82.0	92.3
Polio: 3+ doses	88.0	90.0	93.6	93.6	91.5	94.3	90.6	96.5
Measles, mumps, rubella vaccine	90.0	91.0	92.1	91.3	92.0	92.8	95.8	94.7
Hib: 3+ doses [4]	92.0	93.0	90.9	90.8	88.6	91.9	88.9	92.6
Hepatitis B: 3+ doses	68.0	90.0	93.5	93.4	92.1	93.7	91.5	97.5
Varicella [5]	(NA)	68.0	90.7	89.8	90.4	91.8	93.8	94.2
PCV: 3+ doses [6]	(X)	(X)	92.8	92.8	90.9	94.1	86.7	91.2
4+ DTP/3+ polio/1+ MMR/3+ Hib [7]	74.0	76.0	79.6	79.3	75.8	80.7	79.3	84.8
4+ DTP/3+ polio/1+ MMR/3+ Hib/3+ HepB [8]	55.1	72.8	78.2	77.8	74.2	79.4	78.7	84.2

NA Not available. X Not applicable. [1] Children in the Q1²2008–Q4²2008 National Immunization Survey were born between January 2005 and June 2007. [2] Non-Hispanic. [3] Children of Hispanic ethnicity may be any race. [4] Haemophilus influenzae type B. [5] Data collection for varicella (chicken pox) began in July 1996. [6] PCV = Pneumococcal conjugate vaccine. [7] MMR = Measles, mumps, and rubella. [8] Children are considered immunized with this series.

Source: U.S. Centers for Disease Control and Prevention, Atlanta, GA, National Immunization Program, Data and Statistics, *Immunization Coverage in the U.S.* See also <http://www.cdc.gov/vaccines/stats-surv/imz-coverage.htm#nis>.

Table 189. Asthma Incidence Among Children Under 18 Years of Age by Selected Characteristics: 2008

[In thousands, except percent (73,859 represents 73,859,000). Based on the National Health Interview Survey, a sample survey of the civilian noninstitutionalized population; see Appendix III]

Selected characteristic	Total	Ever told had asthma Number [1]	Ever told had asthma Percent [2]	Still have asthma Number [1]	Still have asthma Percent [2]
Total [3]	73,859	10,190	13.9	6,953	9.5
SEX [4]					
Male	37,750	6,184	16.5	4,293	11.5
Female	36,109	4,006	11.2	2,660	7.4
AGE					
0 to 4 years old	20,800	1,499	7.2	1,276	6.2
5 to 11 years old	28,250	4,573	16.2	3,159	11.2
12 to 17 years old	24,809	4,118	16.6	2,518	10.2
RACE					
Race Alone [4, 5]	71,151	9,702	13.7	6,608	9.4
White	55,555	6,837	12.4	4,544	8.2
Black or African American	11,337	2,384	21.2	1,753	15.6
American Indian or Alaska Native	1,178	[6] 218	18.2	[6] 193	15.8
Asian	2,911	191	6.5	107	3.6
Native Hawaiian or Other Pacific Islander	170	(B)	42.6	(B)	(B)
Two or more races [4, 7]	2,708	488	19.7	345	13.7
HISPANIC ORIGIN AND RACE: [4, 8]					
Hispanic or Latino	15,803	1,725	11.2	1,055	6.8
Mexican or Mexican American	10,766	1,044	9.9	638	6.0
Not Hispanic or Latino	58,056	8,465	14.6	5,898	10.2
White, single race	41,294	5,356	13.0	3,638	8.8
Black or African American, single race	10,837	2,283	21.2	1,698	15.7

B Figure too small to meet statistical standards for reliability of a derived figure. [1] Unknowns for the columns are not included in the frequencies, but they are included in the "Total" column. [2] Unknowns for the column variables are not included in the denominators when calculating percentages. [3] Includes other races not shown separately. [4] Estimates are age-adjusted to the 2000 projected U.S. standard population using age groups 0–4 years, 5–11 years, and 12–17 years. [5] Refers to persons who indicated only a single race group. [6] Figures do not meet standard of reliability or precision. [7] Refers to all persons who indicated more than one race group. [8] Persons of Hispanic or Latino origin may be of any race or combination of races.

Source: National Center for Health Statistics, Summary Health Statistics for U.S. Children: *National Health Interview Survey, 2008*, Vital and Health Statistics, Series 10, Number 244, 2009. See also <http://www.cdc.gov/nchs/data/series/sr_10/sr10_244.pdf>.

Table 190. Nursing Homes, Beds, Residents, and Occupancy Rate by State: 2008

[Based on a census of certified nursing facilities]

State	Nursing homes	Beds	Residents	Occupancy rate [1]	State	Nursing homes	Beds	Residents	Occupancy rate [1]
U.S.....	**15,730**	**1,703,846**	**1,412,540**	**82.9**	MO.......	516	55,028	37,510	68.2
AL......	232	26,824	23,205	86.5	MT.......	91	7,081	5,137	72.5
AK......	15	725	616	85.0	NE......	224	16,198	12,899	79.6
AZ......	133	16,033	12,201	76.1	NV......	48	5,675	4,724	83.2
AR......	232	24,477	17,753	72.5	NH......	80	7,718	6,953	90.1
CA......	1,255	122,554	103,487	84.4	NJ......	361	51,132	45,946	89.9
CO......	212	19,956	16,464	82.5	NM......	70	6,780	5,695	84.0
CT......	241	29,678	26,819	90.4	NY......	652	120,336	110,940	92.2
DE......	45	4,870	3,999	82.1	NC......	422	43,770	38,025	86.9
DC......	18	2,645	2,437	92.1	ND......	83	6,395	5,847	91.4
FL......	676	82,067	71,833	87.5	OH......	955	93,039	81,395	87.5
GA......	359	39,762	35,276	88.7	OK......	323	29,786	19,518	65.5
HI......	48	4,256	3,840	90.2	OR......	138	12,473	8,113	65.0
ID......	78	6,034	4,522	74.9	PA......	711	87,878	79,710	90.7
IL......	791	101,790	76,282	74.9	RI......	86	8,868	7,955	89.7
IN......	510	57,107	39,536	69.2	SC......	175	18,798	17,004	90.5
IA......	451	33,658	26,292	78.1	SD......	110	6,591	6,528	99.0
KS......	346	26,011	19,301	74.2	TN......	319	36,943	32,288	87.4
KY......	287	25,769	23,233	90.2	TX......	1,145	126,732	90,385	71.3
LA......	285	36,096	25,875	71.7	UT......	93	7,967	5,456	68.5
ME......	112	7,243	6,591	91.0	VT......	40	3,268	2,992	91.6
MD......	230	29,231	25,243	86.4	VA......	281	31,908	28,279	88.6
MA......	433	49,323	43,684	88.6	WA......	238	22,314	18,760	84.1
MI......	425	47,323	40,224	85.0	WV......	130	10,895	9,710	89.1
MN......	390	34,117	31,056	91.0	WI......	393	37,385	32,325	86.5
MS......	203	18,346	16,246	88.6	WY......	39	2,993	2,431	81.2

[1] Percentage of beds occupied (number of nursing home residents per 100 nursing home beds).
Source: U.S. National Center for Health Statistics, *Health, United States, 2009.* See also <http://www.cdc.gov/nchs/hus.htm>.

Table 191. Insufficient Rest or Sleep by Number of Days and Selected Characteristics: 2008

[In percent. Age-adjusted to 2000 projected U.S. population. Respondents were asked, "During the past 30 days, for about how many days have you felt you did not get enough sleep?"]

Characteristic	Number [1]	Days without enough rest or sleep			
		0 days	1–13 days	14–29 days	30 days
Total.............................	**403,981**	**30.7**	**41.3**	**16.8**	**11.1**
Sex:					
Male............................	152,513	33.6	40.9	15.6	9.9
Female..........................	251,468	28.1	41.5	18	12.4
Age:					
18 to 24 years old	13,881	23.2	45.5	19.7	11.6
25 to 34 years old	38,978	21.8	44.1	20.4	13.8
35 to 44 years old	61,350	22.8	45.2	20.1	12.0
45 to 64 years old	169,906	30.5	42.4	16.3	10.9
65 years old or over..............	119,866	56.7	28.3	7.6	7.4
Race/ethnicity:					
White, non-Hispanic..............	318,694	27.9	42.7	18.2	11.2
Black, non-Hispanic..............	31,513	30.4	40.4	16.0	13.3
Other, non-Hispanic [2]............	22,108	35.4	37.2	15.8	11.6
Hispanic [3]......................	28,045	38.8	37.7	13.0	10.5
Employment status:					
Employed........................	215,127	28.7	44.2	17.1	9.9
Unemployed......................	16,797	32.5	36.7	16.9	13.9
Retired..........................	106,325	43.8	33.2	13.4	9.5
Unable to work...................	25,956	24.3	28.4	21.6	25.8
Homemaker or student	38,395	31.3	41.7	15.9	11.1
Education:					
Less than high school	39,395	37.9	33.6	14.2	14.3
High school or GED [4].............	121,346	33.8	37.3	15.7	13.2
Some college or college graduate.........	242,194	28.0	44.5	17.9	9.6
Marital status:					
Married	226,418	30.9	42.1	15.9	11.1
Divorced, widowed, or separated	119,372	30.4	35.1	18.6	16.0
Member of unmarried couple.............	8,945	28.4	42.8	16.7	12.1
Never married	48,016	31.6	41.0	16.7	10.6

[1] Unweighted sample. Categories may not sum to total due to missing responses. [2] Asian, Hawaiian or other Pacific Islander, American Indian/Alaska Native, or multiracial. [3] Persons of Hispanic origin may be any race. [4] General Education Development certificate.
Source: U.S. Centers for Disease Control and Prevention, Atlanta, GA, *Morbidity and Mortality Weekly Report*, Vol. 58, No. 42, 2009. See also <http://www.cdc.gov/mmwr/index2009.html>.

Table 192. Persons 18 Years and Over With Selected Diseases and Conditions by Selected Characteristics: 2008

[In thousands (225,227 represents 225,227,000). Based on National Health Interview Survey, a sample survey of the civilian noninstitutionalized population; see Appendix III]

Selected characteristics	Total persons	Persons with selected diseases and conditions					
		Diabe-tes [1,2]	Ulcers [1]	Kidney dis-ease [3,4]	Liver dis-ease [3]	Arthritis diag-nosis [5]	Chronic joint symp-toms [5]
Total [6]	225,227	18,651	19,321	3,731	3,262	51,233	61,656
SEX							
Male	108,755	8,934	8,481	1,769	1,591	20,136	27,733
Female	116,472	9,717	10,840	1,962	1,671	31,097	33,922
AGE							
18 to 44 years	110,615	2,553	6,065	795	1,060	8,306	18,481
45 to 64 years	77,335	9,223	8,045	1,372	1,680	23,900	27,067
65 to 74 years	19,869	3,940	2,719	601	330	9,574	8,533
75 years and over	17,409	2,935	2,493	963	192	9,454	7,573
RACE							
Race alone [7]	222,430	18,344	19,042	3,688	3,210	50,550	60,657
White	182,651	14,537	16,424	3,002	2,750	43,617	52,421
Black or African American	26,765	2,756	1,866	501	253	5,370	6,365
American Indian or Alaska Native	2,178	262	213	(B)	[8] 52	378	494
Asian	10,501	741	523	153	156	1,132	1,358
Native Hawaiian or other Pacific Islander	334	(B)	(B)	–	–	(B)	(B)
Two or more races [9]	2,798	307	280	[8] 43	[8] 52	683	999
HISPANIC ORIGIN AND RACE [10]							
Hispanic or Latino	30,583	2,524	1,857	483	531	3,726	5,483
Mexican or Mexican American	19,089	1,629	1,191	257	350	2,138	3,291

– Represents zero. B Figure too small to meet statistical standards for reliability of a derived figure. [1] Respondents were asked if they had ever been told by a health professional that they had an ulcer or diabetes. A person may be represented in more than one column. [2] Excludes borderline diabetes. [3] Respondents were asked if they had been told in the last 12 months by a health professional that they had weak or failing kidneys or any kind of liver condition. [4] Excludes kidney stones, bladder infections, or incontinence. [5] Respondents were asked if they had ever been told by a health professional that they had some form of arthritis, rheumatoid arthritis, gout, lupus or fibromyalgia. Those that answered "yes" were classified as having an arthritis diagnosis. Respondents with joint symptoms (excluding back and neck) that began more than 3 months prior to interview were classified as having chronic joint symptoms. [6] Total includes other races not shown separately. [7] Refers to persons who indicated only a single race group. [8] Figures do not meet standard of reliability or precision. [9] Refers to all persons who indicated more than one race group. [10] Persons of Hispanic or Latino origin may be of any race or combination of races.

Source: National Center for Health Statistics, *Summary Health Statistics for U.S. Adults: National Health Interview Survey, 2008*, Vital and Health Statistics, Series 10, Number 242, 2009, <http://www.cdc.gov/nchs/data/series/sr_10/sr10_242.pdf>.

Table 193. Persons 18 Years of Age and Over With Selected Circulatory Diseases by Selected Characteristics: 2008

[In thousands (225,227 represents 225,227,000). In separate questions, respondents were asked if they had ever been told by a doctor or other health professional that they had: hypertension (or high blood pressure); coronary heart disease, angina (or angina pectoris); heart attack (or myocardial infarction); any other heart condition or disease not already mentioned; or a stroke. A person may be represented in more than one column. Based on National Health Interview Survey, a sample survey of the civilian noninstitutionalized population; see Appendix III]

Characteristic	Total persons	Selected circulatory diseases			
		Heart disease		Hyper-tension [3]	Stroke
		All types [1]	Coronary [2]		
Total [4]	225,227	26,628	14,428	56,159	6,460
SEX					
Male	108,755	13,170	8,439	26,031	2,965
Female	116,472	13,457	5,989	30,128	3,495
AGE					
18 to 44 years	110,615	5,067	1,258	9,643	714
45 to 64 years	77,335	9,469	5,205	25,126	2,260
65 to 74 years	19,869	5,287	3,337	10,774	1,248
75 years and over	17,409	6,805	4,628	10,616	2,238
RACE					
Race alone [5]	222,430	26,233	14,210	55,482	6,360
White	182,651	23,082	12,511	45,054	5,286
Black or African American	26,765	2,436	1,307	7,900	832
American Indian or Alaska Native	2,178	230	[6] 119	478	[6] 80
Asian	10,501	472	261	1,985	153
Native Hawaiian or Other Pacific Islander	334	(B)	(B)	(B)	(B)
Two or more races [7]	2,798	395	218	677	[6] 100
HISPANIC ORIGIN AND RACE [8]					
Hispanic or Latino	30,583	1,817	1,217	4,913	562
Mexican or Mexican American	19,089	1,032	668	2,838	341

B Figure too small to meet statistical standards for reliability of a derived figure. [1] Heart disease includes coronary heart disease, angina pectoris, heart attack, or any other heart condition or disease. [2] Coronary heart disease includes coronary heart disease, angina pectoris, or heart attack. [3] Persons had to have been told on two or more different visits that they had hypertension, or high blood pressure, to be classified as hypertensive. [4] Includes other races not shown separately. [5] Refers to persons who indicated only a single race group. [6] Figures do not meet standard of reliability or precision. [7] Refers to all persons who indicated more than one race group. [8] Persons of Hispanic or Latino origin may be any race or combination of races.

Source: National Center for Health Statistics, *Summary Health Statistics for the U.S. Population: National Health Interview Survey*, 2008, Vital and Health Statistics, Series 10, Number 242, 2009. See also <http://www.cdc.gov/nchs/data/series/sr_10/sr10_242.pdf>.

Health and Nutrition 129

Table 194. Selected Respiratory Diseases Among Persons 18 Years of Age and Over by Selected Characteristics: 2008

[In thousands (225,227 represents 225,227,000). Respondents were asked in two separate questions if they had ever been told by a doctor or other health professional that they had emphysema or asthma. Respondents who had been told they had asthma were asked if they still had asthma. Respondents were asked in three separate questions if they had been told by a doctor or other health professional in the past 12 months that they had hay fever, sinusitis, or bronchitis. Based on the National Health Interview Survey, a sample survey of the civilian noninstitutionalized population; see Appendix III]

Selected characteristic	Total persons	Emphy-sema	Asthma Ever	Asthma Still	Hay fever	Sinusitis	Chronic bronchitis
Total [2]	**225,227**	**3,789**	**28,260**	**16,380**	**18,022**	**30,621**	**9,832**
SEX							
Male	108,755	1,769	11,705	6,136	7,463	10,080	3,121
Female	116,472	2,020	16,555	10,244	10,559	20,541	6,711
AGE							
18 to 44 years	110,615	222	14,888	7,949	7,379	12,850	3,486
45 to 64 years	77,335	1,573	9,265	5,768	7,823	12,072	4,251
65 to 74 years	19,869	1,124	2,376	1,548	1,537	3,362	1,172
75 years and over	17,409	870	1,731	1,116	1,283	2,337	922
RACE							
Race alone. [3]	222,430	3,708	27,538	15,881	17,709	30,237	9,649
White	182,651	3,443	22,650	13,032	15,130	25,593	8,442
Black or African American	26,765	217	3,627	2,163	1,699	3,645	1,020
American Indian or Alaska Native	2,178	(B)	263	148	[4] 132	227	[4] 52
Asian	10,501	(B)	966	506	723	740	[4] 124
Native Hawaiian or other Pacific Islander	334	–	(B)	(B)	(B)	(B)	(B)
Two or more races [5]	2,798	[4] 81	722	499	313	384	183
HISPANIC ORIGIN AND RACE [6]							
Hispanic or Latino	30,583	191	2,950	1,639	1,554	2,693	631
Mexican or Mexican American	19,089	[4] 93	1,546	825	872	1,526	304
Not Hispanic or Latino	194,645	3,598	25,310	14,741	16,468	27,928	9,201
White, single race	154,483	3,258	19,951	11,542	13,647	23,112	7,834
Black or African American, single race	26,051	214	3,525	2,107	1,666	3,582	1,011

– Represents zero. B Figure too small to meet statistical standards for reliability of a derived figure. [1] A person may be represented in more than one column. [2] Total includes other races not shown separately. [3] Refers to persons who indicated only a single race group. [4] Figure does not meet standard of reliability or precision. [5] Refers to all persons who indicated more than one race group. [6] Persons of Hispanic or Latino origin may be any race or combination of races.

Source: National Center for Health Statistics, *Summary Health Statistics for the U.S. Population: National Health Interview Survey, 2008*, Vital and Health Statistics, Series 10, Number 242, 2009. See also <http://www.cdc.gov/nchs/data/series /sr_10/sr10_242.pdf>.

Table 195. Persons 18 Years of Age and Over With Migraines and Pains in the Neck, Lower Back, Face, or Jaw by Selected Characteristics: 2008

[In thousands (225,227 represents 225,227,000). Based on National Health Interview Survey, a sample survey of the civilian noninstitutionalized population, Appendix III]

Selected characteristic	Total persons	Migraine or severe headache [2]	Pain in neck [3]	Pain in lower back [3]	Pain in face or jaw [3]
Total [4]	**225,227**	**30,262**	**31,447**	**61,719**	**9,753**
SEX					
Male	108,755	8,886	12,385	27,342	3,051
Female	116,472	21,376	19,062	34,377	6,701
AGE					
18 to 44 years	110,615	18,352	14,017	27,136	5,092
45 to 64 years	77,335	10,260	12,744	22,778	3,523
65 to 74 years	19,869	1,121	2,618	6,359	649
75 years and over	17,409	529	2,068	5,447	489
RACE					
Race alone [5]	222,430	29,671	30,791	60,637	9,569
White	182,651	24,921	26,709	51,792	8,399
Black or African American	26,765	3,524	2,789	6,272	904
American Indian or Alaska Native	2,178	342	351	663	[6] 63
Asian	10,501	844	929	1,822	[6] 196
Native Hawaiian or other Pacific Islander	334	(B)	(B)	[6] 88	(B)
Two or more races [7]	2,798	591	655	1,082	183
HISPANIC ORIGIN AND RACE [8]					
Hispanic or Latino	30,583	4,050	4,082	7,453	1,033
Mexican or Mexican American	19,089	2,501	2,255	4,167	637
Not Hispanic or Latino	194,645	26,212	27,365	54,266	8,719
White, single race	154,483	21,309	23,025	45,183	7,494
Black or African American, single race	26,051	3,319	2,668	6,032	853

B Figure to small to meet statistical standards for reliability of a derived figure. [1] A person may be represented in more than one column. [2] Respondents were asked, "During the past 3 months, did you have a severe headache or migraine?" Respondents were instructed to report pain that had lasted a whole day or more and, conversely, not to report fleeting or minor aches or pains. [3] Respondents were asked, "During the past 3 months, did you have a neck pain; or low back pain; or facial ache or pain in the jaw muscles or the joint in front of the ear?" Respondents were instructed to report pain that had lasted a whole day or more and, conversely, not to report fleeting or minor aches or pains. [4] Total includes other races not shown separately. [5] Refers to persons who indicated only a single race group. [6] Figure does not meet standard of reliability or precision. [7] Refers to all persons who indicated more than one race group. [8] Persons of Hispanic or Latino origin may be any race or combination of races.

Source: National Center for Health Statistics, *Summary Health Statistics for the U.S. Population: National Health Interview Survey, 2008*, Vital and Health Statistics, Series 10, Number 242, 2009. See also <http://www.cdc.gov/nchs/data/series /sr_10/sr10_242.pdf>.

Table 196. Injury and Poisoning Episodes and Conditions by Age and Sex: 2008

[33,255 represents 33,255,000. Covers all medically attended injuries and poisonings occurring during the 5–week period prior to the survey interview. Age adjustment is used to adjust for differences in the age distribution of populations being compared. There may be more than one condition per episode. Based on the National Health Interview Survey, a sample survey of the civilian noninstitutionalized population; see Appendix III]

External cause and nature of injury	Both sexes								Male	Female
	Total	Total, age-adjusted [1]	Under 12 years	12 to 21 years	22 to 44 years	45 to 64 years	65 years and over		Male	Female
EPISODES										
Number (1,000)	33,255	(X)	4,573	6,497	10,653	7,370	4,161		16,692	16,563
Annual rate per 1,000 population, total [2]	111.2	111.9	93.2	156.9	113.4	95.1	112.1		113.9	108.6
Fall.	42.8	42.7	52.9	41.0	31.4	41.8	62.7		34.9	50.4
Struck by or against a person or an object	12.3	12.4	14.1	22.0	10.4	9.8	[4] 9.2		13.4	11.3
Transportation [3]	14.1	14.4	[4] 2.7	21.3	21.4	8.2	[4] 15.2		15.3	13.0
Overexertion	13.5	13.5	[4] 5	21.8	15.4	13.9	[4] 10.0		14.3	12.8
Cutting, piercing instruments. .	7.2	7.3	[4] 3.2	[4] 11.7	11.0	[4] 5.1	[4] 2.0		8.8	5.6
Poisoning [5]	[4] 2.1	2.0	[4] 1.4	[4] 1.8	[4] 1.7	[4] 3.9	–		[4] 3.0	[4] 1.2
CONDITIONS										
Annual rate per 1,000 population, total [2]	155.6	155.9	107.9	207.9	151.7	143.1	196.1		148.3	162.6
Sprains/strains.	50.5	50.6	16.6	98.5	52.8	49.3	38.7		46.9	54.0
Open wounds	18.3	18.7	30.2	12.5	18.8	9.5	[4] 26.1		21.2	15.6
Fractures.	20.9	20.9	22.6	23.1	15.2	19.2	34.5		20.8	21.0
Contusions.	29.4	29.3	[4] 13.0	29.6	28.8	30.2	50.8		19.7	38.8

– Represents or rounds to zero. X Not applicable. [1] Data were age-adjusted using the 2000 standard population using age groups: under 12 years, 12–21 years, 22–44 years, 45–64 years, and 65 years and over. [2] Includes other items not shown separately. [3] Includes the categories "Motor vehicle traffic"; "Pedal cycle, other"; "Pedestrian, other"; and "Transport, other." [4] Figure does not meet standard of reliability or precision. [5] Poisoning episodes are assumed to have a single condition resulting from the episode.

Source: U.S. National Center for Health Statistics, Vital and Health Statistics, unpublished data.

Table 197. Injuries Associated With Selected Consumer Products: 2008

[Estimates calculated from a representative sample of hospitals with emergency treatment departments in the United States. Data are estimates of the number of emergency room treated cases nationwide associated with various products. Product involvement does not necessarily mean the product caused the accident. Products were selected from the U.S. Consumer Product Safety Commission's National Electronic Injury Surveillance System (NEISS)]

Product	Number	Product	Number
Home workshop equipment:		Floors or flooring materials	1,209,603
Saws (hand or power)	91,701	Other doors [2]	313,122
Hammers.	33,053	Home entertainment equipment:	
Household packaging and containers:		Televisions.	57,612
Household containers and packaging	217,943	Computers (equip. & electronic games). . . .	24,721
Bottles and jars	79,406	Personal use items:	
Housewares:		Footwear	154,981
Knives	415,539	Wheelchairs.	126,958
Tableware and flatware	98,456	Crutches, canes, walkers.	100,414
Drinking glasses	77,287	Jewelry	83,571
Home furnishing		Yard and garden equipment:	
Beds	563,922	Lawn mowers.	80,188
Chairs	338,948	Sports and recreation equipment:	
Tables [1]	317,856	Bicycles	516,261
Household cabinets, racks, and shelves . . .	276,285	Skateboards	149,577
Bathtubs and showers.	260,635	Trampolines.	104,752
Home structures, construction:		Minibikes or trail bikes	75,589
Stairs or steps	1,213,555	Swings or swing sets	60,884

[1] Excludes baby-changing and television tables or stands. [2] Excludes glass doors and garage doors.
Source: National Safety Council, Itasca, IL, Injury Facts, annual (copyright). See also <http://www.nsc.org/lrs/statstop.htm>.

Table 198. Costs of Unintentional Injuries: 2008

[701.9 represents $701,900,000,000. Covers costs of deaths or disabling injuries together with vehicle accidents and fires]

Cost	Amount (bil. dol.)					Percent distribution				
	Total [1]	Motor vehicle	Work	Home	Other	Total [1]	Motor vehicle	Work	Home	Other
Total	**701.9**	**255.7**	**183.0**	**182.3**	**103.0**	**100.0**	**100.0**	**100.0**	**100.0**	**100.0**
Wage and productivity losses [2]	354.9	88.7	88.4	116.9	65.3	50.6	34.7	48.3	64.1	63.4
Medical expense	145.1	41.8	38.3	41.2	26.1	20.7	16.3	20.9	22.6	25.3
Administrative expenses [3]	122.4	81.2	37.7	9.8	6.6	17.4	31.8	20.6	5.4	6.4
Motor vehicle damage	41.7	41.7	2.1	(NA)	(NA)	5.9	16.3	1.1	(NA)	(NA)
Employer uninsured cost [4]	22.3	2.3	12.7	4.9	2.8	3.2	0.9	6.9	2.7	2.7
Fire loss.	15.5	(NA)	3.8	9.5	2.2	2.2	(NA)	2.1	5.2	2.1

NA Not available. [1] Excludes duplication between work and motor vehicle: $22.1 billion in 2008. [2] Actual loss of wages and household production, and the present value of future earnings lost. [3] Home and other costs may include costs of administering medical treatment claims for some motor vehicle injuries filed through health insurance plans. [4] Estimate of the uninsured costs incurred by employers, representing the money value of time lost by noninjured workers.
Source: National Safety Council, Itasca, IL, Injury Facts, annual (copyright). See also <http://www.nsc.org/Pages/Home.aspx>.

Table 199. Use of Mammography for Women 40 Years Old and Over by Patient Characteristics: 2000 to 2008

[Percent of women having a mammogram within the past 2 years. Covers civilian noninstitutional population. Based on National Health Interview Survey; see Appendix III]

Characteristic	2000 [1]	2005 [1]	2008 [1]	Characteristic	2000 [1]	2005 [1]	2008 [1]
Total [2]	**70.4**	**66.8**	**67.6**	Years of school completed:			
40 to 49 years old	64.3	63.5	61.5	No high school diploma or GED ...	57.7	52.8	53.8
50 years old and over	73.6	68.4	70.5	High school diploma or GED......	69.7	64.9	65.2
50 to 64 years old	78.7	71.8	74.2	Some college or more	76.2	72.7	73.4
65 years old and over	67.9	63.8	65.5				
White, non-Hispanic	72.2	68.4	68.7	Poverty status: [4]			
Black, non-Hispanic.........	67.9	65.2	68.3	Below poverty	54.8	48.5	51.4
Hispanic origin [3]...........	61.2	58.8	61.2	At or above poverty	72.1	68.8	(NA)

NA Not available. [1] Adjusted data—data have been reweighted using the 2000 Census population controls. [2] Includes other races not shown separately and unknown education level and poverty status. [3] Persons of Hispanic origin may be of any race or combination of races. [4] For explanation of poverty level, see text, Section 13.

Source: U.S. National Center for Health Statistics, *Health, United States, 2010.* See also <http://www.cdc.gov/nchs/hus.htm>.

Table 200. Current Cigarette Smoking: 1990 to 2008

[In percent. Prior to 1992, a current smoker is a person who has smoked at least 100 cigarettes and who now smokes. Beginning 1992, definition includes persons who smoke only "some days." Excludes unknown smoking status. For definition of age adjustment, see text, Section 2. Based on National Health Interview Survey; for details, see Appendix III]

Sex, age, and race	1990 [1]	2000	2005	2008	Sex, age, and race	1990 [1]	2000	2005	2008
Total smokers,					Black, total............	32.5	26.2	26.5	25.3
age-adjusted [2]	**25.3**	**23.1**	**20.8**	**20.6**	18 to 24 years	21.3	20.9	21.6	[4] 17.0
Male..................	28.0	25.2	23.4	22.8	25 to 34 years	33.8	23.2	29.8	25.9
Female.................	22.9	21.1	18.3	18.5	35 to 44 years	42.0	30.7	23.3	21.8
					45 to 64 years	36.7	32.2	32.4	33.6
White male..............	27.6	25.4	23.3	23.0	65 years and over	21.5	14.2	16.8	17.5
Black male..............	32.8	25.7	25.9	24.7	Female, total	22.8	20.9	18.1	18.3
					18 to 24 years	22.5	24.9	20.7	19.0
White female	23.5	22.0	19.1	19.5	25 to 34 years	28.2	22.3	21.5	21.4
Black female	20.8	20.7	17.1	17.4	35 to 44 years	24.8	26.2	21.3	20.9
					45 to 64 years	24.8	21.7	18.8	20.5
Total smokers [3].........	**25.5**	**23.2**	**20.9**	**20.6**	65 years and over	11.5	9.3	8.3	8.3
Male, total	28.4	25.6	23.9	23.1	White, total............	23.4	21.4	18.7	19.1
18 to 24 years	26.6	28.1	28.0	23.6	18 to 24 years	25.4	28.5	22.6	20.1
25 to 34 years	31.6	28.9	27.7	28.5	25 to 34 years	28.5	24.9	23.1	23.1
35 to 44 years	34.5	30.2	26.0	24.3	35 to 44 years	25.0	26.6	22.2	22.6
45 to 64 years	29.3	26.4	25.2	24.8	45 to 64 years	25.4	21.4	18.9	20.9
65 years and over	14.6	10.2	8.9	10.5	65 years and over	11.5	9.1	8.4	8.6
White, total.............	28.0	25.7	23.6	23.1	Black, total............	21.2	20.8	17.3	17.8
18 to 24 years	27.4	30.4	29.7	25.2	18 to 24 years	[4] 10.0	14.2	14.2	16.6
25 to 34 years	31.6	29.7	27.7	29.5	25 to 34 years	29.1	15.5	16.9	17.6
35 to 44 years	33.5	30.6	26.3	24.9	35 to 44 years	25.5	30.2	19.0	19.6
45 to 64 years	28.7	25.8	24.5	24.0	45 to 64 years	22.6	25.6	21.0	21.3
65 years and over	13.7	9.8	7.9	9.9	65 years and over	11.1	10.2	10.0	8.1

[1] Data prior to 2000 are not strictly comparable with data for later years due to the 1997 questionnaire redesign. [2] Data are age-adjusted to the year 2000 standard using five age groups: 18–24 years, 25–34 years, 35–44 years, 45–64 years, 65 years and over. [3] Crude, not age-adjusted. [4] Figure does not meet standard of reliability or precision.

Source: U.S. National Center for Health Statistics, *Health, United States, 2010.* See also <http://www.cdc.gov/nchs/hus.htm>.

Table 201. Current Cigarette Smoking by Sex and State: 2008

[In percent. Current cigarette smoking is defined as persons 18 years and older who reported having smoked 100 or more cigarettes during their lifetime and who currently smoke every day or some days. Based on the Behavioral Risk Factor Surveillance System, a telephone survey of health behaviors of the civilian, noninstitutionalized U.S. population, 18 years old and over; for details, see source]

State	Total	Male	Female	State	Total	Male	Female	State	Total	Male	Female
U.S. [1]...	**18.4**	**20.4**	**16.7**								
AL	22.2	25.2	19.4	KY	25.3	26.3	24.3	ND	18.2	20.4	15.9
AK	21.7	23.9	19.3	LA	20.5	23.4	17.7	OH	20.2	21.5	19.0
AZ	15.9	18.2	13.7	ME.....	18.2	21.6	15.0	OK.....	24.8	26.5	23.1
AR	22.4	24.4	20.4	MD.....	14.9	16.1	13.9	OR.....	16.3	17.4	15.3
CA	14.0	17.8	10.3	MA.....	16.1	16.9	15.4	PA	21.4	23.4	19.6
CO......	17.6	19.8	15.5	MI......	20.4	22.5	18.4	RI......	17.4	17.9	16.9
CT	16.0	17.3	14.8	MN.....	17.6	19.3	15.8	SC	20.1	21.6	18.7
DE	17.8	20.4	15.4	MS.....	22.7	25.4	20.3	SD	17.6	19.0	16.2
DC	16.4	19.4	13.8	MO.....	25.0	27.3	22.9	TN	23.2	26.7	20.0
FL	17.5	18.7	16.4	MT	18.5	18.7	18.4	TX	18.6	22.5	14.9
GA	19.5	21.7	17.4	NE	18.4	20.1	16.8	UT	9.2	10.6	7.9
HI......	15.4	18.2	12.7	NV	22.3	24.5	20.0	VT	16.8	18.4	15.2
ID.......	16.9	18.4	15.4	NH	17.0	18.1	16.0	VA	16.5	17.1	15.9
IL	21.3	25.4	17.5	NJ	14.8	17.4	12.4	WA.....	15.7	17.0	14.4
IN.......	26.1	28.5	23.9	NM	19.4	22.0	16.9	WV.....	26.6	26.1	27.1
IA.......	18.8	21.0	16.7	NY	16.8	17.9	15.8	WI	19.9	21.7	18.2
KS	17.9	19.8	16.1	NC	20.9	23.7	18.3	WY	19.4	20.0	18.9

[1] Represents median value among the states and DC. For definition of median, see Guide to Tabular Presentations.

Source: U.S. Centers for Disease Control and Prevention, *Morbidity and Mortality Weekly Report,* Vol. 58, No. 44, Atlanta, GA, 2009. See also <http://www.cdc.gov/mmwr>.

Table 202. Substance Abuse Treatment Facilities and Clients: 1995 to 2009

[As of October 2 (1995); as of October 1 (1997–2000), as of March 29 (2002), and as of March 31 (2003–2006), and March 30, 2007. Based on the Uniform Facility Data Set (UFDS)/National Survey of Substance Abuse Treatment Services (N-SSATS) survey, a census of all known facilities that provide substance abuse treatment in the United States and associated jurisdictions. Selected missing data for responding facilities were imputed]

Primary focus	Number	Primary focus	Number	Type of care and type of problem	Number of clients
FACILITIES		CLIENTS		**2009, total [1,2]**	**1,182,077**
1995.	10,746	1995.	1,009,127		
2000.	13,428	2000.	1,000,896	Outpatient rehabilitation.	1,053,776
2003.	13,623	2003.	1,092,546	Outpatient detoxification	10,786
2004.	13,454	2004.	1,072,251	24-hour rehabilitation.	105,021
2005.	13,371	2005.	1,081,049	24-hour detoxification	12,494
2006.	13,771	2006.	1,130,881		
2007.	13,648	2007.	1,135,425	**2009, total [1,2]**	**1,179,387**
2008.	13,688	2008.	1,192,490	Drug only	441,128
2009, total [2]	**13,513**	**2009, total [2]**	**1,182,077**	Alcohol only	220,373
Substance abuse treatment		Substance abuse treatment		Both alcohol & drug	517,887
services.	8,257	services.	792,815		
Mental health services.	878	Mental health services.	43,137	Total with a drug	
General health care	169	General health care	13,933	problem [3]	959,015
Both substance abuse and		Both substance abuse and		Total with an alcohol	
mental health.	4,091	mental health.	327,166	problem [4]	738,260
Other	118	Other	5,026		

[1] Excludes clients at facilities that did not provide data on type of substance abuse problem treated. [2] Data for 2009 is based on preliminary data and is subject to change. [3] The sum of clients with a drug problem and clients with both diagnoses. [4] The sum of clients with an alcohol problem and clients with both diagnoses.

Source: U.S. Substance Abuse and Mental Health Services Administration, *Uniform Facility Data Set (UFDS): Annual surveys for 1995–1999*, and Office of Applied Studies, Substance Abuse and Mental Health Services Administration, *National Survey of Substance Abuse Treatment Services* (N-SSATS), 2000–2009, <http://oas.samhsa.gov/oasftp.cfm#Data>.

Table 203. Drug Use by Type of Drug and Age Group: 2003 and 2008

[In percent. Data comes from the National Survey on Drug Use and Health (NSDUH). Current users are those who used drugs at least once within month prior to this study. Based on a representative sample of the U.S. population 12 years old and over, including persons living in households and in some group quarters such as dormitories and homeless shelters. Estimates are based on computer-assisted interviews of about 68,000 respondents. Subject to sampling variability; see source]

Age and type of drug	Ever used 2003	Ever used 2008	Current user 2003	Current user 2008	Age and type of drug	Ever used 2003	Ever used 2008	Current user 2003	Current user 2008
12 YEARS OLD AND OVER					**18 TO 25 YEARS OLD**				
Any illicit drug [1]	46.4	47.0	8.2	8.0	Any illicit drug [1]	60.5	56.6	20.3	19.6
Marijuana and hashish	40.6	41.0	6.2	6.1	Marijuana and hashish	53.9	50.4	17.0	16.5
Cocaine	14.7	14.7	1.0	0.7	Cocaine	15.0	14.4	2.2	1.5
Crack	3.3	3.4	0.3	0.1	Hallucinogens	23.3	17.7	1.7	1.7
Heroin	1.6	1.5	0.1	0.1	Inhalants	14.9	10.4	0.4	0.3
Hallucinogens	14.5	14.4	0.4	0.4	Any psychotherapeutic [2,3]	29.0	29.2	6.0	5.9
LSD	10.3	9.4	(NA)	0.1	Alcohol	87.1	85.6	61.4	61.2
Ecstasy	4.6	5.2	0.2	0.2	"Binge" alcohol use [4]	(NA)	(NA)	41.6	41.8
Inhalants	0.7	8.0	0.2	0.3	Cigarettes	70.2	64.2	40.2	35.7
Any psychotherapeutic [2,3]	20.1	20.8	2.7	2.5	Smokeless tobacco	22.0	20.3	4.7	5.4
Pain relievers	13.1	14.0	2.0	1.9	Cigars	45.2	41.4	11.4	11.3
Tranquilizers.	8.5	8.6	0.8	0.7	**26 TO 34 YEARS OLD**				
Stimulants [3]	8.8	8.5	0.5	0.4	Any illicit drug [1]	57.3	58.2	10.7	11.2
Methamphetamine [3]	6.4	5.0	0.3	0.1	Marijuana and hashish	51.0	51.3	8.4	8.8
Sedatives.	4.0	3.6	0.1	0.1	Cocaine	18.1	16.7	1.5	1.5
Alcohol.	83.1	82.2	50.1	51.6	Hallucinogens	20.3	22.2	0.5	0.6
"Binge" alcohol use [4]	(NA)	(NA)	22.6	23.3	Inhalants	13.6	12.8	–	0.1
Cigarettes	68.7	65.1	25.4	23.9	Any psychotherapeutic [2,3]	24.7	28.0	3.4	3.2
Smokeless tobacco	19.4	18.4	3.3	3.5	**35 YEARS OLD AND OVER**				
Cigars	37.1	35.8	5.4	5.3	Any illicit drug [1]	43.4	45.7	4.4	4.7
Pipe tobacco	16.9	14.6	0.7	0.8	Marijuana and hashish	38.9	40.6	3.0	3.2
12 TO 17 YEARS OLD					Cocaine	15.9	16.4	0.6	0.4
Any illicit drug [1]	30.5	26.2	11.2	9.3	Hallucinogens	12.8	13.6	0.1	0.0
Marijuana and hashish	19.6	16.5	7.9	6.7	Inhalants	7.4	7.7	0.1	0.1
Cocaine	2.6	1.9	0.6	0.4	Any psychotherapeutic [2,3]	18.3	18.9	1.5	1.6
Hallucinogens	5.0	3.9	1.0	1.0	**26 YEARS OLD AND OVER**				
Inhalants	10.7	9.3	1.3	1.1	Alcohol.	88.0	87.3	52.5	54.8
Any psychotherapeutic [2,3]	13.4	11.1	4.0	2.9	"Binge" alcohol use [4]	(NA)	(NA)	21.0	22.1
Alcohol.	42.9	38.3	17.7	14.6	Cigarettes	73.6	70.7	24.7	23.8
"Binge" alcohol use [4]	(NA)	(NA)	10.6	8.8	Smokeless tobacco	20.6	19.5	3.2	3.3
Cigarettes	31.0	22.9	12.2	9.1	Cigars	38.7	37.8	4.5	4.4
Smokeless tobacco	7.6	7.2	2.0	2.2					
Cigars	15.1	12.4	4.5	3.8					

NA Not available. – Represents or rounds to zero. [1] Illicit drugs include marijuana/hashish, cocaine (including crack), heroin, hallucinogens, inhalants, or prescription-type psychotherapeutics used nonmedically. [2] Nonmedical use of prescription-type psychotherapeutics includes the nonmedical use of pain relievers, tranquilizers, stimulants, or sedatives and does not include over-the-counter drugs. [3] Includes data from new methamphetamine items added in 2006 and 2007. Previous estimates have been adjusted to be comparable with new data and differ from those in reports prior to the 2007 data year. [4] Binge alcohol use is defined as drinking five or more drinks on the same occasion (i.e., at the same time or within a couple of hours of each other) on at least 1 day in the past 30 days.

Source: U.S. Substance Abuse and Mental Health Services Administration, National Survey on Drug Use and Health, 2003 and 2008, <http://oas.samhsa.gov/nhsda.htm>.

Table 204. Estimated Use of Selected Drugs by State: 2007 to 2008

[19,966 represents 19,966,000. Data in this table cover a 2-year period. Data is based on the National Survey on Drug Use and Health (NSDUH). Current users are those persons 12 years old and over who used drugs at least once within month prior to this study. Based on national sample of respondents (see also headnote, Table 203). The state estimates were produced by combining the prevalence rate based on the state sample data and the prevalence rate based on a national regression model applied to local-area county and census block group/tract-level estimates from the state (i.e., a survey-weighted hierarchical Bayes estimation approach). The parameters of the regression model are estimated from the entire national sample. For comparison purposes, the data shown here display estimates for all 50 states and the District of Columbia utilizing the modeled estimates for all 51 areas]

State	Estimated current users (1,000)					Current users as percent of population				
	Any illicit drug [1]	Mari-juana	Any illicit drug other than mari-juana [1]	Ciga-rettes	Binge alcohol [2]	Any illicit drug [1]	Mari-juana	Any illicit drug other than mari-juana [1]	Ciga-rettes	Binge alcohol [2]
U.S. . . .	19,966	14,825	8,917	59,918	57,938	8.0	6.0	3.6	24.1	23.3
AL	258	175	146	1,040	733	6.7	4.6	3.8	27.2	19.2
AK	64	50	21	131	131	11.8	9.2	3.9	24.2	24.2
AZ	463	300	230	1,240	1,202	9.0	5.8	4.5	23.9	23.2
AR	185	127	100	723	503	8.0	5.5	4.3	31.1	21.6
CA	2,715	1,998	1,179	5,794	6,466	9.1	6.7	3.9	19.4	21.6
CO	470	370	183	1,007	1,072	11.7	9.2	4.6	25.1	26.7
CT	240	189	95	638	760	8.2	6.5	3.3	21.9	26.1
DE	66	51	30	189	176	9.1	7.1	4.2	26.4	24.5
DC	61	48	23	136	151	12.1	9.6	4.5	27.0	29.9
FL	1,193	853	535	3,677	3,500	7.8	5.6	3.5	24.0	22.9
GA	560	415	236	2,001	1,671	7.3	5.4	3.1	26.0	21.7
HI	104	71	44	227	241	9.9	6.7	4.2	21.6	23.0
ID	97	69	43	262	228	8.0	5.7	3.5	21.7	18.8
IL	758	574	311	2,667	2,824	7.2	5.4	3.0	25.2	26.7
IN	458	326	219	1,437	1,201	8.8	6.3	4.2	27.6	23.0
IA	102	80	45	588	674	4.1	3.2	1.8	23.7	27.2
KS	153	115	80	572	563	6.8	5.1	3.6	25.3	24.9
KY	295	196	154	1,129	696	8.4	5.6	4.4	32.2	19.9
LA	253	177	139	936	840	7.2	5.0	3.9	26.5	23.8
ME	102	92	34	297	244	9.1	8.2	3.0	26.4	21.7
MD	339	249	150	998	1,030	7.3	5.4	3.2	21.5	22.1
MA	484	388	184	1,087	1,404	8.9	7.1	3.4	19.9	25.7
MI	748	587	298	2,130	2,040	9.0	7.0	3.6	25.5	24.4
MN	356	307	133	1,087	1,297	8.2	7.1	3.1	25.2	30.1
MS	151	103	73	595	467	6.4	4.4	3.1	25.3	19.9
MO	358	264	188	1,321	1,154	7.4	5.4	3.9	27.2	23.8
MT	81	67	31	188	215	10.0	8.3	3.9	23.3	26.8
NE	93	72	42	357	367	6.4	5.0	2.9	24.7	25.3
NV	196	130	93	560	508	9.4	6.2	4.5	26.6	24.2
NH	119	100	40	249	289	10.7	9.0	3.6	22.3	25.9
NJ	464	350	197	1,614	1,645	6.4	4.8	2.7	22.4	22.8
NM	141	99	57	365	353	8.7	6.2	3.6	22.7	21.9
NY	1,469	1,130	576	3,463	3,784	9.0	6.9	3.5	21.3	23.3
NC	576	446	261	1,976	1,593	7.8	6.0	3.5	26.6	21.4
ND	31	27	12	133	173	5.9	5.0	2.3	25.1	32.6
OH	724	557	314	2,678	2,430	7.6	5.9	3.3	28.1	25.5
OK	237	140	142	802	633	8.1	4.8	4.9	27.3	21.6
OR	385	271	174	769	739	12.2	8.6	5.5	24.4	23.4
PA	685	499	325	2,592	2,539	6.6	4.8	3.1	24.8	24.3
RI	119	97	52	220	247	13.3	10.9	5.9	24.7	27.7
SC	244	181	113	992	782	6.7	5.0	3.1	27.3	21.5
SD	41	34	15	160	186	6.3	5.2	2.3	24.6	28.5
TN	421	298	219	1,448	958	8.2	5.8	4.3	28.3	18.7
TX	1,194	845	629	4,465	4,427	6.3	4.4	3.3	23.4	23.2
UT	130	89	65	320	315	6.2	4.3	3.1	15.3	15.1
VT	62	54	21	120	135	11.6	10.2	4.0	22.5	25.3
VA	462	365	197	1,465	1,492	7.3	5.8	3.1	23.2	23.7
WA	518	399	202	1,224	1,140	9.6	7.4	3.7	22.7	21.1
WV	104	73	58	447	296	6.8	4.8	3.8	29.1	19.3
WI	406	302	194	1,281	1,317	8.7	6.5	4.2	27.4	28.2
WY	30	24	13	119	107	6.8	5.6	3.0	27.3	24.7

[1] Illicit drugs include marijuana/hashish, cocaine (including crack), heroin, hallucinogens, inhalants, or prescription-type psychotherapeutics used nonmedically. Illicit drugs other than marijuana include cocaine (including crack), heroin, hallucinogens, inhalants, or prescription-type psychotherapeutics used nonmedically. [2] Binge alcohol use is defined as drinking five or more drinks on the same occasion (i.e., at the same time or within a couple of hours of each other) on at least 1 day in the past 30 days.

Source: U.S. Substance Abuse and Mental Health Services Administration, *National Survey on Drug Use and Health, 2007 and 2008*. See also <http://www.oas.samhsa.gov/nhsda.htm>.

Table 205. Cumulative Percent Distribution of Population by Height and Sex: 2007 to 2008

[Data are based on National Health and Nutrition Examination Survey (NHANES), a sample of the civilian noninstitutional population. For this survey, the respondent participates in an interview and a physical examination. For persons 20 years old and over. Height was measured without shoes. Based on sample and subject to sampling variability; see source]

Height	Males						Females					
	20–29 years	30–39 years	40–49 years	50–59 years	60–69 years	70–79 years	20–29 years	30–39 years	40–49 years	50–59 years	60–69 years	70–79 years
Percent under—												
4'10"	–	–	–	(B)	–	–	–	[1] 1.7	–	[1] 1.0	–	[1] 3.3
4'11"	–	–	–	(B)	(B)	–	[1] 2.6	3.1	[1] 1.6	2.1	[1] 3.6	8.7
5'	(B)	–	–	(B)	(B)	–	5.7	6.0	5.0	8.0	9.0	16.0
5'1"	(B)	(B)	(B)	(B)	[1] 0.4	(B)	12.3	11.6	10.8	16.7	14.7	26.0
5'2"	(B)	(B)	(B)	(B)	(B)	(B)	20.8	19.7	19.8	23.3	23.4	36.9
5'3"	(B)	[1] 3.1	[1] 1.9	(B)	[1] 2.3	(B)	30.4	31.3	30.8	36.3	38.4	51.9
5'4"	3.7	[1] 4.4	3.8	[1] 4.3	4.4	5.8	43.5	46.6	46.0	50.7	52.8	69.9
5'5"	7.2	6.7	5.6	7.6	7.8	12.8	54.1	61.2	58.0	68.4	66.6	82.8
5'6"	11.6	13.1	9.8	12.2	14.7	23.0	72.4	74.0	72.2	79.7	83.3	89.3
5'7"	20.6	19.6	19.4	18.6	23.7	35.1	82.3	84.9	83.0	88.4	93.3	95.4
5'8"	33.1	32.2	30.3	30.3	37.7	47.7	90.3	91.8	91.2	95.2	97.0	98.4
5'9"	42.2	45.4	40.4	41.2	50.2	60.3	94.1	96.1	94.7	97.3	97.8	99.6
5'10"	58.6	58.1	54.4	54.3	65.2	75.2	97.6	98.9	97.8	98.9	99.6	99.6
5'11"	70.7	69.4	69.6	70.0	75.0	85.8	99.6	98.9	99.4	100.0	99.8	100.0
6'	79.9	78.5	79.1	81.2	84.3	91.0	100.0	99.4	99.5	100.0	99.9	100.0
6'1"	89.0	89.0	87.4	91.6	93.6	94.9	100.0	99.9	99.5	100.0	99.9	100.0
6'2"	94.1	94.0	92.5	93.7	97.8	98.6	100.0	100.0	99.5	100.0	100.0	100.0
6'3"	98.3	95.8	97.7	96.6	99.9	100.0	100.0	100.0	99.5	100.0	100.0	100.0
6'4"	100.0	97.6	99.0	99.5	100.0	100.0	100.0	100.0	99.5	100.0	100.0	100.0
6'5"	100.0	99.4	99.4	99.6	100.0	100.0	100.0	100.0	100.0	100.0	100.0	100.0
6'6"	100.0	99.5	99.9	100.0	100.0	100.0	100.0	100.0	100.0	100.0	100.0	100.0

– Represents zero. B Base figure too small to meet statistical standards of reliability of a derived figure. [1] Figure does not meet standard for reliability or precision.

Source: U.S. National Center for Health Statistics, unpublished data, <http://www.cdc.gov/nchs/nhanes.htm>.

Table 206. Cumulative Percent Distribution of Population by Weight and Sex: 2007 to 2008

[See headnote, Table 205. Data are based on National Health and Nutrition Examination Survey (NHANES). Weight was measured without shoes. Pregnant females were excluded from the analyses. Based on sample and subject to sampling variability; see source]

Weight	Males						Females					
	20–29 years	30–39 years	40–49 years	50–59 years	60–69 years	70–79 years	20–29 years	30–39 years	40–49 years	50–59 years	60–69 years	70–79 years
Percent under—												
100 lbs	–	–	(B)	(B)	–	–	[1] 2.0	1.3	(B)	[1] 0.4	0.2	(B)
110 lbs	(B)	–	(B)	(B)	(B)	(B)	4.9	4.7	3.7	[1] 4.0	(B)	6.1
120 lbs	(B)	(B)	(B)	[1] 1.1	(B)	1.5	16.3	10.5	7.8	7.9	7.2	12.4
130 lbs	4.3	[1] 2.1	[1] 2.5	[1] 2.3	2.8	3.5	27.8	18.9	16.0	17.1	13.5	22.5
140 lbs	11.1	6.4	4.7	5.6	5.3	5.2	39.4	29.8	26.4	27.3	27.4	30.1
150 lbs	20.9	11.5	7.6	8.6	10.0	9.7	49.7	40.6	37.5	38.7	37.4	43.1
160 lbs	31.3	20.4	15.1	13.9	16.5	17.7	57.5	51.1	49.8	49.7	46.1	53.7
170 lbs	43.6	30.5	21.3	22.0	24.9	27.4	63.2	59.8	59.3	56.9	58.9	65.6
180 lbs	55.7	40.9	33.6	33.2	33.4	40.1	72.6	68.7	65.6	63.7	72.4	74.0
190 lbs	65.0	50.6	43.7	44.5	42.6	50.1	76.3	73.6	75.0	70.3	79.4	81.2
200 lbs	73.5	59.3	58.0	55.7	55.5	65.7	80.0	79.4	80.0	75.3	84.6	87.3
210 lbs	79.4	70.0	66.2	64.6	64.4	71.6	82.8	83.7	82.8	81.9	88.4	90.5
220 lbs	83.8	76.1	75.6	74.0	73.4	80.0	84.9	89.0	87.2	85.9	91.1	93.4
230 lbs	86.5	81.7	84.6	78.8	81.2	83.5	88.6	91.3	90.6	89.5	93.7	96.4
240 lbs	89.7	85.5	88.1	85.6	85.1	87.3	90.0	94.1	93.0	91.4	95.6	97.0
250 lbs	93.2	89.6	89.7	88.0	88.2	90.6	92.3	95.2	95.5	92.9	96.7	98.4
260 lbs	94.7	92.0	92.8	91.3	90.7	93.1	93.3	95.8	96.7	96.5	97.6	98.6
270 lbs	95.1	93.3	94.6	93.5	93.0	96.4	95.7	96.4	97.5	97.2	98.0	98.6
280 lbs	96.1	95.1	95.4	94.2	94.8	97.5	97.0	97.2	97.8	98.2	99.0	99.4
290 lbs	96.8	96.4	96.4	95.8	97.2	98.5	97.2	97.5	98.2	98.9	99.0	99.6
300 lbs	97.5	96.9	98.1	98.1	97.8	99.4	97.7	98.4	98.3	99.4	99.3	100.0
320 lbs	98.1	98.2	98.8	99.0	98.5	99.4	98.9	99.1	98.7	99.7	99.9	100.0
340 lbs	99.5	98.8	98.8	99.1	99.0	100.0	99.6	99.5	99.4	99.8	99.9	100.0
360 lbs	99.5	99.4	99.3	99.8	99.0	100.0	99.6	99.7	99.8	99.9	99.9	100.0
380 lbs	99.7	99.7	99.5	99.8	99.1	100.0	99.6	99.9	99.8	100.0	100.0	100.0
400 lbs	99.7	99.7	99.5	99.9	99.5	100.0	99.6	100.0	99.8	100.0	100.0	100.0
420 lbs	99.7	99.7	99.5	100.0	99.5	100.0	99.6	100.0	99.9	100.0	100.0	100.0
440 lbs	99.8	99.9	99.5	100.0	99.5	100.0	99.6	100.0	100.0	100.0	100.0	100.0

– Represents zero. B Base figure too small to meet statistical standards of reliability of a derived figure. [1] Figure does not meet standard of reliability or precision.

Source: U.S. National Center for Health Statistics, unpublished data, <http://www.cdc.gov/nchs/nhanes.htm>.

U.S. Census Bureau, Statistical Abstract of the United States: 2011

Table 207. Age-Adjusted Percent Distributions of Body Mass Index (BMI) Among Persons 18 Years Old and Over by Selected Characteristics: 2007 to 2008

[See headnote, Table 205. Body Mass Index (BMI) is a measure that adjusts body weight for height. It is calculated as weight in kilograms divided by height in meters squared. For both men and women, underweight is indicated by a BMI under 18.5; healthy weight is indicated by a BMI greater than or equal to 18.5 and less than 25.0; overweight is indicated by a BMI greater than or equal to 25.0 and less than 30.0; obesity is indicated by a BMI greater than or equal to 30.0. BMI is calculated from the measurement of the participants' weight and height during the examination. For definition of age adjustment, see text, Section 2. Based on the National Health and Nutrition Examination Survey (NHANES)]

Selected characteristic	Underweight	Healthy weight	Above healthy weight		
			Total	Overweight	Obese
Total [1] (age-adjusted)	1.8	31.6	66.6	33.9	32.6
Total [1] (crude)	1.8	31.2	67.0	34.0	33.0
Age: [2]					
18 to 44 years old	2.1	35.5	62.4	32.2	30.3
45 to 64 years old	[3] 1.6	26.9	71.5	34.2	37.3
65 to 74 years old	(B)	25.7	73.3	36.5	36.8
75 years old and over	1.7	30.3	68.0	41.7	26.2
Sex:					
Male...............................	1.1	28.2	70.7	39.9	30.8
Female............................	2.5	34.8	62.7	28.2	34.5
Race/ethnicity and sex:					
Not Hispanic or Latino:					
White, male............................	[3] 1.2	27.8	71.1	40.5	30.5
White, female..........................	2.6	37.3	60.0	27.7	32.3
Black alone or African American, male	[3] 1.6	31.4	67.0	31.1	36.0
Black alone or African American, female..........	2.8	21.1	76.0	27.9	48.1
Mexican or Mexican American, male................	(B)	20.9	78.6	44.0	34.6
Mexican or Mexican American, female	(B)	25.2	73.6	31.0	42.6
Education: [4]					
Less than a high school diploma..................	2.2	25.1	72.6	34.4	38.3
High school diploma or GED....................	1.5	27.6	70.9	36.1	34.8
Some college, bachelor's degree, or higher	1.0	31.6	67.4	35.1	32.3

B Base figure too small to meet statistical standards for reliability of a derived figure. [1] Total includes other race/ethnicities not shown separately and persons with unknown race/ethnicity. [2] Estimates for age groups are not age adjusted. [3] Figure does not meet standard of reliability or precision. [4] Education is shown only for persons 25 years old and over.

Source: U.S. National Center for Health Statistics, unpublished data, <http://www.cdc.gov/nchs/nhanes.htm>.

Table 208. Age-Adjusted Percentage of Persons Engaging in Physical Activity and Fitness by Selected Characteristics: 2008

[In percent. Covers persons 18 years old and over. Based on the National Health Interview Survey, a sample survey of the civilian noninstitutionalized population. Leisure-time physical activity is assessed by asking respondents a series of questions about participation in moderate and vigorous-intensity physical activities. For definition of age adjustment, see text, Section 2. To assess muscle-strengthening activities, respondents were asked about leisure-time physical activities specifically designed to strengthen their muscles]

Characteristic	No leisure-time physical activity [1]	Regular physical activity-moderate or vigorous [2]	Muscular strength and endur-ance [3]	Characteristic	No leisure-time physical activity [1]	Regular physical activity-moderate or vigorous [2]	Muscular strength and endur-ance [3]
Total.................	36.2	32.5	21.9	Two or more races	32.3	29.2	23.0
SEX				HISPANIC ORIGIN			
Male...................	33.9	34.7	25.7	AND RACE			
Female.................	38.2	30.5	18.3	Hispanic or Latino	47.4	25.1	15.0
AGE [4]				Not Hispanic or Latino.....	34.3	33.8	23.2
18 to 29 years old	28.7	38.4	29.3	White, non-Hispanic......	31.9	35.8	24.2
30 to 44 years old	31.7	35.5	24.6	Black, non-Hispanic......	47.9	24.8	19.2
45 to 64 years old	37.2	31.7	19.9				
65 to 74 years old	45.8	26.1	16.3	Education level (persons			
75 years old and over	55.9	18.4	11.5	aged 25 years			
RACE				and over):			
Race alone				Less than 9th grade......	64.3	14.6	6.3
White	34.6	33.8	22.6	Grades 9 thru 11	56.3	18.0	9.2
Black or African				High School graduate	47.0	25.0	14.4
American..............	47.3	25.0	19.4	Some college or AA			
American Indian or				degree...............	33.0	31.8	22.4
Alaska Native..........	49.2	25.0	11.2	College graduate or			
Asian or Pacific				above...............	20.7	45.2	31.8
Islander	(NA)	(NA)	(NA)				

[1] Persons with no moderate- or vigorous-intensity activity for at least 10 minutes at a time. [2] Regular physical activity is moderate-intensity physical activity at least 5 times a week for 30 minutes at a time or vigorous-intensity physical activity for at least 3 times a week for 20 minutes at a time. [3] Persons who participated in muscle strengthening activities at least 2 times a week. [4] Age data are not age-adjusted.

Source: National Center for Health Statistics, National Health Interview Survey—United States, 2008, Hyattsville, MD. See also <http://wonder.cdc.gov/data2010/>.

Table 209. High School Students Engaged in Physical Activity by Sex: 2007

[In percent. For students in grades 9 to 12. Based on the Youth Risk Behavior Survey, a school-based survey and subject to sampling error; for details, see source]

Characteristic	Met currently recommended levels of physical activity [1]	Did not participate in 60+ min. of physical activity on any day [2]	Attended physical education class		Played on at least one sports team [5]	Injured while exercising or playing sports [6]	Used computers 3 or more hours/day [7]	Watched 3 or more hours/day of TV [8]
			Total [3]	Attended daily [4]				
All students	**34.7**	**24.9**	**53.6**	**30.3**	**56.3**	**21.9**	**24.9**	**35.4**
Male.	**43.7**	**18.0**	**57.7**	**33.2**	**62.1**	**24.1**	**29.1**	**37.5**
Grade 9	44.4	17.1	68.3	39.7	63.4	26.0	30.5	42.0
Grade 10	45.1	16.3	62.3	35.7	64.7	24.5	30.0	38.1
Grade 11	45.2	18.0	51.4	27.9	63.0	23.8	29.5	35.4
Grade 12	38.7	21.5	44.6	27.5	56.2	20.9	25.6	32.8
Female	**25.6**	**31.8**	**49.4**	**27.3**	**50.4**	**19.3**	**20.6**	**33.2**
Grade 9	31.5	26.1	65.1	40.4	54.7	21.7	24.9	37.2
Grade 10	24.4	31.7	51.2	26.1	50.8	20.8	22.6	35.9
Grade 11	24.6	34.3	38.8	19.8	52.5	18.2	17.9	29.6
Grade 12	20.6	36.2	38.5	20.2	41.9	14.8	14.8	28.9

[1] Were physically active doing any kind of physical activity that increased their heart rate and made them breathe hard some of the time for a total of at least 60 minutes/day for at least 5 or more days out of the 7 days preceding the survey. [2] Did not participate in 60 or more minutes of any kind of physical activity that increased their heart rate and made them breathe hard some of the time on at least 1 day during the 7 days before the survey. [3] On one or more days in an average week when they were in school. [4] 5 days in an average week when they were in school. [5] Run by their school or community groups during the 12 months before the survey. [6] Students who saw a doctor or nurse for an injury that happened while exercising or playing sports during the 30 days before the survey, among 79.6% of students nationwide who exercised or played sports. [7] For something that was not schoolwork. [8] On an average school day.

Source: U.S. Centers for Disease Control and Prevention, Atlanta, GA, "Youth Risk Behavior Surveillance—United States, 2007," *Morbidity and Mortality Weekly Report*, Vol. 57, No. SS-4, June 2008. See also <http://www.cdc.gov/mmwr/preview /mmwrhtml/ss5704a1.htm>.

Table 210. Households and Persons Having Problems With Access to Food: 2004 to 2008

[112,967 represents 112,967,000. Food-secure means that a household had access at all times to enough food for an active healthy life for all household members, with no need for recourse to socially unacceptable food sources or extraordinary coping behaviors to meet their basic food needs. Food-insecure households had limited or uncertain ability to acquire acceptable foods in socially acceptable ways. Households with very low food security (a subset of food-insecure households) were those in which food intake of one or more household members was reduced and normal eating patterns disrupted due to inadequate resources for food. The severity of food insecurity in households is measured through a series of questions about experiences and behaviors known to characterize households that are having difficulty meeting basic food needs. These experiences and behaviors generally occur in an ordered sequence as the severity of food insecurity increases. As resources become more constrained, adults in typical households first worry about having enough food, then they stretch household resources and juggle other necessities, then decrease the quality and variety of household members' diets, then decrease the frequency and quantity of adults' food intake, and finally decrease the frequency and quantity of children's food intake. All questions refer to the previous 12 months and include a qualifying phrase reminding respondents to report only those occurrences that resulted from inadequate financial resources. Restrictions to food intake due to dieting or busy schedules are excluded. The omission of homeless persons may be a cause of underreporting. Data are from the Food Security Supplement to the Current Population Survey (CPS); for details about the CPS, see text, Section 1 and Appendix III]

Household food	Number (1,000)					Percent distribution				
	2004	2005	2006	2007	2008	2004	2005	2006	2007	2008
Households, total.	**112,967**	**114,437**	**115,609**	**117,100**	**117,565**	**100.0**	**100.0**	**100.0**	**100.0**	**100.0**
Food-secure	99,473	101,851	102,961	104,089	100,416	88.1	89.0	89.1	88.9	85.4
Food-insecure	13,494	12,586	12,648	13,011	17,149	11.9	11.0	10.9	11.1	14.6
With low food security [1]	9,045	8,158	8,031	8,262	10,426	8.0	7.1	6.9	7.0	8.9
With very low food security [2]	4,449	4,428	4,617	4,749	6,723	3.9	3.9	4.0	4.1	5.7
With very low food security among children [3]	274	270	221	323	506	0.7	0.7	0.6	0.8	1.3
Adult members	**215,564**	**217,897**	**220,423**	**223,467**	**225,461**	**100.0**	**100.0**	**100.0**	**100.0**	**100.0**
In food-secure households	191,236	195,172	197,536	199,672	193,026	88.7	89.6	89.6	89.4	85.6
In food-insecure households	24,328	22,725	22,887	23,795	32,435	11.3	10.4	10.4	10.6	14.4
With low food security	16,946	15,146	15,193	15,602	20,320	7.9	7.0	6.9	7.0	9.0
With very low food security [2]	7,382	7,579	7,694	8,193	12,115	3.4	3.5	3.5	3.7	5.4
Child members.	**73,039**	**73,604**	**73,587**	**73,575**	**74,106**	**100.0**	**100.0**	**100.0**	**100.0**	**100.0**
In food-secure households	59,171	61,201	60,959	61,140	57,433	81.0	83.1	82.8	83.1	77.5
In food-insecure households	13,868	12,403	12,628	12,435	16,673	19.0	16.9	17.2	16.9	22.5
With very low food security among children [3]	545	606	430	691	1,077	0.7	0.8	0.6	0.9	1.5

[1] Prior to 2006, USDA described these households as food insecure without hunger. [2] Food intake of one or more members in these households was reduced and normal eating patterns disrupted at some time during the year because of the household's food insecurity. Prior to 2006, USDA described these households as food insecure with hunger. [3] Percentages omit households with no children. The food security survey measures food security status at the household level. Not all children residing in food-insecure households were directly affected by the households' food insecurity. Similarly, not all children in households classified as having very low food security among children were subject to the reductions in food intake and disruptions in eating patterns that characterize this condition. Young children, in particular, are often protected from effects of the households' food insecurity.

Source: U.S. Department of Agriculture, Economic Research Service, *Household Food Security in the United States, 2008*, Economic Research Report Number 83, 2009. See also <http://www.ers.usda.gov/publications/err83/>

Health and Nutrition 137

Table 211. Per Capita Consumption of Selected Beverages by Type: 1980 to 2008

[In gallons. See headnote, Table 213. Per capita consumption uses U.S. resident population, July 1, for all beverages except coffee, tea, and fruit juices which use U.S. total population (Resident plus Armed Forces overseas), July 1]

Beverages	1980 [1]	1990	1995	2000	2004	2005	2006	2007	2008
Nonalcoholic	132.5	140.2	132.4	139.8	(NA)	(NA)	(NA)	(NA)	(NA)
Milk (plain and flavored).	27.5	25.7	23.9	22.5	21.3	21.0	21.0	20.6	20.8
Whole.	17.0	10.5	8.6	8.1	7.3	7.0	6.7	6.4	6.1
Reduced-fat, light, and skim	10.5	15.2	15.3	14.4	14.0	14.1	14.2	14.3	14.6
Tea.	7.3	6.9	7.9	7.8	8.0	8.0	8.4	8.4	8.0
Coffee	26.7	26.8	20.2	26.3	24.7	24.3	24.4	24.6	24.2
Bottled water	(NA)	(NA)	(NA)	(NA)	(NA)	(NA)	(NA)	(NA)	(NA)
Carbonated soft drinks	35.1	46.2	47.4	49.3	(NA)	(NA)	(NA)	(NA)	(NA)
Diet	5.1	10.7	10.9	11.6	(NA)	(NA)	(NA)	(NA)	(NA)
Regular	29.9	35.6	36.5	37.7	(NA)	(NA)	(NA)	(NA)	(NA)
Fruit juices	7.4	7.0	8.1	8.9	8.5	8.1	8.0	7.9	6.9
Alcoholic	28.5	27.6	24.9	25.0	25.3	25.2	25.6	25.7	25.7
Beer.	24.4	24.1	21.9	21.7	21.7	21.5	21.8	21.8	21.7
Wine.	2.1	2.0	1.8	2.0	2.3	2.3	2.4	2.5	2.5
Distilled spirits	2.0	1.5	1.2	1.3	1.4	1.4	1.4	1.4	1.4

NA Not available. [1] Excludes wine coolers.

Source: U.S. Department of Agriculture, Economic Research Service, *Food Consumption, Prices, and Expenditures, 1970–1997*; Food Consumption (Per Capita) Data System, <http://www.ers.usda.gov/data/foodconsumption/>.

Table 212. Nutrition—Nutrients in Foods Available for Civilian Consumption Per Capita Per Day: 1970 to 2006

[Computed by the Center for Nutrition Policy and Promotion (CNPP). Based on Economic Research Service (ERS) estimates of per capita quantities of food available for consumption from "Food Consumption, Prices, and, Expenditures," on imputed consumption data for foods no longer reported by ERS, and on CNPP estimates of quantities of produce from home gardens. Food supply estimates do not reflect loss of food or nutrients from further marketing or home processing. Enrichment and fortification levels of iron, zinc, thiamin, riboflavin, niacin, folate, vitamin A, vitamin B_6, vitamin B_{12}, and Vitamin C are included]

Nutrient	Unit	1970–79	1980–89	1990–99	2000	2006
Food energy	Kilocalories	3,200	3,400	3,600	3,900	3,900
Carbohydrate.	Grams	395	421	478	495	474
Fiber	Grams	20	22	24	24	25
Protein.	Grams	96	100	108	111	111
Total fat [1]	Grams	143	151	150	169	178
Saturated.	Grams	49	50	48	52	54
Monounsaturated.	Grams	57	61	64	75	77
Polyunsaturated.	Grams	27	30	31	35	39
Cholesterol	Milligrams	430	420	400	410	420
Vitamin A.	Micrograms RAE [2]	1,050	1,050	1,100	1,090	940
Carotene	Micrograms	560	600	710	690	690
Vitamin E.	Milligrams a-TE [3]	14	16	17	20	21
Vitamin C.	Milligrams	109	115	118	121	106
Thiamin.	Milligrams	2	3	3	3	3
Riboflavin.	Milligrams	3	3	3	3	3
Niacin.	Milligrams	25	29	31	32	32
Vitamin B_6	Milligrams	2	2	2	2	2
Folate [4].	Micrograms DFE [5]	341	383	504	902	874
Vitamin B_{12}.	Micrograms	9	8	8	8	8
Calcium	Milligrams	930	930	980	980	960
Phosphorus.	Milligrams	1,540	1,590	1,690	1,720	1,700
Magnesium	Milligrams	340	360	390	400	400
Iron	Milligrams	17	20	23	23	23
Zinc	Milligrams	13	14	15	15	16
Copper.	Milligrams	2	2	2	2	2
Potassium	Milligrams	3,510	3,550	3,720	3,780	3,620
Sodium [6]	Milligrams	1,210	1,210	1,240	1,230	1,150
Selenium	Micrograms	133	143	163	179	181

[1] Includes other types of fat not shown separately. [2] Retinol activity equivalents. [3] Alpha-Tocopherol equivalents. [4] Reflects new terminology from Institute of Medicine's Dietary Reference Intakes reports. [5] Dietary Folate Equivalents (DFE). [6] Does not include amount from processed foods; underestimates actual availability.

Source: U.S. Department of Agriculture, Center for Nutrition Policy and Promotion, *Nutrient Content of the U.S. Food Supply, 1909–2006*. Data also published by Economic Research Service, *Food Consumption, Prices, and Expenditures*, annual. See also <http://www.usda.gov/cnpp/>.

Table 213. Per Capita Consumption of Major Food Commodities: 1980 to 2008

[In pounds, retail weight, except as indicated. Consumption represents the residual after exports, nonfood use and ending stocks are subtracted from the sum of beginning stocks, domestic production, and imports. Based on Census Bureau estimated resident population as of April 1; 2005, 2007, 2008 as of July 1]

Commodity	Unit	1980	1990	1995	2000	2005	2007	2008
Red meat, total (boneless, trimmed weight) [1, 2]	Pounds	126.4	112.2	113.6	113.7	110.3	110.7	108.3
Beef	Pounds	72.1	63.9	63.5	64.5	62.5	62.2	61.2
Veal	Pounds	1.3	0.9	0.8	0.5	0.4	0.3	0.3
Lamb and mutton	Pounds	1.0	1.0	0.9	0.8	0.8	0.8	0.7
Pork	Pounds	52.1	46.4	48.4	47.8	46.6	47.3	46.0
Poultry (boneless, trimmed weight) [2]	Pounds	40.8	56.2	62.1	67.9	73.7	73.7	72.6
Chicken	Pounds	32.7	42.4	48.2	54.2	60.6	59.9	58.8
Turkey	Pounds	8.1	13.8	13.9	13.7	13.2	13.8	13.9
Fish and shellfish (boneless, trimmed weight)	Pounds	12.4	14.9	14.8	15.2	16.2	16.3	16.0
Eggs	Number	271	234	232	251	255	249	247
Shell	Number	236	186	172	172	172	170	170
Processed	Number	35	48	60	79	83	79	77
Dairy products, total [3]	Pounds	543.1	568.0	576.2	591.1	597.9	603.8	600.5
Fluid milk products [4]	Gallons	27.9	26.2	24.6	23.2	22.2	22.0	22.1
Beverage milks	Gallons	27.6	25.7	23.9	22.5	21.0	20.6	20.8
Plain whole milk	Gallons	16.5	10.2	8.3	7.7	6.7	6.1	5.9
Plain reduced-fat milk (2%)	Gallons	6.3	9.1	8.0	7.1	6.9	6.9	7.3
Reduced fat milk (1%) and skim milk	Gallons	3.1	4.9	6.1	6.1	5.6	5.7	5.7
Flavored whole milk	Gallons	0.6	0.3	0.3	0.4	0.3	0.3	0.2
Flavored milks other than whole	Gallons	0.6	0.8	0.8	1.0	1.4	1.4	1.4
Buttermilk	Gallons	0.5	0.4	0.3	0.3	0.2	0.2	0.2
Yogurt (excl. frozen)	1/2 pints	4.6	7.8	11.4	12.0	19.1	21.3	21.9
Fluid cream products [5]	1/2 pints	10.5	14.3	15.6	18.3	24.1	24.7	23.9
Cream [6]	1/2 pints	6.3	8.7	9.4	11.6	14.9	15.7	15.3
Sour cream and dips	1/2 pints	3.4	4.7	5.4	6.1	8.3	8.2	7.9
Condensed and evaporated milks	Pounds	7.0	7.9	6.8	5.8	5.9	7.6	7.5
Whole milk	Pounds	3.8	3.1	2.3	2.0	2.2	2.0	2.4
Skim milk	Pounds	3.3	4.8	4.5	3.8	3.7	5.6	5.1
Cheese [7]	Pounds	17.5	24.6	26.9	29.8	31.6	33.1	32.4
American [8]	Pounds	9.6	11.1	11.7	12.7	12.7	12.8	13.0
Cheddar	Pounds	6.8	9.0	9.0	9.7	10.3	10.0	9.9
Italian [8]	Pounds	4.4	9.0	10.3	12.1	13.3	14.5	14.0
Mozzarella	Pounds	3.0	6.9	8.0	9.3	10.2	11.0	10.6
Other [8]	Pounds	3.3	4.3	5.0	5.0	5.6	6.1	5.4
Swiss	Pounds	1.3	1.4	1.1	1.0	1.3	1.3	1.2
Cream and Neufchatel	Pounds	0.9	1.6	2.2	2.4	2.4	2.6	2.5
Cottage cheese, total	Pounds	4.5	3.4	2.7	2.6	2.7	2.6	2.3
Lowfat	Pounds	0.8	1.2	1.2	1.3	1.4	1.4	1.3
Frozen dairy products	Pounds	26.4	28.5	29.0	30.0	25.8	25.5	25.0
Ice cream	Pounds	17.5	15.8	15.5	16.7	14.6	14.2	13.9
Lowfat ice cream	Pounds	7.1	7.7	7.4	7.3	6.7	7.0	6.8
Sherbet	Pounds	1.2	1.2	1.3	1.2	1.2	1.3	1.2
Frozen yogurt	Pounds	(NA)	2.8	3.4	2.0	1.3	1.1	1.1
Fats and oils:								
Total, fat content only	Pounds	56.9	62.3	64.2	81.7	85.5	84.9	85.2
Butter (product weight)	Pounds	4.5	4.4	4.4	4.5	4.5	4.7	5.0
Margarine (product weight)	Pounds	11.3	10.9	9.1	8.2	4.0	4.5	4.2
Lard (direct use)	Pounds	2.3	0.9	0.4	0.8	1.6	1.6	1.0
Edible beef tallow (direct use)	Pounds	1.1	0.6	2.7	4.0	3.8	2.9	2.9
Shortening	Pounds	18.2	22.2	22.2	31.5	29.0	21.0	18.0
Salad and cooking oils	Pounds	21.2	25.2	26.5	33.7	42.8	50.2	54.3
Other edible fats and oils	Pounds	1.5	1.2	1.6	1.5	1.6	1.7	1.7
Flour and cereal products [9]	Pounds	144.9	181.0	188.7	199.3	192.3	197.3	196.5
Wheat flour	Pounds	116.9	135.9	140.0	146.3	134.4	138.3	136.6
Rice, milled	Pounds	9.5	15.8	17.1	19.1	20.8	20.8	21.0
Corn products	Pounds	12.9	21.4	24.9	28.4	31.4	32.4	33.0
Oat products	Pounds	3.9	6.5	5.5	4.3	4.6	4.7	4.8
Caloric sweeteners, total [10]	Pounds	120.2	132.4	144.1	148.9	142.3	136.2	136.3
Sugar, refined cane and beet	Pounds	83.6	64.4	64.9	65.5	63.2	62.0	65.7
Corn sweeteners [11]	Pounds	35.3	66.8	77.9	81.8	77.7	72.9	69.2
High-fructose corn syrup	Pounds	19.0	49.6	57.6	62.6	59.2	56.2	53.1
Other:								
Cocoa beans	Pounds	3.4	5.4	4.5	5.9	6.5	6.0	5.6
Coffee (green beans)	Pounds	10.3	10.3	7.9	10.3	9.5	9.6	9.5
Peanuts (shelled)	Pounds	5.1	6.1	5.7	5.8	6.7	6.3	6.4
Tree nuts (shelled)	Pounds	1.8	2.5	1.9	2.6	2.6	3.5	3.5

NA Not available. [1] Excludes edible offals. [2] Excludes shipments to Puerto Rico and the other U.S. possessions. [3] Milk-equivalent, milk-fat basis. Includes butter. [4] Fluid milk figures are aggregates of commercial sales and milk produced and consumed on farms. [5] Includes eggnog, not shown separately. [6] Heavy cream, light cream, and half-and-half. [7] Excludes full-skim American, cottage, pot, and baker's cheese. [8] Includes other cheeses, not shown separately. [9] Includes rye flour and barley products, not shown separately. Excludes quantities used in alcoholic beverages. [10] Dry weight. Includes edible syrups (maple, molasses, etc.) and honey, not shown separately. [11] Includes glucose and dextrose, not shown separately.

Source: U.S. Department of Agriculture, Economic Research Service, "Food Consumption, Prices, and Expenditures, Food Availability (Per Capita) Data System," <http://www.ers.usda.gov/data/foodconsumption/>.

Health and Nutrition 139

Table 214. Per Capita Utilization of Selected Commercially Produced Fruits and Vegetables: 1980 to 2008

[In pounds, farm weight. Domestic food use of fresh fruits and vegetables reflects the fresh-market share of commodity production plus imports and minus exports. Based on Census Bureau estimated resident population as of April 1; 2004 to 2008 as of July 1]

Commodity	1980	1990	1995	2000	2004	2005	2006	2007	2008
Fruits and vegetables, total [1]	**603.4**	**648.4**	**688.2**	**710.9**	**703.1**	**685.4**	**672.5**	**670.1**	**643.6**
Fruits, total	264.9	256.8	273.7	286.0	278.3	270.1	268.8	261.7	250.9
Fresh fruits	106.2	116.5	123.1	128.5	127.7	125.3	127.9	123.6	126.8
Noncitrus	80.1	95.2	99.3	105.0	105.0	103.7	106.3	105.6	106.1
Apples	19.2	19.6	18.7	17.5	18.8	16.7	17.7	16.4	16.2
Bananas	20.8	24.3	27.1	28.4	25.8	25.2	25.1	26.0	25.1
Cantaloupes	5.8	9.2	9.0	11.1	9.8	9.6	9.3	9.6	8.9
Grapes	4.0	7.8	7.4	7.4	7.8	8.6	7.6	8.0	8.5
Peaches and nectarines	7.1	5.5	5.3	5.3	5.1	4.8	4.6	4.5	5.1
Pears	2.6	3.2	3.4	3.4	3.0	2.9	3.2	3.1	3.1
Pineapples	1.5	2.0	1.9	3.2	4.4	4.9	5.2	5.0	5.1
Plums and prunes	1.5	1.5	0.9	1.2	1.1	1.1	1.0	1.0	0.9
Strawberries	2.0	3.2	4.1	4.9	5.5	5.8	6.1	6.3	6.5
Watermelons	10.7	13.3	15.2	13.8	13.0	13.6	15.1	14.4	15.4
Other [2]	5.1	5.4	6.3	8.7	10.7	10.5	11.3	11.4	11.4
Fresh citrus	26.1	21.4	23.8	23.5	22.7	21.6	21.7	17.9	20.6
Oranges	14.3	12.4	11.8	11.7	10.8	11.4	10.3	7.5	9.9
Grapefruit	7.3	4.4	6.0	5.1	4.1	2.7	2.3	2.8	3.2
Other [3]	4.5	4.6	6.0	6.7	7.7	7.5	9.1	7.6	7.5
Processed fruits	158.7	140.3	150.7	157.5	150.6	144.7	140.8	138.1	124.1
Frozen fruits [4]	3.3	4.3	4.3	4.6	4.3	5.2	5.0	5.3	4.9
Dried fruits [5]	11.2	12.1	12.7	10.4	9.3	10.1	10.4	10.0	10.1
Canned fruits [6]	24.4	20.8	17.2	17.5	16.9	16.5	15.4	16.0	15.3
Fruit juices [7]	119.0	102.7	116.2	124.6	119.7	112.4	109.3	106.4	93.0
Vegetables, total	338.6	391.6	414.5	424.9	424.8	415.4	403.7	408.4	392.7
Fresh vegetables	151.6	176.4	188.1	200.7	204.8	196.8	194.1	194.7	187.7
Asparagus (all uses)	0.3	0.6	0.6	1.0	1.1	1.1	1.1	1.2	1.2
Broccoli	1.4	3.4	4.3	5.9	5.3	5.3	5.8	5.6	5.9
Cabbage	8.0	8.3	8.1	8.9	8.0	7.8	7.8	8.0	8.2
Carrots	6.2	8.3	11.2	9.2	8.7	8.7	8.1	8.1	8.1
Cauliflower	1.1	2.2	1.6	1.7	1.6	1.8	1.7	1.7	1.6
Celery (all uses)	7.4	7.2	6.9	6.3	6.2	5.9	6.0	6.2	6.2
Corn	6.5	6.7	7.8	9.0	9.0	8.7	8.3	9.2	9.2
Cucumbers	3.9	4.7	5.6	6.4	6.4	6.2	6.1	6.4	6.7
Head lettuce	25.6	27.7	22.2	23.5	21.3	20.9	20.1	18.4	16.9
Mushrooms	1.2	2.0	2.0	2.6	2.6	2.6	2.6	2.5	2.4
Onions	11.4	15.1	17.8	18.9	21.9	20.9	19.9	21.6	19.2
Snap beans	1.3	1.1	1.6	2.0	1.9	1.8	2.1	2.2	2.1
Bell peppers (all uses)	2.9	5.9	7.0	8.2	8.6	9.2	9.5	9.4	9.8
Potatoes	51.1	46.7	49.2	47.1	45.9	41.4	38.6	39.1	36.7
Sweet potatoes (all uses)	4.4	4.4	4.2	4.2	4.6	4.5	4.6	5.1	5.0
Tomatoes	12.8	15.5	16.8	19.0	20.0	20.2	19.8	19.2	18.5
Other fresh vegetables [8]	6.1	16.6	21.1	27.0	31.6	29.9	32.1	30.9	29.9
Processed vegetables	187.0	215.2	226.4	224.1	220.0	218.6	209.6	213.8	205.0
Selected vegetables for freezing [9]	51.5	66.8	78.8	79.3	78.9	76.6	74.6	76.2	73.1
Selected vegetables for canning [10]	102.5	110.3	108.2	103.2	102.6	105.0	94.5	97.2	95.2
Vegetables for dehydrating [11]	10.5	14.6	14.5	17.3	15.3	13.9	14.2	14.1	13.9
Potatoes for chips	16.5	16.4	16.4	15.9	16.6	16.2	18.8	18.7	15.9
Pulses [12]	5.9	7.2	8.4	8.5	6.7	6.9	7.5	7.6	7.0

[1] Excludes wine grapes. [2] Apricots, avocados, cherries, cranberries, kiwifruit, mangoes, papayas, and honeydew melons.
[3] Lemons, limes, tangerines, and tangelos. [4] Apples, apricots, blackberries, blueberries, boysenberries, cherries, loganberries, peaches, plums, prunes, raspberries, and strawberries. [5] Apples, apricots, dates, figs, peaches, pears, prunes, and raisins.
[6] Apples, apricots, cherries, olives, peaches, pears, pineapples, plums, and prunes. [7] Apple, cranberry, grape, grapefruit, lemon, lime, orange, pineapple, and prunes. [8] Artichokes, brussels sprouts, eggplant, escarole, endive, garlic, romaine, leaf lettuce, radishes, spinach, and squash. Beginning 2000, includes collard greens, kale, mustard greens, okra, pumpkin, and turnip greens.
[9] Asparagus, snap beans, lima beans, broccoli, carrots, cauliflower, sweet corn, green peas, potatoes, spinach, and miscellaneous vegetables. [10] Asparagus, snap beans, beets, cabbage, carrots, chili peppers, sweet corn, cucumbers for pickling, green peas, lima beans, mushrooms, spinach, and tomatoes. [11] Onions and potatoes. [12] Dry peas, lentils, and dry edible beans.

Source: U.S. Department of Agriculture, Economic Research Service, "Food Consumption, Prices, and Expenditures, Food Availability (Per Capita) Data System," <http://www.ers.usda.gov/data/foodconsumption/>.

Section 4
Education

This section presents data primarily concerning formal education as a whole, at various levels, and for public and private schools. Data shown relate to the school–age population and school enrollment, educational attainment, education personnel, and financial aspects of education. In addition, data are shown for charter schools, security measures used in schools, computer usage in schools, and adult education. The chief sources are the decennial census of population and the Current Population Survey (CPS), both conducted by the U.S. Census Bureau (see text, Section 1, Population); annual, biennial, and other periodic surveys conducted by the National Center for Education Statistics (NCES), a part of the U.S. Department of Education; and surveys conducted by the National Education Association.

The censuses of population have included data on school enrollment since 1840 and on educational attainment since 1940. The CPS has reported on school enrollment annually since 1945 and on educational attainment periodically since 1947.

The NCES is continuing the pattern of statistical studies and surveys conducted by the U.S. Office of Education since 1870. The annual *Digest of Education Statistics* provides summary data on pupils, staff, finances, including government expenditures, and organization at the elementary, secondary, and higher education levels. It is also a primary source for detailed information on federal funds for education, projections of enrollment, graduates, and teachers. The *Condition of Education*, issued annually, presents a summary of information on education of particular interest to policymakers. NCES also conducts special studies periodically.

The census of governments, conducted by the Census Bureau every 5 years (for the years ending in "2" and "7"), provides data on school district finances and state and local government expenditures for education. Reports published by the Bureau of Labor Statistics contain data relating

civilian labor force experience to educational attainment (see also Tables 592, 618, and 626 in Section 12, Labor Force, Employment, and Earnings).

Types and sources of data— The statistics in this section are of two general types. One type, exemplified by data from the Census Bureau, is based on direct interviews with individuals to obtain information about their own and their family members' education. Data of this type relate to school enrollment and level of education attained, classified by age, sex, and other characteristics of the population. The school enrollment statistics reflect attendance or enrollment in any regular school within a given period; educational attainment statistics reflect the highest grade completed by an individual, or beginning 1992, the highest diploma or degree received.

Beginning in 2001, the CPS used Census 2000 population controls. From 1994 to 2000, the CPS used 1990 census population controls plus adjustment for undercount. Also the survey changed from paper to computer-assisted technology. For years 1981 through 1993, 1980 census population controls were used; 1971 through 1980, 1970 census population controls had been used. These changes had little impact on summary measures (e.g., medians) and proportional measures (e.g., enrollment rates); however, use of the controls may have significant impact on absolute numbers.

The second type, generally exemplified by data from the NCES and the National Education Association, is based on reports from administrators of educational institutions and of state and local agencies having jurisdiction over education. Data of this type relate to enrollment, attendance, staff, and finances for the nation, individual states, and local areas.

Unlike the NCES, the Census Bureau does not regularly include specialized vocational, trade, business, or correspondence

U.S. Census Bureau, Statistical Abstract of the United States: 2011

schools in its surveys. The NCES includes nursery schools and kindergartens that are part of regular grade schools in their enrollment figures. The Census Bureau includes all nursery schools and kindergartens. At the higher education level, the statistics of both agencies are concerned with institutions granting degrees or offering work acceptable for degree-credit, such as junior colleges.

School attendance—All states require that children attend school. While state laws vary as to the ages and circumstances of compulsory attendance, generally they require that formal schooling begin by age 6 and continue to age 16.

Schools—The NCES defines a school as "a division of the school system consisting of students composing one or more grade groups or other identifiable groups, organized as one unit with one or more teachers to give instruction of a defined type, and housed in a school plant of one or more buildings. More than one school may be housed in one school plant, as is the case when the elementary and secondary programs are housed in the same school plant."

Regular schools are those which advance a person toward a diploma or degree. They include public and private nursery schools, kindergartens, graded schools, colleges, universities, and professional schools.

Public schools are schools controlled and supported by local, state, or federal governmental agencies; private schools are those controlled and supported mainly by religious organizations or by private persons or organizations.

The Census Bureau defines *elementary* schools as including grades 1 through 8; *high* schools as including grades 9 through 12; and *colleges* as including junior or community colleges, regular 4-year colleges, and universities and graduate or professional schools. Statistics reported by the NCES and the National Education Association by type of organization, such as elementary level and secondary level, may not be strictly comparable with those from the Census Bureau because the grades included at the two levels vary, depending on the level assigned to the middle or junior high school by the local school systems.

School year—Except as otherwise indicated in the tables, data refer to the school year which, for elementary and secondary schools, generally begins in September of the preceding year and ends in June of the year stated. For the most part, statistics concerning school finances are for a 12-month period, usually July 1 to June 30. Enrollment data generally refer to a specific point in time, such as fall, as indicated in the tables.

Statistical reliability—For a discussion of statistical collection, estimation, and sampling procedures and measures of statistical reliability applicable to the Census Bureau and the NCES data, see Appendix III.

Table 215. School Enrollment: 1980 to 2019

[In thousands (58,306 represents 58,306,000). As of fall]

Year	All levels			Pre-kindergarten through grade 8		Grades 9 through 12		College [1]	
	Total	Public	Private	Public	Private	Public	Private	Public	Private
1980............	58,306	50,335	7,971	27,647	3,992	13,231	1,339	9,457	2,640
1985............	57,226	48,901	8,325	27,034	4,195	12,388	1,362	9,479	2,768
1989............	59,279	51,120	8,159	29,152	4,035	11,390	1,163	10,578	2,961
1990............	60,269	52,061	8,208	29,878	4,084	11,338	1,150	10,845	2,974
1991............	62,087	53,357	8,730	30,506	4,518	11,541	1,163	11,310	3,049
1992............	62,987	54,208	8,779	31,088	4,528	11,735	1,148	11,385	3,102
1993............	63,438	54,654	8,784	31,504	4,536	11,961	1,132	11,189	3,116
1994............	64,385	55,245	9,139	31,896	4,856	12,215	1,138	11,134	3,145
1995............	65,020	55,933	9,087	32,338	4,756	12,502	1,163	11,092	3,169
1996............	65,911	56,732	9,180	32,762	4,755	12,849	1,178	11,121	3,247
1997............	66,574	57,323	9,251	33,071	4,759	13,056	1,185	11,196	3,306
1998............	67,033	57,676	9,357	33,344	4,776	13,195	1,212	11,138	3,369
1999............	67,667	58,167	9,500	33,486	4,789	13,371	1,229	11,309	3,482
2000............	68,685	58,956	9,729	33,686	4,906	13,517	1,264	11,753	3,560
2001............	69,919	59,905	10,014	33,936	5,023	13,736	1,296	12,233	3,695
2002............	71,015	60,935	10,080	34,114	4,915	14,069	1,306	12,752	3,860
2003............	71,551	61,399	10,152	34,201	4,788	14,339	1,311	12,859	4,053
2004............	72,154	61,776	10,379	34,178	4,756	14,618	1,331	12,980	4,292
2005............	72,674	62,135	10,539	34,204	4,724	14,909	1,349	13,022	4,466
2006............	73,066	62,496	10,570	34,235	4,631	15,081	1,360	13,180	4,579
2007............	73,451	62,783	10,668	34,205	4,546	15,087	1,364	13,491	4,757
2008, proj. [2]	74,337	63,237	11,100	34,316	4,574	14,949	1,395	13,972	5,131
2009, proj...........	74,807	63,723	11,084	34,505	4,580	14,807	1,389	14,410	5,114
2010, proj...........	74,991	63,879	11,112	34,730	4,582	14,657	1,382	14,492	5,149
2011, proj...........	75,227	64,093	11,135	34,974	4,598	14,580	1,363	14,539	5,174
2012, proj...........	75,648	64,458	11,190	35,206	4,622	14,589	1,340	14,663	5,229
2013, proj...........	76,293	64,994	11,299	35,437	4,657	14,651	1,318	14,906	5,324
2014, proj...........	77,150	65,699	11,452	35,636	4,702	14,810	1,294	15,253	5,456
2015, proj...........	77,940	66,349	11,591	35,881	4,757	14,946	1,275	15,522	5,560
2016, proj...........	78,709	66,977	11,733	36,205	4,801	14,993	1,274	15,778	5,658
2017, proj...........	79,488	67,611	11,877	36,526	4,844	15,058	1,282	16,027	5,751
2018, proj...........	80,269	68,237	12,032	36,838	4,885	15,108	1,298	16,291	5,849
2019, proj...........	80,998	68,831	12,167	37,156	4,927	15,186	1,321	16,489	5,919

[1] Data beginning 1996 based on new classification system. See footnote 1, Table 274. [2] Pre-K through 12 are projections; college data are actual.

Source: U.S. National Center for Education Statistics, *Digest of Education Statistics*, annual, and *Projections of Education Statistics*, annual. See also <http://www.nces.ed.gov/annuals>.

Table 216. School Expenditures by Type of Control and Level of Instruction in Constant (2008 to 2009) Dollars: 1980 to 2009

[In millions of dollars (442,613 represents $442,613,000,000). For school years ending in year shown. Data shown reflect historical revisions. Total expenditures for public elementary and secondary schools include current expenditures, interest on school debt and capital outlay. Data deflated by the Consumer Price Index, all urban consumers, on a school-year basis (supplied by the National Center for Education Statistics). See also Appendix III. Based on survey of state education agencies; see source for details]

Year	Total	Elementary and secondary schools			Colleges and universities [1]		
		Total	Public	Private	Total	Public	Private
1980..........	442,613	285,245	265,337	19,908	157,368	104,430	52,938
1985..........	485,772	303,213	278,047	25,166	182,559	118,352	64,208
1990..........	618,447	390,804	359,698	31,106	227,642	145,000	82,643
1991..........	633,662	399,495	367,757	31,738	234,167	149,009	85,158
1992..........	649,130	406,545	374,395	32,150	242,585	153,525	89,061
1993..........	662,199	413,328	380,947	32,381	248,871	157,494	91,377
1994..........	676,428	421,935	389,491	32,445	254,492	160,475	94,017
1995..........	692,419	431,292	398,181	33,110	261,128	164,788	96,339
1996..........	706,527	441,885	407,984	33,901	[2] 264,642	166,064	[2] 98,578
1997..........	727,901	457,866	423,014	34,851	[2] 270,035	170,175	[2] 99,860
1998..........	757,108	479,922	443,691	36,232	277,186	176,309	100,877
1999..........	787,766	501,790	464,218	37,572	285,975	183,344	102,632
2000..........	823,324	523,088	484,161	38,927	300,236	193,144	107,092
2001..........	864,331	545,326	503,643	41,683	319,005	208,838	110,167
2002..........	906,832	568,670	524,459	44,210	338,162	220,975	117,187
2003..........	937,913	580,891	536,217	44,674	357,022	232,242	124,780
2004..........	957,746	592,373	547,040	45,333	365,374	236,548	128,826
2005..........	980,937	605,780	559,420	46,360	375,157	241,648	133,509
2006..........	998,590	617,177	570,360	46,817	381,413	244,386	137,027
2007 [2]	1,034,911	640,019	591,228	48,791	394,892	251,137	143,755
2008 [2, 3]	1,068,000	654,000	604,000	50,000	414,000	265,000	149,000
2009 [2, 3]	1,093,000	661,000	611,000	50,000	432,000	271,000	161,000

[1] Data beginning 1996 based on new classification system. See footnote 1, Table 274. [2] Estimated. [3] Detail may not add to total due to rounding.

Source: U.S. National Center for Education Statistics, *Digest of Education Statistics*, annual. See also <http://www.nces.ed.gov/programs/digest/>.

Education 143

Table 217. School Enrollment, Faculty, Graduates, and Finances—Projections: 2009 to 2015

[As of fall, except as indicated (55,234 represents 55,234,000)]

Item	Unit	2009	2010	2011	2012	2013	2014	2015
ELEMENTARY AND SECONDARY SCHOOLS								
School enrollment, total................	1,000	55,234	55,282	55,350	55,515	55,757	56,063	56,442
Pre-kindergarten through grade 8......	1,000	38,890	39,086	39,312	39,572	39,828	40,094	40,338
Grades 9 through 12.................	1,000	16,345	16,196	16,038	15,943	15,929	15,969	16,104
Public............................	1,000	49,265	49,312	49,386	49,554	49,795	50,088	50,446
Pre-kindergarten through grade 8.....	1,000	34,316	34,505	34,730	34,974	35,206	35,437	35,636
Grades 9 through 12................	1,000	14,949	14,807	14,657	14,580	14,589	14,651	14,810
Private...........................	1,000	5,969	5,970	5,964	5,961	5,962	5,975	5,995
Pre-kindergarten through grade 8.....	1,000	4,574	4,580	4,582	4,598	4,622	4,657	4,702
Grades 9 through 12................	1,000	1,395	1,389	1,382	1,363	1,340	1,318	1,294
Classroom teachers, total FTE [1]........	1,000	3,612	3,617	3,633	3,662	3,701	3,747	3,805
Public............................	1,000	3,157	3,161	3,174	3,198	3,232	3,271	3,322
Private...........................	1,000	455	457	460	464	469	475	483
High school graduates, total [2]..........	1,000	3,319	3,306	3,252	3,222	3,200	3,176	3,171
Public............................	1,000	3,005	2,991	2,937	2,906	2,891	2,868	2,872
Public schools: [2]								
Average daily attendance (ADA).......	1,000	45,979	46,024	46,093	46,249	46,474	46,748	47,082
Current dollars: [3]								
Current school expenditure..........	Bil. dol	498	499	509	525	544	(NA)	(NA)
Per pupil in fall enrollment..........	Dollar.....	10,105	10,126	10,300	10,591	10,930	(NA)	(NA)
Constant (2007–2008) dollars: [3,4]								
Current school expenditure..........	Bil. dol	491	488	490	495	504	514	530
Per pupil in fall enrollment..........	Dollar.....	9,967	9,899	9,920	9,987	10,119	10,268	10,500
HIGHER EDUCATION								
Enrollment, total.....................	1,000	19,103	19,525	19,641	19,713	19,892	20,230	20,709
Male.............................	1,000	8,189	8,451	8,511	8,513	8,539	8,624	8,757
Full-time.........................	1,000	5,234	5,433	5,479	5,483	5,501	5,558	5,652
Part-time.........................	1,000	2,955	3,019	3,032	3,030	3,037	3,066	3,105
Female...........................	1,000	10,914	11,073	11,130	11,200	11,353	11,607	11,952
Full-time.........................	1,000	6,513	6,609	6,660	6,716	6,806	6,941	7,123
Part-time.........................	1,000	4,401	4,465	4,471	4,484	4,547	4,666	4,828
Public............................	1,000	13,972	14,410	14,492	14,539	14,663	14,906	15,253
Four-year institutions..............	1,000	7,332	7,567	7,623	7,658	7,730	7,860	8,042
Two-year institutions	1,000	6,640	6,843	6,870	6,881	6,933	7,046	7,210
Private...........................	1,000	5,131	5,114	5,149	5,174	5,229	5,324	5,456
Four-year institutions..............	1,000	4,800	4,785	4,818	4,842	4,894	4,985	5,109
Two-year institutions	1,000	331	329	331	332	334	339	347
Undergraduate.....................	1,000	16,366	16,706	16,814	16,871	17,003	17,261	17,636
Postbaccalaureate..................	1,000	2,737	2,819	2,827	2,841	2,889	2,969	3,073
Full-time equivalent	1,000	14,394	14,733	14,837	14,901	15,036	15,280	15,629
Public............................	1,000	10,062	10,396	10,466	10,507	10,595	10,762	11,002
2-year	1,000	3,922	4,050	4,068	4,076	4,105	4,168	4,262
4-year	1,000	6,140	6,346	6,398	6,431	6,491	6,594	6,741
Private...........................	1,000	4,332	4,337	4,371	4,394	4,440	4,518	4,627
2-year	1,000	302	301	302	303	305	310	317
4-year	1,000	4,030	4,036	4,068	4,091	4,135	4,208	4,310
Degrees conferred, total [2]	1,000	3,189	3,285	3,373	3,431	3,479	3,532	3,603
Associate's.......................	1,000	773	797	818	833	845	858	876
Bachelor's	1,000	1,607	1,652	1,696	1,725	1,744	1,762	1,786
Master's..........................	1,000	649	670	687	696	709	727	750
Doctoral..........................	1,000	66	69	72	75	78	81	83
First-professional..................	1,000	94	97	101	102	103	105	107

NA Not available. [1] Full-time equivalent. [2] For school year ending in June the following year. [3] Limited financial projections are shown due to the uncertain behavior of inflation over the long term. [4] Based on the Consumer Price Index (CPI) for all urban consumers, U.S. Bureau of Labor Statistics. CPI adjusted to a school year basis by NCES.

Source: U.S. National Center for Education Statistics, *Projections of Education Statistics to 2019*. See also <http://www.nces.ed.gov/surveys/AnnualReports/>.

Table 218. Federal Funds for Education and Related Programs: 2005 to 2009

[In millions of dollars (146,207.0 represents $146,207,000,000), except percent. For fiscal years ending in September. Figures represent on-budget funds]

Level, agency, and program	2005	2008	2009 [1]
Total, all programs	**146,207.0**	**147,275.5**	**(NA)**
Percent of federal budget outlays	5.9	4.9	(NA)
Elementary/secondary education programs	**68,957.7**	**71,626.7**	**82,896.1**
Department of Education [2]	37,477.6	38,330.4	44,867.1
Grants for the disadvantaged	14,635.6	14,872.5	15,924.2
School improvement programs	7,918.1	7,077.7	12,475.4
Indian education	121.9	115.8	114.6
Special education	10,940.3	12,280.1	11,734.1
Vocational and adult education	1,967.1	1,894.7	2,174.7
Education reform—Goals 2000	-35.0	(X)	(X)
Department of Agriculture [2]	12,577.3	15,139.6	16,592.1
Child nutrition programs	[3] 11,901.9	[3] 13,932.1	[3] 15,552.1
Agricultural Marketing Service—commodities [3]	399.3	940.0	670.0
Department of Defense [2]	1,786.3	1,863.8	1,918.4
Overseas dependents schools	1,060.9	1,110.1	1,137.6
Section VI schools [4]	410.2	400.9	410.0
Department of Health and Human Services	8,003.3	8,003.3	9,731.8
Head Start	6,842.3	6,877.0	8,502.0
Social security student benefits	1,161.0	1,126.3	1,229.8
Department of Homeland Security	0.5	2.6	2.9
Department of the Interior [2]	938.5	679.2	696.8
Mineral Leasing Act and other funds	140.0	123.7	121.3
Indian Education	797.5	554.5	574.6
Department of Justice	554.5	769.8	828.1
Inmate programs	554.5	768.8	827.2
Department of Labor	5,654.0	5,070.0	6,321.0
Job Corps	1,521.0	763.0	1,664.0
Department of Veterans Affairs	1,815.0	1,628.1	1,789.2
Vocational rehab for disabled veterans	1,815.0	1,628.1	1,789.2
Other agencies and programs	153.2	139.9	148.6
Higher education programs	**38,587.3**	**36,460.8**	**37,221.1**
Department of Education [2]	31,420.0	28,838.8	27,712.9
Student financial assistance	15,209.5	17,751.1	23,172.1
Federal Family Education Loans [5]	10,777.5	3,288.5	352.1
Department of Agriculture	62.0	66.7	73.2
Department of Commerce	(NA)	(NA)	(NA)
Department of Defense	1,858.3	1,946.4	2,180.4
Tuition assistance for military personnel	608.1	603.6	678.6
Service academies [6]	300.8	330.2	352.7
Senior ROTC	537.5	549.6	646.8
Professional development education	411.9	463.0	502.3

Level, agency, and program	2005	2008	2009 [1]
Department of Health and Human Services [2]	1,433.5	1,184.9	1,250.1
Health professions training programs	581.7	318.2	354.3
National Health Service Corps scholarships	45.0	40.0	40.0
National Institutes of Health training grants [7]	756.0	770.5	790.2
Department of Homeland Security	36.4	52.4	55.7
Department of the Interior	249.2	180.5	183.4
Shared revenues, Mineral Leasing Act and other receipts—estimated education share	146.2	52.7	51.3
Indian programs	103.0	127.8	132.1
Department of State	424.0	522.0	538.0
Department of Transportation	73.0	72.0	83.0
Department of Veterans Affairs [2]	2,478.6	2,996.9	4,290.8
Post-Vietnam veterans	1.1	0.9	0.8
All-volunteer-force educational assistance	2,071.0	2,166.0	3,452.0
Other agencies and programs [2]	552.2	600.4	853.6
National Endowment for the Humanities	29.3	36.5	36.0
National Science Foundation	490.0	531.0	776.0
Other education programs	**6,908.5**	**7,882.2**	**8,581.7**
Department of Education [2]	3,538.9	4,545.0	5,255.1
Administration	548.8	1,252.5	1,314.8
Rehabilitative services and handicapped research	2,973.3	3,242.3	3,914.0
Department of Agriculture	468.6	517.2	541.8
Department of Health and Human Services	313.0	323.0	331.0
Department of Homeland Security	278.2	264.5	277.0
Department of Justice	26.1	28.4	30.0
Department of State	109.3	116.3	117.0
Other agencies and programs [2]	2,174.3	2,087.6	2,029.6
Agency for International Development	574.0	608.4	620.0
Library of Congress	430.0	434.0	439.0
National Endowment for the Arts	2.5	3.2	3.3
National Endowment for the Humanities	88.0	87.7	89.0
Research programs at universities and related institutions [2]	**31,753.5**	**31,305.7**	**(NA)**
Department of Agriculture	709.7	543.4	(NA)
Department of Defense	2,675.9	2,453.8	(NA)
Department of Energy	4,339.9	4,631.1	(NA)
Department of Health and Human Services	16,358.0	15,959.3	(NA)
National Aeronautics and Space Administration	2,763.1	2,404.2	(NA)
National Science Foundation	3,503.2	4,107.6	(NA)

NA Not available. X Not applicable. [1] Estimated except U.S. Department of Education [1], which are actual budget reports. [2] Includes other programs and agencies, not shown separately. [3] Purchased under Section 32 of the Act of August 1935 for use in child nutrition programs. [4] Program provides for the education of dependents of federal employees residing on federal property where free public education is unavailable in the nearby community. [5] Includes Federal Direct Loans. [6] Instructional costs only including academics, audiovisual, academic computer center, faculty training, military training, physical education, and libraries. [7] Includes alcohol, drug abuse, and mental health training programs.

Source: U.S. National Center for Education Statistics, *Digest of Education Statistics* annual. See also <http://www.nces.ed.gov/programs/digest/>.

Table 219. School Enrollment by Age: 1970 to 2008

[As of October (60,357 represents 60,357,000). Covers civilian noninstitutional population enrolled in nursery school and above. Based on Current Population Survey; see text, Section 1 and Appendix III]

Age	1970	1980	1985	1990	1995	2000	2005	2006	2007	2008
ENROLLMENT (1,000)										
Total, 3 to 34 years old.......	**60,357**	**57,348**	**58,013**	**60,588**	**66,939**	**69,560**	**72,768**	**72,270**	**72,970**	**73,275**
3 and 4 years old............	1,461	2,280	2,801	3,292	4,042	4,097	4,383	4,534	4,491	4,458
5 and 6 years old............	7,000	5,853	6,697	7,207	7,901	7,648	7,486	7,628	7,792	7,651
7 to 13 years old	28,943	23,751	22,849	25,016	27,003	28,296	27,936	27,504	27,532	27,681
14 and 15 years old..........	7,869	7,282	7,362	6,555	7,651	7,885	8,375	8,252	8,137	7,965
16 and 17 years old..........	6,927	7,129	6,654	6,098	6,997	7,341	8,472	8,203	8,205	8,202
18 and 19 years old..........	3,322	3,788	3,716	4,044	4,274	4,926	5,109	5,306	5,566	5,607
20 and 21 years old..........	1,949	2,515	2,708	2,852	3,025	3,314	4,069	3,839	3,916	4,052
22 to 24 years old	1,410	1,931	2,068	2,231	2,545	2,731	3,254	3,256	3,375	3,488
25 to 29 years old	1,011	1,714	1,942	2,013	2,216	2,030	2,340	2,373	2,577	2,764
30 to 34 years old	466	1,105	1,218	1,281	1,284	1,292	1,344	1,376	1,379	1,407
35 years old and over	(NA)	1,290	1,766	2,439	2,830	2,653	3,013	2,927	2,997	3,079
ENROLLMENT RATE										
Total, 3 to 34 years old.......	**56.4**	**49.7**	**48.3**	**50.2**	**53.7**	**55.8**	**56.5**	**56.0**	**56.1**	**56.2**
3 and 4 years old............	20.5	36.7	38.9	44.4	48.7	52.1	53.6	55.7	54.5	52.8
5 and 6 years old............	89.5	95.7	96.1	96.5	96.0	95.6	95.4	94.6	94.7	93.8
7 to 13 years old	99.2	99.3	99.2	99.6	98.9	98.2	98.6	98.3	98.4	98.7
14 and 15 years old..........	98.1	98.2	98.1	99.0	98.9	98.7	98.0	98.3	98.7	98.6
16 and 17 years old..........	90.0	89.0	91.7	92.5	93.6	92.8	95.1	94.6	94.3	95.2
18 and 19 years old..........	47.7	46.4	51.6	57.3	59.4	61.2	67.6	65.5	66.8	66.0
20 and 21 years old..........	31.9	31.0	35.3	39.7	44.9	44.1	48.7	47.5	48.4	50.1
22 to 24 years old	14.9	16.3	16.9	21.0	23.2	24.6	27.3	26.7	27.3	28.2
25 to 29 years old	7.5	9.3	9.2	9.7	11.6	11.4	11.9	11.7	12.4	13.2
30 to 34 years old	4.2	6.4	6.1	5.8	6.0	6.7	6.9	7.2	7.2	7.3
35 years old and over	(NA)	1.4	1.6	2.1	2.2	1.9	2.0	1.9	1.9	2.0

NA Not available.

Source: U.S. Census Bureau, Current Population Reports, PPL-148, P-20, and earlier reports, and "School Enrollment," <http://www.census.gov/population/www/socdemo/school.html>.

Table 220. School Enrollment by Race, Hispanic Origin, and Age: 2000 to 2008

[(54,257 represents 54,257,000). See headnote, Table 219]

Age	White [1]			Black [1]			Hispanic [2]		
	2000	2005	2008	2000	2005	2008	2000	2005	2008
ENROLLMENT (1,000)									
Total, 3 to 34 years old...........	**54,257**	**55,715**	**55,886**	**11,115**	**10,885**	**10,944**	**9,928**	**12,502**	**13,590**
3 and 4 years old	3,091	3,380	3,318	725	655	723	518	773	892
5 and 6 years old	5,959	5,707	5,893	1,219	1,144	1,101	1,390	1,532	1,718
7 to 13 years old	22,061	21,310	21,080	4,675	4,317	4,218	4,373	5,394	5,725
14 and 15 years old	6,176	6,429	6,098	1,260	1,321	1,217	1,093	1,431	1,513
16 and 17 years old	5,845	6,520	6,212	1,106	1,281	1,272	959	1,357	1,449
18 and 19 years old	3,924	4,006	4,420	716	707	790	617	681	848
20 and 21 years old	2,688	3,262	3,197	416	430	507	311	447	450
22 to 24 years old	2,101	2,411	2,728	393	475	416	309	419	443
25 to 29 years old	1,473	1,740	2,006	353	307	418	198	310	381
30 to 34 years old	939	950	934	252	248	282	160	158	171
35 years old and over	2,087	2,299	2,357	387	499	478	235	307	379
ENROLLMENT RATE									
Total, 3 to 34 years old...........	**55.1**	**55.9**	**55.5**	**59.0**	**58.4**	**57.8**	**51.3**	**50.9**	**51.9**
3 and 4 years old	50.2	54.2	52.0	59.9	52.2	54.6	35.9	43.0	43.6
5 and 6 years old	95.3	95.3	94.0	96.3	95.9	93.1	94.3	93.8	91.8
7 to 13 years old	98.2	98.6	98.6	98.0	98.6	98.9	97.5	97.6	97.9
14 and 15 years old	98.4	98.3	98.7	99.6	95.8	97.9	96.2	97.3	98.7
16 and 17 years old	92.8	95.4	95.4	91.4	93.1	94.2	87.0	92.6	93.8
18 and 19 years old	61.3	68.0	67.1	57.2	62.8	59.2	49.5	54.3	55.1
20 and 21 years old	44.9	49.3	51.2	36.6	37.6	40.3	26.1	30.0	32.1
22 to 24 years old	23.7	26.0	28.1	24.2	28.0	24.9	18.2	19.5	19.8
25 to 29 years old	10.4	11.3	12.3	14.3	11.7	14.7	7.4	7.8	9.2
30 to 34 years old	6.0	6.2	6.2	9.6	10.0	11.5	5.6	4.2	4.2
35 years old and over	1.8	1.8	1.8	2.6	3.1	2.8	2.0	2.0	2.2

[1] Starting 2005, data are for persons who selected this race group only. See footnote 2, Table 225. [2] Persons of Hispanic origin may be any race.

Source: U.S. Census Bureau, Current Population Reports, PPL-148, P-20, and earlier reports, and "School Enrollment," <http://www.census.gov/population/www/socdemo/school.html>.

Table 221. Enrollment in Public and Private Schools: 1970 to 2008

[In millions (52.2 represents 52,200,000), except percent. As of October. For civilian noninstitutional population. For 1970 to 1985, persons 3 to 34 years old; beginning 1990, for 3 years old and over. For enrollment 35 years old and over, see Table 219]

Year	Public						Private					
	Total	Nursery	Kinder-garten	Elemen-tary	High school	College	Total	Nursery	Kinder-garten	Elemen-tary	High school	College
1970........	52.2	0.3	2.6	30.0	13.5	5.7	8.1	0.8	0.5	3.9	1.2	1.7
1975........	52.8	0.6	2.9	27.2	14.5	7.7	8.2	1.2	0.5	3.3	1.2	2.0
1980........	(NA)	0.6	2.7	24.4	(NA)	(NA)	(NA)	1.4	0.5	3.1	(NA)	(NA)
1985........	49.0	0.9	3.2	23.8	12.8	8.4	9.0	1.6	0.6	3.1	1.2	2.5
1990 [1]......	53.8	1.2	3.3	26.6	11.9	10.7	9.2	2.2	0.6	2.7	0.9	2.9
1992........	55.0	1.1	3.5	27.1	12.3	11.1	9.4	1.8	0.6	3.1	1.0	3.0
1993........	56.0	1.2	3.5	27.7	12.6	10.9	9.4	1.8	0.7	2.9	1.0	3.0
1994........	58.6	1.9	3.3	28.1	13.5	11.7	10.7	2.3	0.6	3.4	1.1	3.3
1995........	58.7	2.0	3.2	28.4	13.7	11.4	11.1	2.4	0.7	3.4	1.2	3.3
1996........	59.5	1.9	3.4	28.1	14.1	12.0	10.8	2.3	0.7	3.4	1.2	3.2
1997........	61.6	2.3	3.3	29.3	14.6	12.1	10.5	2.2	0.7	3.1	1.2	3.3
1998........	60.8	2.3	3.1	29.1	14.3	12.0	11.3	2.3	0.7	3.4	1.2	3.6
1999........	60.8	2.3	3.2	29.2	14.4	11.7	11.4	2.3	0.7	3.6	1.3	3.5
2000........	61.2	2.2	3.2	29.4	14.4	12.0	11.0	2.2	0.7	3.5	1.3	3.3
2001........	62.4	2.2	3.1	29.8	14.8	12.4	10.8	2.1	0.6	3.4	1.2	3.5
2002........	62.8	2.2	3.0	29.7	15.1	12.8	11.3	2.2	0.6	3.5	1.3	3.7
2003........	63.8	2.6	3.1	29.2	15.8	13.1	11.1	2.4	0.6	3.4	1.3	3.5
2004........	64.3	2.5	3.4	29.2	15.5	13.7	11.3	2.3	0.6	3.4	1.3	3.7
2005........	64.2	2.5	3.3	29.0	15.8	13.4	11.5	2.1	0.6	3.4	1.4	4.0
2006........	64.1	2.5	3.6	29.0	15.6	13.5	11.1	2.2	0.5	3.1	1.5	3.8
2007........	65.1	2.6	3.7	29.1	15.8	14.1	10.8	2.1	0.5	3.1	1.3	3.9
2008........	65.5	2.6	3.6	29.2	15.4	14.7	10.8	2.0	0.5	3.2	1.3	4.0
Percent White:												
1970........	84.5	59.5	84.4	83.1	85.6	90.7	93.4	91.1	88.2	94.1	96.1	92.8
1980........	(NA)	68.2	80.7	80.9	(NA)	(NA)	(NA)	89.0	87.0	90.7	(NA)	(NA)
1990........	79.8	71.7	78.3	78.9	79.2	84.1	87.4	89.6	83.2	88.2	89.4	85.0
2000........	77.0	69.4	77.3	76.7	78.0	78.0	83.5	84.9	82.8	85.9	84.6	79.8
2005 [2].....	75.7	71.3	78.0	75.2	76.0	76.7	81.4	83.6	79.0	83.0	83.6	78.4
2006 [2].....	75.6	72.1	76.0	75.7	74.9	76.8	80.9	83.4	78.4	81.9	83.1	78.0
2007 [2].....	75.4	73.2	77.6	75.3	75.2	77.1	80.4	80.9	81.3	82.1	86.1	76.6
2008 [2].....	75.7	69.5	76.8	75.4	75.2	77.6	79.9	83.2	79.5	80.6	83.6	76.4

NA Not available. [1] Beginning 1990, based on a revised edit and tabulation package. [2] Beginning 2005, for persons who selected this race group only. See footnote 2, Table 225.

Source: U.S. Census Bureau, Current Population Reports, PPL-148, P-20, and earlier reports, and "School Enrollment," <http://www.census.gov/population/www/socdemo/school.html>.

Table 222. School Enrollment by Sex and Level: 1970 to 2008

[In millions (60.4 represents 60,400,000). As of October. For the civilian noninstitutional population. Prior to 1980, persons 3 to 34 years old; beginning 1980, 3 years old and over. Elementary includes kindergarten and grades 1–8; high school, grades 9–12; and college, 2-year and 4-year colleges, universities, and graduate and professional schools. Data for college represent degree-credit enrollment. See headnote, Table 219]

Year	All levels [1]			Elementary			High school			College		
	Total	Male	Female	Total	Male	Female	Total	Male	Female	Total	Male	Female
1970.......	60.4	31.4	28.9	37.1	19.0	18.1	14.7	7.4	7.3	7.4	4.4	3.0
1980.......	58.6	29.6	29.1	30.6	15.8	14.9	14.6	7.3	7.3	11.4	5.4	6.0
1985.......	59.8	30.0	29.7	30.7	15.7	15.0	14.1	7.2	6.9	12.5	5.9	6.6
1990 [2].....	63.0	31.5	31.5	33.2	17.1	16.0	12.8	6.5	6.4	13.6	6.2	7.4
1991.......	63.9	32.1	31.8	33.8	17.3	16.4	13.1	6.8	6.4	14.1	6.4	7.6
1992.......	64.6	32.2	32.3	34.3	17.7	16.6	13.3	6.8	6.5	14.0	6.2	7.8
1993.......	65.4	32.9	32.5	34.8	17.9	16.9	13.6	7.0	6.6	13.9	6.3	7.6
1994.......	69.3	34.6	34.6	35.4	18.2	17.2	14.6	7.4	7.2	15.0	6.8	8.2
1995.......	69.8	35.0	34.8	35.7	18.3	17.4	15.0	7.7	7.3	14.7	6.7	8.0
1996.......	70.3	35.1	35.2	35.5	18.3	17.3	15.3	7.9	7.4	15.2	6.8	8.4
1997.......	72.0	35.9	36.2	36.3	18.7	17.6	15.8	8.0	7.7	15.4	6.8	8.6
1998.......	72.1	36.0	36.1	36.4	18.7	17.7	15.6	7.9	7.6	15.5	6.9	8.6
1999.......	72.4	36.3	36.1	36.7	18.8	17.9	15.9	8.2	7.7	15.2	7.0	8.2
2000.......	72.2	35.8	36.4	36.7	18.9	17.9	15.8	8.1	7.7	15.3	6.7	8.6
2001.......	73.1	36.3	36.9	36.9	19.0	17.9	16.1	8.2	7.8	15.9	6.9	9.0
2002.......	74.0	36.8	37.3	36.7	18.9	17.8	16.4	8.3	8.0	16.5	7.2	9.3
2003.......	74.9	37.3	37.6	36.3	18.7	17.6	17.1	8.6	8.4	16.6	7.3	9.3
2004.......	75.5	37.4	38.0	36.5	19.0	17.6	16.8	8.4	8.4	17.4	7.6	9.8
2005.......	75.8	37.4	38.4	36.4	18.6	17.7	17.4	8.9	8.5	17.5	7.5	9.9
2006.......	75.2	37.2	38.0	36.1	18.5	17.6	17.1	8.8	8.4	17.2	7.5	9.7
2007.......	76.0	37.6	38.4	36.3	18.6	17.7	17.1	8.8	8.3	18.0	7.8	10.1
2008.......	76.3	37.8	38.6	36.4	18.6	17.7	16.8	8.5	8.2	18.6	8.3	10.3

[1] Includes nursery schools, not shown separately. [2] Data beginning 1990, based on a revised edit and tabulation package.

Source: U.S. Census Bureau, Current Population Reports, PPL-148, P-20, and earlier reports, and "School Enrollment," <http://www.census.gov/population/www/socdemo/school.html>.

Table 223. School Enrollment by Control and Level: 1980 to 2009

[In thousands (58,305 represents 58,305,000). As of fall. Data below college level are for regular day schools and exclude subcollegiate departments of colleges, federal schools, and home-schooled children. College data include degree-credit and nondegree-credit enrollment. Based on survey of state education agencies; see source for details. For more projections, see Tables 215 and 217]

Control of school and level	1980	1990	1995	2000	2004	2005	2006	2007	2008, proj.	2009, proj.
Total	58,305	60,269	65,020	68,685	72,154	72,674	73,066	73,451	74,337	74,807
Public.	50,335	52,061	55,933	58,956	61,776	62,135	62,496	62,783	63,237	63,723
Private	7,971	8,208	9,087	9,729	10,379	10,539	10,570	10,668	11,100	11,084
Pre-kindergarten through 8	31,639	33,962	37,094	38,592	38,933	38,928	38,866	38,751	38,890	39,086
Public.	27,647	29,878	32,338	33,686	34,178	34,204	34,235	34,205	34,316	34,505
Private	3,992	4,084	4,756	1 4,906	1 4,756	4,724	1 4,631	4,546	1 4,574	4,580
Grades 9 through 12	14,570	12,488	13,665	14,781	15,949	16,258	16,441	16,451	16,345	16,196
Public.	13,231	11,338	12,502	1 13,517	1 14,618	14,909	1 15,081	15,087	1 14,949	14,807
Private	1,339	1,150	1,163	1,264	1,331	1,349	1,360	1,364	1,395	1,389
College 2	12,097	13,819	14,262	15,312	17,272	17,487	17,759	18,248	19,103	19,525
Public.	9,457	10,845	11,092	11,753	12,980	13,022	13,180	13,491	3 13,972	3 14,410
Private	2,640	2,974	3,169	3,560	4,292	4,466	4,579	4,757	5,131	5,114
Not-for-profit	2,528	2,760	2,929	3,109	3,412	3,455	3,513	3,571	3,662	(NA)
For profit	112	214	240	450	880	1,011	1,066	1,186	1,469	(NA)

NA Not available. 1 Estimated. 2 Data beginning 2000, reflects new classification system. See footnote 1, Table 274. 3 Data are actual.

Source: U.S. National Center for Education Statistics, *Digest of Education Statistics*, annual, and *Projections of Education Statistics*, annual. See also <http://www.nces.ed.gov/annuals>.

Table 224. Students Who Are Foreign Born or Who Have Foreign-Born Parents: 2008

[In thousands (49,059 represents 49,059,000), except percent. As of October. Covers civilian noninstitutional population enrolled in elementary school and above. Based on Current Population Survey, see text, Section 1 and Appendix III]

Characteristic	All students	Students with at least one foreign-born parent					
		Total		Foreign-born student		Native student	
		Number	Percent	Number	Percent	Number	Percent
ELEMENTARY AND HIGH SCHOOL							
Total 1	49,059	10,874	22.2	2,494	5.1	8,380	17.1
White 2	37,239	7,601	20.4	1,683	4.5	5,918	15.9
White, non-Hispanic.	28,133	1,892	6.7	404	1.4	1,488	5.3
Black 2	7,632	1,023	13.4	260	3.4	763	10.0
Asian 2, 3	1,976	1,704	86.2	490	24.8	1,214	61.4
Hispanic 4	9,934	6,104	61.4	1,362	13.7	4,742	47.7
COLLEGE, 1 TO 4 YEARS							
Total 1	14,956	3,354	22.4	1,544	10.3	1,810	12.1
White 2	11,593	2,034	17.5	824	7.1	1,210	10.4
White, non-Hispanic.	9,745	873	9.0	378	3.9	495	5.1
Black 2	2,121	451	21.3	268	12.6	183	8.6
Asian 2, 3	799	723	90.5	407	51.0	316	39.6
Hispanic 4	1,979	1,248	63.1	484	24.5	764	38.6
GRADUATE SCHOOL							
Total 1	3,676	1,001	27.2	577	15.7	424	11.5
White 2	2,812	458	16.3	205	7.3	252	9.0
White, non-Hispanic.	2,579	323	12.5	142	5.5	181	7.0
Black 2	361	90	24.9	64	17.7	26	7.2
Asian 2, 3	421	410	97.4	297	70.5	113	26.8
Hispanic 4	248	145	58.5	67	27.0	77	31.0

1 Includes other races not shown separately. 2 For persons who selected this race group only. See footnote 2, Table 225.
3 Data are for Asians only, excludes Pacific Islanders. 4 Persons of Hispanic origin may be any race.

Source: U.S. Census Bureau, Current Population Survey, unpublished data, <http://www.census.gov/population/www/socdemo/school.html>.

Table 225. Educational Attainment by Race and Hispanic Origin: 1970 to 2009

[In percent. For persons 25 years old and over. 1970 and 1980 as of April 1 and based on sample data from the censuses of population. Other years as of March and based on the Current Population Survey; see text, Section 1 and Appendix III. See Table 226 for data by sex]

Year	Total [1]	White [2]	Black [2]	Asian and Pacific Islander [2]	Hispanic [3] Total [4]	Mexican	Puerto Rican	Cuban
HIGH SCHOOL GRADUATE OR MORE [5]								
1970.	52.3	54.5	31.4	62.2	32.1	24.2	23.4	43.9
1980.	66.5	68.8	51.2	74.8	44.0	37.6	40.1	55.3
1990.	77.6	79.1	66.2	80.4	50.8	44.1	55.5	63.5
1995.	81.7	83.0	73.8	(NA)	53.4	46.5	61.3	64.7
2000.	84.1	84.9	78.5	85.7	57.0	51.0	64.3	73.0
2005.	85.2	85.8	81.1	[6] 87.6	58.5	52.2	72.4	73.3
2006.	85.5	86.1	80.7	87.4	59.3	53.1	72.3	74.9
2007.	85.7	86.2	82.3	87.8	60.3	53.9	73.5	79.8
2008.	86.6	87.1	83.0	88.7	62.3	55.2	76.4	80.0
2009.	86.7	87.1	84.1	88.2	61.9	55.7	76.6	78.5
COLLEGE GRADUATE OR MORE [5]								
1970.	10.7	11.3	4.4	20.4	4.5	2.5	2.2	11.1
1980.	16.2	17.1	8.4	32.9	7.6	4.9	5.6	16.2
1990.	21.3	22.0	11.3	39.9	9.2	5.4	9.7	20.2
1995.	23.0	24.0	13.2	(NA)	9.3	6.5	10.7	19.4
2000.	25.6	26.1	16.5	43.9	10.6	6.9	13.0	23.0
2005.	27.7	28.1	17.6	[6] 50.2	12.0	8.2	13.8	24.6
2006.	28.0	28.4	18.5	49.7	12.4	8.5	15.1	24.4
2007.	28.7	29.1	18.5	52.1	12.7	9.0	16.4	27.2
2008.	29.4	29.8	19.6	52.6	13.3	9.1	15.5	28.1
2009.	29.5	29.9	19.3	52.3	13.2	9.5	16.5	27.9

NA Not available. [1] Includes other races not shown separately. [2] Beginning 2005, for persons who selected this race group only. The 2003 Current Population Survey (CPS) allowed respondents to choose more than one race. Beginning 2003, data represent persons who selected this race group only and exclude persons reporting more than one race. The CPS in prior years only allowed respondents to report one race group. See also comments on race in the text for Section 1. [3] Persons of Hispanic origin may be any race. [4] Includes persons of other Hispanic origin not shown separately. [5] Through 1990, completed 4 years of high school or more and 4 years of college or more. [6] Starting in 2005, data are for Asians only, excludes Pacific Islanders.

Source: U.S. Census Bureau, U.S. Census of Population, 1970 and 1980, Vol. 1; Current Population Reports, P20-550, and earlier reports; and "Educational Attainment," <http://www.census.gov/population/www/socdemo/educ-attn.html>.

Table 226. Educational Attainment by Race, Hispanic Origin, and Sex: 1970 to 2009

[In percent. See Table 225 for headnote and totals for both sexes]

Year	All races [1] Male	Female	White [2] Male	Female	Black [2] Male	Female	Asian and Pacific Islander [2] Male	Female	Hispanic [3] Male	Female
HIGH SCHOOL GRADUATE OR MORE [4]										
1970.	51.9	52.8	54.0	55.0	30.1	32.5	61.3	63.1	37.9	34.2
1980.	67.3	65.8	69.6	68.1	50.8	51.5	78.8	71.4	45.4	42.7
1990.	77.7	77.5	79.1	79.0	65.8	66.5	84.0	77.2	50.3	51.3
1995.	81.7	81.6	83.0	83.0	73.4	74.1	(NA)	(NA)	52.9	53.8
2000.	84.2	84.0	84.8	85.0	78.7	78.3	88.2	83.4	56.6	57.5
2005.	84.9	85.5	85.2	86.2	81.0	81.2	[5] 90.4	[5] 85.2	57.9	59.1
2006.	85.0	85.9	85.5	86.7	80.1	81.2	89.6	85.5	58.5	60.1
2007.	85.0	86.4	85.3	87.1	81.9	82.6	89.8	85.9	58.2	62.5
2008.	85.9	87.2	86.3	87.8	81.8	84.0	90.8	86.9	60.9	63.7
2009.	86.2	87.1	86.5	87.7	84.0	84.1	90.4	86.2	60.6	63.3
COLLEGE GRADUATE OR MORE [4]										
1970.	13.5	8.1	14.4	8.4	4.2	4.6	23.5	17.3	7.8	4.3
1980.	20.1	12.8	21.3	13.3	8.4	8.3	39.8	27.0	9.4	6.0
1990.	24.4	18.4	25.3	19.0	11.9	10.8	44.9	35.4	9.8	8.7
1995.	26.0	20.2	27.2	21.0	13.6	12.9	(NA)	(NA)	10.1	8.4
2000.	27.8	23.6	28.5	23.9	16.3	16.7	47.6	40.7	10.7	10.6
2005.	28.9	26.5	29.4	26.5	16.0	18.8	[5] 54.0	[5] 46.8	11.8	12.1
2006.	29.2	26.9	29.7	27.1	17.2	19.4	52.5	47.1	11.9	12.9
2007.	29.5	28.0	29.9	28.3	18.0	19.0	55.2	49.3	11.8	13.7
2008.	30.1	28.8	30.5	29.1	18.7	20.4	55.8	49.8	12.6	14.1
2009.	30.1	29.1	30.6	29.3	17.8	20.6	55.7	49.3	12.5	14.0

NA Not available. [1] Includes other races not shown separately. [2] Beginning 2005, for persons who selected this race group only. See footnote 2, Table 225. [3] Persons of Hispanic origin may be any race. [4] Through 1990, completed 4 years of high school or more and 4 years of college or more. [5] Starting in 2005, data are for Asians only, excludes Pacific Islanders.

Source: U.S. Census Bureau, U.S. Census of Population, 1970 and 1980, Vol. 1; Current Population Reports P20-550, and earlier reports; and "Educational Attainment," <http://www.census.gov/population/www/socdemo/educ-attn.html>.

Education 149

Table 227. Educational Attainment by Selected Characteristics: 2009

[For persons 25 years old and over (198,285 represents 198,285,000). As of March. Based on the Current Population Survey; see text, Section 1 and Appendix III. For composition of regions, see map, inside front cover]

| Characteristic | Population (1,000) | Percent of population— | | | | | |
		Not a high school graduate	High school graduate	Some college, but no degree	Associate's degree [1]	Bachelor's degree	Advanced degree
Total persons	**198,285**	**13.3**	**31.1**	**17.1**	**9.0**	**19.0**	**10.6**
Age:							
25 to 34 years old	40,520	11.7	28.0	19.2	8.9	22.8	9.3
35 to 44 years old	41,322	11.7	28.7	16.6	10.2	21.4	11.4
45 to 54 years old	44,366	10.9	32.2	17.0	10.8	18.8	10.4
55 to 64 years old	34,289	11.1	30.2	17.8	9.2	18.6	13.1
65 to 74 years old	20,404	17.7	36.4	15.5	5.9	13.9	10.5
75 years old or over	17,384	26.3	36.6	13.7	4.9	11.4	7.0
Sex:							
Male	95,518	13.8	31.4	16.8	7.9	19.0	11.1
Female	102,767	12.9	30.8	17.3	10.0	19.0	10.1
Race:							
White [2]	162,079	12.9	31.2	16.9	9.1	19.3	10.7
Black [2]	22,598	15.9	35.4	20.3	9.0	12.7	6.6
Other	13,608	14.3	22.3	13.9	7.8	25.8	16.0
Hispanic origin:							
Hispanic	25,956	38.1	29.3	13.3	6.1	9.6	3.6
Non-Hispanic	172,329	9.6	31.3	17.6	9.4	20.4	11.6
Region:							
Northeast	36,572	11.8	33.3	13.1	8.6	19.9	13.3
Midwest	43,163	10.2	34.4	17.7	9.8	18.2	9.7
South	72,720	15.0	31.8	16.9	8.6	17.9	9.8
West	45,829	14.8	25.1	19.9	9.1	20.7	10.5
Marital status:							
Never married	34,386	14.6	30.3	17.7	7.9	20.3	9.2
Married, spouse present	118,712	10.8	29.9	16.3	9.4	21.0	12.5
Married, spouse absent [3]	3,021	27.4	28.7	12.2	6.8	15.6	9.3
Separated	4,943	24.2	34.3	17.5	9.1	10.6	4.3
Widowed	14,217	27.2	38.1	14.7	6.2	8.9	4.9
Divorced	23,006	11.6	33.4	21.9	10.3	15.2	7.5
Civilian labor force status:							
Employed	121,526	8.4	28.1	17.4	10.4	22.6	13.0
Unemployed	10,597	17.4	36.7	18.8	8.5	13.7	4.9
Not in the labor force	65,444	21.9	35.8	16.0	6.5	13.0	6.8

[1] Includes vocational degrees. [2] For persons who selected this race group only. See footnote 2, Table 225. [3] Excludes those separated.

Source: U.S. Census Bureau, Current Population Survey, unpublished data, <http://www.census.gov/population/www/socdemo/educ-attn.html>.

Table 228. Mean Earnings by Highest Degree Earned: 2008

[In dollars. For persons 18 years old and over with earnings. Persons as of March the following year. Based on Current Population Survey; see text, Section 1 and Appendix III. For definition of mean, see Guide to Tabular Presentation]

| Characteristic | Total persons | Mean earnings by level of highest degree (dollars) | | | | | | | |
		Not a high school graduate	High school graduate only	Some college, no degree	Associate's	Bachelor's	Master's	Professional	Doctorate
All persons [1]	**42,588**	**21,023**	**31,283**	**32,555**	**39,506**	**58,613**	**70,856**	**125,019**	**99,697**
Age:									
25 to 34 years old	37,233	20,471	28,224	31,956	35,541	48,445	55,636	79,785	83,219
35 to 44 years old	49,605	23,793	35,233	41,416	42,611	66,332	76,480	130,730	102,837
45 to 54 years old	51,696	25,598	36,916	42,559	44,996	70,053	84,495	147,878	111,843
55 to 64 years old	50,947	27,393	35,338	41,741	43,062	64,807	72,604	141,584	105,255
65 years old and over	36,273	18,550	27,532	32,218	28,255	43,378	45,802	112,449	74,518
Sex:									
Male	51,148	24,831	36,753	39,635	48,237	72,868	88,450	147,518	116,574
Female	32,922	14,521	24,329	25,296	32,253	44,078	54,517	87,723	70,898
White [2]	43,666	21,590	32,126	33,298	40,317	59,866	72,125	127,968	99,943
Male	52,672	25,386	37,852	40,744	49,655	75,053	91,251	151,669	116,613
Female	33,115	14,370	24,610	25,335	32,411	43,848	54,308	85,545	71,702
Black [2]	32,874	18,123	27,265	28,570	34,494	46,527	58,311	104,656	92,998
Male	36,507	22,344	30,985	31,910	40,790	51,691	66,085	(B)	(B)
Female	29,734	13,976	23,195	25,982	30,538	42,858	52,919	(B)	(B)
Hispanic [3]	30,291	21,310	27,020	29,610	36,830	48,081	74,122	81,969	96,070
Male	34,240	24,340	30,618	34,721	46,877	56,980	92,644	99,804	(B)
Female	24,646	14,960	21,725	23,979	28,058	39,231	54,385	(B)	(B)

B Base figure too small to meet statistical standards for reliability of a derived figure. [1] Includes other races not shown separately. [2] For persons who selected this race group only. See footnote 2, Table 225. [3] Persons of Hispanic origin may be any race.

Source: U.S. Census Bureau, Current Population Survey, unpublished data, <http://www.census.gov/population/www/socdemo/educ-attn.html>.

150 Education

Table 229. Educational Attainment by State: 1990 to 2008

[In percent. 1990 and 2000 as of April. 2008 represents annual averages for calendar year. For persons 25 years old and over. Based on the 1990 and 2000 Census of Population and the American Community Survey, which includes the household population and the population living in institutions, college dormitories, and other group quarters. See text, Section 1 and Appendix III]

State	1990			2000			2008		
	High school graduate or more	Bachelor's degree or more	Advanced degree or more	High school graduate or more	Bachelor's degree or more	Advanced degree or more	High school graduate or more	Bachelor's degree or more	Advanced degree or more
United States	**75.2**	**20.3**	**7.2**	**80.4**	**24.4**	**8.9**	**85.0**	**27.7**	**10.2**
Alabama	66.9	15.7	5.5	75.3	19.0	6.9	81.9	22.0	7.7
Alaska	86.6	23.0	8.0	88.3	24.7	8.6	91.6	27.3	9.7
Arizona	78.7	20.3	7.0	81.0	23.5	8.4	83.8	25.1	9.2
Arkansas	66.3	13.3	4.5	75.3	16.7	5.7	82.0	18.8	6.3
California	76.2	23.4	8.1	76.8	26.6	9.5	80.2	29.6	10.8
Colorado	84.4	27.0	9.0	86.9	32.7	11.1	88.9	35.6	12.7
Connecticut	79.2	27.2	11.0	84.0	31.4	13.3	88.6	35.6	15.2
Delaware	77.5	21.4	7.7	82.6	25.0	9.4	87.2	27.5	10.8
District of Columbia	73.1	33.3	17.2	77.8	39.1	21.0	85.8	48.2	26.7
Florida	74.4	18.3	6.3	79.9	22.3	8.1	85.2	25.8	9.0
Georgia	70.9	19.3	6.4	78.6	24.3	8.3	83.9	27.5	9.7
Hawaii	80.1	22.9	7.1	84.6	26.2	8.4	90.3	29.1	9.9
Idaho	79.7	17.7	5.3	84.7	21.7	6.8	87.9	24.0	7.4
Illinois	76.2	21.0	7.5	81.4	26.1	9.5	85.9	29.9	11.2
Indiana	75.6	15.6	6.4	82.1	19.4	7.2	86.2	22.9	8.1
Iowa	80.1	16.9	5.2	86.1	21.2	6.5	90.3	24.3	7.3
Kansas	81.3	21.1	7.0	86.0	25.8	8.7	89.5	29.6	10.1
Kentucky	64.6	13.6	5.5	74.1	17.1	6.9	81.3	19.7	7.9
Louisiana	68.3	16.1	5.6	74.8	18.7	6.5	81.2	20.3	6.5
Maine	78.8	18.8	6.1	85.4	22.9	7.9	89.7	25.4	8.9
Maryland	78.4	26.5	10.9	83.8	31.4	13.4	88.0	35.2	15.4
Massachusetts	80.0	27.2	10.6	84.8	33.2	13.7	88.7	38.1	16.4
Michigan	76.8	17.4	6.4	83.4	21.8	8.1	88.1	24.7	9.4
Minnesota	82.4	21.8	6.3	87.9	27.4	8.3	91.6	31.5	10.0
Mississippi	64.3	14.7	5.1	72.9	16.9	5.8	79.9	19.4	6.8
Missouri	73.9	17.8	6.1	81.3	21.6	7.6	86.5	25.0	9.1
Montana	81.0	19.8	5.7	87.2	24.4	7.2	90.9	27.1	8.4
Nebraska	81.8	18.9	5.9	86.6	23.7	7.3	90.1	27.1	8.6
Nevada	78.8	15.3	5.2	80.7	18.2	6.1	83.5	21.9	7.0
New Hampshire	82.2	24.4	7.9	87.4	28.7	10.0	90.9	33.3	12.0
New Jersey	76.7	24.9	8.8	82.1	29.8	11.0	87.4	34.4	12.8
New Mexico	75.1	20.4	8.3	78.9	23.5	9.8	82.4	24.7	10.7
New York	74.8	23.1	9.9	79.1	27.4	11.8	84.1	31.9	13.8
North Carolina	70.0	17.4	5.4	78.1	22.5	7.2	83.6	26.1	8.6
North Dakota	76.7	18.1	4.5	83.9	22.0	5.5	89.6	26.9	6.6
Ohio	75.7	17.0	5.9	83.0	21.1	7.4	87.6	24.1	8.7
Oklahoma	74.6	17.8	6.0	80.6	20.3	6.8	85.6	22.2	7.2
Oregon	81.5	20.6	7.0	85.1	25.1	8.7	88.6	28.1	10.1
Pennsylvania	74.7	17.9	6.6	81.9	22.4	8.4	87.5	26.3	10.0
Rhode Island	72.0	21.3	7.8	78.0	25.6	9.7	83.7	30.0	11.3
South Carolina	68.3	16.6	5.4	76.3	20.4	6.9	83.2	23.7	8.5
South Dakota	77.1	17.2	4.9	84.6	21.5	6.0	90.3	25.1	7.3
Tennessee	67.1	16.0	5.4	75.9	19.6	6.8	83.0	22.9	8.0
Texas	72.1	20.3	6.5	75.7	23.2	7.6	79.6	25.3	8.3
Utah	85.1	22.3	6.8	87.7	26.1	8.3	90.4	29.1	9.4
Vermont	80.8	24.3	8.9	86.4	29.4	11.1	90.6	32.1	12.2
Virginia	75.2	24.5	9.1	81.5	29.5	11.6	85.9	33.7	13.8
Washington	83.8	22.9	7.0	87.1	27.7	9.3	89.6	30.7	10.9
West Virginia	66.0	12.3	4.8	75.2	14.8	5.9	82.2	17.1	6.7
Wisconsin	78.6	17.7	5.6	85.1	22.4	7.2	89.6	25.7	8.6
Wyoming	83.0	18.8	5.7	87.9	21.9	7.0	91.7	23.6	7.9

Source: U.S. Census Bureau, 1990 Census of Population, CPH-L-96; 2000 Census of Population, P37, "Sex by Educational Attainment for the Population 25 Years and Over"; 2008 American Community Survey, R1501, "Percent of Persons 25 Years and Over Who Have Completed High School"; R1502, "Percent of Persons 25 Years and Over Who Have Completed a Bachelor's Degree"; and R1503, "Percent of Persons 25 Years and Over Who Have Completed an Advanced Degree," <http://factfinder.census.gov/>, accessed February 2010.

Education 151

Table 230. Children With Parental Involvement in Home Literacy Activities: 1993 to 2007

[In percent, except number of children (8,579 represents 8,579,000). For children 3 to 5 years old not yet enrolled in kindergarten who participated in activities with a family member. Based on the School Readiness Early Childhood Program Participation Surveys of the National Household Education Surveys Program; see source and Appendix III. See also Table 231]

Characteristic	Children (1,000)		Read to [1]		Told a story [1]		Taught letters, words, or numbers [1]		Visited a library [2]	
	1993	2007	1993	2007	1993	2005	1993	2005	1993	2007
Total..............................	8,579	8,686	78	83	43	54	58	77	38	36
Age:										
3 years old...........................	3,889	3,755	79	84	46	54	57	75	34	36
4 years old...........................	3,713	3,738	78	83	41	53	58	77	41	35
5 years old...........................	976	1,193	76	83	36	55	58	80	38	39
Race/ethnicity:										
White, non-Hispanic...................	5,902	4,664	85	91	44	53	58	76	42	41
Black, non-Hispanic..................	1,271	1,312	66	78	39	54	63	81	29	25
Hispanic [3]...........................	1,026	1,899	58	68	38	50	54	74	26	27
Other	381	812	73	87	50	64	59	82	43	46
Mother's home language: [4]										
English..............................	7,805	7,244	81	88	44	55	58	78	39	38
Not English	603	1,312	42	57	36	45	52	69	26	24
Mother's highest education: [4]										
Less than high school	1,036	808	60	56	37	39	56	70	22	20
High school	3,268	2,048	76	74	41	51	56	78	31	29
Vocational ed or some college.........	2,624	2,658	83	86	45	57	60	79	44	33
College degree	912	1,849	90	95	48	56	56	75	55	43
Graduate/professional training or degree	569	1,194	90	95	50	64	60	76	59	53

[1] Three or more times in the past week. [2] At least once in the past month. [3] Persons of Hispanic origin may be any race. [4] Excludes children with no mother in the household and no female guardian.

Source: U.S. National Center for Education Statistics, Statistical Brief, NCES 2000–026, November 1999; the Early Childhood Program Participation Survey, National Household Education Surveys Program (NHES), 2005, unpublished data; and the NHES School Readiness Survey, 2007, unpublished data, <http://nces.ed.gov/nhes>.

Table 231. Children's School Readiness Skills: 1993 to 2007

[In percent. For children 3 to 5 years old not yet enrolled in kindergarten. Based on the School Readiness Surveys of the National Household Education Survey Program; see source for details. See also Table 230]

Characteristic	Recognizes all letters		Counts to 20 or higher		Writes name		Reads or pretends to read storybooks		Has 3 to 4 skills	
	1993	2007	1993	2007	1993	2007	1993	2005	1993	2005
Total	21	32	52	63	50	60	72	70	35	42
Age:										
3 years old........................	11	17	37	47	22	34	66	67	15	24
4 years old........................	28	38	62	73	70	76	75	73	49	55
5 years old........................	36	59	78	84	84	88	81	72	65	66
Sex:										
Male...............................	19	31	49	61	47	56	68	70	32	40
Female............................	23	33	56	65	53	63	76	71	39	45
Race/ethnicity:										
White, non-Hispanic................	23	36	56	69	52	64	76	75	39	47
Black, non-Hispanic................	18	37	53	69	45	58	63	67	31	44
Hispanic [1]........................	10	15	32	41	42	49	59	55	22	26
Other	22	39	49	69	52	61	70	79	36	48
Mother's employment status: [2]										
Employed..........................	23	34	57	66	52	63	75	72	39	46
Unemployed.......................	17	14	41	42	46	41	67	61	29	32
Not in the labor force	18	31	49	60	47	58	68	69	32	39
Family type:										
Two parents	22	33	54	64	51	62	74	72	37	44
None or one parent	18	27	49	57	47	52	65	65	31	36
Poverty status: [3]										
Above threshold....................	24	35	57	67	53	64	74	75	40	47
Below threshold....................	12	21	41	48	41	46	64	54	23	26

[1] Persons of Hispanic origin may be any race. [2] Excludes children with no mother in the household and no female guardian. [3] Children are considered poor if they lived in households with incomes below the poverty threshold, which is a dollar amount determined by the federal government to meet the household's need, given its size and composition. For more information about the poverty threshold, see text, section 13.

Source: U.S. Department of Education, U.S. National Center for Education Statistics, *Home Literacy Activities and Signs of Children's Emerging Literacy*, 1993, NCES 2000–026, November 1999; the Early Childhood Program Participation Survey, National Household Education Surveys Program (NHES), 2005, unpublished data; and the NHES School Readiness Survey, 2007, unpublished data, <http://nces.ed.gov/nhes>.

Table 232. Children Who Speak a Language Other Than English at Home by Region: 2008

[In thousands (10,872 represents 10,872,000), except percent. For children 5 to 17 years old. For more on languages spoken at home, see Tables 54–55. Based on the American Community Survey; see text, Section 1 and Appendix III. For composition of regions, see map, inside front cover]

Characteristic	U.S.	Northeast	Midwest	South	West
Children who speak another language at home	10,872	1,867	1,324	3,471	4,209
Percent of children 5 to 17 years old	20.5	20.6	11.4	17.7	33.1
Speak Spanish	7,781	1,002	796	2,733	3,251
Speak English "very well"	5,774	790	577	1,973	2,434
Speak English less than "very well"	2,008	211	219	760	818
Speak other Indo-European languages	1,513	538	290	375	309
Speak English "very well"	1,237	435	229	312	260
Speak English less than "very well"	276	103	61	63	49
Speak Asian and Pacific Island languages	1,153	232	145	255	522
Speak English "very well"	839	164	102	192	380
Speak English less than "very well"	314	67	43	63	141
Speak other languages	424	96	93	107	127
Speak English "very well"	342	79	74	89	100
Speak English less than "very well"	82	17	20	19	27
Have difficulty speaking English [1]	2,680	399	342	905	1,035
Language spoken at home in linguistically isolated households [2]	2,889	453	322	952	1,162
Speak only English	164	39	18	54	52
Speak Spanish	2,120	243	205	757	915
Speak other Indo-European languages	217	79	42	55	42
Speak Asian and Pacific Island languages	320	76	38	70	135
Speak other languages	68	15	18	17	18

[1] Children aged 5 to 17 who speak English less than "very well." [2] A household in which no person aged 14 or over speaks English at least "very well."

Source: U.S. Census Bureau, 2008 American Community Survey, B16003, "Age by Language Spoken at Home for the Population 5 Years and Over," and C16004, "Age By Language Spoken at Home For the Population 5 Years and Over in Linguistically Isolated Households," <http://factfinder.census.gov>, accessed February 2010.

Table 233. Preprimary School Enrollment—Summary: 1970 to 2008

[As of October. Civilian noninstitutional population (10,949 represents 10,949,000). Includes public and nonpublic nursery school and kindergarten programs. Excludes 5-year-olds enrolled in elementary school. Based on Current Population Survey. See text, Section 1 and Appendix III]

Item	1970	1980	1990	1995	2000	2005	2006	2007	2008
NUMBER OF CHILDREN (1,000)									
Population, 3 to 5 years old	10,949	9,284	11,207	12,518	11,858	12,134	12,187	12,325	12,583
Total enrolled [1]	4,104	4,878	6,659	7,739	7,592	7,801	8,009	8,056	7,928
Nursery	1,094	1,981	3,378	4,331	4,326	4,529	4,636	4,569	4,570
Public	332	628	1,202	1,950	2,146	2,409	2,481	2,532	2,609
Private	762	1,353	2,177	2,381	2,180	2,120	2,156	2,037	1,961
Kindergarten	3,010	2,897	3,281	3,408	3,266	3,272	3,373	3,487	3,358
Public	2,498	2,438	2,767	2,799	2,701	2,804	2,960	3,087	2,982
Private	511	459	513	608	565	468	413	400	376
White [2]	3,443	3,994	5,389	6,144	5,861	6,025	6,145	6,191	6,011
Black [2]	586	725	964	1,236	1,265	1,148	1,225	1,213	1,231
Hispanic [3]	(NA)	370	642	1,040	1,155	1,494	1,624	1,751	1,645
3 years old	454	857	1,205	1,489	1,540	1,715	1,716	1,717	1,654
4 years old	1,007	1,423	2,086	2,553	2,556	2,668	2,817	2,774	2,804
5 years old	2,643	2,598	3,367	3,697	3,496	3,418	3,476	3,565	3,470
ENROLLMENT RATE									
Total enrolled [1]	37.5	52.5	59.4	61.8	64.0	64.3	65.7	65.4	63.0
White [2]	37.8	52.7	59.7	63.0	63.2	65.1	66.0	68.7	65.1
Black [2]	34.9	51.8	57.8	58.9	68.5	62.0	66.7	69.7	66.2
Hispanic [3]	(NA)	43.3	49.0	51.1	52.6	56.1	59.8	63.0	57.6
3 years old	12.9	27.3	32.6	35.9	39.2	41.3	42.4	41.5	39.3
4 years old	27.8	46.3	56.0	61.6	64.9	66.2	68.8	67.8	66.1
5 years old	69.3	84.7	88.8	87.5	87.6	86.4	85.8	87.1	83.8

NA Not available. [1] Includes races not shown separately. [2] Beginning 2005, for persons who selected this race group only. See footnote 2, Table 225. [3] Persons of Hispanic origin may be any race. The method of identifying Hispanic children was changed in 1980 from allocation based on status of mother to status reported for each child. The number of Hispanic children using the new method is larger.

Source: U.S. Census Bureau, Current Population Reports, PPL-148; earlier PPL and P-20 reports and unpublished data; and "School Enrollment," <http://www.census.gov/population/www/socdemo/school.html>.

Education 153

Table 234. Type of School Attended by Student and Household Characteristics: 1996 and 2007

[In percent, except total in thousands (34,600 represent 34,600,000). For students in grades 1 to 12. Includes homeschooled students enrolled in public or private school 9 or more hours per week. Based on the Parent and Family Involvement Survey of the National Household Education Survey Program; see source and Appendix III for details]

Characteristic	Public Assigned 1996	Public Assigned 2007	Public Chosen 1996	Public Chosen 2007	Private Church related 1996	Private Church related 2007	Private Not church related 1996	Private Not church related 2007
Total students (1,000)	34,600	34,700	6,200	7,400	3,700	4,100	1,000	1,200
Percent distribution	76.0	73.2	13.7	15.5	8.0	8.7	2.3	2.6
Grade level:								
1 to 5	74.1	71.4	14.8	17.0	8.9	8.7	2.2	2.8
6 to 8	79.4	77.0	11.2	11.9	7.4	8.6	2.0	2.5
9 to 12	75.9	72.6	14.1	16.4	7.3	8.6	2.7	2.3
Race/ethnicity:								
White, non-Hispanic	77.1	73.6	11.1	12.5	9.2	10.8	2.7	3.1
Black, non-Hispanic	72.9	68.9	21.5	23.7	4.2	5.5	1.4	1.8
Other, non-Hispanic	69.3	72.7	19.0	17.4	9.5	6.4	2.2	3.5
Hispanic [1]	76.4	75.8	16.1	17.4	6.3	5.6	1.3	1.2
Family type:								
Two-parent household	76.3	72.7	11.7	14.4	9.5	10.0	2.4	2.9
One-parent household	74.6	74.9	18.4	17.7	5.0	5.4	1.9	2.0
Nonparent guardians	80.2	72.8	14.6	22.7	2.3	3.9	2.9	0.6
Parents' education:								
Less than high school	78.8	85.4	17.4	12.4	2.0	1.5	1.8	0.6
High school diploma or equivalent	82.1	79.8	12.3	15.4	5.0	3.5	0.7	1.3
Some college, including vocational/technical	76.4	75.4	14.7	16.3	7.1	7.3	1.8	1.0
Bachelor's degree	70.7	70.7	13.1	15.3	13.0	11.6	3.3	2.4
Graduate/professional degree	66.1	62.2	12.6	15.8	15.3	15.1	6.0	6.8
Region: [2]								
Northeast	74.3	72.3	12.9	13.3	9.2	10.9	3.6	3.4
South	78.7	75.2	12.5	14.0	6.4	8.5	2.4	2.3
Midwest	75.4	73.6	12.4	15.0	10.9	9.9	1.3	1.5
West	74.0	70.6	17.7	20.1	6.3	6.1	2.0	3.3

[1] Persons of Hispanic origin may be of any race. [2] For composition of regions see map, inside front cover.
Source: U.S. National Center for Education Statistics, *Condition of Education, 2009*, NCES 2009-081, June 2009.

Table 235. Public Charter and Traditional Schools—Selected Characteristics: 2007 to 2008

[47,432 represents 47,432,000. A public charter school is a public school that, in accordance with an enabling state statute, has been granted a charter exempting it from selected state and local rules and regulations]

Characteristic	All schools Traditional	All schools Public charter	Elementary Traditional	Elementary Public charter	Secondary Traditional	Secondary Public charter	Combined Traditional	Combined Public charter
Number of schools	87,190	3,560	60,390	2,050	20,720	920	6,080	590
Enrollment (1,000)	47,432	1,047	29,194	619	16,513	229	1,725	200
PERCENT DISTRIBUTION OF STUDENTS								
Race/ethnicity	100.0	100.0	100.0	100.0	100.0	100.0	100.0	100.0
White, non-Hispanic	58.2	41.0	56.2	35.9	60.3	43.5	71.3	54.0
Black, non-Hispanic	15.7	29.0	15.8	36.1	15.8	(S)	12.2	17.6
Hispanic [1]	20.3	23.8	22.1	21.6	18.0	31.5	11.5	22.0
Asian/Pacific Islander	4.4	3.8	4.5	3.8	4.7	3.5	1.3	(S)
American Indian/Alaska Native	1.4	2.3	1.4	2.6	1.2	1.5	3.8	(S)
PERCENT DISTRIBUTION OF SCHOOLS								
Size of enrollment	100.0	100.0	100.0	100.0	100.0	100.0	100.0	100.0
Less than 300 students	28.1	64.2	24.1	59.3	28.9	81.1	65.8	54.9
300 to 599 students	40.6	25.8	49.2	29.2	20.8	14.8	22.8	31.2
600 to 999 students	20.8	7.4	22.5	10.0	19.9	(S)	7.5	6.9
1,000 students or more	10.5	2.7	4.3	(S)	30.4	(S)	4.0	(S)
Percent minority enrollment	100.0	100.0	100.0	100.0	100.0	100.0	100.0	100.0
Less than 10.0	28.7	(S)	27.7	(S)	30.2	(S)	33.8	(S)
10.0 to 24.9	17.9	17.0	18.1	15.7	18.4	(S)	14.5	30.7
25.0 to 49.9	19.7	18.0	19.5	15.1	21.3	20.8	17.4	23.9
50.0 to 74.9	12.6	14.1	13.1	11.8	11.4	20.7	12.2	(S)
75.0 or more	21.0	42.7	21.7	50.4	18.7	39.2	22.1	21.2
Percent of students eligible for free or reduced-price lunch [2]	100.0	100.0	100.0	100.0	100.0	100.0	100.0	100.0
Less than 15.0	4.0	24.5	1.7	16.2	8.5	35.8	11.0	35.3
15.0 to 29.9	27.6	9.9	27.4	9.4	32.7	(S)	11.9	(S)
30.0 to 49.9	27.7	18.8	26.5	16.6	30.9	28.7	28.6	(S)
50.0 to 74.9	21.4	21.4	23.2	25.9	15.6	(S)	22.6	27.5
75.0 or more	19.4	25.5	21.2	31.9	12.2	16.6	25.9	16.9

S Figure does not meet publication standards. [1] Persons of Hispanic origin may be any race. [2] Excludes data for schools not providing information on eligibility for free or reduced-price lunch.
Source: U.S. National Center for Education Statistics, Common Core of Data, "Public Elementary/Secondary School Universe Survey," 2007–08; <http://www.nces.ed.gov/ccd/>.

Table 236. Students Who are Homeschooled by Selected Characteristics: 2007

[As of spring. (51,135 represents 51,135,000). For students 5 to 17 with a grade equivalent of K–12. Homeschoolers are students whose parents reported them to be schooled at home instead of a public or private school. Excludes students who were enrolled in school for more than 25 hours a week or were homeschooled due to a temporary illness. Based on the Parent and Family Involvement Survey of the National Household Education Surveys Program; see source and Appendix III for details]

Characteristic	Number of students			Percent distribution		
	Total (1,000)	Home-schooled (1,000)	Percent home-schooled	Total	Home-schooled	Non-Home-schooled
Total..............................	51,135	1,508	2.9	100.0	100.0	100.0
Grade equivalent: [1]						
K–5......................	23,529	717	3.0	46.0	47.6	46.0
Kindergarten........................	3,669	114	3.1	7.2	7.6	7.2
Grades 1 to 3........................	11,965	406	3.4	23.4	26.9	23.3
Grades 4 to 5........................	7,895	197	2.5	15.4	13.1	15.5
Grades 6 to 8........................	12,435	359	2.9	24.3	23.8	24.3
Grades 9 to 12........................	15,161	422	2.8	29.6	28.0	29.7
Sex:						
Male........................	26,286	633	2.4	51.4	41.9	51.7
Female........................	24,849	875	3.5	48.6	58.1	48.3
Race/ethnicity:						
White, non-Hispanic.....................	29,815	1,159	3.9	58.3	76.8	57.7
Black, non-Hispanic....................	7,523	61	0.8	14.7	4.0	15.0
Hispanic [2].............................	9,589	147	1.5	18.8	9.8	19.0
Other........................	4,208	141	3.3	8.2	9.3	8.2
Number of children in the household:						
One child............................	8,463	187	2.2	16.6	12.4	16.7
Two children........................	20,694	412	2.0	40.5	27.3	40.9
Three or more children...............	21,979	909	4.1	43.0	60.3	42.5
Number of parents in the household:						
Two parents........................	37,262	1,348	3.6	72.9	89.4	72.4
One parent........................	11,734	115	1.0	22.9	7.6	23.4
Nonparental guardians...............	2,139	45	2.1	4.2	3.0	4.2
Parents' participation in the labor force:						
Two parents—one in labor force...........	26,075	509	2.0	51.0	33.8	51.5
Two parents—both in labor force...........	10,776	808	7.5	21.1	53.6	20.1
One parent in labor force................	9,989	127	1.3	19.5	8.4	19.9
No parent in labor force.................	4,296	64	1.5	8.4	1.3	0.5
Household income:						
$25,000 or less.....................	11,544	239	2.1	22.6	15.9	22.8
$25,001 to 50,000.....................	10,592	364	3.4	20.7	24.1	20.6
$50,001 to 75,000.....................	10,289	405	3.0	20.1	26.8	19.9
$75,001 or more.....................	18,710	501	2.7	36.6	33.2	36.7
Parents' highest educational attainment:						
High school diploma or less................	14,303	206	1.4	28.0	13.7	28.4
Voc/tech degree or some college...........	14,584	549	3.8	28.5	36.4	28.3
Bachelor's degree.......................	12,321	502	4.1	24.1	33.3	23.8
Graduate/professional school..............	9,927	251	2.5	19.4	16.6	19.5

[1] Excludes those ungraded. [2] Persons of Hispanic origin may be of any race.

Source: U.S. National Center for Education Statistics, "Parent and Family Involvement in Education Survey", National Household Education Surveys Program, 2007, unpublished data. See also <http://nces.ed.gov/nhes>.

Table 237. Public Elementary and Secondary Schools by Type and Size of School: 2007 to 2008

[Enrollment in thousands (48,910 represents 48,910,000). Data reported by schools, rather than school districts. Based on the Common Core of Data Survey; see source for details]

Enrollment size of school	Number of schools					Enrollment [1]				
	Total	Elementary [2]	Secondary [3]	Combined [4]	Other [5]	Total	Elementary [2]	Secondary [3]	Combined [4]	Other [5]
Total...............	98,916	68,114	24,269	6,222	311	48,910	31,194	16,096	1,593	27
PERCENT										
Total................	100.00	100.00	100.00	100.00	100.00	100.00	100.00	100.00	100.00	100.00
Under 100 students......	10.90	5.97	18.29	39.44	50.81	0.97	0.64	1.13	5.51	13.82
100 to 199 students......	9.53	8.38	11.15	16.37	25.95	2.76	2.70	2.32	7.89	24.67
200 to 299 students......	11.55	12.69	8.53	10.31	10.27	5.63	6.84	2.99	8.39	17.47
300 to 399 students......	13.86	16.36	8.11	7.66	5.95	9.41	12.22	3.99	8.88	15.06
400 to 499 students......	13.64	16.71	6.35	6.83	5.41	11.84	15.96	4.02	10.16	16.34
500 to 599 students......	11.10	13.45	5.81	4.84	0.54	11.77	15.67	4.52	8.82	2.15
600 to 699 students......	8.13	9.55	5.01	4.06	0.54	10.19	13.15	4.61	8.81	2.52
700 to 799 students......	5.60	6.46	3.89	2.45	–	8.10	10.26	4.12	6.11	–
800 to 999 students......	6.40	6.50	6.93	3.12	–	11.00	12.24	8.78	9.20	–
1,000 to 1,499 students...	5.44	3.53	11.58	3.20	–	12.61	8.71	20.17	12.68	–
1,500 to 1,999 students...	2.10	0.33	7.55	0.83	–	6.99	1.18	18.51	4.68	–
2,000 to 2,999 students...	1.42	0.08	5.54	0.62	0.54	6.51	0.38	18.54	4.98	7.97
3,000 or more students ...	0.32	–	1.26	0.26	–	2.22	0.03	6.30	3.88	–
Average enrollment [1]	516	469	706	300	147	516	469	706	300	147

– Represents zero. [1] Exclude data for schools not reporting enrollment. [2] Includes schools beginning with grade 6 or below and with no grade higher than 8. [3] Includes schools with no grade lower than 7. [4] Includes schools beginning with grade 6 or below and ending with grade 9 or above. [5] Includes special education, alternative, and other schools not classified by grade span.

Source: U.S. National Center for Education Statistics, Digest of Education Statistics, annual. See also <http://www.nces.ed.gov/programs/digest/>.

Table 238. Public Elementary and Secondary Schools—Summary: 1980 to 2008

[For school year ending in year shown, except as indicated (48,041 represents 48,041,000). Data are estimates]

Item	Unit	1980	1990	2000	2005	2006	2007	2008
School districts, total	**Number**	**16,044**	**15,552**	**15,403**	**15,731**	**15,730**	**15,500**	**15,582**
ENROLLMENT								
Population 5–17 years old [1]	1,000	48,041	44,949	52,811	53,249	53,265	53,397	53,419
Percent of resident population...........	Percent ...	21.4	18.2	18.8	18.2	18.0	17.9	17.7
Fall enrollment [2]	1,000	41,778	40,527	46,577	48,417	48,723	48,750	48,888
Percent of population 5–17 years old.....	Percent ...	87.0	90.2	88.2	90.9	91.5	91.3	91.5
Elementary [3]	1,000	24,397	26,253	29,243	29,632	29,732	29,747	29,884
Secondary [4]	1,000	17,381	14,274	17,334	18,784	18,992	19,003	19,004
Average daily attendance (ADA)	1,000	38,411	37,573	43,313	45,088	45,508	45,687	45,863
High school graduates..................	1,000	2,762	2,327	2,544	2,803	2,843	2,906	3,016
INSTRUCTIONAL STAFF								
Total [5]	**1,000**	**2,521**	**2,685**	**3,273**	**3,509**	**3,558**	**3,619**	**3,672**
Classroom teachers...................	1,000	2,211	2,362	2,891	3,072	3,125	3,172	3,201
Average salaries:								
Instructional staff....................	Dollar....	16,715	32,638	43,837	49,135	50,650	52,724	54,503
Classroom teachers..................	Dollar ...	15,970	31,367	41,807	47,516	49,086	51,052	52,800
REVENUES								
Revenue receipts.....................	Mil. dol.. ...	97,635	208,656	369,754	477,371	506,245	533,029	558,877
Federal.............................	Mil. dol.. ...	9,020	13,184	26,346	42,908	46,052	46,021	47,615
State	Mil. dol.. ...	47,929	100,787	183,986	225,142	237,234	253,686	270,614
Local	Mil. dol.. ...	40,686	94,685	159,421	209,321	222,960	233,321	240,649
EXPENDITURES								
Total..........................	**Mil. dol.**....	**96,105**	**209,698**	**374,782**	**496,199**	**521,554**	**549,002**	**575,727**
Current expenditures (day schools)........	Mil. dol.. ...	85,661	186,583	320,954	422,346	443,382	465,801	485,647
Other current expenditures [6]	Mil. dol.. ...	1,859	3,341	6,618	8,710	9,053	9,442	9,817
Capital outlay.......................	Mil. dol.. ...	6,504	16,012	37,552	48,757	52,733	56,059	62,356
Interest on school debt	Mil. dol.. ...	2,081	3,762	9,659	16,385	16,386	17,700	17,905
In current dollars:								
Revenue receipts per pupil enrolled	Dollar.....	2,337	5,149	7,939	9,860	10,390	10,934	11,432
Current expenditures per pupil enrolled ...	Dollar.....	2,050	4,604	6,891	8,723	9,100	9,555	9,934
In constant (2008) dollars: [7]								
Revenue receipts per pupil enrolled	Dollar.....	6,376	8,582	9,927	10,888	11,053	11,341	11,432
Current expenditures per pupil enrolled ...	Dollar.....	5,594	7,674	8,617	9,633	9,681	9,911	9,934

[1] Estimated resident population as of July 1 of the previous year, except 1980, 1990, and 2000 population enumerated as of April 1. Estimates reflect revisions based on the 2000 Census of Population. [2] Fall enrollment of the previous year. [3] Kindergarten through grade 6. [4] Grades 7 through 12. [5] Full-time equivalent. [6] Current expenses for summer schools, adult education, post-high school vocational education, personnel retraining, etc., when operated by local school districts and not part of regular public elementary and secondary day-school program. [7] Compiled by U.S. Census Bureau. Deflated by the Consumer Price Index, all urban consumers (for school year July through June) supplied by U.S. National Center for Education Statistics.

Source: Except as noted, National Education Association, Washington, DC, Estimates of School Statistics Database (copyright).

Table 239. Public Elementary and Secondary School Enrollment by Grade: 1980 to 2007

[In thousands (40,877 represents 40,877,000). As of fall of year. Based on survey of state education agencies; see source for details]

Grade	1980	1990	1995	2000	2001	2002	2003	2004	2005	2006	2007
Pupils enrolled [1]	**40,877**	**41,217**	**44,840**	**47,204**	**47,672**	**48,183**	**48,540**	**48,795**	**49,113**	**49,299**	**49,293**
Pre-kindergarten to 8 [1]	27,647	29,878	32,341	33,688	33,938	34,116	34,202	34,178	34,205	34,221	34,205
Pre-K and Kindergarten.....	2,689	3,610	4,173	4,158	4,244	4,349	4,453	4,534	4,656	4,706	4,691
First....................	2,894	3,499	3,671	3,636	3,614	3,594	3,613	3,663	3,691	3,750	3,750
Second	2,800	3,327	3,507	3,634	3,593	3,565	3,544	3,560	3,606	3,640	3,704
Third....................	2,893	3,297	3,445	3,676	3,653	3,623	3,611	3,580	3,586	3,627	3,659
Fourth	3,107	3,248	3,431	3,711	3,695	3,669	3,619	3,612	3,578	3,585	3,624
Fifth	3,130	3,197	3,438	3,707	3,727	3,711	3,685	3,635	3,633	3,601	3,600
Sixth....................	3,038	3,110	3,395	3,663	3,769	3,788	3,772	3,735	3,670	3,660	3,628
Seventh	3,085	3,067	3,422	3,629	3,720	3,821	3,841	3,818	3,777	3,715	3,701
Eighth	3,086	2,979	3,356	3,538	3,616	3,709	3,809	3,825	3,802	3,765	3,709
Grades 9 to 12 [1]	13,231	11,338	12,500	13,340	13,577	14,067	14,338	14,617	14,909	15,078	15,087
Ninth	3,377	3,169	3,704	3,963	4,012	4,105	4,190	4,281	4,287	4,260	4,200
Tenth	3,368	2,896	3,237	3,491	3,528	3,584	3,675	3,750	3,866	3,881	3,863
Eleventh.................	3,195	2,612	2,826	3,083	3,174	3,229	3,277	3,369	3,455	3,551	3,558
Twelfth	2,925	2,381	2,487	2,803	2,863	2,990	3,046	3,094	3,180	3,276	3,375

[1] Includes unclassified students not shown separately.

Source: U.S. National Center for Education Statistics, *Digest of Education Statistics*, annual. See also <http://www.nces.ed.gov /programs/digest/>.

Table 240. Public Elementary and Secondary Schools and Enrollment—States: 2007 to 2008

[For schools with membership (48,910 represents 48,910,000). Based on the Common Core of Data Program; see source for details]

State	Total number of schools with member- ship	Total number of students (1,000)	Regular Number of schools	Regular Percent of students	Special education [1] Number of schools	Special education [1] Percent of students	Vocational education [2] Number of schools	Vocational education [2] Percent of students	Alternative education [3] Number of schools	Alternative education [3] Percent of students
Total.	98,916	48,910	88,274	98.1	2,267	0.4	1,409	0.3	6,966	1.2
Alabama	1,605	744	1,373	99.3	40	0.2	73	(Z)	119	0.5
Alaska	501	131	448	89.5	1	(Z)	3	0.5	49	10.0
Arizona	2,135	1,087	1,880	98.5	10	0.1	166	0.3	79	1.1
Arkansas	1,121	479	1,082	99.6	4	(Z)	24	0.1	11	0.3
California	9,983	6,070	8,438	96.8	144	0.5	76	(Z)	1,325	2.7
Colorado	1,757	802	1,650	98.3	9	0.1	5	0.1	93	1.5
Connecticut	1,117	568	1,019	97.0	36	0.5	17	1.8	45	0.7
Delaware	235	123	177	92.0	19	1.7	6	5.3	33	1.0
District of Columbia	244	78	210	87.8	15	5.6	5	2.2	14	4.4
Florida	3,935	2,667	3,268	97.7	159	0.6	51	0.1	457	1.5
Georgia	2,452	1,650	2,196	99.5	70	0.1	3	0.1	183	0.4
Hawaii	287	180	283	99.8	3	0.1	–	–	1	0.1
Idaho	727	272	622	97.9	11	(Z)	11	(Z)	83	2.0
Illinois.	4,399	2,113	3,927	98.2	227	1.2	55	0.2	190	0.5
Indiana.	1,970	1,046	1,883	99.7	37	(Z)	29	–	21	0.2
Iowa.	1,511	482	1,431	98.9	10	0.2	–	–	70	0.9
Kansas.	1,422	468	1,406	99.9	14	0.1	1	–	1	(Z)
Kentucky	1,528	666	1,231	98.8	10	0.1	126	–	161	1.1
Louisiana	1,470	681	1,267	95.6	41	0.2	6	–	156	4.2
Maine.	670	191	640	100.0	3	(Z)	27	–	–	–
Maryland	1,453	846	1,303	97.0	50	0.7	24	1.0	76	1.3
Massachusetts.	1,878	963	1,790	95.5	27	0.6	39	3.6	22	0.4
Michigan	4,096	1,666	3,489	96.6	252	1.3	55	0.1	300	2.0
Minnesota	2,679	838	1,653	96.1	290	1.7	11	(Z)	725	2.2
Mississippi	1,068	494	913	100.0	4	(Z)	89	–	62	–
Missouri.	2,417	917	2,190	99.3	65	0.3	63	0.2	99	0.2
Montana.	831	143	824	99.9	2	(Z)	–	–	5	0.1
Nebraska	1,143	291	1,102	99.0	38	0.4	–	–	3	(Z)
Nevada	610	429	571	98.5	8	0.2	1	(Z)	30	1.3
New Hampshire	488	201	488	100.0	–	–	–	–	–	–
New Jersey	2,591	1,380	2,343	97.4	74	0.6	55	1.7	119	0.2
New Mexico	851	328	803	98.4	6	0.2	2	0.1	40	1.3
New York	4,631	2,765	4,447	97.3	127	1.0	29	1.4	28	0.3
North Carolina	2,516	1,458	2,385	99.1	33	0.2	10	(Z)	88	0.7
North Dakota	528	95	487	99.9	35	0.1	6	–	–	–
Ohio.	3,924	1,822	3,754	99.5	75	0.4	75	(Z)	20	(Z)
Oklahoma	1,798	642	1,788	99.8	5	(Z)	–	–	5	0.2
Oregon.	1,295	559	1,247	98.9	3	(Z)	–	–	45	1.1
Pennsylvania	3,246	1,788	3,133	98.9	13	0.1	87	0.9	13	0.1
Rhode Island	328	146	298	97.2	3	0.1	12	1.3	15	1.4
South Carolina.	1,195	712	1,122	99.7	10	0.1	40	–	23	0.2
South Dakota.	730	120	692	99.0	9	(Z)	–	–	29	0.9
Tennessee	1,718	964	1,651	99.5	20	0.2	22	0.3	25	0.1
Texas	8,758	4,673	7,317	98.3	23	(Z)	1	–	1,417	1.6
Utah.	1,010	576	827	95.9	82	1.3	8	–	93	2.8
Vermont.	329	92	313	100.0	–	–	15	–	1	(Z)
Virginia.	2,027	1,231	1,856	99.8	12	(Z)	31	–	128	0.2
Washington	2,311	1,030	1,863	95.5	117	0.4	11	(Z)	320	4.1
West Virginia	762	283	696	99.6	7	0.1	31	(Z)	28	0.3
Wisconsin	2,268	874	2,159	99.4	9	(Z)	8	0.1	92	0.6
Wyoming	368	86	339	98.3	5	0.1	–	–	24	1.7

– Represents zero. Z Less than 0.05 percent. [1] Focuses on special education with materials and instructional approaches adapted to meet the students' needs. [2] Focuses on vocational, technical, or career education and provides education and training in at least one semi-skilled or technical occupation. [3] Addresses the needs of students that typically cannot be met in the regular school setting and provides nontraditional education.

Source: U.S. National Center for Education Statistics, Common Core of Data, "Public Elementary/Secondary School Universe Survey," 2007–08, Version 1b, <http://www.nces.ed.gov/ccd/>.

Table 241. Selected Statistics for the Largest Public School Districts: 2006 to 2007

[For the 50 largest districts by enrollment size. Based on reports from state education agencies in the spring 2007. Data from the Common Core Data Program; see source for details. School district boundaries are not necessarily the same as city or county boundaries]

School district	City	County	Number of students [1]	Number of full-time equivalent (FTE) teachers	Number of 2005–06 com- pleters [2]	Number of schools
New York City Public Schools, NY	New York	New York	999,150	70,889	46,870	1,429
Los Angeles Unified, CA	Los Angeles	Los Angeles	707,627	34,365	28,322	815
Puerto Rico Department of Education, PR	Hato Rey	San Juan	544,138	40,163	(NA)	1,515
City of Chicago School District, IL	Chicago	Cook	413,694	18,966	17,065	633
Dade County School District, FL	Miami	Miami-Dade	353,790	20,656	18,740	442
Clark County School District, NV	Las Vegas	Clark	303,448	15,930	12,433	319
Broward County School District, FL	Fort Lauderdale	Broward	262,813	15,234	14,866	293
Houston Independent School District, TX	Houston	Harris	202,936	12,057	7,853	296
Hillsborough County School District, FL	Tampa	Hillsborough	193,517	10,210	10,124	280
Hawaii Department of Education, HI	Honolulu	Honolulu	180,728	11,270	11,119	286
Philadelphia City School District, PA	Philadelphia	Philadelphia	178,241	9,917	(NA)	274
Orange County School District, FL	Orlando	Orange	175,245	10,975	9,644	230
Palm Beach County School District, FL.	West Palm Beach	Palm Beach	171,431	10,633	9,288	263
Fairfax County Public Schools, VA	Falls Church	Fairfax	163,952	13,384	11,056	207
Dallas Independent School District, TX	Dallas	Dallas	159,144	10,643	6,343	242
Gwinnett County, GA	Lawrenceville	Gwinnett	152,043	10,341	7,413	108
Montgomery County Public Schools, MD	Rockville	Montgomery	137,814	9,613	9,944	204
Prince George's County Public Schools, MD . .	Upper Marlboro	Prince George's	131,014	8,880	7,832	213
San Diego Unified, CA.	San Diego	San Diego	130,983	7,135	6,588	223
Charlotte-Mecklenburg Schools, NC	Charlotte	Mecklenburg	128,789	9,408	(NA)	158
Wake County Schools, NC	Raleigh	Wake	128,748	9,178	(NA)	147
Duval County School District, FL.	Jacksonville	Duval	125,176	7,776	6,205	176
Detroit City School District, MI.	Detroit	Wayne	117,609	7,127	5,866	233
Memphis City School District, TN	Memphis	Shelby	117,349	7,020	6,341	194
Pinellas County School District, FL	Largo	Pinellas	109,915	7,015	5,945	173
Cobb County, MD	Marietta	Cobb	107,274	7,739	6,353	114
Baltimore County Public Schools, GA	Baltimore	Baltimore	105,839	7,420	7,380	169
DeKalb County, GA	Decatur	Dekalb	101,396	7,134	5,329	150
Albuquerque Public Schools, NM	Albuquerque	Bernalillo	95,493	6,241	4,776	164
Polk County School District, FL.	Bartow	Polk	92,801	6,478	4,374	152
Jefferson County, KY	Louisville	Jefferson	92,659	5,971	(NA)	171
Cypress–Fairbanks Independent School District, TX.	Houston	Harris	92,135	5,838	4,768	75
Long Beach Unified, CA	Long Beach	Los Angeles	90,663	4,213	4,896	91
Milwaukee, WI	Milwaukee	Milwaukee	89,912	5,116	(NA)	224
Jefferson County, CO	Golden	Jefferson	86,154	4,809	5,906	160
Baltimore City Public Schools, MD	Baltimore	Baltimore	84,515	5,928	4,184	198
Fulton County, GA	Atlanta	Fulton	83,861	5,955	4,450	94
Northside Independent School District, TX	San Antonio	Bexar	82,587	5,226	4,259	95
Austin Independent School District, TX.	Austin	Travis	82,140	5,714	3,862	116
Fort Worth Independent School District, TX . . .	Fort Worth	Tarrant	79,457	4,839	3,556	147
Lee County School District, FL	Fort Myers	Lee	78,981	4,648	3,834	105
Jordan District, UT.	Sandy	Salt Lake	78,299	3,206	(NA)	96
Fresno Unified, CA	Fresno	Fresno	77,555	3,894	3,735	110
Brevard County School District, FL	Viera	Brevard	74,785	4,723	4,631	127
Mesa Unified District, AZ.	Mesa	Maricopa	74,128	3,854	4,034	89
Nashville-Davidson County School District, TN.	Nashville	Davidson	73,731	4,981	3,454	133
Anne Arundel County Public Schools, MD	Annapolis	Anne Arundel	73,066	4,893	4,769	121
Denver County, CO	Denver	Denver	72,561	4,107	2,843	149
Virginia Beach City Public Schools, VA	Virginia Beach	Virginia Beach	72,538	5,967	4,709	88
Guilford County Schools, NC.	Greensboro	Guilford	71,722	5,405	(NA)	117

NA Not available. [1] Number of students receiving educational services from the school district. [2] Includes high school diploma recipients and other completers (for example certificates of attendance) but does not include high school equivalents (GEDs).

Source: U.S. Department of Education, National Center for Education Statistics, Common Core of Data (CCD), "Public Elementary/Secondary School Universe Survey," 2006–07, Version 1b; "Local Education Agency Universe Survey," 2006–07, Version 1b; and "Local Education Universe Survey Dropout and Completion Public-Use Data File," 2005–06, Version 1b., <http://www.nces.ed.gov/ccd/>.

Table 242. Public Elementary and Secondary School Enrollment by State: 1990 to 2007

[In thousands (29,878 represents 29,878,000), except rate. As of fall. Includes unclassified students. Based on survey of state education agencies; see source for details]

State	Prekindergarten through grade 8 [1]					Grades 9 through 12 [1]				
	1990	2000	2005	2006	2007	1990	2000	2005	2006	2007
United States	**29,878**	**33,688**	**34,205**	**34,235**	**34,205**	**11,338**	**13,515**	**14,908**	**15,081**	**15,087**
Alabama	527	539	529	529	527	195	201	212	215	218
Alaska	85	94	91	90	89	29	39	42	42	42
Arizona	479	641	740	760	771	161	237	355	309	316
Arkansas	314	318	336	337	340	123	132	138	140	139
California	3,615	4,408	4,466	4,410	4,329	1,336	1,733	1,971	1,997	2,015
Colorado	420	517	550	559	566	154	208	230	235	236
Connecticut	347	406	400	398	394	122	156	175	177	177
Delaware	73	81	85	85	85	27	34	36	37	38
District of Columbia	61	54	56	52	56	19	15	21	20	23
Florida	1,370	1,760	1,873	1,867	1,856	492	675	802	805	811
Georgia	849	1,060	1,145	1,167	1,179	303	385	453	463	471
Hawaii	123	132	127	126	126	49	52	55	55	54
Idaho	160	170	183	187	191	61	75	79	80	81
Illinois.	1,310	1,474	1,480	1,478	1,473	512	575	631	641	640
Indiana.	676	703	724	730	730	279	286	311	316	317
Iowa.	345	334	326	326	330	139	161	157	157	156
Kansas.	320	323	321	326	327	117	147	147	143	142
Kentucky	459	471	487	487	469	177	194	192	196	197
Louisiana	586	547	482	492	500	199	197	172	184	181
Maine.	155	146	133	132	131	60	61	62	62	66
Maryland	527	609	589	579	576	188	244	271	273	269
Massachusetts.	604	703	675	671	667	230	273	297	298	296
Michigan	1,145	1,222	1,191	1,171	1,137	440	498	551	552	556
Minnesota	546	578	558	558	558	211	277	281	282	279
Mississippi	372	364	358	356	354	131	134	137	139	141
Missouri.	588	645	635	634	632	228	268	283	286	285
Montana.	111	105	98	97	96	42	50	48	47	46
Nebraska.	198	195	195	106	200	76	91	92	92	91
Nevada	150	251	296	303	308	51	90	116	122	122
New Hampshire.	126	147	139	136	134	46	61	67	67	66
New Jersey	784	968	971	963	954	306	346	425	425	428
New Mexico	208	225	230	230	230	94	95	97	98	99
New York	1,828	2,029	1,909	1,887	1,856	770	853	906	922	909
North Carolina	783	945	1,003	1,027	1,072	304	348	413	417	417
North Dakota	85	72	66	64	63	33	37	33	32	32
Ohio.	1,258	1,294	1,261	1,253	1,241	514	541	578	584	586
Oklahoma	425	445	457	460	463	154	178	178	179	179
Oregon.	340	379	380	381	384	132	167	173	182	182
Pennsylvania	1,172	1,258	1,228	1,220	1,205	400	550	603	651	597
Rhode Island	102	114	104	102	99	37	44	50	50	48
South Carolina.	452	493	498	501	505	170	184	204	207	208
South Dakota.	95	88	84	83	83	34	41	38	38	38
Tennessee	598	668	677	692	682	226	241	277	286	283
Texas.	2,511	2,943	3,268	3,320	3,375	872	1,117	1,257	1,280	1,300
Utah.	325	333	358	371	410	122	148	151	152	166
Vermont.	71	70	65	64	63	25	32	32	32	31
Virginia.	728	816	841	842	850	270	329	372	379	380
Washington	613	694	699	695	697	227	310	333	332	333
West Virginia	224	201	197	198	199	98	85	84	84	84
Wisconsin	566	595	584	585	585	232	285	291	292	289
Wyoming	71	60	57	58	59	27	30	27	27	27

[1] Includes unclassified.

Source: U.S. National Center for Education Statistics, *Digest of Education Statistics*, annual. See also <http://www.nces.ed.gov/programs/digest/>.

Education 159

Table 243. Public Schools Reporting Incidents of Crime by Incident Type and Selected School Characteristic: 2007 to 2008

[For school year. Includes incidents that happen in school buildings, on school grounds, on school buses, and at places that hold school-sponsored events or activities. Based on sample; see source for details]

School characteristic	Total number of schools	Percent of schools with—				Rate per 1,000 students			
		Violent incidents [1]	Serious violent incidents [2]	Theft [3]	Other incidents [4]	Violent incidents [1]	Serious violent incidents [2]	Theft [3]	Other incidents [4]
All public schools [5]	**83,000**	**75.5**	**17.2**	**47.3**	**67.4**	**27.9**	**1.2**	**5.6**	**9.2**
Level: [6]									
Primary	49,200	65.1	13.0	30.6	55.1	25.6	1.0	2.1	4.9
Middle	15,300	94.3	22.0	69.5	84.0	41.3	1.9	8.3	12.3
High school	11,900	94.0	28.9	83.7	93.5	22.3	1.1	9.9	14.8
Enrollment size:									
Less than 300	19,200	60.6	12.3	33.3	47.6	34.4	[7] 1.8	5.4	9.1
300 to 499	24,300	69.1	11.4	35.6	62.1	24.3	0.8	3.2	6.5
500 to 999	30,200	83.4	19.8	54.0	75.5	30.0	1.2	5.1	7.7
1,000 or more	9,300	97.0	34.0	84.9	95.5	25.5	1.4	8.3	13.4
Percent minority enrollment: [8]									
Less than 5 percent	13,700	66.7	15.0	46.1	60.6	21.7	0.8	5.9	7.4
5 to 20 percent	21,400	72.7	13.7	43.0	62.0	18.8	0.6	5.5	7.3
20 to 50 percent	20,300	77.3	15.2	45.8	70.0	27.1	0.8	5.2	8.4
50 percent or more	27,600	80.5	22.5	52.4	72.9	36.6	2.0	5.9	11.7

[1] Violent incidents include rape, sexual battery other than rape, physical attack or fight with or without a weapon, threat of physical attack with or without a weapon, and robbery with or without a weapon. [2] Serious violent incidents include rape, sexual battery other than rape, physical attack or fight with a weapon, threat of physical attack with a weapon, and robbery with or without a weapon. [3] Theft or larceny (taking things worth over $10 without personal confrontation). Includes pocket picking, stealing purse or backpack (if left unattended or no force was used to take from owner), theft from motor vehicles, etc. [4] Other incidents include possession of a firearm or explosive device, possession of knife or sharp object, distribution of illegal drugs, possession or use of alcohol or illegal drugs, and vandalism. [5] Includes combined schools, not shown separately, which include all other combination of grades, including K–12 schools. [6] Primary schools are defined as schools in which the lowest grade is not higher than grade 3 and the highest grade is not higher than grade 8. Middle schools are defined as schools in which the lowest grade is not lower than grade 4 and the highest grade is not higher than grade 9. High schools are defined as schools in which the lowest grade is not lower than grade 9 and the highest grade is not higher than grade 12. [7] Interpret data with caution. [8] These estimates exclude data from Tennessee because schools in this state did not report estimates of student race.

Source: U.S. Department of Education, U.S. National Center for Education Statistics, School Survey on Crime and Safety, 2008.

Table 244. Percent of Public Schools Reporting Selected Types of Disciplinary Problems Occurring at School by Selected School Characteristics: 2007 to 2008

[In percent. For school year. "At school" includes activities that happen in school buildings, on school grounds, on school buses, and at places that hold school-sponsored events or activities. Based on sample; see source for details]

School characteristic	Happens daily or at least once a day						Happens at all	
	Student racial tensions	Student bullying	Student sexual harassment of other students [1]	Student verbal abuse of teachers	Widespread disorder in classrooms	Student acts of disrespect for teachers	Undesirable gang activities [2]	Undesirable cult or extremist group activities [3]
All public schools	**3.7**	**25.3**	**3.0**	**6.0**	**10.5**	**4.0**	**19.8**	**2.6**
Level: [4]								
Primary	2.6	20.5	[5] 1.3	3.7	7.7	3.1	10.0	[5] 0.6
Middle	5.6	43.5	6.5	9.8	17.7	6.6	35.4	3.1
High school	5.3	21.7	5.7	12.1	16.9	4.8	43.1	8.0
Combined	[5] 4.3	24.9	(S)	[5] 2.9	[5] 3.8	(S)	14.3	[5] 6.4
Enrollment size:								
Less than 300	[5] 3.2	18.7	[5] 2.7	[5] 4.5	[5] 5.6	[5] 3.2	9.8	[5] 1.3
300 to 499	[5] 1.4	20.8	[5] 1.8	3.1	8.4	[5] 2.6	12.8	[5] 1.0
500 to 999	5.3	30.6	3.4	6.4	11.9	5.1	21.8	2.6
1,000 or more	5.5	33.2	5.7	15.3	22.0	6.1	52.4	9.4
Percent minority enrollment: [6]								
Less than 5 percent	[5] 1.2	25.6	[5] 2.7	[5] 2.8	5.6	[5] 2.0	3.9	(S)
5 to 20 percent	2.7	24.9	2.5	2.6	5.6	2.1	9.9	[5] 1.7
20 to 50 percent	3.0	22.1	2.2	5.5	11.5	[5] 2.3	21.3	2.7
50 percent or more	6.2	27.6	4.2	10.5	16.1	7.8	34.2	3.6

S Figure does not meet publication standards. [1] Sexual harassment includes "unsolicited, offensive behavior that inappropriately asserts sexuality over another person. This behavior may be verbal or nonverbal." [2] Gang includes an "ongoing loosely organized association of three or more persons, whether formal or informal, that has a common name, signs, symbols, or colors, whose members engage, either individually or collectively, in violent or other forms of illegal behavior." [3] Cult or extremist group includes "a group that espouses radical beliefs and practices, which may include a religious component, that are widely seen as threatening the basic values and cultural norms of society at large." [4] Primary schools are defined as schools in which the lowest grade is not higher than grade 3 and the highest grade is not higher than grade 8. Middle schools are defined as schools in which the lowest grade level is not lower than grade 4 and the highest grade is not higher than grade 9. High schools are defined as schools in which the lowest grade is not lower than grade 9 and the highest grade is not higher than grade 12. Combined schools include all other combinations of grades, including K–12 schools. [5] Intepret data with caution. [6] These estimates exclude data from Tennessee because schools in this state did not report estimates of student race.

Source: U.S. Department of Education, National Center for Education Statistics, "2007–08 School Survey on Crime and Safety," 2008.

Table 245. Students Who Reported Being Threatened or Injured With a Weapon on School Property by Selected Student Characteristics: 1993 to 2007

[In percent. For students in grades 9 to 12. Data are for previous 12 months. "On school property" was not defined for survey respondents]

Characteristic	1993	1995	1997	1999	2001	2003	2005	2007
Total	**7.3**	**8.4**	**7.4**	**7.7**	**8.9**	**9.2**	**7.9**	**7.8**
Sex:								
Male	9.2	10.9	10.2	9.5	11.5	11.6	9.7	10.2
Female	5.4	5.8	4.0	5.8	6.5	6.5	6.1	5.4
Race/ethnicity: [1]								
White	6.3	7.0	6.2	6.6	8.5	7.8	7.2	6.9
Black	11.2	11.0	9.9	7.6	9.3	10.9	8.1	9.7
Hispanic	8.6	12.4	9.0	9.8	8.9	9.4	9.8	8.7
Asian	[2]	[2]	[2]	7.7	11.3	11.5	4.6	[3] 7.6
American Indian/Alaska Native	11.7	[3] 11.4	[3] 12.5	[3] 13.2	[3] 15.2	22.1	9.8	5.9
Pacific Islander/Native Hawaiian	[2]	[2]	[2]	15.6	24.8	16.3	[3] 14.5	[3] 8.1
More than one race	[2]	[2]	[2]	9.3	10.3	18.7	10.7	13.3
Grade:								
9th	9.4	9.6	10.1	10.5	12.7	12.1	10.5	9.2
10th	7.3	9.6	7.9	8.2	9.1	9.2	8.8	8.4
11th	7.3	7.7	5.9	6.1	6.9	7.3	5.5	6.8
12th	5.5	6.7	5.8	5.1	5.3	6.3	5.8	6.3

[1] Race categories exclude persons of Hispanic ethnicity. [2] The response categories for race/ethnicity changed in 1999 making comparisons of some categories with earlier years problematic. In 1993, 1995, and 1997, Asian students and Pacific Islander students were not categorized separately and students were not given the option of choosing more than one race. [3] Interpret data with caution.

Source: U.S. National Center for Education Statistics and U.S. Department of Justice, Bureau of Justice Statistics, *Indicators of School Crime and Safety: 2009*, NCES 2010–2012. See also <http://www.nces.ed.gov/programs/crimeindicators/crimeindicators2009/>.

Table 246. Public Schools Using Selected Safety and Security Measures by School Characteristics: 2000 to 2008

[In percent. For school year ending in year shown. Based on survey of principals or persons knowledgeable about discipline issues at the school. Refers only to those times during normal school hours or when school activities or events were in session. Based on the School Survey on Crime and Safety and subject to sampling error; for details see source]

Measure	2000	2004	2006	2008
Controlled access during school hours:				
Buildings (locked or monitored doors)	74.6	83.0	84.9	89.5
Grounds (locked or monitored gates)	33.7	36.2	41.1	42.6
Closed the campus for most students during lunch	64.6	66.0	66.1	65.0
Drug testing:				
Any students	4.1	5.3	(NA)	(NA)
Athletes	(NA)	4.2	5.0	6.4
Students in extracurricular activities other than athletes	(NA)	2.6	3.4	4.5
Any other students	(NA)	(NA)	3.0	3.0
Prohibited all tobacco use on school grounds	90.1	88.8	90.3	91.4
Required to wear badges or picture IDs:				
Students	3.9	6.4	6.1	7.6
Faculty and staff	25.4	48.0	47.8	58.3
Metal detector checks on students:				
Random checks [1]	7.2	5.6	4.9	5.3
Required to pass through daily	0.9	1.1	1.1	1.3
Sweeps and technology:				
Random dog sniffs to check for drugs [1]	20.6	21.3	23.0	21.5
Random sweeps for contraband [1,2]	11.8	12.8	13.1	11.4
Provided telephones in most classrooms	44.6	60.8	66.8	71.6
Used security cameras to monitor school [1]	19.4	36.0	42.8	55.0
Provided two-way radios	(NA)	71.2	70.8	73.1
Visitor requirements:				
Sign-in or check-in	96.6	98.3	97.6	98.7
Pass through metal detectors	0.9	0.9	1.0	(NA)
Dress code:				
Required students to wear uniforms	11.8	13.8	13.8	17.5
Enforced a strict dress code	47.4	55.1	55.3	54.8
School supplies and equipment:				
Required clear book bags or banned book bags on school grounds	5.9	6.2	6.4	6.0
Provided school lockers to students	46.5	49.5	50.6	48.9

NA Not available. [1] One or more. [2] For example, drugs or weapons. Does not include dog sniffs.

Source: U.S. National Center for Education Statistics and U.S. Department of Justice, Bureau of Justice Statistics, *Indicators of School Crime and Safety, 2009*, December 2009, NCES 2010-012. See also <http://www.nces.ed.gov/programs/crimeindicators/crimindicators2009/>.

Education 161

Table 247. Students Who Reported Being Bullied at School or Cyber-Bullied by Student Characteristics: 2007

[In percent. For students aged 12 through 18. For school year ending in 2007. "At school" includes the school building, on school property, on a school bus, or going to and from school. For more information, see Appendix A of source]

Characteristic	Total [1]	Bullied at school					Cyber-bullying anywhere [2]
		Total bullying at school	Made fun of, called names, or insulted	Subject of rumors	Threatened with harm	Pushed, shoved, tripped, spit on	
Total	32.2	31.7	21.0	18.1	5.8	11.0	3.7
Sex:							
Male	30.6	30.3	20.3	13.5	6.0	12.2	2.0
Female	33.7	33.2	21.7	22.8	5.6	9.7	5.3
Race/ethnicity: [3]							
White	34.6	34.1	23.5	20.3	6.3	11.5	4.2
Black	30.9	30.4	19.5	15.7	5.8	11.3	3.2
Hispanic	27.6	27.3	16.1	14.4	4.9	9.9	2.9
Asian	18.1	18.1	10.6	8.2	(S)	[4] 3.8	(S)
Other	34.6	34.1	20.1	20.8	7.7	14.4	[4] 2.4
Grade:							
6th	42.9	42.7	31.2	21.3	7.0	17.6	3.1
7th	35.7	35.6	27.6	20.2	7.4	15.8	3.4
8th	37.3	36.9	25.1	19.7	6.9	14.2	3.3
9th	30.8	30.6	20.3	18.1	4.6	11.4	2.5
10th	28.4	27.7	17.7	15.0	5.8	8.6	4.6
11th	29.3	28.5	15.3	18.7	4.9	6.5	5.1
12th	23.5	23.0	12.1	14.1	4.3	4.1	3.5

S Reporting standards not met. [1] Bullying types do not sum to total because students could have experienced more than one type of bullying. Also, total includes other types of bullying not shown separately. [2] Cyber-bullied includes students who responded that another student "made unwanted contact, for example, threatened or insulted (the respondent) via text (SMS) messaging." This category did not meet reporting standards to be reported separately. [3] Race categories exclude persons of Hispanic ethnicity. Other includes American Indian, Alaska Native, Pacific Islander, and more than one race. [4] Interpret data with caution.

Source: U.S. National Center for Education Statistics and U.S. Department of Justice, Bureau of Justice Statistics, *Indicators of School Crime and Safety: 2009*, December 2009, NCES 2010-012 . See also <http://www.nces.ed.gov/programs/crimeindicators /crimeindicators2009/>.

Table 248. Parent Participation in School-Related Activities by Selected School, Student, and Family Characteristics: 2007

[In percent, except as noted (51,600 represents 51,600,000). For school year ending in 2007. Covers parents with children in kindergarten through grade 12. Homeschooled students are excluded]

Characteristic	Number of students in grades K through 12 (thousands)	Participation in school activities by parent or other household member				
		Attended a general school or PTO/PTA [1] meeting	Attended regularly scheduled parent-teacher conference	Attended a school or class event	Volunteered or served on school committee	Participated in school fundraising
Total	51,600	89	78	74	46	65
School type: [2]						
Public, assigned	37,168	89	76	72	42	63
Public, chosen	7,951	88	81	74	45	62
Private, religious	4,560	96	86	86	73	85
Private, nonreligious	1,438	97	90	86	68	72
Student's sex:						
Male	26,875	89	79	71	45	65
Female	24,725	90	77	78	48	66
Student's race/ethnicity:						
White, non-Hispanic	29,832	91	78	80	54	72
Black, non-Hispanic	7,837	87	77	65	35	58
Hispanic [3]	9,767	87	80	65	32	51
Asian or Pacific Islander, non-Hispanic	1,566	90	80	72	46	62
Other, non-Hispanic	2,598	90	74	76	47	62
Student's grade level: [4]						
K–2nd grade	11,516	93	90	78	63	72
3rd–5th grade	11,519	94	92	83	57	71
6th–8th grade	12,058	91	76	72	38	63
9th–12th grade	16,503	83	61	68	34	57
Parents' highest education level:						
Less than high school	3,504	75	70	48	20	34
High school graduate or equivalent	11,070	84	74	65	33	55
Vocational/technical or some college	14,844	89	77	72	42	67
Bachelor's degree	11,353	94	81	83	56	72
Graduate or professional school	10,829	95	82	87	64	77
Parents' language at home:						
Both/only parent(s) speak(s) English	45,219	90	78	77	49	69
One of two parents speaks English	1,022	82	75	63	42	54
No parent speaks English	5,359	84	82	57	22	38

[1] Parent Teacher Organization (PTO) or Parent Teacher Association (PTA) meeting. [2] Variables for school characteristics (school type and school size) have a certain number of missing cases due to school non-report; therefore, the number of students across the categories for each school variable does not sum to the total number of students. [3] Persons of Hispanic origin may be any race. [4] Students whose parents reported the student's grade equivalent as "ungraded" were excluded from the analyses of grade level.

Source: U.S. Department of Education, National Center for Education Statistics, Parent and Family Involvement in Education Survey of the National Household Education Surveys Program (NHES), 2007.

162 Education

Table 249. School Enrollment Below Postsecondary—Summary by Sex, Race, and Hispanic Origin: 2008

[In thousands (57,721 represents 57,721,000), except percent and rate. As of October. Covers civilian noninstitutional population enrolled in nursery school through high school. Based on Current Population Survey, see text, Section 1 and Appendix III]

Characteristic	Total			Race and Hispanic origin				
				White [2]				
	Number [1]	Male	Female	Total	Non-Hispanic	Black [2]	Asian [2]	Hispanic [3]
All students	**57,721**	**29,444**	**28,277**	**43,839**	**33,049**	**8,939**	**2,325**	**11,739**
Nursery	4,614	2,317	2,296	3,479	2,708	706	205	844
Full day	2,214	1,101	1,113	1,525	1,189	481	102	372
Part day	2,400	1,216	1,183	1,954	1,519	225	103	472
Kindergarten	4,047	2,144	1,902	3,121	2,206	601	143	961
Elementary	32,344	16,504	15,840	24,552	18,349	4,993	1,356	6,742
High school	16,715	8,477	8,238	12,687	9,783	2,639	620	3,192
Students in public schools	50,768	25,958	24,810	38,149	27,923	8,282	1,961	11,093
Nursery	2,632	1,342	1,289	1,830	1,212	547	109	666
Full day	1,239	611	627	793	540	347	38	272
Part day	1,393	731	662	1,036	673	200	71	394
Kindergarten	3,578	1,869	1,709	2,748	1,883	546	119	909
Elementary	29,162	14,933	14,228	21,986	16,029	4,665	1,168	6,450
High school	15,397	7,813	7,583	11,584	8,797	2,524	564	3,066
Population 15 to 17 years old	12,289	6,263	6,026	9,658	7,534	1,994	507	2,321
Percent below modal grade [4]	31.7	34.5	28.6	30.8	29.3	39.5	20.0	35.7
Students, 10th to 12th grade	11,750	5,999	5,751	8,942	7,079	1,868	429	2,062
Annual dropout rate	3.3	2.9	3.8	2.8	2.2	6.1	3.9	4.9
Population 18 to 24 years old	28,950	14,559	14,390	22,530	17,839	4,265	1,113	5,176
Percent dropouts	9.3	9.9	8.7	5.3	5.4	12.1	3.8	22.3
Percent high school graduates	84.8	83.7	86.0	85.8	89.9	79.4	91.3	70.2
Percent enrolled in college	39.6	37.0	42.3	40.6	44.3	31.6	58.8	25.9

[1] Includes other races not shown separately. [2] For persons who selected this race group only. See footnote 2, Table 225. [3] Persons of Hispanic origin may be any race. [4] The modal grade is the grade most common for a given age.

Source: U.S. Census Bureau, Current Population Survey, unpublished data, <http://www.census.gov/population/www/socdemo/school.html>.

Table 250. Elementary and Secondary Schools—Teachers, Enrollment, and Pupil-Teacher Ratio: 1970 to 2008

[In thousands (2,292 represents 2,292,000), except ratios. As of fall. Data are for full-time equivalent teachers. Based on surveys of state education agencies and private schools; see source for details]

Year	Teachers			Enrollment			Pupil-teacher ratio		
	Total	Public	Private	Total	Public	Private	Total	Public	Private
1970	2,292	2,059	233	51,257	45,894	5,363	22.4	22.3	20.0
1975	2,453	2,198	255	49,819	44,819	5,000	20.3	20.4	19.6
1980	2,485	2,184	301	46,208	40,877	5,331	18.6	18.7	17.7
1984	2,508	2,168	340	44,908	39,208	5,700	17.9	18.1	16.8
1985	2,549	2,206	343	44,979	39,422	5,557	17.6	17.9	16.2
1986	2,592	2,244	348	45,205	39,753	5,452	17.4	17.7	15.7
1987	2,631	2,279	352	45,487	40,008	5,479	17.3	17.6	15.6
1988	2,668	2,323	345	45,430	40,189	5,242	17.0	17.3	15.2
1989	2,713	2,357	356	45,741	40,543	5,198	17.0	17.2	15.7
1990	2,759	2,398	361	46,451	41,217	5,234	17.0	17.2	15.6
1991	2,797	2,432	365	47,728	42,047	5,681	17.1	17.3	15.6
1992	2,827	2,459	368	48,500	42,823	5,677	17.2	17.4	15.4
1993	2,874	2,504	370	49,133	43,465	5,668	17.1	17.4	15.3
1994 [1]	2,925	2,552	373	49,898	44,111	5,787	17.1	17.3	15.5
1995	2,974	2,598	376	50,759	44,840	5,918	17.1	17.3	15.7
1996 [1]	3,051	2,667	384	51,544	45,611	5,933	16.9	17.1	15.5
1997	3,138	2,746	391	52,071	46,127	5,944	16.6	16.8	15.2
1998 [1]	3,230	2,830	400	52,525	46,539	5,988	16.3	16.4	15.0
1999	3,319	2,911	408	52,876	46,857	6,018	15.9	16.1	14.7
2000 [1]	3,366	2,941	424	53,373	47,204	6,169	15.9	16.0	14.5
2001	3,440	3,000	441	53,992	47,672	6,320	15.7	15.9	14.3
2002 [1]	3,476	3,034	442	54,403	48,183	6,220	15.7	15.9	14.1
2003	3,490	3,049	441	54,639	48,540	6,099	15.7	15.9	13.8
2004 [1]	3,536	3,091	445	54,882	48,795	6,087	15.5	15.8	13.7
2005	3,593	3,143	450	55,187	49,113	6,073	15.4	15.6	13.5
2006 [1]	3,622	3,166	456	55,307	49,316	5,991	15.3	15.6	13.2
2007 [2]	3,634	3,178	456	55,203	49,293	5,910	15.2	15.5	13.0
2008 [2]	3,689	3,233	456	55,500	49,623	5,878	15.0	15.3	12.9

[1] Private school numbers are estimated based on data from the Private School Universe Survey. [2] Projection.

Source: U.S. National Center for Education Statistics, *Digest of Education Statistics*, annual, and *Projections of Educational Statistics*. See also <http://www.nces.ed.gov/annuals>.

U.S. Census Bureau, Statistical Abstract of the United States: 2011

Table 251. Public Elementary and Secondary School Teachers—Selected Characteristics: 2007 to 2008

[For school year (509 represents 509,000). Based on the 2007–2008 Schools and Staffing Survey and subject to sampling error; for details, see source at <http://nces.ed.gov/surveys/sass/>. Excludes prekindergarten teachers. See Table 262 for similar data on private school teachers]

Characteristic	Unit	Age					Sex		Race/ethnicity		
		Under 30 years old	30 to 39 years old	40 to 49 years old	50 to 59 years old	Over 60 years old	Male	Female	White [1]	Black [1]	His-panic
Total teachers [2]	**1,000**	**509**	**661**	**953**	**786**	**93**	**821**	**2,584**	**2,829**	**239**	**240**
Highest degree held:											
Bachelor's	Percent	70.1	46.8	43.7	38.4	35.0	47.0	47.5	46.8	47.0	56.3
Master's	Percent	28.0	46.1	47.3	50.4	51.1	43.9	44.8	45.7	41.4	34.1
Education specialist	Percent	1.5	6.0	7.3	8.7	9.6	5.5	6.7	6.0	8.7	7.7
Doctorate	Percent	0.1	0.4	0.7	1.5	3.2	1.6	0.7	0.8	2.0	1.1
Full-time teaching experience:											
Less than 3 years	Percent	44.1	10.3	7.4	3.4	2.9	13.6	13.4	13.0	13.1	18.0
3 to 9 years	Percent	55.9	53.5	25.1	11.4	8.5	33.2	33.7	32.6	38.0	39.0
10 to 20 years	Percent	(X)	36.3	45.2	29.5	22.4	28.5	29.5	29.7	27.0	28.3
20 years or more	Percent	(X)	(X)	22.3	55.7	66.2	24.7	23.4	24.8	22.0	14.7
Full-time teachers	1,000	568	824	737	(NA)	(NA)	773	2,342	2,571	226	228
Earned income	Dollars	43,560	50,050	54,410	(NA)	(NA)	56,890	52,020	53,230	52,460	53,200
Salary	Dollars	39,820	46,380	50,920	(NA)	(NA)	50,630	49,300	49,630	49,050	49,360

X Not applicable. NA Not available. [1] Non-Hispanic. [2] Includes teachers with no degrees and associate's degrees not shown separately.

U.S. Department of Education, National Center for Education Statistics, Schools and Staffing Survey, "Public Teacher Questionnaire" and "Private Teacher Questionnaire," 2007–08.

Table 252. Public Elementary and Secondary Schools—Number and Average Salary of Classroom Teachers, 1990 to 2008, and by State, 2008

[Estimates for school year ending in June of year shown (2,362 represents 2,362,000). Schools classified by type of organization rather than by grade-group; elementary includes kindergarten]

Year and state	Teachers [1] (1,000)			Avg. salary ($1,000)			Year and state	Teachers			Avg. salary ($1,000)		
	Total	Ele-men-tary	Sec-ond-ary	All teach-ers	Ele-men-tary	Sec-ond-ary		Total	Ele-men-tary	Sec-ond-ary	All teach-ers	Ele-men-tary	Sec-ond-ary
1990	2,362	1390	972	31.4	30.8	32.0	MD	60.2	35.0	25.2	60.1	59.8	60.4
1995	2,565	1,517	1,048	36.7	36.1	37.5	MA	71.2	30.6	40.6	63.8	63.8	63.8
2000	2,891	1,696	1,195	41.8	41.3	42.5	MI	94.1	52.1	42.0	56.1	56.1	56.1
2001	2,947	1,735	1,213	43.4	42.9	44.1	MN	52.9	26.9	26.0	50.6	50.6	50.6
2002	2,992	1,751	1,240	44.7	44.2	45.3	MS	33.5	19.9	13.7	42.4	42.4	42.4
2003	3,020	1,769	1,251	45.7	45.4	46.1	MO	66.6	34.0	32.6	43.2	43.2	43.2
2004	3,042	1,782	1,260	46.5	46.2	47.0	MT	10.5	7.0	3.4	42.9	42.9	42.9
2005	3,072	1,799	1,273	47.5	47.1	47.7	NE	21.7	14.0	7.7	43.6	43.6	43.6
2006	3,125	1,811	1,313	49.1	48.6	49.5	NV	22.9	13.4	9.6	47.7	47.7	47.7
2007	3,172	1,848	1,324	51.1	50.7	51.5	NH	15.4	10.6	4.9	48.3	48.3	48.3
2008, U.S.	**3,201**	**1,860**	**1,341**	**52.8**	**52.4**	**53.3**	NJ	109.9	42.7	67.2	61.3	60.4	63.0
AL	48.0	26.7	21.3	46.6	46.1	47.1	NM	21.7	14.8	6.8	45.1	44.7	46.0
AK	8.6	5.8	2.8	56.8	57.9	56.8	NY	225.1	98.2	126.9	65.5	65.7	65.3
AZ	53.6	38.1	15.6	45.8	44.4	49.0	NC	97.7	69.1	28.6	47.4	47.4	47.4
AR	34.6	16.9	17.7	45.8	45.8	45.8	ND	7.6	5.2	2.4	40.3	40.6	39.6
CA	300.5	211.6	88.9	65.8	65.8	65.8	OH	120.2	80.7	39.5	53.4	53.9	53.2
CO	47.7	24.6	23.2	47.5	47.1	47.9	OK	42.2	27.6	14.6	43.6	43.2	44.3
CT	43.3	29.1	14.2	62.0	62.0	62.0	OR	29.7	19.1	10.5	52.7	52.4	53.2
DE	8.2	4.1	4.1	56.0	55.8	56.2	PA	123.6	60.5	63.1	56.1	56.1	56.1
DC	5.7	3.7	2.0	60.6	60.6	60.6	RI	15.3	9.6	5.7	57.2	57.2	57.2
FL	172.4	88.1	84.3	46.9	46.9	46.9	SC	49.2	34.1	15.1	45.8	43.8	44.7
GA	117.2	70.9	46.2	51.5	51.0	52.3	SD	9.0	6.4	2.6	36.7	36.8	36.4
HI	11.5	6.2	5.3	53.4	53.4	53.4	TN	63.3	44.3	18.9	44.8	44.8	44.8
ID	15.0	7.9	7.1	44.1	44.0	44.2	TX	321.7	164.8	157.0	46.2	45.8	46.6
IL	135.1	92.3	42.8	60.5	57.0	63.8	UT	22.5	12.1	10.4	41.6	41.6	41.6
IN	62.2	33.4	28.8	49.2	49.7	48.6	VT	9.1	4.7	4.4	46.6	46.6	46.6
IA	35.7	23.6	12.2	45.7	45.9	45.3	VA	104.0	60.2	43.8	46.7	46.6	46.8
KS	34.3	16.7	17.6	44.8	44.8	44.8	WA	54.2	29.7	24.5	49.9	49.9	49.9
KY	41.5	29.4	12.1	47.2	47.0	47.6	WV	19.9	14.4	5.5	42.5	42.3	43.2
LA	48.2	33.8	14.5	47.0	47.0	47.0	WI	59.1	40.5	18.6	49.1	49.2	48.8
ME	16.6	11.1	5.4	43.4	43.4	43.4	WY	6.9	3.5	3.4	53.0	52.7	53.2

[1] Full-time equivalent.

Source: National Education Association, Washington, DC, Estimates of School Statistics Database (copyright).

Table 253. Teacher Stayers, Movers, and Leavers by Selected Characteristics: 1988 to 1989 and 2004 to 2005

[2,386.5 represents 2,386,500. Data compare the teaching status of teacher between one school year and the prior year. Stayers are teachers who were teaching in the same school in both years. Movers are teachers who were still teaching in the current school year but in a different school. Leavers are teachers who left the teaching profession. Based on the School and Staffing Survey; see source for details]

Characteristic	Public				Private			
	Total [1]	Stayers	Movers	Leavers	Total [1]	Stayers	Movers	Leavers
NUMBER (1,000)								
1988–89	2,386.5	2,065.8	188.4	132.3	311.9	242.5	29.7	39.7
2004–05	3,214.9	2,684.2	261.1	269.6	465.3	374.6	27.6	63.1
PERCENT DISTRIBUTION								
Total, 2004–05	100.0	83.5	8.1	8.4	100.0	80.5	5.9	13.6
Age:								
Less than 30 years old	100.0	76.3	14.7	9.0	100.0	68.1	11.8	20.1
30 to 39 years old	100.0	84.2	9.0	6.8	100.0	80.6	5.2	14.2
40 to 49 years old	100.0	87.6	7.1	5.3	100.0	84.3	5.0	10.7
50 years old or more	100.0	83.7	4.5	11.8	100.0	84.7	3.8	[2] 11.5
Sex:								
Male	100.0	83.9	8.3	7.7	100.0	80.5	5.2	14.2
Female	100.0	83.4	8.1	8.6	100.0	80.5	6.1	13.4
Race/ethnicity:								
White, non-Hispanic	100.0	83.9	7.9	8.2	100.0	81.3	5.7	13.0
Black, non-Hispanic	100.0	79.3	9.7	11.0	100.0	67.8	9.2	[2] 23.0
Hispanic, single or more than one race	100.0	80.6	10.1	9.3	100.0	70.3	7.6	22.1
Asian, Native Hawaiian, or Other Pacific Islander, non-Hispanic	100.0	81.8	7.9	[2] 10.3	100.0	89.7	2.7	7.6
American Indian/Alaska Native, non-Hispanic	100.0	93.1	5.0	1.9	100.0	65.5	[2] 18.5	[2] 16.0
More than one race, non-Hispanic	100.0	88.1	6.6	[2] 5.3	100.0	65.8	[2] 13.4	[2] 20.8
Full-time teaching experience:								
No full-time teaching experience	100.0	63.3	17.1	19.6	100.0	73.6	4.0	22.3
1 to 3 years experience	100.0	77.1	14.8	8.1	100.0	71.0	10.1	18.9
4 to 9 years experience	100.0	82.7	9.4	7.9	100.0	77.2	6.7	16.1
10 to 19 years experience	100.0	88.2	6.3	5.5	100.0	88.3	3.8	7.8
20 years or more experience	100.0	84.9	3.9	11.2	100.0	89.7	3.3	7.0
Main assignment field:								
Early childhood/general elementary	100.0	84.5	7.4	8.1	100.0	81.1	6.8	12.2
Special education	100.0	78.9	11.1	10.0	100.0	72.2	[2] 7.4	20.4
Arts/music	100.0	84.7	9.3	6.0	100.0	77.6	4.4	18.0
English/language arts	100.0	83.2	9.0	7.8	100.0	81.1	5.6	13.3
Mathematics	100.0	84.6	8.6	6.8	100.0	83.8	5.4	10.7
Natural sciences	100.0	88.5	5.6	5.9	100.0	84.0	5.9	10.1
Social sciences	100.0	85.6	6.0	8.4	100.0	81.8	4.8	13.4
Other	100.0	81.3	8.0	10.7	100.0	79.2	5.3	15.5

[1] Total teachers prior school year. [2] Interpret data with caution. The standard error for this estimate is equal to 50 percent.

Source: U.S. National Center for Education Statistics, *Teacher Attrition and Mobility: Results for the 2004–05 Teacher Follow-up Survey*, NCES 2007-307, January 2007.

Table 254. Public and Private School Teachers Who Moved to a Different School or Left Teaching by Reason: 2004 to 2005

[In percent. Movers are teachers who were still teaching in the current year but had moved to a different school after the 2003–04 school year. Leavers are teachers who left the teaching profession after the 2003–04 school year. Based on the School and Staffing Survey; see source for details]

Reason for moving	Movers		Reason for leaving	Leavers	
	Public	Private		Public	Private
New school is closer to home	26.2	22.8	Changed residence	11.2	17.4
Better safety and benefits	16.5	46.4	Pregnancy or child rearing	18.7	24.6
Higher job security	19.1	33.4	Health	11.8	13.2
Opportunity for a better teaching assignment	38.1	33.1	Retirement	31.4	10.2
Dissatisfaction with workplace conditions at previous school	32.7	21.4	School staffing action [1]	14.6	17.7
Dissatisfaction with support from administrators at previous school	37.2	27.0	Better salary or benefits	14.2	21.8
Dissatisfaction with changes in job description or responsibilities	18.3	17.5	To pursue a position other than that of a K–12 teacher	25.3	29.5
Laid off or involuntarily transferred	18.7	19.2	To take courses to improve career opportunities within the field of education	8.9	9.8
Did not have enough autonomy over classroom at previous school	10.4	7.6	To take courses to improve career opportunities outside the field of education	5.3	7.3
Dissatisfaction with opportunities for professional development at previous school	12.8	19.7	Dissatisfied with teaching as a career	14.6	10.8
Other dissatisfaction with previous school	31.2	29.7	Dissatisfied with previous school or teaching assignment	16.0	18.1
			Other family or personal reasons	20.4	30.6

[1] For example reduction in force, lay-off, school closing, school reorganization, reassignment.

Source: U.S. National Center for Education Statistics, *Teacher Attrition and Mobility: Results for the 2004–05 Teacher Follow-up Survey*, NCES 2007-307, January 2007.

Table 255. Average Salary and Wages Paid in Public School Systems: 1985 to 2009

[In dollars. For school year ending in year shown. Data reported by a stratified sample of school systems enrolling 300 or more pupils. Data represent unweighted means of average salaries paid school personnel reported by each school system]

Position	1985	1990	1995	2000	2005	2006	2007	2008	2009
ANNUAL SALARY									
Central-office administrators:									
Superintendent (contract salary)....	56,954	75,425	90,198	112,158	128,770	134,436	141,191	148,387	155,634
Deputy/assoc. superintendent......	52,877	69,623	81,266	97,251	116,186	122,078	128,307	134,245	136,832
Assistant superintendent..........	48,003	62,698	75,236	88,913	103,212	106,492	111,963	116,833	119,755
Administrators for—..............									
Finance and business...........	40,344	52,354	61,323	73,499	83,678	86,390	91,718	96,490	98,590
Instructional services..........	43,452	56,359	66,767	79,023	88,950	91,094	95,025	99,748	102,322
Public relations/information.......	35,287	44,926	53,263	60,655	70,502	72,378	77,121	80,534	83,235
Staff personnel services.........	44,182	56,344	65,819	76,608	86,966	90,097	94,761	98,190	100,620
Technology...................	(X)	(X)	(X)	(X)	76,308	78,249	81,809	86,085	87,898
Subject area supervisors.........	34,422	45,929	54,534	63,103	68,714	71,984	75,982	78,309	80,290
School building administrators:									
Principals:									
Elementary	36,452	48,431	58,589	69,407	76,182	79,496	82,414	85,907	88,062
Junior high/middle.............	39,650	52,163	02,311	73,877	81,514	84,685	87,866	91,334	93,478
Senior high	42,094	55,722	66,596	79,839	86,938	90,260	92,965	97,486	99,365
Assistant principals:									
Elementary	30,496	40,916	48,491	56,419	63,140	65,770	67,735	71,192	71,893
Junior high/middle.............	33,793	44,570	52,942	60,842	67,600	70,268	73,020	76,053	77,476
Senior high	35,491	46,486	55,556	64,811	71,401	73,622	75,121	79,391	81,083
Classroom teachers............	23,587	31,278	37,264	42,213	45,884	48,160	49,294	51,329	52,900
Auxiliary professional personnel:									
Counselors	27,593	35,979	42,486	48,195	52,500	53,744	55,930	57,618	58,775
Librarians....................	24,981	33,469	40,418	46,732	50,720	53,331	54,881	56,933	57,974
School nurses	19,944	26,090	31,066	35,540	40,520	41,746	43,277	46,025	46,476
Secretarial/clerical personnel:									
Central office:									
Secretaries	15,343	20,238	23,935	28,405	32,716	34,132	35,629	36,657	37,785
Accounting/payroll clerks........	15,421	20,088	24,042	28,498	33,217	34,812	35,991	37,732	39,031
Typists/data entry clerks	12,481	16,125	18,674	22,853	26,214	26,899	28,940	30,072	31,718
School building level:									
Secretaries	12,504	16,184	19,170	22,630	25,381	26,396	27,398	28,810	29,480
Library clerks................	9,911	12,152	14,381	16,509	18,443	19,125	19,806	21,004	21,190
HOURLY WAGE RATE									
Other support personnel:									
Teacher aides:									
Instructional.................	5.89	7.43	8.77	10.00	11.35	11.77	12.32	12.86	13.23
Noninstructional..............	5.60	7.08	8.29	9.77	11.23	11.75	12.19	12.70	13.13
Custodians...................	6.90	8.54	10.05	11.35	12.61	13.20	13.78	14.19	14.59
Cafeteria workers	5.42	6.77	7.89	9.02	10.33	10.70	11.16	11.60	11.94
Bus drivers..................	7.27	9.21	10.69	12.48	14.18	14.81	15.48	16.56	16.44

X Not applicable.

Source: Educational Research Service, Arlington, VA, *National Survey of Salaries and Wages in Public Schools*, annual (copyright).

Table 256. Public School Employment: 1990 and 2008

[In thousands (3,181 represents 3,181,000). Covers all public elementary-secondary school districts with 100 or more full-time employees]

Occupation	1990					2008				
	Total	Male	Female	White [1]	Black [1]	Total	Male	Female	White [1]	Black [1]
All occupations [2]...............	**3,181**	**914**	**2,267**	**2,502**	**463**	**4,772**	**1,213**	**3,559**	**3,562**	**617**
Officials, administrators............	43	28	15	37	4	76	36	41	60	8
Principals and assistant principals	90	56	34	70	13	190	86	104	125	35
Classroom teachers [3]	1,746	468	1,278	1,469	192	2,544	613	1,930	2,055	240
Elementary schools...............	875	128	747	722	103	1,218	152	1,066	978	107
Secondary schools...............	662	304	358	570	66	1,007	394	614	828	92
Other professional staff	227	58	170	187	30	386	71	315	298	49
Teachers' aides [4]	324	54	270	208	69	555	72	483	372	96
Clerical, secretarial staff	226	5	221	181	24	323	11	312	230	37
Service workers [5].................	524	245	279	348	129	761	352	409	454	164

[1] Excludes individuals of Hispanic origin. [2] 2008 Includes other occupations not shown separately. [3] Includes other classroom teachers not shown separately. [4] Includes technicians. [5] Includes craftworkers and laborers.

Source: U.S. Equal Employment Opportunity Commission, *Elementary-Secondary Staff Information (EEO-5)*, biennial.

Table 257. Public Elementary and Secondary School Finances by Enrollment-Size Group: 2007 to 2008

[In millions of dollars (582,126 represents $582,126,000,000). Data are based on the Annual Government Finance Survey. For details, see source. See also Appendix III]

Item	All school systems	School systems with enrollment of— 50,000 or more	25,000 to 49,999	15,000 to 24,999	7,500 to 14,999	5,000 to 7,499	3,000 to 4,999	Under 3,000
TOTAL AMOUNT								
General revenue	582,126	125,933	72,128	53,295	82,864	51,402	68,609	127,893
From federal sources	47,071	11,554	6,055	4,110	6,397	3,252	4,584	11,120
Through state	43,359	10,939	5,687	3,895	5,819	2,974	4,249	9,798
Child nutrition programs	9,916	2,475	1,426	1,023	1,377	762	1,018	1,836
Direct	3,712	615	368	215	579	278	335	1,322
From state sources [1]	280,927	58,744	36,581	28,658	40,949	23,250	30,848	61,897
General formula assistance	188,068	35,582	24,995	19,845	28,094	15,851	20,812	42,889
Compensatory programs	6,914	1,443	1,322	894	1,220	618	578	839
Special education	16,341	3,983	1,742	1,294	2,059	1,339	1,953	3,971
From local sources	254,128	55,635	29,492	20,528	35,518	24,900	33,177	54,876
Taxes	169,097	28,438	20,421	14,169	25,211	17,883	23,844	39,131
Contributions from parent government	43,824	19,415	3,908	2,746	4,718	3,504	4,594	4,939
From other local governments	5,492	517	656	334	497	518	775	2,195
Current charges	14,819	2,654	1,709	1,341	2,118	1,294	1,776	3,927
School lunch	7,014	1,072	840	703	1,104	706	947	1,641
Other	20,896	4,612	2,798	1,938	2,974	1,701	2,189	4,684
General expenditure	593,175	130,823	74,302	54,849	83,957	52,600	68,096	128,549
Current spending	506,771	109,697	61,519	46,362	71,828	44,994	59,292	113,080
By function:								
Instruction	304,751	68,096	36,793	27,913	43,340	27,366	35,782	65,461
Support services	175,909	35,926	21,429	15,908	24,821	15,469	20,618	41,737
Other current spending	26,112	5,675	3,297	2,542	3,667	2,158	2,892	5,882
By object:								
Total salaries and wages	301,658	65,322	37,946	28,491	43,442	26,968	35,178	64,311
Total employee benefits	103,221	22,113	11,847	9,545	15,010	9,506	12,537	22,663
Other	101,893	22,262	11,726	8,327	13,376	8,520	11,576	26,106
Capital outlay	68,653	17,105	10,390	6,897	9,556	5,930	6,799	11,976
Interest on debt	16,044	3,743	2,319	1,560	2,364	1,464	1,815	2,778
Payments to other governments	1,707	277	75	30	209	212	190	715
Debt outstanding	377,419	84,737	52,402	37,288	55,397	34,992	44,650	67,953
Long-term	369,433	83,857	51,545	36,700	54,031	34,212	43,607	65,481
Short-term	7,986	880	857	588	1,366	780	1,043	2,472
Long-term debt issued	50,058	13,408	6,303	4,707	7,582	4,146	5,387	8,526
Long-term debt retired	31,216	8,132	4,361	2,580	3,985	2,603	3,750	5,804
PER PUPIL AMOUNTS								
Fall enrollment (1,000)	48,396	10,182	6,514	4,908	7,204	4,278	5,622	9,688
General revenue	12,028	12,368	11,073	10,859	11,503	12,016	12,204	13,201
From federal sources	973	1,135	930	837	888	760	815	1,148
From state sources [1]	5,805	5,769	5,616	5,839	5,684	5,435	5,487	6,389
General formula assistance	3,886	3,495	3,837	4,043	3,900	3,705	3,702	4,427
Special education	338	391	267	264	286	313	347	410
From local sources [1]	5,251	5,464	4,527	4,183	4,930	5,821	5,901	5,664
Taxes	3,494	2,793	3,135	2,887	3,500	4,180	4,241	4,039
Contributions from parent government	906	1,907	600	559	655	819	817	510
Current charges	306	261	262	273	294	303	316	405
School lunch	145	105	129	143	153	165	168	169
General expenditure [1]	12,044	12,583	11,219	11,003	11,471	12,086	11,906	13,049
Current spending	10,259	10,508	9,256	9,274	9,787	10,308	10,340	11,452
By function:								
Instruction	6,211	6,566	5,577	5,637	5,947	6,297	6,268	6,682
Support services	3,635	3,528	3,290	3,241	3,446	3,616	3,667	4,308
By object:								
Total salaries and wages	6,233	6,415	5,825	5,805	6,030	6,304	6,257	6,638
Total employee benefits	2,133	2,172	1,819	1,945	2,084	2,222	2,230	2,339
Capital outlay	1,419	1,680	1,595	1,405	1,327	1,386	1,209	1,236
Interest on debt	332	368	356	318	328	342	323	287
Debt outstanding	7,799	8,322	8,044	7,597	7,690	8,180	7,942	7,014
Long-term	7,634	8,236	7,913	7,478	7,500	7,997	7,756	6,759

[1] Includes other sources not shown separately.

Source: U.S. Census Bureau, *Public Education Finances, 2008*, June 2010, <http://www.census.gov/govs/school>.

Table 258. Public Elementary and Secondary Estimated Finances: 1980 to 2008, and by State, 2008

[In millions of dollars (101,724 represents $101,724,000,000), except as noted. For school years ending in June of year shown]

	Receipts						Expenditures				
	Revenue receipts							Current expenditures			
		Source								Average per pupil in ADA [4]	
Year and state	Total	Total	Federal	State	Local	Non-revenue receipts [1]	Total [2]	Per capita [3] (dol.)	Elementary and secondary day schools	Amount (dol.)	Rank
1980	101,724	97,635	9,020	47,929	40,686	4,089	96,105	428	85,661	2,230	(X)
1985	146,976	141,013	9,533	69,107	62,373	5,963	139,382	591	127,230	3,483	(X)
1990	218,126	208,656	13,184	100,787	94,685	9,469	209,698	850	186,583	4,966	(X)
1995	288,501	273,255	18,764	129,958	124,533	15,246	276,584	1,051	242,995	5,957	(X)
2000	390,861	369,754	26,346	183,986	159,421	21,106	374,782	1,343	320,954	7,410	(X)
2004	488,959	455,013	40,629	215,480	198,904	33,946	469,623	1,618	400,931	8,930	(X)
2005	519,291	477,371	42,908	225,142	209,321	41,921	496,199	1,693	422,346	9,367	(X)
2006	550,345	506,245	46,052	237,234	222,960	44,100	521,554	1,763	443,382	9,743	(X)
2007	582,604	533,029	46,021	253,686	233,321	49,575	549,002	1,839	465,801	10,196	(X)
2008, total	**600,077**	**558,877**	**47,615**	**270,614**	**240,649**	**41,199**	**575,727**	**1,909**	**485,647**	**10,589**	**(X)**
Alabama	7,958	7,650	731	4,659	2,260	308	7,819	1,686	6,796	9,569	37
Alaska	1,536	1,366	171	868	327	170	1,508	2,211	1,403	12,045	13
Arizona	8,891	8,882	697	4,628	3,557	9	7,458	1,172	6,139	6,139	50
Arkansas	4,872	4,595	527	2,568	1,500	278	4,845	1,705	4,373	11,417	18
California	84,194	74,256	6,609	46,834	20,812	9,938	69,217	1,911	53,887	8,883	43
Colorado	8,941	7,790	608	3,331	3,851	1,151	9,023	1,863	7,493	10,066	30
Connecticut	8,644	8,630	565	3,298	4,767	14	8,634	2,475	7,723	13,744	8
Delaware	1,947	1,746	143	1,099	504	201	1,928	2,230	1,564	13,407	9
District of Columbia	898	898	114	–	785	–	1,259	2,148	996	19,077	(X)
Florida	31,499	29,491	2,548	11,390	15,553	2,008	31,589	1,728	24,086	9,619	35
Georgia	19,631	18,775	1,646	8,226	8,903	856	18,119	1,900	15,776	10,240	26
Hawaii	2,542	2,542	311	2,154	77	–	2,343	1,835	2,123	12,774	10
Idaho	2,378	2,171	208	1,440	523	206	2,446	1,632	2,050	8,033	46
Illinois	25,416	22,362	1,949	6,023	14,390	3,054	24,986	1,955	23,129	11,940	15
Indiana	11,045	10,444	865	5,508	4,071	601	11,801	1,859	9,868	10,174	28
Iowa	5,410	5,108	339	2,479	2,289	302	5,179	1,739	4,328	9,837	33
Kansas	5,811	5,378	344	3,139	1,895	433	5,538	1,995	4,524	10,995	23
Kentucky	6,691	6,680	711	3,907	2,062	11	6,619	1,555	6,024	10,121	29
Louisiana	9,149	7,859	1,318	3,523	3,018	1,290	8,029	1,835	6,822	10,809	24
Maine	2,706	2,539	265	993	1,281	167	2,706	2,054	2,478	13,762	7
Maryland	11,453	11,382	761	4,469	6,152	71	10,876	1,930	9,537	12,014	14
Massachusetts	14,687	14,686	753	6,180	7,753	1	14,217	2,187	13,188	14,547	6
Michigan	20,286	19,947	1,618	11,314	7,015	339	19,748	1,965	18,272	11,615	16
Minnesota	11,063	9,759	769	7,293	1,697	1,304	11,020	2,123	8,700	11,227	20
Mississippi	4,231	4,123	652	2,209	1,262	108	3,929	1,345	3,554	7,492	47
Missouri	10,811	9,622	933	3,077	5,612	1,190	8,834	1,495	7,625	9,179	39
Montana	1,437	1,411	175	674	562	26	1,340	1,400	1,290	10,621	25
Nebraska	2,785	2,748	216	1,059	1,473	37	2,898	1,637	2,537	9,617	36
Nevada	4,969	3,242	248	1,055	1,939	1,728	4,133	1,610	3,150	7,342	48
New Hampshire	2,569	2,546	137	987	1,423	22	2,528	1,919	2,338	12,593	11
New Jersey	22,181	22,179	727	8,017	13,435	1	22,147	2,565	21,427	15,432	3
New Mexico	3,941	3,631	500	2,559	571	311	3,787	1,924	3,150	9,968	32
New York	44,825	44,644	3,413	20,285	20,947	180	46,710	2,405	41,643	15,932	2
North Carolina	13,387	12,226	1,242	7,962	3,022	1,161	13,799	1,522	12,225	9,161	40
North Dakota	1,099	1,042	130	379	532	58	1,007	1,578	823	9,351	38
Ohio	18,459	18,459	1,510	8,039	8,910	–	19,684	1,709	16,818	10,212	27
Oklahoma	5,887	5,482	646	2,974	1,862	405	5,452	1,509	4,976	8,343	44
Oregon	6,427	6,156	554	3,198	2,403	272	6,353	1,702	5,493	11,041	22
Pennsylvania	25,516	25,316	1,780	9,210	14,326	200	24,920	1,990	21,007	12,431	12
Rhode Island	2,266	2,266	170	908	1,187	–	2,510	2,379	2,339	14,993	5
South Carolina	8,352	7,787	716	3,950	3,122	564	8,092	1,829	6,443	9,801	34
South Dakota	1,298	1,208	186	410	613	90	1,168	1,465	1,038	9,051	41
Tennessee	8,113	7,801	883	3,563	3,355	312	7,737	1,253	7,227	8,036	45
Texas	54,312	45,680	4,605	20,549	20,526	8,632	51,159	2,146	39,166	8,986	42
Utah	4,240	3,601	413	1,898	1,291	638	3,508	1,317	2,792	6,278	49
Vermont	1,493	1,471	115	1,274	82	22	1,446	2,330	1,301	17,258	1
Virginia	15,755	14,880	939	6,019	7,922	875	15,792	2,046	12,942	11,369	19
Washington	11,946	11,180	979	7,066	3,135	767	13,890	2,149	9,600	9,980	31
West Virginia	3,465	3,152	403	1,878	870	314	3,446	1,903	2,933	11,135	21
Wisconsin	11,057	10,485	670	5,245	4,571	572	11,030	1,969	9,334	11,568	17
Wyoming	1,604	1,603	102	846	655	1	1,518	2,900	1,198	15,015	4

– Represents or rounds to zero. X Not applicable. [1] Amount received by local education agencies from the sales of bonds and real property and equipment, loans, and proceeds from insurance adjustments. [2] Includes interest on school debt and other current expenditures not shown separately. [3] Based on U.S. Census Bureau estimated resident population, as of July 1, the previous year, except 1990, and 2000 population enumerated as of April 1. [4] Average daily attendance.
Source: National Education Association, Washington, DC, Estimates of School Statistics Database (copyright).

U.S. Census Bureau, Statistical Abstract of the United States: 2011

Table 259. Computers for Student Instruction in Elementary and Secondary Schools: 2005 to 2006

[54,848 represents 54,848,000. Market Data Retrieval collects student use computer information in elementary and secondary schools nationwide through a comprehensive annual technology survey that utilizes mail, telephone, and Internet data methods]

Level	Total schools	Total enroll- ment (1,000)	Number of com- puters [1] (1,000)	Students per com- puter	Schools with a wireless network (percent)	Schools with distance learning programs for students [2] (percent)	Schools with laptop comput- ers [3] (percent)	Schools with com- puters with high speed Internet access [4] (percent)	Schools with video- stream- ing (percent)
U.S. total	**114,749**	**54,848**	**14,165**	**3.9**	**54.2**	**19.1**	**59.7**	**84.3**	**43.4**
Public schools, total	91,977	49,567	12,914	3.8	54.4	20.3	60.0	85.7	45.0
Elementary	53,245	23,805	5,612	4.2	49.1	11.2	55.4	85.0	41.3
Middle/junior high	14,310	9,376	2,503	3.7	61.6	15.6	66.2	85.8	53.2
Senior high	17,282	14,028	4,067	3.4	64.0	43.8	67.9	87.5	50.4
K to 12/other	7,140	2,358	733	3.2	54.7	43.2	61.7	85.9	41.0
Catholic schools, total	7,673	2,481	554	4.5	51.0	7.1	60.3	74.0	29.7
Elementary	6,326	1,797	358	5.0	46.5	3.8	57.9	71.6	27.3
Secondary	1,179	621	179	3.5	67.7	20.8	70.0	83.8	38.8
K to 12/other	168	63	17	3.8	73.1	7.7	65.4	73.1	38.5
Other private schools, total	15,099	2,800	697	4.0	52.1	6.5	50.1	66.4	24.1
Elementary	7,426	1,171	283	4.1	52.9	2.0	51.4	67.6	26.5
Secondary	1,274	265	77	3.4	67.5	18.1	54.2	68.7	24.1
K to 12/other	6,399	1,363	338	4.0	47.1	9.5	47.4	64.2	20.8

[1] Includes estimates for schools not reporting number of computers. [2] Distance learning programs as determined by respondents. [3] For student instruction. [4] Statistics based on responses to those indicating type of Internet connection. High speed includes Internet connection types: T1, T3, and cable modem.

Source: Market Data Retrieval, Shelton, CT, unpublished data (copyright).

Table 260. Public School Districts Offering Various Technology Resources to All or Some Elementary School or Secondary School Students by District Characteristics: 2008

[In percent. As of Fall. Percents are based on the percent of public school districts with students at that level (97 percent of districts have elementary students and 88 percent have secondary students). For composition of regions, see map, inside front cover]

Characteristic	Electronic storage space on a server				Online access to the library catalogue				Online curriculum			
	Elementary		Secondary		Elementary		Secondary		Elementary		Secondary	
	All	Some	All	Some	All	Some	All	Some	All	Some	All	Some
All public school districts	62	17	83	7	72	6	82	2	47	19	53	25
District enrollment size:												
Less than 2,500	63	15	85	3	69	5	80	[1] 1	46	17	53	23
2,500 to 9,999	59	22	78	14	79	7	87	3	50	23	54	28
10,000 or more	58	23	74	17	84	7	87	6	49	26	51	34
Community type:												
City	52	32	75	16	80	14	89	5	47	28	46	36
Suburban	67	15	84	7	76	7	87	2	40	23	46	30
Town	63	18	84	7	82	4	88	2	44	26	51	31
Rural	60	16	83	6	66	5	77	1	52	14	57	20
Region:												
Northeast	73	16	90	4	78	8	88	3	41	22	42	36
Southeast	43	20	64	18	74	4	82	3	52	16	59	20
Central	67	14	91	2	71	4	82	(S)	45	20	56	21
West	53	22	75	10	69	6	77	2	55	17	54	23
Poverty concentration:												
Less than 10 percent	76	12	92	3	82	6	92	[1] 1	45	22	51	30
10 to 19 percent	60	19	85	7	69	5	82	2	44	20	51	28
20 percent or more	50	21	72	10	66	6	72	2	54	14	56	18

S Reporting standards not met. [1] Interpret data with caution; the coefficient of variation is greater than 50 percent.

Source: U.S. National Center for Education Statistics, Educational Technology in Public School Districts: Fall 2008, NCES 2010-003, December 2009.

U.S. Census Bureau, Statistical Abstract of the United States: 2011

Table 261. Private Schools: 2007 to 2008

[4,997 represents 4,997,000. Based on the Private School Survey, conducted every 2 years; see source for details. For composition of regions, see map, inside front cover]

Characteristic	Schools				Students (1,000)				Teachers (1,000) [1]			
	Number	Elementary	Secondary	Combined	Total	Elementary	Secondary	Combined	Total	Elementary	Secondary	Combined
Total	**28,218**	**16,348**	**2,932**	**8,938**	**4,997**	**2,438**	**827**	**1,732**	**442**	**193**	**69**	**180**
School type:												
Catholic	7,401	5,966	1,093	342	2,154	1,452	595	107	146	94	42	9
Parochial	3,363	3,126	161	76	873	786	63	24	56	50	5	2
Diocesan	3,064	2,470	501	93	905	598	281	26	61	39	19	2
Private	973	370	431	172	377	68	252	57	30	6	18	5
Other religious	13,955	7,166	836	5,952	1,909	695	128	1,087	180	64	13	103
Conservative Christian	4,907	1,692	176	3,040	770	196	26	548	68	17	2	49
Affiliated	2,539	1,602	238	699	449	202	43	204	45	20	5	20
Unaffiliated	6,508	3,873	422	2,213	690	298	58	334	67	27	6	34
Nonsectarian	6,863	3,216	1,003	2,645	934	291	104	539	116	35	14	67
Regular	2,879	1,447	377	1,055	632	168	68	396	73	19	9	46
Special emphasis	2,457	1,545	371	541	195	109	23	63	24	14	3	7
Special education	1,527	224	254	1,049	106	13	13	80	19	2	2	14
Program emphasis:												
Regular elem/sec	22,905	14,040	2,151	6,714	4,589	2,282	775	1,532	388	173	63	152
Montessori	1,345	1,179	(B)	160	87	72	(B)	14	11	9	(B)	1
Special program emphasis	863	476	99	288	119	51	14	54	14	6	2	6
Special education	1,738	271	272	1,196	117	15	14	88	21	3	2	16
Vocational/tech	(B)	(B)	(B)	(B)	(B)	(B)	(B)	(B)	(B)	(B)	(B)	(B)
Alternative	1,210	256	401	554	76	11	23	42	8	1	2	5
Early childhood	152	126	(X)	(B)	7	6	(X)	(B)	1	(Z)	(B)	(B)
Size:												
Less than 50	8,944	5,048	842	3,053	228	131	19	78	35	17	4	14
50 to 149	8,421	5,053	655	2,714	777	477	62	238	88	49	8	31
150 to 299	5,964	4,087	458	1,420	1,269	863	100	306	105	64	10	31
300 to 499	2,800	1,629	383	788	1,078	626	149	303	85	42	13	29
500 to 749	1,237	456	289	491	746	269	177	300	58	16	13	28
750 or more	853	75	304	473	900	72	320	508	71	5	21	46
Region:												
Northeast	6,531	3,776	965	1,790	1,202	594	277	332	115	48	25	42
Midwest	7,070	4,979	649	1,442	1,176	731	223	222	92	53	17	22
South	8,902	4,247	643	4,012	1,653	613	165	875	156	54	14	88
West	5,716	3,346	675	1,695	966	501	162	304	80	38	13	29

B Does not meet standard of reliability or precision. X Not applicable. Z Less than 500. [1] Full-time equivalents.
Source: U.S. National Center for Education Statistics, "Private School Universe Survey, 2007–2008," <http://nces.ed.gov/surveys/pss/>.

Table 262. Private Elementary and Secondary School Teachers—Selected Characteristics: 2004 to 2005

[For school year (63 represents 63,000). Based on the 2004–2005 Teacher Follow–up Survey, a component of the School and Staffing Survey, and subject to sampling error; for details, see source. Excludes prekindergarten teachers. See Table 251 for similar data on public school teachers]

Characteristic	Unit	Age				Sex		Race/ethnicity		
		Under 30 years old	30 to 39 years old	40 to 49 years old	50 years old and over	Male	Female	White [1]	Black [1]	Hispanic [2]
Total teachers [3]	**1,000**	**63**	**91**	**100**	**148**	**90**	**312**	**359**	**13**	**13**
Highest degree held:										
Bachelor's	Percent	78.2	64.4	58.2	49.1	4.4	8.1	58.4	66.4	78.3
Master's	Percent	13.6	22.1	29.2	38.0	55.5	60.5	30.2	13.6	12.6
Education specialist	Percent	(X)	1.1	2.4	4.0	33.3	27.0	2.3	3.7	–
Doctorate	Percent	(X)	2.1	3.1	3.7	1.3	2.6	2.2	–	3.3
Full–time teaching experience:										
Less than 3 years	Percent	24.3	6.7	4.0	1.5	9.6	6.1	6.4	10.4	8.9
3 to 9 years	Percent	75.7	60.4	33.3	12.5	35.4	39.3	38.2	51.2	32.6
10 to 20 years	Percent	(X)	32.8	43.6	25.8	23.4	29.1	28.3	8.1	36.0
20 years or more	Percent	(X)	(X)	19.1	60.2	31.7	25.6	27.1	30.3	22.5
Full–time teachers	1,000	55	73	74	125	68	259	292	12	9
Earned income	Dol	30,455	33,200	36,413	40,448	42,618	34,577	36,212	29,414	44,844
Salary	Dol	29,489	32,335	35,325	39,391	40,981	33,737	35,164	28,919	43,414

– Represents or rounds to zero. X Not applicable. [1] Non-Hispanic. [2] Persons of Hispanic origin may be any race. [3] Includes teachers with no degrees and associate's degrees, not shown separately.
Source: U.S. National Center for Education Statistics, "Teacher Follow-up Survey, 2004–05," unpublished data.

Table 263. SAT Scores and Characteristics of College-Bound Seniors: 1970 to 2009

[For school year ending in year shown. Data are for the SAT I: Reasoning Tests. SAT I: Reasoning Test replaced the SAT in March 1994. Scores between the two tests have been equated to the same 200–800 scale and are thus comparable. Scores for 1995 and prior years have been recentered and revised]

Type of test and characteristic	Unit	1970	1980	1990	1995	2000	2005	2006	2007	2008	2009
AVERAGE TEST SCORES [1]											
Critical reading, total [2]	Point.....	537	502	500	504	505	508	503	502	502	501
Male	Point.....	536	506	505	505	507	513	505	504	504	503
Female	Point.....	538	498	496	502	504	505	502	502	500	498
Math, total [2]	Point.....	512	492	501	506	514	520	518	515	515	515
Male	Point.....	531	515	521	525	533	538	536	533	533	534
Female	Point.....	493	473	483	490	498	504	502	499	500	499
Writing	Point.....	(X)	(X)	(X)	(X)	(X)	(X)	497	494	494	493
Male	Point.....	(X)	(X)	(X)	(X)	(X)	(X)	491	489	488	486
Female	Point.....	(X)	(X)	(X)	(X)	(X)	(X)	502	500	501	499
PARTICIPANTS											
Total [3]	1,000....	(NA)	922	1,026	1,068	1,260	1,476	1,466	1,495	1,519	1,530
Male	Percent ..	(NA)	48.2	47.8	46.4	46.2	46.5	46.4	46.4	46.4	46.5
White	Percent ..	(NA)	82.1	73.0	69.2	66.4	62.3	62.1	60.8	59.8	58.1
Black	Percent ..	(NA)	9.1	10.0	10.7	11.2	11.6	11.3	11.7	12.1	12.8
Obtaining scores [1] of—											
600 or above:											
Critical reading	Percent ..	(NA)	(NA)	20.3	21.9	21.1	22.5	21.4	21.2	21.0	20.5
Math	Percent ..	(NA)	(NA)	20.4	23.4	24.2	26.5	25.8	24.5	25.0	25.7
Writing	Percent ..	(X)	(X)	(X)	(X)	(X)	(X)	18.9	18.4	18.3	18.7
Below 400:											
Critical reading	Percent ..	(NA)	(NA)	17.3	16.4	15.9	15.5	16.6	16.5	17.0	17.4
Math	Percent ..	(NA)	(NA)	15.8	16.0	14.7	13.8	14.3	14.8	15.0	15.3
Writing	Percent ..	(X)	(X)	(X)	(X)	(X)	(X)	17.8	18.4	18.5	19.4

NA Not available. X Not applicable. [1] Minimum score, 200; maximum score, 800. [2] 1970 estimates based on total number of persons taking SAT. For 2009, based on 1,530,128 test takers. [3] 922 represents 922,000.

Source: The College Board, *College-Bound Seniors 2009* (copyright 1967 to 2009), <http://www.collegeboard.com>. Reproduced with permission.

Table 264. ACT Program Scores and Characteristics of College Bound Students: 1970 to 2009

[For academic year ending in year shown. Except as indicated, test scores and characteristics of college-bound students. Through 1980, data based on 10 percent sample; thereafter, based on all ACT tested graduating seniors]

Type of test and characteristic	Unit	1970	1980	1990 [1]	1995 [1]	2000 [1]	2005 [1]	2006 [1]	2007 [1]	2008 [1]	2009 [1]
TEST SCORES [2]											
Composite	Point......	19.9	18.5	20.6	20.8	21.0	20.9	21.1	21.2	21.1	21.1
Male	Point......	20.3	19.3	21.0	21.0	21.2	21.1	21.2	21.2	21.2	21.3
Female	Point......	19.4	17.9	20.3	20.7	20.9	20.9	21.0	21.0	21.0	20.9
English	Point......	18.5	17.9	20.5	20.2	20.5	20.4	20.6	20.7	20.6	20.6
Male	Point......	17.6	17.3	20.1	19.8	20.0	20.0	20.1	20.2	20.1	20.2
Female	Point......	19.4	18.3	20.9	20.6	20.9	20.8	21.0	21.0	21.0	20.9
Math	Point......	20.0	17.4	19.9	20.2	20.7	20.7	20.8	21.0	21.0	21.0
Male	Point......	21.1	18.9	20.7	20.9	21.4	21.3	21.5	21.6	21.6	21.6
Female	Point......	18.8	16.2	19.3	19.7	20.2	20.2	20.3	20.4	20.4	20.4
Reading [3]	Point......	19.7	17.2	(NA)	21.3	21.4	21.3	21.4	21.5	21.4	21.4
Male	Point......	20.3	18.2	(NA)	21.1	21.2	21.0	21.1	21.2	21.2	21.3
Female	Point......	19.0	16.4	(NA)	21.4	21.5	21.5	21.6	21.6	21.5	21.4
Science reasoning [4]	Point......	20.8	21.1	(NA)	21.0	21.0	20.9	20.9	21.0	20.8	20.9
Male	Point......	21.6	22.4	(NA)	21.6	21.6	21.4	21.2	21.4	21.3	21.4
Female	Point......	20.0	20.0	(NA)	20.5	20.6	20.5	21.0	20.5	20.4	20.4
PARTICIPANTS [5]											
Total [6]	1,000.....	788	822	817	945	1,065	1,186	1,206	1,301	1,422	1,480
Male	Percent ...	52	45	46	44	43	44	44	45	45	45
White	Percent ...	(NA)	83	73	69	72	66	63	60	63	64
Black	Percent ...	4	8	9	9	10	12	12	12	13	13
Obtaining composite scores of— [7]											
27 or above	Percent ...	14	13	12	13	14	14	14	15	16	16
18 or below	Percent ...	21	33	35	34	32	34	33	32	33	34

NA Not available. [1] Beginning 1990, not comparable with previous years because a new version of the ACT was introduced. Estimated average composite scores for prior years: 1989, 20.6; 1988, 1987, and 1986, 20.8. [2] Minimum score, 1; maximum score, 36. [3] Prior to 1990, social studies; data not comparable with previous years. [4] Prior to 1990, natural sciences; data not comparable with previous years. [5] Beginning 1985, data are for seniors who graduated in year shown and had taken the ACT in their junior or senior years. Data by race are for those responding to the race question. [6] 788 represents 788,000. [7] Prior to 1990, 26 or above and 15 or below.

Source: ACT, Inc., Iowa City, IA, *High School Profile Report*, annual.

Table 265. Proficiency Levels on Selected NAEP Tests for Students in Public Schools by State: 2009

[Represents percent of public school students scoring at or above basic and proficient levels. Basic denotes mastery of the knowledge and skills that are fundamental for proficient work at a given grade level. Proficient represents solid academic performance. Students reaching this level demonstrated competency over challenging subject matter. For more detail, see <http://www.nagb.org /pubs/pubs.html>. Based on the National Assessment of Educational Progress (NAEP) tests which are administered to a representative sample of students in public schools, private schools, and Department of Defense schools. Data shown here are for public school students only]

State	Grade 4 Math		Grade 8 Math		Grade 4 Reading		Grade 8 Reading	
	At or above Basic	At or above Proficient	At or above Basic	At or above Proficient	At or above Basic	At or above Proficient	At or above Basic	At or above Proficient
U.S. average	**82**	**39**	**73**	**34**	**67**	**33**	**75**	**32**
Alabama	70	24	58	20	62	28	66	24
Alaska	78	38	75	33	59	27	72	27
Arizona	71	28	67	29	56	25	68	27
Arkansas	80	36	67	27	63	29	69	27
California	72	30	59	23	54	24	64	22
Colorado	84	45	76	40	72	40	78	32
Connecticut	86	46	78	40	76	42	81	43
Delaware	84	36	75	32	73	35	78	31
District of Columbia	56	17	40	11	44	17	51	14
Florida	86	40	70	29	73	36	76	32
Georgia	78	34	67	27	63	29	72	27
Hawaii	77	37	65	25	57	26	67	22
Idaho	85	41	78	38	69	32	77	33
Illinois	80	38	73	33	65	32	77	33
Indiana	87	42	78	36	70	34	79	32
Iowa	87	41	76	34	69	34	77	32
Kansas	89	46	79	39	72	35	80	33
Kentucky	81	37	70	27	72	36	79	33
Louisiana	72	23	62	20	51	18	64	20
Maine	87	45	78	35	70	35	80	35
Maryland	85	44	75	40	70	37	77	36
Massachusetts	92	57	85	52	80	47	83	43
Michigan	78	35	68	31	64	30	72	31
Minnesota	89	54	83	47	70	37	82	38
Mississippi	69	22	54	15	55	22	62	19
Missouri	83	41	77	35	70	36	79	34
Montana	88	45	82	44	73	35	84	38
Nebraska	82	38	75	35	70	35	80	35
Nevada	79	32	63	25	57	24	65	22
New Hampshire	92	56	82	43	77	41	81	39
New Jersey	88	49	80	44	76	40	83	42
New Mexico	72	26	59	20	52	20	66	22
New York	83	40	73	34	71	36	75	33
North Carolina	87	43	74	36	65	32	70	29
North Dakota	91	45	86	43	76	35	86	34
Ohio	85	45	76	36	71	36	80	37
Oklahoma	82	33	68	24	65	28	73	26
Oregon	80	37	75	37	65	31	76	33
Pennsylvania	84	46	78	40	70	37	81	40
Rhode Island	81	39	68	28	69	36	72	28
South Carolina	78	34	69	30	62	28	68	24
South Dakota	86	42	83	42	70	33	84	37
Tennessee	74	28	65	25	63	28	73	28
Texas	85	38	78	36	65	28	73	27
Utah	81	41	75	35	67	31	78	33
Vermont	89	51	81	43	75	41	84	41
Virginia	85	43	76	36	74	38	78	32
Washington	84	43	78	39	68	33	78	36
West Virginia	77	28	61	19	62	26	67	22
Wisconsin	85	45	79	39	67	33	78	34
Wyoming	87	40	78	35	72	33	82	34

Source: U.S. Department of Education, National Center for Education Statistics, National Assessment of Educational Progress (NAEP), 2009 Mathematics and Reading Assessments. See also <http://nces.ed.gov/nationsreportcard/>, accessed April 2010.

Table 266. Public High School Graduates by State: 1980 to 2008

[In thousands (2,747.7 represents 2,747,700). For school year ending in year shown]

State	1980	1990	2000	2008, proj.	State	1980	1990	2000	2008, proj.
United States	**2,747.7**	**2,320.3**	**2,553.8**	**3,010.9**					
Alabama	45.2	40.5	37.8	39.4	Missouri	62.3	49.0	52.8	60.5
Alaska	5.2	5.4	6.6	8.0	Montana	12.1	9.4	10.9	10.3
Arizona	28.6	32.1	38.3	52.1	Nebraska	22.4	17.7	20.1	20.7
Arkansas	29.1	26.5	27.3	29.5	Nevada	8.5	9.5	14.6	18.2
California	249.2	236.3	309.9	385.3	New Hampshire	11.7	10.8	11.8	14.6
Colorado	36.8	33.0	38.9	48.0	New Jersey	94.6	69.8	74.4	95.1
Connecticut	37.7	27.9	31.6	38.4	New Mexico	18.4	14.9	18.0	17.8
Delaware	7.6	5.6	6.1	7.5	New York	204.1	143.3	141.7	169.7
District of Columbia [1]	5.0	3.6	2.7	3.3	North Carolina	70.9	64.8	62.1	81.2
Florida	87.3	88.9	106.7	148.2	North Dakota	9.9	7.7	8.6	7.2
Georgia	61.6	56.6	62.6	79.7	Ohio	144.2	114.5	111.7	122.6
Hawaii	11.5	10.3	10.4	11.0	Oklahoma	39.3	35.6	37.6	37.3
Idaho	13.2	12.0	16.2	16.8	Oregon	29.9	25.5	30.2	36.4
Illinois	135.6	108.1	111.8	133.1	Pennsylvania	146.5	110.5	114.0	151.7
Indiana	73.1	60.0	57.0	63.0	Rhode Island	10.9	7.8	8.5	10.3
Iowa	43.4	31.8	33.9	35.3	South Carolina	38.7	32.5	31.6	35.1
Kansas	30.9	25.4	29.1	30.0	South Dakota	10.7	7.7	9.3	8.2
Kentucky	41.2	38.0	36.8	40.7	Tennessee	49.8	46.1	41.6	54.2
Louisiana	46.3	36.1	38.4	34.1	Texas	171.4	172.5	212.9	259.5
Maine	15.4	13.8	12.2	13.2	Utah	20.0	21.2	32.5	30.8
Maryland	54.3	41.6	47.8	58.3	Vermont	6.7	6.1	6.7	7.1
Massachusetts	73.8	55.9	53.0	63.9	Virginia	66.6	60.6	65.6	77.1
Michigan	124.3	93.8	97.7	109.4	Washington	50.4	45.9	57.6	62.6
Minnesota	64.9	49.1	57.4	60.9	West Virginia	23.4	21.9	19.4	17.5
Mississippi	27.6	25.2	24.2	24.9	Wisconsin	69.3	52.0	58.5	66.0
					Wyoming	6.1	5.8	6.5	5.4

[1] Beginning in 1990, graduates from adult programs are excluded.

Source: U.S. National Center for Education Statistics, Digest of Education Statistics, annual. See also <http://www.nces.ed.gov/programs/digest/>.

Table 267. High School Dropouts by Race and Hispanic Origin: 1980 to 2008

[In percent. As of October]

Item	1980	1985	1990 [1]	1995	2000	2002	2003	2004	2005	2006	2007	2008
EVENT DROPOUTS [2]												
Total [3]	6.0	5.2	4.5	5.4	4.5	3.3	3.8	4.4	3.6	3.5	3.3	3.3
White [4]	5.6	4.8	3.9	5.1	4.3	3.0	3.7	4.2	3.1	3.5	2.8	2.8
Male	6.4	4.9	4.1	5.4	4.7	3.0	4.9	3.4	3.9	2.8	2.7
Female	4.9	4.7	3.8	4.8	4.0	3.0	3.4	3.5	3.7	3.1	3.7	3.0
Black [4]	8.3	7.7	7.7	6.1	5.6	4.4	4.5	5.2	6.9	3.7	4.3	6.0
Male	8.0	8.3	6.9	7.9	7.6	5.1	4.1	4.8	7.5	3.2	4.9	4.6
Female	8.5	7.2	8.6	4.4	3.8	3.8	4.9	5.7	6.2	4.3	3.6	7.6
Hispanic [5]	11.5	9.7	7.7	11.6	6.8	5.3	6.5	8.0	4.7	6.4	5.5	4.9
Male	16.9	9.3	7.6	10.9	7.1	6.2	7.7	11.5	5.6	6.3	5.5	4.2
Female	6.9	9.8	7.7	12.5	6.5	4.4	5.4	4.6	3.9	6.6	5.6	5.6
STATUS DROPOUTS [6]												
Total [3]	15.6	13.9	14.4	13.9	12.4	12.3	11.8	12.1	11.3	11.0	10.2	9.3
White [4]	14.4	13.5	14.1	13.6	12.2	12.2	11.6	11.9	11.3	10.8	10.0	8.8
Male	15.7	14.7	15.4	14.3	13.5	13.7	13.3	13.7	13.2	12.4	11.7	9.8
Female	13.2	12.3	12.8	13.0	10.9	10.6	9.8	10.0	9.4	9.2	8.3	7.8
Black [4]	23.5	17.6	16.4	14.4	15.3	14.6	14.2	15.1	12.9	13.0	10.2	12.0
Male	26.0	18.8	18.6	14.2	17.4	16.9	16.7	17.9	14.8	11.2	10.0	10.2
Female	21.5	16.6	14.5	14.6	13.5	12.0	12.7	11.2	14.7	10.3	13.7
Hispanic [5]	40.3	31.5	37.7	34.7	32.3	30.1	28.4	28.0	27.3	26.2	25.3	22.3
Male	42.6	35.8	40.3	34.2	36.8	33.8	31.7	33.5	32.1	31.0	29.2	24.3
Female	38.1	27.0	35.0	35.4	27.3	25.6	24.7	21.7	21.8	21.0	21.1	20.2

[1] Beginning 1990, reflects new editing procedures for cases with missing data on school enrollment. [2] Percent of students who drop out in a single year without completing high school. For grades 10 to 12. [3] Includes other races, not shown separately. [4] Beginning 2003, for persons who selected this race group only. See footnote 2, Table 225. [5] Persons of Hispanic origin may be any race. [6] Percent of the population who have not completed high school and are not enrolled, regardless of when they dropped out. For persons 18 to 24 years old.

Source: U.S. Census Bureau, Current Population Reports, PPL-148, P-20 and earlier reports, and "School Enrollment," <http://www.census.gov/population/www/socdemo/school.html>.

U.S. Census Bureau, Statistical Abstract of the United States: 2011

Table 268. High School Dropouts by Age, Race, and Hispanic Origin: 1980 to 2008

[As of October (5,212 represents 5,212,000). For persons 14 to 24 years old. See Table 270 for definition of dropouts. Based on Current Population Survey; see text, Section 1 and Appendix III]

Age and race	Number of dropouts (1,000)					Percent of population				
	1980	1990	2000	2005	2008	1980	1990	2000	2005	2008
Total dropouts [1,2]	**5,212**	**3,854**	**3,883**	**3,597**	**3,118**	**12.0**	**10.1**	**9.1**	**7.9**	**6.8**
16 to 17 years	709	418	460	303	416	8.8	6.3	5.8	3.4	2.5
18 to 21 years	2,578	1,921	2,005	1,669	1,452	15.8	13.4	12.9	10.5	8.8
22 to 24 years	1,798	1,458	1,310	1,485	1,249	15.2	13.8	11.8	12.4	10.1
White [2,3]	4,169	3,127	3,065	2,785	2,290	11.3	10.1	9.1	7.9	6.5
16 to 17 years	619	334	366	223	298	9.2	6.4	5.8	3.3	2.3
18 to 21 years	2,032	1,516	1,558	1,299	1,071	14.7	13.1	12.6	10.4	8.4
22 to 24 years	1,416	1,235	1,040	1,167	920	14.0	14.0	11.7	12.6	9.5
Black [2,3]	934	611	705	616	596	16.0	10.9	10.9	9.2	8.6
16 to 17 years	80	73	84	64	82	6.9	6.9	7.0	4.7	3.1
18 to 21 years	486	345	383	281	290	23.0	16.0	16.0	12.4	11.2
22 to 24 years	346	185	232	231	224	24.0	13.5	14.3	13.6	13.4
Hispanic [2,4]	919	1,122	1,499	1,467	1,252	29.5	26.8	23.5	18.6	15.0
16 to 17 years	92	89	121	93	96	16.6	12.9	11.0	6.3	3.1
18 to 21 years	470	502	733	672	588	40.3	32.9	30.0	24.5	20.0
22 to 24 years	323	523	602	663	567	40.6	42.8	35.5	30.8	25.4

[1] Includes other groups not shown separately. [2] Includes persons 14 to 15 years not shown separately. [3] Beginning 2005, for persons who selected this race group only. See footnote 2, Table 225. [4] Persons of Hispanic origin may be any race.

Source: U.S. Census Bureau, Current Population Reports, PPL-148, P-20 and earlier reports, and "School Enrollment," <http://www.census.gov/population/www/socdemo/school.html>.

Table 269. Enrollment Status by Race, Hispanic Origin, and Sex: 2000 and 2008

[As of October (15,553 represents 15,553,000). For persons 18 to 21 years old. For the civilian noninstitutional population. Based on the Current Population Survey; see text, Section 1 and Appendix III]

Characteristic	Total persons 18 to 21 years old (1,000)		Percent distribution							
			Enrolled in high school		High school graduates				Not high school graduates and not enrolled in high school	
					Total		In college			
	2000	2008	2000	2008	2000	2008	2000	2008	2000	2008
Total [1]	**15,553**	**16,575**	**9.4**	**9.6**	**77.6**	**81.6**	**43.5**	**48.3**	**12.9**	**8.8**
White [2]	12,383	12,828	8.9	8.8	78.5	82.8	44.4	50.2	12.6	8.4
Black [2]	2,389	2,593	12.6	13.7	71.3	75.4	34.7	36.2	16.0	10.9
Hispanic [3]	2,439	2,941	12.5	12.3	57.2	68.1	25.3	31.4	30.0	19.6
Male [1]	7,814	8,434	11.0	10.4	74.7	80.8	38.9	45.1	14.3	8.8
White [2]	6,313	6,581	10.6	9.3	75.7	81.7	39.8	46.8	13.7	9.0
Black [2]	1,096	1,262	14.9	14.8	66.0	77.2	27.4	33.4	19.1	8.0
Hispanic [3]	1,269	1,509	14.4	13.6	51.8	67.1	21.9	29.2	33.7	19.3
Female [1]	7,739	8,141	7.9	8.9	80.6	82.4	48.1	51.6	11.5	8.8
White [2]	6,070	6,247	7.1	8.3	81.3	83.9	49.3	53.8	11.4	7.8
Black [2]	1,293	1,332	10.7	12.7	75.9	73.6	40.9	38.9	13.5	13.7
Hispanic [3]	1,169	1,432	10.6	11.0	63.1	69.1	28.9	33.7	26.1	20.0

[1] Includes other races not shown separately. [2] For 2008, for persons who selected this race group only. See footnote 2, Table 225. [3] Persons of Hispanic origin may be any race.

Source: U.S. Census Bureau, Current Population Reports, PPL-148, P-20 and earlier reports, and "School Enrollment," <http://www.census.gov/population/www/socdemo/school.html>.

Table 270. Employment Status of High School Graduates and Dropouts Not Enrolled in School by Sex and Race: 1980 to 2009

[In thousands (11,622 represents 11,622,000), except percent. As of October. For civilian noninstitutional population 16 to 24 years old. Based on Current Population Survey; see text, Section 1 and Appendix III]

Employment status, sex, and race	Graduates [1]				Dropouts [3]			
	1980	1990	2000 [2]	2009 [2]	1980	1990	2000 [2]	2009 [2]
Civilian population	**11,622**	**8,370**	**7,351**	**6,994**	**5,254**	**3,800**	**3,776**	**3,030**
In labor force	9,795	7,107	6,195	5,340	3,549	2,506	2,612	1,911
Percent of population.	84.3	84.9	84.3	76.3	67.5	66.0	69.2	63.1
Employed.	8,567	6,279	5,632	4,071	2,651	1,993	2,150	1,308
Percent of labor force	87.5	88.3	90.9	76.2	74.7	79.5	82.3	68.4
Unemployed.	1,228	828	563	1,269	898	513	463	603
Unemployment rate, total [4]	12.5	11.7	9.1	23.8	25.3	20.5	17.7	31.5
Male.	13.5	11.1	9.3	24.8	23.5	18.8	16.3	31.8
Female.	11.5	12.3	8.8	22.2	28.7	23.5	20.3	31.0
White [5]	10.8	9.0	7.2	21.3	21.6	17.0	15.0	29.2
Black [5]	26.1	26.0	18.1	34.9	43.9	44.3	33.2	45.0
Not in labor force	1,827	1,262	1,156	1,655	1,705	1,294	1,163	1,119
Percent of population.	15.7	15.1	15.7	23.7	32.5	34.1	30.8	36.9

[1] For persons not enrolled in college who have completed 4 years of high school only. [2] Data not strictly comparable with data for earlier years. See text, this section, and February 2000 and 2009 issues of Employment and Earnings. [3] For persons not in regular school and who have not completed the 12th grade nor received a general equivalency degree. [4] Includes other races not shown separately. [5] 2009 data are for persons who selected this race group only. See footnote 2, Table 225.

Source: U.S. Bureau of Labor Statistics, News Release, USDL 10-0533, April 2010, and unpublished data. See also <http://www.bls.gov/news.release/hsgec.toc.htm>.

Table 271. General Educational Development (GED) Credentials Issued: 1980 to 2008

[GEDs issued in thousands (479 represents 479,000). For the 50 states and DC]

Year	GEDs issued	Percent distribution of GED test takers				
		19 years old or under	20 to 24 years old	25 to 29 years old	30 to 34 years old	35 years old and over
1980.	479	37	27	13	8	15
1985.	413	32	26	15	10	16
1990.	410	36	25	13	10	15
1995.	504	38	25	13	9	15
2000.	487	45	25	11	7	13
2002.	330	49	25	10	6	11
2003.	387	47	26	10	7	11
2004.	406	46	26	11	6	10
2005.	424	45	26	12	7	11
2006.	464	46	25	12	6	11
2007.	495	46	24	12	7	11
2008.	539	41	24	13	8	14

Source: U.S. National Center for Education Statistics, *Digest of Education Statistics*, annual. See also <http://www.nces.ed.gov/programs/digest/>.

Table 272. College Enrollment of Recent High School Completers: 1970 to 2008

[2,758 represents 2,758,000. For persons 16 to 24 years old who graduated from high school in the preceding 12 months. Includes persons receiving GEDs. Based on surveys and subject to sampling error; data will not agree with data in other tables]

Year	Number of high school completers (1,000)						Percent enrolled in college [5]					
	Total [1]	Male	Female	White [2]	Black [2,3]	His-panic [3,4]	Total [1]	Male	Female	White [2]	Black [2,3]	His-panic [3,4]
1970. . .	2,758	1,343	1,415	2,461	(NA)	(NA)	52	55	49	52	(NA)	(NA)
1975. . .	3,185	1,513	1,672	2,701	302	132	51	53	49	51	42	58
1980. . .	3,088	1,498	1,589	2,554	350	130	49	47	52	50	43	52
1985. . .	2,668	1,287	1,381	2,104	332	141	58	59	57	60	42	51
1990. . .	2,362	1,173	1,189	1,819	331	121	60	58	62	63	47	43
1995. . .	2,599	1,238	1,361	1,861	349	288	62	63	61	64	51	54
1999. . .	2,897	1,474	1,423	1,978	436	329	63	61	64	66	59	42
2000. . .	2,756	1,251	1,505	1,938	393	300	63	60	66	66	55	53
2001. . .	2,549	1,277	1,273	1,834	381	241	62	60	63	64	55	52
2002. . .	2,796	1,412	1,384	1,903	382	344	65	62	68	69	59	54
2003. . .	2,677	1,306	1,372	1,832	327	314	64	61	67	66	58	59
2004. . .	2,752	1,327	1,425	1,854	398	286	67	61	72	69	63	62
2005. . .	2,675	1,262	1,414	1,799	345	390	69	67	70	73	56	54
2006. . .	2,692	1,328	1,363	1,805	318	382	66	66	66	69	55	58
2007. . .	2,955	1,511	1,444	2,043	416	355	67	66	68	70	56	64
2008. . .	3,151	1,640	1,511	2,091	416	458	69	66	72	72	56	64

NA Not available. [1] Includes other races not shown separately. [2] Beginning 2003, for persons of this race group only. See footnote 2, Table 225. [3] Due to small sample size, data are subject to relatively large sampling errors. [4] Persons of Hispanic origin may be any race. [5] As of October.

Source: U.S. National Center for Education Statistics, *Digest of Education Statistics*, annual. See also <http://www.nces.ed.gov/programs/digest/>.

Table 273. College Enrollment by Sex and Attendance Status: 2005 to 2009

[As of fall. In thousands (17,487 represents 17,487,000). Includes enrollment at branch campuses, some additional (primarily 2-year) colleges and excludes a few institutions that did not award degrees. Includes enrollment at institutions that were eligible to participate in Title IV federal financial aid programs. Includes unclassified students, (students taking courses for credit, but are not candidates for degrees)]

Sex and age	2005		2006		2007		2008		2009, proj.	
	Total	Part-time	Total	Part-time	Total	Part-time	Total	Part-time	Total	Part-time
Total.	**17,487**	**6,690**	**17,759**	**6,802**	**18,248**	**6,979**	**19,103**	**7,355**	**19,525**	**7,483**
Male.	7,456	2,653	7,575	2,696	7,816	2,787	8,189	2,955	8,451	3,019
14 to 17 years old	78	41	82	16	75	17	92	19	87	21
18 to 19 years old	1,592	235	1,705	297	1,805	273	1,850	278	1,913	304
20 to 21 years old	1,778	318	1,673	341	1,633	288	1,792	342	1,846	350
22 to 24 years old	1,355	405	1,470	466	1,551	544	1,558	485	1,607	506
25 to 29 years old	978	539	1,051	488	1,020	435	1,177	602	1,216	593
30 to 34 years old	545	306	557	325	659	430	640	414	659	413
35 years old and over	1,130	809	1,037	762	1,074	799	1,080	814	1,123	831
Female.	10,032	4,038	10,184	4,106	10,432	4,192	10,914	4,401	11,073	4,465
14 to 17 years old	121	27	149	48	104	9	101	12	114	20
18 to 19 years old	2,018	338	2,064	318	2,173	327	2,240	357	2,293	370
20 to 21 years old	2,000	430	1,975	363	2,129	452	2,137	409	2,169	428
22 to 24 years old	1,717	571	1,724	634	1,811	685	1,922	703	1,918	708
25 to 29 years old	1,406	709	1,350	696	1,502	824	1,560	818	1,571	822
30 to 34 years old	809	499	852	480	770	449	842	547	835	519
35 years old and over	1,960	1,464	2,070	1,567	1,943	1,446	2,112	1,554	2,173	1,598

Source: U.S. National Center for Education Statistics, *Digest of Education Statistics*, annual. See also <http://www.nces.ed.gov/programs/digest/>.

Education 175

Table 274. Higher Education—Institutions and Enrollment 1980 to 2008

[As of fall (686 represents 686,000). Covers universities,colleges, professional schools, junior and teachers' colleges, both publicly and privately controlled, regular session. Includes estimates for institutions not reporting. See also Appendix III]

Item	Unit	1980	1990	2000	2004	2005	2006	2007	2008
ALL INSTITUTIONS									
Number of institutions [1]	**Number...**	**3,231**	**3,559**	**4,182**	**4,216**	**4,276**	**4,314**	**4,352**	**(NA)**
4-year	Number ...	1,957	2,141	2,450	2,533	2,582	2,629	2,675	(NA)
2-year	Number ...	1,274	1,418	1,732	1,683	1,694	1,685	1,677	(NA)
Instructional staff—									
(lecturer or above) [2]	**1,000 .....**	**686**	**817**	**(NA)**	**(NA)**	**1,290**	**(NA)**	**1,371**	**(NA)**
Percent full-time	Percent ...	66	61	(NA)	(NA)	52	(NA)	51	(NA)
Total enrollment [3,4]	**1,000 .....**	**12,097**	**13,819**	**15,312**	**17,272**	**17,487**	**17,759**	**18,248**	**19,103**
Male	1,000	5,874	6,284	6,722	7,387	7,456	7,575	7,816	8,189
Female	1,000	6,223	7,535	8,591	9,885	10,032	10,184	10,432	10,914
4-year institutions	1,000	7,571	8,579	9,364	10,726	10,999	11,240	11,630	12,131
2-year institutions	1,000	4,526	5,240	5,948	6,546	6,488	6,519	6,618	6,971
Full-time	1,000	7,098	7,821	9,010	10,610	10,797	10,957	11,270	11,748
Part-time	1,000	4,999	5,998	6,303	6,662	6,690	6,802	6,978	7,355
Public	1,000	9,457	10,845	11,753	12,980	13,022	13,180	13,491	13,972
Private	1,000	2,640	2,974	3,560	4,292	4,466	4,579	4,757	5,131
Not-for-profit	1,000	2,528	2,760	3,109	3,412	3,455	3,513	3,571	3,662
For profit	1,000	112	213	450	880	1,011	1,066	1,186	1,469
Undergraduate [4]	1,000	10,475	11,959	13,155	14,781	14,964	15,184	15,604	16,366
Men	1,000	5,000	5,380	5,778	6,340	6,409	6,513	6,728	7,067
Women	1,000	5,475	6,579	7,377	8,441	8,555	8,671	8,876	9,299
First-time freshmen	1,000	2,588	2,257	2,428	2,630	2,657	2,707	2,776	3,025
First professional	1,000	278	273	307	335	337	343	351	(NA)
Men	1,000	199	167	164	168	170	174	178	(NA)
Women	1,000	78	107	143	166	167	170	173	(NA)
Graduate [4]	1,000	1,343	1,586	1,850	2,157	2,186	2,231	2,294	(NA)
Men	1,000	675	737	780	879	877	887	910	(NA)
Women	1,000	670	849	1,071	1,278	1,309	1,344	1,383	(NA)
2-YEAR INSTITUTIONS									
Number of institutions [1]	**Number...**	**1,274**	**1,418**	**1,732**	**1,683**	**1,694**	**1,685**	**1,677**	**(NA)**
Public	Number ...	945	972	1,076	1,061	1,053	1,045	1,032	(NA)
Private	Number ...	329	446	656	622	641	640	645	(NA)
Instructional staff—									
(lecturer or above) [2]	**1,000 .....**	**192**	**(NA)**	**(NA)**	**(NA)**	**373**	**(NA)**	**381**	**(NA)**
Enrollment [3,4]	**1,000 ....**	**4,526**	**5,240**	**5,948**	**6,546**	**6,488**	**6,519**	**6,618**	**6,971**
Public	1,000	4,329	4,996	5,697	6,244	6,184	6,225	6,324	6,640
Private	1,000	198	244	251	302	304	293	294	331
Male	1,000	2,047	2,233	2,559	2,698	2,680	2,705	2,771	2,936
Female	1,000	2,479	3,007	3,390	3,848	3,808	3,814	3,847	4,035
4-YEAR INSTITUTIONS									
Number of institutions [1]	**Number...**	**1,957**	**2,141**	**2,450**	**2,533**	**2,582**	**2,629**	**2,675**	**(NA)**
Public	Number ...	552	595	622	639	640	643	653	(NA)
Private	Number ...	1,405	1,546	1,828	1,894	1,942	1,986	2,022	(NA)
Instructional staff—									
(lecturer or above) [2]	**1,000 .....**	**494**	**(NA)**	**(NA)**	**(NA)**	**917**	**(NA)**	**991**	**(NA)**
Enrollment [3,4]	**1,000 .....**	**7,571**	**8,579**	**9,364**	**10,726**	**10,999**	**11,240**	**11,630**	**12,131**
Public	1,000	5,129	5,848	6,055	6,737	6,838	6,955	7,167	7,332
Private	1,000	2,442	2,730	3,308	3,990	4,162	4,285	4,464	4,800
Male	1,000	3,827	4,051	4,163	4,690	4,776	4,870	5,045	5,253
Female	1,000	3,743	4,527	5,201	6,037	6,224	6,370	6,585	6,878

NA Not available. [1] Number of institutions includes count of branch campuses. Due to revised survey procedures, data beginning 1990 are not comparable with previous years. Beginning 2000, data reflect a new classification of institutions; this classification includes some additional, primarily 2-year, colleges and excludes a few institutions that did not award degrees. Includes institutions that were eligible to participate in Title IV federal financial aid programs. Includes schools accredited by the National Association of Trade and Technical Schools. [2] Due to revised survey methods, data beginning 1990 not comparable with previous years. [3] Branch campuses counted according to actual status, e.g., 2-year branch in 2-year category. [4] Includes unclassified students. (Students taking courses for credit, but are not candidates for degrees.)

Source: U.S. National Center for Education Statistics, *Digest of Education Statistics*, annual, and unpublished data. See also <http://www.nces.ed.gov/programs/digest/>.

Table 275. College Enrollment by Selected Characteristics: 1990 to 2008

[In thousands (13,818.6 represents 13,818,600). As of fall. Nonresident alien students are not distributed among racial/ethnic groups]

Characteristic	1990	2000 [1]	2004 [1]	2005 [1]	2006 [1]	2007 [1]	2008 [1]
Total.	**13,818.6**	**15,312.3**	**17,272.0**	**17,487.5**	**17,758.9**	**18,248.1**	**19,102.8**
Male.	6,283.9	6,721.8	7,387.3	7,455.9	7,574.8	7,815.9	8,188.9
Female.	7,534.7	8,590.5	9,884.8	10,031.6	10,184.1	10,432.2	10,913.9
Public.	10,844.7	11,752.8	12,980.1	13,021.8	13,180.1	13,490.8	13,972.2
Private.	2,973.9	3,559.5	4,291.9	4,465.6	4,578.7	4,757.3	5,130.7
2-year	5,240.1	5,948.4	6,545.9	6,488.1	6,518.5	6,617.9	6,971.4
4-year	8,578.6	9,363.9	10,726.2	10,999.4	11,240.3	11,630.2	12,131.4
Undergraduate.	11,959.2	13,155.4	14,780.6	14,964.0	15,184.3	15,603.8	16,365.7
Graduate	1,586.2	1,850.3	2,156.9	2,186.5	2,231.1	2,293.6	(NA)
First professional	273.4	306.6	334.5	337.0	343.4	350.8	(NA)
White [2]	10,722.5	10,462.1	11,422.8	11,495.4	11,572.4	11,756.2	12,088.8
Male.	4,861.0	4,634.6	4,988.0	5,007.2	5,046.2	5,146.1	5,302.9
Female.	5,861.5	5,827.5	6,434.8	6,488.2	6,526.2	6,610.1	6,785.9
Public.	8,385.4	7,963.4	8,546.3	8,518.2	8,540.5	8,640.3	8,817.7
Private.	2,337.0	2,498.7	2,876.5	2,977.3	3,032.0	3,116.0	3,271.1
2-year	3,954.3	3,804.1	4,063.8	3,998.6	3,969.1	3,975.2	4,101.6
4-year	6,768.1	6,658.0	7,359.0	7,496.9	7,603.4	7,781.0	7,987.1
Undergraduate.	9,272.6	8,983.5	9,771.3	9,828.6	9,885.4	10,046.6	10,339.2
Graduate	1,228.4	1,258.5	1,413.3	1,428.7	1,445.3	1,465.0	(NA)
First professional	221.5	220.1	238.2	238.1	241.7	244.7	(NA)
Black [2]	1,247.0	1,730.3	2,164.7	2,214.6	2,279.6	2,383.4	2,584.5
Male.	484.7	635.3	758.4	774.1	795.4	838.1	911.8
Female.	762.3	1,095.0	1,406.3	1,440.4	1,484.2	1,545.3	1,672.7
Public.	976.4	1,319.2	1,574.6	1,580.4	1,612.6	1,667.6	1,759.2
Private.	270.6	411.1	590.1	634.2	667.0	715.7	825.3
2-year	524.3	734.9	905.8	901.1	917.9	941.7	1,019.5
4-year	722.8	995.4	1,258.9	1,313.4	1,361.7	1,441.7	1,565.0
Undergraduate.	1,147.2	1,548.9	1,918.5	1,955.4	2,005.7	2,092.6	2,269.3
Graduate	83.9	157.9	220.4	233.2	247.2	263.5	(NA)
First professional	15.9	23.5	25.9	26.0	26.8	27.3	(NA)
Hispanic.	782.4	1,461.8	1,809.6	1,882.0	1,964.3	2,076.2	2,272.9
Male.	353.9	627.1	745.1	774.6	810.0	861.6	946.7
Female.	428.5	834.7	1,064.5	1,107.3	1,154.3	1,214.5	1,326.1
Public.	671.4	1,229.3	1,477.4	1,525.6	1,594.3	1,685.4	1,832.4
Private.	111.0	232.5	332.2	356.4	370.1	390.7	440.5
2-year	424.2	843.9	972.4	981.5	1,014.3	1,067.4	1,180.7
4-year	358.2	617.9	837.2	900.5	950.0	1,008.7	1,092.2
Undergraduate.	724.6	1,351.0	1,666.9	1,733.6	1,810.1	1,915.9	2,103.5
Graduate	47.2	95.4	125.8	130.7	135.8	140.9	(NA)
First professional	10.7	15.4	17.0	17.7	18.4	19.3	(NA)
American Indian/ Alaska Native.	102.8	151.2	176.1	176.3	181.1	190.0	193.3
Male.	43.1	61.4	68.6	68.4	71.2	74.4	76.9
Female.	59.7	89.7	107.5	107.9	110.0	115.6	116.4
Public.	90.4	127.3	144.4	143.0	145.9	153.3	153.0
Private.	12.4	23.9	31.8	33.3	35.2	36.7	40.3
2-year	54.9	74.7	82.2	80.7	81.1	81.4	85.5
4-year	47.9	76.5	93.9	95.6	100.0	108.6	108.6
Undergraduate.	95.5	138.5	160.3	160.4	164.2	171.3	175.6
Graduate	6.2	10.3	13.4	13.4	14.5	16.1	(NA)
First professional	1.1	2.3	2.4	2.5	2.5	2.6	(NA)
Asian/Pacific Islander	572.4	978.2	1,108.7	1,134.4	1,165.5	1,217.9	1,302.8
Male.	294.9	465.9	511.6	522.0	536.0	562.5	597.4
Female.	277.5	512.3	597.1	612.4	629.5	655.4	705.4
Public.	461.0	770.5	866.1	881.9	903.8	942.5	982.9
Private.	111.5	207.7	242.6	252.4	261.7	275.4	319.9
2-year	215.2	401.9	430.7	434.4	442.8	456.4	479.4
4-year	357.2	576.3	678.0	700.0	722.7	761.5	823.4
Undergraduate.	500.5	845.5	949.9	971.4	997.9	1,042.1	1,117.9
Graduate	53.2	95.8	115.9	118.4	121.9	127.8	(NA)
First professional	18.7	36.8	42.9	44.6	45.7	48.0	(NA)
Nonresident alien.	391.5	528.7	590.2	584.8	595.9	624.5	660.6
Male.	246.3	297.3	315.6	309.5	316.1	333.2	353.3
Female.	145.2	231.4	274.6	275.3	279.8	291.2	307.3
Public.	260.0	343.1	371.4	372.8	383.1	401.7	427.0
Private.	131.4	185.6	218.8	212.0	212.8	222.8	233.6
2-year	67.1	89.0	90.9	91.8	93.4	95.8	104.7
4-year	324.3	439.7	499.2	493.1	502.5	528.7	555.9
Undergraduate.	218.7	288.0	313.8	314.7	321.0	335.3	360.3
Graduate	167.3	232.3	268.1	262.1	266.4	280.3	(NA)
First professional	5.4	8.4	8.2	8.1	8.4	8.8	(NA)

NA Not available. [1] Data beginning 2000 reflect a new classification of institutions; see footnote 1, Table 274. [2] Non-Hispanic.

Source: U.S. National Center for Education Statistics, *Digest of Education Statistics*, annual. See also <http://www.nces.ed.gov/programs/digest/>.

Education 177

Table 276. Degree-Granting Institutions, Number and Enrollment by State: 2007

[18,248 represents 18,248,000. Number of institutions beginning in academic year. Opening fall enrollment of resident and extension students attending full-time or part-time. Excludes students taking courses for credit by mail, radio, or TV, and students in branches of U.S. institutions operated in foreign countries. See Appendix III]

State	Num-ber of institu-tions [1]	Enrollment (1,000)							Minority			Non-resi-dent alien
		Total	Male	Female	Public	Private	Full-time	White [2]	Total [3]	Black [2]	His-panic	
United States......	4,409	18,248	7,816	10,432	13,491	4,757	11,270	11,756	5,867	2,383	2,076	624
Alabama	72	268	110	158	238	31	177	174	88	77	5	6
Alaska	7	31	12	19	29	1	13	21	8	1	1	1
Arizona	75	624	243	381	332	292	420	391	212	74	95	22
Arkansas	50	152	61	91	136	17	97	113	36	29	4	3
California	426	2,530	1,124	1,406	2,136	393	1,277	1,055	1,395	196	698	80
Colorado	80	311	137	174	228	83	195	232	74	20	36	5
Connecticut	46	179	76	104	114	65	117	127	44	19	16	8
Delaware	10	52	21	32	39	13	34	36	14	10	2	2
District of Columbia ...	16	115	45	70	6	110	64	53	55	42	6	7
Florida	188	914	383	531	683	230	524	507	377	163	178	29
Georgia	135	454	183	271	360	94	303	263	177	143	14	13
Hawaii	21	67	28	39	50	16	39	17	44	1	2	6
Idaho	14	79	35	44	61	18	53	69	7	1	4	2
Illinois...........	180	837	359	478	551	286	498	538	272	121	99	27
Indiana...........	107	380	169	211	279	102	265	310	56	34	12	14
Iowa.............	66	256	107	150	155	102	160	216	33	17	9	7
Kansas...........	66	194	86	108	170	24	114	155	30	12	10	9
Kentucky	73	258	112	147	211	47	156	223	31	24	3	4
Louisiana	85	225	91	134	193	31	160	140	79	66	6	6
Maine............	30	67	27	40	48	19	42	62	4	1	1	1
Maryland	57	328	135	192	270	58	177	184	130	92	14	14
Massachusetts.......	124	463	198	266	199	265	319	330	105	38	31	28
Michigan	106	643	277	367	519	124	376	484	135	89	19	24
Minnesota	114	392	163	229	250	142	238	315	67	35	9	11
Mississippi	40	155	60	95	140	15	119	88	65	61	1	2
Missouri...........	131	384	162	222	223	161	234	300	74	49	12	11
Montana..........	23	47	22	26	43	5	35	40	6	(Z)	1	1
Nebraska..........	42	127	57	70	97	31	83	109	15	6	5	3
Nevada	21	116	52	65	105	11	55	70	44	10	19	3
New Hampshire......	28	71	30	41	42	29	50	63	6	1	2	2
New Jersey	63	398	176	222	318	80	243	233	149	56	57	16
New Mexico	42	134	57	78	125	10	69	57	74	4	55	4
New York	307	1,173	496	677	652	520	835	696	402	162	138	74
North Carolina......	133	502	202	300	411	92	317	335	156	121	15	12
North Dakota	22	50	24	26	43	7	37	42	5	1	1	2
Ohio..............	209	630	274	357	460	170	432	504	109	78	14	18
Oklahoma	59	206	90	116	178	29	133	144	53	19	8	9
Oregon...........	60	203	90	113	165	38	122	162	34	5	12	6
Pennsylvania	262	725	316	410	397	329	523	563	137	78	25	26
Rhode Island	13	83	36	47	42	41	61	65	15	5	6	3
South Carolina.......	69	218	86	132	180	37	148	146	69	60	4	3
South Dakota........	24	50	21	28	39	11	32	43	5	1	1	1
Tennessee.........	105	298	123	174	209	89	215	220	71	58	6	7
Texas.............	218	1,269	550	719	1,110	159	706	631	590	159	351	49
Utah..............	38	204	103	101	148	56	126	174	23	3	11	6
Vermont...........	25	42	19	23	25	17	31	38	3	1	1	1
Virginia............	114	478	204	274	370	108	290	320	146	95	20	13
Washington	78	352	154	198	302	50	216	263	78	15	22	11
West Virginia	44	117	55	61	88	29	77	102	13	8	3	2
Wisconsin	75	344	148	196	274	70	224	292	45	19	11	7
Wyoming	11	35	16	19	34	2	19	31	3	(Z)	2	1
U.S. military [4]	5	15	12	3	15	(X)	15	12	3	1	1	(Z)

X Not applicable. Z Fewer than 500. [1] Branch campuses counted as separate institutions. [2] Non-Hispanic. [3] Includes other races not shown separately. [4] Service schools.

Source: U.S. National Center for Education Statistics, *Digest of Education Statistics*, annual. See also <http://www.nces.ed.gov/programs/digest/>.

Table 277. College Enrollment by Sex, Age, Race, and Hispanic Origin: 1980 to 2008

[In thousands (11,387 represents 11,387,000). As of October for the civilian noninstitutional population, 14 years old and over. Based on the Current Population Survey; see text, Section 1 and Appendix III]

Characteristic	1980	1990 [1]	1995	2000	2002	2003	2004	2005	2006	2007	2008
Total [2]	**11,387**	**13,621**	**14,715**	**15,314**	**16,497**	**16,638**	**17,383**	**17,472**	**17,020**	**17,770**	**18,632**
Male [3]	5,430	6,192	6,703	6,682	7,240	7,318	7,575	7,539	7,427	7,749	8,311
18 to 24 years	3,604	3,922	4,089	4,342	4,629	4,697	4,866	4,972	4,874	5,156	5,383
25 to 34 years	1,325	1,412	1,561	1,361	1,460	1,590	1,604	1,486	1,571	1,625	1,806
35 years old and over	405	772	985	918	1,071	970	1,033	1,019	982	968	989
Female [3]	5,957	7,429	8,013	8,631	9,258	9,319	9,808	9,933	9,593	10,021	10,321
18 to 24 years	3,625	4,042	4,452	5,109	5,404	5,667	5,742	5,859	5,712	6,004	6,083
25 to 34 years	1,378	1,749	1,788	1,846	1,941	1,904	2,091	2,115	2,087	2,212	2,207
35 years old and over	802	1,546	1,684	1,589	1,797	1,660	1,850	1,838	1,793	1,804	1,922
White [3, 4]	9,925	11,488	12,021	11,999	12,781	12,870	13,381	13,467	13,112	13,693	14,405
18 to 24 years	6,334	6,635	7,011	7,566	7,921	8,150	8,354	8,499	8,298	8,780	9,141
25 to 34 years	2,328	2,698	2,686	2,339	2,515	2,545	2,748	2,647	2,725	2,769	2,859
35 years old and over	1,051	2,023	2,208	1,978	2,236	2,075	2,143	2,206	2,090	2,144	2,234
Male	4,804	5,235	5,535	5,311	5,719	5,714	5,944	5,844	5,772	5,989	6,570
Female.................	5,121	6,253	6,486	6,689	7,062	7,155	7,438	7,624	7,340	7,705	7,834
Black [3, 4]	1,163	1,393	1,772	2,164	2,278	2,144	2,301	2,297	2,304	2,473	2,481
18 to 24 years	688	894	988	1,216	1,227	1,225	1,238	1,229	1,321	1,395	1,349
25 to 34 years	289	258	426	567	542	503	522	520	502	629	646
35 years old and over	156	207	334	361	454	388	502	448	480	449	451
Male	476	587	710	815	802	798	776	864	886	1,006	919
Female.................	686	807	1,062	1,349	1,476	1,346	1,525	1,435	1,418	1,468	1,562
Hispanic origin [3, 5]	443	748	1,207	1,426	1,656	1,714	1,975	1,942	1,914	2,131	2,227
18 to 24 years	315	435	745	899	979	1,115	1,223	1,216	1,182	1,375	1,338
25 to 34 years	118	168	250	309	414	380	460	438	461	487	500
35 years old and over	(NA)	130	193	195	249	207	271	257	271	269	338
Male	222	364	568	619	705	703	852	804	789	864	1,042
Female.................	221	384	639	807	951	1,011	1,123	1,139	1,125	1,267	1,185

NA Not available. [1] Beginning 1990, based on a revised edit and tabulation package. [2] Includes other races not shown separately. [3] Includes persons 14 to 17 years old not shown separately. [4] Beginning 2003, for persons who selected this race group only. See footnote 2, Table 225. [5] Persons of Hispanic origin may be any race.

Source: U.S. Census Bureau, Current Population Reports, PPL-148, P-20 and earlier reports, and "School Enrollment," <http://www.census.gov/population/www/socdemo/school.html>.

Table 278. Foreign (Nonimmigrant) Student Enrollment in College: 1980 to 2009

[In thousands (286 represents 286,000). For fall of the previous year]

Region of origin	1980	1990	1995	1998	1999	2000	2001	2002	2003	2004	2005	2006	2007	2008	2009
All regions	**286**	**387**	**453**	**481**	**491**	**515**	**548**	**583**	**586**	**573**	**565**	**565**	**583**	**624**	**672**
Africa	36	25	21	23	26	30	34	38	40	38	36	36	36	36	37
Nigeria............	16	4	2	2	3	4	4	4	6	6	6	6	6	6	6
Asia [1, 2]	165	245	292	308	308	315	339	363	367	356	356	346	367	405	444
China [3]............	1	33	39	47	51	54	60	63	65	62	63	63	68	81	98
Taiwan [3]	18	31	36	31	31	29	29	29	28	26	26	28	29	29	28
Hong Kong	10	11	13	10	9	8	8	8	8	7	7	8	8	8	8
India	9	26	34	34	37	42	55	67	75	80	80	77	84	95	103
Indonesia	2	9	12	13	12	11	12	12	10	9	8	8	7	8	8
Iran	51	7	3	2	2	2	2	2	2	2	2	2	3	3	4
Japan	12	30	45	47	46	47	46	47	46	41	42	39	35	34	29
Malaysia	4	14	14	15	12	9	8	7	7	6	6	6	5	5	6
Saudi Arabia	10	4	4	5	5	5	5	6	4	4	3	3	8	10	13
South Korea	5	22	34	43	39	41	46	49	52	52	53	59	62	69	75
Thailand..........	7	7	11	15	12	11	11	12	10	9	9	9	9	9	9
Europe [4]...........	23	46	65	72	74	78	81	82	78	74	72	85	83	84	88
Latin America [1, 5]	42	48	47	51	55	62	64	68	69	66	68	65	65	64	68
Mexico	6	7	9	10	10	11	11	13	13	13	13	14	14	15	15
Venezuela	10	3	4	5	5	5	5	6	5	6	5	5	5	4	5
North America	16	19	23	23	23	24	26	27	27	28	29	29	29	29	30
Canada	15	18	23	22	23	24	25	27	27	27	28	28	28	29	30
Oceania...........	4	4	4	4	4	5	5	5	5	5	4	5	4	5	5

[1] Includes countries not shown separately. [2] Beginning 2006, excludes Cyprus and Turkey. [3] With the establishment of diplomatic relations with China on January 1, 1979, the U.S. government recognized the People's Republic of China as the sole legal government of China and acknowledged the Chinese position that there is only one China and that Taiwan is part of China. [4] Beginning 2006, includes Cyprus and Turkey. [5] Includes Mexico, Central America, Caribbean, and South America.

Source: Institute of International Education, New York, NY, *Open Doors Report on International Educational Exchange*, annual (copyright).

U.S. Census Bureau, Statistical Abstract of the United States: 2011

Table 279. College Enrollment—Summary by Sex, Race, and Hispanic Origin: 2008

[In thousands (18,632 represents 18,632,000), except percent. As of October. Covers civilian noninstitutional population 15 years old and over enrolled in colleges and graduate schools. Based on Current Population Survey. See text, Section 1 and Appendix III]

Characteristic	Total			Race and Hispanic origin				
				White [2]				
	Number [1]	Male	Female	Total	Non-Hispanic	Black [2]	Asian [2]	Hispanic [3]
Total enrollment...........	18,632	8,311	10,321	14,404	12,324	2,481	1,219	2,227
15 to 17 years old	241	133	108	171	121	36	27	53
18 to 19 years old	4,126	1,909	2,217	3,353	2,850	479	172	528
20 to 21 years old	3,920	1,908	2,013	3,119	2,734	462	246	407
22 to 24 years old	3,420	1,566	1,854	2,669	2,309	407	236	402
25 to 29 years old	2,657	1,229	1,428	1,952	1,625	376	245	359
30 to 34 years old	1,356	577	779	907	779	269	136	141
35 years old and over	2,911	989	1,922	2,234	1,906	451	156	338
Type of school:								
2-year	5,344	2,330	3,013	4,108	3,194	839	246	970
15 to 19 years old	1,731	775	956	1,426	1,148	205	55	290
20 to 24 years old	1,727	857	870	1,345	1,008	250	95	352
25 years old and over	1,886	698	1,187	1,337	1,038	384	96	329
4-year	9,610	4,406	5,204	7,485	6,551	1,281	553	1,009
15 to 19 years old	2,615	1,255	1,361	2,082	1,810	309	139	288
20 to 24 years old	4,735	2,238	2,497	3,741	3,363	561	295	424
25 years old and over	2,260	913	1,346	1,662	1,378	410	119	296
Graduate school	3,676	1,574	2,103	2,812	2,579	360	421	248
15 to 24 years old	898	391	507	718	685	59	98	37
25 to 34 years old	1,583	708	876	1,162	1,046	163	220	121
35 years old and over	1,195	475	720	932	847	138	102	90
Public...................	14,738	6,608	8,130	11,432	9,630	1,975	918	1,918
2-year	5,006	2,206	2,800	3,874	3,009	766	227	922
4-year	7,333	3,392	3,942	5,695	4,944	984	435	803
Graduate	2,399	1,010	1,389	1,863	1,677	225	256	193
Percent of students:								
Employed full-time.........	17.2	16.2	18.0	17.3	17.4	17.9	15.0	16.4
Employed part-time	16.2	14.0	18.2	17.7	19.3	9.9	15.5	10.6

[1] Includes other races not shown separately. [2] For persons who selected this race group only. See footnote 2, Table 225.
[3] Persons of Hispanic origin may be any race.
Source: U.S. Census Bureau, unpublished data.

Table 280. Higher Education Enrollments in Languages Other Than English: 1970 to 2006

[As of fall (1,111.5 represents 1,111,500). For credit enrollment]

Enrollment	1970	1980	1983	1986	1990	1995	1998	2002	2006
Registrations [1] (1,000)........	**1,111.5**	**924.8**	**966.0**	**1,003.2**	**1,184.1**	**1,138.8**	**1,193.8**	**1,397.3**	**1,577.8**
By selected language (1,000):									
Spanish.....................	389.2	379.4	386.2	411.3	533.9	606.3	656.6	746.3	823.0
French......................	359.3	248.4	270.1	275.3	272.5	205.4	199.1	202.0	206.4
German.....................	202.6	126.9	128.2	121.0	133.3	96.3	89.0	91.1	94.3
Italian.......................	34.2	34.8	38.7	40.9	49.7	43.8	49.3	63.9	78.4
American Sign Language	(X)	(X)	(X)	(X)	1.6	4.3	11.4	60.8	78.8
Japanese....................	6.6	11.5	16.1	23.5	45.7	44.7	43.1	52.2	66.6
Chinese.....................	6.2	11.4	13.2	16.9	19.5	26.5	28.5	34.2	51.6
Latin........................	27.6	25.0	24.2	25.0	28.2	25.9	26.1	29.8	32.2
Russian.....................	36.2	24.0	30.4	34.0	44.6	24.7	23.8	23.9	24.8
Hebrew	16.6	19.4	18.2	15.6	13.0	13.1	15.8	22.8	23.8
Ancient Greek	16.7	22.1	19.4	17.6	16.4	16.3	16.4	20.4	22.8
Arabic......................	1.3	3.5	3.4	3.4	3.5	4.4	5.5	10.6	24.0
Portuguese	5.1	4.9	4.4	5.1	6.2	6.5	6.9	8.4	10.3
Korean......................	0.1	0.4	0.7	0.9	2.3	3.3	4.5	5.2	7.1
Index (1965 = 100)	107.3	89.3	93.2	96.8	114.3	109.9	115.2	134.9	152.3

X Not applicable. [1] Includes other languages not shown separately.
Source: Furman, Nelly, David Goldberg, and Natalia Lusin. Enrollments in Languages Other Than English in United States Institutions of Higher Education, Fall 2006. Modern Language Association, November 13, 2007 (copyright). For 1968 to 2002, consult prior Association of Departments of Foreign Languages (ADFL) Bulletins.

Table 281. College Freshmen—Summary Characteristics: 1980 to 2009

[In percent, except as indicated (24.5 represents $24,500). As of fall for first-time full-time freshmen in 4-year colleges and universities. Based on sample survey and subject to sampling error; see source]

Characteristic	1980	1990	1995	2000	2005	2006	2007	2008	2009
Sex:									
Male	48.8	46.9	45.6	45.2	45.0	45.1	45.2	45.4	45.9
Female	51.2	53.1	54.4	54.8	55.0	54.9	54.8	54.6	54.1
Applied to more than three colleges	31.5	42.9	44.4	50.5	55.4	56.5	56.5	60.1	61.9
Average grade in high school:									
A– to A+	26.6	29.4	36.1	42.9	46.6	46.0	45.9	47.2	48.1
B– to B+	58.2	57.0	54.2	50.5	48.0	49.4	49.0	48.0	47.5
C to C+	14.9	13.4	9.6	6.5	5.4	4.6	5.0	4.7	4.4
D	0.2	0.2	0.1	0.1	0.1	0.1	0.1	0.1	0.1
Political orientation:	(NA)	(NA)	(NA)	67.4	79.7	74.2	75.9	(NA)	77.0
Liberal	21.0	24.6	22.9	24.8	27.1	28.4	29.3	31.0	29.0
Middle of the road	57.0	51.7	51.3	51.9	45.0	43.3	43.4	43.3	44.4
Conservative	19.0	20.6	21.8	18.9	22.6	23.9	23.1	20.7	21.8
Probable field of study:									
Arts and humanities	10.5	10.5	11.2	12.1	12.8	13.1	12.8	13.5	13.3
Biological sciences	4.5	4.9	8.3	6.6	7.6	8.3	8.6	9.3	9.7
Business	21.2	21.1	15.4	16.7	17.4	17.9	17.7	16.8	14.3
Education	8.4	10.3	10.1	11.0	9.9	9.5	9.2	8.2	8.1
Engineering	11.2	9.7	8.1	8.7	8.3	8.0	7.5	9.4	9.7
Physical science	3.2	2.8	3.1	2.6	3.1	3.1	3.2	3.2	3.4
Social science	8.2	11.0	9.9	10.0	10.7	11.2	11.1	11.5	11.7
Professional	15.5	13.0	16.5	11.6	14.6	13.0	14.5	13.8	14.4
Technical	3.1	1.1	1.2	2.1	1.2	1.1	1.0	1.0	1.1
Data processing/computer programming	1.7	0.7	0.8	1.5	0.5	0.5	0.6	0.5	0.6
Other [1]	14.0	15.8	16.0	17.9	14.1	14.2	14.2	13.2	14.3
Communications	2.4	2.9	1.8	2.7	2.0	2.2	1.8	1.8	1.9
Computer science	2.6	1.7	2.2	3.7	1.1	1.1	1.1	1.0	1.0
Personal objectives—very important or essential:									
Being very well off financially	62.5	72.3	72.8	73.4	74.5	73.4	74.4	76.8	78.1
Developing a meaningful philosophy of life	62.5	45.9	45.4	42.4	45.0	46.3	49.2	51.4	48.0
Keeping up to date with political affairs	45.2	46.6	32.3	28.1	36.4	37.2	37.2	39.5	36.0
Median family income ($1,000)	24.5	46.6	54.8	64.4	73.2	76.2	77.9	77.5	76.6

NA Not available. [1] Includes other fields not shown separately.

Source: The Higher Education Research Institute, University of California, Los Angeles, CA, *The American Freshman: National Norms*, annual.

Table 282. Students Reported Disability Status by Selected Characteristic: 2007 to 2008

[20,928 represents 20,928,000. Disabled students reported that they had one or more of the following conditions a specific learning disability, a visual handicap, hard of hearing, deafness, a speech disability, an orthopedic handicap, or a health impairment. Based on the 2007–2008 National Postsecondary Student-Aid Study; see source for details. Includes Puerto Rico. See also Appendix III]

Student characteristic	Undergraduate			Graduate and first-professional		
	All students	Disabled students	Nondisabled students	All students	Disabled students	Nondisabled students
Total students (1,000)	**20,928**	**2,266**	**18,662**	**3,456**	**261**	**3,195**
PERCENT DISTRIBUTION						
Total	**100.0**	**10.8**	**89.2**	**100.0**	**7.6**	**92.4**
Age:						
15 to 23 years old	59.7	54.0	60.4	11.4	7.8	11.7
24 to 29 years old	17.3	20.1	17.0	39.9	36.2	40.2
30 years or older	23.0	25.9	22.7	48.7	56.0	48.1
Sex:						
Male	43.1	42.7	43.1	40.1	39.2	40.2
Female	56.9	57.3	56.9	59.9	60.8	59.8
Race/ethnicity of student:						
White, non-Hispanic	61.8	66.3	61.2	66.6	63.6	66.9
Black, non-Hispanic	14.0	12.7	14.1	11.7	19.0	11.1
Hispanic	14.1	12.3	14.4	8.0	7.4	8.0
Asian/Pacific Islander	6.6	4.8	6.8	11.1	7.3	11.4
American Indian/Alaska Native	0.8	0.8	0.9	0.3	0.5	0.3
Other	2.7	3.2	2.6	2.3	2.3	2.3
Attendance status:						
Full-time, full-year	39.3	34.7	39.8	34.1	32.6	34.2
Part-time or part-year	60.7	65.3	60.2	65.9	67.4	65.8
Student housing status:						
On-campus	14.2	11.1	14.5	(NA)	(NA)	(NA)
Off-campus	54.0	56.3	53.7	(NA)	(NA)	(NA)
With parents or relatives	31.9	32.6	31.8	(NA)	(NA)	(NA)
Dependency status:						
Dependent	53.0	46.8	53.7	(S)	(S)	(S)
Independent, unmarried	15.3	19.5	14.7	50.0	52.7	49.8
Independent, married	6.4	6.9	6.3	16.9	12.9	17.2
Independent with dependents	25.4	26.7	25.2	33.1	34.4	33.0

NA Not available. S Figure does not meet publication standards.

Source: U.S. National Center for Education Statistics, *Digest of Education Statistics*, annual.

U.S. Census Bureau, Statistical Abstract of the United States: 2011

Table 283. Average Total Price of Attendance of Undergraduate Education: 2007 to 2008

[In dollars. Excludes students attending more than one institution. Price of attendance includes tuition and fees, books and supplies, room and board, transportation, and personal and other expenses allowed for federal cost of attendance budgets. Based on the 2007–2008 National Postsecondary Student-Aid Study; see source for details. Includes Puerto Rico. See also Appendix III]

Student characteristic	All institu-tions [1]	Public 2-year	Public 4-year		Private not-for-profit 4-year		Private for-profit
			Non-doctorate	Doctorate	Non-doctorate	Doctorate	
Total..........................	14,006	7,033	12,657	16,615	25,194	31,628	20,636
Age: [2]							
18 years or younger.................	17,065	12,630	16,664	19,888	32,586	38,311	19,868
19 to 23 years.....................	16,059	6,830	10,128	12,513	17,861	22,540	20,376
24 to 29 years.....................	11,551	8,035	11,188	13,833	17,823	21,294	20,275
30 to 39 years.....................	10,994	3,854	5,739	7,319	8,446	10,419	21,305
40 years or older..................	9,269	8,268	14,912	18,501	31,809	37,581	21,265
Sex:							
Male................................	13,957	7,406	13,778	17,661	30,099	35,206	21,765
Female.............................	14,044	6,856	10,701	13,005	17,458	20,772	20,133
Race:							
One race:							
White..............................	14,446	6,546	9,690	12,452	15,561	17,839	20,888
Black or African American..........	13,235	5,992	9,062	10,623	14,722	14,452	20,141
Asian..............................	15,122	7,121	12,668	16,486	25,512	31,163	22,203
American Indian/Alaska Native.......	12,150	7,013	13,170	16,707	26,717	32,236	25,013
Native Hawaiian or other Pacific Islander................	12,904	6,974	12,824	15,891	21,412	26,817	23,122
Other race.........................	12,788	6,990	10,511	15,513	19,548	27,808	24,076
More than one race.................	15,077	7,313	13,285	18,271	29,162	36,973	23,245
Hispanic or Latino [3]...............	12,419	6,920	12,644	16,757	24,765	32,182	19,753
Attendance pattern:							
Full-time, full-year................	22,368	7,330	10,436	15,078	27,614	(S)	28,638
Full-time, part-year................	12,227	6,718	12,988	16,878	18,659	40,521	16,653
Part-time, full-year................	10,655	6,759	10,879	15,650	16,534	(S)	19,259
Part-time, part-year................	5,231	7,495	13,028	17,256	28,172	34,460	11,810

S Data do not meet publication standards. [1] Includes public less-than-2-year and private not-for-profit less-than-4-year. [2] As of December 31, 2007. [3] Persons of Hispanic origin may be any race.

Source: U.S. National Center for Education Statistics, "Student Financial Aid Estimates for 2007–08," NCES 2009-166, April 2009, <http://nces.ed.gov/surveys/npsas/>.

Table 284. Average Amount of Aid Received by Aided Undergraduates: 2007 to 2008

[In dollars, except percent. Excludes students attending more than one institution. Types of financial aid are grants, loans, and work-study programs. Based on the 2007–2008 National Postsecondary Student-Aid Study; see source for details. Includes Puerto Rico. See also Appendix III]

Student characteristic	Percent of under-graduates receiving aid	Amount of aid received by type of institution						
		All institu-tions [1]	Public 2-year	Public 4-year		Private not-for-profit 4 year		Private for-profit
				Non-doctorate	Doctorate	Non-doctorate	Doctorate	
Total..........................	65.3	9,127	3,395	8,041	10,097	16,006	18,962	10,821
Age: [2]								
18 years or younger....................	70.6	10,718	3,563	8,365	10,485	19,836	21,538	12,051
19 to 23 years........................	66.0	10,481	3,516	8,612	10,358	19,114	21,171	11,077
24 to 29 years........................	65.7	7,788	3,675	7,682	9,603	10,798	13,840	10,853
30 to 39 years........................	66.1	6,817	3,190	6,625	8,898	9,182	10,889	10,418
40 years or older.....................	55.9	5,702	2,774	5,531	7,027	8,540	8,393	10,293
Sex:								
Male..................................	61.0	9,309	3,346	8,024	10,094	15,678	19,152	11,772
Female................................	68.6	9,003	3,427	8,055	10,099	16,241	18,816	10,397
Race:								
One race:								
White................................	63.2	9,425	3,492	8,176	9,615	16,947	19,039	10,943
Black or African American.............	75.8	8,971	3,511	9,604	11,905	14,226	18,369	10,608
Asian.................................	52.6	9,700	3,156	7,496	10,752	17,611	19,508	11,652
American Indian/Alaska Native ...	71.4	7,089	3,549	6,864	9,401	17,673	(S)	9,809
Native Hawaiian or other Pacific Islander ...	61.6	8,355	2,884	6,710	12,843	16,473	15,889	11,928
Other race............................	62.7	7,802	2,866	(S)	11,819	(S)	(S)	9,200
More than one race....................	68.3	10,264	3,865	8,387	10,951	19,422	22,496	11,415
Hispanic or Latino [3]..................	68.7	7,924	2,949	6,213	10,275	11,851	18,270	10,646
Attendance pattern:								
Full-time, full-year...................	80.1	12,902	5,432	9,867	11,548	19,956	22,363	13,051
Full-time, part-year...................	70.8	7,520	3,113	6,082	7,304	10,548	13,655	9,902
Part-time, full-year...................	61.0	6,159	3,378	6,460	8,823	10,867	12,449	11,383
Part-time, part-year...................	43.6	3,657	1,840	4,100	5,057	5,861	6,820	7,160

S Data do not meet publication standards. [1] Includes public less-than-2-year and private not-for-profit less-than-4-year. [2] As of 31 December 2007. [3] Persons of Hispanic origin may be any race.

Source: U.S. National Center for Education Statistics, "Student Financial Aid Estimates for 2007–08," NCES 2009-166, April 2009, <http://nces.ed.gov/surveys/npsas/>.

Table 285. Average Out-of-Pocket Net Price of Attendance for Undergraduates: 2007 to 2008

[In dollars. Excludes students attending more than one institution. Net Price of attendance is the price that students pay to receive postsecondary education after taking financial aid into account. Based on net tuition and net price for all students. Based on the 2007–2008 National Postsecondary Student-Aid Study; see source for details. Includes Puerto Rico. See also Appendix III]

| Student characteristic | All institu-tions [1] | Type of Institution | | | | | |
| | | Public 2-year | Public 4-year | | Private not-for-profit 4 year | | Private for-profit |
			Non-doctorate	Doctorate	Non-doctorate	Doctorate	
Total.	8,769	5,645	7,801	10,627	12,772	18,103	11,647
Age: [2]							
18 years or younger	10,219	6,612	8,927	11,313	15,067	20,967	9,974
19 to 23 years	9,974	5,995	8,488	11,509	14,672	20,217	11,460
24 to 29 years	7,160	5,303	6,559	7,508	9,755	11,380	11,239
30 to 39 years	7,073	5,168	5,916	7,360	8,858	9,832	12,353
40 years or older	6,487	4,998	5,933	7,180	9,365	8,822	12,379
Sex:							
Male.	8,985	5,705	8,061	11,042	12,946	19,016	11,942
Female.	8,603	5,599	7,586	10,248	12,644	17,313	11,517
Race:							
One race:							
White	9,211	5,674	8,266	11,196	13,550	18,899	11,858
Black or African American	7,286	5,192	6,039	7,318	10,564	12,319	11,109
Asian	10,613	6,386	9,518	12,615	17,147	24,543	12,809
American Indian/Alaska Native	7,715	5,493	6,047	8,115	(S)	(S)	16,623
Native Hawaiian or other Pacific Islander	8,445	5,627	8,840	9,499	7,855	29,807	11,896
Other race	8,286	5,435	(S)	7,968	(S)	(S)	15,868
More than one race	8,867	5,854	7,581	10,100	11,828	17,450	13,817
Hispanic or Latino [3]	7,567	5,638	6,941	8,657	9,761	12,824	11,028
Attendance pattern:							
Full-time, full-year	13,218	9,428	9,654	12,419	15,659	21,293	16,875
Full-time, part-year	7,751	5,442	6,672	8,522	10,386	14,220	8,825
Part-time, full-year	7,410	6,544	7,588	9,030	9,561	12,597	9,174
Part-time, part-year	3,906	3,348	4,193	5,297	5,498	6,791	5,933

S Date do not meet publication standards. [1] Includes public less-than-2-year and private not-for-profit less-than-4-year. [2] As of 31 December 2007. [3] Persons of Hispanic origin may be of any race.

Source: U.S. National Center for Education Statistics, "Student Financial Aid Estimates for 2007–08," NCES 2009-166, April 2009, <http://nces.ed.gov/surveys/npsas/>.

Table 286. Higher Education Price Indexes: 2002 to 2009

[1983 = 100. For years ending June 30. The Higher Education Price Index (HEPI), calculated for the July–June academic fiscal year, reflects prices paid by colleges and universities for the following eight cost factors: faculty salaries, administrative salaries, clerical and service employees, fringe benefits, miscellaneous services, supplies and materials, and utilities. Minus sign (–) indicates decrease]

| Item and year | Total | Personnel compensation | | | | | Contracted services, supplies, and equipment | | |
		Faculty salaries	Admin-istrative salaries	Clerical salaries	Service employ-ees salaries	Fringe benefits	Miscel-laneous services	Supplies and materials	Utilities
INDEXES									
2002.	212.7	222.7	236.4	205.4	189.6	277.1	205.8	128.2	118.1
2003.	223.5	229.4	255.7	211.1	193.9	292.3	209.5	132.2	157.6
2004.	231.7	234.2	263.3	217.1	197.6	312.8	216.4	135.6	176.4
2005.	240.8	240.7	274.0	223.4	201.4	327.2	222.7	145.5	200.2
2006.	253.1	248.2	287.7	229.5	205.5	343.7	228.8	158.1	255.7
2007.	260.3	257.6	299.2	237.7	213.6	360.8	238.3	165.3	220.6
2008.	273.2	268.1	314.0	245.0	220.4	380.7	246.5	180.0	252.0
2009.	279.3	277.3	330.9	251.6	226.7	394.4	253.1	181.6	213.8
ANNUAL PERCENT CHANGE [1]									
2002.	3.0	3.8	3.1	3.9	3.8	5.9	3.0	–2.7	–30.5
2003.	5.1	3.0	8.2	2.8	2.3	5.5	1.8	3.1	33.5
2004.	3.7	2.1	3.0	2.8	1.9	7.0	3.3	2.6	11.9
2005.	3.9	2.8	4.1	2.9	1.9	4.6	2.9	7.3	13.5
2006.	5.1	3.1	5.0	2.7	2.0	5.0	2.7	8.7	27.7
2007.	2.8	3.8	4.0	3.6	4.0	5.0	4.2	4.5	–13.7
2008.	5.0	4.1	5.0	3.1	3.2	5.5	3.4	8.9	14.2
2009.	2.3	3.4	5.4	2.7	2.9	3.6	2.7	0.9	–15.1

[1] Percent change from the immediate prior year.

Source: The Commonfund Institute, Wilton, CT, (copyright), <http://www.commonfund.org>.

U.S. Census Bureau, Statistical Abstract of the United States: 2011

Table 287. Federal Student Financial Assistance: 1995 to 2010

[For award years July 1 of year shown to the following June 30 (35,477 represents $35,477,000,000). Funds utilized exclude operating costs, etc., and represent funds given to students]

Type of assistance	1995	2000	2005	2007	2008, est.	2009, est.	2010, est.
FUNDS UTILIZED (mil. dol.)							
Total	**35,477**	**44,007**	**72,634**	**83,046**	**97,478**	**129,148**	**145,241**
Federal Pell Grants	5,472	7,956	12,693	14,676	18,291	28,213	32,295
Academic Competitiveness Grants	(X)	(X)	(X)	309	340	503	548
SMART [1] Grants	(X)	(X)	(X)	205	200	361	384
TEACH Grants [2]	(X)	(X)	(X)	(X)	25	72	80
Federal Supplemental Educational Opportunity Grant	764	907	1,084	1,068	1,039	959	959
Federal Work-Study	764	939	1,050	1,063	1,113	1,417	1,171
Federal Perkins Loan	1,029	1,144	1,593	1,383	961	1,106	1,042
Federal Direct Student Loan (FDSL)	8,296	10,348	12,930	13,022	18,213	29,738	73,529
Federal Family Education Loans (FFEL)	19,152	22,712	43,284	51,320	57,296	66,778	35,234
NUMBER OF AWARDS (1,000)							
Total	**13,667**	**15,043**	**21,317**	**23,084**	**25,713**	**31,945**	**34,890**
Federal Pell Grants	3,612	3,899	5,167	5,543	6,157	7,738	8,355
Academic Competitiveness Grants	(X)	(X)	(X)	396	438	716	786
SMART [1] Grants	(X)	(X)	(X)	65	64	139	150
TEACH Grants [2]	(X)	(X)	(X)	(X)	8	31	32
Federal Supplemental Educational Opportunity Grant	1,083	1,175	1,419	1,450	1,451	1,303	1,303
Federal Work-Study	702	713	710	697	678	930	768
Federal Perkins Loan	688	639	727	650	488	521	490
Federal Direct Student Loan (FDSL)	2,339	2,739	2,971	2,764	3,730	6,109	14,790
Federal Family Education Loans (FFEL)	5,243	5,878	10,323	11,519	12,698	14,459	8,216
AVERAGE AWARD (dol.)							
Total	**2,596**	**2,925**	**3,407**	**3,598**	**3,791**	**4,043**	**4,163**
Federal Pell Grants	1,515	2,041	2,456	2,648	2,971	3,646	3,865
Academic Competitiveness Grants/SMART [1] Grants	(X)	(X)	(X)	779	774	703	697
SMART [1] Grants	(X)	(X)	(X)	3,137	3,107	2,597	2,560
TEACH Grants [2]	(X)	(X)	(X)	(X)	3,125	2,369	2,500
Federal Supplemental Educational Opportunity Grant	705	772	764	736	716	736	736
Federal Work-Study	1,088	1,318	1,478	1,524	1,642	1,524	1,524
Federal Perkins Loan	1,496	1,790	2,190	2,125	1,968	2,125	2,125
Federal Direct Student Loan (FDSL)	3,547	3,778	4,352	4,711	4,882	4,867	4,971
Federal Family Education Loans (FFEL)	3,653	3,864	4,193	3,941	4,512	4,618	4,289
COHORT DEFAULT RATE [3]							
Federal Perkins Loan	12.6	9.9	8.1	8.3	10.4	(NA)	(NA)

NA Not available. X Not applicable. [1] National Science and Mathematics Access to Retain Talent. [2] Teacher Education Assistance for College and Higher Education (TEACH) Grant Program. [3] As of June 30. Represents the percent of borrowers entering repayment status in year shown who defaulted in the following year.

Source: U.S. Department of Education, Office of Postsecondary Education, unpublished data.

Table 288. State and Local Financial Support for Higher Education by State: 2006 to 2009

[For 2008-2009 fiscal year, except as indicated (10,839.9 represents 10,839,900). Data for the 50 states]

State	2008–2009 FTE enrollment [1] (thousands)	2008–2009 Educational appropriations per FTE enrollment [2] (dollars)	State	2008–2009 FTE enrollment [1] (thousands)	2008–2009 Educational appropriations per FTE enrollment [2] (dollars)
Total	**10,839.9**	**6,904**			
AL	195.9	5,768	MT	36.4	5,087
AK	19.0	15,362	NE	77.8	7,486
AZ	235.8	7,684	NV	65.7	8,451
AR	108.5	6,474	NH	34.7	3,505
CA	1,789.8	7,043	NJ	246.2	7,546
CO	167.9	4,687	NM	89.5	8,337
CT	80.4	10,294	NY	542.3	8,923
DE	32.4	7,104	NC	385.8	8,260
FL	561.9	6,340	ND	36.4	5,480
GA	330.9	8,265	OH	407.4	5,210
HI	37.1	13,739	OK	127.1	7,240
ID	44.7	8,611	OR	141.7	5,172
IL	388.2	7,937	PA	353.5	5,722
IN	241.8	5,439	RI	30.7	5,192
IA	117.3	6,530	SC	153.2	5,209
KS	129.4	6,156	SD	31.0	3,924
KY	144.1	7,134	TN	178.1	7,317
LA	169.6	7,596	TX	822.1	7,001
ME	35.8	6,883	UT	107.6	6,504
MD	210.0	8,030	VT	20.7	2,962
MA	152.9	6,740	VA	294.4	5,666
MI	398.9	5,908	WA	236.7	6,787
MN	200.7	6,502	WV	74.9	5,120
MS	120.3	5,963	WI	224.1	6,810
MO	184.8	6,288	WY	23.6	13,706

[1] Full-time equivalent. Includes degree enrollment and enrollment in public postsecondary programs resulting in a certificate or other formal recognition. Includes summer sessions. Excludes medical enrollments. [2] State and local appropriations for general operating expenses of public postsecondary education. Includes American Recovery and Reinvestment Act of 2009 (ARRA) funds, state-funded financial aid to students attending in-state public institutions. Excludes sums for research, agricultural extension, and teaching hospitals and medical schools.

Source: State Higher Education Executive Officers, Boulder, CO (copyright), <http://www.sheeo.org>.

Table 289. Institutions of Higher Education—Average Charges: 1985 to 2009

[In dollars. Estimated. For the entire academic year ending in year shown. Figures are average charges per full-time equivalent student. Room and board are based on full-time students]

Academic control and year	Tuition and required fees [1]				Board rates [2]				Dormitory charges			
	All institu- tions	2-yr. col- leges	4-yr. univer- sities	Other 4-yr. schools	All institu- tions	2-yr. col- leges	4-yr. univer- sities	Other 4-yr. schools	All institu- tions	2-yr. col- leges	4-yr. univer- sities	Other 4-yr. schools
Public:												
1985........	971	584	1,386	1,117	1,241	1,302	1,276	1,201	1,196	921	1,237	1,200
1990........	1,356	756	2,035	1,608	1,635	1,581	1,728	1,561	1,513	962	1,561	1,554
1995........	2,057	1,192	2,977	2,499	1,949	1,712	2,108	1,866	1,959	1,232	1,992	2,044
2000........	2,506	1,338	3,768	3,091	2,364	1,834	2,628	2,239	2,440	1,549	2,516	2,521
2004........	3,319	1,702	5,363	4,141	2,823	2,233	3,084	2,724	3,107	2,086	3,232	3,198
2005........	3,629	1,849	5,939	4,512	2,931	2,353	3,222	2,809	3,304	2,174	3,427	3,413
2006........	3,874	1,935	6,399	4,765	3,035	2,306	3,372	2,899	3,545	2,251	3,654	3,672
2007........	4,102	2,018	6,842	5,020	3,191	2,390	3,498	3,083	3,757	2,407	3,875	3,881
2008........	4,291	2,061	7,173	5,285	3,331	2,409	3,668	3,221	3,952	2,506	4,079	4,083
2009, prel....	4,544	2,137	7,630	5,618	3,554	2,777	3,911	3,412	4,185	2,654	4,335	4,313
Private:												
1985........	5,315	3,485	6,843	5,135	1,462	1,294	1,647	1,405	1,426	1,424	1,753	1,309
1990........	8,147	5,196	10,348	7,778	1,948	1,811	2,339	1,823	1,923	1,663	2,411	1,774
1995........	11,111	6,914	14,537	10,653	2,509	2,023	3,035	2,362	2,587	2,233	3,469	2,347
2000........	14,081	8,235	19,307	13,361	2,882	2,922	3,157	2,790	3,224	2,808	4,070	2,976
2004........	17,327	11,546	24,128	16,298	3,364	4,432	3,778	3,222	3,945	3,581	4,979	3,647
2005........	18,154	12,122	25,643	17,050	3,485	3,728	3,855	3,370	4,171	4,243	5,263	3,854
2006........	18,862	12,450	26,954	17,702	3,647	4,726	4,039	3,517	4,380	3,994	5,517	4,063
2007........	20,048	12,708	28,580	18,848	3,785	3,429	4,166	3,672	4,606	4,613	5,691	4,302
2008........	21,462	13,126	30,251	20,190	3,992	4,074	4,376	3,875	4,804	4,484	6,006	4,466
2009, prel....	23,201	11,789	30,251	21,451	3,994	3,272	4,376	3,880	4,725	3,796	6,006	4,347

[1] For in-state students. [2] Beginning 1990, rates reflect 20 meals per week, rather than meals served 7 days a week.

Source: U.S. National Center for Education Statistics, *Digest of Education Statistics*, annual. See also <http://www.nces.ed.gov /programs/digest/>.

Table 290. Voluntary Financial Support of Higher Education: 1990 to 2009

[For school years ending in years shown (9,800 represents $9,800,000,000). Voluntary support, as defined in Gift Reporting Standards, excludes income from endowment and other invested funds as well as all support received from federal, state, and local governments and their agencies and contract research]

Item	Unit	1990	1995	2000	2005	2006	2007	2008	2009
Estimated support, total............	Mil. dol.	9,800	12,750	23,200	25,600	28,000	29,750	31,600	27,850
Individuals.....................	Mil. dol.	4,770	6,540	12,220	12,100	14,100	13,920	14,820	12,125
Alumni....................	Mil. dol.	2,540	3,600	6,800	7,100	8,400	8,270	8,700	7,130
Business corporations............	Mil. dol.	2,170	2,560	4,150	4,400	4,600	4,800	4,900	4,620
Foundations...................	Mil. dol.	1,920	2,460	5,080	7,000	7,100	8,500	9,100	8,235
Fundraising consortia and other organizations...................	Mil. dol.	700	940	1,380	1,730	1,825	2,150	2,400	2,545
Religious organizations...........	Mil. dol.	240	250	370	370	375	300	380	325
Current operations..............	Mil. dol.	5,440	7,230	11,270	14,200	15,000	16,100	17,070	16,955
Capital purposes...............	Mil. dol.	4,360	5,520	11,930	11,400	13,000	13,650	14,530	10,895
Support per student.............	Dollars.....	724	893	1,568	1,482	1,601	1,675	1,732	1,489
In 2009 dollars................	Dollars.....	1,187	1,256	1,953	1,627	1,703	1,732	1,724	1,489
Expenditures, higher education.....	Bil. dol.	134.7	183.0	236.8	335.0	353.6	369.0	386.0	387.1
Expenditures per student.........	Dollars.....	9,946	12,814	16,008	19,396	20,219	20,778	21,153	20,700
In 2009 dollars................	Dollars.....	16,316	18,028	19,932	21,293	21,503	21,487	21,065	20,700
Institutions reporting support.......	Number	1,056	1,086	945	997	1,014	1,023	1,052	1,027
Total support reported............	Mil. dol.	8,214	10,992	19,419	20,953	23,475	25,247	27,323	23,693
Private 4-year institutions........	Mil. dol.	5,072	6,500	11,047	11,011	12,857	13,675	14,296	12,351
Public 4-year institutions	Mil. dol.	3,056	4,382	8,254	9,780	10,421	11,321	12,766	11,141
2-year colleges	Mil. dol.	85	110	117	163	197	251	261	201

Source: Council for Aid to Education, New York, NY, *Voluntary Support of Education*, annual.

Table 291. Average Salaries for College Faculty Members: 2008 to 2010

[In thousands of dollars (73.2 represents $73,200). For academic year ending in year shown. Figures are for 9 months teaching for full-time faculty members in 2-year and 4-year institutions with ranks. Fringe benefits averaged in 2008, $20,178 in public institutions and $24,193 in private institutions; in 2009, $21,691 in public institutions and $25,374 in private institutions; and in 2010, $22,258 in public institutions and $25,516 in private institutions]

Type of control and academic rank	2008	2009	2010	Type of control and academic rank	2008	2009	2010
Public: All ranks	73.2	77.0	78.0	Private: [1] All ranks	88.2	92.3	92.9
Professor...................	98.3	104.5	105.7	Professor...................	122.2	128.3	128.7
Associate professor..........	72.2	75.2	75.7	Associate professor..........	79.2	82.9	82.9
Assistant professor	60.8	63.4	64.0	Assistant professor	65.8	69.0	69.5
Instructor..................	43.4	44.7	46.5	Instructor..................	49.9	51.6	52.8

[1] Excludes church-related colleges and universities.

Source: American Association of University Professors, Washington, DC, *AAUP Annual Report on the Economic Status of the Profession*.

U.S. Census Bureau, Statistical Abstract of the United States: 2011

Table 292. Employees in Higher Education Institutions by Sex and Occupation: 1995 to 2007

[In thousands (2,662.1 represents 2,662,100). As of fall. Based on complete census taken every other year; see source]

Year and status	Total	Professional staff										Non-professional staff, total
		Total	Executive, administrative, and managerial		Faculty [1]		Research/instruction assistants		Other			
			Male	Female	Male	Female	Male	Female	Male	Female		
1995, total	**2,662.1**	**1,744.9**	**82.1**	**65.3**	**562.9**	**368.8**	**124.0**	**91.9**	**177.2**	**272.7**		**917.2**
Full–time	1,801.4	1,066.5	79.2	61.8	360.2	190.7	–	–	151.5	223.2		734.9
Part–time	860.7	678.4	2.9	3.6	202.7	178.1	124.0	91.9	25.6	49.5		182.3
2005, total [2]	**3,379.1**	**2,459.9**	**95.2**	**101.1**	**714.5**	**576.0**	**167.5**	**149.6**	**262.8**	**393.2**		**919.2**
Full–time	2,179.9	1,432.1	92.9	97.2	401.5	274.1	–	–	231.4	335.0		747.8
Part–time	1,199.2	1,027.8	2.4	3.9	312.9	301.9	167.5	149.6	31.4	58.2		171.4
2007, total	**3,561.4**	**2,629.4**	**102.3**	**115.3**	**743.8**	**627.6**	**173.1**	**155.9**	**282.9**	**428.6**		**932.0**
Full–time	2,281.2	1,526.8	99.6	110.7	409.1	294.3	–	–	248.5	364.6		754.4
Part–time	1,280.2	1,102.6	2.7	4.6	334.7	333.2	173.1	155.9	34.4	64.0		177.6

– Represents zero. [1] Instruction and research. [2] Beginning 2005, data reflect the new classification of institutions. See footnote 1, Table 274.

Source: U.S. National Center for Education Statistics, *Digest of Education Statistics*, annual. See also <http://www.nces.ed.gov/programs/digest>.

Table 293. Faculty in Institutions of Higher Education: 1980 to 2007

[In thousands (686 represents 686,000), except percent. As of fall. Based on complete census taken every other year; see source]

Year	Total	Employment status		Control		Level		Percent		
		Full-time	Part-time	Public	Private	4-Year	2-Year or less	Part-time	Public	2-Year or less
1980 [1] . . .	686	450	236	495	191	494	192	34	72	28
1985 [1] . . .	715	459	256	503	212	504	211	36	70	30
1991 [2] . . .	826	536	291	581	245	591	235	35	70	28
1995	932	551	381	657	275	647	285	41	70	31
1997 [3] . . .	990	569	421	695	295	683	307	43	70	31
1999 [3] . . .	1,028	591	437	713	315	714	314	43	69	31
2001 [3] . . .	1,113	618	495	771	342	764	349	44	69	31
2003 [3] . . .	1,174	630	544	792	382	814	359	46	67	31
2005 [3] . . .	1,290	676	615	841	449	917	373	48	65	29
2007 [3] . . .	1,371	703	668	877	494	991	381	49	64	28

[1] Estimated on the basis of enrollment. [2] Data beginning 1991 not comparable to prior years. [3] Beginning 1997, data reflect the new classification of institutions. See footnote 1, Table 274.

Source: U.S. National Center for Education Statistics, *Digest of Education Statistics*, annual. See also <http://www.nces.ed.gov/programs/digest/>.

Table 294. Salary Offers to Candidates for Degrees: 2005 to 2009

[In dollars. Data are average beginning salaries based on offers made by business, industrial, government, nonprofit, and educational employers to graduating students. Data from representative colleges throughout the United States]

Field of study	Bachelor's			Master's [1]			Doctoral		
	2005	2008	2009	2005	2008	2009	2005	2008	2009
Accounting.	42,940	48,020	48,471	45,992	50,124	48760	(NA)	(NA)	(NA)
Business administration/ management [2]	39,480	46,171	44,607	[3] 50,513	61,353	[3] 63,615	[3] 66,500	[3] 91,734	[3] 82,429
Marketing.	36,409	41,506	42,260	[3] 47,000	[3] 43,300	(NA)	(NA)	(NA)	(NA)
Engineering:									
Civil	43,774	51,780	52,287	48,619	56,300	[3] 53,311	[3] 59,216	[3] 60,981	[3] 60,351
Chemical	53,639	63,773	65,675	62,845	[3] 66,338	[3] 70,484	[3] 73,317	82,419	[3] 85,250
Computer.	52,242	60,280	60,844	58,631	[3] 75,712	[3] 72,771	[3] 69,625	[3] 96,235	[3] 104,286
Electrical	51,773	57,603	60,509	64,781	72,814	70,921	[3] 75,066	85,045	[3] 89,715
Mechanical	50,175	57,024	59,222	60,223	65,121	66,961	69,757	72,068	[3] 75,186
Nuclear [4]	[3] 51,225	58,531	60,209	[3] 59,059	[3] 62,109	[3] 69,100	(NA)	(NA)	(NA)
Petroleum	62,236	75,621	85,417	[3] 65,000	[3] 87,000	(NA)	(NA)	(NA)	(NA)
Engineering technology. . . .	45,790	53,511	55,023	(NA)	(NA)	(NA)	(NA)	(NA)	(NA)
Chemistry	38,635	43,951	39,354	(NA)	[3] 54,093	[3] 49,800	55,874	66,985	62,785
Mathematics	43,304	49,759	50,461	[3] 34,500	[3] 68,400	[3] 58,200	[3] 55,047	[3] 68,095	[3] 70,226
Physics	[3] 44,700	49,616	[3] 53,939	[3] 62,500	(NA)	[3] 98,425	[3] 54,897	[3] 54,827	[3] 74,333
Humanities.	31,565	[3] 40,702	[3] 38,292	[3] 35,212	[3] 39,099	[3] 42,380	[3] 43,728	[3] 41,400	[3] 47,491
Social sciences [5]	31,621	39,476	36,217	[3] 40,575	[3] 52,605	[3] 47,000	[3] 46,838	[3] 56,509	[3] 54,870
Computer science	50,664	61,110	61,467	64,840	73,826	[3] 68,627	[3] 84,025	[3] 87,216	[3] 84,080

NA Not available. [1] Candidates with 1 year or less of full-time nonmilitary employment. [2] For master's degree, offers are after nontechnical undergraduate degree. [3] Fewer than 50 offers reported. [4] Includes engineering physics. [5] Excludes economics.

Source: National Association of Colleges and Employers, Bethlehem, PA (copyright). Reprinted with permission from Fall 2005, 2008, and 2009 Salary Survey. All rights reserved.

186 Education

Table 295. Degrees Earned by Level and Sex: 1960 to 2008

[In thousands (477 represents 477,000), except percent. Based on survey; see Appendix III]

Year ending	All degrees Total	All degrees Percent male	Associate's Male	Associate's Female	Bachelor's Male	Bachelor's Female	Master's Male	Master's Female	First professional Male	First professional Female	Doctoral Male	Doctoral Female
1960 [1]	477	65.8	(NA)	(NA)	254	138	51	24	(NA)	(NA)	9	1
1970.	1,271	59.2	117	89	451	341	126	83	33	2	26	4
1975.	1,666	56.0	191	169	505	418	162	131	49	7	27	7
1980.	1,731	51.1	184	217	474	456	151	147	53	17	23	10
1985.	1,828	49.3	203	252	483	497	143	143	50	25	22	11
1990.	1,940	46.6	191	264	492	560	154	171	44	27	24	14
1992.	2,108	45.6	207	297	521	616	162	191	45	29	26	15
1993.	2,167	45.5	212	303	533	632	169	200	45	30	26	16
1994.	2,206	45.1	215	315	532	637	176	211	45	31	27	17
1995.	2,218	44.9	218	321	526	634	179	219	45	31	27	18
1996 [2]	2,248	44.2	220	336	522	642	179	227	45	32	27	18
1997 [2]	2,288	43.6	224	347	521	652	181	238	46	33	27	19
1998 [2]	2,298	43.2	218	341	520	664	184	246	45	34	27	19
1999 [2]	2,323	42.7	218	342	519	682	186	254	44	34	25	19
2000 [2]	2,385	42.6	225	340	530	708	192	265	44	36	25	20
2001 [2]	2,416	42.4	232	347	532	712	194	274	43	37	25	20
2002 [2]	2,494	42.2	238	357	550	742	199	283	43	38	24	20
2003 [2]	2,621	42.1	253	380	573	775	211	301	42	39	24	22
2004 [2]	2,755	41.8	260	405	595	804	230	329	42	41	25	23
2005 [2]	2,850	41.6	268	429	613	826	234	341	44	43	27	26
2006 [2]	2,936	41.3	270	443	631	855	238	356	44	44	29	27
2007 [2]	3,093	41.2	283	468	668	895	246	379	46	45	31	32
2008 [2]	3,144	41.2	286	470	681	918	250	381	47	46	32	33

NA Not available. [1] First-professional degrees are included with bachelor's degrees. [2] Beginning 1996, data reflect the new classification of institutions. See footnote 1, Table 274.

Source: U.S. National Center for Education Statistics, *Digest of Education Statistics*, annual. See also <http://www.nces.ed.gov/programs/digest/>.

Table 296. Degrees Earned by Level and Race/Ethnicity: 1990 to 2008

[For school year ending in year shown. Based on survey; see Appendix III]

Level of degree and race/ethnicity	Total 1990	Total 2000 [1]	Total 2005 [1]	Total 2007 [1]	Total 2008 [1]	Percent distribution 1990	Percent distribution 2000 [1]	Percent distribution 2008 [1]
Associate's degrees, total.	**455,102**	**564,933**	**696,660**	**728,114**	**750,164**	**100.0**	**100.0**	**100.0**
White, non-Hispanic.	376,816	408,772	475,513	491,572	501,079	82.8	72.4	66.8
Black, non-Hispanic.	34,326	60,221	86,402	91,529	95,702	7.5	10.7	12.8
Hispanic.	21,504	51,573	78,557	85,410	91,274	4.7	9.1	12.2
Asian or Pacific Islander	13,066	27,782	33,669	37,266	38,843	2.9	4.9	5.2
American Indian/Alaska Native	3,430	6,497	8,435	8,583	8,849	0.8	1.2	1.2
Nonresident alien.	5,960	10,088	14,084	13,754	14,417	1.3	1.8	1.9
Bachelor's degrees, total	**1,051,344**	**1,237,875**	**1,439,264**	**1,524,092**	**1,563,069**	**100.0**	**100.0**	**100.0**
White, non-Hispanic.	887,151	929,106	1,049,141	1,099,850	1,122,675	84.4	75.1	71.8
Black, non-Hispanic.	61,046	108,013	130,122	146,653	152,457	5.8	8.7	9.8
Hispanic.	32,829	75,059	101,124	114,936	123,048	3.1	6.1	7.9
Asian or Pacific Islander	39,230	77,912	97,209	105,297	109,058	3.7	6.3	7.0
American Indian/Alaska Native	4,390	8,719	10,307	11,455	11,509	0.4	0.7	0.7
Nonresident alien.	26,698	39,066	45,361	45,901	44,322	2.5	3.2	2.8
Master's degrees, total	**324,301**	**457,056**	**574,618**	**604,607**	**625,023**	**100.0**	**100.0**	**100.0**
White, non-Hispanic.	254,299	320,485	379,350	399,267	409,312	78.4	70.1	65.5
Black, non-Hispanic.	15,336	35,874	54,482	62,574	65,062	4.7	7.8	10.4
Hispanic.	7,892	19,253	31,485	34,822	36,801	2.4	4.2	5.9
Asian or Pacific Islander	10,439	23,218	32,783	36,134	37,408	3.2	5.1	6.0
American Indian/Alaska Native	1,090	2,246	3,295	3,575	3,758	0.3	0.5	0.6
Nonresident alien.	35,245	55,980	73,223	68,235	72,682	10.9	12.2	11.6
Doctoral degrees, total	**38,371**	**44,808**	**52,631**	**60,616**	**63,712**	**100.0**	**100.0**	**100.0**
White, non-Hispanic.	26,221	27,843	30,261	34,071	36,390	68.3	62.1	57.1
Black, non-Hispanic.	1,149	2,246	3,056	3,727	3,906	3.0	5.0	6.1
Hispanic.	780	1,305	1,824	2,034	2,279	2.0	2.9	3.6
Asian or Pacific Islander	1,225	2,420	2,911	3,541	3,618	3.2	5.4	5.7
American Indian/Alaska Native	98	160	237	249	272	0.3	0.4	0.4
Nonresident alien.	8,898	10,834	14,342	16,994	17,247	23.2	24.2	27.1
First-professional degrees, total . . .	**70,988**	**80,057**	**87,289**	**90,064**	**91,309**	**100.0**	**100.0**	**100.0**
White, non-Hispanic.	60,487	59,637	63,429	64,546	65,383	85.2	74.5	71.6
Black, non-Hispanic.	3,409	5,555	6,313	6,474	6,400	4.8	6.9	7.0
Hispanic.	2,425	3,865	4,445	4,700	4,840	3.4	4.8	5.3
Asian or Pacific Islander	3,362	8,584	10,501	11,686	11,846	4.7	10.7	13.0
American Indian/Alaska Native	257	564	564	681	675	0.4	0.7	0.7
Nonresident alien.	1,048	1,852	2,037	1,977	2,165	1.5	2.3	2.4

[1] Beginning 2000, data reflect the new classification of institutions. See footnote 1, Table 274.

Source: U.S. National Center for Education Statistics, *Digest of Education Statistics*, annual. See also <http://www.nces.ed.gov/programs/digest/>.

Education 187

Table 297. Degrees and Awards Earned Below Bachelor's by Field: 2008

[Covers associate's degrees and other awards based on postsecondary curriculums of less than 4 years in institutions of higher education. Based on survey; see Appendix III]

Field of study	Less than 1-year awards		1- to less than 4-year awards		Associate degree	
	Total	Women	Total	Women	Total	Women
Total [1]	**260,629**	**141,244**	**190,086**	**117,636**	**750,164**	**467,643**
Agriculture and natural resources, total	3,433	895	1,636	614	5,738	2,140
Architecture and related services	224	79	201	138	568	308
Area, ethnic, cultural, and gender studies	406	285	99	65	169	110
Biological and biomedical sciences	66	34	41	27	2,200	1,533
Business, management, and marketing	33,831	22,972	15,145	11,313	104,566	69,792
Communications and communications technologies	1,392	738	1,234	417	6,857	2,618
Computer and information sciences	9,322	3,192	4,530	1,590	28,296	7,105
Construction trades	9,425	452	8,018	293	4,309	203
Education	3,343	2,888	1,809	1,640	13,108	11,194
Engineering and engineering technologies	9,336	1,588	6,580	850	31,620	4,373
English language and literature/letters	875	557	294	164	1,402	918
Family and consumer sciences	11,200	9,429	3,350	2,702	8,613	8,269
Foreign languages and literatures	837	629	417	375	1,258	1,042
Health professions and related sciences	96,669	77,434	88,865	76,869	155,816	132,882
Nursing	1,730	1,566	4,224	3,648	73,277	64,044
Legal professions and studies	1,382	1,198	2,104	1,814	9,465	8,455
Liberal arts and sciences, general studies, and humanities	328	252	4,631	2,988	254,012	158,574
Library science	181	162	63	57	117	91
Mathematics	28	2	3	–	855	280
Mechanics and repairers	17,776	1,044	20,578	854	15,297	763
Military technologies	3	–	–	–	851	157
Multi/interdisciplinary studies	692	349	957	611	16,255	9,706
Parks, recreation, leisure, and fitness studies	357	168	279	163	1,344	535
Personal and culinary services	7,216	5,530	9,987	8,081	16,592	8,121
Philosophy and religion	11	7	91	48	458	321
Physical sciences and science technologies	306	144	384	146	3,388	1,434
Precision production trades	7,312	418	5,513	232	1,968	130
Psychology	75	51	46	36	2,412	1,858
Public administration and social services	930	718	672	542	4,192	3,623
Security and protective services	20,163	4,738	5,191	1,343	29,590	13,539
Social sciences and history	442	223	187	77	7,812	5,053
Theology and religious vocations	149	95	360	177	582	300
Transportation and material moving	17,394	1,543	883	76	1,550	242
Visual and performing arts	5,525	3,430	5,938	3,334	18,890	11,963

– Represents zero. [1] Includes other fields of study, not shown separately.

Source: U.S. National Center for Education Statistics, *Digest of Education Statistics*, annual. See also <http://www.nces.ed.gov/programs/digest>.

Table 298. Bachelor's Degrees Earned by Field: 1980 to 2008

[The new Classification of Instructional Programs was introduced in 2002–2003. Data for previous years has been reclassified where necessary to conform to the new classifications. Based on survey; see Appendix III]

Field of study	1980	1990	2000	2005	2007	2008
Total [1]	**929,417**	**1,051,344**	**1,237,875**	**1,439,264**	**1,524,092**	**1,563,069**
Agriculture and natural resources	22,802	12,900	24,238	23,002	23,133	24,113
Architecture and related services	9,132	9,364	8,462	9,237	9,717	9,805
Area, ethnic, cultural, and gender studies	2,840	4,447	6,212	7,569	8,194	8,454
Biological and biomedical sciences	46,190	37,204	63,005	64,611	75,151	77,854
Business	186,264	248,568	256,070	311,574	327,531	335,254
Communication, journalism, and related programs [2]	28,616	51,572	57,058	75,238	78,420	81,048
Computer and information sciences	11,154	27,347	37,788	54,111	42,170	38,476
Education	118,038	105,112	108,034	105,451	105,641	102,582
Engineering and engineering technologies	69,387	82,480	73,419	79,743	82,072	83,853
English language and literature/letters	32,187	46,803	50,106	54,379	55,122	55,038
Family and consumer sciences/human sciences	18,411	13,514	16,321	20,074	21,400	21,870
Foreign languages, literatures, and linguistics	12,480	13,133	15,886	18,386	20,275	20,977
Health professions and related clinical sciences	63,848	58,983	80,863	80,685	101,810	111,478
Legal professions and studies	683	1,632	1,969	3,161	3,596	3,771
Liberal arts and sciences, general studies, and humanities	23,196	27,985	36,104	43,751	44,255	46,940
Mathematics and statistics	11,378	14,276	11,418	14,351	14,954	15,192
Multi/interdisciplinary studies	11,457	16,557	28,561	30,243	33,792	36,149
Parks, recreation, leisure, and fitness studies	5,753	4,582	17,571	22,888	27,430	29,931
Philosophy and religious studies	7,069	7,034	8,535	11,584	11,969	12,257
Physical sciences and science technologies	23,407	16,056	18,331	18,905	21,073	21,934
Psychology	42,093	53,952	74,194	85,614	90,039	92,587
Public administration and social services	16,644	13,908	20,185	21,769	23,147	23,493
Security and protective services	15,015	15,354	24,877	30,723	39,206	40,235
Social sciences and history	103,662	118,083	127,101	156,892	164,183	167,363
Theology and religious vocations	6,170	5,185	6,789	9,284	8,696	8,992
Transportation and materials moving	213	2,387	3,395	4,904	5,657	5,203
Visual and performing arts	40,892	39,934	58,791	80,955	85,186	87,703

[1] Includes other fields of study, not shown separately. [2] Includes technologies.

Source: U.S. National Center for Education Statistics, *Digest of Education Statistics*, annual and unpublished data. See also <http://www.nces.ed.gov/programs/digest/>.

Table 299. Master's and Doctoral Degrees Earned by Field: 1980 to 2008

[The new Classification of Instructional Programs was introduced in 2002–2003. Data for previous years has been reclassified where necessary to conform to the new classifications. Based on survey; see Appendix III]

Field of study	1980	1990	2000	2005	2007	2008
MASTER'S DEGREES						
Total [1]	**298,081**	**324,301**	**457,056**	**574,618**	**604,607**	**625,023**
Agriculture and natural resources	3,976	3,382	4,360	4,746	4,623	4,684
Architecture and related services	3,139	3,499	4,268	5,674	5,951	6,065
Area, ethnic, cultural, and gender studies	852	1,191	1,544	1,755	1,699	1,778
Biological and biomedical sciences	6,322	4,906	6,781	8,199	8,747	9,565
Business	55,008	76,676	111,532	142,617	150,211	155,637
Communication, journalism, and related programs [2]	3,082	4,353	5,525	7,195	7,272	7,546
Computer and information sciences	3,647	9,677	14,990	18,416	16,232	17,087
Education	101,819	84,890	123,045	167,490	176,572	175,880
Engineering and engineering technologies	16,765	25,294	26,726	35,133	32,162	34,592
English language and literature/letters	6,026	6,317	7,022	8,468	8,742	9,161
Family and consumer sciences/human sciences	2,690	1,679	1,882	1,827	2,080	2,199
Foreign languages, literatures, and linguistics	3,067	3,018	3,037	3,407	3,443	3,565
Health professions and related clinical sciences	15,374	20,406	42,593	46,703	54,531	58,120
Legal professions and studies	1,817	1,888	3,750	4,170	4,486	4,754
Liberal arts and sciences, general studies, and humanities	2,646	1,999	3,256	3,680	3,634	3,797
Library science	5,374	4,341	4,577	6,213	6,767	7,162
Mathematics and statistics	2,860	3,624	3,208	4,477	4,884	4,980
Multi/interdisciplinary studies	2,494	3,182	3,487	4,252	4,762	5,289
Parks, recreation, leisure, and fitness studies	647	529	2,322	3,740	4,110	4,440
Philosophy and religious studies	1,204	1,327	1,376	1,647	1,716	1,879
Physical sciences and science technologies	5,167	5,410	4,810	5,678	5,839	5,899
Psychology	9,938	10,730	15,740	18,830	21,037	21,431
Public administration and social services	17,560	17,399	25,594	29,552	31,131	33,029
Security and protective services	1,805	1,151	2,609	3,991	4,906	5,760
Social sciences and history	12,176	11,634	14,066	16,952	17,665	18,495
Theology and religious vocations	3,872	4,941	5,534	5,815	6,446	6,996
Visual and performing arts	8,708	8,481	10,918	13,183	13,767	14,164
DOCTORAL DEGREES						
Total [1]	**32,615**	**38,371**	**44,808**	**52,631**	**60,616**	**63,712**
Agriculture and natural resources	991	1,295	1,168	1,173	1,272	1,257
Architecture and related services	79	103	129	179	178	199
Area, ethnic, cultural, and gender studies	151	125	205	189	233	270
Biological and biomedical sciences	3,527	3,837	5,180	5,578	6,354	6,918
Business	767	1,093	1,194	1,498	2,029	2,084
Communication, journalism, and related programs [2]	193	272	357	468	480	496
Computer and information sciences	240	627	779	1,119	1,595	1,698
Education	7,314	6,503	6,409	7,681	8,261	8,491
Engineering and engineering technologies	2,546	5,030	5,421	6,601	8,123	8,167
English language and literature/letters	1,196	986	1,470	1,212	1,178	1,262
Family and consumer sciences/human sciences	192	273	327	331	337	323
Foreign languages, literatures and linguistics	657	810	1,086	1,027	1,059	1,078
Health professions and related clinical sciences	821	1,449	2,053	5,868	8,355	9,886
Legal professions and studies	40	111	74	98	143	172
Liberal arts and sciences, general studies, and humanities	192	63	83	109	77	76
Mathematics and statistics	724	917	1,075	1,176	1,351	1,360
Multi/interdisciplinary studies	318	442	792	983	1,093	1,142
Parks, recreation, leisure, and fitness studies	21	35	134	207	218	228
Philosophy and religious studies	374	445	598	586	637	635
Physical sciences and science technologies	3,044	4,116	3,963	4,114	4,846	4,804
Psychology	3,395	3,811	4,731	5,106	5,153	5,296
Public administration and social services	342	508	537	673	726	760
Security and protective services	18	38	52	94	85	88
Social sciences and history	3,230	3,010	4,095	3,819	3,844	4,059
Theology and religious vocations	1,315	1,317	1,630	1,422	1,573	1,446
Visual and performing arts	655	849	1,127	1,278	1,364	1,453

[1] Includes other fields of study, not shown separately. [2] Includes technologies.

Source: U.S. National Center for Education Statistics, *Digest of Education Statistics*, annual and unpublished data. See also <http://www.nces.ed.gov/programs/digest/>.

U.S. Census Bureau, Statistical Abstract of the United States: 2011

Table 300. First Professional Degrees Earned in Selected Professions: 1970 to 2008

[First professional degrees include degrees which require at least 6 years of college work for completion (including at least 2 years of preprofessional training). Based on survey; see Appendix III]

Type of degree and sex of recipient	1970	1980	1985	1990	1995	2000	2005	2006	2007	2008
Medicine (M.D.):										
Institutions conferring degrees	86	112	120	124	119	118	120	119	120	120
Degrees conferred, total	8,314	14,902	16,041	15,075	15,537	15,286	15,461	15,455	15,730	15,646
Percent to women	8.4	23.4	30.4	34.2	38.8	42.7	47.3	48.9	49.2	49.3
Dentistry (D.D.S. or D.M.D.):										
Institutions conferring degrees	48	58	59	57	53	54	53	54	55	55
Degrees conferred, total	3,718	5,258	5,339	4,100	3,897	4,250	4,454	4,389	4,596	4,795
Percent to women	0.9	13.3	20.7	30.9	36.4	40.1	43.8	44.5	44.6	44.5
Law (LL.B. or J.D.):										
Institutions conferring degrees	145	179	181	182	183	190	198	197	200	201
Degrees conferred, total	14,916	35,647	37,491	36,485	39,349	38,152	43,423	43,440	43,486	43,769
Percent to women	5.4	30.2	38.5	42.2	42.6	45.9	48.7	48.0	47.6	47.0
Theological (B.D., M.Div., M.H.L.):										
Institutions conferring degrees	(NA)	(NA)	(NA)	(NA)	192	198	(NA)	(NA)	(NA)	(NA)
Degrees conferred, total	5,298	7,115	7,221	5,851	5,978	6,129	5,533	5,666	5,990	5,751
Percent to women	2.3	13.8	18.5	24.8	25.7	29.2	35.6	33.6	33.2	34.3

NA Not available.

Source: U.S. National Center for Education Statistics, *Digest of Education Statistics*, annual. See also <http://www.nces.ed.gov/programs/digest/>.

Table 301. Academic Libraries by Selected Characteristics: 2008

[As of Fall of year shown. For information on public libraries, see Tables 1151 and 1152]

Institution characteristic	Number of libraries	Circulation (1,000) General collection	Circulation (1,000) Reserve collection	Expenditures (mil. dol.)	Paid staff [1] Total [2]	Paid staff [1] Librarians	Paid staff [1] Other professional staff	Paid staff [1] Student assistants
All U.S. academic libraries . . .	**3,827**	**138,103**	**40,663**	**6,786**	**93,438**	**27,030**	**7,491**	**24,110**
Control:								
Public.	1,576	88,140	27,745	4,031	56,019	15,666	4,355	13,572
Private	2,251	49,962	12,918	2,754	37,419	11,364	3,136	10,537
Level: [3]								
Total 4-year and above	2,393	120,659	34,859	6,145	80,431	22,797	6,433	21,315
Doctor's	721	88,575	24,553	4,751	56,617	15,367	4,964	13,822
Master's	911	21,614	6,789	991	16,716	5,143	984	5,158
Bachelor's	730	10,168	3,333	355	6,572	2,093	456	2,200
Less than 4-year	1,434	17,444	5,805	640	13,007	4,233	1,058	2,794
Size (FTE enrollment): [4]								
Less than 1,000.	1,455	7,255	1,310	329	6,692	2,331	640	2,232
1,000 to 2,999	1,136	19,700	6,072	856	14,630	4,534	1,018	4,569
3,000 to 4,999	475	11,348	3,803	558	9,298	2,955	670	2,414
5,000 to 9,999	405	17,603	7,147	1,017	14,665	4,443	976	3,610
10,000 to 19,999	238	30,325	10,942	1,642	20,625	5,541	1,586	4,838
20,000 or more	118	51,872	11,389	2,384	27,528	7,226	2,601	6,446

[1] Full-time equivalent (FTE) staff is calculated by dividing the total number of hours for all part-time positions by the number of hours the library defines as a full-time position. [2] Includes other staff not shown separately. [3] Level refers to the highest level of any degree offered by the institution. Doctoral, master's, and bachelor's level institutions do not sum to total number of 4-year and above institutions because there are 4-year and above institutions that grant "other" degrees and are thus not included in the breakdown. [4] Full-time equivalent (FTE) enrollment is calculated by adding one-third of part-time enrollment to full-time enrollment.

Source: U.S. National Center for Education Statistics, Academic Libraries Survey (ALS), 2008. See also <http://nces.ed.gov/surveys/libraries/academic.asp>.

Section 5
Law Enforcement, Courts, and Prisons

This section presents data on crimes committed, victims of crimes, arrests, and data related to criminal violations and the criminal justice system. The major sources of these data are the Bureau of Justice Statistics (BJS), the Federal Bureau of Investigation (FBI), and the Administrative Office of the U.S. Courts. BJS issues many reports—see our Guide to Sources for a complete listing. The Federal Bureau of Investigation's major annual reports are *Crime in the United States, Law Enforcement Officers Killed and Assaulted*, annual, and *Hate Crimes*, annual, which present data on reported crimes as gathered from state and local law enforcement agencies.

Legal jurisdiction and law enforcement— Law enforcement is, for the most part, a function of state and local officers and agencies. The U.S. Constitution reserves general police powers to the states. By act of Congress, federal offenses include only offenses against the U.S. government and against or by its employees while engaged in their official duties and offenses which involve the crossing of state lines or an interference with interstate commerce. Excluding the military, there are 52 separate criminal law jurisdictions in the United States: one in each of the 50 states, one in the District of Columbia, and the federal jurisdiction. Each of these has its own criminal law and procedure and its own law enforcement agencies. While the systems of law enforcement are quite similar among the states, there are often substantial differences in the penalties for like offenses.

Law enforcement can be divided into three parts: Investigation of crimes and arrests of persons suspected of committing them; prosecution of those charged with crime; and the punishment or treatment of persons convicted of crime.

Crime—The U.S. Department of Justice administers two statistical programs to measure the magnitude, nature, and impact of crime in the nation: the Uniform Crime Reporting (UCR) Program and the National Crime Victimization Survey (NCVS). Each of these programs produces valuable information about aspects of the nation's crime problem. Because the UCR and NCVS programs are conducted for different purposes, use different methods, and focus on somewhat different aspects of crime, the information they produce together provides a more comprehensive panorama of the nation's crime problem than either could produce alone.

Uniform Crime Reports (UCR)— The FBI's UCR Program, which began in 1929, collects information on the following crimes reported to law enforcement authorities—Part 1 offenses (detail data reported): murder and nonnegligent manslaughter, forcible rape, robbery, aggravated assault, burglary, larceny-theft, motor vehicle theft, and arson. For Part 2 offenses, law enforcement agencies report only arrest data for 21 additional crime categories. For UCR definitions of criminal offenses (including those listed), please go to: <www.fbi.gov/ucr/cius2008/about/offense_definitions.html>.

The UCR Program compiles data from monthly law enforcement reports or individual crime incident records transmitted directly to the FBI or to centralized state agencies that then report to the FBI. The Program thoroughly examines each report it receives for reasonableness, accuracy, and deviations that may indicate errors. Large variations in crime levels may indicate modified records procedures, incomplete reporting, or changes in a jurisdiction's boundaries. To identify any unusual fluctuations in an agency's crime counts, the Program compares monthly reports to previous submissions of the agency and with those for similar agencies.

The UCR Program presents crime counts for the nation as a whole, as well as for regions, states, counties, cities, towns, tribal law enforcement, and colleges and universities. This permits studies among neighboring jurisdictions and among

U.S. Census Bureau, Statistical Abstract of the United States: 2011

those with similar populations and other common characteristics.

The UCR Program annually publishes its findings in a preliminary release in the spring of the following calendar year, followed by a detailed annual report, *Crime in the United States*, issued in the fall. In addition to crime counts and trends, this report includes data on crimes cleared, persons arrested (age, sex, and race), law enforcement personnel (including the number of sworn officers killed or assaulted), and the characteristics of homicides (including age, sex, and race of victims and offenders; victim-offender relationships; weapons used; and circumstances surrounding the homicides). Other periodic reports are also available from the UCR Program.

National Crime Victimization Survey (NCVS)—The 2006 national crime victimization estimates are not comparable to 2005 and previous years and 2007–2008 because of changes in methodology. The methodological changes included: a new sample, a change in the method of handling first time interviews with households, and a change in the method of interviewing. For more information on methodology, go to <http://www.ojp .usdoj.gov/bjs /abstract /cv06.htm>.

A second perspective on crime is provided by this survey of the Bureau of Justice Statistics (BJS). The NCVS is an annual data collection (interviews of persons aged 12 or older), conducted by the U.S. Census Bureau for the BJS. As an ongoing survey of households, the NCVS measures crimes of violence and property both reported and not reported to police. It produces national rates and levels of personal and property victimization. No attempt is made to validate the information against police records or any other source.

The NCVS measures rape/sexual assault, robbery, assault, pocket-picking, purse snatching, burglary, and motor vehicle theft. The NCVS includes crimes reported to the police, as well as those not reported. Murder and kidnapping are not covered. The so-called victimless crimes, such as drunkenness, drug abuse, and prostitution, also are excluded, as are crimes for which it is difficult to identify

knowledgeable respondents or to locate data records.

Crimes of which the victim may not be aware also cannot be measured effectively. Buying stolen property may fall into this category, as may some instances of embezzlement. Attempted crimes of many types probably are under recorded for this reason. Events in which the victim has shown a willingness to participate in illegal activity also are excluded.

In any encounter involving a personal crime, more than one criminal act can be committed against an individual. For example, a rape may be associated with a robbery, or a household offense, such as a burglary, can escalate into something more serious in the event of a personal confrontation. In classifying the survey measured crimes, each criminal incident has been counted only once—by the most serious act that took place during the incident and ranked in accordance with the seriousness classification system used by the FBI. The order of seriousness for crimes against persons is as follows: rape, robbery, assault, and larceny. Personal crimes take precedence over household offenses.

A *victimization*, basic measure of the occurrence of crime, is a specific criminal act as it affects a single victim. The number of victimizations is determined by the number of victims of such acts. Victimization counts serve as key elements in computing rates of victimization. For crimes against persons, the rates are based on the total number of individuals aged 12 and over or on a portion of that population sharing a particular characteristic or set of traits. As general indicators of the danger of having been victimized during the reference period, the rates are not sufficiently refined to represent true measures of risk for specific individuals or households.

An *incident* is a specific criminal act involving one or more victims; therefore the number of incidents of personal crimes is lower than that of victimizations.

Courts—Statistics on criminal offenses and the outcome of prosecutions are incomplete for the country as a whole, although data are available for many states individually.

192 Law Enforcement, Courts, and Prisons

Since 1982, through its National Judicial Reporting Program, the BJS has surveyed a nationally representative sample of 300 counties every 2 years and collected detailed information on demographic characteristics of felons, conviction offenses, type of sentences, sentence lengths, and time from arrest to conviction and sentencing.

The bulk of civil and criminal litigation in the country is commenced and determined in the various state courts. Only when the U.S. Constitution and acts of Congress specifically confer jurisdiction upon the federal courts may civil or criminal litigation be heard and decided by them. Generally, the federal courts have jurisdiction over the following types of cases: suits or proceedings by or against the United States; civil actions between private parties arising under the Constitution, laws, or treaties of the United States; civil actions between private litigants who are citizens of different states; civil cases involving admiralty, maritime, or private jurisdiction; and all matters in bankruptcy.

There are several types of courts with varying degrees of legal jurisdiction. These jurisdictions include original, appellate, general, and limited or special. A court of original jurisdiction is one having the authority initially to try a case and pass judgment on the law and the facts; a court of appellate jurisdiction is one with the legal authority to review cases and hear appeals; a court of general jurisdiction is a trial court of unlimited original jurisdiction in civil and/or criminal cases, also called a "major trial court"; a court of limited or special jurisdiction is a trial court with legal authority over only a particular class of cases, such as probate, juvenile, or traffic cases.

The 94 federal courts of original jurisdiction are known as the U.S. district courts. One or more of these courts is established in every state and one each in the District of Columbia, Puerto Rico, the Virgin Islands, the Northern Mariana Islands, and Guam. Appeals from the district courts are taken to intermediate appellate courts of which there are 13, known as U.S. courts of appeals and the United States Court of Appeals for the Federal Circuit. The Supreme Court of the United States is the final and highest appellate court in the federal system of courts.

Juvenile offenders—For statistical purposes, the FBI and most states classify as juvenile offenders persons under the age of 18 years who have committed a crime or crimes.

Delinquency cases are all cases of youths referred to a juvenile court for violation of a law or ordinance or for seriously "anti-social" conduct. Several types of facilities are available for those adjudicated delinquents, ranging from the short-term physically unrestricted environment to the long-term very restrictive atmosphere.

Prisoners and jail inmates—
BJS started to collect annual data in 1979 on prisoners in federal and state prisons and reformatories. Adults convicted of criminal activity may be given a prison or jail sentence. A *prison* is a confinement facility having custodial authority over adults sentenced to confinement of more than 1 year. A *jail* is a facility, usually operated by a local law enforcement agency, holding persons detained pending adjudication and/or persons committed after adjudication to 1 year or less.

Data on inmates in local jails were collected by the BJS for the first time in 1970. Since then, BJS has conducted censuses of facilities and inmates every 5 to 6 years. In 1984, BJS initiated an annual survey of jails conducted in noncensus years.

Statistical reliability—For discussion of statistical collection, estimation and sampling procedures, and measures of statistical reliability pertaining to the National Crime Victimization Survey and Uniform Crime Reporting Program, see Appendix III.

Table 302. Crimes and Crime Rates by Type of Offense: 1980 to 2008

[(1,345 represents 1,345,000). Data include offenses actually reported to law enforcement and also offense estimations for nonreporting and partially reporting agencies within each state. Rates are based on Census Bureau estimated resident population as of July 1; 1980, 1990, and 2000, enumerated as of April 1. See source for details. For definitions of types of crimes, go to <http://www.fbi.gov/ucr/cius2008/about/offense_definitions.html>]

Item and year	All crimes	Violent crime					Property crimes			
		Total	Murder [1]	Forcible rape	Robbery	Aggra-vated assault	Total	Burglary	Larceny/ theft	Motor vehicle theft
Number of offenses (1,000):										
1980	13,408	1,345	23.0	83.0	566	673	12,064	3,795	7,137	1,132
1985	12,430	1,328	19.0	87.7	498	723	11,103	3,073	6,926	1,103
1990	14,476	1,820	23.4	102.6	639	1,055	12,655	3,074	7,946	1,636
1994	13,990	1,858	23.3	102.2	619	1,113	12,132	2,713	7,880	1,539
1995	13,863	1,799	21.6	97.5	581	1,099	12,064	2,594	7,998	1,472
1996	13,494	1,689	19.6	96.3	536	1,037	11,805	2,506	7,905	1,394
1997	13,195	1,636	18.2	96.2	499	1,023	11,558	2,461	7,744	1,354
1998	12,486	1,534	17.0	93.1	447	977	10,952	2,333	7,376	1,243
1999	11,634	1,426	15.5	89.4	409	912	10,208	2,101	6,956	1,152
2000	11,608	1,425	15.6	90.2	408	912	10,183	2,051	6,972	1,160
2001 [2]	11,877	1,439	16.0	90.9	424	909	10,437	2,117	7,092	1,228
2002	11,879	1,424	16.2	95.2	421	891	10,455	2,151	7,057	1,247
2003	11,827	1,384	16.5	93.9	414	859	10,443	2,155	7,027	1,261
2004	11,679	1,360	16.1	95.1	401	847	10,319	2,144	6,937	1,238
2005	11,565	1,391	16.7	94.3	417	862	10,175	2,155	6,783	1,236
2006	11,402	1,418	17.0	92.8	447	861	9,984	2,184	6,607	1,193
2007	11,252	1,408	16.9	90.4	445	856	9,843	2,179	6,569	1,096
2008	11,150	1,382	16.3	89.0	442	835	9,768	2,222	6,589	957
Rate per 100,000 population:										
1980	5,950	597	10.2	36.8	251	299	5,353	1,684	3,167	502
1985	5,225	558	8.0	36.8	209	304	4,666	1,292	2,911	464
1990	5,803	730	9.4	41.1	256	423	5,073	1,232	3,185	656
1991	5,898	758	9.8	42.3	273	433	5,140	1,252	3,229	659
1994	5,374	714	9.0	39.3	238	428	4,660	1,042	3,027	591
1995	5,276	685	8.2	37.1	221	418	4,591	987	3,043	560
1996	5,087	637	7.4	36.3	202	391	4,451	945	2,980	526
1997	4,930	611	6.8	35.9	186	382	4,316	919	2,892	506
1998	4,619	568	6.3	34.5	166	361	4,053	863	2,730	460
1999	4,267	523	5.7	32.8	150	334	3,744	770	2,551	423
2000	4,125	507	5.5	32.0	145	324	3,618	729	2,477	412
2001 [2]	4,163	505	5.6	31.8	149	319	3,658	742	2,486	431
2002	4,125	494	5.6	33.1	146	310	3,631	747	2,451	433
2003	4,067	476	5.7	32.3	143	295	3,591	741	2,417	434
2004	3,977	463	5.5	32.4	137	289	3,514	730	2,362	422
2005	3,899	469	5.6	31.8	141	291	3,432	727	2,288	417
2006	3,808	474	5.7	31.0	149	288	3,335	729	2,207	398
2007	3,730	467	5.6	30.0	148	284	3,264	723	2,178	363
2008	3,667	455	5.4	29.3	145	275	3,213	731	2,167	315

[1] Includes nonnegligent manslaughter. [2] The murder and nonnegligent homicides that occurred as a result of the events of September 11, 2001, were not included in this table.

Source: U.S. Department of Justice, Federal Bureau of Investigation, "Crime in the United States," September 2009, <http://www.fbi.gov/ucr/cius2008/index.html>

Table 303. Crimes and Crime Rates by Type and Area: 2008

[In thousands (1,382.0 represents 1,382,000), except rate. Rate per 100,000 population; based on Census Bureau estimated resident population as of July 1. See headnote, Table 302. For definitions of types of crimes, go to <http://www.fbi.gov /ucr/cius2008/about/offense_definitions.html>]

Type of crime	United States		Metropolitan statistical area [1]		Cities outside metropolitan areas		Nonmetropolitan counties	
	Total	Rate	Total	Rate	Total	Rate	Total	Rate
Violent crime	1,382.0	454.5	1,242.0	489.0	78.2	392.0	61.7	205.1
Murder and nonnegligent manslaughter	16.3	5.4	14.6	5.7	0.7	3.5	1.0	3.4
Forcible rape	89.0	29.3	74.3	29.3	7.6	38.2	7.0	23.4
Robbery	441.9	145.3	423.3	166.7	13.4	67.1	5.2	17.1
Aggravated assault	834.9	274.6	729.8	287.3	56.5	283.3	48.5	161.1
Property crime	9,767.9	3,212.5	8,514.2	3,352.0	747.7	3,746.5	506.0	1,681.1
Burglary	2,222.2	730.8	1,894.5	745.8	162.4	813.9	165.3	549.2
Larceny-theft	6,588.9	2,167.0	5,732.1	2,256.7	553.4	2,772.6	303.4	1,008.0
Motor vehicle theft	956.8	314.7	887.6	349.5	31.9	159.9	37.3	124.0

[1] For definition, see Appendix II.

Source: U.S. Department of Justice, Federal Bureau of Investigation, "Crime in the United States," September 2009, <http://www.fbi.gov/ucr/cius2008/index.html/>.

Table 304. Crime Rates by State, 2007 and 2008, and by Type, 2008

[Rates per 100,000 population. Data include offenses actually reported to law enforcement and also offense estimations for nonreporting and partially reporting agencies within each state. Based on Census Bureau estimated resident population as of **July 1**. For definitions of types of crimes, go to <http://www.fbi.gov/ucr/cius2008/about/offense_definitions.html>]

State	Violent crime 2007, total	Violent crime 2008 Total	Murder	Forcible rape	Robbery	Aggra-vated assault	Property crime 2007, total	Property crime 2008 Total	Burglary	Larceny/ theft	Motor vehicle theft
Alabama	448	466	8.0	35.1	167.8	255	3,972	4,193	1,111	2,782	299
Alaska	661	654	4.0	64.8	94.7	491	3,380	2,920	471	2,212	238
Arizona	483	479	7.0	33.1	150.7	288	4,414	3,806	893	2,324	589
Arkansas	529	516	5.9	50.5	99.1	361	3,953	3,911	1,197	2,481	233
California	523	504	5.8	24.2	188.8	285	3,033	2,940	647	1,770	524
Colorado	348	344	3.2	43.4	67.7	230	3,006	2,819	560	1,989	269
Connecticut	256	307	3.8	19.4	115.5	168	2,400	2,491	432	1,805	254
Delaware	689	709	6.5	42.5	211.5	448	3,370	3,595	777	2,525	293
District of Columbia [1]	1,414	1,438	31.4	31.4	748.5	626	4,914	5,105	640	3,372	1,092
Florida	723	689	6.4	32.6	198.0	452	4,089	4,141	1,028	2,766	347
Georgia	493	496	7.1	24.5	198.8	266	3,901	4,069	1,067	2,563	439
Hawaii	273	273	2.0	28.2	84.2	158	4,225	3,567	730	2,439	397
Idaho	239	239	1.5	37.7	15.6	185	2,247	2,089	441	1,540	108
Illinois [2,3]	533	(NA)	8.9	(NA)	284.7	384	2,936	3,498	729	2,419	350
Indiana	334	376	5.7	28.5	135.9	205	3,397	3,571	823	2,448	300
Iowa	295	298	2.6	32.3	43.6	220	2,616	2,522	571	1,800	151
Kansas	453	415	3.6	44.6	55.0	312	3,679	3,385	685	2,470	230
Kentucky	295	307	4.9	34.7	99.7	167	2,518	2,705	707	1,814	184
Louisiana	730	658	12.7	27.1	141.7	477	4,076	3,780	1,012	2,455	313
Maine	118	119	2.4	28.8	25.3	63	2,429	2,464	498	1,876	90
Maryland	642	628	8.8	20.0	234.3	365	3,432	3,516	689	2,377	450
Massachusetts	432	466	2.6	27.0	109.8	327	2,392	2,393	558	1,639	197
Michigan	536	522	5.7	45.1	135.2	336	3,066	2,970	756	1,850	363
Minnesota [3]	289	(NA)	2.1	(NA)	82.4	149	3,037	2,893	515	2,180	198
Mississippi	291	329	8.9	32.7	124.4	163	3,201	3,287	945	2,096	245
Missouri	505	505	7.8	27.4	126.1	344	3,738	3,682	778	2,551	354
Montana	288	302	3.3	35.6	21.2	242	2,765	2,733	381	2,169	184
Nebraska	302	323	4.0	33.9	77.2	208	3,161	2,952	497	2,207	247
Nevada	751	728	6.3	42.5	249.0	430	3,778	3,456	931	1,913	612
New Hampshire	137	166	1.1	30.6	34.5	100	1,892	2,218	334	1,772	112
New Jersey	329	326	4.3	12.9	146.2	163	2,213	2,291	465	1,594	232
New Mexico	664	671	7.6	57.2	112.3	494	3,726	3,924	1,066	2,441	418
New York	414	402	4.3	14.4	165.1	218	1,979	2,005	338	1,537	130
North Carolina	466	487	6.7	25.7	167.5	287	4,087	4,156	1,231	2,623	302
North Dakota	142	201	0.9	46.3	12.2	141	1,890	2,143	378	1,615	149
Ohio	343	385	4.9	41.8	184.0	154	3,455	3,597	961	2,363	273
Oklahoma	500	540	5.9	41.0	104.2	389	3,526	3,525	979	2,240	306
Oregon	288	265	2.3	31.5	72.0	159	3,526	3,350	559	2,485	305
Pennsylvania	417	417	5.8	28.4	155.5	227	2,361	2,425	479	1,762	184
Rhode Island	227	253	3.0	26.8	83.7	139	(NA)	2,845	549	1,992	305
South Carolina	788	726	6.9	37.5	146.4	535	4,272	4,211	1,018	2,802	392
South Dakota	169	301	4.8	76.5	19.2	200	1,652	1,881	347	1,413	121
Tennessee	753	722	6.6	33.3	173.7	508	4,089	4,028	1,044	2,676	308
Texas	511	508	5.6	33.1	155.3	314	4,121	3,986	946	2,689	351
Utah	235	226	1.5	33.6	52.7	138	3,500	3,395	542	2,586	268
Vermont	124	141	2.8	21.8	15.4	101	2,323	2,620	577	1,947	97
Virginia	270	258	4.8	23.1	96.4	134	2,466	2,536	415	1,949	172
Washington	333	332	3.0	40.1	97.8	191	4,031	3,784	806	2,539	439
West Virginia	275	300	4.2	23.7	54.2	218	2,525	2,718	650	1,878	190
Wisconsin	291	277	2.6	20.1	92.4	162	2,838	2,770	490	2,074	206
Wyoming	239	246	2.3	34.5	16.1	193	2,866	2,720	413	2,172	136

NA Not Available. [1] Includes offenses reported by the Zoological Police and the Metro Transit Police. [2] Limited data for 2007 and 2008 were available for Illinois. [3] The data collection methodology for the offense of forcible rape used by the Illinois and the Minnesota state Uniform Crime Reporting (UCR) Programs (with the exception of Rockford, Illinois, and Minneapolis and St. Paul, Minnesota) does not comply with national UCR guidelines. Consequently, their state figures for forcible rape and violent crime (of which forcible rape is a part) are not published in this table.

Source: U.S. Department of Justice, Federal Bureau of Investigation, "Crime in the United States," September 2009, <http://www.fbi.gov/ucr/cius2008/index.html/>

U.S. Census Bureau, Statistical Abstract of the United States: 2011

Table 305. Crime Rates by Type—Selected Large Cities: 2008

[Offenses known to law enforcement per 100,000 population. Based on U.S. Census Bureau estimated resident population. For definitions of types of crimes, go to <http://www.fbi.gov/ucr/cius2008/index.html>]

Cities ranked by population size, 2008	Violent crime					Property crime			
	Total	Murder	Forcible rape	Robbery	Aggra-vated assault	Total	Burglary	Larceny-theft	Motor vehicle theft
New York, NY	580	6.3	10.7	266	298	1,797	238	1,410	149
Los Angeles, CA	690	10.0	24.6	349	306	2,618	512	1,518	587
Chicago, IL	(¹)	18.0	(¹)	589	602	4,632	920	3,041	670
Houston, TX	1,107	13.1	33.5	474	587	4,947	1,204	3,064	680
Phoenix, AZ	660	10.5	30.3	304	315	5,214	1,184	3,070	960
Philadelphia, PA	1,441	23.0	72.0	667	679	4,343	891	2,823	629
Las Vegas MPD, NV	985	8.9	53.9	364	557	3,929	1,101	1,985	843
San Antonio, TX	718	8.6	31.4	203	475	7,220	1,399	5,229	592
Dallas, TX	895	13.3	39.1	507	336	5,936	1,657	3,322	957
San Diego, CA	476	4.3	29.6	159	283	3,174	609	1,726	840
San Jose, CA	385	3.3	23.3	119	240	2,359	366	1,440	553
Honolulu, HI	284	2.0	22.4	102	157	3,506	703	2,369	434
Detroit, MI	1,924	33.8	36.4	675	1,179	5,862	1,967	2,080	1,815
Indianapolis, IN	1,204	14.1	58.8	498	634	6,084	1,765	3,522	797
Jacksonville, FL	996	14.3	32.5	364	585	5,731	1,490	3,741	500
San Francisco, CA	845	12.3	20.8	515	297	4,548	677	3,150	721
Charlotte-Mecklenburg PD, NC	932	10.9	35.8	393	492	6,186	1,573	3,919	694
Austin, TX	522	3.1	36.2	177	306	5,945	1,139	4,457	349
Columbus, OH	774	14.5	81.8	477	200	6,421	1,956	3,759	706
Fort Worth, TX	656	7.0	49.9	243	356	5,037	1,286	3,360	391
Memphis, TN	1,925	20.5	54.5	712	1,138	8,011	2,362	4,843	806
Baltimore, MD	1,589	36.9	21.6	634	896	4,818	1,234	2,715	868
Louisville Metro, KY	684	11.3	34.9	280	358	4,672	1,156	3,100	416
El Paso, TX	461	2.8	29.6	74	355	3,217	339	2,428	450
Boston, MA	1,104	10.3	39.2	397	658	3,711	578	2,735	398
Nashville, TN	1,396	12.6	50.0	396	937	5,372	1,051	3,946	375
Milwaukee, WI	1,219	11.8	34.5	533	640	6,072	1,064	3,922	1,086
Seattle, WA	576	4.8	21.1	270	281	5,488	1,087	3,786	614
Denver, CO	567	6.7	47.6	160	352	3,258	873	1,779	607
Washington, DC	1,375	31.4	31.4	702	610	4,859	639	3,174	1,046
Portland, OR	623	4.7	45.2	205	368	5,288	779	3,905	604
Oklahoma City, OK	977	10.3	57.6	276	634	5,894	1,670	3,519	706
Atlanta, GA	1,389	19.7	23.6	621	725	7,313	1,874	4,221	1,218
Tucson, AZ	804	12.3	46.5	274	471	(²)	975	(²)	1,098
Albuquerque, NM	894	7.2	70.1	256	561	6,066	1,180	4,000	886
Fresno, CA	585	8.4	16.8	207	353	4,636	877	2,965	794
Sacramento, CA	998	10.5	36.0	377	574	4,817	1,117	2,649	1,051
Long Beach, CA	676	8.6	25.7	318	324	2,781	659	1,507	615
Mesa, AZ	501	3.5	35.2	144	319	3,834	627	2,759	448
Kansas City, MO	1,389	25.5	54.9	463	845	6,264	1,654	3,647	963
Omaha, NE	606	10.1	41.2	217	337	4,298	726	2,949	623
Virginia Beach, VA	240	3.2	16.8	124	97	2,904	442	2,314	148
Cleveland, OH	1,429	23.5	97.6	878	430	5,784	2,100	2,465	1,219
Miami, FL	1,335	14.7	9.8	565	746	5,190	1,155	3,177	857
Oakland, CA	1,968	28.6	84.2	827	1,028	5,351	1,118	2,220	2,013
Raleigh, NC	578	8.7	24.4	264	281	3,401	796	2,361	244
Tulsa, OK	1,285	13.1	65.8	286	920	5,946	1,756	3,589	600
Colorado Springs, CO	528	6.3	88.5	137	297	4,246	899	3,050	297
Minneapolis, MN ¹	1,268	9.8	97.4	532	629	5,515	1,484	3,391	640
Arlington, TX	602	6.1	37.5	185	374	5,361	1,187	3,762	412
Wichita, KS	852	8.3	76.7	133	635	5,525	1,124	3,888	513
St. Louis, MO	2,073	46.9	66.5	739	1,220	8,547	2,042	4,865	1,640
Santa Ana, CA	508	8.8	19.4	248	232	2,055	323	1,280	452
Tampa, FL	883	8.0	24.6	313	537	4,600	1,216	2,864	520
Anaheim, CA	393	3.3	24.9	172	193	2,496	481	1,688	328
Cincinnati, OH	1,264	21.9	80.9	727	434	6,092	1,903	3,706	483
Bakersfield, CA	637	7.7	14.7	217	397	4,956	1,278	2,906	772
Toledo, OH	1,141	5.7	41.6	436	658	5,882	2,055	3,362	465
Aurora, CO	513	5.7	59.4	175	272	3,370	701	2,259	410
Pittsburgh, PA	1,084	23.2	43.9	497	519	4,076	1,003	2,666	406
Riverside, CA	642	6.3	36.4	242	357	3,694	738	2,415	541
Stockton, CA	1,475	8.2	38.2	532	897	6,126	1,485	3,788	853
Corpus Christi, TX	777	6.6	67.0	171	532	6,160	1,209	4,712	239
Lexington, KY	632	4.3	48.7	188	392	3,455	803	2,444	209
New Orleans, LA	1,019	63.6	23.1	386	547	5,287	1,631	2,516	1,140
Anchorage, AK	945	3.6	93.9	194	653	3,289	425	2,590	274
Newark, NJ	951	23.9	18.2	496	413	3,485	715	1,428	1,342
St. Paul, MN ¹	796	6.5	53.2	277	460	4,174	1,063	2,452	658
Buffalo, NY	1,375	13.7	64.4	569	727	5,725	1,521	3,516	688
Plano, TX	227	2.6	18.1	54	152	3,060	583	2,322	155
Glendale, AZ	518	6.6	25.7	229	257	5,235	1,038	3,269	928
Henderson, NV	207	2.0	35.1	83	87	2,270	602	1,344	324
Chandler, AZ	317	2.4	22.1	95	197	3,155	559	2,279	317
Lincoln, NE	510	1.6	44.9	85	378	4,042	624	3,280	138
Fort Wayne, IN	325	10.0	38.2	191	86	4,106	959	2,881	265
Mobile, AL ³	480	16.7	10.8	349	104	5,515	1,317	3,772	427

¹ The data collection methodology for the offense of forcible rape used by the Illinois and Minnesota state programs (with the exception of Rockford, Illinois, and Minneapolis and St. Paul, Minnesota) does not comply with national Uniform Crime Reporting (UCR) Program guidelines. Consequently, their figures for forcible rape and violent crime (of which forcible rape is a part) are not published in this table. ² It was determined that the agency did not follow the national UCR program guidelines for reporting an offense. Consequently, this figure is not included in this table. ³ The population for the city of Mobile, Alabama, includes 60,536 inhabitants from the jurisdiction of the Mobile County Sheriff's Department.

Source: U.S. Department of Justice, Federal Bureau of Investigation, Uniform Crime Reporting Program, see <http://www.fbi.gov/ucr/cius2008/data/table_08.html>.

Table 306. Murder Victims—Circumstances and Weapons Used or Cause of Death: 2000 to 2008

[The Uniform Crime Reporting (UCR) Program defines murder and nonnegligent manslaughter as the willful (nonnegligent) killing of one human being by another. The classification of this offense is based solely on police investigation as opposed to the determination of a court, medical examiner, coroner, jury, other judicial body. For more information on murder, go to <http://www.fbi.gov/ucr/cius2008/offenses/violent_crime/murder_homicide.html/>]

Characteristic	2000	2005	2007	2008	Characteristic	2000	2005	2007	2008
Murders, total	**13,230**	**14,965**	**14,916**	**14,299**	Institutional killings	10	12	11	15
					Sniper attack	8	2	1	4
CIRCUMSTANCES					Other, not specified	1,901	1,938	2,187	2,014
Felonies, total	2,229	2,189	2,184	2,101					
Rape	58	45	32	23	Unknown	4,070	5,635	5,479	5,000
Robbery	1,077	930	935	924					
Burglary	76	91	86	87	TYPE OF WEAPON OR CAUSE OF DEATH				
Larceny/theft	23	12	10	16					
Motor vehicle theft	25	32	20	19					
Arson	81	39	59	26	Total firearms	8,661	10,158	10,129	9,484
Prostitution and					Handguns	6,778	7,565	7,398	6,755
commercialized vice	6	13	11	7	Rifles	411	445	453	375
Other sex offenses	10	9	10	11	Shotguns	485	522	457	444
Narcotic drug laws	589	597	590	501	Other not specified or	53	138	116	79
Gambling	12	2	4	10	type unknown				
Other, not specified	272	419	447	477					
Suspected felony type	60	45	67	104	Firearms, type not				
					stated	934	1,488	1,705	1,831
Other than felony type,					Knives or cutting				
total	6,871	7,096	7,165	7,014	instruments	1,782	1,920	1,817	1,897
Romantic triangle	122	118	105	104	Blunt objects [1]	617	608	647	614
Child killed by					Personal weapons [2]	927	905	869	861
babysitter	30	26	35	51	Poison	8	9	10	10
Brawl due to influence					Explosives	9	2	1	10
of alcohol	188	123	118	125	Fire	134	125	131	86
Brawl due to influence					Narcotics	20	46	52	33
of narcotics	99	97	65	68	Drowning	15	20	12	15
Argument over money					Strangulation	166	118	134	88
or property	206	210	192	192	Asphyxiation	92	90	109	89
Other arguments	3,589	3,718	3,695	3,586					
Gangland killings	65	96	78	133	All other [3]	799	958	1,005	993
Juvenile gang killings	653	756	678	711					

[1] Refers to club, hammer, etc. [2] Hands, fists, feet, pushed, etc. [3] Includes poison, explosives, narcotics, drowning, and unknown.

Source: U.S. Department of Justice, Federal Bureau of Investigation, "Uniform Crime Reporting Program Supplementary Homicide Report," <http://www.fbi.gov/ucr/cius2008/offenses/violent_crime/murder_homicide.html>.

Table 307. Murder Victims by Age, Sex, and Race: 2008

[See headnote, Table 306]

Age	Total	Sex			Race			
		Male	Female	Unknown	White	Black	Other	Unknown
Murders, total	**14,299**	**11,154**	**3,103**	**42**	**6,907**	**6,826**	**325**	**241**
Percent of total	100.0	78.0	21.7	0.3	48.3	47.7	2.3	1.7
Under 18 years old [1]	1,502	1,044	451	7	736	699	38	28
18 years old and over [1]	12,565	9,961	2,598	6	6,077	6,054	282	153
Infant (under 1 year old)	223	114	105	4	145	65	7	6
1 to 4 years old	346	197	147	2	179	143	15	9
5 to 8 years old	71	37	33	1	42	19	5	5
9 to 12 years old	72	39	33	–	40	30	3	1
13 to 16 years old	448	360	88	–	193	246	7	2
17 to 19 years old	1,343	1,164	179	–	540	773	17	12
20 to 24 years old	2,457	2,108	348	1	962	1,435	42	18
25 to 29 years old	2,163	1,822	341	–	868	1,224	45	26
30 to 34 years old	1,624	1,334	290	–	688	866	39	31
35 to 39 years old	1,208	941	267	–	595	565	31	17
40 to 44 years old	1,030	745	270	6	560	430	24	16
45 to 49 years old	971	709	262	–	574	367	18	12
50 to 54 years old	694	515	179	–	419	251	17	7
55 to 59 years old	491	348	143	–	312	154	20	5
60 to 64 years old	291	209	82	–	220	59	8	4
65 to 69 years old	206	131	75	–	143	45	13	5
70 to 74 years old	146	76	70	–	112	25	7	2
75 years old and over	283	146	137	–	220	56	2	2
Age unknown	232	149	54	29	94	73	5	60

– Represents zero. [1] Does not include unknown ages.

Source: U.S. Department of Justice, Federal Bureau of Investigation, "Uniform Crime Reporting Program Supplementary Homicide Reports." See also <http://www.fbi.gov/ucr/cius2008/offenses/violent_crime/murder_homicide.html>.

Law Enforcement, Courts, and Prisons 197

Table 308. Homicide Trends: 1980 to 2007

[Not all agencies which report offense information to the FBI also submit supplemental data on homicides. To account for the total number of homicide victims, the data were weighted to match national and state estimates prepared by the FBI; hence, detail may not equal total. For more information on the methodology, go to <http://www.ojp.usdoj.gov/bjs/homicide/homtrnd.htm#contents>]

Year	Number of victims						Rate [1]					
	Total	Male	Female	White	Black	Other	Total	Male	Female	White	Black	Other
1980.......	23,040	17,803	5,237	12,275	9,767	327	10.2	16.1	4.5	6.3	37.7	5.7
1985.......	18,980	14,095	4,885	10,590	7,891	399	7.9	12.2	4.0	5.2	27.6	5.5
1990.......	23,440	18,320	5,121	11,278	11,489	400	9.4	15.1	4.0	5.4	37.6	4.2
1995.......	21,610	16,579	5,030	10,376	10,444	581	8.2	12.7	3.7	4.8	31.6	4.9
1996.......	19,650	15,175	4,475	9,483	9,476	512	7.4	11.5	3.3	4.3	28.3	4.1
1997.......	18,210	14,079	4,132	8,620	8,842	524	6.8	10.5	3.0	3.9	26.0	4.1
1998.......	16,970	12,812	4,158	8,389	7,931	393	6.3	9.5	3.0	3.8	23.0	2.9
1999.......	15,522	11,718	3,804	7,777	7,139	458	5.7	8.6	2.7	3.5	20.5	3.3
2000.......	15,586	11,844	3,742	7,560	7,425	399	5.5	8.6	2.6	3.3	20.3	2.7
2001.......	16,037	12,256	3,782	7,884	7,522	424	5.6	8.8	2.6	3.4	20.2	2.8
2002.......	16,204	12,432	3,772	7,784	7,759	437	5.6	8.8	2.6	3.3	20.6	2.8
2003.......	16,528	12,828	3,700	7,932	7,893	468	5.7	9.0	2.5	3.4	20.7	2.9
2004.......	16,148	12,596	3,552	7,944	7,562	417	5.5	8.7	2.4	3.3	19.6	2.5
2005.......	16,740	13,169	3,571	8,045	8,015	443	5.6	9.0	2.4	3.3	20.5	2.6
2006.......	17,030	13,433	3,597	7,906	8,428	461	5.7	9.1	2.4	3.3	21.3	2.6
2007.......	16,929	13,286	3,643	7,924	8,352	402	5.6	8.9	2.4	3.3	20.9	2.2

[1] Rate is per 100,000 inhabitants.

Source: U.S. Department of Justice, Bureau of Justice Statistics, *Homicide Trends in the United States, 1976–2007.* See also <http://bjs.ojp.usdoj.gov/content/homicide/homtrnd.cfm>.

Table 309. Homicide Victims by Race and Sex: 1980 to 2006

[Rates per 100,000 resident population in specified group. Excludes deaths to nonresidents of United States. Effective with data for 1999, causes of death are classified by The Tenth Revision International Classification of Diseases (ICD-10), replacing the Ninth Revision (ICD-9) used for 1979–98 data. In ICD-9, the category Homicide also includes death as a result of legal intervention. ICD-10 has two separate categories for these two causes of death. Some caution should be used in comparing data between 1998 and 1999. See text, Section 2]

Year	Homicide victims					Homicide rate [2]				
		White		Black			White		Black	
	Total [1]	Male	Female	Male	Female	Total [1]	Male	Female	Male	Female
1980.......	24,278	10,381	3,177	8,385	1,898	10.7	10.9	3.2	66.6	13.5
1985.......	19,893	8,122	3,041	6,616	1,666	8.3	8.2	2.9	48.4	11.0
1990.......	24,932	9,147	3,006	10,083	2,124	9.6	8.5	2.6	65.1	12.4
1994.......	24,926	9,055	2,921	10,083	2,124	9.6	8.5	2.6	65.1	12.4
1995.......	22,895	8,336	3,028	8,847	1,936	8.7	7.8	2.7	56.3	11.1
1996.......	20,971	7,570	2,747	8,183	1,800	7.9	7.0	2.5	51.5	10.2
1997.......	19,846	7,343	2,570	7,601	1,652	7.4	6.7	2.3	47.1	9.3
1998.......	18,272	6,707	2,534	6,873	1,547	6.8	6.1	2.2	42.1	8.6
1999.......	16,889	6,162	2,466	6,214	1,434	6.2	5.6	2.2	37.5	7.8
2000.......	16,765	5,925	2,414	6,482	1,385	6.1	5.3	2.1	38.6	7.5
2001.......	20,308	8,254	3,074	6,780	1,446	7.1	7.2	2.6	38.3	7.4
2002.......	17,638	6,282	2,403	6,896	1,391	6.1	5.4	2.0	38.4	7.0
2003.......	17,732	6,337	2,372	7,083	1,309	6.1	5.4	2.0	38.9	6.6
2004.......	17,357	6,302	2,341	6,839	1,296	5.9	5.3	1.9	37.1	6.4
2005.......	18,124	6,457	2,313	7,412	1,257	6.1	5.4	1.9	39.7	6.2
2006.......	18,573	6,514	2,346	7,677	1,355	6.2	5.4	1.9	40.6	6.6

[1] Includes races not shown separately. [2] Rate based on enumerated population figures as of April 1 for 1980, 1990, and 2000; estimated resident population as of July 1 for other years.

Source: U.S. National Center for Health Statistics, *Vital Statistics of the United States*, annual; and National Vital Statistics Reports (NVSR) (formerly Monthly Vital Statistics Report); and unpublished data.

Table 310. Forcible Rape—Number and Rate: 1980 to 2007

[For definition of rape, go to http://www.fbi.gov/ucr/cius2007/about/offense_definitions.html]

Item	1980	1990	1995	2000	2002	2003	2004	2005	2006	2007
NUMBER										
Total.................	82,990	102,560	97,460	90,186	95,235	93,883	95,089	94,347	92,757	90,427
By force...............	63,599	86,541	85,249	81,111	86,655	85,837	87,147	86,597	85,266	83,333
Attempt	19,391	16,019	12,211	9,075	8,580	8,046	7,942	7,750	7,491	7,094
RATE										
Per 100,000 population	36.8	41.1	37.1	32.0	33.1	32.3	32.4	31.8	31.0	30.0
Per 100,000 females	71.6	80.5	72.5	62.7	65.0	63.5	63.8	62.5	60.9	59.1

Source: U.S. Department of Justice, Federal Bureau of Investigation, "Violent Crime, Forcible Rape", <http://www.fbi.gov/ucr/cius2007/offenses/violent_crime/forcible_rape.html>.

Table 311. Criminal Victimizations and Victimization Rates: 1995 to 2008

[(39,926 represents 39,926,000). Based on National Crime Victimization Survey; see text, this section and Appendix III. For definitions of crimes, see also <http://www.ojp.usdoj.gov/index.cfm?ty=tdtp&tid=3>]

Type of crime	Number of victimizations (1,000)				Victimization rates [1]			
	1995	2000	2005	2008	1995	2000	2005	2008
All crimes, total	**39,926**	**25,893**	**23,441**	**21,312**	(X)	(X)	(X)	(X)
Population: Aged 12 or older (1,000)	215,709	226,805	244,505	252,243	(X)	(X)	(X)	(X)
Personal crimes [2]	**10,436**	**6,597**	**5,401**	**4,993**	46.2	29.1	22.1	19.8
Crimes of violence	10,022	6,323	5,174	4,856	44.5	27.9	21.2	19.3
Completed violence	2,960	2,044	1,659	1,362	12.9	9.0	6.8	5.4
Attempted/threatened violence	7,061	4,279	3,515	3,494	31.6	18.9	14.4	13.9
Rape/sexual assault	363	261	192	204	1.6	1.2	0.8	0.8
Rape/attempted rape	252	147	130	123	1.1	0.6	0.5	0.5
Rape	153	92	69	52	0.7	0.4	0.3	0.2
Attempted rape	99	55	61	70	0.4	0.2	0.2	0.3
Sexual assault	112	114	62	81	0.5	0.5	0.3	0.3
Robbery	1,171	732	625	552	5.3	3.2	2.6	2.2
Completed/property taken	753	520	415	372	3.5	2.3	1.7	1.5
With injury	224	160	143	142	1.0	0.7	0.6	0.6
Without injury	529	360	272	231	2.4	1.6	1.1	0.9
Attempted to take property	418	212	210	180	1.8	0.9	0.9	0.7
With injury	84	66	64	64	0.4	0.3	0.3	0.3
Without injury	335	146	145	115	1.4	0.6	0.6	0.5
Assault	8,487	5,330	4,357	4,101	37.6	23.5	17.8	16.3
Aggravated	2,050	1,293	1,052	840	8.8	5.7	4.3	3.3
With injury	533	346	331	253	2.4	1.5	1.4	1
Threatened with weapon	1,517	946	722	587	6.4	4.2	3.0	2.3
Simple	6,437	4,038	3,305	3,261	28.9	17.8	13.5	12.9
With minor injury	1,426	989	795	616	6.0	4.4	3.3	2.4
Without injury	5,012	3,048	2,510	2,645	22.9	13.4	10.3	10.5
Personal theft [3]	414	274	227	137	1.7	1.2	0.9	0.5
Total number of households (1,000)	101,888	108,353	117,100	121,141	(X)	(X)	(X)	(X)
Property crimes	**29,490**	**19,297**	**18,040**	**16,319**	279.5	178.1	154.0	134.7
Household burglary	5,004	3,444	3,456	3,189	47.4	31.8	29.5	26.3
Completed	4,232	2,909	2,900	2,599	40.0	26.9	24.8	21.5
Attempted forcible entry	773	534	556	590	7.4	4.9	4.7	4.9
Motor vehicle theft	1,717	937	978	795	16.2	8.6	8.4	6.6
Completed	1,163	642	775	593	10.8	5.9	6.6	4.9
Attempted	554	295	203	202	5.5	2.7	1.7	1.7
Theft	22,769	14,916	13,606	12,335	215.9	137.7	116.2	101.8
Completed [4]	21,857	14,300	13,116	11,741	207.6	132.0	112.0	96.9
Attempted	911	616	489	595	8.4	5.7	4.2	4.9

X Not applicable [1] Per 1,000 persons aged 12 or older for "Personal crime"; per 1,000 households for "Property crime."
[2] The victimization survey cannot measure murder because of the inability to question the victim. [3] Includes pocket picking, purse snatching, and attempted purse snatching. [4] Includes thefts in which the amount taken was not ascertained.

Source: U.S. Department of Justice, Bureau of Justice Statistics, National Crime Victimization Survey, *Criminal Victimization*, annual, and series NCJ-227777, September 2009. See also <http://www.ojp.usdoj.gov/index.cfm?ty=tdtp&tid=3>.

Table 312. Victimization Rates by Type of Crime and Characteristics of the Victim: 2008

[Rate per 1,000 persons aged 12 years or older. Based on the National Crime Victimization Survey. See headnote, Table 311]

Characteristic of the victim	Population	All crimes	Crimes of violence						Personal theft [1]
			Total	Rape/ sexual assault	Robbery	Assault			
						Total	Aggra- vated	Simple	
Total	**252,242,520**	**19.8**	**19.3**	**0.8**	**2.2**	**16.3**	**3.3**	**12.9**	**0.5**
Male	123,071,020	21.9	21.3	[2] 0.3	2.7	18.3	3.9	14.5	0.5
Female	129,171,510	17.8	17.3	1.3	1.7	14.3	2.8	11.5	0.5
12 to 15 years old	16,414,550	43.6	42.2	[2] 1.6	5.5	35.2	6.1	29	[2] 1.4
16 to 19 years old	17,280,270	37.4	37.0	2.2	4.8	30.0	5.6	24.5	[2] 0.4
20 to 24 years old	20,547,620	38.4	37.8	2.1	5.4	30.3	8.7	21.5	[2] 0.6
25 to 34 years old	40,649,500	23.8	23.4	0.7	2.3	20.5	4.0	16.5	[2] 0.4
35 to 49 years old	65,123,030	17.4	16.7	0.8	1.9	14.1	2.7	11.4	0.6
50 to 64 years old	55,116,320	11.1	10.7	[2] 0.2	0.8	9.7	2.0	7.7	[2] 0.4
65 years old and over	37,111,240	3.5	3.1	[2] 0.2	[2] 0.2	2.7	0.4	[2] 2.3	[2] 0.5
White	204,683,500	18.6	18.1	0.6	1.6	15.9	3.0	12.8	0.5
Black	30,709,860	26.6	25.9	[2] 1.9	5.5	18.5	5.2	13.3	[2] 0.7
Other [3]	13,952,240	15.5	15.2	[2] 0.9	[2] 3.0	11.3	2.8	8.5	[2] 0.4
Hispanic	34,506,680	17.1	16.4	[2] 0.6	3.4	12.4	3.5	8.9	[2] 0.7
Non-Hispanic	217,351,750	20.3	19.7	0.8	2.0	16.9	3.3	13.6	0.5
Household income:									
Less than $7,500	6,760,710	44.0	43.5	[2] 4.4	5.9	33.1	9.3	23.8	[2] 0.5
$7,500 to $14,999	10,261,320	41.3	40.4	[2] 2.1	4.8	33.5	8.6	24.9	[2] 0.9
$15,000 to $24,999	17,538,250	26.5	26.0	[2] 1.0	3.0	22.0	5.3	16.8	[2] 0.6
$25,000 to $34,999	19,522,830	25.7	25.4	[2] 0.6	3.7	21.2	3.4	17.8	[2] 0.2
$35,000 to $49,999	28,963,880	23.1	22.4	[2] 1.0	2.0	19.3	3.8	15.5	[2] 0.7
$50,000 to $74,999	33,797,170	16.5	15.9	[2] 0.0	1.3	14.6	3.0	11.6	[2] 0.6
$75,000 or more	59,992,830	12.9	12.6	[2] 0.5	1.4	10.7	1.9	8.8	[2] 0.3

[1] Includes pocket picking, completed purse snatching, and attempted purse snatching. [2] Based on 10 or fewer sample cases.
[3] Includes American Indians, Alaska Natives, Asians, Native Hawaiians, and other Pacific Islanders.

Source: U.S. Department of Justice, Bureau of Justice Statistics, National Crime Victimization Survey, *Criminal Victimization*, annual, and series NCJ-227777, September 2009. See also <http://bjs.ojp.usdoj.gov/index.cfm?ty=pbdetail&iid=1975>.

Table 313. Victim-Offender Relationship in Crimes of Violence by Characteristics of the Criminal Incident: 2008

[In percent, except as indicated. Covers only crimes of violence. An incident is a specific criminal act involving one or more victims and offenders. For example, if two people are robbed at the same time and place, this is classified as two robbery victimizations but only one robbery incident. See headnote, Table 311]

Selected characteristics of incident	Number of incidents	Total	Rape/ sexual assault	Robbery	Assault Total	Assault Aggra-vated [1]	Assault Simple
Total.	**4,581,260**	**100**	**100**	**100**	**100**	**100**	**100**
Victim/offender relationship: [2]							
Relatives	508,620	10.5	[3] 5.9	7.8	11.1	9.5	11.5
Well-known	1,222,550	25.2	46.0	17.1	25.2	25.0	25.3
Casual acquaintance	674,380	13.9	[3] 13.5	[3] 6.4	14.9	13.9	15.2
Stranger	1,755,980	36.2	26.9	54.3	34.2	37.0	33.5
Time of day: [4]							
6 a.m. to 6 p.m.	2,455,980	53.6	42.5	48.5	54.8	44.6	57.4
6 p.m. to midnight	1,429,040	31.2	32.8	32.3	31.0	41.5	28.4
Midnight to 6 a.m.	516,970	11.3	21.7	17.5	9.9	10.9	9.7
Location of crime:							
At or near victim's home or lodging	1,609,400	35.2	42.6	32.8	35.1	35.6	35.0
Friend's/relative's/neighbor's home	418,180	9.1	[3] 10.3	8.5	8.7	11.0	8.2
Commercial places	552,250	12.1	[3] 6.0	[3] 5.0	13.3	10.1	14.1
Parking lots/garages	320,470	7.0	-	17.0	6.1	10.0	5.1
School	609,360	13.3	[3] 12.1	[3] 5.9	14.3	7.3	16.1
Streets other than near victim's home	622,500	13.6	[3] 10.9	25.6	12.2	15.9	11.3
Other [5]	449,110	9.7	10.1	5.3	10.3	10.1	10.4
Victim's activity: [6]							
At work or traveling to or from work	858,170	18.7	[3] 8.3	14.1	(NA)	16.4	20.7
School	694,080	15.2	[3] 18.5	11.7	(NA)	7.3	17.4
Activities at home	1,162,070	25.4	39.0	18.2	(NA)	27.1	25.2
Shopping/errands	234,950	5.1	[3] 1.6	9.5	(NA)	7.4	4.1
Leisure activities away from home	943,930	20.6	[3] 17.7	22.6	(NA)	23.1	19.9
Traveling	337,330	7.4	[3] 8.2	13.4	(NA)	10.1	5.7
Other [7]	285,390	6.2	[3] 6.6	9.0	(NA)	5.3	5.9
Distance from victim's home: [8]							
Inside home or lodging	841,690	18.4	35.0	16.0	17.8	16.4	18.2
Near victim's home	819,440	17.9	[3] 13.5	18.1	18.1	21.6	17.2
1 mile or less	821,040	17.9	23.5	28.2	16.3	18.9	15.7
5 miles or less	960,700	21.0	[3] 16.3	12.6	22.3	19.0	23.1
50 miles or less	923,810	20.2	[3] 9.9	19.7	20.8	19.0	21.2
More than 50 miles	175,700	3.8	[3] 1.7	[3] 5.4	3.7	[3] 4.4	3.6
Weapons:							
No weapons present	897,230	69.5	79.6	49.3	76.5	8.0	93.5
Weapons present	326,730	25.3	[3] 1.4	39.9	18.1	91.2	(X)

- Represents zero. NA Not available. X Not applicable. [1] An aggravated assault is any assault in which an offender possesses or uses a weapon or inflicts serious injury. [2] Excludes "don't know" relationships. [3] Based on 10 or fewer sample cases. [4] Excludes "not known and not available" time of day. [5] Includes areas on public transportation or inside station, in apartment yard, park, field, playground, or other areas. [6] Excludes "don't know" and "not available" victim activity. [7] Includes sleeping. [8] Excludes "don't know" and "not available" distance from victim's home.

Source: U.S. Department of Justice, Bureau of Justice Statistics, National Crime Victimization Survey, *Criminal Victimization*, annual, and series NCJ-227777, September 2009. See also <http://bjs.ojp.usdoj.gov/index.cfm?ty=pbdetail&iid=1975>.

Table 314. Violence by Intimate Partners by Sex, 1995 to 2007, and by Type of Crime, 2007

[Violence includes rape and sexual assault, robbery, aggravated assault, simple assault and homicide. Intimate partners are defined as spouses, ex-spouses, current boy/girlfriends, and ex-boy/girlfriends. See headnote, Table 311]

Year and type of crime	All persons Number	All persons Rate per 1,000 [1]	Female victims Number	Female victims Rate per 1,000 [1]	Male victims Number	Male victims Rate per 1,000 [1]
1995	975,510	4.5	858,100	7.7	117,410	1.1
2000	670,900	3.0	560,230	4.8	110,670	1.0
2002	588,020	2.5	498,210	4.2	89,810	0.8
2003	540,700	2.3	444,140	3.6	96,560	0.8
2004	612,650	2.5	474,250	3.8	138,400	1.2
2005	493,110	2.0	385,850	3.1	107,260	0.9
2006 [2]	779,040	3.2	617,190	4.9	161,840	1.3
2007, total	**646,790**	**2.6**	**564,430**	**4.4**	**82,360**	**0.7**
Rape or sexual assault	55,110	0.2	55,110	0.4	(B)	(B)
Robbery	43,270	0.2	37,320	0.3	5,960	-
Aggravated assault	85,010	0.3	69,010	0.5	16,000	0.1
Simple assault	446,510	1.8	399,370	3.1	47,140	0.4
Homicide	1,531	0.5	1,185	0.8	346	0.2

- Rounds to zero. B Base figure too small to meet statistical standards for reliability of derived figure. [1] Rates are the number of victimizations per 1,000 persons aged 12 or older. Except for Homicide, the number of victimizations is per 100,000 persons aged 12 or older. [2] Due to changes in methodology, the 2006 national crime victimization rates are not comparable to previous years or to 2007 and cannot be used for yearly trend comparisons. However, the overall patterns of victimization at the national level can be examined.

Source: U.S. Department of Justice, Bureau of Justice Statistics, National Crime Victimization Survey, *Intimate Partner Violence in the United States*, Series NCJ-210675, December 2007, and *Crime Victimization,* annual, Series NCJ-224390. See also <http://bjs.ojp.usdoj.gov/index.cfm?ty=pbdetail&iid=1000>.

Table 315. Stalking and Harassment Victimization in the United States: 2006

[Survey based on population of persons aged 18 or older. The survey defines stalking as a course of conduct directed at a specific person that would cause a reasonable person to feel fear. The survey characterizes individuals as victims of harassment who experience the behaviors associated with stalking but neither reported feeling fear as a result of such conduct nor experienced actions that would cause a reasonable person to feel fear]

Characteristic	Population	Number			Rate per 1,000 persons		
		All	Stalking	Harassment	All	Stalking	Harassment
All victims [1]	**246,500,200**	**5,857,030**	**3,424,100**	**2,432,930**	**23.8**	**13.9**	**9.9**
Gender							
Male.	120,068,420	2,032,460	892,340	1,140,120	16.9	7.4	9.5
Female.	126,431,780	3,824,570	2,531,770	1,292,800	30.3	20.0	10.2
Age							
18 to 19 years old	8,047,540	379,610	238,990	140,620	47.2	29.7	17.5
20 to 24 years old	20,346,940	929,710	576,870	352,840	45.7	28.4	17.3
25 to 34 years old	39,835,680	1,198,195	805,260	392,930	30.1	20.2	9.9
35 to 49 years old	65,886,490	1,971,290	1,139,320	831,970	29.9	17.3	12.6
50 to 64 years old	51,400,990	1,046,650	534,870	511,780	20.4	10.4	10.0
65 years old and over . . .	35,515,670	331,580	128,790	202,790	9.3	3.6	5.7
Race							
White.	200,874,080	4,835,270	2,860,810	1,974,460	24.1	14.2	9.8
Black.	29,853,700	678,230	363,280	314,950	22.7	12.2	10.5
American Indian/ Alaska Native	1,695,400	55,890	[2] 33,150	[2] 22,740	33.0	[2] 19.6	[2] 13.4
Asian/Pacific Islander	11,317,780	151,670	79,790	71,890	13.4	7.0	6.4
More than one race [3]	2,759,240	135,960	87,080	48,880	49.3	31.6	17.7
Hispanic origin							
Hispanic.	29,522,670	487,320	312,490	174,830	16.5	10.6	5.9
Non-Hispanic.	215,025,170	5,308,010	3,089,570	2,218,440	24.7	14.4	10.3
Marital status							
Never married	79,715,080	2,143,400	1,321,870	821,530	26.9	16.6	10.3
Married	123,633,560	2,078,830	1,071,630	1,007,200	16.8	8.7	8.1
Divorced or separated . . .	26,334,200	1,363,540	895,620	467,920	51.8	34.0	17.8
Widowed	14,318,190	229,450	107,730	121,720	16.0	7.5	8.5
Household Income							
Less than $7,500	8,418,570	395,740	266,800	128,940	47.0	31.7	15.3
$7,500 to $14,999	14,562,850	583,840	399,620	184,210	40.1	27.4	12.6
$15,000 to $24,999	22,428,240	724,270	474,220	250,050	32.3	21.1	11.1
$25,000 to $34,999	22,000,000	625,000	362,180	263,500	27.4	15.8	11.5
$35,000 to $49,999	30,345,140	765,580	480,750	284,830	25.2	15.8	9.4
$50,000 to $74,999	37,956,910	877,660	476,420	401,230	23.1	12.6	10.6
$75,000 or more	56,633,800	1,063,860	542,730	521,130	18.8	9.6	9.2

[1] Table excludes missing data. [2] Based on 10 or fewer sample cases. [3] Includes all persons of any race, including persons who identify two or more races.

Source: U.S. Department of Justice, Bureau of Justice Statistics, National Crime Victimization Survey, Supplemental Victimization Survey, *Stalking Victimization in the United States*, Series NCJ-224527, January 2009. See <http://bjs.ojp.usdoj.gov/index.cfm?ty=dcdetail&iid=245>.

Table 316. Property Victimization Rates by Selected Household Characteristics: 2008

[(121,141 represents 121,141,000). Households headed by persons aged 12 years or older. Based on National Crime Victimization Survey (NCVS); see text, this section and Appendix III. See headnote, Table 311]

Characteristic	Number of house-holds (1,000)	Number of victimizations (1,000)				Victimization rate per 1,000 households			
		Total	Burglary	Motor vehicle theft	Theft	Total	Burglary	Motor vehicle theft	Theft
Total	**121,141**	**16,319**	**3,189**	**795**	**12,335**	**134.7**	**26.3**	**6.6**	**101.8**
Race:									
White	98,421	12,818	2,320	530	9,968	130.2	23.6	5.4	101.3
Black	15,538	2,454	653	196	1,605	158.0	42.0	12.6	103.3
Other	5,927	672	121	46	505	113.4	20.4	7.8	85.2
Ethnicity:									
Hispanic.	13,716	2,571	470	161	1,940	187.5	34.3	11.7	141.4
Non-Hispanic.	107,190	13,744	2,718	634	10,391	128.2	25.4	5.9	96.9
Household income:									
	4,115	840	233	38	569	204.2	56.6	9.4	138.3
$7,500 to $14,999	6,362	1,113	334	49	729	175.0	52.6	7.8	114.6
$15,000 to $24,999	9,413	1,522	304	58	1,160	161.7	32.3	6.2	123.2
$25,000 to $34,999	9,902	1,490	326	60	1,104	150.5	33.0	6.0	111.5
$35,000 to $49,999	13,497	1,926	361	101	1,464	142.7	26.8	7.5	108.5
$50,000 to $74,999	14,601	1,837	308	112	1,417	125.8	21.1	7.6	97.0
$75,000 or more	24,115	3,217	393	141	2,682	133.4	16.3	5.9	111.2
Number of persons in household:									
1.	34,561	3,467	948	162	2,357	100.3	27.4	4.7	68.2
2 or 3	60,022	7,337	1,328	366	5,642	122.2	22.1	6.1	94.0
4 or 5	22,868	4,505	761	209	3,535	197.0	33.3	9.1	154.6
6 or more	3,690	1,010	151	58	801	273.9	41.0	15.7	217.1

Source: U.S. Department of Justice, Office of Justice Programs, Bureau of Justice Statistics, National Crime Victimization Survey, *Criminal Victimization*, annual, and series NCJ-227777, September 2009; See also <http://bjs.ojp.usdoj.gov/index.cfm?ty=pbdetail&iid=1975>

Table 317. Robbery and Property Crimes by Type and Selected Characteristics: 1990 to 2008

[(639 represents 639,000.) For definitions of types of crimes, see http://www.fbi.gov/ucr/cius2008/about/offense_definitions.html>]

Characteristic of offense	Number of offenses (1,000)				Rate per 100,000 population				Average value lost (dol.)			
	1990	2000	2005	2008	1990	2000	2005	2008	1990	2000	2005	2008
Robbery, total [1]	**639**	**408**	**417**	**360**	**256.3**	**144.9**	**140.7**	**138.2**	**631**	**1,127**	**1,239**	**1,313**
Type of crime:												
Street or highway	359	188	184	157	144.2	66.7	62.1	59.6	511	858	1,020	1,013
Commercial house	73	57	60	49	29.5	20.1	20.1	18.9	945	1,685	1,662	1,644
Gas station	18	12	12	9	7.1	4.1	4.0	3.5	423	679	1,104	1,006
Convenience store	39	26	24	20	15.6	9.3	8.0	7.6	344	566	677	712
Residence	62	50	59	58	25.1	17.7	20.0	22.4	828	1,243	1,332	1,665
Bank	9	9	9	7	3.8	3.1	3.0	2.8	2,885	4,379	4,113	4,808
Weapon used:												
Firearm	234	161	175	143	94.1	57.0	59.0	59.5	(NA)	(NA)	(NA)	(NA)
Knife or cutting instrument	76	36	37	26	30.7	12.8	12.5	10.8	(NA)	(NA)	(NA)	(NA)
Other weapon	61	53	39	29	24.5	18.9	13.2	12.1	(NA)	(NA)	(NA)	(NA)
Strong-arm	268	159	166	133	107.7	56.4	56.0	55.5	(NA)	(NA)	(NA)	(NA)
Burglary, total	**3,074**	**2,050**	**2,154**	**1,900**	**1,232.2**	**728.4**	**726.7**	**735.1**	**1,014**	**1,458**	**1,771**	**2,085**
Forcible entry [2]	2,150	1,297	1,310	1,077	864.5	460.7	440.0	447.4	(NA)	(NA)	(NA)	(NA)
Unlawful entry [2]	678	615	701	567	272.8	218.7	237.5	235.3	(NA)	(NA)	(NA)	(NA)
Attempted forcible entry [2]	245	138	133	110	98.7	49.0	45.2	45.8	(NA)	(NA)	(NA)	(NA)
Residence	2,033	1,335	1,417	1,335	817.4	474.3	477.9	516.7	1,037	1,378	1,813	1,596
Nonresidence	1,041	715	738	566	418.5	254.1	248.8	218.4	967	1,610	1,687	2,096
Occurred during the night [2]	1,135	699	708	608	456.4	248.3	238.9	236.5	(NA)	(NA)	(NA)	(NA)
Occurred during the day [2]	1,151	836	890	879	462.8	297.2	328.8	341.2	(NA)	(NA)	(NA)	(NA)
Larceny-theft, total	**7,946**	**6,972**	**6,783**	**5,564**	**3,185.1**	**2,477.3**	**2,286.3**	**2,143.2**	**426**	**727**	**857**	**1,013**
Pocket picking	81	36	29	24	32.4	12.7	9.8	9.1	384	437	346	541
Purse snatching	82	37	42	28	32.8	13.2	14.2	10.8	228	387	404	430
Shoplifting	1,291	959	940	903	519.1	340.7	317.0	346.3	104	185	184	196
From motor vehicles	1,744	1,754	1,752	1,455	701.3	623.3	590.6	558.5	461	692	704	717
Motor vehicle accessories	1,185	677	693	545	476.3	240.6	233.6	208.5	297	451	482	530
Bicycles	443	312	249	188	178.2	110.9	83.9	72.1	188	273	267	288
From buildings	1,118	914	852	633	449.4	324.6	287.3	245.3	673	1,184	1,738	1,529
From coin-operated machines	63	46	41	23	25.4	16.2	13.8	8.7	144	272	232	256
Other	1,940	2,232	2,184	1,765	780.0	793.0	736.1	684.0	615	957	1,137	1,730
Motor vehicles, total [3]	**1,636**	**1,160**	**1,236**	**824**	**655.8**	**412.2**	**417.4**	**315.9**	**5,117**	**6,581**	**6,204**	**6,729**
Automobiles	1,304	877	907	547	524.3	311.5	304.5	227.1	(NA)	(NA)	(NA)	(NA)
Trucks and buses	238	209	219	137	95.5	74.1	76.2	56.7	(NA)	(NA)	(NA)	(NA)

NA Not available. [1] Includes other crimes not shown separately. [2] Unknown data not included. [3] Includes other types of motor vehicles, not shown separately.
Source: U.S. Department of Justice, Federal Bureau of Investigation, "Crime in the United States." See <http://www.fbi.gov/ucr/cius2008/offenses/index.html>.

U.S. Census Bureau, Statistical Abstract of the United States: 2011

Table 318. Hate Crimes—Number of Incidents, Offenses, Victims, and Known Offenders by Bias Motivation: 2000 to 2008

[The FBI collected statistics on hate crimes from 13,690 law enforcement agencies representing over 269 million inhabitants in 2008. Hate crime offenses cover incidents motivated by race, religion, sexual orientation, ethnicity/national origin, and disability]

Bias motivation	Incidents reported	Offenses	Victims [1]	Known offenders [2]
2000, total	8,213	9,619	10,117	7,690
2005, total	7,163	8,380	8,804	6,804
2006, total	7,722	9,080	9,652	7,330
2007, total	7,624	9,006	9,535	6,965
2008, total	**7,783**	**9,168**	**9,691**	**6,927**
Bias motive:				
Race, total	**3,992**	**4,704**	**4,934**	**3,723**
Anti-White	716	812	829	811
Anti-Black	2,876	3,413	3,596	2,596
Anti-American Indian/Alaska native	54	59	63	61
Anti-Asian/Pacific Islander	137	162	170	140
Anti-multiracial group	209	258	276	115
Ethnicity/national origin, total	**894**	**1,148**	**1,226**	**1,034**
Anti-Hispanic	561	735	792	711
Anti-other ethnicity/national origin	333	413	434	323
Religion, total	**1,519**	**1,606**	**1,732**	**632**
Anti-Jewish	1,013	1,055	1,145	353
Anti-Catholic	75	75	89	35
Anti-Protestant	56	60	62	34
Anti-Islamic	105	123	130	85
Anti-other religious group	191	212	222	90
Anti-multi-religious group	65	67	70	33
Anti-atheism/agnosticism/etc.	14	14	14	2
Sexual orientation, total	**1,297**	**1,617**	**1,706**	**1,460**
Anti-male homosexual	776	948	981	921
Anti-female homosexual	154	194	198	156
Anti-homosexual	307	415	466	336
Anti-heterosexual	33	33	34	25
Anti-bisexual	27	27	27	22
Disability, total	**78**	**85**	**85**	**72**
Anti-physical	22	28	28	26
Anti-mental	56	57	57	46
Multiple bias [3]	**3**	**8**	**8**	**6**

[1] The term "victim" may refer to a person, business, institution, or a society as a whole. [2] The term "known offender" does not imply that the identity of the suspect is known, but only that an attribute of the suspect has been identified which distinguishes him/her from an unknown offender. [3] In a "multiple-bias incident" two conditions must be met: more than one offense type must occur in the incident and at least two offense types must be motivated by different biases.

Source: U.S. Department of Justice, Federal Bureau of Investigation, Uniform Crime Reports, "About Hate Crime Statistics, 2008," <http://www.fbi.gov/ucr/hc2008/victims.html/>.

Table 319. Hate Crimes Reported by State: 2008

[(269,382 represents 269,382,000). See headnote, Table 318]

State	Number of participating agencies	Population covered (1,000)	Agencies submitting incidents	Incidents reported	State	Number of participating agencies	Population covered (1,000)	Agencies submitting incidents	Incidents reported
United States [1]	**13,690**	**269,382**	**2,145**	**7,783**					
Alabama	163	2,803	5	11	Montana	99	957	12	24
Alaska	2	287	2	8	Nebraska	193	809	8	11
Arizona	89	6,439	26	185	Nevada	34	2,600	6	94
Arkansas	260	2,768	36	91	New Hampshire	144	1,137	26	44
California	730	36,757	269	1,381	New Jersey	512	8,676	202	744
Colorado	210	4,803	48	149	New Mexico	49	1,187	4	9
Connecticut	101	3,501	57	164	New York	339	17,527	76	570
Delaware	54	873	17	58	North Carolina	495	9,129	46	124
District of Columbia	2	592	2	42	North Dakota	80	601	11	16
Florida	487	18,236	72	153	Ohio	545	9,071	106	345
Georgia	6	554	2	9	Oklahoma	303	3,642	20	51
Idaho	106	1,519	12	30	Oregon	166	3,775	37	187
Illinois	308	8,048	44	120	Pennsylvania	1,241	12,276	31	68
Indiana	131	3,063	17	61	Rhode Island	48	1,051	14	35
Iowa	228	2,974	15	33	South Carolina	480	4,478	65	153
Kansas	351	2,312	48	113	South Dakota	108	687	8	42
Kentucky	315	3,822	23	64	Tennessee	461	6,214	81	255
Louisiana	87	2,446	10	67	Texas	1,000	24,305	69	246
Maine	134	1,316	28	63	Utah	117	2,694	18	40
Maryland	158	5,634	23	100	Vermont	82	607	12	20
Massachusetts	351	6,397	91	333	Virginia	407	7,768	75	263
Michigan	590	9,754	171	560	Washington	251	6,538	61	239
Minnesota	248	4,304	48	164	West Virginia	294	1,637	23	43
Mississippi	60	752	1	4	Wisconsin	379	5,628	29	92
Missouri	630	5,905	32	00	Wyoming	62	520	0	0

[1] No data available for Hawaii.

Source: U.S. Department of Justice, Federal Bureau of Investigation, Uniform Crime Reports, "About Hate Crime Statistics, 2008," <http://www.fbi.gov/ucr/hc2008/victims.html>.

Table 320. Persons Arrested by Offense, Sex, and Race: 2008

[In thousands (10,709.4 represents 10,709,400). Represents arrests (not charges) reported by 11,711 agencies with a total 2008 population of almost 231 million as estimated by the FBI. Age and sex data are mandatory, while race data are optional and not always reported with arrest data; hence, two different total number of arrests. See source for details, <http://www.fbi.gov/ucr/cius2008/about/offense_definitions.html>]

Offense	Total arrests	Male	Female	Total	White	Black	American Indian or Alaska Native	Asian or Pacific Islander
Total [1]	10,709.4	8,086.7	2,622.7	10,662.2	7,382.1	3,015.9	142.9	121.3
Murder and nonnegligent manslaughter . . .	9.9	8.8	1.1	9.9	4.7	4.9	0.1	0.1
Forcible rape	16.9	16.7	0.2	16.8	11.0	5.4	0.2	0.2
Robbery.	100.7	89.0	11.7	100.5	42.0	56.9	0.7	0.9
Aggravated assault	329.9	259.1	70.8	328.7	208.1	112.3	4.5	3.9
Burglary.	236.2	201.8	34.4	235.4	157.3	74.0	2.1	2.1
Larceny-theft	983.0	577.5	405.5	979.1	666.4	286.8	12.7	13.3
Motor vehicle theft	75.1	62.2	12.9	74.9	44.7	28.5	0.8	0.9
Arson.	10.8	9.1	1.7	10.7	8.1	2.3	0.1	0.1
Violent crime [2]	457.5	373.7	83.8	456.0	265.8	179.6	5.4	5.1
Property crime [3]	1,305.1	850.6	454.5	1,300.2	876.4	391.6	15.7	16.4
Other assaults	994.8	740.0	254.8	991.2	645.9	319.5	14.2	11.6
Forgery and counterfeiting.	69.0	42.9	26.1	68.6	46.4	21.1	0.3	0.8
Fraud.	174.6	98.7	75.9	173.6	117.2	53.5	1.4	1.4
Embezzlement.	16.5	8.0	8.5	16.3	10.5	5.5	0.1	0.2
Stolen property—buying, receiving, possessing.	85.6	68.2	17.4	85.4	52.7	31.3	0.7	0.7
Vandalism	219.1	181.5	37.5	218.2	164.3	48.0	3.4	2.5
Weapons—carrying, possessing, etc.	138.3	127.9	10.4	137.9	78.1	57.5	1.0	1.3
Prostitution and commercialized vice	58.8	18.0	40.8	58.7	32.7	24.0	0.5	1.5
Sex offenses (except forcible rape and prostitution)	60.8	55.6	5.2	60.6	44.6	14.5	0.6	0.8
Drug abuse violations	1,304.1	1,063.5	240.6	1,299.7	829.4	452.6	8.4	9.3
Gambling.	7.6	7.0	0.6	7.6	1.7	5.7	0.0	0.2
Offenses against the family and children. . .	87.2	64.9	22.3	86.1	57.3	26.5	1.6	0.6
Driving under the influence	1,110.1	872.4	237.7	1,104.3	964.6	110.7	14.7	14.4
Liquor laws	478.8	346.0	132.8	475.2	401.0	54.9	14.0	5.3
Drunkenness.	474.4	397.9	76.5	472.6	390.1	71.0	8.9	2.6
Disorderly conduct.	529.9	391.2	138.7	527.6	334.7	180.1	8.6	4.2
Vagrancy	26.3	20.4	5.9	26.3	15.7	9.9	0.5	0.1
Suspicion.	1.3	1.0	0.3	1.2	0.6	0.6	0.0	0.0
Curfew and loitering law violations	104.2	71.7	32.5	104.0	65.7	36.2	0.8	1.3
Runaways	84.1	36.9	47.1	83.8	55.4	22.7	1.6	4.0
All other offenses (except traffic)	2,921.5	2,248.8	672.7	2,907.3	1,931.3	898.9	40.2	36.8

[1] These data represent the number of persons arrested; however, some persons may be arrested more than once during a year. Therefore, the statistics in this table could, in some cases, represent multiple arrests of the same person. [2] Violent crimes are offenses of murder and nonnegligent manslaughter, forcible rape, robbery, and aggravated assault. [3] Property crimes are offenses of burglary, larceny-theft, motor vehicle theft, and arson.

Source: U.S. Department of Justice, Federal Bureau of Investigation, "Crime in the United States, Arrests," September 2009, <http://www.fbi.gov/ucr/cius2008/arrests/index.html>.

Table 321. Juvenile Arrests for Drug Abuse Offenses: 1980 to 2008

[169,439 represents 169,439,000. Juveniles are persons under 18 years of age]

Offense	1980	1990	1995	2000	2003	2004	2005	2006	2007	2008
Number of contributing agencies	8,178	10,765	10,037	9,904	11,368	11,437	11,778	13,650	12,357	12,285
Population covered (1,000) . . .	169,439	204,543	206,762	204,965	219,562	222,147	230,176	245,902	235,486	240,183
NUMBER										
Drug abuse, total [1]	86,685	66,300	149,236	146,594	134,746	135,056	137,809	145,153	143,270	134,661
Sale and manufacturing.	13,004	24,575	34,077	26,432	21,987	21,136	21,607	22,466	21,493	19,467
Heroin/cocaine.	1,318	17,511	19,187	11,000	7,848	7,852	7,863	8,261	7,334	6,288
Marijuana.	8,876	4,372	10,682	11,792	10,463	9,743	9,845	10,333	10,640	9,678
Synthetic narcotics	465	346	701	945	1,043	1,119	1,071	1,262	1,162	1,093
Dangerous nonnarcotic drugs	2,345	2,346	3,507	2,695	2,633	2,422	2,828	2,610	2,357	2,408
Possession	73,681	41,725	115,159	120,432	112,759	113,920	116,202	122,687	121,777	115,194
Heroin/cocaine.	2,614	15,194	21,253	12,586	9,932	10,805	11,131	12,024	9,756	7,944
Marijuana.	64,465	20,940	82,015	95,962	87,909	87,717	88,909	95,120	97,671	93,042
Synthetic narcotics	1,524	1,155	2,047	2,052	2,872	3,279	3,235	3,337	3,142	3,286
Dangerous nonnarcotic drugs	5,078	4,436	9,844	9,832	12,046	12,119	12,927	12,206	11,208	10,922

[1] These data represent the number of persons arrested; however, some persons may be arrested more than once during a year. Therefore, the statistics in this table could, in some cases, represent multiple arrests of the same person.

Source: U.S. Department of Justice, Federal Bureau of Investigation, "Crime in the United States, Arrest," September 2009, <http://www.fbi.gov/ucr/cius2008/arrests/index.html\>.

Table 322. Arrests—18 Years and Older: 2008

[11,713 agencies; 2008 estimated population 230,897,506. See head note, Table 320. See Table 323, for "Total arrest data"]

Offense charged	Ages 18 and over	18–19	20–24	25–29	30–34	35–39	40–44	45–49	50 and over
Total [1]	9,086,278	1,048,246	2,072,179	1,523,228	1,053,380	938,036	864,786	747,575	838,848
Murder and nonnegligent manslaughter	8,914	1,392	2,568	1,689	918	753	555	416	623
Forcible rape	14,411	1,645	3,165	2,362	1,838	1,638	1,453	1,027	1,283
Robbery	73,216	17,520	21,624	11,645	6,695	5,511	4,579	3,258	2,384
Aggravated assault	286,944	25,868	61,756	51,324	36,843	31,859	28,370	24,052	26,872
Burglary	171,801	34,503	43,783	27,075	17,530	15,705	13,965	10,642	8,598
Larceny-theft	731,514	122,238	164,978	107,996	76,180	71,665	67,382	57,205	63,870
Motor vehicle theft	56,067	9,411	13,801	9,843	6,781	5,946	4,748	3,252	2,285
Arson	5,763	901	1,299	823	642	497	515	455	631
Violent crime [2]	383,485	46,425	89,113	67,020	46,294	39,761	34,957	28,753	31,162
Property crime [3]	965,145	167,053	223,861	145,737	101,133	93,813	86,610	71,554	75,384
Other assaults	817,285	67,157	170,771	146,974	107,287	97,040	85,328	69,806	72,922
Forgery and counterfeiting	66,973	5,347	14,508	13,426	9,604	8,374	6,503	4,861	4,350
Fraud	168,907	10,424	29,810	29,729	25,030	23,262	19,263	14,553	16,836
Embezzlement	15,465	2,424	4,113	2,378	1,843	1,484	1,292	905	1,026
Stolen property; buying, receiving, possessing	69,524	10,811	16,829	11,972	8,287	7,197	6,147	4,365	3,916
Vandalism	136,618	26,379	38,156	22,752	13,697	11,280	9,568	7,397	7,389
Weapons; carrying, possessing, etc.	107,451	17,997	30,741	19,677	11,189	8,183	6,569	5,701	7,394
Prostitution and commercialized vice	57,626	4,150	11,392	9,438	7,538	7,758	7,260	5,393	4,697
Sex offenses (except forcible rape and prostitution)	49,775	4,667	8,929	6,677	5,611	5,424	5,431	4,814	8,222
Drug abuse violations	1,166,140	164,731	301,655	207,658	130,463	106,789	96,509	81,548	76,787
Gambling	6,337	1,154	1,765	937	535	446	359	368	773
Offenses against the family and children	82,819	3,618	12,081	15,135	13,728	13,439	10,799	7,558	6,461
Driving under the influence	1,098,082	56,114	244,022	204,165	136,200	117,761	107,844	98,831	133,145
Liquor laws	377,956	163,695	101,804	21,049	15,170	14,940	17,350	19,030	24,918
Drunkenness	462,444	27,071	90,993	70,782	50,128	48,925	53,301	54,514	66,730
Disorderly conduct	384,997	45,371	99,231	63,228	40,516	35,539	34,180	31,377	35,555
Vagrancy	23,227	2,200	3,215	2,345	2,020	2,479	3,235	3,355	4,378
All other offenses (except traffic)	2,644,973	221,258	578,929	461,983	327,005	294,051	272,209	232,825	256,713
Suspicion	1,049	200	261	166	102	91	72	67	90

[1] See Table 320, footnote 1. [2] Violent crimes are offenses of murder and nonnegligent manslaughter, forcible rape, robbery, and aggravated assault. [3] Property crimes are offenses of burglary, larceny-theft, motor vehicle theft, and arson.

Source: U.S. Department of Justice, Federal Bureau of Investigation, "Crime in the United States, Arrest," September 2009, <http://www.fbi.gov/ucr/cius2008/arrests/index.html>.

Table 323. Arrest—Ages Under 18 Years: 2008

[11,713 agencies; 2008 estimated population 230,897,506. See headnote, Table 320]

Offense charged	Total all ages	Ages under 18	Under 10	10–12	13–14	15	16	17
Total [1]	10,709,361	1,623,083	11,226	88,568	342,244	318,635	404,507	457,903
Murder and nonnegligent manslaughter	9,888	974	1	8	70	150	296	449
Forcible rape	16,916	2,505	8	216	636	462	540	643
Robbery	100,738	27,522	61	672	4,651	5,517	7,717	8,904
Aggravated assault	329,913	42,969	399	3,176	9,777	8,273	10,050	11,294
Burglary	236,219	64,418	554	3,692	14,292	13,252	15,634	16,994
Larceny-theft	982,997	251,483	1,480	15,687	55,754	49,373	62,106	67,083
Motor vehicle theft	75,135	19,068	20	401	3,398	4,489	5,359	5,401
Arson	10,784	5,021	291	885	1,646	901	695	603
Violent crime [2]	457,455	73,970	469	4,072	15,134	14,402	18,603	21,290
Property crime [3]	1,305,135	339,990	2,345	20,665	75,090	68,015	83,794	90,081
Other assaults	994,804	177,519	1,932	16,571	48,054	35,107	38,762	37,093
Forgery and counterfeiting	68,976	2,003	9	47	183	223	489	1,052
Fraud	174,598	5,691	42	149	734	845	1,489	2,432
Embezzlement	16,458	993	4	3	21	43	287	635
Stolen property; buying, receiving, possessing	85,584	16,060	58	578	3,083	3,155	4,333	4,853
Vandalism	219,059	82,441	1,543	8,282	23,405	15,779	16,745	16,687
Weapons; carrying, possessing, etc.	138,255	30,804	391	2,376	6,928	5,607	7,171	8,331
Prostitution and commercialized vice	58,784	1,158	8	7	114	172	329	528
Sex offenses (except forcible rape and prostitution)	60,804	11,029	240	1,487	3,502	1,934	1,913	1,953
Drug abuse violations	1,304,098	137,958	192	2,176	17,989	23,031	37,641	56,929
Gambling	7,632	1,295	3	10	169	262	333	518
Offenses against the family and children	87,197	4,378	84	228	901	833	1,119	1,213
Driving under the influence	1,110,083	12,001	39	20	137	460	2,777	8,568
Liquor laws	478,800	100,844	128	695	8,388	14,843	28,652	48,138
Drunkenness	474,378	11,934	59	59	1,155	1,795	2,915	5,951
Disorderly conduct	529,929	144,932	881	11,920	39,844	30,326	32,183	29,778
Vagrancy	26,325	3,098	6	148	759	825	954	406
All other offenses (except traffic)	2,921,526	276,553	1,764	10,700	52,399	55,648	71,710	84,332
Suspicion	1,259	210	1	9	41	47	55	57
Curfew and loitering law violations	104,168	104,168	402	4,231	22,095	23,898	29,124	24,418
Runaways	84,054	84,054	626	4,135	22,119	21,385	23,129	12,660

[1] See Table 320, footnote 1. [2] Violent crimes are offenses of murder and nonnegligent manslaughter, forcible rape, robbery, and aggravated assault. [3] Property crimes are offenses of burglary, larceny-theft, motor vehicle theft, and arson.

Source: U.S. Department of Justice, Federal Bureau of Investigation, "Crime in the United States, Arrest"; September 2009 <http://www.fbi.gov/ucr/cius2008/arrests/index.html>..

U.S. Census Bureau, Statistical Abstract of the United States: 2011

Table 324. Drug Arrest Rates for Drug Abuse Violations, 1990 to 2008, and by Region, 2008

[Rate per 100,000 inhabitants. Based on Census Bureau estimated resident population as of July 1, except 1990 and 2000, enumerated as of April 1. For composition of regions, see map, inside front cover]

Offense	1990	2000	2005	2008 Total	North east	Midwest	South	West
Drug arrest rate, total	435.3	587.1	600.9	523.6	487.1	387.1	568.7	594.3
Sale and/or manufacture	139.0	122.7	109.9	93.2	106.2	74.1	95.8	95.8
Heroin or cocaine [1]	93.7	60.8	47.8	40.1	64.1	21.6	42.9	34.7
Marijuana..............................	26.4	34.2	29.6	29.3	28.6	31.2	26.1	32.2
Synthetic or manufactured drugs..........	2.7	6.4	8.6	7.9	5.8	4.6	14.6	3.7
Other dangerous nonnarcotic drugs	16.2	21.3	23.9	15.9	7.6	16.7	12.2	25.3
Possession	296.3	464.4	490.9	430.4	380.9	315.0	472.9	498.4
Heroin or cocaine [1]	144.4	138.7	131.5	103.9	101.7	48.3	117.3	131.1
Marijuana..............................	104.9	244.4	228.9	233.6	226.9	203.6	283.6	198.9
Synthetic or manufactured drugs..........	6.6	12.0	21.0	18.1	12.8	14.4	25.4	15.4
Other dangerous nonnarcotic drugs	40.4	69.4	109.6	74.8	39.5	48.6	46.7	153.1

[1] Includes other derivatives such as morphine, heroin, and codeine.

Source: U.S. Department of Justice, Federal Bureau of Investigation, "Crime in the United States," annual <http://www.fbi.gov/ucr/cius2008/arrests/index.html> and unpublished data.

Table 325. Federal Drug Arrests and Seizures by Type of Drug: 2000 to 2009

[For fiscal years ending in year shown. The data have all been revised. In years past, the data for the amount of drugs seized at the Federal level was obtained from the Federal-wide Drug Seizure System (FDSS). A new system has been created called the National Seizure System (NSS). This system will broaden the scope of data collected for the amount of drugs seized (in pounds) at the national level. The data for "Seizure in (pounds)" for years shown are from NSS]

Drug	2000	2002	2003	2004	2005	2006	2007	2008	2009
Number of Arrests, total [1, 2]	36,845	27,031	26,019	26,852	28,106	27,314	27,462	25,650	26,749
Heroin	3,622	2,560	2,527	2,489	2,450	2,361	2,167	2,599	3,026
Cocaine	16,375	12,353	11,389	11,972	13,040	13,097	12,868	12,102	11,607
Marijuana.............	8,572	5,721	6,031	6,310	6,113	6,002	6,883	6,234	7,416
Methamphetamine......	8,276	6,397	6,072	6,081	6,503	5,854	5,544	4,715	4,700
Seizure in (pounds), total..............	1,446,534	3,144,438	3,750,422	3,320,613	2,909,176	3,000,619	4,011,379	3,484,144	4,805,081
Cocaine	56,341	122,548	106,530	104,836	112,076	143,397	126,076	109,824	127,528
Heroin	1,590	6,812	5,968	4,159	4,004	4,412	3,711	4,339	5,355
Marijuana.............	1,383,020	3,004,965	3,622,318	3,198,468	2,779,543	2,838,631	3,868,269	3,355,360	4,654,709
Methamphetamine)	5,582	10,114	15,607	13,149	13,553	14,179	13,323	14,621	17,489

[1] Arrests are for Drug Enforcement Administration only. [2] Includes other drug-related arrests not shown.

Source: U.S. Drug Enforcement Administration, *Stats and Facts*, and unpublished data from the National Seizure System (NSS). See also <www.usdoj.gov/dea/statistics.html>.

Table 326. Background Checks for Firearm Transfers: 1994 to 2008

[In thousands (97,080 represents 97,080,000), except rates]

Inquiries and rejections	Total 1994–2008 [1]	Interm period 1994–1998 [2]	Permanent Brady [3] 1998 [4]	1999	2000	2003	2004	2005	2006	2007	2008
Applications and denials:											
Applications received.........	97,080	12,740	893	8,621	7,699	7,831	8,084	8,278	8,612	8,658	9,901
Applications denied	1,778	312	20	204	153	126	126	132	135	136	147
Denied (percent)	1.8	2.4	2.2	2.4	2.0	1.6	1.6	1.6	1.6	1.6	1.5
Selective reasons for rejection:											
Felony indictment/conviction ...	341	44	(NA)	147	88	53	53	57	52	49	77
Other	268	18	(NA)	57	65	73	73	75	83	87	70
Felony denials per 1,000 applications	(NA)	(NA)	(NA)	17.0	11.4	6.8	6.6	6.9	6.0	5.7	7.2

NA Not available. [1] Number of applications and estimates of denials for firearm transfers or permits since the inception of the Brady Act, 1994–2007. [2] Background checks on applicants were conducted by state and local agencies, mainly on handgun transfers. See "Presale Handgun Checks, the Brady Interim Period, 1994–98"(NCJ 175034). [3] The period beginning November 30, 1998 is the effective date for the Brady Handgun Violence Prevention Act, P.L. 103–159, 1993. The National Instant Criminal Background Check System (NICS) began operations. Checks on handgun and long gun transfers are conducted by the Federal Bureau of Investigation (FBI), and by state and local agencies. Totals combine Firearm Inquiry Statistics (FIST) estimates for state and local agencies with transactions and denials reported by the FBI. [4] For the period of November 30 to December 31, 1998. Counts are from the NICS operations report and may include multiple transactions for the same application.

Source: U.S. Department of Justice, Office of Justice Programs, Bureau of Justice Statistics, "Background Checks for Firearm Transfers, 2008," Series NCJ 227471, August 2009, <http://bjs.ojp.usdoj.gov/index.cfm?ty=pbdetail&iid=1706>.

Table 327. Law Enforcement Officers Killed and Assaulted: 1990 to 2008

[Contains statistics on felonious and accidental deaths of duly sworn local, state, tribal, and federal law enforcement officers. For composition of regions, see map, inside front cover]

Item	1990	1995	2000	2003	2004	2005	2006	2007	2008
OFFICERS KILLED									
Total killed	**132**	**133**	**134**	**133**	**139**	**122**	**114**	**141**	**109**
Geographical region:									
Northeast	13	16	13	13	18	12	12	13	14
Midwest	20	19	32	20	25	23	20	20	14
South	68	63	67	66	66	58	48	78	52
West	23	32	19	31	24	24	31	28	26
Puerto Rico	8	2	3	3	5	5	3	1	2
Island Areas, foreign countries	–	1	–	–	1	–	–	1	1
Total feloniously killed	65	74	51	52	57	55	48	58	41
Firearms	56	63	47	45	54	50	46	56	35
Handgun	47	44	33	34	36	42	36	39	25
Rifle	8	14	10	10	13	3	8	8	6
Shotgun	1	5	4	1	5	5	2	8	4
Type of firearm not reported	–	–	–	–	–	–	–	1	–
Blunt instrument	–	–	–	1	–	–	–	–	–
Bomb	–	8	–	–	–	–	–	–	2
Knife/cutting instrument	3	1	1	–	1	–	–	–	–
Personal weapons [1]	2	–	–	–	–	–	–	–	–
Vehicle	1	2	3	6	2	5	2	2	4
Other	3	–	–	–	–	–	–	–	–
Total accidentally killed	67	59	83	81	82	67	66	83	68
OFFICERS ASSAULTED									
Population covered (1,000) [2]	197,426	191,759	204,599	225,770	226,273	222,874	227,361	234,734	226,611
Number of—									
Reporting agencies	9,343	8,503	8,940	10,539	10,589	10,119	10,596	10,973	10,110
Officers employed	410,131	428,379	452,531	501,738	501,462	489,393	504,147	523,944	518,120
Total assaulted	**72,091**	**57,762**	**58,398**	**58,600**	**59,692**	**57,820**	**59,396**	**61,257**	**58,792**
Firearm	3,651	2,354	1,749	1,879	2,114	2,157	2,290	2,216	2,244
Knife/cutting instrument	1,647	1,356	1,015	1,084	1,123	1,059	1,055	1,028	935
Other dangerous weapon	7,423	6,414	8,132	8,180	8,645	8,379	8,611	8,692	8,161
Personal weapons [1]	59,370	47,638	47,502	47,457	47,810	46,225	47,440	49,321	47,452

– Represents zero. [1] Includes hands, fists, feet, etc. [2] Represents the number of persons covered by agencies shown.
Source: U.S. Department of Justice, Federal Bureau of Investigation, "Law Enforcement Officers Killed and Assaulted," annual, <http://www.fbi.gov/ucr/killed/2008/index.html/>.

Table 328. U.S. Supreme Court—Cases Filed and Disposition: 1980 to 2009

[Statutory term of court begins first Monday in October]

Action	1980	1990	1995	2000	2005	2006	2007	2008	2009
Total cases on docket	**5,144**	**6,316**	**7,565**	**8,965**	**9,608**	**10,256**	**9,602**	**8,966**	**9,302**
Appellate cases on docket	2,749	2,351	2,456	2,305	2,025	2,069	1,969	1,941	1,908
From prior term	527	365	361	351	354	346	355	345	328
Docketed during present term	2,222	1,986	2,095	1,954	1,671	1,723	1,614	1,596	1,580
Cases acted upon	2,324	2,042	2,130	2,024	1,703	1,736	1,666	1,654	1,607
Granted review	167	114	92	85	63	62	85	78	69
Denied, dismissed, or withdrawn	1,999	1,802	1,945	1,842	1,554	1,611	1,529	1,505	1,452
Summarily decided	90	81	62	63	46	39	30	29	45
Cases not acted upon	425	309	326	281	322	333	303	287	301
Pauper cases on docket	2,371	3,951	5,098	6,651	7,575	8,181	7,628	7,021	7,388
Cases acted upon [1]	2,027	3,436	4,514	5,736	6,533	7,186	6,753	6,214	6,524
Granted review	17	27	13	14	15	15	10	9	8
Denied, dismissed, or withdrawn	1,968	3,369	4,439	5,658	6,459	6,925	6,562	6,136	6,465
Summarily decided	32	28	55	61	58	239	175	65	46
Cases not acted upon	344	515	584	915	1,042	995	875	807	864
Original cases on docket	24	14	11	9	8	6	5	4	6
Cases disposed of during term	7	3	5	2	4	1	1	1	2
Total cases available for argument	**264**	**201**	**145**	**138**	**122**	**108**	**125**	**136**	**125**
Cases disposed of	162	131	93	89	87	80	78	88	86
Cases argued	154	125	90	86	88	78	75	87	82
Cases dismissed or remanded without argument	8	6	3	3	1	2	3	1	4
Cases remaining	102	70	52	49	31	28	47	48	40
Cases decided by signed opinion	144	121	87	83	82	74	72	83	77
Cases decided by per curiam opinion	8	4	3	4	5	4	2	3	4
Number of signed opinions	123	112	75	77	69	67	67	74	73

[1] Includes cases granted review and carried over to next term, not shown separately.
Source: Office of the Clerk, Supreme Court of the United States, unpublished data.

Table 329. U.S. District Courts—Civil Cases Commenced and Pending: 2000 to 2009

[For years ending June 30]

Type of case	Cases commenced				Cases pending			
	2000	2005	2008	2009	2000	2005	2008	2009
Cases total [1]	**263,049**	**282,758**	**256,354**	**257,204**	**249,692**	**267,270**	**286,193**	**297,257**
Contract actions [1]	54,494	28,590	34,818	35,229	38,262	26,712	30,696	30,019
Recovery of overpayments [2]	25,636	3,380	3,491	3,214	12,107	1,953	1,686	1,625
Real property actions	6,481	4,541	5,607	5,413	4,249	4,512	4,525	4,719
Tort actions	40,877	75,273	59,588	61,936	63,116	76,821	105,763	116,918
Personal injury	36,867	52,215	55,777	57,332	59,232	72,716	101,181	111,747
Personal injury product liability [1]	15,349	35,615	39,664	43,055	31,772	46,575	74,440	86,662
Asbestos	7,893	1,628	23,726	25,861	4,949	1,073	35,857	47,552
Other personal injury	21,518	16,600	16,113	14,277	27,460	26,141	26,741	25,085
Personal property damage	4,010	23,058	3,811	4,604	3,884	4,105	4,582	5,171
Actions under statutes [1]	161,187	171,922	156,277	154,572	144,053	157,357	145,077	145,512
Civil rights [1]	41,226	36,724	31,632	33,188	44,259	40,596	34,652	35,629
Employment	21,404	17,998	13,036	13,778	24,456	21,344	15,452	15,500
Bankruptcy suits	3,378	3,428	2,630	2,334	2,555	2,650	1,793	1,570
Commerce (ICC rates, etc.)	1,007	492	373	(NA)	444	395	217	168
Environmental matters	894	726	900	735	1,355	1,193	1,219	1,236
Prisoner petitions	57,706	62,698	55,374	52,237	43,560	47,870	46,229	46,080
Forfeiture and penalty	2,246	2,214	2,324	2,322	1,772	2,156	2,237	2,066
Labor laws	14,229	18,643	16,685	17,153	11,267	15,725	15,171	14,954
Protected property rights [3]	8,745	11,809	9,636	8,714	7,858	10,507	9,019	8,234
Securities commodities and exchanges	2,500	2,371	1,669	1,720	3,578	5,192	3,621	3,469
Social security laws	14,365	16,066	13,329	13,222	13,667	15,420	13,181	13,216
Tax suits	938	1,348	1,448	1,411	1,068	1,222	1,366	1,306
Freedom of information	335	426	294	279	380	378	365	370

NA Not available. [1] Includes other types not shown separately. [2] Includes enforcement of judgments in student loan cases, and overpayments of veterans' benefits. [3] Includes copyright, patent, and trademark rights.

Source: Administrative Office of the U.S. Courts, *Statistical Tables for the Federal Judiciary*, annual. See also <http://www.uscourts.gov/>.

Table 330. U.S. District Courts—Offenders Convicted and Sentenced to Prison and Length of Sentence: 2000 and 2006

Selected most serious offense of conviction	Offenders convicted [1]		Offenders sentenced to prison [1, 2]		Mean length of sentence for incarceration (months) [3]	
	2000	2006	2000	2006	2000	2006
Total	**68,156**	**79,904**	**50,451**	**63,699**	**56.7**	**63.7**
Violent offenses [4]	2,557	2,452	2,360	2,311	86.5	108.0
Murder [5]	283	146	249	140	94.2	123.6
Assault	253	514	188	446	33.0	53.0
Robbery	1579	1323	1,532	1,290	93.0	104.8
Property offenses	12,454	11,303	7,462	6,781	24.2	30.2
Fraudulent	10,396	9,906	6,272	5,987	22.5	29.2
Embezzlement	917	544	506	295	14.8	19.2
Fraud [6]	8,177	8,280	5,008	5,007	23.5	30.5
Forgery	86	50	41	20	19.1	17.2
Counterfeiting	1,216	1,032	717	665	20.8	24.3
Other [4]	2,058	1,397	1,190	794	33.2	37.3
Larceny [7]	1,394	935	689	434	27.3	18.5
Arson	158	187	134	156	71.8	96.0
Transportation of stolen property	272	142	200	108	33.4	34.6
Drug offenses [4]	24,206	27,361	22,352	25,425	75.5	87.2
Public-order offenses [4]	4,585	6,045	2,989	4,481	45.8	59.3
Regulatory	1,376	805	647	396	28.4	37.7
Other	3,209	5,240	2,342	4,085	46.5	61.4
Tax law violations [8]	655	503	355	334	18.5	25.5
Escape	487	1,010	447	647	19.2	21.0
Racketeering and extortion	951	1,660	778	1,406	81.5	74.6
Nonviolent sex offenses	475	1,277	429	1,236	47.1	80.6
Obscene material [9]	28	16	7	12	(B)	87.1
Weapon offenses [10]	4,196	8,831	3,834	8,201	91.4	88.4
Immigration offenses [10]	11,125	17,017	10,073	15,307	29.5	25.9
Misdemeanors [11]	8,961	6,895	1,356	1,193	10.4	5.1

B Base figures too small to meet statistical standards for reliability of a derived figure. [1] Total may not equal the sum of individual sanctions. [2] All sentences to incarceration, including split, mixed, life and indeterminate sentences. [3] Excludes sentences of life, death, and indeterminate sentences. [4] Includes offenses not shown separately. [5] Includes nonnegligent manslaughter. [6] Excludes tax fraud. [7] Excludes transportation of stolen property. [8] Includes tax fraud. [9] Denotes the mail or transport thereof. [10] Beginning in 2001, "Weapon and Immigration" offenses became major offense categories. Previously, these offenses were classified within "Public-order offenses." [11] Includes misdemeanors, petty offenses, unknown offense levels, and drug possession.

Source: U.S. Department of Justice, Office of Justice Programs, Bureau of Justice Statistics, *Federal Justice Statistics, 2006*, Series NCJ 225711, September 2009. See also <http://bjs.ojp.usdoj.gov/index.cfm?ty=pbdetail&iid=980>.

Table 331. Suspects in Matters Investigated by U.S. Attorneys by Offense: 1995 to 2006

[The most serious offense investigated is based on the criminal lead charge as determined by the assistant U.S. attorney responsible for the criminal matter]

Most serious offense investigated	1995	1997	1998	1999 [1]	2000	2001	2002	2003	2004	2005	2006
All offenses [2] ...	102,220	110,034	115,692	117,994	123,559	121,818	124,335	130,078	141,212	143,640	133,935
Violent offenses [3]..	5,720	7,354	7,527	5,768	6,036	6,225	6,392	5,688	5,714	5,485	5,011
Property offenses .	31,759	29,916	30,125	28,011	28,423	28,608	27,321	27,375	24,956	25,570	25,008
Fraudulent [4]	27,836	25,854	26,328	24,200	24,679	25,275	24,019	24,261	22,182	23,052	22,588
Other [5]	3,923	4,062	3,797	3,811	3,744	3,333	3,302	3,114	2,774	2,518	2,420
Drug offenses	31,686	34,027	36,355	37,313	38,959	37,944	38,150	37,416	37,501	40,038	35,210
Public-order offenses	19,036	22,857	21,244	22,816	24,180	23,980	23,472	23,717	21,277	21,583	20,158
Regulatory.....	5,371	5,423	6,541	6,332	5,737	5,411	4,738	5,366	4,959	5,037	4,488
Other	13,665	17,434	14,703	16,484	18,443	18,569	18,734	18,351	16,318	16,546	15,670
Weapon offenses [6].......	5,376	4,870	4,907	6,982	8,589	8,989	11,200	14,022	14,398	13,689	12,321
Immigration offenses [6].......	7,256	9,366	14,114	15,539	16,495	15,378	16,699	20,341	35,858	36,559	34,894
Unknown or indeterminable offenses	1,387	1,644	1,420	1,565	877	694	1,101	1,519	1,508	716	1,333

[1] Starting in 1999 and through the current year of data, nonviolent sex offenses were reclassified from "Violent offenses" to "Public-order offenses." [2] Includes suspects whose offense category could not be determined. See Methodology for a listing of detailed offense categories within each major offense category. [3] In this table, "Violent offenses" may include nonnegligent manslaughter. [4] Fraudulent property excludes tax fraud. [5] Excludes fraudulent property and includes destruction of property and trespassing. [6] Beginning in 2001, "Weapon" and "Immigration" offenses became major offense categories. Previously, these offenses were classified within "Public-order offenses."

Source: U.S. Department of Justice, Office of Justice Programs, Bureau of Justice Statistics, *Federal Justice Statistics, 2006*, Series NCJ 225711, September 2009. See also <http://bjs.ojp.usdoj.gov/index.cfm?ty=pbdetail&iid=980>.

Table 332. Criminal Appeals Filed by Offense: 1995 to 2005

[Appeals were classified into the offense category that represents the offense of conviction. Offenses represent the statutory offense charged against a defendant in a criminal appeal]

Most serious offense of convinction	1995	1996	1997	1998	1999 [1]	2000	2001	2002	2003	2004	2005
All offenses [2]	10,162	10,889	10,521	10,535	10,251	9,162	11,281	11,569	11,968	12,517	14,644
Violent offenses [3]........	700	685	739	742	559	490	591	606	601	673	710
Property offenses	1,707	2,093	1,972	1,947	1,739	1,482	1,681	1,726	1,842	1,873	2,104
Fraudulent [4]	1,323	1,581	1,519	1,439	1,338	1,164	1,299	1,389	1,478	1,524	1,673
Other [5]..............	444	512	453	508	401	318	382	337	364	349	431
Drug offenses	4,499	5,099	4,750	4,845	4,513	3,843	4,529	4,689	4,565	4,678	5,778
Public-order offenses.....	886	985	1,050	878	954	827	1,024	876	894	955	1,025
Regulatory...........	220	196	224	178	162	150	144	128	137	142	159
Other	666	789	826	700	792	677	880	642	757	813	866
Weapon offenses [6].......	1,034	1,183	1,135	982	1,070	872	1,266	1,386	1,681	2,024	2,242
Immigration offenses [6]....	277	353	417	693	934	1,179	1,654	1,679	1,821	1,856	2,373
Unknown or indeterminble offenses..............	999	491	458	448	482	469	536	607	564	458	374

[1] Starting in 1999 and through the current data year, nonviolent sex offenses were reclassified from "Violent offenses" to "Public-order offenses." [2] Include suspects whose offense category could not be determined. See Methodology for a listing of detailed offense categories within each major offense category. [3] In this table, "Violent offenses" may include nonnegligent manslaughter. [4] Fraudulent property excludes tax fraud. [5] Excludes fraudulent property and includes destruction of property and trespassing. [6] Beginning in 2001, "Weapon" and "Immigration" offenses became major offense categories. Previously, these offenses were classified within "Public-order offenses."

Source: U.S. Department of Justice, Office of Justice Programs, Bureau of Justice Statistics, *Federal Justice Statistics, 2006*, Series NCJ 225711, September 2009. See also <http://bjs.ojp.usdoj.gov/index.cfm?ty=pbdetail&iid=980>.

U.S. Census Bureau, Statistical Abstract of the United States: 2011

Table 333. Fraud and Identity Theft—Consumer Complaints by State: 2009

[Rate per 100,000 population. As of December 31. Based on Census Bureau population estimate. Federal Trade Commission (FTC) has developed and maintained a complaint database called the Consumer Sentinel. This database collects information about consumer fraud and identity theft from the FTC and over 115 other organizations and makes the information available to law enforcement. See appendixes in the annual report for list of contributing organizations]

Consumer state	Fraud complaints		Identity theft victims		Consumer state	Fraud complaints		Identity theft victims	
	Number	Rate	Number	Rate		Number	Rate	Number	Rate
U.S. [1]	**939,085**	**305.9**	**266,461**	**86.8**	MO........	20,780	347.1	3,850	64.3
AL	13,942	296.1	3,586	76.2	MT........	3,085	316.4	408	41.8
AK	2,638	377.7	313	44.8	NE	4,878	271.5	938	52.2
AZ	23,266	352.7	7,875	119.4	NV	10,912	412.9	2,802	106.0
AR	6,430	222.5	1,862	64.4	NH	5,261	397.2	584	44.1
CA........	122,824	332.3	42,209	114.2	NJ	26,682	306.4	7,361	84.5
CO........	20,722	412.4	4,775	95.0	NM	5,550	276.2	1,969	98.0
CT........	10,012	284.6	2,682	76.2	NY	51,454	263.3	18,906	96.7
DE........	3,269	369.3	725	81.9	NC	26,941	287.2	6,798	72.5
DC........	3,171	528.8	902	150.4	ND	1,287	199.0	192	29.7
FL........	67,083	361.9	22,664	122.3	OH........	33,411	289.5	7,525	65.2
GA........	31,611	321.6	9,556	97.2	OK........	9,371	254.2	2,633	71.4
HI........	4,559	352.0	584	45.1	OR........	14,987	391.7	2,583	67.5
ID........	4,747	307.1	755	48.8	PA	37,872	300.5	9,887	78.4
IL........	36,103	279.9	12,113	93.8	RI........	2,711	257.4	672	63.8
IN........	18,452	287.3	4,163	64.8	SC	12,402	271.9	3,070	67.3
IA........	7,153	237.8	1,179	39.2	SD	1,588	195.5	236	29.1
KS	7,843	278.2	1,906	67.6	TN	18,594	295.3	4,370	69.4
KY........	9,779	226.7	2,088	48.4	TX	69,546	280.6	28,844	116.4
LA........	11,998	267.1	3,252	72.4	UT	8,168	293.3	1,738	62.4
ME........	3,555	269.7	511	38.8	VT	1,787	287.4	277	44.6
MD........	22,431	393.6	5,232	91.8	VA	28,911	366.8	5,741	72.8
MA........	19,187	291.0	4,551	69.0	WA	25,062	376.1	5,145	77.2
MI........	26,381	264.6	7,525	75.5	WV	4,187	230.1	841	46.2
MN........	14,563	276.5	2,877	54.6	WI	14,751	260.9	2,777	49.1
MS........	5,551	188.0	2,161	73.2	WY........	1,607	295.3	268	49.2

[1] Fraud and other complaints reported by state consumers. Identity theft reported by state victims.

Source: U.S. Federal Trade Commission, *Consumer Sentinel Network Data book*, Consumer Fraud and Identity Theft complaint data, January–December 2009, February 2010. See also <http://www.ftc.gov/sentinel/reports.shtml>.

Table 334. Authorized Intercepts of Communication—Summary: 1980 to 2009

[As of December 31. Data for jurisdictions with statutes authorizing or approving interception of wire or oral communication]

Item	1980	1990	1995	2000	2004	2005	2006	2007	2008	2009
Jurisdictions: [1]										
With wiretap statutes	28	40	41	45	47	47	47	47	47	47
Reporting interceptions	22	25	19	26	20	23	24	25	23	24
Intercept applications authorized...	564	872	1,156	1,266	1,710	1,773	1,839	2,208	1,891	2,376
Intercept installations [2]	524	812	1,024	1,139	1,633	1,694	1,714	2,119	1,809	1,764
Federal.....................	79	321	527	472	723	624	461	454	384	337
State	445	491	497	667	910	1,070	1,253	1,665	1,425	1,427
Intercepted communications,										
average [3]	1,058	1,487	2,028	1,769	3,017	2,835	2,685	3,106	2,707	3,673
Incriminating average [3]	315	321	459	402	619	629	547	920	514	688
Persons arrested [4]	1,871	2,057	2,577	3,411	4,506	4,674	4,376	4,830	4,133	4,537
Convictions [4]	259	420	494	736	634	776	711	984	810	678
Major offense specified:										
Gambling.....................	199	116	95	49	90	42	56	55	54	35
Drugs........................	282	520	732	894	1,308	1,433	1,473	1,792	1,593	2,046
Homicide and assault	13	21	30	72	48	82	119	132	92	82
Racketeering	(NA)	(NA)	98	76	138	94	90	98	58	61

NA Not available. [1] Jurisdictions include federal government, 44 states and the Virgin Islands, and District of Columbia. [2] Based on the number of orders for which intercept devices were installed as reported by the prosecuting official. [3] Average per authorized installation. [4] Based on information received from intercepts installed in year shown; additional arrests/convictions will occur in subsequent years but are not shown here.

Source: Administrative Office of the U.S. Courts, *Report on Applications for Orders Authorizing or Approving the Interception of Wire, Oral or Electronic Communications* (Wiretap Report), annual. See also <http://www.uscourts.gov/Statistics/WiretapReports/WiretapReport2009.aspx>.

Table 335. Federal Prosecutions of Public Corruption: 1990 to 2008

[As of Dec. 31. Prosecution of persons who have corrupted public office in violation of Federal Criminal Statutes]

Prosecution status	1990			2000			2005			2008		
	Charged	Con-victed	Await-ing trial	Charged	Con-victed	Await-ing trial	Charged	Con-victed	Await-ing trial	Charged	Con-victed	Await-ing trial
Total [1]	1,176	1,084	300	1,000	938	327	1,163	1,027	451	1,304	1,129	489
Federal officials ...	615	583	103	441	422	92	445	390	118	518	458	117
State officials.....	96	79	28	92	91	37	96	94	51	144	123	61
Local officials.....	257	225	98	211	183	89	309	232	148	287	246	127
Others involved ...	208	197	71	256	242	109	313	311	134	355	302	184

[1] Includes individuals who are neither public officials nor employees, but were involved with public officials or employees in violating the law, not shown separately.

Source: U.S. Department of Justice, Criminal Division, *Report to Congress on the Activities and Operations of the Public Integrity Section.* See also <http://www.justice.gov/criminal/pin/>.

Table 336. Financial Crimes: 2003 to 2009

[For the year ending September 30. The FBI focuses its financial crimes investigations on such criminal activities as corporate fraud, securities and commodities fraud, health care fraud, mortgage fraud, insurance fraud, mass marketing fraud, and money laundering. These are the identified priority crime problem areas of the Financial Crimes Section (FCS) of the FBI. The mission of the FCS is to oversee the investigation of financial fraud, and to facilitate the forfeiture of assets from those engaging in federal crimes. For more information on financial fraud types including mortgage fraud, go to <http://www.fbi.gov/publications/financial /fcs_report2009/financial_crime_2009.htm>. For more detailed information on mortgage fraud, go to <http://www.fbi.gov /publications/fraud/mortgage_fraud09.htm>]

Type of financial fraud	Unit indicator	2003	2004	2005	2006	2007	2008	2009
Corporate fraud:								
Cases pending	Number	279	332	423	486	529	545	592
Indictments	Number	150	192	178	176	183	160	161
Convictions	Number	143	126	150	134	181	134	162
Restitution	Bil. dol.	–	0.4	5.6	1.1	12.6	8.2	6.1
Recoveries	1,000 dol.	37.0	28.0	68.0	41,400.0	27,400.0	6,590.0	16,100.0
Fines	Mil. dol.	3.0	117.1	122.4	14.2	38.6	193.7	5.3
Seizures	Mil. dol.	(NA)	20.8	12.6	82.4	70.1	9.3	40.6
Securities/Commodities fraud:								
Cases pending	Number	937	987	1,139	1,165	1,217	1,210	1510
Indictments	Number	358	393	327	320	408	359	412
Convictions	Number	320	305	363	279	321	302	309
Restitution	Bil. dol.	1.6	0.9	2.3	2.1	1.5	3.0	2.1
Recoveries	Mil. dol.	28.6	13.0	76.3	20.6	25.4	43.7	47.3
Fines	Mil. dol.	16.7	12.5	14.8	80.7	202.8	128.5	7.4
Seizures	Mil. dol.	(NA)	11.9	281.9	41.8	83.0	77.5	85.0
Insurance fraud:								
Cases pending	Number	326	289	270	233	209	177	152
Indictments	Number	111	100	72	56	39	73	43
Convictions	Number	172	77	79	66	47	60	42
Restitution	Mil. dol.	101.9	121.6	171.7	30.4	27.6	553.7	22.9
Recoveries	1,000 dol.	115.0	34,200.0	913.0	14.0	21.0	10,400.0	31,400.0
Fines	1,000 dol.	810.0	330.0	112.0	212.0	447.0	31.0	138.0
Seizures	Mil. dol.	0.3	15.7	10.7	3.5	15.9	25.3	2.2
Mass marketing fraud:								
Cases pending	Number	236	192	161	147	127	100	92
Indictments	Number	94	66	28	15	13	50	9
Convictions	Number	93	64	43	46	11	23	23
Restitution	Mil. dol.	154.2	23.0	503.8	273.2	30.6	4.2	4.4
Recoveries	1,000 dol.	125.0	1,900.0	4.0	468.0	542.0	173.0	–
Fines	1,000 dol.	4,900.0	11,100.0	362.0	86,900.0	121.0	23.0	2.1
Seizures	Mil. dol.	9.6	1.8	8.1	12.7	(Z)	–	(Z)
Health care fraud:								
Cases pending	Number	2,262	2,468	2,547	2,423	2,493	2,434	2,494
Indictments	Number	523	693	589	588	847	851	982
Convictions	Number	414	564	550	535	642	707	674
Restitution	Bil. dol.	1.1	1.0	1.1	0.4	1.1	1.1	1.3
Recoveries	Mil. dol.	10.0	28.8	115.0	1,600.0	439.8	102.4	517.1
Fines	Mil. dol.	79.0	610.0	40.4	172.0	33.7	25.6	68.9
Seizures	Mil. dol.	79.7	60.4	52.7	28.9	86.1	48.3	55.7
Money laundering:								
Cases pending	Number	496	509	507	473	443	404	350
Indictments	Number	105	127	126	264	140	114	63
Convictions	Number	61	69	91	112	115	134	96
Restitution	Mil. dol.	13.2	282.9	313.0	17.1	69.4	222.4	81.9
Recoveries	Mil. dol.	2.9	0.8	9.3	3.2	2.7	20.9	0.6
Fines	Mil. dol.	2.4	0.9	0.3	0.4	11.4	34.1	1.5
Seizures	Mil. dol.	8.2	5.1	7.8	6.4	10.9	24.2	4.5
Mortgage fraud:								
Cases pending	Number	(NA)	(NA)	721	881	1,211	1,644	2,794
Indictments	Number	(NA)	(NA)	93	138	328	574	822
Convictions	Number	(NA)	(NA)	60	123	283	354	494
Restitution	Mil. dol.	(NA)	(NA)	151.2	308.3	600.6	825.2	2,540.0
Recoveries	Mil. dol.	(NA)	(NA)	(Z)	1.2	21.8	3.3	7.5
Fines	Mil. dol.	(NA)	(NA)	44.0	300.8	1.6	3.1	58.4
Seizures	Mil. dol.	(NA)	(NA)	(NA)	(NA)	5.1	6.6	5.0
Suspicious Activity Reports (SARs) [1,2]								
Mortgage fraud related—								
Number of violations:								
Mortgage fraud	Number	6,936	17,127	21,994	35,617	46,717	63,713	67,190
Commercial loan	Number	1,850	1,724	2,126	2,409	3,240	4,189	4,514
False statement	Number	4,569	6,784	11,611	21,023	28,692	37,622	38,159
Dollars losses reported on:								
Mortgage fraud SARs	Bil. dol.	0.2	0.4	1.0	0.9	0.8	1.5	2.8
Reported on commercial loan SARs	Bil. dol.	1.0	1.1	0.7	0.5	1.0	1.9	1.7
False statement SARs	Bil. dol.	0.4	0.5	1.0	1.4	0.8	2.5	2.1

– Represents zero. NA Not available. Z represents a value less than 50 thousand. [1] Reports filed by federally-insured financial institutions. [2] SARs are cataloged according to the year in which they are submitted and the information contained within them may describe activity that occurred in previous month or years.

Source: U.S. Department of Justice, Federal Bureau of Investigation, *Financial Crimes Report to the Public* and 2009 Mortgage Fraud Report, "Year in Review."

Table 337. Delinquency Cases Disposed by Juvenile Courts by Reason for Referral: 1990 to 2007

[In thousands (1,337 represents 1,337,000), except rate. A delinquency offense is an act committed by a juvenile for which an adult could be prosecuted in a criminal court. Disposition of a case involves taking a definite action such as waiving the case to criminal court, dismissing the case, placing the youth on probation, placing the youth in a facility for delinquents, or such actions as fines, restitution, and community service]

Reason for referral	1990	1995	1998	1999	2000	2001	2002	2003	2004	2005	2006	2007
All delinquency offenses ...	**1,337**	**1,800**	**1,795**	**1,721**	**1,713**	**1,692**	**1,683**	**1,694**	**1,704**	**1,694**	**1,655**	**1,666**
Case rate [1]	52.1	62.9	60.1	56.9	55.7	54.5	53.7	53.8	54.1	53.7	52.7	53.5
Person offenses [2]	256	398	403	398	392	401	402	410	418	428	413	409
Criminal homicide	2	3	2	2	2	1	1	1	1	1	1	1
Forcible rape	4	6	5	4	4	4	4	4	4	4	4	4
Robbery	28	42	30	26	22	22	21	21	22	25	30	31
Aggravated assault	53	73	59	53	52	50	48	49	50	52	50	50
Property offenses [2]	776	901	779	708	680	645	640	631	623	601	580	594
Burglary	146	149	135	117	112	109	107	106	101	100	103	105
Larceny-theft	344	429	357	326	316	294	294	288	289	268	242	256
Motor vehicle theft	70	53	44	38	37	37	37	38	34	32	29	27
Arson	7	10	9	9	9	9	9	8	9	8	9	8
Drug law violations	71	161	193	187	192	196	188	189	191	188	187	190
Public order offenses [2]	233	340	419	429	449	450	453	465	472	477	475	472
Obstruction of justice	88	135	210	205	217	217	213	219	213	214	213	215
Disorderly conduct	56	91	89	97	100	105	114	117	125	129	125	125
Weapons offenses	30	47	42	39	37	35	34	37	41	43	44	41
Liquor law violations	18	17	21	27	36	34	34	35	35	34	36	37
Nonviolent sex offenses	11	10	12	12	13	14	14	13	13	13	12	11

[1] Number of cases disposed per 1,000 youth (aged 10 to 17) at risk of referral to juvenile court. [2] Total include other offenses not shown.

Source: National Center for Juvenile Justice, Pittsburgh, PA, Juvenile Court Statistics, annual. See also <http://ojjdp.ncjrs.gov/ojstatbb/default.asp>.

Table 338. Delinquency Cases and Case Rates by Sex and Race: 1995 to 2007

[See headnote, Table 337]

Sex, race, and offense	Number of cases disposed				Case rate [1]			
	1995	2000	2005	2007	1995	2000	2005	2007
Male, total	**1,395,900**	**1,276,300**	**1,228,100**	**1,217,100**	**94.7**	**80.9**	**76.1**	**76.4**
Person	299,700	283,100	301,100	288,300	20.3	18.0	18.6	18.1
Property	697,100	507,300	436,400	435,100	47.3	32.2	27.0	27.3
Drugs	138,000	159,500	150,600	155,000	9.4	10.1	9.3	9.7
Public order	261,100	326,500	340,000	338,800	17.7	20.7	21.1	21.3
Female, total	**404,000**	**436,500**	**465,500**	**448,900**	**28.9**	**29.2**	**30.3**	**29.6**
Person	98,600	109,200	127,200	120,900	7.1	7.3	8.3	8.0
Property	203,400	173,000	164,200	159,400	14.6	11.6	10.7	10.5
Drugs	23,400	32,100	37,300	35,100	1.7	2.1	2.4	2.3
Public order	78,600	122,200	136,800	133,600	5.6	8.2	8.9	8.8
White, total	**1,208,800**	**1,168,800**	**1,087,900**	**1,060,900**	**52.9**	**48.4**	**44.4**	**43.8**
Person	236,000	243,800	243,000	230,800	10.3	10.1	9.9	9.5
Property	643,500	475,200	405,200	395,300	28.2	19.7	16.5	16.3
Drugs	106,000	142,100	138,000	137,800	4.6	5.9	5.6	5.7
Public order	223,100	307,700	301,700	297,000	9.8	12.7	12.3	12.3
Black, total	**541,300**	**494,200**	**556,500**	**558,100**	**124.3**	**102.2**	**107.9**	**110.6**
Person	152,300	138,200	174,400	167,900	35.0	28.6	33.8	33.3
Property	229,000	180,800	174,900	179,900	52.6	37.4	33.9	35.7
Drugs	52,600	45,100	44,800	47,500	12.1	9.3	8.7	9.4
Public order	107,400	130,000	162,400	162,900	24.7	26.9	31.5	32.3
Other races, total	**568,400**	**520,100**	**581,400**	**582,300**	**33.4**	**28.6**	**26.5**	**25.0**
Person	157,400	143,600	180,200	173,600	6.7	5.9	5.8	5.6
Property	244,000	193,100	184,900	189,400	18.8	13.9	11.1	10.3
Drugs	54,100	47,600	47,800	50,300	1.8	2.5	2.7	2.6
Public order	112,900	135,700	168,500	169,100	6.1	6.3	6.8	6.6

[1] Cases per 1,000 youth (aged 10 to 17) at risk.

Source: National Center for Juvenile Justice, Pittsburgh, PA, Juvenile Court Statistics, annual. See also <http://ojjdp.ncjrs.gov/ojstatbb/default.asp>.

U.S. Census Bureau, Statistical Abstract of the United States: 2011

Table 339. Child Abuse and Neglect Cases Substantiated and Indicated— Victim Characteristics: 2000 to 2008

[Based on reports alleging child abuse and neglect that were referred for investigation by the respective child protective services agency in each state. The reporting period may be either calendar or fiscal year. The majority of states provided duplicated counts. Also, varying number of states reported the various characteristics presented below. A substantiated case represents a type of investigation disposition that determines that there is sufficient evidence under state law to conclude that maltreatment occurred or that the child is at risk of maltreatment. An indicated case represents a type of disposition that concludes that there was a reason to suspect maltreatment had occurred]

Item	2000 Number	2000 Percent	2005 [1] Number	2005 [1] Percent	2007 [1] Number	2007 [1] Percent	2008 [5] Number	2008 [5] Percent
TYPES OF SUBSTANTIATED MALTREATMENT [2]								
Victims, total.............	864,837	116.5	900,642	113.1	760,863	114.0	773,792	115.0
Neglect	517,118	59.8	566,277	62.9	533,995	70.2	549,399	71.0
Physical abuse..............	167,713	19.4	149,328	16.6	122,383	16.1	125,971	16.3
Sexual abuse..............	87,770	10.2	83,786	9.3	71,115	9.3	71,162	9.2
Emotional maltreatment.......	66,965	7.7	63,438	7.0	55,223	7.3	55,236	7.1
Medical neglect	25,498	3.0	17,653	2.0	16,279	2.1	16,783	2.2
Other and unknown..........	146,184	16.9	137,946	15.3	68,054	8.9	71,237	9.2
SEX OF VICTIM [3, 4]								
Victims, total.............	864,837	100.0	882,239	100.0	758,587	100.0	770,868	100.0
Male.....................	413,744	47.8	426,019	48.3	366,587	48.3	373,889	48.5
Female...................	446,230	51.6	456,220	51.7	392,000	51.7	396,979	51.5
AGE OF VICTIM [3, 4]								
Victims, total.............	864,837	100.0	881,058	100.0	755,164	100.0	770,907	100.0
1 year and younger	133,094	15.4	154,399	17.3	144,257	19.1	150,866	19.5
2 to 5 years old	205,790	23.8	222,387	24.7	190,206	25.2	194,342	25.2
6 to 9 years old	212,186	24.5	193,089	21.4	166,853	22.1	168,055	21.8
10 to 13 years old	176,071	20.4	171,776	19.0	135,416	17.9	135,838	17.6
14 to 17 years old	126,207	14.6	138,934	15.4	118,021	15.6	121,164	15.8
18 years old and over	992	0.1	473	0.1	411	0.1	642	0.1

[1] Data have been revised. [2] A child may be a victim of more than one maltreatment. Therefore, the total for this item adds up to more than 100 percent. [3] The increase in unknown age, sex, and race in 2005 is due to some states reporting summary data without breakdown of corresponding fields. [4] Unknown data not shown. [5] Data have been updated since the release of the annual report.

Source: U.S. Department of Health and Human Services, Administration for Children and Families, Statistics and Research, *Child Maltreatment 2008*, annual, <http://www.acf.hhs.gov/programs/cb/pubs/cm08/index.htm>.

Table 340. Child Abuse and Neglect Cases Reported and Investigated by State: 2008

[See headnote, Table 339]

State and outlying area	Population under 18 years of age	Number of reports [1]	Number of children subject of an investi- gation [2]	Number of child victims [3]	State and outlying area	Population under 18 years of age	Number of reports [1]	Number of children subject of an investi- gation [2]	Number of child victims [3]
Total	**74,924,121**	**2,024,094**	**3,674,250**	**773,792**					
					MT.......	220,358	7,988	13,366	1,625
AL	1,121,877	19,605	28,952	9,217	NE.......	446,995	12,472	29,327	4,668
AK	179,876	7,845	13,269	4,522	NV	667,801	14,332	29,760	4,877
AZ	1,707,221	20,572	67,159	3,516	NH.......	293,358	8,031	11,868	1,129
AR	702,481	27,824	57,925	9,289	NJ	2,047,582	53,895	83,064	9,089
CA.......	9,364,530	244,194	470,368	84,848	NM.......	502,450	14,469	23,178	5,656
CO.......	1,207,135	34,164	53,392	11,247	NY	4,408,016	159,556	265,561	84,089
CT.......	812,213	24,409	36,480	9,641	NC.......	2,243,677	69,428	139,640	24,618
DE.......	206,229	6,274	15,026	2,278	ND.......	143,048	4011	6984	1285
DC.......	112,016	4,694	11,529	2,645	OH.......	2,730,377	83,827	129,952	36,106
FL	4,004,271	173,218	374,276	51,271	OK.......	906,035	34,940	62,682	11,169
GA.......	2,548,841	32,430	77,466	26,330	OR.......	867,575	27485	43703	11042
HI.......	285,243	2,508	4,576	1,902	PA.......	2,762,004	25,051	25,051	4,055
ID.......	412,640	6,783	10,631	1,836	RI.......	228,540	6,356	9,821	3,082
IL	3,179,260	67,021	147,280	29,788	SC	1,066,227	18,206	41,398	12,549
IN........	1,584,681	66,690	104,005	21,846	SD	198,309	3,589	6,865	1,394
IA........	712,613	21,661	33,080	11,200	TN	1,478,594	61,346	99,918	11,586
KS	700,485	16,823	25,031	1,685	TX	6,725,771	169,628	288,034	70,976
KY	1,008,064	49,976	77,119	18,252	UT	849,635	19,922	31,382	13,179
LA	1,107,973	21,405	34,420	10,173	VT	128,930	2,359	2,948	677
ME.......	274,867	6,216	10,319	4,033	VA	1,823,201	28,969	59,956	5,912
MD.......	1,340,583	27,314	38,775	15,519	WA.......	1,541,175	35,693	52,972	6,738
MA.......	1,427,033	44,307	89,003	41,596	WV.......	386,158	23,103	52,418	6,077
MI........	2,390,198	71,820	177,871	29,643	WI	1,314,412	26,382	38,557	5,787
MN.......	1,254,644	18,608	26,483	5,824	WY	128,457	2,405	4,880	713
MS.......	766,720	19,063	29,888	7,976					
MO.......	1,421,469	49,129	70,743	5,528	PR	982,273	17,098	35,899	14,109

[1] The number of investigations includes assessments. The number of investigations is based on the total number of investigations that received a disposition in 2008. [2] The number of "Children Subject of an Investigation" is based on the total number of children who were included in an investigation or assessment [3] Victims are defined as children subject of a substantiated, indicated, or alternative response-victim maltreatment.

Source: U.S. Department of Health and Human Services, Administration for Children and Families, Statistics and Research, *Child Maltreatment 2008*, annual, <http://www.acf.hhs.gov/programs/cb/pubs/cm08/index.htm\>.

Table 341. Employment by State and Local Law Enforcement Agencies by Type of Agency and Employee: 2004

[As of September 30]

Type of agency	Number of agencies	Number of employees					
		Full-time			Part-time		
		Total	Sworn	Civilian	Total	Sworn	Civilian
Total [1]	17,876	1,076,897	731,903	344,994	105,252	45,982	59,270
Local police	12,766	573,152	446,974	126,178	62,693	28,712	33,981
Sheriffs' offices	3,067	326,531	175,018	151,513	27,004	11,784	15,220
Primary State...........	49	89,265	58,190	31,075	708	31	677
Special jurisdiction........	1,481	85,126	49,398	35,728	14,342	5,063	9,279
Constable/marshal.......	513	2,823	2,323	500	505	392	113

[1] Excludes agencies with less than one full-time officer or the equivalent in part-time officers.

Source: U.S. Bureau of Justice Statistics, Census of State and Local Law Enforcement Agencies, 2004, Series NCJ 212749, June 2007. See also <http://bjs.ojp.usdoj.gov/index.cfm?ty=pbdetail&iid=539>.

Table 342. State and Local Government Expenditures Per Capita by Criminal Justice Function and State: 2006

[In dollars. See Table 463 for more details]

State	Total justice system	Police protec-tion	Judicial and legal	Correc-tions	State	Total justice system	Police protec-tion	Judicial and legal	Correc-tions
Total..............	597	264	123	210	Missouri.........	417	202	77	138
Alabama	420	201	78	141	Montana.........	519	201	132	185
Alaska	894	318	263	313	Nebraska........	436	190	81	166
Arizona	643	275	137	232	Nevada	757	357	177	223
Arkansas...........	443	180	78	186	New Hampshire...	422	209	87	126
California...........	871	355	214	301	New Jersey......	728	347	159	221
Colorado	562	252	99	210	New Mexico......	636	262	129	245
Connecticut	604	259	168	177	New York	828	393	170	265
Delaware	795	335	173	287	North Carolina....	452	216	62	174
District of Columbia ...	1,325	848	124	353	North Dakota.....	376	166	94	116
Florida.............	669	328	117	224	Ohio............	551	235	142	174
Georgia	519	210	95	214	Oklahoma	443	188	79	177
Hawaii	550	218	192	140	Oregon..........	604	254	100	250
Idaho	468	189	101	178	Pennsylvania.....	548	204	118	225
Illinois.............	523	294	94	136	Rhode Island.....	596	270	143	183
Indiana.............	380	165	67	148	South Carolina....	396	197	55	143
Iowa...............	409	192	97	121	South Dakota.....	423	167	78	178
Kansas.............	472	230	105	137	Tennessee.......	432	199	86	147
Kentucky	399	157	92	150	Texas...........	483	208	85	189
Louisiana...........	631	275	121	235	Utah............	498	211	114	173
Maine.............	385	168	76	140	Vermont.........	475	219	93	163
Maryland	667	286	120	261	Virginia..........	542	227	95	219
Massachusetts.......	577	260	140	177	Washington	535	208	105	222
Michigan	571	231	114	227	West Virginia	378	131	107	141
Minnesota...........	513	251	118	143	Wisconsin	586	257	99	229
Mississippi..........	391	194	68	130	Wyoming	837	323	163	351

Source: U.S. Department of Justice, Office of Justice Programs, Bureau of Justice Statistics, Expenditures and Employment Statistics, Series NCJ 224394. See also <http://bjs.ojp.usdoj.gov/index.cfm?ty=pbdetail&iid=1022>

Table 343. Felony Convictions in State Courts: 2000 to 2006

[In 2006, an estimated 1,205,273 persons were convicted of a felony (federal and state courts). Of that number, 1,132,290 were convicted in state courts, the vast majority (94 percent) of whom pleaded guilty. At the time of sentencing, about 3 out of 4 felons sentenced (77 percent) were sentenced for a single felony]

Most serious conviction	Felony convictions in state courts							
	2000		2002		2004		2006	
	Number	Percent	Number	Percent	Number	Percent	Number	Percent
All offenses	924,700	100	1,051,000	100	1,078,920	100	1,132,290	100.0
Violent offenses..........	173,200	18.7	197,030	18.8	194,570	18.0	206,140	18.2
Murder [1]	8,600	0.9	8,990	0.9	8,400	0.8	8,670	0.8
Rape/Sexual assault	31,500	3.4	35,500	3.4	33,190	3.1	33,200	2.9
Robbery...............	36,800	4.0	38,430	3.7	38,850	3.6	41,740	3.7
Aggravated assault	79,400	8.6	95,600	9.1	94,380	8.7	100,560	8.9
Other violent [2]	17,000	1.8	18,510	1.8	19,750	1.8	21,980	1.9
Property offenses	262,000	28.3	325,200	30.9	310,680	28.8	321,570	28.4
Burglary...............	79,300	8.6	100,640	9.6	93,870	8.7	99,910	8.8
Larceny [3]	100,000	10.8	124,320	11.8	119,340	11.1	125,390	11.1
Fraud/forgery [4]..........	82,700	8.9	100,240	9.5	97,470	9.0	96,260	8.5
Drug offenses	319,700	34.6	340,330	32.4	362,850	33.6	377,860	33.4
Possession	116,300	12.6	127,530	12.1	161,090	14.9	165,360	14.6
Trafficking.............	203,400	22.0	212,810	20.2	201,760	18.7	212,490	18.8
Weapon offenses..........	28,200	3.1	32,470	3.1	33,010	3.1	38,010	3.4
Other offenses [5].........	141,600	15.3	155,970	14.8	177,810	16.5	188,730	16.7

[1] A small number of cases were classified as nonnegligent manslaughter when it was unclear if the conviction offense was murder or nonnegligent manslaughter. [2] Includes offenses such as negligent manslaughter and kidnapping. [3] When vehicle theft could not be distinguished from other theft, the case was coded as "other theft." This results in a conservative estimate of vehicle thefts. [4] Includes embezzlement. [5] Composed of nonviolent offenses such as receiving stolen property and vandalism.

Source: U.S. Department of Justice, Office of Justice Programs, Bureau of Justice Statistics, Criminal Sentencing Statistics, Series NCJ 226846, December 2009. See <http://bjs.ojp.usdoj.gov/index.cfm?ty=pbdetail&iid=2152>.

Table 344. Prisoners Under Jurisdiction of Federal or State Correctional Authorities—Summary by State: 1990 to 2008

[For years ending December 31. To have jurisdiction over a prisoner, a state or the federal system must have legal authority over the prisoner]

State	1990	2000	2005	2007	2008
U.S. [1]	**773,919**	**1,391,261**	**1,527,929**	**1,598,245**	**1,609,606**
Federal....	65,526	145,416	187,618	199,618	201,280
State	708,393	1,245,845	1,340,311	1,398,627	1,408,326
AL	15,665	26,332	27,888	29,412	30,508
AK [2]	2,622	4,173	4,812	5,167	5,014
AZ [3]	14,261	26,510	33,565	37,746	39,589
AR	7,322	11,915	13,541	14,314	14,716
CA	97,309	163,001	170,676	174,282	173,670
CO	7,671	16,833	21,456	22,841	23,274
CT [2]	10,500	18,355	19,442	20,924	20,661
DE [2]	3,471	6,921	6,966	7,276	7,075
DC [4,5]	9,947	7,456	(NA)	(NA)	(NA)
FL	44,387	71,319	89,768	98,219	102,388
GA [3]	22,411	44,232	48,749	54,256	52,719
HI [2]	2,533	5,053	6,146	5,978	5,955
ID	1,961	5,535	6,818	7,319	7,290
IL	27,516	45,281	44,919	45,215	45,474
IN	12,736	20,125	24,455	27,132	28,322
IA [3]	3,967	7,955	8,737	8,732	8,766
KS	5,775	8,344	9,068	8,696	8,539
KY	9,023	14,919	19,662	22,457	21,706
LA	18,599	35,207	36,083	37,540	38,381
ME	1,523	1,679	2,023	2,148	2,195
MD	17,848	23,538	22,737	23,433	23,324
MA	8,345	10,722	10,701	11,436	11,408
MI	34,267	47,718	49,546	50,233	48,738
MN.......	3,176	6,238	9,281	9,468	9,406

State	1990	2000	2005	2007	2008
MS	8,375	20,241	20,515	22,431	22,754
MO	14,943	27,543	30,823	29,857	30,186
MT......	1,425	3,105	3,532	3,462	3,607
NE	2,403	3,895	4,455	4,505	4,520
NV [6]	5,322	10,063	11,782	13,400	12,743
NH	1,342	2,257	2,530	2,943	2,904
NJ	21,128	29,784	27,359	26,827	25,953
NM......	3,187	5,342	6,571	6,466	6,402
NY	54,895	70,199	62,743	62,620	60,347
NC......	18,411	31,266	36,365	37,970	39,482
ND	483	1,076	1,385	1,416	1,452
OH......	31,822	45,833	45,854	50,731	51,686
OK	12,285	23,181	26,676	25,849	25,864
OR	6,492	10,580	13,411	13,948	14,167
PA	22,290	36,847	42,380	45,969	49,307
RI [2]	2,392	3,286	3,654	4,018	4,045
SC	17,319	21,778	23,160	24,239	24,326
SD	1,341	2,616	3,463	3,311	3,342
TN	10,388	22,166	26,369	26,267	27,228
TX	50,042	166,719	169,003	171,790	172,506
UT	2,496	5,637	6,382	6,515	6,546
VT [2]	1,049	1,697	2,078	2,145	2,116
VA	17,593	30,168	35,344	38,069	38,276
WA	7,995	14,915	17,382	17,772	17,926
WV......	1,565	3,856	5,312	6,056	6,059
WI	7,465	20,754	22,697	23,743	23,380
WY......	1,110	1,680	2,047	2,084	2,084

NA Not available. [1] U.S. total includes federal prisoners not distributed by state. This total includes all inmates held in public and private adult correctional facilities. [2] Data include both total jail and prison population. Prisons and jails form one integrated system. [3] Numbers are for custody rather than jurisdiction counts. [4] The transfer of responsibility for sentenced felons from the District of Columbia to the federal system was completed by the year end 2001. [5] The District of Columbia inmates sentenced to more than 1 year are now under the responsibility of the Bureau of Prisons. [6] Estimated data for 2007.

Source: U.S. Department of Justice, Bureau of Justice Statistics, *Prisoners in 2008*, Series NCJ 228417 and earlier reports. See also <http://bjs.ojp.usdoj.gov/index.cfm?ty=pbdetail&iid=1763>.

Table 345. Adults on Probation or Parole, Incarcerated in Jail or Prison: 1980 to 2008

[As of December 31, except jail counts as of June 30]

Year	Total [1]	Supervision rate per 100,000 adults	Community supervision — Probation	Community supervision — Parole	Incarceration — Jail	Incarceration — Prison	Male [2]	Female [2]
1980.........	1,840,400	1.1	1,118,097	220,438	182,288	319,598	(NA)	(NA)
1990.........	4,350,343	2.3	2,670,234	531,407	405,320	743,382	3,746,300	601,700
1993.........	4,944,000	2.6	2,903,061	676,100	455,500	909,381	4,215,800	728,200
1994.........	5,141,300	2.7	2,981,022	690,371	479,800	990,147	4,377,400	763,900
1995.........	5,342,900	2.8	3,077,861	679,421	507,044	1,078,542	4,513,000	822,100
1996.........	5,482,700	2.8	3,164,996	679,733	510,400	1,127,528	4,629,900	852,800
1997......	5,725,800	2.9	3,296,513	694,787	557,974	1,176,564	4,825,300	900,500
1998.........	6,126,100	3.1	3,670,441	696,385	584,372	1,224,469	(NA)	(NA)
1999.........	6,331,400	3.1	3,779,922	714,457	596,485	1,287,172	(NA)	(NA)
2000 [3]	6,445,100	3.1	3,826,209	723,898	621,149	1,316,333	5,376,300	1,068,800
2001 [3]	6,581,700	3.1	3,931,731	732,333	631,240	1,330,007	5,468,900	1,112,800
2002 [3]	6,758,800	3.1	4,024,067	750,934	665,475	1,367,547	5,579,500	1,179,300
2003 [3,4]	6,924,500	3.2	4,120,012	769,925	691,301	1,390,279	5,724,200	1,200,300
2004 [3]	6,995,100	3.2	4,143,792	771,852	713,990	1,421,345	5,767,300	1,227,800
2005 [3]	7,051,900	3.1	4,166,757	780,616	747,529	1,448,344	5,823,200	1,228,700
2006 [5]	7,182,100	3.2	4,215,361	799,875	765,819	1,492,973	5,885,900	1,296,200
2007 [6,7]	7,274,300	3.2	4,234,471	821,177	780,174	1,517,867	5,984,300	1,290,000
2008 [8]	7,308,200	3.2	4,270,917	828,169	785,556	1,518,559	6,006,800	1,301,400

NA Not available. [1] Totals may not add due to individuals having multiple correctional statuses. [2] Estimated. [3] The jail population includes juveniles held as adults. [4] Due to changes in reporting, total probation and parole counts include estimated counts for Massachusetts, Pennsylvania, and Washington. [5] Illinois did not provide prison or parole data for 2006, therefore, all prison and parole data for Illinois were estimated. [6] Illinois and Nevada did not provide prison data for 2007; therefore, all prison data for these states were estimated. [7] Oklahoma did not provide probation or parole data for 2007, therefore, all probation and parole data were estimated. [8] Virginia did not provide parole data, therefore the data were estimated.

Source: U.S. Department of Justice, Bureau of Justice Statistics (BJS), Prisoners Inmates at Midyear 2008—Statistical Tables; Jail inmates at Midyear 2008—Statistical Tables; *Probation and Parole in the United States, 2008*; and *Prisoners in 2008*. See also <http://bjs.ojp.usdoj.gov/index.cfm?ty=tp&tid=1>.

U.S. Census Bureau, Statistical Abstract of the United States: 2011

Table 346. Jail Inmates by Sex, Race, and Hispanic Origin: 1990 to 2008

[As of June 30. Data based on the Annual Survey of Jails, a sample survey and subject to sampling variability]

Characteristic	1990	1995	2000	2005	2006	2007	2008
Total inmates [1,2]	**405,320**	**507,044**	**621,149**	**747,529**	**765,819**	**780,174**	**785,556**
Incarceration rate per 100,000 residents	163	193	220	252	256	259	258
Rated capacity [3,4]	389,171	545,763	677,787	786,954	794,984	810,543	828,413
Adult	403,019	499,300	613,534	740,770	759,717	773,341	777,852
Male	365,821	448,000	543,120	646,807	661,164	673,346	678,677
Female	37,198	51,300	70,414	93,963	98,552	99,995	99,175
Juveniles [5]	2,301	7,800	7,615	6,759	6,102	6,833	7,703
White, non-Hispanic	169,600	203,300	260,500	331,000	336,500	338,200	333,300
Black, non-Hispanic	172,300	220,600	256,300	290,500	295,900	301,700	308,000
Hispanic/Latino	58,100	74,400	94,100	111,900	119,200	125,500	128,500
Other [6]	5,400	8,800	10,200	13,000	13,500	13,900	14,000

[1] Total does not include offenders who were supervised outside of jail facilities. [2] Race\Hispanic origin data do not include the two or more race data. [3] Beginning 1995, rated capacity subject to sampling error. [4] Rated capacity is the number of beds or inmates assigned by a rating official to facilities within each jurisdiction. [5] Juveniles are persons held under the age of 18. Includes juveniles who were tried or awaiting trial as adults. [6] Excludes persons of Hispanic or Latino origin. Includes American Indians, Alaska Natives, Asians, and Pacific Islanders.

Source: U.S. Department of Justice, Bureau of Justice Statistics, *Prison and Jail Inmates at Midyear*, Series NCJ 225709, annual. See also <http://bjs.ojp.usdoj.gov/index.cfm?ty=pbdetail&iid=1004>.

Table 347. Prisoners Under Federal or State Jurisdiction by Sex: 1980 to 2008

[Prisoners, as of December 31. Includes all persons under jurisdiction of federal or state authorities rather than those in the custody of such authorities. Represents inmates sentenced to maximum term of more than a year]

Year	Total [1]	Rate [2]	State	Male	Female	Year	Total [1]	Rate [2]	State	Male	Female
1980	315,974	139	295,363	303,643	12,331	1998	1,245,402	461	1,141,720	1,167,802	77,600
1985	480,568	202	447,873	459,223	21,345	1999	1,304,074	476	1,189,799	1,221,611	82,463
1989	680,907	276	633,739	643,643	37,264	2000	1,331,278	[3] 470	1,204,323	1,246,234	85,044
1990	739,980	297	689,577	699,416	40,564	2001	1,345,217	470	1,208,708	1,260,033	85,184
1991	789,610	313	732,914	745,808	43,802	2002	1,380,516	476	1,237,476	1,291,450	89,066
1992	846,277	332	780,571	799,776	46,501	2003	1,408,361	482	1,256,442	1,315,790	92,571
1993	932,074	359	857,675	878,037	54,037	2004	1,433,728	486	1,274,591	1,337,730	95,998
1994	1,016,691	389	936,896	956,566	60,125	2005	1,462,866	491	1,296,693	1,364,178	98,688
1995	1,085,022	411	1,001,359	1,021,059	63,963	2006	1,504,660	501	1,331,127	1,401,317	103,343
1996	1,137,722	427	1,048,907	1,068,123	69,599	2007	1,532,850	506	1,353,646	1,427,064	105,786
1997	1,195,498	445	1,100,511	1,121,663	73,835	2008	1,540,036	504	1,357,703	1,434,784	105,252

[1] Includes prisoners under the legal authority of state or federal correctional officials. [2] Rate per 100,000 estimated population. Based on U.S. Census Bureau estimated resident population. [3] Decrease in incarceration rate from 1999 to 2000 due to use of new Census numbers.

Source: U.S. Department of Justice, Bureau of Justice Statistics, *Prisoners in 2008*, Series NCJ 228417, annual. See also <http://bjs.ojp.usdoj.gov/index.cfm?ty=pbdetail&iid=1763>.

Table 348. Prisoners Under Sentence of Death by Characteristic: 1980 to 2008

[As of December 31. Excludes prisoners under sentence of death who remained within local correctional systems pending exhaustion of appellate process or who had not been committed to prison]

Characteristic	1980	1990	1995	2000	2001	2002	2003	2004	2005	2006	2007	2008
Total [1,2]	**688**	**2,346**	**3,064**	**3,601**	**3,577**	**3,562**	**3,377**	**3,320**	**3,245**	**3,233**	**3,215**	**3,207**
White	418	1,368	1,732	1,989	1,968	1,939	1,882	1,856	1,802	1,806	1,806	1,798
Black and other	270	978	1,332	1,612	1,609	1,623	1,495	1,464	1,443	1,427	1,409	1,409
Under 20 years old	11	8	20	11	4	4	1	1	–	–	1	–
20 to 24 years old	173	168	264	237	192	153	133	95	61	51	42	44
25 to 34 years old	334	1,110	1,068	1,103	1,099	1,058	965	896	816	735	680	610
35 to 54 years old	186	1,006	1,583	2,019	2,043	2,069	1,969	1,977	2,012	2,043	2,060	2,076
55 years old and over	10	64	119	223	243	273	306	345	365	399	437	477
Years of school completed:												
7 years or less	68	178	191	214	212	215	213	207	192	186	183	176
8 years	74	186	195	233	236	234	227	221	206	195	189	185
9 to 11 years	204	775	979	1,157	1,145	1,130	1,073	1,053	1,030	1,015	989	977
12 years	162	729	995	1,184	1,183	1,173	1,108	1,091	1,105	1,098	1,089	1,094
More than 12 years	43	209	272	315	304	294	270	262	256	248	248	247
Unknown	163	279	422	490	501	511	483	480	465	486	522	528
Marital status:												
Never married	268	998	1,412	1,749	1,763	1,746	1,641	1,622	1,586	1,577	1,558	1,552
Married	229	632	718	739	716	709	684	658	649	626	635	630
Divorced [3]	217	726	924	1,105	1,102	1,102	1,049	1,034	1,019	1,025	1,027	1,025
Time elapsed since sentencing:												
Less than 12 months	185	231	287	208	151	147	137	117	122	105	110	106
12 to 47 months	389	753	784	786	734	609	495	421	399	382	352	339
48 to 71 months	102	438	423	507	476	468	451	388	299	262	262	244
72 months and over	38	934	1,560	2,092	2,220	2,333	2,291	2,388	2,434	2,479	2,496	2,518
Legal status at arrest:												
Not under sentence	384	1,345	1,764	2,202	2,189	2,165	2,048	2,026	1,979	1,952	1,963	1,961
Parole or probation [4]	115	578	866	921	918	909	845	809	792	778	760	753
Prison or escaped	45	128	110	126	135	141	137	145	144	142	143	146
Unknown	170	305	314	344	339	342	344	334	339	356	354	347

– Represents zero. [1] Revisions to the total number of prisoners were not carried to the characteristics except for race. [2] Includes races not shown separately. [3] Includes persons married but separated, widows, widowers, and unknown. [4] Includes prisoners on mandatory conditional release, work release, other leave, AWOL or bail. Covers 28 prisoners in 1990; 33 in 1995; 26 in 1998; 21 in 1999 and 2000; 17 in 2001, 2002, and 2003; 15 in 2004; and 14 in 2005, 2006, and 2007.

Source: U.S. Department of Justice, Bureau of Justice Statistics, *Capital Punishment*, annual, Series NCJ 228662. See also <http://bjs.ojp.usdoj.gov/index.cfm?ty=pbdetail&iid=1757>.

Table 349. Prisoners Executed Under Civil Authority by Sex and Race: 1930 to 2009

[Excludes executions by military authorities]

Year or period	Total [1]	Male	Female	White	Black	Executed for murder Total [1]	Executed for murder White	Executed for murder Black
All years, 1930–2009 . . .	**5,047**	**5,004**	**43**	**2,510**	**2,480**	**4,522**	**2,423**	**2,044**
1960 to 1967	191	190	1	98	93	155	87	68
1968 to 1976	–	–	–	–	–	–	–	–
1977 to 2009	927	917	10	599	315	927	599	315
1985.	18	18	–	11	7	18	11	7
1990.	23	23	–	16	7	23	16	7
1995.	56	56	–	33	22	56	33	22
1997.	74	74	–	45	27	74	45	27
1998.	68	66	2	48	18	68	48	18
1999.	98	98	–	61	33	98	61	33
2000.	85	83	2	49	35	85	49	35
2001.	66	63	3	48	17	66	48	17
2002.	71	69	2	53	18	71	53	18
2003.	65	65	–	44	20	65	44	20
2004.	59	59	–	39	19	59	39	19
2005.	60	59	1	41	19	60	41	19
2006.	53	53	–	32	21	53	32	21
2007.	42	42	–	28	14	42	28	14
2008.	37	37	–	20	17	37	20	17
2009.	52	52	–	31	21	52	31	21

– Represents zero. [1] Includes races other than White or Black.

Source: Through 1978, U.S. Law Enforcement Assistance Administration; thereafter, U.S. Department of Justice, Office of Justice Programs, Bureau of Justice Statistics, *Capital Punishment*, Series NCJ 228662, annual. See also <http://bjs.ojp.usdoj.gov/index.cfm?ty=pbdetail&iid=1757>.

Table 350. Prisoners Under Sentence of Death and Executed Under Civil Authority by State: 1977 to 2009

[Alaska, District of Columbia, Hawaii, Iowa, Maine, Massachusetts, Michigan, Minnesota, New Jersey, North Dakota, Rhode Island, Vermont, West Virginia, and Wisconsin are jurisdictions without a death penalty]

State	1977 to 2009	2005	2007	2008	2009	State	1977 to 2009	2005	2007	2008	2009	State	1977 to 2009	2005	2007	2008	2009
U.S. . . .	**1,188**	**60**	**42**	**37**	**52**	IL	12	–	–	–	–	OH . . .	33	4	2	2	5
						IN	20	5	2	–	1	OK . . .	91	4	3	2	3
AL	44	4	3	–	6	KY . . .	3	–	–	1	–	OR . . .	2	–	–	–	–
AZ	23	–	1	–	–	LA . . .	27	–	–	–	–	PA . . .	3	–	–	–	–
AR	27	1	–	–	–	MD . . .	5	1	–	–	–	SC . . .	42	3	1	3	2
CA	13	2	–	–	–	MS . . .	10	1	–	2	–	OD . . .	I	–	1	–	–
OO	I	–	–	–	–	MO . . .	67	5	–	–	1	TN . . .	6	–	2	–	2
CT	1	1	–	–	–	MT . . .	3	–	–	–	–	TX . . .	447	19	26	18	24
DE	14	1	–	–	–	NE . . .	3	–	–	–	–	UT . . .	6	–	–	–	–
FL	68	1	–	2	2	NV . . .	12	–	–	–	–	VA . . .	105	–	–	4	3
GA	46	3	1	3	3	NM . . .	1	–	–	–	–	WA . . .	4	–	–	–	–
ID	I	–	–	–	–	NC . . .	43	5	–	–	–	WY . . .	1	–	–	–	–

– Represents zero.

Source: Through 1978, U.S. Law Enforcement Assistance Administration; thereafter, U.S. Department of Justice, Office of Justice Programs, Bureau of Justice Statistics, *Capital Punishment*, Series NCJ 228662, annual. See <http://bjs.ojp.usdoj.gov/index.cfm?ty=pbdetail&iid=1757>.

Table 351. Fire Losses—Total and Per Capita: 1980 to 2008

[5,579 represents $5,579,000,000. Includes allowance for uninsured and unreported losses but excludes losses to government property and forests. Represents incurred losses]

Year	Total (mil. dol.)	Per capita [1] (dol.)	Year	Total (mil. dol.)	Per capita [1] (dol.)	Year	Total (mil. dol.)	Per capita [1] (dol.)
1980.	5,579	24.56	1993.	11,331	43.96	2001 [2]	17,118	[3] 60.05
1985.	7,753	32.70	1994.	12,778	49.08	2002.	17,586	[3] 61.12
1987.	8,504	34.96	1995.	11,887	45.23	2003.	21,129	[3] 72.81
1988.	9,626	39.11	1996.	12,544	47.29	2004.	17,344	[3] 59.22
1989.	9,514	38.33	1997.	12,940	48.32	2005.	20,427	[3] 69.11
1990.	9,495	38.07	1998.	11,510	45.59	2006.	20,340	[3] 68.17
1991.	11,302	44.82	1999.	12,428	45.58	2007.	[3] 24,399	[3] 80.98
1992.	13,588	53.28	2000.	13,457	47.69	2008.	30,561	[3] 100.51

[1] Based on U.S. Census Bureau estimated resident population as of July 1. Enumerated population as of April 1 for 1080, 1990, and 2000. [2] Does not include insured fire losses related to terrorism. [3] Data have been revised.

Source: Insurance Information Institute, New York, NY. *The III Insurance Fact Book*, annual, and *Financial Services Fact Book*, annual (copyright). Data from ISO. See also <http://www.iii.org>.

Law Enforcement, Courts, and Prisons 217

Table 352. The U.S. Fire Service: Departments and Personnel: 1990 to 2008

[(In thousands 1,025.7 represents 1,025,700.) A fire department is a public or private organization that provides fire prevention, fire suppression, and associated emergency and non-emergency services to a jurisdiction such as a county, municipality, or organized fire district. For 2008, there was an estimated 30,170 fire departments in the United States. These fire departments have an estimated 52,400 fire stations, 68,200 pumpers, 6,725 aerial apparatus and 75,300 other suppression vehicles. A fire department responds to a fire every 22 seconds]

Items	1990	1995	2000	2003	2004	2005	2006	2007	2008
Fire departments (Number)........									
Total.........................	**30,391**	**31,197**	**30,339**	**30,542**	**30,400**	**30,300**	**30,635**	**30,185**	**30,170**
All career.....................	1,949	1,831	2,178	2,018	1,917	2,087	2,321	2,263	2,315
Mostly career.................	1,338	1,660	1,667	1,582	1,242	1,766	1,731	1,765	1,790
Mostly volunteer	4,000	4,581	4,523	5,271	4,084	4,902	5,134	4,989	4,830
All volunteer..................	23,104	23,125	21,971	21,671	23,157	21,575	21,449	21,168	21,235
Fire Department personnel (1,000)...	1,025.7	1,098.1	1,064.2	1,096.9	1,100.8	1,136.7	1,140.9	1,148.5	1,148.9
Career[1]	253.0	260.9	286.8	296.9	305.2	313.3	317.0	323.4	321.7
Volunteer[2]	772.7	838.0	777.4	800.1	795.6	823.7	824.0	825.5	827.2

[1] Career firefighters include full-time uniform firefighters regardless of assignment (i.e., suppression, administrative, prevention/inspection, etc.). Career firefighters do not include firefighters who work for the state or federal government or in private fire brigades. [2] Volunteer firefighters include any active part-time (call or volunteer) firefighters.

Source: National Fire Protection Association, Quincy, MA, October 2009 Annual Fire Department Profile Report and prior issues (copyright 2009), <http://www.nfpa.org/categoryList.asp?categoryID=955&URL=Research/Fire%20statistics/The%20U.S.%20fire%20service\>.

Table 353. Fires—Number and Loss by Type and Property Use: 2005 to 2008

[1,602 represents 1,602,000 and property loss of 10,672 represents $10,672,000,000. Based on annual sample survey of fire departments. No adjustments were made for unreported fires and losses]

Type and property use	Number (1,000)				Direct property loss (mil. dol.) [1]			
	2005	2006	2007	2008	2005	2006	2007	2008
Fires, total	**1,602**	**1,642**	**1,557**	**1,451**	**10,672**	**11,307**	**14,639**	**15,478**
Structure	511	524	531	515	9,193	9,636	10,638	12,361
Outside of structure [2]............	78	82	85	71	93	262	707	129
Brush and rubbish..............	594	627	561	523	–	–	–	–
Vehicle.......................	290	278	257	236	1,318	1,319	1,411	1,494
Other........................	129	131	123	106	68	90	[3] 1,883	[4] 1,494
Structure by property use:								
Public assembly...............	13	13	15	14	320	444	498	518
Educational	6	6	6	6	67	105	100	66
Institutional	8	8	7	7	40	42	41	22
Stores and offices	23	20	21	20	687	691	642	684
Residential...................	396	413	414	403	6,875	6,990	7,546	8,550
1–2 family homes [5]	287	304	300	291	5,781	5,936	6,225	6,892
Apartments	94	92	99	96	948	896	1,164	1,351
Other residential [6]	15	17	15	16	146	158	157	307
Storage	30	29	31	30	590	650	670	661
Industry, utility, defense [7]........	12	12	12	10	376	573	779	[8] 1,401
Special structures	23	23	25	25	238	141	362	459

– Represents zero. [1] Direct property damage figures do not include indirect losses, like business interruption, and adjustments for inflation. [2] Includes outside storage, crops, timber, etc. [3] Includes California Fire Storm 2007 with an estimated $1.8 billion in property loss. [4] Includes California Wildfires 2008 with an estimated $1.4 billion in property loss. [5] Includes mobile homes. [6] Includes hotels and motels, college dormitories, boarding houses, etc. [7] Data underreported as some incidents were handled by private fire brigades or fixed suppression systems which do not report. [8] Includes three industrial property incidents that resulted in $775 million in property loss.

Source: National Fire Protection Association, Quincy, MA, "2008 U.S. Fire Loss," NFPA Journal, September 2009, and prior issues (copyright 2009), <http://www.nfpa.org/assets/files/PDF/OS.fireloss.pdf>.

Table 354. Fires and Property Loss for Incendiary and Suspicious Fires and Civilian Fire Deaths and Injuries by Selected Property Type: 2005 to 2008

[511 represents 511,000. Based on sample survey of fire departments]

Characteristic	2005	2006	2007	2008	Characteristic	2005	2006	2007	2008
NUMBER (1,000)					One- and two-family dwellings	2,575	2,155	2,350	2,365
Structure fires, total.	**511**	**524**	**531**	**515**	Apartments	460	425	515	390
Structure fires that were intentionally set	32	31	32	31	Vehicles.............	520	490	385	365
PROPERTY LOSS [1] (mil. dol.)					CIVILIAN FIRE INJURIES				
Structure fires, total.	9,193	9,636	10,638	12,361	**Injuries, total [2]**	**17,925**	**16,400**	**17,675**	**16,705**
Structure fires that were intentionally set	664	775	773	866	Residential property ...	13,825	12,925	14,000	13,560
CIVILIAN FIRE DEATHS					One- and two-family dwellings	10,300	8,800	9,650	9,185
Deaths, total [2].............	**3,675**	**3,245**	**3,430**	**3,320**	Apartments..	3,000	3,700	3,950	3,975
Residential property ...	3,055	2,620	2,895	2,780	Vehicles.............	1,650	1,200	1,675	1,065

[1] Direct property loss only. [2] Includes other not shown separately.

Source: National Fire Protection Association, Quincy, MA, "2008 U.S. Fire Loss," NFPA Journal, September 2009, and prior issues (copyright 2008), <http://www.nfpa.org/assets/files/PDF/OS.fireloss.pdf>.

This section presents a variety of information on the physical environment of the United States, starting with basic area measurement data and ending with climatic data for selected weather stations around the country. The subjects covered between those points are mostly concerned with environmental trends but include related subjects such as land use, water consumption, air pollutant emissions, toxic releases, oil spills, hazardous waste sites, municipal waste and recycling, threatened and endangered wildlife, and the environmental industry.

The information in this section is selected from a wide range of federal agencies that compile the data for various administrative or regulatory purposes, such as the Environmental Protection Agency (EPA), U.S. Geological Survey (USGS), National Oceanic and Atmospheric Administration (NOAA), Natural Resources Conservation Service (NRCS), and National Atlas® of the United States. New information on the greenhouse gases and earthquakes may be found in Tables 372 and 385.

Area—For the 2000 census and 2008, area measurements were calculated by computer based on the information contained in a single, consistent geographic database, the Topologically Integrated Geographic Encoding & Referencing system (TIGER®) database. The 2008 area measurements may be found in Table 355.

Geography—The USGS conducts investigations, surveys, and research in the fields of geography, geology, topography, geographic information systems, mineralogy, hydrology, and geothermal energy resources as well as natural hazards. The USGS provides United States cartographic data through the Earth Sciences Information Center, water resources data through the *Water Resources of the United States* at <http://water.usgs.gov/pubs/>. In a joint project with the U.S. Census Bureau, during the 1980s, the USGS provided the basic information on geographic features for input into a national geographic and cartographic database prepared by the Census Bureau, called TIGER® database. Since then, using a variety of sources, the Census Bureau has updated these features and their related attributes (names, descriptions, etc.) and inserted current information on the boundaries, names, and codes of legal and statistical geographic entities. The 2008 area measures, land and water, including their classifications, reflect base feature updates made in the Master Address File (MAF)/TIGER database through May 1, 2008. The boundaries of the states and equivalent areas are as of January 1, 2008. Maps prepared by the Census Bureau using the TIGER® database show the names and boundaries of entities and are available on a current basis.

An inventory of the nation's land resources by type of use/cover was conducted by the National Resources Inventory Conservation Services (NRCS) every 5 years beginning in 1977 through 2007. The most recent survey results, which were published for the year 2007, covered all nonfederal land for the contiguous 48 states.

Environment—The principal federal agency responsible for pollution abatement and control activities is the Environmental Protection Agency (EPA). It is responsible for establishing and monitoring national air quality standards, water quality activities, solid and hazardous waste disposal, and control of toxic substances. Many of these series now appear in the Envirofacts portion of the EPA Web site at <http://www.epa.gov/enviro/>.

The Clean Air Act, which was last amended in 1990, requires the EPA to set National Ambient Air Quality Standards (NAAQS) (40 CFR part 50) for pollutants considered harmful to public health and the environment. The Clean Air Act established two types of national air quality standards. **Primary standards** set limits to protect public health,

U.S. Census Bureau, Statistical Abstract of the United States: 2011

including the health of "sensitive" populations such as asthmatics, children, and the elderly. **Secondary standards** set limits to protect public welfare, including protection against decreased visibility, damage to animals, crops vegetation, and buildings. See <http://www.epa.gov/air/criteria.html>. The EPA Office of Air Quality Planning and Standards (OAQPS) has set National Ambient Air Quality Standards for six principal pollutants, which are called "criteria" pollutants. These pollutants are: Carbon Monoxide, Lead, Nitrogen Dioxide, Particulate Matter (PM2.5 and 10), Ozone, and Sulfur Dioxide. NAAQS are periodically reviewed and revised to include any additional or new health or welfare data. Table 368 gives some of the health-related standards for the six air pollutants having NAAQS. Data gathered from state networks are periodically submitted to EPA's National Aerometric Information Retrieval System (AIRS) for summarization in annual reports on the nationwide status and trends in air quality. For details, see "Air Trends" on the EPA Web site at <http://www.epa.gov /airtrends/index .html>.

The Toxics Release Inventory (TRI), published by the EPA, is a valuable source of information on approximately 650 chemicals that are being used, manufactured, treated, transported, or released into the environment. Sections 313 of the Emergency Planning and Community Right-to- Know Act (EPCRA) and 6607 of the Pollution Prevention Act (PPA), mandate that a publicly-accessible toxic chemical database be developed and maintained by EPA. This database, known as the TRI, contains information concerning waste management activities and the release of toxic chemicals by facilities that manufacture, process, or otherwise use said materials. Data on the release of

these chemicals are collected from about 22,000 facilities and facilities added in 1998 that have the equivalent of 10 or more full time employees and meet the established thresholds for manufacturing, processing, or "other use" of listed chemicals. Facilities must report their releases and other waste management quantities. Since 1994 federal facilities have been required to report their data regardless of industry classification. In May 1997, EPA added seven new industry sectors that reported to the TRI for the first time in July 1999 for the 1998 reporting year. More current information on this program can be found at <http://www.epa.gov/tri /index.htm>.

Climate—NOAA, through the National Weather Service and the National Environmental Satellite, Data, and Information Service, is responsible for climate data. NOAA maintains about 11,600 weather stations, of which over 3,000 produce autographic precipitation records, about 600 take hourly readings of a series of weather elements, and the remainder record data once a day. These data are reported monthly in the Climatological Data and Storm Data, published monthly and annually in the Local Climatological Data (published by location for major cities).

The normal climatological temperatures, precipitation, and degree days listed in this publication are derived for comparative purposes and are averages for the 30-year period, 1971–2000. For stations that did not have continuous records for the entire 30 years from the same instrument site, the normals have been adjusted to provide representative values for the current location. The information in all other tables is based on data from the beginning of the record at that location through 2007.

Table 355. Land and Water Area of States and Other Entities: 2008

[One square mile = 2.59 square kilometers. Table data have been revised. The area measurements were derived from the Census Bureau's Master Address File/Topologically Integrated Geographic Encoding and Referencing (MAF/TIGER) geographic database. The boundaries of the states and equivalent areas are as of January 1, 2008. The land and water areas, including their classifications, reflect base feature updates made in the MAF/TIGER database through May 1, 2008. These updates show increases in total water area and decrease in land area for nearly every state. For more details, see <http://www.census.gov/geo/www/tiger/tgrshp2008/tgrshp2008.html>]

State and other areas	Total area Sq. mi.	Total area Sq. km.	Land area Sq. mi.	Land area Sq. km.	Water area Total Sq. mi.	Water area Total Sq. km.	Inland (sq. mi.)	Coastal (sq. mi.)	Great Lakes (sq. mi.)	Territorial (sq. mi.)
Total..........	3,805,142	9,855,318	3,535,846	9,157,841	269,296	697,477	86,478	43,201	59,959	76,392
United States	3,795,951	9,831,513	3,531,822	9,147,420	264,129	684,094	86,409	43,185	59,959	74,575
Alabama	52,420	135,768	50,644	131,168	1,776	4,600	1,057	518	(X)	201
Alaska	664,988	1,722,319	570,665	1,478,022	94,323	244,297	20,028	28,162	(X)	46,133
Arizona	113,990	295,235	113,595	294,211	396	1,026	396	–	(X)	–
Arkansas	53,178	137,732	52,030	134,758	1,149	2,976	1,149	–	(X)	–
California	163,694	423,967	155,766	403,434	7,928	20,534	2,842	222	(X)	4,864
Colorado	104,094	269,604	103,641	268,430	454	1,176	454	–	(X)	–
Connecticut	5,544	14,358	4,840	12,536	703	1,821	164	539	(X)	–
Delaware	2,489	6,445	1,949	5,048	539	1,396	74	372	(X)	93
District of Columbia	68	177	61	158	7	18	7	–	(X)	–
Florida	65,758	170,312	53,603	138,832	12,154	31,479	5,373	1,128	(X)	5,653
Georgia	59,425	153,911	57,501	148,928	1,924	4,983	1,420	49	(X)	455
Hawaii	10,926	28,300	6,428	16,649	4,499	11,652	40	–	(X)	4,459
Idaho	83,568	216,442	82,643	214,045	926	2,398	926	–	(X)	–
Illinois...........	57,916	150,002	55,518	143,792	2,398	6,211	836	–	1,562	–
Indiana.........	36,417	94,321	35,823	92,782	594	1,538	361	–	233	–
Iowa.............	56,273	145,746	55,858	144,672	415	1,075	415	–	(X)	–
Kansas.........	82,278	213,101	81,762	211,764	516	1,336	516	–	(X)	–
Kentucky	40,411	104,665	39,492	102,284	919	2,380	919	–	(X)	–
Louisiana........	51,988	134,649	43,199	111,885	8,789	22,764	4,433	1,951	(X)	2,405
Maine..........	35,384	91,644	30,841	79,878	4,543	11,766	2,282	613	(X)	1,647
Maryland	12,406	32,131	9,705	25,136	2,700	6,993	736	1,854	(X)	111
Massachusetts.....	10,554	27,336	7,801	20,205	2,754	7,133	461	977	(X)	1,316
Michigan	96,713	250,486	56,528	146,408	40,185	104,079	2,164	–	38,021	–
Minnesota	86,935	225,163	79,607	206,182	7,328	18,980	4,782	–	2,546	–
Mississippi.......	48,432	125,438	46,920	121,523	1,512	3,916	772	591	(X)	149
Missouri........	69,702	180,529	68,716	177,974	987	2,556	987	–	(X)	–
Montana.........	147,039	380,831	145,541	376,951	1,498	3,880	1,498	–	(X)	–
Nebraska........	77,349	200,334	76,825	198,977	524	1,357	524	–	(X)	–
Nevada.........	110,572	286,382	109,780	284,330	792	2,051	792	–	(X)	–
New Hampshire....	9,348	24,210	8,952	23,186	396	1,026	328	–	(X)	68
New Jersey	8,723	22,592	7,354	19,047	1,369	3,546	458	402	(X)	509
New Mexico.......	121,590	314,919	121,297	314,159	293	759	293	–	(X)	–
New York	54,555	141,298	47,126	122,056	7,429	19,241	1,979	977	3,990	482
North Carolina.....	53,819	139,391	48,619	125,923	5,200	13,468	4,044	–	(X)	1,157
North Dakota	70,698	183,109	69,001	178,713	1,697	4,395	1,697	–	(X)	–
Ohio	44,826	110,097	40,858	105,822	3,967	10,275	467	–	3,500	–
Oklahoma	69,899	181,038	68,603	177,682	1,296	3,357	1,296	–	(X)	–
Oregon..........	98,379	254,801	95,985	248,601	2,394	6,200	1,063	74	(X)	1,256
Pennsylvania......	46,055	119,281	44,739	115,874	1,316	3,408	567	–	749	–
Rhode Island......	1,545	4,001	1,034	2,678	511	1,323	187	9	(X)	315
South Carolina.....	32,021	82,934	30,070	77,881	1,951	5,053	1,044	74	(X)	832
South Dakota	77,116	199,730	75,811	196,350	1,305	3,380	1,305	–	(X)	–
Tennessee	42,144	109,154	41,235	106,799	910	2,357	910	–	(X)	–
Texas	268,597	695,666	261,226	676,575	7,371	19,091	5,607	406	(X)	1,358
Utah............	84,897	219,883	82,191	212,875	2,706	7,009	2,706	–	(X)	–
Vermont.........	9,616	24,906	9,217	23,872	400	1,036	400	–	(X)	–
Virginia..........	42,775	110,787	39,493	102,287	3,282	8,500	1,106	1,729	(X)	447
Washington	71,298	184,661	66,449	172,103	4,849	12,559	1,646	2,537	(X)	666
West Virginia	24,230	62,755	24,038	62,258	192	497	192	–	(X)	–
Wisconsin	65,496	169,636	54,154	140,259	11,342	29,376	1,984	–	9,358	–
Wyoming	97,812	253,334	97,088	251,458	724	1,875	724	–	(X)	–
Puerto Rico	5,325	13,791	3,424	8,868	1,901	4,924	68	16	(X)	1,817
Island Areas:.......	3,866	10,013	600	1,554	3,266	8,459	(NA)	(NA)	(X)	(NA)
American Samoa...	583	1,510	77	199	506	1,311	(NA)	(NA)	(X)	(NA)
Guam...........	571	1,479	210	544	361	935	(NA)	(NA)	(X)	(NA)
No. Mariana Islands........	1,975	5,115	179	464	1,796	4,652	(NA)	(NA)	(X)	(NA)
U.S. Virgin Islands..........	738	1,911	134	347	604	1,564	(NA)	(NA)	(X)	(NA)

– Represents or rounds to zero. NA Not available. X Not applicable.
Source: U.S. Census Bureau, unpublished data from the Census TIGER "R" database.

Geography and Environment 221

Table 356. Great Lakes Profile

[The Great Lakes contain the largest supply of freshwater in the world, holding about 18% of the world's total freshwater and about 90% of the United States' total freshwater. The Lakes are a series of five interconnecting large lakes, one small lake, four connecting channels, and the St. Lawrence Seaway. Combined, the lakes cover an area of over 94,000 square miles (245,000 square kilometers) and contain over 5,400 cubic miles (23,000 cubic kilometers) of water]

Characteristics	Unit	Lake Superior	Lake Michigan	Lake Huron	Lake Erie	Lake Ontario
Length	Miles	350	307	206	241	193
Breadth	Miles	160	118	183	57	53
Depth						
Average	Feet	489	279	159	62	283
Maximum	Feet	1,333	923	750	210	802
Volume	Cubic miles	2,935	1,180	849	116	393
Water Surface Area [1]	Square miles	31,700	22,300	23,000	9,910	7,340
Surface area in U.S	Square miles	20,598	22,300	9,111	4,977	3,560
Retention/Replacement Time [2]	Years	191	99	22	3	6

[1] Includes surface area in both U.S. and Canada. [2] The amount of time it takes for lakes to get rid of pollutants.

Source: Department of Commerce, National Oceanic and Atmospheric Administration, Great Lakes Environmental Research Laboratory, "About Our Great Lakes, Lake by Lake Profiles," June 2004, <http://www.glerl.noaa.gov/pr/ourlakes/intro.html\>.

Table 357. Great Lakes Length of Shoreline in Separate Basin

[In statute miles]

	Total	Canada	U.S.	MI	MN	WI	IL	IN	OH	PA	NY
Total	10,368	5,127	5,241	3,288	189	820	63	45	312	51	473
Lake Superior	2,980	1,549	1,431	917	189	325	–	–	–	–	–
St. Marys River	297	206	91	91	–	–	–	–	–	–	–
Lake Michigan	1,661	–	1,661	1,058	–	495	63	45	–	–	–
Lake Huron	3,350	2,416	934	934	–	–	–	–	–	–	–
St. Clair River	128	47	81	81	–	–	–	–	–	–	–
Lake St. Clair	160	71	89	89	–	–	–	–	–	–	–
Detroit River	107	43	64	64	–	–	–	–	–	–	–
Lake Erie	860	366	494	54	–	–	–	–	312	51	77
Niagara River	99	34	65	–	–	–	–	–	–	–	65
Lake Ontario	726	395	331	–	–	–	–	–	–	–	331

– Represents zero.

Source: State of Michigan, Department of Environment Quality, "Great Lakes, Shorelines of the Great Lakes," <http://www.michigan.gov/deq/0,1607,7-135-3313_3677---,00.html\>.

Table 358. Largest Lakes in the United States

[The list of lakes include manmade lakes and those that are only partially within the United States]

Lake	Location	Area in sq. mi.	Lake	Location	Area in sq. mi.
Lake Superior	MI-MN-WI-Ontario	31,700	Lake Pontchartrain	Louisiana	631
Lake Huron	MI-Ontario	23,000	Lake Sakakawea [1]	North Dakota	520
Lake Michigan	IL-IN-MI-WI	22,300	Lake Champlain	NY-VT-Quebec	490
Lake Erie	MI-NY-OH-PA-Ontario	9,910	Becharof Lake	Alaska	453
Lake Ontario	NY-Ontario	7,340	Lake St. Clair	MI-Ontario	430
Great Salt Lake	Utah	2,117	Red Lake	Minnesota	427
Lake of the Woods	MN-Manitoba-Ontario	1,485	Selawik Lake	Alaska	404
Iliamna Lake	Alaska	1,014	Fort Peck Lake [1]	Montana	393
Lake Oahe [1]	ND-SD	685	Salton Sea	California	347
Lake Okeechobee	Florida	662	Rainy Lake	MN-Ontario	345

[1] Manmade lakes.

Source: U.S. Geological Survey, 2003, and National Oceanic and Atmospheric Administration, "Great Lakes, 2002" and The National Atlas of the United States of America, Lakes, <http://nationalatlas.gov/articles/mapping/a_general.html\>.

Table 359. U.S.–Canada and U.S.–Mexico Border Lengths

[In statue miles. Each statue mile equals one mile. For 2008, there were over 57 million personal vehicle passengers entering the United States from Canada, and almost 158 million personal vehicle passengers entering the United States from Mexico]

State	Length of international border	State	Length of international border
United States–Canada total	**5,525**	Ohio...........................	146
Alaska...............................	1,538	Pennsylvania...................	42
Idaho................................	45	Vermont	90
Maine................................	611	Washington.....................	427
Michigan.............................	721		
Minnesota............................	547	**United States–Mexico total.**.............	**1,933**
Montana.............................	545	Arizona	373
New Hampshire.......................	58	California.......................	140
New York............................	445	New Mexico.....................	180
North Dakota.........................	310	Texas..........................	1,241

Source: U.S.–Canada lengths: International Boundary Commission, 2003; U.S. Mexico lengths: U.S. Geological Survey; and The National Atlas of the United States, 1976, *Borders*, <http://nationalatlas.gov/articles/mapping/a_general.html>.

Table 360. Coastline and Shoreline of the United States by State

[In statue miles. Each statue mile equals one mile. The term **coastline** is used to describe the general outline of the seacoast. For the table below, United States coastline measurements were made from small-scale maps, and the coastline was generalized. The coastlines of large sounds and bays were included. Measurements were made in 1948. **Shoreline** is the term used to describe a more detailed measure of the seacoast. The tidal shoreline figures in the table below were obtained in 1939–1940 from the largest-scale charts and maps then available. Shoreline of the outer coast, offshore islands, sounds, and bays was included, as well as the tidal portion of rivers and creeks. Only states with coastline or shoreline are included in the following table]

State	General coastline	Tidal shoreline	State	General coastline	Tidal shoreline
United States	**12,383**	**88,633**	Mississippi	44	359
Alabama........................	53	607	New Hampshire	13	131
Alaska..........................	6,640	33,904	New Jersey....................	130	1,792
California	840	3,427	New York.......................	127	1,850
Connecticut.....................	–	618	North Carolina	301	3,375
Delaware	28	381	Oregon........................	296	1,410
Florida..........................	1,350	8,426	Pennsylvania	–	89
Georgia.........................	100	2,344	Rhode Island	40	384
Hawaii..........................	750	1,052	South Carolina	187	2,876
Louisiana	397	7,721	Texas	367	3,359
Maine...........................	228	3,478	Virginia	112	3,315
Maryland........................	31	3,190	Washington....................	157	3,026
Massachusetts	192	1,519			

– Represents zero.

Source: National Oceanic Atmospheric Administration, 1975 and The National Atlas of the United States, *Coastline and Shoreline*, <http://nationalatlas.gov/articles/mapping/a_general.html>.

Table 361. Flows of Largest U.S. Rivers—Length, Discharge, and Drainage Area

River	Location of mouth	Source stream (name and location)	Length (miles) [1]	Average discharge at mouth (1,000 cubic feet per second)	Drainage area (1,000 sq. miles)
Missouri	Missouri..............	Red Rock Creek, MT	[3] 2,540	76.2	[2] 529
Mississippi	Louisiana	Mississippi River, MN	2,340	[4] 593	[2, 5] 1,150
Yukon..........	Alaska	McNeil River, Canada	1,980	225	[2] 328
St. Lawrence ...	Canada	North River, MN	1,900	348	[2] 396
Rio Grande	Mexico-Texas.........	Rio Grande, CO..............	1,900	[7]	336
Arkansas	Arkansas	East Fork Arkansas River, CO ...	1,460	41	161
Colorado	Mexico...............	Colorado River, CO............	1,450	[7]	246
Atchafalaya [6] ...	Louisiana	Tierra Blanca Creek, NM	1,420	58	95.1
Ohio	Illinois-Kentucky	Allegheny River, PA	1,310	281	203
Red [6]	Louisiana	Tierra Blanca Creek, NM	1,290	56	93.2
Brazos	Texas................	Blackwater Draw, NM	1,280	[7]	45.6
Columbia	Oregon-Washington ...	Columbia River, Canada	1,240	265	[2] 258
Snake	Washington	Snake River, WY	1,040	56.9	108
Platte	Nebraska	Grizzly Creek, CO	990	[7]	84.9
Pecos.........	Texas................	Pecos River, NM	926	[7]	44.3
Canadian......	Oklahoma	Canadian River, CO...........	906	[7]	46.9
Tennessee	Kentucky	Courthouse Creek, NC	886	68	40.9

[1] From source to mouth. [2] Drainage area includes both the United States and Canada. [3] The length from the source of the Missouri River to the Mississippi River and thence to the Gulf of Mexico is about 3,710 miles. [4] Includes about 167,000 cubic feet per second diverted from the Mississippi into the Atchafalaya River but excludes the flow of the Red River. [5] Excludes the drainage areas of the Red and Atchafalaya Rivers. [6] In east-central Louisiana, the Red River flows into the Atchafalaya River, a distributary of the Mississippi River. Data on average discharge, length, and drainage area include the Red River, but exclude all water diverted into the Atchafalaya from the Mississippi River. [7] Less than 15,000 cubic feet per second.

Source: U.S. Geological Survey, *Largest Rivers in the United States*, September 2005, <http://pubs.usgs.gov/of/1987/ofr87-242\>.

Geography and Environment 223

Table 362. Extreme and Mean Elevations by State and Other Areas

[One foot = .305 meter. There are 2,130 square miles of the United States below sea level (Death Valley is the lowest point). There are 20,230 square miles above 10,000 feet (Mount McKinley is the highest point in the United States). Minus sign (–) indicates below sea level]

State and other areas	Highest point			Lowest point			Approximate mean elevation	
	Name	Elevation		Name	Elevation			
		Feet	Meters		Feet	Meters	Feet	Meters
U.S.	**Mt. McKinley (AK)**	**20,320**	**6,198**	**Death Valley (CA)**	**−282**	**−86**	**2,500**	**763**
AL	Cheaha Mountain	2,407	734	Gulf of Mexico	(¹)	(¹)	500	153
AK	Mount McKinley	20,320	6,198	Pacific Ocean	(¹)	(¹)	1,900	580
AZ	Humphreys Peak	12,633	3,853	Colorado River	70	21	4,100	1,251
AR	Magazine Mountain	2,753	840	Ouachita River	55	17	650	198
CA	Mount Whitney	14,494	4,419	Death Valley	−282	−86	2,900	885
CO	Mt. Elbert	14,433	4,402	Arikaree River	3,315	1,011	6,800	2,074
CT	Mt. Frissell on south slope	2,380	726	Long Island Sound	(¹)	(¹)	500	153
DE ²	Ebright Road ²	448	137	Atlantic Ocean	(¹)	(¹)	60	18
DC	Tenleytown at Reno Reservoir	410	125	Potomac River	1	(Z)	150	46
FL	Britton Hill	345	105	Atlantic Ocean	(¹)	(¹)	100	31
GA	Brasstown Bald	4,784	1,459	Atlantic Ocean	(¹)	(¹)	600	183
HI	Pu'u Wekiu, Mauna Kea	13,796	4,208	Pacific Ocean	(¹)	(¹)	3,030	924
ID	Borah Peak	12,662	3,862	Snake River	710	217	5,000	1,525
IL	Charles Mound	1,235	377	Mississippi River	279	85	600	183
IN	Hoosier Hill	1,257	383	Ohio River	320	98	700	214
IA	Hawkeye Point	1,670	509	Mississippi River	480	146	1,100	336
KS	Mount Sunflower	4,039	1,232	Verdigris River	679	207	2,000	610
KY	Black Mountain	4,145	1,264	Mississippi River	257	78	750	229
LA	Driskill Mountain	535	163	New Orleans	−8	−2	100	31
ME	Mount Katahdin	5,268	1,607	Atlantic Ocean	(¹)	(¹)	600	183
MD	Hoye Crest	3,360	1,025	Atlantic Ocean	(¹)	(¹)	350	107
MA	Mount Greylock	3,491	1,065	Atlantic Ocean	(¹)	(¹)	500	153
MI	Mount Arvon	1,979	604	Lake Erie	571	174	900	275
MN	Eagle Mountain	2,301	702	Lake Superior	601	183	1,200	366
MS	Woodall Mountain	806	246	Gulf of Mexico	(¹)	(¹)	300	92
MO	Taum Sauk Mountain	1,772	540	St. Francis River	230	70	800	244
MT	Granite Peak	12,799	3,904	Kootenai River	1,800	549	3,400	1,037
NE	Panorama Point	5,424	1,654	Missouri River	840	256	2,600	793
NV	Boundary Peak	13,140	4,007	Colorado River	479	146	5,500	1,678
NH	Mount Washington	6,288	1,918	Atlantic Ocean	(¹)	(¹)	1,000	305
NJ	High Point	1,803	550	Atlantic Ocean	(¹)	(¹)	250	76
NM	Wheeler Peak	13,161	4,014	Red Bluff Reservoir	2,842	867	5,700	1,739
NY	Mount Marcy	5,344	1,630	Atlantic Ocean	(¹)	(¹)	1,000	305
NC	Mount Mitchell	6,684	2,039	Atlantic Ocean	(¹)	(¹)	700	214
ND	White Butte	3,506	1,069	Red River of the North	750	229	1,900	580
OH	Campbell Hill	1,550	473	Ohio River	455	139	850	259
OK	Black Mesa	4,973	1,517	Little River	289	88	1,300	397
OR	Mount Hood	11,239	3,428	Pacific Ocean	(¹)	(¹)	3,300	1,007
PA	Mount Davis	3,213	980	Delaware River	(¹)	(¹)	1,100	336
RI	Jerimoth Hill	812	248	Atlantic Ocean	(¹)	(¹)	200	61
SC	Sassafras Mountain	3,560	1,086	Atlantic Ocean	(¹)	(¹)	350	107
SD	Harney Peak	7,242	2,209	Big Stone Lake	966	295	2,200	671
TN	Clingmans Dome	6,643	2,026	Mississippi River	178	54	900	275
TX	Guadalupe Peak	8,749	2,668	Gulf of Mexico	(¹)	(¹)	1,700	519
UT	Kings Peak	13,528	4,126	Beaverdam Wash	2,000	610	6,100	1,861
VT	Mount Mansfield	4,393	1,340	Lake Champlain	95	29	1,000	305
VA	Mount Rogers	5,729	1,747	Atlantic Ocean	(¹)	(¹)	950	290
WA	Mount Rainier	14,411	4,395	Pacific Ocean	(¹)	(¹)	1,700	519
WV	Spruce Knob	4,863	1,483	Potomac River	240	73	1,500	458
WI	Timms Hill	1,951	595	Lake Michigan	579	177	1,050	320
WY	Gannett Peak	13,804	4,210	Belle Fourche River	3,099	945	6,700	2,044
Other areas:								
Puerto Rico	Cerro de Punta	4,390	1,339	Atlantic Ocean	(¹)	(¹)	1,800	549
American Samoa	Lata Mountain	3,160	964	Pacific Ocean	(¹)	(¹)	1,300	397
Guam	Mount Lamlam	1,332	406	Pacific Ocean	(¹)	(¹)	330	101
U.S. Virgin Islands	Crown Mountain	1,556	475	Atlantic Ocean	(¹)	(¹)	750	229

Z Less than .5 meter. ¹ Sea level. ² At DE–PA state line.

Source: For highest and lowest points, see U.S. Geological Survey, "Elevations and Distances in the United States," <http://egsc.usgs.gov/isb/pubs/booklets/elvadist/elvadist.html\>, released April 2005. For mean elevations, see *Elevations and Distances in the United States*, 1983 edition.

Table 363. Land Cover/Use by Type: 1982 to 2003

[In millions of acres (1,937.7 represents 1,937,700,000), except percent. Excludes Alaska, Hawaii, and District of Columbia. For inventory-specific glossary of key terms, see <http://www.nrcs.usda.gov/technical/NRI/glossaries.html>]

Year	Total surface area	Nonfederal rural land						Developed land	Water areas	Federal land
		Rural land total [1]	Crop- land	Pasture- land	Range- land	Forest land	Other rural land			
Land										
1982.............	1,937.7	1,417.2	420.4	131.4	414.5	402.6	48.3	72.8	48.6	399.1
1992.............	1,937.6	1,400.2	381.2	125.1	406.6	404.0	49.3	86.5	49.4	401.5
2001.............	1,937.7	1,379.3	369.6	116.9	404.7	404.9	51.4	106.3	50.3	401.8
2002.............	1,937.7	1,378.1	368.4	117.3	405.3	404.9	50.6	107.3	50.4	401.9
2003.............	1,937.7	1,377.3	367.9	117.0	405.1	405.6	50.2	108.1	50.4	401.9
Percent of total land										
1982.............	100.0	73.1	21.7	6.8	21.4	20.8	2.5	3.8	2.5	20.6
1992.............	100.0	72.3	19.7	6.5	21.0	20.9	2.5	4.5	2.5	20.7
2001.............	100.0	71.2	19.1	6.0	20.9	20.9	2.7	5.5	2.6	20.7
2002.............	100.0	71.1	19.0	6.1	20.9	20.9	2.6	5.5	2.6	20.7
2003.............	100.0	71.1	19.0	6.0	20.9	20.9	2.6	5.6	2.6	20.7

[1] Includes Conservation Reserve Program (CRP) land not shown separately. CRP is a federal program established under the Food Security Act of 1985 to assist private landowners to convert highly erodible cropland to vegetative cover for 10 years.

Source: U.S. Department of Agriculture, Natural Resources and Conservation Service, *2003 Annual National Resources Inventory*. See also <http://www.nrcs.usda.gov/technical/NRI>.

Table 364. Wetlands on Nonfederal Land and Water Areas by Land Cover/Use and Farm Production Region: 2003

[In thousands of acres (110,760 represents 110,760,000). Represents palustrine and estuarine wetlands; see source]

Farm production region [1]	Total	Cropland [2]	Forest land	Range- land	Other rural land	Developed land	Water area
Wetlands, total.........	**110,760**	**16,730**	**65,440**	**7,740**	**15,800**	**1,590**	**3,460**
Lake states..............	22,460	2,710	15,480	–	3,880	160	230
Southeast..............	22,360	940	16,010	970	3,460	420	560
Delta states.............	17,950	3,240	11,020	270	2,730	190	500
Northeast...............	14,150	1,250	10,890	–	1,550	240	220
Northern plains..........	7,640	3,020	210	2,870	1,090	80	370
Appalachian.............	7,460	400	6,080	–	570	110	300
Southern plains	6,600	970	2,350	970	520	230	550
Mountain...............	4,780	1,570	220	2,010	820	30	130
Corn belt..............	4,690	1,330	2,440	–	380	100	440
Pacific.................	3,680	1,300	740	650	800	30	160

– Represents or rounds to zero. [1] Ten regions established by USDA, Economic Research Service, that group states according to differences in soils, slope of land, climate, distance to market, and storage and marketing facilities. [2] Includes pastureland and Conservation Reserve Program (CRP) lands.

Source: U.S. Department of Agriculture, Natural Resources Conservation Service, *2003 Annual National Resources Inventory*. See also <http://www.nrcs.usda.gov/technical/NRI/>.

Table 365. Land Cover/Use by State: 2003

[In thousands of acres (1,937,664 represents 1,937,664,000), except percent. Excludes Alaska, District of Columbia, Hawaii, and Island Areas]

State	Total surface area	Selected nonfederal rural land, percent of total			State	Total surface area	Selected nonfederal rural land, percent of total		
		Crop- land	Range- land	Forest land			Crop- land	Range- land	Forest land
United States........	**1,937,664**	**19.0**	**20.9**	**20.9**					
Alabama.............	33,424	7.5	0.2	64.4	Nebraska...........	49,510	39.5	46.6	1.6
Arizona.............	72,964	1.3	44.2	5.7	Nevada.............	70,763	0.9	11.7	0.4
Arkansas............	34,037	22.1	0.1	44.1	New Hampshire.......	5,941	2.1	–	65.6
California...........	101,510	9.3	17.5	13.7	New Jersey..........	5,216	10.1	–	30.8
Colorado............	66,625	12.5	37.2	4.9	New Mexico.........	77,823	2.0	51.3	7.0
Connecticut..........	3,195	5.4	–	53.4	New York...........	31,361	17.1	–	56.1
Delaware...........	1,534	29.8	–	22.2	North Carolina.......	33,709	16.4	–	45.9
Florida.............	37,534	7.7	7.2	33.9	North Dakota........	45,251	53.6	24.5	1.0
Georgia............	37,741	11.0	–	58.0	Ohio...............	26,445	42.5	–	27.3
Idaho..............	53,488	10.2	12.0	7.5	Oklahoma...........	44,738	20.1	31.6	16.5
Illinois.............	36,059	66.5	–	11.0	Oregon.............	62,161	6.0	15.1	20.5
Indiana.............	23,158	57.5	–	16.5	Pennsylvania........	28,995	17.7	–	53.9
Iowa...............	36,017	70.8	–	6.4	Rhode Island........	813	2.5	–	45.9
Kansas.............	52,661	50.3	30.1	2.9	South Carolina.......	19,939	11.9	–	56.0
Kentucky............	25,863	21.2	–	40.6	South Dakota........	49,358	34.6	44.7	1.0
Louisiana...........	31,377	17.3	0.9	42.5	Tennessee..........	26,974	17.6	–	44.3
Maine..............	20,966	1.8	–	84.0	Texas..............	171,052	14.9	56.2	6.2
Maryland............	7,870	19.3	–	30.1	Utah...............	54,339	3.1	19.6	3.5
Massachusetts........	5,339	4.7	–	49.9	Vermont............	6,154	9.5	–	67.1
Michigan............	37,349	21.7	–	44.7	Virginia............	27,087	10.6	–	48.7
Minnesota...........	54,010	39.1	–	30.3	Washington.........	44,035	14.7	13.3	28.9
Mississippi..........	30,527	16.3	–	54.9	West Virginia........	15,508	5.3	–	68.1
Missouri............	44,614	30.7	0.2	28.1	Wisconsin..........	35,920	28.7	–	40.4
Montana............	94,110	15.4	39.0	5.7	Wyoming...........	62,603	3.5	44.0	1.5

– Represents zero.

Source: U.S. Department of Agriculture, Natural Resources and Conservation Service, *Summary Report, 2003 Annual National Resources Inventory*. See also <http://www.nrcs.usda.gov/technical/NRI/>.

U.S. Census Bureau, Statistical Abstract of the United States: 2011

Table 366. U.S. Wetland Resources and Deepwater Habitats by Type: 1998 to 2004

[In thousands of acres (148,618.8 represents 148,618,800). Wetlands and deepwater habitats are defined separately because the term wetland does not include permanent water bodies. Deepwater habitats are permanently flooded land lying below the deepwater boundary of wetlands. Deepwater habitats include environments where surface water is permanent and often deep, so that water, rather than air, is the principal medium within which the dominant organisms live, whether or not they are attached to the substrate. As in wetlands, the dominant plants are hydrophytes; however, the substrates are considered nonsoil because the water is too deep to support emergent vegetation. In general terms, wetlands are lands where saturation with water is the dominant factor determining the nature of soil development and the types of plant and animal communities living in the soil and on its surface. The single feature that most wetlands share is soil or substrate that is at least periodically saturated with or covered by water. Wetlands are lands transitional between terrestrial and aquatic systems where the water table is usually at or near the surface or the land is covered by shallow water. For more information on wetlands, see the "Classification of Wetlands and Deepwater Habitats of the United States" at <http://www.fws.gov/wetlands/_documents/gNSDI/ClassificationWetlandsDeepwaterHabitatsUS.pdf>]

Wetland or deepwater category	Estimated area, 1998	Estimated area, 2004	Change, 1998 to 2004
All wetlands and deepwater habitats, total	**148,618.8**	**149,058.5**	**439.7**
All deepwater habitats, total	41,046.6	41,304.5	247.9
Lacustrine [1]	16,610.5	16,773.4	162.9
Riverine [2]	6,765.5	6,813.3	47.7
Estuarine Subtidal [3]	17,680.5	17,717.8	37.3
All wetlands, total	107,562.3	107,754.0	191.8
Intertidal wetlands [4]	5,328.7	5,300.3	−28.4
Marine intertidal	130.4	128.6	−1.9
Estuarine intertidal nonvegetated	594.1	600.0	5.9
Estuarine intertidal vegetated	4,604.2	4,571.7	−32.4
Freshwater wetlands	102,233.6	102,453.8	220.2
Freshwater nonvegetated	5,918.7	6,633.9	715.3
Freshwater vegetated	96,414.9	95,819.8	−495.1
Freshwater emergent [5]	26,289.6	26,147.0	−142.6
Freshwater forested [6]	51,483.1	52,031.4	548.2
Freshwater shrub [7]	18,542.2	17,641.4	−900.8

[1] The lacustrine system includes deepwater habitats with all of the following characteristics: (1) situated in a topographic depression or a dammed river channel; (2) lacking trees, shrubs, persistent emergents, emergent mosses or lichens with greater than 30 percent coverage; and (3) total area exceeds 20 acres (8 hectares). [2] The riverine system includes deepwater habitats contained within a channel, with the exception of habitats with water containing ocean derived salts in excess of 0.5 parts per thousand. [3] The estuarine system consists of deepwater tidal habitats and adjacent tidal wetlands that are usually semi-enclosed by land but have open, partly obstructed, or sporadic access to the open ocean, and in which ocean water is at least occasionally diluted by freshwater runoff from the land. Subtidal is where the substrate is continuously submerged by marine or estuarine waters. [4] Intertidal is where the substrate is exposed and flooded by tides. Intertidal includes the splash zone of coastal waters. [5] Emergent wetlands are characterized by erect, rooted, herbaceous hydrophytes, excluding mosses and lichens. This vegetation is present for most of the growing season in most years. These wetlands are usually dominated by perennial plants. [6] Forested wetlands are characterized by woody vegetation that is 20 feet tall or taller. [7] Shrub wetlands include areas dominated by woody vegetation less than 20 feet tall. The species include true shrubs, young trees, and trees or shrubs that are small or stunted because of environmental conditions.

Source: U.S. Fish and Wildlife Service, *Status and Trends of Wetlands in the Conterminous United States, 1998 to 2004*, December 2005. See also <http://www.fws.gov/wetlands/_documents/gSandT/NationalReports /StatusTrendsWetlandsConterminousUS1998to2004.pdf>.

Table 367. U.S. Water Withdrawals Per Day by End Use: 1950 to 2005

[(180 represents 180,000,000,000). Includes the District of Columbia, Puerto Rico and U.S. Virgin Islands. Withdrawal signifies water physically withdrawn from a source. Includes fresh and saline water; excludes water used for hydroelectric power. Table has been changed and data have been revised. For information on "Changes for the 2005 report," see "Trends in Estimated Water Use in the United States, Table 14"]

Year	Total with-drawals	Public supply	Rural domestic and livestock — Self supplied domestic	Rural domestic and livestock — Live-stock	Irri-gation	Thermo electric power	Other — Self supplied domestic	Other — Mining	Other — Com-mercial	Other — Aqua-culture
1950 [1]	180	14	2.1	1.5	89	40	37	(5)	(5)	(5)
1955 [2]	240	17	2.1	1.5	110	72	39	(5)	(5)	(5)
1960 [3]	270	21	2.0	1.6	110	100	38	(5)	(5)	(5)
1965 [4]	310	24	2.3	1.7	120	130	46	(5)	(5)	(5)
1970 [4]	370	27	2.6	1.9	130	170	47	(5)	(5)	(5)
1975 [3]	420	29	2.8	2.1	140	200	45	(5)	(5)	(5)
1980 [3]	430	33	3.4	2.2	150	210	45	(5)	(5)	(5)
1985 [3]	397	36.4	3.32	2.23	135	187	25.9	3.44	1.23	2.24
1990 [3]	404	38.8	3.39	2.25	134	194	22.6	4.93	2.39	2.25
1995 [3]	399	40.2	3.39	2.28	130	190	22.4	3.72	2.89	3.22
2000 [3]	413	43.2	3.58	2.38	139	195	19.7	4.50	(NA)	5.77
2005 [3]	410	44.2	3.83	2.14	128	201	18.2	4.02	(NA)	8.78

NA Not available. [1] Population covered: 48 states, District of Columbia, and Hawaii. [2] Population covered: 48 states, [3] Population covered: 50 states, District of Columbia, Puerto Rico, and the Virgin Islands. [4] Population covered: 50 states, District of Columbia, and Puerto Rico. [5] Included in "Self-Supplied Industrial."

Source: 1940–1960, U.S. Bureau of Domestic Business Development, based principally on committee prints, *Water Resources Activities in the United States*, for the Senate Committee on National Water Resources, U.S. Senate, thereafter, U.S. Geological Survey, *Estimated Use of Water in the United States in 2005*, circular I344. See also <http://pubs.usgs.gov/circ/1344/> (October 2009).

226 Geography and Environment

Table 368. National Ambient Air Pollutant Concentrations by Type of Pollutant: 2001 to 2007

[Data represent annual composite averages of pollutant based on daily 24-hour averages of monitoring stations, except carbon monoxide which is based on the second-highest, nonoverlapping, 8-hour average; ozone, the fourth-highest maximum 8-hour value; and lead, the maximum quarterly average of ambient lead levels. Based on data from the Air Quality System. @mg/m³ = micrograms of pollutant per cubic meter of air; ppm = parts per million]

Pollutant	Unit	Monitoring stations, number	Air quality standard [1]	2001	2002	2003	2004	2005	2006	2007
Carbon monoxide	ppm	322	[2] 9	3.3	2.9	2.7	2.5	2.3	2.2	2.0
Ozone	ppm	1,013	[3] 0.075	0.081	0.085	0.080	0.074	0.079	0.077	0.077
Sulfur dioxide	ppm	406	[4] 0.03	0.005	0.004	0.004	0.004	0.004	0.004	0.004
Particulates (PM-10)	µmg/m³	734	[5] 150	86.5	86.8	84.4	69.6	65.2	75.6	68.5
Fine particulates (PM2.5) annual average	µmg/m³	725	[6] 15	13.2	12.7	12.3	11.9	12.9	11.6	11.9
Fine particulates (PM2.5) daily average	µmg/m³	725	[7] 35	34.1	32.9	30.8	30.5	33.5	28.7	30.9
Nitrogen dioxide	ppm	313	[8] 0.053	0.015	0.015	0.014	0.013	0.013	0.013	0.012
Lead	µmg/m³	103	[9] 0.15	0.35	0.17	0.17	0.21	0.16	0.14	0.155

[1] Refers to the primary National Ambient Air Quality Standard. [2] Based on 8-hour standard of 9 ppm. [3] Based on annual standard of 0.03 ppm. [4] Based on 8-hour standard of 0.075 ppm. On March 12, 2008, EPA revised the level of the primary and secondary 8-hour ozone standards to 0.075 ppm. [5] Based on 24-hour (daily) standard of 150 mg/m³. The particulates (PM-10) standard replaced the previous standard for total suspended particulates in 1987. In 2006, EPA revoked the annual PM-10 standard. [6] Based on annual standard of 15 mg/m³. The PM-2.5 national monitoring network was deployed in 1999. National trend data prior to that time is not available. [7] Based on daily standard of 35 mg/m³. The PM-2.5 national monitoring network was deployed in 1999. National trend data prior to that time is not available. [8] Based on annual standard of 0.053 ppm. [9] Based on 3-month standard of 1.5 µmg/m³. On October 15, 2008, EPA revised the form of the primary and secondary lead standards and revised the level to 0.15 mg/m³.

Source: U.S. Environmental Protection Agency, *Latest Findings on National Air Quality—Status and Trends through 2007*, released November 2008, <http://www.epa.gov/air/airtrends/2008/index.html>.

Table 369. Selected National Air Pollutant Emissions: 1970 to 2008

[In thousands of tons (4,320 represents 4,320,000), except as indicated. The methodology used to estimate emission data for 1970 thru 1984 and for 1985 thru the current year is different. Beginning with 1985, the methodology for more recent years is described in the document available at <http://www.epa.gov/ttn/chief/net/2005inventory.html>]

Year	Ammonia	Carbon monoxide	Nitrogen oxide	PM-10 [1]	PM-10 [2]	PM-2.5 [1]	PM-2.5 [2]	Sulfur dioxide	V.O.C. [3]
1970	(NA)	204,042	26,882	13,022	13,022	(NA)	(NA)	31,218	34,659
1980	(NA)	185,408	27,080	7,013	7,013	(NA)	(NA)	25,926	31,107
1990	4,320	154,188	25,527	27,753	27,753	7,560	7,560	23,077	24,108
1995	4,659	126,778	24,955	25,820	25,820	6,929	6,929	18,619	22,042
2000	4,907	114,465	22,599	23,748	22,962	7,287	6,503	16,348	17,511
2004	4,101	99,041	19,793	21,211	18,321	5,497	3,044	14,820	19,789
2005	4,085	93,034	19,122	21,153	18,266	5,457	3,015	14,844	18,422
2006	4,071	87,917	18,111	19,037	16,150	5,269	2,861	13,656	17,590
2007	4,057	82,800	17,318	16,921	14,034	5,080	2,707	13,006	16,759
2008	4,043	77,683	16,366	14,805	11,918	4,892	2,553	11,502	15,927

NA Not available. [1] PM=Particular Matter; PM-10 is equal to or less than ten microns in diameter; PM-2.5 to or less than 2.5 microns effective diameter. [2] Without condensibles. [3] Volatile organic compound.

Source: U.S. Environmental Protection Agency, *National Emissions Inventory (NEI) Air Pollution Emissions Trends Data, 1970–2002*. See <http://www.epa.gov/ttn/chief/trends/index.html#tables>, *Air and Radiation; Air Trends*, <http://www.epa.gov/airtrends/index.html>.

Table 370. Selected Air Pollutant Emissions by Pollutant and Source: 2008

[In thousands of tons, except as indicated (4,043 represents 4,043,000). See headnote, Table 369]

Source	Ammonia	Carbon monoxide	Nitrogen oxide	PM-10 [1]	PM-2.5 [1]	Sulfur dioxide	V.O.C. [2]
Total emissions	4,043	77,683	16,366	14,805	4,892	11,502	15,927
Fuel combustion, stationary sources	68	5,283	5,597	1,330	1,006	9,872	1,450
Electric utilities	34	699	3,033	534	410	7,624	50
Industrial	16	1,216	1,838	330	175	1,670	130
Other fuel combustion	18	3,369	727	466	421	578	1,269
Industrial processes	206	3,767	1,047	1,461	751	1,025	7,142
Chemical and allied product manufacturing	22	265	67	39	29	255	228
Metals processing	3	947	68	78	52	203	46
Petroleum and related industries	3	355	350	24	17	206	561
Other	151	500	418	967	355	329	404
Solvent utilization	–	2	6	8	7	–	4,226
Storage and transport	1	115	18	57	22	4	1,303
Waste disposal and recycling	26	1,584	120	288	267	27	374
Highway vehicles	308	38,866	5,206	171	110	64	3,418
Off highway [3]	3	18,036	4,255	304	283	456	2,586
Miscellaneous [4]	3,457	11,731	260	11,540	2,742	85	1,332

– Rounds to zero. [1] PM=Particular Matter. [2] Volatile organic compound. [3] Includes emissions from farm tractors and other farm machinery, construction equipment, industrial machinery, recreational marine vessels, and small general utility engines such as lawn mowers. [4] Includes emissions such as from forest fires and other kinds of burning, various agricultural activities, fugitive dust from paved and unpaved roads, and other construction and mining activities, and natural sources.

Source: U.S. Environmental Protection Agency, *National Emissions Inventory (NEI) Air Pollution Emissions Trends Data, 1970–2002*, <http://www.epa.gov/ttn/chief/trends/index.html#tables>, *Air and Radiation, Air Trends*, <http://www.epa.gov/airtrends/index.html>.

Table 371. Emissions of Greenhouse Gases by Type and Source: 1990 to 2008

[In millions of metric tons (6,187.4 represents 6,187,400,000). Metric ton = 2,204.6 lbs. Emission estimates were mandated by Congress through Section 1605(a) of the Energy Policy Act of 1992 (Title XVI). Data shown below, by type and source, are measured in terms of their carbon dioxide equivalent. Data have been revised for years shown]

Type and source	1990	1995	2000	2004	2005	2006	2007	2008 [1]
CARBON DIOXIDE EQUIVALENT								
Total emissions	**6,187.4**	**6,522.3**	**7,009.8**	**7,152.1**	**7,182.6**	**7,100.8**	**7,209.8**	**7,052.6**
Carbon dioxide, total	5,022.3	5,341.5	5,886.4	6,009.9	6,029.0	5,928.7	6,017.0	5,839.3
From energy use by sector								
Residential............	958.6	1,035.5	1,179.8	1,221.9	1,254.5	1,186.7	1,235.1	1,220.1
Commercial.............	785.1	845.1	1,013.1	1,043.3	1,059.6	1,034.9	1,070.3	1,075.1
Industrial..............	1,689.5	1,739.5	1,784.7	1,728.5	1,671.4	1,657.8	1,655.2	1,589.1
Transportation	1,586.9	1,682.2	1,872.7	1,958.9	1,988.7	2,014.3	2,025.7	1,930.1
Adjustments to energy [2].....	−82.9	−63.1	−61.7	−44.6	−48.8	−70.9	−74.9	−79.0
Adjusted energy subtotal.....	4,937.2	5,239.1	5,788.7	5,907.9	5,925.5	5,822.8	5,911.5	5,735.5
Other sources	85.1	102.3	97.8	102.0	103.5	106.0	105.6	103.8
Methane...................	783.5	756.2	683.0	686.6	691.8	706.3	722.7	737.4
Energy sources	294.4	284.8	277.6	278.9	274.2	276.7	282.8	295.7
Agricultural sources........	201.5	219.1	211.1	212.5	218.8	221.8	222.6	225.0
Waste management........	283.0	246.8	188.6	189.6	193.7	202.6	212.1	212.1
Industrial processes........	4.6	5.6	5.7	5.6	5.1	5.2	5.2	4.7
Nitrous oxide	279.3	305.6	289.8	302.2	304.0	305.2	299.8	300.3
Agricultural sources........	196.4	199.2	199.1	213.9	217.9	220.8	213.9	217.9
Energy use	51.6	70.4	71.0	71.4	68.8	67.1	66.8	63.9
Industrial processes........	28.8	33.1	16.7	13.7	14.0	14.0	15.9	15.1
Waste management........	2.6	2.8	3.1	3.2	3.3	3.3	3.4	3.4
High-GWP gases [3]..........	102.3	119.0	150.5	153.5	157.8	160.5	170.3	175.6

[1] 2008 preliminary data. [2] Carbon dioxide (CO2) emissions from U.S. Territories are added to the U.S. total, and CO2 emissions from fuels used for international transport (both ocean-going vessels and airplanes) are subtracted to derive total U.S. greenhouse as emissions. [3] High global warming potential gases: hyrdofluorocarbons (HFCs), perfluorocarbons (PFCs), and sulfur hexafluoride (SF6).

Source: U.S. Energy Information Administration, *Greenhouse Gas Emissions in the United States, 2008*, Series DOE/EIA-0573 (2008), annual. See also <http://www.eia.doe.gov/oiaf/1605/ggrpt/index.html>.

Table 372. Carbon Dioxide Emissions by Sector and Source: 1990 to 2008

[In million metric tons (5,022.3 represents 5,022,300,000), except as noted. Data below measured in terms of carbon dioxide equivalent. Data have been revised for years shown]

Sector	1990	2000	2003	2004	2005	2006	2007	2008 [1]
Total [2]	**5,022.3**	**5,886.4**	**5,908.8**	**6,009.9**	**6,029.0**	**5,928.7**	**6,017.0**	**5,839.3**
Petroleum [3]	5,020.1	5,850.4	5,838.6	5,952.5	5,974.3	5,893.7	5,986.4	5,814.4
Natural gas	2,185.9	2,461.3	2,516.7	2,605.4	2,625.7	2,594.9	2,588.6	2,436.0
Coal	1,024.7	1,240.6	1,194.6	1,195.4	1,176.1	1,157.1	1,231.7	1,241.8
Residential	**958.6**	**1,179.8**	**1,224.9**	**1,221.9**	**1,254.5**	**1,186.7**	**1,235.1**	**1,220.1**
Petroleum	99.2	108.6	106.8	107.2	101.1	85.5	86.7	80.1
Natural gas	238.3	270.8	277.5	264.5	262.7	237.5	256.8	265.0
Coal....................	3.0	1.1	1.2	1.1	0.8	0.6	0.7	0.7
Electricity [4].............	618.2	799.3	839.5	849.1	889.9	863.0	890.9	874.4
Commercial	**785.1**	**1,013.1**	**1,026.1**	**1,043.3**	**1,059.6**	**1,034.9**	**1,070.3**	**1,075.1**
Petroleum [5]	70.1	54.7	55.8	54.9	52.4	44.8	44.3	41.4
Natural gas	142.3	172.5	173.7	170.0	163.2	154.0	164.2	169.9
Coal....................	11.8	8.8	7.8	9.8	9.2	6.2	6.7	6.4
Electricity [4].............	560.8	777.2	788.7	808.6	834.8	830.0	855.2	857.3
Industrial	**1,689.5**	**1,784.7**	**1,690.3**	**1,728.5**	**1,671.4**	**1,657.8**	**1,655.2**	**1,589.1**
Petroleum	367.2	373.1	396.5	421.1	419.2	432.5	417.2	385.3
Natural gas	432.5	480.7	431.7	432.0	397.9	394.3	403.6	409.0
Coal....................	256.8	210.0	190.2	190.7	182.0	178.3	173.7	167.5
Electricity [4].............	632.5	713.4	666.1	668.9	667.2	645.8	657.7	622.6
Transportation	**1,586.9**	**1,872.7**	**1,897.4**	**1,958.9**	**1,988.7**	**2,014.3**	**2,025.7**	**1,930.1**
Petroleum [6]	1,547.7	1,833.4	1,859.5	1,922.2	1,950.7	1,976.4	1,985.1	1,889.4
Natural gas	36.1	35.7	33.4	32.0	33.1	33.2	35.4	35.9
Electricity [4].............	3.2	3.6	4.5	4.7	4.9	4.7	5.2	4.9
Electric power sector [7]	**1,814.6**	**2,293.5**	**2,298.8**	**2,331.3**	**2,396.8**	**2,343.5**	**2,409.1**	**2,359.1**
Petroleum	101.8	91.5	98.1	100.1	102.3	55.6	55.3	39.7
Natural gas	175.5	280.9	278.3	296.8	319.1	338.2	371.7	362.0
Coal....................	1,531.2	1,910.8	1,910.7	1,922.9	1,963.9	1,937.8	1,970.6	1,945.9

[1] Preliminary. [2] Includes other items, not shown separately. [3] This includes carbon dioxide from international bunker fuels, both civilian and military, which are excluded from the accounting of carbon dioxide emissions under the United Nations convention. [4] Share of total electric power sector carbon dioxide emissions weighted by sales to this sector. [5] Includes small amounts of petroleum coke. [6] Includes lease and plant fuel. [7] Includes electricity-only and combined heat and power plants whose primary business is to sell electricity, or electricity and heat, to the public. Beginning 2005, also includes emissions from municipal solid waste and geothermal electricity generation. Emissions from the electric power sector are apportioned to each end-use sector according to their share of electricity sales.

Source: "State Energy Data Report"; 1990 to 2000, "Emissions of Greenhouse Gases in the U.S., 2006"; and after, *Annual Energy Outlook*. See also <http://www.eia.doe.gov>.

228 Geography and Environment

Table 373. Municipal Solid Waste Generation, Materials Recovery, Combustion With Energy Recovery, and Discards: 1980 to 2008

[In millions of tons (151.6 represents 151,600,000), except as indicated. Covers post-consumer residential and commercial solid wastes which comprise the major portion of typical municipal collections. Excludes mining, agricultural and industrial processing, demolition and construction wastes, sewage sludge and junked autos and obsolete equipment wastes. Based on material-flows estimating procedure and wet weight as generated]

Item and material	1980	1990	2000	2005	2006	2007	2008
Waste generated	151.6	205.2	239.1	249.7	254.2	254.6	249.6
Per person per day (lb.)	3.7	4.5	4.7	4.6	4.7	4.6	4.5
Total materials recovery	14.5	33.2	69.4	79.2	82.2	84.2	82.9
Per person per day (lb.)	0.4	0.7	1.4	1.5	1.5	1.5	1.5
Recovery for recycling	14.5	29.0	52.9	58.6	61.4	62.5	60.8
Per person per day (pounds)	0.35	0.64	1.03	1.08	1.08	1.14	1.10
Recovery for composting [1]	(Z)	4.2	16.5	20.6	20.8	21.7	22.1
Per person per day (pounds)	(Z)	0.09	0.32	0.38	0.38	0.39	0.40
Combustion with energy recovery	2.7	29.7	33.7	31.6	31.9	32.0	31.6
Per person per day (lb.)	0.07	0.70	0.66	0.58	0.60	0.58	0.57
Discards to landfill, other disposal	134.4	142.3	136.0	138.9	140.1	138.4	135.1
Per person per day (lb.)	3.2	3.1	2.6	2.6	2.6	2.5	2.4
PERCENT DISTRIBUTION OF GENERATION							
Percent of total generation	71.8	71.4	74.5	73.5	73.6	73.3	72.6
Paper and paperboard	36.4	35.4	36.7	34.0	33.6	32.4	31.0
Glass	10.0	6.4	5.3	5.0	5.3	4.9	4.9
Metals	10.2	8.1	7.9	8.0	8.1	8.2	8.4
Plastics	4.5	8.3	10.7	11.7	11.7	12.1	12.0
Rubber and leather	2.8	2.8	2.8	2.9	2.9	3.0	3.0
Textiles	1.7	2.8	3.9	4.6	4.7	4.7	5.0
Wood	4.6	6.0	5.5	5.6	5.5	6.3	6.6
Other	1.7	1.6	1.7	1.7	1.7	1.7	1.8
Total other waste	28.2	28.6	25.5	26.3	26.4	26.7	27.4
Food scraps	8.6	10.1	11.2	12.1	12.2	12.4	12.7
Yard trimmings	18.1	17.1	12.8	12.8	12.7	12.8	13.2
Miscellaneous organic wastes	1.5	1.4	1.5	1.5	1.5	1.5	1.5

Z Less than 5,000 tons or 0.05 percent. [1] Composting of yard trimmings, food scraps, and other municipal solid waste.

Source: Franklin Associates, a Division of ERG, Prairie Village, KS, *Municipal Solid Waste in the United States: 2008 Facts and Figures.* Prepared for the U.S. Environmental Protection Agency. See also <www.epa.gov/osw/nonhaz/municipal/msw99.htm>.

Table 374. Generation and Recovery of Selected Materials in Municipal Solid Waste: 1980 to 2008

[In millions of tons (151.6 represents 151,600,000), except as indicated. Covers post-consumer residential and commercial solid wastes which comprise the major portion of typical municipal collections. Excludes mining, agricultural and industrial processing, demolition and construction wastes, sewage sludge, and junked autos and obsolete equipment wastes. Based on material-flows estimating procedure and wet weight as generated]

Item and material	1980	1990	2000	2005	2006	2007	2008
Waste generated, total [1]	**151.6**	**205.2**	**239.0**	**249.7**	**254.2**	**254.6**	**249.6**
Paper and paperboard	55.2	72.7	87.7	84.8	83.4	82.5	77.4
Glass	15.1	13.1	12.8	12.5	13.5	12.5	12.2
Metals: Ferrous	12.6	12.6	14.1	15.0	15.5	15.6	15.7
Aluminum	1.7	2.8	3.2	3.3	3.4	3.4	3.4
Other nonferrous	1.2	1.1	1.6	1.7	1.8	1.8	1.8
Plastics	6.8	17.1	25.5	29.2	29.8	30.7	30.1
Food scraps	13.0	20.8	26.8	30.2	31.0	31.7	31.8
Yard trimmings	27.5	35.0	30.5	32.1	32.4	32.6	32.9
Materials recovered, total [1]	**14.5**	**33.2**	**69.3**	**79.2**	**82.2**	**84.2**	**82.9**
Paper and paperboard	11.7	20.2	37.6	42.0	43.9	44.5	42.9
Glass	0.8	2.6	2.9	2.6	2.9	2.9	2.8
Metals: Ferrous	0.4	2.2	4.7	5.0	5.3	5.3	5.3
Aluminum	0.3	1.0	0.9	0.7	0.7	0.7	0.7
Other nonferrous	0.5	0.7	1.1	1.2	1.2	1.2	1.2
Plastics	0.2	0.4	1.5	1.8	2.1	2.1	2.1
Food scraps	(Z)	(Z)	0.7	0.7	0.7	0.8	0.8
Yard trimings	(Z)	4.2	15.8	19.9	20.1	20.9	21.3
Percent of generation recovered, total [1]	**9.6**	**16.2**	**29.0**	**31.7**	**32.3**	**33.1**	**33.2**
Paper and paperboard	21.3	27.8	42.8	49.5	51.4	53.9	55.5
Glass	5.0	20.1	22.6	20.7	21.3	23.0	23.1
Metals: Ferrous	2.9	17.6	33.2	33.6	33.9	33.8	33.7
Aluminum	17.9	35.9	26.9	20.7	20.3	21.7	21.1
Other nonferrous	46.6	66.4	66.3	69.0	69.3	69.7	68.8
Plastics	0.3	2.2	5.8	6.0	6.9	6.8	7.1
Food scraps	(Z)	(Z)	2.5	2.3	2.2	2.6	2.5
Yard trimmings	(Z)	12.0	51.7	61.9	62.0	64.1	64.7

Z Less than 5,000 tons or 0.05 percent. [1] Includes products not shown separately.

Source: Franklin Associates, a Division of ERG, Prairie Village, KS, *Municipal Solid Waste in the United States: 2008 Facts and Figures.* Prepared for the U.S. Environmental Protection Agency. See also <www.epa.gov/osw/nonhaz/municipal /msw99.htm>.

Geography and Environment 229

Table 375. Municipal Solid Waste—Generation, Recovery, and Discards by Selected Type of Product: 2008

[See headnote, Table 374]

Type of product	Generation (1,000 tons)	Recovery Products recovered (1,000 tons)	Recovery Percent of generation	Discards (1,000 tons)
Paper and paperboard products [1]	77,410	42,940	55.5	34,470
Nondurable goods	39,120	17,860	45.7	21,260
Newsprint.	6,290	5,510	87.6	780
Groundwood inserts	2,510	2,220	88.4	290
Magazines.	2,050	820	40.0	1,230
Office-type papers.	6,050	4,290	70.9	1,760
Standard mail	5,510	2,240	40.7	3,270
Other commercial printing	5,130	2,200	42.9	2,930
Containers and packaging	38,290	25,080	65.5	13,210
Corrugated boxes	29,710	22,760	76.6	6,950
Folding cartons	5,340	1,880	35.2	3,460
Glass products [1]	12,150	2,810	23.1	9,340
Containers and packaging	10,050	2,810	28.0	7,240
Beer and soft drink bottles.	6,350	2,260	35.6	4,090
Wine and liquor bottles	1,610	240	14.9	1,370
Food and other bottles and jars.	2,090	310	14.8	1,780
Metal products [1].	20,850	7,220	34.6	13,630
Ferrous	15,680	5,290	33.7	10,390
Aluminum.	3,410	720	21.1	2,690
Other nonferrous	1,760	1,210	68.8	550
Plastics [1]	30,050	2,120	7.1	27,930
Plastics in durable goods.	10,520	390	3.7	10,130
Plastics in nondurable goods.	6,520	(Z)	(Z)	6,520
Plastics in containers and packaging	13,010	1,730	13.3	11,280
Rubber and leather [1]	7,410	1,060	14.3	6,350
Rubber in tires.	3,000	1,060	35.3	1,940

Z Less than 5,000 tons or 0.05 percent. [1] Includes products not shown separately.

Source: Franklin Associates, a Division of ERG, Prairie Village, KS, *Municipal Solid Waste in he United States: 2008 Facts and Figures*. Prepared for the U.S. Environmental Protection Agency. See also <www.epa.gov/osw/nonhaz/municipal/msw99.htm>.

Table 376. Environmental Industry—Revenues and Employment by Industry Segment: 2000 to 2009

[211.2 represents $211,200,000,000. Covers approximately 30,000 private and public companies engaged in revenue-generating environmental activities]

Industry segment	Revenue (bil. dol.) 2000	2005	2008	2009	Employment 2000	2005	2008	2009
Industry total	**211.2**	**255.1**	**308.9**	**309.2**	**1,371,600**	**1,548,200**	**1,775,000**	**1,745,100**
Analytical services [1].	1.8	1.8	1.9	1.9	20,200	20,000	21,100	19,700
Wastewater treatment works [2].	28.7	35.6	40.7	41.7	118,800	141,100	164,200	160,000
Solid waste management [3]	39.4	47.8	53.1	54.0	221,400	256,500	300,200	280,700
Hazardous waste management [4].	8.2	8.7	9.2	9.1	44,800	45,000	45,900	44,400
Remediation/industrial services.	10.1	11.0	12.5	12.0	100,200	96,600	111,100	100,600
Consulting and engineering.	17.4	22.4	26.7	26.6	184,000	220,800	270,400	251,300
Water equipment and chemicals	19.8	24.8	28.5	28.7	130,500	153,000	179,800	169,400
Instrument manufacturing	3.8	4.8	5.9	5.7	30,200	35,500	43,300	39,600
Air pollution control equipment [5]	19.0	18.8	18.0	16.7	129,600	123,400	113,900	107,600
Waste management equipment [6].	10.0	10.1	11.4	11.0	75,500	72,900	78,500	73,800
Process and prevention technology.	1.2	1.5	1.9	1.8	29,000	28,100	34,300	28,600
Water utilities [7].	29.9	35.1	39.2	39.5	130,000	145,200	163,300	157,500
Resource recovery [8]	16.0	21.0	28.5	24.7	127,000	156,600	204,900	170,200
Clean energy systems and power [9].	5.9	11.9	31.4	35.8	30,400	53,500	126,800	141,700

[1] Covers environmental laboratory testing and services. [2] Mostly revenues collected by municipal entities for sewage or wastewater plants. [3] Covers such activities as collection, transportation, transfer stations, disposal, landfill ownership and management for solid waste and recyclables. [4] Transportation and disposal of hazardous, medical, and nuclear waste. [5] Includes stationary and mobile sources. [6] Includes vehicles, containers, liners, processing, and remediation equipment. [7] Revenues generated from the sale of water, majority in public sector. [8] Revenues generated from the sale of recovered metals, paper, plastic, etc. [9] Revenues generated from the sale of equipment and systems and electricity.

Source: Environmental Business International, Inc., San Diego, CA, *Environmental Business Journal*, monthly (copyright). See also <http://www.ebiusa.com/>.

Table 377. Toxic Chemical Releases and Transfers by Media: 2003 to 2008

[In millions of pounds (4,447.7 represents 4,447,700,000), except as indicated. Based on reports filed as required by Section 313 of the Emergency Planning and Community Right-to-Know Act (EPCRA, or Title III of the Superfund Amendments and Reauthorization Act of 1986), Public Law 99-499. The Pollution Prevention Act (PPA)of 1990 mandates collection of data on toxic chemicals that are treated on-site, recycled, and combusted for energy recovery. Owners and operators of facilities that are classified within North American Industrial Classification Code groups 31 through 33, 2121, 2122, 2211, 4246, 4247 and 562; have 10 or more full-time employees, and that manufacture, process, or otherwise use any listed toxic chemical in quantities greater than the established threshold in the course of a calendar year are covered and required to report. Includes all Persistent, Toxic (PBT) chemicals and vanadium and vanadium compounds. Does not include off-site disposal or other releases transferred to other TRI facilities that reported the amounts as on-site disposal or other releases. Data for all the years have been revised]

Media	2003	2004	2005	2006	2007	2008
Total facilities reporting	24,593	24,428	24,140	23,543	22,775	21,695
Total on- and off-site disposal or other releases	4,447.7	4,253.6	4,364.7	4,322.7	4,118.7	3,861.3
On-site releases	3,961.5	3,738.1	3,829.5	3,784.6	3,559.8	3,372.4
Air emissions [1]	1,586.3	1,544.1	1,516.4	1,413.5	1,319.8	1,140.9
Surface water discharges	230.8	253.3	256.7	250.0	238.7	246.8
Underground injection class I	207.2	210.3	211.5	199.8	184.1	168.7
Underground injection class II-V	22.0	27.7	20.2	20.1	21.5	18.2
RCRA subtitle C landfills [2]	196.3	151.9	155.2	151.8	150.6	123.0
Other landfills	268.0	267.8	266.9	263.1	267.2	291.4
Land treatment/application farming	18.1	21.5	23.7	26.8	22.0	24.7
Surface impoundments	822.6	719.3	782.0	822.2	764.9	736.4
Other land disposal	610.2	542.1	596.9	637.3	590.9	622.4
Off-site releases	486.2	515.5	535.2	538.1	558.8	488.9
Total transfers offsite for further waste management	3,711.0	4,006.4	3,944.6	3,989.0	3,885.1	3,458.4
Tranfers to recycling	1,916.1	2,085.0	2,095.8	2,181.6	2,142.3	1,935.9
Transfers to energy recovery	649.8	650.4	609.0	555.3	525.4	441.9
Transfers to treatment	279.6	326.6	335.4	328.1	286.5	254.9
Transfers to POTWs (non metals)[3]	270.1	259.9	264.6	260.1	252.5	251.5
Transfers to POTWs metal and metal compounds [3]	1.9	1.7	1.8	1.8	2.0	1.3
Other off-site transfers	0.9	71.5	0.4	0.5	0.2	0.1
Transfers off-site for disposal or other releases	592.5	611.3	637.6	661.5	676.3	572.7
Total production-related waste managed	25,080.0	25,863.8	24,863.3	24,305.5	24,377.3	22,574.6
Recycled on-site	7,143.2	7,135.9	6,719.6	6,822.9	6,878.2	6,649.5
Recycled off-site	1,918.2	2,085.3	2,100.7	2,185.2	2,121.5	1,935.6
Energy recovery on-site	2,649.1	2,617.1	2,462.9	2,392.7	2,286.9	2,164.6
Energy recovery off-site	649.6	649.5	608.9	554.6	523.3	440.7
Treated on-site	7,616.6	8,447.8	7,918.0	7,314.6	7,755.4	6,962.0
Treated off-site	520.0	566.2	574.9	555.7	515.1	477.7
Quantity disposed or otherwise release of on and off site	4,583.4	4,362.1	4,478.3	4,479.9	4,296.9	3,944.6
Non-production-related waste managed	24.8	19.3	24.1	18.1	14.3	37.8

[1] Air emissions include both fugitive and point source. [2] RCRA=Resource Conservation and Recovery Act. [3] POTW (Publicly Owned Treatment Work) is a wastewater treatment facility that is owned by a state or municipality.

Source: U.S. Environmental Protection Agency, Toxic Release Inventory (TRI) Program, *2008 TRI National Analysis*. See also <http://www.epa.gov/tri/tridata/tri08/national_analysis/index.htm>.

Table 378. Toxic Chemical Releases by Industry: 2008

[In millions of pounds (3,861.3 represents 3,861,300,000), except as indicated. See headnote, Table 377]

Industry	2002 NAICS [1] code	Total on- and off-site releases	On-site releases Total	On-site releases Air emissions	On-site releases Other surface impound- ments	Off-site releases/ transfers to disposal [2]
Total [3]	(X)	3,861.3	3,372.4	1,140.9	732.2	488.9
Coal mining	2121	13.5	13.5	0.7	0.3	(Z)
Metal mining	2122	1,157.7	1,154.7	3.7	574.9	3.0
Electric utilities	2211	904.8	819.8	524.6	107.4	85.0
Food/beverages/tobacco	311/312	166.8	158.0	46.8	0.1	8.8
Textiles	313/314	2.4	1.8	1.4	0.1	0.6
Apparel	315	–	(Z)	(Z)	–	(Z)
Leather	316	1.3	0.4	0.3	–	0.9
Wood products	321	14.4	13.4	13.1	(Z)	1.0
Paper	322	186.1	178.8	139.4	3.6	7.4
Printing and publishing	323/51	10.3	10.0	10.0	–	0.3
Petroleum	324	72.8	68.6	41.1	(Z)	4.2
Chemicals	325	468.0	419.6	166.3	13.5	48.4
Plastics and rubber	326	49.2	38.8	38.4	(Z)	10.4
Stone/clay/glass	327	25.4	22.3	18.2	0.1	3.1
Cement	32731	9.1	9.0	7.4	(Z)	0.1
Primary metals	331	440.6	193.4	41.0	30.2	247.2
Fabricated metals	332	54.5	31.3	27.1	(Z)	23.3
Machinery	333	9.9	7.4	7.3	–	2.5
Computers/electronic products	334	7.7	5.0	2.1	–	2.7
Electrical equipment	335	7.0	2.8	2.8	(Z)	4.2
Transportation equipment	336	38.4	31.2	30.5	(Z)	7.2
Furniture	337	6.9	6.7	6.7	–	0.2
Miscellaneous Manufacturing	339	5.3	3.2	3.2	–	2.0
Chemical wholesalers	4246	1.6	1.2	1.2	–	0.4
Petroleum bulk terminals	4247	5.2	5.1	5.0	(Z)	0.1
Hazardous waste	562	167.1	143.0	0.6	0.5	24.1
No codes [3]	(X)	35.5	33.7	2.0	1.4	1.9

– Represents zero. X Not applicable. Z less than 50,000 lbs. [1] North American Industry Classification System, see text, Section 12. [2] Includes off-site disposal to underground injection for Class I wells, Class II to V wells, other surface impoundments, land releases, and other releases, not shown separately. [3] Includes industries with no specific industry identified.

Source: U.S. Environmental Protection Agency, *2008 TRI National Analysis*. See also <http://www.epa.gov/tri/tridata/tri08/national_analysis/index.htm>.

Geography and Environment 231

Table 379. Toxic Chemical Releases by State and Outlying Area: 2008

[In millions of pounds (3,861.3 represents 3,861,300,000). Based on reports filed as required by Section 313 of the EPCRA. See headnote, Table 377]

State and outlying areas	Total on-and off-site releases	On-site Releases or other Disposal			Off-site releases/ trans-fers to disposal	State and outlying areas	Total on-and off-site releases	On-site Releases or other Disposal			Off-site releases/ trans-fers to disposal
		Total [1]	Air emis-sions	Other surface im-pound-ments				Total [1]	Air emis-sions	Other surface im-pound-ments	
Total.....	3,861.3	3,372.4	1,140.9	732.2	488.9	MT	47.1	45.7	3.4	14.0	1.3
U.S. total ...	3,855.0	3,366.7	1,135.5	732.2	488.4	NE	33.7	30.3	8.4	(Z)	3.5
AL	113.3	86.8	40.0	17.8	26.6	NV	202.3	200.5	1.3	105.9	1.8
AK	567.8	567.6	0.6	221.7	0.2	NH	3.1	2.8	2.8	(Z)	0.3
AZ	95.1	93.8	3.6	17.8	1.3	NJ	18.0	15.6	6.1	–	2.4
AR	40.5	36.4	16.2	2.1	4.1	NM	19.1	19.0	1.1	1.3	0.1
CA	42.3	38.5	12.5	(Z)	3.8	NY	32.5	24.3	11.2	3.1	8.2
CO	21.6	17.2	2.8	3.6	4.4	NC	92.9	84.6	56.8	5.1	8.3
CT	4.0	2.5	2.2	(Z)	1.5	ND	22.5	14.6	4.3	5.9	7.9
DE	12.6	9.4	5.8	(Z)	3.1	OH	224.0	180.8	90.1	11.5	43.2
DC	0.1	0.1	(Z)	0.1	(Z)	OK	33.4	29.5	13.7	0.4	3.9
FL	77.6	73.5	46.1	0.6	4.2	OR	18.9	17.5	9.4	(Z)	1.4
GA	104.6	102.3	71.5	16.7	2.3	PA	150.7	96.3	73.7	0.5	54.4
HI	3.2	2.9	2.3	–	0.2	RI.	0.4	0.2	0.2	–	0.2
ID	69.2	68.3	3.7	15.0	1.0	SC	65.0	55.9	42.1	3.6	9.1
IL	115.1	79.2	37.3	5.6	35.9	SD	7.6	7.0	1.6	(Z)	0.6
IN........	209.3	112.2	55.0	6.7	97.1	TN	112.3	95.4	43.2	26.9	16.9
IA........	43.0	34.9	22.4	1.5	8.1	TX	207.1	184.0	69.1	4.2	23.1
KS	24.6	20.4	10.0	0.4	4.1	UT	215.0	212.3	9.2	141.8	2.6
KY	92.7	81.9	56.4	8.2	10.9	VT	0.3	0.2	(Z)	–	0.1
LA	139.3	129.9	51.8	4.5	9.4	VA	64.8	59.1	34.5	1.4	5.7
ME	10.4	9.1	4.6	–	1.3	WA	30.7	24.9	7.5	12.1	5.7
MD......	49.9	46.0	40.6	(Z)	4.0	WV	71.8	64.7	46.5	2.6	7.2
MA......	5.8	3.9	3.8	(Z)	1.9	WI	42.8	26.4	17.5	(Z)	16.4
MI........	95.7	67.7	45.3	6.4	28.0	WY	20.0	18.8	2.2	1.1	1.2
MN......	26.1	23.2	10.8	2.4	3.0						
MS......	67.7	64.7	19.3	10.7	3.0	Puerto Rico ..	5.2	4.7	4.6	–	0.5
MO......	87.5	84.2	15.1	49.1	3.3						

– Represents zero. Z Less than 50,000 lbs. [1] Includes other types of release not shown separately.

Source: U.S. Environmental Protection Agency, Toxic Release Inventory (TRI) Program, *2008 TRI National Analysis*. See also <http://www.epa.gov/tri/tridata/tri08/national_analysis/index.htm>.

Table 380. Hazardous Waste Sites on the National Priority List by State and Outlying Area: 2008

[As of December 31. Includes both proposed and final sites listed on the National Priorities List for the Superfund program as authorized by the Comprehensive Environmental Response, Compensation, and Liability Act (CERCLA) of 1980 and the Superfund Amendments and Reauthorization Act (SARA) of 1986. For information on CERCLA and SARA, see also <http://www.epa.gov/superfund/policy/cercla.htm>]

State and outlying areas	Total sites	Rank	Per-cent distri-bution	Federal	Non-fed-eral	State and outlying areas	Total sites	Rank	Per-cent distri-bution	Fed-eral	Non-fed-eral
Total............	1,318	(X)	(X)	163	1,155	Missouri.........	29	16	2.3	3	26
United States	1,301	(X)	(X)	161	1,140	Nebraska........	13	32	1.0	1	12
Alabama	15	26	1.2	3	12	Nevada	1	49	0.1	–	1
Alaska	5	45	0.4	5	–	New Hampshire...	21	19	1.7	1	20
Arizona	9	39	0.7	2	7	New Jersey	116	1	9.3	8	108
Arkansas..........	9	40	0.7	–	9	New Mexico......	14	29	1.1	1	13
California..........	97	2	7.8	24	73	New York	86	4	6.9	4	82
Colorado	20	20	1.6	3	17	North Carolina....	32	13	2.6	2	30
Connecticut	15	24	1.2	1	14	North Dakota.....	–	50	–	–	–
Delaware	14	27	1.1	1	13	Ohio.............	40	10	3.2	5	35
District of Columbia...	1	(X)	0.1	1	–	Oklahoma	9	42	0.7	1	8
Florida............	52	6	4.2	6	46	Oregon..........	12	36	1.0	2	10
Georgia...........	16	23	1.3	2	14	Pennsylvania.....	96	3	7.7	6	90
Hawaii	3	46	0.2	2	1	Rhode Island.....	12	37	1.0	2	10
Idaho.............	9	41	0.7	2	7	South Carolina....	26	17	2.1	2	24
Illinois............	49	7	3.9	5	44	South Dakota.....	2	47	0.2	1	1
Indiana............	31	14	2.5	–	31	Tennessee.......	14	30	1.1	4	10
Iowa..............	12	33	1.0	1	11	Texas...........	49	8	3.9	4	45
Kansas............	12	34	1.0	1	11	Utah............	19	22	1.5	4	15
Kentucky..........	14	28	1.1	1	13	Vermont.........	11	38	0.9	0	11
Louisiana..........	13	31	1.0	1	12	Virginia..........	30	15	2.4	11	19
Maine.............	12	35	1.0	3	9	Washington	48	9	3.8	13	35
Maryland..........	19	21	1.5	10	9	West Virginia	9	43	0.7	2	7
Massachusetts.......	32	12	2.6	6	26	Wisconsin.......	38	11	3.0	–	38
Michigan	67	5	5.4	1	66	Wyoming	2	48	0.2	1	1
Minnesota	25	18	2.0	2	23						
Mississippi.........	6	44	0.5	–	6	Puerto Rico	13	(X)	(X)	1	12

– Represents zero. X Not applicable.

Source: U.S. Environmental Protection Agency, Supplementary Materials: CERCLIS3/WasteLan Database, published July 2009. See also <http://www.epa.gov/osw/inforesources/data/biennialreport/>.

Table 381. Hazardous Waste Generated, Shipped, and Received by State and Other Areas: 2007

[In thousands of tons (32,269.7 represents 32,269,700). Covers hazardous waste regulated under the Resource Conservation and Recovery Act (RCRA) of 1976 as amended. The data have been revised. See source for exclusions of data from the 2007 National Biennial RCRA Hazardous Waste Report]

State and other areas	Hazardous waste quantity (1,000) tons			State and other areas	Hazardous waste quantity (1,000) tons		
	Generated	Shipped	Received		Generated	Shipped	Received
Total.............	**32,269.7**	**7,010.7**	**7,176.1**	Nebraska..........	38.7	39.9	32.4
				Nevada...........	10.0	14.5	112.7
United States.......	**32,206.3**	**655.0**	**713.3**	New Hampshire.....	5.4	5.4	–
				New Jersey........	596.1	596.8	220.8
Alabama..........	898.1	206.1	136.9	New Mexico........	5.6	6.2	4.8
Alaska...........	2.5	2.1	–	New York.........	1,267.6	274.6	201.0
Arizona...........	56.7	54.1	46.5	North Carolina......	96.9	103.1	18.6
Arkansas..........	495.8	324.4	358.5	North Dakota......	538.6	1.2	0.3
California..........	540.9	631.6	491.0	Ohio..............	1,612.0	717.7	804.0
Colorado..........	54.9	40.0	34.4	Oklahoma.........	134.4	42.3	69.2
Connecticut.........	30.4	38.3	42.2	Oregon...........	75.0	64.2	65.1
Delaware..........	19.7	19.4	0.1	Pennsylvania.......	388.8	295.7	437.8
District of Columbia....	0.8	0.8	–	Rhode Island.......	4.6	9.4	6.4
Florida...........	152.7	55.8	23.7	South Carolina.....	151.4	189.2	187.8
Georgia...........	102.6	53.2	5.7	South Dakota......	0.8	0.9	0.1
Hawaii...........	1.1	1.1	0.2	Tennessee........	220.0	56.9	31.0
Idaho.............	5.6	8.1	456.6	Texas.............	13,406.4	706.2	493.9
Illinois...........	1,122.9	235.9	420.4	Utah.............	82.8	88.6	134.8
Indiana...........	958.0	404.8	510.0	Vermont..........	3.0	2.5	0.3
Iowa.............	49.0	48.8	0.4	Virginia...........	94.9	83.8	18.0
Kansas...........	125.6	121.0	221.2	Washington........	147.2	65.7	40.8
Kentucky..........	139.9	167.6	75.1	West Virginia......	76.6	49.5	13.5
Louisiana..........	5,010.8	474.1	352.3	Wisconsin........	310.3	155.6	55.4
Maine.............	5.3	5.1	0.6	Wyoming..........	4.0	4.0	–
Maryland..........	43.6	46.8	43.2				
Massachusetts........	185.6	60.9	94.3	Guam............	0.1	0.1	0.1
Michigan..........	340.5	237.4	430.3	Navajo Nation.....	–	–	–
Minnesota.........	94.4	56.2	249.7	Puerto Rico.......	60.0	42.8	2.7
Mississippi..........	2,239.7	21.5	55.7	Virgin Islands......	3.2	3.1	–
Missouri..........	228.1	66.4	175.7				
Montana...........	29.5	9.4	–				

– Represents or rounds to zero.

Source: U.S. Environmental Protection Agency, *The National Biennial RCRA Hazardous Waste Report (Based on 2007 Data),* Series EPA530-R-03-007. See also <http://www.epa.gov/epawaste/inforesources/data/biennialreport/index.htm>.

Table 382. Oil Spills in U.S. Water—Number and Volume: 2000 to 2009

[These summary statistics are based on reported discharges of oil and petroleum based products into U.S. navigable waters, including territorial waters (extending 3 to 12 miles from the coastline), tributaries, the contiguous zone, onto shoreline, or into other waters that threaten the marine environment. Spills associated with Hurricanes Katrina and Rita have been excluded]

Spill characteristic	Number of spills				Spill volume (millions)			
	2000	2005	2008	2009	2000	2005	2008	2009
Total.................	**8,354**	**4,073**	**3,633**	**3,492**	**1,431,370**	**2,364,169**	**777,039**	**195,189**
Size of spill (gallons):								
1 to 100...............	8,058	3,857	3,474	3,351	39,355	33,041	25,335	24,428
101 to 1,000............	219	166	130	123	78,779	62,357	50,486	46,062
1,001 to 3,000..........	37	26	12	9	67,529	46,019	22,130	20,907
3,001 to 5,000..........	12	9	8	2	45,512	36,803	30,396	6,872
5,001 to 10,000.........	16	7	3	3	112,415	58,453	21,800	21,400
10,001 to 50,000........	6	5	3	4	108,400	106,870	73,600	75,520
50,001 to 100,000.......	4	1	1	–	266,380	84,000	82,274	–
100,001 to 1,000,000......	2	1	2	–	713,000	110,000	471,018	–
1,000,000 and over.......	–	1	–	–	–	1,826,626	–	–
Source:								
Tankship................	111	40	36	34	608,176	2,975	1,338	14,415
Tankbarge..............	229	130	184	166	133,540	2,006,774	288,029	5,678
All other vessels.........	5,220	1,789	1,577	1,585	291,927	115,906	263,632	92,388
Facilities................	1,054	996	1,048	963	311,604	92,399	170,299	38,299
Pipelines...............	25	20	18	17	17,021	111,253	14,494	1,739
All other nonvessels.......	566	264	297	312	45,136	13,422	29,056	27,557
Unknown...............	1,149	834	473	415	23,966	21,440	10,191	15,113

– Represents zero.

Source: U.S. Coast Guard, *Pollution Incidents In and Around U.S. Waters, A Spill/Release Compendium: 1969–2004,* and *2004–2009: U.S. Coast Guard Marine Information for Safety and Law Enforcement (MISLE).* Data are unpublished. See <http://homeport.uscg.mil/mycg/portal/ep/home.do\>.

Geography and Environment 233

Table 383. Threatened and Endangered Wildlife and Plant Species: 2010

[As of April. Endangered species: One in danger of becoming extinct throughout all or a significant part of its natural range. Threatened species: One likely to become endangered in the foreseeable future]

Item	Mammals	Birds	Reptiles	Amphibians	Fishes	Snails	Clams	Crustaceans	Insects	Arachnids	Plants
Total listings.............	360	281	119	34	152	36	72	22	64	12	762
Endangered species, total ...	**325**	**258**	**79**	**22**	**85**	**25**	**64**	**19**	**54**	**12**	**616**
United States..............	70	76	13	14	74	24	62	19	50	12	615
Foreign	255	182	66	8	11	1	2	–	4	–	1
Threatened species, total	**35**	**23**	**40**	**12**	**67**	**11**	**8**	**3**	**10**	**–**	**146**
United States..............	15	16	24	11	66	11	8	3	10	–	146
Foreign	20	7	16	1	1	–	–	–	–	–	–

– Represents zero.

Source: U.S. Fish and Wildlife Service, *Endangered Species Bulletin*, bimonthly. See also <http://ecos.fws.gov /tess_public/pub/listedanimals.jsp>, accessed May 2010.

Table 384. Tornadoes, Floods, Tropical Storms, and Lightning: 1995 to 2008

Weather type	1995	2000	2001	2002	2003	2004	2005	2006	2007	2008
Tornadoes: [1]										
Number	1,235	1,071	1,216	941	1,376	1,819	1,264	1,106	1,098	1,691
Lives lost	30	41	40	55	54	35	38	67	81	126
Injuries.................	650	882	743	968	1,087	396	537	990	659	1,714
Property loss (mil. dol.)	411	424	630	801	1,263	537	422	752	1,408	1,844
Floods and flash floods:										
Lives lost	80	38	48	49	85	82	43	76	70	82
Injuries.................	57	47	277	88	65	128	38	23	51	46
Property loss (mil. dol.)	1,251	1,255	1,220	655	2,541	1,696	1,538	3,768	1,278	3,406
North Atlantic tropical										
cyclones and hurricanes [2] ..	19	15	15	12	21	16	27	9	17	17
Hurricanes	11	8	9	4	7	9	15	5	6	8
Lives lost...............	17	–	24	51	14	34	1,016	–	1	12
Property loss (bil.dol.).....	5.9	8.1	5.2	1.1	1.9	18.9	93.0	2.4	38.8	7.6
Lightning:										
Deaths.................	85	51	44	51	44	32	38	48	45	27
Injuries.................	433	364	371	256	237	280	309	246	138	216

– Represents zero. [1] Source: U.S. National Weather Service, <http://www.spc.noaa.gov/climo/torn/monthlytornstats.html>. A violent, rotating column of air descending from a cumulonimbus cloud in the form of a tubular- or funnel-shaped cloud, usually characterized by movements along a narrow path and wind speeds from 100 to over 300 miles per hour. Also known as a "twister" or "waterspout." [2] Source: National Hurricane Center (NHC), Coral Gables, FL, unpublished data. For data on individual hurricanes, see <http://www.nhc.noaa.gov/>.

Source: Except as noted, U.S. National Oceanic and Atmospheric Administration (NOAA), National Weather Service (NWS), *Office of Climate, Water, and Weather Services, Natural Hazard Statistics*, monthly. See also <http://www.nws.noaa.gov /om/hazstats.shtml>.

Table 385. Number of Earthquakes in the United States: 2000 to 2009

[The United States Geological Survey (USGS) detects but does not generally locate mine blasts (explosions) throughout the United States on any given business day. For more information, see "Routine United States Mining Seismicity." For information on "Top Earthquake States," see <http://earthquake.usgs.gov/earthquakes/states/top_states.php>]

Magnitude	2000	2001	2002	2003	2004	2005	2006	2007	2008	2009 [1]	Top earthquake states	1974–2003 [2]
Total	**2,342**	**2,261**	**3,876**	**2,946**	**3,550**	**3,685**	**2,783**	**2,791**	**3,618**	**4,256**	**Total**	**21,080**
8.0 to 9.9	–	–	–	–	–	–	–	–	–	–	AK	[3] 12,053
7.0 to 7.9	–	1	1	2	–	1	–	1	–	–	CA	4,895
6.0 to 6.9	6	5	4	7	2	4	7	9	9	4	HI	1,533
5.0 to 5.9	63	41	63	54	25	47	51	72	85	52	NE	778
4.0 to 4.9	281	290	536	541	284	345	346	366	432	296	WA	424
3.0 to 3.9	917	842	1,535	1,303	1,362	1,475	1,213	1,137	1,486	1,491	ID	404
2.0 to 2.9	660	646	1,228	704	1,336	1,738	1,145	1,173	1,573	2,370	WY	217
1.0 to 1.9	–	2	2	2	1	2	7	11	13	26	MT	186
0.1 to 0.9	–	–	–	–	–	–	1	–	–	1	UT	139
No magnitude ...	415	434	507	333	540	73	13	22	20	16	OR	73

– Represents zero. [1] Data are as of July 20, 2010. [2] The total number represents earthquakes of a magnitude range of 3.5 and greater. [3] The number of earthquakes is underreported. Events in the magnitude range of 3.5 to 4.0 in the Aleutian Islands are not recorded on enough seismograph stations to be located.

Source: U.S. Geological Survey, *Earthquake Facts and Statistics*. See <http://earthquake.usgs.gov/earthquakes/eqarchives /year/eqstats.php>

Table 386. Wildland Fires, Number, and Acres: 1970 to 2009

[In thousands (3,279 represents 3,279,000), except as indicated. As of December 31. There are three distinct types of wildland fires: wildfire, wildland fire use, and prescribed fire. Wildland fire is any nonstructure fire that occurs in the wildland]

Year	Total [1] Fires (number)	Total [1] Acres (1,000)	Year	Total [1] Fires (number)	Total [1] Acres (1,000)	State	Wildland [1] Fires	Wildland [1] Acres	Prescribed [2] Fires	Prescribed [2] Acres
1970.....	121,736	3,279	2000.....	92,250	7,393	Total....	78,792	5,921,786	12,429	2,531,133
1975.....	134,872	1,791	2001.....	84,079	3,571	AK.....	527	2,951,597	1	290
1980.....	234,892	5,261	2002.....	73,457	7,185	TX.....	16,614	753,261	151	172,826
1985.....	82,591	2,896	2003.....	63,629	3,961	NM.....	1,278	421,481	76	99,132
1990.....	66,481	4,622	2004 [3]...	65,461	8,098	CA.....	9,159	405,585	841	93,940
1994.....	79,107	4,074	2005.....	66,753	8,689	AZ.....	2,371	263,358	2,097	147,531
1995.....	82,234	1,841	2006.....	96,385	9,874	OK.....	1,773	153,948	14	5,383
1996.....	96,363	6,066	2007.....	85,705	9,328	FL.....	2,797	124,401	1,090	512,350
1997.....	66,196	2,857	2008.....	78,979	5,292	UT.....	1,136	112,753	147	28,173
1998.....	81,043	1,330	2009.....	78,792	5,922	OR.....	1,488	100,668	750	130,654
1999.....	92,487	5,626				WA.....	1,976	77,250	135	26,419

[1] Data are for wildland fires only. The data do not include wildland fire use and prescribed fires. [2] Prescribed fire is any fire which are ignited by management action under certain predetermined conditions to meet specific objectives related to hazardous fuels or habitat improvement. [3] 2004 fires and acres do not include state lands for North Carolina.

Source: National Interagency Coordination Center, "Wildland Fires and Acres (1960–2009)," <http://www.nifc.gov/fire_info /fires_acres.htm\>, accessed February 2010.

Table 387. Highest and Lowest Temperatures by State Through 2003

State	Highest temperatures Station	Highest temperatures Temperature (F)	Highest temperatures Date	Lowest temperatures Station	Lowest temperatures Temperature (F)	Lowest temperatures Date
AL	Centerville	112	Sep. 5, 1925	New Market	−27	Jan. 30, 1966
AK	Fort Yukon	100 [1]	Jun. 27, 1915	Prospect Creek Camp...	−80	Jan. 23, 1971
AZ	Lake Havasu City........	128	Jun. 29, 1994	Hawley Lake	−40	Jan. 7, 1971
AR	Ozark.................	120	Aug. 10, 1936	Pond	−29	Feb. 13, 1905
CA	Greenland Ranch	134	Jul. 10, 1913	Boca	−45	Jan. 20, 1937
CO	Bennett	118	Jul. 11, 1888	Maybell	−61	Feb. 1, 1985
CT	Danbury...............	106	Jul. 15, 1995	Coventry	−32 [2]	Jan. 22, 1961
DE	Millsboro	110	Jul. 21, 1930	Millsboro	−17	Jan. 17, 1893
FL	Monticello	109	Jun. 29, 1931	Tallahassee	−2	Feb. 13, 1899
GA	Greenville	112	Aug. 20, 1983	CCC Camp F-16	−17 [1]	Jan. 27, 1940
HI	Pahala	100	Apr. 27, 1931	Mauna Kea Obs. 111.2 ..	12	May 17, 1979
ID	Orofino...............	118	Jul. 28, 1934	Island Park Dam	−60	Jan. 18, 1943
IL	East St. Louis..........	117	Jul. 14, 1954	Congerville	−36	Jan. 5, 1999
IN	Collegeville	116	Jul. 14, 1936	New Whiteland.........	−36	Jan. 19, 1994
IA	Keokuk...............	118	Jul. 20, 1934	Elkader	−47 [2]	Feb. 3, 1996
KS	Alton (near)	121 [2]	Jul. 24, 1936	Lebanon..............	−40	Feb. 13, 1905
KY	Greensburg	114	Jul. 28, 1930	Shelbyville	−37	Jan. 19, 1994
LA	Plain Dealing	114	Aug. 10, 1936	Minden...............	−16	Feb. 13, 1899
ME......	North Bridgton..........	105 [2]	Jul. 10, 1911	Van Buren	18	Jan. 19, 1925
MD......	Cumberland & Frederick ..	109 [2]	Jul. 10, 1936	Oakland..............	−40	Jan. 13, 1912
MA......	New Bedford & Chester...	107	Aug. 2, 1975	Chester	−35	Jan. 12, 1981
MI.......	Mio..................	112	Jul. 13, 1936	Vanderbilt............	−51	Feb. 9, 1934
MN......	Moorhead	114 [2]	Jul. 6, 1936	Tower................	−60	Feb. 2, 1996
MS......	Holly Springs	115	Jul. 29, 1930	Corinth..............	−19	Jan. 30, 1966
MO......	Warsaw & Union	118 [2]	Jul. 14, 1954	Warsaw	−40	Feb. 13, 1905
MT......	Medicine Lake	117	Jul. 5, 1937	Rogers Pass	−70	Jan. 20, 1954
NE......	Minden...............	118 [2]	Jul. 24, 1936	Oshkosh	−47 [2]	Dec. 22, 1989
NV......	Laughlin..............	125 [2]	Jun. 29, 1994	San Jacinto	−50	Jan. 8, 1937
NH......	Nashua	106	Jul. 4, 1911	Mt. Washington	−47	Jan. 29, 1934
NJ	Runyon	110	Jul. 10, 1936	River Vale	−34	Jan. 5, 1904
NM......	Waste Isolat Pilot Plt	122	Jun. 27, 1994	Gavilan	−50	Feb. 1, 1951
NY	Troy.................	108	Jul. 22, 1926	Old Forge............	−52 [2]	Feb. 18, 1979
NC	Fayetteville............	110	Aug. 21, 1983	Mt. Mitchell...........	−34	Jan. 21, 1985
ND	Steele	121	Jul. 6, 1936	Parshall	−60	Feb. 15, 1936
OH	Gallipolis (near)	113 [2]	Jul. 21, 1934	Milligan	−39	Feb. 10, 1899
OK	Tipton................	120	Jun. 27, 1994	Watts	−27 [2]	Jan. 18, 1930
OR	Pendleton.............	119 [2]	Aug. 10, 1898	Seneca	−54 [2]	Feb. 10, 1933
PA	Phoenixville...........	111 [2]	Jul. 10, 1936	Smethport	−42 [1]	Jan. 5, 1904
RI.......	Providence............	104	Aug. 2, 1975	Greene..............	−25	Feb. 5, 1996
SC	Camden...............	111 [2]	Jun. 28, 1954	Caesars Head	−19	Jan. 21, 1985
SD	Gannvalley............	120	Jul. 5, 1936	McIntosh	−58	Feb. 17, 1936
TN	Perryville	113 [2]	Aug. 9, 1930	Mountain City..........	−32	Dec. 30, 1917
TX	Monahans	120 [2]	Jun. 28, 1994	Seminole	−23 [2]	Feb. 8, 1933
UT	Saint George	117	Jul. 5, 1985	Peter's Sink	−69	Feb. 1, 1985
VT	Vernon...............	105	Jul. 4, 1911	Bloomfield	−50	Dec. 30, 1933
VA	Balcony Falls	110	Jul. 15, 1954	Mtn. Lake Bio. Stn.	−30	Jan. 22, 1985
WA......	Ice Harbor Dam	118 [2]	Aug. 5, 1961	Mazama & Winthrop	−48	Dec. 30, 1968
WV......	Martinsburg...........	112 [2]	Jul. 10, 1936	Lewisburg	−37	Dec. 30, 1917
WI	Wisconsin Dells	114	Jul. 13, 1936	Couderay............	−55	Feb. 4, 1996
WY	Basin................	115	Aug. 8, 1983	Riverside R.S.	−66	Feb. 9, 1933

[1] Also on earlier dates at the same or other places [2] Estimated.

Source: U.S. National Oceanic and Atmospheric Administration, National Environmental Satellite, Data, and Information Services (NESDIS), National Climatic Data Center (NCDC), *Temperature Extremes and Drought,*<http://www.ncdc .noaa.gov/oa/climate/severeweather/temperatures.html\>.

U.S. Census Bureau, Statistical Abstract of the United States: 2011

Table 388. Major U.S. Weather Disasters: 2006 to 2009

[5.0 represents $5,000,000,000. Covers only weather-related disasters costing $1 billion or more]

Event	Description	Time period	Estimated cost [1] (bil.dol.)	Deaths (number)
2009 Southwest/Great Plains drought....	Drought conditions occurred during much of the year causing agricultural losses in TX, OK, KS, CA, NM, and AZ. The largest losses occurred in TX and CA.	Entire year 2009	Over 5.0	–
Western wildfires..............	Residual and sustained drought conditions across western and south-central states resulted in thousands of fires. Most affected states include CA, AZ, NM, TX, OK, and UT.	Summer–Fall 2009	Over 1.0	10
Midwest, South, and Eastern severe weather	Sustained outbreak of thunderstorms and high winds in TX, OK, MO, NE, KS, AR, AL, MS, TN, NC, SC, KY, and PA.	June 2009	Over 1.1	–
South/Southeast tornadoes and severe weather	Outbreak of tornadoes, hail and severe thunderstorms in AL, AR, GA, KY, MO, SC, TN—with 85 tornadoes confirmed.	April 2009	Over 1.2	6
Midwest/Southeast tornadoes ...	Outbreak of tornadoes in NE, KS, OK, IA, TX LA, MS, AL, GA, TN, KY—with 56 tornadoes confirmed.	March 2009	Over 1.0	–
Southeast/Ohio Valley severe weather	Complex of severe thunderstorms and high winds in TN, KY, OK, OH, VA, WV, and PA. The majority of the damage occurred in OK and OH.	February 2009	Over 1.4	10
2008 widespread drought	Severe drought and heat caused agricultural losses in areas of the South and West. Record low lake levels. Also occurred in areas of the Southeast. Includes states of CA, GA, NC, SC, TN, and TX.	Entire year 2008	Over 2.0	–
Hurricane Ike	Category 2 hurricane made landfall in Texas as the largest (in size) Atlantic hurricane on record, causing wind and considerable surge in coastal and significant flooding damage in AR, IL, IN, KY, LA, MO, OH, PA, and TX.	September 2008	Over 27.0	82
Hurricane Gustav.............	Category 2 hurricane made landfall in Louisiana causing significant wind, storm surge and flood damage in AL, AR, LA, and MS.	September 2008	5.0	43
Hurricane Dolly	Category 2 hurricane made landfall in southern Texas causing considerable wind and flooding damage in TX and NM.	July 2008	Over 1.2	3
U.S. wildfires	Drought conditions across numerous Western, Central and Southeastern states (15) resulted in thousands of wildfires, national acreage burned exceeding 5.2 million acres (mainly in the West).	Summer–Fall 2008	Over 2.0	16
Midwest flood.............	Heavy rainfall and flooding caused significant agricultural loss and property damage in seven states with Iowa being hardest hit with widespread rainfall totals ranging from 4 to 16 inches.	June 2008	Over 15.0	24
Midwest/Mid-Atlantic storms	An outbreak of tornadoes and thunderstorms over the states of IA, IL, IN, KS, NE, MD, MI, MN, MO, OK, VA, WI, WV.	June 2008	Over 1.1	18
Midwest/Ohio Valley storms.......	Outbreak of tornadoes over the Midwest/Ohio Valley over the region (IL, IN, IA KS, MN, NE, OK, WY, and CO)—with 235 tornadoes confirmed.	May 2008	Over 2.4	13
Southeast/Midwest tornadoes	Series of tornadoes and severe thunderstorms across the Southeast and Midwest states (AL, AR, IN, KY, MS, OH, TN, TX)—with 87 tornadoes confirmed.	February 2008	Over 1.0	57
Great Plains and Eastern drought. ...	Severe drought with periods of extreme heat resulting in major reductions in crop yields, along with very low stream flows, and lake levels.	Entire year 2007	5.0	[2]
Western wildfires.............	Continued drought conditions and high winds over much of the Western United States, resulting in numerous wildfires.	Summer–Fall 2007	Over 1.0	12
Spring freeze.............	Widespread severe freeze over much of the East and Midwest causing losses in fruit crops, field crops, and in the ornamental industry.	April 2007	2.0	–
Severe storms and tornadoes	Flooding, hail, tornadoes and severe thunderstorms across numerous Eastern and Southern states.	April 2007	1.5	9
Freeze	Widespread agricultural freeze over a good portion of California, destroying numerous agricultural crops.	January 2007	1.4	1
Widespread drought	Rather severe drought affected crops in states especially during the spring-summer, centered over the Great Plains region, with other areas affected across portions of the South and Far West.	Spring–Summer 2006	Over 6.0	[2]
Severe storms and tornadoes	Outbreak of tornadoes over portions of the Midwest and South during a week-long period.	March 2006	Over 1.0	10+
Numerous wildfires	Wildfires mainly over the Western half of the country, due to dry weather and high wind burning nearly 10 million.	Entire year 2006	Over 1.0	28+

– Represents zero. [1] Represents actual dollar costs at the time of event and is not adjusted for inflation. [2] Some deaths reported due to heat but not beyond typical annual averages.
Source: U.S. National Oceanic and Atmospheric Administration, National Climatic Data Center, "Billion Dollar U.S. Weather Disasters, 1980–2009" (released January 2010).
See also <http://www.ncdc.noaa.gov/oa/reports/billionz.html>.

236 Geography and Environment

Table 389. Normal Daily Mean, Maximum, and Minimum Temperatures— Selected Cities

[In Fahrenheit degrees. Airport data, except as noted. Based on standard 30-year period, 1971–2000]

State	Station	Daily mean temperature January	July	Annual average	Daily maximum temperature January	July	Annual average	Daily minimum temperature January	July	Annual average
AL	Mobile	50.1	81.5	66.8	60.7	91.2	77.4	39.5	71.8	56.2
AK	Juneau.	25.7	56.8	41.5	30.6	64.3	47.6	20.7	49.2	35.3
AZ	Phoenix	56.1	94.8	74.2	67.3	106.6	86.4	44.8	82.9	61.9
AR	Little Rock	40.1	82.4	62.1	49.5	92.8	72.7	30.8	72.0	51.5
CA	Los Angeles.	57.1	69.3	63.3	65.6	75.3	70.6	48.6	63.3	56.1
	Sacramento.	46.3	75.4	61.1	53.8	92.4	73.7	38.8	58.3	48.4
	San Diego	57.8	70.9	64.4	65.8	75.8	70.8	49.7	65.9	58.1
	San Francisco	49.4	62.8	57.3	55.9	71.1	65.1	42.9	54.5	49.6
CO	Denver.	29.2	73.4	50.1	43.2	88.0	64.2	15.2	58.7	35.8
CT	Hartford	25.7	73.7	50.2	34.1	84.9	60.5	17.2	62.4	40.0
DE	Wilmington.	31.5	76.6	54.4	39.3	86.0	63.5	23.7	67.3	45.1
DC	Washington	34.9	79.2	57.5	42.5	88.3	66.4	27.3	70.1	48.6
FL	Jacksonville	53.1	81.6	68.0	64.2	90.8	78.4	41.9	72.4	57.6
	Miami.	68.1	83.7	76.7	76.5	90.9	84.2	59.6	76.5	69.1
GA	Atlanta	42.7	80.0	62.1	51.9	89.4	72.0	33.5	70.6	52.3
HI	Honolulu	73.0	80.8	77.5	80.4	87.8	84.7	65.7	73.8	70.2
ID	Boise	30.2	74.7	51.9	36.7	89.2	62.6	23.6	60.3	41.3
IL	Chicago	22.0	73.3	49.1	29.6	83.5	58.3	14.3	63.2	39.8
	Peoria	22.5	75.1	50.8	30.7	85.7	60.7	14.3	64.6	40.9
IN	Indianapolis	26.5	75.4	52.5	34.5	85.6	62.3	18.5	65.2	42.7
IA	Des Moines	20.4	76.1	50.0	29.1	86.0	59.8	11.7	66.1	40.2
KS	Wichita.	30.2	81.0	56.4	40.1	92.9	67.4	20.3	69.1	45.2
KY	Louisville	33.0	78.4	56.9	41.0	87.0	66.0	24.9	69.8	47.9
LA	New Orleans	52.6	82.7	68.8	61.8	91.1	78.0	43.4	74.2	59.6
ME	Portland	21.7	68.7	45.7	30.9	78.8	55.2	12.5	58.6	36.3
MD	Baltimore	32.3	76.5	54.6	41.2	87.2	65.1	23.5	65.8	44.2
MA	Boston	29.3	73.9	51.6	36.5	82.2	59.3	22.1	65.5	43.9
MI	Detroit	24.5	73.5	49.7	31.1	83.4	58.4	17.8	63.6	41.0
	Sault Ste. Marie	13.2	63.9	40.1	21.5	75.7	49.6	4.9	52.0	30.5
MN	Duluth	8.4	65.5	39.1	17.9	76.3	48.7	−1.2	54.6	29.3
	Minneapolis St. Paul . . .	13.1	73.2	45.4	21.9	83.3	54.7	4.3	63.0	35.9
MS	Jackson	45.0	81.4	64.1	55.1	91.4	75.0	35.0	71.4	53.2
MO	Kansas City	26.9	78.5	54.2	36.0	88.8	64.3	17.8	68.2	44.0
	St. Louis.	29.6	80.2	56.3	37.9	89.8	65.7	21.2	70.6	46.9
MT	Great Falls	21.7	66.2	43.7	32.1	82.0	56.4	11.3	50.4	31.1
NE	Omaha.	21.7	76.7	50.7	31.7	87.4	61.5	11.6	65.9	39.8
NV	Reno	33.6	71.3	51.3	45.5	91.2	67.4	21.8	51.4	35.2
NH	Concord.	20.1	70.0	45.9	30.6	82.9	57.7	9.7	57.1	34.1
NJ	Atlantic City	32.1	75.3	53.5	41.4	85.1	63.6	22.8	65.4	43.3
NM	Albuquerque	35.7	78.5	56.8	47.6	92.3	70.4	23.8	64.7	43.2
NY	Albany	22.2	71.1	47.5	31.1	82.2	57.6	13.3	60.0	37.5
	Buffalo	24.5	70.8	47.9	31.1	79.6	56.0	17.0	62.1	39.9
	New York [1]	32.1	76.5	54.6	38.6	84.2	61.7	26.2	68.8	47.5
NC	Charlotte	41.7	80.3	61.4	51.3	90.1	71.7	32.1	70.6	51.0
	Raleigh	39.7	78.8	59.6	49.8	89.1	70.6	29.6	68.5	48.6
ND	Bismarck	10.2	70.4	42.3	21.1	84.5	54.5	−0.6	56.4	30.1
OH	Cincinnati.	29.7	76.3	54.2	38.0	86.4	64.0	21.3	66.1	44.3
	Cleveland.	25.7	71.9	49.6	32.6	81.4	58.1	18.8	62.3	41.2
	Columbus	28.3	75.1	52.9	36.2	85.3	62.6	20.3	64.9	43.2
OK	Oklahoma City	36.7	82.0	60.1	47.1	93.1	71.1	26.2	70.8	49.2
OR	Portland	39.9	68.1	53.5	45.6	79.3	62.1	34.2	56.9	44.8
PA	Philadelphia.	32.3	77.6	55.3	39.0	85.5	63.2	25.5	69.7	47.4
	Pittsburgh	27.5	72.6	50.9	35.1	82.7	60.4	19.9	62.4	41.5
RI	Providence.	28.7	73.3	51.1	38.9	90.9	75.9	20.3	64.1	42.0
SC	Columbia	44.6	82.0	63.6	55.1	92.1	74.8	34.0	71.8	52.5
SD	Sioux Falls	14.0	73.0	45.1	25.2	85.6	57.2	2.9	60.3	33.0
TN	Memphis	39.9	82.5	62.3	48.6	92.1	72.1	31.3	72.9	52.5
	Nashville	36.8	79.1	58.9	45.6	88.7	69.0	27.9	69.5	48.8
TX	Dallas-Fort Worth	44.1	85.0	65.5	54.1	95.4	75.8	34.0	74.6	55.1
	El Paso	45.1	83.3	64.7	57.2	94.5	77.1	32.9	72.0	52.1
	Houston.	51.8	83.6	68.8	62.3	93.6	79.4	41.2	73.5	58.2
UT	Salt Lake City	29.2	77.0	52.0	37.0	90.6	62.9	21.3	63.4	41.2
VT	Burlington	18.0	70.6	45.2	26.7	81.4	54.5	9.3	59.8	35.8
VA	Norfolk.	40.1	79.1	59.6	47.8	86.8	67.8	32.3	71.4	51.4
	Richmond	36.4	77.9	57.6	45.3	87.5	67.8	27.6	68.3	47.4
WA	Seattle-Tacoma	40.9	65.3	52.3	45.8	75.3	59.8	35.9	55.3	44.8
	Spokane	27.3	68.6	47.3	32.8	82.5	57.4	21.7	54.6	37.2
WV	Charleston.	33.4	73.9	54.5	42.6	84.9	65.4	24.2	62.9	43.5
WI	Milwaukee	20.7	72.0	47.5	28.0	81.1	55.9	13.4	62.9	39.2
WY	Cheyenne	25.9	67.7	44.9	37.1	81.9	57.6	14.8	53.4	32.3
PR	San Juan	76.6	82.2	79.9	82.4	87.4	85.5	70.8	76.9	74.2

[1] City office data.

Source: U.S. National Oceanic and Atmospheric Administration, Comparative Climatic Data. See also <http://www.ncdc.noaa.gov/oa/climate/online/ccd/nrmmax.txt>; <http://www.ncdc.noaa.gov/oa/climate/online/ccd/nrmmin.txt>; and <http://www.ncdc.noaa.gov/oa/climate/online/ccd/nrmavg.txt>.

U.S. Census Bureau, Statistical Abstract of the United States: 2011

Table 390. Highest Temperature of Record—Selected Cities

[In Fahrenheit degrees. Airport data, except as noted. For period of record through 2008]

State	Station	Length of record (years)	Jan.	Feb.	Mar.	Apr.	May	June	July	Aug.	Sept.	Oct.	Nov.	Dec.	Annual [1]
AL	Mobile	67	84	82	90	94	100	102	104	105	99	93	87	81	105
AK	Juneau	64	57	57	61	74	82	86	90	84	73	61	56	54	90
AZ	Phoenix	71	88	92	100	105	113	122	121	116	118	107	95	88	122
AK	Little Rock	67	83	85	91	95	98	105	112	109	106	97	86	80	112
CA	Los Angeles	73	91	92	95	102	97	104	97	98	110	106	101	94	110
	Sacramento	58	70	76	88	95	105	115	114	110	108	104	87	72	115
	San Diego	68	88	90	93	98	96	101	99	98	111	107	97	88	111
	San Francisco	81	72	78	85	92	97	106	105	100	103	99	85	75	106
CO	Denver	66	73	77	84	90	96	104	105	104	97	89	80	75	105
CT	Hartford	54	72	73	89	96	99	100	102	102	99	91	81	76	102
DE	Wilmington	61	75	78	86	94	96	100	102	101	100	91	85	75	102
DC	Washington	67	79	82	89	95	99	101	104	105	101	94	86	79	105
FL	Jacksonville	67	85	88	91	95	100	103	105	102	100	96	88	84	105
	Miami	66	88	89	93	96	96	98	98	98	97	95	91	87	98
GA	Atlanta	60	79	80	89	93	95	101	105	104	98	95	84	79	105
HI	Honolulu	39	88	88	88	91	93	92	94	93	95	94	93	80	95
ID	Boise	69	63	71	81	92	99	109	111	110	102	94	78	65	111
IL	Chicago	50	65	72	88	91	93	104	104	101	99	91	78	71	104
	Peoria	69	70	72	86	92	94	105	104	103	100	93	81	71	105
IN	Indianapolis	69	71	76	85	89	93	102	104	102	100	91	81	74	104
IA	Des Moines	69	67	73	91	93	98	103	105	108	101	95	81	69	108
KS	Wichita	56	75	87	89	96	100	110	113	110	108	97	86	83	113
KY	Louisville	61	77	77	86	91	95	102	106	105	104	93	84	76	106
LA	New Orleans	62	83	85	89	92	96	100	101	102	101	94	87	84	102
ME	Portland	68	67	64	88	85	94	98	99	103	95	88	74	71	103
MD	Baltimore	58	75	79	89	94	98	101	104	105	100	94	83	77	105
MA	Boston	57	69	70	89	94	95	100	102	102	100	90	79	76	102
MI	Detroit	50	64	70	81	89	93	104	102	100	98	91	77	69	104
	Sault Ste. Marie	68	45	49	75	85	89	93	97	98	95	81	68	62	98
MN	Duluth	67	52	55	78	88	90	94	97	97	95	86	71	55	97
	Minneapolis-St. Paul	70	58	61	83	95	97	102	105	102	98	90	77	68	105
MS	Jackson	45	83	85	89	94	99	105	106	107	104	95	88	84	107
MO	Kansas City	36	71	78	86	93	95	105	107	109	106	95	82	74	109
	St. Louis	51	78	76	85	89	93	94	102	107	107	104	94	85	76	107
MT	Great Falls	71	67	70	78	89	93	101	105	106	98	91	76	69	106
NE	Omaha	72	69	78	89	97	99	105	114	110	104	96	83	72	114
NV	Reno	67	71	75	83	89	97	103	108	105	101	91	77	70	108
NH	Concord	67	69	67	89	95	97	98	102	101	98	90	80	73	102
NJ	Atlantic City	65	78	75	87	94	99	106	104	103	99	90	84	77	106
NM	Albuquerque	69	69	76	85	89	98	107	105	101	100	91	77	72	107
NY	Albany	62	71	68	89	92	94	99	100	99	100	89	82	71	100
	Buffalo	65	72	71	81	94	91	96	97	99	98	87	80	74	99
	New York [2]	140	72	75	86	96	99	101	106	104	102	94	84	75	106
NC	Charlotte	69	79	81	90	93	100	103	103	104	104	98	85	80	104
	Raleigh	64	80	84	92	95	97	104	105	105	104	98	88	81	105
ND	Bismarck	69	63	69	81	93	98	111	112	109	105	95	79	65	112
OH	Cincinnati	47	69	75	84	89	93	102	103	102	98	91	81	75	103
	Cleveland	67	73	74	83	88	92	104	103	102	101	90	82	77	104
	Columbus	69	74	75	85	89	94	102	100	101	100	91	80	76	102
OK	Oklahoma City	55	80	92	93	100	104	105	110	110	108	96	87	86	110
OR	Portland	68	66	71	80	90	100	102	107	107	105	92	73	65	107
PA	Philadelphia	67	74	74	87	95	97	100	104	101	100	96	81	73	104
	Pittsburgh	56	72	76	82	89	91	98	103	100	97	87	82	74	103
RI	Providence	55	69	72	85	98	95	97	102	104	100	86	78	77	104
SC	Columbia	61	84	84	91	94	101	107	107	107	101	101	90	83	107
SD	Sioux Falls	63	66	70	87	94	100	110	108	108	104	94	81	63	110
TN	Memphis	67	79	81	86	94	99	104	108	107	103	95	86	81	108
	Nashville	69	78	84	86	91	97	106	107	106	105	94	84	79	107
TX	Dallas-Fort Worth	55	88	95	96	101	103	113	110	109	111	102	89	89	113
	El Paso	69	80	83	89	98	105	114	112	108	104	96	87	80	114
	Houston	39	84	91	91	95	99	103	104	107	109	96	89	85	109
UT	Salt Lake City	80	63	69	78	89	99	104	107	106	100	89	75	69	107
VT	Burlington	65	66	62	84	91	93	100	100	101	98	85	75	67	101
VA	Norfolk	60	80	82	88	97	100	101	103	104	99	95	86	80	104
	Richmond	79	81	83	93	96	100	104	105	104	103	99	86	81	105
WA	Seattle-Tacoma	64	64	70	78	85	93	96	100	99	98	89	74	64	100
	Spokane	61	59	63	71	90	96	101	103	108	98	86	67	56	108
WV	Charleston	61	79	79	89	94	93	98	104	104	102	93	85	80	104
WI	Milwaukee	68	63	68	82	91	93	101	103	103	98	89	77	68	103
WY	Cheyenne	73	66	71	74	83	91	100	100	98	95	83	75	69	100
PR	San Juan	54	92	96	96	97	96	97	95	97	97	98	96	94	98

[1] Represents the highest observed temperature in any month. [2] City office data.
Source: U.S. National Oceanic and Atmospheric Administration, *Comparative Climatic Data*. See also <http://www.ncdc.noaa .gov/oa/climate/online/ccd/lowtmp.txt>.

Table 391. Lowest Temperature of Record—Selected Cities

[In Fahrenheit degrees. Airport data, except as noted. For period of record through 2008]

State	Station	Length of record (years)	Jan.	Feb.	Mar.	Apr.	May	June	July	Aug.	Sept.	Oct.	Nov.	Dec.	Annual [1]
AL	Mobile	67	3	11	21	32	43	49	60	59	42	30	22	8	3
AK	Juneau.	64	−22	−22	−15	6	25	31	36	27	23	11	−5	−21	−22
AZ	Phoenix	71	17	22	25	32	40	50	61	60	47	34	25	22	17
AR	Little Rock	67	−4	−5	11	28	40	46	54	52	37	29	17	−1	−5
CA	Los Angeles.	73	23	32	34	39	43	48	49	51	47	41	34	32	23
	Sacramento.	58	21	23	26	31	36	41	48	49	42	36	26	18	18
	San Diego	68	29	36	39	41	48	51	55	57	51	43	38	34	29
	San Francisco	81	24	25	30	31	36	41	43	42	38	34	25	20	20
CO	Denver	66	−25	−30	−11	−2	21	30	43	41	17	3	−8	−25	−30
CT	Hartford	54	−26	−21	−6	9	28	35	44	36	30	17	1	−14	−26
DE	Wilmington.	61	−14	−6	2	18	30	41	48	43	36	24	14	−7	−14
DC	Washington	67	−5	4	11	24	34	47	54	49	39	29	16	1	−5
FL	Jacksonville	67	7	19	23	31	45	47	61	59	48	33	21	11	7
	Miami.	66	30	32	32	46	53	60	69	68	68	51	39	30	30
GA	Atlanta	60	−8	5	10	26	37	46	53	55	36	28	3	0	−8
HI	Honolulu	39	53	53	55	57	60	65	66	67	66	61	57	54	53
ID	Boise	69	−17	−15	6	19	22	31	35	34	23	11	−3	−25	−25
IL	Chicago	50	−27	−19	−8	7	24	36	40	41	28	17	1	−25	−27
	Peoria	69	−25	−19	−10	14	25	39	47	41	26	19	−2	−23	−25
IN	Indianapolis	69	−27	−21	−7	16	28	37	44	41	28	17	−2	−23	−27
IA	Des Moines	69	−24	−26	−22	9	30	38	47	40	26	14	−4	−22	−26
KS	Wichita.	56	−12	−21	−2	15	31	43	51	48	31	18	1	−16	−21
KY	Louisville	61	−22	−19	−1	22	31	42	50	46	33	23	−1	−15	−22
LA	New Orleans	62	14	16	25	32	41	50	60	60	42	35	24	11	11
ME	Portland	68	−26	−39	−21	8	23	33	40	33	23	15	3	−21	−39
MD	Baltimore	58	−7	−3	6	20	32	40	50	45	35	25	13	0	−7
MA	Boston	57	−12	−4	5	16	34	45	50	47	38	28	15	−7	−12
MI	Detroit	50	−21	−15	−4	10	25	36	41	38	29	17	9	−10	−21
	Sault Ste. Marie.	68	−36	−35	−24	−2	18	26	36	29	25	16	−10	−31	−36
MN	Duluth	67	−39	−39	−29	−5	17	27	35	32	22	8	−23	−34	−39
	Minneapolis-St. Paul . . .	70	−34	−32	−32	2	18	34	43	39	26	13	−17	−29	−34
MS	Jackson	45	2	10	15	27	38	47	51	51	35	26	17	1	2
MO	Kansas City	36	−17	−19	−10	12	30	42	51	43	31	17	1	−23	−23
	St. Louis.	51	−18	−12	−5	22	31	43	51	47	36	23	1	−16	−18
MT	Great Falls	71	−37	−35	−29	−8	15	31	36	30	16	−11	−25	−43	−43
NE	Omaha.	72	−23	−21	−16	5	27	38	44	43	25	13	−9	−23	−23
NV	Reno	67	−16	−16	−2	13	18	21	33	24	20	8	1	−16	−16
NH	Concord.	67	−33	−37	−16	8	21	30	35	29	21	10	−5	−22	−37
NJ	Atlantic City	65	−10	−11	4	12	25	37	42	40	32	20	10	−7	−11
NM	Albuquerque	69	−17	−5	8	19	16	40	52	50	37	21	−7	−7	−17
NY	Albany	62	−28	−21	−21	10	26	36	40	34	24	16	5	−22	−28
	Buffalo	65	−16	−20	−7	12	26	35	43	38	32	20	9	−10	−20
	New York [2]	140	−6	−15	3	12	32	44	52	50	39	28	5	−13	−15
NC	Charlotte	69	−5	5	4	21	32	45	53	50	39	24	11	2	−5
	Raleigh	64	−9	0	11	23	31	38	48	46	37	19	11	4	−9
ND	Bismarck	69	−44	−43	−31	−12	15	30	35	33	11	−10	−30	−43	−44
OH	Cincinnati.	47	−25	−11	−11	15	27	39	47	43	31	16	1	−20	−25
	Cleveland.	67	−20	−15	−5	10	25	31	41	38	32	19	3	−15	−20
	Columbus	69	−22	−13	−6	14	25	35	43	39	31	20	5	−17	−22
OK	Oklahoma City.	55	−4	−3	3	20	37	47	53	51	36	16	11	−8	−8
OR	Portland	68	−2	−3	19	29	29	39	43	44	34	26	13	6	−3
PA	Philadelphia.	67	−7	−4	7	19	28	44	51	44	35	25	15	1	−7
	Pittsburgh	56	−22	−12	−1	14	26	34	42	39	31	16	−1	−12	−22
RI	Providence.	55	−13	−7	1	14	29	41	48	40	33	20	6	−10	−13
SC	Columbia	61	−1	5	4	26	34	44	54	53	40	23	12	4	−1
SD	Sioux Falls	63	−36	−31	−23	5	17	33	38	34	22	9	−17	−28	−36
TN	Memphis	67	−4	−11	12	28	38	48	52	48	36	25	9	−13	−13
	Nashville	69	−17	−13	2	23	34	42	51	47	36	26	−1	−10	−17
TX	Dallas-Fort Worth	55	4	7	15	29	41	51	59	56	43	29	20	−1	−1
	El Paso	69	−8	8	14	23	31	46	57	56	41	25	1	5	−8
	Houston.	39	12	3	22	31	44	52	62	60	48	29	19	7	3
UT	Salt Lake City	80	−22	−30	2	14	25	35	40	37	27	16	−14	−21	−30
VT	Burlington	65	−30	−30	−20	2	24	33	39	35	25	15	−2	−26	−30
VA	Norfolk.	60	−3	8	18	28	36	45	54	49	45	27	20	7	−3
	Richmond	79	−12	−10	11	23	31	40	51	46	35	21	10	−1	−12
WA	Seattle-Tacoma	64	0	1	11	29	28	38	43	44	35	28	6	6	0
	Spokane	61	−22	−24	−7	17	24	33	37	35	22	7	−21	−25	−25
WV	Charleston.	61	−16	−12	0	19	26	33	46	41	34	17	6	−12	−16
WI	Milwaukee	68	−26	−26	−10	12	21	33	40	44	28	18	−5	−20	−26
WY	Cheyenne	73	−29	−34	−21	−8	16	25	38	36	8	−1	−16	−28	−34
PR	San Juan	54	61	62	60	64	66	69	69	70	69	46	66	59	46

[1] Represents the lowest observed temperature in any month. [2] City office data.

Source: U.S. National Oceanic and Atmospheric Administration, Comparative Climatic Data. See also <http://www.ncdc.noaa.gov/oa/climate/online/ccd/lowtmp.txt>.

U.S. Census Bureau, Statistical Abstract of the United States: 2011

Table 392. Normal Monthly and Annual Precipitation—Selected Cities

[In inches. Airport data, except as noted. The table data are the 30-year average values computed from the data recorded during the period 1971–2000]

State	Station	Jan.	Feb.	Mar.	Apr.	May	June	July	Aug.	Sept.	Oct.	Nov.	Dec.	Annual
AL	Mobile	5.75	5.10	7.20	5.06	6.10	5.01	6.54	6.20	6.01	3.25	5.41	4.66	66.29
AK	Juneau	4.81	4.02	3.51	2.96	3.48	3.36	4.14	5.37	7.54	8.30	5.43	5.41	58.33
AZ	Phoenix	0.83	0.77	1.07	0.25	0.16	0.09	0.99	0.94	0.75	0.79	0.73	0.92	8.29
AR	Little Rock	3.61	3.33	4.88	5.47	5.05	3.95	3.31	2.93	3.71	4.25	5.73	4.71	50.93
CA	Los Angeles	2.98	3.11	2.40	0.63	0.24	0.08	0.03	0.14	0.26	0.36	1.13	1.79	13.15
	Sacramento	3.84	3.54	2.80	1.02	0.53	0.20	0.05	0.06	0.36	0.89	2.19	2.45	17.93
	San Diego	2.28	2.04	2.26	0.75	0.20	0.09	0.03	0.09	0.21	0.44	1.07	1.31	10.77
	San Francisco	4.45	4.01	3.26	1.18	0.38	0.11	0.03	0.07	0.20	1.04	2.49	2.89	20.11
CO	Denver	0.51	0.49	1.28	1.93	2.32	1.56	2.16	1.82	1.14	0.99	0.98	0.63	15.81
CT	Hartford	3.84	2.96	3.88	3.86	4.39	3.85	3.67	3.98	4.13	3.94	4.06	3.60	46.16
DE	Wilmington	3.43	2.81	3.97	3.39	4.15	3.59	4.28	3.51	4.01	3.08	3.19	3.40	42.81
DC	Washington	3.21	2.63	3.60	2.77	3.82	3.13	3.66	3.44	3.79	3.22	3.03	3.05	39.35
FL	Jacksonville	3.69	3.15	3.93	3.14	3.48	5.37	5.97	6.87	7.90	3.86	2.34	2.64	52.34
	Miami	1.88	2.07	2.56	3.36	5.52	8.54	5.79	8.63	8.38	6.19	3.43	2.18	58.53
GA	Atlanta	5.03	4.68	5.38	3.62	3.95	3.63	5.12	3.67	4.09	3.11	4.10	3.82	50.20
HI	Honolulu	2.73	2.35	1.89	1.11	0.78	0.43	0.50	0.46	0.74	2.18	2.27	2.85	18.29
ID	Boise	1.39	1.14	1.41	1.27	1.27	0.74	0.39	0.30	0.76	0.76	1.38	1.38	12.19
IL	Chicago	1.75	1.63	2.65	3.68	3.38	3.63	3.51	4.62	3.27	2.71	3.01	2.43	36.27
	Peoria	1.50	1.67	2.83	3.56	4.17	3.84	4.02	3.16	3.12	2.77	2.99	2.40	36.03
IN	Indianapolis	2.48	2.41	3.44	3.61	4.36	4.13	4.42	3.82	2.88	2.76	3.61	3.03	40.95
IA	Des Moines	1.03	1.19	2.21	3.58	4.25	4.57	4.18	4.51	3.15	2.62	2.10	1.33	34.72
KS	Wichita	0.84	1.02	2.71	2.57	4.16	4.25	3.31	2.94	2.96	2.45	1.82	1.35	30.38
KY	Louisville	3.28	3.25	4.41	3.91	4.88	3.76	4.30	3.41	3.05	2.79	3.81	3.69	44.54
LA	New Orleans	5.87	5.47	5.24	5.02	4.62	6.83	6.20	6.15	5.55	3.05	5.09	5.07	64.16
ME	Portland	4.09	3.14	4.14	4.26	3.82	3.28	3.32	3.05	3.37	4.40	4.72	4.24	45.83
MD	Baltimore	3.47	3.02	3.93	3.00	3.89	3.43	3.85	3.74	3.98	3.16	3.12	3.35	41.94
MA	Boston	3.92	3.30	3.85	3.60	3.24	3.22	3.06	3.37	3.47	3.79	3.98	3.73	42.53
MI	Detroit	1.91	1.88	2.52	3.05	3.05	3.55	3.16	3.10	3.27	2.23	2.66	2.51	32.89
	Sault Ste. Marie	2.64	1.60	2.41	2.57	2.50	3.00	3.14	3.47	3.71	3.32	3.40	2.91	34.67
MN	Duluth	1.12	0.83	1.69	2.09	2.95	4.25	4.20	4.22	4.13	2.46	2.12	0.94	31.00
	Minneapolis-St. Paul	1.04	0.79	1.86	2.31	3.24	4.34	4.04	4.05	2.69	2.11	1.94	1.00	29.41
MS	Jackson	5.67	4.50	5.74	5.98	4.86	3.82	4.69	3.66	3.23	3.42	5.04	5.34	55.95
MO	Kansas City	1.15	1.31	2.44	3.38	5.39	4.44	4.42	3.54	4.64	3.33	2.30	1.64	37.98
	St. Louis	2.14	2.28	3.60	3.69	4.11	3.76	3.90	2.98	2.96	2.76	3.71	2.86	38.75
MT	Great Falls	0.68	0.51	1.01	1.40	2.53	2.24	1.45	1.65	1.23	0.93	0.59	0.67	14.89
NE	Omaha	0.77	0.80	2.13	2.94	4.44	3.95	3.86	3.21	3.17	2.21	1.82	0.92	30.22
NV	Reno	1.06	1.06	0.86	0.35	0.62	0.47	0.24	0.27	0.45	0.42	0.80	0.88	7.48
NH	Concord	2.97	2.36	3.04	3.07	3.33	3.10	3.37	3.21	3.16	3.46	3.57	2.96	37.60
NJ	Atlantic City	3.60	2.85	4.06	3.45	3.38	2.66	3.86	4.32	3.14	2.86	3.26	3.15	40.59
NM	Albuquerque	0.49	0.44	0.61	0.50	0.60	0.65	1.27	1.73	1.07	1.00	0.62	0.49	9.47
NY	Albany	2.71	2.27	3.17	3.25	3.67	3.74	3.50	3.68	3.31	3.23	3.31	2.76	38.60
	Buffalo	3.16	2.42	2.99	3.04	3.35	3.82	3.14	3.87	3.84	3.19	3.92	3.80	40.54
	New York [1]	4.13	3.15	4.37	4.28	4.69	3.84	4.62	4.22	4.23	3.85	4.36	3.95	49.69
NC	Charlotte	4.00	3.55	4.39	2.95	3.66	3.42	3.79	3.72	3.83	3.66	3.36	3.18	43.51
	Raleigh	4.02	3.47	4.03	2.80	3.79	3.42	4.29	3.78	4.26	3.18	2.97	3.04	43.05
ND	Bismarck	0.45	0.51	0.85	1.46	2.22	2.59	2.58	2.15	1.61	1.28	0.70	0.44	16.84
OH	Cincinnati	2.92	2.75	3.90	3.96	4.59	4.42	3.75	3.79	2.82	2.96	3.46	3.28	42.60
	Cleveland	2.48	2.29	2.94	3.37	3.50	3.89	3.52	3.69	3.77	2.74	3.38	3.14	38.71
	Columbus	2.53	2.20	2.89	3.25	3.88	4.08	4.62	3.72	2.92	2.31	3.19	2.93	38.52
OK	Oklahoma City	1.28	1.56	2.90	2.90	5.44	4.63	2.94	2.48	3.98	3.64	2.11	1.89	35.85
OR	Portland	5.07	4.18	3.71	2.64	2.38	1.59	0.72	0.93	1.65	2.88	5.61	5.71	37.07
PA	Philadelphia	3.52	2.74	3.81	3.49	3.89	3.29	4.39	3.82	3.88	2.75	3.16	3.31	42.05
	Pittsburgh	2.70	2.37	3.17	3.01	3.80	4.12	3.96	3.38	3.21	2.25	3.02	2.86	37.85
RI	Providence	4.37	3.45	4.43	4.16	3.66	3.38	3.17	3.90	3.70	3.69	4.40	4.14	46.45
SC	Columbia	4.66	3.84	4.59	2.98	3.17	4.99	5.54	5.41	3.94	2.89	2.88	3.38	48.27
SD	Sioux Falls	0.51	0.51	1.81	2.65	3.39	3.49	2.93	3.01	2.58	1.93	1.36	0.52	24.69
TN	Memphis	4.24	4.31	5.58	5.79	5.15	4.30	4.22	3.00	3.31	3.31	5.76	5.68	54.65
	Nashville	3.97	3.69	4.87	3.93	5.07	4.08	3.77	3.28	3.59	2.87	4.45	4.54	48.11
TX	Dallas-Fort Worth	1.90	2.37	3.06	3.20	5.15	3.23	2.12	2.03	2.42	4.11	2.57	2.57	34.73
	El Paso	0.45	0.39	0.26	0.23	0.38	0.87	1.49	1.75	1.61	0.81	0.42	0.77	9.43
	Houston	3.68	2.98	3.36	3.60	5.15	5.35	3.18	3.83	4.33	4.50	4.19	3.69	47.84
UT	Salt Lake City	1.37	1.33	1.91	2.02	2.09	0.77	0.72	0.76	1.33	1.57	1.40	1.23	16.50
VT	Burlington	2.22	1.67	2.32	2.88	3.32	3.43	3.97	4.01	3.83	3.12	3.06	2.22	36.05
VA	Norfolk	3.93	3.34	4.08	3.38	3.74	3.77	5.17	4.79	4.06	3.47	2.98	3.03	45.74
	Richmond	3.55	2.98	4.09	3.18	3.96	3.54	4.67	4.18	3.98	3.60	3.06	3.12	43.91
WA	Seattle-Tacoma	5.13	4.18	3.75	2.59	1.78	1.49	0.79	1.02	1.63	3.19	5.90	5.62	37.07
	Spokane	1.82	1.51	1.53	1.28	1.60	1.18	0.76	0.68	0.76	1.06	2.24	2.25	16.67
WV	Charleston	3.25	3.19	3.90	3.25	4.30	4.09	4.86	4.11	3.45	2.67	3.66	3.32	44.05
WI	Milwaukee	1.85	1.65	2.59	3.78	3.06	3.56	3.58	4.03	3.30	2.49	2.70	2.22	34.81
WY	Cheyenne	0.45	0.44	1.05	1.55	2.48	2.12	2.26	1.82	1.43	0.75	0.64	0.46	15.45
PR	San Juan	3.02	2.30	2.14	3.71	5.29	3.52	4.16	5.22	5.60	5.06	6.17	4.57	50.76

[1] City office data.

Source: U.S. National Oceanic and Atmospheric Administration, Climatography of the United States, No. 81. See also <http://www.ncdc.noaa.gov/oa/climate/online/ccd/nrmpcp.txt>.

Table 393. Snow, Hail, Ice Pellets, and Sleet—Selected Cities

[In inches. Airport data, except as noted. For period of record through 2008. T denotes trace. Stations may show snowfall (hail) during the warm months]

State	Station	Length of record (years)	Jan.	Feb.	Mar.	Apr.	May	June	July	Aug.	Sept.	Oct.	Nov.	Dec.	Annual
AL	Mobile	66	0.1	0.1	0.1	T	T	–	T	–	–	–	T	0.1	0.4
AK	Juneau	64	25.9	18.7	15.3	3.5	T	T	–	–	T	1.1	12.3	21.4	97.4
AZ	Phoenix	62	T	–	T	T	T	–	–	–	–	T	–	T	–
AR	Little Rock	57	2.4	1.5	0.5	T	T	T	–	–	–	T	0.2	0.6	5.2
CA	Los Angeles	62	T	T	T	–	–	–	–	–	–	–	–	T	–
	Sacramento	50	T	T	T	–	T	–	–	–	–	–	–	T	–
	San Diego	60	T	–	T	T	–	–	–	–	–	–	T	T	–
	San Francisco	69	–	T	T	–	–	–	–	–	–	–	–	–	–
CO	Denver	64	8.0	7.4	12.2	8.6	1.6	–	T	T	1.6	3.8	8.8	7.9	60.3
CT	Hartford	51	13.2	12.5	10.0	1.5	–	T	–	–	–	0.1	2.1	10.9	50.3
DE	Wilmington	58	6.7	6.6	3.2	0.2	T	T	T	–	–	0.1	0.9	3.4	21.3
DC	Washington	65	5.3	5.5	2.3	2.3	T	T	T	T	–	–	0.8	3.0	19.4
FL	Jacksonville	60	T	–	–	T	–	T	T	–	–	–	–	–	–
	Miami	59	–	–	–	–	T	–	–	–	–	–	–	–	–
GA	Atlanta	69	1.0	0.5	0.4	T	–	–	T	–	–	T	T	0.2	2.1
HI	Honolulu	52	–	–	–	–	–	–	–	–	–	–	–	–	–
ID	Boise	69	6.4	3.7	1.7	0.6	0.1	T	T	T	T	0.1	2.3	5.8	20.3
IL	Chicago	49	11.2	8.2	6.6	1.6	0.1	T	T	T	T	0.4	2.1	8.6	38.2
	Peoria	65	6.5	5.3	4.2	0.8	T	T	T	–	T	0.1	2.1	6.3	25.1
IN	Indianapolis	77	6.9	5.7	3.5	0.5	T	T	T	–	T	0.2	1.9	5.5	24.2
IA	Des Moines	65	8.3	7.5	6.1	1.9	T	T	T	–	T	0.3	3.1	6.7	33.6
KS	Wichita	55	4.0	4.1	2.7	0.2	T	T	T	T	T	–	1.4	3.6	16.0
KY	Louisville	61	5.1	4.2	3.2	0.1	T	T	T	–	T	0.1	1.0	2.5	16.1
LA	New Orleans	51	T	0.1	T	T	T	–	–	–	–	–	T	0.1	0.2
ME	Portland	68	19	16.6	13.3	3.1	0.2	–	–	–	T	0.2	3.3	15.1	70.4
MD	Baltimore	58	6.1	7.1	3.6	0.1	T	T	T	–	–	T	1.0	3.3	21.4
MA	Boston	71	12.7	12.0	8.1	0.9	–	T	T	T	–	T	1.3	8.2	43.2
MI	Detroit	50	11.0	9.4	7.1	1.9	T	–	–	–	T	0.2	2.5	10.2	41.4
	Sault Ste. Marie	61	29.3	18.8	14.5	6.0	0.5	T	T	T	0.1	2.4	15.8	31.0	117.4
MN	Duluth	65	17.7	12.3	14.0	6.9	0.7	T	T	T	0.1	1.6	12.5	15.9	81.7
	Minneapolis-St. Paul	66	10.4	8.1	10.7	2.8	0.1	T	T	T	T	0.5	7.6	9.6	49.7
MS	Jackson	38	0.5	0.2	0.2	T	–	–	–	T	–	–	T	0.1	1.0
MO	Kansas City	74	5.4	4.5	3.4	0.8	T	T	T	T	T	0.1	1.3	4.5	19.9
	St. Louis	72	5.3	4.6	3.8	0.5	T	T	T	–	–	T	1.4	4.1	19.5
MT	Great Falls	71	9.3	8.6	10.6	7.2	1.9	0.4	T	0.1	1.5	3.5	7.5	8.3	58.4
NE	Omaha	73	7.6	6.9	6.2	1.1	0.1	T	T	T	T	0.3	2.6	5.7	30.6
NV	Reno	59	6.1	5.2	4.2	1.2	0.8	–	–	–	–	0.3	2.5	4.6	24.9
NH	Concord	67	17.9	14.4	11.5	2.8	0.1	T	–	–	T	0.1	3.8	14.5	64.5
NJ	Atlantic City	59	5.0	5.6	2.5	0.3	T	T	T	–	–	T	0.4	2.4	16.2
NM	Albuquerque	69	2.5	2.1	1.8	0.6	T	T	T	T	T	0.1	1.2	3.0	11.3
NY	Albany	62	16.9	13.6	11.6	2.8	0.1	T	T	–	T	0.2	3.9	14.9	64.1
	Buffalo	65	24.2	18.0	12.7	3.2	0.2	T	T	T	T	0.7	10.9	21.4	93.7
	New York [1]	140	7.7	8.7	5.1	0.9	T	–	T	–	–	T	0.9	5.6	28.9
NC	Charlotte	69	2.2	1.8	1.2	T	T	T	–	–	–	T	0.1	0.5	5.8
	Raleigh	64	2.8	2.6	1.3	T	T	T	T	–	–	–	0.1	0.8	7.6
ND	Bismarck	69	7.6	6.9	8.3	4.0	0.9	T	T	T	0.2	1.9	6.8	7.4	43.7
OH	Cincinnati	61	7.1	5.6	4.2	0.5	–	T	T	T	–	0.3	2.0	3.8	23.5
	Cleveland	67	14.3	12.6	11.1	2.9	0.1	T	T	–	T	0.6	5.1	12.6	58.9
	Columbus	61	8.7	6.3	4.8	1.0	T	T	T	–	T	0.1	2.2	5.3	28.2
OK	Oklahoma City	69	3.2	2.4	1.5	T	T	T	T	T	T	T	0.6	1.9	9.6
OR	Portland	55	3.2	1.1	0.4	T	–	–	–	T	T	–	0.4	1.4	6.5
PA	Philadelphia	66	6.0	7.0	3.4	0.3	T	T	–	–	–	T	0.7	3.4	21
	Pittsburgh	56	11.8	9.5	8.2	1.8	0.1	T	T	T	T	0.4	3.4	8.3	43.6
RI	Providence	55	9.6	9.8	7.3	0.7	0.2	–	–	–	–	0.1	1.3	7.3	36.4
SC	Columbia	60	0.6	0.8	0.2	T	–	T	T	–	–	–	T	0.3	1.9
SD	Sioux Falls	63	6.9	8.0	9.4	3.2	T	T	T	T	T	0.9	6.0	7.1	41.2
TN	Memphis	51	2.2	1.4	0.9	T	T	T	–	–	–	T	0.1	0.6	5.1
	Nashville	62	3.7	3.0	1.5	–	–	T	–	T	–	–	0.4	1.4	10.0
TX	Dallas-Fort Worth	50	1.1	1.0	0.2	T	T	–	–	–	–	T	0.1	0.2	2.6
	El Paso	59	1.3	0.8	0.4	0.3	T	T	–	T	–	T	1.0	1.6	5.4
	Houston	74	0.2	0.2	T	T	T	T	T	–	–	–	T	–	0.4
UT	Salt Lake City	80	13.4	10.0	9.0	4.9	0.6	T	T	T	0.1	1.3	6.8	12.2	58.1
VT	Burlington	65	19.3	17.0	13.9	4.1	0.2	–	T	T	T	0.2	6.6	19.0	79.8
VA	Norfolk	58	3.0	2.9	1.0	–	T	T	–	T	–	–	–	1.0	7.9
	Richmond	69	4.9	3.8	2.4	0.1	T	–	T	–	–	T	0.4	2.0	13.7
WA	Seattle-Tacoma	52	4.9	1.6	1.3	0.1	T	–	T	–	–	–	1.1	2.4	11.4
	Spokane	61	15.5	7.4	4.0	0.7	0.1	T	–	–	T	0.4	6.2	14.9	47.8
WV	Charleston	54	10.6	8.6	5.3	0.9	–	T	T	T	T	0.2	2.4	5.2	33.3
WI	Milwaukee	68	14.0	9.7	8.4	2.0	0.1	T	T	T	T	0.2	3.0	11.1	47.5
WY	Cheyenne	73	6.0	6.4	11.8	9.2	3.4	0.2	–	T	1.1	3.8	7.2	6.7	56.1
PR	San Juan	53	–	–	–	–	–	–	–	T	–	–	–	–	–

– Represents zero. [1] City office data.

Source: U.S. National Oceanic and Atmospheric Administration, Comparative Climatic Data, annual. See also ‹http://www.ncdc.noaa.gov/oa/climate/online/ccd/avgsnf.txt›.

Table 394. Cloudiness, Average Wind Speed, Heating and Cooling Degree Days, and Average Relative Humidity—Selected Cities

[Airport data, except as noted. For period of record through 2008, except as noted. M=morning. A=afternoon]

State	Station	Cloudiness-average percentage of days [1] — Length of record (yr.)	Annual	Average wind speed (mph) — Length of record (yr.)	Annual	Jan.	July	Heating degree days	Cooling degree days	Avg. rel. humidity — Length of record (yr.)	Annual M	Annual A	Jan. M	Jan. A	July M	July A
AL	Mobile	47	72.1	60	8.8	10.1	6.9	1,681	2,539	46	86	65	81	67	89	68
AK	Juneau	47	87.9	63	8.2	8.0	7.5	8,574	–	42	80	70	78	75	79	68
AZ	Phoenix	57	42.5	63	6.2	5.3	7.1	1,027	4,364	48	49	23	63	31	42	20
AR	Little Rock	35	67.7	66	7.7	8.4	6.7	3,084	2,086	44	82	63	78	66	85	62
CA	Los Angeles	60	60.0	60	7.5	6.7	7.9	1,274	679	49	79	66	71	61	86	68
	Sacramento	49	48.5	58	7.8	6.9	8.9	2,666	1,248	22	83	46	90	69	77	29
	San Diego	55	60.0	68	7.0	6.0	7.5	1,063	866	48	77	63	72	58	82	66
	San Francisco	68	56.2	81	10.6	7.2	13.6	2,862	142	49	84	63	86	68	86	60
CO	Denver	61	68.5	52	8.7	8.7	8.3	6,128	696	40	67	40	63	49	67	33
CT	Hartford	41	77.5	54	8.4	8.9	7.3	6,104	759	49	77	53	72	56	78	51
DE	Wilmington	47	73.4	60	9.0	9.8	7.8	4,888	1,125	61	78	55	75	50	79	54
DC	Washington	48	74.0	60	9.4	10.0	8.3	4,055	1,531	48	75	53	70	55	76	53
FL	Jacksonville	47	74.2	59	7.8	8.1	7.0	1,354	2,627	72	89	56	87	57	88	58
	Miami	46	79.5	59	9.2	9.5	7.9	149	4,361	44	83	61	83	59	82	63
GA	Atlanta	61	70.1	70	9.1	10.4	7.7	2,827	1,810	48	82	56	78	58	87	58
HI	Honolulu	47	75.3	59	11.2	9.4	13.1	–	4,561	39	72	56	80	61	67	51
ID	Boise	56	67.1	69	8.7	7.9	8.4	5,727	807	69	69	43	80	70	53	21
IL	Chicago	37	77.0	50	10.3	11.6	8.4	6,498	830	50	80	65	77	70	81	61
	Peoria	52	73.7	65	9.8	10.9	7.8	6,097	998	49	82	67	79	72	85	65
IN	Indianapolis	64	76.2	60	9.6	10.9	7.5	5,521	1,042	49	83	61	81	70	86	59
IA	Des Moines	46	71.5	59	10.7	11.4	8.9	6,436	1,052	47	79	66	76	70	82	64
KS	Wichita	39	64.9	55	12.2	11.9	11.2	4,765	1,658	55	79	61	78	66	78	56
KY	Louisville	47	74.8	61	8.3	9.5	6.8	4,352	1,443	48	81	58	77	64	83	57
LA	New Orleans	47	72.3	60	8.2	9.3	6.1	1,417	2,773	60	87	67	83	69	90	70
ME	Portland	54	72.3	68	8.7	9.0	7.6	7,318	347	68	79	59	75	60	79	59
MD	Baltimore	45	71.2	58	8.7	9.2	7.5	4,720	1,147	55	77	53	72	56	79	52
MA	Boston	60	73.2	51	12.3	13.7	11.0	5,630	777	44	72	58	68	58	73	57
MI	Detroit	37	79.5	50	10.2	11.8	8.5	6,422	736	50	81	59	80	69	81	53
	Sault Ste. Marie . . .	54	81.9	67	9.2	9.6	7.8	9,224	145	67	85	66	81	73	87	61
MN	Duluth	47	79.2	59	11.0	11.6	9.4	9,724	189	47	81	68	77	73	84	65
	Minneapolis-St. Paul	57	74.0	70	10.5	10.5	9.4	7,876	699	49	78	64	75	70	79	60
MS	Jackson	30	69.6	45	6.9	8.2	5.2	2,401	2,264	45	89	65	84	69	92	67
MO	Kansas City	23	67.1	36	10.6	11.1	9.2	5,249	1,325	36	80	67	76	69	83	67
	St. Louis	47	72.6	59	9.6	10.6	8.0	4,758	1,561	48	80	64	79	69	82	62
MT	Great Falls	57	78.4	67	12.5	14.8	10.0	7,828	288	47	68	46	66	60	67	30
NE	Omaha	49	69.6	72	10.5	10.9	8.8	6,311	1,095	44	80	66	78	69	83	65
NV	Reno	53	56.7	66	6.6	5.6	7.2	5,600	493	45	68	31	79	50	57	18
NH	Concord	54	75.3	66	6.7	7.2	5.7	7,478	442	43	81	53	76	58	82	51
NJ	Atlantic City	37	74.2	50	9.8	10.7	8.3	5,113	935	44	81	56	78	58	82	56
NM	Albuquerque	56	54.2	69	8.9	8.0	8.9	4,281	1,290	48	58	29	67	39	58	27
NY	Albany	57	81.1	70	8.9	9.8	7.5	6,860	544	43	80	58	77	63	80	55
	Buffalo	52	85.2	69	11.8	13.9	10.2	6,692	548	48	80	63	79	72	78	55
	New York [2]	42	71.0	71	9.1	10.4	7.5	4,754	1,151	74	72	56	67	59	74	55
NC	Charlotte	49	70.4	59	7.4	7.8	6.6	3,162	1,681	48	82	53	77	54	85	56
	Raleigh	47	69.9	59	7.5	8.2	6.7	3,465	1,521	44	84	53	78	54	88	57
ND	Bismarck	56	74.5	69	10.2	10.0	9.2	8,802	471	49	80	63	76	71	82	56
OH	Cincinnati	44	77.8	61	9.0	10.4	7.2	5,148	1,064	46	82	60	79	68	85	57
	Cleveland	54	81.9	67	10.5	12.2	8.6	6,121	702	48	79	62	78	70	80	56
	Columbus	46	80.3	59	8.3	9.8	6.5	5,492	951	49	80	59	77	67	83	55
OK	Oklahoma City	44	61.9	60	12.2	12.5	10.8	3,663	1,907	43	79	62	76	64	78	58
OR	Portland	47	81.1	60	7.9	9.9	7.6	4,400	390	68	85	59	85	75	81	44
PA	Philadelphia	55	74.5	68	9.5	10.3	8.2	4,759	1,235	49	76	54	73	58	77	53
	Pittsburgh	43	83.8	56	9.0	10.4	7.3	5,829	726	48	80	58	77	66	82	54
RI	Providence	42	73.2	55	10.4	10.9	9.4	5,754	714	45	75	55	71	56	76	55
SC	Columbia	48	68.5	60	6.8	7.2	6.3	2,594	2,074	42	86	51	81	53	87	53
SD	Sioux Falls	50	71.2	60	11.0	10.9	9.8	7,812	747	45	81	67	78	72	83	62
TN	Memphis	43	67.7	60	8.8	10.0	7.5	3,041	2,187	69	80	61	77	65	83	61
	Nashville	54	71.8	67	8.0	9.1	6.5	3,677	1,652	43	82	64	77	67	86	64
TX	Dallas-Fort Worth .	42	63.0	55	10.7	11.0	9.7	2,370	2,568	45	79	62	77	65	77	56
	El Paso	53	47.1	66	8.8	8.3	8.3	2,543	2,254	48	56	27	63	34	60	29
	Houston	26	75.3	39	7.6	8.1	6.6	1,525	2,893	39	88	68	84	70	90	67
UT	Salt Lake City	69	65.8	79	8.8	7.5	9.5	5,631	1,066	48	67	43	79	69	50	21
VT	Burlington	52	84.1	65	9.0	9.7	8.0	7,665	489	43	77	58	73	64	78	53
VA	Norfolk	47	71.2	60	10.5	11.4	8.9	3,368	1,612	60	78	58	74	58	81	59
	Richmond	50	72.9	60	7.7	8.1	6.9	3,919	1,435	74	82	53	79	56	84	55
WA	Seattle-Tacoma . . .	51	84.4	60	8.8	9.5	8.1	4,797	173	49	84	62	82	74	81	49
	Spokane	48	76.4	61	8.9	8.7	8.6	6,820	394	49	78	52	86	79	64	26
WV	Charleston	47	82.2	61	5.8	6.9	4.8	4,644	978	61	84	56	78	63	90	59
WI	Milwaukee	55	75.3	68	11.5	12.6	9.7	7,087	616	48	79	68	75	70	80	65
WY	Cheyenne	60	71.2	51	12.9	15.1	10.4	7,388	273	49	65	45	57	50	68	37
PR	San Juan	40	80.0	53	8.3	8.3	9.6	–	5,426	53	81	65	78	67	79	65

– Represents zero. [1] Percent of days that are either partly cloudy or cloudy. [2] Airport data for sunshine.

Source: U.S. National Oceanic and Atmospheric Administration, *Comparative Climatic Data*, annual. See also <http://www.ncdc.noaa.gov/oa/climate/online/ccd/clpcdy.txt>; <http://www.ncdc.noaa.gov/oa/climate/online/ccd/wndspd.txt>; <http://www.ncdc.noaa.gov/oa/climate/online/ccd/nrmhdd.txt>; <http://www.ncdc.noaa.gov/oa/climate/online/ccd/nrmcdd.txt>; <http://www.ncdc.noaa.gov/oa/climate/online/ccd/relhum.txt>.

Section 7
Elections

This section relates primarily to presidential, congressional, and gubernatorial elections. Also presented are summary tables on congressional legislation; state legislatures; Black, Hispanic, and female officeholders; population of voting age; voter participation; and campaign finances.

Official statistics on federal elections, collected by the Clerk of the House, are published biennially in *Statistics of the Presidential and Congressional Election and Statistics of the Congressional Election.* Federal and state elections data appear also in *America Votes*, a biennial volume published by CQ Press (a division of Congressional Quarterly, Inc.), Washington, DC. Federal elections data also appear in the U.S. Congress, *Congressional Directory*, and in official state documents. Data on reported registration and voting for social and economic groups are obtained by the U.S. Census Bureau as part of the Current Population Survey (CPS) and are published in Current Population Reports, Series P20 (see text, Section 1).

Almost all federal, state, and local governmental units in the United States conduct elections for political offices and other purposes. The conduct of elections is regulated by state laws or, in some cities and counties, by local charter. An exception is that the U.S. Constitution prescribes the basis of representation in Congress and the manner of electing the president and grants to Congress the right to regulate the times, places, and manner of electing federal officers. Amendments to the Constitution have prescribed national criteria for voting eligibility. The 15th Amendment, adopted in 1870, gave all citizens the right to vote regardless of race, color, or previous condition of servitude. The 19th Amendment, adopted in 1919, further extended the right to vote to all citizens regardless of sex. The payment of poll taxes as a prerequisite to voting in federal elections was banned by the 24th Amendment in 1964. In 1971, as a result of the 26th Amendment, eligibility to vote

in national elections was extended to all citizens, 18 years old and over.

Presidential election— The Constitution specifies how the president and vice president are selected. Each state elects, by popular vote, a group of electors equal in number to its total of members of Congress. The 23rd Amendment, adopted in 1961, grants the District of Columbia three presidential electors, a number equal to that of the least populous state. Subsequent to the election, the electors meet in their respective states to vote for president and vice president. Usually, each elector votes for the candidate receiving the most popular votes in his or her state. A majority vote of all electors is necessary to elect the president and vice president. If no candidate receives a majority, the House of Representatives, with each state having one vote, is empowered to elect the president and vice president, again, with a majority of votes required.

The 22nd Amendment to the Constitution, adopted in 1951, limits presidential tenure to two elective terms of 4 years each or to one elective term for any person who, upon succession to the presidency, has held the office or acted as President for more than 2 years.

Congressional election— The Constitution provides that representatives be apportioned among the states according to their population, that a census of population be taken every 10 years as a basis for apportionment, and that each state have at least one representative. At the time of each apportionment, Congress decides what the total number of representatives will be. Since 1912, the total has been 435, except during 1960 to 1962 when it increased to 437, adding one representative each for Alaska and Hawaii. The total reverted to 435 after reapportionment following the 1960 census. Members are elected for 2-year terms, all terms covering the same period. The District of Columbia, American Samoa, Guam, and the Virgin Islands

Elections 243

each elect one nonvoting delegate, and Puerto Rico elects a nonvoting resident commissioner.

The Senate is composed of 100 members, two from each state, who are elected to serve for a term of 6 years. One-third of the Senate is elected every 2 years. Senators were originally chosen by the state legislatures. The 17th Amendment to the Constitution, adopted in 1913, prescribed that senators be elected by popular vote.

Voter eligibility and participation— The Census Bureau publishes estimates of the population of voting age and the percent casting votes in each state for presidential and congressional election years. These voting-age estimates include a number of persons who meet the age requirement but are not eligible to vote, (e.g. aliens and some institutionalized persons). In addition, since 1964, voter participation and voter characteristics data have been collected during November of election years as part of the CPS. These survey data include noncitizens in the voting-age population estimates, but exclude members of the Armed Forces and the institutional population.

Statistical reliability— For a discussion of statistical collection and estimation, sampling procedures, and measures of statistical reliability applicable to Census Bureau data, see Appendix III.

Figure 7.1
Vote Cast for President by Major Political Party: 2000 to 2008

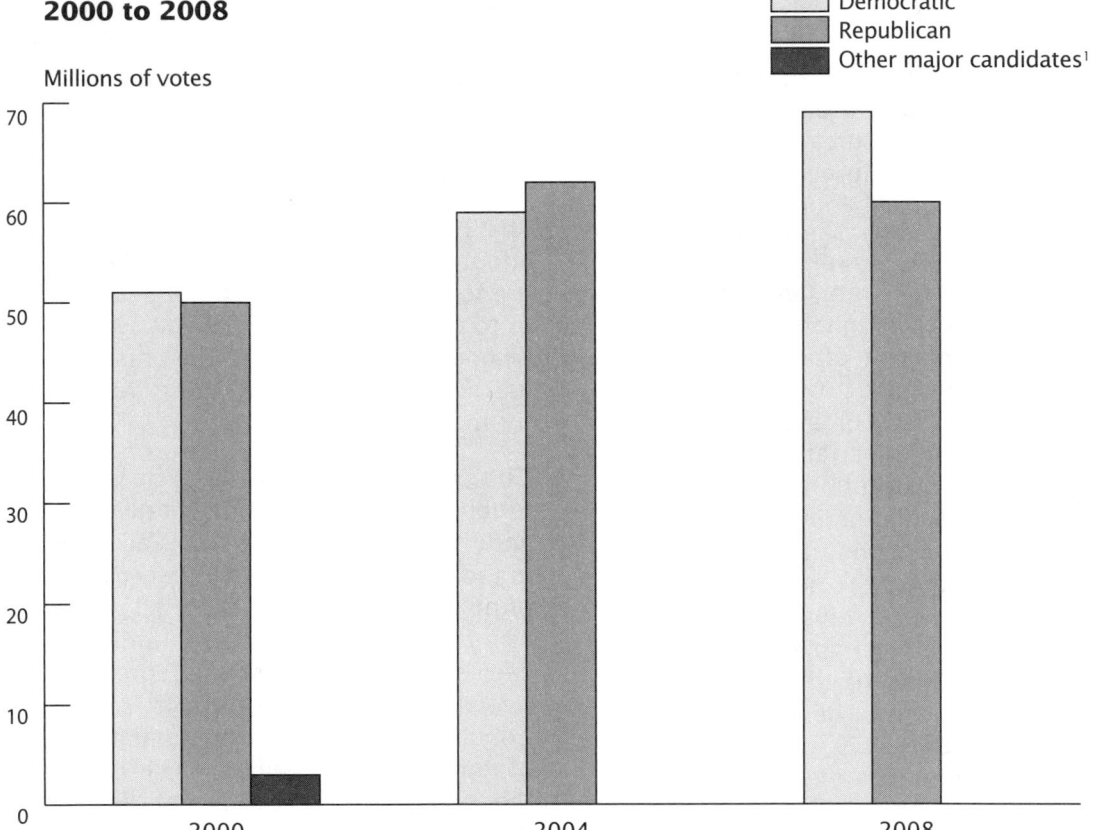

¹Candidates with 1 million or more votes: 2000—Green, Ralph Nader.

Source: Chart prepared by U.S. Census Bureau. For data, see Tables 395 and 396.

U.S. Census Bureau, Statistical Abstract of the United States: 2011

Table 395. Vote Cast for President by Major Political Party: 1952 to 2008

[In thousands (61,552 represents 61,552,000), except percent and electoral vote. Prior to 1960, excludes Alaska and Hawaii; prior to 1964, excludes DC. Vote cast for major party candidates includes the votes of minor parties cast for those candidates]

Year	Candidates for President		Vote cast for President						
	Democratic	Republican	Total popular vote [1] (1,000)	Democratic			Republican		
				Popular vote		Electoral vote	Popular vote		Electoral vote
				Number (1,000)	Percent		Number (1,000)	Percent	
1952....	Stevenson	Eisenhower ...	61,552	27,315	44.4	89	33,779	54.9	442
1956....	Stevenson	Eisenhower ...	62,027	26,739	43.1	73	35,581	57.4	457
1960....	Kennedy......	Nixon........	68,836	34,227	49.7	303	34,108	49.5	219
1964....	Johnson......	Goldwater	70,098	42,825	61.1	486	27,147	38.7	52
1968....	Humphrey	Nixon........	73,027	30,989	42.4	191	31,710	43.4	301
1972....	McGovern	Nixon........	77,625	28,902	37.2	17	46,740	60.2	520
1976....	Carter	Ford........	81,603	40,826	50.0	297	39,148	48.0	240
1980....	Carter	Reagan	86,497	35,481	41.0	49	43,643	50.5	489
1984....	Mondale......	Reagan	92,655	37,450	40.4	13	54,167	58.5	525
1988....	Dukakis	Bush	91,587	41,717	45.5	111	48,643	53.1	426
1992....	Clinton	Bush	104,600	44,858	42.9	370	38,799	37.1	168
1996....	Clinton	Dole.........	96,390	47,402	49.2	379	39,198	40.7	159
2000....	Gore........	Bush	105,594	50,996	48.3	266	50,465	47.8	271
2004....	Kerry	Bush	122,349	58,895	48.1	251	61,873	50.6	286
2008....	Obama.......	McCain	131,407	69,498	52.9	365	59,948	45.6	173

[1] Include votes for minor party candidates, independents, unpledged electors, and scattered write-in votes.

Source: U.S. House of Representatives, Office of the Clerk, *Statistics of the Presidential and Congressional Election*, 2009, biennial. See also <http://clerk.house.gov/member_info/election.html>.

Table 396. Vote Cast for Leading Minority Party Candidates for President: 1952 to 2008

[In thousands (135 represents 135,000). See headnote, Table 395. Data do not include write-ins, scatterings, or votes for candidates who ran on party tickets not shown]

Year	Candidate	Party	Popular vote (1,000)	Candidate	Party	Popular vote (1,000)
1952.....	Vincent Hallinan......	Progressive	135	Stuart Hamblen .	Prohibition	73
1956 [1]	T. Coleman Andrews	States' Rights	91	Eric Hass...........	Socialist Labor.....	41
1960.....	Eric Hass...........	Socialist Labor........	46	Rutherford Decker	Prohibition	46
1964.....	Eric Hass...........	Socialist Labor........	43	Clifton DeBerry	Socialist Workers...	22
1968.....	George Wallace......	American Independent ..	9,446	Henning Blomen	Socialist Labor......	52
1972 [1]	John Schmitz........	American.............	993	Benjamin Spock......	People's...........	9
1976.....	Eugene McCarthy	Independent...........	680	Roger McBride.......	Libertarian........	172
1980.....	John Anderson	Independent...........	5,251	Ed Clark...........	Libertarian........	920
1984.....	David Bergland	Libertarian	227	Lyndon H. LaRouche ..	Independent.......	79
1988.....	Ron Paul	Libertarian	410	Lenora B. Fulani	New Alliance......	129
1992.....	H. Ross Perot.......	Independent...........	19,722	Andre Marrou........	Libertarian	281
1996.....	H. Ross Perot........	Reform...............	7,137	Ralph Nader	Green...........	527
2000.....	Ralph Nader	Green...............	2,530	Pat Buchanan	Reform..........	324
2004.....	Ralph Nader	Independent........	156	Michael Badnarik.....	Libertarian........	369
2008.....	Ralph Nader	Independent...........	739	Bob Barr	Libertarian........	515

[1] Data include write-ins, scatterings, and/or votes for candidates who ran on party tickets not shown.

Source: U.S. House of Representatives, Office of the Clerk, *Statistics of the Presidential and Congressional Election*, 2009, biennial. See also <http://clerk.house.gov/member_info/election.html>.

Table 397. Democratic and Republican Percentages of Two-Party Presidential Vote by Selected Characteristics of Voters: 2004 and 2008

[In percent. Covers citizens of voting age living in private housing units in the contiguous United States. Percentages for Democratic Presidential vote are computed by subtracting the percentage Republican vote from 100 percent; third-party or independent votes are not included as valid data. Data are from the National Election Studies and are based on a sample and subject to sampling variability; for details, see source]

| Characteristic | 2004 | | 2008 | | Characteristic | 2004 | | 2008 | |
	Demo-cratic	Republi-can	Demo-cratic	Republi-can		Demo-cratic	Republi-can	Demo-cratic	Republi-can
Total [1]	**50**	**50**	**55**	**45**	Race:				
					White	42	58	44	56
Year of birth:					Black	90	10	99	1
1975 or later	66	34	65	35	Education:				
1959 to 1974	45	55	56	44	Less than high school...	69	31	72	28
1943 to 1958	44	56	54	46	High school diploma/				
1927 to 1942	51	49	41	59	equivalent	46	54	57	43
1911 to 1926	52	48	52	48	Some college,				
1895 to 1910	–	–	–	–	no degree	47	53	53	47
					College	50	50	51	49
Sex:									
Male............	46	54	52	48	Union household	64	36	60	40
Female..........	53	47	57	43	Nonunion household	46	54	54	46

– Represents zero. [1] Includes other characteristics, not shown separately.

Source: American National Election Studies, <http://www.electionstudies.org/>.

Elections 245

Table 398. Electoral Vote Cast for President by Major Political Party—States: 1968 to 2008

[D = Democratic, R = Republican. For composition of regions, see map, inside front cover]

State	1968 [1]	1972 [2]	1976 [3]	1980	1984	1988 [4]	1992	1996	2000 [5]	2004 [6]	2008 [7]
Democratic......	**191**	**17**	**297**	**49**	**13**	**111**	**370**	**379**	**266**	**251**	**365**
Republican......	**301**	**520**	**240**	**489**	**525**	**426**	**168**	**159**	**271**	**286**	**173**
Northeast:											
Democratic	102	14	86	4	–	53	106	106	102	101	101
Republican........	24	108	36	118	113	60	–	–	4	–	–
Midwest:											
Democratic	31	–	58	10	10	29	100	100	68	57	97
Republican........	118	145	87	135	127	108	29	29	61	66	27
South:											
Democratic	45	3	149	31	3	8	68	80	15	16	71
Republican........	77	165	20	138	174	168	116	104	168	173	118
West:											
Democratic	13	–	4	4	–	21	96	93	81	77	96
Republican........	82	102	97	98	111	90	23	26	38	47	28
AL	(¹)	R-9	D-9	R-9	R-9	R-9	R-9	R-9	R-9	R-9	R-9
AK	R-3	R-3	R-3	R-3	R-3	R-3	R-3	R-3	R-3	R-3	R-3
AZ	R-5	R-6	R-6	R-6	R-7	R-7	R-8	D-0	R-8	R-10	R-10
AR	(¹)	R-6	D-6	R-6	R-6	R-6	D-6	D-6	R-6	R-6	R-6
CA	R-40	R-45	R-45	R-45	R-47	R-47	D-54	D-54	D-54	D-55	D-55
CO	R-6	R-7	R-7	R-7	R-8	R-8	D-8	R-8	R-8	R-9	D-9
CT	D-8	R-8	R-8	R-8	R-8	R-8	D-8	D-8	D-8	D-7	D-7
DE	R-3	R-3	D-3	R-3	R-3	R-3	D-3	D-3	D-3	D-3	D-3
DC	D-3	D-3	D-3	D-3	D-3	D-3	D-3	D-3	⁵ D-2	D-3	D-3
FL	R-14	R-17	D-17	R-17	R-21	R-21	R-25	D-25	R-25	R-27	D-27
GA	(¹)	R-12	D-12	D-12	R-12	R-12	D-13	R-13	R-13	R-15	R-15
HI	D-4	R-4	D-4	D-4	R-4	D-4	D-4	D-4	D-4	D-4	D-4
ID	R-4	R-4	R-4	R-4	R-4	R-4	R-4	R-4	R-4	R-4	R-4
IL	R-26	R-26	R-26	R-26	R-24	R-24	D-22	D-22	D-22	D-21	D-21
IN	R-13	R-13	R-13	R-13	R-12	R-12	R-12	R-12	R-12	R-11	D-11
IA	R-9	R-8	R-8	R-8	R-8	D-8	D-7	D-7	D-7	R-7	D-7
KS	R-7	R-7	R-7	R-7	R-7	R-7	R-6	R-6	R-6	R-6	R-6
KY	R-9	R-9	D-9	R-9	R-9	R-9	D-8	D-8	R-8	R-8	R-8
LA	(¹)	R-10	D-10	R-10	R-10	R-10	D-9	D-9	R-9	R-9	R-9
ME	D-4	R-4	R-4	R-4	R-4	R-4	D-4	D-4	D-4	D-4	D-4
MD	D-10	R-10	D-10	D-10	R-10	R-10	D-10	D-10	D-10	D-10	D-10
MA	D-14	D-14	D-14	R-14	R-13	D-13	D-12	D-12	D-12	D-12	D-12
MI	D-21	R-21	R-21	R-21	R-20	R-20	D-18	D-18	D-18	D-17	D-17
MN	D-10	R-10	D-10	D-10	D-10	D-10	D-10	D-10	D-10	⁶ D-9	D-10
MS	(¹)	R-7	D-7	R-7	R-7	R-7	R-7	R-7	R-7	R-6	R-6
MO	R-12	R-12	D-12	R-12	R-11	R-11	D-11	D-11	R-11	R-11	R-11
MT	R-4	R-4	R-4	R-4	R-4	R-4	D-3	R-3	R-3	R-3	R-3
NE	R-5	R-5	R-5	R-5	R-5	R-5	R-5	R-5	R-5	R-5	⁷ R-4
NV	R-3	R-3	R-3	R-3	R-4	R-4	D-4	D-4	R-4	R-5	D-5
NH	R-4	R-4	R-4	R-4	R-4	R-4	D-4	D-4	R-4	D-4	D-4
NJ	R-17	R-17	R-17	R-17	R-16	R-16	D-15	D-15	D-15	D-15	D-15
NM	R-4	R-4	R-4	R-4	R-5	R-5	D-5	D-5	D-5	R-5	D-5
NY	D-43	R-41	D-41	R-41	R-36	D-36	D-33	D-33	D-33	D-31	D-31
NC	¹ R-12	R-13	D-13	R-13	R-13	R-13	R-14	R-14	R-14	R-15	D-15
ND	R-4	R-3	R-3	R-3	R-3	R-3	R-3	R-3	R-3	R-3	R-3
OH	R-26	R-25	D-25	R-25	R-23	R-23	D-21	D-21	R-21	R-20	D-20
OK	R-8	R-8	R-8	R-8	R-8	R-8	R-8	R-8	R-8	R-7	R-7
OR	R-6	R-6	R-6	R-6	R-7	D-7	D-7	D-7	D-7	D-7	D-7
PA	D-29	R-27	D-27	R-27	R-25	R-25	D-23	D-23	D-23	D-21	D-21
RI	D-4	R-4	D-4	D-4	R-4	D-4	D-4	D-4	D-4	D-4	D-4
SC	R-8	R-8	D-8	R-8	R-8	R-8	R-8	R-8	R-8	R-8	R-8
SD	R-4	R-4	R-4	R-4	R-3	R-3	R-3	R-3	R-3	R-3	R-3
TN	R-11	R-10	D-10	R-10	R-11	R-11	D-11	D-11	R-11	R-11	R-11
TX	D-25	R-26	D-26	R-26	R-29	R-29	R-32	R-32	R-32	R-34	R-34
UT	R-4	R-4	R-4	R-4	R-5	R-5	R-5	R-5	R-5	R-5	R-5
VT	R-3	R-3	R-3	R-3	R-3	R-3	D-3	D-3	D-3	D-3	D-3
VA	R-12	² R-11	R-12	R-12	R-12	R-12	R-13	R-13	R-13	R-13	D-13
WA	D-9	R-9	³ R-8	R-9	R-10	D-10	D-11	D-11	D-11	D-11	D-11
WV	D-7	R-6	D-6	D-6	R-6	⁴ D-5	D-5	D-5	R-5	R-5	R-5
WI	R-12	R-11	D-11	R-11	R-11	D-11	D-11	D-11	D-11	D-10	D-10
WY	R-3	R-3	R-3	R-3	R-3	R-3	R-3	R-3	R-3	R-3	R-3

– Represents zero. ¹ Excludes 46 electoral votes cast for American Independent George C. Wallace as follows: AL 10, AR 6, GA 12, LA 10, MS 7, and NC 1. ² Excludes one electoral vote cast for Libertarian John Hospers in Virginia. ³ Excludes one electoral vote cast for Ronald Reagan in Washington. ⁴ Excludes one electoral vote cast for Lloyd Bentsen for President in West Virginia. ⁵ Excludes one electoral vote left blank by a Democratic elector in the District of Columbia. ⁶ Excludes one electoral vote cast for Democratic vice presidential nominee John Edwards in Minnesota. ⁷ Excludes one electoral vote for Barack Obama in Nebraska.

Source: U.S. House of Representatives, Office of the Clerk, *Statistics of the Presidential and Congressional Election*, 2009, biennial. See also <http://clerk.house.gov/member_info/election.html>.

U.S. Census Bureau, Statistical Abstract of the United States: 2011

Table 399. Popular Vote Cast for President by Political Party—States: 2004 and 2008

[In thousands (122,349 represents 122,349,000), except percent]

State	2004 Total [1]	2004 Democratic party	2004 Republican party	2004 Percent of total vote Democratic party	2004 Percent of total vote Republican party	2008 Total [1]	2008 Democratic party	2008 Republican party	2008 Percent of total vote Democratic party	2008 Percent of total vote Republican party
United States	**122,349**	**58,895**	**61,873**	**48.1**	**50.6**	**131,407**	**69,498**	**59,948**	**52.9**	**45.6**
Alabama	1,883	694	1,176	36.8	62.5	2,100	813	1,267	38.7	60.3
Alaska	313	111	191	35.5	61.1	326	124	194	37.9	59.4
Arizona	2,013	894	1,104	44.4	54.9	2,293	1,035	1,230	45.1	53.6
Arkansas	1,055	470	573	44.5	54.3	1,087	422	638	38.9	58.7
California	12,421	6,745	5,510	54.3	44.4	13,562	8,274	5,012	61.0	37.0
Colorado	2,130	1,002	1,101	47.0	51.7	2,401	1,289	1,074	53.7	44.7
Connecticut	1,579	857	694	54.3	43.9	1,647	998	629	60.6	38.2
Delaware	375	200	172	53.3	45.8	412	255	152	61.9	36.9
District of Columbia	228	203	21	89.2	9.3	266	246	17	92.5	6.5
Florida	7,610	3,584	3,965	47.1	52.1	8,391	4,282	4,046	51.0	48.2
Georgia	3,302	1,366	1,914	41.4	58.0	3,924	1,844	2,049	47.0	52.2
Hawaii	429	232	194	54.0	45.3	456	326	121	71.5	26.4
Idaho	598	181	409	30.3	68.4	655	236	403	36.1	61.5
Illinois	5,274	2,892	2,346	54.8	44.5	5,522	3,419	2,031	61.9	36.8
Indiana	2,468	969	1,479	39.3	59.9	2,751	1,374	1,346	49.9	48.9
Iowa	1,507	742	752	49.2	49.9	1,537	829	682	53.9	44.4
Kansas	1,188	435	736	36.6	62.0	1,236	515	700	41.7	56.6
Kentucky	1,796	713	1,069	39.7	59.5	1,827	752	1,048	41.2	57.4
Louisiana	1,943	820	1,102	42.2	56.7	1,961	783	1,148	39.9	58.6
Maine	741	397	330	53.6	44.6	731	422	295	57.7	40.4
Maryland	2,384	1,334	1,025	56.0	43.0	2,632	1,629	960	61.9	36.5
Massachusetts	2,927	1,804	1,071	61.6	36.6	3,103	1,904	1,109	61.4	35.7
Michigan	4,839	2,479	2,314	51.2	47.8	5,002	2,873	2,049	57.4	41.0
Minnesota	2,828	1,445	1,347	51.1	47.6	2,910	1,573	1,275	54.1	43.8
Mississippi	1,140	458	673	40.2	59.0	1,290	555	725	43.0	56.2
Missouri	2,731	1,259	1,456	46.1	53.3	2,925	1,442	1,446	49.3	49.4
Montana	450	174	266	38.6	59.1	490	232	243	47.3	49.5
Nebraska	778	254	513	32.7	65.9	801	333	453	41.6	56.5
Nevada	830	397	419	47.9	50.5	968	534	413	55.1	42.7
New Hampshire	678	341	331	50.2	48.8	711	385	317	54.1	44.5
New Jersey	3,612	1,911	1,670	52.9	46.2	3,868	2,215	1,613	57.3	41.7
New Mexico	756	371	377	49.0	49.8	830	472	347	56.9	41.8
New York	7,448	4,181	2,807	56.1	37.7	7,722	4,805	2,753	62.2	35.6
North Carolina	3,501	1,526	1,961	43.6	56.0	4,298	2,143	2,128	49.8	49.5
North Dakota	313	111	197	35.5	62.9	317	141	169	44.6	53.3
Ohio	5,628	2,741	2,860	48.7	50.8	5,708	2,940	2,678	51.5	46.0
Oklahoma	1,464	504	960	34.4	65.6	1,463	502	960	34.4	65.6
Oregon	1,837	943	867	51.3	47.2	1,828	1,037	738	56.7	40.4
Pennsylvania	5,770	2,938	2,794	50.9	48.4	6,013	3,276	2,656	54.5	44.2
Rhode Island	437	260	169	59.4	38.7	472	297	165	62.9	35.1
South Carolina	1,618	662	938	40.9	58.0	1,921	862	1,035	44.9	53.9
South Dakota	388	149	233	38.4	59.9	382	171	203	44.7	53.2
Tennessee	2,437	1,036	1,384	42.5	56.8	2,600	1,087	1,479	41.8	56.9
Texas	7,411	2,833	4,527	38.2	61.1	8,078	3,529	4,479	43.7	55.5
Utah	928	241	664	26.0	71.5	952	328	596	34.4	62.6
Vermont	312	184	121	58.9	38.8	325	219	99	67.5	30.4
Virginia	3,195	1,455	1,717	45.5	53.7	3,723	1,960	1,725	52.6	46.3
Washington	2,859	1,510	1,305	52.8	45.6	3,037	1,751	1,229	57.7	40.5
West Virginia	756	327	424	43.2	56.1	713	304	397	42.6	55.7
Wisconsin	2,997	1,490	1,478	49.7	49.3	2,983	1,677	1,262	56.2	42.3
Wyoming	244	71	168	29.0	68.7	255	83	165	32.5	64.7

[1] Includes other parties.

Source: U.S. House of Representatives, Office of the Clerk, *Statistics of the Presidential and Congressional Election*, 2009, biennial. See also <http://clerk.house.gov/member_info/election.html>.

U.S. Census Bureau, Statistical Abstract of the United States: 2011

Table 400. Vote Cast for U.S. Senators, 2006 and 2008, and Incumbent Senators, 2010—States

[1,527 represents 1,527,000. D = Democrat, R = Republican, I = Independent]

State	2006 Total[2] (1,000)	2006 Percent for leading party	2008 Total[2] (1,000)	2008 Percent for leading party	Incumbent senators and year term expires[1] — Name, party, and year	Incumbent senators and year term expires[1] — Name, party, and year
Alabama	(X)	(X)	2,060	R-63.4	Jeff Sessions (R) 2015	Richard Shelby (R) 2011
Alaska	(X)	(X)	318	D-47.8	Lisa Murkowski (R) 2011	Mark Begich (D) 2015
Arizona	1,527	R-53.3	(X)	(X)	Jon Kyl (R) 2013	John McCain (R) 2011
Arkansas	(X)	(X)	1,012	D-79.5	Blanche L. Lincoln (D) 2011	Mark L. Pryor (D) 2015
California	8,541	D-59.4	(X)	(X)	Barbara Boxer (D) 2011	Dianne Feinstein (D) 2013
Colorado	(X)	(X)	2,332	D-52.8	Mark Udall (D) 2015	Michael F. Bennett [3] (D) 2011
Connecticut	1,135	D-39.7	(X)	(X)	Christopher J. Dodd (D) 2011	Joseph I. Lieberman (I) 2013
Delaware	243	D-70.2	398	D-64.7	Edward E. Kaufman [4] (D) 2015	Thomas R. Carper (D) 2013
Florida	4,794	D-60.3	(X)	(X)	George S. LeMieux [5] (R) 2011	Bill Nelson (D) 2013
Georgia	(X)	(X)	2,266	R-54.2	Saxby Chambliss (R) 2015	Johnny Isakson (R) 2011
Hawaii	343	D-61.3	(X)	(X)	Daniel K. Akaka (D) 2013	Daniel K. Inouye (D) 2011
Idaho	(X)	(X)	645	R-57.7	James E. Risch (R) 2015	Mike Crapo (R) 2011
Illinois	(X)	(X)	5,330	D-67.8	Richard J. Durbin (D) 2015	Roland W. Burris [6] (D) 2011
Indiana	1,341	R-87.4	(X)	(X)	Evan Bayh (D) 2011	Richard G. Lugar (R) 2013
Iowa	(X)	(X)	1,503	D-62.7	Chuck Grassley (R) 2011	Tom Harkin (D) 2015
Kansas	(X)	(X)	1,211	R-60.1	Sam Brownback (R) 2011	Pat Roberts (R) 2015
Kentucky	(X)	(X)	1,801	R-53.0	Jim Bunning (R) 2011	Mitch McConnell (R) 2015
Louisiana [7]	(X)	(X)	1,897	D-52.1	Mary L. Landrieu (D) 2015	David Vitter (R) 2011
Maine	545	R-74.4	724	R-61.3	Susan M. Collins (R) 2015	Olympia J. Snowe (R) 2013
Maryland	1,781	D-54.2	(X)	(X)	Barbara A. Mikulski (D) 2011	Benjamin L. Cardin (D) 2013
Massachusetts	2,244	D-66.9	3,103	D-63.6	Scott P. Brown [8] (R) 2013	John F. Kerry (D) 2015
Michigan	3,780	D-56.9	4,849	D-62.7	Carl Levin (D) 2015	Debbie Stabenow (D) 2013
Minnesota	2,203	D-58.1	2,888	D-42.0	Al Franken (D) 2015	Amy Klobuchar (D) 2013
Mississippi	611	R-63.6	1,247	R-61.4	Thad Cochran (R) 2015	Roger F. Wicker (R) 2013
Missouri	2,128	D-49.6	(X)	(X)	Christopher S. Bond (R) 2011	Claire McCaskill (D) 2013
Montana	407	D-49.2	478	D-72.9	Max Baucus (D) 2015	John Tester (D) 2013
Nebraska	592	D-63.9	793	R-57.5	Mike Johanns (R) 2015	Ben Nelson (D) 2013
Nevada	583	R-55.4	(X)	(X)	John Ensign (R) 2013	Harry Reid (D) 2011
New Hampshire	(X)	(X)	695	D-51.6	Judd Gregg (R) 2011	Jeanne Shaheen (D) 2015
New Jersey	102	D-57.2	3,482	D-56.0	Robert Menendez (D) 2013	Frank R. Lautenberg (D) 2015
New Mexico	559	D-70.6	824	D-61.3	Jeff Bingaman (D) 2013	Tom Udall (D) 2015
New York	4,701	D-57.4	(X)	(X)	Kirsten E. Gillibrand [9] (D) 2013	Charles E. Schumer (D) 2011
North Carolina	(X)	(X)	4,272	D-52.7	Richard Burr (R) 2011	Kay R. Hagan (D) 2015
North Dakota	218	D-68.8	(X)	(X)	Kent Conrad (D) 2013	Byron L. Dorgan (D) 2011
Ohio	4,019	D-56.2	(X)	(X)	Sherrod Brown (D) 2013	George V. Voinovich (R) 2011
Oklahoma	(X)	(X)	1,347	R-56.7	Tom Coburn (R) 2011	James M. Inhofe (R) 2015
Oregon	(X)	(X)	1,768	D-48.9	Jeff Merkley (D) 2015	Ron Wyden (D) 2011
Pennsylvania	4,081	D-58.6	(X)	(X)	Robert P. Casey Jr. (D) 2013	Arlen Specter (D) 2011
Rhode Island	385	D-53.5	439	D-73.1	Sheldon Whitehouse (D) 2013	Jack Reed (D) 2015
South Carolina	(X)	(X)	1,871	R-57.5	Jim DeMint (R) 2011	Lindsey Graham (R) 2015
South Dakota	(X)	(X)	381	D-62.5	Tim Johnson (D) 2015	John Thune (R) 2011
Tennessee	1,834	R-50.7	2,425	R-65.1	Lamar Alexander (R) 2015	Bob Corker (R) 2013
Texas	4,315	R-61.7	7,912	R-54.8	John Cornyn (R) 2015	Kay Hutchinson (R) 2013
Utah	571	R-62.4	(X)	(X)	Robert F. Bennett (R) 2011	Orrin G. Hatch (R) 2013
Vermont	262	R-32.4	(X)	(X)	Bernard Sanders (I) 2013	Patrick J. Leahy (D) 2011
Virginia	2,370	D-49.6	3,643	D-65.0	Jim Webb (D) 2013	Mark R. Warner (D) 2015
Washington	2,084	D-56.9	(X)	(X)	Maria Cantwell (D) 2013	Patty Murray (D) 2011
West Virginia	207	D-77.0	702	D-63.7	Carte P. Goodwin [10] (D) 2013	John D. Rockefeller IV (D) 2015
Wisconsin	2,138	D-67.3	(X)	(X)	Russell D. Feingold (D) 2011	Herb Kohl (D) 2013
Wyoming	196	R-68.9	250	D-75.6	Michael B. Enzi (R) 2015	John Barrasso (R) 2013

X Not applicable. [1] As of 3 August 2010. [2] Includes vote cast for minor parties. [3] Appointed January 21, 2009, to fill vacancy due to resignation of Ken Salazar, January 20, 2009. [4] Appointed January 15, 2009, to fill vacancy due to resignation of Joseph R. Biden, Jr., January 15, 2009. [5] Appointed August 28, 2009, to fill vacancy due to resignation of Mel Martinez, September 9, 2009. [6] Appointed December 31, 2008, to fill vacancy due to resignation of Barack Obama, November 16, 2009. [7] Louisiana holds an open-primary election with candidates from all parties running on the same ballot. Any candidate who receives a majority is elected. [8] Elected in the January 19, 2010 special election to fill seat previously held by appointed Senator Paul G. Kirk, Jr. 2006 data represents votes cast for Edward M. Kennedy. [9] Appointed January 23, 2009, to fill vacancy due to resignation of Hillary Rodham Clinton, January 21, 2009. [10] Appointed July 16, 2010, to fill vacancy due to death of Robert C. Byrd, June 28, 2010.

Source: U.S. House of Representatives, Office of the Clerk, *Statistics of the Presidential and Congressional Election,* 2009, biennial. See also <http://clerk.house.gov/member_info/election.html>.

U.S. Census Bureau, Statistical Abstract of the United States: 2011

Table 401. Vote Cast for U.S. Representatives by Major Political Party—States: 2004 to 2008

[In thousands (113,192 represents 113,192,000), except percent. R = Republican, D = Democrat, and I = Independent. In each state, totals represent the sum of votes cast in each Congressional District or votes cast for Representative-at-Large in states where only one member is elected. In all years there are numerous districts within the state where either the Republican or Democratic party had no candidate. In some states the Republican and Democratic vote includes votes cast for the party candidate by endorsing parties]

State	2004				2006				2008			
	Total [1]	Demo-cratic	Republi-can	Percent for leading party	Total [1]	Demo-cratic	Republi-can	Percent for leading party	Total [1]	Demo-cratic	Republi-can	Percent for leading party
U.S.	113,192	52,745	55,713	R-49.2	80,976	42,082	35,675	D-52.0	122,586	64,888	51,953	D-52.9
AL	1,793	708	1,080	R-60.2	1,140	502	628	R-55.0	1,855	718	1,121	R-60.4
AK	300	67	213	R-71.1	235	94	133	R-56.6	317	143	159	R-50.1
AZ	1,871	598	1,128	R-60.3	1,493	627	771	R-51.7	2,156	1,055	1,022	D-49.0
AR [2]	791	426	358	R-53.9	763	457	306	D-59.8	787	415	215	D-52.8
CA	11,624	6,224	5,031	D-53.5	8,296	4,720	3,314	D-56.9	12,322	7,381	4,516	D-59.9
CO	2,039	995	992	D-48.8	1,539	833	624	D-54.1	2,284	1,260	991	D-55.2
CT	1,429	786	630	D-55.0	1,075	649	420	D-60.4	1,527	909	505	D-59.5
DE	356	106	246	R-69.1	252	98	144	R-57.2	385	146	235	R-61.1
FL [2]	5,627	2,212	3,319	R-59.0	3,852	1,600	2,183	R-56.7	7,421	3,435	3,792	R-51.1
GA	2,961	1,141	1,820	R-61.5	2,070	932	1,138	R-55.0	3,655	1,858	1,797	D-50.8
HI	417	262	148	D-62.9	338	220	118	D-65.0	456	320	83	D-70.2
ID	572	171	401	R-70.1	445	177	248	R-55.7	638	260	377	R-59.2
IL	4,989	2,675	2,272	D-53.6	3,453	1,986	1,423	D-57.5	5,248	3,176	1,961	D-60.5
IN	2,416	999	1,382	R-57.2	1,667	812	832	R-49.9	2,677	1,389	1,241	D-51.9
IA	1,458	625	823	R-56.4	1,033	493	522	R-50.6	1,482	759	698	D-51.3
KS	1,156	387	724	R-62.6	845	369	459	R-54.3	1,208	470	690	R-57.1
KY	1,635	602	1,017	R-62.2	1,254	602	612	R-48.8	1,750	761	955	R-54.6
LA [2]	1,259	478	780	R-62.0	916	309	580	R-63.3	1,046	398	594	R-56.8
ME	710	418	283	D-58.9	536	351	163	D-65.4	710	432	278	D-60.8
MD	2,254	1,311	896	D-58.2	1,701	1,099	547	D-64.6	2,498	1,677	763	D-67.2
MA	2,927	2,060	435	D-70.4	2,244	1,632	199	D-72.7	3,103	2,246	318	D-72.4
MI	4,631	2,242	2,289	R-49.4	3,646	1,923	1,625	D-52.7	4,811	2,517	2,114	D-52.3
MN	2,722	1,400	1,236	D-51.4	2,179	1,153	925	D-52.9	2,803	1,612	1,069	D-57.5
MS	1,116	335	659	R-59.0	601	260	304	R-50.7	1,265	732	527	D-57.9
MO	2,667	1,193	1,430	R-53.6	2,097	992	1,049	R-50.0	2,821	1,413	1,313	D-50.1
MT	444	146	286	R-64.4	406	159	239	R-58.9	481	156	308	R-64.1
NE	705	231	515	R-67.3	596	262	334	R-56.1	775	265	511	R-65.8
NV	791	334	421	R-53.2	575	288	260	D-50.1	908	457	384	D-50.4
NH	652	244	396	R-60.8	403	209	190	D-52.0	675	365	295	D-54.1
NJ	3,285	1,721	1,515	D-52.4	2,137	1,208	903	D-56.5	3,438	1,912	1,462	D-55.6
NM	743	385	358	D-51.8	561	313	248	D-55.8	815	457	321	D-56.1
NY	7,448	3,457	2,209	D-46.4	4,687	2,538	1,160	D-54.1	7,722	4,006	1,800	D-51.9
NC	3,413	1,670	1,743	R-51.1	1,941	1,027	914	D-52.9	4,215	2,294	1,902	D-54.4
ND	311	185	126	D-59.6	218	140	75	D-65.7	314	195	119	D-62.0
OH	5,184	2,515	2,650	R-51.1	3,961	2,082	1,870	D-52.6	5,374	2,752	2,491	D-51.2
OK	1,375	389	875	R-63.7	905	373	518	R-57.2	1,337	504	803	R-60.0
OR	1,772	952	762	D-53.7	1,357	766	557	D-56.4	1,683	1,036	436	D-61.6
PA	5,151	2,478	2,565	R-49.8	4,013	2,229	1,732	D-55.5	5,788	3,209	2,521	D-55.4
RI	402	279	113	D-69.5	373	265	42	D-71.0	438	304	119	D-69.3
SC	1,439	486	913	R-63.5	1,086	473	600	R-55.2	1,874	920	940	R-50.1
SD	389	208	179	D-53.4	334	230	98	D-69.1	379	256	123	D-67.6
TN	2,219	1,032	1,161	R-52.3	1,715	861	800	D-50.2	2,302	1,196	978	D-51.9
TX	6,959	2,714	4,013	R-57.7	4,141	1,831	2,094	R-50.6	7,529	2,979	4,204	R-55.8
UT	909	362	520	R-57.3	570	244	292	R-51.3	937	394	504	R-53.8
VT	305	22	74	I-67.5	263	140	117	D-53.2	298	248	(X)	D-83.2
VA	3,004	1,023	1,817	R-60.5	2,297	947	1,223	R-53.2	3,495	1,853	1,591	D-53.0
WA	2,730	1,609	1,095	D-58.9	2,054	1,244	798	D-60.6	2,914	1,725	1,189	D-59.2
WV	722	415	303	D-57.6	455	264	191	D-58.0	646	432	213	D-66.9
WI	2,822	1,369	1,381	R-48.9	2,063	1,003	1,040	R-50.4	2,775	1,384	1,275	D-49.9
WY	239	100	132	R-55.2	196	92	93	R-47.6	250	107	131	R-52.6

X Not applicable. [1] Includes votes cast for minor parties. [2] State law does not require tabulation of votes for unopposed candidates.

Source: U.S. House of Representatives, Office of the Clerk, *Statistics of the Presidential and Congressional Election,* 2009, biennial. See also <http://clerk.house.gov/member_info/election.html>.

U.S. Census Bureau, Statistical Abstract of the United States: 2011

Table 402. Vote Cast for U.S. Representatives by Major Political Party—Congressional Districts: 2008

[As of December 2008. Does not include special elections, see <http://clerk.house.gov/member_info/vacancies.html>. In some states the Democratic and Republican vote includes votes cast for the party candidate by endorsing parties]

State and disrict	Democratic candidate Name	Percent of total	Republican candidate Name	Percent of total	State and district	Democratic candidate Name	Percent of total	Republican candidate Name	Percent of total
AL.....	(X)	(X)	(X)	(X)	47th...	Sanchez	69.49	Avila	25.43
1st....	(¹)	(¹)	Bonner	98.27	48th...	Young	40.67	Campbell	55.61
2d.....	Bright	50.23	Love	49.61	49th...	Hamilton	37.45	Issa	58.30
3d.....	Segall	45.84	Rogers	54.03	50th...	Leibham	45.18	Bilbray	50.24
4th....	Sparks	25.11	Aderholt	74.76	51st...	Filner	72.75	Joy	24.21
5th....	Griffith	51.52	Parker	47.94	52d....	Lumpkin	38.95	Hunter	56.37
6th....	(¹)	(¹)	Bachus	97.79	53d....	Davis	68.49	Crimmins	27.45
7th....	Davis	98.63	(¹)	(¹)	**CO**....	(X)	(X)	(X)	(X)
AK....	Berkowitz	44.97	Young	50.14	1st....	DeGette	71.94	Lilly	23.78
AZ.....	(X)	(X)	(X)	(X)	2d....	Polis	62.60	Starin	33.86
1st....	Kirkpatrick	55.88	Hay	39.43	3d....	Salazar	61.61	Wolf	38.39
2d.....	Thrasher	37.16	Franks	59.44	4th....	Markey	56.20	Musgrave	43.80
3d.....	Lord	42.07	Shadegg	54.08	5th....	Bidlack	37.04	Lamborn	60.03
4th....	Pastor	72.11	Karg	21.25	6th....	Eng	39.33	Coffman	60.67
5th....	Mitchell	53.16	Schweikert	43.57	7th....	Perlmutter	63.48	Lerew	36.52
6th....	Schneider	34.55	Flake	62.42	**CT**....	(X)	(X)	(X)	(X)
7th....	Grijalva	63.26	Sweeney	32.79	1st....	Larson	65.81	Visconti	26.01
8th....	Giffords	54.72	Bee	42.82	2d....	Courtney	61.60	Sullivan	32.37
AR.....	(X)	(X)	(X)	(X)	3d....	DeLauro	68.86	Itshaky	19.70
1st....	Berry	(²)	(¹)	(¹)	4th....	Himes	48.37	Shays	47.56
2d.....	Snyder	76.54	(¹)	(¹)	5th....	Murphy	53.25	Cappiello	38.96
3d.....	(¹)	(¹)	Boozman	78.53	**DE**....	Hartley-Nagle	37.99	Castle	61.08
4th....	Ross	86.17	(¹)	(¹)	**FL**....	(X)	(X)	(X)	(X)
CA.....	(X)	(X)	(X)	(X)	1st....	Bryan	29.82	Miller	70.18
1st....	Thompson	68.10	Starkewolf	23.36	2d....	Boyd	61.88	Mulligan	38.08
2d.....	Morris	42.11	Herger	57.89	3d....	Brown	(²)	(¹)	(¹)
3d.....	Durston	43.93	Lungren	49.49	4th....	McGovern	34.75	Crenshaw	65.25
4th....	Brown	49.76	McClintock	50.24	5th....	Russell	38.85	Brown-Waite	61.15
5th....	Matsui	74.27	Smith	20.80	6th....	Cunha	39.11	Stearns	60.89
6th....	Woolsey	71.69	Halliwell	24.06	7th....	Armitage	38.00	Mica	62.00
7th....	Miller	72.82	Petersen	21.79	8th....	Grayson	52.01	Keller	47.99
8th....	Pelosi	71.87	Walsh	9.68	9th....	Mitchell	36.27	Bilirakis	62.17
9th....	Lee	86.06	Hargrave	9.70	10th...	Hackworth	39.32	Young	60.68
10th...	Tauscher	65.12	Gerber	31.13	11th...	Castor	71.66	Adams, Jr	28.34
11th...	McNerney	55.27	Andal	44.72	12th...	Tudor	42.54	Putnam	57.46
12th...	Speier	75.11	Conlon	18.46	13th...	Jennings	37.49	Buchanan	55.54
13th...	Stark	76.43	Chui	23.57	14th...	Neeld	24.77	Mack	59.44
14th...	Eshoo	69.77	Santana	22.22	15th...	Blythe	41.99	Posey	53.10
15th...	Honda	71.66	Cordi	23.26	16th...	Mahoney	39.91	Rooney	60.09
16th...	Lofgren	71.34	Winston	24.06	17th...	Meek	(²)	(¹)	(¹)
17th...	Farr	73.88	Taylor	25.82	18th...	Taddeo	42.13	Ros-Lehtinen	57.87
18th...	Cardoza	100.00	(¹)	(¹)	19th...	Wexler	66.16	Lynch	27.24
19th...	(¹)	(¹)	Radanovich	98.43	20th...	Schultz	77.48	(¹)	(¹)
20th...	Costa	74.33	Lopez	25.67	21st...	Martinez	42.10	Diaz-Balart	57.90
21st...	Johnson	31.61	Nunes	68.39	22d...	Klein	54.68	West	45.32
22d....	(¹)	(¹)	McCarthy	100.00	23d...	Hastings	82.18	Thorpe, Jr	17.80
23d....	Capps	68.07	Kokkonen	31.93	24th...	Kosmas	57.20	Feeney	41.11
24th...	Jorgensen	41.85	Gallegly	58.15	25th...	Garcia	46.95	Diaz-Balart	53.05
25th...	Conaway	42.27	McKeon	57.73	**GA**....	(X)	(X)	(X)	(X)
26th...	Warner	40.44	Dreier	52.64	1st....	Gillespie	33.47	Kingston	66.53
27th...	Sherman	68.51	Singh	24.83	2d....	Bishop, Jr	68.95	Ferrell	31.05
28th...	Berman	99.89	(¹)	(¹)	3d....	Camp	34.30	Westmore-land	65.69
29th...	Schiff	68.91	Hahn	26.74	4th....	Johnson, Jr	99.91	(¹)	(¹)
30th...	Waxman	100.00	(¹)	(¹)	5th....	Lewis	99.95	(¹)	(¹)
31st...	Becerra	100.00	(¹)	(¹)	6th....	Jones	31.52	Price	68.48
32d....	Solis	99.99	(¹)	(¹)	7th....	Heckman	37.97	Linder	62.03
33d....	Watson	87.57	Crowley II	12.43	8th....	Marshall	57.24	Goddard	42.76
34th...	Roybal-Allard	77.09	Balding	22.91	9th....	Scott	24.49	Deal	75.51
35th...	Waters	82.58	Hayes	13.24	10th...	Saxon	39.27	Broun	60.73
36th...	Harman	68.64	Gibson	31.36	11th...	Gammon	31.81	Gingrey	68.19
37th...	Richardson	74.94	(¹)	(¹)	12th...	Barrow	66.00	Stone	34.00
38th...	Napolitano	81.73	(¹)	(¹)	13th...	Scott	69.04	Honeycutt	30.96
39th...	Sanchez	69.67	Lenning	30.33	**HI**.....	(X)	(X)	(X)	(X)
40th...	Avalos	37.45	Royce	62.55	1st....	Abercrombie	70.60	Tataii	17.45
41st...	Prince	38.35	Lewis	61.65	2d....	Hirono	69.75	Evans	18.70
42d....	Chau	39.84	Miller	60.16	**ID**.....	(X)	(X)	(X)	(X)
43d....	Baca	69.14	Roberts	30.86	1st....	Minnick	50.61	Sali	49.39
44th...	Hedrick	48.81	Calvert	51.19	2d....	Holmes	28.90	Simpson	70.89
45th...	Bornstein	41.71	Mack	58.29					
46th...	Cook	43.08	Rohrabacher	52.52					

See footnotes at end of table.

[See headnote, p. 250]

State and district	Democratic candidate — Name	Percent of total	Republican candidate — Name	Percent of total
IL......	(X)	(X)	(X)	(X)
1st....	Rush	85.87	Members	14.13
2d....	Jackson, Jr.	89.41	Williams	10.59
3d....	Lipinski	73.28	Hawkins	21.37
4th....	Gutierrez	80.60	Cunningham	11.48
5th....	Emanuel	73.94	Hanson	22.04
6th....	Morgenthaler	42.43	Roskam	57.57
7th....	Davis	85.02	Miller	14.98
8th....	Bean	60.72	Greenberg	39.28
9th....	Schakowsky	74.66	Younan	21.99
10th...	Seals	47.44	Kirk	52.56
11th...	Halvorson	58.40	Ozinga	34.48
12th...	Costello	71.40	Richardson, Jr	24.95
13th...	Harper	43.65	Biggert	53.55
14th...	Foster	57.75	Oberweis	42.25
15th...	Cox	35.81	Johnson	64.19
16th...	Abboud	36.08	Manzullo	60.87
17th...	Hare	99.77	(1)	(1)
18th...	Callahan	37.94	Schock	58.88
19th...	Davis	33.38	Shimkus	64.46
IN......	(X)	(X)	(X)	(X)
1st....	Visclosky	70.90	Leyva	27.18
2d....	Donnelly	67.09	Puckett	30.23
3d....	Montagano	39.70	Souder	55.04
4th....	Ackerson	40.13	Buyer	59.87
5th....	Ruley	34.45	Burton	65.55
6th....	Welsh	33.38	Pence	63.95
7th....	Carson	65.08	Campo	34.92
8th....	Ellsworth	64.74	Goode	35.26
9th....	Hill	57.77	Sodrel	38.41
IA......	(X)	(X)	(X)	(X)
1st....	Braley	64.61	Hartsuch	35.39
2d....	Loebsack	57.24	Miller-Meeks	38.80
3d....	Boswell	56.40	Schmett	42.13
4th....	Greenwald	39.43	Latham	60.57
5th....	Hubler	37.38	King	59.84
KS......	(X)	(X)	(X)	(X)
1st....	Bordonaro	13.27	Moran	81.88
2d....	Boyda	46.21	Jenkins	50.61
3d....	Moore	56.44	Jordan	39.66
4th....	Betts, Jr	32.38	Tiahrt	63.41
KY......	(X)	(X)	(X)	(X)
1st....	Ryan	35.65	Whitfield	64.35
2d....	Boswell	47.43	Guthrie	52.57
3d....	Yarmuth	59.37	Northup	40.63
4th....	Kelley	36.97	Davis	63.03
5th....	(1)	(1)	Rogers	84.11
6th....	Chandler	64.66	Larson	35.34
LA[3]....	(X)	(X)	(X)	(X)
1st....	Harlan	34.32	Scalise	65.68
2d[4]...	Jefferson	46.83	Cao	49.54
3d....	Melancon	(2)	(1)	(1)
4th[4]...	Carmouche	47.69	Fleming	48.07
5th....	(1)	(1)	Alexander	(2)
6th....	Cazayoux, Jr	40.29	Cassidy	48.12
7th....	Cravins, Jr	34.33	Boustany, Jr	61.88
ME......	(X)	(X)	(X)	(X)
1st....	Pingree	54.90	Summers	45.10
2d....	Michaud	67.44	Frary	32.56
MD......	(X)	(X)	(X)	(X)
1st....	Kratovil, Jr	49.12	Harris	48.33
2d....	Ruppersberger	71.86	Matthews	24.81
3d....	Sarbanes	69.66	Harris	30.08
4th....	Edwards	85.83	James	12.85
5th....	Hoyer	73.65	Bailey	23.97
6th....	Dougherty	38.79	Bartlett	57.76
7th....	Cummings	79.50	Hargadon	18.58
8th....	Hollen	75.07	Hudson	21.68
MA......	(X)	(X)	(X)	(X)
1st....	Olver	69.67	Bech	25.86
2d....	Neal	76.39	(1)	(1)
3d....	McGovern	75.04	(1)	(1)
4th....	Frank	64.30	Sholley	23.94
5th....	Tsongas	74.72	(1)	(1)
6th....	Tierney	66.79	Baker	28.00
7th....	Markey	70.48	Cunningham	22.57
8th....	Capuano	76.03	(1)	(1)
9th....	Lynch	76.29	(1)	(1)
10th...	Delahunt	75.02	(1)	(1)
MI......	(X)	(X)	(X)	(X)
1st....	Stupak	65.04	Casperson	32.74
2d....	Johnson	34.81	Hoekstra	62.36
3d....	Sanchez	35.37	Ehlers	61.11
4th....	Concannon	35.68	Camp	61.94
5th....	Kildee	70.36	Sawicki	26.96
6th....	Cooney	38.56	Upton	58.86
7th....	Schauer	48.78	Walberg	46.47
8th....	Alexander	40.23	Rogers	56.53
9th....	Peters	52.08	Knollenberg	42.63
10th...	Denison	31.17	Miller	66.30
11th...	Larkin	45.37	McCotter	51.41
12th...	Levin	72.07	Copple	23.87
13th...	Kilpatrick	74.13	Gubics	19.08
14th...	Conyers, Jr	92.40	(1)	(1)
15th...	Dingell	70.70	Lynch	24.95
MN......	(X)	(X)	(X)	(X)
1st....	Walz	62.50	Davis	32.93
2d....	Sarvi	42.55	Kline	57.29
3d....	Madia	40.85	Paulsen	48.48
4th....	McCollum	68.44	Matthews	31.31
5th....	Ellison	70.88	White	22.00
6th....	Tinklenberg	43.43	Bachmann	46.41
7th....	Peterson	72.20	Menze	27.67
8th....	Oberstar	67.69	Cummins	32.15
MS......	(X)	(X)	(X)	(X)
1st....	Childers	54.47	Davis	43.88
2d....	Thompson	69.05	Cook	30.95
3d....	Gill	37.46	Harper	62.54
4th....	Taylor	74.54	McCay III	25.46
MO......	(X)	(X)	(X)	(X)
1st....	Clay	86.86	(1)	(1)
2d....	Haas	35.41	Akin	62.28
3d....	Carnahan	66.37	Sander	30.41
4th....	Skelton	65.91	Parnell	34.09
5th....	Cleaver	64.37	Turk	35.63
6th....	Barnes	36.86	Graves	59.43
7th....	Monroe	28.16	Blunt	67.76
8th....	Allen	26.16	Emerson	71.44
9th....	Baker	47.49	Luetkemeyer	49.99
MT....	Driscoll	32.42	Rehberg	64.14
NE....	(X)	(X)	(X)	(X)
1st....	Yashirin	29.64	Fortenberry	70.36
2d....	Esch	48.07	Terry	51.93
3d....	Stoddard	23.13	Smith	76.87
NV.....	(X)	(X)	(X)	(X)
1st....	Berkley	67.65	Wegner	28.32
2d....	Derby	41.44	Heller	51.82
3d....	Titus	47.43	Porter	42.29
NH.....	(X)	(X)	(X)	(X)
1st....	Shea-Porter	51.76	Bradley	45.86
2d....	Hodes	56.44	Horn	41.42
NJ.....	(X)	(X)	(X)	(X)
1st....	Andrews	72.40	Glading	25.95
2d....	Kurkowski	39.09	LoBiondo	59.06
3d....	Adler	52.08	Myers	47.92
4th....	Zeitz	32.63	Smith	66.21
5th....	Shulman	42.40	Garrett	55.87
6th....	Pallone, Jr	66.95	McLeod	31.61
7th....	Stender	42.22	Lance	50.22
8th....	Pascrell, Jr	71.11	Straten	28.17
9th....	Rothman	67.53	Micco	31.04
10th...	Payne	98.92	(1)	(1)
11th...	Wyka	37.01	Frelinghuysen	61.84
12th...	Holt	63.12	Bateman	35.32
13th...	Sires	75.36	Turula	21.74

See footnotes at end of table.

U.S. Census Bureau, Statistical Abstract of the United States: 2011

Table 402. Vote Cast for U.S. Representatives by Major Political Party—Congressional Districts: 2008—Con.

[See headnote, p. 250]

State and district	Democratic candidate Name	Percent of total	Republican candidate Name	Percent of total	State and district	Democratic candidate Name	Percent of total	Republican candidate Name	Percent of total
NM.....	(X)........	(X)	(X)........	(X)	3d....	Blumenauer...	74.54	Lopez........	20.84
1st....	Heinrich.....	55.65	White........	44.35	4th....	DeFazio......	82.34	(¹).........	(¹)
2d....	Teague......	55.96	Tinsley......	44.04	5th....	Schrader.....	54.25	Erickson.....	38.33
3d....	Lujan.......	56.74	East........	30.47	**PA**.....	(X)........	(X)	(X)........	(X)
NY.....	(X)........	(X)	(X)........	(X)	1st....	Brady........	90.76	Muhammad....	9.24
1st....	Bishop......	43.52	Zeldin.......	30.72	2d....	Fattah.......	88.93	Lang........	11.07
2d....	Israel.......	48.71	Stalzer......	23.77	3d....	Dahlkemper...	51.25	English......	48.75
3d....	Long.......	29.18	King........	46.62	4th....	Altmire......	55.86	Hart........	44.14
4th....	McCarthy....	50.82	Martins......	28.27	5th....	McCracken....	41.04	Thompson.....	56.72
5th....	Ackerman...	51.43	Berney......	20.92	6th....	Roggio......	47.90	Gerlach......	52.10
6th....	Meeks......	67.12	(¹).........	(¹)	7th....	Sestak.......	59.59	Williams.....	40.41
7th....	Crowley.....	60.29	Britt, Jr.....	10.25	8th....	Murphy.......	56.77	Manion......	41.63
8th....	Nadler......	60.08	Lin........	14.57	9th....	Barr........	36.08	Shuster......	63.92
9th....	Weiner.....	52.25	(¹).........	(¹)	10th...	Carney......	56.33	Hackett......	43.67
10th...	Towns......	67.80	Grupico.....	3.59	11th...	Kanjorski.....	51.63	Barletta.....	48.37
11th...	Clarke......	68.50	Carr........	5.04	12th...	Murtha......	57.85	Russell......	42.15
12th...	Velazquez...	63.56	Romaguera..	6.86	13th...	Schwartz.....	62.79	Kats........	34.53
13th...	McMahon....	47.89	Straniere....	27.78	14th...	Doyle.......	91.26	(¹).........	(¹)
14th...	Maloney.....	64.25	Heim.......	15.80	15th...	Bennett.....	41.43	Dent........	58.57
15th...	Rangel.....	69.49	Daniels.....	6.39	16th...	Slater......	39.39	Pitts........	55.82
16th...	Serrano.....	72.75	Mohamed....	2.33	17th...	Holden......	63.68	Gilhooley....	36.32
17th...	Engel.......	61.40	Goodman....	14.77	18th...	O'Donnell....	35.93	Murphy......	64.07
18th...	Lowey......	55.41	Russell......	24.25	19th...	Avillo, Jr.....	33.35	Platts.......	66.65
19th...	Hall.......	44.05	Lalor.......	32.39	**RI**.....	(X)........	(X)	(X)........	(X)
20th...	Gillibrand....	53.48	Treadwell....	29.86	1st....	Kennedy.....	68.52	Scott.......	24.22
21st...	Tonko......	51.24	Buhrmaster..	27.34	2d....	Langevin.....	70.02	Zaccaria.....	29.81
22d...	Hinchey.....	50.75	Phillips......	26.39	**SC**.....	(X)........	(X)	(X)........	(X)
23d...	Oot.......	26.81	McHugh.....	46.23	1st....	Ketner......	47.89	Brown, Jr....	51.93
24th...	Arcuri......	43.01	Hanna......	36.64	2d....	Miller......	46.18	Wilson......	53.74
25th...	Maffei......	46.03	Sweetland...	33.10	3d....	Dyer.......	35.23	Barrett......	64.69
26th...	Kryzan.....	33.91	Lee........	38.62	4th....	Corden......	36.91	Inglis.......	60.09
27th...	Higgins.....	57.65	Humiston...	17.18	5th....	Spratt, Jr....	61.64	Spencer.....	36.99
28th...	Slaughter....	57.16	Crimmen...	15.45	6th....	Clyburn.....	67.48	Harrelson....	32.47
29th...	Massa.....	42.80	Kuhl, Jr.....	37.79	**SD**.....	Sandlin......	67.56	Lien.......	32.44
NC.....	(X)........	(X)	(X)........	(X)	**TN**.....	(X)........	(X)	(X)........	(X)
1st....	Butterfield...	70.28	Stephens....	29.72	1st....	Russell......	24.54	Roe........	71.82
2d....	Etheridge....	66.93	Mansell.....	31.27	2d....	Scott.......	21.89	Duncan, Jr...	78.11
3d....	Weber.....	34.10	Jones......	65.90	3d....	Vandagriff...	27.40	Wamp......	69.37
4th....	Price.......	63.32	Lawson.....	36.68	4th....	Davis.......	58.76	Lankford.....	37.81
5th....	Carter.....	41.63	Foxx.......	58.37	5th....	Cooper......	65.84	Donovan.....	31.01
6th....	Bratton......	33.00	Coble......	67.00	6th....	Gordon......	74.42	(¹).........	(¹)
7th....	McIntyre.....	68.84	Breazeale...	31.16	7th....	Morris......	31.42	Blackburn....	68.58
8th....	Kissell.....	55.38	Hayes......	44.62	8th....	Tanner......	99.97	(¹).........	(¹)
9th....	Taylor......	35.89	Myrick......	62.37	9th....	Cohen......	87.85	(¹).........	(¹)
10th...	Johnson.....	42.45	McHenry....	57.55	**TX**.....	(X)........	(X)	(X)........	(X)
11th...	Shuler......	61.96	Mumpower...	35.83	1st....	(¹).........	(¹)	Gohmert.....	87.58
12th...	Watt.......	71.56	Cobb, Jr.....	28.44	2d....	(¹).........	(¹)	Poe.........	88.92
13th...	Miller......	65.93	Webster.....	34.07	3d....	Daley.......	38.03	Johnson.....	59.75
ND.....	Pomeroy....	61.97	Sand.......	38.03	4th....	Melancon.....	29.28	Hall.......	68.80
OH.....	(X)........	(X)	(X)........	(X)	5th....	(¹).........	(¹)	Hensarling....	83.59
1st....	Driehaus....	52.47	Chabot......	47.48	6th....	Otto.......	35.61	Barton.......	62.02
2d....	Wulsin......	37.46	Schmidt.....	44.83	7th....	Skelly......	42.36	Culberson....	55.90
3d....	Mitakides....	36.68	Turner......	63.32	8th....	Hargett......	24.79	Brady.......	72.56
4th....	Carroll.....	34.83	Jordan......	65.17	9th....	Green.......	93.65	(¹).........	(¹)
5th....	Mays.......	35.91	Latta.......	64.09	10th...	Doherty.....	43.15	McCaul......	53.89
6th....	Wilson.....	62.28	Stobbs.....	32.84	11th...	(¹).........	(¹)	Conaway.....	88.33
7th....	Neuhardt....	41.78	Austria.....	58.22	12th...	Smith.......	30.60	Granger.....	67.59
8th....	Von Stein....	32.10	Boehner.....	67.90	13th...	Waun.......	22.35	Thornberry....	77.65
9th....	Kaptur.....	74.37	Leavitt......	25.63	14th...	(¹).........	(¹)	Paul........	100.00
10th...	Kucinich....	57.02	Trakas......	39.13	15th...	Hinojosa.....	65.71	Zamora......	31.95
11th...	Fudge......	85.22	Pekarek.....	14.71	16th...	Reyes.......	82.14	(¹).........	(¹)
12th...	Robinson....	42.24	Tiberi......	54.79	17th...	Edwards.....	52.98	Curnock......	45.50
13th...	Sutton.....	64.70	Potter......	35.29	18th...	Jackson-Lee..	77.32	Faulk........	20.34
14th...	O'Neill.....	38.74	LaTourette...	58.32	19th...	Fullingim....	24.95	Neugebauer....	72.44
15th...	Kilroy......	45.94	Stivers......	45.18	20th...	Gonzalez.....	71.90	Litoff........	25.18
16th...	Boccieri.....	55.36	Schuring.....	44.64	21st...	(¹).........	(¹)	Smith.......	80.00
17th...	Ryan.......	78.15	Grassell.....	21.85	22d...	Lampson.....	45.36	Olson.......	52.43
18th...	Space......	59.87	Dailey......	40.13	23d...	Rodriguez....	55.76	Larson......	41.92
OK.....	(X)........	(X)	(X)........	(X)	24th...	Love.......	41.07	Marchant.....	55.98
1st....	Oliver......	33.83	Sullivan.....	66.17	25th...	Doggett.....	65.83	Morovich.....	30.45
2d....	Boren......	70.47	Wickson.....	29.53	26th...	Leach.......	36.43	Burgess......	60.17
3d....	Robbins.....	23.57	Lucas......	69.72	27th...	Ortiz.......	57.95	Vaden.......	38.38
4th....	Cummings...	29.21	Cole.......	66.02	28th...	Cuellar......	68.71	Fish........	29.22
5th....	Perry......	34.11	Fallin......	65.89	29th...	Green.......	74.65	Story.......	23.89
OR.....	(X)........	(X)	(X)........	(X)	30th...	Johnson.....	82.48	Wood.......	15.87
1st....	Wu........	71.50	(¹).........	(¹)	31st...	Ruiz.......	36.58	Carter.......	60.27
2d....	Lemas......	25.75	Walden......	69.50	32d...	Roberson.....	40.57	Sessions.....	57.25

See footnotes at end of table.

252 Elections

Table 402. Vote Cast for U.S. Representatives by Major Political Party—Congressional Districts: 2008—Con.

[See headnote, p. 250]

State and district	Democratic candidate Name	Democratic candidate Percent of total	Republican candidate Name	Republican candidate Percent of total	State and district	Democratic candidate Name	Democratic candidate Percent of total	Republican candidate Name	Republican candidate Percent of total
UT	(X)	(X)	(X)	(X)	4th . . .	Fearing	36.91	Hastings.	63.09
1st	Bowen	30.47	Bishop	64.85	5th . . .	Mays	34.72	Rodgers.	65.28
2d. . . .	Matheson. . .	63.35	Dew	34.47	6th . . .	Dicks	66.86	Cloud.	33.14
3d. . . .	Spencer. . . .	28.28	Chaffetz	65.61	7th . . .	McDermott. . .	83.65	Beren.	16.35
VT	Welch.	83.25	(¹)	(¹)	8th . . .	Burner	47.22	Reichert.	52.78
VA	(X)	(X)	(X)	(X)	9th . . .	Smith	65.45	Postma.	34.55
1st	Day, Jr	41.75	Wittman	56.58	**WV**	(X)	(X)	(X)	(X)
2d.	Nye III	52.40	Drake.	47.46	1st . . .	Mollohan	99.93	(¹)	(¹)
3d.	Scott	97.02	(¹)	(¹)	2d. . .	Barth	42.92	Capito	57.07
4th	Miller	40.37	Forbes	59.51	3d. . .	Rahall II	66.92	Gearheart	33.08
5th	Perriello	50.09	Goode, Jr. . . .	49.86	**WI**	(X)	(X)	(X)	(X)
6th	Rasoul	36.61	Goodlatte. . . .	61.57	1st . . .	Krupp.	34.69	Ryan	63.97
7th	Hartke	37.10	Cantor	62.72	2d. . .	Baldwin	69.33	Theron	30.56
8th	Moran	67.94	Ellmore	29.68	3d. . .	Kind	63.19	Stark	34.44
9th	Boucher. . . .	97.07	(¹)	(¹)	4th . . .	Moore	87.63	(¹)	(¹)
10th . . .	Feder.	38.83	Wolf	58.80				Sensenbrenner,	
11th . . .	Connolly. . . .	54.69	Fimian	43.05	5th . . .	(¹)	(¹)	Jr.	79.58
WA.	(X)	(X)	(X)	(X)	6th . . .	Kittelson.	36.21	Petri	63.71
1st	Inslee.	67.76	Ishmael	32.24	7th . . .	Obey	60.79	Mielke	39.14
2d.	Larsen	62.39	Bart	37.61	8th . . .	Kagen	54.00	Gard.	45.90
3d.	Baird	64.01	Delavar	35.99	**WY**	Trauner	42.78	Lummis	52.59

X Not applicable. ¹ No candidate. ² According to state law, it is not required to tabulate votes for unopposed candidates.
³ Louisiana holds an open-primary election with candidates from all parties running on the same ballot. Any candidate who receives a majority is elected; if no candidate receives 50 percent, there is a run-off election in November between the top two finishers.
⁴ Reflects votes cast in the run-off election held on December 6, 2008.

Source: U.S. House of Representatives, Office of the Clerk, *Statistics of the Presidential and Congressional Election*, 2009, biennial. See also <http://clerk.house.gov/member_info/election.html>.

Table 403. Composition of Congress by Political Party: 1975 to 2010

[D = Democratic, R = Republican. As of beginning of first session of each Congress, except as noted. Data reflect immediate result of elections. Vacancies and third party candidates are noted]

Year	Party and president	Congress	House Majority party	House Minority party	House Other	Senate Majority party	Senate Minority party	Senate Other
1975 [1]	R (Ford)	94th	D-291	R-144	–	D-61	R-37	2
1977 [2]	D (Carter)	95th	D-292	R-143	–	D-61	R-38	1
1979 [2]	D (Carter)	96th	D-277	R-158	–	D-58	R-41	1
1981 [2]	R (Reagan)	97th	D-242	R-192	1	R-53	D-46	1
1983.	R (Reagan)	98th	D-269	R-166	–	R-54	D-46	–
1985.	R (Reagan)	99th	D-253	R-182	–	R-53	D-47	–
1987.	R (Reagan)	100th	D-258	R-177	–	D-55	R-45	–
1989.	R (Bush)	101st	D-260	R-175	–	D-55	R-45	–
1991 [3]	R (Bush)	102d.	D-267	R-167	1	D-56	R-44	–
1993 [3]	D (Clinton)	103d.	D-258	R-176	1	D-57	R-43	–
1995 [3]	D (Clinton)	104th	R-230	D-204	1	R-52	D-48	–
1997 [4]	D (Clinton)	105th	R-226	D-207	2	R-55	D-45	–
1999 [3]	D (Clinton)	106th	R-223	D-211	1	R-55	D-45	–
2001 [4]	R (Bush)	107th	R-221	D-212	2	D-50	R-50	–
2003 [5, 6]	R (Bush)	108th	R-229	D-204	1	R-51	D-48	1
2005 [5]	R (Bush)	109th	R-232	D-202	1	R-55	D-44	1
2007 [7]	R (Bush)	110th	D-233	R-202	–	D-49	R-49	2
2009 [6, 7, 8]	D (Obama)	111th	D-256	R-178	–	D-55	R-41	2
2010 [7, 9]	D (Obama)	111th	D-255	R-178	–	D-57	R-41	2

– Represents zero. ¹ Senate had one Independent and one Conservative-Republican. ² Senate had one Independent. ³ House had one Independent-Socialist. ⁴ House had one Independent-Socialist and one Independent. ⁵ House and Senate each had one Independent. ⁶ House had one vacancy. ⁷ Senate had two Independents. ⁸ Senate had two vacancies. ⁹ As of beginning of second session, January 5, 2010.

Source: U.S. House of Representatives, Office of the Clerk, *Official List of Members, 2010*, annual. See also <http://clerk.house.gov/member_info/olm_111.pdf>

Elections 253

Table 404. Composition of Congress by Political Party Affiliation—States: 2005 to 2010

[Figures are for the beginning of the first session, except as noted. Dem. = Democratic; Rep. = Republican]

State	Representatives								Senators							
	109th Cong.,[1,2,3] 2005		110th Cong., 2007		111th Cong.,[4] 2009		111th Cong.,[5,6] 2010		109th Cong.,[3,7] 2005		110th Cong.,[8] 2007		111th Cong.,[8,9] 2009		111th Cong.,[5,8] 2010	
	Dem.	Rep.	Dem.	Rep.	Dem.	Rep.	Dem.	Rep.	Dem.	Rep.	Dem.	Rep.	Dem.	Rep.	Dem.	Rep.
U.S. . . .	202	231	233	202	256	178	255	178	44	55	49	49	55	41	57	41
AL	2	5	2	5	3	4	2	5	–	2	–	2	–	2	–	2
AK	–	1	–	1	–	1	–	1	–	2	–	2	1	1	1	1
AZ	2	6	4	4	5	3	5	3	–	2	–	2	–	2	–	2
AR	3	1	3	1	3	1	3	1	2	–	2	–	2	–	2	–
CA	33	20	34	19	34	19	34	19	2	–	2	–	2	–	2	–
CO	3	4	4	3	5	2	5	2	1	1	1	1	2	–	2	–
CT	2	3	4	1	5	–	5	–	2	–	1	–	1	–	1	–
DE	–	1	–	1	–	1	–	1	2	–	2	–	2	–	2	–
FL	7	18	9	16	10	15	10	15	1	1	1	1	1	1	1	1
GA	6	7	6	7	6	7	6	7	–	2	–	2	–	2	–	2
HI	2	–	2	–	2	–	1	1	2	–	2	–	2	–	2	–
ID	–	2	–	2	1	1	1	1	–	2	–	2	–	2	–	2
IL	10	9	10	9	11	7	12	7	2	–	2	–	1	–	2	–
IN	2	7	5	4	5	4	5	3	1	1	1	1	1	1	1	1
IA	1	4	3	2	3	2	3	2	1	1	1	1	1	1	1	1
KS	1	3	2	2	1	3	1	3	–	2	–	2	–	2	–	2
KY	1	5	2	4	2	4	2	4	–	2	–	2	–	2	–	2
LA	2	5	2	5	1	6	1	6	1	1	1	1	1	1	1	1
ME	2	–	2	–	2	–	2	–	–	2	–	2	–	2	–	2
MD	6	2	6	2	7	1	7	1	2	–	2	–	2	–	2	–
MA	10	–	10	–	10	–	10	–	2	–	2	–	2	–	1	1
MI	6	9	6	9	8	7	8	7	2	–	2	–	2	–	2	–
MN	4	4	5	3	5	3	5	3	1	1	1	1	1	–	2	–
MS	2	2	2	2	3	1	3	1	–	2	–	2	–	2	–	2
MO	4	5	4	5	4	5	4	5	–	2	1	1	1	1	1	1
MT	–	1	–	1	–	1	–	1	1	1	2	–	2	–	2	–
NE	–	3	–	3	–	3	–	3	1	1	1	1	1	1	1	1
NV	1	2	1	2	2	1	2	1	1	1	1	1	1	1	1	1
NH	–	2	2	–	2	–	2	–	–	2	–	2	1	1	1	1
NJ	7	6	7	6	8	5	8	5	2	–	2	–	2	–	2	–
NM	1	2	1	2	3	–	3	–	1	1	1	1	2	–	2	–
NY	20	9	23	6	26	3	26	2	2	–	2	–	2	–	2	–
NC	6	7	7	6	8	5	8	5	–	2	–	2	1	1	1	1
ND	1	–	1	–	1	–	1	–	2	–	2	–	2	–	2	–
OH	6	11	7	11	10	8	10	8	–	2	1	1	1	1	1	1
OK	1	4	1	4	1	4	1	4	–	2	–	2	–	2	–	2
OR	4	1	4	1	4	1	4	1	1	1	1	1	2	–	2	–
PA	7	12	11	8	12	7	12	7	–	2	1	1	1	1	2	–
RI	2	–	2	–	2	–	2	–	1	1	2	–	2	–	2	–
SC	2	4	2	4	2	4	2	4	–	2	–	2	–	2	–	2
SD	1	–	1	–	1	–	1	–	1	1	1	1	1	1	1	1
TN	5	4	5	4	5	4	5	4	–	2	–	2	–	2	–	2
TX	11	21	13	19	12	20	12	20	–	2	–	2	–	2	–	2
UT	1	2	1	2	1	2	1	2	–	2	–	2	–	2	–	2
VT	–	–	1	–	1	–	1	–	1	–	1	–	1	–	1	–
VA	3	8	3	8	6	5	6	5	–	2	1	1	2	–	2	–
WA	6	3	6	3	6	3	6	3	2	–	2	–	2	–	2	–
WV	2	1	2	1	2	1	2	1	2	–	2	–	2	–	2	–
WI	4	4	5	3	5	3	5	3	2	–	2	–	2	–	2	–
WY	–	1	–	1	–	1	–	1	–	2	–	2	–	2	–	2

– Represents zero. [1] Vermont had one Independent-Socialist representative. [2] Ohio had one vacancy due to the resignation of Rob Portman, April 29, 2005. [3] As of June 28, 2005. [4] One vacancy due to the resignation of Rahm Emanuel, January 6, 2009 [5] As of second session, July 20, 2010. [6] Two vacancies—one in Indiana due to the resignation of Mark E. Souder, May 21, 2010, and one in New York due to the resignation of Eric J. J. Massa, March 8, 2010. [7] Vermont had one Independent senator. [8] Vermont and Connecticut both had one Independent senator. [9] Two vacancies—one in Illinois due to the resignation of Barack Obama, November 16, 2008, and one in Minnesota due to election dispute between Norm Coleman and Al Franken.

Source: U.S. House of Representatives, Office of the Clerk, *Official List of Members*, annual. See also <http://clerk.house.gov/member_info/olm_111.pdf>.

U.S. Census Bureau, Statistical Abstract of the United States: 2011

Table 405. Members of Congress—Selected Characteristics: 1995 to 2009

[As of beginning of first session of each Congress, except as noted. Figures for Representatives exclude vacancies]

Members of Congress and year	Male	Female	Black[1]	API[2]	His-panic[3]	Age[4] (in years) Under 40	40 to 49	50 to 59	60 to 69	70 and over	Seniority[5,6] Less than 2 yrs.	2 to 9 yrs.	10 to 19 yrs.	20 to 29 yrs.	30 yrs. or more
REPRESENTATIVES															
104th Cong., 1995...	388	47	[7]40	7	17	53	155	135	79	13	92	188	110	36	9
106th Cong., 1999...	379	56	[7]39	6	19	23	116	173	87	35	41	236	104	46	7
107th Cong., 2001...	376	59	[7]39	7	19	14	97	167	117	35	44	155	158	63	14
108th Cong., 2003...	376	59	[7]39	5	22	19	86	174	121	32	54	178	140	48	13
109th Cong., 2005...	369	65	[7]42	4	23	22	96	175	113	28	37	173	158	48	18
110th Cong., 2007...	361	74	[7]42	4	23	20	91	172	118	34	62	159	160	37	17
111th Cong., 2009...	366	72	[7]41	8	(NA)	24	84	156	126	44	66	166	142	42	18
SENATORS															
104th Cong., 1995...	92	8	1	2	–	1	14	41	27	17	12	38	30	15	5
106th Cong., 1999...	91	9	–	2	–	–	14	38	35	13	8	39	33	14	6
107th Cong., 2001...	87	13	–	2	–	–	8	39	33	18	11	34	30	14	9
108th Cong., 2003...	86	14	–	2	–	1	12	29	34	24	9	42	29	13	7
109th Cong., 2005...	86	14	1	2	2	–	17	29	33	21	9	41	29	14	7
110th Cong., 2007...	84	16	1	2	3	–	11	31	34	24	12	42	24	13	9
111th Cong., 2009[8]..	83	17	1	1	(NA)	–	7	31	38	22	9	34	28	17	10

– Represents zero. NA Not available. [1] Source: Joint Center for Political and Economic Studies, Washington, DC, *Black Elected Officials: Statistical Summary*, annual (copyright). [2] Asian and Pacific Islanders. Source: Prior to 2005, Library of Congress, Congressional Research Service, "Asian Pacific Americans in the United States Congress," Report 94-767 GOV; starting 2005, U.S. House of Representatives, "House Press Gallery," <http://www.house.gov/daily/> (as of May 25, 2009) and U.S. Senate, "Minorities in the Senate," <http://www.senate.gov/artandhistory/history/common/briefing/minority_senators.htm> (August 30, 2010). [3] Source: National Association of Latino Elected and Appointed Officials, Washington, DC, *National Roster of Hispanic Elected Officials*, annual. [4] Some members do not provide date of birth. [5] Represents consecutive years of service. [6] Some members do not provide years of service. [7] Includes District of Columbia and Virgin Islands delegate. [8] Excludes vacancies.

Source: Except as noted, compiled by U.S. Census Bureau from data published in *Congressional Directory*, biennial. See also <http://www.gpoaccess.gov/cdirectory/browse.html>.

Table 406. U.S. Congress—Measures Introduced and Enacted and Time in Session: 1993 to 2009

[Excludes simple and concurrent resolutions]

Item	103d Cong., 1993–94	104th Cong., 1995–96	105th Cong., 1997–98	106th Cong., 1999–00	107th Cong., 2001–02	108th Cong., 2003–04	109th Cong., 2005–06	110th Cong., 2007–08	111th Cong., 2009
Measures introduced........	8,544	6,808	7,732	9,158	9,130	8,625	10,703	11,228	7,415
Bills.................	7,883	6,545	7,532	8,968	8,953	8,468	10,560	11,081	7,324
Joint resolutions..........	661	263	200	190	177	157	143	147	91
Measures enacted..........	473	337	404	604	337	504	590	460	125
Public[1].................	465	333	394	580	331	498	589	460	125
Private[2]...............	8	4	10	24	6	6	1	–	–
HOUSE OF REPRESENTATIVES									
Number of days............	265	290	251	272	265	243	241	283	159
Number of hours...........	1,887	2,445	2,001	2,179	1,694	1,894	1,917	2,138	1,247
Number of hours per day.....	7.1	8.4	8.0	8.0	6.4	7.8	8.0	7.6	7.8
SENATE									
Number of days............	291	343	296	303	322	300	297	374	191
Number of hours...........	2,514	2,876	2,188	2,200	2,279	2,486	2,250	2,364	1,421
Number of hours per day.....	8.6	8.4	7.4	7.3	7.1	8.3	7.6	6.3	7.4

– Represents zero. [1] Laws on public matters that apply to all persons. [2] Laws designed to provide legal relief to specified persons or entities adversely affected by laws of general applicability.

Source: U.S. Congress, *Congressional Record and Daily Calendar*, selected issues. See also <http://www.senate.gov/pagelayout/reference/two_column_table/Resumes.htm>.

Table 407. Congressional Bills Vetoed: 1961 to 2010

Period	President	Total vetoes	Regular vetoes	Pocket vetoes	Vetoes sustained	Bills passed over veto
1961–63.............	John F. Kennedy	21	12	9	21	–
1963–69.............	Lyndon B. Johnson	30	16	14	30	–
1969–74.............	Richard M. Nixon......	43	26	17	36	7
1974–77.............	Gerald R. Ford........	66	48	18	54	12
1977–81.............	Jimmy Carter.........	31	13	18	29	2
1981–89.............	Ronald W. Reagan.....	78	39	39	69	9
1989–93.............	George Bush.........	44	29	15	43	1
1993–2001...........	William J. Clinton......	37	36	1	34	2
2001–2009...........	George W. Bush.......	10	10	–	7	3
2009–2010[1]	Barack Obama........	1	–	1	1	–

– Represents zero. [1] For the period January 20, 2009 through May 11, 2010.

Source: U.S. Congress, Senate Library, *Presidential Vetoes ... 1789–1968*; U.S. Congress, *Calendars of the U.S. House of Representatives and History of Legislation*, annual. See also <http://clerk.house.gov/art_history/house_history/vetoes.html>.

Elections 255

Table 408. Number of Governors by Political Party Affiliation: 1975 to 2010

[Reflects figures after inaugurations for each year]

Year	Demo-cratic	Republi-can	Inde-pendent/ other	Year	Demo-cratic	Republi-can	Inde-pendent/ other	Year	Demo-cratic	Republi-can	Inde-pendent/ other
1975....	36	13	1	1999....	17	31	1	2005....	22	28	–
1980....	31	19	–	2000....	18	30	2	2006....	22	28	–
1985....	34	16	–	2001....	19	29	2	2007....	28	22	–
1990....	29	21	–	2002....	22	27	1	2008....	28	22	–
1995....	19	30	1	2003....	23	27	–	2009....	28	22	–
1998....	17	32	1	2004....	22	28	–	2010....	26	24	–

– Represents zero.

Source: National Governors Association, Washington, DC, 1970–87 and 1991–2010, *Directory of Governors of the American States, Commonwealths & Territories*, annual, and 1988–90, *Directory of Governors*, annual (copyright).

Table 409. Vote Cast for and Governor Elected by State: 2006 to 2009

[In thousands (1,250 represents 1,250,000), except percent. D = Democratic, R = Republican]

State	Current governor [1]	Year of election	Total vote [2]	Republican	Democratic	Percent leading party
Alabama	Bob Riley	2006	1,250	718	520	R-57.4
Alaska	Sean Parnell [3]	2006	238	115	97	R-48.1
Arizona	Jan Brewer [4]	2006	1,534	544	960	D-62.6
Arkansas	Mike Beebe	2006	774	315	430	D-55.5
California	Arnold Schwarzenegger	2006	8,679	4,850	3,377	R-55.9
Colorado	Bill Ritter	2006	1,558	626	888	D-57.0
Connecticut	M. Jodi Rell	2006	1,123	710	398	R-63.2
Delaware	Jack Markell	2008	395	127	267	D-67.5
Florida	Charlie Crist	2006	4,829	2,520	2,178	R-52.2
Georgia	Sonny Perdue	2006	2,122	1,230	811	R-57.9
Hawaii	Linda Lingle	2006	349	215	122	R-61.7
Idaho	C.L. "Butch" Otter	2006	489	276	199	R-52.7
Illinois	Patrick Quinn [5]	2006	3,586	1,369	1,736	D-48.4
Indiana	Mitch Daniels	2008	2,704	1,564	1,082	R-57.8
Iowa	Chet Culver	2006	1,059	467	569	D-53.7
Kansas	Mark Parkinson [6]	2006	850	344	492	D-57.9
Kentucky	Steven L. Beshear	2007	1,055	436	620	D-58.7
Louisiana	Bobby Jindal	2007	1,298	699	398	R-54.0
Maine	John E. Baldacci	2006	551	166	210	D-38.1
Maryland	Martin O'Malley	2006	1,717	825	942	D-52.7
Massachusetts	Deval L. Patrick	2006	2,244	784	1,235	D-55.0
Michigan	Jennifer Granholm	2006	3,801	1,608	2,143	D-56.3
Minnesota	Tim Pawlenty	2006	2,218	1,029	1,007	R-46.4
Mississippi	Haley Barbour	2007	744	431	313	R-57.9
Missouri	Jay Nixon	2008	2,878	1,136	1,681	D-58.4
Montana	Brian Schweitzer	2008	487	158	319	D-65.5
Nebraska	Dave Heineman	2006	593	436	145	R-73.3
Nevada	James A. Gibbons	2006	582	279	256	R-47.9
New Hampshire	John Lynch	2008	683	189	479	D-70.2
New Jersey	Christopher J. Christie	2009	2,452	1,174	1,088	R-47.9
New Mexico	Bill Richardson	2006	559	174	385	D-68.8
New York	David A. Paterson [7]	2006	4,698	1,106	2,741	D-58.3
North Carolina	Beverly Perdue	2008	4,269	2,001	2,146	D-50.3
North Dakota	John Hoeven	2008	316	235	74	R-74.4
Ohio	Ted Strickland	2006	4,184	1,471	2,428	D-58.0
Oklahoma	Brad Henry	2006	926	310	616	R-66.5
Oregon	Ted Kulongoski	2006	1,400	534	579	D-41.3
Pennsylvania	Edward G. Rendell	2006	4,093	1,622	2,471	D-60.4
Rhode Island	Don Carcieri	2006	388	197	190	R-51.0
South Carolina	Mark Sanford	2006	1,092	602	489	R-55.1
South Dakota	Mike Rounds	2006	336	207	121	R-61.7
Tennessee	Phil Bredesen	2006	1,819	541	1,247	D-68.6
Texas	Rick Perry	2006	4,399	1,717	1,310	R-39.0
Utah	Gary Herbert [8]	2008	907	701	175	R-77.9
Vermont	Jim Douglas	2008	319	170	70	R-53.4
Virginia	Robert McDonnell	2009	1,982	1,164	819	R-59.0
Washington	Christine Gregoire	2008	3,003	1,404	1,599	D-53.2
West Virginia	Joe Manchin III	2008	706	182	493	D-69.8
Wisconsin	Jim Doyle	2006	2,162	979	1,139	D-52.7
Wyoming	Dave Freudenthal	2006	194	58	136	D-69.8

[1] As of September 3, 2010. Source: National Governors Association, Washington, DC. See also <http://www.nga.org>.
[2] Includes minor party and scattered votes. [3] Data are for Sarah Palin, who resigned July 26, 2009. [4] Data are for Janet Napolitano, who was appointed U.S. Secretary of Homeland Security January 21, 2009. [5] Data are for Rod Blagojevich, who was removed from office January 29, 2009. [6] Data are for Kathleen Sebelius, who resigned April 28, 2009. [7] Data are for Eliot Spitzer, who resigned March 17, 2008. [8] Data are for Jon Huntsman, who resigned August 7, 2009.

Source: Except as noted, The Council of State Governments, Lexington, KY, *The Book of States 2010*, annual (copyright).

Table 410. Political Party Control of State Legislatures by Party: 1985 to 2010

[As of beginning of year. Nebraska has a nonpartisan legislature]

Year	Democratic control	Split control or tie	Republican control	Year	Democratic control	Split control or tie	Republican control	Year	Democratic control	Split control or tie	Republican control
1985....	27	11	11	1996....	16	15	18	2004....	17	11	21
1989[1] ..	28	13	8	1997....	20	11	18	2005....	19	10	20
1990....	29	11	9	1999....	20	12	17	2006....	19	10	20
1992....	29	14	6	2000....	16	15	18	2007....	22	12	15
1993....	25	16	8	2001....	16	15	18	2008....	23	14	12
1994....	24	17	8	2002....	17	15	17	2009....	27	8	14
1995....	18	12	19	2003....	16	12	21	2010....	27	8	14

[1] A party change during the year by a Democratic representative broke the tie in the Indiana House of Representatives, giving the Republicans control of both chambers.

Source: National Conference of State Legislatures, Denver, CO, *State Legislatures*, periodic.

Table 411. Composition of State Legislatures by Political Party Affiliation: 2009 and 2010

[Data as of March and reflect February election results in year shown, except as noted. Figures reflect immediate results of elections, including holdover members in state houses which do not have all of their members running for reelection. Dem. = Democrat, Rep. = Republican, Vac. = Vacancies. In general, Lower House refers to body consisting of state representatives and Upper House, of state senators]

State	Lower House 2009 Dem.	Rep.	Other	Vac.	Lower House 2010 Dem.	Rep.	Other	Vac.	Upper House 2009 Dem.	Rep.	Other	Vac.	Upper House 2010 Dem.	Rep.	Other	Vac.
U.S........	3,041	2,346	18	6	3,028	2,356	21	6	1,021	890	2	9	1,026	893	2	1
AL[1]........	62	43	–	–	60	45	–	–	19	13	–	3	21	14	–	–
AK[2]........	18	22	–	–	18	22	–	–	10	10	–	–	10	10	–	–
AZ[3]........	24	36	–	–	25	35	–	–	12	18	–	–	12	18	–	–
AR[2]........	71	28	1	–	71	28	1	–	27	8	–	–	27	8	–	–
CA[2]........	51	29	–	–	49	29	1	1	25	14	–	1	25	14	–	1
CO[2]........	38	27	–	–	38	27	–	–	21	14	–	–	21	14	–	–
CT[3]........	114	36	–	1	114	37	–	–	24	12	–	–	24	12	–	–
DE[2]........	24	17	–	–	24	17	–	–	16	5	–	–	15	6	–	–
FL[2]........	44	76	–	–	44	76	–	–	14	26	–	–	14	26	–	–
GA[3]........	73	107	–	–	74	105	1	–	22	34	–	–	22	34	–	–
HI[2]........	45	6	–	–	45	6	–	–	23	2	–	–	23	2	–	–
ID[3]........	18	52	–	–	18	52	–	–	7	28	–	–	7	28	–	–
IL[4]........	70	48	–	–	70	48	–	–	37	22	–	–	37	22	–	–
IN[2]........	52	48	–	–	52	48	–	–	17	33	–	–	17	33	–	–
IA[2]........	56	44	–	–	56	44	–	–	32	18	–	–	32	18	–	–
KS[2]........	49	76	–	–	49	76	–	–	9	31	–	–	9	31	–	–
KY[2]........	65	35	–	–	65	35	–	–	15	21	1	1	17	20	1	–
LA[1]........	51	50	3	1	52	50	3	–	22	15	–	2	24	15	–	–
ME[3]........	95	55	1	–	96	54	1	–	20	15	–	–	20	15	–	–
MD[1]........	104	36	1	–	104	36	1	–	33	14	–	–	33	14	–	–
MA[3]........	142	16	1	1	143	16	1	–	35	5	–	–	35	5	–	–
MI[2]........	67	43	–	–	66	43	–	1	16	21	–	1	16	22	–	–
MN[2]........	87	47	–	–	87	47	–	–	46	21	–	–	46	21	–	–
MS[1]........	74	48	–	–	74	48	–	–	27	25	–	–	27	25	–	–
MO[2]........	74	89	–	–	74	88	–	1	11	23	–	–	11	23	–	–
MT[2]........	50	50	–	–	50	50	–	–	23	27	–	–	23	27	–	–
NE[5]........	(5)	(5)	(5)	(5)	(5)	(5)	(5)	(5)	(5)	(5)	(5)	(5)	(5)	(5)	(5)	(5)
NV[2]........	28	14	–	–	28	14	–	–	12	9	–	–	12	9	–	–
NH[3]........	224	175	–	1	225	175	–	–	14	10	–	–	14	10	–	–
NJ[2]........	48	32	–	–	47	33	–	–	23	16	–	1	23	17	–	–
NM[2]........	45	25	–	–	45	25	–	–	27	15	–	–	27	15	–	–
NY[3]........	108	41	1	–	105	43	2	–	32	30	–	–	32	30	–	–
NC[3]........	68	52	–	–	68	52	–	–	30	20	–	–	30	20	–	–
ND[1]........	36	58	–	–	36	58	–	–	21	26	–	–	21	26	–	–
OH[2]........	53	46	–	–	53	46	–	–	12	21	–	–	12	21	–	–
OK[2]........	40	61	–	–	40	61	–	–	22	26	–	–	22	26	–	–
OR[2]........	36	24	–	–	36	24	–	–	18	12	–	–	18	12	–	–
PA[2]........	104	99	–	–	103	97	–	3	21	29	–	–	20	30	–	–
RI[3]........	69	6	–	–	69	6	–	–	33	4	1	–	33	4	1	–
SC[2]........	52	71	–	1	51	73	–	–	19	27	–	–	19	27	–	–
SD[3]........	24	46	–	–	24	46	–	–	14	21	–	–	14	21	–	–
TN[2]........	49	50	–	–	48	51	–	–	14	19	–	–	14	19	–	–
TX[2]........	74	76	–	–	73	77	–	–	12	19	–	–	12	19	–	–
UT[2]........	22	53	–	–	22	53	–	–	8	21	–	–	8	21	–	–
VT[3]........	95	48	7	–	95	48	7	–	23	7	–	–	23	7	–	–
VA[2]........	45	53	2	–	39	59	2	–	21	19	–	–	22	18	–	–
WA[2]........	61	36	–	1	61	37	–	–	31	18	–	–	31	18	–	–
WV[2]........	71	29	–	–	71	29	–	–	26	8	–	–	26	8	–	–
WI[2]........	52	46	1	–	52	46	1	–	18	15	–	–	18	15	–	–
WY[2]........	19	41	–	–	19	41	–	–	7	23	–	–	7	23	–	–

– Represents zero. [1] Members of both houses serve 4-year terms. [2] Upper house members serve 4-year terms and lower house members serve 2-year terms. [3] Members of both houses serve 2-year terms. [4] Illinois—4- and 2-year term depending on district. [5] Nebraska—4-year term and only state to have a nonpartisan legislature.

Source: The Council of State Governments, Lexington, KY, *The Book of States 2010*, annual (copyright).

Elections 257

Table 412. Women Holding State Public Offices by Office and State: 2009

[As of January. For data on women in U.S. Congress, see Table 405. For women in parliament by country, see Table 1364]

State	Total	Statewide elective executive office [1]	State legislature Total	State legislature Percent [2]	State	Total	Statewide elective executive office [1]	State legislature Total	State legislature Percent [2]
U.S.	**1,868**	**71**	**1,797**	**25**	MO	44	2	42	21
					MT	43	4	39	26
AL	24	6	18	13	NE	11	1	10	(3)
AK	13	–	13	22	NV	23	3	20	32
AZ	31	3	28	31	NH	159	–	159	38
AR	32	1	31	23	NJ	36	–	36	30
CA	34	1	33	28	NM	37	3	34	30
CO	39	2	37	37	NY	52	–	52	25
CT	63	4	59	32	NC	50	6	44	26
DE	18	2	16	26	ND	24	1	23	16
FL	38	1	37	23	OH	30	2	28	21
GA	47	1	46	19	OK	21	4	17	11
HI	26	1	25	33	OR	26	2	24	27
ID	27	1	26	25	PA	37	–	37	15
IL	50	1	49	28	RI	26	1	25	22
IN	33	1	32	21	SC	17	–	17	10
IA	36	1	35	23	SD	21	–	21	20
KS	49	1	48	29	TN	24	–	24	18
KY	23	1	22	16	TX	45	2	43	24
LA	23	–	23	16	UT	23	–	23	22
ME	54	–	54	29	VT	68	1	67	37
MD	58	–	58	31	VA	24	–	24	17
MA	53	1	52	26	WA	49	1	48	33
MI	39	2	37	25	WV	23	1	22	16
MN	73	3	70	35	WI	31	2	29	22
MS	25	–	25	14	WY	16	1	15	17

– Represents zero. [1] Excludes women elected to the judiciary, women appointed to state cabinet-level positions, women elected to executive posts by the legislature, and elected members of university Board of Trustees or Board of Education.
[2] Calculated by U.S. Census Bureau based on total (male and female) state legislature (both upper and lower houses) data from Table 411. [3] Nebraska—4-year term and only state to have a nonpartisan legislature.

Source: Center for the American Woman and Politics, Eagleton Institute of Politics, Rutgers University, New Brunswick, NJ, information releases, (copyright).

Table 413. Black Elected Officials by Office, 1970 to 2002, and State, 2002

[As of January 2002, no Black elected officials had been identified in Montana or South Dakota]

State	Total	U.S. and state legislatures [1]	City and county offices [2]	Law enforcement [3]	Education [4]	State	Total	U.S. and state legislatures [1]	City and county offices [2]	Law enforcement [3]	Education [4]
1970 (Feb.)	1,469	179	715	213	362	MD	192	40	101	41	10
1980 (July)	4,890	326	2,832	526	1,206	MA	79	6	60	2	11
1990 (Jan.)	7,335	436	4,485	769	1,645	MI	353	24	153	62	114
1995 (Jan.)	8,385	604	4,954	987	1,840	MN	20	2	4	10	4
1999 (Jan.)	8,896	618	5,354	997	1,927	MS	950	46	646	121	137
2000 (Jan.)	9,001	621	5,420	1,037	1,923	MO	206	19	145	17	25
2001 (Jan.)	9,061	633	5,456	1,044	1,928	NE	9	1	5	–	3
						NV	13	5	4	2	2
2002 (Jan.)	**9,430**	**636**	**5,753**	**1,081**	**1,960**	NH	5	5	–	–	–
AL	757	36	569	56	96	NJ	269	18	162	–	89
AK	2	1	1	–	–	NM	4	1	0	2	1
AZ	13	1	1	6	5	NY	328	34	90	84	120
AR	535	15	374	17	129	NC	523	28	369	31	95
CA	234	10	78	76	70	ND	1	–	1	–	–
CO	17	4	5	8	–	OH	305	21	197	35	52
CT	69	14	46	3	6	OK	115	6	85	4	20
DE	29	4	18	–	7	OR	5	3	1	1	–
DC	174	[5] 2	169	–	3	PA	215	19	85	75	36
FL	275	25	180	43	27	RI	8	7	1	–	–
GA	640	53	413	48	126	SC	547	32	345	12	158
HI	1	1	–	–	–	TN	195	18	118	28	31
ID	1	–	1	–	–	TX	466	19	306	47	94
IL	619	28	327	59	205	UT	5	1	3	1	–
IN	94	13	54	13	14	VT	1	1	–	–	–
IA	12	1	8	1	2	VA	248	16	132	16	84
KS	16	7	4	3	2	WA	24	2	9	11	2
KY	62	5	45	6	6	WV	19	2	13	3	1
LA	739	32	408	132	167	WI	33	8	15	5	5
ME	2	–	1	–	1	WY	1	–	1	–	–

– Represents zero. [1] Includes elected state administrators. [2] County commissioners and councilmen, mayors, vice mayors, aldermen, regional officials, and other. [3] Judges, magistrates, constables, marshals, sheriffs, justices of the peace, and other.
[4] Members of state education agencies, college boards, school boards, and other. [5] Includes one shadow senator (an elected official who lobbied Congress on D.C. issues, but is not sworn in at the federal level and has no voting privileges).

Source: Joint Center for Political and Economic Studies, Washington, DC, *Black Elected Officials: A Statistical Summary*, annual (copyright), <http://www.jointcenter.org/publications_recent_publications/black_elected_officials>.

Table 414. Hispanic Public Elected Officials by Office, 1985 to 2008, and State, 2008

[As of January of year shown. For states not shown, no Hispanic public officials had been identified]

State	Total	State executives and legislators[1]	County and municipal officials	Judicial and law enforcement	Education and school boards	State	Total	State executives and legislators[1]	County and municipal officials	Judicial and law enforcement	Education and school boards
1985	3,147	129	1,316	517	1,185	MD	11	4	6	–	1
1990	4,004	144	1,819	583	1,458	MA	20	4	9	–	7
2000	5,019	217	1,852	447	2,503	MI	14	3	2	4	5
2001	5,205	223	1,846	454	2,682	MN	5	3	1	1	–
2002	4,303	227	1,960	532	1,603	MO	2	1	1	–	–
2003	4,432	231	1,958	549	1,694	MT	3	1	–	2	–
2004	4,651	253	2,059	638	1,723	NE	3	1	1	–	1
2005	4,853	266	2,149	678	1,760	NV	12	6	2	3	1
2006	4,932	244	2,151	693	1,835	NH	4	3	1	–	–
2007	4,954	270	2,152	685	1,847	NJ	117	10	61	–	46
2008	**5,240**	**283**	**2,266**	**738**	**1,952**	NM	654	49	338	105	162
AK	1	–	1	–	–	NY	61	19	27	13	2
AZ	362	19	135	53	155	NC	4	2	2	–	–
CA	1,127	35	416	42	634	ND	1	–	1	–	–
CO	152	9	104	8	31	OH	6	–	5	1	–
CT	28	6	18	–	4	OK	2	–	–	–	2
DE	2	1	1	–	–	OR	12	2	5	5	–
FL	150	21	87	35	7	PA	9	1	5	2	1
GA	6	3	1	2	–	RI	7	3	4	–	–
HI	2	1	1	–	–	SC	1	1	–	–	–
ID	2	2	–	–	–	TN	3	1	2	–	–
IL	111	13	60	8	30	TX	2,245	44	918	441	842
IN	17	1	11	3	2	UT	8	3	3	2	–
IA	1	–	1	–	–	VA	3	1	1	–	1
KS	10	4	6	–	–	WA	35	3	19	–	13
KY	2	–	1	–	1	WI	9	1	3	4	1
LA	10	–	3	4	3	WY	5	2	3	–	–

– Represents zero. [1] Includes U.S. Senators and Representatives, not shown separately.

Source: National Association of Latino Elected and Appointed Officials (NALEO) Educational Fund, Washington, DC, *National Directory of Latino Elected Officials*, annual.

Table 415. Reported Voting and Registration Among Native and Naturalized Citizens by Race and Hispanic Origin: 2008

[In thousands, except percent. (206,072 represents 206,072,000). As of November]

Nativity status, race, and Hispanic origin	Total citizen population	U.S. Citizen							
		Reported registered		Not registered		Reported voted		Did not vote	
		Number	Percent	Number	Percent	Number	Percent	Number	Percent
Total:									
All races [1]	206,072	146,311	71.0	59,761	29.0	131,144	63.6	74,928	36.4
White alone [2]	169,438	122,020	72.0	47,418	28.0	109,100	64.4	60,338	35.6
Black alone [2]	24,930	17,375	69.7	7,555	30.3	16,133	64.7	8,797	35.3
Asian alone [2]	7,059	3,901	55.3	3,159	44.7	3,357	47.6	3,702	52.4
Hispanic [3]	19,537	11,608	59.4	7,930	40.6	9,745	49.9	9,792	50.1
Native citizen:									
All races [1]	190,683	137,001	71.8	53,682	28.2	122,839	64.4	67,844	35.6
White alone [2]	160,266	116,375	72.6	43,891	27.4	104,005	64.9	56,262	35.1
White alone, non-Hispanic	146,906	108,438	73.8	38,467	26.2	97,538	66.4	49,367	33.6
Black alone [2]	23,442	16,431	70.1	7,011	29.9	15,249	65.0	8,193	35.0
Asian alone [2]	2,654	1,353	51.0	1,301	49.0	1,194	45.0	1,460	55.0
Hispanic [3]	14,461	8,574	59.3	5,886	40.7	6,995	48.4	7,466	51.6
White alone or in combination [4]	162,511	117,910	72.6	44,601	27.4	105,341	64.8	57,170	35.2
Black alone or in combination [4]	24,211	16,965	70.1	7,246	29.9	15,738	65.0	8,472	35.0
Asian alone or in combination [4]	3,114	1,641	52.7	1,473	47.3	1,433	46.0	1,681	54.0
Naturalized citizen:									
All races [1]	15,390	9,310	60.5	6,080	39.5	8,305	54.0	7,085	46.0
White alone [2]	9,171	5,645	61.6	3,526	38.4	5,095	55.6	4,076	44.4
White alone, non-Hispanic	4,415	2,776	62.9	1,639	37.1	2,504	56.7	1,912	43.3
Black alone [2]	1,488	943	63.4	544	36.6	884	59.4	604	40.6
Asian alone [2]	4,405	2,548	57.8	1,857	42.2	2,163	49.1	2,242	50.9
Hispanic [3]	5,077	3,033	59.8	2,043	40.2	2,751	54.2	2,326	45.8
White alone or in combination [4]	9,287	5,718	61.6	3,569	38.4	5,159	55.6	4,128	44.4
Black alone or in combination [4]	1,557	995	63.9	562	36.1	936	60.1	621	39.9
Asian alone or in combination [4]	4,448	2,584	58.1	1,864	41.9	2,194	49.3	2,254	50.7

[1] Includes other races, not shown separately. [2] Beginning with the 2003 Current Population Survey (CPS), respondents could choose more than one race. Data shown represent persons who selected this race group only and exclude persons reporting more than one race. [3] Persons of Hispanic origin may be any race. [4] In combination with one or more races.

Source: U.S. Census Bureau, *Voting and Registration in the Election of November 2008,* Current Population Reports P20-562, 2010. See also <http://www.census.gov/hhes/www/socdemo/voting/index.html>.

U.S. Census Bureau, Statistical Abstract of the United States: 2011

Table 416. Voting-Age Population—Reported Registration and Voting by Selected Characteristics: 1996 to 2008

[193.7 represents 193,700,000. As of November. Covers civilian noninstitutional population 18 years old and over. Includes aliens. Figures are based on Current Population Survey (see text, Section 1 and Appendix III) and differ from those in Table 418 based on population estimates and official vote counts]

| Characteristic | Voting-age population (mil.) | | | | | | | Percent reporting they registered | | | | | | | Percent reporting they voted | | | | | | |
| | | | | | | | | Presidential election years | | | | Congressional election years | | | Presidential election years | | | | Congressional election years | | |
	1996	1998	2000	2002	2004	2006	2008	1996	2000	2004	2008	1998	2002	2006	1996	2000	2004	2008	1998	2002	2006
Total[1]	**193.7**	**198.2**	**202.6**	**210.4**	**215.7**	**220.6**	**225.5**	**65.9**	**63.9**	**65.9**	**64.9**	**62.1**	**60.9**	**61.6**	**54.2**	**54.7**	**58.3**	**58.2**	**41.9**	**42.3**	**43.6**
18 to 20 years old	10.8	11.4	11.9	11.7	11.5	11.6	11.7	45.6	40.5	50.7	49.3	32.1	32.6	37.0	31.2	28.4	41.0	41.0	13.5	15.1	17.1
21 to 24 years old	13.9	14.1	14.9	15.6	16.4	16.2	16.6	51.2	49.3	52.1	56.5	35.0	42.5	44.9	33.4	35.4	42.5	46.6	19.2	18.7	21.9
25 to 34 years old	40.1	38.6	37.3	38.5	39.0	39.4	40.2	56.9	54.7	55.6	56.5	52.4	50.2	50.3	43.1	43.7	46.9	48.5	28.0	27.1	28.3
35 to 44 years old	43.3	44.4	44.5	43.7	43.1	42.6	41.5	66.5	63.8	64.2	61.4	62.4	60.0	59.3	54.9	55.0	56.9	55.2	40.7	40.2	40.1
45 to 64 years old	53.7	57.4	61.4	66.9	71.0	75.0	78.1	73.5	71.2	72.7	70.4	71.1	69.4	69.6	64.4	64.1	66.6	65.0	53.6	53.1	54.3
65 years old and over	31.9	32.3	32.8	33.9	34.7	35.8	37.5	77.0	76.1	76.9	75.0	75.4	75.8	75.4	67.0	67.6	68.9	68.1	59.5	61.0	60.5
Male	92.6	95.2	97.1	100.9	103.8	106.5	109.0	64.4	62.2	64.0	62.6	60.6	58.9	59.5	52.8	53.1	56.3	55.7	41.4	41.4	42.4
Female	101.0	103.0	105.5	109.5	111.9	114.1	116.5	67.3	65.6	67.6	67.0	63.5	62.8	63.5	55.5	56.2	60.1	60.4	42.4	43.0	44.7
White[2]	162.8	165.8	168.7	174.1	176.6	179.9	183.2	67.7	65.6	67.9	66.6	63.9	63.1	64.0	56.0	56.4	60.3	59.6	43.3	44.1	45.8
Black[2]	22.5	23.3	24.1	24.4	24.9	25.7	26.5	63.5	63.6	64.4	65.5	60.2	58.8	57.4	50.6	53.5	56.3	60.8	39.6	39.7	38.6
Asian[2,3]	(NA)	(NA)	8.0	9.6	9.3	9.9	10.5	(NA)	30.7	34.9	37.3	(NA)	30.7	32.9	(NA)	25.4	29.8	32.1	(NA)	19.4	21.8
Hispanic[4]	18.4	20.3	21.6	25.2	27.1	29.0	30.9	35.7	34.9	34.3	37.6	33.7	32.6	32.1	26.7	27.5	28.0	31.6	20.0	18.9	19.3
Region:[5]																					
Northeast	38.3	38.5	38.9	41.1	41.0	41.2	41.5	64.7	63.7	65.3	63.7	60.8	60.8	60.3	54.5	55.2	58.6	57.4	41.2	41.4	42.8
Midwest	45.2	45.9	46.4	48.8	48.4	49.1	49.4	71.6	70.2	72.8	70.6	68.2	66.5	68.3	59.3	60.9	65.0	63.4	47.3	47.1	50.7
South	68.1	70.1	71.8	74.2	77.2	80.0	82.4	65.9	64.5	65.5	65.5	62.7	61.6	62.0	52.2	53.5	56.4	57.7	38.6	41.6	40.3
West	42.1	43.7	45.5	46.3	49.1	50.4	52.2	60.8	56.9	60.1	59.4	56.0	54.0	55.4	51.8	49.9	54.4	54.6	42.3	39.0	42.4
School years completed:																					
8 years or less	14.1	13.3	12.9	12.3	12.6	12.1	11.1	40.7	36.1	32.5	30.1	40.2	32.4	29.5	28.1	26.8	23.6	23.4	24.6	19.4	17.1
High school:																					
Less than high school graduate	21.0	21.0	20.1	20.9	20.7	20.2	19.1	47.9	45.9	45.8	43.2	43.4	41.6	39.6	33.8	33.6	34.6	33.7	25.0	23.3	22.8
High school graduate or GED[6]	65.2	65.6	66.3	68.9	68.5	70.0	70.4	62.2	60.1	61.5	59.5	58.6	57.1	57.5	49.1	49.4	52.4	50.9	37.1	37.1	37.6
College:																					
Some college or associate's degree	50.9	52.9	55.3	57.3	58.9	60.2	63.8	72.9	70.0	73.7	72.0	68.3	66.7	68.3	60.5	60.3	66.1	65.0	46.2	45.8	47.3
Bachelor's or advanced degree	42.5	45.4	48.0	51.0	54.9	58.2	61.1	80.4	77.3	78.1	76.8	75.1	74.4	73.9	73.0	72.0	74.2	73.3	57.2	58.5	59.5
Employed	125.6	130.5	133.4	134.9	138.8	143.8	143.2	67.0	64.7	67.1	66.4	62.6	61.7	62.7	55.2	55.5	60.0	60.1	41.2	42.1	43.9
Unemployed	6.4	5.2	4.9	7.7	7.3	6.2	9.5	52.5	46.1	56.3	57.2	48.5	48.1	48.5	37.2	35.1	46.4	48.8	28.4	27.2	28.0
Not in labor force	61.6	62.5	64.2	67.8	69.6	70.5	72.8	65.1	63.8	64.4	62.9	62.1	60.9	60.7	54.1	54.5	56.2	55.5	44.5	44.2	44.3

NA Not available. [1] Includes other races, not shown separately. [2] Beginning with the 2003 Current Population Survey (CPS), respondents could choose more than one race. 2004, 2006, and 2008 data represent persons who selected this race group only and exclude persons reporting more than one race. The CPS in prior years only allowed respondents to report one race group. See also comment on race in the text for Section 1. [3] Prior to 2004, this category was "Asian and Pacific Islanders," therefore rates are not comparable with prior years. [4] Persons of Hispanic origin may be any race. [5] For composition of regions, see map, inside cover. [6] The General Educational Development (GED) Test measures how well a non-high school graduate has mastered the skills and general knowledge that are acquired in a 4-year high school education. Successfully passing the exam is a credential generally considered to be equivalent to a high school diploma.

Source: U.S. Census Bureau, Voting and Registration in the Election of November 2008, Current Population Reports, P20-562, 2010, and earlier reports, and unpublished data, <http://www.census.gov/hhes/www/socdemo/voting/index.html>.

Table 417. Persons Reported Registered and Voted by State: 2008

[225,499 represents 225,499,000. As of November. See headnote, Table 416]

State	Voting-age population (1,000)	Percent of voting-age population Registered	Percent of voting-age population Voted	State	Voting-age population (1,000)	Percent of voting-age population Registered	Percent of voting-age population Voted
U.S.	225,499	64.9	58.2	MO	4,430	72.8	64.2
AL	3,497	69.7	60.8	MT	731	70.6	64.7
AK	488	70.8	62.4	NE	1,308	71.8	64.5
AZ	4,688	61.3	53.3	NV	1,946	59.0	52.8
AR	2,108	62.5	51.8	NH	1,015	74.5	69.8
CA	26,993	55.1	51.2	NJ	6,489	62.0	56.0
CO	3,694	66.0	62.5	NM	1,473	63.6	57.4
CT	2,651	66.4	60.8	NY	14,665	57.7	51.5
DE	648	69.1	63.0	NC	6,845	71.6	63.8
DC	469	69.0	65.3	ND	484	82.3	66.3
FL	14,069	62.4	56.5	OH	8,499	71.9	64.5
GA	7,018	65.9	59.6	OK	2,667	67.4	56.5
HI	977	53.5	46.8	OR	2,904	67.5	62.6
ID	1,095	66.0	58.8	PA	9,449	68.3	60.8
IL	9,521	64.6	57.1	RI	804	70.6	63.0
IN	4,686	66.3	58.8	SC	3,313	72.0	63.4
IA	2,244	72.6	66.9	SD	590	74.9	66.1
KS	2,037	65.9	59.8	TN	4,692	62.3	53.6
KY	3,179	71.1	61.4	TX	17,295	58.5	48.8
LA	3,161	75.7	68.0	UT	1,859	56.8	50.5
ME	1,020	78.5	70.2	VT	487	70.9	63.2
MD	4,218	67.0	61.9	VA	5,720	69.1	63.8
MA	4,962	66.4	61.3	WA	4,912	67.2	62.6
MI	7,487	73.9	65.0	WV	1,395	65.7	53.1
MN	3,898	75.2	70.8	WI	4,212	73.5	68.5
MS	2,109	75.3	68.2	WY	397	67.9	62.9

Source: U.S. Census Bureau, *Voting and Registration in the Election of November 2008,* Current Population Reports, P20-562, 2010, and earlier reports, and unpublished data, <http://www.census.gov/hhes/www/socdemo/voting/index.html>.

Table 418. Participation in Elections for President and U.S. Representatives: 1932 to 2008

[75,768 represents 75,768,000. As of November, except as noted. Estimated resident population 21 years old and over, 1932–70, except as noted, and 18 years old and over thereafter; includes Armed Forces stationed in the U.S. Prior to 1958, excludes Alaska and prior to 1960, excludes Hawaii. District of Columbia is included in votes cast for President beginning 1964]

Year	Resident population (includes aliens) of voting age [1] (1,000)	For President (1,000)	Percent of voting-age population	For U.S. Representatives (1,000)	Percent of voting-age population	Year	Resident population (includes aliens) of voting age [1] (1,000)	For President (1,000)	Percent of voting-age population	For U.S. Representatives (1,000)	Percent of voting age population
1932	75,768	39,817	52.6	(NA)	(NA)						
1934	77,997	(X)	(X)	32,804	42.1	1972	140,777	77,625	55.1	71,188	50.6
1936	80,174	45,647	56.9	(NA)	(NA)	1974	146,338	(X)	(X)	52,313	35.7
1938	82,354	(X)	(X)	(NA)	(NA)	1976	152,308	81,603	53.6	74,259	48.8
1940	84,728	49,815	58.8	(NA)	(NA)	1978	158,369	(X)	(X)	54,584	34.5
1942	86,465	(X)	(X)	28,074	32.5	1980	163,945	86,497	52.8	77,874	47.5
1944	85,654	48,026	56.1	45,110	52.7	1982	169,643	(X)	(X)	63,881	37.7
1946	92,659	(X)	(X)	34,410	37.1	1984	173,995	92,655	53.3	82,422	47.4
1948	95,573	48,834	51.1	46,220	48.4	1986	177,922	(X)	(X)	59,758	33.6
1950	98,134	(X)	(X)	40,430	41.2	1988	181,956	91,587	50.3	81,682	44.9
1952	99,929	61,552	61.6	57,571	57.6	1990	185,812	(X)	(X)	62,355	33.6
1954	102,075	(X)	(X)	42,583	41.7	1992	189,493	104,600	55.2	97,198	51.3
1956	104,515	62,027	59.3	58,886	56.3	1994	193,010	(X)	(X)	70,494	36.5
1958	106,447	(X)	(X)	45,719	43.0	1996	196,789	96,390	49.0	90,233	45.9
1960	109,672	68,836	62.8	64,124	58.5	1998	201,270	(X)	(X)	66,605	33.1
1962	112,952	(X)	(X)	51,242	45.4	2000	[2] 209,787	105,594	50.3	98,800	47.1
1964	114,090	70,098	61.4	65,879	57.7	2002	[2] 214,755	(X)	(X)	74,707	34.8
1966	116,638	(X)	(X)	52,902	45.4	2004	[2] 219,553	122,349	55.7	113,192	51.6
1968	120,285	73,027	60.7	66,109	55.0	2006	[2] 224,583	(X)	(X)	80,976	36.1
1970	124,498	(X)	(X)	54,259	43.6	2008	[2] 229,945	131,407	57.1	122,586	53.3

NA Not available. X Not applicable. [1] Population 18 and over in Georgia, 1944–70, and in Kentucky, 1956–70; 20 and over in Alaska and 20 and over in Hawaii, 1960–70. Source: Through 1990, U.S. Census Bureau, "Table 4. Participation in Elections for President and U.S. Representatives: 1930 to 1992," May 1994, <http://www.census.gov/population/socdemo/voting/p25-1117/tab03-04.pdf>. For 1992–1998, "Estimates and Projections of the Voting-Age Population, 1992 to 2000, and Percent Casting Votes for President, by State: November 1992 and 1996," July 2000, <http://www.census.gov/population/socdemo/voting/proj00/tab03.txt>. Starting 2000, "Annual Estimates of the Resident Population by Sex and Selected Age Groups for the United States: April 1, 2000 to July 1, 2009," (NC-EST2009-02), June 2010, <http://www.census.gov/popest/national/asrh/NC-EST2009/NC-EST2009-02.xls/>. [2] As of July 1.

Source: Except as noted, U.S. House of Representatives, Office of the Clerk, *Statistics of the Presidential and Congressional Election*, 2009, biennial. See also <http://clerk.house.gov/member_info/election.html>.

Elections 261

Table 419. Resident Population of Voting Age and Percent Casting Votes— States: 2000 to 2008

[209,787 represents 209,787,000. Estimated population, 18 years old and over. Includes Armed Forces stationed in each state, aliens, and institutional population]

| State | Voting-age population (1,000) [1] | | | | Percent casting votes for— | | | | | |
| | | | | | Presidential electors | | | U.S. Representatives | | |
	2000	2004	2006	2008	2000	2004	2008	2000	2006	2008
U.S.	209,787	219,553	224,583	229,945	50.3	55.7	57.1	47.1	36.1	53.3
AL	3,330	3,403	3,476	3,548	50.0	55.3	59.2	43.2	32.8	52.3
AK	437	475	493	508	65.3	65.8	64.3	62.8	47.6	62.5
AZ	3,791	4,232	4,550	4,782	40.4	47.6	48.0	38.7	32.8	45.1
AR	1,998	2,063	2,117	2,161	46.1	51.1	50.3	31.7	36.0	36.4
CA	24,723	26,078	26,534	27,156	44.4	47.6	49.9	42.2	31.3	45.4
CO	3,221	3,448	3,576	3,725	54.1	61.8	64.5	50.4	43.0	61.3
CT	2,570	2,632	2,656	2,689	56.8	60.0	61.3	51.1	40.5	56.8
DE	591	627	649	669	55.4	59.9	61.6	52.9	38.8	57.6
DC	457	464	469	477	44.2	49.1	55.7	(X)	(X)	(X)
FL	12,390	13,455	14,023	14,353	48.1	56.6	58.5	40.4	27.5	51.7
GA	6,052	6,550	6,852	7,132	42.7	50.4	55.0	39.9	30.2	51.2
HI	917	959	985	998	40.1	44.7	45.7	37.1	34.3	45.7
ID	929	1,010	1,064	1,112	54.0	59.3	58.9	53.0	41.8	57.4
IL	9,192	9,417	9,514	9,660	51.6	56.0	57.2	47.8	36.3	54.3
IN	4,517	4,639	4,715	4,796	48.7	53.2	57.4	47.8	35.4	55.8
IA	2,195	2,229	2,253	2,281	61.6	67.6	67.4	58.1	45.9	64.9
KS	1,979	2,031	2,060	2,097	54.2	58.5	58.9	52.3	41.0	57.6
KY	3,054	3,153	3,213	3,272	50.6	57.0	55.8	47.0	39.0	53.5
LA	3,252	3,319	3,175	3,331	54.3	58.6	58.9	37.0	28.9	31.4
ME	976	1,017	1,031	1,044	66.8	72.8	70.0	65.4	52.0	68.0
MD	3,954	4,158	4,236	4,302	51.2	57.3	61.2	48.7	40.2	58.1
MA	4,861	4,966	5,009	5,105	56.2	58.9	60.8	56.2	44.8	60.8
MI	7,359	7,548	7,598	7,610	57.5	64.1	65.7	55.3	48.0	63.2
MN	3,645	3,808	3,883	3,968	66.9	74.3	73.3	64.9	56.1	70.6
MS	2,074	2,122	2,137	2,173	47.9	53.7	59.4	47.6	28.1	58.2
MO	4,178	4,335	4,429	4,521	56.5	63.0	64.7	55.7	47.4	62.4
MT	673	706	727	748	61.0	63.8	65.6	61.0	55.9	64.3
NE	1,263	1,296	1,315	1,334	55.2	60.0	60.1	54.1	45.3	58.1
NV	1,502	1,729	1,848	1,939	40.6	48.0	49.9	39.1	31.1	46.8
NH	930	985	1,009	1,028	61.2	68.9	69.2	59.8	39.9	65.6
NJ	6,342	6,495	6,536	6,610	50.3	55.6	58.5	47.1	32.7	52.0
NM	1,313	1,394	1,442	1,481	45.6	54.3	56.1	44.8	38.9	55.0
NY	14,311	14,677	14,819	15,015	48.6	50.7	51.4	48.6	31.6	51.4
NC	6,112	6,446	6,703	6,993	47.7	54.3	61.5	45.5	29.0	60.3
ND	481	489	493	498	59.9	63.9	63.5	59.4	44.1	63.0
OH	8,478	8,642	8,710	8,789	55.5	65.1	64.9	54.1	45.5	61.1
OK	2,562	2,633	2,682	2,737	48.2	55.6	53.4	42.4	33.8	48.9
OR	2,583	2,725	2,817	2,912	59.4	67.4	62.8	55.7	48.2	57.8
PA	9,367	9,530	9,641	9,771	52.4	60.5	61.5	48.6	41.6	59.2
RI	803	825	823	824	51.0	53.0	57.3	47.9	45.3	53.2
SC	3,013	3,172	3,289	3,428	45.9	51.0	56.0	43.9	33.0	54.7
SD	553	578	591	606	57.2	67.2	63.0	56.9	56.4	62.5
TN	4,304	4,486	4,622	4,749	48.2	54.3	54.7	43.1	37.1	48.5
TX	15,038	16,159	16,851	17,538	42.6	45.9	46.1	39.8	24.6	42.9
UT	1,523	1,679	1,781	1,877	50.6	55.2	50.7	49.8	32.0	49.9
VT	462	479	486	492	63.6	65.2	66.0	61.3	54.0	60.5
VA	5,363	5,662	5,818	5,957	51.1	56.4	62.5	45.2	39.5	58.7
WA	4,395	4,662	4,835	5,008	56.6	61.3	60.6	54.2	42.5	58.2
WV	1,406	1,414	1,419	1,427	46.1	53.5	50.0	41.2	32.0	45.2
WI	4,005	4,170	4,243	4,311	64.9	71.9	69.2	62.6	48.6	64.4
WY	365	380	389	404	58.5	64.1	63.1	58.1	50.4	61.8

X Not applicable. [1] As of July 1. Source: U.S. Census Bureau, "Annual Estimates of the Resident Population by Sex and Age for States: April 1, 2000 to July 1, 2009," (SC-EST2009-02), June 2010, <http://www.census.gov/popest/states/asrh /SC-EST2009-02.html>.

Source: Except as noted, U.S. House of Representatives, Office of the Clerk, *Statistics of the Presidential and Congressional Election*, 2009, biennial. See also <http://clerk.house.gov/member_info/electionInfo/index.html>.

U.S. Census Bureau, Statistical Abstract of the United States: 2011

Table 420. Political Action Committees—Number by Committee Type: 1980 to 2009

[As of December 31, except 2009 as of May 22]

Committee type	1980	1990	1995	2000	2005	2006	2007	2008	2009
Total.....................	2,551	4,172	4,016	3,907	4,210	4,183	4,234	4,611	4,481
Corporate	1,206	1,795	1,674	1,545	1,622	1,582	1,601	1,598	1,574
Labor......................	297	346	334	317	290	273	273	272	275
Trade/membership/health	576	774	815	860	925	937	925	995	1,104
Nonconnected..............	374	1,062	1,020	1,026	1,233	1,254	1,300	1,594	1,390
Cooperative.................	42	59	44	41	37	37	38	49	43
Corporation without stock	56	136	129	118	103	100	97	103	95

Source: U.S. Federal Election Commission, press release, May 2009.

Table 421. Political Action Committees—Financial Activity Summary by Committee Type: 2003 to 2008

[In millions of dollars (915.7 represents $915,700,000). Covers financial activity during 2-year calendar period indicated]

Committee type	Receipts			Disbursements [1]			Contributions to candidates		
	2003–04	2005–06	2007–08	2003–04	2005–06	2007–08	2003–04	2005–06	2007–08
Total.....................	915.7	477.4	1,212.4	842.9	394.1	1,180.0	310.5	141.1	412.8
Corporate	239.0	131.2	313.4	221.6	116.3	298.6	115.6	56.5	158.3
Labor......................	191.7	100.3	262.1	182.9	73.1	265.0	52.1	21.1	62.7
Trade/membership/health	181.8	95.4	372.7	170.1	74.6	364.6	83.2	38.0	66.6
Nonconnected..............	289.4	141.6	241.0	255.2	122.6	229.5	52.5	22.0	112.9
Cooperative.................	4.2	2.7	10.3	3.9	1.9	9.9	2.9	1.4	6.9
Corporation without stock	9.6	6.1	13.0	9.2	5.7	12.4	4.2	2.1	5.5

[1] Comprises contributions to candidates, independent expenditures, and other disbursements.
Source: U.S. Federal Election Commission, *FEC Reports on Financial Activity, Final Report, Party and Non-party Political Committees*, biennial.

Table 422. Presidential Campaign Finances—Federal Funds for General Election: 1996 to 2008

[In millions of dollars (152.6 represents $152,600,000). Based on FEC certifications, audit reports, and Dept. of Treasury reports]

1996		2000		2004		2008	
Candidate	Amount	Candidate	Amount	Candidate	Amount	Candidate	Amount
Total........	152.6	Total.......	147.7	Total.......	150.1	Total.......	84.2
Clinton.......	61.8	Bush	67.6	Bush	74.6	Obama......	–
Dole.........	61.8	Gore........	67.6	Kerry	74.6	McCain	84.1
Perot	29.0	Buchanan ...	12.0	Nader.......	0.9	Nader.......	0.1

– Represents zero.
Source: U.S. Federal Election Commission, periodic press releases.

Table 423. Presidential Campaign Finances—Primary Campaign Receipts and Disbursements: 1999 to 2008

[In millions of dollars (351.6 represents $351,600,000). Covers campaign finance activity during 2-year calendar period indicated. Covers candidates who received federal matching funds or who had significant financial activity]

Item	Total [1]			Democratic			Republican		
	1999–00	2003–04	2007–08 [2, 3]	1999–00	2003–04	2007–08 [2]	1999–00	2003–04	2007–08 [3]
Receipts, total [4]	351.6	673.9	1,346.6	96.6	401.8	950.1	236.7	269.6	392.6
Individual contributions	238.2	611.4	1,325.6	66.7	351.0	932.6	159.1	258.9	390.0
Federal matching funds.....	61.6	28.0	21.0	29.3	27.2	17.5	26.5	–	2.6
Disbursements..........	343.5	661.1	1,414.6	92.2	389.7	1,043.9	233.2	268.9	450.2

– Represents zero. [1] Includes other parties, not shown separately. [2] Obama activity includes both Primary and General election funds because he used a single committee for both elections. Dodd received $1,961,742 in matching funds; however his committee reported the receipt of $1,447,568. Gravel received an additional $115,966 in matching funds in early 2009. [3] Tancredo received an additional $83,775 in matching funds in early 2009. [4] Includes other types of receipts, not shown separately.
Source: U.S. Federal Election Commission, *FEC Reports on Financial Activity, Final Report, Presidential Pre-Nomination Campaigns*, quadrennial.

U.S. Census Bureau, Statistical Abstract of the United States: 2011

Table 424. Congressional Campaign Finances—Receipts and Disbursements: 2003 to 2008

[708.5 represents $708,500,000. Covers all campaign finance activity during 2-year calendar period indicated for primary, general, run-off, and special elections. Data have been adjusted to eliminate transfers between all committees within a campaign. For further information on legal limits of contributions, see Federal Election Campaign Act of 1971, as amended]

Item	House of Representatives						Senate					
	Amount (mil. dol.)			Percent distribution			Amount (mil. dol.)			Percent distribution		
	2003–04	2005–06	2007–08	2003–04	2005–06	2007–08	2003–04	2005–06	2007–08	2003–04	2005–06	2007–08
Total receipts [1]	**708.5**	**875.4**	**1,005.2**	**100**	**100**	**100**	**497.6**	**564.6**	**434.1**	**100**	**100**	**100**
Individual contributions	396.7	478.9	538.8	56	55	54	324.1	383.2	267.0	65	68	62
Other committees	225.4	279.8	300.4	32	32	30	63.7	68.9	78.2	13	12	18
Candidate loans	47.4	56.1	77.6	7	6	8	39.8	47.0	24.2	8	8	6
Candidate contributions	7.8	14.7	32.4	1	2	3	38.2	37.5	5.7	8	7	1
Democrats	307.4	417.5	561.0	43	48	56	250.6	291.8	237.3	50	52	55
Republicans	399.2	453.6	440.8	56	52	44	246.1	245.8	196.1	49	44	45
Others	1.9	4.2	3.4	(Z)	(Z)	(Z)	0.9	26.9	0.7	(Z)	5	(Z)
Incumbents	452.6	532.6	581.7	64	61	58	171.7	278.4	234.1	35	49	54
Challengers	118.2	188.7	252.2	17	22	25	79.5	186.6	135.0	16	33	31
Open seats [2]	137.8	154.1	171.3	19	18	17	246.4	99.6	65.1	50	18	15
Total disbursements	**660.3**	**854.8**	**929.9**	**100**	**100**	**100**	**496.4**	**562.9**	**449.4**	**100**	**100**	**100**
Democrats	288.5	395.5	491.0	44	46	53	254.6	288.6	229.6	51	51	51
Republicans	370.0	455.2	435.6	56	53	47	241.0	249.3	202.0	49	44	45
Others	1.8	4.1	3.3	(Z)	(Z)	(Z)	0.8	25.0	17.9	(Z)	4	4
Incumbents	410.1	519.2	527.6	62	61	57	171.7	274.3	251.2	35	49	56
Challengers	116.6	185.6	246.7	18	22	27	76.6	187.1	132.9	15	33	30
Open seats [2]	133.6	150.0	155.6	20	18	17	248.1	101.5	65.4	50	18	15

Z Less than $50,000 or 0.5 percent. [1] Includes other types of receipts, not shown separately. [2] Elections in which an incumbent did not seek reelection.

Source: U.S. Federal Election Commission, *FEC Reports on Financial Activity, Final Report, U.S. Senate and House Campaigns*, biennial.

Table 425. Contributions to Congressional Campaigns by Political Action Committees (PAC) by Type of Committee: 1997 to 2008

[In millions of dollars (158.7 represents $158,700,000). Covers amounts given to candidates in primary, general, run-off, and special elections during the 2-year calendar period indicated. For number of political action committees, see Table 420]

Type of committee	Total [1]	Democrats	Republicans	Incumbents	Challengers	Open seats [2]
HOUSE OF REPRESENTATIVES						
1997–98	158.7	77.6	80.9	124.0	14.9	19.8
1999–00	193.4	98.2	94.7	150.5	19.9	23.0
2001–02	206.9	102.6	104.2	161.0	13.8	32.1
2003–04	225.4	98.6	126.6	187.3	15.6	22.5
2005–06	279.8	125.0	154.8	232.0	24.4	23.5
2007–08, total [3]	**300.4**	**184.3**	**116.1**	**245.7**	**35.8**	**18.9**
Corporate	108.0	56.7	51.3	99.4	5.0	3.6
Trade association [4]	85.6	47.6	38.0	73.6	7.2	4.8
Labor	53.4	49.7	3.7	37.5	11.3	4.6
Nonconnected [5]	43.9	25.1	18.8	27.0	11.6	5.4
SENATE						
1997–98	48.1	20.7	27.3	34.3	6.6	7.2
1999–00	51.9	18.7	33.2	33.5	7.1	11.3
2001–02	59.2	25.4	33.8	37.0	14.2	8.1
2003–04	63.7	28.4	35.3	39.3	5.6	18.8
2005–06	68.9	28.6	37.5	50.0	9.9	8.7
2007–08, total [3]	**78.2**	**33.5**	**44.3**	**56.6**	**12.8**	**9.0**
Corporate	32.4	11.2	21.2	26.8	2.5	3.1
Trade association [4]	19.4	7.2	12.2	14.9	2.5	2.0
Labor	7.0	6.5	0.5	2.8	2.9	1.2
Nonconnected [5]	17.5	7.8	9.7	10.7	4.4	2.5

[1] Includes other parties, not shown separately. [2] Elections in which an incumbent did not seek reelection. [3] Includes other types of political action committees, not shown separately. [4] Includes membership organizations and health organizations.
[5] Represents "ideological" groups as well as other issue groups not necessarily ideological in nature.

Source: U.S. Federal Election Commission, *FEC Reports on Financial Activity, Party and Non-Party Political Committees, Final Report*, biennial.

U.S. Census Bureau, Statistical Abstract of the United States: 2011

Section 8
State and Local Government Finances and Employment

This section presents data on revenues, expenditures, debt, and employment of state and local governments. Nationwide statistics relating to state and local governments, their numbers, finances, and employment are compiled primarily by the U.S. Census Bureau through a program of censuses and surveys. Every fifth year (for years ending in "2" and "7"), the Census Bureau conducts a census of governments involving collection of data for all governmental units in the United States. In addition, the Census Bureau conducts annual surveys which cover all the state governments and a sample of local governments.

Annually, the Census Bureau releases information on the Internet which presents financial data for the federal government, nationwide totals for state and local governments, and state-local data by states. Also released annually is a series on state, city, county, and school finances and on state and local public employment. There is also a series of quarterly data releases covering tax revenue and finances of major public employee retirement systems.

Basic information for Census Bureau statistics on governments is obtained by mail canvass from state and local officials; however, financial data for each of the state governments and for many of the large local governments are compiled from their official records and reports by Census Bureau personnel. In over two-thirds of the states, all or part of local government financial data are obtained through central collection arrangements with state governments. Financial data on the federal government are primarily based on the *Budget* published by the Office of Management and Budget (see text, Section 9, Federal Government Finances and Employment).

Governmental units—The governmental structure of the United States includes, in addition to the federal government and the states, thousands of local governments— counties, municipalities, townships, school districts, and many "special districts." In 2007, 89,527 local governments were identified by the census of governments (see Tables 426–428). As defined by the census, governmental units include all agencies or bodies having an organized existence, governmental character, and substantial autonomy. While most of these governments can impose taxes, many of the special districts—such as independent public housing authorities and numerous local irrigation, power, and other types of districts—are financed from rentals, charges for services, benefit assessments, grants from other governments, and other non-tax sources. The count of governments excludes semi-autonomous agencies through which states, cities, and counties sometimes provide for certain functions—for example, "dependent" school systems, state institutions of higher education, and certain other "authorities" and special agencies which are under the administrative or fiscal control of an established governmental unit.

Finances—The financial statistics relate to government fiscal years ending June 30 or at some date within the 12 previous months. The following governments are exceptions and are included as though they were part of the June 30 group; ending September 30, the state governments of Alabama and Michigan, the District of Columbia, and Alabama school districts; and ending August 31, the state governments of Nebraska, Texas, and Chicago school districts. New York State ends its fiscal year on March 31. The federal government ended the fiscal year June 30 until 1976 when its fiscal year, by an act of

U.S. Census Bureau, Statistical Abstract of the United States: 2011

Congress, was revised to extend from Oct. 1 to Sept. 30. A 3-month quarter (July 1 to Sept. 30, 1976) bridged the transition.

Nationwide government finance statistics have been classified and presented in terms of uniform concepts and categories, rather than according to the highly diverse terminology, organization, and fund structure utilized by individual governments.

Statistics on governmental finances distinguish among general government, utilities, liquor stores, and insurance trusts. *General government* comprises all activities except utilities, liquor stores, and insurance trusts. Utilities include government water supply, electric light and power, gas supply, and transit systems. Liquor stores are operated by 17 states and by local governments in 6 states. Insurance trusts relate to employee retirement, unemployment compensation, and other social insurance systems administered by the federal, state, and local governments.

Data for cities or counties relate only to municipal or county and their dependent agencies and do not include amounts for other local governments in the same geographic location. Therefore, expenditure figures for "education" do not include spending by the separate school districts which administer public schools within most municipal or county areas. Variations in the assignment of governmental

responsibility for public assistance, health, hospitals, public housing, and other functions to a lesser degree also have an important effect upon reported amounts of city or county expenditure, revenue, and debt.

Employment and payrolls— These data are based mainly on mail canvassing of state and local governments. Payroll includes all salaries, wages, and individual fee payments for the month specified, and employment relates to all persons on governmental payrolls during a pay period of the month covered—including paid officials, temporary help, and (unless otherwise specified) part-time as well as full-time personnel. Effective with the 1997 Census of Governments, the reference period for measuring government employment was changed from October of the calendar year to March of the calendar year. As a result, there was no annual survey of government employment covering the October 1996 period. The prior reference month of October was used from 1958 to 1995. Figures shown for individual governments cover major dependent agencies such as institutions of higher education, as well as the basic central departments and agencies of the government.

Statistical reliability— For a discussion of statistical collection and estimation, sampling procedures, and measures of statistical reliability applicable to Census Bureau data, see Appendix III.

Table 426. Number of Governmental Units by Type: 1962 to 2007

Type of government	1962	1967	1972	1977	1982	1987	1992	1997	2002	2007
Total units.........	**91,237**	**81,299**	**78,269**	**79,913**	**81,831**	**83,237**	**85,006**	**87,504**	**87,576**	**89,527**
U.S. government......	1	1	1	1	1	1	1	1	1	1
State government.....	50	50	50	50	50	50	50	50	50	50
Local governments....	91,186	81,248	78,218	79,862	81,780	83,186	84,955	87,453	87,525	89,476
County............	3,043	3,049	3,044	3,042	3,041	3,042	3,043	3,043	3,034	3,033
Municipal..........	18,000	18,048	18,517	18,862	19,076	19,200	19,279	19,372	19,429	19,492
Township and town...	17,142	17,105	16,991	16,822	16,734	16,691	16,656	16,629	16,504	16,519
School district.......	34,678	21,782	15,781	15,174	14,851	14,721	14,422	13,726	13,506	13,051
Special district.......	18,323	21,264	23,885	25,962	28,078	29,532	31,555	34,683	35,052	37,381

Source: U.S. Census Bureau, *Census of Governments*, Volume 1, Number 1, Government Organization, Series GC07(1)-1), quinquennial. See also <http://www.census.gov/govs/cog/>.

Table 427. Number of Local Governments by Type—States: 2007

[Governments in existence in January. Limited to governments actually in existence. Excludes, therefore, a few counties and numerous townships and "incorporated places" existing as areas for which statistics can be presented as to population and other subjects, but lacking any separate organized county, township, or municipal government. See Appendix III]

State	All govern-mental units [1]	County	Municipal	Town-ship [1]	School district	Special district [2] Total [3]	Natural resources	Fire protection	Housing [4]
United States......	**89,476**	**3,033**	**19,492**	**16,519**	**13,051**	**37,381**	**7,227**	**5,873**	**3,463**
Alabama...........	1,185	67	458	–	131	529	69	11	150
Alaska.............	177	14	148	–	–	15	–	–	14
Arizona............	645	15	90	–	239	301	78	150	–
Arkansas...........	1,548	75	502	–	247	724	250	81	119
California..........	4,344	57	478	–	1,044	2,765	473	353	70
Colorado..........	2,416	62	270	–	180	1,904	180	252	89
Connecticut........	649	–	30	149	17	453	1	72	114
Delaware..........	338	3	57	–	19	259	238	–	3
District of Columbia....	2	–	1	–	–	1	–	–	–
Florida............	1,623	66	411	–	95	1,051	125	61	94
Georgia...........	1,439	154	535	–	180	570	38	2	191
Hawaii.............	10	3	1	–	–	15	14	–	–
Idaho.............	1,240	44	200	–	116	880	174	150	10
Illinois.............	6,994	102	1,299	1,432	912	3,249	1,026	841	113
Indiana............	3,231	91	567	1,008	293	1,272	139	1	65
Iowa..............	1,954	99	947	–	380	528	247	66	23
Kansas............	3,931	104	627	1,353	316	1,531	258	1	197
Kentucky..........	1,346	118	419	–	175	634	126	156	13
Louisiana..........	526	60	303	–	68	95	8	3	–
Maine.............	850	16	22	466	98	248	15	–	34
Maryland..........	256	23	157	–	–	76	38	–	20
Massachusetts.......	861	5	45	306	82	423	16	16	252
Michigan..........	2,893	83	533	1,242	579	456	79	25	–
Minnesota.........	3,520	87	854	1,788	341	456	144	–	162
Mississippi.........	1,000	82	296	–	164	458	249	33	55
Missouri...........	3,723	114	952	312	536	1,809	329	357	124
Montana...........	1,273	54	129	–	332	758	132	220	13
Nebraska..........	2,659	93	530	454	288	1,294	83	417	168
Nevada............	198	16	19	–	17	146	33	18	5
New Hampshire......	545	10	13	221	164	137	10	16	21
New Jersey.........	1,383	21	324	242	549	247	15	196	–
New Mexico.........	863	33	101	–	96	633	576	–	6
New York..........	3,403	57	618	929	680	1,119	3	891	–
North Carolina.......	963	100	548	–	–	315	145	–	94
North Dakota.......	2,699	53	357	1,320	198	771	78	281	35
Ohio..............	3,702	88	938	1,308	668	700	106	85	77
Oklahoma..........	1,880	77	594	–	567	642	100	30	137
Oregon............	1,546	36	242	–	234	1,034	204	271	21
Pennsylvania........	4,871	66	1,016	1,546	515	1,728	5	–	90
Rhode Island........	134	–	8	31	4	91	4	37	25
South Carolina.......	698	46	268	–	85	299	48	83	43
South Dakota........	1,983	66	309	916	166	526	103	84	49
Tennessee..........	928	92	347	–	14	475	109	1	96
Texas.............	4,835	254	1,209	–	1,081	2,291	442	139	387
Utah..............	599	29	242	–	40	288	82	18	17
Vermont...........	733	14	45	237	293	144	14	16	10
Virginia............	511	95	229	–	1	186	47	–	–
Washington.........	1,845	39	281	–	296	1,229	178	375	43
West Virginia........	663	55	232	–	55	321	14	–	37
Wisconsin..........	3,120	72	592	1,259	441	756	251	–	177
Wyoming...........	726	23	99	–	55	549	131	64	–

– Represents zero. [1] Includes "town" governments in the six New England States and in Minnesota, New York, and Wisconsin.
[2] Single function districts. [3] Includes other special districts not shown separately. [4] Includes community development.

Source: U.S. Census Bureau, *Census of Governments*, Volume 1, Number 1, Government Organization, Series GC07(1)–1), quinquennial. See also <http://www.census.gov/cog/>.

Table 428. State and Local Government Current Receipts and Expenditures in the National Income and Product Accounts: 1990 to 2009

[In billions of dollars (737.8 represents $737,800,000,000). For explanation of national income, see text, Section 13. Minus sign (–) indicates net loss]

Item	1990	1995	2000	2004	2005	2006	2007	2008	2009
Current receipts	**738.0**	**991.9**	**1,322.6**	**1,601.0**	**1,730.4**	**1,829.7**	**1,927.3**	**1,974.2**	**1,995.5**
Current tax receipts	519.1	672.1	893.2	1,059.4	1,163.1	1,249.0	1,313.4	1,336.3	1,263.1
Personal current taxes	122.6	158.1	236.7	248.6	276.7	302.5	322.8	330.0	273.0
Income taxes	109.6	141.7	217.4	224.7	251.7	276.1	295.5	302.4	245.0
Other	13.0	16.4	19.4	23.8	25.0	26.4	27.3	27.6	28.0
Taxes on production and imports	374.1	482.4	621.3	769.1	831.4	887.4	934.0	955.3	931.6
Sales taxes	184.3	242.7	316.8	370.7	402.2	430.4	446.3	443.9	422.7
Property taxes	161.5	202.6	254.7	326.7	346.9	370.1	396.3	410.6	421.8
Other	28.3	37.0	49.8	71.7	82.3	86.9	91.5	100.9	87.0
Taxes on corporate income	22.5	31.7	35.2	41.7	54.9	59.2	56.5	51.0	58.5
Contributions for government social insurance	10.0	13.6	10.8	24.1	24.8	21.8	19.8	21.1	21.9
Income receipts on assets	68.5	68.5	94.3	77.1	88.3	103.5	114.2	113.9	116.1
Interest receipts	64.1	63.0	86.7	66.7	76.4	90.9	101.2	100.1	101.8
Dividends	0.2	1.0	1.4	2.0	2.1	2.3	2.5	2.9	2.8
Rents and royalties	4.2	4.5	6.3	8.5	9.8	10.3	10.5	11.0	11.6
Current transfer receipts	133.5	224.2	313.9	439.4	454.3	456.7	483.9	506.1	597.5
Federal grants-in-aid	111.4	184.2	247.3	349.2	361.2	359.0	378.9	391.7	476.6
From business (net)	7.1	13.5	28.6	36.5	36.5	38.4	41.3	45.6	47.9
From persons	14.9	26.5	38.0	53.7	56.5	59.2	63.7	68.8	73.1
Current surplus of government enterprises	6.9	13.5	10.4	1.0	0.1	–1.3	–3.9	–3.2	–3.2
Current expenditures	**731.8**	**982.7**	**1,281.3**	**1,609.3**	**1,704.5**	**1,778.6**	**1,905.6**	**2,014.4**	**2,014.6**
Consumption expenditures	547.0	701.3	930.6	1,139.1	1,212.0	1,282.3	1,366.1	1,452.4	1,430.5
Government social benefit payments to persons	127.7	217.6	271.4	384.3	404.8	402.9	433.7	455.0	475.9
Interest payments	56.8	63.5	78.8	85.6	87.3	93.0	98.7	103.9	106.8
Subsidies	0.4	0.3	0.5	0.4	0.4	0.4	7.1	3.0	1.4
Net state and local government saving	**6.2**	**9.2**	**41.3**	**-8.4**	**25.9**	**51.0**	**21.7**	**-40.2**	**-19.2**
Social insurance funds	2.0	4.0	2.0	6.9	7.4	4.7	1.9	2.0	1.9
Other	4.2	5.1	39.3	-15.3	18.5	46.4	19.8	-42.2	-21.1

Source: U.S. Bureau of Economic Analysis, *Survey of Current Business*, April 2010. See also <http://www.bea.gov/national/nipaweb/SelectTable.asp?selected=N>.

Table 429. Federal Grants-in-Aid to State and Local Governments: 1990 to 2010

[135,325 represents $135,325,000,000, except as indicated. For year ending Sept. 30. Minus sign (–) indicates decrease]

Year	Total grants (mil. dol.)	Annual percent change [1]	Grants to individuals, total (mil. dol.)	Percent of total grants	State and local government expenditures from own sources [2]	Federal outlays	Gross domestic product	Total grants (bil. dol.)	Annual percent change [1]
					(Grants as percent of—)			*(Constant (2000) dollars)*	
1990	135,325	11.0	77,264	57.1	25.2	10.8	2.4	198.1	6.3
1995	224,991	8.8	144,427	64.2	31.5	14.8	3.1	283.6	6.3
1996	227,811	1.3	146,493	64.3	30.8	14.6	3.0	280.5	–1.1
1997	234,160	2.8	148,236	63.3	30.2	14.6	2.9	283.1	0.9
1998	246,128	5.1	160,305	65.1	30.3	14.9	2.8	293.9	3.8
1999	267,886	8.8	172,384	64.3	31.2	15.7	2.9	314.8	7.1
2000	285,874	6.7	182,592	63.9	27.4	16.0	2.9	326.8	3.8
2001	318,542	11.4	203,920	64.0	28.4	17.1	3.1	354.9	8.6
2002	352,895	10.8	227,373	64.4	29.5	17.5	3.3	387.4	9.2
2003	388,542	10.1	246,570	63.5	30.5	18.0	3.5	416.2	7.4
2004	407,512	4.9	262,177	64.3	30.9	17.8	3.5	424.3	1.9
2005	428,018	5.0	273,898	64.0	30.8	17.3	3.4	428.0	0.9
2006	434,099	1.4	272,585	62.8	29.7	16.3	3.3	417.3	–2.5
2007	443,797	2.2	284,362	64.1	28.4	16.3	3.2	413.0	–1.0
2008	461,317	3.9	300,820	65.2	27.4	15.5	3.2	411.7	–0.3
2009	537,991	16.6	356,692	66.3	33.2	15.3	3.8	482.9	17.3
2010, est...	653,665	21.5	394,502	60.4	(NA)	17.6	4.5	572.3	18.5

NA Not available. [1] Average annual percent change from prior year shown. For explanation, see Guide to Tabular Presentation. For 1990, change from 1989. [2] Expenditures from own sources as defined in the national income and product accounts.

Source: U.S. Office of Management and Budget, *Budget of the United States Government, Historical Tables*, annual. See also <http://www.whitehouse.gov/omb/budget>.

Table 430. Total Outlays for Grants to State and Local Governments—Selected Programs: 1990 to 2010

[In millions of dollars (135,325 represents $135,325,000,000). For year ending Sept. 30. Includes trust funds]

Program	1990	2000	2005	2006	2007	2008	2009	2010, est.
Total outlays for grants	**135,325**	**285,874**	**428,018**	**434,099**	**443,797**	**461,317**	**537,991**	**653,665**
Energy	461	433	636	651	667	524	999	5,927
Natural resources and environment	3,745	4,595	5,858	6,062	6,060	5,902	6,285	8,836
Environmental Protection Agency [1]	2,874	3,490	3,734	3,966	4,016	3,854	3,580	6,119
Agriculture	1,285	724	933	749	803	862	937	1,231
Transportation	19,174	32,222	43,368	46,681	47,945	51,216	55,438	72,249
Grants for airports [1]	1,220	1,624	3,530	3,841	3,874	3,808	3,759	3,265
Federal-aid highways [2]	13,854	24,711	30,915	32,703	33,222	35,429	36,049	38,910
Urban mass transportation [1]	3,728	5,262	–	–	8,984	9,847	11,182	15,283
Community and regional development	4,965	8,665	20,167	21,285	20,653	19,221	17,368	21,221
Rural community advance program	139	479	814	773	760	5	(NA)	(NA)
Community development fund	2,818	4,955	4,985	5,012	10,867	8,935	6,408	7,230
Homeland Security	1,184	2,439	13,541	14,731	8,267	8,630	9,068	10,353
State and local programs	(NA)	(NA)	2,116	2,601	2,385	2,870	2,529	2,870
Firefighter assistance grants	(NA)	(NA)	1,185	228	499	(NA)	(NA)	(NA)
Operations, planning, and support	11	192	132	(NA)	(NA)	(NA)	(NA)	(NA)
Mitigation grants	(NA)	13	39	34	32	33	11	(NA)
Disaster relief	1,173	2,234	10,069	11,868	5,351	5,724	6,525	(NA)
Education, training, employment, social services	21,780	36,672	57,247	60,512	58,077	58,904	73,986	111,715
Education for the disadvantaged [3]	4,437	8,511	14,539	14,604	14,409	14,799	15,797	22,157
School improvement programs [3]	1,080	2,394	6,569	5,589	5,299	5,208	5,247	5,442
Special education	1,485	4,696	10,661	11,582	11,585	12,078	12,536	16,553
Social services-block grant	2,749	1,827	1,822	1,848	1,956	1,843	1,854	2,118
Children and family services programs	2,618	5,843	8,490	8,492	8,496	8,633	8,793	12,118
Training and employment services	3,042	2,957	3,372	4,566	3,006	3,052	3,768	5,357
Health	43,890	124,843	197,848	197,347	208,311	218,025	268,320	294,613
Substance abuse and mental health services [3]	1,241	1,931	3,203	3,183	3,179	2,847	2,888	2,870
Grants to states for Medicaid [3]	41,103	117,921	181,720	180,625	190,624	201,426	250,924	275,383
State children's health insurance fund [3]	(NA)	1,220	5,129	5,451	6,000	6,900	7,547	8,903
Income security	36,768	68,653	90,885	89,816	90,971	96,102	103,169	121,818
SNAP (formerly Food Stamp Program) [3]	2,130	3,508	1,385	1,600	4,002	4,935	5,624	6,627
Child nutrition programs [3]	4,871	9,060	11,726	12,263	12,871	13,761	15,083	17,136
Temporary assistance for needy families [3]	(NA)	15,464	17,357	16,897	16,876	17,532	17,861	17,754
Veterans benefits and services [3]	134	434	552	625	639	695	809	935
Administration of justice	574	5,203	4,784	4,961	4,603	4,201	4,810	5,783

– Represents zero. NA Not available. [1] Grants include trust funds. [2] Trust funds. [3] Includes grants for payments to individuals.

Source: U.S. Office of Management and Budget, *Budget of the United States Government, Historical Tables*, annual. See also <http://www.whitehouse.gov/omb/budget>.

Table 431. Federal Aid to State and Local Governments by State: 2000 to 2008

[In millions of dollars (291,943 represents $291,943,000,000). For fiscal year ending September 30]

State	2000	2005	2007	2008	State	2000	2005	2007	2008
U.S. [1]	**291,943**	**403,660**	**439,794**	**469,773**	MO	5,671	7,407	7,955	8,273
AL	4,570	6,306	6,869	6,994	MT	1,439	2,021	1,835	2,109
AK	2,260	2,671	2,431	2,604	NE	1,682	2,250	2,328	2,439
AZ	4,501	7,965	8,672	9,940	NV	1,244	2,213	2,320	2,450
AR	2,657	4,179	4,474	4,733	NH	1,116	1,483	1,626	1,692
CA	33,158	46,029	49,976	53,818	NJ	8,212	10,479	11,929	11,580
CO	3,273	4,538	4,900	5,321	NM	2,774	4,097	4,347	5,381
CT	3,771	4,539	4,963	5,279	NY	30,038	43,438	43,297	44,454
DE	818	1,142	1,225	1,363	NC	7,911	11,568	12,448	12,906
DC	2,963	3,450	2,137	11,946	ND	1,155	1,394	1,281	1,402
FL	11,676	19,046	20,033	20,659	OH	10,560	13,726	15,731	15,230
GA	7,192	8,914	10,465	10,675	OK	3,587	4,935	5,516	5,922
HI	1,221	1,731	1,971	2,120	OR	3,597	4,808	5,003	5,498
ID	1,229	1,814	2,031	2,688	PA	12,765	18,103	18,981	18,832
IL	11,271	14,616	16,141	16,267	RI	1,526	1,937	2,105	2,037
IN	5,142	6,483	7,258	8,272	SC	4,017	5,326	5,863	6,035
IA	2,639	3,594	3,688	4,014	SD	1,131	1,336	1,280	1,473
KS	2,315	2,872	3,415	3,514	TN	6,160	9,083	9,031	9,201
KY	4,720	5,779	6,370	6,867	TX	17,350	25,622	28,104	30,580
LA	5,248	7,148	13,278	12,457	UT	1,910	2,633	2,845	3,160
ME	1,850	2,623	2,546	2,695	VT	900	1,213	1,546	1,441
MD	5,538	6,800	7,372	7,473	VA	4,615	6,330	7,173	7,724
MA	7,500	9,989	11,224	11,402	WA	5,707	7,681	8,050	8,668
MI	9,486	12,113	12,822	13,587	WV	2,542	3,482	3,571	3,557
MN	4,599	5,878	7,001	7,533	WI	4,504	6,563	6,719	7,000
MS	3,420	5,168	8,239	7,484	WY	1,014	2,243	1,898	2,334

[1] Includes Island Areas and amounts not distributed to the states.

Source: U.S. Census Bureau, *Federal Aid to States for Fiscal Year 2008*. See also <http://www.census.gov/prod/2009pubs/fas-08.pdf>.

Table 432. Federal Aid to State and Local Governments—Selected Programs by State: 2008

[In millions of dollars (469,773 represents $469,773,000,000). For fiscal year ending September 30. Negative amounts (–) are refunds (from the recipients) of advances from a prior year, or represent reductions in the amount of funds originally obligated to the recipients for the particular program or program category during the fiscal year]

| State and Island Areas | Federal aid total [1] | Department of Agriculture | | | | | Department of Education | | | | |
| | | | Food and Nutrition Service | | | | | | Office of Elementary and Secondary Education | | |
		Total	Child nutrition programs	Supplemental Nutrition Assistance Program (SNAP)[2]	Special supplemental food program (WIC)	Other	Special education programs	Total	No Child Left Behind Act	Title 1 programs	Other
United States, total ..	469,773	27,759	13,671	4,913	6,162	3,012	36,040	12,005	4,655	11,318	8,061
Alabama	6,994	466	266	33	107	60	576	179	80	199	118
Alaska	2,604	135	39	12	24	60	152	1	3	–	148
Arizona	9,940	547	297	60	131	60	903	253	95	267	287
Arkansas	4,733	328	178	34	65	51	377	123	51	128	74
California	53,818	3,407	1,659	520	990	238	4,917	1,451	668	1,679	1,119
Colorado	5,321	287	136	40	64	47	567	222	68	127	151
Connecticut	5,279	194	101	32	46	15	357	135	47	107	69
Delaware	1,363	85	45	10	15	16	129	47	25	33	26
District of Columbia	11,946	62	30	12	14	6	119	28	16	39	36
Florida	20,659	1,267	763	96	336	71	1,997	806	242	531	418
Georgia	10,675	960	583	70	226	80	102	6	4	–	93
Hawaii	2,120	116	45	14	34	23	227	63	24	40	101
Idaho	2,688	152	63	14	27	48	187	60	29	42	57
Illinois	16,267	917	507	120	210	80	1,691	679	201	540	271
Indiana	8,272	466	265	51	97	53	641	246	73	231	92
Iowa	4,014	254	120	25	49	60	350	159	39	76	76
Kansas.............	3,514	241	133	21	45	42	98	12	4	–	81
Kentucky	6,867	439	232	43	98	65	615	226	80	188	120
Louisiana	12,457	542	302	62	113	66	46	1	5	–	40
Maine..............	2,695	101	45	13	18	25	179	58	31	44	45
Maryland	7,473	344	177	43	91	33	649	239	69	212	129
Massachusetts........	11,402	382	212	49	91	30	759	333	92	211	123
Michigan	13,587	759	350	111	189	109	1,195	390	182	422	202
Minnesota	7,533	431	204	73	100	54	512	201	68	115	126
Mississippi	7,484	405	224	31	79	71	492	123	72	176	122
Missouri	8,273	452	248	59	84	60	106	14	10	–	82
Montana	2,109	116	39	13	15	50	202	55	32	38	78
Nebraska...........	2,439	171	87	18	30	35	248	96	33	53	67
Nevada............	2,450	144	75	15	37	18	260	68	31	88	73
New Hampshire	1,692	63	27	7	13	17	158	64	29	35	29
New Jersey	11,580	511	272	97	114	28	956	435	114	248	158
New Mexico..........	5,381	255	129	36	47	44	445	101	46	117	180
New York	44,454	1,708	877	345	384	102	3,203	959	412	1,351	481
North Carolina	12,906	814	445	82	177	110	1,093	447	121	309	217
North Dakota	1,402	82	31	10	12	29	150	39	26	31	54
Ohio..............	15,230	835	423	136	191	85	87	5	11	–	72
Oklahoma	5,922	436	223	50	92	71	578	197	71	133	178
Oregon.............	5,498	416	139	74	70	132	489	193	76	122	98
Pennsylvania	18,832	841	407	183	165	86	1,302	394	191	522	195
Rhode Island........	2,037	75	37	8	19	10	21	5	–	–	16
South Carolina........	6,035	398	238	22	92	46	609	237	79	195	98
South Dakota	1,473	100	40	14	16	30	76	12	2	–	62
Tennessee	9,201	544	297	60	124	63	746	289	96	231	131
Texas	30,580	2,455	1,552	179	582	141	3,397	1,018	430	1,166	782
Utah	3,160	198	105	27	37	29	330	161	35	52	83
Vermont............	1,441	70	18	21	13	17	120	39	23	29	30
Virginia	7,724	417	195	83	82	57	875	360	92	210	213
Washington	8,668	502	217	60	132	94	627	217	77	169	164
West Virginia	3,557	179	89	12	35	42	265	75	45	95	49
Wisconsin	7,000	381	191	48	83	59	722	278	86	195	163
Wyoming	2,334	50	19	6	9	16	125	39	24	26	36
Island Areas:											
American Samoa.....	142	30	15	5	7	3	26	7	1	–	19
Micronesia..........	92	–	–	–	–	–	4	4	–	–	–
Guam..............	303	23	8	2	8	5	47	21	1	–	25
Marshall Islands......	209	–	–	–	–	–	2	2	–	–	–
Northern Marianas ...	174	19	7	9	3	1	17	5	–	–	12
Palau	23	–	–	–	–	–	3	1	–	–	2
Puerto Rico	5,745	2,134	228	1,633	222	52	908	127	194	496	92
Virgin Islands........	281	40	19	10	7	5	5	3	–	–	2
Undistributed amounts..	1,725	13	–	–	–	13	–	–	–	–	–

See footnotes at end of table.

U.S. Census Bureau, Statistical Abstract of the United States: 2011

Table 432. Federal Aid to State and Local Governments—Selected Programs by State: 2008—Con.

[See headnote, page 270]

State and Island Areas	FEMA [3] total	Department of Housing and Urban Development						Department of Labor			
		Total	Community development block grants	Public housing programs			Other	State unemployment insurance and employment		Workforce investment	Other
				Low rent housing assistance	Housing certificate program	Capital program		Total	service		
United States, total	**4,330**	**47,344**	**9,038**	**25,266**	**2,647**	**3,277**	**7,116**	**8,707**	**4,003**	**3,026**	**1,678**
Alabama	45	484	75	248	11	72	78	106	49	32	25
Alaska	16	105	18	37	3	3	46	58	29	12	17
Arizona	6	443	75	164	14	10	179	127	44	49	34
Arkansas	44	218	36	114	17	22	29	97	49	27	21
California	328	4,424	606	2,773	210	129	706	1,061	512	392	157
Colorado	8	413	44	248	33	17	72	113	55	38	20
Connecticut	3	721	52	454	87	45	83	113	67	27	19
Delaware	2	95	10	49	18	4	14	22	13	5	4
District of Columbia	–	7,265	621	4,756	241	289	1,359	160	19	12	129
Florida	515	1,633	244	951	47	74	317	259	126	91	42
Georgia	47	1,002	106	521	20	101	255	183	100	63	19
Hawaii	13	152	15	92	6	10	29	44	18	8	18
Idaho	2	85	16	40	10	1	18	46	29	10	8
Illinois	34	1,895	180	1,087	146	214	267	403	201	146	56
Indiana	17	472	71	290	15	34	61	181	90	63	28
Iowa	68	230	43	143	6	7	31	83	40	19	24
Kansas	324	171	38	86	8	13	26	64	27	29	8
Kentucky	15	426	44	246	9	51	77	123	54	43	26
Louisiana	1,235	3,653	3,113	354	20	71	95	126	49	61	16
Maine	16	217	23	114	35	8	38	42	19	11	11
Maryland	9	887	62	530	57	68	170	208	78	33	97
Massachusetts	6	1,690	129	1,099	221	73	168	179	93	58	28
Michigan	4	945	153	426	164	47	156	471	226	170	76
Minnesota	26	540	67	263	95	34	81	135	77	33	25
Mississippi	383	1,092	855	160	10	27	40	120	37	69	15
Missouri	84	511	64	302	17	44	83	156	62	66	28
Montana	11	70	10	02	4	4	20	33	14	7	11
Nebraska	68	138	20	75	4	13	26	37	24	5	7
Nevada	4	168	24	98	5	8	33	51	35	10	7
New Hampshire	7	171	18	100	18	6	29	30	18	8	4
New Jersey	18	1,415	110	838	201	99	167	232	133	73	25
New Mexico	11	179	35	92	7	6	38	59	25	18	16
New York	152	4,603	593	2,608	199	667	536	502	234	196	71
North Carolina	16	818	77	515	20	69	137	281	155	73	53
North Dakota	7	98	10	66	2	3	17	23	13	5	6
Ohio	40	1,369	168	793	84	102	222	350	157	153	39
Oklahoma	111	309	43	145	12	19	90	73	30	25	17
Oregon	23	325	43	190	15	12	65	148	64	52	32
Pennsylvania	31	1,703	253	842	164	185	260	347	187	112	48
Rhode Island	1	242	18	153	27	17	28	37	22	10	6
South Carolina	10	388	43	234	10	28	73	167	69	76	22
South Dakota	16	107	19	40	12	3	33	23	11	6	6
Tennessee	7	497	53	271	24	61	88	165	82	62	22
Texas	187	1,889	327	1,017	92	155	300	522	180	258	84
Utah	8	138	20	80	5	5	28	58	31	14	12
Vermont	7	103	12	66	12	4	9	26	12	6	8
Virginia	12	799	69	423	84	111	111	231	72	34	126
Washington	61	622	62	391	5	29	135	227	110	71	45
West Virginia	6	188	39	114	12	10	13	50	22	18	10
Wisconsin	20	438	60	204	68	22	83	163	93	39	31
Wyoming	5	33	5	15	3	2	10	22	11	5	6
Island Areas:											
American Samoa	–	1	1	–	–	–	1	1	–	1	1
Micronesia	2	–	–	–	–	–	–	1	–	1	–
Guam	30	34	4	26	–	2	2	5	–	3	1
Marshall Islands	–	–	–	–	–	–	–	–	–	–	–
Northern Marianas	2	5	2	3	–	–	–	2	–	1	1
Palau	–	–	–	–	–	–	–	–	–	–	–
Puerto Rico	11	676	133	270	36	162	75	152	33	111	8
Virgin Islands	–	33	3	20	1	6	4	8	3	3	2
Undistributed amounts	190	4	–	–	–	–	3	–	–	–	–

See footnotes at end of table.

Table 432. Federal Aid to State and Local Governments—Selected Programs by State: 2008—Con.

[See headnote, page 270]

State and Island Areas	Department of Health and Human Services						Department of Transportation				Other, federal aid [4]
	Administration for Children and Families				Centers for Medicare and Medicaid Services	Other					
	Total	Children & family services (Head Start)	Foster care and adoption assistance	Temporary assistance for needy families			Total	Highway trust fund	Federal Transit Administration	Other	
United States, total ...	267,604	8,593	6,731	17,467	206,108	28,706	53,239	34,913	10,275	8,051	24,750
Alabama	3,681	133	48	118	2,961	421	1,206	1,060	68	78	430
Alaska	990	46	21	56	723	144	746	399	85	262	402
Arizona	6,623	186	137	243	5,304	753	890	600	188	102	401
Arkansas	3,002	84	54	77	2,537	251	487	384	24	79	181
California	32,910	1,098	1,662	3,918	22,773	3,459	4,798	2,735	1,303	760	1,972
Colorado	2,625	189	95	149	1,725	466	774	574	135	65	533
Connecticut	3,174	76	106	271	2,373	349	534	429	77	29	182
Delaware	744	17	7	21	595	104	167	141	9	17	119
District of Columbia	1,497	49	31	59	1,076	282	1,933	284	328	1,321	910
Florida	11,410	339	252	681	8,680	1,460	2,768	2,172	323	273	808
Georgia	6,511	213	128	438	5,047	685	1,468	1,143	189	137	402
Hawaii	1,093	38	39	139	748	129	334	245	30	58	142
Idaho	1,113	42	14	31	894	133	922	272	623	28	181
Illinois	9,325	344	260	605	6,968	1,147	1,402	1,243	14	145	600
Indiana	5,098	126	91	226	4,216	439	1,124	953	84	87	273
Iowa	2,318	72	61	134	1,803	247	501	410	42	50	210
Kansas	1,901	71	32	99	1,488	211	557	490	32	35	159
Kentucky	4,215	151	94	230	3,463	276	696	614	39	43	338
Louisiana	5,355	179	74	182	4,450	470	801	427	19	354	699
Maine	1,748	42	27	81	1,438	160	245	146	65	34	148
Maryland	4,327	111	142	252	3,233	589	626	527	19	81	422
Massachusetts	7,252	151	114	464	5,797	725	716	471	188	57	418
Michigan	8,197	299	192	640	6,097	968	1,461	988	324	149	556
Minnesota	4,567	123	76	257	3,588	524	950	627	139	184	373
Mississippi	3,751	195	16	104	3,101	335	946	493	180	273	295
Missouri	5,580	165	97	228	4,609	481	998	854	16	127	386
Montana	873	47	18	41	605	161	540	399	99	42	252
Nebraska	1,319	55	32	48	993	192	295	249	17	28	163
Nevada	1,097	33	33	58	744	228	437	247	128	63	288
New Hampshire	898	23	19	46	694	116	213	165	16	32	152
New Jersey	6,443	147	100	405	5,024	767	1,539	801	609	129	467
New Mexico	3,149	85	47	140	2,290	586	348	266	42	40	936
New York	29,437	590	707	2,390	23,695	2,056	3,551	1,446	1,967	138	1,297
North Carolina	8,244	276	114	335	6,750	769	1,264	872	279	113	374
North Dakota	577	37	15	26	375	126	266	229	11	25	200
Ohio	10,456	315	414	1,078	7,701	949	1,561	1,176	201	184	532
Oklahoma	3,325	136	70	167	2,560	392	757	664	48	45	334
Oregon	2,915	118	88	225	2,148	336	780	451	249	79	402
Pennsylvania	11,762	294	336	656	9,400	1,076	2,184	1,515	514	155	661
Rhode Island	1,303	25	22	93	1,039	123	223	176	25	22	135
South Carolina	3,763	108	43	117	3,105	390	447	359	44	45	253
South Dakota	700	48	8	22	458	164	291	239	14	37	161
Tennessee	5,807	167	74	206	4,845	513	867	679	80	108	567
Texas	17,376	643	284	583	13,956	1,910	3,406	2,578	476	351	1,348
Utah	1,562	60	26	61	1,180	235	492	302	127	63	374
Vermont	835	25	19	48	656	88	176	146	15	16	103
Virginia	3,855	136	89	167	2,965	497	1,142	846	204	92	393
Washington	4,866	172	139	345	3,566	644	1,247	724	388	135	516
West Virginia	2,185	64	52	88	1,773	208	478	413	18	47	205
Wisconsin	4,206	130	111	322	3,166	476	745	629	56	60	326
Wyoming	434	22	2	22	300	88	245	208	9	29	1,419
Island Areas:											
American Samoa	22	4	–	–	9	8	15	7	1	6	46
Micronesia	3	–	–	–	–	3	–	–	–	–	81
Guam	45	6	–	2	16	21	31	10	1	20	90
Marshall Islands	2	–4	–	–	–	2	137	–	–	137	68
Northern Marianas	9	–	–	–	5	4	74	1	60	13	45
Palau	3	1	–	–	–	2	–	–	–	–	16
Puerto Rico	1,064	271	2	68	388	334	171	142	–	28	629
Virgin Islands	45	10	–	3	10	22	28	20	–	8	122
Undistributed amounts...	18	6	–	–	–	12	1,239	275	34	931	261

– Represents or rounds to zero. [1] Total includes programs, not shown separately. [2] For Puerto Rico, amount shown is for nutritional assistance grant program, all other amounts are grant payments for food stamp administration. [3] FEMA = Federal Emergency Management Agency. FEMA is part of the U.S. Department of Homeland Security. [4] Represents aid for other programs, not shown.

Source: U.S. Census Bureau, Federal Aid to States for Fiscal Year 2008. See also <http://www.census.gov/prod/2009pubs/fas-08.pdf>.

Table 433. State and Local Governments—Summary of Finances: 1990 to 2007

[In millions of dollars (1,032,115 represents $1,032,115,000,000) except as indicated. For fiscal year ending in year shown; see text, this section. Local government amounts are estimates subject to sampling variation; see Appendix III and source]

Item	1990	2000	2004	2005	2006	2007
Revenue [1]	**1,032,115**	**1,942,328**	**2,435,084**	**2,528,912**	**2,736,542**	**3,072,645**
From federal government	**136,802**	**291,950**	**425,683**	**438,432**	**452,233**	**467,949**
Public welfare	59,961	148,549	217,176	225,691	225,605	237,220
Highways	14,368	24,414	30,692	33,672	34,559	36,295
Education	23,233	45,873	71,010	74,136	79,397	79,514
Health and hospitals	5,904	15,611	23,316	22,725	23,819	24,555
Housing and community development	9,655	17,690	26,560	28,018	29,121	32,766
Other and unallocable	23,683	39,812	56,929	54,191	59,732	57,599
From state and local sources	**895,313**	**1,650,379**	**2,009,401**	**2,090,479**	**2,186,018**	**2,604,695**
General, net intergovernmental	712,700	1,249,373	1,464,058	1,588,292	1,733,785	1,867,945
Taxes	501,619	872,351	1,010,277	1,099,200	1,195,254	1,283,283
Property	155,613	249,178	318,242	335,981	359,109	389,573
Sales and gross receipts	177,885	309,290	360,629	384,383	412,114	439,586
Individual income	105,640	211,661	215,215	242,273	268,599	289,827
Corporation net income	23,566	36,059	33,716	43,138	52,931	60,592
Other	38,915	66,164	82,475	93,425	102,500	103,705
Charges and miscellaneous	211,081	377,022	453,781	489,093	538,531	584,662
Utility and liquor stores	58,642	89,546	114,054	119,607	131,642	141,234
Water supply system	17,674	30,515	36,087	37,377	40,274	43,652
Electric power system	29,268	42,436	55,980	59,157	65,387	70,494
Gas supply system	5,216	8,049	9,783	6,937	8,724	8,698
Transit system	3,043	3,954	6,506	10,146	10,881	11,568
Liquor stores	3,441	4,592	5,698	5,990	6,377	6,823
Insurance trust revenue [2]	123,970	311,460	431,289	382,580	418,881	595,516
Employee retirement	94,268	273,881	365,265	316,576	352,521	532,154
Unemployment compensation	18,441	23,366	38,362	35,367	36,989	34,186
Direct expenditure	**972,695**	**1,742,914**	**2,260,330**	**2,368,692**	**2,500,583**	**2,661,210**
By function:						
Direct general expenditure [2]	831,573	1,502,768	1,903,194	2,012,422	2,121,946	2,258,229
Education [2]	288,148	521,612	655,361	689,057	727,967	774,373
Elementary and secondary	202,009	365,181	452,055	473,406	500,528	534,905
Higher education	73,418	134,352	173,086	182,146	191,758	204,706
Highways	61,057	101,336	118,179	124,602	135,412	144,713
Public welfare	107,287	233,350	335,257	362,932	370,325	384,769
Health	24,223	51,366	63,125	66,971	71,110	74,196
Hospitals	50,412	75,976	96,551	103,404	110,455	118,876
Police protection	30,577	56,798	69,707	74,727	79,066	84,088
Fire protection	13,186	23,102	28,330	31,439	34,167	36,828
Natural resources	12,330	20,235	23,299	25,057	25,482	28,717
Sanitation and sewerage	28,453	45,261	55,908	58,069	61,900	67,016
Housing and community development	15,479	26,590	37,221	39,969	41,980	45,937
Parks and recreation	14,326	25,038	30,467	31,941	34,769	37,526
Financial administration	16,217	29,300	36,163	36,519	37,441	39,631
Interest on general debt [3]	49,739	69,814	81,723	81,119	85,660	93,586
Utility and liquor stores [3]	77,801	114,916	159,732	160,682	174,679	189,330
Water supply system	22,101	35,789	44,806	45,799	47,752	54,331
Electric power system	30,997	39,719	59,299	58,612	66,308	69,736
Gas supply system	2,989	3,724	6,717	7,075	9,064	12,073
Transit system	18,788	31,883	44,237	44,310	46,327	47,587
Liquor stores	2,926	3,801	4,673	4,885	5,228	5,603
Insurance trust expenditure [2]	63,321	125,230	197,405	195,588	203,958	213,652
Employee retirement	38,355	95,679	137,537	145,796	156,180	166,975
Unemployment compensation	16,499	18,648	43,278	29,849	28,097	28,934
By character and object:						
Current operation	700,131	1,288,746	1,662,510	1,764,453	1,863,023	1,977,229
Capital outlay	123,102	217,063	269,976	277,200	295,368	324,467
Construction	89,144	161,694	209,395	216,254	229,529	253,858
Equipment, land, and existing structures	33,958	55,369	60,581	60,947	65,839	1,977,229
Assistance and subsidies	27,227	31,375	36,922	39,469	41,035	324,467
Interest on debt (general and utility)	58,914	80,499	93,518	91,981	97,198	253,858
Insurance benefits and repayments	63,321	125,230	197,405	195,588	203,958	213,652
Expenditure for salaries and wages [4]	*340,654*	*548,796*	*666,041*	*693,146*	*721,255*	*761,991*
Debt outstanding, year end	**858,006**	**1,451,815**	**1,951,661**	**2,085,597**	**2,200,892**	**2,411,298**
Long-term	838,700	1,427,524	1,913,286	2,054,838	2,167,684	2,379,359
Short-term	19,306	24,291	38,374	30,759	33,208	31,939
Long-term debt:						
Issued	108,468	184,831	346,813	321,960	339,333	386,465
Retired	64,831	121,897	241,111	223,862	227,682	227,545

[1] Aggregates exclude duplicative transactions between state and local governments; see source. [2] Includes amounts not shown separately. [3] Interest on utility debt included in "utility and liquor stores expenditure." For total interest on debt, see "Interest on debt (general and utility)." [4] Included in items above.

Source: U.S. Census Bureau, 2007 Census of Government Finances. See also http://www.census.gov/govs/cog /how_data_collected.html. Data users who create their own estimates from this table should cite the U.S. Census Bureau as the source of the original data only.

Table 434. State and Local Governments—Revenue and Expenditures by Function: 2006 and 2007

[In millions of dollars (2,736,542 represents $2,736,542,000,000) For fiscal year ending in year shown; see text, this section. Local government amounts are estimates subject to sampling variation; see Appendix III and source]

Item	2006 Total	2006 State	2006 Local	2007 Total	2007 State	2007 Local
Revenue [1]	**2,736,542**	**1,773,208**	**1,406,440**	**3,072,645**	**2,000,366**	**1,539,014**
Intergovernmental revenue [1]	452,233	419,143	476,196	467,949	430,278	504,407
Total revenue from own sources [1]	2,284,309	1,354,064	930,244	2,604,695	1,570,088	1,034,607
General revenue from own sources	1,733,785	966,233	767,552	1,867,945	1,027,524	840,421
Taxes [2]	1,195,254	710,864	484,390	1,283,283	757,471	525,813
Property	359,109	11,794	347,315	389,573	12,621	376,952
Individual income	268,599	245,883	22,717	289,827	265,863	23,964
Corporation income	52,931	47,466	5,465	60,592	52,915	7,677
Sales and gross receipts	412,114	332,972	79,142	439,586	352,706	86,880
General sales	282,179	226,712	55,467	299,650	238,304	61,346
Selective sales [2]	129,936	106,260	23,675	139,936	114,402	25,534
Motor fuel	36,972	35,702	1,270	37,904	36,543	1,361
Alcoholic beverages	5,369	4,925	444	5,620	5,166	453
Tobacco products	14,975	14,499	476	15,834	15,299	535
Public utilities	23,669	11,426	12,243	27,105	14,333	12,772
Motor vehicle and operators' licenses	22,599	21,087	1,512	23,195	21,613	1,582
Death and gift	4,875	4,745	130	5,111	4,924	187
Charges and miscellaneous [2]	538,531	255,369	283,162	584,662	270,054	314,608
Current charges [2]	334,841	137,401	197,440	351,824	141,573	210,251
Education [2]	96,898	74,306	22,592	103,736	80,180	23,557
School lunch sales	6,745	22	6,723	6,920	22	6,898
Higher education	82,127	73,195	8,932	88,433	79,060	9,373
Natural resources	3,548	2,449	1,099	4,047	2,480	1,567
Hospitals	83,658	31,718	51,939	91,432	33,838	57,594
Sewerage	33,804	49	33,754	36,157	44	36,113
Solid waste management	13,633	476	13,157	14,458	432	14,025
Parks and recreation	8,659	1,462	7,197	8,812	1,495	7,317
Housing and community development	5,075	622	4,452	5,435	675	4,760
Airports	15,471	1,152	14,320	16,583	1,216	15,366
Sea and inland port facilities	3,699	1,066	2,633	3,867	1,137	2,730
Highways	16,302	10,326	5,976	10,640	6,086	4,554
Interest earnings	71,495	38,207	33,288	92,170	47,199	44,971
Special assessments	7,094	779	6,316	8,157	889	7,268
Sale of property	3,941	1,115	2,826	4,590	1,142	3,448
Utility and liquor store revenue	131,642	21,246	110,397	141,234	22,535	118,699
Insurance trust revenue	418,881	366,586	52,296	595,516	520,029	75,487
Expenditure [1]	**2,507,086**	**1,551,555**	**1,390,867**	**2,665,881**	**1,635,747**	**1,499,268**
Intergovernmental expenditure [1]	6,504	428,925	12,915	4,671	459,605	14,200
Direct expenditure [1]	2,500,583	1,122,631	1,377,952	2,661,210	1,176,142	1,485,068
General expenditure [2]	2,121,946	918,205	1,203,740	2,258,229	964,590	1,293,639
Education [2]	727,967	202,474	525,493	774,373	213,868	560,505
Elementary and secondary education	500,528	6,025	494,503	534,905	8,305	526,600
Higher education	191,758	160,769	30,990	204,706	170,801	33,905
Public welfare	370,325	324,714	45,611	384,769	336,510	48,259
Hospitals	110,455	44,320	66,135	118,876	47,953	70,923
Health	71,110	32,994	38,115	74,196	37,321	36,875
Highways	135,412	84,289	51,123	144,713	88,333	56,380
Police protection	79,066	10,838	68,228	84,088	11,383	72,706
Fire protection	34,167	–	34,167	36,828	–	36,828
Corrections	62,667	40,413	22,254	68,092	44,021	24,071
Natural resources	25,482	18,146	7,336	28,717	19,752	8,964
Sewerage	39,220	1,266	37,955	44,197	1,364	42,834
Solid waste management	22,679	3,254	19,425	22,819	2,226	20,593
Housing and community development	41,980	5,153	36,827	45,937	8,712	37,225
Governmental administration	111,335	46,814	64,521	119,396	49,236	70,160
Parks and recreation	34,769	4,876	29,893	37,526	5,181	32,345
Interest on general debt	85,660	37,808	47,852	93,586	41,594	51,992
Utility	169,451	24,904	144,547	183,727	24,530	159,196
Liquor store expenditure	5,228	4,338	890	5,603	4,664	939
Insurance trust expenditure	203,958	175,183	28,775	213,652	182,358	31,294
By character and object:						
Current operation	1,863,023	774,651	1,088,372	1,977,229	809,535	1,167,694
Capital outlay	295,368	101,432	193,936	324,467	110,044	214,423
Construction	229,529	83,858	145,672	253,858	90,788	163,070
Equipment, land, and existing structures	65,839	17,575	48,264	70,608	19,256	51,352
Assistance and subsidies	41,035	31,644	9,391	39,802	30,621	9,181
Interest on debt (general and utility)	97,198	39,720	57,478	106,061	43,584	62,476
Insurance benefits and repayments	203,958	175,183	28,775	213,652	182,358	31,294
Expenditure for salaries and wages [3]	*721,255*	*203,164*	*518,091*	*761,991*	*217,018*	*544,973*

– Represents or rounds to zero. [1] Aggregates exclude duplicative transactions between levels of government; see source.
[2] Includes other items, not shown separately. [3] Included in items shown above.

Source: U.S. Census Bureau, *State and Local Government Finances*, 2006–07, July 2010. See also <http://www.census.gov/govs/>.

Table 435. State and Local Governments—Capital Outlays: 1990 to 2007

[In millions of dollars (123,102 represents $123,102,000,000), except percent. For fiscal year ending in year shown; see text, this section. Local government amounts are subject to sampling variation; see Appendix III and source]

Level and function	1990	2000	2002	2003	2004	2005	2006	2007
State & local governments: total	**123,102**	**217,063**	**257,071**	**263,198**	**269,976**	**277,200**	**295,368**	**324,467**
Percent of direct expenditure	12.7	12.5	12.6	12.2	11.9	11.7	11.8	12.2
By function:								
Education [1]	25,997	60,968	71,680	70,813	74,597	77,779	82,505	91,466
Elementary and secondary	18,057	45,150	53,294	51,118	52,977	54,509	59,256	65,467
Higher education	7,441	15,257	17,652	19,044	21,121	22,782	22,798	25,356
Highways	33,867	56,439	66,017	65,523	65,964	69,642	76,371	83,289
Health and hospitals	3,848	5,502	6,126	7,158	7,241	7,711	8,538	9,737
Natural resources	2,545	4,347	4,247	4,244	4,657	4,543	4,473	6,372
Housing and community development	3,997	6,184	6,939	7,660	7,578	7,880	8,130	7,991
Air transportation	3,434	6,717	8,551	9,066	9,731	9,326	9,064	9,851
Sea and inland port facilities [2]	924	1,618	1,691	3,721	1,798	1,598	1,850	2,140
Sewerage	8,356	10,093	11,574	12,467	14,068	14,170	15,336	17,683
Parks and recreation	3,877	6,916	9,093	9,224	7,866	8,151	9,267	10,085
Utilities	16,601	24,847	30,241	34,538	37,432	34,879	36,795	38,230
Water	6,873	10,542	11,831	13,536	13,651	14,402	14,356	16,960
Electric	3,976	4,177	6,538	6,438	7,173	6,055	7,793	7,981
Gas	310	400	358	422	582	544	520	508
Transit	5,443	9,728	11,514	14,142	16,026	13,879	14,126	12,781
Other	19,657	33,431	40,912	38,784	39,044	41,520	43,039	47,624
State governments: Total	**45,524**	**76,233**	**89,767**	**91,943**	**90,950**	**94,181**	**101,432**	**110,044**
Percent of direct expenditure	11.5	10.1	9.8	9.4	8.9	8.8	9.0	9.4
By function:								
Education [1]	7,253	14,077	16,589	17,727	19,632	20,632	20,623	23,752
Elementary and secondary	388	521	490	643	716	442	580	1,734
Higher education	6,366	12,995	15,365	16,433	18,417	19,702	19,593	21,375
Highways	24,850	41,651	49,119	48,719	48,566	51,578	57,025	61,218
Health and hospitals	1,531	2,228	2,241	2,930	2,763	3,278	3,469	3,972
Natural resources	1,593	2,758	2,766	2,788	2,957	2,670	2,588	3,324
Housing and community development	119	860	582	774	222	338	196	505
Air transportation	339	561	525	846	795	615	519	655
Sea and inland port facilities [2]	202	310	346	410	388	367	493	573
Sewerage	333	403	405	405	881	486	650	740
Parks and recreation	601	1,044	1,483	1,098	945	931	1,146	1,176
Utilities	2,605	4,232	5,145	7,084	5,211	4,319	5,907	4,859
Water	20	197	222	174	321	83	83	89
Electric	464	296	1,011	964	1,089	685	1,826	983
Gas	–	–	–	–	–	–	–	–
Transit	2,121	3,740	3,911	5,945	3,800	3,550	3,998	3,788
Other	6,098	8,108	10,567	9,163	8,589	8,967	8,817	9,272
Local governments: total	**77,578**	**140,830**	**167,304**	**171,255**	**179,026**	**183,020**	**193,936**	**214,423**
Percent of direct expenditure	13.5	14.3	14.8	14.5	14.4	14.1	14.1	14.4
By function:								
Education [1]	18,744	46,890	55,091	53,087	54,965	57,147	61,882	67,714
Elementary and secondary	17,669	44,629	52,804	50,475	52,261	54,068	58,677	63,733
Higher education	1,076	2,261	2,286	2,612	2,704	3,079	3,205	3,981
Highways	9,017	14,789	16,898	16,804	17,398	18,064	19,346	22,071
Health and hospitals	2,316	3,274	3,886	4,228	4,478	4,433	5,069	5,765
Natural resources	952	1,589	1,481	1,456	1,699	1,873	1,885	3,048
Housing and community development	3,878	5,324	6,358	6,886	7,356	7,542	7,934	7,486
Air transportation	3,095	6,156	8,026	8,221	8,936	8,712	8,545	9,196
Sea and inland port facilities [2]	722	1,308	1,345	3,310	1,410	1,231	1,357	1,567
Sewerage	8,023	9,690	11,169	12,062	13,186	13,684	14,687	16,943
Parks and recreation	3,276	5,872	7,611	8,126	6,921	7,221	8,122	8,909
Utilities	13,996	20,615	25,096	27,455	32,221	30,560	30,888	33,371
Other	13,559	25,323	30,345	29,621	30,454	32,553	34,222	38,352

– Represents or rounds to zero. [1] Includes other education, not shown separately. [2] Includes terminals.

Source: U.S. Census Bureau, *State and Local Government Finances*, 2006–07, July 2010, and unpublished data. See also <http://www.census.gov/govs/>.

Table 436. State and Local Governments—Expenditures for Public Works: 2000 to 2007

[In millions of dollars (230,569 represents $230,569,000,000), except percent. Public works include expenditures for current operations and capital outlays on highways, airports, Sea and inland port facilities, sewerage, solid waste management, water supply, and mass transit systems. Represents direct expenditures excluding intergovernmental grants]

Item	Total	Highways	Air transportation	Sea and inland port facilities	Sewerage	Solid waste management	Water supply	Mass transit
2000, Total	**230,569**	**101,336**	**13,160**	**3,141**	**28,052**	**17,208**	**35,789**	**31,883**
State	74,974	61,942	1,106	863	955	2,347	354	7,407
Local	155,595	39,394	12,054	2,277	27,098	14,861	35,435	24,476
Capital expenditures (percent)	41.9	55.7	51.0	51.5	36.0	8.9	29.5	30.5
2005, Total	**294,638**	**124,602**	**17,962**	**3,896**	**36,599**	**21,469**	**45,799**	**44,310**
State	92,823	76,575	1,406	1,156	1,109	3,184	319	9,074
Local	201,815	48,026	16,556	2,740	35,491	18,285	45,480	35,237
Capital expenditures (percent)	42.4	55.9	51.9	41.0	38.7	9.3	31.4	31.3
2007, Total	**338,467**	**144,713**	**20,061**	**4,759**	**44,197**	**22,819**	**54,331**	**47,587**
State	105,649	88,333	1,613	1,485	1,364	2,226	365	10,264
Local	232,818	56,300	18,448	3,275	42,834	20,593	53,966	37,323
Capital expenditures (percent)	42.8	57.6	49.1	45.0	40.0	10.1	31.2	26.9

Source: U.S. Census Bureau, *State and Local Government Finances*, 2006–07, July 2010, and unpublished data. See also <http://www.census.gov/govs>.

U.S. Census Bureau, Statistical Abstract of the United States: 2011

Table 437. State and Local Governments—Indebtedness: 1990 to 2007

[In billions of dollars (858.0 represents $858,000,000,000). For fiscal year ending in year shown; see text, this section. Local government amounts are estimates subject to sampling variation; see Appendix III and source]

Item	Debt outstanding Total	Cash and security holdings	Long-term Total	Long-term Public debt for private purposes	Long-term All other	Short-term	Long-term Net long-term [1]	Long-term Debt issued	Long-term Debt retired
1990: Total	**858.0**	**1,490.8**	**838.7**	**294.1**	**544.6**	**19.3**	**474.4**	**108.5**	**64.8**
State	318.3	963.3	315.5	154.4	161.1	2.8	125.5	43.5	22.9
Local	539.8	527.5	523.2	139.7	383.5	16.5	348.9	65.0	42.0
1995: Total	**1,115.4**	**2,058.5**	**1,088.3**	**300.6**	**787.7**	**27.0**	**697.3**	**129.3**	**95.1**
State	427.2	1,393.9	421.1	176.8	244.4	6.1	205.3	52.6	37.5
Local	688.1	664.6	667.2	123.9	543.3	20.9	491.9	76.8	57.6
1996: Total	**1,169.7**	**2,261.7**	**1,145.7**	**312.6**	**833.0**	**24.0**	**751.6**	**141.1**	**106.5**
State	452.4	1,562.9	446.5	186.4	260.2	5.8	220.3	60.2	42.4
Local	717.3	698.8	699.1	126.3	572.8	18.2	531.3	80.9	64.1
1997: Total	**1,224.5**	**2,546.9**	**1,207.9**	**329.0**	**878.9**	**16.6**	**797.7**	**151.3**	**109.3**
State	456.7	1,785.1	454.5	193.7	260.8	2.1	222.6	54.4	41.1
Local	767.9	761.8	753.4	135.3	618.1	14.5	575.1	96.8	68.2
1998: Total	**1,283.6**	**2,890.2**	**1,266.3**	**335.8**	**930.5**	**17.3**	**842.6**	**204.4**	**144.6**
State	483.1	2,058.6	480.9	202.3	278.7	2.2	237.2	83.4	58.1
Local	800.4	831.6	785.4	133.6	651.8	15.1	605.4	120.9	86.5
1999: Total	**1,369.3**	**3,168.5**	**1,351.4**	**351.1**	**1,000.3**	**17.8**	**907.3**	**229.4**	**153.1**
State	510.5	2,265.9	507.8	213.9	293.9	2.7	249.4	83.2	55.6
Local	858.8	902.5	843.6	137.2	706.4	15.2	657.9	146.2	97.5
2000: Total	**1,451.8**	**3,503.7**	**1,427.5**	**372.6**	**1,054.9**	**24.3**	**959.6**	**184.8**	**121.9**
State	547.9	2,518.9	541.5	227.3	314.2	6.4	266.9	75.0	44.4
Local	903.9	984.8	886.0	145.3	740.7	17.9	692.7	109.8	77.5
2001: Total	**1,554.0**	**3,592.1**	**1,531.9**	**395.1**	**1,136.8**	**22.1**	**1,038.6**	**199.6**	**130.6**
State	576.5	2,537.7	572.8	238.2	334.7	3.7	287.4	81.3	50.7
Local	977.5	1,054.3	959.1	157.0	802.1	18.5	751.2	118.3	79.9
2002: Total	**1,681.4**	**3,650.7**	**1,638.1**	**417.7**	**1,220.5**	**43.2**	**1,121.0**	**262.7**	**161.9**
State	636.8	2,555.4	618.2	258.5	359.6	18.6	311.8	104.2	64.9
Local	1,044.6	1,095.3	1,020.0	159.2	860.8	24.6	809.2	158.5	97.0
2003: Total	**1,812.7**	**3,696.1**	**1,772.2**	**431.4**	**1,340.8**	**40.5**	**1,242.7**	**345.8**	**215.2**
State	697.9	2,594.2	681.8	267.3	414.5	16.1	366.2	148.8	85.9
Local	1,114.7	1,101.9	1,090.4	164.1	926.3	24.3	876.5	196.9	129.3
2004: Total	**1,951.7**	**4,120.1**	**1,913.3**	**448.4**	**1,464.9**	**38.4**	**1,349.6**	**346.8**	**241.1**
State	754.2	2,930.1	740.4	268.4	472.0	13.7	412.2	158.4	107.1
Local	1,197.5	1,189.9	1,172.9	180.0	992.9	24.6	937.4	188.5	134.0
2005: Total	**2,085.6**	**4,439.4**	**2,054.8**	**480.6**	**1,574.2**	**30.8**	**1,441.1**	**322.0**	**231.8**
State	813.8	3,156.4	808.3	296.1	512.2	5.6	444.7	131.5	101.8
Local	1,271.8	1,283.0	1,246.5	184.5	1,062.0	25.2	996.4	190.5	130.0
2006: Total	**2,200.9**	**4,807.1**	**2,167.7**	**505.1**	**1,662.6**	**33.2**	**1,519.5**	**339.3**	**227.7**
State	870.9	3,436.4	860.3	315.9	544.4	10.6	473.4	147.0	95.0
Local	1,330.0	1,370.7	1,307.4	189.1	1,118.2	22.6	1,046.0	192.4	132.7
2007: Total	**2,411.3**	**5,470.7**	**2,379.4**	**553.8**	**1,825.6**	**31.9**	**1,673.3**	**386.5**	**227.5**
State	936.5	3,922.4	929.9	354.7	575.3	6.6	499.7	161.4	92.7
Local	1,474.8	1,548.3	1,449.4	199.1	1,250.3	25.4	1,173.6	225.0	134.8

[1] Net long-term debt outstanding is the amount of long-term debt held by a government for which no funds have been set aside for its repayment.

Source: U.S. Census Bureau, 1990, *Government Finances*, Series GF, No. 5, annual; thereafter, *State and Local Government Finances*, 2006–07, July 2010, and unpublished data. See also <http://www.census.gov/govs>.

Table 438. New Security Issues, State and Local Governments: 1990 to 2009

[In billions of dollars (122.9 represents 122,900,000,000)]

Type of issue, issuer, or use	1990	1995	2000	2003	2004	2005	2006	2007	2008	2009
All issues, new and refunding [1]	**122.9**	**145.7**	**180.4**	**384.3**	**357.9**	**409.6**	**389.5**	**426.2**	**390.6**	**410.9**
By type of issue:										
General obligation	39.5	57.0	64.5	144.1	130.5	145.8	115.1	130.5	112.5	156.6
Revenue	83.3	88.7	115.9	238.0	227.4	263.8	274.4	295.7	278.1	254.3
By type of issuer:										
State	15.0	14.7	19.9	49.8	47.4	31.6	28.3	35.0	32.2	61.8
Special district of statutory authority [2]	75.9	93.5	121.2	253.5	234.2	298.6	293.4	315.3	285.4	269.1
Municipality, county, or township	32.0	37.5	39.3	79.0	76.3	79.4	67.9	75.9	73.0	80.0
Issues for new capital	**97.9**	**102.4**	**154.3**	**264.7**	**228.4**	**223.8**	**262.5**	**275.3**	**215.0**	**262.8**
By use of proceeds:										
Education	17.1	24.0	38.7	70.4	65.4	71.0	70.3	70.9	57.3	62.6
Transportation	11.8	11.9	19.7	23.8	20.5	25.4	30.2	27.9	24.8	35.6
Utilities and conservation	10.0	9.6	11.9	10.3	9.2	9.9	7.8	11.4	12.7	12.1
Industrial aid	6.6	6.6	7.1	22.3	19.1	18.6	35.0	38.1	24.9	33.4
Other purposes	31.7	30.8	47.3	97.7	80.4	60.6	72.7	82.9	64.9	91.0

[1] Par amounts of long-term issues based on date of sale. [2] Includes school districts.

Source: Board of Governors of the Federal Reserve System, *Statistical Supplement to the Federal Reserve Bulletin*, monthly. Based on data from Securities Data Company. See also <http://www.federalreserve.gov/econresdata/releases/govsecure/current.htm>.

Table 439. State and Local Governments—Total Revenue and Expenditures by State: 2000 to 2007

[In millions of dollars (1,942,328 represents $1,942,328,000,000), except as indicated. For fiscal year ending in year shown; see text, this section. These data cannot be used to compute the deficit or surplus for any single government, as these are estimates for all state and local governments within a state area. For further information, see the 2006 Government Finance and Employment Classification Manual at <http://www.census.gov/govs/classification/>]

State	Revenue				Expenditures			
	2000	2005	2006	2007	2000	2005	2006	2007
United States	1,942,328	2,528,912	2,736,542	3,072,645	1,746,943	2,373,309	2,507,086	2,665,881
Alabama	25,726	33,377	35,697	40,959	25,319	33,241	35,276	36,198
Alaska	10,525	11,404	13,247	15,460	8,628	10,027	10,788	11,663
Arizona	27,778	41,103	45,324	51,271	27,293	39,300	42,763	47,164
Arkansas	13,833	18,866	20,798	22,543	12,245	17,224	18,503	19,124
California	270,380	381,504	404,541	473,951	236,645	344,532	365,041	390,452
Colorado	29,603	38,915	41,158	46,709	26,173	35,063	37,107	40,478
Connecticut	25,828	30,490	33,554	37,417	24,011	29,649	31,502	32,672
Delaware	6,224	7,637	8,467	9,227	5,153	7,595	8,292	8,702
District of Columbia	6,383	10,043	11,075	11,389	6,527	8,860	10,091	10,585
Florida	92,402	135,562	151,624	172,872	84,301	130,858	140,638	148,513
Georgia	49,310	60,297	65,307	76,001	43,517	58,905	63,053	73,615
Hawaii	8,488	11,000	11,999	13,575	8,254	10,534	11,018	12,274
Idaho	7,590	10,004	10,850	12,347	6,404	8,915	9,330	9,967
Illinois.	80,695	99,826	108,037	120,026	74,727	97,745	100,995	108,910
Indiana.	32,716	44,261	51,062	49,162	31,250	42,048	44,033	46,814
Iowa.	17,220	23,204	24,840	27,670	17,275	21,486	23,102	24,248
Kansas.	16,235	19,990	21,602	24,269	14,419	18,948	20,295	21,799
Kentucky	25,200	28,044	31,152	33,817	21,473	26,963	29,514	31,716
Louisiana	27,109	35,858	39,729	46,815	25,018	32,578	35,314	39,298
Maine.	8,554	11,383	11,700	12,481	7,652	10,207	10,713	10,862
Maryland	33,949	45,075	48,367	54,271	30,598	41,373	44,280	47,764
Massachusetts.	46,103	62,109	66,603	70,530	44,362	59,312	61,910	64,752
Michigan	70,112	81,055	88,461	91,423	61,506	75,980	77,016	81,004
Minnesota	38,785	45,465	48,830	54,341	35,424	42,936	44,820	47,216
Mississippi	16,672	21,113	24,015	29,627	15,379	20,041	22,109	24,768
Missouri.	31,635	41,340	44,201	49,755	27,953	37,186	39,551	42,037
Montana.	5,043	7,438	8,019	9,183	4,983	6,412	6,948	7,448
Nebraska.	11,650	15,905	17,006	18,271	10,831	14,332	15,320	16,839
Nevada	11,885	18,953	20,363	23,207	11,230	17,405	18,818	20,017
New Hampshire.	6,948	8,911	9,380	10,366	6,222	8,679	9,030	9,416
New Jersey	62,331	79,126	85,517	95,276	54,590	79,845	82,928	87,088
New Mexico.	13,073	16,656	18,452	20,972	11,195	15,596	16,404	18,123
New York	188,907	234,681	266,263	292,764	171,858	226,951	240,996	249,961
North Carolina	50,542	64,813	67,479	75,949	46,135	60,747	64,330	68,131
North Dakota	4,495	5,239	5,772	6,346	4,041	4,794	4,926	5,234
Ohio.	80,074	102,498	107,494	121,412	68,418	91,959	97,514	100,220
Oklahoma	18,760	24,552	26,811	30,228	15,962	22,005	23,967	26,062
Oregon.	28,644	32,400	36,149	41,861	24,086	29,084	30,549	32,261
Pennsylvania	80,546	103,692	109,300	121,211	75,624	101,484	104,228	106,958
Rhode Island	7,427	9,731	10,271	11,244	6,432	9,226	9,667	10,021
South Carolina.	23,467	33,278	34,676	39,435	23,436	33,011	34,234	36,645
South Dakota.	4,277	5,857	6,062	7,034	3,760	4,973	5,210	5,552
Tennessee	33,625	44,863	47,256	52,613	32,010	42,708	44,399	49,098
Texas	120,666	162,748	176,919	195,732	109,634	151,927	160,532	171,092
Utah.	14,954	19,183	20,781	23,380	13,044	17,269	18,527	19,985
Vermont.	4,019	5,393	5,732	6,366	3,766	5,179	5,390	5,806
Virginia.	44,175	56,658	61,647	70,485	38,092	51,529	55,853	59,041
Washington	46,372	57,510	63,055	72,165	41,794	55,800	56,588	62,268
West Virginia	10,760	14,576	14,044	14,814	9,990	12,120	12,387	12,612
Wisconsin	43,003	48,235	47,967	55,882	34,559	43,146	45,316	46,692
Wyoming	7,030	7,084	7,885	8,539	3,743	5,619	5,972	6,719

Source: U.S. Census Bureau, Annual Survey of State & Local Government Finances, 2000–2007, July 2010, <http://www.census.gov/govs>.

U.S. Census Bureau, Statistical Abstract of the United States: 2011

Table 440. State and Local Governments—Revenue by State: 2007

[In millions of dollars (3,072,645 represents $3,072,645,000,000). For fiscal year ending in year shown; see text, this section]

State	Total revenue	General revenue from own sources								
		Total	Intergov- ernmental from federal govern- ment	General revenue from own sources	Select taxes					
					Total [1]	Property	Sales and gross receipt	Indi- vidual income	Corpor- ation income	Other taxes
United States ...	3,072,645	2,335,894	467,949	1,867,945	1,283,283	389,573	439,586	289,827	60,592	82,662
Alabama	40,959	31,571	7,823	23,748	13,530	2,095	6,422	3,140	506	1,137
Alaska	15,460	12,982	2,547	10,435	4,944	1,036	483	–	814	2,542
Arizona	51,271	41,202	8,713	32,488	23,335	6,221	11,299	3,747	986	843
Arkansas	22,543	17,691	4,507	13,184	9,179	1,348	4,886	2,168	363	282
California	473,951	316,410	55,362	261,047	179,855	48,642	54,207	53,318	11,158	9,886
Colorado	46,709	35,335	5,646	29,689	18,635	5,665	6,594	4,795	479	843
Connecticut	37,417	30,764	4,561	26,203	21,516	8,070	5,319	6,335	894	695
Delaware	9,227	7,633	1,264	6,370	3,658	569	462	1,073	302	1,217
District of Columbia........	11,389	9,747	2,999	6,748	5,192	1,516	1,330	1,313	417	590
Florida	172,872	133,716	22,956	110,760	72,974	26,846	35,687	–	2,443	6,807
Georgia	76,001	62,305	13,797	48,509	33,088	9,519	12,773	8,799	1,017	689
Hawaii	13,575	11,223	2,242	8,981	6,545	1,137	3,388	1,560	101	142
Idaho	12,347	9,442	1,978	7,464	4,762	1,114	1,699	1,406	188	222
Illinois...........	120,026	91,714	17,004	74,711	55,079	20,451	18,612	9,408	2,936	2,293
Indiana..........	49,162	42,025	8,229	33,796	21,323	6,170	8,035	5,219	987	661
Iowa............	27,670	21,868	4,562	17,306	10,933	3,616	3,460	2,741	325	372
Kansas..........	24,269	19,970	3,353	16,617	11,354	3,459	4,022	2,747	527	421
Kentucky	33,817	26,965	6,724	20,241	13,705	2,580	5,083	4,042	1,110	649
Louisiana	46,815	39,414	13,298	26,116	17,593	2,611	9,341	3,214	753	1,562
Maine...........	12,481	10,362	2,523	7,838	5,743	2,059	1,690	1,469	184	254
Maryland	54,271	43,947	8,089	35,858	27,065	6,547	6,332	10,743	782	2,200
Massachusetts.....	70,530	55,147	10,653	44,494	32,120	11,042	6,171	11,400	2,107	1,100
Michigan	91,423	71,849	14,390	57,460	37,086	14,530	11,879	6,911	1,786	1,070
Minnesota	54,341	41,449	7,333	34,117	23,661	6,116	7,527	7,231	1,184	1,088
Mississippi	29,627	23,815	9,729	14,086	8,819	2,206	4,269	1,402	369	448
Missouri..........	49,755	37,539	8,653	28,886	19,171	5,258	7,172	5,168	391	918
Montana..........	9,183	7,137	2,017	5,120	3,272	1,107	535	833	179	462
Nebraska........	18,271	13,388	2,710	10,678	7,211	2,381	2,387	1,651	213	448
Nevada	23,207	17,838	2,471	15,368	10,444	2,875	6,078	–	–	1,321
New Hampshire....	10,366	8,550	1,684	6,865	4,743	2,912	735	107	596	307
New Jersey	95,276	78,612	11,778	66,834	51,428	21,483	12,287	11,727	2,887	2,595
New Mexico.......	20,972	16,366	4,480	11,886	7,455	1,009	3,499	1,178	460	1,106
New York	292,764	222,609	45,141	177,468	134,027	38,076	32,517	42,663	12,410	7,425
North Carolina.....	75,949	62,329	14,316	48,013	32,422	7,306	11,026	10,589	1,566	1,287
North Dakota......	6,346	5,364	1,332	4,032	2,600	698	909	317	136	481
Ohio.............	121,412	84,571	18,206	66,365	45,695	13,315	14,384	13,742	1,211	2,066
Oklahoma	30,228	23,995	5,684	18,311	11,822	1,931	4,553	2,775	561	1,390
Oregon..........	41,861	26,931	5,914	21,017	12,749	3,958	1,105	5,612	463	1,150
Pennsylvania	121,211	93,161	19,024	74,137	52,108	14,915	15,036	13,632	2,287	5,420
Rhode Island	11,244	8,794	2,103	6,691	4,786	1,964	1,370	1,086	179	136
South Carolina.....	39,435	31,288	7,054	24,234	13,795	4,293	4,864	3,239	312	901
South Dakota......	7,034	5,097	1,414	3,684	2,390	819	1,294	–	77	142
Tennessee........	52,613	38,872	8,916	29,956	18,818	4,524	10,784	249	1,120	1,674
Texas............	195,732	155,716	31,044	124,672	82,036	34,193	38,340	–	–	7,753
Utah.............	23,380	18,279	3,458	14,822	9,093	2,038	3,484	2,561	399	307
Vermont..........	6,366	5,479	1,433	4,047	2,935	1,237	856	581	83	101
Virginia..........	70,485	54,930	7,463	47,467	32,374	10,018	8,538	10,239	880	2,185
Washington	72,165	50,027	8,911	41,116	27,542	7,368	17,083	–	–	2,599
West Virginia	14,814	13,277	3,417	9,860	6,102	1,136	2,310	1,361	539	668
Wisconsin	55,882	40,078	7,166	32,913	23,329	8,397	6,394	6,334	923	914
Wyoming	8,539	7,118	1,878	5,241	3,247	1,197	1,072	–	–	895

See footnotes at end of table

U.S. Census Bureau, Statistical Abstract of the United States: 2011

Table 440. State and Local Governments—Revenue by State: 2007—Con.

[See headnote page 278]

State	General revenue from own sources—Con.								Utility and liquor stores	Insurance trust revenue
	Current charges and miscellaneous revenue									
		Current charges				Miscellaneous revenue				
	Total	Total [1]	Education	Hospitals	Sewerage	Total [1]	Interest earnings	Special assessments		
United States	584,662	351,824	103,736	91,432	36,157	232,837	92,170	8,157	141,234	595,516
Alabama	10,218	7,205	2,243	3,714	367	3,013	1,086	34	2,826	6,563
Alaska	5,490	1,099	183	192	65	4,391	1,711	9	302	2,177
Arizona	9,154	5,041	1,852	687	629	4,113	1,615	124	3,985	6,085
Arkansas	4,005	2,682	1,036	896	218	1,323	580	25	792	4,059
California	81,193	51,644	9,132	13,070	5,178	29,549	12,296	1,494	25,730	131,811
Colorado	11,053	6,877	2,497	1,458	638	4,177	1,713	361	2,187	9,186
Connecticut	4,687	2,540	1,003	404	286	2,147	894	39	723	5,931
Delaware	2,711	1,266	560	16	144	1,446	321	434	383	1,211
District of Columbia	1,555	639	41	–	186	916	280	1	813	829
Florida	37,787	22,652	3,916	5,263	2,395	15,135	5,024	1,818	8,418	30,738
Georgia	15,421	10,381	2,437	4,046	1,012	5,040	1,576	65	4,314	9,382
Hawaii	2,436	1,510	285	408	192	926	385	32	249	2,103
Idaho	2,702	1,911	424	707	161	791	326	41	324	2,581
Illinois.............	19,632	10,679	4,037	1,257	995	8,953	3,989	417	3,259	25,052
Indiana............	12,473	7,549	3,191	2,571	783	4,924	1,728	46	1,956	5,181
Iowa..............	6,373	4,431	1,551	1,843	334	1,942	884	18	1,044	4,759
Kansas............	5,262	3,575	1,195	1,378	298	1,687	695	63	1,166	3,133
Kentucky	6,535	4,246	1,454	1,370	369	2,289	1,162	20	1,406	5,447
Louisiana..........	8,523	4,819	1,119	2,057	325	3,704	1,634	38	1,214	6,187
Maine.............	2,096	1,147	430	73	141	949	314	12	114	2,006
Maryland	8,793	5,320	2,436	165	756	3,473	1,119	76	919	9,405
Massachusetts.......	12,374	6,136	2,243	488	851	6,239	2,779	441	2,974	12,408
Michigan	20,374	12,731	5,077	2,908	1,471	7,643	2,615	221	2,944	16,629
Minnesota	10,456	6,415	2,317	1,370	624	4,040	1,507	381	2,007	10,884
Mississippi..........	5,267	3,963	1,032	2,300	185	1,304	439	9	1,045	4,766
Missouri............	9,714	5,821	2,249	1,724	571	3,894	1,862	45	1,702	10,515
Montana...........	1,848	1,012	477	62	74	836	359	61	173	1,874
Nebraska..........	3,467	2,219	782	734	146	1,248	455	68	2,938	1,946
Nevada	4,924	2,964	574	595	374	1,959	743	83	993	4,375
New Hampshire.......	2,123	1,132	567	11	95	991	505	1	520	1,207
New Jersey	15,406	9,195	3,139	1,036	1,317	6,211	2,402	7	1,671	14,993
New Mexico..........	4,431	1,695	556	534	131	2,736	1,097	27	496	4,110
New York	43,441	23,263	4,320	6,220	1,786	20,178	7,264	115	12,933	57,222
North Carolina.......	15,591	10,555	2,936	4,144	1,185	5,037	2,066	22	4,041	9,580
North Dakota	1,432	842	427	5	40	590	316	61	116	866
Ohio..............	20,671	12,768	5,456	2,844	1,515	7,902	3,328	239	3,032	33,809
Oklahoma	6,489	4,079	1,736	1,013	256	2,410	819	16	1,420	4,813
Oregon.............	8,000	4,000	1,440	1,019	741	3,468	1,051	96	1,727	13,202
Pennsylvania	22,029	12,862	4,567	1,842	1,950	9,167	4,631	129	4,026	24,024
Rhode Island	1,905	874	411	5	87	1,031	458	4	193	2,257
South Carolina........	10,439	7,639	1,961	3,950	441	2,800	1,040	65	2,954	5,193
South Dakota........	1,294	652	288	38	58	641	330	20	253	1,684
Tennessee..........	11,138	6,474	1,783	2,408	562	4,664	1,077	110	7,767	5,974
Texas..............	42,636	24,087	7,895	6,789	2,718	18,549	8,324	222	10,626	29,391
Utah...............	5,729	3,783	1,302	931	279	1,946	918	60	1,893	3,207
Vermont............	1,112	619	434	–	51	493	211	4	249	638
Virginia.............	15,093	9,555	3,196	2,458	922	5,538	1,971	145	2,220	13,336
Washington	13,574	9,359	2,366	2,469	1,388	4,215	1,726	183	6,311	15,827
West Virginia	3,758	1,897	752	267	193	1,861	519	29	274	1,262
Wisconsin	9,584	6,146	2,258	1,041	627	3,439	1,464	114	1,381	14,422
Wyoming	1,994	1,074	176	650	47	920	561	9	223	1,197

– Represents or rounds to zero. [1] Includes items not shown separately.
Source: U.S. Census Bureau, *State Government Finances 2006–2007*, July 2010, <http://www.census.gov/govs>.

U.S. Census Bureau, Statistical Abstract of the United States: 2011

Table 441. State and Local Governments—Expenditures and Debt by State: 2007

[In millions of dollars (2,665,881 represents $2,665,881,000,000), except as indicated. For fiscal year ending in year shown; see text, this section]

State	Total expenditures	General expenditures Total [1]	Direct general expenditures Total [1]	Education	Public welfare	Health	Hospitals	Highways	Police protection	Corrections
United States	2,665,881	2,262,900	2,258,229	774,373	384,769	74,196	118,876	144,713	84,088	68,092
Alabama	36,198	30,987	30,987	12,031	4,758	886	3,646	1,957	976	768
Alaska	11,663	10,340	10,340	2,604	1,427	184	229	1,400	236	241
Arizona	47,164	39,288	39,288	12,972	6,577	1,620	1,021	2,706	2,046	1,545
Arkansas	19,124	17,053	17,053	6,777	3,639	271	927	1,156	480	448
California	390,452	318,341	314,791	98,462	46,933	12,507	17,175	14,186	13,875	12,625
Colorado	40,478	33,550	33,547	11,544	3,814	1,061	1,788	2,116	1,345	1,176
Connecticut	32,672	28,390	28,390	10,674	4,763	685	1,284	1,218	907	660
Delaware	8,702	7,751	7,750	2,710	1,316	389	63	481	309	266
District of Columbia . . .	10,585	8,480	8,480	1,546	2,161	387	145	105	500	226
Florida	148,513	130,630	130,630	39,515	18,569	4,168	6,587	9,805	6,288	4,230
Georgia	73,615	63,714	63,714	23,258	9,390	1,968	4,774	6,438	2,136	2,210
Hawaii	12,274	10,995	10,995	3,240	1,526	649	455	502	305	197
Idaho	9,967	8,990	8,990	2,970	1,513	203	742	803	300	270
Illinois	108,910	91,124	91,124	30,630	14,547	2,765	2,414	6,661	4,061	1,867
Indiana	46,814	42,132	42,132	15,465	7,164	759	2,989	2,431	1,118	975
Iowa	24,248	21,634	21,634	8,099	3,610	476	2,158	1,863	586	436
Kansas	21,799	19,377	19,377	7,069	3,000	376	1,570	1,665	678	383
Kentucky	31,716	27,110	27,108	9,693	5,763	661	1,434	2,356	629	657
Louisiana	39,298	34,646	34,646	10,109	4,856	744	2,851	2,213	1,212	1,067
Maine	10,862	10,059	10,045	3,091	2,457	504	125	727	232	198
Maryland	47,764	42,760	42,760	15,655	7,013	1,593	481	2,760	1,782	1,661
Massachusetts	64,752	54,615	54,421	16,797	12,291	1,048	1,375	2,272	1,825	1,285
Michigan	81,004	69,937	69,937	28,208	11,027	3,309	3,081	3,791	2,337	2,371
Minnesota	47,216	40,932	40,932	13,882	9,405	1,004	1,704	3,204	1,412	840
Mississippi	24,768	22,161	22,161	6,717	4,041	402	2,623	1,877	573	431
Missouri	42,037	36,645	36,645	12,794	5,892	1,428	2,411	2,967	1,401	801
Montana	7,448	6,648	6,648	2,333	853	366	100	730	206	181
Nebraska	16,839	12,537	12,508	4,717	2,077	416	806	1,010	356	326
Nevada	20,017	17,231	17,225	5,679	1,872	369	899	1,790	985	662
New Hampshire	9,416	8,469	8,469	3,261	1,546	140	56	625	296	164
New Jersey	87,088	74,972	74,972	29,611	12,038	1,651	2,176	3,512	3,058	2,029
New Mexico	18,123	16,215	16,215	5,552	3,221	496	852	1,323	598	468
New York	249,961	204,645	204,016	60,844	44,639	5,651	11,553	9,430	7,642	5,660
North Carolina	68,131	59,236	59,236	21,572	9,799	2,756	4,929	3,330	2,033	1,743
North Dakota	5,234	4,737	4,737	1,744	737	90	18	599	106	89
Ohio	100,220	84,718	84,715	29,965	17,220	3,929	3,333	4,697	2,956	1,628
Oklahoma	26,062	22,743	22,698	8,676	4,419	674	1,018	1,748	719	667
Oregon	32,261	26,335	26,335	8,653	3,801	948	1,274	1,946	967	990
Pennsylvania	106,958	91,686	91,525	31,552	20,333	3,669	2,173	6,939	2,669	3,042
Rhode Island	10,021	8,564	8,537	2,797	2,006	171	94	363	327	220
South Carolina	36,645	31,134	31,134	11,395	5,368	1,105	3,901	1,362	901	661
South Dakota	5,552	4,958	4,958	1,613	768	144	96	706	137	140
Tennessee	49,098	35,993	35,993	11,430	7,619	1,535	2,851	2,282	1,355	953
Texas	171,092	147,303	147,303	59,001	20,359	3,561	9,489	11,671	5,246	4,712
Utah	19,985	16,762	16,762	6,374	2,180	514	818	1,169	583	476
Vermont	5,806	5,272	5,272	2,154	1,204	156	18	437	141	114
Virginia	59,041	53,133	53,132	20,966	7,672	1,531	2,768	3,002	1,911	1,941
Washington	62,268	49,629	49,624	16,537	7,097	2,094	3,508	3,521	1,413	1,581
West Virginia	12,612	11,806	11,806	4,543	2,418	315	324	1,057	268	272
Wisconsin	46,692	40,489	40,489	14,879	7,447	1,576	1,122	3,207	1,494	1,366
Wyoming	6,719	6,042	6,042	2,010	623	294	649	595	175	171

See footnotes at end of table.

U.S. Census Bureau, Statistical Abstract of the United States: 2011

[See headnote, page 280]

State	General expenditures—Con.								Utility and liquor store expenditures	Insurance trust expenditures	Total debt outstanding
	Direct general expenditures—Con.										
	Natural resources	Parks and recreation	Housing and community development	Sewerage	Solid waste	Governmental administration	Interest on general debt	Other direct general expenditures			
United States....	28,717	37,526	45,937	44,197	22,819	119,396	93,586	208,832	189,330	213,652	2,411,298
Alabama	282	422	452	305	252	1,339	952	1,752	2,776	2,435	24,586
Alaska	277	122	271	89	77	724	441	2,175	473	850	9,997
Arizona	626	1,030	472	1,204	361	2,404	1,354	3,115	4,890	2,985	39,330
Arkansas	230	205	171	295	181	885	451	962	852	1,218	12,208
California	6,104	5,516	8,686	6,144	3,531	20,991	12,841	34,813	35,357	36,753	330,359
Colorado	358	1,076	697	806	139	2,292	1,695	3,343	3,349	3,579	46,478
Connecticut	106	242	682	385	375	1,678	1,459	2,892	1,111	3,172	32,727
Delaware	130	95	118	190	127	656	316	678	480	471	7,372
District of Columbia	18	370	449	228	296	528	375	984	1,974	130	8,916
Florida	4,681	3,155	2,137	2,455	2,440	7,957	4,749	15,551	10,035	7,847	134,438
Georgia	481	981	1,062	1,467	744	3,133	1,297	3,933	5,511	4,390	48,470
Hawaii	152	253	216	263	218	661	607	1,760	401	878	10,304
Idaho	243	129	47	212	133	571	218	742	306	672	5,223
Illinois...........	569	2,813	1,904	1,459	522	4,471	5,207	9,851	6,215	11,570	116,526
Indiana..........	356	692	649	881	211	1,913	1,703	4,519	2,330	2,352	41,556
Iowa............	294	326	167	335	168	917	644	1,653	1,116	1,498	14,772
Kansas..........	266	234	202	301	130	917	821	1,787	1,177	1,244	19,957
Kentucky	375	285	285	463	221	1,241	1,321	1,709	1,748	2,859	37,713
Louisiana	641	621	3,295	500	293	1,788	1,417	3,204	1,632	3,020	27,879
Maine...........	178	79	251	158	117	509	337	1,134	131	672	7,986
Maryland	609	942	1,038	700	587	2,328	1,625	3,797	1,559	3,445	36,348
Massachusetts.....	310	407	1,708	1,081	404	2,548	3,962	6,440	4,408	5,729	89,414
Michigan	401	845	970	1,936	481	3,152	2,919	4,584	3,568	7,499	73,128
Minnesota	587	826	844	620	353	1,989	1,575	2,920	2,346	3,939	38,706
Mississippi........	300	153	217	226	185	807	459	3,236	1,068	1,539	12,556
Missouri..........	375	555	616	761	149	1,466	1,729	3,056	2,062	3,330	38,816
Montana..........	266	68	102	80	80	482	234	741	198	602	6,313
Nebraska.........	254	174	198	201	97	521	275	1,158	3,736	565	11,491
Nevada	229	686	226	267	21	1,343	715	1,243	1,566	1,220	22,083
New Hampshire....	71	92	175	112	114	463	462	792	482	465	10,253
New Jersey	435	1,076	1,074	1,171	1,175	3,402	3,320	8,813	3,011	9,105	85,692
New Mexico.......	290	304	146	192	145	932	496	1,252	657	1,250	12,195
New York	609	2,533	4,840	3,551	2,545	9,483	9,519	23,220	22,305	23,011	259,599
North Carolina	744	969	883	1,418	694	2,319	1,538	4,456	4,749	4,146	50,213
North Dakota	190	104	60	51	46	235	206	619	147	350	3,632
Ohio............	398	1,082	1,953	2,583	493	4,955	3,272	5,121	3,516	11,986	66,817
Oklahoma	211	331	263	383	204	1,195	646	1,362	1,440	1,878	16,565
Oregon..........	500	534	536	791	142	1,721	1,127	2,399	2,141	3,785	29,063
Pennsylvania	692	933	1,761	2,011	746	5,018	4,521	5,537	5,550	9,722	112,446
Rhode Island	45	67	179	113	108	591	453	800	281	1,176	10,460
South Carolina.....	280	371	360	434	328	1,789	1,186	1,631	3,196	2,314	35,870
South Dakota......	145	125	102	115	34	284	174	464	273	321	4,853
Tennessee........	310	517	666	629	329	1,718	1,000	2,527	10,993	2,112	33,961
Texas............	1,487	1,894	1,836	2,615	1,032	5,632	7,337	10,815	12,847	10,942	187,701
Utah.............	244	414	301	353	133	1,305	498	1,402	2,200	1,022	15,924
Vermont..........	73	37	122	75	39	242	191	303	286	247	4,105
Virginia..........	261	968	984	923	595	2,867	1,751	4,244	2,640	3,268	51,080
Washington	892	935	1,069	1,490	544	2,152	2,022	4,693	7,823	4,816	62,107
West Virginia	181	141	134	263	72	751	327	834	369	437	9,083
Wisconsin	732	654	339	835	356	1,738	1,748	3,147	1,787	4,416	41,792
Wyoming	229	142	25	78	53	390	91	666	261	415	2,239

[1] Includes items not shown separately.

Source: U.S. Census Bureau, *State and Local Government Finances, 2006–2007*, July 2010, <http://www.census.gov/govs/>.

Table 442. State Resources, Expenditures, and Balances: 2008 and 2009

[In millions of dollars (1,502,492 represents $1,502,492,000,000). For fiscal year ending in year shown; see text; this section. General funds exclude special funds earmarked for particular purposes, such as highway trust funds and federal funds; they support most on-going broad-based state services, and are available for appropriation to support any governmental activity. Minus sign (–) indicates deficit]

State	Expenditures by fund source			State general fund					
	Total, 2008 actual	2009 [1] estimated		Resources [3, 4]		Expenditures [4]		Balance [5, 6]	
		Total [2]	General fund	Federal fund	2008	2009 [1]	2008	2009 [1]	2008	2009 [1]
United States ...	1,502,492	1,592,818	664,421	478,369	734,875	674,794	687,269	663,890	34,550	8,165
Alabama	40,159	46,558	16,496	13,704	8,748	7,515	8,612	7,465	219	50
Alaska	12,322	14,315	5,899	3,434	9,723	6,659	5,463	5,152	–	–
Arizona	24,721	27,070	9,111	10,662	10,038	8,277	10,037	8,775	1	–499
Arkansas	16,899	18,403	4,400	5,516	4,353	4,435	4,353	4,435	–	–
California	194,276	208,864	91,547	76,629	105,361	87,733	102,986	91,547	2,376	–3,379
Colorado	25,129	26,928	7,730	6,247	7,767	7,605	7,440	7,456	327	148
Connecticut	24,536	25,010	16,779	1,982	16,419	15,880	16,319	16,828	99	–948
Delaware	8,621	8,741	3,296	1,256	3,948	3,674	3,422	3,296	526	379
Florida	64,379	65,517	24,803	18,853	28,029	24,274	27,708	23,973	321	301
Georgia	36,762	36,203	18,076	12,105	21,655	19,638	19,438	17,455	2,217	2,183
Hawaii	11,160	11,822	5,375	1,919	5,737	5,338	5,407	5,375	330	–37
Idaho	5,930	6,780	2,744	2,460	3,033	2,720	2,794	2,720	240	50
Illinois	46,877	48,379	19,830	14,417	30,301	29,285	27,153	29,961	141	279
Indiana	24,239	25,720	13,037	9,061	14,144	14,113	12,730	13,019	1,050	964
Iowa	16,129	17,716	5,961	4,970	6,084	5,934	5,888	5,934	48	–
Kansas	12,689	13,375	6,349	3,366	6,628	6,236	6,102	6,164	527	73
Kentucky	22,995	24,057	9,031	8,233	9,816	9,263	9,450	9,158	86	40
Louisiana	29,995	32,823	9,468	16,139	11,326	10,370	9,633	7,382	866	76
Maine	7,427	8,092	3,020	2,778	3,131	3,100	3,129	3,018	1	52
Maryland	29,798	31,586	14,315	7,791	14,926	14,396	14,439	14,309	487	87
Massachusetts	44,146	45,523	27,499	2,841	35,261	33,256	33,035	32,421	2,226	835
Michigan	43,982	48,347	9,383	19,464	10,343	8,731	9,885	8,520	458	210
Minnesota	28,446	31,632	17,572	8,910	18,925	17,456	17,005	16,918	1,920	538
Mississippi	15,599	19,380	4,842	9,165	5,181	4,967	5,145	5,178	36	7
Missouri	21,179	22,426	8,448	6,280	8,910	8,712	8,074	8,454	836	258
Montana	4,477	4,533	1,753	1,827	2,502	2,250	2,069	1,858	434	392
Nebraska	8,712	10,836	3,595	3,128	3,832	3,753	3,248	3,329	584	424
Nevada	9,240	8,300	4,203	2,203	3,752	3,783	3,436	3,570	316	213
New Hampshire	4,806	4,871	1,467	1,600	1,546	1,491	1,528	1,560	17	–
New Jersey	48,704	49,255	30,515	11,980	35,324	30,369	33,112	29,612	1,303	734
New Mexico	14,790	15,455	6,030	4,946	6,858	6,750	6,008	6,051	735	481
New York	116,056	121,571	54,607	38,425	56,139	56,555	53,385	54,607	2,754	1,948
North Carolina	41,587	40,277	19,653	11,855	21,190	19,745	20,521	19,653	599	92
North Dakota	3,597	4,050	1,254	1,405	1,657	1,807	1,204	1,237	453	362
Ohio	56,763	57,794	26,783	10,342	28,092	28,367	26,410	27,632	1,682	735
Oklahoma	19,962	20,415	5,868	9,930	6,737	6,567	6,447	6,534	290	33
Oregon	22,644	24,482	5,786	5,790	6,985	5,854	6,980	5,843	5	11
Pennsylvania	58,696	63,009	27,184	20,552	27,551	25,054	26,968	27,084	583	–2,030
Rhode Island	7,097	7,587	3,001	2,415	3,364	2,938	3,405	2,999	–41	–61
South Carolina	20,787	20,543	6,006	7,621	7,473	5,869	7,149	5,748	324	121
South Dakota	3,150	3,496	1,137	1,396	1,177	1,154	1,176	1,153	–	–
Tennessee	26,324	28,518	11,886	10,953	11,972	10,893	10,973	10,802	348	–
Texas	82,156	89,907	42,629	29,051	48,922	45,823	39,647	42,629	7,034	2,134
Utah	12,420	11,601	4,816	3,205	5,943	5,016	5,784	4,817	–	–
Vermont	5,308	5,341	1,168	1,694	1,230	1,168	1,200	1,146	–	–
Virginia	35,330	36,963	15,020	6,772	17,576	16,082	17,263	15,943	313	139
Washington	31,732	32,817	14,617	7,623	15,405	14,811	14,616	14,617	790	194
West Virginia	18,710	20,362	3,928	3,878	4,361	4,479	3,757	3,980	550	481
Wisconsin	36,091	38,445	12,744	9,711	13,678	12,817	13,526	12,744	131	90
Wyoming	4,958	7,123	3,760	1,885	1,823	1,835	1,813	1,830	10	5

– Represents zero. [1] Estimated. [2] Includes bonds and other state funds, not shown separately. [3] Includes funds budgeted, adjustments, and balances from previous year. [4] May or may not include budget stabilization fund transfers, depending on state accounting practices. [5] Resources less expenditures. [6] Ending balance is held in a budget stabilization fund.

Source: National Association of State Budget Officers, Washington, DC, *2008 State Expenditure Report*, and *State General Fund from NASBO, Fiscal Survey of the States, semiannual* (copyright), <http://www.nasbo.org/publications.php>.

Table 443. Bond Ratings for State Governments by State: 2009

[As of fourth quarter. Key to investment grade ratings are in declining order of quality. The ratings from AA to CCC may be modified by the addition of a (+) or (–) sign to show relative standing within the major rating categories. *S&P*: AAA, AA, A, BBB, BB, B, CCC, CC, C; *Moody's*: Aaa, Aa, A, Baa, Ba, B, Caa, Ca, C; Numerical modifiers 1, 2, and 3 are added to letter-rating. *Fitch*: AAA, AA, A, BBB, BB, B, CCC, CC, C]

State	Standard & Poor's	Moody's	Fitch	State	Standard & Poor's	Moody's	Fitch
Alabama	AA	Aa2	AA	Montana	AA	Aa2	AA
Alaska	AA+	A1	AA	Nebraska	¹ AA+ (ICR)	(²)	(NA)
Arizona	¹ AA–(ICR)	A1	(NA)	Nevada	AA+	Aa2	AA
Arkansas	AA	Aa2	(NA)	New Hampshire	AA	Aa2	AA
California	A–	Baa1	BBB	New Jersey	AA	Aa3	AA–
Colorado	¹ AA (ICR)	Aa2	(NA)	New Mexico	AA+	Aa1	(NA)
Connecticut	AA	Aa3	AA	New York	AA	Aa3	AA–
Delaware	AAA	Aaa	AAA	North Carolina	AAA	Aaa	AAA
Florida	AAA	Aa1	AA+	North Dakota	¹ AA+ (ICR)	Aa2	(NA)
Georgia	AAA	Aaa	AAA	Ohio	AA+	Aa2	AA
Hawaii	AA	Aa2	AA	Oklahoma	AA+	Aa3	AA
Idaho	¹ AA(ICR)	Aa2	(NA)	Oregon	AA	Aa2	AA
Illinois	A+	A2	A	Pennsylvania	AA	Aa2	AA
Indiana	¹ AAA(ICR)	Aa1	(NA)	Rhode Island	AA	Aa3	AA–
Iowa	¹ AAA(ICR)	Aa1	AA+	South Carolina	AA+	Aaa	AAA
Kansas	1 AA+	Aa1	(NA)	South Dakota	¹ AA (ICR)	(²)	(NA)
Kentucky	¹ AA–(ICR)	Aa2	(NA)	Tennessee	AA+	Aa1	AA+
Louisiana	AA–	A1	AA–	Texas	AA+	Aa1	AA+
Maine	AA	Aa3	AA	Utah	AAA	Aaa	AAA
Maryland	AAA	Aaa	AAA	Vermont	AA+	Aaa	AA+
Massachusetts	AA	Aa2	AA	Virginia	AAA	Aaa	AAA
Michigan	AA–	Aa3	A+	Washington	AA+	Aa1	AA
Minnesota	AAA	Aa1	AAA	West Virginia	AA	Aa3	AA–
Mississippi	AA	Aa3	AA	Wisconsin	AA	Aa3	AA–
Missouri	AAA	Aaa	AAA	Wyoming	¹ AA+ (ICR)	(²)	(NA)

NA Not available. ¹ Standard and Poor's Issue Credit Rating (ICR) is a current opinion of an obliger with respect to a specific financial obligation, a specific class of financial obligations, or a specific financial program. ² Not rated.

Source: Standard & Poor's, New York, NY (copyright), <http://www2.standardandpoors.com/portal/site/sp/en/us/page.home/home/0,0,0,0,0,0,0,0,0,0,0,0,0,0,0,0.html>; Moody's Investors Service, New York, NY (copyright), <http://www.moodys.com/cust/default_alt.asp>; Fitch Ratings, New York, NY (copyright), <http://www.fitchratings.com>.

Table 444. Bond Ratings for City Governments by Largest Cities: 2009

[As of fourth quarter. See headnote in Table 443]

Cities ranked by 2000 population	Standard & Poor's	Moody's	Fitch	Cities ranked by 2000 population	Standard & Poor's	Moody's	Fitch
New York, NY	AA	Aa3	AA–	Oakland, CA	AA–	A1	A+
Los Angeles, CA	AA–	Aa2	AA–	Mesa, AZ	AA	A1	(NA)
Chicago, IL	AA–	Aa3	AA	Tulsa, OK	AA	Aa2	(NA)
Houston, TX	AA	Aa3	AA–	Omaha, NE	AAA	Aa1	(NA)
Philadelphia, PA	BBB	Baa1	BBB	Minneapolis, MN	AAA	Aa1	AAA
Phoenix, AZ	AAA	Aa1	(NA)	Honolulu, HI	AA	Aa2	AA
San Diego, CA	A	A2	A+	Miami, FL	A+	A2	A
Dallas, TX	AA+	Aa1	(NA)	Colorado Springs, CO	AA– (Lease)	Aa3	(NA)
San Antonio, TX	AAA	Aa1	AA+	St. Louis, MO	A+	A2	A
Detroit, MI	BB	Ba3	BB	Wichita, KS	AA+	Aa2	(NA)
San Jose, CA	AAA	Aa1	AA+	Santa Ana, CA	(¹)	(²)	(NA)
Indianapolis, IN	AAA	Aa1	(NA)	Pittsburgh, PA	BBB	Baa1	BBB+
San Francisco, CA	AA–	Aa2	AA–	Arlington, TX	AA+	Aa2	(NA)
Jacksonville, FL	AA–	Aa2	AA	Cincinnati, OH	AA+	Aa1	(NA)
Columbus, OH	AAA	Aaa	AAA	Anaheim, CA	AA	Aa2	(NA)
Austin, TX	AAA	Aa1	(NA)	Toledo, OH	A	Baa1	(NA)
Baltimore, MD	AAA	Aa3	(NA)	Tampa, FL	(¹)	Aa2	(NA)
Memphis, TN	AA	A1	A+	Buffalo, NY	A–	Baa2	(NA)
Milwaukee, WI	AA	Aa2	AA+	St. Paul, MN	AAA	Aa2	(NA)
Boston, MA	AA+	Aa1	AA	Corpus Christi, TX	AA–	A1	AA–
Washington, DC	A+	A1	A+	Aurora, CO	AA	Aa2	(NA)
El Paso, TX	AA	Aa3	AA–	Raleigh, NC	AAA	Aaa	AAA
Seattle, WA	AAA	Aaa	AAA	Newark, NJ	AA	Baa2	(NA)
Denver, CO	AAA	Aa1	AA+	Lexington–Fayette, KY	(¹)	Aa2	(NA)
Nashville-Davidson, TN	AA	Aa2	AA	Anchorage, AK	AA	Aa3	AA
Charlotte, NC	AAA	Aaa	AAA	Louisville, KY	(¹)	Aa2	(NA)
Fort Worth, TX	AA+	Aa2	AA	Riverside, CA	AA–	(²)	AA
Portland, OR	NR	Aaa	(NA)	St Petersburg, FL	(¹)	A1	(NA)
Oklahoma City, OK	AA+	Aa1	(NA)	Bakersfield, CA	(¹)	(²)	(NA)
Tucson, AZ	AA–	Aa3	AA	Stockton CA	³ A+(ICR)	A2	(NA)
New Orleans, LA	BBB	Baa3	BBB	Birmingham, AL	AA	Aa3	AA–
Las Vegas, NV	AA	Aa2	AA	Jersey City, NJ	(¹)	Baa2	BBB
Cleveland, OH	A (Lease)	A2	A+	Norfolk, VA	AA	A1	AA
Long Beach, CA	AA–	Aa3	(NA)	Baton Rouge, LA	(¹)	Aa3	(NA)
Albuquerque, NM	AAA	Aa2	AA	Hialeah, FL	(¹)	(²)	(NA)
Kansas City, MO	AA	Aa3	AA+	Lincoln, NE	AAA	Aaa	(NA)
Fresno, CA	AA	A1	AA–	Greensboro, NC	AAA	Aaa	AAA
Virginia Beach, VA	AAA	Aa1	AA+	Plano, TX	AAA	Aaa	AAA
Atlanta, GA	A	A1	(NA)	Rochester, NY	A	A2	(NA)
Sacramento, CA	A+	Aa3	(NA)				

NA Not available. ¹ Not reviewed. ² Issuer Rating/No General Obligation. ³ Standard and Poor's Issue Credit Rating (ICR) is a current opinion of an obliger with respect to a specific financial obligation, a specific class of financial obligations, or a specific financial program.

Source: Standard & Poor's, New York, NY (copyright),<http://www2.standardandpoors.com/portal/site/sp/en/us/page.home/home/0,0,0,0,0,0,0,0,0,0,0,0,0,0,0,0.html>; Moody's Investors Service, New York, NY (copyright); <http://www.moodys.com/cust/default_alt.asp>; Fitch Ratings, New York, NY (copyright), <http://www.fitchratings.com>.

Table 445. Estimated State and Local Taxes Paid by a Family of Three for Largest City in Selected States: 2008

[Data based on average family of three (two wage earners and one school age child) owning their own home and living in a city where taxes apply. Comprises state and local sales, income, auto, and real estate taxes. For definition of median, see Guide to Tabular Presentation]

City	Total taxes paid by gross family income level (dollars)					Total taxes paid as percent of income				
	$25,000	$50,000	$75,000	$100,000	$150,000	$25,000	$50,000	$75,000	$100,000	$150,000
Albuquerque, NM.......	2,478	3,849	5,787	7,895	11,184	9.9	7.7	7.7	7.9	7.5
Atlanta, GA	3,241	4,423	6,929	9,666	14,139	13.0	8.8	9.2	9.7	9.4
Baltimore, MD	2,183	4,749	7,293	10,087	14,836	8.7	9.5	9.7	10.1	9.9
Boston, MA	3,113	4,897	6,757	8,787	12,020	12.5	9.8	9.0	8.8	8.0
Charlotte, NC..........	3,170	4,245	6,799	9,604	13,994	12.7	8.5	9.1	9.6	9.3
Chicago, IL...........	3,274	6,226	8,093	10,037	12,855	13.1	12.5	10.8	10.0	8.6
Columbus, OH........	3,017	5,183	7,516	10,196	14,921	12.1	10.4	10.0	10.2	9.9
Denver, CO	2,828	3,277	5,055	7,324	10,337	11.3	6.6	6.7	7.3	6.9
Detroit, MI	2,871	5,769	8,385	11,069	15,430	11.5	11.5	11.2	11.1	10.3
Honolulu, HI..........	3,213	2,545	4,441	6,701	10,931	12.9	5.1	5.9	6.7	7.3
Houston, TX..........	2,479	3,047	4,228	5,357	6,532	9.9	6.1	5.6	5.4	4.4
Indianapolis, IN	3,184	5,044	7,189	9,611	13,563	12.7	10.1	9.6	9.6	9.0
Jacksonville, FL	2,594	2,323	3,006	4,000	5,183	10.4	4.6	4.1	4.0	3.5
Kansas City, MO	3,021	4,181	6,477	8,908	13,089	12.1	8.4	8.6	8.9	8.7
Las Vegas, NV........	2,455	3,243	4,046	4,988	5,949	9.8	6.5	5.4	5.0	4.0
Los Angeles, CA	2,665	4,993	6,417	8,508	13,317	10.7	10.0	8.6	8.5	8.9
Memphis, TN	2,738	3,005	4,155	5,194	6,473	11.0	6.0	5.5	5.2	4.3
Milwaukee, WI	2,316	5,058	7,224	9,898	14,141	9.3	10.1	9.6	9.9	9.4
New Orleans, LA.......	2,713	3,198	5,207	7,469	10,533	10.9	6.4	6.9	7.5	7.0
New York City, NY	2,890	4,542	7,337	10,689	17,520	11.6	9.1	9.8	10.7	11.7
Oklahoma City, OK	2,719	3,627	5,901	8,180	11,788	10.9	7.3	7.9	8.2	7.9
Omaha, NE	2,406	4,227	6,412	9,348	13,804	9.6	8.5	8.5	9.3	9.2
Philadelphia, PA........	4,103	6,864	9,293	11,839	16,175	16.4	13.7	12.4	11.8	10.8
Phoenix, AZ...........	2,911	2,962	4,327	6,290	8,786	11.6	5.9	5.8	6.3	5.9
Portland, OR	2,695	4,264	6,847	9,935	15,080	10.8	8.5	9.1	9.9	10.1
Seattle, WA	2,831	3,790	4,865	5,636	6,274	11.3	7.6	6.5	5.6	4.2
Virginia Beach, VA......	2,600	3,682	5,734	7,936	11,420	10.4	7.4	7.6	7.9	7.6
Washington, DC........	2,564	3,311	5,620	7,938	12,430	10.3	6.6	7.5	7.9	8.3
Wichita, KS	2,503	3,522	5,995	8,862	12,903	10.0	7.0	8.0	8.6	8.6
Average [1]...........	$2,720	4,084	6,024	8,179	11,749	10.9	8.2	8.0	8.2	7.8
Median [1]...........	$2,703	3,849	5,995	8,207	12,596	10.8	7.7	8.0	8.2	8.4

[1] Based on selected cities and District of Columbia. For complete list of cities, see Table 446.

Source: Government of the District of Columbia, Office of the Chief Financial Officer, "Tax Rates and Revenues, Tax Burden Comparisons, Nationwide Comparison," annual. See also <http://www.cfo.dc.gov/cfo>.

Table 446. Residential Property Tax Rates for Largest City in Each State: 2008

[The real property tax is a function of housing values, real estate tax rates, assessment levels, homeowner exemptions and credits. Effective rate is the amount each jurisdiction considers based upon assessment level used. Assessment level is ratio of assessed value to assumed market value. Nominal rates represent the "announced" rates levied by the jurisdiction]

City	Effective tax rate per $100		Assessment level (percent)	Nominal rate per $100	City	Effective tax rate per $100		Assessment level (percent)	Nominal rate per $100
	Rank	Rate				Rank	Rate		
Indianapolis, IN	1	2.93	100.0	2.93	Sioux Falls, SD	28	1.49	85.0	1.27
Bridgeport, CT........	2	3.87	70.0	2.71	Louisville, KY.........	29	1.24	100.0	1.24
Philadelphia, PA.......	3	8.26	32.0	2.64	Oklahoma City, OK	30	10.98	11.0	1.21
Houston, TX..........	4	2.52	100.0	2.52	Kansas City, MO	31	6.32	19.0	1.20
Milwaukee, WI........	5	2.42	100.0	2.42	Salt Lake City, UT	32	1.19	100.0	1.19
Providence, RI........	6	2.37	100.0	2.37	Las Vegas, NV........	33	3.27	35.0	1.14
Baltimore MD.........	7	2.27	100.0	2.27	Minneapolis, MN	34	1.2	92.5	1.11
Detroit, MI	8	6.58	32.1	2.11	Los Angeles, CA	35	1.1	100.0	1.10
Des Moines, IA	9	4.5	45.0	2.03	Charlotte, NC.........	36	1.3	82.9	1.08
Fargo, ND	10	45.54	4.4	2.00	Columbia, SC	37	26.26	4.0	1.05
Columbus, OH........	11	5.94	33.4	1.98	Boston, MA	38	1.02	100.0	1.02
Omaha, NE	12	2.05	96.0	1.97	Portland, OR	39	1.95	52.1	1.02
Burlington, VT	13	1.78	100.0	1.78	New York City, NY	40	15.43	6.0	0.93
Memphis, TN	14	7.47	23.3	1.74	Virginia Beach, VA.....	41	0.89	100.0	0.89
Jackson, MS	15	17.16	10.0	1.72	Phoenix, AZ..........	42	8.75	10.0	0.88
Anchorage, AK	16	1.72	100.0	1.72	Charleston, WV	43	1.44	60.0	0.87
Manchester, NH.......	17	1.69	98.6	1.66	Washington, DC.......	44	0.85	100.0	0.85
Atlanta, GA	18	4.1	40.0	1.64	Seattle, WA	45	0.94	83.4	0.79
Portland, ME	19	1.77	91.0	1.61	Birmingham, AL.......	46	7.53	10.0	0.75
Jacksonville, FL.......	20	1.6	100.0	1.6	Cheyenne, WY........	47	7.1	9.5	0.67
Wilmington, DE	21	3.38	47.2	1.59	Chicago, IL...........	48	6.72	10.0	0.67
Newark, NJ	22	2.6	60.0	1.56	Billings, MT	49	1.86	34.0	0.63
Wichita, KS	23	12.32	11.5	1.42	Denver, CO	50	7.06	8.0	0.56
Little Rock, AR........	24	7.05	20.0	1.41	Honolulu, HI..........	51	0.33	100.0	0.33
Albuquerque, NM......	25	4.52	30.0	1.36					
Boise, ID	26	1.32	100.5	1.32	Unweighted average ...	(X)	5.63	58.2	1.45
New Orleans, LA......	27	12.93	10.0	1.29	Median..............	(X)	2.6	(X)	(X)

X Not applicable.

Source: Government of the District of Columbia, Office of the Chief Financial Officer, "Tax Rates and Revenues, Tax Burden Comparisons, Nationwide Comparison" annual. See also <http://www.cfo.dco.gov/cfo>.

U.S. Census Bureau, Statistical Abstract of the United States: 2011

Table 447. Gross Revenue From Parimutuel and Amusement Taxes and Lotteries by State: 2005 to 2007

[In millions of dollars (72,695.9 represents $72,695,900,000). For fiscal years; see text, this section]

State	2005, total gross revenue	2006, total gross revenue	2007 Total gross revenue	2007 Amusement taxes [1]	2007 Parimutuel taxes	Lottery revenue Total [2]	Apportionment of funds Prizes	Apportionment of funds Administration	Apportionment of funds Proceeds available from ticket sales
United States	72,695.9	78,521.2	82,218.1	6,055.2	232.1	75,930.8	55,959.9	2,297.5	17,673.4
Alabama	3.2	3.3	3.1	0.1	3.0	–	–	–	–
Alaska	2.5	2.4	2.4	2.4	(X)	–	–	–	–
Arizona	372.1	438.7	432.1	0.6	–	431.1	257.5	34.2	139.4
Arkansas	4.8	5.5	8.1	2.7	5.4	–	–	–	–
California	3,139.6	3,371.3	3,123.3	(X)	37.5	3,085.8	1,765.6	157.4	1,162.7
Colorado	513.9	533.1	568.9	112.5	3.0	453.4	298.1	32.1	123.2
Connecticut	1,307.4	1,383.2	1,377.8	465.7	8.7	903.4	579.9	37.8	285.8
Delaware	6,842.4	7,144.4	7,904.3	(X)	–	7,904.1	7,544.1	48.5	311.6
Florida	3,307.1	3,739.9	3,923.4	(X)	28.1	3,895.3	2,484.5	150.6	1,260.2
Georgia	2,546.6	2,751.9	2,957.8	(X)	(X)	2,957.8	1,978.4	127.7	851.7
Hawaii	(X)	(X)	(X)	(X)	(X)	–	–	–	–
Idaho	105.3	122.5	121.9	(X)	1.9	120.0	78.9	9.1	32.0
Illinois...........	2,521.8	2,656.7	2,839.6	832.1	8.5	1,999.0	1,159.6	63.8	775.6
Indiana..........	1,486.5	1,569.9	1,557.2	830.3	4.6	722.3	477.8	33.0	211.5
Iowa............	419.4	486.6	499.2	276.1	2.7	220.4	133.4	29.0	58.0
Kansas..........	198.4	216.0	229.3	0.5	2.8	226.0	134.2	22.6	69.2
Kentucky	676.7	710.5	702.5	–	5.8	696.5	456.4	41.8	198.3
Louisiana	848.0	970.5	1,065.3	726.1	4.6	334.5	179.4	28.8	126.3
Maine...........	199.1	227.9	235.6	19.9	3.5	212.2	145.5	16.3	50.4
Maryland	1,401.1	1,470.9	1,474.7	7.5	2.0	1,465.1	927.0	54.2	483.9
Massachusetts.....	4,222.7	4,208.9	4,196.0	3.8	3.9	4,188.4	3,225.0	92.0	871.4
Michigan	2,035.1	2,191.4	2,511.1	159.4	9.2	2,342.6	1,355.3	64.3	923.0
Minnesota	420.8	453.1	429.6	49.1	1.5	378.9	263.7	22.5	92.7
Mississippi........	223.1	145.7	185.8	185.8	(X)	–	–	–	–
Missouri..........	1,064.5	1,201.2	1,217.0	339.6	(X)	877.4	584.0	33.5	259.9
Montana.........	85.1	94.9	94.4	60.2	0.1	34.1	21.4	6.5	6.2
Nebraska........	100.1	112.1	113.1	5.5	0.2	107.3	65.4	13.3	28.6
Nevada	934.6	1,045.8	1,089.1	1,089.1	(X)	–	–	–	–
New Hampshire.....	220.6	252.1	253.0	–	3.1	249.6	155.9	15.9	77.8
New Jersey	2,623.2	2,774.6	2,669.8	450.1	(X)	2,219.7	1,319.0	81.2	819.5
New Mexico.......	177.5	201.7	214.9	70.9	1.4	142.6	89.5	18.7	34.5
New York	5,873.5	6,321.7	6,608.5	0.7	28.1	6,579.8	3,970.7	282.5	2,326.5
North Carolina.....	11.2	225.2	839.5	15.9	(X)	823.6	475.7	45.8	302.1
North Dakota......	28.2	31.1	30.8	8.9	0.3	21.6	11.3	3.6	6.7
Ohio............	2,039.9	2,091.7	2,131.6	(X)	12.1	2,119.4	1,338.4	109.0	672.1
Oklahoma	6.2	195.3	214.6	11.1	1.8	201.6	116.0	15.5	70.2
Oregon..........	1,735.3	2,216.4	2,665.4	–	2.6	2,662.8	1,933.0	72.6	657.2
Pennsylvania	2,453.4	2,838.2	3,103.4	255.1	24.7	2,823.6	1,832.6	74.5	916.5
Rhode Island.....	1,460.8	1,542.7	1,619.7	(X)	2.9	1,616.8	1,288.2	9.4	319.2
South Carolina.....	925.6	1,100.2	956.2	38.1	(X)	918.1	600.1	43.0	275.0
South Dakota......	564.1	580.6	587.0	7.8	0.3	578.9	452.2	6.7	120.0
Tennessee........	789.4	930.9	989.2	(X)	(X)	989.2	658.4	52.2	278.6
Texas...........	3,511.1	3,619.8	3,618.3	26.4	10.9	3,581.0	2,315.3	172.4	1,093.3
Utah............	(X)	(X)	(X)	(X)	(X)	–	–	–	–
Vermont..........	87.2	98.7	98.4	(X)	(X)	98.4	66.2	8.9	23.3
Virginia..........	1,258.4	1,289.2	1,286.0	–	(X)	1,285.9	791.8	66.1	428.0
Washington	431.3	449.5	463.5	–	2.0	461.4	304.8	41.3	115.2
West Virginia	13,094.2	14,027.7	14,545.6	(X)	3.1	14,542.5	13,833.7	30.3	678.4
Wisconsin	422.4	475.4	460.0	–	1.0	458.7	292.1	28.9	137.6
Wyoming	0.4	0.2	–	(X)	–	–	–	–	–

– Represents or rounds to zero. X Not applicable. [1] Represents nonlicense taxes. [2] Excludes commissions.
Source: U.S. Census Bureau, *State Government Finances, Lottery*, and unpublished data, <http://www.census.gov/govs>.

Table 448. Lottery Sales—Type of Game and Use of Proceeds: 1990 to 2009

[In millions of dollars (20,017 represents $20,017,000,000). For fiscal years]

Game	1990	1995	2000	2005	2006	2007	2008	2009
Total ticket sales	20,017	31,931	37,201	47,364	51,595	52,414	53,360	53,062
Instant [1]	5,204	11,511	15,459	25,946	28,342	29,736	30,471	30,324
Three-digit [2].....................	4,572	5,737	5,341	5,428	5,456	5,586	5,544	5,518
Four-digit [2]......................	1,302	1,941	2,711	3,300	3,400	3,499	3,605	3,781
Lotto [3]	8,563	10,594	9,160	9,707	11,015	10,014	10,292	9,989
Other [4]	376	2,148	4,530	2,983	3,382	3,579	3,448	3,451
State proceeds (net income) [5]	7,703	11,100	11,404	15,779	17,220	17,627	17,877	17,601

[1] Player scratches a latex section on ticket which reveals instantly whether ticket is a winner. [2] Players choose and bet on three or four digits, depending on game, with various payoffs for different straight order or mixed combination bets. [3] Players typically select six digits out of a large field of numbers. Varying prizes are offered for matching three through six numbers drawn by lottery. [4] Includes break-open tickets, spiel, keno, video lottery, etc. [5] Sales minus prizes and expenses equal net government income.

Source: TLF Publications, Inc., Boyds, MD, *2009 World Lottery Almanac* (copyright). See <http://www.lafleurs.com>.

Table 449. State Governments—Summary of Finances: 1990 to 2007

[In millions of dollars (673,119 represents $673,119,000,000). For fiscal year ending in year shown; see text, this section]

Item	1990	2000	2002	2003	2004	2005	2006	2007
Borrowing and revenue	**673,119**	**1,336,798**	**1,205,999**	**1,430,303**	**1,727,347**	**1,757,221**	**1,906,455**	**2,138,574**
Borrowing	40,948	75,968	108,170	134,644	140,682	115,264	133,247	138,208
Total revenue	632,172	1,260,829	1,097,829	1,295,659	1,586,665	1,641,957	1,773,208	2,000,366
General revenue	517,429	984,783	1,062,305	1,112,349	1,194,056	1,286,714	1,385,376	1,457,803
Taxes	300,489	539,655	535,241	548,991	590,414	650,612	710,864	757,471
Sales and gross receipts	147,069	252,147	262,361	273,811	293,326	312,584	332,972	352,706
General	99,702	174,461	179,665	184,597	197,949	212,921	226,712	238,304
Motor fuels	19,379	29,968	31,968	32,269	33,762	34,567	35,702	36,543
Alcoholic beverages	3,191	4,104	4,249	4,399	4,593	4,706	4,925	5,166
Tobacco products	5,541	8,391	8,902	11,482	12,303	12,917	14,499	15,299
Other	19,256	35,222	37,576	41,065	44,718	47,474	51,134	57,393
Licenses	18,842	32,598	35,391	35,863	39,679	42,584	45,241	46,697
Motor vehicles	9,848	15,099	15,641	16,009	17,336	18,221	19,015	19,470
Corporations in general	3,099	6,460	5,842	6,129	6,339	7,148	7,579	8,570
Other	5,895	11,039	13,908	13,725	16,004	17,216	18,648	18,657
Individual income	96,076	194,573	185,697	181,933	196,255	221,597	245,883	265,863
Corporation net income	21,751	32,522	25,123	28,384	30,229	38,691	47,466	52,915
Property	5,848	10,996	9,702	10,471	10,714	11,342	11,794	12,621
Other	10,902	16,819	16,967	18,529	20,211	23,813	27,509	26,668
Charges and miscellaneous	90,612	170,747	191,641	201,741	209,029	220,242	255,369	270,054
Intergovernmental revenue	126,329	274,382	335,423	361,617	394,613	407,860	419,143	430,278
From federal government	118,353	259,114	317,581	343,308	374,694	386,283	397,597	410,184
Public welfare	59,397	147,150	181,517	196,954	214,528	222,909	222,916	233,479
Education	21,271	42,086	51,103	56,362	64,913	68,275	73,493	73,411
Highways	13,931	23,790	29,641	29,481	29,606	32,677	33,536	35,173
Health and hospitals	5,475	14,223	17,875	19,559	20,377	20,443	21,144	21,592
Other	18,279	31,865	37,445	40,951	45,270	41,980	46,508	46,530
From local governments	7,976	15,268	17,842	18,309	19,919	21,576	21,546	20,094
Utility revenue	3,305	4,513	11,935	12,518	12,955	14,627	15,816	16,736
Liquor store revenue	2,907	3,895	4,288	4,518	4,866	5,118	5,430	5,799
Insurance trust revenue [1]	108,530	267,639	19,301	166,274	374,788	335,498	366,586	520,029
Employee retirement	78,898	230,166	-25,244	110,839	308,896	269,617	300,350	456,789
Unemployment compensation	18,370	23,260	26,960	35,191	38,230	35,243	36,864	34,063
Expenditure and debt redemption	**592,213**	**1,125,828**	**1,334,969**	**1,426,715**	**1,497,114**	**1,555,611**	**1,627,579**	**1,710,221**
Total expenditure	572,318	1,084,097	1,280,290	1,359,048	1,406,175	1,471,936	1,551,555	1,635,747
General expenditure	508,284	964,723	1,109,227	1,163,968	1,209,436	1,277,979	1,347,130	1,424,195
Education	184,935	346,465	389,390	411,094	429,341	454,364	481,877	514,147
Public welfare	104,971	238,890	287,016	314,407	339,409	370,219	378,605	393,690
Health	20,029	42,066	50,293	50,221	49,559	48,957	51,121	57,388
Hospitals	22,637	32,578	37,393	38,395	40,426	43,103	44,800	48,916
Highways	44,249	74,415	84,198	85,726	86,166	91,063	99,519	103,201
Police protection	5,166	9,788	10,706	11,144	10,766	11,426	12,233	12,876
Corrections	17,266	35,129	38,918	39,188	39,314	40,592	42,720	46,498
Natural resources	9,909	15,967	17,821	18,577	18,652	18,850	20,034	22,038
Housing and community development	2,856	4,726	5,989	8,112	7,191	7,708	7,918	12,475
Other and unallocable	96,267	164,698	187,504	187,106	188,613	191,697	208,302	212,964
Utility expenditure	7,131	10,723	20,279	22,405	21,676	21,824	24,904	24,530
Liquor store expenditure	2,452	3,195	3,498	3,697	3,924	4,082	4,338	4,664
Insurance trust expenditure [1]	54,452	105,456	147,286	168,979	171,139	168,052	175,183	182,358
Employee retirement	29,562	75,971	91,971	103,049	111,376	118,333	127,493	135,760
Unemployment compensation	16,423	18,583	42,017	51,411	43,174	29,776	28,009	28,854
By character and object:								
Intergovernmental expenditure	175,028	327,070	364,789	382,197	389,706	403,488	428,925	459,605
Direct expenditure	397,291	757,027	915,501	976,852	1,016,469	1,068,449	1,122,631	1,176,142
Current operation	258,046	523,114	620,763	656,989	691,652	739,988	774,651	809,535
Capital outlay	45,524	76,233	89,919	91,943	90,950	94,181	101,432	110,044
Construction	34,803	59,681	71,035	72,374	73,372	77,039	83,858	90,788
Land and existing structure	3,471	4,681	5,305	6,945	6,576	6,259	6,135	19,256
Equipment	7,250	11,871	13,579	12,623	11,002	10,883	11,440	(NA)
Assistance and subsidies	16,902	22,136	24,313	25,901	28,104	30,181	31,644	30,621
Interest on debt	22,367	30,089	33,220	33,040	34,624	36,047	39,720	43,584
Insurance benefits [2]	54,452	105,456	147,286	168,979	171,139	168,052	175,183	182,358
Debt redemption	19,895	41,730	54,678	67,666	90,939	83,675	76,024	74,474
Debt outstanding, year-end	**318,254**	**547,876**	**642,202**	**697,929**	**754,150**	**813,846**	**870,939**	**936,524**
Long-term [3]	315,490	541,497	623,558	681,796	740,414	808,293	860,310	929,947
Full-faith and credit	74,972	138,525	159,502	179,372	209,385	(NA)	(NA)	(NA)
Nonguaranteed	240,518	402,972	464,056	502,424	531,030	(NA)	(NA)	(NA)
Short-term	2,764	6,379	18,644	16,133	13,736	5,553	10,629	6,577
Net long-term [4]	125,524	266,870	317,829	366,207	412,194	444,685	473,447	499,709
Full-faith and credit only	63,481	128,384	149,580	170,137	200,295	(NA)	(NA)	(NA)

NA Not available. [1] Includes other items not shown separately. [2] Includes repayments. [3] As of fiscal year 2005, the Census Bureau no longer collects government debt information by the character of long-term debt. For further information, see the 2006 Government Finance and Employment Classification Manual at <http://www.census.gov/govs/www/classification/>. [4] Less cash and investment assets specifically held for redemption of long-term debt.

Source: U.S. Census Bureau, 2007 Survey of State Government Finances, <http://www.census.gov/govs>.

Table 450. State Governments—Revenue by State: 2007

[In millions of dollars (2,000,366 represents $2,300,366,000,000), except as noted. For fiscal year ending in year shown. See text, this section. Includes local shares of state imposed taxes]

State	Total revenue [1,2]	General revenue Total	Intergovernmental revenue Total [1]	Intergovernmental revenue From federal govern- ment	General revenue from own sources Total	General revenue from own sources Total taxes	General revenue from own sources Current charges	General revenue from own sources Miscel- laneous general revenue	Utilities and liquor store revenue	Insur- ance trust revenue
United States . . .	**2,000,366**	**1,457,803**	**430,278**	**410,184**	**1,027,524**	**757,471**	**141,573**	**128,481**	**22,535**	**520,029**
Alabama	27,752	21,503	7,732	6,952	13,771	8,868	3,192	1,711	236	6,013
Alaska	12,724	10,582	2,289	2,283	8,293	3,688	540	4,065	17	2,124
Arizona	31,886	26,192	8,124	7,770	18,068	14,405	1,599	2,064	28	5,666
Arkansas	18,176	14,161	4,286	4,266	9,875	7,392	1,752	731	–	4,015
California	299,448	189,043	49,890	47,251	139,153	114,737	13,878	10,538	5,920	104,484
Colorado	26,892	18,492	4,733	4,655	13,759	9,217	2,638	1,904	–	8,400
Connecticut	25,841	20,731	4,167	4,154	16,564	13,272	1,614	1,678	27	5,082
Delaware	7,433	6,313	1,242	1,196	5,071	2,906	935	1,231	12	1,108
Florida	98,081	69,044	19,190	18,925	49,855	38,819	5,626	5,410	23	29,015
Georgia	45,157	36,404	13,005	12,766	23,399	18,253	2,991	2,155	0	8,753
Hawaii	11,173	9,070	2,064	2,060	7,006	5,090	1,158	757	–	2,103
Idaho	9,100	6,413	1,843	1,828	4,571	3,537	562	472	106	2,580
Illinois.	71,207	52,330	14,234	13,726	38,095	30,066	3,895	4,135	–	18,878
Indiana.	32,657	27,565	7,979	7,804	19,586	14,199	3,136	2,251	–	5,092
Iowa	19,053	14,120	4,379	4,152	9,741	6,470	2,064	1,207	180	4,753
Kansas.	15,605	12,610	3,156	3,117	9,454	6,893	1,797	764	–	2,995
Kentucky	25,425	20,058	6,338	6,306	13,720	9,895	2,513	1,311	–	5,367
Louisiana	33,373	27,498	12,395	12,328	15,103	10,973	1,841	2,290	5	5,870
Maine.	9,549	7,543	2,394	2,383	5,149	3,696	661	791	0	2,006
Maryland	35,167	27,554	7,199	6,926	20,355	15,094	2,838	2,423	116	7,496
Massachusetts.	49,684	38,967	9,606	9,228	29,361	20,695	3,537	5,129	172	10,545
Michigan	61,887	47,601	13,083	12,807	34,518	23,849	6,136	4,533	743	13,543
Minnesota	38,733	28,464	6,681	6,571	21,784	17,768	2,228	1,787	–	10,269
Mississippi.	22,490	17,488	9,111	8,969	8,377	6,482	1,246	649	235	4,766
Missouri.	32,729	23,099	8,005	7,846	15,094	10,706	2,299	2,089	–	9,630
Montana.	7,128	5,190	1,814	1,806	3,377	2,320	497	559	64	1,874
Nebraska.	9,793	8,187	2,533	2,471	5,654	4,122	833	699	–	1,606
Nevada	14,184	9,734	2,091	1,948	7,642	6,305	663	675	75	4,375
New Hampshire	7,172	5,472	1,775	1,556	3,697	2,175	737	785	439	1,261
New Jersey	65,909	50,160	11,495	10,897	38,665	29,488	4,909	4,268	774	14,975
New Mexico	17,103	12,994	4,220	4,117	8,774	5,527	992	2,255	–	4,110
New York	178,884	130,375	47,300	39,570	83,075	63,162	8,034	11,880	7,655	40,854
North Carolina	51,899	42,398	13,288	12,517	29,109	22,613	3,634	2,862	0	9,501
North Dakota	4,786	3,942	1,228	1,196	2,714	1,783	577	354	–	844
Ohio.	87,317	53,035	16,692	16,189	36,344	25,698	6,606	4,039	688	33,594
Oklahoma	22,203	17,107	5,100	5,279	11,701	8,141	1,930	1,631	476	4,619
Oregon.	30,676	17,099	4,945	4,900	12,154	7,743	2,210	2,202	376	13,200
Pennsylvania	83,112	59,114	16,094	15,949	43,020	30,838	6,648	5,535	1,349	22,649
Rhode Island	8,418	6,279	2,087	1,963	4,192	2,766	569	858	32	2,107
South Carolina.	27,531	20,942	7,098	6,691	13,845	8,689	3,574	1,582	1,401	5,187
South Dakota	4,920	3,299	1,276	1,256	2,023	1,266	278	479	–	1,627
Tennessee	29,489	24,831	8,342	8,246	16,489	11,390	1,870	3,229	0	4,658
Texas	114,589	88,724	28,278	27,374	60,447	40,315	9,544	10,587	–	25,865
Utah.	16,055	12,654	3,081	3,073	9,573	6,076	2,359	1,138	194	3,207
Vermont	5,442	4,790	1,380	1,375	3,411	2,564	458	389	41	611
Virginia.	47,233	35,222	6,865	6,390	28,357	18,667	5,887	3,803	502	11,508
Washington	47,043	31,226	7,893	7,582	23,333	17,706	3,488	2,139	505	15,313
West Virginia	11,933	10,636	3,257	3,186	7,380	4,642	1,232	1,505	70	1,227
Wisconsin	40,228	26,723	6,769	6,608	19,953	14,483	3,216	2,255	–	13,506
Wyoming	6,091	4,820	1,947	1,776	2,873	2,025	150	698	74	1,197

– Represents or rounds to zero. [1] Includes amounts for categories not shown separately. [2] Duplicate intergovernmental transactions are excluded.

Source: U.S. Census Bureau, "Survey of State Government Finances, 2006." See also <http://www.census.gov/govs/www/state.html>.

U.S. Census Bureau, Statistical Abstract of the United States: 2011

Table 451. State Government Tax Collections by State: 2007

[In millions of dollars (757,471 represents $757,471,000,000]

State	All taxes	Total property taxes	Total general sales and gross receipts		Selective sales and gross receipts						
					Total	Selective sales tax					
						Alcoholic beverage sales	Insurance premiums	Motor fuels sales	Public utilities	Tobacco products	Other
			Total	gross receipts							
United States	757,471	12,621	352,706	238,304	114,402	5,166	15,413	36,543	14,333	15,299	27,647
Alabama	8,868	274	4,390	2,278	2,112	159	277	568	745	151	213
Alaska	3,688	66	236	–	236	35	55	39	4	74	28
Arizona	14,405	925	8,290	6,612	1,677	63	441	769	45	358	1
Arkansas	7,392	633	3,855	2,904	950	47	139	462	–	148	155
California	114,737	2,304	40,504	32,669	7,835	334	2,178	3,433	687	1,079	124
Colorado	9,217	–	3,450	2,196	1,254	34	182	685	10	228	116
Connecticut	13,272	–	5,317	3,030	2,286	40	234	440	234	254	1,085
Delaware	2,906	–	459	–	459	15	110	117	48	88	81
Florida	38,819	41	30,616	22,849	7,767	654	786	2,306	3,024	454	543
Georgia	18,253	79	7,855	5,916	1,939	160	342	1,083	–	243	112
Hawaii	5,090	–	3,228	2,558	670	46	99	90	124	86	226
Idaho	3,537	–	1,669	1,278	391	7	86	232	2	55	9
Illinois.	30,066	60	14,915	7,817	7,098	156	329	1,454	1,879	639	2,642
Indiana.	14,199	5	7,943	5,424	2,519	40	191	881	203	361	845
Iowa.	6,470	–	2,768	1,787	981	14	105	447	–	135	279
Kansas.	6,893	73	3,057	2,242	815	101	130	431	1	121	31
Kentucky	9,895	494	4,590	2,818	1,773	102	148	571	53	178	722
Louisiana	10,973	39	5,482	3,481	2,000	54	402	617	18	147	763
Maine.	3,696	38	1,689	1,055	634	17	85	233	24	159	116
Maryland	15,094	595	5,812	3,448	2,364	29	385	754	133	278	786
Massachusetts.	20,695	3	6,006	4,076	1,930	72	397	676	24	438	323
Michigan	23,849	2,323	11,602	7,983	3,619	136	224	1,034	21	1,132	1,072
Minnesota	17,768	675	7,302	4,471	2,831	72	318	644	–	448	1,348
Mississippi.	6,482	48	4,178	3,156	1,023	42	192	449	2	56	282
Missouri.	10,706	26	4,814	3,273	1,542	31	295	737	–	109	370
Montana.	2,320	202	530	–	530	26	63	211	41	91	99
Nebraska.	4,122	2	2,004	1,484	519	26	37	321	54	72	11
Nevada	6,305	184	5,126	3,213	1,913	40	259	328	11	138	1,137
New Hampshire.	2,175	385	735	–	735	13	87	129	73	139	294
New Jersey	29,488	4	12,181	8,610	3,571	103	479	562	927	784	717
New Mexico.	5,527	56	2,647	1,937	710	42	121	244	30	47	227
New York	63,162	–	19,506	10,880	8,626	194	1,172	516	774	982	4,987
North Carolina	22,613	–	8,866	5,202	3,664	246	487	1,609	372	241	708
North Dakota	1,783	2	809	484	324	6	30	139	35	24	89
Ohio.	25,698	–	12,448	7,751	4,697	92	448	1,720	1,106	986	346
Oklahoma	8,141	–	2,940	1,964	976	80	197	397	30	231	41
Oregon.	7,743	22	783	–	783	14	56	417	22	271	3
Pennsylvania	30,838	64	14,483	8,662	5,821	265	694	2,143	1,299	1,018	402
Rhode Island	2,766	1	1,357	876	481	11	57	132	102	120	59
South Carolina.	8,689	9	4,577	3,234	1,344	147	123	533	40	32	468
South Dakota.	1,266	–	1,020	711	309	13	59	123	3	47	63
Tennessee.	11,390	–	8,364	6,772	1,592	112	375	860	8	136	102
Texas.	40,315	–	31,811	20,435	11,377	736	1,292	3,075	995	1,331	3,948
Utah.	6,076	–	2,625	1,954	671	36	124	382	30	62	37
Vermont.	2,564	889	845	334	511	19	55	87	10	64	274
Virginia.	18,667	21	6,096	3,635	2,461	168	385	919	140	172	678
Washington	17,706	1,689	13,852	10,861	2,991	253	392	1,129	444	445	328
West Virginia	4,642	4	2,213	1,130	1,084	9	111	349	153	111	351
Wisconsin	14,483	120	6,037	4,159	1,878	52	157	996	351	314	9
Wyoming	2,025	266	826	698	128	3	24	72	3	25	1

See footnotes at end of table.

U.S. Census Bureau, Statistical Abstract of the United States: 2011

Table 451. State Government Tax Collections by State: 2007—Con.

[See headnote, page 288]

State	License taxes Total [1]	Selected license taxes Corporation	Selected license taxes Motor vehicle operators	Selected license taxes Occupancy and business, n.e.c.[2]	Income taxes Total	Income taxes Individual income	Income taxes Corporation net income	Other taxes Total [1]	Selected other taxes Death and gift	Selected other taxes Severance
United States	46,697	8,570	2,144	11,849	318,779	265,863	52,915	26,668	4,924	11,064
Alabama	477	99	16	125	3,525	3,020	506	202	1	144
Alaska	136	1	–	39	814	–	814	2,437	–	2,437
Arizona	413	22	27	99	4,734	3,747	986	44	–	44
Arkansas	298	23	15	92	2,531	2,168	363	74	–	22
California	7,415	64	228	3,469	64,476	53,318	11,158	38	6	32
Colorado	354	9	10	35	5,275	4,795	479	137	1	137
Connecticut	364	18	38	87	7,229	6,335	894	362	178	–
Delaware	1,006	624	3	241	1,328	1,025	302	113	1	–
Florida	1,875	196	173	239	2,443	–	2,443	3,845	43	46
Georgia	486	30	63	73	9,817	8,799	1,017	17	1	–
Hawaii	153	1	–	26	1,661	1,560	101	48	–	–
Idaho	264	2	7	56	1,595	1,406	188	9	–	7
Illinois...........	2,381	201	71	700	12,345	9,408	2,936	364	264	–
Indiana...........	496	7	229	39	5,603	4,616	987	151	150	1
Iowa.............	615	36	7	92	2,992	2,667	325	95	78	–
Kansas...........	303	56	20	25	3,272	2,745	527	188	56	132
Kentucky	459	77	17	111	4,030	3,042	988	322	44	275
Louisiana.........	570	315	12	95	3,967	3,214	753	915	11	904
Maine............	232	8	12	97	1,653	1,469	184	84	55	–
Maryland	722	74	26	146	7,461	6,679	782	504	224	–
Massachusetts......	694	25	82	162	13,507	11,400	2,107	485	250	–
Michigan	1,375	20	51	152	8,229	6,443	1,786	320	1	82
Minnesota	973	7	48	297	8,415	7,231	1,184	404	108	35
Mississippi........	403	126	31	80	1,771	1,402	369	82	–	82
Missouri..........	631	77	17	166	5,225	4,835	391	8	–	–
Montana..........	308	3	9	85	1,012	833	179	268	1	265
Nebraska.........	207	7	9	63	1,864	1,651	213	45	27	2
Nevada	523	72	16	155	–	–	–	472	1	62
New Hampshire.....	210	37	13	51	703	107	596	142		–
New Jersey	1,497	321	39	507	14,614	11,727	2,887	1,192	605	–
New Mexico........	244	3	4	24	1,638	1,178	460	942	–	942
New York	1,328	72	157	149	39,996	34,580	5,416	2,332	1,053	–
North Carolina.....	1,338	399	127	162	12,154	10,589	1,566	254	178	2
North Dakota......	128	–	4	51	453	317	136	391	–	391
Ohio.............	2,322	649	82	608	10,849	9,723	1,126	79	72	7
Oklahoma	836	50	14	86	3,336	2,775	561	1,028	67	942
Oregon...........	833	11	32	275	6,002	5,590	406	104	80	13
Pennsylvania	2,847	777	58	723	12,099	9,813	2,287	1,344	737	–
Rhode Island......	94	4	1	33	1,265	1,086	179	49	36	–
South Carolina.....	471	67	52	142	3,551	3,239	312	80	2	–
South Dakota......	164	3	2	75	77	–	77	5	1	5
Tennessee........	1,270	635	45	259	1,370	249	1,120	386	111	2
Texas............	5,736	3,215	117	763	–	–	–	2,768	5	2,763
Utah.............	389	5	10	37	2,960	2,561	399	102	–	102
Vermont..........	111	5	5	17	665	581	83	54	18	–
Virginia...........	674	57	46	161	11,118	10,239	880	758	153	2
Washington	895	24	61	233	–	–	–	1,270	183	49
West Virginia	184	9	3	42	1,900	1,361	539	341	–	328
Wisconsin	861	17	31	303	7,257	6,334	923	208	121	5
Wyoming	126	10	2	19	–	–	–	806	3	804

– Represents zero or rounds to zero. [1] Includes other items not shown separately. [2] n.e.c. means not elsewhere classified.

Source: U.S. Census Bureau, *Tax collections, State government tax collections*, annual. See also <http://www.census.gov/govs/statetax>.

Table 452. State Governments—Expenditures and Debt by State: 2007

[In millions of dollars (1,635,747 represents $1,635,747,000,000) except as indicated. For fiscal year ending in year shown; see text, this section]

State	Total expend-itures	General expenditures		Direct expenditures						
		Total	Inter-govern-mental	Total	Educa-tion	Public welfare	Health	Hospi-tals	High-ways	Police protec-tion
United States ...	1,635,747	1,424,195	459,605	964,590	213,868	336,510	37,321	47,953	88,333	11,383
Alabama	23,493	20,974	6,089	14,885	4,909	4,711	619	1,198	1,142	144
Alaska	9,192	8,291	1,366	6,925	1,095	1,423	118	30	1,200	73
Arizona	28,828	25,969	10,342	15,628	3,311	6,296	1,382	70	1,249	243
Arkansas	14,949	13,762	4,300	9,462	2,395	3,625	237	743	733	71
California	232,450	197,414	92,416	104,998	20,873	31,930	2,613	6,245	6,675	1,429
Colorado	21,244	17,981	6,001	11,980	3,809	3,176	674	395	785	111
Connecticut	21,598	18,493	3,832	14,661	2,719	4,673	574	1,284	740	205
Delaware	6,736	6,214	1,158	5,056	1,089	1,316	352	63	398	103
Florida	73,018	65,974	19,681	46,294	7,490	17,291	3,297	698	6,273	456
Georgia	41,845	37,750	10,516	27,234	6,261	9,204	1,069	731	5,009	245
Hawaii	9,840	8,970	138	8,832	3,240	1,494	602	455	306	13
Idaho	6,910	6,160	1,932	4,229	950	1,485	135	44	501	45
Illinois...........	59,767	51,502	14,260	37,242	7,008	13,905	2,092	953	3,969	404
Indiana..........	28,861	26,574	8,179	18,395	5,459	6,643	542	247	1,659	230
Iowa............	15,462	13,843	3,892	9,950	2,519	3,511	127	1,017	1,002	86
Kansas..........	13,824	12,623	3,870	8,753	1,915	2,957	150	928	1,069	94
Kentucky	23,738	20,921	4,527	16,394	4,282	5,710	435	999	1,950	164
Louisiana	27,839	24,999	6,175	18,824	3,751	4,823	588	844	1,564	211
Maine...........	7,932	7,260	1,273	5,987	919	2,423	476	55	471	70
Maryland	31,695	28,454	7,568	20,886	4,062	6,846	1,277	481	1,842	354
Massachusetts.....	44,488	39,863	9,365	30,498	4,672	12,225	933	513	1,551	464
Michigan	54,772	48,066	19,395	28,671	8,420	9,928	836	2,055	1,577	276
Minnesota	31,880	28,163	10,686	17,477	4,622	7,826	439	328	1,144	245
Mississippi	18,630	16,900	5,086	11,814	2,022	4,020	312	861	1,291	97
Missouri	25,193	22,316	5,501	16,815	3,104	5,759	1,051	1,211	1,870	199
Montana.........	5,553	4,895	1,176	3,719	887	809	275	43	571	34
Nebraska........	7,834	7,436	1,794	5,642	1,413	1,996	358	225	558	63
Nevada	10,755	9,459	3,827	5,632	1,545	1,552	249	241	706	92
New Hampshire....	6,226	5,382	1,408	3,973	865	1,342	111	56	409	48
New Jersey	56,080	44,925	10,671	34,253	8,160	11,007	1,264	1,831	2,392	492
New Mexico.......	14,907	13,641	4,145	9,496	2,041	3,116	447	735	972	164
New York	151,550	124,894	50,528	74,366	10,359	34,428	2,102	4,600	4,239	766
North Carolina....	44,009	39,736	12,646	27,090	7,722	8,416	1,205	1,372	2,770	491
North Dakota	3,778	3,441	742	2,700	775	690	52	15	370	22
Ohio............	66,494	54,240	18,043	36,198	8,834	14,222	1,510	1,959	2,510	222
Oklahoma	18,052	15,794	4,015	11,779	3,260	4,384	520	167	1,024	145
Oregon..........	20,606	16,703	5,047	11,656	2,493	3,538	290	1,002	1,059	169
Pennsylvania......	68,130	58,348	17,009	41,339	7,791	16,792	659	2,155	5,347	713
Rhode Island	7,071	5,909	1,063	4,846	775	1,998	162	94	264	60
South Carolina.....	24,825	20,887	4,871	16,016	4,111	5,345	944	1,310	1,035	178
South Dakota......	3,570	3,262	652	2,610	502	755	111	55	485	28
Tennessee........	24,860	23,197	6,035	17,163	3,773	7,478	1,205	394	1,589	141
Texas............	90,624	80,768	21,920	58,848	14,658	20,045	1,821	3,287	7,979	606
Utah............	12,774	11,611	2,601	9,010	2,840	2,091	312	767	772	115
Vermont..........	4,994	4,687	1,416	3,271	840	1,203	147	18	276	71
Virginia..........	36,774	33,652	10,459	23,193	6,596	6,312	616	2,541	2,246	284
Washington	36,823	31,671	8,602	23,069	6,269	6,973	1,187	1,598	2,143	227
West Virginia	9,724	9,247	2,074	7,172	1,814	2,413	257	89	974	62
Wisconsin	31,004	26,912	9,748	17,165	4,208	5,798	366	951	1,262	120
Wyoming	4,536	4,062	1,569	2,493	443	610	222	2	408	38

See footnotes at end of table.

U.S. Census Bureau, Statistical Abstract of the United States: 2011

Table 452. State Governments—Expenditures and Debt by State: 2007—Con.

[See headnote, page 290]

State	General expenditures—Con.							Expenditures			
	Direct expenditures—Con.										
	Corrections	Parks and recreation	Housing and community development	Sewerage	Solid waste management	Government administration	Interest on general debt	Other	Utility and liquor store	Insurance trust	Cash and security holdings	Total debt outstanding
United States . . .	44,021	5,181	8,712	1,364	2,226	49,236	41,594	76,889	29,194	182,358	3,922,371	936,524
Alabama	487	29	8	–	2	550	284	802	199	2,319	43,865	7,059
Alaska	237	13	133	–	–	525	321	1,757	75	825	59,081	6,553
Arizona	898	103	72	–	5	659	466	873	31	2,828	51,214	9,546
Arkansas	331	44	11	–	9	527	175	562	–	1,187	27,390	4,509
California	7,787	397	271	156	1,020	8,368	5,360	11,874	5,640	29,397	579,171	114,702
Colorado	748	71	82	2	1	674	701	751	28	3,235	64,491	14,906
Connecticut	660	22	161	–	159	1,093	1,143	1,226	318	2,787	45,089	23,836
Delaware	266	57	56	–	110	472	253	521	89	433	14,162	5,391
Florida	2,542	188	70	–	228	2,893	1,391	3,477	98	6,946	192,315	36,483
Georgia	1,422	187	214	5	60	711	554	1,563	42	4,053	78,739	11,406
Hawaii	197	78	127	12	–	424	458	1,426	–	878	19,552	5,959
Idaho	202	36	13	–	–	297	135	386	80	670	17,390	2,807
Illinois	1,199	123	208	18	34	1,175	2,742	3,413	–	8,265	136,240	54,535
Indiana	604	67	256	11	6	668	866	1,138	37	2,250	63,338	19,180
Iowa	256	31	27	–	3	500	340	530	123	1,496	35,280	6,727
Kansas	272	29	53	–	4	417	307	557	–	1,202	22,256	5,894
Kentucky	451	106	144	22	47	749	474	861	–	2,817	44,731	11,646
Louisiana	522	289	2,912	–	–	776	852	1,694	4	2,835	59,460	14,019
Maine	130	11	132	2	1	278	238	781	–	672	20,428	5,327
Maryland	1,347	262	244	85	20	1,242	970	1,854	552	2,689	63,166	20,912
Massachusetts	1,010	186	384	336	11	1,641	3,366	3,209	248	4,378	99,126	68,448
Michigan	1,766	79	503	–	9	967	1,183	1,071	604	6,101	110,439	28,586
Minnesota	469	166	64	–	25	803	491	854	104	3,613	64,495	8,867
Mississippi	301	39	12	–	–	261	227	2,372	191	1,539	35,074	5,858
Missouri	625	38	175	–	11	484	1,049	1,239	–	2,877	74,552	18,716
Montana	147	12	42	2	1	316	188	392	56	602	16,586	4,801
Nebraska	213	32	1	5	9	187	91	491	–	399	14,485	2,332
Nevada	293	23	9	–	–	340	190	391	77	1,220	27,766	4,141
New Hampshire	109	11	91	3	11	209	364	342	388	456	13,194	7,690
New Jersey	1,423	406	233	3	41	1,707	1,931	3,361	2,060	9,096	111,844	51,385
New Mexico	341	71	59	–	1	486	335	728	16	1,250	47,611	7,323
New York	3,016	513	645	–	109	4,953	3,594	5,043	12,541	14,115	347,377	110,085
North Carolina	1,268	218	162	–	11	1,033	607	1,817	151	4,122	97,917	19,246
North Dakota	54	22	21	–	–	128	142	410	–	336	11,135	1,792
Ohio	1,176	82	281	546	20	1,754	1,395	1,678	431	11,824	199,957	26,065
Oklahoma	569	90	13	7	15	488	435	662	428	1,830	38,543	8,667
Oregon	597	76	108	–	4	895	509	915	202	3,700	79,486	11,334
Pennsylvania	1,665	229	24	1	37	2,327	1,768	1,831	1,317	8,465	150,326	37,079
Rhode Island	178	9	42	32	62	381	377	411	125	1,037	16,967	8,380
South Carolina	466	104	122	–	–	951	550	901	1,627	2,311	44,820	14,981
South Dakota	102	28	40	–	–	147	122	235	–	308	12,948	3,232
Tennessee	595	145	32	17	12	655	202	925	5	1,657	38,495	4,142
Texas	3,177	80	26	4	67	1,431	1,044	4,624	–	9,856	297,794	23,909
Utah	310	53	65	13	–	738	274	658	141	1,022	31,346	5,927
Vermont	113	14	73	11	10	158	160	176	66	241	7,294	3,104
Virginia	1,106	131	153	42	3	903	822	1,437	470	2,652	79,118	19,684
Washington	1,090	70	87	–	13	695	940	1,777	494	4,657	85,562	21,059
West Virginia	233	51	15	28	10	422	176	629	71	406	12,480	5,628
Wisconsin	931	26	23	–	13	610	971	1,886	6	4,086	99,482	21,461
Wyoming	117	33	12	–	3	167	60	377	59	415	18,793	1,205

– Represents or rounds to zero.

Source: U.S. Census Bureau, *State Government Finances, 2007*, July 2010, <http://www.census.gov/govs>.

Table 453. Local Governments—Revenue by State: 2007

[In millions of dollars (1,539,014 represents $1,539,014,000,000), except as noted. For fiscal year ending in year shown; see text, this section]

State	Total revenue	General revenue, total	Inter-govern-mental revenue	Total	Total	Property	Sales and gross receipt	Indi-vidual income	Corpo-ration income	Other taxes
United States	**1,539,014**	**1,344,828**	**504,407**	**840,421**	**525,813**	**376,952**	**86,880**	**23,964**	**7,677**	**30,340**
Alabama	19,650	16,511	6,534	9,977	4,661	1,822	2,032	120	–	687
Alaska	3,960	3,623	1,481	2,142	1,256	970	248	–	–	39
Arizona	28,995	24,619	10,198	14,420	8,930	5,296	3,009	–	–	624
Arkansas	8,399	7,562	4,252	3,309	1,787	715	1,031	–	–	41
California	266,702	219,565	97,671	121,894	65,118	46,337	13,703	–	–	5,077
Colorado	24,855	21,882	5,952	15,930	9,419	5,665	3,144	–	–	610
Connecticut	15,723	14,179	4,540	9,639	8,244	8,070	2	–	–	173
Delaware	3,074	2,600	1,301	1,298	752	569	3	48	–	133
District of Columbia	11,389	9,747	2,999	6,740	5,192	1,516	1,330	1,313	417	616
Florida	96,597	86,479	25,573	60,906	34,155	26,805	5,071	–	–	2,278
Georgia	41,718	36,776	11,666	25,110	14,834	9,440	4,918	–	–	476
Hawaii	2,632	2,383	408	1,975	1,454	1,137	160	–	–	157
Idaho	5,213	4,994	2,101	2,893	1,225	1,114	31	–	–	80
Illinois	64,761	55,327	18,712	36,615	25,013	20,391	3,697	–	–	925
Indiana	24,498	22,452	8,243	14,210	7,124	6,165	92	603	–	264
Iowa	12,662	11,793	4,228	7,565	4,464	3,616	693	75	–	80
Kansas	12,360	11,056	3,893	7,163	4,461	3,385	965	2	–	110
Kentucky	12,591	11,106	4,585	6,521	3,810	2,086	493	1,000	122	108
Louisiana	18,837	17,311	6,298	11,013	6,620	2,572	3,859	–	–	189
Maine	4,269	4,155	1,465	2,690	2,047	2,021	2	–	–	24
Maryland	25,480	22,768	7,265	15,503	11,971	5,952	521	4,064	–	1,434
Massachusetts	31,017	26,352	11,219	15,133	11,425	11,039	165	–	–	222
Michigan	47,726	42,439	19,497	22,942	13,237	12,208	277	468	–	284
Minnesota	25,813	23,190	10,857	12,333	5,893	5,441	225	–	–	227
Mississippi	11,555	10,744	5,035	5,709	2,337	2,159	91	–	–	87
Missouri	22,466	19,880	6,088	13,791	8,465	5,232	2,358	333	–	543
Montana	3,141	3,031	1,288	1,743	952	905	5	–	–	41
Nebraska	10,288	7,011	1,987	5,023	3,088	2,379	384	–	–	325
Nevada	13,641	12,723	4,998	7,725	4,139	2,690	952	–	–	497
New Hampshire	4,745	4,629	1,460	3,169	2,568	2,526	–	–	–	41
New Jersey	41,211	40,295	12,126	28,169	21,940	21,479	106	–	–	355
New Mexico	7,656	7,160	4,048	3,112	1,928	953	852	–	–	122
New York	166,271	144,625	50,232	94,393	70,866	38,076	13,012	8,083	6,994	4,700
North Carolina	36,699	32,580	13,676	18,904	9,809	7,306	2,160	–	–	342
North Dakota	2,259	2,121	803	1,318	817	697	101	–	–	19
Ohio	52,889	50,330	20,308	30,022	19,997	13,315	1,936	4,019	86	641
Oklahoma	12,052	10,914	4,304	6,610	3,681	1,931	1,613	–	–	137
Oregon	16,336	14,983	6,121	8,863	5,006	3,936	322	16	57	674
Pennsylvania	56,995	52,944	21,827	31,117	21,271	14,851	554	3,819	–	2,047
Rhode Island	4,086	3,774	1,275	2,498	2,020	1,962	13	–	–	45
South Carolina	16,571	15,013	4,624	10,389	5,106	4,284	286	–	–	536
South Dakota	2,735	2,424	764	1,661	1,124	819	273	–	–	32
Tennessee	28,727	19,643	6,177	13,466	7,428	4,524	2,420	–	–	484
Texas	104,900	90,748	26,523	64,225	41,721	34,193	6,529	–	–	1,000
Utah	9,982	8,282	3,034	5,249	3,017	2,038	859	–	–	120
Vermont	2,302	2,067	1,431	636	371	348	11	–	–	12
Virginia	33,704	30,159	11,049	19,109	13,707	9,997	2,442	–	–	1,268
Washington	34,480	28,160	10,377	17,783	9,836	5,680	3,231	–	–	925
West Virginia	4,889	4,650	2,169	2,480	1,459	1,132	96	–	–	231
Wisconsin	25,468	23,171	10,212	12,959	8,846	8,277	357	–	–	212
Wyoming	4,048	3,899	1,531	2,368	1,221	930	246	–	–	45

See footnotes at end of table.

U.S. Census Bureau, Statistical Abstract of the United States: 2011

Table 453. Local Governments—Revenue by State: 2007—Con.

[See headnote, page 292]

State	General revenue—Con. General revenue from own sources—Con. Current charges and miscellaneous general revenue	Current charges Total [1]	Current charges Education	Current charges Hospitals	Current charges Sewerage	Miscellaneous general revenue Total [1]	Miscellaneous general revenue Interest earnings	Miscellaneous general revenue Special assessment	Utility revenue	Liquor store revenue	Insurance trust revenue
United States	314,608	210,251	23,557	57,594	36,113	104,357	44,971	7,268	117,675	1,024	75,487
Alabama	5,316	4,013	326	2,670	367	1,303	515	34	2,590	–	549
Alaska . . .	886	559	25	188	65	326	201	9	285	–	52
Arizona . . .	5,491	3,442	531	687	629	2,049	906	124	3,956	–	420
Arkansas	1,522	930	146	188	218	592	266	25	792	–	44
California	56,776	37,766	2,513	8,540	5,178	19,010	8,413	1,451	19,810	–	27,327
Colorado	6,511	4,239	408	1,168	638	2,272	783	361	2,187	–	786
Connecticut	1,395	925	133	–	286	469	212	39	695	–	848
Delaware	546	331	18	–	144	215	62	31	371	–	103
District of Columbia . . .	1,555	639	41	–	186	916	280	1	813	–	829
Florida	26,751	17,026	1,955	4,896	2,395	9,725	3,254	1,818	8,395	–	1,723
Georgia	10,276	7,391	530	3,644	1,012	2,885	1,212	65	4,313	–	628
Hawaii	521	352	–	–	192	169	124	21	249	–	–
Idaho	1,668	1,349	90	681	161	320	128	41	218	–	1
Illinois	11,602	6,783	1,250	804	995	4,819	1,987	417	3,259	–	6,175
Indiana	7,085	4,413	390	2,560	783	2,672	643	46	1,956	–	90
Iowa	3,101	2,366	488	1,044	334	735	334	18	863	–	6
Kansas	2,702	1,779	371	620	298	923	413	63	1,166	–	138
Kentucky	2,711	1,732	129	450	369	978	707	20	1,406	–	79
Louisiana	4,393	2,979	62	1,664	325	1,414	718	38	1,210	–	316
Maine	643	485	45	69	141	158	62	12	114	–	–
Maryland	3,532	2,482	582	–	756	1,050	295	76	580	223	1,909
Massachusetts	3,708	2,598	306	479	851	1,110	357	34	2,802	–	1,863
Michigan	9,705	6,595	1,141	922	1,471	3,110	1,331	221	2,201	–	2,086
Minnesota . . . . , ,	6,440	4,187	110	1,109	624	2,253	906	381	1,748	259	615
Mississippi	3,372	2,717	370	1,820	185	654	225	9	810	–	–
Missouri	5,326	3,521	669	1,171	571	1,804	787	45	1,702	–	885
Montana	792	515	67	55	71	277	94	61	109	–	–
Nebraska	1,935	1,386	213	567	146	550	215	68	2,938	–	340
Nevada	3,586	2,302	129	572	374	1,284	402	81	919	–	–
New Hampshire	601	395	54	–	95	206	80	3	90	–	26
New Jersey	6,229	4,286	1,107	299	1,296	1,943	659	7	897	–	18
New Mexico	1,185	703	100	87	131	481	188	27	496	–	–
New York	23,527	15,229	1,361	3,390	1,786	8,298	3,270	115	5,278	–	16,368
North Carolina	9,095	6,921	540	3,290	1,185	2,174	863	22	3,520	520	79
North Dakota	501	265	46	0	40	236	68	61	116	–	22
Ohio	10,025	6,162	1,114	1,033	1,512	3,863	2,088	239	2,344	–	215
Oklahoma	2,929	2,149	306	842	256	780	317	16	943	–	194
Oregon	3,857	2,590	464	244	741	1,266	570	96	1,351	–	2
Pennsylvania	9,847	6,215	858	26	1,950	3,632	2,067	129	2,677	–	1,374
Rhode Island	478	305	33	–	86	173	61	4	162	–	150
South Carolina	5,283	4,065	248	2,644	441	1,218	522	65	1,553	–	5
South Dakota	537	374	64	38	58	162	68	20	232	21	57
Tennessee	6,039	4,604	411	2,354	562	1,435	688	110	7,767	–	1,316
Texas	22,504	14,542	2,016	3,906	2,706	7,962	4,739	222	10,626	–	3,526
Utah	2,231	1,424	80	46	279	808	334	59	1,700	–	–
Vermont	265	161	23	–	51	104	37	4	208	–	27
Virginia	5,402	3,668	397	256	922	1,735	733	145	1,717	–	1,828
Washington	7,947	5,871	340	1,569	1,388	2,076	927	183	5,806	–	514
West Virginia	1,021	665	39	199	188	356	163	29	204	–	35
Wisconsin	4,113	2,929	508	70	627	1,184	586	92	1,381	–	916
Wyoming	1,146	925	68	649	47	221	108	9	149	–	–

– Represents or rounds to zero. [1] Includes items not shown separately.

Source: U.S. Census Bureau, *State Government Finances*, 2007, July 2010, <http://www.census.gov/govs/>.

Table 454. Local Governments—Expenditures and Debt by State: 2007

[In millions of dollars (1,499,268 represents $1,499,268,000,000), except as indicated. For fiscal year ending in year shown; see text, this section]

State	Total expendi-tures	General expenditures							
		Direct expenditures							
		Total [1]	Total	Educa-tion	Public welfare	Health	Hospi-tals	High-ways	Police protec-tion
United States	1,499,268	1,307,839	1,293,639	560,505	48,259	36,875	70,923	56,380	72,706
Alabama	18,809	16,117	16,102	7,123	47	267	2,448	815	832
Alaska	3,838	3,416	3,415	1,508	4	66	198	200	163
Arizona	28,928	23,912	23,661	9,661	281	238	951	1,458	1,802
Arkansas	8,484	7,600	7,591	4,383	14	33	184	423	409
California	247,178	210,104	209,793	77,589	15,003	9,894	10,929	7,511	12,445
Colorado	25,287	21,622	21,567	7,735	639	387	1,393	1,332	1,234
Connecticut	14,916	13,739	13,729	7,955	90	111	–	478	702
Delaware	3,123	2,694	2,694	1,621	–	36	–	82	207
District ofColumbia ...	10,585	8,480	8,480	1,546	2,161	387	145	105	500
Florida	95,441	84,602	84,337	32,025	1,277	870	5,889	3,533	5,832
Georgia	42,325	36,519	36,480	16,997	187	900	4,043	1,429	1,892
Hawaii	2,564	2,163	2,163	–	32	47	–	196	292
Idaho	4,991	4,763	4,761	2,020	27	68	699	302	255
Illinois	63,415	53,895	53,882	23,623	642	673	1,461	2,692	3,657
Indiana	26,240	23,845	23,737	10,006	521	218	2,742	771	888
Iowa	12,771	11,776	11,684	5,580	98	349	1,141	861	500
Kansas	11,870	10,650	10,624	5,154	43	226	642	595	584
Kentucky	12,506	10,717	10,713	5,411	53	226	435	406	464
Louisiana	17,647	15,835	15,822	6,358	33	156	2,007	650	1,001
Maine	4,191	4,059	4,058	2,173	34	28	71	255	162
Maryland	23,964	22,200	21,874	11,593	167	316	–	917	1,428
Massachusetts	30,200	24,689	23,923	12,126	67	115	863	722	1,361
Michigan	45,867	41,505	41,266	19,788	1,100	2,473	1,025	2,215	2,061
Minnesota	26,151	23,583	23,455	9,260	1,579	564	1,376	2,060	1,167
Mississippi	11,225	10,348	10,347	4,695	22	91	1,763	585	476
Missouri	22,346	19,831	19,830	9,690	133	377	1,200	1,097	1,202
Montana	3,072	2,930	2,928	1,446	44	91	57	158	172
Nebraska	10,772	6,869	6,866	3,305	81	58	580	453	293
Nevada	13,090	11,601	11,593	4,134	320	120	658	1,083	893
New Hampshire	4,670	4,567	4,496	2,396	204	29	–	216	248
New Jersey	42,058	41,098	40,719	21,451	1,031	387	345	1,120	2,566
New Mexico	7,390	6,749	6,719	3,511	105	49	117	351	433
New York	156,259	137,599	129,650	50,485	10,211	3,549	6,953	5,191	6,876
North Carolina	37,516	32,895	32,147	13,850	1,384	1,551	3,558	560	1,542
North Dakota	2,207	2,046	2,038	968	47	38	3	228	84
Ohio	52,116	48,868	48,517	21,131	2,997	2,420	1,374	2,187	2,734
Oklahoma	11,981	10,921	10,919	5,416	35	155	851	724	574
Oregon	16,716	14,692	14,679	6,160	264	658	272	887	799
Pennsylvania	56,013	50,522	50,186	23,762	3,541	3,010	19	1,592	1,956
Rhode Island	3,985	3,691	3,691	2,022	8	9	–	99	267
South Carolina	16,720	15,147	15,118	7,284	23	161	2,591	327	723
South Dakota	2,634	2,348	2,348	1,111	13	33	41	221	109
Tennessee	30,278	18,835	18,830	7,657	141	330	2,458	693	1,215
Texas	103,842	89,908	88,455	44,344	313	1,740	6,203	3,693	4,640
Utah	9,826	7,767	7,752	3,534	89	202	51	397	468
Vermont	2,228	2,002	2,001	1,314	1	9	–	160	70
Virginia	32,755	29,968	29,939	14,371	1,360	915	227	756	1,626
Washington	34,095	26,607	26,554	10,267	124	906	1,910	1,378	1,186
West Virginia	4,966	4,637	4,633	2,729	5	57	235	83	206
Wisconsin	25,467	23,356	23,324	10,671	1,650	1,210	171	1,944	1,374
Wyoming	3,753	3,550	3,549	1,567	13	72	647	186	137

See footnotes at end of table.

U.S. Census Bureau, Statistical Abstract of the United States: 2011

Table 454. Local Governments—Expenditures and Debt by State: 2007—Con.

[See headnote, page 294]

State	General expenditures—Con.										Debt out-standing
	Direct expenditures—Con.									Insurance trust expenditures	
	Corrections	Sewerage	Solid waste	Parks and recreation	Housing and community development	Governmental administration	Interest on general debt	Other	Utility expenditures		
United States	24,071	42,834	20,593	32,345	37,225	70,160	51,992	168,771	160,135	31,294	1,474,775
Alabama	281	305	250	394	443	789	668	1,440	2,576	116	17,526
Alaska	3	89	77	109	138	199	121	539	397	25	3,443
Arizona	647	1,204	356	927	400	1,745	888	3,102	4,859	157	29,784
Arkansas	117	295	172	161	160	358	277	605	852	32	7,699
California	4,838	5,989	2,511	5,119	8,415	12,623	7,481	29,445	29,718	7,356	215,657
Colorado	428	804	137	1,005	615	1,618	994	3,247	3,321	343	31,573
Connecticut	–	385	215	220	521	585	316	2,151	793	384	8,891
Delaware	–	190	16	38	62	184	63	193	391	38	1,982
District ofColumbia ...	226	228	296	370	449	528	375	1,164	1,974	130	8,916
Florida	1,687	2,455	2,212	2,967	2,067	5,064	3,359	15,100	9,938	901	97,954
Georgia	787	1,461	684	794	848	2,422	743	3,294	5,469	337	37,064
Hawaii	–	251	218	175	89	237	149	477	401	–	4,345
Idaho	68	212	133	93	34	274	83	493	226	2	2,416
Illinois...........	668	1,441	488	2,690	1,696	3,296	2,465	8,390	6,215	3,305	61,991
Indiana..........	371	870	206	625	393	1,245	837	4,045	2,292	103	22,376
Iowa............	181	334	165	295	140	417	304	1,319	992	2	8,045
Kansas..........	111	301	126	204	149	501	514	1,475	1,177	42	14,063
Kentucky	206	441	174	179	141	492	847	1,238	1,748	41	26,067
Louisiana........	545	500	293	332	383	1,013	564	1,986	1,628	185	13,860
Maine...........	68	156	116	68	119	231	99	478	131	–	2,659
Maryland	314	615	567	681	794	1,086	655	2,741	1,007	756	15,436
Massachusetts.....	275	745	393	221	1,324	908	596	4,210	4,160	1,351	20,966
Michigan	604	1,936	472	766	467	2,185	1,737	4,437	2,964	1,398	44,541
Minnesota	370	620	328	660	780	1,185	1,084	2,420	2,241	326	29,839
Mississippi........	130	226	185	114	205	546	232	1,079	877	–	6,698
Missouri..........	176	761	138	517	441	982	680	2,437	2,062	453	20,100
Montana.........	35	78	79	55	60	167	46	441	142	–	1,512
Nebraska........	113	196	89	142	197	334	193	843	0,730	167	9,160
Nevada	009	267	21	663	217	1,003	525	1,320	1,489	–	17,942
New Hampshire......	54	109	103	81	84	254	98	620	94	8	2,563
New Jersey	606	1,168	1,134	670	841	1,695	1,389	6,317	951	10	34,307
New Mexico	127	192	144	233	87	446	161	763	641	–	4,872
New York	2,645	3,551	2,436	2,019	4,195	4,530	5,925	21,083	9,764	8,896	149,514
North Carolina......	476	1,418	682	751	721	1,287	931	3,436	4,598	23	30,968
North Dakota.......	36	51	46	82	39	107	64	245	147	13	1,839
Ohio.............	452	2,036	465	1,000	1,672	3,201	1,877	4,972	3,085	162	40,752
Oklahoma	98	377	189	241	250	707	211	1,092	1,012	49	7,898
Oregon...........	393	791	138	458	427	826	618	1,988	1,939	85	17,729
Pennsylvania.......	1,377	2,010	709	705	1,736	2,691	2,753	4,327	4,233	1,257	75,368
Rhode Island.......	42	81	46	58	138	210	75	637	155	139	2,079
South Carolina......	196	434	328	267	238	838	635	1,073	1,570	4	20,888
South Dakota.......	38	115	34	97	62	137	52	284	273	13	1,620
Tennessee.........	358	613	317	371	633	1,063	798	2,182	10,988	455	29,820
Texas............	1,534	2,611	966	1,814	1,809	4,202	6,293	8,293	12,847	1,086	163,792
Utah.............	166	340	133	362	236	567	224	983	2,060	–	9,998
Vermont..........	–	64	29	24	49	83	31	167	220	6	1,001
Virginia..........	835	880	592	837	831	1,964	929	3,816	2,170	617	31,397
Washington.......	491	1,490	531	865	982	1,457	1,082	3,885	7,329	159	41,049
West Virginia	39	235	62	90	119	329	151	292	298	31	3,455
Wisconsin	435	835	343	628	317	1,128	777	1,842	1,781	330	20,331
Wyoming	54	78	49	109	13	223	32	368	202	–	1,034

– Represents or rounds to zero. [1] Includes other items not shown seperately.
Source: U.S. Census Bureau, *State Government Finances, 2007*, July 2010, <http://www.census.gov/govs>.

Table 455. City Governments—Revenue for Largest Cities: 2006

[In millions of dollars (83,520 represents $83,520,000,000). For fiscal years ending in year shown; see text, this section. Cities ranked by estimated resident population as of July 1. Data reflect inclusion of fiscal activity of dependent school systems where applicable. Regarding intercity comparisons, see text, this section. See Appendix III]

Cities ranked by 2006 population	Total revenue	General revenue: Total	Intergov.: Total	Intergov.: From federal govt.	Intergov.: From state/local govt.	Intergov.: From local govt.	Own sources: Total	Taxes: Total [1]	Taxes: Property	Sales & gross receipts: Total [1]	Sales & gross receipts: General sales	Sales & gross receipts: Public utilities	Current charges: Total [1]	Current charges: Parks and recreation	Current charges: Sewerage	Misc.: Total [1]	Misc.: Interest earnings	Utility revenue [2]	Insurance trust revenue
New York, NY [3]	83,520	70,823	25,957	3,722	22,045	191	44,866	35,104	12,754	5,953	4,439	516	6,380	63	1,151	3,382	1,153	3,472	9,224
Los Angeles, CA	14,199	7,863	952	282	670	–	6,911	3,233	1,090	1,362	552	673	2,413	105	599	1,264	461	3,143	3,193
Chicago, IL	8,812	7,257	1,325	449	876	–	5,933	2,179	429	1,454	275	555	2,872	–	144	881	248	347	1,207
Houston, TX	4,449	3,119	550	195	328	27	2,569	1,492	781	664	423	187	808	26	330	269	153	341	989
Phoenix, AZ	3,377	2,903	1,115	581	488	46	1,788	1,023	261	692	537	84	581	26	232	184	137	288	186
Philadelphia, PA [3]	7,345	5,809	2,478	653	1,712	113	3,332	2,450	394	225	125	27	698	1	240	184	105	1,007	529
San Antonio, TX	3,283	1,469	191	54	120	17	1,278	612	292	287	200	–	431	24	280	234	107	1,573	242
San Diego, CA	3,266	2,100	411	175	216	20	1,690	744	313	323	173	45	694	63	396	252	110	332	833
Dallas, TX	3,027	2,277	164	123	36	6	2,112	857	488	329	198	89	861	35	185	394	144	207	543
San Jose, CA	1,924	1,498	217	50	141	27	1,281	660	285	238	106	112	440	15	241	181	100	20	406
Honolulu, HI [3]	1,483	1,337	197	117	79	–	1,140	807	591	114	–	62	284	23		50	29	146	–
Detroit, MI	3,184	2,132	694	97	543	54	1,439	867	309	218	–	61	452	4	351	119	47	314	739
Jacksonville, FL [3]	3,292	1,829	323	72	251	10	1,506	745	365	371	213	106	383	16	158	379	207	1,187	276
Indianapolis, IN [3]	3,749	3,014	646	86	550	10	2,367	1,638	1,486	47	–	1	506	26	74	224	94	687	48
San Francisco, CA [3]	7,955	5,647	2,155	87	1,664	404	3,492	2,047	923	598	327	91	1,045	25	165	400	178	426	1,882
Columbus, OH	1,227	1,058	198	82	103	13	860	560	40	20	–	7	228	11	172	72	26	169	–
Austin, TX	2,272	1,037	108	54	30	24	929	457	255	186	124	30	378	23	166	94	26	1,032	203
Louisville/Jefferson, KY [3]	1,090	975	170	73	89	8	805	515	124	55	–	4	117	11	–	173	93	115	–
Memphis, TN	3,777	1,882	1,149	63	557	529	733	449	301	135	99	5	150	11	102	134	86	1,587	308
Ft. Worth, TX	1,132	712	56	–	56	–	656	417	236	144	102	32	153	5	120	85	32	184	237
Baltimore, MD [3]	3,339	2,922	1,504	262	1,205	38	1,418	1,023	558	87	–	56	261	10	149	134	48	109	308
Charlotte City, NC	1,613	1,507	351	76	114	161	1,157	366	286	39	2	–	398	–	199	392	50	80	26
El Paso, TX	822	627	91	74	17	–	535	339	178	141	107	32	134	3	71	62	20	81	115
Boston, MA	3,626	3,103	1,368	100	1,264	3	1,735	1,333	1,255	40	–	32	194	–	122	209	48	112	411
Seattle, WA	2,481	1,424	144	41	100	3	1,279	784	284	307	146	124	387	42	288	108	23	882	176
Washington, DC.	9,248	8,674	2,589	2,589	–	–	6,085	4,545	1,214	1,257	817	214	574	26	178	966	205	96	369
Milwaukee, WI	1,392	931	442	69	306	67	489	250	237	–	–	26	191	4	109	48	17	59	402
Denver, CO [3]	2,472	2,121	237	17	219	2	1,884	849	226	534	460	54	810	45	70	225	72	166	185
Las Vegas, NV	883	882	401	22	272	107	481	233	121	60	–	15	185	11	78	63	15	–	–
Nashville-Davidson, TN [3]	3,237	1,955	446	8	438	–	1,509	1,101	720	327	271	31	236	9	82	172	99	1,008	275
Oklahoma City, OK	1,069	950	96	56	39	2	854	451	45	358	319	–	268	12	84	135	33	78	41
Portland, OR	1,053	961	181	54	71	56	780	419	254	65	–	49	294	24	205	67	33	91	1
Tucson, AZ	953	756	265	79	170	15	492	305	54	243	196	28	149	21	38	37	6	126	72
Albuquerque, NM.	1,146	1,047	321	28	259	33	727	414	102	248	219	19	239	15	98	74	43	98	–
Atlanta, GA	1,696	1,517	323	118	114	90	1,194	354	186	110	–	38	650	31	148	190	155	146	34

– Represents or rounds to zero. [1] Includes revenue sources not shown separately. [2] Includes water, electric, and transit. [3] Represents, in effect, city-county consolidated government.
Source: U.S. Census Bureau, Federal, State, and Local Governments, *State Government Finances, 2006*, July 2009. See also <http://www.census.gov/govs/>.

Table 456. City Governments—Expenditures and Debt for Largest Cities: 2006

[In millions of dollars (82,454 represents $82,454,000,000). For fiscal year ending in year shown; see headnote, Table 455]

Cities ranked by 2006 population	Total expenditures [1]	Total direct expenditures [1]	General expenditures Total [1]	Education	Housing and community development	Public welfare	Health and hospitals	Police protection	Fire protection	Corrections	Highways	Parks and recreation	Sewerage	Solid waste management	Governmental administration [2]	Interest on general debt	Utility expenditures [3]	Insurance trust expenditures [3]	Debt outstanding
New York, NY [4]	82,454	77,456	66,237	17,472	3,710	9,811	8,976	3,971	1,519	1,314	1,526	559	2,161	1,100	1,178	3,205	8,699	7,517	85,234
Los Angeles, CA	12,315	12,315	7,252	1	275	202	202	1,659	589	–	561	332	498	238	842	410	3,675	1,388	15,723
Chicago, IL	7,622	7,544	6,033	–	257	135	178	1,175	390	20	454	77	101	183	153	756	316	1,272	15,862
Houston, TX	3,982	3,953	3,295	1	255	–	98	571	381	–	139	129	384	67	139	357	307	381	11,403
Phoenix, AZ	3,362	3,349	2,592	18	100	–	–	367	187	13	127	577	198	99	114	251	672	97	7,373
Philadelphia, PA [4]	6,745	6,660	5,077	23	234	555	1,292	510	172	350	71	94	189	98	332	114	1,054	614	5,825
San Antonio, TX	3,625	3,625	1,546	45	35	43	43	242	161	–	112	157	248	57	52	81	2,010	70	6,055
San Diego, CA	2,431	2,418	1,803	–	339	–	44	336	160	9	82	142	290	52	88	70	413	215	2,795
Dallas, TX	2,713	2,704	2,194	–	41	7	27	268	143	8	121	124	196	67	80	229	276	242	8,557
San Jose, CA	1,894	1,866	1,703	–	186	–	15	227	116	–	95	138	144	79	192	204	36	156	4,368
Honolulu, HI [4]	1,473	1,473	1,228	–	46	16	26	180	82	–	107	100	159	137	98	100	246	–	3,155
Detroit, MI	3,349	3,248	2,168	35	98	47	66	447	192	62	146	79	402	107	157	147	627	554	7,515
Jacksonville, FL [4]	3,474	3,343	1,847	–	33	–	84	206	96	75	200	77	198	86	97	217	1,447	180	11,022
Indianapolis, IN	3,412	3,398	2,592	–	268	91	619	188	70	75	110	149	301	40	173	193	741	79	4,125
San Francisco, CA [4]	6,908	6,908	5,305	102	148	605	1,246	317	211	170	143	200	155	–	714	406	1,008	595	8,738
Columbus, OH	1,152	1,144	1,012	–	3	–	32	212	144	10	94	60	193	34	72	93	140	110	1,703
Austin, TX	2,304	2,304	1,159	–	35	10	124	176	88	–	83	96	137	43	58	80	1,036	–	3,887
Louisville/Jefferson, KY [4]	925	924	868	–	39	17	75	130	47	41	15	38	–	18	31	102	57	–	2,520
Memphis, TN	3,508	3,479	1,815	999	36	–	11	180	132	–	65	56	33	43	45	62	1,502	191	2,747
Ft. Worth, TX	1,047	1,047	766	–	21	–	15	161	81	–	85	58	76	35	31	26	197	83	1,231
Baltimore, MD [4]	3,289	3,212	2,930	1,029	86	2	147	348	134	–	192	391	147	69	128	58	101	259	2,287
Charlotte City, NC	1,448	1,436	1,019	–	42	–	5	151	77	–	96	52	253	40	21	44	413	16	2,665
El Paso, TX	725	725	476	–	22	16	16	81	52	–	35	25	44	13	27	25	187	61	1,005
Boston, MA	3,341	3,038	2,813	950	82	150	184	279	160	106	51	34	215	58	55	57	171	357	1,459
Seattle, WA	2,424	2,311	1,400	–	45	36	14	190	135	13	113	195	175	114	67	52	932	93	3,465
Washington, DC	8,543	8,291	8,256	1,478	560	1,846	669	493	176	206	96	332	237	266	434	320	169	118	7,824
Milwaukee, WI	1,302	1,274	1,026	–	123	32	32	218	99	–	132	4	66	76	37	37	72	203	1,199
Denver, CO [4]	2,415	2,357	2,110	–	103	98	55	165	87	75	86	216	79	–	132	289	199	106	5,845
Las Vegas, NV	747	745	745	–	18	1	–	124	105	39	90	80	40	5	117	16	–	1	352
Nashville-Davidson, TN [4]	3,270	3,269	2,046	679	9	28	168	158	101	52	38	72	109	21	105	148	1,084	140	3,837
Oklahoma City, OK	1,115	1,115	960	–	9	–	–	125	111	–	91	83	146	31	137	30	138	17	1,049
Portland, OR	1,210	1,210	1,059	–	54	–	–	137	79	–	162	89	192	3	52	85	71	80	2,524
Tucson, AZ	874	874	694	–	43	–	–	134	56	–	70	71	70	36	71	46	146	35	1,090
Albuquerque, NM	843	843	760	–	32	19	9	122	66	49	55	107	29	45	31	37	83	–	777
Atlanta, GA	2,025	1,979	1,552	–	5	–	–	152	66	36	43	103	185	45	61	87	407	65	6,425

– Represents or rounds to zero. [1] Includes expenditure sources, not shown separately. [2] Excludes public buildings. [3] Includes water, electric, and transit. [4] Represents, in effect, city-county consolidated government.
Source: U.S. Census Bureau, State Government Finances, 2006, July 2009. See also <http://www.census.gov/govs/>.

Table 457. County Governments—Revenue for Largest Counties: 2006

[In millions of dollars (21,586 represents $21,586,000,000). For fiscal year ending in year shown; see text, this section. See Appendix III]

Counties ranked by 2006 population	Total revenue [1]	General revenue Total	Intergov. Total	From federal gov. Total [1]	Housing and community development	From state gov. Total [1]	Public welfare	Health and hospitals	From local government	Own sources Total	Taxes Total [1]	Property	Sales Total	General sales	Current charges Total [1]	Parks and recreation	Sanitation [2]	Hospitals	Misc. Total [1]	Interest earnings
Los Angeles, CA	21,586	17,015	9,177	386	4	8,556	4,815	1,311	235	7,838	3,285	3,009	127	42	3,802	95	83	2,220	751	235
Cook, IL	3,378	2,851	606	41	–	564	287	216	1	2,245	1,536	810	702	358	577	47	–	333	132	49
Harris, TX	3,165	3,165	647	91	23	471	174	216	85	2,518	1,318	1,232	56	–	815	3	–	256	385	245
Maricopa, AZ	2,015	2,015	952	55	9	869	167	27	28	1,062	781	604	144	144	80	4	114	–	202	128
Orange, CA	4,439	3,464	1,926	51	8	1,800	650	172	75	1,538	626	536	46	43	622	42	–	–	289	181
San Diego, CA	5,117	4,027	2,880	167	120	2,447	986	473	266	1,147	686	585	27	18	259	3	24	1,084	201	110
Dade, FL	6,528	6,263	1,353	896	254	413	–	55	44	4,910	1,871	1,283	480	119	2,477	36	508	545	562	289
Dallas, TX	1,662	1,623	254	9	–	233	150	19	12	1,369	649	597	12	–	608	7	–	184	111	29
Riverside, CA	3,399	3,400	1,898	61	13	1,683	904	208	154	1,502	666	534	43	35	581	7	71	331	255	99
San Bernardino, CA	3,919	3,290	2,043	134	18	1,826	918	240	83	1,247	383	326	25	17	680	7	73	10	183	62
Wayne, MI	1,991	1,848	1,117	122	8	862	14	522	134	731	448	423	16	–	229	4	75	–	54	19
King, WA	2,239	2,108	520	135	16	266	–	178	119	1,588	1,005	446	534	431	499	7	333	–	84	51
Broward, FL	2,336	2,270	466	119	10	203	38	6	144	1,804	927	780	124	–	676	16	–	475	201	111
Clark, NV	4,446	3,980	1,051	87	16	792	971	23	173	2,928	1,333	577	484	113	1,082	66	172	688	513	83
Santa Clara, CA	3,497	3,497	1,717	37	3	1,603	7	180	78	1,779	800	605	143	140	872	4	96	146	107	37
Tarrant, TX	1,150	1,150	273	51	24	219	101	189	4	877	515	478	15	–	203	–	3	389	158	124
Bexar, TX	1,113	1,113	203	6	2	188	275	44	9	909	396	363	27	–	421	10	–	–	93	70
Suffolk, NY	2,744	2,592	580	29	7	538	737	153	13	2,012	1,701	556	1,119	1,114	174	24	–	341	137	50
Alameda, CA	3,198	2,696	1,468	31	3	1,399	811	311	38	1,228	480	399	26	15	609	13	24	–	139	66
Sacramento, CA	3,235	2,559	1,563	46	–	1,457	397	202	60	997	428	275	89	63	373	23	–	–	195	65
Nassau, NY	3,347	3,347	769	73	21	696	503	136	0	2,578	1,903	906	965	953	431	2	83	247	244	39
Cuyahoga, OH	2,170	2,170	964	20	19	940	–	260	4	1,206	565	336	184	169	383	5	2	341	258	198
Palm Beach, FL	1,873	1,823	239	102	9	136	282	–	1	1,584	967	685	154	–	421	13	5	–	196	37
Allegheny, PA	1,486	1,419	1,026	63	47	961	6	467	2	393	302	262	38	23	64	4	199	4	27	6
Oakland, MI	1,162	1,051	574	201	6	218	45	61	155	477	350	326	9	–	85	9	–	0	42	15
Hillsborough, FL	1,836	1,663	259	75	32	183	353	–	1	1,404	901	605	274	199	395	2	18	284	108	44
Hennepin, MN	1,843	1,843	854	50	8	785	193	169	19	989	478	459	–	–	388	4	78	3	123	30
Franklin, OH	1,158	1,156	459	14	4	419	5	128	26	696	459	334	104	85	97	3	70	–	140	124
Orange, FL	1,753	1,704	285	85	–	199	391	–	–	1,420	941	506	225	155	322	47	3	–	156	95
Contra Costa, CA	2,506	2,071	899	113	102	705	146	113	81	1,173	406	342	24	10	670	45	24	404	96	33
Fairfax, VA	5,137	4,343	1,024	122	68	874	1	76	28	3,319	2,673	2,117	326	–	426	1	232	–	220	127
St Louis, MO	727	683	71	17	11	54	–	5	–	612	512	152	347	312	78	1	4	–	21	6
Salt Lake, UT	532	532	76	15	–	51	–	–	9	456	346	203	112	79	70	7	12	–	40	5
Fulton, GA	1,162	1,000	102	29	23	70	32	14	10	898	733	522	178	164	71	–	46	–	94	37
Westchester, NY	2,468	2,459	508	14	–	484	245	116	10	1,951	1,041	607	426	407	838	31	30	563	73	46

– Represents or rounds to zero. [1] Includes revenue sources, not shown separately. [2] Includes fee for sewerage and solid waste management.
Source: U.S. Census Bureau, *Survey of State & Local Government Finances, 2006*, July 2009, <http://www.census.gov/govs/>.

Table 458. County Governments—Expenditures and Debt for Largest Counties: 2006

[In millions of dollars (18,720 represents $18,720,720,000,000). For fiscal year ending in year shown; see text, this section and Appendix III]

Counties ranked by 2006 population	Total expenditures[1]	Total direct expenditures[1]	General expenditures: Total[1]	Education	Housing and community development	Public welfare	Health	Hospitals	Police protection	Correction	Highways	Parks and recreation	Natural resources	Sewage and solid waste management	Governmental administration	General public building	Interest on general debt	Utility expenditures[2]	Employee retirement expenditures	Debt outstanding
Los Angeles, CA	18,720	18,439	16,859	890	5	4,515	1,925	2,454	1,213	1,128	273	248	424	66	1,572	114	63	1,798	2,713	3
Cook, IL	3,048	3,036	2,665	–	10	8	41	916	85	350	119	118	–	–	620	149	–	383	3,246	3
Harris, TX	3,207	3,207	3,207	–	12	43	208	888	364	70	266	24	142	–	329	450	–	–	8,538	8
Maricopa, AZ	1,813	1,517	1,813	34	13	376	81	–	69	354	138	8	90	6	391	108	–	–	1,880	2
Orange, CA	3,482	3,428	3,217	244	14	764	528	–	282	253	54	20	67	100	433	174	–	265	2,856	3
San Diego, CA	4,205	3,843	3,879	425	102	989	518	1,380	207	237	175	278	47	29	523	125	587	326	1,845	2
Dade, FL	6,931	6,921	6,344	–	295	298	71	1,010	425	229	153	3	–	502	273	620	–	–	10,985	10
Dallas, TX	1,547	1,547	1,533	4	32	7	42	–	32	99	43	3	–	1	131	22	–	13	423	1
Riverside, CA	3,156	2,994	3,156	367	78	660	325	271	265	177	162	10	66	66	277	74	–	204	1,298	1
San Bernardino, CA	3,335	3,187	3,131	379	9	799	219	376	242	203	74	18	56	71	247	116	–	–	1,912	2
Wayne, MI	1,828	1,771	1,717	–	8	153	474	49	65	250	124	67	46	67	330	50	–	111	643	3
King, WA	2,226	2,180	1,785	–	30	2	344	1	121	127	112	53	9	413	246	163	441	–	3,167	3
Broward, FL	2,215	2,160	2,068	–	15	46	39	–	353	190	43	127	19	149	183	165	147	–	3,225	3
Clark, NV	4,013	3,953	3,487	–	22	187	30	495	467	156	483	319	11	42	268	218	526	–	5,865	5
Santa Clara, CA	3,350	3,274	3,350	214	9	624	365	905	105	258	102	31	4	3	336	58	–	–	910	1
Tarrant, TX	1,034	1,034	1,034	–	23	7	35	446	34	98	35	–	36	–	136	114	–	–	1,981	2
Bexar, TX	1,029	1,004	1,029	–	1	43	52	578	42	73	11	2	1	–	89	67	–	–	933	1
Suffolk, NY	2,750	2,454	2,568	161	7	504	337	–	431	124	42	43	32	79	116	65	182	216	1,797	2
Alameda, CA	2,563	2,559	2,303	39	6	557	319	394	87	271	27	1	36	–	281	41	44	183	1,327	3
Sacramento, CA	2,804	2,741	2,603	154	10	741	430	–	224	253	133	34	4	94	240	81	18	–	2,167	3
Nassau, NY	3,633	3,243	3,631	181	23	573	298	380	683	215	127	61	2	111	189	153	2	–	3,532	3
Cuyahoga, OH	2,131	2,112	2,131	–	20	438	327	576	26	94	54	–	7	13	260	201	–	–	3,338	3
Palm Beach, FL	1,777	1,690	1,686	32	57	72	50	–	216	102	112	92	37	169	193	63	91	60	1,818	3
Allegheny, PA	1,477	1,385	1,416	10	63	351	461	–	32	73	29	62	–	–	106	24	–	36	613	1
Oakland, MI	988	964	926	–	9	7	266	8	52	102	123	9	30	98	131	13	27	–	339	–
Hillsborough, FL	1,911	1,781	1,718	–	32	89	154	–	165	132	109	78	55	75	222	56	193	–	2,174	2
Hennepin, MN	1,856	1,847	1,849	–	23	458	268	480	85	83	108	3	–	52	112	25	7	–	544	1
Franklin, OH	1,164	1,126	1,160	–	7	289	320	–	30	53	47	20	–	6	162	118	3	–	2,178	2
Orange, FL	1,689	1,652	1,675	–	30	79	42	–	142	153	159	36	20	232	128	128	14	–	3,074	3
Contra Costa, CA	2,253	2,198	2,054	127	106	379	189	437	89	116	100	–	28	23	155	58	1	198	1,106	1
Fairfax, VA	4,831	4,759	4,328	2,195	162	227	178	–	196	37	37	144	9	259	174	177	197	306	3,701	4
St Louis, MO	725	495	696	–	10	24	47	–	77	20	83	30	–	4	66	16	4	25	410	–
Salt Lake, UT	519	519	519	–	1	46	26	–	32	63	25	78	5	14	92	6	–	–	197	1
Fulton, GA	1,111	909	952	–	8	62	35	78	65	83	26	4	1	62	259	14	100	59	749	1
Westchester, NY	2,629	2,311	2,586	95	–	455	277	591	41	134	43	56	1	146	107	53	44	–	1,594	1

– Represents or rounds to zero. [1] Includes expenditure categories, not shown separately. [2] Includes water, gas, electric, and transit.

Source: U.S. Census Bureau, State and Local Governments, State & Local Government Finances, 2006, July 2009, <http://www.census.gov/govs/>.

Table 459. Governmental Employment and Payrolls: 1982 to 2008

[Employees in thousands (15,841 represents 15,841,000), payroll in millions of dollars (23,173 represents $23,173,000,000). Data are for the month of October through 1992. Beginning with the 1997 survey, data are for the month of March. Covers both full-time and part-time employees. Local government data are estimates subject to sampling variation; see Appendix III and source]

Type of government	1982	1987	1992	1997	2000	2004	2005	2006	2007	2008
EMPLOYEES (1,000)										
Total.............	**15,841**	**17,212**	**18,745**	**19,540**	**20,876**	**21,493**	**21,725**	**22,048**	**22,116**	**22,462**
Federal (civilian) [1].....	2,848	3,091	3,047	2,807	2,899	2,733	2,720	2,721	2,730	2,769
State and local	12,993	14,121	15,698	16,733	17,976	18,759	19,004	19,327	19,386	19,693
Percent of total	82	82	84	86	86	87	87	88	88	88
State	3,744	4,116	4,595	4,733	4,877	5,041	5,078	5,128	5,200	5,270
Local	9,249	10,005	11,103	12,000	13,099	13,718	13,926	14,199	14,186	14,423
Counties	1,824	1,963	2,253	2,425	(NA)	(NA)	(NA)	(NA)	(NA)	(NA)
Municipalities	2,397	2,493	2,665	2,755	(NA)	(NA)	(NA)	(NA)	(NA)	(NA)
School districts	4,194	4,627	5,134	5,675	(NA)	(NA)	(NA)	(NA)	(NA)	(NA)
Townships	356	393	424	455	(NA)	(NA)	(NA)	(NA)	(NA)	(NA)
Special districts	478	529	627	691	(NA)	(NA)	(NA)	(NA)	(NA)	(NA)
PAYROLLS (mil. dol.)										
Total.............	**23,173**	**32,669**	**43,120**	**49,156**	**58,166**	**68,759**	**71,599**	**74,638**	**78,583**	**83,268**
Federal (civilian) [1].....	5,959	7,924	9,937	9,744	11,485	12,844	13,475	13,896	14,427	15,472
State and local	17,214	24,745	33,183	39,412	46,681	55,914	58,123	60,741	64,156	67,796
Percent of total	74	76	77	80	80	81	81	81	82	81
State	5,022	7,263	9,828	11,413	13,279	15,477	16,062	16,769	17,789	18,726
Local	12,192	17,482	23,355	27,999	33,402	40,437	42,062	43,972	46,368	49,070
Counties	2,287	3,270	4,698	5,750	(NA)	(NA)	(NA)	(NA)	(NA)	(NA)
Municipalities	3,428	4,770	6,207	7,146	(NA)	(NA)	(NA)	(NA)	(NA)	(NA)
School districts	5,442	7,961	10,394	12,579	(NA)	(NA)	(NA)	(NA)	(NA)	(NA)
Townships	370	522	685	869	(NA)	(NA)	(NA)	(NA)	(NA)	(NA)
Special districts	665	959	1,370	1,654	(NA)	(NA)	(NA)	(NA)	(NA)	(NA)

NA Not available. [1] Includes employees outside the United States.

Source: U.S. Census Bureau, Federal, State, and Local Governments, "Government Employment and Payroll Data," May 2010, <http://www.census.gov/govs/apes/>.

Table 460. All Governments—Employment and Payroll by Function: 2008

[Employees in thousands (22,462 represents 22,462,000); payroll in millions of dollars (83,268 represents $83,268,000,000). See headnote, Table 459]

Function	Employees (1,000)					Payrolls (mil. dol.)				
	Employees, total	Federal (civilian) [1]	State and local			Federal (civilian) [1]		State and local		
			Total	State	Local	Total		Total	State	Local
Total	**22,462**	**2,769**	**19,693**	**5,270**	**14,423**	**83,268**	**15,472**	**67,796**	**18,726**	**49,070**
National defense [2]	723	723	(X)	(X)	(X)	3,313	3,313	(X)	(X)	(X)
Postal Service	729	729	(X)	(X)	(X)	3,438	3,438	(X)	(X)	(X)
Space research and technology	18	18	(X)	(X)	(X)	163	163	(X)	(X)	(X)
Elem. and secondary education	7,916	(X)	7,916	65	7,851	25,623	–	25,623	237	25,387
Higher education	3,001	(X)	3,001	2,426	575	8,749	(X)	8,749	7,256	1,492
Other education	111	10	101	101	(X)	459	68	390	390	(X)
Health	634	150	484	192	291	2,851	1,064	1,787	750	1,036
Hospitals	1,274	190	1,084	441	643	5,575	1,297	4,277	1,757	2,521
Public welfare	554	8	546	248	299	1,955	63	1,892	868	1,024
Social insurance administration......	147	66	81	81	(X)	711	388	322	320	3
Police protection	1,196	177	1,019	110	909	5,745	1,046	4,699	541	4,159
Fire protection	449	(X)	449	(X)	449	1,895	(X)	1,895	(X)	1,895
Correction	796	37	759	486	274	3,182	198	2,984	1,921	1,063
Streets & highways	565	3	562	242	320	2,176	21	2,155	1,012	1,143
Air transportation................	96	47	49	3	46	629	405	224	16	209
Water transport/terminals	19	5	14	5	9	80	13	67	25	43
Solid waste management	123	(X)	123	2	121	412	(X)	412	10	402
Sewerage.......................	136	(X)	136	2	134	543	(X)	543	10	532
Parks & recreation................	433	25	408	40	368	998	126	872	115	756
Natural resources	392	182	209	159	50	1,920	1,172	748	588	160
Housing & community development ..	135	16	120	–	120	570	107	463	–	463
Water supply	186	–	186	1	185	730	–	730	4	726
Electric power	81	–	81	4	77	471	–	471	26	445
Gas supply.....................	12	–	12	–	12	46	–	46	–	46
Transit	245	(X)	245	33	212	1,164	(X)	1,164	183	981
Libraries........................	199	4	196	1	195	447	27	420	2	418
State liquor stores	9	(X)	9	9	(X)	23	(X)	23	23	(X)
Financial administration............	562	110	452	177	275	2,390	702	1,688	719	969
Other government administration	485	25	460	61	399	1,357	147	1,210	243	967
Judicial and legal.................	518	62	456	181	276	2,397	419	1,978	862	1,116
Other & unallocable..............	716	183	533	199	334	3,257	1,293	1,965	847	1,118

– Represents or rounds to zero. X Not applicable. [1] Includes employees outside the United States. [2] Includes international relations.

Source: U.S. Census Bureau, Federal, State, and Local Governments, "2008 Annual Survey of Public Employment and Payroll," May 2010. See also <http://www.census.gov/govs/apes/>.

Table 461. State and Local Government—Employer Costs Per Hour Worked: 2010

[In dollars. As of March. Based on a sample; see source for details. Collection of severance pay and supplemental unemployment plans, which comprised "other benefits" and was published in all tables, was discontinued beginning with the March 2006 estimates]

Occupation and industry	Total compen-sation	Wages and salaries	Benefit cost					
			Total	Paid leave	Supple-mental pay	Insur-ance	Retire-ment and savings	Legally required benefits
Total workers	**39.81**	**26.25**	**13.56**	**3.00**	**0.33**	**4.68**	**3.16**	**2.39**
Occupational group:								
Management, professional, and related	48.34	33.09	15.26	3.34	0.25	5.21	3.72	2.73
Professional and related	47.49	32.65	14.84	3.03	0.23	5.22	3.69	2.66
Teachers [1]	54.83	38.85	15.98	2.82	0.14	5.72	4.34	2.96
Primary, secondary, and special education school teachers	53.58	37.96	15.62	2.52	0.15	6.05	4.13	2.78
Sales and office	27.63	16.96	10.67	2.50	0.20	4.23	2.02	1.74
Office and administrative support	27.82	17.03	10.79	2.53	0.19	4.29	2.04	1.73
Service	29.51	17.81	11.70	2.61	0.55	3.77	2.79	1.98
Industry group:								
Education and health services	41.85	28.50	13.35	2.72	0.20	4.92	3.15	2.36
Educational services	42.84	29.38	13.46	2.64	0.15	5.00	3.29	2.37
Elementary and secondary schools	42.49	29.22	13.27	2.29	0.15	5.17	3.36	2.30
Junior colleges, colleges, and universities	44.28	30.13	14.15	3.80	0.13	4.51	3.11	2.59
Health care and social assistance	34.90	22.29	12.61	3.25	0.61	4.31	2.16	2.28
Hospitals	37.01	23.69	13.33	3.48	0.74	4.53	2.19	2.38
Public administration	37.69	23.24	14.46	3.61	0.56	4.44	3.41	2.44

[1] Includes postsecondary teachers; primary, secondary, and special education teachers; and other teachers and instructors.

Source: U.S. Bureau of Labor Statistics, *National Compensation Survey, Benefits, Archives, 2010 National Survey Compensation Publications List, Employer Costs for Employee Compensation*, News Release, March 2010, <http://www.bls.gov/ncs/ncspubs.htm>.

Table 462. State and Local Government—Full-Time Employment and Salary by Sex and Race and Ethnic Group: 1980 to 2007

[As of June 30. (2,350 represents 2,350,000). Excludes school systems and educational institutions. Based on reports from state governments (42 in 1980; 47 in 1983; 42 in 1980; 47 in 1983; 49 in 1981 and 1984 through 1987; 49 in 1981 and 1984 through 1987; and 50 in 1989 through 1991) and a sample of county, municipal, township, and special district jurisdictions employing 15 or more nonelected, nonappointed full-time employees. Beginning 1993, only for state and local governments with 100 or more employees. For definition of median, see Guide to Tabular Presentation]

Year and occupation	Employment (1,000)						Median annual salary ($1,000)					
				Minority						Minority		
	Male	Female	White[1]	Total[2]	Black[1]	His-panic[3]	Male	Female	White[1]	Total[2]	Black[1]	His-panic[3]
1980	2,350	1,637	3,146	842	619	163	15.2	11.4	13.8	11.8	11.5	12.3
1981	2,740	1,925	3,591	1,074	780	205	17.7	13.1	16.1	13.5	13.3	14.7
1983	2,674	1,818	3,423	1,069	768	219	20.1	15.3	18.5	15.9	15.6	17.3
1984	2,700	1,880	3,458	1,121	799	233	21.4	16.2	19.6	17.4	16.5	18.4
1985	2,789	1,952	3,563	1,179	835	248	22.3	17.3	20.6	18.4	17.5	19.2
1986	2,797	1,982	3,549	1,230	865	259	23.4	18.1	21.5	19.6	18.7	20.2
1987	2,818	2,031	3,600	1,249	872	268	24.2	18.9	22.4	20.9	19.3	21.1
1989	3,030	2,227	3,863	1,394	961	308	26.1	20.6	24.1	22.1	20.7	22.7
1990	3,071	2,302	3,918	1,456	994	327	27.3	21.8	25.2	23.3	22.0	23.8
1991	3,110	2,349	3,965	1,494	1,011	340	28.4	22.7	26.4	23.8	22.7	24.5
1993	2,820	2,204	3,588	1,436	948	341	30.6	24.3	28.5	25.9	24.2	26.8
1995	2,960	2,355	3,781	1,534	993	379	33.5	27.0	31.4	26.3	26.8	28.6
1997	2,898	2,307	3,676	1,529	973	392	34.6	27.9	32.2	30.2	27.4	29.5
1999	2,939	2,393	3,723	1,609	1,012	417	37.0	29.9	34.8	31.1	29.6	31.2
2001	3,080	2,554	3,888	1,746	1,077	471	39.8	32.1	37.5	34.0	31.5	33.8
2003	3,134	2,610	3,919	1,826	1,097	508	42.2	34.7	40.0	35.9	33.6	36.6
2005	3,185	2,644	3,973	1,856	1,100	532	44.1	36.4	41.5	37.7	35.3	38.9
2007, total	3,383	2,823	4,156	2,051	1,138	661	(NA)	(NA)	(NA)	(NA)	(NA)	(NA)
Officials/administrators	243	154	316	80	46	23	(NA)	(NA)	(NA)	(NA)	(NA)	(NA)
Professionals	709	923	1,148	485	249	133	(NA)	(NA)	(NA)	(NA)	(NA)	(NA)
Technicians	288	208	340	156	76	54	(NA)	(NA)	(NA)	(NA)	(NA)	(NA)
Protective service	1,019	250	876	392	222	142	(NA)	(NA)	(NA)	(NA)	(NA)	(NA)
Paraprofessionals	107	290	226	171	109	48	(NA)	(NA)	(NA)	(NA)	(NA)	(NA)
Admiminstrative support	135	829	610	354	186	129	(NA)	(NA)	(NA)	(NA)	(NA)	(NA)
Skilled craft	426	23	320	129	70	46	(NA)	(NA)	(NA)	(NA)	(NA)	(NA)
Service/maintenance	456	146	319	283	180	85	(NA)	(NA)	(NA)	(NA)	(NA)	(NA)

NA Not available [1] Non-Hispanic. [2] Includes other minority groups, not shown separately. [3] Persons of Hispanic origin may be any race.

Source: U.S. Equal Employment Opportunity Commission, 1980–1991, "State and Local Government Information Report," annual; beginning 1993, biennial.

Table 463. State and Local Government Full-Time Equivalent Employment by Selected Function and State: 2008

[In thousands (1,780.3 represents 1,780,300). For March. Local government amounts are estimates subject to sampling variation; see Appendix III and source]

State	Education Total [1] State	Education Total [1] Local	Education Elementary and secondary State	Education Elementary and secondary Local	Education Higher education State	Education Higher education Local	Public welfare State	Public welfare Local	Health State	Health Local	Hospitals State	Hospitals Local
United States	1,780.3	7,135.3	53.0	6,804.9	1,633.7	330.5	242.9	280.1	185.7	260.4	414.5	583.7
Alabama	41.3	104.6	–	104.6	38.0	–	4.4	1.2	6.1	5.3	11.8	25.8
Alaska	8.8	16.7	3.3	16.6	5.3	0.1	1.8	0.2	0.7	0.3	0.2	0.7
Arizona	31.8	149.2	–	136.6	28.4	12.6	5.7	2.4	3.3	4.1	0.7	3.0
Arkansas	25.9	69.9	–	69.7	24.3	0.1	4.0	0.1	4.9	0.3	5.9	1.8
California	154.5	763.6	–	692.5	150.3	71.1	3.8	66.9	12.3	48.3	40.9	63.0
Colorado	38.1	103.1	–	101.8	36.8	1.2	2.2	6.1	1.2	4.2	5.2	9.7
Connecticut	21.3	88.9	–	88.9	18.5	–	5.8	1.6	2.1	1.4	9.9	–
Delaware	8.1	17.7	–	17.7	7.7	–	1.8	–	2.3	0.4	1.8	–
District of Columbia	–	11.9	–	11.1	–	0.8	–	2.1	–	0.9	–	1.9
Florida	60.9	364.6	–	337.0	57.2	27.6	9.4	6.5	22.9	10.1	3.0	50.8
Georgia	56.5	252.7	–	252.7	53.2	–	8.8	1.6	5.5	10.4	7.8	20.3
Hawaii	37.5	–	28.4	–	9.0	–	0.9	0.1	2.4	0.2	4.3	–
Idaho	8.7	32.7	–	31.3	8.2	1.4	1.8	0.1	1.2	1.1	0.8	6.5
Illinois.	58.8	307.7	–	285.0	56.7	22.7	10.0	6.0	2.6	8.0	10.9	11.2
Indiana.	56.9	149.1	–	149.1	55.8	–	4.9	1.2	1.9	3.5	2.6	26.1
Iowa.	26.2	79.9	–	72.9	25.0	7.1	3.1	1.0	0.4	2.0	8.3	11.7
Kansas.	21.2	94.8	–	86.8	20.6	8.0	2.5	1.0	1.3	3.3	3.1	8.4
Kentucky	37.5	112.1	–	112.1	34.9	–	6.5	0.5	2.2	5.4	5.4	4.3
Louisiana	36.7	103.5	1.2	103.5	29.7	–	6.0	0.9	4.0	1.7	14.7	17.3
Maine.	7.8	38.2	–	38.2	7.5	–	3.1	0.4	1.1	0.3	0.6	0.8
Maryland	29.2	136.2	–	125.5	26.9	10.8	6.7	3.5	6.9	4.5	4.8	–
Massachusetts.	31.4	149.5	0.1	149.4	30.1	0.1	7.1	2.7	7.8	3.1	7.8	4.0
Michigan	70.2	211.4	0.1	197.6	69.6	13.8	9.6	2.6	2.0	9.0	18.7	8.9
Minnesota	40.0	118.9	–	118.9	36.2	–	3.0	10.3	2.4	3.9	5.4	10.0
Mississippi	21.1	82.3	–	75.4	19.5	6.9	2.5	0.2	2.9	0.3	12.1	17.9
Missouri	29.9	148.5	–	141.6	28.2	6.9	8.1	2.8	2.8	4.3	11.6	11.9
Montana.	7.3	21.6	–	21.3	6.9	0.3	1.7	0.5	0.9	0.9	0.6	0.8
Nebraska	13.0	50.5	–	47.6	12.4	2.9	2.6	0.8	0.7	0.7	3.9	4.8
Nevada	10.8	45.2	–	45.2	10.7	–	1.6	0.9	1.3	0.8	1.5	4.4
New Hampshire.	6.9	35.7	–	35.7	6.6	–	1.6	2.7	1.0	0.2	0.8	–
New Jersey	55.1	217.4	19.3	206.5	32.7	10.9	9.1	10.0	4.2	4.6	18.9	2.5
New Mexico	20.4	51.7	–	48.1	19.2	3.6	1.9	0.9	2.4	0.5	6.9	1.0
New York	55.2	500.3	–	475.6	50.5	24.6	6.5	49.6	10.0	20.1	45.9	63.0
North Carolina	59.1	250.4	–	230.6	56.0	19.8	2.1	15.9	5.0	15.6	17.6	41.4
North Dakota	8.2	14.5	–	14.5	7.9	–	0.5	0.9	1.3	0.6	0.9	–
Ohio.	72.1	257.1	–	252.0	69.5	5.1	2.9	24.0	3.6	17.8	15.4	12.1
Oklahoma	32.5	91.6	–	91.3	30.5	0.4	7.1	0.3	6.0	1.3	2.9	10.5
Oregon.	21.2	75.3	–	67.3	20.4	7.9	6.9	1.0	1.5	4.3	5.0	2.5
Pennsylvania	62.1	265.8	–	255.8	57.7	9.9	12.0	20.2	1.8	5.1	11.8	0.8
Rhode Island	7.0	20.2	0.6	20.2	5.8	–	1.6	0.1	1.2	0.1	1.1	–
South Carolina.	32.2	107.4	–	107.4	29.4	–	4.5	0.4	6.3	2.4	7.4	21.9
South Dakota.	5.1	19.7	–	19.2	4.7	0.5	1.1	0.2	0.7	0.2	0.9	0.4
Tennessee	35.6	128.1	–	128.1	33.3	–	8.2	2.0	5.1	4.4	6.5	22.8
Texas	119.1	710.0	–	669.9	114.3	40.2	24.4	3.7	13.3	24.9	29.0	51.1
Utah.	24.1	51.9	–	51.9	22.9	–	3.2	0.6	1.8	1.3	7.0	0.5
Vermont	5.7	19.3	–	19.3	5.1	–	1.4	–	0.7	–	0.3	–
Virginia.	57.5	198.1	–	196.6	54.5	1.5	2.7	8.4	5.4	6.0	15.2	2.6
Washington	56.4	102.8	–	102.8	54.3	–	10.0	1.5	5.3	4.2	9.8	15.3
West Virginia	14.4	42.4	–	42.4	13.1	–	3.3	–	0.8	1.2	1.6	2.5
Wisconsin	35.0	130.1	–	120.5	33.9	9.6	1.5	12.9	1.6	6.4	3.4	1.0
Wyoming	3.9	20.6	–	18.6	3.7	2.0	0.8	0.1	0.7	0.5	0.9	5.7

See footnote at end of table.

U.S. Census Bureau, Statistical Abstract of the United States: 2011

Table 463. State and Local Government Full-Time Equivalent Employment by Selected Function and State: 2008—Con.

[See headnote, page 302]

States	Highways		Police protection		Fire protection		Corrections		Parks and recreation	
	State	Local	State	Local	State	Local	State	Local	State	Local
United States	**237.0**	**302.7**	**108.0**	**844.1**	**(X)**	**349.6**	**481.4**	**266.2**	**34.9**	**236.9**
Alabama	4.6	7.0	1.4	12.3	(X)	5.8	5.1	3.3	0.6	4.1
Alaska	3.0	0.7	0.4	1.3	(X)	0.8	1.8	0.1	0.1	0.6
Arizona	3.0	4.6	2.2	19.7	(X)	10.6	10.5	5.9	0.4	6.8
Arkansas	3.6	3.6	1.2	7.1	(X)	2.6	5.2	2.2	0.7	1.1
California	20.8	24.7	13.2	97.7	(X)	36.4	60.7	34.0	3.4	35.5
Colorado	3.2	5.9	1.2	13.2	(X)	6.3	7.2	3.9	0.3	7.3
Connecticut	3.1	3.5	2.1	8.8	(X)	4.4	7.7	–	0.2	2.0
Delaware	1.6	0.6	1.0	1.5	(X)	0.2	3.0	–	0.3	0.3
District of Columbia	–	0.7	–	3.7	(X)	2.1	–	0.9	–	1.0
Florida	7.4	14.7	4.4	65.1	(X)	27.3	29.0	17.5	1.4	19.1
Georgia	5.9	8.8	2.1	25.6	(X)	12.2	20.4	10.0	2.5	5.8
Hawaii	0.9	0.9	–	3.9	(X)	1.9	2.4	–	0.2	1.9
Idaho	1.6	1.8	0.5	3.7	(X)	1.6	2.0	1.4	0.2	0.8
Illinois	6.6	11.9	3.9	42.9	(X)	17.7	12.1	9.6	0.6	15.5
Indiana	4.6	6.1	2.1	15.9	(X)	7.9	7.5	6.1	0.2	3.2
Iowa	2.4	5.7	1.0	6.0	(X)	1.9	3.4	1.4	0.1	2.0
Kansas	3.4	5.2	1.1	8.4	(X)	3.3	3.8	3.2	0.6	2.9
Kentucky	4.6	3.2	2.3	7.9	(X)	4.5	4.1	4.6	1.3	2.1
Louisiana	4.8	5.5	1.7	16.8	(X)	5.9	7.7	6.9	1.0	4.2
Maine	2.4	1.8	0.5	2.7	(X)	2.0	1.3	0.8	0.2	0.7
Maryland	4.8	5.0	2.4	15.0	(X)	6.7	12.3	3.5	0.4	6.3
Massachusetts	3.6	6.8	6.7	19.3	(X)	14.9	6.1	2.8	0.6	2.5
Michigan	2.9	8.9	2.7	19.7	(X)	8.2	16.0	6.0	0.3	3.9
Minnesota	4.4	6.9	1.0	10.6	(X)	2.7	4.1	5.0	0.6	4.6
Mississippi	3.3	4.7	1.3	8.0	(X)	3.3	3.6	1.8	0.4	1.2
Missouri	6.5	7.3	2.4	16.2	(X)	6.8	12.3	3.2	0.6	4.5
Montana	2.2	1.4	0.5	2.1	(X)	0.7	1.2	0.6	0.1	0.5
Nebraska	2.1	2.9	0.7	4.0	(X)	1.4	2.9	1.5	0.3	1.0
Nevada	1.8	1.4	0.8	8.0	(X)	2.8	3.8	2.9	0.2	3.8
New Hampshire	1.8	1.6	0.5	3.5	(X)	1.9	1.3	0.7	0.2	0.5
New Jersey	7.0	10.5	4.6	31.6	(X)	8.8	10.3	7.1	2.2	5.7
New Mexico	2.6	2.0	0.7	5.4	(X)	2.2	4.1	2.1	0.8	2.5
New York	12.7	29.0	6.7	80.2	(X)	25.2	34.2	26.3	2.7	12.1
North Carolina	11.1	4.0	4.0	23.2	(X)	8.8	21.7	5.0	1.1	6.3
North Dakota	1.1	1.0	0.2	1.3	(X)	0.3	0.7	0.3	0.2	0.8
Ohio	7.1	13.3	2.7	30.4	(X)	17.4	16.6	9.5	0.6	8.4
Oklahoma	3.0	5.4	2.0	9.3	(X)	4.1	5.7	1.2	0.9	1.9
Oregon	3.4	3.8	1.3	7.8	(X)	3.9	5.5	3.6	0.5	3.3
Pennsylvania	13.4	12.0	6.4	27.9	(X)	6.1	17.5	13.3	1.7	3.6
Rhode Island	0.8	0.8	0.3	3.1	(X)	2.3	1.7	–	0.1	1.0
South Carolina	4.9	2.4	2.1	11.5	(X)	5.1	8.1	2.8	0.6	3.2
South Dakota	1.0	1.4	0.3	1.7	(X)	0.5	0.9	0.6	0.1	0.5
Tennessee	4.3	7.2	2.3	17.6	(X)	7.7	7.4	5.9	1.2	3.1
Texas	15.6	20.6	4.3	62.1	(X)	24.1	44.6	27.9	1.2	16.4
Utah	1.7	1.5	0.9	5.3	(X)	2.2	3.3	2.1	0.3	2.8
Vermont	1.0	1.2	0.6	0.9	(X)	0.4	1.2	–	0.1	0.2
Virginia	8.8	5.2	3.2	20.9	(X)	10.4	15.0	8.9	1.0	8.9
Washington	7.8	7.2	2.0	13.4	(X)	8.8	9.5	4.7	0.7	5.8
West Virginia	5.2	0.9	1.0	2.8	(X)	1.0	3.4	0.2	0.6	0.9
Wisconsin	1.7	8.6	0.9	15.4	(X)	5.0	10.5	3.9	0.2	2.8
Wyoming	1.9	0.8	0.3	1.8	(X)	0.5	1.0	0.6	0.1	0.8

- Represents or rounds to zero. X Not applicable. [1] Includes other categories, not shown separately.

Source: U.S. Census Bureau, "2008 Annual Survey of Public Employment and Payroll," May 2010. See also <http://www.census.gov/govs/apes/>.

Table 464. State and Local Government Employment and Average Monthly Earnings by State: 2000 to 2008

[4,083 represents 4,083,000. As of March. Full-time equivalent employment is a derived statistic that provides an estimate of a government's total full-time employment by converting part-time employees to a full-time amount]

State	Full-time equivalent employment (1,000)						Average monthly earnings [2] (dol.)					
	State			Local [1]			State			Local [1]		
	2000	2007	2008	2000	2007	2008	2000	2007	2008	2000	2007	2008
United States	4,083	4,307	4,363	10,995	12,147	12,305	3,374	4,276	4,445	3,169	3,945	4,124
Alabama	80	89	89	182	196	199	2,841	3,785	3,990	2,431	3,017	3,155
Alaska	23	26	26	25	27	28	3,842	4,565	4,659	3,818	4,442	4,652
Arizona	65	68	73	182	232	251	3,055	4,004	4,257	2,942	4,074	4,161
Arkansas	49	59	61	96	106	105	2,842	3,301	3,459	2,175	2,779	2,866
California	355	387	394	1,322	1,448	1,452	4,451	5,684	5,913	4,062	5,392	5,652
Colorado	66	68	69	164	195	195	3,779	4,722	4,901	3,076	3,858	4,067
Connecticut	66	62	66	111	126	125	3,909	5,187	5,480	3,856	4,545	4,843
Delaware	24	26	27	21	25	24	3,222	4,117	4,177	3,163	3,875	4,494
District of Columbia.....	(X)	(X)	(X)	45	47	47	(X)	(X)	(X)	3,923	5,174	5,403
Florida	185	189	189	580	702	720	3,149	3,734	3,808	2,865	3,801	4,010
Georgia	120	126	130	334	393	409	2,899	3,590	3,724	2,677	3,261	3,391
Hawaii	55	57	60	14	14	15	2,926	3,981	4,065	3,352	4,464	4,791
Idaho	23	22	23	51	58	59	3,022	3,976	4,106	2,478	3,088	3,258
Illinois	128	125	129	493	520	519	3,441	4,802	4,914	3,307	4,075	4,272
Indiana	83	90	91	232	250	263	2,990	3,752	4,073	2,711	3,322	3,423
Iowa	55	53	55	121	129	128	3,656	4,927	5,165	2,727	3,328	3,511
Kansas..............	43	45	46	128	143	149	3,071	3,753	3,895	2,491	3,149	3,242
Kentucky	74	80	81	149	167	165	3,051	3,609	3,878	2,339	2,786	2,996
Louisiana	95	85	92	185	180	190	2,807	3,663	4,007	2,278	2,896	3,104
Maine...............	21	23	23	51	54	55	2,983	3,838	3,967	2,609	3,209	3,280
Maryland	91	90	89	182	210	211	3,312	4,371	4,492	3,535	4,595	4,910
Massachusetts........	96	96	98	232	239	245	3,683	4,758	4,823	3,403	4,380	4,518
Michigan	142	145	141	351	349	334	3,934	4,672	4,746	3,518	4,173	4,417
Minnesota	73	78	79	206	203	201	3,892	4,808	5,070	3,255	4,043	4,265
Mississippi	56	56	57	133	133	134	2,752	3,283	3,365	2,121	2,745	2,865
Missouri	91	90	89	208	238	239	2,678	3,213	3,291	2,678	3,158	3,307
Montana	18	20	20	34	36	35	2,931	3,797	3,822	2,546	3,052	3,261
Nebraska.............	30	32	32	78	81	85	2,514	3,522	3,695	2,779	3,506	3,669
Nevada	22	29	28	61	82	86	3,444	4,657	4,752	3,817	4,675	4,942
New Hampshire	19	20	20	46	53	52	3,079	4,048	4,367	2,830	3,521	3,776
New Jersey	133	156	156	316	357	350	4,075	5,375	5,580	3,967	4,914	5,158
New Mexico...........	48	52	49	70	81	81	2,811	3,577	3,767	2,494	2,946	3,191
New York............	251	253	255	924	979	981	3,859	4,908	5,052	3,961	4,736	4,858
North Carolina	123	143	146	328	399	421	3,012	3,722	3,931	2,708	3,319	3,496
North Dakota	16	18	18	23	24	23	2,826	3,409	3,639	2,778	3,537	3,662
Ohio................	136	143	143	459	470	478	3,369	4,459	4,635	3,118	3,745	3,897
Oklahoma	64	70	72	134	146	144	2,821	3,594	3,699	2,280	2,849	2,924
Oregon..............	53	60	60	124	131	130	3,269	4,055	4,463	3,332	4,019	4,210
Pennsylvania	150	160	162	388	434	434	3,436	4,138	4,188	3,296	3,885	4,021
Rhode Island	20	20	20	36	33	32	3,772	4,795	4,853	3,550	4,471	4,631
South Carolina........	79	76	78	155	178	183	2,741	3,376	3,530	2,474	3,069	3,374
South Dakota	13	14	13	28	30	30	2,777	3,538	3,591	2,359	2,903	3,028
Tennessee	81	85	86	218	240	242	2,786	3,515	3,794	2,631	3,189	3,276
Texas	269	290	290	909	1,054	1,081	3,095	3,868	4,057	2,643	3,277	3,465
Utah	49	51	51	73	81	84	2,880	3,963	4,152	2,836	3,576	3,857
Vermont..............	14	15	15	23	25	25	3,153	4,193	4,333	2,534	3,384	3,525
Virginia	119	125	128	269	317	323	3,229	4,054	4,163	2,928	3,687	3,829
Washington	112	120	123	193	220	227	3,551	4,405	4,581	3,835	4,783	5,050
West Virginia	32	38	39	61	63	63	2,694	3,210	3,347	2,517	2,932	2,942
Wisconsin	64	69	69	220	213	214	3,710	4,617	4,780	3,210	3,876	3,958
Wyoming	11	13	13	29	35	36	2,589	3,613	3,727	2,660	3,598	3,858

X Not applicable. [1] Estimates subject to sampling variation; see Appendix III and source. [2] For full-time employees.
Source: U.S. Census Bureau, "2008 Annual Survey of Public Employment and Payroll," May 2010. See also <http://www.census.gov/govs/apes/>.

Table 465. City Government Employment and Payroll—Largest Cities: 2000 to 2008

[In thousands (458.1 represents 458,100), except as noted. As of March. See footnote 2, Table 455, for those areas representing city-county consolidated governments. See headnote, Table 464 for full-time equivalent employment definition]

Cities ranked by 2007 population [1]	Total employment (1,000)			Full-time equivalent employment total (1,000)			Payroll (mil. dol.)			Average earnings for full-time employees (dol.)		
	2000	2007	2008	2000	2007	2008	2000	2007	2008	2000	2007	2008
New York, NY	458.1	448.5	467.0	429.3	422.5	430.3	1,708.8	2,067.8	2,166.3	4,150	5,044	5,091
Los Angeles, CA	49.4	57.0	56.2	48.4	55.8	52.1	230.1	358.4	364.5	4,793	6,484	7,264
Chicago, IL	41.3	40.0	38.7	40.7	39.5	37.9	171.3	172.5	191.5	4,239	4,395	5,072
Houston, TX	25.2	21.7	22.1	24.9	21.5	21.7	75.2	80.3	89.2	3,037	3,753	4,100
Phoenix, AZ	13.0	16.1	18.1	12.7	16.0	17.2	50.3	113.0	104.8	4,024	7,278	6,285
Philadelphia, PA	31.1	31.1	31.1	30.0	30.2	30.3	109.2	139.0	144.3	3,637	4,618	4,786
San Antonio, TX	16.9	16.6	16.1	15.7	15.8	15.5	48.0	59.0	60.6	3,160	3,818	3,998
San Diego, CA	12.3	11.6	11.4	11.4	10.7	10.6	46.9	57.6	60.2	4,201	5,517	5,847
Dallas, TX	15.6	15.2	15.7	15.2	14.9	15.3	50.4	68.5	71.8	3,332	4,663	4,763
San Jose, CA	7.6	7.4	7.8	6.9	6.6	6.8	36.3	47.5	50.8	5,569	7,593	7,847
Detroit, MI	40.7	13.9	13.8	36.1	13.7	13.7	132.1	53.9	57.6	3,693	3,953	4,225
Honolulu, HI	9.8	9.3	9.5	9.1	8.6	8.9	30.9	38.6	42.1	3,435	4,575	4,827
Jacksonville, FL	10.1	10.5	14.5	9.7	10.3	13.7	35.6	43.2	61.3	3,815	4,248	4,533
Indianapolis, IN	12.4	17.2	15.5	12.0	15.9	14.6	36.7	57.8	55.4	3,115	3,617	3,803
San Francisco, CA	27.7	29.5	30.8	27.7	28.0	29.1	141.6	196.6	210.6	5,112	7,253	7,482
Columbus, OH	9.1	8.7	8.8	8.8	8.4	8.4	30.1	38.8	40.9	3,478	4,688	4,904
Austin, TX	10.6	12.3	13.0	10.1	11.9	12.6	31.2	54.2	58.9	3,128	4,583	4,718
Louisville, KY	4.6	8.1	7.9	4.3	7.8	7.6	11.8	28.1	29.1	2,844	3,707	3,909
Ft. Worth, TX	6.1	6.1	7.0	5.7	5.8	6.7	18.9	25.1	29.2	3,394	4,470	4,446
Memphis, TN	28.2	28.5	25.9	26.9	25.7	24.7	80.3	95.2	84.0	3,024	3,796	3,459
Charlotte, NC	5.2	6.5	6.7	5.1	6.3	6.5	17.1	26.6	28.2	3,408	4,265	4,377
Baltimore, MD	30.8	29.3	28.4	29.2	27.6	26.9	95.3	121.0	128.0	3,361	4,463	4,866
El Paso, TX	5.9	5.9	5.9	5.8	5.7	5.8	15.6	18.3	21.1	2,701	3,225	3,703
Milwaukee, WI	7.9	6.9	7.2	7.7	6.7	7.0	28.5	29.2	34.6	3,706	4,387	5,036
Boston, MA	23.3	21.3	21.8	22.0	20.3	20.5	80.2	100.6	107.0	3,734	5,019	5,283
Seattle, WA	11.4	11.8	14.0	10.3	10.9	12.6	48.3	60.3	67.7	4,726	5,773	5,556
Nashville, TN	20.6	23.2	23.3	19.6	21.7	21.6	62.3	85.3	87.2	3,235	4,010	4,167
Denver, CO	14.5	13.3	13.6	13.7	12.6	12.7	47.3	61.1	68.8	3,534	4,953	5,549
Washington, DC	37.7	38.4	38.9	36.5	36.8	37.3	139.4	185.2	193.7	3,863	5,150	5,309
Las Vegas, NV	2.6	3.2	3.3	2.5	3.0	3.1	11.2	19.3	20.0	4,681	6,548	6,687
Portland, OR	6.2	6.7	6.9	5.4	5.8	6.0	23.4	31.6	32.8	4,416	5,624	5,680
Oklahoma City, OK	5.1	4.7	4.6	4.8	4.4	4.4	16.0	20.8	21.6	3,457	4,790	5,033
Tucson, AZ	7.1	6.3	6.4	5.8	5.8	5.9	16.0	26.2	27.4	2,787	4,697	4,836
Atlanta, GA	8.8	10.0	7.9	8.6	9.6	7.9	25.6	36.2	29.8	2,974	3,795	3,749
Albuquerque, NM	7.1	8.0	7.2	6.6	7.6	6.8	18.3	18.5	23.1	2,868	2,523	3,507
Fresno, CA	3.2	4.9	4.7	3.1	4.3	4.4	12.7	20.3	22.2	4,073	4,857	5,350
Long Beach, CA	6.1	5.8	6.4	5.7	5.4	6.0	25.7	29.9	32.8	4,855	5,816	5,806
Sacramento, CA	4.4	5.6	5.6	4.0	4.8	4.9	17.0	31.5	30.0	4,400	7,208	6,537
Mesa, AZ	3.5	4.7	4.0	3.3	4.5	3.8	13.4	23.2	20.7	4,072	5,270	5,494
Kansas, MO	6.8	6.7	6.8	6.6	6.7	6.4	21.3	27.2	29.2	3,246	4,114	4,283
Cleveland, OH	10.1	7.8	8.1	9.4	7.6	7.9	27.8	31.5	35.4	2,989	4,133	4,470
Virginia Beach, VA	19.7	19.7	19.3	17.4	18.0	17.8	43.4	61.8	60.9	2,679	3,715	3,724
Omaha, NE	3.4	3.1	3.0	2.9	2.8	2.8	10.6	13.5	13.5	3,874	4,974	5,147
Miami, FL	3.8	4.3	4.1	3.6	4.2	4.0	15.1	21.9	23.0	4,276	5,381	5,977
Oakland, CA	4.2	5.2	5.4	4.2	5.2	5.4	24.8	35.1	37.7	5,861	6,825	7,044
Tulsa, OK	4.5	4.4	4.4	4.5	4.3	4.3	13.7	16.9	17.2	3,126	3,930	4,062
Minneapolis, MN	6.3	6.0	5.5	5.8	5.5	5.2	21.3	25.4	25.1	3,866	4,747	4,957
Colorado Springs, CO	7.4	7.7	7.7	6.9	7.1	7.2	25.3	33.4	34.8	3,747	4,738	4,905
Raleigh, NC	3.2	4.1	4.1	2.9	3.6	3.6	8.9	13.5	13.9	3,114	3,978	4,040
Arlington, TX	3.0	2.7	2.9	2.4	2.4	2.5	7.1	10.7	11.8	3,090	4,733	4,941
Wichita, KS	3.6	3.9	4.0	3.1	3.2	3.3	9.3	12.0	13.3	3,072	3,772	4,165
St. Louis, MO	8.0	6.7	6.8	7.6	6.5	6.5	24.1	24.8	27.1	3,176	3,806	4,170
Santa Ana, CA	2.5	1.9	2.1	2.2	1.7	1.8	10.1	12.1	13.3	5,606	7,597	7,813
Tampa, FL	4.3	4.8	4.6	4.2	4.8	4.5	14.1	20.3	20.5	3,370	4,341	4,589
Anaheim, CA	3.2	3.8	3.7	2.5	2.7	2.8	11.5	16.8	17.5	5,267	7,403	7,591
Cincinnati, OH	6.5	6.4	5.9	6.4	5.8	5.6	21.3	24.4	26.4	3,504	4,481	4,967
Bakersfield, CA	1.3	1.6	1.6	1.2	1.5	1.6	5.3	8.2	8.3	4,469	5,439	5,400
Aurora, CO	2.5	2.8	2.7	2.5	2.8	2.7	9.0	13.4	13.7	3,682	4,823	5,105
Pittsburgh, PA	4.4	3.2	5.1	4.3	3.2	5.1	15.3	14.8	23.6	3,593	4,665	4,712
Toledo, OH	2.8	2.9	3.0	2.8	2.9	3.0	10.0	13.2	13.2	3,628	4,611	4,406
Riverside, CA	2.1	2.6	2.7	1.9	2.3	2.5	8.0	13.5	14.5	4,625	6,160	6,325
Stockton, CA	2.3	2.2	2.2	1.9	1.8	1.8	7.1	10.3	10.6	4,054	5,938	6,187
Corpus Christi, TX	3.5	3.2	3.2	3.3	3.1	3.2	8.6	10.6	11.5	2,675	3,486	3,608
Newark, NJ	5.5	4.2	4.4	5.2	3.7	3.7	22.3	16.7	17.5	4,371	4,678	4,926
Anchorage, AK	10.1	10.9	10.9	9.0	9.8	9.8	34.6	44.8	45.8	3,973	4,731	4,760
Lexington, KY	4.0	4.8	4.9	3.6	4.2	4.3	10.2	14.8	15.6	2,910	3,784	4,008
St. Paul, MN	4.2	3.2	3.3	3.2	3.0	3.0	13.3	14.6	15.2	4,189	5,143	5,283
Buffalo, NY	11.4	12.6	10.8	10.5	11.5	9.9	43.4	48.0	45.4	4,457	4,275	4,747
Plano, TX	2.0	2.4	2.6	1.8	2.2	2.3	6.4	10.7	10.5	3,702	5,155	4,843
Glendale, AZ	1.5	1.9	2.1	1.4	1.9	2.1	4.7	9.2	10.6	3,275	4,834	5,231
Lincoln, NE	2.7	2.9	2.9	2.5	2.7	2.6	8.2	11.6	12.0	3,382	4,436	4,734
St. Petersburg, FL	3.2	4.2	4.1	3.0	4.1	3.9	9.9	16.0	16.5	3,366	4,119	4,405
Chandler, AZ	1.4	1.8	1.9	1.2	1.6	1.8	3.9	8.7	9.7	3,204	5,397	5,724

[1] 2007 based on estimated resident population as of July 1.

Source: U.S. Census Bureau, "2008 Annual Survey of Public Employment and Payroll," May 2010. See also <http://www.census.gov/govs/apes/>.

Table 466. County Government Employment and Payroll—Largest Counties: 2000 to 2008

[In thousands (98.8 represents 98,800). As of March. See text, this section. See headnote, Table 464, for full-time equivalent employment definition]

Counties ranked by 2007 population [1]	Total employment (1,000)			Total full-time equivalent employment (1,000)		Payroll (mil. dol.)			Average monthly earnings for full-time employees (dol.)	
	2000	2005	2008	2000	2008	2000	2005	2008	2000	2008
Los Angeles, CA	98.8	99.5	109.5	94.2	105.6	396.7	475.0	594.1	4,274	5,698
Cook, IL	28.9	27.8	22.7	28.9	22.7	99.3	126.3	108.6	3,445	4,782
Harris, TX.	19.8	21.7	24.1	19.4	23.1	59.5	77.4	102.9	3,063	4,449
Maricopa, AZ	15.3	16.4	14.6	15.0	14.1	43.7	54.9	58.7	2,934	4,198
Orange, CA	24.3	25.0	22.8	22.5	21.9	81.4	104.9	110.4	3,623	4,985
San Diego, CA.	19.5	19.7	24.4	18.2	22.9	66.3	83.9	115.5	3,651	5,069
Dade, FL	36.0	43.8	46.9	35.1	45.8	130.3	190.8	274.3	3,817	6,089
Dallas, TX	12.5	15.2	15.8	12.0	15.0	36.4	54.5	66.7	3,055	4,430
Riverside, CA.	16.6	20.1	21.9	15.4	21.4	54.2	90.6	114.0	3,534	5,326
San Bernardino, CA. . . .	20.6	19.9	21.6	18.8	20.6	67.6	84.0	103.4	3,664	5,125
Wayne, MI	6.7	5.8	5.6	6.7	5.5	25.8	25.1	28.1	3,914	5,103
King, WA	15.8	14.5	14.8	14.2	14.0	52.1	64.6	76.1	3,812	5,618
Clark, NV	16.6	19.1	22.3	15.2	20.2	60.3	88.4	120.2	4,169	6,142
Broward, FL.	11.0	12.9	13.3	10.8	12.9	37.0	48.4	59.0	3,437	4,634
Santa Clara, CA.	14.9	18.0	19.2	14.3	18.2	65.3	100.4	125.2	4,655	6,995
Tarrant, TX.	6.9	9.4	10.4	6.8	10.2	19.0	34.4	41.2	2,811	4,081
Bexar, TX.	9.5	10.1	11.4	9.1	11.0	23.6	27.9	41.0	2,619	3,715
Alameda, CA	12.1	11.3	12.9	11.1	12.3	51.1	60.9	83.3	4,619	6,849
Suffolk, NY.	12.9	14.2	15.9	11.3	14.2	51.9	68.2	80.9	4,686	5,744
Sacramento, CA	13.3	14.9	14.7	12.6	14.3	50.3	71.0	75.4	4,094	5,313
Nassau, NY	18.9	16.8	21.1	16.9	19.0	71.3	76.6	92.1	4,295	4,968
Cuyahoga, OH.	16.1	15.7	16.6	16.1	16.3	49.2	57.1	69.3	3,065	4,171
Palm Beach, FL.	8.6	10.5	11.5	8.5	11.1	27.0	40.4	58.1	3,200	5,334
Allegheny, PA.	7.0	6.8	6.9	6.8	6.8	17.6	20.2	22.3	2,605	3,330
Oakland, MI	4.5	4.6	6.2	4.3	5.8	15.6	18.9	25.4	3,697	4,436
Hillsborough, FL	16.2	13.9	11.7	12.2	10.7	34.4	39.1	46.9	2,993	4,447
Hennepin, MN	13.0	11.4	8.7	11.0	8.1	41.5	49.3	44.3	3,815	5,647
Franklin, OH.	6.6	6.7	6.7	6.5	6.4	19.2	21.7	23.6	2,962	3,734
Orange, FL	9.9	10.5	12.4	9.3	11.5	28.0	35.7	50.2	3,092	4,400
Contra Costa, CA	10.7	10.0	9.9	9.5	9.3	44.7	41.6	57.0	4,779	6,175
Fairfax, VA	35.3	44.7	43.2	32.3	36.4	117.5	165.4	181.9	3,746	5,071
St. Louis, MO.	4.2	3.9	4.0	4.1	3.9	12.9	14.0	15.7	3,215	4,054
Fulton, GA	7.9	7.6	8.9	7.7	8.6	25.0	29.2	37.6	3,356	4,595
Travis, TX.	3.5	4.6	5.0	3.5	4.9	10.6	15.7	20.1	3,057	4,074
Pima, AZ	8.0	7.2	8.4	7.2	7.7	20.0	22.5	30.1	2,859	4,034
Westchester, NY	6.9	7.3	11.5	6.3	10.5	26.6	29.8	43.4	4,240	4,145
Milwaukee, WI	8.5	9.3	7.4	8.1	7.0	26.5	35.7	30.1	3,314	4,321
Montgomery, MD	37.4	40.6	43.4	28.8	36.2	123.1	175.3	214.4	4,619	6,376
Du Page, IL	3.9	3.6	3.6	3.6	3.4	11.8	14.1	12.6	3,360	3,727
Pinellas, FL	6.2	6.6	7.0	6.1	6.8	18.5	25.7	30.2	3,039	4,441
Erie, NY.	10.9	11.3	11.4	9.8	10.2	33.4	37.4	42.1	3,578	4,253
Shelby, TN	13.1	14.2	14.5	12.4	13.9	35.1	45.4	53.2	2,842	3,839
Fresno, CA.	8.6	9.2	9.1	8.2	8.4	26.0	32.9	37.1	3,293	4,414
Bergen, NJ.	5.8	5.7	5.6	4.1	4.9	13.0	23.7	25.2	3,178	5,336
Mecklenburg, NC.	23.8	27.1	29.4	21.1	26.5	58.2	82.1	101.7	2,834	3,944
Hamilton, OH.	5.9	6.1	6.1	5.7	5.9	15.3	20.5	22.1	2,679	3,724
Wake, NC	17.8	21.0	24.2	15.8	23.0	44.7	65.3	85.8	2,876	3,738
Macomb, MI.	3.0	3.2	3.3	2.8	3.0	8.9	12.0	12.7	3,333	4,357
Prince Georges, MD . . .	29.4	32.2	37.6	26.3	33.1	90.8	112.1	154.6	3,564	5,024
Ventura, CA.	8.6	8.6	9.1	8.3	8.7	31.5	43.2	54.2	3,829	6,296
Kern, CA	9.2	10.3	11.2	8.6	10.4	30.3	40.7	50.1	3,504	4,874
Baltimore, MD	23.3	27.5	30.0	20.7	25.9	63.8	92.9	114.7	3,227	4,665
Middlesex, NJ	4.5	4.3	4.7	4.0	4.0	14.4	16.6	19.8	3,881	5,157
Gwinnett, GA.	3.8	4.5	5.4	3.5	5.1	11.4	16.7	21.3	3,243	4,263
Montgomery, PA	3.5	4.1	4.1	3.4	4.0	9.2	12.4	12.4	2,783	3,154
Essex, NJ	5.6	5.0	5.4	5.0	4.8	19.3	21.0	23.7	4,048	5,053
Pierce, WA.	3.4	3.6	3.9	3.2	3.7	13.0	16.6	20.1	4,216	5,554
Dekalb, GA	6.5	7.1	7.6	6.2	7.4	19.5	25.1	27.2	3,170	3,717
El Paso, TX	4.0	4.7	5.0	4.0	4.9	10.4	15.3	18.5	2,685	3,849
Collin, TX.	1.1	1.4	1.8	1.1	1.8	2.8	5.0	7.1	2,557	3,915
Monroe, NY	7.0	6.9	6.9	5.9	6.0	20.4	22.8	24.2	3,430	4,110
Hidalgo, TX	1.9	2.2	2.7	1.9	2.7	4.0	5.6	8.1	2,174	2,993
Lake, IL	3.2	3.3	3.3	2.9	3.0	9.6	13.0	13.7	3,277	4,573
San Mateo, CA	6.2	7.2	7.8	5.8	7.4	24.6	35.5	42.3	4,415	6,578
Multnomah, OR	6.0	5.0	4.9	5.2	4.5	15.0	16.6	20.3	3,050	4,571
Oklahoma City, OK	2.6	2.3	2.3	2.3	2.1	4.4	5.7	6.1	1,860	2,898
Cobb, GA.	3.9	4.7	6.1	3.8	5.2	11.9	16.2	20.5	3,353	4,084
Snohomish, WA.	2.4	3.2	3.0	2.4	3.0	9.3	13.5	15.1	3,906	5,138
San Joaquin, CA	7.4	7.7	8.1	6.8	7.2	22.6	30.4	37.3	3,509	5,201
Jackson, MO	2.1	1.9	1.9	2.0	1.8	5.0	5.8	5.9	2,519	3,202
Jefferson, AL.	4.8	4.5	4.4	4.7	4.3	14.7	16.9	16.4	3,122	3,806
Norfolk, MA	0.6	0.5	0.5	0.5	0.5	1.6	2.0	2.4	2,977	5,051

[1] 2007 based on estimated resident population as of July 1.

Source: U.S. Census Bureau Federal, State, and Local Governments "2008 Annual Survey of Public Employment and Payroll," May 2010. See also <http://www.census.gov/govs/apes/>.

U.S. Census Bureau, Statistical Abstract of the United States: 2011

Federal Government Finances and Employment

This section presents statistics relating to the financial structure and the civilian employment of the federal government. The fiscal data cover taxes, other receipts, outlays, and debt. The principal sources of fiscal data are the *Budget of the United States Government* and related documents, published annually by the Office of Management and Budget (OMB), and the U.S. Department of the Treasury's *United States Government Annual Report* and its *Appendix*. Detailed data on tax returns and collections are published annually by the Internal Revenue Service. The personnel data relate to staffing and payrolls. They are published by the Office of Personnel Management and the Bureau of Labor Statistics. Data on federally owned land and real property are collected by the General Services Administration and presented in its annual "Federal Real Property Report."

Budget concept—Under the unified budget concept, all federal monies are included in one comprehensive budget. These monies comprise both federal funds and trust funds. Federal funds are derived mainly from taxes and borrowing and are not restricted by law to any specific government purpose. Trust funds, such as the Unemployment Trust Fund, collect certain taxes and other receipts for use in carrying out specific purposes or programs in accordance with the terms of the trust agreement or statute. Fund balances include both cash balances with the Treasury and investments in U.S. securities. Part of the balance is obligated, part unobligated. Prior to 1985, the budget totals, under provisions of law, excluded some federal activities—including the Federal Financing Bank, the Postal Service, the Synthetic Fuels Corporation, and the lending activities of the Rural Electrification Administration. The Balanced Budget and Emergency Deficit Control Act of 1985 (P.L.99-177) repealed the off-budget status of these entities and placed social security (Federal Old-Age and Survivors Insurance and the federal disability insurance trust funds) off-budget. Though

social security is now off-budget and, by law, excluded from coverage of the congressional budget resolutions, it continues to be a federal program. Receipts arising from the government's sovereign powers are reported as governmental receipts and all other receipts, i.e., from business-type or market-oriented activities, are offset against outlays. Outlays are reported on a checks-issued (net) basis (i.e., outlays are recorded at the time the checks to pay bills are issued).

Debt concept—For most of U.S. history, the total debt consisted of debt borrowed by the Treasury (i.e., public debt). The present debt series includes both public debt and agency debt. The *gross federal debt* includes money borrowed by the Treasury and by various federal agencies; it is the broadest generally used measure of the federal debt. *Total public debt* is covered by a statutory debt limitation and includes only borrowing by the Treasury.

Treasury receipts and outlays—All receipts of the government, with a few exceptions, are deposited to the credit of the U.S. Treasury regardless of ultimate disposition. Under the Constitution, no money may be withdrawn from the Treasury unless appropriated by the Congress.

The day-to-day cash operations of the federal government clearing through the accounts of the U.S. Treasury are reported in the *Daily Treasury Statement*. Extensive detail on the public debt is published in the *Monthly Statement of the Public Debt of the United States.*

Budget receipts such as taxes, customs duties, and miscellaneous receipts, which are collected by government agencies, and outlays represented by checks issued and cash payments made by disbursing officers as well as government agencies are reported in the *Daily Treasury Statement of Receipts and Outlays of the United States Government* and in the Treasury's *United States Government Annual Report* and its *Appendix*. These deposits in and payments from accounts maintained by government agencies are on the same basis as the unified budget.

The quarterly *Treasury Bulletin* contains data on fiscal operations and related Treasury activities, including financial statements of government corporations and other business-type activities.

Income tax returns and tax collections—Tax data are compiled by the Internal Revenue Service of the Treasury Department. The annual *Internal Revenue Service Data Book* gives a detailed account of tax collections by kind of tax. The agency's annual *Statistics of Income* reports present detailed data from individual income tax returns and corporation income tax returns. The quarterly *Statistics of Income Bulletin* presents data on such diverse subjects as tax-exempt organizations, unincorporated businesses, fiduciary income tax and estate tax returns, sales of capital assets by individuals, international income and taxes reported by corporations and individuals, and estate tax wealth.

Employment and payrolls—The Office of Personnel Management collects employment and payroll data from all departments and agencies of the federal government, except the Central Intelligence Agency, the National Security Agency, and the Defense Intelligence Agency. Employment figures represent the number of persons who occupied civilian positions at the end of the report month shown and who are paid for personal services rendered for the federal government, regardless of the nature of appointment or method of payment. Federal payrolls include all payments for personal services rendered during the report month and payments for accumulated annual leave of employees who separate from the service. Since most federal employees are paid on a biweekly basis, the calendar month earnings are partially estimated on the basis of the number of work days in each month where payroll periods overlap.

Federal employment and payroll figures are published by the Office of Personnel Management in its *Federal Civilian Workforce Statistics—Employment and Trends*. It also publishes biennial employment data for minority groups, data on occupations of white- and blue-collar workers, and data on employment by geographic area; reports on salary and wage distribution of federal employees are published annually. General schedule is primarily white-collar; wage system primarily blue-collar. Data on federal employment are also issued by the Bureau of Labor Statistics in its *Monthly Labor Review* and in Employment and Earnings and by the U.S. Census Bureau in its annual publication *Public Employment*.

U.S. Census Bureau, Statistical Abstract of the United States: 2011

Figure 9.1
Federal Budget Summary: 1990 to 2010

Receipts, outlays, and surplus or deficit

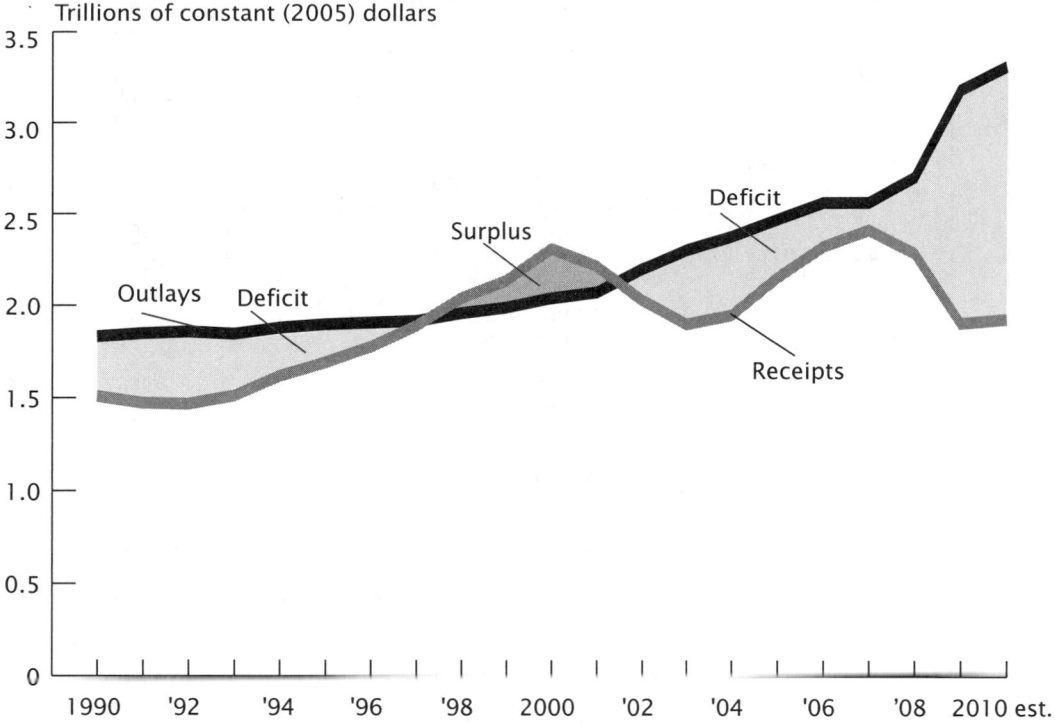

Outlays and federal debt as a percent of gross domestic product (GDP)

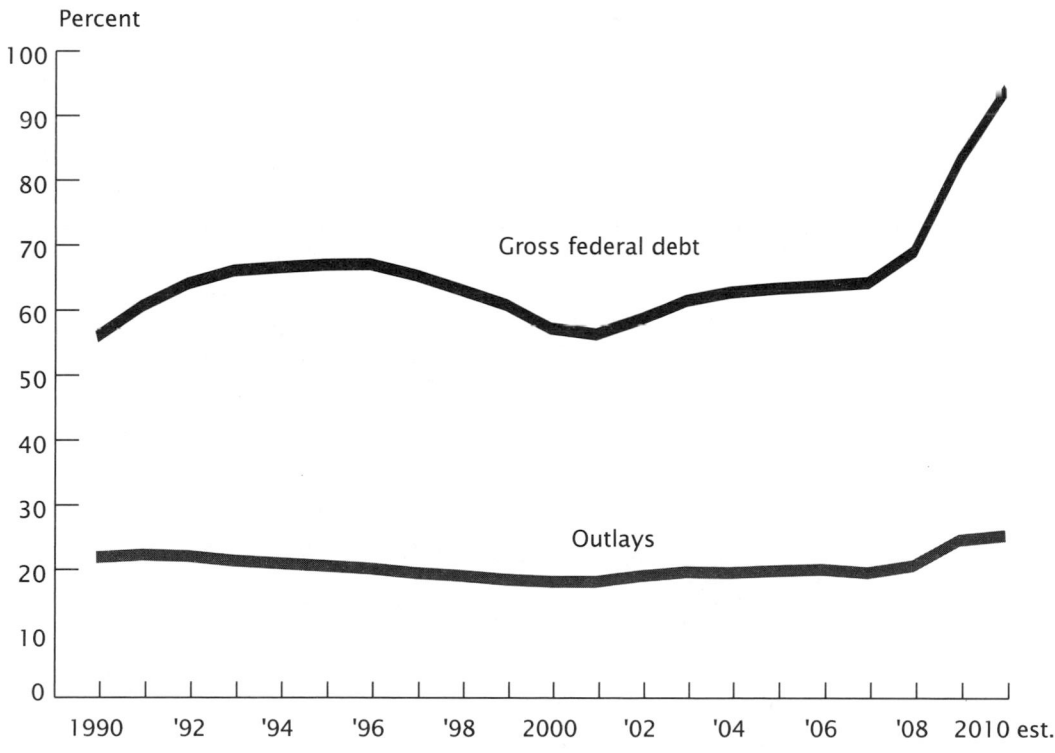

Source: Charts prepared by U.S. Census Bureau. For data, see Tables 467 & 468.

Table 467. Federal Budget—Receipts and Outlays: 1960 to 2010

[92.5 represents $92,500,000,000. For fiscal years ending in year shown; see text, Section 8. See also headnote, Table 469]

Fiscal year	In current dollars (billion dollars)			In constant (2005) dollars (bil. dol.)			As percentage of GDP [1]		
	Receipts	Outlays	Surplus or deficit (−)	Receipts	Outlays	Surplus or deficit (−)	Receipts	Outlays	Surplus or deficit (−)
1960.	92.5	92.2	0.3	630.9	628.9	2.1	17.8	17.8	0.1
1970.	192.8	195.6	−2.8	968.4	982.7	−14.3	19.0	19.3	−0.3
1980.	517.1	590.9	−73.8	1,197.6	1,368.6	−171.0	19.0	21.7	−2.7
1985.	734.0	946.3	−212.3	1,250.9	1,612.7	−361.8	17.7	22.8	−5.1
1990.	1,032.0	1,253.0	−221.0	1,508.7	1,831.9	−323.2	18.0	21.9	−3.9
1991.	1,055.0	1,324.2	−269.2	1,473.0	1,849.0	−375.9	17.8	22.3	−4.5
1992.	1,091.2	1,381.5	−290.3	1,467.5	1,857.9	−390.4	17.5	22.1	−4.7
1993.	1,154.3	1,409.4	−255.1	1,511.5	1,845.5	−334.0	17.5	21.4	−3.9
1994.	1,258.6	1,461.8	−203.2	1,617.7	1,878.9	−261.2	18.0	21.0	−2.9
1995.	1,351.8	1,515.8	−164.0	1,691.4	1,896.6	−205.1	18.4	20.6	−2.2
1996.	1,453.1	1,560.5	−107.4	1,775.5	1,906.8	−131.3	18.8	20.2	−1.4
1997.	1,579.2	1,601.1	−21.9	1,889.9	1,916.1	−26.2	19.2	19.5	−0.3
1998.	1,721.7	1,652.5	69.3	2,040.9	1,958.8	82.1	19.9	19.1	0.8
1999.	1,827.5	1,701.8	125.6	2,136.4	1,989.5	146.8	19.8	18.5	1.4
2000.	2,025.2	1,789.0	236.2	2,310.0	2,040.6	269.5	20.6	18.2	2.4
2001.	1,991.1	1,862.9	128.2	2,215.3	2,072.7	142.7	19.5	18.2	1.3
2002.	1,853.1	2,010.9	−157.8	2,028.6	2,201.3	−172.7	17.6	19.1	−1.5
2003.	1,782.3	2,159.9	−377.6	1,901.1	2,303.9	−402.8	16.2	19.7	−3.4
2004.	1,880.1	2,292.9	−412.7	1,949.5	2,377.5	−428.0	16.1	19.6	−3.5
2005.	2,153.6	2,472.0	−318.3	2,153.6	2,472.0	−318.3	17.3	19.9	−2.6
2006.	2,406.9	2,655.1	−248.2	2,324.1	2,563.8	−239.6	18.2	20.1	−1.9
2007.	2,568.0	2,728.7	−160.7	2,414.0	2,565.1	−151.1	18.5	19.6	−1.2
2008.	2,524.0	2,982.6	−458.6	2,288.5	2,704.3	−415.8	17.5	20.7	−3.2
2009	2,105.0	3,517.7	−1,412.7	1,906.7	3,186.3	−1,279.6	14.8	24.7	−9.9
2010, est.	2,165.1	3,720.7	−1,555.6	1,929.2	3,315.2	−1,386.1	14.8	25.4	−10.6

[1] Gross domestic product; see text, Section 13.

Source: U.S. Office of Management and Budget, *Budget of the United States Government, Historical Tables*, annual. See also <http://www.whitehouse.gov/omb/budget>.

Table 468. Federal Budget Debt: 1960 to 2010

[290.5 represents $290,500,000,000. As of the end of the fiscal year. See text, Section 8]

Fiscal year	Total (bil. dol.)					As percentages of GDP [1]				
	Gross federal debt	Federal government accounts	Held by the public			Gross federal debt	Federal government accounts	Held by the public		
			Total	Federal Reserve System	Other			Total	Federal Reserve System	Other
1960.	290.5	53.7	236.8	26.5	210.3	56.0	10.3	45.6	5.1	40.5
1970.	380.9	97.7	283.2	57.7	225.5	37.6	9.6	28.0	5.7	22.3
1980.	909.0	197.1	711.9	120.8	591.1	33.4	7.2	26.1	4.4	21.7
1985.	1,817.4	310.2	1,507.3	169.8	1,337.5	43.8	7.5	36.4	4.1	32.3
1986.	2,120.5	379.9	1,740.6	190.9	1,549.8	48.2	8.6	39.5	4.3	35.2
1987.	2,346.0	456.2	1,889.8	212.0	1,677.7	50.4	9.8	40.6	4.6	36.1
1988.	2,601.1	549.5	2,051.6	229.2	1,822.4	51.9	11.0	41.0	4.6	36.4
1989.	2,867.8	677.1	2,190.7	220.1	1,970.6	53.1	12.5	40.6	4.1	36.5
1990.	3,206.3	794.7	2,411.6	234.4	2,177.1	55.9	13.9	42.1	4.1	38.0
1991.	3,598.2	909.2	2,689.0	258.6	2,430.4	60.7	15.3	45.3	4.4	41.0
1992.	4,001.8	1,002.1	2,999.7	296.4	2,703.3	64.1	16.1	48.1	4.7	43.3
1993.	4,351.0	1,102.6	3,248.4	325.7	2,922.7	66.1	16.7	49.3	4.9	44.4
1994.	4,643.3	1,210.2	3,433.1	355.2	3,077.9	66.6	17.3	49.2	5.1	44.1
1995.	4,920.6	1,316.2	3,604.4	374.1	3,230.3	67.0	17.9	49.1	5.1	44.0
1996.	5,181.5	1,447.4	3,734.1	390.9	3,343.1	67.1	18.8	48.4	5.1	43.3
1997.	5,369.2	1,596.9	3,772.3	424.5	3,347.8	65.4	19.4	45.9	5.2	40.8
1998.	5,478.2	1,757.1	3,721.1	458.2	3,262.9	63.2	20.3	43.0	5.3	37.7
1999.	5,605.5	1,973.2	3,632.4	496.6	3,135.7	60.9	21.4	39.4	5.4	34.1
2000.	5,628.7	2,218.9	3,409.8	511.4	2,898.4	57.3	22.6	34.7	5.2	29.5
2001.	5,769.9	2,450.3	3,319.6	534.1	2,785.5	56.4	24.0	32.5	5.2	27.2
2002.	6,198.4	2,658.0	3,540.4	604.2	2,936.2	58.8	25.2	33.6	5.7	27.8
2003.	6,760.0	2,846.6	3,913.4	656.1	3,257.3	61.6	25.9	35.6	6.0	29.7
2004.	7,354.7	3,059.1	4,295.5	700.3	3,595.2	62.9	26.2	36.8	6.0	30.8
2005.	7,905.3	3,313.1	4,592.2	736.4	3,855.9	63.5	26.6	36.9	5.9	31.0
2006.	8,451.4	3,622.4	4,829.0	768.9	4,060.0	63.9	27.4	36.5	5.8	30.7
2007.	8,950.7	3,915.6	5,035.1	779.6	4,255.5	64.4	28.2	36.2	5.6	30.6
2008.	9,986.1	4,183.0	5,803.1	491.1	5,311.9	69.2	29.0	40.2	3.4	36.8
2009.	11,875.9	4,331.1	7,544.7	769.2	6,775.5	83.4	30.4	53.0	5.4	47.6
2010, est.	13,786.6	4,489.0	9,297.7	(NA)	(NA)	94.3	30.7	63.6	(NA)	(NA)

NA Not available. [1] Gross domestic product; see text, Section 13.

Source: U.S. Office of Management and Budget, *Budget of the United States Government, Historical Tables*, annual. See also <http://www.whitehouse.gov/omb/budget>.

Table 469. Federal Budget Outlays by Type: 1990 to 2010

[1,253.0 represents $1,253,000,000,000. For years ending September 30. Given the inherent imprecision in deflating outlays, the data shown in constant dollars present a reasonable perspective—not precision. The deflators and the categories that are deflated are as comparable over time as feasible. Minus sign (–) indicates offset]

Type	Unit	1990	2000	2005	2007	2008	2009	2010, est.
Current dollar outlays	**Bil. dol**	**1,253.0**	**1,789.0**	**2,472.0**	**2,728.7**	**2,982.6**	**3,517.7**	**3,720.7**
National defense [1]	Bil. dol	299.3	294.4	495.3	551.3	616.1	661.0	719.2
Nondefense, total	Bil. dol	953.7	1,494.6	1,976.7	2,177.4	2,366.5	2,856.6	3,001.5
Payments for individuals	Bil. dol	585.7	1,054.5	1,490.2	1,689.4	1,824.6	2,093.0	2,392.4
Direct payments [2]	Bil. dol	507.0	867.7	1,212.1	1,401.0	1,520.0	1,732.2	1,988.2
Grants to State and local governments	Bil. dol	78.7	186.8	278.1	288.4	304.7	360.7	404.3
All other grants	Bil. dol	56.4	99.1	149.9	155.4	156.6	177.2	249.3
Net interest [2]	Bil. dol	184.3	222.9	184.0	237.1	252.8	186.9	187.8
All other [2]	Bil. dol	163.9	160.7	217.8	177.8	218.7	492.2	251.7
Undistributed offsetting receipts [2]	Bil. dol	−36.6	−42.6	−65.2	−82.2	−86.2	−92.6	−79.7
Constant (2005) dollar outlays	**Bil. dol**	**1,831.9**	**2,040.6**	**2,472.0**	**2,565.1**	**2,704.3**	**3,186.3**	**3,315.2**
National defense [1]	Bil. dol	461.2	361.3	495.3	509.2	548.6	580.3	626.2
Nondefense, total	Bil. dol	1,370.6	1,679.3	1,976.7	2,055.7	2,155.7	2,606.2	2,688.8
Payments for individuals	Bil. dol	815.4	1,172.3	1,490.2	1,602.4	1,667.0	1,927.6	2,155.5
Direct payments [2]	Bil. dol	705.7	964.4	1,212.1	1,329.1	1,388.9	1,595.7	1,792.0
Grants to state and local governments	Bil. dol	109.6	207.9	278.1	273.3	278.1	331.9	363.6
All other grants	Bil. dol	87.9	118.5	149.9	139.9	133.8	151.2	209.1
Net interest [2]	Bil. dol	255.7	250.8	184.0	222.8	232.1	169.1	168.4
All other [2]	Bil. dol	278.8	190.5	217.8	166.8	200.2	440.3	225.8
Undistributed offsetting receipts [2]	Bil. dol	−67.1	−52.9	−65.2	−76.1	−77.5	−82.0	−70.0
Outlays as percent of GDP [3]	**Percent**	**21.9**	**18.2**	**19.9**	**19.6**	**20.7**	**24.7**	**25.4**
National defense [1]	Percent	5.2	3.0	4.0	4.0	4.3	4.6	4.9
Nondefense, total	Percent	16.6	15.2	15.9	15.7	16.4	20.1	20.5
Payments for individuals	Percent	10.2	10.7	12.0	12.2	12.6	14.7	16.4
Direct payments [2]	Percent	8.8	8.8	9.7	10.1	10.5	12.2	13.6
Grants to state and local governments	Percent	1.4	1.9	2.2	2.1	2.1	2.5	2.8
All other grants	Percent	1.0	1.0	1.2	1.1	1.1	1.2	1.7
Net interest [2]	Percent	3.2	2.3	1.5	1.7	1.8	1.3	1.3
All other [2]	Percent	2.9	1.6	1.7	1.3	1.5	3.5	1.7
Undistributed offsetting receipts [2]	Percent	−0.6	−0.4	−0.5	−0.6	−0.6	−0.7	−0.5

[1] Includes a small amount of grants to state and local governments and direct payments for individuals. [2] Includes some off-budget amounts; most of the off-budget amounts are direct payments for individuals (social security benefits). [3] Gross domestic product; see text, Section 13.

Source: U.S. Office of Management and Budget, *Budget of the United States Government, Historical Tables*, annual. See also <http://www.whitehouse.gov/omb/budget>.

Table 470. Federal Budget Outlays by Agency: 1990 to 2010

[In billions of dollars (1,253.0 represents $1,253,000,000,000). For years ending September 30]

Department or other unit	1990	2000	2005	2007	2008	2009	2010, est.
Outlays, total [1]	**1,253.0**	**1,789.0**	**2,472.0**	**2,728.7**	**2,982.6**	**3,517.7**	**3,720.7**
Legislative Branch	2.2	2.9	4.0	4.3	4.4	4.7	5.4
The Judiciary Branch	1.6	4.1	5.5	6.0	6.3	6.6	7.2
Agriculture	45.9	75.1	85.3	84.4	90.8	114.4	142.0
Commerce	3.7	7.8	6.1	6.5	7.7	10.7	16.7
Defense—Military	289.7	281.0	474.4	528.6	594.7	636.8	692.0
Education	23.0	33.5	72.9	66.4	66.0	53.4	106.9
Energy	12.1	15.0	21.3	20.1	21.4	23.7	38.3
Health and Human Services	175.5	382.3	581.4	672.0	700.4	796.3	868.8
Homeland Security	7.2	13.2	38.7	39.2	40.7	51.7	52.9
Housing and Urban Development	20.2	30.8	42.5	45.6	49.1	61.0	62.5
Interior	5.8	8.0	9.3	10.5	9.8	11.8	12.0
Justice	5.9	16.8	22.4	23.3	26.5	27.7	30.3
Labor	26.1	31.9	46.9	47.5	58.8	138.2	209.3
State	4.8	6.7	12.7	13.7	17.5	21.4	25.7
Transportation	25.6	41.6	56.6	61.7	64.9	73.0	90.9
Treasury	253.9	390.5	410.2	490.6	548.8	701.8	503.0
Veterans Affairs	29.0	47.0	69.8	72.8	84.7	95.5	124.6
Corps of Engineers	3.3	4.2	4.7	3.9	5.1	6.8	10.5
Other Defense—Civil Programs	21.7	32.8	43.5	47.1	45.8	57.3	54.3
Environmental Protection Agency	5.1	7.2	7.9	8.3	7.9	8.1	11.3
Executive Office of the President	0.2	0.3	7.7	3.0	1.2	0.7	0.7
International Assistance Programs	10.1	12.1	15.0	12.8	11.4	14.8	23.9
National Aeronautics and Space Administration	12.4	13.4	15.6	15.9	17.8	19.2	19.1
National Science Foundation	1.8	3.4	5.4	5.5	5.8	6.0	7.8
Office of Personnel Management	31.9	48.7	59.5	58.4	64.4	72.3	71.6
Social Security Administration (on-budget)	17.3	45.1	54.6	54.9	58.6	78.7	85.1
Social Security Administration (off-budget)	245.0	396.2	506.8	566.8	599.2	648.9	683.9
Undistributed offsetting receipts	−98.9	173.0	226.2	−260.2	−277.8	−274.2	−271.1

[1] Includes other agencies, not shown separately.

Source: U.S. Office of Management and Budget, *Budget of the United States Government, Historical Tables*, annual. See also <http://www.whitehouse.gov/omb/budget>.

Table 471. Federal Outlays by Detailed Function: 1990 to 2010

[In billions of dollars (1,253.0 represents $1,253,000,000,000). For years ending September 30. Minus sign (−) indicates decrease]

Superfunction and function	1990	2000	2004	2005	2006	2007	2008	2009	2010, est.
Total outlays	**1,253.0**	**1,789.0**	**2,292.9**	**2,472.0**	**2,655.1**	**2,728.7**	**2,982.6**	**3,517.7**	**3,720.7**
National defense [1]	299.3	294.4	455.8	495.3	521.8	551.3	616.1	661.0	719.2
Department of Defense-Military	289.7	281.0	436.4	474.1	499.3	528.5	594.6	636.7	692.0
Military personnel	75.6	76.0	113.6	127.5	127.5	127.5	138.9	147.3	155.0
Operation and maintenance	88.3	105.8	174.0	188.1	203.8	216.6	244.8	259.3	279.4
Procurement	81.0	51.7	76.2	82.3	89.8	99.6	117.4	129.2	147.2
Research, development, test, and evaluation	37.5	37.6	60.8	65.7	68.6	73.1	75.1	79.0	79.3
Military construction	5.1	5.1	6.3	5.3	6.2	7.9	11.6	17.6	23.8
Atomic energy defense activities	9.0	12.1	16.6	18.0	17.5	17.1	17.1	17.6	20.0
International affairs [1]	13.8	17.2	26.9	34.6	29.5	28.5	28.9	37.5	51.1
International development and humanitarian assistance	5.5	6.5	13.8	17.7	16.7	15.5	14.1	22.1	26.5
International security assistance	8.7	6.4	8.4	7.9	7.8	8.0	9.5	6.2	9.9
Conduct of foreign affairs	3.0	4.7	7.9	9.1	8.6	8.4	10.4	12.2	13.2
General science, space, and technology	14.4	18.6	23.0	23.6	23.6	25.5	27.7	29.4	33.0
General science and basic research	2.8	6.2	8.4	8.8	9.1	10.3	10.5	11.1	14.5
Space flight, research, and supporting activities	11.6	12.4	14.6	14.8	14.5	15.3	17.2	18.4	18.6
Energy	3.3	−0.8	−0.2	0.4	0.8	−0.9	0.6	4.7	19.0
Energy supply	2.0	−1.8	−1.6	−0.9	0.2	−2.0	−0.4	2.0	8.8
Natural resources and environment [1]	17.1	25.0	30.7	28.0	33.0	31.7	31.8	35.6	47.0
Water resources	4.4	5.1	5.6	5.7	8.0	5.1	6.1	8.1	12.4
Conservation and land management	4.0	6.8	9.8	6.2	7.8	9.6	8.7	9.8	12.5
Recreational resources	1.4	2.5	2.9	3.0	3.0	3.0	3.2	3.6	4.0
Pollution control and abatement	5.2	7.4	8.5	8.1	8.6	8.4	8.1	8.3	11.5
Agriculture	11.8	36.5	15.4	26.6	26.0	17.7	18.4	22.2	26.6
Farm income stabilization	9.7	33.4	11.2	22.0	21.4	13.1	13.8	17.6	21.3
Agricultural research and services	2.1	3.0	4.3	4.5	4.6	4.6	4.6	4.6	5.3
Commerce and housing credit [1]	67.6	3.2	5.3	7.6	6.2	0.5	27.9	291.5	−25.3
Mortgage credit	3.8	−3.3	2.7	−0.9	−0.6	−5.0	0.0	99.8	55.7
Postal service	2.1	2.1	−4.1	−1.2	−1.0	−3.2	−3.1	−1.0	1.0
Deposit insurance	57.9	−3.1	−2.0	−1.4	−1.1	−1.5	18.8	22.6	−26.6
Transportation [1]	29.5	46.9	64.6	67.9	70.2	72.9	77.6	84.3	106.5
Ground transportation	19.0	31.7	40.7	42.3	45.2	46.8	50.0	54.1	72.7
Air transportation	7.2	10.6	16.7	18.8	18.0	18.1	19.4	20.8	22.7
Water transportation	3.2	4.4	6.9	6.4	6.7	7.7	8.1	9.1	10.4
Community and regional development [1]	8.5	10.6	15.8	26.3	54.5	29.6	24.0	27.7	28.5
Community development	3.5	5.5	6.2	5.9	5.8	11.8	10.2	7.7	9.8
Disaster relief and insurance	2.1	2.6	7.3	17.7	46.0	15.2	11.2	16.7	16.5
Education, training, employment, and social services [1]	37.2	53.8	88.0	97.6	118.5	91.7	91.3	79.7	142.5
Elementary, secondary, and vocational education	9.9	20.6	34.4	38.3	39.7	38.4	38.9	53.2	84.1
Higher education	11.1	10.1	25.3	31.4	50.5	24.6	23.6	−3.3	20.4
Research and general education aids	1.6	2.5	3.0	3.1	3.0	3.2	3.2	3.5	3.8
Training and employment	5.6	6.8	7.9	6.9	7.2	7.1	7.2	7.7	10.9
Social services	8.1	12.6	15.9	16.3	16.5	16.7	16.8	17.0	21.4
Health	57.7	154.5	240.1	250.5	252.7	266.4	280.6	334.3	372.3
Health care services	47.6	136.2	210.1	219.6	220.8	233.9	247.7	300.0	335.2
Health research and training	8.6	16.0	27.1	28.1	28.8	29.3	29.9	30.6	32.7
Consumer and occupational health and safety	1.5	2.3	2.9	2.9	3.1	3.2	3.0	3.8	4.4
Medicare	98.1	197.1	269.4	298.6	329.9	375.4	390.8	430.1	457.2
Income security [1]	148.7	253.7	333.1	345.8	352.5	366.0	431.3	533.2	685.9
General retirement and disability insurance (excluding social security)	5.1	5.2	6.6	7.0	4.6	7.8	8.9	8.2	8.0
Federal employee retirement and disability	52.0	77.2	88.7	93.4	98.3	103.9	109.0	118.1	120.6
Unemployment compensation	18.9	23.0	45.0	35.4	33.8	35.1	45.3	122.5	194.3
Housing assistance	15.9	28.9	36.8	37.9	38.3	39.7	40.6	50.9	77.0
Food and nutrition assistance	24.0	32.5	46.0	50.8	53.9	54.5	60.7	79.1	99.3
Social security	248.6	409.4	495.5	523.3	548.5	586.2	617.0	683.0	721.5
Veterans benefits and services [1]	29.0	47.0	59.7	70.1	69.8	72.8	84.7	95.4	124.7
Income security for veterans	15.3	24.9	30.8	35.8	35.8	35.7	41.3	46.0	63.1
Veterans education, training, and rehabilitation	0.2	1.3	2.6	2.8	2.6	2.7	2.7	3.5	9.0
Hospital and medical care for veterans	12.1	19.5	26.9	28.8	29.9	32.3	37.0	41.9	46.2
Veterans housing	0.5	0.4	−2.0	0.9	−1.2	−0.9	−0.4	−0.6	0.6
Administration of justice	10.2	28.5	45.6	40.0	41.0	41.2	47.1	51.5	55.0
Federal law enforcement activities	4.8	12.1	19.1	19.9	20.0	19.6	24.6	27.6	28.8
Federal litigative and judicial activities	3.6	7.8	9.7	9.6	10.1	11.0	11.8	12.1	12.9
Federal correctional activities	1.3	3.7	5.5	5.9	6.2	6.3	6.9	7.3	7.7
Criminal justice assistance	0.5	4.9	11.3	4.6	4.8	4.3	3.9	4.6	5.6
General government	10.5	13.0	22.3	17.0	18.2	17.4	20.3	22.0	29.3
Net interest [1]	184.3	222.9	160.2	184.0	226.6	237.1	252.8	186.9	187.8
Interest on Treasury debt securities (gross)	264.7	361.9	321.7	352.3	405.9	430.0	451.1	383.1	425.1
Interest received by on-budget trust funds	−46.3	−69.3	−67.8	−69.2	−71.6	−72.0	−77.8	−63.6	−73.0
Interest received by off-budget trust funds	−16.0	−59.8	−86.2	−91.8	−97.7	−106.0	−113.7	−118.0	−118.4
Allowances	−	−	−	−	−	−	−	−	18.8
Undistributed offsetting receipts	−36.6	−42.6	−58.5	−65.2	−68.3	−82.2	−86.2	−92.6	−79.7

− Represents or rounds to zero. [1] Includes functions not shown separately.

Source: U.S. Office of Management and Budget, *Budget of the United States Government, Historical Tables*, annual. See also <http://www.whitehouse.gov/omb/budget>.

Table 472. Outlays for Payments for Individuals by Category and Major Program: 1990 to 2010

[In billions of dollars (585.7 represents 585,700,000,000). For fiscal years ending September 30]

Category and program	1990	2000	2005	2006	2007	2008	2009	2010, est.
Total, payments for individuals.	**585.7**	**1,054.5**	**1,490.9**	**1,592.8**	**1,690.4**	**1,825.8**	**2,094.1**	**2,393.4**
Social security and railroad retirement	250.5	410.5	523.4	554.5	586.7	617.4	681.0	721.1
Social security:								
Old age and survivors insurance	221.9	351.4	434.0	457.7	483.3	506.6	561.4	590.4
Disability insurance	24.4	54.4	84.2	91.2	97.5	104.7	115.5	124.2
Railroad retirement (excl. social security)	4.1	4.6	5.3	5.6	5.8	6.1	4.1	6.6
Federal employees retirement and insurance	64.1	100.3	126.9	132.3	138.0	148.2	161.7	181.2
Military retirement	21.5	32.8	39.0	41.1	43.5	45.8	50.0	50.8
Civil service retirement	31.0	45.1	54.7	57.8	60.9	63.5	67.5	70.0
Veterans service-connected compensation	10.7	20.8	30.9	31.0	31.1	36.3	40.4	57.2
Other	0.8	1.7	2.4	2.4	2.6	2.7	3.8	3.2
Unemployment assistance	17.4	21.1	33.1	31.9	33.2	43.4	119.8	190.7
Medical care	164.3	362.7	562.5	606.0	682.4	714.9	813.8	883.3
Medicare:								
Hospital insurance	65.9	127.9	182.8	183.9	204.9	223.6	240.0	249.3
Supplementary medical insurance	41.5	87.2	151.0	191.7	230.1	231.1	257.6	279.4
State children's health insurance	–	1.2	5.1	5.5	6.0	6.9	7.5	9.1
Medicaid	41.1	117.9	181.7	180.6	190.6	201.4	250.9	275.4
Indian health	1.1	2.4	3.1	3.3	3.3	3.3	3.6	4.5
Hospital and medical care for veterans	12.0	19.3	23.1	24.4	30.5	31.1	35.3	38.5
Health resources and services	1.4	3.9	5.9	6.1	5.9	6.3	6.5	7.6
Substance abuse and mental health services	1.2	2.5	3.2	3.2	3.2	3.1	3.4	3.3
Health care tax credit	–	–	0.1	0.1	0.1	0.1	0.1	0.2
Uniformed Services retiree health care fund	–	–	6.3	7.1	7.6	7.9	8.4	8.6
Other	(Z)	0.3	0.2	0.2	0.2	0.2	0.5	1.8
Assistance to students	11.2	10.9	32.1	51.7	31.0	31.1	30.6	55.0
Veterans education benefits	0.8	1.6	3.2	3.3	3.4	3.6	4.3	9.7
Student assistance, Department of Education and other	10.4	9.2	28.9	48.4	27.5	27.5	26.3	45.3
Housing assistance	15.9	24.1	31.8	32.1	33.0	33.4	43.6	68.3
Food and nutrition assistance	23.9	32.4	50.7	53.8	54.3	60.5	78.9	99.1
Food stamp program (including Puerto Rico)	15.9	18.3	32.6	34.6	34.9	39.3	55.6	72.5
Child nutrition and special milk programs	5.0	9.2	11.9	12.4	13.0	13.9	15.3	17.3
Supplemental feeding programs (WIC [1] and CSFP [2])	2.1	4.0	5.0	5.1	5.3	6.2	6.5	7.7
Commodity donations and other	0.8	0.9	1.2	1.7	1.1	1.1	1.6	1.6
Public assistance and related programs	34.9	88.3	123.3	125.1	126.3	168.6	156.0	188.2
Supplemental security income program	11.5	29.5	35.3	34.3	32.8	38.0	41.4	44.0
Family support payments to states and TANF [3]	12.2	18.4	21.3	20.9	21.1	21.8	22.0	22.5
Low income home energy assistance	1.3	1.5	2.1	2.6	2.5	2.7	4.5	5.0
Earned income tax credit	4.4	26.1	34.6	36.2	38.3	40.6	42.4	49.5
Legal services	0.3	0.3	0.3	0.3	0.3	0.3	0.4	0.4
Payments to states for daycare assistance	–	3.3	4.9	5.3	5.1	5.0	5.3	6.3
Veterans non-service-connected pensions	3.6	3.0	3.7	3.5	3.4	3.8	4.2	4.4
Payments to states for foster care/adoption assistance	1.6	5.5	6.4	6.4	6.6	6.8	6.9	7.4
Payment where child credit exceeds tax liability	–	0.8	14.6	15.5	16.2	34.0	24.3	23.4
Other public assistance	–	–	(Z)	0.1	0.1	15.6	3.8	24.8
All other payments for individuals	3.5	4.3	7.1	5.6	5.6	8.1	8.7	6.4
Coal miners and black lung benefits	1.5	1.0	0.7	0.7	0.6	0.6	3.0	0.5
Veterans insurance and burial benefits	1.4	1.4	1.4	1.4	1.3	1.4	1.4	1.4
D.C. employee retirement	–	0.4	2.2	0.5	0.5	0.5	0.5	0.5
Aging services programs	–	0.9	1.4	1.4	1.4	1.4	1.5	1.6
Energy employees compensation fund	–	–	0.6	0.9	1.0	1.1	1.0	1.0
September 11th victim compensation	–	–	(Z)	(Z)	–	–	–	–
Refugee assistance and other	0.6	0.6	0.8	0.8	0.8	3.2	1.2	1.4

– Represents zero. Z Less than $50,000,000. [1] WIC means Women, Infants, and Children. [2] CSFP means Commodity Supplemental Food Program. [3] TANF means Temporary Assistance for Needy Families.

Source: U.S. Office of Management and Budget, *Budget of the United States Government, Historical Tables*, annual. See also <http://www.whitehouse.gov/omb/budget>.

U.S. Census Bureau, Statistical Abstract of the United States: 2011

Table 473. Federal Budget Receipts by Source: 1990 to 2010

[In billions of dollars (1,032.0 represents $1,032,000,000,000). For years ending September 30. Receipts reflect collections. Covers both federal funds and trust funds; see text, this section]

Source	1990	2000	2005	2006	2007	2008	2009	2010, est.
Total federal receipts	**1,032.0**	**2,025.2**	**2,153.6**	**2,406.9**	**2,568.0**	**2,524.0**	**2,105.0**	**2,165.1**
Individual income taxes	466.9	1,004.5	927.2	1,043.9	1,163.5	1,145.7	915.3	935.8
Corporation income taxes	93.5	207.3	278.3	353.9	370.2	304.3	138.2	156.7
Social insurance and retirement receipts	380.0	652.9	794.1	837.8	869.6	900.2	890.9	875.8
Excise taxes	35.3	68.9	73.1	74.0	65.1	67.3	62.5	73.2
Other	56.2	91.7	80.9	97.3	99.6	106.4	98.1	123.6
Social insurance and retirement receipts	**380.0**	**652.9**	**794.1**	**837.8**	**869.6**	**900.2**	**890.9**	**875.8**
Employment and general retirement	353.9	620.5	747.7	790.0	824.3	856.5	848.9	819.8
Old-age and survivors insurance (off-budget)	255.0	411.7	493.6	520.1	542.9	562.5	559.1	543.0
Disability insurance (off-budget)	26.6	68.9	83.8	88.3	92.2	95.5	94.9	92.2
Hospital insurance	68.6	135.5	166.1	177.4	184.9	194.0	190.7	180.5
Railroad retirement/pension fund	2.3	2.7	2.3	2.3	2.3	2.4	2.3	2.3
Unemployment insurance funds	21.6	27.6	42.0	43.4	41.1	39.5	37.9	51.5
Other retirement	4.5	4.8	4.5	4.4	4.3	4.2	4.1	4.4
Federal employees retirement-employee share	4.4	4.7	4.4	4.3	4.2	4.1	4.1	4.4
Excise taxes, total	**35.3**	**68.9**	**73.1**	**74.0**	**65.1**	**67.3**	**62.5**	**73.2**
Federal funds [1]	15.6	22.7	22.5	22.5	11.1	15.7	13.9	22.0
Alcohol	5.7	8.1	8.1	8.5	8.6	9.3	9.9	9.9
Tobacco	4.1	7.2	7.9	7.7	7.6	7.6	12.8	17.4
Telephone	3.0	5.7	6.0	4.9	−2.1	1.0	1.1	0.9
Transportation fuels	–	0.8	−0.8	−2.4	−3.3	−5.1	−10.3	−8.4
Trust funds [1]	19.8	46.2	50.5	51.5	54.0	51.6	48.6	51.2
Highway	13.9	35.0	37.9	38.5	39.4	36.4	35.0	36.2
Airport and airway	3.7	9.7	10.3	10.4	11.5	12.0	10.6	11.8
Black lung disability	0.7	0.5	0.6	0.6	0.6	0.7	0.6	0.6
Inland waterway	0.1	0.1	0.1	0.1	0.1	0.1	0.1	0.1
Oil spill liability	0.1	0.2	–	0.1	0.5	0.3	0.4	0.4
Aquatic resources	0.2	0.3	0.4	0.5	0.6	0.6	0.6	0.6
Tobacco assessments	–	–	0.9	0.9	0.9	1.1	1.0	1.0
Vaccine injury compensation	0.2	0.1	0.1	0.2	0.2	0.3	0.2	0.3

– Represents zero. [1] Includes other funds, not shown separately.

Source: U.S. Office of Management and Budget, *Budget of the United States Government, Historical Tables*, annual. See also <http://www.whitehouse.gov/omb/budget>.

Table 474. Federal Trust Fund Income, Outlays, and Balances: 2009 to 2011

[In billions of dollars (11.0 represents $11,000,000,000). For years ending September 30. Receipts deposited. Outlays on a checks-issued basis less refunds collected. Balances: That which have not been spent. See text, this section, for discussion of the budget concept and trust funds. Minus sign (−) indicates a negative balance]

Description	Income 2009	Income 2010, est.	Income 2011, est.	Outlays 2009	Outlays 2010, est.	Outlays 2011, est.	Balances [1] 2009	Balances [1] 2010, est.	Balances [1] 2011, est.
Airport and airway trust fund	11.0	12.2	12.9	11.9	10.6	12.9	8.8	10.4	10.4
Federal civilian employees' retirement funds	93.1	99.3	101.5	67.7	70.2	72.4	754.3	783.4	812.5
Federal employees' health benefits fund	37.2	39.7	42.8	37.4	40.2	42.9	15.3	14.7	14.7
Foreign military sales trust fund	24.9	24.9	25.5	21.9	24.7	24.5	17.2	17.3	18.3
Highway trust fund	42.3	36.5	37.4	45.0	50.5	51.2	14.1	0.1	−13.8
Medicare:									
Hospital insurance (HI) trust fund	234.3	224.2	238.0	243.4	253.5	269.6	309.8	280.6	248.9
Supplemental medical insurance trust fund	265.1	282.1	309.7	262.8	282.9	315.0	61.4	60.6	55.3
Military retirement fund	75.1	93.8	100.1	50.0	50.8	51.7	276.1	319.1	367.5
Railroad retirement trust funds	8.5	9.8	10.3	10.9	11.2	11.4	21.2	19.7	18.8
Social security: Old-age, survivors, and disability insurance trust funds	807.1	793.0	835.7	669.8	708.4	735.7	2,503.8	2,588.4	2,688.4
Unemployment trust funds	58.7	128.7	81.6	117.3	186.0	107.1	22.8	16.1	15.7
Veterans' life insurance trust funds	1.1	1.0	0.9	1.7	1.7	1.6	10.9	10.3	9.6
Other trust funds	34.1	28.8	31.2	25.5	25.1	25.8	73.3	76.3	81.0

[1] Balances available on a cash basis (rather than an authorization basis) at the end of the year. Balances are primarily invested in federal debt securities.

Source: U.S. Office of Management and Budget, *Budget of the United States Government, Analytical Perspectives*, annual. See also <http://www.whitehouse.gov/omb/budget>.

Table 475. Tax Expenditures Estimates Relating to Individual and Corporate Income Taxes by Selected Function: 2009 to 2012

[In millions of dollars (11,930 represents $11,930,000,000). For years ending September 30. Tax expenditures are defined as revenue losses attributable to provisions of the federal tax laws which allow a special exclusion, exemption, or deduction from gross income or which provide a special credit, a preferential rate of tax, or a deferral of liability. Minus sign (–) indicates decrease]

Function and provision	2009	2010	2011	2012
National Defense:				
Exclusion of benefits and allowances to armed forces personnel	11,930	12,570	11,530	11,570
International affairs:				
Exclusion of income earned abroad by U.S. citizens	5,320	5,590	5,870	6,160
Deferral of income from controlled foreign corporations (normal tax method)	31,580	30,960	32,720	33,870
Deferred taxes for financial firms on certain income earned overseas	5,570	5,460	5,770	5,980
General science, space, and technology:				
Expensing of research and experimentation expenditures (normal tax method)	3,820	3,500	4,560	5,720
Credit for increasing research activities	8,010	5,890	3,850	3,080
Energy:				
Alternative fuel production credit	60	50	20	10
Commerce and housing:				
Financial institutions and insurance:				
Exclusion of interest on life insurance savings	20,280	21,140	23,070	24,700
Housing:				
Deductibility of mortgage interest on owner-occupied homes	79,400	92,180	104,540	116,620
Deductibility of state and local property tax on owner-occupied homes	29,010	18,860	23,710	29,730
Capital gains exclusion on home sales	23,500	23,860	31,300	39,510
Exclusion of net imputed rental income	27,040	32,530	37,630	40,810
Exception from passive loss rules for $25,000 of rental loss	6,020	5,910	7,330	8,510
Credit for low-income housing investments	3,800	5,680	6,170	6,660
Accelerated depreciation on rental housing (normal tax method)	3,860	4,640	5,870	7,100
Commerce:				
Capital gains (except agriculture, timber, iron ore, and coal)	52,590	45,360	44,290	41,090
Step-up basis of capital gains at death	41,370	36,740	44,520	53,270
Accelerated depreciation of machinery and equipment (normal tax method)	57,400	10,470	1,170	14,120
Expensing of certain small investments (normal tax method)	–130	410	–3,200	–2,820
Graduated corporation income tax rate (normal tax method)	2,720	2,860	3,120	3,070
Deduction for U.S. production activities	9,020	11,530	13,640	14,420
Transportation:				
Exclusion of reimbursed employee parking expenses	2,960	3,020	3,100	3,190
Education, training, employment, and social services:				
Education:				
HOPE tax credit	2,920	–	840	4,250
Lifetime Learning tax credit	3,860	2,910	3,360	4,780
Exclusion of interest on bonds for private nonprofit educational facilities	1,780	1,610	2,220	2,720
Parental personal exemption for students age 19 years or over	4,440	2,710	2,780	3,140
Deductibility of charitable contributions (education)	4,170	4,290	4,940	5,370
Training, employment, and social services:				
Child credit	25,640	23,450	18,550	10,870
Credit for child and dependent care expenses	4,330	3,750	2,200	1,890
Deductibility of charitable contributions, other than education and health	36,710	37,720	43,850	47,730
Health:				
Exclusion of employer contributions for medical insurance premiums [1]	144,412	159,868	176,964	191,540
Self-employed medical insurance premiums	4,870	5,250	5,740	6,150
Deductibility of medical expenses	8,760	9,090	10,030	10,980
Exclusion of interest on hospital construction bonds	2,690	2,440	3,350	4,110
Deductibility of charitable contributions (health)	4,150	4,260	4,950	5,380
Income security:				
Exclusion of workers' compensation benefits	5,810	5,870	5,940	6,070
Net exclusion of pension contributions and earnings:				
Employer plans	40,670	41,360	44,630	47,870
401(k) plans	44,126	53,549	67,061	70,168
Individual Retirement Accounts	12,090	12,780	14,080	15,770
Keogh plans	12,770	13,890	15,120	17,190
Exclusion of other employee benefits:				
Premiums on group term life insurance	2,160	2,110	2,160	2,280
Earned income tax credit	4,420	6,190	6,200	8,380
Social security:				
Exclusion of social security benefits:				
Social security benefits for retired workers	20,970	21,410	20,240	21,380
Social security benefits for disabled	6,460	6,950	7,160	7,450
Social security benefits for dependents and survivors	3,650	3,850	3,140	3,150
Veterans' benefits and services:				
Exclusion of veterans' death benefits and disability compensation	3,900	4,130	4,370	4,630
General purpose fiscal assistance:				
Exclusion of interest on public purpose state and local bonds	22,990	20,810	28,660	35,130
Deductibility of nonbusiness state and local taxes other than on owner-occupied homes	45,310	33,920	46,500	58,100
Addendum: Aid to state and local governments:				
Deductibility of:				
Property taxes on owner-occupied homes	29,010	18,860	23,710	29,730
Nonbusiness state and local taxes other than on owner-occupied homes	45,310	33,920	46,500	58,100
Exclusion of interest on State and local bonds for:				
Public purposes	22,990	20,810	28,660	35,130
Private nonprofit educational facilities	1,780	1,610	2,220	2,720
Hospital construction	2,690	2,440	3,350	4,110

– Represents zero. [1] Includes medical care.

Source: U.S. Office of Management and Budget, *Budget of the United States Government, Analytical Perspectives*, annual. See also <http://www.whitehouse.gov/omb/budget>.

Table 476. U.S. Savings Bonds: 1990 to 2009

[In billions of dollars (122.5 represents $122,500,000,000), except percent. As of September 30]

Item	Unit	1990	1995	2000	2002	2003	2004	2005	2006	2007	2008	2009
Amounts outstanding, total [1] . . .	Bil. dol	122.5	181.5	177.7	185.5	192.6	194.1	189.9	189.2	181.5	177.8	175.6
Sales	Bil. dol	7.8	7.2	5.6	12.5	13.2	10.3	6.5	8.5	3.6	3.6	3.0
Accrued discounts	Bil. dol	8.0	9.5	6.9	7.7	7.3	6.9	6.7	7.5	7.2	7.1	6.9
Redemptions [2]	Bil. dol	7.5	11.8	14.5	12.5	12.2	14.6	13.8	16.0	10.8	10.7	9.9
Percent of total outstanding	Percent . . .	6.1	6.5	8.2	6.7	6.3	7.5	7.3	8.5	6.0	6.0	5.7

[1] Interest-bearing debt only for amounts at end of year. [2] Matured and unmatured bonds.

Source: U.S. Department of the Treasury, Bureau of Public Debt, <http://www.treasurydirect.gov/govt/reports/pd/pd_sbntables _downloadable_files.htm>, accessed January 2010.

Table 477. Federal Funds—Summary Distribution by State: 2008

[In millions of dollars (2,792,611 represents $2,792,611,000,000), except as indicated. For year ending September 30. Data for grants, salaries and wages, and direct payments to individuals are on an expenditures basis; procurement data are on an obligation basis]

State and Island Areas	Federal funds Total	Federal funds Per capita [1] (dollars)	Agency Defense	Agency Non-defense	Object category Direct payments	Object category Procure-ment	Object category Grants	Object category Salaries and wages
United States [2]	**2,792,611**	**9,042**	**488,726**	**2,303,885**	**1,449,874**	**514,117**	**574,659**	**253,962**
Alabama	47,966	10,289	11,412	36,553	26,623	10,253	7,242	3,847
Alaska	9,423	13,730	3,629	5,794	2,036	2,480	2,702	2,206
Arizona	54,314	8,356	14,677	39,637	25,992	13,832	10,325	4,166
Arkansas	23,857	8,355	1,962	21,894	15,540	1,331	5,050	1,936
California	299,923	8,160	48,763	251,160	143,626	52,045	82,219	22,033
Colorado	38,015	7,696	8,263	29,752	18,383	7,709	6,524	5,399
Connecticut	38,879	11,104	12,772	26,106	16,922	12,856	7,378	1,723
Delaware	6,623	7,585	671	5,952	4,224	366	1,435	598
District of Columbia	47,203	79,757	6,732	40,471	5,473	16,541	6,163	19,027
Florida	149,872	8,177	20,175	129,697	101,535	16,625	20,226	11,486
Georgia	74,165	7,657	14,176	59,988	38,462	11,069	14,569	10,065
Hawaii	15,009	11,651	6,107	8,902	6,138	2,456	2,283	4,133
Idaho	11,227	7,368	742	10,485	6,044	2,003	2,133	1,047
Illinois	100,672	7,803	11,307	89,365	57,546	13,197	22,737	7,192
Indiana	52,813	8,282	9,509	43,304	31,844	8,922	8,857	3,189
Iowa	23,927	7,969	1,596	22,332	15,512	1,870	5,057	1,488
Kansas	25,129	8,968	5,055	20,074	13,692	4,102	4,280	3,054
Kentucky	52,264	12,242	8,590	43,675	31,923	7,729	8,312	4,300
Louisiana	44,496	10,088	6,412	38,085	22,857	6,240	12,337	3,062
Maine	11,974	9,096	1,516	10,459	6,891	1,130	2,930	1,023
Maryland	77,905	13,829	17,295	60,610	30,036	25,602	10,528	11,739
Massachusetts	72,115	11,098	12,430	59,685	34,213	13,350	20,427	4,124
Michigan	82,933	8,290	7,393	75,540	50,795	8,612	19,205	4,322
Minnesota	38,246	7,326	2,726	35,519	22,849	3,363	9,230	2,804
Mississippi	30,098	10,242	5,883	24,215	15,545	5,539	6,790	2,224
Missouri	60,829	10,290	14,514	46,315	30,997	14,450	10,372	5,010
Montana	8,843	9,141	701	8,142	5,083	572	2,185	1,004
Nebraska	15,739	8,825	1,685	14,054	9,339	1,208	3,733	1,459
Nevada	17,260	6,638	2,303	14,957	9,801	2,701	3,107	1,651
New Hampshire	10,311	7,837	1,942	8,369	5,779	1,914	1,877	742
New Jersey	72,085	8,302	8,873	63,212	41,975	8,961	16,204	4,946
New Mexico	23,846	12,017	2,711	21,135	9,115	6,914	5,531	2,287
New York	174,071	8,931	12,222	161,849	94,833	13,732	54,421	11,085
North Carolina	70,203	7,612	9,742	60,461	41,309	5,794	15,165	7,934
North Dakota	7,323	11,415	734	6,589	4,237	552	1,660	872
Ohio	90,592	7,887	9,774	80,818	57,330	9,096	17,769	6,397
Oklahoma	31,758	8,719	4,833	26,925	18,862	2,853	6,216	3,828
Oregon	27,530	7,264	2,202	25,328	16,836	2,375	6,132	2,187
Pennsylvania	121,551	9,764	16,368	105,183	73,866	18,294	21,678	7,713
Rhode Island	9,841	9,365	1,187	8,654	5,702	865	2,441	833
South Carolina	38,832	8,668	7,490	31,342	21,764	7,621	6,422	3,025
South Dakota	8,552	10,634	795	7,758	5,249	653	1,794	855
Tennessee	58,672	9,441	5,047	53,625	31,321	9,876	14,188	3,288
Texas	210,005	8,633	63,546	146,458	92,405	60,703	38,300	18,597
Utah	17,117	6,255	3,346	13,771	8,007	3,030	3,536	2,544
Vermont	6,080	9,787	611	5,469	2,911	564	2,103	502
Virginia	118,527	15,256	52,155	66,372	40,183	53,868	8,776	15,699
Washington	56,436	8,617	10,780	45,656	28,097	10,386	11,023	6,929
West Virginia	18,002	9,922	771	17,231	11,243	1,328	3,711	1,720
Wisconsin	40,137	7,132	3,989	36,148	24,859	4,487	8,431	2,358
Wyoming	5,969	11,207	515	5,455	2,431	529	2,422	588

[1] Based on U.S. Census Bureau estimated resident population as of July 1. [2] Includes Island Areas, not shown separately.

Source: U.S. Census Bureau, *Consolidated Federal Funds Report for Fiscal Year 2008,* July 2009. See also <http://www. census.gov/gov/cffr /index.html>.

Table 478. Internal Revenue Gross Collections by Type of Tax: 2005 to 2009

[2,269 represents $2,269,000,000,000. For years ending September 30. See text, this section, for information on taxes]

Type of tax	Gross collections (bil. dol.)					Percent of total				
	2005	2006	2007	2008	2009	2005	2006	2007	2008	2009
United States, total	**2,269**	**2,519**	**2,692**	**2,745**	**2,345**	**100.0**	**100.0**	**100.0**	**100.0**	**100.0**
Individual income taxes	1,108	1,236	1,366	1,400	1,175	48.8	49.1	50.8	51.0	50.1
Withheld by employers	787	849	929	971	881	34.7	33.7	34.5	35.4	37.6
Tax payments [1]	321	387	438	430	295	14.1	15.4	16.3	15.7	12.6
Estate and trust income tax	(NA)	(NA)	(NA)	26	15	(NA)	(NA)	(NA)	0.9	0.6
Employment taxes	771	815	850	883	858	34.0	32.4	31.6	32.2	36.6
Old-age and disability insurance	760	803	838	871	847	33.5	31.9	31.1	31.7	36.1
Unemployment insurance	7	8	7	7	7	0.3	0.3	0.3	0.3	0.3
Railroad retirement	5	5	5	5	5	0.2	0.2	0.2	0.2	0.2
Corporation income taxes	307	381	396	354	225	13.5	15.1	14.7	12.9	9.6
Estate and gift taxes	24	27	25	27	22	1.0	1.1	0.9	1.0	0.9
Excise taxes	57	58	53	52	47	2.5	2.3	2.0	1.9	2.0

NA Not available. [1] Includes estimated income tax collections and payments made with tax filings. Also includes estate and trust income tax for 2004–2007.

Source: U.S. Internal Revenue Service, *IRS Data Book* (Publication 55B), annual. See also <http://www.irs.gov/taxstats/index.html>.

Table 479. Individual Income Tax Returns Filed—Examination Coverage: 1995 to 2009

[114,683 represents 114,683,000. See the annual *IRS Data Book* (Publication 55B) for a detailed explanation]

Year	Returns filed [1] (1,000)	Returns examined		Total recommended additional tax [3] ($1,000)	Average recommended additional tax per return (dollars) [3]
		Total [2] (1,000)	Percent coverage		
1995	114,683	1,919	1.7	7,756,954	4,041
1997	118,363	1,519	1.3	8,363,918	5,505
1998	120,342	1,193	1.0	6,095,698	5,110
1999	122,547	1,100	0.9	4,458,474	4,052
2000	124,887	618	0.5	3,388,905	5,486
2001	127,097	732	0.6	3,301,860	4,512
2002	129,445	744	0.6	3,636,486	4,889
2003	130,341	849	0.7	4,559,902	5,369
2004	130,134	997	0.8	6,201,693	6,220
2005	130,577	1,199	0.9	13,355,087	11,138
2006	132,276	1,284	1.0	13,045,221	10,160
2007	134,543	1,385	1.0	15,705,155	11,343
2008	137,850	1,392	1.0	12,462,770	8,956
2009 [4]	138,950	1,426	1.0	14,940,892	10,478

[1] Returns generally filed in previous calendar year. [2] Includes taxpayer examinations by correspondence. [3] For 1995 to 1997, amount includes associated penalties. [4] Excludes returns filed by individuals only to receive an Economic Stimulus Payment and who had no other reason to file.

Source: U.S. Internal Revenue Service, *IRS Data Book* (Publication 55B), annual. See also <http://www.irs.gov/taxstats/index.html>.

Table 480. Federal Individual Income Tax Returns—Adjusted Gross Income, Taxable Income, and Total Income Tax: 2006 and 2007

[138,395 represents 138,395,000. For tax years. Based on a sample of returns, see source and Appendix III]

Year	2006		2007		Percent change in amount, 2006–07
	Number of returns (1,000)	Amount (mil. dol.)	Number of returns (1,000)	Amount (mil. dol.)	
Adjusted gross income (less deficit)	138,395	8,030,843	142,979	8,687,719	8.2
Exemptions [1]	275,257	891,912	282,613	943,171	5.7
Taxable income	106,667	5,579,145	110,533	6,063,264	8.7
Total income tax	92,741	1,023,920	96,270	1,115,602	9.0
Alternative minimum tax	3,967	21,565	4,109	24,110	11.8

[1] The number of returns columns represent the number of exemptions.

Source: U.S. Internal Revenue Service, *Statistics of Income Bulletin*, fall issues. See also <http://www.irs.gov/taxstats/index.html>.

Table 481. Federal Individual Income Tax Returns—Adjusted Gross Income (AGI) by Selected Source of Income and Income Class: 2007

[In millions of dollars (8,687,719 represents $8,687,719,000,000), except as indicated. For the tax year. Minus sign (–) indicates net loss was greater than net income. Based on sample; see Appendix III]

Item	Total [1]	Under $10,000	$10,000 to $19,999	$20,000 to $29,999	$30,000 to $39,999	$40,000 to $49,999	$50,000 to $99,999	$100,000 and over
Number of all returns (1,000)	142,979	25,953	22,976	18,969	14,741	11,151	31,195	17,993
Adjusted gross income [2]	8,687,719	11,673	342,106	470,883	512,920	499,464	2,210,446	4,640,226
Salaries and wages	5,842,270	117,238	259,234	388,428	425,047	407,111	1,722,349	2,522,862
Interest received	268,058	12,181	10,155	9,601	9,934	9,175	47,653	169,359
Dividends in AGI	237,052	5,231	4,385	4,523	4,350	4,991	30,848	182,724
Business, profession, net profit less loss	279,736	4,179	27,107	15,684	13,695	13,337	54,660	151,075
Sales of property, net gain less loss [3]	912,013	11,064	3,720	4,398	4,494	5,340	40,936	842,060
Pensions and annuities in AGI....	490,581	9,309	32,311	36,220	37,597	36,930	173,861	164,354
Rents and royalties, net income less loss [4]	453,451	–59,296	–749	370	719	1,809	18,030	492,566

[1] Includes a small number of returns with no adjusted gross income. [2] Includes other sources, not shown separately. [3] Includes sales of capital assets and other property; net gain less loss. [4] Excludes rental passive losses disallowed in the computation of AGI; net income less loss.

Source: U.S. Internal Revenue Service, *Statistics of Income*, fall issues. See also <http://www.irs.gov/taxstats/index.html>.

Table 482. Federal Individual Income Tax Returns—Total and Selected Sources of Adjusted Gross Income: 2006 and 2007

[138,395 represents 138,395,000. For tax years. Based on a sample of returns, see source and Appendix III. Minus sign (–) indicates decrease]

Item	2006 Number of returns (1,000)	2006 Amount (mil. dol.)	2007 Number of returns (1,000)	2007 Amount (mil. dol.)	Change in amount, 2006–07 Net change (mil. dol.)	Change in amount, 2006–07 Percent change
Adjusted gross income (less deficit) [1]	138,395	8,030,843	142,979	8,687,719	656,876	8.2
Salaries and wages.............................	116,379	5,469,370	120,845	5,842,270	372,900	6.8
Taxable interest................................	62,401	222,707	64,505	268,058	45,351	20.4
Ordinary dividends	31,620	199,359	32,006	237,052	37,693	18.9
Qualified dividends	26,584	137,196	27,145	155,872	18,676	13.6
Business or profession net income (less loss).........	21,656	281,527	22,629	279,736	–1,791	–0.6
Net capital gain	26,668	779,462	27,156	907,656	128,194	16.4
Capital gain distributions [2].....................	14,511	59,417	15,714	86,397	26,980	45.4
Sales of property other than capital assets, net gain (less loss)............................	1,779	4,202	1,751	4,357	155	3.7
Sales of property other than capital assets, net gain	895	14,021	893	15,113	1,092	7.8
Taxable social security benefits...................	13,749	144,404	15,012	167,187	22,783	15.8
Total rental and royalty net income (less net loss) [3].....	9,988	23,427	10,334	20,639	–2,788	–11.9
Partnership and S corporation net income (less loss)...	7,619	425,477	7,945	414,705	–10,772	–2.5
Estate and trust net income (less loss)	596	17,183	591	18,107	923	5.4
Farm net income (less loss)	1,958	–15,331	1,978	–14,693	638	4.2
Farm net income	552	7,684	556	9,931	2,247	29.2
Unemployment compensation......................	7,378	26,524	7,622	29,415	2,891	10.9
Taxable pensions and annuities...................	24,098	450,454	25,181	490,581	40,127	8.9
Taxable Individual Retirement Account distributions	9,965	124,706	10,683	147,959	23,254	18.6
Other net income (less loss) [4].....................	(NA)	29,938	(NA)	36,140	6,202	20.7
Gambling earnings	1,871	27,902	2,009	30,139	2,237	8.0

NA Not available. [1] Includes sources of income, not shown separately. [2] Includes both Schedule D and non-Schedule D capital gain distributions. [3] Includes farm rental net income (less loss). [4] Other net income (less loss) represents data reported on Form 1040, line 21, except net operating loss, the foreign-earned income exclusion, and gambling earnings.

Source: U.S. Internal Revenue Service, *Statistics of Income Bulletin*, fall issues. See also <http://www.irs.gov/taxstats/index.html>.

Table 483. Federal Individual Income Tax Returns—Net Capital Gains and Capital Gain Distributions From Mutual Funds: 1989 to 2007

[15,060 represents 15,060,000. For tax years. Based on a sample of returns, see source and Appendix III. Minus sign (–) indicates decrease]

Tax year	Net capital gain (less loss)				Capital gain distributions [2]			
	Number of returns (1,000)	Current dollars (mil. dol.)	Constant (1982–1984) dollars [1]		Number of returns (1,000)	Current dollars (mil. dol.)	Constant (1982–1984) dollars [1]	
			Amount (mil. dol.)	Percent change			Amount (mil. dol.)	Percent change
1989.....	15,060	145,631	117,444	–9.6	5,191	5,483	4,422	34.9
1990.....	14,288	114,231	87,400	–25.6	5,069	3,905	2,988	–32.4
1991.....	15,009	102,776	75,460	–13.7	5,796	4,665	3,425	14.6
1992.....	16,491	118,230	84,269	11.7	5,917	7,426	5,293	54.5
1993.....	18,409	144,172	99,773	18.4	9,998	11,995	8,301	56.8
1994.....	18,823	142,288	96,011	–3.8	9,803	11,322	7,640	–8.0
1995.....	19,963	170,415	111,821	16.5	10,744	14,391	9,443	23.6
1996.....	22,065	251,817	160,495	43.5	12,778	24,722	15,757	66.9
1997.....	24,240	356,083	221,859	38.2	14,969	45,132	28,120	78.5
1998.....	25,690	446,084	273,671	23.4	16,070	46,147	28,311	0.7
1999.....	27,701	542,758	325,785	19.0	17,012	59,473	35,698	26.1
2000.....	29,521	630,542	366,169	12.4	17,546	79,079	45,923	28.6
2001.....	25,956	326,527	184,375	–49.6	12,216	13,609	7,685	–83.3
2002.....	24,189	238,789	132,734	–28.0	7,567	5,343	2,970	–61.4
2003.....	22,985	294,354	159,975	20.5	7,265	4,695	2,552	–14.1
2004.....	25,267	473,662	250,747	56.7	10,733	15,336	8,119	218.1
2005.....	26,196	668,015	342,046	36.4	13,393	35,581	18,219	124.4
2006.....	26,668	779,462	386,638	13.0	14,511	59,417	29,473	61.8
2007.....	27,156	907,656	437,758	13.2	15,714	86,397	41,669	41.4

[1] Constant dollars were calculated using the U.S. Bureau of Labor Statistics consumer price index for urban consumers (CPI-U, 1982–84 = 100). See Table 724. [2] Capital gain distributions are included in net capital gain (less loss). For 1989–1996, and 1999 and later years, capital gain distributions from mutual funds are the sum of the amounts reported on the Form 1040 and Schedule D. For 1997 and 1998, capital gain distributions were reported entirely on the Schedule D.

Source: U.S. Internal Revenue Service, *Statistics of Income Bulletin*, fall issues. See also <http://www.irs.gov/taxstats/index.html>.

Table 484. Alternative Minimum Tax: 1986 to 2007

[609 represents 609,000. For tax years. Based on a sample of returns, see source and Appendix III]

Tax year	Highest statutory alternative minimum tax rate (percent)	Alternative minimum tax		Tax year	Highest statutory alternative minimum tax rate (percent)	Alternative minimum tax	
		Number of returns (1,000)	Amount (mil. dol.)			Number of returns (1,000)	Amount (mil. dol.)
1986........	20	609	6,713	1997........	28	618	4,005
1987........	21	140	1,675	1998........	[1] 28	853	5,015
1988........	21	114	1,028	1999........	[1] 28	1,018	6,478
1989........	21	117	831	2000........	[1] 28	1,304	9,601
1990........	21	132	830	2001........	[1] 28	1,120	6,757
1991........	24	244	1,213	2002........	[1] 28	1,911	6,854
1992........	24	287	1,357	2003........	[1] 28	2,358	9,470
1993........	28	335	2,053	2004........	[1] 28	3,096	13,029
1994........	28	369	2,212	2005........	[1] 28	4,005	17,421
1995........	28	414	2,291	2006........	[1] 28	3,967	21,565
1996........	28	478	2,813	2007........	[1] 28	4,109	24,110

[1] Top rate on most long-term capital gains was 20 percent; beginning 2003, the rate was 15 percent.

Source: U.S. Internal Revenue Service, *Statistics of Income Bulletin*, fall issue. See also <http://www.irs.gov/taxstats/index.html>

Table 485. Federal Individual Income Tax Returns—Sources of Net Losses Included in Adjusted Gross Income: 2005 to 2007

[5,308 represents 5,308,000. For tax years. Based on a sample of returns, see source and Appendix III]

Item	2005 Number of returns (1,000)	2005 Amount (mil. dol.)	2006 Number of returns (1,000)	2006 Amount (mil. dol.)	2007 Number of returns (1,000)	2007 Amount (mil. dol.)
Total net losses	(NA)	319,587	(NA)	343,271	(NA)	390,035
Business or profession net loss	5,308	45,016	5,447	48,738	5,697	54,849
Net capital loss [1]	10,023	22,137	8,642	18,752	7,558	16,508
Net loss, sales of property other than capital assets	877	9,180	884	9,819	858	10,756
Total rental and royalty net loss [2]	4,554	43,988	4,658	49,927	4,886	56,288
Partnership and S corporation net loss	2,539	89,694	2,597	102,747	2,799	132,696
Estate and trust net loss	36	1,654	45	1,942	47	2,505
Farm net loss	1,371	20,653	1,406	23,015	1,422	24,625
Net operating loss [3]	863	79,452	917	80,796	923	86,369
Other net loss [4]	346	7,811	347	7,535	228	5,438

NA Not available. [1] Includes only the portion of capital losses allowable in the calculation of adjusted gross income. Only $3,000 of net capital loss per return ($1,500 for married filing separately) are allowed to be included in negative total income. Any excess is carried forward to future years. [2] Includes farm rental net loss. [3] Net operating loss is a carryover of the loss from a business when taxable income from a prior year was less than zero. [4] Other net loss represents losses reported on Form 1040, line 21, except net operating loss and the foreign-earned income exclusion.

Source: U.S. Internal Revenue Service, *Statistics of Income Bulletin*, fall issues. See also <http://www.irs.gov/taxstats/index.html>.

Table 486. Federal Individual Income Tax Returns—Number, Income Tax, and Average Tax by Size of Adjusted Gross Income: 2000 and 2007

[129,374 represents 129,374,000. Based on sample of returns; see Appendix III]

Size of adjusted gross income	Number of returns (1,000) 2000	2007	Adjusted gross income (AGI) (bil. dol.) 2000	2007	Income tax total [1] (bil. dol.) 2000	2007	Taxes as a percent of AGI (for taxable returns only) 2000	2007	Average tax (for taxable returns only) (dol.) 2000	2007
Total	129,374	142,979	6,365	8,688	981	1,116	16	14	10,129	11,590
Less than $1,000 [2]	2,966	3,687	−58	−110	−	−	(X)	−2	648	2,959
$1,000 to $2,999	5,385	4,853	11	10	−	−	7	3	134	67
$3,000 to $4,999	5,599	5,298	22	21	−	−	4	4	179	174
$5,000 to $6,999	5,183	4,839	31	29	1	−	5	2	297	121
$7,000 to $8,999	4,972	4,965	40	40	1	−	4	3	331	254
$9,000 to $10,999	5,089	4,650	51	47	1	−	5	2	470	225
$11,000 to $12,999	4,859	4,814	58	58	2	1	6	3	704	348
$13,000 to $14,999	4,810	4,760	67	67	3	1	6	4	883	507
$15,000 to $16,999	4,785	4,546	76	73	3	1	7	4	1,052	673
$17,000 to $18,999	4,633	4,345	83	78	4	2	7	5	1,279	842
$19,000 to $21,999	6,502	6,327	133	130	7	4	8	5	1,565	1,060
$22,000 to $24,999	5,735	5,808	135	136	8	5	8	6	1,815	1,367
$25,000 to $29,999	8,369	9,005	229	247	16	10	8	6	2,248	1,783
$30,000 to $39,999	13,548	14,741	471	513	40	28	9	7	3,094	2,428
$40,000 to $49,999	10,412	11,151	466	499	46	34	10	8	4,462	3,441
$50,000 to $74,999	17,076	19,451	1,045	1,196	116	97	11	9	6,824	5,289
$75,000 to $99,999	8,597	11,744	738	1,015	100	94	14	9	11,631	8,117
$100,000 to $199,999 . . .	8,083	13,458	1,066	1,793	184	229	17	13	22,783	17,089
$200,000 to $499,999 . . .	2,136	3,492	614	1,005	146	196	24	20	68,628	56,397
$500,000 to $999,999 . . .	396	651	269	441	76	103	28	23	192,092	158,858
$1,000,000 or more	240	392	817	1,401	226	310	28	22	945,172	792,395

− Represents or rounds to zero. X Not applicable. [1] Consists of income tax after credits (including alternative minimum tax). [2] In addition to low income taxpayers, this size class (and others) includes taxpayers with "tax preferences," not reflected in adjusted gross income or taxable income which are subject to the "alternative minimum tax" (included in total income tax).

Source: U.S. Internal Revenue Service, *Statistics of Income Bulletin*, quarterly and fall issues. See also <http://www.irs.gov/taxstats/index.html>.

Table 487. Federal Individual Income Tax Returns—Selected Itemized Deductions and the Standard Deduction: 2006 and 2007

[49,124 represents 49,124,000. For tax years. Based on a sample of returns, see source and Appendix III. Minus sign (–) indicates decrease]

Item	2006		2007		Percent change, 2006–07	
	Number of returns [1] (1,000)	Amount (mil. dol.)	Number of returns [1] (1,000)	Amount (mil. dol.)	Number of returns [1] (percent)	Amount (percent)
Total itemized deductions before limitation ...	**49,124**	**1,264,390**	**50,544**	**1,372,138**	**2.9**	**8.5**
Medical and dental expenses after 7.5 percent AGI limitation............................	10,209	70,704	10,520	76,347	3.0	8.0
Taxes paid [2]..............................	48,661	432,774	50,119	465,881	3.0	7.6
State and local income taxes.................	35,666	246,382	36,683	269,351	2.9	9.3
State and local general sales taxes...........	11,249	18,924	11,936	18,522	6.1	–2.1
Interest paid [3].............................	40,285	470,475	41,283	524,790	2.5	11.5
Home mortgage interest	39,831	443,152	40,777	491,432	2.4	10.9
Charitable contributions [4].....................	41,438	186,647	41,119	193,604	–0.8	3.7
Other than cash contributions	24,748	52,631	23,854	58,747	–3.6	11.6
Casualty and theft losses	206	5,136	107	2,337	–48.1	–54.5
Miscellaneous deductions after 2-percent AGI limitation.............................	12,314	76,666	12,734	85,218	3.4	11.2
Total unlimited miscellaneous deductions	1,606	21,988	1,692	23,961	5.4	9.0
Itemized deductions in excess of limitation	6,789	35,152	7,131	39,102	5.0	11.2
Total itemized deductions after limitation.........	49,124	1,229,237	50,544	1,333,037	2.9	8.4
Total standard deduction...................	86,584	607,464	90,511	654,182	4.5	7.7
Total deductions (after itemized deduction limitation)	135,707	1,836,701	141,055	1,987,218	3.9	8.2

[1] Returns with no adjusted gross income are excluded from the deduction counts. For this reason, the sum of the number of returns with total itemized deductions and the number of returns with total standard deduction is less than the total number of returns for all filers. [2] Includes real estate taxes, personal property taxes, and other taxes not shown separately. [3] Includes investment interest and deductible mortgage "points" not shown separately. [4] For more information See Table 582.

Source: U.S. Internal Revenue Service, *Statistics of Income Bulletin*, Fall issues. See also <http://www.irs.gov/taxstats/index.html>.

Table 488. Federal Individual Income Tax Returns—Statutory Adjustments: 2006 and 2007

[33,981 represents 33,981,000. For tax years. Based on a sample of returns, see source and Appendix III. Minus sign (–) indicates decrease]

Item	2006		2007		Percent change in amount, 2006–07
	Number of returns (1,000)	Amount (mil. dol.)	Number of returns (1,000)	Amount (mil. dol.)	
Total statutory adjustments	**33,981**	**113,845**	**36,050**	**123,020**	**8.1**
Payments to an Individual Retirement Account........	3,231	12,534	3,300	12,877	2.7
Educator expenses deduction......................	3,167	806	3,654	926	14.9
Moving expenses adjustment	1,083	3,159	1,119	2,903	–8.1
Student loan interest deduction.....................	8,541	6,157	9,091	7,464	21.2
Tuition and fees deduction.........................	4,016	9,621	4,543	10,579	10.0
Self-employment tax deduction.....................	17,075	23,925	17,840	24,760	3.5
Self-employment health insurance deduction	3,804	20,303	3,839	21,283	4.8
Payments to a self-employed retirement (Keogh) plan ..	1,228	22,012	11,191	22,262	1.1
Forfeited interest penalty..........................	1,164	430	1,164	353	–17.9
Alimony paid	585	9,116	600	9,497	4.2
Other adjustment [1]...............................	(NA)	1,245	(NA)	1,415	13.7

NA Not available. [1] Includes foreign housing adjustment, Medical Savings Accounts deduction, jury duty pay deduction, and other adjustments for 2006 and 2007.

Source: U.S. Internal Revenue Service, *Statistics of Income Bulletin*, Fall issues. See also <http://www.irs.gov/taxstats/index.html>.

Table 489. Federal Individual Income Tax Returns—Itemized Deductions and Statutory Adjustments by Size of Adjusted Gross Income: 2007

[50,544 represents 50,544,000. Based on a sample of returns, see Appendix III]

Item	Unit	Total	Adjusted gross income class						
			Under $10,000	$10,000 to $19,999	$20,000 to $29,999	$30,000 to $39,999	$40,000 to $49,999	$50,000 to $99,999	$100,000 and over
Returns with itemized deductions:									
Number of returns [1,2]	1000....	50,544	905	2,267	3,254	4,308	4,529	19,305	15,976
Amount [1,2]	Mil. dol..	1,333,037	14,431	34,532	49,674	67,360	74,965	387,273	704,802
Medical and dental expenses: [3]									
Returns	1000....	10,520	555	1,314	1,326	1,448	1,206	3,588	1,083
Amount	Mil. dol..	119,154	4,362	11,331	11,434	12,275	11,722	43,098	24,932
Taxes paid:									
Returns [2]	1000....	50,119	852	2,190	3,178	4,246	4,482	19,218	15,953
Amount, total	Mil. dol..	465,881	2,495	6,052	9,714	14,429	17,451	112,245	303,495
State and local income taxes: [4]									
Returns	1000....	48,619	739	1,985	2,998	4,064	4,302	18,773	15,759
Amount	Mil. dol..	287,874	617	1,493	3,283	5,753	7,795	57,508	211,426
Real estate taxes:									
Returns	1000....	43,604	642	1,640	2,358	3,365	3,631	17,014	14,953
Amount	Mil. dol..	166,885	1,797	4,260	5,793	8,045	8,892	50,916	87,182
Interest paid:									
Returns	1000....	41,283	615	1,454	2,262	3,235	3,559	16,381	13,776
Amount	Mil. dol..	524,790	6,616	13,671	20,904	29,578	33,818	174,638	245,565
Home mortgage interest:									
Returns	1000....	40,777	606	1,431	2,236	3,214	3,539	16,278	13,472
Amount	Mil. dol..	491,432	6,509	13,472	20,503	29,140	33,270	171,927	216,611
Charitable contributions:									
Returns	1000....	41,119	508	1,417	2,205	3,079	3,368	15,910	14,632
Amount	Mil. dol..	193,603	563	2,457	4,376	6,453	7,291	41,774	130,690
Unreimbursed employee business expenses:									
Returns	1000....	16,479	86	363	919	1,428	1,591	7,242	4,850
Amount	Mil. dol..	82,106	345	1,792	4,785	7,505	8,259	33,620	25,800
Returns with statutory adjustments:									
Number of returns [2]	1000....	36,050	4,580	4,404	3,453	3,261	2,992	9,971	7,390
Amount of adjustments	Mil. dol..	123,020	6,526	6,287	6,227	6,322	6,857	26,356	64,445
Payments to IRAs: [4]									
Returns	1000....	3,300	85	206	340	367	358	1,217	728
Amount	Mil. dol..	12,877	225	502	990	1,161	1,236	4,804	3,958
Deduction for self-employment tax:									
Returns	1000....	17,840	3,380	3,015	1,618	1,303	1,136	3,848	3,541
Amount	Mil. dol..	24,760	1,486	2,344	1,593	1,412	1,372	5,372	11,181
Self-employment health insurance:									
Returns	1000....	3,839	368	361	333	287	280	890	1,319
Amount	Mil. dol..	21,283	1,365	1,305	1,280	1,274	1,223	4,520	10,316
Payments to Keogh plans:									
Returns	1000....	1,191	18	22	28	30	37	243	813
Amount	Mil. dol..	22,262	92	131	114	189	346	2,126	19,265

[1] After limitations. [2] Includes other deductions and adjustments, not shown separately. [3] Before limitation. [4] State and local taxes include income taxes and sales taxes.

Source: U.S. Internal Revenue Service, *Statistics of Income Bulletin*, Fall issues. See also <http://www.irs.gov/taxstats/index.html>.

Table 490. Federal Individual Income Tax Returns—Selected Tax Credits: 2005 to 2007

[42,246 represents 42,246,000. For tax years. Based on a sample of returns, see source and Appendix III]

Item	2005		2006		2007	
	Number of returns (1,000)	Amount (mil. dol.)	Number of returns (1,000)	Amount (mil. dol.)	Number of returns (1,000)	Amount (mil. dol.)
Total tax credits [1]	**42,246**	**55,316**	**46,092**	**58,939**	**48,091**	**63,779**
Child care credit	6,501	3,462	6,467	3,487	6,492	3,483
Earned income credit [2]	2,896	745	2,960	797	3,420	934
Foreign tax credit	5,398	9,362	6,418	10,958	7,643	15,435
General business credit	251	878	387	1,302	231	846
Minimum tax credit	290	1,081	359	1,032	395	1,035
Child tax credit [3]	25,951	32,048	25,742	31,742	25,889	31,556
Education credits	7,057	6,120	7,725	7,022	7,435	6,910
Retirement savings contribution credit	5,294	945	5,192	894	5,862	977

[1] Includes credits not shown separately. [2] Represents portion of earned income credit used to offset income tax before credits. [3] Excludes refundable portion.

Source: U.S. Internal Revenue Service, *Statistics of Income Bulletin*, Fall issues. See also <http://www.irs.gov/taxstats/index.html>.

Table 491. Federal Individual Income Tax Returns by State: 2007

[154,708 represents 154,708,000. For tax year. Data will not agree with data in other tables due to differing survey methodology used to derive state data]

State	Total number of returns (1,000)	Adjusted gross income (mil. dol.)			Itemized deductions (mil. dol.)				Income tax (mil. dol.)
		Total [1]	Salaries and wages	Net capital gain [2]	Total [1]	State and local income tax	Real estate taxes	Mortgage interest paid	
U.S.	154,708	8,564,745	5,857,279	819,566	1,354,091	274,719	169,443	542,643	1,112,906
AL	2,354	102,787	71,928	7,148	13,142	2,322	641	5,164	11,572
AK	371	19,988	13,857	1,058	1,959	23	299	1,046	2,570
AZ	2,899	154,964	105,416	14,854	27,127	4,023	1,993	13,532	18,461
AR	1,393	54,796	38,951	3,453	7,028	1,653	338	2,178	6,073
CA	17,601	1,109,534	748,654	118,595	235,683	54,337	24,827	107,531	148,426
CO	2,455	151,057	100,657	17,161	24,295	4,685	1,857	12,112	19,593
CT	1,868	158,353	102,564	21,006	25,110	6,956	4,314	8,923	26,619
DE	455	25,626	17,596	2,044	3,971	859	297	1,772	3,112
DC	316	23,740	14,963	3,209	4,407	1,337	276	1,523	3,736
FL	9,688	530,465	316,464	77,024	80,377	2,614	11,278	36,947	72,449
GA	4,560	230,079	166,296	17,928	41,257	8,161	3,708	17,157	27,393
HI	694	35,510	23,977	2,881	5,978	1,251	315	2,906	3,998
ID	722	33,553	22,380	3,445	5,602	1,215	420	2,342	3,608
IL	6,559	392,665	267,880	38,792	56,849	8,421	10,518	23,185	54,217
IN	3,243	150,942	109,317	9,067	18,995	4,046	1,990	7,165	17,043
IA	1,539	71,961	50,471	4,296	9,167	2,149	993	2,905	7,851
KS	1,401	72,231	50,127	5,108	9,479	2,298	1,051	3,033	8,656
KY	2,137	88,681	63,239	5,438	12,031	3,178	936	4,220	9,515
LA	2,146	92,468	66,880	5,073	10,412	1,861	457	3,680	10,691
ME	730	31,232	21,374	2,478	4,630	1,179	628	1,669	3,284
MD	2,943	194,552	137,671	15,614	40,720	10,658	4,045	16,248	25,045
MA	3,462	243,829	161,987	28,518	37,955	9,850	5,538	14,555	36,134
MI	5,022	246,805	173,839	14,438	37,547	6,286	5,885	15,149	28,555
MN	2,734	156,772	110,901	11,664	26,405	6,579	2,946	11,122	19,321
MS	1,441	52,429	38,382	2,689	7,056	1,132	356	2,076	5,249
MO	3,011	141,955	99,256	9,755	20,163	4,548	2,045	7,426	16,516
MT	514	22,344	14,015	2,332	3,256	703	298	1,201	2,412
NE	918	44,820	31,075	3,930	6,115	1,349	825	1,850	5,148
NV	1,348	80,657	51,402	11,616	14,945	427	1,187	7,482	10,630
NH	724	42,846	29,979	4,366	5,020	455	1,387	2,612	5,527
NJ	4,577	329,024	233,513	26,108	60,975	14,747	12,946	20,722	48,589
NM	980	42,803	28,876	3,375	5,423	936	397	2,337	4,759
NY	9,919	676,036	434,170	91,076	115,145	40,286	16,873	31,952	104,833
NC	4,602	219,982	154,464	16,140	35,697	9,694	3,042	13,761	24,971
ND	344	15,749	10,526	1,001	1,357	205	190	425	1,800
OH	6,119	282,439	202,482	16,196	39,853	10,689	5,308	14,241	32,353
OK	1,772	82,317	54,687	7,175	10,578	2,001	711	3,089	9,911
OR	1,911	96,000	63,240	8,559	18,549	4,733	1,953	7,420	10,757
PA	6,697	346,909	240,538	26,535	46,062	10,253	7,401	16,275	43,829
RI	568	29,958	20,660	2,505	4,852	1,084	804	1,910	3,677
SC	2,257	98,962	68,050	7,855	15,430	3,337	969	5,869	10,622
SD	417	19,186	12,206	1,817	1,691	60	200	632	2,364
TN	3,162	143,315	101,746	11,893	16,524	452	1,444	7,508	17,283
TX	11,279	606,393	429,068	54,363	63,575	1,154	11,049	24,066	82,113
UT	1,190	63,719	44,150	6,069	12,112	2,308	809	4,772	6,842
VT	345	16,859	10,986	1,817	2,259	517	420	814	1,908
VA	4,016	246,080	174,228	19,359	43,319	8,886	4,651	20,532	31,527
WA	3,371	206,825	136,978	23,742	29,800	700	3,943	15,975	27,185
WV	926	34,353	24,834	1,571	3,152	835	172	1,134	3,530
WI	2,958	149,072	105,343	10,440	23,063	5,848	3,957	7,916	17,118
WY	284	18,951	10,493	3,551	1,836	110	121	729	2,750
Other [3]	1,765	81,775	74,546	13,440	5,358	1,111	436	1,852	10,775

[1] Includes other items, not shown separately. [2] Less loss. [3] Includes returns filed from Army Post Office and Fleet Post Office addresses by members of the armed forces stationed overseas; returns by other U.S. citizens abroad; and returns filed by residents of Puerto Rico with income from sources outside of Puerto Rico or with income earned as U.S. government employees.

Source: U.S. Internal Revenue Service, *Statistics of Income Bulletin*, Spring issues. See also <http://www.irs.gov/taxstats/index .html>.

Table 492. Federal Individual Income Tax—Tax Liability and Effective and Marginal Tax Rates for Selected Income Groups: 2000 to 2009

[Refers to income after exclusions but before deductions for itemized or standard deductions and for personal exemptions. Tax liability is after reductions for tax credits. As a result of the tax credits, tax liability can be negative, which means that the taxpayer receives a payment from the government. The effective rate represents tax liability, which may be negative as a result of the tax credits, divided by stated income. The marginal tax rate is the percentage of the first additional dollar of income which would be paid in income tax. Tax credits which increase with income can result in negative marginal tax rates. Computations assume itemized deductions (in excess of floors) of 18 percent of adjusted gross income or the standard deduction, whichever is greater. All income is assumed to be from wages and salaries. Does not include social security and Medicare taxes imposed on most wages and salaries]

Adjusted gross income	2000	2005	2006	2007	2008 [1]	2009
TAX LIABILITY (dol.)						
Single person, no dependents:						
$5,000	[2]−353	[2]−383	[2]−383	[2]−383	[1,2]−683	[2,5]−693
$10,000	[2]391	[2]46	[2]−7	[2]−73	[1,2]−415	[2,5]−598
$20,000	1,920	1,405	1,355	1,296	[1]656	[5]780
$30,000	3,270	2,845	2,818	2,789	[1]2,156	[5]2,280
$40,000	4,988	4,075	4,048	4,019	[1]3,394	[5]3,555
$50,000	7,284	6,115	5,983	5,824	[1]5,119	[5]5,125
$75,000	13,024	11,240	11,108	10,949	[1]10,244	[5]10,250
$100,000	19,233	16,571	16,368	16,119	[1]15,969	[5]15,775
Married couple, two dependents, with one spouse working:						
$5,000	−2,000	[2]−2,000	[2]−2,000	[2]−2,000	[1,2]−3,200	−2,610
$10,000	−3,888	[2]−4,000	[2]−4,000	[2]−4,000	[1,2,4]−5,425	−5,670
$20,000	−2,349	[2,4]−4,986	[2,4]−5,169	[2,5]−5,404	[1,2,4]−7,484	−7,828
$30,000	475	[2,3,4]−2,810	[2,3,4]−3,108	[2,4,5]−3,490	[1,2,3,4]−5,143	−5,621
$40,000	2,218	[3,4]−150	[3,4]−280	[4,5]−428	[1,2,3,4]−2,637	−2,515
$50,000	3,470	[3]1,350	[3]1,200	[4]1,073	[1,3]−838	−35
$75,000	7,384	[3]4,575	[3]4,490	[4]4,403	[1,3]2,523	3,400
$100,000	13,124	[3]8,630	[3]8,315	[4]7,948	[1,3]5,888	6,475
EFFECTIVE RATE (percent)						
Single person, no dependents:						
$5,000	−7.1	[2]−7.7	[2]−7.7	[2]−7.7	[1,2]−13.7	[2,5]−13.9
$10,000	3.9	[2]0.5	[2]−0.1	[2]−0.7	[1,2]−4.2	[2,5]−6
$20,000	9.6	7.0	6.8	6.5	[1]3.3	[5]3.9
$30,000	10.9	9.5	9.4	9.3	[1]7.2	[5]7.6
$40,000	12.5	10.2	10.1	10.1	[1]8.5	[5]8.9
$50,000	14.6	12.2	12.0	11.6	[1]10.2	[5]10.3
$75,000	17.4	15	14.8	14.6	[1]13.7	[5]13.7
$100,000	19.2	16.6	16.4	16.1	16.0	15.8
Married couple, two dependents, with one spouse working:						
$5,000	[2]−40.0	[2]−40.0	[2]−40.0	[2]−40.0	[1,2]−64	[2,4,5]−52.2
$10,000	[2]−38.9	[2]−40.0	[2]−39.3	[2]−40.0	[1,2,4]−54.3	[2,4,5]−56.7
$20,000	[2,3]−11.7	[2,4]−24.9	[2,4]−21.2	[2,5]−27.0	[1,2,4]−37.4	[2,4,5]−39.1
$30,000	[2,3]1.6	[2,3,4]−9.4	[2,3,4]−4.3	[2,4,5]−11.6	[1,2,3,4]−17.1	[2,3,4,5]−18.7
$40,000	[3]5.5	[3,4]−0.4	[3,4]1.6	[4,5]−1.1	[1,2,3,4]−6.6	[2,3,4,5]−6.3
$50,000	[3]6.9	[3]2.7	[3]4.2	[4]2.1	[1,3]−1.7	[3,5]−0.1
$75,000	[3]9.8	[3]6.1	[3]6.9	[4]5.9	[1,3]3.4	[3,5]4.5
$100,000	[3]13.1	[3]8.6	[3]10.4	[4]7.9	[1,3]5.9	[3,5]6.5
MARGINAL TAX RATE (percent)						
Single person, no dependents:						
$5,000	−	[2]−7.7	[2]−7.7	[2]−7.7	[2]−7.7	[2,5]−13.9
$10,000	[2]22.7	[2]17.7	[2]17.7	[2]17.7	[2]17.7	[2]17.7
$20,000	15.0	15.0	15.0	15.0	15.0	15.0
$30,000	15.0	15.0	15.0	15.0	15.0	15.0
$40,000	28.0	15.0	15.0	15.0	15.0	15.0
$50,000	28.0	25.0	25.0	25.0	25.0	25.0
$75,000	28.0	25.0	25.0	25.0	25.0	[5]27.0
$100,000	31.0	28.0	28.0	28.0	25.0	25.0
Married couple, two dependents, with one spouse working:						
$5,000	[2]−40.0	[2]−40.0	[2]−40.0	[2]−40.0	[2]−40.0	[2,4,5]−61.2
$10,000	−	[2]−40.0	[2]−40.0	[2]−40.0	[2,4]−55	[2,4,5]−61.2
$20,000	[2,3]21.1	[2,4]6.1	[2,4]6.1	[2,5]6.1	[2,4]6.1	−
$30,000	[2]36.1	[2,3,4]31.1	[2,3,4]31.1	[2,4,5]31.1	[2,3,4]31.1	[2]31.1
$40,000	15.0	[3,4]15	[3,4]15	[4,5]15	[2,3,4]31.1	[2]31.1
$50,000	15.0	15.0	15.0	15.0	15.0	15.0
$75,000	28.0	15.0	15.0	15.0	15.0	15.0
$100,000	28.0	25.0	25.0	25.0	25.0	15.0

− Represents zero. [1] Includes effect of the Recovery Rebate paid in 2008 under the Economic Stimulus Act of 2008 (P.L. 110–185). [2] Includes effect from the refundable earned income credit. [3] Includes effect from the child tax credit. [4] Includes effect from the additional (refundable) child tax credit. [5] Includes effect from the (refundable) Making Work Pay tax credit.

Source: U.S. Department of the Treasury, Office of Tax Analysis, unpublished data.

Table 493. Federal Individual Income Tax—Current Income Equivalent to 2000 Constant Income for Selected Income Groups: 2000 to 2009

[Constant 2000 incomes calculated by using the U.S. Bureau of Labor Statistics Consumer Price Index for Urban Consumers (CPI–U); see Table 724, Section 14. See also headnote, Table 492]

Adjusted gross income (constant 2000 dollars)	2000	2005	2006	2007	2008 [1]	2009
REAL INCOME EQUIVALENT (dol.)						
$5,000	5,000	5,670	5,850	6,020	6,250	6,230
$10,000	10,000	11,340	11,710	12,040	12,500	12,460
$20,000	20,000	22,680	23,410	24,080	25,010	24,920
$30,000	30,000	34,020	35,120	36,120	37,510	37,380
$40,000	40,000	45,370	46,830	48,160	50,010	49,830
$50,000	50,000	56,710	58,540	60,200	62,520	62,290
$75,000	75,000	85,060	87,800	90,310	93,770	93,440
$100,000	100,000	113,410	117,070	120,410	125,030	124,590
TAX LIABILITY (dol.)						
Single person, no dependents:						
$5,000	[2] –353	[2] –399	[2] –412	[2] –428	[1,2] –738	[2,5] –843
$10,000	[2] 391	[2] 283	[2] 295	[2] 287	[1,2] –29	[2,5] –164
$20,000	1,920	1,807	1,867	1,908	[1] 1,408	[5] 1,518
$30,000	3,270	3,339	3,447	3,542	[1] 3,087	[5] 3,233
$40,000	4,988	5,166	5,333	5,447	[1] 5,121	[5] 5,090
$50,000	7,284	7,491	7,733	7,915	[1] 7,685	[5] 7,644
$75,000	13,024	13,302	13,732	14,087	[1] 14,692	[5] 14,399
$100,000	19,233	19,649	20,287	20,805	[1] 21,705	[5] 21,304
Married couple, 2 dependents with one spouse working:						
$5,000	[2] –2,000	[2] –2,268	–2,340	[2] –2,408	[1,2] –3,700	[2,4,5] –3,363
$10,000	[2] –3,888	[2,4] –4,451	–4,598	[2] –4,760	[1,2,4] –6,624	[2,4,5] –7,176
$20,000	[2,3] –2,349	[2,4] –4,823	–4,963	[2,4] –5,157	[1,2,3,4] –6,693	[2,4,5] –7,091
$30,000	[2,3] 475	[2,3,4] –1,561	–1,518	[2,3,4] –1,589	[1,2,3,4] –3,410	[2,3,4,5] –3,329
$40,000	[2] 2,218	[3] 656	745	[3,4] 797	[1,3] –836	[3,5] –60
$50,000	[3] 3,470	[3] 2,325	2,465	[3] 2,582	[1,3] 987	[3,5] 1,809
$75,000	[3] 7,384	[3] 5,812	6,064	[3] 6,286	[1,3] 4,831	[3,5] 5,668
$100,000	[3] 13,124	[3] 11,579	12,214	[3] 12,682	[1,3] 11,819	[3,5] 12,216
EFFECTIVE TAX RATE (percent)						
Single person, no dependents:						
$5,000	[2] –7.1	[a] –7.0	[2] –7.0	[2] –7.10	[1,2] –11.8	[2,5] –13.5
$10,000	[2] 3.9	[2] 2.5	[2] 2.5	[2] 2.38	[1,2] –0.2	[2,5] –1.3
$20,000	9.6	8.0	8.0	7.9	[1] 5.6	[5] 0.1
$30,000	10.9	9.8	9.8	9.8	[1] 8.2	[5] 8.6
$40,000	12.5	11.4	11.4	11.3	[1] 10.2	[5] 10.2
$50,000	14.6	13.2	13.2	13.1	[1] 12.3	[5] 12.3
$75,000	17.4	15.6	15.6	15.6	[1] 15.7	[5] 15.4
$100,000	19.2	17.3	17.3	17.3	[1] 17.4	17.1
Married couple, 2 dependents with one spouse working:						
$5,000	[2] –40	[2] –40	[2] –40	[2] –40	[1,2] –60.2	[2,4,5] –54
$10,000	[2] –38.9	[2,4] –39.3	[2,4] –39.3	[2] –39.5	[1,2,4] –53	[2,4,5] –57.6
$20,000	[2,3] –11.7	[2,4] –21.3	[2,4] –21.2	[2,4] –21.4	[1,2,3,4] –26.8	[2,4,5] –28.5
$30,000	[2,3] 1.6	[2,3,4] –4.6	[2,3,4] –4.2	[2,3,4] –4.40	[1,2,3,4] –9.1	[2,3,4,5] –8.9
$40,000	[3] 5.5	[3] 1.4	[3] 1.6	[3,4] 1.65	[1,3] –1.7	[3,5] –0.1
$50,000	[3] 6.9	[3] 4.1	[3] 4.2	[3] 4.28	[1,3] 1.6	[3,5] 2.9
$75,000	[3] 9.8	[3] 6.8	[3] 6.9	[3] 6.96	[1,3] 5.2	[3,5] 6.1
$100,000	[3] 13.1	[3] 10.2	[3] 10.4	[3] 10.5	[1,3] 9.5	[3,5] 9.8
MARGINAL TAX RATE (percent)						
Single person, no dependents:						
$5,000	–	–	–	–	–	[5] –6.2
$10,000	[2] 22.7	[2] 17.7	[2] 17.7	[2] 17.7	[2] 7.7	[2] 17.7
$20,000	15.0	15.0	15.0	15.0	15.0	15.0
$30,000	15.0	15.0	15.0	15.0	15.0	15.0
$40,000	28.0	25.0	25.0	25.0	25.0	25.0
$50,000	28.0	25.0	25.0	25.0	25.0	25.0
$75,000	28.0	25.0	25.0	25.0	25.0	[5] 27
$100,000	31.0	28.0	28.0	28.0	28.0	28.0
Married couple, 2 dependents with one spouse working:						
$5,000	[2] –40.0	[2] –40.0	[2] –40.0	[2] –40.0	[2] –40.0	[2,4,5] –61.2
$10,000	–	[4] –15.0	[4] –15.0	[4] –15.0	[4] –15.0	[2,4,5] –61.2
$20,000	[2,3] 21.1	[2,4] 6.1	[2,4] 6.1	[2,3,4] 6.1	[2,3,4] 31.1	[2] 21.1
$30,000	[2] 36.1	[2,3,4] 31.1	[2,3,4] 31.1	[2,3,4] 31.1	[2,3,4] 31.1	[2] 31.1
$40,000	15.0	15.0	15.0	15.0	15.0	15.0
$50,000	15.0	15.0	15.0	15.0	15.0	15.0
$75,000	28.0	15.0	15.0	15.0	15.0	15.0
$100,000	28.0	[3] 30.1	[3] 30.1	[3] 30.1	[3] 30.1	[3] 30.1

– Represents zero. [1] Includes effect of the Recovery Rebate paid in 2008 under the Economic Stimulus Act of 2008 (P.L. 110–185). [2] Includes effect from the refundable earned income credit. [3] Includes effect from the child tax credit. [4] Includes effect from the additional (refundable) child tax credit. [5] Includes effect from the (refundable) Making Work Pay tax credit.

Source: U.S. Department of the Treasury, Office of Tax Analysis, unpublished data.

U.S. Census Bureau, Statistical Abstract of the United States: 2011

Table 494. Federal Civilian Employment and Annual Payroll by Branch: 1970 to 2009

[2,997 represents 2,997,000. For fiscal year ending in year shown. See text, Section 8. Includes employees in U.S. territories and foreign countries. Data represent employees in active-duty status, including intermittent employees. Annual employment figures are averages of monthly figures. Excludes Central Intelligence Agency, National Security Agency, and as of November 1984, the Defense Intelligence Agency; and as of October 1996, the National Imagery and Mapping Agency]

| Year | Employment | | | | | | Payroll (mil. dol.) | | | | |
| | Total (1,000) | Percent of U.S. em- ployed [1] | Executive (1,000) | | Legis- lative (1,000) | Judicial (1,000) | Total | Executive | | Legis- lative | Judicial |
			Total	Defense				Total	Defense		
1970....	[2] 2,997	3.81	2,961	1,263	29	7	27,322	26,894	11,264	338	89
1975....	2,877	3.35	2,830	1,044	37	10	39,126	38,423	13,418	549	154
1980....	[2] 2,987	3.01	2,933	971	40	14	58,012	56,841	18,795	883	288
1985....	3,001	2.80	2,944	1,080	39	18	80,599	78,992	28,330	1,098	509
1990....	[2] 3,233	2.72	3,173	1,060	38	23	99,138	97,022	31,990	1,329	787
1995....	2,943	2.36	2,880	852	34	28	118,304	115,328	31,753	1,598	1,379
2002....	2,699	1.98	2,635	671	31	34	136,611	132,893	28,845	1,781	1,938
2003....	2,743	1.99	2,677	669	31	34	143,380	139,506	29,029	1,908	1,966
2004....	2,714	1.95	2,649	668	30	34	148,037	144,134	29,128	1,977	1,927
2005....	2,709	1.91	2,645	671	30	34	152,222	148,275	29,331	2,048	1,900
2006....	2,700	1.87	2,636	676	30	34	160,570	156,543	29,580	2,109	1,918
2007....	2,695	1.85	2,632	674	30	33	161,394	157,010	29,025	2,119	2,265
2008....	2,730	1.88	2,666	682	30	34	167,166	162,675	29,749	2,162	2,328
2009....	2,804	2.00	2,740	714	30	34	174,804	170,349	30,995	2,203	2,252

[1] Civilian employed only. See Table 584, Section 12. [2] Includes temporary census workers.

Source: U.S. Office of Personnel Management, *Federal Civilian Workforce Statistics—Employment and Trends*, bimonthly, and unpublished data, <http://www.opm.gov/feddata>.

Table 495. Full-Time Federal Civilian Employment—Employees and Average Pay by Pay System: 2000 to 2009

[As of March 31 (1,671 represents 1,671,000). Excludes employees of Congress and federal courts, maritime seamen of U.S. Department of Commerce, and small number for whom rates were not reported. See text, this section, for explanation of general schedule and wage system]

| Pay system | Employees (1,000) | | | | Average annual pay (dol.) | | | |
	2000	2007	2008	2009	2000	2007	2008	2009
Total, excluding postal ...	**1,671**	**1,845**	**1,885**	**1,798**	**50,429**	**65,825**	**69,061**	**63,678**
General Schedule	1,216	1,330	1,265	1,083	49,428	65,856	68,674	59,330
Wage system.............	205	200	200	189	37,082	46,317	47,652	50,223
Other..................	250	315	420	526	66,248	78,134	80,444	77,433
Postal pay system [1]	788	685	663	623	37,627	48,752	50,294	52,510

[1] Source: Career employees—U.S. Postal Service, *Annual Report of the Postmaster General*. See also <http://www.usps.com/financials/cspo/welcome.html>. Average pay—U.S. Postal Service, *Comprehensive Statement of Postal Operations*, annual.

Source: Except as noted, U.S. Office of Personnel Management, "Pay Structure of the Federal Civil Service," annual (publication discontinued) and unpublished data, <http://www.opm.gov/feddata>.

Table 496. Paid Civilian Employment in the Federal Government by State: 2000 and 2008

[As of December 31. In thousands (2,766 represents 2,766,000). Excludes Central Intelligence Agency, Defense Intelligence Agency, seasonal and on-call employees, and National Security Agency]

State	2000	2008	State	2000	2008	State	2000	2008
U.S. [1].....	**2,766**	**1,860**	KY	30	22	OH.......	84	49
AL	48	38	LA	33	21	OK.......	43	34
AK	14	12	ME.......	13	10	OR.......	29	20
AZ	43	38	MD.......	130	117	PA	107	67
AR	20	14	MA.......	53	27	RI........	10	7
CA	248	157	MI........	58	28	SC	26	20
CO	51	37	MN.......	34	17	SD	9	8
CT	21	8	MS.......	24	19	TN	50	26
DE	5	3	MO.......	54	36	TX	162	130
DC	181	149	MT.......	11	10	UT	30	27
FL	113	84	NE.......	15	10	VT	6	4
GA	89	74	NV.......	13	11	VA	145	138
HI........	23	23	NH.......	8	4	WA.......	62	51
ID........	11	9	NJ.......	62	30	WV.......	18	18
IL........	94	49	NM.......	25	24	WI.......	30	14
IN........	37	22	NY.......	134	69	WY.......	6	5
IA........	18	9	NC.......	57	39			
KS	25	16	ND.......	8	6			

[1] Includes employees outside the United States and in states not specified, not shown separately.

Source: U.S. Office of Personnel Management, "Employment by Geographic Area," biennial (publication discontinued) and unpublished data, <http://www.opm.gov/feddata>.

Table 497. Federal Civilian Employment by Branch and Agency: 1990 to 2009

[For years ending September 30. Annual averages of monthly figures. Excludes Central Intelligence Agency, National Security Agency; the Defense Intelligence Agency; and as of October 1996, the National Imagery and Mapping Agency]

Agency	1990	2000	2005	2007	2008	2009
Total, all agencies	**3,128,267**	**2,708,101**	**2,708,753**	**2,694,929**	**2,730,040**	**2,803,909**
Legislative Branch	37,495	31,157	30,303	29,573	29,919	29,997
Judicial Branch	23,605	32,186	33,690	32,921	33,682	33,754
Executive Branch	3,067,167	2,644,758	2,644,764	2,632,435	2,666,440	2,740,158
Executive Office of the President	1,731	1,658	1,736	1,719	1,717	1,723
Executive Departments	2,065,542	1,592,200	1,689,914	1,696,893	1,740,979	1,850,913
State	25,288	27,983	33,808	34,657	35,779	36,762
Treasury	158,655	143,508	114,194	111,577	111,335	110,686
Defense	1,034,152	676,268	670,790	673,722	682,142	714,483
Justice	83,932	125,970	105,102	106,946	107,970	111,214
Interior	77,679	73,818	73,599	70,256	70,515	71,536
Agriculture	122,594	104,466	104,989	99,629	98,720	97,803
Commerce [1]	69,920	47,652	38,927	40,163	41,339	74,305
Labor	17,727	16,040	15,599	15,855	16,269	16,316
Health & Human Services [2]	123,959	62,605	60,944	61,217	62,344	65,389
Housing & Urban Development	13,596	10,319	10,086	9,718	9,599	9,636
Transportation [3]	67,364	63,598	55,975	53,536	54,676	56,310
Energy	17,731	15,692	15,050	14,696	14,857	15,613
Education	4,771	4,734	4,429	4,146	4,210	4,097
Veterans Affairs	248,174	219,547	236,363	245,537	265,390	289,335
Homeland Security [3]	(X)	(X)	149,977	155,397	165,839	177,428
Independent agencies [4]	999,894	1,050,900	953,113	[4] 933,833	923,744	887,522
Board of Governors Federal Reserve System	1,525	2,372	1,851	1,874	1,873	1,873
Environmental Protection Agency	17,123	18,036	17,964	19,153	18,127	18,301
Equal Employment Opportunity Commission	2,880	2,780	2,421	2,191	2,209	2,226
Federal Communications Commission	1,778	1,965	1,936	1,827	1,809	1,849
Federal Deposit Insurance Corporation	17,641	6,958	4,998	4,573	4,726	5,478
Federal Trade Commission	988	1,019	1,046	1,094	1,131	1,131
General Services Administration	20,277	14,334	12,685	12,099	11,929	12,157
National Archives & Records Administration	3,120	2,702	3,048	2,973	3,068	3,298
National Aeronautics & Space Administration	24,872	18,819	19,105	19,378	18,531	18,441
National Labor Relations Board	2,263	2,054	1,822	1,772	1,670	1,631
National Science Foundation	1,318	1,247	1,325	1,356	1,383	1,430
Nuclear Regulatory Commission	3,353	2,858	3,230	3,609	3,833	4,114
Office of Personnel Management	6,636	3,780	4,333	5,201	5,375	5,408
Peace Corps	1,179	1,065	1,064	1,077	1,035	978
Railroad Retirement Board	1,772	1,176	1,010	990	977	957
Securities & Exchange Commission	2,302	2,955	3,933	3,534	3,562	3,715
Small Business Administration	5,128	4,150	4,288	4,234	3,813	4,087
Smithsonian Institution	5,092	5,065	4,981	5,008	4,929	4,930
Social Security Administration [2]	(X)	64,474	65,861	62,769	62,337	65,085
Tennessee Valley Authority	28,392	13,145	12,721	12,293	11,727	11,688
U.S. Information Agency	8,555	2,436	2,212	2,046	2,052	1,959
U.S. International Development Cooperation Agency	4,698	2,552	2,644	2,761	2,515	2,515
U.S. Postal Service	816,886	860,726	767,972	753,254	744,405	703,658

X Not applicable. [1] Includes enumerators for the 1990 and 2000 census. [2] Sizeable changes in 1995 due to the Social Security Administration which was separated from the Department of Health and Human Services to become an independent agency effective April 1995. [3] See text, Section 10, National Security and Veteran Affairs, concerning the development of the Department of Homeland Security. [4] Includes agencies with fewer than 1,000 employees in 2005, not shown separately.

Source: U.S. Office of Personnel Management, Federal Civilian Workforce Statistics—Employment and Trends, bimonthly. See <http://www.opm.gov/feddata>.

Table 498. Federal Employees—Summary Characteristics: 1990 to 2007

[As of September 30. In percent, except as indicated. For civilian employees, excluding U.S. Postal Service employees]

Characteristics	1990	1995	2000	2002	2003	2004	2005	2006	2007
Average age (years) [1]	42.3	44.3	46.3	46.5	46.7	46.8	46.9	46.9	47.0
Average length of service (years)	13.4	15.5	17.1	16.8	16.8	16.6	16.4	16.3	16.1
Retirement eligible: [2]									
Civil Service Retirement System	8	10	17	23	27	30	33	37	41
Federal Employees Retirement System	3	5	11	11	12	13	13	13	13
Bachelor's degree or higher	35	39	41	41	41	42	43	43	45
Sex: Male	57	56	55	55	55	56	56	56	56
Female	43	44	45	45	45	44	44	44	44
Race and national origin:									
Total minorities	27.4	28.9	30.4	30.8	31.1	31.4	31.7	32.1	32.5
Black	16.7	16.8	17.1	17.0	17.0	17.0	17.0	17.2	17.3
Hispanic	5.4	5.9	6.6	6.9	7.1	7.3	7.4	7.5	7.6
Asian/Pacific Islander	3.5	4.2	4.5	4.7	4.8	5.0	5.1	5.1	5.4
American Indian/Alaska Native	1.8	2.0	2.2	2.2	2.1	2.1	2.1	2.1	2.1
Disabled	7.0	7.0	7.0	7.0	7.0	7.0	7.0	7.0	7.0
Veterans preference	30.0	26.0	24.0	23.0	22.0	22.0	22.0	22.0	22.0
Vietnam era veterans	17.0	17.0	14.0	13.0	13.0	12.0	11.0	10.0	9.0
Retired military	4.9	4.2	3.9	4.4	4.6	4.9	5.4	5.7	6.0
Retired officers	0.5	0.5	0.5	0.7	0.8	0.9	1.0	1.1	1.2

[1] For full-time permanent employees. [2] Represents full-time permanent employees under the Civil Service Retirement System (excluding hires since January 1984), and the Federal Employees Retirement System (since January 1984).

Source: U.S. Office of Personnel Management, Office of Workforce Information, The Fact Book, Federal Civilian Workforce Statistics, annual. See also <http://www.opm.gov/feddata>.

Table 499. Federal Executive Branch (Nonpostal) Employment by Race and National Origin: 1990 to 2007

[As of September 30. Covers total employment for only executive branch agencies participating in OPM's Central Personnel Data File (CPDF). For information on the CPDF, see <http://www.opm.gov/feddata/acpdf.pdf>]

Pay system	1990	1995	2000	2004	2005	2006	2007
All personnel [1]	**2,150,359**	**1,960,577**	**1,755,689**	**1,851,349**	**1,856,966**	**1,848,339**	**1,862,404**
White, non-Hispanic	1,562,846	1,394,690	1,224,836	1,270,366	1,267,922	1,254,308	1,254,131
General schedule and related	1,218,188	1,101,108	961,261	972,737	973,767	948,740	878,182
Grades 1 to 4	132,028	79,195	55,067	48,798	46,671	43,450	42,135
Grades 5 to 8	337,453	288,755	239,128	231,765	227,387	219,168	208,180
Grades 9 to 12	510,261	465,908	404,649	405,825	408,111	399,400	367,195
Grades 13 to 15	238,446	267,250	262,417	286,349	291,598	286,722	260,672
Total executive/senior pay levels	9,337	13,307	14,332	16,337	16,409	16,118	20,718
Wage pay system	244,220	186,184	146,075	134,821	135,383	133,942	132,290
Other pay systems	91,101	94,091	103,168	146,471	142,363	155,508	222,941
Black	356,867	327,302	298,701	313,099	315,644	317,697	323,470
General schedule and related	272,657	258,586	241,135	244,736	246,691	246,248	236,721
Grades 1 to 4	65,077	41,381	26,895	20,797	19,774	18,326	17,692
Grades 5 to 8	114,993	112,962	99,937	95,798	94,655	93,717	89,903
Grades 9 to 12	74,985	79,795	82,809	88,813	90,809	91,869	88,042
Grades 13 to 15	17,602	24,448	31,494	39,328	41,453	42,336	41,084
Total executive/senior pay levels	479	942	1,180	1,238	1,270	1,218	1,510
Wage pay system	72,755	55,637	42,590	37,798	37,666	37,378	37,685
Other pay systems	10,976	12,137	13,796	29,327	30,017	32,853	47,554
Hispanic	115,170	115,964	115,247	135,533	138,507	138,596	141,968
General schedule and related	83,218	86,762	89,911	102,612	104,927	105,236	102,613
Grades 1 to 4	15,738	11,081	8,526	7,969	7,768	6,854	6,454
Grades 5 to 8	28,727	31,152	31,703	34,380	33,653	33,834	33,738
Grades 9 to 12	31,615	34,056	36,813	43,868	46,268	46,951	45,309
Grades 13 to 15	7,138	10,473	12,869	16,395	17,238	17,597	17,112
Total executive/senior pay levels	154	382	547	656	682	699	1,070
Wage pay system	26,947	22,128	16,926	15,915	15,945	15,822	15,652
Other pay systems	4,851	6,692	7,863	16,350	16,953	16,839	22,633
American Indian, Alaska Native, Asian, and Pacific Islander	115,476	122,621	116,905	132,351	134,893	136,593	141,138
General schedule and related	81,499	86,768	86,074	96,014	97,866	97,870	95,008
Grades 1 to 4	15,286	11,854	9,340	8,528	8,357	7,877	7,938
Grades 5 to 8	24,960	26,580	25,691	27,601	27,417	26,986	26,292
Grades 9 to 12	31,346	33,810	33,167	37,172	38,276	38,492	36,664
Grades 13 to 15	9,907	14,524	17,876	22,713	23,816	24,515	24,114
Total executive/senior pay levels	148	331	504	760	804	873	2,630
Wage pay system	24,927	21,553	17,613	16,760	16,938	16,728	16,661
Other pay systems	8,902	13,969	12,714	18,817	19,285	21,122	26,839

[1] Beginning 2006, includes persons classified as multiracial, not shown separately.
Source: U.S. Office of Personnel Management, Central Personnel Data File, <http://www.opm.gov/feddata>.

Table 500. Area of Federally Owned Buildings in the United States by State: 2008

[3,260.7 represents 3,260,700,000. As of September 30. For executive branch agencies. For data on federal land by state, see Table 362]

State	Total building area [1] (mil. sq. ft.)	Owned building area (mil. sq. ft.)	Leased building area (mil. sq. ft.)	State	Total building area [1] (mil. sq. ft.)	Owned building area (mil. sq. ft.)	Leased building area (mil. sq. ft.)
U.S. [2]	**3,260.7**	**2,589.0**	**550.6**	MO	52.8	42.6	7.9
AL	55.2	47.8	4.4	MT	18.0	14.9	2.3
AK	49.9	46.8	2.8	NE	15.2	12.6	1.6
AZ	54.2	49.8	3.6	NV	31.5	28.4	2.3
AR	24.1	19.7	1.2	NH	4.3	2.9	0.5
CA	287.0	262.9	20.2	NJ	46.3	38.7	5.3
CO	54.1	47.0	6.5	NM	62.1	55.7	5.0
CT	13.8	10.8	1.3	NY	98.8	81.6	12.9
DE	6.0	5.1	0.4	NC	79.0	72.4	4.4
DC	88.0	62.8	24.7	ND	22.5	20.0	1.0
FL	107.5	94.2	10.1	OH	69.1	61.6	5.3
GA	107.7	98.7	7.3	OK	61.5	52.6	6.8
HI	47.9	46.5	0.7	OR	24.9	20.1	2.5
ID	21.7	18.3	2.7	PA	77.9	66.7	8.4
IL	69.3	59.8	6.0	RI	12.5	11.6	0.5
IN	43.2	31.5	9.2	SC	53.2	49.2	1.9
IA	15.7	11.1	1.7	SD	17.9	14.4	2.0
KS	35.3	31.0	2.5	TN	66.3	59.1	4.3
KY	47.4	42.3	3.2	TX	194.1	169.5	21.0
LA	46.1	34.0	5.0	UT	33.8	28.8	3.0
ME	11.7	10.2	0.6	VT	4.1	2.5	1.0
MD	120.3	96.8	21.4	VA	165.5	135.4	28.8
MA	35.5	30.0	3.1	WA	81.6	73.3	6.6
MI	31.4	23.3	4.0	WV	20.0	15.9	2.5
MN	20.9	14.4	1.9	WI	24.6	19.6	2.4
MS	39.5	32.0	1.9	WY	15.2	13.4	0.8

[1] Includes otherwised managed square feet, not shown separately. [2] Includes location not reported, not shown separately.
Source: U.S. General Services Administration, Federal Real Property Council, "Federal Real Property Report 2008." See also <http://www.gsa.gov/portal/content/102880>.

Section 10
National Security and Veterans Affairs

This section displays data for national security (national defense and homeland security) and benefits for veterans. Data are presented on national defense and its human and financial costs; active and reserve military personnel; and federally sponsored programs and benefits for veterans, and funding, budget and selected agencies for homeland security. The principal sources of these data are the annual *Selected Manpower Statistics* and the *Atlas/Data Abstract for the United States, Annual Report of Secretary of Veterans Affairs*, U.S. Department of Veterans Affairs (VA), Budget in Brief, U.S. Department of Homeland Security; and *The Budget of the United States Government*, Office of Management and Budget. For data on international expenditures and personnel, see Table 1407, Section 30.

Department of Defense (DoD)— The U.S. Department of Defense is responsible for providing the military forces of the United States. It includes the Office of the Secretary of Defense, the Joint Chiefs of Staff, the Army, the Navy, the Air Force, and the defense agencies. The President serves as Commander-in-Chief of the Armed Forces; from him, the authority flows to the Secretary of Defense and through the Joint Chiefs of Staff to the commanders of unified and specified commands (e.g., U.S. Strategic Command).

Reserve components—The Reserve Components of the Armed Forces consist of the Army National Guard of the United States, Army Reserve, Naval Reserve, Marine Corps Reserve, Air National Guard, Air Force Reserve, and Coast Guard Reserve. They provide trained personnel and units available for active duty in the Armed Forces during times of war or national emergency, and at such other times as national security may require. The National Guard has dual federal/state responsibilities and uses jointly provided equipment, facilities, and budget support. The President is empowered to mobilize the National Guard and to use such of the Armed Forces as he considers necessary to enforce federal authority in any state. There is in each Armed Force a ready reserve, a standby reserve, and a retired reserve. The Ready Reserve includes the Selected Reserve, which provides trained and ready units and individuals to augment the active forces during times of war or national emergency, or at other times when required; and the Individual Ready Reserve, which is a manpower pool that can be called to active duty during times of war or national emergency and would normally be used as individual fillers for active, guard, and reserve units, and as a source of combat replacements. Most of the Ready Reserve serves in an active status. See Table 511 for Standby Reserve and Retired Reserve detail.

Department of Veterans Affairs (VA)—A veteran is someone 18 years and older (there are a few 17-year-old veterans) who is not currently on active duty, but who once served on active duty in the United States Army, Navy, Air Force, Marine Corps, or Coast Guard, or who served in the Merchant Marine during World War II. There are many groups whose active service makes them veterans including: those who incurred a service-connected disability during active duty for training in the Reserves or National Guard, even though that service would not otherwise have counted for veteran status; members of a national guard or reserve component who have been ordered to active duty by order of the President or who have a full-time military job. The latter are called AGRs (Active Guard and Reserve). No one who has received a dishonorable discharge is a veteran.

The VA administers laws authorizing benefits for eligible former and present members of the Armed Forces and for the beneficiaries of deceased members. Veterans' benefits available under various acts of Congress include compensation for service-connected disability or death; pensions for non-service-connected disability

U.S. Census Bureau, Statistical Abstract of the United States: 2011

or death; vocational rehabilitation, education and training; home loan insurance; life insurance; health care; special housing and automobiles or other conveyances for certain disabled veterans; burial and plot allowances; and educational assistance to families of deceased or totally disabled veterans, servicemen missing in action, or prisoners of war. Since these benefits are legislated by Congress, the dates they were enacted and the dates they apply to veterans may be different from the actual dates the conflicts occurred. VA estimates of veterans cover all persons discharged from active U.S. military service under conditions other than dishonorable.

Department of Homeland Security (DHS)— The creation of DHS, which began operations in March 2003, represents a fusion of 22 federal agencies (legacy agencies, Coast Guard and Secret Service remained intact) to coordinate and centralize the leadership of many homeland security activities under a single department. The largest organizations under DHS include: Customs and Border Protection (CBP), Immigration and Customs Enforcement (ICE), Transportation Security Administration (TSA), Federal Emergency Management Agency (FEMA), and the Coast Guard.

Coast Guard—With more than 218 years of service to the Nation, the Coast Guard is a military, multi-mission, maritime organization that promotes safety and safeguards U.S. economic and security interests throughout the maritime environment. As one of the five Armed Services of the United States, it is the only military organization within the DHS. Unlike its sister services in the Department of Defense (DoD), the Coast Guard is also a law enforcement and regulatory agency with broad domestic authorities.

Federal Emergency Management Agency (FEMA)—FEMA manages and coordinates the federal response to and recovery from major domestic disasters and emergencies of all types in accordance with the Robert T. Stafford Disaster Relief and Emergency Assistance Act. The agency ensures the effectiveness of emergency response providers at all levels of government in responding to terrorist attacks, major disasters, and other emergencies. Through the Disaster Relief Fund, FEMA provides individual and public assistance to help families and communities impacted by declared disasters rebuild and recover. FEMA is also the principal component for preparing state and local governments to prevent or respond to threats or incidents of terrorism and other catastrophic events, through their state and local programs.

The Customs and Border Protection (CBP) is responsible for managing, securing, and controlling U.S. borders. This includes carrying out traditional border-related responsibilities, such as stemming the tide of illegal drugs and illegal aliens; securing and facilitating legitimate global trade and travel; and protecting the food supply and agriculture industry from pests and disease. CBP is composed of the Border Patrol and Inspections (both moved from INS) along with Customs (absorbed from the U.S. Department of Treasury) and Animal and Plant Health Inspections Services (absorbed from the U.S. Department of Agriculture).

The Immigration and Customs Enforcement (ICE) mission is to protect America and uphold public safety by targeting the people, money, and materials crossing the nation's borders that support terrorist and criminal activities. ICE is the largest investigation arm of DHS. ICE is composed of five law enforcement divisions: Investigations, Intelligence, Federal Protective Service, International Affairs, and Detention and Removal Operations. ICE investigates a wide range of national security, financial and smuggling violations including drug smuggling, human trafficking, illegal arms exports, financial crimes, commercial fraud, human smuggling, document fraud, money laundering, child pornography/exploitation, and immigration fraud.

The Transportation Security Administration (TSA) was created as part of the Aviation and Transportation Security Act on November 19, 2001. TSA was originally part of the U.S. Department of Transportation, but was moved to DHS. TSA's mission is to provide security to our nation's transportation systems with a primary focus on aviation security.

U.S. Census Bureau, Statistical Abstract of the United States: 2011

Figure 10.1
Officers and Enlisted Personnel by Military Branch: 2008

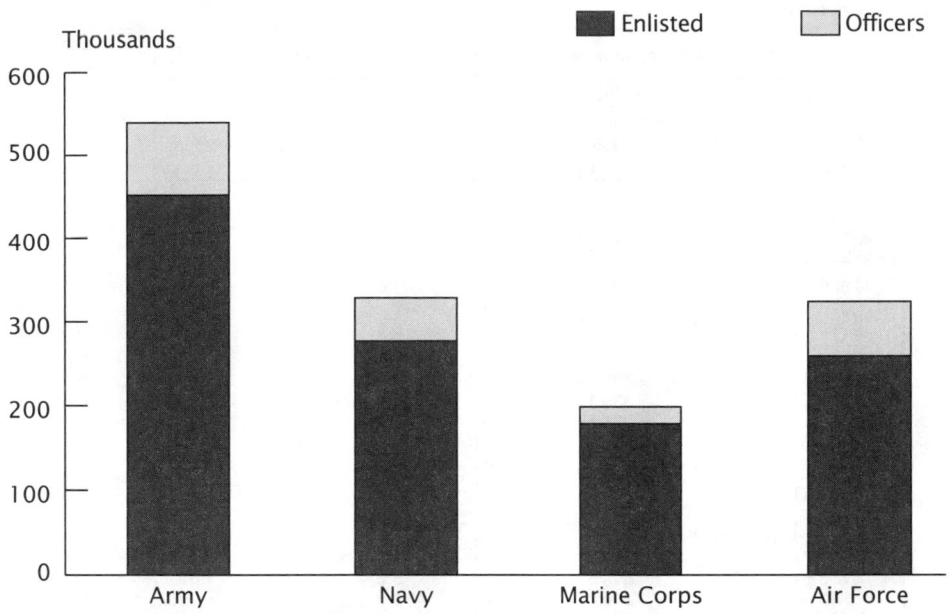

Source: Chart prepared by U.S. Census Bureau. For data, see Table 508.

Figure 10.2
Department of Defense Personnel by Sex: 2008

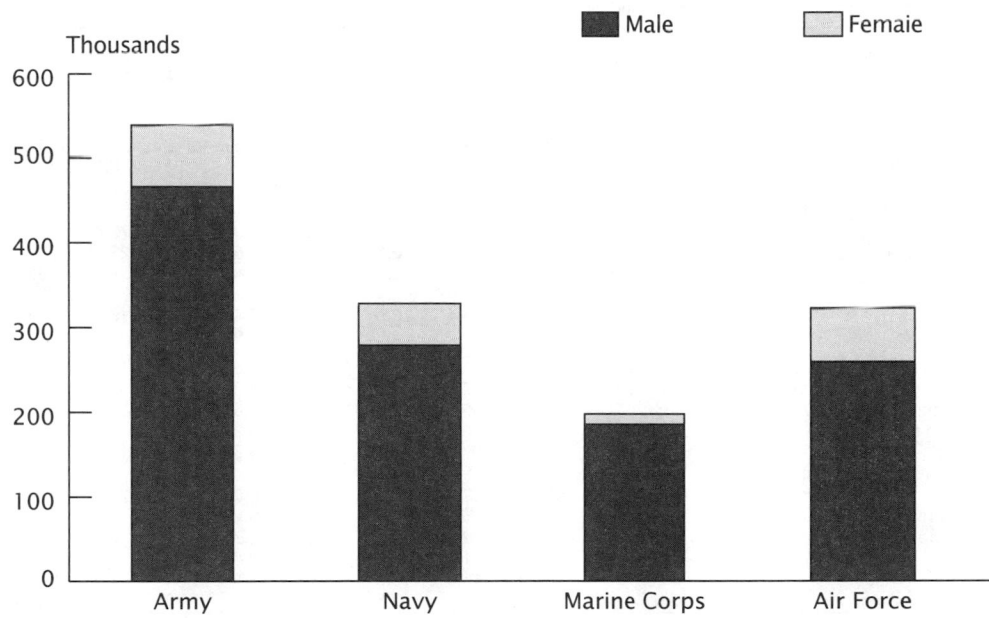

Source: Chart prepared by U.S. Census Bureau. For data, see Table 508.

U.S. Census Bureau, Statistical Abstract of the United States: 2011

Table 501. National Defense Outlays and Veterans' Benefits: 1960 to 2011

[In billions of dollars (53.5 represents $53,500,000,000), except percent. For fiscal year ending in year shown, see text, Section 8. Includes outlays of Department of Defense, Department of Veterans Affairs, and other agencies for activities primarily related to national defense and veterans programs. For explanation of average annual percent change, see Guide to Tabular Presentation. Minus sign (–) indicates decrease]

Year	National defense and veterans' outlays				Annual percent change [1]			Defense outlays, percent of—	
		Defense outlays							
	Total outlays	Current dollars	Constant (FY2005) dollars	Veterans' outlays	Total outlays	Defense outlays	Veterans' outlays	Federal outlays	Gross domestic product [2]
1960.........	53.5	48.1	328.1	5.4	2.5	2.4	3.1	52.2	9.3
1970.........	90.4	81.7	410.3	8.7	0.3	–1.0	13.6	41.8	8.1
1980.........	155.1	134.0	310.3	21.1	13.9	15.2	6.3	22.7	4.9
1985.........	279.0	252.7	430.6	26.3	10.3	11.1	2.7	26.7	6.1
1990.........	328.4	299.3	437.6	29.1	–1.6	–1.4	–3.2	23.9	5.2
1995.........	310.0	272.1	340.0	37.9	–2.9	–3.4	0.8	17.9	3.7
1998.........	310.0	268.2	317.9	41.8	0.1	–0.8	6.3	16.2	3.1
1999.........	320.2	274.8	321.2	43.2	3.3	2.5	3.4	16.1	3.0
2000.........	341.5	294.4	335.8	47.1	6.6	7.1	9.0	16.5	3.0
2001.........	349.8	304.8	339.1	45.0	2.4	3.5	4.3	16.4	3.0
2002.........	399.5	348.5	381.5	51.0	14.2	14.3	13.2	17.3	3.4
2003.........	461.8	404.8	431.8	57.0	15.6	16.2	11.8	18.7	3.7
2004.........	515.6	455.8	472.7	59.8	11.7	12.6	4.8	19.9	4.0
2005.........	565.5	495.3	495.3	70.2	9.7	8.7	17.4	20.0	4.0
2006.........	591.7	521.8	503.9	69.8	4.6	5.4	–0.4	19.7	4.0
2007.........	624.1	551.3	518.2	72.8	5.5	5.6	4.3	20.2	4.0
2008.........	700.7	616.1	558.6	84.7	12.3	11.8	16.2	20.7	4.9
2009.........	756.5	661.0	598.8	95.4	8.0	7.3	12.7	17.3	5.2
2010, est.	843.8	719.2	640.8	124.7	11.5	8.8	30.6	19.9	5.5
2011, est.	874.3	749.7	658.8	124.5	3.6	4.3	–0.1	19.6	4.9

[1] Change from immediate prior year; for 1960, change from 1955. [2] Represents fiscal year GDP; for definition, see text, Section 13.

Source: U.S. Office of Management and Budget, "Budget of the United States Government, Historical Tables," annual, <http://www.whitehouse.gov/omb/budget/>.

Table 502. National Defense Budget Authority and Outlays for Defense Functions: 1990 to 2010

[In billions of dollars (303.3 represents $303,300,000,000). For year ending September 30. Data includes defense budget authority and outlays by other departments. Minus sign (–) indicates decrease]

Function	1990	1995	2000	2003	2004	2005	2006	2007	2008	2009	2010, est.
Total budget authority	**303.3**	**266.4**	**304.0**	**456.0**	**490.6**	**505.8**	**556.3**	**625.8**	**696.2**	**697.8**	**722.1**
Department of Defense—Military	293.0	255.7	290.3	437.7	470.9	483.9	532.9	603.0	674.7	667.5	696.9
Military personnel	78.9	71.6	73.8	109.1	116.1	121.3	128.5	131.8	139.0	149.3	156.4
Operation and maintenance	88.4	93.7	108.7	178.3	189.8	179.2	213.5	240.2	256.2	271.6	297.3
Procurement	81.4	43.6	55.0	78.5	83.1	96.6	105.4	133.8	165.0	135.4	134.5
Research, development, test, and evaluation	36.5	34.5	38.7	58.1	64.6	68.8	72.9	77.5	79.6	80.0	80.6
Military construction.	5.1	5.4	5.1	6.7	6.1	7.3	9.5	14.0	22.1	26.8	22.9
Family housing.	3.1	3.4	3.5	4.2	3.8	4.1	4.4	4.0	2.9	3.9	2.3
Other	–0.4	3.4	5.5	2.9	7.4	6.6	–1.3	1.6	9.9	0.6	2.9
Atomic energy defense activities.....	9.7	10.1	12.4	16.4	16.8	17.9	17.4	17.2	16.6	23.0	17.8
Defense-related activities	0.7	1.0	1.3	2.0	2.8	4.0	5.9	5.7	4.9	7.3	7.4
Total outlays.................	**299.3**	**272.1**	**294.4**	**404.8**	**455.8**	**495.3**	**521.8**	**551.3**	**616.1**	**661.0**	**719.2**
Department of Defense—Military	289.8	259.4	281.1	387.2	436.5	474.1	499.3	528.6	594.6	636.7	692.0
Military personnel	75.6	70.8	76.0	106.7	113.6	127.5	127.5	127.5	138.9	147.3	155.0
Operation and maintenance	88.3	91.0	105.8	151.4	174.0	188.1	203.8	216.6	244.8	259.3	279.4
Procurement	81.0	55.0	51.7	67.9	76.2	82.3	89.8	99.6	117.4	129.2	147.2
Research, development, test, and evaluation	37.5	34.6	37.6	53.1	60.8	65.7	68.6	73.1	75.1	79.0	79.3
Military construction.	5.1	6.8	5.1	5.9	6.3	5.3	6.2	7.9	11.6	17.6	23.8
Family housing.	3.5	3.6	3.4	3.8	3.9	3.7	3.7	3.5	3.6	2.7	4.0
Other	–1.2	–2.4	1.5	–1.6	1.6	1.5	–0.4	0.2	3.2	1.5	3.3
Atomic energy activities.	9.0	11.8	12.1	16.0	16.6	18.0	17.5	17.1	17.1	17.6	20.0
Defense-related activities	0.6	0.9	1.2	1.6	2.8	3.2	5.1	5.7	4.3	6.8	7.2

Source: U.S. Office of Management and Budget, "Budget of the United States Government, Historical Tables, Budget Authority by Function and Subfunction, Outlay by Function and Subfunction," annual, <http://www.whitehouse.gov/omb/budget>.

Table 503. Military Expenditures: 2000 to 2008

[In millions of dollars (229,072 represents $229,072,000,000). For year ending September 30. For definitions, see headnote, Tables 504 and 506]

Item	2000	2004	2005	2006	2007	2008
Expenditures, total	229,072	345,891	381,290	408,249	455,769	501,032
Payroll outlays	103,447	139,490	141,018	146,858	154,326	146,781
Active duty military pay	36,872	50,489	50,482	55,829	61,918	52,159
Civilian pay	29,935	36,234	43,798	45,105	43,587	46,170
Reserve and National Guard pay	4,646	10,303	11,087	10,123	12,325	11,068
Retired military pay	31,994	42,465	35,651	35,801	36,496	37,384
Total contracts [1]	123,295	203,388	236,986	257,456	297,363	349,557
Army	32,615	59,249	74,432	79,962	98,171	139,437
Navy & Marine Corps	38,963	57,659	62,775	70,351	82,321	92,679
Air Force	35,369	51,533	51,671	58,552	66,240	59,262
Other Defense activities	16,348	34,947	48,108	48,592	50,630	58,178
Grants	2,330	3,012	3,285	3,934	4,080	4,694

[1] Represents contract awards over $25,000.

Source: U.S. Department of Defense, DoD Personnel and Procurement Statistics, Personnel, Publications, *Atlas/Data Abstract for the United States and Selected Areas*, annual, <http://siadapp.dmdc.osd.mil>.

Table 504. Department of Defense Payroll and Contract Awards—States: 2008

[(In millions of dollars (146,781 represents $146,781,000,000). For year ending September 30. Payroll outlays include the gross earnings of civilian, active duty military personnel, reserve and national guard, and retired military for services rendered to the government and for cash allowances for benefits. Excludes employer's share of employee benefits, accrued military retirement benefits and most permanent change of station costs. Contracts refer to awards made in year specified; expenditures relating to awards may extend over several years. Military awards for supplies, services, and construction. Net value of contracts of over $25,000 for work in each state and DC. Figures reflect impact of prime contracting on state distribution of defense work. The state in which a prime contractor is located is not often the state where the subcontracted work is done. Undistributed civilians and military personnel, their payrolls, and prime contract awards for performance in classified locations are excluded]

State	Payroll — Total	Payroll — Active duty military	Contract awards	Grants	State	Payroll — Total	Payroll — Active duty military	Contract awards	Grants
U.S.	146,781	52,159	349,557	4,694	MO	2,489	708	12,212	87
AL	3,831	721	8,442	116	MT	435	164	247	53
AK	1,753	1,211	2,016	46	NE	956	381	789	38
AZ	2,653	927	12,248	50	NV	1,231	518	1,131	25
AR	1,292	336	828	51	NH	334	52	1,606	32
CA	12,563	4,113	37,820	463	NJ	2,160	404	7,194	89
CO	3,584	1,675	4,877	72	NM	1,428	470	1,508	31
CT	580	156	12,208	75	NY	3,011	1,340	9,398	175
DE	461	189	225	30	NC	6,653	3,668	3,647	89
DC	2,584	1,098	4,770	72	ND	533	301	188	31
FL	8,376	2,391	12,394	190	OH	3,248	498	6,938	109
GA	7,811	3,633	7,407	95	OK	3,209	1,040	2,032	124
HI	4,488	2,715	2,259	57	OR	800	86	1,343	76
ID	584	217	164	34	PA	3,365	318	13,588	226
IL	2,490	575	9,180	154	RI	637	85	602	25
IN	1,669	188	7,006	102	SC	2,825	1,007	4,973	46
IA	497	75	1,071	69	SD	398	159	404	20
KS	2,227	1,273	3,000	74	TN	1,772	180	3,475	27
KY	3,160	2,080	5,677	37	TX	13,172	6,151	51,905	342
LA	1,853	833	4,840	57	UT	1,810	311	1,895	42
ME	822	95	870	50	VT	177	37	347	19
MD	5,421	1,421	13,138	304	VA	15,024	4,525	39,384	118
MA	1,170	221	11,283	202	WA	5,799	2,512	5,598	129
MI	1,447	147	6,188	121	WV	421	61	357	42
MN	796	113	1,913	81	WI	734	121	3,303	60
MS	1,730	503	4,392	20	WY	320	150	206	19

Source: U.S. Department of Defense, DoD Personnel and Procurement Statistics, Personnel, Publications, *Atlas/Data Abstract for the United States and Selected Areas*, annual, <http://siadapp.dmdc.osd.mil/>.

Table 505. Expenditures and Personnel by Selected Major Locations: 2009

[In thousands of dollars (8,406,173 represents $8,406,173,000), except for personnel. For year ending September 30. See headnote, Table 508]

Major locations	Expenditures — Total	Expenditures — Payroll outlays	Expenditures — Contracts/ grants	Major locations	Military and civilian personnel — Total	Military and civilian personnel — Active duty military	Military and civilian personnel — Civilian
Washington, DC. . .	8,406,173	3,599,245	4,806,928	Fort Hood, TX	60,309	54,309	6,000
Fort Hood, TX	6,478,403	6,075,895	402,508	Camp Pendleton, CA. . .	49,114	46,242	2,872
San Diego, CA. . . .	6,413,361	1,884,891	4,528,470	Camp Lejeune, NC	44,286	40,789	3,497
Oshkosh, WI	5,780,785	20,929	5,759,856	Fayetteville, NC	36,223	36,198	25
Huntsville, AL.	5,744,462	366,537	5,377,925	Fort Lewis, WA.	35,250	32,220	3,030
Arlington, VA	5,279,716	2,946,069	2,333,647	Fort Campbell, KY	33,971	32,799	1,172
Tucson, AZ.	4,879,568	326,019	4,553,549	Fort Carson, CO	26,759	23,796	2,963
Fayetteville, NC . . .	4,658,633	4,623,376	35,257	Arlington, VA	26,335	9,305	17,030
St. Louis, MO.	4,623,210	203,614	4,419,596	Fort Benning, GA.	26,101	22,123	3,978
Louisville, KY	4,436,075	167,250	4,268,825	Fort Bragg, NC	23,843	15,580	8,263

Source: U.S. Department of Defense, DoD Personnel and Procurement Statistics, Personnel, Publications, *Atlas/Data Abstract for the United States and Selected Areas*, annual, <http://siadapp.dmdc.osd.mil/>.

U.S. Census Bureau, Statistical Abstract of the United States: 2011

Table 506. Military and Civilian Personnel in Installations: 2009

[As of September 30. Civilian personnel includes United States citizens and foreign national direct-hire civilians subject to Office of Management and Budget (OMB) ceiling controls and civilian personnel involved in civil functions in the United States. Excludes indirect-hire civilians and those direct-hire civilians not subject to OMB ceiling controls. Military personnel include active duty personnel based ashore or afloat, excludes personnel temporarily shore-based in a transient status]

State	Active military personnel				Reserve and National Guard, total [1]	Civilian personnel			
	Total [1]	Army	Navy/ Marine Corps	Air Force		Total [1]	Army	Navy/ Marine Corps	Air Force
United States	**1,088,465**	**537,407**	**264,375**	**286,683**	**819,318**	**709,265**	**274,140**	**186,135**	**160,339**
Alabama	11,896	8,121	403	3,372	22,099	24,794	19,768	84	2,472
Alaska	23,178	14,087	113	8,978	4,747	5,356	3,049	20	1,938
Arizona	21,343	5,531	4,118	11,694	13,728	9,591	4,471	637	3,408
Arkansas	6,717	1,219	109	5,389	13,051	4,168	3,073	6	973
California	117,806	11,097	88,370	18,339	57,792	61,365	9,278	34,798	10,720
Colorado	35,404	25,471	715	9,218	12,491	11,585	4,187	65	5,675
Connecticut	1,914	624	1,172	118	6,369	2,625	618	1,120	257
Delaware	3,870	246	15	3,609	4,881	1,622	292	5	1,248
District of Columbia . . .	13,424	7,831	3,040	2,553	6,378	16,088	4,708	9,617	853
Florida	42,642	5,363	13,782	23,497	34,653	28,429	4,070	11,871	10,297
Georgia	73,988	59,892	3,724	10,372	29,358	37,012	14,169	4,757	15,222
Hawaii	40,874	22,435	13,642	4,797	9,276	18,400	5,532	9,605	2,188
Idaho	4,967	526	41	4,400	5,892	1,716	893	51	711
Illinois	10,111	2,212	2,805	5,094	25,084	15,770	9,016	1,842	3,688
Indiana	3,108	2,612	209	287	21,073	10,932	2,403	3,243	952
Iowa	1,296	997	118	181	12,390	1,733	1,157	8	525
Kansas	25,482	21,994	117	3,371	11,479	7,800	6,296	6	1,103
Kentucky	43,138	42,532	279	327	13,126	8,962	7,655	164	248
Louisiana	17,398	10,223	1,553	5,622	18,011	6,647	4,045	793	1,476
Maine	730	334	265	131	4,153	6,946	402	5,580	287
Maryland	29,160	8,239	12,652	8,269	16,000	34,966	14,460	15,826	2,384
Massachusetts	3,205	1,157	574	1,474	15,335	6,918	2,632	192	3,171
Michigan	2,858	1,708	743	407	17,618	8,972	6,456	46	892
Minnesota	1,897	1,291	378	228	19,256	2,752	1,766	23	798
Mississippi	9,895	1,443	1,394	7,058	17,332	9,124	3,878	2,428	2,515
Missouri	17,925	12,053	2,028	3,844	23,769	9,982	7,569	490	1,246
Montana	3,623	397	12	3,214	4,748	1,596	686	1	862
Nebraska	6,845	653	450	5,742	7,498	3,785	1,468	15	2,197
Nevada	10,034	545	584	8,905	6,087	2,319	561	285	1,316
New Hampshire	675	307	198	170	4,251	1,047	568	34	304
New Jersey	6,673	1,538	277	4,858	17,312	15,217	10,798	2,122	1,575
New Mexico	11,038	1,094	166	9,778	5,199	7,029	3,041	46	3,460
New York	29,553	26,568	1,676	1,309	30,362	12,318	7,561	151	2,528
North Carolina	116,073	53,231	54,942	7,900	22,542	20,426	8,975	7,669	1,472
North Dakota	7,209	416	14	6,779	4,669	1,910	617	3	1,214
Ohio	8,261	1,939	684	5,638	28,523	25,001	1,884	91	13,671
Oklahoma	21,673	12,216	926	8,531	15,640	22,115	5,739	91	14,794
Oregon	1,615	815	336	464	10,470	3,561	2,893	26	615
Pennsylvania	5,215	3,270	1,443	502	32,297	27,107	10,606	6,469	1,290
Rhode Island	1,490	420	905	165	4,438	4,372	289	3,777	209
South Carolina	32,518	11,074	12,613	8,831	19,102	10,406	3,875	3,868	1,912
South Dakota	3,910	406	1	3,503	4,982	1,388	565	3	775
Tennessee	3,511	1,610	1,422	479	20,606	7,967	4,767	1,202	1,227
Texas	131,548	88,346	4,606	38,596	56,367	48,057	27,585	1,404	15,271
Utah	6,237	1,614	170	4,453	11,999	14,818	2,470	45	11,244
Vermont	565	347	32	186	3,952	729	403	3	290
Virginia	63,160	24,386	25,171	13,603	25,109	89,713	23,532	39,844	4,983
Washington	46,161	34,557	4,907	6,697	19,470	27,980	9,471	15,577	1,980
West Virginia	1,199	677	317	205	9,303	2,146	1,431	97	605
Wisconsin	2,046	1,522	163	361	15,833	2,810	2,138	34	522
Wyoming	3,407	221	1	3,185	3,218	1,193	374	1	776

[1] Includes Other Defense Activities (ODA), not shown separately.

Source: U.S. Department of Defense, DoD Personnel and Procurement Statistics, Personnel, Publications, *Atlas/Data Abstract for the United States and Selected Areas*, annual, <http://siadapp.dmdc.osd.mil/>.

Table 507. Military Personnel on Active Duty by Location: 1980 to 2009

[In thousands (2,051 represents 2,051,000). As of September 30]

Location	1980	1990	1995	2000	2004	2005	2006	2007	2008	2009
Total	**2,051**	**2,046**	**1,518**	**1,384**	**1,427**	**1,389**	**1,385**	**1,380**	**1,402**	**1,419**
Shore-based [1]	1,840	1,794	1,351	1,237	1,291	1,262	1,263	1,264	1,294	1,313
Afloat [2]	211	252	167	147	136	127	121	115	108	105
United States [3]	1,562	1,437	1,280	1,127	1,139	1,098	1,100	1,085	1,113	1,156
Foreign countries	489	609	238	258	288	291	285	295	289	263

[1] Includes Navy personnel temporarily on shore. [2] Includes Marine Corps. [3] Includes Puerto Rico and Island Areas.

Source: U.S. Department of Defense, DoD Personnel and Procurement Statistics, Personnel, Publications, *Atlas/Data Abstract for the United States and Selected Areas*, annual, <http://siadapp.dmdc.osd.mil/>.

Table 508. Department of Defense Personnel: 1960 to 2008

[In thousands (2,475 represents 2,475,000). As of end of fiscal year; see text, Section 8. Includes National Guard, Reserve, and retired regular personnel on extended or continuous active duty. Excludes Coast Guard. Other officer candidates are included under enlisted personnel]

Year	Total [1,2]	Army Total [1]	Army Male Officers	Army Male Enlisted	Army Female Officers	Army Female Enlisted	Navy [2] Total [1]	Navy Male Officers	Navy Male Enlisted	Navy Female Officers	Navy Female Enlisted	Marine Corps Total [1]	Marine Male Officers	Marine Male Enlisted	Marine Female Officers	Marine Female Enlisted	Air Force Total [1]	AF Male Officers	AF Male Enlisted	AF Female Officers	AF Female Enlisted
1960	2,475	873	97	762	4.3	8.3	617	67	540	2.7	5.4	171	16	153	0.1	1.5	815	126	677	3.7	5.7
1965	2,654	969	108	846	3.8	8.5	670	75	583	2.6	5.3	190	17	172	0.1	1.4	825	128	685	4.1	4.7
1970	3,065	1,323	162	1,142	5.2	11.5	691	78	600	2.9	5.8	260	25	233	0.3	2.1	791	125	648	4.7	9.0
1975	2,128	784	98	640	4.6	37.7	535	62	449	3.7	17.5	196	19	174	0.3	2.8	613	100	478	5.0	25.2
1980	2,051	777	91	612	7.6	61.7	527	58	430	4.9	30.1	189	18	164	0.5	6.2	558	90	404	8.5	51.9
1981	2,083	781	94	610	8.3	65.3	540	60	435	5.3	34.6	191	17	165	0.5	7.1	570	90	413	9.1	54.4
1982	2,109	780	94	609	9.0	64.1	553	61	444	5.7	37.3	192	18	165	0.6	7.9	583	92	421	9.9	54.5
1983	2,123	780	97	602	9.5	66.5	558	62	444	6.3	40.8	194	19	166	0.6	8.3	592	94	428	10.6	55.3
1984	2,138	780	98	601	10.2	67.1	565	62	448	6.6	42.6	196	19	167	0.6	8.6	597	95	430	11.2	55.9
1985	2,151	781	99	599	10.8	68.4	571	64	449	6.9	45.7	198	19	169	0.7	9.0	602	96	431	11.9	58.1
1986	2,169	781	99	597	11.3	69.7	581	65	457	7.3	47.2	200	19	170	0.6	9.2	608	97	434	12.4	61.2
1987	2,174	781	96	596	11.6	71.6	587	65	462	7.2	47.7	200	19	170	0.6	9.1	607	94	432	12.6	63.2
1988	2,138	772	95	588	11.8	72.0	593	65	466	7.3	49.7	197	19	168	0.7	9.0	576	92	405	12.9	61.5
1989	2,130	770	95	584	12.2	74.3	593	65	464	7.5	52.1	197	19	168	0.7	9.0	571	91	399	13.4	63.7
1990	2,044	732	92	553	12.4	71.2	579	64	451	7.8	52.1	197	19	168	0.7	8.7	535	87	370	13.3	60.8
1991	1,986	711	91	535	12.5	67.8	570	63	444	8.0	51.4	194	19	166	0.7	8.3	510	84	350	13.3	59.1
1992	1,807	610	83	449	11.7	61.7	542	61	417	8.3	51.0	185	18	157	0.6	7.9	470	77	320	12.7	56.1
1993	1,705	572	77	420	11.1	60.2	510	58	390	3.3	49.3	178	17	153	0.6	7.2	444	72	302	12.3	54.5
1994	1,610	541	74	394	10.9	59.0	469	54	355	3.0	47.9	174	17	149	0.6	7.0	426	69	287	12.3	54.0
1995	1,518	509	72	365	10.8	57.3	435	51	324	7.9	47.9	175	17	150	0.7	7.4	400	66	266	12.1	52.1
1996	1,472	491	70	347	10.6	59.0	417	50	308	7.8	46.9	174	17	149	0.8	7.8	389	64	256	12.0	52.8
1997	1,439	492	69	346	10.4	62.4	396	48	290	7.8	44.8	173	17	148	0.8	8.5	377	62	246	12.0	53.8
1998	1,407	484	68	340	10.4	61.4	382	47	280	7.8	42.9	173	17	146	0.9	8.9	368	60	237	12.0	54.2
1999	1,386	479	67	337	10.5	61.5	373	46	271	7.7	43.9	173	17	145	0.9	9.3	361	58	232	11.8	54.6
2000	1,384	482	66	339	10.8	62.9	373	46	272	7.8	43.8	173	17	146	0.9	9.5	356	57	227	11.8	55.0
2001	1,385	481	65	337	11.0	63.4	378	46	273	8.0	46.6	173	17	145	1.0	9.6	354	57	224	12.0	55.6
2002	1,414	487	66	341	11.5	63.2	385	47	279	8.2	47.3	174	17	146	1.0	9.5	368	59	233	12.9	58.6
2003	1,434	499	68	352	12.0	63.5	382	47	276	8.1	47.3	178	18	149	1.1	9.6	375	61	237	13.5	60.0
2004	1,427	500	69	358	12.3	61.0	373	46	273	8.1	46.1	178	18	149	1.1	9.7	377	61	242	13.6	60.2
2005	1,389	493	69	353	12.4	57.9	363	45	266	7.8	44.5	180	18	151	1.0	9.8	354	60	225	13.4	55.6
2006	1,385	505	71	365	12.5	58.5	350	44	255	7.6	43.2	180	18	151	1.1	10.0	349	58	223	12.8	55.8
2007	1,380	522	71	379	13.0	58.8	338	44	244	7.6	42.2	186	18	156	1.1	10.5	333	54	214	11.8	53.4
2008	1,402	544	74	392	13.5	59.7	332	44	235	7.7	41.4	199	19	167	1.2	11.1	327	53	207	11.9	51.4

[1] Includes cadets, midshipmen, and others, not shown separately. [2] Beginning 1980, excludes Navy Reserve personnel on active duty for Training and Administration of Reserves (TARS).

Source: U.S. Department of Defense, *Selected Manpower Statistics*, annual, and unpublished data.

Table 509. Military Personnel on Active Duty by Rank or Grade: 1990 to 2009

[In thousands (2,043.7 represents 2,043,700). As of September 30]

Rank/grade	1990	2000	2005	2006	2007	2008	2009
Total	**2,043.7**	**1,384.3**	**1,389.4**	**1,385.0**	**1,379.6**	**1,401.8**	**1,418.5**
Total Officers	**296.6**	**217.2**	**226.6**	**223.2**	**221.3**	**223.7**	**228.25**
General-Admiral	(Z)	(Z)	(Z)	(Z)	(Z)	(Z)	(Z)
Lieutenant General-Vice Admiral	0.1	0.1	0.1	0.1	0.1	0.1	0.2
Major General-Rear Admiral (U)	0.4	0.3	0.3	0.3	0.3	0.3	0.3
Brigadier General-Rear Admiral (L)	0.5	0.4	0.4	0.5	0.4	0.5	0.5
Colonel-Captain	14.0	11.3	11.4	11.3	11.3	11.6	12.0
Lieutenant Colonel-Commander	32.3	27.5	28.1	27.5	27.7	28.1	28.4
Major-LT Commander	53.2	43.2	44.4	45.1	44.2	43.4	43.9
Captain-Lieutenant	106.6	68.1	72.5	71.9	70.6	71.0	72.5
1st Lieutenant-Lieutenant (JG)	37.9	24.7	27.5	24.9	23.4	23.9	24.9
2nd Lieutenant-Ensign	31.9	26.4	25.9	25.2	26.0	26.4	26.9
Chief Warrant Officer W-5	(Z)	0.1	0.5	0.6	0.6	0.6	0.7
Chief Warrant Officer W-4	3.0	2.0	2.2	2.4	2.9	3.1	3.1
Chief Warrant Officer W-3	5.0	3.8	4.6	4.6	4.6	4.7	4.7
Chief Warrant Officer W-2	8.4	6.7	6.2	6.0	5.7	6.4	7.1
Warrant Officer W-1	3.2	2.1	2.5	2.9	3.4	3.4	3.2
Total Enlisted	**1,733.8**	**1,154.6**	**1,149.9**	**1,148.6**	**1,145.0**	**1,164.7**	**1,176.7**
E-9	15.3	10.2	10.5	10.4	10.6	10.5	10.4
E-8	38.0	26.0	27.1	26.7	27.4	27.4	27.4
E-7	134.1	97.7	97.8	99.3	97.1	97.2	98.5
E-6	239.1	164.9	172.4	170.3	168.4	170.3	170.5
E-5	361.5	229.5	248.5	248.8	247.4	249.0	248.5
E-4	427.8	251.0	261.7	261.4	260.1	266.1	280.2
E-3	280.1	196.3	201.7	185.4	192.5	194.9	205.9
E-2	140.3	99.0	70.8	83.5	79.9	83.6	84.8
E-1	97.6	80.0	59.5	62.8	61.7	65.6	50.4
Cadets and Midshipmen	**13.3**	**12.5**	**12.9**	**13.2**	**13.2**	**13.4**	**13.6**

Z Fewer than 50.

Source: U.S. Department of Defense, DoD Personnel and Procurement Statistics, Personnel, Military, *Military Personnel Statistics*, annual, <http://siadapp.dmdc.osd.mil\>.

Table 510. Military Retirement System: 2009

[Payment in millions of dollars (3,849 represents $3,849,000,000). As of September 30. The data published in this report are produced from the files maintained by the Defense Manpower Data Center (DMDC). This report compiles data primarily from the "Retiree Pay and Survivor Pay" files. Any grouping of members by address reflects mailing, not necessarily residence address. Only those members in plans administered by the Department of Defense (DoD) are included in this table. The data are preliminary because of reporting delays due to the information about many members who retired or died within one month of the September 30 reporting date. These data were not processed in time to be included in this report. For more information, please see *Introduction* and *Overview* at <http://www.defenselink.mil/actuary/statbook2009.pdf]

State	Retired military personnel [1]			Monthly payment	State	Retired military personnel [1]			Monthly payment
	Total	Disabled [2]	Non-disabled			Total	Disabled [2]	Non-disabled	
Total [3]	**2,022,166**	**191,397**	**1,830,769**	**3,849**	MO	36,836	3,813	33,023	62
U.S.	1,981,364	179,260	1,802,104	3,778	MT	8,713	826	7,887	15
AL	56,077	4,564	51,513	105	NE	13,865	1,031	12,834	27
AK	9,600	646	8,954	18	NV	27,302	1,852	25,450	53
AZ	54,139	4,591	49,548	107	NH	9,512	791	8,721	18
AR	25,745	2,411	23,334	44	NJ	20,333	2,654	17,679	31
CA	167,181	15,683	151,498	325	NM	21,385	1,692	19,693	43
CO	48,672	3,896	44,776	107	NY	38,003	5,812	32,191	53
CT	10,723	1,312	9,411	18	NC	85,111	7,375	77,736	164
DE	8,247	555	7,692	14	ND	4,829	369	4,460	8
DC	2,870	408	2,462	6	OH	44,442	5,667	38,775	74
FL	185,661	15,219	170,442	378	OK	34,743	2,888	31,855	61
GA	89,738	7,606	82,132	168	OR	21,247	2,516	18,731	37
HI	16,088	1,056	15,032	33	PA	49,495	5,902	43,593	81
ID	12,828	1,131	11,697	23	RI	5,549	523	5,026	10
IL	35,723	4,502	31,221	62	SC	55,433	4,250	51,183	103
IN	24,163	3,088	21,075	37	SD	7,234	581	6,653	12
IA	11,926	1,285	10,641	18	TN	51,333	4,659	46,674	91
KS	20,796	1,719	19,077	39	TX	187,755	15,997	171,758	378
KY	26,759	2,854	23,905	46	UT	15,095	1,145	13,950	27
LA	25,653	2,749	22,904	44	VT	3,746	340	3,406	6
ME	12,108	1,130	10,978	20	VA	145,957	7,963	137,994	370
MD	51,258	3,839	47,419	107	WA	70,717	5,233	65,484	138
MA	19,176	2,517	16,659	30	WV	10,882	1,333	9,549	17
MI	27,925	4,182	23,743	41	WI	19,796	2,378	17,418	29
MN	17,668	2,036	15,632	26	WY	5,004	407	4,597	9
MS	26,323	2,284	24,039	44					

[1] Represents military personnel (officers and enlisted) receiving and not receiving pay from DoD. [2] A disabled military member is entitled to disability retired pay if the disability is not the result of the member's intentional misconduct or willful neglect, was not incurred during a period of unauthorized absence, and either: (1) the member has at least 20 years of service; or (2) at the time of determination, the disability is at least 30 percent (under a standard schedule of rating disabilities by the Veterans Administration) and one of three additional conditions are met. For the continuation of this footnote, see U.S. Census Bureau, Statistical Abstract, National Security and Veterans Affairs, Military Personnel and Expenditures, Military Retirement System, <http://www.census.gov /compendia/statab/>. [3] Includes states, U.S. territories, and retirees living in foreign countries.

Source: U.S. Department of Defense, Office of the Actuary, *Statistical Report, Fiscal Year 2009* (issued May 2010), <http://www.defenselink.mil/actuary/>.

Table 511. Military Reserve Personnel: 1995 to 2009

[As of September 30. The Ready Reserve data include the Selected Reserve which is scheduled to augment active forces during times of war or national emergency, and the Individual Ready Reserve, which, during times of war or national emergency, would be used to fill out Active, Guard, and Reserve units, and which would also be a source for casualty replacements. Ready Reservists serve in an active status (except for the Inactive National Guard—a very small pool within the Army National Guard). The Standby Reserve cannot be called to active duty, other than for training, unless authorized by Congress under "full mobilization," and a determination is made that there are not enough qualified members in the Ready Reserve in the required categories who are readily available. The Retired Reserve represents a lower potential for involuntary mobilization]

Reserve status and branch of service	1995	2000	2005	2006	2007	2008	2009
Total reserves [1]	**1,674,164**	**1,276,843**	**1,136,200**	**1,119,902**	**1,109,805**	**1,099,915**	**1,094,071**
Ready reserve	**1,648,388**	**1,251,452**	**1,113,427**	**1,101,565**	**1,088,587**	**1,080,617**	**1,079,627**
Army [2]	999,462	725,771	636,355	631,856	621,422	626,892	645,394
Navy	267,356	184,080	140,821	131,802	128,421	123,159	109,271
Marine Corps	103,668	99,855	99,820	100,522	100,787	95,748	95,199
Air Force [3]	263,011	229,009	223,551	224,637	226,806	224,545	220,364
Coast Guard	14,891	12,737	12,880	12,748	11,151	10,273	9,399
Standby reserve	**25,776**	**25,391**	**22,773**	**18,337**	**21,218**	**19,298**	**25,808**
Army	1,128	701	1,668	1,586	[4] 5,294	2,136	2,072
Navy	12,707	7,213	4,038	4,514	3,046	3,310	[4] 10,036
Marine Corps	216	895	1,129	1,210	1,372	1,691	1,205
Air Force	11,453	16,429	15,897	10,932	10,154	10,384	10,530
Coast Guard	272	153	41	95	1,352	1,777	1,965
Retired reserve	**505,905**	**573,305**	**627,424**	**637,262**	**648,346**	**658,251**	**707,060**
Army	259,553	296,004	321,312	325,288	330,121	334,258	378,603
Navy	97,532	109,531	117,093	118,803	120,859	122,000	123,292
Marine Corps	11,319	12,937	14,693	15,000	15,264	15,558	15,948
Air Force	137,501	154,833	174,326	178,171	182,102	186,435	189,217

[1] Less retired reserves. [2] Includes Army National Guard. [3] Includes Air National Guard. [4] The Army for FY2007 and the Navy for FY2009 did a "scrub" of their Individual Ready Reserve (IRR) category and dropped personnel awaiting retirement or discharge into the Standby Reserve. This action was done in order to give them a better perspective on actual IRR members cleared for mobilization, if required.

Source: U.S. Department of Defense, DoD Personnel and Procurement Statistics, Personnel, Publications, *Atlas/Data Abstract for the United States and Selected Areas, Selected Manpower Statistics*. See also <http://siadapp.dmdc.osd.mil>.

Table 512. Ready Reserve Personnel by Race, Hispanic Origin, and Sex: 1990 to 2009

In thousands (1,658.7 represents 1,658,700). As of September 30]

Year	Total [1]	Race				Hispanic [2]	Sex			
		White	Black	Asian	American Indian		Officer		Enlisted	
							Male	Female	Male	Female
1990	1,658.7	1,304.6	272.3	14.9	7.8	83.1	226.8	40.5	1,204.7	186.7
1995	1,648.4	1,267.7	274.5	22.0	8.8	96.2	209.9	44.7	1,196.8	196.9
1998	1,353.4	1,033.9	210.4	21.7	7.8	88.2	175.9	40.3	964.1	173.1
1999	1,288.8	980.0	202.6	22.6	7.6	88.9	166.2	38.4	911.2	173.1
2000	1,251.5	942.2	199.6	26.7	8.4	91.8	159.4	36.9	879.9	175.3
2001	1,224.1	912.7	198.4	27.9	8.5	94.3	158.0	36.6	852.2	177.3
2002	1,199.3	891.3	193.2	27.9	8.8	96.0	152.1	35.6	835.2	176.4
2003	1,167.1	865.7	187.5	25.4	8.5	98.0	145.1	34.0	813.7	174.3
2004	1,145.0	845.3	181.3	26.2	9.1	100.2	141.9	33.6	799.7	169.8
2005	1,113.4	825.4	169.9	26.9	9.5	99.8	139.2	33.3	778.0	162.9
2006	1,101.6	822.4	163.5	27.7	10.1	101.1	136.7	33.1	769.4	162.3
2007	1,088.6	818.1	156.6	28.1	10.8	102.7	130.0	31.8	766.5	160.2
2008	1,080.6	815.2	153.4	29.0	10.9	102.6	128.0	31.2	760.8	160.6
2009	1,070.2	810.6	149.4	30.1	10.8	99.9	126.4	30.8	754.3	158.7

[1] Includes other races, not shown separately. [2] Persons of Hispanic origin may be any race.

Source: U.S. Department of Defense, DoD Personnel and Procurement Statistics, Personnel, Publications, *Atlas/Data Abstract for the United States and Selected Areas*, annual, <http://siadapp.dmdc.osd.mil>.

Table 513. National Guard by Sex and Race: 1995 to 2009

[In thousands (375 represents 375,000). As of September 30]

Year	Army National Guard					Air National Guard				
	Total	Male [1]	Female	White	Black	Total	Male [1]	Female	White	Black
1995	375	344	31	299	59	110	94	16	96	9
2000	353	313	40	278	55	106	88	18	90	10
2003	351	307	44	277	52	108	89	19	91	10
2004	343	299	44	271	50	107	88	19	89	10
2005	333	290	43	264	46	106	87	19	89	9
2006	346	300	47	276	47	106	87	19	88	9
2007	353	304	49	283	47	106	87	19	88	9
2008	360	309	51	288	49	108	88	20	89	9
2009	358	308	50	288	47	109	89	20	90	9

[1] Male population includes unknown sex.

Source: U.S. Department of Defense, DoD Personnel and Procurement Statistics, Personnel, Publications, *Atlas/Data Abstract for the United States and Selected Areas, Selected Manpower Statistics*, annual. See also <http://siadapp.dmdc.osd.mil>.

Table 514. U.S. Active Duty Military Deaths by Manner of Death: 1980 to 2009

[As of December 31]

Manner of death	1980–2009	1980	1990	1995	2000	2003	2004	2005	2006	2007	2008	2009
Deaths, total	**17,715**	**2,392**	**1,507**	**1,040**	**758**	**1,410**	**1,873**	**1,940**	**1,882**	**1,953**	**1,442**	**1,518**
Accident	7,226	1,556	880	538	397	581	607	647	561	559	485	415
Hostile action	4,120	–	–	–	–	339	738	739	769	847	353	335
Homicide	704	174	74	67	34	44	46	53	47	52	46	67
Illness	2,798	419	277	174	139	234	271	291	257	236	238	262
Pending	258	–	–	–	–	1	1	1	8	25	49	173
Self-inflicted	2,350	231	232	250	151	189	202	183	213	211	247	241
Terrorist attack	26	1	1	7	17	–	–	–	–	–	–	–
Undetermined	233	11	43	4	20	22	8	26	27	23	24	25
Deaths per 100,000 of personnel strength	**(X)**	**110.7**	**66.8**	**62.5**	**49.5**	**81.4**	**109.4**	**116.7**	**116.8**	**121.4**	**85.6**	**92.5**
Accident	(X)	72.0	39.0	32.4	25.9	33.5	35.5	38.9	34.8	34.8	28.8	25.3
Hostile action	(X)	–	–	–	–	19.6	43.1	44.4	47.7	52.7	21.0	20.4
Homicide	(X)	8.1	3.3	4.0	2.2	2.5	2.7	3.2	2.9	3.2	2.7	4.1
Illness	(X)	19.4	12.3	10.5	9.1	13.5	15.8	17.5	15.9	14.7	14.1	16.0
Pending	(X)	–	–	–	–	0.1	0.1	0.1	0.5	1.6	2.9	10.5
Self-inflicted	(X)	10.7	10.3	15.0	9.9	10.9	11.8	11.0	13.2	13.1	14.7	14.7
Terrorist attack	(X)	–	–	0.4	1.1	–	–	–	–	–	–	–
Undetermined	(X)	0.5	1.9	0.2	1.3	1.3	0.5	1.6	1.7	1.4	1.4	1.5

– Represents zero. X Not applicable.

Source: Department of Defense Personnel and Procurement, DoD Personnel and Military Casualty Statistics, "Military Casualty Information," <http://siadapp.dmdc.osd.mil/personnel/CASUALTY/castop.htm>.

Table 515. U.S. Military Personnel on Active Duty in Selected Foreign Countries: 1995 to 2009

[As of September 30]

Country	1995	2000	2004	2005	2006	2007	2008	2009
In foreign countries [1]	**238,064**	**257,817**	**287,802**	**290,997**	**284,967**	**295,003**	**288,550**	**262,793**
Ashore	208,836	212,858	265,594	268,214	262,586	272,124	269,260	242,291
Afloat	29,228	44,959	20,208	22,783	22,381	22,879	19,290	20,502
Australia	314	175	196	196	347	140	140	139
Bahrain	618	949	1,712	1,641	1,357	1,495	1,545	1,507
Belgium	1,689	1,554	1,474	1,366	1,361	1,328	1,266	1,267
Bosnia and Herzegovina	1	5,708	951	263	232	209	14	11
Canada	214	156	156	150	133	141	134	128
Colombia	44	224	55	52	104	123	114	77
Cuba (Guantanamo)	5,129	688	682	950	953	932	969	926
Diego Garcia [2]	897	625	816	683	157	260	244	253
Djibouti	7	2	412	622	1,375	2,100	1,780	1,207
Egypt	1,123	499	348	410	360	250	284	265
Germany	73,280	69,203	76,058	66,418	64,319	57,080	55,140	52,658
Greece	489	678	473	428	395	363	366	361
Greenland	131	125	133	146	137	126	134	144
Honduras	193	351	448	438	414	403	429	416
Italy	12,007	11,190	12,606	11,841	10,449	9,855	9,601	9,707
Japan	39,134	40,159	36,365	35,571	33,453	32,803	33,286	35,965
Korea, South	36,016	36,565	40,840	30,983	29,086	27,014	25,062	(NA)
Kuwait	771	4,602	(3)	(3)	(3)	(3)	(3)	(3)
Netherlands	687	659	701	583	591	579	547	510
Portugal	1,066	1,005	1,006	970	922	826	783	716
Qatar	2	52	273	463	446	411	433	463
Saudi Arabia	1,077	7,053	235	258	282	243	284	269
Senegal	13	10	9	42	7	11	7	9
Singapore	166	411	237	169	164	125	129	125
Spain	2,799	2,007	2,012	1,660	1,521	1,286	1,220	1,365
Turkey	3,111	2,006	1,762	1,780	1,810	1,594	1,575	1,616
United Kingdom	12,131	11,207	11,469	10,752	10,331	9,825	9,426	9,199
DEPLOYMENTS								
Operation Enduring Freedom (OEF) [4]	(X)	(X)	(NA)	19,500	21,500	25,240	32,300	66,400
Operation Iraqi Freedom (OIF) [5]	(X)	(X)	170,647	192,600	185,500	218,500	190,400	164,100

X Not applicable. NA Not available. [1] Includes items not shown separately. [2] British Indian Ocean Territory. [3] Military personnel data for Kuwait are included with the Operation Iraqi Freedom (OIF) data. [4] Total (in/around Afghanistan as of September 30) includes Reserve/National Guard. [5] Total (in/around Iraq as of September 30) includes Reserve/National Guard.

Source: U.S. Department of Defense, DoD Personnel and Procurement Statistics, "Active Duty Military Personnel Strengths by Regional Area and by Country." See also <http://siadapp.dmdc.osd.mil>.

Table 516. U.S. Military Sales and Assistance to Foreign Governments: 1995 to 2008

[In millions of dollars (8,495 represents $8,495,000,000). For year ending September 30. Department of Defense (DoD) sales deliveries cover deliveries against sales orders authorized under Arms Export Control Act, as well as earlier and applicable legislation. For details regarding individual programs, see source]

Item	1995	2000	2002	2003	2004	2005	2006	2007	2008
Military sales agreements	8,495	10,705	11,922	12,690	13,442	9,505	17,970	18,667	28,985
Military construction sales agreements . . .	24	284	70	223	684	308	173	485	187
Military sales deliveries [1]	12,100	10,886	10,420	9,739	11,404	11,184	11,602	12,566	11,885
Military construction sales deliveries	(NA)	183	216	245	281	350	323	197	267
Military financing program	3,712	4,333	4,032	5,955	4,584	4,956	4,450	4,519	4,506
Commercial exports licensed under arms export control act [2]	(NA)	478	341	2,728	7,895	30,146	31,605	8,874	(NA)
Military assistance program delivery [3]	20	16	31	182	27	62	46	14	2
IMET program/deliveries [4]	26	50	70	79	89	88	85	84	84

NA Not available. [1] Includes military construction sales deliveries. [2] The total dollar value of deliveries made against purchases of munitions-controlled items by foreign governments directly from U.S. manufacturers. [3] Includes Military Assistance Service Funded (MASF) program data and Section 506(a) drawdown authority. [4] International Military Education & Training. Includes military assistance service funded and emergency drawdowns.

Source: U.S. Department of Defense, Defense Security Cooperation Agency, "DSCA Data and Statistics." See also <http://www.dsca.osd.mil/data_stats.htm>.

Table 517. U.S. Military Sales Deliveries by Selected Country: 1995 to 2008

[In millions of dollars (12,100 represents $12,100,000,000). For year ending September 30. Represents Department of Defense military sales]

Country	1995	2000	2002	2003	2004	2005	2006	2007	2008
Total [1]	**12,100**	**10,886**	**10,420**	**9,739**	**11,404**	**11,184**	**11,602**	**12,566**	**11,885**
Australia.	303	332	216	208	193	350	350	781	933
Bahrain	40	55	84	90	88	65	55	84	44
Belgium	8	61	68	71	42	49	53	49	44
Canada	127	84	85	155	144	150	183	247	470
Denmark	54	44	23	14	22	40	49	63	58
Egypt	1,479	1,092	1,702	1,078	1,514	1,422	1,198	1,227	859
France	64	217	206	276	99	69	42	47	57
Germany	257	131	221	241	264	208	149	205	173
Greece.	220	389	469	1,324	1,225	468	180	204	198
Israel	327	585	630	927	121	1,524	1,284	1,318	1,335
Italy	54	52	103	185	281	127	288	153	76
Japan.	693	458	465	430	392	410	769	651	613
Jordan	47	52	67	69	104	141	102	170	264
Korea, South	442	1,399	533	560	601	604	599	732	808
Kuwait	471	321	131	143	209	278	542	463	247
Netherlands.	153	278	406	224	277	178	231	241	256
Norway.	25	64	87	123	80	106	92	163	88
Portugal.	88	20	28	116	30	84	83	46	70
Saudi Arabia	3,567	1,975	1,308	1,011	1,223	994	978	1,015	898
Singapore	59	131	407	168	205	229	355	173	168
Spain	193	141	317	159	433	127	105	151	169
Taiwan [2]	1,332	784	1,392	710	917	1,402	1,069	779	618
Thailand.	356	114	171	153	100	92	83	46	41
Turkey	368	216	281	277	290	190	247	195	337
United Arab Emirates	345	42	93	87	155	169	201	70	84
United Kingdom.	419	347	386	350	453	382	294	424	303

[1] Includes countries not shown. [2] See footnote 4, Table 1331.

Source: U.S. Department of Defense, Defense Security Cooperation Agency, "DSCA Data and Statistics." See also <http://www.dsca.osd.mil/data_stats.htm>.

Table 518. Veterans by Selected Period of Service and State: 2009

[In thousands (22,848 represents 22,848,000). As of September 30. VetPop2007 is the Department of Veterans Affairs (VA) latest official estimate and projection of the veteran population. It is based on detailed tabulations of Census 2000 data (prepared for the VA Office of the Actuary by the Census Bureau) and on recent American Community Survey data. VetPop2007 also uses administrative data and projections of service member separations from active duty provided by the Department of Defense (the Defense Manpower Data Center and the Office of the Actuary), as well as VA administrative data on veterans benefits]

State	Total [1,2]	Gulf War [3]	Vietnam era	State	Total [1,2]	Gulf War [3]	Vietnam era
United States	**22,848**	**5,460**	**7,583**	Missouri	515	115	174
Alabama	410	110	139	Montana	103	24	36
Alaska	76	27	27	Nebraska	148	36	51
Arizona	561	132	181	Nevada	245	60	87
Arkansas	258	63	88	New Hampshire	130	24	46
California	2,026	486	659	New Jersey	464	76	145
Colorado	424	112	153	New Mexico	177	48	58
Connecticut	238	39	80	New York	988	172	315
Delaware	79	19	25	North Carolina	770	215	253
District of Columbia	38	10	12	North Dakota	57	15	18
Florida	1,684	384	517	Ohio	913	187	309
Georgia	773	233	260	Oklahoma	330	90	110
Hawaii	117	35	36	Oregon	340	69	121
Idaho	137	35	47	Pennsylvania	995	176	328
Illinois	803	182	258	Rhode Island	74	14	25
Indiana	501	107	169	South Carolina	409	112	140
Iowa	240	49	81	South Dakota	73	19	24
Kansas	229	60	76	Tennessee	502	122	177
Kentucky	340	85	115	Texas	1,702	499	570
Louisiana	312	89	98	Utah	155	38	51
Maine	141	29	50	Vermont	53	9	19
Maryland	476	133	151	Virginia	819	290	260
Massachusetts	409	67	133	Washington	637	166	225
Michigan	723	134	254	West Virginia	171	38	57
Minnesota	391	67	142	Wisconsin	428	84	144
Mississippi	209	59	67	Wyoming	56	15	21

[1] Veterans serving in more than one period of service are counted only once in the total. [2] Current civilians discharged from active duty, other than for training only without service-connected disability. [3] Service from August 2, 1990 to the present.

Source: U.S. Department of Veterans Affairs, Veteran Data and Information, Veteran Demographics, <http://www1.va.gov/vetdata/index.asp>.

Table 519. Veterans Living by Period of Service, Age, and Sex: 2009

[In thousands (23,067 represents 23,067,000). As of September 30. Includes those veterans living outside the United States]

Age	Total veterans	Wartime veterans					Peacetime veterans
		Total [1]	Gulf War [2]	Vietnam era	Korean conflict	World War II	
Total	**23,067**	**17,175**	**5,507**	**7,653**	**2,621**	**2,272**	**5,892**
Under 20 years old	10	10	10	–	–	–	–
20 to 24 years old	302	302	302	–	–	–	–
25 to 29 years old	773	773	773	–	–	–	–
30 to 34 years old	868	868	868	–	–	–	–
35 to 39 years old	1,109	1,049	1,049	–	–	–	60
40 to 44 years old	1,480	919	919	–	–	–	560
45 to 49 years old	1,846	643	643	–	–	–	1,203
50 to 54 years old	1,938	785	436	389	–	–	1,153
55 to 59 years old	2,135	1,828	285	1,689	–	–	307
60 to 64 years old	3,411	3,292	156	3,250	–	–	118
65 to 69 years old	2,358	1,630	45	1,624	–	–	727
70 to 74 years old	1,952	674	14	402	313	–	1,278
75 to 79 years old	1,971	1,580	5	177	1,512	23	391
80 to 84 years old	1,566	1,494	1	85	677	947	71
85 years & over	1,348	1,325	–	37	119	1,303	23
Female, total	**1,824**	**1,276**	**881**	**253**	**64**	**110**	**548**

– Represents or rounds to zero. [1] Veterans who served in more than one wartime period are counted only once in the total. [2] Service from August 2, 1990 to the present.

Source: U.S. Department of Veterans Affairs, VA Office of the Actuary, *VetPop 2007*, <http://www1.va.gov/vetdata/>.

Table 520. Veterans by Sex, Race, and Hispanic or Latino Origin: 2008

[Data are based on the American Community Survey (ACS). The survey universe includes the household population and the population living in institutions, college dormitories, and other group quarters. Based on a sample and subject to sampling variability; see text, this section and Appendix III]

Characteristics	Total number	18 to 64 years	65 years and over
Total	**22,424,712**	**13,367,171**	**9,057,541**
Male	20,919,824	12,129,050	8,790,774
Female	1,504,888	1,238,121	266,767
White alone	19,062,247	10,776,191	8,286,056
Male	17,937,608	9,898,031	8,039,577
Female	1,124,639	878,160	246,479
Black or African American alone	2,319,937	1,799,375	520,562
Male	2,040,725	1,532,057	508,668
Female	279,212	267,318	11,894
American Indian/Alaska Native alone	160,471	122,413	38,058
Male	144,986	108,356	36,630
Female	15,485	14,057	1,428
Asian alone	276,079	182,659	93,420
Male	253,788	163,337	90,451
Female	22,291	19,322	2,969
Native Hawaiian and Other Pacific Islander alone	26,810	21,529	5,281
Male	23,971	18,884	5,087
Female	2,839	2,645	194
Some other race alone	266,513	221,132	45,381
Male	243,138	198,960	44,178
Female	23,375	22,172	1,203
Two or more races	312,655	243,872	68,783
Male	275,608	209,425	66,183
Female	37,047	34,447	2,600
Hispanic or Latino origin [1]	1,149,579	863,186	286,393
Male	1,056,255	776,512	279,743
Female	93,324	86,674	6,650

[1] Persons of Hispanic or Latino origin may be any race.

Source: U.S. Census Bureau, 2008 American Community Survey, B21001, B21001A, B21001B, B21001C, B21001D, B21001E, B21001F, and B21001, <http://factfinder.census.gov/>.

Table 521. Veterans Benefits—Expenditures by Program and Compensation for Service-Connected Disabilities: 1990 to 2009

[In millions of dollars (28,998 represents $28,998,000,000). For years ending September 30. Minus sign (–) indicates decrease]

Program	1990	1995	2000	2005	2006	2007	2008	2009
Total expenditures	**28,998**	**37,775**	**47,086**	**69,667**	**69,950**	**72,805**	**84,855**	**95,559**
Medical programs	11,582	16,255	19,637	29,433	31,308	33,705	38,396	43,100
Construction	661	641	466	483	497	704	1,088	1,325
General operating expenses	811	954	1,016	1,294	1,545	1,476	1,628	1840
Compensation and pension	14,674	17,765	22,012	34,694	34,681	34,600	40,241	44,735
Vocational rehabilitation and education	452	1,317	1,610	2,937	3,163	3,180	3,210	3,875
All other [1]	818	844	2,345	826	−1,244	−860	292	384
Compensation for service-connected disabilities [2]	9,284	11,644	15,511	24,515	26,551	28,200	31,393	35,340

[1] Includes insurance, indemnities, and miscellaneous funds and expenditures and offsets from public receipts. (Excludes expenditures from personal funds of patients.) [2] Represents veterans receiving compensation for service-connected disabilities.

Source: U.S. Department of Veterans Affairs, *Expenditures and Workload*, annual; <http://www1.va.gov/vetdata/>.

Table 522. Veterans Compensation and Pension Benefits—Number on Rolls by Period of Service and Status: 1990 to 2009

[In thousands (3,584 represents 3,584,000), except as indicated. As of September 30. Living refers to veterans receiving compensation for disability incurred or aggravated while on active duty and war veterans receiving pension and benefits for nonservice-connected disabilities. Deceased refers to deceased veterans whose dependents were receiving pensions and compensation benefits]

Period of service and veteran status	1990	1995	2000	2005	2006	2007	2008	2009
Total	**3,584**	**3,330**	**3,236**	**3,503**	**3,582**	**3,691**	**3,801**	**3,919**
Living veterans	2,746	2,669	2,672	2,973	3,056	3,167	3,268	3,384
Service-connected	2,184	2,236	2,308	2,637	2,726	2,844	2,952	3,070
Nonservice-connected	562	433	364	336	330	323	316	314
Deceased veterans	838	662	564	530	527	524	533	535
Service-connected	320	307	307	323	326	330	338	341
Nonservice-connected	518	355	257	207	201	195	196	194
World War I	198	89	34	13	11	9	8	7
Living	18	3	(Z)	(Z)	(Z)	(Z)	(Z)	(Z)
World War II	1,723	1,307	968	718	674	634	598	559
Living	1,294	961	676	466	430	397	362	329
Korean conflict [1]	390	368	323	295	290	287	282	276
Living	305	290	255	231	226	223	218	213
Vietnam era [2]	774	868	969	1,218	1,260	1,305	1,347	1,393
Living	685	766	848	1,068	1,104	1,142	1,175	1,214
Gulf War [3]	(X)	138	334	630	716	819	923	1,028
Living	(X)	134	326	617	701	802	904	1,007
Peacetime	495	559	607	627	631	637	644	655
Living	444	514	567	591	596	602	609	621

X Not applicable. Z Fewer than 500. [1] Service during period June 27, 1950 to January 31, 1955. [2] Service from August 5, 1964 to May 7, 1975. [3] Service from August 2, 1990 to the present.

Source: U.S. Department of Veterans Affairs, 1990 to 1995, *Annual Report of the Secretary of Veterans Affairs*; beginning 2000, *Annual Accountability Report* and unpublished data, <http://www1.va.gov/vetdata/>.

Table 523. Homeland Security Funding by Agency: 2008 to 2010

[In millions of dollars. (61,227.8 represents 61,227,800,000). A total of 31 agencies comprise federal homeland security funding. Department of Homeland Security (DHS) is the designated department to coordinate and centralize the leadership of many homeland security activities under a single department. In addition to DHS, the Departments of Defense (DoD), Energy (DoE), Justice (DoJ), Health and Human Services (HHS), and the U.S. State Department account for most of the total government-wide homeland security funding]

Agency	2008	2009	2010
Total budget authority, excluding BioShield [1,2].	61,227.8	70,445.3	70,829.2
Department of Agriculture.	574.6	513.0	599.4
Department of Commerce.	206.9	258.8	254.4
Department of Defense	17,374.4	19,413.5	19,040.6
Department of Education.	27.1	31.8	28.5
Department of Energy.	1,827.3	1,938.8	2,018.0
Department of Health and Human Services	4,300.6	4,627.1	4,803.9
Department of Homeland Security [3]	29,755.8	36,036.5	35,840.0
Department of Housing and Urban Development	1.9	4.8	4.9
Department of the Interior.	50.2	49.9	51.5
Department of Justice.	3,277.5	3,650.4	4,106.9
Department of Labor.	47.8	48.5	52.9
Department of State	1,719.1	1,809.2	1,767.1
Department of Transportation	205.3	220.9	229.6
Department of the Treasury.	120.0	133.3	124.2
Department of Veterans Affairs	308.9	309.9	426.8
Corps of Engineers	42.0	40.0	37.0
Environmental Protection Agency	138.1	157.0	155.1
Executive Office of the President.	21.0	19.1	12.0
General Services Administration.	143.0	125.4	214.0
National Aeronautics and Space Administration	205.2	214.3	218.0
National Science Foundation.	365.1	377.2	390.0
Office of Personnel Management	2.3	1.9	2.2
Social Security Administration.	184.2	181.5	209.3
District of Columbia.	3.4	39.0	15.0
Federal Communications Commission	2.3	2.2	1.7
Intelligence Community Management Account.	122.0	32.8	15.5
National Archives and Records Administration	17.7	19.6	20.0
Nuclear Regulatory Commission.	72.1	72.8	65.4
Securities and Exchange Commission	13.4	15.0	17.0
Smithsonian Institution	91.0	92.3	98.5
United States Holocaust Memorial Museum	8.0	9.0	10.0

[1] The federal spending estimates are for the Executive Branch's homeland security efforts. These estimates do not include the efforts of the Legislative or Judicial Branches. [2] The Department of Homeland Security Appropriations Act, 2004, provided $5.6 billion for Project BioShield, to remain available through 2013. Including this uneven funding stream can distort year-over-year comparisons. [3] Not all activities carried out by DHS constitute homeland security funding (e.g. response to natural disasters and Coast Guard search and rescue activities). DHS estimates in this table do not represent the entire DHS budget. See Table 524.

Source: U.S. Office of Management and Budget, Budget of the United States Government Fiscal Year 2011, The Budget Documents, *Analytical Perspectives, Budget of the United States Government Fiscal Year 2011, Crosscutting Programs, Homeland Security Funding Analysis*, <http://www.whitehouse.gov/omb/budget/>.

Table 524. Department of Homeland Security Total Budget Authority and Personnel by Organization: 2009 and 2010

[In thousands of dollars (52,771,076 represents $52,771,076,000). For the fiscal year ending September 30. Not all activities carried out by the Department of Homeland Security (DHS) constitute homeland security funding (e.g., Coast Guard search and rescue activities)]

Organization	Budget authority		Full-time employees	
	2009	2010	2009	2010
Total.	52,771,076	55,388,333	205,870	212,130
Departmental operations [1].	659,109	802,931	1,303	1,626
Analysis and operations	327,373	335,030	594	682
Office of the Inspector General	114,513	113,874	577	632
U.S. Customs & Border Protection	11,250,652	11,449,283	55,520	58,223
U.S. Immigration & Customs Enforcement	5,968,015	5,741,752	20,215	20,252
Transportation Security Administration	6,992,778	7,656,066	51,618	51,628
U.S. Coast Guard.	9,624,179	10,122,963	49,403	51,114
U.S. Secret Service	1,640,444	1,702,644	6,806	7,055
National Protection and Program Directorate	1,188,263	2,432,755	830	1352
Office of Health Affairs.	157,621	139,250	71	84
Federal Emergency Management Agency (FEMA).	5,971,159	6,194,268	6,917	6,913
FEMA Grants [2].	4,220,858	4,165,200	([3])	([3])
U.S. Citizenship & Immigration Services	2,876,348	2,859,997	10,362	10,835
Federal Law Enforcement Training Center.	332,986	282,812	1,143	1,196
Science & Technology Directorate (S&T)	932,587	1,006,471	381	408
Domestic Nuclear Detection Office	514,191	383,037	130	130

[1] Departmental operations is comprised of the Office of the Secretary & Executive Management, the Office of the Federal Coordinator for Gulf Coast Rebuilding, the Office of the Undersecretary for Management, the Office of the Chief Financial Officer, and the Office of the Chief Information Officer. [2] Includes the following FEMA appropriations: State and Local Programs & Emergency Management Perf. Grants, and Assistance to Firefighters Grants. [3] Employee data are included in the FEMA full-time employees.

Source: U.S. Department of Homeland Security, "Budget-in-Brief, Fiscal Year 2011," <http://www.dhs.gov/xabout/budget/>, accessed May 2010.

Table 525. Homeland Security Grants by State/Territories: 2008 and 2009

[In thousands of dollars (1,697,314 represents 1,697,314,000). For years ending September 30. Grants consist of the following programs: State Homeland Security Program (SHSP), Urban Areas Security Initiative (UASI), Metropolitan Medical Response System (MMRS), and Citizen Corps Program (CCP)]

State/territory	2008	2009	State/territory	2008	2009	State/territory	2008	2009
Total.......	1,697,314	1,714,172	KY..........	11,885	11,668			
			LA..........	23,663	24,735	OR..........	17,035	15,360
U.S.........	1,682,304	1,698,443	ME..........	6,317	6,671	PA..........	56,291	54,042
AL..........	12,698	12,062	MD..........	30,145	28,544	RI..........	11,646	11,750
AK..........	6,941	7,296	MA..........	32,252	31,243	SC..........	9,538	9,026
AZ..........	31,292	29,997	MI..........	36,984	35,561	SD..........	6,302	6,657
AR..........	6,682	7,036	MN..........	21,367	20,134	TN..........	20,688	20,417
CA..........	260,824	262,998	MS..........	6,695	7,038	TX..........	142,270	138,552
CO..........	20,708	19,190	MO..........	30,884	28,431	UT..........	9,162	9,925
CT..........	14,845	15,631	MT..........	6,307	6,661	VT..........	6,297	6,652
DE..........	6,304	6,659	NE..........	6,973	7,327	VA..........	33,540	32,347
DC..........	71,247	68,543	NV..........	18,925	17,068	WA..........	31,379	30,479
FL..........	77,483	72,345	NH..........	6,638	6,993	WV..........	6,332	6,686
GA..........	37,127	35,171	NJ..........	63,770	61,845	WI..........	16,044	15,358
HI..........	11,642	11,746	NM..........	6,657	7,011	WY..........	6,294	6,649
ID..........	6,322	6,677	NY..........	233,090	271,463	AS [1].......	1,888	1,468
IL..........	81,622	86,917	NC..........	22,435	21,651	GU [1].......	1,891	1,471
IN..........	21,063	19,671	ND..........	6,298	6,652	NM [1].......	1,889	1,469
IA..........	6,687	7,040	OH..........	43,168	42,083	PR [1].......	8,352	9,850
KS..........	8,362	8,112	OK..........	13,182	14,674	VI [1].......	1,890	1,470

[1] AS—American Samoa, GU—Guam, NM—Northern Mariana Islands, PR—Puerto Rico, VI—Virgin Islands.

Source: U.S. Department of Homeland Security, State Contacts and Grants Award Administration, <http://www.fema.gov/government/grant/hsgp/index09.shtml/> (released June 2009).

Table 526. Urban Areas Security Initiative (UASI) Grant Program: 2009

[In thousands of dollars (798,631 represents $798,631,000). For year ending September 30. The UASI Program provides financial assistance to address the unique multi-disciplinary planning, operations, equipment, training, and exercise needs of high-threat, high-density urban areas. The 60 highest risk urban areas were eligible for funding. The seven highest risk urban areas are designated Tier 1. For a listing of all grant programs and their descriptions, see <http://www.dhs.gov/xgovt/grants/index.shtm>]

State/territory	Urban area	Amount	State/territory	Urban area	Amount	State/territory	Urban area	Amount
Total...		798,631						
				Jacksonville	5,355	OH....	Cincinnati	4,969
TIER 1				Miami	11,040		Cleveland	5,087
CA....	Bay Area	40,638		Orlando	5,083		Columbus	4,247
	Los Angeles/Long Beach	68,290		Tampa	7,815		Toledo	2,288
DC....	National Capital	58,007	GA....	Atlanta	13,509	OK....	Oklahoma City	4,405
IL.....	Chicago	52,321	HI.....	Honolulu	4,755		Tulsa	2,161
NJ....	Jersey City/Newark	35,298	IN.....	Indianapolis	7,105	OR....	Portland	7,179
NY....	New York City	145,138	KY....	Louisville	2,202	PA....	Philadelphia	17,951
TX....	Houston	39,555	LA....	Baton Rouge	2,973		Pittsburgh	6,396
				New Orleans	5,430	PR....	San Juan	3,104
TIER 2			MD....	Baltimore	10,975	RI.....	Providence	4,764
AZ....	Phoenix	10,820	MA....	Boston	14,565	TN....	Memphis	4,167
	Tucson	4,515	MI.....	Detroit	13,482		Nashville	2,837
CA....	Anaheim/Santa Ana	12,773	MN....	Twin Cities	8,248	TX....	Austin	2,923
	Oxnard	2,503	MO....	Kansas City	7,706		Dallas/Fort Worth/Arlington	19,306
	Riverside	5,277		St. Louis	8,533		El Paso	5,390
	Sacramento	3,938	NV....	Las Vegas	8,150		San Antonio	6,230
	San Diego	16,209	NY....	Albany	1,924	UT....	Salt Lake City	2,894
CO....	Denver	7,053		Buffalo	5,545	VA....	Norfolk	7,372
CT....	Bridgeport	2,807		Rochester	2,308		Richmond	2,670
	Hartford	2,747		Syracuse	1,869	WA....	Seattle	11,031
FL....	Fort Lauderdale	6,063	NC....	Charlotte	4,580	WI....	Milwaukee	4,160

Source: Department of Homeland Security, FEMA, FY 2009 Homeland Security Grant Program (HSGP), <http://www.fema.gov/government/grant/hsgp/index09.shtml/> (released June 2009).

Table 527. Preparedness Grant Programs: 2007 to 2009

[In dollars. For years ending September 30. Program formally called the Infrastructure Protection Programs]

Program [1]	2007	2008	2009
Total	655,230,003	803,916,250	968,585,000
Transit Security Grant Program	257,770,670	388,600,000	348,600,000
Freight Rail Security Grant Program	–	15,000,000	15,000,000
Intercity passenger Rail (AMTRAK)..........	13,409,537	25,000,000	25,000,000
Port Security Grant Program	312,269,796	388,600,000	388,600,000
Intercity Bus Security Grant Program	11,640,000	11,172,250	11,658,000
Trucking Security Program	11,640,000	15,544,000	7,772,000
Buffer Zone Protection Program	48,500,000	48,575,000	48,575,000

– Represents zero. [1] Total Includes programs not listed.

Source: U.S. Department of Homeland Security, State Contacts and Grants Award Administration, <http://www.fema.gov/pdf/government/grant/2010/fy_10_grants_overview.pdf>

U.S. Census Bureau, Statistical Abstract of the United States: 2011

Table 528. Deportable Aliens Located by Program and Border Patrol Sector: 2000 to 2008

[As of the end of September. For purposes of statistical reporting there is no difference between the terms "apprehension" and "deportable alien located." For definitions for Immigration statistics, see <http://www.dhs.gov/files/statistics/dtadefstd.shtm>]

Program and sector	2000	2004	2005	2006	2007	2008
Total	**1,814,729**	**1,264,232**	**1,291,142**	**1,206,457**	**960,756**	**791,568**
Investigations [1]	138,291	103,837	102,034	101,854	53,562	33,573
Detention and Removal Operations [2]	(X)	(X)	(X)	15,467	30,407	34,155
Border Patrol	1,676,438	1,160,395	1,189,108	1,089,136	876,787	723,840
All southwest sectors	**1,643,679**	**1,139,282**	**1,171,428**	**1,072,018**	**858,722**	**705,022**
San Diego, CA	151,681	138,608	126,909	142,122	152,459	162,392
El Centro, CA	238,126	74,467	55,726	61,469	55,881	40,962
Yuma, AZ	108,747	98,060	138,438	118,537	37,994	8,363
Tucson, AZ	616,346	491,771	439,090	392,104	378,323	317,709
El Paso, TX	115,696	104,399	122,689	122,261	75,464	30,310
Marfa, TX	13,689	10,530	10,536	7,517	5,537	5,390
Del Rio, TX	157,178	53,794	68,510	42,634	22,919	20,761
Laredo, TX	108,973	74,706	75,342	74,843	56,715	43,659
Rio Grande Valley, TX	133,243	92,947	134,188	110,531	73,430	75,476
All other sectors	**32,759**	**21,113**	**17,680**	**17,118**	**18,065**	**18,818**
Blaine, WA	2,581	1,354	1,001	809	749	951
Buffalo, NY	1,570	671	400	1,517	2,190	3,338
Detroit, MI	2,057	1,912	1,792	1,282	902	961
Grand Forks, ND	562	1,225	754	517	500	542
Havre, MT	1,568	986	949	567	486	427
Houlton, ME	489	263	233	175	95	81
Livermore, CA [3]	6,205	1,850	117	(X)	(X)	(X)
Miami, FL	6,237	4,602	7,243	6,032	7,121	6,020
New Orleans, LA	6,478	2,889	1,358	3,054	4,018	4,303
Ramey, PR	1,731	1,813	1,619	1,436	548	572
Spokane, WA	1,324	847	279	185	337	340
Swanton, VT	1,957	2,701	1,935	1,544	1,119	1,283

X Not applicable. [1] The Immigration and Customs Enforcement (ICE) Office of Investigations focuses on the enforcement of a wide variety of laws that include immigration and customs statutes. [2] Include arrests of fugitive and nonfugitive aliens under the Office of Detention and Removal Operations (DRO), National Fugitive Operations Program. [3] Livermore sector closed July 30, 2004.

Source: U.S. Department of Homeland Security, Office of Immigration Statistics, *Yearbook of Immigration Statistics, 2008*. See also <http://www.dhs.gov/files/statistics/publications/>.

Table 529. U.S. Border Patrol Apprehensions by Border, Gender, Age, and Leading Country of Nationality: 2005 to 2008

[As of the end of September. See headnote, Table 528]

Characteristic	2005 Number	2005 Percent	2006 Number	2006 Percent	2007 Number	2007 Percent	2008 Number	2008 Percent
Border total	**1,189,031**	**100.0**	**1,089,096**	**100.0**	**876,803**	**100.0**	**723,840**	**100.0**
Southwest	1,171,391	98.5	1,071,979	98.4	858,737	97.9	705,022	97.4
Coastal	10,291	0.9	10,521	1.0	11,687	1.3	10,895	1.5
Northern	7,349	0.6	6,596	0.6	6,379	0.7	7,923	1.1
Gender								
Total	**1,189,031**	**100.0**	**1,089,096**	**100.0**	**876,803**	**100.0**	**723,840**	**100.0**
Male	969,879	81.6	893,380	82	730,217	83.3	606,761	83.8
Female	219,123	18.4	195,699	18	146,574	16.7	117,061	16.2
Unknown	29	–	17	–	12	–	18	–
Age								
Total	**1,189,031**	**100.0**	**1,089,096**	**100.0**	**876,803**	**100.0**	**723,840**	**100.0**
17 years and under	114,222	9.6	101,778	9.3	77,778	8.9	59,578	8.2
18 to 24 years	442,755	37.2	403,320	37.0	325,901	37.2	257,409	35.6
25 to 34 years	411,743	34.6	377,401	34.7	301,002	34.3	255,261	35.3
35 to 44 years	162,069	13.6	151,422	13.9	127,285	14.5	112,941	15.6
45 to 54 years	47,158	4.0	45,001	4.1	36,661	4.2	32,003	4.4
55 years and over	9,569	0.8	9,093	0.8	7,384	0.8	6,235	0.9
Unknown	1,515	0.1	1,081	0.1	792	0.1	413	0.1
Country of Nationality								
Total	**1,189,031**	**100.0**	**1,089,096**	**100.0**	**876,803**	**100.0**	**723,840**	**100.0**
Mexico	1,023,888	86.1	981,069	90.1	808,773	92.2	661,773	91.4
Honduras [1]	52,741	4.4	28,709	2.6	22,914	2.6	19,351	2.7
Guatemala	22,594	1.9	19,925	1.8	17,337	2.0	16,395	2.3
El Salvador [1]	39,309	3.3	41,391	3.8	14,114	1.6	12,684	1.8
Cuba	3,263	0.3	4,021	0.4	4,295	0.5	3,351	0.5
Ecuador	1,343	0.1	1,143	0.1	958	0.1	1,579	0.2
Nicaragua	3,921	0.3	2,736	0.3	1,646	0.2	1,467	0.2
Brazil [1]	31,063	2.6	1,460	0.1	1,214	0.1	977	0.1
China, People's Republic	2,200	0.2	2,179	0.2	837	0.1	836	0.1
Dominican Republic	1,406	0.1	1,023	0.1	562	0.1	819	0.1
Canada	1,020	0.1	876	0.1	554	0.1	610	0.1
Other	6,283	0.5	4,564	0.4	3,599	0.4	3,998	0.6

– Represents zero. [1] Between 2005 and 2008, the percentage of persons apprehended who were from Honduras, El Salvador, and Brazil declined substantially. These decreases reflect the end of "catch and release," the practice of apprehending illegal aliens from countries other than Mexico and releasing them on their own recognizance pending a removal hearing.

Source: U.S. Dept. of Homeland Security, Office of Immigration Statistics, *Fact Sheets*, <http://www.dhs.gov/xlibrary/assets /statistics/publications/ois_apprehensions_fs_2005-2008.pdf>.

Table 530. Deportable Aliens Located: 1925 to 2008

[See headnote, Table 528. Detention and Removal Operations (DRO) data are included beginning in Fiscal Year 2006]

Year	Number	Year	Number	Year	Number	Year	Number
1925.	22,199	1974.	788,145	1986.	1,767,400	1998.	1,679,439
1930.	20,880	1975.	766,600	1987.	1,190,488	1999.	1,714,035
1935.	11,016	1976 [1]	1,097,739	1988.	1,008,145	2000.	1,814,729
1940.	10,492	1977.	1,042,215	1989.	954,243	2001.	1,387,486
1945.	69,164	1978.	1,057,977	1990.	1,169,939	2002.	1,062,279
1950.	468,339	1979.	1,076,418	1991.	1,197,875	2003.	1,046,422
1955.	254,096	1980.	910,361	1992.	1,258,481	2004.	1,264,232
1960.	70,684	1981.	975,780	1993.	1,327,261	2005.	1,291,142
1965.	110,371	1982.	970,246	1994.	1,094,719	2006.	1,206,457
1970.	345,353	1983.	1,251,357	1995.	1,394,554	2007.	960,756
1972.	505,949	1984.	1,246,981	1996.	1,649,986	2008.	791,568
1973.	655,968	1985.	1,348,749	1997.	1,536,520		

[1] Includes the 15 months from July 1, 1975 to September 30, 1976, because the end date of fiscal years was changed from June 30 to September 30.

Source: U.S. Department of Homeland Security, Office of Immigration Statistics, *Yearbook of Immigration Statistics, 2008*. See also <http://www.dhs.gov/files/statistics/publications/>.

Table 531. Aliens Returned or Removed by Crime Categories and Country of Nationality: 2003 to 2008

[As of the end of September. For definitions of immigration enforcement terms, see "Immigration Enforcement Actions, 2008 Yearbook of Immigration Statistics"; "Crime categories" and "Countries of nationality" ranked by latest data year]

Crime category and country of nationality	2003	2004	2005	2006	2007	2008
Total aliens returned or removed:	**1,152,725**	**1,403,508**	**1,343,351**	**1,324,355**	**1,210,772**	**1,170,122**
Returns [1]	945,294	1,166,576	1,096,920	1,043,381	891,390	811,236
Removals [2]	207,431	236,932	246,431	280,974	319,382	358,886
Noncriminal	125,097	146,029	154,706	183,609	219,458	261,753
Criminal [3]	82,334	90,903	91,725	97,365	99,924	97,133
Leading crime categories:						
Dangerous drugs.	32,441	34,071	34,215	33,485	33,449	34,882
Immigration	11,790	15,174	17,106	23,176	21,538	17,542
Assault.	8,878	9,654	9,633	9,574	11,048	7,485
Burglary.	3,324	3,406	3,351	3,506	3,466	3,202
Robbery.	2,887	2,921	3,023	2,915	2,908	3,101
Larceny	2,606	2,830	2,742	2,757	2,878	3,282
Sexual assault	2,316	2,777	2,649	2,571	2,786	2,929
Family offenses	2,277	2,478	2,172	2,262	2,410	2,343
Stolen vehicles	1,577	1,797	1,806	1,934	1,875	(NA)
Sex offenses	1,631	1,984	1,922	1,868	1,874	(NA)
Other	12,607	13,808	13,106	13,371	15,692	(NA)
Leading country of nationality of criminals removed:						
Mexico	64,641	70,113	70,178	72,157	75,243	71,650
Honduras	1,996	2,483	2,659	5,674	5,032	4,944
El Salvador	2,066	2,768	2,808	3,731	4,669	4,795
Guatemala.	1,565	1,937	1,935	3,649	6,477	4,061
Dominican Republic.	2,194	2,556	2,370	2,277	2,108	2,128
Colombia	1,380	1,493	1,393	1,322	1,226	1,098
Jamaica	1,522	1,670	1,506	1,260	1,160	1,246
Nicaragua	323	407	357	593	498	495
Canada	474	565	590	537	521	476
Brazil	220	763	1,433	563	328	354
Other	5,953	6,148	6,496	5,602	7,343	5,886

NA Not available. [1] Returns are the confirmed movement of an inadmissible or deportable alien out of the United States not based on an order of removal. Most of the voluntary departures are of Mexican nationals who have been apprehended by the U.S. Border Patrol and are returned to Mexico. [2] Removals are the compulsory and confirmed movement of an inadmissible or deportable alien out of the United States based on an order of removal. An alien who is removed has administrative or criminal consequences placed on subsequent reentry owing to the fact of the removal. [3] Refers to persons removed based on a criminal charge or those with a criminal conviction.

Source: U.S. Department of Homeland Security, Office of Immigration Statistics, *Yearbook of Immigration Statistics, 2008*, and unpublished data. See also <http://www.dhs.gov/ximgtn/statistics/publications/yearbook.shtm>.

Table 532. Coast Guard Migrant Interdictions by Nationality of Alien: 2000 to 2009

[For the year ending September 30]

Year	Total	Haiti	Dominican Republic	China [1]	Cuba	Mexico	Ecuador	Other
2000.	4,210	1,113	499	261	1,000	49	1,244	44
2004.	10,899	3,229	5,014	68	1,225	86	1,189	88
2005.	9,455	1,850	3,612	32	2,712	55	1,149	45
2006.	7,886	1,198	3,011	31	2,810	52	693	91
2007.	6,338	1,610	1,469	73	2,868	26	125	167
2008.	4,802	1,582	688	1	2,199	47	220	65
2009.	3,467	1,782	727	35	799	77	6	41

[1] See footnote 4, Table 1331.

Source: U.S. Department of Homeland Security, United States Coast Guard, "USCG Migrant Interdiction Statistics," <http://www.uscg.mil/hq/cg5/cg531/amio/flowstats/currentstats.asp/>, accessed June 2010.

Table 533. Customs and Border Protection (CBP)—Processed and Cleared Passengers, Planes, Vehicles, and Containers: 2000 to 2007

[In thousands (80,519 represents 80,519,000). For year ending September 30]

Characteristic	2000	2003	2004	2005	2006	2007
Air						
Passengers	80,519	72,959	80,866	86,123	87,906	91,574
Commercial planes [1]	829	790	824	866	881	916
Private planes	146	132	140	135	139	139
Land						
Passengers [2, 3]	397,312	329,998	326,693	317,765	289,048	299,004
Autos [2]	127,095	120,376	121,419	121,654	119,372	112,428
Rail containers.	2,157	2,472	2,588	2,655	2,735	2,737
Truck containers [4]	10,397	11,163	11,252	11,308	11,489	11,459
Sea						
Passengers [5]	10,990	15,127	22,234	26,228	26,223	27,059
Vessels [6]	211	204	142	113	168	170
Vessel containers [7]	5,813	9,092	9,796	11,341	11,622	11,703

[1] A commercial aircraft is any aircraft transporting passengers and/or cargo for some payment or other consideration, including money or services rendered. [2] See Table 1269 for more details. [3] Includes pedestrians. [4] Truck containers—number of trucks entering the U.S. [5] Does not include passengers on ferries. [6] Includes every description of water craft or other contrivance used or capable of being used as a means of transportation on water, does not include aircraft. [7] Number of vessel containers.

Source: U.S. Department of Homeland Security, Customs and Border Protection, *About CBP, Statistics and Accomplishments, National Workload Statistics, 2000–2007* and unpublished data.

Table 534. Prohibited Items Intercepted at U.S. Airport Screening Checkpoints: 2004 to 2008

[Passengers boarding aircraft in thousands (702,921 represents 702,921,000). For the calendar year. Transportation Security Administration (TSA) assumed responsibility for airport security on February 17, 2002, and by November 19, 2002, TSA assumed control over all passenger screenings from private contractors]

Year	2004	2005	2006	2007	2008
Passengers boarding aircraft, total [1]	**702,921**	**738,327**	**744,242**	**769,370**	**741,450**
Domestic	640,698	670,418	671,796	693,374	664,714
International.	62,222	67,908	72,445	75,996	76,735
Total prohibited items (number)	**7,104,095**	**15,886,404**	**13,709,684**	**6,516,026**	**(NA)**
Knife [2]	2,055,404	1,822,892	1,607,125	1,056,691	(9)
Other cutting items [3]	3,409,888	3,276,941	163,419	101,387	(9)
Club [4]	28,998	20,531	12,296	9,443	(9)
Box cutter	22,430	21,319	15,999	11,908	(9)
Firearm [5]	254	850	820	1,416	902
Incendiary [6]	697,606	374,487	94,097	73,670	116,200
Lighters [7]	178	9,420,991	11,616,688	5,124,344	(9)
Other [8]	889,337	949,243	200,060	137,167	(9)

NA Not available. [1] Data come from the Air Transport Association. Data are for U.S. passenger and cargo airlines only. [2] Knife includes any length and type except round-bladed, butter, and plastic cutlery. [3] Other cutting instruments refer to, e.g., scissors, screwdrivers, swords, sabers, and ice picks. [4] Club refers to baseball bats, night sticks, billy clubs, bludgeons, etc. [5] Firearm refers to items like pistols, revolvers, rifles, automatic weapons, shotguns, parts of guns and firearms. [6] Incendiaries refer to categories of ammunition and gunpowder, flammables/irritants, and explosives. [7] As of April 14, 2005, passengers are prohibited from carrying all lighters on their person or in carry-on luggage or onboard an airplane. [8] Other refers to categories of ammunition and gunpower, dangerous objects, fireworks, replica weapons, and tools. [9] The data for this prohibited item category are no longer collected as of August 8, 2008.

Source: U.S. Department of Homeland Security, Transportation Security Administration, unpublished data, June 2009, <http://www.tsa.gov>; Air Transport Association of America, Washington, DC; Annual Traffic and Operations: U.S. Airlines, <http://www.airlines.org/pages/home.aspx/>.

Table 535. Seizure Statistics for Intellectual Property Rights (IPR) by Commodity and Trading Partner: 2008 and 2009

[In thousands of dollars (272,729 represents $272,729,000, except as indicated). Customs and Border Protection (CBP) is dedicated to protecting against the importation of goods which infringe/violate Intellectual Property Rights (IPR) by devoting substantial resources toward identifying and seizing shipments of infringing articles]

Commodity	2008	2009	Trading partner	2008	2009
Number of IPR Seizures	14,992	14,841	China.	221,662	204,656
Total domestic value of IPR seizures [1]. . . .	272,729	260,698	Hong Kong.	13,434	26,887
Footwear	102,317	99,779	India.	16,258	3,047
Consumer electronics [2]	22,998	31,774	Taiwan	2,632	2,454
Handbags/wallets/backpacks	29,609	21,502	Korea, South	1,028	1,510
Wearing apparel	25,120	21,462	Paraguay	(NA)	1,496
Watches /parts.	(NA)	15,534	Philippines.	(NA)	1,480
Computers/Technology Components . . .	7,590	12,546	Switzerland	(NA)	1,278
Media [3].	5,967	11,100	Pakistan.	780	711
Pharmaceuticals	28,107	11,058	Vietnam	748	604
All other commodities	29,942	35,943	All other countries	13,938	16,575

NA Not available. [1] Domestic value is the cost of the seized goods, plus the costs of shipping and importing the goods into the U.S. and an amount for profit. [2] Consumer electronics includes cell phones and accessories, radios, power strips, electrical tools and appliances. [3] Includes motion pictures on tape, laser disc, and DVD; interactive and computer software on CD-ROM and floppy discs; and music on CD or tape.

Source: U.S. Department of Homeland Security, Customs and Border Protection, "Import, Commercial Enforcement, Intellectual Property Rights, Seizure Statistics," <http://www.cbp.gov/xp/cgov/trade/priority_trade/ipr/seizure/>.

Social Insurance and Human Services

This section presents data related to governmental expenditures for social insurance and human services; governmental programs for Old-Age, Survivors, Disability, and Health Insurance (OASDHI); governmental employee retirement; private pension plans; government unemployment and temporary disability insurance; federal supplemental security income payments and aid to the needy; child and other welfare services; and federal food programs. Also included here are selected data on workers' compensation and vocational rehabilitation, child support, child care, charity contributions, and philanthropic trusts and foundations.

The principal source for these data is the Social Security Administration's *Annual Statistical Supplement to the Social Security Bulletin* which presents current data on many of the programs.

Social insurance under the Social Security Act—

Programs established by the Social Security Act provide protection against wage loss resulting from retirement, prolonged disability, death, or unemployment, and protection against the cost of medical care during old age and disability. The federal OASDI program provides monthly benefits to retired or disabled insured workers and their dependents and to survivors of insured workers. To be eligible, a worker must have had a specified period of employment in which OASDI taxes were paid. The age of eligibility for full retirement benefits had been 65 years old for many years. However, for persons born in 1938 or later that age gradually increases until it reaches age 67 for those born after 1959. Reduced benefits may be obtained as early as age 62. The worker's spouse is under the same limitations. Survivor benefits are payable to dependents of deceased insured workers. Disability benefits are payable to an insured worker under full retirement age with a prolonged disability and to the disabled worker's dependents on the same basis as dependents of retired workers. Disability benefits are provided at age 50 to the disabled widow or widower of a deceased worker who was fully insured at the time of death. Disabled children, aged 18 or older, of retired, disabled, or deceased workers are also eligible for benefits. A lump sum benefit is generally payable on the death of an insured worker to a spouse or minor children. For information on the Medicare program, see Section 3, Health and Nutrition.

Retirement, survivors, disability, and hospital insurance benefits are funded by a payroll tax on annual earnings (up to a maximum of earnings set by law) of workers, employers, and the self-employed. The maximum taxable earnings are adjusted annually to reflect increasing wage levels (see Table 542). Effective January 1994, there is no dollar limit on wages and self-employment income subject to the hospital insurance tax. Tax receipts and benefit payments are administered through federal trust funds. Special benefits for uninsured persons; hospital benefits for persons aged 65 and over with specified amounts of social security coverage less than that required for cash benefit eligibility; and that part of the cost of supplementary medical insurance not financed by contributions from participants are financed from federal general revenues.

Unemployment insurance is presently administered by the U.S. Employment and Training Administration and each state's employment security agency. By agreement with the U.S. Secretary of Labor, state agencies also administer unemployment compensation for eligible ex-military personnel and federal employees. Under state unemployment insurance laws, benefits related to the individual's past earnings are paid to unemployed eligible workers. State laws vary concerning the length of time benefits are paid and their amount. In most states, benefits are payable for 26 weeks

U.S. Census Bureau, Statistical Abstract of the United States: 2011

and, during periods of high unemployment, extended benefits are payable under a federal-state program to those who have exhausted their regular state benefits. Some states also supplement the basic benefit with allowances for dependents.

Unemployment insurance is funded by a federal unemployment tax levied on the taxable payrolls of most employers. Taxable payroll under the federal act and 12 state laws is the first $7,000 in wages paid each worker during a year. Forty-one states have taxable payrolls above $7,000. Employers are allowed a percentage credit of taxable payroll for contributions paid to states under state unemployment insurance laws. The remaining percent of the federal tax finances administrative costs, the federal share of extended benefits, and advances to states. About 97 percent of wage and salary workers are covered by unemployment insurance.

Retirement programs for government employees—

The Civil Service Retirement System (CSRS) and the Federal Employees' Retirement System (FERS) are the two major programs providing age and service, disability, and survivor annuities for federal civilian employees. In general, employees hired after December 31, 1983, are covered under FERS and the social security program (OASDHI), and employees on staff prior to that date are members of CSRS and are covered under Medicare. CSRS employees were offered the option of transferring to FERS during 1987 and 1998. There are separate retirement systems for the uniformed services (supplementing OASDHI) and for certain special groups of federal employees. State and local government employees are covered for the most part by state and local retirement systems similar to the federal programs. In many jurisdictions these benefits supplement OASDHI coverage.

Workers' compensation—

All states provide protection against work-connected injuries and deaths, although some states exclude certain workers (e.g., domestic workers). Federal laws cover federal employees, private employees in the District of Columbia, and longshoremen and harbor workers. In addition, the Department of Labor administers "black lung" benefits programs for coal miners disabled by pneumoconiosis and for specified dependents and survivors. Specified occupational diseases are compensable to some extent. In most states, benefits are related to the worker's salary. The benefits may or may not be augmented by dependents' allowances or automatically adjusted to prevailing wage levels.

Income support—

Income support programs are designed to provide benefits for persons with limited income and resources. The Supplemental Security Income (SSI) program and Temporary Assistance for Needy Families (TANF) program are the major programs providing monthly payments. In addition, a number of programs provide money payments or in-kind benefits for special needs or purposes. Several programs offer food and nutritional services. Also, various federal-state programs provide energy assistance, public housing, and subsidized housing to individuals and families with low incomes. General assistance may also be available at the state or local level.

The SSI program, administered by the Social Security Administration, provides income support to persons aged 65 or older and blind or disabled adults and children. Eligibility requirements and federal payment standards are nationally uniform. Most states supplement the basic SSI payment for all or selected categories of persons.

The Personal Responsibility and Work Opportunity Reconciliation Act of 1996 contained provisions that replaced the Aid to Families With Dependent Children (AFDC), Job Opportunities and Basic Skills (JOBS), and Emergency Assistance programs with the Temporary Assistance for Needy Families block grant program. This law contains strong work requirements, comprehensive child support enforcement, support for families moving from welfare to work, and other features. The TANF became effective as soon as each state submitted a complete plan implementing TANF, but no later than

July 1, 1997. The AFDC program provided cash assistance based on need, income, resources, and family size.

Federal food stamp program—
Under the food stamp program, single persons and those living in households meeting nationwide standards for income and assets may receive coupons redeemable for food at most retail food stores or provides benefits through electronic benefit transfer. The monthly amount of benefits or allotments a unit receives is determined by household size and income. Households without income receive the determined monthly cost of a nutritionally adequate diet for their household size. This amount is updated to account for food price increases. Households with income receive the difference between the amount of a nutritionally adequate diet and 30 percent of their income, after certain allowable deductions.

To qualify for the program, a household must have less than $2,000 in disposable assets ($3,000 if one member is aged 60 or older), gross income below 130 percent of the official poverty guidelines for the household size, and net income below 100 percent of the poverty guidelines. Households with a person aged 60 or older or a disabled person receiving SSI, social security, state general assistance, or veterans' disability benefits may have gross income exceeding 130 percent of the poverty guidelines. All households in which all members receive TANF or SSI are categorically eligible for food stamps without meeting these income or resource criteria. Households are certified for varying lengths of time, depending on their income sources and individual circumstances.

Health and welfare services—
Programs providing health and welfare services are aided through federal grants to states for child welfare services, vocational rehabilitation, activities for the aged, maternal and child health services, maternity and infant care projects, comprehensive health services, and a variety of public health activities. For information about the Medicaid program, see Section 3, Health and Nutrition.

Noncash benefits—
The U.S. Census Bureau annually collects data on the characteristics of recipients of noncash (in-kind) benefits to supplement the collection of annual money income data in the Current Population Survey (see text, Section 1, Population, and Section 13, Income, Expenditures, Poverty, and Wealth). Noncash benefits are those benefits received in a form other than money which serve to enhance or improve the economic well-being of the recipient. As for money income, the data for noncash benefits are for the calendar year prior to the date of the interview. The major categories of noncash benefits covered are public transfers (e.g., food stamps, school lunch, public housing, and Medicaid) and employer or union-provided benefits to employees.

Statistical reliability—
For discussion of statistical collection, estimation, and sampling procedures and measures of statistical reliability applicable to HHS and Census Bureau data, see Appendix III.

U.S. Census Bureau, Statistical Abstract of the United States: 2011

Table 536. Selected Payments to Individuals by Function: 1970 to 2008

[In billions of dollars (108 represents $108,000,000,000). The employee benefit system is composed of voluntary and mandatory programs which are employment-based and financed primarily from employment-based contributions]

Source and sector	1970	1980	1990	1995	1999	2000	2001	2002	2003	2004	2005	2006	2007	2008
All benefits	**108**	**422**	**1,027**	**1,492**	**1,792**	**1,909**	**2,077**	**2,251**	**2,393**	**2,559**	**2,721**	**2,912**	**3,082**	**3,297**
Retirement income benefits	51	202	482	661	812	864	920	977	1,023	1,092	1,158	1,265	1,335	1,395
Social security—old-age, survivors, and disability insurance	31	119	244	328	380	401	425	447	464	486	513	544	576	606
Private employer pension and profit sharing	7	35	136	191	253	271	290	311	323	355	376	433	451	461
Public employer retirement plans	12	48	102	142	179	192	205	219	237	252	269	287	308	328
Federal civilian employee retirement [1]	3	16	32	40	47	50	52	53	55	58	62	67	72	74
State and local government retirement	4	15	41	66	91	100	110	121	133	142	151	162	175	188
Military retirement [2]	3	13	22	28	32	33	35	36	41	43	46	49	52	55
Railroad retirement	2	5	7	8	8	8	8	9	9	9	9	10	10	10
Health benefits	22	99	300	454	550	596	655	705	767	834	901	986	1,044	1,110
Medicare hospital insurance and supplementary medical insurance	7	36	108	179	209	219	243	259	277	305	332	399	428	465
Group health insurance	15	62	191	274	340	376	411	444	488	528	567	585	613	643
Military health insurance [3]	–	–	2	1	1	1	1	2	2	2	2	3	2	3
Other employee benefits	17	51	88	103	113	113	129	156	162	148	147	148	156	180
Unemployment insurance [4]	4	16	18	22	21	21	32	54	53	36	32	30	33	51
Workers' compensation [5]	3	13	38	43	47	48	52	53	56	57	56	55	57	58
Group life insurance	3	7	12	16	20	17	17	18	18	18	19	20	21	22
Miscellaneous disability [6]	1	3	4	3	3	4	4	4	4	5	5	5	6	6
Veterans' benefits [7]	7	13	16	19	22	23	25	28	30	32	35	37	40	44
Public assistance [8]	18	70	157	275	318	336	373	413	441	485	515	513	548	611

– Represents or rounds to zero. [1] Consists of civil service, foreign service, Public Health Service officers, Tennessee Valley Authority, and several small retirement programs. [2] Includes the U.S. Coast Guard. [3] Consists of payments for medical services for dependents of active duty military personnel at nonmilitary facilities. [4] Consists of state, railroad employee, and federal employee unemployment benefits; special unemployment benefits; and supplemental unemployment benefits. [5] Includes payments from private, federal, and state and local workers' compensation funds. [6] Includes federal black-lung payments and payments from state and local temporary disability insurance. [7] Consists of pension and disability, readjustment, and other veterans' benefits. [8] Consists of federal benefits (food stamp benefits, Supplemental Security Income, direct relief, earned income credit, payments to nonprofit institutions, aid to students, and payments for medical services for retired military personnel and their dependents at nonmilitary facilities) and state benefits (medical care, Aid to Families with Dependent Children, Supplemental Security Income, general assistance, emergency assistance, and medical insurance premium payments on behalf of indigents). Financed from state and federal general revenues.

Source: Employee Benefit Research Institute, Washington, DC, *EBRI Databook on Employee Benefits, 12th Ed.*, and unpublished data (copyright). EBRI tabulations based on U.S. Department of Commerce, Bureau of Economic Analysis. See also <http://www.ebri.org/publications/books/index.cfm?fa=databook>.

Table 537. Government Transfer Payments to Individuals—Summary: 1990 to 2008

[In billions of dollars (566.1 represents $566,100,000,000)]

Year	Transfer payments, total	Retirement and disability insurance benefits	Medical payments	Income maintenance benefits	Unemployment insurance benefits	Veterans benefits	Federal education and training assistance payments [1]	Other [2]
1990.	566.1	263.9	188.8	63.5	18.2	17.7	12.3	1.7
1995.	849.8	350.0	338.6	100.4	21.8	20.5	17.2	1.2
1997.	919.2	378.9	377.6	100.5	20.3	22.3	18.2	1.4
1998.	940.9	391.2	383.4	101.1	19.9	23.3	20.5	1.6
1999.	975.7	402.4	400.7	104.8	20.7	24.1	21.3	1.7
2000.	1,027.8	424.5	427.2	106.3	21.0	25.0	21.9	2.0
2001.	1,126.7	449.8	480.8	109.4	32.1	26.6	25.4	2.6
2002.	1,232.1	474.4	523.8	120.7	53.7	29.5	27.9	2.1
2003.	1,299.0	493.5	555.8	133.2	53.6	31.8	28.5	2.7
2004.	1,381.2	517.1	610.3	144.2	37.1	34.0	31.2	7.3
2005.	1,465.1	545.4	653.2	159.6	32.3	36.4	33.8	4.5
2006.	1,565.6	576.9	717.0	163.4	30.9	38.9	35.9	2.7
2007.	1,669.5	609.7	771.8	171.7	33.4	41.7	39.1	2.2
2008.	1,824.4	640.8	824.4	183.6	51.8	45.1	45.1	33.5

[1] See footnote 9, Table 538. [2] See footnote 10, Table 538.

Source: U.S. Bureau of Economic Analysis, "Regional Accounts Data, Annual State Personal Income," <http://www.bea.gov/bea/regional/spi/>, accessed March 2009.

Table 538. Government Transfer Payments to Individuals by Type: 1990 to 2008

[In millions of dollars (566,100 represents $566,100,000,000)]

Item	1990	2000	2004	2005	2006	2007	2008
Total.	566,100	1,027,827	1,381,205	1,465,125	1,565,646	1,669,454	1,824,404
Retirement & disability insurance benefit payments.	263,888	424,461	517,060	545,361	576,904	609,651	640,843
Old-age, survivors, & disability insurance.	244,135	401,393	485,512	512,728	544,096	575,648	605,571
Railroad retirement and disability.	7,221	8,267	9,007	9,191	9,519	9,813	10,068
Workers' compensation payments (federal & state).	8,618	10,898	15,570	15,866	15,650	16,058	16,658
Other government disability insurance & retirement [1].	3,914	3,903	6,971	7,576	7,639	8,102	8,546
Medical payments	188,808	427,194	610,305	653,193	717,010	771,771	824,378
Medicare.	107,638	219,117	304,659	331,924	399,193	428,097	464,716
Public assistance medical care [2].	78,176	205,021	299,842	315,032	310,977	336,753	352,170
Military medical insurance [3].	2,994	3,056	5,804	6,237	6,840	6,921	7,492
Income maintenance benefit payments.	63,481	106,285	144,218	159,624	163,418	171,688	183,602
Supplemental Security Income (SSI).	16,670	31,675	37,095	38,285	39,892	42,059	44,062
Family assistance [4].	19,187	18,440	18,371	18,216	18,226	18,457	18,874
Food stamps.	14,741	14,565	25,946	29,492	29,390	30,920	36,442
Other income maintenance [5].	12,883	41,605	62,806	73,631	76,010	80,252	84,224
Unemployment insurance benefit payments.	18,208	20,989	37,083	32,276	30,900	33,382	51,835
State unemployment insurance compensation . . .	17,644	20,223	35,598	31,001	29,594	32,006	50,218
Unemployment compensation for federal civilian employees.	215	226	281	224	218	216	256
Unemployment compensation for railroad employees.	89	81	79	72	78	83	84
Unemployment compensation for veterans.	144	181	430	446	449	407	468
Other unemployment compensation [6].	116	278	695	533	561	670	809
Veterans benefit payments.	17,687	25,004	34,047	36,371	38,877	41,655	45,127
Veterans pension and disability.	15,550	21,966	30,194	32,505	35,018	37,720	40,797
Veterans readjustment [7].	257	1,322	2,159	2,256	2,290	2,398	2,781
Veterans life insurance benefits.	1,868	1,706	1,682	1,596	1,554	1,520	1,527
Other assistance to veterans [8].	12	10	12	14	15	17	22
Federal education & training assistance payments [9].	12,286	21,851	31,202	33,796	35,859	39,127	45,142
Other payments to individuals [10].	1,742	2,043	7,290	4,504	2,678	2,180	33,477

[1] Consists largely of temporary disability payments, pension benefit guaranty payments, and black lung payments. [2] Consists of medicaid and other medical vendor payments. [3] Consists of payments made under the TriCare Management Program (formerly called CHAMPUS) for the medical care of dependents of active duty military personnel and of retired military personnel and their dependents at nonmilitary medical facilities. [4] Through 1990, consists of emergency assistance and aid to families with dependent children. Beginning with 2000, consists of benefits—generally known as temporary assistance for needy families—provided under the Personal Responsibility and Work Opportunity Reconciliation Act of 1996. [5] Consists largely of general assistance, expenditures for food under the supplemental program for women, infants, and children; refugee assistance; foster home care and adoption assistance; earned income tax credits; and energy assistance. [6] Consists of trade readjustment allowance payments, Redwood Park benefit payments, public service employment benefit payments, and transitional benefit payments. [7] Consists largely of veterans' readjustment benefit payments, educational assistance to spouses and children of disabled or deceased veterans, payments to paraplegics, and payments for autos and conveyances for disabled veterans. [8] Consists largely of state and local government payments to veterans. [9] Excludes veterans. Consists largely of federal fellowship payments (National Science Foundation fellowships and traineeships, subsistence payments to state maritime academy cadets, and other federal fellowships), interest subsidy on higher education loans, basic educational opportunity grants, and Job Corps payments. [10] Consists largely of Bureau of Indian Affairs payments, education exchange payments, Alaska Permanent Fund dividend payments, compensation of survivors of public safety officers, compensation of victims of crime, disaster relief payments, compensation for Japanese internment, and other special payments to individuals.

Source: U.S. Bureau of Economic Analysis, "Regional Accounts Data, Annual State Personal Income," <http://www.bea.gov/bea/regional/spi>, accessed March 2010.

Table 539. Government Transfer Payments to Individuals by State: 2000 to 2008

[In millions of dollars (1,027,827 represents $1,027,827,000,000)]

State	2000, total	2007, total	2008 Total	Retirement and disability insurance benefits	Medical payments	Income maintenance benefits	Unemployment insurance benefits	Veterans benefits	Federal education and training assistance payments [1]	Other [2]
U.S.	1,027,827	1,669,454	1,824,404	640,843	824,378	183,602	51,835	45,127	45,142	33,477
AL	16,803	27,914	30,524	11,409	12,781	3,277	417	1,118	730	792
AK	2,950	3,965	5,215	844	1,536	494	110	153	38	2,041
AZ	15,948	32,326	36,317	12,908	16,920	3,003	559	1,051	1,164	712
AR	10,168	17,589	19,258	7,061	8,244	1,908	444	706	483	413
CA	114,879	187,151	204,236	64,703	92,326	26,273	7,954	3,760	5,945	3,275
CO	11,144	19,197	21,272	8,343	8,973	1,672	519	846	571	348
CT	14,222	20,736	22,797	8,113	11,345	1,574	857	311	382	215
DE	2,908	5,172	5,727	2,143	2,673	421	157	118	135	80
DC	2,695	3,890	4,251	813	2,458	607	92	124	91	65
FL	64,580	108,601	119,486	44,235	53,428	10,773	2,290	3,558	2,980	2,222
GA	24,190	42,684	47,819	16,445	19,495	6,048	1,266	1,654	1,493	1,419
HI	3,887	6,396	7,049	2,617	2,967	793	240	237	89	105
ID	3,868	6,921	7,719	3,189	3,105	578	259	256	192	140
IL	42,291	67,533	71,398	25,509	30,918	8,075	2,735	1,046	1,895	1,220
IN	20,472	33,491	37,005	14,685	15,491	3,165	1,224	695	1,127	618
IA	10,242	15,841	17,231	7,064	7,256	1,252	485	378	569	227
KS	9,091	13,958	15,069	6,066	6,562	1,121	383	388	309	239
KY	16,058	25,943	28,243	10,202	11,985	3,073	716	802	991	473
LA	16,744	26,103	29,126	8,710	14,191	3,707	268	726	736	788
ME	5,351	8,524	9,543	3,299	4,633	793	177	390	149	102
MD	17,140	28,123	30,787	10,753	14,767	2,494	837	732	753	449
MA	26,575	42,485	46,773	13,664	23,721	5,518	2,011	773	705	380
MI	36,987	58,395	64,208	24,359	27,582	5,925	2,812	1,067	1,525	938
MN	16,106	27,486	29,745	10,662	14,041	2,062	1,025	757	848	350
MS	10,916	18,000	20,114	6,495	9,291	2,493	245	484	481	626
MO	21,121	34,068	37,027	13,739	17,072	3,169	702	934	792	620
MT	3,197	5,081	5,573	2,378	2,181	415	118	234	151	97
NE	5,753	9,100	9,776	3,817	4,250	821	136	354	249	148
NV	5,580	10,821	12,183	4,744	4,973	945	670	418	198	235
NH	4,003	6,567	7,120	3,056	3,077	417	150	211	138	72
NJ	33,512	50,426	54,884	20,095	25,677	3,776	2,853	750	1,090	641
NM	6,035	10,962	12,294	3,906	5,704	1,263	206	498	364	354
NY	96,578	140,929	150,614	42,745	80,912	16,793	3,323	1,684	3,246	1,911
NC	28,335	50,080	55,309	19,875	24,142	5,773	1,534	1,849	983	1,153
ND	2,339	3,421	3,642	1,544	1,506	254	58	117	96	67
OH	43,906	68,029	73,517	27,727	32,211	6,934	1,797	1,365	2,367	1,116
OK	12,064	20,755	22,631	8,272	9,897	2,130	254	1,117	526	435
OR	12,330	19,800	21,968	9,000	8,587	1,938	982	791	376	295
PA	55,370	82,738	89,131	32,803	41,421	7,002	3,401	1,509	1,972	1,023
RI	4,702	7,121	7,734	2,639	3,695	644	346	154	165	91
SC	14,601	25,527	28,621	10,591	11,634	3,026	709	1,006	1,006	649
SD	2,499	3,951	4,304	1,702	1,853	339	32	174	92	113
TN	21,977	36,282	39,591	14,173	17,676	4,279	739	1,027	908	790
TX	60,244	109,410	120,684	38,733	55,345	14,280	2,014	4,186	2,716	3,410
UT	5,025	8,758	9,663	3,999	3,853	759	223	246	381	201
VT	2,308	3,940	4,219	1,463	2,025	354	124	105	109	40
VA	20,239	35,284	38,871	15,154	15,828	4,044	644	1,605	926	670
WA	21,190	33,274	36,360	14,825	14,437	3,052	1,238	1,316	1,025	466
WV	8,909	13,147	14,097	5,584	6,007	1,306	231	508	275	187
WI	18,185	28,965	30,841	12,746	12,535	2,638	1,215	746	548	413
WY	1,613	2,598	2,837	1,245	1,190	151	54	95	63	40

[1] Excludes veterans. Consists largely of federal fellowship payments (National Science Foundation, fellowships and traineeships, subsistence payments to state maritime academy cadets, and other federal fellowships), interest subsidy on higher education loans, basic educational opportunity grants, and Job Corps payments. [2] Consists largely of Bureau of Indian Affairs payments, education exchange payments, Alaska Permanent Fund dividend payments, compensation of survivors of public safety officers, compensation of victims of crime, disaster relief payments, compensation for Japanese internment, and other special payments to individuals.

Source: U.S. Bureau of Economic Analysis, "Regional Accounts Data, Annual State Personal Income," <http://www.bea.gov/bea/regional/spi>.

Table 540. Number of Persons With Income by Specified Sources of Income: 2008

[In thousands (211,831 represents 211,831,000). Persons 15 years and over as of March of following year. Based on Current Population Survey; see text, Sections 1 and 13, and Appendix III]

Source of income	Total persons with income	Under 65 years	65 years and over	White [1]	Black [2]	Hispanic origin [3]
Total	**211,831**	**175,325**	**36,506**	**173,809**	**23,948**	**26,684**
Earnings	158,577	150,965	7,611	129,761	17,731	22,138
Wages and salary	149,315	142,790	6,525	121,678	17,159	20,948
Nonfarm self-employment	12,323	11,214	1,109	10,637	867	1,452
Farm self-employment	1,975	1,723	252	1,782	108	120
Unemployment compensation	8,067	7,770	297	6,511	1,073	1,157
State or local only	7,699	7,415	284	6,230	1,012	1,096
Combinations	368	355	13	281	61	61
Workers' compensation	1,604	1,458	147	1,357	169	224
State payments	553	510	43	454	67	91
Employment insurance	661	608	53	580	59	93
Own insurance	46	42	4	40	2	3
Other	398	337	61	322	52	44
Social Security	42,963	10,557	32,406	36,823	4,294	2,920
Supplemental Security Income (SSI)	5,541	4,403	1,139	3,683	1,455	847
Public assistance, total	1,984	1,921	63	1,187	640	443
TANF/Welfare (AFDC) only [4]	1,347	1,315	33	775	477	302
Other assistance only	620	590	30	404	156	136
Both	17	17	–	8	8	5
Veterans benefits	2,737	1,667	1,070	2,232	389	156
Disability only	1,683	1,142	541	1,379	246	109
Survivors only	231	77	154	186	31	7
Pension only	539	245	294	423	83	20
Education only	55	55	–	46	7	1
Other only	117	68	49	105	8	3
Combinations	112	80	31	94	13	16
Means-tested	601	375	226	473	103	41
Nonmeans-tested	2,136	1,292	844	1,760	286	115
Survivors Benefits	2,888	948	1,939	2,550	244	99
Company or Union	1,273	276	997	1,135	104	46
Federal government	307	80	227	255	37	10
Military retirement	171	53	118	151	10	8
Disability benefits	1,505	1,313	192	1,181	236	173
Workers' compensation	102	00	19	80	15	11
Company or union	360	308	51	280	63	30
Federal government	136	113	23	116	14	14
Military retirement	50	39	11	48	2	3
State or local government	240	211	29	198	26	45
Pension income	16,810	5,387	11,424	14,879	1,376	692
Company or union retirement	11,465	3,139	8,326	10,161	929	477
Federal government retirement	1,783	611	1,172	1,511	189	76
Military retirement	1,293	766	527	1,147	100	65
State or local government retirement	4,470	1,814	2,656	3,944	386	207
Property income [5]	99,826	79,635	20,192	87,483	6,135	6,084
Interest	94,580	75,367	19,213	82,885	5,830	5,667
Dividends	28,685	22,108	6,577	25,964	1,008	922
Rents, royalties, estates or trusts	10,454	7,833	2,621	9,301	540	693
Educational assistance	7,634	7,607	27	5,850	1,121	857
Pell grant only	1,909	1,900	9	1,264	456	274
Other government only	1,159	1,156	4	909	162	142
Scholarships only	2,382	2,378	4	1,925	210	240
Child support	4,869	4,831	38	3,797	839	684
Alimony	430	373	57	387	27	43
Financial assistance from outside the household	2,359	2,170	189	1,802	251	278
Other income, n.e.c.	1,026	823	203	843	96	50
Combinations of income types:						
Government transfer payments	63,380	29,605	33,775	52,228	7,938	5,751
Public assistance or SSI or both	7,280	6,088	1,191	4,724	2,009	1,252

– Represents or rounds to zero. [1] Beginning with the 2003 CPS, respondents could choose one or more races. For example, "White" refers to people who reported White and did not report any other race category. The use of this single-race population does not imply that it is the preferred method of presenting or analyzing data. Information on people who reported more than one race, such as "Asian and Black or African American," is available from Census 2000 through American FactFinder. [2] "Black" refers to people who reported Black and did not report any other race category. [3] Persons of Hispanic origin may be of any race. [4] TANF—Temporary Assistance for Needy Families program; AFDC—Aid to Families with Dependent Children program. [5] Includes estates and trusts reported as survivor benefits.

Source: U.S. Census Bureau: "Table PINC-09. Source of Income in 2008—Number With Income and Mean Income of Specified Type in 2008 of People 15 Years Old and Over, by Race, Hispanic Origin and Sex" (published October 2009), <http://www.census.gov/hhes/www/cpstables/032009/perinc/new09_000.htm>.

Table 541. Persons Living in Households Receiving Selected Noncash Benefits: 2008

[In thousands (301,041 represents 301,041,000), except percent. Persons, as of March 2009, who lived with someone (a nonrelative or a relative) who received aid. Not every person tallied here received the aid themselves. Persons living in households receiving more than one type of aid are counted only once. Excludes members of the Armed Forces except those living off post or with their families on post. Population controls for 2008 based on Census 2000 and an expanded sample of households. Based on Current Population Survey; see text, Section 1 and Appendix III]

Age, sex, and race	Total	In household that received means-tested assistance [1]		In household that received means-tested cash assistance		In household that received food stamps		In household in which one or more persons were covered by Medicaid		Lived in public or authorized housing	
		Number	Percent	Number	Percent	Number	Percent	Number	Percent	Number	Percent
Total.	301,041	83,906	27.9	19,484	6.5	27,644	9.2	66,729	22.2	10,838	3.6
Under 18 years	74,068	30,934	41.8	5,591	7.5	11,582	15.6	25,019	33.8	3,896	5.3
18 to 24 years	28,688	8,640	30.1	1,952	6.8	2,882	10.0	7,117	24.8	1,120	3.9
25 to 34 years	40,520	11,688	28.8	2,268	5.6	4,023	9.9	9,596	23.7	1,307	3.2
35 to 44 years	41,322	10,496	25.4	2,139	5.2	2,984	7.2	8,137	19.7	993	2.4
45 to 54 years	44,366	9,293	20.9	2,914	6.6	2,806	6.3	7,301	16.5	1,048	2.4
55 to 59 years	18,755	3,370	18.0	1,337	7.1	974	5.2	2,591	13.8	463	2.5
60 to 64 years	15,534	2,642	17.0	1,064	6.9	693	4.5	2,028	13.1	376	2.4
65 years and over	37,788	6,843	18.1	2,218	5.9	1,700	4.5	4,940	13.1	1,635	4.3
65 to 74 years	20,404	3,612	17.7	1,170	5.7	978	4.8	2,730	13.4	777	3.8
75 years and over . . .	17,384	3,231	18.6	1,048	6.0	722	4.2	2,210	12.7	858	4.9
Male.	147,862	39,075	26.4	9,000	6.1	12,051	8.2	31,082	21.0	4,279	2.9
Female.	153,179	44,832	29.3	10,484	6.8	15,593	10.2	35,647	23.3	6,559	4.3
White alone [2]	240,548	58,393	24.3	12,463	5.2	17,410	7.2	46,872	19.5	5,416	2.3
Black alone [2]	37,966	18,394	48.4	5,306	14.0	8,165	21.5	14,093	37.1	4,372	11.5
Asian alone [2]	13,310	3,194	24.0	659	5.0	590	4.4	2,636	19.8	481	3.6
Hispanic [3].	47,398	23,814	50.2	3,962	8.4	7,163	15.1	18,751	39.6	2,292	4.8
White alone, Non-Hispanic [2]	196,940	36,562	18.6	8,937	4.5	10,960	5.6	29,689	15.1	3,451	1.8

[1] Means-tested assistance includes means-tested cash assistance, food stamps, Medicaid, and public or authorized housing. [2] Refers to people who reported specific race and did not report any other race category. [3] People of Hispanic origin may be of any race.

Source: U.S. Census Bureau, Current Population Reports, P60-235. See also <http://www.census.gov/prod/2009pubs/p60-236.pdf>.

Table 542. Social Security—Covered Employment, Earnings, and Contribution Rates: 1990 to 2009

[164.7 represents 164,700,000. Includes Puerto Rico, Virgin Islands, American Samoa, and Guam. Represents all reported employment. Data are estimated. OASDHI = Old-age, survivors, disability, and health insurance; SMI = Supplementary medical insurance]

Item	Unit	1990	1995	2000	2004	2005	2006	2007	2008	2009
Workers with insured status [1]	Million . . .	164.7	173.6	185.8	193.7	195.8	198.4	200.9	203.4	(NA)
Male.	Million . . .	86.8	90.6	96.0	99.3	100.4	101.5	102.6	103.8	(NA)
Female.	Million . . .	77.9	83.1	89.9	94.4	95.7	96.9	98.3	99.7	(NA)
Under 25 years	Million . . .	21.2	18.9	20.8	20.2	20.2	20.2	20.1	20.3	(NA)
25 to 34 years	Million . . .	41.6	39.5	36.6	36.4	36.5	36.6	37.0	37.6	(NA)
35 to 44 years	Million . . .	36.5	40.7	42.6	41.4	41.1	40.7	40.1	39.5	(NA)
45 to 54 years	Million . . .	23.0	29.7	36.1	39.5	40.4	41.2	41.9	42.4	(NA)
55 to 59 years	Million . . .	8.9	9.9	12.3	15.4	16.3	16.8	17.1	17.5	(NA)
60 to 64 years	Million . . .	8.8	8.6	9.6	11.4	11.9	12.5	13.4	14.1	(NA)
65 to 69 years	Million . . .	8.1	8.0	7.9	8.7	8.9	9.2	9.7	10.3	(NA)
70 years and over	Million . . .	16.5	18.5	19.8	20.6	20.9	21.2	21.5	21.8	(NA)
Workers reported with—										
Taxable earnings [2]	Million . . .	133	141	154	156	159	161	163	162	156
Maximum earnings [2]	Million . . .	8	8	10	9	10	10	10	10	8
Earnings in covered employment [2]	Bil. dol . . .	2,716	3,407	4,842	5,399	5,691	6,049	6,398	6,509	6,197
Reported taxable [2].	Bil. dol . . .	2,359	2,920	4,009	4,554	4,766	5,042	5,263	5,434	5,288
Percent of total.	Percent . .	86.8	85.7	82.8	84.4	83.7	83.4	82.3	83.5	85.3
Average per worker:										
Total earnings [2]	Dollars . . .	20,417	24,198	31,342	34,572	35,904	37,583	39,236	40,058	39,721
Taxable earnings [2]	Dollars . . .	17,731	20,733	25,951	29,163	30,067	31,329	32,278	33,444	33,896
Annual maximum taxable earnings [3].	Dollars . . .	51,300	61,200	76,200	87,900	90,000	94,200	97,500	102,000	106,800
Contribution rates for OASDHI: [4]										
Each employer and employee . .	Percent . .	7.65	7.65	7.65	7.65	7.65	7.65	7.65	7.65	7.65
Self-employed [5].	Percent . .	15.30	15.30	15.30	15.30	15.30	15.30	15.30	15.30	15.30
SMI, monthly premium [6]	Dollars . . .	28.60	46.10	45.50	66.60	78.20	88.50	93.50	96.40	96.40

NA Not available. [1] Estimated number fully insured for retirement and/or survivor benefits as of end of year. [2] Includes self-employment. Averages per worker computed with unrounded earnings and worker amounts and may not agree with rounded table and amounts. [3] Beginning 1995, upper limit on earnings subject to HI taxes was repealed. [4] As of January 1, 2006, each employee and employer pays 7.65 percent and the self-employed pay 15.3 percent. [5] Self-employed pays 15.3 percent and half of the tax is deductible for income tax purposes and for computing self-employment income subject to social security tax. [6] As of January 1.

Source: U.S. Social Security Administration, *Annual Statistical Supplement to the Social Security Bulletin* and unpublished data (released March 2010). See also <http://www.ssa.gov/policy/docs/statcomps/supplement/2009>.

354 Social Insurance and Human Services

Table 543. Social Security (OASDI)—Benefits by Type of Beneficiary: 1990 to 2009

[39,832 represents 39,832,000. A person eligible to receive more than one type of benefit is generally classified or counted only once as a retired-worker beneficiary. OASDI = Old-age, survivors, and disability insurance. See also headnote, Table 544, and Appendix III]

Type of beneficiary	1990	1995	2000	2003	2004	2005	2006	2007	2008	2009
Number of benefits [1] (1,000)	**39,832**	**43,387**	**45,415**	**47,038**	**47,688**	**48,434**	**49,123**	**49,865**	**50,898**	**52,523**
Retired workers [2] (1,000)	24,838	26,673	28,499	29,532	29,953	30,461	30,976	31,528	32,274	33,514
Disabled workers [3] (1,000)	3,011	4,185	5,042	5,874	6,198	6,519	6,807	7,099	7,427	7,788
Wives and husbands [2,4] (1,000)	3,367	3,290	2,963	2,773	2,722	2,680	2,632	2,585	2,525	2,502
Children (1,000)	3,187	3,734	3,803	3,961	3,986	4,025	4,041	4,051	4,132	4,231
Under age 18	2,497	2,956	2,976	3,080	3,097	3,130	3,133	3,120	3,118	3,158
Disabled children [5]	600	686	729	753	759	769	777	795	871	921
Students [6]	89	92	98	128	130	127	131	136	142	152
Of retired workers	422	442	459	480	483	488	490	494	525	561
Of deceased workers	1,776	1,884	1,878	1,910	1,905	1,903	1,899	1,892	1,915	1,921
Of disabled workers	989	1,409	1,466	1,571	1,599	1,633	1,652	1,665	1,692	1,748
Widowed mothers [7] (1,000)	304	275	203	190	184	178	171	165	160	160
Widows and widowers [2,8] (1,000)	5,111	5,226	4,901	4,707	4,643	4,569	4,494	4,436	4,380	4,327
Parents [2] (1,000)	6	4	3	2	2	2	2	2	2	2
Special benefits [9] (1,000)	7	1	(Z)	(Z)	(Z)	(Z)	(Z)	(Z)	(Z)	(Z)
AVERAGE MONTHLY BENEFIT, CURRENT DOLLARS										
Retired workers [2]	603	720	844	922	955	1,002	1,044	1,079	1,153	1,164
Retired worker and wife [2]	1,027	1,221	1,420	1,535	1,586	1,660	1,726	1,776	1,894	1,913
Disabled workers [3]	587	682	786	862	894	938	978	1,004	1,063	1,064
Wives and husbands [2,4]	298	354	416	450	464	485	502	516	551	556
Children of retired workers	259	322	395	444	465	493	518	538	568	570
Children of deceased workers	406	469	550	603	625	656	684	704	745	747
Children of disabled workers	164	183	228	254	265	279	290	299	318	318
Widowed mothers [7]	409	478	595	664	689	725	757	782	835	842
Widows and widowers, nondisabled [2]	556	680	810	888	920	967	1,008	1,040	1,112	1,124
Parents [2]	482	591	704	779	810	851	892	918	979	988
Special benefits [9]	167	192	217	232	238	247	256	261	276	276
AVERAGE MONTHLY BENEFIT, CONSTANT (2007) DOLLARS [10]										
Retired workers [2]	909	947	979	1,010	1,013	1,027	1,087	1,079	1,184	1,164
Retired worker and wife [2]	1,549	1,605	1,647	1,681	1,682	1,702	1,796	1,776	1,946	1,913
Disabled workers [3]	885	897	912	943	948	962	1,017	1,004	1,092	1,064
Wives and husbands [2,4]	449	465	482	493	492	497	523	516	566	556
Children of deceased workers	612	617	638	660	663	673	711	704	766	747
Widowed mothers [7]	617	628	690	727	731	743	787	782	858	842
Widows and widowers, nondisabled [2]	839	894	939	972	976	991	1,049	1,040	1,142	1,124
Number of benefits awarded (1,000)	**3,717**	**3,882**	**4,290**	**4,322**	**4,459**	**4,672**	**4,621**	**4,711**	**5,135**	**5,728**
Retired workers [2]	1,665	1,609	1,961	1,791	1,883	2,000	1,999	2,036	2,279	2,740
Disabled workers [3]	468	646	622	777	796	830	799	805	877	971
Wives and husbands [2,4]	379	322	385	353	367	379	378	364	395	429
Children	695	809	777	852	859	908	897	902	961	1,008
Widowed mothers [7]	58	52	40	39	40	38	36	34	33	33
Widows and widowers [2,8]	452	445	505	508	514	517	512	570	590	547
Parents [2]	(Z)	(Z)	(Z)	(Z)	(Z)	(Z)	(Z)	(Z)	(Z)	(Z)
Special benefits [9]	(Z)	(Z)	(Z)	(Z)	(Z)	(Z)	(Z)	(Z)	(Z)	(Z)
BENEFIT PAYMENTS DURING YEAR (bil. dol.)										
Total [11]	**247.8**	**332.6**	**407.6**	**470.8**	**493.3**	**520.8**	**552.8**	**585.0**	**615.4**	**675.5**
Monthly benefits [12]	247.6	332.4	407.4	470.6	493.1	520.6	552.6	584.8	615.2	675.3
Retired workers [2]	156.8	205.3	253.5	291.5	304.3	321.7	342.9	364.3	384.0	424.0
Disabled workers [3]	22.1	36.6	49.8	64.8	71.7	78.4	85.0	91.3	98.1	109.5
Wives and husbands [2,4]	14.5	17.9	19.4	20.4	20.6	20.5	21.5	22.1	22.6	24.2
Children	12.0	16.1	19.3	22.3	23.3	24.5	25.8	27.0	28.2	30.2
Under age 18	9.0	11.9	14.1	16.2	17.0	17.9	18.8	19.5	20.1	21.2
Disabled children [5]	2.5	3.6	4.6	5.2	5.5	5.8	6.1	6.5	6.9	7.8
Students [6]	0.5	0.6	0.7	0.8	0.9	0.8	1.0	1.0	1.1	1.2
Of retired workers	1.3	1.7	2.1	2.6	2.7	2.9	3.1	3.3	3.5	3.9
Of deceased workers	8.6	10.7	12.5	14.1	14.5	15.1	15.8	16.5	17.0	18.1
Of disabled workers	2.2	3.7	4.7	5.7	6.1	6.5	6.9	7.3	7.7	8.2
Widowed mothers [7]	1.4	1.6	1.4	1.5	1.5	1.5	1.6	1.6	1.6	1.6
Widows and widowers [2,8]	40.7	54.8	63.9	70.1	71.7	73.4	75.9	78.5	80.7	85.6
Parents [2]	(Z)	(Z)	(Z)	(Z)	(Z)	(Z)	(Z)	(Z)	(Z)	(Z)
Special benefits [9]	(Z)	(Z)	(Z)	(Z)	(Z)	(Z)	(Z)	(Z)	(Z)	(Z)
Lump sum	0.2	0.2	0.2	0.2	0.2	0.2	0.2	0.2	0.2	0.2

Z Fewer than 500 or less than $50 million. [1] Number of benefit payments in current-payment status, i.e., actually being made at a specified time with no deductions or with deductions amounting to less than a month's benefit. [2] 62 years and over. [3] Disabled workers under age 65. [4] Includes wife beneficiaries with entitled children in their care and entitled divorced wives. [5] 18 years old and over. Disability began before age 18. [6] Full-time students aged 18 and 19. [7] Includes surviving divorced mothers with entitled children in their care and widowed fathers with entitled children in their care. [8] Includes widows aged 60–61, surviving divorced wives aged 60 and over, disabled widows and widowers aged 50 and over; and widowers aged 60–61. [9] Benefits for persons aged 72 and over not insured under regular or transitional provisions of Social Security Act. [10] Constant dollar figures are based on the consumer price index (CPI-U) for December as published by the U.S. Bureau of Labor Statistics. [11] Represents total disbursements of benefit checks by the U.S. Department of the Treasury during the years specified. [12] Distribution by type estimated.

Source: U.S. Social Security Administration, *Annual Statistical Supplement to the Social Security Bulletin*, 2009, and unpublished data. See also <http://www.ssa.gov/policy>.

Social Insurance and Human Services   355

Table 544. Social Security—Beneficiaries, Annual Payments, and Average Monthly Benefit, 1990 to 2009, and by State and Other Areas, 2009

[Number of beneficiaries in current-payment status (39,832 represents 39,832,000) and average monthly benefit as of December. Data based on 10-percent sample of administrative records. See also headnote, Table 543, and Appendix III]

Year, state, and other area	Number of beneficiaries (1,000)				Annual payments [2] (mil. dol.)				Average monthly benefit (dol.)		
	Total	Retired workers and dependents [1]	Survivors	Disabled workers and dependents	Total	Retired workers and dependents [1]	Survivors	Disabled workers and dependents	Retired workers [3]	Disabled workers	Widows and widowers [4]
1990..............	39,832	28,369	7,197	4,266	247,796	172,042	50,951	24,803	603	587	557
2000..............	45,417	31,761	6,981	6,675	407,431	274,645	77,848	54,938	845	787	810
2005..............	48,446	33,488	6,650	8,307	520,561	345,094	90,073	85,394	1,002	938	967
2006..............	49,123	33,945	6,566	8,612	552,636	366,952	93,300	92,384	1,044	978	1,007
2007..............	49,865	34,454	6,495	8,916	584,764	389,123	96,555	99,086	1,079	1,004	1,040
2008..............	50,898	35,169	6,456	9,273	615,152	409,503	99,348	106,301	1,153	1,063	1,112
2009, total [5]	**52,523**	**36,419**	**6,410**	**9,694**	**675,288**	**451,579**	**105,380**	**118,329**	**1,164**	**1,064**	**1,124**
United States	**51,177**	**35,530**	**6,188**	**9,459**	**664,187**	**445,269**	**102,971**	**115,947**	**(NA)**	**(NA)**	**(NA)**
Alabama	983	592	134	257	12,209	7,119	2,042	3,048	1,130	1,044	1,058
Alaska	75	51	10	14	907	591	143	173	1,111	1,051	1,070
Arizona	1,028	747	111	171	13,457	9,429	1,845	2,183	1,189	1,103	1,163
Arkansas	620	380	77	162	7,480	4,468	1,147	1,865	1,097	1,016	1,037
California	4,835	3,502	551	782	61,960	42,779	9,245	9,936	1,157	1,085	1,142
Colorado	664	481	76	107	8,472	5,855	1,283	1,334	1,149	1,067	1,144
Connecticut	611	456	63	92	8,663	6,293	1,181	1,189	1,275	1,102	1,261
Delaware	168	119	18	31	2,294	1,581	316	397	1,237	1,123	1,216
District of Columbia ..	73	50	9	14	846	562	127	157	1,038	948	952
Florida	3,669	2,726	384	559	47,205	33,803	6,462	6,940	1,158	1,071	1,151
Georgia	1,413	935	184	294	17,750	11,386	2,816	3,548	1,145	1,061	1,080
Hawaii	220	172	22	27	2,813	2,117	357	339	1,152	1,097	1,094
Idaho	259	184	29	46	3,237	2,217	481	539	1,136	1,038	1,151
Illinois	1,993	1,413	254	326	26,766	18,246	4,437	4,083	1,202	1,086	1,197
Indiana	1,158	792	146	220	15,595	10,408	2,532	2,655	1,224	1,067	1,203
Iowa	574	420	71	84	7,463	5,241	1,235	987	1,161	1,013	1,160
Kansas	478	339	58	81	6,311	4,344	1,008	959	1,191	1,035	1,193
Kentucky	870	508	121	241	10,643	5,961	1,839	2,843	1,108	1,041	1,038
Louisiana	770	458	138	175	9,307	5,195	2,069	2,043	1,088	1,048	1,035
Maine	293	194	31	68	3,521	2,250	501	770	1,079	984	1,085
Maryland	827	594	101	131	10,991	7,600	1,706	1,685	1,191	1,095	1,157
Massachusetts	1,118	775	117	226	14,610	9,842	2,043	2,725	1,175	1,051	1,171
Michigan	1,905	1,301	236	368	26,291	17,442	4,196	4,653	1,258	1,122	1,218
Minnesota	858	628	95	135	11,237	7,953	1,647	1,637	1,182	1,053	1,156
Mississippi	584	345	83	155	6,948	4,002	1,174	1,772	1,086	1,013	1,004
Missouri	1,138	761	140	237	14,493	9,397	2,274	2,822	1,149	1,036	1,133
Montana	187	135	22	30	2,311	1,584	367	360	1,107	1,018	1,124
Nebraska	304	220	37	47	3,894	2,714	631	549	1,147	1,009	1,153
Nevada	391	287	39	64	5,092	3,585	660	847	1,167	1,126	1,168
New Hampshire	246	171	23	51	3,262	2,230	410	622	1,208	1,080	1,206
New Jersey	1,441	1,062	158	220	20,623	14,749	2,900	2,974	1,286	1,167	1,235
New Mexico	348	235	44	69	4,165	2,706	648	811	1,091	1,023	1,041
New York	3,215	2,269	353	593	43,521	29,823	6,153	7,545	1,225	1,109	1,179
North Carolina	1,699	1,147	189	362	21,555	14,210	2,915	4,430	1,155	1,056	1,080
North Dakota	119	85	17	16	1,455	986	287	182	1,085	986	1,074
Ohio	2,074	1,422	293	359	27,058	17,772	5,020	4,266	1,172	1,034	1,156
Oklahoma	689	455	92	142	8,595	5,459	1,444	1,692	1,123	1,035	1,096
Oregon	687	504	73	109	8,952	6,299	1,281	1,372	1,171	1,068	1,181
Pennsylvania	2,530	1,772	316	442	33,898	22,905	5,565	5,428	1,200	1,070	1,179
Rhode Island	200	140	19	41	2,601	1,782	330	489	1,169	1,028	1,169
South Carolina	890	592	106	192	11,299	7,316	1,610	2,373	1,157	1,074	1,074
South Dakota	150	110	19	21	1,820	1,277	306	237	1,083	987	1,064
Tennessee	1,213	788	155	270	15,226	9,630	2,391	3,205	1,147	1,034	1,081
Texas	3,320	2,216	470	634	41,291	26,383	7,429	7,479	1,134	1,051	1,090
Utah	312	224	37	50	3,993	2,777	622	594	1,174	1,053	1,195
Vermont	125	87	13	25	1,580	1,081	219	280	1,163	996	1,136
Virginia	1,246	860	149	238	16,059	10,684	2,419	2,956	1,165	1,072	1,103
Washington	1,049	757	112	181	14,011	9,752	1,974	2,285	1,211	1,078	1,203
West Virginia	436	255	66	115	5,616	3,078	1,069	1,469	1,148	1,105	1,086
Wisconsin	1,033	746	116	171	13,691	9,604	2,036	2,051	1,196	1,057	1,187
Wyoming	89	64	11	14	1,148	800	179	169	1,162	1,056	1,162
Puerto Rico	776	450	116	211	6,874	3,552	1,193	2,129	777	931	687
Guam.............	14	9	3	2	117	70	28	19	773	914	769
American Samoa....	6	2	1	2	45	17	13	15	762	831	674
Virgin Islands........	19	14	2	2	207	150	29	28	1,012	1,072	884
Northern Mariana Islands...........	2	1	1	(Z)	16	9	5	2	649	710	540
Abroad.............	529	412	97	17	3,842	2,512	1,141	189	628	967	699

NA Not available. Z Less than 500. [1] Includes special benefits for persons aged 72 years and over not insured under regular or transitional provisions of Social Security Act. [2] Unnegotiated checks not deducted. 1990 and 1995 include lump-sum payments to survivors of deceased workers. [3] Excludes persons with special benefits. [4] Nondisabled only. [5] Includes those with state or area unknown.

Source: U.S. Social Security Administration, *Annual Statistical Supplement to the Social Security Bulletin, 2009,* February 2010. See also <http://www.ssa.gov/policy/docs/statcomps/supplement/2009/supplement09.pdf>.

Table 545. Social Security Trust Funds: 1990 to 2009

[In billions of dollars (272.4 represents $272,400,000,000)]

Type of trust fund	1990	1995	2000	2004	2005	2006	2007	2008	2009
Old-age and survivors insurance (OASI):									
Net contribution income [1,2]	272.4	310.1	433.0	487.4	520.7	534.8	560.9	574.6	570.4
Interest received [2]	16.4	32.8	57.5	79.0	84.0	91.8	97.0	105.3	107.9
Benefit payments [3]	223.0	291.6	352.7	415.0	435.4	454.5	489.1	509.3	557.2
Assets, end of year	214.2	458.5	931.0	1,500.6	1,663.0	1,844.3	2,023.6	2,202.9	2,336.8
Disability insurance (DI):									
Net contribution income [1,2]	28.7	54.7	71.8	81.4	87.2	90.8	95.2	97.8	96.9
Interest received [2]	0.9	2.2	6.9	10.0	10.3	10.6	13.2	11.0	10.5
Benefit payments [3]	24.8	40.9	55.0	78.2	85.4	91.7	95.9	106.0	118.3
Assets, end of year	11.1	37.6	118.5	186.2	195.6	203.8	214.9	215.8	203.6

[1] Includes deposits by states and deductions for refund of estimated employee-tax overpayment. Includes government contributions on deemed wage credits for military service 1957–2001. Includes taxation of benefits. [2] In 1990, includes interest on advance tax transfers. Includes interest on reimbursement for unnegotiated checks. [3] Includes payments for vocational rehabilitation services furnished to disabled persons receiving benefits because of their disabilities. Amounts reflect deductions for unnegotiated benefit checks.

Source: U.S. Social Security Administration, *Annual Report of Board of Trustees, OASI, DI, HI, and SMI Trust Funds*; <http://www.ssa.gov/OACT/TR/2009/index.html>. Also published in *Social Security Bulletin*, quarterly.

Table 546. Public Employee Retirement Systems—Participants and Finances: 1980 to 2008

[4,629 represents 4,629,000. For fiscal year of retirement system, except data for the Thrift Savings Plan which is for calendar year.] For a definition of defined benefit, see headnote, Table 550]

Retirement plan	Unit	1980	1990	2000	2003	2004	2005	2006	2007	2008, proj.
TOTAL PARTICIPANTS [1]										
Federal retirement systems:										
Defined benefit:										
Civil Service Retirement System	1,000...	4,629	4,167	3,256	3,133	3,035	2,958	2,878	2,789	2,650
Federal Employees Retirement System [2]	1,000...	(X)	1,180	1,935	2,140	2,104	2,196	2,290	2,371	2,572
Military Service Retirement System [3]	1,000...	3,380	3,763	3,397	3,457	3,545	3,536	3,560	3,585	3,657
Thrift Savings Plan [4]	1,000...	(X)	1,625	2,500	3,200	3,400	3,600	3,700	3,900	4,000
State and local retirement systems [5,6]	1,000...	(NA)	16,858	16,834	17,650	17,800	17,002	10,484	18,583	19,097
ACTIVE PARTICIPANTS										
Federal retirement systems:										
Defined benefit:										
Civil Service Retirement System	1,000...	2,700	1,020	978	854	788	722	650	580	477
Federal Employees Retirement System [2]	1,000...	(X)	1,136	1,668	1,808	1,882	1,952	2,014	2,066	2,195
Military Service Retirement System [3]	1,000...	2,050	2,130	1,437	1,468	1,480	1,445	1,443	1,438	1,461
Thrift Savings Plan [4]	1,000...	(X)	1,419	1,900	2,400	2,500	2,800	2,600	2,600	2,700
State and local retirement systems [5,6]	1,000...	(NA)	11,345	13,917	14,249	14,181	14,116	14,529	14,422	14,701
ASSETS										
Total	Bil. dol...	258	1,047	2,950	3,092	3,472	3,697	4,023	4,533	4,380
Federal retirement systems	Bil. dol...	73	326	782	920	977	1,039	1,111	1,156	1,190
Defined benefit	Bil. dol...	73	318	684	791	825	866	904	924	987
Civil Service Retirement System	Bil. dol...	73	220	395	425	433	440	442	426	423
Federal Employees Retirement System [2]	Bil. dol...	(X)	18	126	183	204	228	254	280	311
Military Service Retirement System [3]	Bil. dol...	(7)	80	163	103	188	198	208	218	253
Thrift Savings Plan [4]	Bil. dol...	(X)	8	98	129	152	173	207	232	203
State and local retirement systems [5]	Bil. dol...	185	721	2,168	2,172	2,495	2,658	2,912	3,377	3,190
CONTRIBUTIONS										
Total	Bil. dol...	83	103	143	161	187	189	205	224	260
Federal retirement systems	Bil. dol...	19	61	78	86	95	98	108	117	141
Defined benefit	Bil. dol...	19	59	69	72	79	82	88	96	119
Civil Service Retirement System	Bil. dol...	19	28	33	29	34	33	34	36	35
Federal Employees Retirement System [2]	Bil. dol...	(X)	4	8	11	13	13	15	17	19
Military Service Retirement System [3]	Bil. dol...	(7)	27	28	32	32	38	39	43	65
Thrift Savings Plan [4]	Bil. dol...	(X)	2	9	14	16	16	20	21	22
State and local retirement systems [5]	Bil. dol...	64	42	65	75	92	91	97	107	119
BENEFITS										
Total	Bil. dol...	39	89	172	211	226	240	258	282	295
Federal retirement systems	Bil. dol...	27	53	81	89	93	99	106	120	120
Defined benefit	Bil. dol...	27	53	78	86	89	94	99	112	112
Civil Service Retirement System	Bil. dol...	15	31	44	48	50	52	55	57	59
Federal Employees Retirement System [2]	Bil. dol...	(X)	(Z)	1	2	2	3	3	4	4
Military Service Retirement System [3]	Bil. dol...	12	22	33	36	37	39	41	43	49
Thrift Savings Plan [4]	Bil. dol...	(X)	(Z)	3	3	4	5	7	8	8
State and local retirement systems [5]	Bil. dol...	12	36	91	122	133	141	152	162	175

NA Not available. X Not applicable. Z Less than $500 million. [1] Includes active, separated vested, retired employees and survivors. [2] The Federal Employees Retirement System was established June 6, 1986. [3] Includes nondisability and disability retirees, surviving families, and all active personnel with the exception of active reserves. [4] The Thrift Savings Plan (a defined contribution plan) was established April 1, 1987. [5] Excludes state and local plans that are fully supported by employee contributions. [6] Not adjusted for double counting of individuals participating in more than one plan. [7] The Military Retirement System was unfunded until October 1, 1984.

Source: Employee Benefit Research Institute, Washington, DC, *EBRI Databook on Employee Benefits*, 12th ed., and unpublished data (copyright). See also <http://www.ebri.org>.

Social Insurance and Human Services 357

Table 547. Federal Civil Service Retirement: 1990 to 2009

[As of September 30 or for year ending September 30 (2,945 represents 2,945,000). Covers both Civil Service Retirement System and Federal Employees Retirement System]

Item	Unit	1990	1995	2000	2004	2005	2006	2007	2008	2009
Employees covered [1]	1,000	2,945	2,668	2,764	2,670	2,674	2,611	2,618	2,613	2,672
Annuitants, total	1,000	**2,143**	**2,311**	**2,376**	**2,404**	**2,433**	**2,449**	**2,463**	**2,471**	**2,481**
Age and service	1,000	1,288	1,441	1,501	1,544	1,568	1,602	1,625	1,643	1,662
Disability	1,000	297	263	242	231	229	226	222	218	216
Survivors	1,000	558	607	633	629	636	621	616	610	603
Receipts, total [2]	Mil. dol ..	**52,689**	**65,684**	**75,967**	**82,412**	**83,691**	**87,164**	**89,860**	**90,892**	**93,061**
Employee contributions	Mil. dol ...	4,501	4,498	4,637	4,483	4,353	4,304	4,205	4,111	4,083
Federal government contributions	Mil. dol ...	27,368	33,130	37,722	42,240	43,093	46,427	48,397	49,547	51,789
Disbursements, total [3]	Mil. dol ..	**31,416**	**38,435**	**45,194**	**52,277**	**54,790**	**57,983**	**78,146**	**63,687**	**67,669**
Age and service annuitants [4]	Mil. dol ...	26,495	32,070	37,546	43,727	46,029	48,895	68,776	54,202	57,782
Survivors	Mil. dol ...	4,366	5,864	7,210	8,127	8,338	8,642	8,905	9,011	9,463
Average monthly benefit:										
Age and service	Dollars ...	1,369	1,643	1,885	2,154	2,240	2,363	2,473	2,550	2,710
Disability	Dollars ...	1,008	1,164	1,240	1,305	1,327	1,366	1,394	1,409	1,469
Survivors	Dollars ...	653	819	952	1,073	1,106	1,157	1,200	1,232	1,309
Cash and security holdings	Bil. dol ...	238.0	366.2	508.1	631.8	660.8	690.0	701.7	728.9	754.3

[1] Excludes employees in leave-without-pay status. [2] Includes interest on investments. [3] Includes refunds, death claims, and administration. [4] Includes disability annuitants.

Source: U.S. Office of Personnel Management, *Civil Service Retirement and Disability Trust Fund Annual Report*.

Table 548. State and Local Government Retirement Systems—Beneficiaries and Finances: 1990 to 2008

[In billions of dollars (111.3 represents $111,300,000,000), except as indicated. For fiscal years closed during the 12 months ending June 30. Minus sign (–) indicates negative earnings on investment]

Year and level of government	Number of ben- eficiaries (1,000)	Receipts					Benefits and withdrawals			Cash and security holdings
		Total	Em- ployee contribu- tions	Government contributions State	Government contributions Local	Earn- ings on invest- ments	Total	Benefits	With- drawals	
1990: All systems	4,026	111.3	13.9	14.0	18.6	64.9	38.4	36.0	2.4	721
State-administered	3,232	89.2	11.6	14.0	11.5	52.0	29.6	27.6	2.0	575
Locally administered	794	22.2	2.2	(Z)	7.0	12.9	8.8	8.4	0.4	145
1995: All systems	4,979	148.8	18.6	16.6	24.4	89.2	61.5	58.8	2.7	1,118
State-administered	4,025	123.3	15.7	16.2	15.4	76.0	48.0	45.8	2.2	914
Locally administered	954	25.5	2.9	0.4	9.0	13.3	13.5	13.0	0.5	204
2000: All systems	6,292	297.0	25.0	17.5	22.6	231.9	95.7	91.3	4.4	2,169
State-administered	4,786	247.4	20.7	17.2	16.7	192.8	76.0	72.2	3.8	1,798
Locally administered	1,506	49.7	4.3	0.4	5.9	39.1	19.8	19.1	0.7	371
2005: All systems	6,946	353.5	31.5	24.0	35.7	262.2	156.0	142.1	3.7	2,672
State-administered	5,846	293.4	26.8	23.6	22.1	220.9	126.8	115.2	3.1	2,226
Locally administered	1,100	60.1	4.8	0.4	13.6	41.3	29.3	26.9	0.5	445
2007: All systems	7,464	580.5	34.1	30.6	42.3	473.5	183.0	162.7	5.2	3,377
State-administered	6,353	486.8	29.1	30.0	26.4	401.3	148.4	131.2	4.6	2,819
Locally administered	1,110	93.7	5.0	0.6	15.9	72.2	34.6	31.5	0.7	558
2008: All systems	7,744	79.6	36.9	36.3	45.7	–39.3	193.8	175.4	4.6	3,190
State-administered	6,596	56.4	31.6	35.8	28.1	–39.1	157.4	143.5	3.2	2,664
Locally administered	1,148	23.2	5.3	0.5	17.6	–0.2	36.4	32.0	1.4	526

Z Less than $50 million.

Source: U.S. Census Bureau, through 1990, *Finances of Employee-Retirement Systems of State and Local Governments*, Series GF, No. 2, annual; beginning 2000, "Federal, State, and Local Governments, State and Local Government Public Employee Retirement Systems," <http://www.census.gov/govs/retire.html>.

Table 549. Percent of Workers Participating In Retirement Benefits by Worker Characteristics: 2005 to 2009

[Based on National Compensation Survey, a sample survey of 10,370 private industry establishments of all sizes, representing over 105 million workers; see Appendix III. Survey covers all 50 states and the District of Columbia. For a definition of defined benefit and defined contribution, see headnote, Table 550. See also Table 655]

Characteristic	Total [1]				Defined benefit				Defined contribution			
	2005	2007	2008	2009	2005	2007	2008	2009	2005	2007	2008	2009
Total	**50**	**51**	**51**	**51**	**21**	**20**	**20**	**20**	**42**	**43**	**43**	**43**
White-collar occupations	61	69	68	69	24	28	28	28	53	60	60	60
Blue-collar occupations	51	51	52	53	26	25	25	26	38	40	41	41
Service occupations	22	25	25	26	7	7	8	8	18	20	20	21
Full-time	60	60	60	61	25	23	24	24	50	50	51	51
Part-time	19	23	23	22	9	9	10	9	14	18	18	16
Union	85	81	80	82	72	67	67	66	43	41	42	44
Nonunion	46	47	48	48	15	15	15	15	41	43	43	43

[1] Total is less than the sum of the individual retirement items because many employees participated in both types of plans.

Source: U.S. Bureau of Labor Statistics, *Employee Benefits in Private Industry in the United States, March 2010*. See also <http://www.bls.gov/ncs/ebs/benefits/2009/ownership_private.htm>.

Table 550. Private Pension Plans—Summary by Type of Plan: 1990 to 2007

[712.3 represents 712,300. **"Pension plan"** is defined by the Employee Retirement Income Security Act (ERISA) as "any plan, fund, or program which was heretofore or is hereafter established or maintained by an employer or an employee organization, or by both, to the extent that such plan (a) provides retirement income to employees, or (b) results in a deferral of income by employees for periods extending to the termination of covered employment or beyond, regardless of the method of calculating the contributions made to the plan, the method of calculating the benefits under the plan, or the method of distributing benefits from the plan." A **defined benefit** plan provides a definite benefit formula for calculating benefit amounts—such as a flat amount per year of service or a percentage of salary times years of service. A **defined contribution** plan is a pension plan in which the contributions are made to an individual account for each employee. The retirement benefit is dependent upon the account balance at retirement. The balance depends upon amounts contributed, investment experience, and, in the case of profit sharing plans, amounts which may be allocated to the account due to forfeitures by terminating employees. Employee Stock Ownership Plans (ESOP) and 401(k) plans are included among defined contribution plans. Data are based on Form 5500 series reports filed with the U.S. Department of Labor and exclude (1) most pension plans qualified under sections 403(b), 457(b) and 457(f) of the Internal Revenue Code, (2) most SARSEP, SEP and SIMPLE IRA plans, (3) unfunded excess benefit plans, (4) most church plans, (5) top hat plans, (6) individual retirement accounts, and (7) governmental plans]

Item	Unit	Total				Defined contribution plan				Defined benefit plan			
		1990	2000	2005	2007	1990	2000	2005	2007	1990	2000	2005	2007
Number of plans [1]	1,000	712.3	735.7	679.1	707.8	599.2	686.9	631.5	658.8	113.1	48.8	47.6	49.0
Total participants [2]	Million ...	76.9	103.3	117.4	123.9	38.6	61.7	75.5	81.6	38.8	41.6	41.9	42.3
Active participants [3]	Million ...	61.5	73.1	82.7	86.3	35.6	50.9	62.4	66.9	26.2	22.2	20.3	19.4
Assets [4]	Bil. dol ...	1,674	4,203	5,062	6,090	834	2,216	2,808	3,444	962	1,986	2,254	2,647
Contributions [5]	Bil. dol ...	98.8	231.9	341.4	368.1	80.9	198.5	248.8	299.8	24.7	33.4	92.7	68.3
Benefits [6]	Bil. dol ...	129.4	341.0	354.5	452.8	64.0	213.5	218.0	294.1	66.4	127.5	136.6	158.7

[1] Excludes all plans covering only one participant. [2] Includes active, retired, and separated vested participants not yet in pay status. Also includes double counting of workers in more than one plan. [3] Includes any workers currently in employment covered by a plan and who are earning or retaining credited service under a plan. Also includes any nonvested former employees who have not yet incurred breaks in service. [4] Asset amounts shown exclude funds held by life insurance companies under allocated group insurance contracts for payment of retirement benefits. These excluded funds make up roughly 10 to 15 percent of total private fund assets. [5] Includes both employer and employee contributions. [6] Includes benefits paid directly from trust and premium payments made from plans to insurance carriers. Excludes benefits paid directly by insurance carriers.

Source: U.S. Department of Labor, Employee Benefits Security Administration, *Private Pension Plan Bulletin.* See also <http://www.dol.gov/ebsa/pdf/1975–2007historicaltables.pdf>.

Table. 551. Defined Benefit Retirement Plans—Selected Features: 2009

[In percent. Covers full-time employees in private industry. Based on National Compensation Survey, a sample survey of 3,227 private industry establishments of all sizes, representing over 102 million workers; see Appendix III. For definition of defined benefit, see headnote, Table 550. See also Table 655]

Feature	All workers	Goods producing	Service producing	1 to 99 workers	100 workers or more	Union	Nonunion
Benefit formula:							
Percent of terminal earnings	35	27	37	38	33	22	42
Percent of career earnings	11	3	(NA)	15	(NA)	6	14
Dollar amount formula	24	39	19	17	27	45	(NA)
Percent of contribution formula	6	15	(NA)	11	(NA)	13	(NA)
Cash balance.	23	13	27	18	25	11	31
Pension equity	(NA)	(NA)	(NA)	(NA)	(NA)	(NA)	(NA)

NA Not available.

Source: U.S. Bureau of Labor Statistics, *National Compensation Survey: Employee Benefits in Private Industry in the United States* and unpublished data.

Table 552. Percent of U.S. Households Owning Individual Retirement Accounts (IRAs): 2000 to 2009

[Incidence of IRA ownership is based on an annual tracking survey of 3,000 randomly selected, representative U.S. households; see source for details]

Year and characteristic	Any type of IRA [1]	Tradi- tional IRA	Roth IRA	Employer- spon- sored IRA [2]	Year and characteristic	Any type of IRA [1]	Tradi- tional IRA	Roth IRA	Employer- spon- sored IRA [2]
2000.......	35.7	28.7	9.2	6.8	2009, total	39.3	31.2	14.5	8.2
2001.......	36.2	28.9	9.8	8.0	Under 35 years	28.0	17.0	12.0	7.0
2002.......	34.8	28.2	10.8	7.7	35 to 44 years	38.0	27.0	18.0	10.0
2003.......	36.7	29.6	12.5	7.5	45 to 54 years	44.0	34.0	18.0	12.0
2004.......	36.5	29.6	11.6	8.0	55 to 64 years	49.0	44.0	16.0	7.0
2005.......	37.9	30.0	12.8	7.4	65 years and over ...	39.0	37.0	8.0	4.0
2006.......	38.3	31.7	13.4	7.7					
2007.......	39.8	32.5	14.9	7.9					
2008.......	40.5	32.1	15.9	8.6					

[1] Excludes ownership of Coverdell Education Savings Accounts, which were referred to as Education IRAs before July 2001.
[2] Employee-sponsored Individual Retirement Accounts (IRAs) include SIMPLE IRAs, Simplified Employee Pension IRAs (SEP-IRAs), and SAR-SEP IRAs (SEP IRAs with salary reduction plans included).

Source: Investment Company Institute , Washington, DC, *Research Fundamentals,* "Appendix: Additional Data on IRA Ownership in 2009"; Vol 19, No. 1A, January 2010 (copyright). See also <http://www.ici.org/pdf/fm-v19n1-appendix.pdf>.

Table 553. Characteristics of U.S. Households Owning Individual Retirement Accounts (IRAs): 2009

[Incidence of IRA ownership is based on an annual tracking survey of 3,000 randomly selected, representative U.S. households; see source for details]

Characteristic	Households owning IRAs			Households not owning IRAs
	Total [1]	Traditional IRA	Roth IRA	
MEDIAN PER HOUSEHOLD				
Age of household sole or co-decisionmaker for investing	52	54	45	47
Household income [2]...................................	75,000	75,000	90,000	35,000
Household financial assets [3]............................	150,000	180,000	150,000	25,000
Household financial assets in all types of IRAs..............	30,000	40,000	35,000	(X)
Share of household financial assets in type of IRA indicated ...	33	28	10	(X)
PERCENT OF HOUSEHOLDS				
Household has defined contribution account or defined benefit plan coverage (total) [4]....................	80	79	88	47
Defined contribution retirement plan account	69	66	78	39
Defined benefit plan coverage...........................	50	50	56	22
Types of IRAs owned: [4]				
Traditional IRA..	79	100	63	(X)
Roth IRA...	37	29	100	(X)
Employer-sponsored IRA [1]	21	15	17	(X)

X Not applicable. [1] Employer-sponsored IRAs include SIMPLE IRAs, SEP IRAs, and SAR-SEP IRAs. [2] Total reported is household income before taxes in 2008. [3] Household financial assets include assets in employer-sponsored retirement plans but exclude the household's primary residence. [4] Multiple responses are included.

Source: Investment Company Institute, Washington, DC, *Research Fundamentals*, "Appendix: Additional Data on IRA Ownership in 2009," Vol. 19, No. 1A, January 2010 (copyright). See also <http://www.ici.org/pdf/fm-v19n1_appendix.pdf>.

Table 554. Percent Distribution of Assets in Individual Retirement Accounts (IRAs) by Type of IRA: 2009

[Incidence of IRA ownership is based on an annual tracking survey of 3,000 randomly selected, representative U.S. households; see source for details]

Assets in type of IRA	Unit	Total assets in IRAs	Type of IRA owned	
			Traditional IRAs	Roth IRAs
PERCENT DISTRIBUTION OF ASSETS IN IRAs				
Less than $10,000.	Percent	23	23	35
$10,000 to $24,999 .	Percent	20	22	34
$25,000 to $49,999 .	Percent	17	16	13
$50,000 to $99,999 .	Percent	16	16	9
$100,000 to $249,999 .	Percent	15	15	4
$250,000 or more .	Percent	9	8	5
TOTAL ASSETS IN IRAs				
Mean.	Dollars	89,800	86,500	40,700
Median.	Dollars	30,000	30,000	12,500

Source: Investment Company Institute, Washington, DC, *Research Fundamentals*, "Appendix: Additional Data on IRA Ownership in 2009," Vol. 19, No. 1A, January 2010 (copyright). See also <http://www.ici.org/pdf/fm-v19h1_appendix.pdf>.

Table 555. 401(k) Plans—Participants, Assets, Contributions, and Benefits by Type of Plan: 2007

Type of plan [1]	Total plans [2]	Total participants (thousands) [3]	Total assets (millions)	Total contributions (millions) [4]	Total benefits (millions) [5]
Total	**490,917**	**72,178**	**2,981,522**	**273,235**	**262,108**
Profit Sharing and thrift-savings	489,333	70,412	2,887,360	267,082	253,991
Stock bonus.	314	1,075	800	5,130	7,063
Target benefit.	66	1	11	3	30
Money Purchase	986	619	13,430	951	954
Annuity—403(b)(1)	171	5	59	9	3
Custodial account—403(b)(7)	27	36	765	61	68

[1] About 1 percent of defined contribution plans report more than one plan typo. [2] Excludes plans covering only one participant. [3] Includes active, retired, and separated vested participants not yet in pay status. [4] Includes both employer and employee contributions. [5] Amounts shown include benefits paid directly from trust funds and premium payments made by plans to insurance carriers.

Source: U.S. Department of Labor, *Private Pension Plan Bulletin: 2007*. See also <http://www.dol.gov/ebsa/PDF/2007pensionplanbulletin.pdf>.

Table 556. State Unemployment Insurance—Summary: 1990 to 2008

[2,522 represents 2,522,000. Includes unemployment compensation for state and local government employees where covered by state law]

Item	Unit	1990	1995	2000	2003	2004	2005	2006	2007	2008
Insured unemployment, average weekly . . .	1,000	2,522	2,572	2,110	3,531	2,950	2,661	2,475	2,571	3,306
Percent of covered employment [1]	Percent	2.4	2.3	1.7	2.8	2.3	2.1	1.9	2.0	2.5
Percent of civilian unemployed	Percent	35.8	34.7	37.6	40.7	36.8	35.7	35.3	36.3	36.3
Unemployment benefits, average weekly . .	Dollars	161	187	221	262	263	267	277	288	233
Percent of weekly wage.	Percent	36.0	35.5	32.9	36.5	35.2	34.6	34.3	35.1	35.1
Weeks compensated.	Million	116.2	118.3	96.0	163.2	135.1	121.2	112.2	116.3	149.5
Beneficiaries, first payments	1,000	8,629	8,035	7,033	9,935	8,369	7,922	7,350	7,641	10,053
Average duration of benefits [2]	Weeks	13.4	14.7	13.7	16.4	16.1	15.3	15.2	15.3	14.9
Claimants exhausting benefits.	1,000	2,323	2,662	2,144	4,417	3,532	2,856	2,676	2,670	3,424
Percent of first payment [3].	Percent	29.4	34.3	31.8	43.4	39.0	35.9	35.4	35.3	41.5
Contributions collected [4]	Bil. dol.	15.2	22.0	19.9	25.3	31.2	34.8	34.1	34.5	30.0
Benefits paid	Bil. dol.	18.1	21.2	20.5	41.4	34.4	31.2	29.8	30.1	40.7
Funds available for benefits [5].	Bil. dol.	37.9	35.4	53.4	23.4	23.0	29.0	35.8	32.5	29.0
Average employer contribution rate [6].	Percent	1.95	2.44	1.75	2.20	2.68	2.86	2.68	2.61	2.25

[1] Insured unemployment as percent of average covered employment in preceding year. [2] Weeks compensated divided by first payment. [3] Based on first payments for 12-month period ending June 30. [4] Contributions from employers; also employees in states which tax workers. [5] End of year. Sum of balances in state clearing accounts, benefit-payment accounts, and state accounts in federal unemployment trust funds. [6] As percent of taxable wages.

Source: U.S. Department of Labor, Employment and Training Administration, *Unemployment Insurance Financial Data Handbook*. See also <http://www.ows.doleta.gov/unemploy/hb394.asp>.

Table 557. State Unemployment Insurance by State and Other Area: 2008

[10,053 represents 10,053,000. See headnote, Table 556. For state data on insured unemployment, see Table 628]

State and other areas	Beneficiaries, first payments (1,000)	Benefits paid (mil. dol.)	Avg. weekly unemployment benefits (dol.)	State and other areas	Beneficiaries, first payments (1,000)	Benefits paid (mil. dol.)	Avg. weekly unemployment benefits (dol.)
Total........	**10,053**	**40,690**	**297**	MT.........	30	98	255
AL..........	148	299	196	NE.........	38	101	241
AK..........	38	99	202	NV.........	129	569	292
AZ..........	137	432	218	NH.........	34	118	272
AR..........	105	319	265	NJ.........	368	2,215	377
CA..........	1,389	6,655	307	NM.........	38	170	278
CO..........	96	416	341	NY.........	579	2,528	307
CT..........	153	693	322	NC.........	354	1,022	287
DE..........	30	125	257	ND.........	15	47	286
DC..........	21	105	291	OH.........	357	1,441	303
FL..........	510	1,709	238	OK.........	53	182	272
GA..........	311	917	273	OR.........	198	784	302
HI...........	39	213	413	PA.........	562	2,607	335
ID...........	71	211	272	RI.........	46	276	370
IL...........	445	2,209	312	SC.........	157	474	240
IN...........	261	952	298	SD.........	9	25	239
IA...........	126	409	302	TN.........	194	548	221
KS..........	76	260	316	TX.........	405	1,487	303
KY..........	139	539	300	UT.........	47	188	312
LA..........	75	212	209	VT.........	28	105	294
ME..........	39	136	265	VA.........	150	501	282
MD.........	140	610	305	WA.........	233	1,008	355
MA.........	257	1,499	391	WV.........	49	160	242
MI..........	513	2,149	300	WI.........	321	998	273
MN.........	164	836	347	WY.........	10	50	308
MS.........	77	177	183	PR.........	110	222	112
MO.........	176	569	244	VI.........	2	12	328

Source: U.S. Employment and Training Administration, *Unemployment Insurance Financial Data Handbook.* See also <http://www.ows.doleta.gov/unemploy/hb394.asp\>.

Table 558. Persons With Work Disability by Selected Characteristics: 2008

[In thousands, except percent (20,213 represents 20,213,000). As of March. Covers civilian noninstitutional population and members of Armed Forces living off post or with their families on post. Persons are classified as having a work disability if they (1) have a health problem or disability which prevents them from working or which limits the kind or amount of work they can do; (2) have a service-connected disability or ever retired or left a job for health reasons; (3) did not work in survey reference week or previous year because of long-term illness or disability; or (4) are under age 65, and are covered by Medicare or receive supplemental security income. Based on Current Population Survey; see text, Section 1 and Appendix III]

Age and participation status in assistance programs	Total [1]	Male	Female	White alone [2]	Black alone [3]	Hispanic [4]
Persons with work disability	**20,213**	**9,861**	**10,352**	**15,219**	**3,841**	**2,255**
16 to 24 years old	1,562	757	805	1,073	380	230
25 to 34 years old	2,176	1,083	1,094	1,509	536	290
35 to 44 years old	3,522	1,764	1,758	2,621	698	472
45 to 54 years old	5,711	2,679	3,032	4,289	1,100	597
55 to 64 years old	7,242	3,578	3,664	5,727	1126	666
Percent work disabled of total population—						
16 to 24 years old	4.2	4.0	4.3	3.7	6.8	3.5
25 to 34 years old	5.5	5.4	5.5	4.9	10.3	3.6
35 to 44 years old	8.4	8.5	8.3	7.9	13.4	6.9
45 to 54 years old	13.0	12.5	13.5	12.0	21.3	12.2
55 to 64 years old	21.8	22.3	21.3	20.5	33.4	23.9
Percent of work disabled—						
Receiving social security income...........	35.5	36.0	35.0	36.7	31.7	26.7
Receiving food stamps	19.3	15.0	23.3	16.6	29.5	22.6
Covered by Medicaid....................	65.4	68.9	62.0	67.8	60.7	56.6
Residing in public housing...............	5.9	4.7	7.1	4.4	11.1	7.5
Residing in subsidized housing............	3.4	2.3	4.4	2.7	6.1	4.4

[1] Includes other races, not shown separately. [2] Beginning with the 2003 Current Population Survey asked respondents to choose one or more races. White alone refers to people who reported White and did not report any other race category. The use of this single-race population does not imply reported more than one race, such as "White and American Indian and Alaska Native" or "Asian and Black or African American," is available from Census 2000 through American FactFinder. About 2.6 percent of people reported more than one race in 2000. [3] Black alone refers to people who reported Black and did not report any other race category. [4] Hispanic persons may be of any race.
Source: U.S. Census Bureau, unpublished data.

Table 559. Workers' Compensation Payments: 1990 to 2007

[In billions of dollars, except as indicated (53.1 represents $53,100,000,000). See headnote, Table 560]

Item	1990	1995	2000	2001	2002	2003	2004	2005	2006	2007
Workers covered (mil.)............	106	113	127	127	126	125	126	128	130	132
Premium amounts paid [1]........	**53.1**	**57.1**	**60.1**	**66.6**	**73.4**	**82.0**	**86.8**	**88.8**	**87.3**	**85.0**
Private carriers [1]	35.1	31.6	35.7	37.8	41.4	45.3	48.0	50.9	51.7	50.8
State funds	8.0	10.5	8.8	11.5	14.6	17.8	19.1	18.2	15.8	14.3
Federal programs [2]	2.2	2.6	3.6	3.8	3.9	4.0	4.1	4.1	4.1	4.2
Self-insurers	7.9	12.5	11.9	13.6	13.6	14.9	15.8	15.7	15.6	15.6
Annual benefits paid [1]..........	**38.2**	**42.1**	**47.7**	**50.8**	**52.4**	**55.1**	**52.7**	**55.5**	**54.3**	**55.4**
By private carriers [1]	22.2	20.1	26.9	27.9	28.2	28.6	28.1	28.0	27.3	28.4
From state funds [3]	8.8	10.8	10.3	11.1	12.5	13.7	11.0	10.9	10.7	10.4
Employers' self-insurance [4]	7.2	11.2	10.5	11.8	11.8	12.8	13.6	13.2	13.1	13.3
Type of benefit:										
Medical/hospitalization	15.2	16.7	20.9	23.1	24.3	25.8	26.4	26.3	26.3	27.2
Compensation payments..........	23.1	25.4	26.8	27.7	28.1	29.2	29.7	29.2	28.0	28.3
Percent of covered payroll: [1]										
Workers' compensation costs [5,6]	2.18	1.82	1.34	1.45	1.59	1.74	1.75	1.71	1.58	1.45
Benefits [6]	1.53	1.34	1.06	1.10	1.14	1.17	1.13	1.07	0.98	0.95

[1] Premium and benefit amounts include estimated payments under insurance policy deductible provisions. Deductible benefits are allocated to private carriers and state funds. [2] Years 1990–1995 includes federal employer compensation program and that portion of federal black lung benefits program financed from employer contributions. Years 1997–2000 includes federal employer compensation program only due to changes in reporting methods. [3] Net cash and medical benefits paid by competitive and exclusive state funds and by federal workers' compensation programs. [4] Cash and medical benefits paid by self-insurers, plus value of medical benefits paid by employers carrying workers' compensation policies that exclude standard medical coverage. [5] Premiums written by private carriers and state funds, and benefits paid by self-insurers increased by 5–10 prior to 1995 and by 11 percent for 1995–2002 for administrative costs. Also includes benefits paid and administrative costs of federal system for government employees. [6] Excludes programs financed from general revenue—black lung benefits and supplemental pensions in some states.

Source: National Academy of Social Insurance, Washington, DC, *Workers' Compensation: Benefits, Coverage, and Costs*, annual. See also <http://www.nasi.org>.

Table 560. Workers' Compensation Payments by State: 2000 to 2007

[In millions of dollars (47,699 represents $47,699,000,000). Calendar-year data. Payments represent compensation and medical benefits and include insurance losses paid by private insurance carriers (compiled from state workers' compensation agencies and A.M. Best Co.); disbursements of state funds (compiled from the A.M. Best Co. and state workers' compensation agencies); and self-insurance payments (compiled from state workers' compensation agencies and authors' estimates)]

State	2000	2004	2005	2006	2007	State	2000	2004	2005	2006	2007
Total............	**47,699**	**56,053**	**55,510**	**54,686**	**55,427**	Montana...........	155	223	239	248	241
Alabama	529	576	609	609	585	Nebraska..........	230	287	302	263	291
Alaska	139	185	183	182	184	Nevada	347	359	386	394	378
Arizona	498	548	543	608	647	New Hampshire.....	177	213	218	214	200
Arkansas..........	214	228	208	219	243	New Jersey	1,378	1,503	1,619	1,672	1,968
California	9,449	12,453	10,934	10,149	9,916	New Mexico	144	198	231	238	240
Colorado	810	845	889	871	830	New York	2,761	3,335	3,191	3,324	3,204
Connecticut	638	711	708	713	726	North Carolina......	865	1,167	1,391	1,358	1,340
Delaware	118	160	173	207	195	North Dakota.......	70	83	82	81	92
District of Columbia..	78	97	91	92	88	Ohio..............	2,099	2,435	2,447	2,384	2,478
Florida	2,577	2,730	2,794	2,533	2,685	Oklahoma	485	578	589	628	656
Georgia	965	1,126	1,199	1,210	1,339	Oregon............	425	536	550	613	586
Hawaii	231	271	251	243	247	Pennsylvania.......	2,379	2,594	2,678	2,685	2,748
Idaho	114	237	246	238	276	Rhode Island.......	127	145	139	156	155
Illinois............	1,944	2,261	2,399	2,488	2,722	South Carolina......	515	688	770	796	771
Indiana...........	545	594	608	615	644	South Dakota.......	63	77	86	91	119
Iowa.............	343	452	482	492	510	Tennessee.........	774	815	863	794	765
Kansas...........	323	371	385	398	394	Texas.............	2,160	1,633	1,553	1,398	1,423
Kentucky	584	730	701	710	648	Utah..............	172	217	239	245	268
Louisiana..........	547	726	667	579	580	Vermont...........	101	124	122	124	119
Maine............	245	268	272	283	271	Virginia............	597	759	855	838	1,059
Maryland	641	777	767	815	831	Washington	1,527	1,836	1,846	1,927	1,995
Massachusetts......	801	969	904	935	888	West Virginia	661	794	694	696	700
Michigan	1,474	1,517	1,474	1,464	1,502	Wisconsin	765	898	1,170	1,043	1,094
Minnesota	798	916	922	921	936	Wyoming	89	120	117	117	127
Mississippi	293	311	312	341	332	**Federal total** [1].....	**2,957**	**3,256**	**3,258**	**3,270**	**3,340**
Missouri..........	780	1,120	1,156	1,175	854	Federal employees ..	2,119	2,445	2,462	2,455	2,587

[1] Federal benefits include: those paid under the Federal Employees' Compensation Act for civilian employees; the portion of the Black Lung benefit program that is financed by employers; and a portion of benefits under the Longshore and Harbor Workers' Compensation Act that are not reflected in state data, namely, benefits paid by self-insured employers and by special funds under the LHWCA. See Appendix H of source for more information about federal programs.

Source: National Academy of Social Insurance, Washington, DC, *Workers' Compensation: Benefits, Coverage, and Costs*, annual. See also <http://www.nasi.org>.

Table 561. Supplemental Security Income—Recipients and Payments: 1990 to 2008

[In thousands (4,817 represents 4,817,000), except as noted. Recipients and monthly payment as of December. Payments for calendar year. Persons with a federal SSI payment and/or federally administered state supplementation. See also Appendix III]

Program	Unit	1990	1995	2000	2003	2004	2005	2006	2007	2008
Recipients, total	1,000	4,817	6,514	6,602	6,902	6,988	7,114	7,236	7,360	7,521
Aged	1,000	1,454	1,446	1,289	1,233	1,211	1,214	1,212	1,205	1,203
Blind	1,000	84	84	79	77	76	75	73	72	70
Disabled	1,000	3,279	4,984	5,234	5,593	5,701	5,825	5,951	6,083	6,247
Payments, total [1]	Mil. dol.	16,133	27,037	30,672	34,693	36,065	37,236	38,889	41,205	43,040
Aged	Mil. dol.	3,559	4,239	4,540	4,857	4,894	4,965	5,116	5,301	5,379
Blind	Mil. dol.	329	367	386	409	412	414	409	419	416
Disabled	Mil. dol.	12,245	22,431	25,746	29,429	30,745	31,857	33,364	35,485	37,246
Average monthly payment, total	Dollars	276	335	379	417	428	439	455	468	478
Aged	Dollars	208	250	300	342	351	360	373	384	393
Blind	Dollars	319	355	413	455	463	475	488	500	508
Disabled	Dollars	303	358	398	433	444	455	471	485	494

[1] Includes payments not distributed by reason for eligibility.

Source: U.S. Social Security Administration, *Social Security Bulletin*, quarterly, and *Annual Statistical Supplement to the Social Security Bulletin* (released March 2010). See also <http://www.ssa.gov/policy/docs/statcomps/supplement>.

Table 562. Supplemental Security Income (SSI)—Recipients and Payments by State and Other Area: 2000 to 2008

[Recipients as of December; payments for calendar year (6,602 represents 6,602,000). Data cover federal SSI payments and/or federally administered state supplementation. For explanation of methodology, see Appendix III]

State and other area	Recipients (1,000) 2000	Recipients (1,000) 2008	Payments for the year (mil. dol.) 2000	Payments for the year (mil. dol.) 2005	Payments for the year (mil. dol.) 2008	State and other area	Recipients (1,000) 2000	Recipients (1,000) 2008	Payments for the year (mil. dol.) 2000	Payments for the year (mil. dol.) 2005	Payments for the year (mil. dol.) 2008
Total	6,602	7,521	30,672	37,236	43,040	MO	112	124	471	573	662
U.S.	6,601	7,520	30,669	37,232	43,035	MT	14	16	57	70	82
AL	159	167	659	776	875	NE	21	24	85	103	123
AK	9	12	37	53	61	NV	25	37	108	163	198
AZ	81	103	355	482	554	NH	12	16	49	67	84
AR	85	99	333	407	511	NJ	146	160	672	763	877
CA	1,088	1,272	6,386	8,146	8,986	NM	47	58	193	248	298
CO	54	60	228	264	319	NY	617	658	3,197	3,561	4,028
CT	49	55	216	260	303	NC	191	208	732	894	1,067
DE	12	15	50	66	79	ND	8	8	30	33	38
DC	20	23	93	113	131	OH	240	265	1,114	1,295	1,527
FL	377	445	1,621	2,031	2,321	OK	72	88	302	381	469
GA	197	213	785	944	1,123	OR	52	66	228	298	356
HI	21	24	104	119	139	PA	284	340	1,367	1,659	1,956
ID	18	25	76	106	129	RI	28	32	130	161	180
IL	249	266	1,174	1,337	1,500	SC	107	107	429	488	550
IN	88	108	382	488	601	SD	13	13	48	55	64
IA	40	45	158	193	232	TN	164	165	664	752	879
KS	36	42	151	187	230	TX	409	566	1,575	2,191	2,801
KY	174	187	741	862	988	UT	20	25	87	110	133
LA	166	165	715	771	867	VT	13	14	51	63	76
ME	30	34	116	146	176	VA	132	142	535	632	720
MD	88	101	400	481	565	WA	101	125	484	616	733
MA	168	182	807	902	1,058	WV	71	80	318	376	434
MI	210	233	988	1,157	1,332	WI	85	99	357	437	528
MN	64	81	272	355	438	WY	6	6	23	26	30
MS	129	122	512	572	624	N. Mariana	1	1	3	4	5

Source: U.S. Social Security Administration, *Annual Statistical Supplement to the Social Security Bulletin*. See also <http://www.ssa.gov/policy/docs/statcomps/supplement>.

Table 563. Temporary Assistance for Needy Families (TANF)—Families and Recipients: 1980 to 2008

[In thousands (3,712 represents 3,712,000). Average monthly families and recipients for calendar year. Prior to TANF, the cash assistance program to families was called Aid to Families with Dependent Children (1980–1996). Under the new welfare law (Personal Responsibility and Work Opportunity Reconciliation Act of 1996), the program became TANF. See text, this section. Includes Puerto Rico, Guam, and Virgin Islands]

Year	Families	Recipients	Year	Families	Recipients	Year	Families	Recipients
1980	3,712	10,774	1992	4,829	13,773	2000	2,215	5,778
1985	3,701	10,855	1993	5,012	14,205	2001	2,104	5,359
1986	3,763	11,038	1994	5,033	14,161	2002	2,048	5,069
1987	3,776	11,027	1995	4,791	13,418	2003	2,024	4,929
1988	3,749	10,915	1996	4,434	12,321	2004	1,979	4,748
1989	3,799	10,993	1997	3,740	10,376	2005	1,894	4,469
1990	4,057	11,695	1998	3,050	8,347	2006	1,777	4,148
1991	4,497	12,930	1999	2,554	6,824	2007	1,674	3,897
						2008	1,633	3,795

Source: U.S. Department of Health and Human Services, Administration for Children and Families, unpublished data.

Table 564. Temporary Assistance for Needy Families (TANF)—Recipients by State and Other Areas: 2000 to 2008

[In thousands (2,265 represents 2,265,000). Average monthly families and recipients for calendar year. See headnote, Table 563]

State or other area	Families 2000	2005	2008	Recipients 2000	2005	2008	State or other area	Families 2000	2005	2008	Recipients 2000	2005	2008
Total ...	2,265	1,921	1,635	5,943	4,549	3,795	MT	5	4	52	13	12	8
U.S.	2,181	1,876	1,622	5,678	4,418	2,355	NE	9	10	5	24	25	17
AL	19	20	29	45	47	41	NV	6	6	3	16	15	18
AK	7	4	10	21	11	8	NH	6	6	0	14	14	9
AZ	33	42	10	84	96	78	NJ	50	43	29	125	104	79
AR	12	8	20	29	18	19	NM	23	18	52	69	45	36
CA	489	461	46	1,262	1,078	1,217	NY	250	140	9	695	321	256
CO	11	15	65	28	39	21	NC	45	33	17	98	64	46
CT	27	19	22	64	39	37	ND	3	3	–	7	7	5
DE	6	6	11	12	13	12	OH	95	82	–	235	177	178
DC	17	17	35	45	41	12	OK	14	11	–	35	26	18
FL	65	58	3	142	100	83	OR	17	19	–	38	44	43
GA	52	39	7	125	82	38	PA	88	97	–	241	254	120
HI	14	8	5	46	19	14	RI	16	10	–	44	26	19
ID	1	2	33	2	3	2	SC	18	16	–	42	36	35
IL	78	38	14	234	96	55	SD	3	3	–	7	6	6
IN	37	44	116	101	124	84	TN	57	70	–	147	184	136
IA	20	17	24	53	42	39	TX	129	82	–	347	189	115
KS	13	18	2	32	46	31	UT	8	9	–	21	22	12
KY	38	34	82	87	74	59	VT	6	5	–	16	11	7
LA	27	15	8	71	36	22	VA	31	10	–	69	28	65
ME.....	11	9	19	28	25	24	WA.....	56	57	–	148	136	122
MD.....	29	23	50	71	53	46	WV.....	13	12	–	33	26	20
MA.....	43	48	12	100	102	91	WI	17	19	–	38	44	37
MI.......	72	81	8	198	215	166	WY.....	1	–	–	1	1	1
MN.....	39	28	15	114	71	48	PR	30	15	–	88	41	1
MS.....	15	15	3	34	33	23	GU	3	3	7	10	9	32
MO.....	47	40	53	125	96	85	VI	1	–	–	3	1	1

– Represents or rounds to zero.
Source: U.S. Department of Health and Human Services, Administration for Children and Families, unpublished data.

Table 565. Temporary Assistance for Needy Families (TANF)—Expenditures by State: 2000 to 2008

[In millions of dollars (24,781 represents $24,781,000,000). Represents federal and state funds expended in fiscal year]

State	2000, total	2005, total	2008 Total [1]	2008 Expenditures on assistance	State	2000, total	2005, total	2008 Total [1]	2008 Expenditures on assistance
U.S.	24,781	25,580	28,130	10,047	MO	321	299	332	114
AL	96	123	143	46	MT	44	44	39	18
AK .	93	74	62	10	NE	79	78	94	23
AZ	261	299	349	123	NV	69	70	85	31
AR	139	67	144	14	NH	73	63	85	31
CA	6,481	5,882	6,687	3,750	NJ	321	994	955	244
CO	205	214	231	45	NM	149	127	129	58
CT	436	459	496	107	NY	3,512	3,970	4,423	1,791
DE	55	61	68	15	NC	440	448	447	81
DC	157	156	161	21	ND	33	34	37	18
FL	781	868	948	175	OH	995	990	1,501	318
GA	386	520	615	116	OK	130	174	176	61
HI	162	128	229	49	OR	169	269	309	151
ID	43	40	35	6	PA	1,327	1,190	962	238
IL	879	998	1,013	63	RI	172	168	109	42
IN	342	307	308	75	SC	245	230	170	38
IA	163	162	173	73	SD	21	30	29	21
KS	151	154	176	68	TN	293	233	290	118
KY	203	216	193	124	TX	727	851	822	145
LA	118	186	173	48	UT	100	108	86	33
ME	108	127	127	96	VT	62	68	72	32
MD	336	349	405	113	VA	418	290	271	99
MA	690	689	915	293	WA........	535	525	705	268
MI	1,264	1,175	1,230	361	WV	134	124	115	50
MN	381	392	435	71	WI	382	446	453	89
MS.........	62	79	91	25	WY........	34	32	27	16

[1] Includes other items not shown separately.
Source: U.S. Administration for Children and Families, Temporary Assistance for Needy Families (TANF) Program, *Annual Report to Congress*. See also <http://www.acf.hhs.gov/programs/cb/stats_research>.

Table 566. Child Support—Award and Recipiency Status of Custodial Parent: 2007

[In thousands except as noted (13,743 represents 13,743,000). Custodial parents 15 years and older with own children under 21 years of age present from absent parents as of spring 2008. Covers civilian noninstitutionalized population. Based on Current Population Survey; see text, Section 1 and Appendix III. For definition of mean, see Guide to Tabular Presentation]

Award and recipiency status	All custodial parents				Custodial parents below the poverty level			
	Total				Total			
	Number	Percent distribu- tion	Mothers	Fathers	Number	Percent distribu- tion	Mothers	Fathers
Total	**13,743**	(X)	**11,356**	**2,387**	**3,375**	(X)	**3,067**	**308**
With child support agreement or award [1]	7,428	(X)	6,463	965	1,580	(X)	1,464	116
Supposed to receive payments in 2007	6,375	100.0	5,551	825	1,278	100.0	1,185	93
Actually received payments in 2007	4,864	76.3	4,253	611	886	69.3	811	75
Received full amount	2,986	46.8	2,615	371	514	40.2	471	43
Received partial payments	1,878	29.5	1,638	240	372	29.1	340	32
Did not receive payments in 2007	1,511	23.7	1,298	213	392	30.7	374	18
Child support not awarded	6,315	(X)	4,893	1,422	1,796	(X)	1,603	193
MEAN INCOME AND CHILD SUPPORT								
Received child support payments in 2007:								
Mean total money income (dol.)	34,068	(X)	32,271	46,574	8,849	(X)	8,652	10,966
Mean child support received (dol.)	4,395	(X)	4,379	4,510	3,393	(X)	3,413	3,177
Received the full amount due:								
Mean total money income (dol.)	37,266	(X)	35,135	52,294	9,309	(X)	9,115	11,430
Mean child support received (dol.)	5,736	(X)	5,694	6,032	4,462	(X)	4,481	4,259
Received partial payments:								
Mean total money income (dol.)	28,983	(X)	27,696	37,751	8,213	(X)	8,011	10,347
Mean child support received (dol.)	2,264	(X)	2,279	2,163	1,916	(X)	1,934	1,734
Received no payments in 2007:								
Mean total money income (dol.)	29,261	(X)	27,377	40,712	8,598	(X)	8,523	10,142
Without child support agreement or award:								
Mean total money income (dol.)	28,515	(X)	23,242	46,659	6,934	(X)	6,793	8,103

X Not applicable. [1] As of April of following year (e.g., 2007 data is as of April 2008).

Source: U.S. Census Bureau, unpublished data, <http://www.census.gov/hhes/www/childsupport/cs07.html>.

Table 567. Child Support Enforcement Program—Caseload and Collections: 1990 to 2009

[For years ending September 30 (12,796 represents 12,796,000). Includes Puerto Rico, Guam, and the Virgin Islands. The child support enforcement program locates absent parents, establishes paternity of children born out of wedlock, and establishes and enforces support orders. By law, these services are available to all families that need them. The program is operated at the state and local government level, but 66 percent of administrative costs are paid by the federal government. Child support (CS) collected for families not receiving Temporary Assistance for Needy Families (TANF) goes to the family to help it remain self-sufficient. Most of the child support collected on behalf of TANF families goes to federal and state governments to offset TANF payments. Some states pass-through a portion of the CS collections to help families become self-sufficient. Based on data reported by state agencies. Minus sign (–) indicates net outlay]

Item	Unit	1990	2000	2004	2005	2006	2007	2008	2009, prel.
Total cases [1]	**1,000**	**12,796**	**17,334**	**15,854**	**15,861**	**15,844**	**15,755**	**15,676**	**15,798**
Paternities established, total [2]	1,000	393	867	692	690	675	640	629	643
Support orders established, total [3]	1,000	1,022	1,175	1,181	1,180	1,159	1,178	1,193	1,267
FINANCES									
Collections, total	**Mil. dol.**	**6,010**	**17,854**	**21,861**	**23,006**	**23,933**	**24,855**	**26,561**	**26,386**
TANF/FC collections [4]	Mil. dol.	1,750	2,593	2,221	2,191	2,112	2,050	2,254	1,971
State share	Mil. dol.	620	1,080	927	911	875	852	948	741
Estimated incentive payments to states	Mil. dol.	264	353	361	365	402	431	(NA)	541
Federal share [5]	Mil. dol.	533	968	1,147	1,129	1,086	1,054	1,170	945
Current assistance medical support collections	Mil. dol.	(NA)	27	12	11	12	11	12	13
Current assistance payments to families or foster care	Mil. dol.	(NA)	165	136	140	139	133	124	155
Non-TANF collections	Mil. dol.	4,260	15,261	19,641	20,815	21,822	22,804	24,307	24,415
Administrative expenditures, total	Mil. dol.	1,606	4,526	5,322	5,353	5,561	5,594	5,878	5,850
State share	Mil. dol.	545	1,519	1,803	1,813	1,884	1,902	2,221	1,964
Federal share	Mil. dol.	1,061	3,006	3,519	3,540	3,677	3,692	3,657	3,886
Program savings, total	Mil. dol.	–190	–2,125	–3,249	–3,312	–3,600	–3,687	–3,780	(NA)
State share	Mil. dol.	338	–87	–515	–537	–607	–619	–700	(NA)
Federal share	Mil. dol.	–528	–2,038	–2,734	–2,776	–2,993	–3,068	–3,080	(NA)

NA Not available. [1] Passage of the Personal Responsibility and Work Opportunity Reconciliation Act of 1996 (PRWORA) mandated new categories in 1999 and cases were no longer double counted resulting in a 2 million case reduction. [2] Does not include in-hospital paternities. [3] Includes modifications to orders. [4] Collections for current assistance cases where the children are: (1) recipients of TANF under title IV-A of the Social Security Act or (2) entitled to foster care (FC) maintenance under title IV-E of the Social Security Act plus collections distributed as assistance reimbursements. Includes assistance reimbursements, which are collections that will be divided between the state and federal governments to reimburse their respective shares of either Title IV-A assistance payments or Title IV-E foster care maintenance payments. [5] Prior to fiscal year 2002, incentives were paid out of the federal share of collections and the net federal share was reported.

Source: U.S. Department of Health and Human Services, Office of Child Support Enforcement, *Annual Report to Congress*.

Table 568. Federal Food Programs: 1990 to 2009

[20.0 represents 20,000,000, except as noted. For years ending September 30. Program data include Puerto Rico, Virgin Islands, Guam, American Samoa, Northern Marianas, and the former Trust Territory when a federal food program was operated in these areas. Participation data are average monthly figures except as noted. Participants are not reported for programs. Cost data are direct federal benefits to recipients; they exclude federal administrative payments and applicable state and local contributions. Federal costs for commodities and cash in-lieu of commodities are shown separately from direct cash benefits for those programs receiving both]

Program	Unit	1990	2000	2004	2005	2006	2007	2008	2009
Supplemental nutrition assistance program (SNAP): [1]									
Participants	Million ...	20.0	17.2	23.9	25.7	26.7	26.5	28.4	33.7
Federal cost	Mil. dol...	14,143	14,983	24,619	28,568	30,187	30,373	34,608	50,360
Monthly average coupon value per recipient	Dollars ...	58.78	72.62	85.99	92.57	94.32	95.63	101.52	124.45
Nutrition assistance program for Puerto Rico: [2]									
Federal cost	Mil. dol...	937	1,268	1,413	1,495	1,518	1,551	1,623	2,001
National school lunch program (NSLP):									
Free lunches served	Million ...	1,662	2,205	2,397	2,477	2,496	2,506	2,611	2,724
Reduced-price lunches served	Million ...	273	409	462	479	488	501	521	519
Children participating [3]	Million ...	24.1	27.3	29.0	29.6	30.1	30.5	31.0	31.3
Federal cost	Mil. dol...	3,214	5,493	6,663	7,055	7,389	7,707	8,265	8,873
School breakfast (SB):									
Children participating [3]	Million ...	4.1	7.6	8.9	9.4	9.8	10.1	10.6	11.1
Federal cost	Mil. dol...	596	1,393	1,776	1,927	2,043	2,164	2,366	2,582
Special supplemental food program (WIC): [4]									
Participants	Million ...	4.5	7.2	7.9	8.0	8.1	8.3	8.7	9.1
Federal cost	Mil. dol...	1,637	2,853	3,562	3,603	3,598	3,882	4,534	4,642
Child and adult care (CAC): [5]									
Participants [6]	Million ...	1.5	2.7	3.0	3.1	3.1	3.2	3.3	3.3
Federal cost	Mil. dol...	719	1,500	1,812	1,904	1,944	2,023	2,169	2,289
Federal cost of commodities donated to— [7] Child nutrition									
(NSLP, CACFP, SFS, and SBP) [8]	Mil. dol...	644	704	1,028	1,045	875	1,110	1,138	(NA)
Emergency feeding [9]	Mil. dol...	282	182	361	314	243	198	227	(NA)

NA Not available. [1] The program name was changed from Food Stamp to Supplemental Nutrition Assistance (SNAP) in October 2008. [2] Puerto Rico receives a grant in lieu of SNAP benefits. [3] Average monthly participation (excluding summer months of June through August). Includes children in public and private elementary and secondary schools and in residential child care institutes. [4] WIC serves pregnant and postpartum women, infants, and children up to age 5. [5] CACFP provides year-round subsidies to feed preschool children in child care centers and family day care homes. Certain care centers serving disabled or elderly adults also receive meal subsidies. [6] Average quarterly daily attendance at participating institutions. [7] Includes the federal cost of commodity entitlements, cash-in-lieu of commodities, and bonus foods. [8] Includes NSLP, CACFP and Summer Food Service. [9] Provides free (bonus) commodities to needy persons for home consumption through food banks, hunger centers, soup kitchens, and similar nonprofit agencies. Includes The Emergency Food Assistance Program (TEFAP), the commodity purchases for soup kitchens/food banks program (FY 1989–96), and commodity disaster relief. Does not include SNAP disaster assistance.

Source: U.S. Department of Agriculture, Food and Nutrition Service, "Food and Nutrition Service, Program Data," <http://www.fns.usda.gov/pd>, updated monthly.

Table 569. Federal Supplemental Nutrition Assistance Program by State: 2000 to 2009

[For years ending September 30. Participation data are average monthly number participating in year ending September 30. (26,619 represents 26,619,000); institutions. Food stamp costs are for benefits only and exclude administrative expenditures]

State	Persons (1,000)			Benefits (million dollars)			State	Persons (1,000)			Benefits (million dollars)		
	2000	2005	2009	2000	2005	2009		2000	2005	2009	2000	2005	2009
Total [1]	17,194	25,628	33,490	14,983	28,568	50,360	MS	276	435	506	226	463	691
U.S.	17,156	25,588	33,442	14,927	27,352	48,075	MO	423	677	801	358	736	1,136
AL	396	559	679	344	616	971	MT	59	81	92	51	89	135
AK	38	56	64	46	80	130	NE	82	117	134	61	120	179
AZ	259	550	814	240	634	1,224	NV	61	122	200	57	129	286
AR	247	374	411	206	401	570	NH	36	52	79	28	51	116
CA	1,831	1,992	2,670	1,639	2,315	4,382	NJ	345	392	500	304	437	750
CO	156	246	319	127	313	503	NM	169	241	291	140	251	411
CT	165	204	258	138	223	417	NY	1,439	1,755	2,323	1,361	2,136	3,955
DE	32	62	91	31	65	129	NC	488	800	1,137	403	856	1,625
DC	81	89	103	77	103	160	ND	32	42	53	25	45	80
FL	882	1,382	1,952	771	1,598	2,968	OH	610	1,007	1,357	520	1,155	2,167
GA	559	921	1,286	489	1,048	1,944	OK	253	424	473	208	440	666
HI	118	94	115	166	156	274	OR	234	429	581	198	456	831
ID	58	93	136	46	103	201	PA	777	1,043	1,338	656	1,105	1,901
IL	817	1,158	1,462	777	1,400	2,323	RI	74	76	102	59	79	170
IN	300	556	707	268	627	1,071	SC	295	521	688	249	566	1,002
IA	123	207	295	100	220	420	SD	43	56	74	37	61	111
KS	117	178	219	83	180	302	TN	496	850	1,072	415	942	1,604
KY	403	570	702	337	611	1,002	TX	1,333	2,442	3,003	1,215	2,659	4,399
LA	500	808	724	448	979	1,119	UT	82	133	185	68	141	263
ME	102	153	201	81	162	293	VT	41	45	72	32	45	99
MD	219	289	454	199	320	669	VA	336	488	652	263	500	923
MA	232	368	628	182	363	926	WA	295	508	761	241	539	1,047
MI	603	1,048	1,450	457	1,099	2,107	WV	227	262	306	185	258	408
MN	196	260	345	165	275	473	WI	193	346	548	129	317	680
							WY	22	25	27	19	27	37

[1] Includes Guam and the Virgin Islands. Several outlying areas receive nutrition assistance grants in lieu of food stamps (Puerto Rico, American Samoa, and the Northern Marianas).

Source: U.S. Department of Agriculture, Food and Nutrition Service, "Food and Nutrition Service, Program Data," <http://www.fns.usda.gov/pdf>, updated monthly.

Table 570. Selected Characteristics of Food Stamp Households and Participants: 1990 to 2008

[7,811 represents 7,811,000. For years ending September 30. Data for 1990 exclude Guam and the Virgin Islands. Based on a sample of households from the Food Stamp Quality Control System]

Year	Households				Participants		
	Total [1] (1,000)	Percent of total			Total [1] (1,000)	Percent of total	
		With children	With elderly [2]	With disabled [3]		Children	Elderly [2]
1990.........	7,811	60.3	18.1	8.9	20,440	49.6	7.7
1995.........	10,883	59.7	16.0	18.9	26,955	51.5	7.1
2000.........	7,335	53.9	21.0	27.5	17,091	51.3	10.0
2004.........	10,070	54.3	17.3	22.9	23,486	50.2	8.2
2005.........	10,854	53.8	17.1	23.1	24,881	50.0	8.2
2006.........	11,315	52.2	17.9	23.1	25,595	49.2	8.7
2007.........	11,563	51.3	17.9	23.9	25,926	49.1	8.7
2008.........	12,465	50.9	18.5	22.6	27,791	48.6	9.1

[1] Total does not include those who are ineligible or those receiving disaster benefits. [2] Persons 60 years old and over. [3] The substantial increase in 1995 and decrease in 2003 are due in part to the changes in definition of a disabled household. Prior to 1995, disabled households were defined as households with SSI income but no members over age 59. In 1995, that definition changed to households with at least one member under 65 who received SSI, or at least one member aged 18–61 who received Social Security, veterans' benefits, or other government benefits as a result of a disability. Because of changes to the QC data in 2003, the definition of a disabled household changed to households either SSI income or a medical expense deduction and without an elderly person, and households containing a nonelderly adult who does not appear to be working and who is receiving Social Security, veterans' benefits, or workers' compensation.

Source: U.S. Department of Agriculture, Food and Nutrition Service. Percentages obtained from *Characteristics of Food Stamp Households: Fiscal Year 200*8, September 2008. See also <http://www.fns.usda.gov/ora/MENU/Published/snap/SNAPParthh.htm>.

Table 571. Food Stamp Households and Participants—Summary: 2008

[12,465 represents 12,465,000. For year ending September 30. Based on a sample of households from the Food Stamp Quality Control System. Figures are lower than official participation counts because they do not include ineligible participants or those receiving disaster food stamp assistance]

Household type and income source	Households		Age, sex, race, and Hispanic origin	Participants	
	Number (1,000)	Percent		Number (1,000)	Percent
Total......................	12,465	100.0	Total......................	27,791	100.0
With children...................	6,342	50.9	Children......................	13,496	48.6
Single-parent households.......	3,876	31.1	Under 5 years old..............	4,656	16.8
Married-couple households......	1,057	8.5	5 to 17 years old..............	8,840	31.8
Other.......................	1,409	11.3	Adults........................	14,294	51.4
With elderly....................	2,312	18.5	18 to 35 years old.............	6,117	22.0
Living alone...................	1,865	15.0	36 to 59 years old.............	5,658	20.4
Not living alone...............	447	3.6	60 years old and over..........	2,519	9.1
Disabled......................	2,821	22.6			
Living alone...................	1,581	12.7	Male.........................	11,537	41.5
Not living alone...............	1,240	9.9	Female.......................	16,254	58.5
Earned income.................	3,640	29.2			
Wages and salaries............	3,222	25.8	White, non-Hispanic..........	8,417	30.3
			Black, non-Hispanic............	6,270	22.6
Unearned income..............	8,171	65.6	Hispanic......................	4,112	14.8
TANF [1].......................	1,321	10.6	Asian........................	693	2.5
Supplemental security income....	3,278	26.3	Native American..............	1,192	4.3
Social security...............	3,064	24.6	Other [2]......................	7,108	25.6
No income....................	1,986	15.9			

[1] Temporary Assistance for Needy Families (TANF) program. [2] For FY 2008, this category includes respondents who recorded more than one race, and those with no racial/ethnic data.

Source: U.S. Department of Agriculture, Food and Nutrition Service, *Characteristics of Food Stamp Households: Fiscal Year 2008*, September 2009. See also <http://www.fns.usda.gov/ora/menu/Published/snap/SNAPParthh.htm>.

Table 572. Head Start—Summary: 1980 to 2009

[For years ending September 30 (376 represents 376,000)]

Year	Enrollment (1,000)	Appro-priation (mil. dol.)	Age and race	Enrollment, 2009 (percent)	Item	Number
1980......	376	735	Under 3 years old	10	Average cost per child:	
1990......	541	1,552	3 years old............	36	1995..................	$4,534
1995......	751	3,534	4 years old............	51	2000..................	$5,951
1999......	826	4,658	5 years old and over	3	2009..................	$7,600
2000......	858	5,267				
2001......	905	6,200	White................	40	Paid staff (1,000):	
2002......	912	6,537	Black.................	30	1995..................	147
2003......	910	6,668	Hispanic..............	36	2000..................	180
2004......	906	6,775	American Indian/.......		2009..................	212
2005......	907	6,843	Alaska Native	4	Volunteers (1,000):	
2006......	909	6,872	Asian................	2	1995..................	1,235
2007......	908	6,888	Hawaiian/		2000..................	1,252
2008......	907	6,878	Pacific Islander........	1	2009..................	1,274
2009......	904	7,113				

Source: U.S. Department of Health and Services, Administration for Children and Families, "Head Start Statistical Fact Sheet"; <http://www.acf.hhs.gov/programs/ohs/about>.

Table 573. Number of Emergency and Transitional Beds in Homeless Assistance Systems Nationwide: 2008

[Data include beds located in Puerto Rico, Guam, and the Virgin Islands. Data are based on a nationally representative sample of 80 jurisdictions that collect data from emergency shelters and transitional providers. The data estimate homeless persons who used emergency shelters or transitional housing from January 1 through June 30, 2008. As a compliment to the survey, a "Continuum of Care" community was derived from each jurisdiction in order to estimate the number of unsheltered homeless persons and the number of emergency shelter and transitional housing beds available on a single night in January 2008. The data do not include homeless individuals living outside a sampled jurisdiction or homeless individuals not using an emergency shelter or a transitional housing program. For more information on data collection and methodology, see Appendix B of source]

Homeless programs	Year-round units/beds [1]			Total year-round beds	Other beds	
	Family units	Family beds	Individual beds		Seasonal beds [2]	Overflow/ voucher [3]
Emergency shelters............	30,117	98,703	112,519	211,222	20,413	37,141
Transitional housing............	35,470	110,973	94,089	205,062	(NA)	(NA)
Total inventory...............	65,587	209,676	206,608	416,284	20,413	37,141
Permanent supportive housing......	26,729	76,581	119,143	195,724	(NA)	(NA)

NA Not available. [1] Year-round beds are available for use throughout the year and are considered part of the stable inventory of beds for homeless persons. [2] Seasonal beds are typically available during particularly high-demand seasons of the year (e.g. winter months in the North or summer months in the South) to accommodate increased need for emergency shelters to prevent illness or death due to the weather. [3] Overflow beds are typically used during unanticipated emergencies (e.g., precipitous temperature drops or a natural disaster that displaces residents). Voucher beds are made available in a hotel or motel, and often function like overflow beds.

Source: U.S. Department of Housing and Urban Development, *The Fourth Annual Homeless Assessment Report to Congress.* See also <http://www.hudhre.info/documents/4thHomelessAssessmentReport.pdf>.

Table 574. Social Assistance Services—Revenue for Employer Firms: 2000 to 2008

[In millions of dollars (77,032 represents $77,032,000,000). Based on the North American Industry Classification System, 2002, (NAICS); see text, Section 15 and Appendix III]

Kind of business	2002 NAICS code	2000, total	2005, total	2008		
				Total	Taxable firms	Tax-exempt firms
Social assistance, total..................	**624**	**77,032**	**110,483**	**131,912**	**34,823**	**97,089**
Individual and family services..................	6241	37,311	52,797	64,843	11,330	53,513
Child and youth services.....................	62411	7,517	10,397	11,845	1,452	10,393
Services for elderly and disabled persons.........	62412	12,804	19,309	24,878	5,258	19,620
Other individual and family services.............	62419	16,990	23,091	28,120	4,620	23,500
Community, emergency and other relief services....	6242	12,281	18,934	20,354	220	20,134
Community food services.....................	62421	2,835	3,784	4,351	47	4,304
Community housing services..................	62422	4,888	6,683	8,017	148	7,869
Emergency and other relief services.............	62423	4,558	8,467	7,986	(S)	7,961
Vocational rehabilitation services	6243	9,458	13,921	14,037	2,958	11,079
Child day care services.......................	6244	17,982	24,831	32,678	20,315	12,363

S Figure does not meet publication standards.
Source: U.S. Census Bureau, *Service Annual Survey*, 2008. See also <http://www.census.gov/svsd/www/services/sas/sas_data/sas62.htm>.

Table 575. Social Assistance—Nonemployer Establishments and Receipts: 2000 to 2007

[Receipts in millions of dollars (7,539 represents $7,539,000,000). Includes only firms subject to federal income tax. Nonemployers are businesses with no paid employees. Data for 2000 based on the North American Industry Classification System (NAICS), 1997; 2007 based on NAICS 2002; see text, Section 15]

Kind of business	NAICS code	Establishments			Receipts		
		2000	2005	2007	2000	2005	2007
Social assistance, total....................	**624**	**642,946**	**807,729**	**829,550**	**7,539**	**10,265**	**11,539**
Individual and family services..................	6241	72,433	112,909	121,633	1,106	1,920	2,242
Community/emergency and other relief services ...	6242	3,560	5,533	5,766	54	81	101
Vocational rehabilitation services	6243	7,314	11,022	10,862	151	245	260
Child day care services.......................	6244	559,639	678,265	691,289	6,228	8,018	8,936

Source: U.S. Census Bureau, "Nonemployer Statistics," <http://www.census.gov/econ/nonemployer/index.html> (released July 2009).

Table 576. Child Care Arrangements of Preschool Children by Type of Arrangement: 1991 to 2005

[In percent, except as indicated (8,428 represents 8,428,000). Estimates are based on children 3 to 5 years old who have not entered kindergarten. Based on interviews from a sample survey of the civilian, noninstitutionalized population in households with telephones; see source for details. See also Appendix III]

Characteristic	Children		Type of nonparental arrangement [1] (percent)			With parental care only (percent)
	Number (1,000)	Percent distribution	In relative care	In non-relative care	In center-based program [2]	
1991, total	8,428	100.0	16.9	14.8	52.8	31.0
1995, total	9,232	100.0	19.4	16.9	55.1	25.9
2005, total..............	**9,066**	**100.0**	**22.6**	**11.6**	**57.2**	**26.3**
Age:						
3 years old..............	4,070	44.9	24.0	14.4	42.5	33.4
4 years old..............	3,873	42.7	20.8	9.2	69.2	20.6
5 years old..............	1,123	12.4	23.8	9.9	68.7	20.4
Race-ethnicity:						
White, non-Hispanic........	5,177	57.1	21.4	15.0	59.1	24.1
Black, non-Hispanic........	1,233	13.6	25.0	5.2	66.5	19.5
Hispanic.................	1,822	20.1	22.7	8.1	43.4	38.0
Other	834	9.2	26.4	8.1	61.5	24.7
Household income:						
Less than $10,001........	795	8.8	25.1	8.6	53.4	33.4
$10,001 to $20,000	978	10.8	26.0	7.8	49.2	27.2
$20,001 to $30,000	1,183	13.1	25.4	6.3	43.9	38.5
$30,001 to $40,000	1,124	12.4	23.8	6.9	48.7	33.4
$40,001 to $50,000	808	8.9	21.8	11.6	50.0	35.4
$50,001 to $75,000	1,849	20.4	21.1	13.3	57.1	25.5
$75,001 or more	2,329	25.7	19.8	18.0	75.1	11.4

[1] Columns do not add to 100.0 because some children participated in more than one type of nonparental arrangement.
[2] Center-based programs include day care centers, Head Start programs, preschools, prekindergarten, and nursery schools.
Source: U.S. Department of Education, National Center for Education Statistics, Early Childhood Program Participation Survey of the National Household Education Surveys Program (NHES), 2005.

Table 577. Children in Foster Care and Awaiting Adoption: 2000 and 2008

[Data are preliminary and cover the period from October 1 of prior year through September 30 of year shown]

Characteristic	In foster care		Entered foster care		Exited foster care		Waiting to be adopted		Adopted from foster care	
	2000	2008 [1]	2000	2008 [1]	2000	2008 [1]	2000	2008 [1]	2000	2008 [1]
Total	**552,000**	**463,000**	**293,000**	**273,000**	**272,000**	**285,000**	**131,000**	**123,000**	**51,000**	**55,000**
AGE										
Under 1 year	22,839	26,812	37,996	44,365	11,025	13,328	3,957	4,628	939	1,098
1 to 5 years	134,378	133,049	72,365	76,987	70,667	91,509	44,126	46,667	23,135	29,725
6 to 10 years	136,003	91,416	63,346	50,689	63,228	57,855	44,980	32,467	17,831	14,753
11 to 15 years	160,077	113,510	86,555	67,488	65,550	55,187	33,143	29,529	7,946	7,591
16 to 20 years [1]	98,701	98,213	32,737	33,471	61,531	67,121	4,793	9,708	1,149	1,834
RACE										
White [2]	207,970	183,149	136,214	119,242	121,322	124,688	44,898	47,392	19,462	24,377
Black [2]	217,615	142,502	84,460	70,378	84,065	75,441	57,345	36,913	19,566	13,687
Asian [2]	4,370	2,631	3,565	2,269	3,307	2,316	664	587	290	303
Hispanic [3].	81,823	92,464	42,769	54,802	39,909	56,741	17,050	26,223	7,430	11,441
SEX										
Male...............	289,187	243,740	(NA)	(NA)	(NA)	(NA)	68,620	64,725	25,472	27,718
Female............	262,813	219,260	(NA)	(NA)	(NA)	(NA)	62,380	58,275	25,528	27,282

NA Not available. [1] For children waiting to be adopted, includes ages 16 to 17 years only. [2] Beginning with the 2000 census, respondents could choose more than one race. Data represent persons who selected this race group only and exclude persons reporting more than one race. The census in prior years only allowed respondents to report one race group. See also comments on race in text, Section 1. [3] Hispanic persons may be any race.
Source: U.S. Department of Health and Human Services, Administration for Children and Families, Adoption and Foster Care Analysis and Reporting System Reports, annual. See also <http://www.acf.hhs.gov/programs/cb/stats_research/index.htm#afcars>.

Table 578. Private Philanthropy Funds by Source and Allocation: 1990 to 2008

[In billions of dollars (101.4 represents $101,400,000,000). Estimates for sources of funds based on U.S. Internal Revenue Service reports of individual charitable deductions and household surveys of giving by Independent Sector and the Center on Philanthropy at Indiana University. For corporate giving, data are corporate charitable deductions from the U.S. Internal Revenue Service and the contributions made by corporate foundations as reported by the Foundation Center. Data about foundation donations are based upon surveys of foundations and data provided by the Foundation Center. Estimates of the allocation of funds were derived from surveys of nonprofits conducted by various sources]

Source and allocation	1990	1995	1999	2000	2001	2002	2003	2004	2005	2006	2007	2008
Total funds	**101.4**	**123.7**	**202.7**	**229.7**	**231.1**	**231.5**	**236.3**	**260.5**	**293.8**	**294.9**	**306.4**	**307.7**
Individuals	81.0	95.4	154.6	174.5	172.4	172.8	180.2	202.2	221.4	223.0	229.0	229.3
Foundations [1]	7.2	10.6	20.5	24.6	27.2	27.0	26.8	28.4	32.4	34.9	38.5	41.2
Corporations	5.5	7.4	10.2	10.7	11.6	10.8	11.1	11.4	16.6	15.4	15.7	14.5
Charitable bequests.	7.6	10.4	17.4	19.9	19.8	20.9	18.2	18.5	23.5	21.7	23.2	22.7
Allocation:												
Religion	49.8	58.1	71.3	77.0	79.9	82.9	84.6	88.0	93.0	97.7	102.3	106.9
Health	9.9	13.9	15.2	16.4	18.3	17.8	17.8	20.2	22.5	22.0	23.2	21.6
Education.	12.4	15.6	27.2	29.7	32.7	30.0	30.0	33.8	37.3	40.7	43.3	40.9
Human service	11.8	9.7	17.9	20.0	21.8	24.4	24.4	24.4	26.1	27.4	29.6	25.9
Arts, culture, and humanities. . . .	7.9	5.7	9.2	10.5	11.4	10.8	10.8	11.8	11.8	12.7	13.7	12.8
Public/societal benefit	4.9	11.3	13.0	15.4	16.5	18.0	16.4	18.8	21.3	21.4	22.7	23.8
Environment/wildlife.	2.5	2.3	4.2	4.8	5.3	5.3	5.4	5.5	6.0	6.3	7.0	6.6
International.	1.3	3.0	6.6	7.2	8.3	8.7	9.8	11.6	15.2	11.4	13.2	13.3
Gifts to foundations [1]	3.8	8.5	28.8	24.7	25.7	19.2	21.6	20.3	27.5	30.6	27.7	32.7
Unallocated [2]	−3.0	−4.4	9.4	24.2	11.3	14.6	13.8	26.2	33.2	24.8	23.7	19.4

[1] Data are from the Foundation Center through 2001. [2] Money deducted as a charitable contribution by donors but not allocated to sources. May include gifts to governmental entities, in-kind giving, and gifts to new charities.

Source: Giving USA Foundation, Glenview, IL, researched and written by the Center on Philanthropy at Indiana University, *Giving USA*, annual (copyright).

Table 579. Foundations—Number and Finances by Asset Size: 1990 to 2008

[Figures are for latest year reported by foundations (142,500 represents $142,500,000,000). Covers nongovernmental nonprofit organizations with funds and programs managed by their own trustees or directors, whose goals were to maintain or aid social, educational, religious, or other activities deemed to serve the common good. Excludes organizations that make general appeals to the public for funds, act as trade associations for industrial or other special groups, or do not currently award grants]

Asset size	Number	Assets (mil. dol.)	Gifts received (mil. dol.)	Total giving [1] (mil. dol.)
1990.	32,401	142,500	5,000	8,700
2000.	56,582	486,100	27,600	27,600
2005.	71,095	550,600	31,500	36,400
2007.	75,187	682,222	46,844	44,394
2008, total	**75,595**	**564,951**	**39,554**	**46,781**
Under $50,000.	12,795	200	2,635	2,846
$50,000–$99,999.	5,319	394	165	231
$100,000–$249,999.	10,261	1,716	456	621
$250,000–$499,999.	9,873	3,589	517	726
$500,000–$999,999.	10,727	7,739	1,290	1,504
$1,000,000–$4,999,999.	17,059	38,632	3,221	4,322
$5,000,000–$9,999,999.	3,908	27,547	2,400	2,935
$10,000,000–$49,999,999.	4,191	88,305	7,614	8,394
$50,000,000–$99,999,999.	724	50,445	4,030	3,722
$100,000,000–$249,999,999.	465	72,168	5,867	4,925
$250,000,000 or more.	273	274,216	11,360	16,466

[1] Includes grants, scholarships, and employee matching gifts; excludes set-asides, loans, program-related investments (PRIs), and program expenses.

Source: The Foundation Center, New York, NY, *Foundation Yearbook*, annual (copyright).

Table 580. Domestic Private Foundations—Information Returns: 1990 to 2006

[In billions (122.4 represents $122,400,000,000). Minus sign (−) indicates loss]

Item	1990	1995	1998	1999	2000	2001	2002	2003	2004	2005	2006
Number of returns	40,105	47,917	56,658	62,694	66,738	70,787	73,255	76,348	76,897	79,535	81,850
Nonoperating foundations [1]	36,880	43,966	52,460	58,840	61,501	63,650	67,101	70,004	70,613	72,800	74,364
Operating foundations [2]	3,226	3,951	4,198	3,854	5,238	7,137	6,154	6,344	6,284	6,734	7,486
Total assets, book value	122.4	195.6	325.7	384.6	409.5	413.6	383.5	418.5	455.5	481.8	569.3
Total assets, fair market value	151.0	242.9	397.1	466.9	471.6	455.4	413.0	475.0	509.9	545.9	645.8
Investments in securities	115.0	190.7	317.9	363.4	361.4	329.4	294.4	344.3	361.2	373.1	403.7
Total revenue	19.0	30.8	59.7	83.3	72.8	45.3	27.8	48.4	58.7	76.4	94.1
Total expenses.	11.3	17.2	25.9	33.9	37.4	36.7	34.4	35.1	36.6	42.8	48.8
Contributions, gifts, and grants paid.	8.6	12.3	19.4	22.8	27.6	27.4	26.3	26.7	27.6	31.9	34.9
Excess of revenue over expenses (net).	7.7	13.6	33.8	49.4	35.3	8.6	−6.6	13.3	22.1	33.5	45.3
Net investment income [3]	11.9	20.4	39.3	57.1	48.8	25.7	17.6	25.2	34.0	44.3	54.2

[1] Generally provide charitable support through grants and other financial means to charitable organizations; the majority of foundations are nonoperating. [2] Generally conduct their own charitable activities, e.g., museums. [3] Represents income not considered related to a foundation's charitable purpose, e.g., interest, dividends, and capital gains. Foundations could be subject to an excise tax on such income.

Source: Internal Revenue Service, Statistics of Income, SOI Tax Stats—Charities & Other Tax-Exempt Organizations, February 2010, <http://www.irs.gov/taxstats/charitablestats/article/0,,id=96996,00.html#2>.

Table 581. Nonprofit Charitable Organizations—Information Returns: 2000 and 2006

[In billions of dollars (1,562.5 represents $1,562,500,000,000), except as indicated. Categories based on The National Taxonomy of Exempt Entities (NTEE), a classification system that uses 26 major field areas that are aggregated into 10 categories. Includes data reported by organizations described in Internal Revenue Code, Section 501(3), excluding private foundations and most religious organizations. Organizations with receipts under $25,000 were not required to file]

Year and major category	Number of returns (1,000)	Total assets (billions)	Total fund balance or net worth (billions)	Revenue Total	Revenue Program service revenue [1]	Revenue Contributions, gifts, and grants	Total expenses (billions)	Excess of revenue over expenses (net)
2000.	230.2	1,562.5	1,023.2	866.2	579.1	199.1	796.4	69.8
2006, total	**301.2**	**2,549.7**	**1,617.7**	**1,370.9**	**920.2**	**303.2**	**1,230.4**	**140.5**
Arts, culture, and humanities. . .	30.6	99.0	80.9	32.2	7.5	17.5	26.3	6.0
Education.	54.9	856.4	641.8	275.6	135.1	81.2	217.6	58.0
Environment, animals	13.3	37.7	31.4	13.6	2.6	8.9	10.4	3.2
Health	36.2	967.5	522.6	759.4	659.3	55.4	716.4	43.0
Human services.	114.3	275.4	138.1	178.6	91.6	70.2	169.5	9.0
International, foreign affairs. . . .	5.0	22.1	16.1	20.8	1.7	18.0	19.0	1.8
Mutual, membership benefit . . .	27.5	249.8	159.0	77.8	19.3	45.2	60.6	17.2
Public, societal benefit.	18.4	24.0	19.2	10.0	1.5	6.6	8.2	1.8
Religion related	0.9	17.9	8.5	2.9	1.6	0.2	2.3	0.5

[1] Represents fees collected by organizations in support of their tax-exempt purposes, and income such as tuition and fees at educational institutions, hospital patient charges, and admission and activity fees collected by museums and other nonprofit organizations or institutions.

Source: Internal Revenue Service, Statistics of Income, SOI Tax Stats—Charities & Other Tax-Exempt Organizations Statistics. See also <http://www.irs.gov/taxstats/charitablestats/article/0,,id=97176,00.html>, accessed January 2010.

Table 582. Individual Charitable Contributions by State: 2007

[In million of dollars (189,952 represents $189,952,000,000. For tax year. Data will not agree with data in other tables due to differing survey methodology used to derive state data]

State	Number of returns (1,000)	Amount (mil. dol.)	State	Number of returns (1,000)	Amount (mil. dol.)	State	Number of returns (1,000)	Amount (mil. dol.)	State	Number of returns (1,000)	Amount (mil. dol.)
U.S.[1,2] . . .	**41,088**	**189,952**	IL	1,835	7,857	NE . . .	227	1,004	SD . . .	62	487
AL	558	3,036	IN	728	3,078	NV . . .	368	1,423	TN . . .	607	3,811
AK	71	311	IA	372	1,400	NH . . .	193	655	TX . . .	2,160	12,857
AZ	846	3,206	KS . . .	344	1,717	NJ . . .	1,653	5,869	UT . . .	401	3,104
AR	249	1,490	KY . . .	475	1,896	NM . . .	189	750	VT . . .	75	260
CA	5,167	24,548	LA . . .	363	1,730	NY . . .	3,006	17,154	VA . . .	1,277	5,480
CO	775	3,313	ME . . .	159	480	NC . . .	1,299	5,885	WA . . .	927	4,076
CT	661	3,180	MD . . .	1,173	5,203	ND . . .	51	220	WV . . .	110	461
DE	134	538	MA . . .	1,101	4,680	OH . . .	1,497	5,285	WI . . .	854	2,735
DC	104	806	MI . . .	1,422	5,322	OK . . .	383	2,679	WY . . .	47	519
FL	2,311	11,696	MN . . .	907	3,432	OR . . .	576	2,148			
GA	1,398	6,847	MS . . .	262	1,460	PA . . .	1,652	6,779			
HI	182	724	MO . . .	707	3,013	RI	165	463			
ID	191	889	MT . . .	119	456	SC . . .	570	2,790			

[1] The sum for the states does not add to the total because other components are not shown in this table. [2] U.S. totals do not agree with Table 487 in Section 9 because this table also includes (1) "substitutes for returns," whereby the IRS constructs returns for certain nonfilers on the basis of available information and imposes and income tax on the resulting estimate of the tax base and (2) returns of nonresident or departing aliens. In addition, in this table, income tax includes the alternative minimum tax, but differs from total income tax in Table 487 in that it is after subtraction of all tax credits except a portion of the earned income credit.

Source: Internal Revenue Service, Statistics of Income Bulletin, Spring issue. See also <http://www.irs.gov/taxstats/article/0,,id=171535,00.html>.

Table 583. Volunteers by Selected Characteristics: 2009

[In percent, except as noted. Data on volunteers relate to persons who performed unpaid volunteer activities for an organization at any point from September 1, 2008 through September 2009. Data represent the percent of the population involved in the activity]

Type of main organization [1]	Total, both sexes	Sex Male	Sex Female	Educational attainment [2] Less than a high school diploma	Educational attainment [2] High school graduate, no college [3]	Educational attainment [2] Less than a bachelor's degree [4]	Educational attainment [2] College graduates
Total volunteers (1,000)	**63,361**	**26,655**	**36,706**	**2,242**	**11,408**	**15,931**	**25,490**
Percent of population	26.8	23.3	30.1	8.6	18.8	30.5	42.8
Median annual hours [5]	50	52	50	45	48	50	54
Civic and political [6]	5.5	6.7	4.6	3.1	5.4	5.1	6.3
Educational or youth service	26.1	24.2	27.5	24.2	22.7	25.6	26.8
Environmental or animal care . . .	2.2	2.1	2.3	1.4	1.2	2.2	2.6
Hospital or other health	8.5	6.7	9.7	4.6	7.7	9.0	8.4
Public safety	1.2	2.0	0.6	1.5	1.4	1.4	0.7
Religious	34.0	33.7	34.2	47.1	40.4	34.7	31.3
Social or community service	13.9	14.9	13.2	11.7	13.9	13.1	14.3
Sport and hobby [7]	3.4	4.0	2.9	0.9	2.4	3.4	4.2

[1] Main organization is defined as the organization for which the volunteer worked the most hours during the year. See headnote for more details. [2] Data refer to persons 25 years and over. [3] Includes high school diploma or equivalent. [4] Includes the categories, "some college, no degree" and "associate's degree." [5] At all organizations. For those reporting annual hours. [6] Includes professional and/or international. [7] Includes cultural and/or arts.

Source: U.S. Bureau of Labor Statistics, News Release, USDL 10-0097, January 2010. See also <http://www.bls.gov/news.release/pdf/volun.pdf>.

Section 12
Labor Force, Employment, and Earnings

This section presents statistics on the labor force; its distribution by occupation and industry affiliation; and the supply of, demand for, and conditions of labor. The chief source of these data is the Current Population Survey (CPS) conducted by the U.S. Census Bureau for the Bureau of Labor Statistics (BLS). Comprehensive historical and current data are available from the BLS Internet site at <http://www.bls.gov/cps/>. These data are published on a current basis in the BLS monthly publication *Employment and Earnings Online*. Detailed data on the labor force are also available from the Census Bureau's decennial census of population.

Types of data—Most statistics in this section are obtained by two methods: household interviews or questionnaires and reports of establishment payroll records. Each method provides data that the other cannot suitably supply. Population characteristics, for example, are readily obtainable only from the household survey, while detailed industrial classifications can be readily derived only from establishment records.

Household data are obtained from a monthly sample survey of the population. The CPS is used to gather data for the calendar week including the 12th of the month and provides current comprehensive data on the labor force (see text, Section 1, Population). The CPS provides information on the work status of the population without duplication since each person is classified as employed, unemployed, or not in the labor force. Employed persons holding more than one job are counted only once, according to the job at which they worked the most hours during the survey week.

Monthly, quarterly, and annual data from the CPS are published by the BLS in *Employment and Earnings Online*. Data presented include national totals of the number of persons in the civilian labor force by sex, disability status, race, Hispanic origin, and age; the number

employed; hours of work; industry and occupational groups; usual weekly earnings; and the number unemployed, reasons for, and duration of unemployment. Annual data shown in this section are averages of monthly figures for each calendar year, unless otherwise specified. Historical national CPS data are available at <http://www.bls.gov/cps/>.

The CPS also produces annual estimates of employment and unemployment for each state, 50 large metropolitan statistical areas, and selected cities. These estimates are published by the BLS in its annual *Geographic Profile of Employment and Unemployment* available at <http://www.bls.gov/gps/>. More detailed geographic data (e.g., for counties and cities) are provided by the decennial population censuses.

Data based on establishment records are compiled by the BLS and cooperating state agencies as part of an ongoing Current Employment Statistics program. The BLS collects survey data monthly from a probability-based sample of nonfarm, business establishments through electronic data interchange, touchtone data entry, and computer-assisted telephone interviews, Internet, other electronic media, fax, or mail. CES data are adjusted annually to data from government unemployment insurance administrative records, which are supplemented by data from other government agencies. The estimates exclude self-employed persons, private household workers, unpaid family workers, agricultural workers, and members of the Armed Forces. In March 2009, reporting establishments employed 2.9 million manufacturing workers (24 percent of the total manufacturing employment at the time), 20.1 million workers in private nonmanufacturing industries (20.9 percent of the total in private nonmanufacturing), and 15.5 million federal, state, and local government employees (67 percent of total government).

U.S. Census Bureau, Statistical Abstract of the United States: 2011

The establishment survey counts workers each time they appear on a payroll during the reference period (the payroll period that includes the 12th of the month). Thus, unlike the CPS, a person with two jobs is counted twice. The establishment survey is designed to provide estimates of nonfarm wage and salary employment, average weekly hours, and average hourly and weekly earnings by detailed industry for the nation, states, and selected metropolitan areas. Establishment survey data also are published in *Employment and Earnings Online*. Historical national data are available at <http://www.bls.gov/ces/>. Historical data for states and metropolitan areas are available at <http://www.bls.gov/sae/>. CES estimates are currently classified by the 2007 North American Industry Classification System (NAICS). All published series for the nation have a NAICS–based history extending back to at least 1990. Employment series for total nonfarm and other high-level aggregates start in 1939.

In June 2003, the BLS completed a comprehensive sample redesign of the establishment survey begun in June 2000, changing from a quota-based sample to a probability-based sample. Also in June 2003, all establishment survey employment, hours, and earnings series were converted from being classified by the 1987 Standard Industrial Classification (SIC) system to being classified by the 2002 North American Industry Classification System (NAICS). The NAICS conversion resulted in major definitional changes to many of the previously published SIC-based series. All establishment survey historical time series were reconstructed as part of the NAICS conversion process and all published series have a NAICS-based history extending back to at least 1990. For total nonfarm industries and other high-level aggregates, NAICS history was reconstructed back to the previously existing start date for the series, 1939 in most cases. More information on the sample redesign, the conversion to NAICS, and other changes to the establishment survey implemented in June 2003 appears in "Revisions to the Current Employment Statistics National Estimates Effective May

2003" in the June 2003 issue of *Employment and Earnings*, as well as the Establishment Data portion of the Explanatory Notes and Estimates of Error section of *Employment and Earnings Online*.

The completion of the sample redesign and the conversion to NAICS for state and metropolitan area establishment survey data were implemented in March 2003 with the release of January 2003 estimates. For a discussion of the changes to the state and area establishment survey data, see "Revisions to the Current Employment Statistics State and Area Estimates Effective January 2003" in the March 2003 issue of *Employment and Earnings Online*.

Labor force—According to the CPS definitions, the civilian labor force comprises all civilians in the noninstitutionalized population 16 years and over classified as "employed" or "unemployed" according to the following criteria: Employed civilians comprise (a) all civilians, who, during the reference week, did any work for pay or profit (minimum of an hour's work) or worked 15 hours or more as unpaid workers in a family enterprise and (b) all civilians who were not working but who had jobs or businesses from which they were temporarily absent for noneconomic reasons (illness, weather conditions, vacation, labor-management dispute, etc.) whether they were paid for the time off or were seeking other jobs. Unemployed persons comprise all civilians who had no employment during the reference week, who made specific efforts to find a job within the previous 4 weeks (such as applying directly to an employer or to a public employment service or checking with friends) and who were available for work during that week, except for temporary illness. Persons on layoff from a job and expecting recall also are classified as unemployed. All other civilian persons, 16 years old and over, are classified as "not in the labor force."

Various breaks in the CPS data series have occurred over time due to the introduction of population adjustments and other changes. For details on these breaks in series and the effect that they had on the CPS data, see the BLS Web site at

<www.bls.gov.cps/documentation
.htm#concepts.>.

Beginning in January 2009, the CPS data reflect the introduction of revised population controls. The effect of the revised population controls on the monthly CPS estimates was to decrease the December 2008 employment level by 407,000 and the civilian noninstitutional population by 483,000. The updated controls had little or no effect on unemployment rates and other ratios. For additional information on the effects of the revised population controls on estimates from the CPS, see <www.bls .gov.cps/documentation.htm#pop>.

Hours and earnings—Average hourly earnings, based on establishment data, are gross earnings (i.e., earnings before payroll deductions) and include overtime premiums; they exclude irregular bonuses and value of payments in kind. Hours are those for which pay was received. Wages and salaries from the CPS consist of total monies received for work performed by an employee during the income year. It includes wages, salaries, commissions, tips, piece-rate payments, and cash bonuses earned before deductions were made for taxes, bonds, union dues, etc. Persons who worked 35 hours or more are classified as working full-time.

Industry and occupational groups— Industry data derived from the CPS for 1983–91 utilize the 1980 census industrial classification developed from the 1972 SIC. CPS data from 1971 to 1982 were based on the 1970 census classification system, which was developed from the 1967 SIC. Most of the industry categories were not affected by the change in classification.

The occupational classification system used in the 1980 census and in the CPS for 1983–91, evolved from the 1980 Standard Occupational Classification (SOC) system, first introduced in 1977. Occupational categories used in the 1980 census classification system are so radically different from the 1970 census system used in the CPS through 1982, that their implementation represented a break in historical data series.

Beginning in January 1992, the occupational and industrial classification systems used in the 1990 census were introduced into the CPS. (These systems were largely based on the 1980 SOC and the 1987 SIC systems, respectively.)

Beginning in 2003, the 2002 Census Bureau occupational and industrial classification systems were introduced into the CPS. These systems were derived from the 2000 SOC and the 2002 NAICS. The composition of detailed occupational and industrial classifications in the new classification systems was substantially changed from the previous systems in use, as was the structure for aggregating them into broad groups. Consequently, the use of the new classification systems created breaks in existing data series at all levels of aggregation. CPS data using the new classification systems are available beginning 2000. Additional information on the 2002 Census Bureau occupational and industrial classifications systems and details on the changes over time appear on the BLS Web site at <www.bls.gov/cps/documentation .htm#oi >. Establishments responding to the establishment survey are classified according to the 2007 NAICS. Previously they were classified according to the SIC manual. See text, Section 15, Business Enterprise, for information about the SIC manual and NAICS.

Productivity—BLS publishes data on productivity as measured by output per hour (labor productivity), output per combined unit of labor and capital input (multifactor productivity), and, for industry groups and industries, output per combined unit of capital, labor, energy, materials, and purchased service inputs. Labor productivity and related indexes are published for the business sector as a whole and its major subsectors: nonfarm business, manufacturing, and nonfinancial corporations, and for over 200 detailed industries. Productivity indexes that take into account capital, labor, energy, materials, and service inputs are published for 18 major manufacturing industry groups, 86 detailed manufacturing industries, utility services, and air and railroad transportation. The major sector data are published in the BLS quarterly news release *Productivity and Costs* and in the annual *Multifactor Productivity Trends* release. Industry productivity measures are updated and published annually in the news releases *Productivity and Costs by Industry* and *Multifactor Productivity Trends by Industry*. The latest data are available at the Labor Productivity and Costs Web site at <http://www.bls.gov/lpc/> and the Multifactor Productivity Web site at <http://www .bls.gov/mfp>. Detailed information on methods, limitations, and data sources appears in the BLS *Handbook of Methods*, BLS Bulletin 2490 (1997), Chapters 10 and 11 at <http://www.bls .gov/opub/hom /home.htm>.

Unions—As defined here, unions include traditional labor unions and employee associations similar to labor unions. Data on union membership status provided by BLS are for employed wage and salary workers and relate to their principal job. Earnings by union membership status are usual weekly earnings of full-time wage and salary workers. The information is collected through the Current Population Survey.

Work stoppages—Work stoppages include all strikes and lockouts known to BLS that last for at least 1 full day or shift and involve 1,000 or more workers. All stoppages, whether or not authorized by a union, legal or illegal, are counted. Excluded are work slowdowns and instances where employees report to work late or leave early to attend mass meetings or mass rallies.

Seasonal adjustment—Many economic statistics reflect a regularly recurring seasonal movement that can be estimated on the basis of past experience. By eliminating that part of the change which can be ascribed to usual seasonal variation (e.g., climate or school openings and closings), it is possible to observe the cyclical and other nonseasonal movements in the series. However, in evaluating deviations from the seasonal pattern—that is, changes in a seasonally adjusted series—it is important to note that seasonal adjustment is merely an approximation based on past experience. Seasonally adjusted estimates have a broader margin of possible error than the original data on which they are based, since they are subject not only to sampling and other errors, but also are affected by the uncertainties of the adjustment process itself. Consistent with BLS practices, annual estimates will be published only for not seasonally-adjusted data.

Statistical reliability—For discussion of statistical collection, estimation, sampling procedures, and measures of statistical reliability applicable to Census Bureau and BLS data, see Appendix III.

Table 584. Civilian Population—Employment Status: 1970 to 2009

[In thousands (137,085 represents 137,085,000), except as indicated. Annual averages of monthly figures. Civilian noninstitutionalized population 16 years old and over. Based on Current Population Survey; see text, Section 1 and Appendix III]

Year	Civilian noninsti-tutional population	Civilian labor force				Unemployed		Not in labor force	
		Total	Percent of population	Employed	Employ-ment/ population ratio [1]	Number	Percent of labor force	Number	Percent of population
1970	137,085	82,771	60.4	78,678	57.4	4,093	4.9	54,315	39.6
1980	167,745	106,940	63.8	99,303	59.2	7,637	7.1	60,806	36.2
1990 [2]	189,164	125,840	66.5	118,793	62.8	7,047	5.6	63,324	33.5
1992..........	192,805	128,105	66.4	118,492	61.5	9,613	7.5	64,700	33.6
1993..........	194,838	129,200	66.3	120,259	61.7	8,940	6.9	65,638	33.7
1994 [2]	196,814	131,056	66.6	123,060	62.5	7,996	6.1	65,758	33.4
1995	198,584	132,304	66.6	124,900	62.9	7,404	5.6	66,280	33.4
1996..........	200,591	133,943	66.8	126,708	63.2	7,236	5.4	66,647	33.2
1997 [2]	203,133	136,297	67.1	129,558	63.8	6,739	4.9	66,837	32.9
1998 [2]	205,220	137,673	67.1	131,463	64.1	6,210	4.5	67,547	32.9
1999 [2]	207,753	139,368	67.1	133,488	64.3	5,880	4.2	68,385	32.9
2000 [2]	212,577	142,583	67.1	136,891	64.4	5,692	4.0	69,994	32.9
2001..........	215,092	143,734	66.8	136,933	63.7	6,801	4.7	71,359	33.2
2002..........	217,570	144,863	66.6	136,485	62.7	8,378	5.8	72,707	33.4
2003 [2]	221,168	146,510	66.2	137,736	62.3	8,774	6.0	74,658	33.8
2004 [2]	223,357	147,401	66.0	139,252	62.3	8,149	5.5	75,956	34.0
2005 [2]	226,082	149,320	66.0	141,730	62.7	7,591	5.1	76,762	34.0
2006 [2]	228,815	151,428	66.2	144,427	63.1	7,001	4.6	77,387	33.8
2007 [2]	231,867	153,124	66.0	146,047	63.0	7,078	4.6	78,743	34.0
2008 [2]	233,788	154,287	66.0	145,362	62.2	8,924	5.8	79,501	34.0
2009 [2]	235,801	154,142	65.4	139,877	59.3	14,265	9.3	81,659	34.6

[1] Civilian employed as a percent of the civilian noninstitutional population. [2] Data not strictly comparable with data for earlier years. See text, this section, and February 1994, March 1996, February 1997–99, and February 2003–09 issues of Employment and Earnings.

Source: U.S. Bureau of Labor Statistics, "Employment and Earnings Online," January 2010, <http://www.bls.gov/opub/ee/home.htm> and <http://www.bls.gov/cps/home.htm>.

Table 585. Civilian Labor Force and Participation Rates With Projections: 1980 to 2018

[106.9 represents 106,900,000. Civilian noninstitutionalized population 16 years old and over. Annual averages of monthly figures. Rates are based on annual average civilian noninstitutional population of each specified group and represent proportion of each specified group in the civilian labor force. Based on Current Population Survey; see text, Section 1 and Appendix III]

Race, Hispanic origin, sex, and age	Civilian labor force (millions)						Participation rate (percent) [1]					
	1980	1990 [2]	2000 [2]	2005 [2]	2009 [2]	2018, proj.	1980	1990 [2]	2000 [2]	2005 [2]	2009 [2]	2018, proj.
Total [3]	106.9	125.8	142.6	149.3	154.1	166.9	63.8	66.5	67.1	66.0	65.4	64.5
White [4]	93.6	107.4	118.5	122.3	125.6	132.5	64.1	66.9	67.3	66.3	65.8	64.5
Male................	54.6	59.6	64.5	66.7	68.1	71.7	78.2	77.1	75.5	74.1	72.8	71.1
Female............	39.1	47.8	54.1	55.6	57.6	60.8	51.2	57.4	59.5	58.9	59.1	58.2
Black [4]	10.9	13.7	16.4	17.0	17.6	20.2	61.0	64.0	65.8	64.2	62.4	63.3
Male................	5.6	6.8	7.7	8.0	8.3	9.6	70.3	71.0	69.2	67.3	65.0	65.7
Female............	5.3	6.9	8.7	9.0	9.4	10.7	53.1	58.3	63.1	61.6	60.3	61.2
Asian [4,5]	(NA)	(NA)	6.3	6.5	7.2	9.3	(NA)	(NA)	67.2	66.1	66.0	65.0
Male................	(NA)	(NA)	3.4	3.5	3.9	4.9	(NA)	(NA)	76.1	74.8	74.6	73.7
Female............	(NA)	(NA)	2.9	3.0	3.3	4.4	(NA)	(NA)	59.2	58.2	58.2	57.4
Hispanic [6]...........	6.1	10.7	16.7	19.8	22.4	29.3	64.0	67.4	69.7	68.0	68.0	67.3
Male................	3.8	6.5	9.9	12.0	13.3	17.1	81.4	81.4	81.5	80.1	78.8	78.2
Female............	2.3	4.2	6.8	7.8	9.0	12.3	47.4	53.1	57.5	55.3	56.5	56.4
Male...............	61.5	69.0	76.3	80.0	82.1	88.7	77.4	76.4	74.8	73.3	72.0	70.6
16 to 19 years	5.0	4.1	4.3	3.6	3.2	2.9	60.5	55.7	52.8	43.2	37.3	33.2
20 to 24 years	8.6	7.9	7.5	8.1	7.8	8.1	85.9	84.4	82.6	79.1	76.2	75.2
25 to 34 years	17.0	19.9	17.8	17.8	18.2	20.2	95.2	94.1	93.4	91.7	90.3	90.6
35 to 44 years	11.8	17.5	20.1	19.5	18.5	19.1	95.5	94.3	92.7	92.1	91.7	92.0
45 to 54 years	9.9	11.1	16.3	18.1	19.0	18.0	91.2	90.7	88.6	87.7	87.4	87.1
55 to 64 years	7.2	6.6	7.8	10.0	11.7	14.5	72.1	67.8	67.3	69.3	70.2	71.2
65 years and over ...	1.9	2.0	2.5	3.0	3.6	5.9	19.0	16.3	17.7	19.8	21.9	26.7
Female.............	45.5	56.8	66.3	69.3	72.0	78.2	51.5	57.5	59.9	59.3	59.2	58.7
16 to 19 years	4.4	3.7	4.0	3.6	3.2	2.9	52.9	51.6	51.2	44.2	37.7	34.4
20 to 24 years	7.3	6.8	6.7	7.1	7.1	7.2	68.9	71.3	73.1	70.1	69.6	67.3
25 to 34 years	12.3	16.1	14.9	14.5	15.1	16.6	65.5	73.5	76.1	73.9	75.0	74.2
35 to 44 years	8.6	14.7	17.5	16.5	15.7	15.7	65.5	76.4	77.2	75.8	75.9	74.6
45 to 54 years	7.0	9.1	14.8	16.3	17.2	16.3	59.9	71.2	76.8	76.0	76.0	76.6
55 to 64 years	4.7	4.9	6.6	8.9	10.8	14.3	41.3	45.2	51.9	57.0	60.0	65.3
65 years and over ...	1.2	1.5	1.8	2.3	2.9	5.2	8.1	8.6	9.4	11.5	13.6	18.9

NA Not available. [1] Civilian labor force as a percent of the civilian noninstitutional population. [2] See footnote 2, Table 584.
[3] Includes other races, not shown separately. [4] The 2003 Current Population Survey (CPS) allowed respondents to choose more than one race. Beginning 2003, data represent persons who selected this race group only and exclude persons reporting more than one race. Prior to 2003 the CPS only allowed respondents to report one race group. See also comments on race in the text for Section 1. [5] Prior to 2005, includes Pacific Islanders. [6] Persons of Hispanic or Latino origin may be any race.

Source: U.S. Bureau of Labor Statistics,"Employment and Earnings Online," January 2010; "Monthly Labor Review," November 2009; and "Employment Projections Program," <http://www.bls.gov/emp/ep_data_labor_force.htm>.

Table 586. Civilian Population—Employment Status by Sex, Race, and Ethnicity: 1970 to 2009

[In thousands (64,304 represents 64,304,000), except as indicated. Annual averages of monthly figures. See Table 584 for U.S. totals and coverage]

Year, sex, race, and Hispanic origin	Civilian noninstitutionalized population	Civilian labor force				Unemployed		Not in labor force	
		Total	Percent of population	Employed	Employment/population ratio [1]	Number	Percent of labor force	Number	Percent of population
Male:									
1970	64,304	51,228	79.7	48,990	76.2	2,238	4.4	13,076	20.3
1980	79,398	61,453	77.4	57,186	72.0	4,267	6.9	17,945	22.6
1990 [2]	90,377	69,011	76.4	65,104	72.0	3,906	5.7	21,367	23.6
2000 [2]	101,964	76,280	74.8	73,305	71.9	2,975	3.9	25,684	25.2
2005 [2]	109,151	80,033	73.3	75,973	69.6	4,059	5.1	29,119	26.7
2007 [2]	112,173	82,136	73.2	78,254	69.8	3,882	4.7	30,036	26.8
2008 [2]	113,113	82,520	73.0	77,486	68.5	5,033	6.1	30,593	27.0
2009 [2]	114,136	82,123	72.0	73,670	64.5	8,453	10.3	32,013	28.0
Female:									
1970	72,782	31,543	43.3	29,688	40.8	1,855	5.9	41,239	56.7
1980	88,348	45,487	51.5	42,117	47.7	3,370	7.4	42,861	48.5
1990 [2]	98,787	56,829	57.5	53,689	54.3	3,140	5.5	41,957	42.5
2000 [2]	110,613	66,303	59.9	63,586	57.5	2,717	4.1	44,310	40.1
2005 [2]	116,931	69,288	59.3	65,757	56.2	3,531	5.1	47,643	40.7
2007 [2]	119,694	70,988	59.3	67,792	56.6	3,196	4.5	48,707	40.7
2008 [2]	120,675	71,767	59.5	67,876	56.2	3,891	5.4	48,908	40.5
2009 [2]	121,665	72,019	59.2	66,208	54.4	5,811	8.1	49,646	40.8
White: [3]									
1980	146,122	93,600	64.1	87,715	60.0	5,884	6.3	52,523	35.9
1990 [2]	160,625	107,447	66.9	102,261	63.7	5,186	4.8	53,178	33.1
2000 [2]	176,220	118,545	67.3	114,424	64.9	4,121	3.5	57,675	32.7
2005 [2]	184,446	122,299	66.3	116,949	63.4	5,350	4.4	62,148	33.7
2007 [2]	188,253	124,935	66.4	119,792	63.6	5,143	4.1	63,319	33.6
2008 [2]	189,540	125,635	66.3	119,126	62.8	6,509	5.2	63,905	33.7
2009 [2]	190,902	125,644	65.8	114,996	60.2	10,648	8.5	65,258	34.2
Black: [3]									
1980	17,824	10,865	61.0	9,313	52.2	1,553	14.3	6,959	39.0
1990 [2]	21,477	13,740	64.0	12,175	56.7	1,565	11.4	7,737	36.0
2000 [2]	24,902	16,397	65.8	15,156	60.9	1,241	7.6	8,505	34.2
2005 [2]	26,517	17,013	64.2	15,313	57.7	1,700	10.0	9,504	35.8
2007 [2]	27,485	17,496	63.7	16,051	58.4	1,445	8.3	9,989	36.3
2008 [2]	27,843	17,740	63.7	15,953	57.3	1,788	10.1	10,103	36.3
2009 [2]	28,241	17,632	62.4	15,025	53.2	2,606	14.8	10,609	37.6
Asian: [3, 4]									
2000	9,330	6,270	67.2	6,043	64.8	227	3.6	3,060	32.8
2005 [2]	9,842	6,503	66.1	6,244	63.4	259	4.0	3,339	33.9
2007 [2]	10,633	7,067	66.5	6,839	64.3	229	3.2	3,566	33.5
2008 [2]	10,751	7,202	67.0	6,917	64.3	285	4.0	3,549	33.0
2009 [2]	10,842	7,156	66.0	6,635	61.2	522	7.3	3,685	34.0
Hispanic: [5]									
1980	9,598	6,146	64.0	5,527	57.6	620	10.1	3,451	36.0
1990 [2]	15,904	10,720	67.4	9,845	61.9	876	8.2	5,184	32.6
2000 [2]	23,938	16,689	69.7	15,735	65.7	954	5.7	7,249	30.3
2005 [2]	29,133	19,824	68.0	18,632	64.0	1,191	6.0	9,310	32.0
2007 [2]	31,383	21,602	68.8	20,382	64.9	1,220	5.6	9,781	31.2
2008 [2]	32,141	22,024	68.5	20,346	63.3	1,678	7.6	10,116	31.5
2009 [2]	32,891	22,352	68.0	19,647	59.7	2,706	12.1	10,539	32.0
Mexican:									
1990 [2]	9,752	6,707	68.8	6,146	63.0	561	8.4	3,045	31.2
2000 [2]	15,333	10,783	70.3	10,144	66.2	639	5.9	4,550	29.7
2005 [2]	18,523	12,671	68.4	11,887	64.2	784	6.2	5,851	31.6
2007 [2]	19,770	13,672	69.2	12,908	65.3	764	5.6	6,098	30.8
2008 [2]	20,474	14,009	68.4	12,931	63.2	1,078	7.7	6,465	31.6
2009 [2]	20,923	14,210	67.9	12,478	59.6	1,732	12.2	6,713	32.1
Puerto Rican:									
1990 [2]	1,718	960	55.9	870	50.6	91	9.5	758	44.1
2000 [2]	2,193	1,411	64.3	1,318	60.1	92	6.6	783	35.7
2005 [2]	2,654	1,619	61.0	1,492	56.2	126	7.8	1,035	39.0
2007 [2]	2,711	1,684	62.1	1,551	57.2	133	7.9	1,027	37.9
2008 [2]	2,854	1,822	63.9	1,634	57.3	188	10.3	1,032	36.2
2009 [2]	2,962	1,850	62.4	1,594	53.8	256	13.8	1,113	37.6
Cuban:									
1990 [2]	918	603	65.7	559	60.9	44	7.2	315	34.3
2000 [2]	1,174	740	63.1	707	60.3	33	4.5	434	37.0
2005 [2]	1,259	755	60.0	730	58.0	25	3.3	503	40.0
2007 [2]	1,421	898	63.2	862	60.7	36	4.0	523	36.8
2008 [2]	1,422	897	63.1	841	59.1	57	6.3	525	36.9
2009 [2]	1,442	877	60.8	795	55.1	82	9.4	565	39.2

[1] Civilian employed as a percent of the civilian noninstitutional population. [2] See footnote 2, Table 584. [3] Beginning 2005, for persons in this race group only. See footnote 4, Table 585. [4] Prior to 2003, includes Pacific Islanders. [5] Persons of Hispanic or Latino ethnicity may be any race. Includes persons of other Hispanic or Latino ethnicity, not shown separately.

Source: U.S. Bureau of Labor Statistics, "Employment and Earnings Online," January 2010, <www.bls.gov/opub/ee/home.htm> and <http://www.bls.gov/cps/home.htm>.

Table 587. Foreign-Born and Native-Born Populations—Employment Status by Selected Characteristics: 2009

[235,801 represents 235,801,000. For civilian noninstitutional population 16 years old and over, except as indicated. The foreign born are persons who reside in the United States but who were born outside the country or one of its outlying areas to parents who were not U.S. citizens. The foreign born include legally admitted immigrants, refugees, temporary residents such as students and temporary workers and undocumented immigrants. Annual averages of monthly figures. Based on Current Population Survey; see text, Section 1 and Appendix III]

Characteristic	Civilian noninstitu-tionalized population (1,000)	Civilian labor force				
		Total (1,000)	Participation rate [1]	Employed (1,000)	Unemployed	
					Number (1,000)	Unemploy-ment rate
Total	**235,801**	**154,142**	**65.4**	**139,877**	**14,265**	**9.3**
Male	114,136	82,123	72.0	73,670	8,453	10.3
Female	121,665	72,019	59.2	66,208	5,811	8.1
FOREIGN BORN						
Total [2]	**35,216**	**23,926**	**67.9**	**21,608**	**2,317**	**9.7**
Male	17,628	14,190	80.5	12,765	1,426	10.0
Female	17,588	9,735	55.4	8,844	891	9.2
Age:						
16 to 24 years old	3,542	1,986	56.1	1,681	304	15.3
25 to 34 years old	7,637	5,907	77.3	5,330	577	9.8
35 to 44 years old	8,379	6,847	81.7	6,210	637	9.3
45 to 54 years old	6,819	5,588	81.9	5,096	491	8.8
55 to 64 years old	4,321	2,838	65.7	2,590	249	8.8
65 years old and over	4,517	760	16.8	701	59	7.8
Race and Hispanic ethnicity:						
White non-Hispanic	7,249	4,334	59.8	4,002	332	7.7
Black non-Hispanic	2,812	2,037	72.4	1,807	231	11.3
Asian non-Hispanic	7,876	5,332	67.7	4,967	365	6.8
Hispanic [3]	16,933	11,982	70.8	10,612	1,370	11.4
Educational attainment:						
Total, 25 years old and over	31,674	21,940	69.3	19,927	2,013	9.2
Less than a high school diploma	9,542	5,862	61.4	5,122	740	12.6
High school graduates, no college [4]	7,992	5,371	67.2	4,875	496	9.2
Some college or associate's degree	5,070	3,735	73.7	3,406	328	8.8
Bachelor's degree and higher [5]	9,070	6,972	76.9	6,524	448	6.4
NATIVE BORN						
Total [2]	**200,585**	**130,216**	**64.9**	**118,269**	**11,947**	**9.2**
Male	96,508	67,933	70.4	60,905	7,028	10.3
Female	104,077	62,284	59.8	57,364	4,920	7.9
Age:						
16 to 24 years old	34,025	19,375	56.9	15,920	3,455	17.8
25 to 34 years old	32,643	27,392	83.9	24,684	2,707	9.9
35 to 44 years old	32,540	27,391	84.2	25,307	2,085	7.6
45 to 54 years old	37,546	30,617	81.5	28,517	2,101	6.9
55 to 64 years old	30,349	19,667	64.8	18,429	1,238	6.3
65 years old and over	33,481	5,774	17.2	5,413	362	6.3
Race and Hispanic ethnicity:						
White non-Hispanic	153,104	100,525	65.7	92,681	7,844	7.8
Black non-Hispanic	24,466	14,971	61.2	12,700	2,271	15.2
Asian non-Hispanic	2,756	1,681	61.0	1,542	138	8.2
Hispanic [3]	15,958	10,370	65.0	9,034	1,336	12.9
Educational attainment:						
Total, 25 years and over	166,560	110,842	66.5	102,349	8,492	7.7
Less than a high school diploma	16,587	6,284	37.9	5,249	1,035	16.5
High school graduates, no college [4]	53,477	32,815	61.4	29,612	3,203	9.8
Some college or associate's degree	46,657	33,080	70.9	30,482	2,599	7.9
Bachelor's degree and higher [5]	49,839	38,662	77.6	37,007	1,655	4.3

[1] Civilian labor force as a percent of the civilian noninstitutionalized population. [2] Includes other races, not shown separately. [3] Persons of Hispanic origin may be any race. [4] Includes persons with a high school diploma or equivalent. [5] Includes persons with bachelor's, master's, professional, and doctoral degrees.

Source: U.S. Bureau of Labor Statistics, *Foreign-Born Workers: Labor Force Characteristics in 2009*, News Release, USDL-10-0319, March 2010. See also <http://www.bls.gov/news.release/forbrn.toc.htm>.

Table 588. Employment Status of Persons 18 Years Old and Over by Veteran Status, Period of Service, and Sex: 2009

[In thousands (226,857 represents 226,857,000). For civilian noninstitutional population 18 years old and over. Veterans are defined as men and women who have previously served on active duty in the U.S. Armed Forces and who were civilians at the time they were surveyed. See text, Section 10. Annual averages of monthly figures. Based on Current Population Survey; see text, Section 1 and Appendix III]

Veteran status, period of service, and sex	Civilian non-institutionalized population	Civilian labor force						Not in labor force
		Total	Percent of population	Employed		Unemployed		
				Total	Percent of population	Total	Percent of labor force	
Total, 18 years and over.............	**226,857**	**151,915**	**67.0**	**138,227**	**60.9**	**13,688**	**9.0**	**74,942**
Veterans	22,182	12,102	54.6	11,119	50.1	983	8.1	10,080
Gulf War era, total	4,855	4,177	86.0	3,817	78.6	360	8.6	678
Gulf War era I [1]	2,915	2,556	87.7	2,361	81.0	195	7.6	358
Gulf War era II [2]	1,940	1,620	83.5	1,455	75.0	165	10.2	319
WW II, Korean War, and Vietnam era [3] ...	11,390	4,356	38.2	4,029	35.4	327	7.5	7,034
Other service periods [4]	5,937	3,569	60.1	3,273	55.1	296	8.3	2,368
Nonveterans [5]	204,676	139,813	68.3	127,108	62.1	12,706	9.1	64,862
Male, 18 years and over	**109,588**	**81,020**	**73.9**	**72,884**	**66.5**	**8,136**	**10.0**	**28,568**
Veterans	20,425	10,968	53.7	10,076	49.3	892	8.1	9,457
Gulf War era, total	4,057	3,558	87.7	3,254	80.2	305	8.6	499
Gulf War era I [1]	2,464	2,195	89.1	2,026	82.2	169	7.7	269
Gulf War era II [2]	1,593	1,363	85.6	1,228	77.1	136	9.9	230
WW II, Korean War, and Vietnam era [3] ...	11,008	4,223	38.4	3,903	35.5	320	7.6	6,785
Other service periods [4]	5,360	3,187	59.5	2,919	54.5	267	8.4	2,173
Nonveterans [5]	89,163	70,052	78.6	62,807	70.4	7,245	10.3	19,111
Female, 18 years and over	**117,269**	**70,895**	**60.5**	**65,343**	**55.7**	**5,552**	**7.8**	**46,374**
Veterans	1,757	1,134	64.5	1,042	59.3	91	8.0	623
Gulf War era, total	797	618	77.5	563	70.6	55	9.0	179
Gulf War era I [1]	451	361	80.0	335	74.4	26	7.1	90
Gulf War era II [2]	347	257	74.1	228	65.6	30	11.5	89
WW II, Korean War, and Vietnam era [3] ...	382	133	34.8	126	32.9	7	5.4	249
Other service periods [4]	577	382	66.2	354	61.3	29	7.5	195
Nonveterans [5]	115,512	69,761	60.4	64,301	55.7	5,461	7.8	45,751

[1] Gulf War era I: August 1990–August 2001. [2] Gulf War era II: September 2001–present. [3] World War II: December 1941–December 1945. Korea War: July 1950–January 1955. Vietnam era: August 1964–April 1975. [4] Other service periods; all other time periods. [5] Nonveterans are men and women who never served on active duty in the U.S Armed Forces.

Source: Bureau of Labor Statistics, *Employment Situation of Veterans—2009*, New Release, USDL-10-0285, March 2010. See also <http://www.bls.gov/news.release/vet.nr0.htm>.

Table 589. Labor Force Status of Persons With and Without a Disability: 2009

[26,981 represents 26,981,000. For civilian noninstitutionalized population 16 years old and over, except as indicated. Persons with a disability are those who have a physical, mental, or emotional condition that causes serious difficulty with their daily activities. Annual averages of monthly figures. Based on Current Population Survey; see text, Section 1 and Appendix III]

Characteristic	Civilian non-institutional-ized popula-tion (1,000)	Civilian labor force					Not in the labor force
		Total (1,000)	Participation rate	Employed (1,000)	Unemployed		
					Number (1,000)	Unemploy-ment rate	
WITH DISABILITY							
Total	26,981	6,050	22.4	5,174	876	14.5	20,931
Male [1].................	12,184	3,221	26.4	2,735	486	15.1	8,963
Female [1]...............	14,797	2,829	19.1	2,439	390	13.8	11,968
Both Sexes 65 and over....	4,950	476	9.6	441	35	7.4	4,474
WITHOUT DISABILITY							
Total	208,820	148,092	70.9	134,703	13,389	9.0	60,728
Male [1].................	101,952	78,902	77.4	70,935	7,967	10.1	23,050
Female [1]...............	106,868	69,190	64.7	63,769	5,421	7.8	37,678
Both Sexes 65 and over....	11,464	3,121	27.2	2,916	205	6.6	8,343

[1] For ages 16 to 64.

Source: U.S. Bureau of Labor Statistics, Current Population Survey, "Data on the Employment Status of People With a Disability," <http://www.bls.gov/cps/cpsdisability.htm>, and unpublished data.

Table 590. Labor Force Status of Persons With a Work Disability by Age: 2008

[In percent, except as indicated (24,504 represents 24,504,000). As of March. For civilians 16 to 74 years who have a condition which prevents them from working or limits the amount of work they can do. Data from 2008 Annual Social and Economic Supplement of the Current Population Survey; see text, Section 1 and Appendix III]

Labor force status	Total	Age						
		16 to 24 years	25 to 34 years	35 to 44 years	45 to 54 years	55 to 64 years	65 to 69 years	70 to 74 years
Number (1,000)........	**24,504**	**1,562**	**2,176**	**3,522**	**5,710**	**7,242**	**2,406**	**1,885**
In labor force	21.4	29.4	32.4	30.9	24.6	17.2	9.9	6.0
Employed.............	18.8	22.3	27.7	27.2	21.6	15.8	9.1	5.3
Full-time.............	10.9	8.7	16.9	17.9	13.7	8.9	3.0	1.9
Not in labor force	78.6	70.6	67.6	69.1	75.4	82.8	90.1	94.0
Unemployment rate	12.3	24.2	14.5	11.9	12.1	8.1	7.6	10.2

Source: U.S. Census Bureau, "Disability Data from the March Current Population Survey," <http://www.census.gov/hhes/www/disability/disabcps.html>.

Table 591. Civilian Labor Force—Percent Distribution by Sex and Age: 1980 to 2009

[106,940 represents 106,940,000. Civilian noninstitutionalized population 16 years old and over. Annual averages of monthly figures. Based on Current Population Survey; see text, Section 1 and Appendix III]

Year and sex	Civilian labor force (1,000)	Percent distribution						
		16 to 19 years	20 to 24 years	25 to 34 years	35 to 44 years	45 to 54 years	55 to 64 years	65 years and over
Total: 1980	**106,940**	**8.8**	**14.9**	**27.3**	**19.1**	**15.8**	**11.2**	**2.9**
1990 [1]	125,840	6.2	11.7	28.6	25.5	16.1	9.2	2.7
2000 [1]	142,583	5.8	10.0	23.0	26.3	21.8	10.1	3.0
2005 [1]	149,320	4.8	10.1	21.7	24.1	23.0	12.7	3.5
2009 [1]	154,142	4.1	9.7	21.6	22.2	23.5	14.6	4.2
Male: 1980	61,453	8.1	14.0	27.6	19.3	16.1	11.8	3.1
1990 [1]	69,011	5.9	11.4	28.8	25.3	16.1	9.6	2.9
2000 [1]	76,280	5.6	9.9	23.4	26.3	21.3	10.2	3.3
2005 [1]	80,033	4.5	10.1	22.3	24.4	22.6	12.6	3.7
2009 [1]	82,123	3.9	9.5	22.2	22.5	23.1	14.3	4.4
Female: 1980	45,487	9.6	16.1	26.9	19.0	15.4	10.4	2.6
1990 [1]	56,829	6.5	12.0	28.3	25.8	16.1	8.7	2.6
2000 [1]	66,303	6.0	10.2	22.5	26.4	22.3	9.9	2.7
2005 [1]	69,288	5.2	10.2	20.9	23.9	23.6	12.9	3.3
2009 [1]	72,019	4.4	9.9	20.9	21.8	23.9	15.0	4.1

[1] See footnote 2, Table 584.

Source: U.S. Bureau of Labor Statistics, "Employment and Earnings Online," January 2010, <http://www.bls.gov/opub/ee/home.htm> and <http://www.bls.gov/cps/home.htm>.

Table 592. Civilian Labor Force and Participation Rates by Educational Attainment, Sex, Race, and Hispanic Origin: 2000 to 2009

[120,061 represents 120,061,000. Civilian noninstitutional population 25 years old and over. Annual averages of monthly figures. See Table 626 for unemployment data. Rates are based on annual average civilian noninstitutional population of each specified group and represent proportion of each specified group in the civilian labor force]

Year, sex, and race	Civilian labor force					Participation rate [1]				
		Percent distribution								
	Total (1,000)	Less than a high school diploma	High school graduate, no college	Less than a bachelor's degree	College graduate	Total	Less than a high school diploma	High school graduate, no college	Less than a bachelor's degree	College graduate
Total: [2]										
2000 [3]	120,061	10.4	31.4	27.7	30.5	67.3	43.5	64.4	73.9	79.4
2005 [3]	127,030	10.0	30.1	27.5	32.4	67.1	45.5	63.2	72.5	77.9
2008 [3]	132,255	9.2	28.9	27.8	34.1	67.4	46.6	62.6	71.8	77.8
2009 [3]	132,781	9.1	28.8	27.7	34.4	67.0	46.5	62.1	71.2	77.5
Male:										
2000 [3]	64,490	11.8	31.1	25.9	31.2	76.1	56.0	75.1	80.9	84.4
2005 [3]	68,389	11.7	30.9	25.4	32.1	75.4	58.6	73.6	79.3	82.9
2008 [3]	70,982	11.0	30.1	25.7	33.3	75.3	60.0	72.9	78.3	82.4
2009 [3]	71,058	10.9	30.2	25.7	33.3	74.6	59.2	72.1	77.5	81.8
Female:										
2000 [3]	55,572	8.8	31.8	29.7	29.7	59.4	32.3	55.5	68.0	74.0
2005 [3]	58,641	8.0	29.2	30.0	32.8	59.4	32.9	53.8	66.8	72.9
2008 [3]	61,273	7.1	27.6	30.2	35.1	60.0	33.3	53.1	66.4	73.4
2009 [3]	61,723	7.2	27.1	30.1	35.6	59.9	33.8	52.8	65.9	73.3
White: [4]										
2000 [3]	99,964	10.1	31.4	27.5	31.0	67.0	44.1	63.6	73.1	79.0
2005 [3]	104,240	9.8	29.9	27.6	32.7	66.9	46.4	62.5	72.0	77.5
2008 [3]	107,849	9.1	28.8	27.7	34.4	67.2	47.7	62.0	71.2	77.5
2009 [3]	108,354	9.1	31.2	27.6	34.6	66.9	48.0	61.7	70.8	77.0
Black: [4]										
2000 [3]	13,582	12.4	36.0	31.2	20.5	68.2	39.3	69.9	79.3	84.4
2005 [3]	14,252	11.2	36.4	30.2	22.2	67.2	39.8	67.9	75.6	82.0
2008 [3]	14,973	9.6	34.7	31.8	23.8	67.3	39.8	65.7	75.2	81.5
2009 [3]	14,941	9.3	34.0	32.4	24.3	66.2	38.2	64.6	73.4	80.9
Asian: [4, 5]										
2000 [3]	5,402	9.1	20.7	20.2	50.1	70.9	46.0	65.6	76.4	79.1
2005 [3]	5,805	8.0	17.7	17.3	57.0	69.4	45.3	61.8	71.6	77.5
2008 [3]	6,518	7.2	18.3	16.9	57.6	70.5	45.6	64.4	72.7	77.4
2009 [3]	6,540	7.5	17.0	16.9	58.7	69.9	44.6	60.8	71.8	78.4
Hispanic: [6]										
2000 [3]	12,975	36.7	29.3	20.6	13.4	71.5	61.9	75.0	80.8	83.5
2005 [3]	16,135	35.5	29.4	20.9	14.2	70.8	61.4	74.3	78.8	81.7
2008 [3]	18,235	32.4	30.6	21.5	15.5	71.6	61.9	74.1	78.6	83.0
2009 [3]	18,643	32.5	30.3	21.6	15.5	71.3	62.1	73.1	78.9	81.7

[1] See footnote 1, Table 585. [2] Includes other races, not shown separately. [3] See footnote 2, Table 584. [4] Beginning 2005, for persons in this race group only. See footnote 4, Table 585. [5] 2000 data include Pacific Islanders. [6] Persons of Hispanic or Latino origin may be any race.

Source: U.S. Bureau of Labor Statistics, "Employment and Earnings Online," January 2010, <http://www.bls.gov/opub/ee/home.htm> and <http://www.bls.gov/cps/home.htm>.

Table 593. Characteristics of the Civilian Labor Force by State: 2009

[In thousands (154,142 represents 154,142,000), except ratio and rate. Civilian noninstitutionalized population 16 years old and over. Annual averages of monthly figures. Data for states may not sum to national totals due to rounding]

State	Total		Employed		Employ-ment/population ratio [1]	Unemployed					Participation rate [3]	
						Total		Rate [2]				
	Number	Female	Total	Female		Number	Female	Total	Male	Female	Male	Female
United States	**154,142**	**72,019**	**139,877**	**66,208**	**59.3**	**14,265**	**5,811**	**9.3**	**10.3**	**8.1**	**72.0**	**59.2**
Alabama	2,151	1,014	1,911	900	52.7	240	114	11.2	11.1	11.2	66.2	53.1
Alaska	362	167	333	156	64.7	29	11	7.9	9.0	6.7	74.9	65.6
Arizona	3,152	1,414	2,836	1,302	57.3	317	112	10.0	11.8	7.9	71.3	56.2
Arkansas	1,373	642	1,266	595	57.4	107	47	7.8	8.2	7.3	69.1	55.9
California	18,250	8,218	16,190	7,396	57.8	2,060	823	11.3	12.3	10.0	72.7	57.7
Colorado	2,727	1,225	2,526	1,147	65.8	201	78	7.4	8.2	6.4	78.6	63.5
Connecticut	1,890	914	1,737	844	63.2	153	70	8.1	8.5	7.6	74.0	63.9
Delaware	438	213	400	198	58.3	37	15	8.5	10.1	6.9	69.0	59.0
District of Columbia	337	169	305	154	62.6	32	16	9.5	9.8	9.2	74.7	64.4
Florida	9,093	4,303	8,152	3,911	55.8	942	392	10.4	11.5	9.1	68.2	56.8
Georgia	4,798	2,219	4,329	2,016	59.3	469	203	9.8	10.3	9.2	74.0	58.2
Hawaii	632	297	585	278	59.0	47	19	7.4	8.4	6.3	69.4	58.3
Idaho	750	335	686	313	59.8	64	22	8.5	10.0	6.7	73.0	57.9
Illinois	6,606	3,083	5,945	2,814	60.1	661	269	10.0	11.1	8.7	73.3	60.6
Indiana	3,199	1,511	2,879	1,391	58.6	320	121	10.0	11.8	8.0	70.7	59.8
Iowa	1,688	810	1,581	766	67.8	107	44	6.3	7.2	5.4	77.0	68.0
Kansas	1,529	718	1,425	674	66.9	103	43	6.8	7.4	6.0	78.0	65.9
Kentucky	2,064	967	1,846	871	55.4	218	96	10.6	11.1	10.0	68.7	55.8
Louisiana	2,076	983	1,929	922	56.8	147	60	7.1	7.9	6.1	68.2	54.7
Maine	695	335	638	312	59.9	57	23	8.1	9.3	6.9	70.2	60.6
Maryland	3,036	1,489	2,821	1,397	64.0	215	91	7.1	8.0	6.1	74.3	64.0
Massachusetts	3,485	1,690	3,193	1,571	61.0	293	119	8.4	9.7	7.0	71.6	61.9
Michigan	4,908	2,306	4,253	2,063	54.7	655	243	13.3	15.8	10.6	69.1	57.4
Minnesota	2,933	1,395	2,703	1,308	66.2	230	87	7.8	9.3	6.2	76.4	67.4
Mississippi	1,266	609	1,149	564	52.2	117	44	9.2	11.0	7.3	63.6	52.1
Missouri	3,067	1,481	2,779	1,359	60.3	288	122	9.4	10.5	8.2	71.7	61.7
Montana	497	235	462	222	60.3	35	13	7.1	8.5	5.5	69.0	60.9
Nebraska	982	469	937	451	68.8	45	19	4.6	5.1	4.0	76.7	67.6
Nevada	1,352	598	1,199	544	59.9	153	55	11.3	13.0	9.2	74.7	60.4
New Hampshire	743	353	695	334	65.8	48	20	6.4	7.2	5.6	75.3	65.5
New Jersey	4,554	2,134	4,138	1,950	61.0	416	184	9.1	9.6	8.6	74.0	60.8
New Mexico	938	443	866	413	56.9	72	30	7.6	8.4	6.8	67.4	56.2
New York	9,722	4,607	8,913	4,256	57.9	809	351	8.3	9.0	7.6	69.7	57.3
North Carolina	4,574	2,162	4,096	1,977	57.5	478	185	10.4	12.1	8.6	71.1	57.9
North Dakota	364	171	349	165	69.4	15	6	4.2	4.7	3.7	77.3	67.7
Ohio	5,920	2,851	5,313	2,605	59.2	608	247	10.3	11.8	8.6	71.3	61.1
Oklahoma	1,779	832	1,668	789	60.1	111	43	6.2	7.2	5.1	70.7	57.8
Oregon	1,966	919	1,741	833	57.9	225	87	11.5	13.3	9.4	71.0	59.9
Pennsylvania	6,397	3,036	5,893	2,827	59.2	503	209	7.9	8.8	6.9	70.5	58.6
Rhode Island	564	274	501	246	59.8	63	28	11.2	12.1	10.3	72.6	62.6
South Carolina	2,133	1,042	1,881	937	53.8	251	106	11.8	13.4	10.1	66.1	56.5
South Dakota	447	214	425	205	68.9	22	9	5.0	5.7	4.2	76.7	68.3
Tennessee	3,030	1,428	2,704	1,299	55.5	326	128	10.8	12.3	9.0	68.8	56.2
Texas	11,904	5,271	11,007	4,887	60.8	897	384	7.5	7.7	7.3	74.9	57.0
Utah	1,382	595	1,280	559	64.9	101	36	7.3	8.3	6.0	79.7	60.4
Vermont	359	178	336	168	66.4	23	10	6.5	7.3	5.7	73.4	68.8
Virginia	4,130	1,989	3,856	1,870	64.1	274	119	6.6	7.3	6.0	74.6	63.3
Washington	3,532	1,650	3,216	1,528	62.2	317	122	9.0	10.3	7.4	74.0	62.9
West Virginia	819	369	754	348	51.8	66	21	8.0	9.8	5.8	63.9	49.2
Wisconsin	3,099	1,494	2,837	1,392	64.3	262	102	8.4	10.0	6.8	74.0	66.5
Wyoming	299	133	279	127	66.9	19	7	6.5	7.8	4.9	78.9	64.2

[1] Civilian employment as a percent of civilian noninstitutionalized population. [2] Percent unemployed of the civilian labor force. [3] Percent of civilian noninstitutionalized population of each specified group in the civilian labor force.

Source: U.S. Bureau of Labor Statistics, Local Area Unemployment Statistics, "Geographic Profile of Employment and Unemployment, 2009 Annual Averages," <http://www.bls.gov/gps/>.

U.S. Census Bureau, Statistical Abstract of the United States: 2011

Table 594. Civilian Labor Force Status by Selected Metropolitan Area: 2009

[154,142 represents 154,412,000. Civilian noninstitutional population 16 years old and over. Annual averages of monthly figures. Data are derived from the Local Area Unemployment Statistics program. For metro areas with a Census 2000 population of one million or more. For definitions of metropolitan areas, see Appendix II. Metropolitan areas defined as of December 2009]

Metropolitan areas ranked by population, 2000	Civilian labor force (1,000)	Unemployment rate [1]	Metropolitan areas ranked by population, 2000	Civilian labor force (1,000)	Unemployment rate [1]
U.S. total, ...	154,142	9.3	Kansas City, MO-KS.	1,048	8.6
New York-Northern New Jersey-Long Island, NY-NJ-PA.	9,507	8.8	Sacramento—Arden-Arcade—Roseville, CA.	1,058	11.2
Los Angeles-Long Beach-Santa Ana, CA	6,490	10.9	San Jose-Sunnyvale-Santa Clara, CA	903	11.1
Chicago-Joliet-Naperville, IL-IN-WI	4,863	10.0	San Antonio-New Braunfels, TX	965	6.7
Philadelphia-Camden-Wilmington, PA-NJ-DE-MD	2,999	8.3	Orlando-Kissimmee-Sanford, FL	1,119	10.5
Dallas-Fort Worth-Arlington, TX.	3,162	7.8	Columbus, OH	973	8.4
Miami-Fort Lauderdale-Pompano Beach, FL. . . .	2,851	10.2	Virginia Beach-Norfolk-Newport News, VA-NC.	829	6.8
Washington-Arlington-Alexandria, DC-VA-MD-WV	3,055	6.0	Indianapolis-Carmel, IN	894	8.4
Houston-Sugar Land-Baytown, TX	2,850	7.6	Milwaukee-Waukesha-West Allis, WI	797	8.7
Boston-Cambridge-Quincy, MA-NH NECTA [2]	2,531	7.8	Las Vegas-Paradise, NV.	982	12.0
Detroit-Warren-Livonia, MI.	2,103	15.1	Charlotte-Gastonia-Rock Hill, NC-SC.	851	11.7
Atlanta-Sandy Springs-Marietta, GA	2,700	9.6	New Orleans-Metairie-Kenner, LA	534	6.7
San Francisco-Oakland-Fremont, CA	2,255	9.7	Nashville-Davidson—Murfreesboro—Franklin, TN	796	9.3
Riverside-San Bernardino-Ontario, CA	1,778	13.3	Providence-Fall River-Warwick, RI-MA NECTA [2]	704	11.4
Phoenix-Mesa-Glendale, AZ.	2,103	8.5	Austin-Round Rock-San Marcos, TX	886	6.9
Seattle-Tacoma-Bellevue, WA	1,890	8.7	Memphis, TN-MS-AR	612	10.0
Minneapolis-St. Paul-Bloomington, MN-WI	1,856	7.8	Buffalo-Niagara Falls, NY	587	8.4
San Diego-Carlsbad-San Marcos, CA.	1,557	9.7	Louisville-Jefferson County, KY-IN	637	10.1
St. Louis, MO-IL.	1,441	9.9	Jacksonville, FL	686	10.0
Baltimore-Towson, MD	1,398	7.4	Richmond, VA.	658	7.5
Pittsburgh, PA	1,227	7.4	Oklahoma City, OK	574	5.9
Tampa-St. Petersburg-Clearwater, FL	1,309	11.0	Hartford-West Hartford-East Hartford, CT NECTA [2]	599	8.3
Denver-Aurora-Broomfield, CO	1,381	7.9	Birmingham-Hoover, AL	514	9.4
Cleveland-Elyria-Mentor, OH.	1,079	9.1	Rochester, NY	534	7.9
Cincinnati-Middletown, OH-KY-IN	1,133	9.3			
Portland-Vancouver-Hillsboro, OR-WA	1,176	10.6			

[1] Percent unemployed of the civilian labor force. [2] New England City and Town Areas, See appendix II.

Source: U.S. Bureau of Labor Statistics, Local Area Unemployment Statistics program (LAUS), <http://www.bls.gov/lau/data.htm\>.

Table 595. School Enrollment and Labor Force Status: 2009

[In thousands (37,616 represents 37,569,000), except percent. As of October. Based on Current Population Survey; see text, Section 1 and Appendix III]

Characteristic	Population	Civilian labor force	Employed	Unemployed Total	Unemployed Rate [1]	Not in labor force
Total, 16 to 24 years [2]	37,616	20,764	16,945	3,820	18.4	16,851
Enrolled in school [2]	21,854	8,411	7,098	1,314	15.6	13,443
Enrolled in high school	9,612	2,125	1,576	548	25.8	7,488
Male.	4,965	1,055	760	295	28.0	3,910
Female.	4,647	1,069	817	253	23.6	3,578
Enrolled in college	12,242	6,287	5,521	766	12.2	5,955
Enrolled in 2 year college	3,512	2,129	1,772	358	16.8	1,383
Enrolled in 4 year college	8,729	4,158	3,750	408	9.8	4,571
Race/ethnicity:						
White [3]	16,685	6,902	5,928	974	14.1	9,784
Enrolled in high school	7,225	1,757	1,359	398	22.6	5,468
Enrolled in college	9,461	5,145	4,569	576	11.2	4,316
Black or African American [3]	3,237	946	703	243	25.7	2,291
Enrolled in high school	1,608	266	141	125	46.9	1,342
Enrolled in college.	1,630	680	562	119	17.4	949
Asian [3]	1,112	284	250	34	12.0	827
Enrolled in high school	335	30	21	9	(5)	305
Enrolled in college	777	254	229	25	9.9	522
Hispanic [4]	3,306	1,106	877	229	20.7	2,200
Enrolled in high school	1,805	314	187	127	40.4	1,491
Enrolled in college	1,501	792	690	102	12.9	709
Not enrolled [2]	15,762	12,353	9,847	2,506	20.3	3,409
White [3]	12,330	9,913	8,140	1,773	17.9	2,417
Black [3]	2,438	1,679	1,126	553	33.0	759
Asian [3]	348	280	224	56	20.0	68
Hispanic [4]	3,503	2,631	2,023	608	23.1	872

[1] Percent unemployed of civilian labor force in each category. [2] Includes other races, not shown separately.
[3] Data for persons in this race group only. See footnote 4, Table 585. [4] Persons of Hispanic or Latino origin may be any race.
[5] Data not shown where base is less than 75,000.

Source: U.S. Bureau of Labor Statistics, College Enrollment and Work Activity of High School Graduates, News Release, USDL 10-0533, April 2010. See also <http://www.bls.gov/news.release/hsgec.toc.htm>.

Table 596. Labor Force Participation Rates by Marital Status, Sex, and Age: 1970 to 2009

[For the civilian noninstitutional population 16 years old and over. Annual averages of monthly figures. See Table 585 for definition of participation rate. Based on Current Population Survey; see text, Section 1 and Appendix III]

Marital status and year	Male participation rate							Female participation rate						
	Total	16–19 years	20–24 years	25–34 years	35–44 years	45–64 years	65 years and over	Total	16–19 years	20–24 years	25–34 years	35–44 years	45–64 years	65 years and over
Single:														
1970......	65.5	54.6	73.8	87.9	86.2	75.7	25.2	56.8	44.7	73.0	81.4	78.6	73.0	19.7
1980......	72.6	59.9	81.3	89.2	82.2	66.9	16.8	64.4	53.6	75.2	83.3	76.9	65.6	13.9
1990 [1]	74.8	55.1	81.6	89.9	84.5	67.3	15.7	66.7	51.7	74.5	80.9	80.8	66.2	12.1
2000 [1]	73.6	52.5	80.5	89.4	82.9	69.7	17.3	68.9	51.1	76.1	83.9	80.9	69.9	10.8
2002......	71.7	47.2	78.7	88.7	83.1	69.6	16.9	67.4	47.3	74.5	83.3	79.9	69.6	14.3
2003 [1]	70.4	44.0	77.9	87.7	82.9	67.6	19.4	66.2	44.8	72.9	82.2	79.8	69.9	15.2
2004 [1]	70.2	43.6	77.7	87.9	82.7	67.8	20.3	65.9	43.8	73.1	81.8	80.5	70.9	14.7
2005 [1]	70.1	42.9	77.0	87.9	82.9	68.6	18.8	66.0	44.2	72.6	81.4	80.7	70.9	15.5
2006 [1]	70.7	43.4	77.8	87.7	83.5	69.9	19.3	65.7	43.7	71.8	81.4	79.8	70.5	15.0
2007 [1]	70.1	40.8	76.9	88.5	84.0	70.3	22.6	65.3	41.4	72.6	82.1	78.0	70.4	18.4
2008 [1]	69.9	39.8	77.1	87.9	84.3	69.5	24.7	65.3	40.3	71.9	82.6	79.6	70.4	20.5
2009 [1]	68.3	37.1	74.6	86.5	83.7	68.5	26.1	64.2	37.5	71.4	81.6	79.5	69.3	19.7
Married: [2]														
1970......	86.1	92.3	94.7	98.0	98.1	91.2	29.9	40.5	37.8	47.9	38.8	46.8	44.0	7.3
1980......	80.9	91.3	96.9	97.5	97.2	84.3	20.5	49.8	49.3	61.4	58.8	61.8	46.9	7.3
1990 [1]	78.6	92.1	95.6	96.9	96.7	82.6	17.5	58.4	49.5	66.1	69.6	74.0	56.5	8.5
2000 [1]	77.3	79.5	94.1	96.7	95.8	83.0	19.2	61.1	53.2	63.8	70.3	74.8	65.4	10.1
2002......	77.4	81.1	93.3	95.7	95.1	83.8	19.4	61.0	49.6	63.4	69.3	73.8	66.5	10.7
2003 [1]	77.3	76.6	93.2	95.3	95.1	83.5	19.9	61.0	46.7	62.6	68.5	73.3	67.4	11.3
2004 [1]	77.1	77.4	92.4	95.6	95.1	83.1	20.4	60.5	41.1	60.9	67.6	72.7	67.0	11.6
2005 [1]	77.2	71.4	93.4	95.3	95.2	83.6	21.4	60.7	44.1	61.1	68.4	73.0	67.0	12.5
2006 [1]	77.1	79.2	93.3	95.5	95.2	83.6	21.8	61.0	39.6	59.8	69.0	73.3	67.8	12.4
2007 [1]	76.9	86.9	92.9	95.7	95.3	83.6	21.8	61.0	43.3	61.7	68.6	73.1	67.7	13.6
2008 [1]	76.8	83.4	92.0	95.3	95.2	84.0	22.8	61.4	38.0	62.3	69.5	73.8	68.3	14.1
2009 [1]	76.3	75.8	91.2	94.7	94.8	83.8	23.3	61.4	44.7	61.8	69.4	73.7	68.5	14.9
Other: [3]														
1970......	60.7	(B)	90.4	93.7	91.1	78.5	19.3	40.3	48.6	60.3	64.6	68.8	61.9	10.0
1980......	67.5	(B)	92.6	94.1	91.9	73.3	13.7	43.6	50.0	68.4	76.5	77.1	60.2	8.2
1990 [1]	68.9	(B)	93.1	93.0	90.7	74.9	12.0	47.2	53.9	65.4	77.0	82.1	65.0	8.4
2000 [1]	66.8	60.5	88.1	93.2	89.9	73.9	12.9	49.0	46.0	74.0	83.1	82.9	69.8	8.7
2002......	65.5	57.5	87.4	91.2	89.6	74.1	13.2	49.2	46.2	74.7	80.7	82.7	69.7	8.9
2003 [1]	65.0	45.6	88.0	91.4	89.3	72.4	14.3	49.6	44.1	71.4	79.1	81.9	70.7	9.8
2004 [1]	64.9	53.1	87.2	90.6	88.6	72.8	14.3	49.6	48.7	70.0	79.4	81.7	69.8	10.4
2005 [1]	64.9	54.9	86.4	90.4	89.4	72.7	15.1	49.4	46.8	67.4	78.1	80.9	69.4	10.5
2006 [1]	65.6	47.8	86.0	91.5	88.9	73.8	16.3	49.6	45.3	71.5	78.2	80.9	69.3	10.9
2007 [1]	65.6	43.4	82.5	92.1	89.4	73.7	16.1	49.5	44.6	63.8	78.4	81.4	69.3	11.4
2008 [1]	65.0	43.2	84.9	90.7	89.4	73.2	16.8	49.2	39.7	64.9	77.4	81.4	69.1	12.1
2009 [1]	63.7	42.6	78.6	88.5	88.5	72.8	17.0	49.3	39.0	68.3	78.2	80.5	69.7	12.1

B Percentage not shown where base is less than 35,000. [1] See footnote 2, Table 584. [2] Spouse present. [3] Widowed, divorced, and married (spouse absent).

Source: U.S. Bureau of Labor Statistics, Bulletin 2217 and Basic Tabulations, Table 12.

Table 597. Marital Status of Women in the Civilian Labor Force: 1960 to 2009

[23,240 represents 23,240,000. For civilian noninstitutional population 16 years and over. Annual averages of monthly figures. Based on the Current Population Survey; see text, Section 1 and Appendix III]

Year	Female civilian labor force (1,000)				Female participation rate [3]			
	Total	Never married	Married [1]	Other [2]	Total	Never married	Married [1]	Other [2]
1960.......	23,240	5,410	12,893	4,937	37.7	58.6	31.9	41.6
1970.......	31,543	7,265	18,475	5,804	43.3	56.8	40.5	40.3
1980.......	45,487	11,865	24,980	8,643	51.5	64.4	49.8	43.6
1990 [4]	56,829	14,612	30,901	11,315	57.5	66.7	58.4	47.2
2000 [4]	66,303	17,849	35,146	13,308	59.9	68.9	61.1	49.0
2001.......	66,848	18,021	35,236	13,592	59.8	68.1	61.2	49.0
2002.......	67,363	18,203	35,477	13,683	59.6	67.4	61.0	49.2
2003 [4]	68,272	18,397	36,046	13,828	59.5	66.2	61.0	49.6
2004 [4]	68,421	18,616	35,845	13,961	59.2	65.9	60.5	49.6
2005 [4]	69,288	19,183	35,941	14,163	59.3	66.0	60.7	49.4
2006 [4]	70,173	19,474	36,314	14,385	59.4	65.7	61.0	49.6
2007 [4]	70,988	19,745	36,881	14,362	59.3	65.3	61.0	49.5
2008 [4]	71,767	20,231	37,194	14,342	59.5	65.3	61.4	49.2
2009 [4]	72,019	20,224	37,264	14,531	59.2	64.2	61.4	49.3

[1] Husband present. [2] Widowed, divorced, or separated. [3] See footnote 3, Table 593 for definition of participation rate. [4] See footnote 2, Table 584.

Source: U.S. Bureau of Labor Statistics, *Women in the Labor Force: A Databook*, Report 1018, September 2009, and unpublished Basic Tabulations, Table 12. See also <http://www.bls.gov/cps/wlf-databook2009.htm>.

Table 598. Employment Status of Women by Marital Status and Presence and Age of Children: 1970 to 2009

[As of March (7.0 represents 7,000,000). Annual Social and Economic Supplement (ASEC) includes Civilian noninstitutionalized population, 16 years old and over. Based on the Current Population Survey; see text, Section 1 and Appendix III]

Item	Total			With any children								
				Total			Children 6 to 17 years only			Children under 6 years		
	Single	Mar-ried[1]	Other[2]	Single	Mar-ried[1]	Other[2]	Single	Mar-ried[1]	Other[2]	Single	Mar-ried[1]	Other[2]
IN LABOR FORCE (mil.)												
1970.........	7.0	18.4	5.9	(NA)	10.2	1.9	(NA)	6.3	1.3	(NA)	3.9	0.6
1980.........	11.2	24.9	8.8	0.6	13.7	3.6	0.2	8.4	2.6	0.3	5.2	1.0
1990.........	14.0	31.0	11.2	1.5	16.5	4.2	0.6	9.3	3.0	0.9	7.2	1.2
2000.........	17.8	35.0	13.2	3.1	18.2	4.5	1.2	10.8	3.4	1.8	7.3	1.1
2005[3].........	18.6	35.7	14.3	3.4	18.0	4.6	1.4	10.8	3.4	1.9	7.2	1.2
2008[3].........	19.9	37.1	14.6	3.5	17.9	4.5	1.5	10.6	3.3	2.0	7.3	1.2
2009[3].........	19.8	37.5	14.5	3.7	18.0	4.5	1.5	10.8	3.3	2.1	7.2	1.1
PARTICIPATION RATE[4]												
1970.........	53.0	40.8	39.1	(NA)	39.7	60.7	(NA)	49.2	66.9	(NA)	30.3	52.2
1980.........	61.5	50.1	44.0	52.0	54.1	69.4	67.6	61.7	74.6	44.1	45.1	60.3
1990.........	66.4	58.2	46.8	55.2	66.3	74.2	69.7	73.6	79.7	48.7	58.9	63.6
2000.........	68.6	62.0	50.2	73.9	70.6	82.7	79.7	77.2	84.9	70.5	62.8	76.6
2005[3].........	65.1	60.2	49.8	72.9	68.1	79.8	79.7	75.0	82.2	68.5	59.8	73.5
2008[3].........	64.6	61.7	49.5	71.0	69.4	79.4	78.7	76.2	81.5	66.0	61.6	73.9
2009[3].........	63.7	61.7	49.0	72.0	69.8	79.2	78.9	76.7	83.0	67.8	61.6	69.8
EMPLOYMENT (mil.)												
1970.........	6.5	17.5	5.6	(NA)	9.6	1.8	(NA)	6.0	1.2	(NA)	3.6	0.6
1980.........	10.1	23.6	8.2	0.4	12.8	3.3	0.2	8.1	2.4	0.2	4.8	0.9
1990.........	12.9	29.9	10.5	1.2	15.8	3.8	0.5	8.9	2.7	0.7	6.9	1.1
2000.........	16.4	34.0	12.7	2.7	17.6	4.3	1.1	10.6	3.2	1.6	7.1	1.1
2005[3].........	17.0	34.6	13.5	2.9	17.4	4.3	1.3	10.4	3.2	1.6	7.0	1.1
2008[3].........	18.4	35.9	13.8	3.1	17.3	4.3	1.4	10.3	3.2	1.7	7.0	1.1
2009[3].........	17.7	35.5	13.2	3.1	17.0	4.0	1.1	10.2	3.0	1.8	6.8	1.0
UNEMPLOYMENT RATE[5]												
1970.........	7.1	4.8	4.8	(NA)	6.0	7.2	(NA)	4.8	5.0	(NA)	7.9	9.8
1980.........	10.3	5.3	6.4	23.2	5.9	9.2	15.6	4.4	7.9	29.2	8.3	12.8
1990.........	8.2	3.5	5.7	18.4	4.2	8.5	14.5	3.8	7.7	20.8	4.8	10.2
2000.........	7.3	2.7	4.3	11.0	2.9	5.1	8.7	2.6	4.8	12.6	3.5	5.9
2005[3].........	8.9	3.0	5.3	15.1	3.1	6.9	10.9	2.9	5.8	18.2	3.4	9.8
2008[3].........	7.6	3.1	5.4	11.5	3.4	6.0	8.3	3.1	5.3	14.0	3.9	8.0
2009[3].........	10.5	5.3	8.9	15.4	5.4	11.2	11.9	5.1	9.9	17.9	5.9	15.1

NA Not available. [1] Husband present. [2] Widowed, divorced, or separated (including married, spouse absent) [3] See footnote 2, Table 584. [4] Percent of women in each specific category in the labor force. [5] Unemployed as a percent of civilian labor force in specified group.

Source: U.S. Bureau of Labor Statistics, Bulletin 2307 and unpublished data.

Table 599. Labor Force Participation Rates for Wives, Husband Present, by Age of Own Youngest Child: 1990 to 2008

[As of March. Annual Social and Economic Supplement (ASEC) includes Civilian noninstitutionalized population, 16 years old and over, and military personnel who live in households with at least one other civilian adult. Armed Forces includes only those Armed Forces members living on or off post with their families; all other members of the Armed Forces are excluded. Data refer to persons in primary families. Based on Current Population Survey; see text, Section 1 and Appendix III]

Presence and age of child	1990	2000[1]	2005[1]	2007	2008[1]				
					Total	White[2]	Black[2]	Asian[2,3]	Hispanic[4]
Wives, total..............	**58.3**	**62.2**	**60.4**	**61.8**	**61.9**	**61.4**	**67.5**	**63.0**	**55.0**
No children under 18 years	51.1	54.8	54.1	55.7	56.1	55.6	59.2	58.9	52.2
With children under 18 years...	66.5	70.9	68.3	69.4	69.7	69.2	77.3	66.6	56.6
Under 6 years, total.........	59.1	63.1	60.3	61.6	62.0	61.4	70.2	59.3	48.0
Under 3 years	55.9	59.4	57.3	58.8	59.1	59.0	61.9	57.9	44.6
1 year or under	53.9	58.4	55.8	57.8	58.9	58.9	61.2	57.8	43.7
2 years.................	60.9	61.9	60.8	61.4	59.5	59.1	63.9	58.3	46.4
3 to 5 years	64.1	68.6	64.8	65.6	66.3	65.1	81.0	61.0	52.6
3 years.................	63.0	66.0	62.7	64.4	65.3	63.5	84.6	63.9	52.8
4 years.................	65.0	69.6	64.9	63.4	66.5	65.2	82.1	59.9	50.2
5 years.................	64.4	70.7	67.5	69.4	67.2	66.8	75.9	58.5	55.5
6 to 13 years	73.1	76.0	73.2	74.5	74.8	74.4	82.5	69.9	65.9
14 to 17 years	75.0	80.8	79.6	79.8	79.2	78.9	82.2	79.5	66.1

[1] See footnote 2, Table 584. [2] Beginning 2003, for persons in this race group only. See footnote 4, Table 585. [3] Excludes Pacific Islanders. [4] Persons of Hispanic or Latino origin may be any race.

Source: U.S. Bureau of Labor Statistics, Bulletin 2307 and unpublished data.

Table 600. Married-Couple Households by Labor Force Status of Spouse: 1990 to 2009

[52,317 represents 52,317,000. Data represent married-couple households. Based on the Current Population Survey; see text Section 1 and Appendix III]

Year	Number (1,000)					Percent distribution			
	All married couples	In labor force			Husband and wife not in labor force	In labor force			Husband and wife not in labor force
		Husband and wife	Husband only	Wife only		Husband and wife	Husband only	Wife only	
TOTAL									
1990................	52,317	28,056	13,013	2,453	8,794	53.6	24.9	4.7	16.8
2000................	55,311	31,095	11,815	3,301	9,098	56.2	21.4	6.0	16.4
2002................	56,747	31,637	12,327	3,388	9,395	55.8	21.7	6.0	16.6
2003................	57,320	31,951	12,443	3,553	9,373	55.7	21.7	6.2	16.4
2004................	57,719	31,536	12,980	3,684	9,519	54.6	22.5	6.4	16.5
2005................	57,975	31,398	13,385	3,641	9,551	54.2	23.1	6.3	16.5
2006................	58,179	31,783	12,990	3,754	9,652	54.6	22.3	6.5	16.6
2007................	60,676	33,337	13,351	4,031	9,958	54.9	22.0	6.6	16.4
2008................	60,129	32,988	13,141	4,118	9,882	54.8	21.8	6.8	16.4
2009................	60,844	33,249	13,207	4,314	10,074	54.6	21.7	7.1	16.6
WITH CHILDREN UNDER 18									
1990................	24,537	15,768	7,667	558	544	64.3	31.2	2.3	2.2
2000................	25,248	17,116	6,950	795	387	67.8	27.5	3.1	1.5
2002................	25,792	17,233	7,301	777	482	66.8	28.3	3.0	1.9
2003................	25,914	17,065	7,499	893	457	65.9	28.9	3.4	1.8
2004................	25,793	16,691	7,715	952	433	64.7	29.9	3.7	1.7
2005................	25,919	16,789	7,806	925	400	64.8	30.1	3.6	1.5
2006................	25,982	16,909	7,754	900	420	65.1	29.9	3.5	1.6
2007................	26,802	17,670	7,743	920	469	65.9	28.9	3.4	1.7
2008................	25,778	16,977	7,398	932	471	65.9	28.7	3.6	1.8
2009................	25,799	17,054	7,284	963	501	66.1	28.2	3.7	1.9
WITH CHILDREN UNDER 6									
1990................	12,051	6,932	4,692	192	235	57.5	38.9	1.6	2.0
2000................	11,393	6,984	4,077	211	121	61.3	35.8	1.9	1.1
2002................	11,531	6,796	4,311	250	175	58.9	37.4	2.2	1.5
2003................	11,743	6,747	4,507	298	191	57.5	38.4	2.5	1.6
2004................	11,711	6,657	4,579	317	158	56.8	39.1	2.7	1.3
2005................	11,802	6,813	4,553	299	137	57.7	38.6	2.5	1.2
2006................	11,984	6,939	4,572	324	149	57.9	38.2	2.7	1.2
2007................	12,468	7,337	4,633	331	167	58.8	37.2	2.7	1.3
2008................	11,848	6,976	4,382	321	168	58.9	37.1	2.7	1.4
2009................	11,760	6,917	4,330	329	185	58.8	36.8	2.8	1.6

Source: U.S. Census Bureau, Table MC-1, "Married Couples by Labor Force Status of Spouses: 1986 to Present," <http://www.census.gov/population/www/socdemo/hh-fam.html>.

Table 601. Employed Civilians and Weekly Hours: 1980 to 2009

[In thousands (99,303 represents 99,303,000), except as indicated. Annual averages of monthly figures. Civilian noninstitutionalized population 16 years old and over. Based on Current Population Survey; see text, Section 1 and Appendix III]

Item	1980	1990 [1]	2000 [1]	2005 [1]	2007 [1]	2008 [1]	2009 [1]
Total employed...................	**99,303**	**118,793**	**136,891**	**141,730**	**146,047**	**145,362**	**139,877**
Age:							
16 to 19 years old	7,710	6,581	7,189	5,978	5,911	5,573	4,837
20 to 24 years old	14,087	13,401	13,229	13,792	13,964	13,629	12,764
25 to 34 years old	27,204	33,935	31,549	30,680	31,586	31,383	30,014
35 to 44 years old	19,523	30,817	36,433	34,630	34,302	33,457	31,517
45 to 54 years old	16,234	19,525	30,310	33,207	34,562	34,529	33,613
55 to 64 years old	11,586	11,189	14,002	18,349	20,108	20,812	21,019
65 years old and over	2,960	3,346	4,179	5,094	5,613	5,979	6,114
Class of worker:							
Nonagricultural industries	95,938	115,570	134,427	139,532	143,952	143,194	137,775
Wage and salary worker [2]	88,525	106,598	125,114	129,931	134,283	133,882	128,713
Self-employed	7,000	8,719	9,205	9,509	9,557	9,219	8,995
Unpaid family workers	413	253	108	93	112	93	66
Agriculture and related industries	3,364	3,223	2,464	2,197	2,095	2,168	2,103
Wage and salary worker [2]	1,425	1,740	1,421	1,212	1,220	1,279	1,242
Self-employed	1,642	1,378	1,010	955	856	860	836
Unpaid family workers	297	105	33	30	19	28	25
Weekly hours:							
Nonagricultural industries:							
Wage and salary workers [2]	38.1	39.2	39.6	39.1	39.2	39.0	38.0
Self-employed	41.2	40.8	39.7	38.4	38.0	37.0	35.6
Unpaid family workers	34.7	34.0	32.5	32.2	33.4	33.4	30.7
Agriculture and related industries:							
Wage and salary workers [2]	41.6	41.2	43.2	43.6	42.1	42.3	41.8
Self-employed	49.3	46.8	45.3	44.0	45.2	44.2	42.6
Unpaid family workers	38.6	38.5	38.3	41.1	32.7	41.0	36.1

[1] See footnote 2, Table 584. [2] Includes the incorporated self-employed.

Source: U.S. Bureau of Labor Statistics, "Employment and Earnings Online," January 2010, <http://www.bls.gov/opub/ee/home.htm> and <http://www.bls.gov/cps/home.htm>.

Table 602. Persons at Work by Hours Worked: 2009

[In thousands (134,444 represents 134,444,000), except as indicated. Annual averages of monthly figures. Persons "at work" are a subgroup of employed persons "at work," excluding those absent from their jobs during reference period for reasons such as vacation, illness, or industrial dispute. Civilian noninstitutionalized population 16 years old and over. Based on Current Population Survey; see text, Section 1, and Appendix III. See headnote Table 605, regarding industries]

Hours of work	Persons at work (1,000)			Percent distribution		
	Total	Agriculture and related industries	Non-agricultural industries	Total	Agriculture and related industries	Non-agricultural industries
Total..............................	134,444	2,018	132,425	100.0	100.0	100.0
1 to 34 hours........................	37,614	573	37,041	28.0	28.4	28.0
1 to 4 hours........................	1,607	52	1,555	1.2	2.6	1.2
5 to 14 hours.......................	5,622	139	5,484	4.2	6.9	4.1
15 to 29 hours......................	17,720	252	17,469	13.2	12.5	13.2
30 to 34 hours......................	12,665	131	12,534	9.4	6.5	9.5
35 hours and over...................	96,830	1,445	95,385	72.0	71.6	72.0
35 to 39 hours......................	9,936	98	9,838	7.4	4.8	7.4
40 hours...........................	54,570	536	54,035	40.6	26.5	40.8
41 hours and over...................	32,324	812	31,512	24.0	40.2	23.8
41 to 48 hours......................	11,327	135	11,191	8.4	6.7	8.5
49 to 59 hours......................	12,321	244	12,077	9.2	12.1	9.1
60 hours and over...................	8,676	432	8,243	6.5	21.4	6.2
Average weekly hours: Persons at work ...	37.9	42.1	37.8	(X)	(X)	(X)
Persons usually working full-time [1]......	41.9	48.3	41.8	(X)	(X)	(X)

X Not applicable. [1] Full-time workers are those who usually worked 35 hours or more (at all jobs).

Source: U.S. Bureau of Labor Statistics, "Employment and Earnings Online," January 2010, <http://www.bls.gov/opub/ee/home.htm> and <http://www.bls.gov/cps/home.htm>.

Table 603. Persons With a Job, But Not at Work: 1980 to 2009

[In thousands (5,881 represents 5,881,000), except percent. For civilian noninstitutionalized population 16 years old and over. Annual averages of monthly figures. Based on Current Population Survey; see text, Section 1 and Appendix III]

Reason for not working	1980	1990 [1]	2000 [1]	2002	2003 [1]	2004 [1]	2005 [1]	2006 [1]	2007 [1]	2008 [1]	2009 [1]
All industries, number	5,881	6,160	5,681	5,394	5,469	5,482	5,511	5,746	5,719	5,539	5,434
Percent of employed	5.9	5.2	4.2	4.0	4.0	3.9	3.9	4.0	3.9	3.8	3.9
Reason for not working:											
Vacation................	3,320	3,529	3,109	2,929	2,922	2,923	2,892	3,101	3,056	2,916	2,806
Illness	1,420	1,341	1,156	1,072	1,090	1,058	1,088	1,096	1,064	1,026	993
Bad weather............	155	90	89	97	123	133	145	117	140	141	126
Industrial dispute.........	105	24	14	7	18	10	6	7	10	7	6
All other................	876	1,177	1,313	1,289	1,316	1,358	1,381	1,425	1,449	1,449	1,503

[1] See footnote 2, Table 584.

Source: U.S. Bureau of Labor Statistics, unpublished data, <http://www.bls.gov/cps/home.htm>.

Table 604. Class of Worker by Sex and Selected Characteristics: 2009

[In percent, except as indicated (9,831 represents 9,831,000). Civilian noninstitutionalized population 16 years old and over. Annual averages of monthly figures. Based on Current Population Survey; see text, Section 1 and Appendix III]

Characteristic	Unincorporated self-employed			Incorporated self-employed			Wage and salary workers [1]		
	Total	Male	Female	Total	Male	Female	Total	Male	Female
Total (1,000)	9,831	6,140	3,691	5,466	3,955	1,511	124,849	63,539	60,950
PERCENT DISTRIBUTION	100.0	100.0	100.0	100.0	100.0	100.0	100.0	100.0	100.0
Age: 16 to 19 years old	0.8	0.8	0.7	0.1	0.1	0.1	3.8	3.6	4.1
20 to 24 years old	2.7	2.7	2.7	0.9	0.9	0.8	10.0	9.9	10.1
25 to 34 years old	13.9	14.1	13.6	10.5	10.3	11.1	22.5	23.5	21.5
35 to 44 years old	21.9	21.3	22.9	23.5	23.5	23.4	22.5	23.1	22.0
45 to 54 years old	28.0	28.2	27.7	32.7	32.6	33.2	23.3	22.7	24.0
55 to 64 years old	21.4	21.1	21.9	23.8	23.8	23.6	14.1	13.6	14.7
65 years old and over	11.3	11.7	10.5	8.6	8.8	8.0	3.6	3.6	3.7
Race/ethnicity: White [2]..................	86.9	87.5	85.9	88.7	89.3	87.2	84.2	86.9	81.9
Black [2]............................	6.8	6.5	7.4	4.0	4.0	4.0	12.0	10.7	13.5
Asian [2]............................	4.4	4.3	4.7	6.0	5.5	7.1	4.9	5.1	4.8
Hispanic [3].........................	12.3	13.4	10.4	7.0	7.3	6.2	15.0	17.4	12.5
Country of birth: U.S. born..............	83.7	82.7	85.4	(NA)	(NA)	(NA)	(NA)	(NA)	(NA)
Foreign-born	16.3	17.3	14.6	(NA)	(NA)	(NA)	(NA)	(NA)	(NA)

NA Not available. [1] Excludes the incorporated self-employed. [2] For persons in this race group only. [3] Persons of Hispanic or Latino origin may be any race.

Source: U.S. Bureau of Labor Statistics, Current Population Survey, unpublished data.

Table 605. Self-Employed Workers by Industry and Occupation: 2000 to 2009

[In thousands (10,214 represents 10,214,000). Civilian noninstitutionalized population 16 years old and over. Annual averages of monthly figures. Data represent the unincorporated self-employed; the incorporated self-employed are considered wage and salary workers. Based on the occupational and industrial classification derived from those used in the 2000 census. See text, this section. Based on the Current Population Survey; see text, Section 1 and Appendix III]

Item	2000	2005 [1]	2006 [1]	2007 [1]	2008 [1]	2009 [1]
Total self-employed	**10,214**	**10,464**	**10,586**	**10,413**	**10,080**	**9,831**
Industry:						
Agriculture and related industries	1,010	955	901	856	860	836
Mining	12	11	10	19	15	18
Construction	1,728	1,830	1,910	1,890	1,817	1,701
Manufacturing	334	327	326	348	308	324
Wholesale and retail trade	1,221	1,251	1,139	1,116	1,059	963
Transportation and utilities	348	442	428	405	405	402
Information	139	126	120	135	125	145
Financial activities [2]	735	785	841	829	749	667
Professional and business services [2]	1,927	1,957	1,992	2,009	1,980	1,996
Education and health services [2]	1,107	1,071	1,158	1,102	1,071	1,102
Leisure and hospitality [2]	660	674	685	679	693	636
Other services [3]	993	1,036	1,076	1,026	997	1,039
Occupation:						
Management, professional, and related occupations	4,169	4,085	4,069	4,024	4,043	4,079
Service occupations	1,775	1,774	1,905	1,872	1,847	1,879
Sales and office occupations	1,982	1,986	1,971	1,936	1,771	1,663
Natural resources, construction, and maintenance occupations	1,591	1,864	1,879	1,860	1,707	1,535
Production, transportation, and material moving occupations	698	756	763	721	712	674

[1] See footnote 2, Table 584. [2] For composition of industries, see Table 624. [3] Includes private households.

Source: U.S. Bureau of Labor Statistics, "Employment and Earnings Online," January 2010, <http://www.bls.gov/opub/ee/home.htm> and <http://www.bls.gov/cps/home.htm>.

Table 606. Type of Work Flexibility Provided to Employees: 2008

[In percent. The National Study of Employers does not ask employers to report on whether they have "written policies," but rather whether their organization "allows employees to" … or "provides the following benefits or programs …" The wording is used for two reasons. First, employers may have written policies, but not "allow" employees to use them. Second, smaller employers are less likely to have written policies than larger ones. For methodology, see source]

Type of work flexibility provided (to employee)	Employer allows all or most employees	Employer size	
		50 to 99 employees	1,000 or more employees
FLEX TIME AND PLACE			
Periodically change starting and quitting times within some range of hours	37	40	37
Change starting and quitting times on a daily basis	10	11	7
Compress workweek by working longer hours on fewer days for at least part of the year	8	10	5
Work some regular paid hours at home occasionally	3	3	2
Work some regular paid hours at home on regular basis	1	1	1
CHOICES IN MANAGING TIME			
Have control over when to take breaks	55	54	51
Have choices about and control over which shifts to work	16	16	16
Have control over paid and unpaid overtime hours	13	14	15
REDUCED TIME			
Move from full time to part time and back again while remaining in same position or level	13	12	12
Share jobs	8	9	5
Work part year (work reduced time on annual basis)	11	10	11
CAREGIVING LEAVE			
Return to work gradually after childbirth or adoption	57	56	54
TIME OFF			
Family or personal time off without loss of pay	45	46	47
Compensatory time off program	18	21	9
Do volunteer work during regular work hours	21	24	20
FLEX CAREERS			
Phase into retirement by working reduced hours overtime prior to full retirement	25	25	20
Take sabbaticals (paid or unpaid for six months or more)	21	24	14
Take paid or unpaid time off for education or job training skills	40	41	33
Take extended career breaks for caregiving or other personal or family reasons	47	48	44
Receive special consideration when returning to the organization after an extended career break	28	29	21

Source: Families and Work Institute, "2008 National Study of Employers" (copyright), <http://familiesandwork.org/site/research/reports/main.html>.

Table 607. Persons on Flexible Schedules: 2004

[In thousands, except percent. (99,778 represents 99,778,000.) As of May. For employed full-time wage and salary workers 16 years old and over. Excludes all self-employed persons, regardless of whether or not their businesses were incorporated. Data related to the primary job. Based on the Current Population Survey; see text, Section 1 and Appendix III]

Item	Total			Male			Female		
	Total [1]	With flexible schedules [2]		Total [1]	With flexible schedules [2]		Total [1]	With flexible schedules [2]	
		Number	Percent		Number	Percent		Number	Percent
Total...............	99,778	27,411	27.5	56,412	15,853	28.1	43,366	11,558	26.7
AGE									
16 to 19 years old	1,427	336	23.6	903	185	20.5	524	151	28.9
20 years and over	98,351	27,075	27.5	55,509	15,668	28.2	42,842	11,406	26.6
20 to 24 years old	9,004	2,058	22.9	5,147	1,065	20.7	3,856	993	25.8
25 to 34 years old	24,640	6,902	28.0	14,358	4,051	28.2	10,283	2,851	27.7
35 to 44 years old	26,766	7,807	29.2	15,424	4,605	29.9	11,342	3,202	28.2
45 to 54 years old	24,855	6,651	26.8	13,440	3,769	28.0	11,415	2,882	25.2
55 to 64 years old	11,745	3,181	27.1	6,383	1,865	29.2	5,361	1,316	24.5
65 years old and over	1,341	475	35.4	757	314	41.4	585	161	27.6
RACE AND HISPANIC ORIGIN									
White [3].........................	80,498	23,121	28.7	46,222	13,582	29.4	34,276	9,539	27.8
Black [3].........................	12,578	2,476	19.7	6,447	1,193	18.5	6,131	1,283	20.9
Asian [3].........................	4,136	1,132	27.4	2,300	720	31.3	1,836	412	22.4
Hispanic [4]......................	14,110	2,596	18.4	8,621	1,430	16.6	5,489	1,166	21.2
MARITAL STATUS									
Married, spouse present	57,630	16,270	28.2	34,926	10,382	29.7	22,704	5,888	25.9
Not married	42,148	11,141	26.4	21,486	5,471	25.5	20,662	5,670	27.4
Never married	25,144	6,693	26.6	14,469	3,605	24.9	10,676	3,088	28.9
Other marital status..............	17,004	4,448	26.2	7,018	1,866	26.6	9,986	2,582	25.9
PRESENCE AND AGE OF CHILDREN									
Without own children under 18	61,761	16,759	27.1	34,680	9,410	27.1	27,081	7,349	27.1
With own children under 18.......	38,018	10,652	28.0	21,733	6,443	29.6	16,285	4,209	25.8
With youngest child 6 to 17	21,739	5,960	27.4	11,477	3,341	29.1	10,262	2,619	25.5
With youngest child under 6	16,279	4,692	28.8	10,256	3,102	30.2	6,023	1,590	26.4

[1] Includes persons who did not provide information on flexible schedules. [2] Allowed to vary or make changes in time work begins or ends. [3] For persons in the race group only. See footnote 4, Table 585. [4] Persons of Hispanic origin may be any race.

Source: U.S. Bureau of Labor Statistics, *Workers on Flexible and Shift Schedules in May 2004*, News Release, USDL 05-1198, July 2005. See also <http://www.bls.gov/bls/newsrels.htm#OEUS>.

Table 608. Employed Workers With Alternative and Traditional Work Arrangements: 2005

[In thousands (138,952 represents 138,952,000). As of February. For employed workers 16 years old and over. Based on the Current Population Survey; see text, Section 1 and Appendix III]

Characteristic	Total employed [1]	Workers with alternative arrangements				Workers with traditional arrangements
		Independent contractors	On-call workers	Temporary help agency workers	Workers provided by contract firms	
Total employed..................	138,952	10,342	2,454	1,217	813	123,843
16 to 19 years old	5,510	89	133	33	7	5,194
20 to 24 years old	13,114	356	355	202	87	12,055
25 to 34 years old	30,103	1,520	535	362	205	27,427
35 to 44 years old	34,481	2,754	571	253	196	30,646
45 to 54 years old	32,947	2,799	417	200	186	29,324
55 to 64 years old	17,980	1,943	267	135	114	15,496
65 years old and over	4,817	881	175	33	18	3,701
Male.........................	73,946	6,696	1,241	574	561	64,673
16 to 19 years old	2,579	32	82	24	7	2,389
20 to 24 years old	6,928	194	200	107	61	6,331
25 to 34 years old	16,624	1,006	299	185	138	14,950
35 to 44 years old	18,523	1,824	252	120	140	16,130
45 to 54 years old	17,193	1,764	209	71	143	15,003
55 to 64 years old	9,485	1,287	108	52	70	7,954
65 years old and over	2,615	589	91	16	3	1,917
Female........................	65,006	3,647	1,212	643	252	59,170
16 to 19 years old	2,931	57	52	9	–	2,805
20 to 24 years old	6,186	162	155	95	27	5,724
25 to 34 years old	13,480	514	236	177	67	12,477
35 to 44 years old	15,958	930	319	133	57	14,516
45 to 54 years old	15,754	1,035	208	129	43	14,322
55 to 64 years old	8,495	656	158	83	44	7,542
65 years old and over	2,202	292	84	17	15	1,785
Full-time workers	113,798	7,732	1,370	979	695	102,889
Part-time workers	25,154	2,611	1,084	238	119	20,954

– Represents zero. [1] Includes day laborers (an alternative arrangement) and a small number of workers who were both "on call" and "provided by contract firms," not shown separately.

Source: U.S. Bureau of Labor Statistics, *Contingent and Alternative Employment Arrangements, February 2005*, News Release, USDL 05-1443, July 2005. See also <http://www.bls.gov/bls/newsrels.htm#OEUS\>.

Table 609. Multiple Jobholders: 2009

[Annual average of monthly figures (7,271 represents 7,271,000). Civilian noninstitutionalized population 16 years old and over. Multiple jobholders are employed persons who, either 1) had jobs as wage or salary workers with two employers or more; 2) were self-employed and also held a wage and salary job; or 3) were unpaid family workers and also held a wage and salary job. Based on the Current Population Survey; see text, Section 1 and Appendix III]

Characteristic	Total		Male		Female	
	Number (1,000)	Percent of employed	Number (1,000)	Percent of employed	Number (1,000)	Percent of employed
Total [1]	7,271	5.2	3,530	4.8	3,741	5.6
Age:						
16 to 19 years old	186	3.8	71	3.1	115	4.6
20 to 24 years old	710	5.6	307	4.7	403	6.4
25 to 54 years old	5,124	5.4	2,524	5.0	2,599	5.8
55 to 64 years old	1,039	4.9	507	4.7	532	5.2
65 years old and over	212	3.5	120	3.6	92	3.3
Race and Hispanic ethnicity:						
White [2]	6,166	5.4	3,016	4.9	3,150	5.9
Black [2]	714	4.8	319	4.7	395	4.8
Asian [2]	210	3.2	111	3.1	100	3.2
Hispanic [3]	643	3.3	354	3.0	289	3.6
Marital status:						
Married, spouse present	3,993	5.0	2,212	5.0	1,781	5.1
Widowed, divorced, or separated	1,289	5.8	429	4.7	861	6.5
Single, never married	1,989	5.2	890	4.3	1,099	6.2
Full- or part-time status:						
Primary job full-time, secondary job part-time	3,868	(X)	2,042	(X)	1,825	(X)
Both jobs part-time	1,821	(X)	599	(X)	1,222	(X)
Both jobs full-time	249	(X)	157	(X)	92	(X)
Hours vary on primary or secondary job	1,287	(X)	704	(X)	583	(X)

X Not applicable. [1] Includes a small number of persons who work part-time on their primary job and full-time on their secondary job(s), not shown separately. Includes other races, not shown separately. [2] For persons who selected this race group only. See footnote 4, Table 585. [3] Persons of Hispanic or Latino ethnicity may be any race.

Source: U.S. Bureau of Labor Statistics, "Employment and Earnings Online," January 2010, <http://www.bls.gov/opub/ee /home.htm> and <http://www.bls.gov/cps/home.htm>.

Table 610. Average Number of Jobs Held From Ages 18 to 42: 1978 to 2006

[For persons aged 41 to 50 in 2006–07. A job is an uninterrupted period of work with a particular employer. Educational attainment as of 2006–07. Based on the National Longitudinal Survey of Youth 1979; see source for details]

Sex and educational attainment	Total [1]	Number of jobs held by age				
		18 to 22 years	23 to 27 years	28 to 32 years	33 to 37 years	38 to 42 years
Total [2]	10.8	4.4	3.3	2.6	2.2	1.9
Less than a high school diploma	10.9	3.9	3.2	2.6	2.2	1.9
High school graduates, no college	10.5	4.2	3.1	2.6	2.2	1.9
Some college or associate's degree	11.1	4.5	3.4	2.7	2.3	2.0
Bachelor's degree or more	11.1	5.0	3.6	2.6	2.1	1.9
Male	11.0	4.6	3.5	2.8	2.3	2.0
Less than a high school diploma	12.5	4.6	3.8	3.0	2.4	2.0
High school graduate, no college	10.7	4.5	3.4	2.8	2.2	1.9
Some college or associate's degree	11.1	4.5	3.5	2.8	2.4	2.0
Bachelor's degree or more	10.7	4.6	3.4	2.6	2.2	1.9
Female	10.6	4.3	3.1	2.4	2.1	1.9
Less than a high school diploma	8.7	2.9	2.3	2.1	1.9	1.6
High school graduate, no college	10.2	3.9	2.7	2.3	2.2	1.9
Some college or associate's degree	11.0	4.5	3.3	2.5	2.2	1.9
Bachelor's degree or more	11.5	5.3	3.7	2.6	2.0	1.8
White, non-Hispanic	10.9	4.6	3.3	2.6	2.2	1.9
Less than a high school diploma	11.5	4.2	3.3	2.7	2.3	1.9
High school graduate, no college	10.4	4.4	3.1	2.6	2.2	1.9
Some college or associate's degree	11.3	4.7	3.4	2.7	2.3	1.9
Bachelor's degree or more	11.1	5.1	3.6	2.6	2.1	1.8
Black, non-Hispanic	10.4	3.6	3.1	2.6	2.3	2.0
Less than a high school diploma	9.8	2.9	2.9	2.6	2.0	1.8
High school graduate, no college	10.6	3.5	3.0	2.6	2.3	2.0
Some college or associate's degree	10.4	3.8	3.1	2.7	2.4	2.1
Bachelor's degree or more	10.9	4.2	3.6	2.8	2.4	2.2
Hispanic or Latino [3]	10.5	4.1	3.0	2.5	2.2	1.9
Less than a high school diploma	10.4	4.0	2.8	2.4	2.0	1.7
High school graduate, no college	10.6	4.0	3.0	2.5	2.2	1.9
Some college or associate's degree	10.3	4.2	3.0	2.5	2.2	2.1
Bachelor's degree or more	10.7	4.4	3.3	2.7	2.3	1.9

[1] Jobs held in more than one age category were counted in each category, but only once in the total. [2] Includes other races, not shown separately. [3] Persons of Hispanic or Latino origin may be any race.

Source: U.S. Bureau of Labor Statistics, Number of Jobs Held, Labor Market Activity, and *Earnings Growth Among the Youngest Baby Boomers: Results from a Longitudinal Survey*, News Release, USDL 08-0860, June 2008. See also <http://www.bls.gov/nls/home.htm>.

Table 611. Distribution of Workers by Tenure With Current Employer by Selected Characteristics: 2008

[129,276 represents 129,276,000. As of January. For employed wage and salary workers 16 years old and over. Data exclude the incorporated and unincorporated self–employed. Based on the Current Population Survey; see source and Appendix III]

Characteristic	Number employed (1,000)	Percent distribution by tenure with current employer								Median years [1]
		12 months or less	13 to 23 months	2 years	3 to 4 years	5 to 9 years	10 to 14 years	15 to 19 years	20 years or more	
Total [2]	**129,276**	**22.9**	**7.4**	**5.6**	**16.9**	**20.2**	**10.6**	**6.2**	**10.3**	**4.1**
AGE AND SEX										
16 to 19 years old	5,200	73.8	11.5	7.5	7.0	0.3	–	–	–	(NA)
20 to 24 years old	13,139	49.9	13.2	10.2	20.4	6.4	(Z)	–	–	1.3
25 to 34 years old	29,097	28.2	10.4	8.5	23.4	23.5	5.4	0.6	(Z)	2.7
35 to 44 years old	30,150	17.1	6.6	4.8	18.1	25.3	15.3	8.2	4.5	4.9
45 to 54 years old	30,151	12.9	4.4	3.5	13.7	21.6	14.4	9.9	19.4	7.6
55 to 64 years old	17,242	9.4	4.3	2.6	11.2	19.7	14.1	10.9	27.8	9.9
65 years old and over	4,297	8.9	2.5	2.8	10.6	18.9	16.6	10.4	29.2	10.2
Male	66,660	22.4	6.9	5.6	16.9	19.9	10.7	6.1	11.5	4.2
16 to 19 years old	2,423	72.5	11.8	8.4	7.0	0.3	–	–	–	(NA)
20 to 24 years old	6,856	49.6	12.2	10.2	21.3	6.6	–	–	–	1.4
25 to 34 years old	15,709	27.4	9.7	8.3	23.3	24.6	5.8	0.9	(Z)	2.8
35 to 44 years old	15,755	16.7	6.0	4.8	17.6	24.4	16.6	8.7	5.3	5.2
45 to 54 years old	15,289	12.7	3.9	3.3	13.1	20.4	14.0	10.0	22.7	8.2
55 to 64 years old	8,513	8.5	4.7	2.3	11.6	18.8	13.4	9.9	30.7	10.1
65 years old and over	2,115	8.5	2.7	2.0	10.5	17.6	15.8	9.1	33.9	10.4
Female	62,616	23.5	7.8	5.7	16.9	20.4	10.5	6.2	9.0	3.9
16 to 19 years old	2,776	74.9	11.2	6.8	6.9	0.3	–	–	–	(NA)
20 to 24 years old	6,283	50.2	14.2	10.1	19.3	6.1	0.1	–	–	1.3
25 to 34 years old	13,388	29.2	11.2	8.6	23.5	22.3	5.0	0.3	–	2.6
35 to 44 years old	14,395	17.5	7.4	4.8	18.7	26.3	13.9	7.6	3.8	4.7
45 to 54 years old	14,862	13.2	5.1	3.8	14.4	22.9	15.0	9.8	16.0	7.0
55 to 64 years old	8,729	10.3	3.9	2.8	10.8	20.5	14.9	11.8	25.1	9.8
65 years old and over	2,182	9.3	2.3	3.6	10.6	20.3	17.4	11.7	24.7	9.9
RACE AND HISPANIC ORIGIN										
White [3]	105,246	22.6	7.3	5.4	16.4	20.2	10.8	6.4	10.8	4.2
Male	55,008	22.0	6.8	5.4	16.5	19.8	10.9	6.4	12.2	4.4
Female	50,238	23.2	7.9	5.5	16.3	20.6	10.7	6.4	9.3	4.0
Black [3]	14,497	24.5	7.1	6.8	18.0	19.7	10.3	4.7	8.8	3.6
Male	6,704	25.4	7.2	6.7	17.0	19.5	10.6	4.0	9.6	3.5
Female	7,793	23.7	7.0	6.9	18.9	19.9	10.1	5.4	8.2	3.7
Asian [3]	6,283	21.5	7.6	5.4	21.8	22.4	0.6	5.5	8.2	3.7
Male	3,316	19.8	7.5	5.0	23.2	24.0	9.5	5.6	5.4	3.9
Female	2,967	23.4	7.7	5.8	20.3	20.5	9.7	5.3	7.2	3.5
Hispanic [4]	18,645	26.9	7.1	7.2	19.9	20.2	9.3	4.5	4.9	3.2
Male	10,886	25.9	6.3	7.6	20.5	20.1	9.2	4.8	5.6	3.3
Female	7,759	28.3	8.2	6.8	19.1	20.4	9.4	4.0	3.9	3.1

– Represents zero. NA Not available. Z Less than .05 percent. [1] For definition of median, see Guide to Tabular Presentation.
[2] Includes other races, not shown separately. [3] For persons in this race group only. See footnote 4, Table 585. [4] Persons of Hispanic or Latino ethnicity may be any race.

Source: U. S. Bureau of Labor Statistics, *Employee Tenure in 2008*, News Release, USDL 08–1344, September 2008. See also <http://www.bls.gov/news.release/tenure.toc.htm>.

Table 612. Part-Time Workers by Reason: 2009

[In thousands (37,614 represents 37,614,000), except hours. For persons working 1 to 34 hours per week. For civilian noninstitutionalized population 16 years old and over. Annual average of monthly figures. Based on the Current Population Survey; see text, Section 1 and Appendix III]

Reason	All industries			Nonagricultural industries		
		Usually work—			Usually work—	
	Total	Full-time	Part-time	Total	Full-time	Part-time
Total working fewer than 35 hours	**37,614**	**12,853**	**24,761**	**37,041**	**12,679**	**24,362**
Economic reasons	8,913	2,861	6,051	8,791	2,801	5,990
Slack work or business conditions	6,648	2,632	4,015	6,556	2,586	3,970
Could find only part time work	1,966	(S)	1,966	1,955	(S)	1,955
Seasonal work	192	122	70	174	109	65
Job started or ended during the week	108	108	(S)	107	107	(S)
Noneconomic reasons	28,701	9,991	18,710	28,250	9,878	18,372
Child-care problems	713	57	656	709	57	652
Other family or personal obligations	4,916	644	4,272	4,844	636	4,208
Health or medical limitations	793	(S)	793	773	(S)	773
In school or training	5,714	81	5,634	5,654	79	5,575
Retired or social security limit on earnings	2,200	(S)	2,200	2,098	(S)	2,098
Vacation or personal day	3,626	3,626	(S)	3,592	3,592	(S)
Holiday, legal, or religious	2,834	2,834	(S)	2,822	2,822	(S)
Weather-related curtailment	420	420	(S)	393	393	(S)
Other	7,485	2,329	5,156	7,364	2,299	5,065
Average hours per week:						
Economic reasons	22.7	23.6	22.2	22.7	23.7	22.2
Noneconomic reasons	21.9	26.1	19.6	21.9	26.1	19.7

S No data or data do not meet publication standards.
Source: U.S. Bureau of Labor Statistics, "Employment and Earnings Online," January 2010, <http://www.bls.gov/opub/ee /home.htm> and <http://www.bls.gov/cps/home.htm>.

Labor Force, Employment, and Earnings **391**

Table 613. Displaced Workers by Selected Characteristics: 2008

[In percent, except total (3,641 represents 3,641,000). As of January. For persons 20 years old and over with tenure of 3 years or more who lost or left a job between January 2005 and December 2007 because of plant closings or moves, slack work, or the abolishment of their positions. Based on Current Population Survey; see source and Appendix III]

Characteristic	Total (1,000)	Employment status in January 2008			Reason for job loss, 2005–2007		
		Employed	Unemployed	Not in the labor force	Plant or company closed down or moved	Slack/ insufficient work	Position or shift abolished
Total [1]	**3,641**	**67.1**	**18.0**	**15.0**	**45.3**	**23.9**	**30.8**
20 to 24 years old	127	67.5	22.8	9.7	42.4	39.8	17.7
25 to 54 years old	2,602	72.6	17.4	10.0	44.8	25.2	30.0
55 to 64 years old	708	60.8	20.7	18.5	45.7	17.6	36.7
65 years old and over	204	18.4	12.6	69.0	52.2	19.2	28.5
Males	2,024	69.9	18.8	11.2	43.6	27.9	28.5
20 to 24 years old	75	66.4	22.5	11.1	34.2	52.6	13.2
25 to 54 years old	1,490	74.4	19.1	6.5	42.0	29.1	28.9
55 to 64 years old	356	68.0	17.9	14.0	49.7	18.7	31.6
65 years old and over	103	14.4	15.4	70.2	52.3	24.3	23.4
Females	1,617	63.5	16.9	19.6	47.4	19.0	33.6
20 to 24 years old	53	(2)	(2)	(2)	(2)	(2)	(2)
25 to 54 years old	1,112	70.1	15.1	14.8	48.5	20.1	31.4
55 to 64 years old	352	53.4	23.6	23.0	41.6	16.5	41.9
65 years old and over	101	22.4	9.8	67.8	52.2	14.1	33.8
White [3]	3,032	67.9	16.8	15.3	45.4	23.5	31.1
Male	1,684	70.8	18.2	11.0	43.5	27.8	28.7
Female	1,348	64.4	14.9	20.7	47.9	18.1	34.1
Black [3]	408	58.6	28.2	13.3	46.6	26.9	26.4
Male	221	60.5	25.7	13.8	41.8	31.0	27.2
Female	187	56.3	31.1	12.6	52.4	22.1	25.5
Asian [3]	122	67.3	11.7	21.0	44.7	15.7	39.5
Male	65	(2)	(2)	(2)	(2)	(2)	(2)
Female	57	(2)	(2)	(2)	(2)	(2)	(2)
Hispanic [4]	423	68.4	17.4	14.1	43.5	39.5	17.0
Male	270	70.1	23.4	6.6	41.0	47.5	11.5
Female	153	65.5	6.9	27.6	47.9	25.4	26.6

[1] Includes other races, not shown separately. [2] Data not shown where base is less than 75,000. [3] For persons in this race group only. See footnote 3, Table 585. [4] Persons of Hispanic or Latino origin may be any race.

Source: U.S. Bureau of Labor Statistics, *Worker Displacement, 2005–2007*, News Release, USDL 08-1183, August 2008. See also <http://www.bls.gov/news.release/disp.toc.htm>.

Table 614. Persons Not in the Labor Force: 2009

[In thousands (81,659 represents 81,659,000). Annual average of monthly figures. Civilian noninstitutionalized population 16 years old and over. Based on the Current Population Survey; see text, Section 1 and Appendix III]

Status and reason	Total	Age			Sex	
		16 to 24 years old	25 to 54 years old	55 years old and over	Male	Female
Total not in the labor force	**81,659**	**16,207**	**21,823**	**43,629**	**32,013**	**49,646**
Do not want a job now [1]	75,765	14,263	19,199	42,303	29,234	46,531
Want a job now	5,894	1,944	2,624	1,325	2,779	3,115
In the previous year—						
Did not search for a job	3,075	960	1,241	874	1,344	1,731
Did search for a job [2]	2,818	983	1,383	452	1,435	1,384
Not available for work now	592	275	256	61	251	341
Available for work now, not looking for work [3]	2,226	708	1,127	391	1,184	1,043
Reason for not currently looking for work:						
Discouraged over job prospects [4]	778	200	427	151	485	293
Family responsibilities	209	38	131	41	50	159
In school or training	306	234	65	7	163	144
Ill health or disability	136	19	68	49	70	66
Other [5]	798	219	435	144	417	381

[1] Includes some persons who are not asked if they want a job. [2] Persons who had a job in the prior 12 months must have searched since the end of that job. [3] Persons who have searched for work in the previous year and are available to work now also are referred to as "marginally attached to the labor force." [4] Includes such things as believes no work available, could not find work, lacks necessary schooling or training, employer thinks too young or old, and other types of discrimination. [5] Includes such things as child care and transportation problems.

Source: U.S. Bureau of Labor Statistics, "Employment and Earnings Online," January 2010, <http://www.bls.gov/opub/ee /home.htm> and <http://www.bls.gov/cps/tables.htm#annual>.

Table 615. Employed Civilians by Occupation, Sex, Race, and Hispanic Origin: 2009

[139,877 represents 139,877,000. Civilian noninstitutionalized population 16 years old and over. Annual average of monthly figures. Based on Current Population Survey; see text, Section 1 and Appendix III. Occupational classifications are those used in the 2000 census]

Occupation	Total employed (1,000)	Percent of total			
		Female	Black [1]	Asian [1]	Hispanic [2]
Total, 16 years and over.................................	**139,877**	**47.3**	**10.7**	**4.7**	**14.0**
Management, professional and related occupations..............	**52,219**	**51.4**	**8.4**	**6.2**	**7.3**
Management, business, and financial operations occupations........	21,529	42.7	7.0	4.9	7.6
Management occupations [3]................................	15,447	37.4	6.2	4.4	7.5
Chief executives......................................	1,631	25.0	2.9	4.2	4.6
General and operations managers...........................	1,004	30.0	5.5	4.6	6.0
Advertising and promotions managers.......................	78	56.5	6.3	2.7	11.1
Marketing and sales managers.............................	938	42.8	4.4	3.7	7.2
Administrative services managers..........................	118	40.9	6.8	2.6	9.8
Computer and information systems managers..................	471	29.0	6.1	7.0	6.2
Financial managers.....................................	1,183	54.7	8.5	6.1	9.1
Human resources managers...............................	283	66.8	7.6	3.3	7.6
Industrial production managers............................	240	16.4	4.4	2.9	11.2
Purchasing managers...................................	198	50.3	8.7	4.0	3.7
Transportation, storage, and distribution managers.............	234	16.4	7.3	2.0	9.4
Farm, ranch, and other agricultural managers.................	226	17.5	1.5	2.0	7.9
Farmers and ranchers..................................	729	25.2	1.4	0.5	1.7
Construction managers..................................	1,099	5.9	3.3	1.7	8.2
Education administrators.................................	808	62.6	10.7	2.6	7.2
Engineering managers...................................	124	8.1	2.9	8.7	5.4
Food service managers..................................	1,003	45.7	6.9	10.4	14.2
Lodging managers......................................	160	48.2	8.4	14.7	9.4
Medical and health services managers.......................	533	69.5	9.9	4.6	7.0
Property, real estate, and community association managers.......	597	46.7	8.1	2.8	9.3
Social and community service managers.....................	343	69.4	11.5	1.5	8.5
Business and financial operations occupations [3]...............	6,082	56.3	9.3	6.1	8.0
Wholesale and retail buyers, except farm products.............	167	55.9	4.3	5.8	16.4
Purchasing agents, except wholesale, retail, and farm products.....	239	55.5	6.8	3.3	10.7
Claims adjusters, appraisers, examiners, and investigators........	280	60.6	13.7	2.7	7.3
Compliance officers, except agriculture, construction, health and safety, and transportation.............................	200	50.6	12.0	1.7	6.8
Cost estimators.......................................	117	11.4	1.1	0.3	13.5
Human resources, training, and labor relations specialists.........	843	71.1	12.1	3.2	9.6
Management analysts....................................	640	42.8	7.4	4.8	5.0
Accountants and auditors................................	1,754	61.8	8.0	10.3	6.3
Appraisers and assessors of real estate.....................	99	28.9	5.2	1.7	6.0
Financial analysts.....................................	94	30.9	5.8	10.3	6.4
Personal financial advisors..............................	400	32.1	6.9	6.4	7.7
Insurance underwriters..................................	97	62.8	13.6	3.2	11.5
Loan counselors and officers.............................	346	55.8	11.4	5.6	9.9
Tax preparers..	99	65.9	11.8	7.1	10.1
Professional and related occupations [3]......................	30,690	57.5	9.4	7.1	7.1
Computer and mathematical occupations [3]..................	3,481	24.8	6.7	15.7	5.4
Computer scientists and systems analysts..................	759	26.9	7.5	14.7	6.1
Computer programmers................................	498	20.2	5.0	13.0	5.4
Computer software engineers...........................	952	20.2	5.3	26.6	3.5
Computer support specialists...........................	384	26.7	11.7	8.3	7.5
Database administrators...............................	110	35.3	5.1	14.0	7.3
Network and computer systems administrators..............	207	22.3	5.6	7.0	7.6
Network systems and data communications analysts..........	401	24.7	6.2	9.4	5.5
Operations research analysts...........................	108	46.9	10.7	8.4	5.8
Architecture and engineering occupations [3].................	2,740	13.8	5.5	9.9	7.2
Architects, except naval..............................	204	25.3	2.5	4.8	6.9
Aerospace engineers.................................	136	10.0	6.1	7.8	8.3
Chemical engineers..................................	65	18.4	11.0	7.8	2.6
Civil engineers.....................................	338	7.1	4.1	10.6	7.3
Computer hardware engineers..........................	61	8.6	6.2	26.8	7.7
Electrical and electronics engineers.....................	314	9.4	5.1	17.0	5.1
Industrial engineers, including health and safety............	186	17.4	2.9	12.4	9.5
Mechanical engineers................................	302	5.9	4.0	10.1	5.8
Drafters...	149	24.7	6.8	2.9	9.9
Engineering technicians, except drafters..................	365	19.6	9.4	4.0	8.3
Surveying and mapping technicians......................	80	7.8	1.4	2.2	10.3
Life, physical, and social science occupations [3].............	1,328	46.8	6.0	12.7	5.9
Biological scientists.................................	98	45.1	4.7	13.6	5.1
Medical scientists...................................	170	56.9	4.5	33.3	4.3
Chemists and materials scientists.......................	113	30.0	7.2	19.6	6.6
Environmental scientists and geoscientists................	91	29.5	1.0	2.7	1.2
Market and survey researchers.........................	127	37.4	2.1	18.6	4.1
Psychologists......................................	161	68.8	6.3	3.2	6.2
Community and social services occupations [3]................	2,341	62.9	19.8	2.7	9.7
Counselors...	697	70.5	22.9	2.0	9.4
Social workers......................................	725	80.7	22.5	2.5	9.6
Miscellaneous community and social service specialists........	349	65.2	21.4	2.5	15.7
Clergy..	427	17.0	12.4	4.0	5.3

See footnotes at end of table.

U.S. Census Bureau, Statistical Abstract of the United States: 2011

Table 615. Employed Civilians by Occupation, Sex, Race, and Hispanic Origin: 2009—Con.

[139,877 represents 139,877,000. Civilian noninstitutional population 16 years old and over. Annual average of monthly figures. Based on Current Population Survey; see text, Section 1, and Appendix III. Occupational classifications are those used in the 2000 census]

Occupation	Total employed (1,000)	Percent of total			
		Female	Black [1]	Asian [1]	Hispanic [2]
Legal occupations	1,710	49.8	6.5	3.6	5.0
Lawyers	1,043	32.4	4.7	4.1	2.8
Paralegals and legal assistants	354	85.9	9.8	1.4	8.3
Miscellaneous legal support workers	240	73.8	9.7	4.7	8.8
Education, training, and library occupations [3]	8,627	74.3	9.2	3.9	7.8
Postsecondary teachers	1,321	49.2	5.3	11.3	4.6
Preschool and kindergarten teachers	691	97.8	14.2	2.6	10.3
Elementary and middle school teachers	2,862	81.9	9.3	2.4	7.1
Secondary school teachers	1,212	54.9	7.8	2.1	6.6
Special education teachers	385	86.0	6.8	2.3	4.8
Other teachers and instructors	758	68.3	9.5	3.9	8.6
Librarians	206	81.8	5.3	3.0	6.8
Teacher assistants	1,006	91.5	14.5	2.4	14.7
Arts, design, entertainment, sports, and media occupations [3]	2,724	46.6	6.7	3.6	8.8
Artists and related workers	213	45.5	0.8	3.9	9.3
Designers	764	54.3	5.1	4.6	7.9
Producers and directors	138	40.1	11.6	4.1	10.1
Athletes, coaches, umpires, and related workers	258	31.5	10.4	3.1	9.2
Musicians, singers, and related workers	168	31.5	12.2	0.8	8.3
News analysts, reporters and correspondents	80	42.8	1.8	0.9	4.0
Public relations specialists	137	60.7	6.2	3.3	6.0
Editors	169	55.8	3.7	5.4	1.3
Writers and authors	178	62.7	7.3	1.3	3.1
Photographers	188	44.8	4.1	3.9	7.6
Healthcare practitioner and technical occupations [3]	7,738	74.6	11.1	8.3	6.3
Dentists	164	30.2	1.4	10.8	7.9
Pharmacists	267	49.3	8.9	14.7	3.5
Physicians and surgeons	914	32.2	5.7	16.4	6.3
Registered nurses	2,839	92.0	11.5	8.1	4.6
Occupational therapists	106	87.0	3.8	6.3	2.6
Physical therapists	175	64.7	6.1	8.4	4.5
Respiratory therapists	119	59.9	11.4	4.6	10.8
Speech-language pathologists	140	95.8	2.4	1.7	5.6
Clinical laboratory technologists and technicians	349	74.7	13.2	11.2	8.8
Dental hygienists	137	96.6	4.3	6.0	4.5
Diagnostic-related technologists and technicians	342	74.4	8.0	5.3	6.7
Emergency medical technicians and paramedics	156	30.1	7.8	1.2	5.5
Health diagnosing and treating practitioner support technicians	476	79.8	14.5	6.0	11.1
Licensed practical and licensed vocational nurses	633	91.4	22.4	3.5	8.8
Medical records and health information technicians	103	88.7	17.8	4.3	18.6
Service occupations	**24,598**	**57.2**	**15.4**	**4.6**	**20.6**
Healthcare support occupations [3]	3,309	89.4	25.3	3.9	13.8
Nursing, psychiatric, and home health aides	2,002	88.4	34.0	3.7	12.4
Massage therapists	150	85.7	5.1	8.3	10.0
Dental assistants	286	97.6	5.3	5.3	17.9
Medical assistants and other healthcare support occupations	776	90.7	16.2	3.1	16.9
Protective service occupations [3]	3,164	22.3	18.8	1.8	12.3
Fire-fighters	284	3.4	7.5	0.7	8.8
Bailiffs, correctional officers, and jailers	435	26.9	22.0	1.3	12.9
Detectives and criminal investigators	141	26.4	14.9	3.2	10.3
Police and sheriff's patrol officers	714	15.5	14.1	1.5	12.7
Security guards and gaming surveillance officers	942	21.9	28.6	2.2	16.2
Lifeguards and other protective service workers	167	53.3	5.2	1.0	5.4
Food preparation and serving related occupations	7,733	55.7	11.4	5.4	21.6
Chefs and head cooks	348	20.7	12.6	13.8	20.6
First-line supervisors/managers of food preparation and serving workers	597	56.9	15.4	3.6	15.8
Cooks	2,004	41.5	15.5	4.8	32.1
Food-preparation workers	748	58.0	11.2	5.4	22.8
Bartenders	404	56.4	5.6	2.1	11.3
Combined food preparation and serving workers, including fast food	341	67.0	13.3	4.0	15.4
Counter attendants, cafeteria, food concession, and coffee shop	264	65.8	12.7	4.3	12.9
Waiters and waitresses	2,005	71.5	6.2	6.4	15.0
Food servers, nonrestaurant	169	65.7	18.9	4.9	18.4
Dining room and cafeteria attendants and bartender helpers	320	54.1	13.7	6.6	28.8
Dishwashers	263	20.9	10.9	3.5	39.5
Hosts and hostesses, restaurant, lounge, and coffee shop	258	86.4	8.0	2.8	12.5
Building and grounds cleaning and maintenance occupations	5,349	40.4	13.8	2.9	34.1
First-line supervisors/managers of housekeeping and janitorial workers	276	40.6	13.5	2.8	21.0
First-line supervisors/managers of landscaping, lawn service, and groundskeeping workers	263	5.0	3.9	1.2	22.2
Janitors and building cleaners	2,149	32.2	17.3	2.9	29.4
Maids and housekeeping cleaners	1,428	89.8	16.1	4.3	41.7
Grounds maintenance workers	1,178	5.3	7.0	1.5	39.6

See footnotes at end of table.

[139,877 represents 139,877,000. Civilian noninstitutional population 16 years old and over. Annual average of monthly figures. Based on Current Population Survey; see text, Section 1, and Appendix III. Occupational classifications are those used in the 2000 census]

Occupation	Total employed (1,000)	Percent of total			
		Female	Black [1]	Asian [1]	Hispanic [2]
Personal care and service occupations [3]	5,043	78.1	14.5	7.4	14.3
First-line supervisors/managers of gaming workers	154	46.0	4.8	5.4	6.1
First-line supervisors/managers of personal service workers	212	72.3	7.6	17.3	6.3
Nonfarm animal caretakers	163	66.3	4.4	1.7	11.2
Gaming services workers	127	49.1	11.0	26.0	11.2
Barbers	93	18.6	35.0	1.8	19.8
Hairdressers, hairstylists, and cosmetologists	800	90.4	11.9	4.3	12.1
Baggage porters, bellhops, and concierges	74	22.2	27.1	5.7	19.8
Transportation attendants	133	72.3	17.9	4.3	15.0
Child care workers	1,292	95.0	16.8	2.7	18.4
Personal and home care aides	926	85.2	21.1	7.3	19.0
Recreation and fitness workers	369	65.0	9.0	3.0	10.3
Sales and office occupations	**33,787**	**63.0**	**11.2**	**4.2**	**12.4**
Sales and related occupations [3]	15,641	49.6	9.6	4.8	11.9
First-line supervisors/managers of retail sales workers	3,311	44.1	7.7	5.8	10.3
First-line supervisors/managers of non retail sales workers	1,291	28.0	6.1	4.5	9.0
Cashiers	3,056	74.4	15.6	6.3	17.2
Counter and rental clerks	142	48.5	14.1	5.4	10.1
Parts salespersons	102	13.2	6.9	0.2	11.9
Retail salespersons	3,182	51.8	10.9	5.0	14.0
Advertising sales agents	209	49.6	6.8	1.3	3.5
Insurance sales agents	548	46.3	6.3	2.1	9.5
Securities, commodities, and financial services sales agents	329	27.9	5.6	4.5	7.8
Travel agents	72	79.7	11.8	3.3	10.7
Sales representatives, services, all other	514	33.4	8.6	3.7	11.4
Sales representatives, wholesale and manufacturing	1,317	27.4	4.7	2.6	8.2
Real estate brokers and sales agents	860	54.6	5.7	4.8	7.4
Telemarketers	122	66.7	21.7	1.1	10.6
Door-to-door sales workers, news and street vendors, and related workers	217	64.0	10.0	2.2	19.5
Office and administrative support occupations [3]	18,146	74.5	12.7	3.6	12.7
First-line supervisors/managers of office and administrative support workers	1,632	71.3	9.8	2.9	10.7
Bill and account collectors	195	68.6	19.9	2.0	15.7
Billing and posting clerks and machine operators	481	89.9	13.4	2.9	13.9
Bookkeeping, accounting, and auditing clerks	1,306	92.2	6.6	3.7	7.5
Payroll and timekeeping clerks	150	86.7	15.1	3.9	14.4
Tellers	432	87.0	10.4	5.0	13.7
Court, municipal, and license clerks	105	73.6	18.1	5.0	10.3
Customer service representatives	1,862	67.9	18.0	3.9	15.6
File clerks	324	81.8	14.6	4.5	13.8
Hotel, motel, and resort desk clerks	143	65.5	15.9	6.7	13.2
Interviewers, except eligibility and loan	145	81.2	14.7	5.0	18.2
Library assistants, clerical	129	84.2	8.8	1.8	7.7
Loan interviewers and clerks	113	81.0	10.3	3.3	13.2
Order clerks	102	63.8	12.2	8.5	19.6
Receptionists and information clerks	1,277	91.5	9.8	2.5	15.1
Reservation and transportation ticket agents and travel clerks	111	57.9	16.5	5.5	9.0
Couriers and messengers	255	17.5	16.0	2.7	16.0
Dispatchers	278	55.7	15.4	1.6	14.0
Postal service clerks	154	49.6	28.3	13.7	9.4
Postal service mail carriers	355	35.0	14.9	7.7	9.1
Production, planning, and expediting clerks	281	54.1	8.6	4.2	4.9
Shipping, receiving, and traffic clerks	483	33.8	14.4	2.7	23.0
Stock clerks and order fillers	1,397	36.4	15.8	4.4	17.5
Secretaries and administrative assistants	3,176	96.8	8.3	1.9	9.2
Computer operators	115	52.3	21.5	4.2	14.4
Data entry keyers	375	79.1	14.8	5.2	13.3
Word processors and typists	163	92.2	17.1	3.7	19.0
Insurance claims and policy processing clerks	252	82.7	16.7	1.8	12.9
Mail clerks and mail machine operators, except postal service	104	50.0	24.3	5.3	10.1
Office clerks, general	1,002	81.9	13.1	5.5	13.9
Natural resources, construction, and maintenance occupations	**13,323**	**4.4**	**6.8**	**2.0**	**24.2**
Farming, fishing, and forestry occupations [3]	926	20.5	5.0	1.4	40.7
Construction and extraction occupations [3]	7,439	2.6	6.0	1.4	28.5
First-line supervisors/managers of construction trades and extraction workers	735	3.7	5.0	0.8	16.1
Brickmasons, blockmasons, and stonemasons	151	0.1	10.3	1.1	31.3
Carpenters	1,264	1.6	4.5	1.5	24.2

See footnotes at end of table.

Table 615. Employed Civilians by Occupation, Sex, Race, and Hispanic Origin: 2009—Con.

[139,877 represents 139,877,000. Civilian noninstitutional population 16 years old and over. Annual average of monthly figures. Based on Current Population Survey; see text, Section 1, and Appendix III. Occupational classifications are those used in the 2000 census]

Occupation	Total employed (1,000)	Percent of total			
		Female	Black [1]	Asian [1]	Hispanic [2]
Carpet, floor, and tile installers and finishers	223	2.3	2.3	1.8	44.5
Cement masons, concrete finishers, and terrazzo workers.........	74	0.6	4.9	–	51.5
Construction laborers	1,427	2.7	7.4	1.9	44.2
Operating engineers and other construction equipment operators ...	377	1.5	5.5	0.8	13.7
Drywall installers, ceiling tile installers, and tapers	170	2.2	3.2	–	56.6
Electricians	776	2.2	6.7	1.7	15.3
Painters, construction and maintenance	522	6.9	6.6	1.6	39.9
Pipelayers, plumbers, pipefitters, and steamfitters	536	1.3	6.5	1.4	18.0
Roofers	216	0.5	4.4	0.9	47.7
Sheet metal workers	132	2.5	7.5	1.5	11.1
Structural iron and steel workers	63	3.7	2.7	1.2	9.0
Helpers, construction trades	64	3.7	5.9	0.3	48.6
Construction and building inspectors	99	6.3	7.3	2.6	10.8
Highway maintenance workers	108	2.3	13.6	0.1	12.3
Installation, maintenance, and repair occupations [3]	4,957	4.2	8.4	3.1	14.6
First-line supervisors/managers of mechanics, installers, and repairers	342	8.7	7.0	2.0	9.8
Computer, automated teller, and office machine repairers	329	13.0	9.9	4.9	11.4
Radio and telecommunications equipment installers and repairers	179	8.3	12.6	3.3	12.5
Security and fire alarm systems installers	71	3.5	2.9	–	13.0
Aircraft mechanics and service technicians	142	3.8	7.0	6.9	15.5
Automotive body and related repairers	163	1.5	7.3	1.1	30.5
Automotive service technicians and mechanics	799	1.8	8.0	3.3	18.7
Bus and truck mechanics and diesel engine specialists	330	0.8	7.1	3.3	13.0
Heavy vehicle and mobile equipment service technicians and mechanics..	223	1.6	5.8	1.4	9.7
Heating, air conditioning, and refrigeration mechanics and installers	376	0.7	6.1	1.8	18.7
Industrial and refractory machinery mechanics	418	3.5	9.2	3.2	11.3
Maintenance and repair workers, general	415	2.6	11.0	2.9	15.2
Electrical power-line installers and repairers	126	1.3	10.0	0.7	10.8
Telecommunications line installers and repairers	183	3.7	14.2	3.0	15.4
Production, transportation, and material moving occupations	**15,951**	**21.4**	**13.5**	**3.7**	**21.1**
Production occupations [3]..................................	7,654	28.1	11.5	4.9	21.9
First-line supervisors/managers of production and operating workers	739	18.1	9.3	4.9	14.8
Electrical, electronics, and electromechanical assemblers	147	59.4	11.6	13.2	28.8
Bakers	193	56.0	6.3	4.5	32.7
Butchers and other meat, poultry, and fish processing workers	302	22.8	16.7	7.8	35.9
Food batchmakers	87	50.0	7.0	1.8	32.5
Cutting, punching, and press machine setters, operators, and tenders, metal and plastic	81	25.1	10.0	1.6	18.1
Machinists..	372	5.4	5.1	5.7	15.0
Welding, soldering, and brazing workers	459	4.0	9.0	3.4	18.1
Printing machine operators	155	21.9	7.7	2.9	18.6
Laundry and dry-cleaning workers	192	57.3	17.8	9.3	30.6
Sewing machine operators	197	72.9	10.0	13.3	41.7
Tailors, dressmakers, and sewers	74	76.3	8.6	16.5	24.3
Cabinetmakers and bench carpenters	50	3.7	4.7	0.9	24.1
Stationary engineers and boiler operators	98	2.7	10.4	3.1	([4])
Water and liquid waste treatment plant and system operators	72	5.8	18.9	2.9	6.3
Crushing, grinding, polishing, mixing, and blending workers	108	13.1	11.5	2.1	27.2
Cutting workers......................................	81	25.6	10.6	5.3	29.9
Inspectors, testers, sorters, samplers, and weighers	612	34.0	11.0	4.5	14.5
Medical, dental, and ophthalmic laboratory technicians	96	51.8	6.7	5.9	16.4
Packaging and filling machine operators and tenders	237	54.7	15.8	4.0	45.1
Painting workers	153	10.4	14.8	0.7	22.1
Transportation and material-moving occupations [3]	8,297	15.3	15.3	2.6	20.4
Supervisors, transportation and material-moving workers	221	22.6	13.2	2.2	15.0
Aircraft pilots and flight engineers	126	1.3	2.3	1.6	3.9
Bus drivers	655	51.5	24.9	2.0	13.3
Driver/sales workers and truck drivers	3,151	5.2	13.4	1.8	18.7
Taxi drivers and chauffeurs	377	14.6	25.7	12.6	15.3
Parking lot attendants	84	11.8	24.4	8.5	22.2
Service station attendants	89	13.0	9.3	4.7	14.1
Industrial truck and tractor operators	507	6.9	22.4	1.7	26.6
Cleaners of vehicles and equipment	316	11.2	16.4	1.7	37.1
Laborers and freight, stock, and material movers, hand	1,707	17.2	14.0	2.7	21.9
Packers and packagers, hand	378	56.4	12.3	4.8	43.7
Refuse and recyclable material collectors	83	5.8	17.0	0.2	25.9

– Represents or rounds to zero. [1] The Current Population Survey (CPS) allows respondents to choose more than one race. Data represent persons who selected this race group only and exclude persons reporting more than one race. The CPS in prior years only allowed respondents to report one race group. See also comments on race in the text for Section 1. [2] Persons of Hispanic or Latino ethnicity may be any race. [3] Includes other occupations, not shown separately. [4] Data not shown where base is less than 75,000.

Source: U.S. Bureau of Labor Statistics, "Employment and Earnings Online," January 2010, <http://www.bls.gov/opub/ee /home.htm> and <http://www.bls.gov/cps/home.htm>.

Table 616. Employed Civilians by Occupation—States: 2009

[In thousands (139,877 represents 139,877,000). Based on the Current Population Survey see text, Section 1 and Appendix III]

| State | Management, professional, and related occupations | | | Service occupations | Sales and office occupations | | Natural resources, construction, and maintenance occupations | | | Production, transportation, and material-moving occupations | |
	Total	Management, business, and financial operations	Professional and related occupations		Sales and related occupations	Office and administrative occupations	Farming, fishing, and forestry occupations	Construction and extraction occupations	Installation, maintenance, and repair occupations	Production occupations	Transportation and material-moving occupations
Total....	139,877	21,529	30,690	24,598	15,641	18,146	926	7,439	4,957	7,654	8,297
AL	1,911	222	411	284	214	268	14	139	98	136	126
AK	333	50	72	57	31	44	4	23	16	12	24
AZ	2,836	438	599	516	351	404	12	143	103	112	157
AR	1,266	177	238	180	146	161	23	77	59	113	92
CA	16,190	2,583	3,597	2,942	1,854	2,028	182	797	509	817	882
CO......	2,526	454	602	400	297	316	11	144	77	105	119
CT	1,737	299	456	283	188	221	2	85	48	80	75
DE	400	61	90	72	44	58	3	20	13	17	24
DC......	305	72	110	46	20	33	(Z)	7	3	3	11
FL	8,152	1,315	1,710	1,504	1,043	1,116	25	417	323	265	435
GA	4,329	693	926	686	542	534	28	244	170	210	297
HI.......	585	82	110	137	72	79	5	35	19	16	29
ID.......	686	107	133	121	87	86	14	30	26	36	46
IL.......	5,945	902	1,290	1,076	632	796	25	261	178	351	432
IN.......	2,879	403	582	476	349	327	14	145	113	269	202
IA.......	1,581	246	320	251	154	219	15	60	59	138	119
KS.......	1,425	230	313	243	152	178	10	74	63	87	75
KY.......	1,846	236	380	316	203	215	20	105	81	142	147
LA.......	1,929	275	399	336	212	252	16	130	88	105	115
ME.......	638	97	145	108	70	75	10	39	24	35	36
MD.......	2,821	515	775	461	267	356	7	150	83	83	124
MA.......	3,193	528	887	550	321	409	8	143	90	127	130
MI.......	4,253	595	997	789	445	543	24	180	153	275	252
MN.......	2,703	448	661	407	200	340	20	108	88	179	152
MS.......	1,149	132	235	225	96	156	12	76	41	102	75
MO......	2,779	415	534	484	309	399	15	152	106	182	182
MT.......	462	79	92	90	52	53	9	29	16	18	24
NE.......	937	144	201	146	102	124	11	44	32	75	57
NV	1,199	178	199	289	144	165	3	75	45	31	71
NH	695	119	162	106	88	85	2	33	23	42	34
NJ	4,138	707	984	700	483	569	5	183	97	175	235
NM......	866	109	197	153	87	118	8	70	44	43	37
NY	8,913	1,261	2,084	1,770	1,004	1,166	21	485	265	330	527
NC	4,096	647	886	709	475	478	20	239	166	256	221
ND	349	60	68	63	34	43	7	22	13	20	19
OH......	5,313	741	1,000	1035	562	700	17	222	197	415	357
OK......	1,668	265	324	267	182	230	14	109	80	95	102
OR......	1,741	299	379	295	190	232	29	74	52	92	99
PA	5,893	834	1,302	1,042	591	811	34	298	225	344	413
RI.......	501	66	123	93	54	69	2	22	14	33	25
SC	1,881	248	381	332	225	254	6	96	93	152	95
SD	425	77	77	72	47	57	9	21	14	26	24
TN	2,704	387	542	485	296	352	7	165	102	192	177
TX	11,007	1,644	2,138	1,917	1,284	1,419	75	779	435	615	703
UT	1,280	204	264	182	158	188	8	84	44	78	70
VT	336	53	85	54	37	38	4	20	10	20	15
VA	3,856	728	979	610	400	444	23	197	123	165	186
WA......	3,216	513	754	563	335	399	51	171	99	137	194
WV......	754	94	156	129	81	109	2	58	33	38	54
WI	2,837	431	601	478	301	373	28	129	82	247	166
WY......	279	43	47	46	26	34	3	27	17	11	24

Z Less than 500.

Source: U.S. Bureau of Labor Statistics, *Geographic Profile of Employment and Unemployment, 2009*, Bulletin 2748, July 2010. See also <http://www.bls.gov/opub/gp/gpsec11.htm>.

U.S. Census Bureau, Statistical Abstract of the United States: 2011

Table 617. Employment Projections by Occupation: 2008 to 2018

[In thousands (16.0 represents 16,000), except percent and rank. Estimates based on the Current Employment Statistics Program; the Occupational Employment Statistics Survey; and the Current Population Survey. See source for methodological assumptions. Occupations based on the 2000 Standard Occupational Classification system]

Occupation	Employment (1,000)		Change, 2008–2018		Quartile rank by 2008 median annual earn-ings [1]	Most significant source of postsecondary education or training
	2008	2018	Num-ber (1,000)	Per-cent		
FASTEST GROWING						
Biomedical engineers	16.0	27.6	11.6	72.0	VH	Bachelor's degree
Network systems and data communications analyst.	292.0	447.8	155.8	53.4	VH	Bachelor's degree
Home health aides.	921.7	1,382.6	460.9	50.0	VL	Short-term on-the-job training
Personal and home care aides	817.2	1,193.0	375.8	46.0	VL	Short-term on-the-job training
Financial examiners.	27.0	38.1	11.1	41.2	VH	Bachelor's degree
Medical scientists, except epidemiologists	109.4	153.6	44.2	40.4	VH	Doctoral degree
Physician assistants	74.8	103.9	29.2	39.0	VH	Master's degree
Skin care specialists	38.8	53.5	14.7	37.9	L	Postsecondary vocational award
Biochemists and biophysicists.	23.2	31.9	8.7	37.4	VH	Doctoral degree
Athletic trainers	16.3	22.4	6.0	37.0	H	Bachelor's degree
Physical therapist aides.	46.1	62.8	16.7	36.3	L	Short-term on-the-job training
Dental hygienists	174.1	237.0	62.9	36.1	VH	Associate degree
Veterinary technologists and technicians	79.6	108.1	28.5	35.8	L	Associate degree
Dental assistants	295.3	400.9	105.6	35.8	L	Moderate-term on-the-job training
Computer software engineers, applications	514.8	689.9	175.1	34.0	VH	Bachelor's degree
Medical assistants.	483.6	647.5	163.9	33.9	L	Moderate-term on-the-job training
Physical therapist assistants	63.8	85.0	21.2	33.3	H	Associate degree
Veterinarians	59.7	79.4	19.7	33.0	VH	First professional degree
Self-enrichment education teachers	253.6	334.9	81.3	32.0	H	Work experience in a related occupation
Compliance officers, except agriculture, construc-tion, health and safety, and transportation.	260.2	341.0	80.8	31.1	H	Long-term on-the-job training
Occupational therapist aides.	7.8	10.2	2.4	30.7	L	Short-term on-the-job training
Environmental engineers.	54.3	70.9	16.6	30.6	VH	Bachelor's degree
Pharmacy technicians	326.3	426.0	99.8	30.6	L	Moderate-term on-the-job training
Computer software engineers, systems software .	394.8	515.0	120.2	30.4	VH	Bachelor's degree
Survey researchers	23.4	30.5	7.1	30.4	H	Bachelor's degree
Physical therapists.	185.5	241.7	56.2	30.3	VH	Master's degree
Environmental engineering technicians.	21.2	27.5	6.4	30.1	H	Associate degree
Occupational therapist assistants	26.6	34.6	7.9	29.8	H	Associate degree
Fitness trainers and aerobics instructors.	261.1	337.9	76.8	29.4	L	Postsecondary vocational award
LARGEST JOB GROWTH						
Registered nurses	2,618.7	3,200.2	581.5	22.2	VH	Associate degree
Home health aides.	921.7	1,382.6	460.9	50.0	VL	Short-term on-the-job training
Customer service representatives.	2,252.4	2,651.9	399.5	17.7	L	Moderate-term on-the-job training
Combined food preparation and serving workers, including fast food	2,701.7	3,096.0	394.3	14.6	VL	Short-term on-the-job training
Personal and home care aides	817.2	1,193.0	375.8	46.0	VL	Short-term on-the-job training
Retail salespersons.	4,489.2	4,863.9	374.7	8.4	VL	Short-term on-the-job training
Office clerks, general.	3,024.4	3,383.1	358.7	11.9	L	Short-term on-the-job training
Accountants and auditors	1,290.6	1,570.0	279.4	21.7	VH	Bachelor's degree
Nursing aides, orderlies, and attendants.	1,469.8	1,745.8	276.0	18.8	L	Postsecondary vocational award
Postsecondary teachers	1,699.2	1,956.1	256.9	15.1	VH	Doctoral degree
Construction laborers	1,248.7	1,504.6	255.9	20.5	L	Moderate-term on-the-job training
Elementary school teachers, except special education.	1,549.5	1,793.7	244.2	15.8	H	Bachelor's degree
Truck drivers, heavy and tractor-trailer	1,798.4	2,031.3	232.9	13.0	H	Short-term on-the-job training
Landscaping and groundskeeping workers.	1,205.8	1,422.9	217.1	18.0	L	Short-term on-the-job training
Bookkeeping, accounting, and auditing clerks . . .	2,063.8	2,276.2	212.4	10.3	H	Moderate-term on-the-job training
Executive secretaries and administrative assistants.	1,594.4	1,798.8	204.4	12.8	H	Work experience in a related occupation
Management analysts	746.9	925.2	178.3	23.9	VH	Bachelor's or higher degree, plus work experience
Computer software engineers, applications	514.8	689.9	175.1	34.0	VH	Bachelor's degree
Receptionists and information clerks.	1,139.2	1,312.1	172.9	15.2	L	Short-term on-the-job training
Carpenters.	1,284.9	1,450.3	165.4	12.9	H	Long-term on-the-job training
Medical assistants.	483.6	647.5	163.9	33.9	L	Moderate-term on-the-job training
First-line supervisors/managers of office and administrative support workers	1,457.2	1,617.5	160.3	11.0	H	Work experience in a related occupation
Network systems and data communications analysts.	292.0	447.8	155.8	53.4	VH	Bachelor's degree
Licensed practical and licensed vocational nurses	753.6	909.2	155.6	20.7	H	Postsecondary vocational award

[1] Quartile ranks based on the Occupational Employment Statistics annual wages. VH = very high ($51,540 and over), H = high ($32,390 to $51,530), L = low ($21,590 to $32,380), and VL = very low (under $21,590). The rankings were based on quartiles using one-fourth of total employment to define each quartile. Wages are for wage and salary workers.

Source: U.S. Bureau of Labor Statistics "Occupational employment projections to 2018," *Monthly Labor Review*, Volume 132, Number 11, November 2009, <http://www.bls.gov/opub/mlr/2009/11/art5exc.htm>.

Table 618. Occupations of the Employed by Selected Characteristic: 2009

[In thousands (122,277 represents 122,277,000). Annual averages of monthly figures. Civilian noninstitutional population 25 years old and over. Based on Current Population Survey; see text, Section 1 and Appendix III. See headnote, Table 605, regarding occupations]

Race and educational attainment	Total employed	Managerial, professional, and related	Service	Sales and office	Natural resources, construction, and maintenance	Production, transportation, and material-moving
Total [1]	122,277	49,236	18,964	28,159	11,799	14,118
Less than a high school diploma	10,371	701	3,350	1,395	2,335	2,590
High school graduates, no college	34,487	5,770	7,278	9,465	5,126	6,848
Less than a bachelor's degree	33,888	11,315	5,696	10,055	3,359	3,463
College graduates	43,531	31,450	2,640	7,244	978	1,218
White [2]	100,419	41,163	14,243	23,291	10,428	11,295
Less than a high school diploma	8,497	584	2,538	1,129	2,091	2,155
High school graduates, no college	28,372	4,965	5,318	8,004	4,575	5,510
Less than a bachelor's degree	27,697	9,526	4,330	8,211	2,927	2,702
College graduates	35,854	26,089	2,056	5,946	835	927
Black [2]	13,110	4,126	3,193	3,016	830	1,944
Less than a high school diploma	1,096	67	505	157	125	241
High school graduates, no college	4,375	554	1,420	1,016	369	1,016
Less than a bachelor's degree	4,277	1,212	977	1,271	270	546
College graduates	3,363	2,294	291	572	66	140
Asian [2]	6,110	3,091	996	1,229	250	544
Less than a high school diploma	448	32	184	69	34	128
High school graduates, no college	1,028	152	356	259	79	182
Less than a bachelor's degree	1,013	313	219	298	76	107
College graduates	3,622	2,594	236	602	62	127
Hispanic [3]	16,687	3,498	4,207	3,180	2,826	2,977
Less than a high school diploma	5,233	200	1,802	512	1,383	1,336
High school graduates, no college	5,069	585	1,374	1,121	901	1,087
Less than a bachelor's degree	3,656	1,016	738	1,074	416	412
College graduates	2,729	1,697	292	472	126	142

[1] Includes other races not shown separately. [2] For persons in this race group only. See footnote 4, Table 585. [3] Persons of Hispanic or Latino ethnicity may be any race.

Source: U.S. Bureau of Labor Statistics, Current Population Survey, unpublished data.

Table 619. Employment by Industry: 2000 to 2009

[In thousands (136,891 represents 136,891,000), except percent. See headnote, Table 605]

Industry	2000	2005 [1]	2008 [1]	2009 [1]	2009, percent [1] Female	Black [2]	Asian [2]	Hispanic [3]
Total employed	136,891	141,730	145,362	139,877	47.3	10.7	4.7	14.0
Agriculture and related industries	2,464	2,197	2,168	2,103	23.6	3.1	1.1	20.3
Mining	475	624	819	707	13.3	4.4	1.3	15.4
Construction	9,931	11,197	10,974	9,702	9.5	5.2	1.6	00.6
Manufacturing	19,611	18,230	15,904	14,202	28.7	8.8	5.5	15.3
Durable goods	12,519	10,333	10,273	8,927	24.7	7.5	5.8	12.9
Nondurable goods	7,125	5,919	5,631	5,275	35.4	11.1	5.0	19.5
Wholesale trade	4,216	4,579	4,052	3,808	29.1	7.3	4.2	14.7
Retail trade	15,763	16,825	16,533	15,877	49.2	10.3	4.9	13.8
Transportation and utilities	7,380	7,360	7,727	7,245	22.9	15.7	3.9	13.9
Transportation and warehousing	6,096	6,184	6,501	6,012	23.7	17.0	4.2	14.8
Utilities	1,284	1,176	1,225	1,233	19.3	9.7	2.1	9.7
Information	4,059	3,402	3,481	3,239	42.0	11.1	5.4	9.5
Financial activities	9,374	10,203	10,228	9,622	54.0	9.2	4.7	10.2
Finance and insurance	6,641	7,035	7,279	6,826	57.5	9.4	5.1	9.3
Real estate and rental and leasing	2,734	3,168	2,949	2,796	45.5	8.7	3.6	12.3
Professional and business services	13,649	14,294	15,540	15,008	41.7	8.9	5.7	13.9
Professional and technical services	8,266	8,584	9,362	9,159	43.8	5.9	8.0	7.2
Management, administrative, and waste services	5,383	5,709	6,178	5,849	38.6	13.6	2.2	24.4
Education and health services	26,188	29,174	31,402	31,819	75.2	14.0	4.8	10.0
Educational services	11,255	12,264	13,169	13,188	69.4	10.4	3.7	9.1
Health care and social assistance	14,933	16,910	18,233	18,632	79.3	16.6	5.5	10.6
Hospitals	5,202	5,719	6,241	6,265	77.0	15.9	6.9	8.8
Health services, except hospitals	7,009	8,332	8,865	9,213	78.9	15.9	5.1	10.8
Social assistance	2,722	2,860	3,127	3,154	85.0	19.8	3.7	13.5
Leisure and hospitality	11,186	12,071	12,767	12,736	51.5	10.4	6.3	19.1
Arts, entertainment, and recreation	2,539	2,765	2,972	3,018	46.3	8.7	5.1	10.7
Accommodation and food services	8,647	9,306	9,795	9,717	53.1	11.0	6.7	21.7
Other services	6,450	7,020	7,005	6,935	52.1	9.7	5.7	17.5
Other services, except private households	5,731	6,208	6,200	6,152	47.2	10.0	6.0	14.9
Private households	718	812	805	783	90.6	7.1	3.5	37.8
Government workers	6,113	6,530	6,763	6,875	45.5	15.6	3.7	10.1

[1] See footnote 2, Table 584. [2] Persons in this race group only. See footnote 4, Table 585. [3] Persons of Hispanic or Latino origin may be any race.

Source: U.S. Bureau of Labor Statistics, "Employment and Earnings Online," January 2010, <http://www.bls.gov/opub/ee/home.htm> and <http://www.bls.gov/cps/home.htm>.

Labor Force, Employment, and Earnings 399

Table 620. Employment Projections by Industry: 2008 to 2018

[7,214.9 represents 7,214,900. Estimates based on the Current Employment Statistics program. See source for methodological assumptions. Minus sign (–) indicates decline]

Industry	2007 NAICS code [1]	Employment		Change, 2008–2018 (1,000)	Average annual rate of change 2008–2018
		2008 (1,000)	2018 (1,000)		
LARGEST GROWTH					
Construction	23	7,214.9	8,552.0	1,337.1	1.7
Offices of health practitioners	6211, 6212, 6213	3,713.3	4,978.6	1,265.3	3.0
Management, scientific, and technical consulting services	5416	1,008.9	1,844.1	835.2	6.2
Food services and drinking places	722	9,631.9	10,370.7	738.8	0.7
Computer systems design and related services	5415	1,450.3	2,106.7	656.4	3.8
Retail trade	44, 45	15,356.4	16,010.4	654.0	0.4
General local government educational services compensation	(X)	8,075.6	8,728.3	652.7	0.8
Nursing and residential care facilities	623	3,008.0	3,644.8	636.8	1.9
Employment services	5613	3,144.4	3,744.1	599.7	1.8
Hospitals	622	4,641.2	5,191.9	550.7	1.1
Individual and family services	6241	1,108.6	1,638.8	530.2	4.0
Home health care services	6216	958.0	1,399.4	441.4	3.9
Services to buildings and dwellings	5617	1,847.1	2,182.6	335.5	1.7
Architectural, engineering, and related services	5413	1,444.7	1,769.5	324.8	2.0
Other educational services	6114–7	578.9	894.9	316.0	4.5
Outpatient, laboratory, and other ambulatory care services	6214, 6215, 6219	989.5	1,297.9	308.4	2.8
Wholesale trade	42	5,963.9	6,219.8	255.9	0.4
Junior colleges, colleges, universities, and professional schools	6112, 6113	1,602.7	1,857.4	254.7	1.5
Legal services	5411	1,163.7	1,416.8	253.1	2.0
General government, other compensation	(X)	4,224.1	4,464.0	239.9	0.6
FASTEST GROWTH					
Management, scientific, and technical consulting services	5416	1,008.9	1,844.1	835.2	6.2
Other educational services	6114–7	578.9	894.9	316.0	4.5
Individual and family services	6241	1,108.6	1,638.8	530.2	4.0
Home health care services	6216	958.0	1,399.4	441.4	3.9
Specialized design services	5414	143.1	208.7	65.6	3.8
Data processing, hosting, related services, and other information services	518, 519	395.2	574.1	178.9	3.8
Computer systems design and related services	5415	1,450.3	2,106.7	656.4	3.8
Lessors of nonfinancial intangible assets (except copyright works)	533	28.2	37.9	9.7	3.0
Offices of health practitioners	6211, 6212, 6213	3,713.3	4,978.6	1,265.3	3.0
Personal care services	8121	621.6	819.1	197.5	2.8
Outpatient, laboratory, and other ambulatory care services	6214, 6215, 6219	989.5	1,297.9	308.4	2.8
Facilities support services	5612	132.7	173.6	40.9	2.7
Software publishers	5112	263.7	342.8	79.1	2.7
Independent artists, writers, and performers	7115	50.4	64.8	14.4	2.5
Local government passenger transit	(X)	268.6	342.6	74.0	2.5
Elementary and secondary schools	6111	854.9	1,089.7	234.8	2.5
Scientific research and development services	5417	621.7	778.9	157.2	2.3
Waste management and remediation services	562	360.2	451.0	90.8	2.3
Other miscellaneous manufacturing	3399	321.0	399.4	78.4	2.2
Community and vocational rehabilitation services	6242, 6243	540.9	672.0	131.1	2.2
MOST RAPIDLY DECLINING					
Cut and sew apparel manufacturing	3152	155.2	66.7	–88.5	–8.1
Apparel knitting mills	3151	26.2	12.5	–13.7	–7.1
Textile and fabric finishing and fabric coating mills	3133	48.3	23.5	–24.8	–7.0
Fabric mills	3132	65.4	35.0	–30.4	–6.1
Audio and video equipment manufacturing	3343	27.0	14.6	–12.4	–6.0
Apparel accessories and other apparel manufacturing	3159	17.0	9.2	–7.8	–6.0
Fiber, yarn, and thread mills	3131	37.4	20.7	–16.7	–5.7
Textile furnishings mills	3141	75.4	41.9	–33.5	–5.7
Railroad rolling stock manufacturing	3365	28.4	17.5	–10.9	–4.7
Footwear manufacturing	3162	15.8	10.0	–5.8	–4.5
Pulp, paper, and paperboard mills	3221	126.1	81.9	–44.2	–4.2
Basic chemical manufacturing	3251	152.1	99.9	–52.2	–4.1
Semiconductor and other electronic component manufacturing	3344	432.4	286.8	–145.6	–4.0
Computer and peripheral equipment manufacturing	3341	182.8	124.7	–58.1	–3.8
Other textile product mills	3149	72.2	49.4	–22.8	3.0
Federal enterprises except the Postal Service and electric utilities	(X)	63.5	44.9	–18.6	–3.4
Leather and hide tanning and finishing, and other leather and allied product manufacturing	3161, 3169	17.8	13.0	–4.8	–3.1
Cutlery and handtool manufacturing	3322	49.1	35.9	–13.2	–3.1
Manufacturing and reproducing magnetic and optical media	3346	34.9	26.0	–8.9	–2.9
Ventilation, heating, air–conditioning, and commercial refrigeration equipment manufacturing	3334	149.5	112.8	–36.7	–2.8

X Not applicable. [1] Based on the North American Industry Classification System, 2007; see text, Section 15.

Source: U.S. Bureau of Labor Statistics, "Industry output and employment projections to 2018," *Monthly Labor Review*, Vol. 132, No. 11, November 2009, <http://www.bls.gov/opub/mlr/2009/11/art4exc.htm>.

Table 621. Unemployed Workers—Summary: 1980 to 2009

[In thousands (7,637 represents 7,637,000), except as indicated. For civilian noninstitutionalized population 16 years old and over. Annual averages of monthly figures. Based on the Current Population Survey; see text, Section 1 and Appendix III. For data on unemployment insurance, see Table 556]

Item	1980	1990 [1]	2000 [1]	2005 [1]	2006 [1]	2007 [1]	2008 [1]	2009 [1]
UNEMPLOYED								
Total [2]	**7,637**	**7,047**	**5,692**	**7,591**	**7,001**	**7,078**	**8,924**	**14,265**
16 to 19 years old	1,669	1,212	1,081	1,186	1,119	1,101	1,285	1,552
20 to 24 years old	1,835	1,299	1,022	1,335	1,234	1,241	1,545	2,207
25 to 34 years old	2,024	1,995	1,207	1,661	1,521	1,544	1,949	3,284
35 to 44 years old	940	1,328	1,133	1,400	1,279	1,225	1,604	2,722
45 to 54 years old	676	723	762	1,195	1,094	1,135	1,473	2,592
55 to 64 years old	399	386	355	630	595	642	803	1,487
65 years and over	94	105	132	184	159	190	264	421
Male	4,267	3,906	2,975	4,059	3,753	3,882	5,033	8,453
16 to 19 years old	913	667	599	667	622	623	736	898
20 to 24 years old	1,076	715	547	775	705	721	920	1,329
25 to 34 years old	1,137	1,092	602	844	810	856	1,119	1,988
35 to 44 years old	482	711	557	715	642	634	875	1,600
45 to 54 years old	357	413	398	624	569	591	804	1,558
55 to 64 years old	243	249	189	331	318	349	425	840
65 years and over	58	59	83	102	88	108	153	241
Female	3,370	3,140	2,717	3,531	3,247	3,196	3,891	5,811
16 to 19 years old	755	544	483	519	496	478	549	654
20 to 24 years old	760	584	475	560	530	520	625	878
25 to 34 years old	886	902	604	817	711	688	830	1,296
35 to 44 years old	459	617	577	685	637	591	730	1,121
45 to 54 years old	318	310	364	571	524	544	669	1,034
55 to 64 years old	155	137	165	299	277	293	377	647
65 years and over	36	46	50	82	71	81	111	180
White [3]	5,884	5,186	4,121	5,350	5,002	5,143	6,509	10,648
Black [3]	1,553	1,565	1,241	1,700	1,549	1,445	1,788	2,606
Asian [3,4]	(NA)	(NA)	227	259	205	229	285	522
Hispanic [5]	620	876	954	1,191	1,081	1,220	1,678	2,706
UNEMPLOYMENT RATE [6] (percent)								
Total [2]	**7.1**	**5.6**	**4.0**	**5.1**	**4.6**	**4.6**	**5.8**	**9.3**
16 to 19 years old	17.8	15.5	13.1	16.6	15.4	15.7	18.7	24.3
20 to 24 years old	11.5	8.8	7.2	8.8	8.2	8.2	10.2	14.7
25 to 34 years old	6.9	5.6	3.7	5.1	4.7	4.7	5.0	9.9
35 to 44 years old	4.6	4.1	3.0	3.9	3.6	3.4	4.6	7.9
45 to 54 years old	4.0	3.6	2.5	3.5	3.1	3.2	4.1	7.2
55 to 64 years old	3.3	3.3	2.5	3.3	3.0	3.1	3.7	6.6
65 years and over	3.1	3.0	3.1	3.5	2.9	3.3	4.2	6.4
Male	6.9	5.7	3.9	5.1	4.6	4.7	6.1	10.3
16 to 19 years old	18.3	16.3	14.0	18.6	16.9	17.6	21.2	27.8
20 to 24 years old	12.5	9.1	7.3	9.6	8.7	8.9	11.4	17.0
25 to 34 years old	6.7	5.5	3.4	4.7	4.6	4.7	6.1	10.9
35 to 44 years old	4.1	4.1	2.8	3.7	3.3	3.3	4.6	8.6
45 to 54 years old	3.6	3.7	2.4	3.5	3.1	3.1	4.2	8.2
55 to 64 years old	3.4	3.8	2.4	3.3	3.0	3.2	3.8	7.2
65 years and over	3.1	3.0	3.3	3.4	2.8	3.4	4.5	6.7
Female	7.4	5.5	4.1	5.1	4.6	4.5	5.4	8.1
16 to 19 years old	17.2	14.7	12.1	14.5	13.8	13.8	16.2	20.7
20 to 24 years old	10.4	8.5	7.1	7.9	7.6	7.3	8.8	12.3
25 to 34 years old	7.2	5.6	4.1	5.6	4.9	4.6	5.5	8.6
35 to 44 years old	5.3	4.2	3.3	4.1	3.9	3.6	4.5	7.1
45 to 54 years old	4.5	3.4	2.5	3.5	3.1	3.2	3.9	6.0
55 to 64 years old	3.3	2.8	2.5	3.3	2.9	3.0	3.7	6.0
65 years and over	3.1	3.1	2.7	3.5	3.0	3.1	3.9	6.1
White [3]	6.3	4.8	3.5	4.4	4.0	4.1	5.2	8.5
Black [3]	14.3	11.4	7.6	10.0	8.9	8.3	10.1	14.8
Asian [3,4]	(NA)	(NA)	3.6	4.0	3.0	3.2	4.0	7.3
Hispanic [5]	10.1	8.2	5.7	6.0	5.2	5.6	7.6	12.1
Percent without work for—								
Fewer than 5 weeks	43.2	46.3	44.9	35.1	37.3	35.9	32.8	22.2
5 to 14 weeks	32.3	32.0	31.9	30.4	30.3	31.5	31.4	26.8
15 to 26 weeks	13.8	11.7	11.8	14.9	14.7	15.0	16.0	19.5
27 weeks and over	10.7	10.0	11.4	19.6	17.6	17.6	19.7	31.5
Unemployment duration, average (weeks)	11.9	12.0	12.6	18.4	16.8	16.8	17.9	24.4

NA Not available. [1] See footnote 2, Table 584. [2] Includes other races not shown separately. [3] See footnote 4, Table 585. [4] Prior to 2004, includes Pacific Islanders. [5] Persons of Hispanic or Latino origin may be any race. [6] Unemployed as percent of civilian labor force in specified group.

Source: U.S. Bureau of Labor Statistics, "Employment and Earnings Online," January 2010, <http://www.bls.gov/opub/ee/home.htm> and <http://www.bls.gov/cps/home.htm>.

Table 622. Unemployed Jobseekers' Job Search Activities: 2009

[14,265 represents 14,265,000. For the civilian noninstitutionalized population 16 years old and over. Annual averages of monthly data. Based on the Current Population Survey; see text, Section 1 and Appendix III]

Characteristic	Population (1,000)		Jobseekers' job search methods (percent)							Average number of methods used
	Total unemployed	Total jobseekers [1]	Employer directly	Sent out a resume or filled out applications	Placed or answered ads	Friends or relatives	Public employment agency	Private employment agency	Other activities	
Total, 16 years and over [2] ...	**14,265**	**12,635**	**55.2**	**54.0**	**18.2**	**28.7**	**22.6**	**8.9**	**16.1**	**2.04**
16 to 19 years old	1,552	1,475	52.9	60.1	12.0	19.5	10.3	3.3	10.2	1.69
20 to 24 years old	2,207	2,043	55.2	55.7	16.9	25.5	19.9	6.6	14.3	1.95
25 to 34 years old	3,284	2,918	55.5	54.3	18.8	29.9	24.1	9.3	15.3	2.08
35 to 44 years old	2,722	2,353	55.2	53.1	19.8	31.5	26.6	10.9	18.0	2.16
45 to 54 years old	2,592	2,228	57.1	52.6	20.1	31.2	26.5	10.7	18.6	2.18
55 to 64 years old	1,487	1,269	54.8	51.6	20.5	31.4	24.7	11.4	19.7	2.15
65 years old and over	421	349	52.2	41.6	15.1	30.1	16.6	7.0	16.7	1.80
Male..................	8,453	7,304	56.6	51.8	18.0	30.4	23.2	9.1	16.2	2.06
16 to 19 years old	898	851	54.0	58.8	11.9	20.7	11.5	3.6	9.9	1.71
20 to 24 years old	1,329	1,206	56.5	53.2	16.4	26.6	20.7	6.7	13.4	1.94
25 to 34 years old	1,988	1,703	56.8	52.2	18.7	32.2	24.4	9.7	14.6	2.09
35 to 44 years old	1,600	1,336	56.9	49.9	19.4	33.5	27.5	11.8	18.5	2.18
45 to 54 years old	1,558	1,304	58.1	50.8	20.7	33.1	27.1	10.8	19.8	2.21
55 to 64 years old	840	703	57.3	48.9	19.9	32.7	25.2	11.2	21.4	2.18
65 years old and over	241	201	53.2	40.4	13.4	31.8	15.1	5.6	17.6	1.77
Female..................	5,811	5,331	53.3	57.1	18.4	26.3	21.7	8.5	15.9	2.02
16 to 19 years old	654	624	51.5	61.9	12.1	17.8	8.7	3.0	10.6	1.66
20 to 24 years old	878	837	53.4	59.1	17.6	23.8	18.8	6.6	15.6	1.96
25 to 34 years old	1,296	1,215	53.8	57.2	19.0	26.7	23.7	8.7	16.3	2.06
35 to 44 years old	1,121	1,017	53.0	57.4	20.3	28.8	25.4	9.6	17.2	2.13
45 to 54 years old	1,034	924	55.6	55.1	19.3	28.6	25.8	10.5	16.9	2.13
55 to 64 years old	647	566	51.7	54.9	21.2	29.9	23.9	11.7	17.5	2.12
65 years old and over	180	147	50.8	43.2	17.6	27.7	18.6	9.0	15.5	1.83
White [3]	10,648	9,260	55.7	54.8	18.8	28.6	21.6	8.9	16.6	2.06
Male...................	6,421	5,429	57.3	52.5	18.7	30.3	22.2	9.1	16.9	2.08
Female.................	4,227	3,831	53.4	58.0	19.0	26.2	20.7	8.6	16.0	2.03
Black [3]	2,606	2,450	54.3	51.3	16.4	28.3	27.5	8.5	13.9	2.01
Male...................	1,448	1,348	54.7	49.1	15.7	29.8	28.6	8.7	13.0	2.00
Female.................	1,159	1,102	53.9	54.1	17.2	26.4	26.1	8.2	15.0	2.01
Asian [3]	522	484	50.3	51.6	17.8	33.9	16.8	11.6	19.3	2.02
Male...................	306	282	52.2	50.0	17.8	35.7	16.7	12.1	18.8	2.04
Female.................	216	201	47.8	53.8	17.8	31.3	17.0	10.9	20.0	1.99
Hispanic [4]...............	2,706	2,377	56.5	46.3	13.4	33.8	22.3	9.0	12.8	1.95
Male...................	1,670	1,430	58.4	43.9	13.5	35.5	22.9	8.9	13.0	1.97
Female.................	1,036	946	53.6	49.8	13.3	31.3	21.3	9.1	12.6	1.91

[1] Excludes persons on temporary layoff. [2] Includes other races not shown separately. [3] Data for this race group only. See footnote 4, Table 585. [4] Persons of Hispanic or Latino origin may be any race.

Source: U.S. Bureau of Labor Statistics, "Employment and Earnings Online," January 2010, <http://www.bls.gov/opub/ee /home.htm> and <http://www.bls.gov/cps/home.htm>.

Table 623. Unemployed Persons by Sex and Reason: 1980 to 2009

[In thousands (4,267 represents 4,267,000). For civilian noninstitutionalized population 16 years old and over. Annual averages of monthly figures. Based on Current Population Survey; see text, Section 1 and Appendix III]

Sex and reason	1980	1990 [1]	2000 [1]	2001	2002	2003 [1]	2004 [1]	2005 [1]	2006 [1]	2007 [1]	2008 [1]	2009 [1]
Male, total	**4,267**	**3,906**	**2,975**	**3,690**	**4,597**	**4,906**	**4,456**	**4,059**	**3,753**	**3,882**	**5,033**	**8,453**
Job losers [2]	2,649	2,257	1,516	2,119	2,820	3,024	2,603	2,188	2,021	2,175	3,055	5,967
Job leavers	438	528	387	422	434	422	437	445	406	408	458	438
Reentrants........	776	806	854	925	1,068	1,141	1,070	1,067	1,015	956	1,128	1,504
New entrants	405	315	217	223	274	320	346	359	312	343	393	545
Female, total.....	**3,370**	**3,140**	**2,717**	**3,111**	**3,781**	**3,868**	**3,694**	**3,531**	**3,247**	**3,196**	**3,891**	**5,811**
Job losers [2]	1,297	1,130	1,001	1,356	1,787	1,814	1,595	1,479	1,300	1,340	1,735	3,193
Job leavers	453	513	393	413	432	397	421	427	421	385	438	444
Reentrants........	1,152	1,124	1,107	1,105	1,300	1,336	1,338	1,319	1,223	1,186	1,345	1,683
New entrants	468	373	217	237	262	321	340	306	304	285	374	491

[1] See footnote 2, Table 584. [2] Beginning 2000, persons who completed temporary jobs are identified separately and are included as job losers.

Source: U.S. Bureau of Labor Statistics, "Employment and Earnings Online," January 2010, <http://www.bls.gov/opub/ee /home.htm> and <http://www.bls.gov/cps/home.htm>.

Table 624. Unemployment Rates by Industry and by Sex: 2000 to 2009

[In percent. Civilian noninstitutionalized population 16 years old and over. Annual averages of monthly figures. Rate represents unemployment as a percent of labor force in each specified group. Based on Current Population Survey; see text, Section 1 and Appendix III. See also headnote, Table 605, regarding industries]

Industry	2000	2005 [1]	2008 [1]	2009 [1]	Male 2000	Male 2009 [1]	Female 2000	Female 2009 [1]
All employed [2]	4.0	5.1	5.8	9.3	3.9	10.3	4.1	8.1
Wage and salary workers:								
Agriculture and related industries	9.0	8.3	9.2	14.3	8.3	14.1	11.5	15.3
Mining , quarrying, and oil and gas extraction	4.4	3.1	3.1	11.6	4.6	12.2	2.8	7.2
Construction	6.2	7.4	10.6	19.0	6.4	19.6	5.1	13.8
Manufacturing	3.5	4.9	5.8	12.1	3.0	11.8	4.5	12.7
Wholesale trade	3.3	4.0	4.5	7.2	2.8	6.9	4.4	7.8
Retail trade	4.6	5.7	6.2	9.5	4.0	9.6	5.1	9.3
Transportation and utilities	3.4	4.1	5.1	8.9	3.2	8.9	4.2	8.9
Transportation and warehousing	3.8	4.5	5.6	9.7	1.9	9.9	4.6	9.0
Utilities	1.9	1.9	2.6	4.8	2.8	3.9	2.1	8.6
Information	3.2	5.0	5.0	9.2	2.7	8.5	3.7	10.3
Telecommunications	2.3	5.2	4.4	8.4	1.5	7.4	3.3	10.0
Financial activities	2.4	2.9	3.9	6.4	2.1	6.5	2.6	6.3
Finance and insurance	2.2	2.7	3.6	5.8	1.7	5.6	2.5	5.9
Real estate and rental and leasing	3.1	3.3	4.8	8.1	2.9	8.5	3.2	7.7
Professional and business services	4.8	6.2	6.5	10.8	4.4	10.2	5.2	11.6
Professional and technical services	2.5	3.5	3.8	6.7	2.2	6.0	2.9	7.6
Management, administrative, and waste services	8.1	10.2	10.5	16.7	7.6	15.8	8.8	18.3
Education and health services	2.5	3.4	3.5	5.3	2.2	5.5	2.5	5.2
Educational services	2.4	3.7	4.8	6.6	2.1	6.8	2.5	6.6
Health care and social assistance	2.5	3.3	3.2	4.9	2.3	5.0	2.5	4.9
Leisure and hospitality	6.6	7.8	8.6	11.7	6.2	11.6	7.0	11.8
Arts, entertainment, and recreation	5.9	6.9	8.2	11.1	6.1	11.6	5.7	10.5
Accommodation and food services	6.8	8.0	8.8	11.8	6.2	11.6	7.3	12.0
Other services [3]	3.9	4.8	5.3	7.5	3.7	8.3	4.0	6.8
Government workers	2.1	2.6	2.4	3.6	2.1	3.9	2.2	3.4

[1] See footnote 2, Table 584. [2] Includes the self-employed, unpaid family workers, and persons with no previous work experience, not shown separately. [3] Includes private household workers.

Source: U.S. Bureau of Labor Statistics, "Employment and Earnings Online," January 2010, <http://www.bls.gov/opub/ee/home.htm> and <http://www.bls.gov/cps/home.htm>.

Table 625. Unemployment by Occupation, 2000 to 2009, and by Sex, 2009

[5,602 represents 5,692,000. Civilian noninstitutionalized population 16 years old and over. Annual averages of monthly data. Rate represents unemployment as a percent of the labor force for each specified group. Based on Current Population Survey; see text, Section 1 and Appendix III. See also headnote, Table 605, regarding occupations]

Occupation	Number (1,000) 2000	Number (1,000) 2005 [1]	Number (1,000) 2009 [1]	Unemployment rate 2000	Unemployment rate 2005 [1]	2009 [1] Total	2009 [1] Male	2009 [1] Female
Total [2]	5,692	7,591	14,265	4.0	5.1	9.3	10.3	8.1
Management, professional, and related occupations	827	1,172	2,531	1.8	2.3	4.6	4.7	4.5
Management, business, and financial operations	320	464	1,105	1.6	2.2	4.9	4.6	5.3
Management	214	322	740	1.5	2.1	4.6	4.4	4.9
Business and financial operations	106	142	365	2.0	2.4	5.7	5.4	5.9
Professional and related occupations	507	708	1,427	1.9	2.4	4.4	4.8	4.2
Computer and mathematical	74	96	192	2.2	2.9	5.2	5.1	5.7
Architecture and engineering	51	60	203	1.7	2.1	6.9	6.7	8.0
Life, physical, and social science	18	39	63	1.4	2.7	4.5	5.0	4.0
Community and social services	40	52	105	2.0	2.4	4.3	4.0	4.5
Legal	18	27	60	1.2	1.6	3.4	2.3	4.5
Education, training, and library	136	210	368	1.8	2.5	4.1	4.2	4.1
Arts, design, entertainment, sports, and media	97	135	251	3.5	4.7	8.4	7.8	9.1
Healthcare practitioner and technical	73	90	184	1.2	1.3	2.3	1.9	2.5
Service occupations	1,132	1,587	2,605	5.2	6.4	9.6	10.5	8.9
Healthcare support	101	154	240	4.0	4.7	6.8	9.3	6.4
Protective service	70	121	177	2.7	4.0	5.3	5.1	6.2
Food preparation and serving-related	469	615	1,011	6.6	7.7	11.6	12.3	11.0
Building and grounds cleaning and maintenance	301	429	736	5.8	7.6	12.1	13.0	10.8
Personal care and service	190	268	441	4.4	5.6	8.0	9.3	7.7
Sales and office occupations	1,446	1,820	3,143	3.8	4.8	8.5	8.8	8.4
Sales and related	673	874	1,501	4.1	5.0	8.8	8.0	9.6
Office and administrative support	773	946	1,642	3.6	4.6	8.3	10.1	7.7
Natural resources, construction, and maintenance	758	1,069	2,464	5.3	6.5	15.6	15.6	16.2
Farming, fishing, and forestry	133	103	179	10.2	9.6	16.2	15.3	19.6
Construction and extraction	507	751	1,825	6.2	7.6	19.7	19.7	21.1
Installation, maintenance, and repair	119	214	459	2.4	3.9	8.5	8.5	7.3
Production, transportation, and material moving occupations	1,081	1,245	2,453	5.1	6.5	13.3	12.8	15.2
Production	575	677	1,322	4.8	6.7	14.7	14.1	16.3
Transportation and material moving	505	568	1,131	5.6	6.2	12.0	11.8	13.2

[1] See footnote 2, Table 584. [2] Includes persons with no previous work experience and those whose last job was in the Armed Forces.

Source: U.S. Bureau of Labor Statistics, "Employment and Earnings Online," January 2010, <http://www.bls.gov/opub/ee/home.htm> and <http://www.bls.gov/cps/home.htm>.

Table 626. Unemployed and Unemployment Rates by Educational Attainment, Sex, Race, and Hispanic Origin: 1992 to 2009

[3,589 represents 3,589,000. Annual averages of monthly figures. Civilian noninstitutionalized population 25 years old and over. See Table 592 for civilian labor force and participation rate data. Based on Current Population Survey; see text, Section 1 and Appendix III]

Year, sex, and race	Unemployed (1,000)					Unemployment rate [1]				
	Total	Less than a high school diploma	High school graduate, no college	Some college or associate's degree	Bachelor's degree or more	Total	Less than a high school diploma	High school graduate, no college	Some college or associate's degree	Bachelor's degree or more
Total: [2]										
2000 [3]	3,589	791	1,298	890	610	3.0	6.3	3.4	2.7	1.7
2005 [3]	5,070	967	1,798	1,349	955	4.0	7.6	4.7	3.9	2.3
2009 [3]	10,505	1,775	3,699	2,927	2,103	7.9	14.6	9.7	8.0	4.6
Male:										
2000 [3]	1,829	411	682	427	309	2.8	5.4	3.4	2.6	1.5
2005 [3]	2,617	514	973	636	494	3.8	6.4	4.6	3.7	2.3
2009 [3]	6,227	1,147	2,357	1,600	1,123	8.8	14.9	11.0	8.8	4.7
Female:										
2000 [3]	1,760	380	616	463	301	3.2	7.8	3.5	2.8	1.8
2005 [3]	2,453	453	826	713	461	4.2	9.7	4.8	4.0	2.4
2009 [3]	4,279	629	1,342	1,327	980	6.9	14.2	8.0	7.1	4.5
White: [4]										
2000 [3]	2,644	564	924	667	489	2.6	5.6	2.9	2.4	1.6
2005 [3]	3,627	669	1,257	973	729	3.5	6.5	4.0	3.4	2.1
2009 [3]	7,934	1,374	2,800	2,177	1,583	7.3	13.9	9.0	7.3	4.2
Black: [4]										
2000 [3]	731	179	315	169	68	5.4	10.7	6.4	4.0	2.5
2005 [3]	1,075	231	440	295	110	7.5	14.4	8.5	6.9	3.5
2009 [3]	1,830	297	710	557	266	12.3	21.3	14.0	11.5	7.3
Asian: [4, 5]										
2000 [3]	146	28	34	35	49	2.7	5.7	3.0	3.2	1.8
2005 [3]	203	26	47	32	99	3.5	5.5	4.6	3.2	3.0
2009 [3]	430	41	83	92	214	6.6	8.4	7.5	8.3	5.6
Hispanic: [6]										
2000 [3]	569	297	150	85	38	4.4	6.2	3.9	3.2	2.2
2005 [3]	773	354	216	138	66	4.8	6.2	4.5	4.1	2.9
2009 [3]	1,956	831	589	370	166	10.5	13.7	10.4	9.2	5.7

[1] Percent unemployed of the civilian labor force. [2] Includes other races, not shown separately. [3] See footnote 2, Table 584.
[4] Beginning 2005 data are for persons in this race group only. See footnote 4, Table 585. [5] 2000 data include Pacific Islanders.
[6] Persons of Hispanic or Latino origin may be any race.

Source: U.S. Bureau of Labor Statistics, "Employment and Earnings Online," January 2010, <http://www.bls.gov/opub/ee/home.htm> and <http://www.bls.gov/cps/home.htm>.

Table 627. Unemployed Persons by Age, Sex, and Reason for Unemployment: 2009

[14,265 represents 14,265,000. Annual averages of monthly data. Based on Current Population Survey; see text Section 1 and Appendix III]

Age, sex, and reason	Total unemployed (1,000)	Percent distribution by duration				
		Less than 5 weeks	5 to 14 weeks	15 weeks and over		
				Total	15 to 26 weeks	27 weeks or longer
Total 16 years old and over	**14,265**	**22.2**	**26.8**	**51.0**	**19.5**	**31.5**
16 to 19 years old	1,552	31.8	32.4	35.9	16.5	19.4
Total 20 years old and over	**12,712**	**21.0**	**26.2**	**52.8**	**19.8**	**33.0**
Males	7,555	20.8	26.0	53.2	20.3	33.0
Job losers and persons who completed temporary jobs	5,796	21.9	26.4	51.7	20.5	31.3
On temporary layoff	1,103	44.6	33.1	22.3	14.6	7.7
Not on temporary layoff	4,694	16.5	24.8	58.6	21.9	36.8
Permanent job losers	3,794	15.3	24.5	60.2	22.4	37.8
Persons who completed temporary jobs	899	21.9	26.1	52.1	19.7	32.4
Job leavers	407	19.9	26.8	53.3	19.9	33.4
Reentrants	1,190	16.7	23.9	59.4	19.6	39.8
New entrants	162	14.8	23.7	61.5	19.3	42.2
Females	5,157	21.3	26.5	52.2	19.2	33.1
Job losers and persons who completed temporary jobs	3,093	21.3	26.3	52.4	19.6	32.8
On temporary layoff	450	50.9	30.9	18.2	10.8	7.4
Not on temporary layoff	2,642	16.3	25.5	58.2	21.1	37.1
Permanent job losers	2,202	15.2	24.9	59.9	21.2	38.8
Persons who completed temporary jobs	440	21.8	28.3	49.9	20.9	28.9
Job leavers	419	23.5	27.8	48.7	19.1	29.6
Reentrants	1,449	21.1	26.4	52.5	18.2	34.3
New entrants	196	18.8	26.8	54.4	18.9	35.6

Source: U.S. Bureau of Labor Statistics, "Employment and Earnings Online," January 2010, <http://www.bls.gov/opub/ee/home.htm> and <http://www.bls.gov/cps/home.htm>.

[5,692 represents 5,692,000. Civilian noninstitutionalized population 16 years old and over. Annual averages of monthly figures. State total unemployment estimates come from the Local Area Unemployment Statistics program, while U.S. totals come from the Current Population Survey; see text, Section 1 and Appendix III. U.S. totals derived by independent population controls; therefore state data may not add to U.S. totals. Unemployment data are based on population controls from Census 2000]

| State | Total unemployed | | | | | | | | Insured unemployed [3] | | | |
| | Number (1,000) | | | | Percent [1] | | | | Number (1,000) | | Percent [4] | |
	2000 [2]	2005 [2]	2008 [2]	2009 [2]	2000 [2]	2005 [2]	2008 [2]	2009 [2]	2000	2009	2000	2009
United States	**5,692**	**7,591**	**8,924**	**14,265**	**4.0**	**5.1**	**5.8**	**9.3**	[5] **2,130.2**	[5] **5,756.2**	[5] **1.7**	[5] **4.3**
Alabama	87	81	112	212	4.1	3.8	5.2	10.1	29.4	71.2	1.6	3.8
Alaska	20	24	23	29	6.2	6.9	6.5	8.0	12.2	15.1	4.9	5.1
Arizona	100	134	183	284	4.0	4.7	5.9	9.1	20.5	100.1	1.0	3.9
Arkansas	53	69	72	100	4.2	5.1	5.2	7.3	24.2	57.2	2.2	5.0
California	833	953	1,313	2,086	4.9	5.4	7.2	11.4	339.6	784.1	2.4	5.1
Colorado	65	133	132	208	2.7	5.1	4.9	7.7	14.7	70.0	0.7	3.1
Connecticut	39	88	104	156	2.3	4.9	5.6	8.2	28.9	82.5	1.8	4.9
Delaware	14	17	22	35	3.3	4.0	4.9	8.1	6.0	15.6	1.5	3.7
District of Columbia ...	18	21	22	34	5.7	6.5	6.6	10.2	5.5	7.6	1.3	1.5
Florida	300	330	578	966	3.8	3.8	6.3	10.5	70.8	290.3	1.1	3.8
Georgia	148	241	302	457	3.5	5.2	6.2	9.6	34.8	155.5	0.9	3.9
Hawaii	24	17	26	43	4.0	2.8	4.0	6.8	8.4	20.1	1.7	3.4
Idaho	31	27	37	60	4.6	3.7	4.9	8.0	12.3	33.7	2.3	5.3
Illinois............	291	371	428	665	4.5	5.8	6.4	10.1	105.7	281.3	1.8	4.9
Indiana...........	92	172	189	320	2.9	5.4	5.8	10.1	32.3	127.3	1.1	4.5
Iowa..............	45	70	73	100	2.8	4.3	4.4	6.0	19.5	52.8	1.4	3.6
Kansas............	53	75	66	102	3.8	5.1	4.4	6.7	15.9	48.8	1.3	3.6
Kentucky	83	121	135	218	4.2	6.0	6.6	10.5	25.4	73.1	1.5	4.2
Louisiana	101	139	92	141	5.0	6.7	4.5	6.8	24.2	53.7	1.3	2.9
Maine.............	22	34	38	57	3.3	4.9	5.3	8.0	8.9	21.2	1.6	3.6
Maryland	100	122	133	209	3.6	4.1	4.4	7.0	29.0	83.3	1.3	3.4
Massachusetts.......	92	164	183	293	2.7	4.8	5.3	8.4	59.9	148.9	1.9	4.7
Michigan	190	346	413	665	3.7	6.8	8.3	13.6	83.3	262.4	1.9	6.5
Minnesota	87	120	158	236	3.1	4.2	5.4	8.0	31.8	104.2	1.3	3.9
Mississippi	74	103	89	123	5.7	7.8	6.8	9.6	19.9	43.5	1.8	3.9
Missouri...........	98	162	186	283	3.3	5.4	6.1	9.3	43.8	105.0	1.7	3.9
Montana...........	22	17	23	31	4.8	3.6	4.6	6.2	7.7	19.5	2.2	4.6
Nebraska	27	38	33	45	2.8	3.9	3.3	4.6	7.4	19.8	0.9	2.2
Nevada	48	55	90	161	4.5	4.5	6.7	11.8	19.6	71.9	2.1	5.8
New Hampshire......	19	26	29	47	2.7	3.6	3.9	6.3	3.1	21.2	0.5	3.4
New Jersey	157	197	246	418	3.7	4.5	5.5	9.2	84.6	197.7	2.3	5.1
New Mexico	42	47	43	69	5.0	5.2	4.5	7.2	9.5	28.3	1.4	3.4
New York	416	474	514	813	4.5	5.0	5.3	8.4	147.4	349.2	1.8	4.1
North Carolina	155	229	283	484	3.7	5.3	6.2	10.6	55.0	203.6	1.5	5.1
North Dakota	10	12	12	16	2.9	3.4	3.2	4.3	3.9	6.5	1.3	1.9
Ohio..............	234	344	393	611	4.0	5.9	6.6	10.2	72.8	228.3	1.4	4.4
Oklahoma	52	77	64	114	3.1	4.5	3.7	6.4	12.2	41.6	0.9	2.8
Oregon............	90	113	126	217	5.1	6.2	6.5	11.1	41.6	110.8	2.7	6.6
Pennsylvania	255	312	342	519	4.2	5.0	5.3	8.1	131.4	328.5	2.5	5.9
Rhode Island	23	28	43	64	4.2	5.1	7.6	11.2	12.3	23.0	2.8	5.0
South Carolina.......	71	140	147	255	3.6	6.8	6.9	11.7	27.6	93.6	1.6	5.1
South Dakota........	11	16	14	21	2.7	3.7	3.1	4.8	2.1	5.8	0.6	1.5
Tennessee..........	115	164	204	317	4.0	5.6	6.7	10.5	42.9	98.5	1.7	3.7
Texas	452	599	576	911	4.4	5.4	4.9	7.6	107.4	267.1	1.2	2.6
Utah..............	38	53	51	90	3.4	4.1	3.7	6.6	10.7	36.7	1.1	3.1
Vermont...........	9	12	16	25	2.7	3.5	4.5	6.9	4.8	13.2	1.7	4.5
Virginia............	82	138	162	278	2.3	3.5	3.9	6.7	22.5	83.0	0.7	2.4
Washington	151	180	186	314	5.0	5.5	5.4	8.9	70.1	139.8	2.7	4.9
West Virginia	44	39	34	63	5.5	4.9	4.3	7.9	14.2	27.3	2.1	4.0
Wisconsin	101	146	148	262	3.4	4.8	4.8	8.5	54.1	158.5	2.0	5.8
Wyoming	10	10	9	19	3.8	3.7	3.2	6.4	2.9	8.2	1.3	3.0

[1] Total unemployment as percent of civilian labor force. [2] See footnote 2, Table 584. [3] Number of jobless workers who are receiving state unemployment benefits. Source: U.S. Employment and Training Administration, Unemployment Insurance, Financial Handbook, annual updates. See <http://www.ows.doleta.gov/unemploy/claims.asp>. [4] Those currently collecting unemployment insurance as a percent of the total number of eligible workers. [5] U.S. totals include Puerto Rico and the Virgin Islands.

Source: Except as noted, U.S. Bureau of Labor Statistics, Local Area Unemployment Statistics program <http://www.bls.gov/lau/>.

Table 629. Nonfarm Establishments—Employees, Hours, and Earnings by Industry: 1990 to 2009

[Annual averages of monthly data. (109,487 represents 109,487,000). Based on data from establishment reports. Includes all full- and part-time employees who worked during, or received pay for, any part of the pay period reported. Excludes proprietors, the self-employed, farm workers, unpaid family workers, private household workers, and Armed Forces. Establishment data shown here conform to industry definitions in the 2007 North American Industry Classification System (NAICS) and are adjusted to March 2009 employment benchmarks. Based on the Current Employment Statistics Program; see source and Appendix III]

Item and year	Total nonfarm	Private industry																Government
		Total [1]	Construction	Manufacturing	Wholesale trade	Retail trade	Transportation and warehousing	Utilities	Information	Finance and insurance	Real estate and rental and leasing	Professional, scientific, and technical services	Administrative and waste services	Educational services	Health care and social assistance	Arts, entertainment and recreation	Accommodations and food services	
EMPLOYEES (1,000)																		
1990	109,487	91,072	5,263	17,695	5,268	13,182	3,476	740	2,688	4,976	1,637	4,538	4,643	1,688	9,296	1,132	8,156	18,415
2000	131,785	110,995	6,787	17,263	5,933	15,280	4,410	601	3,630	5,677	2,011	6,702	8,168	2,390	12,718	1,788	10,074	20,790
2005	133,703	111,899	7,336	14,226	5,764	15,280	4,361	554	3,061	6,019	2,134	7,025	8,170	2,836	14,536	1,892	10,923	21,804
2006	136,086	114,113	7,691	14,155	5,905	15,353	4,470	549	3,038	6,156	2,173	7,357	8,398	2,901	14,925	1,929	11,181	21,974
2007	137,598	115,380	7,630	13,879	6,015	15,520	4,541	553	3,032	6,132	2,169	7,660	8,416	2,941	15,380	1,969	11,457	22,218
2008	136,790	114,281	7,162	13,406	5,943	15,283	4,508	559	2,984	6,015	2,130	7,799	8,032	3,040	15,798	1,970	11,466	22,509
2009	130,920	108,371	6,037	11,883	5,625	14,528	4,235	561	2,807	5,763	1,995	7,509	7,215	3,090	16,101	1,915	11,188	22,549
WEEKLY EARNINGS [2] (dol.)																		
1990	(NA)	349.75	513.43	436.16	444.48	235.62	471.72	670.40	479.50	(NA)	(NA)	504.83	273.60	(NA)	319.80	219.02	147.89	(NA)
2000	(NA)	481.01	685.78	590.77	631.40	333.38	562.31	955.66	700.86	(NA)	(NA)	745.77	387.49	(NA)	449.27	273.79	207.44	(NA)
2005	(NA)	544.33	750.22	673.33	685.00	377.58	618.58	1,095.90	805.08	(NA)	(NA)	862.79	431.92	(NA)	560.43	330.19	226.48	(NA)
2006	(NA)	567.87	781.21	691.02	718.63	383.02	636.97	1,135.34	850.42	(NA)	(NA)	907.74	464.97	(NA)	581.55	332.66	236.70	(NA)
2007	(NA)	590.04	816.66	711.56	748.94	385.11	654.95	1,182.65	874.65	(NA)	(NA)	956.42	485.15	(NA)	606.74	348.35	251.52	(NA)
2008	(NA)	607.95	842.61	724.46	769.62	386.21	670.37	1,230.69	908.99	(NA)	(NA)	995.66	500.14	(NA)	630.06	354.52	259.93	(NA)
2009	(NA)	617.11	852.45	725.87	784.75	388.72	677.44	1,243.76	931.93	(NA)	(NA)	1,036.37	517.38	(NA)	643.13	359.89	261.68	(NA)
WEEKLY HOURS [2]																		
1990	(NA)	34.3	38.3	40.5	38.4	30.6	37.7	41.5	35.8	(NA)	(NA)	36.1	32.3	(NA)	31.8	26.1	25.9	(NA)
2000	(NA)	34.3	39.2	41.3	38.8	30.7	37.4	42.0	36.8	(NA)	(NA)	36.2	33.1	(NA)	32.1	25.6	26.2	(NA)
2005	(NA)	33.8	38.6	40.7	37.7	30.6	37.0	41.1	36.5	(NA)	(NA)	35.7	32.8	(NA)	32.9	25.7	25.7	(NA)
2006	(NA)	33.9	39.0	41.1	38.0	30.5	36.9	41.4	36.6	(NA)	(NA)	35.9	33.4	(NA)	32.8	25.2	25.8	(NA)
2007	(NA)	33.9	39.0	41.2	38.2	30.2	37.0	42.4	36.5	(NA)	(NA)	36.0	33.5	(NA)	32.8	24.7	25.6	(NA)
2008	(NA)	33.6	38.5	40.8	38.2	30.0	36.4	42.7	36.7	(NA)	(NA)	35.8	33.6	(NA)	32.8	24.1	25.4	(NA)
2009	(NA)	33.1	37.6	39.8	37.6	29.9	36.0	42.1	36.6	(NA)	(NA)	35.7	33.3	(NA)	32.4	23.8	25.0	(NA)
HOURLY EARNINGS [2] (dol.)																		
1990	(NA)	10.20	13.42	10.78	11.58	7.71	12.50	16.14	13.40	(NA)	(NA)	13.99	8.48	(NA)	10.05	8.41	5.70	(NA)
2000	(NA)	14.02	17.48	14.32	16.28	10.86	15.05	22.75	19.07	(NA)	(NA)	20.61	11.69	(NA)	13.98	10.68	7.92	(NA)
2005	(NA)	16.13	19.46	16.56	18.16	12.36	16.70	26.68	22.06	(NA)	(NA)	24.15	13.16	(NA)	17.05	12.85	8.80	(NA)
2006	(NA)	16.76	20.02	16.81	18.91	12.57	17.28	27.40	23.23	(NA)	(NA)	25.27	13.93	(NA)	17.75	13.21	9.19	(NA)
2007	(NA)	17.43	20.95	17.26	19.59	12.75	17.72	27.88	23.96	(NA)	(NA)	26.58	14.47	(NA)	18.48	14.10	9.82	(NA)
2008	(NA)	18.08	21.87	17.75	20.13	12.87	18.41	28.83	24.78	(NA)	(NA)	27.82	14.87	(NA)	19.23	14.73	10.23	(NA)
2009	(NA)	18.62	22.67	18.23	20.85	13.02	18.80	29.56	25.45	(NA)	(NA)	29.03	15.52	(NA)	19.83	15.10	10.48	(NA)

NA Not available. [1] Includes other industries not shown separately. [2] Average hours and earnings of production workers for mining and logging, manufacturing, and construction; average hours and earnings of nonsupervisory workers for the service-providing industries.

Source: U.S. Bureau of Labor Statistics, Current Employment Statistics, "Employment, Hours, and Earnings—National," <http://www.bls.gov/ces/home.htm>.

Table 630. Employees in Nonfarm Establishments—States: 2009

[In thousands (130,920 represents 130,920,000). Includes all full- and part-time employees who worked during, or received pay for, any part of the pay period reported. Excludes proprietors, the self-employed, farm workers, unpaid family workers, private household workers, and Armed Forces. National totals differ from the sum of the state figures because of differing benchmarks among states and differing industrial and geographic stratification. Compiled from data supplied by cooperating state agencies. Based on North American Industry Classification System, 2007; see text, section 15]

State	Total [1]	Con-struction	Manu-facturing	Trade transpor-tation and utilities	Infor-mation	Fin-ancial activi-ties [2]	Profes-sional and business ser-vices [3]	Educa-tion and health ser-vices [4]	Leisure and hospita-lity [5]	Other ser-vices [6]	Govern-ment
U.S.	130,920	6,037	11,883	24,949	2,807	7,758	16,580	19,191	13,102	5,364	22,549
AL	1,885.7	91.4	247.8	365.6	24.8	95.7	204.7	210.6	170.0	80.0	383.4
AK	321.2	16.1	13.0	63.3	6.6	14.7	26.1	39.1	31.4	11.5	84.2
AZ	2,426.4	128.8	153.1	479.9	39.3	166.5	345.9	329.4	256.1	93.8	422.6
AR	1,165.2	51.8	164.1	234.9	16.2	50.7	112.7	162.8	100.2	45.0	216.6
CA	14,079.0	620.1	1,280.9	2,636.5	446.8	797.1	2,051.6	1,740.2	1,499.0	484.3	2,497.3
CO	2,244.0	130.5	129.5	403.3	74.8	147.1	329.6	257.4	262.5	94.2	390.8
CT	1,627.2	54.8	171.8	293.1	35.1	137.7	187.8	302.4	134.0	61.5	248.4
DE	415.8	[7] 19.9	27.9	75.3	6.6	43.9	55.8	63.7	40.6	19.9	62.3
DC	703.3	[7] 11.7	1.4	26.9	19.0	26.5	148.4	104.5	58.0	64.7	242.1
FL	7,260.1	392.9	323.0	1,470.3	143.0	482.5	1,044.1	1,057.7	909.8	313.2	1,118.2
GA	3,876.6	166.5	357.0	818.2	104.8	210.4	506.7	475.6	380.9	157.8	689.5
HI	591.5	[7] 31.5	13.7	110.9	9.0	27.8	71.1	74.7	101.0	26.1	125.7
ID	610.0	34.2	54.7	122.3	10.0	29.6	75.1	81.0	59.1	21.1	119.6
IL	5,657.6	219.1	577.6	1,140.4	106.4	371.8	784.9	817.1	516.2	257.4	857.4
IN	2,787.2	121.2	440.0	549.6	37.6	131.5	261.1	414.9	276.6	108.1	440.1
IA	1,478.2	64.7	203.7	301.9	30.4	101.9	117.6	211.0	132.6	57.6	254.7
KS	1,344.6	58.1	167.6	256.4	35.2	71.1	139.5	180.1	113.9	52.6	262.1
KY	1,769.5	73.3	213.2	362.3	27.1	88.1	171.8	247.0	168.8	69.9	324.1
LA	1,899.0	130.0	142.3	369.2	24.6	90.8	193.5	266.1	195.3	68.2	368.3
ME	595.0	25.0	52.5	118.4	9.2	31.6	54.8	118.9	59.3	19.5	103.4
MD	2,520.8	[7] 154.4	118.6	439.9	46.0	144.5	384.4	393.8	230.5	115.9	492.7
MA	3,173.0	111.3	258.6	540.0	84.7	212.4	460.9	650.3	298.5	118.5	436.5
MI	3,876.1	127.3	462.4	717.0	55.7	190.9	608.7	613.2	379.5	168.1	646.6
MN	2,650.1	92.8	300.1	496.3	54.9	172.3	306.6	453.0	237.3	115.3	416.6
MS	1,096.7	51.1	141.2	214.3	12.8	45.8	86.9	130.5	119.9	35.4	250.4
MO	2,688.1	119.0	255.7	518.9	63.3	163.2	316.2	401.2	274.3	118.0	453.6
MT	429.3	24.0	17.4	88.4	7.5	21.1	38.6	62.2	57.0	16.9	89.2
NE	944.4	[7] 47.6	93.5	197.6	17.5	68.2	100.2	134.3	81.5	35.6	168.5
NV	1,148.5	81.5	40.2	213.0	13.1	55.6	136.1	97.5	307.7	33.8	158.4
NH	624.1	22.6	67.6	134.2	12.5	36.4	62.7	106.7	62.2	21.5	96.8
NJ	3,891.7	139.0	267.3	816.4	84.2	255.3	583.7	598.2	335.8	161.6	648.7
NM	812.5	47.8	30.1	135.5	14.9	33.4	102.1	118.6	84.7	28.8	199.2
NY	8,555.9	323.9	477.1	1,450.0	253.7	677.9	1,096.3	1,665.2	711.2	365.1	1,523.9
NC	3,915.7	190.9	447.7	719.7	69.8	201.9	463.5	542.4	393.4	164.7	715.7
ND	366.3	20.7	23.6	77.7	7.5	20.2	29.1	53.2	34.1	15.4	77.7
OH	5,073.6	181.4	629.2	968.3	80.6	278.6	616.5	826.3	477.5	213.1	790.4
OK	1,538.7	68.8	129.6	280.8	27.5	81.2	165.6	201.6	140.2	62.0	338.3
OR	1,612.0	73.8	167.3	312.8	33.1	95.6	178.8	223.2	163.1	57.5	299.8
PA	5,608.5	225.3	573.6	1,078.9	99.9	318.9	670.5	1,119.9	493.8	249.7	755.9
RI	459.0	17.2	41.7	73.0	10.1	31.1	52.3	100.8	48.6	22.0	62.0
SC	1,821.3	87.5	213.8	349.2	27.7	101.6	201.7	207.5	209.5	69.4	349.3
SD	403.7	21.7	37.9	80.8	6.7	30.5	26.5	63.3	43.0	15.7	77.7
TN	2,618.9	109.5	309.7	558.9	47.2	140.4	293.0	366.7	263.2	102.2	428.1
TX	10,311.0	595.5	840.0	2,063.8	205.2	629.1	1,249.3	1,335.0	1,006.4	361.0	1,819.8
UT	1,191.8	71.0	112.5	235.3	29.7	72.0	150.4	151.2	110.5	34.2	214.2
VT	296.9	13.5	31.2	56.0	5.5	12.4	22.0	59.9	31.6	9.5	54.6
VA	3,636.8	190.5	239.0	623.4	81.0	180.3	638.8	449.6	340.0	186.7	697.3
WA	2,825.5	159.6	265.9	524.3	103.6	142.8	325.5	373.0	268.5	107.3	549.1
WV	744.1	34.1	50.7	135.9	10.4	28.4	59.6	118.5	71.6	55.5	149.8
WI	2,748.2	102.0	435.6	515.6	47.9	160.1	255.3	414.0	251.9	138.0	424.8
WY	286.4	23.9	9.2	53.5	4.0	11.2	17.3	25.5	32.9	11.8	71.6

[1] Includes mining and logging, not shown separately. [2] Finance and insurance; real estate and rental and leasing. [3] Professional, scientific, and technical services; management of companies and enterprises; administrative and support and waste management and remediation services. [4] Education services; health care and social assistance. [5] Arts, entertainment, and recreation; accommodations and food services. [6] Includes repair and maintenance; personal and laundry services; and membership associations and organizations. [7] Mining and logging included with construction.

Source: U.S. Bureau of Labor Statistics, Current Employment Statistics (CES), "State and Metro Area Employment, Hours, and Earnings (SAE)," <http://www.bls.gov/sae/data.htm>.

U.S. Census Bureau, Statistical Abstract of the United States: 2011

Table 631. Nonfarm Industries—Employees and Earnings: 1990 to 2009

[Annual averages of monthly figures (109,487 represents 109,487,000). Covers all full- and part-time employees who worked during, or received pay for, any part of the pay period including the 12th of the month. See also headnote, Table 629]

Industry	2007 NAICS code [1]	All employees (1,000)					Average hourly earnings [2] (dol.)		
		1990	2000	2005	2008	2009	2000	2005	2009
Total nonfarm	**(X)**	**109,487**	**131,785**	**133,703**	**136,790**	**130,920**	**(NA)**	**(NA)**	**(NA)**
Goods-producing [3]	(X)	23,723	24,649	22,190	21,334	18,620	15.27	17.60	19.90
Service-providing [4]	(X)	85,764	107,136	111,513	115,456	112,300	(NA)	(NA)	(NA)
Total private	**(X)**	**91,072**	**110,995**	**111,899**	**114,281**	**108,371**	**14.02**	**16.13**	**18.62**
Mining and logging	**(X)**	**765**	**599**	**628**	**767**	**700**	**16.55**	**18.72**	**23.29**
Logging	1133	85	79	65	57	50	13.70	15.74	17.00
Mining	**21**	**680**	**520**	**562**	**710**	**650**	**16.94**	**19.04**	**23.83**
Oil and gas extraction	211	190	125	126	161	162	19.43	19.34	27.60
Mining, except oil and gas	212	302	225	213	226	212	18.07	20.18	23.38
Support activities for mining	213	188	171	224	323	277	14.55	17.89	22.80
Construction	**23**	**5,263**	**6,787**	**7,336**	**7,162**	**6,037**	**17.48**	**19.46**	**22.67**
Construction of buildings	236	1,413	1,633	1,712	1,642	1,366	16.74	19.05	22.32
Residential building	2361	673	823	960	816	639	15.18	17.72	19.63
Nonresidential building	2362	741	809	752	826	726	18.18	20.55	24.50
Heavy and civil engineering construction [6]	237	813	937	951	965	847	16.80	19.60	22.99
Highway, street, and bridge construction	2373	289	340	351	327	286	18.17	20.12	23.14
Specialty trade contractors	238	3,037	4,217	4,673	4,556	3,824	17.91	19.55	22.70
Building foundation and exterior contractors	2381	703	919	1,083	979	781	16.93	18.44	21.06
Building equipment contractors	2382	1,282	1,897	1,918	2,020	1,768	19.52	21.01	24.35
Building finishing contractors	2383	665	857	992	900	725	16.44	18.82	21.45
Manufacturing	**31–33**	**17,695**	**17,263**	**14,226**	**13,406**	**11,883**	**14.32**	**16.56**	**18.23**
Durable goods	(X)	10,737	10,877	8,956	8,463	7,309	14.92	17.33	19.35
Wood products	321	541	613	559	456	361	11.63	13.16	14.93
Nonmetallic mineral products	327	528	554	505	465	398	14.53	16.61	17.28
Cement and concrete products	3273	195	234	240	220	188	14.64	16.68	17.83
Primary metals	331	689	622	466	442	365	16.64	18.94	20.08
Iron and steel mills and ferroalloy production	3311	187	135	96	99	85	20.97	23.55	24.84
Foundries	3315	214	217	164	148	115	14.72	17.50	18.69
Fabricated metal products	332	1,610	1,753	1,522	1,528	1,318	13.77	15.80	17.49
Architectural and structural metals	3323	357	428	398	406	348	13.43	15.10	17.07
Machine shops and threaded products	3327	309	365	345	361	312	14.53	16.43	18.33
Machinery	333	1,410	1,457	1,166	1,188	1,029	15.21	17.02	18.38
Agricultural, construction, and mining machinery	3331	229	222	208	242	216	14.21	15.91	17.16
Heating, ventilation and air conditioning, and commercial refrigeration equipment	3334	165	194	154	150	127	13.10	14.60	16.19
Metalworking machinery	3335	267	274	202	191	158	16.66	17.86	19.14
Computer and electronic products	334	1,903	1,820	1,316	1,244	1,136	14.73	18.39	21.88
Computer and peripheral equipment	3341	367	302	205	183	166	18.39	22.75	21.34
Communications equipment	3342	223	239	141	127	121	14.39	18.05	22.48
Semiconductors and electronic components	3344	574	676	452	432	377	13.46	17.03	20.39
Electronic instruments	3345	635	488	441	441	421	15.80	17.71	23.85
Electrical equipment and appliances	335	633	591	434	424	377	13.23	15.24	16.27
Household appliances	3352	114	106	85	71	60	(NA)	(NA)	(NA)
Electrical equipment	3353	244	210	152	159	147	13.28	15.31	16.11
Transportation equipment [5]	336	2,135	2,057	1,772	1,608	1,353	18.89	22.09	24.93
Motor vehicles	3361	271	291	248	192	143	24.45	29.01	27.69
Motor vehicle parts	3363	653	840	678	544	419	17.95	21.10	20.85
Aerospace products and parts	3364	841	517	455	507	493	20.52	24.82	32.25
Ship and boat building	3366	174	154	154	156	132	14.84	17.26	21.29
Furniture and related products	337	604	683	568	480	386	11.73	13.45	15.04
Household and institutional furniture	3371	401	443	383	307	246	11.39	13.15	14.73
Miscellaneous manufacturing	339	686	728	647	629	587	11.93	14.07	16.13
Medical equipment and supplies	3391	283	305	300	311	308	12.70	14.71	16.87
Nondurable goods	(X)	6,958	6,386	5,271	4,943	4,574	13.31	15.27	16.56
Food manufacturing	311	1,507	1,553	1,478	1,481	1,459	11.77	13.04	14.40
Fruit and vegetable preserving and specialty	3114	218	197	174	173	172	11.90	12.81	14.60
Fruit and vegetable canning and drying	31142	127	96	85	87	88	13.23	13.70	15.36
Animal slaughtering and processing	3116	427	507	504	510	499	10.27	11.47	12.79
Bakeries and tortilla manufacturing	3118	292	306	280	281	273	11.45	12.57	14.01
Beverages and tobacco products [5]	312	218	207	192	198	188	17.40	18.76	20.49
Beverages	3121	173	175	167	177	169	(NA)	(NA)	(NA)
Textile mills	313	492	378	218	151	126	11.23	12.38	13.71
Textile product mills	314	236	230	176	147	127	10.43	11.61	11.44
Apparel	315	903	484	251	199	170	8.60	10.26	11.37
Cut and sew apparel	3152	750	380	193	155	134	8.40	10.05	11.34
Leather and allied products	316	133	69	40	33	29	10.35	11.50	13.90
Paper and paper products	322	647	605	484	445	407	15.91	17.99	19.28
Pulp, paper, and paperboard mills	3221	238	191	142	126	117	20.62	22.99	24.64
Converted paper products	3222	409	413	343	319	291	13.58	15.71	16.96
Printing and related support activities	323	809	807	646	594	524	14.09	15.74	16.75
Petroleum and coal products	324	153	123	112	117	115	22.80	24.47	29.63
Chemicals	325	1,036	980	872	847	803	17.09	19.67	20.30
Basic chemicals	3251	249	188	150	152	145	21.06	23.80	24.09
Resin, rubber, and artificial fibers	3252	158	136	108	104	93	17.09	19.03	21.08
Pharmaceuticals and medicines	3254	207	274	288	291	285	17.27	21.31	21.12
Plastics and rubber products	326	825	951	802	729	627	12.70	14.80	16.01
Plastics products	3261	618	737	634	585	505	12.04	14.01	15.70
Rubber products	3262	207	214	168	145	122	14.83	17.58	17.16

See footnotes at end of table.

408 Labor Force, Employment, and Earnings

Table 631. Nonfarm Industries—Employees and Earnings: 1990 to 2009—Con.

[Annual averages of monthly figures (109,487 represents 109,487,000). Covers all full- and part-time employees who worked during, or received pay for, any part of the pay period including the 12th of the month. See also headnote, Table 629]

Industry	2007 NAICS code [1]	All employees (1,000)					Average hourly earnings [2] (dol.)		
		1990	2000	2005	2008	2009	2000	2005	2009
Trade, transportation, and utilities	(X)	**22,666**	**26,225**	**25,959**	**26,293**	**24,949**	**13.31**	**14.92**	**16.50**
Wholesale trade	**42**	**5,268**	**5,933**	**5,764**	**5,943**	**5,625**	**16.28**	**18.16**	**20.85**
Durable goods	423	2,834	3,251	2,999	3,052	2,827	16.71	18.88	20.55
Motor vehicles and parts	4231	309	356	344	338	316	14.27	16.18	16.99
Lumber and construction supplies	4233	181	227	254	235	205	13.61	16.78	17.99
Commercial equipment	4234	597	722	639	654	617	20.29	23.67	24.54
Electric goods	4236	357	425	342	349	326	19.43	21.78	23.24
Hardware and plumbing	4237	216	247	245	252	231	15.07	16.47	19.29
Machinery and supplies	4238	690	725	659	684	643	16.47	18.71	20.61
Nondurable goods	424	1,900	2,065	2,022	2,048	1,980	14.33	16.15	19.12
Paper and paper products	4241	162	177	152	139	131	15.65	17.23	21.27
Druggists' goods	4242	136	192	213	209	201	18.98	19.20	23.62
Apparel and piece goods	4243	152	163	148	149	138	14.58	17.53	19.90
Grocery and related products	4244	623	689	699	730	714	13.57	15.38	18.40
Electronic markets and agents and brokers	425	535	618	743	843	818	20.79	20.71	26.32
Retail trade	**44,45**	**13,182**	**15,280**	**15,280**	**15,283**	**14,528**	**10.86**	**12.36**	**13.02**
Motor vehicle and parts dealers	441	1,494	1,847	1,919	1,831	1,640	14.94	16.33	16.52
Automobile dealers	4411	983	1,217	1,261	1,177	1,022	16.95	17.85	17.68
Auto parts, accessories, and tire stores	4413	418	499	491	492	482	11.04	12.74	14.04
Furniture and home furnishings stores	442	432	544	576	531	450	12.33	14.23	15.17
Furniture stores	4421	244	289	298	262	224	13.37	14.87	15.99
Home furnishings stores	4422	188	254	278	269	226	11.06	13.46	14.12
Electronics and appliance stores	443	382	564	536	541	487	13.67	17.73	16.74
Building material and garden supply stores	444	891	1,142	1,276	1,248	1,163	11.25	13.14	14.02
Building material and supplies dealers	4441	753	982	1,134	1,111	1,035	11.30	13.24	14.03
Food and beverage stores	445	2,779	2,993	2,818	2,862	2,829	9.76	10.85	11.87
Grocery stores	4451	2,406	2,582	2,446	2,503	2,475	9.71	10.80	11.91
Specialty food stores	4452	232	270	236	221	217	9.97	11.04	11.26
Beer, wine, and liquor stores	4453	141	141	136	138	137	10.40	11.48	12.00
Health and personal care stores	446	792	928	954	1,003	984	11.68	14.03	16.83
Gasoline stations	447	910	936	871	842	827	8.05	8.92	9.79
Clothing & clothing accessories stores	448	1,313	1,322	1,115	1,400	1,009	9.90	11.07	11.66
Clothing stores	4481	930	954	1,066	1,121	1,050	9.88	10.63	10.88
Shoe stores	4482	216	193	180	188	181	8.96	10.05	12.65
Jewelry, luggage, and leather goods stores	4483	167	175	169	158	138	11.48	14.10	14.98
Sporting goods, hobby, book, and music stores	451	532	686	647	651	616	9.33	10.35	11.58
Sporting goods and musical instrument stores	4511	352	437	447	478	461	9.55	10.68	11.66
Book, periodical, and music stores	4512	180	249	200	174	155	8.91	9.59	11.32
General merchandise stores	452	2,500	2,820	2,934	3,026	2,956	9.22	10.53	10.80
Department stores	4521	1,494	1,755	1,595	1,541	1,471	(NA)	(NA)	(NA)
Miscellaneous store retailers	453	738	1,007	900	843	785	10.20	11.22	11.87
Florists	4531	121	130	101	86	75	8.95	9.88	10.72
Office supplies, stationery, and gift stores	4532	358	471	391	348	319	10.46	11.65	13.01
Used merchandise stores	4533	56	107	113	119	118	8.07	8.96	9.89
Nonstore retailers	454	419	492	435	438	422	13.22	14.56	17.29
Electronic shopping and mail-order houses	4541	157	257	240	252	245	13.38	14.52	17.71
Transportation and warehousing	**48,49**	**3,476**	**4,410**	**4,361**	**4,508**	**4,235**	**15.05**	**16.70**	**18.80**
Air transportation	481	529	614	501	491	460	13.57	17.77	24.11
Scheduled air transportation	4811	503	570	456	444	415	(NA)	(NA)	(NA)
Rail transportation	482	272	232	228	231	219	(NA)	(NA)	(NA)
Water transportation	483	57	56	61	67	64	18.07	19.04	23.08
Truck transportation	484	1,122	1,406	1,398	1,389	1,266	15.86	16.74	18.03
General freight trucking	4841	807	1,013	981	976	885	16.37	17.20	17.90
Specialized freight trucking	4842	315	393	417	413	381	14.51	15.60	18.35
Transit and ground passenger transportation	485	274	372	389	423	419	11.88	13.00	14.07
Urban transit, interurban and rural bus transportation	4851,2	46	59	60	63	62	(NA)	(NA)	(NA)
Taxi and limousine service	4853	57	72	66	71	67	(NA)	(NA)	(NA)
School and employee bus transportation	4854	114	152	169	182	184	11.42	12.74	13.10
Pipeline transportation	486	60	46	38	42	42	19.86	24.33	27.56
Scenic and sightseeing transportation	487	16	28	29	28	28	12.49	13.75	15.72
Support activities for transportation	488	364	537	552	592	549	14.57	17.66	20.68
Support activities for air transportation	4881	96	141	148	168	150	13.42	15.07	17.66
Support activities for water transportation	4883	91	97	94	99	93	19.57	27.08	32.70
Support activities for road transportation	4884	35	66	79	85	82	13.98	15.41	15.79
Freight transportation arrangement	4885	111	178	177	187	176	13.46	16.94	19.87
Couriers and messengers	492	375	605	571	573	547	13.51	15.33	17.65
Couriers and express delivery services	4921	340	546	522	523	500	(NA)	(NA)	(NA)
Warehousing and storage	493	407	514	595	672	642	14.46	15.06	15.38
Utilities	**22**	**740**	**601**	**554**	**559**	**561**	**22.75**	**26.68**	**29.56**
Power generation and supply	2211	550	434	401	404	405	23.13	27.63	30.86
Natural gas distribution	2212	155	121	107	107	109	23.41	26.86	27.71
Water, sewage and other systems	2213	35	46	45	48	47	16.93	17.70	22.94

See footnotes at end of table.

Table 631. Nonfarm Industries—Employees and Earnings: 1990 to 2009—Con.

[Annual averages of monthly figures (109,487 represents 109,487,000). Covers all full- and part-time employees who worked during, or received pay for, any part of the pay period including the 12th of the month. See also headnote, Table 629]

Industry	2007 NAICS code [1]	All employees (1,000)					Average hourly earnings [2] (dol.)		
		1990	2000	2005	2008	2009	2000	2005	2009
Information	51	**2,688**	**3,630**	**3,061**	**2,984**	**2,807**	**19.07**	**22.06**	**25.45**
Publishing industries, except Internet	511	871	1,035	904	880	796	20.18	24.20	26.41
Newspaper, book, and directory publishers	5111	773	774	666	617	540	15.06	18.57	20.33
Software publishers	5112	98	261	238	264	256	28.48	38.11	37.63
Motion picture and sound recording industries	512	255	383	378	371	350	21.25	18.75	21.58
Broadcasting, except Internet	515	284	344	328	319	301	16.74	21.22	24.21
Radio and television broadcasting	5151	232	253	239	233	216	(NA)	(NA)	(NA)
Cable and other subscription programming	5152	52	91	89	86	85	(NA)	(NA)	(NA)
Telecommunications	517	980	1,397	1,071	1,019	975	18.59	22.13	26.10
Wired telecommunications carriers	5171	673	922	690	666	635	18.62	22.46	25.77
Wireless telecommunications carriers (except satellite)	5172	36	186	191	201	194	14.40	20.40	26.43
Data processing, hosting and related services	518	211	316	263	260	250	16.97	19.97	25.10
Financial activities	(X)	**6,614**	**7,687**	**8,153**	**8,145**	**7,758**	**14.98**	**17.94**	**20.83**
Finance and insurance	52	**4,979**	**5,680**	**6,023**	**6,015**	**5,763**	**(NA)**	**(NA)**	**(NA)**
Monetary authorities—central bank	521	24	23	21	22	21	(NA)	(NA)	(NA)
Credit intermediation and related activities	522	2,425	2,548	2,869	2,733	2,597	13.14	15.85	17.61
Depository credit intermediation [5]	5221	1,909	1,681	1,769	1,815	1,761	11.97	14.13	17.19
Commercial banking	52211	1,362	1,251	1,296	1,358	1,319	11.83	13.79	16.99
Nondepository credit intermediation	5222	398	644	770	633	572	15.30	19.24	18.91
Activities related to credit intermediation	5223	119	222	330	285	265	15.39	16.48	17.36
Securities, commodity contracts, investments	523	458	805	786	864	810	20.20	26.59	31.84
Securities and commodity contracts brokerage and exchanges	5231,2	338	566	499	516	476	20.07	27.68	32.91
Other financial investment activities	5239	120	239	287	348	334	20.48	24.69	30.18
Insurance carriers and related activities	524	2,016	2,221	2,259	2,305	2,247	17.37	20.66	23.64
Insurance carriers	5241	1,338	1,433	1,386	1,397	1,366	17.92	21.67	24.94
Insurance agencies, brokerages, and related services	5242	678	788	874	909	881	16.28	18.88	21.43
Funds, trusts, and other financial vehicles	525	56	85	88	91	88	17.66	21.12	21.93
Real estate and rental and leasing	53	**1,637**	**2,011**	**2,134**	**2,130**	**1,995**	**(NA)**	**(NA)**	**(NA)**
Real estate	531	1,107	1,312	1,457	1,485	1,417	12.24	14.67	16.96
Lessors of real estate	5311	564	607	600	596	574	11.16	13.75	16.19
Offices of real estate agents and brokers	5312	217	281	356	343	305	12.57	14.90	17.01
Activities related to real estate	5313	327	424	502	546	537	13.60	15.64	17.73
Rental and leasing services	532	514	667	646	617	552	11.69	14.05	15.75
Automotive equipment rental and leasing	5321	163	208	199	193	169	10.70	13.64	14.46
Consumer goods rental	5322	220	292	275	246	225	9.53	12.39	13.90
Professional and business services	(X)	**10,848**	**16,666**	**16,954**	**17,735**	**16,580**	**15.52**	**18.08**	**22.35**
Professional and technical services	54	**4,557**	**6,734**	**7,053**	**7,799**	**7,509**	**20.61**	**24.15**	**29.03**
Legal services	5411	944	1,066	1,168	1,162	1,122	21.38	23.96	30.35
Accounting and bookkeeping services	5412	664	866	849	951	920	14.42	17.45	20.61
Architectural and engineering services	5413	942	1,238	1,311	1,439	1,325	20.49	23.96	29.20
Computer systems design and related services	5415	410	1,254	1,195	1,440	1,426	27.13	31.64	36.77
Management and technical consulting services	5416	305	673	824	1,002	993	20.83	23.97	26.92
Scientific research and development services	5417	494	515	577	620	614	21.39	28.33	34.66
Advertising and related services	5418	382	497	446	462	421	16.99	19.49	23.00
Other professional and technical services	5419	317	462	524	584	562	13.55	15.53	18.40
Management of companies and enterprises	55	**1,667**	**1,796**	**1,759**	**1,905**	**1,856**	**15.28**	**18.08**	**23.05**
Administrative and waste services	56	**4,624**	**8,136**	**8,142**	**8,032**	**7,215**	**11.69**	**13.16**	**15.52**
Administrative and support services [5]	561	4,395	7,823	7,804	7,675	6,864	11.53	12.93	15.30
Office administrative services	5611	211	264	345	403	400	14.68	17.82	22.34
Employment services [5]	5613	1,494	3,817	3,578	3,133	2,498	11.89	13.04	15.96
Temporary help services	56132	1,156	2,636	2,549	2,348	1,828	11.79	12.00	14.24
Business support services	5614	505	787	766	832	817	11.08	13.14	14.54
Travel arrangement and reservation services	5615	250	299	224	223	196	12.72	14.55	16.87
Investigation and security services	5616	507	689	737	805	790	9.78	11.64	13.84
Services to buildings and dwellings	5617	1,175	1,571	1,738	1,840	1,749	10.02	11.44	12.93
Waste management and remediation services [5]	562	229	313	338	357	351	15.29	17.69	19.16
Waste collection	5621	82	100	124	140	136	12.97	15.54	17.43
Waste treatment and disposal	5622	77	119	103	99	98	15.02	17.76	20.20

See footnotes at end of table.

U.S. Census Bureau, Statistical Abstract of the United States: 2011

Table 631. Nonfarm Industries—Employees and Earnings: 1990 to 2009—Con.

[Annual averages of monthly figures (109,487 represents 109,487,000). Covers all full- and part-time employees who worked during, or received pay for, any part of the pay period including the 12th of the month. See also headnote, Table 629]

Industry	2007 NAICS code [1]	All employees (1,000)					Average hourly earnings [2] (dol.)		
		1990	2000	2005	2008	2009	2000	2005	2009
Education and health services	(X)	**10,984**	**15,109**	**17,372**	**18,838**	**19,191**	**13.95**	**16.71**	**19.49**
Educational services	61	**1,688**	**2,390**	**2,836**	**3,040**	**3,090**	**(NA)**	**(NA)**	**(NA)**
Elementary and secondary schools	6111	461	716	837	858	862	(NA)	(NA)	(NA)
Junior colleges	6112	44	79	100	81	81	(NA)	(NA)	(NA)
Colleges and universities	6113	939	1,196	1,393	1,518	1,554	(NA)	(NA)	(NA)
Business, computer, and management training	6114	60	86	77	77	76	(NA)	(NA)	(NA)
Technical and trade schools	6115	72	91	102	115	120	(NA)	(NA)	(NA)
Other schools and instruction	6116	96	184	250	297	300	(NA)	(NA)	(NA)
Educational support services	6117	17	39	78	93	99	(NA)	(NA)	(NA)
Health care and social assistance	62	**9,296**	**12,718**	**14,536**	**15,798**	**16,101**	**13.98**	**17.05**	**19.83**
Ambulatory health care services	621	2,842	4,320	5,114	5,647	5,777	14.99	17.86	20.95
Offices of physicians	6211	1,278	1,840	2,094	2,253	2,280	15.65	18.95	22.75
Offices of dentists	6212	513	688	774	818	818	15.96	19.40	22.37
Offices of other health practitioners	6213	276	438	549	627	651	14.24	16.70	19.99
Outpatient care centers	6214	261	386	473	533	543	15.29	18.96	21.97
Medical and diagnostic laboratories	6215	129	162	198	217	216	15.74	18.67	23.42
Home health care services	6216	288	633	821	961	1,024	12.86	14.42	16.41
Hospitals	622	3,513	3,954	4,345	4,627	4,677	16.71	21.30	25.05
General medical and surgical hospitals	6221	3,305	3,745	4,096	4,337	4,378	16.75	21.40	25.22
Psychiatric and substance abuse hospitals	6222	113	86	93	102	105	14.97	17.79	18.97
Nursing and residential care facilities	623	1,856	2,583	2,855	3,016	3,081	10.67	12.37	14.07
Nursing care facilities	6231	1,170	1,514	1,577	1,619	1,644	11.08	13.08	14.97
Residential mental health facilities	6232	269	437	497	542	561	9.96	11.30	13.23
Community care facilities for the elderly	6233	330	478	615	687	712	9.83	11.33	12.73
Social assistance	624	1,085	1,860	2,222	2,508	2,565	9.78	11.35	12.77
Individual and family services	6241	389	678	921	1,112	1,165	10.57	12.44	13.32
Emergency and other relief services	6242	67	117	129	138	137	10.95	13.48	14.45
Vocational rehabilitation services	6243	242	370	383	400	406	9.57	10.67	12.49
Child day care services	6244	388	696	790	859	857	8.88	10.14	11.91
Leisure and hospitality	(X)	**9,288**	**11,862**	**12,816**	**13,436**	**13,102**	**8.32**	**9.38**	**11.11**
Arts, entertainment, and recreation	71	**1,132**	**1,788**	**1,892**	**1,970**	**1,915**	**10.68**	**12.85**	**15.10**
Performing arts and spectator sports [5]	711	273	382	376	406	397	13.11	18.67	21.11
Museums, historical sites, zoos, and parks	712	68	110	121	132	130	12.21	13.67	15.44
Amusements, gambling, and recreation	713	791	1,296	1,395	1,433	1,387	9.86	11.08	13.20
Accommodation and food services	72	**8,156**	**10,074**	**10,923**	**11,400**	**11,188**	**7.92**	**8.80**	**10.48**
Accommodation	721	1,616	1,884	1,819	1,869	1,760	9.48	10.75	13.17
Traveler accommodation and other longer-term accommodation	7211	1,582	1,837	1,765	1,815	1,705	9.49	10.78	13.23
Food services and drinking places	722	6,540	8,189	9,104	9,598	9,428	7.49	8.34	9.86
Full-service restaurants	7221	3,070	3,845	4,316	4,576	4,481	7.78	8.84	10.54
Limited-service eating places	7222	2,765	3,462	3,889	4,125	4,076	6.87	7.49	8.83
Special food services	7223	392	491	538	546	525	9.45	10.48	11.52
Drinking places, alcoholic beverages	7224	312	391	361	351	310	7.24	7.89	9.96
Other services	81	**4,261**	**5,168**	**5,395**	**5,515**	**5,364**	**12.73**	**14.34**	**16.59**
Repair and maintenance	811	1,009	1,242	1,236	1,227	1,154	13.28	14.82	16.57
Automotive repair and maintenance	8111	659	888	886	856	806	12.45	14.11	15.27
Electronic equipment repair and maintenance	8112	100	107	103	103	98	16.31	16.65	20.09
Commercial machinery repair and maintenance	8113	161	161	170	192	178	15.53	16.89	20.60
Personal and laundry services	812	1,120	1,243	1,277	1,323	1,282	10.18	11.81	12.95
Personal care services	8121	430	490	577	616	604	10.18	12.44	13.40
Death care services	8122	123	136	137	135	135	13.04	15.34	16.81
Dry-cleaning and laundry services	8123	371	388	347	332	311	9.17	10.18	11.60
Dry-cleaning and laundry services, except coin-operated	81232	215	211	180	164	151	8.14	9.14	10.34
Other personal services	8129	196	229	216	239	232	10.52	11.29	11.92
Pet care services, except veterinary	81291	23	31	44	57	59	12.12	10.61	12.01
Parking lots and garages	81293	68	93	103	114	111	8.81	9.89	11.00
Membership associations & organizations [5]	813	2,132	2,683	2,882	2,966	2,928	13.66	15.20	18.17
Grantmaking and giving services	8132	113	116	137	155	151	14.65	18.80	22.25
Social advocacy organizations	8133	126	143	174	198	202	12.08	13.89	16.81
Civic and social organizations	8134	377	404	409	412	396	9.85	11.16	12.04
Professional and similar organizations	8139	379	473	492	514	485	15.98	18.60	22.59
Government	(X)	**18,415**	**20,790**	**21,804**	**22,509**	**22,549**	**(NA)**	**(NA)**	**(NA)**
Federal	(X)	3,196	2,865	2,732	2,762	2,828	(NA)	(NA)	(NA)
State	(X)	4,305	4,786	5,032	5,177	5,180	(NA)	(NA)	(NA)
Local	(X)	10,914	13,139	14,041	14,571	14,542	(NA)	(NA)	(NA)

NA Not available. X Not applicable. [1] Based on the North American Industry Classification System, 2007. See text, Section 15. [2] Production employees in the goods-producing industries and nonsupervisory employees in service-providing industries. See footnotes 3 and 4. [3] Mining and logging, construction, and manufacturing. [4] Trade, transportation and utilities, information, financial activities, professional and business services, education and health services, leisure and hospitality, other services, and government. [5] Includes other industries not shown separately.

Source: U.S. Bureau of Labor Statistics, Current Employment Statistics, "Employment, Hours, and Earnings—National," <http://www.bls.gov/ces/data.htm\>.

Table 632. Women Employees on Nonfarm Payrolls by Major Industry: 1980 to 2009

[(37,813 represents 37,813,000). Annual averages of monthly data. For coverage, see headnote, Table 629]

Industry	Women employees (1,000)				Percent of total employees			
	1980	1990	2000	2009	1980	1990	2000	2009
Total nonfarm [1]	**37,813**	**51,587**	**63,223**	**65,234**	**41.8**	**47.1**	**48.0**	**49.8**
Total private	29,783	41,732	51,452	52,339	40.2	45.8	46.4	48.3
Construction	458	656	846	804	10.3	12.5	12.5	13.3
Manufacturing	5,676	5,702	5,359	3,400	30.3	32.2	31.0	28.6
Trade, transportation, and utilities	6,799	9,363	10,859	10,244	36.9	41.3	41.4	41.1
Wholesale trade	1,179	1,611	1,827	1,717	25.9	30.6	30.8	30.5
Retail trade	4,980	6,696	7,680	7,361	48.6	50.8	50.3	50.7
Transportation and warehousing	506	879	1,202	1,024	17.1	25.3	27.3	24.2
Utilities	134	177	151	142	20.6	24.0	25.1	25.4
Information	1,118	1,324	1,697	1,172	47.4	49.3	46.7	41.8
Financial activities	2,848	4,055	4,638	4,600	56.7	61.3	60.3	59.3
Professional and business services	3,096	5,105	7,680	7,472	41.0	47.1	46.1	45.1
Professional and technical services	(NA)	2,209	3,146	3,582	(NA)	48.7	46.9	47.7
Management of companies and enterprises	(NA)	849	924	948	(NA)	50.9	51.4	51.1
Administrative and waste services	(NA)	2,048	3,610	2,942	(NA)	44.1	44.2	40.8
Education and health services	5,459	8,422	11,586	14,851	77.2	76.7	76.7	77.4
Educational services	(NA)	958	1,417	1,897	(NA)	56.8	59.3	61.4
Health care and social assistance	(NA)	7,464	10,168	12,955	(NA)	80.3	79.9	80.5
Leisure and hospitality	3,021	4,829	6,082	6,877	44.9	52.0	51.3	52.5
Arts, entertainment, and recreation	(NA)	516	815	904	(NA)	45.6	45.6	47.2
Accommodation and food services	(NA)	4,312	5,267	5,972	(NA)	52.9	52.3	53.4
Other services	1,185	2,164	2,614	2,821	43.0	50.8	50.6	52.6
Government	8,029	9,855	11,771	12,895	49.0	53.5	56.6	57.2
Federal	1,136	1,378	1,231	1,255	37.9	43.1	43.0	44.4
State government	1,641	2,137	2,464	2,634	45.5	49.6	51.5	50.8
Local government	5,252	6,340	8,076	9,006	53.8	58.1	61.5	61.9

NA Not available [1] Includes other industries, not shown separately.

Source: U.S. Bureau of Labor Statistics, Current Employment Statistics, "Employment, Hours, and Earnings—National," <http://www.bls.gov/ces/data.htm>.

Table 633. Private Nonfarm Extended Mass Layoff Activity by Industry and Reason for Layoff: 2000 to 2009

[Covers layoffs of at least 31 days duration that involve 50 or more individuals from a single employer. Based on administrative records of unemployment filings and establishment classifications, supplemented with employer confirmation of layoffs, plant closings, and additional employer provided data. See source for more information]

Industry	2007 NAICS code [1]	Extended mass layoff events	Separations	Initial claimants [2]
2000	(X)	4,591	915,962	846,267
2001	(X)	7,375	1,524,832	1,457,512
2002	(X)	6,337	1,272,331	1,218,143
2003	(X)	6,181	1,216,886	1,200,811
2004	(X)	5,010	993,909	903,079
2005	(X)	4,881	884,661	834,533
2006	(X)	4,885	935,969	951,155
2007	(X)	5,363	965,935	978,712
2008	(X)	8,259	1,516,978	1,670,042
Total, 2009	**(X)**	**11,827**	**2,108,803**	**2,439,840**
Mining, quarrying, and gas extraction	21	196	31,825	31,188
Utilities	22	21	3,647	4,264
Construction	23	2,021	245,770	312,787
Manufacturing	31–33	3,835	668,279	893,502
Wholesale trade	42	339	46,431	47,220
Retail trade	44,45	768	176,134	188,626
Transportation and warehousing	48,49	655	131,781	130,674
Information	51	315	54,191	73,317
Finance and Insurance	52	479	98,629	101,746
Real estate and rental and leasing	53	95	12,538	13,364
Professional and technical services	54	448	87,501	81,193
Management of companies and enterprises	55	54	9,098	11,578
Administrative and waste services	56	1,083	246,258	279,691
Educational services	61	77	10,915	11,368
Health care and social assistance	62	393	53,861	51,006
Arts, entertainment, and recreation	71	254	57,874	39,232
Accommodation and food services	72	644	154,146	149,143
Other services	81	148	19,660	19,676
Unclassified	(X)	2	265	265
Reason for layoff:				
Business demand	(X)	5,404	825,083	1,140,737
Disaster/safety	(X)	19	3,985	2,431
Financial issues	(X)	1,075	228,737	244,644
Organizational changes	(X)	573	120,233	136,415
Production specific	(X)	62	12,866	10,876
Seasonal	(X)	2,211	409,787	394,620
Other/miscellaneous	(X)	2,483	508,112	510,117

X Not applicable. [1] Based on North American Industry Classification System, 2007. See text, Section 15. [2] A person who files any notice of unemployment to initiate a request either for a determination of entitlement to and eligibility for compensation, or for a subsequent period of unemployment within a benefit year or period of eligibility.

Source: U.S. Bureau of Labor Statistics, Mass Layoff Statistics, May 2010, <http://www.bls.gov/mls/home.htm>.

Table 634. Private Sector Gross Job Gains and Job Losses: 2000 to 2009

[In thousands (16,096 represents 16,096,000). For year ending in March. Based on the Quarterly Census of Employment and Wages (QCEW). Excludes self-employed and certain nonprofit organizations. Minus sign (–) indicates a decrease in employment and come from either closing establishments or contracting establishments]

Year and industry	Gross job gains			Gross job losses			Net change [1]
	Total	Expanding establish-ments	Opening establish-ments	Total	Contracting establish-ments	Closing establish-ments	
2000.	16,096	10,618	5,478	13,118	8,284	4,834	2,978
2001.	15,177	10,147	5,030	14,330	9,249	5,081	847
2002.	13,630	8,631	4,999	16,359	11,027	5,332	–2,729
2003.	13,196	8,604	4,592	13,928	9,290	4,638	–732
2004.	13,310	8,951	4,359	12,432	8,237	4,195	878
2005.	13,766	9,410	4,356	11,774	7,671	4,103	1,992
2006.	14,019	9,625	4,394	11,438	7,711	3,727	2,581
2007.	13,441	9,238	4,203	11,941	8,246	3,695	1,500
2008.	12,704	8,714	3,990	12,609	8,772	3,837	95
2009, Total private	**10,088**	**6,683**	**3,405**	**15,939**	**11,651**	**4,288**	**–5,851**
Goods producing.	1,617	1,168	449	4,232	3,341	891	–2,615
Natural resources and mining.	208	148	60	278	215	63	–70
Construction.	842	564	278	1,937	1,383	554	–1,095
Manufacturing.	567	456	111	2,017	1,743	274	–1,450
Service providing.	8,469	5,514	2,955	11,707	8,308	3,399	–3,238
Wholesale trade.	471	329	142	802	577	225	–331
Retail trade.	1,161	713	448	1,990	1,434	556	–829
Transportation and warehousing.	323	232	91	582	432	150	–259
Utilities.	32	27	5	24	19	5	8
Information.	262	194	68	408	306	102	–146
Financial activities.	720	494	226	1,080	734	346	–360
Professional and business services.	1,947	1,332	615	3,161	2,348	813	–1,214
Education and health services.	1,506	1,154	352	1,141	799	342	365
Leisure and hospitality.	1,473	765	708	1,921	1,290	631	–448
Other services.	419	266	153	544	361	183	–125

[1] Net change is the difference between total gross job gains and total gross job losses.

Source: Bureau of Labor Statistics, Business Employment Dynamics, "Annual Business Employment Dynamics Data," <http://www.bls.gov/bdm/bdmann.htm#TOTAL\>.

Table 635. Private Sector Gross Job Gains and Job Losses by State: 2009

[In thousands (10,088 represents 10,0088,000). For year ending in March. Based on the Quarterly Census of Employment and Wages (QCEW). Excludes self-employed and certain nonprofit organizations. Minus sign (–) indicates a decrease in employment and come from either closing establishments or contracting establishments]

State	Gross job gains			Gross job losses			Net change [1]	State	Gross job gains			Gross job losses			Net change [1]
	Total	Expanding estab-lish-ments	Open-ing estab-lish-ments	Total	Con-tracting estab-lish-ments	Clos-ing estab-lish-ments			Total	Expand-ing estab-lish-ments	Open-ing estab-lish-ments	Total	Con-tract-ing estab-lish-ments	Clos-ing estab-lish-ments	
U.S.	**10,088**	**6,683**	**3,405**	**15,939**	**11,651**	**4,288**	**–5,851**	MO.	211	144	67	310	222	88	–99
AL	135	88	47	237	184	53	–102	MT	32	22	10	52	37	15	–20
AK	25	18	7	26	19	7	–1	NE	64	45	19	85	65	20	–21
AZ	205	126	79	389	285	104	–184	NV	98	65	33	210	163	46	–111
AR	94	62	33	131	97	34	–37	NH	45	32	14	67	50	17	–21
CA	1,216	794	421	2,017	1,445	572	–802	NJ	294	190	104	455	337	118	–161
CO	188	123	65	284	205	79	–96	NM	62	41	21	94	67	27	–32
CT	107	78	29	169	136	33	–63	NY	633	427	206	861	622	240	–229
DE	31	18	13	53	39	14	–22	NC	306	193	114	526	386	140	–220
DC	49	36	14	55	39	16	–5	ND	26	19	7	28	22	7	–2
FL	714	385	329	1,245	790	455	–531	OH	339	248	91	584	453	131	–246
GA	345	204	141	571	386	184	–225	OK	133	86	47	171	119	52	–37
HI	40	26	14	73	55	18	–33	OR	111	73	38	226	170	56	–115
ID	49	29	20	90	65	25	–41	PA	378	269	108	543	413	130	–165
IL	353	242	111	602	459	143	–248	RI	31	21	10	53	38	15	–22
IN	197	132	65	357	276	81	–161	SC	128	84	44	240	183	57	–113
IA	99	72	27	140	107	33	–41	SD	27	19	8	35	27	8	–7
KS	106	71	35	146	107	38	–40	TN	185	126	59	347	274	73	–162
KY	127	87	41	206	157	49	–79	TX	892	610	282	1,111	829	283	–219
LA	178	122	56	204	149	56	–26	UT	99	63	36	160	115	45	–61
ME	42	26	15	62	44	18	–20	VT	20	14	6	30	22	8	–10
MD	200	137	63	286	205	81	–86	VA	278	184	94	394	292	102	–116
MA	209	151	58	314	236	78	–105	WA	220	158	61	346	260	85	–126
MI	259	175	85	550	409	141	–291	WV	59	42	17	71	50	21	–12
MN	173	119	55	282	199	83	–109	WI	167	117	49	285	223	62	–119
MS	83	55	28	136	99	36	–53	WY	25	17	8	32	22	10	–8

[1] Net change is the difference between total gross job gains and total gross job losses.

Source: Bureau of Labor Statistics, Business Employment Dynamics, "Annual Business Employment Dynamics Data," <http://www.bls.gov/bdm/bdmann.htm#TOTAL\>.

Labor Force, Employment, and Earnings 413

Table 636. Hires and Separations Affecting Establishment Payrolls: 2006 to 2009

[64,906 represents 64,906,000. Hires represent any additions to payrolls, including new and rehired employees, full- and part-time workers, short-term and seasonal workers, etc. Separations represent terminations of employment, including quits, layoffs, and discharges, etc. Based on a monthly survey of private nonfarm establishments and governmental entities]

Industry	Annual hires (1,000)				Annual separations (1,000)			
	2006	2007	2008	2009	2006	2007	2008	2009
Total	64,906	63,404	56,204	48,696	62,661	62,125	59,640	53,679
Total private industry	60,481	58,843	52,486	45,237	58,467	57,882	56,111	50,112
Mining and logging	311	346	364	214	255	310	332	310
Construction	5,396	4,813	4,564	3,882	5,232	4,972	5,303	4,930
Manufacturing	4,601	4,613	3,671	2,906	4,762	4,873	4,543	4,277
Durable goods	2,735	2,685	2,110	1,513	2,770	2,884	2,736	2,600
Nondurable goods	1,864	1,928	1,558	1,391	1,988	1,989	1,808	1,677
Trade, transportation, and utilities	13,805	13,212	11,600	10,009	13,442	12,893	12,708	11,030
Wholesale trade.................	2,045	2,208	1,905	1,648	1,894	2,129	2,161	1,900
Retail trade	9,602	9,121	7,897	6,658	9,513	8,931	8,612	7,172
Transportation, warehousing, and utilities	2,160	1,882	1,801	1,704	2,034	1,835	1,935	1,955
Information.......................	1,123	985	805	760	1,139	997	919	928
Financial activities	3,099	3,160	2,629	2,136	2,940	3,260	2,845	2,528
Finance and insurance	1,991	2,092	1,697	1,274	1,864	2,177	1,849	1,545
Real estate and rental and leasing	1,107	1,066	932	861	1,081	1,082	997	984
Professional and business services	11,955	11,474	9,983	8,428	11,424	11,187	10,784	9,146
Education and health services	6,382	6,440	6,499	6,156	5,908	5,913	6,035	5,850
Educational services	879	915	934	888	835	852	840	855
Health care and social assistance......	5,503	5,524	5,565	5,268	5,074	5,060	5,196	4,994
Leisure and hospitality...............	11,258	11,208	9,981	8,313	10,861	10,940	10,208	8,568
Arts, entertainment, and recreation	1,581	1,648	1,471	1,246	1,497	1,602	1,496	1,319
Accommodation and food services	9,677	9,561	8,509	7,066	9,364	9,338	8,711	7,249
Other services	2,559	2,595	2,386	2,430	2,498	2,537	2,438	2,549
Government workers	4,427	4,562	3,720	3,457	4,195	4,243	3,528	3,564
Federal.........................	714	853	333	452	715	819	329	391
State and local....................	3,711	3,709	3,387	3,007	3,478	3,426	3,199	3,174

Source: U.S. Bureau of Labor Statistics, *Job Openings and Labor Turnover*, News Release, USDL 10-0282, March 2010. See also <http://www.bls.gov/news.release/archives/jolts-03092010.htm>.

Table 637. Type of Separations Affecting Establishment Payrolls: 2009

[21,964 represents 21,964,000. Covers all private nonfarm establishments. Separations are the total number of terminations of employment occurring at any time during the reference month, and are reported by type of separation—quits, layoffs and discharges, and other separations. Annual rate estimates are computed by dividing annual levels by the Current Employment Statistics (CES) annual average employment level, see Table 631, and multiplying that quotient by 100]

Industry	Number (1,000)			Rate		
	Annual quits level [1]	Annual layoffs and discharge levels [2]	Annual other separations [3]	Annual quits level [1]	Annual layoffs and discharge levels [2]	Annual other separations [3]
Total...........................	21,964	27,790	3,921	16.8	21.2	3.0
Private industry	20,689	26,154	3,273	19.1	24.1	3.0
Mining and logging	90	193	26	12.9	27.6	3.7
Construction	906	3,891	131	15.0	64.5	2.2
Manufacturing	1,064	2,929	288	9.0	24.6	2.4
Durable goods	519	1,892	190	7.1	25.9	2.6
Nondurable goods	544	1,035	97	11.9	22.6	2.1
Trade, transportation, and utilities	4,911	5,185	931	19.7	20.8	3.7
Wholesale trade.................	551	1,171	182	9.8	20.8	3.2
Retail trade	3,615	2,960	597	24.9	20.4	4.1
Transportation, warehousing, and utilities.........................	744	1,055	155	15.5	22.0	3.2
Information.......................	409	438	76	14.6	15.6	2.7
Financial activities	918	1,389	221	11.8	17.9	2.8
Finance and insurance	593	784	165	10.3	13.6	2.9
Real estate and rental and leasing	325	603	55	16.3	30.2	2.8
Professional and business services	3,398	5,115	632	20.5	30.9	3.8
Education and health services	3,057	2,255	538	15.9	11.8	2.8
Educational services	328	469	55	10.6	15.2	1.8
Health care and social assistance.....	2,729	1,785	481	16.9	11.1	3.0
Leisure and hospitality..............	4,808	3,467	295	36.7	26.5	2.3
Arts, entertainment, and recreation ...	421	859	39	22.0	44.9	2.0
Accommodation and food services	4,386	2,607	254	39.2	23.3	2.3
Other services	1,128	1,291	130	21.0	24.1	2.4
Government workers.................	1,278	1,634	650	5.7	7.2	2.9
Federal.........................	65	217	109	2.3	7.7	3.9
State and local...................	1,214	1,419	541	6.2	7.2	2.7

[1] Quits are voluntary separations by employees (except for retirements, which are reported as other separations). [2] Layoffs and discharges are involuntary separations initiated by the employer and include layoffs with no intent to rehire; formal layoffs lasting or expected to last more than seven days; discharges resulting from mergers, downsizing, or closings, firings or other discharges for cause; terminations of permanent or short-term employees; and terminations of seasonal employees. [3] Other separations include retirements, transfers to other locations, deaths, and separations due to disability.

Source: U.S. Bureau of Labor Statistics, *Job Openings and Labor Turnover*, News Release, USDL 10-0282, March 2010. See also <http://www.bls.gov/news.release/archives/jolts-03092010.htm>.

414 Labor Force, Employment, and Earnings

Table 638. Average Hours Per Week Spent Doing Unpaid Household Work and Paid Work by Sex and Age: 2003–2007

[In hours. Data for persons in the civilian noninstitutionalized population 15 years old and over for 2003 through 2007. Unpaid household work is defined as activities that are unpaid, for which market substitutes exist, and done for one's own household]

Type of work	Total, 15 years and over	Age						
		15–24 years	25–34 years	35–44 years	45–54 years	55–64 years	65–74 years	75 years and over
MEN								
Total paid work and unpaid household work . . .	**47.4**	**29.9**	**57.2**	**60.0**	**57.6**	**47.9**	**30.2**	**21.2**
Unpaid household work.	15.9	8.9	15.8	18.3	17.0	17.8	19.9	18.1
Household activities	9.2	4.6	7.4	9.1	10.6	12.3	13.4	12.8
Food and drink preparation	1.9	0.8	1.7	2.2	2.1	2.2	2.3	3.0
Cleaning	1.2	0.9	1.2	1.3	1.2	1.2	1.2	1.4
Laundry and sewing	0.4	0.3	0.5	0.5	0.5	0.4	0.4	0.4
Household management	0.8	0.4	0.6	0.8	0.9	1.1	1.2	1.2
Lawn and garden care.	1.9	0.5	1.0	1.5	2.2	3.2	3.9	3.6
Maintenance and repair.	2.4	1.4	1.8	2.3	2.8	3.2	3.5	2.3
Caring for and helping household members.	2.0	0.7	3.4	4.1	1.6	0.6	0.6	0.7
Purchasing goods and services	2.4	1.9	2.5	2.4	2.2	2.6	3.3	2.7
Travel related to unpaid household work	2.4	1.8	2.4	2.7	2.5	2.3	2.6	1.9
Paid work.	31.4	20.9	41.4	41.7	40.6	30.1	10.3	3.1
WOMEN								
Total paid work and unpaid household work . . .	**47.7**	**33.4**	**58.0**	**60.4**	**55.8**	**48.0**	**33.7**	**25.1**
Unpaid household work.	26.7	15.9	31.7	33.1	26.7	26.2	28.1	23.8
Household activities	15.5	7.1	13.9	17.0	17.3	18.1	20.9	18.8
Food and drink preparation	5.3	2.2	5.3	6.1	5.6	5.9	7.0	6.4
Cleaning	4.0	2.3	4.2	4.4	4.0	4.3	5.0	4.5
Laundry and sewing	2.5	0.9	2.0	2.8	3.0	2.9	3.6	3.1
Household management	1.1	0.8	0.8	1.1	1.2	1.3	1.6	1.5
Lawn and garden care.	0.9	0.2	0.5	0.8	1.1	1.5	1.7	1.6
Maintenance and repair.	0.8	0.4	0.5	0.8	1.1	1.1	0.9	0.7
Caring for and helping household members.	4.4	3.1	10.3	8.1	2.4	1.1	0.8	0.5
Purchasing goods and services	3.7	3.3	3.8	4.1	3.8	4.1	3.9	2.8
Travel related to unpaid household work	3.1	2.4	3.7	4.0	3.1	2.9	2.5	1.7
Paid work.	21.0	17.4	26.3	27.3	29.1	21.8	5.7	1.2

Source: U.S. Bureau of Labor Statistics, "Measuring time spent in unpaid household work: results from the American Time Use Survey," Monthly Labor Review, July 2009, Vol. 132, No. 7, <http://www.bls.gov/opub/mlr/2009/07/contents.htm>.

Table 639. Average Hours Worked Per Day by Employed Persons: 2009

[148,720 represents 148,720,000). Civilian noninstitutionalized population 15 years old and over, except as indicated. Includes work at main and any other job(s). Excludes travel related to work. Based on the American Time Use Survey. See source for details]

Characteristic	Total employed (1,000)	Employed persons who worked on their diary day [1]			Worked at workplace		Worked at home [2]	
		Number (1,000)	Percent of employed	Hours of work	Percent of employed [3]	Hours of work	Percent of employed [3]	Hours of work
Total	**148,720**	**101,379**	**68.2**	**7.48**	**84.1**	**7.82**	**23.6**	**2.98**
Work status: [4].								
Full-time workers [5].	114,618	82,511	72.0	7.97	85.3	8.24	23.5	3.13
Part-time workers [5]	34,102	18,868	55.3	5.34	79.0	5.81	24.2	2.35
Male [4].	78,264	55,676	71.1	7.90	85.2	8.17	23.4	3.12
Full-time workers [5].	65,641	48,043	73.2	8.29	85.9	8.51	23.1	3.24
Part-time workers [5]	12,623	7,633	60.5	5.47	80.2	5.93	25.6	2.49
Female [4].	70,456	45,703	64.9	6.97	82.8	7.38	23.8	2.81
Full-time workers [5].	48,977	34,468	70.4	7.53	84.4	7.87	24.0	2.99
Part-time workers [5]	21,479	11,235	52.3	5.25	78.2	5.74	23.3	2.24
Jobholding status:								
Single jobholders.	132,834	88,563	66.7	7.48	84.5	7.81	22.4	3.13
Multiple jobholders.	15,886	12,816	80.7	7.51	81.1	7.88	32.0	2.24
Educational attainment: [6].								
Less than high school	9,087	5,968	65.7	7.75	92.8	7.92	10.2	(B)
High school diploma [7]	36,852	24,251	65.8	8.03	88.9	8.14	13.0	4.97
Some college.	33,136	23,045	69.5	7.76	85.7	8.07	20.7	3.02
Bachelor's degree or higher. . .	47,722	34,855	73.0	7.20	75.7	7.82	40.3	2.64

B Percent not shown where base is less than 1.2 million. [1] Individuals may have worked at more than one location. [2] "Working at home" includes any time persons did work at home and is not restricted to persons whose usual workplace is their home. [3] Percent of employed who worked on their diary day. [4] Includes workers whose hours vary. [5] Full-time workers usually worked 35 or more hours per week at all jobs combined; part-time workers fewer than 35 hours per week. [6] For those 25 years old and over. [7] Includes persons with a high school diploma or equivalent.

Source: U.S. Bureau of Labor Statistics, American Time Use Survey—2009 Results, News Release, USDL 10-0855, June 2010. See also <http://www.bls.gov/tus/home.htm#news>.

Table 640. Productivity and Related Measures for Selected NAICS Industries: 1987 to 2008 and 2001 to 2008

[For a discussion of productivity measures and methodology, see text, this section and BLS Handbook of Methods, <http://www.bls.gov/opub/hom/homch11_a.htm>. Minus sign (−) indicates decrease]

| Industry | 2007 NAICS code [1] | Average annual percent change [2] | | | | | | | |
| | | 1987–2008 [3] | | | | 2001–2008 | | | |
		Output per hour	Output	Hours	Unit labor costs	Output per hour	Output	Hours	Unit labor costs
Mining	21	−0.4	−0.2	0.2	5.7	−4.4	−0.7	3.9	11.1
Oil and gas extraction	2111	0.5	−0.8	−1.3	6.5	−4.2	−0.9	3.5	11.7
Mining, except oil and gas	212	2.0	0.8	−1.1	1.4	−0.7	–	0.7	4.8
Support activities for mining	2131	3.1	5.6	2.4	3.2	4.9	12.2	7.0	2.3
Utilities:									
Power generation and supply	2211	2.4	1.1	−1.3	1.6	0.3	−0.4	−0.7	3.5
Natural gas distribution	2212	2.8	1.3	−1.5	2.0	1.3	0.5	−0.8	2.3
Manufacturing:									
Food	311	1.1	1.4	0.3	1.7	0.9	0.6	−0.2	2.1
Animal slaughtering and processing	3116	0.9	2.3	1.4	1.5	1.8	1.6	−0.2	2.0
Bakeries and tortilla manufacturing	3118	0.4	0.3	−0.2	2.1	−0.7	−0.9	−0.2	1.5
Beverages and tobacco products	312	0.6	−0.3	−0.9	1.9	−0.1	−1.7	−1.5	3.2
Textile mills	313	3.5	−2.6	−5.9	–	4.8	−6.3	−10.6	−0.3
Textile product mills	314	0.8	−1.1	−1.9	2.0	−0.1	−4.6	−4.5	2.2
Apparel	315	−1.3	−8.1	−6.9	3.1	−10.1	−18.6	−9.4	9.6
Leather and allied products	316	2.2	−4.5	−6.6	1.8	−0.5	−7.7	−7.2	3.1
Wood products	321	1.3	0.1	−1.3	2.5	2.6	−1.3	−3.8	2.1
Other wood products	3219	1.1	0.1	−1.0	3.0	3.1	−0.4	−3.4	2.0
Paper and paper products	322	2.0	0.2	−1.7	1.3	2.7	−0.9	−3.5	0.3
Converted paper products	3222	1.5	0.5	−1.0	1.9	2.6	−0.4	−3.0	0.7
Printing and related support activities	3231	1.5	0.1	−1.3	1.6	3.3	−1.0	−4.1	0.5
Petroleum and coal products	3241	2.6	1.2	−1.3	2.7	1.2	1.0	−0.2	4.8
Chemicals	325	1.8	1.0	−0.7	2.3	2.4	0.5	−1.8	2.1
Pharmaceuticals and medicines	3254	0.7	3.0	2.4	3.4	0.1	0.4	0.3	5.2
Plastics and rubber products	326	2.0	1.7	−0.3	1.3	1.4	−1.2	−2.6	1.2
Plastics products	3261	1.9	2.0	0.1	1.4	1.1	−1.1	−2.2	1.5
Nonmetallic mineral products	327	1.2	0.7	−0.5	1.8	1.7	−0.4	−2.1	1.7
Primary metals	331	2.6	0.5	−2.1	0.7	4.8	0.8	−3.8	−0.4
Fabricated metal products	332	1.6	1.5	−0.2	1.6	2.2	1.0	−1.2	1.7
Architectural and structural metals	3323	1.1	1.8	0.7	2.3	1.5	1.0	−0.5	3.3
Machine shops and threaded products	3327	2.5	3.3	0.8	1.3	2.0	2.3	0.3	1.0
Other fabricated metal products	3329	1.7	0.9	−0.8	1.2	4.3	2.5	−1.7	−0.3
Machinery	333	2.5	1.9	−0.6	0.6	3.4	1.8	−1.6	−0.3
Agriculture, construction, and mining machinery	3331	3.0	3.6	0.6	−0.1	4.3	6.5	2.1	−0.9
Other general purpose machinery	3339	2.6	1.9	−0.7	1.1	3.9	1.8	−2.0	0.3
Computer and electronic products	334	12.2	9.8	−2.2	−7.7	8.5	3.9	−4.3	−5.1
Semiconductors and electronic components	3344	16.8	15.2	−1.4	−11.2	9.8	4.0	−5.2	−5.6
Electronic instruments	3345	4.4	2.5	−1.8	−0.3	5.5	4.9	−0.6	−1.2
Electrical equipment and appliances	335	2.7	0.5	−2.1	1.1	2.3	−1.0	−3.2	1.2
Transportation equipment	336	2.9	1.4	−1.4	−0.2	4.2	1.4	−2.7	−0.9
Motor vehicles	3361	3.4	1.2	−2.2	−0.3	5.0	−0.3	−5.0	−1.0
Motor vehicle parts	3363	2.9	2.0	−0.8	−0.8	3.1	−2.1	−5.0	−1.2
Aerospace products and parts	3364	1.7	−0.5	−2.1	1.2	1.0	0.9	−0.1	2.5
Furniture and related products	337	1.9	0.6	−1.2	1.7	2.9	−1.3	−4.1	1.2
Household and institutional furniture	3371	1.8	0.3	−1.5	1.9	2.6	−1.8	−4.3	1.5
Miscellaneous manufacturing	339	3.0	3.0	0.0	1.4	3.5	2.1	−1.4	1.4
Medical equipment and supplies	3391	3.6	5.0	1.3	0.9	3.8	4.4	0.6	1.1
Other miscellaneous manufacturing	3399	2.2	1.3	−0.9	1.9	2.7	−0.3	−2.9	1.8
Wholesale trade	42	3.0	3.7	0.7	1.1	2.1	2.4	0.3	1.3
Durable goods	423	4.9	5.4	0.5	−0.6	4.1	3.7	−0.4	−0.9
Nondurable goods	424	0.9	1.3	0.4	3.5	0.7	0.5	−0.2	2.9
Electronic markets and agents and brokers	4251	2.0	4.7	2.6	0.2	−1.8	3.6	5.5	5.5
Retail trade	44–45	3.0	3.7	0.6	0.1	3.0	2.7	−0.4	−0.3
Motor vehicle and parts dealers	441	2.0	2.8	0.8	0.9	0.4	0.1	−0.3	1.2
Automobile dealers	4411	1.8	2.7	0.8	1.1	0.1	−0.4	−0.4	1.0
Other motor vehicle dealers	4412	3.3	5.3	2.0	0.3	2.4	5.4	3.0	−0.4
Auto parts, accessories, and tire stores	4413	2.0	2.6	0.5	0.8	1.1	0.3	−0.7	2.1
Furniture and home furnishings stores	442	3.8	4.3	0.4	−0.8	4.5	3.2	−1.2	−2.4
Furniture stores	4421	3.3	3.7	0.4	−0.6	3.5	2.7	−0.8	−2.3
Home furnishings stores	4422	4.6	5.1	0.5	−1.0	5.5	3.9	−1.6	−2.6
Electronics and appliance stores	4431	13.5	15.0	1.3	−8.9	15.6	14.9	−0.6	−12.6
Building material and garden supply stores	444	3.0	4.4	1.3	−0.3	2.9	3.3	0.5	0.1
Building material and supplies dealers	4441	2.7	4.4	1.6	–	2.2	2.9	0.7	0.7
Lawn and garden equipment and supplies stores	4442	5.2	4.7	−0.5	−2.0	7.3	6.0	−1.2	−3.9
Food and beverage stores	445	0.4	0.3	−0.1	3.0	2.3	0.6	−1.6	1.5
Grocery stores	4451	0.3	0.3	–	3.2	2.0	0.4	−1.6	2.2
Specialty food stores	4452	−0.1	−0.4	−0.3	2.6	3.3	0.9	−2.3	−2.2
Beer, wine, and liquor stores	4453	2.2	1.0	−1.2	1.6	4.7	2.8	−1.8	−2.3
Health and personal care stores	4461	2.4	3.8	1.4	1.5	2.5	3.5	0.9	1.9
Gasoline stations	4471	2.0	1.2	−0.7	1.3	1.6	–	−1.6	0.8
Clothing and clothing accessories stores	448	4.9	4.5	−0.3	−1.3	5.1	4.6	−0.5	−1.4
Clothing stores	4481	5.2	5.2	−0.1	−1.6	6.0	5.6	−0.4	−1.9
Shoe stores	4482	3.7	2.6	−1.1	−0.8	3.4	2.4	−1.0	−1.1
Jewelry, luggage, and leather goods stores	4483	3.9	3.5	−0.4	−0.4	2.2	1.8	−0.4	1.1

See footnotes at end of table.

[For a discussion of productivity measures and methodology, see text, this section and BLS Handbook of Methods, <http://www.bls.gov/opub/hom/homch11_a.htm>. Minus sign (–) indicates decrease]

Industry	2007 NAICS code [1]	Average annual percent change [2]							
		1987–2008 [3]				2001–2008			
		Output per hour	Output	Hours	Unit labor costs	Output per hour	Output	Hours	Unit labor costs
Retail Trade—Con.									
Sporting goods, hobby, book, and music stores . . .	451	4.1	4.7	0.6	–0.8	4.5	3.1	–1.3	–2.3
Sporting goods and musical instrument stores . . .	4511	4.7	5.5	0.7	–1.3	5.3	5.1	–0.2	–3.2
Book, periodical, and music stores	4512	2.6	2.9	0.3	0.3	2.7	–1.6	–4.2	–0.5
General merchandise stores	452	3.4	5.3	1.8	–1.2	2.6	4.9	2.3	–0.8
Department stores	4521	0.6	2.1	1.4	0.6	–0.6	–0.9	–0.3	1.2
Other general merchandise stores	4529	6.9	9.2	2.2	–3.2	4.2	9.6	5.2	–0.7
Miscellaneous store retailers	453	4.5	4.6	0.1	–1.9	5.4	2.0	–3.2	–3.1
Florists	4531	3.5	1.0	–2.5	–0.3	6.5	–0.5	–6.6	–2.2
Office supplies, stationery, and gift stores	4532	6.0	5.8	–0.2	–2.8	6.7	2.0	–4.4	–4.4
Used merchandise stores	4533	5.8	6.6	0.7	–2.9	8.2	5.0	–2.9	–5.8
Other miscellaneous store retailers	4539	2.5	3.9	1.3	–1.3	2.4	1.8	–0.6	–0.9
Nonstore retailers	454	8.5	8.7	0.2	–4.5	8.1	7.1	–0.9	–3.2
Electronic shopping and mail-order houses	4541	11.2	15.2	3.6	–6.4	10.6	11.2	0.6	–5.1
Vending machine operators	4542	2.1	–0.7	–2.7	2.2	6.3	0.5	–5.4	–0.9
Direct selling establishments	4543	3.1	1.5	–1.6	–	0.7	–0.7	–1.4	3.1
Transportation and warehousing:									
Air transportation	481	2.9	3.1	0.2	–0.2	6.4	3.0	–3.2	–4.7
General freight trucking	4841	1.3	2.5	1.1	1.4	1.1	1.6	0.5	1.1
Used household and office goods moving	48421	–0.6	–0.2	0.4	2.7	1.6	–1.7	–3.3	–1.1
Postal service	4911	0.9	0.7	–0.2	3.3	0.6	–1.6	–2.1	4.1
Couriers and messengers	492	–0.2	2.2	2.4	2.5	1.1	–1.4	–2.6	0.5
Warehousing and storage	4931	2.7	6.1	3.4	–0.1	0.2	4.6	4.4	2.3
Information:									
Publishing	511	3.8	4.1	0.3	1.5	2.6	–0.2	–2.8	1.4
Newspaper, book, and directory publishers	5111	–	–1.0	–1.0	4.4	–0.1	–3.3	–3.1	4.3
Software publishers	5112	14.4	21.9	6.5	–7.9	5.6	3.6	–1.9	–2.0
Motion picture and video exhibition	51213	1.2	1.9	0.7	1.7	2.0	–0.5	–2.5	3.2
Broadcasting, except Internet	515	1.6	2.7	1.1	2.2	4.9	4.3	–0.5	–0.5
Radio and television broadcasting	5151	0.4	0.6	0.1	3.4	2.6	1.9	–0.7	0.5
Cable and other subscription programming	5152	3.6	8.3	4.5	2.0	8.2	8.1	–0.1	0.8
Wired telecommunications carriers	5171	4.4	3.8	–0.5	–0.9	4.7	–0.4	4.8	–
Wireless telecommunications carriers	5172	9.5	22.4	11.9	–5.6	14.8	15.3	0.4	–5.5
Finance and insurance:									
Commercial banking	52211	3.5	3.5	–	1.9	1.8	2.7	0.9	3.1
Real estate and rental and leasing:									
Passenger car rental	532111	1.8	2.9	1.1	2.8	2.7	–0.4	–3.0	1.8
Truck, trailer, and RV rental and leasing	53212	3.7	2.9	–0.8	0.6	2.0	–0.4	–2.3	2.9
Video tape and disc rental	53223	4.2	4.4	0.2	–1.3	4.7	–2.1	–6.5	–1.3
Professional and technical services:									
Tax preparation services	541213	0.7	3.3	2.6	1.3	0.3	1.5	1.1	5.0
Architectural services	54131	1.5	3.9	2.3	2.1	1.6	3.0	1.4	1.7
Engineering services	54133	1.8	4.0	2.2	2.7	4.0	5.7	1.7	0.6
Advertising agencies	54181	2.0	2.4	0.4	2.5	4.4	4.4	–	–2.3
Photography studios, portrait	541921	0.1	2.3	2.2	2.3	–0.3	0.9	1.2	1.3
Administrative and waste services:									
Employment placement agencies	561311	7.6	8.9	1.2	–1.5	13.8	10.4	–3.0	–8.8
Travel agencies	56151	6.2	5.1	–1.0	–1.0	15.5	9.9	–4.9	–9.9
Janitorial services	56172	2.2	4.2	2.0	1.7	2.1	3.4	1.3	0.6
Health care and social assistance:									
Medical and diagnostic laboratories	6215	4.3	7.4	3.0	–1.2	2.8	6.0	3.1	0.2
Medical laboratories	621511	3.6	6.1	2.4	–0.7	2.4	4.7	2.2	1.0
Diagnostic imaging centers	621512	5.0	9.4	4.2	–1.5	2.6	8.1	5.3	–0.6
Arts, entertainment, and recreation:									
Amusement and theme parks	71311	0.1	3.0	2.9	3.5	2.9	2.0	–0.9	1.8
Bowling centers	71395	0.4	–1.5	–1.9	2.8	2.9	0.1	–2.7	1.2
Accommodation and food services	72	0.9	2.4	1.5	3.0	1.0	2.3	1.3	2.1
Accommodation	721	1.7	2.9	1.2	2.4	1.7	2.2	0.5	0.9
Traveler accommodation	7211	1.7	2.9	1.2	2.3	1.7	2.2	0.5	0.9
Food services and drinking places	722	0.6	2.3	1.6	3.2	0.8	2.3	1.5	2.6
Full-service restaurants	7221	0.6	2.3	1.7	4.0	0.2	1.8	1.6	3.4
Limited-service eating places	7222	0.6	2.5	1.8	2.8	1.0	2.9	1.9	1.9
Special food services	7223	1.7	2.9	1.1	1.2	1.6	2.8	1.1	2.3
Drinking places, alcoholic beverages	7224	–0.4	–0.6	–0.1	2.9	3.5	0.2	–3.2	0.2
Other services:									
Automotive repair and maintenance	8111	1.0	1.6	0.6	2.4	–0.4	–1.5	–1.1	3.5
Reupholstery and furniture repair	81142	–0.2	–2.0	–1.8	3.2	–0.5	–4.1	–3.6	3.9
Hair, nail, and skin care services	81211	2.3	3.1	0.8	2.1	2.4	3.1	0.7	1.8
Funeral homes and funeral services	81221	–0.5	–0.2	0.4	4.5	0.1	–2.0	–2.1	3.9
Drycleaning and laundry services	8123	0.9	0.6	–0.3	2.5	0.9	–0.5	–1.4	2.5
Photofinishing	81292	0.7	–4.8	–5.4	2.6	4.5	–7.7	–11.6	–2.7

– Represents zero or rounds to less than half the unit of measurement shown. [1] North American Industry Classification System, 2007 (NAICS); see text, section 15. [2] Average annual percent changes based on compound rate formula. Rates of change are calculated using index numbers to three decimal places. [3] For NAICS industries 4931, 49311, and 49312, annual percent changes are for 1992–2008, and for NAICS industries 4841, 561311, 6215, and 621512, annual percent changes are for 1994–2008.

Source: U.S. Bureau of Labor Statistics, Labor Productivity and Costs, <http://www.bls.gov/lpc/data.htm>, accessed July 2010.

Table 641. Productivity and Related Measures: 1990 to 2009

[See text, this section. Minus sign (–) indicates decrease]

Item	1990	2000	2003	2004	2005	2006	2007	2008	2009
INDEXES (1992=100)									
Output per hour, business sector	94.5	117.2	131.0	134.9	137.2	138.5	141.0	144.0	149.4
Nonfarm business	94.7	116.8	130.3	134.0	136.2	137.5	140.1	142.9	148.3
Manufacturing	93.9	139.2	160.6	164.3	172.0	173.4	179.2	181.2	184.4
Output, [1] business sector	97.1	141.9	150.3	156.5	161.8	166.8	170.5	170.5	164.5
Nonfarm business	97.3	142.2	150.6	156.8	162.0	167.1	171.0	170.7	164.5
Manufacturing	98.5	144.3	137.5	140.0	144.9	147.2	149.5	145.1	129.0
Hours, [2] business sector	102.7	121.0	114.7	116.1	118.0	120.4	120.9	118.4	110.1
Nonfarm business	102.7	121.7	115.5	117.0	118.9	121.5	122.1	119.4	110.9
Manufacturing	104.9	103.7	85.6	85.2	84.3	84.9	83.4	80.1	70.0
Compensation per hour, [3] business sector	90.3	134.6	152.3	157.6	163.8	170.1	177.3	182.5	185.7
Nonfarm business	90.2	134.1	151.4	156.6	162.8	169.0	176.1	181.4	184.7
Manufacturing	90.1	132.5	156.7	157.9	163.2	166.4	173.5	179.0	187.1
Real hourly compensation, [3] business sector	96.0	111.9	118.6	119.5	120.2	120.8	122.4	121.4	124.0
Nonfarm business	95.8	111.5	117.9	118.7	119.4	120.0	121.6	120.7	123.3
Manufacturing	95.7	110.2	122.0	119.7	119.7	118.2	119.9	119.0	124.9
Unit labor costs, [4] business sector	95.6	114.8	116.2	116.9	119.5	122.8	125.7	126.8	124.3
Nonfarm business	95.2	114.8	116.2	116.8	119.5	122.9	125.7	126.9	124.6
Manufacturing	96.0	95.2	97.6	96.1	94.9	96.0	96.8	98.8	101.5
ANNUAL PERCENT CHANGE [5]									
Output per hour, business sector	2.1	3.5	3.8	2.9	1.7	1.0	1.8	2.1	3.8
Nonfarm business	1.8	3.4	3.7	2.8	1.7	1.0	1.8	2.0	3.7
Manufacturing	2.2	4.1	6.3	2.3	4.7	0.8	3.4	1.1	1.8
Output, [1] business sector	1.5	4.5	3.1	4.2	3.4	3.1	2.2	–	−3.5
Nonfarm business	1.4	4.4	3.0	4.1	3.4	3.1	2.3	−0.1	−3.6
Manufacturing	−0.3	2.7	1.1	1.8	3.6	1.6	1.6	−3.0	−11.1
Hours, [2] business sector	−0.6	1.0	−0.7	1.2	1.6	2.1	0.4	−2.1	−7.0
Nonfarm business	−0.4	1.0	−0.6	1.3	1.7	2.1	0.5	−2.1	−7.1
Manufacturing	−2.5	−1.3	−4.9	−0.5	−1.1	0.8	−1.7	−4.0	−12.6
Compensation per hour, [3] business sector	6.4	7.4	4.8	3.5	4.0	3.8	4.2	3.0	1.8
Nonfarm business	6.2	7.4	4.8	3.4	4.0	3.8	4.2	3.0	1.8
Manufacturing	4.8	7.7	8.0	0.8	3.3	2.0	4.3	3.1	4.6
Real hourly compensation, [3] business sector	1.4	3.9	2.5	0.8	0.6	0.5	1.3	−0.8	2.1
Nonfarm business	1.1	4.0	2.5	0.7	0.6	0.5	1.3	−0.8	2.2
Manufacturing	−0.1	4.2	5.6	−1.9	–	−1.2	1.4	−0.7	5.0
Unit labor costs, [4] business sector	4.2	3.7	0.9	0.6	2.2	2.8	2.4	0.8	−1.9
Nonfarm business	4.3	3.9	1.1	0.5	2.3	2.8	2.3	1.0	−1.9
Manufacturing	2.6	3.5	1.6	−1.4	−1.3	1.2	0.9	2.0	2.7

– Represents zero. [1] Refers to gross sectoral product, a chain-type, current-weighted index.
[2] Hours at work of all persons engaged in the business and nonfarm business sectors (employees, proprietors, and unpaid family workers); employees' and proprietors' hours in manufacturing. [3] Wages and salaries of employees plus employers' contributions for social insurance and private benefit plans. Also includes an estimate of same for self-employed. Real compensation deflated by the consumer price index research series, see text, Section 14. [4] Hourly compensation divided by output per hour. [5] All changes are from the immediate prior year.

Source: U.S. Department of Labor, Bureau of Labor Statistics, *Productivity and Costs*, News Release, USDL 10-0747, June 2010. See also <http://www.bls.gov/lpc/home.htm>.

Table 642. Annual Total Compensation and Wages and Salary Accruals Per Full-Time Equivalent Employee by Industry: 2000 to 2008

[In dollars. Wage and salary accruals include executives' compensation, bonuses, tips, and payments-in-kind; total compensation includes in addition to wages and salaries, employer contributions for social insurance, employer contributions to private and welfare funds, director's fees, jury and witness fees, etc. Based on the 2002 North American Industry Classification System (NAICS); see text, section 15]

Industry	Total annual compensation				Annual salary and wages			
	2000	2005	2007	2008	2000	2005	2007	2008
Compensation of employees	47,059	56,620	61,162	62,899	39,243	45,729	49,844	51,187
Domestic industries	46,946	56,371	60,874	62,589	39,157	45,537	49,619	50,945
Private industries	45,772	54,139	58,424	59,909	38,862	44,717	48,828	50,028
Agriculture, forestry, fishing, and hunting	25,799	34,322	35,928	37,366	22,154	28,600	29,521	30,769
Mining	69,644	86,560	97,150	102,280	57,983	73,161	83,212	88,558
Utilities	80,304	104,284	114,090	116,442	64,742	77,409	84,570	86,306
Construction	46,145	53,139	57,994	60,940	38,563	43,948	48,817	51,189
Manufacturing	53,285	64,534	69,596	71,392	43,933	50,909	55,345	56,409
Wholesale trade	59,059	68,006	73,986	75,511	50,853	57,922	63,812	65,022
Retail trade	31,110	35,468	36,995	37,322	26,585	29,230	30,730	30,911
Transportation and warehousing	47,985	55,737	58,841	59,543	39,057	43,865	47,260	47,736
Information	71,023	83,067	90,636	92,485	62,582	68,330	74,895	76,495
Finance and insurance	75,339	92,949	103,019	104,246	64,561	77,981	87,723	88,094
Real estate and rental and leasing	43,195	50,768	55,653	55,101	37,146	43,708	48,395	47,824
Professional, scientific, and technical services	71,541	81,862	88,805	91,385	62,568	69,767	76,784	79,064
Management of companies and enterprises [1]	89,918	106,577	120,979	121,497	74,201	87,971	100,044	100,715
Administrative and waste management services	28,934	36,942	39,723	41,647	25,035	31,370	34,132	35,663
Educational services	34,085	41,730	45,000	46,397	29,243	34,844	37,730	39,126
Health care and social assistance	41,701	51,850	55,186	56,747	35,269	42,286	45,471	46,948
Arts, entertainment, and recreation	37,296	43,210	46,617	48,950	32,479	37,149	40,329	42,564
Accommodation and food services	20,801	24,809	26,572	27,014	18,047	21,018	22,865	23,353
Other services, except government	30,118	35,781	38,547	39,738	25,989	30,465	33,094	34,243
Government	53,344	68,229	74,080	76,747	40,767	49,894	53,887	55,794
Federal	69,842	99,230	107,606	111,446	46,470	64,184	68,447	70,330
State and local	48,707	60,161	65,451	67,812	39,164	46,174	50,139	52,051

[1] Consists of offices of bank and other holding companies and of corporate, subsidiary, and regional managing offices.
Source: U.S. Bureau of Economic Analysis, *Survey of Current Business*, April 2010. See also <http://www.bea.gov/national/nipaweb/Index.asp>.

Table 643. Average Hourly and Weekly Earnings by Private Industry Group: 1990 to 2009

[In dollars. Average earnings include overtime. Data are for production employees in mining and logging, manufacturing, and construction, and nonsupervisory employees in the service providing industries. See headnote, Table 624]

Private industry group	Current dollars					Constant (1982–84) dollars [1]				
	1990	2000	2005	2008	2009	1990	2000	2005	2008	2009
AVERAGE HOURLY EARNINGS										
Total private	**10.20**	**14.02**	**16.13**	**18.08**	**18.62**	**7.91**	**8.30**	**8.45**	**8.57**	**8.88**
Mining and logging	13.40	16.55	18.72	22.50	23.29	10.39	9.80	9.80	10.66	11.11
Construction	13.42	17.48	19.46	21.87	22.67	10.40	10.35	10.19	10.36	10.81
Manufacturing	10.78	14.32	16.56	17.75	18.23	8.36	8.48	8.67	8.41	8.70
Trade, transportation, and utilities [2]	9.83	13.31	14.92	16.16	16.50	7.62	7.88	7.81	7.66	7.87
Information	13.40	19.07	22.06	24.78	25.45	10.39	11.29	11.55	11.74	12.14
Financial activities [2]	9.99	14.98	17.95	20.28	20.83	7.74	8.87	9.40	9.61	9.94
Professional and business services [2]	11.14	15.52	18.08	21.18	22.35	8.64	9.19	9.47	10.04	10.66
Education and health services [2]	10.00	13.95	16.71	18.87	19.49	7.75	8.26	8.75	8.94	9.30
Leisure and hospitality [2]	6.02	8.32	9.38	10.84	11.11	4.67	4.93	4.91	5.14	5.30
Other services	9.08	12.73	14.34	16.09	16.59	7.04	7.54	7.51	7.62	7.91
AVERAGE WEEKLY EARNINGS										
Total private	**350**	**481**	**544**	**608**	**617**	**271**	**285**	**285**	**288**	**294**
Mining and logging	603	735	854	1,015	1,008	467	435	447	481	481
Construction	513	686	750	843	852	398	406	393	399	407
Manufacturing	436	591	673	724	726	338	350	353	343	346
Trade, transportation, and utilities	332	450	498	536	542	257	266	261	254	259
Information	480	701	805	909	932	372	415	422	431	445
Financial activities [2]	355	537	645	727	751	275	318	338	345	358
Professional and business services [2]	381	535	619	738	776	295	317	324	350	370
Education and health services [2]	319	449	545	614	629	248	266	285	291	300
Leisure and hospitality [2]	156	217	241	273	276	121	129	126	130	132
Other services	298	413	443	496	506	231	245	232	235	242

[1] Earnings in current dollars divided by the Consumer Price Index (CPI-W) on a 1982–84 base; see text, Section 14.
[2] For composition of industries, see Table 624.

Source: U.S. Bureau of Labor Statistics, Current Employment Statistics, "Employment, Hours, and Earnings—National." See also <http://www.bls.gov/ces/data.htm>.

Table 644. Mean Hourly Earnings and Weekly Hours by Selected Characteristics: 2009

[Covers civilian workers in private industry establishments and state and local governments in the 50 states and DC. Excludes private households, federal government and agriculture. See source and Appendix III for details about the National Compensation Survey]

Item	Mean hourly earnings (dollars) [1]			Mean weekly hours		
	Total	Private industry	State and local government	Total	Private industry	State and local government
Total	**20.99**	**20.18**	**25.74**	**35.3**	**35.1**	**36.2**
WORKER CHARACTERISTIC						
Management, professional and related	33.90	34.35	32.61	36.8	37.1	35.9
Management, business, and financial	37.77	38.30	34.86	39.4	39.8	37.5
Professional and related	32.14	32.16	32.08	35.7	35.7	35.6
Service	12.01	10.50	19.05	30.9	30.0	36.4
Sales and office	16.40	16.33	17.19	34.8	34.7	36.4
Sales and related	17.13	17.14	16.42	32.5	32.5	34.0
Office and administrative support	16.01	15.84	17.21	36.2	36.2	36.5
Natural resources, construction, and maintenance	21.03	21.06	20.67	39.1	39.1	38.8
Construction and extraction	20.98	21.10	19.92	39.1	39.2	38.6
Installation, maintenance, and repair	21.20	21.16	21.59	39.2	39.2	39.2
Production, transportation, and material moving	15.85	15.73	19.14	37.1	37.2	34.4
Production	16.16	16.07	21.33	38.8	38.8	39.6
Transportation and material moving	15.54	15.37	18.46	35.6	35.7	33.1
Full-time [3]	22.36	21.61	26.40	39.5	39.6	38.9
Part-time [3]	12.03	11.70	16.27	20.7	20.9	18.3
Union [4]	25.47	22.71	29.13	36.6	36.4	37.0
Nonunion	20.19	19.90	23.01	35.0	35.0	35.6
Time [5]	20.76	19.87	25.74	35.1	34.9	36.2
Incentive [5]	25.29	25.27	(S)	38.3	38.3	(S)
ESTABLISHMENT CHARACTERISTIC						
Goods producing [6]	(S)	21.86	(S)	(X)	39.4	(X)
Service producing [6]	(S)	19.75	(S)	(X)	34.1	(X)
1 to 49 workers	17.57	17.51	19.57	33.8	33.8	33.0
50 to 99 workers	19.18	19.07	20.90	34.7	34.6	35.8
100 to 499 workers	20.61	20.17	23.90	35.9	35.9	36.0
500 workers or more	26.51	26.04	27.35	36.9	37.0	36.7

S Figure does not meet publication standards. X Not applicable. [1] Earnings are straight time hourly wages or salary, including incentive pay, cost-of-living adjustments, and hazard pay. Excludes premium pay for overtime, vacations and holidays, nonproduction bonuses and tips. [2] Mean weekly hours are the hours an employee is scheduled to work in a week exclusive of overtime [3] Based on definition used by each establishment. [4] Workers whose wages are determined through collective bargaining. [5] Time worker wages are based solely on an hourly rate or salary. Incentive workers wages are based at least in part on productivity payments such as piece rates or commissions. [6] For private industry only. See footnotes 3 and 4, Table 631, for composition of goods and service producing industries.

Source: U.S. Bureau of Labor Statistics, *National Compensation Survey: Occupational Earnings in the United States*, Bulletin 2738, July 2010. See also <http://www.bls.gov/ncs/ncswage2009.htm#Wage_Tables>.

Table 645. Employment and Wages: 2000 to 2008

[(129,877 represents 129,877,000). See headnote, Table 646]

Employment and wages	Unit	2000	2003	2004	2005	2006	2007	2008
Average annual employment:								
Total	1,000	129,877	127,796	129,278	131,572	133,834	135,366	134,806
Excluding federal	1,000	127,006	125,032	126,539	128,838	131,105	132,640	132,044
Private	1,000	110,015	107,066	108,490	110,611	112,719	114,012	113,189
State government	1,000	4,370	4,482	4,485	4,528	4,566	4,611	4,643
Local governments	1,000	12,620	13,484	13,564	13,699	13,820	14,016	14,212
Federal government	1,000	2,871	2,764	2,740	2,734	2,729	2,726	2,762
Annual wages:								
Total	Bil. dol.	4,588	4,826	5,088	5,352	5,693	6,018	6,142
Excluding federal	Bil. dol.	4,455	4,676	4,929	5,188	5,523	5,841	5,959
Private	Bil. dol.	3,888	4,016	4,246	4,480	4,781	5,058	5,135
State government	Bil. dol.	159	180	184	191	200	212	223
Local governments	Bil. dol.	409	481	499	517	541	572	601
Federal government	Bil. dol.	133	150	158	164	170	177	183
Average wage per employee:								
Total	Dol.	35,323	37,765	39,354	40,677	42,535	44,458	45,563
Excluding federal	Dol.	35,077	37,401	38,955	40,270	42,124	44,038	45,129
Private	Dol.	35,337	37,508	39,134	40,505	42,414	44,362	45,371
State government	Dol.	36,296	40,057	41,118	42,249	43,875	45,903	47,980
Local governments	Dol.	32,387	35,669	36,805	37,718	39,179	40,790	42,274
Federal government	Dol.	46,228	54,239	57,782	59,864	62,274	64,871	66,293
Average weekly wage per employee:								
Total	Dol.	679	726	757	782	818	855	876
Excluding federal	Dol.	675	719	749	774	810	847	868
Private	Dol.	680	721	753	779	816	853	873
State government	Dol.	698	770	791	812	844	883	923
Local governments	Dol.	623	686	708	725	753	784	813
Federal government	Dol.	889	1,043	1,111	1,151	1,198	1,248	1,275

Source: U.S. Bureau of Labor Statistics, *Employment and Wages Annual Averages 2008*, Bulletin 2718, January 2010. See also <http://www.bls.gov/cew/cewbultn08.htm>.

Table 646. Average Annual Wage, by State: 2007 and 2008

[In dollars, except percent change. Based on federal-state cooperative program, The Quarterly Census of Employment and Wages (QCEW), also referenced as ES-202. Includes workers covered by state unemployment insurance laws and for federal civilian workers covered by unemployment compensation for federal employees, approximately 97 percent of employees on non-farm payrolls in 2007. Excludes most agricultural workers on small farms, all Armed Forces, elected officials in most states, railroad employees, most domestic workers, most student workers at school, value of meals and lodging, and tips and other gratuities]

State	Average wage per employee 2007	Average wage per employee 2008	Percent change, 2007–2008	State	Average wage per employee 2007	Average wage per employee 2008	Percent change, 2007–2008
United States	**44,458**	**45,563**	**2.5**	Missouri	38,603	40,361	4.6
Alabama	37,492	38,734	3.3	Montana	32,224	33,305	3.4
Alaska	43,972	45,805	4.2	Nebraska	35,238	36,243	2.9
Arizona	41,551	42,518	2.3	Nevada	42,149	42,984	2.0
Arkansas	34,118	34,919	2.3	New Hampshire	43,863	44,912	2.4
California	50,538	51,487	1.9	New Jersey	53,853	55,280	2.7
Colorado	45,396	46,614	2.7	New Mexico	36,379	37,910	4.2
Connecticut	58,029	58,395	0.6	New York	59,439	60,288	1.4
Delaware	47,308	47,569	0.6	North Carolina	38,909	39,740	2.1
District of Columbia	73,450	76,518	4.2	North Dakota	33,086	35,075	6.0
Florida	39,746	40,568	2.1	Ohio	39,917	40,784	2.2
Georgia	42,178	42,585	1.0	Oklahoma	35,491	37,284	5.1
Hawaii	39,466	40,675	3.1	Oregon	39,565	40,500	2.4
Idaho	33,544	33,897	1.1	Pennsylvania	43,239	44,381	2.6
Illinois	47,685	48,719	2.2	Rhode Island	41,646	43,029	3.3
Indiana	37,528	38,403	2.3	South Carolina	35,393	36,252	2.4
Iowa	35,738	36,964	3.4	South Dakota	31,655	32,822	3.7
Kansas	37,044	38,178	3.1	Tennessee	39,082	39,996	2.3
Kentucky	36,480	37,434	2.6	Texas	44,695	45,939	2.8
Louisiana	38,229	40,381	5.6	Utah	37,054	37,980	2.5
Maine	35,129	36,317	3.4	Vermont	36,956	38,328	3.7
Maryland	48,241	49,535	2.7	Virginia	45,995	47,241	2.7
Massachusetts	55,244	56,746	2.7	Washington	45,021	46,569	3.4
Michigan	43,357	44,245	2.0	West Virginia	34,106	35,987	5.5
Minnesota	44,375	45,826	3.3	Wisconsin	38,050	39,119	2.8
Mississippi	32,291	33,508	3.8	Wyoming	39,254	41,487	5.7

Source: U.S. Bureau of Labor Statistics, *Employment and Wages Annual Averages 2008*, Bulletin 2718, January 2010, and computed by U.S. Census Bureau. See also <http://www.bls.gov/cew/cewbultn08.htm>.

Table 647. Full-Time Wage and Salary Workers—Number and Earnings by Sex, Race, Ethnicity, and Occupation: 2000 to 2009

[In current dollars of usual weekly earnings. Data represent annual averages (101,210 represents 101,210,000). Full time workers are those who usually worked 35 hours or more at all jobs combined. Based on the Current Population Survey; see text, Section 1 and Appendix III. For definition of median, see Guide to Tabular Presentation]

Characteristic	Number of workers (1,000)			Median weekly earnings (dollars)		
	2000	2005 [1]	2009 [1]	2000	2005 [1]	2009 [1]
All workers [2]	**101,210**	**103,560**	**99,820**	**576**	**651**	**739**
Male	57,107	58,406	55,108	641	722	819
Female	44,103	45,154	44,712	493	585	657
White [3]	83,228	84,110	80,873	590	672	757
Black [3]	12,410	12,388	11,713	474	520	601
Asian [3,4]	4,598	4,651	4,923	615	753	880
Hispanic [5]	12,761	14,673	14,624	399	471	541
OCCUPATION						
Management, professional and related occupations	34,831	36,908	39,080	810	937	1,044
Management, business, and financial operations	14,240	14,977	15,879	877	997	1,138
Professional and related occupations	20,590	21,931	23,201	770	902	994
Computer and mathematical occupations	3,051	2,924	3,151	938	1,132	1,253
Architecture and engineering occupations	2,781	2,509	2,397	949	1,105	1,266
Life, physical, and social science occupations	989	1,164	1,106	811	965	1,059
Community and social services occupations	1,641	1,797	1,913	629	725	783
Legal occupations	1,039	1,162	1,217	919	1,052	1,200
Education, training, and library occupations	5,467	6,066	6,426	704	798	887
Arts, design, entertainment, sports, and media	1,488	1,488	1,416	724	819	888
Healthcare practitioner and technical occupations	4,134	4,821	5,575	727	878	970
Service occupations	12,595	14,123	14,299	365	413	470
Healthcare support occupations	1,731	2,085	2,293	358	410	472
Protective service occupations	2,281	2,549	2,705	591	678	747
Food preparation and serving-related occupations	3,483	4,007	3,809	317	356	398
Building and grounds cleaning and maintenance	3,354	3,425	3,298	351	394	444
Personal care and service occupations	1,746	2,057	2,193	351	409	440
Sales and office occupations	25,606	25,193	23,503	492	575	624
Sales and related occupations	9,650	10,031	9,489	525	622	665
Office and administrative support occupations	15,956	15,161	14,014	480	550	612
Natural resources, construction, and maintenance occupations	10,958	12,086	10,216	582	623	719
Farming, fishing, and forestry occupations	842	755	707	310	372	416
Construction and extraction occupations	5,852	6,826	5,267	580	604	718
Installation, maintenance, and repair occupations	4,263	4,504	4,242	628	705	781
Production, transportation, and material-moving occupations	17,221	15,251	12,722	475	540	605
Production occupations	10,378	8,403	6,576	471	538	610
Transportation and material-moving occupations	6,843	6,848	6,145	481	543	599

[1] See footnote 2, Table 584. [2] Includes other races, not shown separately. [3] Beginning 2005, for persons in this race group only. See footnote 4, table 585. [4] 2000, includes Pacific Islanders. [5] Persons of Hispanic or Latino ethnicity may be any race.

Source: U.S. Bureau of Labor Statistics, "Employment and Earnings Online," January 2010, <http://www.bls.gov/opub/ee /home.htm> and <http://www.bls.gov/cps/home.htm>.

Table 648. Median Usual Weekly Earnings of Full-Time Wage and Salary Workers by Sex: 1980 to 2009

[In current dollars, except as indicated. For wage and salary workers 25 years and over. Based on Current Population Survey; see text, Section 1 and Appendix III. Wages and salaries are collected before taxes and other deductions and include overtime pay, commissions, or tips usually received at principal job. Earnings reported on basis other than weekly are converted to a weekly equivalent. Excludes all incorporated and unincorporated self employed]

Year and sex	Total	Less than a high school diploma	High school, no college [1]	Some college or associate's degree	Bachelor's degree and higher [2]
CURRENT DOLLARS					
Male					
1980	339	267	327	358	427
1990 [3]	512	349	459	542	741
2000 [3]	693	406	591	691	1,020
2009 [3]	873	500	716	835	1,327
Female					
1980	213	164	201	231	290
1990 [3]	369	240	315	395	535
2000 [3]	516	304	420	505	756
2009 [3]	687	382	542	630	970
WOMEN'S EARNINGS AS PERCENT OF MEN'S					
1980	62.8	61.4	61.5	64.5	67.9
1990 [3]	72.1	68.8	68.6	72.9	72.2
2000 [3]	74.5	74.9	71.1	73.1	74.1
2009 [3]	78.7	76.4	75.7	75.4	73.1

[1] Includes persons with a high school diploma or equivalent. [2] Includes persons with a bachelor's, master's, professional, or doctoral degree. [3] Data not strictly comparable to data for earlier years. See text this section and <http://www.bls.gov/cps /eetech_methods.pdf>.

Source: U.S. Bureau of Labor Statistics, "Highlights of Women's Earnings in 2009," Report 1025, July 2010, <http://www.bls.gov /cps/cpswom2009.pdf>.

Table. 649. Workers With Earnings by Occupation of Longest Held Job and Sex: 2008

[As of March. (60,714 represents 60,714,000). For definition of median, see Guide to Tabular Presentation. Annual Social and Economic Supplement (ASEC) includes Civilian noninstitutional population, 15 years old and over, and military personnel who live in households with at least one other civilian adult. Based on Current Population Survey; see text, Section 1, and Appendix III]

Major occupation group of longest job held in 2008	All workers				Full-time, year-round			
	Female		Male		Female		Male	
	Number (1,000)	Median earnings (dol.)	Number (1,000)	Median earnings (dol.)	Number (1,000)	Median earnings (dol.)	Number (1,000)	Median earnings (dol.)
Total	**60,714**	**25,616**	**84,039**	**36,568**	**44,156**	**35,745**	**59,861**	**46,367**
Management, business, and financial occupations	8,339	46,039	12,953	65,278	7,787	51,073	11,097	70,924
Professional and related occupations	15,504	38,649	13,651	60,123	11,944	46,761	10,609	67,105
Service occupations	12,577	13,229	11,753	20,344	7,247	22,945	6,740	30,660
Sales and office occupations	20,313	23,161	14,014	32,039	14,258	30,950	9,735	41,826
Natural resources, construction, and maintenance	605	17,688	15,633	31,687	389	31,408	10,417	40,045
Production, transportation, and material-moving occupations	3,317	19,703	15,283	30,525	2,482	25,549	10,567	36,391
Armed Forces	59	(B)	752	45,385	49	(B)	696	46,569

B Data not shown where base is less than 75,000.

Source: U.S. Census Bureau, *Income, Poverty, and Health Insurance in the United States: 2008*, Current Population Reports, P60-236, and "Detailed Tables—Table PINC-06," September 2009. See also <http://www.census.gov/hhes/www/income/data/incpovhlth/2008/index.html>.

Table. 650. Employment Cost Index (ECI) by Total Compensation and Occupation and Industry: 2006 to 2009

[As of December. (2005 = 100). The ECI is a measure of the rate of change in compensation (wages, salaries, and employer costs for employee benefits). Data are not seasonally adjusted. Based on North American Industry Classification System (NAICS) for classifying by industry. Based on the 2000 Standard Occupational Classification (SOC) for classifying by occupation]

Occupational group and industry	Indexes (December 2005 = 100)				Percent change for 12 months ending December			
	2006	2007	2008	2009	2006	2007	2008	2009
Civilian workers [1]	**103.3**	**106.7**	**109.5**	**111.1**	**3.3**	**3.3**	**2.6**	**1.5**
State and local government	**104.1**	**108.4**	**111.6**	**114.3**	**4.1**	**4.1**	**3.0**	**2.4**
Workers, by occupational group:								
Management, professional and related occupations	104.0	108.3	111.6	113.9	4.0	4.1	3.0	2.1
Sales and office occupations	104.1	108.6	111.3	114.7	4.1	4.3	2.5	3.1
Service occupations	104.5	109.1	112.4	115.6	4.5	4.4	3.0	2.8
Workers, by industry division:								
Service-providing industries								
Education and health services	104.3	108.2	111.5	114.0	4.3	3.7	3.0	2.2
Schools	104.1	108.0	111.2	113.7	4.1	3.7	3.0	2.2
Health care and social assistance	105.7	109.3	113.2	115.8	5.7	3.4	3.6	2.3
Hospitals	104.3	108.2	111.3	114.5	4.3	3.7	2.9	2.9
Public administration [2]	103.8	109.1	112.0	115.1	3.8	5.1	2.7	2.8
Private industry workers [3]	**103.2**	**106.3**	**108.9**	**110.2**	**3.2**	**3.0**	**2.4**	**1.2**
Workers, by occupational group:								
Management, professional, and related occupations	103.5	106.8	109.9	110.7	3.5	3.2	2.9	0.7
Sales and office occupations	102.9	106.1	107.9	109.2	2.9	3.1	1.7	1.2
Natural resources, construction, and maintenance occupations	103.6	106.7	109.6	111.2	3.6	3.0	2.7	1.5
Production, transportation, and material moving occupations	102.3	104.5	106.9	108.9	2.3	2.2	2.3	1.9
Service occupations	103.1	107.0	109.8	111.8	3.1	3.8	2.6	1.8
Workers, by industry division:								
Goods-producing industries [4]	102.5	105.0	107.5	108.6	2.5	2.4	2.4	1.0
Construction	103.6	107.6	110.9	111.7	3.6	3.9	3.1	0.7
Manufacturing	101.8	103.8	105.9	107.0	1.8	2.0	2.0	1.0
Service-providing industries [5]	103.4	106.7	109.4	110.8	3.4	3.2	2.5	1.3
Trade, transportation, and utilities	103.0	105.5	107.5	108.8	3.0	2.4	1.9	1.2
Information	103.2	106.1	107.4	108.3	3.2	2.8	1.2	0.8
Financial activities	102.5	105.6	107.1	108.6	2.5	3.0	1.4	1.4
Professional and business services	103.5	107.5	111.6	112.4	3.5	3.9	3.8	0.7
Education and health services	104.1	107.7	110.6	112.8	4.1	3.5	2.7	2.0
Leisure and hospitality	103.7	108.1	111.4	112.7	3.7	4.2	3.1	1.2
Bargaining status								
Union	103.0	105.1	108.0	111.1	3.0	2.0	2.8	2.9
Nonunion	103.2	106.5	109.1	110.1	3.2	3.2	2.4	0.9

[1] Includes private industry and state and local government workers and excludes farm, household, and federal government workers. [2] Consists of executive, legislative, judicial, administrative, and regulatory activities. [3] Excludes farm and household workers. [4] Includes the following NAICS industries: construction and manufacturing. [5] Includes all other service industries, not shown separately. For a description of NAICS industries, see text, Section 15.

Source: U.S. Bureau of Labor Statistics, "Employment Cost Index Historical Listing Current-dollar," <http://www.bls.gov/ncs/ect/home.htm>.

Table 651. Federal and State Minimum Wage Rates: 1950 to 2010

[In current dollars. Where an employee is subject to both the state and federal minimum wage laws, the employee is entitled to the higher minimum wage rate]

Year	Federal minimum wage rates per hour	State	2010 minimum wage rates per hour	State	2010 minimum wage rates per hour	State	2010 minimum wage rates per hour
1950........	0.75	AL	(¹)	KY	7.25	ND	7.25
1955........	0.75	AK	7.75	LA	(¹)	OH	⁸7.30
1960........	1.00	AZ	7.25	ME	7.50	OK	⁹7.25/2.00
1965........	1.25	AR	²6.25	MD	7.25	OR	8.40
1970........	1.60	CA	8.00	MA	8.00	PA	7.25
1975........	2.10	CO	7.24	MI..........	⁴7.4	RI..........	7.40
1980........	3.10	CT	8.25	MN.........	⁵6.15/5.25	SC	(¹)
1985........	3.35	DE	7.25	MS.........	(¹)	SD	7.25
1990........	3.80	DC	8.25	MO	7.25	TN	(¹)
1995........	4.25	FL	7.25	MT	⁶7.25	TX	7.25
2000........	5.15	GA	³5.15	NE	²7.25	UT	7.25
2005........	5.15	HI	7.25	NV	⁷7.55/6.55	VT	⁴8.06
2006........	5.15	ID	7.25	NH	7.25	VA	²7.25
2007........	5.85	IL	²8.25	NJ	7.25	WA	8.55
2008........	6.55	IN	⁴7.25	NM.........	7.50	WV	³7.25
2009........	7.25	IA	7.25	NY	7.25	WI..........	7.25
2010........	7.25	KS	7.25	NC	7.25	WY	5.15

¹ No state minimum wage law. ² Employers of 4 or more, Illinois excluding family members. ³ Employers of 6 or more. ⁴ Employers of 2 or more. ⁵ Large employer (receipts of $625.000 or more) and small employer (with annual receipts of less than $625,000). ⁶ Except businesses with gross annual sales of $110,000 or less. ⁷ $7.55 with no health insurance benefits provided by employer. $6.55 with health insurance provided by employer and received by employee. ⁸ $7.25 for those employers grossing $276,000 or less. ⁹ Employees of 10 or more full time employees at any one location and employers with gross sales over $100,000 regardless of number of full-time employees. All other employers $2.00.

Source: U.S. Department of Labor, Wage and Hour Division, "Minimum Wage Laws in the States—January 1, 2010," <http://www.dol.gov/esa/minwage/america.htm> and <http://www.dol.gov/whd/minimumwage.htm>.

Table 652. Workers Paid Hourly Rates by Selected Characteristics: 2009

[Data are annual averages (72,611 represents 72,611,000). For employed wage and salary workers, excluding the incorporated self-employed. Based on the Current Population Survey; see text, Section 1 and Appendix III]

Characteristic	Number of workers paid hourly rates (1,000)				Percent of workers paid hourly rates			
		At or below federal minimum wage				At or below federal minimum wage		
	Total	Total	Below prevailing federal minimum wage	At prevailing federal minimum wage	Total	Total	Below prevailing federal minimum wage	At prevailing federal minimum wage
Total, 16 years and over ¹	72,611	3,572	2,592	980	4.9	1.3	3.6	
16 to 24 years	14,389	1,737	1,229	500	12.1	3.5	8.5	
25 years and over	58,222	1,835	1363	472	3.2	0.8	2.3	
Male, 16 years old and over	35,185	1,358	990	368	3.9	1.0	2.8	
16 to 24 years	7,045	674	460	214	9.6	3.0	6.5	
25 years and over	28,140	684	530	154	2.4	0.5	1.9	
Female, 16 years old and over ...	37,426	2,215	1,603	612	5.9	1.6	4.3	
16 to 24 years	7,344	1,064	769	295	14.5	4.0	10.5	
25 years and over	30,082	1,151	833	318	3.8	1.1	2.8	
White ²	58,633	2,857	2,094	763	4.9	1.3	3.6	
Men	28,873	1,074	774	300	3.7	1.0	2.7	
Women	29,760	1,783	1,320	463	6.0	1.6	4.4	
Black ²	9,269	495	327	168	5.3	1.8	3.5	
Men	4,038	192	142	50	4.8	1.2	3.5	
Women	5,231	302	185	117	5.8	2.2	3.5	
Asian ²	2,718	117	96	21	4.3	0.8	3.5	
Men	1,258	47	41	6	3.7	0.5	3.3	
Women	1,460	70	55	15	4.8	1.0	3.8	
Hispanic ³	12,740	622	439	183	4.9	1.4	3.4	
Men	7,291	290	210	80	4.0	1.1	2.9	
Women	5,449	331	229	102	6.1	1.9	4.2	
Full-time workers	52,454	1,272	952	320	2.4	0.6	1.8	
Men	28,388	579	442	137	2.0	0.5	1.6	
Women	24,066	694	511	183	2.9	0.8	2.1	
Part-time workers ⁴	20,027	2,281	1,625	656	11.4	3.3	8.1	
Men	6,721	769	540	229	11.4	3.4	8.0	
Women	13,307	1,513	1,085	428	11.4	3.2	8.2	
Private sector industries	62,885	3,349	2,430	919	5.3	1.5	3.9	
Public sector industries	9,725	223	162	61	2.3	0.6	1.7	

¹ Includes races not shown separately. Also includes a small number of multiple jobholders whose full- or part-time status cannot be determined for their principal job. ² For persons in this race group only. See footnote 4, Table 585. ³ Persons of Hispanic or Latino origin may be any race. ⁴ Working fewer than 35 hours per week.

Source: U.S. Bureau of Labor Statistics, CPS Reports and Summaries, "Characteristics of Minimum Wage Workers: 2009," March 2010, <http://www.bls.gov/cps/minwage2009.htm>.

Labor Force, Employment, and Earnings 423

Table 653. Employer Costs for Employee Compensation Per Hour Worked: 2009

[In dollars. As of December. Based on a sample of establishments from the National Compensation Survey; see source for details. Compensation levels in state and local government should not be directly compared with levels in private industry, Differences between these sectors stem from factors such as variation in work activities and occupational structures. See source for details. See also Appendix III]

Compensation component	Total civilian workers	State and local government workers	Private Industry workers						
			Total	Goods producing [1]	Service providing [2]	Union workers	Non-union workers	1–99 workers	100 workers or more
Total compensation	**29.37**	**39.60**	**27.42**	**32.14**	**26.43**	**36.32**	**26.37**	**22.82**	**32.70**
Wages and salaries	20.49	26.11	19.41	21.60	18.96	22.75	19.04	16.81	22.41
Total benefits	8.88	13.49	8.00	10.54	7.47	13.88	7.33	6.01	10.29
Paid leave	2.04	2.99	1.86	2.08	1.81	2.71	1.76	1.26	2.54
Vacation	0.98	1.13	0.95	1.11	0.92	1.41	0.90	0.63	1.32
Holiday	0.64	0.90	0.60	0.74	0.57	0.80	0.57	0.43	0.78
Sick	0.32	0.76	0.23	0.17	0.24	0.37	0.21	0.15	0.33
Supplemental pay	0.74	0.33	0.82	1.21	0.74	1.13	0.78	0.63	1.03
Overtime [3]	0.25	0.17	0.26	0.57	0.20	0.73	0.21	0.19	0.34
Insurance	2.54	4.61	2.15	3.00	1.97	4.50	1.88	1.52	2.87
Health insurance	2.40	4.45	2.01	2.80	1.85	4.21	1.76	1.43	2.67
Retirement and savings	1.29	3.19	0.92	1.36	0.83	2.42	0.75	0.56	1.33
Defined benefit	0.78	2.86	0.38	0.74	0.30	1.70	0.23	0.20	0.58
Defined contributions	0.51	0.33	0.55	0.62	0.53	0.71	0.53	0.36	0.76
Legally required	2.27	2.36	2.25	2.89	2.12	3.11	2.16	2.03	2.52
Social security and Medicare	1.67	1.84	1.63	1.85	1.59	1.99	1.59	1.40	1.90
Social security [4]	1.33	1.43	1.31	1.49	1.28	1.61	1.28	1.13	1.53
Medicare	0.34	0.42	0.32	0.36	0.31	0.39	0.31	0.27	0.38
Federal unemployment	0.03	–	0.03	0.03	0.03	0.03	0.03	0.04	0.03
State unemployment	0.13	0.07	0.15	0.20	0.14	0.21	0.14	0.15	0.15
Workers' compensation	0.44	0.45	0.44	0.81	0.36	0.88	0.39	0.44	0.44

– Represents or rounds to zero. [1] Based on the North American Industry Classification System, 2002 (NAICS). See text, this section. Includes mining, construction, and manufacturing. The agriculture, forestry, farming, and hunting sector is excluded. [2] Based on the 2002 NAICS. Includes utilities; wholesale and retail trade; transportation and warehousing; information; finance and insurance; real estate and rental and leasing; professional and technical services; management of companies and enterprises, administrative and waste services; education services; health care and social assistance; arts, entertainment, and recreation; accommodations and food services; and other services, except public administration. [3] Includes premium pay for work in addition to regular work schedule, such as, overtime, weekends, and holidays. [4] Comprises the Old-Age, Survivors, and Disability Insurance Program (OASDI).

Source: U.S. Bureau of Labor Statistics, *Employer Costs for Employee Compensation—December 2009*, News Release, USDL 10-0283, March 2010. See also <http://www.bls.gov/ncs/ect/home.htm>.

Table 654. Percent of Workers in Private Industry With Access to Retirement and Health Care Benefits by Selected Characteristics: 2009

[In percent (All workers = 100 percent) As of March. Based on National Compensation Survey (NCS). See headnote, Table 655]

Characteristic	Retirement benefits			Healthcare benefits			
	All plans [1]	Defined benefit [2]	Defined contribution [2]	Medical care	Dental care	Vision care	Outpatient prescription drug coverage
Total	**67**	**21**	**61**	**71**	**46**	**27**	**69**
WORKER CHARACTERISTICS							
Management, professional, and related occupations	80	30	75	86	61	36	84
Service occupations	45	8	41	46	28	18	44
Sales and office occupations	71	20	67	72	47	24	70
Natural resources, construction, and maintenance occupations	68	26	58	77	44	31	73
Production, transportation, and material moving occupations	69	26	60	77	49	30	74
Full-time [3]	76	25	70	86	56	33	83
Part-time [3]	39	11	34	24	16	10	23
Union [4]	87	68	54	90	69	54	88
Nonunion [4]	65	16	62	69	44	24	67
AVERAGE HOURLY WAGE [5]							
Less than $7.85	35	5	33	25	13	(S)	24
$7.85 to under $10.13	43	8	39	38	22	12	37
$10.13 to under $15.00	69	16	64	77	49	26	75
$15.00 to under $23.25	76	25	69	86	54	32	83
$23.25 to under $34.79	84	39	77	89	66	41	87
$34.79 or greater	86	39	81	90	69	41	89
ESTABLISHMENT CHARACTERISTIC							
Goods producing [6]	75	31	67	85	55	33	82
Service producing [6]	65	19	60	68	44	26	66

S Figure does not meet publication standards. [1] Employees may have access to both defined benefit and defined contribution plans. Total excludes duplication. [2] A defined benefit plan is a retirement plan that uses a specific, predetermined formula to calculate the amount of an employee's guaranteed future benefit. A defined contribution plan is a type of retirement plan in which the employer makes specified contributions to individual employee accounts, but the amount of the retirement benefit is not specified. [3] Employees are classified as working either a full-time or part-time schedule based on the definition used by each establishment. [4] See footnote 6, Table 655. [5] The National Compensation Survey—Benefits program presents wage data in percentiles rather than dollar amounts; for calculation detail, see "Technical Note" in source. [6] See Table 631 for composition of goods and service producing industries.

Source: U.S. Bureau of Labor Statistics, *Employee Benefits in the United States, March 2009*, News Release, USDL 09-0872, July 2009. See also <http://www.bls.gov/ncs/ebs/home.htm>.

Table 655. Percent of Workers in Private Industry With Access to Selected Employee Benefits: 2009

[As of March. Based on National Compensation Survey (NCS). Excludes agricultural establishments, private households, and the self-employed. The NCS benefits survey obtained data from 12,872 private industry establishments of all sizes, representing over 107 million workers. An employee has access to a benefit plan if the plan is made available by the employer, regardless of whether the employee actually participates in the plan. See Appendix III]

Characteristic	Paid holidays	Paid sick leave	Paid vacation	Paid jury duty leave	Paid military leave	Employer assistance for child care [1]	Flexible work-place [2]	Subsidized commuting [3]	All non-production bonuses [4]	Cash profit-sharing bonus [5]	Stock options [8]
Total	77	61	78	70	(NA)	9	5	6	46	5	8
WORKER CHARACTERISTIC											
Management, professional, and related occupations	89	84	87	86	(NA)	17	12	11	55	7	14
Service occupations	53	42	61	51	(NA)	8	1	2	33	1	2
Sales and office occupations	81	66	80	73	(NA)	7	5	6	49	5	10
Natural resources, construction, and maintenance occupations	77	49	76	56	(NA)	3	2	4	47	5	6
Production, transportation, and material moving occupations	84	52	83	70	(NA)	5	1	3	47	8	8
Full-time [5]	89	73	91	78	(NA)	10	6	7	52	6	9
Part-time [5]	39	26	38	44	(NA)	4	2	2	30	1	5
Union [6]	86	69	85	83	(NA)	15	2	7	38	8	9
Nonunion [6]	76	61	77	68	(NA)	8	5	6	47	5	8
AVERAGE HOURLY WAGE [7]											
Less than $7.85	36	21	42	37	(NA)	5	1	2	27	1	4
$7.85 to under $10.13	52	33	55	47	(NA)	5	1	2	33	2	4
$10.13 to under $15.00	84	64	85	73	(NA)	7	2	4	48	4	7
$15.00 to under $23.25	89	73	89	78	(NA)	9	5	7	51	6	9
$23.25 to under $34.79	88	81	88	85	(NA)	16	12	12	56	9	12
$34.79 or greater	88	84	88	88	(NA)	19	15	14	58	11	18
ESTABLISHMENT CHARACTERISTIC											
Goods producing [8]	87	52	86	70	(NA)	7	5	2	52	11	8
Service producing [8]	75	63	76	70	(NA)	9	5	7	45	4	8
GEOGRAPHIC AREA [9]											
New England	78	70	77	30	(NA)	9	5	8	52	5	8
Middle Atlantic	81	67	79	79	(NA)	7	6	7	45	3	6
East North Central	77	56	78	71	(NA)	10	5	4	47	8	9
West North Central	75	62	77	67	(NA)	9	4	6	47	6	7
South Atlantic	78	59	80	71	(NA)	8	4	4	50	6	9
East South Central	77	55	79	68	(NA)	(10)	3	2	50	(10)	5
West South Central	80	61	79	67	(NA)	8	4	4	46	5	9
Mountain	74	59	75	63	(NA)	7	4	7	43	4	7
Pacific	74	65	77	61	(NA)	10	5	10	42	7	11

NA No: available. [1] Employer assistance of child care includes employer provided funds, on-site and off-site child care, and child care resource and referral services. [2] Arrangements permitting employees to work at home several days of the workweek. [3] Employers subsidize employees' cost of commuting to and from work via public transportation, company-sponsored van pool, discounted subway fares, for example. [4] All nonproduction bonuses include cash profit sharing bonuses, holiday bonuses, referral bonuses, and stock options. [5] Employees are classified as working either a full-time or part-time schedule based on the definition used by each establishment. [6] Union workers are those workers whose wages are determined through collective bargaining. [7] The National Compensation Survey-Benefits program presents wage data in percentiles rather than dollar amounts; see "Technical Note" in source. [8] See Table 631 for composition of goods and service producing industries. [9] Composition of divisions: New England = Connecticut, Maine, Massachusetts, New Hampshire, Rhode Island, and Vermont; Middle Atlantic = New Jersey, New York, and Pennsylvania; East North Central = Illinois, Indiana, Michigan, Ohio, and Wisconsin; West North Central = Iowa, Kansas, Minnesota, Nebraska, North Dakota, and Missouri; South Atlantic = Delaware, District of Columbia, Florida, Georgia, Maryland, North Carolina, South Carolina, Virginia, and West Virginia; East South Central = Alabama, Kentucky, Mississippi, and Tennessee; West South Central = Arkansas, Louisiana, Oklahoma, and Texas; Mountain = Arizona, Colorado, Idaho, Montana, Nevada, New Mexico, Utah, and Wyoming; and Pacific = Alaska, California, Hawaii, Oregon, and Washington. [10] No workers in category or data did not meet publication criteria.

Source: U.S. Bureau of Labor Statistics, Employee Benefits in the United States, March 2009, Bulletin 2731, September 2009. See also <http://www.bls.gov/ncs/ebs/benefits/2009/benefits.htm>.

Table 656. Workers Killed or Disabled on the Job: 1970 to 2008

[Data for 2008 are preliminary estimates (1.7 represents 1,700). Excludes homicides and suicides. Estimates based on data from the U.S. National Center for Health Statistics, state vital statistics departments, state industrial commissions and beginning 1995, Bureau of Labor Statistics, Census of Fatal Occupational Injuries. Numbers of workers based on data from the U.S. Bureau of Labor Statistics]

Year	Deaths				Disabling injuries [2] (mil.)	Year and industry group	Deaths, 2008		Disabling injuries 2008 [2] (1,000)
	Manufacturing		Nonmanufacturing						
	Number (1,000)	Rate [1]	Number (1,000)	Rate [1]			Number (1,000)	Rate [1]	
1970....	1.7	9	12.1	21	2.2	Total, 2008 [3]...................	4,303	2.9	3,200
1980....	1.7	8	11.5	15	2.2	Agriculture [4]......................	623	29.0	60
1990....	1.0	5	9.1	9	3.9	Mining [5].........................	172	21.1	10
1995....	0.6	3	4.4	4	3.6	Construction.....................	932	8.9	260
1997....	0.7	3	4.5	4	3.8	Manufacturing....................	358	2.3	390
1998....	0.6	3	4.5	4	3.8	Wholesale trade..................	152	3.8	80
1999....	0.6	3	4.6	4	3.8	Retail trade......................	149	0.9	380
2000....	0.6	3	4.4	4	3.9	Transportation & warehousing.......	691	13.0	160
2001....	0.5	3	4.5	4	3.9	Utilities.........................	36	4.0	20
2002....	0.5	3	4.2	3	3.7	Information.......................	34	1.0	30
2003....	0.4	2	4.3	4	3.4	Financial activities [6].............	65	0.6	70
2004 ...	0.4	3	4.6	4	3.7	Professional & business services [6]...	339	2.2	150
2005....	0.4	2	4.6	4	3.7	Educational & health services.......	107	0.5	510
2006....	0.4	3	4.7	4	3.7	Leisure & hospitality [6]..............	114	0.9	270
2007....	0.4	2	4.4	3	3.5	Other services [7]....................	127	1.8	110
2008....	0.4	2	3.9	3	3.2	Government.......................	397	1.8	700

[1] Per 100,000 workers. [2] Disabling injury defined as one which results in death, some degree of physical impairment, or renders the person unable to perform regular activities for a full day beyond the day of the injury. Due to change in methodology, data beginning 1992 not comparable with prior years. [3] Includes deaths where industry is not known. [4] Includes forestry, fishing, and hunting. [5] Includes oil and gas extraction. [6] For composition of industry, see Table 631. [7] Excludes public service administration.

Source: National Safety Council, Itasca, IL, *Accident Facts*, annual through 1998 edition; thereafter, *Injury Facts*, annual (copyright).

Table 657. Worker Deaths, Injuries, and Production Time Lost: 2000 to 2008

[47.0 represents 47,000. Data may not agree with Table 659 because data here are not revised]

Item	Deaths (1,000)			Disabling injuries [1] (mil.)			Production time lost (mil. days)					
							In current year			In future years [2]		
	2000	2005	2008	2000	2005	2008	2000	2005	2008	2000	2005	2008
All accidents	**47.0**	**54.3**	**56.6**	**10.5**	**11.9**	**12.6**	**240**	**275**	**295**	**460**	**535**	**565**
On the job...............	5.2	5.0	4.3	3.9	3.7	3.2	80	80	70	60	65	55
Off the job...............	41.8	49.3	52.3	6.6	8.2	9.4	160	195	225	400	470	510
Motor vehicle............	22.8	24.1	20.9	1.2	1.3	1.1	(NA)	(NA)	(NA)	(NA)	(NA)	(NA)
Public nonmotor vehicle....	8.3	10.0	8.7	2.8	3.3	2.9	(NA)	(NA)	(NA)	(NA)	(NA)	(NA)
Home..................	10.7	15.2	22.7	2.6	3.6	5.4	(NA)	(NA)	(NA)	(NA)	(NA)	(NA)

NA Not available. [1] Disabling injury defined as one which results in death, some degree of physical impairment, or renders the person unable to perform regular activities for a full day beyond the day of the injury. [2] Based on an average of 5,850 days lost in future years per fatality and 565 days lost in future years per permanent injury.

Source: National Safety Council, Itasca, IL, *Injury Facts*, annual (copyright).

Table 658. Industries With the Highest Total Case Incidence Rates for Nonfatal Injuries and Illnesses: 2008

[Private industry unless otherwise noted. Incidence rates refer to any Occupational Safety & Health Administration (OSHA) recordable occupational injury or illness, whether or not it resulted in days away from work, job transfer, or restriction. Incidence rates were calculated as: Number of injuries and illnesses divided by total hours worked by all employees during the year multiplied by 200,000 as base for 100 full-time equivalent workers (working 40 hours per week, 50 weeks per year)]

Industry	2002 NAICS code [1]	Incidence rate	Industry	2002 NAICS code [1]	Incidence rate
All Industries [2]......................	**(X)**	**4.2**	Hospitals [4]..............................	622	11.9
			Ambulance services	62191	11.4
Fire protection [3].........................	92216	14.8	Iron and steel forging	332111	10.9
Police protection [3].......................	92212	14.5	Leather and hide tanning and finishing.......	3161	10.8
Skiing facilities	71392	14.2	Motor home manufacturing	336213	10.7
Secondary smelting and alloying of			Travel trailer and camper manufacturing......	336214	10.6
aluminum	331314	13.7	Animal (except poultry) slaughtering	311611	10.3
Steel foundries (except investment)	331513	13.7	Prefabricated wood building manufacturing ...	321992	10.3
Sports teams and clubs	711211	13.4	Aluminum foundries (except die-casting)	331524	10.2
Heavy and civil engineering construction [3] ...	237	12.9	Manufactured home (mobile home)		
Sawmill and woodworking machinery			manufacturing..........................	321991	10.0
manufacturing	33321	12.8	Fabricated structural metal manufacturing	332312	9.9
Nursing and residential care facilities [4]......	623	12.5	Truck trailer manufacturing	336212	9.8
Iron foundries	331511	12.0	Special food services	7223	9.7

X Not applicable [1] Based on the North American Industry Classification System (NAICS), 2002. See text, Section 15.
[2] Includes state and local government and excludes farms with fewer than 11 employees. [3] Local government. [4] State government.

Source: U.S. Bureau of Labor Statistics, *Workplace Injuries and Illnesses—2008*, News Release, USDL 09-1302, October 2009. See also <http://www.bls.gov/iif/oshsum.htm#08Summary%20News%20Release>.

Table 659. Nonfatal Occupational Injuries and Illnesses: 2008

[Rates per 100 full-time employees. Except as noted, data refer to any Occupational Safety and Health Administration (OSHA) recordable occupational injury or illness, whether or not it resulted in days away from work, job transfer, or restriction. Incidence rates were calculated as: Number of injuries and illnesses divided by total hours worked by all employees during the year multiplied by 200,000 as base for 100 full-time equivalent workers (working 40 hours, per week, 50 weeks per year)]

Industry	2002 NAICS code [1]	Incidence rate of cases	Industry	2002 NAICS code [1]	Incidence rate of cases
Total [2]	(X)	4.2	Transit and ground passenger transportation	485	5.2
Private industry [3]	(X)	3.9	Support activities for transportation	488	4.0
Agriculture, forestry, fishing hunting [2]	11	5.3	Couriers and messengers	492	8.7
Crop production [3]	111	5.3	Warehousing and storage	493	6.8
Animal production [3]	112	6.9	Utilities [2]	22	3.5
Mining [4]	21	2.9	Information [2]	51	2.0
Construction [2]	23	4.7	Telecommunications	517	2.6
Construction of buildings	236	4.0	Finance and insurance	52	0.9
Heavy and civil engineering construction	237	4.2	Real estate and rental and leasing [2]	53	3.1
Manufacturing [2]	31–33	5.0	Real estate	531	2.7
Food manufacturing	311	6.2	Rental and leasing services	532	4.1
Beverage and tobacco product manufacturing	312	6.8	Professional, scientific, and technical services	54	1.1
Wood product manufacturing	321	7.2	Management of companies and enterprises	55	1.6
Petroleum and coal products manufacturing	324	1.9	Administrative and support and waste management and remediation services [2]	56	3.1
Chemical manufacturing	325	2.7	Administrative and support services	561	2.9
Plastics and rubber products manufacturing	326	5.7	Waste management and remediation services	562	5.5
Nonmetallic mineral product manufacturing	327	5.9	Educational services	61	2.3
Primary metal manufacturing	331	7.2	Health care and social assistance [2]	62	5.4
Fabricated metal product manufacturing	332	6.8	Ambulatory health care services	621	2.7
Machinery manufacturing	333	5.6	Hospitals	622	7.6
Transportation equipment manufacturing	336	6.0	Nursing and residential care facilities	623	8.4
Furniture and related product manufacturing	337	5.8	Social assistance	624	3.5
Miscellaneous manufacturing	339	3.6	Arts, entertainment, and recreation [2]	71	5.1
Wholesale trade	42	3.7	Performing arts, spectator sports, and related industries	711	6.1
Retail trade [2]	44–45	4.4	Amusement, gambling, and recreation industries	713	4.9
Motor vehicle and parts dealers	441	4.2	Accommodation and food services	72	4.1
Furniture and home furnishings stores	442	4.1	Accommodation	721	5.6
Building material and garden equipment and supplies dealers	444	5.8	Food services and drinking places	722	3.7
Food and beverage stores	445	5.7	Other services, except public administration	81	3.1
Gasoline stations	447	3.4	State and local government [3]	(X)	6.3
Clothing and clothing accessories stores	448	2.4			
Sporting goods, hobby, book, and music stores	451	3.4			
General merchandise stores	452	5.7			
Transportation and warehousing [2,5]	48–49	5.7			
Air transportation	481	8.7			
Truck transportation	484	5.2			

X Not applicable. [1] North American Industry Classification System, 2002; see text, section 15. [2] Excludes farms with fewer than 11 employees. [3] Includes other industries, not shown separately. [4] Data for Mining (Sector 21 in the North American Industry Classification System—United States, 2002) include establishments not governed by the Mine Safety and Health Administration rules and reporting, such as those in Oil and Gas Extraction and related support activities. Data for mining operators in coal, metal, and nonmetal mining are provided to BLS by the Mine Safety and Health Administration, U.S. Department of Labor. Independent mining contractors are excluded from the coal, metal, and nonmetal mining industries. These data do not reflect the changes the Occupational Safety and Health Administration made to its recordkeeping requirements effective January 1, 2002; therefore, estimates for these industries are not comparable to estimates in other industries. [5] Data for employers in railroad transportation are provided to BLS by the Federal Railroad Administration, U.S. Department of Transportation.

Source: U.S. Bureau of Labor Statistics, *Workplace Injuries and Illnesses—2008*, News Release, USDL 09-1302, October 2009. See also <http://www.bls.gov/news.release/osh.nr0.htm>.

Table 660. Fatal Work Injuries by Event or Exposure: 2008

[For the 50 states and DC. Based on the Census of Fatal Occupational Injuries. For details, see source. Due to methodological differences, data differ from National Safety Council data]

Event or exposure	Number of fatalities	Percent distribution	Event or exposure	Number of fatalities	Percent distribution
Total	5,214	100	Contacts with objects and equipment [1]	937	18.0
			Struck by object or equipment [1]	520	10.0
Transportation incidents [1]	2,130	40.9	Struck by falling object or equipment	356	6.8
Highway incident [1]	1,215	23.3	Struck by flying object	51	1.0
Collision between vehicles, mobile equipment	597	11.4	Caught in or compressed by equipment or objects	302	5.8
Noncollision incidents	275	5.3	Caught in or crushed in collapsing materials	100	1.9
Nonhighway incident (farm, industrial premises)	284	5.4	Falls	700	13.4
Aircraft accidents	191	3.7	Exposure to harmful substances or environments [1]	439	8.4
Workers struck by a vehicle	329	6.3	Contact with electric current	192	3.7
Water vehicle accidents	76	1.5	Exposure to caustic, noxious or allergenic substances	130	2.5
Railway accidents	34	0.7	Oxygen deficiency	79	1.5
Assaults and violent acts [1]	816	15.7	Drowning, submersion	60	1.2
Homicides [1]	526	10.1	Fires and explosions	174	3.3
Shooting	421	8.1	Other events and exposures	18	(Z)
Stabbing	33	0.6			
Self-inflicted injury	263	5.0			

Z Less than 0.5 percent. [1] Includes other events or exposures, not shown separately.

Source: U.S. Bureau of Labor Statistics, "Census of Fatal Occupational Injuries (CFOI)—Current and Revised Data," <http://www.bls.gov/iif/oshcfoi1.htm>.

Table 661. Workplace Violence Incidents and Security Measures: 2005

[In percent. Covers period September 2004 to June 2006. Based on establishment survey; see source for details]

Incident or security measure	Total	Industry			Employment size				
		Private indus- try [1]	State govern- ment	Local govern- ment	1 to 10 employ- ees	11 to 49 employ- ees	50 to 249 employ- ees	250 to 999 employ- ees	1,000 or more employ- ees
Any workplace violence incidents	5.3	4.8	32.2	14.7	2.4	9.1	16.0	28.8	49.9
Criminal.........................	2.2	2.1	8.7	3.7	1.4	3.5	4.7	6.8	17.2
Customer or client................	2.2	1.9	15.4	10.3	1.0	3.9	6.4	12.2	28.3
Co-worker	2.3	2.1	17.7	4.3	0.6	4.6	8.1	16.8	34.1
Domestic violence	0.9	0.8	5.5	2.1	0.1	2.0	2.9	9.0	24.1
No incident......................	92.1	92.5	65.3	85.1	95.6	87.8	77.8	63.9	43.8
Selected types of security provided:									
Intruder/burglar systems	41.8	42.1	29.1	35.5	35.7	53.9	57.5	54.2	61.0
Surveillance cameras	22.6	22.2	45.2	32.7	17.0	29.2	47.9	69.1	77.9
Motion detectors	26.9	27.1	14.8	21.3	24.0	32.9	33.7	28.3	36.4
Metal detectors	0.9	0.7	16.0	4.3	0.5	1.1	2.5	7.2	15.7
Electronic badges [2]	6.3	6.0	35.6	9.0	3.9	7.2	20.8	45.1	60.1
Security guards	9.5	9.1	48.6	10.5	6.4	11.7	24.8	53.9	65.3
Limited access [3].................	30.7	30.0	50.0	50.7	26.0	35.9	52.5	68.3	83.2
Physical barriers [4]	13.4	13.1	27.2	23.6	10.2	18.2	24.5	33.5	46.5
Lighting of work areas.............	39.1	38.7	55.8	48.5	32.2	50.0	62.1	71.9	80.4
Workplace violence training provided:									
Any training.....................	20.8	20.2	58.0	32.3	14.6	29.1	45.7	64.2	67.8
No training......................	78.4	78.9	42.0	67.6	84.3	70.5	54.0	35.6	32.0

[1] Excludes farms with fewer than 11 employees. [2] Or ID scanner at entry or exit. [3] Secured entry/locked doors [4] Between work areas and the public.

Source: U.S. Bureau Labor Statistics, *Survey of Workplace Violence and Prevention—2005*, News Release, USDL 06-1860, October 2006. See also <http://www.bls.gov/iif/home.htm>.

Table 662. Work Stoppages: 1960 to 2009

[896 represents 896,000. Excludes work stoppages involving fewer than 1,000 workers and lasting less than 1 day. The term "major work stoppage" includes both worker-initiated strikes and employer-initiated lockouts that involve 1,000 workers or more. Information is based on reports of labor disputes appearing in daily newspapers, trade journals, and other public sources. The parties to the disputes are contacted by telephone, when necessary, to clarify details of the stoppages]

Year	Number of work stop- pages [1]	Workers involved [2] (1,000)	Days idle		Year	Number of work stop- pages [1]	Workers involved [2] (1,000)	Days idle	
			Number [3] (1,000)	Percent estimated working time [4]				Number [3] (1,000)	Percent estimated working time [4]
1960......	222	896	13,260	0.09	1991.....	40	392	4,584	0.02
1965......	268	999	15,140	0.10	1992.....	35	364	3,989	0.01
1970......	381	2,468	52,761	0.29	1993.....	35	182	3,981	0.01
1975......	235	965	17,563	0.09	1994.....	45	322	5,021	0.02
1976......	231	1,519	23,962	0.12	1995.....	31	192	5,771	0.02
1977......	298	1,212	21,258	0.10	1996.....	37	273	4,889	0.02
1978......	219	1,006	23,774	0.11	1997.....	29	339	4,497	0.01
1979......	235	1,021	20,409	0.09	1998.....	34	387	5,116	0.02
1980......	187	795	20,844	0.09	1999.....	17	73	1,996	0.01
1981......	145	729	16,908	0.07	2000.....	39	394	20,419	0.06
1982......	96	656	9,061	0.04	2001.....	29	99	1,151	(Z)
1983......	81	909	17,461	0.08	2002.....	19	46	660	(Z)
1984......	62	376	8,499	0.04	2003.....	14	129	4,091	0.01
1985......	54	324	7,079	0.03	2004.....	17	171	3,344	0.01
1986......	69	533	11,861	0.05	2005.....	22	100	1,736	0.01
1987......	46	174	4,481	0.02	2006.....	20	70	2,688	0.01
1988......	40	118	4,381	0.02	2007.....	21	189	1,265	(Z)
1989......	51	452	16,996	0.07	2008.....	15	72	1,954	0.01
1990......	44	185	5,926	0.02	2009.....	5	13	124	(Z)

Z Less than 0.005 percent. [1] Beginning in year indicated. [2] Workers counted more than once if involved in more than one stoppage during the year. [3] Resulting from all stoppages in effect in a year, including those that began in an earlier year. [4] Agricultural and government employees are included in the total working time; private household and forestry and fishery employees are excluded.

Source: U.S. Bureau of Labor Statistics, *Major Work Stoppages in 2009*, News Release, USDL 10-0170, February 2010. See also <http://www.bls.gov/wsp/>.

Table 663. Labor Union Membership by Sector: 1985 to 2009

[Annual averages of monthly figures (16,996 represents 16,996,000). For wage and salary workers in agriculture and non-agriculture. Data represent union members by place of residence. Based on the Current Population Survey and subject to sampling error. For methodological details, see source]

Sector	1985	1990	1995	2000	2005	2006	2007	2008	2009
TOTAL (1,000)									
Wage and salary workers:									
Union members..................	16,996	16,740	16,360	16,258	15,685	15,359	15,670	16,098	15,327
Covered by unions................	19,358	19,058	18,346	17,944	17,223	16,860	17,243	17,761	16,904
Public sector workers:									
Union members.................	5,743	6,485	6,927	7,111	7,430	7,378	7,557	7,832	7,897
Covered by unions...............	6,921	7,691	7,987	7,976	8,262	8,172	8,373	8,676	8,678
Private sector workers:									
Union members.................	11,253	10,255	9,432	9,148	8,255	7,981	8,114	8,265	7,431
Covered by unions...............	12,438	11,366	10,360	9,969	8,962	8,688	8,870	9,084	8,226
PERCENT									
Wage and salary workers:									
Union members..................	18.0	16.1	14.9	13.5	12.5	12.0	12.1	12.4	12.3
Covered by unions................	20.5	18.3	16.7	14.9	13.7	13.1	13.3	13.7	13.6
Public sector workers:									
Union members.................	35.7	36.5	37.7	37.5	36.5	36.2	35.9	36.8	37.4
Covered by unions...............	43.1	43.3	43.5	42.0	40.5	40.1	39.8	40.7	41.1
Private sector workers:									
Union members.................	14.3	11.9	10.3	9.0	7.8	7.4	7.5	7.6	7.2
Covered by unions...............	15.9	13.2	11.3	9.8	8.5	8.1	8.2	8.4	8.0

Source: The Bureau of National Affairs (BNA), Inc., Arlington, VA, *Union Membership and Earnings Data Book: Compilations from the Current Population Survey (2010 edition)*, (copyright by BNA PLUS); authored by Barry Hirsch of Georgia State University and David Macpherson of Trinity University. See also <http://unionstats.gsu.edu> and <http://bnaplus.bna.com/LaborReports.aspx>.

Table 664. Union Members by Selected Characteristics: 2009

[Annual averages of monthly data (124,490 represents 124,490,000). Covers employed wage and salary workers 16 years old and over. Excludes self-employed workers whose businesses are incorporated although they technically qualify as wage and salary workers. Based on Current Population Survey; see text, Section 1 and Appendix III]

Characteristic	Employed wage and salary workers			Median usual weekly earnings [3] (dollars)			
		Percent					
	Total (1,000)	Union members [1]	Repre-sented by union [2]	Total	Union members [1]	Repre-sented by union [2]	Not repre-sented by union
Total [4]	**124,490**	**12.3**	**13.6**	**739**	**908**	**901**	**710**
16 to 24 years old	17,173	4.7	5.5	442	598	586	433
25 to 34 years old	28,067	10.5	11.6	678	834	827	653
35 to 44 years old	28,066	13.1	14.4	817	941	936	789
45 to 54 years old	29,054	15.7	17.2	838	959	952	807
55 to 64 years old	17,599	16.6	18.1	841	958	957	800
65 years and over	4,530	9.4	10.7	684	837	831	662
Men	63,539	13.3	14.4	819	957	953	786
Women	60,951	11.3	12.7	657	840	833	628
White [5]	101,581	12.1	13.4	757	934	926	728
Men	52,691	13.1	14.3	845	981	976	811
Women	48,889	11.1	12.4	669	859	852	639
Black [5]	14,127	13.9	15.4	601	749	745	581
Men	6,257	15.4	16.7	621	780	781	599
Women	7,870	12.7	14.3	582	717	710	560
Asian [5]	5,847	11.4	12.5	880	907	919	870
Men	3,075	10.8	12.0	952	888	906	959
Women	2,772	12.0	13.0	779	936	938	756
Hispanic [6]	18,034	10.2	11.3	541	774	763	516
Men	10,518	10.5	11.4	569	824	813	535
Women	7,515	9.7	11.1	509	683	674	493
INDUSTRY [7]							
Private sector industry	103,357	7.2	8.0	711	856	845	697
Mining	662	8.6	9.5	1,050	1013	1,015	1,058
Construction.....................	6,613	14.5	15.0	744	1,072	1,052	698
Manufacturing....................	13,454	10.9	11.9	767	800	799	762
Wholesale and retail trade	17,851	5.3	5.8	611	648	641	609
Transportation and utilities	5,162	22.2	23.4	798	975	964	748
Information	2,790	10.0	11.2	905	1,105	1,083	883
Financial activities	8,236	1.8	2.3	839	843	831	839
Professional and business services ...	11,325	2.3	2.8	864	761	748	868
Education and health services	19,269	8.6	9.9	715	839	838	698
Leisure and hospitality	11,352	3.1	3.6	464	583	576	458
Other services	5,598	2.9	3.2	605	886	862	599
Public sector	21,133	37.4	41.1	865	947	943	782
Federal..........................	3,594	28.0	33.2	1,002	981	989	1,019
State	6,294	32.2	35.3	829	906	899	767
Local	11,244	43.3	46.8	834	956	948	720

[1] Members of a labor union or an employee association similar to a labor union. [2] Members of a labor union or an employee association similar to a union as well as workers who report no union affiliation but whose jobs are covered by a union or an employee association contract. [3] For full-time employed wage and salary workers. [4] Includes races not shown separately. Also includes a small number of multiple jobholders whose full- and part-time status cannot be determined for their principal job. [5] For persons in this race group only. See footnote 4, Table 585. [6] Persons of Hispanic or Latino ethnicity may be any race. [7] For composition of industries, see Table 631.

Source: U.S. Bureau of Labor Statistics, *Union Members in 2009*, News Release, USDL-10-0069, January 2010. See also <http://www.bls.gov/news.release/union2.nr0.htm>.

Labor Force, Employment, and Earnings 429

Table 665. Labor Union Membership by State: 1985 and 2009

[Annual averages of monthly figures (16,996.1 represents 16,996,100). For wage and salary workers in agriculture and non-agriculture. Data represent union members by place of residence. Based on the Current Population Survey and subject to sampling error. For methodological details, see source]

| State | Union members (1,000) | | Workers covered by unions (1,000) | | Percent of workers | | | | | |
| | | | | | Union members | | Covered by unions | | Private sector union members | |
	1985	2009	1985	2009	1985	2009	1985	2009	1985	2009
United States	**16,996.1**	**15,327.3**	**19,358.1**	**16,903.6**	**18.0**	**12.3**	**20.5**	**13.6**	**14.3**	**7.2**
Alabama [1]	226.6	191.3	254.9	211.6	15.7	10.9	17.6	12.0	13.5	6.0
Alaska	47.7	65.2	53.4	69.2	25.0	22.3	28.0	23.6	17.0	10.3
Arizona [1]	115.6	161.7	145.7	194.3	9.5	6.5	12.0	7.9	7.9	3.6
Arkansas [1]	91.6	46.5	108.4	54.6	11.2	4.2	13.3	5.0	9.5	2.8
California	2,123.1	2,453.4	2,485.8	2,622.3	20.4	17.2	23.9	18.3	15.8	9.5
Colorado	165.2	153.2	191.1	180.7	11.8	7.0	13.7	8.3	8.9	4.5
Connecticut	306.5	265.5	325.9	282.4	20.9	17.3	22.2	18.4	14.4	8.5
Delaware	45.6	43.7	50.9	47.1	16.6	11.9	18.5	12.8	12.8	5.8
District of Columbia	45.2	28.6	58.2	34.6	16.5	10.4	21.2	12.5	13.9	6.5
Florida [1]	395.2	410.9	515.7	489.2	9.1	5.8	11.9	6.9	5.3	2.0
Georgia [1]	239.5	176.7	273.1	226.5	10.0	4.6	11.4	5.9	9.l	2.8
Hawaii	109.6	123.5	121.2	127.8	27.8	23.5	30.8	24.3	19.7	14.7
Idaho [1]	41.7	36.3	48.4	45.6	11.7	6.3	13.6	7.9	9.8	3.2
Illinois...............	1,031.7	950.6	1,124.9	996.5	22.2	17.5	24.3	18.3	19.2	10.9
Indiana..............	476.7	277.3	524.4	318.8	21.3	10.6	23.4	12.2	20.8	7.6
Iowa [1]	181.7	155.6	212.8	185.3	17.0	11.1	20.0	13.3	14.5	6.9
Kansas [1]	129.0	77.2	157.3	104.4	12.8	6.2	15.6	8.4	11.4	4.0
Kentucky	219.2	142.4	250.8	173.2	16.5	8.6	18.8	10.5	16.4	6.8
Louisiana [1]	147.9	98.8	172.8	110.5	9.6	5.8	11.2	6.5	7.9	3.7
Maine...............	77.5	63.4	90.0	74.2	17.1	11.7	19.8	13.7	11.2	5.1
Maryland	329.9	322.8	412.9	366.5	16.7	12.6	20.9	14.3	13.0	7.3
Massachusetts........	495.4	476.0	548.4	515.6	18.5	16.6	20.4	18.0	13.0	8.8
Michigan	1,004.5	710.0	1,071.0	751.7	28.4	18.8	30.3	19.9	23.5	12.2
Minnesota	407.5	361.9	452.7	376.9	22.6	15.1	25.1	15.7	16.7	8.5
Mississippi [1]	81.3	49.1	94.5	66.3	9.3	4.8	10.8	6.4	8.4	4.4
Missouri.............	378.3	233.6	418.9	263.8	18.7	9.4	20.7	10.6	19.1	8.0
Montana.............	57.3	52.1	66.9	67.6	19.4	13.9	22.7	18.1	14.9	6.5
Nebraska [1]	78.8	75.8	99.0	94.0	12.7	9.2	16.0	11.4	10.3	4.2
Nevada [1]	89.7	172.6	102.1	188.4	21.6	15.7	24.6	17.2	19.5	12.7
New Hampshire	48.8	66.7	54.8	75.6	10.7	10.8	12.0	12.3	6.9	4.5
New Jersey	821.0	721.0	937.2	741.5	24.9	19.3	28.4	19.9	19.0	10.5
New Mexico	49.4	51.1	62.4	77.4	10.0	6.7	12.7	10.2	8.9	3.1
New York	2,102.3	2,018.8	2,298.3	2,181.8	30.2	25.2	33.0	27.2	21.3	14.0
North Carolina [1]	167.0	115.1	209.5	161.6	6.4	3.1	8.0	4.4	4.7	1.5
North Dakota [1]	27.9	20.6	34.2	29.5	11.4	6.8	14.0	9.8	6.4	4.3
Ohio................	999.0	684.9	1,090.9	742.3	23.6	14.2	25.7	15.4	20.7	8.9
Oklahoma [2]	128.4	83.1	151.0	106.6	10.5	5.7	12.3	7.3	8.2	2.7
Oregon..............	231.6	250.3	260.8	272.2	22.7	17.0	25.6	18.5	16.7	8.9
Pennsylvania	1,055.4	781.7	1,174.7	844.0	22.8	15.0	25.4	16.2	19.1	9.4
Rhode Island	90.2	79.6	97.7	83.2	21.1	17.9	22.9	18.7	12.7	8.8
South Carolina [1]	58.8	75.1	72.5	91.1	4.5	4.5	5.6	5.4	3.8	2.8
South Dakota [1]	27.9	19.8	34.5	23.7	11.2	5.5	13.8	6.6	7.5	3.0
Tennessee [1]	236.8	121.3	281.8	156.5	13.1	5.1	15.6	6.6	10.9	2.8
Texas [1]	474.8	508.1	626.2	615.4	7.4	5.1	9.7	6.2	5.6	3.1
Utah [1]	69.9	78.9	91.9	90.4	11.4	6.9	14.9	8.0	8.0	4.3
Vermont.............	28.5	35.1	35.4	40.3	12.8	12.3	15.9	14.1	7.1	5.3
Virginia [1]	236.0	165.9	296.7	190.8	9.7	4.7	12.2	5.4	8.6	2.6
Washington	405.8	574.1	469.2	612.1	25.0	20.2	28.9	21.5	18.6	12.6
West Virginia	134.7	97.3	148.3	107.9	22.7	13.9	25.0	15.4	22.2	10.3
Wisconsin	435.9	384.7	463.9	400.4	22.3	15.2	23.8	15.8	17.8	8.3
Wyoming [1]	26.8	18.5	34.2	19.9	13.8	7.7	17.6	8.3	11.2	5.2

[1] Right to work state. [2] Passed right to work law in 2001.

Source: The Bureau of National Affairs (BNA), Inc., Arlington, VA, Union Membership and Earnings Data Book: Compilations from the Current Population Survey (2010 edition), (copyright by BNA PLUS); authored by Barry Hirsch of Georgia State University and David Macpherson of Trinity University. See also <http://unionstats.gsu.edu> and <http://bnaplus.bna.com/LaborReports.aspx>.

Section 13
Income, Expenditures, Poverty, and Wealth

This section presents data on gross domestic product (GDP), gross national product (GNP), national and personal income, saving and investment, money income, poverty, and national and personal wealth. The data on income and expenditures measure two aspects of the U.S. economy. One aspect relates to the National Income and Product Accounts (NIPA), a summation reflecting the entire complex of the nation's economic income and output and the interaction of its major components; the other relates to the distribution of money income to families and individuals or consumer income.

The primary source for data on GDP, GNP, national and personal income, gross saving and investment, and fixed assets and consumer durables is the *Survey of Current Business*, published monthly by the Bureau of Economic Analysis (BEA). A comprehensive revision to the NIPA was released beginning in July 2009. Discussions of the revision appeared in the March, August, September, October, and November 2009 issues of the *Survey of Current Business*. Summary historical estimates appeared in the August 2009 issue of the *Survey of Current Business*. Detailed historical data can be found on BEA's Web site at <http://www.bea.gov/>.

Sources of income distribution data are the decennial censuses of population, the Current Population Survey (CPS), and the American Community Survey, all products of the U.S. Census Bureau (see text, Section 1 and Section 4). Annual data on income of families, individuals, and households are presented in *Current Population Reports, Consumer Income*, P60 Series, in print. Many data series are also found on the Census Web site at <http://www.census.gov/hhes /www/income/income.html>. Data on the household sector's saving and assets are published by the Board of Governors of the Federal Reserve System in the quarterly statistical release *Flow of Funds Accounts*. The Federal Reserve Board also periodically conducts the *Survey of Consumer Finances*, which presents financial information on family assets and net worth. The most recent survey is available at <http://www.federalreserve.gov/pubs /oss/oss2/scfindex.html>. Detailed information on personal wealth is published periodically by the Internal Revenue Service (IRS) in *SOI Bulletin*.

National income and product— GDP is the total output of goods and services produced by labor and property located in the United States, valued at market prices. GDP can be viewed in terms of the expenditure categories that comprise its major components: personal consumption expenditures, gross private domestic investment, net exports of goods and services, and government consumption expenditures and gross investment. The goods and services included are largely those bought for final use (excluding illegal transactions) in the market economy. A number of inclusions, however, represent imputed values, the most important of which is the rental value of owner-occupied housing. GDP, in this broad context, measures the output attributable to the factors of production located in the United States. GDP by state is the gross market value of the goods and services attributable to labor and property located in a state. It is the state counterpart of the nation's GDP.

The featured measure of real GDP is an index based on chain-type annual weights. Changes in this measure of real output and prices are calculated as the average of changes based on weights for the current and preceding years. (Components of real output are weighted by price, and components of prices are weighted by output.) These annual changes are "chained" (multiplied) together to form a time series that allows for the effects of changes in relative prices and changes in the composition of output over time. Quarterly and monthly changes are based on quarterly and monthly weights, respectively.

U.S. Census Bureau, Statistical Abstract of the United States: 2011

The output indexes are expressed as 2005 = 100, and for recent years, in 2005 dollars; the price indexes are also based to 2005 = 100. For more information on chained–dollar indexes, see the article on this subject in the November 2003 issue of the *Survey of Current Business*.

Chained (2005) dollar estimates of most components of GDP are not published for periods prior to 1990, because during periods far from the base period, the levels of the components may provide misleading information about their contributions to an aggregate. Values are published in index form (2005 = 100) for 1929 to the present to allow users to calculate the percent changes for all components, which are accurate for all periods. In addition, BEA publishes estimates of contributions of major components to the percent change in GDP for all periods.

Gross national product measures the output attributable to all labor and property supplied by United States residents. GNP differs from "national income" mainly in that GNP includes allowances for depreciation—that is, consumption of fixed capital.

National income includes all net incomes net of consumption of fixed capital (CFC), earned in production. National income is the sum of compensation of employees, proprietors' income with inventory valuation adjustment (IVA) and capital consumption adjustment (CCAdj), rental income of persons with CCAdj, corporate profits with IVA and CCAdj, net interest and miscellaneous payments, taxes on production and imports, business current transfer payments (net), and current surplus of government enterprises, less subsidies.

Capital consumption adjustment for corporations and for nonfarm sole proprietorships and partnerships is the difference between capital consumption based on income tax returns and capital consumption measured using empirical evidence on prices of used equipment and structures in resale markets, which have shown that depreciation for most types of assets approximates a geometric pattern. The tax return data are valued at

historical costs and reflect changes over time in service lives and depreciation patterns as permitted by tax regulations. Inventory valuation adjustment represents the difference between the book value of inventories used up in production and the cost of replacing them.

Personal income is the current income received by persons from all sources minus their personal contributions for government social insurance. Classified as "persons" are individuals (including owners of unincorporated firms), nonprofit institutions that primarily serve individuals, private trust funds, and private noninsured welfare funds. Personal income includes personal current transfer receipts (payments not resulting from current production) from government and business such as social security benefits, public assistance, etc., but excludes transfers among persons. Also included are certain nonmonetary types of income chiefly, estimated net rental value to owner-occupants of their homes and the value of services furnished without payment by financial intermediaries. Capital gains (and losses) are excluded.

Disposable personal income is personal income less personal current taxes. It is the income available to persons for spending or saving. Personal current taxes are tax payments (net of refunds) by persons (except personal contributions for government social insurance) that are not chargeable to business expense. Personal taxes include income taxes, personal property taxes, motor vehicle licenses, and other miscellaneous taxes.

Gross domestic product by industry—The BEA also prepares estimates of value added by industry. *Value added* is a measure of the contribution of each private industry and of government to the nation's GDP. It is defined as an industry's gross output (which consists of sales or receipts and other operating income, commodity taxes, and inventory change) minus its intermediate inputs (which consists of energy, raw materials, semi-finished goods, and services that are purchased from domestic industries or from foreign sources). These estimates of value added are produced for

61 private industries and for 4 government classifications—federal general government and government enterprises and state and local general government and government enterprises.

The estimates by industry are available in current dollars and are derived from the estimates of gross domestic income, which consists of three components— the compensation of employees, gross operating surplus, and taxes on production and imports, less subsidies. Real, or inflation-adjusted, estimates are also prepared.

Regional Economic Accounts—
These accounts consist of estimates of state and local area personal income and of gross domestic product by state and are consistent with estimates of personal income and gross domestic product in the Bureau's national economic accounts. BEA's estimates of state and local area personal income provide a framework for analyzing individual state and local economies, and they show how the economies compare with each other. The *personal income* of a state and/or local area is the income received by, or on behalf of, the residents of that state or area. Estimates of labor and proprietors' earnings by place of work indicate the economic activity of business and government within that area, and estimates of personal income by place of residence indicate the income within the area that is available for spending. BEA prepares estimates for states, counties, metropolitan areas, and BEA economic areas.

Gross domestic product by state estimates measure the value added to the nation's production by the labor and property in each state. GDP by state is often considered the state counterpart of the nation's GDP. The GDP by state estimates provide the basis for analyzing the regional impacts of national economic trends. GDP by state is measured as the sum of the distributions by industry and state of the components of gross domestic income; that is, the sum of the costs incurred and incomes earned in the production of GDP by state. The GDP estimates are presented in current dollars and in real (chained dollars) for 63 industries.

Consumer Expenditure Survey—
The Consumer Expenditure Survey program was begun in 1980. The principal objective of the survey is to collect current consumer expenditure data, which provide a continuous flow of data on the buying habits of American consumers. The data are necessary for future revisions of the Consumer Price Index.

The survey conducted by the Census Bureau for the Bureau of Labor Statistics consists of two components: (1) an interview panel survey in which the expenditures of consumer units are obtained in five interviews conducted every 3 months, and (2) a diary or recordkeeping survey completed by participating households for two consecutive 1-week periods.

Each component of the survey queries an independent sample of consumer units representative of the U.S. total population. Over 52 weeks of the year, 7,000 consumer units are sampled for the diary survey. Each consumer unit keeps a diary for two 1-week periods yielding approximately 14,000 diaries a year. The interview sample is selected on a rotating panel basis, targeted at 7,000 consumer units per quarter. Data are collected in 91 areas of the country that are representative of the U.S. total population. The survey includes students in student housing. Data from the two surveys are combined; integration is necessary to permit analysis of total family expenditures because neither the diary nor quarterly interview survey was designed to collect a complete account of consumer spending.

Distribution of money income to families and individuals—
Money income statistics are based on data collected in various field surveys of income conducted since 1936. Since 1947, the Census Bureau has collected the data on an annual basis and published them in *Current Population Reports*, P60 Series. In each of the surveys, field representatives interview samples of the population with respect to income received during the previous year. *Money income* as defined by the Census Bureau differs from the BEA concept of "personal income." Data on consumer income

Income, Expenditures, Poverty, and Wealth 433

collected in the CPS by the Census Bureau cover money income received (exclusive of certain money receipts such as capital gains) before payments for personal income taxes, social security, union dues, medicare deductions, etc. Therefore, money income does not reflect the fact that some families receive part of their income in the form of noncash benefits (see Section 11) such as food stamps, health benefits, and subsidized housing; that some farm families receive noncash benefits in the form of rent-free housing and goods produced and consumed on the farm; or that noncash benefits are also received by some nonfarm residents, which often take the form of the use of business transportation and facilities, full or partial payments by business for retirement programs, medical and educational expenses, etc. These elements should be considered when comparing income levels. None of the aggregate income concepts (GDP, national income, or personal income) is exactly comparable with money income, although personal income is the closest.

Poverty—Families and unrelated individuals are classified as being above or below poverty following the Office of Management and Budget's Statistical Policy Directive 14. The Census Bureau uses a set of thresholds that vary by family size and composition.

The poverty calculation is based solely on money income and does not reflect the fact that many low-income persons receive noncash benefits such as food stamps, medicaid, and public housing.

The original thresholds were based on the U.S. Department of Agriculture's 1961 Economy Food Plan and reflected the different consumption requirements of families. The poverty thresholds are updated every year to reflect changes in the Consumer Price Index. The following technical changes to the thresholds were made in 1981: (1) distinctions based on sex of householder were eliminated, (2) separate thresholds for farm families were dropped, and (3) the matrix was expanded to families of nine or more persons from the old cutoff of seven or more persons. These changes were incorporated in the calculation of poverty data beginning with 1981. Besides the Census Bureau Web site at <http://www.census.gov/hhes/www/poverty/poverty.html>, information on poverty guidelines and research may be found at the U.S. Department of Human Services Web site at <http://aspe.hhs.gov/poverty/index.shtml>.

In the recent past, the Census Bureau has published a number of technical papers and reports that presented experimental poverty estimates based on income definitions that counted the value of selected government noncash benefits. The Census Bureau has also published reports on after–tax income.

Statistical reliability—For a discussion of statistical collection and estimation, sampling procedures, and measures of statistical reliability pertaining to Census Bureau data, see Appendix III.

Table 666. Gross Domestic Product in Current and Chained (2005) Dollars: 1970 to 2009

[In billions of dollars (1,038 represents $1,038,000,000,000). For explanation of gross domestic product and chained dollars, see text, this section. Minus sign (−) indicates decline in inventories or net imports]

Item	1970	1980	1990	1995	1997	1998	1999	2000	2001	2002	2003	2004	2005	2006	2007	2008	2009
CURRENT DOLLARS																	
Gross domestic product	**1,038**	**2,788**	**5,801**	**7,415**	**8,332**	**8,794**	**9,354**	**9,952**	**10,286**	**10,642**	**11,142**	**11,868**	**12,638**	**13,399**	**14,078**	**14,441**	**14,256**
Personal consumption expenditures	648	1,756	3,836	4,987	5,571	5,919	6,343	6,830	7,149	7,439	7,804	8,285	8,819	9,323	9,826	10,130	10,089
Durable goods	90	226	497	636	716	780	857	916	946	992	1,015	1,062	1,106	1,133	1,161	1,035	1,035
Nondurable goods	229	573	994	1,180	1,291	1,330	1,433	1,543	1,588	1,618	1,713	1,831	1,968	2,089	2,205	2,308	2,220
Services	330	956	2,344	3,172	3,564	3,809	4,053	4,371	4,615	4,829	5,077	5,393	5,745	6,101	6,461	6,727	6,834
Gross private domestic investment	152	479	861	1,144	1,389	1,511	1,642	1,772	1,662	1,647	1,730	1,969	2,172	2,327	2,289	2,136	1,629
Fixed investment	150	486	846	1,113	1,318	1,447	1,581	1,718	1,700	1,635	1,713	1,904	2,122	2,267	2,269	2,171	1,750
Change in private inventories	2	−6	15	31	71	64	61	55	−38	12	16	65	50	60	19	−35	−121
Net exports of goods and services	4	−13	−78	−91	−101	−162	−262	−382	−371	−427	−504	−619	−723	−769	−714	−708	−392
Exports	60	281	552	812	954	954	989	1,093	1,028	1,003	1,041	1,180	1,305	1,471	1,656	1,831	1,564
Imports	56	294	630	903	1,056	1,116	1,251	1,475	1,399	1,430	1,545	1,799	2,028	2,240	2,370	2,539	1,957
Government consumption expenditures and gross investment	234	566	1,182	1,374	1,474	1,526	1,631	1,731	1,846	1,983	2,113	2,233	2,370	2,518	2,677	2,883	2,931
Federal	113	244	508	519	531	531	555	576	612	681	757	825	876	932	977	1,083	1,145
National defense	88	168	374	349	350	346	361	371	393	438	498	551	589	625	662	738	779
Nondefense	26	76	134	170	181	185	194	205	219	243	259	274	287	307	315	345	366
State and local	120	322	674	855	944	995	1,076	1,155	1,235	1,303	1,356	1,408	1,494	1,587	1,700	1,801	1,786
CHAINED (2005) DOLLARS																	
Gross domestic product	**4,270**	**5,839**	**8,034**	**9,094**	**9,854**	**10,284**	**10,780**	**11,226**	**11,347**	**11,553**	**11,841**	**12,264**	**12,638**	**12,976**	**13,254**	**13,312**	**12,987**
Personal consumption expenditures	2,740	3,766	5,316	6,079	6,523	6,866	7,241	7,608	7,814	8,022	8,248	8,533	8,819	9,074	9,314	9,291	9,235
Durable goods	(NA)	(NA)	(NA)	512	595	667	754	820	864	930	986	1,051	1,106	1,150	1,200	1,146	1,101
Nondurable goods	(NA)	(NA)	(NA)	1,438	1,523	1,580	1,661	1,715	1,746	1,780	1,846	1,905	1,968	2,024	2,075	2,057	2,037
Services	(NA)	(NA)	(NA)	4,208	4,465	4,662	4,853	5,093	5,219	5,318	5,418	5,578	5,745	5,900	6,041	6,083	6,088
Gross private domestic investment	475	718	994	1,259	1,541	1,695	1,844	1,970	1,832	1,807	1,872	2,058	2,172	2,230	2,146	1,989	1,528
Fixed investment	(NA)	(NA)	(NA)	1,236	1,471	1,630	1,782	1,914	1,878	1,798	1,856	1,993	2,122	2,171	2,126	2,018	1,648
Change in private inventories	(NA)	(NA)	(NA)	32	77	72	69	60	−42	13	17	66	50	59	20	−26	−108
Net exports of goods and services	(NA)	(NA)	(NA)	−99	−140	−253	−357	−452	−472	−549	−604	−688	−723	−729	−648	−494	−356
Exports	176	352	600	846	1,025	1,049	1,094	1,188	1,122	1,099	1,117	1,223	1,305	1,422	1,546	1,629	1,472
Imports	237	345	673	945	1,165	1,301	1,451	1,640	1,594	1,648	1,721	1,911	2,028	2,151	2,194	2,124	1,828
Government consumption expenditures and gross investment	1,234	1,359	1,864	1,389	1,944	1,985	2,056	2,098	2,178	2,280	2,331	2,362	2,370	2,402	2,443	2,518	2,565
Federal	(NA)	(NA)	(NA)	704	689	681	695	698	727	780	831	865	876	895	906	976	1,027
National defense	(NA)	(NA)	(NA)	477	457	448	456	454	471	505	549	580	589	598	612	659	695
Nondefense	(NA)	(NA)	(NA)	228	232	234	239	244	256	274	282	285	287	297	295	316	332
State and local	(NA)	(NA)	(NA)	1,184	1,254	1,304	1,362	1,400	1,452	1,501	1,500	1,497	1,494	1,507	1,537	1,544	1,541
Residual	−118	−11	−67	−176	−119	−88	−50	–	−29	−20	−12	–	–	−2	–	20	18

– Represents or rounds to zero. NA Not available.

Source: U.S. Bureau of Economic Analysis, *Survey of Current Business*, April 2010. See also <http://www.bea.gov/national/nipaweb/SelectTable.asp?Selected=N>.

Income, Expenditures, Poverty, and Wealth **435**

Table 667. Real Gross Domestic Product, Chained (2005) Dollars—Annual Percent Change: 1990 to 2009

[Change from immediate previous year; for example, 1990, change from 1989. Minus sign (–) indicates decrease]

Component	1990	2000	2002	2003	2004	2005	2006	2007	2008	2009
Gross domestic product (GDP)	**1.9**	**4.1**	**1.8**	**2.5**	**3.6**	**3.1**	**2.7**	**2.1**	**0.4**	**−2.4**
Personal consumption expenditures	2.0	5.1	2.7	2.8	3.5	3.4	2.9	2.6	−0.2	−0.6
Durable goods	−0.4	8.8	7.6	6.0	6.6	5.2	4.1	4.3	−4.5	−3.9
Nondurable goods	1.2	3.2	2.0	3.7	3.2	3.4	2.8	2.5	−0.8	−1.0
Services	3.0	5.0	1.9	1.9	2.9	3.0	2.7	2.4	0.7	0.1
Gross private domestic investment	−3.4	6.8	−1.4	3.6	10.0	5.5	2.7	−3.8	−7.3	−23.2
Fixed investment	−2.1	7.4	−4.2	3.2	7.3	6.5	2.3	−2.1	−5.1	−18.3
Nonresidential	0.5	9.8	−7.9	0.9	6.0	6.7	7.9	6.2	1.6	−17.8
Structures	1.5	7.8	−17.7	−3.8	1.1	1.4	9.2	14.9	10.3	−19.8
Equipment and software	–	10.5	−4.2	2.5	7.7	8.5	7.4	2.6	−2.6	−16.6
Residential	−8.6	1.0	5.2	8.2	9.8	6.2	−7.3	−18.5	−22.9	−20.5
Exports	9.0	8.6	−2.0	1.6	9.5	6.7	9.0	8.7	5.4	−9.6
Goods	8.4	11.1	−3.6	1.8	8.5	7.5	9.4	7.4	5.9	−12.2
Services	10.5	2.7	1.9	1.2	11.9	5.0	7.9	11.8	4.2	−4.1
Imports	3.6	13.0	3.4	4.4	11.0	6.1	6.1	2.0	−3.2	−13.9
Goods	2.9	13.4	3.7	4.9	11.0	6.8	5.9	1.7	−3.9	−16.0
Services	6.5	11.0	1.8	1.9	11.2	2.8	7.1	3.5	0.7	−3.6
Government consumption expenditures and gross investment	3.2	2.0	4.7	2.2	1.4	0.3	1.4	1.7	3.1	1.8
Federal	2.0	0.5	7.3	6.6	4.1	1.3	2.1	1.3	7.7	5.2
National defense	–	−0.5	7.4	8.7	5.7	1.5	1.6	2.2	7.8	5.4
Nondefense	8.2	2.4	7.2	2.8	1.0	0.9	3.2	−0.6	7.3	4.8
State and local	4.1	2.8	3.3	−0.1	−0.2	−0.2	0.9	2.0	0.5	−0.2

– Represents or rounds to zero.

Source: U.S. Bureau of Economic Analysis, *Survey of Current Business*, April 2010. See also <http://www.bea.gov/national/nipaweb/SelectTable.asp?Selected=N>.

Table 668. Gross Domestic Product in Current and Chained (2005) Dollars by Type of Product and Sector: 1990 to 2009

[In billions of dollars (5,801 represents $5,801,000,000,000). For explanation of chained dollars, see text, this section]

Type of product and sector	1990	2000	2003	2004	2005	2006	2007	2008	2009
CURRENT DOLLARS									
Gross domestic product	**5,801**	**9,952**	**11,142**	**11,868**	**12,638**	**13,399**	**14,078**	**14,441**	**14,256**
PRODUCT									
Goods	1,923	3,125	3,170	3,334	3,473	3,661	3,814	3,784	3,699
Durable goods	981	1,770	1,707	1,785	1,891	1,977	2,048	2,042	1,815
Nondurable goods	942	1,355	1,463	1,549	1,582	1,683	1,766	1,742	1,884
Services [1]	3,344	5,878	6,892	7,319	7,802	8,286	8,811	9,265	9,396
Structures	534	949	1,080	1,215	1,363	1,453	1,453	1,392	1,161
SECTOR									
Business	4,454	7,716	8,503	9,085	9,696	10,284	10,789	10,953	10,666
Nonfarm	4,377	7,642	8,410	8,966	9,594	10,191	10,673	10,821	10,560
Farm	77	74	92	118	102	93	116	132	106
Households and institutions	624	1,157	1,347	1,424	1,506	1,603	1,687	1,800	1,830
General government	723	1,079	1,292	1,359	1,437	1,512	1,602	1,688	1,760
Federal	259	315	383	412	439	461	486	515	559
State and local	464	764	909	947	998	1,051	1,116	1,173	1,201
CHAINED (2005) DOLLARS									
Gross domestic product	**8,034**	**11,226**	**11,841**	**12,264**	**12,638**	**12,976**	**13,254**	**13,312**	**12,987**
PRODUCT									
Goods	1,920	3,056	3,164	3,326	3,473	3,653	3,790	3,805	3,621
Durable goods	(NA)	1,625	1,671	1,778	1,891	1,989	2,087	2,116	1,886
Nondurable goods	(NA)	1,430	1,494	1,548	1,582	1,663	1,703	1,691	1,724
Services [1]	5,269	6,919	7,416	7,613	7,802	7,985	8,193	8,315	8,351
Structures	942	1,245	1,264	1,326	1,363	1,341	1,281	1,205	1,024
SECTOR									
Business	5,815	8,501	9,006	9,380	9,696	9,992	10,215	10,215	9,855
Nonfarm	5,760	8,418	8,915	9,282	9,594	9,892	10,124	10,109	9,741
Farm	56	84	92	98	102	99	92	103	111
Households and institutions	1,010	1,376	1,418	1,457	1,506	1,540	1,574	1,599	1,601
General government	1,266	1,349	1,418	1,427	1,437	1,445	1,466	1,498	1,525
Federal	484	411	432	436	439	438	442	459	487
State and local	789	939	987	991	998	1,007	1,024	1,038	1,038

NA Not available. [1] Includes government consumption expenditures, which are for services (such as education and national defense) produced by government. In current dollars, these services are valued at their cost of production.

Source: U.S. Bureau of Economic Analysis, *Survey of Current Business*, April 2010. See also <http://www.bea.gov/national/nipaweb/SelectTable.asp?Selected=N>.

Table 669. Gross Domestic Product in Current and Chained (2005) Dollars by Industry: 2000 to 2009

[In billions of dollars (9,952 represents $9,952,000,000,000). Data are based on the 2002 North American Industry Classification System (NAICS), see text, Section 15. Data include nonfactor charges (capital consumption allowances, indirect business taxes, etc.) as well as factor charges against gross product; corporate profits and capital consumption allowances have been shifted from a company to an establishment basis]

Industry	Current dollars				Chained (2005) dollars			
	2000	2005	2008	2009	2000	2005	2008	2009
Gross domestic product	**9,952**	**12,638**	**14,441**	**14,256**	**11,226**	**12,638**	**13,312**	**12,987**
Private industries	8,736	11,053	12,588	12,324	9,786	11,053	11,620	11,314
Agriculture, forestry, and fishing	96	127	163	136	104	127	132	138
Farms	74	102	132	(NA)	84	102	103	(NA)
Agricultural services	22	25	31	(NA)	21	25	28	(NA)
Mining	109	192	307	231	233	192	199	206
Oil and gas extraction	68	129	204	(NA)	155	129	131	(NA)
Mining, except oil and gas	28	36	49	(NA)	45	36	32	(NA)
Mining support activities	14	27	55	(NA)	29	27	35	(NA)
Utilities	174	206	255	269	223	206	221	228
Construction	467	612	639	578	655	612	552	497
Manufacturing	1,416	1,568	1,670	1,569	1,397	1,568	1,647	1,551
Durable goods	839	878	923	847	748	878	978	905
Wood products	28	33	27	(NA)	33	33	36	(NA)
Nonmetallic mineral products	42	45	41	(NA)	45	45	38	(NA)
Primary metals	46	54	59	(NA)	62	54	40	(NA)
Fabricated metal products	121	120	136	(NA)	130	120	127	(NA)
Machinery	111	110	124	(NA)	111	110	122	(NA)
Computer and electronic products	172	183	195	(NA)	82	183	273	(NA)
Electrical equipment, appliances, and components	44	40	50	(NA)	43	40	46	(NA)
Motor vehicles, bodies & trailers, & parts	117	113	89	(NA)	94	113	113	(NA)
Other transportation equipment	66	76	94	(NA)	78	76	91	(NA)
Furniture and related products	34	34	30	(NA)	35	34	29	(NA)
Miscellaneous manufacturing	58	70	79	(NA)	60	70	78	(NA)
Nondurable goods	577	690	746	722	650	690	674	648
Food & beverage & tobacco	165	172	190	(NA)	176	172	190	(NA)
Textile mills and textile product mills	28	24	17	(NA)	27	24	16	(NA)
Apparel and leather and allied products	21	16	14	(NA)	20	16	15	(NA)
Paper products	62	61	60	(NA)	58	61	61	(NA)
Printing and related support activities	40	38	37	(NA)	38	38	37	(NA)
Petroleum and coal products	44	139	149	(NA)	74	139	123	(NA)
Chemical products	152	183	213	(NA)	170	183	184	(NA)
Plastics and rubber products	65	66	67	(NA)	66	66	61	(NA)
Wholesale trade	618	725	821	793	606	725	762	754
Retail trade	686	839	866	842	751	839	823	786
Transportation and warehousing	301	370	405	394	318	370	388	377
Air transportation	53	56	57	(NA)	43	56	56	(NA)
Rail transportation	23	27	32	(NA)	27	27	25	(NA)
Water transportation	8	9	14	(NA)	7	9	21	(NA)
Truck transportation	97	119	126	(NA)	107	119	128	(NA)
Transit & ground passenger transport	18	21	22	(NA)	21	21	22	(NA)
Pipeline transportation	9	10	14	(NA)	9	10	12	(NA)
Other transportation & support	68	92	99	(NA)	76	92	90	(NA)
Warehousing and storage	26	35	41	(NA)	29	35	37	(NA)
Information	418	593	623	634	397	593	643	653
Publishing industries (includes software)	100	151	146	(NA)	102	151	143	(NA)
Motion picture and sound recording	37	56	61	(NA)	43	56	57	(NA)
Broadcasting and telecommunications	257	311	345	(NA)	227	311	366	(NA)
Information and data processing services	24	74	71	(NA)	24	74	78	(NA)
Finance and insurance	762	1,029	1,200	1,198	841	1,029	1,117	1,086
Real estate and rental and leasing	1,236	1,578	1,843	1,860	1,422	1,578	1,704	1,666
Professional, scientific, and technical services	662	876	1,071	1,078	745	876	958	941
Legal services	139	195	210	(NA)	176	195	175	(NA)
Computer systems design, related services	114	129	170	(NA)	102	129	168	(NA)
Miscellaneous services	410	552	691	(NA)	467	552	617	(NA)
Management of companies & enterprises	171	218	261	252	215	218	222	216
Admin/support waste management/remediation services	283	369	417	394	312	369	395	370
Educational services	86	120	146	153	116	120	126	125
Health care and social assistance	592	833	992	1,036	709	833	912	928
Ambulatory health care services	288	406	486	(NA)	326	406	453	(NA)
Hospitals, nursing, residential care	253	354	419	(NA)	322	354	381	(NA)
Social assistance	52	73	86	(NA)	62	73	78	(NA)
Arts, entertainment, and recreation	99	117	138	138	115	117	127	124
Performing arts, spectator sports, museums, and related activities	48	64	75	(NA)	59	64	68	(NA)
Amusements, gambling, & recreation	50	54	63	(NA)	55	54	60	(NA)
Accommodation and food services	283	364	407	408	328	364	370	357
Accommodation	89	109	119	(NA)	100	109	110	(NA)
Food services and drinking places	194	256	288	(NA)	227	256	260	(NA)
Other services, except government	278	319	366	361	347	319	332	310
Government	1,215	1,586	1,853	1,933	1,507	1,586	1,647	1,678
Federal	378	502	579	626	483	502	515	544
State and local	837	1,084	1,275	1,307	1,025	1,084	1,132	1,133

NA Not available.

Source: U.S. Bureau of Economic Analysis, *Survey of Current Business*, May 2010. See also <http://www.bea.gov/newsreleases/industry/gdpindustry/gdpindnewsrelease.htm>.

Income, Expenditures, Poverty, and Wealth 437

Table 670. Gross Domestic Product by State in Current and Chained (2000) Dollars: 2000 to 2008

[In billions of dollars (9,749.1 represents $9,749,100,000,000). For definition of gross domestic product by state or chained dollars, see text, this section]

State	Current dollars					Chained (2000) dollars				
	2000	2005	2006	2007	2008	2000	2005	2006	2007	2008
United States [1]	9,749.1	12,339.0	13,090.8	13,715.7	14,165.6	9,749.1	10,912.2	11,218.8	11,439.2	11,523.6
Alabama	114.6	150.6	158.9	164.5	170.0	114.6	132.3	134.9	136.1	137.1
Alaska	27.0	39.4	43.3	44.9	47.9	27.0	29.3	30.6	30.6	30.0
Arizona	158.5	215.2	236.4	246.0	248.9	158.5	196.2	208.6	211.6	210.2
Arkansas	66.8	86.5	90.7	95.1	98.3	66.8	76.5	77.5	78.7	79.2
California	1,287.1	1,628.6	1,727.6	1,801.8	1,846.8	1,287.1	1,467.9	1,512.9	1,539.4	1,546.1
Colorado	171.9	212.6	225.1	235.8	248.6	171.9	188.4	193.4	197.3	203.0
Connecticut	160.4	190.5	201.6	212.3	216.2	160.4	169.1	174.3	178.5	177.7
Delaware	41.5	57.6	59.2	61.5	61.8	41.5	49.9	49.6	50.1	49.2
District of Columbia	58.7	83.4	88.1	92.5	97.2	58.7	70.0	71.4	72.6	74.8
Florida	471.3	670.0	721.4	741.9	744.1	471.3	589.3	613.6	613.4	603.5
Georgia	290.9	359.5	375.6	391.2	397.8	290.9	322.6	326.5	331.3	329.5
Hawaii	40.2	54.0	50.1	62.0	63.8	40.2	46.9	48.7	49.4	49.8
Idaho	35.0	46.6	48.6	52.1	52.7	35.0	42.9	43.8	45.5	45.5
Illinois	464.2	553.0	588.9	617.4	633.7	464.2	490.3	505.3	514.8	516.1
Indiana	194.4	232.9	239.9	249.2	254.9	194.4	208.1	208.3	211.1	209.9
Iowa	90.2	115.8	121.1	129.9	135.7	90.2	102.6	104.5	108.1	110.4
Kansas	82.8	102.9	109.9	117.0	122.7	82.8	90.0	93.1	96.0	98.1
Kentucky	111.9	138.6	146.4	152.1	156.4	111.9	122.9	125.8	127.0	127.0
Louisiana	131.5	183.0	197.6	207.4	222.2	131.5	140.3	143.1	144.4	144.9
Maine	35.5	44.5	46.3	48.0	49.7	35.5	39.0	39.4	39.8	40.3
Maryland	180.4	241.5	253.0	264.4	273.3	180.4	211.4	214.2	217.9	220.9
Massachusetts	274.9	317.4	334.5	352.2	365.0	274.9	289.9	297.6	306.5	312.5
Michigan	337.2	372.0	375.1	379.9	382.5	337.2	339.9	334.8	331.0	326.1
Minnesota	185.1	232.8	240.9	252.5	262.8	185.1	208.4	209.4	212.8	217.0
Mississippi	64.3	79.5	83.8	87.7	91.8	64.3	68.4	69.6	70.5	71.7
Missouri	176.7	213.2	219.7	229.0	237.8	176.7	189.1	188.8	191.2	193.8
Montana	21.4	29.8	31.8	34.3	35.9	21.4	25.2	25.8	26.8	27.3
Nebraska	55.5	71.0	75.0	80.4	83.3	55.5	62.2	63.8	65.7	66.6
Nevada	73.7	112.4	121.7	129.3	131.2	73.7	97.2	101.1	103.9	103.2
New Hampshire	43.5	53.5	56.1	57.8	60.0	43.5	48.5	49.3	49.6	50.6
New Jersey	344.8	425.5	445.7	461.3	474.9	344.8	379.1	384.6	388.0	390.4
New Mexico	50.7	68.0	71.8	75.2	79.9	50.7	57.6	59.0	60.2	61.4
New York	777.2	956.4	1,034.1	1,105.0	1,144.5	777.2	865.7	912.9	949.5	964.8
North Carolina	273.7	348.4	378.6	390.5	400.2	273.7	309.7	326.9	329.1	329.4
North Dakota	17.8	24.3	25.4	28.5	31.2	17.8	20.9	21.1	22.6	24.3
Ohio	372.0	438.8	449.0	462.5	471.5	372.0	390.6	387.3	388.3	385.6
Oklahoma	89.8	120.6	129.6	136.4	146.4	89.8	99.2	102.2	104.1	106.9
Oregon	112.4	138.0	151.2	158.3	161.6	112.4	129.4	139.6	144.8	147.1
Pennsylvania	389.6	482.0	509.0	533.2	553.3	389.6	422.5	431.0	438.9	443.7
Rhode Island	33.6	43.1	45.5	46.7	47.4	33.6	37.8	38.5	38.5	38.1
South Carolina	112.5	138.6	146.5	151.7	156.4	112.5	122.8	125.2	126.3	127.1
South Dakota	23.1	30.7	31.2	35.2	37.0	23.1	27.4	27.1	29.3	30.3
Tennessee	174.9	223.8	236.1	245.2	252.1	174.9	200.9	206.4	209.1	210.2
Texas	727.2	982.1	1,070.3	1,148.5	1,223.5	727.2	828.4	869.4	907.4	925.5
Utah	67.6	89.1	98.3	105.6	109.8	67.6	77.8	82.7	86.5	87.7
Vermont	17.8	22.8	23.7	24.6	25.4	17.8	20.7	21.0	21.3	21.7
Virginia	260.7	350.9	368.0	384.1	397.0	260.7	309.3	314.5	320.3	324.5
Washington	222.0	272.7	289.1	310.3	322.8	222.0	241.8	248.5	259.4	264.6
West Virginia	41.5	52.9	55.8	57.9	61.7	41.5	44.7	44.9	45.2	46.3
Wisconsin	175.7	214.8	224.9	233.4	240.4	175.7	191.7	195.0	197.0	198.3
Wyoming	17.3	26.4	30.1	31.5	35.3	17.3	19.3	20.7	20.8	21.8

[1] For chained (2000) dollar estimates, states will not add to U.S. total.

Source: U.S. Bureau of Economic Analysis, *Survey of Current Business,* June 2009, and "Gross Domestic Product by State," June 2009, <http://www.bea.gov/regional/gsp/>.

Table 671. Gross Domestic Product by Selected Industries and State: 2008

[In billions of dollars (14,165.6 represents $14,165,600,000,000). Preliminary data. For definition of gross domestic product by state, see text, this section. Industries based on 1997 North American Industry Classification System; see text, Section 15]

State	Total [1]	Manu-facturing	Whole-sale trade	Retail trade	Infor-mation	Finance and insur-ance	Real estate, rental, and leasing	Profes-sional and technical services	Health care and social assis-tance	Govern-ment [2]
United States	14,165.6	1,637.7	818.8	885.5	622.0	1,064.9	1,783.5	1,095.6	1,019.7	1,740.9
Alabama	170.0	29.3	9.9	13.2	4.4	9.1	15.1	10.6	12.3	27.8
Alaska	47.9	1.0	0.9	2.0	1.0	1.3	3.5	1.7	2.4	8.4
Arizona	248.9	19.5	13.9	19.5	6.7	17.7	40.0	15.7	19.4	32.4
Arkansas	98.3	17.1	6.4	7.2	3.9	3.7	8.4	3.9	7.7	13.7
California	1,846.8	181.1	105.1	118.6	112.8	107.6	308.7	174.6	115.6	216.8
Colorado	248.6	15.9	13.8	14.7	21.1	14.7	31.5	24.3	14.9	30.6
Connecticut	216.2	28.9	11.3	11.9	8.2	33.7	27.4	16.9	17.0	20.4
Delaware	61.8	4.6	2.0	2.6	1.3	20.0	7.5	4.0	3.6	5.4
District of Columbia	97.2	0.2	0.9	1.2	5.6	4.0	9.7	21.0	4.3	31.7
Florida	744.1	35.7	46.6	55.8	30.5	47.4	134.0	50.7	57.6	90.6
Georgia	397.8	43.3	31.0	26.0	25.3	23.9	45.3	29.2	24.6	55.4
Hawaii	63.8	1.1	2.1	4.5	1.4	2.5	11.4	3.0	4.2	15.1
Idaho	52.7	5.2	2.8	4.5	1.2	2.5	6.5	4.0	3.9	7.5
Illinois............	633.7	78.8	44.0	35.2	23.1	58.0	79.2	57.6	42.9	61.3
Indiana...........	254.9	63.8	14.4	15.9	5.6	14.8	23.4	11.1	20.1	25.9
Iowa.............	135.7	28.2	7.7	7.9	3.9	14.2	10.4	4.6	9.2	15.8
Kansas...........	122.7	18.6	7.6	8.1	7.2	6.9	10.0	6.8	8.8	17.4
Kentucky	156.4	28.8	9.7	10.4	4.1	7.4	12.9	6.9	13.0	24.6
Louisiana.........	222.2	40.5	9.7	13.6	4.4	6.7	15.6	9.8	12.8	24.6
Maine............	49.7	5.5	2.5	4.4	1.3	3.1	6.8	2.6	5.6	7.0
Maryland	273.3	15.2	13.5	16.1	10.1	15.3	38.6	30.5	21.4	51.1
Massachusetts........	365.0	34.8	20.7	17.7	17.6	35.5	51.8	44.5	34.6	33.1
Michigan	382.5	61.8	23.3	25.8	10.5	23.1	44.0	32.5	32.9	44.5
Minnesota	262.8	33.7	18.4	15.0	9.1	23.0	30.6	17.3	22.8	27.8
Mississippi..........	91.8	13.7	4.5	7.5	2.1	3.8	7.6	3.4	6.7	16.1
Missouri...........	237.8	32.0	15.3	16.1	11.1	13.4	22.7	16.1	18.8	29.6
Montana...........	35.9	1.5	1.9	2.5	0.9	1.7	3.9	1.9	3.3	5.6
Nebraska..........	83.3	9.9	4.7	5.0	2.8	6.2	6.7	4.2	6.1	11.7
Nevada	131.2	5.7	5.1	9.9	2.4	10.0	18.6	6.8	6.6	13.4
New Hampshire.......	60.0	6.5	3.7	4.7	2.2	4.9	8.9	4.5	5.5	5.8
New Jersey	474.0	43.9	37.7	29.6	22.1	36.4	74.4	45.8	35.5	49.3
New Mexico..........	79.9	5.3	2.7	5.2	2.1	2.4	7.7	6.5	5.4	13.9
New York	1,144.5	69.1	53.2	57.3	80.1	187.2	176.0	103.1	82.6	117.5
North Carolina	400.2	78.0	21.7	25.0	12.1	39.9	36.7	21.7	26.6	56.0
North Dakota	31.2	2.8	2.2	2.1	1.0	1.7	2.5	1.1	2.6	4.4
Ohio..............	471.5	84.1	30.1	30.3	12.4	34.7	46.7	29.0	40.2	54.1
Oklahoma	146.4	15.7	7.1	9.8	4.5	6.2	11.3	6.5	9.9	23.0
Oregon............	161.6	30.2	10.5	8.7	5.4	7.9	21.2	8.6	13.0	20.7
Pennsylvania	553.3	75.5	33.0	33.3	20.2	40.3	65.3	43.6	53.6	54.0
Rhode Island	47.4	4.7	2.4	2.8	1.8	5.3	7.0	2.7	4.5	6.1
South Carolina........	156.4	25.2	9.0	12.3	4.3	7.3	16.5	8.2	9.7	27.1
South Dakota........	37.0	3.5	2.0	2.5	1.0	6.5	2.4	1.0	3.2	4.5
Tennessee.........	252.1	40.6	17.0	20.6	8.4	14.4	24.3	14.8	22.9	28.6
Texas	1,223.5	158.8	76.4	72.0	46.3	66.8	104.6	83.3	69.5	130.0
Utah..............	109.8	13.0	5.5	8.0	3.8	9.5	12.3	7.9	6.2	15.2
Vermont...........	25.4	2.9	1.2	2.1	0.9	1.5	3.1	1.6	2.6	3.5
Virginia............	397.0	34.1	16.5	22.7	18.8	23.1	50.3	52.6	22.5	72.9
Washington	322.8	32.0	19.5	22.7	25.5	17.1	45.3	22.0	22.5	46.9
West Virginia	61.7	6.6	2.9	4.6	1.5	2.5	5.1	2.5	5.7	11.0
Wisconsin	240.4	48.9	13.6	14.6	7.3	17.7	27.5	11.3	20.9	26.5
Wyoming	35.3	1.1	1.2	1.9	0.5	0.9	2.5	1.0	1.4	4.5

[1] Includes industries not shown separately. [2] Includes federal civilian and military and state and local government.

Source: U.S. Bureau of Economic Analysis, *Survey of Current Business,* June 2009, and "Gross Domestic Product by State," June 2009, <http://www.bea.gov/regional/gsp/>.

U.S. Census Bureau, Statistical Abstract of the United States: 2011

Table 672. Relation of GDP, GNP, Net National Product, National Income, Personal Income, Disposable Personal Income, and Personal Saving: 1990 to 2009

[In billions of dollars (5,801 represents $5,801,000,000,000). For definitions, see text, this section. Minus sign (–) indicates deficit or net disbursement]

Item	1990	2000	2004	2005	2006	2007	2008	2009
Gross domestic product (GDP)	**5,801**	**9,952**	**11,868**	**12,638**	**13,399**	**14,078**	**14,441**	**14,256**
Plus: Income receipts from the rest of the world	189	381	449	573	721	862	809	589
Less: Income payments to the rest of the world	154	343	357	476	649	746	667	485
Equals: Gross national product (GNP)	**5,835**	**9,989**	**11,959**	**12,736**	**13,471**	**14,193**	**14,583**	**14,361**
Less: Consumption of fixed capital	691	1,184	1,433	1,541	1,661	1,760	1,847	1,864
Equals: Net national product	**5,144**	**8,805**	**10,526**	**11,194**	**11,811**	**12,433**	**12,736**	**12,497**
Less: Statistical discrepancy	*84*	*–134*	*–8*	*–80*	*–221*	*–15*	*101*	*209*
Equals: National income	**5,060**	**8,939**	**10,534**	**11,274**	**12,031**	**12,448**	**12,635**	**12,288**
Less: Corporate profits [1]	434	819	1,247	1,456	1,608	1,542	1,360	1,309
Taxes on production and imports less subsidies	398	663	817	869	936	974	994	964
Contributions for government social insurance	410	706	827	873	922	959	991	967
Net interest and miscellaneous payments on assets	444	539	462	543	652	739	815	788
Business current transfer payments (net)	40	87	82	96	83	102	119	134
Current surplus of government enterprises	2	9	1	–4	–4	–7	–7	–8
Wage accruals less disbursements	–	–	–15	5	1	–6	–5	5
Plus: Personal income receipts on assets	921	1,361	1,409	1,542	1,830	2,032	1,994	1,793
Personal current transfer receipts	595	1,083	1,416	1,509	1,605	1,718	1,876	2,105
Equals: Personal income	**4,847**	**8,559**	**9,937**	**10,486**	**11,268**	**11,894**	**12,239**	**12,026**
Less: Personal current taxes	593	1,232	1,048	1,209	1,352	1,491	1,432	1,103
Equals: Disposable personal income	**4,254**	**7,327**	**8,889**	**9,277**	**9,916**	**10,403**	**10,806**	**10,924**
Less: Personal outlays	3,977	7,114	8,586	9,150	9,681	10,224	10,520	10,459
Equals: Personal saving	**277**	**213**	**304**	**128**	**235**	**179**	**286**	**465**

– Represents or rounds to zero. [1] Corporate profits with inventory valuation and capital consumption adjustments.

Source: U.S. Bureau of Economic Analysis, *Survey of Current Business,* April 2010. See also <http://www.bea.gov/national/nipaweb/SelectTable.asp?Selected=N>.

Table 673. Gross Saving and Investment: 1990 to 2009

[In billions of dollars (918 represents $918,000,000,000)]

Item	1990	2000	2004	2005	2006	2007	2008	2009
Gross saving	**918**	**1,800**	**1,724**	**1,903**	**2,174**	**2,040**	**1,824**	**1,508**
Net saving	226	616	291	362	514	280	–23	–356
Net private saving	397	389	679	619	667	495	660	888
Personal saving	277	213	304	128	235	179	286	465
Undistributed corporate profits with IVA and CCA [1]	120	176	391	486	430	322	378	418
Wage accruals less disbursements	–	–	–15	5	1	–6	–5	5
Net government saving	–170	227	–388	–257	–153	–215	–683	–1,244
Federal	–176	185	–380	–283	–204	–237	–643	–1,225
State and local	6	41	–8	26	51	22	–40	–19
Consumption of fixed capital	691	1,184	1,433	1,541	1,661	1,760	1,847	1,864
Private	560	987	1,201	1,291	1,391	1,470	1,536	1,539
Domestic business	470	824	979	1,046	1,123	1,189	1,252	1,258
Households and institutions	91	163	222	245	268	281	284	281
Government	131	198	232	251	269	290	311	325
Federal	68	88	95	100	107	113	120	126
State and local	63	110	137	150	163	178	191	200
Gross domestic investment, capital acct. transactions, and net lending	**1,002**	**1,666**	**1,716**	**1,824**	**1,954**	**2,025**	**1,925**	**1,713**
Gross domestic investment	1,077	2,077	2,341	2,564	2,752	2,750	2,632	2,143
Gross private domestic investment	861	1,772	1,969	2,172	2,327	2,289	2,136	1,629
Gross government investment	216	304	372	392	425	462	496	514
Capital account transactions (net) [2]	7	1	–1	–11	4	2	–	3
Net lending or net borrowing	–82	–412	–624	–730	–803	–727	–707	–433
Statistical discrepancy	84	–134	–8	–80	–221	–15	101	209
Addenda:								
Gross private saving	957	1,376	1,880	1,910	2,058	1,965	2,196	2,427
Gross government saving	–40	424	–156	–7	117	76	–372	–919
Federal	–109	273	–285	–183	–97	–124	–523	–1,099
State and local	69	151	129	176	214	200	151	180
Net domestic investment	386	892	908	1,023	1,092	990	785	279
Gross saving as a percentage of gross national income	16.0	17.8	14.4	14.9	15.9	14.4	12.6	10.7
Net saving as a percentage of gross national income	3.9	6.1	2.4	2.8	3.8	2.0	–0.2	–2.5

– Represents or rounds to zero. [1] IVA and CCA = Inventory valuation adjustment and capital consumption adjustment.
[2] Consists of capital transfers and the acquisition and disposal of nonproduced nonfinancial assets.

Source: U.S. Bureau of Economic Analysis, *Survey of Current Business,* April 2010. See also <http://www.bea.gov/national/nipaweb/SelectTable.asp?Selected=N>.

Table 674. Flow of Funds Accounts—Composition of Individuals' Savings: 1990 to 2009

[In billions of dollars (510.6 represents $510,600,000,000). Combined statement for households, farm business, and nonfarm noncorporate business. Minus sign (−) indicates decrease]

Composition of savings	1990	2000	2004	2005	2006	2007	2008	2009
Net acquisition of financial assets............	510.6	374.0	1,385.3	1,212.9	1,227.4	1,583.5	849.2	21.1
Foreign deposits.........................	1.4	7.6	5.4	2.4	5.2	15.8	−21.2	−10.5
Checkable deposits and currency............	−8.4	−74.0	68.1	−50.7	32.2	−0.8	146.3	6.1
Time and savings deposits	33.1	348.8	450.3	510.5	506.8	492.1	190.6	55.3
Money market fund shares	30.6	152.4	−53.2	47.6	168.4	234.4	237.9	−265.3
Securities..............................	201.4	−641.0	145.2	39.8	−299.7	−33.7	37.8	362.7
Open market paper	5.8	12.4	6.4	14.7	19.0	−10.2	−101.3	−1.4
U.S. savings bonds	8.5	−1.7	0.6	0.7	−2.7	−6.0	−2.4	−2.8
Other Treasury securities................	89.3	−204.3	31.3	−93.6	−84.3	−81.4	172.0	530.1
Agency and GSE-backed securities [1]	35.3	34.1	80.6	101.6	−60.8	349.5	99.9	−618.6
Municipal securities....................	34.7	4.5	40.3	78.7	51.9	24.6	40.3	60.6
Corporate and foreign bonds.............	47.1	84.7	39.6	119.6	167.6	241.9	−193.4	−149.1
Corporate equities [2].....................	−50.8	−637.5	−269.9	−409.9	−596.3	−795.1	28.2	126.9
Mutual fund shares	31.5	66.7	216.4	228.1	205.9	243.0	−5.4	416.9
Life insurance reserves	26.5	50.2	33.1	16.1	65.6	34.2	67.0	46.6
Pension fund reserves.....................	191.8	273.0	303.8	253.3	234.1	172.1	79.6	63.8
Miscellaneous and other assets	34.3	256.9	432.6	393.8	514.7	669.4	111.2	−237.5
Gross investment in tangible assets........	803.3	1,500.2	1,912.9	2,047.8	2,075.2	1,995.5	1,791.1	1,559.1
Minus: Consumption of fixed capital	572.9	917.4	1,140.4	1,214.8	1,287.0	1,343.5	1,382.9	1,377.2
Equals: Net investment in tangible assets	230.4	582.7	772.6	833.0	788.2	651.9	408.2	181.9
Net increase in liabilities..................	230.2	930.5	1,508.0	1,699.7	1,836.8	1,499.8	155.0	−490.5
Mortgage debt on nonfarm homes	207.1	422.8	1,005.3	1,101.0	1,051.7	692.9	−109.8	−202.0
Other mortgage debt [3].....................	−1.9	109.2	158.8	120.6	237.3	301.1	139.6	−68.9
Consumer credit	15.1	176.5	117.2	100.4	95.4	139.3	38.8	−112.7
Policy loans	4.1	2.8	1.6	0.8	3.3	3.6	5.9	1.3
Security credit	−3.7	7.2	81.5	−31.6	59.7	33.4	−160.7	38.1
Other liabilities [3].......................	9.5	211.9	143.7	408.5	389.4	329.4	241.2	−146.3
Personal saving with consumer durables [4]	526.6	61.8	646.2	311.2	195.5	738.8	1,090.9	682.5
Personal saving without consumer durables [4]....	448.7	−174.4	404.0	72.2	−32.2	517.1	955.9	600.1
Personal saving (NIPA, excludes consumer durables) [5].............................	276.7	213.1	303.7	127.7	235.0	178.9	286.4	471.5

[1] GSE = government-sponsored enterprises. [2] Only directly held and those in closed-end and exchange-traded funds. Other equities are included in mutual funds and life insurance and pension reserves. [3] Includes corporate farms. [4] Flow of Funds measure. [5] National Income and Product Accounts measure.

Source: Board of Governors of the Federal Reserve System, "Federal Reserve Statistical Release, Z.1, Flow of Funds Accounts of the United States," March, 2010, <http://www.federalreserve.gov/releases/z1/20100311/>.

Table 675. Government Consumption Expenditures and Gross Investment by Level of Government and Type: 2000 to 2009

[In billions of dollars (1,731.0 represents $1,731,000,000,000). Government consumption expenditures are services (such as education and national defense) produced by government that are valued at their cost of production. Excludes government sales to other sectors and government own-account investment (construction and software). Gross government investment consists of general government and government enterprise expenditures for fixed assets; inventory investment is included in government consumption expenditures. For explanation of national income and chained dollars, see text, Section 13]

Item	Current Dollars				Chained (2005) dollars			
	2000	2005	2008	2009	2000	2005	2008	2009
Government consumption expenditures and gross investment, total	1,731.0	2,369.9	2,883.2	2,930.7	2,097.8	2,369.9	2,518.1	2,564.6
Consumption expenditures	1,426.6	1,977.9	2,386.9	2,416.9	1,750.6	1,977.9	2,085.9	2,124.1
Gross investment...................	304.3	392.0	496.3	513.8	347.5	392.0	432.1	440.3
Structures	189.6	246.5	315.5	329.7	239.4	246.5	255.4	260.3
Equipment and software	114.7	145.5	180.8	184.1	109.8	145.5	178.7	181.9
Federal	576.1	876.3	1,082.6	1,144.8	698.1	876.3	975.9	1,026.6
Consumption expenditures	496.0	765.8	934.4	986.4	616.4	765.8	835.1	876.0
Gross investment......................	80.1	110.5	148.2	158.4	82.0	110.5	141.4	151.5
Structures	13.7	15.7	24.6	30.1	17.2	15.7	20.9	25.4
Equipment and software	66.4	94.7	123.6	128.4	65.2	94.7	120.5	125.6
National defense	371.0	589.0	737.9	779.0	453.5	589.0	659.4	695.0
Consumption expenditures	321.8	514.8	634.0	666.6	403.9	514.8	561.6	589.3
Gross investment.....................	49.2	74.2	103.9	112.4	50.3	74.2	98.4	106.6
Structures	5.4	7.5	12.9	16.7	6.9	7.5	11.0	14.2
Equipment and software	43.8	66.8	91.0	95.7	43.6	66.8	87.2	91.9
Nondefense	205.0	287.3	344.7	365.8	244.4	287.3	316.4	331.5
Consumption expenditures	174.2	251.0	300.4	319.7	212.4	251.0	273.5	286.7
Gross investment.....................	30.9	36.3	44.3	46.1	31.6	36.3	43.0	44.8
Structures	8.3	8.3	11.7	13.3	10.4	8.3	9.9	11.2
Equipment and software	22.6	28.0	32.5	32.7	21.5	28.0	33.2	33.5
State and local........................	1,154.9	1,493.6	1,800.6	1,785.9	1,400.1	1,493.6	1,543.7	1,541.0
Consumption expenditures	930.6	1,212.0	1,452.4	1,430.5	1,133.7	1,212.0	1,251.5	1,249.4
Gross investment.....................	224.3	281.6	348.2	355.4	266.6	281.6	292.3	291.3
Structures	176.0	230.8	290.9	299.6	222.2	230.8	234.6	235.2
Equipment and software	48.3	50.8	57.3	55.7	44.3	50.8	58.0	56.1

Source: U.S. Bureau of Economic Analysis, *Survey of Current Business*, April 2010. See also <http://www.bea.gov/national/nipaweb/SelectTable.asp?Selected=N>.

U.S. Census Bureau, Statistical Abstract of the United States: 2011

Table 676. Personal Consumption Expenditures by Function: 2000 to 2008

[In billions of dollars (6,830.4 represents $6,830,400,000,000). For definition of "chained" dollars, see text, this section]

Function	Current dollars				Chained (2005) dollars			
	2000	2005	2007	2008	2000	2005	2007	2008
Personal consumption expenditures [1]	**6,830.4**	**8,819.0**	**9,826.4**	**10,129.9**	**7,608.1**	**8,819.0**	**9,313.9**	**9,290.9**
Food and nonalcoholic beverages purchased for off-premises consumption	463.1	569.5	629.9	669.4	519.1	569.5	594.5	593.5
Alcoholic beverages purchased for off-premises consumption	74.0	95.1	109.8	114.5	81.1	95.1	105.8	106.9
Clothing, footwear, and related services	297.3	331.8	359.1	355.6	276.8	331.8	362.5	360.9
Clothing	250.4	280.3	303.9	300.2	230.3	280.3	307.3	306.3
Footwear [2]	46.9	51.5	55.2	55.4	46.6	51.5	55.3	54.6
Housing [1]	1,010.5	1,328.9	1,480.0	1,543.1	1,174.2	1,328.9	1,377.5	1,397.2
Rental of tenant-occupied nonfarm housing [3]	227.9	264.7	311.9	330.3	267.9	264.7	288.9	295.4
Imputed rental of owner-occupied nonfarm housing [4]	768.9	1,044.5	1,143.5	1,186.8	890.7	1,044.5	1,068.9	1,082.2
Household utilities and fuels	204.0	275.0	307.2	327.2	265.4	275.0	274.1	265.8
Water supply and sanitation	50.4	63.6	72.9	77.1	61.9	63.6	66.1	66.0
Electricity, gas, and other fuels	153.5	211.4	234.3	250.2	203.4	211.4	208.0	199.9
Furnishings, household equipment, and routine household maintenance [1]	342.5	423.9	456.2	449.9	332.4	423.9	455.9	446.6
Furniture, furnishings, and floor coverings [5]	114.4	143.0	150.8	143.4	106.2	143.0	154.7	149.6
Household appliances [6]	37.6	47.6	51.0	50.4	36.7	47.6	48.0	46.8
Tools and equipment for house and garden	17.1	22.3	23.5	23.2	17.1	22.3	23.2	23.1
Medical products, appliances, and equipment	191.2	285.5	320.8	324.0	224.0	285.5	304.6	301.3
Pharmaceutical and other medical products [7]	159.0	247.3	277.6	279.4	189.6	247.3	263.1	258.9
Therapeutic appliances and equipment	32.2	38.2	43.2	44.6	34.1	38.2	41.5	42.5
Outpatient services	436.6	636.5	707.3	747.2	490.2	636.5	669.6	691.8
Physician services [8]	229.2	332.4	365.6	381.8	248.7	332.4	347.9	359.5
Dental services	63.6	89.0	99.3	103.5	79.7	89.0	89.8	89.0
Paramedical services	143.8	215.1	242.3	261.9	162.6	215.1	232.1	243.7
Hospital and nursing home services	481.8	679.5	762.3	807.0	592.8	679.5	705.9	724.7
Transportation	798.4	979.3	1,051.6	1,036.5	901.0	979.3	971.6	897.7
Motor vehicles	321.4	361.6	347.8	289.9	311.4	361.6	353.6	300.6
New motor vehicles	210.7	248.9	233.3	184.5	202.8	248.9	237.3	190.5
Net purchases of used motor vehicles	110.7	112.7	114.5	105.4	108.5	112.7	116.3	110.1
Motor vehicle operation [1]	404.0	541.0	620.5	660.4	524.9	541.0	540.4	517.7
Motor vehicle parts and accessories	41.8	48.0	52.5	52.4	45.2	48.0	48.8	46.3
Motor vehicle fuels, lubricants, and fluids	172.9	283.8	343.9	386.4	261.3	283.8	280.9	271.7
Motor vehicle maintenance and repair	127.4	154.9	162.0	158.5	148.7	154.9	150.4	140.3
Public transportation	73.0	76.8	83.3	86.2	72.7	76.8	77.6	74.5
Telephone and facsimile equipment	5.5	7.5	8.7	9.0	3.3	7.5	10.3	11.2
Postal and delivery services	9.9	9.3	9.7	9.5	11.9	9.3	8.9	8.2
Recreation [1]	639.9	807.4	906.5	928.0	600.6	807.4	926.7	949.2
Video and audio equipment	83.1	107.8	116.6	117.7	59.1	107.8	143.7	159.1
Information processing equipment	44.1	55.9	65.3	66.3				
Services related to video and audio goods and computers	57.2	75.7	87.9	92.2	66.9	75.7	83.6	85.6
Sports and recreational goods and related services	147.9	188.4	209.3	211.5	135.6	188.4	214.4	216.1
Membership clubs, sports centers, parks, theaters, and museums	91.9	110.6	125.1	128.3	106.9	110.6	117.0	116.9
Magazines, newspapers, books, and stationery	81.0	93.1	103.4	105.6	84.8	93.1	101.4	101.5
Pets, pet products, and related services	39.7	53.1	61.6	65.1	45.8	53.1	56.9	55.7
Education [1]	134.3	180.7	206.8	220.8	188.2	180.7	183.8	185.4
Higher education	76.8	108.8	125.0	135.0	109.9	108.8	110.2	112.1
Food services	354.9	455.3	507.9	525.2	408.0	455.3	474.7	470.3
Accommodations [9]	55.2	70.0	80.0	83.5	62.4	70.0	72.9	75.1
Financial services	370.0	427.2	515.1	520.9	405.0	427.2	485.1	473.8
Insurance	199.9	285.4	309.2	314.7	259.6	285.4	287.3	286.0
Personal care [10]	132.2	169.1	189.5	198.8	142.8	169.1	180.5	184.0
Personal items [11]	63.7	72.6	80.4	78.9	57.3	72.6	74.0	67.0
Social services and religious activities [12]	85.0	118.7	135.9	144.4	98.7	118.7	127.4	131.4
Legal services	65.4	89.7	102.1	102.9	81.7	89.7	93.9	91.0
Funeral and burial services	15.8	19.0	18.5	18.7	19.2	19.0	16.7	16.1
Tobacco	68.5	71.1	75.1	77.1	80.3	71.1	68.1	65.9
Net foreign travel and expenditures abroad by U.S. residents [1]	−13.3	−0.1	−3.2	−13.5	−3.0	−0.1	−5.7	−18.3
Foreign travel by U.S. residents	84.3	99.8	114.0	118.8	106.8	99.8	102.7	99.0
Less: Expenditures in the United States by nonresidents	100.8	104.9	123.3	138.6	115.0	104.9	113.2	121.3

NA Not available. [1] Includes other expenditures not shown separately. [2] Consists of shoes and other footwear, and of repair and hire of footwear. [3] Consists of space rent (see footnote 4) and rent for appliances, furnishings, and furniture. [4] Consists of rent for space and for heating and plumbing facilities, water heaters, lighting fixtures, kitchen cabinets, linoleum, storm windows and doors, window screens, and screen doors, but excludes rent for appliances and furniture and purchases of fuel and electricity. [5] Includes clocks, lamps, lighting fixtures, and other household decorative items; also includes repair of furniture, furnishings, and floor coverings. [6] Consists of major household appliances, small electric household appliances, and repair of household appliances. [7] Excludes drug preparations and related products dispensed by physicians, hospitals, and other medical services. [8] Consists of offices of physicians, health maintenance organization medical centers, and freestanding ambulatory surgical and emergency centers. [9] Consists of transient hotels, motels, other traveler accommodations, clubs, and housing at schools. [10] Consists of cosmetics and toiletries, electric appliances for personal care, hairdressing salons, and miscellaneous personal care services. [11] Consists of jewelry, watches, luggage, and similar personal items. [12] Consists of household purchases of goods and services from business, government, and nonprofit institutions providing social services and religious activities. Purchases from nonprofit establishments exclude unrelated sales, secondary sales, and sales to businesses, government, and the rest of the world, but include membership dues and fees.

Source: U.S. Bureau of Economic Analysis, *Survey of Current Business*, April 2010. See also <http://www.bea.gov/national/nipaweb/SelectTable.asp?Selected=N>.

Table 677. Personal Income and Its Disposition: 1990 to 2009

[In billions of dollars (4,847 represents $4,847,000,000,000), except as indicated. For definition of personal income and chained dollars, see text, this section]

Item	1990	2000	2004	2005	2006	2007	2008	2009
Personal income	**4,847**	**8,559**	**9,937**	**10,486**	**11,268**	**11,894**	**12,239**	**12,026**
Compensation of employees, received	3,326	5,789	6,708	7,060	7,476	7,863	8,042	7,787
Wage and salary disbursements	2,741	4,828	5,426	5,701	6,069	6,409	6,546	6,284
Supplements to wages and salaries	585	961	1,283	1,359	1,407	1,454	1,497	1,503
Proprietors' income [1]	365	818	1,034	1,070	1,133	1,096	1,106	1,041
Farm	32	30	50	44	29	39	49	29
Nonfarm	333	788	984	1,026	1,104	1,057	1,058	1,012
Rental income of persons [1]	50	215	198	178	147	145	210	268
Personal income receipts on assets	921	1,361	1,409	1,542	1,830	2,032	1,994	1,793
Personal interest income	752	984	860	987	1,128	1,266	1,308	1,239
Personal dividend income	169	377	548	555	702	765	686	554
Personal current transfer receipts	595	1,083	1,416	1,509	1,605	1,718	1,876	2,105
Government social benefits to persons	573	1,041	1,399	1,483	1,584	1,688	1,843	2,072
Old-age, survivors, disability, and health insurance benefits	352	621	790	845	943	1,004	1,070	1,157
Other current transfer receipts, from business (net)	22	42	17	26	21	30	33	33
Less: Contributions for government social insurance	410	706	827	873	922	959	991	967
Less: Personal current taxes	*593*	*1,232*	*1,048*	*1,209*	*1,352*	*1,491*	*1,432*	*1,103*
Equals: Disposable personal income	**4,254**	**7,327**	**8,889**	**9,277**	**9,916**	**10,403**	**10,806**	**10,924**
Less: Personal outlays	*3,977*	*7,114*	*8,586*	*9,150*	*9,681*	*10,224*	*10,520*	*10,459*
Personal consumption expenditures	3,836	6,830	8,285	8,819	9,323	9,826	10,130	10,089
Personal interest payments [2]	111	200	190	211	230	257	238	214
Personal current transfer payments	31	83	110	120	128	141	152	156
Equals: Personal saving	**277**	**213**	**304**	**128**	**235**	**179**	**286**	**465**
Personal saving as a percentage of disposable personal income	6.5	2.9	3.4	1.4	2.4	1.7	2.7	4.3
Addenda:								
Disposable personal income:								
Total, billions of chained (2005) dollars	5,896	8,162	9,155	9,277	9,651	9,861	9,911	9,999
Per capita:								
Current dollars	17,004	25,944	30,287	31,318	33,157	34,445	35,450	35,526
Chained (2005) dollars	23,568	28,899	31,193	31,318	32,271	32,648	32,514	32,519

[1] With inventory valuation adjustments and capital consumption adjustment. [2] Consists of nonmortgage interest paid by households.

Source: U.S. Bureau of Economic Analysis, *Survey of Current Business,* April 2010. See also <http://www.bea.gov/national/nipaweb/SelectTable.asp?Selected=N>.

Table 678. Selected Per Capita Income and Product Measures in Current and Chained (2005) Dollars: 1960 to 2009

[In dollars. Based on U.S. Census Bureau estimated population including Armed Forces abroad; based on quarterly averages. For explanation of chained dollars, see text, this section]

Year	Current dollars					Chained (2005) dollars				
	Gross domestic product	Gross national product	Personal income	Dispos- able personal income	Personal consump- tion expen- ditures	Gross domestic product	Gross national product	Dispos- able personal income	Personal consump- tion expen- ditures
1960	2,912	2,930	2,275	2,020	1,836	15,661	15,770	10,865	9,871
1970	5,063	5,094	4,089	3,586	3,161	20,820	20,964	15,158	13,361
1975	7,583	7,643	6,180	5,497	4,786	22,592	22,786	17,091	14,881
1980	12,243	12,394	10,107	8,794	7,710	25,640	25,967	18,863	16,538
1985	17,683	17,794	14,661	12,911	11,394	28,717	28,904	21,571	19,037
1990	23,185	23,323	19,373	17,004	15,331	32,112	32,304	23,568	21,249
1992	24,686	24,799	20,813	18,436	16,491	32,255	32,408	23,958	21,430
1993	25,616	25,736	21,393	18,909	17,226	32,747	32,900	24,044	21,904
1994	26,893	26,985	22,299	19,678	18,033	33,671	33,784	24,517	22,466
1995	27,813	27,924	23,260	20,470	18,708	34,112	34,245	24,951	22,803
1996	29,062	29,180	24,439	21,355	19,553	34,977	35,115	25,475	23,325
1997	30,526	30,612	25,648	22,255	20,408	36,102	36,202	26,061	23,899
1998	31,843	31,905	27,251	23,534	21,432	37,238	37,312	27,299	24,861
1999	33,486	33,585	28,321	24,356	22,707	38,592	38,708	27,805	25,923
2000	35,237	35,370	30,308	25,944	24,185	39,750	39,901	28,899	26,939
2001	36,049	36,231	31,133	26,805	25,054	39,768	39,969	29,299	27,385
2002	36,935	37,106	31,444	27,799	25,819	40,096	40,283	29,976	27,841
2003	38,310	38,546	32,244	28,805	26,832	40,711	40,964	30,442	28,357
2004	40,435	40,746	33,857	30,287	28,228	41,784	42,107	31,193	29,072
2005	42,664	42,992	35,398	31,318	29,771	42,664	42,992	31,318	29,771
2006	44,805	45,047	37,679	33,157	31,174	43,391	43,625	32,271	30,341
2007	46,611	46,994	39,381	34,445	32,535	43,884	44,244	32,648	30,838
2008	47,375	47,841	40,149	35,450	33,231	43,671	44,098	32,514	30,479
2009	46,364	46,706	39,112	35,526	32,812	42,238	42,551	32,519	30,034

Source: U.S. Bureau of Economic Analysis, *Survey of Current Business,* April 2010. See also <http://www.bea.gov/national/nipaweb/SelectTable.asp?Selected=N>.

Table 679. Personal Income in Current and Constant (2005) Dollars by State: 2000 to 2009

[In billions of dollars (8,554.9 represents $8,554,900,000,000). Represents a measure of income received from all sources during the calendar year by residents of each state. Data exclude federal employees overseas and U.S. residents employed by private U.S. firms on temporary foreign assignment. Totals may differ from those in Tables 672, 677, and 678]

State	Current dollars					Constant (2005) dollars [1]				
	2000	2005	2007	2008	2009, prel.	2000	2005	2007	2008	2009, prel.
United States	8,554.9	10,476.7	11,879.8	12,225.6	12,015.5	9,529.0	10,476.7	11,260.3	11,212.9	10,998.5
Alabama	107.2	135.6	152.1	157.4	155.8	119.4	135.6	144.2	144.4	142.6
Alaska	19.2	24.6	28.0	30.2	29.8	21.3	24.6	26.6	27.7	27.2
Arizona	135.7	188.2	218.6	223.2	217.2	151.1	188.2	207.2	204.7	198.8
Arkansas	60.5	77.5	89.6	92.5	92.3	67.4	77.5	84.9	84.8	84.5
California	1,135.3	1,387.7	1,572.3	1,604.1	1,564.4	1,264.6	1,387.7	1,490.3	1,471.2	1,432.0
Colorado	147.1	179.7	205.5	212.3	207.7	163.8	179.7	194.8	194.7	190.2
Connecticut	143.0	168.7	194.1	197.0	191.4	159.3	168.7	183.9	180.7	175.2
Delaware	24.4	31.1	34.5	35.4	35.2	27.2	31.1	32.7	32.4	32.3
District of Columbia	23.1	32.2	37.6	39.1	39.6	25.8	32.2	35.6	35.9	36.2
Florida	466.6	633.2	713.5	719.7	700.4	519.8	633.2	676.3	660.1	641.1
Georgia	234.8	292.6	330.0	338.0	332.1	261.6	292.6	312.8	310.0	304.0
Hawaii	35.2	45.3	52.3	54.2	54.4	39.2	45.3	49.5	49.7	49.8
Idaho	32.1	42.2	49.2	50.4	48.9	35.7	42.2	46.7	46.2	44.8
Illinois............	405.9	472.2	533.2	546.3	534.6	452.1	472.2	505.4	501.1	489.4
Indiana............	167.3	195.6	213.9	220.7	216.6	186.3	195.6	202.7	202.4	198.3
Iowa..............	79.9	95.4	106.5	112.3	110.5	89.0	95.4	100.9	103.0	101.2
Kansas............	76.7	90.9	103.8	108.8	106.9	85.4	90.9	98.4	99.8	97.8
Kentucky	100.4	119.0	132.2	136.9	137.5	111.8	119.0	125.3	125.6	125.9
Louisiana	105.3	135.3	154.7	160.7	159.5	117.3	135.3	146.6	147.4	146.0
Maine.............	34.1	42.0	46.1	48.0	48.4	38.0	42.0	43.7	44.0	44.3
Maryland	184.2	237.5	264.4	272.5	275.2	205.1	237.5	250.6	250.0	251.9
Massachusetts........	243.1	282.4	322.7	333.0	328.9	270.8	282.4	305.8	305.5	301.0
Michigan	292.6	325.7	343.6	349.6	339.2	325.9	325.7	325.7	320.7	310.5
Minnesota	160.8	193.9	216.4	224.7	218.8	179.1	193.9	205.1	206.1	200.3
Mississippi	61.4	77.8	86.3	89.3	88.9	68.4	77.8	81.8	81.9	81.3
Missouri............	156.4	186.7	207.6	216.5	213.6	174.2	186.7	196.7	198.6	195.5
Montana............	21.2	28.2	32.5	33.5	33.2	23.6	28.2	30.8	30.7	30.3
Nebraska............	49.0	60.1	67.1	69.8	68.4	54.6	60.1	63.6	64.0	62.6
Nevada	62.5	91.8	105.1	107.1	102.0	69.7	91.8	99.6	98.2	93.3
New Hampshire.......	42.3	50.0	56.2	57.4	56.7	47.1	50.0	53.3	52.6	51.9
New Jersey	326.0	379.9	434.9	445.9	438.1	363.1	379.9	412.3	409.0	401.0
New Mexico..........	41.4	55.3	63.2	66.3	66.3	46.1	55.3	59.9	60.8	60.7
New York	657.9	786.6	925.1	950.2	917.6	732.8	786.6	876.8	871.5	839.9
North Carolina........	225.5	277.7	316.0	326.0	323.2	251.2	277.7	299.5	299.0	295.8
North Dakota.........	16.4	20.6	23.4	25.6	25.6	18.3	20.6	22.2	23.5	23.4
Ohio..............	326.1	372.1	405.2	413.7	408.4	363.2	372.1	384.1	379.5	373.8
Oklahoma	85.0	107.6	123.9	131.1	130.0	94.7	107.6	117.4	120.2	119.0
Oregon............	98.5	117.7	133.4	137.6	136.4	109.7	117.7	126.4	126.2	124.9
Pennsylvania	369.9	432.0	485.1	499.7	498.9	412.0	432.0	459.8	458.3	456.6
Rhode Island	31.0	38.6	42.4	43.5	43.2	34.5	38.6	40.1	39.9	39.5
South Carolina........	100.9	124.4	141.2	146.3	145.0	112.4	124.4	133.9	134.2	132.8
South Dakota........	20.0	25.8	29.0	31.1	30.0	22.2	25.8	27.5	28.5	27.5
Tennessee	152.2	187.6	210.8	217.4	214.6	169.6	187.6	199.8	199.4	196.5
Texas..............	597.0	756.7	878.1	918.9	904.2	665.0	756.7	832.3	842.8	827.6
Utah..............	55.0	71.5	84.7	87.4	86.0	61.3	71.5	80.3	80.2	78.7
Vermont............	17.2	20.7	23.4	24.0	23.9	19.1	20.7	22.2	22.0	21.9
Virginia............	224.8	294.2	333.2	343.6	345.8	250.4	294.2	315.8	315.1	316.6
Washington	191.6	230.0	271.0	280.7	278.2	213.4	230.0	256.9	257.4	254.7
West Virginia	40.1	48.1	54.6	57.4	58.6	44.6	48.1	51.7	52.7	53.7
Wisconsin	156.6	186.6	207.2	212.6	208.2	174.4	186.6	196.4	194.9	190.6
Wyoming	14.5	20.0	24.5	25.9	24.9	16.1	20.0	23.2	23.7	22.8

[1] Constant dollar estimates are computed by the U.S. Census Bureau using the national implicit price deflator for personal consumption expenditures from the Bureau of Economic Analysis. Any regional differences in the rate of inflation are not reflected in these constant dollar estimates.

Source: Except as noted, U.S. Bureau of Economic Analysis, *Survey of Current Business,* April 2010, and unpublished data. See also <http://www.bea.gov/regional/spi>.

Table 680. Personal Income Per Capita in Current and Constant (2005) Dollars by State: 2000 to 2009

[In dollars, except as indicated. 2009 preliminary. See headnote, Table 679]

State	Current dollars				Constant (2005) dollars [1]				Income rank	
	2000	2005	2008	2009	2000	2005	2008	2009	2000	2009
United States	**30,318**	**35,424**	**40,166**	**39,138**	**33,770**	**35,424**	**36,839**	**35,896**	(X)	(X)
Alabama	24,069	29,838	33,655	33,096	26,810	29,838	30,867	30,355	44	41
Alaska	30,531	36,764	43,922	42,603	34,008	36,764	40,284	39,074	15	9
Arizona	26,262	31,491	34,339	32,935	29,252	31,491	31,495	30,207	37	43
Arkansas	22,577	27,908	32,257	31,946	25,148	27,908	29,585	29,300	48	45
California	33,398	38,767	43,852	42,325	37,201	38,767	40,220	38,819	8	10
Colorado	33,977	38,555	43,021	41,344	37,846	38,555	39,458	37,919	7	15
Connecticut	41,920	48,503	56,245	54,397	46,693	48,503	51,586	49,891	1	1
Delaware	31,007	37,001	40,375	39,817	34,538	37,001	37,031	36,519	13	17
District of Columbia	40,484	55,268	66,316	66,000	45,094	55,268	60,823	60,533	(X)	(X)
Florida	29,080	35,605	39,064	37,780	32,391	35,605	35,828	34,651	21	24
Georgia	28,531	32,164	34,849	33,786	31,780	32,164	31,962	30,988	26	39
Hawaii	29,071	35,804	42,078	42,009	32,381	35,804	38,593	38,529	22	11
Idaho	24,683	29,606	32,994	31,632	27,494	29,606	30,261	29,012	41	48
Illinois.	32,636	37,255	42,540	41,411	36,352	37,255	39,016	37,981	9	14
Indiana.	27,460	31,279	34,543	33,725	30,587	31,279	31,682	30,932	32	40
Iowa.	27,293	32,331	37,509	36,751	30,401	32,331	34,402	33,707	33	27
Kansas.	28,477	33,136	38,886	37,916	31,720	33,136	35,665	34,775	28	23
Kentucky	24,786	28,446	31,936	31,883	27,608	28,446	29,291	29,242	40	46
Louisiana	23,570	30,086	36,091	35,507	26,254	30,086	33,102	32,566	45	32
Maine.	26,696	32,008	36,368	36,745	29,736	32,008	33,356	33,701	34	28
Maryland	34,681	42,547	48,164	48,285	38,630	42,547	44,175	44,286	4	4
Massachusetts.	38,210	43,770	50,897	49,875	42,561	43,770	46,681	45,744	3	3
Michigan	29,392	32,274	34,953	34,025	32,739	32,274	32,058	31,207	18	37
Minnesota	32,597	37,978	42,953	41,552	36,309	37,978	39,395	38,110	10	13
Mississippi	21,555	26,819	30,383	30,103	24,009	26,819	27,866	27,610	50	50
Missouri.	27,891	32,158	36,356	35,676	31,067	32,158	33,345	32,721	31	30
Montana.	23,470	30,144	34,622	34,004	26,143	30,144	31,754	31,187	46	38
Nebraska	28,598	34,318	39,182	38,081	31,854	34,318	35,937	34,927	25	22
Nevada	30,986	38,117	40,936	38,578	34,514	38,117	37,545	35,383	14	20
New Hampshire	34,087	38,386	43,423	42,831	37,969	38,386	39,826	39,283	6	8
New Jersey	38,666	44,060	51,473	50,313	43,069	44,060	47,210	46,146	2	2
New Mexico.	22,751	28,876	33,389	32,992	25,342	28,876	30,623	30,259	47	42
New York	34,630	40,690	48,809	46,957	38,573	40,690	44,766	43,068	5	5
North Carolina	27,914	32,035	35,249	34,453	31,093	32,035	32,329	31,599	30	35
North Dakota	25,624	32,346	39,874	39,530	28,542	32,346	36,571	36,256	38	19
Ohio.	28,694	32,429	35,889	35,381	31,961	32,429	32,916	32,450	24	33
Oklahoma	24,605	30,469	35,969	35,268	27,407	30,469	32,990	32,347	42	34
Oregon.	28,718	32,525	36,365	35,667	31,988	32,525	33,353	32,713	23	31
Pennsylvania	30,110	34,791	39,762	39,578	33,550	34,791	36,469	36,300	16	18
Rhode Island	29,484	36,214	41,261	41,003	32,841	36,214	37,843	37,607	17	16
South Carolina	25,081	29,223	32,495	31,799	27,937	29,223	29,803	29,165	39	47
South Dakota.	26,427	33,117	38,644	36,935	29,436	33,117	35,443	33,876	36	25
Tennessee	26,691	31,294	34,833	34,089	29,730	31,294	31,948	31,265	35	36
Texas	28,504	33,185	37,809	36,484	31,750	33,185	34,677	33,462	27	29
Utah.	24,517	28,617	32,050	30,875	27,309	28,617	29,395	28,318	43	49
Vermont.	28,183	33,441	38,700	38,503	31,392	33,441	35,494	35,314	29	21
Virginia.	31,640	38,892	44,075	43,874	35,243	38,892	40,424	40,240	12	7
Washington	32,407	36,734	42,747	41,751	36,097	36,734	39,206	38,293	11	12
West Virginia	22,174	26,686	31,634	32,219	24,699	26,686	29,014	29,550	49	44
Wisconsin	29,139	33,673	37,770	36,822	32,457	33,673	34,642	33,772	20	26
Wyoming	29,281	39,446	48,580	45,705	32,615	39,446	44,556	41,919	19	6

X Not applicable. [1] Constant dollar estimates are computed by the U.S. Census Bureau using the national implicit price deflator for personal consumption expenditures from the Bureau of Economic Analysis. Any regional differences in the rate of inflation are not reflected in these constant dollar estimates.

Source: Except as noted, U.S. Bureau of Economic Analysis, *Survey of Current Business,* April 2010, and unpublished data. See also <http://www.bea.gov/bea/regional/spi>.

Table 681. Disposable Personal Income Per Capita in Current and Constant (2005) Dollars by State: 2000 to 2009

[In dollars, except percent. 2009 preliminary. Disposable personal income is the income available to persons for spending or saving; it is calculated as personal income less personal tax and nontax payments. See headnote, Table 679]

State	Current dollars				Constant (2005) dollars [1]				Index, compared to U.S. average	
	2000	2005	2008	2009, prel.	2000	2005	2008	2009, prel.	2000	2009, prel.
United States	**25,955**	**31,342**	**35,464**	**35,553**	**28,911**	**31,342**	**32,527**	**32,544**	**100.0**	**100.0**
Alabama	21,357	27,027	30,438	30,597	23,789	27,027	27,917	28,007	82.3	86.1
Alaska	27,101	33,567	39,945	39,416	30,187	33,567	36,636	36,080	104.4	110.9
Arizona	22,939	28,159	30,964	30,456	25,551	28,159	28,399	27,878	88.4	85.7
Arkansas	20,034	25,344	29,239	29,536	22,315	25,344	26,817	27,036	77.2	83.1
California	27,664	33,811	38,307	38,127	30,814	33,811	35,134	34,900	106.6	107.2
Colorado	28,857	34,161	37,828	37,418	32,143	34,161	34,695	34,251	111.2	105.2
Connecticut	33,837	40,649	46,592	47,154	37,690	40,649	42,733	43,163	130.4	132.6
Delaware	26,427	32,252	35,580	36,097	29,436	32,252	32,633	33,042	101.8	101.5
District of Columbia	33,459	47,829	57,471	59,056	37,269	47,829	52,711	54,057	128.9	166.1
Florida	25,392	31,726	35,172	34,880	28,283	31,726	32,259	31,928	97.8	98.1
Georgia	24,606	28,660	31,093	30,926	27,408	28,660	28,518	28,308	94.8	87.0
Hawaii	25,495	31,764	37,647	38,614	28,398	31,764	34,529	35,346	98.2	108.6
Idaho	21,575	26,585	29,670	29,148	24,032	26,585	27,212	26,681	83.1	82.0
Illinois	27,877	32,981	37,425	37,539	31,051	32,981	34,325	34,362	107.4	105.6
Indiana	23,983	28,026	30,875	30,998	26,714	28,026	28,318	28,374	92.4	87.2
Iowa	24,136	29,261	33,752	33,734	26,884	29,261	30,956	30,879	93.0	94.9
Kansas	24,841	29,705	34,555	34,528	27,670	29,705	31,693	31,605	95.7	97.1
Kentucky	21,726	25,468	28,558	29,204	24,200	25,468	26,193	26,732	83.7	82.1
Louisiana	21,073	27,557	32,894	32,953	23,473	27,557	30,169	30,164	81.2	92.7
Maine	23,227	28,676	32,665	33,859	25,872	28,676	29,959	30,993	89.5	95.2
Maryland	29,231	36,854	41,642	43,125	32,560	36,854	38,193	39,475	112.6	121.3
Massachusetts	30,786	37,559	43,306	44,163	34,292	37,559	39,719	40,425	118.6	124.2
Michigan	25,285	28,916	31,343	31,309	28,164	28,916	28,747	28,659	97.4	88.1
Minnesota	27,780	33,291	37,599	37,493	30,943	33,291	34,485	34,319	107.0	105.5
Mississippi	19,491	24,806	27,994	28,221	21,710	24,806	25,675	25,832	75.1	79.4
Missouri	24,335	28,880	32,487	32,623	27,106	28,880	29,796	29,862	93.8	91.8
Montana	20,781	27,192	31,035	31,123	23,147	27,192	28,464	28,489	80.1	87.5
Nebraska	25,070	30,997	35,159	34,824	27,925	30,997	32,247	31,876	96.6	97.9
Nevada	26,882	33,735	36,804	35,611	29,943	33,735	33,756	32,597	103.6	100.2
New Hampshire	29,273	34,536	38,988	39,436	32,606	34,536	35,759	36,098	112.8	110.9
New Jersey	32,333	38,153	44,397	44,893	36,015	38,153	40,720	41,093	124.6	126.3
New Mexico	20,200	26,242	30,299	30,604	22,500	26,242	27,789	28,014	77.8	86.1
New York	28,623	34,601	40,909	41,068	31,882	34,601	37,521	37,592	110.3	115.5
North Carolina	24,253	28,545	31,258	31,443	27,015	28,545	28,669	28,782	93.4	88.4
North Dakota	23,121	29,681	36,272	36,496	25,754	29,681	33,268	33,407	89.1	102.7
Ohio	24,757	28,738	31,875	32,255	27,576	28,738	29,235	29,525	95.4	90.7
Oklahoma	21,723	27,435	32,248	32,370	24,197	27,435	29,577	29,630	83.7	91.0
Oregon	24,536	28,503	31,798	32,246	27,330	28,503	29,164	29,517	94.5	90.7
Pennsylvania	25,999	30,792	35,041	35,861	28,960	30,792	32,139	32,826	100.2	100.9
Rhode Island	25,340	32,137	36,659	37,460	28,225	32,137	33,623	34,289	97.6	105.4
South Carolina	22,165	26,365	29,312	29,386	24,689	26,365	26,884	26,899	85.4	82.7
South Dakota	23,881	30,619	35,527	34,483	26,600	30,619	32,584	31,564	92.0	97.0
Tennessee	24,011	28,802	31,976	31,964	26,745	28,802	29,327	29,258	92.5	89.9
Texas	25,166	30,175	34,281	33,818	28,032	30,175	31,442	30,956	97.0	95.1
Utah	21,454	25,555	28,585	28,188	23,897	25,555	26,217	25,802	82.7	79.3
Vermont	24,523	29,910	34,443	35,232	27,315	29,910	31,590	32,250	94.5	99.1
Virginia	26,780	33,965	38,596	39,502	29,829	33,965	35,399	36,158	103.2	111.1
Washington	27,951	33,207	38,447	38,472	31,134	33,207	35,262	35,216	107.7	108.2
West Virginia	19,815	24,249	28,703	29,790	22,071	24,249	26,326	27,268	76.3	83.8
Wisconsin	25,078	29,873	33,433	33,452	27,934	29,873	30,664	30,621	96.6	94.1
Wyoming	25,330	35,371	42,827	41,382	28,214	35,371	39,280	37,879	97.6	116.4

[1] Constant dollar estimates are computed by the Census Bureau using the national implicit price deflator for personal consumption expenditures from the Bureau of Economic Analysis. Any regional differences in the rate of inflation are not reflected in these constant dollar estimates.

Source: Except as noted, U.S. Bureau of Economic Analysis, *Survey of Current Business,* April 2010, earlier reports and unpublished data. See also <http://www.bea.gov/regional/spi>.

Table 682. Personal Income by Selected Large Metropolitan Area: 2005 to 2008

[10,476,669 represents $10,476,669,000,000. Metropolitan areas as defined November 2009. MSA = Metropolitan Statistical Area. See Appendix II. Minus sign (–) indicates decrease]

Metropolitan areas ranked by 2008 population	Personal income (mil. dol.)				Personal income per capita			
	2005 (mil. dol.)	2007 (mil. dol.)	2008 (mil. dol.)	Annual percent change, 2007– 2008	2005 (dol.)	2007 (dol.)	2008 (dol.)	Index (U.S.= 100), 2008
United States	10,476,669	11,879,836	12,225,589	2.9	35,424	39,392	40,166	100.0
New York-Northern New Jersey-Long Island, NY-NJ-PA MSA	863,820	1,018,093	1,041,636	2.3	45,952	53,864	54,914	136.7
Los Angeles-Long Beach-Santa Ana, CA MSA.	496,602	555,946	568,435	2.2	38,915	43,801	44,519	110.8
Chicago-Joliet-Naperville, IL-IN-WI MSA . . .	375,515	423,953	431,795	1.8	40,110	44,854	45,377	113.0
Dallas-Fort Worth-Arlington, TX MSA	220,483	254,067	262,549	3.3	37,907	41,267	41,667	103.7
Philadelphia-Camden-Wilmington, PA-NJ-DE-MD MSA.	236,441	265,838	272,829	2.6	40,413	44,961	45,927	114.3
Houston-Sugar Land-Baytown, TX MSA	209,656	248,161	262,484	5.8	39,561	44,333	45,835	114.1
Miami-Fort Lauderdale-Pompano Beach, FL MSA	210,606	234,822	236,645	0.8	38,692	42,967	43,013	107.1
Atlanta-Sandy Springs-Marietta, GA MSA . .	179,151	203,961	206,463	1.2	36,214	38,721	38,336	95.4
Washington-Arlington-Alexandria, DC-VA-MD-WV MSA	262,168	296,134	305,595	3.2	50,135	55,737	56,824	141.5
Boston-Cambridge-Quincy, MA-NH MSA . . .	212,287	243,740	250,811	2.9	47,610	54,117	55,187	137.4
Detroit-Warren-Livonia, MI MSA	164,081	170,963	172,649	1.0	36,508	38,362	39,028	97.2
Phoenix-Mesa-Glendale, AZ MSA	131,597	153,131	155,014	1.2	33,877	36,673	36,156	90.0
San Francisco-Oakland-Fremont, CA MSA. .	227,853	263,201	266,680	1.3	54,910	62,634	62,598	155.8
Riverside-San Bernardino-Ontario, CA MSA.	108,599	122,811	125,379	2.1	28,125	30,332	30,634	76.3
Seattle-Tacoma-Bellevue, WA MSA.	138,212	164,759	169,798	3.1	43,159	49,816	50,586	125.9
Minneapolis-St. Paul-Bloomington, MN-WI MSA.	133,835	150,181	154,282	2.7	42,721	46,870	47,653	118.6
San Diego-Carlsbad-San Marcos, CA MSA.	122,033	136,616	140,847	3.1	41,483	45,911	46,649	116.1
St. Louis, MO-IL MSA	101,080	112,948	117,886	4.4	36,449	40,247	41,823	104.1
Tampa-St. Petersburg-Clearwater, FL MSA. .	91,394	101,211	102,407	1.2	34,634	37,331	37,512	93.4
Baltimore-Towson, MD MSA	111,491	124,418	128,213	3.1	42,079	46,604	47,881	119.2
Denver-Aurora-Broomfield, CO MSA.	101,789	116,354	120,044	3.2	43,250	47,501	48,010	119.5
Pittsburgh, PA MSA	84,947	95,780	99,172	3.5	35,808	40,634	42,104	104.8
Portland-Vancouver-Hillsboro, OR-WA MSA	74,753	85,339	88,022	3.1	35,869	39,443	39,942	99.4
Cincinnati-Middletown, OH-KY-IN MSA.	75,149	82,568	84,330	2.1	35,744	38,434	39,066	97.3
Sacramento-Arden-Arcade-Roseville, CA MSA.	75,038	84,193	86,397	2.6	36,989	40,572	41,119	102.4
Cleveland-Elyria-Mentor, OH MSA	76,115	82,646	84,009	1.6	35,933	39,370	40,118	99.9
Orlando-Kissimmee-Sanford, FL MSA	64,007	72,381	73,612	1.7	32,997	35,570	35,717	88.9
Kansas City, MO-KS MSA.	70,738	80,154	82,653	3.1	36,119	39,841	40,396	100.6
San Antonio-New Braunfels, TX MSA	58,670	68,213	70,047	1.0	31,235	34,368	34,937	87.0
Las Vegas-Paradise, NV MSA	64,175	73,444	75,013	2.1	37,555	39,945	39,920	99.4
San Jose-Sunnyvale-Santa Clara, CA MSA.	89,628	105,576	105,979	0.4	51,590	59,365	58,531	145.7
Columbus, OH MSA	60,969	67,204	68,952	2.6	35,562	38,198	38,741	96.5
Indianapolis-Carmel, IN MSA	60,018	65,586	67,623	3.1	36,485	38,633	39,297	97.8
Charlotte-Gastonia-Rock Hill, NC-SC MSA. .	57,214	66,218	67,612	2.1	37,655	40,108	39,621	98.6
Virginia Beach-Norfolk-Newport News, VA-NC MSA.	56,594	63,748	65,639	3.0	34,107	38,135	39,300	97.8
Austin-Round Rock-San Marcos, TX MSA . .	51,047	59,758	61,800	3.4	34,861	37,477	37,362	93.0
Providence-New Bedford-Fall River, RI-MA MSA	57,416	63,409	65,391	3.1	35,669	39,643	40,887	101.8
Nashville-Davidson-Murfreesboro-Franklin, TN MSA	52,294	60,049	61,893	3.1	36,052	39,378	39,768	99.0
Milwaukee-Waukesha-West Allis, WI MSA . .	58,252	64,768	66,396	2.5	37,917	41,926	42,824	106.6
Jacksonville, FL MSA	45,618	52,267	52,697	0.8	36,538	40,171	40,028	99.7
Memphis, TN-MS-AR MSA	44,054	49,107	50,094	2.0	34,924	38,050	38,577	96.0
Louisville-Jefferson County, KY-IN MSA	41,223	46,378	47,484	2.4	34,083	37,491	37,995	94.6
Richmond, VA MSA.	44,586	50,735	51,918	2.3	37,978	41,844	42,309	105.3
Oklahoma City, OK MSA	38,462	44,274	46,951	6.0	33,298	37,166	38,882	96.8
Hartford-West Hartford-East Hartford, CT MSA.	51,426	59,198	60,458	2.1	43,635	49,900	50,755	126.4
New Orleans-Metairie-Kenner, LA MSA	43,501	48,912	48,775	–0.3	33,119	44,088	41,740	103.9
Buffalo-Niagara Falls, NY MSA	36,232	40,778	42,317	3.8	31,801	36,216	37,647	93.7
Birmingham-Hoover, AL MSA	39,198	43,734	44,798	2.4	35,947	39,299	39,886	99.3
Salt Lake City, UT MSA.	35,347	41,551	42,505	2.3	33,830	38,030	38,237	95.2
Raleigh-Cary, NC MSA	35,209	41,897	43,182	3.1	36,939	40,059	39,602	98.6
Rochester, NY MSA.	35,255	39,852	41,132	3.2	34,114	38,635	39,812	99.1
Tucson, AZ MSA	28,574	33,112	34,393	3.9	30,111	33,225	34,058	84.8
Tulsa, OK MSA	30,734	35,796	37,540	4.9	34,860	39,524	40,981	102.0
Fresno, CA MSA	24,078	27,117	27,994	3.2	27,758	30,472	30,997	77.2
Honolulu, HI MSA	34,264	39,258	40,809	4.0	38,057	43,683	45,205	112.5
Bridgeport-Stamford-Norwalk, CT MSA	60,934	70,748	70,754	(Z)	68,387	79,576	79,108	197.0
Albany-Schenectady-Troy, NY MSA	30,671	34,883	36,327	4.1	36,239	40,941	42,523	105.9
Albuquerque, NM MSA	25,338	28,883	29,982	3.8	31,723	34,604	35,415	88.2
New Haven-Milford, CT MSA.	33,857	38,551	39,673	2.9	40,335	45,697	46,918	116.8
Omaha-Council Bluffs, NE-IA MSA.	31,080	34,979	36,098	3.2	38,347	42,185	43,012	107.1

Source: U.S. Bureau of Economic Analysis, *Survey of Current Business*, April 2010. See also <http://www.bea.gov/regional /reis>.

Table 683. Average Annual Expenditures of All Consumer Units by Selected Major Types of Expenditure: 1990 to 2008

[In dollars, except as indicated (96,968 represents $96,968,000). Based on Consumer Expenditure Survey. Data are averages for the noninstitutional population. Expenditures reported here are out-of-pocket. Consumer units include families, single prsons living alone or sharing a household with others but who are financially independent, or two or more persons living together who share expenses]

Type of expenditure	1990	1995	2000	2004	2005	2006	2007	2008
Number of consumer units (1,000)	96,968	103,123	109,367	116,282	117,356	118,843	120,171	120,770
Expenditures, total [1] (dol.).	**28,381**	**32,264**	**38,045**	**43,395**	**46,409**	**48,398**	**49,638**	**50,486**
Food	4,296	4,505	5,158	5,781	5,931	6,111	6,133	6,443
Food at home [1]	2,485	2,803	3,021	3,347	3,297	3,417	3,465	3,744
Meats, poultry, fish, and eggs	668	752	795	880	764	797	777	846
Dairy products	295	297	325	371	378	368	387	430
Fruits and vegetables	408	457	521	561	552	592	600	657
Other food at home	746	856	927	1,075	1,158	1,212	1,241	1,305
Food away from home	1,811	1,702	2,137	2,434	2,634	2,694	2,668	2,698
Alcoholic beverages.	293	277	372	459	426	497	457	444
Housing [1]	8,703	10,458	12,319	13,918	15,167	16,366	16,920	17,109
Shelter	4,836	5,928	7,114	7,998	8,805	9,673	10,023	10,183
Utilities, fuels, and public services.	1,890	2,191	2,489	2,927	3,183	3,397	3,477	3,649
Apparel and services.	1,618	1,704	1,856	1,816	1,886	1,874	1,881	1,801
Transportation [1]	5,120	6,014	7,417	7,801	8,344	8,508	8,758	8,604
Vehicle purchases	2,129	2,638	3,418	3,397	3,544	3,421	3,244	2,755
Gasoline and motor oil.	1,047	1,006	1,291	1,598	2,013	2,227	2,384	2,715
Other vehicle expenses	1,642	2,015	2,281	2,365	2,339	2,355	2,592	2,621
Health care	1,480	1,732	2,066	2,574	2,664	2,766	2,853	2,976
Entertainment	1,422	1,612	1,863	2,218	2,388	2,376	2,698	2,835
Reading.	153	162	146	130	126	117	118	116
Tobacco products, smoking supplies.	274	269	319	288	319	327	323	317
Personal insurance and pensions	2,592	2,964	3,365	4,823	5,204	5,270	5,336	5,605
Life and other personal insurance	345	373	399	390	381	322	309	317
Pensions and Social Security	2,248	2,591	2,966	4,433	4,823	4,948	5,027	5,288

[1] Includes expenditures not shown separately.

Source: U.S. Bureau of Labor Statistics, *Consumer Expenditures in 2008*, News Release, USDL-09-1208, October 2009. See also <http://stats.bls.gov/cex/home.htm>.

Table 684. Average Annual Expenditures of All Consumer Units by Metropolitan Area: 2007 to 2008

[In dollars. Covers 2-year period, 2007–2008. Metropolitan areas defined June 30, 1983: CMSA = Consolidated Metropolitan Statistical Area; MSA = Metropolitan Statistical Area; PMSA = Primary Metropolitan Statistical Area. See text, Section 1 and Appendix II. See headnote, Table 683]

Metropolitan area	Total expenditures [1]	Food	Housing Total [1]	Housing Shelter	Housing Utility, fuels [2]	Transportation Total [1]	Transportation Vehicle purchases	Transportation Gasoline and motor oil	Health care
Atlanta, GA MSA	46,667	6,005	17,275	10,925	3,811	7,316	2,101	2,821	2,383
Baltimore, MD MSA	52,543	5,979	20,255	12,904	4,170	7,793	2,396	2,665	2,571
Boston-Lawrence-Salem, MA-NH CMSA . .	55,954	7,446	20,677	13,051	4,067	8,067	2,572	2,224	2,936
Chicago-Gary-Lake County, IL-IN-WI CMSA	57,930	7,155	20,830	13,034	4,062	8,947	3,075	2,547	3,324
Cleveland-Akron-Lorain, OH CMSA	48,571	5,659	16,933	9,761	3,839	8,365	2,995	2,384	3,651
Dallas-Fort Worth, TX CMSA	52,985	6,217	17,737	9,876	4,307	10,140	4,196	2,733	2,787
Detroit-Ann Arbor, MI CMSA	48,149	6,899	15,866	9,472	3,654	9,200	2,242	2,946	2,432
Houston-Galveston-Brazoria, TX CMSA . . .	55,703	6,837	18,059	10,359	4,332	10,880	4,070	3,274	3,002
Los Angeles-Long Beach, CA PMSA	59,131	7,641	22,645	15,521	3,364	9,227	2,883	2,913	2,512
Miami-Fort Lauderdale, FL CMSA	47,079	5,629	18,459	12,095	3,576	8,506	3,049	2,863	1,933
Minneapolis-St. Paul, MN-WI MSA	58,246	7,121	19,842	11,718	3,482	9,678	3,950	2,432	3,365
New York-Northern New Jersey-Long Island, NY-NJ-CT CMSA	59,185	7,223	23,441	15,472	4,146	8,249	2,102	2,051	2,829
Philadelphia-Wilmington-Trenton, PA-NJ-DE-MD CMSA	55,706	6,107	20,870	12,637	4,356	8,658	2,455	2,447	2,682
Phoenix-Mesa, AZ MSA	56,847	6,401	19,492	11,711	3,874	11,630	5,074	2,957	3,195
San Diego, CA MSA	51,159	5,556	22,562	15,761	2,861	6,556	1,429	2,593	1,840
San Francisco-Oakland-San Jose, CA CMSA	68,966	8,393	26,111	18,800	3,204	10,591	2,973	2,589	3,321
Seattle-Tacoma, WA CMSA	63,565	7,296	21,515	13,890	3,485	9,643	3,113	2,608	3,373
Washington, DC-MD-VA MSA	70,611	8,144	26,128	17,167	4,001	10,452	3,492	2,666	2,996

[1] Includes expenditures not shown separately. [2] Includes public services.

Source: U.S. Bureau of Labor Statistics, *Consumer Expenditures in 2008*, News Release, USDL-09-1208, October 2009. See also <http://stats.bls.gov/cex/home.htm>.

Table 685. Average Annual Expenditures of All Consumer Units by Race, Hispanic Origin, and Age of Householder: 2008

[In dollars. See headnote, Table 683]

Type	All consumer units [1]	White and all other races	Asian	Black or African American	Hispanic or Latino	Age of householder Under 25 years	Age of householder 65 years old and over
Expenditures, total	**50,486**	**52,265**	**55,430**	**36,721**	**43,052**	**29,325**	**36,844**
Food	6,443	6,676	7,089	4,594	6,596	4,447	4,692
Food at home	3,744	3,865	3,943	2,825	4,039	2,330	3,075
Cereals and bakery products	507	522	562	382	509	281	435
Cereals and cereal products	170	169	256	148	191	103	131
Bakery products	337	353	306	234	318	178	304
Meats, poultry, fish, and eggs [2]	846	839	1,010	848	1,039	573	687
Beef	239	245	200	208	307	165	182
Pork	163	160	193	174	190	108	145
Poultry	159	154	187	190	214	112	112
Fish and seafood	128	118	304	144	152	89	114
Dairy products	430	457	326	263	429	256	362
Fresh milk and cream	168	175	172	116	194	109	136
Other dairy products	261	282	153	147	235	147	225
Fruits and vegetables [2]	657	678	852	447	789	370	577
Fresh fruits	222	231	306	128	284	114	197
Fresh vegetables	212	217	369	130	246	114	184
Processed fruits	116	120	94	98	138	78	106
Other food at home [2]	1,305	1,368	1,193	886	1,274	851	1,015
Sugar and other sweets	129	136	126	80	121	79	121
Nonalcoholic beverages	342	355	316	261	384	246	250
Food away from home	2,698	2,811	3,147	1,768	2,556	2,117	1,617
Alcoholic beverages	444	484	300	205	297	448	251
Housing	17,109	17,456	20,138	13,770	15,582	9,975	12,993
Shelter	10,183	10,345	13,703	7,985	9,688	6,530	6,933
Owned dwellings	6,760	7,095	8,471	3,940	5,334	1,383	4,685
Mortgage interest and charges	3,826	3,951	5,479	2,463	3,525	918	1,288
Property taxes	1,758	1,866	2,168	896	1,217	282	1,766
Maintenance, repair, insurance, other expenses	1,176	1,279	824	581	592	184	1,631
Rented dwellings	2,724	2,484	4,680	3,762	4,065	4,940	1,658
Other lodging	698	766	552	282	289	206	590
Utilities, fuels, and public services	3,649	3,674	3,275	3,598	3,457	1,875	3,314
Natural gas	531	531	536	533	424	211	539
Electricity	1,353	1,351	1,119	1,439	1,305	739	1,232
Fuel oil and other fuels	192	218	[3] 55	58	51	25	279
Telephone	1,127	1,121	1,118	1,168	1,231	732	823
Water and other public services	446	453	447	400	446	167	440
Household operations	998	1,057	931	610	797	326	884
Personal services	383	397	417	279	402	140	218
Other household expenses	614	660	514	331	395	185	667
Housekeeping supplies [2]	654	688	494	461	542	303	627
Laundry and cleaning supplies	148	148	131	153	184	83	115
Postage and stationery	156	168	123	81	107	66	190
Household furnishings and equipment [2]	1,624	1,693	1,735	1,116	1,098	942	1,235
Household textiles	126	129	107	116	93	36	101
Furniture	388	394	393	320	266	204	220
Major appliances	204	215	225	121	164	104	160
Miscellaneous household equipment	749	785	866	458	468	460	579
Apparel and services [2]	1,801	1,767	1,997	1,983	2,119	1,351	1,092
Men and boys	427	425	513	413	468	296	239
Women and girls	718	705	828	778	878	439	487
Footwear	314	292	313	478	395	253	179
Other apparel products and services	248	252	277	214	231	192	159
Transportation	8,604	8,889	9,049	6,520	7,986	5,464	5,620
Vehicle purchases (net outlay) [2]	2,755	2,885	2,414	1,969	2,554	1,988	1,502
Cars and trucks, new	1,305	1,373	1,480	783	802	615	885
Cars and trucks, used	1,315	1,367	905	1,088	1,679	1,114	565
Gasoline and motor oil	2,715	2,790	2,539	2,257	2,717	1,974	1,629
Other vehicle expenses	2,621	2,698	2,815	2,033	2,335	1,273	2,039
Vehicle finance charges	312	319	250	285	316	233	116
Maintenance and repair	731	772	628	476	564	412	555
Vehicle insurance	1,113	1,113	[3] 1,384	1,036	1,078	[3] 427	1,073
Vehicle rental, leases, licenses, other charges	465	494	553	237	378	202	294
Public transportation	513	515	1,280	261	380	229	450
Health care [4]	2,976	3,211	2,233	1,595	1,571	682	4,605
Entertainment [5]	2,835	3,007	3,447	1,478	1,787	1,608	1,914
Personal care products and services	616	630	584	528	545	370	512
Reading	116	127	90	47	38	48	142
Education	1,046	1,096	1,676	508	669	1,691	272
Tobacco products and smoking supplies	317	337	166	223	143	251	161
Miscellaneous	840	884	736	565	586	280	588
Cash contributions	1,737	1,845	1,165	1,171	1,010	427	2,156
Personal insurance and pensions	5,605	5,856	6,760	3,532	4,124	2,283	1,846
Life and other personal insurance	317	325	332	254	116	37	330
Pensions and social security	5,288	5,531	6,428	3,278	4,007	2,246	1,516
Personal taxes	**1,789**	**1,988**	**2,389**	**240**	**362**	**219**	**500**

[1] Includes other races, not shown separately. [2] Includes other types not shown separately. [3] Data are likely to have large sampling errors. [4] For additional health care expenditures, see Table 139. [5] For additional recreation expenditures, see Section 26.

Source: U.S. Bureau of Labor Statistics, *Consumer Expenditures in 2008*, News Release, USDL-09-1208 October 2009. See also <http://www.bls.gov/cex/2008/Standard/race.pdf>; <http://www.bls.gov/cex/2008/Standard/hiopanic.pdf>; and <http://www.bls.gov/cex/2008/Standard/age.pdf>.

Table 686. Average Annual Expenditures of All Consumer Units by Region and Size of Unit: 2008

[In dollars. For composition of regions, see map, inside front cover. See headnote, Table 683]

Type	Region				Size of consumer unit				
	North-east	Mid-west	South	West	One person	Two persons	Three persons	Four persons	Five or more
Expenditures, total	**54,918**	**47,846**	**46,823**	**55,453**	**30,120**	**53,320**	**59,488**	**65,955**	**66,262**
Food	6,959	5,966	6,109	7,037	3,620	6,276	7,598	9,172	9,805
Food at home	4,021	3,528	3,494	4,140	1,975	3,626	4,508	5,279	6,061
Cereals and bakery products	579	483	472	528	262	476	599	754	854
Cereals and cereal products	195	164	152	182	81	154	208	250	313
Bakery products	384	319	320	346	181	321	391	504	541
Meats, poultry, fish, and eggs [1]	920	750	843	888	421	821	1,042	1,153	1,451
Beef	234	223	243	252	110	230	307	317	432
Pork	154	151	174	165	77	162	195	230	274
Poultry	184	135	157	166	78	150	208	216	274
Fish and seafood	167	96	119	143	75	124	149	168	208
Dairy products	461	421	392	473	234	411	507	622	683
Fresh milk and cream	175	160	161	182	92	150	200	252	291
Other dairy products	286	261	231	291	143	261	307	370	392
Fruits and vegetables [1]	725	591	580	792	365	654	791	884	1,007
Fresh fruits	242	199	189	282	122	221	273	299	336
Fresh vegetables	239	175	181	276	118	225	243	272	310
Processed fruits	136	112	104	126	69	106	140	166	186
Other food at home [1]	1,336	1,283	1,207	1,459	693	1,264	1,569	1,866	2,066
Sugar and other sweets	134	139	113	141	68	132	146	175	210
Nonalcoholic beverages	352	315	332	379	179	327	422	497	541
Food away from home	2,938	2,438	2,615	2,897	1,645	2,650	3,090	3,892	3,743
Alcoholic beverages	455	450	389	518	374	527	439	429	402
Housing	19,525	15,550	15,276	19,682	11,507	17,330	19,660	22,266	21,961
Shelter	12,023	8,923	8,479	12,721	7,511	10,143	11,267	13,138	12,513
Owned dwellings	7,889	6,282	5,643	8,130	3,686	6,931	7,824	10,036	9,162
Mortgage interest and charges	3,834	3,218	3,290	5,317	1,811	3,453	4,696	6,549	5,974
Property taxes	2,796	1,924	1,266	1,525	1,025	2,001	1,926	2,295	2,122
Maintenance, repair, insurance, other expenses	1,258	1,140	1,087	1,288	850	1,478	1,201	1,192	1,066
Rented dwellings	3,068	2,000	2,297	3,880	3,480	2,204	2,647	2,398	2,805
Other lodging	1,066	641	539	711	345	1,008	796	704	546
Utilities, fuels, and public services	4,117	3,527	3,661	3,369	2,265	3,798	4,214	4,635	5,050
Natural gas	727	807	297	464	340	560	566	672	759
Electricity	1,302	1,124	1,648	1,154	832	1,393	1,582	1,733	1,896
Fuel oil and other fuels	599	147	83	77	131	260	180	181	177
Telephone	1,134	1,066	1,166	1,121	702	1,118	1,383	1,466	1,561
Water and other public services	355	382	466	554	260	466	503	583	657
Household operations	1,177	863	911	1,128	511	884	1,293	1,667	1,447
Personal services	507	356	336	384	74	176	645	957	804
Other household expenses	670	507	574	744	437	707	649	710	643
Housekeeping supplies [1]	665	678	646	635	347	691	775	910	900
Laundry and cleaning supplies	142	135	156	152	77	140	182	198	257
Postage and stationery	160	169	136	174	114	189	182	172	113
Household furnishings and equipment [1]	1,543	1,559	1,580	1,829	873	1,815	2,111	1,916	2,050
Household textiles	103	103	132	161	60	160	150	168	116
Furniture	419	353	407	366	210	399	542	468	528
Major appliances	208	204	183	236	93	229	261	271	274
Miscellaneous household equipment	659	725	724	888	416	829	974	834	988
Apparel and services [1]	1,974	1,618	1,772	1,888	922	1,710	2,376	2,494	2,847
Men and boys	423	348	427	509	199	389	579	608	739
Women and girls	800	677	714	699	384	718	917	913	1,121
Footwear	344	264	336	307	159	282	413	481	502
Other apparel products and services	314	219	214	280	164	275	282	311	267
Transportation	8,898	8,418	8,482	8,745	4,439	9,225	10,758	11,515	11,602
Vehicle purchases (net outlay) [1]	2,687	2,872	2,726	2,737	1,217	2,987	3,849	3,538	3,800
Cars and trucks, new	1,379	1,274	1,355	1,195	553	1,594	1,774	1,622	1,409
Cars and trucks, used	1,203	1,445	1,263	1,360	605	1,266	1,828	1,754	2,215
Gasoline and motor oil	2,386	2,664	2,937	2,679	1,384	2,789	3,280	3,805	4,057
Other vehicle expenses	3,059	2,472	2,488	2,623	1,523	2,829	3,062	3,609	3,151
Vehicle finance charges	233	289	364	318	121	314	404	489	492
Maintenance and repair	793	692	650	850	443	804	817	947	907
Vehicle insurance	1,363	980	1,181	931	700	1,203	1,288	1,538	1,193
Vehicle rental, leases, licenses, other charges	670	511	294	524	259	508	553	635	558
Public transportation	765	410	331	706	314	620	568	563	594
Health care [2]	3,035	3,049	2,849	3,057	1,821	3,972	2,944	3,039	3,022
Entertainment [3]	2,960	2,758	2,512	3,333	1,655	3,178	3,070	3,714	3,612
Personal care products and services	638	551	580	721	388	638	733	805	777
Reading	141	118	87	140	88	144	123	115	98
Education	1,585	1,029	797	1,019	602	866	1,404	1,626	1,617
Tobacco products and smoking supplies	324	357	324	257	214	326	421	350	385
Miscellaneous	952	725	743	1,020	558	955	1,005	946	888
Cash contributions	1,485	1,705	1,744	1,966	1,314	2,079	1,873	1,603	1,821
Personal insurance and pensions	5,987	5,552	5,158	6,067	2,620	6,095	7,084	7,881	7,426
Life and other personal insurance	384	306	321	265	108	421	399	380	376
Pensions and social security	5,602	5,246	4,837	5,803	2,511	5,674	6,685	7,501	7,050
Personal taxes	**2,258**	**1,270**	**1,389**	**2,584**	**1,205**	**2,413**	**2,414**	**1,890**	**308**

[1] Includes other types not shown separately. [2] For additional health care expenditures, see Table 139. [3] For additional recreation expenditures, see Section 26.

Source: U.S. Bureau of Labor Statistics, *Consumer Expenditures in 2008*, News Release, USDL-09-1208 October 2009. See also <http://www.bls.gov/cex/2008/Standard/cusize.pdf> and <http://www.bls.gov/cex/2008/Standard/region.pdf>.

Table 687. Average Annual Expenditures of All Consumer Units by Income Level: 2008

[In dollars. See headnote, Table 683]

Income level	Total expendi- tures [1]	Food	Housing			Transportation			Health care	Pen- sions and social security
			Total [1]	Shelter	Utilities, fuels [2]	Total [1]	Vehicle pur- chases	Gaso- line and motor oil		
All consumer units	**50,486**	**6,443**	**17,109**	**10,183**	**3,649**	**8,604**	**2,755**	**2,715**	**2,976**	**5,288**
Consumer units with complete reporting:										
Less than $70,000	34,687	4,818	12,499	7,328	3,065	6,127	1,868	2,118	2,446	2,278
$70,000 to $79,999	58,742	7,503	19,617	11,633	4,257	10,449	3,114	3,528	3,503	6,573
$80,000 to $99,999	67,180	8,760	21,360	12,396	4,536	12,227	3,916	3,770	3,695	8,023
$100,000 and over	100,065	11,302	31,784	19,465	5,242	15,674	5,450	4,208	4,471	14,974
$100,000 to $119,999	77,586	9,773	25,002	15,095	4,632	13,424	4,546	3,954	4,037	10,282
$120,000 to $149,999	91,590	10,969	28,058	16,754	5,083	15,720	5,764	4,237	4,316	13,259
$150,000 and over	124,678	13,011	39,909	24,848	5,848	17,486	5,984	4,396	4,931	19,961

[1] Includes expenditures not shown separately. [2] Includes public service.

Source: U.S. Bureau of Labor Statistics, *Consumer Expenditures in 2008*, News Release, USDL-09-1208 October 2009. See also <http://www.bls.gov/cex/2008/share/higherincome.pdf>.

Table 688. Annual Expenditure Per Child by Husband-Wife Families by Family Income and Expenditure Type: 2009

[In dollars. Data are for a child in a two-child family. Excludes expenses for college. Expenditures based on before tax income data from the 2005–2006 Consumer Expenditure Survey updated to 2009 dollars using the Consumer Price Index. For more on the methodology, see report cited below]

Family income and age of child	Expenditure type							
	Total	Housing	Food	Transpor- tation	Clothing	Health care	Child care and educa- tion [1]	Miscella- neous [2]
INCOME: LESS THAN $56,670								
Less than 2 years old	8,570	2,960	1,110	990	630	590	1,870	420
3 to 5 years old	8,630	2,960	1,210	1,030	500	560	1,760	610
6 to 8 years old	8,330	2,960	1,640	1,140	560	620	780	630
9 to 11 years old	9,040	2,960	1,890	1,140	570	670	1,190	620
12 to 14 years old	9,450	2,960	2,040	1,250	680	1,020	810	690
15 to 17 years old	9,450	2,960	2,030	1,380	720	950	830	580
INCOME: $56,670 TO $98,120								
Less than 2 years old	11,700	3,890	1,340	1,420	750	790	2,630	880
3 to 5 years old	11,730	3,890	1,430	1,470	600	750	2,510	1,080
6 to 8 years old	11,650	3,890	2,010	1,570	670	880	1,540	1,090
9 to 11 years old	12,420	3,890	2,290	1,580	690	940	1,940	1,090
12 to 14 years old	13,090	3,890	2,470	1,680	820	1,320	1,750	1,160
15 to 17 years old	13,530	3,890	2,450	1,810	890	1,240	2,210	1,040
INCOME: MORE THAN $98,120								
Less than 2 years old	19,410	7,030	1,820	2,160	1,030	920	4,680	1,770
3 to 5 years old	19,410	7,030	1,910	2,200	870	870	4,560	1,970
6 to 8 years old	19,380	7,030	2,520	2,300	950	1,010	3,590	1,980
9 to 11 years old	20,230	7,030	2,850	2,310	990	1,080	3,990	1,980
12 to 14 years old	21,510	7,030	3,050	2,410	1,150	1,510	4,310	2,050
15 to 17 years old	23,180	7,030	3,040	2,550	1,260	1,430	5,940	1,930

[1] Includes only families with child care and education expenses. [2] Expenses include personal care items, entertainment, and reading materials.

Source: U.S. Department of Agriculture, Center for Nutrition Policy and Promotion, *Expenditures on Children by Families, 2009*, 1528-2009, June 2010. See also <http://www.cnpp.usda.gov/Publications/CRC/crc2009.pdf>.

Table 689. Money Income of Households—Percent Distribution by Income Level, Race, and Hispanic Origin, in Constant (2008) Dollars: 1980 to 2008

[Constant dollars based on CPI-U-RS deflator. Households as of March of following year. (82,368 represents 82,368,000). Based on Current Population Survey, Annual Social and Economic Supplement (ASEC); see text, this section and Section 1, and Appendix III. For data collection changes over time, see <http://www.census.gov/hhes/www/income/histinc/hstchg.html>. For definition of median, see Guide to Tabular Presentation]

Year	Number of house-holds (1,000)	Percent distribution							Median income (dollars)
		Under $15,000	$15,000 to $24,999	$25,000 to $34,999	$35,000 to $49,999	$50,000 to $74,999	$75,000 to $99,999	$100,000 and over	
ALL HOUSEHOLDS [1]									
1980.	82,368	15.4	12.7	12.1	16.3	21.4	11.6	10.6	44,059
1990.	94,312	13.9	11.8	11.1	15.7	19.9	12.3	15.1	47,818
2000 [2]	108,209	11.7	10.9	10.7	14.3	18.4	13.0	21.0	52,500
2007.	116,783	12.8	11.3	10.5	14.0	18.0	12.0	21.4	52,163
2008.	117,181	12.9	11.8	10.9	14.0	17.9	11.9	20.5	50,303
WHITE									
1980.	71,872	13.5	12.1	11.9	16.6	22.3	12.2	11.4	46,482
1990.	80,968	11.9	11.5	11.0	16.0	20.5	13.0	16.1	49,875
2000 [2]	90,030	10.4	10.5	10.4	14.2	18.6	13.6	22.2	54,908
2007 [3, 4]	95,112	11.1	11.0	10.3	13.9	18.3	12.5	22.7	54,117
2008 [3, 4]	95,297	11.4	11.5	10.6	13.9	18.4	12.5	21.7	52,312
BLACK									
1980.	8,847	30.6	17.7	13.6	14.2	14.1	6.4	3.5	26,779
1990.	10,671	29.0	15.0	12.3	14.4	15.3	7.4	6.5	29,825
2000 [2]	13,174	20.4	14.3	13.0	15.2	17.6	9.0	10.5	37,093
2007 [3, 5]	14,551	23.5	14.1	12.5	14.6	16.2	8.6	10.6	35,219
2008 [3, 5]	14,595	23.0	14.5	13.4	15.6	15.4	8.2	10.0	34,218
ASIAN AND PACIFIC ISLANDER									
1990.	1,958	10.7	9.5	8.2	12.5	20.6	14.0	24.6	61,403
2000 [2]	3,963	9.1	7.1	8.0	11.7	17.0	15.0	32.1	69,713
2007 [3, 6]	4,494	10.3	8.1	7.4	11.4	17.1	13.1	32.8	68,643
2008 [3, 6]	4,573	11.8	8.6	7.6	11.8	15.7	12.3	32.3	65,637
HISPANIC [7]									
1980.	3,906	19.9	17.1	15.0	17.8	17.4	7.9	5.1	33,961
1990.	6,220	19.6	16.4	12.9	17.5	18.2	7.9	7.4	35,660
2000 [2]	10,034	13.7	14.7	13.1	17.4	19.0	10.8	11.3	41,470
2007.	13,339	15.5	14.6	13.8	16.4	18.3	10.1	11.2	40,165
2008.	13,425	16.8	14.6	14.5	16.4	16.9	9.2	11.7	37,913

[1] Includes other races, not shown separately. [2] Data reflect implementation of Census 2000-based population controls and a 28,000 household sample expansion to 78,000 households. [3] Beginning with the 2003 Current Population Survey (CPS), the questionnaire allowed respondents to choose more than one race. For 2002 and later, data represent persons who selected this race group only and exclude persons reporting more than one race. The CPS in prior years allowed respondents to report only one race group. See also comments on race in the text for Section 1. [4] Data represent White alone, which refers to people who reported White and did not report any other race category. [5] Data represent Black alone, which refers to people who reported Black and did not report any other race category. [6] Data represent Asian alone, which refers to people who reported Asian and did not report any other race category. [7] People of Hispanic origin may be any race.

Source: U.S. Census Bureau, *Income, Poverty and Health Insurance Coverage in the United States: 2008*, Current Population Reports, P60-236(RV), and Historical Tables—Table H17, September 2009. See also <http://www.census.gov/hhes/www/income/income.html> and <http://www.census.gov/hhes/www/income/data/historical/household/index.html>.

Table 690. Money Income of Households—Median Income by Race and Hispanic Origin, in Current and Constant (2008) Dollars: 1980 to 2008

[In dollars. See headnote, Table 689]

Year	Median income in current dollars					Median income in constant (2008) dollars				
	All house-holds [1]	White [2]	Black [3]	Asian, Pacific Islander [4]	His-panic [5]	All house-holds [1]	White [2]	Black [3]	Asian, Pacific Islander [4]	His-panic [5]
1980.	17,710	18,684	10,764	(NA)	13,651	44,059	46,482	26,779	(NA)	33,961
1990.	29,943	31,231	18,676	38,450	22,330	47,818	49,875	29,825	61,403	35,660
1995 [6]	34,076	35,766	22,393	40,614	22,860	47,803	50,174	31,414	56,975	32,069
2000 [7, 8]	41,990	43,916	29,667	55,757	33,168	52,500	54,908	37,093	69,713	41,470
2001.	42,228	44,517	29,470	53,635	33,565	51,356	54,140	35,840	65,228	40,820
2002 [9]	42,409	45,086	29,026	52,626	33,103	50,756	53,960	34,739	62,984	39,618
2003.	43,318	45,631	29,645	55,699	32,997	50,711	53,419	34,705	65,206	38,629
2004 [10]	44,334	46,658	30,095	57,504	34,271	50,535	53,184	34,304	65,547	39,064
2005.	46,326	48,554	30,858	61,094	35,967	51,093	53,550	34,033	67,380	39,668
2006.	48,201	50,673	31,969	64,238	37,781	51,473	54,113	34,139	68,599	40,346
2007.	50,233	52,115	33,916	66,103	38,679	52,163	54,117	35,219	68,643	40,165
2008.	50,303	52,312	34,218	65,637	37,913	50,303	52,312	34,218	65,637	37,913

NA Not available. [1] Includes other races, not shown separately. [2] Beginning with 2002, data represents White alone, which refers to people who reported White and did not report any other race category. [3] Beginning with 2002, data represents Black alone, which refers to people who reported Black and did not report any other race category. [4] Beginning with 2002, data represents Asian alone, which refers to people who reported Asian and did not report any other race category. [5] People of Hispanic origin may be any race. [6] Data reflect full implementation of the 1990 census-based sample design and metropolitan definitions, 7,000 household sample reduction, and revised race edits. [7] Implementation of Census 2000-based population controls. [8] Implementation of a 28,000 household sample expansion. [9] See footnote 3, Table 689. See also comments on race in the text for Section 1. [10] Data have been revised to reflect a correction to the weights in the 2005 ASEC.

Source: U.S. Census Bureau, *Income, Poverty and Health Insurance Coverage in the United States: 2008*, Current Population Reports, P60-236(RV), and Historical Tables—Table H-5, September 2009. See also <http://www.census.gov/hhes/www/income/income.html> and <http://www.census.gov/hhes/www/income/data/historical/household/index.html>.

Table 691. Money Income of Households—Distribution by Income Level and Selected Characteristics: 2008

[117,181 represents 117,181,000. Households as of March of the following year. Based on Current Population Survey, Annual Social and Economic Supplement (ASEC); see text, this section and Section 1, and Appendix III. For definition of median, see Guide to Tabular Presentation]

Characteristic	Number of households (1,000)								Median house-hold income (dollars)
	Total house-holds	Under $15,000	$15,000 to $24,999	$25,000 to $34,999	$35,000 to $49,999	$50,000 to $74,999	$75,000 to $99,999	$100,000 and over	
Total	**117,181**	**15,224**	**13,800**	**12,733**	**16,432**	**20,977**	**14,004**	**24,013**	**50,303**
Age of householder:									
15 to 24 years	6,357	1,367	1,002	1,035	1,120	978	475	382	32,270
25 to 34 years	19,302	2,046	1,980	2,122	3,185	4,036	2,659	3,275	51,400
35 to 44 years	22,171	1,794	1,824	2,023	2,869	4,524	3,216	5,919	62,954
45 to 54 years	24,633	2,265	1,938	2,019	3,194	4,700	3,539	6,975	64,349
55 to 64 years	19,883	2,381	1,913	1,870	2,562	3,630	2,452	5,073	57,265
65 years and over	24,834	5,371	5,143	3,662	3,502	3,105	1,663	2,388	29,744
Region: [1]									
Northeast	21,309	2,848	2,123	2,135	2,740	3,614	2,603	5,247	54,346
Midwest	26,282	3,266	3,143	3,047	3,651	5,074	3,286	4,818	50,112
South	43,423	6,133	5,727	4,990	6,398	7,604	4,854	7,720	45,590
West	26,166	2,978	2,807	2,561	3,644	4,689	3,259	6,227	55,085
Size of household:									
One person	31,657	9,117	6,342	4,564	4,575	3,951	1,412	1,695	25,642
Two people	39,242	3,025	4,104	4,483	6,057	7,866	5,352	8,355	55,418
Three people	18,606	1,433	1,540	1,621	2,449	3,773	2,761	5,031	63,830
Four people	16,099	923	976	1,072	1,864	3,108	2,693	5,463	75,746
Five people	7,406	471	541	626	933	1,440	1,097	2,300	69,271
Six people	2,640	166	197	216	360	529	431	744	67,158
Seven or more people	1,529	89	101	150	193	310	260	425	67,293
Type of household:									
Family household	78,850	5,685	6,900	7,544	10,766	15,459	11,575	20,920	62,621
Married-couple	59,118	2,261	3,850	4,685	7,400	12,151	9,788	18,982	73,010
Male householder, wife absent	5,252	473	614	678	909	1,079	659	839	49,186
Female householder, husband absent	14,480	2,952	2,436	2,180	2,456	2,227	1,131	1,099	33,073
Nonfamily household	38,331	9,537	6,900	5,187	5,666	5,519	2,427	3,092	30,078
Male householder	17,694	3,442	2,682	2,454	2,822	3,012	1,422	1,861	36,006
Female householder	20,637	6,096	4,219	2,734	2,847	2,507	1,005	1,231	25,014
Educational attainment of householder: [2]									
Total	**110,823**	**13,857**	**12,799**	**11,697**	**15,312**	**19,999**	**13,528**	**23,630**	**51,388**
Less than 9th grade	5,350	1,919	1,123	742	658	537	190	181	21,242
9th to 12th grade (no diploma)	8,650	2,488	1,784	1,322	1,210	1,027	457	364	25,321
High school graduate	32,416	4,779	5,130	4,285	5,370	5,965	3,468	3,415	39,962
Some college, no degree	20,236	2,319	2,186	2,401	3,130	4,207	2,634	3,362	50,323
Associate's degree	10,244	791	908	1,042	1,523	2,212	1,641	2,130	59,163
Bachelor's degree or more	33,928	1,562	1,668	1,905	3,421	6,054	5,138	14,177	85,127
Bachelor's degree	21,403	1,115	1,192	1,329	2,410	4,111	3,324	7,922	78,290
Master's degree	9,031	341	348	447	806	1,510	1,374	4,205	92,642
Professional degree	1,841	38	62	88	97	218	228	1,108	100,000
Doctoral degree	1,654	69	66	43	106	216	212	942	100,000
Number of earners:									
No earners	24,944	10,124	5,755	3,348	2,628	1,713	647	726	18,628
One earner	43,232	4,508	6,554	6,876	8,230	8,251	3,718	5,096	40,772
Two earners and more	49,005	591	1,490	2,508	5,574	11,014	9,636	18,191	82,576
Two earners	39,250	544	1,378	2,251	4,890	9,256	7,569	13,359	78,454
Three earners	7,245	43	94	227	586	1,437	1,536	3,321	94,530
Four earners or more	2,511	3	17	29	100	320	533	1,510	100,000
Work experience of householder:									
Total	**117,181**	**15,224**	**13,800**	**12,733**	**16,432**	**20,977**	**14,004**	**24,013**	**50,303**
Worked	80,627	4,398	6,787	7,864	11,642	16,816	11,941	21,180	62,768
Worked at full-time jobs	67,585	2,263	4,930	6,361	9,774	14,800	10,549	18,911	66,624
50 weeks or more	56,910	1,031	3,464	5,075	8,038	12,776	9,308	17,220	70,763
27 to 49 weeks	6,977	456	932	827	1,144	1,401	910	1,304	51,479
26 weeks or less	3,698	774	534	461	590	623	329	387	36,973
Worked at part-time jobs	13,042	2,136	1,856	1,503	1,870	2,015	1,397	2,269	42,722
50 weeks or more	7,179	920	983	838	1,034	1,193	808	1,404	46,719
27 to 49 weeks	2,777	461	409	311	392	403	315	487	43,129
26 weeks or less	3,087	753	464	354	444	420	271	378	34,325
Did not work	36,554	10,826	7,013	4,867	4,791	4,164	2,062	2,833	25,756
Tenure:									
Owner occupied	78,825	6,362	7,416	7,241	10,259	15,216	11,325	21,004	62,082
Renter occupied	36,761	8,378	6,109	5,260	5,998	5,547	2,568	2,904	31,829
Occupier paid no cash rent	1,595	483	276	230	175	213	109	105	27,307

[1] For composition of regions, see map, inside front cover. [2] People 25 years old and over.

Source: U.S. Census Bureau, *Income, Poverty and Health Insurance Coverage in the United States: 2008*, Current Population Reports, P60-236(RV), and Detailed Tables—Table HINC 01, September 2009. See also <http://www.census.gov/hhes/www/cpstables/032009/hhinc/new01_000.htm>.

Income, Expenditures, Poverty, and Wealth 453

Table 692. Money Income of Households—Number and Distribution by Race and Hispanic Origin: 2008

[Households as of March of the following year. (117,181 represents 117,181,000). Based on Current Population Survey, Annual Social and Economic Supplement (ASEC); see text, this section and Section 1, and Appendix III. The 2009 CPS allowed respondents to choose more than one race. Data represent persons who selected this race group only and excludes persons reporting more than one race. See also comments on race in the text for Section 1]

Income interval	Number of households (1,000)					Percent distribution				
	All races	White alone	Black alone	Asian alone	His-panic [1]	All races	White alone	Black alone	Asian alone	His-panic [1]
All households.........	**117,181**	**95,297**	**14,595**	**4,573**	**13,425**	**100.0**	**100.0**	**100.0**	**100.0**	**100.0**
Under $10,000............	8,377	5,632	2,128	319	1,254	7.1	5.9	14.6	7.0	9.3
$10,000 to $14,999.........	6,847	5,248	1,229	220	1,006	5.8	5.5	8.4	4.8	7.5
$15,000 to $19,999.........	6,716	5,361	1,021	163	949	5.7	5.6	7.0	3.6	7.1
$20,000 to $24,999.........	7,084	5,579	1,089	232	1,008	6.0	5.9	7.5	5.1	7.5
$25,000 to $29,999.........	6,428	5,098	1,009	152	915	5.5	5.3	6.9	3.3	6.8
$30,000 to $34,999.........	6,305	5,008	942	194	1,028	5.4	5.3	6.5	4.2	7.7
$35,000 to $39,999.........	6,000	4,802	851	195	821	5.1	5.0	5.8	4.3	6.1
$40,000 to $44,999.........	5,593	4,459	806	184	789	4.8	4.7	5.5	4.0	5.9
$45,000 to $49,999.........	4,830	3,956	617	161	592	4.1	4.2	4.2	3.5	4.4
$50,000 to $59,999.........	9,234	7,650	1,077	300	1,045	7.9	8.0	7.4	6.6	7.8
$60,000 to $74,999.........	11,743	9,883	1,174	415	1,220	10.0	10.4	8.0	9.1	9.1
$75,000 to $84,999.........	6,465	5,479	596	241	571	5.5	5.7	4.1	5.3	4.3
$85,000 to $99,999.........	7,539	6,464	593	321	661	6.4	6.8	4.1	7.0	4.9
$100,000 to $149,999......	14,286	12,230	998	810	1,031	12.2	12.8	6.8	17.7	7.7
$150,000 to $199,999......	5,250	4,498	309	359	345	4.5	4.7	2.1	7.9	2.6
$200,000 to $249,999......	2,001	1,743	79	152	82	1.7	1.8	0.5	3.3	0.6
$250,000 and above........	2,476	2,207	77	155	108	2.1	2.3	0.5	3.4	0.8

[1] Persons of Hispanic origin may be any race.

Source: U.S. Census Bureau, *Income, Poverty and Health Insurance Coverage in the United States: 2008*, Current Population Reports, P60-236(RV), and Detailed Tables—Table HINC-06, September 2009. See also <http://www.census.gov/hhes/www/cpstables/032009/hhinc/new06_000.htm>.

Table 693. Share of Aggregate Income Received by Each Fifth and Top 5 Percent of Households: 1970 to 2008

[Households as of March of the following year, (64,778 represents 64,778,000). Income in constant 2008 CPI-U-RS-adjusted dollars. The shares method ranks households from highest to lowest on the basis of income and then divides them into groups of equal population size, typically quintiles. The aggregate income of each group is then divided by the overall aggregate income to derive shares. Based on the Current Population Survey, Annual Social and Economic Supplement (ASEC); see text, this section and Section 1, and Appendix III. For data collection changes over time, see <http://www.census.gov/hhes/www/income/data/historical/history.html>]

Year	Number of house-holds (1,000)	Income at selected positions (dollars)					Percent distribution of aggregate income					
		Upper limit of each fifth				Top 5 percent	Lowest 5th	Second 5th	Third 5th	Fourth 5th	Highest 5th	Top 5 percent
		Lowest	Second	Third	Fourth							
1970......	64,778	18,250	34,960	50,849	72,548	114,678	4.1	10.8	17.4	24.5	43.3	16.6
1980......	82,368	18,604	34,889	53,488	78,316	126,035	4.2	10.2	16.8	24.7	44.1	16.5
1990......	94,312	19,962	37,787	57,810	88,161	151,310	3.8	9.6	15.9	24.0	46.6	18.5
1995 [1]	99,627	20,201	37,756	58,922	91,359	158,521	3.7	9.1	15.2	23.3	48.7	21.0
2000 [2, 3] ...	108,209	22,405	41,260	65,233	102,232	181,568	3.6	8.9	14.8	23.0	49.8	22.1
2001......	109,297	21,854	40,515	64,456	101,549	183,030	3.5	8.7	14.6	23.0	50.1	22.4
2002......	111,278	21,442	39,946	63,625	100,552	179,525	3.5	8.8	14.8	23.3	49.7	21.7
2003......	112,000	21,053	39,803	63,747	101,693	180,425	3.4	8.7	14.8	23.4	49.8	21.4
2004 [4]	113,343	21,072	39,525	62,955	100,311	179,133	3.4	8.7	14.7	23.2	50.1	21.8
2005......	114,384	21,151	39,704	63,593	101,141	183,081	3.4	8.6	14.6	23.0	50.4	22.2
2006......	116,011	21,395	40,338	64,073	103,619	185,824	3.4	8.6	14.5	22.9	50.5	22.3
2007......	116,783	21,071	40,602	64,382	103,842	183,801	3.4	8.7	14.8	23.4	49.7	21.2
2008......	117,181	20,712	39,000	62,725	100,240	180,000	3.4	8.6	14.7	23.3	50.0	21.5

[1] Data reflect full implementation of the 1990 census-based sample design and metropolitan definitions, 7,000 household sample reduction, and revised race edits. [2] Implementation of Census 2000-based population controls. [3] Implementation of a 28,000 household sample expansion. [4] Data have been revised to reflect a correction to the weights in the 2005 ASEC.

Source: U.S. Census Bureau, *Income, Poverty and Health Insurance Coverage in the United States: 2008*, Current Population Reports, P60-236RV, and Historical Tables—Tables H1 and H2, September 2009. See also <http://www.census.gov/hhes/www/income/income.html> and <http://www.census.gov/hhes/www/income/data/historical/household/index.html>.

Table 694. Money Income of Families—Number and Distribution by Race and Hispanic Origin: 2008

[Families as of March of the following year. (78,874 represents 78,874,000). Based on Current Population Survey, Annual Social and Economic Supplement (ASEC); see text, this section, Section 1, and Appendix III. The 2009 CPS allowed respondents to choose more than one race. Data represent persons who selected this race group only and excludes persons reporting more than one race. See also comments on race in the text for Section 1]

Income interval	Number of families (1,000)					Percent distribution				
	All races	White alone	Black alone	Asian alone	His-panic [1]	All races	White alone	Black alone	Asian alone	His-panic [1]
All families [1]	**78,874**	**64,183**	**9,359**	**3,494**	**10,503**	**100.0**	**100.0**	**100.0**	**100.0**	**100.0**
Under $10,000	3,787	2,420	1,065	146	880	4.8	3.8	11.4	4.2	8.4
$10,000 to $14,999	2,584	1,805	585	109	648	3.3	2.8	6.3	3.1	6.2
$15,000 to $19,999	3,175	2,285	674	115	713	4.0	3.6	7.2	3.3	6.8
$20,000 to $24,999	3,932	3,062	621	138	791	5.0	4.8	6.6	3.9	7.5
$25,000 to $29,999	3,798	2,959	624	102	704	4.8	4.6	6.7	2.9	6.7
$30,000 to $34,999	3,858	3,022	573	144	792	4.9	4.7	6.1	4.1	7.5
$35,000 to $39,999	3,774	2,966	548	154	648	4.8	4.6	5.9	4.4	6.2
$40,000 to $44,999	3,715	2,957	520	146	642	4.7	4.6	5.6	4.2	6.1
$45,000 to $49,999	3,242	2,647	401	133	472	4.1	4.1	4.3	3.8	4.5
$50,000 to $59,999	6,395	5,257	750	242	851	8.1	8.2	8.0	6.9	8.1
$60,000 to $74,999	8,872	7,495	838	338	1,016	11.2	11.7	9.0	9.7	9.7
$75,000 to $84,999	5,137	4,392	441	188	463	6.5	6.8	4.7	5.4	4.4
$85,000 to $99,999	6,115	5,280	467	258	566	7.8	8.2	5.0	7.4	5.4
$100,000 to $149,999	11,967	10,234	865	679	861	15.2	15.9	9.2	19.4	8.2
$150,000 to $199,999	4,561	3,903	258	331	287	5.8	6.1	2.8	9.5	2.7
$200,000 to $249,999	1,726	1,501	67	132	72	2.2	2.3	0.7	3.8	0.7
$250,000 and above	2,230	1,998	63	138	97	2.8	3.1	0.7	3.9	0.9

[1] Persons of Hispanic origin may be any race.

Source: U.S. Census Bureau, *Income, Poverty and Health Insurance Coverage in the United States: 2008*, Current Population Reports, P60-236RV, and Detailed Tables—Table FINC-07, September 2009. See also <http://www.census.gov/hhes/www/cpstables/032009/faminc/new07_000.htm>.

Table 695. Money Income of Families—Percent Distribution by Income Level in Constant (2008) Dollars: 1980 to 2008

[Constant dollars based on CPI-U-RS deflator. Families as of March of following year, (60,309 represents 60,309,000). Based on Current Population Survey, Annual Social and Economic Supplement (ASEC); see text, this section, Section 1, and Appendix III. For data collection changes over time, see <http://www.census.gov/hhes/www/income/data/historical/history.html>. For definition of median, see Guide to Tabular Presentation]

Year	Number of families (1,000)	Percent distribution							Median income (dollars)
		Under $15,000	$15,000 to $24,999	$25,000 to $34,999	$35,000 to $49,999	$50,000 to $74,999	$75,000 to $99,999	$100,000 and over	
ALL FAMILIES [1]									
1980	60,309	8.8	10.5	11.4	17.1	24.8	14.2	13.2	52,301
1990	66,322	8.6	9.4	10.2	15.6	22.4	14.7	19.1	56,458
2000 [2]	73,778	6.7	8.4	9.5	14.1	19.7	15.4	26.2	63,430
2007	77,908	7.6	8.7	9.4	13.4	19.2	14.4	27.4	63,712
2008	78,874	8.1	0.0	9.7	13.6	19.4	14.3	26.0	61,521
WHITE									
1980	52,710	7.0	9.5	11.1	17.3	25.8	15.0	14.1	54,493
1990	56,803	6.7	8.7	9.9	15.8	23.1	15.5	20.4	58,952
2000 [2]	61,330	5.5	7.7	9.1	14.0	19.9	16.1	27.7	66,302
2007 [3,4]	63,595	6.1	8.1	9.1	13.2	19.5	15.0	29.0	66,903
2008 [3,4]	64,183	6.6	8.3	9.3	13.4	19.9	15.1	27.5	65,000
BLACK									
1980	6,317	22.8	18.2	14.1	15.3	16.7	8.2	4.5	31,530
1990	7,471	24.0	14.6	12.6	14.4	17.5	8.8	8.2	34,212
2000 [2]	8,731	15.1	13.8	13.0	15.7	18.8	10.5	13.0	42,105
2007 [3,5]	9,259	17.9	13.4	12.0	14.6	17.6	10.9	13.7	41,685
2008 [3,5]	9,359	17.7	13.8	12.8	15.7	16.9	9.7	13.4	39,879
ASIAN AND PACIFIC ISLANDER									
1990	1,536	8.1	7.8	8.2	11.5	20.8	15.1	28.5	67,466
2000 [2]	2,982	5.9	6.1	6.8	11.0	17.3	15.9	37.0	78,290
2007 [3,6]	3,302	5.8	6.4	6.8	10.5	18.0	13.7	38.7	80,097
2008 [3,6]	3,494	7.3	7.2	7.1	12.4	16.6	12.8	36.6	73,578
HISPANIC ORIGIN [7]									
1980	3,235	15.8	17.1	15.1	19.1	19.0	8.5	5.4	36,611
1990	4,981	17.0	16.3	13.6	17.2	19.0	8.7	8.2	37,419
2000 [2]	8,017	11.9	14.3	13.4	18.0	19.4	11.0	12.0	43,063
2007	10,397	12.9	14.8	14.2	16.7	19.0	10.2	12.1	42,125
2008	10,503	14.6	14.3	14.2	16.8	17.8	9.8	12.5	40,466

[1] Includes other races, not shown separately. [2] Data reflect implementation of Census 2000-based population controls and a 28,000 household sample expansion to 78,000 households. [3] Beginning with the 2003 Current Population Survey (CPS), the questionnaire allowed respondents to choose more than one race. For 2002 and later, data represent persons who selected this race group only and excludes persons reporting more than one race. The CPS in prior years allowed respondents to report only one race group. See also comments on race in the text for Section 1. [4] Data represent White alone, which refers to people who reported White and did not report any other race category. [5] Data represent Black alone, which refers to people who reported Black and did not report any other race category. [6] Data represent Asian alone, which refers to people who reported Asian and did not report any other race category. [7] People of Hispanic origin may be any race.

Source: U.S. Census Bureau, *Income, Poverty and Health Insurance Coverage in the United States: 2008*, Current Population Reports, P60-236(RV), and Historical Tables—Table F-23, September 2009. See also <http://www.census.gov/hhes/www/income/income.html> and <http://www.census.gov/hhes/www/income/data/historical/families/index.html>.

Table 696. Money Income of Families—Median Income by Race and Hispanic Origin in Current and Constant (2008) Dollars: 1990 to 2008

[In dollars. See headnote, Table 695]

Year	Median income in current dollars					Median income in constant (2008) dollars				
	All families [1]	White [2]	Black [3]	Asian, Pacific Islander [4]	His-panic [5]	All families [1]	White [2]	Black [3]	Asian, Pacific Islander [4]	His-panic [5]
1990.........	35,353	36,915	21,423	42,246	23,431	56,458	58,952	34,212	67,466	37,419
1995 [6].......	40,611	42,646	25,970	46,356	24,570	56,971	59,825	36,432	65,030	34,468
2000 [7,8].......	50,732	53,029	33,676	62,617	34,442	63,430	66,302	42,105	78,290	43,063
2003 [9].......	52,680	55,768	34,369	63,251	34,272	61,671	65,286	40,235	74,047	40,121
2004 [10]........	54,061	56,723	35,148	65,420	35,440	61,623	64,657	40,064	74,570	40,397
2005.........	56,194	59,317	35,464	68,957	37,867	61,976	65,420	39,113	76,052	41,763
2006.........	58,407	61,280	38,269	74,612	40,000	62,372	65,440	40,867	79,677	42,715
2007.........	61,355	64,427	40,143	77,133	40,566	63,712	66,903	41,685	80,097	42,125
2008.........	61,521	65,000	39,879	73,578	40,466	61,521	65,000	39,879	73,578	40,466

[1] Includes other races, not shown separately. [2] Beginning with 2002, data represent White alone, which refers to people who reported White and did not report any other race category. [3] Beginning with 2002, data represent Black alone, which refers to people who reported Black and did not report any other race category. [4] Beginning with 2002, data represent Asian alone, which refers to people who reported Asian and did not report any other race category. [5] People of Hispanic origin may be any race. [6] Data reflect full implementation of the 1990 census-based sample design and metropolitan definitions, 7,000 household sample reduction, and revised race edits. [7] Implementation of Census 2000-based population controls. [8] Implementation of 28,000 household sample expansion. [9] See footnote 3, Table 695. See also comments on race in the text for Section 1. [10] Data have been revised to reflect a correction to the weights in the 2005 ASEC.

Source: U.S. Census Bureau, *Income, Poverty and Health Insurance Coverage in the United States: 2008*, Current Population Reports, P60-236(RV), and Historical Tables—Table F-05, September 2009. See also <http://www.census.gov/hhes/www/income/income.html> and <http://www.census.gov/hhes/www/income/data/historical/families/index.html>.

Table 697. Money Income of Families—Distribution by Family Characteristics and Income Level: 2008

[78,874 represents 78,874,000. See headnote, Table 695. For composition of regions, see map inside front cover]

Characteristic	Number of families (1,000)								Median income (dollars)
	Total	Under $15,000	$15,000 to $24,999	$25,000 to $34,999	$35,000 to $49,999	$50,000 to $74,999	$75,000 to $99,999	$100,000 and over	
All families................	**78,874**	**6,371**	**7,107**	**7,656**	**10,731**	**15,267**	**11,252**	**20,484**	**61,521**
Age of householder:									
15 to 24 years old...............	3,402	844	492	494	539	565	257	212	31,964
25 to 34 years old..............	13,355	1,655	1,394	1,366	1,929	2,646	1,902	2,463	52,845
35 to 44 years old..............	17,551	1,228	1,343	1,453	2,128	3,532	2,683	5,179	68,304
45 to 54 years old..............	18,120	948	1,074	1,231	2,148	3,543	2,955	6,221	75,651
55 to 64 years old..............	13,467	745	911	1,031	1,630	2,625	2,068	4,459	72,444
65 years old and over.............	12,980	950	1,891	2,079	2,362	2,359	1,390	1,949	44,188
Region:									
Northeast......................	14,125	1,013	1,042	1,224	1,776	2,589	2,070	4,411	69,317
Midwest......................	17,561	1,329	1,482	1,752	2,312	3,738	2,723	4,221	61,976
South........................	29,563	2,696	3,136	3,129	4,259	5,676	3,980	6,688	55,877
West.........................	17,625	1,333	1,446	1,550	2,384	3,267	2,482	5,164	65,672
Type of family:									
Married-couple families............	59,137	2,274	3,880	4,702	7,431	12,177	9,758	18,915	72,743
Male householder, no spouse present	5,255	611	695	741	938	1,053	549	667	43,571
Female householder, no spouse present........	14,482	3,485	2,533	2,212	2,364	2,042	944	902	30,129
Unrelated subfamilies..............	452	178	102	73	47	41	2	11	20,097
Educational attainment of householder: Persons 25 years old and over, total........................	75,472	5,527	6,614	7,162	10,194	14,703	10,998	20,272	63,013
Less than 9th grade............	3,408	680	791	591	578	461	172	135	28,798
9th to 12th grade (no diploma).......	5,591	1,090	1,059	928	979	861	367	306	31,383
High school graduate (includes equivalency).....................	22,084	1,905	2,649	2,735	3,893	4,849	3,006	3,050	49,414
Some college, no degree............	13,653	994	998	1,382	2,032	3,182	2,199	2,868	60,355
Associate's degree..............	7,266	347	441	577	1,028	1,615	1,376	1,883	69,232
Bachelor's degree or more..........	23,470	510	679	949	1,687	3,733	3,878	12,030	100,000
Bachelor's degree................	14,774	367	514	682	1,250	2,672	2,545	6,744	92,527
Master's degree.................	6,195	111	114	194	350	819	1,023	3,586	100,000
Professional degree..............	1,372	15	26	52	56	127	155	941	100,000
Doctoral degree.................	1,129	17	27	21	32	118	156	758	100,000
Number of earners:									
No earners......................	11,274	3,194	2,340	1,888	1,641	1,172	478	561	25,491
One earner.....................	25,332	2,744	3,625	3,767	4,591	4,724	2,397	3,486	42,103
Two earners or more..............	42,268	433	1,143	2,000	4,503	9,374	8,379	16,437	85,165

Source: U.S. Census Bureau, *Income, Poverty and Health Insurance Coverage in the United States: 2008*, Current Population Reports, P60-236(RV), and Detailed Tables—Table FINC-01, September 2009. See also <http://www.census.gov/hhes/www/cpstables/032009/faminc/new01_000.htm>.

Table 698. Median Income of Families by Type of Family in Current and Constant (2008) Dollars: 1990 to 2008

[In dollars. See headnote, Table 695. For definition of median, see Guide to Tabular Presentation]

Year	All families	Current dollars					Constant (2008) dollars				
		Married-couple families			Male house-holder, no wife present	Female house-holder, no husband present		Married-couple families			Male house-holder, no wife present	Female house-holder, no husband present
		Total	Wife in paid labor force	Wife not in paid labor force			Total	Total	Wife in paid labor force	Wife not in paid labor force		
1990......	35,353	39,895	46,777	30,265	29,046	16,932	56,458	63,711	74,701	48,332	46,386	27,040
1995 [1]	40,611	47,062	55,823	32,375	30,358	19,691	56,971	66,020	78,311	45,417	42,587	27,623
2000 [2,3]	50,732	59,099	69,235	39,982	37,727	25,716	63,430	73,891	86,564	49,989	47,170	32,153
2003......	52,680	62,281	75,170	41,122	38,032	26,550	61,671	72,911	88,000	48,141	44,523	31,081
2004 [4]	54,061	63,626	76,854	42,215	40,361	26,969	61,623	72,525	87,604	48,120	46,006	30,741
2005......	56,194	65,906	78,755	44,457	41,111	27,244	61,976	72,687	86,858	49,031	45,341	30,047
2006......	58,407	69,404	82,788	45,757	41,844	28,829	62,372	74,115	88,408	48,863	44,684	30,786
2007......	61,355	72,589	86,435	47,329	44,358	30,296	63,712	75,378	89,756	49,148	46,062	31,460
2008......	61,521	72,743	86,621	48,502	43,571	30,129	61,521	72,743	86,621	48,502	43,571	30,129

[1] Data reflect full implementation of the 1990 census-based sample design and metropolitan definitions, 7,000 household sample reduction, and revised race edits. [2] Implementation of Census 2000-based population controls. [3] Implementation of a 28,000 household sample expansion. [4] Data have been revised to reflect a correction to the weights in the 2005 ASEC.

Source: U.S. Census Bureau, *Income, Poverty and Health Insurance Coverage in the United States: 2008*, Current Population Reports, P60-236(RV), and Historical Tables—Table F-7, September 2009. See also <http://www.census.gov/hhes/www/income /income.html> and <http://www.census.gov/hhes/www/income/data/historical/families/index.html>.

Table 699. Married-Couple Families—Number and Median Income by Work Experience of Husbands and Wives and Presence of Children: 2008

[59,137 represents 59,137,000. See headnote, Table 695. For definition of median, see Guide to Tabular Presentation]

Work experience of husband or wife	Number (1,000)					Median income (dollars)				
	All married-couple families	With no related children	One or more related children under 18 years old			All married-couple families	With no related children	One or more related children under 18 years old		
			Total	One child	Two children or more			Total	One child	Two children or more
All married-couple families ..	**59,137**	**32,647**	**28,490**	**10,278**	**16,212**	**72,743**	**68,539**	**77,715**	**79,779**	**76,575**
Husband worked	46,201	21,415	24,786	9,444	15,342	82,922	85,925	80,648	83,282	78,877
Wife worked...............	33,954	15,977	17,977	7,401	10,576	90,592	92,958	88,410	90,273	87,209
Wife did not work	12,247	5,438	6,809	2,043	4,767	60,037	62,457	56,194	55,896	56,353
Husband year-round, full-time										
worker	37,433	16,445	20,988	7,930	13,058	88,458	91,999	85,763	88,369	83,953
Wife worked...............	27,898	12,644	15,254	6,237	9,017	95,522	98,446	92,570	93,813	91,907
Wife did not work	9,535	3,801	5,734	1,000	4,042	64,439	66,550	61,641	62,127	61,450
Husband did not work	12,936	11,232	1,704	834	870	37,862	38,015	36,769	39,376	33,387
Wife worked...............	4,081	3,076	1,004	486	518	50,864	52,578	45,687	47,782	42,469
Wife did not work	8,855	8,156	699	348	351	32,894	33,581	21,764	26,206	16,901

Source: U.S. Census Bureau, *Income, Poverty and Health Insurance Coverage in the United States: 2008*, Current Population Reports, P60-236(RV), and Detailed Tables—Table FINC-04, September 2009. See also <http://www.census.gov/hhes/www /cpstables/032009/faminc/new04_000.htm>.

Table 700. Median Income of People in Constant (2008) Dollars by Sex, Race, and Hispanic Origin: 1990 to 2008

[In dollars. People as of March of following year. People 15 years old and over. Constant dollars based on CPI-U-RS deflator. Based on the Current Population Survey, Annual Social and Economic Supplement (ASEC); see text, this section and Section 1 and Appendix III. For data collection changes over time, see <http://www.census.gov/hhes/www/income/data/historical/history.html>]

Race and Hispanic Origin	Male					Female				
	1990	2000 [1]	2005 [2]	2007	2008	1990	2000 [1]	2005 [2]	2007	2008
All races [3]	**32,407**	**35,437**	**34,493**	**34,472**	**33,161**	**16,081**	**20,084**	**20,487**	**21,726**	**20,867**
White [4]	33,808	37,255	35,490	36,491	35,120	16,476	20,104	20,590	21,879	20,950
Black [5]	20,550	26,685	24,984	26,814	25,254	13,300	19,856	19,445	20,511	20,197
Asian [6]	(NA)	(NA)	37,736	38,622	36,607	(NA)	(NA)	23,868	25,291	23,109
Hispanic [7]............	21,511	24,378	24,362	25,390	24,003	12,028	15,314	16,583	17,392	16,417
White non-Hispanic	35,066	39,394	38,982	38,809	37,409	16,898	20,836	21,452	22,520	21,749

NA Not available. [1] Implementation of Census 2000-based population controls and sample expanded by 28,000 households. [2] Beginning with the 2003 Current Population Survey (CPS), the questionnaire allowed respondents to choose more than one race. For 2005 and later, data represent persons who selected this race group only and excludes persons reporting more than one race. The CPS in prior years allowed respondents to report only one race group. See also comments on race in the text for Section 1. [3] Includes other races, not shown separately. [4] Beginning with 2005, data represent White alone, which refers to people who reported White and did not report any other race category. [5] Beginning with 2005, data represent Black alone, which refers to people who reported Black and did not report any other race category. [6] Beginning with 2005, data represent Asian alone, which refers to people who reported Asian and did not report any other race category. [7] People of Hispanic origin may be any race.

Source: U.S. Census Bureau, *Income, Poverty and Health Insurance Coverage in the United States: 2008,* Current Population Reports, P60-236(RV), and Historical Tables—Table P-2, September 2009. See also <http://www.census.gov/hhes/www/income /income.html> and <http://www.census.gov/hhes/www/income/data/historical/people/index.html>.

Income, Expenditures, Poverty, and Wealth 457

Table 701. Money Income of People—Selected Characteristics by Income Level: 2008

[People as of March 2009, (116,720 represents 116,720,000). Covers people 15 years old and over. Median income in constant dollars based on CPI-U-RS deflator. For definition of median, see Guide to Tabular Presentation. For composition of regions, see map, inside front cover. Based on the Current Population Survey, Annual Social and Economic Supplement (ASEC), see text, this section, Section 1, and Appendix III]

Characteristic	All persons (1,000)	People with income									Median income (current dollars)
		Number (1,000)									
		Total (1,000)	Under $5,000 [1]	$5,000 to $9,999	$10,000 to $14,999	$15,000 to $24,999	$25,000 to $34,999	$35,000 to $49,999	$50,000 to $74,999	$75,000 and over	
MALE											
Total...............	**116,720**	**105,428**	**7,183**	**7,445**	**8,596**	**16,521**	**14,547**	**16,497**	**17,068**	**17,573**	**33,161**
15 to 24 years old	21,202	13,775	4,036	2,480	1,818	2,431	1,559	879	426	147	10,778
25 to 34 years old	20,440	19,316	838	1,110	1,269	3,259	3,466	3,915	3,332	2,133	33,415
35 to 44 years old	20,491	19,733	561	765	1,069	2,330	2,651	3,564	4,236	4,553	44,189
45 to 54 years old	21,772	20,795	724	1,073	1,055	2,427	2,481	3,535	4,197	5,302	45,540
55 to 64 years old	16,506	15,896	637	877	1,027	2,154	1,923	2,493	3,108	3,675	41,757
65 years old and over	16,308	15,913	388	1,139	2,357	3,920	2,466	2,110	1,769	1,764	25,503
Region:											
Northeast..............	21,130	19,210	1,352	1,354	1,370	2,936	2,380	2,862	3,246	3,710	35,768
Midwest...............	25,490	23,361	1,734	1,553	1,788	3,537	3,472	3,867	3,973	3,437	33,263
South.................	42,410	37,859	2,371	2,787	3,437	6,278	5,463	5,900	5,884	5,741	31,675
West.................	27,689	24,999	1,726	1,751	2,001	3,770	3,230	3,869	3,967	4,688	35,057
Educational attainment of householder: [2]											
Total	**95,518**	**91,653**	**3,147**	**4,966**	**6,778**	**14,090**	**12,988**	**15,619**	**16,641**	**17,425**	**37,463**
Less than 9th grade.......	5,399	4,973	274	797	1,015	1,431	737	444	203	73	17,043
9th to 12th grade [3]	7,754	7,158	414	956	1,021	1,903	1,230	897	511	225	20,845
High school graduate [4]	30,025	28,450	1,077	1,707	2,631	5,643	5,036	5,672	4,501	2,186	30,879
Some college, no degree...	16,093	15,523	574	707	994	2,177	2,610	3,110	3,256	2,096	37,297
Associate's degree	7,541	7,375	224	231	358	842	1,025	1,612	1,866	1,219	42,608
Bachelor's degree or more..............	28,706	28,174	585	568	761	2,093	2,349	3,883	6,306	11,627	63,277
Bachelor's degree	18,101	17,726	421	396	568	1,453	1,726	2,768	4,187	6,210	57,278
Master's degree.........	7,009	6,896	115	110	139	417	489	816	1,586	3,225	70,973
Professional degree......	1,953	1,930	28	29	32	140	68	144	250	1,241	100,000
Doctoral degree........	1,643	1,622	21	32	23	85	68	155	284	952	90,575
Tenure:											
Owner-occupied	82,939	75,551	4,992	4,358	5,214	10,330	9,573	12,006	13,652	15,425	38,177
Renter-occupied	32,319	28,588	2,082	2,926	3,251	5,909	4,739	4,316	3,289	2,077	25,204
Occupier paid no cash rent...........	1,462	1,289	110	161	130	281	234	175	127	71	22,744
FEMALE											
Total................	**123,424**	**106,403**	**13,170**	**14,031**	**13,385**	**20,022**	**14,473**	**13,837**	**10,824**	**6,660**	**20,867**
15 to 24 years old	20,657	13,260	4,434	2,687	1,810	2,336	1,055	651	224	62	8,901
25 to 34 years old	20,079	17,445	1,976	1,520	1,638	3,384	3,026	3,082	2,021	797	25,553
35 to 44 years old	20,831	18,477	2,123	1,428	1,648	3,220	2,780	3,068	2,510	1,696	27,371
45 to 54 years old	22,594	20,490	1,916	1,766	1,769	3,603	3,146	3,298	3,034	1,957	28,236
55 to 64 years old	17,783	16,138	1,663	1,807	1,714	2,726	2,357	2,291	2,086	1,496	25,515
65 years old and over	21,480	20,593	1,057	4,821	4,807	4,750	2,108	1,452	948	652	14,559
Region:											
Northeast..............	22,978	20,178	2,485	2,505	2,538	3,456	2,722	2,584	2,336	1,555	21,930
Midwest...............	26,932	24,089	2,892	3,289	2,923	4,695	3,512	3,202	2,328	1,248	20,817
South.................	45,422	38,521	4,624	5,422	5,155	7,446	5,228	5,045	3,542	2,059	20,126
West.................	28,091	23,615	3,169	2,813	2,769	4,424	3,012	3,008	2,619	1,797	21,408
Educational attainment of householder: [2]											
Total	**102,767**	**93,143**	**8,736**	**11,343**	**11,575**	**17,685**	**13,418**	**13,187**	**10,598**	**6,598**	**22,944**
Less than 9th grade.......	5,429	4,201	605	1,329	1,049	835	232	66	61	25	10,625
9th to 12th grade [3]	7,833	6,413	816	1,770	1,390	1,474	606	219	85	51	11,904
High school graduate [4]	31,601	28,217	2,515	4,400	4,540	6,941	4,637	3,199	1,441	545	18,293
Some college, no degree...	17,739	16,329	1,531	1,703	1,980	3,454	2,944	2,530	1,529	656	23,252
Associate's degree	10,297	9,662	821	730	921	1,811	1,761	1,776	1,366	477	27,715
Bachelor's degree or more..............	29,868	28,321	2,446	1,410	1,695	3,170	3,239	5,398	6,117	4,846	40,801
Bachelor's degree	19,534	18,381	1,767	1,048	1,227	2,359	2,366	3,700	3,549	2,362	36,294
Master's degree.........	8,110	7,801	566	307	382	652	737	1,420	2,065	1,670	48,000
Professional degree......	1,253	1,197	57	31	53	85	86	154	269	463	58,364
Doctoral degree........	971	942	55	26	32	76	50	126	231	350	60,619
Tenure:											
Owner-occupied	87,254	76,485	9,528	9,297	8,834	13,576	10,319	10,447	8,782	5,701	22,246
Renter-occupied	34,691	28,694	3,432	4,480	4,350	6,213	4,002	3,294	1,993	930	17,624
Occupier paid no cash rent	1,478	1,224	209	253	201	233	152	98	51	30	13,599

[1] Includes persons with income deficit. [2] Persons 25 years and over. [3] No diploma attained. [4] Includes high school equivalency.
Source: U.S. Census Bureau, *Income, Poverty and Health Insurance Coverage in the United States: 2008*, Current Population Reports, P60-236(RV), and Detailed Tables—Table PINC-01, September 2009. See also <http://www.census.gov/hhes/www/cpstables/032009/perinc/new01_000.htm>.

Table 702. Average Earnings of Year-Round, Full-Time Workers by Educational Attainment: 2008

[In dollars. For people 18 years old and over as of March 2009. See headnote, Table 700]

Sex and age	All workers	Less than 9th grade	High school		College		Bachelor's degree or more
			9th to 12th grade (no diploma)	High school graduate [1]	Some college, no degree	Associate degree	
Male, total	**61,783**	**28,375**	**33,457**	**43,493**	**50,433**	**54,830**	**94,206**
18 to 24 years old	28,246	19,896	21,305	26,218	27,591	31,992	44,888
25 to 34 years old	48,749	24,211	32,212	36,742	44,597	48,089	68,211
35 to 44 years old	65,839	27,366	34,998	47,057	53,937	57,183	97,334
45 to 54 years old	70,869	30,166	34,707	49,003	58,439	60,788	109,260
55 to 64 years old	72,773	34,106	45,244	47,568	56,486	58,959	104,983
65 years old and over	69,489	37,047	34,029	54,235	53,022	53,532	96,309
Female, total	**43,305**	**21,376**	**22,246**	**31,666**	**36,019**	**39,935**	**60,293**
18 to 24 years old	26,391	(B)	17,228	22,814	24,953	26,814	36,320
25 to 34 years old	39,037	17,923	18,107	27,607	31,592	35,091	50,755
35 to 44 years old	46,595	21,641	22,348	30,574	38,391	40,393	67,353
45 to 54 years old	45,984	21,945	24,076	33,187	39,153	43,734	65,631
55 to 64 years old	47,087	24,644	24,744	37,731	41,247	43,065	62,915
65 years old and over	43,382	(B)	27,995	35,335	40,193	39,202	62,399

B Base figure too small to meet statistical standards for reliability of derived figure. [1] Includes equivalency.

Source: U.S. Census Bureau, *Income, Poverty and Health Insurance Coverage in the United States: 2008*, Current Population Reports, series P60-236(RV), and Detailed Tables—Table PINC-04, September 2009. See also <http://www.census.gov/hhes/www /cpstables/032009/perinc/new04_000.htm>.

Table 703. Per Capita Money Income in Current and Constant (2008) Dollars by Race and Hispanic Origin: 1990 to 2008

[In dollars. Constant dollars based on CPI-U-RS deflator. People as of March of following year. Based on the Current Population Survey, Annual Social and Economic Supplement (ASEC); see text, this section, Section 1, and Appendix III. For data collection changes over time, see <http://www.census.gov/hhes/www/income/data/historical/history.html>]

Year	Current dollars					Constant (2008) dollars				
	All races [1]	White [2]	Black [3]	Asian and Pacific Islander [4]	His-panic [5]	All races [1]	White [2]	Black [3]	Asian and Pacific Islander [4]	His-panic [5]
1990	14,387	15,265	9,017	(NA)	8,424	22,976	24,378	14,400	(NA)	13,453
1995 [6]	17,227	18,304	10,982	16,567	9,300	24,167	25,678	15,406	23,241	13,046
2000 [7,8]	22,346	23,582	14,796	23,350	12,651	27,939	29,484	18,499	29,194	15,818
2003 [9]	23,276	24,626	15,775	24,604	13,492	27,240	28,829	18,467	28,803	15,795
2004 [10]	23,857	25,223	16,025	26,165	14,105	27,194	28,751	18,266	29,825	16,078
2005	25,036	26,496	16,874	27,331	14,483	27,612	29,222	18,610	30,143	15,973
2006	26,352	27,821	17,902	30,474	15,421	28,141	29,710	19,117	32,543	16,468
2007	26,804	28,325	18,428	29,901	15,603	27,834	29,413	19,136	31,050	16,203
2008	26,964	28,502	18,406	30,292	15,674	26,964	28,502	18,406	30,292	15,674

NA Not available. [1] Includes other races, not shown separately. [2] Beginning with 2003, data represents White alone, which refers to people who reported White and did not report any other race category. [3] Beginning with 2003, data represents Black alone, which refers to people who reported Black and did not report any other race category. [4] Beginning with 2003, data represents Asian alone, which refers to people who reported Asian and did not report any other race category. [5] People of Hispanic origin may be any race. [6] Data reflect full implementation of the 1990 census-based sample design and metropolitan definitions, 7,000 household sample reduction, and revised race edits. [7] Implementation of Census 2000-based population controls. [8] Implementation of a 28,000 household sample expansion. [9] See footnote 3, Table 695. See also comments on race in the text for Section 1. [10] Data have been revised to reflect a correction to the weights in the 2005 ASEC.

Source: U.S. Census Bureau, *Income, Poverty and Health Insurance Coverage in the United States: 2008*, Current Population Reports, P60-236(RV), and Historical Tables—Table P-1, September 2009. See also <http://www.census.gov/hhes/www/income /income.html> and <http://www.census.gov/hhes/www/income/data/historical/people/index.html>.

Table 704. Money Income of People—Number by Income Level and by Sex, Race, and Hispanic Origin: 2008

[In thousands (116,720 represents 116,720,000). People as of March of the following year. Based on Current Population Survey, Annual Social and Economic Supplement (ASEC); see text, this section, Section 1, and Appendix III]

Income interval	Male					Female				
	All races [1]	White alone	Black alone	Asian alone	His-panic [2]	All races [1]	White alone	Black alone	Asian alone	His-panic [2]
All households	**116,720**	**95,533**	**13,103**	**5,082**	**17,217**	**123,424**	**98,838**	**15,816**	**5,704**	**16,231**
Under $10,000 [3]	25,919	19,062	4,661	1,217	4,791	44,222	34,458	6,079	2,339	8,137
$10,000 to $19,999	16,747	13,624	2,052	603	3,409	24,035	19,547	3,089	829	3,126
$20,000 to $29,999	15,590	12,792	1,806	575	3,073	17,094	13,759	2,314	612	2,057
$30,000 to $39,999	13,638	11,422	1,349	555	2,208	12,334	9,994	1,637	442	1,179
$40,000 to $49,999	10,186	8,546	1,049	360	1,230	8,254	6,719	1,018	374	641
$50,000 to $59,999	8,303	7,063	728	351	813	5,796	4,747	645	287	436
$60,000 to $74,999	8,765	7,603	629	388	732	5,028	4,146	502	282	322
$75,000 to $84,999	4,153	3,584	276	203	261	1,871	1,480	192	166	101
$85,000 to $99,999	3,392	2,950	187	196	194	1,602	1,321	122	125	81
$100,000 to $149,999	5,885	5,131	251	415	305	2,264	1,884	165	182	113
$150,000 to $199,999	2,054	1,856	72	96	101	483	407	28	33	20
$200,000 to $249,999	760	709	7	41	30	214	187	9	16	14
$250,000 and above	1,329	1,190	36	86	69	227	191	16	18	5

[1] Includes races not shown separately. [2] Persons of Hispanic origin may be of any race. [3] Includes persons without income.

Source: U.S. Census Bureau, *Income, Poverty and Health Insurance Coverage in the United States: 2008*, Current Population Reports, P60-236(RV), and Detailed Tables—Table PINC-11, September 2009. See also <http://www.census.gov/hhes/www /cpstables/032009/perinc/new11_000.htm>.

Table 705. Household Income—Distribution by Income Level and State: 2008

[In thousands (113,101 represents 113,101,000), except as indicated. The American Community Survey universe includes the household population and the population living in institutions, college dormitories, and other group quarters. Based on a sample and subject to sampling variability; see text, Section 1 and Appendix III. For definition of median, see Guide to Tabular Presentation]

State	Number of households (1,000)								Median income (dollars)
	Total	Under $25,000	$25,000 to $49,999	$50,000 to $74,999	$75,000 to $99,999	$100,000 to $149,999	$150,000 to $199,999	$200,000 or more	
United States	113,101	26,340	27,747	21,252	14,015	13,921	4,954	4,872	52,029
Alabama	1,816	549	477	331	194	175	47	43	42,666
Alaska	238	33	52	45	39	45	13	11	68,460
Arizona	2,274	512	602	442	287	272	81	78	50,958
Arkansas	1,114	363	320	195	109	85	21	20	38,815
California	12,177	2,440	2,612	2,155	1,538	1,833	791	808	61,021
Colorado	1,898	382	450	366	246	267	95	92	56,993
Connecticut	1,329	235	248	237	184	224	91	110	68,595
Delaware	329	62	81	65	45	47	16	13	57,989
District of Columbia	250	58	52	38	29	31	17	25	57,936
Florida	7,057	1,739	1,922	1,345	812	733	248	258	47,778
Georgia	3,470	835	867	672	416	398	141	141	50,861
Hawaii	437	74	84	83	68	78	26	24	67,214
Idaho	566	133	163	125	67	53	13	11	47,576
Illinois	4,766	1,033	1,093	906	630	642	230	233	56,235
Indiana	2,481	607	678	497	311	261	68	59	47,966
Iowa	1,215	287	331	260	156	120	33	29	48,980
Kansas	1,111	252	301	222	145	120	39	33	50,177
Kentucky	1,686	529	451	302	187	144	37	36	41,538
Louisiana	1,625	483	423	281	179	169	47	44	43,733
Maine	542	141	147	112	65	51	16	11	46,581
Maryland	2,093	317	412	383	309	363	165	143	70,545
Massachusetts	2,467	488	468	430	335	405	169	172	65,401
Michigan	3,811	946	1,005	726	471	423	132	108	48,591
Minnesota	2,089	409	495	425	297	282	94	86	57,288
Mississippi	1,094	377	297	185	105	85	24	21	37,790
Missouri	2,330	594	639	453	282	237	66	60	46,867
Montana	376	104	107	73	40	34	8	9	43,654
Nebraska	704	164	190	148	93	72	19	18	49,693
Nevada	953	176	239	202	138	127	38	32	56,361
New Hampshire	505	87	107	100	76	82	30	24	63,731
New Jersey	3,154	523	604	540	429	553	246	258	70,378
New Mexico	741	212	202	133	80	74	24	17	43,508
New York	7,137	1,658	1,551	1,252	871	960	394	451	56,033
North Carolina	3,595	935	976	686	407	362	120	109	46,549
North Dakota	275	71	78	54	33	25	7	7	45,685
Ohio	4,509	1,144	1,186	897	540	476	147	120	47,988
Oklahoma	1,408	402	397	264	151	128	34	32	42,822
Oregon	1,475	352	382	295	180	169	51	45	50,169
Pennsylvania	4,905	1,182	1,233	950	601	579	183	177	50,713
Rhode Island	399	94	87	72	55	56	20	16	55,701
South Carolina	1,702	482	453	315	198	162	49	42	44,625
South Dakota	320	81	90	69	39	25	8	8	46,032
Tennessee	2,435	689	682	452	259	214	68	72	43,614
Texas	8,422	2,083	2,124	1,527	1,005	978	355	350	50,043
Utah	854	145	218	194	121	117	32	27	56,633
Vermont	250	54	65	54	34	29	8	7	52,104
Virginia	2,961	563	648	541	388	445	185	191	61,233
Washington	2,548	487	605	501	357	364	122	113	58,078
West Virginia	750	252	212	136	75	53	12	10	37,989
Wisconsin	2,250	481	587	475	313	267	67	60	52,094
Wyoming	209	42	55	42	29	27	8	6	53,207

Source: U.S. Census Bureau, 2008 American Community Survey, B19001, "Household Income in the Past 12 Months" and B19013, "Median Household Income in the Past 12 Months (In 2008 Inflation-Adjusted Dollars)," <http://factfinder.census.gov/>, accessed January 2010.

Table 706. Family Income—Distribution by Income Level and State: 2008

[In thousands (75,031 represents 75,031,000), except as indicated. The American Community Survey universe includes the household population and the population living in institutions, college dormitories, and other group quarters. Based on a sample and subject to sampling variability; see text, Section 1 and Appendix III. For definition of median, see Guide to Tabular Presentation]

State	Number of families (1,000)								Median income (dollars)
	Total	Less than $25,000	$25,000 to $49,000	$50,000 to $74,999	$75,000 to $99,999	$100,000 to $149,999	$150,000 to $199,999	$200,000 and over	
United States	75,031	11,765	17,067	15,144	11,048	11,568	4,252	4,185	63,366
Alabama	1,217	249	308	256	165	156	43	39	54,270
Alaska	157	15	29	30	28	36	11	9	79,541
Arizona	1,489	236	369	312	219	219	69	66	60,547
Arkansas	752	174	217	154	94	75	20	18	47,648
California	8,266	1,253	1,684	1,465	1,121	1,438	637	667	70,029
Colorado	1,209	155	249	243	188	214	82	79	70,164
Connecticut	889	92	139	152	136	191	81	98	85,344
Delaware	222	26	49	47	35	40	15	11	68,745
District of Columbia	107	19	24	15	10	14	9	17	66,722
Florida	4,577	768	1,189	957	633	605	207	218	57,455
Georgia	2,364	412	552	486	332	336	122	123	60,268
Hawaii	303	30	56	59	54	63	22	20	78,659
Idaho	396	64	110	98	56	47	12	10	54,695
Illinois.	3,139	440	648	624	491	533	199	203	68,958
Indiana.	1,648	258	412	370	263	230	61	53	59,380
Iowa.	792	108	194	193	133	108	30	26	61,663
Kansas.	736	101	177	164	123	106	36	29	62,462
Kentucky	1,126	245	295	233	160	126	35	32	51,729
Louisiana	1,094	234	274	209	150	145	43	39	53,963
Maine.	344	56	88	81	52	42	14	10	57,719
Maryland	1,396	129	230	250	221	294	142	130	84,415
Massachusetts.	1,569	184	258	271	246	321	143	146	81,569
Michigan	2,525	411	608	532	389	369	117	99	60,615
Minnesota	1,343	145	267	295	237	239	83	76	71,817
Mississippi	755	199	201	148	92	75	21	19	46,668
Missouri.	1,530	251	389	337	235	205	59	53	58,088
Montana.	238	40	62	56	35	29	7	8	56,820
Nebraska.	457	58	111	113	78	64	17	16	62,067
Nevada	615	78	142	137	102	99	30	26	64,910
New Hampshire	345	34	63	72	60	69	27	21	76,710
New Jersey	2,168	216	358	365	324	459	216	231	85,761
New Mexico.	482	102	128	90	65	61	21	15	52,172
New York	4,582	738	938	831	645	757	321	354	67,877
North Carolina	2,398	431	611	506	331	312	107	99	56,588
North Dakota	171	24	43	39	30	23	6	6	61,109
Ohio.	2,936	465	720	655	443	414	131	108	60,061
Oklahoma	937	181	249	206	128	113	31	28	53,862
Oregon.	939	148	223	207	142	140	42	39	61,190
Pennsylvania	3,205	466	746	691	486	496	164	158	63,316
Rhode Island	248	32	51	46	41	48	16	14	71,992
South Carolina.	1,142	224	287	240	167	142	45	37	55,664
South Dakota.	206	30	53	53	35	22	7	7	60,104
Tennessee	1,623	314	432	346	220	188	60	63	53,799
Texas	5,868	1,092	1,400	1,121	811	824	313	308	58,765
Utah	632	69	149	154	105	102	29	25	65,226
Vermont.	160	19	38	38	27	24	7	6	63,438
Virginia.	1,999	247	395	379	295	356	159	167	73,192
Washington	1,637	201	334	343	268	291	105	94	70,498
West Virginia	491	107	144	110	64	47	11	9	49,082
Wisconsin	1,468	178	341	340	260	237	60	53	65,622
Wyoming	136	16	32	30	22	24	7	5	66,504

Source: U.S. Census Bureau, 2008 American Community Survey, B19101, "Family Income in the Past 12 Months" and B19113, "Median Family Income in the Past 12 Months (In 2008 Inflation-Adjusted Dollars)," <http://factfinder.census.gov/>, accessed January 2010.

Income, Expenditures, Poverty, and Wealth 461

Table 707. Household, Family, and Per Capita Income and People and Families Below Poverty Level by City: 2008

[See headnote, Table 708. The American Community Survey universe includes the household population and the population living in institutions, college dormitories, and other group quarters. Based on a sample and subject to sampling variability; see text, Section 1 and Appendix III. For definition of median, see Guide to Tabular Presentation]

City	Median household income (dol.)	Median family income (dol.)	Per capita income (dol.)	Number below poverty level [1] Individuals	Number below poverty level [1] Families	Percent below poverty level [1] Individuals	Percent below poverty level [1] Families
Albuquerque, NM	46,437	61,154	26,024	76,302	12,361	15.0	10.0
Anaheim, CA	61,128	67,357	22,583	42,849	7,205	13.1	10.2
Anchorage municipality, AK	75,637	87,930	36,452	17,474	3,268	6.4	4.8
Arlington, TX	52,777	62,587	25,304	39,831	7,578	11.3	8.7
Atlanta, GA	48,865	60,954	35,128	95,484	11,985	22.4	16.2
Aurora, CO	46,684	57,340	24,234	46,533	8,558	15.4	12.1
Austin, TX	51,372	64,726	30,680	128,941	19,906	17.0	11.9
Bakersfield, CA	50,409	56,728	22,813	53,286	10,246	16.7	13.5
Baltimore, MD	40,313	48,216	22,885	119,340	19,392	19.3	15.4
Boston, MA	51,688	60,543	32,714	108,688	15,957	18.7	14.4
Buffalo, NY	29,973	35,258	19,254	76,419	15,465	30.3	26.5
Charlotte, NC	52,530	65,237	32,402	80,814	14,147	12.0	8.2
Chicago, IL	46,911	54,086	26,924	555,391	96,550	20.6	16.9
Cincinnati, OH	33,562	46,114	23,758	70,491	11,947	25.1	20.4
Cleveland, OH	26,731	33,986	16,545	121,397	22,623	30.5	25.0
Colorado Springs, CO	56,263	67,770	28,674	45,964	7,881	11.8	7.9
Columbus, OH	44,369	54,146	23,604	145,959	24,600	20.1	14.7
Corpus Christi, TX	45,612	54,026	24,325	47,907	9,321	17.2	13.1
Dallas, TX	40,796	43,973	26,436	271,880	51,425	22.6	19.5
Denver, CO	45,831	57,657	30,557	108,567	15,954	18.4	13.5
Detroit, MI	28,730	32,798	14,976	255,559	47,944	33.3	30.3
El Paso, TX	37,600	42,935	17,786	145,285	32,288	24.3	21.4
Fort Wayne, IN	43,212	52,297	23,721	32,138	6,541	13.5	10.5
Fort Worth, TX	48,870	57,220	23,208	110,219	19,660	16.6	12.8
Fresno, CA	40,134	44,633	20,213	119,188	20,798	25.5	20.2
Honolulu, HI [2]	60,531	76,549	33,369	39,298	6,187	10.8	7.1
Houston, TX	44,315	48,887	26,836	391,240	75,055	19.5	16.3
Indianapolis, IN [3]	43,652	56,855	25,471	126,814	22,170	16.4	11.9
Jacksonville, FL	50,476	62,035	25,993	94,806	16,449	11.9	8.2
Kansas City, MO	45,824	57,840	27,298	71,087	13,427	16.4	12.8
Las Vegas, NV	53,097	61,075	27,045	72,011	12,514	12.6	9.1
Lexington-Fayette, KY	50,325	69,223	30,530	42,448	7,620	15.6	10.8
Long Beach, CA	50,975	57,639	25,961	91,765	14,492	19.8	15.3
Los Angeles, CA	48,882	53,577	28,071	723,516	126,421	19.4	16.2
Memphis, TN	37,207	45,540	22,612	143,168	25,999	23.1	18.0
Mesa, AZ	51,433	62,900	24,862	56,381	8,248	11.7	7.4
Miami, FL	28,333	33,613	22,330	86,174	15,709	25.6	20.3
Milwaukee, WI	37,331	43,609	19,237	132,189	23,430	23.4	18.5
Minneapolis, MN	48,724	62,308	30,825	73,704	10,156	21.3	14.1
Nashville-Davidson, TN [3]	45,587	58,347	27,467	101,357	16,911	17.5	12.5
New Orleans, LA	37,751	51,146	21,309	67,861	6,945	22.6	14.9
New York, NY	51,116	56,552	31,245	1,500,484	280,749	18.2	15.3
Newark, NJ	35,296	38,668	17,372	66,022	13,633	26.1	22.8
Oakland, CA	48,699	59,411	30,372	63,375	11,270	17.5	15.4
Oklahoma City, OK	43,821	54,456	24,565	87,773	17,878	16.4	12.9
Omaha, NE	44,358	61,337	25,850	56,981	8,780	15.0	9.7
Philadelphia, PA	36,976	46,363	20,973	336,272	59,082	24.1	18.8
Phoenix, AZ	50,140	57,507	24,296	285,957	42,154	18.9	13.7
Pittsburgh, PA	36,709	51,567	26,140	58,567	8,306	21.2	13.4
Plano, TX	85,003	102,275	40,920	17,249	3,300	6.7	4.9
Portland, OR	50,979	66,645	30,540	78,768	12,430	14.4	9.9
Raleigh, NC	53,825	71,563	30,849	46,137	6,361	13.3	8.1
Riverside, CA	56,859	60,988	22,141	40,415	6,013	13.5	9.3
Sacramento, CA	50,958	57,572	25,313	72,413	11,623	16.1	11.7
San Antonio, TX	42,261	52,666	21,582	243,887	41,116	19.2	14.3
San Diego, CA	62,668	75,867	32,472	176,885	25,222	14.4	9.4
San Francisco, CA	73,798	91,812	47,420	88,154	8,573	11.0	6.2
San Jose, CA	80,616	90,119	33,849	81,063	13,208	8.9	6.4
Santa Ana, CA	54,239	54,187	16,220	56,150	8,880	17.6	14.9
Seattle, WA	61,786	90,835	43,012	64,812	5,386	11.6	4.6
St. Louis, MO	34,078	44,503	21,204	79,163	12,425	22.9	17.7
St. Paul, MN	45,831	61,353	27,120	47,854	7,586	18.4	13.6
St. Petersburg, FL	43,305	53,062	27,452	30,351	4,785	12.5	8.2
Stockton, CA	49,034	54,098	19,658	58,553	11,015	21.6	17.7
Tampa, FL	45,224	56,049	28,547	58,666	10,724	17.8	13.8
Toledo, OH	34,157	42,275	18,804	68,210	13,796	24.7	20.4
Tucson, AZ	36,640	47,698	19,567	108,949	16,372	20.9	14.8
Tulsa, OK	39,657	51,944	25,944	68,899	12,270	18.3	13.2
Virginia Beach, VA	65,776	74,358	31,332	27,527	5,472	6.5	4.8
Washington, DC	57,936	66,722	42,069	96,769	14,675	17.2	13.7
Wichita, KS	44,211	58,130	25,899	51,332	10,580	14.3	11.4

[1] See headnote, Table 708. [2] Data shown for census designated place (CDP). [3] Represents the portion of a consolidated city that is not within one or more separately incorporated places.

Source: U.S. Census Bureau, 2008 American Community Survey, B19013, B19113, B19301, B17001, and B17010, <http://factfinder.census.gov/> accessed February 2010.

Table 708. Individuals and Families Below Poverty Level—Number and Rate by State: 2000 and 2008

[In thousands (33,311 represents 33,311,000), except as indicated. Represents number and percent below poverty in the past 12 months. Prior to 2006, the American Community Survey universe was limited to the household population and excluded the population living in institutions, college dormitories, and other group quarters. Poverty status was determined for all people except institutionalized people, people in military group quarters, people in college dormitories, and unrelated individuals under 15 years old. These groups were excluded from the numerator and denominator when calculating poverty rates. Based on a sample and subject to sampling variability; see Appendix III]

| State | Number below poverty (1,000) | | | | Percent below poverty | | | |
| | Individuals | | Families | | Individuals | | Families | |
	2000	2008	2000	2008	2000	2008	2000	2008
United States	**33,311**	**39,108**	**6,615**	**7,252**	**12.2**	**13.2**	**9.3**	**9.7**
Alabama	672	713	146	146	15.6	15.7	12.4	12.0
Alaska	55	56	11	9	9.1	8.4	6.8	5.7
Arizona	780	939	150	154	15.6	14.7	11.6	10.3
Arkansas	439	481	96	98	17.0	17.3	13.0	13.0
California	4,520	4,778	832	825	13.7	13.3	10.7	10.0
Colorado	363	553	64	95	8.7	11.4	5.7	7.8
Connecticut	254	315	51	59	7.7	9.3	5.8	6.7
Delaware	70	85	14	15	9.3	10.0	6.7	6.9
District of Columbia	94	97	17	15	17.5	17.2	15.4	13.7
Florida	1,987	2,371	387	433	12.8	13.2	9.3	9.5
Georgia	999	1,381	206	263	12.6	14.7	10.0	11.1
Hawaii	103	115	19	18	8.8	9.1	6.8	6.0
Idaho	144	188	26	37	11.4	12.6	7.7	9.4
Illinois.	1,335	1,532	262	283	11.1	12.2	8.6	9.0
Indiana.	592	808	113	158	10.1	13.1	7.1	9.6
Iowa.	281	335	53	58	10.0	11.5	7.0	7.3
Kansas.	247	307	43	57	9.5	11.3	6.2	7.7
Kentucky	640	721	148	147	16.4	17.3	13.5	13.1
Louisiana	862	744	182	146	20.0	17.3	16.0	13.4
Maine.	124	158	22	29	10.1	12.3	6.6	8.6
Maryland	477	443	89	75	9.3	8.1	6.6	5.4
Massachusetts.	586	627	110	112	9.6	10.0	7.1	7.1
Michigan	975	1,410	196	265	10.1	14.4	7.7	10.5
Minnesota	328	491	66	83	6.9	9.6	5.1	6.2
Mississippi.	498	602	104	128	18.2	21.2	14.2	17.0
Missouri.	606	768	118	148	11.2	13.4	7.7	9.7
Montana.	117	140	23	23	13.4	14.8	9.5	9.7
Nebraska	158	187	28	31	9.6	10.8	6.5	6.8
Nevada	194	290	34	49	9.9	11.3	6.9	7.9
New Hampshire.	63	97	11	17	5.3	7.6	3.5	5.0
New Jersey	651	741	126	135	7.9	8.7	6.0	6.2
New Mexico.	320	333	64	61	18.0	17.1	14.2	12.6
New York	2,391	2,581	491	472	13.1	13.6	10.7	10.3
North Carolina	1,018	1,302	203	260	13.1	14.6	9.6	10.9
North Dakota	71	74	14	13	11.6	12.0	8.1	7.9
Ohio.	1,216	1,492	246	289	11.1	13.4	8.4	9.8
Oklahoma	459	562	100	110	13.8	15.9	11.0	11.8
Oregon.	439	506	84	90	13.2	13.6	9.5	9.6
Pennsylvania	1,240	1,458	247	271	10.5	12.1	7.8	8.5
Rhode Island	108	119	23	19	10.7	11.7	8.5	7.7
South Carolina.	557	680	123	132	14.4	15.7	11.7	11.6
South Dakota.	83	96	16	17	11.5	12.5	8.4	8.2
Tennessee	745	938	158	187	13.5	15.5	10.5	11.6
Texas.	3,056	3,760	639	726	15.1	15.8	12.3	12.4
Utah.	192	258	40	42	8.8	9.6	7.2	6.6
Vermont.	63	63	12	10	10.7	10.6	7.5	6.5
Virginia.	630	768	124	147	9.2	10.2	6.8	7.3
Washington	667	728	127	126	11.6	11.3	8.6	7.7
West Virginia	327	301	72	61	18.6	17.0	14.7	12.4
Wisconsin	461	569	75	98	8.9	10.4	5.6	6.7
Wyoming	55	49	10	8	11.4	9.4	7.9	5.7

Source: U.S. Census Bureau, 2008 American Community Survey, B17001, "Poverty Status in the Past 12 Months by Sex and Age" and B17010, "Poverty Status in the Past 12 Months of Families by Family Type by Presence of Related Children under 18 Years by Age of Related Children," <http://factfinder.census.gov/>, accessed February 2010.

Table 709. Poverty Thresholds by Size of Family Unit: 1980 to 2008

[In dollars per year. For information on the official poverty thresholds; see text, this section. For more on poverty, see <http://www.census.gov/hhes/www/poverty/about/overview/measure.html>]

Size of family unit	1980	1990	1995	2000 [1]	2004 [2]	2005	2006	2007	2008
One person (unrelated individual) [3]	4,190	6,652	7,763	8,791	9,646	9,973	10,294	10,590	10,991
Under 65 years old	4,290	6,800	7,929	8,959	9,827	10,160	10,488	10,787	11,201
65 years old and over	3,949	6,268	7,309	8,259	9,060	9,367	9,669	9,944	10,326
Two persons	5,363	8,509	9,933	11,235	12,335	12,755	13,167	13,540	14,051
Householder under 65 years old	5,537	8,794	10,259	11,589	12,714	13,145	13,569	13,954	14,489
Householder 65 years old and over	4,983	7,905	9,219	10,418	11,430	11,815	12,201	12,550	13,030
Three persons	6,565	10,419	12,158	13,740	15,066	15,577	16,079	16,530	17,163
Four persons	8,414	13,359	15,569	17,604	19,307	19,971	20,614	21,203	22,025
Five persons	9,966	15,792	18,408	20,815	22,830	23,613	24,382	25,080	26,049
Six persons	11,269	17,839	20,804	23,533	25,787	26,683	27,560	28,323	29,456
Seven persons	12,761	20,241	23,552	26,750	29,233	30,249	31,205	32,233	33,529
Eight persons	14,199	22,582	26,237	29,701	32,641	33,610	34,774	35,816	37,220
Nine or more persons	16,896	26,848	31,280	35,150	39,062	40,288	41,499	42,739	44,346

[1] Implementation of Census 2000-based population controls and sample expanded by 28,000 households. [2] The 2004 data have been revised to reflect a correction to the weights in the 2005 Annual Social and Economic Supplement (ASEC). [3] A person living alone or with non-relatives.

Source: U.S. Census Bureau, *Income, Poverty, and Health Insurance Coverage in the United States: 2008*, Current Population Reports, P60-236, and Historical Tables—Table 1, September 2009. See also <http://www.census.gov/hhes/www/poverty/poverty.html> and <http://www.census.gov/hhes/www/poverty/data/historical/people.html>.

Table 710. People Below Poverty Level and Below 125 Percent of Poverty Level by Race and Hispanic Origin: 1980 to 2008

[29,272 represents 29,272,000. People as of March of the following year. Based on Current Population Survey, Annual Social and Economic Supplement (ASEC); see text, this section, Section 1, and Appendix III. For data collection changes over time, see <http://www.census.gov/hhes/www/income/data/historical/history.html>]

Year	Number of persons below poverty (1,000)					Percent of persons below poverty					Below 125 percent [6] of poverty level	
	All races [1]	White [2]	Black [3]	Asian and Pacific Islander [4]	His-panic [5]	All races [1]	White [2]	Black [3]	Asian and Pacific Islander [4]	His-panic [5]	Number (1,000)	Percent of total population
1980	29,272	19,699	8,579	(NA)	3,491	13.0	10.2	32.5	(NA)	25.7	40,658	18.1
1985	33,064	22,860	8,926	(NA)	5,236	14.0	11.4	31.3	(NA)	29.0	44,166	18.7
1987 [7]	32,221	21,195	9,520	1,021	5,422	13.4	10.4	32.4	16.1	28.0	43,032	17.9
1988	31,745	20,715	9,356	1,117	5,357	13.0	10.1	31.3	17.3	26.7	42,551	17.5
1989	31,528	20,785	9,302	939	5,430	12.8	10.0	30.7	14.1	26.2	42,653	17.3
1990	33,585	22,326	9,837	858	6,006	13.5	10.7	31.9	12.2	28.1	44,837	18.0
1991	35,708	23,747	10,242	996	6,339	14.2	11.3	32.7	13.8	28.7	47,527	18.9
1992 [8]	38,014	25,259	10,827	985	7,592	14.8	11.9	33.4	12.7	29.6	50,592	19.7
1993 [9]	39,265	26,226	10,877	1,134	8,126	15.1	12.2	33.1	15.3	30.6	51,801	20.0
1994	38,059	25,379	10,196	974	8,416	14.5	11.7	30.6	14.6	30.7	50,401	19.3
1995	36,425	24,423	9,872	1,411	8,574	13.8	11.2	29.3	14.6	30.3	48,761	18.5
1996	36,529	24,650	9,694	1,454	8,697	13.7	11.2	28.4	14.5	29.4	49,310	18.5
1997	35,574	24,396	9,116	1,468	8,308	13.3	11.0	26.5	14.0	27.1	47,853	17.8
1998	34,476	23,454	9,091	1,360	8,070	12.7	10.5	26.1	12.5	25.6	46,036	17.0
1999 [10]	32,791	22,169	8,441	1,285	7,876	11.9	9.8	23.6	10.7	22.7	45,030	16.3
2000 [11]	31,581	21,645	7,982	1,258	7,747	11.3	9.5	22.5	9.9	21.5	43,612	15.6
2001	32,907	22,739	8,136	1,275	7,997	11.7	9.9	22.7	10.2	21.4	45,320	16.1
2002 [12]	34,570	23,466	8,602	1,161	8,555	12.1	10.2	24.1	10.1	21.8	47,084	16.5
2003	35,861	24,272	8,781	1,401	9,051	12.5	10.5	24.4	11.8	22.5	48,687	16.9
2004 [13]	37,040	25,327	9,014	1,201	9,122	12.7	10.8	24.7	9.8	21.9	49,693	17.1
2005	36,950	24,872	9,168	1,402	9,368	12.6	10.6	24.9	11.1	21.8	49,327	16.8
2006	36,460	24,416	9,048	1,353	9,243	12.3	10.3	24.3	10.3	20.6	49,688	16.8
2007	37,276	25,120	9,237	1,349	9,890	12.5	10.5	24.5	10.2	21.5	50,876	17.0
2008	39,829	26,990	9,379	1,576	10,987	13.2	11.2	24.7	11.8	23.2	53,805	17.9

NA Not available. [1] Includes other races, not shown separately. [2] Beginning 2002, data represent White alone, which refers to people who reported White and did not report any other race category. [3] Beginning 2002, data represent Black alone, which refers to people who reported Black and did not report any other race category. [4] Beginning 2002, data represent Asian alone, which refers to people who reported Asian and did not report any other race category. [5] People of Hispanic origin may be any race. [6] Includes those in poverty, plus those who have income above poverty but less than 1.25 times their poverty threshold. [7] Implementation of a new March CPS processing system. [8] Implementation of 1990 census population controls. [9] The March 1994 income supplement was revised to allow for the coding of different income amounts on selected questionnaire items. Limits either increased or decreased in the following categories: earnings increased to $999,999; social security increased to $49,999; supplemental security income and public assistance increased to $24,999; veterans' benefits increased to $99,999; child support and alimony decreased to $49,999. [10] Implementation of Census-2000-based population controls. [11] Implementation of sample expansion by 28,000 households. [12] Beginning with the 2003 Current Population Survey (CPS), the questionnaire allowed respondents to choose more than one race. For 2002 and later, data represent persons who selected this race group only and exclude persons reporting more than one race. The CPS in prior years allowed respondents to report only one race group. See also comments on race in the text for Section 1, Population. [13] Data have been revised to reflect a correction to the weights in the 2005 ASEC.

Source: U.S. Census Bureau, *Income, Poverty, and Health Insurance Coverage in the United States: 2008*, Current Population Reports, series P60-236, and Historical Tables—Tables 2 and 6, September 2009. See also <http://www.census.gov/hhes/www/poverty/poverty.html> and <http://www.census.gov/hhes/www/poverty/data/historical/people.html>.

Table 711. Children Below Poverty Level by Race and Hispanic Origin: 1980 to 2008

[11,114 represents 11,114,000. Persons as of March of the following year. Covers only related children in families under 18 years old. Based on Current Population Survey, Annual Social and Economic Supplement (ASEC); see text, this section, Section 1, and Appendix III. For data collection changes over time, see <http://www.census.gov/hhes/www/income/data/historical/history.html>]

Year	Number of children below poverty level (1,000)					Percent of children below poverty level				
	All races [1]	White [2]	Black [3]	Asian and Pacific Islander [4]	His-panic [5]	All races [1]	White [2]	Black [3]	Asian and Pacific Islander [4]	His-panic [5]
1980........	11,114	6,817	3,906	(NA)	1,718	17.9	13.4	42.1	(NA)	33.0
1985........	12,483	7,838	4,057	(NA)	2,512	20.1	15.6	43.1	(NA)	39.6
1989........	12,001	7,164	4,257	368	2,496	19.0	14.1	43.2	18.9	35.5
1990........	12,715	7,696	4,412	356	2,750	19.9	15.1	44.2	17.0	37.7
1991........	13,658	8,316	4,637	348	2,977	21.1	16.1	45.6	17.1	39.8
1992 [6].....	14,521	8,752	5,015	352	3,440	21.6	16.5	46.3	16.0	39.0
1993 [7].....	14,961	9,123	5,030	358	3,666	22.0	17.0	45.9	17.6	39.9
1994........	14,610	8,826	4,787	308	3,956	21.2	16.3	43.3	17.9	41.1
1995........	13,999	8,474	4,644	532	3,938	20.2	15.5	41.5	18.6	39.3
1996........	13,764	8,488	4,411	553	4,090	19.8	15.5	39.5	19.1	39.9
1997........	13,422	8,441	4,116	608	3,865	19.2	15.4	36.8	19.9	36.4
1998........	12,845	7,935	4,073	542	3,670	18.3	14.4	36.4	17.5	33.6
1999 [8].....	11,678	7,194	3,698	367	3,561	16.6	13.1	32.8	11.5	29.9
2000 [9].....	11,005	6,834	3,495	407	3,342	15.6	12.4	30.9	12.5	27.6
2001........	11,175	7,086	3,423	353	3,433	15.8	12.8	30.0	11.1	27.4
2002 [10].....	11,646	7,203	3,570	302	3,653	16.3	13.1	32.1	11.4	28.2
2003........	12,340	7,624	3,750	331	3,982	17.2	13.9	33.6	12.1	29.5
2004 [11].....	12,473	7,876	3,702	265	3,985	17.3	14.3	33.4	9.4	28.6
2005........	12,335	7,652	3,743	312	3,977	17.1	13.9	34.2	11.0	27.7
2006........	12,299	7,522	3,690	351	3,959	16.9	13.6	33.0	12.0	26.6
2007........	12,802	8,002	3,838	345	4,348	17.6	14.4	34.3	11.8	28.3
2008........	13,507	8,441	3,781	430	4,888	18.5	15.3	34.4	14.2	30.3

NA Not available. [1] Includes other races, not shown separately. [2] Beginning 2002, data represent White alone, which refers to people who reported White and did not report any other race category. [3] Beginning 2002, data represent Black alone, which refers to people who reported Black and did not report any other race category. [4] Beginning 2002, data represent Asian alone, which refers to people who reported Asian and did not report any other race category. [5] People of Hispanic origin may be of any race. [6] Implementation of 1990 census population controls. [7] The March 1994 income supplement was revised to allow for the coding of different income amounts on selected questionnaire items. Limits either increased or decreased in the following categories: earnings increased to $999,999; social security increased to $49,999; supplemental security income and public assistance increased to $24,999; veterans' benefits increased to $99,999; child support and alimony decreased to $49,999. [8] Implementation of Census 2000-based population controls. [9] Implementation of sample expansion to 28,000 households. [10] Beginning with the 2003 Current Population Survey (CPS), the questionnaire allowed respondents to choose more than one race. For 2002 and later, data represent persons who selected this race group only and excludes persons reporting more than one race. The CPS in prior years allowed respondents to report only one race group. See also comments on race in the text for Section 1. [11] Data have been revised to reflect a correction to the weights in the 2005 Annual Social and Economic Supplement (ASEC).

Source: U.S. Census Bureau, *Income, Poverty, and Health Insurance Coverage in the United States: 2008*, Current Population Reports, P60-236, and Historical Tables—Table 3, September 2009. See also <http://www.census.gov/hhes/www/poverty/poverty.html> and <http://www.census.gov/hhes/www/poverty/data/historical/people.html>.

Table 712. People Below Poverty Level by Selected Characteristics: 2008

[39,829 represents 39,829,000. People as of March 2009. Based on Current Population Survey, Annual Social and Economic Supplement (ASEC); see text, this section and Section 1, and Appendix III. The 2009 CPS allowed respondents to choose more than one race. For 2008, data represent persons who selected this race group only and exclude persons reporting more than one race. The CPS in prior years allowed respondents to report only one race group. See also comments on race in the text for Section 1. For composition of regions, see map, inside front cover]

Sex, age, region, nativity	Number below poverty level (1,000)					Percent below poverty level				
	All races [1]	White alone	Black alone	Asian alone	His-panic [2]	All races [1]	White alone	Black alone	Asian alone	His-panic [2]
Total	**39,829**	**26,990**	**9,379**	**1,576**	**10,987**	**13.2**	**11.2**	**24.7**	**11.8**	**23.2**
Male	17,698	12,083	4,045	717	5,116	12.0	10.1	22.9	11.3	21.0
Female...............	22,131	14,907	5,334	859	5,871	14.4	12.3	26.3	12.4	25.5
Under 18 years old	14,068	8,863	3,878	446	5,010	19.0	15.8	34.7	14.6	30.6
18 to 24 years old	5,283	3,650	1,179	203	1,172	18.4	16.4	28.1	17.8	23.1
25 to 34 years old	5,351	3,670	1,219	215	1,672	13.2	11.6	22.7	10.0	20.6
35 to 44 years old	4,277	2,980	914	230	1,347	10.4	9.1	17.7	9.9	19.2
45 to 54 years old	4,047	2,834	884	167	802	9.1	7.8	16.7	8.5	15.6
55 to 59 years old	1,642	1,113	378	87	245	8.8	7.1	18.8	11.0	13.9
60 to 64 years old	1,504	1,109	280	72	214	9.7	8.4	18.4	12.3	17.8
65 years old and over	3,656	2,771	646	157	525	9.7	8.5	20.0	12.1	19.3
65 to 74 years old	1,710	1,246	327	80	288	8.4	7.2	17.6	10.6	17.7
75 years old and over	1,945	1,525	319	77	238	11.2	10.0	23.2	14.1	21.8
Northeast................	6,295	4,142	1,515	440	1,619	11.6	9.5	22.8	15.3	24.8
Midwest.................	8,120	5,501	2,075	168	963	12.4	9.8	30.9	11.3	24.3
South..................	15,862	9,909	5,131	332	3,834	14.3	11.8	24.4	11.1	22.3
West	9,552	7,437	659	636	4,572	13.5	13.0	18.6	10.7	23.2
Native	33,293	22,298	8,797	550	6,740	12.6	10.3	25.3	11.2	22.7
Foreign born	6,536	4,692	582	1,026	4,247	17.8	19.4	18.0	12.2	24.0
Naturalized citizen........	1,577	974	190	356	715	10.2	10.5	13.0	8.0	13.9
Not a citizen............	4,959	3,718	392	670	3,532	23.3	24.9	22.1	16.9	28.1

[1] Includes other races, not shown separately. [2] Persons of Hispanic origin may be any race.

Source: U.S. Census Bureau, *Income, Poverty, and Health Insurance Coverage in the United States: 2008*, Current Population Reports, P60-236, and Detailed Tables—Tables POV01, POV29, and POV41. See also <http://www.census.gov/hhes/www/cpstables/032009/pov/toc.htm>.

Income, Expenditures, Poverty, and Wealth 465

Table 713. Work Experience of People During 2008 by Poverty Status, Sex, and Age: 2008

[104,023 represents 104,023,000. Covers only persons 16 years old and over. Based on Current Population Survey, Annual Social and Economic Supplement (ASEC); see text, this section, Section 1, and Appendix III]

Sex and age	Worked full-time year-round			Did not work full-time year-round			Did not work		
		Below poverty level			Below poverty level			Below poverty level	
	Number (1,000)	Number (1,000)	Percent	Number (1,000)	Number (1,000)	Percent	Number (1,000)	Number (1,000)	Percent
BOTH SEXES									
Total...............	104,023	2,754	2.6	54,294	7,331	13.5	77,707	17,131	22.0
16 to 17 years old	99	6	6.1	2,130	181	8.5	6,822	1,268	18.6
18 to 64 years old	100,626	2,711	2.7	47,837	7,029	14.7	40,723	12,365	30.4
18 to 24 years old	7,284	399	5.5	12,839	2,193	17.1	8,565	2,691	31.4
25 to 34 years old	23,580	875	3.7	10,484	2,011	19.2	6,455	2,465	38.2
35 to 54 years old	53,257	1,226	2.3	17,668	2,264	12.8	14,763	4,834	32.7
55 to 64 years old	16,504	211	1.3	6,846	561	8.2	10,940	2,374	21.7
65 years old and over	3,298	37	1.1	4,327	121	2.8	30,163	3,498	11.6
MALE									
Total...............	59,869	1,586	2.6	24,020	3,124	13.0	30,733	6,593	21.5
16 to 17 years old	55	6	(B)	1,068	91	8.5	3,472	635	18.3
18 to 64 years old	57,792	1,561	2.7	20,790	2,985	14.4	15,137	4,932	32.6
18 to 24 years old	4,158	210	5.0	6,294	882	14.0	4,057	1,184	29.2
25 to 34 years old	13,780	461	3.3	4,757	843	17.7	1,903	762	40.0
35 to 54 years old	30,593	746	2.4	6,892	1,006	14.6	4,778	1,935	40.5
55 to 64 years old	9,261	145	1.6	2,847	255	8.9	4,398	1,051	23.9
65 years old and over	2,023	19	0.9	2,162	47	2.2	12,124	1,026	8.5
FEMALE									
Total...............	44,154	1,168	2.6	30,274	4,207	13.9	46,975	10,537	22.4
16 to 17 years old	44	–	(B)	1,062	90	8.5	3,350	633	18.9
18 to 64 years old	42,834	1,150	2.7	27,047	4,044	15.0	25,586	7,433	29.1
18 to 24 years old	3,127	189	6.0	6,545	1,311	20.0	4,508	1,507	33.4
25 to 34 years old	9,800	415	4.2	5,728	1,169	20.4	4,552	1,703	37.4
35 to 54 years old	22,664	480	2.1	10,776	1,258	11.7	9,984	2,900	29.0
55 to 64 years old	7,243	66	0.9	3,998	307	7.7	6,542	1,323	20.2
65 years old and over	1,275	19	1.5	2,165	73	3.4	18,039	2,472	13.7

– Represents zero. B Base figure too small to meet statistical standards for reliability of a derived figure.

Source: U.S. Census Bureau, *Income, Poverty, and Health Insurance Coverage in the United States: 2008*, Current Population Reports, P60-236, and Detailed Tables—Table POV22, September 2009. See also <http://www.census.gov/hhes/www/cpstables/032009/pov/toc.htm>.

Table 714. Families Below Poverty Level and Below 125 Percent of Poverty by Race and Hispanic Origin: 1980 to 2008

[6,217 represents 6,217,000. Families as of March of the following year. Based on Current Population Survey, Annual Social and Economic Supplement (ASEC); see text, this section and Section 1, and Appendix III. For data collection changes over time, see <http://www.census.gov/hhes/www/income/data/historical/history.html>]

Year	Number of families below poverty (1,000)					Percent of persons below poverty					Below 125 percent [6] of poverty level	
	All races [1]	White [2]	Black [3]	Asian and Pacific Islander [4]	His-panic [5]	All races [1]	White [2]	Black [3]	Asian and Pacific Islander [4]	His-panic [5]	Number (1,000)	Percent
1980.....	6,217	4,195	1,826	(NA)	751	10.3	8.0	28.9	(NA)	23.2	8,764	14.5
1985.....	7,223	4,983	1,983	(NA)	1,074	11.4	9.1	28.7	(NA)	25.5	9,753	15.3
1990.....	7,098	4,622	2,193	169	1,244	10.7	8.1	29.3	11.0	25.0	9,564	14.4
1995.....	7,532	4,994	2,127	264	1,695	10.8	8.5	26.4	12.4	27.0	10,223	14.7
1999 [7] ...	6,792	4,447	1,887	258	1,593	9.3	7.3	21.8	10.3	20.5	9,320	12.9
2000 [8] ...	6,400	4,333	1,686	233	1,540	8.7	7.1	19.3	7.8	19.2	9,032	12.2
2001.....	6,813	4,579	1,829	234	1,649	9.2	7.4	20.7	7.8	19.4	9,525	12.8
2002 [9] ...	7,229	4,862	1,923	210	1,792	9.6	7.8	21.5	7.4	19.7	9,998	13.2
2003.....	7,607	5,058	1,986	311	1,925	10.0	8.1	22.3	10.2	20.8	10,360	13.6
2004 [10] ...	7,835	5,293	2,035	232	1,953	10.2	8.4	22.8	7.4	20.5	10,499	13.7
2005.....	7,657	5,068	1,997	289	1,948	9.9	8.0	22.1	9.0	19.7	10,442	13.5
2006.....	7,668	5,118	2,007	260	1,922	9.8	8.0	21.6	7.8	18.9	10,531	13.4
2007.....	7,623	5,046	2,045	261	2,045	9.8	7.9	22.1	7.9	19.7	10,551	13.5
2008.....	8,147	5,414	2,055	341	2,239	10.3	8.4	22.0	9.8	21.3	11,164	14.2

NA Not available. [1] Includes other races, not shown separately. [2] Beginning 2002, data represent White alone, which refers to people who reported White and did not report any other race category. [3] Beginning 2002, data represent Black alone, which refers to people who reported Black and did not report any other race category. [4] Beginning 2002, data represent Asian alone, which refers to people who reported Asian and did not report any other race category. [5] People of Hispanic origin may be any race. [6] See footnote 6, Table 710. [7] Implementation of Census 2000-based population controls. [8] Implementation of a 28,000 household sample expansion. [9] Beginning with the 2003 Current Population Survey (CPS), the questionnaire allowed respondents to choose more than one race. For 2002 and later, data represent persons who selected this race group only and excludes persons reporting more than one race. The CPS in prior years allowed respondents to report only one race group. See also comments on race in the text for Section 1. [10] Data have been revised to reflect a correction to the weights in the 2005 Annual Social and Economic Supplement (ASEC).

Source: U.S. Census Bureau, *Income, Poverty, and Health Insurance Coverage in the United States: 2008*, Current Population Reports, P60-236, and Historical and Detailed Tables—Tables 4 and POV04. See also <http://www.census.gov/hhes/www/poverty/poverty.html> and <http://www.census.gov/hhes/www/poverty/data/historical/families.html>.

Table 715. Families Below Poverty Level by Selected Characteristics: 2008

[8,147 represents 8,147,000. Families as of March 2009. Based on Current Population Survey, Annual Social and Economic Supplement (ASEC); see text, this section, Section 1, and Appendix III. The 2009 CPS allowed respondents to choose more than one race. For 2008, data represent persons who selected this race group only and exclude persons reporting more than one race. See also comments on race in the text for Section 1. For composition of regions, see map, inside front cover]

Characteristic	Number below poverty level (1,000)					Percent below poverty level				
	All races [1]	White alone	Black alone	Asian alone	His-panic [2]	All races [1]	White alone	Black alone	Asian alone	His-panic [2]
Total families	**8,147**	**5,414**	**2,055**	**341**	**2,239**	**10.3**	**8.4**	**22.0**	**9.8**	**21.3**
Age of householder:										
15 to 24 years old	928	605	261	16	256	28.7	25.3	44.1	13.5	31.2
25 to 34 years old	2,296	1,467	665	60	740	17.2	14.2	34.1	9.1	27.6
35 to 44 years old	1,932	1,272	491	88	611	11.0	9.2	21.4	9.5	21.0
45 to 54 years old	1,265	868	268	70	333	7.0	5.8	12.8	8.7	16.4
55 to 64 years old	868	602	181	56	148	6.4	5.3	13.8	9.8	13.1
65 years old and over	816	572	178	46	133	6.3	5.1	16.7	11.4	15.1
Region:										
Northeast	1,265	800	340	93	360	9.0	6.9	21.1	12.0	24.1
Midwest	1,679	1,109	472	37	192	9.6	7.3	28.2	9.7	22.7
South	3,342	2,084	1,096	71	784	11.3	9.1	20.8	9.1	19.8
West	1,862	1,421	148	140	902	10.6	9.8	18.2	9.0	21.4
Type of family:										
Married couple	3,261	2,548	346	244	1,078	5.5	5.0	7.9	8.6	15.6
Male householder, no spouse present	723	499	161	24	154	13.8	12.5	19.9	10.5	15.1
Female householder, no spouse present	4,163	2,368	1,548	72	1,007	28.7	25.2	37.2	16.7	39.2

[1] Includes other races, not shown separately. [2] Hispanic persons may be any race.

Source: U.S. Census Bureau, *Income, Poverty, and Health Insurance Coverage in the United States: 2008*, Current Population Reports, P60-236, and Detailed Tables—Tables POV04 and POV44, September 2009. See also <http://www.census.gov/hhes/www/cpstables/032009/pov/toc.htm\>.

Table 716. Top Wealth Holders With Gross Assets of $1.5 Million or More—Debts, Mortgages, and Net Worth: 2004

[2,728 represents 2,728,000. Net worth is defined as assets minus liabilities. Figures are estimates based on a sample of federal estate tax returns (Form 706). Based on the estate multiplier technique; for more information on this methodology, see source]

Sex and net worth	Total assets		Debts and mortgages		Net worth	
	Number of top wealth holders (1,000)	Amount [1] (mil. dol.)	Number of top wealth holders (1,000)	Amount (mil. dol.)	Number of top wealth holders (1,000)	Amount (mil. dol.)
Both sexes, total	**2,728**	**11,076,759**	**2,099**	**850,622**	**2,728**	**10,201,246**
Size of net worth:						
Under $1.5 million [2]	531	736,039	468	231,035	531	480,113
$1.5 million under $2.0 million	746	1,386,077	544	98,187	746	1,287,890
$2.0 million under $3.5 million	846	2,316,701	614	147,370	846	2,169,331
$3.5 million under $5.0 million	247	1,082,889	192	58,950	247	1,023,939
$5.0 million under $10.0 million	231	1,668,002	176	104,811	231	1,563,191
$10.0 million under $20.0 million	79	1,155,326	64	69,849	79	1,085,477
$20.0 million or more	47	2,731,726	40	140,421	47	2,591,305
Males, total	**1,555**	**6,471,540**	**1,208**	**583,805**	**1,555**	**5,862,844**
Size of net worth:						
Under $1.5 million [2]	389	528,017	339	184,673	389	318,454
$1.5 million under $2.0 million	359	675,321	258	54,149	359	621,172
$2.0 million under $3.5 million	465	1,289,522	346	96,654	465	1,192,868
$3.5 million under $5.0 million	131	578,304	102	37,496	131	540,808
$5.0 million under $10.0 million	135	989,077	100	74,003	135	915,074
$10.0 million under $20.0 million	47	679,613	38	41,466	47	638,146
$20.0 million or more	30	1,731,686	25	95,364	30	1,636,322
Females, total	**1,173**	**4,605,219**	**891**	**266,817**	**1,173**	**4,338,402**
Size of net worth:						
Under $1.5 million [2]	143	208,021	129	46,362	143	161,659
$1.5 million under $2.0 million	387	710,757	286	44,038	387	666,719
$2.0 million under $3.5 million	380	1,027,179	268	50,716	380	976,463
$3.5 million under $5.0 million	116	504,585	89	21,454	116	483,131
$5.0 million under $10.0 million	96	678,924	77	30,808	96	648,116
$10.0 million under $20.0 million	33	475,713	27	28,382	33	447,331
$20.0 million or more	18	1,000,040	15	45,057	18	954,983

[1] Includes other types of assets, not shown separately. [2] Includes individuals with zero net worth.

Source: U.S. Internal Revenue Service, Statistics of Income Division, "SOI Data Tables," July 2008, <http://www.irs.gov/taxstats/indtaxstats/article/0,,id=96426,00.html>.

Table 717. Top Wealth Holders With Gross Assets of $1.5 Million or More by Type of Property, Sex, and Size of Net Worth: 2004

[2,728 represents 2,728,000. Net worth is defined as assets minus liabilities. Figures are estimates based on a sample of federal estate tax returns (Form 706). Based on the estate multiplier technique; for more information on this methodology, see source]

Sex and net worth	Number of top wealth holders (1,000)	Assets (mil. dol.)				
		Total [1]	Personal residences	Other real estate	Closely held stock	Publicly traded stock
Both sexes, total	**2,728**	**11,076,759**	**1,185,941**	**1,402,029**	**1,127,194**	**2,247,269**
Size of net worth:						
Under $1.5 million [2]	531	736,039	176,105	134,674	42,431	63,062
$1.5 million under $2.0 million	746	1,386,077	229,369	206,626	69,066	219,818
$2.0 million under $3.5 million	846	2,316,701	342,206	329,893	141,272	415,249
$3.5 million under $5.0 million	247	1,082,889	127,444	152,634	95,958	209,459
$5.0 million under $10.0 million	231	1,668,002	148,543	230,146	165,781	373,575
$10.0 million under $20.0 million	79	1,155,326	76,472	137,770	136,144	246,824
$20.0 million or more	47	2,731,726	85,802	210,286	476,542	719,282
Males, total	**1,555**	**6,471,540**	**597,971**	**828,055**	**833,929**	**1,140,665**
Size of net worth:						
Under $1.5 million [2]	389	528,017	117,554	96,796	36,177	42,494
$1.5 million under $2.0 million	359	675,321	97,605	105,224	44,376	94,788
$2.0 million under $3.5 million	465	1,289,522	163,984	179,481	102,116	199,844
$3.5 million under $5.0 million	131	578,304	60,123	80,919	63,006	95,417
$5.0 million under $10.0 million	135	989,077	68,653	151,731	110,961	200,003
$10.0 million under $20.0 million	47	679,613	38,710	75,459	97,601	135,157
$20.0 million or more	30	1,731,686	51,342	138,446	379,692	372,962
Females, total	**1,173**	**4,605,219**	**587,970**	**573,974**	**293,264**	**1,106,604**
Size of net worth:						
Under $1.5 million [2]	143	208,021	58,550	37,879	6,255	20,568
$1.5 million under $2.0 million	387	710,757	131,764	101,402	24,690	125,030
$2.0 million under $3.5 million	380	1,027,179	178,222	150,412	39,155	215,405
$3.5 million under $5.0 million	116	504,585	67,321	71,714	32,953	114,042
$5.0 million under $10.0 million	96	678,924	79,890	78,416	54,820	173,572
$10.0 million under $20.0 million	33	475,713	37,762	62,312	38,543	111,667
$20.0 million or more	18	1,000,040	34,461	71,840	96,849	346,320

[1] Includes other types of assets, not shown separately. [2] Includes individuals with zero net worth.
Source: U.S. Internal Revenue Service, Statistics of Income Division, "SOI Data Tables," July 2008, <http://www.irs.gov/taxstats/indtaxstats/article/0,,id=96426,00.html>.

Table 718. Top Wealth Holders With Net Worth of $1.5 Million or More— Number and Net Worth by State: 2004

[2,196 represents 2,196,000. Estimates based on a sample of federal estate tax returns (Form 706). Estimates of wealth by state can be subject to significant year-to-year fluctuations and this is especially true for individuals at the extreme tail of the net worth distribution and for states with relatively small decedent populations. Based on the estate multiplier technique; for more information on this methodology, see source]

State	Number of top wealth holders (1,000)	Net worth (mil. dol.)	State	Number of top wealth holders (1,000)	Net worth (mil. dol.)
Total [1]	**2,196**	**9,721,133**	Montana...............	7	23,966
Alabama	18	79,123	Nebraska...............	13	83,265
Alaska	1	4,776	Nevada	15	80,768
Arizona	36	139,861	New Hampshire..........	7	27,342
Arkansas	11	94,704	New Jersey	79	324,712
California................	428	1,793,642	New Mexico.............	9	28,107
Colorado	32	163,324	New York	168	942,812
Connecticut..............	47	197,801	North Carolina............	59	223,408
Delaware	8	30,923	North Dakota	1	3,988
District of Columbia	7	27,850	Ohio..................	61	228,532
Florida	199	904,014	Oklahoma	17	58,554
Georgia	56	270,677	Oregon................	15	61,328
Hawaii	7	22,552	Pennsylvania	86	399,312
Idaho	5	23,982	Rhode Island	8	30,782
Illinois..................	101	476,354	South Carolina...........	14	67,856
Indiana.................	32	112,272	South Dakota............	6	18,850
Iowa...................	18	55,332	Tennessee.............	25	100,778
Kansas.................	21	65,084	Texas.................	108	492,663
Kentucky	18	65,404	Utah..................	8	52,674
Louisiana...............	22	92,315	Vermont...............	4	20,584
Maine..................	8	35,173	Virginia................	59	223,984
Maryland	50	191,279	Washington	50	180,008
Massachusetts...........	83	335,482	West Virginia	12	28,415
Michigan	47	261,085	Wisconsin	26	127,515
Minnesota	33	135,682	Wyoming	5	106,698
Mississippi..............	8	61,786			
Missouri................	33	115,716	Other areas [1]	5	28,042

[1] Includes U.S. territories and possessions.
Source: U.S. Internal Revenue Service, Statistics of Income Division, "SOI Data Tables," July 2008, <http://www.irs.gov/taxstats/indtaxstats/article/0,,id=96426,00.html>.

Table 719. Nonfinancial Assets Held by Families by Type of Asset: 2007

[221.5 represents $221,500. Families include one-person units and, as used in this table, are more comparable to the U.S. Census Bureau's household concept. Based on Survey of Consumer Finance; see Appendix III and <http://www.federalreserve.gov/pubs /oss/oss2/papers/measurement.pdf>. For definition of median, see Guide to Tabular Presentation. For data on financial assets, see Table 1169]

Family characteristic	Any financial or non-financial asset	Any non-financial asset	Vehicles	Pri-mary residence	Other resi-dential property	Equity in nonresi-dential property	Bus-iness equity	Other asset
PERCENT OF FAMILIES HOLDING ASSET								
All families, total	97.7	92.0	87.0	68.6	13.7	8.1	13.6	7.2
Age of family head:								
Under 35 years old	97.1	88.2	85.4	40.7	5.6	3.2	8.0	5.9
35 to 44 years old	96.9	91.3	87.5	66.1	12.0	7.5	18.2	5.5
45 to 54 years old	97.6	95.0	90.3	77.3	15.7	9.5	17.2	8.7
55 to 64 years old	99.1	95.6	92.2	81.0	20.9	11.5	18.1	8.5
65 to 74 years old	98.4	94.5	90.6	85.5	18.9	12.3	11.2	9.1
75 years old and over	98.1	87.3	71.5	77.0	13.4	6.8	4.5	5.8
Race or ethnicity or respondent:								
White non-Hispanic	98.9	94.6	89.6	75.6	15.3	9.0	15.8	8.4
Non-White or Hispanic	94.9	85.8	80.9	51.9	10.0	5.9	8.2	4.3
Tenure:								
Owner occupied	100.0	100.0	93.8	100.0	17.5	10.8	17.5	8.0
Renter occupied or other	92.8	74.5	72.3	(B)	5.6	2.1	5.0	5.3
MEDIAN VALUE [1] ($1,000)								
All families, total	221.5	177.4	15.5	200.0	146.0	75.0	92.2	14.0
Age of family head:								
Under 35 years old	38.8	30.9	13.3	175.0	85.0	50.0	35.0	8.0
35 to 44 years old	222.3	182.6	17.4	205.0	150.0	50.0	59.0	10.0
45 to 54 years old	306.0	224.9	18.7	230.0	150.0	80.0	76.8	15.0
55 to 64 years old	347.0	233.1	17.4	210.0	157.0	90.0	100.0	20.0
65 to 74 years old	303.3	212.2	14.6	200.0	150.0	75.0	300.0	20.0
75 years old and over	219.3	157.1	9.4	150.0	100.0	110.0	225.0	25.0
Race or ethnicity of respondent:								
White non-Hispanic	271.0	203.8	17.1	200.0	136.5	75.0	100.0	15.0
Non-White or Hispanic	89.2	102.0	12.0	180.0	175.0	62.7	50.0	8.0
Tenure:								
Owner occupied	344.2	253.5	18.4	200.0	150.0	80.0	100.0	20.0
Renter occupied or other	13.6	10.1	8.6	(B)	85.0	38.0	33.0	5.4

B Base too small to meet statistical standards for reliability of derived figure. [1] Median value of asset for families holding such assets.

Source: Board of Governors of the Federal Reserve System, "2007 Survey of Consumer Finances," May 2009, <http://www.federalreserve.gov/pubs/oss/oss2/2007/scf2007home.html>.

Table 720. Family Net Worth—Mean and Median Net Worth in Constant (2007) Dollars by Selected Family Characteristics: 1998 to 2007

[Net worth in thousands of constant (2007) dollars (359.7 represents $359,700). Constant dollar figures are based on consumer price index for all urban consumers published by U.S. Bureau of Labor Statistics. Families include one-person units and as used in this table are comparable to the U.S. Census Bureau's household concept. Based on Survey of Consumer Finance; see Appendix III. For definition of mean and median, see Guide to Tabular Presentation]

Family characteristic	1998 Mean	1998 Median	2001 Mean	2001 Median	2004 Mean	2004 Median	2007 Mean	2007 Median
All families	359.7	91.3	464.4	101.2	492.3	102.2	556.3	120.3
Age of family head:								
Under 35 years old	81.3	11.6	106.1	13.7	80.7	15.6	106.0	11.8
35 to 44 years old	249.9	80.8	303.7	90.7	328.6	76.2	325.6	86.6
45 to 54 years old	461.5	134.5	568.4	155.4	596.1	158.9	661.2	182.5
55 to 64 years old	677.6	162.8	856.0	216.8	926.7	273.1	935.8	253.7
65 to 74 years old	594.2	186.5	793.5	207.9	758.8	208.8	1,015.2	239.4
75 years old and over	395.7	159.9	548.6	181.6	580.0	179.1	638.2	213.5
Race or ethnicity of respondent:								
White non-Hispanic	429.5	121.9	571.2	143.0	617.0	154.5	692.2	170.4
Non-White or Hispanic	128.0	21.2	137.4	21.0	168.2	27.2	228.5	27.8
Tenure:								
Owner occupied	514.7	168.2	655.5	201.8	686.3	202.6	778.2	234.2
Renter occupied or other	55.3	5.4	64.4	5.6	59.4	4.4	70.6	5.1

Source: Board of Governors of the Federal Reserve System, "2007 Survey of Consumer Finances," May 2009, <http://www.federalreserve.gov/pubs/oss/oss2/2007/scf2007home.html>.

Table 721. Household and Nonprofit Organization Sector Balance Sheet: 1990 to 2009

[In billions of dollars (24,288 represents $24,288,000,000,000). As of December 31. For details of financial assets and liabilities, see Table 1168]

Item	1990	1995	2000	2005	2006	2007	2008	2009
Assets	**24,288**	**32,985**	**50,106**	**71,737**	**77,869**	**78,795**	**65,599**	**68,178**
Tangible assets [1]	9,718	11,464	16,704	28,388	29,735	28,037	23,891	23,063
Real estate	7,601	8,836	13,379	24,128	25,271	23,391	19,112	18,207
Households [2,3]	6,802	8,054	12,137	22,084	22,944	20,978	17,039	16,575
Consumer durable goods [4]	2,039	2,531	3,196	4,077	4,268	4,438	4,559	4,637
Financial assets [1]	14,570	21,520	33,402	43,348	48,134	50,759	41,707	45,115
Deposits [1]	3,326	3,357	4,376	6,155	6,769	7,426	7,901	7,750
Time and savings deposits	2,490	2,300	3,033	4,914	5,400	5,889	6,050	6,130
Money market fund shares	391	472	960	949	1,114	1,347	1,580	1,320
Credit market instruments [1]	1,746	2,235	2,465	3,363	3,478	4,082	4,034	4,203
Agency and GSE-backed securities [5]	117	216	594	488	403	682	701	35
Municipal securities	648	533	531	821	872	897	937	998
Corporate and foreign bonds	238	467	552	1,300	1,523	2,011	1,988	2,236
Corporate equities [2]	1,961	4,434	8,205	7,993	9,493	9,465	5,881	7,698
Mutual fund shares [6]	512	1,253	2,704	3,839	4,388	4,832	3,445	4,417
Security credit	62	128	412	575	656	866	743	668
Life insurance reserves	392	566	819	1,083	1,164	1,202	1,180	1,250
Pension fund reserves	3,310	5,725	9,171	11,374	12,696	13,376	10,432	11,806
Equity in noncorporate business [7]	3,007	3,493	4,871	8,358	8,843	8,798	7,325	6,538
Liabilities [1]	**3,703**	**5,038**	**7,377**	**12,157**	**13,405**	**14,312**	**14,195**	**14,001**
Credit market instruments [1]	3,581	4,841	6,987	11,716	12,890	13,748	13,773	13,536
Home mortgages [8]	2,489	3,319	4,798	8,848	9,825	10,484	10,427	10,262
Consumer credit	824	1,168	1,741	2,321	2,416	2,555	2,594	2,481
Net worth	**20,585**	**27,946**	**42,729**	**59,580**	**64,464**	**64,484**	**51,404**	**54,176**
Replacement cost value of structures:								
Residential [1]	4,618	6,091	8,469	13,475	14,441	14,643	13,981	13,533
Households	4,512	5,975	8,326	13,276	14,229	14,430	13,779	13,337
Nonresidential (nonprofits)	472	591	812	1,175	1,280	1,353	1,424	1,332
Owners' equity in household real estate	4,313	4,735	7,338	13,237	13,118	10,494	6,612	6,313
Owners' equity as percentage of household real estate	63.4	58.8	60.5	59.9	57.2	50.0	38.8	38.1

[1] Includes types of assets and/or liabilities not shown separately. [2] At market value. [3] Includes all types of owner-occupied housing including farm houses and mobile homes, as well as second homes that are not rented, vacant homes for sale, and vacant land. [4] At replacement (current) cost. [5] GSE = Government-sponsored enterprises. [6] Value based on the market values of equities held and the book value of other assets held by mutual funds. [7] Net worth of noncorporate business and owners' equity in farm business and unincorporated security brokers and dealers. [8] Includes loans made under home equity lines of credit and home equity loans secured by junior liens.

Source: Board of Governors of the Federal Reserve System, "Federal Reserve Statistical Release, Z.1, Flow of Funds Accounts of the United States," March 2010, <http://www.federalreserve.gov/releases/z1/Current/>.

Table 722. Net Stock of Fixed Assets and Consumer Durable Goods in Current and Chained (2005) Dollars: 1990 to 2008

[In billions of dollars (18,314 represents $18,314,000,000,000). Estimates as of December 31. For explanation of chained dollars, see text, this section]

Item	1990	1995	2000	2004	2005	2006	2007	2008
CURRENT DOLLARS								
Net stock, total	**18,314**	**22,856**	**30,157**	**38,894**	**42,619**	**45,920**	**47,824**	**48,139**
Fixed assets	16,275	20,325	26,961	35,010	38,542	41,652	43,386	43,581
Private	12,678	15,821	21,241	27,747	30,601	32,871	33,929	34,261
Nonresidential	6,571	8,000	10,573	12,922	14,071	15,189	16,024	17,182
Equipment and software	2,507	3,100	4,134	4,698	4,931	5,243	5,510	5,792
Structures	4,064	4,900	6,439	8,224	9,140	9,946	10,515	11,390
Residential	6,107	7,821	10,668	14,825	16,530	17,682	17,905	17,079
Government	3,598	4,504	5,721	7,264	7,941	8,781	9,457	9,320
Nonresidential	3,449	4,316	5,489	6,958	7,606	8,432	9,111	8,987
Equipment and software	551	675	704	767	802	850	891	959
Structures	2,898	3,641	4,786	6,190	6,804	7,582	8,220	8,027
Residential	149	188	232	306	335	349	346	334
Federal	1,077	1,292	1,435	1,641	1,749	1,867	1,947	1,943
Defense	734	868	904	1,018	1,081	1,152	1,202	1,207
State and local	2,521	3,213	4,285	5,623	6,193	6,914	7,510	7,377
Consumer durable goods	2,039	2,531	3,196	3,883	4,077	4,268	4,438	4,559
Motor vehicles and parts	650	811	1,042	1,269	1,302	1,307	1,319	1,261
Furnishings and durable household equipment	649	787	977	1,174	1,248	1,325	1,380	1,439
Other	322	392	449	521	548	604	649	704
CHAINED (2005) DOLLARS								
Net stock, total	**(NA)**	**30,459**	**35,765**	**40,066**	**41,154**	**42,327**	**43,400**	**44,230**
Fixed assets	(NA)	28,518	32,920	36,203	37,052	38,003	38,863	39,561
Private	(NA)	22,092	25,971	28,658	29,374	30,178	30,891	31,433
Nonresidential	(NA)	10,227	12,340	13,342	13,594	13,928	14,311	14,658
Equipment and software	(NA)	3,044	4,204	4,736	4,901	5,103	5,286	5,400
Structures	(NA)	7,371	8,162	8,606	8,693	8,831	9,035	9,267
Residential	(NA)	11,898	13,626	15,316	15,780	16,249	16,579	16,764
Government	(NA)	6,430	6,949	7,545	7,678	7,825	7,974	8,130
Nonresidential	(NA)	6,149	6,648	7,227	7,357	7,503	7,649	7,803
Equipment and software	(NA)	714	734	772	796	824	850	884
Structures	(NA)	5,422	5,911	6,455	6,561	6,679	6,802	6,923
Residential	(NA)	281	302	318	321	323	325	327
Consumer durable goods	(NA)	2,175	2,943	3,863	4,102	4,332	4,559	4,698

NA Not available.

Source: U.S. Bureau of Economic Analysis, *Survey of Current Business*, October 2009. See also <http://www.bea.gov/national/FA2004/SelectTable.asp>.

470 Income, Expenditures, Poverty, and Wealth

Section 14
Prices

This section presents indexes of producer and consumer prices, actual prices for selected commodities, and energy prices. The primary sources of these data are monthly publications of the U.S. Department of Labor, Bureau of Labor Statistics (BLS), which include *Monthly Labor Review, Consumer Price Index, Detailed Report, Producer Price Indexes*, and *U.S. Import and Export Price Indexes*. The U.S. Department of Commerce, Bureau of Economic Analysis is the source for gross domestic product measures. Cost of living data for many urban and metropolitan areas are provided by The Council for Community and Economic Research, a private organization in Arlington, VA. Table 713 on housing price indexes appears in this edition from the Office of Federal Housing Enterprise Oversight, *Housing Price Index*. Other commodity, housing, and energy prices may be found in the Energy and Utilities, Natural Resources, and Construction and Housing sections.

Consumer price indexes (CPI)—
The CPI is a measure of the average change in prices over time in a "market basket" of goods and services purchased either by urban wage earners and clerical workers or by all urban consumers. In 1919, BLS began to publish complete indexes at semiannual intervals, using a weighting structure based on data collected in the expenditure survey of wage-earner and clerical-worker families in 1917–19 (BLS Bulletin 357, 1924). The first major revision of the CPI occurred in 1940, with subsequent revisions in 1953, 1964, 1978, 1987, and 1998.

Beginning with the release of data for January 1988 in February 1988, most consumer price indexes shifted to a new reference base year. All indexes previously expressed on a base of 1967 = 100, or any other base through December 1981, have been rebased to 1982–84 = 100. The expenditure weights are based upon data tabulated from the Consumer Expenditure Surveys.

The BLS publishes CPIs for two population groups: (1) a CPI for all urban consumers (CPI-U), which covers approximately 80 percent of the total population; and (2) a CPI for urban wage earners and clerical workers (CPI-W), which covers 32 percent of the total population. The CPI-U includes, in addition to wage earners and clerical workers, groups which historically have been excluded from CPI coverage, such as professional, managerial, and technical workers; the self-employed; short-term workers; the unemployed; and retirees and others not in the labor force.

The current CPI is based on prices of food, clothing, shelter, fuels, transportation fares, charges for doctors' and dentists' services, drugs, etc. purchased for day-to-day living. Prices are collected in 87 areas across the country from over 50,000 housing units and 23,000 establishments. Area selection was based on the 1990 census. All taxes directly associated with the purchase and use of items are included in the index. Prices of food, fuels, and a few other items are obtained every month in all 87 locations. Prices of most other commodities and services are collected monthly in the three largest geographic areas and every other month in other areas.

In calculating the index, each item is assigned a weight to account for its relative importance in consumers' budgets. Price changes for the various items in each location are then averaged. Local data are then combined to obtain a U.S. city average. Separate indexes are also published for regions, area size-classes, cross-classifications of regions and size-classes, and for 26 local areas, usually consisting of the Metropolitan Statistical Area (MSA); see Appendix II. Area definitions are those established by the Office of Management and Budget in 1983. Definitions do not include revisions made since 1992. Area indexes do not measure differences in the level of prices among cities; they only measure the average change in prices for each area since the base period. For further detail regarding the CPI, see the BLS *Handbook of Methods*, Bulletin 2490 (June 2008), Chapter 17; the *Consumer Price Index*, and the CPI home page at <http://www.bls.gov/cpi/>. In January 1983, the method of measuring home-ownership costs in the CPI-U was changed to a rental equivalence approach. This treatment calculates homeowner costs of shelter based on the implicit rent owners would pay to rent the homes they own. The rental equivalence approach was introduced into the CPI-W in 1985. The CPI-U was used to prepare the consumer price tables in this section.

Producer price index (PPI)—This index, dating from 1890, is the oldest continuous statistical series published by the BLS. It is designed to measure average changes in prices received by domestic producers of all commodities, at various stages of processing.

The index has undergone several revisions (see *Monthly Labor Review*, February 1962, April 1978, and August 1988). It is now based on approximately 10,000 individual products and groups of products along with about 100,000 quotations per month. Indexes for the net output of manufacturing and mining industries have been added in recent years. Prices used in constructing the index are collected from sellers and generally apply to the first significant large-volume commercial transaction for each commodity—i.e., the manufacturer's or other producer's selling price or the selling price on an organized exchange or at a central market.

The weights used in the index represent the total net selling value of commodities produced or processed in this country. Values are f.o.b. (free on board) production point and are exclusive of excise taxes. Effective with the release of data for January 1988, many important producer price indexes were changed to a new reference base year, 1982 = 100, from 1967 = 100. The reference year of the PPI shipment weights has been taken primarily from the 2002 Census of Manufactures. For further detail regarding the PPI, see the BLS *Handbook of Methods*, Bulletin 2490 (June 2008),

Chapter 14. The PPI Web page is <http://www.bls .gov/ppi/>.

BEA price indexes—Chain-weighted price indexes, produced by the Bureau of Economic Analysis (BEA), are weighted averages of the detailed price indexes used in the deflation of the goods and services that make up the gross domestic product (GDP) and its major components. Growth rates are constructed for years and quarters using quantity weights for the current and preceding year or quarter; these growth rates are used to move the index for the preceding period forward a year or quarter at a time. All chain-weighted price indexes are expressed in terms of the reference year value 2000 = 100.

Personal consumption expenditures (PCE) price and quantity indexes are based on market transactions for which there are corresponding price measures. The price index provides a measure of the prices paid by persons for domestic purchases of goods and services, which may be a useful measure of consumer prices for some analytical purposes. PCEs are defined as market value of spending by individuals and not-for-profit institutions on all goods and services. Personal consumption expenditures also include the value of certain imputed goods and services—such as the rental value of owner-occupied homes and compensation paid in kind—such as employer-paid health and life insurance premiums. More information on this index may be found at <http://www.bea.gov/bea/mp _National .htm>.

Measures of inflation— Inflation is defined as a time of generally rising prices for goods and factors of production. The BLS samples prices of items in a representative market basket and publishes the result as the CPI. The media invariably announce the inflation rate as the percent change in the CPI from month to month. A much more meaningful indicator of inflation is the percent change from the same month of the prior year. The PPI measures prices at the producer level only. The PPI shows the same general pattern of inflation as does the CPI but is more volatile.

The PPI often tends to foreshadow trends that later occur in the CPI.

Other measures of inflation include the gross domestic purchases chain-weighted price index, the index of industrial materials prices; the Futures Price and Spot Market prices from the Commodity Research Bureau; the Employment Cost Index, the Hourly Compensation Index, or the Unit Labor Cost Index found in Section 12, Labor Force, Employment, and Earnings, as a measure of the change in cost of the labor factor of production; and changes in long-term interest rates that are often used to measure changes in the cost of the capital factor of production.

International price indexes—

The BLS International Price Program produces export and import price indexes for nonmilitary goods traded between the United States and the rest of the world.

The export price index provides a measure of price change for all products sold by U.S. residents to foreign buyers. The import price index provides a measure of price change for goods purchased from other countries by U.S. residents. The reference period for the indexes is 2000 = 100, unless otherwise indicated. The product universe for both the import and export indexes includes raw materials, agricultural products, semifinished manufactures, and finished manufactures, including both capital and consumer goods. Price data for these items are collected primarily by mail questionnaire. In nearly all cases, the data are collected directly from the exporter or importer, although in a few cases, prices are obtained from other sources.

To the extent possible, the data gathered refer to prices at the U.S. border for exports and at either the foreign border or the U.S. border for imports. For nearly all products, the prices refer to transactions completed during the first week of the month. Survey respondents are asked to indicate all discounts, allowances, and rebates applicable to the reported prices, so that the price used in the calculation of the indexes is the actual price for which the product was bought or sold.

Table 723. Purchasing Power of the Dollar: 1950 to 2009

[Indexes: PPI, 1982 = $1.00; CPI, 1982-84 = $1.00. Producer prices prior to 1961, and consumer prices prior to 1964, exclude Alaska and Hawaii. Producer prices based on finished goods index. Obtained by dividing the average price index for the 1982 = 100, PPI; 1982-84 = 100, CPI base periods (100.0) by the price index for a given period and expressing the result in dollars and cents. Annual figures are based on average of monthly data]

Year	Annual average as measured by—		Year	Annual average as measured by—	
	Producer prices	Consumer prices		Producer prices	Consumer prices
1950	3.546	4.151	1980	1.136	1.215
1951	3.247	3.846	1981	1.041	1.098
1952	3.268	3.765	1982	1.000	1.035
1953	3.300	3.735	1983	0.984	1.003
1954	3.289	3.717	1984	0.964	0.961
1955	3.279	3.732	1985	0.955	0.928
1956	3.195	3.678	1986	0.969	0.913
1957	3.077	3.549	1987	0.949	0.880
1958	3.012	3.457	1988	0.926	0.846
1959	3.021	3.427	1989	0.880	0.807
1960	2.994	3.373	1990	0.839	0.766
1961	2.994	3.340	1991	0.822	0.734
1962	2.985	3.304	1992	0.812	0.713
1963	2.994	3.265	1993	0.802	0.692
1964	2.985	3.220	1994	0.797	0.675
1965	2.933	3.166	1995	0.782	0.656
1966	2.841	3.080	1996	0.762	0.638
1967	2.809	2.993	1997	0.759	0.623
1968	2.732	2.873	1998	0.765	0.613
1969	2.632	2.726	1999	0.752	0.600
1970	2.545	2.574	2000	0.725	0.581
1971	2.469	2.466	2001	0.711	0.565
1972	2.392	2.391	2002	0.720	0.556
1973	2.193	2.251	2003	0.698	0.543
1974	1.901	2.029	2004	0.673	0.529
1975	1.718	1.859	2005	0.642	0.512
1976	1.645	1.757	2006	0.623	0.496
1977	1.546	1.649	2007	0.600	0.482
1978	1.433	1.532	2008	0.565	0.464
1979	1.289	1.380	2009 [1]	0.579	0.466

[1] PPI data are preliminary.

Source: Bureau of Labor Statistics, CPI Detailed Report, monthly, and at <http://www.bls.gov/cpi/cpi_dr.htm>. See also Monthly Labor Review at <http://www.bls.gov/opub/mlr/welcome.htm> and Producer Price Indexes, monthly and annual.

Table 724. Consumer Price Indexes (CPI-U) by Major Groups: 1990 to 2009

[1982-84 = 100, except as indicated. Represents annual averages of monthly figures. Reflects buying patterns of all urban consumers. Minus sign (–) indicates decrease. See text, this section]

Year	All items	Commodities	Services	Food	Energy	All items less food and energy	Food and beverages	Housing	Apparel	Transportation	Medical care	Education and communication [1]
1990	130.7	122.8	139.2	132.4	102.1	135.5	132.1	128.5	124.1	120.5	162.8	(NA)
1995	152.4	136.4	168.7	148.4	105.2	161.2	148.9	148.5	132.0	139.1	220.5	92.2
1996	156.9	139.9	174.1	153.3	110.1	165.6	153.7	152.8	131.7	143.0	228.2	95.3
1997	160.5	141.8	179.4	157.3	111.5	169.5	157.7	156.8	132.9	144.3	234.6	98.4
1998	163.0	141.9	184.2	160.7	102.9	173.4	161.1	160.4	133.0	141.6	242.1	100.3
1999	166.6	144.4	188.8	164.1	106.6	177.0	164.6	163.9	131.3	144.4	250.6	101.2
2000	172.2	149.2	195.3	167.8	124.6	181.3	168.4	169.6	129.6	153.3	260.8	102.5
2001	177.1	150.7	203.4	173.1	129.3	186.1	173.6	176.4	127.3	154.3	272.8	105.2
2002	179.9	149.7	209.8	176.2	121.7	190.5	176.8	180.3	124.0	152.9	285.6	107.9
2003	184.0	151.2	216.5	180.0	136.5	193.2	180.5	184.8	120.9	157.6	297.1	109.8
2004	188.9	154.7	222.8	186.2	151.4	196.6	186.6	189.5	120.4	163.1	310.1	111.6
2005	195.3	160.2	230.1	190.7	177.1	200.9	191.2	195.7	119.5	173.9	323.2	113.7
2006	201.6	164.0	238.9	195.2	196.9	205.9	195.7	203.2	119.5	180.9	336.2	116.8
2007	207.3	167.5	246.8	202.9	207.7	210.7	203.3	209.6	119.0	184.7	351.1	119.6
2008	215.3	174.8	255.5	214.1	236.7	215.6	214.2	216.3	118.9	195.5	364.1	123.6
2009	214.5	169.7	259.2	218.0	193.1	219.2	218.2	217.1	120.1	179.3	375.6	127.4
PERCENT CHANGE [2]												
1990	5.4	5.2	5.5	5.8	8.3	5.0	5.8	4.5	4.6	5.6	9.0	(NA)
1995	2.8	1.9	3.4	2.8	0.6	3.0	2.8	2.6	-1.0	3.6	4.5	3.8
1996	3.0	2.6	3.2	3.3	4.7	2.7	3.2	2.9	-0.2	2.8	3.5	3.4
1997	2.3	1.4	3.0	2.6	1.3	2.4	2.6	2.6	0.9	0.9	2.8	3.3
1998	1.6	0.1	2.7	2.2	-7.7	2.3	2.2	2.3	0.1	-1.9	3.2	1.9
1999	2.2	1.8	2.5	2.1	3.6	2.1	2.2	2.2	-1.3	2.0	3.5	0.9
2000	3.4	3.3	3.4	2.3	16.9	2.4	2.3	3.5	-1.3	6.2	4.1	1.3
2001	2.8	1.0	4.1	3.2	3.8	2.6	3.1	4.0	-1.8	0.7	4.6	2.6
2002	1.6	-0.7	3.1	1.8	-5.9	2.4	1.8	2.2	-2.6	-0.9	4.7	2.6
2003	2.3	1.0	3.2	2.2	12.2	1.4	2.1	2.5	-2.5	3.1	4.0	1.8
2004	2.7	2.3	2.9	3.4	10.9	1.8	3.4	2.5	-0.4	3.5	4.4	1.6
2005	3.4	3.6	3.3	2.4	17.0	2.2	2.5	3.3	-0.7	6.6	4.2	1.9
2006	3.2	2.4	3.8	2.4	11.2	2.5	2.4	3.8	–	4.0	4.0	2.7
2007	2.8	2.1	3.3	4.0	5.5	2.3	3.9	3.1	-0.4	2.1	4.4	2.4
2008	3.8	4.3	3.5	5.5	13.9	2.3	5.4	3.2	-0.1	5.9	3.7	3.4
2009	-0.4	-2.9	1.4	1.8	-18.4	1.7	1.9	0.4	1.0	-8.3	3.2	3.0

– Represents zero. NA Not available. [1] Dec. 1997 = 100. [2] Change from immediate prior year. 1990 change from 1989.

Source: U.S. Bureau of Labor Statistics, *CPI Detailed Report*, monthly, <http://www.bls.gov/cpi/cpi_dr.htm>. See also *Monthly Labor Review*, <http://www.bls.gov/opub/mlr/welcome.htm>.

Table 725. Annual Percent Changes From Prior Year in Consumer Price Indexes (CPI-U)—Selected Areas: 2009

[Percent changes computed from annual averages of monthly figures published by source. Local area CPI indexes are by-products of the national CPI program. Each local index has a smaller sample size than the national index and is therefore subject to substantially more sampling and other measurement error. As a result, local area indexes show greater volatility than the national index, although their long-term trends are similar. Area definitions are those established by the Office of Management and Budget in 1983. For further detail, see the U.S. Bureau of Labor Statistics Handbook of Methods, Bulletin 2285, Chapter 19, the Consumer Price Index, and Report 751, the CPI: 1987 Revision. Minus sign (–) indicates decrease. See also text, this section and Appendix III]

Area	All items	Food and beverage	Food	Housing	Apparel	Transportation	Medical care	Fuel and other utilities
U.S. city average	**-0.4**	**1.9**	**1.8**	**0.4**	**1.0**	**-8.3**	**3.2**	**-4.2**
Anchorage, AK MSA	1.2	-0.2	0.3	3.7	3.6	-4.8	4.3	12.3
Atlanta, GA MSA	-2.6	0.7	0.8	-1.3	-0.8	-11.3	-0.8	-2.9
Boston, MA MSA	-0.7	2.4	2.3	-1.8	1.8	-8.1	5.1	-17.6
Chicago-Gary, IL-IN CMSA	-1.2	2.3	2.2	-2.2	2.5	-9.4	5.7	-15.9
Cincinnati-Hamilton, OH-KY-IN CMSA	-0.5	2.4	1.7	1.3	1.1	-10.3	1.4	0.3
Cleveland-Akron-Lorain, OH CMSA	-1.2	2.4	2.4	-1.8	-0.6	-9.2	2.5	-12.5
Dallas-Fort Worth, TX CMSA	-0.6	2.1	1.9	-0.1	-1.0	-8.8	5.8	-8.7
Denver-Boulder-Greely, CO CMSA	-0.6	–	-0.3	-0.4	0.2	-6.8	2.3	-9.0
Detroit-Ann Arbor-Flint, MI CMSA	-0.6	2.1	2.1	-0.8	-1.0	-4.7	0.5	0.4
Honolulu, HI MSA	0.5	3.6	3.6	0.4	7.2	-6.4	1.1	-15.4
Houston-Galveston-Brazoria, TX CMSA	0.3	1.2	0.9	3.7	-1.2	-9.9	5.0	–
Kansas City, MO-KS CMSA	-0.1	3.2	3.3	-0.4	3.0	-8.7	2.1	-8.6
Los Angeles-Anaheim-Riverside, CA CMSA	-0.8	1.0	1.0	0.2	1.5	-7.3	3.0	-3.9
Miami-Fort Lauderdale, FL CMSA	-0.3	1.3	1.4	0.8	-8.8	-6.5	3.7	3.1
Milwaukee, WI PMSA	-0.0	1.9	2.0	-0.1	1.8	-9.5	6.8	-7.7
Minneapolis-St. Paul, MN-WI MSA	-0.5	1.6	1.1	0.2	0.5	-8.4	5.5	-12.7
NY-NJ-CT CMSA	0.4	2.3	2.3	0.8	2.7	-6.1	0.9	-6.0
Philadelphia-Wilmington-Trenton, PA-NJ-DE-MD CMSA	-0.4	1.5	1.4	0.3	3.5	-8.4	1.7	-4.4
Pittsburgh, PA MSA	0.4	3.5	3.6	0.1	3.2	-7.6	3.3	-7.8
Portland, OR MSA	0.1	2.6	2.6	2.1	-5.6	-7.5	7.4	3.5
San Diego, CA MSA	-0.0	1.0	0.7	1.7	0.2	-8.0	2.1	13.4
San Francisco-Oakland-San Jose, CA CMSA	0.7	1.4	1.4	1.5	3.6	-5.5	4.2	0.8
Seattle-Tacoma, WA CMSA	0.6	1.1	1.1	1.9	-0.3	-4.3	2.2	3.1
St. Louis-East St. Louis, MO-IL CMSA	-0.1	2.8	2.9	0.6	3.9	-7.1	4.5	-0.4
Tampa-St. Petersburg-Clearwater, FL MSA	-0.1	1.8	1.7	-0.2	5.2	-6.3	0.1	8.3
Washington-Baltimore, DC-MD-VA-WV CMSA	0.2	1.9	1.9	1.7	0.7	-9.0	1.4	-1.3

– Represents zero.

Source: U.S. Bureau of Labor Statistics, *CPI Detailed Report*, monthly, <http://www.bls.gov/cpi/cpi_dr.htm>. See also *Monthly Labor Review*, <http://www.bls.gov/opub/mlr/welcome.htm>.

Table 726. Consumer Price Indexes for All Urban Consumers (CPI-U) for Selected Items and Groups: 2000 to 2009

[1982-84 = 100, except as noted. Annual averages of monthly figures. Minus sign (−) indicates decrease. See headnote, Table 724]

Item	2000	2004	2005	2006	2007	2008	2009	Annual percent change, 2008–2009
All items	**172.2**	**188.9**	**195.3**	**201.6**	**207.3**	**215.3**	**214.5**	**−0.4**
Food and beverages	**168.4**	**186.6**	**191.2**	**195.7**	**203.3**	**214.2**	**218.2**	**1.9**
Food	167.8	186.2	190.7	195.2	202.9	214.1	218.0	1.8
Food at home	167.9	186.2	189.8	193.1	201.2	214.1	215.1	0.5
Cereals and bakery products	188.3	206.0	209.0	212.8	222.1	244.9	252.6	3.2
Cereals and cereal products	175.9	186.2	186.7	187.3	194.7	214.4	221.8	3.4
Rice, pasta, and cornmeal	150.7	164.5	165.3	171.4	181.4	218.8	229.9	5.1
Rice [1][2]	99.3	108.0	108.8	114.9	120.1	152.8	161.0	5.3
Bakery products	194.1	216.2	220.5	226.4	236.6	261.0	268.9	3.0
Bread [2]	107.4	121.1	126.2	130.4	140.1	160.6	162.6	1.3
Cakes, cupcakes, and cookies	187.9	206.4	209.8	214.2	221.7	239.9	250.7	4.5
Other bakery products	191.5	211.8	211.4	215.5	220.5	236.5	245.9	4.0
Meats, poultry, fish and eggs	154.5	181.7	184.7	186.6	195.6	204.7	203.8	−0.4
Meats, poultry, and fish	155.5	182.3	186.7	188.2	195.4	203.6	204.6	0.5
Meats	150.7	183.2	187.5	188.8	195.0	201.8	200.5	−0.6
Beef and veal	148.1	195.3	200.4	202.1	211.1	220.6	218.3	−1.0
Uncooked ground beef	125.2	166.3	175.1	176.3	184.3	196.4	198.5	1.0
Uncooked beef steaks [2]	109.1	144.7	145.1	146.1	151.8	155.3	150.1	−3.4
Pork	156.5	174.2	177.7	177.3	180.9	185.0	181.4	−2.0
Other meats	152.0	173.4	177.5	180.7	184.8	190.6	194.9	2.3
Poultry	159.8	181.7	185.3	182.0	191.4	200.9	204.2	1.7
Chicken [2]	102.5	118.2	120.6	117.6	124.4	130.7	132.6	1.4
Fish and seafood	190.4	194.3	200.1	209.5	219.1	232.1	240.6	3.6
Dairy products	160.7	180.2	182.4	181.4	194.8	210.4	197.0	−6.4
Milk [2]	107.8	125.0	127.0	125.5	140.1	148.5	129.0	−13.2
Cheese and related products	162.8	180.8	183.3	180.8	191.5	214.5	203.5	−5.2
Ice cream and related products	164.4	178.3	177.6	179.3	183.4	192.8	196.6	2.0
Fruits and vegetables	204.6	232.7	241.4	252.9	262.6	278.9	272.9	−2.1
Fresh fruits and vegetables	238.8	274.7	285.3	300.4	312.1	328.3	312.7	−4.8
Fresh fruits	258.3	286.8	297.4	315.2	320.5	345.4	324.4	−6.1
Fresh vegetables	219.4	261.2	271.7	284.3	293.5	309.8	299.3	−3.4
Processed fruits and vegetables [2]	105.6	115.5	119.3	122.8	127.2	139.3	148.6	6.6
Nonalcoholic beverages and beverage materials	137.8	140.4	144.4	147.4	153.4	160.0	163.0	1.9
Juices and nonalcoholic drinks [2]	105.6	108.5	110.6	113.2	117.9	123.1	126.3	2.6
Carbonated drinks	123.4	127.9	131.9	134.2	140.1	147.0	154.1	4.8
Nonfrozen noncarbonated juices and drinks [2]	104.2	105.7	106.5	109.5	112.9	117.5	118.0	0.4
Beverage materials including coffee and tea [2]	97.9	97.6	102.4	104.1	108.2	112.8	113.3	0.4
Other food at home	155.6	164.9	167.0	169.6	173.3	184.2	191.2	3.8
Sugar and sweets	154.0	163.2	165.2	171.5	176.8	186.6	196.9	5.6
Candy and chewing gum [2]	103.8	108.4	109.5	112.2	116.1	123.2	130.2	5.7
Fats and oils	147.4	167.8	167.7	168.0	172.9	196.8	201.2	2.3
Frozen and freeze dried prepared food	148.5	152.5	153.2	153.7	166.7	100.5	168.1	2.8
Snacks	166.3	173.7	178.5	181.2	184.9	199.8	213.2	6.7
Spices, seasonings, condiments, sauces	175.6	185.3	188.0	190.3	195.5	204.6	214.7	4.9
Other miscellaneous food [2]	107.5	110.4	111.3	113.9	115.1	119.9	122.4	2.1
Food away from home	169.0	187.5	193.4	199.4	206.7	215.8	223.3	3.5
Full service meals and snacks [2]	106.8	118.4	121.9	125.7	130.2	135.4	139.2	2.8
Limited service meals and snacks [2]	106.3	118.6	122.4	126.0	130.6	136.9	142.6	4.2
Food at employee sites and schools [2]	104.4	115.5	118.6	122.6	126.8	131.8	137.3	4.2
Food from vending machines and mobile vendors [2]	102.4	109.8	112.6	115.1	118.3	124.1	129.7	4.5
Other food away from home [2]	109.0	125.3	131.3	136.6	144.1	150.6	155.9	3.5
Alcoholic beverages	174.7	192.1	195.9	200.7	207.0	214.5	220.8	2.9
Alcoholic beverages at home	158.1	170.2	172.3	174.9	179.1	184.9	190.3	2.9
Beer, ale, and other malt beverages at home	156.8	174.6	176.4	178.1	184.1	190.3	197.4	3.7
Distilled spirits, excluding whiskey, at home [1]	163.3	175.7	176.8	178.0	178.3	181.9	184.9	1.6
Wine at home	151.6	153.8	156.2	159.8	162.9	168.7	172.1	2.0
Alcoholic beverages away from home	207.1	236.6	244.5	254.6	266.0	277.4	285.6	2.9
Housing	**169.6**	**189.5**	**195.7**	**203.2**	**209.6**	**216.3**	**217.1**	**0.4**
Shelter	193.4	218.8	224.4	232.1	240.6	246.7	249.4	1.1
Rent of primary residence	183.9	211.0	217.3	225.1	234.7	243.3	248.8	2.3
Lodging away from home [2]	117.5	125.9	130.3	136.0	142.8	143.7	134.2	−6.6
Other lodging away from home including hotels and motels	252.4	265.3	274.2	285.6	299.9	301.0	279.3	−7.2
Owners' equivalent rent of primary residence [3]	198.7	224.9	230.2	238.2	246.2	252.4	256.6	1.7
Tenants' and household insurance [2]	103.7	116.2	117.6	116.5	117.0	118.8	121.5	2.2
Fuels and utilities	137.9	161.9	179.0	194.7	200.6	220.0	210.7	−4.2
Household energy	122.8	144.4	161.6	177.1	181.7	200.8	188.1	−6.3
Fuel oil and other fuels	129.7	160.5	208.6	234.9	251.5	334.4	239.8	−28.3
Fuel oil	130.3	160.0	216.4	244.6	262.6	365.0	240.2	−34.2
Propane, kerosene and firewood [4]	155.5	202.1	240.6	268.8	286.0	344.2	293.1	−14.9

See footnotes at end of table.

U.S. Census Bureau, Statistical Abstract of the United States: 2011

Table 726. Consumer Price Indexes for All Urban Consumers (CPI-U) for Selected Items and Groups: 2000 to 2009—Con.

[1982-84 = 100, except as noted. Annual averages of monthly figures. Minus sign (–) indicates decrease. See headnote, Table 724]

Item	2000	2004	2005	2006	2007	2008	2009	Annual percent change 2008–2009
Gas (piped) and electricity	128.0	150.6	166.5	182.1	186.3	202.2	193.6	–4.3
Electricity	128.5	142.1	150.8	169.2	175.8	187.1	192.7	3.0
Utility (piped) gas service	132.0	180.1	215.4	220.8	217.7	247.8	193.7	–21.8
Water and sewer and trash collection services [2]	106.5	124.0	130.3	136.8	143.7	152.1	161.1	5.9
Water and sewerage maintenance	227.5	268.1	283.4	297.2	312.6	331.3	354.4	7.0
Garbage and trash collection [5]	269.8	303.3	314.0	330.1	345.6	364.7	376.4	3.2
Household furnishings and operations	128.2	125.5	126.1	127.0	126.9	127.8	128.7	0.7
Window and floor coverings and other linens [2]	100.9	88.8	87.4	84.2	80.7	78.2	75.3	–3.7
Furniture and bedding	134.4	127.3	125.9	127.0	125.8	124.5	124.8	0.2
Bedroom furniture	138.4	137.3	142.7	145.4	144.7	143.7	143.0	–0.5
Living room, kitchen, and dining room furniture [2]	102.4	95.9	92.7	92.8	91.6	90.5	90.7	0.3
Appliances [2]	96.3	85.9	86.9	88.1	89.8	89.9	91.1	1.3
Other household equipment and furnishings [2]	98.0	87.4	85.5	80.4	76.9	75.6	74.0	–2.1
Clocks, lamps, and decorator items	111.7	91.4	88.0	79.6	73.6	69.9	67.2	–3.8
Nonelectric cookware and tableware [2]	98.4	90.7	91.3	91.1	93.1	95.9	97.1	1.3
Tools, hardware, outdoor equipment and supplies [2]	97.0	93.5	94.4	94.6	94.6	93.5	94.2	0.8
Tools, hardware, and supplies [2]	97.3	94.8	98.1	99.4	99.7	99.0	99.2	0.3
Outdoor equipment and supplies [2]	96.8	92.6	92.4	92.1	92.0	90.7	91.4	0.8
Housekeeping supplies	153.4	157.4	159.9	166.6	169.4	176.5	183.1	3.7
Household cleaning products [2]	105.1	107.0	107.9	111.6	112.3	115.9	121.4	4.8
Household paper products [2]	113.8	120.8	125.4	132.0	135.6	146.8	156.1	6.3
Miscellaneous household products [2]	104.3	105.3	106.4	111.0	113.6	116.3	116.8	0.5
Household operations [2]	110.5	125.0	130.3	136.6	140.6	147.5	150.3	1.8
Domestic services [2]	109.7	123.8	128.3	133.1	138.1	142.8	144.1	0.9
Gardening and lawncare services [2]	111.4	122.9	127.9	136.6	140.5	151.2	156.5	3.5
Apparel	**129.6**	**120.4**	**119.5**	**119.5**	**119.0**	**118.9**	**120.1**	**1.0**
Men's and boy's apparel	129.7	117.5	116.1	114.1	112.4	113.0	113.6	0.5
Men's apparel	133.1	121.4	121.4	119.8	118.2	118.4	118.6	0.2
Men's shirts and sweaters [2]	98.3	85.3	84.2	84.7	82.5	80.4	81.0	0.7
Boys' apparel	116.2	102.6	97.0	93.7	91.7	93.5	95.2	1.8
Women's and girl's apparel	121.5	113.0	110.8	110.7	110.3	107.5	108.1	0.6
Women's apparel	121.9	113.3	111.8	112.5	112.1	109.3	109.9	0.6
Women's suits and separates [2]	98.2	89.8	87.3	88.2	88.9	85.7	84.9	–1.0
Women's underwear, nightwear, sportswear, and accessories [2]	101.8	94.2	95.4	94.4	91.8	90.4	93.1	3.0
Girls' apparel	119.7	111.4	105.3	101.6	101.1	98.5	99.0	0.5
Footwear	123.8	119.3	122.6	123.5	122.4	124.2	126.9	2.2
Men's footwear	129.5	119.7	121.3	123.5	120.9	122.9	126.4	2.8
Women's footwear	119.6	118.4	121.9	122.8	122.5	122.6	123.4	0.7
Jewelry and watches [4]	137.0	129.5	127.6	130.7	137.1	146.5	149.2	1.8
Jewelry [4]	141.2	133.6	131.3	134.8	142.4	153.8	157.0	2.1
Transportation	**153.3**	**163.1**	**173.9**	**180.9**	**184.7**	**195.5**	**179.3**	**–8.3**
Private transportation	149.1	159.4	170.2	177.0	180.8	191.0	174.8	–8.5
New and used motor vehicles [2]	100.8	94.2	95.6	95.6	94.3	93.3	93.5	0.2
New vehicles	142.8	137.1	137.9	137.6	136.3	134.2	135.6	1.1
Used cars and trucks	155.8	133.3	139.4	140.0	135.7	134.0	127.0	–5.2
Leased cars and trucks [7]	(NA)	93.6	92.7	93.1	92.6	95.1	102.4	7.7
Motor fuel	129.3	160.4	194.7	221.0	239.1	279.7	202.0	–27.8
Gasoline (all types)	128.6	159.7	194.7	219.9	238.0	277.5	201.6	–27.4
Motor vehicle parts and equipment	101.5	108.7	111.9	117.3	121.6	128.7	134.1	4.1
Motor vehicle maintenance and repair	177.3	200.2	206.9	215.6	223.0	233.9	243.3	4.1
Motor vehicle maintenance and servicing	162.7	182.8	189.2	195.7	202.1	213.1	222.3	4.3
Motor vehicle repair [2]	108.2	122.7	126.7	132.7	137.4	143.8	149.4	3.9
Motor vehicle insurance	256.7	323.2	329.9	331.8	333.1	341.5	357.0	4.5
Motor vehicle fees [2]	107.3	131.0	134.7	138.8	141.2	145.8	155.7	6.8
State and local registration and license [2]	105.1	131.3	133.2	137.3	138.8	141.9	152.1	7.2
Public transportation	209.6	209.1	217.3	226.6	230.0	250.5	236.3	–5.7
Airline fare	239.4	227.2	236.6	247.3	251.7	282.0	258.0	–8.5
Medical care	**260.8**	**310.1**	**323.2**	**336.2**	**351.1**	**364.1**	**375.6**	**3.2**
Medical care commodities	238.1	269.3	276.0	285.9	290.0	296.0	305.1	3.1
Prescription drugs	285.4	337.1	349.0	363.9	369.2	378.3	391.1	3.4
Nonprescription drugs and medical supplies [4]	149.5	152.3	151.7	154.6	156.8	158.3	161.4	2.0
Internal and respiratory over-the-counter drugs	176.9	180.9	179.7	183.4	186.4	188.7	193.0	2.3
Nonprescription medical equipment and supplies	178.1	179.7	180.6	183.2	185.1	185.6	188.2	1.3
Medical care services	266.0	321.3	336.7	350.6	369.3	384.9	397.3	3.2
Professional medical services	237.7	271.5	281.7	289.3	300.8	311.0	319.4	2.7
Physicians' services	244.7	278.3	287.5	291.9	303.2	311.3	320.8	3.0
Dental services	258.5	306.9	324.0	340.9	358.4	376.9	388.1	3.0
Eyeglasses and eye care [4]	149.7	159.3	163.2	168.1	171.6	174.1	175.5	0.8
Services by other medical professionals [4]	161.9	181.9	186.8	192.2	197.4	205.5	209.8	2.1
Hospital and related services	317.3	417.9	439.9	468.1	498.9	534.0	567.9	6.4
Hospital services [9]	115.9	153.4	161.6	172.1	183.6	197.2	210.7	6.9

See footnotes at end of table.

U.S. Census Bureau, Statistical Abstract of the United States: 2011

[1982-84 = 100, except as noted. Annual averages of monthly figures. Minus sign (−) indicates decrease. See headnote, Table 724]

Item	2000	2004	2005	2006	2007	2008	2009	Annual percent change 2008– 2009
Recreation [2]	**103.3**	**108.6**	**109.4**	**110.9**	**111.4**	**113.3**	**114.3**	**0.9**
Video and audio [2]	101.0	104.2	104.2	104.6	102.9	102.6	101.3	−1.3
Cable and satellite television and radio service [5]	266.8	322.4	331.9	344.9	351.5	359.9	367.6	2.1
Pets, pet products and services [2]	106.1	120.1	123.6	128.4	133.8	144.5	153.4	6.2
Pets and pet products	144.3	154.5	155.8	161.7	166.6	181.9	194.9	7.2
Pet services including veterinary [2]	114.6	142.3	150.3	156.5	165.7	176.0	184.4	4.8
Sporting goods	119.0	115.0	115.5	117.1	116.4	118.4	119.9	1.2
Sports vehicles, including bicycles	130.9	130.8	133.2	138.0	137.9	139.4	140.1	0.5
Other recreational goods [2]	87.8	73.3	69.5	67.2	64.3	62.1	60.2	−3.1
Recreation services [2]	111.7	127.5	130.5	135.1	139.4	142.9	144.6	1.3
Club membership dues and fees for participant sports [2]	108.9	116.7	117.4	121.9	123.7	125.8	125.7	−0.1
Admissions	230.5	272.9	282.3	291.9	303.8	312.3	317.8	1.7
Education and communication [2]	**102.5**	**111.6**	**113.7**	**116.8**	**119.6**	**123.6**	**127.4**	**3.0**
Education [2]	112.5	143.7	152.7	162.1	171.4	181.3	190.9	5.3
Tuition, other school fees, and childcare	324.0	414.3	440.9	468.1	494.1	522.1	549.0	5.1
College tuition and fees	331.9	442.1	475.1	507.0	538.7	572.3	606.7	6.0
Child care and nursery school [6]	156.3	187.1	195.4	206.0	214.9	224.6	232.8	3.6
Communication [2]	93.6	86.7	84.7	84.1	83.4	84.2	85.0	0.9
Information and information processing [2]	92.8	84.6	82.6	81.7	80.7	81.4	81.9	0.7
Telephone services [2]	98.5	95.8	94.9	95.8	98.2	100.5	102.4	1.9
Land-line telephone services, local charges	175.6	204.1	209.6	213.9	222.1	230.0	236.6	2.8
Land-line telephone services, long distance charges [2]	91.8	70.9	67.5	68.3	71.5	74.8	78.1	4.3
Wireless telephone services [2]	76.0	66.2	65.0	64.6	64.4	64.2	64.3	0.0
Information technology, hardware, and services [10]	25.9	14.8	13.6	12.5	10.6	10.1	9.7	−3.9
Other goods and services	**271.1**	**304.7**	**313.4**	**321.7**	**333.3**	**345.4**	**368.6**	**6.7**
Tobacco and smoking products	394.9	478.0	502.8	519.9	554.2	588.7	730.3	24.1
Cigarettes [2]	159.9	193.5	203.5	210.4	224.8	239.0	297.4	24.5
Personal care	165.6	181.7	185.6	190.2	195.6	201.3	204.6	1.6
Personal care products	153.7	153.9	154.4	155.8	158.3	159.3	162.6	2.1
Hair, dental, shaving, and miscellaneous personal care products [2]	103.3	102.1	101.8	102.6	103.6	104.3	105.4	1.0
Cosmetics, perfume, bath, nail preparations and implements	166.8	169.5	171.3	173.1	177.0	178.0	183.6	3.1
Personal care services	178.1	197.6	203.9	209.7	216.6	223.7	227.6	1.8
Haircuts and other personal care services [2]	108.7	120.6	124.4	127.9	132.1	136.5	138.9	1.8
Miscellaneous personal services	252.3	293.9	303.0	313.6	325.0	338.9	344.5	1.6
Legal services [4]	189.3	232.3	241.8	250.0	260.3	270.7	278.1	2.7
Funeral expenses [4]	187.8	221.3	228.8	240.6	252.6	265.4	275.7	3.9
Special aggregate indexes								
Commodities	**149.2**	**154.7**	**160.2**	**164.0**	**167.5**	**174.8**	**169.7**	**−2.9**
Commodities less food and beverages	137.7	136.7	142.5	145.9	147.5	153.0	144.4	−5.6
Nondurables less food and beverages	147.4	157.2	168.4	176.7	182.5	196.2	179.0	−8.8
Nondurables less food, beverages, and apparel	162.5	183.9	202.6	216.3	226.2	248.8	219.6	−11.7
Durables	125.4	114.8	115.3	114.5	112.5	110.9	109.9	−0.9
Services	195.3	222.8	230.1	238.9	246.8	255.5	259.2	1.4
Rent of shelter [3]	201.3	227.9	233.7	241.9	250.8	257.2	259.9	1.1
Transportation services	196.1	220.6	225.7	230.8	233.7	244.1	251.0	2.9
Other services	229.9	261.3	268.4	277.5	285.6	295.8	304.0	2.8
All items less food	173.0	189.4	196.0	202.7	208.1	215.5	214.0	0.7
All items less shelter	165.7	179.3	186.1	191.9	196.6	205.5	203.3	−1.0
All items less medical care	167.3	182.7	188.7	194.7	200.1	207.8	206.6	−0.6
Commodities less food	139.2	138.8	144.5	148.0	149.7	155.3	147.1	−5.3
Nondurables less food	149.1	159.3	170.1	178.2	184.0	197.3	181.5	−8.0
Nondurables less food and apparel	162.9	183.8	201.2	213.9	223.4	244.4	218.7	−10.5
Nondurables	158.2	172.2	180.2	186.7	193.5	205.9	198.5	−3.6
Apparel less footwear	126.2	116.3	114.4	114.1	113.8	113.4	114.2	0.7
Services less rent of shelter [3]	202.9	233.5	243.2	253.3	260.8	273.0	278.1	1.9
Services less medical care services	188.9	214.5	221.2	229.6	236.8	245.0	248.1	1.3
Energy	124.6	151.4	177.1	196.9	207.7	236.7	193.1	−18.4
All items less energy	178.6	194.4	198.7	203.7	208.9	214.8	218.4	1.7
All items less food and energy	181.3	196.6	200.9	205.9	210.7	215.6	219.2	1.7
Commodities less food and energy commodities	144.9	139.6	140.3	140.6	140.1	140.2	142.0	1.3
Energy commodities	129.5	161.2	197.4	223.0	241.0	284.4	205.3	−27.8
Services less energy services	202.1	230.2	236.6	244.7	253.1	261.0	265.9	1.9
Domestically produced farm food	170.1	191.7	195.0	198.1	206.5	220.1	220.4	0.1
Utilities and public transportation	152.6	167.5	176.6	186.7	191.3	202.8	200.3	−1.2

NA Not available. [1] Special indexes based on a substantially smaller sample. [2] December 1997=100. [3] December 1982=100. [4] December 1986=100. [5] December 1983=100. [6] December 1990=100. [7] December 2001=100. [8] December 1993=100. [9] December 1996=100. [10] December 1988=100. [11] December 2007=100

Source: Bureau of Labor Statistics, CPI Detailed Report, monthly; <http://www.bls.gov/cpi/opi_dr.htm> See also Monthly Labor Review; <http://www.bls.gov/opub/mlr/welcome.htm>.

Table 727. Cost of Living Index—Selected Urban Areas: Annual Average 2009

[Data are for a selected urban area within the larger metropolitan area shown. Measures relative price levels for consumer goods and services in participating areas for a mid-management standard of living. The nationwide average equals 100 and each index is read as a percent of the national average. The index does not measure inflation, but compares prices at a single point in time. Excludes taxes. Metropolitan areas as defined by the Office of Management and Budget. For definitions, urban areas, and components of metropolitan areas, see source]

Urban area	Composite index (100%)	Grocery items (13%)	Housing (29%)	Utilities (10%)	Trans- portation (12%)	Health care (4%)	Misc. goods and services (32%)
Akron, OH	97.4	97.2	96.8	106.4	103.3	88.7	93.9
Albany, NY	106.0	98.1	107.4	120.8	104.6	99.7	104.5
Amarillo, TX	89.8	90.5	85.9	82.6	95.8	97.9	92.1
Anchorage, AK	124.9	129.5	137.7	101.9	118.4	127.9	120.6
Asheville, NC	102.1	104.8	102.0	117.4	94.9	103.7	98.8
Atlanta, GA	94.4	100.8	89.0	82.5	97.8	104.0	97.9
Austin, TX	96.7	91.9	84.6	90.3	97.0	95.1	111.8
Baltimore, MD	121.8	108.2	162.8	121.8	101.9	98.4	100.5
Baton Rouge, LA	92.8	100.2	84.2	89.8	94.1	96.9	97.6
Bergen-Passaic, NJ	129.8	111.6	174.5	119.4	102.0	106.5	113.3
Bethesda-Gaithersburg-Frederick, MD	129.5	108.8	182.9	117.7	110.4	105.0	103.5
Boston, MA	131.2	117.1	147.4	156.6	100.8	127.8	126.0
Bradenton, FL	97.0	102.7	92.8	91.5	102.6	100.1	97.7
Brownsville, TX	87.5	89.9	73.2	97.7	94.3	95.0	92.9
Burlington-Chittenden Co, VT	119.6	107.3	137.3	121.4	102.8	103.5	116.4
Camden, SC	95.2	102.5	86.8	102.0	88.3	93.5	100.5
Cedar Rapids, IA	91.4	92.3	80.0	90.0	99.6	103.1	97.2
Champaign-Urbana, IL	98.3	100.4	89.5	99.4	99.0	98.4	104.7
Charleston, WV	92.9	89.2	89.2	96.7	101.5	92.5	93.2
Charleston-N Charleston, SC	99.6	109.7	91.9	90.3	96.3	105.7	106.0
Charlotte, NC	93.4	96.7	80.1	96.9	98.9	107.5	99.3
Cheyenne, WY	100.1	100.1	109.7	90.7	100.4	92.2	95.3
Chicago, IL	113.5	104.6	132.2	114.3	115.6	110.6	99.4
Cincinnati, OH	91.3	88.6	84.8	102.6	102.4	91.6	90.5
Cleveland, OH	99.8	109.4	89.1	113.5	101.5	100.8	100.6
Colorado Springs, CO	92.5	96.2	92.4	84.3	95.0	105.0	91.2
Columbia, SC	97.3	99.9	80.1	101.0	101.9	105.6	107.8
Columbus, OH	94.0	92.2	88.2	113.7	98.6	101.6	91.2
Conroe, TX	89.7	86.7	77.9	93.9	94.5	93.5	98.1
Corpus Christi, TX	91.8	80.8	81.4	123.5	94.0	88.2	95.3
Covington, KY	89.2	83.8	79.8	91.2	102.8	92.8	93.7
Dallas, TX	92.3	96.2	71.6	107.9	99.5	104.4	100.3
Davenport-Moline-Rock Island, IA-IL	96.9	99.5	93.9	81.2	105.3	96.3	100.3
Dayton, OH	92.8	90.6	73.4	109.3	102.3	93.9	102.4
Denver, CO	103.1	101.6	107.9	99.3	94.5	105.5	103.5
Des Moines, IA	90.8	90.2	87.4	89.9	93.1	90.3	93.7
Dover, DE	98.4	99.7	89.5	118.1	97.5	103.4	99.3
Durham, NC	95.9	96.9	82.1	96.4	103.3	104.2	103.9
El Paso, TX	89.8	100.5	82.1	89.3	97.0	95.3	89.3
Eugene, OR	111.3	91.7	136.5	88.8	110.2	117.0	103.3
Fargo-Moorhead, ND-MN	92.6	102.1	84.4	81.3	96.9	102.7	96.7
Fayetteville, AR	91.3	96.1	76.9	89.8	95.3	93.9	101.0
Fort Lauderdale, FL	119.1	109.2	157.6	93.6	108.7	101.7	102.4
Fort Smith, AR	85.0	88.3	71.9	91.3	85.0	92.1	92.8
Fort Worth, TX	90.9	92.9	76.1	103.4	98.2	92.9	96.6
Fresno, CA	120.4	117.5	142.8	113.7	114.9	106.1	107.3
Gastonia, NC	90.6	105.6	74.6	93.9	93.9	92.4	96.5
Grand Rapids, MI	94.9	95.0	91.6	122.9	95.6	87.4	89.8
Green Bay, WI	95.3	90.0	84.0	122.4	101.9	102.5	96.0
Gunnison, CO	116.0	120.2	142.4	98.2	100.3	98.3	104.1
Hampton Roads-SE Virginia, VA	110.9	106.6	121.1	100.9	96.5	108.6	112.2
Harlingen, TX	86.9	85.7	76.2	122.0	90.7	92.2	83.9
Hickory, NC	95.0	98.9	93.5	103.4	91.9	98.9	92.7
Honolulu, HI	166.7	157.8	250.0	140.0	128.3	117.8	123.9
Houston, TX	89.5	84.9	76.6	99.1	95.2	96.1	97.0

See footnotes at end of table.

U.S. Census Bureau, Statistical Abstract of the United States: 2011

Table 727. Cost of Living Index—Selected Urban Areas: Annual Average 2009—Con.

[Data are for a selected urban area within the larger metropolitan area shown. Measures relative price levels for consumer goods and services in participating areas for a mid-management standard of living. The nationwide average equals 100 and each index is read as a percent of the national average. The index does not measure inflation, but compares prices at a single point in time. Excludes taxes. Metropolitan areas as defined by the Office of Management and Budget. For definitions, urban areas, and components of metropolitan areas, see source]

Urban area	Composite index (100%)	Grocery items (13%)	Housing (29%)	Utilities (10%)	Trans-portation (12%)	Health care (4%)	Misc. goods and services (32%)
Huntsville, AL	92.5	94.6	79.4	85.8	99.4	91.8	103.2
Indianapolis, IN	89.0	89.8	83.0	89.6	104.9	96.9	86.9
Jackson, MS	96.2	92.3	89.3	119.6	93.0	101.9	97.3
Jacksonville, FL	94.0	103.2	80.7	91.6	106.7	99.3	97.7
Joliet-Will County, IL	101.6	102.5	101.3	108.3	111.6	105.0	95.4
Kalamazoo, MI	94.3	103.7	86.3	100.6	98.3	96.2	94.0
Kansas City, MO-KS	95.9	94.6	88.7	89.6	97.6	96.7	104.2
Knoxville, TN	89.5	89.5	78.5	99.9	85.9	89.9	97.6
Lafayette, LA	98.6	93.3	106.5	77.5	104.8	88.7	99.3
Las Vegas, NV	104.8	100.5	114.9	91.0	104.4	106.9	101.6
Lawrence, KS	92.4	87.5	90.5	86.7	94.2	96.0	96.7
Little Rock-North Little Rock, AR	94.7	94.4	83.9	104.7	96.5	97.9	100.5
Los Angeles-Long Beach, CA	142.0	107.7	230.2	90.7	115.0	109.6	106.4
Louisville, KY	89.8	81.6	78.9	112.7	99.0	88.7	92.5
Loveland, CO	92.9	100.2	80.3	93.8	96.5	101.4	98.5
Lubbock, TX	88.8	93.7	77.8	76.1	98.9	99.3	95.5
McAllen, TX	87.4	79.5	78.7	112.9	91.1	97.0	87.9
Memphis, TN	88.1	90.3	77.6	85.8	94.1	99.2	93.7
Miami-Dade County, FL	110.1	108.3	121.7	92.2	112.4	107.4	105.4
Middlesex-Monmouth, NJ	123.2	109.0	152.9	124.2	101.3	112.5	111.2
Missoula, MT	102.0	118.0	94.4	94.8	103.0	106.2	103.8
Mobile, AL	92.5	102.8	80.5	107.3	92.2	84.8	95.6
Montgomery, AL	97.8	103.9	91.0	110.3	97.3	90.6	98.6
Murfreesboro-Smyrna, TN	89.8	95.1	75.2	93.6	93.1	99.2	97.1
Myrtle Beach, SC	93.4	104.5	78.2	88.8	97.4	103.8	101.3
Nassau County, NY	144.5	114.3	211.7	132.4	111.3	117.8	115.5
New Haven, CT	120.4	119.3	133.1	124.4	104.9	111.0	115.2
New York (Manhattan), NY	217.9	146.1	401.5	156.9	128.6	131.0	144.4
New York (Queens), NY	157.6	126.1	228.1	159.2	117.8	112.0	126.8
Newark-Elizabeth, NJ	127.6	113.4	165.8	125.1	00.7	105.0	112.8
Oakland, CA	136.6	115.6	194.5	91.3	113.4	116.8	118.1
Oklahoma City, OK	90.1	91.7	82.6	84.8	89.4	98.6	97.0
Olympia, WA	105.4	109.4	99.5	84.7	117.1	121.5	109.1
Omaha, NE	89.5	92.1	77.9	102.5	97.8	95.2	91.0
Orlando, FL	98.6	98.2	87.9	103.9	104.5	96.0	104.8
Palm Springs, CA	123.3	107.7	160.6	108.2	116.7	100.1	105.9
Peoria, IL	100.8	97.5	93.0	111.3	101.9	96.6	106.2
Philadelphia, PA	124.2	123.5	142.6	129.1	104.4	109.9	115.3
Phoenix, AZ	98.6	105.8	95.1	88.5	101.5	97.9	101.0
Pittsburgh, PA	92.1	97.7	73.9	104.3	106.9	90.5	97.1
Plano, TX	94.6	100.1	81.5	106.7	100.3	102.9	97.2
Portland, OR	116.8	115.6	129.3	93.4	112.7	108.8	115.7
Providence, RI	119.2	110.2	122.0	125.8	101.5	118.7	124.8
Raleigh, NC	101.5	109.1	91.5	100.6	99.6	106.3	108.0
Reno-Sparks, NV	106.2	107.4	112.8	97.2	108.9	105.8	101.5
Richmond, VA	106.9	105.4	105.7	115.4	99.6	111.2	108.1
Rio Rancho, NM	96.4	98.3	89.5	89.1	96.8	103.5	103.3
Riverside City, CA	113.6	108.1	138.9	87.9	118.1	105.3	100.2
Roanoke, VA	95.5	92.3	94.7	96.7	93.0	97.0	97.9
Rochester, MN	99.8	89.7	89.3	119.8	100.8	108.8	105.6
Rochester, NY	100.3	93.9	94.1	121.7	108.7	103.6	98.2
Round Rock, TX	92.4	83.4	79.2	112.5	91.8	101.9	100.9
Sacramento, CA	116.2	116.1	139.0	99.8	115.5	109.5	101.9
Salt Lake City, UT	100.2	104.8	106.9	71.1	99.9	96.1	102.0
San Antonio, TX	95.2	85.1	95.2	82.1	98.2	104.0	101.1
San Diego, CA	133.9	105.9	202.2	96.0	114.7	113.3	105.0
San Francisco, CA	163.4	118.8	274.3	92.4	112.8	118.9	127.6
San Jose, CA	155.4	132.7	243.0	128.1	119.5	114.0	112.6
Sarasota, FL	102.4	105.1	105.6	98.4	107.5	105.4	97.2
Savannah, GA	93.0	92.8	86.3	89.3	95.1	96.4	98.9
Seattle, WA	123.6	112.2	151.9	83.0	117.6	122.1	117.8

Source: C2ER, Arlington, VA, ACCRA Cost of Living Index, Annual Average 2009 (copyright). See also <http://www.c2er.org>.

U.S. Census Bureau, Statistical Abstract of the United States: 2011

Table 728. Single-Family Housing Price Indexes by State: 2000 to 2009

[Index 1991, 1st quarter = 100. The index reflects average price changes in repeat sales or refinancings on the same properties. Since the data are for the fourth quarter, the index represents the annual percentage change in home values in the fourth quarter of the year shown relative to the fourth quarter of the previous year. The information is obtained by reviewing repeat mortgage transactions on single-family properties whose mortgages have been purchased or securitized by either Fannie Mae or Freddie Mac; for more information on methodology, see Appendix III. Minus sign (–) indicates decrease]

State	2000	2005	2008	2009	Percent change 2008–2009	State	2000	2005	2008	2009	Percent change 2008–2009
U.S....	**144**	**212**	**199**	**197**	**−1.3**	MO.....	150	197	194	194	–
AL.....	143	182	193	198	2.1	MT.....	180	278	311	302	−2.8
AK.....	136	206	223	217	−2.8	NE.....	162	194	193	197	2.1
AZ.....	155	297	227	198	−12.7	NV.....	129	270	166	137	−17.3
AR.....	141	185	187	190	1.5	NH.....	147	238	208	207	−0.6
CA.....	122	275	171	170	−0.4	NJ.....	133	253	235	227	−3.6
CO.....	216	271	265	272	2.6	NM.....	145	215	237	226	−4.5
CT.....	118	194	184	178	−3.1	NY.....	129	216	216	214	−0.8
DE.....	121	208	201	194	−3.9	NC.....	146	182	194	194	0.2
DC.....	134	325	336	335	−0.1	ND.....	139	194	215	217	1.2
FL.....	140	296	209	192	−8.2	OH.....	149	175	160	162	0.9
GA.....	151	190	176	173	−1.8	OK.....	144	178	190	197	3.4
HI......	92	204	210	183	−13.0	OR.....	184	297	309	286	−7.4
ID......	154	228	244	227	−6.7	PA.....	122	190	196	195	−0.5
IL......	146	204	198	188	−4.8	RI.....	120	236	201	199	−0.8
IN......	142	165	160	162	1.7	SC.....	145	185	191	194	1.2
IA......	158	192	198	200	0.7	SD.....	160	209	224	227	1.6
KS.....	153	187	197	200	1.5	TN.....	147	185	195	193	−0.6
KY.....	150	183	188	191	1.6	TX.....	143	172	191	192	0.8
LA.....	156	212	231	232	0.7	UT.....	195	256	292	269	−7.7
ME.....	133	220	211	213	1.0	VT.....	126	206	213	210	−1.4
MD.....	123	253	229	216	−5.6	VA.....	131	232	215	222	3.1
MA.....	158	254	225	224	−0.2	WA.....	155	243	257	244	−5.2
MI......	174	203	157	153	−3.0	WV.....	137	178	193	188	−2.4
MN.....	172	253	224	222	−1.0	WI.....	167	224	221	218	−1.2
MS.....	142	177	186	183	−1.6	WY.....	171	260	310	292	−6.0

– Represents zero.

Source: Federal Housing Finance Agency, *Housing Price Index, 4th quarter 2009*. See also <http://www.fhfa.gov>.

Table 729. Average Prices of Selected Fuels and Electricity: 1990 to 2009

[In dollars per unit, except electricity, in cents per kWh. Represents price to end-users, except as noted]

Item	Unit	1990	2000	2002	2003	2004	2005	2006	2007	2008	2009
Crude oil, composite [1]	Barrel........	22.22	28.26	24.10	28.53	36.98	50.24	60.24	67.94	94.73	59.27
Motor gasoline: [2]											
Unleaded regular	Gallon	1.16	1.51	1.36	1.59	1.88	2.30	2.59	2.80	3.27	2.35
Unleaded premium	Gallon	1.35	1.69	1.56	1.78	2.07	2.49	2.81	3.03	3.52	2.61
No. 2 heating oil	Gallon	0.73	0.93	0.74	0.93	1.17	1.71	1.98	2.24	2.99	1.96
No. 2 diesel fuel	Gallon	0.73	0.94	0.76	0.94	1.24	1.79	2.10	2.27	3.15	1.83
Propane, consumer grade...	Gallon	0.75	0.60	0.42	0.58	0.84	1.09	1.36	1.49	1.84	1.24
Residual fuel oil	Gallon	0.44	0.60	0.57	0.70	0.74	1.05	1.22	1.37	1.96	1.34
Natural gas, residential	1,000 cu/ft	5.80	7.76	7.89	9.63	10.75	12.70	13.73	13.06	13.89	11.97
Electricity, residential	kWh.........	7.83	8.24	8.44	8.72	8.95	9.45	10.40	10.65	11.26	11.55

[1] Refiner acquisition cost. [2] Average, all service.

Source: U.S. Energy Information Administration, *Monthly Energy Review*. See also <http://www.eia.doe.gov/emeu/mer>.

Table 730. Retail Gasoline Prices—Selected Areas: 2007 to 2009

[In cents per gallon. Prices are annual averages]

Area	Regular 2007	Regular 2008	Regular 2009	Midgrade 2007	Midgrade 2008	Midgrade 2009	Premium 2007	Premium 2008	Premium 2009
Boston, MA	271.0	317.2	230.6	283.6	330.2	243.1	294.2	340.7	253.5
Chicago, IL............	294.1	340.7	246.3	305.1	352.0	257.1	315.4	362.3	267.5
Cleveland, OH	275.9	317.1	232.6	286.4	327.7	243.2	297.2	338.4	254.0
Denver, CO	276.8	315.4	223.4	289.0	327.8	235.8	299.7	338.8	246.8
Houston, TX...........	260.6	308.1	216.7	272.1	321.8	231.7	283.1	334.1	243.8
Los Angeles, CA	304.7	350.6	268.6	315.5	361.6	279.0	325.7	372.0	289.0
Miami, FL.............	286.0	337.7	244.9	299.1	351.9	259.7	309.8	362.6	270.1
New York, NY..........	278.9	327.1	236.5	293.3	344.5	251.2	304.4	355.9	262.1
San Francisco, CA......	317.1	356.4	269.0	329.7	369.3	281.0	340.0	379.7	291.3
Seattle, WA	294.7	339.0	256.2	305.1	350.8	267.9	315.4	361.2	278.4

Source: U.S. Energy Information Administration, *Weekly U.S. Retail Gasoline Prices*, Gasoline Historical Data. See also <http://www.eia.doe.gov/oil_gas/petroleum/data_publications/wrgp/mogas_history.html>.

Table 731. Weekly Food Cost of a Nutritious Diet by Type of Family and Individual: 2009

[In dollars, As of December. Assumes that food for all meals and snacks is purchased at the store and prepared at home. See source for details on estimation procedures]

Family type	Thrifty plan	Low-cost plan	Moderate plan	Liberal plan
FAMILIES				
Family of two:				
19 to 50 years	79.80	101.70	126.70	158.60
51 to 70 years	75.70	97.60	120.50	145.00
Family of four:				
Couple, 19 to 50 years and children—				
2 to 3 and 4 to 5 years	116.20	147.50	182.70	226.30
6 to 8 and 9 to 11 years	133.40	173.40	217.50	264.10
INDIVIDUALS [1]				
Child:				
1 year.	19.80	26.30	30.20	36.40
2 to 3 years	21.50	26.90	32.70	39.70
4 to 5 years	22.20	28.10	34.80	42.40
6 to 8 years	28.30	38.30	47.30	55.70
9 to 11 years	32.50	42.60	55.00	64.20
Male:				
12 to 13 years	34.60	48.70	60.70	71.50
14 to 18 years	35.60	50.10	62.90	71.90
19 to 50 years	38.40	49.50	62.10	76.10
51 to 70 years	35.10	46.80	57.50	69.70
71 years and over	35.30	46.30	57.70	71.00
Female:				
12 to 13 years	34.80	42.20	50.90	61.70
14 to 18 years	34.30	42.50	51.50	63.20
19 to 50 years	34.10	43.00	53.10	68.00
51 to 70 years	33.70	41.90	52.10	62.10
71 years and over	33.30	41.50	51.70	62.30

[1] The costs given are for individuals in 4-person families. For individuals in other size families, the following adjustments are suggested: 1-person, add 20 percent; 2-person, add 10 percent; 3-person, add 5 percent; 5- or 6-person, subtract 5 percent; 7- (or more) person, subtract 10 percent.

Source: U.S. Department of Agriculture, *Official USDA Food Plans: Cost of Food at Home at Four Levels*, monthly. See also <http://www.cnpp.usda.gov/Publications/FoodPlans/2009/CostofFoodDec09.pdf>.

Table 732. Food—Retail Prices of Selected Items: 2000 to 2009

[In dollars per pound, except as indicated. As of December. See Appendix III]

Food	2000	2008	2009	Food	2000	2008	2009
Cereals and bakery products:				Fresh fruits and vegetables:			
Flour, white, all purpose	0.28	0.50	0.46	Apples, Red Delicious	0.82	1.18	1.11
Rice, white, lg. grain, raw	(NA)	0.81	0.75	Bananas	0.49	0.62	0.57
Spaghetti and macaroni	0.88	1.13	1.17	Oranges, navel	0.62	0.93	0.93
Bread, white, pan	0.99	1.42	1.39	Grapefruit	0.58	0.91	0.88
Bread, whole wheat	1.36	1.95	1.76	Grapes, Thompson seedless	2.36	2.46	3.14
Beef:				Lemons	1.11	1.62	1.60
Ground beef, 100% beef	1.63	2.41	2.19	Pears, Anjou	(NA)	1.37	1.28
Ground chuck, 100% beef	1.98	3.00	2.83	Potatoes, white	0.35	0.68	0.56
Ground beef, lean and extra lean . .	2.33	3.44	3.39	Lettuce, iceberg	0.85	0.88	1.19
Round steak, USDA Choice	3.28	4.37	4.18	Tomatoes, field grown	1.57	1.73	1.96
Sirloin steak, boneless	4.81	6.07	5.68	Processed fruits and vegetables:			
Pork:				Orange juice, frozen concentrate,			
Bacon, sliced	3.03	3.67	3.57	12 oz. can, per 16 oz	1.88	2.56	2.53
Chops, center cut, bone-in	3.46	3.54	3.29	Sugar and sweets:			
Ham, boneless, excluding				Sugar, white, all sizes	0.41	0.53	0.60
canned	2.75	3.41	3.10	Sugar, white, 33–80 oz. pkg	0.40	0.50	0.57
Poultry, fish, and eggs:				Fats and oils:			
Chicken, fresh, whole	1.08	1.31	1.27	Margarine, stick	(NA)	1.18	1.11
Chicken legs, bone-in	1.26	1.50	1.46	Margarine, tubs, soft	0.84	1.57	1.66
Turkey, frozen, whole	0.99	1.33	1.37	Peanut butter, creamy, all sizes . . .	1.96	2.15	2.10
Eggs, Grade A, large, (dozen)	0.96	1.83	1.77				
Dairy products:				Nonalcoholic beverages:			
Milk, fresh, whole, fortified				Coffee, 100% ground roast,			
(per gal.)	2.79	3.68	3.11	all sizes	3.21	(NA)	3.67
Butter, salted, grade AA, stick	2.80	3.13	2.67				
American processed cheese	3.69	4.14	3.86	Other prepared foods:			
Cheddar cheese, natural	3.76	4.95	4.55	Potato chips, per 16 oz	3.44	4.48	4.65
Ice cream, prepack., bulk, reg.							
(1/2 gal.)	3.66	4.28	4.23				

NA Not available.

Source: U.S. Bureau of Labor Statistics, *CPI Detailed Report*, monthly, <http://www.bls.gov/cpi/cpi_dr.htm>. See also *Monthly Labor Review*, <http://www.bls.gov/opub/mlr/welcome.htm>.

Table 733. Producer Price Indexes by Stage of Processing: 1990 to 2009

[1982 = 100, except as indicated. Minus sign (–) indicates decrease. See Appendix III]

Year	Crude materials — Total	Crude materials — Foodstuffs and feedstuffs	Crude materials — Fuel	Crude materials — Crude nonfood materials, except fuel	Intermediate materials and supplies, components	Finished goods — Consumer goods	Finished goods — Capital equipment	Finished consumer foods — Crude	Finished consumer foods — Processed	Finished consumer goods, excluding food
1990........	108.9	113.1	84.8	107.3	114.5	118.2	122.9	123.0	124.4	115.3
1995........	102.7	105.8	72.1	105.8	124.9	125.6	136.7	118.8	129.8	124.0
1997........	111.1	112.2	101.3	103.5	125.6	130.2	138.2	126.6	135.1	128.2
1998........	96.8	103.9	86.7	84.5	123.0	128.9	137.6	127.2	134.8	126.4
1999........	98.2	98.7	91.2	91.1	123.2	132.0	137.6	125.5	135.9	130.5
2000........	120.6	100.2	136.9	118.0	129.2	138.2	138.8	123.5	138.3	138.4
2001........	121.0	106.1	151.4	101.5	129.7	141.5	139.7	127.7	142.4	141.4
2002........	108.1	99.5	117.3	101.0	127.8	139.4	139.1	128.5	141.0	138.8
2003........	135.3	113.5	185.7	116.9	133.7	145.3	139.5	130.0	147.2	144.7
2004........	159.0	127.0	211.4	149.2	142.6	151.7	141.4	138.2	153.9	150.9
2005........	182.2	122.7	279.7	176.7	154.0	160.4	144.6	140.2	156.9	161.9
2006........	184.8	119.3	241.5	210.0	161.0	166.0	146.9	151.3	157.1	169.2
2007........	207.1	146.7	236.8	238.7	170.7	173.5	149.5	170.2	166.7	175.6
2008........	251.8	163.4	298.3	308.5	188.3	186.3	153.8	175.5	178.6	189.1
2009 [1]......	175.0	134.4	165.6	211.0	172.6	179.2	156.8	157.8	177.3	179.6
PERCENT CHANGE [2]										
1990........	5.6	1.7	–0.6	12.0	2.2	5.4	3.5	2.8	4.9	5.9
1995........	0.9	–0.7	–12.5	9.1	5.4	1.9	1.9	6.7	1.5	2.0
1997........	–2.4	–7.7	9.4	–2.1	–0.1	0.5	–0.1	–2.0	1.0	0.5
1998........	–12.9	–7.4	–14.4	–18.4	–2.1	–1.0	–0.4	0.5	–0.2	–1.4
1999........	1.4	–5.0	5.2	7.8	0.2	2.4	0.0	–1.3	0.8	3.2
2000........	22.8	1.5	50.1	29.5	4.9	4.7	0.9	–1.6	1.8	6.1
2001........	0.3	5.9	10.6	–14.0	0.4	2.4	0.6	3.4	3.0	2.2
2002........	–10.7	–6.2	–22.5	–0.5	–1.5	–1.5	–0.4	0.6	–1.0	–1.8
2003........	25.2	14.1	58.3	15.7	4.6	4.2	0.3	1.2	4.4	4.3
2004........	17.5	11.9	13.8	27.6	6.7	4.4	1.4	6.3	4.6	4.3
2005........	14.6	–3.4	32.3	18.4	8.0	5.7	2.3	1.4	1.9	7.3
2006........	1.4	–2.8	–13.7	18.8	6.5	3.5	1.6	7.9	0.1	4.5
2007........	12.1	23.0	–1.9	13.7	4.1	4.5	1.8	12.5	6.1	3.8
2008........	21.6	11.4	26.0	29.2	10.3	7.4	2.9	3.1	7.1	7.7
2009 [1]......	–30.5	–17.7	–44.5	–31.6	–8.3	–3.8	2.0	–10.1	–0.7	–5.0

[1] Preliminary. [2] Change from immediate prior year. 1990, change from 1989.
Source: U.S. Bureau of Labor Statistics, *Producer Price Indexes*, monthly and annual. See also *Monthly Labor Review*, <http://www.bls.gov/opub/mlr/welcome.htm>.

Table 734. Commodity Research Bureau Futures Price Index: 1990 to 2009

[1967 = 100. Index computed daily. Represents unweighted geometric average of commodity futures prices (through 6 months forward) of 17 major commodity futures markets. Represents end of year index]

Commodity	1990	1995	2000	2001	2002	2003	2004	2005	2006	2007	2008	2009
All commodities......	**222.6**	**243.2**	**227.8**	**190.6**	**234.5**	**255.3**	**283.9**	**347.9**	**394.9**	**476.1**	**363.1**	**484.42**
Softs [1]	276.0	354.4	254.4	252.8	303.7	250.5	343.5	420.5	475.9	467.5	487.2	(NA)
Industrials	245.5	272.5	211.0	141.8	176.6	256.6	232.1	302.5	368.8	418.3	475.4	(NA)
Grains and oilseeds [2].....	171.2	218.6	174.9	159.0	188.2	225.8	177.0	193.8	279.1	427.0	545.5	(NA)
Energy................	246.0	180.0	355.8	204.9	320.7	358.7	457.3	705.3	591.6	825.1	1,263.2	(NA)
Oilseeds [3]	223.6	277.5	(3)	(3)	(3)	(3)	(3)	(3)	(3)	(3)	(3)	(3)
Livestock and meats	226.2	192.4	253.6	247.4	251.0	237.8	303.6	300.3	294.6	297.7	337.0	(NA)
Metals (precious)........	257.8	276.0	265.7	246.8	289.1	364.1	396.6	478.1	611.9	773.6	894.6	(NA)

NA Not available. [1] Prior to 1997, reported as imported. Softs include commodities that are grown and not mined such as coffee, cocoa, lumber, cotton, and sugar. [2] Prior to 1997, reported as grains. [3] Incorporated into grains and oilseeds beginning 1997.
Source: Commodity Research Bureau (CRB), Chicago, IL, *CRB Commodity Index Report*, weekly (copyright). See <http://www.crbtrader.com>.

Table 735. Indexes of Spot Primary Market Prices: 1990 to 2009

[1967 = 100. Computed daily. Represents unweighted geometric average of price quotations of 23 commodities; much more sensitive to changes in market conditions than is a monthly producer price index]

Item and number	1990	1995	2000	2001	2002	2003	2004	2005	2006	2007	2008	2009
All commodities (23).....	**258.1**	**289.1**	**224.0**	**212.1**	**244.3**	**283.6**	**293.0**	**303.3**	**362.4**	**413.4**	**313.0**	**424.2**
Foodstuffs (10)	206.4	236.4	184.7	201.6	238.1	250.2	256.0	241.7	276.0	335.9	294.2	344.7
Raw industrials (13).......	301.2	332.2	255.8	217.3	248.6	309.1	321.5	354.7	437.3	477.0	326.5	489.4
Livestock and products (5)...	292.7	307.4	265.5	257.2	317.8	365.9	365.0	326.6	378.6	402.6	310.8	407.6
Metals (5)...............	283.2	300.6	214.0	172.5	184.5	276.7	357.7	440.9	693.9	811.9	390.9	809.1
Textiles and fibers (4).......	257.6	274.3	245.7	217.4	230.2	255.2	237.9	252.5	254.4	267.5	241.3	294.0
Fats and oils (4)..........	188.7	226.7	163.6	175.8	234.0	297.2	262.6	223.4	273.9	363.4	268.0	339.7

Source: Commodity Research Bureau, Chicago, IL, *CRB Commodity Index Report*, weekly (copyright). See <http://www.crbtrader.com>.

482 Prices

Table 736. Producer Price Indexes by Stage of Processing and Commodity: 1990 to 2009

[1982=100, except as indicated. See Appendix III]

Stage of processing	1990	1995	2000	2005	2006	2007	2008	2009 [1]
Finished goods	**119.2**	**127.9**	**138.0**	**155.7**	**160.4**	**166.6**	**177.1**	**172.6**
Finished consumer goods	**118.2**	**125.6**	**138.2**	**160.4**	**166.0**	**173.5**	**186.3**	**179.2**
Finished consumer foods	**124.4**	**129.0**	**137.2**	**155.7**	**156.7**	**167.0**	**178.3**	**175.5**
Fresh fruits and melons	118.1	85.8	91.4	102.8	111.0	123.4	122.9	110.4
Fresh and dry vegetables	118.1	144.4	126.7	142.6	153.3	165.5	172.3	162.9
Eggs for fresh use (Dec. 1991 = 100)	(NA)	86.3	84.9	79.6	90.0	132.6	152.4	123.3
Bakery products	141.0	164.3	182.3	201.1	207.7	216.6	237.5	245.9
Milled rice	102.5	113.1	101.2	120.1	136.1	155.0	251.9	205.7
Pasta products (June 1985 = 100)	114.1	125.0	121.6	127.9	128.3	136.3	183.5	180.2
Beef and veal	116.0	100.9	113.7	147.4	142.3	146.1	153.7	142.0
Pork	119.8	101.5	113.4	131.9	128.0	133.3	130.7	115.7
Processed young chickens	111.0	113.5	110.4	136.2	118.1	139.0	143.2	147.8
Processed turkeys	107.6	104.9	98.7	105.1	103.6	110.2	120.3	120.0
Finfish and shellfish	147.2	170.8	198.1	222.6	237.4	242.8	255.4	250.7
Dairy products	117.2	119.7	133.7	154.5	147.5	175.7	182.7	157.2
Processed fruits and vegetables	124.7	122.4	128.6	140.4	148.9	157.4	166.8	176.4
Soft drinks	122.3	133.1	144.1	159.1	162.8	166.7	174.9	181.7
Roasted coffee	113.0	146.5	133.5	151.1	153.6	163.7	179.0	179.2
Shortening and cooking oils	123.2	142.5	132.4	176.7	183.7	211.7	293.2	225.7
Finished consumer goods excluding foods	**115.3**	**124.0**	**138.4**	**161.9**	**169.2**	**175.6**	**189.1**	**179.6**
Alcoholic beverages	117.2	128.5	140.6	158.5	160.1	160.2	166.0	172.0
Apparel	117.5	124.2	127.4	125.6	125.9	127.0	128.0	129.2
Women's/girls/infants' cut & sew apparel (Dec. 2003 = 100)	(NA)	(NA)	(NA)	100.3	100.3	101.1	101.1	102.1
Men's and boy's cut and sew apparel Dec. 2003 = 100)	(NA)	(NA)	(NA)	98.7	98.0	98.6	99.7	101.0
Textile house furnishings	109.5	119.5	122.0	122.9	123.2	125.3	127.0	129.0
Footwear	125.6	139.2	144.9	148.1	149.3	151.6	156.9	159.9
Residential electric power (Dec. 1990 = 100)	(NA)	111.8	110.8	126.4	134.8	138.8	146.1	150.7
Residential gas (Dec. 1990 = 100)	(NA)	104.4	135.5	216.8	226.7	224.9	250.6	205.7
Gasoline	78.7	63.7	94.6	168.6	197.2	221.9	263.0	178.4
Fuel oil No. 2	73.3	56.6	93.5	178.4	207.4	223.7	305.2	163.0
Soaps and synthetic detergents	117.7	122.9	128.2	134.6	142.7	144.9	153.8	161.4
Cosmetics and other toilet preparations	121.6	129.0	137.4	143.0	145.2	147.6	147.9	148.1
Tires, tubes, and tread	96.8	100.2	93.0	108.1	114.7	118.5	128.0	130.9
Sanitary papers and health products	135.3	144.4	146.7	154.6	160.1	161.8	171.5	179.5
Book publishing	153.4	185.0	218.2	264.0	275.2	285.0	(NA)	(NA)
Household furniture	125.1	141.8	152.7	166.5	172.3	174.6	181.0	187.1
Floor coverings	119.0	123.7	129.6	146.4	154.5	156.6	160.6	167.4
Household appliances	110.8	112.4	107.3	103.3	104.1	105.2	107.2	111.1
Home electronic equipment	82.7	78.9	71.8	62.6	60.3	58.2	56.7	53.6
Household glassware	132.5	153.2	166.0	174.7	172.3	177.0	190.7	197.8
Household flatware	122.1	138.3	142.6	147.7	152.7	186.8	194.7	(NA)
Lawn and garden equipment, except tractors	123.0	130.4	132.0	134.5	134.9	137.0	140.4	142.3
Passenger cars	118.3	134.1	132.8	131.8	128.0	126.2	128.9	131.0
Toys, games, and children's vehicles	118.1	124.3	121.9	127.0	128.5	131.0	134.3	143.1
Sporting and athletic goods	112.6	122.0	126.1	124.6	126.1	129.9	129.8	131.9
Tobacco products	221.4	231.3	397.2	457.8	460.0	489.1	508.8	539.2
Mobile homes	117.5	145.6	161.3	200.8	208.8	211.0	218.7	222.5
Jewelry, platinum, and karat gold	122.8	127.8	127.2	138.6	148.6	153.2	164.7	170.0
Costume jewelry and novelties	125.3	135.1	141.6	153.5	154.2	156.7	159.6	159.0
Capital Equipment	**122.9**	**136.7**	**138.8**	**144.6**	**146.9**	**149.5**	**153.8**	**156.8**
Agricultural machinery and equipment	121.7	142.9	153.7	174.7	178.9	184.3	192.9	199.8
Construction machinery and equipment	121.6	136.7	148.6	168.3	175.4	179.6	185.3	191.0
Metal cutting machine tools	129.8	148.0	161.9	155.1	163.4	165.8	170.3	174.2
Metal forming machine tools	128.7	145.7	161.8	178.9	183.3	184.4	192.5	198.6
Pumps, compressors, and equipment	119.2	139.4	154.1	178.5	186.0	195.0	205.4	212.5
Electronic computers (Dec. 2004 = 100)	(NA)	850.1	261.6	85.5	66.5	51.6	40.8	34.1
Textile machinery	128.8	146.7	156.2	160.5	161.7	162.5	164.9	166.3
Paper industries machinery (June 1982 = 100)	134.8	151.0	164.7	178.1	180.6	183.4	188.5	193.5
Printing trades machinery	124.9	133.6	142.1	144.3	146.5	150.5	152.7	157.0
Transformers and power regulators	120.9	128.9	135.8	150.3	172.5	194.9	216.2	210.7
Communication/related equip.(Dec. 1985 = 100)	106.1	112.1	110.6	102.5	102.4	103.2	104.8	105.7
X-ray and electromedical equipment	109.8	111.8	101.5	95.7	94.9	92.8	91.6	90.2
Mining machinery and equipment	121.0	135.6	146.1	175.9	183.9	190.9	205.8	217.0
Office and store machines and equipment	109.5	111.5	112.7	115.1	114.7	114.6	122.1	123.5
Commercial furniture	133.4	148.2	158.4	172.7	177.0	181.5	190.1	196.1
Light motor trucks	130.0	159.0	157.6	148.4	143.3	145.3	146.0	151.9
Heavy motor trucks	120.3	144.1	148.0	162.4	169.1	177.2	182.2	190.3
Truck trailers	110.8	131.7	139.4	157.1	164.5	169.4	177.0	177.7
Civilian aircraft (Dec. 1985 = 100)	115.3	141.8	159.6	202.2	212.4	219.6	230.2	235.3
Ships (Dec. 1985 = 100)	110.1	132.8	146.9	176.6	183.2	192.1	199.4	210.1
Railroad equipment	118.6	134.8	135.7	160.4	169.4	176.4	180.2	182.0
Intermediate materials, supplies, and components	**114.5**	**124.9**	**129.2**	**154.0**	**164.0**	**170.7**	**188.3**	**172.6**
Intermediate foods and feeds	**113.3**	**114.8**	**111.7**	**133.8**	**135.2**	**154.4**	**181.6**	**165.9**
Flour	103.6	123.0	103.8	133.6	145.8	178.4	239.8	182.7
Refined sugar	122.7	119.3	110.6	124.9	149.9	132.6	137.2	158.0
Soft drink beverage bases (December 1985 = 100)	126.2	148.3	167.1	180.4	188.4	196.0	210.3	223.7
Prepared animal feeds	107.4	109.1	102.9	115.6	118.7	142.7	182.7	175.2

See footnotes at end of table.

U.S. Census Bureau, Statistical Abstract of the United States: 2011

Table 736. Producer Price Indexes by Stage of Processing and Commodity: 1990 to 2009—Con.

[1982=100, except as indicated. See Appendix III]

Stage of processing	1990	1995	2000	2005	2006	2007	2008	2009 [1]
Intermediate materials less foods and feeds	**114.5**	**125.5**	**130.1**	**155.1**	**165.4**	**171.5**	**188.7**	**173.1**
Synthetic fibers	106.7	109.4	107.2	112.3	115.0	114.2	116.5	113.4
Processed yarns and threads	112.6	112.8	107.9	111.7	114.0	116.9	123.7	120.1
Leather	177.5	191.4	182.2	219.6	223.7	230.6	234.3	220.9
Liquefied petroleum gas	77.4	65.1	127.1	244.7	268.5	316.1	375.9	233.7
Commercial electric power	115.3	131.7	131.5	149.8	161.3	165.4	173.3	178.8
Industrial electric power	119.6	130.8	131.5	156.2	172.8	180.4	189.1	190.8
Commercial natural gas (Dec. 1990 = 100)	(NA)	96.5	134.7	232.5	239.9	235.6	272.1	212.3
Industrial natural gas (Dec. 1990 = 100)	(NA)	90.9	139.0	249.4	246.2	242.3	283.1	211.3
Natural gas to electric utilities (Dec. 1990 = 100)	(NA)	87.7	120.7	204.0	191.4	186.0	203.4	165.1
Jet fuels	76.0	55.0	88.5	169.6	199.1	211.2	300.1	169.3
No. 2 Diesel fuel	74.1	57.0	93.3	189.1	216.9	235.5	324.9	180.6
Residual fuel	57.7	52.6	84.7	148.9	161.1	173.4	229.7	156.8
Industrial chemicals	113.2	128.4	129.1	188.5	212.4	226.4	274.6	234.9
Prepared paint	124.8	142.1	160.8	187.9	201.3	208.8	223.0	236.3
Fats and oils, inedible	88.1	126.9	70.1	146.9	147.9	189.4	288.3	210.3
Mixed fertilizers	103.3	111.1	112.4	138.9	144.9	161.2	249.2	192.2
Plastic resins and materials	124.1	143.5	141.6	193.0	198.4	195.9	215.0	191.6
Synthetic rubber	111.9	126.3	119.1	151.3	162.0	169.3	206.6	185.7
Plastic construction products	117.2	133.8	135.8	158.8	181.8	179.2	185.6	186.2
Unsupported plastic film, sheet, and shapes	119.0	135.6	133.2	164.8	175.1	176.0	194.2	191.0
Plastic parts and components for manufacturing	112.9	115.9	117.3	119.8	130.3	130.0	132.8	135.8
Softwood lumber	123.8	178.5	178.6	203.6	189.4	170.5	156.3	141.3
Hardwood lumber	131.0	167.0	185.9	196.6	195.3	192.4	184.5	171.3
Plywood	114.2	165.3	157.6	186.8	172.7	176.1	174.7	164.0
Paper	128.8	159.0	149.8	159.6	167.4	169.3	184.3	179.6
Paperboard	135.7	183.1	176.7	175.5	192.0	201.7	217.9	206.7
Paper boxes and containers	129.9	163.8	172.6	183.7	192.5	197.8	208.3	211.9
Building paper and board	112.2	144.9	138.8	184.9	173.0	155.2	163.9	156.6
Commercial printing (June 1982 = 100)	128.0	144.5	155.2	161.6	165.0	166.0	169.2	167.7
Foundry and forge shop products	117.2	129.3	136.5	156.2	163.0	170.7	189.6	185.2
Primary nonferrous metals	133.4	146.8	113.6	158.2	236.0	268.6	269.1	176.9
Nonferrous wire and cable	142.6	151.5	143.7	169.4	226.9	238.7	249.2	223.2
Metal containers	114.0	117.2	106.8	123.9	126.9	133.4	144.0	(NA)
Hardware	125.9	141.1	151.2	168.0	174.0	179.7	189.9	194.0
Plumbing fixtures and brass fittings	144.3	166.0	180.4	197.6	207.2	220.6	226.7	228.9
Heating equipment	131.6	147.5	155.6	179.9	185.7	195.5	208.8	218.9
Fabricated ferrous wire products (June 1982 = 100)	114.6	125.7	130.0	157.1	162.6	166.7	200.7	200.1
Mechanical power transmission equipment	125.3	146.9	163.9	189.5	197.0	205.2	219.7	231.1
Air conditioning and refrigeration equipment	122.1	130.2	135.3	146.2	150.1	157.3	162.7	164.6
Ball and roller bearings	130.6	152.0	168.8	187.1	193.1	199.8	211.9	222.6
Wiring devices	132.2	147.2	152.9	176.6	188.2	194.5	206.4	206.8
Motors, generators, motor generator sets	132.9	143.9	146.2	157.8	165.0	172.9	181.7	187.0
Switchgear and switchboard equipment	124.4	140.3	153.0	170.2	178.6	188.5	195.5	201.0
Electronic components and accessories	118.4	113.6	97.1	87.0	88.5	82.3	77.0	75.5
Internal combustion engines	120.2	135.6	143.8	147.7	152.5	154.7	157.2	162.3
Flat glass	107.5	113.2	109.7	111.0	113.5	114.2	115.9	114.9
Cement	103.7	128.1	150.1	176.4	199.3	209.7	209.7	207.3
Concrete products	113.5	129.4	147.8	177.2	195.1	203.5	210.6	214.1
Asphalt felts and coatings	97.1	100.0	104.1	130.8	144.5	145.7	187.2	220.0
Gypsum products	105.2	154.5	201.4	229.6	274.9	233.0	213.2	213.8
Glass containers	120.4	130.5	127.4	146.4	152.8	162.0	171.8	178.6
Motor vehicle parts	111.2	116.0	113.6	113.1	116.3	117.9	119.7	120.7
Aircraft engines and engine parts (Dec. 1985 = 100)	113.5	132.8	141.0	165.9	172.4	178.9	185.9	193.0
Photographic supplies	127.6	126.8	125.2	120.1	121.6	122.9	125.5	127.9
Medical/surgical/personal aid devices	127.3	141.3	146.0	159.2	161.4	163.1	165.7	167.4
Crude materials for further processing	**108.9**	**102.7**	**120.6**	**182.2**	**184.8**	**207.1**	**251.8**	**175.0**
Crude foodstuffs and feedstuffs	113.1	105.8	100.2	122.7	119.3	146.7	163.4	134.4
Wheat	87.6	118.6	80.3	102.7	116.9	172.1	235.1	149.2
Corn	100.9	109.0	76.4	75.9	95.6	141.5	199.1	146.9
Slaughter cattle	122.5	99.5	104.1	131.5	126.2	136.1	136.1	122.0
Slaughter hogs	94.1	70.2	72.7	82.7	77.2	76.1	78.1	68.9
Slaughter broilers/fryers	119.5	129.1	127.6	181.0	156.1	199.9	210.7	202.6
Slaughter turkeys	116.9	120.3	120.7	131.1	140.5	153.3	165.9	146.7
Fluid milk	100.8	93.6	92.0	113.5	96.7	143.3	137.2	95.2
Soybeans	100.8	102.2	83.4	102.6	96.8	137.9	203.9	175.9
Crude nonfood materials	101.5	96.8	130.4	223.4	230.6	246.3	313.9	197.1
Raw cotton	118.2	156.2	95.2	78.9	79.7	83.1	98.0	80.4
Coal	97.5	95.0	87.9	116.8	126.6	130.7	161.7	182.5
Natural gas	80.4	66.6	155.5	335.4	280.3	273.8	344.0	159.1
Crude petroleum	71.0	51.1	85.2	150.1	176.0	192.6	275.7	161.4
Logs and timber	142.8	220.4	196.4	197.4	201.2	217.1	216.7	188.0
Wastepaper	138.9	371.1	282.5	230.9	234.8	368.7	372.5	235.8
Iron ore	83.3	91.8	94.8	116.9	132.5	128.8	142.5	144.0
Iron and steel scrap	166.0	202.7	142.1	289.8	335.2	406.8	566.8	338.1
Nonferrous metal ores (Dec. 1983 = 100)	98.3	101.6	68.0	150.0	215.9	243.5	251.0	217.5
Copper base scrap	181.3	193.5	123.7	258.6	436.8	485.2	494.3	378.0
Aluminum base scrap	172.6	209.4	177.0	210.1	275.7	274.7	272.8	166.8
Construction sand, gravel, and crushed stone	125.4	142.3	163.1	195.8	213.9	232.4	247.7	259.0
Industrial sand	117.6	132.5	146.0	174.4	183.2	190.9	217.7	238.1

NA Not available. [1] Preliminary data.

Source: U.S. Bureau of Labor Statistics, *Producer Price Indexes*, monthly and annual. See also *Monthly Labor Review*, <http://www.bls.gov/opub/mlr/welcome.htm>.

Table 737. Producer Price Indexes for the Net Output of Selected Industries: 2005 to 2009

[Indexes are based on selling prices reported by establishments of all sizes by probability sampling. Manufacturing industries selected by shipment value. N.e.c.= not elsewhere classified. See text, Section 22. See Appendix III]

Industry	NAICS Code [1]	Index base [2]	2005	2006	2007	2008	2009 [3]
Logging industries	**113310**	**12/81**	**179.2**	**176.7**	**175.1**	**171.6**	**160.5**
Total mining industries	**21**	**12/84**	**201.0**	**208.7**	**220.1**	**274.7**	**178.6**
Crude petroleum & natural gas extraction	211111	06/02	253.5	252.3	261.5	349.2	185.9
Natural gas liquid extraction	211112	06/02	285.4	258.1	286.7	347.6	194.6
Bituminous coal & lignite surface mining	212111	12/01	111.9	117.1	120.9	140.4	149.1
Anthracite mining	212113	12/79	205.4	234.9	240.9	267.0	275.5
Iron ore mining	212210	12/84	115.7	131.2	127.5	141.0	142.6
Gold ore mining	212221	06/85	131.7	177.5	203.0	208.9	235.4
Copper ore & nickel ore mining	212234	06/88	200.8	360.4	397.8	401.7	304.3
Crushed and broken granite mining and quarrying	212313	12/83	217.3	242.5	279.3	305.1	329.0
Construction sand and gravel mining	212321	06/82	209.9	229.1	247.0	262.6	271.3
Clay and ceramic and refractory minerals mining	212325	06/84	148.3	156.9	163.4	174.2	184.4
Drilling oil and gas wells	213111	12/85	258.8	377.7	360.6	366.9	327.7
Nonmetallic minerals support activity (except fuels)	213115	06/85	127.5	137.2	140.2	146.0	148.7
Total manufacturing industries	**31-33**	**12/84**	**150.8**	**156.9**	**162.9**	**175.8**	**167.1**
Dog & cat food mfg	311111	12/85	145.8	147.8	155.2	175.3	186.3
Flour milling	311211	06/83	117.5	127.4	153.9	202.8	160.8
Rice milling	311212	06/84	102.1	114.5	129.2	209.6	170.8
Chocolate & confectionery mfg. from cacao beans	311320	06/83	157.5	161.0	166.0	181.1	194.1
Frozen fruit, juice, & vegetable mfg	311411	06/81	156.0	171.1	174.9	179.0	189.2
Frozen specialty food mfg	311412	12/82	143.6	144.4	145.5	154.1	160.4
Fruit and vegetable canning	311421	06/81	151.4	155.9	165.3	176.8	189.9
Fluid milk	311511	12/82	165.2	163.2	193.7	200.9	179.8
Ice cream and frozen dessert mfg	311520	06/83	168.2	171.8	177.7	184.5	186.0
Animal (except poultry) slaughtering	311611	12/80	141.0	136.4	142.7	149.6	134.8
Meat processed from carcasses	311612	12/82	136.6	137.1	139.5	144.7	144.1
Poultry processing	311615	12/81	135.3	124.1	139.5	145.0	148.3
Coffee and tea manufacturing	311920	06/81	161.0	164.1	173.8	189.4	191.7
Spice and extracts manufacturing	311942	12/03	99.1	99.8	102.3	108.5	115.0
Soft drinks manufacturing	312111	06/81	168.6	173.0	177.4	186.4	194.3
Bottled water manufacturing	312112	12/03	101.5	101.8	99.4	98.9	97.0
Breweries	312120	06/82	158.4	158.4	156.0	163.0	(NA)
Wineries	312130	12/83	144.8	152.7	155.7	159.3	162.3
Distilleries	312140	06/83	165.5	167.8	175.3	187.2	188.6
Tobacco stemming & redrying	312210	06/84	119.9	109.4	112.6	113.4	115.2
Cigarettes	312221	12/82	437.0	440.1	470.2	489.5	520.7
Men's/boys' cut & sew trouser/slack/jean mfg	315224	12/81	123.2	121.5	122.3	122.9	123.9
Women's/girls' cut & sew dress mfg	315233	12/80	123.7	123.4	120.8	123.0	124.5
Sawmills	321113	12/80	162.0	158.3	152.0	143.5	124.8
Wood preservation	321114	06/85	175.7	169.4	163.8	165.6	162.0
Hardwood veneer & plywood manufacturing	321211	06/85	146.2	149.8	151.1	153.0	151.5
Softwood veneer or plywood, mfg	321212	12/80	172.7	151.1	154.9	150.8	135.8
Wood window & door mfg	321911	12/03	103.1	106.6	107.3	107.7	109.2
Manufactured homes (mobile homes) mfg	321991	06/81	204.4	212.4	214.7	222.6	226.4
Paper (except newsprint) mills	322121	12/03	108.4	112.7	116.2	125.2	126.1
Newsprint mills	322122	12/03	115.7	123.9	106.8	119.4	103.7
Paperboard mills	322130	12/82	196.2	213.0	224.4	242.6	230.6
Book printing	323117	12/83	154.9	158.2	158.6	159.0	159.6
Petroleum refineries	324110	06/85	205.3	241.0	266.9	338.3	216.9
Petroleum lubricating oils and greases	324191	12/80	231.2	284.5	304.8	356.6	354.9
Industrial gas manufacturing	325120	12/03	118.3	123.0	123.3	140.9	129.1
Plastics material and resins manufacturing	325211	12/80	228.5	235.5	232.4	255.1	228.6
Synthetic rubber manufacturing	325212	06/81	150.6	161.9	170.2	214.3	202.9
Nitrogenous fertilizer manufacturing	325311	12/79	236.9	245.6	278.5	427.0	276.5
Phosphatic fertilizer manufacturing	325312	12/79	173.3	183.7	257.4	580.3	263.7
Pharmaceutical preparation mfg	325412	06/81	378.7	397.9	413.8	440.7	468.9
Plastics pipe and pipe fitting manufacturing	326122	06/93	171.9	214.1	197.2	215.0	203.0
Cement manufacturing	327310	06/82	175.2	197.7	208.4	207.8	205.0
Lime	327410	12/85	144.6	156.6	166.0	175.5	207.5
Steel investment foundries	331512	06/81	204.8	216.0	235.4	235.4	235.4
Steel foundries (except investment)	331513	06/81	160.1	170.5	183.7	193.4	191.2
Aluminum die-casting foundries	331521	06/91	116.4	125.1	126.4	133.0	119.7
Iron & steel forging	332111	12/83	128.1	133.9	140.4	150.9	148.5
Hand and edge tools, except machine tools and handsaws	332212	06/83	177.0	183.7	188.9	197.0	203.2
Saw blade & handsaw mfg	332213	06/83	146.0	150.2	152.8	158.1	165.1
Metal window and door manufacturing	332321	06/83	175.2	183.5	188.1	196.5	200.4
Sheetmetal work mfg	332322	12/82	165.6	171.6	176.8	187.6	182.2
Heating equipment (except warm air furnaces) mfg	333414	06/80	215.4	222.3	231.2	245.7	255.3
Laboratory apparatus and furniture	339111	12/91	148.1	152.5	158.8	165.3	(NA)
Surgical and medical instrument mfg	339112	06/82	135.2	134.0	134.5	136.3	137.3
Services industries							
Beer, wine, and liquor stores	445310	06/00	111.0	111.3	113.2	120.6	119.8
Gasoline stations with convenience stores	447110	12/03	104.3	110.1	123.0	135.1	128.8
Scheduled passenger air transportation	481111	12/89	217.1	229.6	234.5	257.1	235.9
Scheduled freight air transportation	481112	12/03	104.9	108.4	109.0	127.8	118.9
General freight trucking, long-distance	484121	12/03	108.6	112.0	113.5	119.5	111.2
Pipeline transportation of crude oil	486110	06/86	125.5	135.3	138.9	152.0	156.4
Pipeline transportation of refined petroleum products	486910	06/86	120.3	123.8	131.7	139.2	147.3
Marine cargo handling	488320	12/91	115.1	118.4	122.8	124.7	127.4
United States Postal Service	491110	06/89	155.0	164.7	171.9	178.9	185.0
Nursing care facilities	623110	12/94	161.4	166.2	174.0	180.9	187.0

[1] North American Industry Classification System, 2002. [2] Index base year equals 100. [3] Preliminary data.

Source: U.S. Bureau of Labor Statistics, *Producer Price Indexes*, monthly and annual. See also *Monthly Labor Review*, <http://www.bls.gov/opub/mlr/welcome.htm>.

Prices 485

Table 738. Chain-Type Price Indexes for Personal Consumption Expenditures by Type of Expenditure: 1990 to 2008

[2005 = 100. For explanation of "chain-type", see text Section 13. See also Table 676]

Type of Expenditure	1990	1995	2000	2004	2006	2007	2008
Personal consumption expenditures	**72.1**	**82.0**	**89.8**	**97.1**	**102.7**	**105.5**	**109.0**
Household consumption expenditures [1]	71.7	82.2	89.7	97.1	102.8	105.6	109.2
Food and beverages purchased for off-premises consumption	73.9	80.9	89.5	98.3	101.7	105.6	111.9
Food and nonalcoholic beverages purchased for off-premises consumption	74.1	80.6	89.2	98.2	101.8	105.9	112.8
Alcoholic beverages purchased for off-premises consumption	72.1	83.0	91.2	98.9	101.3	103.8	107.1
Food produced and consumed on farms	93.6	81.6	78.4	97.1	96.4	104.6	103.2
Clothing, footwear, and related services	113.9	112.6	107.4	100.7	99.8	99.0	98.5
Clothing	115.8	113.7	108.7	101.4	99.6	98.9	98.0
Garments	120.1	116.6	110.6	101.6	99.4	98.5	97.2
Women's and girls' clothing	125.4	119.4	109.7	101.9	99.9	99.6	97.0
Men's and boys' clothing	113.2	113.3	111.7	101.2	98.3	96.8	97.4
Children's and infants' clothing	113.9	111.4	111.7	101.5	99.9	97.7	97.5
Footwear [2]	104.2	106.9	100.8	97.2	100.8	99.9	101.4
Housing, utilities, and fuels	64.1	73.4	84.4	96.3	104.4	108.2	112.5
Housing	64.4	74.3	86.1	97.6	103.6	107.4	110.4
Rental of tenant-occupied nonfarm housing [3]	64.2	73.5	85.1	97.1	103.6	108.0	111.8
Imputed rental of owner-occupied nonfarm housing [4]	64.6	74.4	86.3	97.7	103.5	107.0	109.7
Household utilities and fuels	61.9	69.0	76.9	90.4	108.4	112.1	123.1
Water supply and sanitation	53.8	71.0	81.4	95.0	104.9	110.2	116.7
Electricity, gas, and other fuels	64.2	68.5	75.5	89.0	109.5	112.6	125.1
Electricity	78.0	86.0	85.2	94.2	112.1	116.5	123.9
Natural gas	45.1	47.7	61.9	83.6	102.5	101.4	115.2
Fuel oil and other fuels	45.9	40.5	60.7	74.7	114.1	121.9	166.2
Furnishings, household equipment, and routine household maintenance	95.4	100.7	103.0	99.2	100.4	100.1	100.7
Furniture, furnishings, and floor coverings [5]	101.2	107.9	107.8	100.8	99.3	97.5	95.9
Household textiles	133.2	132.4	120.3	102.4	95.4	90.5	87.1
Household appliances [6]	105.7	105.7	102.7	97.0	102.7	106.2	107.7
Glassware, tableware, and household utensils [7]	111.8	115.3	111.9	100.6	96.3	94.6	95.7
Health	58.5	75.8	85.0	97.0	103.2	106.6	109.3
Medical products, appliances, and equipment	62.4	74.9	85.3	97.2	103.8	105.3	107.5
Pharmaceutical and other medical products [8]	60.1	72.7	83.9	97.0	104.0	105.5	108.0
Pharmaceutical products	59.9	72.5	83.7	97.0	104.1	105.6	108.0
Other medical products	79.1	93.2	98.6	99.5	101.5	102.5	102.8
Therapeutic appliances and equipment	74.9	87.5	94.5	98.4	102.3	104.0	104.9
Outpatient services	62.8	79.6	89.1	97.6	101.9	105.6	108.0
Physician services	65.6	85.0	92.2	98.2	101.0	105.1	106.2
Dental services	48.4	63.9	79.8	94.7	105.2	110.6	116.3
Paramedical services	65.9	78.7	88.4	97.7	101.9	104.4	107.4
Hospital and nursing home services	54.0	72.8	81.3	96.3	104.2	108.0	111.4
Hospitals	54.6	74.9	81.3	96.3	104.4	108.0	111.2
Nursing homes	52.1	64.2	81.2	96.4	103.0	107.8	112.0
Transportation	72.2	80.9	88.6	93.1	100.5	105.0	108.2
Motor vehicles	82.7	100.7	103.2	98.5	99.6	98.4	96.4
New motor vehicles	87.5	101.9	103.9	99.5	99.4	98.3	96.8
Net purchases of used motor vehicles	73.0	98.4	102.0	96.2	100.1	98.5	95.7
Motor vehicle operation	62.6	66.3	77.0	89.3	108.4	114.8	127.6
Motor vehicle parts and accessories	94.2	93.9	92.4	97.7	104.1	107.6	113.2
Motor vehicle fuels, lubricants, and fluids	51.8	51.5	66.2	82.1	112.8	122.4	142.2
Public transportation	87.2	92.0	100.4	94.6	106.1	107.4	115.8
Ground transportation	64.4	72.6	81.9	96.0	104.7	106.3	111.4
Air transportation	100.9	102.6	110.3	93.6	107.3	108.5	119.6
Water transportation	113.1	131.5	126.0	98.8	99.6	99.1	97.5
Recreation	110.1	115.2	106.5	101.1	99.1	97.8	97.8
Video and audio equipment, computers, and related services	253.5	214.3	137.6	106.0	93.9	87.7	82.9
Video and audio equipment	208.5	183.1	140.5	107.8	91.1	81.1	74.0
Sports and recreational goods and related services	112.2	118.4	109.1	101.7	99.3	97.6	97.9
Sports and recreational vehicles	84.5	93.6	97.9	98.4	102.4	101.5	102.6
Other sporting and recreational goods	123.2	128.2	113.3	102.9	98.1	96.1	96.1
Magazines, newspapers, books, and stationery	71.5	87.4	95.5	98.9	100.8	102.0	104.0
Education	40.1	56.1	71.4	93.3	106.3	112.5	119.1
Higher education	36.8	55.7	69.9	93.0	106.7	113.4	120.5
Net foreign travel and expenditures abroad by U.S. residents							
Foreign travel by U.S. residents	63.2	75.1	78.9	93.7	104.2	111.0	120.0
Less: Expenditures in the United States by nonresidents	67.4	76.5	87.7	95.3	104.7	108.9	114.2

[1] Consists of household purchases of goods and services from business, government, nonprofit institutions, and the rest of the world. [2] Consists of shoes and other footwear, and of repair and hire of footwear. [3] Consists of space rent (see footnote 4) and rent for appliances, furnishings, and furniture. [4] Consists of rent for space and for heating and plumbing facilities, water heaters, lighting fixtures, kitchen cabinets, linoleum, storm windows and doors, window screens, and screen doors, but excludes rent for appliances and furniture and purchases of fueland electricity. [5] Includes clocks, lamps, lighting fixtures, and other household decorative items;also includes repair of furniture, furnishings, and floor coverings. [6] Consists of major household appliances, small electric household appliances, and repair of household appliances. [7] Consists of dishes, flatware, and non-electric cookware and tableware. [8] Excludes drug preparations and related products dispensed by physicians, hospitals,and other medical services.

Source: U.S. Bureau of Economic Analysis, *Survey of Current Business*, April 2010. See also <http://www.bea.doc.gov/bea /dn/nipaweb/SelectTable.asp?Selected=N>.

Table 739. Chain-Type Price Indexes for Gross Domestic Product: 1990 to 2009

[2005 = 100. For explanation of "chain-type," see text, Section 13]

Component	1990	1995	2000	2004	2006	2007	2008	2009
Gross domestic product	**72.2**	**81.5**	**88.6**	**96.8**	**103.3**	**106.2**	**108.5**	**109.7**
Personal consumption expenditures...	**72.1**	**82.0**	**89.8**	**97.1**	**102.7**	**105.5**	**109.0**	**109.2**
Durable goods.....................	89.7	95.6	97.5	97.9	101.5	102.8	106.2	103.5
Nondurable goods..................	117.3	124.3	111.7	101.0	98.5	96.7	95.5	94.0
Services.........................	76.7	82.1	90.0	96.1	103.2	106.3	112.2	109.0
Gross private domestic investment....	**63.8**	**75.4**	**85.8**	**96.7**	**103.4**	**107.0**	**110.6**	**112.3**
Fixed investment	86.7	90.8	90.0	95.6	104.4	106.7	107.4	106.5
Nonresidential	85.8	90.1	89.8	95.5	104.4	106.7	107.6	106.1
Structures	100.8	102.2	96.2	96.8	103.5	106.2	107.9	107.5
Equipment and software	53.5	60.6	72.3	88.4	112.9	121.3	125.2	122.8
Residential.......................	125.4	122.3	106.1	99.9	100.2	100.7	101.5	102.0
Net exports of goods and services:								
Exports	92.0	96.0	92.0	96.5	103.4	107.1	112.4	106.3
Goods	100.2	101.4	92.9	96.9	103.3	107.0	112.4	104.9
Services........................	74.4	83.9	89.9	95.6	103.7	107.3	112.4	109.2
Imports	93.6	95.6	90.0	94.1	104.1	108.0	119.6	107.0
Goods	99.1	98.9	91.1	93.9	104.2	108.0	120.3	106.2
Services........................	71.0	80.2	84.2	95.6	103.8	107.9	115.7	110.9
Government consumption expenditures and gross investment ..	**63.4**	**72.8**	**82.5**	**94.5**	**104.8**	**109.6**	**114.5**	**114.3**
Federal...........................	63.5	73.7	82.5	95.3	104.1	107.8	110.9	111.5
National defense	63.9	73.2	81.8	94.9	104.4	108.3	111.9	112.1
Nondefense	62.6	74.8	83.9	96.2	103.5	106.7	108.9	110.4
State and local....................	63.5	72.3	82.5	94.1	105.3	110.6	116.6	115.9

Source: U.S. Bureau of Economic Analysis, *Survey of Current Business*, April 2010. See also <http://www.bea.gov/bea/dn/nipaweb/SelectTable.asp?Selected=N>.

Table 740. Import and Export Price Indexes by End-Use Category: 1990 to 2009

[As of June. Import indexes are weighted by the 2000 Tariff Schedule of the United States Annotated, a scheme for describing and reporting product composition and value of U.S. imports. Import prices are based on U.S. dollar prices paid by importer. Export indexes are weighted by 2000 export values according to the Schedule B classification system of the U.S. Census Bureau. Prices used in these indexes were collected from a sample of U.S. manufacturers of exports and are factory transaction prices, except as noted. Minus sign (–) indicates decrease]

Year	Index (2000 = 100)						Percent change [1]					
	Imports			Exports			Imports			Exports		
	Total	Petro-leum imports	Non–petro-leum imports	Total	Agri-cultural exports	Non–agri-cultural exports	Total	Petro-leum imports	Non–petro-leum imports	Total	Agri-cultural exports	Non–agri-cultural exports
1990.....	90.8	55.4	96.4	95.1	107.7	93.5	–0.8	–13.4	0.5	–0.1	–4.0	0.5
1995.....	101.4	62.9	107.6	104.5	117.0	103.3	5.3	9.2	4.9	6.1	7.0	5.9
2000.....	100.2	101.9	99.9	100.1	100.5	100.0	7.9	87.0	1.1	1.9	–0.6	2.1
2002.....	94.1	85.3	96.2	98.0	100.7	97.8	–3.6	–4.6	–2.7	–1.4	–0.2	–1.5
2003.....	96.2	96.4	97.3	99.5	110.0	98.7	2.2	13.0	1.1	1.5	9.2	0.9
2004.....	101.7	129.7	99.7	103.4	127.4	101.5	5.7	34.5	2.5	3.9	15.8	2.8
2005.....	109.2	181.5	102.0	106.7	123.9	105.4	7.4	39.9	2.3	3.2	–2.7	3.8
2006.....	117.3	242.6	104.2	111.2	124.1	110.3	7.4	33.7	2.2	4.2	0.2	4.6
2007.....	120.0	245.6	107.1	116.0	146.7	113.8	2.3	1.2	2.8	4.3	18.2	3.2
2008.....	145.5	450.3	114.9	126.1	195.2	121.2	21.3	83.3	7.3	8.7	33.1	6.5
2009.....	120.0	241.5	107.4	117.8	169.7	114.1	–17.5	–46.4	–6.5	–6.6	–13.1	–5.9

[1] Percent change from immediate prior year.

Source: U.S. Bureau of Labor Statistics, *US Import and Export Price Indexes*, monthly. See also <http://www.bls.gov/web/ximpim.supp.toc.htm#long_tables>.

Table 741. Export Price Indexes—Selected Commodities: 2000 to 2009

[2000 = 100. As of June. Indexes are weighted by 2000 export values according to the Schedule B classification system of the U.S. Census Bureau. Prices used in these indexes were collected from a sample of U.S. manufacturers of exports and are factory transaction prices, except as noted]

Commodity	2000 [1]	2003	2004	2005	2006	2007	2008	2009
All commodities	**100.1**	**99.5**	**103.4**	**106.7**	**111.2**	**116.0**	**126.1**	**118.0**
Animal products	102.2	104.5	121.5	130.9	125.1	153.2	174.5	158.8
Fish	99.1	109.6	105.2	114.2	122.8	124.3	149.1	145.1
Vegetable products	100.0	115.0	140.3	130.3	131.0	159.3	239.3	205.5
Fruit and nuts	94.8	97.3	109.2	126.5	114.5	117.5	123.0	102.3
Cereals	100.0	119.3	143.3	118.1	136.9	179.2	293.6	222.1
Wheat	99.4	121.4	136.2	130.0	154.3	180.4	276.7	(NA)
Corn (maize)	101.0	121.3	146.9	111.8	127.1	189.8	286.4	(NA)
Oilseeds	102.8	121.5	161.0	136.2	121.5	157.4	259.3	238.1
Beverages and tobacco	100.0	102.8	110.7	110.3	112.5	120.5	136.3	142.1
Mineral products	97.8	106.4	129.7	182.3	238.4	243.4	360.5	200.5
Fuels	97.4	106.2	127.9	172.8	219.6	230.5	361.9	195.2
Chemicals and related products	100.3	102.4	107.7	115.3	122.8	130.1	145.4	137.9
Plastics and rubber products	101.5	102.6	105.7	118.4	128.7	131.3	142.2	130.8
Hides, skins, and leather products	95.7	104.3	108.6	113.0	116.8	122.6	117.3	79.1
Wood products	100.0	93.0	103.8	104.3	107.8	113.5	112.3	102.1
Woodpulp and paper products	101.6	95.1	98.1	101.9	105.5	110.6	117.5	107.5
Textiles	100.2	97.7	98.8	100.8	101.9	101.9	108.0	101.9
Stone and glass products	100.7	100.2	99.0	103.5	104.1	110.1	111.1	115.9
Gems and precious metals	98.1	92.1	101.6	106.5	141.8	162.7	183.1	171.3
Base metals	100.5	100.2	119.6	131.8	151.9	169.3	181.2	144.3
Iron and steel	101.7	102.7	152.9	164.0	173.7	209.2	243.3	148.6
Articles of iron and steel	100.2	104.7	115.3	124.8	134.6	148.5	156.6	163.4
Copper	98.7	93.4	122.7	143.1	230.6	243.9	261.2	184.5
Aluminum	98.4	94.6	107.3	113.2	146.0	149.5	150.6	101.6
Machinery	99.9	95.4	94.9	94.9	93.8	94.3	95.3	95.4
Nonelectrical machinery	100.0	99.1	99.9	100.5	101.5	102.7	103.7	105.2
Electrical machinery	99.8	91.2	89.4	88.6	85.3	85.2	86.2	84.7
Transportation equipment	100.0	104.5	106.5	108.8	111.5	113.8	116.6	120.5
Motor vehicles	100.0	101.1	102.4	103.2	104.6	105.6	106.7	107.7
Instruments	100.0	101.2	101.2	101.3	102.4	103.3	107.1	107.7
Miscellaneous manufactured articles	100.4	100.5	99.2	100.6	101.1	104.7	108.6	106.7

NA Not available [1] June 2000 may not equal 100 because indexes were reweighted to an "average" trade value in 2000.

Source: U.S. Bureau of Labor Statistics, *U.S. Import and Export Price Indexes*, monthly. See also <http://stats.bls.gov/news.release/ximpim.toc.htm>.

Table 742. Import Price Indexes—Selected Commodities: 2000 to 2009

[2000 = 100. As of June. Indexes are weighted by the 2000 Tariff Schedule of the United States Annotated, a scheme for describing and reporting product composition and value of U.S. imports. Import prices are based on U.S. dollar prices paid by importer]

Commodity	2000 [1]	2003	2004	2005	2006	2007	2008	2009
All commodities	**100.2**	**96.2**	**101.7**	**109.2**	**117.1**	**120.0**	**145.5**	**120.2**
Animal products	99.9	95.1	107.8	112.7	118.2	127.4	141.6	129.3
Meat	100.5	104.1	130.8	138.7	137.2	146.8	165.4	153.2
Fish	100.2	81.9	83.4	88.3	96.6	100.2	106.3	99.0
Vegetable products	97.1	102.7	103.0	116.9	108.6	129.3	159.5	161.3
Vegetables	93.9	122.7	113.8	136.8	143.6	175.3	202.6	293.1
Fruit and nuts	96.9	96.5	96.3	89.7	81.7	90.9	112.8	104.1
Beverages and tobacco	100.0	105.4	108.9	114.0	119.8	124.3	140.0	134.6
Mineral products	101.3	100.6	130.9	178.1	229.2	234.0	418.5	226.1
Fuels	101.3	99.5	130.0	177.5	229.0	233.7	421.6	222.9
Chemicals and related products	99.8	99.1	103.6	111.3	114.5	123.8	139.2	131.6
Organic chemicals	100.6	97.0	100.1	109.6	118.0	120.5	132.9	123.7
Pharmaceutical products	99.8	101.8	106.9	111.0	106.5	107.6	114.1	113.3
Plastics and rubber products	99.9	103.9	105.9	113.5	120.1	121.7	133.2	129.9
Hides, skins, and leather products	100.2	99.9	101.5	104.0	105.2	107.0	112.4	114.0
Wood products	100.5	96.1	129.5	124.2	120.7	113.5	118.5	109.5
Woodpulp and paper products	100.0	95.2	98.2	102.3	107.9	108.0	115.3	108.2
Textiles	99.7	99.8	100.3	100.4	100.7	102.1	103.5	102.6
Footwear and clothing accessories	99.6	99.4	99.8	99.9	100.6	101.5	105.8	99.3
Footwear	99.6	100.0	100.2	100.3	101.0	101.3	104.7	106.9
Stone and glass products	99.5	102.4	103.8	105.4	108.6	110.4	115.4	125.7
Gems and precious metals	99.3	87.8	93.5	98.3	125.1	132.8	157.1	140.5
Gold	98.3	127.0	137.1	150.7	241.2	238.2	317.4	(NA)
Platinum	(NA)	89.9	116.2	125.7	230.1	257.2	368.6	(NA)
Base metals	101.5	96.5	118.9	132.1	157.9	176.7	206.9	151.5
Iron and steel	104.1	103.3	155.1	170.6	173.8	206.2	308.8	171.9
Articles of iron and steel	100.6	96.8	109.0	122.7	125.1	129.0	159.7	142.1
Copper	97.2	94.3	119.0	142.7	291.6	307.5	326.2	234.9
Aluminum	97.9	96.8	110.5	113.2	150.0	146.8	155.8	105.8
Machinery	100.2	92.8	90.7	89.7	88.1	87.8	88.9	86.7
Nonelectrical machinery	99.8	92.9	90.9	90.1	88.3	88.2	89.3	87.8
Electrical machinery	100.5	92.8	90.5	89.4	87.9	87.5	88.5	85.6
Transportation equipment	100.0	101.0	102.8	104.4	104.9	105.9	109.5	109.7
Motor vehicles	100.1	100.7	102.3	103.8	104.3	105.1	108.7	108.7
Instruments	99.8	99.6	99.1	100.1	99.6	99.4	101.5	101.8
Miscellaneous manufactured articles	99.7	97.5	97.4	99.4	99.5	101.1	106.4	107.7
Furniture	99.5	98.3	99.7	103.4	103.4	104.6	111.9	112.8

NA Not available. [1] June 2000 may not equal 100 because indexes were reweighted to an "average" trade value in 2000.

Source: U.S. Bureau of Labor Statistics, *U.S. Import and Export Price Indexes*, monthly. See also <http://stats.bls.gov/news.release/ximpim.toc.htm>.

Section 15
Business Enterprise

This section relates to the place and behavior of the business firm and to business initiative in the American economy. It includes data on the number, type, and size of businesses; financial data of domestic and multinational U.S. corporations; business investments, expenditures, and profits; and sales and inventories.

The principal sources of these data are the *Survey of Current Business*, published by the Bureau of Economic Analysis (BEA); the Web site of the Board of Governors of the Federal Reserve System at <http://www.federalreserve.gov /econresdata/default.htm>; the annual *Statistics of Income (SOI)* reports of the Internal Revenue Service (IRS); and the U.S. Census Bureau's Economic Census, *County Business Patterns, Quarterly Financial Report for Manufacturing, Mining, and Trade Corporations (QFR), Survey of Business Owners,* and *Annual Capital Expenditures Survey.*

Business firms—A firm is generally defined as a business organization under a single management and may include one or more establishments. The terms firm, business, company, and enterprise are used interchangeably throughout this section. A firm doing business in more than one industry is classified by industry according to the major activity of the firm as a whole.

The IRS concept of a business firm relates primarily to the legal entity used for tax reporting purposes. A sole proprietorship is an unincorporated business owned by one person and may include large enterprises with many employees and hired managers and part-time operators. A partnership is an unincorporated business owned by two or more persons, each of whom has a financial interest in the business. A corporation is a business that is legally incorporated under state laws. While many corporations file consolidated tax returns, most corporate tax returns represent individual corporations, some of which are affiliated through common ownership or control with other corporations filing separate returns.

Economic census—The economic census is the major source of facts about the structure and functioning of the nation's economy. It provides essential information for government, business, industry, and the general public. It furnishes an important part of the framework for such composite measures as the gross domestic product estimates, input/output measures, production and price indexes, and other statistical series that measure short–term changes in economic conditions. The Census Bureau takes the economic census every 5 years, covering years ending in "2" and "7."

The economic census is collected on an establishment basis. A company operating at more than one location is required to file a separate report for each store, factory, shop, or other location. Each establishment is assigned a separate industry classification based on its primary activity and not that of its parent company. Establishments responding to the establishment survey are classified into industries on the basis of their principal product or activity (determined by annual sales volume). The statistics issued by industry in the 2007 Economic Census are classified primarily on the 2007 North American Industry Classification System (NAICS), and, to a lesser extent, on the 2002 NAICS used in the previous census (see below).

More detailed information about the scope, coverage, methodology, classification system, data items, and publications for each of the economic censuses and related surveys is published in the 2007 *Economic Census User Guide* at <http://www.census.gov/econ/census07 /www/user_guide.html>.

Data from the 2007 Economic Census are released through the Census Bureau's American FactFinder® service on the

U.S. Census Bureau, Statistical Abstract of the United States: 2011

Census Bureau Web site. For more information, see <http://www.census.gov/econ/census07/>.

Survey of Business Owners—
The Survey of Business Owners (SBO) provides statistics that describe the composition of U.S. businesses by gender, Hispanic or Latino origin, and race. Data from SBO are published in a series of reports: *American Indian- and Alaska Native-Owned Firms, Asian-Owned Firms, Black-Owned Firms, Hispanic-Owned Firms, Native Hawaiian and Other Pacific Islander-Owned Firms, Women-Owned Firms,* and *Company Summary.* Data are presented by industry classifications and/or geographic area and size of firm (employment and receipts). The reports include totals for all U.S. businesses based on the 2002 Economic Census and estimates of business ownership by gender, Hispanic or Latino origin, and race based on the 2002 SBO. Each owner had the option of selecting more than one race and therefore is included in each race selected. For more information, see <http://www.census.gov/econ/sbo/>.

North American Industry Classification System (NAICS)—
NAICS is the standard used by federal statistical agencies in classifying business establishments for the purpose of collecting, analyzing, and publishing statistical data related to the U.S. business economy. NAICS was developed under the auspices of the Office of Management and Budget (OMB), and adopted in 1997 to replace the Standard Industrial Classification (SIC) system. The official 2007 U.S. NAICS Manual includes definitions for each industry, background information, tables showing changes between 2002 and 2007, and a comprehensive index. For more information, see <http://www.census.gov/eos/www/naics/>.

Changes between 2002 NAICS and 2007 NAICS are relatively minor, but do affect totals for sectors 52 (finance and insurance), 53 (real estate, rental, and leasing), 54 (professional, scientific, and technical services), and 56 (admin/support waste mgt/remediation services). Nearly all industries are comparable from 2002 to 2007 NAICS classifications. Several industries in the Information sector have been consolidated.

Quarterly Financial Report—
The Quarterly Financial Report (QFR) program publishes quarterly aggregate statistics on the financial conditions of U.S. corporations. The QFR requests companies to report estimates from their statements of income and retained earnings, and balance sheets. The statistical data are classified and aggregated by type of industry and asset size. The QFR sample includes manufacturing companies with assets of $250 thousand and above, and mining, wholesale, and retail companies with assets of $50 million and above. The data are available quarterly in the *Quarterly Financial Report for Manufacturing, Mining, and Trade Corporations* at <http://www.census.gov/econ/qfr/index.html>.

Multinational companies—
BEA collects financial and operating data on U.S. multinational companies. These data provide a picture of the overall activities of foreign affiliates and U.S. parent companies, using a variety of indicators of their financial structure and operations. The data on foreign affiliates cover the entire operations of the affiliate, irrespective of the percentage of U.S. ownership. These data cover items such as sales, value added, employment and compensation of employees, capital expenditures, exports and imports, and research and development expenditures. Separate tabulations are available for all affiliates and for affiliates that are majority-owned by their U.S. parent(s). More information is available at <http://www.bea.gov/international/index.htm#omc>.

Statistical reliability—For a discussion of statistical collection, estimation, and sampling procedures and measures of reliability applicable to data from the Census Bureau and the Internal Revenue Service, see Appendix III.

Table 743. Number of Tax Returns, Receipts, and Net Income by Type of Business: 1990 to 2007

[14,783 represents 14,783,000. Covers active enterprises only. Figures are estimates based on sample of unaudited tax returns; see Appendix III]

Item	Number of returns (1,000)			Business receipts [1] (bil. dol.)			Net income (less loss) [2] (bil. dol.)		
	Nonfarm proprietor- ships	Partner- ships	Corpora- tions	Nonfarm proprietor- ships	Partner- ships	Corpora- tions	Nonfarm proprietor- ships	Partner- ships	Corpora- tions
1990........	14,783	1,554	3,717	731	541	10,914	141	17	371
1991........	15,181	1,515	3,803	713	539	10,963	142	21	345
1992........	15,495	1,485	3,869	737	571	11,272	154	43	402
1993........	15,848	1,468	3,965	757	627	11,814	156	67	498
1994........	16,154	1,494	4,342	791	732	12,858	167	82	577
1995........	16,424	1,581	4,474	807	854	13,969	169	107	714
1996........	16,955	1,654	4,631	843	1,042	14,890	177	145	806
1997........	17,176	1,759	4,710	870	1,297	15,890	187	168	915
1998........	17,409	1,855	4,849	918	1,534	16,543	202	187	838
1999........	17,576	1,937	4,936	969	1,829	18,009	208	228	929
2000........	17,905	2,058	5,045	1,021	2,316	19,593	215	269	928
2001........	18,338	2,132	5,136	1,017	2,569	19,308	217	276	604
2002........	18,926	2,242	5,267	1,030	2,669	18,849	221	271	564
2003........	19,710	2,375	5,401	1,050	2,818	19,755	230	301	780
2004........	20,591	2,547	5,558	1,140	3,142	21,717	248	385	1,112
2005........	21,468	2,764	5,671	1,223	3,719	24,060	270	546	1,949
2006........	22,075	2,947	5,841	1,278	4,131	26,070	278	667	1,933
2007........	23,122	3,098	5,869	1,324	4,541	27,335	281	683	1,837

[1] Excludes investment income except for partnerships and corporations in finance, insurance, and real estate before 1998. Beginning 1998, finance and insurance, real estate, and management of companies included investment income for partnerships and corporations. Excludes investment income for S corporations; for definition, see footnote 1, Table 752. [2] Net income (less loss) is defined differently by form of organization, basically as follows: (a) Proprietorships: Total taxable receipts less total business deductions, including cost of sales and operations, depletion, and certain capital expensing, excluding charitable contributions and owners' salaries; (b) Partnerships: Total taxable receipts (including investment income except capital gains) less deductions, including cost of sales and operations and certain payments to partners, excluding charitable contributions, oil and gas depletion, and certain capital expensing; (c) Corporations: Total taxable receipts (including investment income, capital gains, and income from foreign subsidiaries deemed received for tax purposes, except for S corporations) less business deductions, including cost of sales and operations, depletion, certain capital expensing, and officers' compensation excluding S corporation charitable contributions and investment expenses; net income is before income tax.

Source: U.S. Internal Revenue Service, *Statistics of Income*, various publications.

Table 744. Number of Tax Returns and Business Receipts by Size of Receipts: 2000 to 2007

[5,045 represents 5,045,000. Covers active enterprises only. Figures are estimates based on sample of unaudited tax returns; see Appendix III. Minus sign (–) indicates loss]

Size-class of receipts	Returns (1,000)					Business receipts [1] (bil. dol.)				
	2000	2004	2005	2006	2007	2000	2004	2005	2006	2007
Corporations	**5,045**	**5,558**	**5,671**	**5,841**	**5,869**	**19,593**	**21,717**	**24,060**	**26,070**	**27,335**
Under $25,000 [2]...........	1,220	1,317	1,300	1,363	1,391	4	4	4	3	–2
$25,000 to $49,999........	302	334	340	341	356	10	12	12	13	13
$50,000 to $99,999........	477	545	544	554	570	35	40	40	41	42
$100,000 to $499,999......	1,515	1,703	1,755	1,780	1,766	397	424	437	443	445
$500,000 to $999,999......	582	635	644	668	657	407	448	458	473	465
$1,000,000 or more........	946	1,023	1,088	1,135	1,128	18,738	20,788	23,108	25,097	26,372
Partnerships..............	**2,058**	**2,547**	**2,764**	**2,947**	**3,098**	**2,316**	**3,142**	**3,719**	**4,131**	**4,541**
Under $25,000 [2]...........	1,105	1,373	1,465	1,568	1,650	5	5	5	6	6
$25,000 to $49,999........	183	193	218	240	233	7	7	8	9	8
$50,000 to $99,999........	187	226	233	245	275	13	16	17	18	20
$100,000 to $499,999......	353	436	489	498	530	82	102	114	118	125
$500,000 to $999,999......	92	121	131	149	149	66	86	92	106	107
$1,000,000 or more........	137	198	227	248	261	2,143	2,925	3,482	3,875	4,275
Nonfarm proprietorships ...	**17,905**	**20,591**	**21,468**	**22,075**	**23,122**	**1,021**	**1,140**	**1,223**	**1,278**	**1,324**
Under $25,000 [2]...........	11,997	13,916	14,456	14,867	15,752	82	97	100	104	111
$25,000 to $49,999........	2,247	2,536	2,587	2,721	2,796	80	90	92	96	99
$50,000 to $99,999........	1,645	1,792	1,981	1,983	2,027	117	128	140	140	144
$100,000 to $499,999......	1,733	2,020	2,091	2,139	2,173	355	405	425	437	440
$500,000 to $999,999......	190	218	235	236	242	126	147	160	161	165
$1,000,000 or more........	92	109	117	128	132	261	273	306	340	364

[1] Finance and insurance, real estate, and management of companies included investment income for partnerships and corporations. [2] Includes firms with no receipts.

Source: U.S. Internal Revenue Service, *Statistics of Income Bulletin* and unpublished data.

Table 745. Number of Tax Returns, Receipts, and Net Income by Type of Business and Industry: 2007

[23,123 represents 23,123,000. Covers active enterprises only. Figures are estimates based on sample of unaudited tax returns; see Appendix III. Based on the North American Industry Classification System (NAICS), 2007; see text, this section. Minus sign (−) indicates net loss]

Industry	2002 NAICS code	Number of returns (1,000)			Business receipts [1] (bil. dol.)			Net income (less loss) (bil. dol.)		
		Nonfarm proprietorships	Partnerships	Corporations	Nonfarm proprietorships	Partnerships	Corporations	Nonfarm proprietorships	Partnerships	Corporations
Total........................	(X)	**23,122**	**3,098**	**5,869**	**1,324**	**4,541**	**27,335**	**281**	**683**	**1,837**
Agriculture, forestry, fishing, and hunting [2]	11	301	127	142	18	28	140	1	3	4
Mining	21	127	40	39	13	101	351	2	41	54
Utilities..........................	22	10	4	8	1	134	665	(Z)	6	43
Construction	23	2,931	209	781	231	305	1,588	36	9	54
Special trade contractors...........	238	2,347	72	480	160	67	656	28	5	32
Manufacturing	31–33	362	48	274	29	856	7,175	3	64	468
Wholesale and retail trade [3]	(X)	2,777	220	996	249	918	7,337	14	24	211
Wholesale trade..................	42	340	54	382	50	531	3,786	5	21	113
Retail trade [4]	44–45	2,436	167	613	199	388	3,551	9	4	98
Motor vehicle and parts dealers	441	146	20	88	41	121	828	1	1	8
Food and beverage stores.........	445	82	22	95	27	81	497	1	1	12
Gasoline stations...............	447	18	8	42	26	62	320	(Z)	(Z)	1
Transportation and warehousing......	48–49	1,155	46	201	82	119	748	11	7	15
Information [4]	51	352	34	122	10	231	974	3	34	93
Broadcasting (except Internet)	515	[5] 43	2	8	[5] 2	35	110	[5] (Z)	2	9
Telecommunications	517	([5])	6	19	([5])	141	453	([5])	28	37
Finance and insurance	52	726	308	251	94	677	4,135	20	323	601
Real estate and rental and leasing	53	1,393	1,489	657	71	315	268	22	39	55
Professional, scientific, and technical services [4]	54	3,235	176	836	169	345	974	72	82	37
Legal services	5411	363	27	109	39	136	92	17	49	8
Accounting, tax preparation, bookkeeping, and payroll services ..	5412	376	22	77	12	58	38	5	12	1
Management, scientific, and technical consulting services	5416	952	39	234	46	48	211	26	10	14
Management of companies and enterprises..................	55	(NA)	24	48	(NA)	69	1,146	(NA)	26	118
Administrative and support and waste management and remediation services	56	2,251	62	274	60	69	484	16	4	20
Educational services	61	597	12	49	9	4	40	3	(Z)	2
Health care and social assistance.....	62	2,016	68	406	116	161	590	46	20	29
Arts, entertainment, and recreation....	71	1,283	55	123	31	49	91	8	−1	4
Accommodation and food services	72	411	107	288	48	137	424	1	1	20
Accommodation..................	721	51	34	34	6	63	96	(Z)	(Z)	5
Food services and drinking places ...	722	361	73	254	42	74	328	1	1	15
Other services [4]....................	81	2,668	69	372	88	24	205	21	1	7
Auto repair and maintenance	8111	397	24	111	24	9	69	3	(Z)	2
Personal and laundry services	812	1,583	37	155	44	9	78	13	(Z)	3
Religious, grantmaking, civic, professional, and similar organizations.............	813	252	1	49	4	(Z)	13	2	(Z)	(Z)
Unclassified.....................	(X)	527	1	2	5	(Z)	(Z)	2	(Z)	(Z)

NA Not available. X Not applicable. Z Less than $500 million. [1] Includes investment income for partnerships and corporations in finance and insurance, real estate, and management of companies' industries. Excludes investment income for S corporations; for definition, see footnote 1, Table 752. [2] For corporations, represents agricultural services only. [3] For corporations, includes trade business not identified as wholesale or retail. [4] Includes other industries, not shown separately. [5] Broadcasting includes telecommunications.

Source: U.S. Internal Revenue Service, *Statistics of Income*, various publications.

Table 746. Nonfarm Sole Proprietorships—Selected Income and Deduction Items: 1990 to 2007

[In billions of dollars (731 represents $731,000,000,000) except as indicated. All figures are estimates based on samples. Tax law changes have affected the comparability of the data over time; see Statistics of Income reports for a description. See Appendix III]

Item	1990	1995	2000	2002	2003	2004	2005	2006	2007
Number of returns (1,000)	14,783	16,424	17,905	18,926	19,710	20,591	21,468	22,075	23,122
Returns with net income (1,000)	11,222	12,213	13,308	13,751	14,448	15,053	15,750	16,207	16,929
Business receipts	731	807	1,021	1,030	1,050	1,140	1,223	1,278	1,324
Income from sales and operations	719	797	1,008	1,015	1,034	1,122	1,205	1,259	1,304
Business deductions [1]	589	638	806	809	820	892	953	1,001	1,044
Cost of goods sold/operations [1]	291	307	387	352	338	371	397	410	423
Purchases	210	219	269	227	218	239	253	260	264
Labor costs	23	24	29	30	28	32	32	32	35
Materials and supplies	30	34	43	46	47	53	56	60	62
Advertising	(NA)	(NA)	10	11	12	13	14	15	16
Car and truck expenses	22	33	46	50	53	59	71	75	82
Commissions	9	10	12	14	14	13	15	16	15
Contract labor	(NA)	(NA)	(NA)	(NA)	(NA)	25	28	35	37
Depreciation	24	27	32	37	42	43	39	39	40
Insurance	13	13	14	16	17	19	19	19	19
Interest paid [2]	13	10	12	11	11	11	12	14	15
Office expenses	(NA)	(NA)	10	11	12	12	13	13	13
Rent paid [3]	23	28	33	35	36	37	39	41	43
Repairs	9	10	12	13	13	15	15	16	16
Salaries and wages (net)	47	54	63	66	68	71	75	77	79
Supplies	(NA)	(NA)	22	25	26	27	29	32	32
Taxes paid	10	13	14	15	15	16	17	18	18
Utilities	14	17	19	21	22	21	23	24	25
Net income (less loss) [4]	141	169	215	221	230	248	270	278	281
Net income [4]	162	192	245	257	269	291	315	327	335
Constant (2000) Dollars [5]									
Business receipts	896	877	1,021	991	991	1,045	1,085	1,097	1,105
Business deductions	722	693	806	778	774	818	846	859	871
Net income (less loss)	173	184	215	213	217	227	239	239	235
Net income	198	208	245	248	254	266	279	280	280

NA Not available. [1] Includes other amounts not shown separately. [2] Interest paid includes "mortgage interest" and "other interest paid on business indebtedness." [3] Rent paid includes "Rent on machinery and equipment" and "Rent on other business property." [4] After adjustment for the passive loss carryover from prior years. Therefore, "business receipts" minus "total deductions" do not equal "net income." [5] Based on the overall implicit price deflator for gross domestic product.

Source: U.S. Internal Revenue Service, *Statistics of Income Bulletin*.

Table 747. Partnerships—Selected Income and Balance Sheet Items: 1990 to 2007

[In billions of dollars (1,735 represents $1,735,000,000,000), except as indicated. Covers active partnerships only. All figures are estimates based on samples. See Appendix III]

Item	1990	1995	2000	2002	2003	2004	2005	2006	2007
Number of returns (1,000)	1,554	1,581	2,058	2,242	2,375	2,547	2,764	2,947	3,098
Returns with net income (1,000)	854	955	1,261	1,325	1,357	1,441	1,580	1,623	1,659
Number of partners (1,000)	17,095	15,606	13,660	14,328	14,108	15,557	16,212	16,728	18,516
Assets [1,2]	1,735	2,719	6,694	8,867	9,675	11,608	13,734	17,146	20,386
Depreciable assets (net)	681	767	1,487	1,792	1,846	1,988	2,176	2,490	2,865
Inventories, end of year	57	88	150	203	214	276	315	446	339
Land	215	221	359	423	455	509	607	731	820
Liabilities [1,2]	1,415	1,886	3,696	4,972	5,303	6,248	7,483	9,350	10,440
Accounts payable	67	91	230	346	276	336	400	505	430
Short-term debt [3]	88	124	252	283	274	296	373	456	565
Long-term debt [4]	498	544	1,132	1,375	1,389	1,546	1,772	2,227	2,556
Nonrecourse loans	470	466	639	770	800	854	914	1,103	1,210
Partners' capital accounts [2]	320	832	2,999	3,895	4,372	5,360	6,251	7,796	9,946
Receipts [1]	566	890	2,405	2,773	2,923	3,260	3,863	4,301	4,727
Business receipts [5]	483	854	2,316	2,669	2,818	3,142	3,719	4,131	4,541
Interest received	21	31	82	70	71	88	134	193	260
Deductions [1]	550	784	2,136	2,502	2,621	2,876	3,317	3,634	4,043
Cost of goods sold/operations	243	395	1,226	1,430	1,523	1,666	1,976	2,109	2,310
Salaries and wages	56	80	201	238	245	269	293	332	373
Taxes paid	9	13	31	36	39	42	47	53	56
Interest paid	30	43	93	68	65	64	103	137	174
Depreciation	60	23	59	83	84	90	71	79	86
Net income (less loss)	17	107	269	271	301	385	546	667	683
Net income	116	179	410	440	469	566	724	871	976

[1] Includes items not shown separately. [2] Assets, liabilities, and partners' capital accounts are understated because not all partnerships file complete balance sheets. [3] Mortgages, notes, and bonds payable in less than 1 year. [4] Mortgages, notes, and bonds payable in 1 year or more. [5] Excludes investment income except for partnerships in finance, insurance, and real estate in 1995. Beginning 2000, finance and insurance, real estate, and management of companies included investment income for partnerships.

Source: U.S. Internal Revenue Service, *Statistics of Income*, various issues.

Table 748. Partnerships—Selected Items by Industry: 2007

[In billions of dollars (20,386 represents $20,386,000,000,000), except as indicated. Covers active partnerships only. Figures are estimates based on samples. Based on the North American Industry Classification System (NAICS), 2007; see text, this section. See Appendix III. Minus sign (−) indicates net loss]

Industry and year	2002 NAICS code	Number of partnerships (1,000) Total	With net income	With net loss	Total assets [1]	Business receipts [2]	Total deduc- tions	Net income less loss	Net income	Net loss
Total [3]	(X)	3,098	1,659	1,437	20,386	4,541	4,043	683.4	975.9	292.5
Agriculture, forestry, fishing, and hunting	11	127	64	63	143	28	37	2.7	9.9	7.2
Mining	21	40	25	15	241	101	76	40.7	50.8	10.0
Utilities	22	4	1	3	162	134	133	6.0	9.7	3.7
Construction	23	209	109	100	335	305	303	9.3	24.1	14.7
Manufacturing	31–33	48	17	31	598	856	821	64.2	79.3	15.0
Wholesale trade	42	54	31	23	191	531	518	20.5	23.3	2.8
Retail trade	44–45	167	69	98	131	388	394	3.5	10.4	6.9
Transportation and warehousing	48–49	46	27	19	194	119	118	7.2	10.8	3.6
Information	51	34	12	22	586	231	227	34.2	48.0	13.8
Finance and insurance	52	308	220	88	12,264	677	354	322.7	381.8	59.1
Real estate and rental and leasing	53	1,489	760	729	4,354	315	285	39.0	150.0	111.0
Professional, scientific, and technical services	54	176	117	59	185	345	284	82.0	89.0	7.0
Management of companies and enterprises	55	24	13	11	523	69	42	26.2	37.3	11.1
Administrative and support and waste management and remediation services	56	62	34	28	47	69	73	3.9	6.7	2.7
Educational services	61	12	8	4	4	4	4	0.1	0.7	0.6
Health care and social assistance	62	68	43	25	103	161	152	20.1	25.9	5.8
Arts, entertainment, and recreation	71	55	23	32	83	49	56	−0.7	5.5	6.2
Accommodation and food services	72	107	52	55	220	137	142	0.7	10.4	9.6
Other services	81	69	34	35	20	24	24	0.9	2.5	1.6

X Not applicable. [1] Total assets are understated because not all partnerships file complete balance sheets. [2] Finance and insurance, real estate, and management of companies include investment income for partnerships. [3] Includes businesses not allocable to individual industries.

Source: U.S. Internal Revenue Service, *Statistics of Income*, various issues.

Table 749. Nonfarm Noncorporate Business-Sector Balance Sheet: 1990 to 2009

[In billions of dollars (3,685 represents $3,685,000,000,000), except as noted. Represents year-end outstandings]

Item	1990	1995	2000	2004	2005	2006	2007	2008	2009
Assets	3,685	4,120	6,567	8,957	10,929	11,872	12,276	11,131	10,108
Tangible assets	3,328	3,572	5,144	6,852	8,387	8,815	8,743	7,383	6,603
Real estate [1]	3,020	3,222	4,706	6,340	7,839	8,229	8,123	6,734	5,818
Residential	2,100	2,391	3,469	4,909	6,032	6,139	5,954	4,869	4,397
Nonresidential	921	831	1,237	1,431	1,807	2,090	2,169	1,865	1,421
Equipment and software [2]	260	293	369	436	466	499	526	556	697
Residential [3]	28	32	35	40	43	46	48	50	48
Nonresidential	233	261	333	396	423	453	478	507	649
Inventories [2]	47	56	70	76	82	88	94	92	87
Financial assets	356	548	1,423	2,106	2,542	3,057	3,533	3,748	3,505
Checkable deposits and currency	71	105	164	279	355	429	494	517	483
Time and savings deposits	51	71	248	301	324	344	359	389	364
Money market fund shares	7	17	49	67	69	72	74	79	74
Treasury securities	13	24	40	50	56	56	59	63	59
Municipal securities	–	2	2	4	4	6	5	6	5
Mortgages	31	22	23	31	36	35	42	45	42
Trade receivables	98	140	342	364	431	471	526	558	521
Miscellaneous assets	86	167	554	1,010	1,266	1,644	1,973	2,093	1,957
Insurance receivables	39	44	46	60	65	67	69	71	70
Equity investment in GSEs [4]	1	1	2	2	2	2	2	4	5
Other	47	122	506	947	1,198	1,576	1,902	2,018	1,883
Liabilities	1,357	1,404	2,683	3,529	4,064	4,647	5,228	5,480	5,173
Credit market instruments	1,102	1,070	1,806	2,455	2,787	3,196	3,650	3,851	3,545
Bank loans n.e.c. [5]	136	165	361	473	630	743	882	986	794
Other loans and advances	103	100	137	145	150	164	175	208	200
Mortgages	863	805	1,308	1,837	2,008	2,289	2,593	2,657	2,551
Trade payables	60	86	260	277	329	349	379	398	376
Taxes payable	32	33	65	78	87	96	99	102	99
Miscellaneous liabilities	164	215	552	718	861	1,006	1,100	1,130	1,152
Net worth	2,327	2,715	3,884	5,428	6,864	7,226	7,048	5,651	4,936
Debt/net worth (percent)	47.3	39.4	46.5	45.2	40.6	44.2	51.8	68.1	71.8

– Represents or rounds to zero. [1] At market value. [2] At replacement (current) cost. [3] Durable goods in rental properties. [4] GSEs = government-sponsored enterprises. Equity in the Farm Credit System. [5] Not elsewhere classified.

Source: Board of Governors of the Federal Reserve System, "Federal Reserve Statistical Release, Z.1, Flow of Funds Accounts of the United States," March 2010, <http://www.federalreserve.gov/releases/z1/20100311/>.

Table 750. Nonfinancial Corporate Business-Sector Balance Sheet: 1990 to 2009

[In billions of dollars (9,729 represents $9,729,000,000,000). Represents year-end outstandings]

Item	1990	1995	2000	2004	2005	2006	2007	2008	2009
Assets	**9,729**	**11,515**	**19,071**	**21,802**	**24,714**	**27,106**	**28,984**	**27,962**	**26,544**
Tangible assets	6,143	6,544	9,331	10,901	12,853	14,490	15,279	14,211	12,253
Real estate [1]	3,389	3,150	4,881	5,971	7,644	8,935	9,406	8,178	6,336
Equipment and software [2]	1,852	2,325	3,128	3,482	3,651	3,890	4,084	4,287	4,255
Inventories [2]	901	1,070	1,322	1,448	1,557	1,664	1,788	1,746	1,662
Financial assets [3]	3,586	4,971	9,740	10,901	11,862	12,617	13,705	13,751	14,291
Checkable deposits and currency	166	205	246	178	252	135	122	103	273
Time and savings deposits	75	100	272	400	450	497	441	405	532
Money market fund shares	20	60	191	324	366	432	564	736	684
Treasury securities	38	57	18	33	51	44	38	27	46
Mortgages	53	58	44	67	68	60	41	23	4
Consumer credit	67	85	81	59	60	58	59	60	57
Trade receivables	967	1,185	1,939	1,831	2,108	2,090	2,253	2,113	2,040
Mutual fund shares [1]	10	46	122	140	156	204	218	143	163
Liabilities [3]	**4,729**	**6,010**	**9,611**	**10,349**	**11,145**	**11,782**	**12,873**	**13,302**	**13,550**
Credit market instruments	2,543	2,942	4,634	5,180	5,514	5,983	6,776	7,119	7,229
Commercial paper	117	157	278	98	90	113	124	131	59
Municipal securities [4]	115	135	154	169	177	182	190	193	198
Corporate bonds [5]	1,008	1,357	2,271	2,976	3,032	3,248	3,559	3,764	4,145
Bank loans n.e.c. [6]	545	602	853	543	509	518	609	678	554
Other loans and advances	482	477	726	824	933	1,047	1,347	1,370	1,323
Mortgages	275	213	351	571	774	876	946	983	950
Trade payables	626	878	1,541	1,500	1,699	1,813	1,899	1,765	1,681
Taxes payable	38	40	78	88	93	85	36	43	28
Net worth (market value)	**4,999**	**5,505**	**9,460**	**11,453**	**13,569**	**15,324**	**16,111**	**14,660**	**12,993**
Debt/net worth (percent)	50.9	53.4	49.0	45.2	40.6	39.0	42.1	48.6	55.6

[1] At market value. [2] At replacement (current) cost. [3] Includes items not shown separately. [4] Industrial revenue bonds. Issued by state and local governments to finance private investment and secured in interest and principal by the industrial user of the funds. [5] Through 1992, corporate bonds include net issues by Netherlands Antillean financial subsidiaries. [6] Not elsewhere classified.

Source: Board of Governors of the Federal Reserve System, "Federal Reserve Statistical Release, Z.1, Flow of Funds Accounts of the United States," March 2010, <http://www.federalreserve.gov/releases/z1/20100311/>.

Table 751. Corporate Funds—Sources and Uses: 1990 to 2009

[In billions of dollars (242 represents $242,000,000,000). Covers nonfarm nonfinancial corporate business]

Item	1990	1995	2000	2004	2005	2006	2007	2008	2009
Profits before tax	242	431	432	660	954	1,115	1,056	805	807
− Taxes on corporate income	98	140	170	186	271	307	299	237	243
− Net dividends	117	177	250	362	168	466	462	407	361
+ Capital consumption allowance [1]	365	461	637	739	609	639	677	835	782
= U.S. internal funds, book	392	575	649	851	1,124	981	972	996	984
+ Foreign earnings retained abroad	45	53	103	120	−18	149	181	187	163
+ Inventory valuation adjustment (IVA)	−13	−18	−17	−34	−31	−38	−44	−38	(Z)
= Internal funds + IVA	424	610	735	944	1,091	1,092	1,100	1,140	1,149
Gross investment	370	655	929	1,045	968	1,003	975	997	1,066
Capital expenditures	429	621	968	878	987	1,142	1,183	1,190	881
Fixed investment [2]	423	580	922	835	948	1,077	1,174	1,207	997
Inventory change + IVA	12	40	53	53	47	60	19	−26	−112
Nonproduced nonfinancial assets	−6	1	−7	−10	−8	4	−10	9	−4
Net financial investment	−59	33	−39	167	−19	−139	−208	−193	185
Net acquisition of financial assets [3]	124	424	1,199	776	943	697	1,069	267	440
Foreign deposits	(Z)	2	−7	16	7	−11	1	−19	10
Checkable deposits and currency	6	4	15	−13	74	−118	−13	−19	171
Time and savings deposits	−6	3	35	38	50	47	−56	−37	127
Money market fund shares	9	23	37	25	42	66	132	172	−52
Commercial paper	(−Z)	1	10	19	16	12	−53	−59	8
Municipal securities	8	−20	7	−4	(Z)	−4	1	−24	12
Mortgages	−2	2	2	15	2	−8	−18	−18	−18
Mutual fund shares	−1	5	4	1	7	31	2	−7	−7
Trade receivables	29	78	282	129	278	−18	163	−140	−73
Miscellaneous assets [3]	114	318	809	548	435	712	926	433	239
U.S. direct investment abroad [4]	36	90	138	272	25	219	297	264	191
Insurance receivables	13	8	(−Z)	19	21	7	7	10	−5
Net increase in liabilities [3]	184	391	1,237	609	961	836	1,277	460	256
Net funds raised in markets	72	179	245	81	−7	−94	−1	12	36
Net new equity issues	−63	−58	−118	−123	−342	−566	−787	−336	−65
Credit market instruments [3]	135	237	363	203	334	471	786	348	101
Corporate bonds [4]	47	104	164	75	57	216	311	205	381
Bank loans n.e.c [5]	3	75	44	−6	−34	9	85	68	−134
Other loans and advances [6]	55	30	84	55	109	118	300	23	−47
Mortgages	21	7	22	58	203	101	70	43	−34
Trade payables	28	81	313	97	199	110	86	−134	−85
Miscellaneous liabilities [3]	83	131	673	424	764	828	1,242	574	320
Foreign direct investment in U.S	59	55	249	96	99	191	281	214	101

Z Less than $500 million. [1] Consumption of fixed capital plus capital consumption adjustment. [2] Nonresidential fixed investment plus residential fixed investment. [3] Includes other items not shown separately. [4] 1990, corporate bonds include net issues by Netherlands Antillean financial subsidiaries, and U.S. direct investment abroad excludes net inflows from those bond issues. [5] Not elsewhere classified. [6] Loans from rest of the world, U.S. government, and nonbank financial institutions.

Source: Board of Governors of the Federal Reserve System, "Federal Reserve Statistical Release, Z.1, Flow of Funds Accounts of the United States," March 2010, <http://www.federalreserve.gov/releases/z1/20100311/>.

U.S. Census Bureau, Statistical Abstract of the United States: 2011

Table 752. Corporations—Selected Financial Items: 1990 to 2007

[In billions of dollars (18,190 represents $18,190,000,000,000), except as noted. Covers active corporations only. All corporations are required to file returns except those specifically exempt. See source for changes in law affecting comparability of historical data. Based on samples; see Appendix III]

Item	1990	1995	2000	2002	2003	2004	2005	2006	2007
Number of returns (1,000).	3,717	4,474	5,045	5,267	5,401	5,558	5,671	5,841	5,869
Number with net income (1,000)	1,911	2,455	2,819	2,801	2,932	3,116	3,324	3,367	3,368
S Corporation returns [1] (1,000)	1,575	2,153	2,860	3,154	3,342	3,518	3,684	3,873	3,990
Assets [2]	18,190	26,014	47,027	50,414	53,645	60,118	66,445	73,081	81,486
Cash	771	962	1,820	1,923	2,120	2,730	2,823	2,902	3,625
Notes and accounts receivable	4,198	5,307	8,754	8,886	8,995	10,691	11,962	13,611	15,315
Inventories	894	1,045	1,272	1,221	1,267	1,386	1,505	1,613	1,656
Investments in government obligations	921	1,363	1,236	1,527	1,656	1,571	1,613	1,714	1,785
Mortgage and real estate	1,538	1,713	2,822	3,687	4,073	4,627	4,777	5,232	5,177
Other investments	4,137	7,429	17,874	18,728	20,536	22,657	25,162	27,903	30,939
Depreciable assets	4,318	5,571	7,292	7,678	7,805	7,974	8,416	8,817	9,222
Depletable assets	129	154	191	226	237	270	310	382	497
Land.	210	242	303	326	342	363	407	457	493
Liabilities [2]	18,190	26,014	47,027	50,414	53,645	60,118	66,445	73,081	81,486
Accounts payable	1,094	1,750	3,758	4,074	4,338	5,045	6,020	7,779	7,724
Short-term debt [3]	1,803	2,034	4,020	3,814	4,002	4,399	4,192	4,709	4,735
Long-term debt [4]	2,665	3,335	6,184	7,185	7,384	8,154	8,332	9,399	10,786
Net worth [5]	4,739	8,132	17,349	17,545	18,819	20,814	23,525	25,996	28,812
Capital stock	1,585	2,194	3,966	4,000	3,151	2,308	2,482	2,513	2,775
Paid-in or capital surplus	2,814	5,446	12,265	15,287	15,258	16,160	17,828	19,142	21,792
Retained earnings [6]	1,410	2,191	3,627	1,111	2,282	3,278	4,331	5,764	5,970
Receipts [2,7]	11,410	14,539	20,606	19,749	20,690	22,712	25,505	27,402	28,763
Business receipts [7,8]	9,860	12,786	17,637	17,297	18,264	19,976	21,800	23,310	24,217
Interest [9]	977	1,039	1,628	1,282	1,182	1,368	1,773	2,307	2,640
Rents and royalties	133	145	254	252	270	274	290	299	314
Deductions [2,7]	11,033	13,821	19,692	19,199	19,941	21,636	23,613	25,502	26,974
Cost of sales and operations [8]	6,611	8,206	11,135	10,607	11,319	12,498	13,816	14,800	15,513
Compensation of officers.	205	304	401	381	389	417	445	474	479
Rent paid on business property.	185	232	380	411	407	420	439	462	477
Taxes paid	251	326	390	397	417	447	473	497	509
Interest paid.	825	744	1,272	913	818	939	1,287	1,787	2,085
Depreciation	333	437	614	711	692	691	531	564	599
Advertising.	126	163	234	218	225	239	253	277	277
Net income (less loss) [7,10]	371	714	928	564	780	1,112	1,949	1,933	1,837
Net income	553	881	1,337	1,053	1,176	1,456	2,235	2,240	2,253
Deficit.	182	166	409	489	396	344	286	306	416
Income subject to tax.	366	565	760	601	699	857	1,201	1,291	1,248
Income tax before credits [11].	119	194	266	210	244	300	419	453	437
Tax credits	32	42	62	56	66	75	107	100	106
Foreign tax credit.	25	30	49	42	50	57	82	78	87
Income tax after credits [12]	96	156	204	154	178	224	312	353	331

[1] Represents certain small corporations with a limit on the number of shareholders, mostly individuals, electing to be taxed at the shareholder level. [2] Includes items not shown separately. [3] Payable in less than 1 year. [4] Payable in 1 year or more. [5] Net worth is the sum of "capital stock," "additional paid-in capital," "retained earnings, appropriated," "retained earnings, unappropriated" minus "cost of treasury stock." [6] Appropriated and unappropriated and "adjustments to shareholders' equity." [7] Receipts, deductions, and net income of S corporations are limited to those from trade or business. Those from investments are excluded. [8] Includes gross sales and cost of sales of securities, commodities, and real estate by exchanges, brokers, or dealers selling on their own accounts. Excludes investment income. [9] Includes tax-exempt interest in state and local government obligations. [10] Excludes regulated investment companies. [11] Consists of regular (and alternative tax) only. [12] Includes minimum tax, alternative minimum tax, adjustments for prior year credits, and other income-related taxes.

Source: U.S. Internal Revenue Service, *Statistics of Income, Corporation Income Tax Returns*, annual.

Table 753. Corporations by Receipt-Size Class and Industry: 2007

[Number of returns in thousands (5,869 represents 5,869,000); receipts and net income in billions of dollars (27,335 represents $27,335,000,000,000). Covers active enterprises only. Figures are estimates based on a sample of unaudited tax returns; see Appendix III. Numbers in parentheses represent North American Industry Classification System 2007 codes; see text, this section]

Industry	Total	Under $1 mil. [1]	$1 to $4.9 mil.	$5 to $9.9 mil.	$10 to $49.9 mil.	$50 mil. or more
Total: [2]						
Number of returns	5,869	4,740	824	140	130	35
Business receipts [3]	27,335	963	1,782	973	2,682	20,935
Net income (less loss)	1,837	56	69	33	133	1,546
Agriculture, forestry, fishing, and hunting (11):						
Returns	142	124	14	2	1	(Z)
Business receipts [3]	140	21	32	13	24	50
Mining (21):						
Returns	39	30	6	1	1	(Z)
Business receipts [3]	351	5	15	9	22	300
Utilities (22):						
Returns	8	7	1	(Z)	(Z)	(Z)
Business receipts [3]	665	1	1	2	4	657
Construction (23):						
Returns	781	595	141	22	19	3
Business receipts [3]	1,588	142	313	157	383	593
Manufacturing (31–33):						
Returns	274	165	65	18	19	7
Business receipts [3]	7,175	43	149	126	399	6,458
Wholesale and retail trade (42, 44–45):						
Returns	996	662	224	49	49	13
Business receipts [3]	7,337	171	498	338	1,033	5,298
Transportation and warehousing (48–49):						
Returns	201	162	27	6	5	1
Business receipts [3]	748	31	64	41	94	518
Information (51):						
Returns	122	103	13	2	3	1
Business receipts [3]	974	16	31	14	52	861
Finance and insurance (52):						
Returns	251	207	27	5	8	4
Business receipts [3]	4,135	37	59	38	164	3,837
Real estate and rental and leasing (53):						
Returns	657	630	22	2	2	(Z)
Business receipts [3]	268	57	47	17	30	116
Professional, scientific, and technical services (54):						
Returns	836	728	86	11	9	2
Business receipts [3]	974	128	180	80	172	414
Management of companies and enterprises (55):						
Returns	40	41	3	1	2	1
Business receipts [3]	1,146	-2	7	9	48	1,083
Administrative and support and waste management and remediation services (56):						
Returns	274	228	37	5	4	1
Business receipts [3]	484	50	81	30	79	245
Educational services (61):						
Returns	49	46	3	(Z)	(Z)	(Z)
Business receipts [3]	40	7	6	1	6	20
Health care and social assistance (62):						
Returns	406	323	70	7	5	1
Business receipts [3]	590	97	139	46	97	211
Arts, entertainment, and recreation (71):						
Returns	123	113	8	1	1	(Z)
Business receipts [3]	91	19	16	9	11	36
Accommodation and food services (72):						
Returns	288	238	44	4	2	(Z)
Business receipts [3]	424	71	87	26	33	207
Other services (81):						
Returns	372	337	30	3	2	(Z)
Business receipts [3]	205	69	57	18	31	30

Z Less than 500 returns. [1] Includes businesses without receipts. [2] Includes businesses not allocable to individual industries. [3] Includes investment income for corporations in finance and insurance and management of companies' industries. Excludes investment income for S corporations (certain small corporations with up to 75 shareholders, mostly individuals, electing to be taxed at the shareholder level).

Source: U.S. Internal Revenue Service, *Statistics of Income, Corporation Income Tax Returns*, annual.

Table 754. Corporations by Asset-Size Class and Industry: 2007

[In billions of dollars (155 represents $155,000,000,000), except number of returns. Covers active corporations only. Excludes corporations not allocable by industry. Numbers in parentheses represent North American Industry Classification System 2007 codes; see text, this section]

Industry	Total	Asset-size class					
		Under $10 mil.[1]	$10 to $24.9 mil.	$25 to $49.9 mil.	$50 to $99.9 mil.	$100 to $249.9 mil.	$250 mil. and over
Agriculture, forestry, fishing, and hunting (11):							
Returns	142,180	140,937	836	199	115	58	37
Total receipts	155	92	16	5	9	10	23
Mining (21):							
Returns	39,114	37,344	796	336	218	179	241
Total receipts	395	41	11	8	10	15	310
Utilities (22):							
Returns	7,661	7,207	116	79	38	46	174
Total receipts	714	10	1	3	2	7	690
Construction (23):							
Returns	780,606	770,814	6,721	1,766	729	365	211
Total receipts	1,612	886	191	102	82	84	267
Manufacturing (31–33):							
Returns	273,771	257,853	7,695	3,173	1,792	1,385	1,874
Total receipts	7,828	550	224	186	180	281	6,407
Wholesale and retail trade (42, 44–45):							
Returns	995,846	975,953	12,620	3,723	1,670	963	918
Total receipts	7,502	2,034	639	393	307	369	3,759
Transportation and warehousing (48–49):							
Returns	200,651	198,547	1,192	368	194	155	195
Total receipts	777	222	38	22	21	29	447
Information (51):							
Returns	122,370	119,619	1,170	518	356	264	443
Total receipts	1,163	97	19	17	18	27	985
Finance and insurance (52):							
Returns	251,331	231,245	3,996	2,566	2,698	3,368	7,458
Total receipts	4,135	299	27	25	34	62	3,687
Real estate and rental and leasing (53):							
Returns	656,946	648,645	5,088	1,443	763	467	540
Total receipts	392	158	18	14	12	16	173
Professional, scientific, and technical services (54):							
Returns	835,838	831,015	2,668	918	525	388	324
Total receipts	1,017	553	67	38	38	56	264
Management of companies and enterprises (55):							
Returns	47,866	40,935	1,186	995	1,205	1,712	1,832
Total receipts	1,146	26	2	3	6	18	1,091
Administrative and support and waste management and remediation services (56):							
Returns	274,370	273,030	680	225	174	113	149
Total receipts	498	253	27	13	21	24	159
Educational services (61):							
Returns	49,240	49,014	114	32	33	25	21
Total receipts	42	18	2	2	3	4	13
Health care and social assistance (62):							
Returns	405,587	404,420	600	212	148	97	111
Total receipts	614	395	22	14	15	20	147
Arts, entertainment, and recreation (71):							
Returns	123,386	122,494	495	218	67	56	55
Total receipts	101	51	6	4	4	7	29
Accommodation and food services (72):							
Returns	287,949	286,516	782	275	138	94	143
Total receipts	461	216	14	11	14	20	186
Other services (81):							
Returns	372,048	371,442	400	106	53	20	26
Total receipts	212	173	8	5	6	3	18

[1] Includes returns with zero assets.

Source: U.S. Internal Revenue Service, *Statistics of Income, Corporation Income Tax Returns*, annual.

Table 755. Economic Census Summary (NAICS 2002 Basis): 2002 and 2007

[24 represents 24,000. 2007 data are preliminary. Covers establishments with payroll. Data are based on the 2002 and 2007 economic censuses which are subject to nonsampling error. Data for the construction sector are also subject to sampling errors. For details on survey methodology and nonsampling and sampling errors, see Appendix III]

Kind of business	2002 NAICS code [1]	Establish-ments (1,000)		Sales, receipts, or shipments (bil. dol.)		Annual payroll (bil. dol.)		Paid employees [2] (1,000)	
		2002	2007	2002	2007	2002	2007	2002	2007
Mining	21	24	21	183	369	21	37	475	703
Oil & gas extraction	211	8	6	113	231	5	10	99	162
Mining (except oil & gas)	212	7	6	48	81	9	11	196	220
Mining support activities	213	9	8	22	57	7	16	180	322
Utilities	22	17	17	399	582	42	51	663	632
Construction	23	710	725	1,209	1,782	254	348	7,193	7,399
Manufacturing	31–33	351	294	3,915	5,339	568	612	14,664	13,333
Wholesale trade	42	436	432	4,635	6,039	260	336	5,878	6,295
Merchant wholesalers, durable goods	423	260	253	2,171	2,709	157	206	3,357	3,637
Merchant wholesalers, nondurable goods	424	143	133	1,980	2,754	93	117	2,273	2,367
Wholesale electronic markets and agents and brokers	425	32	46	483	576	10	14	249	292
Retail trade	44–45	1,115	1,123	3,056	3,932	302	365	14,648	15,611
Motor vehicle & parts dealers	441	125	126	802	893	65	73	1,845	1,916
Furniture & home furnishings stores	442	65	65	92	110	13	15	535	589
Electronics & appliance stores	443	47	50	82	111	9	11	391	484
Bldg. material & garden equipment & supplies dealers	444	(NA)	90	(NA)	323	(NA)	38	(NA)	1,340
Food & beverage stores	445	149	147	457	541	49	56	2,839	2,879
Health & personal care stores	446	82	87	178	239	20	29	1,024	1,012
Gasoline stations	447	121	117	249	447	14	15	927	887
Clothing & clothing accessories stores	448	150	155	168	213	21	27	1,427	1,689
Sporting goods, hobby, book, & music stores	451	62	57	73	82	9	10	611	626
General merchandise stores	452	41	46	445	578	43	55	2,525	2,770
Miscellaneous store retailers	453	129	120	91	103	13	14	792	791
Nonstore retailers	454	55	61	173	292	17	23	571	628
Transportation & warehousing [3]	48–49	200	218	382	656	116	172	3,651	4,436
Information	51	138	141	892	1,075	195	223	3,736	3,428
Publishing industries (except Internet)	511	32	30	242	273	66	76	1,090	1,028
Motion picture & sound recording industries	512	22	24	78	95	13	17	303	326
Broadcasting (except Internet)	515	10	10	74	99	14	18	291	291
Internet publishing and broadcasting	516	2	3	6	15	2	5	40	55
Telecommunications	517	49	49	412	485	72	72	1,440	1,210
Internet service providers, Web search portals, and data processing	518	19	21	75	101	26	34	514	463
Other information services	519	3	4	5	7	2	2	58	55
Finance & insurance [4]	52	440	503	2,804	3,641	378	494	6,579	6,563
Real estate & rental & leasing [4]	53	323	377	336	452	60	85	1,949	2,249
Professional, scientific, & technical services	54	771	852	887	1,352	376	515	7,244	8,121
Management of companies & enterprises	55	49	(S)	107	(S)	179	(S)	2,605	(S)
Admin/support waste management/remediation services	56	851	882	433	629	206	291	8,742	10,154
Administrative & support services	561	332	360	381	556	194	275	8,410	9,787
Waste management & remediation services	562	19	21	51	73	12	16	332	367
Educational services	61	49	61	31	47	10	15	430	562
Health care and social assistance	62	705	779	1,207	1,697	496	666	15,052	16,860
Ambulatory health care services	621	489	545	489	692	203	280	4,925	5,791
Hospitals	622	6	7	500	713	197	263	5,174	5,536
Nursing & residential care facilities	623	69	76	127	168	59	74	2,831	3,056
Social assistance	624	140	152	91	124	36	48	2,123	2,477
Arts, entertainment, & recreation	71	110	124	142	189	45	58	1,849	2,071
Performing arts, spectator sports, & related industries	711	38	44	58	76	21	27	423	441
Museums, historical sites, & like institutions	712	7	7	9	13	3	4	123	129
Amusement, gambling, & recreation industries	713	66	73	75	99	21	27	1,303	1,500
Accommodation & food services	72	566	627	449	613	128	170	10,121	11,588
Accommodation	721	61	63	128	180	35	46	1,813	1,980
Food services & drinking places	722	505	564	321	433	93	124	8,308	9,608
Other services (except public administration)	81	538	538	307	418	83	100	3,475	3,516
Repair & maintenance	811	231	223	118	143	35	42	1,285	1,305
Personal and laundry services	812	201	208	72	84	23	27	1,297	1,341
Religious/grantmaking/prof/like organizations	813	106	107	117	190	25	31	893	870

NA Not available. S Estimates did not meet publication standards. [1] Based on North American Industry Classification System, 2002; see text, this section. [2] For pay period including March 12. [3] For detailed industries, see Table 1068. [4] For detailed industries, see Table 1162.

Source: U.S. Census Bureau, "2007 Economic Census, Comparative Statistics for United States, Summary Statistics by 2002 NAICS," March 2009, <http://factfinder.census.gov/>.

Table 756. Nonemployer Establishments and Receipts by Industry: 2000 to 2007

[Establishments: 16,530 represents 16,530,000. Includes only firms subject to federal income tax. Nonemployers are businesses with no paid employees. Data originate chiefly from administrative records of the Internal Revenue Service; see Appendix III. Data for 2000 based on the North American Industry Classification System (NAICS), 1997; 2006 based on NAICS 2002; and 2007 based on NAICS 2007; see text, this section]

Kind of business	NAICS code	Establishments (1,000)			Receipts (mil. dol.)		
		2000	2006	2007	2000	2006	2007
All industries	(X)	**16,530**	**20,769**	**21,708**	**709,379**	**970,384**	**991,792**
Forestry, fishing & hunting, & agricultural support services	113–115	223	229	236	9,196	10,670	10,963
Mining	21	86	102	102	5,227	9,026	9,012
Utilities	22	14	17	18	504	698	728
Construction	23	2,014	2,549	2,657	107,538	159,432	159,042
Manufacturing	31–33	285	311	328	13,022	15,469	16,333
Wholesale trade	42	388	387	402	31,684	34,804	35,823
Retail trade	44–45	1,743	1,858	1,980	73,810	83,933	88,143
Transportation & warehousing	48–49	747	1,002	1,083	37,824	62,928	66,633
Information	51	238	318	307	7,620	10,776	10,958
Finance & insurance	52	692	758	764	49,058	52,768	54,351
Real estate & rental & leasing	53	1,696	2,421	2,327	133,398	193,105	183,264
Professional, scientific, & technical services	54	2,420	2,904	3,029	90,272	124,237	130,386
Admin/support waste mgt/remediation services	56	1,032	1,482	1,793	23,754	34,989	39,811
Educational services	61	283	482	528	3,736	6,509	7,215
Health care & social assistance	62	1,317	1,728	1,768	36,550	52,579	55,050
Arts, entertainment, & recreation	71	782	1,002	1,120	17,713	24,782	27,357
Accommodation & food services	72	218	287	303	13,418	15,694	16,071
Other services (except public administration)	81	2,350	2,931	2,965	55,056	77,986	80,653

X Not applicable.

Source: U.S. Census Bureau, "Nonemployer Statistics," June 2009, <http://www.census.gov/econ/nonemployer/>.

Table 757. Establishments, Employees, and Payroll by Employment-Size Class: 1990 to 2007

[6,176 represents 6,176,000. Excludes most government employees, railroad employees, self-employed persons. Employees are for the week including March 12. Covers establishments with payroll. An *establishment* is a single physical location where business is conducted or where services or industrial operations are performed. For statement on methodology, see Appendix III]

Employment-size class	Unit	1990	1995	2000	2003	2004	2005	2006	2007
Establishments, total	1,000	**6,176**	**6,613**	**7,070**	**7,255**	**7,388**	**7,500**	**7,601**	**7,705**
Under 20 employees	1,000	5,354	5,733	6,069	6,240	6,359	6,468	6,533	6,633
20 to 99 employees	1,000	684	730	826	845	856	856	886	892
100 to 499 employees	1,000	122	135	157	151	154	157	163	161
500 to 999 employees	1,000	10	10	12	11	12	12	12	12
1,000 or more employees	1,000	6	6	7	7	7	7	7	7
Employees, total	1,000	**93,476**	**100,335**	**114,065**	**113,398**	**115,075**	**116,317**	**119,917**	**120,604**
Under 20 employees	1,000	24,373	25,785	27,569	28,313	28,701	28,874	29,429	30,057
20 to 99 employees	1,000	27,414	29,202	33,147	33,760	34,288	34,302	35,504	35,615
100 to 499 employees	1,000	22,926	25,364	29,736	28,549	28,976	29,591	30,616	30,453
500 to 999 employees	1,000	6,551	7,021	8,291	7,638	7,815	8,053	8,248	8,284
1,000 or more employees	1,000	12,212	12,962	15,322	15,138	15,295	15,497	16,120	16,196
Annual payroll, total	Bil. dol.	**2,104**	**2,666**	**3,879**	**4,041**	**4,254**	**4,483**	**4,792**	**5,027**
Under 20 employees	Bil. dol	485	608	818	885	926	970	1,021	1,067
20 to 99 employees	Bil. dol	547	696	1,006	1,068	1,124	1,177	1,260	1,313
100 to 499 employees	Bil. dol	518	675	1,031	1,054	1,106	1,176	1,264	1,310
500 to 999 employees	Bil. dol	174	219	336	334	355	376	401	428
1,000 or more employees	Bil. dol	381	467	690	700	743	784	848	910

Source: U.S. Census Bureau, "County Business Patterns," July 2009, <http://www.census.gov/econ/cbp/>.

Table 758. Establishments, Employees, and Payroll by Employment-Size Class and Industry: 2000 to 2007

[Establishments and employees in thousands (7,070.0 represents 7,070,000); payroll in billions of dollars. See headnote, Table 757. Data for 2000 based on the North American Industry Classification System (NAICS), 1997; 2006 and 2007 data based on NAICS 2002. See text, this section]

Industry	NAICS code	2000, total	2006, total	2007					
				Total	Under 20 employ-ees	20 to 99 employ-ees	100 to 499 employ-ees	500 to 999 employ-ees	1,000 or more employ-ees
Establishments, total [1]	(X)	7,070.0	7,601.2	7,705.0	6,632.9	891.6	161.3	12.1	7.1
Forestry, fishing & hunting, & ag support services	113–115	26.1	23.6	23.6	22.2	1.3	0.2	(Z)	(Z)
Mining	21	23.7	26.2	26.2	20.3	4.7	1.0	0.1	(Z)
Utilities	22	17.3	17.2	16.7	11.5	3.8	1.1	0.1	(Z)
Construction	23	709.6	802.3	811.5	739.4	63.3	8.2	0.4	0.2
Manufacturing	31–33	354.5	331.1	331.4	228.4	74.5	25.1	2.4	1.0
Wholesale trade	42	446.2	430.0	434.5	371.8	54.2	7.8	0.5	0.2
Retail trade	44–45	1,113.6	1,120.3	1,123.6	964.0	132.0	27.2	0.4	(Z)
Transportation and warehousing	48–49	190.0	215.1	219.8	183.4	29.0	6.5	0.7	0.3
Information	51	133.6	141.9	143.8	116.9	20.8	5.2	0.6	0.3
Finance and insurance	52	423.7	494.3	508.1	463.0	37.0	6.6	1.0	0.6
Real estate and rental and leasing	53	300.2	382.1	380.1	363.5	14.6	1.8	0.1	(Z)
Professional, scientific, and technical services	54	722.7	846.5	867.6	801.2	56.0	9.1	0.8	0.4
Management of companies and enterprises	55	47.4	48.3	50.6	33.4	11.6	4.5	0.7	0.4
Admin/support waste mgt/remediation services	56	351.5	378.3	384.5	319.9	46.6	15.7	1.5	0.9
Educational services	61	68.0	82.6	86.9	66.7	16.3	3.1	0.4	0.4
Health care and social assistance	62	658.6	762.5	784.2	664.7	94.3	21.5	1.8	2.0
Arts, entertainment, and recreation	71	103.8	123.0	125.2	105.5	16.5	2.9	0.2	0.1
Accommodation and food services	72	542.4	612.3	632.5	452.6	169.7	9.7	0.4	0.2
Other services [2]	81	723.3	736.4	744.3	694.7	45.4	4.0	0.2	0.1
Unclassified establishments	99	99.0	27.0	10.0	9.9	(Z)	(Z)	–	–
Employees, total [1]	(X)	114,065	119,917	120,604	30,057	35,615	30,453	8,284	16,196
Forestry, fishing & hunting, & ag support services	113–115	184	166	172	79	48	32	5	9
Mining	21	456	554	701	100	195	207	90	108
Utilities	22	655	614	623	62	170	225	92	74
Construction	23	6,573	7,339	7,268	2,769	2,457	1,482	270	289
Manufacturing	31–33	16,474	13,632	13,320	1,318	3,276	5,019	1,618	2,089
Wholesale trade	42	6,112	6,031	5,965	1,792	2,119	1,445	318	291
Retail trade	44–45	14,841	15,768	15,760	5,186	5,245	5,012	245	72
Transportation and warehousing	48–49	3,790	4,306	4,395	752	1,195	1,232	474	742
Information	51	3,546	3,396	3,399	526	883	1,047	409	534
Finance and insurance	52	5,963	6,647	6,549	2,017	1,432	1,335	684	1,082
Real estate and rental and leasing	53	1,942	2,217	2,224	1,194	552	329	78	72
Professional, scientific, and technical services	54	6,816	8,054	8,180	2,749	2,185	1,742	510	994
Management of companies and enterprises	55	2,874	2,916	3,121	183	519	971	469	979
Admin/support waste mgt/remediation services	56	9,138	10,004	9,984	1,254	2,035	3,069	1,006	2,620
Educational services	61	2,532	2,980	3,039	321	685	603	289	1,141
Health care and social assistance	62	14,109	16,451	16,798	3,531	3,760	3,966	1,220	4,321
Arts, entertainment, and recreation	71	1,741	1,974	2,009	400	694	544	138	233
Accommodation and food services	72	9,881	11,381	11,565	2,858	6,516	1,512	258	421
Other services [2]	81	5,293	5,459	5,520	2,955	1,648	680	111	126
Unclassified establishments	99	144	30	13	3	1	–	–	–
Annual payroll, total [1]	(X)	3,879	4,792	5,027	1,067	1,313	1,310	428	910
Forestry, fishing & hunting, & ag support services	113–115	5	5	6	3	2	1	(Z)	(Z)
Mining	21	22	37	40	5	11	12	6	7
Utilities	22	41	48	51	4	12	19	9	7
Construction	23	240	322	336	106	119	80	15	15
Manufacturing	31–33	644	620	627	49	136	227	81	134
Wholesale trade	42	270	323	328	89	112	82	21	24
Retail trade	44–45	303	368	375	116	129	120	7	3
Transportation and warehousing	48–49	126	166	175	28	46	48	19	35
Information	51	209	213	223	30	51	71	29	42
Finance and insurance	52	347	481	511	107	116	117	55	115
Real estate and rental and leasing	53	59	88	89	42	25	16	4	3
Professional, scientific, and technical services	54	362	497	533	145	149	132	39	68
Management of companies and enterprises	55	211	266	293	18	45	89	43	98
Admin/support waste mgt/remediation services	56	210	283	300	45	66	82	26	81
Educational services	61	62	88	94	8	18	19	7	41
Health care and social assistance	62	431	627	668	147	133	125	51	212
Arts, entertainment, and recreation	71	43	57	60	15	14	20	5	6
Accommodation and food services	72	126	167	176	41	87	28	7	13
Other services [2]	81	110	134	141	09	43	21	4	4
Unclassified establishments	99	4	1	(Z)	(Z)	(D)	(D)	–	–

– Represents zero. D Data withheld to avoid disclosure. X Not applicable. Z Less than 50 establishments. [1] Totals for 2000 include auxiliaries. Beginning 2006, cases previously classified under NAICS code 95 (auxiliaries) are coded in the operating NAICS sector of the establishment. [2] Except public administration.

Source: U.S. Census Bureau, "County Business Patterns," July 2009, <http://www.census.gov/econ/cbp/>.

Table 759. Employer Firms, Employment, and Annual Payroll by Employment Size of Firm and Industry: 2007

[6,050 represents 6,050,000. A firm is an aggregation of all establishments owned by a parent company (within a geographic location and/or industry) with some annual payroll. A firm may be a single location or it can include multiple locations. Employment is measured in March and payroll is annual leading to some firms with zero employment. Numbers in parentheses represent North American Industry Classification System codes, 2002; see text, this section]

Industry and data type	Unit	Total	All industries—employment size of firm						
			0 to 4	5 to 9	10 to 19	20 to 99	100 to 499	Less than 500	500 or more
Total [1]:									
Firms	1,000	6,050	3,705	1,060	645	532	89	6,031	18
Employment	1,000	120,604	6,139	6,975	8,656	20,923	17,174	59,867	60,737
Annual payroll	Bil. dol	5,027	235	222	292	769	687	2,205	2,822
Construction (23):									
Firms	1,000	800	525	132	76	58	7	799	1
Employment	1,000	7,268	832	863	1,022	2,220	1,254	6,190	1,077
Annual payroll	Bil. dol	336	32	30	41	105	66	273	63
Manufacturing (31–33):									
Firms	1,000	287	115	54	45	56	14	283	4
Employment	1,000	13,320	213	358	612	2,289	2,446	5,918	7,402
Annual payroll	Bil. dol	627	8	12	22	92	103	237	389
Wholesale trade (42):									
Firms	1,000	335	190	57	39	37	8	332	3
Employment	1,000	5,965	325	378	525	1,366	1,041	3,636	2,329
Annual payroll	Bil. dol	328	16	17	25	68	54	180	148
Retail trade (44–45):									
Firms	1,000	713	418	147	81	56	8	711	2
Employment	1,000	15,760	769	968	1,076	2,095	1,231	6,139	9,621
Annual payroll	Bil. dol	375	18	21	26	63	40	169	207
Transportation & warehousing (48–49):									
Firms	1,000	174	112	24	16	15	4	172	2
Employment	1,000	4,395	169	161	220	572	497	1,618	2,777
Annual payroll	Bil. dol	175	6	5	7	20	19	57	118
Information (51):									
Firms	1,000	76	46	11	8	8	2	75	1
Employment	1,000	3,399	68	74	106	306	323	877	2,522
Annual payroll	Bil. dol	223	5	3	5	17	20	49	174
Finance & insurance (52):									
Firms	1,000	264	188	38	17	15	4	262	2
Employment	1,000	6,549	324	241	222	624	724	2,135	4,414
Annual payroll	Bil. dol	511	14	13	15	44	54	139	371
Professional, scientific and technical services (54):									
Firms	1,000	787	571	106	59	41	7	784	3
Employment	1,000	8,180	858	694	785	1,527	1,131	4,995	3,185
Annual payroll	Bil. dol	533	44	34	43	99	79	299	234
Management of companies and enterprises (55):									
Firms	1,000	28	4	1	1	6	9	21	7
Employment	1,000	3,121	4	4	7	78	290	384	2,738
Annual payroll	Bil. dol	293	1	(Z)	1	5	19	26	267
Admin/support waste mgt/ remediation services (56):									
Firms	1,000	329	208	49	30	29	9	325	4
Employment	1,000	9,984	314	322	409	1,161	1,518	3,724	6,259
Annual payroll	Bil. dol	300	12	10	13	37	41	112	188
Educational services (61):									
Firms	1,000	77	38	12	10	13	3	76	1
Employment	1,000	3,039	58	79	133	551	543	1,364	1,676
Annual payroll	Bil. dol	94	2	2	3	14	17	37	57
Health care and social assistance (62):									
Firms	1,000	615	314	142	80	59	16	611	4
Employment	1,000	16,798	582	937	1,066	2,364	3,041	7,990	8,808
Annual payroll	Bil. dol	668	29	37	44	88	95	293	375
Accommodation and food services (72):									
Firms	1,000	477	203	92	85	86	9	475	2
Employment	1,000	11,565	328	617	1,159	3,188	1,563	6,855	4,710
Annual payroll	Bil. dol	176	8	7	14	43	22	94	82
Other services (except public administration) (81):									
Firms	1,000	677	426	137	67	41	4	676	1
Employment	1,000	5,520	795	890	879	1,481	631	4,677	843
Annual payroll	Bil. dol	141	18	20	21	37	19	114	26

Z Less than $500 million. [1] Includes other industries, not shown separately.

Source: U.S. Small Business Administration, Office of Advocacy, "Statistics of U.S. Businesses," <http://www.sba.gov/advo/research/data.html> accessed June 2010.

Table 760. Employer Firms, Employment, and Payroll by Employment Size of Firm and State: 2000 and 2007

[5,652.5 represents 5,652,500. A firm is an aggregation of all establishments owned by a parent company (within a state) with some annual payroll. A firm may be a single location or it can include multiple locations. Employment is measured in March and payroll is annual leading to some firms with zero employment]

State	Employer firms (1,000) 2000 Total	Employer firms (1,000) 2000 Less than 20 employ-ees	Employer firms (1,000) 2007 Total	Employer firms (1,000) 2007 Less than 20 employ-ees	Employer firms (1,000) 2007 Less than 500 employ-ees	Employment, 2007 (mil.) Total	Employment, 2007 (mil.) Less than 20 employ-ees	Employment, 2007 (mil.) Less than 500 employ-ees	Annual payroll, 2007 (bil. dol.) Total	Annual payroll, 2007 (bil. dol.) Less than 20 employ-ees	Annual payroll, 2007 (bil. dol.) Less than 500 employ-ees
U.S.	5,652.5	5,035.0	6,049.7	5,410.4	6,031.3	120.6	21.8	59.9	5,026.8	749.4	2,204.8
AL	79.9	68.2	81.6	69.2	79.3	1.7	0.3	0.8	58.3	8.8	26.4
AK	15.9	14.0	16.8	14.7	16.3	0.2	0.1	0.1	11.4	2.3	5.6
AZ	93.0	79.3	113.3	96.7	110.3	2.4	0.4	1.1	90.8	13.0	38.6
AR	52.4	45.4	53.7	46.2	52.1	1.0	0.2	0.5	33.3	5.1	13.9
CA	664.6	581.1	730.8	645.3	725.0	13.8	2.6	7.1	653.9	102.0	295.4
CO	116.2	101.5	131.9	116.3	128.9	2.1	0.4	1.0	87.8	14.7	39.2
CT	78.5	67.2	77.1	65.8	75.1	1.5	0.3	0.8	81.5	11.9	37.4
DE	20.2	16.6	20.7	16.6	19.3	0.4	0.1	0.2	18.6	2.3	6.9
DC	16.3	12.4	16.9	12.6	15.7	0.5	0.1	0.2	28.8	3.3	12.1
FL	354.0	319.3	432.3	392.9	427.8	7.4	1.3	3.3	267.5	45.1	113.7
GA	160.4	138.3	184.7	160.3	180.7	3.6	0.6	1.7	142.1	20.6	58.3
HI	24.3	20.8	26.9	22.8	26.0	0.5	0.1	0.3	18.3	3.3	9.6
ID	32.2	28.0	40.7	35.7	39.6	0.5	0.1	0.3	17.5	3.9	9.4
IL	254.1	218.1	264.3	228.9	259.9	5.4	0.9	2.6	243.3	34.2	105.1
IN	116.3	98.1	118.2	100.3	115.3	2.6	0.4	1.3	94.8	12.5	40.6
IA	65.6	56.2	65.9	56.4	64.1	1.3	0.2	0.7	43.4	6.3	20.0
KS	61.6	52.4	62.1	52.6	60.1	1.2	0.2	0.6	42.0	6.5	19.8
KY	72.3	61.0	72.8	61.3	70.6	1.6	0.3	0.8	52.4	7.3	22.6
LA	81.7	69.5	83.2	70.4	81.1	1.6	0.3	0.9	59.2	9.5	29.2
ME	34.1	30.1	35.8	31.5	34.8	0.5	0.1	0.3	17.0	3.6	9.4
MD	106.0	90.4	115.3	98.6	112.6	2.2	0.4	1.2	99.5	15.3	47.3
MA	148.2	127.8	144.8	124.7	141.8	3.1	0.5	1.5	157.2	21.7	67.6
MI	193.9	167.2	188.5	164.1	185.4	3.7	0.7	1.9	150.9	22.5	87.2
MN	116.2	99.4	123.7	106.0	121.2	2.5	0.4	1.3	107.2	13.7	44.2
MS	48.3	41.5	48.7	41.6	47.1	0.9	0.2	0.5	28.6	4.7	13.0
MO	118.1	101.1	122.6	105.1	119.8	2.5	0.4	1.2	91.3	12.6	38.5
MT	28.0	25.0	33.0	29.5	32.3	0.4	0.1	0.2	10.6	2.9	6.8
NE	41.4	35.5	42.8	36.7	41.4	0.8	0.1	0.4	27.2	4.0	11.8
NV	40.3	33.4	51.3	42.5	49.2	1.2	0.2	0.5	44.4	6.3	18.8
NH	32.1	27.3	33.0	28.0	31.9	0.6	0.1	0.3	22.8	4.3	11.0
NJ	202.2	178.4	208.0	183.5	204.8	3.7	0.7	1.9	184.2	28.6	80.2
NM	35.5	30.1	38.3	32.3	36.8	0.6	0.1	0.4	21.9	3.9	10.8
NY	424.8	379.2	446.0	400.2	441.7	7.5	1.5	3.9	429.1	60.6	179.1
NC	163.6	142.0	179.8	155.8	176.3	3.6	0.6	1.7	132.0	19.6	55.2
ND	17.2	14.7	17.9	15.1	17.2	0.3	0.1	0.2	9.1	1.7	4.9
OH	212.5	180.5	205.5	174.9	201.7	4.8	0.8	2.3	181.0	23.9	76.5
OK	70.2	61.0	73.6	63.5	71.6	1.3	0.3	0.7	44.6	7.4	21.2
OR	85.1	74.2	94.3	82.4	92.2	1.5	0.3	0.8	56.0	9.9	27.9
PA	237.5	204.6	240.6	207.1	236.6	5.2	0.9	2.6	208.0	28.8	90.5
RI	25.2	21.5	26.4	22.5	25.5	0.4	0.1	0.2	17.0	3.1	8.7
SC	78.4	67.2	85.1	72.9	82.7	1.6	0.3	0.8	53.9	8.8	24.3
SD	20.6	17.7	22.0	18.9	21.3	0.3	0.1	0.2	10.1	2.0	5.6
TN	102.4	86.7	104.7	88.2	101.7	2.5	0.4	1.1	90.1	12.2	37.9
TX	369.0	321.3	397.7	344.7	392.3	9.0	1.4	4.1	373.0	51.4	152.0
UT	46.2	39.3	61.0	52.6	59.2	1.1	0.2	0.5	38.7	6.1	17.7
VT	19.1	16.7	19.5	16.9	18.9	0.3	0.1	0.2	8.8	2.0	5.3
VA	139.7	120.3	157.5	136.1	154.2	3.2	0.6	1.5	136.3	19.5	59.6
WA	138.2	120.9	153.6	135.0	150.8	2.5	0.5	1.4	112.3	17.9	51.5
WV	33.5	28.8	31.9	27.1	30.8	0.6	0.1	0.3	18.1	2.9	8.3
WI	115.6	98.2	117.4	99.9	115.0	2.5	0.4	1.3	92.6	13.0	42.4
WY	15.9	13.9	18.1	15.7	17.5	0.2	0.1	0.1	8.2	1.9	4.7

Source: U.S. Small Business Administration, Office of Advocacy, "Statistics of U.S. Businesses," <http://www.sba.gov/advo/research/data.html>, July 2010.

Table 761. Employer Firms, Establishments, Employment, and Annual Payroll by Firm Size: 1990 to 2007

[In thousands except as noted (5,074 represents 5,074,000). Firms are an aggregation of all establishments owned by a parent company with some annual payroll. Establishments are locations with active payroll in any quarter. This table illustrates the changing importance of enterprise sizes over time, not job growth, as enterprises can grow or decline and change enterprise size cells over time]

Item	Total	All industries—employment size of firm						
		0 to 4 [1]	5 to 9	10 to 19	20 to 99	100 to 499	Less than 500	500 or more
Firms:								
1990................	5,074	3,021	952	563	454	70	5,060	14
1995................	5,369	3,250	981	577	470	76	5,354	15
2000................	5,653	3,397	1,021	617	516	84	5,635	17
2003................	5,767	3,504	1,025	620	515	85	5,750	17
2004................	5,886	3,580	1,043	633	526	87	5,869	17
2005................	5,984	3,678	1,050	630	521	87	5,966	17
2006................	6,022	3,670	1,061	647	536	91	6,004	18
2007................	6,050	3,705	1,060	645	532	89	6,031	18
Establishments:								
1990................	6,176	3,032	971	600	590	255	5,448	728
1995................	6,613	3,260	998	618	630	284	5,799	814
2000................	7,070	3,406	1,035	652	674	312	6,080	990
2003................	7,255	3,510	1,038	655	687	331	6,222	1,033
2004................	7,388	3,586	1,056	667	693	330	6,331	1,056
2005................	7,500	3,684	1,063	662	679	332	6,421	1,079
2006................	7,601	3,677	1,073	679	698	346	6,473	1,129
2007................	7,705	3,711	1,074	682	723	356	6,546	1,159
Employment:								
1990................	93,469	5,117	6,252	7,543	17,710	13,545	50,167	43,302
1995................	100,315	5,395	6,440	7,734	18,422	14,660	52,653	47,662
2000................	114,065	5,593	6,709	8,286	20,277	16,260	57,124	56,941
2003................	113,398	5,768	6,732	8,330	20,187	16,430	57,448	55,950
2004................	115,075	5,845	6,853	8,500	20,643	16,758	58,597	56,477
2005................	116,317	5,937	6,898	8,454	20,444	16,911	58,645	57,672
2006................	119,917	5,960	6,974	8,676	21,077	17,537	60,224	59,693
2007................	120,604	6,139	6,975	8,656	20,923	17,174	59,867	60,737
Annual payroll (bil. dol.):								
1990................	2,104	117	114	144	352	279	1,007	1,097
1995................	2,666	142	137	175	437	361	1,252	1,414
2000................	3,879	186	174	231	608	528	1,727	2,152
2003................	4,041	197	187	247	635	552	1,818	2,222
2004................	4,254	206	196	258	670	588	1,917	2,337
2005................	4,483	220	206	269	700	617	2,013	2,470
2006................	4,792	230	214	282	742	661	2,129	2,664
2007................	5,027	235	222	292	769	687	2,205	2,822

[1] Employment is measured in March, thus some firms (start-ups after March, closures before March, and seasonal firms) will have zero employment and some annual payroll.

Source: U.S. Small Business Administration, Office of Advocacy, "Statistics of U.S. Businesses," <http://www.sba.gov/advo/research/data.html>, accessed June 2010.

Table 762. Number of Active Establishments by Firm Age and Size of Employer: 2005

[In thousands (2,869 represents 2,869,000). A firm may have one establishment (a single unit establishment) or many establishments (a multi-unit firm). Firms are defined at the enterprise level such that all establishments under the operational control of the enterprise are considered part of the firm. These data include nearly all nonfarm private establishments with paid employees as well as some public sector activities. The Business Dynamics Statistics data measure the net change in employment at the establishment level. Data are not to be compared with Table 759, which is shown by industry based on North American Industry Classification System codes. Data are also not comparable to U.S. Small Business Administration data (Tables 760 and 761) due to differing survey methodologies. For more information about concepts and methodology, see <http://www.ces.census.gov/index.php/bds/bds_overview>]

Firm age [1]	Firm size							Share of employ-ment	Share of job creation
	1 to 4	5 to 9	10 to 19	20 to 99	100 to 499	Less than 500	500 or more		
Total.................	**2,869**	**1,088**	**666**	**675**	**328**	**5,626**	**1,030**	**1.00**	**1.00**
Startups................	470	44	18	11	3	546	2	0.08	0.19
1 to 5 years	932	310	159	112	19	1,533	7	0.23	0.15
6 to 10 years	510	213	126	110	31	990	23	0.15	0.10
11 to 20 years	553	267	168	153	58	1,199	85	0.19	0.13
21 years and over	403	253	195	290	218	1,358	913	0.34	0.43
Share of employment	0.05	0.06	0.07	0.18	0.15	0.51	0.49	(X)	(X)
Share of job creation	0.11	0.08	0.08	0.17	0.14	0.58	0.42	(X)	(X)

X Not applicable. [1] Establishment age is computed by taking the difference between the current year of operation and the birth year. Firm age is computed from the age of the establishments belonging to that particular firm. For more information, see <http://www.ces.census.gov/index.php/bds/bds_overview>.

Source: U.S. Census Bureau, Center for Economic Studies, "Business Dynamics Statistics," <http://www.ces.census.gov/index.php/bds/bds_database_list>, accessed August 2010.

504 Business Enterprise

Table 763. Establishment Births, Deaths, and Employment by Sector and Firm Type—Startups, Young, and Mature Firms: 2005

[In thousands (519 represents 519,000). A firm may have one establishment (a single unit establishment) or many establishments (a multi-unit firm). Firms are defined at the enterprise level such that all establishments under the operational control of the enterprise are considered part of the firm. Sectors based on the Standard Industrial Classification System (SIC); see <http://www.osha.gov/pls/imis/sic_manual.html>. These data include nearly all nonfarm private establishments with paid employees as well as some public sector activities. The Business Dynamics Statistics data measure the net change in employment at the establishment level. Data are not to be compared with Tables 759, 761, and 764, which are shown by industry based on North American Industry Classification System codes. Data are also not comparable to U.S. Small Business Administration data due to differing survey methodologies. For more information about concepts and methodology, see <http://www.ces.census.gov/index.php/bds/bds_overview>. Minus sign (−) indicates decrease]

Sector and firm type [1]	Establishments			Number of employees	Change in employment				
	Number	Births [2]	Deaths [3]		Net total	Due to births [2]	Due to deaths [3]	Due to birth and expansion [4]	Due to death and contraction [4]
All sectors: [5]									
Startups [6]	519	519	–	3,444	3,444	3,296	–	3,444	–
Young firms [7]	2,512	100	408	23,990	−996	675	2,473	4,386	5,382
Mature firms [8]	3,533	169	238	87,600	−162	3,072	2,877	10,209	10,371
Agriculture:									
Startups [6]	12	12	–	67	67	67	–	67	–
Young firms [7]	57	3	10	473	36	23	49	142	106
Mature firms [8]	45	2	4	607	−2	22	28	97	100
Mining:									
Startups [6]	1	1	–	12	12	12	–	12	–
Young firms [7]	7	(Z)	1	77	−3	2	11	16	19
Mature firms [8]	14	1	1	392	12	14	11	57	45
Construction:									
Startups [6]	38	38	–	179	179	179	–	179	–
Young firms [7]	269	13	53	2,066	−105	52	235	446	551
Mature firms [8]	246	8	23	3,984	−137	55	167	571	707
Transportation, communication, and utilities:									
Startups [6]	22	22	–	148	148	(Z)	–	148	–
Young firms [7]	104	5	20	993	−64	30	124	180	244
Mature firms [8]	100	12	15	5,383	−16	302	212	724	740
Wholesale:									
Startups [6]	24	24	–	130	130	130	–	130	–
Young firms [7]	147	5	22	1,167	35	28	110	201	236
Mature firms [8]	285	12	17	5,690	4	210	204	692	688
Manufacturing:									
Startups [6]	16	16	–	206	206	206	–	206	–
Young firms [7]	102	3	15	1,450	−53	39	157	253	306
Mature firms [8]	205	5	13	13,482	−153	231	335	1,171	1,324
Retail:									
Startups [6]	118	118	–	960	960	960	–	960	–
Young firms [7]	519	18	95	5,189	−555	124	623	772	1,327
Mature firms [8]	835	37	46	18,760	105	802	481	2,210	2,105
Finance, insurance, and real estate:									
Startups [6]	53	53	–	234	234	234	–	234	–
Young firms [7]	241	10	35	1,552	−66	58	167	291	357
Mature firms [8]	422	39	40	6,688	−85	477	467	1,031	1,116
Services:									
Startups [6]	233	233	–	1,507	1,507	1,507	–	1,507	–
Young firms [7]	1,065	42	157	11,024	−151	315	997	2,084	2,235
Mature firms [8]	1,312	52	80	32,614	109	959	971	3,657	3,548

– Represents zero. Z Less than 500. [1] Establishment type is computed by taking the difference between the current year of operation and the birth year. Firm age is computed from the age of the establishments belonging to that particular firm. For more information, see <http://www.ces.census.gov/index.php/bds/bds_overview>. [2] Birth year is defined as the year an establishment first reports positive employment. [3] Death year is defined as the year an establishment permanently shuts down. [4] For explanation of expansions and contractions, see <http://www.ces.census.gov/index.php/bds/bds_overview>. [5] Excludes government and those sectors not elsewhere classified. [6] Less than 1 year old. [7] 1–10 years old. [8] More than 10 years old.

Source: U.S. Census Bureau, Center for Economic Studies, "Business Dynamics Statistics," <http://www.ces.census.gov/index.php/bds/bds_database_list>, accessed August 2010.

U.S. Census Bureau, Statistical Abstract of the United States: 2011

Table 764. Firm Births and Deaths by Employment Size of Enterprise: 1990 to 2006

[In thousands (541.1 represents 541,100). Data represent activity from March of the beginning year to March of the ending year. Establishments with no employment in the first quarter of the beginning year were excluded. This table provides the number of births and deaths of initial establishments (based on Census ID) as an approximation of firm births and deaths]

Item	Births (initial locations)				Deaths (initial locations)			
	Total	Less than 20 employees	Less than 500 employees	500 employees or more	Total	Less than 20 employees	Less than 500 employees	500 employees or more
Firms:								
1990 to 1991	541.1	515.9	540.9	0.3	546.5	517.0	546.1	0.4
1995 to 1996	597.8	572.4	597.5	0.3	512.4	485.5	512.0	0.4
2000 to 2001	585.1	558.0	584.8	0.3	553.3	524.0	552.8	0.5
2001 to 2002 [1]	569.8	541.5	568.3	1.5	586.9	557.1	586.5	0.4
2002 to 2003	612.3	585.6	612.0	0.3	540.7	514.6	540.3	0.3
2003 to 2004	628.9	601.9	628.7	0.3	541.0	515.0	540.7	0.3
2004 to 2005	644.1	616.0	643.9	0.3	565.7	539.1	565.5	0.3
2005 to 2006	670.1	640.7	669.8	0.2	599.3	573.3	599.1	0.3
Employment:								
1990 to 1991	3,105	1,713	2,907	198	3,208	1,723	3,044	164
1995 to 1996	3,256	1,845	3,056	200	3,100	1,560	2,808	291
2000 to 2001	3,418	1,821	3,109	310	3,262	1,701	3,050	212
2001 to 2002 [1]	3,370	1,748	3,034	336	3,660	1,755	3,257	403
2002 to 2003	3,667	1,856	3,174	493	3,324	1,608	2,880	445
2003 to 2004	3,575	1,889	3,241	334	3,221	1,615	2,868	353
2004 to 2005	3,609	1,931	3,279	330	3,307	1,685	2,981	326
2005 to 2006	3,682	1,999	3,412	270	3,220	1,711	2,964	256

[1] A change in methodology ("based on Census ID" rather than "plant number") has affected the allocation of firms by employment size.

Source: U.S. Small Business Administration, Office of Advocacy, "Firm Size Data, Statistics of U.S. Businesses and Nonemployer Statistics," <http://www.sba.gov/advo/research/data.html>.

Table 765. Establishments and Employment Changes from Births, Deaths, Expansions, and Contractions by Employment Size of Enterprise: 2005 to 2006

[In thousands (6,639 represents 6,639,000), except percent. See headnote, Table 764. An establishment is a single physical location at which business is conducted or where services or industrial operations are performed. An enterprise is a business organization consisting of one or more domestic establishments under common ownership or control. Minus sign (–) indicates decrease]

Employment size of firm	Establish- ments	Births [1]	Deaths [2]	Employ- ment	Change in employ- ment	Percent change in employment due to—			
						Births [1]	Deaths [2]	Births and expan- sions [3]	Deaths and con- tractions [4]
Total.	**6,639**	**825**	**702**	**116,294**	**3,598**	**5.8**	**−4.6**	**16.2**	**−13.2**
1–4.	2,857	514	467	5,932	1,002	15.1	−13.3	37.9	−21.0
5–9.	1,062	85	73	6,893	296	8.0	−6.8	21.6	−17.3
10–19.	662	43	37	8,449	292	6.6	−5.5	18.7	−15.3
20–99.	678	42	31	20,438	590	5.4	−4.3	16.0	−13.1
100–499.	328	29	15	16,910	346	5.3	−3.7	14.5	−12.5
Less than 500	5,587	713	623	58,622	2,526	6.8	−5.5	18.8	−14.5
500 or more.	1,052	112	79	57,672	1,073	4.8	−3.7	13.6	−11.7

[1] Births are establishments that have zero employment in the first quarter of the initial year and positive employment in the first quarter of the subsequent year. [2] Deaths are establishments that have positive employment in the first quarter of the initial year and zero employment in the first quarter of the subsequent year. [3] Expansions are establishments that have positive first quarter employment in both the initial and subsequent years and increase employment during the time period between the first quarter of the initial year and the first quarter of the subsequent year. [4] Contractions are establishments that have positive first quarter employment in both the initial and subsequent years and decrease employment during the time period between the first quarter of the initial year and the first quarter of the subsequent year.

Source: U.S. Small Business Administration, Office of Advocacy, "Statistics of U.S. Businesses," <http://www.sba.gov/advo/research/data.html>, accessed August 2010.

Table 766. Employer Firm Births and Deaths and Business Bankruptcies by State: 2005 to 2008

[Births represent an employing unit which is determined, for the first time, as meeting the definition of "employer" in the state unemployment compensation law or a previously terminated employing unit, which again is determined as meeting the definition of employer]

State	Births			Deaths			Business bankruptcies [1]		
	2005	2007	2008	2005	2007	2008	2005	2007	2008
United States [2]	938,927	923,932	874,816	935,736	926,283	966,647	32,406	23,889	33,822
Alabama	10,575	9,813	9,194	10,168	10,710	11,468	322	285	395
Alaska	1,982	1,777	1,922	2,294	3,615	2,879	67	63	78
Arizona	21,339	18,208	15,847	18,249	16,019	21,219	522	332	691
Arkansas	7,591	8,157	8,499	7,021	7,596	7,511	363	335	429
California	121,482	113,829	103,572	151,944	143,591	150,314	3,576	2,697	4,697
Colorado	26,610	23,035	21,921	14,035	23,080	27,591	748	536	756
Connecticut	9,220	9,265	9,164	11,131	11,052	11,488	104	250	366
Delaware	3,299	2,921	2,980	3,355	2,775	3,698	190	243	361
District of Columbia	4,316	4,302	3,939	3,952	3,378	2,765	46	35	42
Florida	84,890	75,533	72,203	58,737	60,724	72,003	1,278	1,455	2,759
Georgia	29,804	30,062	28,980	29,315	29,517	29,945	2,161	1,316	1,714
Hawaii	3,763	3,611	3,475	3,794	4,185	3,973	55	43	51
Idaho	9,312	8,065	6,854	6,334	6,995	7,273	141	79	167
Illinois	30,445	30,013	31,493	32,846	33,213	35,689	901	868	1,178
Indiana	14,545	13,863	13,959	16,504	12,826	14,380	586	484	692
Iowa	6,004	5,903	5,893	6,802	7,601	7,679	367	227	270
Kansas	7,095	7,799	8,156	7,330	8,376	7,648	313	196	244
Kentucky	9,617	8,816	8,821	8,515	8,320	8,790	297	258	390
Louisiana	9,393	10,356	9,527	9,123	8,334	7,656	683	451	571
Maine	4,251	4,243	4,202	4,711	4,565	5,095	98	118	154
Maryland	22,083	20,168	18,392	21,769	20,835	21,251	493	406	405
Massachusetts	19,723	18,427	18,581	18,878	21,695	20,223	350	297	334
Michigan	24,642	23,166	22,090	26,971	20,359	34,272	757	1,019	1,394
Minnesota	12,555	12,313	11,811	15,302	12,004	12,597	1,400	473	656
Mississippi	6,071	6,871	5,776	6,823	7,550	6,800	186	234	298
Missouri	17,239	15,510	15,061	20,109	19,422	21,290	368	316	534
Montana	4,768	4,751	4,181	4,394	4,476	4,771	116	47	71
Nebraska	5,127	4,752	4,602	4,982	5,092	5,200	265	202	221
Nevada	11,299	11,057	10,202	8,485	9,222	10,771	292	234	395
New Hampshire	4,758	4,588	4,587	5,406	5,523	5,515	441	306	318
New Jersey	33,022	36,381	26,774	32,751	34,183	31,167	661	705	925
New Mexico	5,272	6,158	5,971	5,670	6,003	5,972	755	102	185
New York	62,045	67,577	65,624	62,667	65,500	69,267	1,488	1,236	1,504
North Carolina	25,906	29,042	24,153	22,007	23,570	23,734	537	473	738
North Dakota	1,893	1,812	1,842	2,512	2,192	2,344	74	57	54
Ohio	22,542	21,900	20,361	23,429	23,434	21,038	1,590	1,172	1,436
Oklahoma	8,609	8,961	8,943	7,231	7,777	7,787	751	315	392
Oregon	14,445	14,333	13,952	14,804	13,479	14,182	871	298	283
Pennsylvania	36,609	34,558	35,587	36,989	34,528	42,318	1,159	889	1,078
Rhode Island	3,677	3,460	3,310	4,164	4,536	4,459	75	65	122
South Carolina	12,341	12,554	11,634	10,681	11,603	11,657	163	118	196
South Dakota	2,102	2,124	2,127	2,354	2,442	2,311	149	74	95
Tennessee	17,484	17,619	17,167	17,135	17,602	18,614	542	483	653
Texas	55,858	55,865	55,214	55,039	55,269	36,108	2,964	2,241	2,728
Utah	11,536	13,403	11,238	11,871	11,419	8,105	427	139	302
Vermont	1,911	2,228	2,146	2,346	2,374	2,555	65	56	52
Virginia	25,061	28,174	25,517	21,359	21,726	23,971	527	436	798
Washington	30,353	33,191	33,701	40,944	35,077	37,955	681	439	565
West Virginia	3,493	3,434	3,363	4,869	4,824	4,644	229	117	169
Wisconsin	13,656	12,663	12,905	13,397	12,920	12,711	785	363	525
Wyoming	2,632	2,707	2,593	2,689	2,903	2,703	60	35	42

[1] For year ending June 30. See headnote, Table 771. [2] Includes Puerto Rico and Virgin Islands, not shown separately. Bankruptcy data also includes Guam and Northern Mariana Islands.

Source: U.S. Small Business Administration, unpublished data, and Administrative Office of the U.S. Courts, "Bankruptcy Statistics"; <http://www.uscourts.gov/bnkrpctystats/statistics.htm>.

Table 767. Small Business Administration Loans to Minority-Owned Small Businesses: 2000 to 2009

[3,634 represents $3,634,000,000. For year ending September 30. A small business must be independently owned and operated, must not be dominant in its particular industry, and must meet standards set by the Small Business Administration as to its annual receipts or number of employees]

Minority group	Number of loans					Amount (mil. dol.)				
	2000	2005	2007	2008	2009	2000	2005	2007	2008	2009
Total minority loans	11,999	29,721	36,330	24,851	11,104	3,634	6,132	6,853	5,674	3,304
Percent of all loans	24.8	28.3	32.9	31.7	21.8	29.4	30.2	33.3	31.6	25.2
African American	2,120	6,635	8,919	7,127	2,780	388	627	919	1,009	512
Asian American	5,838	13,457	15,433	10,813	5,331	2,383	4,056	4,324	3,517	2,131
Hispanic American	3,500	8,794	11,049	6,249	2,666	761	1,325	1,482	1,037	612
Native American	541	835	929	662	327	101	123	128	111	49

Source: U.S. Small Business Administration, *Management Information Summary*, unpublished data.

U.S. Census Bureau, Statistical Abstract of the United States: 2011

Table 768. U.S. Firms—Ownership by Women, Race, and Hispanic or Latino Origin: 2002

[22,975 represents 22,975,000. A Hispanic firm may be of any race and therefore may be included in more than one race group. See text, this section]

Group	All firms [1] Firms (1,000)	All firms [1] Sales and receipts (billion dollars)	Firms with paid employees Firms (1,000)	Firms with paid employees Sales and receipts (billion dollars)	Firms with paid employees Employees (1,000)	Firms with paid employees Annual payroll (billion dollars)
All firms [2]	**22,975**	**22,604**	**5,525**	**21,836**	**110,767**	**3,812**
Female-owned	6,489	940	917	803	7,141	174
Male-owned	13,184	7,061	3,525	6,564	42,429	1,320
Equally male-/female-owned	2,693	732	718	627	5,665	130
Publicly held and other firms [3]	494	13,820	353	13,797	55,398	2,186
Hispanic or Latino origin	1,573	222	200	180	1,537	37
Black	1,198	89	95	66	754	18
American Indian and Alaska Native	201	27	24	22	191	5
Asian	1,104	327	319	291	2,214	56
Native Hawaiian and Other Pacific Islander	29	4	4	4	29	1

[1] Both firms with paid employees and firms with no paid employees. [2] U.S. totals are based on the 2002 Economic Census, where as the gender, Hispanic or Latino origin, and race estimates are based on the 2002 Survey of Business Owners. [3] Publicly held and other firms not classifiable by gender, Hispanic or Latino origin, and race.

Source: U.S. Census Bureau, 2002 Economic Census, Survey of Business Owners, Women-Owned Firms: 2002 (SB02-00CS-WMN)(RV); Hispanic-Owned Firms: 2002 (SB02-00CS-HISP)(RV); Black-Owned Firms: 2002 (SB02-00CS-BLK)(RV); American Indian- and Alaska Native-Owned Firms: 2002 (SB02-00CS-AIAN)(RV); Asian-Owned Firms: 2002 (SB02-00CS-ASIAN)(RV); and Native Hawaiian- and Other Pacific Islander-Owned Firms: 2002 (SB02-00CS-NHPI)(RV).

Table 769. Women-Owned and Minority-Owned Firms With Paid Employees by Employment Size: 2002

[917 represents 917,000. Employment reflects number of paid employees during the March 12 pay period. Based on the 2002 Survey of Business Owners; see text, this section]

Item	Unit	Total	Number of employees None [1]	Number of employees 1 to 4	Number of employees 5 to 9	Number of employees 10 to 19	Number of employees 20 to 49	Number of employees 50 to 99	Number of employees 100 to 499	Number of employees 500 or more
WOMEN-OWNED										
Firms	1,000	917	161	462	149	83	43	11	7	1
Sales and receipts	Mil. dol.	802,851	23,539	113,447	96,282	103,160	117,875	74,053	114,484	160,012
Employees	1,000	7,141	–	939	971	1,105	1,269	750	1,194	913
Annual payroll	Mil. dol.	173,529	3,953	20,483	21,360	25,946	31,578	19,316	30,015	20,877
HISPANIC-OWNED										
Firms	1,000	200	37	100	31	18	9	3	1	(Z)
Sales and receipts	Mil. dol.	179,508	6,703	28,292	26,627	26,945	29,496	19,447	27,206	14,792
Employees	1,000	1,537	–	202	205	248	267	185	244	186
Annual payroll	Mil. dol.	36,712	1,153	4,568	4,958	5,705	6,393	4,817	5,900	3,217
BLACK-OWNED										
Firms	1,000	95	19	47	14	7	4	1	1	(Z)
Sales and receipts	Mil. dol.	65,799	2,986	10,679	7,773	7,769	10,912	9,697	11,193	4,790
Employees	1,000	754	–	96	92	100	133	87	162	82
Annual payroll	Mil. dol.	17,550	541	2,251	2,133	2,279	3,034	2,154	3,623	1,535
AMERICAN INDIAN AND ALASKA NATIVE-OWNED										
Firms	1,000	24	5	12	4	2	1	(Z)	(Z)	(Z)
Sales and receipts	Mil. dol.	21,987	1,021	3,378	2,411	2,996	3,814	3,092	2,842	2,433
Employees	1,000	191	–	26	23	28	36	23	26	29
Annual payroll	Mil. dol.	5,135	137	578	528	706	945	675	773	793
ASIAN-OWNED										
Firms	1,000	319	54	161	55	30	15	3	2	(Z)
Sales and receipts	Mil. dol.	291,163	10,287	56,967	46,155	44,109	50,950	30,759	32,955	18,980
Employees	1,000	2,214	–	347	353	393	437	226	302	155
Annual payroll	Mil. dol.	56,045	1,616	7,946	7,992	9,130	10,947	6,048	8,211	4,154
NATIVE HAWAIIAN- AND OTHER PACIFIC ISLANDER-OWNED										
Firms	1,000	4	1	2	1	(Z)	(Z)	(Z)	(Z)	–
Sales and receipts	Mil. dol.	3,502	73	520	413	574	805	420	698	–
Employees	1,000	29	–	4	4	5	7	4	5	–
Annual payroll	Mil. dol.	826	12	133	99	123	228	100	132	–

– Represents zero. Z Less than 500. [1] Firms reported annual payroll but did not report any employees on their payroll during specified period in 2002.

Source: U.S. Census Bureau, 2002 Economic Census, Survey of Business Owners, Women-Owned Firms: 2002 (SB02-00CS-WMN)(RV). Hispanic-Owned Firms: 2002 (SB02-00CS-HISP)(RV); Black-Owned Firms: 2002 (SB02-00CS-BLK)(RV); American Indian- and Alaska Native-Owned Firms: 2002 (SB02-00CS-AIAN)(RV); Asian-Owned Firms: 2002 (SB02-00CS-ASIAN)(RV); and Native Hawaiian- and Other Pacific Islander-Owned Firms: 2002 (SB02-00CS-NHPI)(RV).

Table 770. Bankruptcy Petitions Filed and Pending by Type and Chapter: 1990 to 2009

[For years ending June 30. Covers only bankruptcy cases filed under the Bankruptcy Reform Act of 1978. *Bankruptcy*: legal recognition that a company or individual is insolvent and must restructure or liquidate. Petitions "filed" means the commencement of a proceeding through the presentation of a petition to the clerk of the court; "pending" is a proceeding in which the administration has not been completed]

Item	1990	1995	2000	2004	2005	2006	2007	2008	2009
Total filed	725,484	858,104	1,276,922	1,635,725	1,637,254	1,484,570	751,056	967,831	1,306,315
Business [1]	64,688	51,288	36,910	35,739	32,406	31,562	23,889	33,822	55,021
Nonbusiness [2]	660,796	806,816	1,240,012	1,599,986	1,604,848	1,453,008	727,167	934,009	1,251,294
Chapter 7 [3]	468,171	552,244	864,183	1,146,761	1,174,681	1,142,958	435,064	592,376	870,266
Chapter 11 [4]	2,116	1,755	722	935	847	749	540	780	1,088
Chapter 13 [5]	190,509	252,817	375,107	452,286	429,315	309,298	291,560	340,852	379,939
Voluntary	723,886	856,991	1,276,146	1,635,099	1,636,678	1,484,085	750,577	967,248	(NA)
Involuntary	1,598	1,113	776	626	576	485	479	583	(NA)
Chapter 7 [3]	505,337	581,390	885,447	1,167,101	1,196,212	1,164,815	450,332	615,748	907,603
Chapter 9 [6]	7	12	8	7	6	10	7	4	6
Chapter 11 [4]	19,591	13,221	9,947	11,048	6,703	6,224	5,586	7,293	13,951
Chapter 12 [7]	1,351	904	732	302	290	360	386	314	422
Chapter 13 [5]	199,186	262,551	380,770	457,171	433,945	313,085	294,693	344,421	384,187
Section 304 [8]	12	26	18	96	98	[9] 36	(X)	(X)	(X)
Chapter 15 [9]	(X)	(X)	(X)	(X)	(X)	40	52	51	146
Total pending	961,919	1,090,446	1,400,416	1,697,267	1,750,562	1,411,212	1,312,016	1,325,220	1,521,595

NA Not available. X Not applicable. [1] Business bankruptcies include those filed under chapters 7, 9, 11, 12, 13, or 15. [2] Includes other petitions, not shown separately. [3] Chapter 7, liquidation of nonexempt assets of businesses or individuals. [4] Chapter 11, individual or business reorganization. [5] Chapter 13, adjustment of debts of an individual with regular income. [6] Chapter 9, adjustment of debts of a municipality. [7] Chapter 12, adjustment of debts of a family farmer with regular income, effective November 26, 1986. [8] Chapter 11, U.S.C., Section 304, cases ancillary to foreign proceedings. [9] Chapter 15 was added and Section 304 was terminated by changes in the Bankruptcy Laws effective October 17, 2005.

Source: Administrative Office of the U.S. Courts, *Statistical Tables for the Federal Judiciary* and "Bankruptcy Statistics," <http://www.uscourts.gov/bnkrpctystats/statistics.htm>.

Table 771. Bankruptcy Cases Filed by State: 2000 to 2009

[In thousands (1,276.9 represents 1,276,900). For years ending June 30. Covers only bankruptcy cases filed under the Bankruptcy Reform Act of 1978. *Bankruptcy*: legal recognition that a company or individual is insolvent and must restructure or liquidate. Petitions "filed" means the commencement of a proceeding through the presentation of a petition to the clerk of the court]

State	2000	2005	2008	2009	State	2000	2005	2008	2009
Total [1]	1,276.9	1,637.3	967.8	1,306.3					
					Missouri	26.3	39.2	23.1	28.6
Alabama	31.4	42.6	25.8	33.6	Montana	3.3	4.4	1.7	2.4
Alaska	1.4	1.6	0.7	1.0	Nebraska	5.0	5.0	5.9	7.2
Arizona . .	21.7	82.4	14.3	26.8	Nevada	14.3	16.3	14.4	24.4
Arkansas	16.3	25.5	12.8	15.4	New Hampshire	3.9	4.9	3.5	4.6
California	160.6	122.6	98.7	171.6					
					New Jersey	38.7	40.7	22.9	31.6
Colorado	15.6	30.2	17.9	24.7	New Mexico	7.1	10.1	4.0	5.3
Connecticut	11.4	11.8	7.1	9.2	New York	61.7	81.7	42.4	53.2
Delaware	4.9	3.6	2.3	4.4	North Carolina	25.8	37.5	20.8	25.5
District of Columbia . . .	2.6	1.9	0.8	1.0	North Dakota	2.0	2.5	1.3	1.5
Florida	74.0	85.8	52.7	82.9					
					Ohio	53.6	95.8	54.2	64.5
Georgia	57.9	77.3	55.0	70.0	Oklahoma	19.3	28.2	9.9	12.7
Hawaii	5.0	3.2	1.6	2.7	Oregon	18.1	25.3	10.5	15.9
Idaho	7.3	9.7	4.2	6.7	Pennsylvania	43.8	62.3	31.5	35.6
Illinois	62.3	83.6	48.5	65.0	Rhode Island	4.8	4.4	3.6	4.9
Indiana	37.5	55.9	35.0	44.6					
					South Carolina	11.7	15.2	7.6	9.5
Iowa	8.2	14.3	7.5	9.3	South Dakota	2.1	2.9	1.4	1.7
Kansas	11.4	17.3	8.2	10.1	Tennessee	47.1	60.8	42.9	52.6
Kentucky	20.8	29.2	19.2	23.6	Texas	62.9	97.5	44.2	48.8
Louisiana	23.1	31.1	15.1	16.8	Utah	14.4	20.5	7.7	12.1
Maine	4.1	4.7	2.6	3.5					
					Vermont	1.6	1.7	1.1	1.4
Maryland	31.1	28.5	16.3	21.4	Virginia	37.1	38.8	23.9	33.3
Massachusetts	16.7	19.6	15.0	18.6	Washington	31.2	37.7	18.1	27.1
Michigan	36.4	68.5	51.3	63.8	West Virginia	8.2	12.6	4.9	6.0
Minnesota	15.4	19.4	14.2	19.2	Wisconsin	18.0	29.0	18.8	24.7
Mississippi	17.9	21.8	11.6	13.8	Wyoming	2.0	2.5	0.8	1.1

[1] Includes Island Areas, not shown separately.

Source: Administrative Office of the U.S. Courts, *Statistical Tables for the Federal Judiciary* and "Bankruptcy Statistics," <http://www.uscourts.gov/bnkrpctystats/statistics.htm>.

U.S. Census Bureau, Statistical Abstract of the United States: 2011

Table 772. Patents and Trademarks: 1990 to 2009

[In thousands (99.2 represents 99,200). Calendar year data. Covers U.S. patents issued to citizens of the United States and residents of foreign countries. For data on foreign countries, see Table 1393]

Type	1990	1995	2000	2004	2005	2006	2007	2008	2009
Patents issued	**99.2**	**113.8**	**176.0**	**181.3**	**157.7**	**196.4**	**182.9**	**185.2**	**191.9**
Inventions	90.4	101.4	157.5	164.3	143.8	173.8	157.3	157.8	167.3
Individuals	17.3	17.4	22.4	17.6	14.7	16.6	14.0	12.6	12.6
Corporations:									
United States	36.1	44.0	70.9	73.0	65.2	78.9	70.5	70.0	74.8
Foreign [1]	36.0	39.1	63.3	72.9	63.2	77.4	72.0	74.5	79.3
U.S. government	1.0	1.0	0.9	0.8	0.7	0.8	0.7	0.7	0.7
Designs	8.0	11.7	17.4	15.7	13.0	21.0	24.1	25.6	23.1
Botanical plants	0.3	0.4	0.5	1.0	0.7	1.1	1.0	1.2	1.0
Reissues	0.4	0.3	0.5	0.3	0.2	0.5	0.5	0.6	0.5
U.S. residents	52.8	64.4	96.9	94.1	82.6	102.2	93.7	92.0	95.0
Foreign country residents	46.2	49.4	79.1	87.2	75.2	94.2	89.2	93.2	96.9
Percent of total	46.7	43.4	44.9	48.1	47.6	48.0	48.8	50.3	50.5
Trademarks:									
Applications filed	127.3	181.0	361.8	304.5	334.7	362.3	401.0	390.8	351.9
Issued	60.8	92.5	115.2	146.0	154.8	193.7	218.8	233.9	222.1
Trademarks	53.6	85.6	106.4	113.7	121.6	153.3	170.8	194.4	177.4
Trademark renewals	7.2	6.9	8.8	32.3	33.3	40.4	48.1	39.5	44.7

[1] Includes patents to foreign governments.

Source: U.S. Patent and Trademark Office, "Statistical Reports Available For Viewing, Calendar Year Patent Statistics," <http://www.uspto.gov/web/offices/ac/ido/oeip/taf/reports.htm> and unpublished data.

Table 773. Patents by State and Island Areas: 2009

[Includes only U.S. patents granted to residents of the United States and territories]

State	Total	Inventions	Designs	Botanical plants	Reissues	State	Total	Inventions	Designs	Botanical plants	Reissues
Total	**95,032**	**82,382**	**12,025**	**389**	**236**	Missouri	877	708	164	3	2
						Montana	91	73	18	–	–
Alabama	377	304	57	14	2	Nebraska	226	193	29	4	–
Alaska	55	39	16	–	–	Nevada	426	338	87	–	1
Arizona	1,759	1,562	190	4	3	New Hampshire ...	608	542	62	1	3
Arkansas	154	96	58	–	–	New Jersey	3,259	2,839	405	4	11
California	23,354	20,646	2,506	135	67	New Mexico	329	303	26	–	–
Colorado	1,968	1,716	248	1	3	New York	6,127	5,237	876	4	10
Connecticut	1,661	1,416	238	4	3	North Carolina	2,298	2,012	266	15	5
Delaware	342	311	30	–	1	North Dakota	92	82	10	–	–
District of Columbia ...	62	57	4	–	1	Ohio	3,023	2,341	676	1	5
Florida	2,899	2,197	632	64	6	Oklahoma	445	403	38	2	2
Georgia	1,666	1,415	232	15	4	Oregon	2,014	1,784	199	24	7
Hawaii	96	71	17	8	–	Pennsylvania	3,064	2,656	387	13	8
Idaho	985	941	38	–	6	Rhode Island	305	231	74	–	–
Illinois.	3,615	2,898	699	10	8	South Carolina	579	461	116	2	–
Indiana.	1,246	1,095	147	–	4	South Dakota	56	46	10	–	–
Iowa	730	670	60	–	–	Tennessee	785	647	134	1	3
Kansas.	509	435	73	–	1	Texas	6,436	5,934	486	4	12
Kentucky	457	368	88	–	1	Utah.	855	765	88	–	2
Louisiana	315	257	55	3	–	Vermont	500	452	48	–	–
Maine.	130	118	10	–	2	Virginia.	1,208	1,073	131	1	3
Maryland	1,444	1,277	156	5	6	Washington	4,856	4,310	525	9	12
Massachusetts.	4,038	3,696	330	3	9	West Virginia	102	92	8	2	–
Michigan	3,516	2,983	510	17	6	Wisconsin	1,887	1,467	413	5	2
Minnesota	2,972	2,625	324	10	13	Wyoming	64	59	5	–	–
Mississippi	144	125	16	1	2	Island areas......	26	16	10	–	–

– Represents zero.

Source: U.S. Patent and Trademark Office, "Statistical Reports Available For Viewing, Calendar Year Patent Statistics," <http://www.uspto.gov/web/offices/ac/ido/oeip/taf/reports.htm>.

Table 774. Copyright Registration by Subject Matter: 2000 to 2009

[In thousands (497.6 represents 497,600). For years ending September 30. Comprises claims to copyrights registered for both U.S. and foreign works. Semiconductor chips and renewals are not considered copyright registration claims]

Subject matter	2000	2005	2008	2009	Subject matter	2000	2005	2008	2009
Total copyright claims ...	**497.6**	**515.2**	**232.1**	**381.3**	Musical works [2]	138.9	133.7	65.1	93.3
Monographs [1]	169.7	191.4	78.7	133.3	Works of the visual arts [3]	85.8	82.5	42.1	75.2
Serials	69.0	57.7	22.0	37.5	Semiconductor chip products ...	0.7	0.5	0.2	0.3
Sound recordings	34.2	49.9	24.2	42.0	Renewals	16.8	15.8	0.4	0.5

[1] Includes computer software and machine readable works. [2] Includes dramatic works, accompanying music, choreography, pantomimes, motion pictures, and filmstrips. [3] Two-dimensional works of fine and graphic art, including prints and art reproductions; sculptural works; technical drawings and models; photographs; commercial prints and labels; works of applied arts, cartographic works, and multimedia works.

Source: The Library of Congress, Copyright Office, *Annual Report*.

Table 775. Net Stock of Private Fixed Assets by Industry: 2000 to 2008

[In billions of dollars (21,241 represents $21,241,000,000,000). Estimates as of Dec. 31. Net stock estimates are presented in terms of current cost and cover equipment, software, and structures]

Industry	NAICS code [1]	2000	2005	2007	2008
Private fixed assets	(X)	**21,241**	**30,601**	**33,929**	**34,261**
Agriculture, forestry, fishing, and hunting	11	339	440	485	499
Farms [2]	111, 112	312	404	445	457
Forestry, fishing, and related activities	113-115	27	36	40	42
Mining	21	539	1,024	1,268	1,428
Oil and gas extraction	211	403	845	1,037	1,171
Mining, except oil and gas	212	92	116	141	152
Support activities for mining	213	44	63	90	105
Utilities	22	1,038	1,401	1,613	1,798
Construction	23	174	230	273	295
Manufacturing	31-33	1,768	2,010	2,186	2,313
Durable goods	(X)	1,003	1,139	1,232	1,305
Wood products	321	32	36	41	44
Nonmetallic mineral products	327	56	65	72	77
Primary metals	331	125	128	136	142
Fabricated metal products	332	112	124	133	140
Machinery	333	142	167	188	202
Computer and electronic products	334	247	279	297	310
Electrical equipment, appliances, and components	335	45	50	54	57
Motor vehicles, bodies and trailers, and parts	3361-3363	106	122	125	129
Other transportation equipment	3364, 3365, 3369	80	96	107	117
Furniture and related products	337	16	20	22	23
Miscellaneous manufacturing	339	44	52	58	64
Nondurable goods	(X)	765	872	954	1,008
Food and beverage and tobacco products	311, 312	183	209	227	240
Textile mills and textile product mills	313, 314	44	43	44	44
Apparel and leather and allied products	315, 316	17	18	18	19
Paper products	322	101	102	110	115
Printing and related support activities	323	41	49	55	58
Petroleum and coal products	324	92	116	139	152
Chemical products	325	220	256	278	294
Plastics and rubber products	326	68	77	83	87
Wholesale trade	42	349	467	508	526
Retail trade	44-45	647	898	1,025	1,102
Transportation and warehousing [3]	48-49	827	982	1,072	1,134
Air transportation	481	191	239	253	266
Railroad transportation	482	286	312	330	341
Water transportation	483	40	51	59	62
Truck transportation	484	70	83	94	95
Transit and ground passenger transportation	485	36	41	46	47
Pipeline transportation	486	74	115	137	163
Warehousing and storage	493	22	29	36	39
Information	51	864	1,036	1,175	1,255
Publishing industries (includes software)	511	50	54	61	65
Motion picture and sound recording industries	512	32	36	38	39
Broadcasting and telecommunications	513	763	916	1,040	1,111
Information and data processing services	514	20	30	36	40
Finance and insurance	52	823	1,099	1,258	1,353
Federal Reserve banks	521	11	16	19	21
Credit intermediation and related activities	522	466	613	689	733
Securities, commodity contracts, and investments	523	87	110	131	143
Insurance carriers and related activities	524	164	205	224	237
Funds, trusts, and other financial vehicles	525	96	156	195	220
Real estate and rental and leasing	53	11,539	17,714	19,277	18,534
Real estate	531	11,300	17,358	18,850	18,090
Rental and leasing services and lessors of intangible assets [4]	532, 533	239	356	427	444
Professional, scientific, and technical services [3]	54	214	317	363	388
Legal services	5411	20	26	28	29
Computer systems design and related services	5415	50	68	79	83
Management of companies and enterprises [5]	551111, 551112	271	374	430	471
Admin/support waste mgt	56	153	205	233	246
Administrative and support services	561	85	124	142	151
Waste management and remediation services	562	68	81	91	95
Educational services	61	212	325	384	432
Health care and social assistance	62	689	1,001	1,155	1,209
Ambulatory health care services	621	210	300	343	366
Hospitals	622	425	624	725	751
Nursing and residential care facilities	623	30	44	49	52
Social assistance	624	24	33	38	40
Arts, entertainment, and recreation	71	126	190	223	237
Performing arts, spectator sports, museums, and related activities	711, 712	48	75	91	99
Amusements, gambling, and recreation industries	713	79	115	133	138
Accommodation and food services	72	338	446	511	540
Accommodation	721	177	220	250	254
Food services and drinking places	722	161	226	262	285
Other services, except government	81	331	442	491	501

X Not applicable. [1] Based on North American Industry Classification System, 2002; see text this section. [2] NAICS crop and animal production. [3] Includes other activities, not shown separately. [4] Intangible assets include patents, trademarks, and franchise agreements, but not copyrights. [5] Consists of bank and other holding companies.

Source: U.S. Bureau of Economic Analysis, "Table 3.1ES. Current-Cost Net Stock of Private Fixed Assets by Industry," October 2009, <http://www.bea.gov/bea/dn/FA2004/SelectTable.asp#S3>.

Table 776. Private Domestic Investment in Current and Chained (2005) Dollars: 1990 to 2008

[In billions of dollars (861 represents $861,000,000,000). Covers equipment, software, and structures. Minus sign (–) indicates decrease. For explanation of chained dollars; see text, Section 13]

Item	1990	2000	2003	2004	2005	2006	2007	2008
CURRENT DOLLARS								
Gross private domestic investment	**861**	**1,772**	**1,730**	**1,969**	**2,172**	**2,327**	**2,289**	**2,136**
Less: Consumption of fixed capital	560	987	1,136	1,201	1,291	1,391	1,470	1,536
Equals: Net private domestic investment	301	785	594	768	881	936	819	600
Fixed investment	846	1,718	1,713	1,904	2,122	2,267	2,269	2,171
Less: Consumption of fixed capital	560	987	1,136	1,201	1,291	1,391	1,470	1,536
Equals: Net fixed investment	286	731	577	703	832	876	800	635
Nonresidential	622	1,269	1,136	1,223	1,347	1,505	1,640	1,694
Residential	224	449	578	681	775	762	629	477
Change in private inventories	15	55	16	65	50	60	19	–35
CHAINED (2005) DOLLARS								
Gross private domestic investment	**994**	**1,970**	**1,872**	**2,058**	**2,172**	**2,230**	**2,146**	**1,989**
Less: Consumption of fixed capital	627	1,063	1,205	1,244	1,291	1,341	1,395	1,441
Equals: Net private domestic investment	366	908	667	814	881	889	751	548
Fixed investment	987	1,914	1,856	1,993	2,122	2,171	2,126	2,018
Nonresidential	618	1,319	1,191	1,263	1,347	1,454	1,544	1,570
Residential	386	580	664	730	775	718	585	451
Change in private inventories	17	60	17	66	50	59	20	–26

Source: U.S. Bureau of Economic Analysis, *Survey of Current Business,* April 2010. See also <http://www.bea.gov/national/nipaweb/SelectTable.asp?Selected=N>.

Table 777. Information and Communications Technology (ICT) Equipment and Computer Software Expenditures: 2007 and 2008

[In millions of dollars (92,795 represents $92,795,000,000). Covers only companies with employees. The Information and Communication Technology Survey collects noncapitalized and capitalized data on information and communication technology equipment, including computer software. This survey is sent to a sample of approximately 46,000 private nonfarm employer businesses operating in the United States]

Type of expenditure and industry	NAICS code [1]	Noncapitalized expenditures [2]		Capitalized expenditures [3]	
		2007	2008	2007	2008
Total expenditures for ICT equipment and computer software	**(X)**	**92,795**	**91,412**	**174,039**	**204,849**
Total equipment expenditures	(X)	38,113	35,443	(NA)	(NA)
Purchases	(X)	20,405	18,274	110,310	132,969
Computer and peripheral equipment	(X)	13,659	12,203	59,031	66,083
Information and communication technology equipment	(X)	6,481	5,699	46,142	60,187
Electromedical and electrotherapeutic apparatus	(X)	265	372	5,136	6,700
Operating leases and rental payments	(X)	17,708	17,169	(NA)	(NA)
Computer and peripheral equipment	(X)	11,983	11,822	(NA)	(NA)
Information and communication technology equipment	(X)	4,524	4,434	(NA)	(NA)
Electromedical and electrotherapeutic apparatus	(X)	1,201	913	(NA)	(NA)
Total computer software expenditures	(X)	54,681	55,969	(NA)	(NA)
Purchases and payroll for developing software	(X)	28,810	28,547	63,729	71,880
Software licensing and service/maintenance agreements	(X)	25,872	27,421	(NA)	(NA)
Forestry, fishing, and agricultural services	113–115	64	73	89	159
Mining	21	1,224	1,825	1,343	1,443
Utilities	22	1,378	1,804	2,719	3,736
Construction	23	1,186	902	1,747	1,881
Manufacturing	31–33	17,278	16,108	18,585	19,684
Durable goods industries	321, 327, 33	11,371	10,718	11,131	11,499
Nondurable goods industries	31, 322-326	5,907	5,390	7,454	8,185
Wholesale trade	42	3,018	3,306	6,261	7,117
Retail trade	44–45	4,462	4,164	11,575	14,227
Transportation and warehousing	48–49	1,784	1,798	3,313	3,528
Information	51	12,795	12,923	55,036	69,806
Finance and insurance	52	21,818	20,939	29,262	29,158
Real estate and rental and leasing	53	1,639	1,349	1,920	2,810
Professional, scientific, and technical services	54	11,598	11,353	13,828	15,663
Management of companies and enterprises	55	676	881	1,382	1,829
Admin/support and waste management/remediation services	56	2,210	2,392	4,171	4,742
Educational services	61	1,653	1,734	2,016	2,598
Health care and social assistance	62	6,916	6,440	14,562	17,816
Arts, entertainment, and recreation	71	551	502	1,140	1,173
Accommodation and food services	72	850	803	1,821	3,277
Other services (except public administration)	81	1,373	1,681	2,665	2,683
Equipment expenditures serving multiple industry codes	(X)	320	422	605	1,520

NA Not available. X Not applicable. [1] Based on North American Industry Classification System, 2002; see text, this section. [2] Expenses for ICT equipment including computer software not charged to asset accounts for which depreciation or amortization accounts are ordinarily maintained. [3] Expenses for ICT equipment including computer software chargeable to asset accounts for which depreciation or amortization accounts are ordinarily maintained.

Source: U.S. Census Bureau, "2008 Information and Communication Technology Survey," May 2010, <http://www.census.gov/econ/ict/xls/2008/Full%20Report.htm>.

Table 778. Capital Expenditures: 2000 to 2008

[In billions of dollars (1,161 represents $1,161,000,000,000). Based on a sample survey and subject to sampling error; see source for details]

Item	All companies				Companies with employees				Companies without employees			
	2000	2005	2007	2008	2000	2005	2007	2008	2000	2005	2007	2008
Capital expenditures, total ...	**1,161**	**1,145**	**1,355**	**1,375**	**1,090**	**1,063**	**1,271**	**1,295**	**71**	**82**	**84**	**80**
Structures	364	402	525	565	338	369	491	532	26	33	34	33
New	329	366	481	526	309	341	457	503	20	25	24	23
Used	35	36	44	39	29	28	34	29	6	8	11	10
Equipment and software	797	743	829	810	752	694	780	763	45	49	50	47
New	751	701	790	763	718	665	750	726	32	37	40	37
Used	46	42	39	47	34	29	29	37	12	13	10	10
Capital leases	20	18	20	20	19	18	19	19	(Z)	(Z)	1	1

Z Less than $500 million.

Source: U.S. Census Bureau, "2008 Annual Capital Expenditures Survey," March 2010, <http://www.census.gov/econ/aces/>, and earlier reports.

Table 779. Capital Expenditures by Industry: 2000 and 2008

[In billions of dollars (1,090 represents $1,090,000,000,000). Covers only companies with employees. Data for 2000 based on the North American Industry Classification System (NAICS), 1997; 2007 based on NAICS, 2002; see text this section. Based on a sample survey and subject to sampling error; see source for details]

Industry	NAICS code	2000	2008	Industry	NAICS code	2000	2008
Total expenditures	(X)	**1,090**	**1,295**	Professional, scientific, and technical			
Forestry, fishing, and agricultural				services	54	34	33
services	113–115	1	2	Management of companies and			
Mining	21	43	150	enterprises.	55	5	5
Utilities.......................	22	61	98	Admin/support waste mgt/remediation			
Construction	23	25	42	services.......................	56	18	17
Manufacturing	31–33	215	211	Educational services	61	18	27
Durable goods	321, 327, 33	134	103	Health care and social assistance.....	62	52	90
Nondurable goods	31, 322–326	81	108	Arts, entertainment, and recreation., , ,	71	19	17
Wholesale trade...............	42	34	33	Accommodation and food services	72	26	41
Retail trade	44–45	70	73	Other services (except public			
Transportation and warehousing	48–49	60	80	administration)..................	81	21	28
Information....................	51	160	103	Structure and equipment expenditures			
Finance and insurance	52	134	145	serving multiple industry categories ..	(X)	2	4
Real estate and rental and leasing ..	53	92	96				

X Not applicable.

Source: U.S. Census Bureau, "2008 Annual Capital Expenditures Survey," March 2010, <http://www.census.gov/econ/aces/>, and earlier reports.

Table 780. Business Cycle Expansions and Contractions—Months of Duration: 1945 to 2007

[A trough is the low point of a business cycle; a peak is the high point. Contraction, or recession, is the period from peak to subsequent trough; expansion is the period from trough to subsequent peak. Business cycle reference dates are determined by the National Bureau of Economic Research, Inc.]

Business cycle reference date				Contraction (Peak to trough)	Expansion (Previous trough to peak)	Length of cycle	
Peak		Trough				Trough from previous trough	Peak from previous peak
Month	Year	Month	Year				
February	1945	October	1945	8	[1] 80	[1] 88	[2] 93
November	1948	October	1949	11	37	48	45
July	1953	May	1954	10	45	55	56
August..................	1957	April	1958	8	39	47	49
April....................	1960	February	1961	10	24	34	32
December	1969	November	1970	11	106	117	116
November	1973	March........	1975	16	36	52	47
January	1980	July	1980	6	58	64	74
July	1981	November	1982	16	12	28	18
July	1990	March........	1991	8	92	100	108
March...................	2001	November	2001	8	120	128	128
December	2007				73		81
Average, all cycles:							
1945 to 2001 (10 cycles)....				10	57	67	67

[1] Previous trough: June 1938. [2] Previous peak: May 1937.

Source: National Bureau of Economic Research, Inc., Cambridge, MA, "Business Cycle Expansions and Contractions," <http://www.nber.org/cycles.html>, accessed April 2009.

U.S. Census Bureau, Statistical Abstract of the United States: 2011

Table 781. The Conference Board Leading, Coincident, and Lagging Economic Indexes: 2000 to 2009

[299.4 represents 299,400]

Item	Unit	2000	2005	2006	2007	2008	2009
The Conference Board Leading Economic							
Index (LEI) for the U.S., composite	2004 = 100	86.0	102.9	104.6	104.3	101.5	102.0
Average weekly hours, manufacturing	Hours	41.2	40.6	41.2	41.2	40.8	39.8
Average weekly initial claims for unemployment insurance	1,000	299.4	330.6	312.7	321.6	420.9	571.4
Manufacturers' new orders, consumer goods and materials (1982 dol.)	Mil. dol	152,036	150,268	149,963	152,087	136,408	119,599
Index of supplier deliveries— vendor performance [1]	Percent	53.4	54.1	54.3	51.2	51.6	51.4
Manufacturers' new orders, nondefense capital goods (1982 dol.)	Mil. dol	49,809	45,352	48,782	56,274	47,853	34,311
Building permits, new private housing units	1,000	1,598	2,160	1,844	1,392	896	583
Stock prices, 500 common stocks [1]	1941-43 = 10	1,426.8	1,207.1	1,310.0	1,476.7	1,220.9	946.7
Money supply, M2 (chain 2005 dol.)	Bil. dol	5,325	6,522	6,682	6,918	7,170	7,712
Interest rate spread, 10-year Treasury bonds less federal funds	Percent	−0.21	1.08	−0.17	−0.39	1.74	3.10
Index of consumer expectations [1]	1966:1 = 100	102.7	77.4	75.9	75.6	57.3	64.1
The Conference Board Coincident Economic							
Index (CEI) for the U.S., composite	2004 = 100	98.2	102.4	105.2	106.7	105.4	100.0
Employees on nonagricultural payrolls	1,000	131,794	133,694	136,086	137,588	136,777	130,911
Personal income less transfer payments (chain 2005 dol.)	Bil. dol	8,327	8,981	9,405	9,639	9,500	9,087
Industrial production	2002 = 100	103.7	107.2	109.7	111.3	108.8	98.2
Manufacturing and trade sales (chain 2005 dol.)	Mil. dol	919,657	1,013,268	1,041,901	1,046,022	1,012,423	930,953
The Conference Board Lagging Economic							
Index (LAG) for the U.S., composite	2004 = 100	98.6	103.3	106.3	109.5	113.1	111.2
Average duration of unemployment	Weeks	12.7	18.4	16.8	16.8	17.8	24.3
Inventories to sales ratio, manufacturing and trade (chain 2005 dol.)	Ratio	1.36	1.31	1.31	1.33	1.39	1.43
Change in labor cost per unit of output, manufacturing (six-month change, annual rate)	Percent	2.2	−2.1	0.2	0.6	5.4	−2.0
Average prime rate	Percent	9.2	6.2	8.0	8.1	5.1	3.3
Commercial and industrial loans outstanding (chain 2005 dol.)	Mil. dol	186,935	190,616	191,562	192,654	193,680	194,770
Consumer installment credit to personal income ratio	Percent	14.6	15.0	15.0	15.1	15.2	15.3
Change in consumer price index for services (6-month change, annual rate)	Percent	1.8	1.9	1.9	2.0	2.1	2.1

[1] Data are from private sources and provided through the courtesy of the compilers and are subject to their copyrights: stock prices, Standard & Poor's Corporation; index of consumer expectations, University of Michigan's Survey Research Center; index of supplier deliveries, Institute for Supply Management.

Source: The Conference Board, New York, NY 10022-6601, *Business Cycle Indicators*, monthly, <http://www.conference-board.org/data/monthlybci.cfm>. Reproduced with permission from The Conference Board, Inc. 2010, The Conference Board, Inc. (copyright).

Table 782. Manufacturing and Trade—Sales and Inventories: 1992 to 2009

[In billions of dollars (541 represents $541,000,000,000), except ratios. Based on North American Industry Classification System (NAICS), 2002; see text, this section]

Year	Sales, average monthly [1]				Inventories [2]				Inventory-sales ratio [3]			
	Total	Manufac-turing	Retail trade	Merchant whole-salers	Total	Manufac-turing	Retail trade	Merchant whole-salers	Total	Manufac-turing	Retail trade	Merchant whole-salers
1992	541	242	151	147	837	379	261	197	1.53	1.57	1.67	1.31
1993	568	252	162	154	864	380	280	205	1.50	1.50	1.68	1.30
1994	610	270	176	165	927	400	305	222	1.46	1.44	1.66	1.29
1995	655	290	185	180	986	425	323	238	1.48	1.44	1.72	1.29
1996	687	300	197	190	1,005	430	334	241	1.46	1.43	1.67	1.27
1997	724	320	206	198	1,047	444	345	259	1.42	1.37	1.64	1.26
1998	743	325	216	202	1,079	449	357	272	1.43	1.39	1.62	1.31
1999	787	336	234	217	1,139	464	385	290	1.40	1.35	1.59	1.30
2000	834	351	249	235	1,197	481	407	309	1.41	1.35	1.59	1.29
2001	819	331	256	232	1,120	428	395	297	1.42	1.38	1.58	1.32
2002	824	326	261	236	1,140	423	416	301	1.36	1.28	1.55	1.25
2003	855	335	272	248	1,148	408	432	308	1.34	1.24	1.56	1.22
2004	925	359	290	276	1,240	441	461	339	1.30	1.19	1.56	1.17
2005	1,003	395	308	300	1,311	474	472	365	1.27	1.17	1.51	1.18
2006	1,066	418	323	324	1,406	524	487	396	1.28	1.20	1.49	1.18
2007	1,125	445	334	346	1,483	563	498	421	1.29	1.22	1.48	1.18
2008	1,155	457	330	368	1,474	559	479	436	1.32	1.28	1.51	1.21
2009	1,003	384	306	313	1,329	510	429	390	1.37	1.36	1.45	1.29

[1] Averages of monthly not-seasonally-adjusted figures. [2] Seasonally adjusted end-of-year data. [3] Averages of seasonally-adjusted monthly ratios.

Source: U.S. Council of Economic Advisors, *Economic Indicators*, May 2010.

Table 783. Industrial Production Indexes by Industry: 1990 to 2009

[2002 = 100. Except as noted, based on the North American Industry Classification System (NAICS), 2002; see text, this section]

Industry	NAICS code [1]	1990	2000	2004	2005	2006	2007	2008	2009
Total index	(X)	**69.7**	**103.7**	**103.8**	**107.2**	**109.7**	**111.3**	**108.8**	**98.2**
Manufacturing (SIC) [2]	(X)	**67.0**	**104.4**	**104.3**	**108.5**	**111.2**	**112.7**	**109.1**	**96.7**
Manufacturing (NAICS)	31–33	65.5	103.9	104.7	109.1	112.1	113.8	110.3	97.9
Durable goods	(X)	52.8	105.2	107.0	112.8	117.8	120.2	116.3	96.9
Wood products	321	84.1	103.7	104.4	110.4	110.0	99.2	84.8	66.5
Nonmetallic mineral products	327	83.3	103.6	103.6	108.1	109.9	106.9	100.7	83.1
Primary metals	331	96.7	111.4	110.0	108.0	112.6	110.0	102.4	67.7
Fabricated metal products	332	80.3	110.7	98.9	103.4	109.0	112.1	110.1	89.7
Machinery	333	86.7	117.7	103.7	110.2	115.5	116.4	109.4	85.9
Computers and electronic products	334	13.8	101.4	129.9	144.5	163.8	176.7	192.9	174.0
Electrical equipment, appliances, and components	335	87.5	121.3	99.0	100.7	101.4	104.8	104.5	91.8
Motor vehicles and parts	3361–3	55.8	99.9	103.7	103.9	100.2	97.4	83.3	59.8
Aerospace and other misc. transportation equipment	3364–9	123.0	99.3	94.3	105.0	110.9	121.7	119.3	115.1
Furniture and related products	337	75.2	103.3	100.9	104.6	104.2	101.0	90.4	71.7
Miscellaneous products	339	67.3	96.7	103.2	109.9	113.3	118.3	117.7	113.8
Nondurable goods	(X)	87.7	102.2	102.0	104.8	105.7	106.7	103.6	97.8
Food, beverage, and tobacco products	311,2	90.0	101.2	102.5	106.2	106.7	109.6	109.3	107.2
Textile and product mills	313,4	99.2	111.9	94.6	96.7	88.0	81.2	72.6	60.7
Apparel and leather	315,6	172.4	150.8	82.0	80.4	79.1	79.3	75.9	64.7
Paper	322	97.4	105.3	97.6	97.5	97.6	95.9	92.1	82.1
Printing and related support	323	102.1	113.1	96.9	99.2	99.8	100.6	93.9	80.3
Petroleum and coal products	324	86.9	96.9	106.0	110.1	109.7	109.1	110.0	107.8
Chemical	325	78.3	95.0	105.6	109.3	112.7	114.1	108.8	103.6
Plastics and rubber products	326	67.2	102.9	101.5	102.3	102.9	104.7	99.1	84.4
Other manufacturing (non-NAICS) [3]	1133, 5111	100.9	112.6	97.9	97.6	96.6	95.3	89.9	75.6
Mining	21	**107.8**	**104.2**	**99.6**	**98.3**	**101.5**	**102.1**	**104.2**	**97.9**
Utilities	2211,2	**77.9**	**97.4**	**103.3**	**105.4**	**104.8**	**108.3**	**108.6**	**106.4**
Electric power generation, transmission, and distribution	2211	76.7	97.2	104.2	107.2	107.8	110.5	110.4	107.0
Natural gas distribution	2212	85.6	98.6	98.8	97.1	91.3	98.1	100.5	98.7

X Not applicable. [1] Based on North American Industry Classification System, 2002; see text, this section. [2] Standard Industrial Classification (SIC); see text, this section. [3] Those industries—logging and newspaper, periodical, book, and directory publishing that have traditionally been considered to be manufacturing.

Source: Board of Governors of the Federal Reserve System, *Industrial Production and Capacity Utilization*, Statistical Release G.17, monthly. See also <http://www.federalreserve.gov/releases/g17/>.

Table 784. Index of Industrial Capacity: 1990 to 2009

[2002 output = 100. Annual figures are averages of monthly data. Capacity represents estimated quantity of output relative to output in 2002 which the current stock of plant and equipment was capable of producing]

Year	Index of capacity		Relation of output to capacity (percent)				
				Stage of process			
	Total industry	Manufacturing	Total industry	Crude [1]	Primary and semifinished [2]	Finished [3]	Manufacturing
1990	84.5	82.0	82.5	88.2	82.7	80.6	81.7
1995	95.7	94.3	84.0	89.0	86.6	79.7	83.2
2000	126.9	130.4	81.7	88.5	84.4	77.1	80.1
2001	131.5	135.7	76.1	85.3	77.4	72.5	73.8
2002	134.0	137.6	74.6	82.7	76.6	70.7	72.7
2003	133.7	137.4	75.8	84.4	77.7	71.6	73.7
2004	133.4	137.0	77.9	86.1	79.8	73.3	76.2
2005	133.8	138.1	80.1	86.5	81.7	76.0	78.6
2006	135.7	140.1	80.9	88.3	81.7	77.1	79.4
2007	138.1	142.7	80.6	87.8	81.0	77.5	79.0
2008	140.3	145.4	77.6	86.5	77.3	74.1	75.1
2009	140.1	144.9	70.1	81.8	67.5	68.4	66.8

[1] Crude processing, covers a relatively small portion of total industrial capacity and consists of logging (NAICS 1133), much of mining (excluding stone, sand, and gravel mining, and oil and gas drilling, which are NAICS 21231, 21221–2, and 213111) and some basic manufacturing industries, including basic chemicals (NAICS 3251); fertilizers, pesticides, and other agricultural chemicals (NAICS 32531,2); pulp, paper, and paperboard mills (NAICS 3221); and alumina, aluminum, and other nonferrous production and processing mills (NAICS 3313,4). [2] Primary and semifinished processing loosely corresponds to the previously published aggregate, primary processing. Includes utilities and portions of several 2-digit SIC industries included in the former advanced processing group. These include printing and related support activities (NAICS 3231); paints and adhesives (NAICS 3255); and newspaper, periodical, book, and directory publishers (NAICS 5111). [3] Finished processing generally corresponds to the previously published aggregate, advanced processing. Includes oil and gas well drilling and carpet and rug mills.

Source: Board of Governors of the Federal Reserve System, *Industrial Production and Capacity Utilization*, Statistical Release G.17, monthly. (Based on data from Federal Reserve Board; U.S. Dept. of Commerce; U.S. Bureau of Labor Statistics; McGraw-Hill Information Systems Company, New York, NY; and other sources.)

U.S. Census Bureau, Statistical Abstract of the United States: 2011

Table 785. Corporate Profits, Taxes, and Dividends: 1990 to 2009

[In billions of dollars (434 represents $434,000,000,000). Covers corporations organized for profit and other entities treated as corporations. Represents profits to U.S. residents, without deduction of depletion charges and exclusive of capital gains and losses; intercorporate dividends from profits of domestic corporations are eliminated; net receipts of dividends, reinvested earnings of incorporated foreign affiliates, and earnings of unincorporated foreign affiliates are added. CCA = capital consumption adjustment]

Item	1990	2000	2005	2006	2007	2008	2009
Corporate profits with IVA and CCA [1]	434	819	1,456	1,608	1,542	1,360	1,309
Taxes on corporate income	145	265	412	473	452	292	315
Profits after tax with IVA and CCA [1]	289	554	1,044	1,135	1,090	1,068	994
Net dividends.	169	378	557	705	768	690	576
Undistributed profits with IVA and CCA [1]	120	176	486	430	322	378	418
Cash flow:							
Net cash flow with IVA and CCA [1]	493	861	1,337	1,356	1,303	1,478	1,584
Undistributed profits with IVA and CCA [1]	120	176	486	430	322	378	418
Consumption of fixed capital	373	685	863	926	981	1,037	1,042
Less: Inventory valuation adjustment (IVA)	–13	–17	–31	–38	–44	–38	9
Equals: Net cash flow with CCA	506	878	1,368	1,394	1,347	1,517	1,575

[1] Inventory valuation adjustment and capital consumption adjustment.

Source: U.S. Bureau of Economic Analysis, *Survey of Current Business*, April 2010. See also <http://www.bea.gov/national/nipaweb/Index.asp>.

Table 786. Corporate Profits With Inventory Valuation and Capital Consumption Adjustments—Financial and Nonfinancial Industries: 2000 to 2009

[In billions of dollars (819 represents $819,000,000,000). Based on the North American Industry Classification System, 2002; see text, this section. Minus sign (–) indicates loss. See headnote, Table 785]

Industry group	2000	2005	2006	2007	2008	2009
Corporate profits with IVA/CCA [1]	**819**	**1,456**	**1,608**	**1,542**	**1,360**	**1,309**
Domestic industries	674	1,217	1,352	1,194	983	997
Rest of the world	146	239	257	348	377	312
Corporate profits with IVA [1]	**756**	**1,610**	**1,785**	**1,730**	**1,425**	**1,437**
Domestic industries	610	1,370	1,528	1,383	1,047	1,125
Financial [2]	190	444	448	368	279	331
Nonfinancial.	420	926	1,080	1,015	768	794
Utilities.	26	30	54	49	40	54
Manufacturing	144	247	305	279	176	136
Wholesale trade.	59	92	104	102	75	88
Retail trade	61	123	133	122	78	91
Transportation and warehousing	15	29	42	30	11	6
Information.	-16	81	92	90	85	109
Other nonfinancial [3]	132	324	350	343	303	310
Rest of the world	146	239	257	348	377	312

[1] Inventory valuation adjustment and capital consumption adjustment. [2] Consists of finance and insurance and bank and other holding companies. [3] Consists of agriculture, forestry, fishing, and hunting; mining; construction; real estate and rental and leasing; professional, scientific, and technical services; administrative and waste management services; educational services; health care and social assistance; arts, entertainment, and recreation; accommodation and food services; and other services, except government.

Source: U.S. Bureau of Economic Analysis, *Survey of Current Business*, April 2010. See also <http://www.bea.gov/national/nipaweb/Index.asp>.

Table 787. Corporate Profits Before Taxes by Industry: 2000 to 2008

[In billions of dollars (772 represents $772,000,000,000). Profits are without inventory valuation and capital consumption adjustments. Minus sign (–) indicates loss. See headnote, Table 785]

Industry	2002 NAICS code [1]	2000	2005	2006	2007	2008
Corporate profits before tax	**(X)**	**772**	**1,640**	**1,823**	**1,774**	**1,463**
Domestic industries	(X)	627	1,401	1,566	1,427	1,086
Agriculture, forestry, fishing, and hunting.	11	1	5	5	6	4
Mining	21	15	43	57	57	68
Utilities.	221	26	31	54	49	40
Construction	23	42	85	85	72	61
Manufacturing	31-33	154	260	327	296	192
Wholesale trade.	42	62	101	114	118	86
Retail trade	44–45	63	128	136	128	84
Transportation and warehousing	48–49	15	30	42	31	10
Information.	51	-16	81	93	91	86
Finance and insurance	52	102	282	286	232	142
Real estate and rental and leasing	53	10	29	25	18	5
Professional, scientific, and technical services	54	2	42	52	55	52
Management of companies and enterprises [2]	551111, 551112	88	161	162	136	137
Admin/support waste mgt/remediation services	56	9	24	21	29	24
Educational services	61	2	5	5	5	5
Health care and social assistance.	62	26	54	58	60	56
Arts, entertainment, and recreation.	71	2	7	7	6	5
Accommodation and food services	72	15	22	24	22	17
Other services, except public administration	81	9	12	13	14	10
Rest of the world [3]	(X)	146	239	257	348	377

X Not applicable. [1] Based on North American Industry Classification System, 2002; see text, this section. [2] Consists of bank and other holding companies. [3] Consists of receipts by all U.S. residents, including both corporations and persons, of dividends from foreign corporations, and, for U.S. corporations, their share of reinvested earnings of their incorporated foreign affiliates, and earnings of unincorporated foreign affiliates, net of corresponding payments.

Source: U.S. Bureau of Economic Analysis, *Survey of Current Business*, April 2010. See also <http://www.bea.gov/national/nipaweb/Index.asp>.

516 Business Enterprise

Table 788. Manufacturing, Mining, and Trade Corporations—Profits and Stockholders' Equity by Industry: 2008 and 2009

[Averages of quarterly figures at annual rates. Manufacturing data exclude estimates for corporations with less than $250,000 in assets at time of sample selection. Mining, wholesale and retail trade data excludes estimates for corporations with less than $50 million in assets at time of sample selection. Based on sample; see source for discussion of methodology. Based on North American Industry Classification System (NAICS), 2002; see text, this section. Minus sign (−) indicates loss]

Industry	2002 NAICS code	Ratio of profits after taxes to stockholders' equity (percent)		Profits after taxes per dollar of sales (cents)		Ratio of stockholders' equity to debt	
		2008	2009	2008	2009	2008	2009
Manufacturing	**31–33**	**8.3**	**10.1**	**3.8**	**5.5**	**1.8**	**1.5**
Nondurable manufacturing	(X)	14.5	16.0	6.1	8.5	1.7	1.4
Food	311	14.7	17.8	4.9	5.9	1.3	1.1
Beverage and tobacco products	312	21.0	21.7	12.5	17.4	1.3	1.6
Textile mills and textile product mills	313, 314	−11.4	1.3	−4.5	0.5	1.9	2.1
Apparel and leather products	315, 316	11.8	13.3	4.8	5.3	1.9	1.9
Paper	322	−11.2	10.8	−2.4	3.3	0.8	0.6
Printing and related support activities	323	−6.6	1.8	−0.5	0.3	0.6	0.4
Petroleum and coal products	324	17.3	10.7	4.4	5.3	2.9	2.4
Chemicals	325	15.1	19.4	11.6	16.4	1.7	1.3
Plastics and rubber products	326	3.9	9.3	1.1	2.9	0.9	0.9
Durable manufacturing	(X)	1.9	3.7	3.7	2.1	1.9	1.7
Wood products	321	−3.8	−4.1	−1.7	−1.9	1.3	1.0
Nonmetallic mineral products	327	−0.7	−8.6	−0.6	−5.7	1.1	1.0
Primary metals	331	−7.4	−4.6	−4.0	−3.0	2.1	1.8
Fabricated metal products	332	17.6	8.9	5.9	3.6	1.5	1.4
Machinery	333	14.6	8.5	6.5	4.7	1.8	1.8
Computer and electronic products	334	2.0	7.6	2.2	6.9	3.3	3.0
Electrical equipment, appliances, & components	335	14.5	9.4	11.6	8.5	3.5	3.6
Transportation equipment	336	−77.3	−76.4	−6.1	−4.3	0.8	0.4
Furniture and related products	337	2.5	2.6	0.7	0.8	1.1	1.0
Miscellaneous manufacturing	339	11.0	11.7	8.0	9.4	2.0	2.0
All mining	**21**	**7.5**	**−1.7**	**7.5**	**−2.8**	**1.9**	**1.8**
All wholesale trade	**42**	**6.8**	**5.4**	**0.9**	**0.8**	**1.3**	**1.4**
Durable goods	421	3.7	1.5	0.7	0.3	1.5	1.5
Nondurable goods	422	12.6	12.1	1.0	1.2	1.1	1.2
All retail trade	**44–45**	**7.3**	**12.0**	**1.4**	**2.4**	**1.4**	**1.5**
Food and beverage stores	445	8.8	6.9	1.1	0.8	1.1	1.1
Clothing and general merchandise stores	448, 452	9.1	14.6	2.3	3.5	1.0	1.7
All other retail trade	(X)	5.0	10.7	0.9	2.1	1.3	1.4

X Not applicable.

Source: U.S. Census Bureau, *Quarterly Financial Report for Manufacturing, Mining, and Trade Corporations.*

Table 789. Value Added, Employment, and Capital Expenditures of Nonbank U.S. Multinational Companies: 1999 to 2007

[Value added and capital expenditures in billions of dollars (2,481 represents $2,481,000,000,000); employees in thousands. See headnote, Table 790. MNC = Multinational company. MOFA = Majority-owned foreign affiliate. Minus sign (−) indicates decrease]

Item	1999	2000	2003	2004	2005	2006	2007	Percent change at annual rates 1999 to 2006	Percent change at annual rates 2006 to 2007
VALUE ADDED									
MNCs worldwide:									
Parents and MOFAs	2,481	2,748	2,656	2,992	3,233	3,538	3,706	5.2	4.8
Parents	1,914	2,141	1,958	2,173	2,321	2,537	2,589	4.1	2.0
MOFAs	566	607	698	818	911	1,001	1,118	8.5	11.6
EMPLOYEES									
MNCs worldwide:									
Parents and all affiliates	32,227	33,598	30,762	31,245	32,094	32,766	33,741	0.2	3.0
Parents and MOFAs	30,773	32,057	29,347	29,843	30,573	31,233	32,020	0.2	2.5
Parents	23,007	23,885	21,105	21,177	21,472	21,616	22,003	−0.9	1.8
Affiliates, total	9,220	9,713	9,658	10,068	10,622	11,150	11,738	2.8	5.3
MOFAs	7,766	8,171	8,242	8,667	9,101	9,617	10,017	3.1	4.2
Other	1,454	1,542	1,415	1,402	1,520	1,533	1,721	0.8	12.3
CAPITAL EXPENDITURES									
MNCs worldwide:									
Parents and all affiliates	550	(NA)	(NA)	487	(NA)	(NA)	(NA)	(NA)	(NA)
Parents and MOFAs	519	548	444	463	507	600	652	2.1	8.5
Parents	406	438	335	339	377	445	482	1.3	8.4
Affiliates, total	144	(NA)	(NA)	147	(NA)	(NA)	(NA)	(NA)	(NA)
MOFAs	113	111	110	123	130	155	169	4.6	9.0
Other	31	(NA)	(NA)	24	(NA)	(NA)	(NA)	(NA)	(NA)

NA Not available.

Source: U.S. Bureau of Economic Analysis, *Survey of Current Business*, August 2009. See also <http: www.bea.gov /international/index.htm>.

U.S. Census Bureau, Statistical Abstract of the United States: 2011

Table 790. U.S. Multinational Companies—Selected Characteristics: 2007

[Preliminary. In billions of dollars (18,521 represents $18,521,000,000,000), except as indicated. Consists of nonbank U.S. parent companies and their nonbank foreign affiliates. U.S. parent comprises the domestic operations of a multinational and is a U.S. person that owns or controls, directly or indirectly, 10 percent or more of the voting securities of an incorporated foreign business enterprise, or an equivalent interest in an unincorporated foreign business enterprise. A U.S. person can be an incorporated business enterprise. A majority-owned foreign affiliate (MOFA) is a foreign business enterprise in which a U.S. parent company owns or controls more than 50 percent of the voting securities]

| Industry [1] | 2002 NAICS code | U.S. parents | | | | MOFAs | | |
		Total assets	Capital expenditures	Value added	Employ-ment (1,000)	Capital expenditures	Value added	Employ-ment (1,000)
All industries	(X)	**19,965**	**482.5**	**2,589**	**22,003**	**169.1**	**1,118**	**10,017**
Mining	21	357	39.5	62	182	43.0	152	187
Utilities	22	590	32.2	84	226	3.6	11	45
Manufacturing [2]	31-33	5,240	173.4	1,065	7,292	62.8	510	4,683
Petroleum and coal products	324	721	26.3	154	264	4.6	70	38
Chemicals	325	962	22.2	180	907	12.6	108	615
Transportation equipment	336	1,376	63.8	204	1,751	13.2	71	973
Wholesale trade	42	841	28.2	138	1,074	7.7	152	776
Information [2]	51	1,513	70.2	317	1,919	6.9	45	355
Broadcasting (except Internet) and telecommunications	515, 517	1,115	60.0	218	1,158	4.6	12	82
Finance (except depository institutions) and insurance	52 exc. 521, 522	9,497	40.9	229	1,129	10.7	52	318
Professional, scientific, and technical services	54	382	8.7	154	1,216	4.4	61	622
Other industries [2]	(X)	1,545	89.3	540	8,965	30.0	134	3,032
Retail trade	44–45	423	28.8	207	4,145	6.5	47	975

X Not applicable. [1] Represents 2000 North American Industry Classification System-based industry of U.S. parent or industry of foreign affiliate. [2] Includes other industries, not shown separately.

Source: U.S. Bureau of Economic Analysis, *Survey of Current Business*, August 2009 and unpublished data.

Table 791. U.S. Multinational Companies—Value Added: 2000 and 2007

[In billions of dollars (2,748 represents $2,748,000,000,000). See headnote, Table 790. Data are by industry of U.S. parent. Based on the North American Industry Classification System (NAICS), 2002; see text, this section]

| Industry | 2002 NAICS code | U.S. multinationals | | U.S. parents | | Majority-owned foreign affiliates | |
		2000	2007	2000	2007	2000	2007
All industries	(X)	**2,748**	**3,706**	**2,141**	**2,589**	**607**	**1,118**
Mining	21	39	215	28	62	11	152
Utilities	22	86	95	81	84	5	11
Manufacturing [1]	31–33	1,410	1,575	995	1,065	415	510
Petroleum and coal products	324	232	224	112	154	120	70
Chemicals	325	212	288	141	180	71	108
Transportation equipment	336	271	276	209	204	62	71
Wholesale trade	42	133	290	99	138	34	152
Information [1]	51	325	362	302	317	22	45
Broadcasting (except Internet) and telecommunications	515, 517	(NA)	230	(NA)	218	(NA)	12
Finance (except depository institutions) and insurance	52 exc. 521, 522	181	281	157	229	24	52
Professional, scientific, and technical services	54	141	215	101	154	41	61
Other industries [1]	(X)	433	675	379	540	54	134
Retail trade	44–45	166	255	149	207	18	47

NA Not available. X Not applicable. [1] Includes other industries not shown separately.

Source: U.S. Bureau of Economic Analysis, *Survey of Current Business*, November 2003 and August 2009.

Table 792. U.S. Majority-Owned Foreign Affiliates—Value Added by Industry of Affiliate and Country: 2007

[Preliminary. In millions of dollars (1,117,585 represents $1,117,585,000,000). See headnote, Table 790. Numbers in parentheses represent North American Industry Classification System 2002 codes; see text, this section]

| Country | All industries [1] | Mining (21) | Manufacturing (31-33) | | | Wholesale trade (42) | Professional, scientific, and technical services (54) |
			Total [1]	Chemicals (325)	Transportation equipment (336)		
All countries [2]	**1,117,585**	**152,285**	**509,962**	**107,519**	**71,208**	**151,964**	**61,383**
United Kingdom	172,310	13,501	63,615	8,369	9,142	25,979	14,014
Canada	116,180	19,241	50,880	5,835	11,014	10,602	5,695
Germany	86,649	1,209	58,240	6,528	11,881	9,602	4,335
France	56,196	53	28,960	5,871	3,004	8,160	2,900
Ireland	53,842	181	29,443	16,416	91	5,485	1,967
Australia	44,088	7,163	16,409	2,204	1,678	6,441	3,412
Japan	38,954	4	11,631	4,802	518	7,429	5,442
Italy	32,508	13	20,878	4,129	1,160	4,469	1,793
Mexico	31,327	2,388	18,254	4,029	5,390	1,881	865
Netherlands	29,515	881	17,698	4,423	1,790	3,877	2,080

[1] Includes other industries, not shown separately. [2] Includes other countries, not shown separately.

Source: U.S. Bureau of Economic Analysis, *Survey of Current Business*, August 2009.

518 Business Enterprise

This section presents statistics on scientific, engineering, and technological resources, with emphasis on patterns of research and development (R&D) funding and on scientific, engineering, and technical personnel; education; and employment.

The National Science Foundation (NSF) gathers data chiefly through recurring surveys. Current NSF publications containing data on funds for research and development and on scientific and engineering personnel include detailed statistical tables; info briefs; and annual, biennial, and special reports, see <http://www.nsf.gov/statistics>. Titles or the areas of coverage of these reports include the following: *Science and Engineering Indicators; National Patterns of R&D Resources; Women, Minorities, and Persons with Disabilities in Science and Engineering, Federal Funds for Research and Development; Federal R&D Funding by Budget Function; Federal Support to Universities, Colleges, and Selected Nonprofit Institutions; Research and Development in Industry;* R&D expenditures and graduate enrollment and support in academic science and engineering; and characteristics of doctoral scientists and engineers and of recent graduates in the United States. Statistical surveys in these areas pose problems of concept and definition and the data should therefore be regarded as broad estimates rather than precise, quantitative statements. See sources for methodological and technical details.

The National Science Board's biennial *Science and Engineering Indicators* at <http://www.nsf.gov/statistics/seind10/> contains data and analysis of international and domestic science and technology, including measures of inputs and outputs.

Research and development outlays— NSF defines research as "systematic study directed toward fuller scientific knowledge of the subject studied" and development as "the systematic use of scientific knowledge directed toward the production of useful materials, devices, systems, or methods, including design and development of prototypes and processes."

National coverage of R&D expenditures is developed primarily from periodic surveys in four principal economic sectors: (1) *Government*, made up primarily of federal executive agencies; (2) *Industry*, consisting of manufacturing and nonmanufacturing firms and the federally funded research and development centers (FFRDCs) they administer; (3) *Universities and colleges*, composed of universities, colleges, and their affiliated institutions, agricultural experiment stations, and associated schools of agriculture and of medicine, and FFRDCs administered by educational institutions; and (4) *Other nonprofit institutions*, consisting of such organizations as private philanthropic foundations, nonprofit research institutes, voluntary health agencies, and FFRDCs administered by nonprofit organizations.

The R&D funds reported consist of current operating costs, including planning and administration costs, except as otherwise noted. They exclude funds for routine testing, mapping and surveying, collection of general purpose data, dissemination of scientific information, and training of scientific personnel.

Scientists, engineers, and technicians—Scientists and engineers are defined as persons engaged in scientific and engineering work at a level requiring a knowledge of sciences equivalent at least to that acquired through completion of a 4-year college course. Technicians are defined as persons engaged in technical work at a level requiring knowledge acquired through a technical institute, junior college, or other type of training less extensive than 4-year college training. Craftsmen and skilled workers are excluded.

U.S. Census Bureau, Statistical Abstract of the United States: 2011

Table 793. Research and Development (R&D) Expenditures by Source and Objective: 1980 to 2008

[In millions of dollars (63,224 represents $63,224,000,000), except as indicated]

Year	Total	Sources of funds					Objective (percent of total)			Character of work		
		Federal government	Industry	Universities\ colleges	Non-profit	Nonfederal government [1]	Defense related [2]	Space related [3]	Other	Basic research	Applied research	Development
1980.....	63,224	29,986	30,929	920	871	519	24.3	5.3	70.4	8,745	13,714	40,765
1981.....	72,292	33,739	35,948	1,058	967	581	24.4	5.2	70.4	9,658	16,329	46,305
1982.....	80,748	37,133	40,692	1,207	1,095	621	26.1	4.9	69.0	10,651	18,218	51,879
1983.....	89,950	41,451	45,264	1,357	1,220	658	27.7	4.2	68.1	11,880	20,298	57,771
1984.....	102,244	46,470	52,187	1,514	1,351	721	28.7	3.0	68.3	13,332	22,451	66,461
1985.....	114,671	52,641	57,962	1,743	1,491	834	29.9	3.1	67.0	14,748	25,401	74,522
1986.....	120,249	54,622	60,991	2,019	1,647	969	31.4	3.0	65.6	17,154	27,240	75,855
1987.....	126,360	58,609	62,576	2,262	1,849	1,065	31.7	3.2	65.1	18,481	27,951	79,929
1988.....	133,881	60,131	67,977	2,527	2,081	1,165	30.2	3.5	66.3	19,787	29,528	84,567
1989.....	141,891	60,466	74,966	2,852	2,333	1,274	27.6	3.9	68.5	21,891	32,277	87,723
1990.....	151,993	61,610	83,208	3,187	2,589	1,399	25.1	4.3	70.6	23,020	34,897	94,067
1991.....	160,876	60,783	92,300	3,458	2,852	1,483	22.4	4.5	73.1	27,140	38,631	95,105
1992.....	165,350	60,915	96,229	3,569	3,113	1,525	21.6	4.3	74.1	27,604	37,936	99,811
1993.....	165,730	60,528	96,549	3,709	3,388	1,557	21.2	4.4	74.4	28,743	37,283	99,705
1994.....	169,207	60,777	99,204	3,938	3,665	1,623	19.7	4.5	75.8	29,651	36,618	102,938
1995.....	183,625	62,969	110,871	4,110	3,925	1,751	18.6	4.5	76.9	29,610	40,936	113,079
1996.....	197,346	63,394	123,417	4,436	4,239	1,861	17.6	4.1	78.3	32,799	43,170	121,377
1997.....	212,152	64,574	136,228	4,838	4,590	1,922	16.7	4.1	79.2	36,921	46,554	128,677
1998.....	226,402	66,383	147,846	5,163	5,038	1,972	15.8	3.8	80.4	35,341	46,348	144,712
1999.....	244,922	67,055	164,660	5,619	5,489	2,098	14.6	3.2	82.2	38,887	52,006	154,029
2000.....	267,298	66,417	186,136	6,232	6,267	2,247	13.4	2.3	84.3	42,667	56,826	167,805
2001.....	277,366	72,836	188,440	6,827	6,867	2,397	14.0	2.4	83.6	47,617	64,583	165,167
2002.....	276,022	77,710	180,711	7,344	7,700	2,557	15.6	2.4	82.0	51,174	50,814	174,034
2003.....	288,324	83,618	186,174	7,650	8,140	2,742	16.5	2.3	81.2	54,375	61,563	172,386
2004.....	299,201	88,766	191,376	7,937	8,239	2,883	17.2	2.1	80.7	55,868	70,095	173,238
2005.....	322,104	93,817	207,826	8,579	8,960	2,922	17.1	2.0	80.9	59,462	70,215	192,427
2006.....	347,048	98,038	227,254	9,307	9,429	3,021	16.8	1.8	81.4	61,038	76,428	209,582
2007.....	372,535	101,772	246,927	9,993	10,593	3,249	16.2	1.5	82.3	65,988	83,214	223,333
2008 [4] ...	397,629	103,709	267,847	10,600	12,020	3,453	15.3	1.4	83.3	69,146	88,591	239,891

[1] Nonfederal R&D expenditures to university and college performers. [2] R&D spending by the Department of Defense, including space activities, and a portion of the Department of Energy funds. [3] For the National Aeronautics and Space Administration only. [4] Preliminary.

Source: U.S. National Science Foundation, *National Patterns of R&D Resources*, NSF 10-314, 2010. See also <www.nsf.gov/statistics/nsf10314/>.

Table 794. National Research and Development (R&D) Expenditures as a Percent of Gross Domestic Product by Country: 1990 to 2008

Year	United States	Japan [1]	Germany [2]	France	United Kingdom	Italy	Canada	South Korea	OECD total [3]	Russia [4]	China [5]
1990....	2.65	2.81	2.61	2.32	2.14	1.25	1.51	(NA)	2.25	2.03	(NA)
1995....	2.51	2.71	2.19	2.29	1.94	0.97	1.70	2.27	2.06	0.85	0.57
2000....	2.75	3.04	2.45	2.15	1.85	1.05	1.91	2.30	2.21	1.05	0.90
2001....	2.76	3.12	2.46	2.20	1.82	1.09	2.09	2.47	2.25	1.18	0.95
2002....	2.66	3.17	2.49	2.23	1.82	1.13	2.04	2.40	2.22	1.25	1.07
2003....	2.66	3.20	2.52	2.17	1.78	1.11	2.03	2.49	2.22	1.28	1.13
2004....	2.54	3.17	2.49	2.15	1.69	1.10	2.08	2.68	2.17	1.15	1.23
2005....	2.57	3.32	2.49	2.10	1.73	1.09	2.05	2.79	2.21	1.07	1.34
2006....	2.61	3.41	2.53	2.10	1.76	1.13	1.97	3.01	2.24	1.07	1.42
2007....	2.66	3.44	2.53	2.04	1.82	1.18	1.90	3.21	2.28	1.12	1.44
2008....	2.77	(NA)	(NA)	2.02	1.88	1.18	1.84	(NA)	(NA)	1.04	(NA)

NA Not available. [1] Data on Japanese research and development after 1995 may not be consistent with data in earlier years because of changes in methodology. [2] Data for 1990 are for West Germany only. [3] Organization for Economic Cooperation and Development. [4] As of May 16, 2007 Russia is an OECD accession candidate country. [5] As of 2007 China is an OECD enhanced engagement country.

Source: Organization for Economic Cooperation and Development, *Main Science and Technology Indicators*, 2009/2nd edition (copyright). See also <http://www.oecd.org/>.

Table 795. Performance Sector of Research and Development (R&D) Expenditures: 2000 to 2008

[In millions of dollars (267,298 represents $267,298,000,000). For calendar year. FFRDCs are federally funded research and development centers]

Year	Total	Federal government	Industry Total	Industry Funded by Federal government	Industry Funded by Industry[1]	Industry FFRDCs	Univ. & colleges Total	Univ. Funded by Federal government	Univ. Funded by Non-federal government[2]	Univ. Funded by Industry	Univ. Funded by Universities & colleges	Univ. Funded by Non-profits	University & college FFRDCs[3]	Other nonprofit Total	Nonprofit Funded by Federal government	Nonprofit Funded by Industry	Nonprofit Funded by Non-profits
RESEARCH AND DEVELOPMENT TOTAL																	
2000	267,298	17,917	199,961	17,117	182,844	2,001	30,705	17,727	2,247	2,174	6,232	2,326	5,742	9,506	4,447	1,118	3,941
2004	299,201	22,844	208,301	20,266	188,035	2,465	43,128	27,173	2,883	2,190	7,937	2,946	7,659	12,140	5,695	1,151	5,294
2005	322,104	24,470	226,159	21,909	204,250	2,601	45,197	28,260	2,922	2,323	8,579	3,113	7,817	13,032	5,932	1,253	5,846
2006	347,048	25,556	247,669	24,304	223,355	3,122	46,983	28,815	3,021	2,515	9,307	3,325	7,306	13,469	5,992	1,374	6,103
2007	372,535	25,858	269,267	26,585	242,632	5,165	49,021	29,328	3,249	2,748	9,993	3,703	5,567	14,341	5,954	1,497	6,890
2008[4]	397,629	27,000	289,105	25,795	263,310	6,307	51,163	30,177	3,453	2,908	10,600	4,024	4,717	15,606	5,982	1,629	7,995
BASIC RESEARCH																	
2000	42,667	3,765	7,040	925	6,115	547	22,917	13,966	1,550	1,499	4,298	1,604	2,874	4,908	2,099	621	2,188
2004	55,868	4,697	7,835	1,072	6,763	175	31,994	21,154	1,958	1,488	5,392	2,002	3,730	6,366	2,788	639	2,939
2005	59,462	4,770	8,667	1,108	7,559	135	34,044	22,198	2,043	1,625	6,000	2,177	3,820	6,844	2,903	696	3,246
2006	61,038	4,716	8,384	1,444	6,940	652	35,700	22,736	2,155	1,795	6,641	2,373	3,344	7,001	2,849	763	3,389
2007	65,988	4,600	11,268	2,780	8,488	2,253	37,323	23,070	2,351	1,989	7,233	2,680	1,724	7,466	2,809	831	3,826
2008[4]	69,146	4,734	11,907	2,697	9,209	2,390	38,822	23,508	2,503	2,108	7,685	2,918	1,634	8,229	2,885	904	4,439
APPLIED RESEARCH																	
2000	56,826	6,105	39,176	2,682	36,494	269	6,617	3,315	572	553	1,585	592	1,329	3,113	1,831	283	999
2004	70,095	7,455	45,432	4,775	40,657	1,509	9,335	5,140	759	576	2,087	774	1,920	4,081	2,448	292	1,342
2005	70,215	7,557	45,284	5,289	39,995	1,492	9,333	5,158	721	573	2,114	768	1,912	4,231	2,432	318	1,482
2006	76,428	7,435	51,173	6,140	45,033	1,331	9,557	5,290	710	590	2,186	781	1,874	4,487	2,592	348	1,547
2007	83,214	7,303	57,570	8,945	48,625	1,163	10,003	5,542	736	623	2,264	839	1,354	4,722	2,596	379	1,746
2008[4]	88,591	7,573	61,437	8,679	52,758	1,993	10,556	5,824	779	656	2,390	908	713	4,985	2,546	413	2,026
DEVELOPMENT																	
2000	167,805	8,047	153,745	13,510	140,235	1,185	1,172	447	125	121	348	130	1,539	1,485	517	214	754
2004	173,238	10,692	155,034	14,419	140,615	801	1,799	878	167	126	458	170	2,008	1,692	459	220	1,013
2005	192,427	12,142	172,208	15,512	156,696	974	1,820	904	158	126	464	169	2,085	1,957	598	240	1,119
2006	209,582	13,406	188,112	16,720	171,392	1,139	1,726	789	156	130	480	171	2,088	1,981	551	263	1,168
2007	223,333	13,955	200,429	14,860	185,569	1,738	1,695	716	162	137	497	184	2,488	2,154	549	286	1,318
2008[4]	239,891	14,693	215,761	14,419	201,342	1,949	1,785	746	171	144	525	199	2,370	2,392	551	312	1,530

[1] Includes all nonfederal sources of industry R&D expenditures. [2] Includes all nonfederal sources. [3] Includes all R&D expenditures of FFRDCs administered by academic institutions and funded by the federal government. [4] Preliminary.

Source: National Science Foundation, data derived from: *Research and Development in Industry*, annual; *Academic Research and Development Expenditures*, annual; and *Federal Funds For Research and Development*, annual. See also <http://www.nsf.gov/statistics/nsf10314/>.

Science and Technology **521**

Table 796. Federal Obligations for Research in Current and Constant (2000) Dollars by Field of Science: 2005 to 2009

[In millions of dollars (53,738 represents $53,738,000,000). For years ending September 30. Excludes R&D plant]

Field of science	Current dollars				Constant (2000) dollars [1]			
	2005	2007	2008, prel.	2009, prel.	2005	2007	2008, prel.	2009, prel.
Research, total	53,738	54,094	55,097	54,801	47,682	45,248	45,213	44,081
Basic	27,140	26,866	27,559	28,536	24,082	22,472	22,615	22,954
Applied	26,598	27,228	27,538	26,265	23,601	22,775	22,598	21,127
Life sciences	28,128	29,464	29,675	29,299	24,958	24,645	24,351	23,567
Psychology	1,892	1,838	1,861	1,853	1,679	1,537	1,527	1,490
Physical sciences	5,494	5,136	5,249	5,593	4,875	4,296	4,308	4,499
Environmental sciences	3,503	3,171	3,315	3,352	3,108	2,652	2,720	2,697
Mathematics and computer sciences	2,983	2,946	3,285	3,333	2,647	2,464	2,696	2,681
Engineering	8,553	8,990	9,353	8,907	7,589	7,520	7,676	7,164
Social sciences	1,097	1,147	1,071	1,123	973	960	879	903
Other sciences, n.e.c. [2]	2,089	1,403	1,287	1,341	1,854	1,174	1,056	1,079

[1] Based on gross domestic product implicit price deflator. [2] Not elsewhere classified.

Source: U.S. National Science Foundation, *Federal Funds for Research and Development*, NSF 09-320, 2009. See also <http://www.nsf.gov/statistics/fedfunds/>.

Table 797. Federal Budget Authority for Research and Development (R&D) in Current and Constant (2000) Dollars by Selected Budget Functions: 2005 to 2009

[In millions of dollars (126,601 represents $126,601,000,000). For year ending September 30. Excludes R&D plant. Represents budget authority. Functions shown are those for which $1 billion or more was authorized since 2001]

Function	Current dollars				Constant (2000) dollars [1]			
	2005	2007	2008	2009, prel. [2]	2005	2007	2008	2009, prel. [2]
Total [3]	126,601	138,087	140,113	157,213	112,335	115,506	114,979	126,458
National defense	74,047	82,272	84,713	85,595	65,703	68,818	69,517	68,851
Health	28,824	29,461	29,063	39,826	25,576	24,643	23,849	32,035
Space research and technology	7,300	9,024	8,323	8,629	6,477	7,548	6,830	6,941
Energy	1,296	1,893	1,896	2,921	1,150	1,583	1,556	2,350
General science	6,570	7,809	8,234	11,634	5,830	6,532	6,757	9,358
Natural resources and environment	2,168	1,936	2,106	2,293	1,924	1,619	1,728	1,844
Transportation	1,847	1,361	1,394	1,562	1,639	1,138	1,144	1,256
Agriculture	1,820	1,857	1,864	1,927	1,615	1,553	1,530	1,550

[1] Based on gross domestic product implicit price deflator. [2] Includes ARRA (American Recovery and Reinvestment Act) funds. [3] Includes other functions, not shown separately.

Source: U.S. National Science Foundation, *Federal R&D Funding by Budget Function*, NSF 10-317, 2010. See also <http://www.nsf.gov/statistics/nsf10317/>.

Table 798. Federal Research and Development (R&D) by Federal Agency: Fiscal Year (FY) 2008 and 2009

[In millions of dollars (144,456 represents $144,456,000,000). For years ending September 30. R&D refers to actual research and development activities as well as R&D facilities. R&D facilities (also known as R&D plants) includes construction, repair, or alteration of physical plant used in the conduct of R&D. Based on Office of Management and Budget data]

Federal agency	2008	2009	Federal agency	2008	2009
Total research and development	144,456	145,605			
Defense R&D	85,129	85,309	Department of Veterans Affairs	886	943
Nondefense R&D	59,326	60,297	Department of Homeland Security	995	1,096
			Department of Transportation	875	925
Department of Defense	81,166	81,484	Department of Interior	683	702
Science and technology	13,045	13,967	U.S. Geological Survey	586	615
All other Department of Defense R&D	68,122	67,517	Environmental Protection Agency	548	563
Health and Human Services	29,250	31,058	Department of Education	313	312
National Institute of Health	28,532	29,752	Smithsonian	194	216
All other Health and Human Services R&D	718	1,306	International Assistance Programs	152	152
Department of Energy	9,769	10,301	Department of Housing and Urban Development	50	58
Atomic Energy Defense	3,963	3,825	Department of State	103	103
Office of Science	3,807	4,372	Nuclear Regulatory Commission	71	101
Energy R&D	1,999	2,104	Department of Justice	81	94
NASA	11,183	8,788	Social Security Administration	27	35
National Science Foundation	4,506	4,767	U.S. Postal Service	43	43
Department of Agriculture	2,332	2,437	Tennessee Valley Authority	20	18
Department of Commerce	1,188	1,389	Army Corps of Engineers	11	11
National Oceanic and Atmospheric Administration	633	785	Telecommunications Development Agency	5	6
National Institute of Standards and Technology	498	553	Department of Labor	4	4

Source: American Association for the Advancement of Science (AAAS), AAAS Report XXXIV *Research and Development FY 2010*, annual (copyright). See also <http://www.aaas.org/spp/rd/rdreport2010/>.

Table 799. Research and Development (R&D) Funds in R&D-Performing Manufacturing and Nonmanufacturing Companies by Industry: 2005 to 2007

Industry	NAICS [1] code	Total R&D funds as a percent of net sales			Company R&D funds as a percent of net sales		
		2005	2006	2007	2005	2006	2007
All industries, total	(X)	**3.7**	**3.7**	**3.8**	**3.3**	**3.4**	**3.5**
All manufacturing industries, total	(X)	**4.0**	**4.0**	**4.1**	**3.6**	**3.6**	**3.7**
Food	311	0.7	0.7	(D)	0.7	0.7	0.7
Paper, printing, and support activities	322, 323	(D)	(D)	(D)	1.5	1.2	1.3
Petroleum and coal products	324	(D)	0.3	(D)	0.4	0.3	0.3
Chemicals	325	6.9	7.6	(D)	6.9	7.5	7.9
Plastic and rubber products	326	2.0	2.0	(D)	1.9	1.9	1.5
Nonmetallic mineral products	327	1.8	2.1	1.8	1.8	1.9	1.8
Primary metals	331	0.6	0.5	0.6	0.5	0.5	0.6
Fabricated metal products	332	0.8	1.4	1.7	0.8	1.4	1.6
Machinery	333	3.7	3.6	3.7	3.6	3.6	3.7
Navigational, measuring, electromedical, and control instruments	3345	12.8	13.1	10.2	7.0	7.5	6.1
Electrical equipment, appliances, and components	335	2.4	2.6	3.1	2.3	2.5	3.0
Transportation equipment	336	(D)	(D)	(D)	3.0	2.9	3.1
Motor vehicles, trailers, and parts	3361–3363	(D)	(D)	(D)	2.5	2.4	2.4
Aerospace products and parts	3364	6.6	6.7	7.0	4.8	4.9	5.1
All nonmanufacturing industries, total	(X)	**3.2**	**3.2**	**3.4**	**2.9**	**2.9**	**3.0**
Information	51	5.4	5.3	(D)	5.3	5.2	5.1
Internet service and data processing providers	518	9.1	9.6	(D)	8.7	9.4	9.6
Software publishing	5112	21.9	(D)	(D)	21.9	19.9	19.6
Professional, scientific, and technical services	54	12.2	9.5	11.7	10.0	7.6	9.5
Architectural, engineering, and related services	5413	9.4	14.4	12.0	4.9	10.7	8.1
Computer systems design and related services	5415	10.0	5.3	7.0	9.6	4.9	6.6
Scientific R&D services	5417	35.6	35.1	42.0	27.4	24.2	30.0

D Figure withheld to avoid disclosure of information pertaining to a specific organization or individual. X Not applicable.
[1] North American Industry Classification System 1997 (NAICS); see text, Section 15.
Source: U.S. National Science Foundation, *Research and Development in Industry*, annual. See also <www.nsf.gov /statistics/>.

Table 800. Funds for Performance of Industrial Research and Development (R&D) by Source of Funds and Selected Industries: 2004 to 2007

[In millions of dollars (208,301 represents $208,301,000,000). For calendar years. Covers basic research, applied research, and development. Based on the Survey of Industry Research and Development.

Industry	NAICS [1] code	2004	2005	2006	2007
CURRENT DOLLARS					
Total funds [2]	(X)	**208,301**	**226,159**	**247,669**	**269,267**
Company and other funds	(X)	188,035	204,250	223,365	242,682
Federal funds	(X)	20,266	21,900	24,004	26,585
Petroleum and coal products	324	1,603	(D)	1,432	(D)
Chemicals and allied products	325	(D)	42,995	46,329	(D)
Pharmaceuticals and medicines	3254	31,477	34,839	38,901	(D)
Machinery	333	6,579	8,531	9,848	9,865
Computer and electronic products	334	48,296	(D)	56,773	50,599
Navigational, measuring, electromedical, and control instruments	3345	15,214	15,204	18,300	20,438
Electrical equipment, appliances, and components	335	2,664	2,424	2,281	(D)
Motor vehicles, trailers, and parts	3361–3363	15,677	(D)	(D)	(D)
Aerospace products and parts	3364	13,086	15,055	16,367	18,436
Information	51	22,593	23,836	26,883	(D)
Professional, scientific, and technical services	54	28,709	32,021	38,049	40,533
Computer systems design and related services	5415	11,575	13,592	14,841	14,407
Scientific R&D services	5417	11,355	12,299	14,525	16,849
CONSTANT (2000) DOLLARS [3]					
Total funds [2]	(X)	**190,351**	**200,088**	**212,271**	**224,732**
Company and other funds	(X)	171,831	180,704	191,440	202,544
Federal funds	(X)	18,520	19,383	20,830	22,188
Petroleum and coal products	324	1,465	(D)	1,227	(D)
Chemicals	325	(D)	38,039	39,707	(D)
Pharmaceuticals and medicines	3254	28,765	30,823	33,341	(D)
Machinery	333	6,012	7,548	8,440	8,233
Computer and electronic products	334	44,134	(D)	48,659	48,907
Navigational, measuring, electromedical, and control instruments	3345	13,903	13,451	15,684	17,058
Electrical equipment, appliances, and components	335	2,434	2,145	1,955	(D)
Motor vehicles, trailers, and parts	3361–3363	14,326	(D)	(D)	(D)
Aerospace products and parts	3364	11,958	13,319	14,028	15,387
Information	51	20,646	21,088	23,041	(D)
Professional, scientific, and technical services	54	26,235	28,330	32,611	33,829
Computer systems design and related services	5415	10,578	12,025	12,720	12,024
Scientific R&D services	5417	10,376	10,881	12,449	14,062

D Figure withheld to avoid disclosure of information pertaining to a specific organization or individual. X Not applicable.
[1] 1997 North American Industry Classification System; see text, Section 15. [2] Includes other industries not shown separately.
[3] Based on gross domestic product implicit price deflator.
Source: U.S. National Science Foundation, *Research and Development in Industry*, annual. See also <www.nsf.gov /statistics/>.

Science and Technology 523

Table 801. Academic and Industrial Research and Development (R&D) Performed by State: 2007

[In millions of dollars (49,021 represents 49,021,000,000). For definition of Research and Development, see text, this section]

State	Academic R&D (mil. dol.)	Academic R&D per $1,000 of state GDP	Industry-performed R&D (mil. dol.)	Industry R&D per $1,000 of state GDP	State	Academic R&D (mil. dol.)	Academic R&D per $1,000 of state GDP	Industry-performed R&D (mil. dol.)	Industry R&D per $1,000 of state GDP
U.S.[1]	49,021	3.55	269,267	19.50	MO	941	4.11	2,736	11.95
AL	655	3.98	1,771	[2]10.76	MT	179	5.22	134	3.91
AK	160	3.56	58	1.29	NE	365	4.54	489	6.09
AZ	783	3.18	3,846	15.64	NV	192	1.48	567	4.38
AR	240	2.52	339	3.56	NH	307	5.31	1,814	[3]31.37
CA	6,734	3.74	64,187	35.62					
					NJ	865	1.88	17,892	38.79
CO	873	3.70	5,223	22.15	NM	410	5.45	568	7.55
CT	691	3.26	9,444	44.49	NY	3,964	3.59	10,916	9.88
DE	126	2.05	1,472	23.92	NC	1,885	4.83	6,829	17.49
DC	333	3.60	379	4.10	ND	169	5.93	126	4.42
FL	1,558	2.10	4,569	6.16					
					OH	1,807	3.91	7,265	15.71
GA	1,389	3.55	2,788	7.13	OK	299	2.19	527	3.86
HI	274	4.42	218	3.52	OR	575	3.63	3,629	[3]22.92
ID	114	2.19	726	13.93	PA	2,438	4.57	10,387	19.48
IL	1,867	3.02	11,362	18.40	RI	230	4.93	411	8.80
IN	894	3.59	4,939	19.82					
					SC	569	3.75	1,426	9.40
IA	587	4.52	1,202	9.25	SD	82	2.33	132	3.75
KS	376	3.21	1,304	11.15	TN	761	3.10	1,638	6.68
KY	503	3.31	890	5.85	TX	3,417	2.98	13,889	12.09
LA	604	2.91	373	[2]1.80	UT	415	3.93	1,764	16.71
ME	137	2.85	265	5.52					
					VT	115	4.67	413	16.77
MD	2,542	9.61	3,665	13.86	VA	971	2.53	4,840	12.60
MA	2,172	6.17	19,488	55.34	WA	981	3.16	12,687	40.89
MI	1,510	3.97	15,736	41.42	WV	167	2.89	233	4.03
MN	637	2.52	6,636	26.28	WI	1,067	4.57	3,411	14.61
MS	411	4.69	279	3.18	WY	80	2.54	37	[2]1.17

[1] National totals for calendar year 2007. Includes $3.3 billion of industrial R&D expenditures that year that could not be allocated to specific states. [2] Estimated, more than 50 percent of the industrial R&D value is imputed due to raking of state data. [3] More than 50 percent of the industrial R&D value is imputed.

Source: National Science Foundation, *National Patterns of R&D Resources*, NSF-10-314, 2010. See also <http://www.nsf.gov/statistics/nsf10314/>.

Table 802. Research and Development (R&D) Expenditures in Science and Engineering at Universities and Colleges in Current and Constant (2000) Dollars: 2000 to 2008

[In millions of dollars (30,084 represents $30,084,000,000). Totals may not add due to rounding]

Characteristic	Current dollars				Constant (2000) dollars [1]			
	2000	2005	2007	2008	2000	2005	2007	2008
Total	30,084	45,799	49,554	51,909	30,084	40,638	41,395	42,354
Basic research [2]	22,547	34,368	37,842	39,408	22,547	30,495	31,611	32,154
Applied R&D [2]	7,537	11,432	11,712	12,501	7,537	10,144	9,784	10,200
Source of funds:								
Federal government	17,548	29,209	30,458	31,231	17,548	25,917	25,443	25,482
State and local government	2,200	2,940	3,143	3,418	2,200	2,609	2,626	2,789
Institutions' own funds	5,925	8,266	9,748	10,435	5,925	7,335	8,143	8,514
Industry	2,156	2,291	2,680	2,870	2,156	2,033	2,239	2,342
Other	2,255	3,093	3,525	3,954	2,255	2,744	2,945	3,226
Fields:								
Physical sciences	2,713	3,704	3,859	3,933	2,713	3,287	3,224	3,209
Environmental sciences	1,766	2,555	2,724	2,800	1,766	2,267	2,275	2,285
Mathematical sciences	342	495	573	621	342	439	479	507
Computer sciences	877	1,406	1,421	1,468	877	1,248	1,187	1,198
Life sciences	17,471	27,605	29,838	31,215	17,471	24,494	24,925	25,469
Psychology	517	826	872	929	517	733	728	758
Social sciences	1,300	1,685	1,798	1,940	1,300	1,495	1,502	1,583
Other sciences	543	778	943	1046	543	690	788	853
Engineering	4,557	6,746	7,525	7,957	4,557	5,986	6,286	6,492

[1] Based on gross domestic product implicit price deflator (updated March 2009). [2] Basic research and applied R&D statistics were re-estimated for FY1998 and forward. These data are not directly comparable to those from earlier years.

Source: U.S. National Science Foundation, *Survey of Research and Development Expenditures at Universities and Colleges*, annual. See also <http://www.nsf.gov/statistics/srvyrdexpenditures/>.

Table 803. Federal Research and Development (R&D) Obligations to Selected Universities and Colleges: 2006 and 2007

[In millions of dollars (24,991.8 represents $24,991,800,000). For years ending September 30. For the top 40 institutions receiving federal R&D funds in 2007. Awards to the administrative offices of university systems are excluded from totals for individual institutions because that allocation of funds is unknown, but those awards are included in "total all institutions"]

Major institution ranked by total 2007 federal R&D obligations	2006	2007	Major institution ranked by total 2007 federal R&D obligations	2006	2007
Total, all institutions [1]	24,991.8	24,998.0	Cornell University	299.1	326.1
Johns Hopkins University	1,153.2	1,054.9	Pennsylvania State University	291.8	320.8
University of Washington	612.1	608.0	Case Western Reserve University	277.9	278.9
University of Michigan	516.2	501.5	University Southern California	265.5	260.3
University of Pennsylvania	497.5	498.5	University of Rochester	252.3	255.2
University of California—Los Angeles	477.6	480.0	Northwestern University	222.2	254.2
Duke University	472.5	470.7	University of Chicago	219.8	248.6
University of California—San Francisco	441.9	433.4	Emory University	228.1	247.9
University of California—San Diego	401.2	432.7	University of California—Davis	236.4	243.1
Harvard University	420.8	429.3	University of Alabama—Birmingham	235.4	235.1
University of Pittsburgh	425.4	425.9	Baylor College of Medicine	236.5	227.9
Columbia University—City of NY	467.8	425.7	University of California—Irvine	161.3	219.6
Stanford University	455.9	424.0	Ohio State University	205.9	217.2
Washington University	410.7	407.8	University of California—Berkeley	228.6	214.2
Yale University	361.7	387.3	University of Arizona	200.7	212.0
Massachusetts Institute of Technology	357.1	380.8	University of Illinois—Urbana		
University of Minnesota	331.2	370.7	Champaign	184.6	210.5
University of Wisconsin—Madison	373.7	369.2	Boston University	204.7	208.5
University of North Carolina at Chapel Hill	343.4	353.5	University of Iowa	193.0	208.4
University of Colorado	340.1	330.0	The Scripps Research Institute	217.5	199.0
Vanderbilt University	306.4	329.6	University of Virginia	176.3	198.4

[1] Includes other institutions, not shown separately.

Source: U.S. National Science Foundation, *Federal S&E Support to Universities and Colleges and Nonprofit Institutions*, NSF 09-313, 2009. See also <http://www.nsf.gov/statistics/fedsupport/>.

Table 804. Graduate Science/Engineering Students in Doctorate-Granting Colleges by Characteristic and Field: 1990 to 2007

[In thousands (409.4 represents 409,400). As of fall. Includes outlying areas]

Field of science or engineering	Total			Characteristic							
				Female			Foreign		Part-time		
	1990	2000	2007	1990	2000	2007	2000	2007	1990	2000	2007
Total, all surveyed fields	409.4	443.5	561.4	155.5	201.8	272.3	123.3	151.2	130.8	123.6	151.9
Science/engineering	360.6	374.8	469.5	117.9	150.3	201.7	118.0	143.5	107.5	99.3	119.4
Engineering, total	101.0	98.8	124.4	13.8	19.7	28.6	46.3	57.2	36.7	28.2	33.5
Sciences, total [1]	259.6	275.9	345.1	104.2	130.7	173.1	71.7	86.3	70.8	71.1	85.9
Physical sciences	32.9	29.6	35.8	7.7	8.8	11.6	11.5	14.2	3.9	3.5	3.4
Environmental	13.1	13.0	13.4	3.8	5.3	6.3	2.6	2.6	3.2	2.8	2.8
Mathematical sciences	18.1	14.4	19.2	5.6	5.2	6.9	5.9	7.3	4.7	3.0	4.2
Computer sciences	20.0	10.0	40.0	8.0	11.7	10.8	19.7	20.6	14.1	16.7	15.7
Agricultural sciences	11.0	11.3	12.5	3.2	4.8	6.1	2.4	2.8	2.0	2.4	3.3
Biological sciences	46.7	53.1	67.5	21.4	27.8	38.0	11.6	16.2	7.2	7.6	9.2
Psychology	38.5	40.3	48.1	25.5	29.0	36.1	2.1	2.7	12.0	10.8	13.8
Social sciences	70.0	73.9	91.3	30.1	38.1	48.6	15.8	17.7	23.8	24.3	28.9
Health fields, total	48.8	68.8	91.8	37.6	51.5	70.5	5.4	7.7	23.3	24.3	32.5

[1] For 2007, includes other sciences, not shown separately.

Source: U.S. National Science Foundation, *Survey of Graduate Science Engineering Students and Postdoctorates,* annual. See also <http://www.nsf.gov/statistics/gradpostdoc>.

Table 805. Non-U.S. Citizens Awarded Doctorates in Science and Engineering by Visa Type and Country of Citizenship: 1998 to 2007

[For description of science and engineering fields, see Table 809]

Visa and country	1998	1999	2000	2001	2002	2003	2004	2005	2006	2007
All non-U.S. citizens	9,736	8,894	9,070	9,217	8,867	9,483	10,158	11,519	12,777	13,545
Canada	286	289	294	306	316	324	380	368	362	397
Mexico	176	172	208	206	182	218	181	206	182	182
Brazil	164	164	131	142	126	108	136	156	139	122
France	76	79	83	85	92	87	92	113	124	129
Germany	210	183	229	220	197	192	185	182	176	162
China	2,503	2,234	2,379	2,407	2,402	2,503	2,878	3,482	4,279	4,395
Japan	155	158	201	149	157	201	186	211	222	235
Korea	822	760	754	865	856	958	1,057	1,179	1,220	1,137
Taiwan	910	746	676	539	469	440	394	444	431	462
Thailand	122	134	153	237	264	314	272	252	199	224
India	1,134	915	834	818	681	773	864	1,110	1,525	1,956
Iran	93	92	80	100	59	68	60	136	148	156
Turkey	172	192	275	307	345	374	344	342	357	436
Science	6,678	6,299	6,269	6,129	5,945	6,305	6,605	7,481	8,209	8,676
Engineering	3,058	2,595	2,801	3,088	2,922	3,178	3,553	4,038	4,568	4,869
Permanent visa	1,991	1,654	1,409	1,271	1,173	1,099	1,003	1,113	1,252	1,222
Temporary visa	7,745	7,240	7,661	7,946	7,694	8,384	9,155	10,406	11,525	12,323

Source: U.S. National Science Foundation, *Science and Engineering Doctorate Awards*, NSF 09-311, 2009. See also <http://www.nsf.gov/statistics/nsf09311/>.

Table 806. Science and Engineering (S&E) Degrees Awarded by Degree Level and Sex of Recipient: 1990 to 2008

[For a description of science and engineering degree categories, see source, Appendix B, <http://www.nsf.gov/statistics/nsf07307/content.cfm?pub_id=3634&id=4>]

Academic year ending	Bachelor's degree Total S&E	Men	Women	Percent women	Master's degree Total S&E	Men	Women	Percent women	Doctoral degree Total S&E	Men	Women	Percent women
1990.....	329,094	189,082	140,012	42.5	77,788	51,230	26,558	34.1	22,867	16,498	6,369	27.9
2000.....	400,059	198,060	201,999	50.5	95,194	53,616	41,578	43.7	25,912	16,518	9,394	36.2
2005.....	499,133	246,356	252,777	50.6	121,180	67,067	54,113	44.7	27,941	17,404	10,537	37.7
2006.....	507,175	250,017	257,158	50.7	120,733	66,042	54,691	45.3	29,836	18,367	11,469	38.4
2007.....	514,509	253,934	260,575	50.6	119,685	64,695	54,990	45.9	31,768	19,509	12,259	38.5
2008.....	524,420	258,781	265,639	50.7	125,803	68,352	57,451	45.7	32,804	19,845	12,959	39.5

Source: U.S. National Science Foundation, *Science and Engineering Degrees: 1966–2006*, NSF-08-321, 2008, and unpublished data. See also <http://www.nsf.gov/statistics/degrees/>.

Table 807. Science and Engineering (S&E) Degrees as Share of Higher Education Degrees Conferred by State: 2007

[S&E degrees include physical, computer, agricultural, biological, earth, atmospheric, ocean, and social sciences; psychology; mathematics; and engineering]

State	S&E degrees conferred [1]	All higher education degrees [1]	S&E higher education degrees (percent)	State	S&E degrees conferred [1]	All higher education degrees [1]	S&E higher education degrees (percent)	State	S&E degrees conferred [1]	All higher education degrees [1]	S&E higher education degrees (percent)
U.S....	685,914	2,138,003	32.1								
AL.....	9,920	32,207	30.8	KY.....	7,218	27,152	26.6	ND.....	1,731	7,042	24.6
AK.....	750	2,261	33.2	LA.....	7,767	28,224	27.5	OH.....	24,410	82,584	29.6
AZ.....	13,463	74,778	18.0	ME.....	2,733	8,532	32.0	OK.....	7,442	24,244	30.7
AR.....	3,440	14,835	23.2	MD.....	16,932	41,936	40.4	OR.....	8,387	23,655	35.5
CA.....	89,947	204,838	43.9	MA.....	26,363	78,421	33.6	PA.....	35,314	113,396	31.1
CO.....	13,729	35,981	38.2	MI.....	23,006	75,304	30.6	RI.....	3,875	12,724	30.5
CT.....	9,052	27,781	32.6	MN.....	12,571	45,085	27.9	SC.....	7,649	25,841	29.6
DE.....	2,325	7,642	30.4	MS.....	4,294	16,438	26.1	SD.....	2,204	6,386	34.5
DC.....	8,287	20,489	40.4	MO.....	13,515	53,828	25.1	TN.....	9,272	36,576	25.3
FL.....	27,510	91,561	30.0	MT.....	2,450	6,509	37.6	TX.....	40,387	130,830	30.9
GA.....	16,566	49,495	33.5	NE.....	4,115	15,765	26.1	UT.....	8,787	23,993	36.6
HI.....	2,511	7,330	34.3	NV.....	2,267	7,279	31.1	VT.....	2,880	7,042	40.9
ID.....	2,859	9,614	29.7	NH.....	3,725	11,207	33.2	VA.....	20,679	53,981	38.3
IL.....	30,055	101,537	29.6	NJ.....	16,851	46,676	36.1	WA.....	14,206	37,541	37.4
IN.....	14,442	51,564	28.0	NM.....	3,302	9,748	33.9	WV.....	3,239	13,707	23.6
IA.....	7,893	25,698	30.7	NY.....	55,360	185,736	29.8	WI.....	13,691	41,842	32.7
KS.....	6,552	23,943	27.4	NC.....	19,022	55,071	34.5	WY.....	1,149	2,154	53.3

[1] Includes bachelor's, master's, and doctorate degrees.

Source: National Science Foundation, *Science and Engineering Indicators, 2010*, January 2010. See also <http://www.nsf.gov/statistics/seind10/>.

Table 808. Doctorates Conferred by Characteristics of Recipients: 2000 and 2008

[In percent, except as indicated. Based on the Survey of Earned Doctorate Awards. For description of methodology, see source]

Characteristic	2000, total [1]	2008 All fields [1]	Engineering	Physical sciences [2]	Earth sciences	Mathematics	Computer sciences	Biological sciences [3]	Agricultural	Social sciences [4]	Psychology
Total conferred (number)....	41,365	48,802	7,862	4,081	862	1,400	1,786	7,793	1,090	4,592	3,361
Male.....	56.0	53.8	78.4	72.5	63.5	69.0	77.6	49.5	57.8	51.0	29.7
Female.....	43.8	46.1	21.5	27.5	36.4	30.9	22.4	50.4	42.2	49.0	70.3
RACE/ETHNICITY [5]											
Total conferred (number)....	29,936	30,791	2,948	2,132	533	667	695	5,135	602	2,889	2,886
White [6].....	79.2	75.4	70.9	78.4	88.0	78.3	72.7	74.4	81.2	74.8	75.0
Black [6].....	5.8	6.6	3.8	3.0	1.7	4.5	3.7	3.7	4.7	6.9	5.7
Asian/Pacific [6].....	7.6	8.3	16.7	10.1	4.7	9.0	16.8	11.7	6.1	7.4	5.1
Indian/Alaskan [6].....	0.6	0.4	0.2	0.1	0.4	0.0	0.0	0.4	0.8	0.3	0.5
Hispanic.....	4.4	5.7	4.5	4.7	3.2	4.3	2.9	6.1	4.0	5.9	9.6
Other/unknown [7].....	2.4	3.6	3.9	3.7	2.1	3.9	3.9	3.7	3.2	4.7	4.1

[1] Includes other fields, not shown separately. [2] Astronomy, physics, and chemistry. [3] Biochemistry, botany, microbiology, physiology, zoology, and related fields. [4] Anthropology, sociology, political science, economics, international relations and related fields. [5] Excludes those with temporary visas. [6] Non-Hispanic. [7] 2008 data includes Native Hawaiians and Other Pacific Islanders, respondents choosing multiple races (excluding those selecting an Hispanic ethnicity), and respondents with unknown race/ethnicity.

Source: U.S. National Science Foundation, *Science and Engineering Doctorate Awards*, NSF-10-308, annual. See also <http://www.nsf.gov/statistics/doctorates/>.

Table 809. Doctorates Awarded by Field of Study and Year of Doctorate: 2000 to 2008

Field of Study	2000	2003	2004	2005	2006	2007	2008
Total, all fields	**41,366**	**40,758**	**42,118**	**43,381**	**45,615**	**48,112**	**48,802**
Science and engineering, total	**25,966**	**25,282**	**26,274**	**27,986**	**29,863**	**31,800**	**32,827**
Engineering, total	5,323	5,281	5,777	6,427	7,185	7,744	7,862
Aeronautical/astronautical	214	200	201	219	238	267	265
Chemical	619	568	638	774	799	807	872
Civil	480	552	547	622	655	701	712
Electrical	1,330	1,238	1,389	1,547	1,786	1,968	1,887
Industrial/manufacturing	176	214	217	221	234	280	281
Materials/metallurgical	404	438	474	493	583	648	636
Mechanical	807	752	754	892	1,044	1,072	1,079
Other	1,293	1,319	1,557	1,659	1,846	2,001	2,130
Science, total	20,643	20,001	20,497	21,559	22,678	24,056	24,965
Biological/agricultural sciences	6,890	6,756	6,987	7,404	7,682	8,313	8,883
Agricultural sciences	1,037	1,060	1,045	1,038	1,033	1,134	1,090
Biological sciences	5,853	5,696	5,942	6,366	6,649	7,179	7,793
Earth, atmospheric, and ocean sciences, total	694	683	686	714	757	878	862
Atmospheric	143	139	126	145	146	167	186
Earth/ocean sciences	551	544	560	569	611	711	676
Mathematical/computer sciences, total	1,911	1,860	2,024	2,334	2,778	3,049	3,186
Computer sciences	861	867	948	1,129	1,453	1,656	1,786
Mathematics	1,050	993	1,076	1,205	1,325	1,393	1,400
Physical sciences, total	3,378	3,287	3,335	3,643	3,927	4,102	4,081
Astronomy	185	167	165	186	197	223	248
Chemistry	1,989	2,040	1,986	2,126	2,362	2,325	2,247
Physics	1,204	1,080	1,184	1,331	1,368	1,554	1,586
Psychology	3,615	3,276	3,326	3,323	3,258	3,292	3,361
Social sciences, total	4,155	4,139	4,139	4,141	4,276	4,422	4,592
Economics	1,086	1,050	1,069	1,183	1,143	1,180	1,202
Political science	986	1,025	947	990	1,000	1,038	1,017
Sociology	617	597	580	536	578	576	601
Other social sciences	1,466	1,467	1,543	1,432	1,555	1,628	1,772
Non-science and engineering, total	**15,400**	**15,476**	**15,844**	**15,395**	**15,752**	**16,312**	**15,975**
Education	6,437	6,643	6,633	6,225	6,120	6,444	6,578
Health	1,591	1,633	1,719	1,784	1,905	2,129	2,094
Humanities	5,213	5,020	5,012	4,950	5,125	4,893	4,503
Professional/other/unknown	2,159	2,180	2,480	2,436	2,602	2,846	2,800

Source: U.S. National Science Foundation, *Science and Engineering Doctorate Awards*, annual. See also <http://www.nsf.gov/statistics/doctorates/>.

Table 810. Scientists and Engineers by Selected Demographic Characteristics: 2006

[In thousands (22,630 represents 22,630,000). Scientists and engineers refer to all persons who have received a bachelor's degree or higher in science and engineering (S&E), or S&E related field, plus persons holding a non-S&E degree or higher, employed in S&E or S&E related field]

Characteristic	Both sexes	Female	Male	Characteristic	Both sexes	Female	Male
All scientists and engineers	**22,630**	**10,230**	**12,400**	Highest degree attained:			
				Bachelor's	13,228	6,223	7,005
Age:				Master's	6,411	3,039	3,373
29 or younger	2,732	1,542	1,190	Doctorate	1,018	308	710
30-39 years	5,302	2,596	2,705	Professional	1,973	660	1,312
40-49 years	5,849	2,699	3,150				
50-59 years	5,400	2,303	3,097	Citizenship status:			
60-69 years	2,497	835	1,662	U.S. citizen, native	19,131	8,743	10,387
70 or older	851	254	596	U.S. citizen, naturalized	2,373	1,062	1,311
				Non-U.S. citizen, permanent			
Race/ethnicity:				resident	835	330	505
American Indian/Alaska Native	102	51	50	Non-U.S. citizen, temporary			
Asian	2,255	994	1,261	resident	291	95	196
Black	1,258	738	520				
Native Hawaiian/Other Pacific				Marital status:			
Islander	85	33	53	Married	16,100	6,655	9,445
White	17,420	7,670	9,751	Living in marriage-like			
Multiple race	316	156	159	relationship	892	482	410
Hispanic, any race	1,193	588	605	Widowed	356	245	111
				Separated	243	131	111
Children in the home?				Divorced	1,518	887	631
Yes	10,966	5,015	5,951	Never married	3,521	1,829	1,692
No	11,664	5,215	6,449				

Source: National Science Foundation, Division of Science Resource Statistics, Scientists and Engineers Statistical Data System (SESTAT), <http://www.nsf.gov/statistics/sestat/>, accessed March 2008.

Table 811. Civilian Employment of Scientists, Engineers, and Related Occupations by Occupation and Industry: 2008

[In thousands (293.0 represents 293,000). Standard Occupational Classification system categorize workers in 1 of 801 detailed occupations. Industry classifications correspond to 2007 North American Industry Classification (NAICS) industrial groups. For definition of scientists and engineers, see text this section and Table 802]

Occupation	Total employ-ment, all workers	Wage and salary workers						Self employ-ed [2]
		Mining (NAICS 21) [1]	Con-struction (NAICS 23)	Manu-facturing (NAICS 31–33)	Informa-tion (NAICS 51)	Profes-sional, scientific and technical services (NAICS 54)	Govern-ment (NAICS 99)	
Computer and information systems managers....................	293.0	0.4	0.7	27.5	33.6	73.5	19.0	9.6
Engineering managers	184.0	1.8	5.0	74.9	5.2	59.2	15.7	1.1
Natural science managers..............	44.6	0.2	(NA)	6.9	(NA)	16.2	13.8	(NA)
Computer and mathematical scientists	3,540.4	7.6	(NA)	272.7	422.3	1,121.5	247.4	155.3
Computer specialists..................	3,424.3	7.1	9.8	266.1	415.7	1,096.0	228.2	154.6
Mathematical science occupations	116.1	(NA)	0.2	6.6	6.5	25.5	19.2	0.8
Surveyors, cartographers, and photogrammetrists..................	70.0	0.8	3.8	0.1	(NA)	50.4	10.1	1.8
Engineers [3]	1,571.9	26.1	47.7	559.6	41.5	468.8	190.3	41.8
Aerospace engineers.................	71.6	(NA)	(NA)	38.4	(NA)	17.8	9.5	2.4
Civil engineers.....................	278.4	0.8	31.1	2.5	0.8	141.0	75.4	12.0
Computer and hardware engineers......	74.7	(NA)	(NA)	32.1	3.5	24.5	4.7	1.0
Electrical and electronics engineers	301.5	0.3	4.8	105.3	32.4	76.9	26.4	4.8
Industrial engineers [4].................	240.4	2.4	6.4	155.2	2.5	33.5	6.1	1.8
Mechanical engineers................	238.7	1.3	3.1	121.2	0.2	69.7	12.3	5.5
Drafters, engineering, and mapping technicians [5]	826.2	5.3	26.0	229.8	22.4	315.0	108.5	15.1
Engineering technicians	497.3	3.9	5.1	169.5	18.9	124.3	91.7	3.6
Surveying and mapping technicians	77.0	0.6	(NA)	0.1	0.8	53.0	11.7	4.3
Life, physical, and social science occupations......................	1,460.8	20.1	(NA)	155.6	28.6	376.0	314.5	97.8
Life scientists......................	279.4	(NA)	(NA)	36.5	0.2	71.9	67.9	9.9
Physical scientists..................	275.5	9.4	(NA)	43.3	1.2	100.8	76.3	6.3
Social scientists and related occupations.......................	549.4	0.3	2.6	22.3	26.7	111.0	82.6	78.2
Life, physical, and social science technicians......................	356.5	10.3	0.6	53.4	0.5	92.4	87.7	3.4

NA Not available. [1] Includes oil and gas extraction. [2] Includes secondary jobs and unpaid private household employment. [3] Includes kinds of engineers not shown separately. [4] Includes health and safety engineers. [5] Includes other drafters, technicians, and mapping technicians.

Source: U.S. Bureau of Labor Statistics, National Employment Matrix, December 2009 (data collected biennially). See also <http://www.bls.gov/emp/empoils.htm>.

Table 812. Employment and Earnings in Science and Engineering (S&E) Occupations by Industry: 2006

[As of May 2006. Industries ordered by Science and Engineering share of total employment]

Industry	2002 NAICS code [1]	Workers employed (number)		S&E workers as percent of all employed	Mean earnings in S&E occupations (dollars)
		All occupations	S&E occupations		
Computer systems design and related services ...	5415	1,254,320	609,590	48.6	75,040
Software publishers..........................	5112	240,130	116,260	48.4	79,120
Scientific research and development services	5417	586,220	247,310	42.2	81,220
Computer and peripheral equipment manufacturing.........................	3341	199,370	79,040	39.6	90,710
Internet service providers and Web search portals..................................	5181	119,560	46,120	38.6	69,720
Data processing, hosting, and related services....	5182	264,320	83,470	31.6	70,460
Internet publishing and broadcasting............	5161	33,220	9,810	29.5	69,800
Architectural, engineering, and related services ...	5413	1,361,280	397,910	29.2	74,570
Communications equipment manufacturing	3342	144,200	39,270	27.2	83,400
Navigational, measuring, electromedical, and control instruments manufacturing	3345	435,510	117,950	27.1	82,190
Aerospace product and parts manufacturing......	3364	464,990	114,620	24.6	80,410
Securities and commodity exchanges...........	5232	8,850	1,930	21.8	74,000
Semiconductor and other electronic component manufacturing..........................	3344	452,060	93,940	20.8	83,490
Pharmaceutical and medicine manufacturing	3254	288,270	55,640	19.3	73,710
Other telecommunications....................	5179	5,300	980	18.5	73,820

[1] North American Industry Classification System (NAICS), 2002; see text Section 15.

Source: U.S. National Science Foundation, *Science and Engineering Indicators 2008*, January 2008. See also <http://nsf.gov /statistics/seind08/>.

Table 813. Employment, Mean Earnings, and Growth in Science and Engineering (S&E) Occupations: 2004 to 2008

[Minus sign (–) represents a decrease. Based on data derived from Bureau of Labor Statistics' Occupational Employment Survey (OES)]

Occupation	Employment					Mean earnings	
	2004, total	2008, total	Total growth	Total growth (percent)	Average annual growth rate (percent)	2008 annual earnings (dol.)	Average annual growth rate (percent)
All occupations	128,127,360	135,185,230	7,057,870	5.5	1.3	42,270	3.4
STEM [1]	7,160,770	7,852,710	691,940	9.7	2.3	74,950	3.6
S&E.	5,085,740	5,781,460	695,720	13.7	3.3	76,680	3.5
Engineers	1,487,810	1,626,330	138,520	9.3	2.3	84,120	3.7
Mathematical and computer scientists	2,566,170	2,972,940	406,770	15.9	3.7	74,420	3.4
Life scientists.	275,500	319,520	44,020	16.0	3.8	75,130	3.7
Physical scientists	273,360	301,500	28,140	10.3	2.5	76,710	3.8
Social scientists.	482,900	561,160	78,260	16.2	3.8	67,980	2.9
Technicians, programmers, and S&E managers	2,075,020	2,071,260	–3,760	–0.2	(Z)	70,170	3.6
S&E related	6,914,070	7,737,490	823,420	11.9	2.9	(NA)	(NA)
Healthcare practitioners and technicians.	6,769,900	7,569,040	799,140	11.8	2.8	(NA)	(NA)
Other S&E related	144,170	168,450	24,280	16.8	4.0	(NA)	(NA)
Not STEM or S&E related	114,052,530	119,595,020	5,542,490	4.9	1.2	(NA)	(NA)

NA Not available. Z Less than 0.05. [1] STEM = science, technology, engineering, and mathematics.
Source: National Science Foundation, *Employment in Science and Engineering Occupations Reached 5.8 Million in 2008*, NSF 10-315, 2010. See also <http://www.nsf.gov/statistics/infbrief/nsf10315/>.

Table 814. Research and Development (R&D) Scientists and Engineers—Employment and Cost by Industry: 2005 to 2007

[In thousands (1,104.5 represents 1,104,500). Data are estimates on full-time-equivalent (FTE) basis. Based on the Survey of Industrial Research and Development. The Business R&D and Innovation Survey replaces the Survey of Industrial Research and Development for data available as of December 2010; see <http://www.nsf.gov/statistics/srvyindustry/about/brdis/>]

Industry	NAICS [1] code	Employed scientists and engineers [2] (1,000)			Cost per scientist or engineer, constant (2000) dollars [3,4] ($1,000)		
		2005	2006	2007	2005	2006	2007
All industries [5]	(X)	1,104.5	1,116.6	1,133.0	192.4	201.6	211.9
Chemicals	325	118.3	123.2	134.0	328.5	330.1	356.4
Machinery	333	61.1	62.3	61.9	125.2	141.1	144.4
Electrical equipment, appliances, and components . . .	335	18.7	16.9	15.8	(D)	(D)	(D)
Motor vehicles, trailers, and parts	3361–3363	42.0	42.0	(NA)	(D)	(D)	(D)
Aerospace products and parts	3364	39.7	39.5	40.2	335.4	359.4	380.5
Software publishing.	5112	93.4	46.5	(NA)	162.5	174.0	175.4
Architectural, engineering, and related services	5413	35.8	41.2	48.5	129.3	146.4	113.9
Computer systems design and related services	5415	82.4	93.1	88.1	158.5	157.2	160.3
Scientific R&D services	5417	43.7	44.3	50.4	264.0	298.2	308.7

D Withheld to avoid disclosure. NA Not available. X Not applicable. [1] North American Industry Classification System 2002 (NAICS); see text, Section 15. [2] The mean number of full-time equivalent (R&D) scientists and engineers employed in January of the year shown and the following January. [3] Based on gross domestic product implicit price deflator. [4] Represents the arithmetic mean of the numbers of R&D scientists and engineers reported in each industry for January in 2 consecutive years divided into total R&D expenditures in each industry. [5] Includes other industries not shown separately.
Source: National Science Foundation, *Research and Development in Industry*, NSF 10-319, 2010, and unpublished data. See also <http://www.nsf.gov/statistics/industry/>.

U.S. Census Bureau, Statistical Abstract of the United States: 2011

Table 815. Federal Outlays for General Science, Space, and Other Technology, 1970 to 2009, and Projections, 2010 and 2011

[In billions of dollars (4.5 represents $4,500,000,000). For fiscal years ending in year shown; see text, Section 8]

Year	Current dollars			Constant (2005) dollars		
	Total	General science/basic research	Space and other technologies	Total	General science/basic research	Space and other technologies
1970.............	4.5	0.9	3.6	23.5	4.9	18.5
1980.............	5.8	1.4	4.5	14.6	3.5	11.2
1985.............	8.6	2.0	6.6	16.7	3.9	12.8
1990.............	14.4	2.8	11.6	24.5	4.8	19.7
1995 [1]	16.7	4.1	12.6	22.0	5.4	16.6
2000.............	18.6	6.2	12.4	22.1	7.3	14.7
2001.............	19.7	6.5	13.2	22.7	7.5	15.2
2002.............	20.7	7.2	13.5	23.1	8.1	15.1
2003.............	20.8	7.9	12.9	22.6	8.6	14.0
2004.............	23.0	8.3	14.6	23.9	8.7	15.2
2005.............	23.6	8.8	14.8	23.6	8.8	14.8
2006.............	23.5	9.0	14.5	22.7	8.7	14.0
2007.............	25.5	10.2	15.3	23.9	9.6	14.3
2008.............	27.7	10.5	17.2	25.3	9.6	15.7
2009.............	29.4	11.0	18.4	26.3	9.8	16.5
2010, proj........	32.8	14.3	18.6	29.4	12.8	16.6
2011, proj.........	31.4	14.4	17.1	27.8	12.7	15.1

[1] Due to the effects of the Credit Reform Act of 1990 on the measurement and classification of federal credit activities, the discretionary outlays for years prior to 1995 are not strictly comparable to those for 1995 and after. However, the discretionary outlays shown for 1995 are no more than $1 billion higher than they would have been if measured on the same (pre-credit reform) basis as the 1990 outlays.

Source: U.S. Office of Management and Budget, *Budget of the United States Government: Historical Tables, Fiscal Year 2011*, annual. See also <http://www.gpoaccess.gov/usbudget/fy11/hist.html>.

Table 816. Worldwide Space Launch Events: 2000 to 2009

[In millions of dollars (2,729 represents $2,729,000,000)]

Country	Non-commercial launches				Commercial launches				Launch revenues for commercial launch events (mil. dol.)			
	2000	2005	2008	2009	2000	2005	2008	2009	2000	2005	2008	2009
Total.............	**50**	**37**	**41**	**54**	**35**	**18**	**28**	**24**	**2,729**	**1,190**	**1,971**	**2,410**
United States........	21	11	9	20	7	1	6	4	370	70	215	298
Russia	23	18	15	19	13	8	11	10	671	350	700	742
Europe.............	–	–	1	2	12	5	5	5	1,433	490	581	1,020
China [1].............	5	5	11	5	–	–	–	1	(X)	(X)	(X)	70
India...............	–	1	3	2	–	–	–	–	(X)	(X)	(X)	(X)
Japan..............	1	2	1	3	–	–	–	–	(X)	(X)	(X)	(X)
Iran	–	–	1	1	–	–	–	–	(X)	(X)	(X)	(X)
Korea, North	–	–	–	1	–	–	–	–	(X)	(X)	(X)	(X)
Korea, South	–	–	–	1	–	–	–	–	(X)	(X)	(X)	(X)
Multinational	–	–	–	–	3	4	6	4	255	280	475	280

– Represents zero. X Not applicable. [1] See footnote 4, Table 1331.

Source: Federal Aviation Administration, *Commercial Space Transportation: 2009 Year in Review*, January 2010, and prior years. See also <http://www.faa.gov/about/office_org/headquarters_offices/ast/reports_studies/year_review>.

Table 817. U.S. and Worldwide Commercial Space Industry Revenue by Type: 2000 to 2008

[In billions of dollars (19.3 represents $19,300,000,000). For calendar years]

Industry	United States				World			
	2000	2005	2007	2008	2000	2005	2007	2008
Revenue, total	**19.3**	**30.8**	**(NA)**	**(NA)**	**64.2**	**88.8**	**121.7**	**144.4**
Satellite manufacturing [1]	6.0	3.2	4.8	3.1	11.5	7.8	11.6	10.5
Launch industry.................	2.7	1.5	1.0	1.1	5.3	3.0	3.2	3.9
Satellite services [2]................	10.6	26.1	(NA)	(NA)	28.9	52.8	72.6	84.0
Ground equipment manufacturing [3]...	(NA)	(NA)	(NA)	(NA)	18.5	25.2	34.3	46.0

NA Not available. [1] Includes revenues from the construction and sale of satellites to both commercial and government. [2] Includes revenues derived from transponder leasing and subscription/retail services such as direct-to-home television, satellite radio, remote sensing, and satellite mobile and data communications. [3] Includes revenues from the manufacture of gateways and satellite control stations, satellite news-gathering trucks, very small aperture terminals, direct-to-home television equipment and mobile satellite phones.

Source: Satellite Industry Association/Futron Corporation, *State of the Satellite Industry Report*, June 2009 (copyright). See also <http://sia.org/IndustryReport.htm>.

Section 17
Agriculture

This section presents statistics on farms and farm operators; land use; farm income, expenditures, and debt; farm output, productivity, and marketings; foreign trade in agricultural products; specific crops; and livestock, poultry, and their products.

The principal sources are the reports issued by the National Agricultural Statistics Service (NASS) and the Economic Research Service (ERS) of the U.S. Department of Agriculture (USDA). The information from the 2007 Census of Agriculture is available in printed form in the Volume 1, Geographic Area Series; in electronic format on CD-ROM; and on the Internet at <http://www.agcensus.usda .gov/Publications/2007/Full_Report /index.asp>. The Department of Agriculture publishes annually *Agricultural Statistics*, a general reference book on agricultural production, supplies, consumption, facilities, costs, and returns. The ERS publishes data on farm assets, debt, and income on the Internet at <http://www.ers.usda.gov /briefing/farmincome/>. Sources of current data on agricultural exports and imports include *Outlook for U.S. Agricultural Trade,* published by the ERS; the ERS Internet site at <http://www.ers.usda.gov/briefing /AgTrade/>; and the foreign trade section of the U.S. Census Bureau Web site at <http://www.census.gov/foreign-trade /statistics/index.html>.

The field offices of the NASS collect data on crops, livestock and products, agricultural prices, farm employment, and other related subjects mainly through sample surveys. Information is obtained on crops and livestock items as well as scores of items pertaining to agricultural production and marketing. State estimates and supporting information are sent to the Agricultural Statistics Board of NASS, which reviews the estimates and issues reports containing state and national data. Among these reports are annual summaries such as *Crop Production,*

Crop Values, Agricultural Prices, and Live-stock Production, Disposition and Income.

Farms and farmland—The definitions of a farm have varied through time. Since 1850, when minimum criteria defining a farm for census purposes first were established, the farm definition has changed nine times. The current definition, first used for the 1974 census, is any place from which $1,000 or more of agricultural products were produced and sold, or normally would have been sold, during the census year.

Acreage designated as "land in farms" consists primarily of agricultural land used for crops, pasture, or grazing. It also includes woodland and wasteland not actually under cultivation or used for pasture or grazing, provided it was part of the farm operator's total operation. Land in farms includes acres set aside under annual commodity acreage programs as well as acres in the Conservation Reserve and Wetlands Reserve Programs for places meeting the farm definition. Land in farms is an operating unit concept and includes land owned and operated as well as land rented from others. All grazing land, except land used under government permits on a per-head basis, was included as "land in farms" provided it was part of a farm or ranch.

An evaluation of coverage has been conducted for each census of agriculture since 1945 to provide estimates of the completeness of census farm counts. Beginning with the 1997 Census of Agriculture, census farm counts and totals were statistically adjusted for coverage and reported at the county level. The size of the adjustments varies considerably by state. In general, farms not on the census mail list tended to be small in acreage, production, and sales of farm products. The response rate for the 2007 Census of Agriculture was 85.2 percent as compared with a response rate of 88.0 for the 2002 Census of Agriculture and 86.2 percent for the 1997 Census of Agriculture.

Agriculture 531

For more explanation about census mail list compilation, collection methods, coverage measurement, and adjustments, see Appendix A, 2007 Census of Agriculture, Volume 1 reports <http://www.agcensus.usda.gov/>.

Farm income—The final agricultural sector output comprises cash receipts from farm marketings of crops and livestock, federal government payments made directly to farmers for farm-related activities, rental value of farm homes, value of farm products consumed in farm homes, and other farm-related income such as machine hire and custom work. Farm marketings represent quantities of agricultural products sold by farmers multiplied by prices received per unit of production at the local market. Information on prices received for farm products is generally obtained by the NASS Agricultural Statistics Board from surveys of firms (such as grain elevators, packers, and processors) purchasing agricultural commodities directly from producers. In some cases, the price information is obtained directly from the producers.

Crops—Estimates of crop acreage and production by the NASS are based on current sample survey data obtained from individual producers and objective yield counts, reports of carlot shipments, market records, personal field observations by field statisticians, and reports from other sources. Prices received by farmers are marketing year averages. These averages are based on U.S. monthly prices weighted by monthly marketings during specific periods. U.S. monthly prices are state average prices weighted by marketings during the month. Marketing year average prices do not include allowances for outstanding loans, government purchases, deficiency payments or disaster payments.

All state prices are based on individual state marketing years, while U.S. marketing year averages are based on standard marketing years for each crop. For a listing of the crop marketing years and the participating states in the monthly program, see *Crop Values*. Value of production is computed by multiplying state prices by each state's production. The U.S. value of production is the sum of state values for all states. Value of production figures shown in Tables 852–856 and 858 should not be confused with cash receipts from farm marketings which relate to sales during a calendar year, irrespective of the year of production.

Livestock—Annual inventory numbers of livestock and estimates of livestock, dairy, and poultry production prepared by the Department of Agriculture are based on information from farmers and ranchers obtained by probability survey sampling methods.

Statistical reliability—For a discussion of statistical collection and estimation, sampling procedures, and measures of statistical reliability pertaining to Department of Agriculture data, see Appendix III.

Table 818. Selected Characteristics of Farms by North American Industry Classification System (NAICS): 2007

[297,220,491 represents 297,220,491,000. See text this section and Appendix III]

Industry	2007 NAICS code [1]	Farms	Land in farms (acres)	Harvested cropland (acres)	Market value of agricultural products sold (1,000)		
					Total	Crops	Livestock [2]
Total........................	(X)	**2,204,792**	**922,095,840**	**309,607,601**	**297,220,491**	**143,657,928**	**153,562,563**
Crop production..................	111	1,051,889	416,961,540	244,213,836	141,921,405	135,806,093	6,115,312
Oilseed and grain farming	1111	338,237	266,831,616	194,191,397	74,559,692	69,851,934	4,707,758
Soybean farming..............	11111	62,923	22,094,100	17,599,156	5,637,504	5,532,934	104,570
Oilseed (except soybean) farming....	11112	515	458,591	306,033	62,238	61,081	1,157
Dry pea and bean farming.........	11113	526	382,071	269,759	79,297	78,454	844
Wheat farming.................	11114	35,232	55,992,672	29,062,744	6,157,944	5,821,678	336,267
Corn farming	11115	161,874	103,071,231	86,627,715	39,675,674	38,524,804	1,150,870
Rice farming	11116	3,853	4,233,156	3,396,230	1,936,574	1,915,447	21,127
Other grain farming	11119	73,314	80,599,795	56,929,760	21,010,459	17,917,536	3,092,923
Vegetable and melon farming.......	11121	40,589	9,272,945	6,018,702	14,975,322	14,850,087	125,235
Potato farming.................	111211	2,182	2,577,795	1,992,430	2,885,906	2,854,320	31,586
Other vegetable (except potato) and melon farming	111219	38,407	6,695,150	4,026,272	12,089,416	11,995,767	93,649
Fruit and tree nut farming	1113	98,281	12,141,683	5,339,755	18,351,629	18,225,583	126,046
Orange groves..................	11131	8,771	1,535,483	800,921	2,423,976	2,382,844	41,131
Citrus (except orange) groves	11132	3,429	402,617	205,522	783,426	778,099	5,326
Noncitrus fruit and tree nut farming...	11133	86,081	10,203,583	4,333,312	15,144,228	15,064,639	79,589
Apple orchards	111331	11,550	2,078,125	488,273	2,259,839	2,251,555	8,284
Grape vineyards	111332	17,036	2,067,987	1,061,070	3,890,152	3,883,341	6,811
Strawberry farming	111333	1,503	149,972	55,461	1,185,736	1,182,263	3,473
Berry (except strawberry) farming ...	111334	8,535	870,154	220,530	1,211,820	1,209,450	2,370
Tree nut farming	111335	22,821	3,239,199	1,652,915	3,655,251	3,626,067	29,184
Fruit and tree nut combination farming	111336	995	292,842	106,488	301,611	286,946	14,666
Other noncitrus fruit farming........	111339	23,641	1,505,304	748,575	2,639,819	2,625,018	14,801
Greenhouse,nursery, and floriculture production	1114	54,889	3,974,530	1,698,564	16,967,123	16,930,975	36,147
Food crops grown under cover	11141	2,044	85,809	18,712	1,552,287	1,550,756	1,531
Nursery and floriculture production ...	11142	52,845	3,888,721	1,679,852	15,414,835	15,380,219	34,616
Nursery and tree production........	111421	34,532	3,287,008	1,505,323	8,901,860	8,875,417	26,443
Floriculture production	111422	18,313	601,713	174,529	6,512,975	6,504,801	8,173
Other crop farming	1119	519,893	124,740,766	36,965,418	17,067,639	15,947,514	1,120,126
Tobacco farming	11191	9,020	2,518,097	1,219,827	1,147,173	1,077,481	69,692
Cotton farming.................	11192	9,968	13,081,671	9,778,279	4,357,082	4,300,124	56,958
Sugarcane farming	11193	614	1,299,318	969,321	885,028	881,698	3,330
Hay farming..................	11194	254,042	49,923,443	18,606,436	6,488,172	5,807,594	680,578
All other crop farming	11199	245,643	57,917,637	6,391,555	4,190,184	3,880,617	309,568
Animal production	112	1,152,903	505,134,300	65,393,765	155,299,086	7,851,835	147,447,251
Cattle ranching and farming	1121	744,858	413,261,549	55,185,767	92,538,429	5,109,567	87,428,862
Beef cattle ranching and farming including feedlots...	11211	687,610	301,000,700	41,093,929	57,784,399	3,895,789	53,888,610
Beef cattle ranching and farming	112111	656,475	376,170,540	36,675,357	27,535,096	2,626,582	24,908,514
Cattle feedlots.................	112112	31,065	15,820,229	5,218,572	30,249,303	1,269,207	28,980,096
Dairy cattle and milk production	11212	57,318	21,270,780	13,291,838	34,754,031	1,213,778	33,540,252
Hog and pig farming..............	1122	30,546	6,949,176	4,747,504	18,127,114	1,614,030	16,513,083
Poultry and egg production..........	1123	64,570	7,040,000	2,140,320	37,797,542	547,736	37,249,806
Chicken egg production............	11231	35,651	2,259,774	477,371	7,546,997	104,546	7,442,452
Broilers and other meat-type chicken production	11232	17,888	3,370,828	1,209,528	22,400,358	306,268	22,094,090
Turkey production	11233	3,405	836,551	396,096	4,643,075	127,009	4,516,067
Poultry hatcheries	11234	775	69,558	9,985	2,777,612	1,790	2,775,822
Other poultry production	11239	6,851	503,289	47,340	429,499	8,124	421,375
Sheep and goat farming............	1124	67,254	11,963,667	429,300	554,107	21,374	532,732
Sheep farming	11241	30,974	8,971,952	324,835	435,107	18,396	416,711
Goat farming	11242	36,280	2,991,715	104,465	119,000	2,979	116,021
Animal aquaculture................	1125	4,777	2,451,244	70,954	1,407,750	18,384	1,389,366
Other animal production	1129	240,898	63,468,664	2,819,920	4,874,144	540,743	4,333,401
Apiculture.....................	11291	7,979	503,609	92,280	263,268	19,827	243,440
Horse and other equine production ...	11292	168,694	22,370,495	675,383	2,088,845	17,332	2,071,512
Fur-bearing animal and rabbit production	11293	2,252	89,224	16,894	154,325	2,744	151,581
All other animal production	11299	61,973	40,505,336	2,035,363	2,367,706	500,839	1,866,867

X Not applicable [1] North American Industry Classification System (NAICS) 2007; see text, Section 15. [2] Includes poultry, and their products sold.

Source: U.S. Department of Agriculture, National Agricultural Statistics Service, *2007 Census of Agriculture*, Vol. 1, February 2009. See also <http://www.agcensus.usda.gov/Publications/2007/Full_Report/index.asp>.

Table 819. Farms—Number and Acreage: 1990 to 2009

[As of June 1 (2,146 represents 2,146,000). Based on 1974 census definition; for definition of farms and farmland, see text, this section. Activities included as agriculture have undergone changes in recent years. Data for period 2000 to 2008 are not directly comparable with data for 1990. Data for 2002 and 2007 have been adjusted for underenumeration]

Year	Unit	1990	2000	2003	2004	2005	2006	2007	2008	2009
Number of farms	1,000	2,146	2,167	2,127	2,113	2,099	2,089	2,205	2,200	2,200
Land in farms.	Mil. acres	987	945	937	932	928	926	921	920	920
Average per farm	Acres	460	436	440	441	442	443	418	418	418

Source: U.S. Department of Agriculture, National Agricultural Statistics Service, *Farms and Land in Farms, Final Estimates, 1988–1992*; *Farms and Land in Farms, Final Estimates, 1993–1997*; *Farm Numbers and Land in Farms, Final Estimates, 1998–2002*; *Farms and Land in Farms, Final Estimates, 2003-2007*; and *Farms, Land in Farms, and Livestock Operations, February 2010*. See also <http://www.nass.usda.gov/Publications/index.asp>.

Table 820. Farms—Number and Acreage by State: 2000 to 2009

[As of June 1 (2,167 represents 2,167,000). See headnote, Table 819]

State	Farms (1,000) 2000	Farms (1,000) 2009	Land in farms (mil. acres) 2000	Land in farms (mil. acres) 2009	Acreage per farm 2000	Acreage per farm 2009	State	Farms (1,000) 2000	Farms (1,000) 2009	Land in farms (mil. acres) 2000	Land in farms (mil. acres) 2009	Acreage per farm 2000	Acreage per farm 2009
United States . . .	**2,167**	**2,200**	**945**	**920**	**436**	**418**							
Alabama	47	49	9	9	191	186	Montana.	28	30	59	61	2,133	2,040
Alaska	1	1	1	1	1,569	1,294	Nebraska.	52	47	46	46	887	966
Arizona	11	16	27	26	2,514	1,684	Nevada	3	3	6	6	2,065	1,916
Arkansas	48	49	15	14	304	277	New Hampshire. . . .	3	4	(Z)	(Z)	133	113
California	83	82	28	25	337	312	New Jersey	10	10	1	1	86	71
Colorado	30	36	32	31	1,053	865	New Mexico.	18	21	45	43	2,494	2,098
Connecticut	4	5	(Z)	(Z)	86	82	New York	38	37	8	7	205	194
Delaware	3	2	1	(Z)	215	198	North Carolina. . . .	56	52	9	9	166	164
Florida	44	48	10	9	236	195	North Dakota	31	32	39	40	1,279	1,238
Georgia	49	48	11	10	222	216	Ohio.	79	75	15	14	187	184
Hawaii	6	8	1	1	251	149	Oklahoma	85	87	34	35	400	406
Idaho	25	26	12	11	486	447	Oregon.	40	39	17	16	433	425
Illinois.	77	76	28	27	357	352	Pennsylvania	59	63	8	8	130	123
Indiana.	63	62	15	15	240	241	Rhode Island	1	1	(Z)	(Z)	75	57
Iowa.	94	93	33	31	346	333	South Carolina. . . .	24	27	5	5	203	181
Kansas.	65	66	48	46	736	705	South Dakota	32	32	44	44	1,358	1,387
Kentucky	90	86	14	14	152	164	Tennessee	88	79	12	11	134	139
Louisiana.	29	30	8	8	277	268	Texas	228	248	131	130	573	527
Maine.	7	8	1	1	190	167	Utah.	16	17	12	11	748	669
Maryland	12	13	2	2	172	160	Vermont	7	7	1	1	192	174
Massachusetts. . . .	6	8	1	1	89	68	Virginia.	49	47	9	8	180	170
Michigan	53	55	10	10	192	182	Washington	37	40	16	15	420	375
Minnesota	81	81	28	27	344	332	West Virginia	21	23	4	4	173	159
Mississippi	42	42	11	11	266	261	Wisconsin	78	78	16	15	206	195
Missouri.	109	108	30	29	277	269	Wyoming	9	11	35	30	3,750	2,745

Z Less than 500,000 acres.

Source: U.S. Department of Agriculture, National Agricultural Statistics Service, *Farm Numbers and Land in Farms, Final Estimates, 1998–2002* and *Farms, Land in Farms, and Livestock Operations, February 2010*. See also <http://www.nass.usda.gov/Publications/index.asp>.

Table 821. Farms by Size and Type of Organization: 1978 to 2007

[2,258 represents 2,258,000. For comments on adjustment, see text, this section]

Size and type of organization	Unit	Not adjusted for coverage 1978	Not adjusted for coverage 1982	Not adjusted for coverage 1987	Not adjusted for coverage 1992	Not adjusted for coverage 1997	Adjusted for coverage 1997 [1]	Adjusted for coverage 2002 [1]	Adjusted for coverage 2007 [1]
Farms	1,000	2,258	2,241	2,088	1,925	1,912	2,216	2,129	2,205
Land in farms.	Mil. acres	1,015	987	964	946	932	955	938	922
Average size of farm	Acres	449	440	462	491	487	431	441	418
Farms by size:									
1 to 9 acres	1,000	151	188	183	166	154	205	179	233
10 to 49 acres	1,000	392	449	412	388	411	531	564	620
50 to 179 acres	1,000	759	712	645	584	593	694	659	661
180 to 499 acres	1,000	582	527	478	428	403	428	389	368
500 to 999 acres	1,000	213	204	200	186	176	179	162	150
1,000 to 1,999 acres	1,000	98	97	102	102	101	103	99	93
2,000 acres or more	1,000	63	65	67	71	75	74	78	80
Farms by type of organization:									
Family or individual	1,000	1,966	1,946	1,809	1,653	1,643	1,923	1,910	1,906
Partnership	1,000	233	223	200	187	169	186	130	174
Corporation	1,000	50	60	67	73	84	90	74	96
Other [2]	1,000	9	12	12	12	15	17	16	28

[1] Data have been adjusted for coverage; see text, this section. [2] Cooperative, estate or trust, institutional, etc.

Source: U.S. Department of Agriculture, National Agricultural Statistics Service, *2007 Census of Agriculture*, Vol. 1. See also <http://www.agcensus.usda.gov/Publications/2007/Full_Report/index.asp>.

534 Agriculture

Table 822. Farms—Number and Acreage by Size of Farm: 2002 and 2007

[2,129 represents 2,129,000. Data have been adjusted for coverage; see text, this section]

Size of farm	Number of farms (1,000)		Land in farms (mil. acres)		Cropland harvested (mil. acres)		Percent distribution, 2007		
	2002	2007	2002	2007	2002	2007	Number of farms	All land in farms	Cropland harvested
Total.	2,129	2,205	938.3	922.1	302.7	309.6	100.0	100.0	100.0
Under 10 acres	179	233	0.8	1.1	0.2	0.3	10.6	0.1	0.1
10 to 49 acres	564	620	14.7	15.9	4.1	4.3	28.1	1.7	1.4
50 to 69 acres	152	154	8.8	8.9	2.5	2.5	7.0	1.0	0.8
70 to 99 acres	191	192	15.7	15.8	4.7	4.5	8.7	1.7	1.5
100 to 139 acres	175	175	20.2	20.3	6.1	5.8	7.9	2.2	1.9
140 to 179 acres	142	139	22.3	22.0	7.3	6.6	6.3	2.4	2.1
180 to 219 acres	91	88	18.0	17.3	6.2	5.6	4.0	1.9	1.8
220 to 259 acres	72	68	17.1	16.3	6.5	5.7	3.1	1.8	1.9
260 to 499 acres	226	213	80.6	75.9	34.1	30.4	9.6	8.2	9.8
500 to 999 acres	162	150	112.4	104.1	56.7	51.6	6.8	11.3	16.7
1,000 to 1,999 acres	99	93	135.7	127.6	72.8	69.8	4.2	13.8	22.6
2,000 acres or more	78	80	491.9	496.9	101.6	122.5	3.6	53.9	39.6

Source: U.S. Department of Agriculture, National Agricultural Statistics Service, *2007 Census of Agriculture*, Vol. 1. See also <http://www.agcensus.usda.gov/Publications/2007/Full_Report/index.asp>.

Table 823. Farms—Number, Acreage, and Value by Tenure of Principal Operator and Type of Organization: 2002 and 2007

[2,129 represents 2,129,000. Full owners own all the land they operate. Part owners own a part and rent from others the rest of the land they operate. A principal operator is the person primarily responsible for the on-site, day-to-day operation of the farm or ranch business. Data have been adjusted for coverage; see text, this section]

Item and year	Unit	Total [1]	Tenure of operator			Type of organization		
			Full owner	Part owner	Tenant	Family or individual	Partner-ship	Corpora-tion
NUMBER OF FARMS								
2002.	1,000	2,129	1,428	551	150	1,910	130	74
2007.	1,000	2,205	1,522	542	141	1,906	174	96
Under 50 acres	1,000	853	739	70	44	774	45	26
50 to 179 acres	1,000	661	492	130	38	588	45	18
180 to 499 acres	1,000	368	198	143	27	312	34	16
500 to 999 acres	1,000	150	51	84	14	118	18	12
1,000 acres or more	1,000	173	41	114	17	114	32	24
LAND IN FARMS								
2002.	Mil. acres	938	357	495	87	622	146	100
2007.	Mil. acres	922	344	496	82	574	161	125
Value of land and buildings, 2007 [2]	Bil. dol	1,744	726	868	150	1,203	277	227
Value of farm products sold, 2007	Bil. dol	297	117	148	32	148	62	84

[1] Includes other types, not shown separately. [2] Based on a sample of farms.

Source: U.S. Department of Agriculture, National Agricultural Statistics Service, *2007 Census of Agriculture*, Vol. 1. See also <http://www.agcensus.usda.gov/Publications/2007/Full_Report/index.asp>

Table 824. Corporate Farms—Characteristics by Type: 2007

[125.3 represents 125,300,000. Data have been adjusted for coverage; see text, this section and Appendix III]

Item	Unit	All corpora-tions	Family held corporations			Other corporations		
			Total	1 to 10 stock-holders	11 or more stock-holders	Total	1 to 10 stock-holders	11 or more stock-holders
Farms	Number	96,074	85,837	83,796	2,041	10,237	9,330	907
Percent distribution	Percent	100	89	87	2	11	10	1
Land in farms.	Mil. acres	125.3	114.3	106.4	7.8	11.1	7.7	3.3
Average per farm.	Acres	1,304	1,331	1,270	3,834	1,080	829	3,657
Value of—								
Land and buildings [1]	Bil. dol	226.6	200.6	189.5	11.0	26.0	20.2	5.8
Average per farm.	$1,000	2,358	2,336	2,262	5,399	2,542	2,170	6,371
Farm products sold	Bil. dol	84.1	65.8	58.9	6.9	18.3	12.2	6.2
Average per farm.	$1,000	876	766	703	3,378	1,791	1,305	6,787

[1] Based on a sample of farms.

Source: U.S. Department of Agriculture, National Agricultural Statistics Service, *2007 Census of Agriculture*, Vol. 1. See also <http://www.agcensus.usda.gov/Publications/2007/Full_Report/index.asp>.

Agriculture 535

Table 825. Farm Operators—Tenure and Characteristics: 2002 and 2007

[In thousands, except as indicated (3,054 represents 3,054,000). An "operator" is a person who operates a farm, either doing the work or making day-to-day decisions. A family operation may have more than one operator. A principal operator is the person primarily responsible for the on-site, day-to-day operation of the farm or ranch business. Data on operator characteristics were collected up to a maximum of three operators per farm, though operations were asked to report the total number of operators. Data have been adjusted for coverage; see text, this section and Appendix III]

Tenure and characteristic	Total operators, 2002	2007		
		Total operators	Principal operators	Other operators
Total operators	**3,054**	**3,282**	**2,205**	**1,077**
White alone	2,966	3,141	2,114	1,026
Black or African American alone	36	40	31	9
American Indian or Alaska Native alone	24	56	35	21
Asian alone	13	18	11	7
Native Hawaiian or Other Pacific Islander alone	2	2	1	1
More than one race reported	12	25	13	12
Operators of Hispanic origin [1]	72	82	56	27
Female	822	985	306	679
Under 25 years old	60	54	12	42
25 to 34 years old	201	209	107	103
35 to 44 years old	590	469	269	200
45 to 54 years old	838	878	565	312
55 to 64 years old	690	848	596	252
65 to 74 years old	439	533	412	121
75 years old and over	236	290	243	47
Average age (years)	53.2	54.9	57.1	(NA)
Full owner	(NA)	(NA)	1,522	(NA)
Part owner	(NA)	(NA)	542	(NA)
Tenant	(NA)	(NA)	141	(NA)
Principal occupation:				
Farming	1,658	1,400	994	406
Other	1,396	1,882	1,211	671
Place of residence:				
On farm operated	2,391	2,492	1,693	799
Not on farm operated	662	789	511	278
Years on present farm:				
2 years or less	143	163	85	78
3 to 4 years	251	240	139	101
5 to 9 years	587	593	360	233
10 years or more	2,073	2,286	1,622	664
Average years on present farm	(NA)	(NA)	22	(NA)
Days worked off farm:				
None	1,354	1,118	778	340
1 to 49 days	183	364	238	125
50 to 99 days	102	181	116	65
100 to 199 days	224	305	197	108
200 days or more	1,190	1,314	876	438

NA Not available. [1] Operators of Hispanic origin may be any race.

Source: U.S. Department of Agriculture, National Agricultural Statistics Service, *2007 Census of Agriculture*, Vol. 1. See also <http://www.agcensus.usda.gov/Publications/2007/Full_Report/index.asp>.

Table 826. Farm Type, Acreage, and Production: 2000 to 2008

[(2,166 represents 2,166,000). Based on Agricultural Resource Management Survey (ARMS) Phase III]

Type of farm	Unit	2000	2001	2002	2003	2004	2005	2006	2007	2008
Total farms										
Number of farms	1,000	2,166	2,149	2,152	2,121	2,108	2,095	2,083	2,197	2,192
Total value of production	Mil dol.	177,286	193,390	182,461	186,644	225,698	215,295	226,045	289,530	310,407
Total acres operated	Mil.	995	979	955	912	990	916	893	878	894
Acres operated per farm	Acres	459	455	444	430	470	437	429	400	408
Commercial farms [1]										
Number of farms	1,000	178	202	188	188	205	216	219	257	272
Total value of production	Mil dol.	121,202	138,799	126,242	134,627	170,130	166,566	178,104	241,728	258,972
Total acres operated	Mil.	392	417	347	341	429	418	382	424	429
Acres operated per farm	Acres	2,205	2,068	1,843	1,815	2,096	1,939	1,747	1,650	1,580
Intermediate farms [2]										
Number of farms	1,000	668	710	649	607	624	550	566	546	583
Total value of production	Mil dol.	41,813	42,843	41,981	37,894	38,438	33,872	32,533	30,933	34,158
Total acres operated	Mil.	392	376	384	349	342	307	318	237	253
Acres operated per farm	Acres	587	529	591	576	547	558	561	434	434
Rural residence farms [3]										
Number of farms	1,000	1,320	1,238	1,315	1,326	1,279	1,329	1,298	1,394	1,338
Total value of production	Mil dol.	14,272	11,747	14,238	14,124	17,130	14,856	15,408	16,869	17,277
Total acres operated	Mil.	211	186	224	221	219	191	193	217	212
Acres operated per farm	Acres	160	150	170	167	172	144	149	156	158

[1] Includes farms with sales of $250,000 or more. [2] Small familly farms whose operators report farming as their major occupation. [3] Includes retirement and residential farms.

Source: U.S. Department of Agriculture, Economic Research Service, ARMS Phase III—"Structural Characteristics Report," <http://www.ers.usda.gov/Data/ARMS/beta.htm>.

Table 827. Organic Agriculture—Number of Farms, Acreage, and Value of Sales: 2007

[2,577 represents 2,577,000. Data have been adjusted for coverage; see text, this section and Appendix III]

Size and usage	Number of farms	Acreage (1,000)	Sales value of organically produced commodities and commodity	Number of farms	Value (mil. dol.)
Total acres used for organic production....	20,437	2,577	Organic product sales, total...........	18,211	1,709
1 to 9 organic acres.....................	9,251	29	$1 to $4,999.......................	8,285	13
10 to 49 organic acres..................	4,994	115	$5,000 to $9,999....................	1,935	13
50 to 179 organic acres.................	3,498	348	$10,000 to $24,999..................	2,318	37
180 to 499 organic acres................	1,808	528	$25,000 to $49,999..................	1,515	54
500 organic acres or more..............	886	1,557	$50,000 or more	4,158	1,593
Acres from which organic crops harvested ..	16,778	1,288	Crops [1]............................	14,968	1,122
Acres of organic pastureland............	7,268	975	Livestock and poultry.................	2,496	110
Acres being converted to organic production............................	11,901	616	Livestock and poultry products	3,191	477

[1] Includes nursery and greenhouse crops.

Source: U.S. Department of Agriculture, National Agricultural Statistics Service, *2007 Census of Agriculture*, Vol. 1. See also <http://www.agcensus.usda.gov/Publications/2007/Full_Report/index.asp>.

Table 828. Certified Organic Farmland, Crops, and Livestock: 2000 to 2008

[1,776 represents 1,776,000. Economic Research Service collaborates with over 50 state and private certifiers to calculate U.S. and state-level estimates of certified organic acreage and livestock]

Item	Unit	2000	2001	2002	2003	2004	2005	2006	2007	2008
Farm operations [1]	Number	6,592	6,949	7,323	8,035	8,021	8,493	9,469	11,352	12,941
Average farm size	acres	269	301	263	273	380	477	310	378	372
Total farmland	1,000 acres ...	1,776	2,094	1,926	2,197	3,045	4,054	2,936	4,290	4,816
Total cropland	1,000 acres ...	557	790	626	745	1,593	2,331	1,051	2,005	2,161
Total pasture/rangeland.....	1,000 acres ...	1,219	1,305	1,300	1,452	1,452	1,723	1,885	2,285	2,655
Grains	1,000 acres ...	116	455	490	548	491	608	624	789	908
Corn..................	1,000 acres ...	78	94	96	106	99	131	138	172	195
Wheat.................	1,000 acres ...	181	195	218	234	214	277	225	330	416
Oats	1,000 acres ...	30	33	53	46	43	46	65	59	67
Beans	1,000 acres ...	166	211	145	153	144	156	157	150	164
Soybeans	1,000 acres ...	136	174	127	122	114	122	115	100	126
Oilseeds...............	1,000 acres ...	55	44	33	28	54	46	45	42	69
Hay and silage............	1,000 acres ...	231	254	268	328	357	411	508	677	793
Vegetables..............	1,000 acres ...	62	72	70	79	80	99	107	132	169
Fruits	1,000 acres ...	43	56	61	78	81	97	96	97	121
Herbs, nursery, and greenhouse	1,000 acres ...	41	15	29	25	8	9	18	18	15
Other cropland............	1,000 acres ...	204	197	198	214	239	298	330	380	415
Livestock [2]	1,000	56	72	108	124	157	197	257	363	476
Milk cows	1,000	38	49	67	74	75	87	130	166	250
Poultry [3]	1,000	3,159	5,014	6,270	8,780	7,305	13,757	9,195	12,185	15,518
Layer hens	1,000	1,114	1,612	1,052	1,591	1,788	2,415	3,072	3,872	5,538
Broilers (meat chicken).....	1,000	1,925	3,286	3,032	6,301	4,769	10,406	5,530	7,436	9,016

[1] Number does not include subcontracted organic farm operations. [2] Total livestock includes other and unclassified livestock animals. [3] Total poultry includes other and unclassified poultry animals.

Source: U.S. Department of Agriculture, Economic Research Service, "Briefing Rooms, Organic Agriculture," <http://www.ers.usda.gov/Briefing/Organic/>.

Table 829. Farms—Number, Acreage, and Value of Sales by Size of Sales: 2002 and 2007

[2,129 represents 2,129,000. Data have been adjusted for coverage; see text, this section and Appendix III]

Market value of agricultural products sold	Farms (1,000)	Acreage Total (mil.)	Acreage Average per farm	Value of sales Total (mil. dol.)	Value of sales Average per farm (dol.)	Percent distribution Farms	Percent distribution Acreage	Percent distribution Value of sales
2002								
Total..................	2,129	938.3	441	200,646	94,244	100.0	100.0	100.0
Less than $2,500.........	827	107.0	129	485	586	38.8	11.4	0.2
$2,500 to $4,999.........	213	23.1	108	763	3,582	10.0	2.5	0.4
$5,000 to $9,999.........	223	34.8	156	1,577	7,072	10.5	3.7	0.8
$10,000 to $24,999......	256	69.5	271	4,068	15,891	12.0	7.4	2.0
$25,000 to $49,999......	158	77.9	494	5,594	35,405	7.4	8.3	2.8
$50,000 to $99,999......	140	110.1	784	10,024	71,600	6.6	11.7	5.0
$100,000 to $249,999.....	159	189.4	1,191	25,401	159,755	7.5	20.2	12.7
$250,000 to $499,999.....	82	140.8	1,723	28,530	347,927	3.9	15.0	14.2
$500,000 to $999,999.....	42	94.0	2,241	28,944	689,143	2.0	10.0	14.4
$1,000,000 or more.......	29	91.7	3,198	95,259	3,284,793	1.4	9.8	47.5
2007								
Total..................	2,205	922.1	418	297,220	134,807	100.0	100.0	100.0
Less than $2,500.........	900	121.5	135	435	483	40.8	13.2	0.1
$2,500 to $4,999.........	200	17.5	87	718	3,585	9.1	1.9	0.2
$5,000 to $9,999.........	219	27.6	126	1,553	7,104	9.9	3.0	0.5
$10,000 to $24,999......	248	65.8	265	3,960	15,949	11.3	7.1	1.3
$25,000 to $49,999......	155	59.8	386	5,480	35,419	7.0	6.5	1.8
$50,000 to $99,999......	125	78.2	623	8,961	71,429	5.7	8.5	3.0
$100,000 to $249,999.....	148	147.6	1,000	24,213	164,156	6.7	16.0	8.1
$250,000 to $499,999.....	93	140.7	1,507	33,410	357,811	4.2	15.3	11.2
$500,000 to $999,999.....	61	119.4	1,965	42,691	702,417	2.8	13.0	14.4
$1,000,000 or more.......	56	144.0	2,593	175,800	3,167,050	2.5	15.6	59.1

Source: U.S. Department of Agriculture, National Agricultural Statistics Service, *2007 Census of Agriculture*, Vol. 1. See also <http://www.agcensus.usda.gov/Publications/2007/Full_Report/index.asp>.

Table 830. Farms—Number, Value of Sales, and Government Payments by Economic Class of Farm: 2002 and 2007

[2,129 represents 2,129,000. Economic class of farm is a combination of market value of agricultural products sold and federal farm program payments. Data have been adjusted for coverage; see text, this section and Appendix III]

Economic class	Number of farms (1,000) 2002, total	Number of farms (1,000) 2007 Total	Number of farms (1,000) 2007 Receiving government payments	Market value of agricultural products sold and government payments (mil. dol.) 2002, total	Market value of agricultural products sold and government payments (mil. dol.) 2007 Total	Market value of agricultural products sold and government payments (mil. dol.) 2007 Agricultural products sold	Market value of agricultural products sold and government payments (mil. dol.) 2007 Government payments
Total.....................	2,129	2,205	838	207,192	305,204	297,220	7,984
Less than $1,000............	431	500	42	72	96	77	19
$1,000 to $2,499............	307	271	85	508	448	332	116
$2,500 to $4,999............	243	246	80	870	884	685	199
$5,000 to $9,999............	247	255	87	1,746	1,811	1,488	323
$10,000 to $24,999..........	272	274	110	4,320	4,364	3,810	554
$25,000 to $49,999..........	164	164	87	5,804	5,795	5,286	508
$50,000 to $99,999..........	143	129	83	10,202	9,219	8,644	575
$100,000 to $249,999........	163	149	110	26,119	24,401	23,256	1,145
$250,000 to $499,999........	86	96	75	30,084	34,367	32,980	1,387
$500,000 to $999,999........	44	64	46	30,598	44,578	43,156	1,422
$1,000,000 to $2,499,999.....	21	42	27	31,701	62,751	61,508	1,243
$2,500,000 to $4,999,999.....	5	10	6	16,056	33,190	32,839	352
$5 million or more	3	6	2	49,112	83,300	83,159	141

Source: U.S. Department of Agriculture, National Agricultural Statistics Service, *2007 Census of Agriculture*, Vol. 1. See also <http://www.agcensus.usda.gov/Publications/2007/Full_Report/index.asp>.

Table 831. Farm Production Expenses: 2002 and 2007

[2,129 represents 2,129,000. Data have been adjusted for coverage; see text, this section and Appendix III]

Production expenses	2002 Farms (1,000)	2002 Expenses (mil. dol.)	2002 Percent of total	2007 Farms (1,000)	2007 Expenses (mil. dol.)	2007 Percent of total
Total	2,129	173,199	100.0	2,205	241,114	100.0
Fertilizer.................................	1,190	9,751	5.6	1,148	18,107	7.5
Chemicals.................................	947	7,609	4.4	919	10,075	4.2
Seeds, plants, vines, and trees	875	7,599	4.4	776	11,741	4.9
Livestock and poultry [1]........................	554	27,421	15.8	491	38,004	15.8
Feed	1,241	31,695	18.3	1,136	49,095	20.4
Gasoline and fuel.............................	2,024	6,675	3.9	2,149	12,912	5.4
Utilities..................................	1,241	4,874	2.8	1,103	5,918	2.5
Supplies, repairs, and maintenance	1,899	13,387	7.7	1,992	15,897	6.6
Farm labor [2]..............................	783	22,020	12.7	665	26,392	11.0
Customwork and custom hauling	450	3,314	1.9	362	4,091	1.7
Cash rent for land, buildings and grazing fees.............	498	9,046	5.2	490	13,275	5.5
Rent and lease for machinery, equipment, and farm share...	151	1,468	0.8	109	1,385	0.6
Interest expense	758	9,572	5.5	667	10,881	4.5
Property taxes	1,963	5,351	3.1	1,996	6,223	2.6
Other production expenses........................	1,254	13,418	7.7	1,116	17,119	7.1

[1] Purchased or leased. 2002 does not include breeding livestock leased. [2] Includes hired and contract labor.

Source: U.S. Department of Agriculture, National Agricultural Statistics Service, *2007 Census of Agriculture*, Vol. 1. See also <http://www.agcensus.usda.gov/Publications/2007/Full_Report/index.asp>.

Table 832. Farms—Number, Acreage, and Value by State: 2002 and 2007

[2,129 represents 2,129,000. Data have been adjusted for coverage; see text, this section and Appendix III]

State	Number of farms (1,000)		Land in farms (mil. acres)		Average size of farm (acres)		Total value of land and buildings [1] (bil. dol.)		Market value of agricultural products sold and government payments, 2007 (mil. dol.)	Total number of operators, 2007 (1,000)
	2002	2007	2002	2007	2002	2007	2002	2007		
U.S.	2,129	2,205	938.3	922.1	441	418	1,144.9	1,744.3	305,204	3,337
AL	45	49	8.9	9.0	197	185	15.1	20.7	4,540	71
AK	1	1	0.9	0.9	1,479	1,285	0.3	0.3	59	1
AZ	7	16	26.6	26.1	3,645	1,670	10.6	19.5	3,290	26
AR	47	49	14.5	13.9	305	281	21.2	32.5	7,778	75
CA	80	81	27.6	25.4	346	313	96.1	162.5	34,125	131
CO	31	37	31.1	31.6	991	853	23.8	33.1	6,217	61
CT	4	5	0.4	0.4	85	83	3.5	5.1	556	8
DE	2	3	0.5	0.5	226	200	2.3	5.3	1,092	4
FL	44	47	10.4	9.2	236	195	29.3	52.1	7,831	73
GA	49	48	10.7	10.2	218	212	22.6	31.6	7,337	69
HI	5	8	1.3	1.1	241	149	4.6	8.6	516	11
ID	25	25	11.8	11.5	470	454	15.3	22.7	5,788	40
IL	73	77	27.3	26.8	374	348	66.7	101.5	13,816	111
IN	60	61	15.1	14.8	250	242	38.4	52.9	8,532	92
IA	91	93	31.7	30.7	350	331	64.2	104.2	21,124	136
KS	64	66	47.2	46.3	733	707	32.6	42.2	14,840	97
KY	87	85	13.8	14.0	160	164	25.5	37.5	4,928	124
LA	27	30	7.8	8.1	286	269	12.2	16.7	2,787	44
ME	7	8	1.4	1.3	190	166	2.3	3.0	626	13
MD	12	13	2.1	2.1	170	160	8.5	14.4	1,868	20
MA	6	8	0.5	0.5	85	67	4.6	6.4	494	12
MI	53	56	10.1	10.0	190	179	27.1	34.2	5,872	85
MN	81	81	27.5	26.9	340	332	41.8	69.2	13,626	120
MS	42	42	11.1	11.5	263	273	15.6	21.4	5,108	61
MO	107	108	29.9	29.0	280	269	45.3	63.2	7,832	164
MT	28	30	59.6	61.4	2,130	2,079	23.3	47.6	3,025	47
NE	49	48	45.9	45.5	930	953	35.7	52.7	15,893	72
NV	3	3	6.3	5.9	2,118	1,873	2.8	3.6	517	5
NH	3	4	0.4	0.5	132	113	1.4	2.3	202	7
NJ	10	10	0.0	0.7	81	71	7.4	11.3	994	16
NM	15	21	44.8	43.2	2,954	2,066	10.6	14.6	2,218	32
NY	37	36	7.7	7.2	206	197	12.9	16.3	4,481	58
NC	54	53	9.1	8.5	168	160	28.0	34.7	10,461	77
ND	31	32	39.3	39.7	1,283	1,241	15.8	30.6	6,444	45
OH	78	76	14.6	14.0	187	184	39.6	49.2	7,302	114
OK	83	87	33.7	35.1	404	405	23.8	40.6	6,016	131
OR	40	39	17.1	16.4	427	425	20.4	31.0	4,463	65
PA	58	63	7.7	7.8	133	124	26.3	37.3	5,885	95
RI	1	1	0.1	0.1	71	56	0.6	1.1	67	2
SC	25	26	4.8	4.9	197	189	10.1	14.0	2,420	37
SD	32	31	43.8	43.7	1,380	1,401	19.6	39.1	6,841	47
TN	88	79	11.7	11.0	133	138	28.5	37.1	2,713	117
TX	229	247	129.9	130.4	567	527	100.5	165.6	21,722	373
UT	15	17	11.7	11.1	768	664	9.0	13.9	1,438	26
VT	7	7	1.2	1.2	189	177	2.5	3.6	680	11
VA	48	47	8.6	8.1	181	171	23.3	34.1	2,961	71
WA	36	39	15.3	15.0	426	381	22.4	29.8	6,931	64
WV	21	24	3.6	3.7	172	157	4.8	8.8	595	35
WI	77	78	15.7	15.2	204	194	35.8	49.0	9,163	123
WY	9	11	34.4	30.2	3,651	2,726	10.2	15.5	1,186	19

[1] Based on reports for a sample of farms.

Source: U.S. Department of Agriculture, National Agricultural Statistics Service, *2007 Census of Agriculture*, Vol. 1. See also <http://www.agcensus.usda.gov/Publications/2007/Full_Report/index.asp>.

Table 833. Balance Sheet of the Farming Sector: 1990 to 2008

[In billions of dollars, except as indicated (841 represents $841,000,000,000). As of December 31]

Item	1990	1995	2000	2001	2002	2003	2004	2005	2006	2007	2008
Farms (1,000)	**2,146**	**2,196**	**2,167**	**2,149**	**2,135**	**2,127**	**2,113**	**2,099**	**2,089**	**2,205**	**2,200**
Assets	841	966	1,203	1,256	1,260	1,383	1,588	1,779	1,924	2,055	2,005
Real estate	619	740	946	996	999	1,112	1,305	1,487	1,626	1,751	1,693
Livestock and poultry [1]	71	58	77	79	76	79	79	81	81	81	81
Machinery, motor vehicles [2]	86	88	90	93	96	100	108	113	114	115	116
Crops [3]	23	27	28	25	23	24	24	24	23	23	28
Purchased inputs	3	3	5	4	6	6	6	6	6	7	7
Financial assets	38	49	57	59	60	62	66	67	74	79	82
Debt [4]	131	143	164	171	177	164	182	196	204	214	239
Real estate debt	68	72	85	89	95	83	96	105	108	113	130
Farm Credit System	23	22	30	33	38	33	37	41	43	47	56
Farm Service Agency	7	5	3	3	3	2	2	2	2	2	2
Commercial banks	15	20	30	31	33	29	35	38	40	42	49
Life insurance companies	9	8	11	11	11	10	11	11	12	13	13
Individuals and others	14	16	11	10	10	9	11	12	10	9	9
Nonreal estate debt	63	71	79	82	82	81	86	92	96	101	109
Farm Credit System	10	12	17	20	20	20	22	24	28	32	37
Farm Service Agency	10	5	4	4	4	4	3	3	3	3	3
Commercial banks	31	38	45	45	44	44	46	48	51	54	57
Individuals and others	12	16	13	13	13	14	15	16	14	13	12
Equity	709	823	1,039	1,085	1,082	1,219	1,406	1,583	1,720	1,841	1,767
FINANCIAL RATIOS (percent)											
Farm debt/equity ratio	18.5	17.4	15.8	15.7	16.4	13.5	12.9	12.4	11.8	11.6	13.5
Farm debt/asset ratio	15.6	14.8	13.6	13.6	14.1	11.9	11.5	11.0	10.6	10.4	11.9

[1] Excludes horses, mules, and broilers. [2] Include only farm share value for trucks and autos. [3] All non-CCC crops held on farms plus the value above loan rate for crops held under Commodity Credit Corporation. [4] Includes CCC storage and drying facility loans but excludes debt on operator dwellings and for nonfarm purposes.

Source: U.S. Department of Agriculture, Economic Research Service, "Farm Balance Sheet," <http://www.ers.usda.gov/Data/FarmBalanceSheet/>.

Table 834. Farm Sector Output and Value Added: 1990 to 2008

[In billions of dollars (179.9 represents $179,900,000,000). For definition of value added, see text, Section 13. Minus sign (−) indicates decrease]

Item	1990	1995	2000	2001	2002	2003	2004	2005	2006	2007	2008
CURRENT DOLLARS											
Farm output	**179.9**	**191.9**	**204.3**	**212.3**	**201.9**	**229.8**	**262.0**	**251.5**	**252.7**	**302.9**	**335.3**
Cash receipts from farm marketings	171.9	194.3	197.6	201.9	195.8	218.5	240.4	240.0	242.5	290.4	327.1
Farm products consumed on farms	0.6	0.5	0.3	0.3	0.3	0.3	0.3	0.3	0.4	0.4	0.4
Other farm income	4.9	6.3	8.4	9.6	9.6	10.7	12.3	11.3	13.1	12.6	14.6
Change in farm finished goods inventories	2.4	−9.2	−2.0	0.6	−3.7	0.3	9.0	−	−3.3	−0.4	−6.8
Less: Intermediate goods and services consumed	102.6	122.8	130.7	136.1	129.6	137.4	143.7	149.5	159.6	186.8	203.2
Equals: **Gross farm value added**	**77.3**	**69.1**	**73.6**	**76.2**	**72.3**	**92.4**	**118.3**	**102.0**	**93.1**	**116.2**	**132.1**
Less: Consumption of fixed capital	17.9	19.4	23.3	23.9	24.7	25.8	27.4	29.5	31.3	32.8	34.6
Equals: Net farm value added	59.3	49.7	50.4	52.3	47.7	66.7	90.9	72.5	61.8	83.3	97.4
Compensation of employees	13.4	15.5	19.7	20.9	20.8	20.5	22.3	22.6	23.1	23.5	24.4
Taxes on production and imports	3.8	4.2	4.7	4.7	4.8	5.1	5.2	5.2	5.7	6.9	7.1
Less: Subsidies to operators	7.6	6.1	20.0	20.0	10.8	14.2	11.1	20.9	13.5	10.2	10.3
Net operating surplus	49.8	36.1	45.9	46.7	32.8	55.2	74.4	65.6	46.4	63.1	76.3
CHAINED (2000) DOLLARS [1]											
Farm output, total	**(NA)**	**211.6**	**240.6**	**237.2**	**236.2**	**246.1**	**250.2**	**251.5**	**251.9**	**255.5**	**253.3**
Cash receipts from farm marketings	(NA)	218.2	234.8	227.0	231.2	235.5	230.1	240.0	242.1	244.7	247.4
Farm products consumed on farms	(NA)	0.6	0.4	0.3	0.4	0.3	0.3	0.3	0.4	0.4	0.4
Other farm income	(NA)	6.4	9.3	10.3	9.9	10.6	11.7	11.3	12.3	10.2	9.8
Change in farm finished goods inventories	(NA)	−10.8	−2.5	0.8	−4.5	0.4	8.1	−0.2	−3.4	−0.5	−5.1
Less: Intermediate goods and services consumed	(NA)	164.4	159.2	162.1	157.2	156.0	152.7	149.5	152.6	163.6	149.6
Equals: **Gross farm value added**	**(NA)**	**56.4**	**83.5**	**77.7**	**81.2**	**91.6**	**97.9**	**102.0**	**99.1**	**91.6**	**103.4**
Less: Consumption of fixed capital	(NA)	23.1	26.0	26.3	26.9	27.7	28.5	29.5	30.3	30.9	31.5
Equals: Net farm value added	(NA)	35.0	57.8	51.6	54.5	64.1	69.4	72.5	68.7	60.5	71.1

− Represents zero. NA Not available. [1] See text, Section 13.

Source: U.S. Bureau of Economic Analysis, *Survey of Current Business*, August 2009. See also <http://www.bea.gov/national/nipaweb/SelectTable.asp?Selected=N>.

Table 835. Value Added to Economy by Agricultural Sector: 1990 to 2008

[In billions of dollars (188.5 represents $188,500,000,000). Data are consistent with the net farm income accounts and include income and expenses related to the farm operator dwellings. The concept presented is consistent with that employed by the Organization for Economic Cooperation and Development. Minus sign (–) indicates decrease]

Item	1990	1995	2000	2001	2002	2003	2004	2005	2006	2007	2008
Value of agricultural sector production	**188.5**	**203.6**	**220.4**	**229.3**	**220.2**	**243.5**	**282.7**	**276.7**	**275.4**	**326.5**	**364.9**
Value of crop production	83.2	95.9	94.8	95.0	98.3	108.6	124.4	115.2	118.9	150.9	182.5
Food grains	7.5	10.4	6.5	6.4	6.8	8.0	8.9	8.6	9.1	13.4	20.7
Feed crops	18.7	24.5	20.5	21.5	24.0	24.7	27.4	24.7	29.4	42.3	62.0
Cotton	5.5	6.9	2.9	3.6	3.4	6.4	4.8	6.3	5.6	6.5	5.7
Oil crops	12.3	15.5	13.5	13.3	15.0	18.0	17.9	18.5	18.5	24.6	31.2
Fruits and tree nuts	9.4	11.0	12.4	11.9	12.6	13.4	15.5	17.4	17.3	18.5	18.9
Vegetables	11.3	15.0	15.5	15.4	17.1	16.9	16.2	17.0	18.0	19.3	20.4
All other crops	12.9	15.2	18.7	19.3	20.2	21.0	21.4	22.3	24.5	25.3	24.2
Home consumption	0.1	0.2	0.2	0.2	0.2	0.1	0.1	0.1	0.1	0.1	0.1
Value of inventory adjustment [1]	2.8	–5.3	2.2	1.5	–2.9	–1.6	10.7	–0.8	–3.6	0.9	–0.7
Value of livestock production	90.0	87.8	99.1	106.4	93.5	104.9	124.4	126.5	119.4	138.5	139.7
Meat animals	51.1	44.9	53.0	53.3	48.1	56.2	62.4	64.8	63.7	65.1	64.7
Dairy products	20.2	19.9	20.6	24.7	20.6	21.2	27.4	26.7	23.4	35.5	34.8
Poultry and eggs	15.3	19.1	21.9	24.6	21.1	24.0	29.5	28.7	26.7	33.1	36.8
Miscellaneous livestock	2.5	3.4	4.2	4.1	4.1	4.2	4.3	4.6	4.8	4.9	4.8
Home consumption	0.5	0.3	0.1	0.1	0.1	0.1	0.2	0.3	0.3	0.3	0.3
Value of inventory adjustment [1]	0.4	0.2	–0.6	–0.4	–0.6	–0.8	0.6	1.3	0.5	–0.3	–1.7
Services and forestry	15.3	19.9	26.5	28.0	28.5	30.0	33.9	35.0	37.2	37.1	42.6
Machine hire and custom work	1.8	1.9	2.2	2.1	2.2	3.0	3.4	2.8	2.6	2.7	3.0
Forest products sold	1.8	2.8	2.8	2.6	2.5	2.2	2.4	2.5	0.7	0.7	0.7
Other farm income	4.5	5.8	8.7	10.1	10.2	10.5	11.3	10.9	13.2	12.9	16.0
Gross imputed rental value of farm dwellings	7.2	9.4	12.7	13.1	13.6	14.3	16.8	18.8	20.6	20.8	22.9
Less: Purchased inputs	92.2	108.8	121.8	125.7	123.3	130.3	137.4	144.0	153.7	183.4	201.4
Farm origin	39.5	41.8	47.9	48.2	48.3	53.7	57.5	56.9	61.1	73.4	79.5
Feed purchased	20.4	23.8	24.5	24.8	24.9	27.5	29.7	28.0	31.4	41.9	46.9
Livestock and poultry purchased	14.6	12.5	15.9	15.2	14.4	16.7	18.1	18.5	18.6	18.8	17.5
Seed purchased	4.5	5.5	7.5	8.2	8.9	9.4	9.6	10.4	11.0	12.6	15.1
Manufactured inputs	22.0	26.1	28.7	29.4	28.5	28.8	31.6	35.4	37.5	46.3	55.0
Fertilizers and lime	8.2	10.0	10.0	10.3	9.6	10.0	11.4	12.8	13.3	17.7	22.5
Pesticides	5.4	7.7	8.5	8.6	8.3	8.4	8.6	8.8	9.0	10.5	11.7
Petroleum fuel and oils	5.8	5.4	7.2	6.9	6.6	6.9	8.0	10.0	11.3	13.8	16.2
Electricity	2.6	3.0	3.0	3.6	3.9	3.5	3.4	3.5	3.8	4.3	4.5
Other purchased inputs	30.7	40.9	45.2	48.1	46.6	47.9	48.3	51.6	55.2	63.7	66.9
Repair and maintenance of capital items	8.6	9.6	10.9	11.2	10.5	11.0	11.9	11.9	12.5	14.3	14.8
Machine hire and custom work	3.0	3.9	4.1	4.0	4.0	3.5	3.6	3.5	3.5	3.8	4.1
Marketing, storage, and transportation expenses	4.2	7.2	7.5	7.8	7.6	7.1	7.2	8.8	9.1	10.3	10.1
Contract labor	1.6	2.0	2.7	3.1	2.7	3.3	3.1	3.1	3.0	4.4	4.7
Miscellaneous expenses	13.4	18.2	19.9	21.9	21.7	22.9	22.4	24.4	27.1	30.8	33.2
Plus: Net government transactions [2]	3.1	0.4	15.8	15.0	5.2	9.2	5.4	15.8	6.2	0.9	0.9
Direct Government payments [3]	9.3	7.3	23.2	22.4	12.4	16.5	13.0	24.4	15.8	11.9	12.2
Motor vehicle registration and licensing fees	0.4	0.4	0.5	0.5	0.4	0.5	0.5	0.6	0.6	0.6	0.6
Property taxes	5.8	6.4	6.9	6.9	6.8	6.8	7.0	8.0	9.0	10.3	10.7
Equals: Gross value added	**99.3**	**95.1**	**114.4**	**118.7**	**102.1**	**122.4**	**150.7**	**148.6**	**127.9**	**144.1**	**164.4**
Less: Capital consumption	18.1	18.9	20.1	20.6	20.9	21.4	23.1	24.9	26.2	27.1	28.7
Equals: Net value added	**81.2**	**76.2**	**94.3**	**98.2**	**81.1**	**100.9**	**127.6**	**123.6**	**101.7**	**117.0**	**135.7**
Less: Employee compensation	12.4	14.3	17.9	18.8	19.1	18.7	20.2	20.5	21.2	24.0	24.9
Less: Net rent received by nonoperator landlords	9.0	9.6	11.2	11.2	9.6	10.1	10.0	10.6	7.6	7.0	9.3
Less: Real estate and nonreal estate interest	13.5	12.6	14.6	13.3	12.8	11.6	11.6	13.2	14.4	15.1	14.5
Equals: Net farm income	**46.3**	**39.8**	**50.6**	**54.9**	**39.6**	**60.5**	**85.8**	**79.3**	**58.5**	**70.9**	**87.1**

[1] A positive value of inventory change represents current-year production not sold by December 31. A negative value is an offset to production from prior years included in current-year sales. [2] Direct government payments minus motor vehicle registration and licensing fees and property taxes. [3] Government payments reflect payments made directly to all recipients in the farm sector, including landlords. The nonoperator landlords share is offset by its inclusion in rental expenses paid to these landlords and thus is not reflected in net farm income or net cash income.

Source: U.S. Department of Agriculture, Economic Research Service, "United States and State Farm Income Data Files," <http://www.ers.usda.gov/Briefing/FarmIncome/nationalestimates.htm>.

Table 836. Cash Receipts for Selected Commodities—Leading States: 2008

[In millions of dollars (51,551 represents $51,551,000,000). See headnote Table 837]

State	Value	State	Value	State	Value	State	Value
Corn	**51,551**	**Cattle and calves**	**48,189**	**Dairy products**	**34,773**	**Soybeans**	**29,058**
Iowa	9,703	Nebraska	7,069	California	6,924	Iowa	4,800
Illinois	8,878	Texas	6,896	Wisconsin	4,571	Illinois	4,163
Nebraska	5,712	Kansas	6,240	New York	2,306	Minnesota	2,829
Minnesota	4,673	Colorado	3,058	Pennsylvania	2,102	Indiana	2,432
Indiana	3,952	Iowa	2,882	Idaho	2,101	Nebraska	2,209

Source: U.S. Department of Agriculture, Economic Research Service, "Farm Income Cash Receipts," <http://www.ers.usda.gov/Data/FarmIncome/firkdmuXls.htm#commod>.

Table 837. Farm Income—Cash Receipts From Farm Marketings: 2000 to 2008

[In millions of dollars (192,098 represents $192,098,000,000). Represents gross receipts from commercial market sales as well as net Commodity Credit Corporation loans. The source estimates and publishes individual cash receipt values only for major commodities and major producing states. The U.S. receipts for individual commodities, computed as the sum of the reported states, may understate the value of sales for some commodities, with the balance included in the appropriate category labeled "other" or "miscellaneous." The degree of underestimation in some of the minor commodities can be substantial]

Commodities	2000	2005	2007	2008	Commodities	2000	2005	2007	2008
Total	192,098	241,019	288,488	324,187	Beans, snap	393	414	525	509
Livestock and products	99,597	124,942	138,557	141,090	Broccoli	622	539	695	708
Meat animals	53,012	64,813	65,060	64,709	Carrots	390	592	568	634
Cattle and calves	40,783	49,283	49,843	48,189	Corn, sweet	709	800	883	1,093
Hogs	11,758	14,970	14,750	16,077	Lettuce	1,996	1,855	2,281	1,986
Sheep and lambs	470	560	467	443	Head	1,341	1,012	1,248	1,059
Dairy products	20,587	26,705	35,453	34,773	Onions	713	810	1,111	776
Poultry/eggs	21,854	28,806	33,117	36,771	Peppers, green, fresh	531	535	533	672
Broilers	13,989	20,878	21,514	23,112	Tomatoes	1,845	2,225	2,079	(NA)
Chicken eggs	4,289	4,025	6,719	8,226	Fresh	1,195	1,604	1,178	1,423
Turkeys	2,771	3,026	3,929	4,478	Misc. vegetables	2,051	2,904	3,052	3,051
Miscellaneous livestock	4,144	4,618	4,926	4,837	Fruits/nuts	12,385	17,215	18,522	18,851
Horses/mules	1,218	1,104	1,219	1,165	Grapefruit	377	417	409	308
Aquaculture [1]	798	(NA)	1,281	1,268	Lemons	267	345	425	442
Catfish	501	458	456	411	Oranges	1,775	1,901	1,619	1,969
Other livestock	1,970	2,219	2,229	2,142	Apples	1,466	1,712	2,165	2,668
Crops	92,501	116,077	149,931	183,096	Cherries	327	548	625	653
Food grains	6,525	8,594	13,384	20,676	Grapes	3,100	3,490	3,455	3,346
Rice	837	1,589	2,086	3,214	Wine	1,909	2,317	1,976	2,009
Wheat	5,672	6,989	11,283	17,445	Raisins	487	595	597	671
Feed crops	20,546	24,578	42,330	62,028	Peaches	470	511	502	544
Corn	15,162	18,477	33,977	51,551	Pears	288	296	354	388
Hay	3,855	4,695	6,111	7,403	Strawberries	1,045	1,399	1,755	1,885
Cotton	2,950	6,320	6,467	5,684	Blueberries	223	382	614	592
Tobacco	2,316	1,099	1,290	1,445	Almonds	666	2,526	2,402	2,262
Oil crops	13,478	18,388	24,635	31,216	Walnuts	296	557	751	528
Peanuts	897	843	759	1,052	All other crops	18,645	22,696	24,005	22,774
Soybeans	12,047	16,918	23,096	29,058	Sugar beets	1,113	1,193	1,335	1,128
Vegetables	15,657	17,186	19,300	20,421	Cane for sugar	881	815	885	850
Beans, dry	436	488	680	905	Greenhouse/nursery	13,710	16,988	17,336	16,097
Potatoes	2,369	2,639	3,070	3,689	Mushrooms	860	899	981	959

NA Not available. [1] See also Table 892.

Source: U.S. Department of Agriculture, Economic Research Service, "United States and State Farm Income Data," <http://www.ers.usda.gov/Data/farmincome/finfidmu.htm>.

Table 838. Farm Output, Income, and Government Payments by State: 2007 and 2008

[In millions of dollars (326,529 represents $326,529,000,000). Farm income data are after inventory adjustment and include income and expenses related to the farm operator's dwelling]

State	Final agricultural output 2007	2008	Net farm income 2007	2008	Government payments, 2008	State	Final agricultural output 2007	2008	Net farm income 2007	2008	Government payments, 2008
U.S.	326,529	364,879	70,896	87,074	12,238						
AL	4,888	5,539	1,075	1,391	162	MT	3,349	3,704	588	688	294
AK	42	38	9	5	5	NE	16,179	18,461	2,994	4,026	519
AZ	4,228	4,064	998	751	90	NV	600	685	106	170	13
AR	7,918	9,811	2,086	3,091	383	NH	252	270	38	46	8
CA	38,748	39,012	11,203	7,877	434	NJ	1,292	1,323	338	363	17
CO	7,275	7,164	1,362	1,389	261	NM	3,299	3,389	847	830	75
CT	680	728	139	177	13	NY	4,848	5,116	1,091	1,146	69
DE	1,127	1,257	265	237	24	NC	9,766	11,032	2,469	2,834	519
FL	8,612	8,618	1,997	1,741	159	ND	6,446	8,271	1,462	2,349	511
GA	8,027	8,815	2,167	2,775	398	OH	7,826	8,753	1,524	1,952	275
HI	652	654	144	144	8	OK	6,413	7,001	696	1,027	317
ID	6,357	6,894	1,606	1,836	151	OR	4,778	5,030	880	871	125
IL	13,521	17,832	2,953	5,333	636	PA	6,740	7,027	1,539	1,457	87
IN	8,777	10,919	1,853	3,172	322	RI	82	87	20	17	4
IA	21,257	26,295	4,349	7,026	804	SC	2,358	2,806	340	620	153
KS	13,658	15,481	1,697	3,684	648	SD	7,300	9,202	1,840	3,058	401
KY	5,159	5,897	1,067	1,549	371	TN	3,312	4,076	163	621	225
LA	3,121	3,277	840	790	220	TX	23,126	22,081	4,753	3,218	1,181
ME	733	744	180	167	15	UT	1,843	1,915	325	376	47
MD	2,133	2,423	390	491	57	VT	775	755	225	165	16
MA	648	729	108	179	15	VA	3,604	3,883	447	552	133
MI	6,611	7,671	1,215	2,027	166	WA	8,012	8,993	1,867	1,963	201
MN	14,205	18,218	2,914	5,836	544	WV	708	743	17	13	15
MS	5,169	5,745	1,228	1,298	334	WI	10,378	11,283	2,521	2,577	230
MO	8,502	9,867	1,924	3,035	538	WY	1,195	1,303	39	135	46

Source: U.S. Department of Agriculture, Economic Research Service, "United States and State Farm Income Data," <http://www.ers.usda.gov/Data/farmincome/finfidmu.htm>.

Table 839. Farm Marketings, 2007 and 2008, and Principal Commodities, 2008, by State

[In millions of dollars (288,488 represents $288,488,000,000). Cattle include calves; sheep include lambs; and greenhouse includes nursery]

State	2007 Total	2007 Crops	2007 Livestock and products	2008 Total	2008 Crops	2008 Livestock and products	State rank for total farm marketings and four principal commodities in order of marketing receipts
U.S....	288,488	149,931	138,557	324,187	183,096	141,090	**Corn, cattle and calves, dairy products, soybeans**
AL.....	4,098	709	3,389	4,464	962	3,502	27-Broilers, cattle, chicken eggs, greenhouse,
AK.....	33	26	7	31	25	6	50-Greenhouse/nursery, hay, potatoes, cattle
AZ.....	3,589	1,999	1,590	3,465	1,959	1,505	29-Dairy products, cattle, greenhouse/nursery, lettuce
AR.....	7,338	3,217	4,121	8,347	3,997	4,350	12-Broilers, rice, soybeans, cotton
CA.....	36,355	25,536	10,819	36,187	25,554	10,632	1-Dairy products, greenhouse/nursery, grapes, almonds
CO.....	6,289	2,026	4,262	6,509	2,379	4,131	20-Cattle, dairy products, corn, wheat,
CT.....	566	383	184	601	413	188	43-Greenhouse/nursery, dairy products, chicken eggs
DE.....	976	186	790	1,095	266	828	39-Broilers, corn, soybeans, wheat
FL.....	7,941	6,559	1,382	7,978	6,593	1,385	16-Greenhouse/nursery, oranges, tomatoes, dairy products
GA.....	6,806	2,445	4,361	7,393	2,735	4,658	18-Broilers, chicken eggs, cotton, peanuts
HI......	585	516	69	574	511	63	44-Greenhouse/nursery, sugar cane, macadamia nuts
ID......	5,747	2,464	3,282	6,415	3,011	3,405	21-Dairy products, cattle, potatoes, hay
IL......	12,603	10,491	2,113	16,357	14,232	2,125	5-Corn, soybeans, hogs, cattle
IN......	8,056	5,461	2,594	9,962	7,105	2,856	8-Corn, soybeans, hogs, dairy products
IA......	19,173	10,451	8,722	24,753	14,885	9,868	2-Corn, soybeans, hogs, cattle
KS.....	11,953	4,715	7,238	13,967	6,755	7,213	7-Cattle, wheat, corn, soybeans
KY.....	4,516	1,562	2,954	4,838	1,930	2,908	25-Horses/mules, broilers, corn, cattle
LA.....	2,818	1,838	981	3,035	1,985	1,050	32-Rice, corn, sugar cane, soybeans
ME.....	643	348	295	676	341	335	42-Potatoes, dairy products, chicken eggs, greenhouse
MD.....	1,753	651	1,102	1,965	810	1,156	36-Broilers, greenhouse/nursery, corn, dairy products
MA.....	492	373	119	570	454	115	46-Greenhouse/nursery, cranberries, dairy products
MI......	5,854	3,453	2,401	6,606	4,078	2,528	19-Dairy products, corn, soybeans, greenhouse/nursery,
MN.....	12,822	7,039	5,782	15,838	9,752	6,087	6-Corn, soybeans, hogs, dairy products
MS.....	4,435	1,699	2,735	4,968	2,076	2,892	24-Broilers, soybeans, corn, cotton
MO.....	7,403	3,700	3,703	8,436	4,820	3,616	11-Soybeans, corn, cattle, hogs
MT.....	2,472	1,338	1,134	2,902	1,722	1,180	34-Wheat, cattle, barley, hay
NE.....	14,878	6,418	8,460	17,316	8,996	8,320	4-Cattle, corn, soybeans, hogs
NV.....	542	220	322	572	273	299	45-Cattle, hay, dairy products, onions
NH.....	199	108	91	213	119	94	48-Greenhouse/nursery, dairy products, apples
NJ.....	1,092	912	180	1,110	940	177	38-Greenhouse/nursery, horses/mules, blueberries
NM.....	3,077	713	2,365	3,117	710	2,407	30-Dairy products, cattle, hay, pecans
NY.....	4,390	1,693	2,698	4,694	2,011	2,683	26-Dairy products, greenhouse/nursery, corn, apples
NC.....	8,773	2,872	5,901	9,753	3,291	6,461	10-Broilers, hogs, greenhouse/nursery, tobacco
ND.....	5,807	4,829	978	7,629	6,717	912	17-Wheat, soybeans, corn, cattle
OH.....	6,691	4,155	2,535	7,979	5,236	2,744	15-Corn, soybeans, dairy products, chicken eggs
OK.....	5,210	1,223	3,987	5,838	1,930	3,907	23-Cattle, wheat, hogs, broilers
OR.....	4,071	3,063	1,009	4,375	3,234	1,141	28-Greenhouse/nursery, cattle, dairy products, wheat
PA.....	5,808	1,943	3,865	6,122	2,180	3,942	22-Dairy products, cattle, chicken eggs, corn
RI......	65	55	10	68	57	10	49-Greenhouse/nursery, dairy products, sweet corn
SC.....	2,034	769	1,265	2,360	975	1,385	35-Broilers, greenhouse/nursery, turkeys, cattle
SD.....	6,001	3,318	2,683	8,048	5,366	2,681	14-Corn, cattle, soybeans, wheat
TN.....	2,943	1,489	1,453	3,110	1,780	1,330	31-Cattle, broilers, soybeans, corn
TX.....	18,703	7,317	11,386	19,173	8,142	11,031	3-Cattle, cotton, dairy products, broilers
UT.....	1,417	467	951	1,515	527	987	37-Dairy products, cattle, hay, hogs
VT.....	691	105	586	688	116	572	41-Dairy products, cattle, greenhouse/nursery
VA.....	2,840	890	1,950	2,999	1,043	1,956	33-Broilers, cattle, dairy products, turkeys
WA.....	7,405	5,264	2,141	8,180	6,207	1,974	13-Apples, dairy products, wheat, potatoes
WV.....	507	82	424	525	96	429	47-Broilers, cattle, turkeys, dairy products
WI.....	9,002	2,666	6,336	9,886	3,574	6,311	9-Dairy products, corn, cattle, soybeans
WY.....	1,026	178	848	974	226	748	40-Cattle, hay, hogs, sheep

Source: U.S. Department of Agriculture, Economic Research Service, "U.S. and State income and production expenses by expense category, 1949–2008," <http://www.ers.usda.gov/Data/FarmIncome/FinfidmuXls.htm>.

Table 840. Indexes of Prices Received and Paid by Farmers: 2000 to 2009

[1990–1992 = 100, except as noted]

Item	2000	2005	2008	2009	Item	2000	2005	2008	2009
Prices received, all products ...	96	114	149	131	Feed	102	117	194	187
Crops..................	96	110	169	150	Livestock and poultry.......	110	138	124	115
Food grains	85	111	259	186	Seed	124	168	259	299
Feed grains and hay	86	95	206	163	Fertilizer...............	110	164	392	275
Cotton	82	70	100	81	Agricultural chemicals	120	123	139	150
Tobacco.............	107	94	93	104	Fuels	134	216	344	228
Oil-bearing crops..........	85	106	202	177	Supplies and repairs	124	140	154	157
Fruits and nuts............	98	128	148	132	Autos and trucks	119	114	108	110
Commercial vegetables [1]....	121	130	151	161	Farm machinery...........	139	173	209	222
Potatoes and dry beans.....	93	109	157	154	Building materials	121	142	165	163
All other crops	110	113	123	124	Farm services	119	133	146	159
Livestock and products	97	119	130	112	Rent.................	110	129	165	178
Meat animals.............	94	118	117	105	Interest.................	113	111	147	139
Dairy products............	94	116	140	98	Taxes	123	155	209	238
Poultry and eggs	106	123	151	139	Wage rates	140	165	183	187
Prices paid, total [2]	118	142	183	179					
Production...............	116	140	190	182	Parity ratio (1910-14 = 100) [3]..	38	38	39	35

[1] Excludes potatoes and dry beans. [2] Includes production items, interest, taxes, wage rates, and a family living component. The family living component is the Consumer Price Index for all urban consumers from the Bureau of Labor Statistics. See text, Section 14 and Table 724. [3] Ratio of prices received by farmers to prices paid.

Source: U.S. Department of Agriculture, National Agricultural Statistics Service, "Quick Stats—U.S. & All States Data—Prices," <http://quickstats.nass.usda.gov/>.

Agriculture 543

Table 841. Civilian Consumer Expenditures for Farm Foods: 1990 to 2008

[In billions of dollars, except percent (449.8 represents $449,800,000,000). Excludes imported and nonfarm foods, such as coffee and seafood, as well as food consumed by the military, or exported]

Item	1990	1995	2000	2001	2002	2003	2004	2005	2006	2007	2008
Consumer expenditures, total .	**449.8**	**529.5**	**661.1**	**687.5**	**709.4**	**744.2**	**788.9**	**830.7**	**880.7**	**925.2**	**958.9**
Farm value, total	106.2	113.8	123.3	130.0	132.5	140.2	155.5	157.8	163.2	194.3	192.3
Marketing bill, total [1]	343.6	415.7	537.8	557.5	576.9	604.0	633.4	672.9	717.5	731.0	766.6
Percent of total consumer expenditures	76.4	78.5	81.3	81.1	81.3	81.2	80.3	81.0	81.5	79.0	79.9
At-home expenditures [2]	276.2	316.9	390.2	403.9	416.8	437.2	463.5	488.1	517.5	543.7	563.5
Farm value.	80.2	76.1	79.6	83.9	85.7	91.4	98.5	99.3	103.2	128.3	129.0
Marketing bill [1]	196.0	240.8	310.6	320.0	331.1	345.8	365.0	388.8	414.3	415.4	434.5
Away-from-home expenditures . . .	173.6	212.6	270.9	283.6	292.6	307.0	325.4	342.6	363.2	381.5	395.4
Farm value.	26.0	37.7	43.7	46.1	46.8	48.8	57.0	58.5	60.0	66.0	63.3
Marketing bill [1]	147.6	174.9	227.2	237.5	245.8	258.2	268.4	284.1	303.2	315.5	332.1
Marketing bill cost components:											
Labor cost [3]	154.0	196.6	252.9	263.8	273.1	285.9	303.7	319.8	341.0	347.4	364.3
Packaging materials	36.5	48.2	53.5	55.0	56.8	59.5	63.1	66.5	70.5	71.8	75.3
Rail and truck transport [4]	19.8	22.3	26.4	27.5	28.4	29.7	31.6	33.2	35.2	35.9	37.6
Corporate profits before taxes. . .	13.2	19.5	31.1	32.0	33.0	34.6	35.5	37.4	39.7	40.4	38.9
Fuels and electricity.	15.2	18.6	23.1	24.1	24.9	26.1	27.6	31.6	33.5	34.1	37.4
Advertising.	17.1	19.8	26.1	27.5	28.1	29.4	30.8	32.7	34.9	35.6	37.3
Depreciation	16.3	18.9	24.2	24.5	25.3	26.5	27.8	29.5	31.5	32.1	33.7
Net interest	13.5	11.6	16.9	18.6	19.2	20.1	21.1	22.4	23.9	24.3	25.5
Net rent	13.9	19.8	26.7	29.4	30.3	31.7	33.2	35.3	37.6	38.3	40.2
Repairs	6.2	7.9	10.1	10.6	10.9	11.4	12.0	12.7	13.5	13.8	14.5
Taxes	15.7	19.1	23.5	24.1	24.9	26.1	27.4	29.1	31.0	31.6	33.1
Other	22.2	13.4	23.3	20.4	22.0	23.0	19.6	22.7	25.2	25.7	28.8

[1] The difference between expenditures for domestic farm-originated food products and the farm value or payment farmers received for the equivalent farm products. [2] Food primarily purchased from retail food stores for use at home. [3] Covers employee wages and salaries and their health and welfare benefits. Also includes imputed earnings of proprietors, partners, and family workers not receiving stated remuneration. [4] Excludes local hauling.

Source: U.S. Department of Agriculture, Economic Research Service, *Food Cost Review, 1950–97*, ERS Agricultural Economic Report No. AER780, June 1999 and "ERS/USDA Briefing Room—Food marketing and price spreads: USDA marketing bill," <http://ers.usda.gov/Briefing/FoodMarketingSystem/pricespreads.htm>.

Table 842. Agricultural Exports and Imports—Volume by Principal Commodities: 1990 to 2009

[In thousands (7,703 represents 7,703,000). 1,000 hectoliters equals 264.18 gallons. Includes Puerto Rico, U.S. territories, and shipments under foreign aid programs. Excludes fish, forest products, distilled liquors, manufactured tobacco, and products made from cotton; but includes raw tobacco, raw cotton, rubber, beer and wine, and processed agricultural products]

Commodity	Unit	1990	2000	2005	2006	2007	2008	2009
EXPORTS								
Fruit juices and wine	Hectoliters	7,703	14,356	13,982	14,438	14,470	14,871	13,950
Beef, pork, lamb, and poultry meats [1]	Metric tons. . . .	1,451	4,935	4,343	4,617	5,103	6,573	6,165
Wheat, unmilled.	Metric tons. . . .	27,384	27,568	27,040	23,208	32,991	30,021	21,928
Wheat products	Metric tons. . . .	863	844	313	281	448	389	404
Rice, paddy, milled.	Metric tons. . . .	2,534	3,241	4,388	3,779	3,477	3,800	3,439
Feed grains	Metric tons. . . .	61,066	54,946	50,865	62,555	63,215	59,659	51,530
Feed grain products.	Metric tons. . . .	1,430	2,062	3,442	4,153	4,002	1,286	1,227
Feeds and fodders [2].	Metric tons. . . .	10,974	13,065	11,422	11,372	11,823	14,372	14,586
Fresh fruits and nuts	Metric tons. . . .	2,648	3,450	3,675	3,569	3,553	4,037	4,098
Fruit products.	Metric tons. . . .	390	471	394	419	460	540	506
Vegetables, fresh.	Metric tons. . . .	1,297	2,029	2,077	1,982	1,938	2,020	1,972
Vegetables, frozen and canned	Metric tons. . . .	529	1,112	1,086	1,150	1,261	1,604	1,397
Oilcake and meal	Metric tons. . . .	5,079	6,462	6,905	7,943	8,272	8,405	9,266
Oilseeds.	Metric tons. . . .	15,820	28,017	26,462	29,373	31,077	35,011	41,294
Vegetable oils	Metric tons. . . .	1,226	2,043	1,937	2,222	2,539	2,900	3,032
Tobacco, unmanufactured	Metric tons. . . .	223	180	154	180	187	169	172
Cotton, excluding linters	Metric tons. . . .	1,696	1,485	3,405	3,507	3,258	3,001	2,551
IMPORTS								
Fruit juices	Hectoliters	33,116	31,154	41,488	39,002	49,710	47,299	44,234
Wine	Hectoliters	2,510	4,584	7,262	7,950	8,615	8,487	9,462
Malt beverages	Hectoliters	10,382	23,464	29,947	34,356	34,749	33,668	30,276
Coffee, including products	Metric tons. . . .	1,214	1,370	1,307	1,359	1,393	1,393	1,348
Rubber and allied gums, crude	Metric tons. . . .	840	1,232	1,169	1,012	1,028	1,053	704
Beef, pork, lamb, and poultry meats [1]	Metric tons. . . .	1,169	1,579	1,778	1,608	1,610	1,394	1,430
Grains [3]	Metric tons. . . .	2,071	4,622	3,726	4,718	5,576	6,384	5,588
Biscuits, pasta, and noodles	Metric tons. . . .	300	711	1,001	1,033	1,084	1,038	1,019
Feeds and fodders [2].	Metric tons. . . .	959	1,224	963	1,022	1,236	1,298	1,330
Fruits, nuts, and preparations [4]	Metric tons. . . .	5,401	8,354	9,570	9,897	10,706	10,547	10,275
Vegetables, fresh or frozen	Metric tons. . . .	1,898	3,763	5,183	5,404	5,965	6,124	6,118
Tobacco, unmanufactured	Metric tons. . . .	173	216	233	249	243	221	200
Oilseeds and oilnuts	Metric tons. . . .	509	1,056	818	1,091	1,276	1,555	1,249
Vegetable oils and waxes	Metric tons. . . .	1,204	1,846	2,386	2,897	3,117	3,708	3,523
Oilcake and meal.	Metric tons. . . .	316	1,254	1,541	1,663	1,716	1,964	1,539

[1] Includes variety meats. [2] Excluding oil meal. [3] Includes wheat, corn, oats, barley, and rice. [4] Includes bananas and plantains.
Source: U.S. Department of Agriculture, Economic Research Service, "Foreign Agricultural Trade of the United States (FATUS)," <http://www.ers.usda.gov/data/fatus/> and "Global Agricultural Trade System," <http://www.fas.usda.gov/gats>.

544 Agriculture

Table 843. Agricultural Exports and Imports—Value: 1990 to 2009

[In billions of dollars, except percent (16.6 represents $16,600,000,000). For calender year. Includes Puerto Rico, U.S. territories, and shipments under foreign aid programs. Excludes fish, forest products, distilled liquors, manufactured tobacco, and products made from cotton; but includes raw tobacco, raw cotton, rubber, beer and wine, and processed agricultural products]

Year	Trade balance	Exports, domestic products	Percent of all exports	Imports for con-sumption	Percent of all imports	Year	Trade balance	Exports, domestic products	Percent of all exports	Imports for con-sumption	Percent of all imports
1990....	16.6	39.5	11	22.9	5	2003....	12.0	59.4	9	47.4	4
1995....	26.0	56.3	10	30.3	4	2004....	7.4	61.4	8	54.0	4
1998....	14.9	51.8	8	36.9	4	2005....	3.9	63.2	8	59.3	4
1999....	10.7	48.4	8	37.7	4	2006....	5.6	70.9	8	65.3	4
2000....	12.3	51.3	7	39.0	3	2007....	18.1	90.0	9	71.9	4
2001....	14.3	53.7	8	39.4	3	2008....	34.8	115.3	10	80.5	4
2002....	11.2	53.1	8	41.9	4	2009....	26.9	98.6	11	71.7	5

Source: U.S. Department of Agriculture, Economic Research Service, "Foreign Agricultural Trade of the United States (FATUS)," <http://www.ers.usda.gov/data/fatus/> and U.S. Department of Agriculture, Foreign Agricultural Service, "Global Agricultural Trade System," <http://www.fas.usda.gov/gats>.

Table 844. Agricultural Imports—Value by Selected Commodity: 1990 to 2009

[In millions of dollars (22,918 represents $22,918,000,000). For calender year. Includes Puerto Rico, U.S. territories, and shipments under foreign aid programs. Excludes fish, forest products, distilled liquors, manufactured tobacco, and products made from cotton; but includes raw tobacco, raw cotton, rubber, beer and wine, and processed agricultural products]

Commodity	Value (mil. dol.)							Percent distribution		
	1990	2000	2005	2006	2007	2008	2009	1990	2000	2009
Total [1]	22,918	38,974	59,291	65,326	71,913	80,488	71,699	100.0	100.0	100.0
Cattle, live	978	1,152	1,039	1,546	1,878	1,761	1,299	4.3	3.0	1.8
Beef and veal	1,872	2,399	3,651	3,221	3,285	3,058	2,725	8.2	6.2	3.8
Pork	938	997	1,281	1,197	1,162	1,060	978	4.1	2.6	1.4
Dairy products	891	1,671	2,686	2,711	2,883	3,142	2,533	3.9	4.3	3.5
Grains and feeds	1,188	3,075	4,527	5,321	6,422	8,258	7,436	5.2	7.9	10.4
Fruits and preparations	2,167	3,851	5,842	6,517	7,439	7,899	8,204	9.5	9.9	11.4
Vegetables and preparations [2]	1,979	3,958	6,410	7,008	7,713	8,314	8,044	8.6	10.2	11.2
Sugar and related products	1,213	1,555	2,494	3,046	2,592	2,976	3,086	5.3	4.0	4.3
Wine	917	2,207	3,762	4,155	4,638	4,634	4,020	4.0	5.7	5.6
Malt beverages	923	2,179	3,096	3,583	3,625	3,668	3,338	4.0	5.6	4.7
Oilseeds and products	952	1,773	2,998	3,505	4,329	6,766	4,799	4.2	4.5	6.7
Coffee and products	1,915	2,700	2,976	3,313	3,768	4,412	4,066	0.4	6.9	5.7
Cocoa and products	1,072	1,404	2,751	2,659	2,662	3,299	3,476	4.7	3.6	4.8
Rubber, crude natural	707	842	1,552	2,029	2,119	2,857	1,274	3.1	2.2	1.8

[1] Includes other commodities, not shown separately. [2] Includes pulses.

Source: U.S. Department of Agriculture, Economic Research Service, "Foreign Agricultural Trade of the United States (FATUS)," <http://ers.usda.gov/Data/FATUS>, February 2010, and U.S. Department of Agriculture, Foreign Agricultural Service, "Global Agricultural Trade System," December 2009, <http://www.fas.usda.gov/gats>.

Table 845. Agricultural Imports—Value by Selected Countries of Origin: 1990 to 2009

[In millions of dollars (22,918 represents $22,918,000,000). See headnote Table 843]

Country	Value (mil. dol.)							Percent distribution		
	1990	2000	2005	2006	2007	2008	2009	1990	2000	2009
Total	22,918	38,974	59,291	65,326	71,913	80,488	71,681	100.0	100.0	100.0
Canada	3,171	8,661	12,270	13,432	15,244	18,009	14,710	13.8	22.2	20.5
European Union [1]	5,016	8,303	13,410	14,465	15,282	15,510	13,378	21.9	21.3	18.7
Mexico	2,614	5,077	8,331	9,391	10,169	10,907	11,373	11.4	13.0	15.9
China [2]	273	812	1,872	2,265	2,916	3,451	2,877	1.2	2.1	4.0
Brazil	1,563	1,144	1,952	2,231	2,644	2,615	2,433	6.8	2.9	3.4
Australia	1,174	1,592	2,421	2,487	2,633	2,425	2,316	5.1	4.1	3.2
Chile	481	1,026	1,521	1,777	1,837	2,049	2,145	2.1	2.6	3.0
Indonesia	683	998	1,702	2,042	2,081	2,815	1,787	3.0	2.6	2.5
Colombia	790	1,123	1,437	1,480	1,539	1,769	1,772	3.4	2.9	2.5
New Zealand	855	1,132	1,712	1,669	1,733	1,833	1,608	3.7	2.9	2.2
Thailand	470	779	1,094	1,330	1,507	1,917	1,567	2.0	2.0	2.2
Guatemala	497	710	920	924	1,064	1,314	1,297	2.2	1.8	1.8
Malaysia	308	353	666	829	1,139	1,867	1,295	1.3	0.9	1.8
India	285	826	923	1,042	1,166	1,601	1,236	1.2	2.1	1.7
Costa Rica	400	812	916	1,163	1,236	1,207	1,102	1.7	2.1	1.5
Argentina	389	672	831	992	1,079	1,257	1,091	1.7	1.7	1.5
Ecuador	482	451	596	669	691	746	928	2.1	1.2	1.3
Peru	90	196	448	602	683	818	807	0.4	0.5	1.1
Vietnam	(NA)	200	422	495	663	760	727	(NA)	0.5	1.0
Philippines	418	468	568	640	704	916	724	1.8	1.2	1.0
Rest of world	2,958	3,636	5,281	5,401	5,905	6,701	6,509	12.9	9.3	9.1

NA Not available. [1] For consistency, data for all years are shown on the basis of 27 countries in the European Union; see footnote 5, Table 1377. [2] See footnote 4, Table 1331.

Source: U.S. Department of Agriculture, Foreign Agricultural Service, "Global Agricultural Trade System Online (GATS)," July 2010, <http://www.fas.usda.gov/gats/default.aspx>.

Agriculture **545**

Table 846. Selected Farm Products—U.S. and World Production and Exports: 2000 to 2009

[In metric tons, except as indicated (60.6 represents 60,600,000). Metric ton = 1.102 short tons or .984 long tons]

Commodity	Unit	Amount United States			Amount World			United States as percent of world		
		2000	2005	2009	2000	2005	2009	2000	2005	2009
PRODUCTION [1]										
Wheat	Million	60.6	57.2	60.3	581.4	619.6	679.9	10.4	9.2	8.9
Corn for grain.	Million	251.9	282.3	333.0	590.0	698.5	809.0	42.7	40.4	41.2
Soybeans.	Million	75.1	83.5	91.4	176.0	220.7	259.7	42.6	37.8	35.2
Rice, milled	Million	5.9	7.1	6.9	398.2	418.3	440.6	1.5	1.7	1.6
Cotton [2]	Million bales [3]	17.0	23.3	12.2	87.7	121.4	103	19.3	19.1	11.9
EXPORTS [4]										
Wheat [5]	Million	28.0	27.4	23.6	104.0	113.9	129.3	26.9	24.1	18.3
Corn.	Million	48.3	56.1	49.0	76.4	82.6	85.9	63.3	67.9	57.0
Soybeans.	Million	27.1	25.6	39.7	53.9	63.8	87.6	50.3	40.1	45.4
Rice, milled basis.	Million	2.8	3.9	3.3	22.8	29.2	29.8	12.5	13.2	11.2
Cotton [2]	Million bales [3]	6.8	14.4	12.3	27.1	35.0	35.3	24.9	41.2	34.7

[1] Production years vary by commodity. In most cases, includes harvests from July 1 of the year shown through June 30 of the following year. [2] For production and trade years ending in year shown. [3] Bales of 480 lb. net weight. [4] Trade years may vary by commodity. Wheat, corn, and soybean data are for trade year beginning in year shown. Rice data are for calendar year. [5] Includes wheat flour on a grain equivalent.

Source: U.S. Department of Agriculture, Foreign Agricultural Service, "Production, Supply and Distribution Online," <http://www.fas.usda.gov/psdonline/psdhome.aspx>.

Table 847. Percent of U.S. Agricultural Commodity Output Exported: 1990 to 2008

[In percent. All export shares are estimated from export and production volumes]

Commodity group	1990 to 1994, average	1995 to 1999, average	2000 to 2004, average	2000	2005	2006	2007	2008
Total agriculture [1].	**18.5**	**18.6**	**18.5**	**18.5**	**19.1**	**19.6**	**21.0**	**19.2**
Livestock [2]	4.2	4.5	4.6	4.6	4.4	4.6	5.6	7.7
Red meat.	4.1	7.1	8.0	8.1	7.4	8.7	9.4	11.6
Poultry	6.1	12.6	12.0	12.4	11.8	11.7	13.0	14.7
Dairy	3.5	1.4	1.2	1.2	1.2	1.3	2.3	4.5
Crops [3]	20.6	20.7	20.8	20.8	21.5	22.2	23.5	21.2
Food grains	14.5	12.8	13.3	13.3	14.1	11.8	14.6	11.1
Feed grains	21.4	21.7	19.2	20.7	20.0	20.8	20.0	15.7
Oilseeds.	29.4	31.8	33.6	33.3	28.2	32.9	40.5	40.8
Fruit and nuts.	16.2	15.9	17.5	17.6	17.2	18.9	20.6	21.9
Vegetables	8.9	11.0	11.2	11.2	12.2	12.6	12.2	15.3
Sweeteners	5.0	4.6	4.1	3.9	5.3	6.4	7.8	7.2
Wine and beer	3.8	5.9	7.3	6.3	7.6	9.0	9.7	10.5

[1] Includes food and nonfood agricultural products. [2] Includes animal fat; excludes live animals. [3] Includes vegetable oils, oilseed meal, and miscellaneous plant products.

Source: U.S. Department of Agriculture, Economic Research Service, "Food Availability (Per Capita) Data System, Food Availability: Spreadsheets," <http://www.ers.usda.gov/Data/FoodConsumption/FoodAvailSpreadsheets.htm>; USDA Foreign Agricultural Service, "Production, Supply and Distribution," <http://www.fas.usda.gov/psdonline>; and Global Agricultural Trade System, <http://www.fas.usda.gov/gats>.

Table 848. Top 10 U.S. Export Markets for Selected Commodities: 2009

[In thousands of metric tons (47,502 represents 47,502,000)]

Corn Country	Amount	Wheat [1] Country	Amount	Soybeans Country	Amount	Poultry meat Country	Amount
World, total	**47,502**	**World, total . . .**	**21,920**	**World, total . . . .**	**40,372**	**World, total . . . .**	**3,411**
Japan	15,131	Japan	3,036	China [2]	22,818	Russia.	738
Mexico	7,160	Nigeria	2,935	Mexico	3,281	Mexico	502
Korea, South.	6,040	Mexico	1,921	Japan	2,501	Canada.	157
Taiwan [2]	3,753	Philippines	1,262	Taiwan [2]	1,726	China [2]	361
Egypt	2,273	Korea, South. . .	1,108	Indonesia	1,484	Cuba.	149
Canada.	1,900	Taiwan [2]	862	Egypt	1,131	Hong Kong	88
Venezuela.	1,295	Thailand	603	Germany.	1,117	Iraq	101
Colombia	1,235	Indonesia	670	Turkey	811	Ukraine	87
Dominican Republic . . .	964	Yemen [3]	733	Korea, South. . . .	613	Taiwan [2]	76
Guatemala	651	Colombia	632	Thailand	515	Lithuania.	71
Rest of world	7,101	Rest of world . . .	8,158	Rest of world	4,375	Rest of world	1,078

[1] Unmilled. [2] See footnote 4, Table 1331. [3] Includes Aden and Sanaa.

Source: U.S. Department of Agriculture, Foreign Agricultural Service, "Global Agricultural Trade System Online (GATS)-FATUS Commodity Aggregations," <http://www.fas.usda.gov/gats/Default.aspx>.

Table 849. Agricultural Exports—Value by Principal Commodities: 1990 to 2009

[In millions of dollars (39,495 represents $39,495,000,000). Includes Puerto Rico, U.S. territories, and shipments under foreign aid programs. Excludes fish, forest products, distilled liquors, manufactured tobacco, and products made from cotton; but includes raw tobacco, raw cotton, rubber, beer and wine, and processed agricultural products]

Commodity	Value (mil. dol.)							Percent distribution		
	1990	2000	2005	2006	2007	2008	2009	1990	2000	2009
Total agricultural exports	**39,495**	**51,265**	**63,182**	**70,949**	**89,990**	**115,278**	**98,611**	**100.0**	**100.0**	**100.0**
Animals and animal products [1]	6,636	11,600	12,226	13,495	17,188	21,822	18,089	16.8	22.6	18.3
Meat and meat products	2,558	5,276	4,299	5,183	6,122	8,777	7,745	6.5	10.3	7.9
Poultry and poultry products	910	2,235	3,138	2,932	4,092	5,053	4,786	2.3	4.4	4.9
Grains and feeds [1]	14,386	13,620	16,364	19,144	27,896	36,913	25,333	36.4	26.6	25.7
Wheat and products.	4,035	3,578	4,520	4,359	8,616	11,599	5,680	10.2	7.0	5.8
Corn.	6,037	4,469	4,789	6,992	9,763	13,431	8,775	15.3	8.7	8.9
Fruits and preparations	2,007	2,743	3,468	3,760	4,155	4,839	4,656	5.1	5.4	4.7
Nuts and preparations	978	1,322	2,992	3,153	3,387	3,780	4,077	2.5	2.6	4.1
Vegetables and preparations [2]	1,836	3,112	3,571	3,913	4,307	5,124	5,009	4.6	6.1	5.1
Oilseeds and products [1]	5,725	8,584	10,229	11,307	15,601	23,671	24,099	14.5	16.7	24.4
Soybeans.	3,550	5,258	6,274	6,936	9,992	15,431	16,454	9.0	10.3	16.7
Vegetable oils and waxes	832	1,259	1,656	1,831	2,503	3,900	3,083	2.1	2.5	3.1
Tobacco, unmanufactured	1,441	1,204	990	1,141	1,208	1,238	1,160	3.6	2.3	1.2
Cotton, excluding linters	2,783	1,873	3,921	4,502	4,578	4,798	3,384	7.0	3.7	3.4
Other	3,702	7,207	9,421	10,534	11,670	13,093	12,804	9.4	14.1	13.0

[1] Includes commodities not shown separately. [2] Includes pulses.

Source: U.S. Department of Agriculture, Economic Research Service, "Foreign Agricultural Trade of the United States (FATUS)," <http://ers.usda.gov/Data/FATUS>, February 2010, and U.S. Department of Agriculture, Foreign Agricultural Service, "Global Agricultural Trade System," July 2010 <http://www.fas.usda.gov/gats>.

Table 850. Agricultural Exports—Value by Selected Countries of Destination: 1990 to 2009

[(39,495 represents $39,495,000,000). Includes Puerto Rico, U.S. territories, and shipments under foreign aid programs. Excludes fish, forest products, distilled liquors, manufactured tobacco, and products made from cotton; but includes raw tobacco, raw cotton, rubber, beer and wine, and processed agricultural products]

Country	Value (mil. dol.)							Percent distribution		
	1990	2000	2005	2006	2007	2008	2009	1990	2000	2009
Total agricultural exports [1]	**39,495**	**51,265**	**63,182**	**70,949**	**89,990**	**115,278**	**98,611**	**100.0**	**100.0**	**100.0**
Canada	4,214	7,643	10,618	11,951	14,062	16,253	15,701	10.7	14.9	15.9
Mexico	2,560	6,410	9,429	10,881	12,692	16,025	12,946	6.5	12.5	13.1
Caribbean	1,015	1,408	1,913	2,114	2,575	3,592	3,088	2.6	2.7	3.1
Central America.	483	1,121	1,589	1,832	2,363	3,106	2,556	1.2	2.2	2.6
South America [2]	1,063	1,704	1,943	2,364	3,510	5,334	3,457	2.7	3.3	3.5
Asia, excluding Middle East [2]	15,857	19,877	22,543	25,743	32,427	44,209	40,762	40.1	38.8	41.3
Japan.	8,142	9,292	7,931	8,390	10,159	13,223	11,117	20.6	18.1	11.3
Korea, South	2,650	2,546	2,233	2,851	3,528	5,561	3,923	6.7	5.0	4.0
Taiwan [3]	1,663	1,996	2,301	2,477	3,097	3,419	2,990	4.2	3.9	3.0
China [3,4]	818	1,716	5,233	6,711	8,314	12,115	13,150	2.1	3.3	13.3
Indonesia.	275	668	958	1,102	1,542	2,195	1,797	0.7	1.3	1.8
Europe/Eurasia [2]	8,140	7,654	8,361	8,731	10,598	12,262	9,393	20.6	14.9	9.5
European Union [5]	7,474	6,515	7,052	7,408	8,754	10,080	7,461	18.9	12.7	7.6
Russia	(X)	580	972	820	1,329	1,838	1,441	(X)	1.1	1.5
Middle East [2]	1,728	2,323	2,844	3,332	4,952	6,650	4,747	4.4	4.5	4.8
Africa [2]	1,848	2,308	2,773	3,087	5,187	5,814	4,175	4.7	4.5	4.2
Egypt	687	1,050	819	1,022	1,801	2,050	1,354	1.7	2.0	1.4
Oceania	343	490	742	760	963	1,189	1,282	0.9	1.0	1.3

X Not applicable. [1] Totals include transshipments through Canada, but transshipments are not distributed by country after 1998. [2] Includes areas not shown separately. [3] See footnote 4, Table 1331. [4] China includes Macao. However Hong Kong remains separate economically until 2050 and is not included. [5] For consistency, data for all years are shown on the basis of 27 countries in the European Union; see footnote 5, Table 1377.

Source: U.S. Department of Agriculture, Economic Research Service, "Foreign Agricultural Trade of the United States (FATUS);"<http://ers.usda.gov/Data/FATUS> February 2010, and U.S. Department of Agriculture, Foreign Agricultural Service, "Global Agricultural Trade System," July 2010, <http://www.fas.usda.gov/gats>.

Table 851. Cropland Used for Crops and Acreages of Crops Harvested: 1990 to 2009

[In millions of acres, except as indicated (341 represents 341,000,000)]

Item	1990	1995	2000	2003	2004	2005	2006	2007	2008	2009
Cropland used for crops.	**341**	**332**	**345**	**342**	**336**	**337**	**330**	**335**	**340**	**333**
Index (1977 = 100)	90	88	91	90	89	89	87	89	90	88
Cropland harvested [1]	310	302	314	316	312	314	303	312	316	310
Crop failure	6	8	11	10	9	6	11	8	8	8
Cultivated summer fallow.	25	22	20	16	15	16	15	15	16	15
Cropland idled by all federal programs	62	55	31	34	35	35	37	37	34	31
Acres of crops harvested [2]	**322**	**314**	**325**	**324**	**321**	**321**	**312**	**322**	**325**	**319**

[1] Land supporting one or more harvested crops. [2] Area in principal crops harvested as reported by Crop Reporting Board plus acreages in fruits, vegetables for sale, tree nuts, and other minor crops. Acres are counted twice for land that is doublecropped.

Source: U.S. Department of Agriculture, Economic Research Service, "Major Uses of Land in the United States, 2002," May 2006. Also in *Agricultural Statistics*, annual. Beginning 1991, *Agricultural Resources and Environmental Indicators*, periodic, and "AREI Updates: Cropland Use." See also ERS Briefing Room at <http://www.ers.usda.gov/Briefing /LandUse/majorlandusechapter.htm#trends>.

Agriculture 547

Table 852. Principal Crops—Supply and Use: 2000 to 2009

[72.4 represents 72,400,000. Marketing year beginning January 1 for potatoes, May 1 for hay, June 1 for wheat, August 1 for cotton, September 1 for soybeans and corn. Acreage, production, and yield of all crops periodically revised on basis of census data]

Item	Unit	2000	2004	2005	2006	2007	2008	2009
CORN								
Acreage harvested	Million	72.4	73.6	75.1	70.6	86.5	78.6	79.6
Yield per acre	Bushel	136.9	160.3	147.9	149.1	150.7	153.9	164.9
Production	Mil. bu.	9,915	11,806	11,112	10,531	13,038	12,092	13,131
Imports	Mil. bu.	6.82	10.83	8.81	11.98	20.02	13.53	10.00
Total supply [1]	Mil. bu.	11,639	12,775	13,235	12,510	14,362	13,729	14,814
Ethanol	Mil. bu.	628	1,323	1,603	2,119	3,049	3,677	4,300
Exports	Mil. bu.	1,941	1,818	2,134	2,125	2,437	1,858	1,900
Total use [2]	Mil. bu.	9,740	10,661	11,268	11,207	12,737	12,056	12,915
Ending stocks	Mil. bu.	1,899	2,114	1,967	1,304	1,624	1,673	1,899
Price per unit [3]	Dol./bu.	1.85	2.06	2.00	3.04	4.20	4.06	3.60
Value of production	Mil. dol.	18,499	24,381	22,198	32,083	54,667	49,092	47,270
SOYBEANS								
Acreage harvested	Million	72.4	74.0	71.3	74.6	64.1	74.7	76.4
Yield per acre	Bushel	38.1	42.2	43.1	42.9	41.7	39.7	44.0
Production	Mil. bu.	2,758	3,124	3,068	3,197	2,677	2,967	3,359
Imports	Mil. bu.	4	6	3	9	10	13	15
Total supply [1]	Mil. bu.	3,052	3,242	3,327	3,655	3,261	3,185	3,512
Crushings	Mil. bu.	1,640	1,696	1,739	1,808	1,803	1,662	1,730
Exports	Mil. bu.	996	1,097	940	1,116	1,159	1,283	1,445
Total use [2]	Mil. bu.	2,804	2,986	2,878	3,081	3,056	3,047	3,323
Ending stocks	Mil. bu.	248	256	449	574	205	138	190
Price per unit [3]	Dol./bu.	4.54	5.74	5.66	6.43	10.10	9.97	9.45
Value of production	Mil. dol.	12,520	17,895	17,367	20,555	27,039	29,581	31,743
WHEAT								
Acreage harvested	Million	53.1	50.0	50.1	46.8	51.0	55.7	49.9
Yield per acre	Bushel	42.0	43.2	42.0	38.6	40.2	44.9	44.4
Production	Mil. bu.	2,228	2,157	2,103	1,808	2,051	2,499	2,216
Imports	Mil. bu.	89.8	70.6	81.4	121.9	112.6	127.0	115.0
Total supply [1]	Mil. bu.	3,268	2,774	2,725	2,501	2,620	2,932	2,988
Exports	Mil. bu.	1,062	1,066	1,003	908	1,263	1,015	865
Total use [2]	Mil. bu.	2,392	2,234	2,154	2,045	2,314	2,275	2,038
Ending stocks	Mil. bu.	876	540	571	456	306	657	950
Price per unit [3]	Dol./bu.	2.62	3.40	3.42	4.26	6.48	6.78	4.90
Value of production	Mil. dol.	5,782	7,283	7,171	7,695	13,289	16,944	10,859
COTTON								
Acreage harvested	Million	13.1	13.1	13.8	12.7	10.5	7.6	7.7
Yield per acre	Pounds	632	855	831	814	879	813	758
Production [4]	Mil. bales [5]	17.2	23.3	23.9	21.6	19.2	12.8	12.2
Imports	Mil. bales [5]	–	–	–	–	–	–	–
Total supply [1]	Mil. bales [5]	21.1	26.7	29.4	27.7	28.7	22.9	18.5
Exports	Mil. bales [5]	6.7	14.4	17.5	13.0	13.7	13.3	12.0
Total use [2]	Mil. bales [5]	15.6	21.1	23.4	17.9	18.2	16.9	15.5
Ending stocks	Mil. bales [5]	6.0	5.5	6.1	9.5	10.0	6.3	3.0
Price per unit [3]	Cents/lb.	51.6	41.6	47.7	46.5	59.3	47.8	63.5
Value of production	Mil. dol.	4,260	4.994	5,695	5,013	5,653	3,021	3,736
HAY								
Acreage harvested	Million	60.4	61.9	61.6	60.6	61.0	60.2	59.8
Yield per acre	Sh. tons	2.54	2.55	2.44	2.32	2.41	2.43	2.47
Production	Mil. sh. tons	154	158	150	141	147	146	147
Price per unit [6,7]	Dol./ton	84.60	92.00	98.20	110.00	128.00	152.00	111.00
Value of production	Mil. dol.	11,557	12,198	12,534	13,634	16,842	18,639	14,990
POTATOES								
Acreage harvested	Million	1.3	1.2	1.1	1.1	1.1	1.0	1.0
Yield per acre	Cwt. [8]	381	391	390	393	396	396	413
Production	Mil. cwt. [8]	514	456	424	441	445	415	431
Price per unit [3]	Dol./cwt. [8]	5.08	5.66	7.06	7.31	7.51	8.42	8.00
Value of production	Mil. dol.	2,590	2,581	2,992	3,209	3,340	3,771	3,452

– Represents zero or rounds to less than half the unit of measurement shown. [1] Comprises production, imports, and beginning stocks. [2] Includes feed, residual, and other domestic uses not shown separately. [3] Marketing year average price. U.S. prices are computed by weighting U.S. monthly prices by estimated monthly marketings and do not include an allowance for outstanding loans and government purchases and payments. [4] State production figures, which conform with annual ginning enumeration with allowance for cross-state ginnings, rounded to thousands and added for U.S. totals. [5] Bales of 480 pounds, net weight. [6] Prices are for hay sold baled. [7] Season average prices received by farmers. U.S. prices are computed by weighting state prices by estimated sales. [8] Cwt = hundredweight (100 pounds).

Source: Production—U.S. Department of Agriculture, National Agricultural Statistics Service, In Crop Production, annual, and Crop Values, annual. Supply and disappearance—U.S. Department of Agriculture, Economic Research Service, Feed Situation, quarterly; Fats and Oils Situation, quarterly; Wheat Situation, quarterly; Cotton and Wool Outlook Statistics, periodic; and Agricultural Supply and Demand Estimates, periodic. All data are also in Agricultural Statistics, annual. See also <http://www.nass.usda.gov/Publications/Ag_Statistics/> and "Agricultural Outlook: Statistical Indicators," <http://www.ers.usda.gov/Publications/Agoutlook/AOTables/>.

Table 853. Corn—Acreage, Production, and Value by Leading States: 2007 to 2009

[86,520 represents 86,520,000. One bushel of corn (bu.) = 56 pounds]

State	Acreage harvested (1,000 acres)			Yield per acre (bu.)			Production (mil. bu.)			Price per unit ($/bu)			Value of production (mil. dol.)		
	2007	2008	2009	2007	2008	2009	2007	2008	2009	2007	2008	2009	2007	2008	2009
U.S. [1] . . .	**86,520**	**78,640**	**79,620**	**151**	**154**	**165**	**13,038**	**12,101**	**13,131**	**4.20**	**3.90**	**3.70**	**54,667**	**47,378**	**48,589**
IA	13,900	12,800	13,400	171	171	182	2,377	2,189	2,439	4.29	3.95	3.75	10,197	8,646	9,146
IL	13,050	11,900	11,800	175	179	174	2,284	2,130	2,053	4.09	3.80	3.65	9,341	8,094	7,537
NE	9,200	8,550	8,850	160	163	178	1,472	1,394	1,575	4.14	3.90	3.70	6,094	5,435	5,829
MN	7,850	7,200	7,150	146	164	174	1,146	1,181	1,244	4.13	3.80	3.70	4,733	4,487	4,630
IN	6,370	5,460	5,460	154	160	171	981	874	934	4.39	3.75	3.75	4,307	3,276	3,501
SD	4,480	4,400	4,700	121	133	153	542	585	719	4.17	3.60	3.40	2,260	2,107	2,445
KS	3,680	3,630	3,860	138	134	155	508	486	598	4.13	4.25	3.60	2,097	2,067	2,154
OH	3,610	3,120	3,140	150	135	174	542	421	546	4.29	3.95	3.70	2,323	1,664	2,022
WI	3,280	2,880	2,930	135	137	153	443	395	448	4.11	3.50	3.70	1,820	1,381	1,659
MO	3,270	2,650	2,920	140	144	153	458	382	447	4.17	4.00	3.65	1,909	1,526	1,631
MI	2,340	2,140	2,090	123	138	148	288	295	309	4.37	3.60	3.60	1,258	1,063	1,119
TX	1,970	2,030	1,960	148	125	130	292	254	255	4.35	4.80	4.05	1,268	1,218	1,032
ND	2,350	2,300	1,750	116	124	119	273	285	208	4.06	3.85	3.40	1,107	1,098	708
KY	1,340	1,120	1,150	128	136	165	172	152	190	4.14	4.05	3.75	710	617	712
CO	1,060	1,080	990	140	137	153	148	148	151	3.96	3.95	3.85	588	584	583
PA	980	880	920	124	133	143	122	117	132	4.56	3.75	3.85	554	439	507
NC	1,010	830	800	100	78	117	101	65	94	4.00	4.80	3.85	404	311	360
MS	910	700	695	148	140	126	135	98	88	3.68	4.60	3.70	496	451	324
LA	730	510	610	163	144	132	119	73	81	3.80	4.45	3.55	452	327	286
NY	550	640	595	128	144	134	70	92	80	5.05	4.30	3.95	356	396	315
TN	790	630	590	106	118	148	84	74	87	3.80	4.50	3.65	318	335	319

[1] Includes other states, not shown separately.

Source: U.S. Department of Agriculture, National Agricultural Statistics Service, *Crop Production Annual Summary*, January 2010, and *Crop Values Annual Summary*, February 2010. See also <http://www.nass.usda.gov/Publications/index.asp>.

Table 854. Soybeans—Acreage, Production, and Value by Leading States: 2007 to 2009

[64,146 represents 64,146,000. One bushel of soybeans (bu.) = 60 pounds]

State	Acreage harvested (1,000 acres)			Yield per acre (bu.)			Production (mil. bu.)			Price per unit (¢/bu.)			Value of production (mil. dol.)		
	2007	2008	2009	2007	2008	2009	2007	2008	2009	2007	2008	2009	2007	2008	2009
U.S. [1] . . .	**64,146**	**74,641**	**76,372**	**42**	**40**	**44**	**2,677**	**2,959**	**3,359**	**10.10**	**9.25**	**9.45**	**26,974**	**27,399**	**31,760**
IA	8,630	9,670	9,530	52	46	51	449	445	486	10.50	9.65	9.40	4,712	4,293	4,569
IL	8,280	9,100	9,350	44	47	46	360	428	430	10.40	9.35	9.70	3,746	3,999	4,172
MN	6,290	6,950	7,120	43	38	40	267	264	285	10.20	9.60	9.30	2,727	2,535	2,649
IN	4,790	5,430	5,440	46	45	49	220	244	267	10.20	9.30	9.55	2,247	2,272	2,546
MO	4,670	5,030	5,300	38	38	44	175	191	231	10.10	9.00	9.40	1,769	1,720	2,167
NE	3,850	4,860	4,760	51	47	55	196	226	259	9.92	9.40	9.40	1,948	2,124	2,439
OH	4,240	4,480	4,530	47	36	49	199	161	222	9.93	9.60	9.60	1,979	1,548	2,131
SD	3,240	4,060	4,190	42	34	42	136	138	176	9.60	9.05	9.05	1,306	1,249	1,593
ND	3,060	3,760	3,870	36	28	30	109	105	116	9.63	9.10	9.25	1,046	958	1,074
KS	2,610	3,250	3,650	33	37	44	86	120	161	10.10	8.60	9.25	870	1,034	1,486
AR	2,820	3,250	3,270	36	38	38	102	124	123	9.02	8.85	9.60	916	1,093	1,177
MS	1,440	1,960	2,030	41	40	38	58	78	77	8.36	8.75	9.15	488	686	706
MI	1,790	1,890	1,990	40	37	40	72	70	80	9.69	9.20	9.40	694	643	748
NC	1,380	1,670	1,750	22	33	34	30	55	60	10.10	8.65	9.50	307	477	572

[1] Includes other states, not shown separately.

Source: U.S. Department of Agriculture, National Agricultural Statistics Service, *Crop Production Annual Summary*, January 2010, and *Crop Values Annual Summary*, February 2010. See also <http://www.nass.usda.gov/Publications/index.asp>.

Table 855. Wheat—Acreage, Production, and Value by Leading States: 2007 to 2009

[50,999 represents 50,999,000. One bushel of wheat (bu.) = 60 pounds]

State	Acreage harvested (1,000 acres)			Yield per acre (bu.)			Production (mil. bu.)			Price per unit ($/bu.)			Value of production (mil. dol.)		
	2007	2008	2009	2007	2008	2009	2007	2008	2009	2007	2008	2009	2007	2008	2009
U.S. [1] . . .	**50,999**	**55,685**	**49,868**	**40.2**	**44.9**	**44.4**	**2,051**	**2,500**	**2,216**	**6.48**	**6.80**	**4.85**	**13,289**	**16,568**	**10,626**
KS	8,600	8,900	8,800	33.0	40.0	42.0	284	356	370	5.93	7.15	4.85	1,683	2,545	1,793
ND	8,405	8,640	8,415	35.6	36.0	44.8	299	311	377	7.74	7.20	4.85	2,340	2,299	1,822
MT	5,065	5,470	5,305	29.6	30.1	33.3	150	165	177	7.14	6.55	5.15	1,076	1,091	906
OK	3,500	4,500	3,500	28.0	37.0	22.0	98	167	77	6.22	6.50	4.80	610	1,082	370
SD	3,327	3,420	3,009	43.1	50.5	42.9	144	173	129	6.42	6.80	5.10	899	1,175	662
CO	2,369	1,936	2,479	39.2	30.8	40.6	93	60	101	6.01	6.50	4.50	561	389	452
TX	3,800	3,300	2,450	37.0	30.0	25.0	141	99	61	6.40	7.45	5.25	900	738	322
WA	2,137	2,225	2,225	58.7	52.8	55.3	125	118	123	7.58	6.40	4.80	949	755	585

[1] Includes other states, not shown separately.

Source: U.S. Department of Agriculture, National Agricultural Statistics Service, *Crop Production Annual Summary*, January 2010, and *Crop Values Annual Summary*, February 2010. See also <http://www.nass.usda.gov/Publications/index.asp>.

Agriculture 549

Table 856. Commercial Vegetable and Other Specified Crops—Area, Production, and Value, 2007 to 2009, and Leading Producing States, 2009

[295 represents 295,000. Except as noted, relates to commercial production for fresh market and processing combined. Includes market garden areas but excludes minor producing acreage in minor producing states. Excludes production for home use in farm and nonfarm gardens. Value is for season or crop year and should not be confused with calendar-year income. Hundredweight (cwt.) is the unit used for fresh market yield and production and is equal to one hundred pounds]

Crop	Area harvested (1,000 acres)[1]			Production (1,000 cwt)[2]			Value of production (mil. dol.)[3]			Leading states in order of production, 2009
	2007	2008	2009	2007	2008	2009	2007	2008	2009	
Beans, snap..........	295	289	285	21,577	21,984	21,122	524	485	415	(NA)
Fresh market........	96	90	88	6,502	5,824	4,862	398	308	260	CA, FL, GA
Processed..........	199	198	196	15,075	16,160	16,260	127	177	155	WI, OR, MI
Broccoli	130	127	124	19,188	20,086	19,570	695	721	742	CA, AZ
Cabbage[4]...........	69	66	66	23,886	24,516	22,623	386	355	341	CA, FL, NY
Cantaloupes[4]........	74	72	76	20,426	19,294	19,891	302	357	359	CA, CA, CO
Carrots.............	94	90	82	31,973	32,108	30,198	568	636	589	CA,MI,TX
Cauliflower..........	38	37	35	6,828	6,648	6,501	233	269	287	CA, AZ, NY
Celery	28	28	29	20,011	20,025	19,685	408	370	365	CA, MI
Corn, sweet........	602	594	613	86,453	85,549	93,103	883	1,089	1,171	(NA)
Fresh market........	234	233	234	28,504	28,899	28,421	646	749	836	FL, CA, GA
Processed..........	368	361	380	57,949	56,650	64,682	237	340	336	MN, WA, WI
Cucumbers	152	143	144	20,525	20,185	19,581	415	398	402	FL, GA[5]
Garlic.............	25	25	23	4,104	4,282	3,941	169	187	196	CA, NV, OR
Lettuce, head[4].......	162	149	146	57,474	52,952	53,220	1,248	1,063	1,155	CA, AZ
Lettuce, leaf[4]........	55	52	49	12,240	12,781	11,238	374	412	406	CA, AZ
Lettuce, Romaine[4]....	82	77	79	26,409	22,774	26,030	656	479	614	CA, AZ
Onions.............	160	153	149	79,638	75,120	74,970	816	872	844	CA,AZ
Peas, green[5]........	202	210	205	419,080	411,780	441,580	109	148	141	MN, WA, WI
Peppers, bell	54	51	52	16,100	15,888	15,600	533	637	556	CA, FL, GA
Spinach.............	43	46	50	102,879	109,261	101,899	174	206	249	AZ, CA
Squash.............	42	42	44	6,266	6,687	7,219	174	204	203	MI, CA, FL
Tomatoes.............	422	402	434	286,825	277,253	311,776	2,070	2,398	2,533	(NA)
Fresh market........	108	105	106	33,627	31,137	32,365	1,169	1,415	1,314	CA, FL, OH
Processed..........	314	297	328	253,198	246,116	279,411	902	982	1,219	CA
Watermelons[5]........	129	126	126	37,349	40,003	40,122	423	500	461	FL, CA, GA

NA Not available. [1] Area of crops for harvest for fresh market, including any partially harvested or not harvested because of low prices or other factors, plus area harvested for processing. [2] Excludes some quantities not marketed. [3] Fresh market vegetables valued at f.o.b. shipping point. Processing vegetables are equivalent returns at packinghouse door. [4] Fresh market only. [5] Processed only.

Source: U.S. Department of Agriculture, National Agricultural Statistics Service, *Vegetables 2009 Summary*, January 2010. See also <http://www.nass.usda.gov/Surveys/Guide_to_NASS_Surveys/Vegetables/index.asp>.

Table 857. Fresh Fruits and Vegetables—Supply and Use: 2000 to 2009

[In millions of pounds, except per capita in pounds (8,355 represents 8,355,000,000)]

Year	Utilized production[1]	Imports[2]	Supply,[1] total	Exports[2]	Consumption Total	Consumption Per capita[3]	Ending stocks
FRUITS							
Citrus:							
2000.....................	8,355	720	9,075	2,445	6,630	24	(NA)
2004.....................	8,156	993	9,149	2,495	6,654	23	(NA)
2005.....................	7,320	1,007	8,326	2,042	6,284	21	(NA)
2006.....................	7,304	1,051	8,355	2,025	6,329	21	(NA)
2007.....................	5,811	1,318	7,128	1,790	5,338	18	(NA)
2008.....................	7,311	1,241	8,552	2,363	6,189	20	(NA)
Noncitrus:[4]							
2000.....................	13,850	11,225	25,074	3,389	21,685	77	(NA)
2004.....................	14,335	12,325	26,660	3,079	23,581	80	(NA)
2005.....................	14,369	12,460	26,829	3,477	23,352	79	(NA)
2006.....................	13,882	13,136	27,018	3,064	23,955	80	(NA)
2007.....................	14,016	13,437	27,453	3,329	24,125	80	(NA)
2008.....................	14,417	13,668	28,085	3,753	24,332	80	(NA)
VEGETABLES AND MELONS							
2000.....................	46,995	7,231	55,570	4,200	49,147	174	1,266
2004.....................	48,554	8,900	58,707	4,367	51,731	176	1,492
2005.....................	46,504	9,561	57,556	4,226	51,268	173	1,280
2006.....................	46,592	10,201	58,073	3,952	52,172	175	1,162
2007.....................	46,510	10,913	58,586	3,821	52,420	174	1,472
2008.....................	45,039	11,217	57,728	3,981	51,730	170	1,272
2009.....................	44,422	11,534	57,228	3,752	51,348	167	1,346
POTATOES							
2000.....................	13,185	806	13,990	677	13,313	47	(NA)
2004.....................	13,181	755	13,936	485	13,452	46	(NA)
2005.....................	12,076	788	12,863	639	12,224	41	(NA)
2006.....................	11,348	817	12,165	631	11,535	39	(NA)
2007.....................	11,225	1,106	12,331	640	11,691	39	(NA)
2008.....................	10,995	1,178	12,173	642	11,531	38	(NA)
2009.....................	11,275	936	12,211	728	11,482	37	(NA)

NA Not available. [1] Crop-year basis for fruits. Supply data for vegetables include ending stocks of previous year. [2] Fiscal year for fruits; calendar year for vegetables and potatoes. [3] Based on Census Bureau estimated total population. [4] Includes bananas.

Source: U.S. Department of Agriculture, Economic Research Service, *Fruit and Tree Nuts Situation and Outlook Yearbook* and *Vegetables and Melons Situation and Outlook Yearbook*. See also <http://www.ers.usda.gov/publications/outlook/>.

Table 858. Fruits and Nuts—Utilized Production and Value, 2007 to 2009, and Leading Producing States: 2009

[4,523 represents 4,523,000]

Fruits and nuts	Unit	Utilized production [1]			Value of production (mil. dol.)			Leading states in order of production, 2009
		2007	2008	2009	2007	2008	2009	
FRUITS								
Apples [2]	1,000 tons	4,523	4,770	4,854	2,608	2,215	2,247	WA, NY, MI
Apricots	1,000 tons	89	78	69	42	41	45	CA, WA
Avocados	1,000 tons	193	116	269	341	215	345	CA,FL
Blackberries, cultivated (OR)	1,000 tons	30	23	28	29	28	31	OR
Blueberries, total	1,000 tons	182	219	227	614	592	540	MI, FL, CA
Cherries, sweet	1,000 tons	306	241	376	557	574	506	WA, CA
Cherries, tart	1,000 tons	124	107	160	68	80	63	MI, UT
Cranberries	1,000 tons	328	393	346	332	456	341	WI, MA,
Dates (CA)	1,000 tons	16	21	23	37	26	29	CA
Figs (fresh) (CA)	1,000 tons	48	43	40	19	26	30	CA
Grapefruit	1,000 tons	1,627	1,548	1,331	312	273	234	FL, CA, TX
Grapes (13 states)	1,000 tons	7,056	7,306	7,267	3,453	3,343	3,688	CA, WA
Kiwifruit (CA)	1,000 tons	24	22	24	23	20	35	CA
Lemons	1,000 tons	798	619	950	449	524	343	CA, AZ
Nectarines	1,000 tons	283	303	220	96	111	139	CA, WA
Olives (CA)	1,000 tons	133	67	46	87	47	32	CA
Oranges [3]	1,000 tons	7,625	10,076	9,198	2,216	2,199	1,950	FL, CA
Peaches	1,000 tons	1,116	1,114	1,083	502	546	594	CA, SC, NJ
Pears	1,000 tons	872	869	956	363	396	355	WA, OR, CA
Plums (CA)	1,000 tons	152	160	112	101	57	58	CA
Prunes (dried basis) (CA)	1,000 tons	235	368	496	117	194	199	CA
Raspberries, total	1,000 tons	71	75	89	263	365	363	CA,OR, WA
Strawberries	1,000 tons	1,223	1,266	1,401	1,751	1,918	2,124	CA, FL
Tangerines and mandarins	1,000 tons	361	527	443	156	236	210	CA, FL
NUTS								
Almonds (shelled basis) (CA)	1,000 tons	1,213	1,410	1,181	2,402	2,343	2,294	CA
Hazelnuts (in the shell) (OR)	1,000 tons	37	32	47	75	52	79	OR
Macadamia nuts (HI)	1,000 tons	21	25	21	25	34	29	HI
Pecans (in the shell) (11 states)	1,000 tons	194	97	146	434	260	417	NM, GA, TX
Pistachios (CA)	1,000 tons	208	139	178	587	570	593	CA
Walnuts(in the shell) (CA)	1,000 tons	328	436	437	751	558	739	CA

[1] Excludes quantities not harvested or not marketed. Utilized production is the amount sold plus the quantities used at home or held in storage [2] Production in commercial orchards with 100 or more bearing-age trees. [3] Includes temples and Navel varieties beginning with the 2006-2007 season.

Source: U.S. Department of Agriculture, National Agricultural Statistics Service, *Citrus Fruits 2009 Summary*, September 2009, and *Noncitrus Fruits and Nuts 2009 Summary*, July 2010. See also <http://www.nass.usda.gov/Publications/index.asp>.

Table 859. Nuts—Supply and Use: 2000 to 2008

[In thousands of pounds (shelled) (331,466 represents 331,466,000). For marketing season beginning July 1 for almonds, hazelnuts, pecans; August 1 for walnuts; and September 1 for pistachios]

Year	Beginning stocks	Marketable production [1]	Imports	Supply, total	Consumption	Exports	Ending stocks
Total nuts: [2]							
2000	331,466	1,127,940	293,172	1,752,577	733,921	780,988	237,669
2005	262,995	1,472,240	431,881	2,167,117	779,131	1,120,833	267,153
2006	267,153	1,651,048	438,343	2,356,544	982,397	1,131,015	243,133
2007	243,133	2,070,933	488,241	2,802,306	1,068,014	1,345,224	389,068
2008, total [2]	**389,068**	**2,233,112**	**429,107**	**3,051,287**	**1,076,706**	**1,437,247**	**537,334**
Almonds [3]	214,322	1,566,162	4,233	1,784,717	396,745	980,002	407,970
Pecans	85,438	87,216	55,968	228,621	141,154	44,704	42,763
Pistachios	67,304	135,392	985	203,681	41,694	129,065	32,922
Hazelnuts	2,104	26,173	10,010	38,287	15,223	21,937	1,127
Walnuts	19,900	395,455	1,884	417,238	152,289	212,397	52,553

[1] Utilized production minus inedibles and noncommercial usage. [2] Includes macadamia nuts, Brazil nuts, cashew nuts, pine nuts, chestnuts, and mixed nuts not shown separately. [3] Preliminary.

Source: U.S. Department of Agriculture, Economic Research Service, Fruit and Tree Nuts Situation and Outlook Yearbook. See also <http://www.ers.usda.gov/publications/fts/>.

Table 860. Honey—Number of Bee Colonies, Yield, and Production: 1990 to 2009

[Includes only beekeepers with five or more colonies. Colonies were not included if honey was not harvested]

Year	Honey-producing colonies [1] (1,000)	Yield per colony (pounds)	Production (1,000 pounds)	Average price per pound (cents)	Value of production (1,000 dollars)
1990	3,220	62	198,674	54	106,688
1995	2,655	80	211,073	69	144,585
2000	2,620	84	220,339	60	132,742
2005	2,413	72	174,818	92	160,428
2006	2,393	65	154,907	104	160,484
2007	2,443	61	148,341	108	159,763
2008	2,342	70	163,709	142	232,744
2009	2,462	59	144,108	145	208,236

[1] Honey producing colonies are the maximum number of colonies from which honey was taken during the year. It is possible to take honey from colonies which did not survive the entire year.

Source: U.S. Department of Agriculture, National Agricultural Statistics Service, *Honey*, February 2010.

Table 861. Adoption of Genetically Engineered Crops: 2000 to 2010

[In percent. As of June. Based on June Agricultural Survey conducted by National Agricultural Statistical Services (NASS). Excludes conventionally bred herbicide resistant varieties. Insect resistant varieties include only those containing bacillus thuringiensis (Bt). The Bt varieties include those that contain more than one gene that can resist different types of insects. Stacked gene varieties include only those varieties containing biotech traits for both herbicide and insect resistance]

Genetically engineered crop	2000	2001	2002	2003	2004	2005	2006	2007	2008	2009	2010
Corn.	25	26	34	40	47	52	61	73	80	85	86
Insect resistant.	18	18	22	25	27	26	25	21	17	17	16
Herbicide resistant	6	7	9	11	14	17	21	24	23	22	23
Stacked gene	1	1	2	4	6	9	15	28	40	46	47
Cotton	61	69	71	73	76	79	83	87	86	88	93
Insect resistant.	15	13	13	14	16	18	18	17	18	17	15
Herbicide resistant	26	32	36	32	30	27	26	28	23	23	20
Stacked gene	20	24	22	27	30	34	39	42	45	48	58
Soybean	54	68	75	81	85	87	89	91	92	91	93
Insect resistant.	(X)	(X)	(X)	(X)	(X)	(X)	(X)	(X)	(X)	(X)	(X)
Herbicide resistant	54	68	75	81	85	87	89	91	92	91	93
Stacked gene	(X)	(X)	(X)	(X)	(X)	(X)	(X)	(X)	(X)	(X)	(X)

X Not applicable.

Source: U.S. Department of Agriculture, Economic Research Service, "Adoption of Genetically Engineered Crops in the U.S.," July 2010, <http://www.ers.usda.gov/Data/BiotechCrops/>.

Table 862. Farmers Markets Characteristics: 2005

[In percent. Based on 2006 National Farmers Market Survey. A farmers market is defined as a retail outlet in which two or more vendors sell agricultural products directly to customers through a common marketing channel. Markets included were in business in the 2005 season and conducted 51 percent of their retail sales directly with consumers]

Characteristic	Total, U.S.	Region [1] North- east	Mid- Atlantic	South- east	North Central	South- west	Rocky Mountain	Far West
Number of vendors:								
Less than 10	23.9	42.4	37.4	24.1	17.8	32.3	15.9	9.4
10 to 19	25.3	27.9	28.4	22.8	29.4	29.0	19.3	12.5
20 to 39	29.0	23.6	22.6	29.7	32.3	17.7	28.4	35.6
40 or more	21.8	6.1	11.6	23.4	20.5	21.0	36.4	42.5
Vendor sales:								
$1 to $5,000.	71.4	70.0	61.2	68.1	81.4	71.6	80.4	56.1
$5,001 to $25,000	22.1	26.2	22.8	25.2	15.5	23.0	18.3	31.5
$25,000 to $100,000	5.9	3.8	15.4	4.3	2.9	5.3	1.3	11.8
$100,001 and above	0.6	–	0.7	2.4	0.2	0.2	–	0.6
Months of operation:								
Year-round.	12.1	3.5	13.7	19.6	4.1	17.5	4.3	35.4
Seasonal	87.9	96.5	86.3	80.4	95.9	82.5	95.7	64.6
Less than 4 months	20.0	26.3	15.5	16.9	19.2	22.2	39.6	11.4
4 to 6 months.	59.5	68.0	57.4	42.6	72.0	47.6	52.7	42.9
7 to 9 months.	7.6	2.3	12.9	18.2	4.6	9.5	3.3	8.6
More than 9 months.	12.9	3.4	14.2	22.3	4.2	20.6	4.4	37.1
Source of goods sold:								
Grew products sold (their own products). . .	(NA)	65.0	72.3	69.8	76.8	78.0	60.3	68.6
Organic products	47.0	67.3	37.2	35.5	39.8	30.4	56.8	74.5
Locally grown.	87.9	89.3	84.8	90.5	91.2	80.6	88.1	82.1
Pasture raised/free range	38.4	33.6	40.2	21.6	42.5	32.3	34.3	46.3
Natural.	46.9	39.3	41.1	45.9	50.9	32.3	55.2	50.4
Hormone or antibiotic free	29.3	20.5	27.7	20.3	34.4	19.4	28.4	36.6
Chemical free/pesticide free	47.6	36.9	39.3	45.9	46.9	41.9	56.7	65.0
Other	12.3	13.9	13.4	12.2	7.3	19.4	16.4	17.1

– Represents zero. NA Not available. [1] Composition of regions—Northeast: Connecticut, Maine, Massachusetts, New Hampshire, New York, Rhode Island, and Vermont. Mid-Atlantic: Delaware, District of Columbia, Maryland, New Jersey, Pennsylvania, Virginia, and West Virginia. Southeast: Alabama, Florida, Georgia, Kentucky, Mississippi, North Carolina, South Carolina, and Tennessee. North Central: Illinois, Indiana, Iowa, Kansas, Minnesota, Missouri, Nebraska, North Dakota, Ohio, South Dakota, and Wisconsin. Southwest: Arkansas, Louisiana, Oklahoma, and Texas. Rocky Mountain: Arizona, Colorado, Idaho, New Mexico, Montana, Utah, and Wyoming. Far West: Alaska, California, Hawaii, Nevada, Oregon, and Washington.

Source: United States Department of Agriculture, Agricultural Marketing Service, *National Farmers Market Manager Survey 2006*, May 2009, <http://www.ams.usda.gov/AMSv1.0/FARMERSMARKETS>.

Table 863. Meat Supply and Use: 1990 to 2009

[In millions of pounds (carcass weight equivalent) (62,255 represents 62,255,000,000). 2008 data are forecasts for red meats and 2009 are forecasts for poultry. Carcass weight equivalent is the weight of the animal minus entrails, head, hide, and internal organs; includes fat and bone. Covers federal and state inspected, and farm slaughtered]

Year and type of meat	Production	Imports	Supply [1]	Exports	Consumption [2]	Ending stocks
RED MEAT AND POULTRY						
1990	62,255	3,295	66,673	2,472	62,937	1,263
2000	82,372	4,136	88,480	9,344	77,068	2,069
2005	86,783	4,845	93,819	9,274	82,333	2,212
2006	88,907	4,326	95,445	10,070	83,240	2,135
2007	90,934	4,297	97,365	11,069	84,102	2,194
2008	93,681	4,130	100,004	12,014	85,816	2,174
ALL RED MEATS						
1990	38,787	3,295	42,742	1,250	40,784	707
2000	46,299	4,127	51,340	3,760	46,559	1,021
2005	45,848	4,803	51,838	3,373	47,385	1,080
2006	47,675	4,265	53,020	4,158	47,696	1,166
2007	48,817	4,223	54,206	4,579	48,435	1,192
2008	50,567	4,055	55,814	5,259	48,333	1,222
Beef:						
1990	22,743	2,356	25,434	1,006	24,031	397
2000	26,888	3,032	30,332	2,468	27,338	525
2005	24,787	3,599	29,023	697	27,754	571
2006	26,256	3,085	29,912	1,145	28,137	630
2007	26,523	3,052	30,205	1,431	28,144	630
2008	26,682	2,930	30,242	1,515	28,127	600
Pork:						
1990	15,354	898	16,565	238	16,031	296
2000	18,952	965	20,406	1,287	18,642	478
2005	20,705	1,024	22,272	2,666	19,112	494
2006	21,074	990	22,558	2,995	19,048	514
2007	21,962	968	23,444	3,138	19,763	542
2008	23,554	925	25,021	3,735	20,686	600
Veal:						
1990	327	(NA)	331	(NA)	325	6
2000	225	(NA)	230	(NA)	225	5
2005	165	(NA)	169	(NA)	164	5
2006	156	(NA)	161	(NA)	155	6
2007	146	(NA)	151	(NA)	144	7
2008	150	(NA)	157	(NA)	153	4
Lamb and mutton:						
1990	363	41	412	6	397	8
2000	234	130	372	5	354	13
2005	191	180	375	9	355	10
2006	190	190	390	18	356	16
2007	188	202	406	10	384	13
2008	181	200	394	9	367	18
POULTRY, TOTAL						
1990	23,468	–	23,931	1,222	22,153	556
2000	36,073	9	37,110	5,584	30,508	1,048
2005	40,935	42	41,970	5,902	34,949	1,119
2007	42,143	74	43,174	6,618	35,574	982
2008	43,235	92	44,309	7,785	35,379	1,144
2009	41,219	103	42,466	7,470	34,116	880
Broilers:						
1990	18,430	–	18,651	1,143	17,266	242
2000	30,209	6	31,011	4,918	25,295	798
2005	34,986	34	35,722	5,203	29,609	910
2007	35,772	61	36,565	5,904	29,942	719
2008	36,511	79	37,309	6,961	29,603	745
2009	35,131	85	35,961	6,835	28,509	616
Mature chicken:						
1990	523	–	530	25	496	9
2000	531	2	540	220	311	9
2005	516	1	520	130	388	2
2007	498	5	508	168	337	2
2008	559	5	566	148	415	3
2009	500	5	508	100	406	2
Turkeys:						
1990	4,514	–	4,750	54	4,390	306
2000	5,333	1	5,589	445	4,902	241
2005	5,432	8	5,728	570	4,952	206
2007	5,873	10	6,101	547	5,294	261
2008	6,165	8	6,434	676	5,361	396
2009	5,588	13	5,998	535	5,201	262

– Represents zero. NA Not available. [1] Total supply equals production plus imports plus ending stocks of previous year.
[2] Includes shipments to territories.

Source: U.S. Department of Agriculture, Economic Research Service, *Food Consumption, Prices, and Expenditures, 1970–1997* and "Agricultural Outlook: Statistical Indicators," <http://www.ers.usda.gov/publications/agoutlook/aotables/>.

Agriculture 553

Table 864. Livestock Inventory and Production: 1990 to 2009

[95.8 represents 95,800,000. Production in live weight; includes animals-for-slaughter market, younger animals shipped to other states for feeding or breeding purposes, farm slaughter and custom slaughter consumed on farms where produced, minus livestock shipped into states for feeding or breeding with an adjustment for changes in inventory]

Type of livestock	Unit	1990	1995	2000	2003	2004	2005	2006	2007	2008	2009
ALL CATTLE [1]											
Inventory: [2] Number on farms . . .	Mil.	95.8	102.8	98.2	96.1	94.4	95.0	96.3	96.6	96.0	94.5
Total value.	Bil. dol.	59.0	63.2	67.1	69.9	77.2	87.0	97.2	89.1	95.1	(NA)
Value per head	Dol.	616	615	683	728	818	916	1,009	922	990	(NA)
Production: Quantity	Bil. lb.	39.2	42.5	43.0	42.2	41.6	41.2	41.8	41.4	41.6	40.9
Beef, price per 100 pounds.	Dol.	74.60	61.80	68.60	79.70	85.80	89.70	87.20	89.90	(NA)	(NA)
Calves, price per 100 pounds.	Dol.	95.60	73.10	104.00	102.00	119.00	135.00	133.00	119.00	(NA)	(NA)
Value of production.	Bil. dol.	29.3	24.7	28.5	32.1	34.9	36.3	35.5	36.0	35.6	31.8
HOGS AND PIGS											
Inventory: [3] Number on farms . . .	Mil.	53.8	59.7	59.3	59.6	60.5	61.0	61.5	62.5	68.2	67.1
Total value.	Bil. dol.	4.3	3.2	4.3	4.2	4.0	6.3	5.8	5.6	5.0	(NA)
Value per head	Dol.	79	53	72	71	67	103	95	90	73	(NA)
Production: Quantity	Bil. lb.	21.3	24.4	25.7	26.3	26.7	27.4	28.2	29.6	31.4	31.1
Price per 100 pounds. . . .	Dol.	53.70	40.50	42.30	37.20	49.30	50.20	40.00	46.60	(NA)	(NA)
Value of production.	Bil. dol.	11.3	9.8	10.8	9.7	13.1	13.6	12.7	13.5	14.5	12.8
SHEEP AND LAMBS											
Inventory: [2] Number on farms . . .	Mil.	11.4	9.0	7.0	6.3	6.1	6.1	6.2	6.1	6.0	5.7
Total value.	Mil. dol.	901	663	670	657	720	798	872	818	823	(NA)
Value per head	Dol.	79	75	95	104	119	130	141	134	138	(NA)
Production: Quantity	Mil. lb.	781	602	512	467	466	472	461	440	417	413
Value of production.	Mil. dol.	374	414	365	389	413	451	368	363	351	357

NA Not available. [1] Includes milk cows. [2] As of January 1. [3] As of December 1 of preceding year.

Source: U.S. Department of Agriculture, National Agricultural Statistics Service, *Meat Animals—Production, Disposition, and Income Final Estimates 1998–2002*, May 2004; *Meat Animals—Production, Disposition, and Income Final Estimates 2003–2007*, May 2009; *Meat Animals Production, Disposition, and Income 2009 Summary, April 2010*. See also <http://www.nass.usda.gov/Publications/index.asp>.

Table 865. Livestock Operations by Size of Herd: 2000 to 2009

[In thousands(1,076 represents 1,076,000). An operation is any place having one or more head on hand at any time during the year]

Size of herd	2000	2005	2008	2009	Size of herd	2000	2005	2008	2009
CATTLE [1]					**MILK COWS** [2]				
Total operations	**1,076**	**983**	**956**	**950**	**Total operations . . . . .**	**105**	**78**	**67**	**65**
1 to 49 head.	671	612	645	642	1 to 49 head.	53	37	33	32
50 to 99 head.	186	164	133	132	50 to 99 head.	31	23	18	17
100 to 499 head.	192	178	148	146	100 head or more	21	15	16	16
500 to 999 head.	19	19	19	19					
1,000 head or more	10	10	11	11	**HOGS AND PIGS**				
					Total operations	**87**	**67**	**73**	**71**
BEEF COWS [2]					1 to 99 head.	50	41	51	50
Total operations	**831**	**770**	**757**	**753**	100 to 499 head.	17	10	7	6
1 to 49 head.	655	597	601	598	500 to 999 head.	8	5	3	3
50 to 99 head.	100	95	83	82	1,000 to 1,999 head. . . .	6	4	4	4
100 to 499 head.	71	73	67	67	2,000 to 4,999 head. . . .	5	5	5	5
500 head or more	6	5	6	6	5,000 head or more. . . .	2	2	3	3

[1] Includes calves. [2] Included in operations with cattle.

Source: U.S. Department of Agriculture, National Agricultural Statistics Service, *Livestock Operations Final Estimates 1998–2002*, April 2004; *Livestock Operations Final Estimates 2003–2007*, March 2009; *Farms, Land in Farms, and Livestock Operations 2009 Summary*, February 2010. See also <http://www.nass.usda.gov/Publications/index.asp>.

Table 866. Hogs and Pigs—Number, Production, and Slaughter by Leading States: 2007 to 2009

[68,177 represents 68,177,000. See headnote, Table 864]

State	Number on farms [1] (1,000)			Quantity produced (mil. lb.)			Value of production (mil. dol.)			Commercial slaughter [2] (mil. lb.)	
	2007	2008	2009	2007	2008	2009	2007	2008	2009	2008	2009
U.S [3] **. . . . .**	**68,177**	**67,148**	**65,327**	**29,606**	**31,411**	**31,131**	**13,468**	**14,457**	**12,762**	**31,199**	**30,723**
IA.	19,400	19,900	19,200	8,444	9,428	9,623	3,632	4,040	3,585	8,744	8,682
NC.	10,200	9,700	9,600	3,815	4,210	4,099	1,931	2,120	1,836	3,160	3,219
MN.	7,700	7,500	7,300	3,540	3,777	3,427	1,646	1,763	1,421	2,594	2,592
IL.	4,350	4,350	4,300	1,513	1,711	1,841	786	917	908	2,989	2,674
IN.	3,700	3,550	3,650	1,607	1,726	1,730	713	818	724	2,182	2,256
MO.	3,150	3,150	3,100	1,806	1,747	1,697	716	765	675	2,160	2,229
NE	3,350	3,350	3,100	1,438	1,385	1,369	727	715	630	2,122	2,068

[1] As of December 1. [2] Includes slaughter in federally inspected and other slaughter plants; excludes animals slaughtered on farms. [3] Includes other states, not shown separately.

Source: U.S. Department of Agriculture, National Agricultural Statistics Service, *Meat Animals—Production, Disposition and Income 2009 Summary*, April 2010, and *Livestock Slaughter 2009 Summary*, April 2010, annual. See also <http://www.nass.usda.gov/Publications/index.asp>.

Table 867. Cattle and Calves—Number, Production, and Value by State: 2008 to 2009

[96,035 represents 96,035,000. Includes milk cows. See headnote, Table 864]

State	Number on farms [1] (1,000)			Production (mil. lb.)			Value of production (mil. dol.)			Commercial slaughter [2] (mil. lb.)	
	2008	2009	2010	2007	2008	2009	2007	2008	2009	2008	2009
U.S. [3]	**96,035**	**94,521**	**93,701**	**41,437**	**41,594**	**40,919**	**35,973**	**35,608**	**31,769**	**43,895**	**42,966**
TX	13,600	13,600	13,300	6,728	7,280	6,924	6,026	6,449	5,481	8,269	8,208
NE	6,450	6,350	6,250	4,697	4,622	4,598	4,246	4,203	3,733	9,415	9,104
KS	6,650	6,300	6,000	4,069	3,892	3,916	3,328	3,321	2,965	8,296	8,175
OK	5,400	5,400	5,450	1,977	2,036	1,984	2,002	1,939	1,747	30	30
CO	2,750	2,600	2,600	1,898	1,783	1,804	1,915	1,737	1,586	3,272	3,119
IA	4,000	3,950	3,850	1,732	1,845	1,787	1,446	1,606	1,437	(4)	(4)
SD	3,700	3,700	3,800	1,472	1,490	1,471	1,410	1,401	1,326	(4)	(4)
MO	4,250	4,250	4,150	1,333	1,394	1,348	1,320	1,275	1,170	108	108
CA	5,450	5,250	5,150	1,977	1,968	1,919	1,289	1,353	1,112	1,999	2,109
MN	2,400	2,400	2,420	1,094	1,108	1,108	886	896	800	1,175	1,167
ID	2,210	2,110	2,140	1,102	1,140	1,046	918	936	798	382	390

[1] As of January 1. [2] Data cover cattle only. Includes slaughter in federally inspected and other slaughter plants; excludes animals slaughtered on farms. [3] Includes other states, not shown separately. [4] Included in U.S. total. Not printed to avoid disclosing individual operation.

Source: U.S. Department of Agriculture, National Agricultural Statistics Service, *Meat Animals—Production, Disposition and Income 2009 Summary*, April 2010, and *Livestock Slaughter 2009 Summary*, April 2010, annual. See also <http://www.nass.usda.gov/Publications/index.asp>.

Table 868. Milk Cows—Number, Production, and Value by State: 2008 to 2009

[9,315 represents 9,315,000]

State	Number on farms [1] (1,000)		Milk produced on farms [2] (mil. lb.)		Milk produced per milk cow [2]		Value of production [3] (mil. dol.)	
	2008	2009	2008	2009	2008	2009	2008	2009
United States [4]	**9,315**	**9,201**	**189,982**	**189,320**	**20,395**	**20,576**	**35,051**	**24,477**
California	1,844	1,796	41,203	39,512	22,344	22,000	6,930	4,510
Wisconsin	1,252	1,257	24,472	25,239	19,546	20,079	4,625	3,306
New York	626	619	12,432	12,424	19,859	20,071	2,387	1,690
Idaho	549	550	12,315	12,150	22,432	22,091	2,106	1,434
Pennsylvania	549	545	10,575	10,561	10,262	10,000	2,113	1,519
Minnesota	464	469	8,782	9,019	18,927	19,230	1,677	1,209
Texas	418	423	8,416	8,840	20,134	20,898	1,574	1,176
Michigan	350	355	7,763	7,968	22,180	22,445	1,490	1,068

[1] Average number during year. Represents cows and heifers that have calved, kept for milk; excluding heifers not yet fresh.
[2] Excludes milk sucked by calves. [3] Valued at average returns per 100 pounds of milk in combined marketings of milk and cream. Includes value of milk fed to calves. [4] Includes other states, not shown separately.

Source: U.S. Department of Agriculture, National Agricultural Statistics Service, *Milk Production, Disposition, and Income 2009 Summary*, April 2010. See also <http://www.nass.usda.gov/Publications/index.asp>.

Table 869. Milk Production and Manufactured Dairy Products: 1990 to 2009

[193 represents 193,000]

Item	Unit	1990	2000	2003	2004	2005	2006	2007	2008	2009
Number of farms with milk cows	1,000	193	105	86	82	78	75	70	67	65
Cows and heifers that have calved, kept for milk	Mil. head . . .	10.0	9.2	9.1	9.0	9.1	9.1	9.2	9.3	9.2
Milk produced on farms	Bil. lb.	148	167	170	171	177	182	186	190	189
Production per cow	1,000 lb.	14.8	18.2	18.8	19.0	19.6	19.9	20.2	20.4	20.6
Milk marketed by producers [1]	Bil. lb.	146	166	169	170	176	181	185	189	188
Value of milk produced	Bil. dol.	20.4	20.8	21.4	27.6	26.9	23.6	35.7	35.1	24.5
Cash receipts from marketing of milk and cream [1]	Bil. dol.	20.1	20.6	21.2	27.4	26.7	23.4	35.5	34.8	24.3
Number of dairy manufacturing plants	Number	1,723	1,164	1,119	1,093	1,088	1,094	1,123	1,125	1,178
Manufactured dairy products:										
Butter (including whey butter)	Mil. lb.	1,302	1,256	1,242	1,247	1,347	1,448	1,533	1,644	1,573
Cheese, total [2]	Mil. lb.	6,059	8,258	8,557	8,873	9,149	9,525	9,777	9,913	10,109
American (excl. full-skim American) . . .	Mil. lb.	2,894	3,642	3,622	3,739	3,808	3,913	3,877	4,109	4,202
Cream and Neufchatel.	Mil. lb.	431	687	677	699	715	756	773	764	767
All Italian varieties	Mil. lb.	2,207	3,289	3,524	3,662	3,803	3,973	4,199	4,121	4,180
Cottage cheese: Creamed [3]	Mil. lb.	832	735	769	788	784	778	774	714	730
Nonfat dry milk [4]	Mil. lb.	902	1,457	1,589	1,412	1,210	1,244	1,298	1,519	1,509
Dry whey [5]	Mil. lb.	1,143	1,188	1,085	1,035	1,041	1,110	1,134	1,082	1,001
Yogurt, plain and fruit-flavored	Mil. lb.	(NA)	1,837	2,507	2,707	3,058	3,301	3,476	3,570	3,832
Ice cream, regular	Mil. gal.	824	980	993	920	960	982	956	931	920
Ice cream, lowfat [6]	Mil. gal.	352	373	398	387	360	377	383	384	381

NA Not available. [1] Comprises sales to plants and dealers, and retail sales by farmers direct to consumers. [2] Includes varieties, not shown separately. [3] Includes partially creamed (low fat). [4] Includes dry skim milk for animal feed through 2000. [5] Includes animal but excludes modified whey production. [6] Includes freezer-made milkshake in most states.

Source: U.S. Department of Agriculture, National Agricultural Statistics Service, Milk Disposition, and Income Final Estimates 2003–2007, May 2009. Dairy Products 2009 Summary, April 2010, and Milk Production, Disposition, and Income 2009 Summary, April 2010, <http://www.nass.usda.gov/Publications/index.asp>.

U.S. Census Bureau, Statistical Abstract of the United States: 2011

Table 870. Milk Production and Commercial Use: 1990 to 2009

[In billions of pounds milkfat basis (147.7 represents 147,700,000,000) except as noted]

Year	Produc-tion	Farm use	Commercial Farm market-ings	Begin-ning stock	Imports	Com-mercial supply, total	Commodity CreditCor-poration net removals [1]	Commercial Ending stock	Exports	Disap-pear-ance [2]	Milk price per 100 pounds [3] (dollars)
1990...	147.7	2.0	145.7	4.1	2.7	152.5	8.5	5.1	(NA)	138.8	13.68
2000...	167.4	1.3	166.1	6.1	4.4	176.7	0.8	6.9	(NA)	169.0	12.40
2005...	176.9	1.1	175.8	7.2	5.0	187.9	–	8.0	3.3	176.7	15.13
2006...	181.8	1.1	180.7	8.0	7.5	196.2	–	9.5	3.4	180.7	12.88
2007...	185.7	1.1	184.6	9.5	7.2	201.3	–	10.4	5.7	185.2	19.13
2008...	190.0	1.1	188.9	10.4	5.3	204.6	–	10.1	8.7	185.7	18.34
2009...	189.3	1.0	188.3	10.1	5.6	204.0	–	11.3	4.1	187.6	12.84

– Represents zero. NA Not available. [1] Removals from commercial supply by Commodity Credit Corporation (CCC) on a fat basis. [2] Prior to 2005, disappearance represents domestic disappearance plus exports. [3] Wholesale price received by farmers for all milk delivered to plants and dealers.

Source: U.S. Department of Agriculture, Economic Research Service, "Agricultural Outlook: Statistical Indicators," <http://www.ers.usda.gov/publications/agoutlook/aotables/>.

Table 871. Broiler, Turkey, and Egg Production: 2000 to 2009

[For year ending November 30 (437 represents 437,000,000), except as noted]

Item	Unit	2000	2001	2002	2003	2004	2005	2006	2007	2008	2009
Chickens:[1]											
Number [2]	Million	437	444	444	450	454	456	458	459	447	450
Value per head [2] ...	Dollars	2.44	2.41	2.38	2.48	2.48	2.52	2.60	2.95	3.39	3.34
Value, total [2].......	Mil. dol.....	1,064	1,069	1,055	1,116	1,126	1,150	1,190	1,352	1,517	1,502
Number sold	Million	218	202	200	190	192	194	174	168	176	175
Price per pound....	Cents.....	5.7	4.5	4.8	4.9	5.8	6.5	5.9	5.6	6.6	7.2
Value of sales	Mil. dol.....	64	47	50	48	58	65	54	51	62	65
PRODUCTION											
Broilers:[3]											
Number	Million	8,284	8,390	8,591	8,493	8,741	8,872	8,868	8,907	9,009	8,551
Weight	Bil. lb..	41.6	42.5	44.1	44.0	45.8	47.9	48.8	49.3	50.4	47.7
Price per pound....	Cents.....	33.6	39.3	30.5	34.6	44.6	43.6	36.3	43.6	46.0	45.7
Production value ...	Mil. dol.....	13,989	16,696	13,437	15,215	20,446	20,878	17,739	21,514	23,203	21,811
Turkeys:											
Number	Million	270	273	275	270	256	250	256	267	273	247
Weight	Bil. lb..	7.0	7.2	7.5	7.2	6.9	7.0	7.2	7.6	7.9	7.1
Price per pound....	Cents.....	40.6	39.0	36.5	34.6	41.5	44.5	48.0	52.3	57.0	50.0
Production value ...	Mil. dol.....	2,828	2,797	2,732	2,504	2,887	3,108	3,468	3,954	4,477	3,574
Eggs:											
Average number of layers..........	Thousand..	327,908	335,012	339,024	338,393	342,279	343,792	347,880	344,385	339,131	337,376
Eggs per layer	Number ...	257	256	257	259	260	262	263	263	266	268
Total production	Billion.....	84.4	85.7	86.7	87.5	89.1	90.9	91.3	90.6	90.0	90.4
Price per dozen	Cents.....	61.6	62.0	58.9	73.1	71.3	54.0	58.3	88.5	109.0	81.7
Production value ...	Mil. dol.....	4,346	4,446	4,281	5,334	5,303	4,067	4,460	6,719	8,216	6,156

[1] Excludes commercial broilers. [2] As of December 1. [3] Young chickens of the heavy breeds and other meat-type birds, to be marketed at 2–5 lbs. live weight and from which no pullets are kept for egg production. Not included in sales of chickens.

Source: U.S. Department of Agriculture, National Agricultural Statistics Service, *Poultry Production and Value Final Estimates 1998–2002*, April 2004; *Turkeys Final Estimates 1998–2002*, April 2004; *Poultry Production and Value Final Estimates 2003–2007*, May 2009; *Chickens and Eggs Final Estimates 1998–2002*, April 2004; *Chickens and Eggs Final Estimates 2003–2007*, March 2009; and *Poultry—Production and Value 2009 Summary, and Chickens and Eggs 2009 Summary*, February 2010. See also <http://www.nass.usda.gov/Publications/index.asp>.

Table 872. Broiler and Turkey Production by State: 2007 to 2009

[In millions of pounds, live weight production (49,331 represents 49,331,000,000)]

State	Broilers 2007	2008	2009	Turkeys 2007	2008	2009	State	Broilers 2007	2008	2009	Turkeys 2007	2008	2009
U.S. [1]....	49,331	50,441	47,727	7,566	7,922	7,150	MS.......	4,614	4,876	4,602	(NA)	(NA)	(NA)
AL	5,625	5,846	5,513	(NA)	(NA)	(NA)	MO.......	(NA)	(NA)	(NA)	646	651	611
AR	6,232	6,380	5,780	572	611	568	NC.......	5,390	5,493	5,317	1,147	1,208	1,090
CA	(NA)	(NA)	(NA)	450	435	390	OH.......	274	328	338	227	230	203
DE	1,598	1,579	1,597	(NA)	(NA)	(NA)	OK.......	1,288	1,260	1,220	(NA)	(NA)	(NA)
FL	418	376	252	(NA)	(NA)	(NA)	PA	847	933	860	199	216	182
GA	7,414	7,469	6,874	(NA)	(NA)	(NA)	SC	1,480	1,516	1,522	382	478	433
IL	(NA)	(NA)	(NA)	77	(NA)	(NA)	SD	(NA)	(NA)	(NA)	173	189	187
IN........	(NA)	(NA)	(NA)	481	519	543	TN	1,050	1,019	968	(NA)	(NA)	(NA)
IA........	(NA)	(NA)	(NA)	325	360	(NA)	TX	3,266	3,460	3,611	(NA)	(NA)	(NA)
KY	1,668	1,653	1,658	(NA)	(NA)	(NA)	UT	(NA)	(NA)	(NA)	(NA)	105	82
MD.......	1,592	1,612	1,401	13	13	(NA)	VA	1,301	1,252	1,204	483	484	449
MI........	(NA)	(NA)	(NA)	192	(NA)	(NA)	WV.......	356	351	331	97	102	97
MN.......	242	238	241	1,218	1,306	(NA)	WI	203	217	192	(NA)	(NA)	(NA)

NA Not available. [1] Includes other states, not shown separately.

Source: U.S. Department of Agriculture, National Agricultural Statistics Service, *Poultry Production and Value Final Estimates 2003–2007*, May 2009, and *Poultry—Production and Value, 2009 Summary*, April 2010. See also <http://www.nass.usda.gov/Publications/index.asp>.

Section 18
Forestry, Fishing, and Mining

This section presents data on the area, ownership, production, trade, reserves, and disposition of natural resources. Natural resources is defined here as including forestry, fisheries, and mining and mineral products.

Forestry—Presents data on the area, ownership, and timber resource of commercial timberland; forestry statistics covering the National Forests and Forest Service cooperative programs; product data for lumber, pulpwood, woodpulp, paper and paperboard, and similar data.

The principal sources of data relating to forests and forest products are *Forest Resources of the United States, 2007; Timber Demand and Technology Assessment; U.S. Timber Production, Trade, Consumption, and Price Statistics, 1965– 2005; Land Areas of the National Forest System,* issued annually by the Forest Service of the U.S. Department of Agriculture; *Agricultural Statistics* issued by the Department of Agriculture; and reports of the annual survey of manufactures, and the annual *Current Industrial Reports,* issued by the U.S. Census Bureau on the Internet and in print in the annual *Manufacturing Profiles.* Additional information is published in the monthly *Survey of Current Business* of the Bureau of Economic Analysis, and the annual *Wood Pulp and Fiber Statistics* and *The Annual Statistics of Paper, Paperboard, and Wood Pulp* of the American Forest and Paper Association, Washington, DC.

The completeness and reliability of statistics on forests and forest products vary considerably. The data for forest land area and stand volumes are much more reliable for areas that have been recently surveyed than for those for which only estimates are available. In general, more data are available for lumber and other manufactured products such as particle board and softwood panels, etc., than for the primary forest products such as poles and piling and fuelwood.

Fisheries—The principal source of data relating to fisheries is *Fisheries of the United States,* issued annually by the National Marine Fisheries Service (NMFS), National Oceanic and Atmospheric Administration (NOAA). The NMFS collects and disseminates data on commercial landings of fish and shellfish. Annual reports include quantity and value of commercial landings of fish and shellfish disposition of landings and number and kinds of fishing vessels and fishing gear. Reports for the fish-processing industry include annual output for the wholesaling and fish processing establishments, annual and seasonal employment. The principal source for these data is the annual *Fisheries of the United States.*

Mining and mineral products—Presents data relating to mineral industries and their products, general summary measures of production and employment, and more detailed data on production, prices, imports and exports, consumption, and distribution for specific industries and products. Data on mining and mineral products may also be found in Sections 19, 21, and 28 of this *Abstract;* data on mining employment may be found in Section 12.

Mining comprises the extraction of minerals occurring naturally (coal, ores, crude petroleum, natural gas) and quarrying, well operation, milling, refining and processing, and other preparation customarily done at the mine or well site or as a part of extraction activity. (Mineral preparation plants are usually operated together with mines or quarries.) Exploration for minerals is included as is the development of mineral properties.

The principal governmental sources of these data are the *Minerals Yearbook* and *Mineral Commodity Summaries,* published by the U.S. Geological Survey, U.S. Department of the Interior, and various monthly and annual publications of the Energy Information Administration, U.S. Department of Energy. See text, Section 19, for a

Forestry, Fishing, and Mining 557

list of Department of Energy publications. In addition, the Census Bureau conducts a census of mineral industries every 5 years.

Nongovernment sources include the *Annual Statistical Report* of the American Iron and Steel Institute, Washington, DC; *Metals Week* and the monthly *Engineering and Mining Journal*, issued by the McGraw-Hill Publishing Co., New York, NY; *The Iron Age*, issued weekly by the Chilton Co., Philadelphia, PA; and the *Joint Association Survey of the U.S. Oil and Gas Industry*, conducted jointly by the American Petroleum Institute, Independent Petroleum Association of America, and Mid-Continent Oil and Gas Association.

Mineral statistics, with principal emphasis on commodity detail, have been collected by the U.S. Geological Survey and the former Bureau of Mines since 1880.

Current data in U.S. Geological Survey publications include quantity and value of nonfuel minerals produced, sold, or used by producers, or shipped; quantity of minerals stocked; crude materials treated and prepared minerals recovered; and consumption of mineral raw materials.

The Economic Census, conducted by the Census Bureau at various intervals since 1840, collects data on mineral industries. Beginning with the 1967 census, legislation provides for a census to be conducted every 5 years for years ending in "2" and "7." The most recent results, published for 2007, are based on the North American Industry Classification System (NAICS). The censuses provide, for the various types of mineral establishments, information on operating costs, capital expenditures, labor, equipment, and energy requirements in relation to their value of shipments and other receipts.

Figure 18.1
Crude Oil Production and Imports: 1990 to 2009

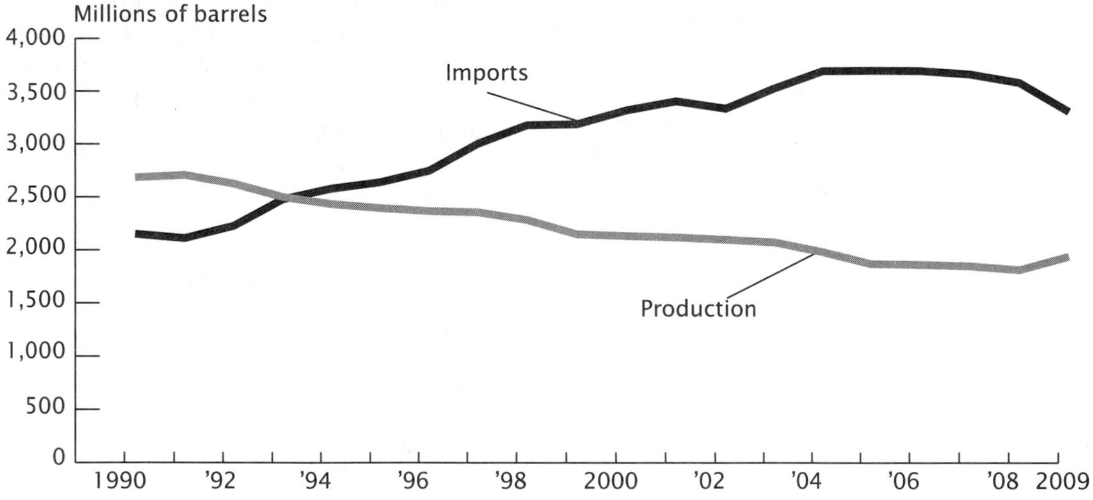

Source: Chart prepared by U.S. Census Bureau. For data, see Table 904.

558 Forestry, Fishing, and Mining

Table 873. Natural Resource-Related Industries—Establishments, Sales, Payroll, and Employees by Industry: 2002 and 2007

[183 represents $183,000,000,000. Includes only establishments of firms with payroll. Data are based on the 2002 and 2007 economic censuses, which are subject to nonsampling error. For details on methodology and nonsampling and sampling errors, see Appendix III]

Industry	2002 NAICS code [1]	Establishments (number)		Value of shipments (bil. dol.)		Annual payroll (bil. dol.)		Paid employees [2] (1,000)	
		2002	2007	2002	2007	2002	2007	2002	2007
Mining	21	24,087	21,169	183	369	21	37	475	703
Oil & gas extraction	211	7,730	6,293	113	231	5	10	99	162
Mining (except oil & gas)	212	7,253	6,465	48	81	9	11	196	220
Mining support activities	213	9,104	8,411	22	57	7	16	180	322
Manufacturing [3]	31–33	350,728	293,919	3,915	5,339	568	612	15	13
Wood product mfg	321	17,192	14,862	89	102	16	17	540	520
Paper mfg	322	5,520	4,803	154	176	21	21	491	417
Petroleum & coal products manufacturing . . .	324	2,268	2,284	216	606	6	8	104	105

[1] North American Industry Classification System, 2002. [2] For pay period including March 12. [3] Includes other industries, not shown separately.

Source: U.S. Census Bureau, 2007 Economic Census, "Comparative Statistics," March 2009, <http://www.census.gov/econ /census07/www/get_data.html>.

Table 874. Natural Resource-Related Industries—Establishments, Employees, and Annual Payroll by Industry: 2000 and 2007

[1,791.3 represents 1,791,300. Excludes government employees, railroad employees, self-employed persons, etc. See "General Explanation" in source for definitions and statement on reliability of data. An establishment is a single physical location where business is conducted or where services or industrial operations are performed]

Industry	2002 NAICS Code [1]	Establishments (number)		Number of employees [2] (1,000)		Annual payroll (bil. dol.)	
		2000	2007	2000	2007	2000	2007
Natural resource related industries, total	(X)	72,932	71,506	1,791.3	1,825.7	66.58	85.09
Forestry, fishing, hunting, and agriculture support. . . .	11	26,076	23,645	183.6	172.1	4.68	5.56
Forestry and logging	113	13,347	10,491	83.1	64.4	2.26	2.26
Timber tract operations	1131	469	450	3.3	2.6	0.13	0.13
Forest nurseries and gathering forest products. . . .	1132	258	231	1.7	2.2	0.07	0.07
Logging	1133	12,620	9,810	78.1	59.6	2.06	2.06
Fishing, hunting and trapping	114	2,671	2,389	10.0	7.1	0.34	0.34
Fishing	1141	2,308	2,062	7.5	5.3	0.27	0.28
Hunting and trapping	1142	363	327	2.5	1.8	0.08	0.06
Agriculture and forestry support activities	115	10,058	10,765	90.4	100.5	2.08	2.97
Crop production support activities	1151	5,061	4,635	57.6	66.3	1.35	1.95
Animal production support activities	1152	3,450	4,375	18.2	20.5	0.38	0.57
Forestry support activities	1153	1,547	1,755	14.7	13.7	0.35	0.45
Mining	21	23,738	26,202	456.1	700.9	22.09	40.44
Oil and gas extraction	211	7,740	7,542	83.0	141.8	5.39	9.60
Mining (except oil and gas)	212	7,231	7,008	204.3	218.0	9.34	11.92
Coal mining	2121	1,253	1,066	70.7	79.8	3.54	4.99
Metal ore mining	2122	522	318	34.8	34.7	1.72	2.23
Nonmetallic mineral mining and quarrying	2123	5,456	5,624	98.8	103.5	4.08	4.70
Mining support activities	213	8,767	11,652	168.8	341.0	7.35	18.92
Timber-related manufacturing	(X)	23,118	21,659	1,151.6	952.7	39.80	39.08
Wood product manufacturing.	321	17,328	16,622	597.7	527.6	16.51	17.51
Sawmills and wood preservation	3211	4,695	4,168	131.4	112.4	3.78	3.89
Veneer, plywood and engineered wood product manufacturing	3212	1,904	1,924	120.6	109.0	3.75	3.91
Other wood product manufacturing	3219	10,729	10,530	345.8	306.1	8.95	9.71
Paper manufacturing	322	5,790	5,037	553.9	425.1	23.29	21.57
Pulp, paper and paperboard mills	3221	597	551	177.1	130.1	9.48	8.24
Converted paper product manufacturing	3222	5,193	4,486	376.8	295.0	13.82	13.33

X Not applicable. [1] North American Industry Classification System, 2002. [2] Covers full- and part-time employees who are on the payroll in the pay period including March 12.

Source: U.S. Census Bureau, "County Business Patterns," July 2009, <http://www.census.gov/econ/cbp/index.html>.

Table 875. Timber-Based Manufacturing Industries—Establishments, Shipments, Payroll, and Employees: 2007

[102,001,662 represents $102,001,662,000. Includes only establishments or firms with payroll. Data for industries with NAICS codes less than 6-digits were derived by summing values with the corresponding 6-digit NAICS codes. See Appendix III]

Industry	2007 NAICS code [1]	Establishments (number)	Value of shipments ($1,000)	Annual payroll ($1,000)	Paid employees [2]
Wood product manufacturing.	321	16,825	102,001,662	17,443,992	524,212
Sawmills and wood preservation	3211	4,094	27,866,369	3,618,616	102,805
Sawmills	321113	3,582	22,040,005	3,123,732	89,507
Wood preservation.	321114	512	5,826,364	494,884	13,298
Veneer, plywood, and engineered wood product manufacturing	3212	1,958	22,258,829	3,829,184	106,848
Other wood product manufacturing	3219	10,773	51,876,464	9,996,192	314,559
Millwork	32191	4,713	28,300,862	5,201,356	153,739
Wood container and pallet manufacturing	32192	2,909	7,235,876	1,519,970	58,467
All other wood product manufacturing	32199	3,151	16,339,726	3,274,866	102,353
Paper manufacturing	322	4,984	176,018,245	20,804,019	417,367
Pulp, paper, and paperboard mills	3221	488	80,114,225	7,876,401	124,747
Pulp mills	32211	39	5,027,395	504,602	7,268
Paper mills.	32212	262	49,732,085	4,919,950	80,838
Paperboard mills	32213	187	25,354,745	2,451,849	36,641
Converted paper product manufacturing	3222	4,496	95,904,020	12,927,618	292,620
Paperboard container manufacturing	32221	2,402	50,900,190	7,387,042	165,839
Paper bag and coated and treated paper manufacturing	32222	891	21,737,348	2,798,096	60,373
Stationery product manufacturing	32223	549	8,242,007	1,197,456	31,628
Other converted paper product manufacturing	32229	654	15,024,475	1,545,024	34,780

[1] North American Industry Classification System, 2007. [2] For pay period including March 12.

Source: U.S. Census Bureau, 2007 Economic Census, "Economy-Wide Key Statistics," August 2010. See also <http://www.census.gov/econ/census07/>.

Table 876. Timber-Based Manufacturing Industries—Employees, Payroll, and Shipments: 2008

[In thousands (12,781 represents 12,781,000). Based on the Annual Survey of Manufactures; see Appendix III]

Selected industry	2007 NAICS code [1]	All employees — Number (1,000)	All employees — Payroll Total (mil. dol.)	All employees — Payroll Per employee (dol.)	Production workers, total (1,000)	Value added by manufactures Total (mil. dol.)	Value added by manufactures Per production worker (dol.)	Value of shipments (mil. dol.)
Manufacturing, all industries [2]	**31–33**	**12,781**	**607,447**	**47,527**	**8,873**	**2,274,367**	**256,327**	**5,486,266**
Timber-based manufacturing, total	**321–322**	**865**	**36,165**	**41,817**	**677**	**113,753**	**167,996**	**266,753**
Percent of total manufacturing	(X)	6.77	5.95	(X)	7.63	5.00	(X)	4.86
Wood product manufacturing	321	462	15,619	33,834	366	34,577	94,592	88,004
Sawmills and wood preservation	3211	92	3,394	37,024	77	7,278	94,704	24,272
Veneer, plywood, and engineered wood product	3212	87	3,225	37,090	68	6,525	95,878	18,381
Other wood product	3219	283	9,000	31,801	221	20,774	94,156	45,352
Millwork	32191	137	4,635	33,821	107	11,029	102,748	24,100
Wood container and pallet	32192	56	1,480	26,401	46	3,469	76,142	7,341
All other wood products	32199	90	2,884	32,088	68	6,276	92,658	13,910
Paper manufacturing	322	403	20,546	50,957	312	79,175	254,115	178,749
Pulp, paper, and paperboard mills	3221	118	7,794	66,142	94	40,476	432,604	82,923
Pulp mills	32211	7	525	70,034	6	2,301	382,939	5,268
Paper mills	32212	76	4,920	64,720	61	26,498	435,894	52,324
Paperboard mills	32213	34	2,350	68,445	27	11,677	436,281	25,331
Converted paper product	3222	285	12,752	44,687	218	38,700	177,513	95,826
Paperboard container	32221	164	7,417	45,134	126	18,403	146,077	51,687
Paper bag and coated and treated paper	32222	58	2,704	46,765	43	9,101	212,356	21,158
Stationery product	32223	29	1,122	38,612	22	3,349	149,053	7,869
Other converted paper products	32229	34	1,510	44,185	27	7,847	293,825	15,111

X Not applicable. [1] North American Industry Classification System, 2007; see text, Section 15. [2] Includes other industries, not shown separately.

Source: U.S. Census Bureau, "Annual Survey of Manufactures, 2008," March 2010, <http://www.census.gov/manufacturing/asm/index.html>.

Table 877. Gross Domestic Product of Natural Resource-Related Industries in Current and Real (2005) Dollars by Industry: 2000 to 2009

[In billions of dollars (9,951.5 represents $9,951,500,000,000). Data are based on the 2002 North American Industry Classification System (NAICS); see text, Section 15. Data include nonfactor charges (capital consumption allowances, indirect business taxes, etc.) as well as factor charges against gross product; corporate profits and capital consumption allowances have been shifted from a company to an establishment basis]

Industry	Current dollars				Chained (2005) dollars			
	2000	2005	2008	2009	2000	2005	2008	2009
All industries, total [1]	**9,951.5**	**12,638.4**	**14,441.4**	**14,256.3**	**11,226.0**	**12,638.4**	**13,312.1**	**12,987.4**
Industries covered	294.5	405.9	556.9	(NA)	427.3	405.9	417.9	(NA)
Percent of all industries	3.0	3.2	3.9	(NA)	3.8	3.2	3.1	(NA)
Agriculture, forestry, fishing, and hunting. . .	95.6	127.1	163.2	136.4	103.7	127.1	132.3	138.4
Farms	73.6	102.0	132.1	(NA)	83.5	102.0	103.4	(NA)
Forestry, fishing, and related activities. . . .	22.0	25.1	31.1	(NA)	20.5	25.1	28.2	(NA)
Mining	108.9	192.0	307.2	231.3	232.5	192.0	199.0	206.3
Oil and gas extraction	67.5	128.6	203.8	(NA)	155.0	128.6	130.5	(NA)
Mining, except oil and gas	27.8	36.3	48.8	(NA)	45.4	36.3	31.7	(NA)
Support activities for mining	13.7	27.2	54.7	(NA)	29.2	27.2	34.5	(NA)
Timber-related manufacturing	90.0	86.8	86.5	(NA)	91.1	86.8	86.6	(NA)
Wood products	28.3	33.0	26.8	(NA)	32.8	33.0	35.9	(NA)
Paper products	61.7	53.8	59.7	(NA)	58.3	53.8	50.7	(NA)

NA Not available. [1] Includes industries not shown separately.

Source: U.S. Bureau of Economic Analysis, *Survey of Current Business*, May 2010. See also <http://www.bea.gov/industry/gdpbyind_data.htm> .

Table 878. Forest Land and Timberland by Type of Owner and Region: 2007

[In thousands of acres (751,228 represents 751,228,000). As of January 1. Forest land is land at least 10 percent stocked by forest trees of any size, including land that formerly had such tree cover and that will be naturally or artificially regenerated. The minimum area for classification of forest land is 1 acre or strips of timber with a crown width of at least 120 feet wide. Timberland is forest land that is producing or is capable of producing crops of industrial wood and that is not withdrawn from timber utilization by statute or administrative regulation]

Region	Forest land, total	Timberland					
		Total	Federal			State, county, and municipal	Private [1]
			Total	National forest	Other		
Total	751,228	514,213	112,733	98,721	14,015	44,994	356,485
North	172,039	164,018	11,897	10,126	1,771	25,252	126,868
Northeast	84,796	79,803	2,971	2,401	570	9,308	67,523
North Central	87,243	84,215	8,926	7,725	1,201	15,944	59,345
South	214,644	204,030	17,164	12,225	4,940	7,880	178,986
Southeast	87,889	85,665	7,559	4,970	2,590	4,689	73,417
South Central	126,756	118,365	9,605	7,255	2,350	3,191	105,569
Rocky Mountains	150,661	70,968	48,612	45,386	3,228	3,185	19,169
Great Plains	5,757	5,287	1,294	1,056	239	198	3,795
Intermountain	144,905	65,681	47,318	44,330	2,989	2,987	15,374
Pacific Coast	213,883	75,197	35,060	30,984	4,076	8,677	31,462
Alaska	126,869	11,865	4,750	3,772	978	4,344	2,771
Pacific Northwest	52,449	43,489	20,403	17,937	2,466	3,704	19,383
Pacific Southwest [2]	34,565	19,843	9,907	9,275	632	629	9,308

[1] Includes Indian lands. [2] Includes Hawaii.

Source: U.S. Forest Service, "RPA Assessment Tables," 2007, <http://www.fs.fed.us/research/rpa/>.

Table 879. National Forest System Lands by State: 2006

[In thousands of acres (232,419 represents 232,419,000). As of September 30, 2006. Data do not include Delaware, District of Columbia, Iowa, Maryland, Massachusetts, New Jersey, or Rhode Island]

State	Total lands	National Forest System lands [1]	Other lands [2]	State	Total lands	National Forest System lands [1]	Other lands [2]
U.S.	**232,419**	**192,822**	**39,596**	NE	442	352	90
				NV	6,275	5,841	434
AL	1,288	667	621	NH	828	735	93
AK	24,359	21,973	2,386	NM	10,455	9,420	1,035
AZ	11,892	11,264	628	NY	16	16	–
AR	3,519	2,595	924	NC	3,165	1,255	1,910
CA	24,435	20,795	3,640	ND	1,108	1,108	–
CO	16,021	14,518	1,503	OH	834	238	596
CT	24	24	–	OK	579	400	179
FL	1,434	1,157	276	OR	17,565	15,726	1,839
GA	1,857	866	991	PA	743	513	230
HI	1	1	–	SC	1,379	628	750
ID	21,651	20,464	1,187	SD	2,370	2,016	354
IL	923	296	627	TN	1,276	707	569
IN	645	201	443	TX	1,994	755	1,239
KS	116	108	8	UT	9,213	8,199	1,014
KY	2,208	814	1,394	VT	817	398	420
LA	1,025	604	420	VA	3,223	1,664	1,559
ME	93	53	40	WA	10,113	9,282	831
MI	4,894	2,872	2,022	WV	1,877	1,043	834
MN	5,467	2,841	2,626	WI	2,023	1,529	494
MS	2,318	1,173	1,145	WY	9,706	9,241	465
MO	3,060	1,491	1,569	PR	56	28	28
MT	19,129	16,948	2,181	VI	–	–	–

– Represents zero. [1] National Forest System is a national significant system of federally owned units of forest, range, and related land consisting of national forests, purchase units, national grasslands, land utilization project areas, experimental forest areas, experimental range areas, designated experimental areas, other land areas; water areas, and interests in lands that are administered by USDA Forest Service or designated for administration through the Forest Service. [2] Other lands are lands within the unit boundaries in private, state, county, and municipal ownership and the federal lands over which the Forest Service has no jurisdiction. Also includes lands offered to the United States and approved for acquisition and subsequent Forest Service administration, but to which title has not yet been accepted by the United States.

Source: U.S. Forest Service. U.S. Timber Production, *Trade, Consumption, and Price Statistics, 1965–2005*, Research Paper RP-FPL-637, and unpublished data. See also <http://www.treesearch.fs.fed.us/pubs/28972>.

Table 880. Timber Volume, Growth, and Removal on Timberland by Species, Group, and Region: 2007

[932,096 represents 932,096,000,000]

Region	Net volume [1]						Timber growth [4] (mil. cu. ft.)			Timber removals [5] (mil. cu. ft.)		
	Growing stock [2] (mil. cu. ft.)			Sawtimber [3] (bil. board ft.)								
	All species	Soft-woods	Hard-woods	All species	Soft-woods	Hard-woods	All species	Soft-woods	Hard-woods	All species	Soft-woods	Hard-woods
Total	**932,096**	**529,203**	**402,893**	**1,013**	**558**	**455**	**26,744**	**15,241**	**11,503**	**15,533**	**9,859**	**5,675**
North	248,007	55,866	192,141	268	60	209	6,576	1,489	5,087	2,820	677	2,143
Northeast	137,585	34,252	103,333	146	37	109	3,249	836	2,412	1,169	353	815
North Central	110,422	21,614	88,808	122	23	99	3,327	652	2,675	1,651	324	1,328
South	288,522	118,471	170,051	325	123	202	13,272	7,632	5,640	9,696	6,317	3,379
Southeast	126,747	56,722	70,025	143	58	84	6,115	3,876	2,239	4,306	2,961	1,345
South Central	161,775	61,749	100,026	182	64	118	7,157	3,756	3,401	5,391	3,357	2,034
Rocky Mountains	137,263	124,809	12,454	159	144	15	1,761	1,577	184	543	521	22
Great Plains	4,539	1,641	2,898	7	2	5	72	27	45	41	25	16
Intermountain	132,724	123,168	9,556	153	142	11	1,689	1,550	139	502	496	6
Pacific Coast	258,304	230,057	28,247	261	232	29	5,135	4,543	593	2,474	2,344	131
Alaska	31,998	29,125	2,873	34	31	3	248	130	118	66	59	7
Pacific Northwest	158,896	146,006	12,890	159	146	13	3,340	3,039	301	1,939	1,818	121
Pacific Southwest [6]	67,410	54,926	12,484	68	55	13	1,548	1,374	174	469	466	3

[1] As of January 1. [2] Live trees of commercial species meeting specified standards of quality or vigor. Cull trees are excluded. Includes only trees 5.0-inches in diameter or larger at 4 1/2 feet above ground. [3] Live trees of commercial species containing at least one 12-foot sawlog or two noncontiguous 8-foot logs, and meeting regional specifications for freedom from defect. Softwood trees must be at least 9.0 inches in diameter and hardwood trees must be at least 11.0-inches in diameter at 4 1/2 feet above ground. [4] The net increase in the volume of trees during a specified year. Components include the increment in net volume of trees at the beginning of the specific year surviving to its end, plus the net volume of trees reaching the minimum size class during the year, minus the volume of trees that died during the year, and minus the net volume of trees that became cull trees during the year. [5] The net volume of trees removed from the inventory during a specified year by harvesting, cultural operations such as timber stand improvement, or land clearing. [6] Includes Hawaii.

Source: U.S. Forest Service, "RPA Assessment Tables," 2007, <http://www.fs.fed.us/research/rpa/>.

Table 881. Timber Removals—Roundwood Product Output by Source and Species Group: 2006

[In million cubic feet (14,990 represents 14,990,000,000)]

Source and species group	Total	Sawlogs	Pulpwood	Veneer logs	Other products [1]	Fuelwood [2]
Total	**14,990**	**7,179**	**4,394**	**1,211**	**798**	**1,408**
Softwoods	9,948	5,289	2,634	1,068	479	477
Hardwoods	5,042	1,890	1,760	143	319	931
Growing stock [3]	13,002	6,781	3,872	1,156	703	490
Softwoods	8,897	5,030	2,345	1,020	417	86
Hardwoods	4,105	1,752	1,527	136	286	404
Other sources [4]	1,988	398	522	55	95	918
Softwoods	1,051	260	289	48	63	391
Hardwoods	937	138	233	7	33	526

[1] Includes such items as cooperage, pilings, poles, posts, shakes, shingles, board mills, charcoal, and export logs. [2] Downed and dead wood volume left on the ground after trees have been cut on timberland. [3] Includes live trees of commercial species meeting specified standards of quality or vigor. Cull trees are excluded. Includes only trees 5.0-inches in diameter or larger at 4 1/2 feet above the ground. [4] Includes salvable dead trees, rough and rotten trees, trees of noncommercial species, trees less than 5.0-inches in diameter at 4 1/2 feet above the ground, tops, and roundwood harvested from nonforest land (for example, fence rows).

Source: U.S. Forest Service, "RPA Assessment Tables," 2007, <http://www.fs.fed.us/research/rpa/>.

Table 882. Timber Products—Production, Foreign Trade, and Consumption by Type of Product: 1990 to 2009

[In millions of cubic feet, roundwood equivalent (15,577 represents 15,577,000,000)]

Type of Product	1990	1995	2000	2002	2003	2004	2005	2006	2007	2008	2009
Industrial roundwood:											
Domestic production	15,577	15,537	15,436	14,902	14,571	15,139	15,465	14,836	13,932	12,493	11,264
Softwoods	10,900	10,191	10,201	10,124	10,290	10,710	11,002	10,413	9,566	8,389	7,213
Hardwoods	4,609	5,347	5,235	4,778	4,282	4,428	4,463	4,423	4,366	4,104	4,052
Imports	3,091	3,907	4,529	4,505	5,096	5,805	5,802	5,292	4,147	3,065	1,986
Exports	2,307	2,282	1,996	1,769	1,535	1,604	1,646	1,596	1,481	1,617	1,240
Consumption	16,361	17,161	17,969	17,637	18,132	19,339	19,622	18,841	16,598	14,041	12,002
Softwoods	11,779	11,961	12,659	12,790	13,398	14,357	14,652	13,732	12,009	9,845	7,941
Hardwoods	4,582	5,200	5,310	4,847	4,734	4,983	4,970	4,799	4,589	4,197	4,062
Lumber:											
Domestic production	7,317	6,815	7,199	7,060	7,131	7,510	7,889	7,552	6,964	5,928	5,020
Imports	1,909	2,522	2,845	3,036	3,193	3,704	3,737	3,415	2,743	1,922	1,336
Exports	589	460	428	353	347	348	389	390	359	345	272
Consumption	8,637	8,877	9,616	9,744	9,977	10,866	11,237	10,577	9,347	7,506	6,084
Plywood and veneer:											
Domestic production	1,423	1,303	1,187	1,074	1,054	1,086	1,068	1,003	912	743	617
Imports	97	107	155	205	240	354	373	339	265	185	177
Exports	109	89	42	31	35	43	37	35	40	45	37
Consumption	1,410	1,321	1,300	1,249	1,259	1,397	1,403	1,308	1,136	882	757
Pulp products:											
Domestic production	5,313	6,079	5,881	5,708	5,557	5,692	5,679	5,470	5,176	4,926	4,818
Imports	1,038	1,248	1,459	1,180	1,579	1,669	1,570	1,440	1,071	918	434
Exports	646	905	842	810	643	680	708	681	526	556	423
Consumption	5,704	6,422	6,498	6,078	6,493	6,680	6,541	6,229	5,721	5,288	4,829
Logs:											
Imports	4	13	68	81	80	73	114	94	67	35	29
Exports	674	451	331	309	356	366	345	339	350	313	321
Pulpwood chips, exports	288	377	353	265	155	168	166	151	205	257	195
Fuelwood consumption	3,019	2,937	2,561	2,581	1,515	1,540	1,550	1,555	1,605	1,510	1,400

Source: U.S. Forest Service, *U.S. Timber Production, Trade, Consumption, and Price Statistics, 1965–2005*, Research Paper RP-FPL-637, and unpublished data. See also <http://www.treesearch.fs.fed.us/pubs/28972>.

Table 883. Selected Timber Products—Imports and Exports: 1990 to 2009

[In million board feet (13,063 represents 13,063,000,000), except as indicated]

Product	Unit	1990	1995	2000	2004	2005	2006	2007	2008	2009
IMPORTS [1]										
Lumber, total [2]	Mil. bd. ft.	13,063	17,524	19,906	25,493	25,738	23,037	18,906	13,042	9,172
From Canada	Percent	91	97	92	83	85	86	89	72	54
Logs, total	Mil. bd. ft. [3]	23	80	435	454	710	585	418	253	179
From Canada	Percent	84	70	96	97	85	85	91	(NA)	(NA)
Paper and board [4]	1,000 tons	12,195	14,292	17,555	21,146	20,438	20,293	18,634	16,872	12,133
Woodpulp	1,000 tons	4,893	5,969	7,227	6,726	6,762	6,939	6,793	6,272	5,044
Plywood	Mil. sq. ft. [5]	1,687	1,951	2,917	5,896	6,325	6,324	4,969	3,722	2,778
EXPORTS										
Lumber, total [2]	Mil. bd. ft.	4,623	2,958	2,700	2,098	2,348	2,359	2,193	2,148	1,690
To: Canada	Percent	14	22	26	12	28	28	27	27	27
Japan	Percent	28	33	12	11	3	4	4	5	4
Europe	Percent	15	17	19	9	15	16	16	5	7
Logs, total	Mil. bd. ft. [3]	4,213	2,820	2,068	2,287	2,157	2,120	2,189	2,240	2,005
To: Canada	Percent	9	25	41	49	54	52	34	33	32
Japan	Percent	62	61	45	28	27	26	26	28	28
China	Percent	9	1	–	3	4	5	7	9	12
Paper and board [4]	1,000 tons	5,163	7,621	10,003	12,566	13,434	13,349	14,582	12,907	12,569
Woodpulp	1,000 tons	5,905	8,261	6,409	6,225	6,413	6,606	6,831	7,790	7,519
Plywood	Mil. sq. ft. [5]	1,766	1,517	754	783	568	749	501	621	473

– Represents zero. NA Not available. [1] Customs value of imports; see text, Section 28. [2] Includes railroad ties. [3] Log scale. [4] Includes paper and board products. Excludes hardboard. [5] 3/8 inch basis.

Source: U.S. Forest Service, *U.S. Timber Production, Trade, Consumption, and Price Statistics, 1965–2005*, Research Paper RP-FPL-637, and unpublished data. See also <http://www.treesearch.fs.fed.us/pubs/28972>.

Table 884. Lumber Consumption by Species Group and End Use: 1995 to 2009

[In billion board feet (59.3 represents 59,300,000,000), except per capita in board feet. Per capita consumption based on estimated resident population as of July 1]

Item	1995	2000	2001	2002	2003	2004	2005	2006	2007	2008	2009
Consumption, total	**59.3**	**66.1**	**64.6**	**67.5**	**67.0**	**73.1**	**75.6**	**71.3**	**62.7**	**49.7**	**40.3**
Per capita	225	240	227	235	230	249	255	238	208	163	131
SPECIES GROUP											
Softwoods	47.6	54.0	53.7	56.4	56.5	62.0	64.4	60.4	52.6	40.7	31.2
Hardwoods	11.7	12.2	11.0	11.1	10.5	11.1	11.2	10.9	10.2	9.0	9.1
END USE											
New housing	18.1	21.1	21.6	22.5	24.0	25.4	27.7	23.8	17.5	11.2	(NA)
Residential upkeep and improvements	15.0	15.3	15.3	16.4	16.2	17.6	18.3	18.6	17.8	16.1	(NA)
New nonresidential construction [1]	4.7	5.5	5.3	4.8	4.4	4.5	4.7	5.2	4.9	5.2	(NA)
Shipping	6.9	7.6	6.9	7.1	7.0	7.7	8.1	8.6	7.9	6.8	(NA)
Other [2]	7.2	8.7	8.9	9.9	9.8	13.2	11.3	9.8	10.0	6.0	(NA)

NA Not available. [1] In addition to new construction, includes railroad ties laid as replacements in existing track and lumber used by railroads for railcar repair. [2] Includes upkeep and improvement of nonresidential buildings and structures; made-at-home projects, such as furniture, boats, and picnic tables; made-on-the-job items such as advertising and display structures; and miscellaneous products and uses.

Source: U.S. Forest Service, *U.S. Timber Production, Trade, Consumption, and Price Statistics, 1965–2005*, Research Paper RP-FPL-637, and unpublished data. See also <http://www.treesearch.fs.fed.us/pubs/28972>.

Table 885. Selected Species—Stumpage Prices in Current and Constant (1996) Dollars: 2000 to 2009

[In dollars per 1,000 board feet. Stumpage prices are based on sales of sawtimber from national forests]

Species	Current dollars				Constant (1996) dollars [1]			
	2000	2005	2008	2009	2000	2005	2008	2009
Softwoods:								
Douglas fir [2]	433	321	(NA)	(NA)	397	260	(NA)	(NA)
Southern pine [3]	258	193	153	105	237	157	103	71
Sugar pine [4]	187	114	75	63	172	93	55	46
Ponderosa pine [4, 5]	155	103	34	38	142	84	23	25
Western hemlock [6]	46	70	(NA)	(NA)	42	57	(NA)	(NA)
Hardwoods:								
All eastern hardwoods [7]	341	415	(NA)	(NA)	313	337	(NA)	(NA)
Oak, white, red, and black [7]	258	329	(NA)	(NA)	237	267	(NA)	(NA)
Maple, sugar [8]	314	648	(NA)	(NA)	288	526	(NA)	(NA)

NA Not available. [1] Deflated by the producer price index, all commodities. [2] Western Washington and western Oregon. [3] Southern region. [4] Pacific Southwest region (formerly California region). [5] Includes Jeffrey pine. [6] Pacific Northwest region. [7] Eastern and Southern regions. [8] Eastern region.

Source: U.S. Forest Service, "RPA Assessment Tables," 2007, <http://www.fs.fed.us/research/rpa/>.

Table 886. Selected Timber Products—Producer Price Indexes: 1990 to 2009

[1982 = 100. For information about producer prices, see text, Section 14]

Product	1990	1995	2000	2004	2005	2006	2007	2008	2009
Lumber and wood products [1]	**129.7**	**178.1**	**178.2**	**195.6**	**196.5**	**194.4**	**192.4**	**191.3**	**183.0**
Lumber	124.6	173.4	178.8	203.6	198.6	188.6	174.7	163.5	149.4
Softwood lumber	123.8	178.5	178.6	209.8	203.6	189.4	170.5	156.3	141.3
Hardwood lumber	131.0	167.0	185.9	199.3	196.6	195.3	192.4	184.5	171.3
Millwork [1]	130.4	163.8	176.4	191.9	197.2	201.8	201.4	204.8	205.6
General millwork	132.0	165.4	178.0	193.1	196.1	201.3	203.9	207.7	210.5
Prefabricated structural members	122.3	163.5	175.1	193.7	206.9	206.6	189.5	189.0	181.2
Plywood	114.2	165.3	157.6	198.5	186.8	172.7	176.1	174.7	164.0
Softwood plywood	119.6	188.1	173.3	250.9	223.5	190.5	197.8	193.1	172.2
Hardwood plywood and related products	102.7	122.2	130.2	134.4	138.1	(NA)	(NA)	(NA)	(NA)
Other wood products [1]	114.7	143.7	130.5	134.3	139.2	142.8	142.1	144.7	142.8
Boxes	119.1	145.0	155.2	163.1	164.9	167.2	170.3	174.6	176.5
Pulp, paper, and allied products [1]	**141.2**	**172.2**	**183.7**	**195.7**	**202.6**	**209.8**	**216.9**	**226.8**	**225.5**
Pulp, paper, and prod., excl. bldg. paper [1]	132.9	163.4	161.4	162.1	169.8	178.4	186.7	199.1	193.9
Woodpulp	151.3	183.2	145.3	132.2	138.0	144.1	161.5	171.4	150.3
Wastepaper	138.9	371.1	282.5	231.4	230.9	234.8	368.7	372.5	235.8
Paper [1]	128.8	159.0	149.8	149.4	159.6	167.4	169.3	184.3	179.6
Writing and printing papers	129.1	158.4	146.6	146.0	156.1	162.8	166.7	181.6	180.8
Newsprint	119.6	161.8	127.5	124.5	138.5	151.8	131.6	148.0	125.7
Paperboard	135.7	183.1	176.7	170.2	175.5	192.0	201.7	217.9	206.7
Converted paper and paperboard products [1]	135.2	157.0	162.7	168.3	176.1	184.1	187.8	199.2	202.8
Office supplies and accessories	121.4	134.9	133.8	137.6	143.1	146.2	151.0	158.3	158.8
Building paper & building board mill prods.	112.2	144.9	138.8	192.4	184.9	173.0	155.2	163.9	156.6

NA Not available. [1] Includes other products not shown separately.
Source: U.S. Bureau of Labor Statistics, *Producer Price Indexes*, monthly.

Table 887. Pulpwood Consumption, Woodpulp Production, and Paper and Board Production and Consumption: 1995 to 2009

[Revised to match data from American Forest and Paper Association and American Pulpwood Association]

Item	Unit	1995	2000	2003	2004	2005	2006	2007	2008	2009
Pulpwood consumption [1]	1,000 cords [2]	97,052	95,904	85,436	87,110	88,595	86,284	84,076	77,442	70,401
Woodpulp production [3]	1,000 tons	67,103	62,758	53,197	54,301	60,267	60,568	56,636	52,899	44,990
Paper and board: [4]										
Production	1,000 tons	89,509	94,491	80,712	83,612	91,031	91,800	91,570	87,619	71,219
Consumption or new supply [5]	1,000 tons	96,126	103,147	94,422	95,068	101,864	102,948	99,825	93,640	79,141
Per capita	Pounds	731	731	629	627	687	688	661	613	515

[1] Includes changes in stocks. [2] One cord equals 128 cubic feet. [3] Excludes defibrated and exploded woodpulp used for hard pressed board. [4] Excludes hardboard. [5] Production plus imports, minus exports (excludes products), changes in inventories not taken into account.

Source: U.S. Forest Service, *U.S. Timber Production, Trade, Consumption and Price Statistics, 1965–2005*, Research Paper FP-FPL-637, and unpublished data. See also <http://www.treesearch.fs.fed.us/pubs/28972>.

Table 888. Paper and Paperboard—Production and New Supply: 1990 to 2008

[In millions of short tons (80.45 represents 80,450,000). 1 short ton = 2,000 lbs.]

Item	1990	1995	2000	2003	2004	2005	2006	2007	2008
Production, total	**80.45**	**91.33**	**96.05**	**89.81**	**93.41**	**92.61**	**93.72**	**92.96**	**88.45**
Paper, total	39.36	42.87	45.52	40.37	41.82	41.40	41.81	41.27	38.96
Paperboard, total	39.32	46.64	48.97	48.02	50.08	49.71	50.41	50.40	48.45
Unbleached kraft	20.36	22.70	21.80	21.73	22.67	22.58	23.41	23.54	22.17
Semichemical	5.64	5.66	5.95	6.10	6.53	6.41	6.22	6.16	5.82
Bleached kraft	4.40	5.30	5.44	5.36	5.65	5.66	5.71	5.81	5.71
Recycled	8.92	12.98	15.79	14.83	15.24	15.05	15.07	14.89	14.69
Wet machine board	0.15	0.15	0.06	0.05	0.05	0.05	0.05	0.03	0.02
Building paper	0.81	0.81	0.64	0.55	0.58	0.57	0.56	0.54	0.44
Insulating board	0.86	0.86	0.86	0.83	0.88	0.88	0.88	0.71	0.57
New supply, all grades, excluding products	**87.68**	**98.16**	**105.02**	**99.76**	**103.74**	**101.81**	**101.69**	**98.85**	**91.99**
Paper, total	49.49	52.77	57.13	53.22	54.88	53.69	52.97	50.88	46.71
Newsprint	13.41	12.76	12.92	11.05	10.84	10.12	9.49	8.35	7.25
Printing/writing papers	25.46	29.55	32.99	31.03	32.68	31.99	31.78	31.05	28.06
Packaging and ind. conv. papers	4.72	4.24	4.27	3.96	4.14	4.05	4.10	4.07	4.05
Tissue	5.90	6.22	6.95	7.18	7.22	7.53	7.60	7.42	7.36
Paperboard, total	36.30	43.45	46.02	44.95	47.20	46.51	47.11	46.61	44.25
Construction and other	1.90	1.95	1.88	1.59	1.66	1.61	1.02	1.36	1.03

Source: American Forest and Paper Association, Washington, DC, *Monthly Statistical Summary of Paper, Paperboard and Woodpulp*.

Table 889. Fishery Products—Domestic Catch, Imports, and Disposition: 1990 to 2008

[Live weight, in millions of pounds (16,349 represents 16,349,000,000). For data on commercial catch for selected countries, see Table 1375, Section 30]

Item	1990	1995	2000	2003	2004	2005	2006	2007	2008
Total	**16,349**	**16,484**	**17,340**	**19,850**	**20,412**	**20,612**	**20,960**	**20,561**	**19,252**
For human food	12,662	13,584	14,738	17,187	17,648	18,147	18,594	18,253	17,089
For industrial use	3,687	2,900	2,599	2,663	2,765	2,382	2,366	2,308	2,163
Domestic catch	**9,404**	**9,788**	**9,069**	**9,507**	**9,683**	**9,707**	**9,483**	**9,309**	**8,326**
For human food	7,041	7,667	6,912	7,521	7,794	7,997	7,842	7,490	6,633
For industrial use	2,363	2,121	2,157	1,986	1,889	1,710	1,641	1,819	1,692
Imports [1]	**6,945**	**6,696**	**8,271**	**10,343**	**10,729**	**10,905**	**11,477**	**11,252**	**10,927**
For human food	5,621	5,917	7,828	9,666	9,854	10,158	10,752	10,763	10,456
For industrial use [2]	1,324	779	443	677	875	747	725	489	471
Exports [1]	**4,627**	**5,166**	**5,758**	**6,756**	**8,203**	**8,420**	**7,710**	**7,057**	**6,353**
For human food	3,832	4,175	4,587	5,392	6,462	6,385	6,250	5,761	5,253
For industrial use [2]	795	991	1,171	1,364	1,741	2,035	1,459	1,296	1,100
Disposition of domestic catch	**9,404**	**9,788**	**9,069**	**9,507**	**9,683**	**9,707**	**9,483**	**9,309**	**8,325**
Fresh and frozen	6,501	7,099	6,657	7,266	7,488	7,776	7,627	7,450	6,538
Canned	751	769	530	498	552	563	573	514	336
Cured	126	90	119	119	137	160	117	121	138
Reduced to meal, oil, etc.	2,026	1,830	1,763	1,624	1,506	1,208	1,166	1,224	1,313

[1] Excludes imports of edible fishery products consumed in Puerto Rico; includes landings of tuna caught by foreign vessels in American Samoa. [2] Fish meal and sea herring.

Source: U.S. National Oceanic and Atmospheric Administration, National Marine Fisheries Service, *Fisheries of the United States*, annual, July 2009. See also <http://www.st.nmfs.noaa.gov/st1/fus/fus08/index.html>.

Table 890. Fisheries—Quantity and Value of Domestic Catch: 1980 to 2008

[In millions of pounds (6,482 represents 6,482,000,000), except as noted]

Year	Quantity (mil. lbs. [1]) Total	For human food	For industrial products [2]	Value (mil. dol.)	Average price per lb. (cents)	Year	Quantity (mil. lbs. [1]) Total	For human food	For industrial products [2]	Value (mil. dol.)	Average price per lb. (cents)
1980	6,482	3,654	2,828	2,237	34.5	2001	9,489	7,311	2,178	3,218	33.9
1985	6,258	3,294	2,964	2,326	37.2	2002	9,397	7,205	2,192	3,092	32.9
1990	9,404	7,041	2,363	3,522	37.5	2003	9,507	7,521	1,986	3,347	35.2
1995	9,788	7,667	2,121	3,770	38.5	2004	9,683	7,794	1,889	3,756	38.8
1997	9,842	7,244	2,598	3,448	35.0	2005	9,707	7,997	1,710	3,942	40.6
1998	9,194	7,173	2,021	3,126	34.0	2006	9,483	7,842	1,641	4,024	42.4
1999	9,339	6,832	2,507	3,467	37.1	2007	9,309	7,490	1,819	4,192	45.0
2000	9,069	6,912	2,157	3,550	39.1	2008	8,325	6,633	1,692	4,383	52.6

[1] Live weight. [2] Meal, oil, solubles, shell products, bait, and animal food.

Source: U.S. National Oceanic and Atmospheric Administration, National Marine Fisheries Service, *Fisheries of the United States*, annual, July 2009. See also <http://www.st.nmfs.noaa.gov/st1/fus/fus08/index.html>.

Table 891. Domestic Fish and Shellfish Catch and Value by Major Species Caught: 2000 to 2008

[In thousands (9,068,985 represents 9,068,985,000)]

Species	Quantity (1,000 lbs.) 2000	2005	2007	2008	Value ($1,000) 2000	2005	2007	2008
Total [1]	**9,068,985**	**9,707,275**	**9,309,203**	**8,325,814**	**3,549,481**	**3,942,376**	**4,192,219**	**4,383,820**
Fish, total [1]	**7,689,661**	**8,462,473**	**8,209,543**	**7,258,070**	**1,594,815**	**1,836,448**	**2,047,796**	**2,235,300**
Cod: Atlantic	25,060	13,920	16,969	18,075	26,384	20,828	27,073	30,635
Pacific	530,505	548,746	487,566	493,952	142,330	150,738	224,301	274,160
Flounder	412,723	419,430	482,889	663,116	109,910	135,176	154,233	184,211
Halibut	75,190	76,263	69,888	66,923	143,826	177,593	227,379	217,735
Herring, Atlantic	160,269	215,565	163,380	173,217	9,972	20,467	19,582	21,306
Herring, Pacific	74,835	87,295	69,329	86,219	12,043	13,799	15,315	23,794
Menhaden	1,760,498	1,243,723	1,483,701	1,341,413	112,403	62,465	92,718	90,725
Pollock, Alaska	2,606,802	3,411,307	3,066,603	2,276,144	160,525	306,972	297,461	323,212
Salmon	628,638	899,457	885,022	658,342	270,213	330,699	381,274	394,595
Tuna	50,779	44,316	50,817	47,903	95,176	85,922	94,105	107,013
Whiting (Atlantic, silver)	26,855	16,561	14,044	13,845	11,370	8,284	7,894	7,547
Whiting (Pacific, hake)	452,718	569,381	455,188	531,418	18,809	29,145	32,603	58,559
Shellfish, total [1]	**1,379,324**	**1,244,802**	**1,066,702**	**1,035,042**	**1,954,666**	**2,105,928**	**2,123,873**	**2,122,284**
Clams	118,482	105,640	115,848	107,772	153,973	173,655	194,154	186,718
Crabs	299,006	299,137	293,959	325,184	405,006	415,057	471,819	562,267
Lobsters: American	83,180	88,032	81,303	81,835	301,300	416,597	375,576	306,177
Oysters	41,146	33,963	37,755	30,162	90,667	110,679	139,245	131,590
Scallops, sea	32,747	56,702	58,559	53,527	164,609	433,512	385,924	369,860
Shrimp	332,486	260,884	280,862	256,597	690,453	406,344	432,740	441,818
Squid, Pacific	259,508	126,107	109,251	82,704	27,077	31,601	29,139	25,569

[1] Includes other species not shown separately.

Source: U.S. National Oceanic and Atmospheric Administration, National Marine Fisheries Service, *Fisheries of the United States*, annual, July 2009. See also <http://www.st.nmfs.noaa.gov/st1/fus/fus08/index.html>.

Table 892. U.S. Private Aquaculture—Trout and Catfish Production and Value: 1990 to 2009

[67.8 represents 67,800,000. Data are for calendar year and foodsize fish (those over 12 inches long)]

Item	Unit	1990	1995	2000	2005	2006	2007	2008	2009
TROUT FOODSIZE									
Number sold	Mil.	67.8	60.2	58.4	55.5	52.5	58.7	40.4	41.1
Total weight	Mil. lb.	56.8	55.6	59.0	59.7	65.3	66.9	52.4	49.1
Total value of sales	Mil. dol.	64.6	60.8	63.3	62.7	72.7	79.5	72.4	68.6
Avg. price received by processors	Dol./lb.	1.14	1.09	1.07	1.05	1.11	1.19	1.38	1.40
Percent sold to processors	Percent	58	68	70	66	69	64	58	62
CATFISH FOODSIZE									
Number sold	Mil.	272.9	321.8	420.1	405.4	370.9	365.8	304.0	266.3
Total weight	Mil. lb.	392.4	481.5	633.8	638.9	587.0	563.9	514.9	476.0
Total value of sales	Mil. dol.	305.1	378.1	468.8	450.2	455.1	423.7	389.3	352.0
Avg. price received by processors	Dol./lb.	0.78	0.79	0.74	0.70	0.78	0.75	0.76	0.74
Fish sold to processors	Mil. lb.	360.4	446.9	593.6	600.7	566.1	496.2	509.6	466.1
Avg. price paid by processors	Cents/lb.	75.8	78.6	75.1	72.5	79.5	76.7	77.6	77.1
Processor sales	Mil. lb.	183.1	227.0	297.2	300.0	284.0	252.5	251.2	229.2
Avg. price received by processors	Dol./lb.	2.24	2.40	2.36	2.29	2.46	2.44	2.44	2.53
Inventory (Jan. 1)	Mil. lb.	9.4	10.9	13.6	13.7	18.2	15.1	15.5	14.5

Source: U.S. Department of Agriculture, National Agricultural Statistics Service, *Trout Production*, February 2010; *Catfish Production*, January 2010; and *Catfish Processing*, February 2010. See also <http://www.nass.usda.gov/Publications/Reports_By_Title/index.asp/>. Also in *Agricultural Statistics*, annual.

Table 893. Supply of Selected Fishery Items: 1990 to 2008

[In millions of pounds (734 represents 734,000,000). Totals available for U.S. consumption are supply minus exports plus imports. Round weight is the complete or full weight as caught]

Species	Unit	1990	1995	2000	2003	2004	2005	2006	2007	2008
Shrimp	Heads-off weight	734	832	1,173	1,608	1,670	1,559	1,879	1,743	1,722
Tuna, canned	Canned weight	856	875	980	982	874	895	858	812	848
Snow crab	Round weight	37	42	122	198	168	171	187	208	197
Clams	Meat weight	152	144	133	143	132	120	125	127	121
Salmon, canned	Canned weight	148	147	95	111	98	123	56	51	26
American lobster	Round weight	94	91	105	128	138	144	150	128	144
Spiny lobster	Round weight	89	89	99	93	93	83	77	78	83
Scallops	Meat weight	74	62	78	94	94	86	94	92	88
Oysters	Meat weight	56	63	71	69	73	65	65	70	54
King crab	Round weight	19	21	41	47	52	78	110	134	71
Crab meat, canned	Canned weight	9	12	29	47	56	59	58	66	68

Source: U.S. National Oceanic and Atmospheric Administration, National Marine Fisheries Service, *Fisheries of the United States*, annual, July 2009. See also <http://www.st.nmfs.noaa.gov/st1/fus/fus08/index.html>.

Table 894. Canned, Fresh, and Frozen Fishery Products—Production and Value: 1990 to 2008

[In millions of pounds (1,178 represents 1,178,000,000). Fresh fishery products exclude Alaska and Hawaii. Canned fishery products data are for natural pack only]

Product	Production (mil. lbs.)					Value (mil. dol.)				
	1990	2000	2005	2007	2008	1990	2000	2005	2007	2008
Canned, total	1,178	1,747	1,082	1,070	1,314	1,562	1,626	1,211	1,324	1,420
Tuna	581	671	446	436	474	902	856	628	702	845
Salmon	196	171	219	142	124	366	288	301	274	225
Clam products	110	127	123	110	105	76	120	127	89	95
Sardines, Maine	13	(Z)	(NA)	(NA)	(NA)	17	(Z)	(NA)	(NA)	(NA)
Shrimp	1	2	1	(Z)	[1] (D)	3	11	3	1	[1] (D)
Crabs	1	(Z)	(Z)	(Z)	(Z)	4	(Z)	(Z)	(Z)	(Z)
Oysters [2]	1	(Z)	(Z)	(Z)	(Z)	1	1	(Z)	(Z)	(Z)
Other	275	776	293	381	611	193	350	152	258	254
Fish fillets and steaks [3]	441	368	615	632	575	843	823	1,136	1,304	1,290
Cod	65	56	47	32	39	132	167	116	102	112
Flounder	54	27	20	21	21	154	71	65	69	70
Haddock	7	6	24	11	9	24	24	89	59	44
Ocean perch, Atlantic	1	(Z)	1	1	1	1	1	4	3	3
Rockfish	33	11	3	2	2	53	25	8	6	4
Pollock, Atlantic	12	2	3	2	3	21	4	6	5	8
Pollock, Alaska	164	160	383	401	284	174	178	404	494	347
Other	105	106	134	162	217	284	353	444	567	702

D Figure withheld to avoid disclosure pertaining to a specific organization or individual. NA Not available. Z Less than 500,000 pounds or $500,000. [1] Included with other. [2] Includes oyster specialities. [3] Fresh and frozen.

Source: U.S. National Oceanic and Atmospheric Administration, National Marine Fisheries Service, *Fisheries of the United States*, annual, July 2009. See also <http://www.st.nmfs.noaa.gov/st1/fus/fus08/index.html>.

Table 895. Mineral Industries—Employment, Hours, and Earnings: 1990 to 2009

[In thousands (680 represents 680,000), except as noted. Based on the Current Employment Statistics Program, see Appendix III]

Industry and item	Unit	1990	1995	2000	2005	2006	2007	2008	2009
All mining: [1]									
All employees	1,000	680	558	520	562	620	664	710	650
Production workers	1,000	469	391	383	419	466	497	526	471
Avg. weekly hours	Number	46.1	46.8	45.5	46.4	46.3	46.2	45.3	43.5
Avg. weekly earnings	Dollars	630	711	771	884	938	989	1,043	1,037
Oil and gas extraction:									
All employees	1,000	190	152	125	126	135	146	161	162
Production workers	1,000	84	73	67	72	78	83	89	86
Avg. weekly hours	Number	44.4	43.6	41.3	44.3	43.0	41.9	41.1	40.6
Avg. weekly earnings	Dollars	591	677	802	856	921	1,015	1,120	1,119
Coal mining:									
All employees	1,000	136	97	72	74	78	77	81	82
Production workers	1,000	110	78	59	61	67	68	71	72
Avg. weekly hours	Number	44.7	45.7	45.6	48.5	49.5	47.9	49.0	47.8
Avg. weekly earnings	Dollars	822	929	945	1,071	1,093	1,052	1,140	1,249
Metal ore mining:									
All employees	1,000	53	48	38	29	32	36	40	35
Production workers	1,000	43	39	29	22	25	28	32	28
Avg. weekly hours	Number	42.5	43.4	43.4	44.2	43.5	45.9	46.1	42.3
Avg. weekly earnings	Dollars	646	788	871	1,001	974	1,077	1,195	1,096
Nonmetallic minerals mining, and quarrying:									
All employees	1,000	113	108	115	110	110	110	105	94
Production workers	1,000	85	81	87	84	82	82	79	73
Avg. weekly hours	Number	45.0	46.3	46.1	45.9	46.1	46.3	43.9	41.9
Avg. weekly earnings	Dollars	532	632	722	830	863	872	839	809

[1] Includes other industries not shown separately.

Source: U.S. Bureau of Labor Statistics, Current Employment Statistics, "Employment, Hours, and Earnings—National," <http://www.bls.gov/ces/home.htm\>, accessed April 2010.

Table 896. Mine Safety: 2000 to 2009

[Reported injury rates per 200,000 employee hours]

Item	All Mines			Coal			Metal and non-metal		
	2000	2008	2009 [1]	2000	2008	2009 [1]	2000	2008	2009 [1]
Number of mines	14,413	14,907	14,574	2,124	2,129	2,064	12,289	12,778	12,510
Number of miners	348,548	392,719	352,595	108,098	133,827	133,433	240,450	258,892	219,162
Fatalities	85	53	34	38	30	18	47	23	16
Fatal injury rate	0.03	0.02	0.01	0.04	0.02	0.01	0.02	0.01	0.01
All injury rate	5.13	3.25	3.01	6.64	3.89	3.67	4.45	2.87	2.55
Coal production (mil. tons)	1,078	1,172	1,072	1,078	1,172	1,072	(X)	(X)	(X)
Total mining area inspection hours/mine	57	56	59	178	227	238	28	21	22
Citations and orders	120,269	174,473	175,079	58,394	107,404	102,660	61,875	67,069	72,419
S&S [2] citations and orders (percent)	36	30	33	42	35	34	31	21	32
Amount assessed [3] (mil. dol.)	24.7	194.3	141.2	12.0	152.7	103.3	12.7	41.6	37.9

X Not applicable. [1] Preliminary. [2] A violation that "significantly and substantially" contributes to the cause and effect of a coal or other mine safety or health hazard. [3] Government penalties or fines.

Source: U.S. Mine Safety and Health Administration, Office of Program Education and Outreach Services, "Mine Safety and Health At a Glance," May 2010, <http://www.msha.gov/MSHAINFO/FactSheets/MSHAFCT10.HTM>.

Table 897. Mining and Primary Metal Production Indexes: 1990 to 2009

[Index 2002 = 100]

Industry group	NAICS [1] code	1990	1995	2000	2004	2005	2006	2007	2008	2009
Mining [2]	21	**107.8**	**105.3**	**104.2**	**99.6**	**98.3**	**101.5**	**102.1**	**104.2**	**97.9**
Oil and gas extraction [2]	211	107.2	104.0	101.0	96.0	92.0	93.5	95.0	97.6	102.2
Crude oil and natural gas	211111	109.2	104.8	100.9	95.9	92.1	93.5	95.0	97.7	102.3
Coal mining	2121	98.3	96.8	99.2	100.8	102.5	105.2	103.6	105.9	97.9
Metal ore mining	2122	113.1	123.8	120.5	98.2	106.1	109.1	106.0	109.8	98.8
Iron ore	21221	109.8	121.8	122.2	106.0	105.2	102.3	100.4	102.1	51.3
Gold ore and silver ore	21222	99.9	106.9	119.0	86.8	86.1	84.5	80.4	76.6	77.1
Copper, nickel, lead, and zinc	21223	122.2	140.0	122.9	100.6	99.2	103.4	102.4	113.2	104.8
Oil and gas drilling	213111	102.3	89.5	114.4	126.9	142.5	164.4	170.3	177.8	104.5
Primary metal manufacturing [2]	331	**96.7**	**106.0**	**111.4**	**110.0**	**108.0**	**112.6**	**110.0**	**102.4**	**67.7**
Iron and steel	3311	95.1	105.6	110.8	118.2	110.1	119.3	115.8	105.2	60.3
Aluminum	3313	103.3	99.1	104.7	96.4	102.7	105.1	102.5	100.3	79.2
Nonferrous metals [2]	3314	111.4	123.9	115.5	103.7	103.4	99.8	101.6	98.6	87.2
Copper	33142	142.5	263.1	133.8	90.7	81.8	68.0	72.2	67.0	66.2

[1] Based on the 2002 North American Industry Classification System (NAICS). [2] Includes other industries not shown separately.
Source: Board of Governors of the Federal Reserve System, *The Statistical Supplement to the Federal Reserve Bulletin*, monthly, and *Industrial Production and Capacity Utilization*, Statistical Release G.17, monthly.

Table 898. Mineral Production: 1990 to 2009

[1,029.1 represents 1,029,100,000. Data represent production as measured by mine shipments, mine sales, or marketable production; see Appendix IV]

Minerals and metals	Unit	1990	2000	2007	2008	2009, est.
FUEL MINERALS						
Coal, total [1]	Mil. sh. tons	1,029.1	1,073.6	1,146.6	1,171.8	1,072.8
Bituminous [1]	Mil. sh. tons	693.2	574.3	542.8	555.3	493.7
Subbituminous	Mil. sh. tons	244.3	409.2	523.7	539.1	504.7
Lignite	Mil. sh. tons	88.1	85.6	78.6	75.7	72.5
Anthracite [1]	Mil. sh. tons	3.5	4.6	1.6	1.7	1.9
Natural gas (marketed production)	Tril. cu. ft.	18.59	20.20	20.20	21.24	21.89
Petroleum (crude)	Mil. bbl. [2]	2,685	2,131	1,848	1,812	1,938
Uranium (recoverable content)	Mil. lb.	8.9	4.0	4.5	3.9	(NA)
NONFUEL MINERALS						
Asbestos (sales)	1,000 metric tons	(D)	5	–	–	–
Barite, primary, sold/used by producers	1,000 metric tons	430	392	455	648	380
Boron minerals, sold or used by producers	1,000 metric tons	1,090	1,070	(D)	(D)	(D)
Bromine, sold or used by producers	1,000 metric tons	177	228	(D)	(D)	(D)
Cement:						
Portland [3]	Mil. metric tons	67	84	91	83	70
Masonry [3]	Mil. metric tons	3	4	4	3	2
Clays	1,000 metric tons	42,900	40,800	36,800	33,200	25,300
Diatomite	1,000 metric tons	631	677	687	764	790
Feldspar [4]	1,000 metric tons	630	790	730	650	530
Fluorspar, finished shipments	1,000 metric tons	64	–	–	(NA)	(NA)
Garnet (industrial)	1,000 metric tons	47	60	61	63	57
Gypsum, crude	Mil. metric tons	15	20	18	14	9
Helium [5]	Mil. cu. meters	65	98	77	80	80
Lime, sold or used by producers	Mil. metric tons	16	20	20	20	15
Mica, scrap & flake, sold/used by producers	1,000 metric tons	109	101	97	84	90
Peat, sales by producers	1,000 metric tons	721	847	694	648	641
Perlite, processed, sold or used	1,000 metric tons	576	672	409	434	380
Phosphate rock (marketable)	Mil. metric tons	46	39	30	30	27
Potash (K_2O equivalent) sales	1,000 metric tons	1,710	1,300	1,100	1,100	840
Pumice & pumicite, producer sales	1,000 metric tons	443	1,050	1,270	791	800
Salt, common, sold/used by producers	Mil. metric tons	37	46	45	47	46
Sand & gravel, sold/used by producer	Mil. metric tons	855	1,148	1,260	1,070	827
Construction	Mil. metric tons	829	1,120	1,230	1,040	800
Industrial	Mil. metric tons	26	20	00	30	27
Sodium carbonate (natural) (soda ash)	1,000 metric tons	9,100	10,200	11,100	11,300	9,300
Sodium sulfate (natural)	1,000 metric tons	349	(NA)	312	319	300
Stone [6]	Mil. metric tons	2,230	2,810	3,570	3,240	2,940
Crushed and broken	Mil. metric tons	1,110	1,560	1,650	1,440	1,110
Dimension [7]	1,000 metric tons	1,120	1,250	1,920	1,800	1,830
Sulfur: Total shipments	1,000 metric tons	11,500	10,700	9,130	9,430	9,700
Sulfur: Frasch mines (shipments)	1,000 metric tons	3,680	900	–	–	–
Talc and pyrophyllite, crude [8]	1,000 metric tons	1,270	851	769	706	527
Vermiculite concentrate	1,000 metric tons	209	150	100	100	110
METALS						
Antimony ore and concentrate	Metric tons	(D)	(D)	(D)	–	–
Aluminum	1,000 metric tons	4,048	3,668	2,554	2,658	1,730
Bauxite (dried)	1,000 metric tons	(D)	(NA)	(NA)	(NA)	(NA)
Copper (recoverable content)	1,000 metric tons	1,590	1,450	1,170	1,310	1,190
Gold (recoverable content)	Metric tons	294	353	238	233	210
Iron ore (gross weight) [9]	Mil. metric tons	57	61	51	54	28
Lead (recoverable content)	1,000 metric tons	484	449	434	399	400
Magnesium metal	1,000 metric tons	139	(D)	(D)	(D)	(D)
Manganiferous ore (gross weight) [10]	1,000 metric ton	(D)	–	(NA)	(NA)	(NA)
Mercury [11]	Metric tons	(NA)	(NA)	(NA)	(NA)	(NA)
Molybdenum (concentrate)	1,000 metric tons	62	41	57	56	50
Nickel ore (recovered Ni content)	1,000 metric tons	330	–	–	–	–
Palladium metal	Kilograms	5,930	10,300	12,800	11,900	12,500
Platinum metal	Kilograms	1,810	3,110	3,860	3,580	3,800
Silicon (Si content)	1,000 metric tons	418	367	[12] 155	[12] 164	[12] 140
Silver (recoverable content)	Metric tons	2,120	1,860	1,280	1,230	1,230
Titanium concentrate (TiO_2 content)	1,000 metric tons	(D)	300	300	200	200
Tungsten ore and concentrate [13]	Metric tons	(D)	–	(D)	(D)	(D)
Zinc (recoverable content)	1,000 metric tons	508	796	769	748	670

– Represents or rounds to zero. D Withheld to avoid disclosing individual company data. NA Not available. [1] Beginning 2007, includes a small amount of refuse recovery. [2] 42 gal. bbl. [3] Excludes Puerto Rico. [4] Beginning 2000, includes aplite. [5] Refined. [6] Excludes abrasive stone, bituminous limestone and sandstone, and ground soapstone, all included elsewhere in table; includes calcareous marl and slate. [7] Includes Puerto Rico in 1990. [8] Includes talc only after 1990. [9] Represents shipments; includes byproduct ores. [10] 5- to 35-percent manganiferous ore. [11] Mercury recovered as a byproduct of gold ores only, 1990. [12] Ferrosilocon only; silicon metal withheld to avoid disclosing proprietary data. [13] Content of ore and concentrate.

Source: Nonfuels, 1990 only, U.S. Bureau of Mines, thereafter, U.S. Geological Survey, *Minerals Yearbook and Mineral Commodities Summaries*, annual. See also <http://minerals.er.usgs.gov/minerals/pubs/mcs/>. Fuels, U.S. Energy Information Administration, *Annual Energy Review, 2009*, August 2010. See also <http://www.eia.doe.gov/emeu/aer/contents.html>.

Table 899. Nonfuel Mineral Commodities—Summary: 2009

[1,730 represents 1,730,000. Preliminary estimates. Average price in dollars per metric tons except as noted]

Mineral	Unit	Mineral disposition				Average price per unit (dollars)	Employment (number)
		Production	Exports	Net import reliance [1] (percent)	Consumption, apparent		
Aluminum.	1,000 metric tons.	1,730	2,710	5	3,110	[2] 0.79	45,000
Antimony (contained).	Metric tons.	[3] –	2,000	93	22,400	[2] 2.36	10
Asbestos	1,000 metric tons.	–	(Z)	100	1	(NA)	–
Barite.	1,000 metric tons.	380	40	80	1,940	[4] 52.00	330
Bauxite and alumina (metal equivalent)	1,000 metric tons.	(NA)	503	100	2,310	[4, 5] 28.00	(NA)
Beryllium (contained).	Metric tons.	120	30	2	120	[2] 120	(NA)
Bismuth (contained).	Metric tons.	–	397	90	1,020	[2] 7.84	(NA)
Boron (B$_2$O$_3$ content).	1,000 metric tons.	(D)	216	([6])	(D)	[4, 7] 430–500	1,200
Bromine (contained).	1,000 metric tons.	(D)	10	([8])	(D)	[9, 10] (NA)	1,000
Cadmium (contained)	Metric tons.	[3] 700	305	([6])	228	[2, 11] 1.22	(NA)
Cement	1,000 metric tons.	[12] 71,800	800	8	73,800	[4] 100	14,000
Chromium	1,000 metric tons.	[13] 160	50	39	260	(NA)	(NA)
Clays	1,000 metric tons.	25,300	3,770	([6])	21,700	(NA)	875
Cobalt (contained)	Metric tons.	[13] 1,700	2,500	75	6,700	[2] 18.00	(NA)
Copper (mine, recoverable)	1,000 metric tons.	1,190	80	24	1,660	[2] 2.41	9.1
Diamond (industrial)	Million carats.	294	74	35	449	[14] 0.17	(NA)
Diatomite.	1,000 metric tons.	790	98	([6])	692	[4] 228	1,020
Feldspar.	1,000 metric tons.	530	4	([6])	528	[4] 65.00	570
Fluorspar.	1,000 metric tons.	(NA)	12	100	460	(NA)	–
Garnet (industrial)	Metric tons.	56,500	8,140	37	89,500	[4] 50–2,000	160
Gemstones	Million dollars.	45.5	9,950	99	4,610	(NA)	1,200
Germanium (contained).	Kilograms.	4,600	13,900	90	(NA)	[9] 950	70
Gold (contained)	Metric tons.	210	385	([6])	(NA)	[15] 950	9,600
Graphite (crude)	1,000 metric tons.	–	8	100	13	[4, 16] 866	(NA)
Gypsum (crude).	1,000 metric tons.	9,400	120	19	21,000	[4] 8.50	4,500
Iodine.	Metric tons.	(D)	1,290	(D)	(D)	[9, 17] 19.88	30
Iron ore (usable)	Million metric tons.	[18] 28	5	([6])	26	[4] 70.00	3,200
Iron and steel scrap (metal).	Million metric tons.	78	22	([6])	(NA)	[4, 19] 195	30,000
Iron and steel slag (metal).	1,000 metric tons.	[20] 13	(Z)	8	13.0	[4] 23.00	2,000
Lead (contained)	1,000 metric tons.	400	360	([6])	1,420	[2] 0.87	2,840
Lime.	1,000 metric tons.	15,000	94	2	15,000	[21] 101	4,800
Magnesium compounds	1,000 metric tons.	255	13	28	352	(NA)	300
Magnesium metal	1,000 metric tons.	(D)	16	35	100	[2] 2.40	400
Manganese (gross weight)	1,000 metric tons.	–	19	100	390	[22] 5.77	(NA)
Mercury	Metric tons.	[13] (NA)	700	([6])	(NA)	[23] 630	(NA)
Mica, scrap and flake.	1,000 metric tons.	90	8	11	101	[4] 146	(NA)
Molybdenum (contained).	Metric tons.	50,000	35,000	([6])	29,000	[8] 25.80	920
Nickel (contained)	Metric tons.	(D)	[24] 99,600	18	88,100	[25] 14,600	–
Niobium (contained).	Metric tons.	–	600	100	2,200	(NA)	(NA)
Nitrogen (fixed)-ammonia	1,000 metric tons.	7,700	50	40	12,800	[26] 250	1,050
Peat.	1,000 metric tons.	610	80	60	1,530	[4] 26.5	610
Perlite	1,000 metric tons.	380	35	21	480	[4] 49.00	97
Phosphate rock	1,000 metric tons.	27,200	–	1	(NA)	[4] 50.00	2,600
Platinum-group metals.	Kilograms.	[27] 16,300	53,780	[28] 89	(NA)	[15, 28, 29] 1,187	1,000
Potash (K$_2$O equivalent)	1,000 metric tons.	840	142	73	3,100	[4, 30] 820	1,075
Pumice and pumicite.	1,000 metric tons.	800	11	3	828	[4] 20.00	110
Salt.	1,000 metric tons.	46,000	1,100	19	56,900	[4, 31] 165	4,100
Silicon (contained) [32].	1,000 metric tons.	[33] (D)	[33] 34	([33, 34])	[35] 200	[36] 77.00	(NA)
Silver (contained).	Metric tons.	1,230	360	63	5,310	[15] 13.37	850
Sodium carbonate (soda ash)	1,000 metric tons.	9,310	4,410	([6])	4,950	[37] 260	2,500
Sodium sulfate.	1,000 metric tons.	300	100	([6])	280	[38] 127	225
Stone (crushed).	Million metric tons.	1,110	1	2	1,160	[4] 9.71	81,000
Sulfur (all forms)	1,000 metric tons.	9,800	1,580	4	10,200	[4, 39] 10.00	2,600
Talc	1,000 metric tons.	527	190	([6])	435	[4] 123	280
Thallium (contained).	Kilograms.	–	350	100	(NA)	[9] 5,700	(NA)
Tin (contained).	Metric tons.	[13] 12,000	3,170	80	49,500	[2] 8.37	(NA)
Titanium dioxide	1,000 metric tons.	1,150	630	([6])	690	[2, 40] 1.10	3,800
Tungsten (contained).	Metric tons.	[13] 4,000	2,620	63	10,800	[41] 150	(NA)
Vermiculite.	1,000 metric tons.	110	6	39	180	[4] 144	80
Zinc (contained).	1,000 metric tons.	690	850	75	920	[2, 42] 0.78	1,540
Zirconium (ZrO$_2$).	Metric tons.	(D)	22,000	([6])	(D)	[4, 43] 830	(NA)

– Represents zero. D Withheld to avoid disclosure. NA Not available. Z Less than 500 metric tons. [1] Calculated as a percent of apparent consumption. [2] Dollars per pound. [3] Refinery production. [4] Dollars per metric ton. [5] Bauxite, average value U.S. imports (f.a.s.). [6] Net exporter. [7] Granulated pentahydrate borax in bulk, f.o.b mine. [8] Less than 25,000 metric tons. [9] Dollars per kilogram. [10] Bulk, purified bromine. [11] 1- to 5-short ton lots. [12] Excludes Puerto Rico. [13] Secondary production. [14] Value of imports, dollars per carat. [15] Dollars per troy ounce. [16] Price of flake imports. [17] C.i.f. value, crude, per kilogram. [18] Shipments of usable ore. [19] Delivered, No. 1 Heavy Melting composite price. [20] Sales include imports and reprocessed slag from past years and decades, and only some from current production. [21] Quicklime only. [22] 46–48 percent Mn metallurgical ore, per unit contained Mn, c.i.f. U.S. ports. [23] Dollars per 76-pound flask. [24] Exports include both primary and secondary materials. [25] London Metal Exchange cash price; dollars per metric ton. [26] F.o.b. Gulf Coast. [27] Platinum and palladium only. [28] Platinum only. [29] Dealer price of platinum. [30] Price of K2O, muriate. [31] Vacuum and open pan, bulk, pellets and packaged, f.o.b. mine and plant. [32] Ferrosilicon statistics include: Production (156,000 tons), exports (6,000 tons), and net import reliance (56%). [33] Silicon metal only. [34] Value is 50% or less. Silicon metal only. [35] Ferrosilicon only. [36] Ferrosilicon, 50 percent; cents per pound. [37] Quoted year-end price, dense, bulk, f.o.b. Green River, WY, dollars per short ton. [38] Quoted price, bulk, f.o.b. works, East, dollars per short ton. [39] Elemental sulfur, f.o.b. plant. [40] Yearend. Unit value based on landed-duty-paid U.S. imports for consumption of pigment with 80 percent or more TiO2. [41] Dollars per metric ton unit WO3 (7.93 kilograms of contained tungsten per metric ton unit). [42] Platt's Metals Week North American price for Special High Grade zinc. [43] Price for imported zircon, f.o.b. U.S. East Coast.

Source: U.S. Geological Survey, *Mineral Commodity Summaries*, annual, January 2010. See also <http://minerals.er.usgs.gov/minerals/pubs/mcs/>.

Table 900. Selected Mineral Products—Average Prices: 1990 to 2009

[Excludes Alaska and Hawaii except as noted]

	Nonfuels								Fuels		
Year	Copper, cathode [1] (cents per lb.)	Plati-num [2] (dol./troy oz.)	Gold (dol./troy oz. [3])	Silver (dol./troy oz. [3])	Lead [4] (cents per lb.)	Tin (New York) [5] (cents per lb.)	Zinc [6] (cents per lb.)	Sulfur, crude [7] (dol./ metric ton)	Bitumi-nous coal [8] (dol./ short ton)	Crude petrol-eum [8] (dol./ bbl.)	Natural gas [8] (dol./ 1,000 cu. ft.)
1990.....	123	467	385	4.82	46	386	75	80.14	27.43	20.03	1.71
1995.....	138	425	386	5.15	42	416	56	44.46	25.56	14.62	1.55
1996.....	109	398	389	5.19	49	412	51	34.11	25.17	18.46	2.17
1997.....	107	397	332	4.89	47	381	65	36.06	24.64	17.23	2.32
1998.....	79	375	295	5.54	45	373	51	29.14	24.87	10.87	1.96
1999.....	76	379	280	5.25	44	366	53	37.81	23.92	15.56	2.19
2000.....	88	549	280	5.00	44	370	56	24.73	24.15	26.72	3.68
2001.....	77	533	272	4.39	44	315	44	10.01	25.36	21.84	4.00
2002.....	76	543	311	4.62	44	292	39	11.84	26.57	22.51	2.95
2003.....	85	694	365	4.91	44	340	41	28.70	26.73	27.56	4.88
2004.....	134	849	411	6.69	55	547	52	32.62	30.56	36.77	5.46
2005.....	174	900	446	7.34	61	483	67	30.88	36.80	50.28	7.33
2006.....	315	1,144	606	11.61	77	565	159	32.85	39.32	59.69	6.39
2007.....	328	1,308	699	13.43	124	899	154	32.49	40.80	66.52	6.25
2008.....	319	1,578	768	15.02	120	1,130	89	262.32	51.39	94.04	7.96
2009.....	241	1,187	950	13.37	87	837	78	10.00	54.25	56.39	3.71

[1] U.S. producer price. [2] Average annual dealer prices. [3] 99.95 percent purity. [4] Nationwide delivered basis.
[5] Composite price. [6] Platt's Metals Week price for North American Special High Grade zinc. Average prices for 1990 are for U.S. High Grade Zinc. [7] F.o.b. (Free on Board) works. [8] Average value at the point of production or domestic first purchase price.

Source: Nonfuels, 1990, U.S. Bureau of Mines, thereafter, U.S. Geological Survey, *Minerals Yearbook* and *Mineral Commodities Summaries*, annual. See also <http://minerals.er.usgs.gov/minerals/pubs/mcs/\>. Fuels, U.S. Energy Information Administration, *Annual Energy Review*. See also <http://www.eia.doe.gov/emeu/mer/prices.html>.

Table 901. Value of Domestic Nonfuel Mineral Production by State: 2000 to 2009

[In millions of dollars (39,400 represents $39,100,000,000). For similar data on fuels, see Table 906]

State	2000	2008 [1]	2009 [1]	State	2000	2008 [1]	2009 [1]
United States [2]	39,400	71,100	57,100				
Alabama	930	1,300	991	Montana.........	596	1,360	1,060
Alaska	1,140	2,660	2,480	Nebraska.........	[3] 84	[3] 152	[3] 118
Arizona	2,510	7,840	5,420	Nevada	2,980	6,290	6,610
Arkansas	484	704	705	New Hampshire....	[3] 57	[3] 101	85
California	3,270	4,200	3,600	New Jersey	[3] 291	[3] 345	279
Colorado	592	2,040	1,960	New Mexico.......	786	1,620	974
Connecticut	[3] 112	[3] 159	[3] 101	New York	1,020	1,480	1,270
Delaware	[3] 14	[3] 21	[3] 14	North Carolina.....	744	1,090	839
Florida	1,820	3,730	2,170	North Dakota......	35	[3] 39	[3] 33
Georgia	1,620	1,800	1,430	Ohio.............	999	1,270	975
Hawaii	[3] 92	162	134	Oklahoma	473	810	696
Idaho	358	1,070	917	Oregon...........	299	398	340
Illinois	913	1,200	874	Pennsylvania......	[3] 1,250	[3] 1,980	1,570
Indiana.............	695	891	776	Rhode Island......	[3] 20	[3] 51	[3] 49
Iowa...............	503	680	518	South Carolina.....	[3] 551	[3] 639	501
Kansas.............	629	1,130	1,100	South Dakota......	233	246	229
Kentucky	501	776	638	Tennessee........	737	856	641
Louisiana...........	325	618	[3] 494	Texas	1,950	3,430	2,900
Maine..............	96	158	120	Utah.............	1,430	4,130	4,000
Maryland	[3] 358	[3] 353	[3] 182	Vermont..........	[3] 67	[3] 111	111
Massachusetts........	[3] 200	[3] 242	219	Virginia..........	710	1,130	954
Michigan	1,640	1,990	1,610	Washington	607	718	586
Minnesota	1,460	[3] 3,320	1,700	West Virginia	172	238	196
Mississippi	149	261	204	Wisconsin	[3] 372	[3] 647	[3] 505
Missouri............	1,370	2,060	1,800	Wyoming	978	2,020	1,940

[1] Preliminary. [2] Includes undistributed not shown separately. [3] Partial data only; excludes values withheld to avoid disclosing individual company data.

Source: U.S. Geological Survey, *Minerals Yearbook*, annual, and *Mineral Commodities Summaries*, annual. See also <http://minerals.er.usgs.gov/minerals/pubs/mcs/>, January 2010.

Table 902. Principal Fuels, Nonmetals, and Metals—World Production and the U.S. Share: 2000 to 2009

[In millions of short tons (4,893 represents 4,893,000,000), except as indicated; see Appendix IV]

Mineral	Unit	World production				Percent U.S. of world			
		2000	2005	2008	2009 [1]	2000	2005	2008	2009 [1]
Fuels: [2]									
Coal	Mil. sh. tons	4,893	6,542	7,271	(NA)	22	17	16	(NA)
Petroleum (crude)	Bil. bbl.	25.0	26.9	26.9	26.4	8	7	7	7
Natural gas (dry, marketable)	Tril. cu. ft.	88.4	100.1	109.8	(NA)	22	18	19	(NA)
Natural gas plant liquids	Bil. bbl.	2.4	2.8	2.9	3.0	30	22	22	24
Nonmetals:									
Asbestos	1,000 metric tons	2,110	2,270	2,090	2,000	–	–	–	–
Barite	1,000 metric tons	6,470	8,110	8,050	5,500	6	6	8	7
Cement	Mil. metric tons	(NA)	2,350	2,840	2,800	(NA)	4	3	3
Feldspar	1,000 metric tons	9,580	16,700	21,900	18,900	8	5	3	3
Fluorspar	1,000 metric tons	4,470	5,280	6,040	5,100	–	–	–	–
Gypsum	Mil. metric tons	106	118	159	152	19	18	9	6
Mica (incl. scrap)	1,000 metric tons	328	359	374	380	31	22	22	24
Nitrogen (N content)	Mil. metric tons	108	122	133	133	11	7	6	6
Phosphate rock (gross wt.)	Mil. metric tons	132	147	161	158	30	25	19	17
Potash (K_2O equivalent)	Mil. metric tons	27	31	35	25	4	4	3	3
Sulfur, elemental basis	Mil. metric tons	58	67	69	70	19	14	14	14
Metals, mine basis:									
Bauxite	Mil. metric tons	136	179	205	200	(NA)	(NA)	(NA)	(NA)
Copper	1,000 metric tons	13,200	15,000	15,400	15,800	11	8	9	8
Gold	Metric tons	2,590	2,470	2,260	2,350	14	10	10	9
Iron ore (gross wt.)	Mil. metric tons	1,070	1,550	2,220	2,300	6	4	2	1
Lead [3]	1,000 metric tons	3,184	3,480	3,840	3,900	15	13	11	10
Mercury	Metric tons	1,350	1,680	1,320	1,280	(NA)	(NA)	(NA)	(NA)
Molybdenum	1,000 metric tons	133	186	218	200	31	31	26	25
Nickel [3]	1,000 metric tons	1,270	1,470	1,600	1,430	(Z)	–	–	–
Silver	1,000 metric tons	18	19	21	21	11	6	6	6
Tantalum concentrates (Ta content)	Metric tons	1,040	1,260	1,170	1,160	–	–	–	–
Titanium mineral concentrates (titanium content) [4]	1,000 metric tons	(NA)	5,200	6,390	5,720	(NA)	6	3	3
Tungsten [3]	1,000 metric tons	44	59	56	58	(NA)	–	(D)	(D)
Vanadium [3]	1,000 metric tons	56	56	56	54	–	–	–	–
Zinc [3]	1,000 metric tons	8,788	10,000	11,500	11,400	10	7	7	6
Metals, smelter basis:									
Aluminum	1,000 metric tons	24,400	31,900	39,000	36,900	15	8	7	5
Cadmium	1,000 metric tons	20	20	20	19	10	7	4	4
Copper	1,000 metric tons	11,000	13,600	14,700	14,600	9	4	4	4
Iron, pig	Mil. metric tons	573	802	932	898	8	8	7	8
Lead [4]	1,000 metric tons	6,580	7,580	8,620	8,800	22	17	15	14
Magnesium [5], [6]	1,000 metric tons	428	622	671	570	(D)	(D)	(D)	(D)
Raw Steel	Mil. metric tons	845	1,140	1,330	919	12	8	8	5
Tin [7]	1,000 metric tons	271	297	299	307	2	–	–	–
Zinc	1,000 metric tons	9,137	10,400	11,800	11,300	4	3	2	2

– Represents or rounds to zero. D Withheld to avoid disclosing company data. NA Not available. Z Less than 0.05 percent.
[1] Preliminary. [2] Source: Energy Information Administration, "International Energy Statistics." [3] Content of ore and concentrate.
[4] Refinery production. [5] Primary production; no smelter processing necessary. [6] Starting 2005, excludes U.S. production.
[7] Production from primary sources only.
   Source: Except as noted, Nonfuels, U.S. Geological Survey, *Minerals Yearbook*, annual, and *Mineral Commodities Summaries*, annual, January 2010, <http://minerals.er.usgs.gov/minerals/pubs/mcs/\>; and fuels, U.S. Energy Information Administration, "International Energy Statistics," <http://tonto.eia.doe.gov/cfapps/ipdbproject/IEDIndex3.cfm> June 2009.

Table 903. Net U.S. Imports of Selected Minerals and Metals as Percent of Apparent Consumption: 1980 to 2009

[In percent. Based on net imports which equal the difference between imports and exports plus or minus government stockpile and industry stock changes]

Minerals and metals	1980	1990	1995	2000	2005	2006	2007	2008	2009 [1]
Bauxite [2]	(NA)	98	99	100	100	100	100	100	100
Fluorspar	87	91	92	100	100	100	100	100	100
Manganese	98	100	100	100	100	100	100	100	100
Strontium	100	100	100	100	100	100	100	100	100
Tantalum	90	86	80	80	100	100	100	100	100
Vanadium	35	(D)	84	100	100	100	100	100	100
Mica (sheet)	100	100	100	100	100	100	100	100	100
Platinum	(NA)	(NA)	(NA)	78	93	90	91	89	89
Tin	79	71	84	88	78	79	81	80	80
Barite	44	71	65	84	84	81	85	80	80
Zinc	60	64	71	72	67	77	73	71	76
Cobalt	93	84	79	78	83	82	80	81	75
Potash	65	68	75	80	80	79	81	84	73
Titanium	(NA)	(NA)	70	79	71	67	76	78	73
Tungsten	53	81	90	66	68	67	68	60	63
Silver	7	(NA)	(NA)	43	72	63	68	67	63
Nickel	76	64	60	52	48	50	22	34	18
Iron and steel	13	13	21	18	15	17	16	13	7
Aluminum	(3)	(3)	23	33	41	31	19	(3)	5
Iron ore	25	21	14	10	4	8	(3)	(3)	(3)

D Withheld to avoid disclosure. NA Not available. [1] Preliminary. [2] Includes alumina. [3] Net exporter.
   Source: Through 1990, U.S. Bureau of Mines; thereafter, U.S. Geological Survey, *Mineral Commodity Summaries* and *Minerals Yearbook*, annual, and *Historical Statistics for Mineral and Material Commodities in the United States*; and import and export data from U.S. Census Bureau.

572 Forestry, Fishing, and Mining

Table 904. Petroleum Industry—Summary: 1990 to 2009

[602 represents 602,000. Includes all costs incurred for drilling and equipping wells to point of completion as productive wells or abandonment after drilling becomes unproductive. Based on sample of operators of different size drilling establishments]

Item	Unit	1990	1995	2000	2005	2006	2007	2008	2009 [1]
Crude oil producing wells, (Dec. 31)	1,000	602	574	534	498	497	500	526	526
Daily output per well [2]	Bbl.	12.2	11.4	10.9	10.4	10.3	10.1	9.4	10.1
Completed wells drilled, total	1,000	27.02	17.97	26.93	39.69	46.69	46.49	51.76	32.57
Crude oil	1,000	12.02	7.66	7.80	10.16	12.63	12.73	16.42	12.42
Natural gas	1,000	10.42	7.52	16.33	26.35	30.41	30.25	31.47	17.73
Dry holes	1,000	4.59	2.79	2.80	3.18	3.65	3.51	3.87	2.43
Average depth per well	Feet	4,602	5,459	4,765	5,407	5,474	5,927	6,195	6,084
Average cost per well	$1,000	384	513	755	1,721	2,102	4,172	5,136	(NA)
Average cost per foot	Dollars	76.07	87.22	142.16	306.50	378.03	688.30	782.31	(NA)
Crude oil production, total [3]	Mil. bbl.	2,685	2,394	2,131	1,890	1,862	1,848	1,812	1,938
Value at wells [3, 4]	Bil. dol.	53.77	35.00	56.93	95.03	111.16	122.96	170.38	109.29
Average price per barrel	Dollars	20.03	14.62	26.72	50.28	59.69	66.52	94.04	56.39
Lower 48 states [5]	Mil. bbl.	2,037	1,853	1,776	1,575	1,592	1,585	1,562	1,703
Alaska	Mil. bbl.	647	542	355	315	270	264	250	235
Onshore	Mil. bbl.	2,290	1,838	1,482	1,265	1,241	1,244	1,310	1,256
Offshore	Mil. bbl.	395	557	649	625	621	605	502	682
Imports: Crude oil [3, 6]	Mil. bbl.	2,151	2,639	3,320	3,696	3,693	3,661	3,581	3,307
Refined petroleum products	Mil. bbl.	775	586	874	1,310	1,310	1,255	1,146	973
Exports: Crude oil [3]	Mil. bbl.	39.7	34.5	18.4	11.6	9.0	10.0	10.5	16.0
Proved reserves	Bil. bbl.	26.3	22.4	22.0	21.8	21.0	21.3	19.1	(NA)
Operable refineries	Number	205	175	158	148	149	149	150	150
Capacity (Jan. 1)	Mil. bbl.	5,684	5,633	6,027	6,251	6,329	6,367	6,422	6,450
Refinery input, total	Mil. bbl.	5,325	5,555	5,964	6,136	6,198	6,205	6,278	6,162
Crude oil [3]	Mil. bbl.	4,894	5,100	5,514	5,555	5,563	5,532	5,361	5,224
Natural gas plant liquids	Mil. bbl.	171	172	139	161	183	184	178	179
Other liquids [7]	Mil. bbl.	260	283	311	420	452	488	739	759
Refinery output, total [8]	Mil. bbl.	5,574	5,838	6,311	6,497	6,561	6,568	6,641	6,520
Motor gasoline [9]	Mil. bbl.	2,540	2,722	2,910	3,036	3,053	3,051	3,129	3,199
Jet fuel [10]	Mil. bbl.	543	517	588	564	541	528	546	510
Distillate fuel oil	Mil. bbl.	1,067	1,152	1,310	1,443	1,475	1,509	1,572	1,477
Residual fuel oil	Mil. bbl.	347	288	255	229	232	246	227	219
Liquefied petroleum gases	Mil. bbl.	182	239	258	209	229	239	230	230
Utilization rate	Percent	87.1	92.0	92.6	90.6	89.7	88.5	85.3	82.8

NA Not available. [1] Preliminary. [2] Based on number of wells producing at end of year. [3] Includes lease condensate. [4] Values based on domestic first purchase price. [5] Excluding Alaska and Hawaii. [6] Includes imports for the Strategic Petroleum Reserve. [7] Unfinished oils (net), other hydrocarbons, hydrogen, aviation and motor gasoline blending components (net). Beginning 1995, also includes oxygenates (net). [8] Includes other products not shown separately [9] Finished motor gasoline. Beginning 1995, also includes ethanol blended into motor gasoline. [10] Prior to 2005, kerosene-type jet fuel is included with kerosene in "Other products." Beginning 2005, naphtha-type jet fuel is also included in "Other products."

Source: U.S. Energy Information Administration, *Annual Energy Review 2009*. See also <http://www.eia.doe.gov/emeu/aer /contents.html>.

Table 905. Supply, Disposition, and Ending Stocks of Crude Oil and Petroleum Products: 2009

[In millions of barrels (1,956.6 represents 1,956,600,000). Minus sign (–) indicates decrease]

Commodity	Supply				Disposition				Ending stocks
	Field produc-tion	Refinery and blender net pro-duction	Imports	Adjust-ments [1]	Stock change	Refinery and blender net inputs	Exports	Products supplied [2]	
Crude oil	1,956.6	(X)	3,289.7	26.5	24.1	5,232.7	16.0	–	1,051.8
Commercial	1,956.6	(X)	3,269.3	26.5	–0.7	(NA)	16.0	–	325.2
Alaskan	235.5	(X)	(NA)	(X)	(NA)	(NA)	(NA)	–	(NA)
Lower 48 states	1,721.1	(X)	(NA)	(X)	(NA)	(NA)	(NA)	–	(NA)
SPR [3]	(X)	(X)	20.4	(X)	24.8	(X)	(NA)	(X)	726.6
Imports by SPR [3]	(X)	(X)	(NA)	(X)	(X)	(X)	(NA)	(X)	(X)
Imports into SPR [3] by others	(X)	(X)	20.4	(X)	(X)	(X)	(NA)	(X)	(X)
Natural gas liquids and LRG [4]	697.1	227.5	70.8	(X)	–14.3	177.2	50.7	776.3	112.6
Pentanes plus	98.9	(X)	4.3	(X)	–3.3	59.1	14.3	27.6	10.5
Liquefied petroleum gases	598.2	227.5	66.5	(X)	–11.0	118.1	36.3	748.7	102.1
Ethane/ethylene	280.6	7.1	0.1	(X)	–6.6	(NA)	(NA)	294.4	21.0
Propane/propylene	199.4	196.0	53.7	(X)	–5.3	(NA)	30.9	423.4	50.1
Normal butane/butylene	49.5	24.1	7.8	(X)	1.1	48.5	5.4	26.4	24.1
Isobutane/isobutylene	68.7	0.2	4.9	(X)	–216.0	69.6	(NA)	4.5	6.9
Finished motor gasoline	(X)	3,206.7	81.5	53.6	–13.4	(X)	71.3	3,283.7	84.9
Kerosene-type jet fuel	(X)	509.7	29.5	(X)	5.4	(X)	25.2	508.5	43.4
Distillate fuel oil [5]	(X)	1,477.5	82.2	–	20.0	(X)	214.4	1,325.3	166.0

– Represents zero. NA Not available. X Not applicable. [1] Includes an adjustment for crude oil, previously referred to as "Unaccounted For Crude Oil." Also included is an adjustment for motor gasoline blending components, fuel ethanol, and distillate fuel oil. See Appendix B of source for more details. [2] Products supplied is equal to field production, plus refinery and blender net production, plus imports, plus adjustments, minus stock change, minus refinery and blender net inputs, minus exports. [3] Strategic Petroleum Reserve. [4] Liquified Refinery Gases (LRGs) are liquefied petroleum gases fractionated from refinery or still gases through compression and/or refrigeration. They are retained in the liquid state. Excludes still gas. [5] Distillate stocks located in the "Northeast Heating Oil Reserve" are not included. For details, see Appendix C of source.

Source: U.S. Energy Information Administration, "Petroleum Supply Annual, Volume 1"; <http://www.eia.doe.gov/oil_gas /petroleum/data_publications/petroleum_supply_annual/psa_volume1/psa_volume1.html>.

Forestry, Fishing, and Mining 573

Table 906. Crude Petroleum and Natural Gas—Production and Value by Major Producing States: 2006 to 2008

[1,862 represents 1,862,000,000 barrels]

State	Crude petroleum Quantity (mil. bbl.)			Crude petroleum Value (mil. dol.)			Natural gas marketed production [1] Quantity (bil. cu. ft.)			Natural gas marketed production [1] Value (mil. dol.)		
	2006	2007	2008	2006	2007	2008	2006	2007	2008	2006	2007	2008
Total [2]	1,862	1,848	1,812	111,158	122,959	170,383	19,410	20,196	21,240	124,074	126,165	169,038
AL	8	7	8	476	510	730	286	270	258	2,168	2,011	2,490
AK [3]	270	264	250	15,380	16,788	22,514	445	433	398	2,576	2,439	2,945
AR	6	6	6	358	387	553	270	270	447	1,739	1,783	3,893
CA	223	217	215	12,813	14,106	19,410	315	307	296	2,039	2,033	2,483
CO	23	23	24	1,492	1,558	2,184	1,203	1,243	1,389	7,362	5,680	9,642
FL	2	2	2	(NA)	(NA)	(NA)	3	2	2	(NA)	(NA)	(NA)
IL	10	10	9	616	631	881	(Z)	1	1	(NA)	(NA)	(NA)
IN	2	2	2	103	113	171	3	4	5	18	21	36
KS	36	36	40	2,165	2,439	3,645	371	366	374	2,082	2,082	2,565
KY	2	3	3	136	170	240	95	95	114	842	701	961
LA	74	77	73	4,745	5,491	7,366	1,361	1,365	1,377	9,429	9,590	12,023
MI	5	5	6	310	348	596	263	265	272	(NA)	(NA)	1,533
MS	17	20	22	1,030	1,400	2,091	61	73	97	414	492	850
MI	36	35	32	2,056	2,251	2,838	113	117	113	624	668	844
NE	2	2	2	134	147	211	1	2	3	(NA)	8	19
NM	60	59	59	3,693	4,056	5,716	1,609	1,518	1,446	9,947	10,448	12,146
NY	(Z)	(Z)	(Z)	(NA)	(NA)	(NA)	56	55	50	399	486	450
ND	40	45	63	2,263	2,942	5,567	55	60	61	361	402	525
OH	5	5	6	341	371	551	86	88	85	669	669	669
OK	63	61	64	3,966	4,225	6,160	1,689	1,784	1,913	10,671	11,129	14,461
PA	4	4	4	232	256	349	176	182	198	(NA)	(NA)	(NA)
TX	397	397	398	24,354	27,108	38,548	5,548	6,123	6,921	36,591	42,734	58,904
UT	18	20	22	1,069	1,220	1,905	348	376	434	1,913	(NA)	2,668
WV	2	2	2	110	106	151	226	231	246	(NA)	(NA)	(NA)
WY	53	54	53	2,817	3,158	4,557	1,816	2,048	2,275	10,627	9,532	15,614
Federal offshore	121	114	103	93,384	103,032	140,547	(NA)	(NA)	(NA)	(NA)	(NA)	(NA)
Lower 48 states	1,592	1,585	1,562	95,778	106,171	147,870	18,965	19,763	20,841	121,498	123,725	166,094

NA Not available. Z Less than 500,000 barrels or 500 million cubic feet. [1] Excludes nonhydrocarbon gases. [2] Includes other states, not shown separately. State production includes state offshore production, as well as extractions from the Gulf not distributed to states. U.S. level totals shown in Tables 904 and 911 may contain revisions not carried to state level. [3] Price data are for North Slope only. Value data were calculated using price data.

Source: U.S. Energy Information Administration, "Petroleum Navigator" and "Natural Gas Navigator," <http://www.eia.gov/dnav/pet/pet_sum_top.asp> and <http://www.eia.gov/dnav/ng/ng_sum_top.asp>, accessed June 2010.

Table 907. Crude Oil, Natural Gas, and Natural Gas Liquids—Reserves by State: 2006 to 2008

[20,972 mil. bbl. represents 20,972,000,000 bbl. As of December 31. Proved reserves are estimated quantities of the mineral, which geological and engineering data demonstrate with reasonable certainty, to be recoverable in future years from known reservoirs under existing economic and operating conditions. Based on a sample of operators of oil and gas wells]

Area	2006 Crude oil proved reserves (mil. bbl.)	2006 Natural gas (bil. cu. ft.)	2006 Natural gas liquids (mil. bbl.)	2007 Crude oil proved reserves (mil. bbl.)	2007 Natural gas (bil. cu. ft.)	2007 Natural gas liquids (mil. bbl.)	2008 Crude oil proved reserves (mil. bbl.)	2008 Natural gas (bil. cu. ft.)	2008 Natural gas liquids (mil. bbl.)
United States [1]	20,972	211,085	8,472	21,317	237,726	9,143	19,121	244,656	9,275
Alabama	45	3,911	56	42	3,994	53	38	3,290	106
Alaska	3,879	10,245	338	4,163	11,917	325	3,507	7,699	312
Arkansas	37	2,269	4	31	3,305	3	30	5,626	2
California	3,389	2,794	132	3,322	2,740	126	2,705	2,406	113
Colorado	274	17,149	478	304	21,851	559	288	23,302	716
Florida	38	45	3	32	108	2	3	1	–
Illinois	89	(NA)	(NA)	101	(NA)	(NA)	54	(NA)	(NA)
Indiana	12	(NA)	(NA)	17	(NA)	(NA)	15	(NA)	(NA)
Kansas	263	3,931	209	206	3,982	198	243	3,557	181
Kentucky	25	2,227	105	24	2,469	89	17	2,714	100
Louisiana	428	10,474	280	458	10,045	303	388	11,573	300
Michigan	63	3,065	42	55	3,630	55	48	3,174	62
Mississippi	186	813	8	200	954	9	249	1,030	9
Montana	419	1,057	10	410	1,052	11	321	1,000	11
Nebraska	14	(NA)	(NA)	12	(NA)	(NA)	8	(NA)	(NA)
New Mexico	705	17,934	861	735	17,245	844	654	16,285	804
New York	(NA)	363	(NA)	(NA)	376	(NA)	(NA)	389	(NA)
North Dakota	412	479	55	482	511	58	573	541	55
Ohio	49	975	(NA)	48	1,027	(NA)	38	985	(NA)
Oklahoma	569	17,464	892	530	19,031	949	581	20,845	1,034
Pennsylvania	20	3,050	(NA)	12	3,361	(NA)	14	3,577	(NA)
Texas	4,871	61,836	3,335	5,122	72,091	3,658	4,555	77,546	3,560
Utah	334	5,146	([2])	355	6,391	108	286	6,643	116
Virginia	(NA)	2,302	(NA)	(NA)	2,529	(NA)	(NA)	2,378	(NA)
West Virginia	23	4,509	110	28	4,729	115	23	5,136	100
Wyoming	706	23,549	[3] 887	690	29,710	1,032	556	31,143	1,121
Federal offshore	4,096	15,360	653	3,905	14,439	624	3,903	13,546	548
Lower 48 states	17,093	200,840	8,134	17,154	225,809	8,818	15,614	236,957	8,963

– Represents zero. NA Not available. [1] Includes other states, not shown separately. [2] Included with Wyoming. [3] Includes Utah.

Source: U.S. Energy Information Administration, "Petroleum Navigator" and "Natural Gas Navigator," <http://www.eia.gov/dnav/pet/pet_sum_top.asp> and <http://www.eia.gov/dnav/ng/ng_sum_top.asp>, accessed March 2010.

Table 908. Federal Offshore Leasing, Exploration, Production, and Revenue: 1990 to 2009

[In millions (56.79 represents 56,790,000), except as indicated. Data presented by fiscal year. See source for explanation of terms and for reliability statement]

Item	Unit	1990	1995	2000	2005	2006	2007	2008	2009
Tracts offered.................	Number ...	10,459	10,995	7,992	11,447	7,905	4,992	19,812	9,893
Tracts leased.................	Number ...	825	835	553	989	763	360	2,121	483
Acres offered.................	Millions....	56.79	59.70	42.89	61.08	42.24	26.63	106.76	52.98
Acres leased.................	Millions....	4.30	4.34	2.92	5.24	4.12	2.01	11.73	2.66
New wells being drilled:									
Active......................	Number ...	120	265	230	149	143	96	132	56
Suspended.................	Number ...	266	155	154	64	60	79	68	67
Cumulative wells (since 1953):									
Wells completed	Number ...	13,167	13,435	13,757	13,393	13,180	12,688	12,055	11,063
Wells plugged and abandoned ...	Number ...	14,677	21,118	26,585	31,427	32,152	33,202	34,175	35,263
Revenue, total [1]................	Bil. dol.....	3.4	2.7	5.2	6.3	7.6	7.0	18.0	5.79
Bonuses....................	Bil. dol.....	0.8	0.4	0.4	0.6	0.9	0.4	9.5	1.18
Oil and gas royalties [1]	Bil. dol.....	2.6	2.1	4.1	5.5	6.5	6.4	8.3	4.38
Rentals	Bil. dol.....	0.09	0.09	0.21	0.22	0.22	0.20	0.24	0.23
Sales value [2]	Bil. dol.....	17.0	13.8	27.4	37.2	45.6	45.5	57.2	32.63
Oil	Bil. dol.....	7.0	6.3	11.5	15.4	24.2	27.8	35.9	23.46
Natural gas	Bil. dol.....	9.5	7.5	15.9	21.8	21.4	17.7	21.3	9.17
Sales volume: [3]									
Oil	Mil. bbl.....	324	409	566	332	391	471	358	425
Natural gas	Bil. cu. ft. ...	5,093	4,692	4,723	3,504	2,581	2,547	1,573	3,539

[1] Includes condensate royalties. [2] Production value is value at time of production, not current value. [3] Excludes sales volumes for gas lost, gas plant products, or sulfur.

Source: U.S. Department of the Interior, Minerals Management Service, *Federal Offshore Statistics*, annual; for revenue, sales value, and sales volume data after 2000, Minerals Revenue Management, Annual Reported Royalty Revenue Statistical Information; <http://www.mrm.mms.gov/MRMWebStats/Home.aspx>.

Table 909. Oil and Gas Extraction Industry—Establishments, Employees, and Payroll by State: 2007

[8,987,718 represents 8,987,718,000. Excludes government employees, railroad employees, self-employed persons, etc. See "General Explanation" in source for definitions and statement on reliability of data. An establishment is a single physical location where business is conducted or where services or industrial operations are performed. See Appendix III]

State	Crude petroleum and natural gas extraction (211111) [1]			State	Natural gas liquid extraction (211112) [1]		
	Establish-ments	Number of employees [2]	Annual pay-roll ($1,000)		Establish-ments	Number of employees [2]	Annual pay-roll ($1,000)
United States [3] ..	**7,221**	**133,286**	**8,987,718**	**United States [3]** ..	**321**	**8,523**	**616,805**
Arkansas..........	88	1,255	78,824	Alabama	2	[4]	(D)
California..........	192	8,903	532,013	Alaska	1	[4]	(D)
Colorado	371	7,458	599,286	California	10	137	10,666
Florida	39	229	9,724	Colorado	18	465	37,591
Illinois............	160	963	34,101	Florida	4	[5]	(D)
Indiana...........	46	195	7,655	Illinois............	3	[6]	(D)
Kansas...........	381	3,087	161,035	Kansas...........	10	[5]	(D)
Kentucky	89	921	44,039	Kentucky	4	[4]	(D)
Louisiana.........	363	12,056	792,842	Louisiana	40	941	65,084
Michigan	95	1,171	72,813	Michigan	6	85	5,160
Mississippi........	76	952	48,950	Minnesota	3	[4]	(D)
Montana..........	72	664	44,294	Mississippi........	3	70	5,308
Nevada	21	[6]	5,547	Missouri	1	[4]	(D)
New Mexico.......	165	2,957	204,651	Montana..........	7	[4]	(D)
New York	46	319	15,240	New Mexico.......	16	670	44,988
North Dakota......	37	1,327	88,150	North Dakota......	6	[6]	(D)
Ohio.............	200	1,537	66,813	Ohio.............	4	[7]	393
Oklahoma	1,100	16,735	1,163,677	Oklahoma	41	[8]	(D)
Pennsylvania......	159	2,387	126,388	Pennsylvania......	12	[5]	(D)
Texas............	2,913	57,662	3,980,159	South Dakota......	4	[4]	(D)
Utah.............	59	1,382	88,323	Texas............	88	2,872	240,803
Virginia...........	16	537	27,884	Utah.............	6	111	5,559
West Virginia	200	2,537	124,300	West Virginia	6	[4]	(D)
Wyoming	170	3,761	282,285	Wyoming	20	665	46,737

D Withheld to avoid disclosing data for individual companies; data are included in higher level totals. [1] North American Industry Classification System, 2002. [2] Covers full- and part-time employees who are on the payroll in the pay period including March 12. [3] Includes other states, not shown separately. [4] 20 to 99 employees. [5] 250 to 499 employees. [6] 100 to 249 employees. [7] 0 to 19 employees. [8] 500 to 999 employees.

Source: U.S. Census Bureau, "County Business Patterns," July 2009, <http://www.census.gov/econ/cbp/index.html>.

Table 910. Natural Gas Plant Liquids—Production and Value: 1990 to 2009

[Barrels of 42 gallons (569 represents 569,000,000)]

Item	Unit	1990	1995	2000	2004	2005	2006	2007	2008	2009
Field production [1]............	Mil. bbl......	569	643	699	662	627	635	651	653	689
Pentanes plus	Mil. bbl......	113	122	112	101	97	96	96	97	97
Liquefied petroleum gases ..	Mil. bbl......	456	521	587	561	529	539	555	556	591
Natural gas processed	Tril. cu. ft....	15	17	17	15	15	15	16	15	(NA)

NA Not available. [1] Includes other finished petroleum products, not shown separately.

Source: U.S. Energy Information Administration, "Petroleum Navigator" and "Natural Gas Navigator"; <http://www.eia.gov/dnav/pet/pet_sum_top.asp> and <http://www.eia.gov/dnav/ng/ng_sum_top.asp>, accessed June 2010.

Forestry, Fishing, and Mining 575

Table 911. Natural Gas—Supply, Consumption, Reserves, and Marketed Production: 1990 to 2009

[269 represents 269,000. Data are for natural gas, plus a small amount of supplemental gaseous fuels. Minus sign (–) indicates debit]

Item	Unit	1990	1995	2000	2004	2005	2006	2007	2008	2009
Producing wells (year-end)	1,000	269	299	342	406	426	441	453	479	496
Production value at wells.	Bil. of dol. . .	31.8	30.2	74.3	106.6	138.7	124.0	126.2	169.1	(NA)
Avg. per 1,000 cu. ft.	Dollars	1.71	1.55	3.68	5.46	7.33	6.39	6.25	7.96	(NA)
Proved reserves [1]	Tril. cu. ft. . . .	169	165	177	193	204	211	238	245	(NA)
Marketed production [2].	**Bil. cu. ft. . . .**	**18,594**	**19,506**	**20,198**	**19,517**	**18,927**	**19,410**	**20,196**	**21,240**	**21,893**
Minus: Extraction losses [3]	Bil. cu. ft. . . .	784	908	1,016	927	876	906	930	953	938
Equals: Dry production	Bil. cu. ft. . . .	17,810	18,599	19,182	18,591	18,051	18,504	19,266	20,286	20,955
Plus: Supplemental gas supplies. . .	Bil. cu. ft. . . .	123	110	90	60	64	66	63	61	64
Equals: Dry production with supplemental gas	Bil. cu. ft. . . .	17,932	18,709	19,272	18,651	18,114	18,570	19,329	20,347	21,019
Plus: Withdrawals from storage	Bil. cu. ft. . . .	1,986	3,025	3,550	3,088	3,107	2,527	3,375	3,417	2,968
Plus: Imports	Bil. cu. ft. . . .	1,532	2,841	3,782	4,259	4,341	4,186	4,608	3,984	3,748
Plus: Balancing item [4]	Bil. cu. ft. . . .	307	396	–305	448	232	89	–209	–133	–549
Equals: Total supply.	Bil. cu. ft. . . .	21,758	24,971	26,299	26,445	25,794	25,372	27,103	27,615	27,186
Minus: Exports	Bil. cu. ft. . . .	86	154	244	854	729	724	822	1,006	1,071
Minus: Additions to storage [5]	Bil. cu. ft. . . .	2,499	2,610	2,721	3,202	3,055	2,963	3,183	3,383	3,281
Equals: Consumption, total	**Bil. cu. ft. . . .**	**19,174**	**22,207**	**23,333**	**22,389**	**22,011**	**21,685**	**23,097**	**23,227**	**22,834**
Lease and plant fuel	Bil. cu. ft. . . .	1,236	1,220	1,151	1,098	1,112	1,142	1,226	1,224	1,261
Pipeline fuel [6].	Bil. cu. ft. . . .	660	700	642	566	584	584	621	648	637
Residential.	Bil. cu. ft. . . .	4,391	4,850	4,996	4,869	4,827	4,368	4,722	4,872	4,761
Commercial [7].	Bil. cu. ft. . . .	2,623	3,031	3,182	3,129	2,999	2,832	3,013	3,136	3,113
Industrial	Bil. cu. ft. . . .	8,255	9,384	9,293	8,341	7,709	7,654	7,874	7,874	7,404
Vehicle fuel	Bil. cu. ft. . . .	(Z)	5	13	21	23	24	25	28	32
Electric power sector	Bil. cu. ft. . . .	3,245	4,237	5,206	5,464	5,869	6,222	6,841	6,668	6,888
World production (dry).	Tril. cu. ft. . . .	73.8	78.1	88.4	97.2	100.1	103.4	105.8	109.8	(NA)
U.S. production (dry).	Tril. cu. ft. . . .	17.8	18.6	19.2	18.6	18.1	18.5	19.1	20.4	21.0
Percent U.S. of world	Percent	24.1	23.8	21.7	19.1	18.0	17.9	18.0	18.6	(NA)

NA Not available. Z Less than 500 million cubic feet. [1] Estimated, end of year. Source: U.S. Energy Information Administration, *U.S. Crude Oil, Natural Gas, and Natural Gas Liquids Reserves*, annual. [2] Marketed production includes gross withdrawals from reservoirs less quantities used for reservoir repressuring and quantities vented or flared. Excludes nonhydrocarbon gases subsequently removed. [3] Volumetric reduction in natural gas resulting from the removal of natural gas plant liquids, which are transferred to petroleum supply. [4] Quantities lost and imbalances in data due to differences among data sources. Since 1980, excludes intransit shipments that cross U.S.-Canada border (i.e., natural gas delivered to its destination via the other country). [5] Underground storage. Through 2004, includes liquefied natural gas (LNG) storage in above-ground tanks. [6] Natural gas consumed in the operation of pipelines and delivery to consumers. [7] Includes deliveries to municipalities and public authorities for institutional heating and other purposes.

Source: Except as noted, U.S. Energy Information Administration, *Annual Energy Review*; "International Energy Annual"; "U.S. Crude Oil, Natural Gas, and Natural Gas Liquids Reserves"; "Natural Gas Annual"; and "International Energy Statistics," <http://www.eia.doe.gov>.

Table 912. Unconventional Dry Natural Gas Production and Proved Reserves: 2007 and 2008

[In billions of cubic feet (1,753 represents 1,753,000). For states not shown, no production or reserves were reported]

State	Production Coalbed methane [1]		Production Shale gas [2]		Proved reserves [3] Coalbed methane [1]		Proved reserves [3] Shale gas [2]	
	2007	2008	2007	2008	2007	2008	2007	2008
U.S.	**1,753**	**1,966**	**1,184**	**2,022**	**21,874**	**20,798**	**21,735**	**32,825**
Alabama	114	107	–	–	2,126	1,727	1	2
Alaska	–	–	–	–	–	–	–	–
Arkansas	3	3	93	279	31	31	1,457	3,831
California	–	–	–	–	–	–	–	–
Colorado	519	497	–	–	7,869	8,238	–	–
Florida	–	–	–	–	–	–	–	–
Kansas.	38	47	–	–	340	301	–	–
Kentucky	–	–	2	2	–	–	20	19
Louisiana	–	1	1	22	7	9	5	832
Michigan	–	–	119	118	–	–	2,761	2,801
Mississippi	–	–	–	–	–	–	–	–
Montana.	13	14	11	11	66	75	124	110
New Mexico	394	443	2	–	4,169	3,991	10	–
New York	–	–	–	–	–	–	–	–
North Dakota	–	–	2	3	–	–	18	22
Ohio	–	–	–	–	1	1	–	–
Oklahoma	82	69	36	151	1,265	511	849	3,458
Pennsylvania	5	11	1	1	108	102	89	83
Texas.	–	–	915	1,433	–	–	16,335	21,595
Utah.	73	71	–	–	922	893	–	–
Virginia.	85	101	–	–	1,948	1,851	–	–
West Virginia	25	28	–	–	255	246	–	14
Wyoming	401	573	–	–	2,738	2,781	–	–

– Represents or rounds to zero. [1] Methane is generated during coal formation and is contained in the coal microstructure. Typical recovery entails pumping water out of the coal to allow the gas to escape. Methane is the principal component of natural gas. Coal bed methane can be added to natural gas pipelines without any special treatment. [2] Natural gas produced from low permeability shale formations. [3] Proved reserves of natural gas as of December 31 of the report year are the estimated quantities which analysis of geological and engineering data demonstrate with reasonable certainty to be recoverable in future years from known reservoirs under existing economic and operating conditions.

Source: U.S. Energy Information Administration, "Natural Gas Navigator," <http://www.eia.gov/dnav/ng/ng_sum_top.asp>, accessed April 8, 2010.

576 Forestry, Fishing, and Mining

Table 913. Coal Supply, Disposition, and Prices: 2000 to 2009

[In millions of short tons (1,073.6 represents 1,073,600,000). 1 short ton = 2,000 lbs.]

Item	2000	2004	2005	2006	2007	2008	2009
United States, total supply	**1,073.6**	**1,112.1**	**1,131.5**	**1,162.8**	**1,146.6**	**1,171.8**	**1,072.8**
Consumption by sector:							
Total	1,084.1	1,107.3	1,126.0	1,112.3	1,128.0	1,120.5	1,000.4
Electric power	985.8	1,016.3	1,037.5	1,026.6	1,045.1	1,040.6	936.5
Coke plants	28.9	23.7	23.4	23.0	22.7	22.1	15.3
Other industrial plants	65.2	62.2	60.3	59.5	56.6	54.4	45.4
Combined heat and power (CHP)	28.0	26.6	25.9	25.3	22.5	23.6	(NA)
Noncombined heat and power	37.2	35.6	34.5	34.2	34.1	31.0	(NA)
Residential/commercial users	4.1	5.1	4.7	3.2	3.5	3.5	3.2
Year-end coal stocks:							
Total [1]	140.0	154.0	144.3	186.9	192.8	205.1	238.8
Electric power	102.0	106.7	101.1	141.0	151.2	161.6	190.0
Coke plants	1.5	1.3	2.6	2.9	1.9	2.3	2.0
Other industrial plants	4.6	4.8	5.6	6.5	5.6	6.0	5.1
Producers/distributors	31.9	41.2	35.0	36.5	34.0	34.7	41.3
U.S. coal trade:							
Net exports [2]	46.0	20.7	19.5	13.4	22.8	47.3	36.5
Exports	58.5	48.0	49.9	49.6	59.2	81.5	59.1
Steam coal	25.7	21.2	21.3	22.1	27.0	39.0	21.8
Metallurgical coal	32.8	26.8	28.7	27.5	32.2	42.5	37.3
Imports	12.5	27.3	30.5	36.2	36.3	34.2	22.6
Average delivered price (dollars per short ton):							
Electric utilities	24.28	27.30	31.22	34.26	36.06	41.32	44.72
Independent power producers	(NA)	27.27	30.39	33.04	33.11	38.98	39.72
Coke plants	44.38	61.50	83.79	92.87	94.97	118.09	143.04
Other industrial plants	31.46	39.30	47.63	51.67	54.42	63.44	64.87
Average free alongside ship (f.a.s.):							
Exports	34.90	54.11	67.10	70.93	70.25	97.68	101.44
Steam coal	29.67	42.03	47.64	46.25	47.90	57.35	73.63
Metallurgical coal	38.99	63.63	81.56	90.81	88.99	134.62	117.73
Imports	30.10	37.52	46.71	49.10	47.64	59.83	63.91

NA Not available. [1] Includes other stocks, not shown separately. [2] Exports minus imports.

Source: U.S. Energy Information Administration, "U.S. Coal Supply and Demand: 2009 Review," annual, April 2010, <http://www.eia.doe.gov/cneaf/coal/page/special/feature.html>.

Table 914. Coal and Coke—Summary: 1990 to 2009

[In millions of short tons (1,029 represents 1,029,000,000), except as indicated. Includes coal consumed at mines. Recoverability varies between 40 and 90 percent for individual deposits; 50 percent or more of overall U.S. coal reserve base is believed to be recoverable]

Item	Unit	1990	1995	2000	2005	2006	2007	2008	2009
COAL									
Coal production, total [1], [2]	Mil. sh. tons	**1,029**	**1,033**	**1,074**	**1,131**	**1,163**	**1,147**	**1,172**	**1,073**
Value [3]	Bil. dol.	22.39	19.45	18.02	26.69	29.25	30.04	36.62	35.31
Anthracite production [2]	Mil. sh. tons	3.5	4.7	4.6	1.7	1.5	1.6	1.7	1.9
Bituminous coal and lignite [4]	Mil. sh. tons	1,026	1,028	1,069	1,130	1,161	1,145	1,170	1,071
Underground	Mil. sh. tons	425	396	374	368	359	352	357	332
Surface [2]	Mil. sh. tons	605	637	700	763	804	795	815	741
Exports	Mil. sh. tons	106	89	58	50	50	59	82	59
Imports	Mil. sh. tons	3	9	13	30	36	36	34	23
Consumption [5]	Mil. sh. tons	904	962	1,084	1,126	1,112	1,128	1,121	1,000
Electric power sector [6]	Mil. sh. tons	783	850	986	1,037	1,027	1,045	1,041	937
Industrial	Mil. sh. tons	115	106	94	84	82	79	77	61
Number of mines	Number	3,243	2,104	1,453	1,415	1,438	1,374	1,458	(NA)
Daily employment	1,000	131	90	72	79	83	81	87	(NA)
Production, by state: [7]									
Alabama	Mil. sh. tons	29	25	19	21	19	19	21	20
Illinois	Mil. sh. tons	60	48	33	32	33	32	33	30
Indiana	Mil. sh. tons	36	26	28	34	35	35	36	36
Kentucky	Mil. sh. tons	173	154	131	120	121	115	120	109
Montana	Mil. sh. tons	38	39	38	40	42	43	45	42
Ohio	Mil. sh. tons	35	26	22	25	23	23	26	25
Pennsylvania	Mil. sh. tons	71	62	75	67	66	65	65	60
Virginia	Mil. sh. tons	47	34	33	28	30	25	25	23
West Virginia	Mil. sh. tons	169	163	158	154	152	153	158	147
Wyoming	Mil. sh. tons	184	264	339	404	447	454	468	422
Other states	Mil. sh. tons	187	192	197	206	196	181	176	158
World production	Mil. sh. tons	5,347	5,077	4,893	6,542	6,769	7,047	7,271	(NA)
Percent U.S. of world	Percent	19.2	20.3	21.9	17.3	17.2	16.3	16.1	(NA)
COKE									
Production	Mil. sh. tons	27.6	23.7	20.8	16.7	16.4	16.2	15.6	11.1
Imports	Mil. sh. tons	0.8	3.8	3.8	3.5	4.1	2.5	3.6	0.3
Exports	Mil. sh. tons	0.6	1.4	1.4	1.7	1.6	1.4	2.0	1.3
Consumption [8]	Mil. sh. tons	27.8	25.8	23.2	18.2	18.8	17.3	17.0	10.3

NA Not available. [1] Includes bituminous coal, subbituminous coal, lignite, and anthracite. [2] Beginning 2005, includes a small amount of refuse recovery. [3] Coal values are based on free-on-board rail/barge prices, which are the free-on-board prices of coal at the point of first sale, excluding freight or shipping and insurance costs. [4] Includes subbituminous. [5] Includes some categories not shown separately. [6] Electricity-only and combined-heat-and-power (CHP) plants whose primary business is to sell electricity and/or heat to the public. [7] Source: U.S. Energy Information, "Weekly Coal Production," Original estimates, August 19, 2010. [8] Consumption is calculated as the sum of production and imports minus exports and stock change.

Source: U.S. Energy Information Administration, Annual Energy Review, "International Energy Annual," "Annual Coal Report," "Monthly Coal Report," and "International Energy Statistics," <http://www.eia.doe.gov>.

Forestry, Fishing, and Mining 577

Table 915. Demonstrated Coal Reserves by Major Producing State: 2007 and 2008

[In millions of short tons (489,395 represents 489,395,000,000), except as number of mines. As of January 1. The demonstrated reserve base represents the sum of coal in both measured and indicated resource categories of reliability. Measured resources of coal are estimates that have a high degree of geologic assurance from sample analyses and measurements from closely spaced and geological well-known sample sites. Indicated resources are estimates based partly from sample and analyses and measurements and partly from reasonable geologic projections]

| State | 2007 | | | | 2008 | | | |
| | Number of mines | Total reserves | Method of mining | | Number of mines | Total reserves | Method of mining | |
			Underground	Surface			Underground	Surface
United States [1]	**1,374**	**489,395**	**333,277**	**156,118**	**1,458**	**487,678**	**332,553**	**155,124**
Alabama	49	4,141	963	3,178	59	4,106	938	3,167
Alaska	1	6,107	5,423	684	1	6,105	5,423	682
Arkansas	2	417	272	144	2	416	272	144
Colorado	12	16,092	11,331	4,761	12	16,033	11,273	4,760
Illinois.	21	104,347	87,811	16,536	19	104,286	87,757	16,529
Indiana.	27	9,379	8,699	681	30	9,325	8,674	651
Iowa.	(NA)	2,189	1,732	457	(NA)	2,189	1,732	457
Kansas.	2	971	(NA)	971	2	971	(NA)	971
Kentucky	417	29,618	16,770	12,848	469	29,416	16,631	12,784
Kentucky, Eastern . . .	394	10,219	990	9,229	446	10,073	902	9,171
Kentucky, Western . . .	23	19,399	15,780	3,619	23	19,342	15,729	3,613
Maryland	19	631	571	60	21	627	569	57
Missouri.	2	5,988	1,479	4,509	2	5,988	1,479	4,509
Montana.	6	119,123	70,957	48,166	6	119,067	70,957	48,110
New Mexico	4	12,057	6,128	5,929	5	12,020	6,114	5,906
North Dakota	4	8,978	(NA)	8,978	4	8,941	(NA)	8,941
Ohio.	57	23,220	17,484	5,736	48	23,174	17,450	5,725
Oklahoma	9	1,549	1,229	320	7	1,547	1,228	319
Pennsylvania	264	27,228	23,006	4,222	266	27,107	22,900	4,207
Anthracite	72	7,195	3,843	3,352	66	7,192	3,842	3,350
Bituminous.	192	20,034	19,164	870	200	19,914	19,057	857
Tennessee	17	766	506	260	23	762	505	258
Texas	11	12,276	(NA)	12,276	11	12,227	(NA)	1,227
Utah.	10	5,295	5,028	268	9	5,246	4,979	268
Virginia.	118	1,598	1,062	536	114	1,555	1,030	525
Washington	(NA)	1,340	1,332	8	(NA)	1,340	1,332	8
West Virginia	282	32,450	28,845	3,605	301	32,187	28,669	3,518
Wyoming	20	62,692	42,493	20,198	20	62,104	42,486	19,618

NA Not available. [1] Includes other states not shown separately.

Source: U.S. Energy Information Administration, *Annual Coal Report, 2008,* September 2009. See also <http://www.eia.doe.gov/cneaf/coal/page/acr/acr_sum.html>.

Table 916. Uranium Concentrate Industry—Summary: 1990 to 2009

[In millions of feet (1.7 represents 1,700,000), except as indicated. See also Section 19, Table 938]

Item	Unit	1990	1995	2000	2004	2005	2006	2007	2008	2009
Exploration and development, surface drilling	Mil. ft.	1.7	1.3	1.0	1.2	1.7	2.7	5.1	5.1	3.7
Expenditures	Mil. dol..	(NA)	2.6	5.6	10.6	18.1	40.1	67.5	81.9	35.4
Number of mines operated . . .	Number	39	12	10	6	10	11	12	17	20
Underground	Number	27	–	1	2	4	5	6	10	14
Openpit	Number	2	–	–	–	–	–	–	–	–
In situ leaching.	Number	7	5	4	3	4	5	5	6	4
Other sources [1]	Number	3	7	5	1	2	1	1	1	2
Mine production	1,000 pounds. . .	5,876	3,528	3,123	2,452	3,045	4,692	4,541	3,879	4,145
Underground	1,000 pounds. . .	(D)	–	(D)	(D)	(D)	(D)	(D)	(D)	(D)
Openpit	1,000 pounds. . .	1,881	–	–	–	–	–	–	–	–
In situ leaching.	1,000 pounds. . .	(D)	3,372	2,995	(D)	2,681	4,259	(D)	(D)	(D)
Other sources [1]	1,000 pounds. . .	3,995	156	128	(D)	(D)	(D)	(D)	(D)	(D)
Uranium concentrate production	1,000 pounds. . .	8,886	6,043	3,958	2,282	2,689	4,106	4,534	3,092	3,708
Concentrate shipments from mills and plants	1,000 pounds. . .	12,957	5,500	3,187	2,280	2,702	3,838	4,050	4,130	3,620
Employment.	Person-years . . .	1,335	1,107	627	420	648	755	1,231	1,563	1,096

– Represents zero. D Data withheld to avoid disclosing figures for individual companies. NA Not available. [1] Includes mine water, mill site cleanup and mill tailings, and well field restoration as sources of uranium.

Source: U.S. Energy Information Administration, through 2002, *Uranium Industry,* annual. Thereafter, "Domestic Uranium Production Report" annual, July 2010. See also <http://www.eia.doe.gov/cneaf/nuclear/dupr/dupr.html>.

Section 19
Energy and Utilities

This section presents statistics on fuel resources, energy production and consumption, electric energy, hydroelectric power, nuclear power, solar and wind energy, wood energy (biomass), and the electric and gas utility industries. The principal sources are the U.S. Department of Energy's Energy Information Administration (EIA), the Edison Electric Institute, Washington, DC, and the American Gas Association, Arlington, VA. The Department of Energy was created in October 1977 and assumed and centralized the responsibilities of all or part of several agencies including the Federal Power Commission (FPC), the U.S. Bureau of Mines, the Federal Energy Administration, and the U.S. Energy Research and Development Administration. For additional data on transportation, see Section 23; on fuels, see Section 18; and on energy–related housing characteristics, see Section 20.

The EIA, in its *Annual Energy Review*, provides statistics and trend data on energy supply, demand, and prices. Information is included on petroleum and natural gas, coal, electricity, hydroelectric power, nuclear power, solar, wind, wood, and geothermal energy. Among its annual reports are *Annual Energy Review; Electric Power Annual; Natural Gas Annual; Petroleum Supply Annual; State Energy Consumption, Price,* and *Expenditure Data; U.S. Crude Oil, Natural Gas,* and *Natural Gas Liquids Reserves; Electric Sales and Revenue; Annual Energy Outlook;* and *International Energy Statistics.* These various reports contain state, national, and international data on production of electricity, net summer capability of generating plants, fuels used in energy production, energy sales and consumption, and hydroelectric power. The EIA also issues the *Monthly Energy Review*, which presents current supply, disposition, and price data and monthly publications on petroleum, coal, natural gas, and electric power. Data on residential energy consumption, expenditures, and conservation activities are available from EIA's Residential Energy Consumption Survey and are published every 4 years.

The Edison Electric Institute's monthly bulletin and annual *Statistical Year Book of the Electric Utility Industry for the Year* contain data on the distribution of electric energy by public utilities; information on the electric power supply, expansion of electric generating facilities, and the manufacture of heavy electric power equipment is presented in the annual *Year-End Summary of the Electric Power Situation in the United States.* The American Gas Association, in its monthly and quarterly bulletins and its yearbook, *Gas Facts*, presents data on gas utilities and financial and operating statistics.

Btu conversion factors—Various energy sources are converted from original units to the thermal equivalent using British thermal units (Btu). A Btu is the amount of energy required to raise the temperature of 1 pound of water 1 degree Fahrenheit (F) at or near 39.2 degrees F. Factors are calculated annually from the latest final annual data available; some are revised as a result. The following list provides conversion factors used in 2008 for production and consumption, in that order, for various fuels: Petroleum, 5.800 and 5.303 mil. Btu per barrel; total coal, 19.973 and 19.753 mil. Btu per short ton; and natural gas (dry), 1,026 Btu per cubic foot for both. The factors for the production of nuclear power and geothermal power were 10,453 and 21,017 Btu per kilowatt-hour, respectively. The fossil fuel steam–electric power plant generation factor of 9,854 Btu per kilowatt-hour— was used for hydroelectric power generation and for wood and waste, wind, photovoltaic, and solar thermal energy consumed at electric utilities.

Electric power industry—In recent years, EIA has restructured the industry categories it once used to gather and report electricity statistics. The electric

U.S. Census Bureau, Statistical Abstract of the United States: 2011

power industry, previously divided into electric utilities and non–utilities, now consists of the Electric Power Sector, the Commercial Sector, and the Industrial Sector.

The Electric Power Sector is composed of electricity-only and combined-heat-and power plants (CHPs) whose primary business is to sell electricity, or electricity and heat, to the public.

Electricity-only plants are composed of traditional electric utilities, and nontraditional participants, including energy service providers, power marketers, independent power producers (IPPs), and the portion of CHPs that produce only electricity.

A utility is defined as a corporation, person, agency, authority, or other legal entity or instrumentality aligned with distribution facilities for delivery of electric energy for use primarily by the public. Electric utilities include investor-owned electric utilities, municipal and state utilities, federal electric utilities, and rural electric cooperatives. In total, there are more than 3,100 electric utilities in the United States.

An independent power producer is an entity defined as a corporation, person, agency, authority, or other legal entity or instrumentality that owns or operates facilities whose primary business is to produce electricity for use by the public. They are not generally aligned with distribution facilities and are not considered electric utilities.

Combined-heat-and-power producers are plants designed to produce both heat and electricity from a single heat source. These types of electricity producers can be independent power producers or industrial or commercial establishments. As some independent power producers are CHPs, their information is included in the data for the combined-heat-and-power sector. There are approximately 2,800 unregulated independent power producers and CHPs in the United States.

The Commercial Sector consists of commercial CHPs and commercial electricity–only plants. Industrial CHPs and industrial electricity–only plants make up the Industrial Sector. For more information, please refer to the *Electric Power Annual 2008* Web site at <http://www.eia.doe.gov/cneaf/electricity/epa/epa_sum.html>.

U.S. Census Bureau, Statistical Abstract of the United States: 2011

Table 917. Utilities—Establishments, Revenue, Payroll, and Employees by Kind of Business: 2007

[584,193 represents $584,193,000,000. Includes only establishments or firms with payroll. Data based on the 2007 Economic Census. See headnote, Table 755 and Appendix III]

Kind of business	NAICS code [1]	Establish- ments (number	Revenue		Annual payroll		Paid employees for pay period including March 12 (number)
			Total (mil. dol.)	Per paid employee (dol.)	Total (mil. dol.)	Per paid employee (dol.)	
Utilities..........................	22	16,578	584,193	916,744	51,654	81,057	637,247
Electric power generation, transmission, & distribution	2211	9,554	445,693	871,368	43,618	85,277	511,487
Electric power generation	22111	1,934	120,968	985,134	11,297	92,001	122,793
Hydroelectric power generation........	221111	295	2,185	534,773	290	71,092	4,086
Fossil fuel electric power generation.....	221112	1,248	85,362	1,140,283	6,413	85,667	74,860
Nuclear electric power generation.......	221113	79	28,996	763,603	4,083	107,525	37,972
Other electric power generation	221119	312	4,425	753,252	511	86,927	5,875
Electric power transmission, control & distribution	22112	7,620	324,726	835,428	32,321	83,153	388,694
Electric bulk power transmission & control	221121	74	4,268	697,997	543	88,795	6,114
Electric power distribution	221122	7,546	320,458	837,625	31,778	83,063	382,580
Natural gas distribution	2212	2,377	128,555	1,542,000	6,038	72,420	83,369
Water, sewage, & other systems..........	2213	4,647	9,944	234,582	1,998	47,125	42,391
Water supply & irrigation systems	22131	3,889	7,623	225,070	1,596	47,115	33,871
Sewage treatment facilities	22132	689	1,309	187,718	297	42,634	6,974
Steam & air-conditioning supply	22133	69	1,012	654,375	105	67,603	1,546

[1] North American Industry Classification System, 2007; see text, Section 15.

Source: U.S. Census Bureau, *2007 Economic Census.* See also <http://www.census.gov/econ/census07/>, accessed September 2010.

Table 918. Utilities—Employees, Annual Payroll, and Establishments by Industry: 2007

[51,125 represents $51,125,000,000. Excludes government employees, railroad employees, self-employed persons, etc. An establishment is a single physical location where business is conducted or where services or industrial operations are performed. See Appendix III]

Industry	2002 NAICS code [1]	Number of employ- ees [2]	Annual payroll (mil. dol.)	Average payroll per employ- ee (dol.)	Establishments by employment size-class				
					Total	Under 20 employ- ees	20 to 99 employ- ees	100 to 499 employ- ees	500 employ- ees and over
Utilities, total	22	622,757	51,125	82,094	16,674	11,545	3,819	1,141	169
Electric power generation, transmission and distribution	2211	503,134	43,266	85,992	9,611	5,557	2,971	929	154
Electric power generation	22111	129,563	12,029	92,840	2,171	1,283	605	235	48
Hydroelectric power generation..	221111	4,651	349	74,976	372	308	58	6	–
Fossil fuel electric power generation................	221112	83,883	7,469	89,038	1,291	642	437	199	13
Nuclear electric power generation................	221113	29,531	3,174	107,474	73	17	15	8	33
Other electric power generation	221119	11,498	1,037	90,221	435	316	95	22	2
Electric power transmission, control & distribution	22112	373,571	31,237	83,617	7,440	4,274	2,366	694	106
Electric bulk power transmission & control	221121	5,085	465	91,527	107	71	21	13	2
Electric power distribution	221122	368,486	30,772	83,508	7,333	4,203	2,345	681	104
Natural gas distribution	2212	79,354	5,924	74,657	2,283	1,575	528	167	13
Water, sewage, & other systems ...	2213	40,269	1,935	48,044	4,780	4,413	320	45	2
Water supply & irrigation systems....................	22131	33,017	1,587	48,054	4,068	3,791	233	43	1
Sewage treatment facilities	22132	5,829	244	41,863	624	557	64	2	1
Steam & air-conditioning supply ..	22133	1,423	104	73,125	88	65	23	–	–

– Represents zero. [1] North American Industry Classification System, 2002; see text, Section 15. [2] Covers full- and part time employees who are on the payroll in the pay period including March 12.

Source: U.S. Census Bureau, "County Business Patterns," July 2009, <http://www.census.gov/econ/cbp/index.html>.

Table 919. Energy Supply and Disposition by Type of Fuel: 1960 to 2009

[In quadrillion British thermal units (Btu) (42.80 represents 42,800,000,000,000,000). For definition of Btu, see source and text, this section]

Year	Production										Consumption						
	Total[1]	Crude oil[2]	Dry natural gas	Coal[3]	Nuclear electric power	Renewable energy[4]					Net imports, total[8]	Total[1]	Petroleum[9]	Dry natural gas[10]	Coal	Nuclear power	Renewable energy[4] total
						Total[1,5]	Hydroelectric power[6]	Biofuel[7]	Solar/photovoltaic	Wind							
1960	42.80	14.93	12.66	10.82	0.01	2.93	1.61	1.32	(NA)	(NA)	2.71	45.09	19.92	12.39	9.84	0.01	2.93
1970	63.50	20.40	21.67	14.61	0.24	4.08	2.63	1.43	(NA)	(NA)	5.71	67.84	29.52	21.79	12.26	0.24	4.08
1975	61.36	17.73	19.64	14.99	1.90	4.72	3.15	1.50	(NA)	(NA)	11.71	72.00	32.73	19.95	12.66	1.90	4.72
1980	67.23	18.25	19.91	18.60	2.74	5.49	2.90	2.48	(NA)	(NA)	12.10	78.12	34.20	20.24	15.42	2.74	5.49
1984	68.92	18.85	18.01	19.72	3.55	6.52	3.39	2.97	(Z)	(Z)	8.68	76.71	31.05	18.39	17.07	3.55	6.52
1985	67.80	18.99	16.98	19.33	4.08	6.19	2.97	3.02	(Z)	(Z)	7.58	76.49	30.92	17.70	17.48	4.08	6.19
1986	67.18	18.38	16.54	19.51	4.38	6.22	3.07	2.93	(Z)	(Z)	10.13	76.76	32.20	16.59	17.26	4.38	6.22
1987	67.66	17.67	17.14	20.14	4.75	5.74	2.63	2.88	(Z)	(Z)	11.59	79.17	32.87	17.64	18.01	4.75	5.74
1988	69.03	17.28	17.60	20.74	5.59	5.57	2.33	3.02	(Z)	(Z)	12.93	82.82	34.22	18.45	18.85	5.59	5.57
1989[11]	69.48	16.12	17.85	21.36	5.60	6.39	2.84	3.16	0.06	0.02	14.11	84.94	34.21	19.60	19.07	5.60	6.39
1990	70.87	15.57	18.33	22.49	6.10	6.21	3.05	2.74	0.06	0.03	14.06	84.65	33.55	19.60	19.17	6.10	6.21
1991	70.53	15.70	18.23	21.64	6.42	6.24	3.02	2.78	0.06	0.03	13.19	84.61	32.85	20.03	18.99	6.42	6.24
1992	70.13	15.22	18.38	21.69	6.48	5.99	2.62	2.93	0.06	0.03	14.44	85.96	33.53	20.71	19.12	6.48	5.99
1993	68.49	14.49	18.58	20.34	6.41	6.26	2.89	2.91	0.07	0.03	17.01	87.60	33.74	21.23	19.84	6.41	6.26
1994	70.89	14.10	19.35	22.20	6.69	6.15	2.68	3.03	0.07	0.04	18.33	89.26	34.56	21.73	19.91	6.69	6.15
1995	71.32	13.89	19.08	22.13	7.08	6.70	3.21	3.10	0.07	0.03	17.75	91.17	34.44	22.67	20.09	7.08	6.70
1996	72.64	13.72	19.34	22.79	7.09	7.17	3.59	3.16	0.07	0.03	19.07	94.17	35.67	23.08	21.00	7.09	7.17
1997	72.63	13.66	19.39	23.31	6.60	7.18	3.64	3.11	0.07	0.03	20.70	94.76	36.16	23.22	21.45	6.60	7.18
1998	73.04	13.24	19.61	24.05	7.07	6.66	3.30	2.93	0.07	0.03	22.28	95.18	36.82	22.83	21.66	7.07	6.65
1999	71.90	12.45	19.34	23.30	7.61	6.68	3.27	2.97	0.07	0.05	23.54	96.81	37.84	22.91	21.62	7.61	6.68
2000	71.49	12.36	19.66	22.74	7.86	6.26	2.81	3.01	0.07	0.06	24.97	98.97	38.26	23.82	22.58	7.86	6.26
2001	71.88	12.28	20.17	23.55	8.03	5.31	2.24	2.62	0.07	0.07	26.39	96.32	38.19	22.77	21.91	8.03	5.31
2002	70.93	12.16	19.44	22.73	8.15	5.89	2.69	2.71	0.06	0.11	25.74	97.85	38.23	23.56	21.90	8.15	5.89
2003	70.20	12.03	19.63	22.09	7.96	6.14	2.82	2.81	0.06	0.11	27.01	98.13	38.81	22.83	22.32	7.96	6.14
2004	70.35	11.50	19.07	22.85	8.22	6.24	2.69	3.00	0.06	0.14	29.11	100.31	40.29	22.91	22.47	8.22	6.25
2005	69.59	10.96	18.56	23.19	8.16	6.39	2.70	3.10	0.07	0.18	30.15	100.45	40.39	22.56	22.80	8.16	6.41
2006	70.96	10.80	19.02	23.79	8.22	6.77	2.87	3.23	0.07	0.26	29.81	99.79	39.96	22.22	22.45	8.22	6.82
2007	71.61	10.72	19.83	23.49	8.46	6.71	2.45	3.49	0.08	0.34	29.24	101.53	39.77	23.70	22.75	8.46	6.72
2008[12]	73.42	10.51	20.83	23.85	8.43	7.38	2.51	3.87	0.10	0.55	25.94	99.40	37.28	23.79	22.39	8.43	7.37
2009	72.97	11.24	21.50	21.58	8.35	7.76	2.68	3.90	0.11	0.70	22.85	94.58	35.27	23.36	19.76	8.35	7.74

NA Not available. Z Less than 5 trillion. [1] Includes other types of fuel, not shown separately. [2] Includes lease condensate. [3] Beginning 1989, includes waste coal supplied. Beginning 2001, also includes a small amount of refuse recovery. [4] Electricity net generation from conventional hydroelectric power, geothermal, solar, and wind; consumption of electricity from wood, waste, and alcohol fuels; geothermal heat pump and direct use energy; and solar thermal direct use energy. [5] Production equals consumption for all renewable energy sources except biofuels. [6] Conventional hydroelectricity net generation. [7] Wood and wood-derived fuels, biomass waste, fuel ethanol, and biodiesel. [8] Imports minus exports. [9] Petroleum products supplied, including natural gas plant liquids and crude oil burned as fuel. [10] Includes supplemental gaseous fuels. [11] There is a discontinuity in this time series between 1989 and 1990. [12] Preliminary.

Source: U.S. Energy Information Administration, *Annual Energy Review 2009*, August 2010. See also <http://www.eia.doe.gov/emeu/aer/overview.html>.

Table 920. Energy Supply and Disposition by Type of Fuel—Estimates, 2007 and 2008, and Projections, 2009 to 2020

[Quadrillion Btu (72.14 represents 72,140,000,000,000,000) per year. Btu = British thermal unit. For definition of Btu, see source and text, this section. Mcf = 1,000 cubic feet. Projections are "reference" or mid level forecasts. See report for methodology and assumptions used in generating projections]

Type of Fuel	2007	2008	Projections			
			2009	2010	2015	2020
Production, total	**72.14**	**74.23**	**73.10**	**73.41**	**77.88**	**81.51**
Crude oil and lease condensate	10.75	10.51	11.30	11.43	12.41	13.19
Natural gas plant liquids	2.41	2.57	2.47	2.40	2.27	2.31
Natural gas, dry	19.62	21.14	21.18	20.57	19.83	20.54
Coal [1]	23.49	23.86	22.13	21.55	23.31	23.71
Nuclear power	8.46	8.46	8.49	8.52	8.75	9.26
Renewable energy [2]	6.59	7.60	7.54	8.40	10.58	11.61
Other [3]	0.81	0.10	-0.01	0.53	0.73	0.89
Imports, total	**34.60**	**32.79**	**30.09**	**29.35**	**29.58**	**29.62**
Crude oil [4]	21.91	21.39	20.05	19.42	19.66	18.95
Petroleum products [5]	6.98	6.38	5.61	5.21	5.54	5.61
Natural gas	4.72	4.06	3.87	3.93	3.59	4.10
Other imports [6]	0.99	0.96	0.56	0.79	0.79	0.96
Exports, total	**5.17**	**6.80**	**6.43**	**6.03**	**6.16**	**6.50**
Petroleum [7]	2.83	3.71	3.92	3.29	3.53	3.74
Natural gas	0.83	1.01	1.03	1.02	1.14	1.44
Coal	1.51	2.07	1.49	1.72	1.49	1.33
Consumption, total	**101.65**	**100.09**	**95.61**	**96.61**	**101.61**	**105.00**
Petroleum products [8]	40.59	38.35	36.82	37.06	38.81	39.36
Natural gas	23.67	23.91	23.23	23.15	22.35	23.27
Coal	22.71	22.41	20.28	20.49	22.35	23.01
Nuclear power	8.46	8.46	8.49	8.52	8.75	9.26
Renewable energy [9]	5.98	6.73	6.58	7.17	9.14	9.91
Other [10]	0.23	0.24	0.21	0.21	0.20	0.20
Net imports of petroleum	**26.06**	**24.06**	**21.74**	**21.34**	**21.67**	**20.83**
Prices (2006 dollars per unit):						
Imported crude oil price [11]	68.69	92.61	56.49	67.40	86.88	98.14
Gas wellhead price (dol. per 1,000 cu. ft.) [12]	6.42	8.07	3.38	4.17	6.35	7.37
Coal minemouth price (dol. per ton) [13]	25.82	31.26	32.13	31.08	33.86	36.67
Average electric price (cents per kWh)	9.10	9.83	9.72	9.41	9.87	11.05

[1] Includes waste coal. [2] Includes grid-connected electricity from conventional hydroelectric; wood and wood waste; landfill gas; municipal solid waste; other biomass; wind; photovoltaic and solar thermal sources; nonelectric energy from renewable sources, such as active and passive solar systems, and wood. Excludes electricity imports using renewable sources and nonmarketed renewable energy. [3] Includes nonbiogenic municipal solid waste, liquid hydrogen, methanol, and some domestic inputs to refineries. [4] Includes imports of crude oil for the Strategic Petroleum Reserve. [5] Includes imports of finished petroleum products, imports of unfinished oils, alcohols, ethers, blending components, and renewable fuels such as ethanol. [6] Includes coal, coal coke (net), and electricity (net). [7] Includes crude oil and petroleum products. [8] Includes petroleum-derived fuels and non-petroleum-derived fuels, such as ethanol, biodiesel, and coal-based synthetic liquids. Petroleum coke, which is a solid, is included. Also included are natural gas plant liquids, crude oil consumed as a fuel, and liquid hydrogen. [9] Includes grid-connected electricity from wood and wood waste, non-electric energy from wood, and biofuels heat and coproducts used in the production of liquid fuels, but excludes the energy content of the liquid fuels. Also includes non-biogenic municipal solid waste and net electricity imports. [10] Includes non-biogenic municipal solid waste and net electricity imports. [11] Weighted average price delivered to U.S. refiners. [12] Represents lower 48 onshore and offshore supplies. [13] Includes reported prices for both open market and captive mines.

Source: U.S. Energy Information Administration, *Annual Energy Outlook 2010*, May 2010. See also <http://www.eia.doe.gov/oiaf/aeo/aeoref_tab.html>.

Table 921. Energy Consumption by End-Use Sector: 1970 to 2009

[67.84 represents 67,840,000,000,000,000 Btu. Btu = British thermal units. For definition of Btu, see source and text, this section. See Appendix III. Total energy consumption in the end-use sectors consists of primary energy consumption, electricity retail sales, and electrical system energy losses]

Year		Residential and commercial [1] (quad. Btu)	Industrial [2] (quad. Btu)	Transportation (quad. Btu)	Percent of total		
	Total (quad. Btu)				Residential and commercial [1]	Industrial [2]	Transportation
1970	67.84	22.11	29.64	16.10	32.6	43.7	23.7
1975	72.00	24.31	29.45	18.24	33.8	40.9	25.3
1980	78.12	26.35	32.08	19.70	33.7	41.1	25.2
1985	76.49	27.53	28.88	20.09	36.0	37.8	26.3
1990	84.65	30.35	31.89	22.42	35.9	37.7	26.5
1995	91.17	33.28	34.05	23.85	36.5	37.3	26.2
2000	98.97	37.66	34.76	26.55	38.1	35.1	26.8
2002	97.85	38.24	32.76	26.84	39.1	33.5	27.4
2003	98.13	38.53	32.61	26.99	39.3	33.2	27.5
2004	100.31	38.83	33.59	27.90	38.7	33.5	27.8
2005	100.45	39.57	32.53	28.35	39.4	32.4	28.2
2006	99.79	38.49	32.47	28.83	38.6	32.5	28.9
2007	101.53	39.91	32.50	29.12	39.3	32.0	28.7
2008	99.40	40.02	31.36	28.03	40.3	31.5	28.2
2009 [3]	94.58	39.35	28.20	27.03	41.6	29.8	28.6

[1] Commercial sector fuel use, including that at commercial combined-heat-and-power (CHP) and industrial electricity-only plants. [2] Industrial sector fuel use, including that at industrial combined-heat-and-power (CHP) and industrial electricity-only plants. [3] Preliminary.

Source: U.S. Energy Information Administration, *Annual Energy Review 2009*, August 2010. See also <http://www.eia.gov/emeu/aer/consump.html>.

Table 922. Energy Consumption—End-Use Sector and Selected Source by State: 2008

[In trillions of Btu (99,382 represents 99,382,000,000,000,000), except as indicated. For definition of Btu, see source and text, this section. Data are preliminary. U.S. totals may not equal sum of states due to independent rounding and/or interstate flows of electricity that are not allocated to the states. For technical notes and documentation, see source <http://www.eia.doe.gov/emeu/states/_seds_tech_notes.html>]

State	Total [1,2]	Per capita [3] (mil. Btu)	End-use sector [4] Residential	End-use sector [4] Commercial	End-use sector [4] Industrial [2]	End-use sector [4] Transportation	Source Petroleum [5]	Source Natural gas (dry) [6]	Source Coal	Source Hydroelectric power [7]	Source Nuclear electric power
U.S.	99,382	327	21,603	18,414	31,356	28,010	38,102	23,847	22,385	2,511	8,427
AL	2,065	441	401	279	905	480	598	420	843	60	408
AK	651	946	55	63	318	215	279	344	15	12	–
AZ	1,553	239	420	369	244	519	576	410	459	72	306
AR	1,125	392	233	167	433	292	376	238	279	46	148
CA	8,381	229	1,569	1,640	1,955	3,218	3,736	2,521	63	238	340
CO	1,498	304	350	300	412	435	504	515	385	20	–
CT	810	231	266	205	90	249	362	170	45	5	161
DE	295	337	66	58	98	73	128	50	61	–	–
DC	180	306	36	121	4	20	20	33	(Z)	–	–
FL	4,447	241	1,295	1,085	540	1,528	1,808	970	693	2	336
GA	3,015	311	745	567	812	891	1,029	437	886	21	331
HI	284	220	37	44	65	138	245	3	20	1	–
ID	529	346	128	86	187	128	159	91	9	92	–
IL	4,089	318	1,026	800	1,237	1,027	1,367	1,015	1,103	1	995
IN	2,857	447	558	377	1,302	620	836	559	1,558	4	–
IA	1,414	472	249	202	654	309	428	324	485	8	55
KS	1,136	406	233	205	420	278	408	293	372	(Z)	89
KY	1,983	462	373	258	891	461	698	233	1,025	19	–
LA	3,488	783	357	276	2,204	651	1,450	1,360	262	10	161
ME	469	356	94	79	177	119	210	65	6	44	–
MD	1,447	256	410	410	175	452	535	203	309	19	153
MA	1,475	225	431	370	185	489	657	382	107	11	61
MI	2,918	292	788	619	756	755	913	797	800	13	329
MN	1,979	378	423	362	615	579	739	410	359	7	136
MS	1,186	403	234	170	421	361	430	364	177	–	98
MO	1,937	325	531	416	406	584	716	298	793	20	98
MT	434	449	84	70	171	110	184	78	203	99	–
NE	782	439	161	141	300	180	226	169	235	3	99
NV	750	287	180	134	199	237	271	275	89	17	–
NH	311	235	90	71	44	106	168	73	40	16	98
NJ	2,637	304	596	630	391	1,020	1,300	635	98	(Z)	337
NM	693	349	115	127	245	207	267	251	284	3	–
NY	3,988	205	1,166	1,275	434	1,113	1,560	1,205	229	263	452
NC	2,702	292	715	582	628	777	953	250	795	30	416
ND	441	687	68	64	214	96	141	66	425	12	–
OH	3,987	346	952	710	1,341	984	1,300	824	1,438	4	183
OK	1,603	440	315	253	559	476	572	691	392	38	–
OR	1,105	292	276	214	283	332	374	275	41	333	–
PA	3,900	310	941	706	1,256	997	1,378	778	1,421	25	822
RI	220	209	70	56	30	65	97	91	–	(Z)	–
SC	1,660	369	362	266	585	447	560	176	445	11	541
SD	350	435	70	61	130	89	117	65	43	29	–
TN	2,261	362	543	383	720	615	763	238	644	56	283
TX	11,552	475	1,616	1,420	5,652	2,865	5,499	3,656	1,606	10	426
UT	799	293	172	156	224	247	291	237	396	7	–
VT	154	249	44	32	27	52	81	9	–	15	51
VA	2,514	322	611	598	536	768	939	311	415	10	292
WA	2,050	312	506	394	528	622	804	307	95	765	97
WV	831	458	165	112	391	163	273	120	956	12	–
WI	1,862	331	430	369	619	445	601	415	481	16	127
WY	542	1,016	48	63	302	129	179	147	500	8	–

– Represents zero. Z Less than 50 billion Btu. [1] Includes other sources, not shown separately. [2] U.S. total energy and U.S. industrial sector include 60.8 trillion Btu of net imports of coal coke that is not allocated to the states. [3] Based on estimated resident population as of July 1. [4] End-use sector data include electricity sales and associated electrical system energy losses. [5] Includes fuel ethanol blended into motor gasoline. [6] Includes supplemental gaseous fuels. [7] Conventional hydroelectric power. Does not include pumped-storage hydroelectricity.

Source: U.S. Energy Information Administration, "State Energy Data, 2008," June 2010, <http://www.eia.doe.gov/emeu/states/_seds.html>.

Table 923. Renewable Energy Consumption Estimates by Source: 1990 to 2009

[In quadrillion Btu (6.21 represents 6,210,000,000,000,000). For definition of Btu, see source and text, this section. Renewable energy is obtained from sources that are essentially inexhaustible, unlike fossil fuels of which there is a finite supply]

Source and sector	1990	2000	2005	2006	2007	2008	2009 [1]
Consumption, total..............	6.21	6.26	6.41	6.82	6.72	7.37	7.74
Conventional hydroelectric power [2].....	3.05	2.81	2.70	2.87	2.45	2.51	2.68
Geothermal energy [3]...............	0.34	0.32	0.34	0.34	0.35	0.36	0.37
Biomass [4].........................	2.74	3.01	3.12	3.28	3.50	3.85	3.88
Solar energy [5].....................	0.06	0.07	0.07	0.07	0.08	0.10	0.11
Wind energy [6].....................	0.03	0.06	0.18	0.26	0.34	0.55	0.70
Residential [7]......................	0.64	0.49	0.51	0.48	0.53	0.57	0.56
Biomass [4].......................	0.58	0.42	0.43	0.39	0.43	0.45	0.43
Geothermal [3].....................	0.01	0.01	0.02	0.02	0.02	0.03	0.03
Solar [5].........................	0.06	0.06	0.06	0.07	0.07	0.09	0.10
Commercial [8].....................	0.10	0.13	0.12	0.12	0.12	0.13	0.13
Biomass [4].......................	0.09	0.12	0.10	0.10	0.10	0.11	0.11
Geothermal [3].....................	(Z)	0.01	0.01	0.01	0.01	0.01	0.02
Hydroelectric [2]....................	(Z)	(Z)	(Z)	(Z)	(Z)	(Z)	(Z)
Industrial [9].......................	1.72	1.93	1.87	1.93	1.96	2.05	2.02
Biomass [4].......................	1.68	1.88	1.84	1.90	1.94	2.03	2.00
Geothermal [3].....................	(Z)	(Z)	(Z)	(Z)	0.01	0.01	(Z)
Hydroelectric [2]....................	0.03	0.04	0.03	0.03	0.02	0.02	0.02
Transportation.....................	0.06	0.14	0.34	0.48	0.60	0.83	0.92
Fuel ethanol [10]....................	0.06	0.14	0.33	0.44	0.56	0.79	0.88
Biodiesel [11]......................	(NA)	(NA)	0.01	0.03	0.05	0.04	0.04
Electric power [12]..................	3.69	3.58	3.57	3.83	3.51	3.80	4.11
Biomass [4].......................	0.32	0.45	0.41	0.41	0.42	0.44	0.43
Geothermal [3].....................	0.33	0.30	0.31	0.31	0.31	0.31	0.32
Hydroelectric [2]....................	3.01	2.77	2.67	2.84	2.43	2.49	2.66
Solar [5].........................	(Z)	0.01	0.01	0.01	0.01	0.01	0.01
Wind [6]..........................	0.03	0.06	0.18	0.26	0.34	0.55	0.70

Z Less than 5 trillion Btu. [1] Preliminary. [2] Power produced from natural stream flow as regulated by available storage. [3] As used at electric power plants, hot water or steam extracted from geothermal reservoirs in the Earth's crust that is supplied to steam turbines at electric power plants that drive generators to produce electricity. [4] Wood and wood-derived fuels, municipal solid waste (from biogenic sources, landfill gas, sludge waste, agricultural byproducts, and other biomass), fuel ethanol, and biodiesel. [5] The radiant energy of the sun, which can be converted into other forms of energy, such as heat or electricity. Solar thermal and photovoltaic electricity net generation and solar thermal direct use energy. [6] Energy present in wind motion that can be converted to mechanical energy for driving pumps, mills, and electric power generators. Wind pushes against sails, vanes, or blades radiating from a central rotating shaft. [7] Consists of living quarters for private households, but excludes institutional living quarters. [8] Consists of service-providing facilities and equipment of businesses, governments, and other private and public organizations. Includes institutional living quarters and sewage treatment facilities. Includes commercial combined-heat-and-power and commercial electricity-only plants. [9] Consists of all facilities and equipment used for producing, processing, or assembling goods. Includes industrial combined-heat-and-power and industrial electricity-only plants. [10] Ethanol primarily derived from corn. [11] Any liquid biofuel suitable as a diesel fuel substitute, additive, or extender. [12] Consists of electricity-only and combined-heat-and-power plants whose primary business is to sell electricity and/or heat to the public. Includes sources not shown separately.

Source: U.S. Energy Information Administration, *Annual Energy Review 2009*, August 2010. See also <http://www.eia.doe.gov/emeu/aer/renew.html>.

Table 924. Fuel Ethanol and Biodiesel—Summary: 1990 to 2009

[110.9 represents 110,900,000,000,000. Data for 1990 are estimates. Beginning 1995, only feedstock data are estimates. Minus sign (–) indicates an excess of exports over imports, except where noted]

Fuel	1990	1995	2000	2004	2005	2006	2007	2008	2009 [1]
FUEL ETHANOL									
Feedstock [2] (tril. Btu)............	110.9	197.7	233.1	483.7	552.4	687.9	914.3	1,299.5	1,493.1
Production:									
1,000 bbl....................	17,802	32,325	38,627	81,058	92,961	116,294	155,263	221,637	256,149
Tril. Btu.....................	63.4	115.2	137.6	288.8	331.2	414.4	553.2	789.7	912.7
Net imports [3] (1,000 bbl.).........	(NA)	387	116	3,542	3,234	17,408	10,457	12,610	4,614
Stocks [4] (1,000 bbl.).............	(NA)	2,186	3,400	6,002	5,563	8,760	10,535	14,226	16,711
Stock change [5] (1,000 bbl.).......	(NA)	–207	–624	24	–439	3,197	1,775	3,691	[6] 2,492
Consumption:									
1,000 bbl....................	17,802	32,919	39,367	84,576	96,634	130,505	163,945	230,556	258,271
Tril. Btu.....................	63.4	117.3	140.3	301.3	344.3	465.0	584.1	821.5	920.2
BIODIESEL									
Feedstock [7] (tril. Btu)............	(NA)	(NA)	(NA)	3.6	11.7	32.4	63.4	87.7	68.8
Production:									
1,000 bbl....................	(NA)	(NA)	(NA)	666	2,162	5,963	11,662	16,145	12,657
Tril. Btu.....................	(NA)	(NA)	(NA)	3.6	11.6	32.0	62.5	86.5	67.8
Net imports [3] (1,000 bbl.).........	(NA)	(NA)	(NA)	–26	1	242	–3,135	–8,626	–4,489
Consumption:									
1,000 bbl....................	(NA)	(NA)	(NA)	640	2,163	6,204	8,528	7,519	8,082
Tril. Btu.....................	(NA)	(NA)	(NA)	3.4	11.6	33.2	45.7	40.3	43.3

NA Not available. [1] Preliminary. [2] Total corn and other biomass inputs to the production of fuel ethanol. [3] Net imports equal imports minus exports. [4] Imports minus exports. Stocks are at end of year. [5] A negative number indicates a decrease in stocks. [6] Derived from preliminary 2008 stock value, not final 2008 value. [7] Total vegetable oil and other biomass inputs to the production of biodiesel.

Source: U.S. Energy Information Administration, *Annual Energy Review 2009*, August, 2010. See also <http://www.eia.doe.gov/emeu/aer/renew.html>.

Table 925. Energy Consumption by Mode of Transportation: 2000 to 2008

[40 represents 40,000,000,000,000. Btu = British thermal unit. For conversion rates for each fuel type, see source]

Mode	Trillion Btu			Physical units			
	2000	2005	2008	Unit	2000	2005	2008
AIR [1]							
Aviation gasoline	40	35	[2] 30	mil. gal.	333	361	[2] 349
Jet fuel	2,138	2,093	[2] 1,940	mil. gal.	14,876	14,733	[2] 14,019
HIGHWAY							
Passenger car and motorcycle	9,159	9,701	8,969	mil. gal.	73,275	74,085	71,497
Other 2-axle 4-tire vehicle	6,617	7,359	7,650	mil. gal.	52,939	65,419	61,199
Single-unit 2-axle 6-tire or more truck	1,326	1,188	1,236	mil. gal.	9,563	9,042	9,889
Combination truck [3]	3,560	3,840	3,719	mil. gal.	25,666	24,411	26,814
Bus	154	155	154	mil. gal.	1,112	1,329	1,110
TRANSIT [4]							
Electricity	19	20	(NA)	mil. kWh	5,382	5,765	6,337
Diesel	109	101	(NA)	mil. gal.	591	480	499
Gasoline and other nondiesel fuels [5]	6	7	(NA)	mil. gal.	24	81	68
Compressed natural gas	8	17	(NA)	mil. gal.	44	94	113
RAIL [6]							
Distillate/diesel fuel	529	581	551	mil. gal.	3,795	4,163	3,949
Electricity	2	2	2	mil. kWh	470	531	582
WATER							
Residual fuel oil	960	775	758	mil. gal.	6,410	5,179	5,066
Distillate/diesel fuel oil	314	278	165	mil. gal.	2,261	2,006	1,187
Gasoline	141	158	142	mil. gal.	1,124	1,261	1,136
PIPELINE							
Natural gas	662	602	668	mil. cu. ft.	642,210	584,026	647,958

NA Not available. [1] Includes general aviation and certified carriers, domestic operations only. Also includes fuel used in air taxi operations, but not commuter operations. [2] Estimate. [3] A power unit (truck tractor) and one or more trailing units (a semitrailer or trailer). [4] Includes light, heavy, and commuter rail; motor bus; trolley bus; van pools; automated guideway; and demand-responsive vehicles. [5] Gasoline and all other nondiesel fuels such as liquefied natural gas, methanol, and propane, except compressed natural gas. [6] Includes Amtrak and freight service carriers that have an annual operating revenue of $250 million or more.

Source: U.S. Department of Transportation Statistics, *National Transportation Statistics, 2010*. See also <http://www.bts.gov/publications/national_transportation_statistics/>, accessed September 2010.

Table 926. Manufacturing Primary Energy Consumption for All Purposes by Type of Fuel and Major Industry Group: 2006

[In trillions of Btu (21,098 represents 21,098,000,000,000). Estimates represent consumption of energy for all purposes. "First Use" represents unduplicated demand for energy by manufacturers. "First Use" includes all energy produced offsite, all energy produced onsite, either directly from captive mines and wells, or as byproducts from nonenergy materials (such as sawdust from furniture production, hydrogen from electrolysis of brine, nut shells from peanut processing). Based on the Manufacturing Energy Consumption Survey and subject to sampling variability]

Industry	NAICS [1] code	Total [2]	Net electricity [3]	Residual fuel oil	Distillate fuel oil [4]	Natural gas [5]	LPG and NGL [6]	Coal	Coke and breeze	Other [7]
All industries, total	(X)	**21,098**	**2,851**	**314**	**143**	**5,911**	**2,376**	**1,433**	**272**	**8,443**
Food	311	1,186	251	26	16	638	3	147	1	105
Beverage and tobacco products	312	107	30	3	1	41	1	20	–	11
Textile mills	313	178	66	2	(Z)	65	(Z)	32	–	12
Textile product mills	314	72	20	(S)	(Z)	46	1	3	–	(Z)
Apparel	315	14	7	(Z)	(Z)	7	(Z)	–	–	(Z)
Leather and allied products	316	3	1	(Z)	(Z)	1	(Z)	–	–	(Z)
Wood products	321	451	91	4	21	87	4	(S)	(S)	228
Paper	322	2,354	247	91	13	474	5	221	–	1,302
Printing and related support	323	85	45	(Z)	(Z)	39	1	–	–	(Z)
Petroleum and coal products	324	6,864	137	58	33	849	29	102	1	5,744
Chemicals	325	5,149	517	87	8	1,746	2,304	182	3	707
Plastics and rubber products	326	337	182	9	3	128	5	(S)	–	(Z)
Nonmetallic mineral products	327	1,114	147	3	30	460	5	320	11	138
Primary metals	331	1,736	458	19	7	627	4	373	253	139
Fabricated metal products	332	396	143	(Z)	2	240	5	–	(S)	(S)
Machinery	333	204	111	(S)	2	84	3	1	–	2
Computer and electronic products	334	142	94	(Z)	1	45	(Z)	–	–	2
Electrical equip., appliances, and components	335	103	44	–	(S)	42	1	(Z)	–	21
Transportation equipment	336	477	195	7	3	249	5	5	(S)	13
Furniture and related products	337	61	32	(Z)	(S)	17	1	3	–	8
Miscellaneous	339	66	33	(Z)	(Z)	25	1	–	–	(S)

– Represents or rounds to zero. D Withheld to avoid disclosing data for individual establishments. S Withheld because Relative Standard Error is greater than 50 percent. X Not applicable. Z Less than 500 billion Btu. [1] North American Industry Classification System 2002 (NAICS); see text, Section 15. [2] Total is the sum of all listed energy sources, including 'other,' minus the shipments of energy sources produced onsite. [3] Net electricity is obtained by aggregating purchases, transfers in, and generation from noncombustible renewable resources minus quantities sold and transferred out. Excludes electricity inputs from onsite cogeneration or generation from combustible fuels because that energy has already been included as generating fuel (for example, coal). [4] Includes No. 1, 2, and 4 fuel oils and No. 1, 2, and 4 diesel fuels. [5] Includes natural gas obtained from utilities, transmission pipelines, and any other supplier such as brokers and producers. [6] Liquid petroleum gas and natural gas liquids. [7] Includes net steam, and other energy that respondents indicated was used to produce heat and power or as feedstock/raw material inputs.

Source: U.S. Energy Information Administration, Manufacturing Energy Consumption Survey (MECS), June 2009, <http://www.eia.doe.gov/emeu/mecs/contents.html>.

Table 927. Fossil Fuel Prices by Type of Fuel: 1980 to 2009

[In dollars per million British thermal units (Btu), except as indicated. For definition of Btu and mineral fuel conversions, see source and text, this section. All fuel prices taken as close to the point of production as possible]

Fuel	1980	1990	1995	2000	2003	2004	2005	2006	2007	2008	2009 [1]
CURRENT DOLLARS											
Composite [2]	2.04	1.84	1.47	2.60	3.09	3.61	4.74	4.73	4.95	6.52	3.97
Crude oil [3]	3.72	3.45	2.52	4.61	4.75	6.34	8.67	10.29	11.47	16.21	9.72
Natural gas [4]	1.45	1.55	1.40	3.32	4.41	4.95	6.64	5.79	5.66	7.24	3.37
Coal [5]	1.10	1.00	0.88	0.80	0.87	0.98	1.16	1.24	1.29	1.55	1.65
CONSTANT (2005) DOLLARS											
Composite [2]	4.28	2.55	1.81	2.93	3.29	3.73	4.74	4.58	4.66	6.01	3.62
Crude oil [3]	7.80	4.78	3.09	5.20	5.05	6.55	8.67	9.97	10.80	14.95	8.86
Natural gas [4]	3.03	2.14	1.72	3.75	4.69	5.11	6.64	5.61	5.33	6.67	3.07
Coal [5]	2.30	1.38	1.08	0.90	0.93	1.01	1.16	1.20	1.21	1.43	1.50

[1] Preliminary. [2] Derived by multiplying the price per Btu of each fossil fuel by the total Btu content of the production of each fossil fuel and dividing this accumulated value of total fossil fuel production by the accumulated Btu content of total fossil fuel production. [3] Domestic first purchase prices. [4] Wellhead prices. [5] Free-on-board (f.o.b.) rail/barge prices, which are the f.o.b. prices of coal at the point of first sale, excluding freight or shipping and insurance costs. Includes bituminous coal, subbituminous coal, and lignite.

Source: U.S. Energy Information Administration, *Annual Energy Review 2009,* August 2010. See also <http://www.eia.gov/emeu/aer/finan.html>.

Table 928. Energy Expenditures and Average Fuel Prices by Source and Sector: 1980 to 2007

[In millions of dollars (374,346 represents $374,346,000,000), except as indicated. For definition of Btu, see text, this section. End-use sector and electric utilities exclude expenditures and prices on energy sources such as hydropower, solar, wind, and geothermal. Also excludes expenditures for reported amounts of energy consumed by the energy industry for production, transportation, and processing operations]

Source and Sector	1980	1990	1995	2000	2003	2004	2005	2006	2007
EXPENDITURES (mil. dol.)									
Total [1, 2, 3]	374,346	472,539	514,049	687,587	754,668	869,112	1,046,466	1,168,183	1,230,050
Natural gas [4]	51,061	65,278	75,020	119,094	144,489	162,702	200,303	190,382	196,482
Petroleum products	237,676	235,368	236,905	359,140	378,967	468,354	595,905	681,448	739,856
Motor gasoline [5]	124,408	126,558	136,647	193,947	209,592	253,218	311,094	357,129	388,561
Coal	22,607	28,602	27,431	28,080	29,402	31,764	36,932	40,005	42,673
Electricity sales	98,095	176,691	205,876	231,577	257,995	268,136	295,789	323,965	340,928
Residential sector [6]	69,418	111,097	128,388	156,061	179,288	190,120	216,016	226,255	238,695
Commercial sector [2, 3]	46,932	79,288	91,788	112,870	129,458	137,903	154,558	166,899	174,108
Industrial sector [2, 3]	94,316	102,411	107,060	139,810	150,740	176,639	208,248	227,319	235,692
Transportation sector [2]	163,680	179,743	186,813	278,846	295,182	364,450	466,643	538,011	584,564
Motor gasoline [5]	121,809	123,845	134,641	191,620	204,878	247,181	303,942	348,544	380,518
Electric utilities [3]	38,027	40,626	39,073	60,054	64,685	71,720	95,975	90,104	100,715
AVERAGE FUEL PRICES (dol. per mil. Btu)									
All sectors	6.89	8.25	8.28	10.31	11.38	12.87	15.52	17.34	18.23
Residential sector [6]	7.46	11.88	12.63	14.27	15.85	17.11	19.22	21.55	21.64
Commercial sector [3]	7.85	11.89	12.64	13.93	15.61	16.60	18.59	20.64	20.74
Industrial sector [3]	4.71	5.23	4.97	6.41	7.39	8.46	10.36	11.33	11.89
Transportation sector	8.60	8.27	8.08	10.78	11.20	13.36	16.84	19.10	20.58
Electric utilities [3]	1.77	1.48	1.29	1.71	1.84	2.00	2.61	2.48	2.68

[1] Includes other sources not shown separately. [2] Through 1990, total also includes ethanol blended into gasoline that is not included in motor gasoline for those years. [3] There are no direct fuel costs for hydroelectric, geothermal, wind, photovoltaic, or solar thermal energy. [4] Excludes supplemental gaseous fuels. [5] Beginning 1995, includes fuel ethanol blended into motor gasoline. [6] There are no direct fuel costs for geothermal, photovoltaic, or solar thermal energy.

Source: U.S. Energy Information Administration, "State Energy Data: Prices and Expenditures," annual, August 2009, <http://www.eia.doe.gov/emeu/states/state.html?q_state_a=us&q_state=UNITED%20STATES>.

Table 929. Energy Expenditures—End-Use Sector and Selected Source by State: 2008

[In millions of dollars (1,411,922 represents $1,411,922,000,000). Data are preliminary. End-use sector and electric utilities exclude expenditures on energy sources such as hydroelectric, photovoltaic, solar thermal, wind, and geothermal. Also excludes expenditures for reported amounts of energy consumed by the energy industry for production, transportation, and processing operations. For technical notes and documentation, see source, <http://www.eia.doe.gov/emeu/states/_seds_tech_notes.html>.]

State	Total [1,2]	End-use sector				Source			
		Resi-dential	Com-mercial	Indus-trial [2]	Transpor-tation	Petroleum products [3]	Natural gas [4]	Coal	Electricity sales
U.S.	1,411,922	256,953	192,249	272,322	690,397	874,865	229,667	49,438	360,573
AL	24,889	4,294	2,839	5,847	11,910	14,281	4,022	2,358	7,496
AK	7,509	774	777	583	5,374	6,332	550	36	921
AZ	22,610	4,340	3,349	2,363	12,558	14,200	3,777	808	6,951
AR	14,715	2,315	1,384	3,689	7,328	9,389	2,298	496	3,407
CA	136,508	20,057	19,333	17,127	79,991	86,486	23,577	169	33,180
CO	19,751	3,531	2,504	3,018	10,698	12,364	3,601	560	4,434
CT	16,460	5,273	3,317	1,357	6,513	9,410	2,196	141	5,508
DE	4,300	946	706	943	1,795	2,461	617	215	1,438
DC	2,529	487	1,525	50	468	515	475	1	1,553
FL	67,907	13,891	10,863	5,289	37,865	42,716	10,173	2,073	24,296
GA	41,568	8,066	5,190	6,718	21,595	24,456	5,595	2,739	11,951
HI	6,850	1,075	1,187	1,052	3,535	5,171	101	46	2,978
ID	6,122	1,055	597	1,237	3,232	3,964	805	21	1,361
IL	55,891	11,561	9,013	9,503	25,813	31,455	11,159	1,819	13,324
IN	33,151	5,605	3,211	8,708	15,626	19,021	5,844	3,553	7,498
IA	16,914	2,770	1,769	4,698	7,677	10,676	3,098	655	3,135
KS	14,569	2,366	1,642	3,987	6,574	9,323	2,519	530	2,923
KY	23,264	3,280	2,055	6,320	11,608	15,000	2,369	2,318	5,777
LA	38,906	3,643	2,742	18,904	13,617	24,359	9,536	620	7,215
ME	7,517	1,838	1,200	1,256	3,223	5,285	743	21	1,615
MD	24,349	5,789	5,028	2,059	11,473	13,520	2,753	1,123	8,232
MA	28,997	7,865	5,608	2,912	12,612	16,513	5,168	317	9,091
MI	39,849	9,011	5,706	6,433	18,700	22,796	8,020	1,727	9,390
MN	26,301	4,478	3,170	4,342	14,312	17,204	3,853	622	5,314
MS	15,503	2,492	1,712	2,896	8,403	9,660	3,135	577	4,183
MO	26,055	4,944	3,089	3,505	14,517	17,118	3,444	1,219	5,768
MT	5,684	911	646	1,353	2,774	3,789	698	275	1,166
NE	9,078	1,454	1,037	2,188	4,398	5,688	1,524	223	1,894
NV	11,192	2,083	1,342	1,765	6,002	6,759	2,462	197	3,417
NH	6,085	1,666	1,060	592	2,766	4,138	818	142	1,608
NJ	46,133	9,171	8,552	4,953	23,458	28,297	8,080	325	11,578
NM	8,893	1,278	1,158	1,314	5,143	6,335	1,302	567	1,796
NY	72,462	20,501	19,447	4,957	27,557	37,267	15,710	617	23,865
NC	37,854	7,406	4,823	5,375	20,249	24,306	3,230	2,602	10,356
ND	4,946	663	494	1,548	2,240	3,414	383	686	824
OH	54,144	10,791	6,949	11,224	25,180	30,461	10,165	3,173	13,254
OK	20,743	3,015	2,114	4,241	11,374	12,905	5,733	530	4,365
OR	14,882	2,516	1,673	2,048	8,645	9,609	2,429	62	3,559
PA	55,531	12,697	7,436	10,435	24,963	32,855	9,385	3,414	13,872
RI	4,223	1,282	846	398	1,698	2,408	1,115	–	1,252
SC	21,438	3,634	2,329	4,270	11,205	13,254	2,051	1,301	6,335
SD	4,233	692	463	856	2,222	2,890	568	78	784
TN	29,365	5,032	3,589	5,304	15,440	17,875	2,649	1,509	8,455
TX	165,334	20,077	14,665	64,067	66,526	113,177	27,433	3,059	37,225
UT	9,901	1,419	1,091	1,261	6,129	6,927	1,543	557	1,810
VT	3,012	831	462	303	1,416	2,177	121	–	708
VA	34,886	6,595	4,698	4,516	19,077	22,935	3,662	1,213	8,762
WA	26,669	4,319	2,962	3,122	16,265	18,312	3,101	215	5,667
WV	9,634	1,397	859	3,445	3,934	6,462	1,055	2,353	1,892
WI	25,444	5,309	3,554	4,841	11,739	14,812	4,515	989	6,262
WY	5,612	463	485	1,685	2,979	4,137	503	589	926

– Represents or rounds to zero. [1] Total expenditures are the sum of purchases for each source (including retail electricity sales) less electric power sector purchases of fuel. [2] Includes sources not shown separately, such as electricity imports and exports and coal coke net imports, which are not allocated to the states. [3] Includes fuel ethanol blended into motor gasoline. [4] Includes supplemental gaseous fuels.

Source: U.S. Energy Information Administration, "State Energy Data, 2008," June 2010, <http://www.eia.doe.gov/emeu/states/_seds.html>.

Table 930. Energy Imports and Exports by Type of Fuel: 1980 to 2009

[In quadrillion of Btu. (12.10 represents 12,100,000,000,000,000 Btu). For definition of Btu, see source and text, this section]

Type of fuel	1980	1990	1995	2000	2003	2004	2005	2006	2007	2008	2009 [1]
Net imports, total [2]	**12.10**	**14.06**	**17.75**	**24.97**	**27.01**	**29.11**	**30.15**	**29.81**	**29.24**	**25.94**	**22.85**
Coal..............	−2.39	−2.70	−2.08	−1.21	−0.49	−0.57	−0.51	−0.36	−0.60	−1.22	−0.95
Natural gas (dry)	0.96	1.46	2.74	3.62	3.36	3.50	3.71	3.56	3.89	3.07	2.76
Petroleum [3]	13.50	15.29	16.89	22.38	24.07	25.99	26.81	26.42	25.79	23.93	20.95
Other [4]	0.04	0.01	0.19	0.18	0.07	0.18	0.13	0.12	0.13	0.15	0.09
Imports, total	15.80	18.82	22.26	28.97	31.06	33.54	34.71	34.67	34.69	32.95	29.78
Coal..............	0.03	0.07	0.24	0.31	0.63	0.68	0.76	0.91	0.91	0.86	0.57
Natural gas (dry)	1.01	1.55	2.90	3.87	4.04	4.37	4.45	4.29	4.72	4.08	3.84
Petroleum [3]	14.66	17.12	18.88	24.53	26.22	28.20	29.25	29.16	28.76	27.64	25.16
Other [4]	0.10	0.08	0.24	0.26	0.17	0.29	0.24	0.25	0.24	0.28	0.19
Exports, total	3.69	4.75	4.51	4.01	4.05	4.43	4.56	4.87	5.45	7.02	6.93
Coal..............	2.42	2.77	2.32	1.53	1.12	1.25	1.27	1.26	1.51	2.07	1.52
Natural gas (dry)	0.05	0.09	0.16	0.25	0.69	0.86	0.74	0.73	0.83	1.02	1.08
Petroleum	1.16	1.82	1.99	2.15	2.15	2.21	2.44	2.75	2.97	3.71	4.21
Other [4]	0.07	0.07	0.05	0.08	0.10	0.11	0.11	0.12	0.10	0.13	0.09

[1] Preliminary. [2] Net imports equals imports minus exports. Minus sign (–) indicates exports are greater than imports. [3] Includes imports into the Strategic Petroleum Reserve. [4] Coal coke, small amounts of electricity transmitted across U.S. borders with Canada and Mexico, and small amounts of biodiesel.

Source: U.S. Energy Information Administration, *Annual Energy Review 2009,* August 2010. See also <http://www.eia.gov/emeu/aer/overview.html>.

Table 931. U.S. Foreign Trade in Selected Mineral Fuels: 1980 to 2009

[985 represents 985,000,000,000 cu. ft. Minus sign (–) indicates trade deficit]

Mineral fuel	Unit	1980	1990	1995	2000	2005	2006	2007	2008	2009 [1]
Natural gas:										
Imports	Bil. cu. ft	985	1,532	2,841	3,782	4,341	4,186	4,608	3,984	3,748
Exports	Bil. cu. ft	49	86	154	244	729	724	822	1,006	1,071
Net trade [2]	Bil. cu. ft	−936	−1,447	−2,687	−3,538	−3,612	−3,462	−3,785	−2,978	−2,677
Crude oil: [3]										
Imports [4]	Mil. bbl	1,926	2,151	2,639	3,320	3,696	3,693	3,661	3,571	3,307
Exports	Mil. bbl	105	40	35	18	12	9	10	10	16
Net trade [2]	Mil. bbl	−1,821	−2,112	−2,604	−3,301	−3,684	−3,684	−3,651	−3,560	−3,291
Petroleum products:										
Imports	Mil. bbl	603	775	586	874	1,310	1,310	1,255	1,143	973
Exports	Mil. bbl	94	273	312	362	414	472	513	647	723
Net trade [2]	Mil. bbl	−508	−502	−274	−512	−896	−838	−742	−496	−249
Coal:										
Imports	Mil. sh. tons ...	1	3	9	13	30	36	36	34	23
Exports	Mil. sh. tons ...	92	106	89	58	50	50	59	82	59
Net trade [2]	Mil. sh. tons ...	90.5	103.1	79.1	46.0	19.5	13.4	22.8	47.3	36.5

[1] Preliminary. [2] Exports minus imports. [3] Includes lease condensate. [4] Includes strategic petroleum reserve imports.

Source: U.S. Energy Information Administration, *Annual Energy Review 2009,* August 2010. See also <http://www.eia.doe.gov/emeu/aer/contents.html>.

Table 932. Crude Oil Imports Into the U.S. by Country of Origin: 1980 to 2009

[In millions of barrels (1,921 represents 1,921,000,000). Barrels contain 42 gallons. Crude oil imports are reported by the Petroleum Administration for Defense (PAD) District in which they are to be processed. A PAD District is a geographic aggregation of the 50 states and D.C. into 5 districts. Includes crude oil imported for storage in the Strategic Petroleum Reserve (SPR). Total OPEC excludes, and Non-OPEC includes, petroleum imported into the United States indirectly from members of OPEC, primarily from Carribean and West European areas, as petroleum products that were refined from crude oil produced by OPEC]

Country of origin	1980	1990	1995	2000	2003	2004	2005	2006	2007	2008	2009
Total imports	**1,921**	**2,151**	**2,639**	**3,311**	**3,521**	**3,674**	**3,670**	**3,685**	**3,656**	**3,571**	**3,307**
OPEC, total [1, 2, 3, 4]	1,410	1,283	1,219	1,659	1,671	2,032	1,738	1,745	1,969	1,984	1,594
Algeria...............	166	23	10	(Z)	41	79	83	130	162	114	101
Angola [2]	(NA)	86	131	108	132	112	164	187	181	184	164
Ecuador [3]	6	(NA)	35	46	50	83	101	99	72	78	64
Iraq	10	188	–	226	171	238	190	202	177	229	164
Kuwait [5]	10	29	78	96	75	88	79	65	64	75	68
Nigeria...............	307	286	227	319	306	389	387	381	395	338	281
Saudi Arabia [5]	456	436	460	556	629	547	525	519	530	551	361
Venezuela	57	243	420	446	436	473	449	416	420	381	352
Non-OPEC, total [2, 3, 4, 6]	511	869	1,419	1,652	1,850	1,838	1,932	1,940	1,687	1,587	1,713
Brazil................	(NA)	–	–	2	17	19	34	49	61	84	107
Canada	73	235	380	492	565	590	600	651	681	707	707
Colombia.............	(NA)	51	76	116	59	51	57	52	50	65	93
Equatorial Guinea	(NA)	(NA)	(NA)	(NA)	(NA)	(NA)	(NA)	21	20	27	32
Mexico...............	185	251	375	479	580	584	566	575	514	434	400
Russia...............	(NA)	(Z)	5	3	54	55	70	39	41	41	85
United Kingdom.........	63	57	124	106	127	86	80	47	37	27	38

– Represents zero. NA Not available. Z Represents less than 500,000 barrels. [1] OPEC (Organization of Petroleum Exporting Countries) includes the nations shown, as well as Iran, Libya, Qatar, United Arab Emirates, and Indonesia. [2] Angola joined OPEC at the beginning of 2007. Prior to 2007, it is included in the non-OPEC total. [3] Ecuador withdrew from OPEC on Dec. 31, 1992; therefore, it is included under OPEC prior to 1995. From 1995 through 2007, it is included in the Non-OPEC total. In Nov. 2007, Ecuador rejoined OPEC; imports for 2008 are included in the OPEC total. [4] Gabon withdrew from OPEC on Dec. 31, 1994; therefore, it is included under OPEC prior to 1995. Beginning 1995, it is included in the Non-OPEC total. [5] Imports from the Neutral Zone between Kuwait and Saudi Arabia are included in Saudi Arabia. [6] Non-OPEC total includes nations not shown.

Source: U.S. Energy Information Administration, "Petroleum Supply Monthly," February 2010, <http://www.eia.gov/pub/oil_gas/petroleum/data_publications/petroleum_supply_monthly/historical/2010/2010_02/psm_2010_02.html>.

U.S. Census Bureau, Statistical Abstract of the United States: 2011

Table 933. Crude Oil and Refined Products—Summary: 1980 to 2009

[13,481 represents 13,481,000 bbl. Barrels (bbl.) of 42 gallons. Data are averages]

Year	Crude oil [1] (1,000 bbl. per day)					Refined oil products (1,000 bbl. per day)			Total oil imports [4] (1,000 bbl. per day)	Crude oil stocks [1, 5] (mil. bbl.)	
	Input to refineries	Domestic production	Imports		Exports	Domestic demand	Imports	Exports		Total	Strategic reserve [6]
			Total [2]	Strategic reserve [3]							
1980......	13,481	8,597	5,263	44	287	17,056	1,646	258	6,909	[7] 466	108
1985......	12,002	8,971	3,201	118	204	15,726	1,866	577	5,067	814	493
1990......	13,409	7,355	5,894	27	109	16,988	2,123	748	8,018	908	586
1995......	13,973	6,560	7,230	–	95	17,725	1,605	855	8,835	895	592
2000......	15,067	5,822	9,071	8	50	19,701	2,389	990	11,459	826	541
2004......	15,475	5,419	10,088	77	27	20,731	3,057	1,021	13,145	961	676
2005......	15,220	5,178	10,126	52	32	20,802	3,588	1,133	13,714	1,008	685
2006......	15,242	5,102	10,118	8	25	20,687	3,589	1,292	13,707	1,001	689
2007......	15,156	5,064	10,031	7	27	20,680	3,437	1,405	13,468	983	691
2008......	14,648	4,950	9,783	19	29	19,498	3,116	1,803	12,915	1,028	703
2009......	14,300	5,315	9,048	(NA)	41	18,682	(NA)	(NA)	11,726	1,054	720

– Represents zero. NA Not available. [1] Includes lease condensate. [2] Includes Strategic Petroleum Reserve. [3] SPR is the Strategic Petroleum Reserve. Through 2000, includes imports by SPR only; beginning in 2004, includes imports by SPR, and imports into SPR by others. [4] Crude oil (including Strategic Petroleum Reserve imports) plus refined products. [5] Crude oil at end of period. Includes commercial and Strategic Petroleum Reserve stocks. [6] Crude oil stocks in the Strategic Petroleum Reserve include non-U.S. stocks held under foreign or commercial storage agreements. [7] Stocks of Alaskan crude oil in transit are included from January 1985 forward.

Source: U.S. Energy Information Administration, "Monthly Energy Review," February 2010, <http://www.eia.gov/emeu/mer/petro.html>.

Table 934. Petroleum and Coal Products Corporations—Sales, Net Profit, and Profit Per Dollar of Sales: 1990 to 2009

[318.5 represents $318,500,000,000. Represents SIC group 29 (NAICS group 324). Through 2000, based on Standard Industrial Classification (SIC) code; beginning 2002, based on North American Industry Classification System (NAICS), 1997. Profit rates are averages of quarterly figures at annual rates. Beginning 1990, excludes estimates for corporations with less than $250,000 in assets]

Item	Unit	1990	1995	2000	2002	2003	2004	2005	2006	2007	2008	2009
Sales..............	Bil. dol....	318.5	283.1	455.2	474.9	597.8	767.7	956.0	1,037.8	1,113.2	1,369.1	847.0
Net profit:												
Before income taxes ..	Bil. dol....	23.1	16.5	55.5	22.4	52.8	89.7	120.2	139.8	127.0	101.6	42.6
After income taxes....	Bil. dol....	17.8	13.9	42.6	19.5	43.6	71.8	96.3	111.0	105.4	81.0	43.7
Depreciation [1]	Bil. dol....	18.7	16.7	15.5	17.8	19.4	18.5	18.6	20.0	22.6	22.9	28.0
Profits per dollar of sales:												
Before income taxes ..	Cents....	7.3	5.8	12.2	4.6	8.8	11.6	12.6	13.4	11.6	5.8	5.2
After income taxes....	Cents....	5.6	4.9	9.4	4.2	7.3	9.3	10.1	10.6	9.6	4.4	5.3
Profits on stockholders' equity:												
Before income taxes ..	Percent ..	16.4	12.6	29.4	9.7	20.8	32.9	38.0	36.3	30.7	21.8	10.4
After income taxes....	Percent ..	12.7	10.6	22.6	8.4	17.1	26.3	30.4	28.8	25.5	17.3	10.7

[1] Includes depletion and accelerated amortization of emergency facilities.

Source: U.S. Census Bureau, *Quarterly Financial Report for Manufacturing, Mining and Trade Corporations.*

Table 935. Major Petroleum Companies—Financial Summary: 1980 to 2009

[32.9 represents $32,900,000,000. Data represent a composite of approximately 42 major worldwide petroleum companies aggregated on a consolidated total company basis. Minus sign (–) indicates deficit]

Item	1980	1990	1995	2000	2004	2005	2006	2007	2008	2009
FINANCIAL DATA (bil. dol.)										
Net income	32.9	26.8	24.3	76.4	120.5	170.6	187.6	237.6	198.1	92.6
Depreciation, depletion, etc.	32.5	38.7	43.1	53.3	76.9	76.5	85.8	114.3	156.8	170.2
Cash flow [1]................	65.4	65.5	67.4	129.7	205.1	239.9	261.2	327.1	440.7	279.6
Dividends paid..........................	9.3	15.9	17.6	23.0	33.5	37.5	39.2	62.2	74.8	72.1
Net internal funds available for investment or debt repayment [2]....................	56.1	49.6	49.8	106.7	171.6	202.4	222.0	264.9	365.9	207.5
Capital and exploratory expenditures	62.1	59.6	59.8	72.8	112.4	140.4	193.1	221.7	328.0	268.0
Long-term capitalization	211.4	300.0	304.3	516.9	700.1	800.4	910.6	1,211.8	1,362.0	1,449.3
Long-term debt	49.8	90.4	85.4	112.8	161.0	165.2	177.4	240.1	299.4	365.7
Preferred stock	2.0	5.2	5.7	5.4	1.3	3.5	3.4	1.9	1.4	1.2
Common stock and retained earnings [3]....	159.6	204.4	213.2	398.7	537.8	631.7	729.8	969.8	1,061.2	1,082.4
Excess of expenditures over cash income [4]..........................	6.0	10.0	10.0	–33.9	–59.2	–62.0	–28.9	–43.2	–37.9	60.5
RATIOS [5] (percent)										
Long-term debt to long-term capitalization ...	23.6	30.1	28.1	21.8	24.1	23.5	19.9	19.1	19.8	21.4
Net income to total average capital	17.0	9.1	8.1	15.7	18.9	23.0	22.3	21.2	15.2	6.6
Net income to average common equity	22.5	13.5	11.6	20.5	24.2	29.3	27.8	26.3	19.2	8.7

[1] Generally represents internally generated funds from operations. Sum of net income and noncash charges such as depreciation, depletion, amortization, ceiling tests, and mark-to-market accounting. [2] Cash flow minus dividends paid. [3] Includes common stock, capital surplus, and earned surplus accounts after adjustments. [4] Capital and exploratory expenditures plus dividends paid minus cash flow. [5] Represents approximate year-to-year comparisons because of changes in the makeup of the group due to mergers and other corporate changes.

Source: Carl H. Pforzheimer & Co., New York, NY, *Comparative Oil Company Statements*, annual.

Table 936. Nuclear Power Plants—Number, Capacity, and Generation: 1980 to 2009

[51.8 represents 51,800,000 kW]

Item	1980	1990	1995	2000	2002	2003	2004	2005	2006	2007	2008	2009
Operable generating units [1,2]	71	112	109	104	104	104	104	104	104	104	104	104
Net summer capacity [2,3] (mil. kW)	51.8	99.6	99.5	97.9	98.7	99.2	99.6	100.0	100.3	100.3	100.8	100.8
Net generation (bil. kWh)	251.1	576.9	673.4	753.9	780.1	763.7	788.5	782.0	787.2	806.4	806.2	798.7
Percent of total electricity net generation	11.0	19.0	20.1	19.8	20.2	19.7	19.9	19.3	19.4	19.4	19.6	20.2
Capacity factor [4] (percent)	56.3	66.0	77.4	88.1	90.3	87.9	90.1	89.3	89.6	91.8	91.1	90.5

[1] Total of nuclear generating units holding full-power licenses, or equivalent permission to operate, at the end of the year. For example, although Browns Ferry 1 was shut down in 1985, the unit remained fully licensed and thus continued to be counted as operable. It was eventually reopened in 2007. [2] As of year-end. [3] Net summer capacity is the peak steady hourly output that generating equipment is expected to supply to system load, exclusive of auxiliary and other power plant, as demonstrated by test at the time of summer peak demand. [4] Weighted average of monthly capacity factors. Monthly factors are derived by dividing actual monthly generation by the maximum possible generation for the month (number of hours in the month multiplied by the net summer capacity at the end of the month).

Source: U.S. Energy Information Administration, "Monthly Energy Review," June 2010, <http://www.eia.doe.gov/emeu/mer/nuclear.html>.

Table 937. Nuclear Power Plants—Number of Units, Net Generation, and Net Summer Capacity by State: 2008

[806,208 represents 806,208,000,000 kWh]

State	Number of units	Nuclear net generation Total (mil. kWh)	Nuclear net generation Percent of total [1]	Nuclear net summer capability Total (mil. kW)	Nuclear net summer capability Percent of total [1]	State	Number of units	Nuclear net generation Total (mil. kWh)	Nuclear net generation Percent of total [1]	Nuclear net summer capability Total (mil. kW)	Nuclear net summer capability Percent of total [1]
U.S.	104	806,208	19.6	100.8	10.0	MS	1	9,397	19.5	1.3	7.9
AL	5	38,993	26.7	5.0	16.0	MO	1	9,379	10.3	1.2	5.7
AZ	3	29,250	24.5	3.9	15.2	NE	2	9,479	29.3	1.3	17.8
AR	2	14,168	25.7	1.8	12.0	NH	1	9,350	40.9	1.2	29.8
CA	4	32,482	15.6	4.4	6.8	NJ	1	32,195	50.6	4.1	22.2
CT	2	15,433	50.8	2.0	25.8	NY	6	43,209	30.8	5.3	13.6
FL	5	32,133	14.6	3.9	7.1	NC	5	39,776	31.0	5.0	17.0
GA	4	31,691	23.3	4.1	11.1	OH	3	17,514	11.4	2.1	6.3
IL	11	95,152	47.7	11.4	26.3	PA	9	78,658	35.4	9.3	20.7
IA	1	5,282	10.0	0.6	4.2	SC	7	51,763	51.3	6.5	27.0
KS	1	8,497	18.2	1.2	9.7	TN	3	27,030	29.8	3.4	16.3
LA	2	15,371	16.6	2.2	8.2	TX	4	40,727	10.1	4.9	4.7
MD	2	14,679	31.0	1.7	13.8	VT	1	4,895	71.8	0.6	55.0
MA	1	5,869	13.8	0.7	5.1	VA	4	27,931	38.4	3.4	14.5
MI	3	31,484	27.4	4.0	13.0	WA	1	9,270	8.4	1.1	3.8
MN	3	12,997	23.7	1.7	11.7	WI	3	12,155	19.1	1.6	9.0

[1] For total generation and capacity, see Table 943.

Source: U.S. Energy Information Administration, "Electric Power Annual 2008," January 2010, <http://www.eia.doe.gov/cneaf/electricity/epa/epa_sprdshts.html>.

Table 938. Uranium Concentrate—Supply, Inventories, and Average Prices: 1990 to 2008

[8.89 represents 8,890,000 pounds (lbs.). Years ending Dec. 31. For additional data on uranium, see Section 18]

Item	Unit	1990	1995	2000	2003	2004	2005	2006	2007	2008
Production [1]	Mil. lb.	8.89	6.04	3.96	2.00	2.28	2.69	4.11	4.53	3.90
Exports [2]	Mil. lb.	2.0	9.8	13.6	13.2	13.2	20.5	18.7	14.8	17.2
Imports [2]	Mil. lb.	23.7	41.3	44.9	53.0	66.1	65.5	64.8	54.1	57.1
Electric plant purchases from domestic suppliers	Mil. lb.	20.5	22.3	24.3	21.7	28.2	27.3	27.9	18.5	20.4
Loaded into U.S. nuclear reactors [3]	Mil. lb.	(NA)	51.1	51.5	62.3	50.1	58.3	51.7	45.5	51.3
Inventories, total	Mil. lb.	129.1	72.5	111.3	85.5	95.2	93.8	106.6	112.4	108.8
At domestic suppliers	Mil. lb.	26.4	13.7	56.5	39.9	37.5	29.1	29.1	31.2	26.9
At electric plants	Mil. lb.	102.7	58.7	54.8	45.6	57.7	64.7	77.5	81.2	81.9
Average price per pound: Purchased imports	Dollars	12.55	10.20	9.84	10.59	12.25	14.83	19.31	34.18	41.30
Domestic purchases	Dollars	15.70	11.11	11.45	10.84	11.91	13.98	18.54	33.13	43.43

NA Not available. [1] Data are for uranium concentrate, a yellow or brown powder obtained by the milling of uranium ore, processing of in situ leach mining solutions, or as a by-product of phosphoric acid production. [2] Includes transactions by uranium buyers (consumers). Buyer imports and exports prior to 1990 are believed to be small. [3] Does not include any fuel rods removed from reactors and later reloaded into the reactor.

Source: U.S. Energy Information Administration, *Annual Energy Review 2009,* August 2010. See also <http://www.eia.doe.gov/emeu/aer/nuclear.html>.

Table 939. Solar Collector Shipments by Type, End Use, and Market Sector: 1980 to 2008

[Shipments in thousands of square feet (19,398 represents 19,398,000). Solar collector is a device for intercepting sunlight, converting the light to heat, and carrying the heat to where it will be either used or stored. 1985 data are not available. Based on the Annual Solar Thermal Collector Manufacturers Survey]

Year	Number of manu-facturers	Total ship-ments [1,2,3]	Collector type		End use			Market sector		
			Low tempera-ture [1,2]	Medium tempera-ture, special/ other [2]	Pool heating	Hot water	Space heating	Resi-dential	Com-merical	Indus-trial
1980........	233	19,398	12,233	7,165	12,029	4,790	1,688	16,077	2,417	488
1990........	51	11,409	3,645	2,527	5,016	1,091	2	5,835	294	22
1995........	36	7,666	6,813	840	6,763	755	132	6,966	604	82
2000........	26	8,354	7,948	400	7,863	367	99	7,473	810	57
2005........	25	16,041	15,224	702	15,041	640	228	14,681	1,160	31
2007........	60	15,153	13,323	1,797	12,076	1,393	189	12,799	931	46
2008........	74	16,963	14,015	2,560	11,973	1,978	186	13,000	1,294	128

[1] Includes shipments of high temperature collectors to the government, including some military, but excluding space applications. Also includes end uses such as process heating, utility, and other market sectors, not shown separately. [2] Includes imputation of shipment data to account for nonrespondents. [3] Total shipments include all domestic and export shipments and may include imported collectors that subsequently were shipped to domestic or foreign customers.

Source: U.S. Energy Information Administration, 1980–1990, "Solar Collector Manufacturing Activity", annual reports; 1995–2002, "Renewable Energy Annual"; thereafter, "Solar Thermal Collector Manufacturing Activities 2008," January 2010, <http://www.eia.doe.gov/cneaf/solar.renewables/page/solarreport/solar.html>.

Table 940. Electricity Net Generation by Sector and Fuel Type: 1990 to 2009

[3,037.8 represents 3,037,800,000,000 kWh. Data are for fuels consumed to produce electricity. Also includes fuels consumed to produce useful thermal output at a small number of electric utility combined-heat-and-power (CHP) plants]

Source and sector	Unit	1990	1995	2000	2005	2008	2009 [1]
Net generation, total	Bil. kWh.......	**3,037.8**	**3,353.5**	**3,802.1**	**4,055.4**	**4,119.4**	**3,953.1**
Electric power sector, total...................	Bil. kWh.......	2,901.3	3,194.2	3,637.5	3,902.2	3,974.3	3,814.3
Electricity-only plants [2].....................	Bil. kWh.......	2,840.0	3,052.8	3,472.9	3,721.8	3,807.4	3,652.7
Combined-heat-and-power plants [3]..........	Bil. kWh.......	61.3	141.5	164.6	180.4	166.9	161.6
Commercial sector [4]	Bil. kWh.......	5.8	8.2	7.9	8.5	7.9	7.6
Industrial sector [5]........................	Bil. kWh.......	130.7	151.0	156.7	144.7	137.1	131.2
Net generation by source, all sectors:							
Fossil fuels, total	Bil. kWh.......	2,103.6	2,293.9	2,692.5	2,909.5	2,926.7	2,734.4
Coal [6].................................	Bil. kWh.......	1,594.0	1,709.4	1,966.3	2,012.9	1,985.8	1,764.5
Petroleum [7]	Bil. kWh.......	126.5	74.6	111.2	122.2	46.2	38.8
Natural gas [8]	Bil. kWh.......	372.8	496.1	601.0	761.0	883.0	920.4
Other gases [9]...........................	Bil. kWh.......	10.4	13.9	14.0	13.5	11.7	10.7
Nuclear electric power.....................	Bil. kWh.......	576.9	673.4	753.9	782.0	806.2	798.7
Hydroelectric pumped storage [10]............	Bil. kWh.......	-3.5	-2.7	-5.5	-6.6	-6.3	-4.3
Renewable energy, total...................	Bil. kWh.......	357.2	384.8	356.5	357.7	381.0	413.2
Conventional hydroelectric power............	Bil. kWh.......	292.9	310.8	275.6	270.3	254.8	272.1
Biomass, total	Bil. kWh.......	45.8	56.9	60.7	54.3	55.0	54.3
Wood [11]...............................	Bil. kWh.......	32.5	36.5	37.6	38.9	37.3	36.2
Waste [12]..............................	Bil. kWh.......	13.3	20.4	23.1	15.4	17.7	18.1
Geothermal	Bil. kWh.......	15.4	13.4	14.1	14.7	15.0	15.2
Solar [13]...............................	Bil. kWh.......	0.4	0.5	0.5	0.6	0.9	0.8
Wind.................................	Bil. kWh.......	2.8	3.2	5.6	17.8	55.4	70.8
Other [14]	Bil. kWh.......	3.6	4.1	4.8	12.8	11.7	11.1
Consumption of fuels for electricity generation:							
Coal [6].................................	Mil. sh. tons	792.5	860.6	994.9	1,041.4	1,042.3	938.1
Petroleum, total.........................	Mil. bbl.........	218.8	132.6	195.2	206.8	80.9	67.9
Distilate fuel oil [15]	Mil. bbl.........	18.1	19.6	31.7	20.7	12.8	12.5
Residual fuel oil [16]	Mil. bbl.........	190.7	95.5	143.4	141.5	38.2	28.4
Other liquids [17].........................	Mil. bbl.........	0.4	0.7	1.4	3.0	2.8	2.7
Petroleum coke	Mil. sh. Tons [18] ..	1.9	3.4	3.7	8.3	5.4	4.9
Natural gas [8]	Bil. cu. ft.	3,691.6	4,737.9	5,691.5	6,036.4	6,895.8	7,104.6
Other gases [9]...........................	Tril. Btu........	111.8	132.5	126.0	109.9	96.8	86.0
Biomass................................	Tril. Btu........	653.5	795.6	825.9	585.3	605.7	576.1
Wood [11]...............................	Tril. Btu........	442.3	479.9	495.8	355.3	338.8	317.5
Waste [12]..............................	Tril. Btu........	211.2	315.7	330.1	230.1	267.0	258.5
Other [14]	Tril. Btu........	36.0	42.0	46.2	173.0	169.9	159.0

[1] Preliminary. [2] Electricity-only plants within the NAICS 22 category whose primary business is to sell electricity to the public. Data also include a small number of electric utility combined-heat-and-power plants (CHP). [3] Combined-heat-and-power plants within the NAICS 22 category whose primary business is to sell electricity and/or heat to the public. Data do not include electric utility CHP plants—these are included under electricity-only plants. [4] Commercial combined-heat-and-power (CHP) and commercial electricity-only plants. [5] Industrial combined-heat-and-power (HCP) and industrial electricity-only plants. [6] Anthracite, bituminous coal, subbituminous coal, lignite, waste coal, and coal synfuel. [7] Distillate fuel oil, residual fuel oil, petroleum coke, jet fuel, kerosene, other petroleum, and waste oil. [8] Includes a small amount of supplemental gaseous fuels that cannot be identified separately. [9] Blast furnace gas, propane gas, and other manufactured and waste gases derived from fossil fuels. [10] Pumped storage facility production minus energy used for pumping. [11] Wood and wood-derived fuels. [12] Municipal solid waste from biogenic sources, landfill gas, sludge waste, tires, agricultural by-products, and other biomass. Through 2000, also includes nonrenewable waste (municipal solid waste from non- biogenic sources, and tire-derived fuels). [13] Solar thermal and photovoltaic energy. [14] Batteries, chemicals, hydrogen, pitch, purchased steam, sulfur, miscellaneous technologies, and beginning 2005, nonrenewable waste (municipal solid waste from nonbiogenic sources, and tire-derived fuels). [15] Fuel oil numbers 1, 2, and 4. Prior to 2005, electric utility data also include small amounts of kerosene and jet fuel. [16] Fuel oil numbers 5 and 6. Prior to 2005, electric utility data also include a small amount of fuel oil number 4. [17] Jet fuel, kerosene, other petroleum liquids, and waste oil. [18] Short tons.

Source: U.S. Energy Information Administration, *Annual Energy Review 2009*, August 2010. See also <http://www.eia.doe.gov /emeu/aer/contents.html>.

592 Energy and Utilities

Table 941. Total Electric Net Summer Capacity, All Sectors: 1990 to 2009

[In million kilowatts (734.1 represents 734,100,000). Data are at end of year. For plants that use multiple sources of energy, capacity is assigned to the predominant energy source]

Source	1990	1995	2000	2004	2005	2006	2007	2008	2009
Net summer capacity, total	**734.1**	**769.5**	**811.7**	**962.9**	**978.0**	**986.2**	**994.9**	**1,010.2**	**1,027.6**
Fossil fuels, total	527.8	554.2	598.9	745.4	757.1	761.6	764.0	770.2	778.2
Coal [1]	307.4	311.4	315.1	313.0	313.4	313.0	312.7	313.3	314.4
Petroleum [2]	77.9	66.6	61.8	59.1	58.5	58.1	56.1	57.4	57.0
Natural gas [3]	140.8	174.5	219.6	371.0	383.1	388.3	392.9	397.4	404.9
Dual fired [4]	113.6	122.0	149.8	172.2	174.7	(NA)	(NA)	(NA)	(NA)
Other gases [5]	1.6	1.7	2.3	2.3	2.1	2.3	2.3	2.0	2.0
Nuclear electric power	99.6	99.5	97.9	99.6	100.0	100.3	100.3	100.8	100.8
Hydroelectric pumped storage	19.5	21.4	19.5	20.8	21.3	21.5	21.9	21.9	21.9
Renewable energy, total	86.8	93.9	94.9	96.4	98.7	101.9	108.0	116.4	125.8
Conventional hydroelectric power	73.9	78.6	79.4	77.6	77.5	77.8	77.9	77.9	78.0
Biomass, total	8.1	10.3	10.0	9.7	9.8	10.1	10.8	11.1	11.4
Wood [6]	5.5	6.7	6.1	6.2	6.2	6.4	6.7	6.9	6.9
Waste [7]	2.5	3.5	3.9	3.5	3.6	3.7	4.1	4.2	4.4
Geothermal	2.7	3.0	2.8	2.2	2.3	2.3	2.2	2.3	2.4
Solar [8]	0.3	0.3	0.4	0.4	0.4	0.4	0.5	0.5	0.6
Wind	1.8	1.7	2.4	6.5	8.7	11.3	16.5	24.7	33.5
Other [9]	0.5	0.5	0.5	0.7	0.9	0.9	0.8	0.9	0.9

NA Not available. [1] Anthracite, bituminous coal, subbituminous coal, lignite, waste coal, and coal synfuel. [2] Distillate fuel oil, residual fuel oil, petroleum coke, jet fuel, kerosene, other petroleum, and waste oil. [3] Includes a small amount of supplemental gaseous fuels that cannot be identified separately. [4] Petroleum and natural gas. [5] Blast furnace gas, propane gas, and other manufactured and waste gases derived from fossil fuels. [6] Wood and wood-derived fuels. [7] Municipal solid waste from biogenic sources, landfill gas, sludge waste, tires, agricultural byproducts, and other biomass. Also includes nonrenewable waste (municipal solid waste from nonbiogenic sources, and tire-derived fuels). [8] Solar thermal and photovoltaic energy. [9] Batteries, chemicals, hydrogen, pitch, purchased steam, sulfur, and miscellaneous technologies.

Source: U.S. Energy Information Administration, *Annual Energy Review 2009,* August 2010. See also <http://www.eia.doe.gov /emeu/aer/elect.html>.

Table 942. Electricity—End Use and Average Retail Prices: 1990 to 2009

[Beginning 2004, the category "other" has been replaced by "transportation," and the categories "commercial" and "industrial" have been redefined. Data represent revenue from electricity retail sales divided by the amount of retail electricity sold (in kilowatt-hours). Prices include state and local taxes, energy or demand charges, customer service charges, environmental surcharges, franchise fees, fuel adjustments, and other miscellaneous charges applied to end-use customers during normal billing operations. Prices do not include deferred charges, credits, or other adjustments, such as fuel or revenue from purchased power, from previous reporting periods. Data are for a census of electric utilities. Beginning in 2000 data also include energy service providers selling to retail customers]

Item	1990	1995	2000	2004	2005	2006	2007	2008	2009 [1]
END USE (Billion kilowatt-hours)									
Total end use [2]	**2,837.1**	**3,164.0**	**3,592.4**	**3,715.9**	**3,811.0**	**3,816.8**	**3,923.8**	**3,906.4**	**3,741.5**
Direct use [3]	124.5	150.7	170.9	168.5	150.0	146.9	159.3	173.5	166.0
Retail sales, total [4]	2,712.6	3,013.3	3,421.4	3,547.5	3,661.0	3,669.9	3,764.6	3,733.0	3,575.5
Residential	924.0	1,042.5	1,192.4	1,292.0	1,359.2	1,351.5	1,392.2	1,380.0	1,362.9
Commercial [5]	838.3	953.1	1,159.3	1,230.4	1,275.1	1,299.7	1,336.3	1,336.0	1,323.0
Industrial [6]	945.5	1,012.7	1,064.2	1,017.8	1,019.2	1,011.3	1,027.8	1,009.3	881.9
Transportation [7]	4.8	5.0	5.4	7.2	7.5	7.4	8.2	7.7	7.7
AVERAGE RETAIL PRICES (Cents per kilowatt-hour)									
Total:									
Nominal	6.57	6.89	6.81	7.61	8.14	8.90	9.13	9.74	9.89
Real	9.10	8.45	7.68	7.86	8.14	8.62	8.60	8.98	9.01
Residential:									
Nominal	7.83	8.40	8.24	8.95	9.45	10.40	10.65	11.26	11.55
Real	10.84	10.30	9.30	9.25	9.45	10.07	10.03	10.38	10.52
Commercial: [8]									
Nominal	7.34	7.69	7.43	8.17	8.67	9.46	9.65	10.36	10.21
Real	10.17	9.43	8.38	8.44	8.67	9.16	9.09	9.55	9.30
Industrial: [6]									
Nominal	4.74	4.66	4.64	5.25	5.73	6.16	6.39	6.83	6.84
Real	6.57	5.72	5.23	5.43	5.73	5.97	6.02	6.30	6.23
Transportation: [7]									
Nominal	(NA)	(NA)	(NA)	7.18	8.57	9.54	9.70	10.74	11.17
Real	(NA)	(NA)	(NA)	7.42	8.57	9.24	9.13	9.90	10.18
Other: [9]									
Nominal	6.40	6.88	6.56	(X)	(X)	(X)	(X)	(X)	(X)
Real	8.86	8.44	7.40	(X)	(X)	(X)	(X)	(X)	(X)

NA Not available. X Not applicable. [1] Preliminary. [2] The sum of "total retail sales" and "direct use." [3] Use of electricity that is 1) self-generated, 2) produced by either the same entity that consumes the power or an affiliate, and 3) used in direct support of a service or industrial process located within the same facility or group of facilities that house the generating equipment. Direct use is exclusive of station use. [4] Electricity retail sales to ultimate customers reported by electric utilities and, beginning in 2000, other energy service providers. [5] Includes public street and highway lighting, interdepartmental sales, and other sales to public authorities. [6] Beginning 2003, includes agriculture and irrigation. [7] Includes sales to railroads and railways. [8] Beginning 2003, includes public street and highway lighting, interdepartmental sales, and other sales to public authorities. [9] Public street and highway lighting, interdepartmental sales, other sales to public authorities, agriculture and irrigation, and transportation including railroads and railways.

Source: U.S. Energy Information Administration, *Annual Energy Review 2009,* August 2010. See also <http://www.eia.doe.gov /emeu/aer/elect.html>.

Table 943. Electric Power Industry—Net Generation and Net Summer Capacity by State: 2000 to 2008

[Capacity as of December 31. 3,802.1 represents 3,802,100,000,000. Covers utilities for public use]

State	Net generation (bil. kWh) 2000	2005	2008 Total (bil. kWh)	Percent from— Petro-leum	Natural gas	Renewable Hydro-electric	Renewable Non-hydro-electric	Nuclear	Coal	Net summer capacity (mil. kW) 2000	2008
U.S.	3,802.1	4,055.4	4,119.4	1.1	21.4	6.2	3.1	19.6	48.2	811.7	1,010.2
AL	124.4	137.9	145.9	0.1	15.3	4.2	2.3	26.7	51.1	23.5	31.2
AK	6.2	6.6	6.8	14.4	59.1	17.3	0.1	–	9.1	2.1	2.0
AZ	88.9	101.5	119.5	(Z)	32.5	6.1	0.1	24.5	36.7	15.3	25.9
AR	43.9	47.8	55.1	0.1	15.4	8.5	2.7	25.7	47.4	9.7	15.3
CA	208.1	200.3	208.0	0.8	57.7	11.6	11.9	15.6	1.1	51.9	64.1
CO	44.2	49.6	53.4	(Z)	25.2	3.8	6.1	–	65.2	8.4	12.5
CT	33.0	33.5	30.4	1.7	26.5	1.8	2.4	50.8	14.4	6.4	7.8
DE	6.0	8.1	7.5	2.9	18.4	–	2.2	–	70.0	2.1	3.4
DC	0.1	0.2	0.1	100.0	–	–	–	–	–	0.8	0.8
FL	191.8	220.3	219.6	5.5	47.1	0.1	2.0	14.6	29.5	41.5	55.5
GA	123.9	136.7	136.2	0.5	9.9	1.6	2.0	23.3	62.8	27.8	36.5
HI	10.6	11.5	11.4	76.2	–	0.7	6.8	–	14.5	2.4	2.4
ID	11.9	10.8	12.0	(Z)	14.2	78.2	6.3	–	0.8	3.0	3.4
IL	178.5	194.1	199.5	0.1	2.1	0.1	1.5	47.7	48.4	36.3	43.2
IN	127.8	130.4	129.5	0.1	2.8	0.3	0.4	–	94.2	23.3	27.1
IA	41.5	44.2	53.1	0.3	4.1	1.5	8.0	10.0	76.1	9.1	13.7
KS	44.8	45.9	46.6	0.3	4.8	(Z)	3.8	18.2	72.9	10.1	12.0
KY	93.0	97.8	97.9	2.9	1.0	2.0	0.5	–	93.6	16.8	19.9
LA	92.9	92.6	92.5	2.5	49.0	1.2	2.9	16.6	26.1	21.0	26.2
ME	14.0	18.8	17.1	3.1	43.2	26.1	23.7	–	2.1	4.2	4.2
MD	51.1	52.7	47.4	0.9	3.9	4.2	1.3	31.0	57.5	10.4	12.6
MA	38.7	47.5	42.5	5.0	50.6	2.7	3.0	13.8	25.0	12.4	13.5
MI	104.2	121.6	115.0	0.4	8.4	1.2	2.3	27.4	60.7	25.8	30.4
MN	51.4	53.0	54.8	0.4	5.2	1.3	10.7	23.7	58.0	10.3	14.2
MS	37.6	45.1	48.2	0.2	42.7	–	2.9	19.5	34.6	9.0	15.9
MO	76.6	90.8	91.0	0.1	5.7	2.2	0.3	10.3	80.8	17.3	20.7
MT	26.5	27.9	29.6	1.4	0.2	33.7	2.8	–	61.9	5.2	5.6
NE	29.1	31.5	32.4	0.1	2.3	1.1	0.8	29.3	66.3	6.0	7.0
NV	35.5	40.2	35.1	(Z)	68.3	5.0	4.4	–	22.3	6.7	11.3
NH	15.0	24.5	22.9	0.6	30.9	7.1	5.1	40.9	15.1	2.9	4.2
NJ	58.1	60.5	63.7	0.5	32.6	(Z)	1.4	50.6	14.2	16.5	18.5
NM	34.0	35.1	37.0	0.1	21.5	0.8	4.5	–	73.0	5.6	8.0
NY	138.1	146.9	140.3	2.7	31.3	19.0	2.4	30.8	13.7	35.6	38.7
NC	122.3	129.7	125.2	0.3	3.3	2.4	1.5	31.8	60.5	24.5	27.7
ND	31.3	31.9	32.7	0.1	(Z)	3.8	5.2	–	90.6	4.7	5.5
OH	149.1	157.0	153.4	0.9	1.6	0.3	0.4	11.4	85.2	28.4	33.5
OK	55.6	68.6	76.3	(Z)	44.2	5.0	3.3	–	47.6	14.1	20.3
OR	51.8	49.3	58.7	(Z)	29.6	57.6	5.8	–	6.9	11.3	13.3
PA	201.7	218.1	222.4	0.4	8.4	1.1	1.3	35.4	52.9	36.7	45.1
RI	6.0	6.1	7.4	0.4	97.4	0.1	2.1	–	–	1.2	1.8
SC	93.3	102.5	101.0	0.2	5.7	1.1	1.8	51.3	41.1	18.7	24.0
SD	9.7	6.5	7.1	0.3	3.2	42.3	2.1	–	51.7	2.8	3.1
TN	95.8	97.1	90.7	0.2	0.5	6.2	1.1	29.8	62.9	19.5	20.9
TX	377.7	396.7	404.8	0.3	47.7	0.3	4.4	10.1	36.3	81.7	105.0
UT	36.6	38.2	46.6	0.1	15.8	1.4	0.6	–	81.6	5.2	7.1
VT	6.3	5.7	6.8	0.1	(Z)	21.9	6.2	71.8	–	1.0	1.1
VA	77.2	78.9	72.7	1.6	12.8	(Z)	3.7	38.4	43.7	19.4	23.5
WA	108.2	102.0	110.8	(Z)	8.9	70.1	4.5	8.4	7.9	26.1	29.5
WV	92.9	93.6	91.1	0.2	0.2	1.4	0.4	–	97.8	15.0	16.4
WI	59.6	61.8	63.5	1.5	8.3	2.5	2.8	19.1	65.7	13.6	17.6
WY	45.5	45.6	46.5	0.1	1.1	1.8	2.1	–	94.2	6.2	7.1

– Represents zero. Z Represents less than 50 million kWh or 50,000 kW.

Source: U.S. Energy Information Administration, "Electric Power Annual 2008," January 2010, <http://www.eia.doe.gov/cneaf/electricity/epa/epa_sprdshts.html>.

U.S. Census Bureau, Statistical Abstract of the United States: 2011

Table 944. Electric Power Industry—Capability, Peak Load, and Capacity Margin: 1980 to 2009

[558,237 represents 558,237,000 kW. Excludes Alaska and Hawaii. Capability represents the maximum kilowatt output with all power sources available and with hydraulic equipment under actual water conditions, allowing for maintenance, emergency outages, and system operating requirements. Capacity margin is the difference between capability and peak load. Minus sign (−) indicates decrease]

| Year | Capability at the time of— | | | | Noncoincident peak load | | Capacity margin | | | |
| | Summer peak load (1,000 kW) | | Winter peak load (1,000 kW) | | | | Summer | | Winter | |
	Amount	Change from prior year	Amount	Change from prior year	Summer (1,000 kW)	Winter (1,000 kW)	Amount (1,000 kW)	Percent of capability	Amount (1,000 kW)	Percent of capability
1980	558,237	13,731	572,195	17,670	427,058	384,567	131,179	23.5	187,628	32.8
1985	621,597	17,357	636,475	14,350	460,503	423,660	161,094	25.9	212,815	33.4
1989	673,316	11,736	685,249	8,309	524,110	496,378	149,206	22.2	188,871	27.6
1990	685,091	11,775	696,757	11,508	546,331	484,231	138,760	20.3	212,526	30.5
1991	690,915	5,824	703,212	6,455	551,418	485,761	139,497	20.2	217,451	30.9
1992	695,436	4,521	707,752	4,540	548,707	492,983	146,729	21.1	214,769	30.3
1993	694,250	−1,186	711,957	4,205	575,356	521,733	118,894	17.1	190,224	26.7
1994	702,985	8,735	715,090	3,133	585,320	518,253	117,665	16.7	196,837	27.5
1995	714,222	11,237	727,679	12,589	620,249	544,684	93,973	13.2	182,995	25.1
1996	730,376	16,154	737,637	9,958	616,790	554,081	113,586	15.6	183,556	24.9
1997	737,855	7,479	736,666	−971	637,677	529,874	100,178	13.6	206,792	28.1
1998	744,670	6,815	735,090	−1,576	660,293	567,558	84,377	11.3	167,532	22.8
1999	765,744	21,074	748,271	13,181	682,122	570,915	83,622	10.9	177,356	23.7
2000	808,054	42,310	767,505	19,234	678,413	588,426	129,641	16.0	179,079	23.3
2001	788,990	−19,064	806,598	39,093	687,812	576,312	101,178	12.8	230,286	28.6
2002	833,380	44,390	850,984	44,386	714,565	604,986	118,815	14.3	245,998	28.9
2003	856,131	22,751	882,120	31,136	709,375	593,874	146,756	17.1	288,246	32.7
2004	875,870	19,739	864,849	−17,271	704,459	618,701	171,411	19.6	246,148	28.5
2005	882,125	6,255	878,110	13,261	758,876	626,365	123,249	14.0	251,745	28.7
2006	891,226	9,101	899,551	21,441	789,475	640,981	101,751	11.4	258,570	28.7
2007	914,007	20,171	910,050	14,000	702,227	607,005	102,170	14.5	275,745	00.2
2008	956,581	42,184	927,781	14,131	752,470	637,905	204,111	21.3	289,876	31.2
2009 [1]	935,965	−20,616	974,499	46,718	779,716	642,383	156,249	16.7	332,116	34.1

[1] Preliminary.
Source: Edison Electric Institute, Washington, DC, *Statistical Yearbook of the Electric Power Industry*, annual.

Table 945. Electric Energy Retail Sales by Class of Service and State: 2008

[In billions of kilowatt-hours (3,733.0 represents 3,733,000,000,000). Data include both bundled and unbundled consumers]

State	Total [1]	Residential	Commercial	Industrial	State	Total [1]	Residential	Commercial	Industrial
United States	3,733.0	1,380.0	1,336.0	1,009.3					
					Missouri	84.4	35.4	31.1	17.9
Alabama	89.7	32.2	22.5	35.0	Montana	15.3	4.7	4.8	5.8
Alaska	6.3	2.1	2.9	1.3	Nebraska	28.8	9.7	9.4	9.6
Arizona	76.3	33.2	30.2	12.9	Nevada	35.2	12.1	9.3	13.8
Arkansas	46.1	17.4	11.7	17.0	New Hampshire	11.0	4.4	4.5	2.1
California	268.2	91.2	125.0	51.0					
					New Jersey	80.5	29.1	40.6	10.5
Colorado	52.1	17.7	20.6	13.8	New Mexico	22.0	6.4	8.8	6.8
Connecticut	31.0	12.7	13.7	4.4	New York	144.1	49.0	77.4	14.7
Delaware	11.7	4.4	4.3	3.0	North Carolina	130.1	55.7	46.5	27.8
District of Columbia	11.9	1.9	9.3	0.3	North Dakota	12.4	4.3	4.5	3.7
Florida	226.2	113.9	93.2	18.9					
					Ohio	159.4	53.4	47.3	58.6
Georgia	135.2	55.6	46.9	32.5	Oklahoma	56.3	21.9	19.0	15.4
Hawaii	10.4	3.1	3.5	3.8	Oregon	49.2	19.9	16.3	12.9
Idaho	23.9	8.5	6.0	9.3	Pennsylvania	150.4	54.1	47.3	48.1
Illinois	144.6	46.8	51.8	45.5	Rhode Island	7.8	3.0	3.7	1.1
Indiana	107.0	34.0	24.6	48.4					
					South Carolina	80.7	29.7	21.7	29.2
Iowa	45.5	14.1	12.2	19.2	South Dakota	11.0	4.4	4.2	2.3
Kansas	39.5	13.4	15.4	10.8	Tennessee	104.2	41.9	29.4	32.8
Kentucky	93.4	27.6	19.7	46.2	Texas	347.1	127.7	113.5	105.8
Louisiana	78.7	28.8	22.9	26.9	Utah	28.2	8.8	10.3	9.1
Maine	11.7	4.4	4.1	3.2					
					Vermont	5.7	2.1	2.0	1.6
Maryland	63.3	27.1	30.0	5.7	Virginia	110.1	44.6	46.9	18.4
Massachusetts	55.9	19.6	26.6	9.3	Washington	87.3	36.3	29.9	21.1
Michigan	105.8	34.3	39.0	32.5	West Virginia	34.2	11.8	7.7	14.7
Minnesota	68.8	22.4	22.6	23.8	Wisconsin	70.1	22.0	23.5	24.7
Mississippi	47.7	10.3	13.2	10.2	Wyoming	10.7	2.7	4.4	9.6

[1] Includes transportation, not shown separately.
Source: U.S. Energy Information Administration, "Electric Sales and Revenue 2008," January 2010, <http://www.eia.doe.gov/cneaf/electricity/esr/esr_sum.html>.

Table 946. Electric Energy Price by Class of Service and State: 2008

[Revenue (in cents) per kilowatt-hour (kWh). Data include both bundled and unbundled consumers]

State	Total [1]	Resi-dential	Com-mercial	Indus-trial	State	Total [1]	Resi-dential	Com-mercial	Indus-trial
United States	**9.74**	**11.26**	**10.36**	**6.83**					
					Missouri	6.84	8.00	6.61	4.92
Alabama	8.59	10.40	9.87	6.11	Montana.	7.72	9.13	8.54	5.90
Alaska	14.73	16.55	13.64	14.17	Nebraska	6.58	7.87	6.68	5.16
Arizona	9.11	10.27	8.93	6.57	Nevada	9.89	11.93	10.07	7.98
Arkansas	7.60	9.27	7.61	5.89	New Hampshire . . .	14.65	15.68	14.32	13.17
California	12.48	13.81	12.54	10.04					
					New Jersey	14.44	15.66	14.48	10.86
Colorado	8.59	10.13	8.57	6.65	New Mexico	8.35	10.01	8.67	6.38
Connecticut	17.79	19.55	17.12	14.93	New York	16.57	18.30	16.84	10.14
Delaware	12.36	13.93	12.07	10.45	North Carolina	7.96	9.52	7.55	5.54
District of Columbia . . .	13.10	12.79	13.23	10.49	North Dakota	6.69	7.51	6.81	5.59
Florida	10.74	11.65	10.14	8.25					
					Ohio	8.39	10.06	9.22	6.19
Georgia	8.84	9.93	9.07	6.67	Oklahoma	7.81	9.09	7.88	5.90
Hawaii	29.20	32.50	29.72	26.05	Oregon.	7.23	8.49	7.29	5.21
Idaho	5.69	6.99	5.72	4.48	Pennsylvania	9.32	11.35	9.38	7.02
Illinois.	9.26	11.07	11.79	4.54	Rhode Island	16.01	17.45	15.36	14.20
Indiana.	7.09	8.87	7.82	5.46					
					South Carolina. . . .	7.85	9.89	8.42	5.37
Iowa.	6.89	9.49	7.18	4.81	South Dakota	7.14	8.27	6.97	5.31
Kansas.	7.45	8.88	7.42	5.69	Tennessee	8.18	8.91	9.24	6.29
Kentucky	6.26	7.94	7.29	4.82	Texas	10.99	13.04	10.75	8.79
Louisiana	9.44	10.28	10.12	7.94	Utah.	6.49	8.26	6.66	4.59
Maine.	13.83	16.20	12.98	11.70					
					Vermont.	12.33	14.48	12.49	9.19
Maryland	13.00	13.84	12.76	10.37	Virginia.	8.00	9.62	7.32	5.82
Massachusetts.	16.27	17.68	15.80	14.85	Washington	6.55	7.54	6.76	4.55
Michigan	8.94	10.75	9.20	6.74	West Virginia	5.61	7.06	6.08	4.20
Minnesota	7.79	9.74	7.88	5.87	Wisconsin	9.00	11.51	9.28	6.51
Mississippi	8.99	10.39	10.02	6.56	Wyoming	5.67	8.21	6.71	4.47

[1] Includes transportation, not shown separately.

Source: U.S. Energy Information Administration, "Electric Sales and Revenue 2008," January 2010, <http://www.eia.doe.gov/cneaf/electricity/esr/esr_sum.html>.

Table 947. Total Electric Power Industry—Generation, Sales, Revenue, and Customers: 1990 to 2009

[2,808 represents 2,808,000,000,000 kWh. Sales and revenue are to and from ultimate customers. Commercial and Industrial are not wholly comparable on a year-to-year basis due to changes from one classification to another. For the 2004 period forward, the Energy Information Administration replaced the "Other" sector with the Transportation sector. The Transportation sector consists entirely of electrified rail and urban transit systems. Data previously reported in "Other" have been relocated to the Commercial sector, except for Agriculture (i.e., irrigation load), which have been relocated to the Industrial sector]

Class	Unit	1990	1995	2000	2004	2005	2006	2007	2008	2009 [1]
Generation [2].	Bil. kWh	2,808	3,353	3,802	3,971	4,055	4,065	4,157	4,119	3,953
Sales [3].	**Bil. kWh. . . .**	**2,713**	**3,013**	**3,421**	**3,548**	**3,661**	**3,670**	**3,765**	**3,733**	**3,575**
Residential or domestic	Bil. kWh	924	1,043	1,192	1,294	1,359	1,352	1,392	1,380	1,363
Percent of total.	Percent	34.1	34.6	34.9	36.5	37.1	36.8	37.0	37.0	38.1
Commercial [4]	Bil. kWh	751	863	1,055	1,229	1,275	1,300	1,336	1,336	1,323
Industrial [5]	Bil. kWh	946	1,013	1,064	1,019	1,019	1,011	1,028	1,009	882
Revenue [3]	**Bil. dol. . . . .**	**178.2**	**207.7**	**233.2**	**270.5**	**298.0**	**326.5**	**343.7**	**363.7**	**353.6**
Residential or domestic	Bil. dol.	72.4	87.6	98.2	116.0	128.4	140.6	148.3	155.4	157.4
Percent of total.	Percent	40.6	42.2	42.1	42.9	43.1	43.1	43.1	42.7	44.5
Commercial [4]	Bil. dol.	55.1	66.4	78.4	100.3	116.5	122.9	128.9	138.5	135.1
Industrial [5]	Bil. dol.	44.9	47.2	49.4	53.7	58.4	62.3	65.7	68.9	60.3
Ultimate customers, Dec. 31 [3]. . .	**Million . . . . .**	**110.6**	**118.3**	**127.6**	**136.1**	**138.4**	**140.4**	**142.1**	**143.3**	**143.9**
Residential or domestic	Million	97.1	103.9	111.7	118.8	120.8	122.5	123.9	124.9	125.6
Commercial [4]	Million	12.1	12.9	14.3	16.6	16.9	17.2	17.4	17.6	17.6
Industrial [5]	Million	0.5	0.6	0.5	0.7	0.7	0.8	0.8	0.8	0.8
Avg. kWh used per customer . . .	**1,000 . . . . . .**	**24.5**	**25.5**	**26.8**	**26.1**	**26.5**	**26.1**	**26.5**	**26.1**	**24.8**
Residential.	1,000	9.5	10.0	10.7	10.9	11.3	11.0	11.2	11.0	10.9
Commercial [4]	1,000	62.2	66.6	73.5	74.0	75.6	75.7	76.9	76.1	75.4
Avg. annual bill per customer . . .	**Dollar . . . . .**	**1,612**	**1,756**	**1,828**	**1,987**	**2,154**	**2,325**	**2,418**	**2,538**	**2,457**
Residential.	Dollar.	745	843	879	977	1,063	1,148	1,196	1,244	1,253
Commercial [4]	Dollar.	4,562	5,124	5,464	6,037	6,551	7,158	7,418	7,884	7,695
Avg. revenue per kWh sold	**Cents. . . . . .**	**6.57**	**6.89**	**6.81**	**7.62**	**8.14**	**8.90**	**9.13**	**9.74**	**9.89**
Residential.	Cents	7.83	8.40	8.24	8.97	9.45	10.40	10.65	11.26	11.55
Commercial [4]	Cents	7.34	7.69	7.43	8.16	8.67	9.46	9.65	10.36	10.21
Industrial [5]	Cents	4.74	4.66	4.64	5.27	5.73	6.16	6.39	6.83	6.84

[1] Preliminary. [2] "Generation" includes batteries, chemicals, hydrogen, pitch, sulfur, purchased steam, and miscellaneous technologies, which are not separately displayed. [3] Includes other types, not shown separately. Data for 1990 are as of December 31, data for following years are average yearly customers. [4] Small light and power. [5] Large light and power.

Source: Edison Electric Institute, Washington, DC, *Statistical Yearbook of the Electric Power Industry*, annual.

Table 948. Revenue and Expense Statistics for Major U.S. Investor-Owned Electric Utilities: 1995 to 2008

[In millions of nominal dollars (199,967 represents $199,967,000,000). Covers approximately 180 investor-owned electric utilities that during each of the last 3 years met any one or more of the following conditions—1 mil. megawatt-hours of total sales; 100 megawatt-hours of sales for resale, 500 megawatt-hours of gross interchange out, and 500 megawatt-hours of wheeling for other. Missing or erroneous respondent data may result in slight imbalances in some of the expense account subtotals]

Item	1995	2000	2004	2005	2006	2007	2008
Utility operating revenues	**199,967**	**233,915**	**238,759**	**265,652**	**275,501**	**278,499**	**298,962**
Electric utility	183,655	213,634	213,012	234,909	246,736	248,278	266,124
Other utility	16,312	20,281	25,747	30,743	28,765	30,221	32,838
Utility operating expenses	**165,321**	**210,250**	**206,960**	**236,786**	**245,589**	**248,039**	**267,263**
Electric utility	150,599	191,564	183,121	207,830	218,445	219,796	236,572
Operation	91,881	132,607	131,560	150,645	158,893	158,971	175,887
Production	68,983	107,554	103,871	120,586	127,494	126,096	140,974
Cost of fuel	29,122	32,407	28,544	36,106	37,945	41,263	47,337
Purchased power	29,981	62,608	67,126	77,902	79,205	76,515	84,724
Other	9,880	12,561	8,226	6,599	10,371	8,337	8,937
Transmission	1,425	2,713	4,531	5,664	6,179	6,102	6,950
Distribution	2,561	3,092	3,287	3,502	3,640	3,824	3,997
Customer accounts	3,613	4,239	4,077	4,229	4,409	4,787	5,286
Customer service	1,922	1,826	2,013	2,291	2,536	2,953	3,567
Sales	348	405	237	219	240	245	225
Administrative and general	13,028	12,768	13,537	14,130	14,580	14,772	14,718
Maintenance	11,767	12,064	11,743	12,033	12,838	13,538	14,192
Depreciation	19,885	20,636	16,322	17,123	17,373	18,480	19,049
Taxes and other	27,065	24,479	22,190	26,805	28,149	27,641	26,202
Other utility	14,722	18,686	23,839	28,956	27,143	28,243	30,692
Net utility operating income	**34,646**	**23,665**	**31,799**	**28,866**	**29,912**	**30,460**	**31,699**

Source: U.S. Energy Information Administration, "Electric Power Annual 2008," January 2010, <http://www.eia.doe.gov/cneaf/electricity/epa/epat8p1.html>.

Table 949. Total Renewable Energy Net Generation of Electricity by Source and State: 2008

[In millions of kilowatt-hours (381,044 represents 381,044,000,000). MSW = municipal solid waste. For more on net generation, see Table 946]

State	Total [1]	Hydro-electric	Bio-mass [2]	Wind	Wood and derived fuels [3]	State	Total [1]	Hydro-electric	Bio-mass [2]	Wind	Wood and derived fuels [3]
U.S.	**381,044**	**254,831**	**17,734**	**55,363**	**37,300**	MO	2,293	2,047	41	203	2
AL	9,493	6,136	34	(NA)	3,324	MT	10,815	10,000	(NA)	593	111
AK	1,177	1,172	5	(Z)	(NA)	NE	622	346	61	214	(NA)
AZ	7,400	7,286	23	(NA)	76	NV	3,289	1,751	(NA)	(NA)	(NA)
AR	6,173	4,660	47	(NA)	1,466	NH	2,808	1,633	155	10	1,010
CA	48,912	24,128	2,362	5,385	3,484	NJ	931	26	882	21	(NA)
CO	5,324	2,039	45	3,221	(Z)	NM	1,974	312	19	1,643	(NA)
CT	1,290	556	732	(NA)	2	NY	30,042	26,723	1,513	1,251	555
DE	163	(NA)	163	(NA)	(NA)	NC	4,956	3,034	120	(NA)	1,800
DC	(NA)	(NA)	(NA)	(NA)	(NA)	ND	2,959	1,253	13	1,693	(NA)
FL	4,509	206	2,334	(NA)	1,969	OH	1,010	386	190	15	418
GA	4,927	2,145	122	(NA)	2,660	OK	6,362	3,811	170	2,358	23
HI	861	84	302	240	(NA)	OR	37,228	33,805	131	2,575	717
ID	10,111	9,363	(NA)	207	455	PA	5,353	2,549	1,416	729	658
IL	3,174	139	697	2,337	1	RI	163	5	158	(NA)	(NA)
IN	948	437	273	238	(NA)	SC	2,939	1,123	120	(NA)	1,696
IA	5,070	819	167	4,084	(Z)	SD	3,140	2,993	2	145	(NA)
KS	1,770	11	(NA)	1,759	(NA)	TN	6,611	5,646	36	50	879
KY	2,377	1,917	109	(NA)	351	TX	18,679	1,039	438	16,225	976
LA	3,774	1,064	71	(NA)	2,639	UT	970	668	24	24	(NA)
ME	8,515	4,457	258	132	3,669	VT	1,918	1,493	(NA)	10	415
MD	2,587	1,974	415	(NA)	198	VA	3,709	1,011	782	(NA)	1,916
MA	2,411	1,156	1,129	4	123	WA	82,575	77,637	168	3,657	1,113
MI	3,956	1,364	740	141	1,710	WV	1,640	1,248	(NA)	392	(-Z)
MN	6,578	727	771	4,355	725	WI	3,370	1,616	492	487	775
MS	1,391	(NA)	5	(NA)	1,386	WY	1,798	835	(NA)	963	(NA)

NA Not available. Z Less than 500,000 million kilowatt-hours. [1] Includes types not shown separately. [2] Includes landfill gas and municipal solid waste biogenic (paper and paper board, wood, food, leather, textiles, and yard trimmings). Also includes agriculture by-products/crops, sludge waste, and other biomass solids, liquids, and gases. Excludes wood and wood waste. [3] Black liquor and wood/woodwaste solids and liquids.

Source: Energy Information Administration, "Renewable Energy Trends in Consumption and Electricity 2008," August 2010, <http://www.eia.doe.gov/fuelrenewable.html>.

Table 950. Gas Utility Industry—Summary: 1990 to 2008

[54,261 represents 54,261,000. Covers natural, manufactured, mixed, and liquid petroleum gas. Based on a questionnaire mailed to all privately and municipally owned gas utilities in the United States, except those with annual revenues less than $25,000]

Item	Unit	1990	1995	2000	2004	2005	2006	2007	2008
End users [1]	**1,000**	**54,261**	**58,728**	**61,262**	**63,297**	**64,395**	**65,020**	**65,389**	**65,487**
Residential	1,000	49,802	53,955	56,494	58,501	59,569	60,147	60,534	60,654
Commercial	1,000	4,246	4,530	4,610	4,641	4,678	4,734	4,718	4,703
Industrial and other	1,000	214	242	159	155	147	140	137	130
Sales [2]	**Tril. Btu** [3]	**9,842**	**9,221**	**9,232**	**8,766**	**8,848**	**8,222**	**8,565**	**8,594**
Residential	Tril. Btu	4,468	4,803	4,741	4,566	4,516	4,117	4,418	4,541
Percent of total	Percent	45	52	51	52	51	50	52	53
Commercial	Tril. Btu	2,192	2,281	2,077	2,075	2,056	1,861	1,943	2,009
Industrial	Tril. Btu	3,010	1,919	1,698	1,763	1,654	1,576	1,522	1,410
Other	Tril. Btu	171	218	715	363	622	668	682	635
Revenues [2]	**Mil. dol.**	**45,153**	**46,436**	**59,243**	**79,929**	**96,909**	**91,928**	**92,131**	**102,641**
Residential	Mil. dol.	25,000	28,742	35,828	47,275	55,680	53,961	55,028	60,195
Percent of total	Percent	55	62	60	59	57	59	60	59
Commercial	Mil. dol.	10,604	11,573	13,339	18,689	22,653	21,557	21,248	23,592
Industrial	Mil. dol.	8,996	5,571	7,432	11,230	13,751	12,006	11,323	13,205
Other	Mil. dol.	553	549	2,645	2,735	4,825	4,405	4,533	5,649
Prices per mil. Btu [3]	**Dollars**	**4.59**	**5.05**	**6.42**	**9.13**	**10.95**	**11.18**	**10.76**	**11.94**
Residential	Dollars	5.60	6.00	7.56	10.37	12.33	13.11	12.46	13.26
Commercial	Dollars	4.84	5.07	6.42	9.01	11.02	11.58	10.93	11.75
Industrial	Dollars	2.99	2.98	4.38	6.37	8.31	7.62	7.44	9.37
Gas mains mileage	**1,000**	**1,189**	**1,278**	**1,369**	**1,462**	**1,438**	**1,534**	**1,520**	**1,525**
Field and gathering	1,000	32	31	27	24	23	20	19	20
Transmission	1,000	292	297	297	299	297	300	300	299
Distribution	1,000	865	950	1,046	1,140	1,118	1,214	1,201	1,206
Construction expenditures [4]	**Mil. dol.**	**7,899**	**10,760**	**8,624**	**16,567**	**10,089**	**10,218**	**10,987**	**14,090**
Transmission	Mil. dol.	2,886	3,380	1,590	3,205	3,368	3,316	4,327	6,388
Distribution	Mil. dol.	3,714	5,394	5,437	11,636	5,129	5,165	4,851	5,427
Production and storage	Mil. dol.	309	367	138	181	179	240	107	174
General	Mil. dol.	770	1,441	1,273	1,271	1,070	1,119	1,146	1,228
Underground storage	Mil. dol.	219	177	185	274	343	379	556	873

[1] Annual average. [2] Excludes sales for resale. [3] For definition of Btu, see text, this section. [4] Includes general.
Source: American Gas Association, Arlington, VA, *Gas Facts*, annual (copyright).

Table 951. Gas Utility Industry—Customers, Sales, and Revenues by State: 2008

[65,487 represents 65,487,000. See headnote, Table 950. For definition of Btu, see text, this section]

State	Customers [1] (1,000) Total	Customers [1] (1,000) Residential	Sales [2] (tril. Btu) Total	Sales [2] (tril. Btu) Residential	Revenues [2] (mil. dol.) Total	Revenues [2] (mil. dol.) Residential	State	Customers [1] (1,000) Total	Customers [1] (1,000) Residential	Sales [2] (tril. Btu) Total	Sales [2] (tril. Btu) Residential	Revenues [2] (mil. dol.) Total	Revenues [2] (mil. dol.) Residential
U.S.	**65,487**	**60,654**	**8,594**	**4,541**	**102,641**	**60,195**							
							MO	1,495	1,352	180	118	2,241	1,524
AL	860	792	100	39	1,417	691	MT	286	253	34	22	379	247
AK	131	119	65	22	446	187	NE	479	438	69	38	690	410
AZ	1,186	1,128	85	40	1,210	677	NV	799	758	91	40	1,000	516
AR	626	557	65	37	808	503	NH	113	98	14	7	224	118
CA	10,936	10,481	703	501	8,449	6,198	NJ	2,757	2,548	328	223	4,593	3,272
CO	1,752	1,607	209	138	1,916	1,309	NM	604	557	53	35	600	416
CT	539	487	86	43	1,291	749	NY	4,026	3,740	477	328	7,194	5,337
DE	160	148	18	10	261	159	NC	1,211	1,095	126	66	1,854	1,059
DC	137	130	14	10	220	166	ND	137	120	33	12	300	119
FL	706	665	40	16	661	322	OH	1,951	1,810	228	166	3,163	2,348
GA	364	330	53	18	674	266	OK	1,016	924	106	68	1,183	816
HI	28	26	3	1	103	22	OR	752	674	92	46	1,099	626
ID	374	336	43	28	454	305	PA	2,663	2,450	314	217	4,760	3,399
IL	3,857	3,600	548	422	6,334	4,940	RI	246	224	26	18	421	299
IN	1,733	1,589	237	150	2,763	1,835	SC	619	561	86	28	1,144	456
IA	971	873	133	78	1,440	898	SD	188	166	29	14	296	154
KS	936	853	105	73	1,267	914	TN	1,212	1,082	160	71	2,024	982
KY	810	727	105	55	1,335	732	TX	4,529	4,204	1,469	199	14,091	2,649
LA	944	886	280	38	2,859	577	UT	855	795	106	68	879	593
ME	27	20	4	1	64	19	VT	41	36	8	3	115	56
MD	998	941	93	70	1,404	1,079	VA	1,147	1,060	127	75	1,840	1,175
MA	1,513	1,389	168	116	2,700	1,930	WA	1,148	1,047	151	87	1,810	1,104
MI	3,253	3,012	463	331	5,242	3,831	WV	381	347	48	28	645	399
MN	1,545	1,413	287	144	2,965	1,574	WI	1,813	1,647	255	145	2,948	1,800
MS	499	443	57	25	694	333	WY	131	117	19	11	174	104

[1] Averages for the year. [2] Excludes sales for resale.
Source: American Gas Association, Arlington, VA, *Gas Facts*, annual (copyright).

Table 952. Privately Owned Gas Utility Industry—Balance Sheet and Income Account: 1990 to 2008

[In millions of dollars (121,686 represents $121,686,000,000). The gas utility industry consists of pipeline and distribution companies. Excludes operations of companies distributing gas in bottles or tanks]

Item	1990	1995	2000	2003	2004	2005	2006	2007	2008
COMPOSITE BALANCE SHEET									
Assets, total	**121,686**	**141,965**	**165,709**	**174,756**	**168,306**	**196,215**	**203,135**	**205,345**	**230,002**
Total utility plant	112,863	143,636	162,206	188,807	180,884	207,976	212,500	213,516	237,140
Depreciation and amortization	*49,483*	*62,723*	*69,366*	*76,642*	*79,889*	*91,794*	*91,804*	*86,244*	*95,211*
Utility plant (net)	63,380	80,912	92,839	112,165	100,996	116,183	120,696	127,272	141,929
Investment and fund accounts	23,872	26,489	10,846	13,430	12,716	16,331	17,309	13,677	11,725
Current and accrued assets	23,268	18,564	35,691	22,905	22,107	32,325	26,955	28,871	31,960
Deferred debits [1]	9,576	13,923	24,279	24,663	31,033	29,574	36,278	34,608	42,922
Liabilities, total	**121,686**	**141,965**	**165,709**	**174,756**	**168,709**	**196,215**	**203,135**	**205,345**	**230,002**
Capitalization, total	74,958	90,581	96,079	112,089	105,579	120,949	126,842	127,609	136,108
Capital stock	43,810	54,402	47,051	57,605	54,252	62,470	66,153	71,038	74,610
Long-term debts	31,148	35,548	48,267	54,179	51,327	58,264	60,632	56,538	61,498
Current and accrued liabilities	29,550	28,272	42,312	28,599	25,515	34,936	32,417	34,017	37,450
Deferred income taxes [2]	11,360	14,393	17,157	23,888	23,944	24,937	27,454	27,009	27,637
Other liabilities and credits	5,818	8,715	10,161	10,179	13,671	15,393	16,422	16,709	28,807
COMPOSITE INCOME ACCOUNT									
Operating revenues, total	**66,027**	**58,390**	**72,042**	**75,527**	**80,194**	**102,018**	**97,156**	**97,195**	**109,547**
Minus: Operating expenses [3]	*60,137*	*50,760*	*64,988*	*66,677*	*71,719*	*89,385*	*87,013*	*85,050*	*97,665*
Operation and maintenance	51,627	37,966	54,602	55,036	59,920	77,673	73,459	71,011	82,386
Federal, state, and local taxes	4,957	6,182	6,163	6,581	6,472	7,513	7,350	7,803	8,477
Equals: Operating income	5,890	7,630	7,053	8,852	8,475	12,632	10,144	12,146	11,882
Utility operating income	6,077	7,848	7,166	9,198	8,619	12,812	10,185	12,472	12,293
Income before interest charges	8,081	9,484	7,589	10,053	9,609	13,972	11,586	14,329	13,313
Net income	4,410	5,139	4,245	6,198	5,942	9,777	6,931	9,758	9,067
Dividends	3,191	4,037	3,239	3,765	2,111	2,419	2,304	2,253	2,427

[1] Includes capital stock discount and expense and reacquired securities. [2] Includes reserves for deferred income taxes. [3] Includes expenses not shown separately.

Source: American Gas Association, Arlington, VA, *Gas Facts*, annual (copyright).

Table 953. Sewage Treatment Facilities: 2007

[Based on the North American Industry Classification System (NAICS), 2002; see text, Section 15]

State	Sewage treatment facilities (NAICS 22132)		State	Sewage treatment facilities (NAICS 22132)	
	Number of establishments	Paid employees		Number of establishments	Paid employees
U.S.	**624**	**5,829**	MO	18	(2)
AL	9	77	MT	(NA)	(NA)
AK	1	(1)	NE	2	(1)
AZ	12	(2)	NV	3	11
AR	4	23	NH	2	(1)
CA	26	(3)	NJ	11	114
CO	8	27	NM	1	(1)
CT	7	(2)	NY	36	293
DE	1	(1)	NC	22	(2)
DC	(NA)	(NA)	ND	(NA)	(NA)
FL	63	840	OH	16	85
GA	10	(4)	OK	9	53
HI	13	(2)	OR	6	(2)
ID	7	(2)	PA	40	346
IL	38	311	RI	2	(2)
IN	34	166	SC	11	51
IA	5	(2)	SD	2	(1)
KS	3	(2)	TN	10	92
KY	9	(4)	TX	48	1,235
LA	20	259	UT	1	(1)
ME	2	(1)	VT	2	(1)
MD	5	(1)	VA	8	82
MA	15	170	WA	9	77
MI	24	(2)	WV	14	73
MN	7	(2)	WI	6	(1)
MS	19	114	WY	3	(1)

NA Not available. [1] 0–19 employees. [2] 20–99 employees. [3] 250–499 employees. [4] 100–249 employees.

Source: U.S. Census Bureau, "County Business Patterns," July 2009, <http://www.census.gov/econ/cbp/index.html>.

Table 954. Public Drinking Water Systems by Size of Community Served and Source of Water: 2009

[As of September. Covers systems that provide water for human consumption through pipes and other constructed conveyances to at least 15 service connections or serve an average of at least 25 persons for at least 60 days a year. Based on reported data in the Safe Drinking Water Information System maintained by the Environmental Protection Agency]

Type of system	Total [1]	Size of community served					Water source	
		500 or fewer persons	501 to 3,300 persons	3,301 to 10,000 persons	10,001 to 100,000 persons	100,001 persons or more	Ground water	Surface water
Total systems	**153,530**	**125,126**	**19,126**	**5,090**	**3,775**	**413**	**139,205**	**14,297**
COMMUNITY WATER SYSTEMS [2]								
Number of systems	51,651	28,804	13,820	4,871	3,746	410	40,025	11,617
Percent of systems	100	56	27	9	7	1	78	22
Population served (1,000)	294,340	4,821	19,807	28,403	106,857	134,453	88,032	206,264
Percent of population	100	2	7	10	36	46	30	70
NONTRANSIENT NONCOMMUNITY WATER SYSTEM [3]								
Number of systems	18,395	15,619	2,625	132	18	1	17,688	702
Percent of systems	100	85	14	1	–	–	96	4
Population served (1,000)	6,243	2,195	2,704	700	441	203	5,416	820
Percent of population	100	35	43	11	7	3	87	13
TRANSIENT NONCOMMUNITY WATER SYSTEM [4]								
Number of systems	83,484	80,703	2,681	87	11	2	81,492	1,978
Percent of systems	100	97	3	–	–	–	98	2
Population served (1,000)	13,303	7,147	2,599	472	361	2,725	10,754	2,548
Percent of population	100	54	20	4	3	20	81	19

– Represents zero. [1] Includes a small number of systems for which the water source (ground vs. surface) is unknown. [2] A public water system that supplies water to the same population year-round. [3] A public water system that regularly supplies water to at least 25 of the same people at least 6 months per year, but not year-round. Some examples are schools, factories, and office buildings which have their own water systems. [4] A public water system that provides water in a place such as a gas station or campground where people do not remain for long periods of time and is open at least 60 day per year.

Source: U.S. Environmental Protection Agency, *Factoids: Drinking Water and Ground Water Statistics for 2009*, November 2009. See also <http://water.epa.gov/scitech/datait/databases/drink/sdwisfed/howtoaccessdata.cfm>.

Table 955. Public Drinking Water Systems—Number and Population Served by State: 2009

[306,898 represents 306,898,000. See headnote, Table 954]

State	Number of systems	Population served (1,000)				State	Number of systems	Population served (1,000)			
		Total	Community [1]	Nontransient, noncommunity [2]	Transient, noncommunity [3]			Total	Community [1]	Nontransient, noncommunity [2]	Transient, noncommunity [3]
U.S. [4]	**151,647**	**306,898**	**287,735**	**5,886**	**13,277**	MO	2,785	5,369	5,176	77	116
AL	619	5,496	5,473	16	7	MT	2,097	972	717	79	176
AK	1,577	755	585	62	108	NE	1,324	1,585	1,479	52	54
AZ	1,592	6,358	6,115	129	113	NV	562	2,594	2,530	42	23
AR	1,095	2,677	2,647	9	21	NH	2,421	1,270	855	97	319
CA	7,134	41,193	39,378	377	1,439	NJ	3,840	9,557	8,786	354	417
CO	2,022	5,589	5,264	74	251	NM	1,239	1,834	1,705	52	77
CT	2,653	2,822	2,650	114	58	NY	9,294	21,112	17,954	313	2,845
DE	489	968	889	26	53	NC	6,337	7,810	7,366	125	318
DC	6	607	607	(Z)	–	ND	508	586	568	4	14
FL	5,721	19,484	18,978	251	255	OH	5,040	11,004	10,351	228	424
GA	2,483	8,427	8,279	66	82	OK	1,571	3,571	3,520	21	30
HI	130	1,453	1,441	11	(Z)	OR	2,630	3,483	3,199	72	212
ID	1,964	1,250	1,091	52	106	PA	9,409	12,058	10,758	521	779
IL	5,731	12,538	12,050	129	359	RI	443	1,053	978	26	49
IN	4,256	5,283	4,711	195	378	SC	1,487	3,903	3,819	42	41
IA	1,950	2,814	2,685	47	81	SD	656	718	687	8	23
KS	1,033	2,598	2,573	21	4	TN	884	6,178	6,095	26	57
KY	479	4,469	4,451	12	6	TX	6,738	25,392	24,631	511	250
LA	1,450	5,004	4,888	56	60	UT	1,023	2,792	2,687	30	76
ME	1,900	914	662	68	184	VT	1,366	592	452	42	98
MD	3,527	5,523	5,146	161	216	VA	2,879	7,033	6,554	308	171
MA	1,729	9,527	9,314	73	139	WA	4,148	6,710	6,172	143	395
MI	11,554	8,972	7,615	337	1,020	WV	1,076	1,570	1,498	39	33
MN	7,262	4,806	4,191	78	536	WI	11,482	4,914	3,988	209	717
MS	1,277	3,169	3,083	75	10	WY	775	543	445	23	75

– Represents zero. Z Less than 500. [1] A public water system that supplies water to the same population year-round. [2] A public water system that regularly supplies water to at least 25 of the same people at least 6 months per year, but not year-round. Some examples are schools, factories, and office buildings which have their own water systems. [3] A public water system that provides water in a place such as a gas station or campground where people do not remain for long periods of time and is open at least 60 days per year. [4] U.S. total does not equal sum of states due to incomplete reporting of a small number of systems.

Source: U.S. Environmental Protection Agency, *Factoids: Drinking Water and Ground Water Statistics for 2009*, November 2009. See also <http://water.epa.gov/scitech/datait/databases/drink/sdwisfed/howtoaccessdata.cfm>.

This section presents data on the construction industry and on various indicators of its activity and costs; on housing units and their characteristics and occupants; and on the characteristics and vacancy rates for commercial buildings. This edition contains data from the 2005 American Housing Survey.

The principal source of these data is the U.S. Census Bureau, which issues a variety of current publications, as well as data from the decennial census. Current construction statistics compiled by the Census Bureau appear in its *New Residential Construction* and *New Residential Sales* press releases and Web site at <http://www.census.gov/const/www/>. Statistics on expenditures by owners of residential properties are issued quarterly and annually in *Expenditures for Residential Improvements and Repairs. Value of New Construction Put in Place* presents data on all types of construction. Reports of the censuses of construction industries (see below) are also issued on various topics.

Other Census Bureau publications include the *Current Housing Reports* series, which comprise the quarterly *Housing Vacancies*, the quarterly *Market Absorption of Apartments*, the biennial *American Housing Survey* (formerly *Annual Housing Survey*), and reports of the censuses of housing and of construction industries.

Other sources include the monthly *Dodge Construction Potentials* of McGraw-Hill Construction, New York, NY, which present national and state data on construction contracts; the National Association of Home Builders with state-level data on housing starts; the NATIONAL ASSOCIATION OF REALTORS®, which presents data on existing home sales; the Bureau of Economic Analysis, which presents data on residential capital and gross housing product; and the U.S. Energy Information Administration, which provides data on commercial buildings through its periodic sample surveys.

Censuses and surveys—Censuses of the construction industry were first conducted by the Census Bureau for 1929, 1935, and 1939; beginning in 1967, a census has been taken every 5 years (through 2002, for years ending in "2" and "7"). The latest reports are part of the 2002 Economic Census. See text, Section 15, Business Enterprise.

The construction sector of the economic census, covers all employer establishments primarily engaged in (1) building construction by general contractors or operative builders; (2) heavy (nonbuilding) construction by general contractors; and (3) construction by special trade contractors. This sector includes construction management and land subdividers and developers. The 2002 census was conducted in accordance with the 2002 North American Industrial Classification System (NAICS). See text, Section 15, Business Enterprise.

From 1850 through 1930, the Census Bureau collected some housing data as part of its censuses of population and agriculture. Beginning in 1940, separate censuses of housing have been taken at 10-year intervals. For the 1970 and 1980 censuses, data on year-round housing units were collected and issued on occupancy and structural characteristics, plumbing facilities, value, and rent; for 1990, such characteristics were presented for all housing units.

The American Housing Survey (*Current Housing Reports* Series H-150 and H-170), which began in 1973, provided an annual and ongoing series of data on selected housing and demographic characteristics until 1983. In 1984, the name of the survey was changed from the Annual Housing Survey. Currently, national data are collected every other year, and data for selected metropolitan areas are collected on a rotating basis. All samples represent a cross section of the housing stock in their respective areas. Estimates are subject to both sampling and nonsampling errors;

U.S. Census Bureau, Statistical Abstract of the United States: 2011

caution should therefore be used in making comparisons between years.

Data on residential mortgages were collected continuously from 1890 to 1970, except 1930, as part of the decennial census by the Census Bureau. Since 1973, mortgage status data, limited to single family homes on less than 10 acres with no business on the property, have been presented in the American Housing Survey. Data on mortgage activity are covered in Section 25, Banking and Finance.

Housing units—In general, a housing unit is a house, an apartment, a group of rooms or a single room occupied or intended for occupancy as separate living quarters; that is, the occupants live separately from any other individual in the building, and there is direct access from the outside or through a common hall. Transient accommodations, barracks for workers, and institutional-type quarters are not counted as housing units.

Statistical reliability—For a discussion of statistical collection and estimation, sampling procedures, and measures of statistical reliability applicable to Census Bureau data, see Appendix III.

Table 956. Construction—Establishments, Employees, and Payroll by Kind of Business (NAICS Basis): 2006 and 2007

[7,339 represents 7,339,000. Covers establishments with payroll. Excludes most government employees, railroad employees, and self-employed persons. Kind-of-business classification based on North American Industry Classification System (NAICS), 2002. For statement on methodology, see Appendix III]

Industry	2002 NAICS code [1]	Establishments		Paid employees [2] (1,000)		Annual payroll (mil. dol.)	
		2006	2007	2006	2007	2006	2007
Construction	**23**	**802,349**	**811,452**	**7,339**	**7,268**	**322,004**	**336,131**
Construction of buildings.....................	236	243,614	244,862	1,708	1,672	82,560	83,317
Residential building construction..............	2361	198,912	198,530	966	905	42,481	39,060
New single-family housing construction (except operative builders)..................	236115	62,108	61,613	305	283	12,546	11,889
Nonresidential building construction	2362	44,702	46,332	742	767	40,079	44,257
Industrial building construction	23621	3,264	3,963	90	97	4,310	5,057
Commercial and institutional building construction...........................	23622	41,438	42,369	652	670	35,769	39,200
Heavy and civil engineering construction	237	51,122	51,421	989	1,016	52,681	56,607
Utility system construction...................	2371	21,232	21,448	497	525	25,067	28,284
Land subdivision	2372	12,469	12,835	77	77	4,098	3,980
Highway, street, and bridge construction........	2373	11,860	11,746	325	323	18,542	19,113
Other heavy and civil engineering construction...	2379	5,561	5,392	90	92	4,974	5,230
Specialty trade contractors	238	507,613	515,169	4,641	4,579	186,763	196,207
Foundation, structure, and building exterior contractors.............................	2381	117,456	115,764	1,168	1,103	41,956	42,369
Poured concrete foundation and structures contractors	23811	26,951	26,342	319	302	12,232	12,301
Structural steel and precast concrete contractors...........................	23812	3,608	3,697	72	79	3,237	3,844
Framing contractors.......................	23813	18,632	17,358	185	148	5,276	4,508
Masonry contractors	23814	27,430	27,122	249	235	8,483	8,426
Glass and glazing contractors...............	23815	5,469	5,584	53	55	2,211	2,472
Roofing contractors.......................	23816	19,660	19,512	195	190	7,127	7,228
Siding contractors	23817	10,543	10,429	52	50	1,679	1,652
Other foundation, structure, and building exterior contractors......................	23819	5,163	5,720	43	45	1,711	1,938
Building equipment contractors...............	2382	182,368	187,856	1,940	1,962	86,667	93,655
Electrical contractors......................	23821	77,558	80,172	815	825	36,296	39,278
Plumbing, heating, and air-conditioning contractors...........................	23822	98,147	100,806	1,001	1,013	43,763	47,154
Other building equipment contractors	23829	6,663	6,878	124	124	6,608	7,223
Building finishing contractors.................	2383	133,343	134,306	975	944	34,454	35,164
Drywall and insulation contractors...........	23831	22,237	22,458	331	320	12,300	12,655
Painting and wall covering contractors	23832	41,477	41,457	243	234	7,791	7,973
Flooring contractors.......................	23833	16,630	16,927	87	85	3,294	3,230
Tile and terrazzo contractors................	23834	11,572	11,965	72	71	2,503	2,517
Finish carpentry contractors	23835	34,738	34,263	174	164	6,009	5,908
Other building finishing contractors...........	23839	6,689	7,236	68	70	2,556	2,881
Other specialty trade contractors..............	2389	74,446	77,243	558	570	23,685	25,019
Site preparation contractors	23891	39,265	41,517	322	331	14,208	14,940
All other specialty trade contractors	23899	35,181	35,726	235	239	9,477	10,079

[1] North American Industry Classification System code, 2002; see text, Section 15. [2] Employees on the payroll for the pay period including March 12.

Source: U.S. Census Bureau, "County Business Patterns," July 2009, <http://www.census.gov/econ/cbp>.

Table 957. Construction Materials—Producer Price Indexes: 1990 to 2009

[1982 = 100, except as noted. Data for 2009 are preliminary. For discussion of producer price indexes, see text, Section 14. This index, more formally known as the special commodity grouping index for construction materials, covers materials incorporated as integral part of a building or normally installed during construction and not readily removable. Excludes consumer durables such as kitchen ranges, refrigerators, etc. This index is not the same as the stage-of-processing index of intermediate materials and components for construction]

Commodity	1990	2000	2003	2004	2005	2006	2007	2008	2009
Construction materials	**119.6**	**144.1**	**147.1**	**161.5**	**169.6**	**180.2**	**183.2**	**196.4**	**189.2**
Interior solvent-based paint	133.0	191.1	198.0	(NA)	(NA)	(NA)	(NA)	(NA)	(NA)
Architectural coatings	132.7	168.7	180.6	187.4	203.3	220.2	230.5	249.0	269.7
Construction products from plastics	117.2	135.8	138.6	144.6	158.8	181.8	179.2	185.6	186.2
Douglas fir, dressed	138.4	185.2	176.7	(NA)	(NA)	(NA)	(NA)	(NA)	(NA)
Southern pine, dressed	111.2	161.0	145.4	(NA)	(NA)	(NA)	(NA)	(NA)	(NA)
Softwood lumber	123.8	178.6	170.8	209.8	203.6	189.4	170.5	156.3	141.3
Millwork	130.4	176.4	181.8	191.9	197.2	201.8	201.4	204.8	205.6
Softwood plywood	119.6	173.3	195.9	250.9	223.5	190.5	197.8	193.1	172.2
Hardwood plywood and related products	102.7	130.2	129.0	134.4	138.1	(NA)	(NA)	(NA)	(NA)
Hardwood veneer and plywood [1]	(NA)	(NA)	(NA)	(NA)	(NA)	101.4	102.4	103.8	103.2
Softwood plywood veneer, excluding reinforced/backed	142.3	182.2	184.1	209.5	206.2	(NA)	(NA)	(NA)	(NA)
Building paper and building board mill products	112.2	138.8	159.9	192.4	184.9	173.0	155.2	163.9	156.6
Steel pipe and tubes [2]	102.6	106.6	113.3	166.3	193.3	200.9	202.4	251.7	215.6
Builders' hardware	133.0	163.8	170.3	172.9	179.2	187.8	198.1	215.1	217.2
Plumbing fixtures and brass fittings	144.3	180.4	183.4	188.3	197.6	207.2	220.6	226.7	228.9
Heating equipment	131.6	155.6	163.2	169.5	179.9	185.7	195.5	208.8	218.9
Metal doors, sash, and trim	131.4	165.1	169.9	175.8	184.9	192.9	197.3	205.6	209.1
Siding, aluminum [3]	(NA)	142.2	152.6	(NA)	(NA)	(NA)	(NA)	(NA)	(NA)
Sheet metal products	129.2	144.0	146.6	162.6	169.4	176.1	181.2	192.5	186.7
Outdoor lighting equipment, including parts [4]	113.0	124.7	126.9	129.4	131.8	137.7	140.1	145.3	146.5
Commercial fluorescent fixtures [5]	113.0	117.7	115.2	113.6	(NA)	(NA)	(NA)	(NA)	(NA)
Commercial and industrial lighting fixtures	127.5	140.3	141.9	142.3	147.0	151.9	158.3	164.9	167.9
Architectural and ornamental metalwork [6]	118.7	139.8	147.2	172.5	185.4	191.5	200.1	227.0	232.5
Fabricated ferrous wire products [2]	114.6	130.0	131.3	149.3	157.1	162.6	166.7	200.7	200.1
Elevators, escalators, and other lifts	110.1	118.7	118.7	120.5	123.5	126.0	129.3	134.7	134.9
Stamped metal switch and receptacle box	158.0	183.0	196.1	205.2	(NA)	(NA)	(NA)	(NA)	(NA)
Electrical conduit and conduit fittings [7]	(NA)	(NA)	(NA)	(NA)	106.5	116.6	112.1	123.4	114.1
Other noncurrent-carrying wiring devices [7]	(NA)	(NA)	(NA)	(NA)	102.3	108.0	114.3	123.2	126.4
Concrete ingredients and related products	115.3	155.6	164.8	170.4	185.3	204.9	220.2	229.7	235.8
Concrete products	113.5	147.8	153.6	161.2	177.2	195.1	203.5	210.6	214.1
Clay construction products excluding refractories	129.9	152.8	154.2	156.6	165.4	176.8	178.7	180.1	179.4
Prep asphalt and tar roofing and siding products	95.8	100.0	110.6	111.3	125.0	137.0	139.7	176.7	217.3
Gypsum products	105.2	201.4	171.5	198.8	229.6	274.9	233.0	213.2	213.8
Insulation materials	108.4	128.6	128.8	137.2	142.2	149.9	145.3	141.7	143.5
Paving mixtures and blocks	101.2	130.4	142.6	144.9	156.9	200.5	218.9	272.4	268.9

NA Not available. [1] December 2005 = 100. [2] June 1982 = 100. [3] December 1982 = 100. [4] June 1985 = 100. [5] Recessed nonair. [6] December 1983 = 100. [7] December 2004 = 100.

Source: U.S. Bureau of Labor Statistics, *Producer Price Indexes*, monthly and annual. See also <http://www.bls.gov/ppi/home.htm>.

Table 958. Value of New Construction Put in Place: 1980 to 2009

[In millions of dollars (273,936 represents $273,936,000,000). Represents value of construction put in place during year; differs from building permit and construction contract data in timing and coverage. Includes installed cost of normal building service equipment and selected types of industrial production equipment (largely site fabricated). Excludes cost of shipbuilding, land, and most types of machinery and equipment. For methodology, see Appendix III. For details, see Tables 959 and 960]

Year	Total	Private			Public		
		Total	Residential buildings	Non-residential	Total	Federal	State and local
1980	273,936	210,290	100,381	109,909	63,646	9,642	54,004
1990	476,778	369,300	191,103	178,197	107,478	12,099	95,379
1992	463,661	347,814	199,393	148,421	115,847	14,376	101,471
1993	502,435	375,073	225,067	150,006	127,362	14,424	112,938
1994	549,420	418,999	258,561	160,438	130,421	14,440	115,981
1995	567,896	427,885	247,351	180,534	140,011	15,751	124,260
1996	623,313	476,638	281,115	195,523	146,675	15,325	131,350
1997	656,171	502,734	289,014	213,720	153,437	14,087	139,350
1998	706,779	552,001	314,607	237,394	154,778	14,318	140,460
1999	768,811	599,729	350,562	249,167	169,082	14,025	155,057
2000	831,075	649,750	374,457	275,293	181,325	14,166	167,157
2001	864,159	662,247	388,324	273,922	201,912	15,081	186,830
2002	847,873	634,435	396,696	237,739	213,438	16,578	196,860
2003	891,497	675,370	446,035	229,335	216,127	17,913	198,214
2004	991,561	771,378	532,900	238,478	220,183	18,342	201,841
2005	1,102,703	868,543	611,899	256,644	234,160	17,300	216,860
2006	1,167,554	912,169	613,731	298,438	255,385	17,555	237,831
2007	1,150,688	861,615	493,246	368,369	289,073	20,580	268,494
2008	1,072,132	766,170	350,078	416,092	305,962	23,840	282,122
2009	935,622	619,277	251,364	367,913	316,345	27,803	288,542

Source: U.S. Census Bureau, "Construction Spending," <http://www.census.gov/const/www/c30index.html>.

Table 959. Value of Private Construction Put in Place: 2000 to 2009

[In millions of dollars (621,431 represents $621,431,000,000). Represents value of construction put in place during year; differs from building permit and construction contract data in timing and coverage. See Appendix III and Tables 958 and 960]

Type of construction	2000	2002	2003	2004	2005	2006	2007	2008	2009
Total construction [1]	**621,431**	**634,435**	**675,370**	**771,378**	**868,543**	**912,169**	**861,615**	**766,170**	**619,277**
Residential	346,138	396,696	446,035	532,900	611,899	613,731	493,246	350,078	251,364
New single family	236,788	265,889	310,575	377,557	433,510	415,997	305,184	185,776	106,288
New multifamily	28,259	32,952	35,116	39,944	47,297	52,803	48,959	44,158	29,264
Improvements [2]	81,091	97,855	100,344	115,399	131,092	144,931	139,103	120,144	115,813
Nonresidential	275,293	237,739	229,335	238,478	256,644	298,438	368,369	416,092	367,913
Lodging	16,304	10,467	9,930	11,982	12,666	17,624	27,481	35,379	25,033
Office [1]	52,407	35,296	30,579	32,879	37,276	45,680	53,815	57,084	40,286
General	49,637	32,356	27,380	28,679	32,962	41,085	48,945	51,939	36,265
Financial	2,689	2,857	3,174	4,186	4,285	4,542	4,785	4,819	3,806
Commercial [1]	64,055	59,008	57,505	63,195	66,584	73,368	85,858	81,495	53,654
Automotive [1]	5,967	5,807	5,039	5,235	5,614	5,528	6,281	5,387	4,608
Sales	1,629	2,235	2,099	2,443	2,834	2,285	2,571	2,279	1,658
Service/parts	3,009	2,308	1,866	1,978	1,805	2,184	2,356	1,846	1,979
Parking	1,330	1,265	1,074	814	975	1,059	1,354	1,262	971
Food/beverage [1]	8,786	7,914	8,369	8,232	7,795	7,442	8,046	8,168	5,174
Food	4,792	4,207	4,234	3,590	3,128	2,752	2,779	3,149	2,132
Dining/drinking	2,935	2,916	3,321	3,937	4,078	3,780	3,957	4,071	2,386
Fast food	1,058	792	813	705	590	910	1,310	948	655
Multiretail [1]	14,911	15,581	15,400	18,828	22,750	29,218	34,751	32,227	20,782
General merchandise	5,100	6,009	5,341	6,416	6,740	5,699	7,572	4,522	4,532
Shopping center	6,803	6,605	6,867	9,256	12,462	18,417	22,197	22,958	12,919
Shopping mall	2,523	2,108	2,231	2,138	2,631	3,616	4,000	3,990	2,459
Other commercial [1]	13,537	12,083	11,249	13,341	11,744	10,874	13,580	12,475	6,789
Drug store	1,682	1,644	1,790	1,427	1,315	1,238	1,500	1,940	1,991
Building supply store	2,592	2,471	2,268	2,521	2,416	2,594	3,507	2,649	1,284
Other stores	8,136	7,145	6,214	8,229	7,075	6,135	7,744	6,806	2,652
Warehouse	14,822	11,908	12,345	12,074	12,827	14,491	16,909	16,838	10,169
General commercial	13,511	10,934	11,004	10,830	11,468	13,493	15,641	15,661	9,165
Farm	5,988	5,611	5,103	5,485	5,854	5,817	6,292	6,401	6,132
Health care	19,455	22,438	24,217	26,272	28,495	32,016	35,588	39,101	36,760
Hospital	10,183	13,925	15,234	16,147	18,250	21,914	24,532	26,421	26,548
Medical building	5,066	4,924	6,068	7,615	8,031	7,165	7,981	8,995	7,032
Special care	4,206	3,538	2,915	2,510	2,213	2,937	3,074	3,684	3,180
Educational [1]	11,683	13,109	13,424	12,701	12,788	13,839	16,691	18,585	16,619
Preschool	770	593	711	674	516	487	704	742	739
Primary/secondary	2,948	3,605	3,204	3,202	2,718	3,240	3,968	3,849	3,204
Higher education [1]	6,333	6,875	7,259	6,496	6,946	7,611	9,424	11,568	10,696
Instructional	3,058	3,619	3,701	3,200	3,556	3,501	4,219	5,507	6,201
Dormitory	1,356	1,528	1,761	1,669	1,537	2,065	2,900	3,747	2,510
Sports/recreation	645	772	677	739	821	858	771	852	848
Other educational	1,318	1,651	1,785	1,998	2,294	2,090	2,167	2,014	1,655
Gallery/museum	920	1,312	1,371	1,335	1,745	1,697	1,939	1,722	1,368
Religious	8,030	8,335	8,559	8,153	7,715	7,740	7,522	7,097	6,287
House of worship	5,656	6,021	6,238	6,015	5,992	6,262	6,270	5,808	5,094
Other religious	2,347	2,312	2,322	2,138	1,723	1,478	1,252	1,289	1,194
Auxiliary building	1,280	1,358	1,296	1,258	1,251	1,219	1,099	1,096	1,060
Public safety	423	217	185	289	408	419	595	650	463
Amusement and recreation [1]	8,768	7,478	7,781	8,432	7,507	9,326	10,193	10,316	7,718
Theme/amusement park	747	230	270	198	200	417	522	275	268
Sports	1,068	1,427	1,306	900	807	959	1,902	2,302	1,695
Fitness	1,152	1,286	1,262	1,141	1,425	2,028	1,945	2,058	1,772
Performance/meeting center	732	900	844	1,054	1,072	737	823	1,097	784
Social center	2,368	2,285	1,996	2,594	1,626	1,538	1,602	1,519	959
Movie theater/studio	1,461	568	855	1,218	1,248	1,309	1,159	572	333
Transportation [1]	6,879	6,773	6,568	6,841	7,124	8,654	9,009	9,896	9,066
Air	1,804	1,281	1,012	869	748	719	732	745	503
Land	4,907	5,325	5,462	5,800	6,214	7,764	8,008	9,009	8,484
Railroad	4,263	4,584	4,851	5,392	5,816	7,313	7,423	8,367	8,019
Communication	18,799	18,384	14,456	15,468	18,846	22,187	27,488	25,496	20,229
Power [1]	29,344	32,608	33,619	27,360	26,304	31,164	47,365	68,702	76,699
Electricity	23,374	24,998	25,592	20,431	19,192	22,804	33,627	50,392	52,789
Gas	4,891	6,080	6,358	5,096	5,239	5,528	7,876	9,396	9,795
Oil	1,003	1,193	1,068	1,579	1,293	1,831	4,779	5,628	6,319
Sewage and waste disposal	508	246	278	331	240	305	408	548	458
Water supply	714	397	393	405	326	477	516	696	345
Manufacturing	37,583	22,744	21,434	23,667	29,886	35,086	45,303	60,784	74,135
Food/beverage/tobacco	3,985	2,817	2,695	3,157	4,677	4,707	4,270	5,033	3,908
Textile/apparel/leather & allied	413	284	218	188	415	144	40	268	343
Wood	483	477	376	485	982	1,465	791	355	573
Paper	479	584	818	548	467	559	506	549	629
Print/publishing	848	666	630	654	777	727	265	295	204
Petroleum/coal	1,255	887	717	1,204	771	1,799	5,719	17,564	31,807
Chemical	3,798	5,625	5,368	5,507	6,588	9,235	14,958	13,719	12,887
Plastic/rubber	1,645	776	659	936	877	884	1,095	1,269	768
Nonmetallic mineral	1,898	536	865	896	1,163	2,603	3,848	3,343	2,547
Primary metal	1,976	241	436	312	836	1,441	1,757	3,846	5,786
Fabricated metal	2,148	833	662	595	699	562	1,050	1,913	1,948
Machinery	864	797	707	645	917	935	550	997	1,409
Computer/electronic/electrical	6,392	1,918	1,444	2,835	4,247	4,347	2,870	2,575	4,472
Transportation equipment	6,318	3,832	3,314	2,610	3,702	2,631	3,626	5,187	4,531
Furniture [3]	148	148	278	217	96	122	180	40	(S)
Miscellaneous	4,398	2,325	2,248	2,878	2,674	2,928	3,781	3,831	2,324

S Suppressed because estimate does not meet publication standards. [1] Includes other types of construction, not shown separately. [2] Private residential improvement does not include expenditures on rental, vacant, or seasonal properties. [3] As of 2009, included in textile apparel/leather/furniture.

Source: U.S. Census Bureau, "Construction Spending," <http://www.census.gov/const/www/c30index.html>.

Table 960. Value of State and Local Government Construction Put in Place: 2000 to 2009

[In millions of dollars (167,157 represents $167,157,000,000). See Tables 958 and 959]

Type of construction	2000	2002	2003	2004	2005	2006	2007	2008	2009
Total construction [1]	**167,157**	**196,860**	**198,214**	**201,841**	**216,860**	**237,831**	**268,494**	**282,122**	**288,542**
Residential	2,962	3,754	3,724	4,110	4,047	4,349	5,094	4,836	6,048
Multifamily	2,945	3,671	3,593	3,956	3,740	3,990	4,476	4,021	5,120
Nonresidential	164,196	193,106	194,490	197,731	212,813	233,482	263,399	277,286	282,493
Office	4,494	6,274	6,116	6,024	5,211	5,588	7,249	8,439	9,227
Commercial [1]	1,820	2,422	2,207	1,979	1,882	1,567	1,777	1,817	2,293
Automotive	1,233	1,714	1,599	1,501	1,490	1,152	1,012	1,266	1,313
Parking	1,143	1,693	1,562	1,356	1,357	1,011	941	1,072	1,171
Warehouse	330	293	318	276	218	230	558	320	481
Health care	2,829	3,490	4,005	5,025	5,059	5,615	7,028	7,065	7,110
Hospital	1,949	2,539	2,685	3,324	3,429	4,085	5,304	5,335	5,526
Medical building	490	509	876	1,211	1,168	919	981	927	914
Special care	390	442	444	490	463	611	743	804	670
Educational [1]	46,818	59,463	59,340	59,741	65,750	69,790	78,376	83,759	83,846
Primary/secondary [1]	33,764	41,972	40,316	40,990	44,184	47,846	55,054	57,456	55,233
Elementary	12,272	15,154	13,430	14,308	14,251	13,870	16,786	18,332	17,308
Middle/junior high	5,820	8,410	7,921	8,132	9,069	10,764	11,719	10,902	10,269
High	13,326	17,142	18,561	17,950	19,892	22,631	25,887	27,679	27,233
Higher education [1]	10,749	14,280	15,451	15,864	18,033	18,961	20,556	23,110	24,803
Instructional	6,317	7,982	9,042	8,699	9,275	9,434	11,300	13,006	14,553
Parking	514	432	508	765	1,013	909	839	721	546
Administration	294	456	236	303	387	657	503	281	279
Dormitory	1,078	1,620	2,074	2,673	2,918	3,409	2,657	2,918	3,334
Library	308	440	544	524	588	493	700	813	860
Student union/cafeteria	322	1,031	702	632	880	1,028	1,547	1,394	1,358
Sports/recreation	966	1,546	1,329	1,370	1,769	1,748	1,726	2,511	2,307
Infrastructure	835	545	613	867	1,138	1,227	1,218	1,231	1,316
Other educational	1,645	2,629	2,687	2,357	2,735	2,312	1,890	2,503	2,928
Library/archive	976	2,118	1,815	1,501	2,098	1,857	1,287	1,575	1,717
Public safety [1]	5,854	5,960	5,844	5,477	6,013	6,608	8,423	9,615	9,408
Correctional	4,754	4,554	4,204	3,771	3,958	4,611	5,384	6,359	5,778
Detention	3,907	3,418	3,148	2,787	2,936	3,305	4,026	4,510	3,456
Police/sheriff	848	1,135	1,056	985	1,022	1,307	1,358	1,850	2,322
Other public safety	1,100	1,406	1,640	1,705	2,055	1,997	3,039	3,256	3,630
Fire/rescue	994	1,227	1,359	1,441	1,675	1,615	2,392	2,360	2,460
Amusement and recreation [1]	7,583	9,215	8,354	7,794	7,340	9,444	10,670	10,826	10,553
Sports	2,289	2,569	2,065	1,746	1,587	1,853	2,040	2,552	2,452
Performance/meeting center	2,075	2,915	2,260	2,061	1,921	2,292	1,706	1,640	1,778
Convention center	1,397	2,130	1,545	1,350	1,350	1,422	1,035	1,047	1,057
Social center	1,152	1,446	1,606	1,476	1,000	1,205	1,373	1,570	1,715
Neighborhood center	886	934	1,221	1,312	866	1,098	1,053	1,218	1,554
Park/camp	1,930	1,928	1,999	2,303	2,728	3,887	5,255	4,932	4,533
Transportation	13,000	17,312	16,483	16,440	16,256	17,695	21,144	21,843	24,284
Air [1]	6,700	8,123	8,146	8,715	8,993	9,676	11,390	11,172	11,793
Passenger terminal	2,930	3,040	3,778	3,972	3,310	3,766	5,224	5,953	6,180
Runway	3,196	4,305	3,793	4,049	4,861	4,898	5,164	4,369	4,765
Land [1]	5,165	7,291	7,207	6,415	5,936	6,629	7,593	9,001	10,935
Passenger terminal	1,253	1,860	2,099	1,368	907	969	1,301	1,587	2,381
Mass transit	1,484	3,375	3,160	3,067	3,208	3,228	3,587	4,203	5,229
Railroad	1,471	674	440	949	552	320	508	585	779
Water [1]	1,136	1,899	1,130	1,309	1,327	1,391	2,161	1,670	1,556
Dock/marina	863	1,203	894	1,028	930	971	1,465	1,279	1,286
Dry dock/marine terminal	236	695	235	281	397	420	697	390	270
Power	5,501	3,771	6,785	7,044	8,320	7,766	11,449	10,623	10,908
Electrical	5,257	3,244	6,041	5,851	7,091	7,195	10,176	9,788	8,591
Distribution	2,087	1,158	2,144	1,856	1,786	2,187	2,818	3,512	3,241
Highway and street [1]	51,574	56,660	56,251	57,351	63,157	71,032	75,455	80,835	83,682
Pavement	37,929	40,962	39,294	40,274	45,177	45,933	47,679	53,231	56,558
Lighting	856	888	1,156	1,146	1,232	1,057	1,709	1,537	1,324
Retaining wall	1,099	742	565	552	675	1,546	1,073	889	1,028
Tunnel	894	657	619	521	373	224	221	259	349
Bridge	9,302	11,741	12,980	13,150	14,244	20,057	22,827	23,704	22,967
Toll/weigh	325	217	180	233	320	657	421	199	285
Maintenance building	293	297	244	170	96	213	102	101	134
Rest facility/streetscape	878	1,155	1,213	1,306	1,042	1,347	1,424	914	1,037
Sewage and waste disposal [1]	14,000	15,334	15,625	17,084	18,336	21,524	23,323	23,839	23,932
Sewage/dry waste [1]	9,338	9,956	9,812	10,836	11,717	13,401	13,891	13,857	13,398
Plant	2,765	2,680	2,735	3,095	3,369	3,410	3,802	3,807	3,363
Line/pump station	6,326	7,082	6,934	7,574	8,243	9,820	9,784	9,787	9,725
Waste water	4,663	5,378	5,813	6,248	6,620	8,124	9,432	9,982	10,534
Plant	3,229	4,227	4,403	4,658	5,231	6,039	7,496	8,616	8,756
Line/drain	1,434	1,151	1,410	1,591	1,389	2,085	1,935	1,366	1,778
Water supply [1]	9,528	11,674	11,711	11,977	13,483	14,299	15,029	15,835	15,128
Plant	3,067	3,824	4,309	4,418	4,943	5,005	5,661	6,475	6,569
Well	378	555	365	318	360	623	661	483	560
Line	4,644	5,195	4,944	5,307	6,234	5,922	6,131	6,029	5,364
Pump station	625	852	767	705	776	1,285	1,124	1,280	1,384
Reservoir	266	463	450	503	502	700	586	634	330
Tank/tower	548	785	876	727	668	764	867	934	921
Conservation and development [1]	933	1,012	1,020	1,466	1,752	2,000	2,198	2,215	1,931
Dam/levee	303	279	231	297	405	591	640	762	730
Breakwater/jetty	270	397	514	654	726	809	627	625	658

[1] Includes other types of construction, not shown separately.

Source: U.S. Census Bureau, "Construction Spending," <http://www.census.gov/const/www/c30index.html>.

Table 961. Construction Contracts—Value of Construction and Floor Space of Buildings by Class of Construction: 1990 to 2009

[246.0 represents $246,000,000,000. Building construction includes new structures and additions; nonbuilding construction includes major alterations to existing structures which affect only valuation, since no additional floor area is created by "alteration"]

Year	Total	Resi-dential build-ings	Nonresidential buildings Total	Com-mer-cial [1]	Manu-factur-ing	Educa-tional [2]	Health	Public build-ings	Reli-gious	Social and recre-ational	Miscel-laneous	Non-building con-struc-tion
VALUE (bil. dol.)												
1990	246.0	100.9	95.4	44.8	8.4	16.6	9.2	5.7	2.2	5.3	3.1	49.7
1995	306.5	127.9	114.2	46.6	13.8	22.9	10.8	6.3	2.8	7.1	3.8	64.4
1998	405.6	179.8	154.5	74.0	12.1	30.1	12.9	6.6	4.3	10.8	3.6	71.3
1999	447.2	195.0	168.7	77.2	11.3	37.1	13.6	8.2	4.5	11.6	5.1	83.5
2000	472.9	208.3	173.3	80.9	8.9	40.9	12.4	7.5	4.6	13.8	4.4	91.3
2001	496.5	219.7	169.1	70.2	8.0	47.0	14.4	7.8	4.8	12.0	4.8	107.7
2002	504.0	248.7	155.1	59.6	5.5	45.3	16.1	7.3	5.1	11.5	4.7	100.2
2003	531.7	283.4	156.1	58.8	6.9	47.7	15.8	7.1	4.5	11.0	4.3	92.3
2004	593.2	333.1	164.4	67.3	8.0	44.0	17.6	7.2	4.5	11.6	4.4	95.6
2005	670.2	384.0	182.4	72.2	10.1	49.1	22.3	7.9	4.1	11.7	5.0	103.8
2006	689.3	342.1	217.1	92.9	13.5	53.8	24.3	8.3	4.1	14.3	5.9	130.1
2007	641.7	262.2	239.4	100.9	20.8	58.1	24.5	12.5	3.8	13.5	5.5	140.1
2008	552.3	161.4	238.8	80.5	29.2	63.7	29.8	13.3	3.6	13.4	5.3	152.1
2009	417.8	111.8	165.7	46.0	9.5	53.1	20.1	15.0	3.3	11.3	7.4	140.3
FLOOR SPACE (mil. sq. ft.)												
1990	3,020	1,817	1,203	694	128	152	69	47	29	51	32	(X)
1995	3,454	2,172	1,281	700	163	186	70	40	33	56	33	(X)
1998	4,812	3,015	1,797	1,107	166	219	96	42	47	85	34	(X)
1999	5,091	3,253	1,838	1,115	141	261	98	49	48	87	39	(X)
2000	4,982	3,113	1,869	1,180	111	273	88	44	49	94	29	(X)
2001	4,828	3,159	1,669	988	93	295	92	44	50	81	27	(X)
2002	4,792	3,356	1,436	810	68	277	97	37	52	71	26	(X)
2003	5,093	3,689	1,404	794	75	270	92	35	45	67	26	(X)
2004	5,518	4,061	1,457	875	86	231	94	34	43	68	27	(X)
2005	5,872	4,345	1,528	927	79	246	108	33	37	67	29	(X)
2006	5,283	3,648	1,635	1,015	83	254	110	34	35	73	33	(X)
2007	4,321	2,651	1,670	1,055	91	247	104	51	31	66	27	(X)
2008	2,950	1,578	1,372	770	79	253	108	49	28	59	27	(X)
2009	1,870	1,107	763	324	36	197	68	47	24	41	25	(X)

X Not applicable. [1] Includes nonindustrial warehouses. [2] Includes science.
Source: McGraw-Hill Construction, a Division of the McGraw-Hill Companies, New York, NY (copyright).

Table 962. Construction Contracts—Value by Region: 2005 to 2009

[In millions of dollars (670,198 represents $670,198,000,000). Represents value of construction in regions in which work was actually done. See headnote, Table 961]

Region	2005	2006	2007	2008	2009 Total [1]	2009 Residential	2009 Nonresiden-tial
U.S.	670,198	689,341	641,745	552,314	417,795	111,832	165,698
New England	25,236	23,277	24,650	20,456	16,884	4,140	7,074
Middle Atlantic	58,872	67,064	65,532	63,789	50,498	9,738	23,650
East North Central	83,652	82,150	72,406	74,837	50,072	11,035	19,579
West North Central	40,848	40,840	43,292	32,970	30,636	7,735	9,539
South Atlantic	172,118	165,355	151,255	113,351	83,848	25,639	33,310
East South Central	35,016	39,801	36,928	37,928	25,509	8,394	9,271
West South Central	75,478	92,124	86,084	84,716	67,800	21,220	25,025
Mountain	74,159	76,382	68,193	51,113	36,499	10,200	14,126
Pacific	104,819	102,350	93,404	73,154	56,048	13,733	24,124

[1] Includes nonbuilding construction, not shown separately.
Source: McGraw-Hill Construction, a Division of the McGraw-Hill Companies, New York, NY, (copyright).

U.S. Census Bureau, Statistical Abstract of the United States: 2011

Table 963. New Privately Owned Housing Units Authorized by State: 2008 and 2009

[905.4 represents 905,400. Based on about 20,000 places in United States having building permit systems in 2008 and 20,000 in 2009]

State	Housing units (1,000) 2008	2009 Total	2009 1 unit	Valuation (mil. dol.) 2008	2009 Total	2009 1 unit	State	Housing units (1,000) 2008	2009 Total	1 unit	Valuation (mil. dol.) 2008	2009 Total	1 unit
U.S...	905.4	583.0	441.1	141,633	95,410	82,357	MO....	13.3	10.1	6.6	1,890	1,434	1,202
AL	17.5	13.3	9.4	2,144	1,664	1,412	MT	2.4	1.7	1.4	359	254	223
AK	0.9	0.9	0.6	209	195	155	NE	6.3	5.2	4.6	860	725	678
AZ	26.1	14.5	12.8	4,483	2,736	2,572	NV	14.9	6.8	4.5	1,653	749	588
AR	8.8	7.1	4.5	994	818	682	NH	3.2	2.3	1.7	593	421	364
CA	62.7	35.1	25.5	12,301	7,758	6,440	NJ	18.4	12.4	7.2	2,801	2,071	1,428
CO	19.0	9.4	7.3	3,999	2,071	1,862	NM	6.1	4.6	4.1	1,066	769	737
CT	5.2	3.8	2.4	1,158	715	608	NY	51.6	18.3	9.7	6,304	3,062	2,132
DE	3.3	3.2	2.7	394	361	326	NC	54.7	33.8	25.4	8,432	5,030	4,446
DC	0.5	1.1	0.2	67	131	28	ND	2.8	3.2	1.7	399	352	291
FL	61.0	35.3	26.6	10,769	6,789	5,900	OH	17.7	13.3	10.6	2,928	2,194	1,997
GA	35.4	18.2	14.7	4,955	2,618	2,342	OK	10.5	8.8	7.3	1,591	1,302	1,206
HI.....	4.1	2.6	2.0	1,171	779	567	OR....	11.7	7.0	5.3	2,247	1,356	1,175
ID.....	6.5	4.9	4.3	1,130	805	756	PA	24.6	18.3	15.3	4,145	3,075	2,759
IL.....	22.5	10.9	7.8	3,783	2,101	1,699	RI.....	1.1	1.0	0.7	232	162	138
IN.....	16.6	12.6	9.7	2,470	1,933	1,705	SC	25.9	15.5	13.4	4,239	2,534	2,360
IA.....	8.4	7.7	5.7	1,319	1,198	1,013	SD	3.9	3.7	2.5	500	464	378
KS	8.2	6.7	4.3	1,173	881	728	TN	22.4	15.0	11.9	3,078	2,079	1,861
KY	10.5	7.4	6.0	1,298	923	838	TX	129.5	84.4	67.1	17,582	12,542	11,246
LA	16.3	12.5	10.8	2,220	1,842	1,729	UT	10.9	10.0	6.3	1,827	1,573	1,208
ME....	3.6	3.1	2.8	582	493	466	VT	1.4	1.4	0.9	241	214	168
MD....	13.0	11.1	8.1	2,230	2,089	1,573	VA	27.6	21.5	16.3	4,078	3,173	2,818
MA....	9.9	7.9	5.1	1,899	1,554	1,236	WA	28.9	17.0	13.0	5,063	3,186	2,771
MI. ...	10.9	6.9	6.2	1,792	1,173	1,117	WV	3.5	2.2	2.0	483	310	295
MN....	11.6	9.4	7.3	2,153	1,712	1,497	WI	15.5	10.8	7.9	2,507	1,753	1,520
MS....	11.4	7.0	5.5	1,274	878	770	WY....	2.7	2.3	1.6	567	407	350

Source: U.S. Census Bureau, Construction Reports, "New Residential Construction." <http://www.census.gov/const/www/newresconstindex.html>.

Table 964. New Privately Owned Housing Units Started—Selected Characteristics: 1970 to 2009

[In thousands (1,434 represents 1,434,000). For composition of regions, see map, inside front cover]

Year	Total units	Structures with— 1 unit	2 to 4 units	5 or more units	Region North-east	Midwest	South	West	Units for sale Total	Single-family	Multi-family
1970	1,434	813	85	536	218	294	612	311	(NA)	(NA)	(NA)
1980.........	1,292	852	110	331	125	218	643	306	689	526	163
1982	1,062	663	80	320	117	149	591	205	549	409	140
1983	1,703	1,068	113	522	168	218	935	382	923	713	210
1984	1,750	1,084	121	544	204	243	866	436	934	728	206
1985.........	1,742	1,072	93	576	252	240	782	468	867	713	154
1986.........	1,805	1,179	84	542	294	296	733	483	925	782	143
1987.........	1,621	1,146	65	409	269	298	634	420	862	732	130
1988.........	1,488	1,081	59	348	235	274	575	404	808	709	99
1989.........	1,376	1,003	55	318	179	266	536	396	735	648	87
1990.........	1,193	895	38	260	131	253	479	329	585	529	56
1991.........	1,014	840	36	138	113	233	414	254	531	490	41
1992.........	1,200	1,030	31	139	127	288	497	288	659	618	41
1993.........	1,288	1,126	29	133	127	298	562	302	760	716	44
1994.........	1,457	1,198	35	224	138	329	639	351	815	763	52
1995.........	1,354	1,076	34	244	118	290	615	331	763	712	51
1996.........	1,477	1,161	45	271	132	322	662	361	833	774	59
1997.........	1,474	1,134	45	296	137	304	670	363	843	784	59
1998.........	1,617	1,271	43	303	149	331	743	395	941	882	59
1999.........	1,641	1,302	32	307	156	347	746	392	981	912	69
2000.........	1,569	1,231	39	299	155	318	714	383	946	871	75
2001.........	1,603	1,273	37	293	149	330	732	391	990	919	71
2002.........	1,705	1,359	39	308	158	350	782	416	1,070	999	71
2003.........	1,848	1,499	34	315	163	374	839	472	1,207	1,120	87
2004.........	1,956	1,611	42	303	175	356	909	516	1,360	1,240	120
2005.........	2,068	1,716	41	311	190	357	996	525	1,508	1,358	150
2006.........	1,801	1,465	43	293	167	280	910	444	1,272	1,121	151
2007.........	1,355	1,046	32	277	143	210	681	321	875	760	115
2008.........	906	622	18	266	121	135	453	196	472	408	64
2009.........	554	445	12	97	62	97	278	117	314	297	17

NA Not available.

Source: U.S. Census Bureau, Construction Reports, "New Residential Construction." <http://www.census.gov/const/www/newresconstindex.html>.

U.S. Census Bureau, Statistical Abstract of the United States: 2011

Table 965. New Privately Owned Housing Units Started: 1991 to 2009

[In thousands of units (1,014 represents 1,014,000) For composition of regions, see map inside front cover]

Year	Total	1 unit	Northeast	Midwest	South	West
1991.	1,014	840	113	233	414	254
1992.	1,200	1,030	127	288	497	288
1993.	1,288	1,126	126	298	562	302
1994.	1,457	1,198	138	329	639	351
1995.	1,354	1,076	118	290	615	331
1996.	1,477	1,161	132	321	662	361
1997.	1,474	1,134	137	304	670	363
1998.	1,617	1,271	148	330	743	395
1999.	1,641	1,303	156	347	746	392
2000.	1,569	1,231	154	318	713	383
2001.	1,603	1,273	149	330	732	391
2002.	1,705	1,359	158	350	781	415
2003.	1,848	1,499	163	374	839	472
2004.	1,956	1,610	175	356	909	516
2005.	2,068	1,716	190	357	996	525
2006.	1,801	1,465	167	280	910	444
2007.	1,355	1,046	143	210	681	321
2008.	905	622	121	135	453	196
2009.	554	445	62	97	278	117

Source: U.S. Bureau of the Census, Construction Reports, Series C-20, "Housing Starts". Prepared by Economics Department, NAHB. Available at <http://www.HousingEconomics.com>.

Table 966. Characteristics of New Privately Owned One-Family Houses Completed: 1990 to 2009

[Percent distribution, except total houses. 966 represents 966,000. Data are percent distribution of characteristics for all houses completed (includes new houses completed, houses built for sale completed, contractor-built and owner-built houses completed, and houses completed for rent). Percents exclude houses for which characteristics specified were not reported]

Characteristic	1990	2000	2005	2009	Characteristic	1990	2000	2005	2009
Total houses (1,000).	966	1,242	1,636	520	Bedrooms.	100	100	100	100
Construction type	100	100	100	100	2 or less.	15	11	12	13
Site built.	(NA)	94	96	96	3.	57	54	49	53
Modular.	(NA)	3	3	2	4 or more.	29	35	39	34
Other.	(NA)	3	2	2	Bathrooms.	100	100	100	100
Exterior wall material	100	100	100	100	1-1/2 or less	13	7	4	8
Brick.	18	20	20	23	2.	42	39	36	37
Wood.	39	14	7	9	2-1/2 or more.	45	54	59	55
Stucco.	18	17	22	19	Heating fuel	100	100	100	100
Vinyl siding [1]	(NA)	39	34	34	Gas.	59	70	66	55
Aluminum siding	5	1	(NA)	(NA)	Electricity.	33	27	31	42
Other [1].	20	7	7	2	Oil.	5	3	2	1
Floor area.	(NA)	100	100	100	Other.	3	1	1	2
Under 1,200 sq. ft	(NA)	14	10	13	Heating system	100	100	100	100
1,200 to 1,599 sq. ft.	(NA)	22	19	20	Warm air furnace.	65	71	67	56
1,600 to 1,999 sq. ft.	(NA)	29	29	27	Electric heat pump.	23	23	29	37
2,000 to 2,399 sq. ft.	(NA)	17	19	17	Other.	12	6	4	7
2,400 sq. ft. and over	(NA)	18	23	23	Central air-conditioning	100	100	100	100
Average (sq. ft.).	2,080	2,266	2,434	2,438	With.	76	85	89	88
Median (sq. ft.).	1,905	2,057	2,227	2,135	Without.	24	15	11	12
Number of stories	100	100	100	100	Fireplaces.	100	100	100	100
1.	46	47	44	47	No fireplace.	34	40	45	49
2 or more.	49	52	55	53	1 or more.	66	59	55	51
Split level.	4	1	(Z)	(Z)	Parking facilities	100	100	100	100
Foundation.	100	100	100	100	Garage.	82	89	91	86
Full or partial basement.	38	37	31	30	Carport	2	1	1	1
Slab.	40	46	53	52	No garage or carport	16	11	8	12
Crawl space.	21	17	16	18					

NA Not available. Z Less than 0.5 percent. [1] Prior to 2000, "other" includes vinyl siding.

Source: U.S. Census Bureau and U.S. Department of Housing and Urban Development "Characteristics of New Housing," <http://www.census.gov/const/www/charindex.html>.

Table 967. Housing Starts and Average Length of Time From Start to Completion of New Privately Owned One-Unit Residential Buildings: 1980 to 2009

[852 represents 852,000. For buildings started in permit issue places]

Year	Total [1]	Purpose of construction			Region [2]			
		Built for sale	Contractor built	Owner built	North-east	Mid-west	South	West
STARTS (1,000)								
1980	852	526	149	164	87	142	428	196
1990	895	529	196	147	104	193	371	226
1995	1,076	712	199	133	102	234	485	256
1997	1,134	784	189	131	111	238	507	278
1998	1,271	882	209	144	122	273	574	303
1999	1,302	912	208	142	126	289	580	308
2000	1,231	871	195	128	118	260	556	297
2001	1,273	919	186	129	111	269	590	303
2002	1,359	999	198	125	118	277	628	336
2003	1,499	1,120	205	127	116	309	686	388
2004	1,611	1,240	198	130	128	306	743	433
2005	1,716	1,358	197	129	138	306	831	441
2006	1,465	1,121	189	119	118	235	757	356
2007	1,046	760	151	104	93	171	540	242
2008	622	408	107	74	63	102	324	133
2009	445	297	83	51	44	76	232	93
COMPLETION (months)								
1980	6.9	6.2	5.5	10.1	7.7	8.0	6.1	7.4
1990	6.4	5.9	5.3	10.3	9.3	5.6	5.7	6.9
1995	5.9	5.2	5.8	9.5	7.4	6.0	5.4	6.0
1997	6.0	5.2	5.9	9.8	7.3	6.2	5.6	5.8
1998	6.0	5.4	6.0	9.5	7.1	6.2	5.5	6.1
1999	6.1	5.5	6.4	9.2	7.0	6.4	5.7	6.3
2000	6.2	5.6	6.5	9.2	7.5	6.4	5.9	6.0
2001	6.2	5.6	7.0	9.2	7.6	6.5	5.8	6.3
2002	6.1	5.5	6.6	9.6	7.3	6.4	5.6	6.2
2003	6.2	5.5	6.8	9.9	7.5	6.7	5.7	6.2
2004	6.2	5.7	7.0	9.1	7.3	6.7	5.8	6.3
2005	6.4	5.9	7.6	9.8	7.7	6.6	6.0	6.8
2006	6.9	6.3	7.8	10.7	8.3	7.1	6.3	7.4
2007	7.1	6.5	7.9	10.2	8.5	7.4	6.5	8.0
2008	7.7	6.8	8.5	11.1	8.9	8.2	6.7	9.0
2009	7.9	6.6	8.7	11.9	10.7	8.2	6.7	9.0

[1] Includes units built for rent not shown separately. [2] For composition of regions, see map, inside front cover.
Source: U.S. Census Bureau, "New Residential Construction," <http://www.census.gov/const/www/newresconstindex.html>.

Table 968. Price Indexes of New One-Family Houses Sold by Region: 1980 to 2009

[2005 = 100. Based on kinds of homes sold in 1996. Includes value of the lot. For composition of regions, see map, inside front cover]

Year	Total	Northeast	Midwest	South	West
1980	38.9	30.2	41.2	44.4	31.9
1982	43.0	34.0	46.4	49.8	34.3
1983	43.9	36.1	46.2	51.2	34.9
1985	46.2	43.1	48.2	53.9	36.4
1986	48.0	49.5	51.0	55.5	37.3
1987	50.6	56.2	54.4	57.6	39.3
1988	52.5	57.6	56.8	58.8	41.4
1989	54.6	59.2	58.1	60.5	44.0
1990	55.7	58.0	58.6	60.6	46.2
1991	56.4	56.2	60.1	61.8	46.4
1992	57.2	60.5	61.2	62.4	46.7
1993	59.4	57.4	65.2	65.5	47.8
1994	62.9	62.1	69.4	68.1	51.9
1995	64.3	62.3	70.9	70.1	52.7
1996	66.0	63.2	72.5	71.2	55.3
1997	67.5	65.9	74.3	72.7	56.5
1998	69.2	66.1	76.0	74.4	58.4
1999	72.8	69.1	79.5	78.1	62.0
2000	75.6	73.0	83.5	80.7	64.4
2001	77.9	76.7	84.4	82.8	67.1
2002	81.4	80.2	86.1	86.3	71.5
2003	86.0	84.3	90.6	89.4	78.2
2004	92.8	91.6	96.7	94.4	88.2
2005	100.0	100.0	100.0	100.0	100.0
2006	104.8	102.6	102.9	105.4	105.2
2007	104.9	101.5	102.8	107.5	102.6
2008	99.5	100.8	98.9	103.7	92.7
2009	95.1	97.1	96.0	101.1	84.0

Source: U.S. Census Bureau, "Construction Price Indexes," <http://www.census.gov/const/www/constpriceindex.html>.

Table 969. New Privately Owned One-Family Houses Sold by Region and Type of Financing, 1980 to 2009, and by Sales-Price Group, 2009

[In thousands (545 represents 545,000). Based on a national probability sample of monthly interviews with builders or owners of one-family houses for which building permits have been issued or, for nonpermit areas, on which construction has started. For details, see source and Appendix III. For composition of regions, see map inside front cover]

Year and sales-price group	Total sales	Region				Financing type			
		Northeast	Midwest	South	West	Conventional [1]	FHA and VA	Rural-Housing Service [2]	Cash
1980	545	50	81	267	145	302	196	14	32
1985	688	112	82	323	171	403	208	11	64
1990	534	71	89	225	149	337	138	10	50
1995	667	55	125	300	187	490	129	9	39
2000	877	71	155	406	244	695	138	4	40
2002	973	65	185	450	273	788	140	4	42
2003	1,086	79	189	511	307	911	130	4	41
2004	1,203	83	210	562	348	1,047	105	6	46
2005	1,283	81	205	638	358	1,150	79	1	52
2006	1,051	63	161	559	267	948	63	1	38
2007	776	65	118	411	181	693	52	2	30
2008	485	35	70	266	114	358	104	(NA)	23
2009	375	31	54	202	87	234	124	(NA)	17
Under $200,000	162	5	30	105	21	(NA)	(NA)	(NA)	(NA)
$200,000 to $299,999	114	10	15	55	34	(NA)	(NA)	(NA)	(NA)
$300,000 to $499,999	69	9	6	30	24	(NA)	(NA)	(NA)	(NA)
$500,000 and over	30	7	3	11	9	(NA)	(NA)	(NA)	(NA)

NA Not available. [1] Includes houses reporting other types of financing. [2] Prior to 2000, the Farmers Home Administration.
Source: U.S. Census Bureau and U.S. Department of Housing and Urban Development "New Residential Sales," <http://www.census.gov/const/www/newressalesindex.html>.

Table 970. Median Sales Price of New Privately Owned One-Family Houses Sold by Region: 1980 to 2009

[In dollars. For definition of median, see Guide to Tabular Presentation. For composition of regions, see map inside front cover. See Appendix III. See also headnote, Table 969]

Year	U.S.	Northeast	Midwest	South	West	Year	U.S.	Northeast	Midwest	South	West
1980	64,600	69,500	63,400	59,600	72,300	2003	195,000	264,500	184,300	168,100	260,900
1985	84,300	103,300	80,300	75,000	92,600	2004	221,000	315,800	205,000	181,100	283,100
1990	122,900	159,000	107,900	99,000	147,500	2005	240,900	343,800	216,900	197,300	332,600
1995	133,900	180,000	134,000	124,500	141,400	2006	246,500	346,000	213,500	208,200	337,700
2000	169,000	227,400	169,700	148,000	196,400	2007	247,900	320,200	208,600	217,700	330,900
2001	175,200	246,400	172,600	155,400	213,600	2008	232,100	343,600	198,900	203,700	294,800
2002	187,600	264,300	178,000	163,400	238,500	2009	216,700	302,500	189,200	194,800	263,700

Source: U.S. Census Bureau and U.S. Department of Housing and Urban Development "New Residential Sales," <http://www.census.gov/const/www/newressalesindex.html>.

Table 971. New Manufactured (Mobile) Homes Placed for Residential Use and Average Sales Price by Region: 1985 to 2009

[283.4 represents 283,400. A mobile home is a moveable dwelling, 8 feet or more wide and 40 feet or more long, designed to be towed on its own chassis, with transportation gear integral to the unit when it leaves the factory, and without need of permanent foundation. Excluded are travel trailers, motor homes, and modular housing. Data are based on a probability sample and subject to sampling variability; see source. For composition of regions, see map, inside front cover]

Year	Units placed (1,000)					Average sales price (dollars)				
	Total	Northeast	Midwest	South	West	U.S.	Northeast	Midwest	South	West
1985	283.4	20.2	38.6	187.6	36.9	21,800	22,700	21,500	20,400	28,700
1990	195.4	18.8	37.7	108.4	30.6	27,800	30,000	27,000	24,500	39,300
1995	319.4	15.0	57.5	203.2	43.7	35,300	35,800	35,700	33,300	44,100
1996	337.7	16.2	58.8	218.2	44.4	37,200	37,300	38,000	35,500	45,000
1997	336.3	14.3	55.3	219.4	47.3	39,800	41,300	40,300	38,000	47,300
1998	373.7	14.7	58.3	250.3	50.4	41,600	42,200	42,400	40,100	48,400
1999	338.3	14.1	53.6	227.2	43.5	43,300	44,000	44,400	41,900	49,600
2000	280.9	14.9	48.7	178.7	38.6	46,400	47,000	47,900	44,300	54,100
2002	174.3	11.8	34.2	101.0	27.2	51,300	53,200	51,700	48,000	62,600
2003	139.8	11.2	25.2	77.2	26.1	54,900	57,300	55,100	50,500	67,700
2004	124.4	11.0	20.6	67.4	25.5	58,200	60,200	58,800	52,300	73,200
2005	122.9	9.2	17.1	68.1	28.5	62,600	67,000	60,600	55,700	79,900
2006	112.4	7.9	14.5	66.1	23.9	64,300	65,300	59,100	58,900	83,400
2007	94.8	7.0	10.8	59.4	17.7	65,400	66,100	64,900	59,900	85,500
2008	79.3	5.0	8.2	53.0	13.1	64,900	68,400	65,700	59,700	85,100
2009	52.5	3.5	5.4	36.5	7.3	62,900	60,700	65,600	59,200	81,700

Source: U.S. Census Bureau, "Manufactured Housing," <http://www.census.gov/const/www/mhsindex.html>.

Table 972. Existing One-Family Homes Sold and Price by Region: 1990 to 2009

[2,914 represents 2,914,000. Includes existing detached single-family homes and townhomes; excludes condos and co-ops. Based on data (adjusted and aggregated to regional and national totals) reported by participating real estate multiple listing services. For definition of median, see Guide to Tabular Presentation. See Table 975 for data on condos and co-ops. For composition of regions, see map inside front cover]

Year	Homes sold (1,000)					Median sales price (dollars)				
	U.S.	North-east	Mid-west	South	West	U.S.	North-east	Mid-west	South	West
1990.......	2,914	513	804	1,008	589	97,300	146,200	76,700	86,300	141,200
1991.......	2,886	516	807	990	573	102,700	149,300	81,000	89,800	147,400
1992.......	3,151	577	907	1,047	620	105,500	149,000	84,600	92,900	143,300
1993.......	3,427	614	961	1,167	685	109,100	149,300	87,600	95,800	144,400
1994.......	3,544	618	961	1,213	752	113,500	149,300	90,900	97,200	151,900
1995.......	3,519	615	940	1,212	752	117,000	146,500	96,500	99,200	153,600
1996.......	3,797	656	986	1,283	872	122,600	147,800	102,800	105,000	160,200
1997.......	3,964	683	1,004	1,356	921	129,000	152,400	108,900	111,300	169,000
1998.......	4,495	745	1,129	1,592	1,029	136,000	157,100	116,300	118,000	179,500
1999.......	4,649	728	1,145	1,704	1,072	141,200	160,700	121,600	122,100	189,400
2000.......	4,603	715	1,116	1,707	1,065	147,300	161,200	125,600	130,300	199,200
2001.......	4,735	710	1,154	1,795	1,076	156,600	169,400	132,300	139,600	211,700
2002.......	4,974	730	1,217	1,872	1,155	167,600	190,100	138,300	149,700	234,300
2003.......	5,446	770	1,323	2,073	1,280	180,200	220,300	143,700	159,700	254,700
2004.......	5,958	821	1,389	2,310	1,438	195,200	254,400	151,500	171,800	289,100
2005.......	6,180	838	1,411	2,457	1,474	219,000	281,600	168,300	181,100	340,300
2006.......	5,677	787	1,314	2,352	1,224	221,900	280,300	164,800	183,700	350,500
2007.......	4,939	723	1,181	2,053	982	217,900	288,100	161,400	178,800	342,500
2008.......	4,350	623	1,022	1,721	984	196,600	271,500	150,500	169,400	276,100
2009.......	4,566	641	1,067	1,745	1,113	172,100	243,200	142,900	155,000	215,400

Source: NATIONAL ASSOCIATION OF REALTORS, Washington, DC, *Real Estate Outlook; Market Trends & Insights*, monthly, (copyright). See also <http://www.realtor.org/research>.

Table 973. Median Sales Price of Existing One-Family Homes by Selected Metropolitan Area: 2005 and 2009

[In thousands of dollars (219.0 represents $219,000). Includes existing detached single-family homes and townhouses. Areas are metropolitan statistical areas defined by Office of Management and Budget as of 2004, except as noted]

Metropolitan area	2005	2009	Metropolitan area	2005	2009
United States, total	**219.0**	**172.1**	NY: Nassau-Suffolk, NY	465.2	383.3
Allentown-Bethlehem-Easton, PA-NJ	243.4	223.4	NY: Newark-Union, NJ-PA	416.8	366.6
Anaheim-Santa Ana-Irvine, CA [1]	691.9	477.2	Norwich-New London, CT	255.9	211.8
Atlantic City, NJ	256.1	221.3	Orlando, FL	243.6	147.4
Baltimore-Towson, MD	265.3	251.2	Palm Bay-Melbourne-Titusville, FL	209.7	107.0
Barnstable Town, MA	398.3	321.0	Philadelphia-Camden-Wilmington,		
Boston-Cambridge-Quincy, MA-NH [2]	413.2	332.6	PA-NJ-DE-MD	215.3	215.9
Boulder, CO	348.4	345.5	Phoenix-Mesa-Scottsdale, AZ	247.4	137.0
Bridgeport-Stamford-Norwalk, CT	482.4	379.2	Pittsfield, MA	207.3	186.4
Cape Coral-Fort Myers, FL	269.2	87.6	Portland-South Portland-Biddeford, ME	246.6	203.5
Charleston-North Charleston, SC	197.0	192.7	Portland-Vancouver-Beaverton, OR-WA	244.9	244.1
Chicago-Naperville-Joliet, IL	264.2	199.2	Providence-New Bedford-Fall River, RI-MA	293.4	218.5
Colorado Springs, CO	205.9	189.8	Raleigh-Cary, NC	194.9	215.4
Deltona-Daytona Beach-Ormond Beach, FL	192.5	124.6	Reno-Sparks, NV	349.9	193.8
Denver-Aurora, CO	247.1	219.9	Richmond, VA	201.9	(NA)
Dover, DE	180.4	197.1	Riverside-San Bernardino-Ontario, CA [1]	374.2	169.7
Eugene-Springfield, OR	197.6	203.7	Sacramento-Arden-Arcade-Roseville,CA [1]	375.9	180.5
Gainesville, FL	184.0	167.6	Salem, OR	177.7	183.7
Hagerstown-Martinsburg, MD-WV	208.7	157.1	San Diego-Carlsbad-San Marcos, CA [1]	604.3	359.5
Hartford-West Hartford-East Hartford, CT	253.3	232.0	San Francisco-Oakland-Fremont, CA [1]	715.7	493.3
Honolulu, HI	590.0	596.2	San Jose-Sunnyvale-Santa Clara, CA [1]	744.5	530.0
Kingston, NY	251.0	208.4	Sarasota-Bradenton-Venice, FL	354.2	170.5
Las Vegas-Paradise, NV	304.7	142.9	Seattle-Tacoma-Bellevue, WA	316.8	306.2
Los Angeles-Long Beach-Santa Ana, CA [1]	529.0	333.9	Springfield, MA	201.8	186.4
Madison, WI	218.3	212.3	Tampa-St.Petersburg-Clearwater, FL	205.3	140.7
Miami-Fort Lauderdale-Miami Beach, FL	363.9	211.2	Trenton-Ewing, NJ	261.1	263.7
Milwaukee-Waukesha-West Allis, WI	215.7	193.4	Tucson, AZ	231.6	172.5
Minneapolis-St. Paul-Bloomington, MN-WI	234.8	177.7	Virginia Beach-Norfolk-Newport News,		
New Haven-Milford, CT	279.1	235.7	VA-NC	197.2	210.0
New York-Northern New Jersey-Long Island,			Washington-Arlington-Alexandria,	425.8	308.6
NY-NJ-PA	445.2	381.4	DC-VA-MD-WV		
New York-Wayne-White Plains, NY-NJ	495.2	437.2	Worcester, MA	290.7	217.7
NY: Edison, NJ	375.5	331.9			

NA Not available. [1] California data supplied by the California Association of REALTORS. [2] Excludes areas in New Hampshire.
Source: NATIONAL ASSOCIATION OF REALTORS, Washington, DC, *Real Estate Outlook: Market Trends & Insights*, monthly, (copyright). See also <http://www.realtor.org/research\>.

U.S. Census Bureau, Statistical Abstract of the United States: 2011

Table 974. Existing Home Sales by State: 2000 to 2009

[In thousands (5,174 represents 5,174,000). Includes condos and co-ops as well as single-family homes. Data shown here reflect revisions from prior estimates]

State	2000	2005	2008	2009	State	2000	2005	2008	2009
United States	**5,174**	**7,076**	**4,913**	**5,156**	Missouri	110.2	142.9	108.7	105.9
Alabama	67.0	128.0	86.0	75.0	Montana	17.4	25.4	19.9	21.7
Alaska	14.3	24.6	23.2	22.4	Nebraska	32.3	41.2	30.9	34.7
Arizona	104.8	199.2	116.1	150.8	Nevada	44.6	98.0	65.5	104.9
Arkansas	45.0	75.3	64.2	61.8	New Hampshire	26.7	(NA)	18.4	19.6
California	573.5	601.1	439.9	510.4	New Jersey	161.1	184.4	112.6	115.3
Colorado	111.5	130.4	106.8	96.2	New Mexico	29.9	57.5	33.3	32.2
Connecticut	61.5	78.0	47.4	46.6	New York	273.3	319.8	255.4	253.8
Delaware	12.9	19.3	11.5	12.6	North Carolina	134.2	215.7	157.1	136.4
District of Columbia	10.6	12.1	7.1	8.4	North Dakota	10.8	15.8	12.4	13.1
Florida	393.6	547.1	262.5	357.8	Ohio	216.4	286.9	229.7	248.7
Georgia	143.6	242.1	174.9	176.6	Oklahoma	67.3	104.6	87.7	83.5
Hawaii	22.1	36.8	20.0	18.4	Oregon	62.6	100.5	54.8	55.0
Idaho	24.1	49.8	26.5	33.8	Pennsylvania	195.9	255.2	174.7	176.5
Illinois	246.8	315.3	183.1	184.4	Rhode Island	17.0	19.8	13.4	15.4
Indiana	111.0	138.3	118.6	104.7	South Carolina	64.3	114.6	80.3	71.1
Iowa	53.3	74.9	55.7	50.0	South Dakota	12.6	18.3	16.3	17.4
Kansas	52.6	77.9	60.4	56.5	Tennessee	100.4	170.9	118.0	107.9
Kentucky	66.0	96.2	75.3	73.8	Texas	381.8	532.5	474.8	443.3
Louisiana	66.8	87.7	59.1	54.8	Utah	35.5	51.7	30.8	31.1
Maine	27.6	33.3	20.6	23.1	Vermont	12.1	15.3	10.7	11.3
Maryland	100.5	135.5	63.8	72.5	Virginia	130.0	182.5	112.7	117.0
Massachusetts	112.3	148.6	103.8	107.9	Washington	112.4	167.8	86.9	82.3
Michigan	185.0	208.6	155.6	167.1	West Virginia	22.9	38.6	25.5	27.6
Minnesota	96.3	134.9	96.2	107.4	Wisconsin	91.6	122.8	84.5	84.5
Mississippi	38.7	61.2	50.4	41.9	Wyoming	9.6	14.3	10.0	9.1

NA Not available.

Source: NATIONAL ASSOCIATION OF REALTORS, Washington, DC, *Real Estate Outlook: Market Trends & Insights*, monthly (copyright). See also <http://www.realtor.org/research>.

Table 975. Existing Apartment Condos and Co-Ops—Units Sold and Median Sales Price by Region: 1990 to 2009

[272 represents 272,000. Data shown here reflect revisions from prior estimates. For definition of median, see Guide to Tabular Presentation. For composition of regions, see map inside front cover]

Year	Units sold (1,000)					Median sales price (dollars)				
	U.S.	Northeast	Midwest	South	West	U.S.	Northeast	Midwest	South	West
1990	272	73	55	80	64	86,900	107,500	70,200	64,200	114,600
1995	333	108	66	96	63	89,000	92,500	90,700	67,800	114,800
2000	571	197	106	160	108	114,000	108,500	121,700	84,200	149,100
2002	657	221	129	193	114	144,900	143,500	148,600	109,900	187,000
2003	732	250	146	211	125	168,500	178,100	162,600	126,900	222,400
2004	820	292	161	230	137	197,100	214,100	181,000	156,600	258,000
2005	896	331	177	245	143	223,900	245,100	189,100	187,300	283,800
2006	801	299	169	211	122	221,900	249,700	190,900	184,000	264,700
2007	713	283	146	182	102	226,300	256,100	195,200	185,100	263,300
2008	563	226	107	144	86	209,800	252,500	188,200	166,800	218,500
2009	590	227	96	169	98	175,600	232,800	157,100	132,700	162,100

Source: NATIONAL ASSOCIATION OF REALTORS, Washington, DC, *Real Estate Outlook: Market Trends & Insights*, monthly (copyright). See <http://www.realtor.org/research>.

Table 976. New Unfurnished Apartments Completed and Rented in 3 Months by Region: 2000 to 2009

[226.2 represents 226,200. Structures with five or more units, privately financed, nonsubsidized, unfurnished rental apartments. Based on sample and subject to sampling variability; see source for details. For composition of regions, see map, inside front cover]

Year and rent	Number (1,000)					Percent rented in 3 months				
	U.S.	North-east	Mid-west	South	West	U.S.	North-east	Mid-west	South	West
2000	226.2	14.8	39.5	125.9	45.9	72	85	76	67	77
2005	113.0	4.7	20.5	57.8	30.0	64	75	64	62	64
2006	117.2	6.0	12.6	69.9	28.6	55	41	58	60	56
2007	104.8	5.6	9.5	61.8	28.0	55	66	58	52	58
2008	146.4	8.9	17.2	88.2	32.1	50	52	58	48	51
2009, prel	**164.3**	**10.2**	**16.9**	**94.5**	**42.7**	**50**	**57**	**70**	**49**	**44**
Less than $850	35.6	1.1	7.5	21.4	5.7	60	85	75	58	45
$850 to $949	21.9	1.8	1.9	14.8	3.4	59	49	78	58	56
$950 to $1,049	22.3	0.5	2.9	15.1	3.9	52	92	67	50	45
$1,050 to $1,149	13.8	1.3	1.0	7.7	3.9	46	55	64	50	33
$1,150 to $1,249	16.8	0.9	0.7	10.4	4.8	45	15	71	43	52
$1,250 or more	53.9	4.7	3.0	25.2	21.0	42	58	57	38	41
Median asking rent (dollars)	1,067	1,204	902	1,023	1,242	(X)	(X)	(X)	(X)	(X)

X Not applicable.

Source: U.S. Census Bureau, Current Housing Reports, Series H130, *Market Absorption of Apartments*, and unpublished data. See also <http://www.census.gov/hhes/www/housing/soma/soma.html>.

Table 977. Total Housing Inventory for the United States: 1990 to 2009

[In thousands (106,283 represents 106,283,000), except percent. Based on the Current Population Survey and the Housing Vacancy Survey and subject to sampling error; see source and Appendix III for details]

Item	1990	1995	2000	2002 [1]	2004	2005	2006	2007	2008	2009
All housing units	**106,283**	**112,655**	**119,628**	**119,297**	**122,187**	**123,925**	**126,012**	**127,958**	**130,113**	**130,159**
Vacant	12,059	12,669	13,908	14,332	15,599	15,694	16,437	17,652	18,704	18,815
Year-round vacant	9,128	9,570	10,439	10,771	11,884	11,916	12,459	13,276	13,936	14,143
For rent	2,662	2,946	3,024	3,347	3,802	3,721	3,737	3,848	4,056	4,393
For sale only	1,064	1,022	1,148	1,220	1,307	1,451	1,836	2,117	2,226	2,020
Rented or sold	660	810	856	842	991	1,060	1,108	1,130	1,075	993
Held off market	4,742	4,793	5,411	5,362	5,784	5,684	5,778	6,181	6,579	6,737
Occasional use	1,485	1,667	1,892	1,819	1,967	1,884	1,858	1,993	2,071	2,068
Usual residence elsewhere	1,068	801	1,037	995	1,068	1,128	1,198	1,139	1,170	1,187
Other	2,189	2,325	2,482	2,548	2,749	2,672	2,722	3,049	3,338	3,482
Seasonal [2]	2,931	3,099	3,469	3,561	3,715	3,778	3,978	4,376	4,768	4,673
Total occupied	94,224	99,985	105,720	104,965	106,588	108,231	109,575	110,306	111,409	111,344
Owner	60,248	64,739	71,250	71,278	73,575	74,553	75,380	75,159	75,566	75,014
Renter	33,976	35,246	34,470	33,687	33,013	33,678	34,195	35,147	35,843	36,330
PERCENT DISTRIBUTION										
All housing units	100.0	100.0	100.0	100.0	100.0	100.0	100.0	100.0	100.0	100.0
Vacant	11.3	11.2	11.6	12.0	12.8	12.7	13.0	13.8	14.4	14.4
Total occupied	88.7	88.8	88.4	88.0	87.2	87.3	87.0	86.2	85.6	85.6
Owner	56.7	57.5	59.6	59.7	60.2	60.2	60.3	58.7	58.1	57.9
Renter	32.0	31.3	28.8	28.2	27.0	27.2	27.5	27.5	27.5	27.9

[1] Revised. Based on 2000 census controls. [2] Includes vacant seasonal mobile homes.

Source: U.S. Census Bureau, "Housing Vacancies and Home Ownership", <http://www.census.gov/hhes/www/housing/hvs/hvs.html>.

Table 978. Occupied Housing Inventory by Age of Householder: 1990 to 2009

[In thousands (94,224 represents 94,224,000). Based on the Current Population Survey and Housing Vacancy Survey; see source for details]

Age of householder	1990	1995	2000	2002 [1]	2004	2005	2006	2007	2008	2009
Total	**94,224**	**99,986**	**105,719**	**104,965**	**106,588**	**108,231**	**109,576**	**110,306**	**111,409**	**111,344**
Under 25 years old	5,143	5,502	6,221	6,372	6,538	6,536	6,578	6,494	6,272	6,106
25 to 29 years old	9,508	8,662	8,482	8,231	8,491	8,790	8,975	9,170	9,094	9,076
30 to 34 years old	11,213	11,206	10,219	10,176	9,865	9,583	9,423	9,349	9,343	9,331
35 to 39 years old	10,914	11,993	11,834	10,924	10,438	10,526	10,520	10,499	10,550	10,185
40 to 44 years old	9,893	11,151	12,377	11,839	11,768	11,722	11,484	11,125	10,974	10,705
45 to 49 years old	8,038	10,080	11,164	11,204	11,583	11,780	11,988	12,007	11,968	11,861
50 to 54 years old	6,532	7,882	9,834	10,123	10,316	10,595	10,896	11,082	11,415	11,605
55 to 59 years old	6,182	6,355	7,602	8,261	8,928	9,504	9,919	10,013	10,217	10,226
60 to 64 years old	6,446	5,860	6,215	6,422	7,112	7,336	7,604	8,108	8,601	8,920
65 to 69 years old	6,407	6,088	5,816	5,644	5,656	5,900	6,074	6,330	6,642	6,822
70 to 74 years old	5,397	5,693	5,567	5,137	5,065	5,016	5,057	5,063	5,114	5,288
75 years old and over	8,546	9,514	10,388	10,632	10,827	10,943	11,058	11,065	11,219	11,220

[1] Revised. Based on 2000 census controls.

Source: U.S. Census Bureau, "Housing Vacancies and Home Ownership," <http://www.census.gov/hhes/www/housing/hvs/hvs.html>.

Table 979. Vacancy Rates for Housing Units—Characteristics: 2000 to 2009

[In percent. Rate is relationship between vacant housing for rent or for sale and the total rental and homeowner supply, which comprises occupied units, units rented or sold and awaiting occupancy, and vacant units available for rent or sale. Based on the Current Population/Housing Vacancy Survey; see source for details. For composition of regions, see map, inside front cover]

Characteristic	Rental Units				Homeowner units			
	2000	2005	2008	2009	2000	2005	2008	2009
Total units	**8.0**	**9.8**	**10.0**	**10.6**	**1.6**	**1.9**	**2.8**	**2.6**
Northeast	5.6	6.5	6.9	7.2	1.2	1.5	2.0	2.0
Midwest	8.8	12.6	10.8	10.7	1.3	2.2	2.9	2.6
South	10.5	11.8	13.0	13.6	1.9	2.1	3.1	2.9
West	5.8	7.3	7.5	9.0	1.5	1.4	2.9	2.6
Units in structure:								
1 unit	7.0	9.9	9.7	9.8	1.5	1.7	2.5	2.3
2 units or more	8.7	10.0	10.4	11.3	4.7	6.2	9.0	8.7
5 units or more	9.2	10.4	11.2	12.3	5.8	6.6	8.7	8.7
Units with—								
3 rooms or less	10.3	12.1	12.4	13.3	10.4	12.0	12.4	14.2
4 rooms	8.2	9.6	10.0	10.9	2.9	3.3	4.9	5.0
5 rooms	6.9	9.3	9.2	9.7	2.0	2.2	3.4	3.1
6 rooms or more	5.2	8.1	8.3	8.3	1.1	1.4	2.2	1.8

Source: U.S. Census Bureau, "Housing Vacancies and Home Ownership," <http://www.census.gov/hhes/www/housing/hvs/hvs.html>.

Table 980. Housing Units and Tenure—States: 2008

[129,060 represents 129,060,000. The American Community Survey universe includes the household population and the population living in institutions, college dormitories, and other group quarters. Based on a sample and subject to sampling variability; see Appendix III]

State	Housing units						Housing tenure			
			Vacant (1,000)		Vacancy rate		Owner-occupied units		Renter-occupied units	
	Total (1,000)	Occu-pied (1,000)	Total	For sea-sonal use[1]	Hom-eowner[2]	Renter[3]	Total (1,000)	Average house-hold size	Total (1,000)	Average house-hold size
United States	**129,060**	**113,101**	**15,959**	**4,612**	**2.7**	**8.0**	**75,373**	**2.70**	**37,728**	**2.44**
Alabama	2,159	1,816	343	72	2.8	10.0	1,289	2.56	527	2.37
Alaska	283	238	46	23	1.4	4.9	154	2.94	83	2.54
Arizona	2,723	2,274	449	169	4.2	11.5	1,549	2.80	725	2.82
Arkansas	1,298	1,114	184	41	2.5	9.7	751	2.55	363	2.37
California	13,394	12,177	1,217	321	2.9	4.8	6,946	3.03	5,230	2.84
Colorado	2,152	1,898	254	98	2.5	7.6	1,281	2.61	617	2.40
Connecticut	1,443	1,329	114	25	1.5	7.4	917	2.69	412	2.25
Delaware	393	329	64	35	3.2	9.7	242	2.65	87	2.41
District of Columbia	285	250	35	1	3.3	6.6	109	2.39	141	2.10
Florida	8,798	7,057	1,741	791	4.4	12.9	4,916	2.55	2,141	2.51
Georgia	4,026	3,470	556	86	3.9	11.1	2,340	2.77	1,130	2.60
Hawaii	513	437	76	30	2.4	10.1	258	2.97	179	2.73
Idaho	642	566	76	31	2.9	7.7	401	2.68	165	2.50
Illinois	5,276	4,766	510	42	2.5	7.0	3,302	2.75	1,464	2.37
Indiana	2,795	2,481	314	36	3.1	9.2	1,782	2.59	699	2.24
Iowa	1,329	1,215	113	19	2.1	6.9	886	2.50	329	2.06
Kansas	1,226	1,111	116	13	2.0	6.3	771	2.57	340	2.17
Kentucky	1,921	1,686	234	33	2.8	8.2	1,173	2.54	514	2.30
Louisiana	1,883	1,625	258	53	1.9	8.3	1,114	2.70	511	2.50
Maine	701	542	158	111	2.2	7.2	391	2.48	151	2.03
Maryland	2,333	2,093	241	47	2.1	8.9	1,454	2.73	639	2.38
Massachusetts	2,736	2,467	268	107	1.5	5.4	1,592	2.73	875	2.19
Michigan	4,536	3,811	725	270	3.9	9.9	2,819	2.65	991	2.30
Minnesota	2,331	2,089	242	111	2.0	5.8	1,560	2.57	530	2.01
Mississippi	1,267	1,094	173	33	2.4	9.4	767	2.63	327	2.52
Missouri	2,664	2,330	334	71	2.7	8.7	1,633	2.57	697	2.23
Montana	438	376	63	32	1.7	5.6	257	2.58	118	2.34
Nebraska	786	704	82	16	1.9	8.3	488	2.59	216	2.15
Nevada	1,127	953	174	37	5.8	11.5	568	2.71	384	2.67
New Hampshire	597	505	92	60	1.8	5.9	365	2.68	140	2.12
New Jersey	3,516	3,154	362	126	2.1	7.3	2,114	2.84	1,040	2.40
New Mexico	872	741	130	44	2.6	7.7	513	2.68	229	2.47
New York	7,977	7,137	840	259	1.9	4.7	3,946	2.82	3,191	2.42
North Carolina	4,200	3,595	605	179	2.7	9.7	2,451	2.54	1,144	2.36
North Dakota	313	275	38	14	1.5	6.4	183	2.42	92	1.87
Ohio	5,080	4,509	571	50	2.9	9.8	3,113	2.59	1,396	2.22
Oklahoma	1,637	1,408	229	37	2.4	9.4	947	2.56	461	2.39
Oregon	1,629	1,475	154	52	2.4	5.8	949	2.62	526	2.32
Pennsylvania	5,497	4,905	592	162	1.8	6.8	3,475	2.58	1,430	2.12
Rhode Island	452	399	53	17	2.3	7.5	249	2.77	150	2.15
South Carolina	2,056	1,702	354	115	3.2	12.5	1,202	2.58	501	2.46
South Dakota	361	320	42	14	1.2	5.5	221	2.55	99	2.12
Tennessee	2,758	2,435	324	59	2.6	10.5	1,700	2.56	735	2.33
Texas	9,599	8,422	1,177	215	2.5	10.4	5,466	2.95	2,956	2.58
Utah	944	854	90	39	2.2	5.4	613	3.25	242	2.89
Vermont	313	250	63	47	1.4	6.1	180	2.51	70	2.12
Virginia	3,306	2,961	345	73	2.2	7.0	2,034	2.61	927	2.38
Washington	2,792	2,548	244	81	2.3	5.1	1,663	2.63	884	2.29
West Virginia	886	750	137	42	2.1	7.6	553	2.45	197	2.11
Wisconsin	2,569	2,250	319	156	2.1	6.4	1,578	2.57	672	2.10
Wyoming	246	209	38	16	1.7	8.3	146	2.59	62	2.23

[1] For seasonal, recreational, or occasional use. [2] Proportion of the homeowner housing inventory which is vacant for sale.
[3] Proportion of the rental inventory which is vacant for rent.

Source: U.S. Census Bureau, 2008 American Community Survey, B25002, "Occupancy Status"; B25003, "Tenure"; B25004, "Vacancy Status"; and B25010, "Average Household Size of Units by Tenure," <http://factfinder.census.gov>, accessed March 2009.

Table 981. Homeownership and Rental Vacancy Rates by State: 2009

[The American Community Survey universe is limited to the household population and excludes the population living in institutions, college dormitories, and other group quarters. Based on a sample and subject to sampling variability, see Appendix III.]

State	Home-owner-ship vacancy rate	Rental vacancy rate	State	Home-owner-ship vacancy rate	Rental vacancy rate	State	Home-owner-ship vacancy rate	Rental vacancy rate
U.S.	2.6	10.6	KS	2.9	10.5	ND	1.7	7.0
			KY	2.6	12.1	OH	3.2	10.7
AL	3.0	14.4	LA	1.5	11.4	OK	2.6	10.8
AK	1.6	7.9	ME	2.1	7.7	OR	3.3	6.2
AZ	3.4	17.7	MD	2.4	11.1	PA	1.6	9.0
AR	3.3	13.0	MA	1.4	6.0	RI	2.2	8.4
CA	2.2	7.6	MI	3.4	13.3	SC	3.0	16.2
CO	3.0	10.9	MN	2.3	8.4	SD	1.4	8.3
CT	1.7	8.3	MS	2.0	16.0	TN	2.5	12.8
DE	2.4	12.4	MO	2.3	11.1	TX	1.9	13.0
DC	3.3	9.9	MT	2.8	6.6	UT	1.9	8.3
FL	4.3	17.8	NE	1.7	8.9	VT	1.4	5.4
GA	3.7	14.3	NV	4.5	14.2	VA	2.3	10.3
HI	1.9	9.2	NH	1.8	7.4	WA	2.6	7.4
ID	2.6	11.0	NJ	2.3	9.7	WV	2.0	9.5
IL	2.5	10.8	NM	1.9	9.5	WI	2.2	9.1
IN	2.5	11.9	NY	2.4	5.7	WY	1.9	6.3
IA	1.6	8.5	NC	3.5	12.8			

Source: U.S. Census Bureau, "Housing Vacancies and Home Ownership," <http://www.census.gov/hhes/www/housing/hvs/annual09/ann09ind.html>.

Table 982. Homeownership and Rental Vacancy Rates by Metropolitan Area: 2009

[Based on the Current Population Survey and the Housing Vacancy Survey, subject to sampling error; see source and Appendix III for details]

Metropolitan area	Home-eowner-ship vacancy rates	Rental vacancy rates	Metropolitan area	Home-eowner-ship vacancy rates	Rental vacancy Rates
Inside Metropolitan Areas	**2.6**	**10.7**			
Akron, OH	3.0	14.1	Minneapolis-St. Paul-Bloomington, MN-WI	2.2	8.5
Albany-Schenectady-Troy, NY	2.4	6.3	Nashville-Davidson-Murfreesboro, TN	1.9	8.3
Albuquerque, NM	1.9	8.0	New Haven-Milford, CT	2.4	8.6
Allenton-Bethleham-Easton, PA-NJ	2.0	7.5	New Orleans-Metairie-Kenner, LA	2.5	18.0
Atlanta-Sandy Springs-Marietta, GA	4.1	16.6	New York-Northern New Jersey-Long Island, NY	2.0	5.9
Austin-Round Rock, TX	1.6	12.2	Oklahoma City, OK	2.8	8.3
Bakersfield, CA	3.4	4.9	Omaha-Council Bluffs, NE-IA	2.0	11.7
Baltimore-Towson, MD	1.9	13.4	Orlando, FL	5.8	22.8
Baton Rouge, LA	2.9	8.5	Oxnard-Thousand Oaks-Ventura, CA	1.5	5.0
Birmingham-Hoover, AL	2.2	13.1	Philadelphia-Camden-Wilmington, PA	1.6	11.4
Boston-Cambridge-Quincy, MA-NH	1.5	6.0	Phoenix-Mesa-Scottsdale, AZ	3.1	18.3
Bridgeport-Stamford-Norwalk, CT	2.0	8.4	Pittsburgh, PA	1.6	9.7
Buffalo-Cheektowaga-Tonawanda, NY	2.9	6.8	Portland-Vancouver-Beaverton, OR-WA	4.8	4.3
Charlotte-Gastonia-Concord, NC-SC	5.1	12.1	Poughkeepsie-Newburg-Middletown, NJ	2.3	12.3
Chicago-Naperville-Joliet, IL	2.9	12.0	Providence-New Bedford-Fall River RI-MA	1.7	8.5
Cincinnati-Middletown, OH-KY-IN	4.0	11.3	Raleigh-Cary, NC	2.8	10.3
Cleveland-Elyria-Mentor, OH	3.0	12.5	Richmond, VA	2.2	18.5
Columbia, SC	3.1	8.4	Riverside-San Bernardino-Ontario, CA	4.0	12.3
Columbus, OH	2.0	7.6	Rochester, NY	1.3	8.0
Dallas-Ft. Worth-Arlington, TX	2.1	11.7	Sacramento-Arden-Arade-Roseville, CA	4.0	10.6
Dayton, OH	4.0	18.8	St. Louis, MO-IL	1.8	11.2
Denver-Aurora, CO	2.7	10.2	Salt Lake City, UT	2.3	10.2
Detroit-Warren-Livonia, MI	3.3	15.8	San Antonio, TX	1.2	12.1
El Paso, TX	2.5	9.6	San Diego-Carlsbad-San Marcos, CA	2.1	8.8
Fresno, CA	1.6	9.7	San Francisco-Oakland-Freemont, CA	1.8	6.7
Grand Rapids-Wyoming, MI	3.7	5.5	San Jose-Sunnyvale-Santa Clara, CA	1.4	7.7
Greensboro-High Point, NC	6.3	15.2	Seattle-Bellevue-Everett, WA	2.8	8.0
Hartford-West Hartford-East Hartford, CT	1.1	8.5	Springfield, MA	1.4	4.4
Honolulu, HI	0.8	6.9	Syracuse, NY	0.8	12.1
Houston-Baytown-Sugar Land, TX	1.9	15.6	Tampa-St. Petersburg-Clearwater, FL	4.1	12.4
Indianapolis, IN	2.6	12.6	Toledo, OH	3.2	13.9
Jacksonville, FL	3.7	15.9	Tucson, AZ	2.7	14.3
Kansas City, MO-KS	3.4	14.4	Tulsa, OK	2.4	15.1
Las Vegas-Paradise, NV	5.0	14.3	Virginia Beach-Norfolk-Newport News, VA	2.3	6.2
Los Angeles-Long Beach-Santa Ana, CA	1.3	6.4	Washington-Arlington-Alexandria, DC-VA-MD-WV	2.3	10.0
Louisville, KY-IN	2.4	12.1	Worcester, MA	1.8	6.3
Memphis, TN-AR-MS	2.4	22.9			
Miami-Fort Lauderdale-Miami Beach, FL	3.2	13.2			
Milwaukee-Waukesha-West Allis, WI	1.4	8.7			

Source: U.S. Census Bureau, "Housing Vacancies and Home Ownership," <http://www.census.gov/hhes/www/housing/hvs/annual09/ann09ind.html>.

Table 983. Housing Units—Characteristics by Tenure and Region: 2009

[In thousands of units (130,112 represents 130,112,000), except as indicated. As of fall. Based on the American Housing Survey; see Appendix III. For composition of regions, see map, inside front cover]

Characteristic	Total housing units	Sea-sonal	Year-round units Occupied Total	Owner	Renter	North-east	Mid-west	South	West	Vacant
Total units	**130,112**	**4,618**	**111,806**	**76,428**	**35,378**	**20,451**	**25,368**	**41,586**	**24,401**	**13,688**
Percent distribution	100.0	3.5	85.9	58.7	27.2	15.7	19.5	32.0	18.8	10.5
Units in structure:										
Single family detached	82,472	2,795	73,079	63,324	9,755	11,431	17,944	28,063	15,642	6,598
Single family attached	7,053	252	5,973	3,952	2,021	1,810	1,055	1,935	1,172	828
2 to 4 units	10,160	167	8,350	1,353	6,998	2,571	1,792	2,096	1,892	1,643
5 to 9 units	6,347	143	5,269	632	4,637	944	1,043	1,818	1,465	935
10 to 19 units	5,722	127	4,661	483	4,178	741	962	1,819	1,139	934
20 or more units	9,588	404	7,634	1,266	6,368	2,415	1,429	1,936	1,854	1,550
Manufactured/mobile home [1]	8,769	730	6,839	5,418	1,421	540	1,145	3,918	1,236	1,201
Year structure built:										
Median year	1974	1975	1974	1975	1971	1958	1970	1979	1976	1973
1980 or later	16,283	615	14,028	9,360	4,668	1,758	2,381	6,438	3,451	1,639
1970 to 1979	24,799	867	21,248	13,167	8,081	2,864	4,681	8,761	4,941	2,684
1960 to 1969	15,261	514	13,326	8,917	4,409	2,451	2,957	4,832	3,086	1,421
1950 to 1959	41,406	1,386	35,399	23,076	12,322	10,828	9,780	8,538	6,252	4,622
Stories in structure: [2]										
1 story	41,537	1,880	35,364	26,216	9,148	1,109	4,072	19,803	10,381	4,292
2 stories	43,447	1,145	37,867	25,210	12,657	6,291	10,192	12,065	9,320	4,435
3 stories	27,574	542	24,508	16,721	7,787	8,689	8,530	4,611	2,678	2,524
4 or more stories	8,785	320	7,228	2,863	4,365	3,823	1,430	1,190	785	1,237
Foundation: [3]										
Full basement	29,104	490	26,713	23,821	2,892	9,022	11,276	4,269	2,145	1,902
Partial building	8,991	170	8,208	7,350	858	2,226	3,280	1,565	1,137	613
Crawlspace	20,955	965	18,022	14,783	3,240	740	2,523	9,517	5,242	1,968
Concrete slab	28,693	1,011	24,917	20,431	4,486	1,146	1,758	13,941	8,071	2,765
Equipment:										
Lacking complete facilities	5,586	667	1,751	378	1,374	487	385	406	474	3,168
With complete facilities	124,526	3,951	110,054	76,050	34,004	19,964	24,984	41,180	23,927	10,520
Kitchen sink	128,769	4,291	111,510	76,329	35,180	20,344	25,308	41,532	24,326	12,968
Refrigerator	126,534	4,056	111,530	76,336	35,193	20,372	25,328	41,502	24,328	10,948
Cooking stove or range	126,744	4,127	111,038	76,153	34,886	20,329	25,207	41,347	24,155	11,579
Dishwasher	82,397	2,111	73,584	57,191	16,393	11,900	15,487	28,691	17,505	6,702
Washing machine	101,387	2,482	93,372	73,826	19,545	15,327	21,537	36,611	19,896	5,534
Clothes dryer	98,657	2,360	90,905	72,562	18,343	14,512	21,327	35,578	19,489	5,392
Disposal in kitchen sink	63,776	1,505	56,531	40,597	15,933	5,332	13,048	20,217	17,934	5,740
Safety Equipment:										
Smoke detector:										
Working	116,141	2,989	104,362	71,797	32,565	19,479	24,153	37,942	22,788	8,789
Powered by:										
Electricity	9,217	267	8,149	5,620	2,528	1,680	1,534	3,238	1,696	801
Batteries	72,868	1,547	66,536	43,210	23,326	12,985	16,379	22,831	14,341	4,785
Both	32,128	983	28,421	22,461	5,960	4,654	5,971	11,370	6,426	2,724
Not working	9,101	824	6,157	3,686	2,472	739	974	3,045	1,399	2,119
Not reported	4,870	804	1,286	945	341	233	241	598	214	2,780
Batteries:										
Replaced in last 6 months	77,933	1,626	71,505	50,073	21,432	14,175	17,336	25,312	14,682	4,803
Not replaced in last 6 months	23,706	579	21,466	14,678	6,788	3,133	4,557	8,179	5,597	1,661
Not reported	3,357	326	1,986	920	1,066	331	457	710	488	1,045
Fire extinguisher purchased or recharged	49,902	(X)	49,902	37,922	11,980	9,405	11,183	19,118	10,196	(X)
Sprinkler system inside home	6,401	246	5,167	2,086	3,081	938	877	1,845	1,507	988
Working carbon monoxide detector	43,494	673	40,698	31,691	9,007	12,483	12,688	9,927	5,600	2,123
Main heating equipment: [4]										
Warm-air furnace	81,629	2,034	71,141	51,691	19,450	8,925	20,671	25,268	16,277	8,454
Steam or hot water system	13,969	259	12,506	7,494	5,012	9,088	2,015	592	811	1,204
Electric heat pump	16,059	868	13,264	9,764	3,500	336	706	10,785	1,436	1,927
Built-in electric units	5,730	320	4,761	2,120	2,641	1,159	1,134	827	1,641	649
Floor, wall, or pipeless furnace	5,525	202	4,802	2,043	2,760	435	388	1,154	2,825	520
Room heaters with flue	1,173	73	950	580	370	124	103	478	244	150
Room heaters without flue	1,365	99	1,109	694	414	24	52	992	41	157
Portable electric heaters	1,405	107	1,167	535	632	29	65	769	304	131
Stoves	1,364	203	1,035	845	190	226	158	341	310	125
Fireplaces [5]	290	42	215	190	25	27	40	53	94	34
None	930	330	386	206	180	3	3	58	321	215
Main cooling equipment:										
Central air conditioning	88,668	2,197	78,437	59,357	19,080	6,931	18,340	39,501	13,665	8,034
One or more room units	26,850	581	24,582	13,707	10,875	10,499	5,478	4,980	3,625	1,687
Source of water:										
Public system or private company	113,489	3,238	98,027	64,372	33,655	17,101	21,435	36,594	22,897	12,224
Well serving 1 to 5 units	15,846	1,070	13,430	11,769	1,660	3,275	3,878	4,821	1,455	1,346
Means of sewage disposal:										
Public sewer	103,155	2,596	89,467	56,736	32,732	16,263	20,432	31,288	21,484	11,092
Septic tank chemical toilet	26,662	1,800	22,307	19,667	2,640	4,185	4,930	10,279	2,913	2,555

X Not applicable. [1] Includes trailers. Includes width not reported, not shown separately. [2] Excludes mobile homes; includes basements and finished attics. [3] Limited to single-family units. [4] Includes other items, not shown separately. [5] With and without inserts.

Source: U.S. Census Bureau, Current Housing Reports, Series H150/09, *American Housing Survey for the United States: 2009*. See also <http://www.census.gov/hhes/www/housing/ahs/nationaldata.html>.

Table 984. Housing Units by Units in Structure and State: 2008

[In percent, except as indicated (129,060 represents 129,060,000). The American Community Survey universe includes the household population and the population living in institutions, college dormitories, and other group quarters. Based on a sample and subject to sampling variability; see Appendix III]

Characteristic	Total housing units (1,000)	Percent of units by units in structures—								
		1-unit detached	1-unit attached	2 units	3 or 4 units	5 or 9 units	10 or 19 units	20 or more units	Mobile homes	Boat, RV, van, etc.
U.S.	129,060	61.9	5.7	3.9	4.5	4.9	4.5	8.0	6.6	0.1
AL	2,159	67.9	1.9	2.2	2.9	4.5	2.9	3.3	14.3	0.1
AK	283	61.0	8.5	4.9	7.6	5.4	2.5	5.3	4.6	0.1
AZ	2,723	63.5	5.3	1.4	3.4	4.3	5.1	5.9	10.7	0.4
AR	1,298	70.5	1.6	3.3	3.4	3.5	3.1	2.3	12.3	0.1
CA	13,394	58.3	7.0	2.6	5.7	6.2	5.2	11.0	3.9	0.1
CO	2,152	63.3	6.8	1.7	3.5	4.9	6.1	9.1	4.6	0.1
CT	1,443	59.1	5.0	8.7	8.8	5.6	3.8	8.2	0.8	(Z)
DE	393	57.5	15.0	1.7	2.2	3.3	5.5	4.6	10.2	(Z)
DC	285	12.6	26.0	2.9	8.2	6.4	11.1	32.8	0.0	0.1
FL	8,798	54.3	6.0	2.3	3.9	5.2	5.9	12.6	9.8	0.1
GA	4,026	66.5	3.6	2.5	2.9	5.0	4.9	4.7	9.9	(Z)
HI	513	53.5	5.9	3.5	4.4	7.0	4.9	20.6	0.2	(Z)
ID	642	72.5	3.1	2.9	4.6	3.0	2.1	2.2	9.3	0.2
IL	5,276	58.6	5.7	6.3	6.7	6.2	4.1	9.7	2.6	(Z)
IN	2,795	72.6	3.4	2.7	3.6	4.8	3.7	3.6	5.5	(Z)
IA	1,329	74.0	3.5	2.7	3.4	3.7	3.6	4.9	4.2	(Z)
KS	1,226	73.4	4.1	2.7	3.5	3.7	3.4	3.8	5.2	(Z)
KY	1,921	67.7	2.2	3.0	3.9	4.6	3.3	2.8	12.6	0.1
LA	1,883	66.3	2.7	3.6	4.4	3.3	2.7	3.5	13.4	0.1
ME	701	68.5	2.0	5.5	5.9	4.3	1.7	3.0	9.1	(Z)
MD	2,333	51.9	21.3	1.8	2.3	5.1	8.5	7.5	1.7	(Z)
MA	2,736	52.9	4.8	10.8	10.4	6.2	4.5	9.5	0.9	(Z)
MI	4,536	71.6	4.7	2.8	2.5	4.4	3.6	4.8	5.7	(Z)
MN	2,331	67.7	7.3	2.5	2.3	2.2	3.5	10.8	3.7	(Z)
MS	1,267	69.9	1.4	2.2	3.1	4.8	1.7	1.5	15.2	0.2
MO	2,664	70.3	3.5	3.9	4.6	3.8	3.5	3.8	6.7	0.1
MT	438	69.3	2.6	3.2	4.1	3.1	2.4	3.3	11.8	(Z)
NE	786	72.9	3.5	2.2	2.8	4.1	4.8	5.9	3.8	(Z)
NV	1,127	59.3	4.8	1.6	6.6	9.0	6.1	6.5	6.0	0.2
NH	597	63.1	4.8	5.8	6.3	5.2	2.7	6.1	0.0	(Z)
NJ	3,516	54.1	8.9	9.3	6.7	4.9	5.1	9.9	1.0	(Z)
NM	872	64.3	3.7	2.2	3.7	3.3	2.2	4.0	16.4	0.1
NY	7,977	41.8	4.8	11.1	7.3	5.4	4.0	23.1	2.5	(Z)
NC	4,200	65.3	3.7	2.2	2.9	4.3	4.0	3.3	14.3	(Z)
ND	313	62.0	5.2	2.5	3.8	4.4	5.4	9.5	7.0	(Z)
OH	5,080	68.5	4.7	4.7	4.5	4.8	3.8	5.1	3.9	(Z)
OK	1,637	73.2	2.1	2.0	3.0	4.1	3.2	3.4	9.0	0.1
OR	1,620	61.0	4.1	3.0	4.4	4.4	3.9	7.1	8.6	0.3
PA	5,497	57.1	18.2	4.8	4.4	3.4	2.5	5.3	4.3	(Z)
RI	452	55.0	2.9	11.0	14.0	5.4	3.3	7.3	1.0	(Z)
SC	2,056	63.0	2.3	2.1	3.1	5.0	3.1	3.3	17.9	0.1
SD	361	69.3	3.2	2.0	3.8	3.6	3.6	5.6	9.0	(Z)
TN	2,758	69.0	3.1	2.9	3.1	4.4	3.7	3.6	10.2	0.1
TX	9,599	66.0	2.6	2.1	3.2	5.1	6.7	6.7	7.4	0.2
UT	944	69.7	5.5	2.9	4.3	3.2	4.4	5.5	4.4	(Z)
VT	313	66.4	3.9	6.3	6.2	5.2	1.9	3.2	6.9	0.1
VA	3,306	63.0	10.2	1.7	2.6	4.7	5.8	6.2	5.8	(Z)
WA	2,792	63.4	3.5	2.8	3.8	4.8	5.4	8.9	7.2	0.2
WV	886	71.7	1.9	2.8	2.6	2.9	1.6	2.4	14.0	(Z)
WI	2,569	66.8	4.3	7.1	3.7	4.7	3.3	6.1	3.8	(Z)
WY	246	66.2	3.6	3.0	5.1	3.1	2.0	2.9	14.0	0.1

Z Less than .05 percent.

Source: U.S. Census Bureau, 2008 American Community Survey, B25024, "Units in Structure," <http://www.factfinder.census.gov>, accessed May 2010.

U.S. Census Bureau, Statistical Abstract of the United States: 2011

Table 985. Housing Units—Size of Units and Lot: 2009

[In thousands (130,112 represents 130,112,000), except as indicated. As of fall. Based on the American Housing Survey; see Appendix III. For composition of regions, see map, inside front cover]

Item	Total housing units	Sea-sonal	Year-round units — Occupied — Total	Owner	Renter	North-east	Mid-west	South	West	Vacant
Total units	**130,112**	**4,618**	**111,806**	**76,428**	**35,378**	**20,451**	**25,368**	**41,586**	**24,401**	**13,688**
Rooms:										
1 room	579	104	352	26	326	111	60	33	149	123
2 rooms	1,423	194	946	68	879	269	130	209	337	283
3 rooms	11,290	697	8,711	1,036	7,675	2,235	1,891	2,461	2,124	1,882
4 rooms	23,036	1,374	17,828	6,475	11,354	3,277	3,889	6,376	4,287	3,834
5 rooms	29,888	1,108	25,444	17,232	8,212	3,854	5,758	10,355	5,476	3,336
6 rooms	27,480	632	24,596	20,364	4,232	4,435	5,400	9,918	4,842	2,252
7 rooms	17,877	315	16,489	14,754	1,735	3,080	3,904	6,110	3,394	1,073
8 rooms or more	18,538	193	17,440	16,474	967	3,189	4,337	6,123	3,791	905
Complete bathrooms:										
No bathrooms	1,678	557	403	175	229	98	93	115	97	717
1 bathroom	46,977	1,899	38,662	15,767	22,894	9,418	9,760	11,847	7,636	6,416
1 and one-half bathrooms	17,233	363	15,656	12,081	3,575	4,066	4,770	4,217	2,603	1,214
2 or more bathrooms	64,223	1,798	57,085	48,405	8,600	6,869	10,746	25,406	14,064	5,340
Square footage of unit:										
Single detached and mobile homes	91,241	3,524	79,918	68,742	11,176	11,971	19,088	31,981	16,878	7,799
Less than 500	988	225	603	383	220	86	104	247	166	161
500 to 749	2,765	462	1,771	1,085	686	249	415	810	298	532
750 to 999	6,440	593	5,014	3,519	1,495	614	1,340	2,086	973	833
1,000 to 1,499	21,224	814	18,419	14,978	3,441	2,047	4,331	7,834	4,207	1,991
1,500 to 1,999	20,636	521	18,519	16,284	2,235	2,458	4,039	7,564	4,457	1,596
2,000 to 2,499	14,361	284	13,190	12,057	1,134	2,000	3,282	5,165	2,743	886
2,500 to 2,999	7,589	141	7,050	6,622	429	1,211	1,594	2,819	1,426	398
3,000 to 3,999	7,252	137	6,692	6,391	301	1,119	1,700	2,488	1,385	424
4,000 or more	4,456	113	4,030	3,787	243	805	994	1,519	712	313
Other [1]	5,529	234	4,630	3,638	992	1,382	1,288	1,449	510	666
Median square footage	1,700	1,150	1,800	1,800	1,300	1,900	1,800	1,700	1,700	1,500
Lot size:										
Single detached and attached units and mobile homes	95,216	3,512	83,466	70,643	12,823	13,297	19,555	33,222	17,392	8,239
Less than one-eighth acre	25,234	946	21,635	16,297	5,338	3,161	4,749	7,268	6,457	2,652
One-eighth to one-quarter acre	13,706	448	11,981	10,581	1,400	1,610	3,063	3,413	3,896	1,277
One-quarter to one-half acre	17,825	518	15,921	13,837	2,084	2,383	4,044	6,523	2,970	1,386
One-half up to one acre	11,292	372	10,036	8,874	1,162	1,974	1,964	4,945	1,153	884
1 up to 5 acres	19,172	754	17,014	14,895	2,120	3,072	3,669	8,310	1,963	1,404
5 up to 10 acres	3,104	120	2,750	2,545	205	464	737	1,106	443	234
10 acres or more	4,885	354	4,127	3,614	513	633	1,329	1,656	509	403
Median acreage	0.27	0.32	0.27	0.32	0.22	0.34	0.28	0.36	0.18	0.25

[1] Represents units not reported or size unknown.

Source: U.S. Census Bureau, Current Housing Reports, Series H150/09, *American Housing Survey for the United States: 2009,* September 2010. See also <http://www.census.gov/hhes/www/housing/ahs/nationaldata.html>.

Table 986. Occupied Housing Units—Tenure by Race of Householder: 1991 to 2009

[In thousands (93,147 represents 93,147,000), except percent. As of fall. Based on the American Housing Survey; see Appendix III]

Race of householder and tenure	1991	1995	1999	2001	2003 [1]	2005	2007	2009
ALL RACES [2]								
Occupied units, total	**93,147**	**97,693**	**102,803**	**106,261**	**105,842**	**108,871**	**110,692**	**111,806**
Owner-occupied	59,796	63,544	68,796	72,265	72,238	74,931	75,647	76,428
Percent of occupied	64.2	65.0	66.9	68.0	68.3	68.8	68.3	68.4
Renter-occupied	33,351	34,150	34,007	33,996	33,604	33,940	35,045	35,378
WHITE [3]								
Occupied units, total	**79,140**	**81,611**	**83,624**	**85,292**	**87,483**	**89,449**	**90,413**	**91,137**
Owner-occupied	53,749	56,507	60,041	62,465	63,126	65,023	65,554	65,935
Percent of occupied	67.9	69.2	71.8	73.2	72.2	72.7	72.5	72.3
Renter-occupied	25,391	25,104	23,583	22,826	24,357	24,426	24,859	25,202
BLACK [3]								
Occupied units, total	**10,832**	**11,773**	**12,936**	**13,292**	**13,004**	**13,447**	**13,856**	**13,993**
Owner-occupied	4,635	5,137	6,013	6,318	6,193	6,471	6,464	6,547
Percent of occupied	42.8	43.6	46.5	47.5	47.6	48.1	46.7	46.8
Renter-occupied	6,197	6,637	6,923	6,974	6,811	6,975	7,392	7,446
HISPANIC ORIGIN [4]								
Occupied units, total	**6,239**	**7,757**	**9,041**	**9,814**	**11,038**	**11,651**	**12,609**	**12,739**
Owner-occupied	2,423	3,245	4,087	4,731	5,106	5,752	6,364	6,439
Percent of occupied	38.8	41.8	45.2	48.2	46.3	49.4	50.5	50.5
Renter-occupied	3,816	4,512	4,955	5,083	5,931	5,899	6,244	6,300

[1] Based on 2000 census controls. [2] Includes other races not shown separately. [3] The 2003 American Housing Survey (AHS) allowed respondents to choose more than one race. Beginning in 2003, data represent householders who selected this race group only and exclude householders reporting more than one race. The AHS in prior years only allowed respondents to report one race group. See also comments on race in the text for Section 1 and the below cited source. [4] Persons of Hispanic origin may be any race.

Source: U.S. Census Bureau, Current Housing Reports, Series H150/91, H150/95RV, H150/99, H150/01, H150/03, H150/05, H150/07, and H150/09, *American Housing Survey for the United States: 2009,* See also <http://www.census.gov/hhes/www/housing/ahs/nationaldata.html>.

Table 987. Homeownership Rates by Age of Householder and Household Type: 1990 to 2009

[In percent. Represents the proportion of owner households to the total number of occupied households. Based on the Current Population Survey and Housing Vacancy Survey; see source and Appendix III for details]

Age of householder and household type	1990	1995	2000	2003	2004	2005	2006	2007	2008	2009
United States	**63.9**	**64.7**	**67.4**	**68.3**	**69.0**	**68.9**	**68.8**	**68.1**	**67.8**	**67.4**
AGE OF HOUSEHOLDER										
Less than 25 years old	15.7	15.9	21.7	22.8	25.2	25.7	24.8	24.8	23.6	23.3
25 to 29 years old	35.2	34.4	38.1	39.8	40.2	40.9	41.8	40.6	40.0	37.7
30 to 34 years old	51.8	53.1	54.6	56.5	57.4	56.8	55.9	54.4	53.5	52.5
35 to 39 years old	63.0	62.1	65.0	65.1	66.2	66.6	66.4	65.0	64.6	63.4
40 to 44 years old	69.8	68.6	70.6	71.3	71.9	71.7	71.2	70.4	69.4	68.7
45 to 49 years old	73.9	73.7	74.7	75.4	76.3	75.0	74.9	74.0	73.6	72.3
50 to 54 years old	76.8	77.0	78.5	77.9	78.2	78.3	77.7	76.9	76.4	76.5
55 to 59 years old	78.8	78.8	80.4	80.9	81.2	80.6	80.4	79.9	79.4	78.6
60 to 64 years old	79.8	80.3	80.3	81.9	82.4	81.9	81.5	81.5	80.9	80.6
65 to 69 years old	80.0	81.0	83.0	82.5	83.2	82.8	82.4	81.7	81.6	82.0
70 to 74 years old	78.4	80.9	82.6	82.0	84.4	82.9	83.0	82.4	81.7	81.9
75 years old and over	72.3	74.6	77.7	78.7	78.8	78.4	79.1	78.7	78.6	78.9
Less than 35 years old	38.5	38.6	40.8	42.2	43.1	43.0	42.6	41.7	41.0	39.7
35 to 44 years old	66.3	65.2	67.9	68.3	69.3	69.3	68.9	67.8	67.0	66.2
45 to 54 years old	75.2	75.2	76.5	76.6	77.2	76.6	76.2	75.4	75.0	74.4
55 to 64 years old	79.3	79.5	80.3	81.4	81.9	81.2	80.9	80.6	80.1	79.5
65 years and over	76.3	78.1	80.4	80.5	81.1	80.6	80.9	80.4	80.1	80.5
TYPE OF HOUSEHOLD										
Family households:										
Married-couple families	78.1	79.6	82.4	83.3	84.0	84.2	84.1	83.8	83.4	82.8
Male householder, no spouse present	55.2	55.3	57.5	57.9	59.6	59.1	58.9	57.4	57.6	56.9
Female householder, no spouse present	44.0	45.1	49.1	49.6	50.9	51.0	51.3	49.9	49.5	49.0
Nonfamily households:										
One-person	49.0	50.5	53.6	55.2	55.8	55.6	55.7	55.2	55.0	55.1
Male householder	42.4	43.8	47.4	50.0	50.5	50.3	50.5	50.2	50.6	50.9
Female householder	53.6	55.4	58.1	59.1	59.9	59.6	59.8	59.1	58.6	58.6
Other:										
Male householder	31.7	34.2	38.0	40.0	41.7	41.7	40.8	40.0	41.3	40.2
Female householder	32.5	33.0	40.6	43.1	43.5	44.8	45.5	42.9	42.5	42.5

Source: U.S. Census Bureau, "Housing Vacancies and Home Ownership," <http://www.census.gov/hhes/www/hvs.html>.

Table 988. Homeownership Rates by State: 1990 to 2009

[In percent. See headnote, Table 987]

State	1990	2000	2005	2007	2008	2009	State	1990	2000	2005	2007	2008	2009
United States	**63.9**	**67.4**	**68.9**	**68.1**	**67.8**	**67.4**	Missouri	64.0	74.2	72.3	70.4	71.4	72.0
Alabama	68.4	73.2	76.6	73.3	73.0	74.1	Montana	69.1	70.2	70.4	67.3	70.3	70.7
Alaska	58.4	66.4	66.0	66.6	66.4	66.8	Nebraska	67.3	70.2	70.2	68.2	69.6	70.2
Arizona	64.5	68.0	71.1	70.4	69.1	68.9	Nevada	55.8	64.0	63.4	63.3	63.6	62.4
Arkansas	67.8	68.9	69.2	69.5	66.9	68.5	New Hampshire	65.0	69.2	74.0	73.8	75.0	76.0
California	53.8	57.1	59.7	58.3	57.5	57.0	New Jersey	65.0	66.2	70.1	68.3	67.3	65.9
Colorado	59.0	68.3	71.0	70.2	69.0	68.4	New Mexico	68.6	73.7	71.4	71.5	70.4	69.1
Connecticut	67.9	70.0	70.5	70.3	70.7	70.5	New York	53.3	53.4	55.9	55.9	55.0	54.4
Delaware	67.7	72.0	75.8	76.8	76.2	76.5	North Carolina	69.0	71.1	70.9	70.3	69.4	70.1
Dist. of Columbia	36.4	41.9	45.8	47.2	44.1	44.9	North Dakota	67.2	70.7	68.5	66.0	66.6	65.7
Florida	65.1	68.4	72.4	71.8	71.1	70.9	Ohio	68.7	71.3	73.3	71.4	70.8	69.7
Georgia	64.3	69.8	67.9	67.6	68.2	67.4	Oklahoma	70.3	72.7	72.9	70.3	70.4	69.6
Hawaii	55.5	55.2	59.8	60.1	59.1	59.5	Oregon	64.4	65.3	68.2	65.7	66.2	68.2
Idaho	69.4	70.5	74.2	74.5	75.0	75.5	Pennsylvania	73.8	74.7	73.3	72.9	72.6	72.2
Illinois	63.0	67.9	70.9	69.4	68.9	69.1	Rhode Island	58.5	61.5	63.1	64.9	64.5	62.9
Indiana	67.0	74.9	75.0	73.8	74.4	72.0	South Carolina	71.4	76.5	73.9	74.1	73.9	74.4
Iowa	70.7	75.2	73.7	74.0	72.4	72.4	South Dakota	66.2	71.2	68.4	70.4	70.4	69.6
Kansas	69.0	69.3	69.5	69.4	68.8	67.4	Tennessee	68.3	70.9	72.4	70.2	71.7	71.1
Kentucky	65.8	73.4	71.6	72.9	72.8	71.2	Texas	59.7	63.8	65.9	66.0	65.5	65.4
Louisiana	67.8	68.1	72.5	71.5	73.5	71.9	Utah	70.1	72.7	73.9	74.9	76.2	74.1
Maine	74.2	76.5	73.9	74.3	73.9	74.0	Vermont	72.6	68.7	74.2	73.7	72.8	74.3
Maryland	64.9	69.9	71.2	71.7	70.6	69.6	Virginia	69.8	73.9	71.2	71.5	70.6	69.7
Massachusetts	58.6	59.9	63.4	64.3	65.7	65.1	Washington	61.8	63.6	67.6	66.8	66.2	65.5
Michigan	72.3	77.2	76.4	76.4	75.9	74.5	West Virginia	72.0	75.9	81.3	77.6	77.8	78.7
Minnesota	68.0	76.1	76.5	73.5	73.1	72.9	Wisconsin	68.3	71.8	71.1	70.5	70.4	70.4
Mississippi	69.4	75.2	78.8	74.0	75.4	75.5	Wyoming	68.9	71.0	72.8	73.2	73.3	73.8

Source: U.S. Census Bureau, "Housing Vacancies and Home Ownership," <http://www.census.gov/hhes/www/hvs.html>.

Construction and Housing 619

Table 989. Occupied Housing Units—Costs by Region: 2009

[76,428 represents 76,428,000. As of fall. See headnote, Table 990, for an explanation of housing costs. Based on the American Housing Survey; see Appendix III. For composition of regions, see map, inside front cover]

Category	Number (1,000)					Percent distribution				
	Total units	North-east	Mid-west	South	West	Total units	North-east	Mid-west	South	West
OWNER-OCCUPIED UNITS										
Total	**76,428**	**13,378**	**18,249**	**29,193**	**15,607**	**100.0**	**100.0**	**100.0**	**100.0**	**100.0**
Monthly housing costs:										
Less than $300	2,635	192	430	1,368	647	3.4	1.4	2.4	4.7	4.1
$300 to $399	5,351	366	1,087	3,026	873	7.0	2.7	6.0	10.4	5.6
$400 to $499	6,022	653	1,549	2,835	984	7.9	4.9	8.5	9.7	6.3
$500 to $599	5,308	738	1,528	2,190	852	6.9	5.5	8.4	7.5	5.5
$600 to $699	8,141	1,682	2,093	3,261	1,105	10.7	12.6	11.5	11.2	7.1
$700 to $799	10,736	1,938	3,071	4,275	1,452	14.0	14.5	16.8	14.6	9.3
$800 to $999	14,984	2,578	4,298	5,563	2,545	19.6	19.3	23.6	19.1	16.3
$1,000 to $1,249	14,867	3,193	3,211	4,565	3,898	19.5	23.9	17.6	15.6	25.0
$1,250 to $1,499	8,383	2,039	982	2,111	3,251	11.0	15.2	5.4	7.2	20.8
Median (dol.) [1]	1,000	1,196	937	827	1,389	(X)	(X)	(X)	(X)	(X)
RENTER-OCCUPIED UNITS										
Total	**35,378**	**7,073**	**7,119**	**12,392**	**8,794**	**100.0**	**100.0**	**100.0**	**100.0**	**100.0**
Monthly housing costs:										
Less than $300										
$300 to $399	976	190	267	351	168	2.8	2.7	3.7	2.8	1.9
$400 to $499	1,381	357	333	408	283	3.9	5.1	4.7	3.3	3.2
$500 to $599	1,359	352	371	441	194	3.8	5.0	5.2	3.6	2.2
$600 to $699	2,094	335	616	783	360	5.9	4.7	8.7	6.3	4.1
$700 to $799	6,793	1,055	1,845	2,712	1,181	19.2	14.9	25.9	21.9	13.4
$800 to $999	9,769	1,727	2,082	3,695	2,265	27.6	24.4	29.2	29.8	25.8
$1,000 to $1,249	7,407	1,819	940	2,271	2,377	20.9	25.7	13.2	18.3	27.0
$1,250 to $1,499	2,965	727	222	648	1,368	8.4	10.3	3.1	5.2	15.6
$1,500 or more	596	169	45	137	245	1.7	2.4	0.6	1.1	2.8
No cash rent	2,037	341	398	945	352	5.8	4.8	5.6	7.6	4.0
Median (dol.) [1]	808	877	691	764	956	(X)	(X)	(X)	(X)	(X)

X Not applicable. [1] For explanation of median, see Guide to Tabular Presentation.

Source: U.S. Census Bureau, Current Housing Reports, Series H150/09, *American Housing Survey for the United States: 2009,* September 2010. See also <http://www.census.gov/hhes/www/housing/ahs/nationaldata.html>.

Table 990. Occupied Housing Units—Financial Summary by Selected Characteristics of the Householder: 2009

[In thousands of units (111,806 represents 111,806,000), except as indicated. As of fall. Housing costs include real estate taxes, property insurance, utilities, fuel, water, garbage collection, homeowner association fees, mobile home fees, and mortgage. Based on the American Housing Survey; see Appendix III]

Characteristic	Total occupied units	Tenure		Black [1]		Hispanic origin [2]		Elderly [3]		Households below poverty level	
		Owner	Renter	Owner	Renter	Owner	Renter	Owner	Renter	Owner	Renter
Total units [4]	**111,806**	**76,428**	**35,378**	**6,547**	**7,446**	**6,439**	**6,300**	**18,472**	**4,623**	**6,405**	**9,334**
Monthly housing costs:											
$199 or less	3,611	2,635	976	322	370	253	132	1,119	261	727	760
$200 to $299	6,732	5,351	1,381	467	422	453	200	2,587	461	1,035	895
$300 to $399	7,381	6,022	1,359	499	357	445	172	2,897	364	818	599
$400 to $499	7,402	5,308	2,094	470	420	371	333	2,395	408	611	823
$500 to $699	14,934	8,141	6,793	801	1,569	503	1,165	3,079	827	777	1,929
$700 to $999	20,505	10,736	9,769	1,041	2,106	910	1,900	2,502	883	893	2,057
$1,000 to $1,499	22,391	14,984	7,407	1,313	1,471	1,186	1,508	1,967	533	722	1,166
$1,500 to $2,499	17,832	14,867	2,965	1,099	348	1,418	593	1,233	277	548	331
$2,500 or more	8,980	8,383	596	537	35	900	58	692	129	275	53
Median amount (dol.) [4]	909	1,000	808	901	746	1,113	854	512	640	502	629
Monthly housing costs as percent of income: [6]											
Less than 5 percent	3,065	2,903	162	133	15	171	35	594	23	8	17
5 to 9 percent	10,334	9,614	721	617	105	561	83	2,658	79	49	21
10 to 14 percent	13,111	11,147	1,964	842	295	711	256	2,932	170	109	47
15 to 19 percent	14,210	10,986	3,224	814	553	719	450	2,410	235	215	87
20 to 24 percent	13,271	9,589	3,682	754	697	716	603	1,966	329	191	159
25 to 29 percent	10,775	7,167	3,608	625	708	586	615	1,481	494	262	366
30 to 34 percent	8,116	5,160	2,956	488	651	579	606	1,024	370	282	360
35 to 39 percent	6,071	3,753	2,317	429	525	370	388	818	312	242	322
40 percent or more	28,695	15,250	13,445	1,743	3,181	1,921	2,808	4,478	2,063	4,245	6,138
Median amount (percent) [5]	24	21	34	25	38	27	38	21	40	89	82

[1] For persons who selected this race group only. See footnote 3, Table 986. [2] Persons of Hispanic origin may be of any race. [3] Householders 65 years old and over. [4] Include units with no cash, not shown separately. [5] For explanation of median, see Guide to Tabular Presentation. [6] Money income before taxes.

Source: U.S. Census Bureau, Current Housing Reports, Series H150/09, *American Housing Survey for the United States: 2009,* September 2010. See also <http://www.census.gov/hhes/www/housing/ahs/nationaldata.html>.

Table 991. Owner-Occupied Housing Units—Value and Costs by State: 2008

[In percent, except as indicated (75,373 represents 75,373,000). The American Community Survey universe includes the household population and the population living in institutions, college dormitories, and other group quarters. Based on a sample and subject to sampling variability; see Appendix III. For definition of median, see Guide to Tabular Presentation]

State	Total (1,000)	Percent of units with value of—			Median value (dol.)	Median selected monthly owner costs [1] (dol.)	Selected monthly owner costs as a percent income in the past 12 months [1]			
		$99,999 or less	$100,000 to $199,999	$200,000 or more			Less than 15 percent	15.0 to 24.9 percent	25.0 to 29.9 percent	30.0 percent or more
U.S.	**75,373**	**21.9**	**28.7**	**49.4**	**197,600**	**1,514**	**17.0**	**32.6**	**12.4**	**37.6**
AL	1,289	41.5	33.4	25.1	121,500	1,089	24.5	35.8	10.5	28.8
AK	154	12.4	24.9	62.7	237,800	1,732	17.8	35.2	14.3	32.5
AZ	1,549	13.6	27.3	59.1	229,200	1,527	15.1	30.3	12.8	41.3
AR	751	47.5	34.1	18.4	105,700	964	25.7	35.8	10.6	27.5
CA	6,946	5.5	6.9	87.6	467,000	2,384	10.6	23.7	11.8	53.3
CO	1,281	9.5	26.1	64.4	242,200	1,620	16.0	33.5	13.2	36.9
CT	917	3.0	16.7	80.3	306,000	2,108	14.4	31.0	13.4	40.9
DE	242	12.1	20.7	67.2	250,900	1,580	17.2	32.4	13.7	36.5
DC	109	2.0	4.8	93.2	474,100	2,218	20.2	31.1	10.9	37.5
FL	4,916	15.7	28.8	55.4	218,700	1,603	12.3	26.2	11.7	49.1
GA	2,340	21.9	39.1	39.1	169,100	1,387	18.7	34.8	12.0	34.0
HI	258	2.3	3.5	94.1	560,200	2,265	12.2	26.3	11.8	49.3
ID	401	16.3	40.0	43.7	183,700	1,198	17.3	34.8	13.7	33.8
IL	3,302	19.0	27.4	53.6	214,900	1,684	15.5	32.6	12.9	38.6
IN	1,782	35.9	42.5	21.6	125,200	1,144	21.7	37.9	12.0	28.1
IA	886	39.0	40.0	21.0	120,700	1,131	23.0	40.6	12.0	24.3
KS	771	39.3	36.9	23.8	125,700	1,212	22.5	40.6	11.5	25.1
KY	1,173	41.4	36.8	21.7	118,400	1,055	23.0	37.6	11.2	27.7
LA	1,114	37.4	36.1	26.5	132,400	1,111	26.2	34.2	10.5	28.6
ME	391	21.8	33.9	44.3	180,200	1,326	16.2	33.5	13.0	37.1
MD	1,454	5.6	12.2	82.2	341,200	1,983	15.6	31.8	13.1	39.2
MA	1,592	3.0	9.8	87.2	353,600	2,105	13.9	30.6	13.3	41.9
MI	2,819	26.8	42.5	30.7	151,300	1,351	16.2	34.3	13.3	35.8
MN	1,560	13.7	31.4	55.0	213,800	1,545	16.3	35.0	14.0	34.4
MS	767	50.1	30.8	19.1	99,700	1,011	22.0	34.1	11.6	30.8
MO	1,633	31.8	40.0	28.3	141,500	1,180	21.1	38.4	11.7	28.4
MT	257	25.3	31.2	43.5	180,300	1,239	19.6	33.5	13.2	33.5
NE	488	35.0	44.4	20.6	126,500	1,235	19.9	40.4	12.0	20.6
NV	500	7.6	18.7	73.8	271,500	1,818	12.1	25.6	12.8	48.9
NH	365	8.1	19.8	72.1	264,700	1,900	12.5	31.3	14.9	41.1
NJ	2,114	4.1	10.6	85.3	364,100	2,360	12.4	27.5	13.4	46.3
NM	513	28.3	32.9	38.9	165,100	1,173	21.8	32.7	10.5	34.4
NY	3,946	17.9	19.0	63.1	318,900	1,936	16.9	29.7	11.9	41.1
NC	2,451	27.4	37.6	35.0	154,500	1,218	20.3	36.0	11.6	31.6
ND	183	43.9	38.4	17.7	112,500	1,140	26.9	37.4	12.3	23.1
OH	3,113	29.0	45.0	26.0	140,200	1,275	18.6	37.3	13.1	30.7
OK	947	47.3	35.8	16.9	105,500	1,064	25.2	37.0	11.0	26.5
OR	949	9.7	17.9	72.4	273,300	1,585	14.1	30.8	13.5	41.4
PA	3,475	28.2	32.3	39.5	164,700	1,389	18.5	35.6	12.4	33.1
RI	249	2.7	11.0	86.3	286,000	1,888	11.9	31.2	14.2	42.2
SC	1,202	35.4	33.2	31.3	138,700	1,142	22.5	34.8	11.3	30.9
SD	221	38.6	39.0	22.5	126,200	1,174	20.0	38.7	13.4	27.8
TN	1,700	32.8	39.0	28.3	138,600	1,149	19.7	36.2	12.5	31.1
TX	5,466	37.0	38.6	24.4	126,800	1,445	20.3	36.2	11.7	31.3
UT	613	7.4	29.0	63.6	236,000	1,445	16.4	34.7	13.7	35.1
VT	180	12.6	32.6	54.8	214,700	1,471	14.1	33.5	13.2	38.8
VA	2,034	13.4	21.2	65.4	269,600	1,715	17.6	33.4	13.2	35.5
WA	1,663	8.0	15.4	76.7	308,100	1,763	13.5	31.2	13.6	41.4
WV	553	52.3	30.1	17.7	95,900	878	28.9	35.8	9.6	25.4
WI	1,578	17.3	42.8	39.8	173,300	1,424	15.1	36.5	14.1	34.1
WY	146	19.6	34.9	45.5	188,200	1,272	23.4	36.6	12.9	27.0

[1] For homes with a mortgage. Includes all forms of debt where the property is pledged as security for repayment of the debt, including deeds of trust, land contracts, home equity loans. Also includes cost of property insurance, utilities, real estate taxes, etc.

Source: U.S. Census Bureau, 2008 American Community Survey, B25075, "Value for Owner-Occupied Housing Units"; B25077, "Median Value for Owner-Occupied Housing Units"; B25088, "Median Selected Monthly Owner Costs by Mortgage Status"; and B25091, "Mortgage Status by Selected Monthly Owner Cost as a Percentage of Household Income," <http://factfinder.census.gov>, accessed May 2010.

Construction and Housing 621

Table 992. Renter-Occupied Housing Units—Gross Rent by State: 2008

[In percent, except as indicated (37,728 represents 37,728,000). The American Community Survey universe includes the household population and the population living in institutions, college dormitories, and other group quarters. Based on a sample and subject to sampling variability; see Appendix III]

State	Total [1] (1,000)	Percent of units with gross rent of—					Median gross rent (dol.)	Gross rent as a percent of household income in the past 12 months			
		$299 or less	$300 to $499	$500 to $749	$750 to $999	$1,000 or more		Less than 15.0 percent	15.0 to 24.9 percent	25.0 to 29.0 percent	30.0 percent or more
U.S.	37,728	5.5	9.8	24.4	22.7	31.9	824	12.0	23.7	10.8	46.1
AL	527	8.0	18.4	31.9	18.5	10.8	631	13.0	21.3	10.3	41.3
AK	83	2.8	4.3	16.2	26.2	39.6	949	13.6	26.9	10.4	38.0
AZ	725	3.1	6.4	25.5	25.6	34.1	866	10.7	24.4	11.0	46.4
AR	363	8.3	18.5	38.0	15.9	8.6	606	12.4	22.6	10.5	42.3
CA	5,230	2.8	4.1	11.4	20.0	58.3	1,135	9.5	22.5	11.2	52.1
CO	617	4.2	7.4	26.0	25.8	33.1	848	10.0	25.2	11.8	47.3
CT	412	6.3	5.9	13.5	25.2	44.8	970	10.4	24.1	11.4	48.2
DE	87	6.5	5.3	15.2	28.5	38.1	917	9.9	23.8	11.2	47.5
DC	141	8.5	4.6	14.8	20.5	49.7	1,011	12.4	25.7	12.1	45.5
FL	2,141	3.6	4.7	17.4	27.5	42.0	947	7.8	20.7	11.2	53.7
GA	1,130	5.3	10.6	26.0	28.5	23.3	787	12.2	23.1	11.0	45.3
HI	179	3.8	3.9	7.4	13.1	64.2	1,298	9.6	20.6	10.3	50.4
ID	165	5.9	13.9	35.7	21.3	16.7	690	13.5	25.2	11.9	41.3
IL	1,464	6.3	8.9	25.2	27.0	28.4	811	13.2	23.7	10.5	45.6
IN	699	6.1	14.6	38.2	23.3	11.5	670	13.1	25.3	10.3	43.5
IA	329	7.6	21.4	37.9	16.7	8.8	607	15.2	26.3	10.2	39.7
KS	340	5.8	18.9	34.5	20.1	14.0	654	15.7	25.9	10.4	40.3
KY	514	10.5	22.5	33.5	16.0	7.3	578	14.6	23.3	9.5	40.7
LA	511	7.2	13.4	29.2	20.5	16.8	698	12.7	20.7	8.0	43.5
ME	151	10.8	11.7	29.8	24.0	16.1	702	9.5	23.2	11.7	47.3
MD	639	4.9	4.0	10.8	22.3	54.4	1,074	10.4	25.6	12.2	46.9
MA	875	8.8	7.5	13.6	19.0	47.4	991	12.3	24.1	11.7	46.5
MI	991	6.6	12.1	34.4	22.7	18.7	706	10.7	22.6	10.1	48.8
MN	530	9.0	11.4	29.5	23.6	22.1	734	12.2	24.6	11.3	46.4
MS	327	8.2	16.6	30.7	18.5	10.3	638	11.1	19.1	8.5	43.0
MO	697	6.6	17.0	35.8	21.8	11.6	657	14.5	25.8	10.2	41.1
MT	118	7.4	21.8	30.8	17.2	12.6	631	15.1	21.9	10.9	40.4
NE	216	7.1	20.7	37.1	17.8	10.7	626	17.4	26.2	10.8	37.7
NV	384	2.0	3.1	14.9	27.6	49.5	1,011	10.3	25.7	12.0	47.3
NH	140	5.0	5.4	18.9	28.1	38.3	914	11.5	25.7	12.4	44.9
NJ	1,040	5.3	3.6	10.2	23.2	54.6	1,068	12.5	24.1	10.8	47.5
NM	229	6.5	15.9	32.8	20.3	15.9	668	14.2	23.1	9.8	42.7
NY	3,191	6.1	7.7	18.0	20.3	44.5	953	13.7	22.5	10.6	47.9
NC	1,144	6.0	12.9	34.9	23.7	14.7	694	13.6	24.7	10.3	41.8
ND	92	8.8	30.7	34.0	11.5	6.2	534	18.3	29.6	8.3	34.4
OH	1,396	7.6	15.2	36.2	22.2	13.5	667	12.8	24.5	10.7	44.1
OK	461	7.1	20.1	35.9	18.1	9.7	614	14.6	25.1	9.7	40.0
OR	526	4.6	8.8	30.0	28.9	23.4	780	11.4	24.5	11.2	47.4
PA	1,430	7.0	13.3	29.5	22.7	21.1	726	13.6	24.7	10.3	43.6
RI	150	11.6	8.6	17.0	28.1	31.7	850	10.5	24.2	13.4	46.5
SC	501	6.2	14.1	34.2	20.7	13.5	675	13.3	23.0	9.5	40.8
SD	99	11.5	23.9	32.3	15.2	7.3	569	18.3	26.8	9.7	34.9
TN	735	7.9	15.5	34.6	20.9	12.8	660	12.4	23.6	10.6	43.0
TX	2,956	4.0	9.1	31.4	26.7	22.9	768	12.7	24.9	10.6	43.9
UT	242	4.0	9.8	29.1	28.7	23.4	784	13.8	28.7	11.5	40.2
VT	70	7.2	8.5	26.1	22.6	27.8	797	8.7	23.1	11.8	47.5
VA	927	4.7	8.3	18.5	20.2	42.0	934	12.2	25.3	11.3	43.7
WA	884	4.7	7.4	22.5	26.0	35.7	874	11.2	26.5	11.8	45.7
WV	197	11.0	26.7	32.8	10.2	4.1	528	15.5	18.8	9.2	38.2
WI	672	5.3	12.5	37.1	25.7	14.8	704	14.0	26.3	11.4	42.5
WY	62	6.3	16.3	33.4	17.7	12.5	636	18.8	23.2	11.1	32.5

[1] Includes units with no cash rent.

Source: U.S. Census Bureau, 2008 American Community Survey, B25063, "Gross Rent"; B25064, "Median Gross Rent"; and B25070, "Gross Rent as a Percentage of Household Income," <http://factfinder.census.gov>, accessed May 2010.

Table 993. Mortgage Characteristics—Owner-Occupied Units: 2009

[In thousands (76,428 represents 76,428,000). As of fall. Based on the American Housing Survey; see Appendix III]

Mortgage characteristic	Total owner occupied units (1,000)	Housing unit characteristics — New construction [1]	Housing unit characteristics — Mobile homes	Household characteristics — Black [2]	Household characteristics — His-panic [3]	Household characteristics — Elderly [4]	Household characteristics — Below poverty level
ALL OWNERS							
Total	**76,428**	**3,830**	**5,418**	**6,547**	**6,439**	**18,472**	**6,405**
Mortgages currently on property: [5]							
None, owned free and clear	24,206	499	3,237	2,073	1,752	12,071	3,466
Regular and home equity mortgages [6]	50,300	3,251	2,107	4,338	4,525	5,804	2,710
Regular mortgage	46,703	3,174	2,002	4,153	4,325	4,604	2,509
Home equity lump sum mortgage	4,022	154	57	241	300	522	156
Home equity line of credit	9,184	297	106	426	579	1,527	334
Number of regular and home equity mortgages:							
1 mortgage	35,274	2,391	1,830	3,329	3,307	4,322	1,940
2 mortgages	10,896	621	98	646	928	833	321
3 mortgages or more	801	20	2	43	67	76	25
Type of mortgage:							
Regular and home equity lump sum	2,779	131	20	152	215	189	76
With home equity line of credit	429	11	2	16	40	52	10
No home equity line of credit	2,341	120	17	135	173	137	65
Regular no home equity lump sum	43,923	3,043	1,982	4,001	4,110	4,415	2,433
With home equity line of credit	6,153	230	36	294	407	527	189
No home equity line of credit	34,513	2,594	1,773	3,390	3,486	3,330	1,835
Home equity lump sum no regular	1,243	22	37	89	85	333	80
With home equity line of credit	248	2	–	20	17	80	14
No home equity line of credit	989	20	37	69	68	252	67
No regular or home equity lump sum	28,483	634	3,379	2,305	2,029	13,535	3,816
With home equity line of credit	2,355	54	68	96	115	867	121
No home equity line of credit	24,458	501	3,247	2,089	1,776	12,312	3,502
OWNERS WITH ONE OR MORE REGULAR OR LUMP SUM HOME EQUITY MORTGAGES							
Total	**47,945**	**3,197**	**2,039**	**4,242**	**4,410**	**4,936**	**2,589**
Type of primary mortgage:							
FHA	6,272	457	112	1,038	801	443	352
VA	3,660	273	207	316	312	356	140
RHS/RD	435	63	36	51	51	49	41
Other types	34,021	2,161	1,490	2,449	3,001	3,463	1,603
Mortgage origination:							
Placed new mortgage(s)	47,616	3,188	2,007	4,212	4,344	4,891	2,556
Primary obtained when property acquired	35,884	3,005	1,744	3,436	3,570	3,010	2,075
Obtained later	11,733	183	263	776	773	1,881	481
Assumed	259	8	28	19	51	40	25
Wrap-around	27	–	4	4	8	–	3
Combination of the above	43	–	–	7	8	5	6
Payment plan of primary mortgage:							
Fixed payment, self amortizing	40,055	2,664	1,713	3,472	3,686	3,820	1,861
Adjustable rate mortgage	1,942	80	58	201	238	187	97
Adjustable term mortgage	80	14	3	3	5	26	15
Graduated payment mortgage	523	48	–	48	62	26	17
Balloon	220	10	14	5	16	21	13
Combination of the above	169	9	–	9	14	21	5
Payment plan of secondary mortgage:							
Units with two or more mortgages	5,520	418	67	404	601	309	159
Fixed payment, self amortizing	4,514	359	58	342	482	221	117
Adjustable rate mortgage	393	15	–	32	53	32	16
Adjustable term mortgage	71	1	–	1	3	15	3
Graduated payment mortgage	71	10	–	3	16	6	–
Balloon	143	20	4	6	8	12	4
Other	2	–	–	–	–	–	–
Combination of the above	101	9	–	–	4	1	6
Reason primary refinanced:							
Units with a refinanced primary mortgage [6]	12,220	224	269	792	947	1,337	429
To get a lower interest rate	9,228	174	172	563	666	832	246
To increase payment period	180	4	9	4	16	6	11
To reduce payment period	573	5	9	25	40	37	19
To renew or extend a loan that has fallen due	123	3	2	7	15	20	8
To receive cash	1,587	16	32	147	153	265	72
Other reason	1,655	32	58	96	170	211	65
Cash received in primary mortgage refinance:							
Units receiving refinance cash	1,587	16	32	147	153	265	72
Median amount received (dol.)	30,000	(B)	(B)	18,000	40,000	50,000	25,000

– Represents or rounds to zero. B means sample too small. [1] Constructed in the past 4 years. [2] For persons who selected this race group only. See footnote 3, Table 986. [3] Persons of Hispanic origin may be any race. [4] 65 years old and over. [5] Regular mortgages include all mortgages not classified as home-equity or reverse. [6] Figures may not add to total because more than one category may apply to a unit.

Source: U.S. Census Bureau, Current Housing Reports, Series H150/09, *American Housing Survey for the United States: 2009*, September 2010. See also <http://www.census.gov/hhes/www/housing/ahs/nationaldata.html>.

Table 994. Home Purchase Loans by Race and Sex: 2008

[Applications in thousands (3,587 represents 3,587,000), amount in millions of dollars (778,333 represents $778,333,000,000). Data is the final 2008 National Aggregates data, see headnote, Table 999]

Race and Gender [1,2,3]	Applications received		Loans originated		Applications approved not accepted		Applications denied		Applications withdrawn		Files closed for incompleteness	
	Number (1,000)	Amount (million dollars)	Number (1,000)	Amount (million dollars)	Number (1,000)	Amount (million dollars)	Number (1,000)	Amount (million dollars)	Number (1,000)	Amount (million dollars)	Number (1,000)	Amount (million dollars)
Total	3,587	778,333	2,144	469,429	338	74,984	680	130,547	333	79,884	93	23,489
White	2,614	543,721	1,641	342,876	236	50,171	450	84,398	225	51,343	62	14,933
Male	913	183,466	525	104,593	87	17,532	192	36,255	83	18,739	26	6,347
Female	561	94,018	332	55,860	53	8,834	114	17,528	48	8,905	14	2,892
Joint (male/female)	1,134	264,970	781	181,802	95	23,694	143	30,329	94	23,499	21	5,645
Black	201	33,851	81	14,133	21	3,370	72	10,956	19	3,647	9	1,744
Male	76	13,103	29	5,024	8	1,293	28	4,650	7	1,402	4	734
Female	84	12,655	33	5,108	9	1,278	31	4,269	8	1,316	4	683
Joint (male/female)	41	7,932	18	3,937	4	780	13	1,992	4	904	1	319
Asian	225	65,691	130	37,031	24	7,610	39	11,385	25	7,364	7	2,301
Male	89	24,348	50	13,182	9	2,824	16	4,578	10	2,818	3	946
Female	54	13,806	30	7,460	6	1,561	11	2,793	6	1,473	2	519
Joint (male/female)	81	27,325	50	16,296	9	3,195	12	3,969	9	3,038	2	828
Native Hawaiian/Other Pacific Islander	14	3,198	7	1,591	1	325	4	786	1	373	–	123
Male	6	1,240	3	595	1	123	2	322	1	144	–	56
Female	4	733	2	336	1	79	1	194	–	90	–	34
Joint (male/female)	5	1,210	2	657	–	120	1	263	–	138	–	32
American Indian/Alaska Native	20	3,208	9	1,498	2	349	6	871	2	385	1	105
Male	9	1,447	4	636	1	160	3	420	1	170	–	61
Female	6	825	2	378	1	88	2	237	1	96	–	26
Joint (male/female)	5	917	2	474	1	99	2	209	–	116	–	18
Two or more minority races	3	599	1	332	–	51	1	125	–	73	–	18
Male	1	259	1	141	–	23	–	59	–	30	–	6
Female	1	154	–	76	–	14	–	38	–	20	–	6
Joint (male/female)	1	180	–	111	–	15	–	27	–	22	–	5
Joint [4]	77	14,713	34	8,222	13	1,893	25	3,038	4	1,278	1	283
Race Not Available [5]	434	113,353	241	63,746	41	11,215	82	18,987	56	15,421	14	3,983
Male	68	16,771	32	7,899	7	1,754	16	3,766	10	2,604	3	748
Female	41	8,459	19	4,040	4	873	10	2,026	6	1,163	1	356
Joint (male/female)	74	20,971	43	12,319	7	2,158	12	3,011	10	2,813	2	670

– Rounds to zero. [1] Applicants are shown in only one race category. [2] Total includes those cases in which gender was reported and that information was not available. [3] Applicants are shown in only one gender category. [4] "Joint" means with two applicants, one reported a single designation of "White" and the other applicant reports one or more minority racial designations. [5] "Not Available" includes situations where information was reported as not provided or not applicable.

Source: Federal Financial Institutions Examination Council, "HMDA National Aggregate Report", annual, <http://www.ffiec.gov/hmdaadwebreport/nataggwelcome.aspx>.

Table 995. Occupied Housing Units—Neighborhood Indicators by Selected Characteristics of the Householder: 2009

[In thousands (111,806 represents 111,806,000). As of fall. Based on the American Housing Survey; see Appendix III]

Characteristic	Total occu-pied units	Tenure Owner	Tenure Renter	Black [1] Owner	Black [1] Renter	Hispanic origin [2] Owner	Hispanic origin [2] Renter	Elderly [3] Owner	Elderly [3] Renter	Households below poverty level Owner	Households below poverty level Renter
Total units	**111,806**	**76,428**	**35,378**	**6,547**	**7,446**	**6,439**	**6,300**	**18,472**	**4,623**	**6,405**	**9,334**
Street noise or traffic present:											
Bothersome street noise or heavy traffic present [4]	111,806	76,428	35,378	6,547	7,446	6,439	6,300	18,472	4,623	6,405	9,334
Yes	25,381	15,223	10,158	1,639	2,460	1,419	1,725	3,497	1,077	1,549	3,110
No	85,122	60,264	24,858	4,836	4,895	4,972	4,545	14,744	3,498	4,692	6,119
Neighborhood crime present											
Serious crime in past 12 months	111,806	76,428	35,378	6,547	7,446	6,439	6,300	18,472	4,623	6,405	9,334
Yes	19,299	11,649	7,650	1,428	2,045	1,223	1,403	2,105	658	951	2,254
No	90,116	63,230	26,886	4,958	5,146	5,129	4,814	15,983	3,853	5,194	6,813
Odors present											
Bothersome smoke, gas, or bad smell [4]	111,806	76,428	35,378	6,547	7,446	6,439	6,300	18,472	4,623	6,405	9,334
Yes	5,434	3,278	2,156	330	614	367	359	663	164	389	727
No	105,015	72,168	32,847	6,142	6,749	6,024	5,907	17,567	4,408	5,843	8,505
Other problems:											
Noise	2,950	1,733	1,217	176	296	165	217	382	95	156	340
Litter or housing deterioration . . .	1,691	1,101	590	196	203	85	127	266	43	121	213
Poor city or county services	694	440	254	80	101	49	37	70	21	72	89
People	4,521	2,706	1,815	298	460	269	297	510	115	249	630
Public transportation: [4]											
With public transportation	60,257	35,616	24,641	3,719	5,856	3,998	4,996	8,283	3,245	2,815	6,562
Household uses public transportation regularly for commuting to school or work	10,212	3,817	6,395	720	1,959	569	1,682	582	564	308	2,089
Household does not use public transportation regularly for commuting to school or work	49,681	31,606	18,075	2,963	3,838	3,411	3,285	7,679	2,670	2,473	4,427
No public transportation	48,532	38,848	9,684	2,689	1,438	2,309	1,217	9,728	1,236	3,337	2,522
Not reported	3,017	1,964	1,053	138	152	132	88	461	142	254	250
Police protection:											
Satisfactory	101,373	69,633	31,740	5,837	6,325	5,742	5,623	16,929	4,294	5,501	8,025
Unsatisfactory	7,356	4,800	2,556	516	835	568	543	1,051	193	608	990
Secured communities: [5]											
Community access secured with walls or fences	10,759	5,337	5,422	367	1,371	656	1,336	1,512	827	440	1,392
Community access not secured	100,124	70,410	29,714	6,124	6,028	5,736	4,930	16,783	3,758	5,831	7,865
Secured multiunits:											
Multiunit access secured	7,211	1,357	5,854	106	1,301	135	998	454	1,426	118	1,503
Multiunit access not secured	16,741	2,151	14,590	216	3,406	237	2,749	608	1,567	163	4,129
Senior citizen communities:											
Households with persons 55 years old and over	45,684	36,591	9,093	3,132	1,842	2,451	1,255	18,472	4,623	3,763	2,645
Community age restricted [6]	3,080	1,457	1,624	89	300	71	169	1,079	1,374	194	588
Access to structure:											
Enter building from outside [4,7] . . .	25,915	3,734	22,181	351	5,056	401	4,212	1,142	3,314	321	6,136
Use of steps not required	9,771	1,532	8,239	91	1,915	186	1,519	565	1,780	149	2,386
Use of steps required	16,136	2,201	13,935	260	3,141	216	2,690	577	1,529	172	3,750
Enter home from outside [8]	85,891	72,694	13,197	6,196	2,391	6,038	2,089	17,330	1,309	6,084	3,198
Use of steps not required	38,011	32,654	5,357	2,706	951	3,354	950	8,253	551	2,668	1,231
Use of steps required	47,752	39,928	7,824	3,487	1,439	2,681	1,139	9,048	751	3,406	1,956
Community quality:											
Some or all activities present	49,962	33,117	16,845	2,570	3,392	2,547	2,647	8,356	2,731	2,468	4,197
Community center or clubhouse	24,410	14,707	9,703	1,181	2,078	1,127	1,347	4,306	1,888	1,177	2,346
Golf in the community	16,709	12,762	3,947	611	471	694	499	3,410	604	832	880
Trails in the community	21,609	15,300	6,309	983	1,017	1,099	876	3,509	826	981	1,369
Shuttle bus	9,933	5,718	4,215	422	702	536	713	2,033	1,258	482	1,161
Daycare	15,883	10,633	5,249	1,157	1,297	795	934	2,392	546	822	1,568
Private or restricted beach, park, or shoreline	21,432	15,124	6,308	925	1,053	1,158	1,145	3,327	731	964	1,466
Trash, litter, or junk on street: [9]											
None	99,010	69,415	29,595	5,639	5,764	5,752	5,211	17,001	4,172	5,507	7,264
Minor accumulation	7,250	3,491	3,759	505	1,064	342	738	673	283	396	1,366
Major accumulation	2,519	1,426	1,093	201	351	193	235	318	72	187	437

[1] For persons who selected this race group only. See footnote 3, Table 986. [2] Persons of Hispanic origin may be of any race. [3] Householders 65 years old and over. [4] Includes those not reporting. [5] Public access is restricted (walls, gates, private security). [6] At least one family member must be 55 years old or older. [7] Restricted to multiunits. [8] Restricted to single units. [9] Or on any properties within 300 feet.

Source: U.S. Census Bureau, Current Housing Reports, Series H150/09, *American Housing Survey for the United States: 2009*, September 2010. See also <http://www.census.gov/hhes/www/housing/ahs/nationaldata.html>.

Table 996. Heating Equipment and Fuels for Occupied Units: 1995 to 2009

[97,693 represents 97,693,000. As of fall. Based on American Housing Survey. See Appendix III]

Type of equipment or fuel	Number (1,000)					Percent distribution	
	1995	2003 [1]	2005	2007	2009	2007	2009
Occupied units, total	**97,693**	**105,842**	**108,871**	**110,692**	**111,806**	**100.0**	**100.0**
Heating equipment:							
Warm air furnace	53,165	65,380	68,275	69,582	71,141	62.9	63.6
Steam or hot water	13,669	13,257	12,880	12,760	12,506	11.5	11.2
Heat pumps	9,406	11,347	12,484	12,996	13,264	11.7	11.9
Built-in electric units	7,035	4,760	4,699	4,802	4,761	4.3	4.3
Floor, wall, or pipeless furnace	4,963	5,322	5,102	4,994	4,802	4.5	4.3
Room heaters with flue	1,620	1,432	1,294	1,135	950	1.0	0.8
Room heaters without flue	1,642	1,509	1,327	1,188	1,109	1.1	1.0
Fireplaces, stoves, portable heaters or other	5,150	2,396	2,411	2,756	2,887	2.5	2.6
None	1,044	439	399	478	386	0.4	0.3
House main heating fuel:							
Electricity	26,771	32,341	34,263	36,079	37,851	32.6	33.9
Utility gas	49,203	54,928	56,317	56,681	56,806	51.2	50.8
Bottled, tank, or LP gas	4,251	6,134	6,228	6,095	5,817	5.5	5.2
Fuel oil, kerosene, etc	12,029	10,136	9,929	9,317	8,813	8.4	7.9
Coal or coke	210	126	95	91	98	(Z)	0.1
Wood and other fuel	4,186	1,735	1,640	1,487	2,035	1.3	1.8
None	1,042	441	398	464	386	0.4	0.3
Cooking fuel:							
Electricity	57,621	62,859	65,297	66,276	67,078	59.9	60.0
Gas [2]	39,218	42,612	43,316	44,194	44,477	39.9	39.8
Other fuel	566	62	51	26	68	(Z)	0.1
None	287	309	206	17	183	(Z)	0.2

Z Less than 0.05 percent. [1] Based on 2000 census controls. [2] Includes utility, bottled, tank, and LP gas.

Source: U.S. Census Bureau, Current Housing Reports, Series H150/95RV, H150/03, H150/05, H150/07, and H150/09, *American Housing Survey for the United States: 2009,* September 2010. See also <http://www.census.gov/hhes/www/housing/ahs/nationaldata.html>.

Table 997. Occupied Housing Units—Housing Indicators by Selected Characteristics of the Householder: 2009

[In thousands of units (111,806 represents 111,806,000) As of fall. Based on the American Housing Survey; see Appendix III]

Characteristic	Total occupied units (1,000)	Tenure		Black [1]		Hispanic origin [2]		Elderly [3]		Households below poverty level	
		Owner	Renter	Owner	Renter	Owner	Renter	Owner	Renter	Owner	Renter
Total units	**111,806**	**76,428**	**35,378**	**6,547**	**7,446**	**6,439**	**6,300**	**18,472**	**4,623**	**6,405**	**9,334**
Amenities:											
Porch, deck, balcony or patio	95,406	70,421	24,984	5,668	5,049	5,732	4,066	16,876	2,836	5,690	6,164
Telephone available	109,325	75,129	34,196	6,388	7,114	6,329	6,123	18,286	4,498	6,245	8,933
Usable fireplace	38,998	34,458	4,540	2,207	659	2,222	625	7,563	314	1,799	626
Separate dining room	53,676	43,717	9,959	3,975	2,298	3,372	1,780	10,171	1,012	2,982	2,163
rooms or rec. rooms	33,912	30,978	2,934	2,156	421	1,773	298	6,842	250	1,444	350
Garage or carport with home	74,236	60,979	13,258	4,257	1,937	5,030	2,382	14,988	1,563	4,275	2,592
Cars and trucks available:											
No cars, trucks, or vans	8,738	2,069	6,669	400	2,141	159	1,238	1,251	1,834	743	3,203
Other households without cars	13,421	9,006	4,415	609	674	934	974	1,789	340	999	1,082
1 car with or without trucks or vans	52,458	35,040	17,418	3,111	3,523	2,663	2,824	10,616	2,095	3,352	4,121
2 cars	28,103	22,384	5,719	1,842	951	1,843	1,027	3,935	320	1,081	791
3 or more cars	9,085	7,929	1,157	584	156	839	236	882	35	231	136
Selected deficiencies:											
Signs of rats in last 3 months	613	354	258	36	87	58	82	96	15	59	90
Signs of mice in last 3 months	6,122	3,984	2,138	356	549	239	464	915	225	445	689
Holes in floors	1,141	581	560	78	177	61	116	115	42	119	223
Open cracks or holes	5,517	3,101	2,416	383	617	288	402	496	149	433	862
paint (interior of unit)	2,378	1,246	1,132	189	306	101	210	269	74	183	423
No electrical wiring	84	57	26	–	2	10	7	2	2	11	4
Exposed wiring	355	221	134	37	31	23	27	52	27	34	46
Rooms without electric outlet	1,274	650	624	88	187	58	121	151	56	86	232
Water leakage from inside structure [4]	9,007	5,170	3,836	480	958	443	620	861	262	424	1,059
Water leakage from outside structure [4]	10,963	7,842	3,121	808	667	562	434	1,548	230	746	874

– Represents or rounds to zero. [1] For persons who selected this race group only. See footnote 3, Table 986. [2] Persons of Hispanic origin may be any race. [3] Householders 65 years old and over. [4] During the 12 months prior to the survey.

Source: U.S. Census Bureau, Current Housing Reports, Series H150/09, *American Housing Survey for the United States: 2009,* September 2010. See also <http://www.census.gov/hhes/www/housing/ahs/nationaldata.html>.

Table 998. Home Remodeling—Number of Households With Work Done by Amount Spent: 2009

[In thousands, except percent (3,008 represents 3,008,000). As of fall 2009. For work done in the prior 12 months. Based on household survey and subject to sampling error; see source]

Remodeling project	Total households with work done [1]		Households with work done by outside contractor	Number of households by amount spent (dol.)		
	Number	Percent of households		Under $1,000	$1,000 to $2,999	Over $3,000
Conversion of garage/attic/basement into living space	3,008	1.33	733	737	676	1,005
Remodel bathroom	15,412	6.82	4,201	6,571	3,357	3,082
Remodel kitchen	9,345	4.14	2,605	2,481	1,796	3,012
Remodel bedroom	8,287	3.67	1,274	4,890	1,020	760
Convert room to home office	2,875	1.27	224	1,707	406	63
Convert room to home theater	753	0.33	116	143	198	166
Remodel other rooms	6,464	2.86	1,286	2,848	1,066	1,115
Add bathroom	1,465	0.65	609	222	283	680
Add/extend garage	1,137	0.50	431	99	50	567
Add other rooms—exterior addition	1,508	0.67	681	150	144	825
Add deck/porch/patio	5,063	2.24	1,861	1,206	1,611	1,313
Roofing	8,649	3.83	5,543	1,169	1,464	4,339
Siding—vinyl/metal	2,957	1.31	1,397	597	536	1,032
Aluminum windows	1,406	0.62	661	336	326	275
Clad-wood/wood windows	895	0.40	414	97	241	292
Vinyl windows	4,789	2.12	2,336	1,126	1,283	1,354
Ceramic tile floors	6,303	2.79	2,148	2,636	1,158	849
Hardwood floors	5,703	2.52	2,310	1,371	1,639	1,485
Laminate flooring	5,278	2.34	1,378	2,528	1,253	506
Vinyl flooring	2,863	1.27	693	1,746	285	81
Carpeting	8,354	3.70	4,707	2,984	2,328	1,278
Kitchen cabinets	4,681	2.07	1,409	1,075	609	1,406
Kitchen counter tops	4,778	2.12	2,285	1,132	855	1,456
Skylights	1,014	0.45	516	404	113	114
Exterior doors	5,924	2.62	2,231	3,653	710	433
Interior doors	4,963	2.20	1,208	3,131	400	267
Garage doors	3,133	1.39	1,675	1,184	796	217
Concrete or masonry work	4,539	2.01	1,991	1492	1,012	1,017
Swimming pool—inground	675	0.30	303	91	29	283
Wall paneling	1,292	0.57	181	729	89	32
Ceramic wall tile	2,531	1.12	707	1,189	216	290

[1] Includes no response and amount unknown.

Source: Mediamark Research Inc., New York, NY, *Top-Line Reports*, (copyright). See also <http://www.mediamark.com>.

Table 999. Home Improvement Loans by Race: 2008

[Applications in thousands (1,404.0 represents 1,404,000), amounts in millions of dollars (100,224.7 represents $100,224,700,000). Data is the final 2008 National Aggregates data. For purposes of categorization, the general rule is: the race (including situation where race was reported as not provided or not applicable) of the application is categorized by the race of the first person listed on the application unless the "joint" race definition applies]

Item	Unit	Total	White, total	Black, total	Asian, total	Joint, total [1]	Race not available, total [2]
Applications received							
Number	1,000	1,404.0	976.3	155.3	26.7	16.4	203.0
Amount	Mil. dol.	100,224.7	71,088.0	9,176.2	3,715.3	1,679.2	12,470.5
Loans originated							
Number	1,000	568.3	445.5	38.7	8.6	5.7	63.4
Amount	Mil. dol.	39,416.4	30,631.2	1,914.5	1,241.3	540.9	4,624.5
Applications approved but not accepted							
Number	1,000	104.6	71.1	9.5	2.4	0.9	19.2
Amount	Mil. dol.	6,745.5	4,754.3	489.8	328.1	87.0	970.7
Applications denied							
Number	1,000	600.1	371.1	94.4	12.2	7.6	99.2
Amount	Mil. dol.	39,438.4	25,680.3	5,528.6	1,500.5	773.7	4,747.5
Applications withdrawn							
Number	1,000	96.1	66.4	9.2	2.4	1.6	14.5
Amount	Mil. dol.	10,943.6	7,601.4	944.6	449.9	216.1	1,481.5
Files closed for incompleteness							
Number	1,000	34.8	22.2	3.6	1.1	0.5	6.8
Amount	Mil. dol.	3,680.9	2,420.8	298.7	195.5	61.5	646.3

[1] Joint means with two applicants, one applicant reports a single designation of "White" and the other applicant reports one or more minority racial designations. [2] "Not available" includes situation where information was not provided or not applicable.

Source: Federal Financial Institutions Examination Council, "HMDA National Aggregate Report," annual. See also <http://www.ffiec.gov/hmdaadwebreport/nataggwelcome.aspx>.

Construction and Housing 627

U.S. Census Bureau, Statistical Abstract of the United States: 2011

Table 1000. Net Stock of Residential Fixed Assets: 1990 to 2008

[In billions of dollars (6,256 represents $6,256,000,000,000). End of year estimates]

Item	1990	1995	2000	2003	2004	2005	2006	2007	2008
Total residential fixed assets ...	**6,256**	**8,009**	**10,899**	**13,516**	**15,131**	**16,865**	**18,031**	**18,251**	**17,413**
By type of owner and legal form of organization:									
Private	6,107	7,821	10,668	13,238	14,825	16,530	17,682	17,905	17,079
Corporate	66	77	105	126	139	156	168	172	164
Noncorporate.	6,041	7,743	10,563	13,112	14,686	16,374	17,514	17,733	16,915
Government.	149	188	232	279	306	335	349	346	334
Federal.	52	62	75	88	95	103	107	105	101
State and local.	97	127	156	191	211	232	242	241	233
By tenure group: [1]									
Owner-occupied	4,512	5,975	8,327	10,514	11,849	13,276	14,229	14,430	13,779
Tenant-occupied	1,719	2,005	2,537	2,959	3,234	3,537	3,747	3,765	3,579

[1] Excludes stocks of other nonfarm residential assets, which consists primarily of dormitories, and of fraternity and sorority houses.

Source: U.S. Bureau of Economic Analysis, "Table 5.1 Current-Cost Net Stock of Residential Fixed Assets by Type of Owner, Legal Form of Organization, Industry, and Tenure Group," <http://www.bea.gov/national/index.htm#fixed>.

Table 1001. Commercial Buildings—Summary: 2003

[4,645 represents 4,645,000. Excludes mall buildings. Building type based on predominant activity in which the occupants were engaged. Based on a sample survey of building representatives conducted in 2003, therefore subject to sampling variability.]

Characteristic	All buildings (1,000)	Total floor-space (mil. sq. ft)	Total workers in all buildings (1,000)	Mean square foot per building [1] (1,000)	Mean square foot per worker [1]	Mean operating hours per week [1]
All buildings.	**4,645**	**64,783**	**72,807**	**13.9**	**890**	**61**
Building floorspace (sq. ft.):						
1,001 to 5,000	2,552	6,789	9,936	2.7	683	57
5,001 to 10,000	889	6,585	7,512	7.4	877	61
10,001 to 25,000	738	11,535	10,787	15.6	1,069	67
25,001 to 50,000	241	8,668	8,881	35.9	976	72
50,001 to 100,000	129	9,057	8,432	70.4	1,074	80
100,001 to 200,000	65	9,064	11,632	138.8	779	89
200,001 to 500,000	25	7,176	6,883	289.0	1,043	100
Over 500,000.	7	5,908	8,744	896.1	676	115
Principal activity within building:						
Education.	386	9,874	12,489	25.6	791	50
Food sales.	226	1,255	1,430	5.6	877	107
Food service	297	1,654	3,129	5.6	528	86
Health care	129	3,163	6,317	24.6	501	59
Inpatient.	8	1,905	3,716	241.4	513	168
Outpatient	121	1,258	2,600	10.4	484	52
Lodging	142	5,096	2,457	35.8	2,074	167
Retail (other than mall)	443	4,317	3,463	9.7	1,246	59
Office.	824	12,208	28,154	14.8	434	55
Public assembly.	277	3,939	2,395	14.2	1,645	50
Public order and safety	71	1,090	1,347	15.5	809	103
Religious worship	370	3,754	1,706	10.1	2,200	32
Service	622	4,050	3,667	6.5	1,105	55
Warehouse and storage	597	10,078	4,369	16.9	2,306	66
Other	79	1,738	1,819	21.9	956	63
Vacant	182	2,567	(NA)	14.1	(NA)	(NA)
Energy sources: [2]						
Electricity.	4,404	63,307	72,708	14.4	871	62
Natural gas	2,391	43,468	51,956	18.2	837	65
Fuel oil.	451	15,157	19,625	33.6	772	68
District heat	67	5,443	10,190	81.4	534	79
District chilled water.	33	2,853	7,189	86.7	397	79
Propane.	502	7,076	5,858	14.1	1,208	60
Wood	62	289	262	4.6	1,105	46

NA Not available. [1] For explanation of mean, see Guide to Tabular Presentation. [2] More than one type may apply.

Source: U.S. Energy Information Administration, "2003 Commercial Buildings Energy Consumption (CBECS)", Detailed Tables, Table B1, <http://www.eia.doe.gov/emeu/cbecs/cbecs2003/detailed_tables_2003/detailed_tables_2003.html>.

This section presents summary data for manufacturing as a whole and more detailed information for major industry groups and selected products. The types of measures shown at the different levels include data for establishments, employment and payroll, value and quantity of production and shipments, value added by manufacture, inventories, and various indicators of financial status.

The principal sources of these data are U.S. Census Bureau reports of the censuses of manufactures conducted every 5 years, the *Annual Survey of Manufactures, and Current Industrial Reports*. Reports on current activities of industries or current movements of individual commodities are compiled by such government agencies as the Bureau of Economic Analysis; Bureau of Labor Statistics; the Department of Commerce, International Trade Administration; and by private research or trade associations.

The Quarterly Financial Report publishes up-to-date aggregate statistics on the financial results and position of U.S. corporations. Based upon a sample survey, the QFR presents estimated statements of income and retained earnings, balance sheets, and related financial and operating ratios for manufacturing corporations with assets of $250,000 or over, and mining, wholesale trade and retail trade corporations with assets of $50 million and over or above industry specific receipt cut-off values. These statistical data are classified by industry and by asset size.

Several private trade associations provide industry coverage for certain sections of the economy. They include the Aluminum Association (Table 1028), American Iron and Steel Institute (Table 1026), Consumer Electronics Association (Table 1032), and the Aerospace Industries Association (Tables 1037 and 1039).

Censuses and annual surveys—
The first census of manufactures covered the year 1809. Between 1809 and 1963, a census was conducted at periodic intervals. Since 1967, it has been taken every 5 years (for years ending in "2" and "7"). Results from the 2002 census are presented in this section utilizing the North American Industry Classification System (NAICS). For additional information see text, Section 15, Business Enterprise, and the Census Bureau Web site at <http://www.census.gov/econ/census07/>. Census data, either directly reported or estimated from administrative records, are obtained for every manufacturing plant with one or more paid employees.

The *Annual Survey of Manufactures* (ASM), conducted for the first time in 1949, collects data for the years between censuses for the more general measure of manufacturing activity covered in detail by the censuses. The annual survey data are estimates derived from a scientifically selected sample of establishments. The Annual Survey of Manufactures is based on a sample of about 50,000 from a universe of 346,000 establishments. These establishments represent all manufacturing establishments of multiunit companies and all single-establishment manufacturing companies mailed schedules in the 2002 Census of Manufactures. For the current panel of the ASM sample, all establishments of companies with 2002 shipments in manufacturing in excess of $500 million were included in the survey with certainty. For the remaining portion of the mail survey, the establishment was defined as the sampling unit. For this portion, all establishments with 500 employees or more and establishments with a very large value of shipments also were included. Therefore, of the 50,000 establishments included in the ASM panel, approximately 24,000 are selected with certainty. Smaller establishments in the remaining portion of the mail survey were selected by sample.

U.S. Census Bureau, Statistical Abstract of the United States: 2011

Establishments and classification—
Each of the establishments covered in the
2002 Economic Census—Manufacturing
was classified in 1 of 480 industries
(473 manufacturing industries and
7 former manufacturing industries) in
accordance with the industry definitions
in the 2002 NAICS manual. In the NAICS
system, an industry is generally defined
as a group of establishments that have
similar production processes. To the
extent practical, the system uses supply-
based or production-oriented concepts in
defining industries. The resulting group
of establishments must be significant
in terms of number, value added by
manufacture, value of shipments, and
number of employees. Establishments
frequently make products classified both
in their industry (primary products) and
other industries (secondary products).
Industry statistics (employment, payroll,
value added by manufacture, value of
shipments, etc.) reflect the activities of
the establishments, which may make both
primary and secondary products. Product
statistics, however, represent the output
of all establishments without regard for
the classification of the producing establishment. For this reason, when relating
the industry statistics, especially the value
of shipments, to the product statistics,
the composition of the industry's output
should be considered.

Establishment—Establishment signifies
a single physical plant site or factory.
It is not necessarily identical to the
business unit or company, which may
consists of one or more establishments.
A company operating establishments
at more than one location is required to
submit a separate report for each location
and include establishments with payroll
at any time during the year. An establishment engaged in distinctly different lines
of activity and maintaining separate
payroll and inventory records is also
required to submit separate reports.

Durable goods—Items with a normal life
expectancy of 3 years or more. Automobiles, furniture, household appliances,
and mobile homes are common examples.

Nondurable goods—Items which generally last for only a short time (3 years or
less). Food, beverages, clothing, shoes,
and gasoline are common examples.

Statistical reliability—For a discussion
of statistical collection and estimation,
sampling procedures, and measures of
statistical reliability applicable to Census
Bureau data, see Appendix III.

Table 1002. Gross Domestic Product in Current and Real (2005) Dollars by Industry: 2000 to 2009

[In billions of dollars (9,951.5 represents $9,951,500,000,000). Data include nonfactor charges (capital consumption allowances, indirect business taxes, etc.) as well as factor charges against gross product; corporate profits and capital consumption allowances have been shifted from a company to an establishment basis]

Industry	2002 NAICS code [1]	2000	2005	2006	2007	2008	2009
CURRENT DOLLARS							
Gross domestic product, total [2]....	(X)	**9,951.5**	**12,638.4**	**13,398.9**	**14,077.6**	**14,441.4**	**14,256.3**
Private industries...................	(X)	8,736.1	11,052.5	11,731.1	12,315.2	12,588.0	12,323.8
Manufacturing	31–33	1,415.6	1,568.0	1,651.5	1,708.6	1,669.6	1,568.6
Durable goods..................	33, 321, 327	839.1	877.6	923.1	947.0	923.4	846.8
Wood products.................	321	28.3	33.0	30.2	28.5	26.8	(NA)
Nonmetallic mineral products	327	41.9	45.3	45.4	45.6	40.5	(NA)
Primary metals	331	46.3	53.7	59.7	60.0	58.5	(NA)
Fabricated metal products........	332	120.7	120.4	125.6	135.9	135.7	(NA)
Machinery	333	110.5	109.5	116.6	122.9	124.0	(NA)
Computer and electronic products...	334	172.1	183.3	200.0	197.7	195.2	(NA)
Electrical equipment, appliances, and components	335	44.1	39.9	45.6	45.9	50.3	(NA)
Motor vehicles, bodies and trailers, and parts.....................	3361–3363	117.4	112.6	107.6	104.6	89.0	(NA)
Other transportation equipment.....	3364–66, 69	65.8	76.0	81.5	93.6	94.0	(NA)
Furniture and related products	337	33.8	34.3	36.6	33.3	30.2	(NA)
Miscellaneous manufacturing	339	58.3	69.6	74.5	79.2	79.2	(NA)
Nondurable goods...............	31, 32 (except 321 and 327)	576.5	690.4	728.4	761.6	746.2	721.8
Food and beverage and tobacco products......................	311, 312	164.8	172.1	181.4	184.8	189.5	(NA)
Textile mills and textile product mills......................	313, 314	27.9	23.5	21.2	21.6	16.9	(NA)
Apparel and leather and allied products......................	315, 316	21.4	16.0	15.5	15.0	14.2	(NA)
Paper products	322	61.7	53.8	59.3	58.9	59.7	(NA)
Printing and related support activities......................	323	40.3	37.5	37.9	38.7	37.1	(NA)
Petroleum and coal products.......	324	43.6	139.3	140.0	146.4	149.2	(NA)
Chemical products...............	325	152.2	182.7	207.9	224.7	212.8	(NA)
Plastics and rubber products.......	326	64.6	65.6	65.1	71.4	66.7	(NA)
CHAINED (2005) DOLLARS							
Gross domestic product, total [2]....	(X)	**11,226.0**	**12,638.4**	**12,976.2**	**13,254.1**	**13,312.1**	**12,987.4**
Private industries...................	(X)	9,785.6	11,052.5	11,385.5	11,633.4	11,619.6	11,313.9
Manufacturing	31–33	1,396.5	1,568.0	1,636.6	1,709.8	1,647.4	1,550.6
Durable goods..................	33, 321, 327	747.5	877.6	937.5	975.8	978.4	904.7
Wood products.................	321	32.8	33.0	32.7	35.9	35.9	(NA)
Nonmetallic mineral products	327	44.7	45.3	40.1	40.5	37.7	(NA)
Primary metals	331	62.2	53.7	46.5	44.0	40.4	(NA)
Fabricated metal products........	332	129.6	120.4	126.1	131.0	126.5	(NA)
Machinery	333	111.3	109.5	116.2	119.8	122.0	(NA)
Computer and electronic products...	334	81.5	183.3	223.8	248.7	273.2	(NA)
Electrical equipment, appliances, and components	335	42.6	39.9	44.9	42.9	46.2	(NA)
Motor vehicles, bodies and trailers, and parts.....................	3361–63	93.5	112.6	121.0	120.6	112.6	(NA)
Other transportation equipment.....	3364–66, 69	78.4	76.0	79.3	90.4	90.8	(NA)
Furniture and related products	337	35.1	34.3	36.1	31.8	28.6	(NA)
Miscellaneous manufacturing	339	60.2	69.6	74.2	77.5	78.0	(NA)
Nondurable goods...............	31, 32 (except 321 and 327)	649.6	690.4	699.7	734.4	673.9	648.0
Food and beverage and tobacco products......................	311, 312	175.7	172.1	193.1	205.1	189.5	(NA)
Textile mills and textile product mills......................	313, 314	27.4	23.5	20.4	21.3	16.4	(NA)
Apparel and leather and allied products	315, 316	19.6	16.0	15.7	15.2	14.7	(NA)
Paper products	322	58.3	53.8	54.8	53.1	50.7	(NA)
Printing and related support activities......................	323	37.5	37.5	36.5	37.5	37.3	(NA)
Petroleum and coal products.......	324	74.1	139.3	120.9	120.9	123.4	(NA)
Chemical products..............	325	169.9	182.7	201.6	218.3	183.5	(NA)
Plastics and rubber products.......	326	65.7	65.6	59.1	66.6	60.5	(NA)

NA Not available. X Not applicable. [1] North American Industry Classification System, 2002; see text, Section 15.

[2] Includes industries, not shown separately. For additional industries, see Table 669.

Source: U.S. Bureau of Economic Analysis, *Survey of Current Business*, May 2010, See also <http://www.bea.gov/scb/index.htm>.

Table 1003. Manufacturing—Selected Industry Statistics by State: 2007

[13,333 represents 13,333,000. Based on the 2007 Economic Census and the 2007 Nonemployer Statistics. See Appendix III]

State	Employers				Nonemployers	
	Number of establishments	Number of employees (1,000)	Annual payroll (mil. dol.)	Sales, shipments, receipts or revenue (mil. dol.)	Number of establishments	Sales, shipments, receipts or revenue (mil. dol.)
U.S.	**293,919**	**13,333**	**612,474**	**5,339,345**	**328,060**	**16,333**
AL	4,928	272	11,352	112,859	4,369	204
AK	544	13	490	8,204	1,087	33
AZ	5,074	172	8,774	57,978	6,524	318
AR	3,088	185	6,518	60,736	2,683	128
CA	44,296	1,448	71,247	491,372	43,798	2,817
CO	5,288	138	6,790	46,332	6,882	284
CT	4,924	191	10,345	58,405	3,776	250
DE	673	35	1,760	25,680	596	36
DC	137	2	81	333	185	8
FL	14,324	355	15,227	104,833	19,505	1,203
GA	8,699	411	16,128	144,281	8,891	425
HI	984	14	511	8,799	2,075	95
ID	1,942	65	2,829	18,011	2,499	91
IL	15,704	664	31,716	257,761	10,347	531
IN	9,015	537	24,475	221,878	6,650	295
IA	3,802	223	9,526	97,592	3,031	117
KS	3,170	178	7,983	76,752	2,739	106
KY	4,165	247	10,773	119,105	3,874	181
LA	3,442	148	7,565	205,055	4,001	190
ME	1,825	59	2,524	16,363	2,652	95
MD	3,680	128	6,454	41,456	4,031	197
MA	7,737	289	15,712	86,429	6,215	315
MI	13,675	582	29,910	234,456	11,725	547
MN	7,951	341	15,999	107,563	7,516	291
MS	2,598	159	5,757	59,869	2,347	103
MO	6,886	295	12,997	110,908	5,987	259
MT	1,324	20	808	10,638	1,959	67
NE	1,984	100	3,789	40,158	1,499	55
NV	2,035	52	2,291	15,736	2,217	138
NH	2,104	82	4,196	18,592	2,287	101
NJ	9,250	311	16,399	116,608	6,503	433
NM	1,574	35	1,560	17,123	3,581	103
NY	18,629	534	24,268	162,720	18,163	933
NC	10,150	506	19,590	205,867	9,828	398
NC	767	26	991	11,350	626	21
OH	16,237	760	35,485	295,891	12,782	640
OK	3,964	142	5,971	60,681	4,099	210
OR	5,717	184	8,139	66,881	6,680	258
PA	15,406	651	29,433	234,840	14,146	767
RI	1,831	54	2,375	12,062	1,290	58
SC	4,335	242	10,061	93,977	3,821	174
SD	1,052	41	1,539	13,051	877	26
TN	6,752	369	15,166	140,448	6,427	306
TX	21,115	894	42,836	593,542	28,790	1,369
UT	3,368	123	5,508	42,432	3,856	171
VT	1,108	36	1,650	10,751	1,738	54
VA	5,777	277	12,170	92,418	5,084	201
WA	7,650	270	13,275	112,053	8,599	343
WV	1,413	60	2,646	25,081	1,363	44
WI	9,659	488	21,850	163,563	6,976	312
WY	596	12	574	8,835	884	32

Source: U.S. Census Bureau, "2007 Economic Census, Geographic Area Series, Detailed Statistics for the State: 2007," April 2010, <http://www.census.gov/econ/census07/>, and "Nonemployer Statistics," August 2009, <http://www.census.gov/econ /nonemployer/index.html>.

Table 1004. Manufacturing—Establishments, Employees, and Annual Payroll by Industry: 2006 and 2007

[(119,917 represents 119,917,000). Excludes self-employed, individual employees on private households, railroad employees, agricultural production employees, and most government employees. See Appendix III]

Industry	2002 NAICS code [1]	Establishments		Employees (1,000) [2]		Payroll (mil. dol.)	
		2006	2007	2006	2007	2006	2007
All industries, total	(X)	7,601,160	7,705,018	119,917	120,604	4,792,430	5,026,778
Manufacturing, total	31–33	331,062	331,355	13,632	13,320	620,224	626,530
Percent of all industries	(X)	4.4	4.3	11.4	11.0	12.9	12.5
Food manufacturing..................	311	25,382	25,796	1,459	1,439	50,219	51,002
Beverage and tobacco products	312	3,684	4,069	155	156	7,552	7,777
Textile mills	313	3,243	3,092	188	164	6,028	5,493
Textile product mills..................	314	6,726	6,732	156	153	4,632	4,772
Apparel manufacturing	315	10,967	10,368	216	197	5,344	5,017
Leather and allied products............	316	1,398	1,392	39	37	1,174	1,134
Wood products	321	16,735	16,622	577	528	18,584	17,507
Paper.............................	322	5,139	5,037	441	425	21,656	21,574
Printing and related support activities	323	33,433	33,281	641	632	25,335	25,436
Petroleum and coal products...........	324	2,448	2,408	103	104	8,151	8,510
Chemical...........................	325	13,247	13,395	805	794	51,084	51,483
Plastics and rubber products...........	326	14,592	14,233	901	855	34,075	33,478
Nonmetallic mineral products	327	17,350	17,472	482	472	20,598	20,380
Primary metal	331	5,285	5,267	450	439	22,784	22,854
Fabricated metal products.............	332	59,064	59,637	1,564	1,566	64,905	67,401
Machinery	333	26,317	26,198	1,127	1,138	55,289	56,797
Computer and electronic products.......	334	14,548	14,478	1,057	1,043	69,826	72,847
Electrical equipment, appliance and component.........................	335	6,109	6,144	420	406	18,416	18,545
Transportation equipment	336	12,707	12,857	1,623	1,574	86,459	85,876
Furniture and related products	337	21,449	21,717	543	517	17,897	17,492
Miscellaneous	339	31,239	31,160	686	681	30,213	31,153

X Not applicable. [1] North American Industry Classification System, 2002; see text, Section 15, [2] Covers full- and part-time employees who are on the payroll in the pay period including March 12.

Source: U.S. Census Bureau, "County Business Patterns," July 2009, <http://www.census.gov/econ/cbp/>.

Table 1005. Manufacturing—Establishments, Employees, and Annual Payroll by State: 2007

[(13,320 represents 13,320,000). Excludes self-employed, individual employees on private households, railroad employees, agricultural production employees, and most government employees. Data are for North American Industry Classification System (NAICS), 2002, codes 31–33. See Appendix III]

State	Establish-ments	Employees (1,000) [1]	Payroll (mil. dol.)	State	Establish-ments	Employees (1,000) [1]	Payroll (mil. dol.)
United States	331,355	13,320	626,530	Missouri............	6,868	303	13,362
Alabama	4,925	282	11,356	Montana............	1,301	20	799
Alaska..............	506	10	460	Nebraska...........	1,990	101	3,824
Arizona	5,038	172	8,693	Nevada............	2,022	50	2,245
Arkansas	3,096	192	6,545	New Hampshire......	2,080	77	4,164
California	44,262	1,403	75,962	New Jersey	9,216	292	16,402
Colorado	5,273	138	7,238	New Mexico.........	1,540	35	1,483
Connecticut	4,924	184	10,583	New York	18,727	534	24,890
Delaware	650	34	1,753	North Carolina.......	10,105	519	20,703
District of Columbia	134	2	86	North Dakota........	758	26	991
Florida..............	14,265	362	15,317	Ohio...............	16,174	761	35,719
Georgia	8,699	409	16,275	Oklahoma	3,961	143	6,002
Hawaii	971	15	519	Oregon............	5,700	185	8,567
Idaho	1,960	65	2,845	Pennsylvania	15,381	645	29,453
Illinois..............	15,692	649	32,009	Rhode Island	1,807	52	2,370
Indiana.............	8,956	544	24,705	South Carolina.......	4,345	265	11,104
Iowa...............	3,796	226	9,694	South Dakota........	1,057	42	1,566
Kansas.............	3,184	176	7,873	Tennessee..........	6,729	376	15,675
Kentucky	4,143	249	10,775	Texas..............	21,045	851	42,293
Louisiana...........	3,399	143	7,373	Utah...............	3,345	123	5,313
Maine..............	1,813	59	2,463	Vermont............	1,085	36	1,598
Maryland	3,626	129	6,791	Virginia.............	5,743	279	12,344
Massachusetts........	7,656	272	15,959	Washington	7,629	254	13,216
Michigan	13,603	580	29,968	West Virginia	1,407	62	2,683
Minnesota	7,940	331	16,284	Wisconsin	9,646	485	21,848
Mississippi..........	2,613	166	5,805	Wyoming	570	12	586

[1] Covers full- and part-time employees who are on the payroll in the pay period including March 12.

Source: U.S. Census Bureau, "County Business Patterns," July 2009, <http://www.census.gov/econ/cbp/>.

Table 1006. Manufactures—Summary by Selected Industry: 2008

[12,781.2 represents 12,781,200. Based on the Annual Survey of Manufactures; see Appendix III]

Industry based on shipments	2002 NAICS code [1]	All employees			Production workers [2] (1,000)	Value added by manufactures [3] (mil. dol.)	Value of shipments [4] (mil. dol.)
		Number [2] (1,000)	Payroll				
			Total (mil. dol.)	Per employee (dol.)			
Manufacturing, total	31–33	12,781.2	607,447	47,527	8,872.9	2,274,367	5,486,266
Food [5]	311	1,437.8	51,818	36,039	1,113.7	246,222	649,056
Grain and oil seed milling	3112	53.2	2,817	52,953	39.5	28,988	94,000
Sugar and confectionery products	3113	61.9	2,625	42,431	47.3	13,184	26,648
Fruit and vegetable preserving and specialty food	3114	167.7	6,232	37,161	138.5	28,045	63,187
Dairy products	3115	132.3	5,899	44,592	95.6	27,072	98,118
Animal slaughtering and processing	3116	505.7	15,217	30,094	438.9	50,823	169,925
Bakeries and tortilla	3118	271.6	9,442	34,760	172.8	34,108	58,701
Beverage and tobacco products	312	152.8	7,322	47,905	87.0	76,292	125,520
Beverage	3121	134.7	6,223	46,196	73.5	44,833	88,085
Textile mills	313	135.6	4,661	34,383	113.1	12,471	31,845
Textile product mills	314	136.3	4,151	30,455	104.9	11,540	26,630
Apparel	315	148.9	3,887	20,112	116.2	9,237	19,596
Cut and sew apparel	3152	118.5	3,075	25,951	92.2	7,385	15,608
Leather and allied products	316	31.7	994	31,361	23.9	2,619	5,411
Wood products [5]	321	461.6	15,619	33,834	365.5	34,577	88,004
Sawmills and wood preservation	3211	91.7	3,394	37,024	76.9	7,278	24,272
Paper	322	403.2	20,546	50,957	311.6	79,175	178,749
Pulp, paper, and paperboard mills	3221	117.8	7,794	66,142	93.6	40,476	82,923
Converted paper products	3222	285.4	12,752	44,687	218.0	38,700	95,826
Printing and related support activities	323	605.9	25,138	41,491	422.4	60,003	99,167
Petroleum and coal products	324	105.9	8,415	79,444	68.2	91,559	769,886
Chemical [5]	325	780.1	50,766	65,074	448.8	355,481	751,030
Basic chemical	3251	151.8	10,880	71,656	92.2	83,629	244,174
Pharmaceutical and medicine	3254	249.1	18,771	75,347	117.8	142,773	194,478
Soap, cleaning compound, and toilet preparation	3256	104.4	5,667	54,259	62.7	46,661	97,431
Plastics and rubber products	326	796.5	31,580	39,651	613.2	91,431	204,679
Plastics products	3261	651.8	25,299	38,815	499.7	76,503	167,423
Rubber product	3262	144.7	6,281	43,415	113.5	14,929	37,256
Nonmetallic mineral products	327	443.4	19,372	43,694	338.0	61,994	115,920
Glass and glass product	3272	93.9	4,227	45,042	74.0	12,562	23,197
Cement and concrete products	3273	213.6	9,106	42,637	161.8	29,774	57,779
Primary metal [5]	331	418.3	22,693	54,245	328.7	93,564	282,141
Iron and steel mills and ferroalloy	3311	109.3	7,668	70,150	87.4	43,036	126,332
Foundries	3315	144.0	6,435	44,689	116.3	15,492	31,842
Fabricated metal products [5]	332	1,572.7	69,231	44,021	1,153.4	188,072	358,363
Forging and stamping	3321	123.5	5,763	46,663	92.0	15,834	34,899
Architectural and structural metals	3323	408.5	17,253	42,239	293.1	44,878	94,980
Machine shops, turned product and screw, nut, and bolt	3327	398.5	17,748	44,537	298.5	39,941	64,064
Coating, engraving, heat treating, and allied activities	3328	136.0	5,360	39,403	104.0	16,432	27,740
Machinery [5]	333	1,127.4	57,212	50,749	726.1	168,153	356,954
Agriculture, construction, and mining machinery	3331	209.2	10,279	49,147	143.0	39,037	94,334
Industrial machinery	3332	127.6	7,648	59,919	67.6	18,703	35,612
Ventilation, heating, air conditioning, and commercial refrigeration equipment	3334	145.8	6,019	41,297	104.7	19,092	40,702
Metalworking machinery	3335	161.3	8,305	51,502	112.1	17,325	29,277
Computer and electronic products [5]	334	1,034.1	66,345	64,156	493.8	234,390	391,082
Computer and peripheral equipment	3341	92.6	5,908	63,792	34.7	38,727	68,110
Communications equipment	3342	132.8	8,961	67,481	53.9	30,504	53,865
Semiconductor and other electronic component	3344	371.6	20,486	55,123	227.9	71,258	116,809
Navigational, measuring, medical, and control instruments	3345	395.1	29,033	73,475	151.3	88,473	139,775
Electrical equipment, appliance, and component	335	411.9	19,038	46,226	285.3	61,975	131,759
Electrical equipment	3353	144.4	6,890	47,705	96.1	21,840	44,301
Transportation equipment [5]	336	1,474.4	82,532	55,976	1,018.6	252,187	666,807
Motor vehicle	3361	163.0	11,318	69,424	139.5	52,337	210,978
Motor vehicle body and trailer	3362	123.5	4,789	38,790	95.0	10,208	29,764
Motor vehicle parts	3363	523.7	24,771	47,297	391.6	62,812	174,646
Aerospace product and parts	3364	439.8	30,892	70,240	235.2	93,036	178,709
Ship and boat building	3366	149.0	6,857	46,016	103.1	16,665	30,430
Furniture and related products [5]	337	459.8	16,344	35,544	343.3	43,965	80,466
Miscellaneous [5]	339	642.9	29,782	46,322	397.1	99,460	153,200
Medical equipment and supplies	3391	313.7	16,151	51,491	188.3	60,424	84,029

[1] North American Industrial Classification System, 2002; see text, Section 15. [2] Includes employment and payroll at administrative offices and auxiliary units. All employees represents the average of production workers plus all other employees for the payroll period ended nearest the 12th of March. Production workers represent the average of the employment for the payroll periods ended nearest the 12th of March, May, August, and November. [3] Adjusted value added; takes into account (a) value added by merchandising operations (that is, difference between the sales value and cost of merchandise sold without further manufacture, processing, or assembly), plus (b) net change in finished goods and work-in- process inventories between beginning and end of year. [4] Includes extensive and unmeasurable duplication from shipments between establishments in the same industry classification. [5] Includes industries not shown separately.

Source: U.S. Census Bureau, Annual Survey of Manufactures, "Statistics for Industry Groups and Industries: 2008," June 2010, <http://www.census.gov/manufacturing/asm/index.html>.

Table 1007. Manufactures—Summary by State: 2008

[12,781.2 represents 12,781,200. Data are for North American Industry Classification System (NAICS) 2002 codes 31–33. Sum of state totals may not add to U.S. total because U.S. and state figures were independently derived. See Appendix III]

State	All employees [1] Number (1,000)	Payroll Total (mil. dol.)	Payroll Per employee (dol.)	Production workers [1] Number (1,000)	Wages (mil. dol.)	Value added by manufactures [2] Total (mil. dol.)	Value added by manufactures [2] Per production worker (dol.)	Value of shipments [3] (mil. dol.)
United States	12,781.2	607,447	47,527	8,873	343,374	2,274,367	256,327	5,486,266
Alabama	266.1	11,444	43,006	203	7,677	43,481	213,897	116,345
Alaska	13.1	473	36,076	11	337	1,629	149,418	9,082
Arizona	163.8	9,036	55,176	99	3,962	32,151	324,741	57,831
Arkansas	173.6	6,451	37,161	138	4,550	23,888	173,270	61,204
California	1,366.2	70,541	51,633	862	32,943	254,497	295,321	520,291
Colorado	136.6	6,797	49,752	92	3,665	23,838	259,239	48,440
Connecticut	177.3	9,983	56,302	108	4,834	33,823	313,834	56,617
Delaware	32.7	1,790	54,778	23	980	8,300	360,660	25,849
District of Columbia . . .	2.0	85	41,860	1	49	196	170,242	345
Florida	318.2	14,373	45,175	208	7,353	51,395	246,841	101,050
Georgia	385.2	15,601	40,501	293	9,941	59,847	204,462	144,326
Hawaii	13.3	502	37,759	8	269	1,708	205,796	8,529
Idaho	59.7	2,745	45,991	45	1,691	9,305	207,827	19,178
Illinois.	640.5	31,688	49,475	437	17,316	104,278	238,419	270,292
Indiana.	493.0	23,240	47,137	363	14,769	99,080	272,870	220,807
Iowa	220.1	9,775	44,413	160	6,036	42,534	265,078	105,581
Kansas.	182.4	8,622	47,265	128	5,283	29,207	227,350	84,290
Kentucky	234.0	10,265	43,861	180	6,985	38,136	212,214	114,082
Louisiana	144.1	7,729	53,633	106	5,010	48,426	454,772	228,209
Maine.	58.3	2,634	45,171	42	1,666	8,808	210,928	16,769
Maryland	121.5	6,285	51,710	75	2,924	20,462	271,422	39,592
Massachusetts.	274.0	15,159	55,325	163	6,605	47,170	288,669	83,278
Michigan	544.5	27,633	50,751	390	17,239	84,530	216,538	210,727
Minnesota	332.4	16,039	48,257	218	8,287	50,656	231,936	116,086
Mississippi	156.6	5,809	37,093	121	3,852	23,122	191,013	62,379
Missouri.	274.1	12,567	45,856	200	7,971	40,515	202,876	110,175
Montana	18.5	838	45,236	12	504	2,891	231,974	12,723
Nebraska.	96.7	3,886	40,174	75	2,621	15,969	214,273	45,949
Nevada	49.6	2,330	46,940	33	1,173	8,950	270,224	16,047
New Hampshire.	79.1	4,249	53,693	49	1,848	9,732	199,674	18,690
New Jersey	291.0	15,844	54,448	183	7,265	54,076	296,283	117,641
New Mexico.	33.0	1,571	47,643	23	919	7,115	314,492	18,588
New York	500.0	24,179	47,729	334	12,665	87,126	260,716	165,293
North Carolina	470.7	18,883	40,116	354	11,963	101,342	285,903	201,714
North Dakota	25.8	1,038	40,303	19	674	4,731	244,763	14,021
Ohio.	732.3	34,201	46,702	526	21,193	121,527	231,088	298,157
Oklahoma	143.9	6,228	43,265	106	3,969	26,934	254,532	73,332
Oregon.	175.3	7,925	45,202	123	4,607	36,308	295,029	64,366
Pennsylvania	628.5	29,763	47,359	443	17,606	109,544	247,407	249,333
Rhode Island	47.5	2,301	48,447	30	1,131	6,488	217,439	12,032
South Carolina.	230.9	10,041	43,486	175	6,464	37,255	213,358	92,710
South Dakota.	41.2	1,617	39,249	31	1,032	5,878	187,431	14,176
Tennessee.	347.2	14,618	42,101	253	9,114	59,548	234,912	138,589
Texas.	853.6	42,778	50,116	579	23,566	192,252	331,920	643,913
Utah.	117.0	5,423	46,362	78	2,965	19,722	253,608	43,302
Vermont.	34.0	1,669	49,038	22	836	4,774	218,693	10,508
Virginia.	265.5	12,178	45,866	186	7,088	48,880	262,180	91,552
Washington	265.5	13,420	50,548	170	6,856	46,168	270,889	111,944
West Virginia	57.6	2,697	46,802	43	1,774	9,928	230,116	26,264
Wisconsin	475.6	21,919	46,089	340	12,940	71,913	211,218	163,420
Wyoming	11.1	584	52,369	8	406	4,330	513,618	10,648

[1] Includes all full-time and part-time employees on the payrolls of operating manufacturing establishments during any part of the pay period that included the 12th of the month. Included are employees on paid sick leave, paid holidays, and paid vacations; not included are proprietors and partners of unincorporated businesses. [2] Value added is derived by subtracting the cost of materials, supplies, containers, fuel, purchased electricity, and contract work from the value of shipments (products manufactured plus receipts for services rendered). The result of this calculation is adjusted by the addition of value added by merchandising operations (i.e., the difference between the sales value and the cost of merchandise sold without further manufacture, processing, or assembly) plus the net change in finished goods and work-in-process between the beginning and end of year inventories. [3] Includes extensive and unmeasurable duplication from shipments between establishments in the same industry classification.

Source: U.S. Census Bureau, Annual Survey of Manufactures, "Geographic Area Statistics: 2008 and 2007," June 2010, <http://www.census.gov/manufacturing/asm/index.html>.

Table 1008. Manufacturers' E-Commerce Shipments by Industry: 2007 and 2008

[(5,338,307 represents $5,338,307,000,000). Based on the 2007 Economic Census—Manufacturing and the 2008 Annual Survey of Manufactures; subject to sampling variability. For businesses with paid employees. E-commerce is the value of goods and services sold online whether over open networks, computer-mediated networks such as the Internet, or proprietary networks running systems such as Electronic Data Interchange (EDI)]

Industry	2002 NAICS Code [1]	2007				2008 [2]			
		Ship-ments, total (mil. dol.)	E-commerce			Ship-ments, total (mil. dol.)	E-commerce		
			Ship-ments, total (mil. dol.)	Percent of total ship-ments	Percent distribu-tion		Ship-ments, total (mil. dol.)	Percent of total ship-ments	Percent distribu-tion
Manufacturing, total	31–33	**5,338,307**	**1,879,424**	**35.2**	**100.0**	**5,486,266**	**2,154,483**	**39.3**	**100.0**
Food products	311	589,859	203,693	34.5	10.8	649,056	245,706	37.9	11.4
Beverage and tobacco	312	128,286	72,038	56.2	3.8	125,520	67,805	54.0	3.1
Textile mills	313	36,185	14,494	40.1	0.8	31,845	12,981	40.8	0.6
Textile product mills	314	28,881	13,470	46.6	0.7	26,630	11,027	41.4	0.5
Apparel	315	24,096	7,072	29.3	0.4	19,596	5,970	30.5	0.3
Leather and allied products	316	5,615	1,281	22.8	0.1	5,411	1,114	20.6	0.1
Wood products	321	102,029	19,468	19.1	1.0	88,004	19,394	22.0	0.9
Paper	322	176,108	62,644	35.6	3.3	178,749	67,843	38.0	3.1
Printing and related support activities	323	103,432	25,649	24.8	1.4	99,167	30,044	30.3	1.4
Petroleum and coal products	324	615,548	195,309	31.7	10.4	769,886	339,652	44.1	15.8
Chemicals	325	724,081	252,390	34.9	13.4	751,030	296,536	39.5	13.8
Plastics and rubber products	326	210,377	62,188	29.6	3.3	204,679	72,915	35.6	3.4
Nonmetallic mineral products	327	128,066	23,173	18.1	1.2	115,920	26,508	22.9	1.2
Primary metals	331	257,277	80,850	31.4	4.3	282,141	109,045	38.6	5.1
Fabricated metal products	332	345,393	84,030	24.3	4.5	358,363	97,801	27.3	4.5
Machinery	333	351,531	111,074	31.6	5.9	356,954	130,251	36.5	6.0
Computer and electronic products	334	403,001	142,777	35.4	7.6	391,082	151,519	38.7	7.0
Electrical equipment, appliances, and components	335	129,737	40,737	31.4	2.2	131,759	44,601	33.9	2.1
Transportation equipment	336	744,893	411,782	55.3	21.9	666,807	360,601	54.1	16.7
Furniture and related products	337	85,534	22,483	26.3	1.2	80,466	25,023	31.1	1.2
Miscellaneous	339	148,377	32,821	22.1	1.7	153,200	38,148	24.9	1.8

[1] North American Industry Classification System, 2002; see text, Section 15. [2] Establishments representing approximately 5 percent of 2007 value of shipments did not have opportunity to report e-commerce receipts.

Source: U.S. Census Bureau, "E-Stats, 2008 E-commerce Multi sector report," May 2010, <http://www.census.gov/eos/www/ebusiness614.htm>.

Table 1009. Manufacturing Employer Costs for Employee Compensation Per Hour Worked: 2000 to 2010

[As of March, for private industry workers. Based on a sample of establishments in the National Compensation Survey; see Appendix III and source for details. See also Table 653, Section 12]

Compensation component	Cost (dol.)					Percent distribution				
	2000	2005	2008	2009	2010	2000	2005	2008	2009	2010
Total compensation	**23.41**	**28.48**	**31.42**	**32.03**	**32.20**	**100.0**	**100.0**	**100.0**	**100.0**	**100.0**
Wages and salaries	16.01	18.26	20.66	21.20	21.26	68.4	64.1	65.7	66.2	66.0
Total benefits	7.40	10.21	10.76	10.83	10.94	31.6	35.9	34.3	33.8	34.0
Paid leave	1.74	2.07	2.38	2.45	2.44	7.4	7.3	7.6	7.7	7.6
Vacation	0.86	1.04	1.25	1.28	1.28	3.7	3.7	4.0	4.0	4.0
Holiday	0.65	0.76	0.86	0.89	0.88	2.8	2.7	2.7	2.8	2.7
Sick	0.13	0.16	0.21	0.23	0.22	0.6	0.6	0.7	0.7	0.7
Other	0.10	0.10	0.05	0.06	0.07	0.4	0.3	0.2	0.2	0.2
Supplemental pay	1.04	1.25	1.35	1.20	1.21	4.4	4.4	4.3	3.8	3.8
Overtime and premium pay	0.58	0.61	0.54	0.53	0.54	2.5	2.1	1.7	1.7	1.7
Shift differentials	0.10	0.12	0.14	0.13	0.13	0.4	0.4	0.4	0.4	0.4
Nonproduction bonuses	0.36	0.53	0.68	0.54	0.55	1.5	1.8	2.10	1.7	1.7
Insurance	1.85	2.68	3.13	3.26	3.34	7.9	9.4	10.0	10.2	10.4
Health insurance	1.69	2.48	2.91	3.03	3.12	7.2	8.7	9.3	9.5	9.7
Retirement and savings	0.75	1.64	1.32	1.30	1.28	3.2	5.8	4.2	4.1	4.0
Defined benefit	0.34	1.13	0.68	0.67	0.66	1.5	4.0	2.1	2.1	2.1
Defined contributions	0.41	0.51	0.65	0.63	0.61	1.8	1.8	2.1	2.0	1.9
Legally required benefits	1.92	2.45	2.58	2.62	2.66	8.2	8.6	8.2	8.2	8.3
Social Security and Medicare	1.38	1.60	1.79	1.84	1.84	5.9	5.6	5.7	5.7	5.7
Federal unemployment	0.03	0.03	0.03	0.03	0.03	0.1	0.1	0.1	0.1	0.1
State unemployment	0.11	0.19	0.18	0.18	0.21	0.5	0.7	0.6	0.6	0.7
Workers compensation	0.40	0.64	0.58	0.57	0.58	1.7	2.2	1.8	1.8	1.8
Other benefits [1]	0.09	0.12	(NA)	(NA)	(NA)	0.4	0.4	(NA)	(NA)	(NA)

NA Not available. [1] Includes severance pay, and supplemental unemployment benefits.

Source: U.S. Bureau of Labor Statistics, *Employer Costs for Employee Compensation—March 2010*, News Release, USDL-10-0774, June 2010. See also <http://www.bls.gov/ncs/>.

Table 1010. Manufacturing Industries—Employees by Industry: 1990 to 2009

[Annual averages of monthly figures (109,487 represents 109,487,000). Covers all full- and part-time employees who worked during, or received pay for, any part of the pay period including the 12th of the month. Minus sign (–) indicates decrease. See also head note, Table 631]

Industry	2007 NAICS code [1]	All employees (1,000)						Percent change	
		1990	2000	2005	2007	2008	2009	1990–2000	2000–2009
All industries	(X)	109,487	131,785	133,703	137,598	136,790	130,920	20.4	–0.7
Manufacturing	31–33	17,695	17,263	14,226	13,879	13,406	11,883	–2.4	–31.2
Percent of all industries	(X)	16	13	11	10	10	9	(X)	(X)
Durable goods	(X)	10,736	10,877	8,956	8,808	8,463	7,309	1.3	–32.8
Wood products [2]	321	541	613	559	515	456	361	13.4	–41.2
Sawmills & wood preservation	3211	148	134	119	111	102	85	–9.6	–36.7
Nonmetallic mineral products [2]	327	528	554	505	501	465	398	4.9	–28.2
Glass & glass products	3272	152	141	108	100	97	84	–7.6	–40.1
Cement & concrete products	3273	195	234	240	242	220	188	20.1	–19.8
Primary metals [2]	331	689	622	466	456	442	365	–9.7	–41.3
Iron & steel mills & ferroalloy production	3311	187	135	96	100	99	85	–27.7	–37.2
Alumina & aluminum production	3313	108	101	73	71	66	56	–7.3	–43.9
Foundries	3315	214	217	164	155	148	115	1.4	–46.8
Fabricated metal products [2]	332	1,610	1,753	1,522	1,563	1,528	1,318	8.9	–24.8
Architectural & structural metals	3323	357	428	398	417	406	348	20.0	–18.6
Machine shops & threaded products	3327	309	365	345	361	361	312	18.4	–14.5
Coating, engraving, & heat treating metals	3328	143	175	145	148	144	120	22.7	–31.2
Machinery [2]	333	1,408	1,457	1,166	1,187	1,188	1,029	3.5	–29.4
Agricultural, construction, & mining machinery	3331	229	222	208	229	242	216	–2.8	–3.0
Commercial & service industry machinery	3333	147	147	111	108	105	96	0.3	–35.0
HVAC & commercial refrigeration equipment	3334	165	194	154	154	150	127	17.9	–34.6
Metalworking machinery	3335	267	274	202	194	191	158	2.5	–42.3
Turbine & power transmission equipment	3336	114	111	98	102	105	95	–2.4	–14.9
Other general purpose machinery	3339	335	344	269	275	274	238	2.7	–30.9
Computer & electronic products	334	1,903	1,820	1,316	1,273	1,244	1,136	–4.3	–37.6
Computer & peripheral equipment	3341	367	302	205	186	183	166	–17.8	–45.0
Communications equipment	3342	232	239	141	128	127	121	3.1	–49.1
Semiconductors & electronic components	3344	574	676	452	448	432	377	17.8	–44.3
Electronic instruments	3345	626	488	441	443	441	421	–22.1	–13.6
Electrical equipment & appliances [2]	335	633	591	434	429	424	377	–6.7	–36.2
Household appliances	3352	114	106	85	76	71	60	–7.0	–43.0
Electrical equipment	3353	244	210	152	157	159	147	–13.9	–30.0
Other electrical equipment & components	3359	195	191	136	138	137	121	–2.3	–36.5
Transportation equipment [2,3]	336	2,133	2,057	1,772	1,712	1,608	1,353	–3.6	–34.2
Motor vehicles	3361	271	291	248	220	192	143	7.4	–51.1
Motor vehicle bodies & trailers	3362	130	183	171	166	140	105	40.8	–42.4
Motor vehicle parts	3363	653	840	678	608	544	419	28.6	–50.1
Aerospace products & parts	3364	841	517	455	489	507	493	–38.5	–4.6
Ship & boat building	3366	173	154	154	160	156	132	–10.7	–14.3
Furniture & related products [2]	337	601	683	568	531	480	386	13.5	–43.5
Household & institutional furniture	3371	398	443	383	349	307	246	11.3	–44.5
Miscellaneous manufacturing	339	690	728	647	642	629	587	5.4	–19.4
Medical equipment & supplies	3391	288	305	300	306	311	308	5.9	1.0
Other miscellaneous manufacturing	3399	403	423	347	336	318	279	5.1	–34.0
Nondurable goods	(X)	6,959	6,386	5,271	5,071	4,943	4,574	–8.2	–28.4
Food manufacturing [2]	311	1,507	1,553	1,478	1,484	1,481	1,459	3.0	–6.1
Fruit & vegetable preserving & specialty	3114	218	197	174	173	173	172	–9.5	–13.0
Dairy products	3115	145	136	132	131	129	131	–5.9	–3.4
Animal slaughtering & processing	3116	427	507	504	508	510	499	18.6	–1.6
Bakeries & tortilla manufacturing	3118	292	306	280	280	281	273	4.9	–11.0
Beverages & tobacco products	312	218	207	192	198	198	188	–4.9	–9.3
Beverages	3121	173	175	167	176	177	169	1.2	–3.1
Textile mills [2]	313	492	378	218	170	151	126	–23.1	–66.8
Fabric mills	3132	270	192	104	75	66	56	–29.0	–70.7
Textile & fabric finishing mills	3133	120	105	63	53	49	39	–12.1	–62.8
Textile product mills [2]	314	209	230	176	158	147	127	9.7	–44.9
Textile furnishings mills	3141	127	129	96	84	75	63	1.3	–51.2
Apparel [2]	315	929	484	251	215	199	170	–48.0	–64.9
Cut & sew apparel	3152	776	380	193	166	155	134	–51.0	–64.8
Leather & allied products [2]	316	133	69	40	34	33	29	–48.3	–57.3
Paper & paper products	322	647	605	484	458	445	407	–6.6	–32.6
Pulp, paper, & paperboard mills	3221	238	191	142	132	126	117	–19.7	–39.1
Converted paper products	3222	409	413	343	326	319	291	1.1	–29.6
Printing & related support activities	323	809	807	646	622	594	524	–0.2	–35.1
Chemicals [2]	325	1,036	980	872	861	847	803	–5.3	–18.1
Basic chemicals	3251	249	188	150	149	152	145	–24.4	–23.1
Resin, rubber, & artificial fibers	3252	158	136	108	106	104	93	–14.2	–31.8
Pharmaceuticals & medicines	3254	207	274	288	295	291	285	32.4	3.7
Other chemical products and preparations	3259	153	127	104	101	95	85	–17.1	–33.1
Plastics & rubber products [2]	326	826	951	802	757	729	627	15.1	–34.0
Plastics products	3261	619	737	634	609	585	505	19.1	–31.4

X Not applicable. [1] Based on the North American Industry Classification System (NAICS), 2007; see text, this section and Section 15. [2] Includes other industries not shown separately. [3] Includes railroad rolling stock manufacturing, not shown separately.

Source: U.S. Bureau of Labor Statistics, Current Employment Statistics Program, "Employment, Hours, and Earnings—National," March, 2010, <http://www.bls.gov/ces/home.htm\>.

Table 1011. Manufacturing Industries—Average Weekly Hours and Average Weekly Overtime Hours of Production Workers: 1990 to 2009

[Covers all full- and part-time employees who worked during, or received pay for, any part of the pay period including the 12th of the month]

Industry	2007 NAICS code [1]	Average weekly hours of production workers					Average weekly overtime hours for production workers				
		1990	1995	2000	2005	2009	1990	1995	2000	2005	2009
Total.	31–33	**40.5**	**41.3**	**41.3**	**40.7**	**39.8**	**3.9**	**4.7**	**4.7**	**4.6**	**2.9**
Durable goods	(X)	41.1	42.1	41.8	41.1	39.9	3.9	5.0	4.8	4.6	2.7
Wood products.	321	40.4	41.0	41.0	40.0	37.4	3.3	3.9	4.1	4.1	2.3
Nonmetallic mineral products	327	40.9	41.8	41.6	42.2	40.9	5.0	5.7	6.1	6.3	3.8
Primary metals	331	42.1	43.4	44.2	43.1	40.7	4.6	5.7	6.5	6.3	3.4
Fabricated metal products	332	41.0	41.9	41.9	41.0	39.4	3.9	4.8	4.9	4.6	2.5
Machinery	333	42.1	43.5	42.3	42.1	40.1	4.0	5.3	5.1	5.0	2.5
Computer and electronic products.	334	41.3	42.2	41.4	40.0	40.4	3.8	4.9	4.6	3.6	2.2
Electrical equipment and appliances	335	41.2	41.9	41.6	40.6	39.3	3.0	3.5	3.7	3.8	2.5
Transportation equipment [2]	336	42.0	43.7	43.3	42.4	41.2	4.5	6.5	5.5	5.3	3.5
Furniture and related products . . .	337	38.0	30.5	30.2	39.2	37.7	2.3	2.8	3.5	3.2	2.0
Miscellaneous manufacturing	339	39.0	39.2	39.0	38.7	38.5	3.0	3.4	3.1	3.3	2.5
Nondurable goods	(X)	39.6	40.1	40.3	39.9	39.8	3.9	4.3	4.5	4.4	3.2
Food manufacturing.	311	39.3	39.6	40.1	39.0	40.0	4.4	4.6	5.0	4.7	4.2
Beverages and tobacco products.	312	38.9	39.3	42.0	40.1	35.7	3.8	4.8	5.8	5.7	1.5
Textile mills	313	40.2	40.9	41.4	40.3	37.7	4.2	5.0	4.8	3.9	2.3
Textile product mills	314	38.5	38.6	38.7	38.9	37.9	2.9	3.3	3.4	4.3	1.7
Apparel	315	34.7	35.3	35.7	35.8	36.0	2.0	2.2	2.1	2.1	0.7
Leather and allied products	316	37.4	37.7	37.5	38.4	33.6	4.0	4.0	4.6	2.2	1.5
Paper and paper products	322	43.6	43.4	42.8	42.5	41.8	4.9	5.5	5.7	5.6	4.1
Printing and related support activities.	323	38.7	39.1	39.2	38.4	38.0	3.6	3.8	3.7	3.3	1.8
Petroleum and coal products	324	44.4	43.7	42.7	45.5	43.4	6.2	6.3	6.5	8.5	6.3
Chemicals	325	42.8	43.3	42.2	42.3	41.4	4.9	5.6	5.0	4.7	3.1
Plastics and rubber products	326	40.6	41.1	40.8	40.0	40.2	3.4	3.9	4.0	4.0	2.9

X Not applicable. [1] Based on the North American Industry Classification System (NAICS), 2007; see text, this section and Section 15.

Source: U.S. Bureau of Labor Statistics, Current Employment Statistics, "Employment Hours, and Earnings—National," March 2010, <http://www.bls.gov/ces/data.htm>.

Table 1012. Indexes of Employment and Hours of All Persons in Manufacturing: 1990 to 2009

[2002 = 100. Based on Current Employment Statistics and supplemented with Current Population Survey. Employment and hours of all persons include those of paid employees, the self employed (partners and proprietors), and unpaid family workers. See text, section 12]

Industry	2007 NAICS code [1]	Employment					Hours				
		1990	1995	2000	2005	2009	1990	1995	2000	2005	2009
Food manufacturing.	311	99.0	102.6	101.6	97.0	96.0	98.5	102.7	103.0	95.6	97.0
Beverage and tobacco products	312	104.3	96.5	99.1	92.2	92.7	106.0	96.7	107.6	93.9	84.1
Textile mills	313	166.1	158.4	128.0	74.2	45.1	164.4	160.6	130.3	74.0	41.7
Textile product mills	314	113.9	117.1	109.5	87.0	66.8	113.6	116.8	109.6	85.8	64.3
Apparel manufacturing	315	250.7	221.0	135.2	72.6	52.2	239.7	214.7	133.1	71.4	51.6
Leather and allied products	316	228.7	182.8	124.2	74.8	55.4	231.1	187.9	127.9	78.7	53.6
Wood product manufacturing.	321	99.5	106.4	111.8	101.7	67.8	100.3	108.7	114.7	101.6	63.3
Paper manufacturing	322	118.0	116.7	110.3	88.4	74.2	122.3	120.4	112.6	89.7	73.1
Printing and related support activities . . .	323	116.7	118.1	114.4	91.8	74.3	117.1	119.8	115.8	91.5	72.8
Petroleum and coal products	324	128.8	117.9	103.7	94.0	97.6	132.6	119.7	103.0	98.3	97.2
Chemical manufacturing	325	111.8	106.7	106.2	94.9	86.6	111.3	108.9	104.6	94.1	84.5
Plastics and rubber products	326	97.8	108.2	112.4	95.0	74.5	97.5	109.6	112.9	93.4	73.2
Nonmetallic mineral products	327	102.8	101.1	107.3	97.7	77.5	100.3	100.2	105.8	97.3	75.6
Primary metal products	331	135.7	126.3	122.0	91.8	71.8	134.7	129.6	127.2	93.8	69.4
Fabricated metal products	332	104.8	105.1	112.7	98.7	85.6	105.6	108.2	116.3	99.3	83.5
Machinery manufacturing	333	115.5	118.1	118.4	94.8	82.4	118.0	125.5	122.9	97.4	81.6
Computer and electronic products.	334	127.6	113.1	121.6	87.5	75.6	132.8	121.4	126.1	88.7	77.2
Electrical equipment and appliances. . . .	335	127.7	119.4	119.0	87.9	76.1	130.9	124.7	123.3	89.2	75.1
Transportation equipment	336	116.4	107.8	112.3	96.5	74.0	115.3	110.0	114.1	96.3	72.5
Furniture and related products	337	100.3	101.1	111.1	94.9	65.1	97.3	99.5	111.0	95.3	62.9
Miscellaneous manufacturing	339	101.8	104.3	107.2	96.8	87.1	101.0	104.2	106.9	95.7	86.3

[1] North American Industry Classification System, 2007; see text, Section 15,

Source: Bureau of Labor Statistics, Labor Productivity and Costs, "Employment and Hours of All Persons for a Comprehensive Set of Industries," Report 1019, September 2009, <http://www.bls.gov/lpc/iprhours09.htm>.

Table 1013. Average Hourly Earnings of Production Workers in Manufacturing Industries by State: 2006 to 2009

[In dollars. Data are based on the North American Industry Classification System (NAICS), 2007. Based on the Current Employment Statistics Program; see headnote, Table 631, and Appendix III]

State	2006	2007	2008	2009	State	2006	2007	2008	2009
United States	**16.81**	**17.26**	**17.75**	**18.23**	Missouri	17.16	16.99	17.70	18.47
Alabama	15.56	15.75	15.68	15.43	Montana	15.90	15.88	16.66	16.85
Alaska	14.31	16.37	16.39	17.42	Nebraska	15.04	15.19	15.26	16.06
Arizona	14.88	15.61	16.44	17.14	Nevada	15.46	15.54	15.53	15.61
Arkansas	13.35	14.06	14.16	14.07	New Hampshire	16.57	17.09	17.30	17.36
California	15.77	16.28	16.79	17.79	New Jersey	16.56	17.22	17.89	18.30
Colorado	16.59	17.77	19.79	21.24	New Mexico	14.06	14.40	14.72	14.59
Connecticut	19.78	20.63	21.42	23.03	New York	18.29	18.49	18.58	18.54
Delaware	18.11	17.83	17.66	17.68	North Carolina	14.57	15.08	15.49	15.88
District of Columbia [1]	(NA)	(NA)	(NA)	(NA)	North Dakota	14.98	14.70	15.15	15.55
Florida	14.75	16.12	18.30	19.60	Ohio	19.17	19.35	19.35	18.63
Georgia	14.74	14.88	14.83	15.42	Oklahoma	14.77	14.56	14.74	14.76
Hawaii	15.89	17.06	18.93	19.06	Oregon	15.57	16.45	16.92	17.68
Idaho	16.89	19.01	19.95	20.30	Pennsylvania	15.38	15.48	15.61	16.28
Illinois	16.03	16.47	16.44	16.61	Rhode Island	13.42	13.78	13.94	14.12
Indiana	18.57	18.70	18.47	18.97	South Carolina	15.03	15.72	15.92	16.29
Iowa	16.40	16.84	16.63	16.73	South Dakota	13.75	14.27	14.64	14.82
Kansas	17.69	18.07	18.73	19.09	Tennessee	14.04	14.39	14.71	14.73
Kentucky	16.92	16.92	17.38	18.11	Texas	14.00	14.07	13.78	15.27
Louisiana	17.94	19.34	19.98	20.48	Utah	15.25	16.71	17.86	18.28
Maine	18.58	19.19	19.71	19.97	Vermont	15.79	16.49	16.51	16.41
Maryland	17.88	17.65	18.04	18.77	Virginia	16.75	17.60	18.33	18.69
Massachusetts	18.26	19.26	20.33	20.57	Washington	19.91	20.51	21.06	23.39
Michigan	21.84	22.06	22.11	21.57	West Virginia	17.89	18.71	19.02	18.69
Minnesota	17.24	17.39	17.74	18.60	Wisconsin	16.54	17.37	17.94	18.14
Mississippi	13.78	13.79	14.43	14.64	Wyoming	17.44	18.02	20.36	20.70

NA Not available. [1] Represents the Washington-Arlington-Alexandria Metropolitan Area.

Source: U.S. Bureau of Labor Statistics, Current Employment Statistics, "State and Metro Area Employment, Hours, and Earnings (SAE)," March, 2010, <http://www.bls.gov/sae/#data.htm>.

Table 1014. Manufacturing Full-Time Equivalent Employees and Wages by Industry: 2000 to 2008

[123,409 represents 123,409,000. Based on National Income and Product Account tables. Full-time equivalent employees equals the number of employees on full-time schedules plus the number of employees for part-time schedules converted to full-time basis]

Industry	2002 NAICS code [1]	Full-time equivalent (FTE) employees (1,000)				Wage and salary accruals (mil. dol.)			
		2000	2005	2007	2008	2000	2005	2007	2008
All domestic industries, total	(X)	**123,409**	**125,444**	**129,178**	**128,533**	**39,157**	**45,537**	**49,619**	**50,945**
Manufacturing	31–33	**16,948**	**13,954**	**13,615**	**13,154**	**43,933**	**50,909**	**55,345**	**56,409**
Percent of all industries	(X)	13.7	11.1	10.5	10.2	112.2	111.8	111.5	110.7
Durable goods	(X)	10,713	8,820	8,662	8,337	46,559	53,124	57,977	59,020
Wood products	321	602	549	507	445	30,350	36,003	37,072	37,603
Nonmetallic mineral products	327	549	494	496	456	38,987	45,741	47,984	48,776
Primary metals	331	611	460	446	434	45,714	53,287	58,373	60,127
Fabricated metal products	332	1,735	1,499	1,528	1,505	37,748	43,660	47,734	49,406
Machinery	333	1,427	1,142	1,169	1,168	46,577	53,650	58,018	58,977
Computer and electronic products	334	1,779	1,293	1,257	1,233	70,397	78,666	87,649	86,458
Electrical equipment, appliances, and components	335	583	428	422	415	40,204	48,883	53,451	55,656
Motor vehicles, bodies and trailers, and parts	3361–3363	1,301	1,095	984	875	48,846	54,026	58,058	57,272
Other transportation equipment	3364–3365	740	671	708	723	53,341	65,931	72,053	73,464
Furniture and related products	337	671	553	519	471	29,571	34,770	37,538	38,525
Miscellaneous manufacturing	339	715	636	626	612	38,724	46,725	51,837	53,369
Nondurable goods	(X)	6,235	5,134	4,953	4,817	39,423	47,103	50,742	51,891
Food and beverage and tobacco products	311–312	1,727	1,617	1,627	1,622	33,922	39,271	41,720	42,946
Textile mills and textile product mills	313–314	588	372	320	292	29,012	34,280	36,490	36,906
Apparel and leather and allied products	315	539	288	241	225	24,198	31,698	35,502	36,892
Paper products	322	598	469	447	430	45,813	53,815	56,651	58,183
Printing and related support activities	323	757	626	612	579	39,141	42,738	44,963	45,665
Petroleum and coal products	324	120	110	113	115	62,322	82,161	94,512	93,817
Chemical products	325	967	862	846	838	61,230	72,920	79,088	79,806
Plastics and rubber products	326	938	788	746	716	35,605	41,181	43,878	44,817

X Not applicable. [1] North American Industry Classification System, 2002; see text, Section 15.

Source: U.S. Bureau of Economic Analysis, *Survey of Current Business*, August 2009. See also <http://www.bea.gov/national/nipaweb/SelectTable.asp?Selected=N>.

Manufactures 639

Table 1015. Manufacturers' Shipments, Inventories, and New Orders: 1995 to 2009

[In billions of dollars (3,480 represents $3,480,000,000,000), except ratio. Based on the Manufacturers' Shipments, Inventories, and Orders (M3) survey. See source for details]

Year	Shipments	Inventories (December 31) [1]	Ratio of inventories to shipments [2]	New orders	Unfilled orders (December 31)
1995........	3,480	415	1.46	3,427	443
1997........	3,835	433	1.39	3,780	508
1998........	3,900	439	1.38	3,808	492
1999........	4,032	453	1.38	3,957	501
2000........	4,209	470	1.37	4,161	545
2001........	3,970	417	1.29	3,873	510
2002........	3,915	412	1.30	3,802	459
2003........	4,015	398	1.22	3,965	475
2004........	4,309	429	1.23	4,256	494
2005........	4,742	461	1.20	4,745	572
2006........	5,016	510	1.25	5,033	659
2007........	5,338	548	1.27	5,473	867
2008........	5,486	545	1.22	5,443	893
2009........	4,610	497	1.33	4,452	793

[1] Inventories are stated at current cost. [2] Ratio based on December seasonally adjusted inventory data.

Source: U.S. Census Bureau, Current Industrial Reports, *Benchmark Report for Manufacturers' Shipments, Inventories, and Orders: January 2004 Through December 2007* and U.S. Census Bureau, "Full Report on Manufacturers' Shipments, Inventories and Orders," February 2009–January 2010, <http://www.census.gov/manufacturing/m3/>.

Table 1016. Ratios of Manufacturers' Inventories to Shipments and Unfilled Orders to Shipments by Industry Group: 2000 to 2009

[Based on the Manufacturers' Shipments, Inventories, and Orders (M3) survey. See source for details]

Industry	2007 NAICS code [1]	2000	2004	2005	2006	2007	2008	2009
INVENTORIES-TO-SHIPMENTS RATIO [2]								
All manufacturing industries	(X)	1.37	1.23	1.20	1.25	1.27	1.22	1.33
Durable goods.................................	(X)	1.55	1.40	1.40	1.49	1.49	1.55	1.61
Wood products.............................	321	1.32	1.26	1.27	1.26	1.36	1.39	1.30
Nonmetallic mineral products	327	1.23	1.16	1.10	1.13	1.19	1.33	1.43
Primary metals	331	1.68	1.60	1.53	1.62	1.57	1.43	1.80
Fabricated metals	332	1.56	1.57	1.53	1.62	1.56	1.59	1.53
Machinery	333	2.08	1.85	1.77	1.93	1.87	1.94	2.18
Computers and electronic products................	334	1.54	1.28	1.45	1.43	1.38	1.48	1.47
Electrical equipment, appliances, and components	335	1.44	1.41	1.36	1.47	1.48	1.48	1.49
Transportation equipment	336	1.35	1.19	1.17	1.32	1.40	1.49	1.57
Furniture and related products	337	1.36	1.23	1.18	1.13	1.13	1.11	1.10
Miscellaneous products.......................	339	1.90	1.70	1.70	1.60	1.69	1.71	1.63
Nondurable goods.............................	(X)	1.14	1.03	0.98	1.01	1.03	0.92	1.07
Food products.............................	311	0.88	0.75	0.75	0.82	0.83	0.77	0.77
Beverages and tobacco products	312	1.51	1.63	1.39	1.49	1.46	1.52	1.60
Textile mills	313	1.48	1.26	1.19	1.25	1.33	1.40	1.42
Textile product mills	314	1.75	1.20	1.18	1.17	1.33	1.48	1.54
Apparel	315	1.89	1.59	1.52	1.27	1.58	1.76	1.81
Leather and allied products....................	316	2.12	1.79	1.75	1.95	2.09	2.14	2.08
Paper products	322	1.11	1.11	1.08	1.06	1.03	1.04	1.04
Printing	323	0.80	0.80	0.80	0.80	0.79	0.81	0.76
Petroleum and coal products....................	324	0.71	0.79	0.75	0.72	0.88	0.55	1.02
Basic chemicals...........................	325	1.40	1.22	1.18	1.23	1.19	1.18	1.24
Plastics and rubber products....................	326	1.21	1.16	1.15	1.16	1.20	1.21	1.23
UNFILLED ORDERS-TO-SHIPMENTS RATIO								
All manufacturing industries	(X)	1.57	1.39	1.45	1.58	1.95	1.95	2.06
Durable goods.................................	(X)	2.78	2.64	2.84	3.09	3.86	4.08	4.33
Primary metals	331	2.42	2.60	2.91	2.97	3.54	2.83	2.62
Fabricated metals	332	5.58	4.91	5.23	5.41	5.98	6.58	6.71
Machinery	333	4.68	3.56	3.79	4.07	4.60	4.34	5.86
Computers and electronic products................	334	5.84	4.62	4.11	4.35	4.40	4.19	4.69
Electrical equipment, appliances, and components	335	0.76	0.70	0.74	0.83	0.84	0.81	0.96
Transportation equipment	336	6.15	8.19	9.74	10.66	15.21	16.71	16.09
Furniture and related products	337	0.69	0.85	0.82	0.70	0.70	0.61	0.71
Miscellaneous products.......................	339	0.11	0.11	0.08	0.10	0.10	0.11	0.12

X Not applicable. [1] Based on the North American Industry Classification System, 2007; see text, this section and Section 15. [2] Ratio based on December seasonally adjusted inventory data.

Source: U.S. Census Bureau, Current Industrial Reports, *Benchmark Report for Manufacturers' Shipments, Inventories, and Orders: January 2004 Through December 2007* and U.S. Census Bureau, "Full Report on Manufacturers' Shipments, Inventories and Orders," February 2009–January 2010, <http://www.census.gov/manufacturing/m3/>.

Table 1017. Value of Manufacturers' Shipments, Inventories, and New Orders by Industry: 2000 to 2009

[In billions of dollars (4,209 represents $4,209,000,000,000). Based on the Manufacturers' Shipments, Inventories, and Orders (M3) survey. See source for details]

Industry	2007 NAICS code [1]	2000	2005	2006	2007	2008	2009
SHIPMENTS							
All manufacturing industries	(X)	**4,209**	**4,742**	**5,015**	**5,338**	**5,486**	**4,610**
Durable goods	(X)	2,374	2,425	2,562	2,696	2,625	2,198
Wood products	321	94	112	112	102	88	79
Nonmetallic mineral products	327	97	115	126	128	116	95
Primary metals	331	157	203	235	257	282	182
Fabricated metals	332	268	289	317	345	358	311
Machinery	333	292	303	326	352	357	275
Computers and electronic products	334	511	373	391	403	391	357
Electrical equipment, appliances, and components	335	125	112	119	130	132	108
Transportation equipment	336	640	691	699	745	667	579
Furniture and related products	337	75	84	86	86	80	65
Miscellaneous products	339	115	143	150	148	153	147
Nondurable goods	(X)	1,835	2,317	2,453	2,642	2,862	2,412
Food products	311	435	532	537	590	649	636
Beverages and tobacco products	312	112	124	124	128	126	120
Textile mills	313	52	42	39	36	32	25
Textile product mills	314	34	35	33	29	27	22
Apparel	315	60	31	30	24	20	16
Leather and allied products	316	10	6	6	6	5	5
Paper products	322	165	162	169	176	179	161
Printing	323	104	97	100	103	99	86
Petroleum and coal products	324	235	476	547	616	770	507
Basic chemicals	325	449	611	724	724	751	660
Plastics and rubber products	326	178	200	210	210	205	175
INVENTORIES (December 31)							
All manufacturing industries	(X)	**470**	**461**	**510**	**548**	**545**	**497**
Durable goods	(X)	298	276	309	327	330	288
Wood products	321	10	12	12	12	10	8
Nonmetallic mineral products	327	10	10	12	12	13	11
Primary metals	331	22	26	32	34	34	27
Fabricated metals	332	34	36	42	44	47	39
Machinery	333	49	43	51	53	56	49
Computers and electronic products	334	63	44	45	45	47	43
Electrical equipment, appliances, and components	335	15	12	14	15	16	13
Transportation equipment	336	69	65	74	83	79	73
Furniture and related products	337	8	8	8	8	7	6
Miscellaneous products	339	18	20	19	20	21	19
Nondurable goods	(X)	172	185	200	221	214	209
Food products	311	32	33	36	41	41	41
Beverages and tobacco products	312	14	14	15	16	16	16
Textile mills	313	6	4	4	4	4	3
Textile product mills	314	5	3	3	3	3	3
Apparel	315	9	4	3	3	3	2
Leather and allied products	316	2	1	1	1	1	1
Paper products	322	15	14	15	15	15	14
Printing	323	6	6	6	6	6	5
Petroleum and coal products	324	13	27	30	41	32	39
Basic chemicals	325	52	58	66	70	72	67
Plastics and rubber products	326	18	19	20	21	21	18
NEW ORDERS							
All manufacturing industries	(X)	**4,161**	**4,745**	**5,038**	**5,473**	**5,443**	**4,452**
Durable goods	(X)	2,327	2,428	2,580	2,831	2,581	2,040
Wood products	321	94	112	112	102	88	79
Nonmetallic mineral products	327	97	115	126	128	116	95
Primary metals	331	154	208	235	259	273	178
Fabricated metals	332	270	297	324	352	358	301
Machinery	333	295	313	342	370	360	262
Computers and electronic products	334	436	297	337	342	321	296
Electrical equipment, appliances, and components	335	126	115	124	132	131	106
Transportation equipment	336	663	745	743	911	701	512
Furniture and related products	337	75	84	85	86	80	65
Miscellaneous products	339	117	142	151	149	153	146
Nondurable goods	(X)	1,835	2,317	2,453	2,642	2,862	2,412

X Not applicable. [1] Based on the North American Industry Classification System, 2007; see text, this section and Section 15.

Source: U.S. Census Bureau, Current Industrial Reports, *Benchmark Report for Manufacturers' Shipments, Inventories, and Orders: January 2004 Through December 2007* and U.S. Census Bureau, "Full Report on Manufacturers' Shipments, Inventories and Orders," February 2009–January 2010, <http://www.census.gov/manufacturing/m3/>.

U.S. Census Bureau, Statistical Abstract of the United States: 2011

Table 1018. Value of Manufacturers' Shipments, Inventories, and New Orders by Market Grouping: 2000 to 2009

[In millions of dollars (4,209 represents $4,209,000,000,000). Based on the Manufacturers' Shipments, Inventories, and Orders (M3) survey. See source for details]

Market grouping	2000	2004	2005	2006	2007	2008	2009
SHIPMENTS							
All manufacturing industries	**4,209**	**4,309**	**4,742**	**5,020**	**5,338**	**5,486**	**4,610**
Consumer goods.....................	1,501	1,701	1,895	1,980	2,108	2,259	1,869
Consumer durable goods	391	419	423	422	423	363	279
Consumer nondurable goods	1,109	1,282	1,473	1,558	1,685	1,895	1,590
Aircraft and parts....................	112	106	114	125	157	156	163
Defense aircraft and parts............	25	41	37	39	43	55	66
Nondefense aircraft and parts..........	87	65	77	86	114	101	97
Construction materials and supplies	445	463	510	510	561	546	472
Motor vehicles and parts	471	495	501	501	500	415	331
Computers and related products.........	110	63	65	65	66	68	64
Information technology industries	400	288	295	295	330	325	300
Nondefense capital goods..............	808	662	731	731	845	846	717
Excluding aircraft..................	758	629	687	687	776	783	655
Defense capital goods................	67	91	92	91	100	113	130
Durables excluding capital goods	1,498	1,512	1,603	1,603	1,752	1,666	1,351
INVENTORIES (December 31)							
All manufacturing industries	**470**	**429**	**461**	**510**	**548**	**545**	**497**
Consumer goods.....................	128	130	140	149	166	157	155
Consumer durable goods	26	25	27	27	27	25	20
Consumer nondurable goods	102	105	113	122	139	133	135
Aircraft and parts....................	36	30	33	39	48	45	44
Defense aircraft and parts............	9	10	12	12	14	11	12
Nondefense aircraft and parts..........	27	20	22	26	34	34	32
Construction materials and supplies	49	50	53	59	61	62	52
Motor vehicles and parts	22	22	23	25	25	22	18
Computers and related products..........	8	4	4	5	5	5	4
Information technology industries	51	32	38	39	39	41	37
Nondefense capital goods..............	127	96	108	120	129	135	119
Excluding aircraft..................	107	82	90	100	103	109	95
Defense capital goods................	17	18	16	17	19	17	18
Durables excluding capital goods	154	143	152	173	180	178	151
NEW ORDERS							
All manufacturing industries	**4,161**	**4,256**	**4,745**	**5,033**	**5,473**	**5,443**	**4,452**
Consumer goods.....................	1,502	1,701	1,894	1,980	2,108	2,258	1,869
Consumer durable goods	393	420	421	422	423	362	279
Consumer nondurable goods	1,109	1,282	1,473	1,558	1,685	1,895	1,590
Aircraft and parts....................	131	106	149	167	296	193	117
Defense aircraft and parts............	31	31	30	38	50	58	62
Nondefense aircraft and parts..........	99	74	119	129	247	135	55
Construction materials and supplies	447	466	518	550	570	547	468
Motor vehicles and parts	468	495	504	503	499	413	330
Computers and related products..........	108	62	64	68	66	69	63
Information technology industries	410	293	297	337	341	325	295
Nondefense capital goods..............	831	674	789	861	1,012	884	646
Excluding aircraft..................	768	630	702	775	816	784	628
Defense capital goods................	80	92	93	88	115	120	116
Durables excluding capital goods	1,416	1,446	1,545	1,632	1,704	1,578	1,278

Source: U.S. Census Bureau, Current Industrial Reports, *Benchmark Report for Manufacturers' Shipments, Inventories, and Orders: January 2004 Through December 2007* and U.S. Census Bureau, "Full Report on Manufacturers' Shipments, Inventories and Orders," February 2009–January 2010, <http://www.census.gov/manufacturing/m3/>.

Table 1019. Finances and Profits of Manufacturing Corporations: 1990 to 2009

[In billions of dollars (4,548 represents $4,548,000,000,000). Data exclude estimates for corporations with less than $250,000 in assets at time of sample selection. See Table 788 for individual industry data]

Item	2000 [1]	2001 [1]	2001 [2]	2003 [2]	2004 [2]	2005 [2]	2006 [2]	2007 [2]	2008 [3]	2009 [3]
Net sales.........................	4,548	4,308	4,295	4,397	4,934	5,411	5,783	6,060	6,374	5,136
Net operating profit	348	185	186	237	320	359	405	416	358	285
Net profit:										
Before taxes......................	381	82	83	306	447	524	605	603	388	360
After taxes......................	275	36	36	237	348	401	470	443	266	284
Cash dividends	132	102	103	115	143	179	178	178	182	161
Net income retained in business	143	-67	-66	122	205	222	292	265	84	123

[1] Based on the Standard Industrial Classification system. [2] Based on the North American Industry Classification System, 2002; see text, Section 15. [3] Based on the North American Industry Classification System, 2007; see text, Section 15.

Source: U.S. Census Bureau, *Quarterly Financial Report for Manufacturing, Mining, and Trade Corporations*. See also Fourth Quarter 2009 QFR Press Release, March 2010, <http://www.census.gov/econ/qfr/>.

Table 1020. Manufacturing Corporations—Assets and Profits by Asset Size: 1990 to 2009

[In millions of dollars (2,629,458 represents $2,629,458,000,000). Corporations and assets as of end of 4th quarter; profits for entire year. Through 2000, based on Standard Industrial Classification code (SIC); beginning 2001, based on the North American Industry Classification System; see text, Section 15. For corporations above a certain asset value based on complete canvass. The asset value for complete canvass was raised in 1988 to $50 million and in 1995 to $250 million. Asset sizes less than these values are sampled, except as noted. For details regarding Survey description, data analysis and methodology, see source, fourth quarter report. Minus sign (–) indicates loss]

Year	Total	Asset–size class						
		Under $10 million [1]	$10 to $25 million	$25 to $50 million	$50 to $100 million	$100 to $250 million	$250 million to $1 billion	$1 billion and over
Assets:								
1990.	2,629,458	142,498	74,477	55,914	72,554	123,967	287,512	1,872,536
1995.	3,345,229	155,618	87,011	68,538	87,262	159,133	370,263	2,417,403
1996.	3,574,407	163,928	87,096	69,722	93,205	156,702	398,651	2,605,102
1997.	3,746,797	167,921	87,398	76,034	85,186	157,130	397,559	2,775,570
1998.	3,967,309	170,068	87,937	69,627	86,816	148,060	419,153	2,985,647
1999.	4,382,814	170,058	85,200	67,352	97,810	138,143	398,881	3,425,370
2000.	4,852,106	171,666	85,482	72,122	90,866	149,714	389,537	3,892,720
2001 [2]	4,747,789	169,701	84,664	67,493	88,088	131,617	393,752	3,812,474
2002.	4,823,219	166,191	82,369	62,654	81,667	134,821	407,423	3,888,095
2003.	5,162,852	161,462	80,681	62,592	77,205	126,826	392,192	4,261,894
2004.	5,538,113	163,072	80,085	71,674	81,741	126,950	414,144	4,600,447
2005.	5,828,716	165,195	85,785	68,731	87,818	142,900	423,917	4,854,370
2006.	6,179,142	168,537	93,786	72,494	91,877	146,651	418,501	5,187,295
2007.	6,891,131	180,319	98,348	80,400	93,017	144,254	433,634	5,861,160
2008.	6,819,681	180,025	99,430	80,757	98,478	137,907	420,104	5,802,981
2009.	7,014,508	171,209	92,616	64,864	97,408	147,678	416,981	6,023,751
Net profit: [3]								
1990.	110,128	8,527	5,160	2,769	2,661	3,525	7,110	80,377
1995.	198,151	13,224	5,668	3,767	5,771	7,000	16,549	146,172
1996.	224,869	15,802	6,872	4,266	5,664	7,935	16,059	168,271
1997.	244,505	17,948	8,383	4,153	4,675	7,074	18,433	183,836
1998.	234,386	18,350	6,421	3,790	4,681	5,610	14,364	181,170
1999.	257,805	17,398	7,618	3,504	4,798	4,795	12,756	206,934
2000.	275,313	16,578	6,820	3,403	2,742	3,510	15,121	227,136
2001 [2]	36,168	8,387	3,366	–408	403	–543	–6,782	31,746
2002.	134,686	10,003	2,784	807	1,699	3,356	–1,227	117,262
2003.	237,041	9,821	3,374	2,005	2,256	2,973	4,115	212,497
2004.	348,151	14,970	5,745	3,858	3,080	5,140	12,787	302,671
2005.	401,344	17,357	6,057	4,066	3,781	7,678	15,967	346,438
2006	470,282	22,301	8,685	5,260	4,601	8,901	21,405	399,131
2007.	442,734	22,930	9,006	4,402	6,518	8,400	17,565	373,915
2008.	266,346	18,182	7,472	5,820	3,739	3,403	2,239	225,492
2009.	284,147	9,861	5,615	4,281	2,954	3,444	2,839	255,154

[1] Excludes estimates for corporations with less than $250,000 in assets at time of sample selection. [2] Beginning 2001, data reported based on the North American Industry Classification System. [3] After taxes.

Source: U.S. Census Bureau, *Quarterly Financial Report for Manufacturing, Mining, and Trade Corporations*. See also Fourth Quarter 2009 QFR Press Release, March 2010, <http://www.census.gov/econ/qfr/>.

Table 1021. Manufacturing Corporations—Selected Finances: 1990 to 2009

[In billions of dollars (2,811 represents $2,811,000,000,000). Data are not necessarily comparable from year to year due to changes in accounting procedures, industry classifications, sampling procedures, etc.; for detail, see source. See head note, Table 1020. Minus sign (–) indicates loss]

Year	All manufacturing corporations			Durable goods			Nondurable goods		
		Profits [1]			Profits [1]			Profits [1]	
	Sales	Before taxes	After taxes	Sales	Before taxes	After taxes	Sales	Before taxes	After taxes
1990.	2,811	158	110	1,357	57	41	1,454	101	69
1995.	3,528	275	198	1,808	131	94	1,721	144	104
1996.	3,758	307	225	1,942	147	106	1,816	160	119
1997.	3,922	331	244	2,076	167	121	1,847	164	123
1998.	3,949	315	234	2,169	175	128	1,781	140	107
1999.	4,149	355	258	2,314	199	140	1,835	157	117
2000.	4,548	381	275	2,457	191	132	2,091	190	144
2001 [2]	4,295	83	36	2,321	–69	–76	1,974	152	112
2002.	4,217	196	135	2,261	45	21	1,955	149	113
2003.	4,397	306	237	2,283	118	88	2,114	188	149
2004.	4,934	447	348	2,537	200	157	2,397	248	192
2005.	5,411	524	401	2,731	211	161	2,681	313	240
2006.	5,783	605	470	2,910	249	193	2,873	356	278
2007.	6,060	603	443	3,016	247	159	3,044	356	283
2008.	6,374	388	266	2,970	98	43	3,405	290	223
2009.	5,136	360	284	2,449	85	54	2,688	275	231

[1] Beginning 1998, profits before and after income taxes reflect inclusion of minority stockholders' interest in net income before and after income taxes. [2] Beginning 2001, data reported based on the North American Industry Classification System.

Source: U.S. Census Bureau, *Quarterly Financial Report for Manufacturing, Mining, and Trade Corporations*. See also Fourth Quarter 2009 QFR Press Release, March 2010, <http://www.census.gov/econ/qfr/>.

Table 1022. Cotton, Wool, and Man made Fibers—Consumption by End-Use: 2005 to 2008

[13,038 represents 13,386,000,000. Based on U.S. Manufactured Fiber, Cotton and Wool End Use Survey. Represents raw fiber which was put into process in order to manufacture end products manufactured by U.S. mills. Excludes glass fiber]

End-use and year	Fiber consumption, total [1] (mil. lb.)	Cotton [2]		Wool [3]		Manufactured fibers					
						Manufactured fibers		Cellulosic [4]		Synthetic [5]	
		Cotton consumption, total (mil. lb.)	Percent of end-use	Wool consumption, total (mil. lb.)	Percent of end-use	Manufactured fibers consumption, total (mil. lb.)	Percent of end-use	Cellulosic consumption, total (mil. lb.)	Percent of end-use	Synthetic consumption, total (mil. lb.)	Percent of end-use
Total:											
2005.........	13,038	2,540	19.5	95	0.7	10,403	79.8	210	1.6	10,697	82.0
2006.........	11,624	1,850	15.9	97	0.8	9,677	83.3	189	1.6	9,869	84.9
2007.........	10,537	1,371	13.0	91	0.9	9,075	86.1	209	2.0	8,866	84.1
2008.........	9,214	1,085	11.8	77	0.8	8,053	87.4	187	2.0	7,866	85.4
Apparel:											
2005.........	2,738	1,414	51.7	51	1.8	1,273	46.5	62	2.3	1,210	44.2
2006.........	2,161	1,037	48.0	51	2.3	1,074	49.7	41	1.9	1,033	47.8
2007.........	1,682	629	37.4	47	2.8	1,007	59.9	40	2.4	967	57.5
2008.........	1,471	507	34.5	38	2.5	927	63.0	29	1.9	898	61.0
Home textiles:											
2005.........	1,465	791	54.0	9	0.6	665	45.4	31	2.1	634	43.3
2006.........	1,109	568	51.2	12	1.0	529	47.7	23	2.0	507	45.7
2007.........	884	420	47.5	10	1.1	454	51.4	22	2.5	432	48.9
2008.........	756	336	44.4	8	1.1	412	54.4	25	3.3	387	51.1
Floor coverings:											
2005.........	4,503	32	0.7	29	0.6	4,442	98.6	–	–	4,442	98.6
2006.........	4,251	32	0.7	29	0.7	4,190	98.6	–	–	4,190	98.6
2007.........	3,847	32	0.8	29	0.8	3,787	98.4	–	–	3,786	98.4
2008.........	3,269	30	0.9	26	0.8	3,213	98.3	–	–	3,213	98.3
Industrial: [6]											
2005.........	4,333	303	7.0	5	0.1	4,024	92.9	112	2.6	3,912	90.3
2006.........	4,102	214	5.2	6	0.1	3,883	94.6	117	2.8	3,766	91.8
2007.........	4,124	290	7.0	5	0.1	3,828	92.8	147	3.6	3,681	89.3
2008.........	3,718	212	5.7	5	0.1	3,502	94.2	133	3.6	3,368	90.6

– Represents or rounds to zero. [1] Includes other fibers such as silk, linen, jute and sisal. [2] Raw cotton. [3] Wool data includes virgin, noils, reprocessed and reused wool and is reported on clean basis. [4] Includes rayon and acetate. [5] Includes acrylic, nylon, polyester, olefin, and spandex. [6] Includes consumer-type products, such as, narrow fabrics, medical, surgical and sanitary, tires, hose, belting, felts, sewing thread, filtration etc.

Source: Fiber Economics Bureau, Inc., Arlington, VA, Fiber Organon, Vol. 80, No. 10, October 2009 (copyright).

Table 1023. Textiles—Production and Foreign Trade: 2009

[515,985 represents 515,985,000. Fabric blends as shown in the report are reported based on the chief weight of the fiber; whereas, fabrics blends as shown for imports and exports are based on the chief value of the fiber]

Product description	Unit	Quantity (1,000)			Value ($1,000)	
		Manufacturers' production	Exports of domestic merchandise [1]	Imports for consumption [2]	Exports of domestic merchandise [1]	Imports for consumption [2, 3]
YARN						
Spun cotton yarns, carded, 85 percent or more cotton.............	Kilograms....	515,985	255,368	12,355	632,805	60,167
Textured, crimped, twisted, or bulked filament yarns, nylon.............	Kilograms....	615,141	19,098	55,870	92,232	238,163
Textured, crimped, twisted, or bulked filament yarns, polyester.............	Kilograms....	247,430	23,544	32,067	72,493	67,808
BROADWOVEN FABRICS [4]						
Yarn dyed fabrics, blue denim.............	Sq. meters...	127,838	108,431	30,566	215,227	79,734
85 percent or more spun yarn fabrics and blends (except yarn dyed), chiefly man made fiber, twills and sateens [5].............	Sq. meters...	135,460	(NA)	21,318	(NA)	24,853
85 percent or more filament yarn fabrics, man made, high tenacity yarn fabrics of nylon, polyester, or rayon.............	Sq. meters...	115,880	21,587	13,013	69,008	44,297
85 percent or more filament yarn fabrics, man made, glass fiber fabrics.............	Sq. meters...	175,554	34,810	47,270	125,735	66,841
85 percent or more filament yarn fabrics, all other man made filament fiber fabrics, including saran, olefin, and carpet backing.............	Sq. meters...	587,716	18,741	484,462	49,090	133,247
KNIT FABRICS						
Pile fabrics.............	Kilograms....	8,460	(S)	116,728	(S)	147,119
Elastic fabrics (over 12 inches in width) (weight 5 percent or more elastomeric yarn or rubber thread)..	Kilograms....	8,942	(S)	19,251	(S)	159,173
Elastic fabrics (12 inches or less in width) (weight 5 percent or more elastomeric yarn or rubber thread)..	Kilograms....	4,634	(S)	658	(S)	4,982

NA Not available. S Withheld because estimate did not meet publication standards [1] Source: U.S. Census Bureau report EM 545, *U.S. Exports.* [2] Source: U.S. Census Bureau report IM 145, *U.S. Imports for Consumption.* [3] Dollar value represents the c.i.f. (cost, insurance, and freight) at the first port of entry in the United States plus calculated import duty. [4] Represents production of gray broad woven fabrics; import and export data represent gray as well as finished broad woven fabrics. [5] Total for man made fiber fabrics does not include chiefly man made/wool blends.

Source: U.S. Census Bureau, Current Industrial Reports, "Textiles," Series MQ313A, <http://www.census.gov/cir/www/313/mq313a.html>.

Table 1024. Pharmaceutical Preparations—Value of Shipments: 1990 to 2009

[In millions of dollars (33,954 represents $33,954,000,000)]

Product description	Product code	1990	2000	2005	2006	2007	2008	2009
Pharmaceutical preparations, except biologicals	(X)	33,954	79,262	118,647	123,118	(NA)	(NA)	(NA)
Affecting neoplasms, endocrine systems, and metabolic disease	3254121	2,743	9,784	23,779	25,721	28,497	33,260	33,791
Acting on the central nervous system and sense organs	3254124	7,219	18,508	25,627	29,882	28,714	26,430	29,605
Acting on the cardiovascular system	3254127	4,815	8,993	10,232	10,874	11,969	11,543	12,963
Acting on the respiratory system	325412A	3,724	10,179	16,367	18,350	16,177	16,573	16,618
Acting on the digestive system	325412D	4,840	10,046	16,829	11,775	9,822	9,949	10,983
Acting on the skin	325412G	1,558	2,941	3,657	3,303	3,498	3,635	3,797
Vitamin, nutrient, and hematitic preparations	325412L	2,588	5,676	7,556	7,711	8,062	8,749	9,033
Affecting parasitic and infective disease	325412P	5,411	11,037	11,228	11,693	11,014	9,403	10,147
Pharmaceutical preparations for veterinary use	325412T	1,057	2,096	3,371	3,808	3,206	3,280	2,970

NA Not available. X Not applicable.

Source: U.S. Census Bureau, Current Industrial Reports, "Pharmaceutical Preparations, Except Biologicals," Series MA325G, <http://www.census.gov/manufacturing/cir/historical_data/ma325g/index.html>.

Table 1025. Inorganic Chemicals and Fertilizers—Production: 2000 to 2009

[In 1,000 short tons (15,809 represents 15,809,000.) 1,000 short tons = 2,000 lb.]

Product description	Product code	2000	2005	2006	2007	2008	2009
FERTILIZERS MQ325B							
Ammonia, synthetic anhydrous	3253111120	15,809	11,181	10,981	11,448	10,549	10,330
Ammonium nitrate (original melt liquor)	3253111201	7,979	7,212	7,068	8,236	7,841	6,943
Ammonium sulfate	3253111240	2,808	2,906	2,870	3,145	2,783	2,499
Urea (original melt liquor)(100%)	3253114101	7,682	5,807	5,934	6,156	5,776	5,604
Nitric acid (100%)	3253111111	8,708	7,398	7,245	8,623	7,370	6,531
Phosphoric acid (100% P2O5)	3253121111	12,192	12,621	11,707	12,001	10,150	9,542
Sulfuric acid, (100%)	3251881100	43,643	40,996	39,578	39,745	34,855	32,126
Superphosphates and other fertilizer materials (100% P2O5)	3253124102	8,899	8,141	7,184	7,241	6,014	6,142
INORGANIC CHEMICALS MQ325A							
Chlorine gas (100 percent)[1]	3251811111	14,000	10,272	12,443	11,895	10,673	9,391
Sodium hydroxide, liquid (caustic soda) (100 percent) all process: liquid [2]	3251814111	11,523	8,517	9,735	8,869	8,111	7,242
Potassium hydroxide (caustic potash) (88-92 percent) liquid [2]	3251817111	539	527	610	621	582	404
Finished sodium bicarbonate (58 percent) NaHCO3	3251817131	536	581	644	663	682	641
Hydrochloric acids (100 percent) by product and other [3]	3251884131	4,717	4,619	4,391	4,331	3,902	3,584
Aluminum oxide, except natural alumina (100 percent A12O3)	3313110100	(D)	(D)	(D)	(D)	(D)	2,918
Aluminum sulfate (commercial) (17 percent aluminum oxide) [4]	3251887151	1,076	967	1,022	967	(S)	831
Sodium chlorite (100 percent)	325188A141	940	523	615	617	607	420
Sodium silicates (soluble silicate glass, liquid and solid) (anhydrous)[5]	325188A181	1,136	1,309	1,270	1,182	1,106	981
Metasilicate anhydrous (100 percent)	325188A187	72	59	28,772	(D)	(D)	(D)
Sodium sulfate (100 percent)	325188A1A7	509	93	101	93	87	47
Granular carbons, activated (dry weight) [6,7]	325998H1E4	95	(D)	24	27	(S)	(S)
Pulverized carbons, activated, (dry weight) [6]	325998H1E7	71	(D)	64	98	(S)	(S)
Hydrogen peroxide (100 percent by weight)	325188G181	1,083	365	390	429	437	377

D Withheld to avoid disclosing data for individual companies. S Does not meet publication standards. [1] Production includes amounts liquefied. [2] Liquid production figures represent total production, including quantities later evaporated to solid caustic. [3] Includes production from salt and acid. [4] Excludes quantities produced and consumed in municipalities. [5] Excludes amounts produced and consumed in making meta, ortho, and sesquisilicates. [6] Excludes reactivated carbon. [7] Includes pelleted carbon.

Source: U.S. Census Bureau, Current Industrial Reports, "Inorganic Chemicals," Series MQ325A, July 2010, and "Fertilizers and Related Chemicals," Series MQ325B, June 2010, <http://www.census.gov/manufacturing/cir/historical_data/mq325a/index.html> and <http://www.census.gov/manufacturing/cir/historical_data/mq325b/index.html>.

Table 1026. Iron and Steel Industry—Summary: 1990 to 2009

[95.5 represents 95,500,000 tons. Comprises carbon, alloy, and stainless steel]

Item	Unit	1990	1995	2000	2005	2006	2007	2008	2009
Steel mill products, apparent supply	Mil. tons [1]	95.5	109.6	131.9	120.8	135.7	121.9	111.0	67.1
Net shipments, total	Mil. tons [1]	85.0	97.5	109.1	105.0	109.5	106.4	98.5	62.2
STEEL MARKETS									
Automotive	Mil. tons [1]	11.1	14.6	16.1	14.5	15.5	13.6	12.8	8.0
Steel service centers, distributors	Mil. tons [1]	21.1	23.8	30.1	30.6	30.1	26.5	25.5	15.2
Construction, including maintenance [2]	Mil. tons [1]	9.2	14.9	20.3	24.0	21.0	23.8	20.4	14.8
Containers, packaging, shipping	Mil. tons [1]	4.5	4.1	3.7	3.0	3.1	2.9	2.8	2.2
Machinery, industrial equipment, tools	Mil. tons [1]	2.4	2.3	1.8	1.7	1.5	1.4	1.1	0.6
Steel for converting and processing	Mil. tons [1]	9.4	10.4	12.7	5.6	8.5	8.0	6.0	3.8
Rail transportation	Mil. tons [1]	1.1	1.4	1.3	1.3	1.4	1.2	1.5	0.9
Contractors' products	Mil. tons [1]	2.9	(2)	(2)	(2)	(2)	(2)	(2)	(2)
Oil and gas industries	Mil. tons [1]	1.9	2.6	2.9	3.1	2.7	2.6	2.4	0.9
Electrical equipment	Mil. tons [1]	2.5	2.4	2.1	1.2	1.1	0.8	0.9	0.5
Appliances, utensils, and cutlery	Mil. tons [1]	1.5	1.6	1.9	1.9	1.7	2.0	1.8	1.2
Other	Mil. tons [1]	17.4	19.3	16.2	18.3	22.8	23.7	23.3	14.1
Exports of steel mill products	Mil. tons [1]	4.3	7.1	6.5	9.4	9.7	11.2	13.5	9.3
Imports of steel mill products	Mil. tons [1]	17.2	24.4	29.4	32.1	45.3	33.2	31.9	16.2
Raw steel production [3]	Mil. tons [1]	98.9	104.9	112.2	104.6	108.2	108.1	101.3	65.5
Basic oxygen furnaces	Percent	58.5	62.5	53.0	45.0	42.9	41.8	43.1	25.0
Electric arc furnaces	Percent	36.9	42.4	47.0	55.0	57.1	58.2	58.2	40.5
Steel employment [4]	(1,000)	169	123	151	122	124	127	129	(NA)

[1] In millions of short tons. Short ton = 2,000 lbs. [2] Beginning 1995, contractors' products included with construction. [3] Raw steel is defined as steel in the first solid state after melting suitable for further processing or sale, including ingots, steel for foundry castings and strand or pressure cast blooms, slabs or other product forms. [4] Covering only those employees engaged in the production and sale of iron and steel products, excludes mining and quarrying operations, transportation, warehousing and other non-steel producing activities.

Source: American Iron and Steel Institute, Washington, DC, Annual Statistical Report (copyright). See also <www.steel.org>.

Table 1027. Metalworking Machinery—Value of Shipments: 2005 to 2009

[In thousands of dollars (2,800,272 represents $2,800,272,000)]

Product description	Product code	2005	2006	2007	2008 [1]	2009 [1]
Metalworking machinery	(X)	**2,800,272**	**3,094,478**	**3,318,208**	**3,435,540**	**1,952,281**
Metal cutting type machine tools	333512 (pt)	2,079,874	2,293,813	2,533,389	2,650,662	1,428,386
Boring and drilling machines	333512A1	110,971	178,487	130,220	161,393	92,612
Gear cutting machines [2]	33351212	(D)	(D)	(D)	(D)	(D)
Grinding and polishing machines	33351221	265,035	259,063	237,928	270,339	165,445
Lathes [3]	33351231	248,240	295,651	375,871	396,793	204,478
Milling machines [4]	33351241	53,582	56,082	81,294	(D)	(D)
Machining centers	33351271	619,563	703,045	807,425	(D)	(D)
Station type machines [5]	33351281	104,481	79,153	(D)	(D)	114,586
Other metal cutting machine tools	33351291	431,962	464,779	585,522	543,791	289,051
Remanufactured metal cutting machine tools	3335126111	93,404	90,172	81,004	(D)	(D)
Metal forming type machine tools	333513 (pt)	720,398	800,665	784,819	784,878	523,895
Punching, shearing, bending, and forming machines	33351311	344,273	403,361	409,791	391,607	256,645
Presses (excluding forging) [6]	33351331	139,924	128,599	135,292	142,282	75,040
All other metal forming type machines [6]	33351351	206,547	228,880	209,309	231,257	163,041
Remanufactured metal forming machine tools	3335137121	(D)	15,081	10,382	19,732	(S)

D Withheld to avoid disclosing data for individual companies. S Figure does not meet publication standards. X Not applicable. [1] Data shown for years 2008 and 2009 do not include metal cutting and forming type machine tools valued under $3,025 each. [2] Data for "Gear cutting machines" are included in total "Metal cutting type." [3] Data for product code 3335123126, "Vertical NC turning machines" are included in total "Metal cutting type," but excluded from product code 33351231. [4] Data for product code 3335124101, "All milling machines valued under $3,025 each" are included in total "Metal cutting type," but excluded from product code 33351241. [5] Data for "Station type machines" are included in total "Metal cutting type." [6] Data for product codes 3335133101 "All presses valued under $3,025 each" and 3335135101 "All other metal forming type machine tools valued under $3,025 each," are included in total "Metal forming type," but excluded from product codes 33351331 and 33351351, respectively.

Source: U.S. Census Bureau, Current Industrial Reports, "Metalworking Machinery," Series MQ333W, August 2010, <http://www.census.gov/manufacturing/cir/historical_data/mq333w/index.html>.

Table 1028. Aluminum—Supply, Shipments, and Foreign Trade: 1990 to 2008

[In millions of pounds (17,334 represents 17,334,000,000)]

Item	1990	1995	2000	2004	2005	2006	2007	2008, prel.
SUPPLY								
Aluminum supply, total	**17,334**	**20,425**	**23,586**	**22,292**	**23,659**	**24,020**	**23,787**	**23,100**
Primary production	8,925	7,441	8,087	5,549	5,468	5,029	5,643	5,862
Recovery from scrap	5,276	7,030	7,606	6,680	6,680	7,842	8,497	7,590
Imports of ingot and mill products	3,133	5,956	7,893	10,063	11,510	11,149	9,648	9,648
Aluminum net shipments, total	**17,188**	**21,019**	**24,496**	**24,924**	**25,520**	**25,967**	**24,656**	**21,869**
PRODUCT [1]								
Mill products, total	13,013	15,716	17,676	17,122	17,738	17,956	16,455	15,281
Sheet, plate, and foil	9,297	11,168	12,116	11,463	11,810	11,794	11,009	10,514
Rod, bar, and wire	370	534	690	631	664	718	702	680
Electrical conductor	542	566	681	763	794	850	818	700
Extruded shapes and tube	2,546	3,102	3,792	3,821	4,018	4,137	3,485	3,030
Powder and paste	106	108	142	155	144	140	151	135
Forgings and impacts	152	238	255	289	308	317	290	222
Ingot for castings and other [2]	4,175	5,303	6,820	7,802	7,782	8,011	8,201	6,588
MARKET [1]								
Domestic, total	14,637	18,152	21,680	22,901	23,064	23,168	21,457	18,595
Building and construction	2,663	2,679	3,204	3,692	3,681	3,627	3,100	2,600
Transportation	3,205	5,749	7,947	8,509	8,685	8,670	7,885	6,092
Consumer durables	1,122	1,369	1,692	1,585	1,561	1,644	1,474	1,357
Electrical	1,309	1,395	1,704	1,580	1,646	1,707	1,679	1,522
Machinery and equipment	992	1,257	1,496	1,610	1,636	1,680	1,623	1,403
Containers and packaging	4,772	5,088	4,992	5,098	5,115	5,113	4,904	4,908
Other	574	615	645	827	740	727	792	713
Exports	2,551	2,867	2,816	2,023	2,456	2,799	3,199	3,274
FOREIGN TRADE [3]								
Exports	3,753	3,846	4,100	4,416	5,629	6,592	6,704	7,621
Imports	3,718	6,899	9,358	11,221	12,607	12,322	10,737	10,126

[1] Statistics on shipments and markets for 1990 to 2000 represent total U.S. producer's shipments plus imports by consumers. Beginning 2001 figures include Canada. [2] Net ingot for foundry castings, export and destructive uses. [3] U.S. imports and exports of aluminum ingot, mill products and scrap.

Source: The Aluminum Association, Inc., Washington, DC, *Aluminum Statistical Review*, annual. See also <http://www.aluminum.org>.

Table 1029. Semiconductors, Electronic Components, and Semiconductor Manufacturing Equipment—Value of Shipments: 2004 to 2008

[In millions of dollars (9,728 represents $9,728,000,000)]

Product description	Product code	2004	2005	2006	2007	2008
Semiconductor machinery	3332950	(NA)	9,728	12,598	13,190	10,064
Transmitting, industrial, and special purpose electron tubes [1]	3344111	641	652	690	734	792
Receiving type electron tubes [2]	3344114	1,049	621	216	(D)	(D)
Electron tubes and parts	3344117	78	72	49	36	31
Bare printed circuit boards	3344120	4,709	4,856	4,933	4,443	4,547
Integrated microcircuits [3]	3344131	60,097	61,631	54,963	49,781	51,585
Transistors	3344134	656	603	679	599	401
Diodes and rectifiers	3344137	305	372	467	457	457
Other semiconductor devices [4]	334413A	7,247	8,330	10,483	10,176	9,122
Capacitors for electronic circuitry	3344140	1,184	1,113	1,064	945	937
Resistors for electronic circuitry	3344150	744	653	660	645	720
Electronic coils, transformers, and other inductors	3344160	1,116	1,216	1,231	1,393	1,389
Connectors for electronic circuitry	3344170	3,416	3,589	3,980	4,189	3,994
Printed circuit assemblies, loaded boards and modules [5]	334418B	19,566	20,106	19,591	20,382	19,999
Crystals, filters, piezoelectric, and other related electronic devices [6]	3344191	654	779	754	689	648
All other miscellaneous transducers [7]	3344194	1,495	1,401	1,323	1,466	1,439
Switches, mechanical types for electronic circuitry	3344197	716	794	645	662	732
Microwave components and devices [8]	334419A	1,326	1,306	1,470	1,541	1,460
All other miscellaneous electronic components	334419E	4,158	4,040	4,346	4,831	4,609

D Figure withheld to avoid disclosure. NA Not available. [1] Except X-ray. [2] Including cathode ray (new and rebuilt). [3] Includes semiconductor networks, microprocessors, and MOS memories. [4] Includes semiconductor parts such as chips, wafers, and heat sinks. [5] Printed circuit boards with inserted electronic components. [6] Except microwave filters. [7] Includes electrical-electronic input/output transducers. [8] Except antennae, tubes, and semiconductors

Source: U.S. Census Bureau, Current Industrial Reports, "Semiconductors, Electronic Components, and Semiconductor Manufacturing Equipment," Series MA334Q, August 2010, <http://www.census.gov/manufacturing/cir/historical_data/ma334q/index.html>.

Table 1030. Computers and Peripheral Equipment—Value of Shipments: 2004 to 2009

[In millions of dollars (37,895 represents $37,895,000,000)]

Product description	Product code	2004	2005	2006	2007	2008	2009
Electronic computers	334111	37,895	38,386	37,657	36,859	37,542	33,013
Host computers, multiusers	3341111	10,993	11,759	(D)	(D)	(D)	(D)
Single user computers, microprocessor-based, capable of supporting attached peripherals	3341117	26,309	25,906	(D)	(D)	(D)	(D)
Personal computers	3341117107	15,690	(D)	(D)	(D)	(D)	(D)
Workstations	3341117109	1,848	(D)	(D)	2,442	(D)	(D)
Mobile computers, including notebooks, subnotebooks, laptop, and tablet PCs	3341117127	8,456	(D)	(D)	(D)	(D)	(D)
Smart handheld devices	3341117129	(D)	(D)	(D)	(D)	(D)	(D)
All other single user computers	3341117130	(D)	(D)	(D)	25	(D)	(D)
Other computers (array, analog, hybrid, and special-use computers)	334111D	593	721	(D)	299	(S)	183
Computer storage devices (except parts, attachments, and accessories)	3341121	5,034	6,100	6,956	7,872	6,367	6,617
Disk subsystem and disk arrays for multiuser computer systems	3341121109	1,362	2,008	(D)	2,531	(D)	(D)
Disk drives (all sizes)	3341121112	69	11	(D)	150	201	298
Storage Area Networks(SANs)	3341121123	(D)	10	(D)	2,892	(D)	2,683
Tape drives (all sizes)	3341121138	278	289	285	239	264	194
Other computer storage devices	3341121150	(D)	3,781	3,795	2,061	1,321	(D)
Parts, attachments, and accessories for computer storage devices	3341124	1,039	1,441	1,929	1,426	1,327	740
Computer terminals (except point-of-sale and funds-transfer devices, parts, attachments, and accessories)	3341131	274	245	268	331	245	128
Parts, attachments, and accessories for computer terminals (except point-of-sale and funds-transfer devices)	3341134	2	(D)	(D)	(D)	(D)	649
All other miscellaneous computer peripheral (input/output) equipment (except parts, attachments and accessories)	3341191	4,705	4,425	4,517	4,427	4,245	3,382
Parts, subassemblies, and accessories for computer peripheral equipment	3341194	2,257	2,743	2,720	3,171	2,600	5,050
Point-of-sale terminals and funds-transfer devices	3341197	513	497	621	1,034	958	440
Parts and attachments for point-of-sale terminals and funds-transfer devices	334119D	(D)	(D)	35	12	9	(S)
Magnetic and optical recording media	3346130	1,586	1,303	1,364	1,381	(S)	841,538

D Withheld to avoid disclosing data for individual companies. S Withheld because estimates did not meet publication standards.

Source: U.S. Census Bureau, Current Industrial Reports, Computers and Peripheral Equipment, Series MA334R (beginning with 2006, MQ334R), August 2010, <http://www.census.gov/manufacturing/cir/historical_data/mq334r/index.html>.

Table 1031. Computers and Peripheral Equipment—Shipments: 2008 and 2009

[27,623,727 represents 27,623,727,000]

Product	Product code	Quantity (1,000)		Value (1,000 dol.)	
		2008	2009	2008	2009
Electronic computers	**334111**	**27,623,727**	**25,584,754**	**37,541,557**	**33,012,655**
Host computers (multiusers)	3341111	(D)	(D)	(D)	(D)
Large-scale systems, including mainframes and super computers	3341111101	(S)	(S)	2,987,089	2,069,263
Midrange servers (all sizes)	3341111104	(S)	(S)	972,994	(S)
Other computers (array, analog, hybrid, and special-use computers)	334111D	(S)	(S)	(S)	182,988
Computer storage devices (except parts, attachments, and accessories)	3341121	(X)	(X)	6,366,977	6,617,433
Disk subsystem and disk arrays for multiuser computer systems	3341121109	(X)	(X)	(D)	(D)
Disk drives (all sizes)	3341121112	(X)	(X)	201,420	298,243
Storage Area Networks(SANs)	3341121123	(X)	(X)	(D)	2,682,722
Tape drives (all sizes)	3341121138	(X)	(X)	264,125	193,704
Other computer storage devices	3341121150	(X)	(X)	1,321,269	(D)
Parts, attachments, and accessories for computer storage devices	3341124	(X)	(X)	1,327,395	739,733
Computer terminals (except point-of-sale and funds transfer devices, parts, attachments, and accessories)	3341131	(X)	(X)	244,501	127,866
All other miscellaneous computer peripheral (input/output) equipment (except parts, attachments and accessories)	3341191	(X)	(X)	4,245,113	3,382,480
Parts, subassemblies, and accessories for computer peripheral equipment	3341194	(X)	(X)	2,600,420	5,050,114
Point-of-sale terminals and funds-transfer devices	3341197	(X)	(X)	957,521	440,478
Parts and attachments for point-of-sale terminals and funds-transfer devices	334119D	(X)	(X)	9,485	(S)
Magnetic and optical recording media	3346130	(X)	(X)	(S)	841,538

D Withheld to avoid disclosing data for individual companies. S Figure does not meet publication standards. X Not applicable. NA Not available. [1] Includes other products, not shown separately.

Source: U.S. Census Bureau, Current Industrial Reports, "Computers and Peripheral Equipment," Series MQ334R <http://www.census.gov/manufacturing/cir/historical_data/mq334r/index.html>.

Table 1032. U.S. Consumer Electronics Sales and Forecasts by Product Category, 2006 to 2009, and Projection, 2010

[In millions of dollars (156,441 represents $156,441,000,000). Represents shipment volumes from manufacturers to U.S. dealers. Includes both domestic production and imports of products to consumer - oriented channels, regardless of retail type, including distribution and direct-to-consumer sales]

Category	2006	2007	2008	2009	2010, proj.
Total	**156,441**	**168,919**	**178,649**	**165,887**	**165,341**
In home technologies total	**76,960**	**79,561**	**82,765**	**75,994**	**74,869**
TV sets and displays	24,042	24,661	25,931	22,617	22,133
Digital TV sets and displays [1]	22,696	24,519	25,931	22,617	22,133
LCD flat panel	8,430	14,520	17,962	16,905	16,881
Plasma flat panel	5,302	4,488	3,689	3,316	2,793
Front projection	2,943	2,996	2,841	1,748	1,679
OLED	(X)	(X)	113	222	700
High-definition TV	18,410	19,439	23,677	21,670	21,322
Video components [1]	4,747	4,911	6,846	7,043	6,773
Component DVD players/recorders	2,228	1,765	1,388	1,688	1,573
Next generation DVD players [2]	65	345	739	1,121	1,394
Set-top boxes [1]	2,409	2,798	4,719	4,234	3,806
Direct broadcast satellite (DBS) receivers	1,278	1,220	1,064	958	863
Cable/multi-system operator (MSO) receivers	874	1,085	1,300	1,448	1,589
Digital Media Adapters (DMAs)	53	152	563	814	909
Audio separates/systems detail [1]	4,810	4,962	4,429	4,041	3,712
Home technologies	2,047	1,996	1,962	1,680	1,778
Home information technologies and security [1]	40,682	42,783	43,547	40,388	40,650
Personal computers	19,553	21,156	20,931	18,251	18,155
Desktop computers	8,956	8,500	6,744	4,844	3,905
Notebook computers	10,597	12,656	14,187	13,407	14,250
Modems/broadband gateways	1,163	1,109	1,090	1,110	1,130
Other computer peripherals	4,561	4,943	5,012	5,142	5,395
Personal computer software	6,655	7,084	7,406	7,256	7,662
Home security systems	2,786	3,204	3,558	3,675	3,775
Communications [1]	2,678	2,244	2,012	1,855	1,601
Phones	968	576	435	346	342
Telephone answering devices	1,162	1,030	954	824	744
VIOP adapters	390	492	517	604	454
In-vehicle technologies total	**10,712**	**12,257**	**12,782**	**7,770**	**8,270**
Entertainment devices	9,358	9,501	8,706	5,870	7,594
Aftermarket autosound equipment [3]	2,654	1,974	1,516	1,279	1,978
Satellite radio receivers	391	156	89	64	58
Mobile video devices [4]	630	713	539	363	337
Factory-installed autosound	6,074	6,814	6,651	4,228	5,128
Information and security [1]	1,354	2,756	4,076	1,900	1,645
Portable and transportable navigation	988	2,387	3,731	1,555	1,303
Anywhere technologies total	**49,588**	**57,900**	**63,546**	**62,995**	**62,690**
Digital imaging [1]	9,827	9,197	9,416	8,746	8,277
Digital cameras	7,819	6,517	6,813	6,267	5,616
All camcorders	1,828	2,112	1,885	1,709	1,889
Digital photo frames	180	568	718	770	772
Portable entertainment [1]	6,722	7,349	7,325	6,732	5,778
Portable Media/MP3 players	5,559	5,968	5,844	5,446	4,469
Electronic gaming [1]	14,662	19,738	23,558	22,793	21,192
Electronic gaming hardware	4,477	6,710	7,780	5,760	4,675
Electronic gaming software	8,450	11,154	14,166	15,582	16,517
e-toys	1,735	1,874	1,612	1,451	1,501
Portable communication [1]	18,377	21,616	23,247	24,724	25,942
Wireless communication technologies [1]	17,836	21,162	22,814	24,051	24,744
Smartphones	5,192	8,645	11,393	14,901	16,908
Consumer electronic enhancements	**19,181**	**19,201**	**19,556**	**19,178**	**19,512**
Accessories [1]	13,614	14,299	14,777	14,443	14,239
Blank media [1]	5,567	4,902	4,779	4,735	5,183
Flash media	3,374	3,441	3,904	4,340	4,603

X Not applicable. [1] Includes categories, not shown separately. [2] Includes HD-DVD. [3] Includes satellite radio receivers, satellite radio accessories and satellite radio kits, does not include Bluetooth headsets. [4] Includes all fixed navigation units.

Source: Consumer Electronics Association, Arlington, VA. U.S. Consumer Electronics Sales and Forecasts, 2005–2010, January 2010 (copyright).

Table 1033. Telecommunication Equipment—Value of Shipments: 2000 to 2009

[In millions of dollars (15,174 represents $15,174,000,000)]

Product description	Product code	2000	2005	2006	2007	2008	2009
Telephone switching and switchboard equipment	3342101	15,174	1,576	1,812	1,959	1,674	1,045
Carrier line equipment and modems	3342104	13,112	2,824	2,912	3,512	3,137	2,851
Wire line voice and data network equipment	3342107	28,971	12,289	18,563	11,181	4,574	3,191
Communication systems and equipment [1]	3342201	36,357	30,272	32,436	(NA)	(NA)	(NA)
Broadcast, studio, and related electronic equipment	3342202	4,029	3,289	3,653	3,350	4,110	4,237
Wireless networking equipment	3342203	(NA)	(NA)	(NA)	6,159	4,845	4,219
Radio station equipment	3342205	(NA)	(NA)	(NA)	17,824	16,456	16,449
Other communications systems equipment	3342209	(NA)	(NA)	(NA)	6,355	10,882	10,705
Alarm systems [2]	3342901	2,755	1,910	1,526	2,044	2,090	1,663
Vehicular and pedestrian traffic control equipment [3]	3342902	838	1,020	1,048	1,239	1,231	(S)
Intercommunications systems [4]	3342903	447	416	433	438	458	389
Modems, consumer type	3344184	95	98	79	82	87	(D)

D Withheld to avoid disclosing data of individual companies. NA Not available. S Estimates did not meet publication standards. [1] Includes microwave and space satellites. [2] Includes electric sirens and horns. [3] Includes electrical railway signals and attachments. [4] Includes inductive paging systems (selective calling), except telephone and telograph.

Source: U.S. Census Bureau, Current Industrial Reports, "Telecommunications," Series MQ334P, <http://www.census.gov/manufacturing/cir/historical_data/mq334p/index.html>.

Manufactures 649

Table 1034. Motor Vehicle Manufactures—Summary by Selected Industry: 2008

[40,878 represents $40,878,000,000. Based on the Annual Survey of Manufactures; see Appendix III]

Industry	2002 NAICS code [1]	All employees [2] Number	Payroll Total (mil. dol.)	Payroll per employee (dol.)	Produc- tion workers [2]	Value of ship- ments [3] (mil. dol.)
Motor vehicle manufacturing, total	3361–3363	**810,222**	**40,878**	**50,453**	**626,154**	**415,388**
Motor vehicle, total.	3361	163,025	11,318	69,424	139,525	210,978
Automobile and light duty motor vehicle	33611	136,534	10,093	73,921	118,700	192,181
Automobile.	336111	62,702	4,599	73,353	54,236	81,693
Light truck and utility vehicle	336112	73,832	5,493	74,404	64,465	110,488
Heavy duty truck	33612	26,491	1,225	46,243	20,825	18,797
Motor vehicle body and trailer	3362	123,456	4,789	38,790	94,997	29,764
Motor vehicle body and trailer manufacturing.	33621	123,456	4,789	38,790	94,997	29,764
Motor vehicle parts	3363	523,741	24,771	47,297	391,632	174,646
Motor vehicle gasoline engine and engine parts	33631	57,344	3,125	54,493	43,538	26,031
Motor vehicle electrical and electronic equipment. . .	33632	64,339	2,966	46,099	43,881	16,419
Motor vehicle steering and suspension	33633	33,887	1,557	45,947	25,517	9,131
Motor vehicle brake system	33634	24,606	933	37,932	18,373	7,986
Motor vehicle transmission and power train parts . . .	33635	66,878	4,144	61,960	52,840	26,860
Motor vehicle seating and interior trim.	33636	46,198	1,930	41,766	33,405	17,038
Motor vehicle metal stamping	33637	86,744	4,319	49,792	67,745	24,228
Other motor vehicle parts	33639	143,746	5,797	40,332	106,332	46,952

[1] North American Industry Classification System, 2002; see text, Section 15, [2] Includes all full-time and part-time employees on the payrolls of operating manufacturing establishments during any part of the pay period that included the 12th of the month specified on the report form. Included are employees on paid sick leave, paid holidays, and paid vacations; not included are proprietors and partners of unincorporated businesses. [3] Includes extensive and unmeasurable duplication from shipments between establishments in the same industry classification.

Source: U.S. Census Bureau, Annual Survey of Manufactures, "Statistics for Industry Groups and Industries: 2008 and 2007," <http://www.census.gov/manufacturing/asm/index.html>.

Table 1035. Motor Vehicle Manufactures—Employees, Payroll, and Shipments by Major State: 2008

[11,317,810 represents 11,317,810,000. Industry based on the North American Industry Classification System (NAICS); see text, Section 15. See footnote 3, Table 1034 for information regarding shipments. Based on the Annual Survey of Manufactures; see Apppendix III]

State	Motor vehicle manufacturing (NAICS 3361) Employees	Payroll (1,000 dol.)	Value of shipments (1,000 dol.)	Motor vehicle parts manufacturing (NAICS 3363) Employees	Payroll (1,000 dol.)	Value of shipments (1,000 dol.)
United States [1]	**163,025**	**11,317,810**	**210,977,683**	**523,741**	**24,771,122**	**174,646,034**
Alabama	11,262	786,903	16,805,982	17,669	771,793	8,327,155
Arizona	–	–	–	2,895	115,986	694,586
Arkansas	(2)	(D)	(D)	5,586	185,456	1,243,220
California	4,246	291,354	3,966,158	20,515	839,882	5,807,443
Connecticut	–	–	–	(4)	(D)	(D)
Florida	–	–	–	4,220	163,279	818,239
Georgia	2,080	152,712	2,883,809	9,405	362,574	3,238,024
Illinois.	6,396	424,885	4,993,500	23,226	1,009,795	6,681,712
Indiana.	12,578	836,192	17,739,679	57,757	2,944,810	17,891,324
Iowa.	–	–	–	5,806	223,674	1,405,030
Kansas.	(3)	(D)	(D)	2,589	88,185	D
Kentucky	14,686	943,513	18,036,453	29,340	1,167,808	10,369,647
Louisiana.	(3)	(D)	(D)	1,377	48,300	272,791
Massachusetts.	–	–	–	2,159	165,349	767,021
Michigan	30,335	2,415,838	45,671,837	101,424	5,563,300	37,965,507
Minnesota	2,031	99,108	(D)	2,935	118,900	655,169
Mississippi.	(4)	(D)	(D)	4,008	169,831	(D)
Missouri	9,361	727,289	12,882,645	11,648	477,129	3,641,752
Nebraska.	–	–	–	4,289	162,816	1,081,278
New Hampshire.	–	–	–	1,072	33,523	228,037
New York	–	–	–	16,005	987,816	5,023,987
North Carolina	4,939	187,079	(D)	16,512	726,930	6,520,462
Ohio.	20,428	1,547,933	30,982,642	70,223	3,647,912	23,460,016
Oklahoma	(3)	(D)	(D)	3,786	111,989	(D)
Oregon.	(3)	(D)	(D)	1,441	64,518	301,883
Pennsylvania	–	–	–	9,918	412,939	2,495,096
South Carolina.	5,262	(D)	(D)	17,792	776,601	5,735,287
South Dakota.	–	–	–	1,125	47,884	255,009
Tennessee.	7,505	506,882	D	32,476	1,380,498	12,801,089
Texas.	7,468	532,811	14,062,771	11,225	469,685	3,591,881
Utah.	–	–	–	3,319	159,573	1,341,895
Virginia.	(3)	(D)	(D)	5,129	216,698	(D)
Washington	–	–	–	2,549	98,696	497,077
West Virginia	–	–	–	1,885	109,279	(D)
Wisconsin	(4)	(D)	(D)	13,664	569,700	4,158,824

– Represents zero. D Withheld to avoid disclosing data on individual companies. [1] Includes states not shown separately. [2] Employee class size of 500 to 999. [3] Employee class size of 1,000 to 2,499. [4] Employee class size of 2,500 to 4,999.

Source: U.S. Census Bureau, Annual Survey of Manufactures, "Geographic Area Statistics: Statistics for all Manufacturing by State: 2008," <http://www.census.gov/manufacturing/asm/index.html>.

Table 1036. Aerospace—Sales, New Orders, and Backlog: 2000 to 2009

[In billions of dollars (109.3 represents $109,300,000,000), except as indicated. Reported by establishments in which the principal business is the development and/or production of aerospace products]

Item	2000	2004	2005	2006	2007	2008	2009
Net sales	**109.3**	**124.3**	**124.2**	**155.9**	**126.8**	**135.2**	**145.8**
U.S. government net sales	41.0	64.2	62.8	69.7	48.4	59.5	59.4
Percent U.S. government	37.5	51.7	50.6	44.7	38.2	44.0	40.7
Complete aircraft and parts	57.2	49.6	49.9	(D)	(D)	(D)	(D)
Aircraft engines and parts	12.5	16.1	18.5	28.6	15.5	(D)	(D)
Missiles and space vehicles, parts	15.6	14.2	(S)	(D)	(D)	(D)	(D)
Other products, services	24.0	44.4	45.8	(D)	43.70	(D)	(D)
Net, new orders	**140.1**	**131.7**	**186.4**	**202.8**	**231.6**	**189.3**	**107.1**
Backlog, December 31	215.0	234.3	290.0	334.5	437.1	482.1	430.7

D Withheld to avoid disclosing data of individual companies. S Does not meet publication standards

Source: U.S. Census Bureau, Current Industrial Reports, "Civil Aircraft and Aircraft Engines; and Aerospace Industry," Series MA336G, <http://www.census.gov/manufacturing/cir/historical_data/ma336g/index.html>.

Table 1037. Net Orders for U.S. Civil Jet Transport Aircraft: 1990 to 2009

[1990 data are net new firm orders; beginning 1995, net announced orders. Minus sign (–) indicates net cancellations. In 1997, Boeing acquired McDonnell Douglas]

Type of aircraft and customer	1990	2000	2004	2005	2006	2007	2008	2009
Total number [1]	**670**	**585**	**267**	**1,004**	**1,058**	**1,417**	**662**	**142**
U.S. customers	259	412	23	220	321	281	112	24
Foreign customers	411	193	204	811	737	1,136	550	118
Unidentified	–	–20	40	–27	–	–	–	–
Boeing 737, total	189	378	142	571	739	846	484	178
U.S. customers	38	302	16	152	242	164	107	34
Foreign customers	151	86	92	439	497	682	377	144
Unidentified	–	–10	34	–20	–	–	–	–
Boeing 747, total	153	24	10	43	72	25	3	2
U.S. customers	24	1	1	13	18	0	0	–2
Foreign customers	129	18	10	30	54	25	3	4
Unidentified	–	5	–1	–	–	–	–	–
Boeing 757, total	66	43	–	–	–	–	–	–
U.S. customers	33	38	–	–	–	–	–	–
Foreign customers	33	14	–	–	–	–	–	–
Unidentified	–	–9	–	–	–	–	–	–
Boeing 767, total	60	6	9	15	10	36	28	2
U.S. customers	23	–2	–	–	–	27	–	–1
Foreign customers	37	14	1	20	10	9	28	3
Unidentified	–	–6	8	–5	–	–	–	0
Boeing 777, total	64	113	42	154	76	141	54	19
U.S. customers	34	60	–	10	35	23	11	–7
Foreign customers	–	53	43	146	41	118	43	26
Unidentified	–	–	–1	–2	–	–	–	–
Boeing 787, total	–	–	56	235	161	369	93	–59
U.S. customers	–	–	–	45	26	67	–6	–
Foreign customers	–	–	56	190	135	302	99	–59
McDonnell Douglas MD–11, total	52	–	–	–	–	–	–	–
U.S. customers	16	–	–	–	–	–	–	–
Foreign customers	36	–	–	–	–	–	–	–
McDonnell Douglas MD–80/90, total	116	–	–	–	–	–	–	–
U.S. customers	91	–	–	–	–	–	–	–
Foreign customers	25	–	–	–	–	–	–	–
McDonnell Douglas MD–95/717, total	–	21	8	–	–	–	–	–
U.S. customers	–	13	6	–	–	–	–	–
Foreign customers	–	8	2	–	–	–	–	–

– Represents zero. [1] Beginning 2000, includes unidentified customers.

Source: Aerospace Industries Association of America, Washington, DC, "Orders: U.S. Civil Jet Transport Aircraft," Statistical Series 22, <http://www.aia–aerospace.org/industry_information/economics/aerospace_statistics/>.

Table 1038. U.S. Aircraft Shipments: 1990 to 2009

[Value in millions of dollars (38,585 represents $38,585,000,000). Data have been revised, see source]

Year	Total		Civil						Military	
			Large transports		General aviation [1]		Rotocraft			
	Units	Value	Units	Value	Units	Value	Units	Value	Units	Value
1990	3,321	38,585	521	22,215	1,144	2,007	603	254	1,053	14,109
1995	2,441	33,658	256	15,263	1,077	2,842	292	194	816	15,359
1996	2,220	37,518	269	18,915	1,115	3,048	278	193	558	15,363
1997	2,780	43,652	374	26,929	1,549	4,593	346	231	511	11,899
1998	3,534	53,728	559	35,663	2,193	5,534	363	252	419	12,280
1999	3,797	56,692	620	38,171	2,475	6,803	345	200	357	11,518
2000	4,113	50,289	485	30,327	2,802	8,040	493	270	333	11,652
2001	3,904	56,221	526	34,155	2,616	7,991	415	247	347	13,828
2002	3,252	49,361	379	27,547	2,196	7,261	318	157	359	14,396
2003	3,261	42,431	281	21,033	2,080	6,205	517	366	383	14,827
2004	3,802	43,555	283	20,484	2,296	6,918	805	515	418	15,639
2005	4,677	51,190	290	22,116	2,853	8,632	947	816	587	19,626
2006	5,426	55,431	398	25,875	3,134	9,550	898	802	996	19,204
2007	5,644	68,878	441	29,160	3,279	11,941	1,009	1,385	915	26,392
2008	5,306	68,307	375	24,076	3,079	13,348	1,094	1,540	758	29,043
2009, proj.	3,262	64,252	381	25,000	1,587	9,082	564	1,170	730	29,000

[1] Excludes off-the-shelf military aircraft.

Source: U.S. Department of Commerce, International Trade Administration, "Shipments of Complete U.S. Aircraft, 1971–2009," <http://trade.gov/mas/manufacturing/OAAI/aero_stats.asp\>.

Manufactures 651

Table 1039. Aerospace Industry Sales by Product Group and Customer: 1990 to 2010

[In billions of dollars (134.4 represents $134,400,000,000). Due to reporting practices and tabulatimg methods, figures may differ from those in Table 1036]

Group	1990	2000	2004	2005 [1]	2006	2007	2008	2009 [2]	2010 [3]
CURRENT DOLLARS									
Total sales	**134.4**	**144.7**	**155.7**	**173.6**	**189.4**	**201.8**	**205.7**	**214.1**	**214.4**
Product group:									
Aircraft, total	71.4	81.6	79.1	112.2	125.4	135.1	137.6	144.1	140.0
Civil [4]	31.3	47.6	32.5	62.1	71.6	80.2	80.6	82.5	76.7
Military	40.1	34.0	46.6	50.1	53.8	54.9	57.0	61.7	63.3
Missiles	14.2	9.3	14.7	10.8	11.7	12.6	13.3	14.8	16.7
Space	26.4	29.7	35.9	33.6	34.9	36.3	38.8	40.4	40.9
Related products and services [5]	22.4	24.1	26.0	17.1	17.3	17.8	16.1	14.8	16.9
Customer group:									
Aerospace products and services, total	112.0	120.6	129.8	156.5	172.0	184.0	189.7	199.3	197.6
DOD [6]	60.5	47.5	70.1	78.2	83.2	86.1	90.5	97.2	100.8
NASA [7] and other agencies	11.1	13.4	16.0	15.0	15.6	16.2	17.4	18.1	18.3
Other customers [8]	40.4	59.7	43.7	63.3	73.2	81.7	81.9	84.1	78.4
Related products and services [5]	22.4	24.1	26.0	17.1	17.3	17.8	16.1	14.8	16.9
CONSTANT (2000) DOLLARS [9]									
Total sales	**123.5**	**144.7**	**141.1**	**151.5**	**159.5**	**164.8**	**162.0**	**164.5**	**161.3**
Product group:									
Aircraft, total	65.6	81.6	71.7	97.9	105.6	110.3	108.4	110.8	105.3
Civil [4]	28.7	47.6	29.5	54.2	60.3	65.5	63.5	63.4	57.6
Military	36.8	34.0	42.2	43.7	45.3	44.9	44.9	47.4	47.6
Missiles	13.0	9.3	13.3	9.4	9.9	10.3	10.4	11.4	12.6
Space	24.3	29.7	32.6	29.3	29.4	29.6	30.6	31.0	30.7
Related products and services [5]	20.6	24.1	23.5	14.9	14.6	14.5	12.7	11.3	12.7
Customer group:									
Aerospace products and services, total	102.9	120.6	117.6	136.6	144.9	150.2	149.4	153.2	148.6
DOD [6]	55.6	47.5	63.5	68.2	70.1	70.3	71.2	74.7	75.8
NASA [7] and other agencies	10.2	13.4	14.5	13.1	13.2	13.3	13.7	13.9	13.8
Other customers [8]	37.1	59.7	39.6	55.2	61.7	66.7	64.5	64.6	59.0
Related products and services [5]	20.6	24.1	23.5	14.9	14.6	14.5	12.7	11.3	12.7

[1] Beginning in 2005, sales numbers for individual product groups are not comparable to figures in prior years due to revised survey methodology. However, total annual sales data remain comparable across all years of the time series. [2] Preliminary. [3] Estimate. [4] All civil sales of aircraft (domestic and export sales of jet transports, commuters, business, and personal aircraft and helicopters). [5] Electronics, software, and ground support equipment, plus sales of non-aerospace products which are produced by aerospace-manufacturing use technology, processes, and materials derived from aerospace products. [6] Department of Defense. [7] National Aeronautics and Space Administration. [8] Includes civil aircraft sales (see footnote 4), commercial space sales, all exports of military aircraft and missiles and related propulsion and parts. [9] Based on Aerospace Industry Association's aerospace composite price deflator (200=100).

Source: Aerospace Industries Association of America, Inc., Washington, DC, *2009 Year-end Review and Forecast.* See also <http://www.aia-aerospace.org>.

Table 1040. Major Household Appliances—Value of Shipments: 2000 to 2009

[In millions of dollars (2,170 represents $2,170,000,000)]

Product description	Product code	2000	2005	2006	2007	2008	2009
Electric household ranges, ovens and surface cooking units, equipment and parts	3352211	2,170	2,577	2,541	2,736	2,506	2,062
Gas household ranges, ovens, and surface cooking units, equipment and parts	3352213	779	1,392	1,363	1,541	1,473	1,126
Other household ranges, cooking equipment and outdoor cooking equipment [1]	3352215	1,251	965	784	491	510	485
Household refrigerators, including combination refrigerator-freezers	3352221	5,396	5,405	5,427	5,440	5,891	5,189
Parts and attachments for household refrigerators and freezers	3352223	(D)	(D)	(D)	159	107	92
Household laundry machines and parts	3352240	4,047	5,236	5,184	5,232	5,835	4,820
Water heaters, electric	3352281	573	638	652	950	953	869
Water heaters, except electric	3352283	844	970	903	1,572	1,547	1,452
Household appliances, n.e.c and parts [2]	3352285	2,066	2,433	2,413	2,717	2,602	2,126

D Withheld to avoid disclosing data of individual companies. [1] Includes parts and accessories. [2] n.e.c. means not elsewhere classified.

Source: U.S. Census Bureau, Current Industrial Reports, "Major Household Appliances," Series MA335F, <http://www.census.gov/manufacturing/cir/historical_data/mq335f/index.html>.

Section 22
Wholesale and Retail Trade

This section presents statistics relating to the distributive trades, specifically wholesale trade and retail trade. Data shown for the trades are classified by kind of business and cover sales, establishments, employees, payrolls, and other items. The principal sources of these data are from the U.S. Census Bureau and include the *2007 Economic Census*, annual and monthly surveys, and the *County Business Patterns* program. These data are supplemented by several tables from trade associations, such as the National Automobile Dealers Association (Table 1056). Several notable research groups are also represented, such as Nielsen Claritas (Table 1058).

Data on wholesale and retail trade also appear in several other sections. For instance, labor force employment and earnings data appear in Section 12, Labor Force, Employment, and Earnings; gross domestic product of the industry (Table 652) appears in Section 13, Income, Expenditures, Poverty, and Wealth; and financial data (several tables) from the quarterly *Statistics of Income Bulletin,* published by the Internal Revenue Service, appear in Section 15, Business Enterprise.

Censuses—Censuses of wholesale trade and retail trade have been taken at various intervals since 1929. Beginning with the 1967 census, legislation provides for a census of each area to be conducted every 5 years (for years ending in "2" and "7"). For more information on the most recent census, see the *Guide to the 2007 Economic Census* found at <http://www .census.gov/econ/census07 /www.user_guide.html>. The industries covered in the censuses and surveys of business are defined in the *North American Industry Classification System*, (NAICS). Retail trade refers to places of business primarily engaged in retailing merchandise to the general public; and *wholesale trade*, to establishments primarily engaged in selling goods to other businesses and normally operating from a warehouse or office that have little or no display of merchandise.

Most Census Bureau tables in this section utilize the 2002 NAICS codes, which replaced the Standard Industrial Classification (SIC) system. NAICS made substantial structural improvements and identifies over 350 new industries. At the same time, it causes breaks in time series far more profound than any prior revision of the previously used SIC system. For information on this system and how it affects the comparability of wholesale and retail statistics historically, see text, Section 15, Business Enterprise, and especially the Census Bureau Web site at <http://www.census.gov/eos/www /naics>. In general, the 2007 Economic Census has three series of publications for these two sectors: 1) subject series with reports such as product lines and establishment and firm sizes, 2) geographic reports with individual reports for each state, and 3) industry series with individual reports for industry groups. For information on these series, see the Census Bureau Web site at <http://www .census.gov/econ/census07/>.

Current surveys—Current sample surveys conducted by the Census Bureau cover various aspects of wholesale and retail trade. Its *Monthly Retail Trade and Food Services* release at <http://www .census.gov/retail/index.html> contains monthly estimates of sales, inventories, and inventory/sales ratios for the United States, by kind of business. Annual figures on retail sales, year-end inventories, purchases, accounts receivable, and gross margins by kind of business are located on the Census Bureau Web site at <http://www.census.gov/econ/retail .htm>. Additionally, annual data for accommodation and food services are located at the same site.

Statistics from the Census Bureau's monthly wholesale trade survey include national estimates of sales, inventories, and inventory/sales ratios for merchant wholesalers excluding manufacturers' sales branches and offices. Data are

Wholesale and Retail Trade 653

presented by major summary groups "durable and nondurable," and 4-digit NAICS industry groups. Merchant wholesalers excluding manufacturers' sales branches and offices are those wholesalers who take title to the goods they sell (e.g., jobbers, exporters, importers, industrial distributors). These data, based on reports submitted by a sample of firms, appear in the *Monthly Wholesale Trade Report* at <http://www.census.gov/wholesale/index.htm>. This report, along with monthly sales, inventories, and inventories/sales ratios, also provides data on annual sales, inventories, and year-end inventories/sales ratios. The Annual Wholesale Trade Survey provides data on merchant wholesalers excluding manufacturer sales branches and offices as well as summary data for all merchant wholesalers. This report also provides separate data for manufacturer sales branches and offices, and electronic markets, agents, brokers, and commission merchants. Also included in the *Monthly Wholesale Trade Report are* data on annual sales, year-end inventories, inventories/sales ratios, operating expenses, purchases, and gross margins. Data are presented by major summary groups "durable and nondurable" and 4-digit NAICS industry groups for sales, end-of-year inventories, and operating expenses. The reports are available as documents on the Census Bureau Web site at <http://www.census.gov/econ/wholesale.htm>.

E-commerce—Electronic commerce (or e-commerce) is sales of goods and services over the Internet and extranet, electronic data interchange (EDI), or other online systems. Payment may or may not be made online. E-commerce data were collected in four separate Census Bureau surveys. These surveys used different measures of economic activity such as shipments for manufacturing, sales for wholesale and retail trade, and revenues for service industries. Consequently, measures of total economic and e-commerce activity vary by economic sector, are conceptually and definitionally different, and therefore, are not additive. This edition has several tables on e-commerce sales, such as Tables 1044, 1054, and 1055 in this section; 1008 in Section 21, Manufactures; and 1277 in Section 27, Accommodation, Food Services, and Other Services.

Statistical reliability—For a discussion of statistical collection and estimation, sampling procedures, and measures of statistical reliability applicable to Census Bureau data, see Appendix III.

Table 1041. Wholesale and Retail Trade—Establishments, Sales, Payroll, and Employees: 2002 and 2007

[435.5 represents $435,500. Covers establishments with payroll. For statement on methodology, see Appendix III]

Kind of business	2002 NAICS code [1]	Establishments (1,000) 2002	Establishments (1,000) 2007	Sales (bil. dol.) 2002	Sales (bil. dol.) 2007	Annual payroll (bil. dol.) 2002	Annual payroll (bil. dol.) 2007	Paid employees (1,000) 2002	Paid employees (1,000) 2007
Wholesale trade	42	435.5	435.0	4,635	6,516	260	336	5,878	6,227
Wholesale trade, durable goods	423	260.4	255.0	2,171	2,898	157	207	3,357	3,619
Wholesale trade, nondurable goods	424	142.7	134.6	1,980	2,991	93	116	2,273	2,320
Wholesale electronic markets and agents and brokers	425	32.4	45.4	483	627	10	13	249	289
Retail trade	44–45	1,114.6	1,128.1	3,056	3,918	302	363	14,648	15,515
Motor vehicle and parts dealers	441	125.1	126.8	802	891	65	73	1,845	1,914
Furniture and home furnishings stores	442	65.2	65.1	92	108	13	15	535	557
Electronics and appliance stores	443	46.8	50.8	82	109	9	11	391	486
Building material and garden equipment and supplies dealers	444	(NA)	91.1	(NA)	318	(NA)	38	(NA)	1,331
Food and beverage stores	445	148.8	146.1	457	539	49	55	2,839	2,827
Health and personal care stores	446	81.8	88.5	178	234	20	28	1,024	1,068
Gasoline stations	447	121.4	118.8	249	450	14	15	927	891
Clothing and clothing accessories stores	448	149.8	156.5	168	216	21	27	1,427	1,644
Sporting goods, hobby, book, and music stores	451	62.2	57.4	73	81	9	9	611	619
General merchandise stores	452	40.7	45.9	445	577	43	54	2,525	2,763
Miscellaneous store retailers	453	129.5	121.9	91	104	13	14	792	792
Nonstore retailers	454	54.9	59.4	173	290	17	23	571	621

NA Not available. [1] North American Industrial Classification System; see text, Section 15.

Source: U.S. Census Bureau, "2007 Economic Census, Comparative Statistics for the United States, (2002 NAICS Basis): 2007 and 2002," July 2010. <http://www.census.gov/econ/census07/>.

Table 1042. Wholesale Trade—Nonemployer Establishments and Receipts by Kind of Business: 2005 to 2007

[34,091 represents $34,091,000,000. Includes only firms subject to federal income tax. Nonemployers are businesses with no paid employees]

Kind of Business	2002 NAICS code [1]	Establishments 2005	Establishments 2006	Establishments 2007	Receipts (mil. dol.) 2005	Receipts (mil. dol.) 2006	Receipts (mil. dol.) 2007
Wholesale trade, total	42	381,137	387,022	401,863	34,091	34,804	35,823
Durable goods merchant wholesalers	423	203,327	203,501	201,713	19,240	19,649	19,804
Motor vehicle and motor vehicle parts and supplies merchant wholesalers	4231	16,470	16,826	16,944	2,300	2,374	2,444
Furniture and home furnishing merchant wholesalers	4232	16,286	16,049	15,317	1,317	1,296	1,259
Lumber and other construction materials merchant wholesalers	4233	7,859	8,704	8,817	1,032	1,037	1,017
Professional and commercial equipment and supplies merchant wholesalers	4234	10,386	10,419	10,755	1,034	1,079	1,121
Metal and mineral (except petroleum) merchant wholesalers	4235	3,175	3,184	3,241	461	494	504
Electrical and electronic goods merchant wholesalers	4236	10,885	11,057	10,948	1,180	1,200	1,282
Hardware and plumbing and heating equipment and supplies merchant wholesalers	4237	5,514	5,429	5,157	557	564	541
Machinery, equipment, and supplies merchant wholesalers	4238	20,318	19,649	19,750	2,627	2,651	2,703
Miscellaneous durable goods merchant wholesalers	4239	112,434	112,184	110,784	8,732	8,956	8,933
Nondurable goods merchant wholesalers	424	150,848	154,295	151,935	12,865	12,936	13,098
Paper and paper product merchant wholesalers	4241	6,831	7,069	7,173	551	544	565
Drugs and druggists' sundries merchant wholesalers	4242	3,180	3,091	2,942	250	239	234
Apparel, piece goods, and notions merchant wholesalers	4243	23,201	23,859	23,504	1,733	1,736	1,744
Grocery and related products merchant wholesalers	4244	27,529	28,085	28,353	3,508	3,559	3,684
Farm product raw material merchant wholesalers	4245	3,936	4,331	4,578	495	485	508
Chemical and allied products merchant wholesalers	4246	4,086	3,940	3,871	441	437	427
Petroleum and petroleum products merchant wholesalers	4247	2,354	2,348	2,327	283	286	301
Beer, wine, and distilled alcoholic beverage merchant wholesalers	4248	3,456	3,778	3,968	320	335	358
Miscellaneous nondurable goods merchant wholesalers	4249	76,275	77,794	75,219	5,285	5,314	5,277
Wholesale electronic markets and agents and brokers	425	26,959	29,226	48,215	1,981	2,219	2,921
Business to business electronics markets	42511	4,738	6,304	6,753	259	328	396

[1] North American Industry Classification System, 2002. See text, Section 15.

Source: U.S. Census Bureau, "Nonemployer Statistics," August 2009, <http://www.census.gov/econ/nonemployer/>

U.S. Census Bureau, Statistical Abstract of the United States: 2011

Table 1043. Wholesale Trade—Establishments, Employees, and Payroll: 2006 and 2007

[430.0 represents 430,000. Covers establishments with payroll. Excludes self-employed individuals, employees of private households, railroad employees, agricultural production employees, and most government employees. For statement on methodology, see Appendix III]

Kind of business	2002 NAICS code [1]	Establishments (1,000)		Employees [2] (1,000)		Payroll (bil. dol.)	
		2006	2007	2006	2007	2006	2007
Wholesale trade, total	42	430.0	434.5	6,031	5,965	323.3	328.0
Merchant wholesalers, durable goods...................	423	244.7	247.3	3,430	3,395	195.0	197.1
Motor vehicle/motor vehicle parts and supply merchant wholesalers......................................	4231	24.5	24.5	368	356	16.0	15.9
Furniture and home furnishing merchant wholesalers	4232	12.6	12.7	158	154	7.3	7.4
Lumber and other construction materials merchant wholesalers......................................	4233	18.9	19.6	275	264	12.9	12.5
Professional and commercial equipment and supplies merchant wholesalers.............................	4234	36.6	36.1	724	706	50.4	49.8
Metal and mineral (except petroleum) merchant wholesalers......................................	4235	10.7	10.7	158	160	9.1	9.4
Electrical goods merchant wholesalers.................	4236	29.2	29.1	466	450	34.6	34.3
Hardware, plumbing and heating equipment and supplies merchant wholesalers......................	4237	19.2	20.1	231	232	11.5	11.9
Machinery, equipment, and supplies merchant wholesalers......................................	4238	59.0	59.7	714	724	38.0	39.8
Miscellaneous durable goods merchant wholesalers	4239	34.0	34.5	336	350	15.2	16.2
Merchant wholesalers, nondurable goods...............	424	130.8	130.6	2,268	2,228	112.4	113.6
Paper and paper product merchant wholesalers..........	4241	11.8	11.4	180	172	9.0	8.8
Drugs and druggists' sundries merchant wholesalers......	4242	7.6	7.6	258	248	20.0	19.9
Apparel, piece goods and notions merchant wholesalers...	4243	15.7	16.2	201	197	10.4	10.3
Grocery and related product merchant wholesalers.......	4244	33.5	33.6	771	768	33.1	34.2
Farm product raw material merchant wholesalers.........	4245	6.6	6.6	62	61	2.4	2.5
Chemical and allied products merchant wholesalers	4246	12.5	12.5	141	139	8.4	8.6
Petroleum and petroleum products merchant wholesalers ..	4247	7.2	7.0	103	95	5.8	5.6
Beer, wine, and distilled alcoholic beverages	4248	4.1	4.2	179	179	8.7	9.1
Miscellaneous nondurable goods merchant wholesalers ...	4249	31.8	31.4	373	368	14.6	14.7
Wholesale electronic markets and agents and brokers......	425	54.5	56.5	333	342	15.8	17.2

[1] North American Industry Classification System, 2002. See text, Section 15. [2] Covers full- and part-time employees who are on the payroll in the pay period including March 12.

Source: U.S. Census Bureau, "County Business Patterns," July 2009, <http://www.census.gov/econ/cbp/>.

Table 1044. Merchant Wholesale Trade Sales—Total and E-Commerce: 2008

[4,410,763 represents $4,410,763,000,000. Covers only businesses with paid employees. Excludes manufacturers' sales branches and offices. Based on the Annual Wholesale Trade Survey, see Appendix III]

Kind of business	2002 NAICS code [1]	2008			
		Value of sales (mil. dol.)		E-commerce as percent of total sales	Percent distribution of E-commerce sales
		Total	E-commerce		
Total merchant wholesale trade	42	4,410,763	719,612	16.3	100.0
Durable goods...............................	423	2,069,702	299,583	14.5	41.6
Motor vehicles, parts and supplies	4231	310,367	102,062	32.9	14.2
Furniture and home furnishings...................	4232	64,001	7,527	11.8	1.0
Lumber and other construction materials	4233	112,584	5,770	5.1	0.8
Professional and commercial equipment and supplies ...	4234	358,487	91,989	25.7	12.8
Computer, peripheral equipment, and software........	42343	172,623	55,686	32.3	7.7
Metals and minerals (except petroleum)	4235	170,837	4,391	2.6	0.6
Electrical goods..............................	4236	350,756	39,747	11.3	5.5
Hardware, and plumbing and heating equipment and supplies..................................	4237	107,738	9,824	9.1	1.4
Machinery, equipment and supplies	4238	353,695	13,497	3.8	1.9
Miscellaneous durable goods	4239	241,237	24,776	10.3	3.4
Nondurable goods.............................	424	2,341,061	420,029	17.9	58.4
Paper and paper products.......................	4241	93,495	17,735	19.0	2.5
Drugs and druggists' sundries....................	4242	364,196	262,129	72.0	36.4
Apparel, piece goods and notions	4243	140,339	30,032	21.4	4.2
Groceries and related products....................	4244	503,861	58,554	11.6	8.1
Farm product raw materials......................	4245	196,147	(S)	(S)	(S)
Chemical and allied products	4246	112,540	4,808	4.3	0.7
Petroleum and petroleum products	4247	611,214	(S)	(S)	(S)
Beer, wine, and distilled alcoholic beverages	4248	105,438	(S)	(S)	(S)
Miscellaneous nondurable goods	4249	213,831	25,604	12.0	3.6

S Figure does not meet publication standards. [1] North American Industry Classification System, 2002. See text, Section 15.

Source: U.S. Census Bureau, "E-Stats, 2008 E-commerce Multi-sector Report," May 2010, <http://www.census.gov/econ/estats/>.

Table 1045. Merchant Wholesalers—Summary: 2000 to 2008

[In billions of dollars (2,814.6 represents $2,814,600,000,000), except ratios. Inventories and inventories/sales ratios, as of December, not seasonally adjusted. Excludes manufacturers' sales branches and offices. Data reflect latest revision. Based on data from the Annual Wholesale Trade Survey and the Monthly Wholesale Trade Survey; see Appendix III]

Kind of business	2002 NAICS code [1]	2000	2003	2004	2005	2006	2007	2008
SALES								
Merchant wholesalers	42	**2,814.6**	**2,971.5**	**3,314.6**	**3,595.6**	**3,889.7**	**4,153.4**	**4,410.8**
Durable goods	423	**1,486.7**	**1,464.1**	**1,685.7**	**1,811.1**	**1,983.6**	**2,065.9**	**2,069.7**
Motor vehicles, parts, and supplies	4231	222.2	260.7	284.8	305.3	337.1	343.0	310.4
Furniture and home furnishings	4232	52.7	55.4	59.6	62.8	69.0	69.1	64.0
Lumber and other construction materials	4233	87.2	105.2	127.7	139.4	142.6	126.7	112.6
Professional, commercial equipment and supplies	4234	282.2	275.9	303.0	316.0	330.7	353.8	358.5
Computer, peripheral equipment and software	42343	174.8	144.1	157.1	162.2	160.0	170.0	172.6
Metal and mineral (except petroleum)	4235	93.8	81.2	120.8	136.1	158.0	162.1	170.8
Electrical and electronic goods	4236	260.0	232.4	264.8	283.6	319.6	346.5	350.8
Hardware, plumbing, heating equipment and supplies	4237	72.1	74.4	84.1	94.8	108.4	111.6	107.7
Machinery, equipment, and supplies	4238	256.1	230.7	259.8	288.2	312.7	326.4	353.7
Miscellaneous durable goods	4239	160.3	148.0	181.1	184.7	205.4	226.8	241.2
Nondurable goods	424	**1,327.9**	**1,507.4**	**1,628.8**	**1,784.5**	**1,906.1**	**2,087.5**	**2,341.1**
Paper and paper products	4241	77.8	73.8	81.5	86.8	90.0	93.3	93.5
Drugs and druggists' sundries	4242	176.0	271.3	291.6	322.4	338.3	346.5	364.2
Apparel, piece goods, and notions	4243	96.5	108.0	115.7	124.4	134.9	143.2	140.3
Grocery and related products	4244	374.7	403.6	406.2	424.1	440.6	482.6	503.9
Farm product raw materials	4245	102.7	111.0	114.0	104.1	110.8	144.9	196.1
Chemical and allied products	4246	62.3	70.7	78.3	89.8	92.5	102.2	112.5
Petroleum and petroleum products	4247	195.8	226.3	276.4	354.7	410.7	470.5	611.2
Beer, wine, and distilled alcoholic beverages	4248	71.3	82.4	86.0	91.0	97.4	102.4	105.4
Miscellaneous nondurable goods	4249	170.9	160.1	179.0	187.0	190.8	202.0	213.8
INVENTORIES								
Merchant wholesalers	42	**309.4**	**309.4**	**339.9**	**366.6**	**397.8**	**424.2**	**438.7**
Durable goods	423	**198.6**	**186.4**	**213.1**	**231.5**	**252.6**	**258.8**	**273.5**
Motor vehicles, parts, and supplies	4231	28.8	31.7	33.9	37.8	40.3	41.9	45.8
Furniture and home furnishings	4232	6.4	6.8	7.2	7.7	8.3	8.4	8.2
Lumber and other construction materials	4233	8.4	10.4	13.3	14.3	14.6	13.7	12.9
Professional, commercial equipment and supplies	4234	27.8	25.0	27.3	27.6	29.5	30.0	30.7
Computer, peripheral equipment and software	42343	12.1	9.5	10.1	10.4	10.6	10.4	10.1
Metal and mineral (except petroleum)	4235	13.4	12.1	18.9	19.5	24.7	23.0	26.4
Electrical and electronic goods	4236	31.1	23.8	27.8	30.2	34.1	36.4	37.7
Hardware, plumbing, heating equipment and supplies	4237	11.5	11.7	13.5	15.3	17.1	17.9	17.2
Machinery, equipment, and supplies	4238	51.2	44.9	50.1	56.0	60.9	63.7	69.7
Miscellaneous durable goods	4239	20.1	18.8	21.0	23.1	23.1	23.8	24.9
Nondurable goods	424	**110.9**	**123.0**	**126.8**	**135.0**	**145.2**	**165.3**	**165.2**
Paper and paper products	4241	6.7	5.5	6.3	6.8	6.9	7.0	7.5
Drugs and druggists' sundries	4242	24.1	33.2	32.9	31.3	32.0	32.9	33.9
Apparel, piece goods, and notions	4243	13.7	13.8	14.5	15.8	17.7	18.6	20.0
Grocery and related products	4244	20.4	20.1	20.6	22.6	24.0	27.0	29.1
Farm product raw materials	4245	11.6	14.1	10.1	11.6	15.9	23.1	17.3
Chemical and allied products	4246	6.0	6.6	7.3	8.2	8.3	9.8	10.3
Petroleum and petroleum products	4247	5.2	6.4	9.2	11.6	12.4	16.1	12.7
Beer, wine, and distilled alcoholic beverages	4248	6.5	7.2	7.7	8.3	8.9	9.9	11.2
Miscellaneous nondurable goods	4249	16.6	16.1	18.3	18.9	18.8	21.0	23.4
INVENTORIES/SALES RATIO								
Merchant wholesalers	42	**1.10**	**1.04**	**1.03**	**1.02**	**1.02**	**1.02**	**0.99**
Durable goods	423	**1.34**	**1.27**	**1.26**	**1.28**	**1.27**	**1.25**	**1.32**
Motor vehicles, parts, and supplies	4231	1.29	1.22	1.19	1.24	1.20	1.22	1.48
Furniture and home furnishings	4232	1.21	1.22	1.20	1.23	1.20	1.21	1.28
Lumber and other construction materials	4233	0.96	0.99	1.04	1.02	1.02	1.08	1.15
Professional, commercial equipment and supplies	4234	0.98	0.91	0.90	0.87	0.89	0.85	0.86
Computer, peripheral equipment and software	42343	0.69	0.66	0.64	0.63	0.66	0.61	0.59
Metal and mineral (except petroleum)	4235	1.43	1.49	1.57	1.43	1.56	1.42	1.55
Electrical and electronic goods	4236	1.20	1.07	1.05	1.07	1.07	1.05	1.07
Hardware, plumbing, heating equipment and supplies	4237	1.60	1.57	1.61	1.61	1.58	1.60	1.59
Machinery, equipment, and supplies	4238	2.00	1.94	1.93	1.94	1.95	1.95	1.97
Miscellaneous durable goods	4239	1.25	1.27	1.16	1.25	1.12	1.05	1.03
Nondurable goods	424	**0.83**	**0.82**	**0.78**	**0.76**	**0.76**	**0.79**	**0.71**
Paper and paper products	4241	0.86	0.74	0.77	0.78	0.76	0.75	0.80
Drugs and druggists' sundries	4242	1.37	1.22	1.13	0.97	0.95	0.95	0.93
Apparel, piece goods, and notions	4243	1.42	1.28	1.25	1.27	1.31	1.30	1.42
Grocery and related products	4244	0.54	0.50	0.51	0.53	0.55	0.56	0.58
Farm product raw materials	4245	1.13	1.27	0.89	1.11	1.44	1.59	0.88
Chemical and allied products	4246	0.97	0.94	0.93	0.91	0.89	0.95	0.92
Petroleum and petroleum products	4247	0.26	0.28	0.33	0.33	0.30	0.34	0.21
Beer, wine, and distilled alcoholic beverages	4248	0.91	0.87	0.89	0.91	0.92	0.97	1.06
Miscellaneous nondurable goods	4249	0.97	1.01	1.02	1.01	0.98	1.04	1.09

[1] North American Industry Classification System, 2002. See text, Section 15.

Source: U.S. Census Bureau, "Annual Revision of Monthly Wholesale Distributors: Sales and Inventories—January 1992 Through January 2009," March 2010, <http://www.census.gov/wholesale/www/historic_releases/annual_historic_releases.html>.

Table 1046. Wholesale and Retail Trade—Establishments, Employees, and Payroll by State: 2006 and 2007

[6,031 represents 6,031,000. Covers establishments with payroll. Excludes self-employed individuals, employees of private households, railroad employees, agricultural production employees, and most government employees. Based on North American Industry Classification System (NAICS) 2002. See text, Section 15. For statement on methodology, see Appendix III]

State	Wholesale trade (NAICS 42)						Retail trade (NAICS 44, 45)					
	Establishments		Employees [1] (1,000)		Annual payroll (mil. dol.)		Establishments		Employees [1] (1,000)		Annual payroll (mil. dol.)	
	2006	2007	2006	2007	2006	2007	2006	2007	2006	2007	2006	2007
U.S.	429,952	434,464	6,031	5,965	323,270	327,991	1,120,319	1,123,629	15,768	15,760	368,278	375,200
AL	5,660	5,669	79	80	3,470	3,606	19,497	19,670	247	245	5,182	5,293
AK	738	741	9	9	413	456	2,655	2,668	35	35	940	974
AZ	6,791	6,965	97	99	4,870	5,239	18,693	19,341	331	342	8,088	8,241
AR	3,514	3,561	49	47	1,987	2,009	11,653	11,795	145	143	2,868	3,019
CA	59,935	60,805	826	820	50,038	50,591	113,307	114,025	1,701	1,713	45,772	46,059
CO	7,350	7,423	100	99	5,681	5,834	19,309	19,368	257	262	6,396	6,630
CT	4,687	4,644	80	75	5,243	4,984	13,752	13,688	201	198	5,313	5,322
DE	1,019	984	20	10	1,511	1,374	3,955	3,920	56	57	1,375	1,394
DC	434	420	6	5	362	335	1,934	1,870	20	20	517	529
FL	31,567	32,283	320	320	15,023	15,148	72,986	73,529	1,057	1,028	25,287	24,721
GA	14,097	14,273	207	206	10,882	11,200	35,371	35,920	478	486	11,045	11,149
HI	1,873	1,886	21	21	819	870	5,045	5,051	73	71	1,770	1,782
ID	2,012	2,076	24	24	976	1,036	6,145	6,379	81	83	1,875	1,936
IL	19,847	20,023	315	303	18,387	17,664	42,941	42,892	652	667	15,412	16,202
IN	8,179	8,283	118	115	5,369	5,326	23,469	23,446	351	334	7,144	7,273
IA	4,857	4,911	64	64	2,686	2,713	13,495	13,285	181	180	3,591	3,672
KS	4,517	4,555	57	57	2,592	2,683	11,367	11,306	151	150	3,126	3,201
KY	4,517	4,521	69	67	2,891	2,929	16,485	16,254	228	216	4,529	4,578
LA	5,533	5,621	72	74	3,312	3,487	16,691	17,037	230	234	5,114	5,247
ME	1,644	1,632	19	18	832	791	6,980	6,951	85	84	1,899	1,921
MD	6,057	5,970	98	95	5,466	5,522	19,590	19,566	307	301	7,544	7,582
MA	8,655	8,720	145	143	9,924	10,021	25,625	25,666	368	367	9,263	9,291
MI	11,785	11,972	174	167	9,338	9,404	38,102	37,709	489	475	10,429	10,288
MN	8,646	8,618	137	137	8,438	8,442	20,868	20,741	313	316	7,165	7,056
MS	2,918	2,913	38	36	1,477	1,449	12,248	12,379	149	144	2,975	2,993
MO	8,259	8,393	128	126	5,504	5,719	23,299	23,148	326	323	7,042	7,181
MT	1,480	1,522	15	14	569	556	5,192	5,224	58	60	1,261	1,356
NE	2,956	3,037	38	38	1,691	1,745	7,981	7,865	109	109	2,204	2,260
NV	2,919	3,001	39	40	1,967	2,058	8,304	8,570	143	144	3,805	3,852
NH	1,965	1,951	25	24	1,414	1,441	6,657	6,569	100	101	2,412	2,427
NJ	16,012	16,005	271	269	17,776	18,078	34,925	34,544	462	467	11,840	12,200
NM	1,991	2,011	22	22	876	927	7,260	7,242	100	100	2,272	2,377
NY	34,864	34,609	405	390	23,058	22,961	76,982	76,516	901	899	22,553	23,016
NC	11,983	12,200	170	174	8,431	8,956	36,148	36,329	467	475	10,292	10,770
ND	1,476	1,483	17	17	688	728	3,419	3,376	45	46	914	951
OH	15,437	15,396	238	233	11,618	11,799	40,312	39,832	609	593	12,795	12,885
OK	4,583	4,617	61	59	2,656	2,744	13,493	13,446	176	176	3,595	3,778
OR	5,681	5,767	77	78	3,876	3,990	14,522	14,699	208	208	5,030	5,081
PA	15,805	15,875	242	237	12,600	12,820	46,660	46,328	679	682	14,873	15,291
RI	1,436	1,468	19	21	947	1,107	4,182	4,168	56	55	1,487	1,497
SC	4,808	4,980	68	64	3,071	2,999	18,598	18,893	229	238	4,860	5,082
SD	1,315	1,389	15	16	552	607	4,220	4,172	51	51	1,053	1,075
TN	7,378	7,496	121	123	5,888	6,234	23,718	24,047	333	326	7,267	7,519
TX	31,411	32,075	464	467	26,082	26,701	76,527	78,111	1,128	1,156	26,068	27,330
UT	3,558	3,681	48	50	2,194	2,397	8,602	8,874	139	142	3,149	3,356
VT	863	859	11	11	441	488	3,878	3,791	41	41	951	964
VA	7,750	7,795	121	116	6,061	6,080	29,345	29,382	441	440	10,074	10,315
WA	9,562	9,656	130	129	6,698	6,923	22,761	22,990	329	328	8,570	8,712
WV	1,625	1,610	21	20	806	845	7,118	7,003	96	95	1,777	1,842
WI	7,241	7,325	115	114	5,487	5,560	21,102	21,065	322	322	6,787	6,946
WY	762	794	7	8	329	412	2,951	2,989	32	33	728	783

[1] Covers full- and part-time employees who are on the payroll in the pay period including March 12.
Source: U.S. Census Bureau, "County Business Patterns," July 2009, <http://www.census.gov/econ/cbp/>.

Table 1047. Retail Trade—Establishments, Employees, and Payroll: 2006 and 2007

[1,120.3 represents 1,120,600. Covers establishments with payroll. Excludes self-employed, employees of private households, railroad employees,agricultural production employees, and most government employees. For statement on methodology, see Appendix III]

Kind of business	2002 NAICS code [1]	Establishments (1,000) 2006	Establishments (1,000) 2007	Employees [2] (1,000) 2006	Employees [2] (1,000) 2007	Payroll (bil. dol.) 2006	Payroll (bil. dol.) 2007
Retail trade, total	**44–45**	**1,120.3**	**1,123.6**	**15,768**	**15,760**	**368.3**	**375.2**
Motor vehicle and parts dealers	441	128.4	127.3	1,948	1,938	75.0	74.7
Automobile dealers	4411	52.2	51.2	1,287	1,274	55.5	55.4
New car dealers	44111	26.0	24.4	1,158	1,138	51.3	50.9
Used car dealers	44112	26.2	26.9	129	136	4.2	4.5
Other motor vehicle dealers	4412	16.8	17.0	167	169	5.9	6.1
Recreational vehicle dealers	44121	3.1	3.0	44	43	1.7	1.7
Motorcycle and boat and other motor vehicle dealers	44122	13.7	14.0	124	126	4.3	4.4
Motorcycle dealers	441221	5.8	6.0	67	69	2.2	2.4
Automotive parts, accessories, and tire stores	4413	59.4	59.1	493	496	13.5	13.2
Automotive parts, accessories and tire stores	44131	40.4	39.6	327	329	8.1	7.8
Tire dealers	44132	19.1	19.5	167	166	5.4	5.5
Furniture and home furnishing stores	442	65.9	65.5	578	597	15.6	15.6
Furniture stores	4421	29.2	29.2	283	272	8.4	8.3
Home furnishings stores	4422	36.6	36.2	295	325	7.3	7.3
Floor covering stores	44221	14.6	14.6	99	95	3.6	3.5
Other home furnishings stores	44229	22.0	21.6	196	230	3.7	3.8
Window treatment stores	442291	2.9	3.1	11	16	0.3	0.4
Electronics and appliance stores	443	49.3	52.5	489	501	13.0	12.5
Appliance, TV, and all other electronics stores	44311	36.4	38.3	379	387	9.8	9.4
Household appliance stores	443111	9.1	9.0	71	69	2.1	2.1
Radio, television, and other electronics stores	443112	27.3	29.3	308	318	7.6	7.3
Computer and software stores	44312	10.7	12.1	95	100	2.8	2.6
Bldg. material & garden equip. & supp. dealers	444	87.8	88.3	1,366	1,374	40.7	39.5
Building material & supplies dealers [3]	4441	67.3	67.9	1,191	1,202	36.2	34.9
Home centers	44411	6.7	7.2	573	(D)	14.9	(D)
Hardware stores	44413	14.0	14.2	142	140	3.0	3.0
Lawn & garden equip, & supplies stores [3]	4442	20.5	20.4	175	172	4.5	4.6
Nursery and garden centers	44422	16.3	16.1	149	145	3.7	3.8
Food & beverage stores	445	152.4	151.0	2,926	2,882	54.5	56.3
Grocery stores	4451	94.2	92.3	2,615	2,565	48.9	50.6
Supermarkets & other grocery (except convenience) stores	44511	66.1	64.1	2,474	2,425	46.8	48.4
Convenience stores	44512	28.1	28.2	142	140	2.2	2.2
Specialty food stores	4452	28.0	28.3	169	175	2.9	3.0
Beer, wine, & liquor stores [4]	4453	30.2	30.4	143	143	2.6	2.7
Health & personal care stores [3]	446	87.0	89.4	1,114	1,069	29.7	32.0
Pharmacies & drug stores	44611	41.8	42.3	851	798	23.2	24.9
Cosmetics, beauty supplies, & perfume stores	44612	13.6	14.2	86	91	1.6	1.7
Optical goods stores	44613	12.6	12.9	66	71	1.8	1.9
Gasoline stations	447	116.9	115.5	913	889	15.0	14.9
Gasoline stations with convenience stores	44711	93.7	95.4	731	725	11.4	11.5
Other gasoline stations	44719	23.1	20.1	183	164	3.6	3.4
Clothing & clothing accessories stores	448	152.0	155.4	1,631	1,648	26.5	27.5
Clothing stores [3]	4481	95.7	99.3	1,260	1,279	18.9	19.7
Men's clothing stores	44811	9.0	8.6	68	66	1.5	1.5
Women's clothing stores	44812	34.5	35.6	336	342	4.9	5.3
Children's & infants' clothing stores	44813	6.4	7.0	74	94	0.9	1.0
Family clothing stores	44814	25.4	27.3	650	635	9.2	9.4
Shoe stores	4482	26.7	27.2	201	206	3.2	3.3
Jewelry, luggage, & leather goods stores	4483	29.7	28.8	171	163	4.4	4.5
Jewelry stores	44831	28.3	27.5	162	154	4.1	4.2
Sporting goods, hobby, book, & music stores	451	60.5	60.1	638	640	10.1	10.2
Sporting goods/hobby/musical instrument stores [3]	4511	43.0	43.5	442	456	7.4	7.5
Sporting goods stores	45111	23.3	23.8	223	236	4.2	4.3
Hobby, toy, and game stores	45112	9.5	9.5	132	136	1.8	1.9
Book, periodical, & music stores [3]	4512	17.5	16.6	196	184	2.7	2.6
Book stores	451211	11.0	10.6	143	145	2.0	1.9
Prerecorded tape, CD, & record stores	45122	4.9	4.5	43	31	0.6	0.6
General merchandise stores	452	46.7	47.5	2,802	2,897	53.4	56.7
Department stores	4521	10.0	10.1	1,532	1,620	28.6	30.4
Discount department stores	452112	6.0	6.1	937	(D)	18.1	(D)
Other general merchandise stores	4529	36.7	37.3	1,270	1,278	24.8	26.3
Warehouse clubs & superstores	45291	3.2	3.3	965	961	20.5	21.9
All other general merchandise stores	45299	33.5	34.1	305	316	4.3	4.4
Miscellaneous store retailers [3]	453	125.1	123.4	840	814	15.5	15.6
Florists	4531	20.2	19.8	98	94	1.4	1.4
Office supplies, stationery, and gift stores	4532	41.2	40.7	338	315	5.7	5.4
Used merchandise stores	4533	17.7	17.7	134	134	2.2	2.3
Other miscellaneous store retailers [3]	4539	46.0	45.2	270	271	6.3	6.4
Nonstore retailers [3]	454	48.3	47.7	522	512	19.3	19.9
Electronic shopping & mail-order houses	4541	16.2	16.7	264	268	10.8	11.5
Direct selling establishments	4543	26.8	25.9	206	194	7.0	7.0
Fuel dealers	45431	10.2	10.5	94	91	3.3	3.5

D Figure withheld to avoid disclosure. [1] Based on North American Industry Classification System (NAICS) 2002. See text, Section 15. [2] See footnote 2, Table 1043. [3] Includes other kinds of business, not shown separately. [4] Includes government employees.

Source: U.S. Census Bureau, "County Business Patterns," July 2009, <http://www.census.gov/econ/cbp/>.

Wholesale and Retail Trade 659

Table 1048. Retail Trade—Nonemployer Establishments and Receipts by Kind of Business: 2005 to 2007

[1,881 represents 1,881,000. Includes only firms subject to federal income tax. Nonemployers are businesses with no paid employees]

Kind of Business	2002 NAICS code [1]	Establishments (1,000)			Receipts (mil. dol.)		
		2005	2006	2007	2005	2006	2007
Retail trade, total	**44–45**	**1,881**	**1,858**	**1,980**	**83,599**	**83,933**	**88,143**
Motor vehicle & parts dealers [2]	441	147	141	176	20,072	19,789	20,762
Furniture & home furnishings stores	442	41	39	49	3,088	2,965	3,115
Electronics and appliance stores	443	27	26	33	1,701	1,645	1,834
Bldg material & garden equip. & supply dealers [2]	444	31	32	41	2,710	2,723	2,993
Building material & supplies dealers	4441	23	23	29	2,141	2,150	2,322
Food & beverage stores [2]	445	89	87	108	9,027	8,983	9,658
Grocery stores	4451	39	38	47	4,518	4,448	4,735
Specialty food stores	4452	39	39	48	2,584	2,607	2,925
Health & personal care stores [2]	446	114	122	146	2,510	2,673	3,383
Cosmetics, beauty supplies, and perfume stores	44612	72	77	87	987	1,066	1,465
Gasoline stations	447	9	8	10	1,517	1,460	1,553
Clothing & clothing accessories stores [2]	448	109	111	142	5,231	5,327	5,945
Clothing stores	4481	73	74	90	3,239	3,319	3,729
Jewelry, luggage, and leather goods stores	4483	32	33	46	1,702	1,712	1,896
Sporting goods, hobby, book, & music stores [2]	451	93	90	90	3,882	3,882	3,883
Book, periodical, and music stores	4512	30	29	29	944	912	909
General merchandise stores	452	36	36	33	1,632	1,640	1,629
Miscellaneous store retailers [2]	453	313	301	296	13,625	13,656	13,779
Office supplies, stationery, and gift stores	4532	75	70	66	2,503	2,439	2,384
Nonstore retailers [2]	454	873	865	856	18,608	19,189	19,610
Electronic shopping & mail-order houses	4541	73	77	84	2,587	2,854	3,227
Direct selling establishments	4543	771	759	743	15,144	15,466	15,483

[1] North American Industry Classification System, 2002. See text, Section 15. [2] Includes other kinds of business, not shown separately.

Source: U.S. Census Bureau, "Nonemployer Statistics," August 2009, <http://www.census.gov/econ/nonemployer/>.

Table 1049. Retail Industries—Employees, Average Weekly Hours, and Average Hourly Earnings: 2000 to 2009

[Annual averages of monthly figures (15,280 represents 15,280,000). Covers all full- and part-time employees who worked during, or received pay for, any part of the pay period including the 12th of the month]

Industry	2007 NAICS code [1]	Employees (1,000)			Average weekly hours			Average hourly earnings (dol.)	
		2000	2005	2009	2000	2005	2009	2000	2009
Retail trade, total	**(X)**	**15,280**	**15,280**	**14,528**	**30.7**	**30.6**	**29.9**	**10.86**	**13.02**
Motor vehicle and parts dealers	441	1,847	1,919	1,640	35.9	35.8	35.9	14.94	16.52
Automobile dealers	4411	1,217	1,261	1,022	35.1	35.8	35.9	16.95	17.68
Other motor vehicle dealers	4412	132	166	136	35.1	34.7	34.2	12.35	16.63
Auto parts, accessories, and tire stores	4413	499	491	482	38.2	36.0	36.5	11.04	14.04
Automotive parts and accessories	44131	339	329	319	38.6	34.8	35.9	10.67	13.64
Furniture and home furnishings stores	442	544	576	450	31.2	30.7	29.1	12.33	15.17
Furniture stores	4421	289	298	224	31.7	31.7	32.6	13.37	15.99
Home furnishings stores	4422	254	278	226	30.7	29.5	25.6	11.06	14.12
Electronics and appliance stores [2]	443	564	536	487	31.4	32.8	30.9	13.67	16.74
Radio, TV, and other electronic stores	443112	236	297	305	31.8	32.9	30.9	13.31	14.52
Building material and garden supply stores	444	1,142	1,276	1,163	35.7	36.8	34.2	11.25	14.02
Building material and supplies dealers	4441	982	1,134	1,035	36.2	37.3	34.3	11.30	14.03
Home centers	44411	479	637	627	36.5	37.8	33.7	10.97	12.87
Lawn and garden equipment and supplies stores	4442	160	142	128	32.5	32.6	32.8	10.89	13.89
Food and beverage stores [2]	445	2,993	2,818	2,829	31.7	30.1	28.9	9.76	11.87
Grocery stores	4451	2,582	2,446	2,475	31.9	30.0	28.8	9.71	11.91
Supermarkets and other grocery stores	44511	2,438	2,301	2,340	31.9	30.0	28.7	9.84	12.06
Specialty food stores	4452	270	236	217	31.6	33.0	30.2	9.97	11.26
Health and personal care stores [2]	446	928	954	984	29.8	29.3	29.5	11.68	16.83
Pharmacies and drug stores	44611	677	695	727	29.7	28.9	29.0	11.89	17.21
Gasoline stations [2]	447	936	871	827	31.6	31.6	30.8	8.05	9.79
Gasoline stations with convenience stores	44711	787	751	726	31.3	31.3	30.5	7.87	9.52
Clothing and clothing accessories stores [2]	448	1,322	1,415	1,369	24.9	24.4	21.0	9.96	11.66
Clothing stores	4481	954	1,066	1,050	24.4	23.1	19.6	9.88	10.88
Jewelry, luggage, and leather goods stores	4483	175	169	138	27.7	31.9	27.8	11.48	14.98
Sporting goods, hobby, book, and music stores	451	686	647	616	26.4	23.3	24.0	9.33	11.58
Sporting goods and musical instrument stores	4511	437	447	461	27.0	23.5	24.5	9.55	11.66
Book, periodical, and music stores	4512	249	200	155	25.4	23.0	22.7	8.91	11.32
General merchandise stores	452	2,820	2,934	2,956	27.8	29.4	30.7	9.22	10.80
Miscellaneous store retailers [2]	453	1,007	900	785	29.2	28.5	27.9	10.20	11.87
Office supplies, stationary, and gift stores	4532	471	391	319	29.7	27.8	27.2	10.46	13.01
Gift, novelty, and souvenir stores	45322	266	213	170	26.0	24.3	22.9	8.28	10.79
Used merchandise stores	4533	107	113	118	26.7	27.8	28.6	8.07	9.89
Pet and pet supplies stores	45391	72	88	102	27.0	28.9	26.7	9.78	10.70
Art dealers	45392	26	24	18	(X)	(X)	(X)	(X)	(X)
Nonstore retailers [2]	454	492	435	422	35.4	34.5	34.8	13.22	17.29
Electronic shopping and mail-order houses	4541	257	240	245	36.2	33.0	35.1	13.38	17.71
Electronic shopping and electronic auctions	454111,2	68	68	96	37.9	35.4	35.2	13.58	20.67
Mail-order houses	454113	189	172	149	35.6	32.1	34.8	13.30	15.97
Direct selling establishments	4543	169	145	135	34.1	36.0	34.6	13.70	16.92
Fuel dealers	45431	106	94	82	37.6	38.2	37.3	13.79	16.69

X Not applicable. [1] Based on the North American Industry Classification System (NAICS), 2007; see text, this section and Section 15. [2] Includes other kind of businesses, not shown separately.

Source: U.S. Bureau of Labor Statistics, Current Employment Statistics, "Employment, Hours, and Earnings—National," <http://www.bls.gov/ces/data.htm>.

Table 1050. Retail Trade and Food Services—Sales by Kind of Business: 2000 to 2009

[In billions of dollars (3,294.2 represents $3,294,200,000) Sales and inventories for leased departments and concessions are tabulated in the kind-of-business category of the leased department or concession]

Kind of Business	2007 NAICS code [1]	2000	2004	2005	2006	2007	2008	2009
Retail sales and food services, total	**44, 45, 722**	**3,294.2**	**3,854.6**	**4,095.5**	**4,305.8**	**4,451.5**	**4,417.3**	**4,130.7**
Retail sales, total	**44, 45**	**2,988.8**	**3,479.8**	**3,697.6**	**3,881.6**	**4,005.2**	**3,959.2**	**3,671.2**
GAFO, total [2]	(X)	863.9	1,005.4	1,061.5	1,114.0	1,148.8	1,147.3	1,113.4
Motor vehicle and parts dealers	441	797.6	867.8	890.0	901.3	911.2	788.7	690.4
Automobile and other motor vehicle dealers	4411, 4412	733.9	800.7	819.6	828.6	836.0	711.6	615.0
Automobile dealers	4411	688.7	738.9	754.2	761.5	767.9	651.7	559.4
New car dealers	44111	630.1	670.4	681.8	685.0	687.3	576.9	492.7
Auto parts, accessories, and tire stores	4413	63.7	67.1	70.4	72.7	75.2	77.1	75.4
Furniture, home furnishings, electronics and appliance stores	442, 443	173.7	198.5	210.7	220.8	221.9	210.1	189.6
Furniture and home furnishings stores	442	91.3	103.9	109.2	112.8	111.2	101.1	89.5
Furniture stores	4421	50.7	55.9	58.8	60.1	59.4	54.1	48.3
Home furnishings stores	4422	40.6	48.0	50.5	52.8	51.8	46.9	41.2
Electronics and appliance stores [3]	443	82.4	94.6	101.5	108.0	110.7	109.1	100.1
Appliances, televisions, and other electronics stores	44311	58.3	72.8	78.4	84.4	86.2	84.7	77.5
Building materials, garden equipment, and supply stores [3]	444	229.3	296.2	321.8	334.9	322.0	306.7	271.3
Hardware stores	44413	16.2	18.3	18.9	20.0	20.6	20.3	18.6
Food and beverage stores [3]	445	445.7	491.0	509.0	526.3	548.9	573.6	575.8
Grocery stores	4451	403.0	441.3	457.6	472.1	491.8	513.8	513.8
Supermarkets and other grocery (except convenience) stores	44511	381.7	418.7	435.2	448.8	468.6	489.2	488.4
Beer, wine and liquor stores	4453	28.7	32.3	33.8	36.3	38.2	40.1	40.4
Health and personal care stores	446	155.4	199.8	210.6	224.0	237.8	247.3	254.6
Pharmacies and drug stores	44611	130.9	169.4	179.4	191.4	202.5	211.0	218.2
Gasoline stations	447	250.0	324.5	379.6	422.9	451.4	499.4	373.1
Clothing and clothing access, stores [3]	448	168.0	190.2	201.7	213.6	221.6	216.6	208.6
Clothing stores [3]	4481	118.2	137.0	146.0	154.7	161.7	158.0	152.2
Women's clothing stores	44812	31.5	34.9	37.1	38.8	40.5	38.6	35.6
Shoe stores [3]	4482	22.9	23.7	25.3	26.7	26.9	27.1	26.1
Jewelry stores	44831	25.0	27.8	20.0	30.3	31.0	29.5	28.3
Sporting goods, hobby, book & music stores [3]	451	76.1	79.6	81.1	83.5	85.0	84.1	83.6
Sporting goods stores	45111	25.4	28.8	30.8	34.0	35.9	37.2	37.7
Hobby, toy, and game stores	45112	17.0	16.4	16.3	16.1	16.5	16.0	17.0
General merchandise stores	452	404.3	497.7	527.9	554.6	578.9	596.9	592.9
Department stores (excluding L.D.) [4]	4521	232.5	215.8	214.5	213.2	209.4	199.6	188.1
Discount department stores	452112	136.2	131.2	130.4	132.7	132.5	128.5	62.4
Department stores (including L.D.) [4]	4521	239.9	222.1	220.8	219.3	215.3	205.1	192.8
Discount department stores	452112	139.6	134.3	133.5	135.8	135.5	131.3	125.7
Warehouse clubs and superstores	45291	139.6	242.4	272.0	298.1	325.0	351.5	357.2
Miscellaneous store retailers	453	108.1	105.7	109.1	115.5	118.1	115.9	112.4
Office supplies, stationery, and gift stores	4532	41.8	39.6	40.1	41.5	41.4	39.5	38.7
Office supplies and stationery stores	45321	22.8	21.8	22.4	22.9	23.3	22.3	20.6
Used merchandise stores	4533	10.1	9.4	9.5	10.5	11.1	11.5	11.6
Nonstore retailers [3]	454	180.7	228.8	256.1	284.2	308.4	319.9	318.9
Electronic shopping and mail-order houses	4541	113.9	153.2	175.6	201.4	222.5	227.1	235.2
Fuel dealers	45431	26.7	30.5	34.6	35.6	37.6	44.4	36.0
Food services and drinking places [5]	**722**	**305.5**	**374.8**	**397.8**	**424.2**	**446.3**	**458.2**	**459.5**

X Not applicable. [1] North American Industry Classification System, 2007; see text, Section 15. [2] GAFO (General Merchandise, Apparel, Furniture, and Office Supplies) represents stores classified in the following NAICS codes: 442, 443, 448, 451, 452, and 4532. [3] Includes other kinds of businesses, not shown separately. [4] L.D. represents leased departments. [5] See also Table 1280.

Source: U.S. Census Bureau, "Annual Revision of Monthly Retail and Food Services: Sales and Inventories—January 1992 Through March 2009," March 2010. See <http://www.census.gov/retail/mrts/www/benchmark/2009/html/annrev09.html>.

Table 1051. Retail Trade Corporations—Sales, Net Profit, and Profit Per Dollar of Sales: 2008 and 2009

[Represents North American Industry Classification System, 2007 (NAICS) groups 44 and 45. Profit rates are averages of quarterly figures at annual rates. Covers corporations with assets of $50,000,000 or more]

Item	Unit	Total retail trade		Food and beverage stores (NAICS 445)		Clothing and general merchandise stores (NAICS 448, 452)		All other retail stores	
		2008	2009	2008	2009	2008	2009	2008	2009
Sales	Bil. dol	2,094	2,023	397	388	749	742	948	892
Net profit:									
Before income taxes	Bil. dol	54.0	75.6	7.6	6.2	27.3	38.5	19.1	30.9
After income taxes	Bil. dol	28.9	48.2	4.2	3.3	16.2	26.2	8.5	18.7
Profits per dollar of sales:									
Before income taxes	Cents	2.6	3.7	1.9	1.6	3.7	5.1	2.0	3.4
After income taxes	Cents	1.4	2.4	1.1	0.8	2.3	3.5	0.9	2.1
Profits on stockholders' equity:									
Before income taxes	Percent	13.7	18.9	15.8	13.1	15.4	21.5	11.3	17.8
After income taxes	Percent	7.3	12.0	8.8	6.9	9.1	14.6	5.0	10.7

Source: U.S. Census Bureau, *Quarterly Financial Report for Manufacturing, Mining and Trade Corporations*, annual, <http://www.census.gov/econ/qfr/>.

Table 1052. Retail Trade and Food Services—Estimated Per Capita Sales by Selected Kind of Business: 2000 to 2008

[Estimates are shown in dollars and are based on data from the Annual Retail Trade Survey and the Census Bureau's Population Estimates Program. Based on estimated resident population estimates as of July 1. For additional information, see <http://www.census.gov/popest/estimates.php>. For statement on methodology, see Appendix III]

Kind of business	2007 NAICS code [1]	2000	2003	2004	2005	2006	2007	2008
Retail and food service sales	44–45,722	**11,675**	**12,465**	**13,154**	**13,847**	**14,421**	**14,761**	**14,512**
Retail sales, total	44–45	**10,592**	**11,256**	**11,875**	**12,502**	**13,000**	**13,281**	**13,007**
Total (excluding motor vehicle and parts dealers	*44–45 ex 441*	*7,765*	*8,353*	*8,913*	*9,493*	*9,981*	*10,260*	*10,416*
Motor vehicle and parts dealers	441	2,827	2,903	2,961	3,009	3,018	3,021	2,591
Furniture and home furnishings stores	442	324	334	355	369	378	369	332
Electronics and appliance stores	443	292	299	323	343	362	367	358
Building material and garden equipment and supplies dealers	444	813	909	1,011	1,088	1,122	1,068	1,008
Food and beverage stores	445	1,579	1,637	1,676	1,721	1,763	1,820	1,885
Health and personal care stores	446	551	663	682	712	750	789	813
Gasoline stations	447	886	948	1,107	1,284	1,416	1,497	1,641
Clothing and clothing accessories stores	448	595	616	649	682	715	735	712
Sporting goods, hobby, book, and music stores	451	270	265	271	274	280	282	276
General merchandise stores	452	1,433	1,615	1,698	1,785	1,858	1,920	1,961
Miscellaneous store retailers	453	383	356	361	369	387	392	381
Nonstore retailers	454	640	710	781	866	952	1,023	1,051
Food services and drinking places	722	**1,083**	**1,209**	**1,279**	**1,345**	**1,421**	**1,480**	**1,505**

[1] North American Industry Classification System, 2007; see text, Section 15.

Source: U.S. Census Bureau, "2008 Annual Retail Trade Survey," March 2010 <http://www.census.gov/retail/>.

Table 1053. Retail Trade—Merchandise Inventories and Inventory/Sales Ratios by Kind of Business: 2000 to 2009

[Inventories in billions of dollars (406.7 represents $406,700,000,000). As of Dec. 31, seasonally adjusted. Estimates exclude food services. Includes warehouses. Adjusted for seasonal variations. Sales data also adjusted for holiday and trading-day differences. Based on data from the Monthly Retail Trade Survey, Annual Retail Trade Survey, and administrative records; see Appendix III. Data have been adjusted using results of the 2007 Economic Census]

Kind of business	2007 NAICS code [1]	Inventories				Inventory/sales ratio			
		2000	2005	2008	2009	2000	2005	2008	2009
Retail Inventories, total [2]	**44–45**	**406.7**	**472.0**	**478.8**	**428.9**	**1.62**	**1.50**	**1.61**	**1.36**
Total excluding motor vehicle and parts dealers	*44–45 ex 441*	*278.4*	*319.0*	*332.7*	*316.5*	*1.49*	*1.33*	*1.38*	*1.24*
Motor vehicle and parts dealers	441	128.3	153.1	146.1	112.4	2.01	2.07	2.61	1.86
Furniture, home furnishings, electronics, and appliance stores	442, 443	25.7	30.7	28.9	27.3	1.85	1.72	1.79	1.73
Building material and garden equipment and supplies dealers	444	34.4	45.1	46.5	43.5	1.75	1.64	1.99	1.95
Food and beverage stores	445	32.2	33.8	37.3	37.1	0.85	0.78	0.79	0.77
Clothing and clothing accessories stores	448	36.8	43.2	46.8	41.9	2.61	2.50	2.78	2.42
General merchandise stores	452	64.9	74.1	73.6	70.8	1.87	1.65	1.50	1.42
Department stores	4521	42.6	37.8	33.6	31.3	2.16	2.13	2.10	2.00

[1] North American Industry Classification System, 2007; see text, Section 15. [2] Includes other kind of businesses, not shown separately.

Source: U.S. Census Bureau, "Annual Revision of Monthly Retail and Food Services: Sales and Inventories—January 1992 Through March 2009," March 2010. See <http://www.census.gov/retail/mrts/www/benchmark/2010/html/annrev10.html>.

Table 1054. Retail Trade Sales—Total and E-Commerce by Kind of Business: 2008

[3,959,157 represents $3,959,157,000,000. Covers retailers with and without payroll. Based on the Annual Retail Trade Survey; see Appendix III]

Kind of business	2007 NAICS code [1]	Value of sales (mil. dol.)		E-commerce as percent of total sales	Percent distribution of E-commerce sales
		Total	E-commerce		
Retail trade, total [2]	**44-45**	**3,959,157**	**141,890**	**3.6**	**100.0**
Motor vehicle and parts dealers	441	788,657	19,996	2.5	14.1
Electronics and appliance stores	443	109,086	1,164	1.1	0.8
Building material and garden equipment and supplies stores	444	306,667	546	0.2	0.4
Food and beverage stores	445	573,619	888	0.2	0.6
Health and personal care stores	446	247,308	(S)	(S)	(S)
Clothing and clothing accessories stores	448	216,584	2,539	1.2	1.8
Sporting goods, hobby, book, and music stores	451	84,067	1,977	2.4	1.4
General merchandise stores	452	596,935	175	(Z)	0.1
Miscellaneous store retailers	453	115,871	2,068	1.8	1.5
Nonstore retailers	454	319,938	110,925	34.7	78.2
Electronic shopping and mail-order houses	45411	227,084	106,821	47.0	75.3

S Data do not meet publication standards because of high sampling variability or poor response quality. Z Less than $500,000 or 0.05 percent. [1] North American Industry Classification System, 2007; see text, Section 15. [2] Includes other kinds of businesses, not shown separately.

Source: U.S. Census Bureau, "E-Stats, 2008 E-commerce Multi-sector Report," May 2010, <http://www.census.gov/econ/estats/>.

Table 1055. Electronic Shopping and Mail-Order Houses—Total and E-Commerce Sales by Merchandise Line: 2007 and 2008

[222,464 represents $222,464,000,000. Represents North American Industry Classification System code 454110 which comprises establishments primarily engaged in retailing all types of merchandise using nonstore means, such as catalogs, toll-free telephone numbers, or electronic media, such as interactive television or computer. Covers businesses with and without paid employees. Based on the Annual Retail Survey; see Appendix III]

Merchandise lines	Value of sales, 2007 (mil. dol.)	2008				
		Value of sales (mil. dol.)		E-commerce as percent of total sales	Percent distribution	
		Total	E-commerce		Total	E-commerce
Total.	**222,464**	**227,084**	**106,821**	**47.0**	**100.0**	**100.0**
Books and magazines	7,495	8,087	5,138	63.5	3.6	4.8
Clothing and clothing accessories (includes footwear)	23,482	24,057	17,058	70.9	10.6	16.0
Computer hardware	25,539	23,127	11,818	51.1	10.2	11.1
Computer software	4,432	4,826	2,522	52.3	2.1	2.4
Drugs, health aids, beauty aids	62,274	65,831	5,510	8.4	29.0	5.2
Electronics and appliances	14,741	16,409	13,018	79.3	7.2	12.2
Food, beer, and wine	4,478	3,882	2,322	59.8	1.7	2.2
Furniture and home furnishings	13,318	13,125	9,811	74.8	5.8	9.2
Music and videos	4,525	5,110	3,972	77.7	2.3	3.7
Office equipment and supplies	8,136	8,111	5,899	72.7	3.6	5.5
Sporting goods	6,068	6,419	3,991	62.2	2.8	3.7
Toys, hobby goods, and games	5,184	5,921	3,344	56.5	2.6	3.1
Other merchandise [1]	31,254	30,486	14,355	47.1	13.4	13.4
Nonmerchandise receipts [2]	11,538	11,693	8,063	69.0	5.1	7.5

[1] Includes other merchandise such as jewelry, collectibles, souvenirs, auto parts and accessories, hardware, and lawn and garden equipment and supplies. [2] Includes nonmerchandise receipts such as auction commissions, shipping and handling, customer training, customer support, and advertising.

Source: U.S. Census Bureau, "E-Stats, 2008 E-commerce Multi-sector Report," May 2010, <http://www.census.gov/econ/estats/>.

Table 1056. Franchised New Car Dealerships—Summary: 1990 to 2009

[316 represents $316,000,000,000]

Item	Unit	1990	2000	2002	2003	2004	2005	2006	2007	2008	2009
Dealerships [1]	Number	24,825	22,250	21,725	21,650	21,640	21,495	21,200	20,770	20,010	18,460
Sales	Bil. dol	316	650	680	699	714	699	675	693	576	487
New cars sold [2]	Millions	9.3	8.8	8.1	7.6	7.5	7.7	7.8	7.6	6.8	5.5
Used vehicles sold	Millions	14.2	20.5	19.4	19.5	19.7	19.7	19.2	18.5	15.0	14.9
Employment	1,000	924	1,114	1,130	1,130	1,130	1,138	1,120	1,115	1,057	913
Dealer pretax profits as a percentage of sales	Percent	1.0	1.6	1.9	1.7	1.7	1.6	1.5	1.5	1.0	1.5
Inventory: [3]											
Domestic: [4]											
Total	1,000	2,537	3,192	2,707	3,003	3,267	2,991	2,943	2,712	2,478	1,619
Days' supply	Days	73	68	63	63	75	70	71	67	80	72
Imported: [4]											
Total	1,000	707	468	521	618	646	566	605	619	687	519
Days' supply	Days	72	50	49	49	59	52	51	51	65	61

[1] At end of year. [2] Data provided by Ward's Automotive Reports. [3] Annual average. Includes light trucks. [4] Classification based on where automobiles are produced (i.e., automobiles manufactured by foreign companies but produced in the U.S., Canada, and Mexico are classified as domestic).

Source: National Automobile Dealers Association, McLean, VA, *NADA Data*, annual.<http://www.nada.org/Publications/NADADATA>.

Table 1057. Retail Sales and Leases of New and Used Vehicles: 1990 to 2008

[In thousands, except as noted (51,390 represents 51,390,000)]

Item	1990	2000	2002	2003	2004	2005	2006	2007	2008
Vehicle sales and leases, total (number of vehicles)	**51,390**	**58,964**	**59,835**	**60,215**	**59,411**	**61,086**	**59,070**	**57,507**	**49,725**
New vehicle sales and leases	13,860	17,344	16,810	16,643	16,866	16,948	16,504	16,089	13,195
New vehicle sales [1]	13,285	13,181	13,639	13,594	13,609	13,551	13,271	12,631	10,933
New vehicle leases [1]	575	4,163	3,171	3,049	3,257	3,397	3,233	3,458	2,262
Used vehicle sales [2]	37,530	41,620	43,025	43,572	42,545	44,138	42,566	41,418	36,530
Vehicle sales, total value (bil. dol.) [3]	**447**	**736**	**721**	**738**	**765**	**776**	**786**	**774**	**642**
New vehicle sales (bil. dol.)	227	380	371	382	407	421	445	435	351
Used vehicle sales (bil. dol.)	220	356	350	356	358	355	341	339	292
Average price (current dol.): [3]									
New vehicle sales	16,350	21,850	22,005	22,894	24,082	24,796	26,854	26,950	26,477
Used vehicle sales	5,857	8,547	8,130	8,180	8,410	8,036	8,009	8,186	7,986

[1] Consumer leases only. [2] Used car sales include sales from franchised dealers, independent dealers, and casual sales. [3] Includes leased vehicles

Source: U.S. Bureau of Transportation Statistics, *National Transportation Statistics*, annual. See also <http://www.bts.gov/publications/national_transportation_statistics/>.

Wholesale and Retail Trade 663

Table 1058. Retail Trade and Food Services—Sales by Type of Store and State: 2009

[In millions of dollars (4,320,921 represents $4,320,921,000,000). Based on North American Industry Classification System (NAICS), 2002; see text, Section 15]

State	Total retail sales plus food services and drinking places (NAICS 44–45, 722)	All retail stores [1] (NAICS 44–45)	Motor vehicle and parts dealers (NAICS 441)	Furniture and home furnishings (NAICS 442)	Electronics and appliances (NAICS 443)	Building and material supply (NAICS 444)	Food and beverage stores (NAICS 445)	Health and personal care (NAICS 446)
U.S.	4,320,921	3,862,237	703,512	92,650	101,451	430,041	589,554	255,813
AL	65,008	59,475	11,511	1,373	1,408	7,702	6,968	4,624
AK	10,966	9,742	1,589	208	173	981	1,681	180
AZ	93,053	83,872	14,690	1,993	3,114	8,240	12,112	4,273
AR	38,330	35,248	7,496	652	1,038	4,380	3,779	2,391
CA	519,572	458,979	79,126	11,009	17,065	44,951	78,820	28,483
CO	75,326	66,795	13,090	1,934	2,044	7,599	11,238	2,531
CT	54,372	48,951	8,299	1,300	1,235	6,002	8,324	3,662
DE	15,502	13,960	2,638	467	400	1,883	2,476	993
DC	6,443	3,885	59	173	88	136	1,214	672
FL	282,928	250,252	49,908	7,425	5,973	23,114	37,840	18,572
GA	130,325	115,515	22,075	2,989	2,775	14,991	16,480	8,028
HI	21,626	18,257	2,622	357	376	1,578	3,270	1,348
ID	21,888	20,139	4,342	558	316	2,617	2,604	753
IL	178,910	157,961	26,198	3,305	4,057	16,330	21,607	8,843
IN	85,301	76,262	14,334	1,558	1,805	9,305	8,798	5,290
IA	40,305	36,856	6,998	759	705	5,367	5,413	1,945
KS	34,823	31,504	5,967	647	686	3,391	5,436	1,726
KY	54,696	49,377	8,213	1,017	768	6,352	6,723	4,153
LA	64,296	58,331	11,018	1,464	1,333	7,672	6,562	4,132
ME	21,639	19,827	3,222	298	328	2,587	3,485	1,010
MD	82,402	73,007	14,219	2,000	1,784	8,751	14,352	4,159
MA	96,567	83,651	14,154	2,331	1,868	9,721	16,679	7,668
MI	128,859	115,837	22,906	2,346	2,932	14,088	14,698	9,053
MN	76,969	69,188	11,589	1,513	2,139	8,819	10,433	3,767
MS	37,956	34,738	6,108	698	514	4,696	3,740	2,652
MO	86,051	77,439	13,510	1,349	1,922	8,605	9,145	4,817
MT	16,919	15,527	2,830	425	460	2,312	1,996	559
NE	26,964	24,724	4,628	563	471	2,999	2,667	1,263
NV	44,768	38,721	6,235	729	1,134	2,923	5,196	1,634
NH	27,433	25,354	4,414	433	811	3,267	4,762	1,132
NJ	131,207	117,522	22,115	2,969	3,123	11,436	25,159	9,195
NM	27,657	24,906	4,598	487	512	2,503	2,542	1,072
NY	267,671	238,440	33,783	6,472	9,058	24,907	41,669	25,298
NC	128,140	115,219	22,563	3,244	2,287	15,817	15,235	8,521
ND	11,602	10,840	2,284	187	249	1,597	1,218	573
OH	145,059	127,801	23,385	2,464	2,901	13,821	20,854	8,451
OK	47,207	42,802	9,429	957	612	5,067	3,973	2,552
OR	54,704	48,539	8,687	1,128	1,563	5,135	8,215	2,113
PA	174,483	157,876	27,985	3,234	2,800	16,439	25,208	12,040
RI	13,968	12,077	1,980	272	182	1,192	3,447	1,532
SC	60,305	53,934	9,322	1,123	768	6,976	7,895	4,389
SD	13,759	12,754	2,604	204	312	1,888	1,278	535
TN	89,524	80,700	14,358	1,786	1,861	9,888	10,778	7,156
TX	336,509	301,778	66,232	8,291	7,244	32,075	42,883	14,208
UT	40,796	38,012	7,352	1,129	878	4,147	4,919	1,004
VT	10,471	9,666	1,664	184	187	1,378	1,728	633
VA	119,784	107,250	18,514	2,743	2,906	12,282	17,666	6,079
WA	97,464	88,375	14,311	2,147	1,936	9,586	13,315	3,985
WV	24,338	22,227	3,870	330	335	2,665	2,593	1,857
WI	76,252	69,110	12,610	1,282	1,839	8,755	9,502	4,096
WY	9,824	9,036	1,879	144	174	1,126	978	213

See footnotes at end of table.

U.S. Census Bureau, Statistical Abstract of the United States: 2011

Table 1058. Retail Trade and Food Services—Sales by Type of Store and State: 2009—Con.

[See headnote page 664]

State	Gasoline service stations (NAICS 447)	Clothing and clothing accessories (NAICS 448)	Sporting goods, hobby, book & music stores (NAICS 451)	General merchandise (NAICS 452)	Miscellaneous stores (NAICS 453)	Nonstore retailers (NAICS 454)	Food services & drinking places (NAICS 722)
U.S.	372,452	210,534	87,343	597,752	114,232	306,904	458,684
AL	6,742	2,777	1,131	11,228	1,565	2,445	5,533
AK	734	391	348	2,479	380	598	1,224
AZ	8,443	3,591	1,674	15,273	2,289	8,178	9,181
AR	4,191	1,262	623	7,377	1,160	900	3,083
CA	36,327	28,033	11,049	71,851	13,002	39,263	60,593
CO	5,202	3,006	2,298	11,315	2,187	4,351	8,531
CT	3,492	3,539	1,237	5,197	1,221	5,442	5,421
DE	926	792	319	1,798	614	655	1,542
DC	167	492	189	287	99	309	2,558
FL	20,663	16,306	5,206	38,553	7,037	19,656	32,675
GA	13,495	6,310	2,305	18,223	3,343	4,501	14,810
HI	1,239	2,269	451	3,660	789	296	3,369
ID	2,548	587	670	3,318	665	1,160	1,749
IL	13,288	8,194	3,477	25,244	4,034	23,383	20,949
IN	9,428	3,765	1,753	13,485	2,353	4,388	9,040
IA	5,059	1,148	693	5,911	710	2,149	3,448
KS	3,692	1,295	674	5,487	808	1,695	3,319
KY	6,630	1,852	847	9,791	1,684	1,345	5,319
LA	7,486	2,741	1,218	10,696	2,084	1,926	5,965
ME	2,268	818	393	2,558	540	2,318	1,812
MD	5,073	4,787	1,775	9,564	1,754	4,790	9,395
MA	6,002	5,598	2,285	7,742	1,952	7,650	12,916
MI	11,010	5,436	2,780	20,330	3,839	6,420	13,021
MN	7,101	3,001	1,570	11,487	1,674	6,095	7,780
MS	5,177	1,783	578	7,131	1,089	573	3,218
MO	10,394	2,911	1,452	13,191	2,339	7,805	8,612
MT	2,659	408	488	2,425	541	423	1,393
NE	2,815	737	714	3,685	501	3,682	2,240
NV	3,167	3,431	789	6,164	1,355	5,964	6,047
NH	1,842	1,164	618	3,299	595	3,018	2,078
NJ	7,791	8,022	2,967	11,005	3,073	10,667	13,685
NM	3,409	854	447	5,178	1,135	2,169	2,751
NY	14,092	23,275	5,981	25,141	10,732	18,033	29,231
NC	12,562	5,054	2,002	17,810	3,277	6,817	10,920
ND	1,771	321	245	1,559	283	553	762
OH	14,727	4,970	2,725	18,675	3,407	11,420	17,258
OK	6,889	1,739	826	8,191	1,877	691	4,405
OR	3,636	2,042	1,400	9,245	1,723	3,652	6,166
PA	14,852	7,245	3,236	20,781	4,542	19,513	16,608
RI	859	608	206	715	298	785	1,892
SC	7,024	3,182	1,008	9,412	1,693	1,140	6,371
SD	1,737	282	211	1,726	292	1,685	1,005
TN	9,542	4,220	1,537	13,396	2,224	3,953	8,824
TX	29,686	15,503	6,808	48,757	8,120	21,972	34,731
UT	3,845	1,356	1,076	5,782	869	5,655	2,784
VT	1,239	328	265	597	316	1,147	806
VA	11,716	5,761	2,400	17,918	2,866	6,401	12,534
WA	6,036	3,742	2,249	15,335	2,699	13,032	9,089
WV	3,076	583	323	4,955	627	1,013	2,111
WI	8,774	2,837	1,642	11,404	1,636	4,732	7,142
WY	1,931	183	185	1,418	339	466	788

[1] Excluding food services and drinking places (NAICS 722). Includes other types of stores, not shown separately.
Source: Nielsen Claritas Retail Market Power, 2010 (copyright).

Wholesale and Retail Trade 665

Table 1059. New Motor Vehicle Sales and Car Production: 1990 to 2009

[In thousands (14,137 represents 14,137,000). Includes leases]

Type of vehicle	1990	2000	2004	2005	2006	2007	2008	2009
New motor vehicle sales	**14,137**	**17,806**	**17,298**	**17,445**	**17,049**	**16,460**	**13,494**	**10,601**
New-car sales and leases	9,300	8,852	7,545	7,720	7,821	7,618	6,814	5,456
Domestic	6,897	6,833	5,396	5,533	5,476	5,253	4,535	3,619
Import	2,403	2,019	2,149	2,187	2,345	2,365	2,278	1,837
New-truck sales and leases	4,837	8,954	9,753	9,725	9,228	8,842	6,680	5,145
Light	4,560	8,492	9,322	9,228	8,683	8,471	6,382	4,945
Domestic	3,957	7,651	8,076	8,013	7,337	7,083	5,285	4,061
Import	603	841	1,246	1,216	1,347	1,388	1,097	884
Other	278	462	432	497	544	371	299	200
Domestic-car production	6,231	5,542	4,230	4,321	4,367	3,924	3,777	2,247
Average expenditure per new car [1] (dol.)	14,371	21,041	22,076	23,017	23,634	23,892	23,417	23,186
Domestic (dol.)	13,936	19,586	20,536	21,593	22,166	22,273	22,166	22,107
Import (dol.)	15,510	25,965	25,941	26,621	27,062	27,487	25,908	25,308

[1] Estimate based on the manufacturer's suggested retail price.

Source: U.S. Bureau of Economic Analysis, "Auto and Truck Seasonal Adjustment," August 2010, <http://www.bea.gov/national/xls/gap_hist.xls>. Data are mainly from "Ward's Automotive Reports," published by Ward's Communications, Southfield, MI.

Table 1060. Shopping Centers—Number and Gross Leasable Area: 1990 to 2009

[As of December 31. A shopping center is a group of architecturally unified commercial establishments built on a site that is planned, developed, owned, and managed as an operating unit related in its location, size, and type of shops to the trade area that the unit serves. The unit provides on-site parking in definite relationship to the types and total size of the stores. The data base attempts to include all centers with three or more stores. Estimates are based on a sample of data available on shopping center properties; for details, contact source]

Year	Total	Gross leasable area (square feet)					
		Less than 100,001	100,001 to 200,000	200,001 to 400,000	400,001 to 800,000	800,001 to 1,000,000	More than 1,000,000
NUMBER							
1990	77,019	64,683	7,790	3,090	876	207	373
1995	81,669	67,764	8,593	3,627	1,059	224	402
2000	88,143	72,509	9,439	4,197	1,301	250	447
2005	97,105	79,735	10,160	4,835	1,607	274	494
2008	104,148	85,654	10,607	5,247	1,818	311	511
2009	104,919	86,248	10,692	5,298	1,853	314	514
Gross Leasable Area (mil. sq. ft.)							
1990	4,788	1,702	1,094	825	482	185	501
1995	5,312	1,813	1,210	972	579	200	539
2000	5,955	1,968	1,328	1,132	705	223	599
2005	6,671	2,160	1,430	1,310	868	244	659
2008	7,164	2,304	1,494	1,427	981	277	682
2009	7,232	2,319	1,506	1,442	999	280	686

Source: CoStar Group, Inc., Bethesda MD, (copyright).

Table 1061. Food and Alcoholic Beverage Sales by Sales Outlet: 1990 to 2009

[In billions of dollars (553.4 represents $553,400,000,000)]

Sales outlet	1990	2000	2003	2004	2005	2006	2007	2008	2009
Food sales, total [1]	**553.4**	**814.6**	**920.1**	**966.1**	**1,021.2**	**1,084.8**	**1,139.3**	**1,172.1**	**1,182.0**
Food at home	305.3	423.2	476.4	494.5	520.9	552.3	578.4	596.7	607.4
Food stores [2]	256.4	303.5	323.8	334.0	347.3	359.9	377.4	397.4	397.4
Other stores [3]	32.3	89.4	122.6	129.4	142.4	160.4	167.3	165.1	176.4
Home-delivered, mail order	5.3	19.2	18.3	18.9	19.5	20.3	21.0	21.0	19.9
Farmers, manufacturers, wholesalers	3.5	4.6	4.8	4.9	5.2	5.4	6.0	6.2	6.5
Home production and donations	7.7	6.5	6.8	7.2	6.5	6.5	6.7	6.9	7.2
Food away from home [4]	248.1	391.5	443.7	471.6	500.3	532.4	560.9	575.4	574.5
Alcoholic beverage sales, total	**72.7**	**111.9**	**126.9**	**139.4**	**146.4**	**159.2**	**167.3**	**168.3**	**167.0**
Packaged alcoholic beverages	38.0	52.7	57.5	59.8	62.3	69.4	72.6	72.5	75.4
Liquor stores	18.6	24.5	26.0	27.7	29.4	31.0	32.6	34.3	35.3
Food stores	10.8	15.9	17.8	18.5	19.3	20.0	20.9	22.0	22.0
All other	8.6	12.3	13.7	13.6	13.6	18.4	19.0	16.2	18.2
Alcoholic drinks away from home	34.7	59.2	69.4	79.6	84.1	89.8	94.7	95.9	91.6
Eating and drinking places [5]	26.7	41.9	45.0	53.0	55.6	59.6	62.5	63.5	65.8
Hotels and motels [5]	3.4	9.9	15.9	17.4	18.8	20.0	21.2	21.2	21.1
All other	4.6	7.4	8.6	9.2	9.6	10.2	10.9	11.2	4.7

[1] Includes taxes and tips. [2] Excludes sales to restaurants and institutions. [3] Includes eating and drinking establishments, trailer parks, commissary stores, and military exchanges. [4] Includes food furnished and donations. [5] Includes tips.

Source: U.S. Department of Agriculture, Economic Research Service, "Food CPI, Prices, and Expenditures: Food Expenditure Tables," June 2010, <http://www.ers.usda.gov/briefing/CPIFoodAndExpenditures/Data>.

This section presents data on civil air transportation, both passenger and cargo, and on water transportation, including inland waterways, oceanborne commerce, the merchant marine, cargo, and vessel tonnages.

This section also presents statistics on revenues, passenger and freight traffic volume, and employment in various revenue-producing modes of the transportation industry, including motor vehicles, trains, and pipelines. Data are also presented on highway mileage and finances, motor vehicle travel, accidents, and registrations; and characteristics of public transit, railroads, and pipelines.

Principal source of transportation data is the annual *National Transportation Statistics* publication of the U.S. Bureau of Transportation Statistics. Principal sources of air and water transportation data are the *Annual Report* issued by the Air Transport Association of America, Washington, DC and the annual *Waterborne Commerce of the United States* issued by the Corps of Engineers of the Department of Army. In addition, the U.S. Census Bureau in its commodity flow survey (part of the census of transportation, taken every 5 years through 2007, for years ending in "2" and "7") provides data on the type, weight, and value of commodities shipped by manufacturing establishments in the United States, by means of transportation, origin, and destination. The advance reports for 2007 are part of the 2007 Economic Census. This census was conducted in accordance with the 2002 North American Industry Classification System (NAICS). See text, Section 15, Business Enterprise, for a discussion of the Economic Census and NAICS.

The Bureau of Transportation Statistics (BTS) was established within the U.S. Department of Transportation (USDOT) in 1992 to collect, report, and analyze transportation data. Today, BTS is a component of the USDOT Research and Innovative Technology Administration

(RITA). BTS products include reports to Congress, the Secretary of Transportation, and stakeholders in the nation's transportation community. These stakeholders include: federal agencies, state and local governments, metropolitan planning organizations, universities, the private sector and general public. Congress requires the BTS to report (congressional mandate, laid out in 49 U.S.C. 111 (1)) on transportation statistics to the President and Congress. *The Transportation Statistics Annual Report* (TSAR), provides a data overview of U.S. transportation issues. As required by Congress, each TSAR has two essential components: a review of the state of transportation statistics with recommendations for improvements and a presentation of the data. The BTS publication *National Transportation Statistics (NTS)*, a companion report to the TSAR, has more comprehensive and longer time-series data. NTS presents information on the U.S. transportation system, including its physical components, safety record, economic performance, energy use, and environmental impacts. The BTS publication *State Transportation Statistics* presents a statistical profile of transportation in the 50 states and the District of Columbia. This profile includes infrastructure, freight movement and passenger travel, system safety, vehicles, transportation-related economy and finance, energy usage and the environment.

The principal compiler of data on public roads and on operation of motor vehicles is the U.S. Department of Transportation's (DOT) Federal Highway Administration (FHWA). These data appear in FHWA's annual *Highway Statistics* and other publications.

The U.S. National Highway Traffic Safety Administration (NHTSA), through its *Traffic Safety Facts FARS/GES Annual Report*, presents descriptive statistics about traffic crashes of all severities, from those that result in property damage to those that result in the loss of human life. The data for this report is a compilation of motor vehicle crash data from the *Fatality Analysis Reporting System (FARS)* and the *General Estimates System (GES)*. For other publications and reports, go to the National Center for Statistics and Analysis (NCSA), Publications and Data Request. The Web site is located at <http://wwnrd .nhtsa.dot.gov/CAT/index.aspx>. DOT's Federal Railroad Administration (FRA), Office of Safety Analysis presents railroad safety information including accidents and incidents, inspections and highway-rail crossing data in its annual report *Railroad Safety Statistics*. The Web site is located at <http://safetydata.fra .dot.gov /officeofsafety>.

Data are also presented in many nongovernment publications. Among them are the weekly and annual *Cars of Revenue Freight Loaded* and the annual *Yearbook of Railroad Facts*, both published by the Association of American Railroads, Washington, DC; *Public Transportation Fact Book*, containing electric railway and motorbus statistics, published annually by the American Public Transportation Association, Washington, DC; and *Injury Facts*, issued by the National Safety Council, Chicago, IL.

Civil aviation—Federal promotion and regulation of civil aviation have been carried out by the Federal Aviation Administration (FAA) and the Civil Aeronautics Board (CAB). The CAB promoted and regulated the civil air transportation industry within the United States and between the United States and foreign countries. The Board granted licenses to provide air transportation service, approved or disapproved proposed rates and fares, and approved or disapproved proposed agreements and corporate relationships involving air carriers. In December 1984, the CAB ceased to exist as an agency. Some of its functions were transferred to the DOT, as outlined below. The responsibility for investigation of aviation accidents resides with the National Transportation Safety Board.

The Office of the Secretary, DOT aviation activities include: negotiation of international air transportation rights, selection of U.S. air carriers to serve capacitycontrolled international markets, oversight of international rates and fares, maintenance

of essential air service to small communities, and consumer affairs. DOT's Bureau of Transportation Statistics (BTS) handles aviation information functions formerly assigned to CAB. Prior to BTS, the Research and Special Programs Administration handled these functions.

The principal activities of the FAA include: the promotion of air safety; controlling the use of navigable airspace; prescribing regulations dealing with the competency of airmen, airworthiness of aircraft and air traffic control; operation of air route traffic control centers, airport traffic control towers, and flight service stations; the design, construction, maintenance, and inspection of navigation, traffic control, and communications equipment; and the development of general aviation.

The CAB published monthly and quarterly financial and traffic statistical data for the certificated route air carriers. BTS continues these publications, including both certificated and noncertificated (commuter) air carriers. The FAA annually publishes data on the use of airway facilities; data related to the location of airmen, aircraft, and airports; the volume of activity in the field of nonair carrier (general aviation) flying; and aircraft production and registration.

General aviation comprises all civil flying (including such commercial operations as small demand air taxis, agriculture application, powerline patrol, etc.) but excludes certificated route air carriers, supplemental operators, large-aircraft commercial operators, and commuter airlines.

Air carriers and service—The CAB previously issued "certificates of public convenience and necessity" under Section 401 of the Federal Aviation Act of 1958 for scheduled and nonscheduled (charter) passenger services and cargo services. It also issued certificates under Section 418 of the Act to cargo air carriers for domestic all-cargo service only. The DOT Office of the Secretary now issues the certificates under a "fit, willing, and able" test of air carrier operations. Carriers operating only a 60-seat-or-less aircraft are given exemption authority to carry passengers, cargo, and mail in scheduled and nonscheduled service under Part 298 of the DOT (formerly CAB) regulations. Exemption authority carriers who offer scheduled passenger service to an essential air service point must meet the "fit, willing, and able" test.

Vessel shipments, entrances, and clearances—Shipments by dry cargo vessels comprise shipments on all types of watercraft, except tanker vessels; shipments by tanker vessels comprise all types of cargo, liquid and dry, carried by tanker vessels. A vessel is reported as entered only at the first port which it enters in the United States, whether or not cargo is unloaded at that port.

A vessel is reported as cleared only at the last port at which clearance is made to a foreign port, whether or not it takes on cargo. Army and Navy vessels entering or clearing without commercial cargo are not included in the figures.

Units of measurement—Cargo (or freight) tonnage and shipping weight both represent the gross weight of the cargo including the weight of containers, wrappings, crates, etc. However, shipping weight excludes lift and cargo vans and similar substantial outer containers. Other tonnage figures generally refer to stowing capacity of vessels, 100 cubic feet being called 1 ton. Gross tonnage comprises the space within the frames and the ceiling of the hull, together with those closed-in spaces above deck available for cargo, stores, passengers, or crew, with certain minor exceptions. Net or registered tonnage is the gross tonnage less the spaces occupied by the propelling machinery, fuel, crew quarters, master's cabin, and navigation spaces. Substantially, it represents space available for cargo and passengers. The net tonnage capacity of a ship may bear little relation to weight of cargo. Deadweight tonnage is the weight in long tons required to depress a vessel from light water line (that is, with only the machinery and equipment on board) to load line. It is, therefore, the weight of the cargo, fuel, etc., which a vessel is designed to carry with safety.

Federal-aid highway systems—The Intermodal Surface Transportation Efficiency Act (ISTEA) of 1991 eliminated the historical Federal-Aid Highway Systems and created the National Highway System (NHS) and other federal aid highway categories. The final NHS was approved by Congress in December of 1995 under the National Highway System Designation Act.

Functional systems—Roads and streets are assigned to groups according to the character of service intended. The functional systems are (1) arterial highways that generally handle the long trips, (2) collector facilities that collect and disperse traffic between the arterials and the lower systems, and (3) local roads and streets that primarily serve direct access to residential areas, farms, and other local areas.

Regulatory bodies— The Federal Energy Regulatory Commission (FERC) is an independent agency that regulates the interstate transmission of electricity, natural gas, and oil. FERC also reviews proposals to build liquefied natural gas (LNG) terminals and interstate natural gas pipelines as well as licensing hydropower projects. The Energy Policy Act of 2005 gave FERC additional responsibilities such as regulating the transmission and wholesale sales of electricity in interstate commerce. See source for more details.

Railroads—The Surface Transportation Board (STB) was created in the Interstate Commerce Commission Termination Act of 1995, Pub. L. No.104-88, 109 Stat. 803 (1995) (ICCTA), and is the successor agency to the Interstate Commerce Commission. The STB is an economic regulatory agency that Congress charged with the fundamental missions of resolving railroad rate and service disputes and reviewing proposed railroad mergers. The STB is decisionally independent, although it is administratively affiliated with the Department of Transportation.

The STB serves as both an adjudicatory and a regulatory body. The agency has jurisdiction over railroad rate and service issues and rail restructuring transactions (mergers, line sales, line construction, and line abandonment); certain trucking company, moving van, and noncontiguous ocean shipping company rate matters; certain intercity passenger bus company

U.S. Census Bureau, Statistical Abstract of the United States: 2011

structure, financial, and operational matters; and rates and services of certain pipelines not regulated by the Federal Energy Regulatory Commission. Other ICC regulatory functions were either eliminated or transferred to the Federal Highway Administration or the Bureau of Transportation Statistics within DOT.

Class I Railroads are regulated by the STB and subject to the Uniform System of Accounts and required to file annual and periodic reports. Railroads are classified based on their annual operating revenues. The class to which a carrier belongs is determined by comparing its adjusted operating revenues for 3 consecutive years to the following scale: Class I, $250 million or more; Class II, $20 million to $250 million; and Class III, $0 to $20 million. Operating revenue dollar ranges are indexed for inflation.

Postal Service—The U.S. Postal Service provides mail processing and delivery services within the United States. The Postal Accountability and Enhancement Act of 2006 was the first major legislative change to the Postal Service since 1971 when the Postal Reorganization Act of 1970 created the Postal Service as an independent establishment of the Federal Executive Branch. The Act of 2006 changed the way the U.S. Postal Service operates and conducts business. Now annual rate increases for market

dominant products are linked to the Consumer Price Index and the Postal Service has more flexibility for pricing competitive products, enabling it to respond to dynamic market conditions and changing customer needs.

Revenue and cost analysis describes the Postal Service's system of attributing revenues and costs to classes of mail and service. This system draws primarily upon probability sampling techniques to develop estimates of revenues, volumes, and weights, as well as costs by class of mail and special service. The costs attributed to classes of mail and special services are primarily incremental costs which vary in response to changes in volume; they account for roughly 60 percent of the total costs of the Postal Service. The balance represents "institutional costs." Statistics on revenues, volume of mail, and distribution of expenditures are presented in the Postal Service's annual report, *Cost and Revenue Analysis*, and its *Annual Report of the Postmaster General* and its annual *Comprehensive Statement on Postal Operations.*

Statistical reliability—For a discussion of statistical collection and estimation, sampling procedures, and measures of statistical reliability applicable to Census Bureau data, see Appendix III.

Table 1062. Transportation-Related Components of U.S. Gross Domestic Product: 2000 to 2008

[In billions of dollars (1,045.3 represents $1,045,300,000,000), except percent. For explanation of chained dollars, see section 13 text]

Item	2000	2004	2005	2006	2007	2008
CURRENT DOLLARS						
Total transportation-related final demand [1]	**1,045.3**	**1,161.2**	**1,266.1**	**1,325.8**	**1,392.2**	**1,375.4**
Total gross domestic product (GDP)	9,951.5	11,867.8	12,638.4	13,398.9	14,077.6	14,441.4
Transportation as a percent of GDP	10.5	9.8	10.0	9.9	9.9	9.5
Personal consumption of transportation	798.4	909.5	979.3	1,008.8	1,051.6	1,036.5
Motor vehicles and parts	363.2	404.7	409.6	397.1	400.3	342.3
Gasoline and oil	172.9	231.6	283.8	314.7	343.9	386.4
Transportation services	262.3	273.2	285.9	297.0	307.4	307.8
Gross private domestic investment	177.6	167.9	188.8	206.9	190.7	142.2
Transportation structures	6.8	6.8	7.1	8.7	9.0	9.9
Transportation equipment	170.8	161.1	181.7	198.2	181.7	132.3
Net exports of transportation-related goods and service [2]	−109.0	−140.2	−136.6	−137.8	−117.6	−87.9
Exports (+)	179.0	191.2	216.6	240.0	271.5	286.0
Civilian aircraft, engines, and parts	48.1	46.1	55.9	64.5	73.0	74.0
Automotive vehicles, engines, and parts	80.4	89.2	98.4	107.3	121.3	121.5
Passenger fares	20.7	18.9	21.0	22.0	25.6	31.6
Other transportation	29.8	37.0	41.3	46.2	51.6	58.9
Imports (−)	288.0	331.4	353.2	377.8	389.1	373.9
Civilian aircraft, engines, and parts	26.4	24.3	25.8	28.4	34.4	35.4
Automotive vehicles, engines, and parts	195.9	228.2	239.4	256.6	259.2	233.8
Passenger fares	24.3	24.7	26.1	27.5	28.4	32.6
Other transportation	41.4	54.2	61.9	65.3	67.1	72.1
Government transportation-related purchases	178.3	224.0	234.6	247.9	267.5	284.6
Federal purchases [3]	19.3	28.9	30.1	32.0	31.9	35.9
State and local purchases [3]	150.0	178.4	188.6	201.0	215.9	230.7
Defense-related purchases [4]	9.0	16.7	15.9	14.9	19.7	18.0
CHAINED (2005) DOLLARS						
Total transportation-related final demand [1]	**1,211.8**	**1,250.8**	**1,266.1**	**1,254.6**	**1,261.7**	**1,167.4**
Total gross domestic product (GDP)	11,226.0	12,263.8	12,638.4	12,976.2	13,254.1	13,312.2
Transportation as a percent of GDP	10.8	10.2	10.0	9.7	9.5	8.8
Personal consumption of transportation	903.6	976.6	979.3	960.5	971.6	893.0
Motor vehicles and parts	356.1	411.3	409.6	396.6	402.4	347.5
Gasoline and oil	261.3	282.1	283.8	278.9	280.9	271.7
Transportation services	286.2	283.2	285.9	285.0	288.3	273.8
Gross private domestic investment	194.1	169.3	188.8	204.9	185.9	137.9
Transportation structures	7.9	7.0	7.1	8.4	8.5	9.0
Transportation equipment	186.2	162.3	181.7	196.5	177.4	128.9
Net exports of transportation-related goods and service [2]	−109.3	−140.2	−136.6	−140.9	−124.7	−90.5
Exports (+)	204.5	199.2	216.6	233.8	256.5	256.5
Civilian aircraft, engines, and parts	58.4	48.1	55.9	62.0	67.1	65.0
Automotive vehicles, engines, and parts	83.2	90.2	98.4	106.0	118.4	117.2
Passenger fares	28.6	20.3	21.0	21.9	23.6	26.4
Other transportation	34.3	40.6	41.3	43.9	47.4	47.9
Imports (−)	313.8	339.4	353.2	374.7	381.2	347.0
Civilian aircraft, engines, and parts	30.7	25.2	25.8	27.3	31.5	30.6
Automotive vehicles, engines, and parts	202.9	230.6	239.4	255.6	255.6	224.8
Passenger fares	29.1	25.7	26.1	26.1	25.3	25.2
Other transportation	51.1	57.9	61.9	65.7	68.8	66.4
Government transportation-related purchases	223.4	245.1	234.6	230.1	228.9	227.0
Federal purchases [3]	23.1	30.1	30.1	30.8	29.6	32.5
State and local purchases [3]	189.1	197.6	188.6	184.9	180.5	179.1
Defense-related purchases [4]	11.2	17.4	15.9	14.4	18.8	15.4

[1] Sum of total personal consumption of transportation, total gross private domestic investment, net exports of transportation-related goods and services, and total government transportation-related purchases. [2] Exports minus imports. [3] Federal purchases and state and local purchases are the sum of consumption expenditures and gross investment. [4] Defense-related purchases are the sum of transportation of material and travel.

Source: U.S. Bureau of Transportation Statistics, "National Transportation Statistics; <http://www.bts.gov/publications/national_transportation_statistics/>

Table 1063. Employment in Transportation and Warehousing: 1990 to 2009

[In thousands (3,476 represents 3,476,000). Annual average of monthly figures. Based on Current Employment Statistics program; see Appendix III]

Industry	2007 NAICS code [1]	1990	1995	2000	2005	2007	2008	2009
Transportation and warehousing	**48–49**	**3,476**	**3,838**	**4,410**	**4,361**	**4,541**	**4,508**	**4,235**
Air transportation	481	529	511	614	501	492	491	460
Rail transportation	482	272	233	232	228	234	231	219
Water transportation	483	57	51	56	61	66	67	64
Truck transportation	484	1,122	1,249	1,406	1,398	1,439	1,389	1,266
Transit and ground	485	274	328	372	389	412	423	419
Pipeline transportation	486	60	54	46	38	40	42	42
Scenic and sightseeing	487	16	22	28	29	29	28	28
Support activities	488	364	430	537	552	584	592	549
Couriers and messengers	492	375	517	605	571	581	573	547
Warehousing and storage	493	407	444	514	595	665	672	642

[1] North American Industry Classification System 2007, see text, Sections 12 and 15.

Source: U.S. Bureau of Labor Statistics, Current Employment Statistics, National, "Employment, Hours, and Earnings." See <http://www.bls.gov/ces/data.htm/>.

U.S. Census Bureau, Statistical Abstract of the United States: 2011

Table 1064. Transportation and Warehousing—Establishments, Employees, and Payroll by Kind of Business (NAICS Basis): 2006 and 2007

[4,306.4 represents 4,306,400. Covers establishments with payroll. Covers establishments with paid employees. Excludes self-employed individuals, employees government employees. of private households, railroad employees, agricultural production employees and most government employees. For statement on methodology, see Appendix III. County Business Patterns excludes rail transportation (NAICS 482) and the National Postal Service (NAICS 491)]

Industry	NAICS code [1]	Establishments		Paid employees (1,000)		Annual payroll (mil. dol.)	
		2006	2007	2006	2007	2006	2007
Transportation & warehousing	**48–49**	**215,117**	**219,806**	**4,306.4**	**4,395.4**	**166,173.9**	**175,479.8**
Air transportation	481	5,610	5,730	474.8	480.6	24,509.7	25,787.0
Scheduled air transportation	4811	3,072	3,084	432.5	435.9	22,141.4	23,042.9
Scheduled passenger air transportation	481111	2,616	2,585	414.4	417.1	21,438.7	22,329.8
Scheduled freight air transportation	481112	456	499	18.1	(NA)	702.7	713.1
Nonscheduled air transportation	4812	2,538	2,646	42.3	44.8	2,368.3	2,744.1
Water transportation	483	1,925	1,928	68.4	68.9	4,084.1	4,467.1
Deep sea, coastal, & Great Lakes water transportation	4831	1,262	1,255	47.5	48.2	2,988.9	3,285.6
Inland water transportation	4832	663	673	20.9	20.8	1,095.2	1,181.5
Inland water freight transportation	483211	396	411	17.2	17.4	949.9	1,029.8
Inland water passenger transportation	483212	267	262	3.7	3.4	145.4	151.7
Truck transportation	484	120,263	121,419	1,532.3	1,476.4	58,935.0	58,867.8
General freight trucking	4841	67,305	68,494	1,050.0	998.7	41,465.8	40,934.5
General freight trucking, local	48411	27,682	28,595	205.1	211.9	7,458.4	7,903.9
General freight trucking, long distance	48412	39,623	39,899	844.9	786.8	34,007.4	33,030.6
Specialized freight trucking	4842	52,958	52,925	482.4	477.7	17,469.2	17,933.3
Used household & office goods moving	48421	8,683	8,502	109.1	105.4	3,430.5	3,365.0
Specialized freight (except used goods) trucking, local	48422	32,598	32,125	218.7	207.0	7,870.5	7,814.9
Specialized freight (except used goods) trucking, long-distance	48423	11,677	12,298	154.6	165.4	6,168.1	6,753.4
Transit & ground passenger transportation	485	17,224	18,322	418.7	440.6	9,079.6	10,019.2
Urban transit systems	4851	912	932	49.4	52.9	1,680.3	1,837.1
Mixed mode systems	485111	63	67	1.3	1.5	40.4	45.8
Commuter rail	485112	25	26	0.5	0.7	20.5	38.0
Bus and other motor vehicle mode systems	485113	778	795	44.6	47.6	1,474.6	1,601.5
Other	485119	46	44	3.0	3.1	144.8	151.8
Interurban & rural bus transportation	4852	475	508	16.5	17.4	464.7	469.8
Taxi & limousine service	4853	7,013	7,493	69.2	72.5	1,542.7	1,652.5
Taxi service	48531	2,878	2,993	30.7	33.4	603.1	658.8
Limousine service	48532	4,135	4,500	38.5	39.1	939.6	993.7
School & employee bus transportation	4854	4,321	4,673	194.8	206.8	3,392.8	3,896.5
Charter bus industry	4855	1,207	1,247	27.9	28.4	647.8	666.2
Other transit & ground passenger transportation	4859	3,296	3,469	60.9	62.6	1,351.3	1,497.1
Special needs transportation	485991	2,166	2,337	45.4	47.7	1,031.6	1,169.6
Pipeline transportation	486	2,653	2,775	39.2	42.4	3,173.5	3,675.3
Pipeline transportation of crude oil	4861	373	374	7.5	8.3	727.8	850.3
Pipeline transportation of natural gas	4862	1,363	1,479	22.2	24.7	1,709.5	2,063.5
Other pipeline transportation	4869	917	922	9.4	9.4	736.2	761.5
Scenic & sightseeing transportation	487	2,720	2,781	26.7	27.5	788.8	808.4
Scenic & sightseeing transportation, land	4871	678	698	9.2	9.7	232.5	247.0
Scenic & sightseeing transportation, water	4872	1,857	1,880	15.3	15.6	463.8	479.4
Scenic & sightseeing transportation, other	4879	185	203	2.2	2.2	92.5	82.0
Support activities for transportation	488	37,083	38,566	579.6	610.6	24,124.8	26,400.8
Support activities for air transportation	4881	5,174	5,430	158.3	165.3	5,431.9	6,229.3
Airport operations	48811	1,619	1,748	70.0	73.0	1,764.6	1,981.3
Air traffic control	488111	171	223	1.7	2.2	63.0	84.1
Other support activities for air transportation	48819	3,555	3,682	88.3	92.3	3,667.3	4,248.0
Support activities for rail transportation	4882	962	1,018	28.1	28.6	1,048.5	1,155.6
Support activities for water transportation	4883	2,331	2,330	91.8	93.4	4,798.3	5,027.8
Port and harbor operations	48831	229	223	7.0	6.6	323.6	318.6
Marine cargo handling	48832	540	552	61.9	62.9	3,262.0	3,428.1
Navigational services to shipping	48833	802	830	12.0	13.0	699.4	756.6
Other	48839	760	725	10.8	10.9	513.4	524.6
Support activities for road transportation	4884	9,545	10,178	71.8	76.5	2,133.2	2,393.8
Motor vehicle towing	48841	7,789	8,267	50.8	53.2	1,524.1	1,617.9
Freight transportation arrangement	4885	17,434	17,903	198.3	212.2	9,452.0	10,157.2
Other support activities for transportation	4889	1,637	1,707	31.2	34.7	1,264.9	1,437.0
Couriers & messengers	492	13,790	13,845	571.4	569.2	19,984.2	21,479.1
Couriers	4921	8,724	9,116	525.6	528.2	18,856.7	20,385.4
Local messengers & local delivery	4922	5,066	4,729	45.8	41.0	1,127.5	1,093.7
Warehousing & storage	493	13,849	14,440	595.3	679.1	21,490.3	23,975.2

NA Not available. [1] Based on the North American Industry Classification System (NAICS), 2002; see text, Section 15.

Source: U.S. Census Bureau, "County Business Patterns" (published July 2009), <http://www.census.gov/econ/cbp/index.html>.

U.S. Census Bureau, Statistical Abstract of the United States: 2011

Table 1065. Transportation and Warehousing—Establishments, Revenue, Payroll, and Employees by Industry: 2002 and 2007

[382,152 represents $382,152,000,000. For establishments with payroll. Based on the 2002 and 2007 Economic Censuses. 2007 data are preliminary. See Appendix III]

Kind of business	NAICS code [1]	Number of establishments	Revenue (mil. dol.)	Annual payroll (mil. dol.)	Paid employees (1,000) [2]
Transportation and warehousing total, 2002....	**48–49**	**199,618**	**382,152**	**115,989**	**3,650.9**
Air transportation [3]	481	3,847	19,735	3,805	99.1
Water transportation	483	1,890	23,331	3,194	66.2
Truck transportation	484	112,642	164,219	47,750	1,435.2
Transit and ground passenger transportation	485	17,260	18,850	7,675	398.4
Pipeline transportation	486	2,188	22,031	2,477	36.8
Scenic and sightseeing transportation	487	2,523	1,859	526	22.5
Support activities for transportation	488	33,942	57,414	16,202	465.6
Couriers and messengers	492	12,655	58,165	17,175	561.5
Warehousing and storage	493	12,671	16,548	17,183	565.5
Transportation and warehousing total, 2007 [4]...	**48–49**	**217,926**	**655,857**	**172,166**	**4,435.8**
Air transportation [3]	481	5,763	146,567	25,639	477.4
Water transportation	483	1,814	36,057	4,048	70.0
Truck transportation	484	119,694	221,737	59,146	1,520.6
Transit and ground passenger transportation	485	17,769	26,967	10,012	453.4
Pipeline transportation	486	2,644	24,666	3,273	38.2
Scenic and sightseeing transportation	487	2,440	2,661	661	24.1
Support activities for transportation	488	41,189	96,256	25,129	615.4
Couriers and messengers	492	12,788	76,286	19,972	550.4
Warehousing and storage	493	13,825	24,660	24,285	686.2

[1] 2002 data based on the 1997 North American Industry Classification System (NAICS); 2007 data are based on the 2002 NAICS; see text, Section 15. [2] Number of paid employees for pay period including March 12. [3] Large certificated air passenger carriers are included in the 2007 data, not included in the 2002 data, affecting comparability for this industry. [4] Railroad transportation and U.S. Postal Service are out of scope for the 2007 Economic Census.

Source: U.S. Census Bureau, "2007 Economic Census, Core Business Statistics Series: Advance Comparative Statistics for the United States (2002 NAICS Basis): 2007 and 2002"; (published 17 March 2009); using American FactFinder; <http://www.census.gov/econ/census07/www/using_american_factfinder/index.html>.

Table 1066. Transportation and Warehousing—Nonemployer Establishments and Receipts by Kind of Business: 2005 to 2007

[962.4 represents 062,100. Includes only firms subject to federal income tax. Nonemployers are businesses with no paid employees. Data originate chiefly from administrative records of the Internal Revenue Service; see Appendix III]

Kind of Business	NAICS code [1]	Establishments (1,000)			Receipts (mil. dol.)		
		2005	2006	2007	2005	2006	2007
Transportation and warehousing	**48–49**	**962.4**	**1,002.0**	**1,083.1**	**58,650**	**62,928**	**66,633**
Air transportation	481	21.1	21.0	21.0	1,291	1,303	1,347
Water transportation	483	6.6	6.7	6.5	496	548	516
Truck transportation	484	509.0	531.8	542.5	43,317	46,653	47,927
General freight trucking	4841	461.3	485.3	489.2	39,456	42,781	43,816
General freight trucking, local	48411	184.3	194.2	193.1	12,790	14,075	14,263
General freight trucking, long-distance	48412	277.0	291.1	296.1	26,666	28,705	29,553
Specialized freight trucking	4842	47.7	46.5	53.3	3,861	3,872	4,111
Transit and ground passenger transportation	485	187.4	193.6	202.1	5,893	6,266	6,759
Urban transit system	4851	1.0	1.1	1.2	37	41	43
Interurban and rural bus transportation	4852	1.7	1.7	1.7	70	76	77
Taxi and limousine service	4853	146.7	151.6	161.4	4,487	4,803	5,270
School and employee bus transportation	4854	7.1	7.3	7.2	188	197	202
Charter bus industry	4855	4.1	4.1	3.8	186	187	194
Other transit and ground passenger transportation	4859	26.8	27.8	26.8	924	962	973
Pipeline transportation	486	0.7	0.8	0.8	74	81	75
Scenic and sightseeing transportation	487	4.0	3.9	5.1	159	167	197
Support activities for transportation	488	59.8	63.2	106.3	3,175	3,387	4,759
Couriers and messengers	492	166.0	172.8	190.5	3,703	3,995	4,513
Warehousing and storage	493	7.9	8.1	8.3	545	529	542

[1] Based on the 2002 North American Industry Classification System (NAICS); see text, Section 15.

Source: U.S. Census Bureau, "Nonemployer Statistics" (June 2009), <http://www.census.gov/econ/nonemployer/index.html>.

U.S. Census Bureau, Statistical Abstract of the United States: 2011

Table 1067. Transportation System Mileage Within the United States: 1980 to 2008

[3,860 represents 3,860,000. Numbers, except where indicated]

System	Unit	1980	1985	1990	1995	2000	2005	2006	2007	2008
Highway [1]	1,000	3,860	3,864	3,867	3,912	3,936	3,996	4,017	4,032	4,043
Class 1 rail [2]	Number	164,822	145,764	119,758	108,264	99,250	95,830	94,942	94,440	94,082
Amtrak	Number	24,000	24,000	24,000	24,000	23,000	22,007	21,708	21,708	21,178
Transit: [3]										
Commuter rail [4]	Number	(NA)	3,574	4,132	4,160	5,209	7,118	6,972	7,135	7,261
Heavy rail [5]	Number	(NA)	1,293	1,351	1,458	1,558	1,622	1,623	1,623	1,623
Light rail [6]	Number	(NA)	384	483	568	834	1,188	1,280	1,341	1,397
Navigable channels	Number	26,000	26,000	26,000	26,000	26,000	26,000	26,000	25,320	25,320
Oil pipeline [7]	Number	218,393	213,605	208,752	181,912	176,996	162,832	162,699	166,972	169,422
Gas pipeline [8]	1,000	1,052	1,111	1,270	1,332	1,377	1,484	1,504	1,523	1,530

NA Not available. [1] All public road and street mileage in the 50 states and the District of Columbia. [2] Data represent miles of road owned (aggregate length of road, excluding yard tracks, sidings, and parallel lines). [3] Transit system length is measured in directional route-miles; see source. [4] Also called metropolitan rail or regional rail. [5] Also called metro, subway, rapid transit, or rapid rail. [6] Also called streetcar, tramway, or trolley. [7] Includes trunk and gathering lines for crude-oil pipeline. [8] Excludes service pipelines.

Source: U.S. Bureau of Transportation Statistics, "National Transportation Statistics," <http://www.bts.gov/publications /national_transportation_statistics>.

Table 1068. U.S. Aircraft, Vehicles, and Other Conveyances: 1980 to 2008

[121,601 represents 121,601,000]

System	1980	1990	1995	2000	2004	2005	2006	2007	2008
Air:									
Air carrier [1]	3,808	6,083	7,411	8,055	8,186	8,225	8,089	8,044	(NA)
General aviation [2] (active fleet)	211,045	198,000	188,089	217,533	219,426	224,352	221,943	231,607	228,663
Highway, registered vehicles (1,000):									
Passenger car	121,601	133,700	128,387	133,621	136,431	136,568	135,400	135,933	137,080
Motorcycle	5,694	4,259	3,897	4,346	5,768	6,227	6,679	7,138	7,753
Van, pick-up, SUV	27,876	48,275	65,738	79,085	91,845	95,337	99,125	101,470	101,235
Truck	5,791	6,196	6,719	8,023	8,171	8,482	8,819	9,028	9,007
Bus	529	627	686	746	795	807	822	834	843
Transit:									
Motor bus	59,411	58,714	67,107	75,013	81,033	82,027	83,080	65,429	66,506
Light rail cars [3]	1,013	910	1,048	1,327	1,622	1,645	1,801	1,810	1,969
Heavy rail cars [4]	9,641	10,567	10,166	10,311	10,858	11,110	11,052	11,222	11,377
Trolley bus	823	610	695	652	597	615	609	559	590
Commuter rail cars and locomotives	4,500	4,982	5,164	5,498	6,228	6,392	6,403	6,391	6,617
Demand response	(X)	16,471	29,352	33,080	37,078	41,958	43,509	64,865	65,799
Other [5]	(NA)	1,197	2,809	5,360	6,406	7,080	8,741	13,877	16,578
Rail:									
Class I, freight cars (1,000)	1,168	659	583	560	474	475	475	460	450
Class I, locomotive	28,094	18,835	18,812	20,028	22,015	22,779	23,732	24,143	24,003
Nonclass I freight cars	102,161	103,527	84,724	132,448	120,169	120,195	120,688	120,463	109,487
Car companies' and shippers' freight cars	440,552	449,832	550,717	688,194	693,978	717,211	750,404	805,074	833,188
Amtrak, passenger train car	2,128	1,863	1,722	1,894	1,211	1,186	1,191	1,164	1,177
Amtrak, locomotive	419	318	313	378	276	258	319	270	278
Water:									
Non-self-propelled vessels [6]	31,662	31,209	31,360	33,152	31,296	32,052	32,211	31,654	31,238
Self-propelled vessels [7]	7,126	8,236	8,281	8,202	8,994	8,976	8,898	9,041	9,063
Ocean-going steam and motor ships (1,000 gross tons and over)	849	635	512	461	412	357	272	275	209
Recreational boats (1,000)	8,578	10,997	11,735	12,782	12,781	12,942	12,746	12,876	12,693

NA Not available. [1] Air carrier aircraft are those carrying passengers or cargo for hire under 14 CFR 121 and 14 CFR 135. [2] Includes air taxi aircraft. [3] Fixed rail streetcar or trolley, for example. [4] Metro, subway, or rapid transit, for example. [5] Includes aerial tramway, automated guideway transit, cablecar, ferry boat, inclined plane, monorail, and vanpool. [6] Includes dry-cargo barges, tank barges, and railroad-car floats. [7] Includes dry-cargo and/or passenger, offshore supply vessels, railroad-car ferries, tankers, and towboats.

Source: U.S. Bureau of Transportation Statistics, "National Transportation Statistics," <http://www.bts.gov/publications /national_transportation_statistics/>.

Table 1069. Shipment Characteristics by Mode of Transportation: 2002 and 2007

[8,397,210 represents $8,397,210,000,000 (except as indicated otherwise). For business establishments in mining, manufacturing, wholesale trade, and selected retail industries. 2002 data are based on the 2002 North American Industry Classification System (NAICS). 2007 data are based on the 2007 NAICS. Selected auxiliary establishments are also included. Based on the 2007 Economic Census; see Appendix III]

Mode of transportation	Value (mil. dol.)		Tons (1,000)		Ton-miles (mil.)		Average miles per shipment	
	2002	2007	2002	2007	2002	2007	2002	2007
All modes	8,397,210	11,684,872	11,667,919	12,543,425	3,137,898	3,344,658	546	619
Single modes...............	7,049,383	9,539,037	11,086,660	11,698,128	2,867,938	2,894,251	240	234
Truck [1]	6,235,001	8,335,789	7,842,836	8,778,713	1,255,908	1,342,104	173	206
For-hire truck	3,757,114	4,955,700	3,657,333	4,075,136	959,610	1,055,646	523	599
Private truck...............	2,445,288	3,380,090	4,149,658	4,703,576	291,114	286,457	64	57
Rail	310,884	436,420	1,873,884	1,861,307	1,261,612	1,344,040	807	728
Water........................	89,344	114,905	681,227	403,639	282,659	157,314	568	520
Shallow draft	57,467	91,004	458,577	343,307	211,501	117,473	450	144
Great lakes	843	(S)	38,041	17,792	13,808	6,887	339	657
Deep draft	31,034	23,058	184,610	42,540	57,350	32,954	664	923
Air (includes truck and air).......	264,959	252,276	3,760	3,611	5,835	4,510	1,919	1,304
Pipeline [2]	149,195	399,646	684,953	650,859	(S)	(S)	(S)	(S)
Multiple modes	1,079,185	1,866,723	216,686	573,729	225,715	416,642	895	975
Parcel, U.S. Postal Service or courier....................	987,746	1,561,874	25,513	33,900	19,004	27,961	894	975
Truck and rail.................	69,929	187,248	42,984	225,589	45,525	196,772	1,413	1,007
Truck and water...............	14,359	58,389	23,299	145,521	32,413	98,396	1,950	1,429
Rail and water	3,329	13,892	105,107	54,878	114,986	47,111	957	1,928
Other multiple modes	3,822	45,320	19,782	113,841	13,788	46,402	(S)	1,182
Other and unknown modes ...	268,642	279,113	364,573	271,567	44,245	33,764	130	116

S Data do not meet publication standards due to high sampling variability or other reasons. [1] Truck as a single mode includes shipments that went by private truck only, for-hire truck only, or a combination of private truck and for-hire truck. [2] Commodity Flow Survey data exclude shipments of crude oil.

Source: U.S. Department of Transportation, Bureau of Transportation Statistics, and U.S. Census Bureau, 2007 Commodity Flow Survey, Transportation Commodity Flow Survey, preliminary; <http://factfinder.census.gov/home/saff/main.html?_lang=en>, accessed December 2009.

Table 1070. Hazardous Shipments by Mode of Transportation: 2002 and 2007

[660,181 represents $660,181,000,000. For business establishments in mining, manufacturing, wholesale trade, and selected retail industries. 2002 data are based on the 2002 North American Industry Classification System (NAICS). 2007 data are based on the 2007 NAICS. Selected auxiliary establishments are also included. Based on the 2007 Economic Census; see Appendix III]

Mode of transportation	Value (mil. dol.)		Tons (1,000)		Ton-miles (mil.)		Average miles per shipment	
	2002	2007	2002	2007	2002	2007	2002	2007
All modes	660,181	1,448,218	2,191,519	2,231,133	326,727	323,457	136	96
Single modes...............	644,489	1,370,615	2,158,533	2,111,622	311,897	279,105	105	65
Truck [1]	419,630	837,074	1,159,514	1,202,825	110,163	103,997	86	59
For-hire truck	189,803	358,792	449,503	495,077	65,112	63,288	285	214
Private truck.................	226,660	478,282	702,186	707,748	44,087	40,709	38	32
Rail	31,339	69,213	109,369	129,743	72,087	92,169	695	578
Water........................	46,856	69,186	228,197	149,794	70,649	37,064	(S)	383
Air (includes truck and air).......	1,643	1,735	64	(S)	85	(S)	2,080	1,095
Pipeline [2]	145,021	393,408	661,390	628,905	(S)	(S)	(S)	(S)
Multiple modes	9,631	71,069	18,745	111,022	12,488	42,886	849	834
Parcel, U.S. Postal Service or courier....................	4,268	7,675	245	236	119	151	837	836
Other multiple modes	5,363	63,394	18,500	110,786	12,369	42,735	1,371	2,749
Other and unknown modes	6,061	6,534	14,241	8,489	2,342	1,466	57	58
Class of material	660,181	1,448,218	2,191,519	2,231,133	326,727	323,457	136	96
Class 1, explosives	7,901	11,754	5,000	3,047	1,568	911	651	738
Class 2, gasses...............	73,932	131,810	213,358	250,506	37,262	55,260	95	51
Class 3, flammable liquids.......	490,238	1,170,455	1,788,986	1,752,814	218,574	181,615	106	91
Class 4, flammable solids.......	6,566	4,067	11,300	20,408	4,391	5,547	158	309
Class 5, oxidizers and organic peroxides....................	5,471	6,695	12,670	14,959	4,221	7,024	407	361
Class 6, toxic (poison)	8,275	21,198	8,459	11,270	4,254	5,667	626	467
Class 7, radioactive materials	5,850	20,633	57	515	44	37	(S)	(S)
Class 8, corrosive materials	38,324	51,475	90,671	114,441	36,260	44,395	301	208
Class 9, miscellaneous dangerous goods.............	23,625	30,131	61,018	63,173	20,153	23,002	368	484

S Data do not meet publication standards due to high sampling variability or other reasons. [1] Truck as a single mode includes shipments that went by private truck only, for-hire truck only, or a combination of private truck and for-hire truck. [2] Commodity Flow Survey Data exclude shipments of crude oil.

Source: U.S. Department of Transportation, Bureau of Transportation Statistics, and U.S. Census Bureau, 2007 Commodity Flow Survey, Transportation Commodity Flow Survey, preliminary; <http://factfinder.census.gov/home/saff/main.html?_lang=en>, accessed February 2010.

Table 1071. Transportation Accidents, Deaths, and Injuries: 1990 to 2008

[6,471 represents 6,471,000. Number, except as indicated]

Mode	Accidents 1990	1995	2000	2005	2008	Deaths 1990	1995	2000	2005	2008	Injuries 1990	1995	2000	2005	2008
Transit type:															
Air:															
Air carrier [1]	24	36	56	40	28	39	168	92	22	3	29	25	29	14	16
Commuter [2]	15	12	12	6	7	6	9	5	–	–	11	17	7	–	2
On-demand [3]	107	75	80	65	56	51	52	71	18	66	36	14	12	23	13
General aviation	2,242	2,056	1,837	1,670	1,559	770	735	596	563	495	409	396	309	267	258
Land:															
Highway crashes (1,000) [4]	6,471	6,699	6,394	6,159	5,811	44.6	41.8	41.9	43.5	37.3	3,231	3,465	3,189	2,699	2,346
Passenger car occupants	5,561	5,594	4,926	4,499	(NA)	24.1	22.4	20.7	18.5	14.6	2,376	2,469	2,052	1,573	1,304
Motorcyclists	103	66	69	101	(NA)	3.2	2.2	2.9	4.6	5.3	84	57	58	87	96
Light truck occupants	2,152	2,750	3,208	3,382	(NA)	8.6	9.6	11.5	13.0	10.8	505	722	887	872	768
Large truck occupants	372	363	438	423	(NA)	0.7	0.6	0.8	0.8	0.7	42	30	31	27	23
Bus occupants	60	59	56	50	(NA)	(Z)	(Z)	(Z)	0.1	(Z)	33	19	18	11	15
Pedestrians	(NA)	(NA)	(NA)	(NA)	(NA)	6.5	5.6	4.8	4.9	4.4	105	86	78	64	69
Pedacyclists	(NA)	(NA)	(NA)	(NA)	(NA)	0.9	0.8	0.7	0.8	0.7	75	67	51	45	52
Other	(NA)	(NA)	(NA)	(NA)	(NA)	0.6	0.5	0.6	0.8	0.8	11	14	15	18	18
Railroad [5]	8,594	7,092	6,485	6,327	4,841	1,297	1,146	937	883	798	25,143	14,440	11,643	9,511	8,789
Highway-rail grade crossing	5,715	4,633	3,502	3,061	2,398	698	579	425	358	285	2,407	1,894	1,219	1,051	949
Railroad [6]	2,879	2,459	2,983	3,266	2,443	599	567	512	525	513	22,736	12,546	10,424	8,460	7,840
Transit [6]	58,002	25,683	24,261	8,151	4,117	339	274	295	236	(NA)	54,556	57,196	56,697	18,131	23,105
Waterborne:															
Waterborne (vessel related) [7]	3,613	5,349	5,403	4,977	(NA)	85	53	53	78	51	175	154	150	140	152
Recreational boating [8]	6,411	8,019	7,740	4,969	4,789	865	829	701	697	709	3,822	4,141	4,355	3,451	3,331
Pipeline: [9]	378	349	380	495	430	9	21	38	16	8	76	64	81	48	65
Hazard liquid	180	188	146	143	139	3	3	1	2	2	7	11	4	2	2
Gas	198	161	234	352	291	6	18	37	11	6	69	53	77	46	63
Hazardous materials [10, 11]	8,879	14,853	17,557	15,929	16,905	8	7	16	34	9	69	53	77	950	219

– Represents or rounds to zero. NA Not available. Z Less than 50. [1] See footnote 1, Table 1077. Injuries classified as serious. [2] See footnote 2, Table 1077. Injuries classified as serious. [3] See footnote 3, Table 1077. Injuries classified as serious. [4] See footnote 4, Table 1077. Injuries classified as serious. Data on deaths are from U.S. National Highway Traffic Safety Administration and are based on deaths within 30 days of the accident. Includes only police reported crashes. For more details, see Table 1102. [5] Accidents which result in damages to railroad property. Grade crossing accidents are also included when classified as a train accident. Deaths exclude fatalities in railroad-highway grade crossing accidents. [6] Includes motor bus, commuter rail, heavy rail, light rail, demand response, van pool, and automated guideway. Starting with 2002, only injuries requiring immediate medical treatment away from the scene now qualify as reportable. [7] Accidents resulting in death, injury, or requiring medical treatment beyond first aid; damages exceeding $500; or a person's disappearance. [8] Covers accidents involving commercial vessels which must be reported to U.S. Coast Guard if there is property damage exceeding $25,000; material damage affecting the seaworthiness or efficiency of a vessel; stranding or grounding; loss of life; or injury causing a person's incapacity for more than 3 days. [9] Beginning 1990, pipeline accidents/incidents are credited to year of occurrence; prior data are credited to the year filed. [10] Incidents, deaths, and injuries involving hazardous materials cover all types of transport, exclude pipelines and bulk, nonpackaged water incidents. [11] The data reported under accident are incident numbers.

Source: U.S. Bureau of Transportation Statistics, "National Transportation Statistics," See <http://www.bts.gov/publications/national_transportation_statistics/>.

Table 1072. U.S. Scheduled Airline Industry—Summary: 1995 to 2009

[For calendar years or December 31, (547.8 represents 547,800,000). For domestic and international operations. Covers carriers certificated under Section 401 of the Federal Aviation Act. Table data have been revised for 2000 through 2008. Minus sign (–) indicates loss]

Item	Unit	1995	2000	2004	2005	2006	2007	2008	2009
SCHEDULED SERVICE									
Revenue passengers enplaned	Mil	547.8	666.1	703.7	738.6	744.7	769.6	743.3	703.9
Revenue passenger miles	Bil	540.7	692.8	734.0	779.0	797.4	829.4	812.4	769.5
Available seat miles	Bil	807.1	957.0	971.9	1,003.3	1,006.3	1,037.7	1,021.3	957.2
Revenue passenger load factor	Percent	67.0	72.4	75.5	77.6	79.2	79.9	79.5	80.4
Mean passenger trip length [1]	Miles	987	1,040	1,043	1,055	1,071	1,078	1,093	1,093
Cargo ton miles	Mil	16,921	23,888	27,978	28,037	29,339	29,570	28,375	25,002
Aircraft departures	1,000	8,062	9,035	11,429	11,564	11,268	11,399	10,896	10,132
FINANCES [2]									
Total operating revenue [3]	**Mil. dol.**	**95,117**	**130,248**	**134,660**	**151,544**	**165,532**	**174,696**	**186,119**	**154,719**
Passenger revenue	Mil. dol.	69,835	93,622	85,669	93,500	101,419	107,678	111,542	91,331
Cargo revenue	Mil. dol.	9,882	14,456	17,146	20,704	22,848	24,531	29,192	22,914
Charter revenue	Mil. dol.	3,742	4,913	5,503	6,074	6,026	5,544	4,338	3,709
Total operating expense	Mil. dol.	89,266	123,234	136,150	151,097	157,892	165,353	189,466	152,310
Operating profit (or loss)	Mil. dol.	5,852	7,014	–1,490	448	7,640	9,344	–3,348	2,409
Interest income (or expense)	Mil. dol.	–2,426	–2,193	–3,715	–4,209	–4,150	–3,915	–3,769	–4,267
Net profit (or loss)	Mil. dol.	2,314	2,533	–9,104	–27,220	18,186	7,691	–23,747	–2,528
Revenue per passenger mile	Cents	12.9	13.5	11.7	12.0	12.7	13.0	13.7	11.9
Operating profit margin	Percent	6.2	5.4	–1.1	0.3	4.6	5.3	–1.8	1.6
Net profit margin	Percent	2.4	1.9	–6.8	–18.0	11.0	4.4	–12.8	–1.6
Adjusted Net Profit (or loss) [4]	Percent	2.4	1.9	–6.8	–18.0	11.0	4.4	–12.8	–1.6
EMPLOYEES [5]									
Total	1,000	547.0	679.7	585.2	576.2	565.0	576.0	559.6	536.2
Pilots and copilots	1,000	55.4	78.4	75.2	78.4	77.8	76.6	77.1	74.8

[1] For definition of mean, see Guide to Tabular Presentation. [2] 2009 data are preliminary. [3] Includes other types of revenues, not shown separately. [4] Excludes special items: bankruptcy-related reorganization charges and fresh-start accounting gains, and special goodwill charges. [5] Average full-time equivalents.

Source: Air Transport Association of America, Washington, DC, *Air Transport Annual Report*.

Table 1073. Airline Cost Indexes: 1980 to 2009

[2000 = 100. To be included in the cost index, carriers must have met the following criteria on an annual basis: 1) must report both passenger revenue and revenue passenger miles (RPMs) and 2) passenger revenue must be greater than or equal to 25% of total operating revenue. Data prior to 1977 excludes passenger airlines with annual revenue less than $100 million. Data for 1980–2008 have been revised]

Index	1980	1990	1995	2000	2001	2002	2003	2004	2005	2006	2007	2008	2009
Composite index [1]	**77.4**	**101.1**	**99.0**	**100.0**	**108.5**	**113.6**	**122.8**	**149.1**	**177.9**	**195.8**	**199.8**	**262.0**	**197.3**
Labor costs	52.0	73.1	91.3	100.0	107.8	118.7	122.7	122.3	117.3	119.0	119.1	119.8	127.4
Fuel	113.7	98.1	69.7	100.0	98.6	89.9	107.9	144.1	206.6	242.8	258.0	374.2	234.9
Aircraft ownership [2]	33.5	71.1	83.0	100.0	102.3	105.2	101.8	103.4	99.1	98.9	94.3	91.0	93.0
Nonaircraft ownership	40.4	88.1	103.3	100.0	139.4	113.0	111.4	104.1	106.1	104.2	106.6	118.8	114.8
Professional services	27.0	67.5	85.4	100.0	102.8	97.3	98.4	103.4	105.5	111.2	115.8	125.4	118.5
Food and beverage	88.5	125.5	106.9	100.0	100.5	87.2	74.6	67.1	61.3	57.9	57.8	60.0	59.7
Landing fees	49.2	81.0	95.8	100.0	109.2	125.2	130.8	131.2	130.7	135.6	136.7	148.6	158.9
Maintenance material	73.3	119.2	94.0	100.0	96.3	84.1	67.3	64.8	59.1	62.2	69.9	77.0	83.3
Aircraft insurance	246.1	161.0	341.5	100.0	163.5	271.0	180.9	174.3	157.1	181.0	152.3	124.0	150.8
Nonaircraft insurance	73.3	68.2	223.8	100.0	171.3	573.7	450.9	373.7	319.9	259.3	222.1	195.4	184.4
Passenger commissions	121.5	227.0	184.8	100.0	86.4	57.8	41.9	37.2	31.6	29.2	28.2	27.0	26.7
Communication	50.3	85.7	86.5	100.0	109.6	102.6	82.0	76.1	73.3	68.5	71.2	79.2	77.1
Advertising and promotion	112.9	165.0	107.8	100.0	93.0	74.7	69.1	77.8	75.5	80.9	67.3	59.0	61.7
Utilities and office supplies	67.9	97.7	87.0	100.0	103.6	92.3	81.0	81.3	87.6	94.3	102.2	108.8	99.8
Transportation-related expenses	46.0	55.0	57.5	100.0	119.1	132.3	256.4	397.4	475.0	508.4	506.7	604.5	524.9
Other operating expenses	56.0	87.4	74.1	100.0	126.4	106.5	94.9	94.3	108.6	108.1	116.1	156.8	123.8
Interest [3]	160.7	182.0	174.6	100.0	98.1	98.8	93.3	96.3	120.6	133.5	120.3	105.6	118.7

[1] Weighted average of all components, including interest. [2] Includes lease, aircraft and engine rentals, depreciation, and amortization. [3] Interest on long-term debt and capital and other interest expense.

Source: Air Transport Association of America, Washington, DC, *U.S. Passenger Airline Cost Index*. See also <http://www.airlines.org/economics/>.

U.S. Census Bureau, Statistical Abstract of the United States: 2011

Table 1074. Top 40 Airports in 2008—Passengers Enplaned: 1998 and 2008

[In thousands (593,144 represents 593,144,000), except rank. For calendar year. Airports ranked by total passengers enplaned by large certificated air carriers on scheduled and nonscheduled operations, 2008]

Airport	1998 Rank	1998 Total	2008 Rank	2008 Total	Airport	1998 Rank	1998 Total	2008 Rank	2008 Total
All airports	(X)	**593,144**	(X)	**699,024**	Fort Lauderdale-Hollywood Intl, FL	32	5,479	21	10,372
Total, top 40	(X)	460,382	(X)	531,820	Baltimore, MD (BWI Intl)	28	6,842	22	10,083
Atlanta, GA (Hartsfield Intl)	1	34,951	1	43,251	Salt Lake City Intl, UT	22	9,096	23	9,992
Chicago, IL (O'Hare Intl)	2	33,002	2	31,358	Washington, DC (Dulles Intl)	33	5,381	24	9,975
Dallas/Ft. Worth Intl, TX	3	28,289	3	26,839	San Diego, CA (Lindbergh Field)	27	6,996	25	8,931
Denver, Intl, CO	5	16,929	4	23,941	Tampa Intl, FL	29	6,276	26	8,692
Los Angeles, Intl, CA	4	22,874	5	22,669	Washington, DC (Ronald Reagan Washington Natl.)	26	7,067	27	8,606
Las Vegas, NV (McCarran Intl)	11	14,033	6	19,897	Chicago, IL (Midway)	36	5,031	28	8,016
Houston, Intercontinental, TX	13	13,784	7	19,414	Honolulu Intl, HI	24	8,605	29	7,786
Phoenix Sky Harbor Intl, AZ	8	15,045	8	19,225	Portland Intl, OR	30	6,208	30	6,959
Charlotte-Douglas Intl, NC	20	10,242	9	17,193	St. Louis, MO (Lambert-St. Louis Intl)	10	14,211	31	6,723
New York, NY (JFK Intl)	21	10,076	10	16,753	Cincinnati, OH (Cincinnati Northern Kentucky Intl)	25	7,783	32	6,640
Detroit, MI (Wayne County)	7	15,113	11	16,752	Oakland Intl, CA	38	4,410	33	5,503
Minneapolis-St. Paul Intl, MN	12	13,909	12	16,317	Memphis Intl, TN	41	4,075	34	5,376
Newark Intl, NJ	9	14,564	13	16,117	Cleveland, OH (Cleveland-Hopkins Intl)	31	5,714	35	5,372
Orlando Intl, FL	16	11,931	14	16,099	Kansas City Intl, MO	34	5,280	36	5,371
San Francisco Intl, CA	6	16,684	15	15,760	Sacramento Intl, CA	45	3,495	37	4,913
Philadelphia Intl, PA	19	10,286	16	15,267	Raleigh, NC (Raleigh-Durham Intl)	48	3,289	38	4,755
Seattle-Tacoma Intl, WA	15	12,243	17	15,231	San Jose Intl, CA	37	4,995	39	4,714
Miami Intl, FL	14	13,265	18	13,578	Nashville, TN (Nashville Intl)	42	3,777	40	4,623
Boston, MA (Logan Intl)	17	10,704	19	11,587					
New York, NY (La Guardia)	18	10,356	20	11,173					

X Not applicable.

Source: U.S. Bureau of Transportation Statisics, Office of Airline Information, BTS Form 41, Schedule T-3, unpublished data.

Table 1075. Domestic Airline Markets: 2009

[In thousands (4,106 represents 4,106,000). For calendar year. Data are for the 25 top markets and include all commercial airports in each metro area. Data represent origin and final destination of travel]

Market	Passengers	Market	Passengers
Los Angeles-New York	4,106	Las Vegas-San Francisco	1,727
Fort Lauderdale-New York	4,093	Orlando-Philadelphia	1,708
Chicago-New York	3,914	Chicago-Orlando	1,703
New York-Orlando	3,675	Dallas/Fort Worth-Houston	1,694
New York-San Francisco	3,140	Dallas/Fort Worth-New York	1,684
New York-Atlanta	3,086	Chicago-Las Vegas	1,674
Los Angeles-San Francisco	2,564	Chicago-Washington	1,664
Miami-New York	2,225	New York-San Juan	1,577
Las Vegas-New York	2,186	Los Angeles-Washington	1,550
New York-West Palm Beach	1,951	Atlanta-Washington	1,544
New York-Tampa	1,815	Chicago-Phoenix	1,520
Chicago-Los Angeles	1,784	Las Vegas-Seattle	1,514
Boston-New York	1,751		

Source: Air Transport Association of America, Washington, DC, *Annual Report*.

Table 1076. Worldwide Airline Fatalities: 1990 to 2008

[For scheduled air transport operations. Excludes accidents due to acts of unlawful interference]

Year	Fatal accidents	Passenger deaths	Death rate [1]	Year	Fatal accidents	Passenger deaths	Death rate [1]
1990........	27	544	0.05	2000.......	18	757	0.04
1992........	28	1,070	0.09	2001.......	13	577	0.03
1993........	33	864	0.07	2002.......	14	791	0.04
1994........	27	1,170	0.09	2003.......	7	466	0.02
1995........	25	711	0.05	2004.......	9	203	0.01
1996........	24	1,146	0.07	2005.......	17	712	0.03
1997........	25	921	0.06	2006.......	23	755	0.02
1998........	20	904	0.05	2007.......	11	587	0.01
1999........	21	499	0.03	2008.......	11	439	0.01

[1] Rate per 100 million passenger kilometers performed. Passenger-kilometers performed (PKPs) is the number of passengers multiplied by the number of kilometers travelled.

Source: International Civil Aviation Organization, Montreal, Canada, *Civil Aviation Statistics of the World*, annual.

Table 1077. Aircraft Accidents: 1990 to 2009

[For years ending December 31]

Item	Unit	1990	1995	2000	2005	2007	2008	2009, prel.
Air carrier accidents, all services [1].......	Number	24	36	56	40	28	28	30
Fatal accidents.....................	Number	6	3	3	3	1	2	2
Fatalities	Number	39	168	92	22	1	3	52
Aboard........................	Number	12	162	92	20	1	1	51
Rates per 100,000 flight hours:								
Accidents......................	Rate......	0.198	0.267	0.306	0.206	0.143	0.147	0.167
Fatal accidents.................	Rate......	0.049	0.022	0.016	0.015	0.005	0.010	0.011
Commuter air carrier accidents [2]........	Number	15	12	12	6	3	7	2
Fatal accidents....................	Number	3	2	1	–	–	–	–
Fatalities	Number ...	6	9	5	–	–	–	–
Aboard........................	Number	4	9	5	–	–	–	–
Rates per 100,000 flight hours:								
Accidents......................	Rate......	0.641	0.457	3.247	2.002	1.028	2.385	0.685
Fatal accidents.................	Rate......	0.128	0.076	0.271	–	–	–	–
On-demand air taxi accidents [3].........	Number	107	75	80	65	62	58	47
Fatal accidents....................	Number	29	24	22	11	14	20	2
Fatalities	Number	51	52	71	18	43	69	17
Aboard........................	Number	49	52	68	16	43	69	14
Rates per 100,000 flight hours:								
Accidents......................	Rate......	4.76	3.02	2.04	1.70	1.54	1.81	1.63
Fatal accidents.................	Rate......	1.29	0.97	0.56	0.29	0.35	0.62	0.07
General aviation accidents [4]	Number	2,242	2,056	1,837	1,670	1,652	1,566	1,474
Fatal accidents....................	Number	444	413	345	321	288	275	272
Fatalities	Number	770	735	596	563	496	494	474
Aboard........................	Number	765	728	585	558	491	485	465
Rates per 100,000 flight hours:								
Accidents......................	Rate......	7.85	8.21	6.57	7.20	6.93	6.86	7.20
Fatal accidents.................	Rate......	1.55	1.63	1.21	1.38	1.20	1.21	1.33

– Represents zero. [1] U.S. air carriers operating under 14 CFR 121. Beginning 2000, includes aircraft with 10 or more seats, previously operating under 14 CFR 135. [2] All scheduled service of U.S. air carriers operating under 14 CFR 135. Beginning 2000, only aircraft with fewer than 10 seats. [3] All nonscheduled service of U.S. air carriers operating under 14 CFR 135. [4] U.S. civil registered aircraft not operated under 14 CFR 121 or 135. Data from 2006 include 154 deaths aboard a foreign registed aircraft when it collided with a business general aviation aircraft over the Brazilian Amazon jungle. There were no fatalities in the general aviation aircraft.

Source: U.S. National Transportation Safety Board, "Aviation Accident Statistics," <http://www.ntsb.gov/aviation/stats.htm>, accessed August 2010.

Table 1078. U.S. Carrier Delays, Cancellations, and Diversions: 1995 to 2008

[In thousands (5,327.4 represents 5,327,400). For calendar year. See headnote, Table 1079]

Item	1995	2000	2001	2002	2003	2004	2005	2006	2007	2008
Total operations......	**5,327.4**	**5,683.0**	**5,967.8**	**5,271.4**	**6,488.5**	**7,129.3**	**7,140.6**	**7,141.9**	**7,455.5**	**7,007.8**
Delays:										
Late departures [1]......	827.9	1,131.7	953.8	717.4	834.4	1,187.6	1,279.4	1,424.8	1,573.0	1,327.2
Late arrivals [2].........	1,039.3	1,356.0	1,104.4	868.2	1,057.8	1,421.4	1,466.1	1,615.5	1,804.0	1,524.6
Cancellations [3]........	91.9	187.5	231.2	65.1	101.5	127.8	133.7	121.9	160.8	137.4
Diversions [4]	10.5	14.3	12.9	8.4	11.4	13.8	14.0	16.2	17.2	17.2

[1] Late departures comprise flights departing 15 minutes or more after the scheduled departure time. [2] Late arrivals comprise flights arriving 15 minutes or more after the scheduled arrival time. [3] A cancelled flight is one that was not operated, but was listed in a carrier's computer reservation system within seven days of the scheduled departure. [4] A diverted flight is one that left from the scheduled departure airport but flew to a destination point other than the scheduled destination point.

Source: U.S. Bureau of Transportation Statistics, "National Transportation Statistics," <http://www.bts.gov/publications/national_transportation_statistics/>.

Transportation 679

Table 1079. On-Time Flight Arrivals and Departures at Major U.S. Airports: 2008

[In percent. Quarterly, based on gate arrival and departure times for domestic scheduled operations of U.S. major airlines. All U.S. airlines with 1 percent or more of total U.S. domestic scheduled airline passenger revenues are required to report on-time data. A flight is considered on time if it operated less than 15 minutes after the scheduled time shown in the carrier's computerized reservation system. See source for data on individual airlines]

Airport	On-time arrivals				On-time departures			
	1st quarter	2nd quarter	3rd quarter	4th quarter	1st quarter	2nd quarter	3rd quarter	4th quarter
Total, all airports	**71.4**	**73.9**	**74.2**	**74.2**	**74.7**	**77.3**	**77.2**	**77.7**
Atlanta, Hartsfield	72.2	79.8	76.8	73.1	72.6	80.3	76.7	77.8
Boston, Logan International	72.6	73.1	71.7	76.3	78.2	80.3	77.8	82.1
Baltimore/Washington International	76.5	80.6	81.4	82.9	76.9	80.0	81.2	82.3
Charlotte, Douglas	74.5	79.2	78.3	81.1	76.3	79.6	79.5	84.2
Cincinnati, Greater Cincinnati	72.4	80.9	82.2	81.8	74.7	81.9	81.6	82.2
Washington, Reagan National	75.5	76.2	78.6	81.6	81.2	81.5	83.0	85.8
Denver International	75.0	76.4	81.6	80.2	75.7	77.9	80.9	80.2
Dallas-Fort Worth International	70.7	70.5	80.9	82.9	69.4	69.3	76.6	80.7
Detroit, Metro Wayne County	71.8	79.9	86.6	82.2	73.4	79.8	85.6	82.9
Newark International	59.6	61.2	66.2	62.6	66.5	67.9	69.7	72.4
Fort Lauderdale-Hollywood International	69.5	77.7	77.9	76.2	74.2	81.4	81.3	81.0
Washington/Dulles	71.1	72.0	74.2	79.6	73.4	73.6	76.0	81.5
Houston, George Bush	74.1	78.4	80.4	80.5	75.7	78.5	79.4	83.2
New York, JFK International	70.1	70.3	61.9	73.0	76.1	78.1	70.6	78.3
Las Vegas, McCarran International	73.4	76.3	84.0	77.4	74.1	77.9	82.7	77.7
Los Angeles International	70.9	74.4	82.4	80.4	75.9	80.6	84.5	82.9
New York, La Guardia	57.9	57.1	65.5	71.7	71.3	71.9	76.2	81.3
Orlando International	72.5	78.8	80.1	80.2	75.9	80.4	81.1	83.9
Chicago, Midway	72.8	81.9	86.5	81.9	67.9	78.9	83.1	77.7
Miami International	66.0	70.7	71.7	75.8	68.6	71.2	70.5	76.8
Minneapolis-St. Paul International	73.5	78.0	85.1	79.5	77.1	82.3	86.4	82.6
Oakland International	74.2	79.1	87.0	82.0	76.4	82.2	87.0	81.5
Chicago, O'Hare	55.5	66.7	74.6	74.6	56.2	68.5	74.7	74.9
Portland International	74.2	76.5	83.2	76.7	81.8	84.1	87.9	81.7
Philadelphia International	71.3	72.8	74.5	73.5	74.5	77.3	78.0	77.9
Phoenix, Sky Harbor International	78.0	80.1	84.1	81.6	78.8	81.1	83.1	82.2
San Diego, Lindbergh Field	73.5	75.7	84.1	79.0	76.9	81.4	86.2	81.7
Seattle-Tacoma International	72.8	74.4	80.4	74.2	78.1	81.0	84.1	79.1
San Francisco International	61.9	68.5	73.6	72.0	69.3	76.5	77.9	77.0
Salt Lake City International	75.5	86.5	89.1	83.4	81.0	89.6	89.5	85.8
St. Louis, Lambert	70.8	75.9	81.4	81.1	73.3	78.2	83.5	81.7
Tampa, Tampa International	73.3	79.0	80.1	80.1	77.7	81.8	82.6	84.0

Source: U.S. Department of Transportation, Aviation Consumer Protection Division, *Air Travel Consumer Report*, monthly. See also <http://airconsumer.ost.dot.gov>.

Table 1080. Consumer Complaints Against U.S. Airlines: 1990 to 2009

[Calendar year data. Represents complaints filed by consumers to the U.S. Department of Transportation, Aviation Consumer Protection Division, regarding service problems with air carrier personnel. See source for data on individual airlines]

Complaint category	1990	2000	2003	2004	2005	2006	2007	2008	2009
Total	**7,703**	**20,564**	**4,601**	**5,839**	**6,900**	**6,452**	**10,960**	**9,194**	**8,819**
Flight problems [1]	3,034	8,698	1,049	1,462	1,942	1,845	4,097	3,247	2,041
Customer service [2]	758	4,074	584	742	800	870	1,214	1,333	1,103
Baggage	1,329	2,753	802	1,085	1,586	1,400	2,154	2,081	1,606
Ticketing/boarding [3]	624	1,405	643	637	679	708	1,136	1,404	1,583
Refunds	701	803	428	376	530	485	745	804	669
Fares [4]	312	708	243	180	219	173	315	389	436
Disability [5]	(NA)	612	325	467	430	368	428	477	517
Oversales [6]	399	759	223	263	284	275	420	432	370
Discrimination [7]	(NA)	(NA)	71	96	100	90	82	115	132
Advertising	96	42	13	41	45	30	34	39	53
Tours	29	25	[8]	[8]	[8]	[8]	[8]	[8]	[8]
Animals	(NA)	1	2	3	3	3	7	5	5
Smoking	74	[9]	[9]	[9]	[9]	[9]	[9]	[9]	[9]
Credit	5	[9]	[9]	[9]	[9]	[9]	[9]	[9]	[9]
Other	342	684	218	487	282	205	328	322	304

NA Not available. [1] Cancellations, delays, etc., from schedule. [2] Unhelpful employees, inadequate meals or cabin service, treatment of delayed passengers. [3] Errors in reservations and ticketing; problems in making reservations and obtaining tickets. Includes disability compliants prior to 1998. [4] Incorrect or incomplete information about fares, discount fare conditions, and availability, etc. [5] Prior to 2000, included in ticketing/boarding. [6] All bumping problems, whether or not airline complied with DOT regulations. [7] Allegations of discrimination by airlines due to factors other than disability, such as race, religion, national origin or sex. [8] Included in "Other" beginning 2002. [9] Included in "Other" beginning 2000.

Source: U.S. Department of Transportation, Aviation Consumer Protection Division, *Air Travel Consumer Report*, monthly. See also <http://airconsumer.ost.dot.gov>.

Table 1081. Commuter/Regional Airline Operations Summary: 2005 to 2009

[154.2 represents 154,200,000. Calendar year data. Commuter/regional airlines operate primarily aircraft of predominately 75 passengers or less and 18,000 pounds of payload capacity serving short haul and small community markets. Represents operations within all North America by U.S. Regional Carriers. Averages are means. For definition of mean, see Guide to Tabular Presentation]

Item	Unit	2005	2006	2007	2008	2009
Passenger carriers operating............	Number.....	75	71	72	(NA)	62
Passengers enplaned..................	Millions......	154.2	153.9	159.0	(NA)	159.5
Average passengers enplaned per carrier...	1,000.......	2,055.6	2,168.0	2,208.5	(NA)	(NA)
Revenue passenger miles (RPM).........	Billions......	73.8	70.8	73.8	(NA)	72.9
Average RPMs per carrier..............	Millions......	983.7	997.2	1,024.7	(NA)	(NA)
Available seat miles..................	Billions......	104.8	94.8	99.0	(NA)	97.6
Average load factor..................	Percent.....	70.4	74.7	74.6	(NA)	74.7
Departures completed.................	Millions......	5.3	5.0	5.0	(NA)	4.1
Airports served.....................	Number.....	846	688	666	(NA)	644
Average trip length..................	Miles.......	478.5	460.0	464.0	(NA)	457.0
Average seating capacity (seats).........	Number.....	54.4	51.0	52.4	(NA)	55.0
Fleet flying hours....................	1,000.......	7,333.0	7,133.1	7,306.7	(NA)	5,146.0

NA Not available.

Source: Compiled by the Regional Airline Association and BACK Aviation from DOT Form 41 data, *Annual Report of the Regional Airline Industry* (copyright). See also <http://www.raa.org/>.

Table 1082. Airports, Aircraft, and Airmen: 1980 to 2008

[As of December 31 or for years ending December 31]

Item	1980	1990	1995	2000	2005	2006	2007	2008
Airports, total [1]..............	**15,161**	**17,490**	**18,224**	**19,281**	**19,854**	**19,990**	**20,060**	**19,653**
Public [1].......................	4,814	5,589	5,415	5,317	5,270	5,233	5,221	5,202
Percent—with lighted runways...	66.2	71.4	74.3	75.9	76.8	77.2	(NA)	(NA)
With paved runways..........	72.3	70.7	73.3	74.3	74.8	75.3	(NA)	(NA)
Private.......................	10,347	11,901	12,809	13,964	14,584	14,757	14,839	14,451
Percent—with lighted runways...	15.2	7.0	6.4	7.2	9.2	9.5	(NA)	(NA)
With paved runways..........	13.3	31.5	33.0	32.0	33.2	33.3	(NA)	(NA)
Certificated [2].................	730	680	667	651	575	604	565	560
Civil......................	(X)	(X)	572	563	575	604	565	560
Civil military.................	(X)	(X)	95	88	(NA)	(NA)	(NA)	(NA)
General aviation...............	14,431	16,810	17,557	18,630	19,279	19,379	19,495	19,103
Active air carrier fleet [3]...........	3,805	6,083	7,411	8,055	8,225	8,089	8,044	(NA)
Fixed wing...................	3,803	6,072	7,293	8,016	8,182	8,042	7,998	(NA)
Helicopter...................	2	11	118	39	43	47	46	(NA)
General aviation fleet [4]...........	211,043	198,000	188,089	217,533	224,352	221,943	231,607	228,663
Fixed-wing...................	200,094	184,500	162,342	183,276	185,373	182,186	186,806	182,961
Turbojet....................	2,992	4,100	4,559	7,001	9,823	10,379	10,385	11,042
Turboprop...................	4,089	5,300	4,995	5,762	7,942	8,063	9,514	8,906
Piston.....................	193,013	175,200	152,788	170,513	167,608	163,743	166,907	163,013
Rotocraft...................	6,001	6,900	5,830	7,150	8,728	9,159	9,567	9,876
Other......................	4,945	6,600	4,741	6,700	6,454	6,277	5,940	5,652
Gliders....................	(X)	(X)	2,182	2,041	2,074	1,975	1,947	1,914
Lighter than air..............	(X)	(X)	2,559	4,660	4,380	4,303	3,993	3,738
Experimental.................	(X)	(X)	15,176	20,407	23,627	23,047	23,228	23,364
Airman certificates held: [5]								
Pilot, total..................	827,071	702,659	639,184	625,581	609,737	597,109	590,349	613,746
Women....................	52,902	40,515	38,032	36,757	36,584	36,101	35,784	37,981
Student....................	199,833	128,663	101,279	93,064	87,213	84,866	84,339	80,989
Recreational.................	(X)	87	232	340	278	239	239	252
Airplane:								
Private...................	357,479	299,111	261,399	251,561	228,619	219,233	211,096	222,596
Commercial................	183,442	149,666	133,980	121,858	120,614	117,610	115,127	124,746
Air transport...............	69,569	107,732	123,877	141,596	141,992	141,935	143,953	146,838
Rotocraft only [6].............	6,030	9,567	7,183	7,775	9,518	10,690	12,290	14,647
Glider only.................	7,039	7,833	11,234	9,387	21,369	21,597	21,274	21,055
Flight instructor certificates.......	60,440	63,775	77,613	80,931	90,555	91,343	92,175	93,202
Instrument ratings.............	260,462	297,073	298,798	311,944	311,828	309,333	309,865	325,247
Nonpilot [7]..................	368,356	492,237	651,341	547,453	644,016	656,227	666,559	678,181
Mechanic..................	250,157	344,282	405,294	344,434	320,293	323,097	322,852	326,276
Repairmen.................	(X)	(X)	61,233	38,208	40,030	40,329	40,277	41,056
Parachute rigger.............	9,547	10,094	11,824	10,477	8,150	8,252	8,186	8,248
Ground instructor............	61,550	66,882	96,165	72,326	74,378	74,849	74,544	74,983
Dispatcher.................	6,799	11,002	15,642	16,340	18,079	18,610	19,043	19,590
Flight navigator.............	1,936	1,290	916	570	298	264	250	222
Flight engineer..............	38,367	58,687	60,267	65,098	57,756	55,952	54,394	53,135

NA Not available. X Not applicable. [1] Existing airports, heliports, seaplane bases, etc., recorded with FAA. Includes military airports with joint civil and military use. Includes U.S. outlying areas. Airport-type definitions: Public—publicly owned and under control of a public agency; private—owned by a private individual or corporation. May or may not be open for public use. [2] Certificated airports serve air-carriers with aircraft seating more than 30 passengers. [3] Air-carrier aircraft are aircraft carrying passengers or cargo for hire under 14 CFR 121 (large aircraft—more than 30 seats) and 14 CFR 135 (small aircraft—30 seats or fewer). [4] Beginning 1995 excludes commuters. [5] Source: U.S. Federal Aviation Administration. See <http://www.faa.gov/data_research/>. Prior years in the *Statistical Handbook of Aviation*, annual. [6] Data for 1980 are for helicopters only. [7] All certificates on record. No medical examination required.

Source: Except as noted, U.S. Bureau of Transportation Statistics, *National Transportation Statistics*, annual. See also <http://www.bts.gov/publications/national_transportation_statistics/>.

Table 1083. Freight Carried on Major U.S. Waterways: 1990 to 2008

[In millions of tons (4.2 represents 4,200,000)]

Item	1990	1995	2000	2004	2005	2006	2007	2008
Atlantic intracoastal waterway . . .	4.2	3.5	3.1	2.3	2.7	2.6	2.5	2.9
Great Lakes	167.1	177.8	187.5	178.4	169.4	173.0	161.0	152.4
Gulf intracoastal waterway.	115.4	118.0	113.8	123.3	116.1	122.6	125.1	115.9
Mississippi River system [1]	659.1	707.2	715.5	699.8	678.0	702.1	699.0	681.6
Mississippi River mainstem	475.3	520.3	515.6	496.9	464.6	497.7	500.5	486.8
Ohio River system [2]	260.0	267.6	274.4	271.5	280.1	270.7	260.2	259.2
Columbia River	51.4	57.1	55.2	53.5	51.5	52.3	58.1	54.8
Snake River	4.8	6.8	6.7	5.7	5.3	5.2	5.4	3.7

[1] Main channels and all tributaries of the Mississippi, Illinois, Missouri, and Ohio Rivers. [2] Main channels and all navigable tributaries and embayments of the Ohio, Tennessee, and Cumberland Rivers.

Source: U.S. Army Corps of Engineers, *Waterborne Commerce of the United States*, annual. See also <http://www.iwr.usace.army.mil/ndc/wcsc/wcsc.htm>, accessed June 2010.

Table 1084. Waterborne Commerce by Type of Commodity: 1995 to 2008

[In millions of short tons (2,240.4 represents 2,240,400,000). One short ton equals 2,000 pounds. Domestic trade includes all commercial movements between United States ports and on inland rivers, Great Lakes, canals, connecting channels of the United States, Puerto Rico, and Virgin Islands]

Commodity	1995	2000	2005	2008 Total	2008 Domestic	2008 Foreign imports	2008 Foreign exports
Total	2,240.4	2,424.6	2,527.6	2,477.1	956.3	998.7	522.1
Coal	324.5	297.0	316.6	348.0	229.9	36.7	81.4
Petroleum and petroleum products	907.1	1,044.0	1,111.4	1,068.3	335.6	629.1	103.5
Crude petroleum	504.6	571.4	602.7	560.7	67.8	492.9	–
Petroleum products [1]	402.5	472.4	508.8	507.6	267.8	136.2	103.5
Gasoline	114.4	125.2	156.1	137.8	69.9	49.9	18.0
Distillate fuel oil	76.7	91.7	141.1	163.6	80.9	47.7	35.0
Residual fuel oil	111.9	131.6	96.1	99.5	73.5	14.0	11.9
Chemicals and related products	153.7	172.4	174.9	168.7	65.5	46.1	57.1
Fertilizers	35.7	35.1	34.5	32.4	12.7	9.0	10.8
Other chemicals and related products	118.0	137.3	140.4	136.3	52.8	37.2	46.4
Crude material, inedible	381.7	380.3	386.0	358.3	194.7	100.8	62.8
Forest products, wood and chips	47.2	33.1	29.4	22.9	7.9	5.4	9.6
Pulp and waste paper	14.9	13.6	18.7	19.8	0.1	2.0	17.8
Soil, sand, gravel, rock, and stone [1]	152.5	165.0	177.9	155.9	111.0	40.8	4.0
Limestone	54.0	67.4	73.5	70.0	49.1	18.0	2.9
Phosphate rock	10.7	3.4	6.0	5.5	2.6	2.9	–
Sand & gravel	77.0	79.0	80.2	67.2	56.3	10.0	0.9
Iron ore and scrap	104.9	97.9	85.7	89.0	54.0	11.6	23.4
Marine shells	0.5	0.3	–	0.1	0.1	–	–
Nonferrous ores and scrap	27.9	29.2	29.2	27.9	7.2	18.1	2.6
Sulphur, clay, and salt	23.4	11.3	8.7	7.1	1.0	1.8	4.4
Slag	1.9	4.0	6.0	4.7	2.3	2.4	0.1
Other nonmetal minerals	8.4	25.9	30.4	30.9	11.2	18.8	0.9
Primary manufactured goods	106.3	153.0	166.4	134.6	38.2	72.1	24.2
Papers products	13.1	12.1	13.7	14.2	0.2	5.8	8.1
Lime, cement, and glass	33.9	55.9	62.4	35.4	16.2	17.5	1.7
Primary iron and steel products	44.1	57.1	52.1	49.3	14.1	31.9	3.3
Primary nonferrous metal products	12.3	25.5	33.5	33.0	7.7	14.6	10.7
Primary wood products	2.9	2.5	4.8	2.7	0.1	2.3	0.4
Food and farm products [1]	303.2	283.3	251.3	277.9	73.4	37.7	166.8
Fish	3.6	2.4	3.0	3.0	0.1	1.8	1.0
Grain [1]	167.9	145.2	124.0	134.7	42.3	1.4	91.0
Wheat	48.5	43.4	36.4	40.4	9.1	0.2	31.0
Corn	105.0	88.2	75.2	82.1	30.2	0.1	51.9
Oilseeds	46.1	57.6	47.2	58.0	19.1	0.3	38.6
Soybeans	42.0	47.3	40.8	49.8	16.5	0.1	33.2
Vegetables products	9.0	8.9	8.3	10.9	1.5	5.3	4.2
Processed grain and animal feed	33.0	23.1	18.4	17.8	4.9	0.7	12.2
Other agricultural products	43.5	46.1	50.5	53.5	5.6	28.2	19.7
All manufactured equip, machinery and products . . .	57.0	83.6	110.3	109.7	17.0	70.7	22.0
Waste and scrap, n.e.c. [2]	5.4	4.3	2.0	1.9	1.9	–	–
Unknown or not elsewhere classified	1.6	6.8	8.7	9.8	0.1	5.5	4.2

– Represents or rounds to zero. [1] Includes commodities not shown separately. [2] Not elsewhere classified.

Source: U.S. Army Corps of Engineers, *Waterborne Commerce of the United States*, annual. See also <http://www.iwr.usace.army.mil/ndc/wcsc/wcsc.htm>, accessed June 2010.

Table 1085. Top U.S. Ports by Tons of Traffic: 2008

[In thousands of short tons (43,413 represents 43,413,000), except rank. One short ton equals 2,000 lbs. For calendar year for the top 30 ports. Represents tons of cargo shipped from or received by the specified port. Excludes cargo carried on general ferries; coal and petroleum products loaded from shore facilities directly onto bunkers of vessels for fuel; and amounts of less than 100 tons of government-owned equipment in support of Corps of Engineers projects]

| Port name | Rank | Total | Foreign | | | Domestic |
			Total	Inbound	Outbound	
Baltimore, MD	17	43,413	30,959	16,613	14,345	12,454
Baton Rouge, LA	14	51,809	15,901	10,885	5,016	35,909
Beaumont, TX	7	69,484	46,796	41,168	5,628	22,688
Corpus Christi, TX	5	76,786	55,355	43,374	11,981	21,431
Duluth-Superior, MN and WI	15	45,342	15,009	486	14,523	30,333
Freeport, TX	26	29,842	25,707	22,971	2,736	4,135
Houston, TX	2	212,208	146,400	92,019	54,381	65,808
Huntington-Tristate [1]	8	69,335	–	–	–	69,335
Lake Charles, LA	12	53,778	31,766	26,009	5,757	22,012
Long Beach, CA	4	80,205	67,271	45,186	22,085	12,934
Los Angeles, CA	11	59,788	52,913	32,733	20,181	6,875
Mobile, AL	9	67,636	38,111	23,806	14,305	29,524
New Orleans, LA	6	73,011	36,481	19,583	16,899	36,530
New York, NY and NJ	3	153,480	91,101	71,460	19,641	62,379
Norfolk Harbor, VA	16	44,593	36,886	9,577	27,310	7,707
Pascagoula, MS	23	33,590	24,137	19,063	5,075	9,453
Paulsboro, NJ	20	36,352	23,870	22,304	1,565	12,482
Philadelphia, PA	24	32,283	20,323	19,657	666	11,960
Pittsburgh, PA	18	41,837	–	–	–	41,837
Plaquemines, LA, Port of	10	63,744	27,931	8,150	19,782	35,813
Port Arthur, TX	25	31,753	21,748	14,835	6,914	10,005
Portland, OR	29	26,668	17,923	4,115	13,808	8,745
Richmond, CA	30	26,357	15,943	13,044	2,899	10,414
Savannah, GA	22	35,394	33,555	19,584	13,971	1,839
South Louisiana, LA, Port of	1	223,987	111,437	47,270	64,168	112,550
St. Louis, MO and IL	27	29,512	–	–	–	29,512
Tacoma, WA	28	27,166	20,279	6,104	14,176	6,886
Tampa, FL	19	39,676	13,380	7,677	5,702	26,296
Texas City, TX	13	52,606	38,710	33,927	4,784	13,896
Valdez, AK	21	35,967	–	–	–	35,967

– Represents zero. [1] The Port of Huntington is the largest inland shipping port in the United States.

Source: U.S. Army Corps of Engineers, *Waterborne Commerce of the United States, 2008*. See also <http://www.iwr.usace.army.mil/ndc/wcsc/wcsc.htm>, accessed June 2010.

Table 1086. Top U.S. Ports/Waterways by Container Traffic: 2008

[In thousands of twenty-foot equivalent units (TEUS). 32,006.9 represents 32,006,900. For calendar year. For the 30 leading ports/waterways in total TEUS. A TEUS is a measure of containerized cargo capacity equal to 1 standard 20 foot length by 8 foot width by 8 foot 6 inch height container]

| Port/waterway name | Rank | Total loaded | Domestic loaded | | | Foreign loaded | |
			Total [1]	Inbound	Outbound	Total	Inbound
Total [2]	(X)	32,006.9	4,918.6	2,054.1	2,054.1	27,898.8	16,913.9
Anchorage, AK	17	288.4	290.9	235.2	52.2	1.1	–
Baltimore, MD	16	505.4	97.9	37.9	39.0	428.4	258.2
Boston, MA	23	163.2	23.8	9.7	8.0	145.5	90.2
Camden-Gloucester, NJ	28	85.0	57.7	20.6	37.0	27.4	24.0
Charleston, SC	9	1,307.4	–	–	–	1,307.4	686.7
Chester, PA	27	93.6	–	–	–	93.6	47.2
Gulfport, MS	21	172.5	–	–	–	172.5	106.9
Honolulu, HI	11	858.9	1,074.8	529.3	295.3	34.4	21.9
Houston, TX	8	1,370.6	50.6	19.2	26.2	1,325.2	566.9
Jacksonville, FL	15	543.7	407.0	59.5	339.6	144.6	49.0
Kahului, Maui, HI	26	94.4	138.7	74.5	19.9	–	–
Kawaihae Harbor, HI	30	57.4	84.0	43.9	13.5	–	–
Long Beach, CA	2	4,843.0	376.0	66.2	269.0	4,507.8	3,104.7
Los Angeles, CA	1	5,521.4	–	–	–	5,521.4	3,956.7
Miami, FL	14	665.2	–	–	–	665.2	313.2
Mobile, AL	29	71.7	–	–	–	71.7	37.3
New Orleans, LA	18	242.3	18.5	5.6	6.5	230.3	79.6
New York, NY and NJ	3	4,102.5	199.8	69.0	108.2	3,925.3	2,530.7
Norfolk Harbor, VA	5	1,644.9	97.9	39.0	37.9	1,568.0	804.2
Oakland, CA	6	1,547.6	241.9	25.7	156.4	1,365.5	722.7
Palm Beach, FL	25	135.4	–	–	–	135.4	35.7
Philadelphia, PA	20	198.7	–	–	–	198.7	137.7
Port Everglades, FL	13	677.3	11.6	–	11.6	665.8	281.7
Portland, OR	19	203.6	18.3	7.7	0.4	195.5	96.4
San Juan, PR	12	800.6	597.0	471.5	117.4	211.6	154.6
Savannah, GA	4	2,086.2	–	–	–	2,086.2	1,083.8
Seattle, WA	10	1,224.4	293.1	42.8	147.4	1,034.2	620.7
Tacoma, WA	7	1,458.3	320.1	66.0	252.7	1,139.6	665.9
Wilmington, DE	22	171.7	–	–	–	171.7	134.9
Wilmington, NC	24	145.4	–	–	–	145.4	88.5

– Represents zero. X Not applicable. [1] Includes empty TEUS. [2] Includes other ports/waterways not shown separately.

Source: U.S. Army Corps of Engineers, *U.S. Waterborne Container Traffic for U.S. Port/Waterway in 2008*. See also <http://www.iwr.usace.army.mil/ndc/wcsc/wcsc.htm>, accessed June 2010.

U.S. Census Bureau, Statistical Abstract of the United States: 2011

Table 1087. Highway Mileage—Urban and Rural by Ownership: 1990 to 2008

[In thousands (3,880 represents 3,880,000). As of Dec. 31. Includes Puerto Rico beginning 2000]

Type and Control	1990	1995	2000	2003	2004	2005	2006	2007	2008
Total mileage [1]	**3,880**	**3,912**	**3,951**	**3,991**	**3,997**	**4,012**	**4,033**	**4,032**	**4,059**
Urban mileage [2]	757	819	859	954	994	1,023	1,043	1,044	1,079
Under state control	96	112	112	127	130	144	148	145	152
Under local control [1]	661	706	746	828	862	874	890	894	920
Rural mileage	3,123	3,093	3,092	3,036	3,003	2,989	2,990	2,988	2,980
Under state control	703	691	664	653	650	637	635	634	633
Under local control [1]	2,242	2,231	2,311	2,263	2,236	2,228	2,231	2,228	2,223
Under federal control	178	170	117	120	118	123	123	126	124

[1] Includes state park, state toll, other state agency, other local agency and other roadways not identified by ownership.
[2] Roadways in federal parks, forest, and reservations that are not part of the state and local highway system.

Source: U.S. Federal Highway Administration, *Highway Statistics*, annual. See <http://www.fhwa.dot.gov/policy/ohpi/hss /index.cfm>.

Table 1088. Highway Mileage by State—Functional Systems and Urban/Rural: 2008

[As of Dec. 31. Excludes Puerto Rico. For definition of functional systems, see text, this section]

State	Total	Functional systems					Urban	Rural
		Interstate	Other freeways and expressways	Arterial	Collector	Local		
U.S.	**4,042,778**	**46,751**	**11,335**	**400,702**	**794,684**	**2,789,306**	**1,065,556**	**2,977,222**
AL	97,325	905	41	9,221	20,571	66,587	21,935	75,390
AK	15,329	1,082	–	1,518	2,807	9,922	2,341	12,988
AZ	60,440	1,168	176	5,730	8,132	45,234	22,917	37,523
AR	99,814	656	101	7,097	20,648	71,312	12,186	87,628
CA	172,511	2,460	1,537	27,367	32,158	108,989	89,029	83,482
CO	88,265	953	312	8,918	16,263	61,819	19,345	68,920
CT	21,363	346	237	2,758	3,201	14,821	15,136	6,227
DE	6,282	41	30	645	1,046	4,520	2,980	3,302
DC	1,506	13	20	266	156	1,051	1,506	–
FL	121,387	1,471	584	12,907	14,289	92,136	81,021	40,366
GA	121,873	1,242	114	14,045	22,881	83,591	38,614	83,259
HI	4,365	55	34	753	838	2,685	2,312	2,053
ID	47,790	612	–	4,197	10,458	32,523	5,662	42,128
IL	139,491	2,182	100	14,593	21,719	100,897	41,290	98,201
IN [1]	95,613	1,171	163	8,290	22,518	63,471	24,315	71,298
IA	114,223	781	–	9,748	31,558	72,136	11,307	102,916
KS	140,611	874	187	9,523	33,541	96,486	12,751	127,860
KY	78,748	762	67	5,867	16,114	55,938	12,535	66,213
LA	61,095	906	50	5,538	10,042	44,559	16,335	44,760
ME	22,828	366	20	2,177	5,937	14,328	2,991	19,837
MD	31,386	481	294	3,790	5,053	21,768	17,333	14,053
MA	36,105	573	314	6,165	4,834	24,219	28,127	7,978
MI	121,667	1,243	329	14,677	24,444	80,974	35,814	85,853
MN [2]	138,242	918	174	13,438	30,489	93,223	20,628	117,614
MS	74,887	698	67	7,522	15,537	51,063	10,958	63,929
MO	129,718	1,181	403	10,215	24,953	92,966	22,953	106,765
MT	74,173	1,192	–	6,036	16,223	50,722	3,057	71,116
NE	93,615	481	21	8,104	20,751	64,258	6,318	87,297
NV	33,907	571	69	3,082	4,995	25,190	7,167	26,740
NH	16,005	225	56	1,533	2,741	11,450	4,908	11,097
NJ	38,753	431	404	5,759	4,152	28,007	31,456	7,297
NM	68,384	1,000	5	5,111	8,535	53,733	7,998	60,386
NY	114,471	1,705	789	13,852	20,685	77,440	48,401	66,070
NC	105,104	1,125	428	9,454	17,620	76,477	33,429	71,675
ND	86,842	571	–	5,913	11,810	68,548	1,897	84,945
OH	122,973	1,574	483	10,958	22,637	87,321	44,713	78,260
OK	113,323	933	191	8,200	25,301	78,698	16,056	97,267
OR	59,252	729	58	7,026	17,669	33,770	12,992	46,260
PA	121,771	1,792	542	13,278	19,824	86,335	45,287	76,484
RI	6,403	72	90	834	882	4,525	5,191	1,212
SC	66,255	843	84	7,146	15,088	43,094	16,422	49,833
SD	82,147	679	11	6,395	19,015	56,047	2,932	79,215
TN	92,175	1,105	153	9,062	17,873	63,982	22,455	69,720
TX	306,404	3,234	1,589	31,425	65,392	204,764	93,406	212,998
UT	44,706	936	20	3,681	7,857	32,212	11,073	33,633
VT	14,421	320	20	1,302	3,113	9,666	1,456	12,965
VA	73,902	1,119	289	8,335	14,069	50,090	23,568	50,334
WA	83,526	764	375	7,758	16,762	57,867	22,743	60,783
WV	38,452	554	10	3,474	8,610	25,804	5,360	33,092
WI	114,844	743	291	12,429	21,703	79,678	22,272	92,572
WY	28,106	913	3	3,590	11,190	12,410	2,678	25,428

– Represents zero. [1] Excludes 788 miles of Federal agency owned roads. [2] Includes 274 miles of miscoded non–Interstate functional system length or rural/urban categorization or both.

Source: U.S. Federal Highway Administration, *Highway Statistics*, annual. See also <http://www.fhwa.dot.gov/policy/ohpi /hss/index.cfm.

684 Transportation

Table 1089. Bridge Inventory—Total Deficient and Obsolete: 1997 to 2009, and by State, 2009

[As of December 2009. Based on the National Bridge Inventory program; for details, see source]

| State and year | Number of bridges | Deficient and obsolete | | | | | |
| | | Total | | Structurally deficient [1] | | Functionally obsolete [2] | |
		number	Percent	Number	Percent	Number	Percent
1997	582,751	175,885	30.2	98,475	16.9	77,410	13.3
1998	582,984	172,582	29.6	93,076	16.0	79,506	13.6
1999	585,542	170,050	29.0	88,150	15.1	81,900	14.0
2000	587,755	167,993	28.6	87,106	14.8	80,887	13.8
2001	590,066	165,099	28.0	83,630	14.2	81,469	13.8
2002	591,220	163,010	27.6	81,437	13.8	81,573	13.8
2003	592,246	160,819	27.2	79,811	13.5	81,008	13.7
2004	593,885	158,318	26.7	77,758	13.1	80,560	13.6
2005	594,616	156,177	26.3	75,871	12.8	80,306	13.5
2006	596,842	153,990	25.8	73,764	12.4	80,226	13.4
2007	599,766	152,316	25.4	72,524	12.1	79,792	13.3
2008	601,411	151,391	25.2	71,469	11.9	79,922	13.3
U.S. total, 2009	**603,245**	**149,647**	**24.8**	**71,179**	**11.8**	**78,468**	**13.0**
Alabama	15,959	3,791	23.8	1,686	10.6	2,105	13.2
Alaska	1,151	275	23.9	129	11.2	146	12.7
Arizona	7,489	879	11.7	210	2.8	669	8.9
Arkansas	12,557	2,809	22.4	933	7.4	1,876	14.9
California	24,462	7,116	29.1	3,228	13.2	3,888	15.9
Colorado	8,476	1,459	17.2	598	7.1	861	10.2
Connecticut	4,186	1,406	33.6	378	9.0	1,028	24.6
Delaware	862	145	16.8	37	4.3	108	12.5
District of Columbia	246	151	61.4	20	8.1	131	53.3
Florida	11,803	1,923	16.3	303	2.6	1,620	13.7
Georgia	14,710	2,777	18.9	949	6.5	1,828	12.4
Hawaii	1,133	493	43.5	144	12.7	349	30.8
Idaho	4,100	787	19.2	367	9.0	420	10.2
Illinois	26,263	4,165	15.9	2,373	9.0	1,792	6.8
Indiana	18,546	4,111	22.2	1,927	10.4	2,184	11.8
Iowa	24,799	6,678	26.9	5,358	21.6	1,320	5.3
Kansas	25,513	5,153	20.2	2,901	11.4	2,252	8.8
Kentucky	13,729	4,426	32.2	1,362	9.9	3,064	22.3
Louisiana	13,328	3,893	29.2	1,723	12.9	2,170	16.3
Maine	2,394	785	32.8	364	15.2	421	17.6
Maryland	5,183	1,343	25.9	372	7.2	971	18.7
Massachusetts	5,037	2,573	51.1	593	11.8	1,980	39.3
Michigan	10,906	2,732	25.1	1,467	13.5	1,265	11.6
Minnesota	13,131	1,601	12.2	1,209	9.2	392	3.0
Mississippi	17,038	4,120	24.2	2,820	16.6	1,300	7.6
Missouri	24,156	7,305	30.2	4,289	17.8	3,016	12.5
Montana	4,984	887	17.8	402	8.1	485	9.7
Nebraska	15,436	3,924	25.4	2,878	18.6	1,046	6.8
Nevada	1,749	215	12.3	44	2.5	171	9.8
New Hampshire	2,403	755	31.4	373	15.5	382	15.9
New Jersey	6,486	2,295	35.4	692	10.7	1,603	24.7
New Mexico	3,890	684	17.6	381	9.8	303	7.8
New York	17,372	6,481	37.3	2,140	12.3	4,341	25.0
North Carolina	18,006	5,124	28.5	2,442	13.6	2,682	14.9
North Dakota	4,437	933	21.0	696	15.7	237	5.3
Ohio	28,119	6,661	23.7	2,795	9.9	3,866	13.7
Oklahoma	23,712	6,902	29.1	5,286	22.3	1,616	6.8
Oregon	7,215	1,665	23.1	477	6.6	1,188	16.5
Pennsylvania	22,293	9,774	43.8	6,060	27.2	3,714	16.7
Rhode Island	739	396	53.6	163	22.1	233	31.5
South Carolina	9,253	2,040	22.0	1,238	13.4	802	8.7
South Dakota	5,920	1,469	24.8	1,231	20.8	238	4.0
Tennessee	19,939	3,932	19.7	1,246	6.2	2,686	13.5
Texas	51,136	9,431	18.4	1,752	3.4	7,679	15.0
Utah	2,905	448	15.4	169	5.8	279	9.6
Vermont	2,707	961	35.5	437	16.1	524	19.4
Virginia	13,529	3,483	25.7	1,241	9.2	2,242	16.6
Washington	7,638	2,025	26.5	405	5.3	1,620	21.2
West Virginia	7,038	2,584	36.7	1,056	15.0	1,528	21.7
Wisconsin	13,917	1,941	13.9	1,207	8.7	734	5.3
Wyoming	3,054	671	22.0	401	13.1	270	8.8
Puerto Rico	2,181	1,070	49.1	227	10.4	843	38.7

[1] Bridges are structurally deficient if they have been restricted to light vehicles, require immediate rehabilitation to remain open, or are closed. [2] Bridges are functionally obsolete if they have deck geometry, load carrying capacity, clearance or approach roadway alignment that no longer meet the criteria for the system of which the bridge is carrying a part.

Source: U.S. Federal Highway Administration, Office of Bridge Technology, "National Bridge Technology," <http://www.fhwa.dot.gov/bridge/nbi.htm>.

Transportation 685

Table 1090. Funding for Highways and Disposition of Highway–User Revenue: 1990 to 2008

[In millions of dollars (75,444 represents $75,444,000,000). Data compiled from reports of state and local authorities]

Type	1990	1995	2000	2003	2004	2005	2006	2007	2008
Total receipts	75,444	96,269	131,115	139,246	145,315	154,690	165,443	192,714	192,718
Current income	69,880	87,620	119,815	124,593	129,521	137,668	147,615	167,983	172,785
Highway-user revenues	44,346	59,331	81,335	79,280	83,006	90,343	93,648	97,916	94,152
Other taxes and fees	19,827	21,732	31,137	37,783	38,956	39,214	44,455	55,584	61,163
Investment income, other receipts. . .	5,707	6,557	7,342	7,530	7,560	8,111	9,512	14,484	17,471
Bond issue proceeds [1]	5,564	8,649	11,301	14,654	15,794	17,022	17,828	24,730	19,933
Funds drawn from or placed in reserves [2]	−36	−2,791	−8,418	4,359	2,174	−1,990	−4,382	−20,961	−10,660
Total funds available	75,408	93,478	122,697	143,605	147,489	152,700	161,061	171,753	182,058
Total disbursements	75,408	93,478	122,697	143,605	147,489	152,700	161,061	171,753	182,058
Current disbursements	72,457	88,994	117,592	136,213	139,478	144,629	153,413	163,721	173,869
Capital outlay.	35,151	44,228	61,323	70,004	70,274	75,162	78,676	81,098	91,144
Maintenance and traffic services. . . .	20,365	24,319	30,636	35,011	36,327	37,882	40,426	45,759	44,972
Administration and research	6,501	8,419	10,020	11,986	12,737	11,126	13,189	14,370	14,711
Highway law enforcement and safety.	7,235	8,218	11,031	13,501	14,322	14,066	14,482	15,074	14,565
Interest on debt	3,205	3,810	4,583	5,711	5,819	6,392	6,639	7,420	8,477
Bond retirement [1]	2,951	4,484	5,105	7,393	8,011	8,071	7,648	8,032	8,189

[1] Proceeds and redemptions of short-term notes and refunding issues are excluded. [2] Negative numbers indicate that funds were placed in reserves.

Source: U.S. Federal Highway Administration, *Highway Statistics*, annual. See also <http://www.fhwa.dot.gov/policy/ohpi/hss/index.cfm>.

Table 1091. Federal Aid to State and Local Governments for Highway Trust Fund by State: 2008

[Year ending Sept. 30. 34,913 represents $34,913,000,000]

State	Total (mil. dol.)	Per capita (dol.) [1]	State	Total (mil. dol.)	Per capita (dol.) [1]	State	Total (mil. dol.)	Per capita (dol.) [1]	State	Total (mil. dol.)	Per capita (dol.) [1]
U.S. [2]	34,913	113	ID	272	178	MT	399	412	RI	176	167
U.S. [3]	34,459	113	IL	1,243	97	NE	249	140	SC	359	80
AL	1,060	227	IN	953	149	NV	247	94	SD	239	297
AK	399	580	IA	410	137	NH	165	125	TN	679	109
AZ	600	92	KS	490	175	NJ	801	92	TX	2,578	106
AR	384	134	KY	614	143	NM	266	134	UT	302	111
CA	2,735	75	LA	427	96	NY	1,446	74	VT	146	235
CO	574	116	ME	146	110	NC	872	94	VA	846	108
CT	429	122	MD	527	93	ND	229	357	WA	724	110
DE	141	161	MA	471	72	OH	1,176	102	WV	413	228
DC	284	481	MI	988	99	OK	664	182	WI	629	112
FL	2,172	118	MN	627	120	OR	451	119	WY	208	389
GA	1,143	118	MS	493	168	PA	1,515	121			
HI	245	191	MO	854	143						

[1] Based on estimated population as of July 1. [2] Includes outlying areas and undistributed funds, not shown separately. [3] For the 50 states and the District of Columbia.

Source: U.S. Census Bureau, *Federal Aid to States for Fiscal Year, 2008,* September 2009. See also <http://www.census.gov/prod/www/abs/fas.html>.

Table 1092. State Motor Fuel Tax Receipts, 2007 and 2008, and Gasoline Tax Rates, 2008

[620 represents $620,000,000. Federal tax rate is 18.4 cents a gallon]

State	Net receipts (mil. dol.) 2007	Net receipts (mil. dol.) 2008	Tax rate, [1] 2008	State	Net receipts (mil. dol.) 2007	Net receipts (mil. dol.) 2008	Tax rate, [1] 2008	State	Net receipts (mil. dol.) 2007	Net receipts (mil. dol.) 2008	Tax rate, [1] 2008
AL	620	666	18.00	KY	563	609	22.50	ND	124	144	23.00
AK	31	30	8.00	LA	640	598	20.00	OH	1,877	1,840	28.00
AZ	717	708	18.00	ME	233	240	28.40	OK	411	371	17.00
AR	462	464	21.50	MD	755	752	23.50	OR	397	398	24.00
CA	3,266	3,254	18.00	MA	668	665	21.00	PA	2,107	2,106	30.00
CO	568	555	22.00	MI	1,010	972	19.00	RI	146	146	30.00
CT	677	678	25.00	MN	659	664	22.50	SC	532	521	16.00
DE	117	118	23.00	MS	431	419	18.40	SD	128	129	22.00
DC	27	23	20.00	MO	704	710	17.00	TN	850	833	20.00
FL	2,233	2,215	15.60	MT	191	194	27.75	TX	3,065	3,043	20.00
GA	934	997	7.50	NE	332	304	26.00	UT	369	364	24.50
HI	85	85	17.00	NV	521	308	24.00	VT	93	88	21.00
ID	233	219	25.00	NH	152	153	19.60	VA	927	935	17.50
IL	1,333	1,314	19.00	NJ	590	588	10.50	WA	1,107	1,168	37.50
IN	880	856	18.00	NM	289	[2] 289	18.88	WV	316	359	32.20
IA	441	435	21.00	NY	2,198	1,607	24.45	WI	986	980	30.90
KS	440	424	24.00	NC	1,654	1,573	30.15	WY	104	106	14.00

[1] State gasoline tax rates in cents per gallon. In effect December 31. [2] 2007 data.

Source: U.S. Federal Highway Administration, *Highway Statistics*, annual. See also <http://www.fhwa.dot.gov/policy/ohpi/hss/index.cfm>.

686 Transportation

Table 1093. Public Obligations for Highways—Changes in Indebtedness During the Year: 1995 to 2008

[In millions of dollars (37,449 represents $37,449,000,000). Table summarizes state indebtedness from all state bond issues, including the toll facility issues and the state issues for local roads. This table is compiled from reports of state authorities. Table also summarizes the change in status of the highway obligations of local governments including toll authorities]

Item	1995	2000	2003	2004	2005	2006	2007	2008
STATE GOVERNMENT								
Obligations outstanding, beginning of year . . .	37,449	56,264	72,175	80,513	82,476	89,642	89,899	102,039
Obligations issued	4,718	9,067	16,571	13,344	19,784	15,651	20,924	20,769
Obligations retired	2,940	3,897	11,541	8,291	14,072	8,780	7,108	12,183
Obligations outstanding, end of year	39,228	61,434	77,205	85,565	88,187	96,513	103,715	110,625
LOCAL GOVERNMENT [1,2]								
Obligations outstanding, beginning of year . . .	26,393	34,904	40,901	42,733	44,406	47,346	50,092	(NA)
Bonds outstanding, beginning of year	25,613	34,229	40,091	41,979	43,403	46,344	48,854	(NA)
Bonds outstanding, end of year	29,505	34,949	41,979	44,368	46,168	49,130	51,049	(NA)
Obligations outstanding, end of year	30,295	35,557	42,734	45,331	47,170	50,366	52,336	(NA)

NA Not available. [1] Short-term notes data not shown. The data are included in beginning and ending year obligations. [2] The number of local government data estimated varied year to year.

Source: U.S. Federal Highway Administration, *Highway Statistics*, annual. See also <http://www.fhwa.dot.gov/policy/ohpi/hss/index.cfm>.

Table 1094. State Disbursements for Highways by State: 1995 to 2008

[In millions of dollars (67,615 represents $67,615,000,000). Comprise disbursements from current revenues or loans for construction, maintenance, interest and principal payments on highway bonds, transfers to local units, and miscellaneous. Includes transactions by state toll authorities. Excludes amounts allocated for collection expenses and nonhighway purposes, and mass transit]

State	1995	2000	2003	2004	2005	2006	2007	2008
United States	67,615	89,832	109,403	104,677	116,517	117,048	130,306	139,584
Alabama	1,002	1,246	1,572	1,562	1,519	1,684	1,752	1,916
Alaska	438	501	618	623	643	654	710	730
Arizona	1,199	2,040	2,453	2,569	2,458	2,662	2,335	2,806
Arkansas	666	817	1,176	1,219	1,078	1,134	1,036	1,051
California	5,966	6,750	9,349	7,967	8,308	10,571	13,288	14,697
Colorado	922	1,392	1,788	1,870	1,652	1,490	1,601	1,695
Connecticut	1,153	1,304	1,743	1,677	1,434	1,223	1,265	1,370
Delaware	441	595	929	798	1,104	804	676	600
District of Columbia	140	244	368	369	327	287	334	335
Florida	3,421	4,208	6,664	5,804	7,369	7,725	8,069	8,698
Georgia	1,437	1,567	1,756	1,935	2,070	2,655	2,878	3,817
Hawaii	060	272	375	314	506	323	352	444
Idaho	350	492	547	568	608	622	758	802
Illinois	3,006	3,447	4,595	4,289	4,201	4,974	5,424	6,299
Indiana	1,433	1,932	2,445	2,578	2,235	2,416	3,251	2,732
Iowa	1,078	1,494	1,419	1,401	1,392	1,515	1,564	1,505
Kansas	1,019	1,206	1,891	1,387	1,394	1,521	1,414	1,487
Kentucky	1,397	1,651	2,152	1,907	1,723	1,635	2,194	2,404
Louisiana	1,198	1,301	1,498	1,576	1,387	1,866	1,923	2,488
Maine	379	488	579	702	616	628	684	739
Maryland	1,289	1,599	1,885	1,831	2,049	2,304	2,689	2,747
Massachusetts	2,501	3,524	3,547	3,612	3,196	2,723	2,815	2,898
Michigan	1,974	2,748	2,799	2,930	3,561	3,263	3,240	3,269
Minnesota	1,210	1,692	1,969	1,995	2,131	2,143	2,168	2,352
Mississippi	662	1,039	1,014	1,087	1,081	1,272	1,647	1,346
Missouri	1,313	1,818	2,120	2,135	2,069	2,430	3,955	2,545
Montana	388	474	578	657	664	696	622	651
Nebraska	578	745	839	859	876	882	1,436	1,352
Nevada	484	651	807	1,045	865	1,144	1,063	906
New Hampshire	328	387	453	389	389	524	693	681
New Jersey	2,102	4,503	6,364	3,849	7,119	5,561	4,018	3,921
New Mexico	535	1,162	862	1,164	911	942	942	860
New York	4,584	5,307	6,592	6,094	9,638	5,659	7,459	7,537
North Carolina	1,871	2,621	3,013	3,557	3,698	3,330	3,385	3,584
North Dakota	270	385	379	388	456	506	441	471
Ohio	2,637	3,351	3,660	3,657	4,040	4,251	4,418	4,631
Oklahoma	828	1,417	1,379	1,175	1,163	2,001	1,282	1,634
Oregon	888	1,010	1,183	1,000	1,628	1,254	1,736	1,364
Pennsylvania	3,153	4,517	5,258	4,283	4,567	5,537	5,999	5,956
Rhode Island	290	256	299	373	407	488	494	419
South Carolina	668	970	1,191	1,254	1,360	1,476	1,472	1,470
South Dakota	286	466	441	455	466	491	402	451
Tennessee	1,230	1,440	1,661	1,549	1,718	1,658	1,657	1,771
Texas	3,593	5,665	6,758	7,134	8,918	9,101	13,136	15,948
Utah	431	1,072	879	1,871	986	1,128	1,335	1,229
Vermont	194	287	312	297	310	335	368	395
Virginia	2,107	2,678	3,419	3,002	3,384	3,195	3,228	3,875
Washington	1,909	1,871	2,288	2,469	2,625	2,656	3,057	3,901
West Virginia	781	1,170	1,169	1,056	1,425	1,117	1,057	1,208
Wisconsin	1,252	1,663	1,904	1,942	2,363	2,161	2,270	2,092
Wyoming	272	396	468	458	429	434	484	574

Source: U.S. Federal Highway Administration, *Highway Statistics*, annual. See also <http://www.fhwa.dot.gov/policy/ohpi/hss/index.cfm>.

Table 1095. State Motor Vehicle Registrations: 1990 to 2008

[In thousands (188,798 represents 188,798,000). Compiled principally from information obtained from state authorities, but it was necessary to draw on other sources and to make numerous estimates in order to complete series. Excludes motorcycles; see Table 1097]

Item	1990	1995	2000	2005	2006	2007	2008
All motor vehicles.........	**188,798**	**201,530**	**221,475**	**241,194**	**244,166**	**247,265**	**248,165**
Private and commercial.......	185,541	197,941	217,567	237,140	240,059	243,094	243,953
Publicly owned..............	3,257	3,589	3,908	4,054	4,106	4,170	4,212
Automobiles [1]...............	133,700	128,387	133,621	136,568	135,400	135,933	137,080
Private and commercial.......	132,164	126,900	132,247	135,192	134,012	134,510	135,638
Publicly owned..............	1,536	1,487	1,374	1,376	1,388	1,423	1,442
Buses.......................	627	686	746	807	822	834	843
Private and commercial.......	275	288	314	331	339	345	350
Publicly owned..............	351	398	432	476	483	490	493
Trucks [1]	54,470	72,458	87,108	103,819	107,944	110,497	110,242
Private and commercial.......	53,101	70,754	85,005	101,616	105,708	108,239	107,965
Publicly owned..............	1,369	1,704	2,103	2,203	2,235	2,258	2,277

[1] Trucks include pickups, panels, and delivery vans. Personal passenger vans, passenger minivans, and utility-type vehicles are no longer included in automobiles but are included in trucks.

Source: U.S. Federal Highway Administration, *Highway Statistics*, annual. See also <http://www.fhwa.dot.gov/policy/ohpi/hss/index.cfm>.

Table 1096. Alternative Fueled Vehicles and Estimated Consumption of Vehicle Fuels by Fuel Type: 2005 to 2008

[In thousands, (420,778 represents 420,778,000). Vehicles in use do not include concept and demonstration vehicles that are not ready for delivery to end users. Vehicles in use represent accumulated acquisitions, less retirements, as of the end of each calendar year]

Vehicles and fuel consumption	Unit	2005	2006	2007	2008
ALTERNATIVE FUELED VEHICLES IN USE					
Total....................................	Number	592,125	634,562	695,766	775,667
Compressed Natural Gas (CNG)..........	Number	117,699	116,131	114,391	113,973
Electric [1].............................	Number	51,398	53,526	55,730	56,901
Ethanol, 85 percent (E85) [2, 3].........	Number	246,363	297,099	364,384	450,327
Hydrogen...............................	Number	119	159	223	313
Liquefied Natural Gas (LNG).............	Number	2,748	2,798	2,781	3,101
Liquefied Petroleum Gas (LPG)..........	Number	173,795	164,846	158,254	151,049
Other fuels [4].........................	Number	3	3	3	3
FUEL CONSUMPTION					
Alternative fuels:......................	1,000 gal.(g-e-g) [5] ...	420,778	417,803	414,715	430,329
Compressed Natural Gas (CNG)..........	1,000 gal.(g-e-g) [5] ...	166,878	172,011	178,565	189,358
Electric [1].............................	1,000 gal.(g-e-g) [5] ...	5,219	5,104	5,037	5,050
Ethanol, 85 percent (E85) [2]...........	1,000 gal.(g-e-g) [5] ...	38,074	44,041	54,091	62,464
Hydrogen...............................	1,000 gal.(g-e-g) [5] ...	25	41	66	117
Liquefied Natural Gas (LNG).............	1,000 gal.(g-e-g) [5] ...	22,409	23,474	24,594	25,554
Liquefied Petroleum Gas (LPG)..........	1,000 gal.(g-e-g) [5] ...	188,171	173,130	152,360	147,784
Other fuels [4].........................	1,000 gal.(g-e-g) [5] ...	2	2	2	2
Biodiesel..............................	1,000 gal.(g-e-g) [5] ...	93,281	267,623	367,764	324,329
Oxygenates:					
Methyl Tertiary Butyl Ether (MTBE)........	1,000 gal.(g-e-g) [5] ...	1,654,500	435,000	–	–
Ethanol in Gasohol	1,000 gal.(g-e-g) [5] ...	2,756,663	3,729,168	4,694,304	6,442,781
Total alternative and replacement fuels......	1,000 gal.(g-e-g) [5] ...	4,925,222	4,849,594	5,476,783	7,197,439
FUEL CONSUMPTION IN NATIVE UNITS					
Alternative fuels:					
Compressed Natural Gas (CNG)..........	million cubic feet	20,106	20,724	21,514	22,814
Electric [1].............................	1,000 kwh	173,967	170,133	167,900	168,333
Ethanol, 85 percent (E85) [2]...........	1,000 gallons.......	52,881	61,168	75,126	86,756
Hydrogen...............................	1,000 kilograms.....	23	37	60	107
Liquefied Natural Gas (LNG).............	1,000 gallons.......	33,953	35,567	37,264	38,718
Liquefied Petroleum Gas (LPG)..........	1,000 gallons.......	254,285	233,959	205,892	199,708
Biodiesel..............................	1,000 gallons.......	90,827	260,584	358,156	315,796
Oxygenates:					
Methyl Tertiary Butyl Ether (MTBE)........	1,000 gallons.......	2,035,320	534,912	–	–
Ethanol in Gasohol	1,000 gallons.......	4,013,679	5,429,217	6,885,690	9,435,428
Total alternative and replacement fuels......	(X)	(X)	(X)	(X)	(X)

– Represents zero. X Not applicable. [1] Excludes gasoline-electric and diesel-electric hybrids because the input fuel is gasoline or diesel rather than an alternative transportation fuel. [2] The remaining portion of E85 percent ethanol is gasoline. Consumption data include the gasoline portion of the fuel. [3] For 2008, the EIA estimates that the number of E85 vehicles that are capable of operating on E85, gasoline, or both, is about 7.1 million. Many of these alternative-fueled vehicles (AFVs) are sold and used as traditional gasoline-powered vehicles. In this table, AFVs in use include only those E85 vehicles believed to be used as AFVs. These are primarily fleet-operated vehicles. [4] May include P-Series fuel or any other fuel designated by the Secretary of Energy as an alternative fuel in accordance with the Energy Policy Act of 1995. [5] Gasoline equivalent gallons.

Source: U.S. Energy Information Administration, "Alternatives to Traditional Transportation Fuels," <http://www.eia.doe.gov/cneaf/alternate/page/atftables/afv_atf.html>.

688 Transportation

Table 1097. State Motor Vehicle Registrations, 1990 to 2008, Motorcycle Registrations and Licensed Drivers by State: 2008

[In thousands (188,798 represents 188,798,000). Motor vehicle registrations cover publicly, privately, and commercially owned vehicles. For uniformity, data have been adjusted to a calendar-year basis as registration years in states differ; figures represent net numbers where possible, excluding reregistrations and nonresident registrations. See also Table 1095]

State	Motor vehicle registrations [1]						2008		Motor cycle registra-tions, [2] 2008	Licensed drivers, 2008
	1990	1995	2000	2005	2006	2007	Total	Auto mobiles (incl. taxis)		
U.S.	188,798	201,530	221,475	241,194	244,166	247,265	248,165	137,080	7,706	208,321
AL	3,744	3,553	3,960	4,545	4,630	4,678	4,730	2,220	127	3,754
AK	477	542	594	673	675	680	691	243	28	503
AZ	2,825	2,873	3,795	3,972	4,182	4,372	4,373	2,235	134	4,316
AR	1,448	1,613	1,840	1,940	1,994	2,010	2,041	957	71	2,055
CA	21,926	22,432	27,698	32,487	33,182	33,935	33,483	19,919	741	23,698
CO	3,155	2,812	3,626	1,808	1,808	1,707	1,618	735	118	3,606
CT	2,623	2,622	2,853	3,059	3,052	3,047	3,094	2,018	65	2,883
DE	526	592	630	737	813	851	868	462	24	652
DC	262	243	242	237	219	218	224	171	1	374
FL	10,950	10,369	11,781	15,691	16,374	16,474	16,462	8,180	667	14,034
GA	5,489	6,120	7,155	8,063	8,286	8,513	8,570	4,260	187	6,257
HI	771	802	738	948	1,009	993	945	488	51	885
ID	1,054	1,043	1,178	1,374	1,275	1,282	1,318	535	64	1,038
IL	7,873	8,973	8,973	9,458	9,876	9,757	9,794	5,780	332	8,261
IN	4,366	5,072	5,571	4,955	4,955	4,956	5,848	3,136	204	5,550
IA	2,632	2,814	3,106	3,398	3,346	3,360	3,431	1,798	182	1,990
KS	2,012	2,085	2,296	2,368	2,389	2,429	2,449	884	84	2,022
KY	2,909	2,631	2,826	3,428	3,558	3,547	3,604	1,973	65	2,933
LA	2,995	3,286	3,557	3,819	3,873	3,927	3,979	1,957	68	2,998
ME	977	967	1,024	1,075	1,072	1,080	1,074	562	55	1,006
MD	3,607	3,654	3,848	4,322	4,488	4,510	4,525	2,651	79	3,787
MA	3,726	4,502	5,265	5,420	5,385	5,367	5,328	3,236	153	4,674
MI	7,209	7,674	8,436	8,247	8,154	8,192	7,945	4,388	270	7,118
MN	3,508	3,882	4,630	4,647	4,705	4,756	4,783	2,544	248	3,190
MS	1,875	2,144	2,289	1,978	1,998	2,008	2,035	1,155	28	1,936
MO	3,905	4,255	4,580	4,589	4,957	4,917	4,866	2,621	99	4,197
MT	783	968	1,026	1,009	1,067	949	927	376	112	739
NE	1,384	1,467	1,619	1,703	1,733	1,739	1,757	817	43	1,346
NV	853	1,047	1,220	1,349	1,367	1,424	1,417	699	65	1,679
NH	946	1,122	1,052	1,174	1,060	1,185	1,214	650	81	1,031
NJ [3]	5,652	5,906	6,390	6,262	5,958	6,247	6,247	3,827	163	5,782
NM	1,301	1,484	1,529	1,548	1,581	1,599	1,570	692	47	1,365
NY	10,196	10,274	10,235	11,863	11,284	11,495	11,089	8,576	340	11,285
NC	5,162	5,682	6,223	6,148	6,301	6,317	6,249	3,572	122	6,457
ND	630	695	694	695	712	711	717	347	31	473
OH	8,410	9,810	10,467	10,634	10,829	10,848	10,933	6,413	369	7,962
OK	2,649	2,856	3,014	3,725	3,202	3,225	3,292	1,654	116	2,302
OR	2,445	2,785	3,022	2,897	2,981	3,088	3,106	1,463	102	2,856
PA	7,071	8,481	9,260	9,804	9,894	9,938	10,366	6,086	397	8,646
RI	672	699	760	812	806	797	794	491	32	748
SC	2,521	2,833	3,095	3,339	3,454	3,521	3,604	1,997	103	3,185
SD	704	709	793	854	844	865	907	347	58	597
TN	4,444	5,400	4,820	4,980	5,091	5,340	5,098	2,834	151	4,451
TX	12,800	13,682	14,070	17,470	17,538	18,072	18,208	8,831	435	15,374
UT	1,206	1,447	1,628	2,210	2,236	2,320	2,439	1,192	58	1,687
VT	462	492	515	508	588	565	581	307	28	542
VA	4,938	5,613	6,046	6,591	6,636	6,614	6,526	3,881	83	5,301
WA	4,257	4,503	5,116	5,598	5,689	5,758	5,980	3,299	234	4,954
WV	1,225	1,425	1,442	1,352	1,441	1,413	1,402	700	48	1,361
WI	3,815	3,993	4,366	4,725	4,971	5,018	4,999	2,659	310	4,076
WY	528	601	586	646	645	652	664	261	31	404

[1] Automobiles, trucks, and buses (excludes motorcycles). Excludes vehicles owned by military services. [2] Private and commercial. [3] 2007 data is used for 2008.

Source: U.S. Federal Highway Administration, *Highway Statistics*, annual. See also <http://www.fhwa.dot.gov/policy/ohpi/hss/hsspubs.htm>.

U.S. Census Bureau, Statistical Abstract of the United States: 2011

Table 1098. Roadway Congestion by Urbanized Area: 2007

[16,437 represents 16,437,000. Various federal, state, and local information sources were used to develop the database with the primary source being the Federal Highway Administration's Highway Performance Monitoring System]

Urbanized area	Freeway daily vehicle miles of travel		Annual person hours of delay		Annual congestion cost [1]		
	Total miles (1,000)	Per lane— mile of freeway	Total hours (1,000)	Per person [2]	Per person (dol.)	Delay and fuel cost (mil. dol.)	Fuel wasted (gal. per person)
Total, average	**16,437**	**16,239**	**39,915**	**22**	**472**	**842**	**15**
Akron, OH	5,530	12,860	3,031	5	102	63	4
Albany-Schenectady, NY	7,005	11,390	6,082	10	220	131	6
Albuquerque, NM	4,875	14,552	11,095	19	416	244	12
Allentown-Bethlehem, PA-NJ	4,935	11,892	7,571	12	247	154	7
Atlanta, GA	47,830	18,943	135,335	30	671	2,981	22
Austin, TX	9,400	16,068	22,777	22	455	471	15
Baltimore, MD	26,670	17,096	56,964	25	550	1,276	18
Beaumont, TX	2,400	11,707	1,425	6	126	28	4
Birmingham, AL	9,715	14,287	12,605	18	373	267	12
Boston, MA-NH-RI	40,000	15,686	91,052	22	475	1,996	15
Bridgeport-Stamford, CT-NY	10,550	17,438	16,077	18	400	350	15
Buffalo, NY	6,760	10,400	6,185	5	119	134	3
Cape Coral, FL	1,845	16,773	7,451	16	331	152	9
Charleston-North, Charleston, SC	3,645	13,500	9,944	21	431	207	13
Charlotte, NC-SC	11,775	14,905	24,237	23	491	525	15
Chicago, IL-IN	55,150	18,507	189,201	22	498	4,207	15
Cincinnati, OH-KY-IN	18,990	15,377	23,832	14	304	508	10
Cleveland, OH	18,120	12,851	12,037	7	134	241	5
Colorado Springs, CO	4,065	12,318	6,457	13	253	129	8
Columbus, OH	15,210	15,844	20,428	17	346	424	12
Dallas-Fort, Worth-Arlington, TX	55,300	17,390	140,744	32	641	2,849	22
Dayton, OH	7,360	13,027	5,800	8	161	120	5
Denver-Aurora, CO	20,395	15,934	61,345	28	569	1,240	19
Detroit, MI	32,780	17,117	116,981	29	610	2,472	19
El Paso, TX-NM	5,505	12,233	7,185	10	210	147	7
Fresno, CA	3,740	12,678	7,032	11	236	151	7
Grand Rapids, MI	5,090	11,311	7,324	12	247	148	7
Hartford, CT	10,840	13,722	10,147	11	227	203	8
Honolulu, HI	6,275	15,120	10,076	14	283	199	10
Houston, TX	48,000	18,824	123,915	32	651	2,482	23
Indianapolis, IN	13,000	14,444	23,505	22	488	522	15
Jacksonville, FL	12,460	15,974	22,491	22	439	457	15
Kansas City, MO-KS	21,015	10,917	12,703	8	175	267	5
Las Vegas, NV	11,510	20,017	34,521	25	502	705	17
Los Angeles-Long Beach-Santa Ana, CA	140,815	23,806	485,022	38	807	10,328	29
Louisville, KY-IN	12,085	15,106	19,015	21	447	409	14
Memphis, TN-MS-AR	8,640	13,292	14,633	14	301	311	9
Miami, FL	41,035	19,494	145,608	27	545	2,955	19
Milwaukee, WI	11,055	14,740	14,860	10	210	307	7
Minneapolis-St. Paul, MN	28,385	17,308	55,287	22	455	1,148	15
Nashville-Davidson, TN	14,150	13,349	20,215	20	428	426	13
New Haven, CT	7,565	14,410	5,728	10	208	117	8
New Orleans, LA	5,340	14,240	11,327	10	222	244	6
New York-Newark, NY-NJ-CT	119,240	16,527	379,328	21	449	8,180	13
Oklahoma City, OK	9,770	12,855	12,826	15	294	257	9
Omaha, NE-IA	4,140	13,143	9,298	14	285	184	9
Orlando, FL	13,540	15,563	41,791	30	605	850	20
Oxnard-Ventura, CA	7,125	18,038	14,258	21	435	298	15
Pensacola, FL-AL	1,520	10,857	5,469	15	300	106	9
Philadelphia, PA-NJ-DE-MD	36,400	15,167	112,074	21	436	2,316	13
Phoenix, AZ	29,450	19,186	80,456	23	552	1,891	17
Pittsburgh, PA	12,405	9,729	15,334	8	168	304	5
Portland, OR-WA	13,625	17,357	34,418	19	395	712	13
Providence, RI-MA	11,735	12,825	19,937	16	310	386	10
Raleigh-Durham, NC	11,300	14,037	19,588	19	411	421	12
Richmond, VA	11,960	11,390	10,212	11	216	202	7
Riverside-San Bernardino, CA	24,210	21,713	48,135	24	534	1,083	19
Sacramento, CA	15,955	19,339	39,197	21	433	806	15
Salem, OR	1,505	12,040	2,069	9	177	41	5
Salt Lake City, UT	7,945	13,939	14,557	15	294	287	10
San Antonio, TX	18,300	16,561	31,026	21	428	621	15
San Diego, CA	38,400	19,296	85,392	29	605	1,786	22
San Francisco-Oakland, CA	49,850	20,101	129,393	29	597	2,675	21
San Jose, CA	16,680	18,330	51,070	30	594	1,013	21
Sarasota-Bradenton, FL	2,575	15,606	9,030	14	264	176	8
Seattle, WA	30,670	16,578	73,636	24	513	1,591	16
St. Louis, MO-IL	29,610	12,600	32,863	15	315	697	9
Tampa-St. Petersburg, FL	14,100	15,932	61,008	26	519	1,205	17
Toledo, OH-MI	4,025	12,015	3,916	8	160	83	5
Tucson, AZ	3,510	14,040	17,321	22	508	393	14
Tulsa, OK	7,140	9,520	9,826	12	237	192	7
Virginia Beach, VA	13,115	13,878	24,665	16	324	501	11
Washington, DC-VA-MD	39,045	18,817	133,862	31	638	2,762	21

[1] Value of extra time (delay) and the extra fuel consumed by vehicles traveling at slower speeds. Fuel cost per gallon is the average price for each state. [2] The hours of extra travel time divided by the number of urban area peak period travelers. This is an annual measure indicating the sum of all extra travel time that would occur during the year for the average traveler.

Source: Texas Transportaton Institute, College Station, Texas, *2009 Urban Mobility Study,* Summer 2009 (copyright). See also <http://mobility.tamu.edu/ums/>.

Table 1099. Commuting to Work by State: 2008

[In percent, except as indicated (143,996 represents 143,996,000). For workers 16 years old and over. The American Community Survey universe includes the household population and the population living in institutions, college dormitories, and other group quarters. Based on a sample and subject to sampling variability; see Appendix III]

State	Total workers (1,000)	Commuted by car, truck, or van		Used public transportation [1]	Walked	Used other means [2]	Worked at home	Mean travel time to work (min.)
		Drove alone	Car-pooled					
U.S.	143,996	75.5	10.7	5.0	2.8	1.8	4.1	25.5
AL	2,052	83.0	11.8	0.5	1.3	1.1	2.3	24.0
AK	341	66.2	14.4	1.7	7.1	4.6	5.9	18.4
AZ	2,901	75.3	13.1	2.3	1.9	2.5	4.9	25.0
AR	1,253	80.2	12.6	0.4	2.0	1.5	3.3	21.3
CA	16,809	72.7	11.9	5.3	2.8	2.5	4.8	27.0
CO	2,552	73.7	11.3	3.4	2.7	2.6	6.3	24.6
CT	1,748	78.7	8.8	4.4	2.9	1.3	4.1	25.1
DE	416	78.6	10.6	3.8	2.4	1.7	3.0	25.0
DC	303	37.2	6.6	35.7	12.1	3.7	4.7	29.5
FL	8,277	79.4	10.3	2.0	1.5	2.3	4.5	25.9
GA	4,508	77.7	11.9	2.4	1.5	1.8	4.8	27.0
HI	656	65.7	16.2	5.9	4.2	3.4	4.6	26.1
ID	714	74.1	12.9	1.0	3.2	3.6	5.3	20.2
IL	6,216	73.3	9.4	8.7	3.0	1.6	4.0	28.5
IN	3,029	81.9	10.1	1.1	2.3	1.5	3.1	23.2
IA	1,569	77.9	11.0	1.2	4.1	1.4	4.4	18.5
KS	1,436	80.9	10.3	0.5	2.6	1.5	4.2	19.1
KY	1,879	81.2	11.3	1.2	2.4	1.0	2.9	22.6
LA	1,959	81.5	10.9	1.3	2.0	1.9	2.4	25.3
ME	650	77.3	10.9	0.7	4.0	1.8	5.2	23.3
MD	2,911	73.2	10.8	8.5	2.3	1.3	3.8	31.5
MA	3,307	72.3	8.6	8.9	4.6	1.7	3.9	27.3
MI	4,461	82.2	9.4	1.4	2.2	1.2	3.5	24.0
MN	2,778	77.7	9.4	3.4	2.9	1.7	4.9	22.6
MS	1,241	81.7	12.3	0.4	1.7	1.7	2.2	24.1
MO	2,846	79.8	11.1	1.0	2.0	1.2	4.2	23.8
MT	477	72.8	11.4	1.1	5.5	2.7	6.5	17.9
NE	944	79.7	10.2	0.7	3.1	1.3	4.9	18.0
NV	1,258	76.8	12.1	3.7	2.4	2.0	3.0	24.0
NH	701	81.0	8.4	0.8	3.3	1.4	5.1	26.0
NJ	4,285	71.7	9.1	10.3	3.3	2.2	3.3	30.1
NM	891	76.6	12.7	1.2	2.6	2.4	4.5	21.9
NY	9,215	53.7	7.7	26.7	6.3	1.7	3.9	31.6
NC	4,371	80.0	11.5	1.1	1.7	1.3	4.3	23.4
ND	348	77.8	10.0	0.6	3.7	1.7	6.1	16.0
OH	5,447	82.6	8.9	1.9	2.2	1.2	3.3	22.9
OK	1,696	80.5	11.9	0.4	2.0	1.7	3.6	21.2
OR	1,796	71.7	10.0	4.5	3.9	3.2	5.9	22.5
PA	5,912	76.2	9.7	5.3	4.0	1.3	3.4	25.8
RI	509	80.8	8.0	2.7	3.1	1.7	3.7	23.1
SC	2,017	81.1	10.9	0.7	1.8	1.8	3.7	23.3
SD	420	78.2	9.8	0.5	4.6	1.6	5.2	16.4
TN	2,855	82.7	10.6	0.7	1.4	1.2	3.4	24.0
TX	11,317	78.3	12.4	1.7	1.7	2.0	3.8	25.1
UT	1,299	75.0	13.1	2.4	3.0	1.9	4.6	21.3
VT	332	73.3	11.1	0.9	6.3	1.7	6.7	21.9
VA	3,927	76.7	10.9	4.3	2.3	1.5	4.3	26.9
WA	3,201	71.5	12.2	5.5	3.6	2.2	5.0	25.4
WV	767	80.9	10.9	0.8	3.1	1.4	3.0	25.4
WI	2,913	79.3	9.8	1.9	3.3	1.9	3.8	21.7
WY	279	74.9	12.7	1.3	3.9	2.4	5.0	18.7

[1] Excluding taxicabs. [2] Includes taxicabs, motorcycles, bicycles, and other means.

Source: U.S. Census Bureau, 2008 American Community Survey, B08006, "Sex of Worker by Means of Transportation to Work" and R0801, "Mean Travel Time to Work of Workers 16 Years Old and Over Who Did Not Work At Home (minutes)," <http://factfinder.census.gov/>, accessed September 2009.

Table 1100. Motor Vehicle Distance Traveled by Type of Vehicle: 1970 to 2008

[1,110 represents 1,110,000,000,000. The travel data by vehicle type and stratification of trucks are estimated by the Federal Highway Administration (FHWA)]

Year	Vehicle—miles of travel (bil.)					Average miles traveled per vehicle (1,000)				
	Total [1]	Cars [1]	Buses [2]	Vans, pickups, SUVs [3]	Trucks [4]	Total [1]	Cars [1]	Buses [2]	Vans, pickups, SUVs [3]	Trucks [4]
1970........	1,110	920	4.5	123	62	10.0	10.0	12.0	8.7	13.6
1980........	1,527	1,122	6.1	291	108	9.5	8.8	11.5	10.4	18.7
1985........	1,775	1,256	4.5	391	124	10.0	9.4	7.5	10.5	20.6
1988........	2,026	1,380	5.5	502	138	10.7	10.0	8.9	11.5	22.5
1989........	2,096	1,412	5.7	536	143	10.9	10.2	9.1	11.7	22.9
1990........	2,144	1,418	5.7	575	146	11.1	10.3	9.1	11.9	23.6
1991........	2,172	1,367	5.8	649	150	11.3	10.3	9.1	12.2	24.2
1992........	2,247	1,381	5.8	707	153	11.6	10.6	9.0	12.4	25.4
1993........	2,296	1,385	6.1	746	160	11.6	10.5	9.4	12.4	26.3
1994........	2,358	1,416	6.4	765	170	11.7	10.8	9.6	12.2	25.8
1995........	2,423	1,438	6.4	790	178	11.8	11.2	9.4	12.0	26.5
1996........	2,486	1,470	6.6	817	183	11.8	11.3	9.4	11.8	26.1
1997........	2,562	1,503	6.8	851	191	12.1	11.6	9.8	12.1	27.0
1998........	2,632	1,550	7.0	868	196	12.2	11.8	9.8	12.2	25.4
1999........	2,691	1,569	7.7	901	203	12.2	11.9	10.5	12.0	26.0
2000........	2,747	1,600	7.6	923	206	12.2	11.9	10.2	11.7	25.7
2001........	2,797	1,628	7.1	943	209	11.9	11.8	9.4	11.2	26.6
2002........	2,856	1,658	6.8	966	215	12.2	12.2	9.0	11.4	27.1
2003	2,890	1,672	6.8	984	218	12.2	12.3	8.7	11.3	28.1
2004........	2,965	1,700	6.8	1,027	221	12.2	12.5	8.5	11.2	27.0
2005........	2,989	1,708	7.0	1,041	223	12.1	12.5	8.6	10.9	26.2
2006........	3,014	1,691	6.8	1,082	223	12.0	12.5	8.3	10.9	25.2
2007........	3,032	1,672	7.0	1,112	227	11.9	12.3	8.4	11.0	25.2
2008........	2,974	1,616	7.1	1,109	227	11.6	11.8	8.4	11.0	25.3

[1] Motorcycles included with cars through 1994; thereafter in total, not shown separately. [2] Includes school buses.
[3] SUV=Sport utility vehicles. [4] Includes combinations.

Source: U.S. Federal Highway Administration, *Highway Statistics*, annual. See also <http://www.fhwa.dot.gov/policy/ohpi/hss/index.cfm>.

Table 1101. Domestic Motor Fuel Consumption by Type of Vehicle: 1970 to 2008

[92.3 represents 92,300,000,000. Comprises all fuel types used for propulsion of vehicles under state motor fuels laws. Excludes federal purchases for military use. Minus sign (–) indicates decrease]

Year	Annual fuel consumption (bil. gal.)						Average miles per gallon				
	All vehicles [1]	Annual percent change [2]	Cars [1]	Buses [3]	Vans, pickups, SUVs [4]	Trucks [5]	All vehicles [1]	Cars [1]	Buses [3]	Vans, pickups, SUVs [4]	Trucks [5]
1970......	92.3	4.8	67.8	0.8	12.3	11.3	12.0	13.5	5.5	10.0	5.5
1980......	115.0	–5.9	70.2	1.0	23.8	20.0	13.3	16.0	6.0	12.2	5.4
1985......	121.3	2.2	71.7	0.8	27.4	21.4	14.6	17.5	5.4	14.3	5.8
1988......	130.1	2.0	73.5	0.9	32.7	22.9	15.6	18.8	5.8	15.4	6.0
1989......	131.9	1.4	74.1	0.9	33.3	23.5	15.9	18.0	6.0	16.1	6.1
1990......	130.8	–0.8	69.8	0.9	35.6	24.5	16.4	20.3	6.4	16.1	6.0
1991......	128.6	–1.7	64.5	0.9	38.2	25.0	16.9	21.2	6.7	17.0	6.0
1992......	132.9	3.3	65.6	0.9	40.9	25.5	16.9	21.0	6.6	17.3	6.0
1993......	137.3	3.3	67.2	0.9	42.9	26.2	16.7	20.6	6.6	17.4	6.1
1994......	140.8	2.5	68.1	1.0	44.1	27.7	16.7	20.8	6.6	17.3	6.1
1995......	143.8	2.1	68.1	1.0	45.6	29.0	16.8	21.1	6.6	17.3	6.1
1996......	147.4	2.5	69.2	1.0	47.4	29.6	16.9	21.2	6.6	17.2	6.2
1997......	150.4	2.0	69.9	1.0	49.4	29.9	17.0	21.5	6.7	17.2	6.4
1998......	155.4	3.3	71.7	1.1	50.5	32.0	16.9	21.6	6.7	17.2	6.1
1999......	161.4	3.9	73.2	1.1	52.8	33.9	16.7	21.4	6.7	17.0	6.0
2000......	162.5	0.7	73.1	1.1	52.9	35.2	16.9	21.9	6.8	17.4	5.8
2001......	163.5	0.6	73.6	1.0	53.5	35.2	17.1	22.1	6.9	17.6	5.9
2002......	168.7	3.2	75.5	1.0	55.2	36.8	16.9	22.0	6.8	17.5	5.8
2003......	170.0	0.8	75.5	1.0	60.7	32.7	17.0	22.2	7.0	16.2	6.7
2004......	173.5	2.1	75.4	1.3	63.4	33.1	17.1	22.5	5.0	16.2	6.7
2005......	174.8	0.7	77.4	1.1	58.9	37.2	17.2	22.1	6.2	17.7	6.0
2006......	175.0	0.1	75.0	1.1	60.7	38.0	17.2	22.5	5.9	17.8	5.9
2007......	176.2	0.7	74.4	1.1	61.8	38.6	17.2	22.5	6.1	18.0	5.9
2008......	170.8	–3.1	71.5	1.1	61.2	36.7	17.4	22.6	6.4	18.1	6.2

[1] Motorcycles included with cars through 1994; thereafter in total, not shown separately. [2] Change from immediate prior year.
[3] Includes school buses. [4] SUV=Sport utility vehicles. [5] Includes combinations.

Source: U.S. Federal Highway Administration, *Highway Statistics*, annual. See also <http://www.fhwa.dot.gov/policy/ohpi/hss/index.cfm>.

Table 1102. Motor Vehicle Accidents—Number and Deaths: 1980 to 2008

[17.9 represents 17,900,000]

Item	Unit	1980	1990	1995	2000	2004	2005	2006	2007	2008
ACCIDENTS										
Motor vehicle accidents [1]	Million ...	17.9	11.5	10.7	13.4	10.9	10.7	10.4	10.6	10.2
DEATHS										
Motor vehicle deaths within 1 yr. [2]	1,000	53.2	46.8	43.4	43.4	44.9	45.3	44.6	43.1	39.0
Noncollision accidents	1,000	(NA)	4.9	4.4	4.8	5.1	5.3	5.3	5.2	4.5
Collision accidents:										
With other motor vehicles	1,000	23.0	19.9	19.0	19.1	19.6	19.4	18.5	17.2	15.1
With pedestrians	1,000	9.7	7.3	6.4	5.9	6.0	6.2	6.1	5.9	5.6
With fixed objects	1,000	(NA)	13.1	12.1	12.3	13.0	13.3	13.4	13.5	12.6
Deaths within 30 days [3]	1,000	51.1	44.6	41.8	41.9	42.8	43.5	42.7	41.3	37.3
Occupants	1,000	36.8	33.9	33.1	33.5	33.3	33.1	32.1	30.5	26.7
Passenger cars	1,000	27.4	24.1	22.4	20.7	19.2	18.5	17.9	16.6	14.6
Light trucks [4]	1,000	7.5	8.6	9.6	11.5	12.7	13.0	12.8	12.5	10.8
Large trucks [4]	1,000	1.3	0.7	0.6	0.8	0.8	0.8	0.8	0.8	0.7
Buses	1,000	(Z)	(Z)	(Z)	(Z)	(Z)	0.1	(Z)	(Z)	0.1
Other/unknown	1,000	0.5	0.5	0.4	0.5	0.6	0.7	0.6	0.6	0.6
Motorcycle riders [5]	1,000	5.1	3.2	2.2	2.9	4.0	4.6	4.8	5.2	5.3
Nonoccupants	1,000	9.2	7.5	6.5	5.6	5.5	5.9	5.8	5.6	5.3
Pedestrians	1,000	8.1	6.5	5.6	4.8	4.7	4.9	4.8	4.7	4.4
Pedalcyclist	1,000	1.0	0.9	0.8	0.7	0.7	0.8	0.8	0.7	0.7
Other/unknown	1,000	0.1	0.1	0.1	0.1	0.1	0.2	0.2	0.2	0.2
Traffic death rates: [3, 6]										
Per 100 million vehicle miles	Rate.....	3.3	2.1	1.7	1.5	1.4	1.5	1.4	1.4	1.3
Per 100,000 licensed drivers	Rate.....	35.2	26.7	23.7	22.0	21.5	21.7	21.1	20.1	17.9
Per 100,000 registered vehicles	Rate.....	34.8	24.2	21.2	19.3	18.0	17.7	17.0	16.1	14.5
Per 100,000 resident population	Rate.....	22.5	17.9	15.9	14.9	14.6	14.7	14.3	13.7	12.3

NA Not available. Z Fewer than 50. [1] Covers only accidents occurring on the road. Data are estimated. Year-to-year comparisons should be made with caution. [2] Deaths that occur within 1 year of accident. Includes collision categories, not shown separately. [3] Within 30 days of accident. Source: U.S. National Highway Traffic Safety Administration, *Traffic Safety Facts*, annual; and unpublished data. See also <http://www-nrd.nhtsa.dot.gov/CATS/index.aspx>. [4] See footnotes 2 and 3 in Table 1106. [5] Includes motorized cycles. [6] Based on 30-day definition of traffic deaths.

Source: Except as noted, National Safety Council, Itasca, IL, *Injury Facts*, annual (copyright). See also <http://www.nsc.org/>.

Table 1103. Traffic Fatalities by State: 1990 to 2008

[For deaths within 30 days of the accident]

State	1990	2000	2005	2008	Fatality rate [1] 1990	Fatality rate [1] 2008	State	1990	2000	2005	2008	Fatality rate [1] 1990	Fatality rate [1] 2008
U.S.	**44,599**	**41,945**	**43,510**	**37,261**	**2.1**	**1.3**	MO	1,097	1,157	1,257	960	2.2	1.4
AL	1,121	996	1,148	966	2.6	1.6	MT	212	237	251	229	2.5	2.1
AK	98	106	73	62	2.5	1.3	NE	262	276	276	208	1.9	1.1
AZ	869	1,036	1,179	937	2.5	1.5	NV	343	323	427	324	3.4	1.6
AR	604	652	654	600	2.9	1.8	NH	158	126	166	139	1.6	1.1
CA	5,192	3,753	4,333	3,434	2.0	1.1	NJ	886	731	747	590	1.5	0.8
CO	544	681	606	548	2.0	1.2	NM	499	432	488	366	3.1	1.4
CT	385	341	278	264	1.5	0.8	NY	2,217	1,460	1,434	1,231	2.1	0.9
DE	138	123	133	121	2.1	1.4	NC	1,385	1,557	1,547	1,433	2.2	1.4
DC	48	48	48	34	1.4	0.9	ND	112	86	123	104	1.9	1.3
FL	2,891	2,999	3,518	2,978	2.6	1.5	OH	1,638	1,366	1,321	1,190	1.8	1.1
GA	1,562	1,541	1,729	1,493	2.2	1.4	OK	641	650	803	749	1.9	1.5
HI	177	132	140	107	2.2	1.0	OR	579	451	487	416	2.2	1.2
ID	244	276	275	232	2.5	1.5	PA	1,646	1,520	1,616	1,468	1.9	1.4
IL	1,589	1,418	1,363	1,043	1.9	1.0	RI	84	80	87	65	1.1	0.8
IN	1,049	886	938	814	2.0	1.2	SC	979	1,065	1,094	920	2.8	1.9
IA	465	445	450	412	2.0	1.3	SD	153	173	186	119	2.2	1.3
KS	444	461	428	385	1.9	1.3	TN	1,177	1,307	1,270	1,035	2.5	1.5
KY	849	820	985	826	2.5	1.7	TX	3,250	3,779	3,536	3,382	2.1	1.4
LA	959	938	963	912	2.5	2.0	UT	272	373	282	275	1.9	1.1
ME	213	169	169	155	1.8	1.1	VT	90	76	73	73	1.5	1.0
MD	707	588	614	591	1.7	1.1	VA	1,079	929	947	824	1.8	1.0
MA	605	433	441	363	1.3	0.7	WA	825	631	649	521	1.8	0.9
MI	1,571	1,382	1,129	980	1.9	1.0	WV	481	411	374	380	3.1	1.8
MN	566	625	559	456	1.5	0.8	WI	769	799	815	605	1.7	1.1
MS	750	949	931	783	3.1	1.8	WY	125	152	170	159	2.1	1.7

[1] Deaths per 100 million vehicle miles traveled.

Source: U.S. National Highway Traffic Safety Administration, *Traffic Safety Facts*, annual. See also <http://www-nrd.nhtsa.dot.gov/CATS/index.aspx>.

U.S. Census Bureau, Statistical Abstract of the United States: 2011

Table 1104. Fatal Motor Vehicle Accidents—National Summary: 1990 to 2008

[Based on data from the Fatality Analysis Reporting System (FARS). FARS gathers data on accidents that result in loss of human life. FARS is operated and maintained by National Highway Traffic Safety Administration's (NHTSA), National Center for Statistics and Analysis (NCSA). FARS data are gathered on motor vehicle accidents that occurred on a roadway customarily open to the public, resulting in the death of a person within 30 days of the accident. Collection of these data depend on the use of police, hospital, medical examiner/coroner, and Emergency Medical Services reports; state vehicle registration, driver licensing, and highway department files; and vital statistics documents and death certificates. See source for further detail]

Item	1990	1995	2000	2004	2005	2006	2007	2008
Fatal crashes, total	**39,836**	**37,241**	**37,526**	**38,444**	**39,252**	**38,648**	**37,435**	**34,017**
One vehicle involved	23,445	21,250	21,117	21,836	22,678	22,701	22,167	20,554
Two or more vehicles involved	16,391	15,991	16,409	16,608	16,574	15,947	15,268	13,463
Persons killed in fatal crashes [1]	**44,599**	**41,817**	**41,945**	**42,836**	**43,510**	**42,708**	**41,259**	**37,261**
Occupants	33,890	33,064	36,348	37,304	37,606	36,956	35,701	31,979
Drivers	22,854	22,370	25,567	26,871	27,491	27,348	26,570	24,175
Passengers	10,931	10,576	10,695	10,355	10,069	9,507	9,036	7,729
Other	105	118	86	78	86	101	95	75
Motorcyclist	3,244	2,227	2,897	4,028	4,576	4,837	5,174	5,290
Nonoccupants	7,465	6,526	5,597	5,532	5,864	5,752	5,504	5,282
Pedestrians	6,482	5,584	4,763	4,675	4,892	4,795	4,654	4,378
Pedalcyclists	859	833	693	727	786	772	698	716
Other	124	109	141	130	186	185	152	188
Occupants killed by vehicle type:								
Passenger cars	24,092	22,423	20,699	19,192	18,512	17,925	16,614	14,587
Mini-compact (95 inches)	3,556	2,207	1,113	599	452	416	347	269
Subcompact (95 to 99 inches)	4,753	4,584	3,660	2,718	2,536	2,228	1,931	1,653
Compact (100 to 104 inches)	5,310	6,899	7,022	6,650	6,288	6,105	5,538	4,737
Intermediate (105 to 109) inches	4,849	4,666	5,204	5,667	5,571	5,461	5,243	4,692
Full-size (110 to 114) inches	2,386	2,116	2,287	2,354	2,491	2,520	2,410	2,170
Largest (115 inches and over)	2,249	1,297	897	807	796	773	780	740
Unknown	989	654	516	397	378	422	365	326
Motorcycles and Other Motorized Cycles . . .	3,129	2,114	2,897	4,028	4,576	4,837	5,174	5,290
Motorcycles	3,014	2,001	2,783	3,827	4,418	4,679	4,986	5,040
Other motorized cycles	115	113	114	201	158	158	188	250
Light trucks [2]	8,601	9,568	11,526	12,674	13,037	12,761	12,458	10,764
Pickup	5,979	5,938	6,003	5,838	6,067	5,993	5,847	5,073
Utility	1,214	1,935	3,358	4,760	4,831	4,928	4,834	4,186
Van	1,154	1,639	2,129	2,046	2,112	1,815	1,764	1,491
Other	254	56	36	30	27	25	13	14
Large trucks [3]	705	648	754	766	804	805	805	677
Medium trucks	134	96	106	99	118	107	112	87
Heavy trucks	571	552	648	667	686	698	693	592
Buses	32	33	22	42	58	27	36	67
Other vehicles	296	307	401	512	492	500	540	520
Unknown	164	85	49	90	167	101	74	74
Persons involved in fatal crashes	**107,777**	**102,102**	**100,716**	**100,760**	**101,262**	**98,356**	**94,338**	**84,026**
Occupants	99,297	94,621	94,325	94,579	94,614	91,860	88,136	78,066
Drivers	58,893	56,164	57,280	58,395	59,220	57,846	56,019	50,186
Passengers	40,229	38,252	36,889	35,992	35,231	33,826	31,919	27,720
Other	175	205	156	192	163	188	198	160
Nonoccupants	8,480	7,481	6,391	6,181	6,648	6,496	6,202	5,960
Vehicle miles traveled (VMT) [4] (bil.)	2,144	2,423	2,747	2,965	2,989	3,014	3,032	2,974
Licensed drivers (1,000)	167,015	176,628	190,625	198,889	200,549	212,810	205,742	208,321
Registered vehicles (1,000)	184,275	197,065	217,028	237,949	245,628	251,415	255,748	257,494
Percent distribution of fatal accidents by the highest driver (BAC) in accident: [5]								
0.00 percent	54.0	62.1	62.7	64.3	63.3	62.6	62.4	62.9
0.01 to 0.07 percent	6.3	5.5	5.6	5.1	5.4	5.7	5.9	5.5
0.08 percent and over	39.4	32.1	31.4	30.4	31.1	31.4	31.5	31.4
Percent distribution of fatal accidents by the highest (BAC) in accident: [5]								
0.00 percent	49.5	57.7	58.7	60.5	59.5	58.4	58.4	58.5
0.01 to 0.07 percent	6.5	5.7	5.9	5.4	5.6	6.0	6.1	5.7
0.08 percent and over	44.0	36.7	35.4	34.2	34.9	35.6	35.6	35.8
Fatalities per 100,000 resident population								
Under 5 years old	4.90	4.30	3.70	3.16	2.94	2.83	2.46	1.96
5 to 9 years old	5.14	4.48	3.55	3.13	3.00	2.64	2.39	1.97
10 to 15 years old	7.60	7.23	5.65	5.43	4.67	4.34	4.28	3.41
16 to 20 years old	36.66	31.59	29.38	28.80	27.48	26.83	25.15	20.89
21 to 24 years old	33.47	29.68	27.02	26.66	27.73	28.08	27.07	23.39
25 to 34 years old	22.78	19.44	17.29	17.28	17.82	17.95	16.91	15.58
35 to 44 years old	16.11	15.10	15.08	14.55	15.08	14.71	14.19	12.74
45 to 54 years old	14.83	13.39	13.79	14.47	14.59	14.43	14.02	12.96
55 to 64 years old	15.00	13.92	13.61	13.19	13.88	13.29	12.59	11.98
65 to 74 years old	17.03	16.64	15.29	14.87	15.16	13.84	13.47	12.24
75 years old and over	25.45	26.09	23.29	21.36	20.47	18.68	18.07	16.37
Fatalities per 100 million VMT [4]	2.08	1.73	1.53	1.44	1.46	1.42	1.36	1.25
Fatalities per 100,000 licensed drivers	26.70	23.68	22.00	21.54	21.70	21.06	20.05	17.89
VMT [5] per registered vehicle	11,637	12,294	12,657	12,461	12,168	11,990	11,855	11,550
Fatalities per 100,000 registered vehicles	24.20	21.22	19.33	18.00	17.71	16.99	16.13	14.47
Fatal crashes per 100 million VMT [4]	2.08	1.73	1.53	1.44	1.46	1.42	1.36	1.25
Fatalities per 100,000 resident population	17.88	15.91	14.87	14.63	14.72	14.31	13.69	12.25

[1] Deaths within 30 days of the accident. Starting with 1995, total does not include motorcyclist data. [2] Trucks with a gross vehicle weight rating of 10,000 pounds or less, including pickups, vans, truck-based station wagons, and utility vehicles. [3] Trucks with a gross vehicle weight rating of over 10,000 pounds. [4] VMT = vehicle miles of travel. [5] BAC = blood alcohol concentration.

Source: U.S. National Highway Traffic Safety Administration, Fatality Analysis Reporting System, annual. See also <http://www-nrd.nhtsa.dot.gov/CATS/index.aspx>.

Table 1105. Motor Vehicle Occupants and Nonoccupants Killed and Injured: 1980 to 2008

[For deaths within 30 days of the accident. (3,231 represents 3,231,000)]

Year	Total	Occupants						Motor-cycle riders [3]	Nonoccupants			
		Total	Pas-senger cars	Light trucks [1]	Large trucks [1]	Buses	Other/un-known [2]		Total	Pedes-trian	Pedal-cyclist	Other/un-known [2]
KILLED												
1980.........	51,091	36,783	27,449	7,486	1,262	46	540	5,144	9,164	8,070	965	129
1985.........	43,825	31,479	23,212	6,689	977	57	544	4,564	7,782	6,808	890	84
1990.........	44,599	33,890	24,092	8,601	705	32	460	3,244	7,465	6,482	859	124
1995.........	41,817	33,064	22,423	9,568	648	33	392	2,227	6,526	5,584	833	109
1998.........	41,501	33,088	21,194	10,705	742	38	409	2,294	6,119	5,228	760	131
1999.........	41,717	33,392	20,862	11,265	759	59	447	2,483	5,842	4,939	754	149
2000.........	41,945	33,451	20,699	11,526	754	22	450	2,897	5,597	4,763	693	141
2001.........	42,196	33,243	20,320	11,723	708	34	458	3,197	5,756	4,901	732	123
2002.........	43,005	34,105	20,569	12,274	689	45	528	3,270	5,630	4,851	665	114
2003.........	42,884	33,627	19,725	12,546	726	41	589	3,714	5,543	4,774	629	140
2004.........	42,836	33,276	19,192	12,674	766	42	602	4,028	5,532	4,675	727	130
2005.........	43,510	33,070	18,512	13,037	804	58	659	4,576	5,864	4,892	786	186
2006.........	42,708	32,119	17,925	12,761	805	27	601	4,837	5,752	4,795	772	185
2007.........	41,259	30,527	16,614	12,458	805	36	614	5,174	5,558	4,699	701	158
2008.........	37,261	26,689	14,587	10,764	677	67	594	5,290	5,282	4,378	716	188
INJURED (1,000)												
1990.........	3,231	2,960	2,376	505	42	33	4	84	187	105	75	7
1995.........	3,465	3,246	2,469	722	30	19	4	57	162	86	67	10
1998.........	3,192	3,012	2,201	763	29	16	4	49	131	69	53	8
1999.........	3,236	3,047	2,138	847	33	22	7	50	140	85	51	3
2000.........	3,189	2,997	2,052	887	31	18	10	58	134	78	51	5
2001.........	3,033	2,841	1,927	861	29	15	9	60	131	78	45	8
2002.........	2,926	2,735	1,805	879	26	19	6	65	126	71	48	7
2003.........	2,889	2,697	1,756	889	27	18	7	67	124	70	46	8
2004.........	2,788	2,594	1,643	900	27	16	7	76	118	68	41	9
2005.........	2,699	2,494	1,573	872	27	11	10	87	118	64	45	8
2006.........	2,575	2,375	1,475	857	23	10	11	88	112	61	44	7
2007.........	2,491	2,264	1,379	841	23	12	8	103	124	70	43	10
2008.........	2,346	2120	1340	768	23	15	9	96	130	69	52	9

[1] See footnotes 2 and 3, Table 1106. [2] Includes combination trucks. [3] Includes motorized cycles.

Source: U.S. National Highway Traffic Safety Administration, *Traffic Safety Facts*, annual, and unpublished data. See also <http://www-nrd.nhtsa.dot.gov/CATS/index.aspx>.

Table 1106. Vehicles Involved in Crashes by Vehicle Type, Rollover Occurrence, and Crash Severity: 2008

[9,997.0 represents 9,997,000. Excludes motorcycles]

Crash severity by vehicle type	Total		Rollover occurrence			
			Yes		No	
	Number (1,000)	Percent	Number (1,000)	Percent	Number (1,000)	Percent
Vehicles involved in all crashes [1]	**9,997.0**	**100.0**	**266.0**	**2.7**	**9,732.0**	**97.3**
Passenger cars	5,575.0	100.0	97.0	1.7	5,477.0	98.3
Light trucks: [2]						
Pickup	1,489.0	100.0	57.0	3.8	1,431.0	96.2
Utility	1,733.0	100.0	83.0	4.8	1,651.0	95.2
Van	669.0	100.0	12.0	1.8	657.0	98.2
Other	72.0	100.0	2.0	2.2	70.0	97.8
Large truck [3]	380.0	100.0	12.0	3.1	368.0	96.9
Bus	60.0	100.0	(Z)	0.1	60.0	99.9
Other/unknown	20.0	100.0	3.0	16.0	17.0	84.0
Fatal crashes	45.0	100.0	9.6	21.3	35.5	78.7
Passenger cars	20.4	100.0	3.4	16.6	17.0	83.4
Light trucks: [2]						
Pickup	9.0	100.0	2.5	28.0	6.5	72.0
Utility	7.3	100.0	2.4	32.9	4.9	67.1
Van	2.8	100.0	4.6	16.7	2.3	83.3
Other	3.5	100.0	0.8	22.9	2.7	77.1
Large truck [3]	4.1	100.0	0.5	13.5	3.5	86.5
Bus	0.2	100.0	(Z)	6.9	0.2	93.1
Other/unknown	1.3	100.0	0.2	18.9	1.0	81.1

Z less than 50. [1] Includes injury and property-only crashes, not shown separately. [2] Trucks of 10,000 pounds gross vehicle weight rating or less, including pickups, vans, truck-based station wagons and utility vehicles. [3] Trucks over 10,000 pounds gross vehicle weight rating.

Source: U.S. National Highway Traffic Safety Administration, *Traffic Safety Facts*, annual. See also <http://www-nrd.nhtsa.dot.gov/CATS/index.aspx\>.

[Speeding consists of exceeding the posted speed limit or driving too fast for the road conditions or any speed-related violation charged (racing, driving above speed limit, speed greater than reasonable, exceeding special speed limit)]

State	Traffic fatalities, total	Total [1]	Interstate Over 55 mph	Interstate At or under 55 mph	Noninterstate 55 mph	50 mph	45 mph	40 mph	35 mph	Under 35 mph
United States	37,261	11,674	1,118	330	2,951	424	1,671	800	1,438	1,322
Alabama	966	447	25	1	106	12	137	48	41	36
Alaska	62	33	9	5	6	1	4	1	2	3
Arizona	937	373	64	9	23	13	81	46	24	44
Arkansas	600	63	3	–	21	2	15	6	12	2
California	3,434	1,141	161	23	237	44	108	97	175	118
Colorado	548	210	18	9	29	8	22	23	40	30
Connecticut	264	83	11	10	5	3	3	6	11	34
Delaware	121	36	1	3	10	14	3	3	–	2
District of Columbia	34	12	–	2	–	–	–	–	–	10
Florida	2,978	553	55	18	83	16	106	52	79	90
Georgia	1,493	309	19	16	91	4	71	11	50	23
Hawaii	107	50	–	5	4	3	5	–	18	14
Idaho	232	74	12	2	6	8	9	2	13	4
Illinois	1,043	385	47	9	154	9	43	17	32	62
Indiana	814	250	24	10	64	10	32	30	35	39
Iowa	412	41	2	–	19	3	2	3	5	4
Kansas	385	96	6	2	34	2	8	5	4	13
Kentucky	826	154	10	5	80	2	20	–	26	9
Louisiana	912	250	18	5	90	12	45	14	31	19
Maine	155	53	3	–	4	8	17	2	10	3
Maryland	591	191	10	12	32	24	7	27	30	43
Massachusetts	363	97	7	7	2	1	7	15	19	30
Michigan	980	232	28	2	122	3	16	1	15	31
Minnesota	456	134	23	6	57	1	7	4	2	23
Mississippi	783	327	30	2	125	11	55	10	38	19
Missouri	960	441	46	16	121	14	27	22	65	52
Montana	229	72	10	–	3	1	5	1	9	6
Nebraska	208	32	6	–	3	2	1	–	3	4
Nevada	324	93	11	–	8	3	22	1	15	13
New Hampshire	139	40	4	–	2	9	4	4	4	12
New Jersey	590	65	2	3	3	15	12	6	6	15
New Mexico	366	70	8	–	10	5	9	2	4	11
New York	1,231	410	9	12	144	8	34	28	18	58
North Carolina	1,433	475	28	1	240	3	126	4	45	11
North Dakota	104	27	5	–	13	1	–	–	2	3
Ohio	1,190	269	26	7	121	7	23	7	43	26
Oklahoma	749	221	27	4	26	2	61	7	15	15
Oregon	416	128	9	4	57	4	12	7	6	8
Pennsylvania	1,468	718	51	35	171	9	127	97	158	63
Rhode Island	65	20	–	–	–	1	2	1	3	9
South Carolina	920	351	35	3	96	11	86	19	52	32
South Dakota	119	37	6	1	15	1	5	–	3	–
Tennessee	1,035	243	20	9	47	14	59	20	28	40
Texas	3,382	1,422	138	54	184	49	143	108	122	136
Utah	275	98	24	–	7	6	4	12	10	8
Vermont	73	25	5	–	–	12	–	1	7	–
Virginia	824	246	20	14	105	4	39	11	23	21
Washington	521	216	13	1	21	27	14	10	58	28
West Virginia	380	97	5	1	36	–	14	2	11	12
Wisconsin	605	198	11	2	103	–	16	3	14	30
Wyoming	159	66	13	–	11	2	3	4	2	4

– Represents zero. [1] Includes fatalities that occurred on roads for which the speed limit was unknown.

Source: U.S. National Highway Traffic Safety Administration, *Traffic Safety Facts, Speeding*, annual. See also <http://www-nrd.nhtsa.dot.gov/CATS/index.aspx>.

Table 1108. Distracted Drivers—Crashes/Road Fatalities and Injuries: 2005 to 2009

["Distraction" is defined as a specific type of inattention that occurs when drivers divert their attention from the driving task to focus on some other activity instead. It is worth noting that "distraction" is a subset of "inattention" (which also includes fatigue, physical conditions of the driver, and emotional conditions of the driver). For more information, see the appendices of the report at <http://www-nrd.nhtsa.dot.gov/Pubs/811379.pdf>]

Description	2005	2008	2009	Description	2005	2008	2009
Fatal crashes [1]				Drivers	4,217	5,477	5,084
				Percentage	7	11	11
Overall:				Fatalities	4,472	5,838	5,474
Crashes	39,252	34,172	30,797	Percentage	10	16	16
Drivers	59,220	50,416	45,230	People injured in crashes: [3]			
Fatalities	43,510	37,423	33,808	Overall	2,699,000	2,346,000	2,217,000
Involving driver distraction: [2]				Involving distraction:			
Crashes	4,026	5,307	4,898	Estimate	604,000	466,000	448,000
Percentage	10	16	16	Percentage of total	22	20	20

[1] Source: NHTSA's Fatality Analysis Reporting System (FARS). [2] For multi-vehicle crashes, the crash was reported as a distracted-driving crash if at least one driver was reported as distracted. In some of these multi-vehicle crashes, multiple drivers were reported as distracted. [3] Source: National Automotive Sampling System (NASS) General Estimates System (GES).

Source: U.S. National Highway Traffic Safety Administration, *Traffic Safety Facts*, Research Note, "An Examination of Driver Distraction as Recorded in the NHTSA Databases." See also <http://www-nrd.nhtsa.dot.gov/CATS/index.aspx>.

Table 1109. Fatalities by Highest Driver Blood Alcohol Concentration (BAC) in the Crash: 1990 to 2008

[g/dl means grams per deciliter. A motor vehicle crash is considered to be alcohol-impaired if at least one driver involved in the crash is determined to have had a BAC of .08 g/dL or higher. Thus, any fatality that occurs in an alcohol-impaired crash is considered an alcohol-impaired-driving fatality. The term "alcohol-impaired" does not indicate that a crash or fatality was caused by the presence of alcohol. A person is considered to be legally impaired with a BAC of .08 g/dl or more]

Item	1990	1995	2000	2004	2005	2006	2007	2008
Total Fatalities [1]	**44,599**	**41,817**	**41,945**	**42,836**	**43,510**	**42,708**	**41,259**	**37,261**
BAC=.00								
Number	23,823	25,768	26,082	27,413	27,423	26,633	25,611	23,317
Percent	53.4	61.6	62.2	64.0	63.0	62.4	62.1	62.6
BAC=.01–.07								
Number	2,901	2,416	2,422	2,212	2,404	2,479	2,494	2,072
Percent	6.5	5.8	5.8	5.2	5.5	5.8	6.1	5.6
Alcohol-Impaired-Driving Fatalities BAC=.08+								
Number	17,705	13,478	13,324	13,099.0	13,582.0	13,491	13,041	11,773
Percent	39.7	32.2	31.8	30.6	31.2	31.6	31.6	31.6

[1] Total fatalities include those in which there was no driver or motorcycle rider present.

Source: U.S. National Highway Traffic Safety Administration, *Traffic Safety Facts*, annual; and unpublished data. See also <http://www-nrd.nhtsa.dot.gov/CATS/index.aspx>.

Table 1110. Traffic Fatalities by State and Highest Driver Blood Alcohol Concentration (BAC) in the Crash: 2008

[See headnote, Table 1109]

State	Traffic fatalities, total	(BAC=.00) Number	(BAC=.00) Percent	(BAC=.01–.07) Number	(BAC=.01–.07) Percent	Alcohol impaired driving fatalities (BAC=.08 or more) Number	Alcohol impaired driving fatalities (BAC=.08 or more) Percent	(BAC=.01 or more) Number	(BAC=.01 or more) Percent
United States	**37,261**	**23,317**	**63**	**2,072**	**6**	**11,773**	**32**	**13,846**	**37**
Alabama	966	596	62	53	5	315	33	367	38
Alaska	62	39	62	3	5	21	33	24	38
Arizona	937	594	63	63	7	266	28	329	35
Arkansas	600	392	65	34	6	171	28	205	34
California	3,434	2,227	65	170	5	1,029	30	1,198	35
Colorado	548	346	63	29	5	173	32	202	37
Connecticut	264	156	59	19	7	86	32	104	40
Delaware	121	72	60	3	3	45	37	49	40
District of Columbia	34	21	61	4	13	9	26	13	39
Florida	2,978	1,930	65	165	6	875	29	1,041	35
Georgia	1,493	997	67	73	5	416	28	489	33
Hawaii	107	56	53	8	7	42	39	50	46
Idaho	232	138	60	14	6	78	34	93	40
Illinois.	1,043	608	58	72	7	362	35	434	42
Indiana.	814	564	69	42	5	208	26	250	31
Iowa.	412	299	73	24	6	89	22	113	27
Kansas.	385	225	59	12	3	145	38	157	41
Kentucky	826	599	73	26	3	200	24	226	27
Louisiana.	912	508	56	66	7	338	37	404	44
Maine.	155	108	70	4	3	43	28	47	30
Maryland	591	405	69	34	6	152	26	186	31
Massachusetts.	363	210	58	27	8	124	34	151	42
Michigan	980	647	66	49	5	282	29	331	34
Minnesota	456	294	64	26	6	135	30	161	35
Mississippi.	783	486	62	32	4	266	34	297	38
Missouri.	960	595	62	53	6	310	32	364	38
Montana.	229	124	54	12	5	91	40	103	45
Nebraska.	208	132	63	20	10	55	27	75	36
Nevada	324	203	63	14	4	107	33	121	37
New Hampshire.	139	87	62	8	6	45	32	53	38
New Jersey	590	392	66	43	7	154	26	197	33
New Mexico.	366	248	68	13	4	105	29	118	32
New York	1,231	821	67	68	5	341	28	409	33
North Carolina	1,433	932	65	77	5	423	30	500	35
North Dakota	104	52	50	5	4	47	46	52	50
Ohio.	1,190	774	65	60	5	356	30	415	35
Oklahoma	749	475	63	29	4	244	33	274	37
Oregon.	416	256	61	23	6	136	33	159	38
Pennsylvania	1,468	886	60	81	6	496	34	578	39
Rhode Island	65	36	55	5	7	25	38	29	45
South Carolina.	920	454	49	60	6	403	44	463	50
South Dakota.	119	74	62	7	6	34	29	41	34
Tennessee.	1,035	648	63	59	6	327	32	386	37
Texas	3,382	1,909	56	195	6	1,269	38	1,463	43
Utah.	275	220	80	9	3	46	17	55	20
Vermont	73	58	79	3	5	12	16	15	21
Virginia.	824	457	55	71	9	294	36	365	44
Washington	521	295	57	43	8	182	35	225	43
West Virginia	380	236	62	15	4	128	34	142	37
Wisconsin	605	355	59	42	7	208	34	250	41
Wyoming	159	84	53	8	5	67	42	75	47

Source: U.S. National Highway Traffic Safety Administration, *Traffic Safety Facts*, annual. See also <http://www-nrd.nhtsa.dot.gov/CATS/index.aspx>.

Table 1111. Crashes by Crash Severity: 1990 to 2008

[6,471 represents 6,471,000. A crash is a police-reported event that produces injury and/or property damage, involves a vehicle in transport and occurs on a trafficway or while the vehicle is in motion after running off the trafficway]

Item	1990	1995	2000	2003	2004	2005	2006	2007	2008
Crashes (1,000)	**6,471**	**6,699**	**6,394**	**6,328**	**6,181**	**6,159**	**5,973**	**6,024**	**5,811**
Fatal	39.8	37.2	37.5	38.5	38.4	39.3	38.6	37.4	34.0
Nonfatal injury	2,122	2,217	2,070	1,925	1,862	1,816	1,746	1,711	1,630
Property damage only	4,309	4,446	4,286	4,365	4,281	4,304	4,189	4,275	4,146
Percent of total crashes:									
Fatal	0.6	0.6	0.6	0.6	0.6	0.6	0.6	0.6	0.6
Nonfatal injury	32.8	33.1	32.4	30.4	30.1	29.5	29.2	28.4	28.1
Property damage only	66.6	66.4	67.0	69.0	69.3	69.9	70.1	71.0	71.4

Source: U.S. National Highway Safety Traffic Administration, *Traffic Safety Facts*, annual. See also <http://www-nrd.nhtsa.dot .gov/CATS/index.aspx>.

Table 1112. Alcohol Involvement for Drivers in Fatal Crashes: 1998 and 2008

[BAC = blood alcohol concentration]

Age, sex, and vehicle type	1998		2008	
	Number of drivers	Percentage with BAC of .08% or greater	Number of drivers	Percentage with BAC of .08% or greater
Total drivers involved in fatal crashes [1]	**56,604**	**20.4**	**50,186**	**21.8**
Drivers by age group:				
Under 16 years old	361	10.8	213	9.9
16 to 20 years old	7,767	16.7	5,729	17.4
21 to 24 years old	5,613	31.6	5,312	34.4
25 to 34 years old	11,925	27.5	9,745	30.8
35 to 44 years old	11,241	24.2	8,762	25.3
45 to 54 years old	7,690	17.6	8,313	20.7
55 to 64 years old	4,478	11.0	5,695	12.4
65 to 74 years old	3,399	6.9	2,913	6.8
75 years old and over	3,291	4.0	2,656	4.0
Drivers by sex:				
Male	40,816	23.4	36,881	24.9
Female	15,089	12.1	12,568	13.1
Drivers by vehicle type:				
Passenger cars	28,907	21.3	20,284	23.1
Light trucks [2]	19,247	22.2	18,989	22.7
Large trucks [2]	4,905	1.5	4,017	1.7
Motorcycles	2,333	34.4	5,383	29.1
Buses	287	4.2	247	0.8

[1] Includes age and sex unknown, and other and unknown types of vehicles. [2] See footnotes 2 and 3, Table 1106.
Source: U.S. National Highway Traffic Safety Administration, *Traffic Safety Facts*, annual. See also <http://www-nrd.nhtsa.dot .gov/CATS/index.aspx>.

Table 1113. Licensed Drivers and Number in Accidents by Age: 2008

[208,100 represents 208,100,000]

Age group	Licensed drivers		Drivers in accidents				Accident rates per number of drivers	
			Fatal		All			
	Number (1,000)	Percent	Number (1,000)	Percent	Number (1,000)	Percent	Fatal [1]	All [2]
Total	**208,100**	**100.0**	**52,500**	**100.0**	**17,300**	**100.0**	**25**	**8**
19 years old and under	10,275	4.9	4,500	8.6	2,130	12.3	44	21
Under 16 years old	491	0.2	200	0.4	180	1.0	(3)	(3)
16 years old	1,334	0.6	600	1.1	330	1.9	45	25
17 years old	2,221	1.1	800	1.5	490	2.8	36	22
18 years old	2,989	1.4	1,400	2.7	580	3.4	47	19
19 years old	3,240	1.6	1,500	2.9	550	3.2	46	17
20 to 24 years old	17,211	8.3	7,400	14.1	2,520	14.6	43	15
20 years old	3,345	1.6	1,500	2.9	490	2.8	45	15
21 years old	3,375	1.6	1,500	2.9	510	2.9	44	15
22 years old	3,442	1.7	1,600	3.0	470	2.7	46	14
23 years old	3,534	1.7	1,400	2.7	450	2.6	40	13
24 years old	3,515	1.7	1,400	2.7	600	3.5	40	17
25 to 34 years old	36,082	17.3	9,900	18.9	3,570	20.6	27	10
35 to 44 years old	38,969	18.7	8,400	16.0	3,260	18.8	22	8
45 to 54 years old	41,560	20.0	8,500	16.2	2,770	16.0	20	7
55 to 64 years old	32,118	15.4	6,200	11.8	1,730	10.0	19	5
65 to 74 years old	18,406	8.8	3,600	6.9	790	4.6	20	4
75 years old and over	13,479	6.5	4,000	7.6	530	3.1	30	4

[1] Per 100,000 licensed drivers. [2] Per 100 licensed drivers. [3] Rates for drivers under age 16 are substantially overstated due to the high proportion of unlicensed drivers involved.
Source: National Safety Council, Itasca, IL, *Injury Facts, annual* (copyright). See also <http://www.nsc.org/>.

Table 1114. Passenger Transit Industry—Summary: 1990 to 2008

[16,053 represents $16,053,000,000. Includes Puerto Rico. Includes aggregate information for all transit systems in the United States. Excludes nontransit services such as taxicab, school bus, unregulated jitney (a small bus or automobile that transport passengers on a route for a small fare), sightseeing bus, intercity bus, and special application mass transportation systems (e.g., amusement parks, airports, island, and urban park ferries). Includes active vehicles only]

Item	Unit	1990	1995	2000	2005	2006	2007	2008
Operating systems.	Number	5,078	5,973	6,000	6,429	6,435	7,700	7,700
Motor bus systems	Number	2,688	2,250	2,262	1,500	1,500	1,200	1,100
Revenue vehicles, active.	Number	93,553	116,473	131,918	150,827	155,195	163,973	169,436
Motor bus.	Number	58,714	67,107	75,013	82,027	83,080	65,249	66,506
Commuter rail	Number	5,007	5,164	5,498	6,392	6,403	6,391	6,617
Demand response [1].	Number	16,471	29,352	33,080	41,958	43,509	64,865	65,799
Heavy rail.	Number	10,419	10,157	10,591	11,110	11,052	11,222	11,377
Light rail.	Number	913	999	1,577	1,645	1,801	1,810	1,969
Trolley bus	Number	832	885	951	615	609	559	590
Other	Number	1,197	2,809	5,208	7,080	8,741	13,877	16,578
Operating funding, total	Mil. dol	16,053	18,241	24,243	31,708	33,713	35,541	37,975
Agency funds.	Mil. dol	6,786	8,069	11,004	12,559	13,545	13,473	14,304
Passenger funding.	Mil. dol	5,891	6,801	8,746	10,269	11,195	11,145	11,860
Other	Mil. dol	895	1,268	2,258	2,290	2,350	2,328	2,444
Government funds [2].	Mil. dol	9,267	10,172	13,239	19,149	20,168	22,068	23,671
Directly generated [3].	Mil. dol	([4])	1,544	1,959	2,694	2,797	2,698	2,448
Local	Mil. dol	5,327	3,981	5,319	6,658	7,105	8,322	8,754
State	Mil. dol	2,970	3,830	4,967	7,495	7,674	8,371	9,795
Federal.	Mil. dol	970	817	994	2,303	2,592	2,678	2,674
Operating expense	Mil. dol	15,742	17,849	22,646	30,295	32,037	33,877	36,398
Vehicle operations	Mil. dol	6,654	8,282	10,111	13,793	14,743	15,560	16,780
Maintenance	Mil. dol	4,631	5,047	6,445	8,259	8,690	9,136	9,651
General administration	Mil. dol	3,450	2,590	3,329	4,075	4,301	4,779	4,983
Purchased transportation	Mil. dol	1,008	1,930	2,761	4,168	4,304	4,402	4,983
Capital expenditures	Mil. dol	(NA)	7,230	9,587	12,383	13,340	14,528	17,765
Vehicle-miles operated	Million	3,242	3,550	4,081	4,601	4,684	5,038	5,204
Motor bus.	Million	2,130	2,184	2,315	2,485	2,495	2,302	2,377
Trolley bus	Million	14	14	14	13	12	11	12
Heavy rail.	Million	537	537	595	646	652	657	674
Light rail.	Million	24	35	53	69	74	84	88
Commuter rail	Million	213	238	271	303	315	326	339
Demand response [1].	Million	306	507	759	978	1,013	1,471	1,495
Other	Million	18	07	74	107	123	186	219
Trips taken.	Million	8,799	7,763	9,363	9,815	10,017	10,247	10,521
Motor bus.	Million	5,677	4,848	5,678	5,855	5,894	5,413	5,573
Trolley bus	Million	126	119	122	107	100	97	101
Heavy rail.	Million	2,346	2,033	2,632	2,808	2,927	3,460	3,547
Light rail.	Million	175	251	320	381	407	419	454
Commuter rail	Million	328	344	413	423	441	459	472
Demand response [1].	Million	68	88	105	125	126	209	191
Other	Million	79	80	93	117	121	190	183
Avg. fare per trip	Cents	67	88	93	102	112	109	113
Employees, number (avg.) [5]. . . .	1,000	273	311	360	367	369	383	387
Payroll, employee	Mil. dol . . .	7,226	8,213	10,400	12,177	12,764	13,205	13,914
Fringe benefits, employee	Mil. dol	3,986	4,484	5,413	8,093	8,424	9,092	9,366

NA Not available. [1] This operation (also called paratransit or dial-a-ride) is comprised of passenger cars, vans or small buses operating in response to calls from passengers or their agents to the transit operator, who then dispatches a vehicle to pick up the passengers and transport them to their destinations. [2] Represents the sum of federal, state, and local assistance, and that portion of directly generated funds that accrue from tax collections, toll transfers from other sectors of operations, and bond proceeds. [3] These are any funds generated from taxes controlled by the transit agency. [4] Funds data are included in local government data through 1993. [5] Through 1990, represents employee equivalents of 2,080 hours = one employee; beginning 1995, equals actual employees.

Source: American Public Transportation Association, Washington, DC, *Public Transportation Fact Book*, annual. See also <http://www.apta.com/resources/statistics/Pages/default.aspx>.

Table 1115. Top Twenty Cities—Transit Savings: 2010

[Individuals who ride public transportation can save on average of $9,330 annually, based on the June 16, 2010 national average gas price and the national unreserved monthly parking rate. On a per month basis, transit riders can save on average $778 per month. See the monthly press release "Riding Public Transit Saves Individuals" dated June 16 at <http://www.apta.com/mediacenter/pressreleases/2010/Pages/default.aspx>. This release and other monthly "Transit Savings" releases contain information and methodology on how savings are calculated. The cities with the highest transit ridership are ranked in order of their transit savings based on the purchase of a monthly public transit pass and factoring in local gas prices for and the local monthly unreserved parking rate]

City	Savings		City	Savings	
	Monthly	Annual		Monthly	Annual
New York	1,159	13,906	Portland	811	9,736
Boston	1,040	12,481	Denver	811	9,727
San Francisco	1,026	12,309	Cleveland	808	9,701
Chicago	955	11,463	Baltimore	789	9,465
Seattle	946	11,346	Washington D.C.	759	9,107
Philadelphia	934	11,203	Miami	756	9,067
Honolulu	902	10,824	Dallas	736	8,834
Los Angeles	847	10,163	Las Vegas	726	8,712
San Diego	834	10,009	Atlanta	725	8,694
Minneapolis	828	9,938	Pittsburgh	685	8,218

Source: American Public Transportation Association, Media Center, Press Releases. See also <http://www.apta.com/resources/statistics/Pages/default.aspx>.

Table 1116. Characteristics of Rail Transit by Transit Authority: 2008

Mode and transit agency	Primary city served	States served	Direc- tional route— miles [1,2]	Number of high- way- rail cross- ings [1]	Number of stations	Number of ADA acces- sible stations [3]
Total [4]	**35**	**32**	**11,219.3**	**5,796**	**3,011**	**1,920**
Heavy rail	**11**	**17**	**1,602.8**	**27**	**1,025**	**492**
Chicago Transit Authority	Chicago	IL, IN	207.8	25	143	86
Greater Cleveland Regional Transit Authority	Cleveland	OH	38.1	–	18	13
L.A. County Metropolitan Transportation Authority	Los Angeles	CA	31.9	–	16	16
Maryland Transit Administration	Baltimore	MD	29.4	–	14	14
Massachusetts Bay Transportation Authority	Boston	MA, NH, RI	76.3	–	53	49
Metropolitan Atlanta Rapid Transit Authority	Atlanta	GA	96.1	–	38	38
Miami-Dade Transit Agency	Miami	FL	45.0	–	22	22
MTA New York City Transit	New York	NY, NJ, CT	493.8	–	468	80
Port Authority Trans-Hudson Corporation	New York	NY, NJ, CT	28.6	2	13	7
Port Authority Transit Corporation	Philadelphia	PA, NJ, DE	31.5	–	13	5
San Francisco Bay Area Rapid Transit District	San Francisco	CA	209.0	–	43	43
Southeastern Pennsylvania Transportation Authority	Philadelphia	PA	74.9	–	75	28
Staten Island Rapid Transit Operating Authority	New York	NY, CT	28.6	–	23	5
Washington Metropolitan Area Transit Authority	Washington	DC, MD, VA	211.8	–	86	86
Commuter rail [5]	**18**	**21**	**8,218.8**	**3,161**	**1,199**	**763**
Alaska Railroad Corporation	Anchorage	AK	958.0	161	10	10
Altamont Commuter Express Authority	San Jose	CA	172.0	127	10	10
Central Puget Sound Regional Transit Authority	Seattle	WA	146.9	44	10	10
Connecticut Department of Transportation	Hartford	CT	101.2	3	8	8
Dallas Area Rapid Transit	Dallas	TX	29.0	15	4	4
Fort Worth Transportation Authority	Fort Worth	TX	43.3	19	5	5
Maryland Transit Administration	Baltimore	MD	400.4	40	42	24
Massachusetts Bay Transportation Authority	Boston	MA, NH, RI	737.5	257	133	95
MTA Long Island Rail Road	New York	NY, NJ, CT	638.2	346	124	100
MTA Metro-North Railroad	New York	NY, NJ, CT	545.7	157	109	42
Northern New England Passenger Rail Authority	Boston	MA, ME, NH	230.4	65	10	10
NE Illinois Regional Commuter Rail Corporation	Chicago	IL, WI	980.4	532	239	165
New Jersey Transit Corporation	New York	NY, NJ, CT	996.8	316	164	70
North County Transit District	San Diego	CA	82.2	34	8	8
Northern Indiana Commuter Transportation District	Chicago	IL, IN	179.8	117	20	13
Peninsula Corridor Joint Powers Board	San Francisco	CA	153.7	46	32	25
Pennsylvania Department of Transportation	Philadelphia	PA	144.4	7	12	4
Regional Transportation Authority	Nashville	TN	62.8	35	6	6
South Florida Regional Transportation Authority	Miami	FL	142.2	73	18	18
Southeastern Pennsylvania Transportation Authority	Philadelphia	PA	446.9	283	154	55
Southern California Regional Rail Authority	Los Angeles	CA	777.8	435	55	55
Virginia Railway Express	Washington	DC, VA, MD	161.5	20	18	18
Utah Transit Authority	Salt Lake City	UT	87.7	29	8	8

– Represents zero. [1] Vehicles operated in maximum services (VOMS) include directly operated (DO) and Purchase Transportation (PT) by mode. [2] The mileage in each direction over which public transportation vehicles travel while in revenue service. The mileage is computed without regard to the number of traffic lanes or rail tracks existing in the right-of-way. [3] Number of stations that comply with the American with Disabilities Act of 1992 (ADA). Additional stations may be wheelchair accessible but not comply with other provisions of the ADA. [4] Includes light rail, not shown separately. [5] Excludes commuter-type services operated independently by Amtrak.

Source: U.S. Bureau of Transportation Statistics, *State Transportation Statistics, 2008*. See also <http://www.bts.gov /publications/state_transportation_statistics/>. National Transit database; Access NTD data; "Top transit cities." See also <http://www.ntdprogram.gov/ntdprogram/data.htm>.

Table 1117. Transit Ridership in Selected Urbanized Areas: 2008

Urbanized areas	Annual unlinked passenger trips [1] (1,000)	Area rank based on trips per capita [2]	Unlinked passenger trips per capita	Percent distribution				
				Motor bus	Heavy rail [3]	Light rail [4]	Commuter rail [5]	Other [6]
U.S. urbanized areas............	10,200,168	(X)	52.6	53.2	34.7	4.4	4.6	3.0
Atlanta, GA....................	162,899	13	46.5	47.9	50.9	–	–	1.2
Austin, TX....................	37,399	14	41.5	97.2	–	–	–	2.8
Baltimore, MD.................	119,141	10	57.4	73.9	11.7	6.6	6.6	1.2
Boston, MA-NH-RI.............	377,999	4	93.7	28.9	39.3	19.5	10.4	1.9
Chicago, IL-IN................	649,604	5	78.2	56.1	30.5	–	12.5	0.9
Cincinnati, OH-KY-IN...........	30,011	28	20.0	98.5	–	–	–	1.5
Cleveland, OH.................	57,681	21	32.3	79.6	13.2	5.7	–	1.5
Dallas-Fort Worth-Arlington, TX.....	76,043	30	18.3	67.2	–	25.6	3.6	3.7
Denver-Aurora, CO.............	101,176	11	51.0	77.6	–	20.4	–	2.0
Detroit, MI...................	53,178	32	13.6	93.7	–	–	–	6.3
Houston, TX...................	100,443	25	26.3	84.3	–	11.7	–	3.9
Indianapolis, IN...............	9,890	35	8.1	97.0	–	–	–	3.0
Kansas City, MO-KS...........	17,821	34	13.1	96.2	–	–	–	3.8
Las Vegas, NV................	66,168	12	50.3	98.5	–	–	–	1.5
Los Angeles-Long Beach-Santa Ana, CA...............	697,825	9	59.2	84.5	6.2	6.2	1.8	1.3
Miami, FL....................	172,464	20	35.1	79.5	10.7	–	2.2	7.5
Milwaukee, WI................	53,703	15	41.0	97.5	–	–	–	2.5
Minneapolis-St. Paul, MN.......	94,799	16	39.7	86.9	–	10.8	–	2.3
New York-Newark, NY-NJ-CT......	4,159,309	1	233.7	31.6	60.6	0.5	6.4	0.9
Philadelphia, PA-NJ-DE-MD.......	361,236	8	70.2	53.1	28.3	8.2	9.6	0.8
Phoenix-Mesa, AZ.............	72,589	26	25.0	96.7	–	–	–	3.3
Pittsburgh, PA................	69,175	17	39.5	85.2	–	10.3	–	4.5
Portland, OR-WA..............	111,693	7	70.6	63.9	–	34.9	–	1.2
Providence, RI-MA.............	22,851	29	19.5	96.2	–	–	–	3.8
Riverside-San Bernardino, CA......	22,605	31	15.0	95.7	–	–	–	4.3
Sacramento, CA...............	37,287	24	26.8	57.2	–	41.5	–	1.2
San Antonio, TX...............	48,349	19	36.4	97.5	–	–	–	2.5
San Diego, CA................	104,806	18	39.2	59.3	–	36.6	1.6	2.5
San Francisco-Oakland, CA	442,185	2	137.0	40.9	26.1	11.4	2.5	19.2
San Jose, CA.................	44,895	22	29.2	74.4	–	–	–	2.4
Seattle, WA..................	195,507	6	72.1	70.8	–	0.7	1.4	27.1
St. Louis, MO-IL...............	56,206	23	27.1	60.0	–	36.0	–	2.0
Tampa-St. Petersburg, FL........	27,710	33	13.4	96.4	–	1.7	–	1.8
Virginia Beach, VA.............	29,268	27	21.0	96.9	–	–	–	3.1
Washington, DC-VA-MD..........	481,776	3	122.5	39.0	59.8	–	0.7	0.4

– Represents zero. X Not applicable. [1] The number of times passengers board public transportation vehicles. A passenger is counted each time he or she boards a vehicle even if the boarding is part of the same journey from origin to destination. [2] As of April 1. Based on the decennial census. [3] Also called metro, subway, rapid transit, or rapid rail. [4] Also called streetcar, tramway, or trolley. [5] Also called metropolitan rail or regional rail. [6] Includes such modes as trolley bus, ferry, cable car, vanpool, automated Guideway, monorail, publico, inclined plane and demand response (see footnote 1, Table 1114).

Source: U.S. Bureau of Transportation Statistics, *State Transportation Statistics, 2008*, <http://www.bts.gov/publications/state_transportation_statistics/>. National Transit database; Access NTD data, Historical Data Files, <http://www.ntdprogram.gov/ntdprogram/data.htm>.

Table 1118. Federal Aid to State and Local Governments for Federal Transit Administration (FTA) by State: 2007

[Year ending Sept. 30. 9,286 represents $9,286,000,000]

State	Total (mil. dol.)	Per capita [1] (dol.)	State	Total (mil. dol.)	Per capita [1] (dol.)	State	Total (mil. dol.)	Per capita [1] (dol.)	State	Total (mil. dol.)	Per capita [1] (dol.)
U.S. [2]...	**9,286**	**31**	ID......	13	9	MT.....	13	14	RI......	30	28
U.S. [3]...	**9,234**	**31**	IL......	546	42	NE.....	20	11	SC.....	36	8
AL.....	64	14	IN......	70	11	NV.....	52	20	SD.....	12	14
AK.....	53	78	IA......	43	14	NH.....	13	10	TN.....	57	9
AZ.....	209	33	KS.....	27	10	NJ.....	676	78	TX.....	450	19
AR.....	22	8	KY.....	54	13	NM.....	31	16	UT.....	128	48
CA.....	1,290	35	LA.....	75	18	NY.....	1,647	85	VT.....	16	25
CO.....	185	38	ME.....	21	16	NC.....	168	19	VA.....	122	16
CT.....	63	18	MD.....	181	32	ND.....	14	21	WA.....	319	49
DE.....	13	15	MA.....	275	43	OH.....	183	16	WV.....	22	12
DC.....	309	525	MI.....	154	15	OK.....	43	12	WI.....	94	17
FL.....	341	19	MN.....	110	21	OR.....	205	55	WY.....	9	17
GA.....	124	13	MS.....	17	6	PA.....	475	38			
HI.....	47	37	HI.....	47	37	MO.....	96	16			

[1] Based on estimated population as of July 1. [2] Includes outlying areas and undistributed funds, not shown separately. [3] For the 50 states and the District of Columbia.

Source: U.S. Census Bureau, Federal, State, and Local Governments, *Federal Aid to States for Fiscal Year, 2007* (published September 2008). See <http://www.census.gov/prod/www/abs/fas.html>.

Table 1119. Truck Transportation, Couriers and Messengers, and Warehousing and Storage—Estimated Revenue: 2003 to 2008

[In millions of dollars (245,766 represents $245,766,000,000). For taxable and tax-exempt employer firms. Estimates have been adjusted to the results of the 2002 Economic Census]

Kind of business	NAICS code [1]	2003	2004	2005	2006	2007	2008
Selected transportation and warehousing industries	**48, 49**	**245,766**	**265,942**	**292,062**	**313,500**	**324,630**	**332,394**
Truck transportation	484	168,486	185,945	206,522	221,719	228,762	233,786
General freight trucking	4841	113,345	124,970	139,157	148,651	152,416	156,196
General freight trucking, local	48411	18,625	20,112	22,491	25,177	25,716	26,218
General freight trucking, long-distance	48412	94,720	104,858	116,666	123,474	126,700	129,978
General freight trucking, long-distance, truckload	484121	68,381	75,854	84,647	89,725	92,752	96,120
General freight trucking, long-distance, less than truckload	484122	26,339	29,004	32,019	33,749	33,948	33,858
Specialized freight trucking	4842	55,141	60,975	67,365	73,068	76,346	77,590
Used household and office goods moving	48421	12,838	13,891	15,136	15,522	15,102	14,803
Specialized freight (except used goods) trucking, local	48422	22,865	25,263	28,003	31,141	33,038	33,673
Specialized freight (except used goods) trucking, long-distance	48423	19,438	21,821	24,226	26,405	28,206	29,114
Couriers and messengers	492	59,825	62,246	66,916	71,635	74,713	75,682
Couriers	4921	56,492	58,797	63,497	68,136	70,983	71,869
Local messengers and local delivery	4922	3,333	3,449	3,419	3,499	3,730	3,813
Warehousing and storage	493	17,455	17,751	18,624	20,146	21,155	22,926
General warehousing and storage	49311	11,174	10,930	11,524	12,732	13,403	14,614
Refrigerated warehousing and storage	49312	2,945	3,167	3,018	3,068	3,256	3,362
Farm product warehousing and storage	49313	748	691	666	673	726	776
Other warehousing and storage	49319	2,588	2,963	3,416	3,673	3,770	4,174

[1] Data for 2003 are based on the 1997 North American Industry Classification System. Data 2004 through 2008 are based on 2002 NAICS; see text, this section and Section 15.

Source: U.S. Census Bureau, "Service Annual Survey, 2008: Truck Transportation, Messenger Services and Warehousing," January 2010, <http://www.census.gov/services/index.html>.

Table 1120. Truck Transportation—Summary: 2003 to 2008

[In millions of dollars (168,486 represents $168,486,000,000), except where noted. For taxable and tax-exempt employer firms. Covers NAICS 484. Estimates have been adjusted to the results of the 2002 Economic Census. Data for 2003 are based on the 1997 North American Industry Classification System (NAICS). Data 2004 through 2008 are based on 2002 NAICS; see text, this section and Section 15]

Item	2003	2004	2005	2006	2007	2008
Total operating revenue	**168,486**	**185,945**	**206,522**	**221,719**	**228,762**	**233,786**
Total motor carrier revenue	156,633	173,354	193,365	207,028	213,702	218,438
Local trucking [1]	52,409	56,666	63,778	69,277	72,785	74,424
Long-distance trucking [1]	104,224	116,688	129,587	137,751	140,917	144,014
Size of shipments:						
Less-than-truckload	37,472	40,218	42,609	51,340	52,736	52,918
Truckload	119,161	133,136	150,756	155,688	160,966	165,520
Commodities handled:						
Agricultural and fish products	14,803	15,650	17,412	18,514	18,953	19,785
Grains, alcohol, and tobacco products	6,047	6,274	7,107	9,139	10,179	10,777
Stone, nonmetallic minerals, and metallic ores	10,256	11,572	13,457	15,516	16,051	15,362
Coal and petroleum products	5,924	6,839	6,921	7,494	8,197	9,273
Pharmaceutical and chemical products	8,615	9,544	10,387	10,949	12,045	11,986
Wood products, textiles, and leathers	14,141	16,420	17,402	17,676	18,776	19,931
Base metal and machinery	12,883	15,029	16,300	18,081	18,536	18,618
Electronic, motorized vehicles,and precision instruments	13,118	13,665	15,133	15,951	15,332	15,453
Used household and office goods	9,309	10,823	11,799	12,346	12,963	12,553
New furniture and miscellaneous manufactured products	17,927	19,522	22,096	22,252	20,778	22,373
Other goods	43,610	48,016	55,351	59,110	61,892	62,327
Hazardous materials	10,109	(S)	16,185	(S)	14,863	14,570
Origin and destination of shipments:						
U.S. to U.S.	150,472	167,338	185,971	198,674	205,090	209,565
U.S. to Canada	1,315	1,375	1,562	1,842	2,007	2,286
U.S. to Mexico	1,477	1,257	1,604	1,698	1,664	1,684
Canada to U.S.	1,032	1,131	1,328	1,336	1,226	1,377
Mexico to U.S	1,134	1,004	1,371	1,818	2,100	1,953
All other destinations	1,203	1,249	1,529	1,660	1,615	1,573
Inventory of revenue-generating equipment (1,000):						
Trucks	208	212	223	249	257	263
Owned and/or leased with drivers	183	189	198	221	228	238
Leased without drivers	26	24	25	27	29	24
Truck-tractors	872	838	882	898	928	903
Owned and/or leased with drivers	731	711	744	749	772	758
Leased without drivers	141	128	138	150	156	146
Trailers	1,863	1,855	1,959	1,979	2,018	2,028
Owned and/or leased with drivers	1,584	1,524	1,604	1,632	1,659	1,688
Leased without drivers	278	331	355	347	360	339
Highway miles traveled (mil.):						
Total	85,279	85,753	91,296	92,632	93,421	91,500
By loaded or partially loaded vehicles	68,506	69,661	73,751	74,655	75,628	73,620
By empty vehicles	16,773	16,093	17,545	17,977	17,794	17,879

S Estimate does not meet publication standards. [1] Local trucking is the carrying of goods within a single metro area and its adjacent nonurban areas; long-distance trucking is the carrying of goods between metro areas.

Source: U.S. Census Bureau, "Service Annual Survey, 2008: Truck Transportation, Messenger Services and Warehousing," January 2010, <http://www.census.gov/services/index.html>.

Table 1121. Railroads, Class I—Summary: 1990 to 2008

[As of December 31, or calendar year data, except as noted (216 represents 216,000). Compiled from annual reports of class I railroads only, except where noted. Minus sign (–) indicates deficit]

Item	Unit	1990	2000	2003	2004	2005	2006	2007	2008
Class I line-hauling companies [1]	Number ...	14	8	7	7	7	7	7	7
Employees [2]	1,000	216	168	155	158	162	168	167	164
Compensation	Mil. dol.	8,654	9,623	9,576	10,337	10,879	11,419	11,599	11,977
Average per hour	Dollars	15.8	21.5	23.4	24.2	25.7	26.0	27.3	28.9
Average per year	Dollars	39,987	57,157	61,920	65,550	66,975	68,141	69,367	72,836
Mileage:									
Railroad line owned [3]	1,000	146	121	117	123	121	120	120	119
Railroad track owned [4]	1,000	244	205	200	211	208	207	207	206
Equipment:									
Locomotives in service	Number ...	18,835	20,028	20,774	22,015	22,779	23,730	24,143	23,999
Average horsepower	1,000 lb.	2,665	3,261	3,415	3,458	3,467	3,485	3,518	3,601
Cars in service:									
Freight train [5]	1,000	1,212	1,381	1,279	1,288	1,312	1,347	1,386	1,393
Freight cars [6]	1,000	659	560	467	474	475	475	460	450
Average capacity	Tons.....	87.5	92.3	93.7	94.3	95.1	96.0	96.7	97.7
Income and expenses:									
Operating revenues	Mil. dol.	28,370	34,102	36,639	40,517	46,118	52,152	54,600	61,243
Operating expenses	Mil. dol.	24,652	29,040	31,440	35,107	37,843	40,980	42,747	47,348
Net revenue from operations	*Mil. dol.*	*3,718*	*5,062*	*5,199*	*5,410*	*8,275*	*11,172*	*11,852*	*13,895*
Income before fixed charges	Mil. dol.	4,627	5,361	5,220	5,523	8,361	11,276	12,084	13,863
Provision for taxes [7]	Mil. dol.	1,088	1,430	1,494	1,543	2,224	3,643	4,108	4,645
Ordinary income	Mil. dol.	1,961	2,501	2,683	2,867	4,917	6,482	6,797	8,102
Net income	Mil. dol.	1,977	2,500	2,687	2,867	4,917	6,482	6,797	8,102
Net railway operating income	Mil. dol.	2,648	3,924	4,078	4,147	6,075	7,560	7,765	9,248
Total taxes [8]	Mil. dol.	3,780	4,379	4,316	4,480	5,176	6,830	7,272	8,069
Indus. return on net investment	Percent ...	8.1	6.5	6.3	6.1	8.5	10.2	9.9	10.7
Gross capital expenditures	Mil. dol.	3,591	5,290	5,989	6,345	7,068	8,159	9,853	10,189
Equipment	Mil. dol.	996	1,508	1,300	1,301	1,026	1,470	2,213	2,315
Roadway and structures	Mil. dol.	2,644	4,549	4,561	4,941	5,364	6,982	6,944	7,907
Other	Mil. dol.	–49	–767	128	102	678	–293	696	–33
Balance sheet:									
Total property investment	Mil. dol.	70,348	106,136	122,902	135,941	141,400	148,320	156,666	164,286
Accrued depreciation and amortization	Mil. dol.	22,222	23,989	29,215	29,771	32,508	35,763	38,702	41,187
Net investment	Mil. dol.	48,126	82,147	93,686	106,170	108,892	112,556	117,963	123,099
Shareholder's equity	Mil. dol.	23,662	32,401	41,151	51,955	55,828	58,901	59,300	62,787
Net working capital	Mil. dol.	–3,505	–5,783	–6,750	–5,171	–4,729	–4,461	–5,482	–3,592
Cash dividends	Mil. dol.	2,074	819	1,406	1,888	1,267	1,089	6,127	3,045
Amtrak passenger traffic:									
Passenger revenue	Mil. dol.	941.9	1,201.6	1,421.1	1,432.6	1,461.7	1,606.0	1,774.7	1,964.7
Revenue passengers carried	1,000	22,382	22,985	24,595	25,215	25,076	24,549	26,550	28,705
Revenue passenger miles	Million ...	6,125	5,574	5,680	5,511	5,381	5,410	5,784	6,179
Averages:									
Revenue per passenger	Dollars	42.1	52.3	57.8	56.8	58.3	65.4	66.8	68.4
Revenue per passenger mile	Cents.....	15.4	21.6	25.0	26.0	27.2	27.2	30.7	31.8
Freight service:									
Freight revenue	Mil. dol.	24,471	33,083	35,413	39,131	44,457	50,315	52,932	59,409
Per ton-mile	Cents.....	2.7	2.3	2.3	2.4	2.6	2.8	3.0	3.3
Per ton originated	Dollar ...	19.3	19.0	19.7	21.2	23.4	25.7	27.3	30.7
Revenue-tons originated	Million ...	1,425	1,738	1,799	1,844	1,899	1,957	1,940	1,934
Revenue-tons carried	Million ...	2,024	2,179	2,240	2,398	2,448	2,517	2,431	2,420
Tons carried one mile	Billion.....	1,034	1,466	1,551	1,663	1,696	1,772	1,771	1,777
Average miles of road operated	1,000	133	121	122	121	121	120	120	119
Revenue ton-miles per mile of road	1,000	7,763	12,156	12,686	13,695	14,071	14,805	14,801	14,887
Revenue per ton-mile	Cents.....	3	2	2	2	3	3	3	3
Train miles	Million ...	380	504	516	535	548	563	543	524
Net ton-miles per train-mile [9]	Number ...	2,755	2,923	3,024	3,126	3,115	3,163	3,274	3,414
Net ton-miles per loaded car-mile [9]	Number ...	69.1	73.1	71.4	78.5	79.0	82	84	87
Train-miles per train-hour	Miles	24	21	20	19	19	18	19	19
Haul per ton, U.S. as a system	Miles	726	843	862	902	893	906	913	919
Accidents/incidents: [10]									
Casualties—all railroads:									
Persons killed	Number ...	1,297	937	868	891	884	903	849	802
Persons injured	Number ...	25,143	11,643	9,264	9,194	9,548	8,784	9,615	8,815
Class I railroads: [11]									
Persons killed	Number ...	1,166	778	754	784	745	788	714	652
Persons injured	Number ...	19,284	7,655	6,246	6,298	6,414	5,817	6,254	5,684

[1] See text, this section, for definition of Class I. [2] Average midmonth count. [3] Represents the aggregate length of roadway of all line-haul railroads. Excludes yard tracks, sidings, and parallel lines. (Includes estimate for Class II and III railroads). [4] Includes multiple main tracks, yard tracks, and sidings owned by both line-haul and switching and terminal. (Includes estimate for Class II and III railroads). [5] Includes cars owned by all railroads, private car companies, and shippers. [6] Class I railroads only. [7] Includes state income taxes. [8] Includes payroll, income, and other taxes. [9] Revenue and nonrevenue freight. [10] Source: Federal Railroad Administration, *Railroad Safety Statistics*, <http://www.fra.dot.gov/>. [11] Includes Amtrak data. Includes highway grade crossing casualties.

Source: Except as noted, Association of American Railroads, Washington, DC, *Industry Information, Industry Statistics, Railroad Statistics*. See also <http://www.aar.org/StatisticsandPublications.aspx>.

Table 1122. Railroads, Class-I Line-Haul-Revenue Freight Originated by Commodity Group: 1990 to 2009

[21,401 represents 21,401,000]

Commodity group	1990	1995	2000	2004	2005	2006	2007	2008	2009
Carloads (1,000) [1]	**21,401**	**23,726**	**27,763**	**30,095**	**31,142**	**32,114**	**31,459**	**30,625**	**26,005**
Farm products	1,689	1,692	1,437	1,519	1,510	1,590	1,681	1,726	1,531
Metallic ores	508	463	322	339	662	674	662	671	527
Coal	5,912	6,095	6,954	7,102	7,202	7,574	7,480	7,713	6,842
Nonmetallic minerals	1,202	1,159	1,309	1,430	1,488	1,470	1,398	1,325	1,054
Food and kindred products	1,307	1,377	1,377	1,461	1,448	1,487	1,493	1,501	1,462
Lumber and wood products	780	719	648	616	611	548	456	391	285
Pulp, paper, allied products	611	628	633	669	679	671	652	666	546
Chemicals, allied products	1,531	1,642	1,820	1,981	1,937	1,943	2,050	2,040	1,895
Petroleum and coal products	573	596	565	651	689	689	691	578	494
Stone, clay, and glass products	539	516	541	594	603	570	513	467	371
Primary metal products	477	575	723	701	680	728	666	634	354
Fabricated metal products	31	32	30	39	36	50	55	58	62
Machinery, exc. electrical	39	41	35	45	42	43	40	44	38
Transportation equipment	1,091	1,473	1,984	1,849	1,923	1,871	1,810	1,521	1,105
Waste and scrap materials	439	623	619	725	706	701	726	729	568
Tons (mil.) [1]	**1,425**	**1,550**	**1,738**	**1,844**	**1,899**	**1,957**	**1,940**	**1,934**	**1,668**
Farm products	147	154	136	142	140	149	152	156	137
Metallic ores	47	44	32	33	60	61	59	60	44
Coal	579	627	758	792	804	852	850	879	787
Nonmetallic minerals	109	110	126	140	146	141	138	132	105
Food and kindred products	81	91	94	100	102	105	105	105	101
Lumber and wood products	53	51	49	47	48	43	36	31	22
Pulp, paper, allied products	33	36	36	38	38	37	35	34	28
Chemicals, allied products	126	138	155	167	165	167	176	175	162
Petroleum and coal products	40	43	42	54	57	57	57	46	39
Stone, clay, and glass products	44	43	48	53	55	52	48	45	35
Primary metal products	38	47	60	59	57	61	56	54	30
Fabricated metal products	1	1	1	1	1	1	1	1	1
Machinery, exc. electrical	1	1	1	1	1	1	1	1	1
Transportation equipment	23	30	42	37	38	36	34	27	19
Waste and scrap materials	28	38	40	46	47	48	48	49	37
Gross revenue (mil. dol.) [1]	**29,775**	**33,782**	**36,331**	**41,622**	**46,743**	**52,639**	**54,637**	**60,513**	**48,041**
Farm products	2,422	3,020	2,673	3,176	3,628	4,205	4,529	5,403	4,413
Metallic ores	408	394	338	317	485	529	542	637	403
Coal	6,954	7,356	7,794	8,418	9,393	10,821	11,471	14,200	12,052
Nonmetallic minerals	885	875	969	1,131	1,293	1,462	1,527	1,749	1,320
Food and kindred products	2,188	2,464	2,424	2,892	3,253	3,730	4,041	4,610	4,261
Lumber and wood products	1,390	1,385	1,524	1,924	2,278	2,335	1,987	1,684	1,095
Pulp, paper, allied products	1,486	1,543	1,526	1,730	1,953	2,124	2,100	2,228	1,656
Chemicals, allied products	3,933	4,553	4,636	5,100	5,432	6,049	6,830	7,655	6,781
Petroleum and coal products	918	997	1,010	1,268	1,500	1,722	1,853	1,930	1,590
Stone, clay, and glass products	931	1,044	1,113	1,323	1,505	1,664	1,607	1,636	1,215
Primary metal products	979	1,199	1,371	1,518	1,734	2,157	2,267	2,572	1,312
Fabricated metal products	42	44	48	50	55	79	86	92	77
Machinery, exc. electrical	67	69	61	72	91	109	126	166	116
Transportation equipment	3,100	3,269	3,843	3,746	3,960	4,228	4,292	3,964	2,677
Waste and scrap materials	504	685	706	956	1,070	1,190	1,276	1,415	1,022

[1] Includes commodity groups and small packaged freight shipments, not shown separately.

Source: Association of American Railroads, Washington, DC, *Freight Commodity Statistics*, annual. See also <http://www.aar.org/NewsAndEvents.asp>.

Table 1123. Railroads, Class-I Cars of Revenue Freight Loaded, 1990 to 2009, and by Commodity Group, 2008 and 2009

[In thousands (16,177 represents 16,177,000). Figures are 52-week totals]

Year	Car-loads [1]	Commodity group	Carloads 2008 [2]	Carloads 2009 [2,3]	Commodity group	Carloads 2008 [2]	Carloads 2009 [2,3]
1990.....	16,177	Coal......................	7,401	6,580	Metals and products..........	569	315
2000 [2]...	16,354	Metallic ores...............	246	101	Stone, clay, and glass products..	415	327
2004 [2]...	16,600	Grain.....................	1,210	1,038	Nonmetallic minerals..........	285	243
2005 [2]...	16,691	Motor vehicles and equipment..	807	535	Waste and scrap materials.....	485	355
2006 [2]...	16,936	Pulp, paper, allied products....	365	294	Lumber, wood products........	178	119
2007 [2]...	16,564	Primary forest products.......	109	79	Coke......................	185	139
2008 [2]...	16,208	Food and kindred products....	443	396	Petroleum products...........	312	278
2009 [2,3].	13,563	Grain mill products..........	445	426	All other carloads............	264	245

[1] Excludes intermodal. [2] Excludes 3 Class I railroads. See text this section for definition of class 1 railroads. [3] 2009 data preliminary.

Source: Association of American Railroads, Washington, DC, *Weekly Railroad Traffic*, annual. See also <http://www.aar.org/NewsAndEvents.aspx>.

Table 1124. Petroleum Pipeline Companies—Characteristics: 1980 to 2008

[173 represents 173,000. Covers pipeline companies operating in interstate commerce and subject to the jurisdiction of the Federal Energy Regulatory Commission]

Item	Unit	1980	1990	1995	2000	2004	2005	2006	2007	2008
Miles of pipeline, total...	1,000.........	173	168	177	152	142	131	140	147	147
Gathering lines.......	1,000.........	36	32	35	18	15	14	12	15	12
Trunk lines...........	1,000.........	136	136	142	134	127	118	129	132	135
Total deliveries........	Mil. Bbl.......	10,600	11,378	12,862	14,450	13,394	12,732	12,768	13,934	12,972
Crude oil............	Mil. Bbl.......	6,405	6,563	6,952	6,923	6,612	6,675	6,668	7,038	6,858
Products............	Mil. Bbl.......	4,195	4,816	5,910	7,527	6,782	6,057	6,101	6,896	6,114
Total trunk line traffic....	Bil. Bbl. miles...	3,405	3,500	3,619	3,508	3,652	3,485	3,536	3,459	3,438
Crude oil............	Bil. Bbl. miles...	1,948	1,891	1,899	1,602	1,604	1,571	1,578	1,451	1,581
Products............	Bil. Bbl. miles	1,458	1,600	1,720	1,900	2,049	1,914	1,958	2,008	1,856
Carrier property value...	Mil. dol.......	19,752	25,828	27,460	29,648	29,552	29,526	32,686	35,863	39,069
Operating revenues.....	Mil. dol.......	6,356	7,149	7,711	7,483	8,020	7,917	8,517	8,996	9,244
Net income..........	Mil. dol.......	1,912	2,340	2,670	2,705	3,323	3,070	3,743	3,757	3,932

Source: PennWell Publishing Co., Houston, Texas, *Oil & Gas Journal*, annual (copyright).

Table 1125. U.S. Postal Service Rates for Letters and Postcards: 1991 to 2010

[In dollars. International rates exclude Canada and Mexico]

Domestic mail date of rate change	Letters First ounce	Letters Each added ounce	Post-cards	Express mail— first 1/2 pound	International air mail date of rate change	Letters— first ounce [1]	Post-cards	Aero-grammes
1991 (Feb. 3)...........	0.29	0.23	0.19	9.95	**First 1/2 ounce**			
1995 (Jan. 1)...........	0.32	0.23	0.20	10.75	1991 (Feb. 3).......	0.50	0.40	0.45
1999 (Jan. 10)..........	0.33	0.22	0.20	11.75	1995 (July 9).......	0.60	0.40	0.45
2001 (Jan. 7)..........	0.34	0.21	0.20	12.25	1999 (Jan. 10)......	0.60	0.50	0.50
2001 (July 1)...........	0.34	0.23	0.21	12.45	**First ounce** [1]			
2002 (June 30).........	0.37	0.23	0.23	13.65	2001 (Jan. 7).......	0.80	0.70	0.70
2006 (Jan. 8)..........	0.39	0.24	0.24	14.40	2006 (Jan. 8).......	0.84	0.75	0.75
2007 (May 14)..........	0.41	0.17	0.26	16.25	2007 (May 14)......	0.90	0.90	(²)
2008 (May 12)..........	0.42	0.17	0.27	[3] 12.60	2008 (May 12)......	0.94	0.94	(²)
2009 (May 11)..........	0.44	0.17	0.28	[4] 13.05	2009 (May 11)......	0.98	0.98	(²)
2010 (January 4)........	0.44	0.17	0.28	[5] 13.65	2010 (no change) ...	0.98	0.98	(²)

[1] International letter prices after the first ounce vary according to the price group that is applicable to each destination country.
[2] Aerogrammes were discontinued on May 14, 2007. [3] On May 12, 2008, the Postal Service initiated a zoned pricing structure for Express Mail. Prices for a mail piece weighing up to a half-pound range from $12.60 to zones 1 and 2 to $19.50 to zone 8.
[4] Express Mail prices increased on January 18, 2009. Prices for a mail piece weighing up to a half-pound range from $13.05 to zones 1 and 2 to $21.20 to zone 8. [5] Express Mail prices increased on January 4, 2010. Prices for a mail piece weighing up to a half-pound range from $13.65 to zones 1 and 2 to $22.20 to zone 8.
Source: U.S. Postal Service, *United States Domestic Postage Rate: Recent History* and unpublished data. See also <http://www.usps.com/prices/welcome.htm>.

Table 1126. U.S. Postal Service—Summary: 1990 to 2009

[166,301 represents 166,301,000,000 except as indicated. For years ending September 30. Includes Puerto Rico and all outlying areas. See text, this section]

Item	1990	1995	2000	2005	2007	2008	2009
Offices, stations, and branches	**40,067**	**39,149**	**38,060**	**37,142**	**36,721**	**36,723**	**36,496**
Number of post offices	28,959	28,392	27,876	27,385	27,276	27,232	27,161
Number of stations and branches	11,108	10,757	10,184	9,757	9,445	9,491	9,335
Delivery Points (mil.)	(NA)	(NA)	135.9	144.3	148.0	149.0	150.1
Residential	(NA)	(NA)	123.9	131.3	134.6	135.7	136.6
City	(NA)	(NA)	76.1	78.5	79.5	79.8	80.2
P.O. Box	(NA)	(NA)	15.9	15.6	15.6	15.6	15.6
Rural/highway contract	(NA)	(NA)	31.9	37.2	39.5	40.2	40.8
Business	(NA)	(NA)	12.1	13.0	13.4	13.5	13.5
Pieces of mail handled (mil.)	**166,301**	**180,734**	**207,882**	**211,743**	**212,234**	**202,703**	**177,058**
Domestic	165,503	179,933	206,782	210,891	210,604	201,128	175,677
First class mail [1]	89,270	96,296	103,526	98,071	96,297	91,697	83,770
Priority mail [2,6]	518	869	1,223	888	(2)	(2)	(2)
Express mail [2,7]	59	57	71	56	(2)	(2)	(2)
Periodicals (formerly 2d class)	10,680	10,194	10,365	9,070	8,796	8,605	7,954
Standard Mail (formerly Standard A)	63,725	71,112	90,057	100,942	103,516	99,084	82,706
Package Services (formerly Standard B)	663	936	1,128	1,166	915	846	730
U.S. Postal Service	538	412	363	621	1,008	824	455
Free for the blind	35	52	47	78	72	72	62
Shipping Services Volume [2]	(X)	(X)	(X)	(X)	1,630	1,575	1,381
International economy mail (surface) [2]	166	106	79	23	(2)	(2)	(2)
International airmail [2]	632	696	1,021	829	(2)	(2)	(2)
Employees, total (1,000)	**843**	**875**	**901**	**803**	**786**	**765**	**712**
Career	761	753	788	705	685	663	623
Headquarters	2	2	2	3	3	3	3
Headquarters support	6	4	6	4	5	4	4
Inspection Service	4	4	4	3	3	3	3
Inspector General	(X)	(X)	1	1	1	1	1
Field Career	749	743	775	693	673	652	612
Postmasters	27	27	26	25	25	25	24
Supervisors/managers	43	35	39	33	33	32	29
Professional, administrative, and technical	10	11	10	9	8	8	6
Clerks	290	274	282	222	204	195	178
Mail handlers	51	57	61	56	58	56	53
City carriers	236	240	241	228	222	212	201
Motor vehicle operators	7	8	9	9	9	9	8
Rural carriers	42	46	57	64	68	69	68
Special delivery messengers	2	2	(X)	(X)	(X)	(X)	(X)
Building and equipment maintenance	33	38	42	40	40	40	40
Vehicle maintenance	5	5	6	5	5	5	5
Other [3]	1	2	2	2	1	1	(Z)
Noncareer	83	122	114	98	101	102	89
Casuals	27	26	30	19	22	12	4
Transitional	(X)	32	13	8	5	18	17
Rural substitutes	43	50	58	57	60	58	55
Relief/Leave replacements	12	13	12	12	12	12	11
Nonbargaining temporary	(Z)	1	1	1	1	1	2
Compensation and employee benefits (mil. dol.)	34,214	41,931	49,532	53,932	64,270	60,992	56,544
Avg. salary per employee (dol.) [4]	37,570	45,001	50,103	62,635	65,905	67,076	70,140
Pieces of mail per employee, (1,000)	197	207	231	264	270	265	249
Total revenue (mil. dol.) [5]	**40,074**	**54,509**	**64,540**	**69,993**	**74,973**	**74,968**	**68,116**
Operating postal revenue	39,201	54,176	64,476	69,798	74,715	74,829	68,043
Mail revenue	37,892	52,490	62,284	66,649	71,035	71,261	65,064
First class mail	24,023	31,955	35,516	36,062	38,405	38,179	35,873
Priority mail [2,6]	1,555	3,075	4,837	4,634	(2)	(2)	(2)
Express mail [2,7]	630	711	996	872	(2)	(2)	(2)
Periodicals (formerly 2d class)	1,509	1,972	2,171	2,161	2,188	2,295	2,038
Standard Mail (formerly Standard A)	8,082	11,792	15,193	18,954	20,779	20,586	17,364
Package Services (formerly Standard B)	919	1,525	1,912	2,201	1,812	1,845	1,683
Shipping Services [2]	(X)	(X)	(X)	(X)	7,852	8,355	8,107
International economy mail (surface) [2]	222	205	180	134	(2)	(2)	(2)
International airmail [2]	941	1,254	1,477	1,631	(2)	(2)	(2)
Service revenue	1,310	1,687	2,191	3,150	3,743	3,671	3,026
Registry [8]	174	118	98	77	53	57	50
Certified [8]	310	560	385	601	698	718	730
Insurance [8]	47	52	109	132	157	145	129
Collect-on-delivery	26	21	22	9	(NA)	(NA)	(NA)
Money orders	155	196	235	208	211	205	190
Other [8]	592	737	1,342	2,122	2,624	2,547	1,928
Operating expenses (million dollars) [9]	40,490	50,730	62,992	68,283	80,105	77,738	71,830

NA Not available. X Not applicable. Z Fewer than 500. [1] Items mailed at 1st class rates and weighing 11 ounces or less. [2] "Volume" and "Mailing & Shipping Revenue" restructured for the "Postal Accountability and Enhancement Act (PAEA) of 2006." [3] Includes discontinued operations, area offices, and nurses. [4] For career bargaining unit employees. Includes fringe benefits. [5] Net revenues after refunds of postage. Includes operating reimbursements, stamped envelope purchases, indemnity claims, and miscellaneous revenue and expenditure offsets. Shown in year which gave rise to the earnings. [6] Provides 2 to 3 day delivery service. [7] Overnight delivery of packages weighing up to 70 pounds. [8] Beginning 2000, return receipt revenue broken out from registry, certified, and insurance and included in "other." [9] Shown in year in which obligation was incurred.

Source: U.S. Postal Service, *Annual Report of the Postmaster General and Comprehensive Statement on Postal Operations*, annual, and unpublished data.

U.S. Census Bureau, Statistical Abstract of the United States: 2011

Section 24
Information and Communications

This section presents statistics on the various information and communications media: publishing, including newspapers, periodicals, books, and software; motion pictures, sound recordings, broadcasting, and telecommunications; and information services, such as libraries. Statistics on computer use and Internet access are also included. Data on the usage, finances, and operations of the U.S. Postal Service previously shown in this section are now presented in Section 23, Transportation.

Information industry—
The U.S. Census Bureau's *Service Annual Survey, Information Services Sector*, provides estimates of operating revenue of taxable firms and revenues and expenses of firms exempt from federal taxes for industries in the information sector of the economy. Similar estimates were previously issued in the *Annual Survey of Communications Services*. Data are based on the North American Industry Classification System (NAICS). The information sector is a newly created economic sector. It comprises establishments engaged in the following processes: (a) producing and distributing information and cultural products, (b) providing the means to transmit or distribute these products as well as data or communications, and (c) processing data. It includes establishments previously classified in the Standard Industrial Classification (SIC) in manufacturing (publishing); transportation, communications, and utilities (telecommunications and broadcasting); and services (software publishing, motion picture production, data processing, online information services, and libraries).

This new sector is comprised of industries which existed previously, were revised from previous industry definitions, or are completely new industries. Among those which existed previously are newspaper publishers, motion picture and video production, and online information services. Revised industries include book publishers, libraries, and archives.

Newly created industries include database and directory publishers, record production, music publishers, sound recording studios, cable networks, wired telecommunications carriers, paging, and satellite telecommunications.

Data from 1998 to 2003 are based on the 1997 NAICS; beginning 2004, data are based on the 2002 NAICS. Major revisions in many communications industries affect the comparability of these data. The following URL contains detailed information about NAICS, see <http://www.census.gov/eos/www/naics/>. See also the text in Section 15, Business Enterprise.

Several industries in the information sectors have been consolidated: paging is now included in Wireless Telecommunications Carriers (except Satellite). Cable and other program distribution and most Internet service providers are now included in Wired Telecommunications Carriers.

The 1997 Economic Census was the first economic census to cover the new information sector of the economy. The census, conducted every 5 years, for the years ending "2" and "7," provides information on the number of establishments, receipts, payroll, and paid employees for the United States and various geographic levels. The most recent reports are from the 2007 Economic Census. This census was conducted in accordance with the 2007 NAICS.

The Federal Communications Commission (FCC), established in 1934, regulates wire and radio communications. Only the largest carriers and holding companies file annual financial reports which are publically available. The FCC has jurisdiction over interstate and foreign communication services but not over intrastate or local services. Also, the gross operating revenues of the telephone carriers reporting publically available data annually to the FCC are estimated to

U.S. Census Bureau, Statistical Abstract of the United States: 2011

cover about 90 percent of the revenues of all U.S. telephone companies. Data are not service comparable with Census Bureau's *Annual Survey* because of coverage and different accounting practices for those telephone companies which report to the FCC.

Reports filed by the broadcasting industry cover all radio and television stations operating in the United States. The private radio services represent the largest and most diverse group of licensees regulated by the FCC. These services provide voice, data communications, point-to-point, and point-to-multipoint radio communications for fixed and mobile communicators. Major users of these services are small businesses, the aviation industry, the maritime trades, the land transportation industry, the manufacturing industry, state and local public safety and govern-mental authorities, emergency medical service providers, amateur radio operators, and personal radio operations (CB and the General Mobile Radio Service). The FCC also licenses entities as private and common carriers. Private and common carriers provide fixed and land mobile communications service on a for-profit basis. Principal sources of wire, radio, and television data are the FCC's Annual Report and its annual *Statistics of Communications Common Carriers* at <http://fcc.gov/wcb/iatd /stats.html/>.

Statistics on publishing are available from the Census Bureau, as well as from various private agencies. Editor & Publisher Co., New York, NY, presents annual data on the number and circulation of daily and Sunday newspapers in its *International Year Book*. The Book Industry Study Group, New York, NY, collects data on books sold and domestic consumer expenditures. Data on academic and public libraries are collected by the Institute of Museums and Library Services. Data on Internet use by adults are collected by the Pew Internet and American Life Project, Washington, DC, and Mediamark Research, Inc., New York, NY.

Advertising—Data on advertising previously shown in this section are now presented in Section 27, Accommodation, Food Services, and Other Services.

Statistical reliability—For a discussion of statistical collection and estimation, sampling procedures, and measures of statistical reliability applicable to Census Bureau data, see Appendix III.

Table 1127. Information Industries—Establishments, Employees, and Payroll: 2006 and 2007

[(3.396.2 represents 3,396,200). Excludes self-employed individuals, employees of private households, railroad employees, agricultural production employees, and most government employees. For statement on methodology, see Appendix III]

Industry	2002 NAICS code [1]	Establishments		Paid employees [2] (1,000)		Annual payroll (mil. dol.)	
		2006	2007	2006	2007	2006	2007
Information industries.	**51**	**141,945**	**143,779**	**3,396.2**	**3,399.3**	**213,277**	**223,098**
Publishing industries	511	31,821	31,508	1,039.7	1,034.7	72,651	78,113
Newspaper, periodical, book, and database publishers	5111	23,080	23,082	699.9	688.0	34,857	35,521
Newspaper publishers	51111	8,547	8,659	372.0	360.3	14,401	14,395
Periodical publishers.	51112	7,932	7,869	161.8	159.0	10,886	11,184
Book publishers	51113	3,335	3,321	83.5	87.0	4,994	5,345
Database and directory publishers	51114	1,834	1,849	56.5	56.3	3,365	3,437
Other publishers	51119	1,432	1,384	26.1	25.4	1,212	1,159
Greeting card publishers	511191	132	126	12.8	11.7	631	602
All other publishers	511199	1,300	1,258	13.4	13.8	581	556
Software publishers	5112	8,741	8,426	339.8	346.7	37,793	42,592
Motion picture and sound recording industries	512	23,961	24,883	331.2	320.6	15,263	15,248
Motion picture and video industries	5121	20,396	21,118	308.8	298.6	13,450	13,406
Motion picture and video production	51211	12,776	13,091	145.4	130.3	10,143	9,509
Motion picture and video distribution	51212	412	456	4.6	10.1	270	602
Motion picture and video exhibition	51213	5,049	5,104	134.5	130.7	1,283	1,351
Motion picture theaters (except drive-ins)	512131	4,771	4,801	132.8	129.0	1,257	1,323
Drive-in motion picture theaters	512132	278	303	1.8	1.7	26	28
Post production and other motion picture and video industries	51219	2,159	2,467	24.3	27.5	1,754	1,944
Teleproduction and other postproduction services.	512191	1,841	2,128	19.6	22.8	1,382	1,598
Other motion picture and video industries	512199	318	339	4.7	4.7	371	346
Sound recording industries	5122	3,565	3,765	22.5	22.0	1,813	1,842
Record production	51221	375	395	1.5	1.5	79	82
Integrated record production/distribution	51222	421	390	8.1	7.2	1,024	989
Music publishers	51223	671	710	4.2	4.4	337	357
Sound recording studios	51224	1,608	1,745	5.5	5.6	235	257
Other sound recording industries	51229	490	525	3.2	3.4	137	157
Broadcasting (except Internet)	515	10,583	10,415	302.0	294.0	18,180	18,133
Radio and television broadcasting	5151	9,910	9,757	262.2	252.3	14,516	14,265
Radio broadcasting	51511	7,611	7,445	120.7	124.2	6,100	6,030
Radio networks	515111	782	858	11.9	12.4	837	782
Radio stations	515112	6,829	6,587	114.8	111.8	5,263	5,247
Television broadcasting	51512	2,299	2,312	135.6	128.1	8,416	8,236
Cable and other subscription programming	5152	673	658	39.7	41.7	3,664	3,867
Internet publishing and broadcasting.	516	2,653	2,746	41.6	46.6	3,164	3,574
Telecommunications	517	47,762	50,078	1,161.8	1,201.9	69,821	73,474
Wired telecommunications carriers	5171	27,159	27,445	634.5	621.7	41,100	10,000
Wireless telecommunications carriers (except satellite)	5172	12,108	11,817	241.4	277.6	13,578	15,964
Paging	517211	623	458	4.8	4.9	240	207
Cellular and other wireless telecommunications	517212	11,485	11,359	236.6	272.7	13,339	15,756
Telecommunications resellers	5173	2,557	3,417	32.4	35.0	1,791	2,104
Satellite telecommunications	5174	581	708	11.5	13.1	1,119	1,111
Cable and other program distribution	5175	4,816	5,326	231.8	240.0	11,586	12,408
Other telecommunications	5179	541	1,365	10.2	14.4	646	958
Internet service providers, Web search portals, and data processing service.	518	21,002	19,922	465.3	446.8	32,151	32,304
Internet service providers and Web search portals	5181	5,572	4,260	80.2	71.3	8,036	7,598
Internet service providers	518111	4,839	3,479	58.0	46.1	4,145	3,498
Web search portals	518112	733	781	22.2	25.2	3,890	4,100
Data processing, hosting, and related services	5182	15,430	15,662	385.1	375.5	24,116	24,707
Other information services	519	4,163	4,227	54.6	54.7	2,047	2,251
News syndicates	51911	764	820	11.6	12.5	746	810
Libraries and archives	51912	2,650	2,521	31.5	30.4	768	794
All other information services	51919	749	886	11.5	11.8	533	647

[1] North American Industry Classification System, 2002. See text, Section 15. [2] Covers full- and part-time employees who are on the pay period including March 12.

Source: U.S. Census Bureau, "County Business Patterns," July 2009, <http://www.census.gov/econ/cbp/index.html>.

U.S. Census Bureau, Statistical Abstract of the United States: 2011

Table 1128. Information Sector Services—Estimated Revenue and Expenses: 2006 to 2008

[In millions of dollars (1,052,274 represents $1,052,274,000,000). For taxable and tax-exempt employer firms. Estimates have been adjusted to the results of the 2002 Economic Census. Based on the Service Annual Survey and administrative data; see Appendix III]

Industry	2002 NAICS code [1]	Operating revenue			Operating expenses		
		2006	2007	2008	2006	2007	2008
Information industries.	**51**	**1,052,274**	**1,114,129**	**1,156,755**	**836,377**	**871,037**	**903,956**
Publishing industries (except Internet)	511	280,794	295,768	300,365	204,111	212,752	215,845
Newspaper, periodical, book, and directory publishers	5111	150,112	152,972	148,657	113,668	115,998	113,355
Newspaper publishers	51111	49,239	47,914	43,918	43,689	41,893	40,389
Periodical publishers	51112	46,827	48,692	47,505	36,461	38,061	35,704
Book publishers	51113	28,240	29,344	30,284	16,131	16,985	18,657
Directory and mailing list publishers	51114	18,886	19,764	20,098	12,804	14,304	14,109
Other publishers	51119	6,920	7,258	6,852	4,583	4,755	4,496
Greeting card publishers	511191	4,630	4,805	4,468	2,816	2,940	2,613
All other publishers	511199	2,290	2,453	2,384	1,767	1,815	1,883
Software publishers	5112	130,682	143,796	151,708	90,443	96,754	102,490
Motion picture and sound recording industries	512	97,199	100,534	101,792	74,044	78,314	81,826
Motion picture and video industries	5121	76,352	80,518	80,668	57,701	62,979	65,895
Motion picture and video production and distribution	51211,12	60,755	64,520	64,577	45,383	50,764	53,632
Motion picture and video exhibition	51213	11,185	11,322	11,453	8,454	8,338	8,350
Motion picture theaters (except drive-ins)	512131	10,974	11,104	11,240	8,343	8,226	8,234
Drive-in motion picture theaters	512132	(S)	(S)	(S)	(S)	112	116
Postproduction services and other motion picture and video industries	51219	4,412	4,676	4,638	3,864	3,877	3,913
Teleproduction and other post-production services	512191	3,501	3,695	3,657	3,044	3,204	3,226
Other motion picture and video industries	512199	911	981	981	820	673	687
Sound recording industries	5122	20,847	20,016	21,124	16,343	15,335	15,931
Record production	51221	285	317	301	313	304	244
Integrated record production/distribution	51222	14,406	13,612	14,931	12,151	10,920	11,822
Music publishers	51223	4,567	4,367	4,231	2,551	2,628	2,343
Sound recording studios	51224	938	1,007	949	801	888	883
Other sound recording industries	51229	651	713	712	527	595	639
Broadcasting (except Internet)	515	93,075	96,453	100,298	69,464	72,521	74,508
Radio and television broadcasting	5151	55,078	55,546	55,247	44,874	46,034	45,886
Radio broadcasting	51511	18,106	18,673	18,027	16,393	16,361	15,638
Radio networks	515111	4,477	5,046	5,315	6,491	6,221	5,818
Radio stations	515112	13,629	13,627	12,712	9,902	10,140	9,820
Television broadcasting	51512	36,972	36,873	37,220	28,481	29,673	30,248
Cable and other subscription programming	5152	37,997	40,907	45,051	24,590	26,487	28,622
Internet publishing and broadcasting	516	12,908	16,683	19,979	11,310	15,604	18,785
Telecommunications	517	462,866	493,609	515,515	393,106	402,804	414,212
Wired telecommunications carriers	5171	195,632	196,981	194,765	173,546	165,524	162,181
Wireless telecommunications carriers (except satellite)	5172	157,491	173,833	184,804	131,114	137,485	143,284
Paging	517211	1,682	1,309	1,245	1,314	946	913
Cellular and other wireless telecommunications	517212	155,809	172,524	183,559	129,800	136,539	142,371
Telecommunications resellers	5173	11,802	12,256	11,619	7,191	7,215	6,636
Satellite telecommunications	5174	6,217	6,296	6,925	4,333	4,452	4,727
Cable and other program distribution	5175	89,713	102,164	115,184	75,205	86,294	95,426
Other telecommunications	5179	2,011	2,079	2,218	1,717	1,834	(S)
Internet service providers, Web search portals, and data processing services	518	98,142	103,462	110,836	78,678	83,283	92,587
Internet service providers and Web search portals	5181	28,061	30,874	33,173	19,247	19,204	20,449
Internet service providers	518111	18,404	18,792	18,803	14,336	13,102	13,505
Web search portals	518112	9,657	12,082	14,370	4,911	6,102	6,944
Data processing, hosting, and related services	5182	70,081	72,588	77,663	59,431	64,079	72,138
Other information services	519	7,290	7,620	7,970	5,664	5,759	6,193
News syndicates	51911	2,198	2,392	2,366	1,795	1,863	1,874
Libraries and archives	51912	2,040	2,194	2,328	1,781	1,914	2,043
Other information services	51919	3,052	3,034	3,276	2,088	1,982	2,276

S Data do not meet publication standards. [1] North American Industry Classification System (NAICS), 2002; see text, Section 15.

Source: U.S. Census Bureau, "Service Annual Survey 2008: Information Sector Services," January 2010, <http://www.census.gov/econ/www/servmenu.html>.

Table 1129. Information Industries—Establishments, Revenue, Payroll, and Employees by Kind of Business: 2007

[For establishments with payroll. (1,072,343, represents $1,072,343,000,000). Based on the 2007 Economic Census; see Appendix III]

Kind of business	2007 NAICS code [1]	Establish- ments	Receipts (mil. dol.)	Annual payroll (mil. dol.)	Paid employees (1,000)
Information industries	51	**141,566**	**1,072,343**	**228,837**	**3,497**
Publishing industries (except Internet)	511	30,958	282,224	80,867	1,093
Newspaper, periodical, book, & directory publishers	5111	22,683	146,823	34,504	706
Software publishers	5112	8,275	135,401	46,363	387
Motion picture & sound recording industries	512	23,891	94,986	17,635	336
Motion picture & video industries	5121	20,164	79,797	15,494	309
Sound recording industries	5122	3,727	15,189	2,142	27
Broadcasting (except Internet)	515	10,188	99,919	18,076	295
Cable & other subscription programming	5152	717	44,926	3,751	46
Telecommunications	517	51,999	491,124	75,401	1,251
Wired telecommunications carriers	5171	33,548	290,781	54,192	885
Wireless telecommunications carriers (except satellite)	5172	11,973	170,584	16,201	289
Satellite telecommunications	5174	823	4,450	793	10
Other telecommunications	5179	5,655	25,309	4,216	67
Data processing, hosting, and related services	518	17,129	66,652	26,428	394
Other information services	519	7,401	37,438	10,428	128

[1] North American Industry Classification System, 2007; see text, this section and Section 15.

Source: U.S. Census Bureau, "2007 Economic Census; Geographic Area Series: Summary Statistics for the United States, EC0751A1, (2007 NAICS Basis)," June 2010, <http://www.census.gov/econ/census07/>.

Table 1130. Media Usage and Consumer Spending: 2003 to 2009

[Estimates for time spent were derived using rating data for television and cable television, survey research for radio, mobile, out-of-home media and yellow pages, and consumer purchase data (units, admissions, access) for books, home video, in-flight entertainment, Internet, newspapers, magazines, box office, recorded music, videogames. Adults 18 and older were the basis for estimates for newspapers, consumer books, consumer magazines, in-flight entertainment, out-of-home media, yellow pages and home video. Persons 12 and older were the basis for the estimates for box office, broadcast TV, cable TV Internet, mobile, radio recorded music and videogames]

Media	2003	2004	2005	2006	2007	2008	2009, proj.
HOURS PER PERSON PER YEAR [1]							
Total	3,445	3,473	3,500	3,515	3,545	3,545	3,532
Television	1,548	1,559	1,606	1,627	1,654	1,693	1,701
Broadcast Television	701	604	660	656	656	640	639
Network—affiliated stations	605	589	565	583	592	578	579
Independent and public stations [2]	96	95	94	73	64	62	60
Cable networks	847	875	946	971	998	1,053	1,081
Basic cable networks	698	722	781	809	840	891	920
Premium cable networks [2]	148	153	165	162	157	161	161
Broadcast and satellite radio	836	823	809	793	784	744	716
Recorded music	183	188	187	183	179	172	165
Newspapers	198	195	191	182	176	169	158
Pure-play internet services [3]	134	145	152	163	174	181	184
Out-of-home media	130	134	135	136	136	133	129
Consumer magazines	125	128	127	129	129	128	126
Consumer books	110	109	109	110	109	104	98
Videogames	80	82	78	80	91	107	121
Home video [4]	61	69	65	66	64	61	59
Yellow Pages	12	12	11	11	11	11	10
Box office	13	13	12	12	12	12	12
Pure-play mobile services [3]	5	7	11	13	17	21	23
In-flight entertainment [3]	2	1	1	1	1	1	1
Educational books [5]	8	8	8	8	8	8	8
CONSUMER SPENDING PER PERSON PER YEAR (dol.)							
Total	739.75	772.47	785.66	819.38	856.14	882.02	900.99
Television	234.26	256.39	280.21	307.58	332.00	357.60	377.34
Cable and satellite TV	234.23	256.30	279.81	306.60	330.14	354.72	373.61
Broadcast Television	0.03	0.09	0.39	0.98	1.86	2.88	3.73
Home video [4]	122.22	125.36	114.82	118.84	113.86	106.77	102.39
Consumer books	93.76	94.60	98.01	99.56	103.60	100.09	95.21
Pure-play Internet services [3]	60.39	60.31	57.88	54.06	55.45	57.46	58.99
Recorded music	49.59	51.37	48.98	46.69	40.75	32.87	25.92
Newspapers	53.59	51.92	50.32	49.23	47.74	45.75	42.59
Consumer magazines	46.54	47.33	47.42	44.46	44.35	43.33	41.63
Box office	37.74	37.50	35.54	36.38	38.01	38.34	41.21
Videogames	34.65	35.66	35.07	38.36	49.05	61.77	72.05
Pure-play mobile services [3]	4.54	7.54	9.59	12.33	15.66	18.55	21.04
Broadcast and satellite radio	0.39	1.19	3.03	5.76	7.67	9.12	10.23

[1] Can include concurrent use of media, such as watching television and reading e-mail simultaneously. Does not include media use at work. [2] Telemundo and Univsion affiliates included in independent and public stations. Pay-per-view, video-on-demand, interactive channels home shopping and audio-only feeds included in premium cable, satellite & RBOC TV services. [3] Online and mobile use and spending on traditional media platforms, such as downloaded music, newspaper websites or info alerts, e-books, cable modems, online video of television programs and Internet radio were included in the traditional media segment, not in pure-play Internet services or pure-play mobile content. Pure-play Internet services and pure-play mobile content included telecommunications access, such as DSL and dial up, but not cable modems, pure play content such as MobiTV, GameSpy, eHarmony, and mobile instant messaging and email alerts. [4] Playback of prerecorded DVD discs and VHS cassettes only. [5] Grades 9–12 and college only. Not included in consumer spending.

Source: Veronis Suhler Stevenson, New York, NY, *Communications Industry Forecast*, annual (copyright).

Information and Communications 711

Table 1131. Utilization and Number of Selected Media: 2000 to 2008

[100.2 represents 100,200,000]

Media	Unit	2000	2001	2002	2003	2004	2005	2006	2007	2008
Households with—										
Telephones [1]	Millions.	100.2	102.2	104.0	107.1	106.4	107.0	108.8	112.2	112.7
Telephone service [1]	Percent	94.1	94.9	95.3	94.7	93.5	92.9	93.4	94.9	95.0
Land line households with										
wireless telephone [2]	Percent	(X)	(X)	(X)	(X)	(X)	42.4	45.6	58.9	58.5
Wireless-only [2]	Percent	(X)	(X)	(X)	(X)	(X)	7.3	10.5	13.6	17.5
Radio [3]	Millions.	100.5	101.9	105.1	106.7	108.3	109.9	110.5	110.5	115.6
Percent of total households	Percent	99.0	99.0	99.0	99.0	99.0	99.0	99.0	99.0	99.0
Average number of sets	Number	5.6	5.6	5.6	8.0	8.0	8.0	8.0	8.0	8.0
Television [4]	Millions.	101	102	106	107	109	110	110	111	113
Percent of total households	Percent	98.2	98.2	98.2	98.2	98.2	98.2	98.2	98.2	98.2
Television sets in homes	Millions.	245	248	254	260	268	287	301	311	310
Average number of sets per home	Number	2.4	2.4	2.4	2.4	2.5	2.6	2.7	2.8	2.8
Time spent watching [5]	Hours/min. . . .	7.35	7.4	7.4	7.6	8.0	8.1	8.1	8.1	8.2
Wired cable television [4]	Percent	70.4	71.0	70.3	68.6	67.5	65.8	64.1	61.3	61.6
Alternative delivery system (ADS)										
households [4]	Percent	9.8	11.9	14.7	16.7	18.8	19.7	21.6	25.8	27.8
Total broadcast stations [6,7]	Number	(NA)	25,890	26,319	26,613	26,254	27,354	27,807	29,593	29,832
Radio stations [8]	Number	(NA)	13,120	13,331	13,563	13,525	13,660	13,837	13,977	14,253
AM stations	Number	(NA)	4,772	4,804	4,794	4,774	4,757	4,754	4,776	4,786
FM commercial	Number	(NA)	6,089	6,173	6,217	6,218	6,231	6,266	6,309	6,427
FM educational	Number	(NA)	2,259	2,354	2,552	2,533	2,672	2,817	2,892	3,040
Television stations: [6]	Number	(NA)	1,695	1,719	1,733	1,748	1,750	1,756	1,759	1,759
Commercial	Number	(NA)	1,316	1,338	1,352	1,366	1,370	1,376	1,379	1,378
Educational	Number	(NA)	379	381	381	382	380	380	380	381
Cable television systems [8]	Number	10,400	10,300	9,900	9,400	8,875	7,926	7,090	6,635	6,101
Cable subscribers	1,000	66,054	64,920	64,556	64,820	65,263	65,296	64,908	65,913	66,218
Cable availability (passed by cable)	1,000	91,700	91,809	90,689	90,779	91,585	92,590	94,060	95,112	95,350
Broadband subscribers: [9]										
Total fixed broadband	Millions.	6.8	12.4	19.4	27.7	37.4	47.8	60.2	70.2	76.9
Mobile broadband	Millions.	(NA)	(NA)	(NA)	(NA)	(NA)	(NA)	(NA)	(NA)	25.1

NA Not available. X Not applicable. [1] As of November. Based on Current Population Survey. For occupied housing units. Source: Federal Communications Commission, *Telephone Subscribership in the United States*, February 2010. See also <www.fcc.gov/wcb/iatd/stats.html/>. [2] From January to June. Based on National Health Interview Survey. For families living in the same housing unit. Source: National Center for Health Statistics, Wireless Substitution: Early Release of Estimates From the National Health Interview Survey, July–December 2008 December 2009, <www.cdc.gov/nchs/data/nhis/earlyrelease /wireless200905.htm#Methods\>. [3] Source: Radio Advertising Bureau New York, NY, *Radio Marketing Guide*, annual (copyright). [4] Source: Television Bureau of Advertising, *TV Basics*, <http://www.tvb.org/nav/build_frameset.aspx>. [5] Annual average per TV, home per day. [6] As of December, 31. Source: Federal Communications Commission, *Broadcast Station Totals Index*, <http://www.fcc.gov/mb/audio/totals/index.html>. [7] Includes Class A, Low Power TV, UHF and VHF Translators, FM Translators and Boosters, and Low Power FM stations. [8] As of January 1. Source: Warren Communications News, Washington DC, *Television and Cable Factbook* (copyright). [9] As of December. Source: Federal Communications Commission, Wireline Competition Bureau, *High-Speed Services for Internet Access: December, 31 2008*, February 2010.

Source: Compiled from sources mentioned in footnotes.

Table 1132. Multimedia Audiences—Summary: 2009

[In percent, except total (225,887 represents 225,887,000). As of fall 2009. For persons 18 years old and over. Represents the percent of persons participating during the prior week, except as indicated. Based on sample and subject to sampling error; see source for details]

Item	Total population (1,000)	Television viewing	Television prime time viewing	Cable viewing [1]	Radio listening	Newspaper reading	Accessed Internet [2]
Total	**225,887**	**93.2**	**83.0**	**82.2**	**82.3**	**70.7**	**74.1**
18 to 24 years old	28,537	89.3	72.7	78.6	85.0	63.3	87.3
25 to 34 years old	40,349	90.1	77.5	77.4	86.4	64.4	84.2
35 to 44 years old	42,375	93.2	83.6	83.4	88.2	69.4	84.2
45 to 54 years old	44,155	94.0	85.1	84.7	87.1	74.1	77.5
55 to 64 years old	33,466	95.0	87.8	85.1	82.5	73.5	70.3
65 years old and over	37,006	96.9	89.3	83.3	63.0	78.4	40.5
Male	109,165	93.2	83.1	81.7	84.3	70.5	73.6
Female	116,722	93.1	82.9	82.7	80.4	71.0	74.5
Not high school graduate	32,257	93.7	81.3	72.3	73.9	54.5	33.6
High school graduate	69,801	94.3	84.4	82.2	81.0	70.6	63.1
Attended college	63,023	93.4	82.7	84.6	85.6	73.2	86.8
College graduate	60,806	91.4	82.5	85.1	84.7	77.0	95.0
Household income:							
Less than $10,000	11,157	90.8	79.8	61.2	72.0	61.5	40.8
$10,000 to $19,999	19,550	92.9	82.1	67.8	70.5	61.0	39.2
$20,000 to $29,999	21,550	93.3	83.2	73.2	75.8	64.6	50.3
$30,000 to $34,999	10,859	93.8	83.5	77.9	77.1	67.0	58.2
$35,000 to $39,999	10,470	92.4	81.6	75.8	79.5	71.2	65.4
$40,000 to $49,999	20,241	92.2	82.6	82.5	81.0	70.0	72.6
$50,000 to $74,999	43,740	93.3	82.3	84.5	85.5	71.5	80.4
$75,000 to $99,999	31,460	93.3	83.8	88.1	86.1	73.2	88.3
$100,000 or more	56,863	94.0	84.2	91.7	88.1	77.2	94.0

[1] In the past 7 days. [2] In the last 30 days.

Source: Mediamark Research & Intelligence, LLC, New York, NY, *Multimedia Audiences*, fall 2009 (copyright).

Table 1133. Publishing Industries—Estimated Revenue by Source and Media Type: 2005 to 2008

[In millions of dollars (267,801 represents $267,801,000,000). For taxable and tax-exempt employer firms. Covers NAICS 51111. Estimates have been adjusted to the results of the 2002 Economic Census. Based on the North American Industry Classification System (NAICS), 2002. See text, Section 15 and Appendix III]

Source of revenue and media type	2005	2006	2007	2008
Publishing industries (except Internet) [1]	**267,801**	**280,794**	**295,768**	**300,365**
Newspaper publishers	**49,594**	**49,239**	**47,914**	**43,918**
General newspapers	41,270	40,730	39,239	35,949
Subscription and sales	8,692	8,673	8,308	8,184
Advertising space	32,578	32,056	30,931	27,765
Specialized newspapers	2,505	2,270	2,449	2,361
Subscription and sales	(S)	(S)	(S)	(S)
Advertising space	2,225	1,930	2,080	2,007
Other operating revenue	5,818	6,239	6,226	5,609
Printing services	1,394	1,317	1,231	1,126
Distribution services	2,105	2,035	1,925	1,620
All other..............................	2,318	2,887	3,069	2,863
Print newspapers........................	41,654	40,953	39,538	35,841
Online newspapers	1,526	1,418	1,645	2,017
Other media newspapers	595	629	504	451
Periodical publishers	**44,241**	**46,827**	**48,692**	**47,505**
General interest periodicals..............	21,985	23,627	23,847	22,152
Subscription and sales	7,372	7,722	7,730	7,109
Advertising space	14,612	15,905	16,116	15,042
Professional and academic periodicals	7,793	7,829	8,119	7,376
Subscription and sales	4,260	4,330	4,335	3,671
Advertising space	3,533	3,499	3,784	3,705
Other periodicals.......................	3,751	3,839	4,178	3,918
Subscription and sales	2,046	2,074	1,869	1,723
Advertising space	1,705	1,764	2,309	2,196
Other operating revenue	10,713	11,533	12,548	14,059
Printing services for others	1,303	1,260	1,273	1,269
Licensing of rights to content.............	394	454	485	477
All other.............................	9,016	9,819	10,789	12,314
Print.................................	30,671	31,567	32,209	28,913
Online	2,307	3,080	2,993	3,507
Other media...........................	550	646	942	1,026
Book publishers	**27,909**	**28,240**	**20,044**	**30,284**
Books, print...........................	24,270	24,504	24,990	25,888
Textbooks............................	9,999	10,346	10,985	11,982
Children's books	3,072	3,097	3,114	3,320
General reference books	1,273	1,081	958	903
Professional, technical, and scholarly books...	3,166	3,256	2,920	3,195
Adult trade books......................	6,760	6,725	7,013	6,488
All other operating revenue	3,639	3,736	4,353	4,396
Print books............................	22,776	22,040	23,090	23,769
Online books..........................	(S)	775	936	1,084
Other media books......................	733	782	958	1,035
Directory and mailing list publishers	**19,413**	**18,886**	**19,764**	**20,098**
Directories............................	13,789	13,520	13,403	12,866
Subscription and sales	361	365	367	381
Advertising space	13,428	13,154	13,036	12,485
Database and other collections	3,426	3,297	4,097	4,502
Subscription and sales	2,736	2,598	3,147	3,227
Advertising space	690	698	949	1,275
Other operating revenue	2,198	2,070	2,264	2,730
Rental or sale of mailing lists.............	582	556	730	740
All other.............................	1,616	1,514	(S)	1,990
Print directories, databases, and other collections of information..................	13,063	12,993	12,854	12,422
Online directories, databases, and other collections of information..................	3,319	3,000	3,700	4,186
Other media directories, databases, and other collections of information..................	833	824	946	760

S Figure does not meet publication standards. [1] Includes other industries not shown separately.

Source: U.S. Census Bureau, "Service Annual Survey 2008: Information Sector Services," January 2010, <http://www.census.gov/econ/www/servmenu.html>.

U.S. Census Bureau, Statistical Abstract of the United States: 2011

Table 1134. Daily and Sunday Newspapers—Number and Circulation: 1970 to 2008

[Number of newspapers as of February 1 the following year. Circulation figures as of September 30 of year shown (62.1 represents 62,100,000). For English language newspapers only]

Type	1970	1980	1990	1995	2000	2002	2003	2004	2005	2006	2007	2008
NUMBER												
Daily: Total [1]	1,748	1,745	1,611	1,533	1,480	1,457	1,456	1,457	1,452	1,437	1,422	1,408
Morning	334	387	559	656	766	777	787	814	817	833	867	872
Evening	1,429	1,388	1,084	891	727	692	680	653	645	614	565	546
Sunday	586	736	863	888	917	913	917	915	914	907	907	902
NET PAID CIRCULATION (mil.)												
Daily: Total [1]	62.1	62.2	62.3	58.2	55.8	55.2	55.2	54.6	53.3	52.3	50.7	48.6
Morning	25.9	29.4	41.3	44.3	46.8	46.6	46.9	46.9	46.1	45.4	44.5	42.8
Evening	36.2	32.8	21.0	13.9	9.0	8.6	8.3	7.7	7.2	6.9	6.2	5.8
Sunday	49.2	54.7	62.6	61.5	59.4	58.8	58.5	57.8	55.3	53.2	51.2	49.1
PER CAPITA CIRCULATION [2]												
Daily: Total [1]	0.30	0.27	0.25	0.22	0.20	0.19	0.19	0.19	0.18	0.18	0.17	0.16
Morning	0.13	0.13	0.17	0.17	0.17	0.16	0.16	0.16	0.16	0.15	0.15	0.14
Evening	0.18	0.14	0.08	0.05	0.03	0.03	0.03	0.03	0.02	0.02	0.02	0.02
Sunday	0.24	0.24	0.25	0.23	0.21	0.21	0.20	0.20	0.19	0.18	0.17	0.16

[1] All-day newspapers are counted in both morning and evening columns but only once in total. Circulation is divided equally between morning and evening. [2] Based on U.S. Census Bureau estimated resident population as of July 1.

Source: Editor & Publisher Co., New York, NY, *Editor & Publisher International Year Book*, annual (copyright).

Table 1135. Daily and Sunday Newspapers—Number and Circulation, 1991 to 2008, and by State, 2008

[Number of newspapers as of February 1 the following year. Circulation as of September 30 (60,687 represents 60,687,000). For English language newspapers only. California, New York, Massachusetts, and Virginia Sunday newspapers include national circulation]

State	Daily Number	Daily Circulation [1] Net paid (1,000)	Daily Circulation [1] Per capita [2]	Sunday Number	Sunday Net paid circulation [1] (1,000s)	State	Daily Number	Daily Circulation [1] Net paid (1,000)	Daily Circulation [1] Per capita [2]	Sunday Number	Sunday Net paid circulation [1] (1,000s)
Total, 1991	1,586	60,687	0.24	875	62,068	KY	23	524	0.12	14	577
Total, 1992	1,570	60,164	0.23	891	62,160	LA	24	573	0.13	18	624
Total, 1993	1,556	59,812	0.23	884	62,566	ME	7	205	0.16	4	168
Total, 1994	1,548	59,305	0.23	886	62,294	MD	10	438	0.08	8	568
Total, 1995	1,533	58,193	0.22	888	61,529	MA	32	1,212	0.19	16	1,154
Total, 1996	1,520	56,983	0.21	890	60,798	MI	48	1,426	0.14	27	1,628
Total, 1997	1,509	56,728	0.21	903	60,484	MN	25	779	0.15	15	976
Total, 1998	1,489	56,182	0.20	898	60,066	MS	22	317	0.11	19	327
Total, 1999	1,483	55,979	0.20	905	59,894	MO	42	817	0.14	21	1,032
Total, 2000	1,480	55,773	0.20	917	59,421	MT	11	180	0.19	7	178
Total, 2001	1,468	55,578	0.19	913	59,090	NE	16	374	0.21	6	357
Total, 2002	1,457	55,186	0.19	913	58,780	NV	7	253	0.10	5	286
Total, 2003	1,456	55,185	0.19	917	58,495	NH	11	193	0.15	8	195
Total, 2004	1,457	54,626	0.19	915	57,753	NJ	18	1,052	0.12	15	1,264
Total, 2005	1,452	53,345	0.18	914	55,270	NM	17	258	0.13	12	257
Total, 2006	1,437	52,329	0.18	907	53,175	NY	59	6,379	0.33	38	4,543
Total, 2007	1,422	50,742	0.17	907	51,246	NC	47	1,164	0.13	39	1,294
						ND	10	148	0.23	7	151
Total, 2008	**1,408**	**48,598**	**0.16**	**902**	**49,115**	OH	82	1,986	0.17	41	2,215
AL	24	575	0.12	20	638	OK	37	532	0.15	30	635
AK	7	98	0.14	4	102	OR	19	592	0.16	12	616
AZ	16	628	0.10	12	754	PA	80	2,353	0.19	42	2,647
AR	26	453	0.16	16	524	RI	6	170	0.16	3	208
CA	83	4,855	0.13	59	5,184	SC	16	550	0.12	14	632
CO	30	887	0.18	15	914	SD	11	141	0.18	4	119
CT	17	579	0.17	13	642	TN	26	781	0.13	19	893
DE	2	117	0.13	2	142	TX	81	2,408	0.10	78	3,004
DC	3	964	1.63	2	904	UT	6	319	0.12	6	353
FL	38	2,672	0.15	36	3,360	VT	8	98	0.16	3	72
GA	34	857	0.09	29	1,108	VA	23	3,115	0.40	17	862
HI	6	259	0.20	6	277	WA	22	894	0.14	16	999
ID	11	200	0.13	7	214	WV	20	351	0.19	14	367
IL	63	1,921	0.15	30	2,119	WI	33	779	0.14	17	950
IN	67	1,178	0.18	25	1,106	WY	9	84	0.16	5	69
IA	37	552	0.18	13	585						
KS	36	356	0.13	13	321						

[1] Circulation figures based on the principal community served by a newspaper which is not necessarily the same location as the publisher's office. [2] Per capita based on estimated resident population as of July 1, except 2000, enumerated resident population as of April 1.

Source: Editor & Publisher Co., New York, NY, *Editor & Publisher International Year Book*, annual (copyright).

Table 1136. Book Publishers' Net Shipments: 2007 to 2010

[In millions (3,126.8 represents 3,126,800,000). Represents net publishers' shipments after returns. Includes all titles released by publishers in the United States and imports which appear under the imprints of American publishers. Multivolume sets, such as encyclopedias, are counted as one unit. Due to changes in methodology and scope, these data are not comparable to those previously published]

Type of publication	2007, est.	2008, est.	2009, proj.	2010, proj.
Total.....................	3,126.8	3,078.9	3,101.3	3,168.9
Trade	2,281.7	2,237.7	2,248.3	2,294.3
Adult	1,380.8	1,348.5	1,360.8	1,393.4
Juvenile	900.9	889.2	887.5	900.8
Religious	274.5	247.1	239.2	246.8
Professional................	245.9	255.8	264.5	269.0
Scholarly	72.1	74.9	76.2	77.5
Elementary and high school	175.0	182.3	188.7	194.1
College	77.6	81.1	84.5	87.2

Source: Book Industry Study Group, Inc., New York, NY, *Book Industry Trends 2009*, annual (copyright).

Table 1137. Software Publishers—Estimated Revenue by Source of Revenue and Software Type: 2005 to 2008

[In millions of dollars (119,856 represents $119,856,000,000). For taxable and tax-exempt employer firms. Covers NAICS 5112. Estimates have been adjusted to the results of the 2002 Economic Census. Based on the North American Industry Classification System (NAICS), 2002. See text, Section 15 and Appendix III]

Item	2005	2006	2007	2008
Operating revenue.............................	**119,856**	**130,682**	**142,796**	**151,708**
Source of revenue:				
System software publishing [1]............................	44,120	46,248	51,327	54,777
Operating system software	16,367	16,189	18,589	19,288
Network software.........................	12,549	13,459	14,504	15,403
Database management software.......................	7,164	8,646	9,773	10,712
Development tools and programming languages software	3,347	3,209	3,126	3,194
Application software publishing [1]......................	43,414	45,750	49,593	50,987
General business productivity and home use applications	20,810	20,281	22,236	23,418
Cross-industry application software......................	11,635	13,349	13,554	13,508
Vertical market application software	6,916	7,099	7,724	7,653
Utilities application software	1,177	1,433	1,528	1,648
Other services [1]....................................	32,322	38,684	41,876	45,944
Customization and integration of packaged software	4,935	4,925	4,268	5,518
Information technology technical consulting services	4,564	5,664	6,348	5,937
Application service provisioning	(S)	(S)	(S)	(S)
Resale of computer hardware and software	2,240	3,256	4,179	5,003
Information technology-related training services.............	1,518	1,740	1,793	1,943
Breakdown of revenue by software sales type:				
System software	44,120	46,248	51,327	54,777
Personal computer software	14,986	15,135	18,158	19,144
Enterprise or network software	16,428	18,214	18,466	18,916
Mainframe computer software	9,087	9,683	10,132	11,038
Other system software.............................	3,618	3,216	4,572	5,679
Application software	43,414	45,750	49,593	50,987
Personal computer software	21,396	(S)	21,564	22,357
Enterprise or network software	15,099	16,979	19,683	20,156
Mainframe computer software	2,721	2,670	2,738	2,386
Other application software.............................	4,197	5,352	5,609	(S)

S Data do not meet publication standards. [1] Includes other sources of revenue and other expenses, not shown separately.

Source: U.S. Census Bureau, "Service Annual Survey 2008: Information Sector Services," January 2010, <http://www.census.gov/econ/www/servmenu.html>.

U.S. Census Bureau, Statistical Abstract of the United States: 2011

Table 1138. Motion Picture and Sound Recording Industries—Estimated Revenue: 2005 to 2008

[In millions of dollars (93,719 represents $93,719,000,000). For taxable and tax-exempt employer firms. Covers NAICS 512. Estimates have been adjusted to the results of the 2002 Economic Census. Based on the North American Industry Classification System (NAICS), 2002. See text, Section 15 and Appendix III]

Kind of business	2005	2006	2007	2008
Operating revenue	**93,719**	**97,199**	**100,534**	**101,792**
Motion picture and video industries	**74,795**	**76,352**	**80,518**	**80,668**
Motion picture and video production and distribution [1]	59,760	60,755	64,520	64,577
Domestic licensing of rights to motion picture films	16,412	16,120	15,592	14,295
Domestic licensing of rights to television programs	9,350	8,747	10,162	9,443
International licensing of rights to motion picture films	6,864	8,370	9,135	8,877
International licensing of rights to television programs	2,949	3,068	3,177	3,428
Sale of audiovisual works for wholesale, retail, and rental markets	7,855	8,061	10,081	10,059
Motion picture and video exhibition [1]	10,789	11,185	11,322	11,453
Feature film exhibition revenue	7,178	7,355	7,528	7,617
Admissions to domestic films	6,996	7,312	7,474	7,557
Admissions to foreign films	182	(S)	55	60
Food and beverage sales	3,049	3,222	3,311	3,332
Postproduction services and other motion picture and video industries [1]	4,246	4,412	4,676	4,638
Audiovisual postproduction services	2,672	2,807	2,902	2,040
Motion picture film laboratory services	463	(S)	461	449
Duplication and copying services	388	414	417	454
Sound recording industries	**18,924**	**20,847**	**20,016**	**21,124**
Integrated record production and distribution [1]	12,856	14,406	13,612	14,931
Licensing of rights to use musical compositions	(S)	1,409	(S)	1,354
Licensing of rights to use musical recordings	528	638	621	879
Sales of recordings	(S)	(S)	11,180	11,814
Music publishers [1]	4,280	4,567	4,367	4,231
Licensing of rights to use musical compositions	2,274	2,391	(S)	2,712
Licensing of rights to use musical recordings	(S)	(S)	(S)	(S)
Print music	1,748	1,894	1,630	1,221
Sound recording studios [1]	804	938	1,007	949
Studio recording	533	595	632	624

S Data do not meet publication standards. [1] Includes other sources of revenue not shown separately.

Source: U.S. Census Bureau, "Service Annual Survey 2008: Information Sector Services," January 2010, <http://www.census.gov/econ/www/servmenu.html>.

Table 1139. Recording Media—Manufacturers' Shipments and Value 2000 to 2009

[1,079.2 represents 1,079,200,000. Based on reports of Recording Industry Association of America members companies who distributed about 84 percent of the prerecorded music in 2009. These data are supplemented by other sources]

Medium	2000	2002	2003	2004	2005	2006	2007	2008	2009
UNIT SHIPMENTS (mil.)									
Total [1]	1,079.2	859.7	798.4	958.0	1,301.8	1,588.5	1,774.3	1,919.2	1,852.1
Physical:									
Compact disks [2]	942.5	803.3	746.0	767.0	705.4	619.7	511.1	368.4	292.9
Music video [3]	18.2	14.7	19.9	32.8	33.8	23.2	27.5	25.1	23.6
Other albums [4]	78.2	33.3	3.2	2.5	2.0	1.3	1.7	3.0	3.2
Other singles [5]	40.3	8.4	12.1	6.6	5.1	3.2	3.2	1.1	1.2
Digital:									
Download single	(X)	(X)	(X)	139.4	366.9	586.4	809.9	1,042.7	1,138.3
Download album	(X)	(X)	(X)	4.6	13.6	27.6	42.5	63.6	76.4
Kiosk [6]	(X)	(X)	(X)	(X)	0.7	1.4	1.8	1.6	1.7
Music video	(X)	(X)	(X)	(X)	1.9	9.9	14.2	20.8	20.4
Mobile [7]	(X)	(X)	(X)	(X)	170.0	315.3	361.0	405.1	305.8
Subscription [8]	(X)	(X)	(X)	(X)	1.3	1.7	1.8	1.6	1.2
VALUE (mil. dol.)									
Total [1]	14,323.7	12,614.2	11,854.4	12,345.0	12,296.9	11,758.2	10,372.1	8,768.4	7,690.0
Physical:									
Compact disks [2]	13,214.5	12,044.1	11,232.9	11,446.5	10,520.2	9,372.6	7,452.3	5,471.3	4,274.1
Music video [3]	281.9	288.4	399.9	607.2	602.2	451.1	484.9	434.6	431.0
Other albums [4]	653.7	238.8	164.2	66.1	48.5	22.1	29.3	57.6	60.2
Other singles [5]	173.6	42.9	57.5	34.9	24.1	17.6	16.2	6.4	5.6
Digital:									
Download single	(X)	(X)	(X)	138.0	363.3	580.6	801.8	1,032.2	1,220.3
Download album	(X)	(X)	(X)	45.5	135.7	275.9	424.9	635.3	763.4
Kiosk [6]	(X)	(X)	(X)	(X)	1.0	1.9	2.6	2.6	6.3
Music video	(X)	(X)	(X)	(X)	3.7	19.7	28.2	41.3	40.6
Mobile [7]	(X)	(X)	(X)	(X)	421.6	774.5	878.9	977.1	728.8
Subscription [8]	(X)	(X)	(X)	(X)	149.2	206.2	200.9	221.4	213.1

X Not applicable [1] Net, after returns. [2] Includes DualDisc. [3] Includes DVD video. [4] Includes cassette, LP/EP, DVD audio, and super audio CD (SACD). [5] Includes CD single and vinyl single. [6] Includes singles and albums. [7] Includes master ringtones, ringbacks, music videos, full length downloads and other mobile. [8] Weighted annual average. Number of units not included in total.

Source: Recording Industry Association of America, Washington, DC, *2009 Year-end Statistics* (copyright). See also <http://www.riaa.com/keystatistics.php>

716 Information and Communications

Table 1140. Radio and Television Broadcasting—Estimated Revenue and Expenses: 2007 and 2008

[In millions of dollars (5,046 represents $5,046,000,000). For taxable and tax-exempt employer firms. Estimates have been adjusted to the results of the 2002 Economic Census. Based on the North American Industry Classification System (NAICS), 2002. See text, Section 15 and Appendix III]

Item	Radio networks (NAICS 515111)		Radio stations (NAICS 515112)		TV broadcasting (NAICS 51512)	
	2007	2008	2007	2008	2007	2008
Operating revenue	**5,046**	**5,315**	**13,627**	**12,712**	**36,873**	**37,220**
Air time	1,305	1,333	11,927	11,066	29,662	29,133
National/regional air time	674	739	2,952	2,940	18,088	17,960
Local air time	631	594	8,976	8,126	11,574	11,173
Other operating revenue	3,742	3,982	1,700	1,646	7,211	8,087
Network compensation	178	213	279	329	1,524	1,442
Public and noncommercial programming services	457	472	(S)	(S)	2,066	2,181
All other operating revenue	3,107	3,297	820	699	3,620	4,464
Operating expenses	**6,221**	**5,818**	**10,140**	**9,820**	**29,673**	**30,248**
Personnel costs	1,210	1,160	5,350	4,642	8,817	8,901
Gross annual payroll	989	943	4,527	3,926	7,402	7,521
Employer's cost for fringe benefits	170	161	650	560	1,254	1,245
Temporary staff and leased employee expense	51	56	173	156	161	135
Expensed materials, parts and supplies (not for resale)	48	28	106	90	207	263
Expensed equipment	(S)	12	35	32	68	84
Expensed purchase of other materials, parts and supplies	37	16	72	58	139	179
Expensed purchased services	(S)	(S)	1,148	1,027	2,016	2,034
Expensed purchases of software	26	27	41	40	88	162
Purchased electricity and fuels (except motor fuel)	24	25	163	177	305	297
Lease and rental payments	127	111	362	355	500	539
Purchased repair and maintenance	28	26	91	70	209	208
Purchased advertising and promotional services	(S)	(S)	492	385	914	827
Other operating expenses	4,369	4,114	3,535	4,062	18,632	19,049
Broadcast rights and music license fees	576	533	793	794	11,229	10,714
Network compensation fees (networks only)	192	212	63	67	343	405
Depreciation and amortization charges	(S)	(S)	473	565	1,630	1,799
Governmental taxes and license fees	19	18	394	370	129	152
All other operating expenses	3,074	2,887	1,811	2,266	5,303	5,978

S Data do not meet publication standards.

Source: U.S. Census Bureau, "Service Annual Survey 2008: Information Sector Services," January 2010, <http://www.census.gov/econ/www/servmenu.html>.

Table 1141. Cable and Premium TV—Summary: 1980 to 2009

[17,500 represents 17,500,000. Cable TV for calendar year. Premium TV as of December 31 of year shown]

	Cable TV				Premium TV					
			Revenue [1]		Units [2]			Monthly rate [4]		
Year	Average basic sub-scribers (1,000)	Average monthly basic rate (dol.)	Total (mil. dol.)	Basic (mil. dol.)	Total premium [3] (1,000)	Premium cable (1,000)	Non-cable delivered premium (1,000)	All premium weighted average [4] (dollars)	Premium cable (dollars)	Non-cable delivered premium (dollars)
1980	17,500	7.69	2,609	1,615	8,581	7,336	(NA)	8.91	8.62	(NA)
1985	35,440	9.73	8,831	4,138	29,885	29,418	(NA)	10.29	10.25	(NA)
1990	50,520	16.78	17,582	10,174	39,902	39,751	(NA)	10.35	10.30	(NA)
1995	60,550	23.07	24,137	16,763	60,098	46,798	8,925	8.32	8.54	6.99
1996	62,300	24.41	26,195	18,249	67,372	49,607	13,265	8.01	8.12	7.50
1997	63,600	26.48	28,931	20,213	72,910	51,600	17,810	8.33	8.43	8.00
1998	64,650	27.81	31,191	21,574	79,483	54,528	21,673	8.60	8.74	8.22
1999	65,500	28.92	34,095	22,732	84,234	57,095	25,864	8.75	8.85	8.50
2000	66,250	30.37	36,427	24,142	94,100	62,715	30,535	8.72	8.81	8.48
2001	66,732	32.87	41,847	26,324	101,676	68,441	33,035	8.97	9.10	8.66
2002	66,472	34.71	47,989	27,690	109,046	71,732	37,314	9.19	9.29	9.00
2003	66,050	36.59	53,242	29,000	108,522	71,841	36,681	9.38	9.45	9.23
2004	65,727	38.14	58,586	30,080	118,151	76,948	41,203	9.91	9.92	9.88
2005	65,337	39.63	64,891	31,075	126,067	81,910	44,157	9.95	9.97	9.93
2006	65,319	41.17	71,887	32,274	132,951	85,194	47,890	10.01	10.02	9.98
2007	65,141	42.72	78,937	33,393	143,009	91,032	51,977	10.05	10.06	10.02
2008	64,274	44.28	85,232	34,151	149,749	92,540	57,209	10.08	10.10	10.06
2009	62,874	46.13	89,470	34,804	150,401	85,975	64,426	10.12	10.13	10.09

NA Not available. [1] Includes installation revenue, subscriber revenue, and nonsubscriber revenue; excludes telephony and high-speed access. [2] Individual program services sold to subscribers. [3] Includes multipoint distribution service (MDS), satellite TV (STV), multipoint multichannel distribution service (MMDS), satellite master antenna TV (SMATV), C-band satellite, DBS satellite and Telco Video for full- and mini-premium services. [4] Includes average premium unit price based on data for major premium movie services.

Source: SNL Kagan, a division of SNL Financial LC. From the Broadband Cable Financial Databook 2004, 2005, 2006, 2007, 2009 (copyright); the Cable Program Investor and Cable TV Investor: Deals & Finance newsletters (monthly); and various other SNL Kagan publications.

Table 1142. Cable and Other Subscription Programming—Estimated Revenue and Expenses: 2005 to 2008

[In millions of dollars (35,400 represents $35,400,000,000). For taxable and tax-exempt employer firms. Covers NAICS 51521. Estimates have been adjusted to the results of the 2002 Economic Census. Based on the North American Industry Classification System (NAICS), 2002. See text, Section 15 and Appendix III]

Item	2005	2006	2007	2008
Operating revenue	35,400	37,997	40,907	45,051
Source of revenue:				
Licensing of rights to broadcast specialty programming [1]	18,254	19,679	21,450	23,777
Air time	15,223	15,900	16,947	18,164
All other operating services revenue	1,923	2,417	2,510	3,110
Operating expenses	23,255	24,590	26,487	28,622
Personnel costs	4,575	4,415	5,096	5,400
Gross annual payroll	3,688	3,461	3,820	4,122
Employer's cost for fringe benefits	575	566	796	796
Temporary staff and leased employee expense	311	388	480	482
Expensed materials, parts and supplies (not for resale)	135	128	125	159
Expensed equipment	52	46	61	73
Expensed purchase of other materials, parts and supplies	83	82	64	85
Expensed purchased services	2,186	2,593	2,243	2,000
Expensed purchases of software	30	37	45	143
Purchased electricity and fuels (except motor fuel)	37	36	36	64
Lease and rental payments	522	460	430	505
Purchased repair and maintenance	80	75	59	108
Purchased advertising and promotional services	1,516	1,985	1,673	1,980
Other operating expenses	16,359	17,454	19,024	20,263
Depreciation and amortization charges	(S)	2,483	2,635	3,023
Government taxes and license fees	107	74	60	61
Program and production costs	10,501	11,330	12,568	13,139
All other operating expenses	3,269	3,566	3,762	4,040

S Data do not meet publication standards. [1] Protected by copyright.

Source: U.S. Census Bureau, "Service Annual Survey 2008: Information Sector Services," January 2010, <http://www.census.gov/econ/www/servmenu.html>.

Table 1143. Internet Publishing and Broadcasting—Estimated Revenue and Expenses: 2005 to 2008

[In millions of dollars (10,391 represents $10,391,000,000). For taxable and tax-exempt employer firms. Covers NAICS 516. Establishments engaged in publishing and/or broadcasting on the Internet exclusively. Estimates have been adjusted to the results of the 2002 Economic Census. Based on the North American Industry Classification System (NAICS), 2002. See text, Section 15 and Appendix III]

Item	2005	2006	2007	2008
Operating revenue	10,391	12,908	16,683	19,979
Source of revenue:				
Publishing and broadcasting of content on the Internet	6,084	7,069	8,728	10,437
Online advertising space	1,994	2,874	3,676	4,604
Licensing of rights to use intellectual property	432	521	569	585
All other operating revenue	1,881	(S)	(S)	4,355
Breakdown of revenue by type of customer:				
Government	(S)	(S)	(S)	(S)
Business firms and not-for-profit organizations	7,329	8,844	11,313	14,269
Household consumers and individual users	2,467	3,361	4,312	4,503
Operating expenses	9,085	11,310	15,604	18,785
Personnel	3,949	4,917	6,319	7,623
Gross annual payroll	3,153	3,935	4,654	5,658
Employer's cost for fringe benefits	561	711	1,029	(S)
Temporary staff and leased employee expense	235	270	(S)	(S)
Expensed materials, parts and supplies (not for resale)	316	361	(S)	(S)
Expensed equipment	133	139	(S)	(S)
Expensed purchase of other materials, parts and supplies	182	222	(S)	(S)
Expensed purchased services	1,544	1,997	(S)	3,245
Expensed purchases of software	194	276	(S)	319
Purchased electricity and fuels (except motor fuel)	16	23	(S)	(S)
Lease and rental payments	343	383	(S)	624
Purchased repair and maintenance	100	108	(S)	(S)
Purchased advertising and promotional services	891	1,208	1,594	2,100
Other operating expenses	3,275	4,035	(S)	7,380
Depreciation and amortization charges	792	909	(S)	(S)
Government taxes and license fees	62	74	96	94

S Data do not meet publication standards.

Source: U.S. Census Bureau, "Service Annual Survey 2008: Information Sector Services," January 2010, <http://www.census.gov/econ/www/servmenu.html>.

Table 1144. Telecommunications Industry—Carriers and Revenue: 2000 to 2007

[Revenue in millions of dollars (292,762 represents $292,762,000,000). Based on annual Telecommunications Reporting Worksheets (FCC Form 499-A) filed by telecommunications providers. Revenues are categorized as those billed to universal service contributors for resale, and those billed to telecommunication providers with annual contributions less than $10,000 and end users.]

Category	Carriers (number)				Telecommunications revenue			
	2000	2005	2006	2007	2000	2005	2006	2007, proj.
Total [1]	**4,879**	**5,005**	**5,312**	**5,114**	**292,762**	**297,921**	**297,268**	**299,451**
Local service providers (fixed local & pay phone)	2,641	2,922	3,119	3,048	128,075	122,609	119,905	115,963
Incumbent local exchange carriers (ILECs)	1,335	1,303	1,311	1,304	116,158	103,561	99,997	93,885
Competitors of Incumbent local exchange carriers	607	1,043	1,227	1,312	10,945	18,568	19,473	21,690
CAPs and CLECs [2]	479	734	780	774	9,814	16,930	17,276	17,476
Interconnected VoIP providers [3]	(NA)	(NA)	145	251	(NA)	(NA)	514	2,394
Private carriers	([4])	([4])	([4])	([4])	39	770	1,080	1,031
Wireless service providers [5]	1,430	905	955	874	63,280	108,809	117,752	124,943
Telephony [6]	783	402	426	428	59,823	107,834	116,971	123,968
Paging service providers	425	300	304	238	3,102	579	555	607
Toll service providers	808	1,178	1,238	1,192	101,407	66,503	59,611	58,545
Interexchange carriers	212	262	270	250	87,311	46,856	44,083	43,701
Operator service providers	20	23	24	23	635	548	631	595
Prepaid service providers	23	69	85	93	727	1,828	1,713	2,195
Satellite service carriers	25	40	39	41	336	714	444	708
Toll resellers	493	721	744	693	10,641	13,362	9,943	8,314
Other toll carriers, including VoIP [3]	35	63	76	92	1,758	3,195	2,798	3,031

NA Not available. [1] Revenue data include adjustments, not shown separately. [2] Competitive access providers (CAPs) and competitive local exchange carriers (CLECs). [3] Voice Over Internet Protocol. [4] Data not available separately. [5] Beginning 2000, includes specialized mobile radio services and other services, not shown separately. [6] Cellular service, personal communications service, and specialized mobile radio.

Source: U.S. Federal Communications Commission, Wireline Competition Bureau, Telecommunications Industry Revenues: 2007, September 2009. See also <http://www.fcc.gov/wcb/iatd/recent.html/>.

Table 1145. Wired and Wireless Telecommunications Carriers—Estimated Revenue: 2005 to 2008

[In millions of dollars (205,652 represents $205,652,000,000). Based on Service Annual Survey and administrative data. For taxable and tax-exempt employer firms. Covers NAICS 5171 Wired Telecommunications, NAICS 517211 Paging, and NAICS 517212 Cellular and Other Wireless. Estimates have been adjusted to the results of the 2002 Economic Census. Based on the North American Industry Classification System (NAICS), 2002. See text Section 15 and Appendix III]

Item	2005	2000	2007	2000
Wired telecommunications carriers operating revenue	**205,652**	**195,632**	**196,981**	**194,765**
Fixed services	93,910	89,575	92,545	89,192
Fixed local	56,905	56,375	59,159	56,325
Fixed long-distance	33,830	31,357	31,420	31,086
Fixed all distance [1]	3,176	1,843	1,966	1,782
Other telecommunication services	96,340	90,874	91,042	92,489
Carrier services	34,572	29,450	26,749	24,861
Private network services	26,852	23,643	23,736	23,905
Subscriber line charges	8,438	7,909	6,167	5,375
Internet access services	16,448	17,516	21,143	23,692
Intrrnet telephony	1,217	1,894	2,145	2,440
Telecommunications network installation services	(S)	6,137	6,494	7,477
Reselling services for telecommunications equipment, retail	3,529	3,352	3,459	3,514
Rental of telecommunications equipment	259	(S)	342	287
Repair and maintenance services for telecommunications equipment	835	761	807	938
All other operating revenue	15,401	15,183	13,395	13,084
Wireless telecommunications carriers operating revenue	**140,030**	**157,491**	**173,833**	**184,804**
Paging	1,995	1,682	1,309	1,245
Messaging (paging) services	1,588	1,277	975	916
Mobile services	111,663	123,414	132,870	138,504
Mobile telephony	57,097	53,804	54,194	58,128
Mobile long distance	4,398	4,808	5,312	4,757
Mobile all-distance	42,292	(S)	57,755	55,963
Other mobile services	7,875	(S)	(S)	19,656
Other telecommunications services	9,508	11,963	14,822	17,127
Internet access services	1,124	2,509	4,541	6,863
Installation services for telecommunications networks	(S)	146	181	301
Reselling services for telecommunications equipment, retail	7,377	8,082	8,689	8,512
Rental of telecommunications equipment	(S)	110	70	71
Repair and maintenance services for telecommunications equipment	732	(S)	(S)	1,380
All other operating revenue	16,865	20,433	24,832	27,928

S Estimate does not meet publication standard. [1] No distinction between local or long distance.

Source: U.S. Census Bureau, "Service Annual Survey 2008: Information Sector Services," January 2010, <http://www.census.gov/econ/www/servmenu.html>.

Table 1146. Telephone Systems—Summary: 1990 to 2007

[130 represents 130,000,000. Covers principal carriers filing annual reports with Federal Communications Commission]

Item	Unit	1990	2000	2001 [1]	2002 [1]	2003 [1]	2004 [1]	2005 [1]	2006 [1]	2007 [1]
LOCAL EXCHANGE CARRIERS [2]										
Carriers [3]	Number ...	51	52	52	53	54	56	56	56	55
Access lines	Millions....	130	245	253	264	275	286	349	379	424
Business access lines	Millions....	36	58	54	53	49	48	47	46	45
Residential access lines	Millions....	89	115	112	104	99	94	89	82	76
Other access lines (public, mobile, special)	Millions....	6	72	87	107	127	144	213	251	303
Number of local calls (originating)	Billions....	402	537	515	454	418	381	330	280	235
Number of toll calls (originating)	Billions....	63	106	98	96	88	82	79	73	70
Average monthly residential local telephone rate	Dollars....	19.24	20.78	22.62	24.07	24.52	24.52	24.64	25.26	25.62
Average monthly single-line business telephone rate	Dollars....	41.21	41.80	42.43	41.95	41.96	43.49	43.75	45.32	48.17
INTERNATIONAL TELEPHONE SERVICE [4]										
Number of U.S. billed calls	Millions....	984	5,742	6,265	5,926	7,839	10,890	13,134	13,673	13,695
Number of U.S. billed minutes	Millions....	8,030	30,135	33,287	35,988	45,904	63,653	70,064	72,440	69,975
End-User U.S. billed revenues	Mil. dol....	8,059	14,909	11,386	9,956	9,294	9,176	7,976	7,907	7,220
U.S. carrier end-user revenue net of settlements with foreign carriers	Mil. dol....	5,188	10,820	7,978	6,822	6,093	5,268	4,515	4,277	3,544

[1] Beginning 2001, detailed financial data are only filed by regional Bell-operating companies. Access lines and calls reported by all subject reporting companies. [2] Gross operating revenues, gross plant, and total assets of reporting carriers estimated at more than 90 percent of total industry. New accounting rules became effective in 1990; prior years may not be directly comparable on a one-to-one basis. Includes Virgin Islands, and prior to 1995, Puerto Rico. [3] The reporting threshold for carriers is $100 million in annual operating revenue. [4] Beginning 1991, data are for all U.S. points, and include calls to and from Alaska, Hawaii, Puerto Rico, Guam, the U.S. Virgin Islands, and offshore U.S. points. Beginning 1991, carriers first started reporting traffic to and from Canada and Mexico. Data for Canada and Mexico in prior years are staff estimates. Beginning 2004, revenue from private-line service includes non-confidential private line service revenue and the total of private line and miscellaneous service revenue for carriers requesting confidential treatment for international telephone service.

Source: U.S. Federal Communications Commission, *Statistics of Communications Common Carriers, Trends in Telephone Service,* and *Trends in the International Telecommunications Industry.* See also <http://www.fcc.gov/wcb/iatd/stats.html>.

Table 1147. Average Annual Telephone Service Expenditures by All Consumer Units: 2001 to 2008

[Based on Consumer Expenditure Survey. A consumer unit is defined as members of a household related by blood, marriage, adoption, or some other legal arrangement; a single person living alone or sharing a household with others, but who is financially independent; or two or more persons living together who share responsibility for at least two out of the three major types of expenses: food, housing, and other expenses]

Year	Average annual telephone service (dol.)				Percent distribution			
	Total telephone services	Residential telephone/ pay phone	Cellular phone service	Other services [1]	Total telephone services	Residential telephone/ pay phone	Cellular phone service	Other services [1]
2001	914	686	210	19	100.0	75.0	23.0	2.0
2002	957	641	294	22	100.0	67.0	30.7	2.3
2003	956	620	316	20	100.0	64.8	33.1	2.1
2004	990	592	378	20	100.0	59.8	38.2	2.0
2005	1,048	570	455	23	100.0	54.4	43.4	2.2
2006	1,087	542	524	21	100.0	49.9	48.2	2.0
2007	1,110	482	608	20	100.0	43.4	54.8	1.8
2008	1,127	467	643	17	100.0	41.4	57.1	1.5

[1] Phone cards, pager services, and beginning in 2007, Voice over Internet Protocol, known as VoIP.

Source: Bureau of Labor Statistics, "Consumer Expenditures in 2008," October 2009, <http://www.bls.gov/cex/cellphones.htm/>.

Table 1148. Cellular Telecommunications Industry: 1990 to 2009

[Calendar year data, except as noted (5,283 represents 5,283,000). Based on a survey sent to facilities-based commercial mobile radio service providers, including cellular, personal communications services, advanced wireless service, and enhanced special mobile radio (ESMR) systems. The number of operational systems beginning 2000 differs from that reported for previous periods as a result of the consolidated operation of ESMR systems in a broader service area instead of by a city-to-city basis]

Item	Unit	1990	2000	2004	2005	2006	2007	2008	2009
Subscribers	1,000	5,283	109,478	182,140	207,896	233,041	255,396	270,334	285,646
Cell sites [1]	Number ..	5,616	104,288	175,725	183,689	195,613	213,299	242,130	247,081
Employees	Number ..	21,382	184,449	226,016	233,067	253,793	266,782	268,528	249,247
Service revenue	Mil. dol ...	4,548	52,466	102,121	113,538	125,457	138,869	148,084	152,552
Roamer revenue [2]	Mil. dol ...	456	3,883	4,210	3,786	3,494	3,742	3,739	3,061
Capital investment [3]	Mil. dol ...	6,282	89,624	173,794	199,025	223,449	244,591	264,761	285,122
Average monthly bill [4]	Dollars ...	80.90	45.27	50.64	49.98	50.56	49.79	50.07	48.16
Average length of call [4]	Minutes ..	2.20	2.56	3.05	3.00	3.03	(NA)	2.27	1.81
Number of text messages [5]	Billions ...	(NA)	(Z)	4.7	9.8	18.7	48.1	110.4	152.7
Number of MMS [5,6]	Billions ...	(NA)	(NA)	(NA)	0.2	0.3	0.8	1.6	5.1

NA Not available. Z Entry less than half the unit of measurement shown. [1] The basic geographic unit of a wireless PCS or cellular system. [2] Service revenue generated by subscribers' calls outside of their system areas. [3] Beginning 2005, cumulative capital investment figure reached by summing the incremental capital investment in year shown with cumulative capital investment of prior year. [4] As of December 31. [5] Number of messages in final month of survey, (December). [6] Multimedia Messaging Service.

Source: CTIA-The Wireless Association, Washington, DC, *Semi-annual Wireless Survey,* (copyright).

720 Information and Communications

Table 1149. Cable and Other Programming Distribution—Estimated Revenue: 2005 to 2008

[In millions of dollars (80,555 represents $80,555,000,000). For taxable and tax-exempt employer firms. Covers NAICS 5175. Estimates have been adjusted to the results of the 2002 Economic Census. Based on the North American Industry Classification System (NAICS), 2002. See text, Section 15 and Appendix III]

Item	2005	2006	2007	2008
Operating revenue..	80,555	89,713	102,164	115,184
Sources of revenue:				
Multichannel programming distribution services	52,676	56,730	61,939	68,384
Basic programming package	40,440	43,394	46,751	51,022
Premium programming package	9,604	10,221	11,550	13,411
Pay-per-view	2,633	3,115	3,638	3,951
Other revenue	27,878	32,983	40,224	46,800
Air time	3,539	3,933	4,005	4,338
Rental and reselling services for program distribution equipment........	2,426	3,067	3,834	4,443
Installation services for connections to program distribution networks	637	721	933	998
Internet access services	11,246	13,415	15,989	18,361
Internet telephony	523	1,599	3,493	5,448
Fixed local telephony.......................................	1,554	1,931	(S)	2,662
Fixed long-distance telephony...............................	646	420	(S)	184
All other operating revenue	7,308	7,898	9,376	10,367
Type of customer:				
Government..	494	463	517	630
Business firms and not for profit organizations	6,581	6,937	8,686	8,856
Household customers and individual customers......................	73,479	82,313	92,961	105,698

S Data do not meet publication standards.

Source: U.S. Census Bureau, "Service Annual Survey 2008: Information Sector Services," January 2010, <http://www.census.gov/econ/www/servmenu.html>.

Table 1150. Internet Service Providers, Web Search Portals, and Data Processing, Hosting and Related Services—Estimated Revenue: 2006 to 2008

[In millions of dollars (18,404 represents $18,404,000,000). For taxable and tax-exempt employer firms. Estimates have been adjusted to the results of the 2002 Economic Census. Based on the North American Industry Classification System (NAICS), 2002. See text, Section 15 and Appendix III]

Item	Internet service providers (NAICS 518111)			Data processing, hosting and related services (NAICS 5182)		
	2006	2007	2008	2006	2007	2008
Operating revenue......................................	18,404	18,792	18,803	(X)	(X)	(X)
Internet access service	12,235	11,121	9,858	(X)	(X)	(X)
Online advertising space	2,304	3,087	4,105	(X)	(X)	(X)
Internet backbone services	306	405	(S)	(X)	(X)	(X)
Internet telephony	(S)	181	(S)	(X)	(X)	(X)
Web site hosting services	1,164	1,028	875	(X)	(X)	(X)
Information technology design and development services	(S)	(S)	(S)	(X)	(X)	(X)
All other operating revenue	(S)	2,707	(S)	(X)	(X)	(X)
Operating revenue......................................	(X)	(X)	(X)	70,081	72,588	77,663
Data processing IT infrastructure provisioning, and hosting services	(X)	(X)	(X)	36,824	36,969	39,784
Business processing management services	(X)	(X)	(X)	19,691	18,313	19,933
Data management services...................................	(X)	(X)	(X)	7,036	7,091	7,357
Application service provisioning	(X)	(X)	(X)	6,338	6,810	7,844
Web site hosting services	(X)	(X)	(X)	2,529	(S)	(S)
Collocation services	(X)	(X)	(X)	(S)	(S)	(S)
Other operating revenue	(X)	(X)	(X)	33,256	35,619	37,879
IT design and development services............................	(S)	(S)	(S)	6,309	6,337	(S)
IT technical support services.................................	(X)	(X)	(X)	1,419	1,406	1,726
IT technical consulting services	(X)	(X)	(X)	1,550	1,882	1,930
Information and document transformation services.................	(X)	(X)	(X)	3,397	3,508	4,028
Software publishing	(X)	(X)	(X)	1,961	2,229	2,740
Reselling services for computer hardware and software, retail	(X)	(X)	(X)	2,081	2,155	(S)
All other operating revenue	(X)	(X)	(X)	16,538	18,101	19,208

S Data do not meet publication standards. X Not applicable.

Source: U.S. Census Bureau, "2008 Service Annual Survey 2008: Information Sector Services," January 2010, <http://www.census.gov/econ/www/servmenu.html>.

Table 1151. Public Libraries, Selected Characteristics: 2008

[11,391 represents $11,391,000,000. Based on survey of public libraries. Data are for public libraries in the 50 states and the District of Columbia. The response rates for these items are between 97 and 100 percent. See source for details]

Population of service area	Number of—		Operating income			Paid staff [3]		Average number of public use Internet computers per station-ary outlet [5]
				Source				
	Public libraries	Stationary outlets [1]	Total [2] (mil. dol.)	State gov-ernment (percent)	Local government (percent)	Total	Librarians with ALA-MLS [4]	
Total...............	9,221	16,671	11,391	8.7	82.7	145,244	32,562	13.2
1,000,000 or more.....	27	1,126	1,764	6.4	82.8	18,678	4,782	24.0
500,000 to 999,000....	57	1,156	1,766	8.5	83.8	20,309	4,991	21.6
250,000 to 499,999....	106	1,141	1,352	11.0	81.4	16,578	4,083	18.6
100,000 to 249,999....	337	2,010	1,791	8.6	84.2	23,134	4,980	17.1
50,000 to 99,999......	557	1,646	1,443	10.6	82.1	18,873	4,301	16.2
25,000 to 49,999......	967	1,705	1,394	8.2	83.9	18,435	4,364	14.7
10,000 to 24,999......	1,763	2,275	1,158	8.2	82.5	16,468	3,531	12.0
5,000 to 9,999........	1,497	1,647	422	9.1	79.4	6,873	1,054	8.5
2,500 to 4,999........	1,340	1,372	174	7.0	77.1	3,176	315	6.2
1,000 to 2,499........	1,573	1,594	100	5.8	75.4	2,050	132	4.6
Fewer than 1,000......	997	999	28	11.1	69.5	671	30	3.5

[1] The sum of central and branch libraries. The total number of central libraries was 9,042; the total of branch libraries was 7,629. [2] Includes income from the federal government (0.4%) and other sources (8.2%), not shown separately. [3] Full-time equivalents. [4] Librarians with master's degrees from a graduate library education program accredited by the American Library Association (ALA). Total librarians, including those without ALA-MLS, were 47,926. [5] The average per stationary outlet was calculated by dividing the total number of public use Internet computers in central and branch outlets by the total number of such outlets.

Source: Institute of Museum and Library Services, "Public Libraries Survey: Fiscal Year 2008," (IMLS-2010–PLS-02), June 2010. See also <http://harvester.census.gov/imls/pubs/pls/index.asp>.

Table 1152. Number of Public Libraries and Library Services by State: 2008

[For Fiscal Year. 1,504,861 represents 1,504,861,000. Based on Public Libraries Survey. Public libraries can have one or more outlets that provide direct service to the public. The three types of outlets include central libraries, branch libraries, and bookmobiles]

State	Number of public libraries [1]	Library visits (1,000s)	Per capita visits [2]	Per capita circula-tion of materi-als [2]	Average number of public use Internet comput-ers per station-ary outlet [3]	State	Number of public libraries [1]	Library visits (1,000s)	Per capita visits [2]	Per capita circula-tion of materi-als [2]	Average number of public use Internet comput-ers per station-ary outlet [3]
U.S.....	9,221	1,504,861	5.1	7.7	13.2	MO......	152	28,353	5.5	9.4	12.8
AL......	210	15,477	3.5	4.4	15.4	MT......	80	4,063	4.5	6.5	7.8
AK......	86	3,473	5.1	6.3	5.5	NE......	270	8,983	6.9	10.5	6.6
AZ......	86	26,196	4.0	7.3	17.8	NV......	22	10,956	4.0	6.5	12.7
AR......	51	9,909	3.7	4.9	8.6	NH......	231	7,302	5.6	8.4	4.9
CA......	181	171,873	4.5	5.8	15.7	NJ.......	303	49,289	5.9	7.3	14.4
CO......	115	30,666	6.3	12.0	15.9	NM......	91	7,487	4.8	6.3	11.9
CT......	195	23,775	6.8	9.4	14.2	NY......	755	117,214	6.2	8.2	13.7
DE......	21	4,361	5.5	10.4	13.9	NC......	77	37,600	4.1	5.8	15.7
DC......	1	2,705	4.6	3.0	12.0	ND......	81	2,426	4.3	7.2	5.6
FL......	80	84,363	4.5	6.2	25.5	OH......	251	92,280	8.0	16.7	15.8
GA......	59	36,980	4.0	4.7	16.4	OK......	115	14,551	4.9	7.0	10.6
HI......	1	5,891	4.6	5.5	10.4	OR......	126	22,267	6.6	15.4	10.6
ID......	104	8,550	6.4	9.4	8.9	PA......	457	48,315	4.0	5.8	11.4
IL......	634	77,553	6.6	9.0	13.3	RI......	48	6,330	6.0	7.0	14.2
IN......	238	41,168	7.2	13.7	16.0	SC......	42	16,770	3.8	5.4	16.0
IA......	539	18,534	6.3	9.6	6.4	SD......	114	3,922	5.6	8.4	6.1
KS......	327	14,671	6.2	11.4	8.0	TN......	187	20,454	3.4	4.1	13.6
KY......	116	18,512	4.4	6.7	16.7	TX......	561	74,221	3.3	4.9	17.2
LA......	68	14,632	3.3	4.0	13.1	UT......	69	17,487	6.7	13.0	13.2
ME......	272	7,188	5.9	7.7	5.2	VT......	183	3,893	6.4	7.7	5.0
MD......	24	32,814	5.9	9.9	20.7	VA......	91	39,888	5.2	9.2	15.0
MA......	370	42,169	6.5	8.4	10.6	WA......	64	42,271	6.5	12.1	13.4
MI......	384	54,390	5.5	8.0	14.8	WV......	97	6,008	3.3	4.2	7.0
MN......	138	28,793	5.5	10.7	12.4	WI......	381	35,467	6.3	10.9	9.9
MS......	50	8,859	3.0	2.9	8.6	WY......	23	3,560	6.8	9.0	9.4

[1] Of the 9,221 public libraries, 7,469 were single outlet libraries and 1,752 were multiple outlet libraries. Single outlet libraries are a central library, bookmobile, or books by mail only outlet. Multiple outlet libraries have to or more direct service outlets including some combination of single outlet libraries. [2] Per capita rate and per 1,000 population based on total unduplicated population of legal service area given by the state library agency of each state. [3] The average per stationary outlet was calculated by dividing the total number of public use Internet computers in central and branch outlets by the total number of such outlets.

Source: Institute of Museum and Library Services, "Public Libraries Survey: Fiscal Year 2008," (IMLS-2010–PLS-02), June 2010. See also <http://harvester.census.gov/imls/pubs/pls/index.asp>.

Table 1153. Public Library Use of the Internet: 2009

[In percent, except number of outlets. As of spring. Kbps = kilobits per second. Mbps = million bits per second. Based on sample survey; see source for details]

Item	Total	Metropolitan status [1] Urban	Metropolitan status [1] Suburban	Metropolitan status [1] Rural	Poverty status [2] Less than 20 percent	Poverty status [2] 20 to 40 percent	Poverty status [2] More than 40 percent
All libraries' outlets [3]	**16,620**	**2,940**	**5,421**	**8,259**	**13,943**	**2,490**	**187**
Connected with public access	98.7	98.7	99.3	98.5	99.0	98.0	100.0
Average number of workstations	11.0	18.7	12.7	7.6	10.4	12.9	22.0
Speed of access:							
Less than 256 kbps	3.4	([4])	2.4	5.1	3.2	4.8	([4])
257 kbps to 768 kbps	9.2	3.2	5.8	13.7	9.4	8.5	5.5
769 kbps to 1.4 mbps	9.3	3.9	7.8	12.2	9.7	7.6	([4])
1.5 mbps	25.5	26.9	27.2	23.8	24.9	28.7	30.7
1.6 mbps to 3 mbps............	10.0	8.0	9.5	11.1	10.0	10.5	5.5
3.1 mbps to 6 mbps............	11.2	14.0	11.6	10.0	11.4	10.2	17.1
6.1 mbps to 10 mbps..........	11.0	16.5	15.7	5.9	11.0	10.8	16.5
Greater than 10 mbps	12.3	23.9	12.4	7.9	11.8	14.1	20.9
Don't know...................	8.1	2.8	7.6	10.3	8.7	4.8	3.7
Public library availability of wireless Internet access:							
Currently available	76.4	83.0	81.9	70.5	77.2	71.9	73.2
Plan to make available within the next year....................	9.2	8.1	7.6	10.7	9.1	9.2	17.7

[1] Urban = inside central city; Suburban = In metro area, outside of a central city; Rural = outside a metro area. [2] Determined by the 2000 poverty status of the service area of the outlet. [3] Central libraries and branches; excludes bookmobiles. [4] Less than 1 percent.

Source: Center for Library and Information Innovation, College of Information Studies, University of Maryland, College Park, MD, *Public Libraries and the Internet 2009: Survey Results and Findings*, by John Carlo Bertot, et al., University of Maryland, College Park, MD. Study funded by the American Library Association.

Table 1154. Household Internet Usage In and Outside of the Home by Selected Characteristics: 2009

[In thousands except percent (119,296 represents 119,296,000). As of October. Based on the Current Population Survey and subject to sampling error. See Appendix III]

Characteristics	Total house-holds	In the home Percent All house-holds	In the home Percent Dial-up	In the home Percent Broad-band	Anywhere Total house-holds	Anywhere Percent of house-holds	No internet use Total house-holds	No internet use Percent of house-holds
All households.................	**119,296**	**68.69**	**4.74**	**63.53**	**91,471**	**76.68**	**27,826**	**23.32**
Age of householder:								
Under 25 years old	6,635	66.96	2.27	64.25	5,502	82.92	1,133	17.08
25 to 34 years old	19,811	74.24	2.50	71.15	16,965	85.63	2,846	14.37
35 to 44 years old	22,180	77.77	4.12	73.26	19,288	86.96	2,892	13.04
45 to 54 years old	25,034	75.83	5.01	70.34	20,966	83.75	4,068	16.25
55 years and older...............	45,636	58.20	6.21	51.66	28,750	63.00	16,886	37.00
Sex of householder:								
Male........................	60,867	71.72	4.58	66.74	48,073	78.98	12,794	21.02
Female......................	58,429	65.53	4.90	60.20	43,398	74.27	15,031	25.73
Race and ethnicity of householder:								
White	83,810	73.31	4.95	67.95	66,945	79.88	16,865	20.12
Black	14,876	54.25	4.40	49.48	10,100	67.89	4,776	32.11
American Indian/Alaskan Native	804	53.41	4.46	48.28	530	65.89	274	34.11
Asian.......................	4,560	80.70	3.00	77.36	3,905	85.65	654	14.35
Hispanic.....................	13,799	52.77	4.35	47.88	8,821	63.92	4,978	36.08
Educational attainment of householder:								
Elementary	5,384	25.18	3.58	21.35	1,802	33.47	3,582	66.53
Some high school	9,339	37.70	4.47	33.15	4,479	47.96	4,860	52.04
High school diploma/GED	34,985	57.18	5.87	50.91	23,333	66.69	11,652	33.31
Some college..................	33,687	75.01	4.98	69.49	28,449	84.45	5,239	15.55
Bachelor's degree or more	35,900	88.54	3.64	84.47	33,407	93.06	2,493	6.94
Family income of householder:								
Less than $15,000...............	15,160	35.90	3.67	31.97	7,431	49.02	7,729	50.98
15,000 to 24,999	11,234	46.75	5.34	41.03	6,551	58.31	4,683	41.69
25,000 to 34,999	12,036	59.92	6.40	53.05	8,611	71.54	3,425	28.46
35,000 to 49,999	13,918	74.20	6.03	67.81	11,604	83.38	2,314	16.62
50,000 to 74,999	17,548	85.55	5.66	79.26	16,131	91.93	1,416	8.07
75,000 to 99,999	10,124	92.13	4.09	87.63	9,725	96.05	400	3.95
100,000 to 149,000	8,818	95.46	1.98	93.10	8,634	97.92	184	2.08
150,000 and over................	6,142	97.38	1.47	95.50	6,052	98.54	90	1.46

Source: U.S. Department of Commerce, National Telecommunications and Information Administration, *Networked Nation: Broadband in America 2007*, January 2008. See also <http://www.ntia.doc.gov/reports/2008/NetworkedNation.html/> and <http://www.ntia.doc.gov/data/CPS2009_Tables.html>.

Information and Communications 723

Table 1155. Household Internet Usage by Type of Internet Connection and State: 2009

[In percent. As of October. See headnote, Table 1154. Based on Current Population Survey. See Appendix III]

State	Any-where	In the home Total	In the home Broad-band	In the home Dial-up	No Internet use	State	Any-where	In the home Total	In the home Broad-band	In the home Dial-up	No Internet use
U.S.	76.68	68.69	63.53	4.74	23.3	MO	73.99	63.67	57.50	5.51	26.01
AL	66.60	56.13	48.44	6.38	33.4	MT	76.73	64.06	58.30	5.60	23.27
AK	86.27	77.26	72.97	3.63	13.7	NE	79.77	70.00	63.89	4.39	20.23
AZ	79.75	72.08	67.16	4.48	20.3	NV	79.23	72.38	67.70	3.75	20.77
AR	66.10	55.88	51.01	4.48	33.9	NH	83.09	78.74	73.21	5.00	16.91
CA	79.88	73.09	67.63	4.85	20.1	NJ	81.05	76.81	72.44	4.19	18.95
CO	82.39	72.91	68.77	3.79	17.6	NM	72.51	61.71	54.62	7.09	27.49
CT	80.62	74.75	70.75	3.69	19.4	NY	75.57	70.65	65.80	4.47	24.43
DE	77.47	71.07	66.70	3.61	22.5	NC	73.21	63.86	59.34	4.35	26.79
DC	80.88	71.78	66.21	5.46	19.1	ND	77.18	67.10	62.54	3.89	22.82
FL	78.35	71.53	66.59	4.66	21.7	OH	75.98	66.85	61.44	5.17	24.02
GA	75.89	67.61	63.94	3.54	24.1	OK	73.40	60.65	55.82	4.69	26.60
HI	79.07	73.33	69.97	3.36	20.9	OR	84.03	76.00	70.08	5.69	15.97
ID	81.39	72.18	67.40	4.42	18.6	PA	73.61	67.31	61.57	5.43	26.39
IL	78.30	68.31	62.54	5.45	21.7	RI	77.01	71.57	69.47	1.80	22.99
IN	70.93	62.51	56.48	5.75	29.1	SC	69.00	58.26	53.30	4.82	31.00
IA	77.24	67.79	62.02	5.40	22.8	SD	74.62	65.49	59.65	5.60	25.38
KS	79.43	70.48	66.78	3.06	20.6	TN	69.80	62.33	55.44	6.47	30.20
KY	69.10	59.49	53.55	5.45	30.9	TX	72.91	63.93	59.92	3.28	27.09
LA	69.67	60.59	57.06	3.05	30.3	UT	86.41	77.86	73.34	4.14	13.59
ME	77.30	70.19	61.35	8.45	22.7	VT	82.58	70.80	60.61	7.73	17.42
MD	80.98	73.37	69.76	3.21	19.0	VA	77.73	71.02	65.01	5.83	22.27
MA	80.78	75.85	72.93	2.19	19.2	WA	86.26	77.93	72.41	5.21	13.74
MI	78.03	68.03	62.32	5.42	22.0	WV	66.30	59.72	52.05	7.52	33.70
MN	82.52	72.38	66.91	5.22	17.5	WI	79.90	71.81	66.95	4.67	20.10
MS	62.58	51.80	41.76	9.31	37.4	WY	79.87	69.79	65.55	3.77	20.13

Source: U.S. Department of Commerce, National Telecommunications and Information Administration, "Current Population Survey (CPS) Internet use 2009," November 2009, <http://www.ntia.doc.gov/data/CPS2009_Tables.html>.

Table 1156. Internet Access and Usage: 2009

[For persons 18 years old and over (225,887 represents 225,887,000. As of fall 2009. Based on sample and subject to sampling error; see source for details]

Characteristic	Total adults	Have Internet access Home or work or other	Have Internet access Home	Have Internet access Work	Used the Internet in the last 30 days Home or work or other	Used the Internet in the last 30 days Home	Used the Internet in the last 30 days Work
Total adults, (1,000) [1]	**225,887**	**195,960**	**167,972**	**84,132**	**167,294**	**150,756**	**73,393**
PERCENT DISTRIBUTION							
Total	100.00	100.00	100.00	100.00	100.00	100.00	100.00
Age:							
18 to 34 years old	30.50	32.49	31.34	32.39	35.20	33.46	31.60
35 to 54 years old	38.31	40.27	42.21	50.12	41.78	42.94	51.45
55 years old and over	31.20	27.24	26.45	17.49	23.02	23.60	16.94
Sex:							
Male	48.33	48.35	48.58	49.63	48.01	47.96	49.42
Female	51.67	51.65	51.42	50.37	51.99	52.04	50.58
Census region: [2]							
Northeast	18.43	19.09	19.81	18.64	19.11	19.67	18.80
Midwest	22.06	22.13	21.71	22.35	22.24	22.04	21.54
South	36.76	35.41	34.43	34.51	34.49	34.03	34.52
West	22.76	23.37	24.05	24.51	24.16	24.26	25.14
Household size:							
1 to 2 persons	46.55	43.81	41.68	41.90	41.99	41.54	42.17
3 to 4 persons	37.23	39.51	41.38	43.28	41.15	41.97	43.19
5 or more persons	16.22	16.68	16.94	14.82	16.85	16.48	14.64
Any child in household	40.02	42.31	43.40	45.93	44.05	44.06	45.95
Marital status:							
Single	25.95	26.66	24.91	24.71	28.06	26.36	23.90
Married	55.01	57.29	60.86	62.05	57.83	60.27	62.93
Other	19.04	16.05	14.22	13.24	14.12	13.37	13.16
Educational attainment:							
Graduated college plus	26.92	30.43	33.93	46.28	34.53	36.78	49.43
Attended college	27.90	30.49	31.41	32.40	32.69	32.66	31.93
Did not attend college	45.18	39.08	34.66	21.32	32.79	30.55	18.64
Employed full-time	49.48	53.69	55.43	86.04	57.36	57.30	87.71
Employed part-time	11.91	12.62	12.83	13.32	13.26	13.29	11.80
Household income:							
Less than $50,000	41.54	35.24	29.12	18.07	30.43	27.04	16.23
$50,000 to $74,999	19.36	20.70	21.46	20.21	21.02	21.19	19.69
$75,000 to $149,999	28.65	32.14	35.80	43.15	35.15	37.27	44.34
$150,000 or more	10.45	11.92	13.62	18.57	13.40	14.50	19.75

[1] Includes other labor force status not shown separately. [2] For composition of regions, see map, inside front cover.

Source: Mediamark Research & Intelligence, LLC, New York, NY, CyberStats, fall 2009 (copyright); <http://www.mriplus.com/pocketpiece.html>.

724 Information and Communications

1157. Adult Computer and Adult Internet Users by Selected Characteristics: 2000 to 2010

[Percent of persons 18 years old and over. Represents persons who use a computer or the Internet at a workplace, school, home, or anywhere else, on at least an occasional basis. Based on telephone surveys of persons with land line telephones. In May 2010, 2,252 persons were interviewed including 744 cell phone users. The response rate for the land line sample was 21.8 percent. The response rate for the cellular sample was 19.3 percent. For 2000, Internet users include persons who have ever gone online to access the Internet or World Wide Web or to send and receive e-mail. For 2005, 2009 and 2010 Internet users include those who at least occasionally use the Internet or send and receive e-mail]

Characteristic	Adult computer users				Adult Internet users				All adults, by type of home connection, 2010	
	2000	2005	2009	2010	2000	2005	2009	2010	Broad-band	Dial-up
Total adults..............	65	71	78	77	53	69	79	79	66	5
Age:										
18 to 29 years old..........	82	83	88	89	72	82	92	95	80	4
30 to 49 years old..........	76	81	87	86	62	80	87	87	75	4
50 to 64 years old..........	61	72	78	78	48	68	79	78	63	6
65 years old and over.......	21	31	42	42	15	28	42	42	31	7
Sex:										
Male....................	66	72	78	78	56	70	81	79	66	5
Female..................	64	70	77	76	51	67	77	79	65	5
Race/ethnicity:										
White, non-Hispanic.........	66	72	78	79	55	70	79	80	67	5
Black, non-Hispanic.........	59	60	66	72	42	54	67	71	56	5
English-speaking Hispanic ...	64	75	84	74	48	73	84	82	66	5
Educational attainment:										
Less than high school.......	28	36	47	43	19	35	50	52	33	4
High school graduate [1]......	56	63	67	67	41	59	69	67	54	6
Some college..............	80	81	89	88	69	80	88	90	76	6
College graduate or higher ...	88	90	94	96	79	88	94	96	86	4
Annual household income:										
Less than $30,000..........	48	52	56	58	35	50	60	63	45	6
$30,000 to $49,999........	74	76	82	82	61	74	80	84	67	8
$50,000 to $74,999........	85	88	93	89	74	86	94	89	79	4
$75,000 or more...........	90	92	95	96	81	91	95	95	87	3

[1] Includes those with a GED certificate.

Source: Pew Internet & American Life Project Surveys from September-December 2000; September and December of 2005; April 2009 and May 2010. <http://www.pewinternet.org/index.asp>.

Table 1158. Internet Activities of Adults by Type of Home Internet Connection: 2010

[In percent. For Internet users 18 years old and over. For persons who have ever performed the activity. Based on telephone surveys of persons with land line telephones, unless otherwise noted. In May 2010, 2,252 persons were interviewed including 744 cell phone users. The response rate for the land line sample was 21.8 percent. The response rate for the cellular sample was 19.3 percent. In January 2010, 2,259 persons were interviewed including 562 cell phone users. The response rate for the land line sample was 22 percent. The response rate for the cellular sample was 20 percent]

Activity	Survey date (month/year)	Percent of American adults performing activity	Percent of Internet users performing activity	Percent of home dial-up users performing activity	Percent of home broadband users performing activity
Send or read e-mail.....................	May, 2010	74	94	91	95
Use a search engine to find information	May, 2010	69	87	61	92
Check weather reports and forecasts online	May, 2010	64	81	70	84
Get news online.......................	May, 2010	59	75	58	79
Buy a product online	May, 2010	29	66	49	71
Visit a local, state, or federal government Web site..........	May, 2010	53	67	57	70
Buy or make a reservation for travel	May, 2010	52	66	45	70
Look for news or information about politics	May, 2010	40	50	33	54
Do any banking online...................	May, 2010	46	58	35	63
Watch a video on a video-sharing site....................	May, 2010	52	66	35	69
Look online for info about a job	May, 2010	43	54	49	56
Look for information on Wikipedia	May, 2010	42	53	26	59
Send instant messages.................	May, 2010	37	47	26	50
Get financial information online.........................	May, 2010	29	37	23	40
Use online classified ads or sites like Craig's List	May, 2010	42	53	39	56
Rate a product, service, or person	May, 2010	25	32	15	35
Use a social networking site...........................	May, 2010	48	61	43	66
Participate in an online auction	May, 2010	21	26	8	30
Look for religious or spiritual information online	May, 2010	25	32	29	34
Download a podcast so you can listen to it or view it later	May, 2010	17	21	15	23
Make a donation to a charity online......................	May, 2010	18	22	9	25
Create or work on your own online journal or blog	January, 2010	11	14	8	15

Source: Pew Internet & American Life Project Surveys, <http://www.pewinternet.org/index.asp>.

U.S. Census Bureau, Statistical Abstract of the United States: 2011

1159. Typical Daily Internet Activities of Adult Internet Users: 2010

[Percent of Internet users 18 years old and over. Represents persons who reported doing the activity "yesterday." Based on telephone surveys of persons with land-line telephones, unless otherwise noted]

Activity	Survey date (month/year)	Total Internet users	Age 18 to 29 years old	Age 30 to 49 years old	Age 50 to 64 years old	Age 65 years old and over	Sex Male	Sex Female
Send or read e-mail	May, 2010	62	62	67	60	55	61	63
Use a search engine to find information	May, 2010	49	55	54	42	34	49	49
Get news online	May, 2010	43	44	45	42	34	48	38
Check weather reports and forecasts online	May, 2010	34	38	37	27	27	37	31
Look for news or information about politics	May, 2010	19	18	22	17	19	23	16
Do any banking online	May, 2010	26	27	30	22	19	27	25
Watch a video on a video-sharing site	May, 2010	23	39	20	12	17	26	20
Use a social networking site	May, 2010	38	60	39	20	13	34	41
Send instant messages	May, 2010	15	24	15	9	4	13	17
Visit a local, state or federal government Web site	May, 2010	12	11	12	12	10	15	9
Get financial information online	May, 2010	12	9	14	13	14	19	6
Buy a product online	May, 2010	8	7	10	6	6	8	7
Look online for info about a job	May, 2010	10	13	10	7	4	10	9
Use online classified ads or sites like Craig's List	May, 2010	11	14	13	6	5	13	8
Create or work on your own online journal or blog	January, 2010	4	6	4	4	4	4	5
Buy or make a reservation for travel	May, 2010	5	5	6	4	3	5	5
Rate a product, service, or person	May, 2010	4	4	4	6	2	4	5
Participate in an online auction	May, 2010	4	5	5	4	2	6	3
Download a podcast so you can listen to it or view it later	May, 2010	3	5	2	3	1	4	2
Make a donation to a charity online	May, 2010	1	2	1	1	1	1	1
Look for information on Wikipedia	May, 2010	17	29	15	11	4	21	14
Look for religious or spiritual information online	May, 2010	5	5	5	6	4	6	4

Source: Pew Internet & American Life Project Surveys, <http://www.pewinternet.org/index.asp>.

1160. Online News Consumption by Selected Characteristics: 2000 to 2010

[Percent of Internet users 18 years old and over. Represents persons who report getting news online "ever" or "yesterday." Based on telephone surveys of persons with land line telephones, unless otherwise noted. In May 2010, 2,252 persons were interviewed including 744 cell phone users. The response rate for the land line sample was 21.8 percent. The response rate for the cellular sample was 19.3 percent]

Characteristic	"Ever" get news online 2000	"Ever" get news online 2009	"Ever" get news online 2010	Got news online "yesterday" 2000	Got news online "yesterday" 2009	Got news online "yesterday" 2010
Total adult Internet users	**60**	**72**	**75**	**22**	**38**	**43**
Age:						
18 to 29 years old	56	74	75	16	35	44
30 to 49 years old	63	76	78	25	44	45
50 to 64 years old	57	71	76	25	37	42
65 years old and over	53	56	62	28	28	34
Sex:						
Male	66	73	77	29	42	48
Female	53	72	74	16	35	38
Race/ethnicity:						
White, non-Hispanic	60	73	75	23	40	43
Black, non-Hispanic	63	72	72	13	32	42
English-speaking Hispanic	57	67	73	23	34	35
Annual household income:						
Less than $30,000	55	59	64	21	28	28
$30,000 to $49,999	57	69	74	20	33	35
$50,000 to $74,999	63	75	78	22	40	47
$75,000 or more	69	84	84	31	53	60
Frequency of Internet use:						
Daily	66	81	82	33	50	54
Several times per week	59	59	64	17	13	14
Less Often	51	30	38	12	2	5

Source: Pew Internet & American Life Project Surveys from March 2000, April 2009, and May 2010, <http://www.pewinternet.org/index.asp>.

Section 25
Banking, Finance, and Insurance

This section presents data on the nation's finances, various types of financial institutions, money and credit, securities, insurance, and real estate. The primary sources of these data are publications of several departments of the federal government, especially the U.S. Treasury Department, and independent agencies such as the Federal Deposit Insurance Corporation, the Board of Governors of the Federal Reserve System, and the Securities and Exchange Commission. National data on insurance are available primarily from private organizations, such as the American Council of Life Insurers and the Insurance Information Institute.

Flow of funds—The flow of funds accounts of the Federal Reserve Board bring together statistics on all of the major forms of financial instruments to present an economy-wide view of asset and liability relationships. In flow form, the accounts relate borrowing and lending to one another and to the nonfinancial activities that generate income and production. Each claim outstanding is included simultaneously as an asset of the lender and as a liability of the debtor. The accounts also indicate the balance between asset totals and liability totals over the economy as a whole. Several publications of the Federal Reserve Board contain information on the flow of funds accounts: Summary data on flows and outstandings, in the statistical release *Flow of Funds Accounts of the United States* (quarterly); and concepts and organization of the accounts in *Guide to the Flow of Funds Accounts* (2000). Data are also available on the Federal Reserve Board's Web site at <http://www.federalreserve.gov/>.

Survey of Consumer Finances (SCF)—The Federal Reserve Board, in cooperation with the Treasury Department, sponsors this survey, which is conducted every 3 years to provide detailed information on the finances of U.S. families. Among the topics covered are the balance sheet, pension, income, and other demographic

characteristics of U.S. families. The survey also gathers information on the use of financial institutions. Since 1992, data for the SCF have been collected by the National Organization for Research at the University of Chicago. Data and information on the survey are available on the Federal Reserve Board's Web site at <http://www.federalreserve.gov/pubs/oss/oss2/scfindex.html>.

Banking system—Banks in this country are organized under the laws of both the states and the federal government and are regulated by several bank supervisory agencies. National banks are supervised by the Comptroller of the Currency. *Reports of Condition* have been collected from national banks since 1863. Summaries of these reports are published in the Comptroller's *Annual Report*, which also presents data on the structure of the national banking system.

The Federal Reserve System was established in 1913 to exercise central banking functions, some of which are shared with the U.S. Treasury. It includes national banks and such state banks that voluntarily join the system. Statements of state bank members are consolidated by the Federal Reserve Board with data for national banks collected by the Comptroller of the Currency into totals for all member banks of the system. Balance sheet data for member banks and other commercial banks are available on the Federal Reserve Board's Web site at <http://www.federalreserve.gov/econresdata/releases/statisticsdata.htm>.

The Federal Deposit Insurance Corporation (FDIC), established in 1933, insures each depositor up to $250,000. Major item balance sheet and income data for all insured financial institutions are published in the *FDIC Quarterly Banking Profile*. This publication is also available on the Internet at the following address: <http://www.fdic.gov>. Quarterly financial information for individual institutions is available through the FDIC and Federal

Financial Institutions Examination Council Web sites at <http://www.fdic.gov> and <http://www.ffiec.gov>.

Credit unions—Federally chartered credit unions are under the supervision of the National Credit Union Administration. State-chartered credit unions are supervised by the respective state supervisory authorities. The administration publishes comprehensive program and statistical information on all federal and federally insured state credit unions in the *Annual Report of the National Credit Union Administration.*

Other credit agencies—Insurance companies, finance companies dealing primarily in installment sales financing, and personal loan companies represent important sources of funds for the credit market. Statistics on loans, investments, cash, etc., of life insurance companies are published principally by the American Council of Life Insurers in its *Life Insurers Fact Book.* Consumer credit data are available on the Federal Reserve Board's Web site at <http://www.federalreserve .gov/econresdata/releases/statisticsdata .htm>. Government corporations and credit agencies make available credit of specified types or to specified groups of private borrowers, either by lending directly or by insuring or guaranteeing loans made by private lending institutions. Data on operations of government credit agencies, along with other government corporations, are available in reports of individual agencies.

Securities—The Securities and Exchange Commission (SEC) was established in 1934 to protect the interests of the public and investors against malpractices in the securities and financial markets and to provide the fullest possible disclosure of information regarding securities to the investing public.

Data on the securities industry and securities transactions are also available from a number of private sources. The Securities Industry and Financial Markets Association, New York, NY, <http://www.sifma .org/>, publishes the *Securities Industry*

Fact Book and *Securities Industry Yearbook.* The Investment Company Institute, Washington, DC, <http://www.ici.org/>, publishes a reference book, research newsletters, and a variety of research reports that examine the industry, its shareholders, or industry issues. The annual *Mutual Fund Fact Book* is a guide to trends and statistics observed in the investment company industry. *Fundamentals* is a newsletter summarizing the findings of major Institute research projects. Institute research reports provide a detailed examination of shareholder demographics and other aspects of fund ownership.

Among the many sources of data on stock and bond prices and sales are the New York Stock Exchange, New York, NY, <http://www.nyse.com/>; NASDAQ, Washington, DC, <http://www.nasdaq.com/>; Global Financial Data, Los Angeles, CA, <http://www.globalfinancialdata.com/>; and Dow-Jones & Company, Inc., New York, NY, <http://www.djindexes.com>.

Insurance—Insuring companies, which are regulated by the various states or the District of Columbia, are classified as either life or property. Both life and property insurance companies may underwrite health insurance. Insuring companies, other than those classified as life, are permitted to underwrite one or more property lines provided they are so licensed and have the necessary capital or surplus. There are a number of published sources for statistics on the various classes of insurance—life, health, fire, marine, and casualty. Organizations representing certain classes of insurers publish reports for these classes. The American Council of Life Insurers publishes statistics on life insurance purchases, ownership, benefit payments, and assets in its *Life Insurers Fact Book.*

Statistical reliability—For a discussion of statistical collection, estimation, and sampling procedures and measures of reliability applicable to data from the Census Bureau and the Federal Reserve Board's Survey of Consumer Finances, see Appendix III.

Figure 25.1
Interest Rates and Bond Yields: 1990 to 2009
(Annual averages)

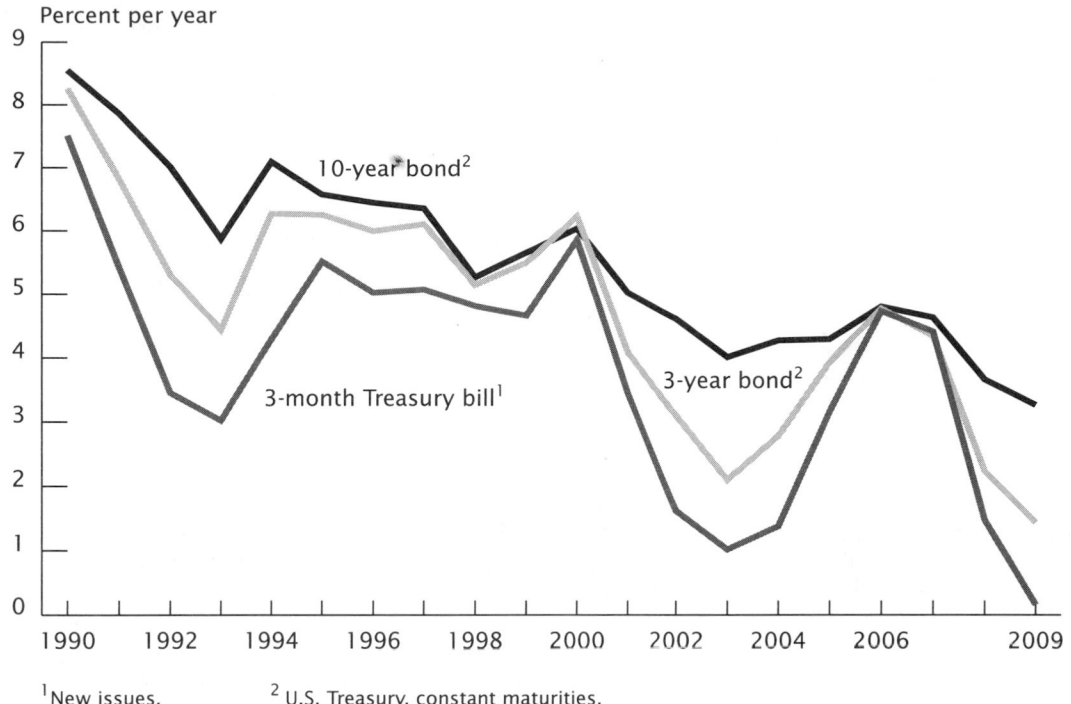

Percent per year

10-year bond[2]

3-month Treasury bill[1]

3-year bond[2]

[1] New issues.   [2] U.S. Treasury, constant maturities.

Source: Chart prepared by U.S. Census Bureau. For data, see Tables 1196 and 1197.

Figure 25.2
Foreign Holdings of U.S. Treasury Securities by Country: 2009
(In billions of dollars)

Total = 3,697.2

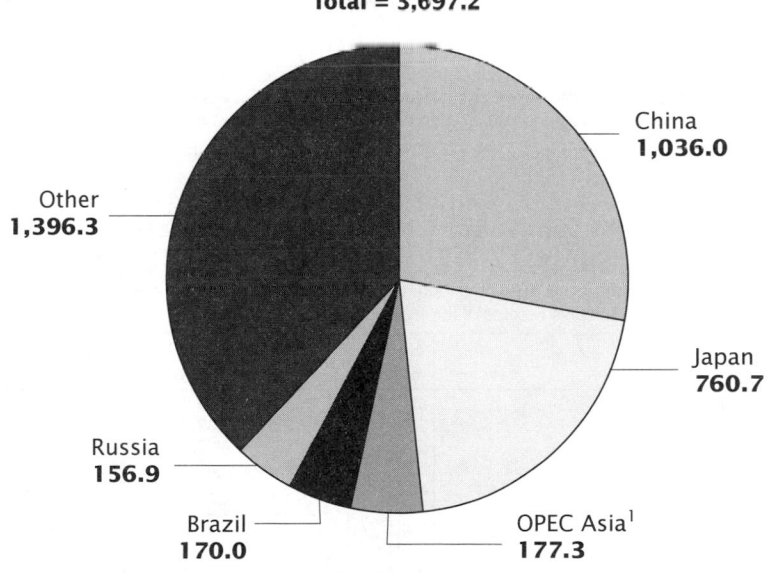

China
1,036.0

Japan
760.7

OPEC Asia[1]
177.3

Brazil
170.0

Russia
156.9

Other
1,396.3

[1] Comprises Iran, Iraq, Kuwait, Qatar, Saudi Arabia, and the United Arab Emirates.

Source: Chart prepared by U.S. Census Bureau. For data, see Table 1205.

U.S. Census Bureau, Statistical Abstract of the United States: 2011

Table 1161. Gross Domestic Product in Finance, Insurance, Real Estate, Rental and Leasing in Current and Chained (2005) Dollars: 2000 to 2009

[In billions of dollars, except percent (762.0 represents $762,000,000,000.) Represents value added by industry. Data for 2000 based on the 1997 North American Classification System (NAICS); beginning 2005 based on 2002 NAICS. See text , Section 15. For definition of gross domestic product and explanation of chained dollars, see text, Section 13, Income]

Industry	NAICS code	Current Dollars				Chained (2005) dollars			
		2000	2005	2008	2009	2000	2005	2008	2009
Finance & insurance, total	52	**762**	**1,029**	**1,200**	**1,198**	**841**	**1,029**	**1,117**	**1,086**
Percent of gross domestic product		7.7	8.1	8.3	8.4	7.5	8.1	8.4	8.4
Monetary authorities–central bank, credit intermediation, and related activities....	521,522	338	471	486	(NA)	371	471	456	(NA)
Security, commodity contracts, & investment activities................	523	126	183	196	(NA)	124	183	160	(NA)
Insurance carriers & related activities	524	274	338	464	(NA)	339	338	450	(NA)
Funds, trusts, & other financial vehicles (part).........................	525	24	37	54	(NA)	20	37	57	(NA)
Real estate & rental & leasing, total...	53	**1,236**	**1,578**	**1,843**	**1,860**	**1,422**	**1,578**	**1,704**	**1,666**
Percent of gross domestic product		12.4	12.5	12.8	13.0	12.7	12.5	12.8	12.8
Real estate	531	1,098	1,425	1,647	(NA)	1,266	1,425	1,524	(NA)
Rental & leasing services and lessors of other nonfinancial intangible assets [1] ...	532,533	138	153	196	(NA)	156	153	180	(NA)

NA Not available. [1] Includes lessors of other nonfinancial intangible assets.

Source: U.S. Bureau of Economic Analysis, *Survey of Current Business*, July 2010, <http://www.bea.gov/Industry/Index.htm>.

Table 1162. Finance and Insurance/Real Estate and Rental and Leasing— Establishments, Revenue, Payroll, and Employees by Kind of Business (2002 NAICS Basis): 2002 and 2007

[2,804 represents $2,804,000,000,000. For establishments with payroll. Based on the 2002 and 2007 Economic Censuses; see Appendix III]

Kind of business	2002 NAICS code [1]	Number of establishments		Revenue (Bil. dol.)		Annual payroll (Bil. dol.)		Paid employees (1,000)	
		2002	2007	2002	2007	2002	2007	2002	2007
Finance & insurance [2]...................	52	**440,268**	**503,156**	**2,804**	**3,641**	**377.8**	**494.5**	**6,579**	**6,563**
Monetary authorities—central bank............	521	47	47	29	45	1.2	1.3	22	19
Credit intermediation & related activities........	522	196,451	235,440	1,056	1,327	151.2	178.1	3,300	3,203
Security, commodity contracts, & like activity	523	72,338	84,829	316	632	103.4	161.1	832	931
Insurance carriers & related activities	524	169,520	182,840	1,380	1,637	120.6	154.0	2,406	2,409
Real estate & rental & leasing	53	**322,815**	**376,799**	**336**	**452**	**60.2**	**85.2**	**1,949**	**2,249**
Real estate	531	256,086	308,004	224	303	41.7	60.8	1,305	1,551
Rental & leasing services	532	64,344	66,067	95	127	16.9	22.1	617	666
Lessors of other nonfinancial intangible assets...	533	2,385	2,728	17	23	1.7	2.4	27	32

[1] Based on the North American Industry Classification System (NAICS); see text, Section 15. [2] Total does not include NAICS 525, Funds, trusts, and other financial vehicles, not published in the 2007 Economic Census.

Source: U.S. Census Bureau, "2007 Economic Census; Core Business Statistics Series: Advance Comparative Statistics for the United States (2002 NAICS Basis): 2007 and 2002," June 2010. See <http://www.census.gov/econ/census07/www/get_data /index.html>.

Table 1163. Finance and Insurance—Nonemployer Establishments and Receipts by Kind of Business: 2005 to 2007

[741.9 represents 741,900. Includes only firms subject to federal income tax. Nonemployers are businesses with no paid employees. Data originate chiefly from administrative records of the Internal Revenue Service; see Appendix III]

Kind of business	NAICS code [1]	Establishments (1,000)			Receipts (mil. dol.)		
		2005	2006	2007	2005	2006	2007
Finance and insurance	52	**741.9**	**758.2**	**763.5**	**47,244**	**52,768**	**54,351**
Credit intermediation & related activities	522	82.5	89.7	92.7	5,046	4,983	4,591
Depository credit intermediation	5221	7.3	7.4	7.6	240	232	278
Nondepository credit intermediation	5222	29.4	30.3	31.7	2,541	2,489	2,376
Activities related to credit intermediation..............	5223	45.8	51.9	53.4	2,265	2,262	1,986
Security, commodity contracts, & like activity	523	276.2	280.3	281.7	23,405	28,113	29,618
Securities & commodity contracts interm & brokerage ...	5231	33.4	32.9	32.6	5,017	4,983	5,496
Investment banking and securities dealing	52311	8.0	8.3	8.1	1,499	1,480	1,596
Securities brokerage	52312	20.5	19.6	19.8	2,872	2,829	2,977
Commodity contracts dealing	52313	1.2	1.3	1.4	211	169	412
Commodity contracts brokerage	52314	3.7	3.7	3.4	435	506	511
Securities & commodity exchanges.................	5232	2.0	2.1	1.9	571	529	578
Other financial investment activities	5239	240.7	246.3	247.1	17,817	22,600	23,544
Insurance carriers & related activities	524	383.3	388.3	389.2	18,793	19,672	20,143
Insurance carriers	5241	0.5	0.5	2.9	37	32	189
Agencies & other insurance-related activities	5242	382.7	387.8	386.2	18,756	19,640	19,954
Insurance agencies & brokerages	52421	256.5	263.0	268.5	13,933	14,593	15,016
Other insurance related activities	52429	126.2	125.2	117.7	4,824	5,047	4,938

[1] Based on the 2002 North American Industry Classification System (NAICS); see text, Section 15.

Source: U.S. Census Bureau, "Nonemployer Statistics" (June 2009), <http://www.census.gov/econ/nonemployer/index.html>.

Table 1164. Finance and Insurance—Establishments, Employees, and Payroll: 2006 and 2007

[494.3 represents 494,300. Covers establishments with payroll. Employees are for the week including March 12. Most government employees are excluded. For statement on methodology, see Appendix III]

Kind of business	NAICS code [1]	Establishments (1,000)		Employees (1,000)		Payroll (bil.dol.)	
		2006	2007	2006	2007	2006	2007
Finance & insurance, total [2]	**52**	**494.3**	**508.1**	**6,647**	**6,549**	**481.0**	**510.6**
Monetary authorities—central bank	521	0.1	0.1	20	20	1.3	1.4
Credit intermediation & related activities	522	224.6	232.7	3,282	3,226	181.3	182.5
Depository credit intermediation [2]	5221	120.6	127.2	2,155	2,138	114.7	121.2
Commercial banking	52211	87.7	93.0	1,634	1,640	91.5	99.0
Savings institutions	52212	16.5	15.9	263	248	13.0	12.4
Credit unions	52213	16.1	18.0	250	242	9.5	9.2
Nondepository credit intermediation [2]	5222	59.4	58.8	765	747	49.5	44.8
Real estate credit	522292	29.9	26.3	402	369	26.5	20.9
Activities related to credit intermediation	5223	44.6	46.8	361	341	17.2	16.5
Security, commodity contracts & like activity	523	86.6	90.1	941	942	148.7	172.3
Security & commodity contracts intermediation & brokerage [2]	5231	39.4	39.7	516	529	89.9	101.7
Investment banking & securities dealing	52311	7.6	9.3	156	184	38.2	46.1
Securities brokerage	52312	29.2	27.7	339	323	49.2	52.1
Securities & commodity exchanges	5232	0.4	(NA)	9	(NA)	1.0	(NA)
Other financial investment activities	5239	46.8	49.9	417	404	57.8	69.2
Insurance carriers & related activities	524	180.2	181.5	2,378	2,327	146.4	151.0
Insurance carriers [2]	5241	34.4	33.6	1,439	1,424	97.1	100.7
Direct life insurance carriers	524113	8.3	8.3	354	359	26.3	28.2
Direct health & medical insurance carriers	524114	4.1	4.1	422	414	27.1	27.8
Direct property & casualty insurance carriers	524126	14.0	13.2	528	533	34.3	36.1
Agencies & other insurance-related activities [2]	5242	145.7	147.9	939	903	49.3	50.3
Insurance agencies & brokerages	52421	132.4	134.3	713	698	37.3	38.5

NA Not available. [1] Based on the 2002 North American Industry Classification System (NAICS); see text, Section 15. [2] Includes industries not shown separately.

Source: U.S. Census Bureau, "County Business Patterns," July 2009, <http://www.census.gov/econ/cbp/index.html>.

Table 1165. Flow of Funds Accounts—Financial Assets of Financial and Nonfinancial Institutions by Holder Sector: 1990 to 2009

[In billions of dollars (35,818 represents $35,818,000,000,000). As of Dec. 31]

Sector	1990	1995	2000	2003	2004	2005	2006	2007	2008	2009
All sectors	**35,818**	**53,494**	**90,088**	**101,759**	**112,771**	**124,017**	**138,676**	**150,852**	**140,250**	**146,086**
Households [1]	14,570	21,520	33,402	35,306	39,263	43,348	48,134	50,759	41,707	45,115
Nonfinancial business	3,970	5,556	11,252	11,908	13,103	14,471	15,748	17,317	17,581	17,878
Farm business	38	49	57	62	66	68	74	79	82	82
Nonfarm noncorporate	356	548	1,423	1,737	2,106	2,542	3,057	3,533	3,748	3,505
Nonfinancial corporations	3,575	4,959	9,772	10,109	10,932	11,862	12,617	13,705	13,751	14,291
State and local government	1,009	1,128	1,002	1,908	2,030	2,247	2,461	2,635	2,612	2,692
U.S. Government	442	432	545	630	610	644	641	687	1,268	1,401
Monetary authorities	342	472	636	797	841	879	908	951	2,271	2,267
Commercial banking	3,337	4,494	6,469	7,825	8,560	9,844	10,821	11,810	14,001	14,138
U.S.-chartered commercial banks	2,644	3,322	4,774	5,838	6,399	7,393	8,190	8,841	10,248	10,046
Foreign banking offices in U.S.	367	666	789	750	633	818	828	1,048	1,625	1,271
Bank-holding companies	298	467	842	1,153	1,429	1,524	1,695	1,813	2,024	2,722
Banks in U.S.-affiliated areas	28	39	63	84	100	109	108	108	105	99
Savings institutions	1,323	1,013	1,218	1,466	1,650	1,789	1,715	1,815	1,524	1,254
Credit unions	217	311	441	617	655	686	716	759	812	885
Life insurance companies	1,351	2,064	3,136	3,773	4,130	4,351	4,685	4,950	4,516	4,819
Property-casualty insurance companies	533	740	862	1,060	1,157	1,246	1,336	1,382	1,306	1,360
Private pension funds	1,629	2,899	4,468	4,520	4,915	5,302	6,010	6,391	4,600	5,457
Defined benefit plans	900	1,466	1,979	1,995	2,132	2,281	2,530	2,666	1,931	2,121
Defined contribution plans	729	1,433	2,489	2,526	2,783	3,021	3,481	3,725	2,670	3,336
State and local government employee retirement funds	730	1,327	2,293	2,349	2,578	2,721	3,108	3,216	2,327	2,673
Federal government retirement funds	340	541	797	958	1,023	1,072	1,141	1,197	1,221	1,324
Money market mutual funds	493	741	1,812	2,016	1,880	2,007	2,312	3,033	3,757	3,259
Mutual funds	608	1,853	4,433	4,654	5,436	6,049	7,068	7,829	5,435	7,002
Closed-end funds	53	136	142	206	246	271	294	317	207	234
Exchange-traded funds	-	1	66	151	227	301	423	608	531	773
Government-sponsored enterprises (GSE)	478	897	1,965	2,794	2,883	2,819	2,873	3,174	3,400	3,029
Agency- and GSE-backed mortgage pools	1,020	1,571	2,493	3,327	3,375	3,542	3,837	4,464	4,961	5,383
Asset-backed securities issuers	268	663	1,497	2,212	2,650	3,388	4,189	4,530	4,096	3,394
Finance companies	596	705	1,213	1,679	1,858	1,857	1,891	1,911	1,852	1,691
Real estate investment trusts	28	33	66	135	251	305	344	317	254	263
Security brokers and dealers	262	568	1,221	1,613	1,845	2,127	2,742	3,092	2,217	2,080
Funding corporations	251	384	1,172	1,065	1,084	1,236	1,313	1,621	2,662	2,294
Rest of the world	1,954	3,452	6,828	8,791	10,523	11,516	13,965	16,091	15,133	15,423

– Represents zero. [1] Includes nonprofit organizations.

Source: Board of Governors of the Federal Reserve System, "Federal Reserve Statistical Release, Z.1, Flow of Funds Accounts of the United States," March 2010, <http://www.federalreserve.gov/releases/z1/20100311>.

U.S. Census Bureau, Statistical Abstract of the United States: 2011

Table 1166. Flow of Funds Accounts—Credit Market Debt Outstanding: 1990 to 2009

[In billions of dollars (13,767 represents $13,767,000,000,000). As of December 31. Excludes corporate equities and mutual fund shares. Represents credit market debt owed by sectors shown]

Item	1990	1995	2000	2003	2004	2005	2006	2007	2008	2009
Credit market debt	**13,767**	**18,469**	**27,138**	**34,624**	**37,799**	**41,267**	**45,329**	**50,044**	**52,525**	**52,417**
Domestic nonfinancial	10,835	13,667	18,166	22,433	24,434	26,764	29,166	31,714	33,577	34,702
Households [1]	3,581	4,841	6,987	9,487	10,548	11,716	12,890	13,748	13,773	13,536
Corporations	2,543	2,942	4,634	4,977	5,180	5,514	5,983	6,776	7,119	7,229
Nonfarm noncorporate business	1,102	1,070	1,806	2,210	2,455	2,787	3,196	3,650	3,850	3,545
Farm business	124	131	156	157	173	190	204	219	219	225
State and local government	987	1,047	1,198	1,568	1,683	1,855	2,008	2,199	2,254	2,362
U.S. government	2,498	3,637	3,385	4,033	4,395	4,702	4,885	5,122	6,362	7,805
Rest of the world	318	568	815	1,253	1,439	1,514	1,883	2,126	1,864	2,063
Financial sectors	2,614	4,234	8,158	10,938	11,926	12,989	14,280	16,204	17,084	15,651
Commercial banking	198	251	509	660	739	824	998	1,261	1,422	1,625
Savings institutions	140	115	301	313	405	427	319	423	356	168
Credit unions	–	–	3	9	11	15	19	32	41	27
Life insurance companies	–	1	2	8	11	11	14	29	55	48
Government-sponsored enterprises (GSE)	399	807	1,826	2,601	2,676	2,592	2,628	2,910	3,182	2,706
Agency- and GSE-backed mortgage pools	1,020	1,571	2,493	3,331	3,375	3,542	3,837	4,464	4,961	5,383
Asset-backed securities issuers	269	666	1,504	2,223	2,662	3,392	4,193	4,533	4,099	3,396
Finance companies	398	500	807	995	1,130	1,109	1,144	1,280	1,200	1,046
Real estate investment trusts	28	45	168	231	340	395	411	421	373	341
Brokers and dealers	15	29	41	47	62	62	69	65	143	93
Funding corporations	147	249	503	518	515	620	648	786	1,253	819

– Represents or rounds to zero. [1] Includes nonprofit organizations.

Source: Board of Governors of the Federal Reserve System, "Federal Reserve Statistical Release, Z.1, Flow of Funds Accounts of the United States," March 2010, <http://www.federalreserve.gov/releases/z1/20100311>.

Table 1167. Flow of Funds Accounts—Financial Assets and Liabilities of Foreign Sector: 1990 to 2009

[In billions of dollars (1,954 represents $1,954,000,000,000). As of December 31]

Type of instrument	1990	1995	2000	2003	2004	2005	2006	2007	2008	2009
Total financial assets [1]	**1,954**	**3,452**	**6,828**	**8,791**	**10,523**	**11,516**	**13,965**	**16,091**	**15,133**	**15,423**
Net interbank assets	53	229	161	110	118	106	97	–57	373	50
U.S. checkable deposits and currency	86	158	236	263	285	300	312	306	361	361
U.S. time deposits	40	40	102	115	149	156	167	208	253	230
Security RPs [2]	20	68	91	460	665	713	1,029	1,109	584	578
Credit market instruments [1]	882	1,465	2,451	3,836	4,635	5,191	6,200	7,273	7,597	7,817
Open market paper	11	43	114	193	230	240	288	278	233	189
Treasury securities	438	817	1,021	1,514	1,814	1,984	2,126	2,376	3,211	3,713
Official	286	490	640	986	1,252	1,341	1,558	1,737	2,326	2,793
Private	152	327	382	527	562	644	568	640	885	921
Agency- and GSE-backed securities [3]	49	123	348	655	875	1,013	1,262	1,582	1,445	1,315
Official	5	18	116	263	373	487	694	954	979	918
Private	44	106	232	392	503	526	568	628	466	397
U.S. corporate bonds [4]	209	355	842	1,330	1,559	1,763	2,321	2,719	2,457	2,357
Loans to U.S. corporate business	172	122	117	125	131	163	169	271	211	182
U.S. corporate equities	243	485	1,422	1,524	1,905	2,039	2,448	2,812	1,776	2,455
Mutual fund shares	–	60	149	146	196	242	317	373	262	338
Trade receivables	46	49	49	50	49	57	63	84	90	139
Miscellaneous assets	584	893	2,155	2,268	2,499	2,688	3,306	3,937	3,776	3,397
Foreign direct investment in U.S. [5]	505	680	1,421	1,581	1,743	1,906	2,154	2,450	2,647	2,786
Other	78	212	734	687	756	782	1,152	1,487	1,129	611
Total liabilities	**1,419**	**2,126**	**3,566**	**4,691**	**5,590**	**6,073**	**7,218**	**8,404**	**8,416**	**7,524**
U.S. official foreign exchange and net IMF [6] position	61	64	46	62	62	46	46	50	57	62
U.S. private deposits	298	419	803	867	957	998	1,085	1,349	996	821
Credit market instruments [1]	318	568	815	1,253	1,439	1,514	1,883	2,126	1,864	2,063
Commercial paper	75	56	121	276	345	384	482	413	342	400
Bonds	145	413	573	869	985	1,012	1,276	1,587	1,393	1,546
Bank loans n.e.c. [7]	19	35	71	66	70	84	98	103	108	97
Trade payables	29	47	51	45	48	54	61	73	63	66
Miscellaneous liabilities [1]	713	1,029	1,851	2,464	3,084	3,461	4,144	4,806	5,435	4,513
U.S. equity in IBRD, [8] etc.	20	27	35	40	42	43	45	47	48	51
Nonofficial foreign currencies	1	2	3	3	3	1	1	24	554	11
U.S. direct investment abroad [4, 5]	630	886	1,532	2,054	2,498	2,652	2,948	3,451	3,699	3,897

– Represents zero. [1] Includes other items not shown separately. [2] Repurchase agreements. [3] GSE = Government-sponsored enterprises. [4] Through 1992, corporate bonds include net issues by Netherlands Antillean financial subsidiaries; U.S. direct investment abroad excludes net inflows from those bond issues. [5] Direct investment is valued on a current-cost basis. [6] IMF = International Monetary Fund. [7] Not elsewhere classified. [8] International Bank for Reconstruction and Development.

Source: Board of Governors of the Federal Reserve System, "Federal Reserve Statistical Release, Z.1, Flow of Funds Accounts of the United States," March 2010, <http://www.federalreserve.gov/releases/z1/20100311>.

Table 1168. Flow of Funds Accounts—Assets of Households and Nonprofit Organizations: 1990 to 2009

[As of December 31 (14,570 represents $14,570,000,000,000). See also Table 721]

Type of instrument	Total (billion dollars)							Percent distribution		
	1990	2000	2005	2006	2007	2008	2009	1990	2000	2009
Total financial assets	**14,570**	**33,402**	**43,348**	**48,134**	**50,759**	**41,707**	**45,115**	**100.0**	**100.0**	**100.0**
Deposits	3,326	4,376	6,155	6,769	7,426	7,901	7,750	22.8	13.1	17.2
Foreign deposits	13	48	60	65	81	60	49	0.1	0.1	0.1
Checkable deposits and currency	433	335	232	189	110	211	251	3.0	1.0	0.6
Time and savings deposits	2,490	3,033	4,914	5,400	5,889	6,050	6,130	17.1	9.1	13.6
Money market fund shares	391	960	949	1,114	1,347	1,580	1,320	2.7	2.9	2.9
Credit market instruments	1,746	2,465	3,363	3,478	4,082	4,034	4,203	12.0	7.4	9.3
Open-market paper	94	97	98	117	107	6	5	0.6	0.3	–
Treasury securities	509	585	508	433	258	264	795	3.5	1.8	1.8
Agency and GSE-backed securities [1]	117	594	488	403	682	701	35	0.8	1.8	0.1
Municipal securities	648	531	821	872	897	937	998	4.4	1.6	2.2
Corporate and foreign bonds	238	552	1,300	1,523	2,011	1,988	2,236	1.6	1.7	5.0
Other loans and advances [2]	–	2	9	8	17	28	32	–	–	0.1
Mortgages	141	103	139	122	109	111	103	1.0	0.3	0.2
Corporate equities [3]	1,961	8,205	7,993	9,493	9,465	5,881	7,698	13.5	24.6	17.1
Mutual fund shares	512	2,704	3,839	4,388	4,832	3,445	4,417	3.5	8.1	9.8
Security credit	62	412	575	656	866	743	668	0.4	1.2	1.5
Life insurance reserves	392	819	1,083	1,164	1,202	1,180	1,250	2.7	2.5	2.8
Pension fund reserves [4]	3,310	9,171	11,374	12,696	13,376	10,432	11,806	22.7	27.5	26.2
Equity in noncorporate business	3,007	4,871	8,358	8,843	8,798	7,325	6,538	20.6	14.6	14.5
Miscellaneous assets	254	379	609	646	712	766	784	1.7	1.1	1.7

– Represents or rounds to zero. [1] GSE = government-sponsored enterprises. [2] Syndicated loans to nonfinancial corporate business by nonprofits and domestic hedge funds. [3] Only those directly held and those in closed-end and exchange-traded funds. Other equities are included in mutual funds and life insurance and pension reserves. [4] See also Table 1216.

Source: Board of Governors of the Federal Reserve System, "Federal Reserve Statistical Release, Z.1, Flow of Funds Accounts of the United States," March 2010, <http://www.federalreserve.gov/releases/z1/20100311>.

Table 1169. Financial Assets Held by Families by Type of Asset: 2004 and 2007

Median value in thousands of constant 2007 dollars (25.3 represents $25,300). All dollar figures are adjusted to 2007 dollars using the "current methods" version of the consumer price index for all urban consumers published by U.S. Bureau of Labor Statistics. Families include one-person units; for definition of family, see text, Section 1. Based on Survey of Consumer Finances; see Appendix III]

Age of family head and family income	Any financial asset [1]	Trans-action accounts [2]	Certifi cates of deposit	Savings bonds	Stocks [3]	Pooled invest-ment funds [4]	Retire-ment accounts [5]	Life insur-ance [6]	Other man-aged [7]
PERCENT OF FAMILIES OWNING ASSET									
2004, total	93.8	91.3	12.7	17.6	20.7	15.0	49.7	24.2	7.3
2007, total	**93.9**	**92.1**	**16.1**	**14.9**	**17.9**	**11.4**	**52.6**	**23.0**	**5.8**
Under 35 years old	89.2	87.3	6.7	13.7	13.7	5.3	41.6	11.1	(B)
35 to 44 years old	93.1	91.0	9.6	16.8	17.0	11.6	57.5	17.5	2.2
45 to 54 years old	93.3	91.7	14.3	19.0	18.6	12.6	64.7	22.3	5.1
55 to 64 years old	97.8	96.4	20.5	16.2	21.3	14.3	60.9	35.2	7.7
65 to 74 years old	96.1	94.6	24.2	10.3	19.1	14.6	51.7	34.4	13.2
75 years old and over	97.4	95.3	37.0	7.9	20.2	13.2	30.0	27.6	14.0
Percentiles of income: [8]									
Less than 20	79.1	74.9	9.4	3.6	5.5	3.4	10.7	12.8	2.7
20 to 39.9	93.2	90.1	12.7	8.5	7.8	4.6	35.6	16.4	4.7
40 to 59.9	97.2	96.4	15.4	15.2	14.0	7.1	55.2	21.6	5.3
60 to 79.9	99.7	99.3	19.3	20.9	23.2	14.6	73.3	29.4	5.7
80 to 89.9	100.0	100.0	19.9	26.2	30.5	18.9	86.7	30.6	7.6
90 to 100	100.0	100.0	27.7	26.1	47.5	35.5	89.6	38.9	13.6
MEDIAN VALUE [9]									
2004, total	25.3	4.1	16.5	1.1	16.5	44.4	38.7	6.6	49.4
2007, total	**28.8**	**4.0**	**20.0**	**1.0**	**17.0**	**56.0**	**45.0**	**8.0**	**70.0**
Under 35 years old	6.8	2.4	5.0	0.7	3.0	18.0	10.0	2.8	(B)
35 to 44 years old	25.8	3.4	5.0	1.0	15.0	22.5	36.0	8.3	24.0
45 to 54 years old	54.0	5.0	15.0	1.0	18.5	50.0	67.0	10.0	45.0
55 to 64 years old	72.4	5.2	23.0	1.9	24.0	112.0	98.0	10.0	59.0
65 to 74 years old	68.1	7.7	23.2	1.0	38.0	86.0	77.0	10.0	70.0
75 years old and over	41.5	6.1	30.0	20.0	40.0	75.0	35.0	5.0	100.0

B Base figure too small. [1] Includes other types of financial assets, not shown separately. [2] Checking, savings, and money market deposit accounts, money market mutual funds, and call accounts at brokerages. [3] Covers only those stocks and bonds that are directly held by families outside mutual funds, retirement accounts, and other managed assets. [4] Excludes money market mutual funds and indirectly held mutual funds and includes all other types of directly held pooled investment funds, such as traditional open-ended and closed-end mutual funds, real estate investment trusts, and hedge funds. [5] The tax-deferred retirement accounts consist of IRAs, Keogh accounts, and certain employer-sponsored accounts. Employer-sponsored accounts include 401(k), 403(b), and thrift saving accounts from current or past jobs; other current job plans from which loans or withdrawals can be made; and accounts from past jobs from which the family expects to receive the account balance in the future. [6] The value of such policies according to their current cash value, not their death benefit. [7] Includes personal annuities and trusts with an equity interest and managed investment accounts. [8] Percentiles of income distribution in 2007 dollars: 20th: $20,600; 40th: $36,500; 60th: $59,600; 80th: $98,200; 90th: $140,900. Percentiles of distribution of net worth in 2007 dollars: 25th: $14,100; 50th: $120,300; 75th: $372,000; 90th: $908,200. Percentile: A value on a scale of zero to 100 that indicates the percent of a distribution that is equal to or below it. [9] Median value of financial asset for families holding such assets.

Source: Board of Governors of the Federal Reserve System, "2007 Survey of Consumer Finances," February 2009, <http://www.federalreserve.gov/pubs/oss/oss2/2007/scf2007home.html>.

Banking, Finance, and Insurance 733

Table 1170. Flow of Funds Accounts—Liabilities of Households and Nonprofit Organizations: 1990 to 2009

[As of December 31 (3,703 represents $3,703,000,000,000). See also Table 721]

Type of instrument	Total (bil. dol.)							Percent distribution		
	1990	2000	2005	2006	2007	2008	2009	1990	2000	2009
Total liabilities	**3,703**	**7,377**	**12,157**	**13,405**	**14,312**	**14,195**	**14,001**	**100.0**	**100.0**	**100.0**
Credit market instruments	3,581	6,987	11,716	12,890	13,748	13,773	13,536	96.7	94.7	96.7
Home mortgages [1]	2,489	4,798	8,848	9,825	10,484	10,427	10,262	67.2	65.0	73.3
Consumer credit	824	1,741	2,321	2,416	2,555	2,594	2,481	22.3	23.6	17.7
Municipal securities	86	138	205	224	241	250	265	2.3	1.9	1.9
Bank loans, not elsewhere classified. . .	18	64	36	86	100	118	151	0.5	0.9	1.1
Other loans and advances.	82	119	119	124	127	133	134	2.2	1.6	1.0
Commercial mortgages	83	127	187	214	240	251	242	2.2	1.7	1.7
Security credit	39	235	232	292	326	165	203	1.0	3.2	1.4
Trade payables	67	135	186	200	215	230	241	1.8	1.8	1.7
Unpaid life insurance premiums [2]	16	20	22	23	24	27	21	0.4	0.3	0.2

[1] Includes loans made under home equity lines of credit and home equity loans secured by junior liens. [2] Includes deferred premiums.

Source: Board of Governors of the Federal Reserve System, "Federal Reserve Statistical Release, Z.1, Flow of Funds Accounts of the United States," March 2010, <http://www.federalreserve.gov/releases/z1/20100311>.

Table 1171. Financial Debt Held by Families by Type of Debt: 2004 and 2007

[Median debt in thousands of constant 2007 dollars (60.7 represents $60,700). See headnote, Table 1169]

Age of family head and family income	Any debt	Secured by residential property		Lines of credit not secured by residential property	Installment loans	Credit card balances [2]	Other [3]
		Primary residence [1]	Other				
PERCENT OF FAMILIES HOLDING DEBT							
2004, total	76.4	47.9	4.0	1.6	46.0	46.2	7.6
2007, total	**77.0**	**48.7**	**5.5**	**1.7**	**46.9**	**46.1**	**6.8**
Under 35 years old	83.5	37.3	3.3	2.1	65.2	48.5	5.9
35 to 44 years old	86.2	59.5	6.5	2.2	56.2	51.7	7.5
45 to 54 years old	86.8	65.5	8.0	1.9	51.9	53.6	9.8
55 to 64 years old	81.8	55.3	7.8	1.2	44.6	49.9	8.7
65 to 74 years old	65.5	42.9	5.0	1.5	26.1	37.0	4.4
75 years old and over	31.4	13.9	0.6	(B)	7.0	18.8	1.3
Percentiles of income: [4]							
Less than 20	51.7	14.9	1.1	(B)	27.8	25.7	3.9
20 to 39.9.	70.2	29.5	1.9	1.8	42.3	39.4	6.8
40 to 59.9.	83.8	50.5	2.6	(B)	54.0	54.9	6.4
60 to 79.9.	90.9	69.7	6.8	2.1	59.2	62.1	8.7
80 to 89.9.	89.6	80.8	8.5	(B)	57.4	55.8	9.6
90 to 100	87.6	76.4	21.9	2.1	45.0	40.6	7.0
MEDIAN DEBT [5]							
2004, total	60.7	104.3	95.6	3.3	12.7	2.4	4.4
2007, total	**67.3**	**107.0**	**100.0**	**3.8**	**13.0**	**3.0**	**5.0**
Under 35 years old	36.2	135.3	78.0	1.0	15.0	1.8	4.5
35 to 44 years old	106.2	128.0	101.6	4.6	13.5	3.5	5.0
45 to 54 years old	95.9	110.0	82.0	6.0	12.9	3.6	4.5
55 to 64 years old	60.3	85.0	130.0	10.0	10.9	3.6	6.0
65 to 74 years old	40.1	69.0	125.0	30.0	10.3	3.0	5.0
75 years old and over	13.0	40.0	50.0	(B)	8.0	0.8	4.5

B Base figure too small. [1] First and second mortgages and home equity loans and lines of credit secured. [2] Families that had an outstanding balance on any of their credit cards after paying their most recent bills. [3] Includes loans on insurance policies, loans against pension accounts, borrowing on margin accounts and unclassified loans. [4] See footnote 8, Table 1169. [5] Median amount of financial debt for families holding such debts.

Source: Board of Governors of the Federal Reserve System, "2007 Survey of Consumer Finances," February 2009, <http://www.federalreserve.gov/pubs/oss/oss2/2007/scf2007home.html>.

Table 1172. Amount of Debt Held by Families—Percent Distribution: 2004 and 2007

[See headnote, Table 1169]

Type of debt	2004	2007	Purpose of debt	2004	2007	Type of lending institution	2004	2007
Total.	**100.0**	**100.0**	**Total. . . . .**	**100.0**	**100.0**	**Total. . . . .**	**100.0**	**100.0**
Secured by residential property:			Primary residence:			Commercial bank.	35.1	37.3
Primary residence	75.2	74.7	Purchase	70.2	69.5	Thrift institution	7.3	4.2
Other	8.5	10.1	Improvement	1.9	2.3	Credit union	3.6	4.2
Lines of credit not secured by residential			Other residential property	9.5	10.8	Finance or loan company	4.1	3.4
property	0.7	0.4	Investments, excluding			Brokerage	2.5	1.6
Installment loans	11.0	10.2	real estate	2.2	1.6	Real estate lender [1]	39.4	41.6
Credit card balances . . .	3.0	3.5	Vehicles	6.7	5.5	Individual lender	1.7	1.4
Other	1.6	1.1	Goods and services. . . .	6.0	6.2	Other nonfinancial	2.0	2.0
			Education.	3.0	3.6	Government.	0.7	0.4
			Other loans	0.6	0.5	Credit card issuer	3.0	3.6
						Other type of lender. . .	0.5	0.4

[1] Includes mortgage lender.

Source: Board of Governors of the Federal Reserve System, "2007 Survey of Consumer Finances," February 2009, <http://www.federalreserve.gov/pubs/oss/oss2/2007/scf2007home.html>.

Table 1173. Ratios of Debt Payments to Family Income: 2001 to 2007

[In percent. All dollar figures are adjusted to 2007 dollars using the "current methods" version of the consumer price index for all urban consumers published by U.S. Bureau of Labor Statistics. Families include one-person units; for definition of family, see text, Section 1. Based on Survey of Consumer Finance; see Appendix III. For definition of median, see Guide to Tabular Presentation]

Age of family head and family income (constant [2007] dollars)	Ratio of debt payments to family income						Percent of debtors with—					
	Aggregate			Median for debtors			Ratios above 40 percent			Any payment 60 days or more past due		
	2001	2004	2007	2001	2004	2007	2001	2004	2007	2001	2004	2007
All families	12.9	14.4	14.5	16.7	18.0	18.6	11.8	12.2	14.7	7.0	8.9	7.1
Under 35 years old	17.2	17.8	19.7	17.7	18.0	17.5	12.0	12.8	15.1	11.9	13.7	9.4
35 to 44 years old	15.1	18.2	18.5	17.8	20.6	20.3	10.1	12.5	12.7	5.9	11.7	8.6
45 to 54 years old	12.8	15.3	14.9	17.4	18.4	19.3	11.6	13.1	16.0	6.2	7.6	7.3
55 to 64 years old	10.9	11.5	12.5	14.3	15.7	17.5	12.3	10.2	14.5	7.1	4.2	4.9
65 to 74 years old	9.2	8.7	9.6	16.0	15.6	17.9	14.7	11.6	15.6	1.5	3.4	4.4
75 years old and over	3.9	7.1	4.4	8.0	12.8	13.0	14.6	10.7	13.9	0.8	3.9	1.0
Percentiles of income: [1]												
Less than 20	16.1	18.2	17.6	19.2	19.7	19.0	29.3	26.8	26.9	13.4	15.9	15.1
20 to 39.9.	15.8	16.6	17.2	16.7	17.4	17.0	16.6	18.5	19.5	11.7	13.8	11.5
40 to 59.9.	17.1	19.4	19.8	17.6	19.5	20.3	12.3	13.7	14.5	7.9	10.4	8.3
60 to 79.9.	16.8	18.5	21.7	18.1	20.6	21.9	6.5	7.1	12.7	4.0	7.1	4.1
80 to 89.9.	17.0	17.3	19.7	17.2	18.1	19.3	3.5	2.4	8.1	2.6	2.3	2.1
90 to 100	8.1	9.3	8.4	11.2	12.7	12.5	2.0	1.8	3.8	1.3	0.3	0.2

[1] See footnote 8, Table 1169.

Source: Board of Governors of the Federal Reserve System, "2007 Survey of Consumer Finances," February 2009, <http://www.federalreserve.gov/pubs/oss/oss2/2007/scf2007home.html>.

Table 1174. Household Debt-Service Payments and Financial Obligations as a Percentage of Disposable Personal Income: 1990 to 2009

[As of end of year, seasonally adjusted. Household debt service ratio is an estimate of the ratio of debt payments to disposable personal income. Debt payments consist of the estimated required payments on outstanding mortgage and consumer debt. The financial obligations ratio adds automobile lease payments, rental payments on tenant-occupied property, homeowners' insurance, and property tax payments to the debt service ratio]

Year	Household debt service ratio	Financial obligations ratio			Year	Household debt service ratio	Financial obligations ratio		
		Total	Renter	Home-owner			Total	Renter	Home-owner
1990	12.03	17.46	24.85	15.57	2005.	13.75	18.44	25.19	17.09
1995.	11.67	17.10	26.67	14.80	2006.	13.85	18.64	25.38	17.31
2000.	12.59	17.65	30.43	15.13	2007.	13.88	18.79	24.99	17.52
2003.	13.19	17.90	26.59	16.17	2008.	13.57	18.56	25.12	17.20
2004.	13.29	17.92	25.41	16.44	2009.	12.60	17.51	24.39	16.08

Source: Board of Governors of the Federal Reserve System, "Household Debt Service and Financial Obligations Ratios," <http://www.federalreserve.gov/releases/housedebt/default.htm\>.

Table 1175. FDIC-Insured Financial Institutions—Deposit Insurance Fund (DIF): 1990 to 2009

[In billions of dollars, except as indicated (4,735 represents $4,735,000,000,000). As of December 31. Includes Island Areas. Includes insured branches of foreign banks]

Item	1990	2000	2003	2004	2005	2006	2007	2008	2009
Number of institutions	15,369	9,920	9,194	8,988	8,845	8,692	8,545	8,315	8,022
Assets, total [1]	4,735	7,472	9,086	10,117	10,894	11,881	13,051	13,900	13,109
Domestic deposits, total [2]	3,415	4,212	5,224	5,725	6,230	6,640	6,922	7,505	7,705
Estimated insured deposits [3]	2,697	3,055	3,452	3,622	3,891	4,154	4,292	4,751	5,392
DIF balance (BIF/SAIF prior to 2006) . . .	4	42	46	48	49	50	52	17	–21
Reserve ratio [4, 5]	0.15	1.36	1.33	1.31	1.25	1.21	1.22	0.36	–0.39
Number of problem institutions	1,496	94	116	80	52	50	76	252	702
Assets of problem institutions	646.8	23.8	29.9	28.2	6.6	8.3	22.2	159.4	402.8
Number of assisted institutions	1	–	–	–	–	–	–	5	8
Assets of assisted institutions	(Z)	–	–	–	–	–	–	1,306.0	1,917.5
Number of failed institutions	381	7	3	4	–	–	3	25	140
Assets of assisted institutions	146.6	0.4	0.9	0.2	–	–	2.6	371.9	169.7

– Represents zero. Z Less than $50 million. [1] Does not include foreign branch assets [2] Excludes foreign office deposits which are uninsured. [3] In general, insured deposits are total domestic deposits minus estimated uninsured deposits. Beginning March 31, 2008, for institutions that file call reports, insured deposits are total assessable deposits minus estimated uninsured deposits. Beginning September 30, 2009, insured deposits include deposits in accounts of $100,000 to $250,000 that are covered by a temporary increase in the FDIC's standard maximum deposit insurance amount (SMDIA). [4] DIF balance as percent of DIF-insured deposits. [5] To provide the FDIC with the funds needed to carry on with the task of resolving failed institutions in 2010 and beyond, but without accelerating the impact of assessments on the industry's earnings and capital, FDIC approved a measure to require insured institutions to prepay 13 quarters worth of deposit insurance premiums. These prepayments—about $46 billion— were collected on December 30, 2009. Cash and marketable securities stood at $66 billion on December 31, 2009. See "Deposit Trend fund trends—Fourth Quarter 2009; Prepaid Assessments."

Source: U.S. Federal Deposit Insurance Corporation, *The FDIC Quarterly Banking Profile.*

Table 1176. FDIC-Insured Financial Institutions—Number, Assets, and Liabilities: 1990 to 2009

[In billions of dollars, except as indicated (4,649 represents $4,649,000,000,000). As of December 31. 2009 data preliminary. Includes Island Areas. Excludes insured branches of foreign banks. Except as noted, includes foreign branches of U.S. banks]

Item	1990	2000	2003	2004	2005	2006	2007	2008	2009
Commercial bank offices, total [1]	**63,205**	**73,174**	**75,985**	**78,473**	**80,967**	**83,860**	**94,081**	**97,474**	**97,423**
Number of main offices	12,347	8,315	7,770	7,631	7,526	7,401	7,283	7,086	6,839
Number of branches	50,858	64,859	68,215	70,842	73,441	76,459	86,798	90,388	90,584
Savings institutions offices, total [2]	**2,815**	**1,589**	**1,411**	**1,345**	**1,307**	**1,279**	**1,251**	**1,219**	**1,173**
Number of financial institutions reporting	15,162	9,905	9,181	8,976	8,833	8,680	8,534	8,305	8,012
Assets, total [3]	**4,649**	**7,462**	**9,075**	**10,106**	**10,878**	**11,862**	**13,034**	**13,841**	**13,109**
Net loans and leases	2,867	4,576	5,349	6,037	6,640	7,156	7,804	7,700	7,059
Real estate loans	1,586	2,396	3,144	3,680	4,141	4,508	4,782	4,705	4,463
1–4 family residential mortgages	859	1,340	1,611	1,833	2,042	2,735	2,853	2,713	2,578
Commercial real estate	328	525	682	752	826	904	969	1,066	1,091
Construction and development	171	197	272	338	450	590	629	591	452
Home equity loans [4]	86	151	346	491	534	559	611	668	661
Commercial and industrial loans	646	1,086	922	968	1,086	1,215	1,439	1,494	1,221
Loans to individuals	451	672	848	930	949	955	1,058	1,089	1,060
Credit cards and related plans	142	266	339	399	396	385	422	445	422
Farm loans	33	49	47	49	52	54	57	60	60
Other loans and leases	245	448	478	496	494	504	629	588	546
Less: Reserve for losses	65	71	86	82	77	78	103	174	227
Less: Unearned income	29	3	3	3	3	2	2	3	4
Securities	890	1,361	1,771	1,860	1,893	1,981	1,954	2,035	2,500
Domestic office assets	4,259	6,702	8,251	9,160	9,824	10,557	11,475	12,321	11,673
Foreign office assets	390	760	824	945	1,054	1,304	1,559	1,520	1,437
Liabilities and capital, total	**4,649**	**7,462**	**9,075**	**10,106**	**10,878**	**11,862**	**13,034**	**13,841**	**13,109**
Noninterest-bearing deposits	511	802	1,028	1,173	1,267	1,270	1,260	1,481	1,618
Interest-bearing deposits	3,127	4,113	4,926	5,412	5,874	6,555	7,156	7,554	7,609
Other borrowed funds	569	1,467	1,735	1,905	2,063	2,121	2,517	2,570	1,782
Subordinated debt	28	90	107	119	131	161	185	185	157
Other liabilities	128	356	450	459	424	507	569	759	476
Equity capital	286	634	831	1,039	1,119	1,248	1,347	1,291	1,447
Domestic office deposits	3,344	4,208	5,213	5,719	6,221	6,631	6,913	7,496	7,697
Foreign office deposits	293	707	741	866	921	1,194	1,503	1,539	1,530

[1] Includes insured branches of foreign banks that file a Call Report. [2] Main offices. [3] Includes other items not shown separately. [4] For one- to four-family residential properties.

Source: U.S. Federal Deposit Insurance Corporation, *The FDIC Quarterly Banking Profile, Historical Statistics on Banking*, annual; *Statistics on Banking*, annual; and *FDIC Quarterly Banking Profile Graph Book*.

Table 1177. FDIC-Insured Financial Institutions—Income and Selected Measures of Financial Condition: 1990 to 2009

[In billions of dollars, except as indicated (437.7 represents $437,700,000,000). 2009 data preliminary. Includes Island Areas. Includes foreign branches of U.S. banks]

Item	1990	2000	2003	2004	2005	2006	2007	2008	2009
Interest income	437.7	511.9	404.2	417.5	522.0	643.5	724.8	603.3	541.2
Interest expense	295.9	276.6	122.3	123.3	205.0	313.4	372.1	245.6	145.4
Net interest income	141.8	235.3	281.9	294.1	317.0	330.1	352.7	357.7	395.8
Provisions for loan losses	41.4	32.1	37.3	29.0	29.8	29.6	69.3	176.2	247.7
Noninterest income	62.2	165.6	202.9	203.6	223.4	240.4	233.1	207.7	260.5
Percent of net operating revenue [1]	30.5	30.7	32.2	31.8	32.9	34.3	35.4	38.6	40.9
Noninterest expense	144.2	242.3	279.7	295.5	317.4	332.3	367.0	368.3	384.6
Income taxes	9.1	43.6	58.9	58.5	64.6	68.1	46.4	6.3	5.5
Net income	11.3	81.5	120.6	122.2	133.8	145.2	100.0	4.5	12.5
PERFORMANCE RATIOS									
Return on assets [2] (percent)	0.24	1.14	1.38	1.28	1.28	1.28	0.81	0.03	0.09
Return on equity [3] (percent)	3.95	13.53	15.05	13.20	12.43	12.30	7.75	0.35	0.90
Net interest margin [4] (percent)	3.47	3.77	3.73	3.52	3.47	3.31	3.29	3.16	3.47
Net charge-offs [5]	34.80	26.30	40.79	32.02	31.59	27.02	44.11	100.36	186.82
Net charge-offs to loans and leases, total (percent)	1.19	0.59	0.78	0.56	0.49	0.39	0.59	1.29	2.49
Net charge-off rate, credit card loans (percent)	3.39	4.36	5.61	4.99	4.74	3.44	4.06	5.44	9.10
CONDITION RATIOS									
Equity capital to assets (percent)	6.16	8.49	9.15	10.28	10.28	10.52	10.34	9.33	11.04
Noncurrent assets plus other real estate owned to assets [6] (percent)	3.16	0.71	0.75	0.53	0.50	0.54	0.95	1.91	3.32

[1] Net operating revenue equals net interest income plus noninterest income. Net operating revenue equals income excluding discretionary transactions such as gains or losses on the sale of investment securities and extraordinary items. Income taxes subtracted from operating income have been adjusted to exclude the portion applicable to securities gains or losses. [2] Net income (including securities transactions and nonrecurring items) as a percentage of average total assets. [3] Net income as a percentage of average total equity capital. [4] Interest income less interest expense as a percentage of average earning assets (i.e. the profit margin a bank earns on its loans and investments). [5] Total loans and leases charged off (removed from balance sheet because of uncollectibility), less amounts recovered on loans and leases previously charged off. [6] Noncurrent assets: the sum of loans, leases, debt securities and other assets that are 90 days or more past due, or in nonaccrual status. Other real estate owned, primarily foreclosed property.

Source: U.S. Federal Deposit Insurance Corporation, *Annual Report*; *Statistics on Banking*, annual; and *FDIC Quarterly Banking Profile*.

Table 1178. FDIC-Insured Financial Institutions by Asset Size: 2009

[(11,846 represents $11,846,000,000,000). Preliminary. Minus sign (–) indicates loss. See headnote, Table 1177]

Item	Unit	Total	Less than $100 million	$100 million to $1 billion	$1 billion to $10 billion	Greater than $10 billion
COMMERCIAL BANKS						
Institutions reporting	Number	6,839	2,525	3,800	429	85
Assets, total.	Bil. dol.	11,846	141	1,113	1,121	9,472
Deposits.	Bil. dol.	8,333	119	918	851	6,445
Net income	Bil. dol.	11	77	(Z)	–4	15
Return on assets	Percent	0.09	0.06	–0.01	–0.35	0.15
Return on equity	Percent	0.85	0.46	–0.15	–3.16	1.44
Equity capital to assets	Percent	11.07	11.65	9.82	10.92	11.23
Noncurrent assets plus other real estate						
owned to assets.	Percent	3.36	2.23	3.36	3.78	3.33
Net charge-offs to loans and leases	Percent	2.57	0.89	1.27	2.04	2.87
Percentage of banks losing money	Percent	29.38	26.73	29.63	39.63	44.71
SAVINGS INSTITUTIONS						
Institutions reporting	Number	1,173	320	695	136	22
Assets, total.	Bil. dol.	1,263	17	243	342	661
Deposits.	Bil. dol.	894	14	188	435	257
Net income	Bil. dol.	2	(–Z)	(Z)	2	(–Z)
Return on assets	Percent	0.14	–0.31	0.01	0.34	–0.12
Return on equity	Percent	1.39	–1.98	0.14	3.29	–1.17
Equity capital to assets	Percent	10.78	15.01	10.50	11.00	10.33
Noncurrent assets plus other real estate						
owned to assets.	Percent	2.96	2.14	2.83	3.03	2.97
Net charge-offs to loans and leases	Percent	1.81	0.63	0.82	2.54	1.34
Percentage of banks losing money	Percent	30.35	34.38	28.49	36.36	29.41

Z Less than $500 million.

Source: U.S. Federal Deposit Insurance Corporation, *Annual Report; Statistics on Banking,* annual; and *FDIC Quarterly Banking Profile.* See also <http://www.fdic.gov/bank/index.html>.

Table 1179. FDIC-Insured Financial Institutions—Number and Assets by State and Island Areas: 2009

[In billions of dollars, except as indicated (13,109.5 represents $13,109,500,000,000). As of December 31. Information is obtained primarily from the Federal Financial Institutions Examination Council (FFIEC) Call Reports and the Office of Thrift Supervision's Thrift Financial Reports. Data are based on the location of each reporting institution's main office. Reported data may include assets located outside of the reporting institution's home state]

State or Island Area	Number of institu-tions	Assets by asset size of bank				State or Island Area	Number of institu-tions	Assets by asset size of bank			
		Total	Less than $1 bil.	$1 bil. to $10 bil.	Greater than $10 bil.			Total	Less than $1 bil.	$1 bil. to $10 bil.	Greater than $10 bil.
Total. . .	**8,012**	**13,109.6**	**1,514.5**	**1,462.7**	**10,132.2**	NV	37	1,240.7	5.6	19.9	1,215.1
AL	152	243.8	31.1	10.1	202.6	NH	24	9.4	8.4	1.0	–
AK	6	4.8	2.2	2.7	–	NJ	123	176.6	31.3	56.8	88.5
AZ	44	15.1	7.8	7.3	–	NM.	54	19.6	10.0	9.6	–
AR	134	55.5	26.4	17.8	11.3	NY	194	629.4	48.2	113.7	467.6
CA	293	451.5	65.0	108.1	278.4	NC	105	2,228.4	23.6	26.6	2,178.2
CO.	145	51.6	29.6	22.0	–	ND	94	23.4	12.6	10.8	–
CT	55	77.6	15.8	23.4	38.3	OH	243	2,256.2	39.8	37.1	2,179.3
DE	30	592.8	4.3	25.4	563.0	OK	252	78.9	33.9	15.8	29.2
DC	6	1.6	1.6	–	–	OR	37	40.6	7.5	17.0	16.1
FL	286	158.6	69.0	65.8	23.8	PA	224	537.9	57.1	100.8	380.1
GA.	305	271.4	65.8	41.3	164.3	RI.	14	148.7	2.5	5.6	140.6
HI.	9	38.8	1.4	11.2	26.1	SC	89	56.8	24.5	20.4	11.9
ID.	18	7.6	5.4	2.3	–	SD	83	728.1	11.0	10.3	706.7
IL.	630	331.4	103.6	76.1	151.7	TN	194	89.0	45.6	17.5	25.8
IN.	148	67.7	29.0	38.7	–	TX	629	371.5	109.5	97.0	165.1
IA.	367	64.9	51.2	13.7	–	UT	64	322.7	12.5	40.9	269.4
KS	339	62.3	42.3	20.1	–	VT	14	5.5	4.1	1.4	–
KY	199	53.6	35.1	18.6	–	VA	119	443.6	30.8	35.3	377.6
LA	158	60.4	36.3	12.2	11.9	WA.	95	76.3	22.8	30.5	23.0
ME.	29	27.7	10.7	6.9	10.1	WV	65	25.3	10.8	14.6	–
MD.	90	35.2	22.1	13.1	–	WI	281	153.9	57.2	23.8	72.8
MA.	171	252.5	46.7	52.1	153.7	WY	37	7.2	7.2	–	–
MI.	146	71.8	28.8	17.6	25.3						
MN.	415	80.2	52.0	10.3	17.9	AS	1	0.1	0.1	–	–
MS.	94	58.6	20.3	25.1	13.2	GU	3	1.2	1.2	–	–
MO.	345	137.6	55.5	43.4	38.7	FM	1	0.1	0.1	–	–
MT	74	21.2	10.9	10.2	–	PR	10	93.0	–	38.2	54.8
NE	236	49.2	26.6	22.6	–	VI.	2	0.2	0.2	–	–

– Represents zero. AS—American Samoa. FM—Federated States of Micronesia. GU—Guam, PR—Puerto Rico. VI—Virgin Islands.

Source: U.S. Federal Deposit Insurance Corporation, *Statistics on Banking,* annual.

Table 1180. FDIC-Insured Financial Institutions—Number of Offices and Deposits by State: 2008

[As of June 30 (7,025.8 represents $7,025,800,000,000). Includes insured U.S. branches of foreign banks. The term "offices" includes both main offices and branches. "Banking office" is defined to include all offices and facilities that actually hold deposits, and does not include loan production offices, computer centers, and other nondeposit installations, such as automated teller machines (ATMs). Several institutions have designated home offices that do not accept deposits; these have been included to provide a more complete listing of all offices. The figures for each geographical area only include deposits of offices located within that area. Based on the Summary of Deposits survey]

State	Number of offices	Total deposits (bil. dol.)	State	Number of offices	Total deposits (bil. dol.)	State	Number of offices	Total deposits (bil. dol.)
Total [1] ...	99,161	7,025.8	IA........	1,639	60.1	NC.......	2,746	219.5
U.S.......	98,525	6,956.6	KS........	1,556	57.9	ND........	445	15.3
			KY........	1,828	64.4	OH........	4,066	227.8
AL........	1,564	76.6	LA........	1,606	74.7	OK........	1,383	63.0
AK........	134	13.7	ME........	518	19.5	OR........	1,104	49.2
AZ........	1,379	78.7	MD........	1,829	96.6	PA........	4,822	271.7
AR........	1,513	47.1	MA........	2,228	185.3	RI........	247	29.6
CA........	7,313	762.8	MI........	3,125	157.2	SC........	1,440	66.5
CO........	1,664	83.1	MN........	1,862	101.1	SD........	482	74.9
CT........	1,305	83.2	MS........	1,181	45.5	TN........	2,302	104.8
DE........	272	176.9	MO........	2,427	110.7	TX........	6,887	404.2
DC........	228	23.4	MT........	387	15.5	UT........	621	229.3
FL........	5,771	380.3	NE........	1,080	38.8	VT........	272	9.9
GA........	2,873	184.3	NV........	603	199.8	VA........	2,649	193.9
HI........	288	26.2	NH........	433	23.0	WA........	1,925	112.3
ID........	541	17.2	NJ........	3,381	227.2	WV........	664	26.9
IL........	5,046	344.6	NM........	512	22.3	WI........	2,389	114.8
IN........	2,401	90.6	NY........	5,364	763.3	WY........	230	11.1

[1] Includes Puerto Rico and other areas not shown separately.

Source: U.S. Federal Deposit Insurance Corporation, *Bank and Thrift Branch Office Data Book*, annual.

Table 1181. U.S. Banking Offices of Foreign Banks—Summary: 1990 to 2009

[In billions of dollars, except as indicated (834 represents $834,000,000,000). As of December. Covers the U.S. offices of foreign banking organizations that are located in the 50 states and the District of Columbia. Offices located in Puerto Rico, American Samoa, Guam, the Virgin Islands and other U.S.-affiliated insular areas are excluded. Foreign-owned institutions are those owned by a bank located outside of the United States and its affiliated insular areas. The U.S. offices of foreign banking organizations consist of U.S. branches and agencies of foreign banks and bank subsidiaries of foreign banking organizations. The latter are U.S. commercial banks of which more than 25 percent are owned by a foreign banking organization or where the relationship is reported as being a controlling relationship by the filer of the FR Y-10 (Report of Changes in Organizational Structure) report form]

Item	1990	2000	2004	2005	2006	2007	2008	2009	Share [1] 1990	2000	2005	2009
Assets...........	834	1,358	1,808	2,123	2,515	2,871	3,032	2,872	20.9	18.9	20.6	21.0
Loans, total........	412	557	656	802	913	1,055	1,167	1,022	17.2	13.5	14.1	14.8
Business........	199	309	231	276	342	412	483	384	27.7	25.0	24.5	28.1
Deposits..........	425	770	1,025	1,162	1,375	1,629	1,606	1,795	14.6	16.5	17.3	19.1

[1] Foreign owned banks plus U.S. branches and offices of foreign banks as percent of all banks in the United States.

Source: Board of Governors of the Federal Reserve System, "Share Data for U.S. Offices of Foreign Banks," March 2010, <http://www.federalreserve.gov/Releases/iba/fboshr.htm>.

Table 1182. Federal and State-Chartered Credit Unions—Summary: 1990 to 2009

[Except as noted, as of December 31 (36,241 represents 36,241,000). Federal data include District of Columbia, Puerto Rico, Guam, and Virgin Islands. Excludes state-insured, privately insured, and noninsured state-chartered credit unions and corporate central credit unions, which have mainly other credit unions as members]

Year	Operating credit unions Federal	State	Number of failed institutions [1]	Members (1,000) Federal	State	Assets (mil. dol.) Federal	State	Loans outstanding (mil. dol.) Federal	State	Savings (mil. dol.) Federal	State
1990........	8,511	4,349	164	36,241	19,454	130,073	68,133	83,029	44,102	117,892	62,082
2000........	6,336	3,980	29	43,883	33,705	242,881	195,363	163,851	137,485	210,188	169,053
2002........	5,953	3,735	15	44,600	36,300	301,238	255,837	181,768	160,881	261,819	222,372
2003........	5,776	3,593	13	46,153	36,287	336,611	273,572	202,898	173,236	291,484	236,856
2004........	5,572	3,442	21	46,858	36,710	358,701	288,294	223,878	190,376	308,317	247,804
2005........	5,393	3,302	27	47,612	36,895	377,804	300,868	249,515	208,728	321,820	255,804
2006........	5,189	3,173	22	48,262	37,487	394,125	315,817	270,420	223,917	333,914	267,275
2007........	5,036	3,065	12	48,474	38,363	417,578	335,885	289,169	237,755	349,100	283,298
2008........	4,847	2,959	19	49,129	39,437	447,484	364,404	309,275	256,721	373,369	307,762
2009........	4,714	2,840	31	49,599	40,333	482,686	402,071	311,154	261,285	408,832	343,835

[1] 1990 for year ending September 30; beginning 2000, reflects calendar year. A failed institution is defined as a credit union which has ceased operation because it was involuntarily liquidated or merged with assistance from the National Credit Union Share Insurance Fund.

Source: National Credit Union Administration, *Annual Report of the National Credit Union Administration*, and unpublished data.

U.S. Census Bureau, Statistical Abstract of the United States: 2011

Table 1183. Noncash Payments by Method of Payment and ATM Cash Withdrawals: 2003 and 2006

[81.4 represents 81,400,000,000. Based on two data collection efforts to estimate the annual number and value of significant types of noncash payments. Estimates of check payments and ATM withdrawals were based on findings from the Depository Institutions Payments Study (2007 DI study). Electronic payments volume estimates were based on findings from the Electronic Payments Study and supplemented by the 2007 DI study. The Depository Institutions Payments Study collected the number and value of different types of payments from deposit accounts at a representative, random sample of depository institutions. A total of 1,437 depository institutions (commercial banks, savings institutions, and credit unions) from a stratified random sample of 2,700 institutions provided data for the survey. The Electronic Payments Study estimated the number and value of electronic payments in the United States for calendar year 2006. Data were collected by surveying payment networks and card issuers. Of the 73 organizations asked to participate, 65 of the largest organizations provided data. Respondents to this study collectively accounted for an estimated 99.8 percent of the electronic transactions and 99.9 percent of the electronic payments value in the United States]

Method of payment	Transactions (billions)		Value (trillion dollars)		Average value per transaction (dollars)	
	2003	2006	2003	2006	2003	2006
Noncash payments, total	**81.4**	**93.3**	**67.6**	**75.8**	**830**	**813**
Checks (paid)	37.3	30.5	41.1	41.6	1,104	1,363
Commercial checks	36.8	30.1	40.8	41.4	1,108	1,371
Commercial banks	29.7	25.1	38.4	39.0	1,293	1,550
Credit unions	4.2	2.7	0.9	0.8	219	288
Savings institutions	3.0	2.3	1.5	1.6	511	696
U.S. Treasury checks	0.3	0.2	0.3	0.2	1,154	1,203
Postal money orders	0.2	0.2	(Z)	(Z)	146	164
Electronic payments	44.1	62.8	26.4	34.1	599	544
Automated Clearing House (ACH)	8.8	14.6	24.1	31.0	2,754	2,122
Debit cards	15.6	25.3	0.6	1.0	40	39
Signature [1]	10.3	16.0	0.4	0.6	42	40
PIN [2]	5.3	9.4	0.2	0.3	38	37
Credit cards [3]	19.0	21.7	1.7	2.1	89	98
Electronic benefits transfer cards	0.8	1.1	(Z)	(Z)	26	27
Memo:						
ATM cash withdrawals	**5.9**	**5.8**	**0.5**	**0.6**	**85**	**99**
Checks (written) [4]	37.6	33.1	41.2	42.4	1,096	1,280
Checks converted to ACH	0.3	2.6	0.1	0.7	187	267

Z Less than $50 million. [1] Signature debit card payments are made like credit card payments, but use funds from transaction deposit accounts. [2] PIN debit card payments also use funds from transaction deposit accounts and typically require the entry of the same personal identification number (PIN) used to access automated teller machines (ATMs). Excludes a portion estimated to have been returned to the customer as cash. [3] Credit cards include both general purpose and private-label cards. [4] Includes the use of checks as source documents to initiate electronic payments.

Source: Board of Governors of the Federal Reserve System, "Recent Payment Trends in the United States," Federal Reserve Bulletin, October 2008, <http://www.federalreserve.gov/pubs/bulletin/2008/default.htm> and "The 2007 Federal Reserve Payments Study," December 2007 <http://www.frbservices.org/files/communications/pdf/research/2007_payments_study.pdf>.

Table 1184. Percentage of Households Using Selected Electronic Banking Technologies: 1995 to 2007

[Covers only those households that access services (other than by check or credit card) at a bank, thrift institution, or credit union. Based on sample surveys. For details on the Survey of Consumer Finances, see Appendix III and the Federal Reserve Board, <www.federalreserve.gov/boarddocs/surveys\>. The Reuters/University of Michigan Surveys of Consumers is based on data from approximately 1,000 respondents. For details, see the University of Michigan Survey Research Center, <http://www.sca.isr.umich.edu/>]

Technology	Survey of Consumer Finances					Reuters/University of Michigan Surveys of Consumers		
	1995	1998	2001	2004	2007	1999	2003	2006
ELECTRONIC								
Direct deposit of any type	53	67	71	75	80	65	70	77
ATM card	35	55	57	65	76	59	65	69
Debit card [1]	20	37	50	62	71	(NA)	54	62
Preauthorized debts	25	40	43	50	49	31	46	57
Automated phone system	(NA)	26	22	20	25	40	44	46
Computer banking	4	7	19	34	53	10	32	51
Smart card [2]	1	2	3	(NA)	(NA)	(NA)	6	12
Prepaid card [3]	(NA)	(NA)	(NA)	(NA)	(NA)	(NA)	73	73
NONELECTRONIC								
In person	87	81	78	78	85	(NA)	(NA)	(NA)
Mail	59	55	51	51	59	(NA)	(NA)	(NA)
Phone (talk in person)	(NA)	43	42	42	57	(NA)	(NA)	(NA)

NA Not available. [1] A debit card is a card that automatically deducts the amount of a purchase from the money in an account. [2] A smart card is a type of payment card containing a computer chip which is set to hold a sum of money. As the card is used, purchases are subtracted from that sum. [3] Prepaid cards are cards that contain a stored value, or a value that has been paid up-front, allowing you to use the card much like cash. As you use the card, the prepaid value is drawn down. Examples are phone cards and gift cards. Smart cards are different from prepaid cards in that you can add money to the card at special machines designed for smart cards or sometimes at ATMs.

Source: Board of Governors of the Federal Reserve System, *Federal Reserve Bulletin*, July 2009, and unpublished data.

Table 1185. Percent of U.S. Households That Use Selected Payment Instruments: 2001 and 2007

[In percent. Based on Survey of Consumer Finances conducted by the Board of Governors of the Federal Reserve System; see Appendix III]

Characteristic of head of household	Any of these instruments		ATM [1]		Debit card		Direct deposit		Automatic bill paying		Software [2]	
	2001	2007	2001	2007	2001	2007	2001	2007	2001	2007	2001	2007
All households	**88.9**	**91.8**	**69.8**	**79.7**	**47.0**	**67.0**	**67.3**	**74.9**	**40.3**	**45.5**	**18.0**	**19.1**
Under 30 years old	83.8	88.6	78.1	84.8	60.6	78.3	48.8	61.3	32.1	35.7	17.0	21.4
30 to 60 years old	89.9	92.4	76.8	85.9	53.4	74.9	64.8	72.6	44.1	48.8	22.0	21.6
61 years old and over	89.4	92.1	48.9	63.5	24.6	43.9	83.2	86.4	35.9	42.9	9.0	12.3
Household income: [3]												
Low income	74.3	79.7	46.8	58.8	29.2	48.1	51.9	60.5	18.2	23.8	6.1	7.7
Moderate income	88.6	91.1	67.4	78.5	46.3	68.0	63.1	68.5	35.1	37.8	10.7	10.7
Middle income	92.5	96.4	75.2	87.5	50.0	75.0	65.7	76.8	45.1	50.2	16.3	18.8
Upper income	97.1	98.4	83.7	91.0	57.8	75.8	80.2	86.6	55.2	61.6	29.9	30.5
No college degree	85.1	88.4	63.7	74.0	42.3	63.7	61.8	68.9	33.7	38.0	10.9	11.9
College degree	96.4	98.2	81.6	90.3	56.2	72.9	78.0	85.9	53.2	59.3	31.8	32.2

[1] The question on ATM cards asked whether any member of the household had an ATM card, not whether the member used it. The other questions asked about usage of other instruments. [2] The question on software asked whether the respondent or spouse/partner uses any type of computer software to help in managing their money. [3] Low income is defined as less than 50 percent of the median household income; moderate income is 50 to 80 income is 80 to 120 percent of the median; and upper income is greater than 120 percent of the median. Each survey refers to income in the previous year. Median income was $41,990 in 2000 and $48,201 in 2006.

Source: Mester, Loretta J., "Changes in the Use of Electronic Means of Payment: 1995-2007," Business Review, Third Quarter 2009, published by Federal Reserve Bank of Philadelphia. See also <http://www.philadelphiafed.org/research-and-data/publications /business-review/2009/q3/brq309_changes-in-electronic-payment.pdf>.

Table 1186. Debit Cards—Holders, Number, Transactions, and Volume, 2000 and 2008, and Projections, 2011

[160 represents 160,000,000]

Type of debit card	Cardholders (mil.)			Number of cards (mil.)			Number of point-of-sale transactions (mil.)			Purchase volume (bil. dol.)		
	2000	2008	2011, proj.	2000	2008	2011, proj.	2000	2008	2011, proj.	2000	2008	2011, proj.
Total [1]	**160**	**181**	**188**	**235**	**491**	**585**	**8,291**	**34,239**	**46,367**	**311**	**1,347**	**1,750**
Bank [2]	137	160	167	137	449	540	5,290	28,464	39,049	210	1,126	1,470
EFT systems [3]	159	180	187	223	276	286	2,979	5,752	7,279	100	219	279
Other [4]	11	12	14	11	12	14	22	23	39	1	1	2

[1] Cardholders may hold more than one type of card. Bank cards and EFT cards are the same pieces of plastic that carry multiple brands. The total card figure shown does not include any duplication. [2] Visa and Master Card debit cards. For 2006 and later, includes Interlink & Master Card PIN debit. [3] Cards issued by financial institution members of regional and national switches such as Star, Interlink (before 2006), Pulse, Nyce, etc. EFT = Electronic funds transfer. [4] Retail cards such as those issued by supermarkets.

Source: The Nilson Report, Carpinteria, CA, Twice-monthly (copyright, used by permission.)

Table 1187. Credit Cards—Holders, Number, Spending, and Debt, 2000 and 2008, and Projections, 2011

[159 represents 159,000,000]

Type of credit card	Cardholders (mil.)			Number of cards (mil.)			Credit card purchase volume (bil. dol.)			Credit card debt outstanding (bil. dol.)		
	2000	2008	2011, proj.	2000	2008	2011, proj.	2000	2008	2011, proj.	2000	2008	2011, proj.
Total [1]	**159**	**176**	**183**	**1,425**	**1,493**	**1,278**	**1,242**	**2,153**	**2,044**	**680**	**976**	**897**
Visa	93	108	104	255	304	282	487	824	803	268	406	375
Master Card	86	100	83	200	260	211	281	547	483	212	305	273
Store	114	114	99	597	539	463	120	143	122	92	101	89
Oil company	76	62	56	98	65	61	45	63	68	5	10	10
Discover	36	42	42	50	58	56	69	106	109	48	55	55
American Express	23	36	36	33	54	54	221	465	455	50	96	91
The Rest [2]	7	6	6	192	160	150	18	5	5	5	3	3

[1] Cardholders may hold more than one type of card. [2] Includes Universal Air Travel Plan (UATP), phone cards, automobile rental, and miscellaneous cards; credit card purchase volume and cardholders excludes phone cards.

Source: The Nilson Report, Carpinteria, CA, Twice-monthly newsletter (copyright, used by permission.)

Table 1188. Usage of General Purpose Credit Cards by Families: 1995 to 2007

[General purpose credit cards include Master Card, Visa, Optima, and Discover cards. Excludes cards used only for business purposes. All dollar figures are given in constant 2007 dollars based on consumer price index data as published by U.S. Bureau of Labor Statistics. Families include one-person units; for definition of family, see text, Section 1. Based on Survey of Consumer Finances; see Appendix III. For definition of median, see Guide to Tabular Presentation]

Age of family head, family income, and housing tenure	Percent having a general purpose credit card	Median number of cards	Median new charges on last month's bill (dollars)	Percent having a balance after last month's bill	Median balance [1] (dollars)	Percent of card holding families who—		
						Almost always pay off the balance	Sometimes pay off the balance	Hardly ever pay off the balance
1995, total	66.4	2	200	56.0	2,000	52.4	20.1	27.5
2001, total	72.7	2	200	53.6	2,100	55.3	19.1	25.6
2004, total	71.5	2	300	56.2	2,300	55.7	20.3	24.0
2007, total	70.2	2	300	58.3	3,000	55.3	19.4	25.4
Under 35 years old	58.9	2	100	70.9	2,000	47.1	22.9	30.0
35 to 44 years old	68.1	2	300	68.2	3,400	46.9	22.5	30.6
45 to 54 years old	74.3	2	300	64.6	4,000	48.8	19.4	31.8
55 to 64 years old	78.9	3	300	58.6	3,500	56.0	20.0	24.0
65 to 74 years old	79.5	2	300	39.9	3,900	70.4	16.7	12.9
75 years old and over	66.0	1	200	23.9	900	80.8	8.8	10.4
Less than $10,000	27.7	2	200	56.8	1,200	59.2	20.7	20.1
$10,000 to $24,999	44.5	2	100	55.9	1,000	54.4	19.4	26.2
$25,000 to $49,999	66.4	2	100	60.3	2,100	49.7	20.5	29.8
$50,000 to $99,999	85.8	2	200	66.2	3,900	50.4	20.7	29.0
$100,000 and more	94.3	3	1,000	47.1	6,000	67.3	16.3	16.3
Owner occupied	81.5	2	300	55.3	4,000	57.5	19.4	23.1
Renter occupied or other	45.4	2	100	70.2	1,400	46.6	19.2	34.2

[1] Among families having a balance.
Source: Board of Governors of the Federal Reserve System, unpublished data.

Table 1189. Consumer Credit Outstanding and Finance Rates: 1990 to 2009

[In billions of dollars, except percent (808 represents $808,000,000,000). Covers most short- and intermediate-term credit extended to individuals, excluding loans secured by real estate. Estimated amounts of seasonally adjusted credit outstanding as of end of year; finance rates, annual averages]

Type of credit	1990	2000	2002	2003	2004	2005	2006	2007	2008	2009
Total	808	1,717	1,971	2,077	2,192	2,292	2,386	2,523	2,561	2,451
Revolving	239	683	751	768	800	831	872	943	958	866
Nonrevolving [1]	570	1,033	1,220	1,308	1,392	1,461	1,513	1,580	1,603	1,585
FINANCE RATES (percent)										
Commercial banks:										
New automobiles (48 months)	11.78	9.34	7.62	6.94	6.60	7.07	7.72	7.77	7.02	6.72
Other consumer goods (24 months)	15.46	13.90	12.54	11.96	11.89	12.06	12.41	12.38	11.37	11.10
Credit card plans	18.17	15.78	13.40	12.30	12.72	12.51	13.21	13.30	12.08	13.40
Finance companies:										
New automobiles	12.54	6.85	4.50	3.81	4.92	6.02	4.99	4.87	5.52	3.82
Used automobiles	15.99	13.47	11.18	9.86	8.81	8.81	9.61	9.24	8.74	9.41

[1] Comprises automobile loans and all other loans not included in revolving credit, such as loans for mobile homes, education, boats, trailers, or vacations. These loans may be secured or unsecured.
Source: Board of Governors of the Federal Reserve System, "Consumer Credit-G.19," March 2010, <http://www.federalreserve.gov/releases/g19/current/g19.htm> and "Finance Companies-G.20," March 2010, <http://www.federalreserve.gov/releases/g20/current/g20.htm>.

Table 1190. Consumer Credit by Type of Holder: 1990 to 2009

[In billions of dollars (824 represents $824,000,000,000). As of December 31. Not seasonally adjusted]

Type of holder	1990	2000	2002	2003	2004	2005	2006	2007	2008	2009
Total	824	1,741	1,997	2,103	2,220	2,321	2,416	2,555	2,594	2,481
Nonfinancial corporations	67	81	75	59	59	60	58	59	60	57
U.S. government	–	60	80	82	86	90	92	98	111	186
Commercial banking	382	551	603	669	704	707	741	804	879	855
Savings institutions	50	65	69	78	91	109	96	91	86	78
Credit unions	92	184	196	206	215	229	235	236	236	237
Government-sponsored enterprises	19	37	37	21	–	–	–	–	–	–
Asset-backed securities issuers	77	528	630	595	572	610	661	684	646	579
Finance companies	138	234	308	393	492	517	534	584	576	489

– Represents or rounds to zero.
Source: Board of Governors of the Federal Reserve System, "Federal Reserve Statistical Release, Z.1, Flow of Funds Accounts of the United States," March 2010, <http://www.federalreserve.gov/releases/z1/20100311>.

U.S. Census Bureau, Statistical Abstract of the United States: 2011

Table 1191. Mortgage Debt Outstanding by Type of Property and Holder: 1990 to 2009

[In billions of dollars (3,781 represents $3,781,000,000,000). As of December 31]

Type of property and holder	1990	2000	2002	2003	2004	2005	2006	2007	2008	2009
Total mortgages [1]	3,781	6,753	8,361	9,365	10,628	12,067	13,464	14,533	14,612	14,307
Home [2]	2,606	5,107	6,413	7,222	8,247	9,356	10,416	11,111	11,000	10,786
Multifamily residential	287	402	483	563	616	687	742	843	903	897
Commercial	820	1,160	1,370	1,497	1,669	1,919	2,199	2,466	2,579	2,485
Farm	68	85	95	83	96	105	108	113	130	138
Household sector	141	103	117	121	131	139	122	109	111	103
State and local government	110	131	124	133	141	152	166	177	171	162
Commercial banking	849	1,660	2,058	2,256	2,596	2,958	3,403	3,644	3,841	3,819
Savings institutions [3]	802	723	781	871	1,057	1,153	1,077	1,094	861	633
Credit unions	33	104	136	160	188	220	250	282	315	317
Life insurance companies	268	236	250	261	273	285	304	326	342	330
Government-sponsored enterprises (GSE)	156	264	357	622	629	589	607	643	701	697
Agency- and GSE-backed mortgage pools	1,020	2,493	3,159	3,331	3,375	3,542	3,837	4,464	4,961	5,383
Asset-backed securities issuers	66	604	836	1,009	1,444	2,131	2,766	2,948	2,593	2,216
Finance companies	114	238	330	370	476	541	594	532	448	401
Real estate investment trusts	8	17	28	49	118	146	136	121	76	60
HOME MORTGAGES [2]										
Total [1]	2,606	5,107	6,413	7,222	8,247	9,356	10,416	11,111	11,000	10,786
State and local government	61	67	63	68	72	77	85	90	88	82
Commercial banking	433	970	1,227	1,360	1,582	1,792	2,082	2,211	2,249	2,261
Savings institutions	600	594	631	703	874	954	868	879	666	449
Credit unions	33	104	136	160	188	220	250	282	315	317
Government-sponsored enterprises (GSE)	119	210	277	519	509	454	458	448	457	439
Agency- and GSE-backed mortgage pools	991	2,426	3,064	3,216	3,256	3,420	3,711	4,319	4,801	5,214
Asset-backed securities issuers	55	385	544	666	1,049	1,622	2,139	2,172	1,859	1,525
Finance companies	80	187	286	320	422	490	538	473	375	331
Memo:										
Home equity loans included above [1, 4]	215	408	501	593	776	915	1,066	1,130	1,113	1,032
Commercial banking	115	235	303	366	484	549	654	692	776	762
Savings institutions	60	73	78	96	121	152	138	180	119	80
Credit unions	20	41	48	52	64	76	87	94	99	94

[1] Includes other holders not shown separately. [2] Mortgages on one- to four-family properties including mortgages on farm houses. [3] Federal Home Loan Bank loans to savings institutions are included in other loans and advances. [4] Loans made under home equity lines of credit and home equity loans secured by junior liens. Excludes home equity loans held by individuals.

Source: Board of Governors of the Federal Reserve System, "Federal Reserve Statistical Release, Z.1, Flow of Funds Accounts of the United States," March 2010, <http://www.federalreserve.gov/releases/z1/20100311>.

Table 1192. Characteristics of Conventional First Mortgage Loans for Purchase of Single-Family Homes: 2000 to 2009

[In percent, except as indicated (234.9 represents $234,900). Annual averages. Covers fully amortized conventional mortgage loans used to purchase single-family nonfarm homes. Excludes refinancing loans, nonamortized and balloon loans, loans insured by the Federal Housing Administration, and loans guaranteed by the Veterans Administration. Based on a sample of mortgage lenders, including savings and loans associations, savings banks, commercial banks, and mortgage companies]

Loan characteristics	New homes						Previously occupied homes					
	2000	2005	2006	2007	2008	2009	2000	2005	2006	2007	2008	2009
Contract interest rate,												
all loans [1]	7.4	5.9	6.5	6.3	5.9	5.0	7.9	5.8	6.5	6.5	6.1	5.1
Fixed-rate loans	8.0	6.1	6.6	6.3	5.9	5.0	8.2	6.0	6.6	6.5	6.1	5.1
Adjustable-rate loans [2]	6.5	5.3	6.2	6.2	5.7	(5)	7.2	5.6	6.4	6.3	5.7	(5)
Initial fees, charges [3]	0.69	0.54	0.67	0.81	0.84	1.00	0.66	0.33	0.33	0.40	0.46	0.55
Effective interest rate,												
all loans [4]	7.5	5.9	6.6	6.4	6.1	5.1	8.1	5.9	6.6	6.5	6.2	5.1
Fixed-rate loans	8.2	6.2	6.7	6.4	6.1	5.2	8.3	6.0	6.6	6.5	6.2	5.2
Adjustable-rate loans [2]	6.5	5.3	6.2	6.3	5.8	(5)	7.2	5.6	6.4	6.4	5.8	(5)
Term to maturity (years)	29.2	29.2	29.5	29.4	29.1	28.8	28.6	28.3	28.9	29.3	28.3	28.1
Purchase price ($1,000)	234.9	328.5	346.4	360.4	350.6	332.3	191.8	291.3	295.9	286.2	296.4	303.6
Loan-to-price ratio	77.4	75.2	75.4	77.1	76.2	73.9	77.9	74.6	76.9	79.9	77.0	74.6
Percent of number of loans with adjustable rates	40	29	21	11	4	(5)	21	30	22	11	8	(5)

[1] Initial interest rate paid by the borrower as specified in the loan contract. [2] Loans with a contractual provision for periodic adjustments in the contract interest rate. [3] Includes all fees, commissions, discounts, and "points" paid by the borrower, or seller, in order to obtain the loan. Excludes those charges for mortgage, credit, life, or property insurance; for property transfer; and for title search and insurance. [4] Contract interest rate plus fees and charges amortized over a ten year period. [5] Insufficient data to report meaningful numbers.

Source: U.S. Federal Housing Finance Agency, *Monthly Interest Rate Survey*, Historical Summary Table, <http://www.fhfa.gov/Default.aspx?Page=252>

Table 1193. Mortgage Originations and Delinquency and Foreclosure Rates: 1990 to 2009

[In percent, except as indicated (459 represents $459,000,000,000). Covers one- to four-family residential nonfarm mortgage loans. Mortgage origination is the making of a new mortgage, including all steps taken by a lender to attract and qualify a borrower, process the mortgage loan, and place it on the lender's books. Based on the National Delinquency Survey which covers 45 million loans on one- to four-unit properties, representing between 80 to 85 percent of all 'first-lien' residential mortgage loans outstanding. Loans surveyed were reported by approximately 120 lenders, including mortgage bankers, commercial banks, and thrifts]

Item	1990	2000	2003	2004	2005	2006	2007	2008	2009
MORTGAGE ORIGINATIONS									
Total (bil. dol.)	**459**	**1,139**	**3,812**	**2,773**	**2,908**	**2,726**	**2,306**	**1,509**	**2,103**
Purchase (bil. dol.)	389	905	1,280	1,309	1,512	1,399	1,140	731	739
Refinance (bil. dol.)	70	234	2,532	1,463	1,397	1,326	1,166	777	1,364
DELINQUENCY RATES [1]									
Total.	**4.7**	**4.4**	**4.7**	**4.5**	**4.5**	**4.6**	**5.4**	**6.9**	**9.3**
Prime conventional loans	(NA)	2.3	2.5	2.3	2.3	2.4	2.9	4.3	6.5
Subprime conventional loans	(NA)	11.9	12.2	10.8	10.8	12.3	15.6	19.9	25.5
Federal Housing Administration loans. . . .	6.7	9.1	12.2	12.2	12.5	12.7	12.7	13.0	14.0
Veterans Administration loans	6.3	6.8	8.0	7.3	7.0	6.7	6.4	7.2	7.9
FORECLOSURE RATES									
Total loans in foreclosure process [2] . . .	**0.9**	**1.2**	**1.3**	**1.2**	**1.0**	**1.2**	**2.0**	**3.3**	**4.6**
Prime conventional loans	(NA)	0.4	0.6	0.5	0.4	0.5	1.0	1.9	3.3
Subprime conventional loans	(NA)	9.4	5.6	3.8	3.3	4.5	8.7	13.7	15.6
Federal Housing Administration loans. . . .	1.3	1.7	2.9	2.7	2.3	1.9	2.3	2.4	3.6
Veterans Administration loans	1.2	1.2	1.6	1.5	1.1	1.0	1.1	1.7	2.5
Loans entering foreclosure process: [3]									
Prime conventional loans	(NA)	0.6	0.8	0.8	0.7	0.8	1.3	2.4	3.9
Subprime conventional loans	(NA)	9.2	6.6	5.9	5.6	7.3	11.7	16.5	16.2
Federal Housing Administration loans. . . .	1.7	2.3	3.6	3.9	3.4	3.3	3.6	3.8	4.8
Veterans Administration loans	1.6	1.5	1.9	2.0	1.5	1.4	1.6	2.3	3.0

NA Not available. [1] Number of loans delinquent 30 days or more as percentage of mortgage loans serviced in survey. Annual average of quarterly figures. Delinquency rate does not include loans in the process of foreclosure. [2] Percentage of loans in the foreclosure process at year-end, not seasonally adjusted. [3] Percentage of loans entering foreclosure process at year-end, not seasonally adjusted.

Source: Mortgage Bankers Association of America, Washington, DC, "MBA Mortgage Originations Estimates," National Delinquency Survey, quarterly, <http://www.mortgagebankers.org/>; and unpublished data.

Table 1194. Delinquency Rates and Charge-Off Rates on Loans at Insured Commercial Banks: 1990 to 2009

[In percent. Annual averages of quarterly figures, not seasonally adjusted. Delinquent loans are those past due 30 days or more and still accruing interest as well as those in nonaccrual status. They are measured as a percentage of end-of-period loans. Charge-offs, which are the value of loans removed from the books and charged against loss reserves, are measured net of recoveries as a percentage of average loans and annualized. Includes only U.S.-chartered commercial banks]

Type of loan	1990	2000	2003	2004	2005	2006	2007	2008	2009
DELINQUENCY RATES									
Total loans	**5.33**	**2.18**	**2.33**	**1.80**	**1.57**	**1.57**	**2.06**	**3.67**	**6.54**
Real estate	6.10	1.89	1.76	1.44	1.37	1.49	2.27	4.67	8.43
Residential [1]	(NA)	2.11	1.83	1.55	1.55	1.73	2.55	5.01	9.10
Commercial [2]	(NA)	1.49	1.54	1.20	1.07	1.12	1.94	4.44	7.90
Consumer	3.83	3.55	3.28	3.08	2.81	2.90	3.13	3.76	4.70
Credit cards	(NA)	4.50	4.47	4.11	3.70	4.01	4.25	5.02	6.52
Other	(NA)	2.98	2.67	2.46	2.24	2.21	2.46	3.00	3.58
Leases	1.97	1.59	1.91	1.34	1.28	1.26	1.20	1.58	2.30
Commercial and industrial . . .	5.34	2.22	3.34	2.18	1.51	1.27	1.22	1.88	3.91
Agricultural.	3.84	2.54	2.50	1.68	1.30	1.11	1.21	1.19	2.37
CHARGE-OFF RATES									
Total loans	**1.44**	**0.66**	**0.86**	**0.60**	**0.54**	**0.42**	**0.61**	**1.43**	**2.64**
Real estate	0.85	0.10	0.17	0.09	0.06	0.09	0.23	1.21	2.27
Residential [1]	(NA)	0.12	0.19	0.10	0.08	0.11	0.26	1.28	2.33
Commercial [2]	(NA)	0.05	0.13	0.07	0.05	0.06	0.20	1.20	2.34
Consumer	1.82	2.36	2.90	2.68	2.75	2.05	2.48	3.52	5.41
Credit cards	3.46	4.46	5.84	5.04	4.84	3.64	3.99	5.52	9.22
Other	1.03	1.14	1.41	1.31	1.38	1.06	1.56	2.34	3.02
Leases	0.66	0.31	0.86	0.42	0.58	0.17	0.24	0.54	1.29
Commercial and industrial . . .	1.29	0.76	1.24	0.53	0.26	0.29	0.49	0.98	2.29
Agricultural.	0.21	0.25	0.35	0.19	0.07	0.10	0.10	0.17	0.53

NA Not available. [1] Residential real estate loans include loans secured by one- to four-family properties, including home equity lines of credit, booked in domestic offices, only. [2] Commercial real estate loans include construction and land development loans, loans secured by multifamily residences, and loans secured by nonfarm, nonresidential real estate, booked in domestic offices, only.

Source: Federal Financial Institutions Examination Council (FFIEC), *Consolidated Reports of Condition and Income* (1990–2000: FFIEC 031 through 034; beginning 2001: FFIEC 031 & 041).

Table 1195. Money Stock: 1990 to 2009

[In billions of dollars (825 represents $825,000,000,000). As of December. Seasonally adjusted averages of daily figures]

Item	1990	2000	2002	2003	2004	2005	2006	2007	2008	2009
M1, total	**825**	**1,088**	**1,220**	**1,307**	**1,377**	**1,375**	**1,368**	**1,376**	**1,595**	**1,693**
Currency [1]	246	531	626	663	698	724	750	760	815	862
Travelers' checks [2]	8	8	8	8	8	7	7	6	6	5
Demand deposits [3]	277	310	307	326	344	325	305	302	460	442
Other checkable deposits [4]	294	238	280	310	328	319	306	308	314	384
M2, total	**3,277**	**4,918**	**5,786**	**6,074**	**6,415**	**6,679**	**7,080**	**7,509**	**8,242**	**8,524**
M1	825	1,088	1,220	1,307	1,377	1,375	1,368	1,376	1,595	1,693
Non-M1 components of M2	2,453	3,830	4,565	4,767	5,038	5,304	5,712	6,134	6,647	6,831
Retail money funds	356	906	897	786	703	707	810	985	1,082	814
Savings deposits (including MMDAs [5])	923	1,878	2,774	3,163	3,507	3,605	3,698	3,876	4,112	4,849
Commercial banks	581	1,424	2,060	2,338	2,632	2,776	2,914	3,047	3,339	4,007
Thrift institutions	342	454	714	825	876	829	784	829	773	842
Small time deposits [6]	1,173	1,046	895	818	828	992	1,204	1,273	1,453	1,169
Commercial banks	611	701	591	542	551	645	779	856	1,074	852
Thrift institutions	563	345	303	276	276	347	425	417	378	317

[1] Currency outside U.S. Treasury, Federal Reserve Banks and the vaults of depository institutions. [2] Outstanding amount of U.S. dollar-denominated travelers' checks of nonbank issuers. Travelers' checks issued by depository institutions are included in demand deposits. [3] Demand deposits at domestically chartered commercial banks, U.S. branches and agencies of foreign banks, and Edge Act corporations (excluding those amounts held by depository institutions, the U.S. government, and foreign banks and official institutions) less cash items in the process of collection and Federal Reserve float. [4] Negotiable order of withdrawal (NOW) and automatic transfer service (ATS) balances at domestically chartered commercial banks, U.S. branches and agencies of foreign banks, Edge Act corporations, and thrift institutions, credit union share draft balances, and demand deposits at thrift institutions. [5] Money market deposit accounts (MMDAs). [6] Small-denomination time deposits are those issued in amounts of less than $100,000. All Individual Retirement Account (IRA) and Keogh account balances at commercial banks and thrift institutions are subtracted from small time deposits.

Source: Board of Governors of the Federal Reserve System, Federal Reserve Statistical Release H.6, weekly.

Table 1196. Money Market Interest Rates and Mortgage Rates: 1990 to 2009

[Percent per year. Annual averages of monthly data, except as indicated]

Type	1990	1995	2000	2002	2003	2004	2005	2006	2007	2008	2009
Federal funds, effective rate	8.10	5.83	6.24	1.67	1.13	1.35	3.22	4.97	5.02	1.92	0.16
Prime rate charged by banks	10.01	8.83	9.23	4.67	4.12	4.34	6.19	7.96	8.05	5.09	3.25
Discount rate [1]	6.98	5.21	5.73	1.17	2.12	2.34	4.19	5.96	5.86	2.39	0.50
Eurodollar deposits, 3-month	8.16	5.93	6.45	1.73	1.14	1.55	3.51	5.19	5.32	3.31	1.03
Large negotiable CDs:											
3-month, secondary market	8.15	5.92	6.46	1.73	1.15	1.57	3.51	5.16	5.27	2.97	0.55
6-month, secondary market	8.17	5.98	6.59	1.81	1.17	1.74	3.73	5.24	5.23	3.14	0.87
Taxable money market funds [2]	7.82	5.48	5.89	1.29	0.64	0.82	2.66	4.51	4.70	2.05	0.18
Tax-exempt money market funds [2]	5.45	3.39	3.54	0.94	0.53	0.66	1.87	2.90	3.13	1.77	0.19
Certificates of deposit (CDs): [3]											
6-month	7.79	4.92	5.09	1.67	1.02	1.14	2.37	3.29	3.46	2.12	0.86
1-year	7.92	5.39	5.46	1.98	1.20	1.45	2.77	3.64	3.65	2.36	1.16
2-year	7.96	5.69	5.64	2.74	1.77	2.21	3.18	3.75	3.65	2.43	1.43
5-year	8.06	6.00	5.97	3.96	2.93	3.34	3.75	4.02	3.89	3.17	2.21
U.S. government securities:											
Secondary market: [4]											
3-month Treasury bill	7.50	5.49	5.82	1.61	1.01	1.37	3.15	4.73	4.36	1.37	0.15
6-month Treasury bill	7.46	5.56	5.90	1.68	1.05	1.58	3.39	4.81	4.44	1.62	0.28
Auction average: [5]											
3-month Treasury bill	7.51	5.51	5.85	1.62	1.02	1.38	3.16	4.73	4.41	1.48	0.16
Home mortgages:											
New-home mortgage yields [6]	10.05	7.85	7.96	6.51	5.73	5.74	5.90	6.60	6.49	6.14	5.14
Conventional, 15 yr. fixed [3]	9.73	7.39	7.76	6.02	5.25	5.23	5.50	6.13	6.11	5.83	4.83
Conventional, 30 yr. fixed [3]	9.97	7.86	8.08	6.56	5.89	5.86	5.93	6.47	6.40	6.23	5.38

[1] Rate for the Federal Reserve Bank of New York. Beginning 2003, the rate charged for discounts made and advances extended under the Federal Reserve's primary credit discount window program, which became effective January 9, 2003. The rate replaced that for adjustment credit, which was discontinued after January 8, 2003. [2] 12-month return for period ending December 31. Source: iMoneyNet, Inc., Westborough, MA, *Money Market Insight*, monthly, (copyright), <http://www.imoneynet.com>. [3] Annual averages. Source: Bankrate, Inc., North Palm Beach, FL, *Bank Rate Monitor*, weekly (copyright), <http://www.bankrate.com>. [4] Averages based on daily closing bid yields in secondary market, bank discount basis. [5] Averages computed on an issue-date basis; bank discount basis. Source: U.S. Council of Economic Advisors, *Economic Indicators*, monthly. [6] Effective rate (in the primary market) on conventional mortgages, reflecting fees and charges as well as contract rate and assumed, on the average, repayment at end of ten years. Source: U.S. Federal Housing Finance Board, *Terms on Conventional Single-Family Mortgages, Annual National Averages, All Homes*.

Source: Except as noted, Board of Governors of the Federal Reserve System, "H15, Selected Interest Rates," <http://www.federalreserve.gov/releases/h15/data.htm>.

Table 1197. Bond Yields: 1990 to 2009

[Percent per year. Annual averages of daily figures, except as indicated]

Type	1990	1995	2000	2002	2003	2004	2005	2006	2007	2008	2009
U.S. Treasury, constant maturities: [1,2]											
1-year	7.89	5.94	6.11	2.00	1.24	1.89	3.62	4.94	4.53	1.83	0.47
2-year	8.16	6.15	6.26	2.64	1.65	2.38	3.85	4.82	4.36	2.01	0.96
3-year	8.26	6.25	6.22	3.10	2.11	2.78	3.93	4.77	4.35	2.24	1.43
5-year	8.37	6.38	6.15	3.82	2.97	3.43	4.05	4.75	4.43	2.80	2.20
7-year	8.52	6.50	6.20	4.30	3.52	3.87	4.15	4.76	4.51	3.17	2.82
10-year	8.55	6.57	6.03	4.61	4.02	4.27	4.29	4.80	4.63	3.66	3.26
20-year	(NA)	6.95	6.23	5.43	4.96	5.05	4.65	4.99	4.91	4.36	4.11
State and local govt. bonds, Aaa rating [3]	6.96	5.79	5.58	4.87	4.52	4.51	4.28	4.15	4.13	4.58	4.27
State and local govt. bonds, Baa rating [3]	7.30	6.05	6.19	5.63	5.20	5.09	4.86	4.71	4.59	5.64	6.34
Municipal (Bond Buyer, 20 bonds)	7.27	5.95	5.71	5.04	4.75	4.68	4.40	4.40	4.40	4.85	4.62
High-grade municipal bonds (Standard & Poor's) [4]	7.25	5.95	5.77	5.05	4.73	4.63	4.29	4.42	4.42	4.80	4.64
Corporate Aaa rating seasoned [3,5]	9.32	7.59	7.62	6.49	5.66	5.63	5.23	5.59	5.56	5.63	5.31
Corporate Baa rating seasoned [3]	10.36	8.20	8.37	7.80	6.76	6.39	6.06	6.48	6.48	7.44	7.29
Corporate seasoned, all industries [3]	9.77	7.83	7.98	7.10	6.24	6.00	5.57	5.98	6.01	6.44	6.12

NA Not available. [1] Yields on actively traded non-inflation-indexed issues adjusted to constant maturities. Data from U.S. Treasury. [2] Through 1995, yields are based on closing bid prices quoted by at least five dealers. Beginning 2000, yields are based on closing indicative prices quoted by secondary market participants. [3] Data from Moody's Investors Service, New York, NY. [4] Source: U.S. Council of Economic Advisors, *Economic Indicators*, monthly. [5] Moody's Aaa rates through December 6, 2001, are average of Aaa utility and Aaa industrial bond rates. As of December 7, 2001, these rates are averages of Aaa industrial bonds only.

Source: Except as noted, Board of Governors of the Federal Reserve System, "H15, Selected Interest Rates," <http://www.federalreserve.gov/releases/h15/data.htm>.

Table 1198. Volume of Debt Markets by Type of Security: 1990 to 2009

[In billions of dollars (1,081 represents $1,081,000,000,000). Covers debt markets as represented by the source]

Type of security	1990	2000	2004	2005	2006	2007	2008	2009
NEW ISSUE VOLUME [1]								
Total	1,081	2,513	5,306	5,296	5,723	5,811	4,602	6,751
U.S. Treasury securities [2]	398	312	953	716	700	752	1,037	2,186
Federal agency securities [3]	55	447	882	669	747	942	985	1,117
Municipal	128	201	360	408	387	429	390	410
Mortgage-backed securities [4]	380	684	1,779	1,967	1,988	2,050	1,344	1,957
Asset-backed securities [5]	44	282	652	754	754	510	140	146
Corporate debt [6]	77	588	781	753	1,059	1,128	707	935
DAILY TRADING VOLUME								
Total	111.2	357.6	818.9	918.7	893.1	1,014.9	1,033.6	814.6
U.S. Treasury securities [2,7]	111.2	206.5	499.0	554.5	524.7	570.2	553.1	407.9
Federal agency securities [7]	(NA)	72.8	78.8	78.8	74.4	83.0	104.5	77.7
Municipal [8]	(NA)	8.8	14.8	16.9	22.5	25.1	19.4	12.5
Mortgage-backed securities [4,7]	(NA)	69.5	207.4	251.8	254.6	320.1	344.9	299.9
Corporate debt [6]	(NA)	(NA)	18.8	16.7	16.9	16.4	11.8	16.8
VOLUME OF SECURITIES OUTSTANDING								
Total	7,745	17,203	24,572	27,124	30,046	32,366	33,735	34,747
U.S. Treasury securities [2]	2,196	3,210	4,407	4,715	4,872	5,082	6,083	7,605
Federal agency securities	435	1,854	2,701	2,616	2,651	2,933	3,205	2,730
Municipal	1,184	1,481	2,000	2,226	2,403	2,619	2,684	2,812
Mortgage-backed securities [4]	1,333	3,566	5,931	7,212	8,635	9,143	9,100	9,188
Asset-backed securities [5]	90	1,072	1,828	1,955	2,130	2,472	2,672	2,429
Money market instruments [9]	1,157	2,663	2,904	3,434	4,009	4,171	3,791	3,128
Corporate debt [6]	1,350	3,358	4,801	4,966	5,345	5,947	6,202	6,856

NA Not available. [1] Covers only long-term issuance. [2] Marketable public debt. [3] Includes overnight discount notes. Beginning 2004, excludes Sallie Mae. [4] Includes only Government National Mortgage Association (GNMA), Federal National Mortgage Association (FNMA), Federal Home Loan Mortgage Corporation (FHLMC) mortgage-backed securities (MBS) and collateralized mortgage obligations (CMOs) and private-label MBS/CMOs. Beginning with 2004, Sallie Mae has been excluded from "Issuance in the U.S. Bond Market" data. [5] Includes auto, credit card, home equity, manufacturing, student loans, and other. [6] Includes non-convertible corporate debt, Yankee bonds, and MTNs (Medium-Term Notes), but excludes all issues with maturities of one year or less, agency debt, and all certificates of deposit. [7] Primary dealer transactions. [8] Beginning 2000, includes customer-to-dealer and dealer-to-dealer transactions. [9] Commercial paper, bankers acceptances, and large time deposits.

Source: The Securities Industry and Financial Markets Association, New York, NY, copyright, <http://www.sifma.org/research/research.aspx?ID=10806>. Based on data supplied by Board of Governors of the Federal Reserve System, U.S. Department of Treasury, Thomson Reuters, FHLMC, FNMA, GNMA, Federal Home Loan Banks, Student Loan Marketing Association, Federal Farm Credit Banks, Tennessee Valley Authority, Bloomberg, Loan Performance, Dealogic and Municipal Securities Rulemaking Board.

U.S. Census Bureau, Statistical Abstract of the United States: 2011

Table 1199. Total Returns of Stocks, Bonds, and Treasury Bills: 1980 to 2009

[In percent. Average annual percent change. Stock return data are based on the Standard & Poor's 500 index. Minus sign (–) indicates loss]

Period	Stocks				Treasury bills, total return	Bonds (10-year), total return
	Total return after inflation	Capital gains	Dividends and reinvestment	Total return after inflation		
1980 to 1989	17.55	12.59	4.40	11.85	9.13	13.01
1990 to 1999	18.21	15.31	2.51	14.85	4.95	8.02
2000 to 2006	1.13	–0.49	1.63	–1.10	3.07	6.76
2000 to 2008	–3.82	–5.40	1.58	–6.68	3.42	6.71
2002.	–22.10	–23.37	1.65	–23.91	1.61	15.37
2003.	28.68	26.38	1.82	26.31	1.03	0.46
2004.	10.88	8.99	1.73	7.38	1.43	4.61
2005.	4.91	3.00	1.85	1.45	3.30	3.09
2006.	15.80	13.62	1.91	11.97	4.97	2.21
2007.	5.49	3.53	1.89	1.35	4.52	10.54
2008.	–37.00	–38.49	1.88	–37.10	1.24	20.23
2009.	26.25	23.45	2.44	23.11	0.15	–9.50

Source: Global Financial Data, Los Angeles, CA, "GFD Guide to Total Returns," <http://www.globalfinancialdata.com>, and unpublished data (copyright).

Table 1200. Equities, Corporate Bonds, and Treasury Securities— Holdings and Net Purchases by Type of Investor: 2000 to 2009

[In billions of dollars (17,575 represents $17,575,000,000,000). Holdings as of December 31. Minus sign (–) indicates net sales]

Type of investor	Holdings					Net purchases				
	2000	2005	2007	2008	2009	2000	2005	2007	2008	2009
EQUITIES [1]										
Total [2]	**17,571**	**20,636**	**25,577**	**15,785**	**20,451**	**5.6**	**–76.6**	**–460.5**	**308.9**	**327.0**
Household sector [3]	8,205	7,993	9,465	5,881	7,698	–637.5	–409.9	–795.1	28.2	126.9
Rest of the world [4]	1,422	2,039	2,812	1,776	2,455	199.7	56.9	218.5	91.2	122.8
Life insurance companies	892	1,162	1,465	1,002	1,142	111.3	65.9	84.1	81.8	21.1
Private pension funds	1,971	2,542	2,863	1,665	1,946	62.8	–4.6	–217.0	–256.7	–159.0
State and local government retirement funds	1,299	1,716	1,986	1,212	1,526	11.6	–5.6	–35.3	–6.7	–8.2
Mutual funds	3,227	4,176	5,477	3,014	4,172	193.1	129.6	91.3	–38.1	85.5
Exchange-traded funds	66	286	574	474	670	42.4	50.0	137.2	154.2	70.5
CORPORATE & FOREIGN BONDS										
Total [2]	**4,827**	**8,695**	**11,424**	**11,134**	**11,506**	**358.9**	**864.2**	**1,227.7**	**–157.1**	**17.1**
Household sector [3]	552	1,300	2,011	1,988	2,236	84.7	119.6	241.9	–193.4	–149.1
Rest of the world [4]	842	1,763	2,719	2,457	2,357	168.2	328.5	424.6	40.0	–99.9
Commercial banking	266	687	978	980	867	56.0	123.4	197.9	1.7	–113.4
Property-casualty insurance companies	188	263	283	268	283	6.4	17.5	5.9	–15.4	16.0
Life insurance companies	1,215	1,825	1,863	1,819	1,956	47.9	74.7	40.0	–43.9	137.4
Private pension funds	266	290	357	400	424	–76.3	22.2	39.7	42.8	23.7
State and local government retirement funds	314	228	288	289	289	4.2	14.5	–9.1	0.8	0.5
Mutual funds	338	663	890	965	1,109	–10.6	65.9	121.6	74.6	144.1
Government-sponsored enterprises . . .	131	466	464	387	311	19.1	50.9	–17.4	–77.7	–33.8
Funding corporations.	25	67	170	667	747	–8.9	–29.4	109.6	497.3	80.6
TREASURY SECURITIES										
Total [2]	**3,358**	**4,678**	**5,099**	**6,338**	**7,782**	**–294.9**	**307.3**	**237.5**	**1,239.0**	**1,443.7**
State and local governments.	310	481	532	492	531	5.5	92.3	14.5	–39.6	39.4
Rest of the world [4]	1,021	1,984	2,376	3,211	3,713	–75.2	245.1	165.2	674.3	502.6
Monetary authority.	512	744	741	476	777	33.7	26.4	–38.3	–264.7	300.7
Money market mutual funds	92	89	178	578	406	–12.9	–9.6	95.5	399.5	–171.3

[1] Excludes mutual fund shares; see Table 1214. [2] Includes other types, not shown separately. [3] Includes nonprofit organizations. [4] Holdings and net purchases of U.S. issues by foreign residents.

Source: Board of Governors of the Federal Reserve System, "Federal Reserve Statistical Release, Z.1, Flow of Funds Accounts of the United States," March 2010, <http://www.federalreserve.gov/releases/z1/20100311>.

Table 1201. New Security Issues of Corporations by Type of Offering: 2000 to 2009

[In billions of dollars (1,082 represents $1,082,000,000,000). Represents gross proceed of issues maturing in more than one year. Figures are the principal amount or the number of units multiplied by the offering price. Excludes secondary offerings, employee stock plans, investment companies other than closed-end, intracorporate transactions, Yankee bonds, and private placements listed. Stock data include ownership securities issued by limited partnerships]

Type of Offering	2000	2005	2008	2009	Type of Offering	2000	2005	2008	2009
Total.	**1,082**	**2,439**	**1,068**	**1,171**	Nonfinancial.	259	216	318	479
					Financial	688	2,108	543	468
Bonds, total	947	2,324	861	947	Stocks, total.	135	115	207	234
Sold in the U.S.	825	2,141	744	784	Nonfinancial.	118	55	45	63
Sold abroad.	123	182	117	163	Financial	17	61	162	171

Source: Board of Governors of the Federal Reserve System, "New Security Issues, U.S. Corporations," May 2010, <http://www.federalreserve.gov/econresdata/releases/corpsecure/current.htm>.

Table 1202. U.S. Purchases and Sales of Foreign Bonds and Stocks, 1990 to 2009, and by Selected Country, 2009

[In billions of dollars (31.2 represents $31,200,000,000). Covers transactions in all types of long-term foreign securities by foreigners as reported to the Treasury International Capital Reporting System by banks, brokers, and other entities in the United States. Data cover new issues of securities, transactions in outstanding issues, and redemptions of securities. Includes transactions executed in the United States for the account of foreigners, and transactions executed abroad for the account of reporting institutions and their domestic customers. Data by country show the country of location of the foreign buyers and sellers who deal directly with reporting institutions in the United States. The data do not necessarily indicate the country of beneficial owner or issuer. The term "foreigner" covers all institutions and individuals domiciled outside the United States, including U.S. citizens domiciled abroad, and the foreign branches, subsidiaries, and other affiliates abroad of U.S. banks and businesses; the central governments, central banks, and other official institutions of foreign countries; and international and regional organizations. "Foreigner" also includes persons in the United States to the extent that they are known by reporting institutions to be acting on behalf of foreigners. Excludes acquisitions of foreign stocks through mergers that involve stock swaps. Including stock swaps, net sales of foreign securities was $199 billion in 2009. Minus sign (–) indicates net sales by U.S. investors or a net inflow of capital into the United States]

Year and country	Net Purchases			Total transactions [1]			Bonds		Stocks	
	Total	Bonds	Stocks	Total	Bonds	Stocks	Purchases	Sales	Purchases	Sales
1990.	31.2	21.9	9.2	907	652	255	337	315	132	123
2000.	17.1	4.1	13.1	5,539	1,922	3,617	963	959	1,815	1,802
2002.	−27.0	−28.5	1.5	5,253	2,716	2,537	1,344	1,372	1,269	1,268
2003.	56.5	−32.0	88.6	5,580	2,883	2,698	1,425	1,457	1,393	1,305
2004.	152.8	67.9	85.0	6,399	2,986	3,413	1,527	1,459	1,749	1,664
2005.	172.4	45.1	127.3	7,572	2,965	4,608	1,505	1,460	2,367	2,240
2006.	250.9	144.5	106.5	11,283	3,904	7,379	2,024	1,880	3,743	3,636
2007.	229.2	133.9	95.3	16,604	6,078	10,527	3,106	2,972	5,311	5,216
2008.	−86.9	−66.4	−20.4	15,332	4,475	10,856	2,204	2,271	5,418	5,438
2009, total [2].	197.6	138.2	59.3	10,442	4,042	6,400	2,090	1,952	3,230	3,170
United Kingdom.	22.3	−1.6	23.9	3,302	1,310	1,992	654	656	1,008	984
Cayman Islands.	−13.6	−15.0	1.3	1,765	625	1,140	305	320	571	570
Canada	41.7	34.5	7.2	818	392	426	213	179	217	209
Hong Kong.	7.7	−1.8	9.5	545	37	509	17	19	259	250
Japan.	−1.9	−4.3	2.5	490	123	367	59	64	184	182
Bermuda	7.9	5.8	2.1	452	269	183	137	132	93	90
France	−16.1	−9.0	−7.0	349	134	215	62	71	104	111
Australia.	54.5	48.6	5.9	294	137	157	93	44	82	76
Germany	−17.8	−15.9	−1.9	193	126	67	55	71	33	35
British Virgin Islands . . .	−1.6	−3.2	1.6	186	20	160	11	15	81	79
Netherlands.	−0.4	0.7	−1.1	162	60	102	30	30	50	51
Bahamas, The	−1.0	−3.1	2.0	147	60	87	29	32	44	42
Switzerland	−61.6	−31.2	−30.4	134	67	67	18	49	18	49
Brazil	27.6	9.9	17.0	127	45	81	28	18	50	32

[1] Total purchases plus total sales. [2] Includes other countries not shown separately.
Source: U.S. Department of Treasury, *Treasury Bulletin*, quarterly.

Table 1203. U.S. Holdings of Foreign Stocks and Bonds by Country: 2007 to 2009

[In billions of dollars (5,248.0 represents $5,248,000,000,000). See also Table 1200]

Country	Stocks			Country	Bonds		
	2007	2008	2009, prel.		2007	2008	2009, prel.
Total holdings.	5,248.0	2,748.4	3,977.4	Total holdings.	1,587.1	1,237.3	1,493.6
Europe [1].	2,569.4	1,378.9	1,888.9	Europe [1].	798.7	571.2	679.7
United Kingdom.	734.7	393.3	583.2	United Kingdom.	296.7	189.0	191.1
Switzerland	281.0	214.3	269.5	Belgium & Luxembourg	48.9	43.4	134.7
France	347.8	212.2	269.3	Germany	76.4	74.9	82.6
Germany	329.2	159.9	197.8	Netherlands.	84.6	75.9	65.2
Netherlands.	154.0	76.6	108.7	France	78.3	52.7	48.2
Spain	106.6	63.3	93.0	Ireland	50.2	22.6	30.0
Italy	96.9	47.0	60.5	Sweden	29.1	20.2	21.8
Sweden	57.4	30.3	47.7	Canada	185.2	165.9	215.5
Belgium and Luxembourg	71.7	31.6	45.8	Caribbean financial centers [1]. . . .	296.3	227.2	227.8
Canada	379.0	180.2	289.2	Cayman Islands.	271.3	202.4	205.4
Caribbean financial centers [1]. . . .	588.6	283.1	390.6	Bermuda	16.7	19.2	27.1
Bermuda	256.1	143.3	193.3	Latin America, excluding			
Cayman Islands.	231.9	95.2	133.1	Caribbean financial centers [1] . . .	79.1	65.9	85.9
Latin America, excluding				Brazil	16.2	18.9	30.6
Caribbean financial centers [1] . . .	293.8	137.3	295.8	Mexico	23.9	19.0	24.1
Brazil	172.6	72.1	185.9	Asia [1].	118.9	103.2	110.4
Mexico	85.4	46.0	74.4	Japan.	49.1	39.7	38.7
Asia [1].	1,193.7	659.2	923.3	Korea, South	9.8	10.5	21.1
Japan.	529.2	347.6	373.2	Africa	9.0	6.1	6.2
Hong Kong.	119.5	61.5	107.2	Other countries [1]	99.8	97.7	168.2
China [2].	95.7	53.3	83.9	Australia.	73.3	71.0	126.9
Korea, South	129.2	45.3	83.3				
Taiwan [2]	81.0	41.2	76.9				
Africa [1].	65.6	35.6	53.1				
South Africa.	49.1	29.6	46.1				
Other countries [1]	157.9	74.1	136.6				
Australia.	138.1	65.2	121.0				

[1] Includes other countries, not shown separately. [2] See footnote 3, Table 1205.
Source: U.S. Bureau of Economic Analysis, *Survey of Current Business*, July 2010.

Table 1204. Foreign Purchases and Sales of U.S. Securities by Type of Security, 1990 to 2009, and by Selected Country, 2009

[In billions of dollars (18.7 represents $18,700,000,000). Covers transactions in all types of long-term domestic securities by foreigners as reported to the Treasury International Capital Reporting System by banks, brokers, and other entities in the United States (except nonmarketable U.S. Treasury notes, foreign series; and nonmarketable U.S. Treasury bonds and notes, foreign currency series). See headnote, Table 1202. Excludes U.S. equities acquired through mergers and reincorporations that involve stock swaps. Also excludes principal repayment flows on foreign holdings of U.S. government agency and corporate asset-backed securities (ABS). Including stock swaps and accounting for ABS repayment flows, net purchases of U.S. securities was $436 billion in 2009. Minus sign (–) indicates net sales by foreigners or a net outflow of capital from the United States]

Year and country	Net purchases					Total transactions [4]				
	Total	Treasury bonds and notes [1]	U.S. government corporations [2] bonds	Corporate bonds [3]	Corporate stocks	Total	Treasury bonds and notes [1]	U.S. government corporations [2] bonds	Corporate bonds [3]	Corporate stocks
1990	18.7	17.9	6.3	9.7	−15.1	4,204	3,620	104	117	362
2000	457.8	−54.0	152.8	184.1	174.9	16,910	7,795	1,305	775	7,036
2001	520.8	18.5	164.0	222.0	116.4	20,003	10,517	2,239	1,260	5,986
2002	547.6	119.9	195.1	182.3	50.2	25,498	14,409	3,261	1,459	6,369
2003	719.9	263.6	155.8	265.7	34.7	26,332	15,739	2,725	1,694	6,174
2004	916.5	352.1	226.4	309.5	28.5	29,441	17,520	2,192	2,033	7,696
2005	1,011.5	338.1	219.3	372.2	82.0	32,425	19,764	1,976	2,182	9,382
2006	1,143.2	195.5	286.5	510.8	150.4	39,725	21,720	2,858	2,846	13,587
2007	1,005.8	198.0	219.0	393.4	195.5	56,624	30,057	3,882	3,433	21,083
2008	411.7	315.0	−39.0	94.2	41.5	60,992	28,941	5,218	2,841	23,992
2009 total [5]	**639.1**	**538.5**	**−11.5**	**−40.7**	**152.8**	**40,324**	**22,648**	**2,098**	**2,420**	**13,158**
United Kingdom	212.8	171.0	20.3	−12.3	33.8	13,902	10,576	462	1,114	1,750
Cayman Islands	2.5	2.4	−23.0	−3.6	26.7	7,828	2,320	410	494	4,604
France	27.0	17.8	13.0	−3.9	0.2	6,426	4,157	60	29	2,181
Canada	48.7	41.3	2.2	6.8	−1.6	1,547	781	60	86	619
Japan	128.2	129.5	−13.5	−1.6	13.8	1,540	1,087	256	69	128
Bermuda	9.5	5.8	3.0	3.3	−2.5	1,169	111	79	75	905
Bahamas, The	0.1	−0.0	−0.7	1.4	−0.7	840	390	8	130	312
British Virgin Islands	3.8	−5.3	−0.2	0.1	9.3	818	176	4	40	599
Anguilla	−1.8	−2.4	−0.7	0.3	0.9	654	32	1	2	619
China [6]	98.8	123.5	−24.7	−4.1	4.0	453	335	71	13	35
Israel	1.9	0.4	0.2	−0.2	1.5	446	409	3	4	29
Ireland	−18.0	−3.0	−4.5	−12.0	1.6	394	187	82	39	87

[1] Marketable bonds and notes. [2] Includes federally sponsored agencies. [3] Includes transactions in directly placed issues abroad by U.S. corporations and issues of states and municipalities. [4] Total purchases plus total sales. [5] Includes other countries not shown separately. [6] See footnote 3, Table 1205.

Source: U.S. Department of Treasury, *Treasury Bulletin*, quarterly.

Table 1205. Foreign Holdings of U.S. Securities by Country: 2007 to 2009

[In billions of dollars (2,376.4 represents $2,376,400,000,000). Covers only private holdings of U.S. securities, except as noted. See also Table 1288]

Country	2007	2008	2009, prel.
U.S. Treasury securities [1],[2]	**2,376.4**	**3,251.4**	**3,697.2**
China [3]	486.8	808.3	1,036.0
Japan	616.8	660.1	760.7
OPEC Asia [4]	116.1	180.6	177.3
Brazil	135.5	140.1	170.0
Russia	41.1	133.8	156.9
Hong Kong	54.5	78.2	148.3
Taiwan [3]	52.6	94.5	115.7
Belgium and Luxembourg	94.6	112.9	104.3
Switzerland	42.0	73.6	89.0
Cayman Islands	50.4	104.8	76.8
Corporate and agency bonds	**3,289.1**	**2,770.6**	**2,841.2**
Europe [2]	2,068.3	1,753.2	1,782.9
Belgium and Luxembourg	753.0	668.9	719.1
United Kingdom	709.3	566.0	543.2
Ireland	168.7	153.0	151.1
Switzerland	97.7	98.8	101.2
Germany	113.4	90.5	88.0
Netherlands	104.2	84.7	80.7
France	58.4	41.0	48.7
Canada	78.0	63.8	64.3
Caribbean financial centers [2]	590.4	480.2	509.7
Cayman Islands	430.7	336.8	349.2
Bermuda	119.8	109.5	120.2
Latin America, excluding Caribbean financial centers [2]	50.0	33.8	30.3
Mexico	24.8	12.4	5.4
Asia [2]	454.2	388.0	398.7
Japan	286.7	265.2	276.7
Taiwan [3]	30.7	36.4	46.6

Country	2007	2008	2009, prel.
Hong Kong	35.1	23.4	28.5
China [3]	56.1	27.8	15.1
OPEC Asia [4]	16.0	13.0	8.5
Africa	3.5	3.4	2.4
Other countries [2]	44.7	48.2	53.0
Australia	32.2	28.9	28.9
Corporate stocks	**2,900.9**	**1,850.2**	**2,445.9**
Europe [2]	1,560.8	964.3	1,244.4
United Kingdom	443.7	282.8	375.7
Belgium and Luxembourg	246.3	147.4	189.5
Switzerland	173.2	118.0	159.2
Netherlands	193.1	124.6	155.6
France	144.1	87.3	104.6
Ireland	82.1	56.0	73.4
Germany	99.2	45.3	54.3
Sweden	50.2	31.4	42.7
Canada	353.0	234.2	293.5
Caribbean financial centers [2]	500.7	305.0	416.6
Cayman Islands	324.3	214.9	295.3
Bermuda	76.0	38.3	43.6
Latin America, excluding Caribbean financial centers	49.4	39.1	55.8
Asia [2]	332.4	239.7	345.0
Japan	217.0	161.9	222.8
Singapore	44.7	20.0	30.5
Africa	9.1	5.1	5.7
Other countries [2]	95.5	62.8	84.9
Australia	88.0	57.3	75.9

[1] Includes foreign official holdings. [2] Includes other countries not shown separately. [3] With the establishment of diplomatic relations with China on January 1, 1979, the U.S. government recognized the People's Republic of China as the sole legal government of China and acknowledged the Chinese position that there is only one China and that Taiwan is part of China. [4] Comprises Indonesia, Iran, Iraq, Kuwait, Qatar, Saudi Arabia, and the United Arab Emirates.

Source: U.S. Bureau of Economic Analysis, *Survey of Current Business*, July 2010.

Table 1206. Stock Prices and Yields: 2000 to 2009

[Closing values as of end of December, except as noted]

Index	2000	2004	2005	2006	2007	2008	2009
STOCK PRICES							
Standard & Poor's indices: [1]							
S&P 500 composite (1941–43 = 10)	1,320	1,212	1,248	1,418	1,468	903	1,115
S&P 400 MidCap Index (1982 = 100)	517	663	738	804	858	538	727
S&P 600 SmallCap Index (Dec. 31, 1993 = 100)	220	329	351	400	395	269	333
S&P 500 Citigroup Value Index (Dec. 31, 1974 = 35)	636	626	648	764	761	447	525
S&P 500 Citigroup Growth Index (Dec. 31, 1974 = 35)	688	582	597	653	703	451	582
Russell indices: [2]							
Russell 1000 (Dec. 31, 1986 = 130)	700	651	679	770	800	488	612
Russell 2000 (Dec. 31, 1986 = 135)	484	652	673	788	766	499	625
Russell 3000 (Dec. 31, 1986 = 140)	726	694	723	822	849	521	653
N.Y. Stock Exchange common stock index:							
Composite (Dec. 31, 2002 = 5000)	6,946	7,250	7,754	9,139	9,740	5,757	7,185
Yearly high	7,165	7,373	7,868	9,188	10,387	9,713	7,288
Yearly low	6,095	6,211	6,903	7,708	8,344	4,607	4,182
American Stock Exchange Composite Index (Dec. 29, 1995 = 550)	898	1,434	1,759	2,056	2,410	1,398	1,825
NASDAQ Composite Index (Feb. 5, 1971 = 100)	2,471	2,175	2,205	2,415	2,653	1,577	2,269
Nasdaq-100 (Jan. 31, 1985 = 125)	2,342	1,621	1,645	1,757	2,085	1,212	1,860
Industrial (Feb. 5, 1971 = 100)	1,483	1,858	1,860	2,090	2,179	1,191	1,748
Banks (Feb. 5, 1971 = 100)	1,939	3,218	3,078	3,417	2,663	2,026	1,651
Computers (Oct. 29, 1993 = 200)	1,295	965	992	1,053	1,283	684	1,168
Transportation (Feb. 5, 1971 = 100)	1,160	2,229	2,438	2,582	2,673	1,885	1,951
Telecommunications (Oct. 29, 1993 = 200)	463	198	184	235	257	146	217
Biotech (Oct. 29, 1993 = 200)	1,085	769	790	798	835	730	844
Dow-Jones and Co., Inc.:							
Composite (65 stocks)	3,317	3,396	3,638	4,121	4,394	3,086	3,567
Industrial (30 stocks)	10,787	10,783	10,718	12,463	13,265	8,776	10,428
Transportation (20 stocks)	2,947	3,798	4,196	4,560	4,571	3,537	4,100
Utility (15 stocks)	412	335	405	457	533	371	398
Dow-Jones Wilshire 5000 Composite Index [3] (December 31, 1980 = 1,405) [3]	12,176	11,971	12,518	14,258	14,820	9,007	11,497
COMMON STOCK YIELDS (percent)							
Standard & Poor's Composite Index (500 stocks): [4]							
Dividend-price ratio [5]	1.15	1.72	1.83	1.87	1.86	2.37	2.01
Earnings-price ratio [6]	3.63	4.00	5.30	5.78	5.29	3.54	4.55

[1] Standard & Poor's Indices are market-value weighted and are chosen for market size, liquidity, and industry group representation. The S&P 500 index represents 500 large publicly-traded companies. The S&P MidCap Index tracks mid-cap companies. The S&P SmallCap Index consists of 600 domestic small-cap stocks. [2] The Russell 1000 and 3000 indices show respectively the 1000 and 3000 largest capitalization stocks in the United States. The Russell 2000 index shows the 2000 largest capitalization stocks in the United States after the first 1000. [3] Dow-Jones Wilshire 5000 Composite Index (full-cap) measures the performance of all U.S. headquartered equity securities with readily available prices. Source: Dow-Jones & Company, Inc., New York, NY, Dow-Jones Indexes, (copyright) [4] Source: U.S. Council of Economic Advisors, Economic Indicators, monthly. [5] Aggregate cash dividends (based on latest known annual rate) divided by aggregate market value based on Wednesday closing prices. Averages of monthly figures. [6] Averages of quarterly ratios which are ratio of earnings (after taxes) for 4 quarters ending with particular quarter-to-price index for last day of that quarter.

Source: Except as noted, Global Financial Data, Los Angeles, CA, (copyright), <http://www.globalfinancialdata.com/>.

Table 1207. Dow Jones U.S. Total Market Index by Industry: 2000 to 2009

[As of end of year]

Industry	2000	2004	2005	2006	2007	2008	2009
U.S. Total Market Index, total	**306.88**	**289.38**	**302.37**	**343.25**	**357.48**	**219.66**	**276.57**
Basic materials	154.49	200.33	205.79	236.22	307.92	147.91	239.44
Consumer goods	219.82	266.44	265.88	298.60	320.39	231.71	278.07
Consumer services	279.11	306.85	298.62	338.32	310.76	211.93	278.96
Oil and gas	272.96	319.76	422.12	510.72	679.31	429.60	494.01
Financial	440.91	492.54	510.02	592.98	474.23	226.52	258.79
Health care	360.18	295.22	315.50	332.38	354.89	268.73	320.51
Industrials	276.11	272.24	280.72	314.41	351.44	207.77	255.47
Technology	749.01	499.78	513.48	561.85	645.98	365.85	595.55
Telecommunications	210.38	136.84	126.90	168.11	179.65	115.34	119.63
Utilities	177.80	136.79	152.41	178.78	204.52	137.79	148.29

Source: Dow-Jones & Company, Inc., New York, NY, Dow-Jones Indexes (copyright).

Table 1208. Transaction Activity in Equities, Options, and Security Futures, 1990 to 2009, and by Exchange, 2009

[In billions of dollars (2,229 represents $2,229,000,000,000). Market value of all sales of equities and options listed on an exchange or subject to last-sale reporting. Also reported are the value of such options that were exercised and the value of single-stock futures that were delivered. Excludes options and futures on indexes]

Year and exchange	Market value of sales (billion dollars)			Option exercises and futures deliveries
	Total	Equity trading	Option trading	
1990.	2,229	2,154	27	48
2000.	36,275	35,557	485	233
2002.	23,028	22,658	161	209
2003.	22,737	22,292	164	282
2004.	27,876	27,158	223	495
2005.	34,568	33,223	350	995
2006.	43,941	41,798	531	1,611
2007.	66,136	63,064	861	2,211
2008.	82,012	78,653	1,096	2,264
2009, total [1].	**59,850**	**57,566**	**710**	**1,574**
BATS Exchange, Inc. [2].	6,523	6,523	–	–
The Boston Stock Exchange.	980	900	24	56
Chicago Board Options Exchange, Inc.	667	138	165	364
FINRA, Inc. [3].	16,348	16,348	–	–
International Securities Exchange, Inc.	1,361	798	173	390
The Nasdaq Stock Market LLC.	14,401	14,338	19	43
National Stock Exchange.	300	300	–	–
New York Stock Exchange, Inc.	7,807	7,807	–	–
NYSE Arca, Inc. [4].	10,382	10,023	110	249
Philadelphia Stock Exchange, Inc.	532	–	170	362

– Represents zero. [1] Includes other exchanges not shown separately. [2] Better Alternative Trading System [3] Financial Industry Regulatory Authority. [4] NYSE Arca, formerly Archipelago, is a fully electronic stock exchange.

Source: U.S. Securities and Exchange Commission, "Select SEC and Market Data," <http://www.sec.gov/about.shtml>.

Table 1209. Volume of Trading on New York Stock Exchange: 1990 to 2009

[39,946 represents 39,946,000,000. Round lot: A unit of trading or a multiple thereof. On the NYSE the unit of trading is generally 100 shares in stocks. For some inactive stocks, the unit of trading is 10 shares. Odd lot: An amount of stock less than the established 100-share unit or 10-share unit of trading]

Item	Unit	1990	2000	2003	2004	2005 [1]	2006	2007	2008	2009
Shares traded	**Million**	**39,946**	**265,499**	**356,767**	**372,718**	**523,811**	**597,720**	**671,402**	**806,883**	**738,193**
Round lots	Million	39,665	262,478	352,398	367,099	516,743	588,127	664,020	802,170	738,193
Average daily shares	Million	157	1,042	1,398	1,457	2,051	2,343	2,645	3,171	2,929
High day	Million	292	1,561	1,886	2,690	3,628	3,853	5,505	7,342	5,043
Low day	Million	57	403	360	509	694	797	917	849	585
Odd lots	Million	282	3,021	4,370	5,619	7,068	9,593	7,383	4,713	([2])
Value of shares traded	**Bil. dol.**	**1,336**	**11,205**	**9,847**	**11,841**	**18,174**	**22,247**	**28,805**	**28,272**	**17,562**
Round lots	Bil. dol.	1,325	11,060	9,692	11,618	17,858	21,790	28,428	28,080	17,562
Odd lots	Bil. dol.	11	145	154	223	316	458	378	192	([2])

[1] Beginning 2005, reflects trades of NYSE Group. [2] This is a discontinued data series because this data in no longer collected due to the rescinding of the rules 440F & 440G.

Source: New York Stock Exchange, Inc., New York, NY, "Facts & Figures," <http://www.nyxdata.com/factbook> (copyright).

Table 1210. Stock Ownership by Age of Head of Family and Family Income: 2001 to 2007

[Median value in thousands of constant 2007 dollars (40.4 represents $40,400). Constant dollar figures are based on consumer price index data published by U.S. Bureau of Labor Statistics. Families include one-person units; for definition of family, see text, Section 1. Based on Survey of Consumer Finance; see Appendix III. For definition of median, see Guide to Tabular Presentation]

Age of family head and family income (constant (2007) dollars)	Families having direct or indirect stock holdings [1] (percent)			Median value among families with holdings			Stock holdings share of total financial assets (percent)		
	2001	2004	2007	2001	2004	2007	2001	2004	2007
All families.	**52.2**	**50.2**	**51.1**	**40.4**	**35.7**	**35.0**	**56.1**	**51.3**	**53.3**
Under 35 years old	49.0	40.8	38.6	8.2	8.8	7.0	52.5	40.3	44.3
35 to 44 years old	59.5	54.5	53.5	32.2	22.0	26.0	57.2	53.5	53.7
45 to 54 years old	59.3	56.5	60.4	58.5	54.9	45.0	59.1	53.8	53.0
55 to 64 years old	57.4	62.8	58.9	94.2	78.0	78.0	56.2	55.0	55.0
65 to 74 years old	40.0	46.9	52.1	175.8	76.9	57.0	55.4	51.5	55.3
75 years old and over	35.7	34.8	40.1	128.7	94.3	41.0	51.8	39.3	48.1
Percentiles of income: [2]									
Less than 20	12.9	11.7	13.6	8.8	8.2	6.5	37.4	32.0	39.0
20 to 39.9.	34.1	29.6	34.0	9.1	11.0	8.8	35.6	30.9	34.3
40 to 59.9.	52.5	51.7	49.5	17.5	16.5	17.7	46.8	43.4	38.3
60 to 79.9.	75.7	69.9	70.5	33.5	28.7	34.1	52.0	41.7	52.5
80 to 89.9.	82.0	83.8	84.4	75.6	60.9	62.0	57.3	48.8	49.3
90 to 100	89.7	92.7	91.0	289.7	225.2	219.0	60.5	57.5	57.6

[1] Indirect holdings are those in retirement accounts and other managed assets. [2] See footnote 8, Table 1169.

Source: Board of Governors of the Federal Reserve System, "2007 Survey of Consumer Finances," February 2009, <http://www.federalreserve.gov/pubs/oss/oss2/2007/scf2007home.html\>.

Table 1211. Households Owning Mutual Funds by Age and Income: 2000 and 2009

[In percent. Ownership includes money market, stock, bond, and hybrid mutual funds, variable annuities, and mutual funds owned through Individual Retirement Accounts (IRAs), Keoghs, and employer-sponsored retirement plans. In 2009, an estimated 51,200,000 households own mutual funds. The May 2009 survey included a sample of 4,201 randomly selected households; for details, see source. For definition of mutual fund, see headnote, Table 1213]

Age of household head and household income [1,2]	Percent distribution, 2009	As a percent of all households		Age of household head and household income [1,2]	Percent distribution, 2009	As a percent of all households	
		2000	2009			2000	2009
Total..................	100	45	43	Less than $25,000.........	6	13	10
Less than 35 years old	17	36	33	$25,000 to $34,999........	5	33	20
35 to 44 years old	21	55	49	$35,000 to $49,999........	13	46	39
45 to 54 years old	27	59	54	$50,000 to $74,999........	21	66	50
55 to 64 years old	19	50	48	$75,000 to $99,999........	19	75	68
65 years old and over	16	26	33	$100,000 to $199,999.....	29	84	76
				$200,000 and over........	7	56	77

[1] Age is based on the sole or co-decision maker for household saving and investing. [2] Total reported is household income before taxes in prior year.

Source: Investment Company Institute, Washington, DC, *Fundamentals, Investment Company Institute Research in Brief*, Vol. 18, No. 17, December 2009 (copyright).

Table 1212. Characteristics of Mutual Fund Owners: 2009

[In percent, except as indicated. Mutual fund ownership includes holdings of money market, stock, bond, and hybrid mutual funds; and funds owned through variable annuities, Individual Retirement Accounts (IRAs), Keoghs, and employer-sponsored retirement plans. Based on a national probability sample of 1,805 primary financial decision-makers in households with mutual fund investments. For definition of mutual fund, see headnote, Table 1213. For definition of median, see Guide to Tabular Presentation]

Characteristic	Total	Age			Household income			
		Under 40 years old	40 to 64 years old	65 years old and over	Less than $50,000	$50,000 to $99,000	$100,000 to $149,000	$150,000 or more
Median age [1] (years).............	50	33	51	72	54	49	40	48
Median household income [2] (dol.)...	80,000	76,000	87,500	50,000	35,000	72,000	113,400	190,000
Median household financial assets [3] (dollars)......................	150,000	50,000	200,000	320,000	45,000	100,000	200,000	500,000
Own an IRA....................	67	57	70	70	02	64	70	77
Household with defined contribution retirement plan(s) [4]	78	89	82	47	59	82	90	82
401(k) plan....................	65	79	69	28	47	68	72	72
403(b), state, local, or federal government plan	31	32	32	27	23	31	37	37
Median mutual fund assets (dol.) ...	80,000	30,000	100,000	150,000	30,000	60,000	100,000	250,000
Own:								
Equity funds...................	77	77	79	60	00	78	79	87
Bond funds	49	47	49	50	36	50	49	64

[1] See Table 1211, footnote 1. [2] See Table 1211, footnote 2. [3] Includes assets in employer-sponsored retirement plans but excludes value of primary residence. [4] For definition of defined contribution plan, see headnote, Table 550.

Source: Investment Company Institute, Washington, DC, *Profile of Mutual Fund Shareholders, 2009*, Winter 2010 (copyright).

Table 1213. Mutual Funds—Summary: 1990 to 2009

[Number of funds and assets as of December 31 (1,065 represents $1,065,000,000,000). A mutual fund is an open-end investment company that continuously issues and redeems shares that represent an interest in a pool of financial assets. Excludes data for funds that invest in other mutual funds. Minus sign (−) indicates net redemptions]

Type of fund	Unit	1990	2000	2003	2004	2005	2006	2007	2008	2009
Number of funds, total	Number...	3,079	8,155	8,126	8,041	7,975	8,117	8,026	8,022	7,691
Equity funds.....................	Number ...	1,099	4,385	4,599	4,547	4,586	4,769	4,763	4,828	4,659
Hybrid funds	Number ...	193	523	508	510	505	508	489	493	474
Bond funds	Number ...	1,046	2,208	2,045	2,041	2,013	1,993	1,969	1,918	1,853
Money market funds, taxable [1]	Number ...	506	703	662	639	595	574	546	535	478
Money market funds, tax-exempt [2] ...	Number ...	235	336	312	304	276	273	259	248	227
Assets, total..................	Bil. dol....	1,065	6,965	7,414	8,107	8,905	10,397	12,001	9,603	11,121
Equity funds.....................	Bil. dol.....	239	3,962	3,684	4,384	4,940	5,911	6,516	3,704	4,958
Hybrid funds	Bil. dol.....	36	346	430	519	567	653	719	499	641
Bond funds	Bil. dol.....	291	811	1,248	1,290	1,357	1,494	1,680	1,567	2,206
Money market funds, taxable [1]	Bil. dol.....	415	1,607	1,764	1,603	1,707	1,972	2,621	3,341	2,919
Money market funds, tax-exempt [2] ...	Bil. dol.....	84	238	288	310	334	366	465	491	397
Net sales:										
Equity, hybrid and bond funds	Bil. dol.....	51	300	282	293	303	369	405	−9	512
Money market funds, taxable [1]	Bil. dol.....	36	192	−252	−157	67	255	623	604	−425
Money market funds, tax-exempt [2] ...	Bil. dol.....	7	31	7	16	24	33	90	26	−87

[1] Funds invest in short-term, high-grade securities sold in the money market. [2] Funds invest in municipal securities with relatively short maturities.

Source: Investment Company Institute, Washington, DC, *Mutual Fund Fact Book*, annual (copyright).

Table 1214. Mutual Fund Shares—Holdings and Net Purchases by Type of Investor: 2000 to 2009

[In billions of dollars (4,433 represents $4,433,000,000,000). Holdings as of Dec. 31. For definition of mutual fund, see headnote, Table 1213. Excludes money market mutual funds. Minus sign (–) indicates net sales]

Type of investor	Holdings					Net purchases				
	2000	2005	2007	2008	2009	2000	2005	2007	2008	2009
Total................................	**4,433**	**6,049**	**7,829**	**5,435**	**7,002**	**237.6**	**260.2**	**364.7**	**31.0**	**494.6**
Households, nonprofit organizations..........	2,704	3,839	4,832	3,445	4,417	66.7	228.1	243.0	–5.4	416.9
Nonfinancial corporate business..............	122	156	218	143	163	3.5	6.7	2.0	–6.8	–6.8
State and local governments.................	31	30	34	27	44	1.2	0.8	2.2	8.6	11.2
Rest of the world..........................	149	242	373	262	338	–9.2	32.2	38.2	5.3	23.8
Commercial banking	15	17	30	20	47	2.5	–1.8	3.6	1.3	15.4
Credit unions.............................	2	2	2	2	1	–0.3	–1.0	–	–	–0.7
Property-casualty insurance companies	3	6	7	4	5	0.4	0.3	–0.5	–0.4	0.1
Life insurance companies	97	109	188	121	141	5.6	–9.9	31.3	–10.7	–
Private pension funds	1,132	1,399	1,848	1,230	1,619	117.3	10.2	50.2	39.9	36.1
State and local government retirement funds ...	178	248	296	181	228	49.9	–5.5	–5.3	–0.8	–1.4

– Represents or rounds to zero.
Source: Board of Governors of the Federal Reserve System, "Federal Reserve Statistical Release, Z.1, Flow of Funds Accounts of the United States," March 2010, <http://www.federalreserve.gov/releases/z1/20100311>.

Table 1215. Retirement Assets by Type of Asset: 1990 to 2009

[In billions of dollars, except as indicated (3,923 represents $3,923,000,000,000). As of December 31]

Institution	1990	2000	2004	2005	2006	2007	2008	2009
Retirement assets, total	**3,923**	**11,696**	**13,782**	**14,862**	**16,748**	**18,021**	**13,989**	**15,963**
IRA assets............................	637	2,629	3,299	[1] 3,652	[2] 4,207	[2] 4,784	[1] 3,579	[1] 4,230
Bank and thrift deposits [3]...............	266	250	269	278	313	340	391	431
Life insurance companies [4]..............	40	203	283	308	318	[1] 325	[1] 310	[1] 303
Mutual funds.........................	139	1,239	1,509	1,688	2,015	2,288	1,585	1,953
Securities held in brokerage accounts [5]	191	937	1,238	[1] 1,378	[2] 1,562	[2] 1,831	[1] 1,293	[1] 1,544
Traditional	(NA)	2,407	2,957	[1] 3,259	[2] 3,722	[2] 4,223	[1] 3,167	[1] 3,722
Roth................................	(X)	78	140	[1] 160	[2] 196	[2] 233	[1] 173	[1] 215
SEP and SAR-SEP [6]...................	(NA)	134	169	[1] 191	[2] 236	[2] 266	[1] 193	[1] 235
SIMPLE [7]...........................	(X)	10	34	[1] 42	[2] 52	[2] 63	[1] 46	[1] 58
Defined contribution plans...............	892	2,970	3,344	3,622	4,145	4,441	3,453	4,088
401(k) plans..........................	(NA)	1,725	2,189	2,396	2,768	2,982	[1] 2,275	[1] 2,754
403(b) plans..........................	(NA)	518	572	617	689	731	611	682
457 plans............................	(NA)	110	130	143	158	173	140	169
Other defined contribution plans [8].........	(NA)	618	453	466	531	555	427	483
State and local government pension plans ...	742	2,340	2,621	2,763	3,175	3,315	2,425	2,766
Private defined benefit plans..............	922	2,009	2,162	2,310	2,557	2,691	1,957	2,148
Federal pension plans [9].................	340	797	1,023	1,072	1,141	1,197	1,221	1,324
Annuities [10]	391	951	1,332	1,443	1,521	1,592	1,355	1,407
Memo:								
Mutual fund retirement assets............	206	2,530	3,143	3,526	4,174	4,697	3,224	4,054
Percent of total retirement assets	5	22	23	24	25	26	23	25
Percent of all mutual funds	19	36	39	40	40	39	34	36

NA Not available. X Not applicable. [1] Data are estimated. [2] Data are preliminary. [3] Includes Keogh deposits. [4] Annuities held by IRAs, excluding variable annuity mutual fund IRA assets. [5] Excludes mutual fund assets held through brokerage accounts, which are included in mutual funds. [6] Simplified Employee Pension IRAs and salary reduction (SAR) SEP IRAs. [7] Savings Incentive Match Plan for Employees (SIMPLE) IRAs. [8] Includes Keoghs and other defined contribution plans (profit-sharing, thrift-savings, stock bonus, and money purchase) without 401(k) features. [9] Federal pension plans include U.S. Treasury security holdings of the civil service retirement and disability fund, the military retirement fund, the judicial retirement funds, the Railroad Retirement Board, and the foreign service retirement and disability fund. These plans also include securities held in the National Railroad Retirement Investment Trust and Federal Employees Retirement System (FERS) Thrift Savings Plan (TSP). [10] Annuities include all fixed and variable annuity reserves at life insurance companies less annuities held by IRAs, 403(b) plans, 457 plans, and private pension funds. Some of these annuity reserves represent assets of individuals held outside retirement plan arrangements and IRAs; however, information to separate out such reserves is not available.
Source: Investment Company Institute, Washington, DC, Research Fundamentals, "*The U.S. Retirement Market, 2009,*" Vol. 19, No. 3, May 2010. See also <http://www.ici.org/pdf/fm-v19n3.pdf>.

Table 1216. Assets of Private and Public Pension Funds by Type of Fund: 1990 to 2009

[In billions of dollars (3,269 represents $3,269,000,000,000). As of end of year. Except for corporate equities, represents book value. Excludes social security trust funds; see Table 545]

Type of pension fund	1990	2000	2003	2004	2005	2006	2007	2008	2009
Total, all types	**3,269**	**9,084**	**9,631**	**10,551**	**11,292**	**12,592**	**13,243**	**10,299**	**11,677**
Private funds	2,199	5,994	6,323	6,950	7,500	8,342	8,829	6,751	7,679
Insured [1]	570	1,526	1,803	2,028	2,197	2,332	2,438	2,151	2,222
Noninsured [2, 3]	1,629	4,468	4,520	4,922	5,302	6,010	6,391	4,600	5,457
Credit market instruments [3]	464	622	653	655	700	758	861	951	976
Agency- and GSE-backed securities [4]	133	197	224	235	252	269	297	318	290
Corporate and foreign bonds	158	266	275	268	290	318	357	400	424
Corporate equities	606	1,971	2,097	2,338	2,542	2,875	2,863	1,665	1,946
Mutual fund shares	40	1,132	1,127	1,278	1,399	1,658	1,848	1,230	1,619
Unallocated insurance contracts [5]	215	308	317	328	338	388	444	352	458
State and local government employee retirement funds [3]	730	2,293	2,349	2,578	2,721	3,108	3,216	2,327	2,673
Credit market instruments [3]	402	743	658	675	693	825	856	851	835
Agency- and GSE-backed securities [4]	63	179	235	259	258	311	334	341	331
Corporate and foreign bonds	142	314	207	214	228	297	288	289	289
Corporate equities	285	1,299	1,421	1,601	1,716	1,926	1,986	1,212	1,526
Federal government retirement funds [6]	340	797	958	1,023	1,072	1,141	1,197	1,221	1,324

[1] Annuity reserves held by life insurance companies, excluding unallocated contracts held by private pension funds. [2] Private defined benefit plans and defined contribution plans (including 401(k) type plans). [3] Includes other types of assets not shown separately. [4] GSE = Government-sponsored enterprises. [5] Assets held at life insurance companies (e.g., guaranteed investment contracts (GICs), variable annuities). [6] Includes the Federal Employees Retirement System Thrift Savings Plan, the National Railroad Retirement Investment Trust, and nonmarketable government securities held by federal government retirement funds.

Source: Board of Governors of the Federal Reserve System, "Federal Reserve Statistical Release, Z.1, Flow of Funds Accounts of the United States," March 2010, <http://www.federalreserve.gov/releases/z1/20100311>.

Table 1217. Annual Revenues of Selected Securities Industries: 2003 to 2008

[In millions of dollars (311,525 represents $311,525,000,000). For taxable and tax-exempt employer firms only. Based on Service Annual Survey. Estimates have been adjusted to the results of the 2002 Economic Census. See Appendix III]

Kind of business	NAICS code [1]	2003	2004	2005	2006	2007	2008
Total	**523x**	**311,525**	**349,166**	**384,401**	**461,403**	**464,494**	**296,630**
Securities and commodity contracts	5231	225,299	250,080	271,976	330,590	317,789	159,276
Investment banking & securities dealing	52311	108,306	127,257	140,371	175,820	162,575	22,762
Securities brokerage	52312	110,689	115,626	123,195	144,598	143,038	123,444
Commodity contracts dealing	52313	3,329	3,858	5,086	5,907	7,144	7,864
Commodity contracts brokerage	52314	2,975	(S)	3,224	4,273	5,032	5,206
Other financial investment activities [2]	5239x	86,226	99,086	112,525	130,805	146,705	137,354
Portfolio management	52392	71,535	80,872	90,682	104,278	117,393	109,331
Investment advice	52393	14,691	18,214	21,843	26,527	29,312	28,023

S Estimate does not meet publication standards. [1] Data for 2003 are based on the 1997 North American Industry Classification System. Data 2004 through 2008 are based on 2002 NAICS; see text, this section and Section 15. [2] Excludes NAICS 52391 (miscellaneous intermediation) and NAICS 52399 (all other financial investment activities).

Source: U.S. Census Bureau, "Service Annual Survey: 2008," January 2010, <http://www.census.gov/services/index.html>.

Table 1218. Securities Industry—Financial Summary: 1990 to 2008

[In billions of dollars, except as indicated. (71.4 represents $71,400,000,000). Minus sign (–) indicates negative gain]

Type	1990	2000	2002	2003	2004	2005	2006	2007	2008
Number of firms	8,437	7,258	6,768	6,565	6,284	6,016	5,808	5,562	5,178
Revenues, total	**71.4**	**349.5**	**221.8**	**219.0**	**242.9**	**332.5**	**458.5**	**496.5**	**296.6**
Commissions	12.0	54.1	45.0	45.5	47.6	46.8	49.7	54.4	55.2
Trading/investment gains	15.7	70.8	24.2	38.8	30.7	30.7	55.2	4.1	–55.3
Underwriting profits	3.7	18.7	14.7	17.2	19.1	19.9	23.6	26.5	16.3
Margin interest	3.2	24.5	6.4	5.3	7.0	13.3	23.7	32.3	18.1
Mutual fund sales	3.2	19.4	15.7	16.2	18.5	20.7	23.3	26.2	22.1
Other	33.4	161.9	115.8	96.0	120.1	201.2	282.9	353.0	240.2
Expenses, total	**70.6**	**310.4**	**206.5**	**193.3**	**219.7**	**311.3**	**419.9**	**491.5**	**320.1**
Interest expense	28.1	131.9	56.4	44.4	59.7	140.2	226.1	282.2	122.7
Compensation	22.9	95.2	74.9	77.4	83.5	88.8	103.4	106.3	95.0
Commissions/clearance paid	3.0	15.5	15.0	16.3	17.4	18.6	22.0	25.9	26.4
Other	16.6	67.8	60.3	55.1	59.2	63.6	68.4	77.0	76.0
Net income, pretax	**0.8**	**39.1**	**15.3**	**25.7**	**23.2**	**21.2**	**38.6**	**5.1**	**–23.6**
Pre-tax profit margin (percent)	1.1	11.2	6.9	11.7	9.5	6.4	8.4	1.0	–7.9
Pre-tax return on equity (percent)	2.2	31.1	10.7	17.6	15.0	13.1	22.1	2.7	–12.8
Assets	657	2,866	3,261	3,980	4,831	5,215	6,222	6,777	4,441
Liabilities	623	2,728	3,119	3,831	4,671	5,051	6,037	6,591	4,261
Ownership equity	34	138	142	149	160	164	185	186	181

Source: U.S. Securities and Exchange Commission, "Select SEC and Market Data Fiscal 2009," forthcoming, <http://www.sec.gov/about/secstats2009.pdf>.

Table 1219. Life Insurance in Force and Purchases in the United States— Summary: 1990 to 2008

[As of December 31 or calendar year, as applicable (389 represents 389,000,000). Covers life insurance with life insurance companies only. Data represents all life insurance in force on lives of U.S. residents whether issued by U.S. or foreign companies]

Year	Number of policies, total (millions)	Life insurance in force Value (bil. dol.) Total [1]	Individual	Group	Life insurance purchases [2] Number (1,000) Total	Individual	Group	Amount (bil. dol.) Total	Individual	Group
1990.........	389	9,393	5,391	3,754	28,791	14,199	14,592	1,529	1,070	459
2000.........	369	15,953	9,376	6,376	34,882	13,345	21,537	2,515	1,594	921
2002.........	375	16,346	9,312	6,876	38,713	14,692	24,020	2,767	1,753	1,014
2003.........	379	17,044	9,655	7,236	35,767	13,821	21,946	2,823	1,773	1,050
2004.........	373	17,508	9,717	7,631	38,453	12,581	25,872	2,948	1,846	1,102
2005.........	373	18,399	9,970	8,263	34,519	11,407	23,112	2,836	1,796	1,040
2006.........	375	19,112	10,057	8,906	29,287	10,908	18,378	2,835	1,813	1,022
2007.........	374	19,539	10,232	9,158	30,788	10,826	19,962	2,994	1,891	1,103
2008.........	335	19,120	10,254	8,717	28,599	10,207	18,392	2,943	1,870	1,073

[1] Includes other types of policies not shown separately. [2] Excludes revivals, increases, dividend additions, and reinsurance acquired. Includes long-term credit insurance (life insurance on loans of more than 10 years' duration).
Source: American Council of Life Insurers, Washington, DC, *Life Insurers Fact Book*, annual (copyright).

Table 1220. U.S. Life Insurance Companies—Summary: 1990 to 2008

[As of December 31 or calendar year, as applicable (402.2 represents $402,200,000,000). Covers domestic and foreign business of U.S. companies. Beginning 2000, includes annual statement data for companies that primarily are health insurance companies. Beginning 2003, includes fraternal benefit societies]

Item	Unit	1990	2000	2002	2003	2004	2005	2006	2007	2008
U.S. companies [1].............	Number ...	2,195	1,269	1,284	1,227	1,179	1,119	1,072	1,009	976
Income.....................	**Bil. dol....**	**402.2**	**811.5**	**734.0**	**727.0**	**756.8**	**779.0**	**883.6**	**950.4**	**940.6**
Life insurance premiums.......	Bil. dol.....	76.7	130.6	134.5	127.3	139.7	142.3	149.2	142.7	147.2
Annuity considerations [2].......	Bil. dol.....	129.1	306.7	269.3	268.6	276.7	277.1	302.7	314.2	328.1
Health insurance premiums.....	Bil. dol.....	58.3	105.6	108.7	115.8	125.8	118.3	141.2	151.5	165.0
Investment and other..........	Bil. dol.....	138.2	268.5	221.5	215.3	214.7	241.4	290.4	342.0	300.3
Payments under life insurance and annuity contracts........	Bil. dol.....	88.4	375.2	301.3	307.1	331.7	365.7	422.7	461.0	445.1
Payments to life insurance beneficiaries...............	Bil. dol.....	24.6	44.1	48.2	51.7	51.6	53.0	55.7	58.0	59.9
Surrender values under life insurance [3]................	Bil. dol.....	18.0	27.2	32.9	35.9	35.5	39.2	38.5	47.7	58.6
Surrender values under. annuity contracts [3, 4].............	Bil. dol.....	(NA)	214.0	142.9	140.3	162.9	190.3	237.8	262.3	236.7
Policyholder dividends.........	Bil. dol.....	12.0	20.0	21.0	20.8	19.0	17.9	18.4	19.5	19.1
Annuity payments [4]...........	Bil. dol.....	32.6	68.7	55.0	57.1	61.2	63.9	71.1	72.3	69.6
Matured endowments..........	Bil. dol.....	0.7	0.6	0.6	0.6	0.6	0.6	0.6	0.6	0.6
Other payments..............	Bil. dol.....	0.6	0.6	0.6	0.7	0.9	0.7	0.6	0.6	0.6
Health insurance benefit payments..................	Bil. dol.....	40.0	78.8	78.7	81.9	88.5	79.6	97.0	106.1	118.9
BALANCE SHEET										
Assets.....................	**Bil. dol....**	**1,408**	**3,182**	**3,380**	**3,887**	**4,253**	**4,482**	**4,823**	**5,092**	**4,648**
Government bonds...........	Bil. dol.....	211	364	481	538	563	590	579	561	634
Corporate securities.........	Bil. dol.....	711	2,238	2,266	2,666	2,965	3,136	3,413	3,628	3,104
Percent of total assets......	Percent ...	50	70	67	69	70	70	71	71	67
Bonds....................	Bil. dol.....	583	1,241	1,475	1,644	1,785	1,850	1,882	1,957	1,968
Stocks....................	Bil. dol.....	128	997	791	1,022	1,180	1,285	1,531	1,670	1,136
Mortgages..................	Bil. dol.....	270	237	251	269	283	295	314	336	353
Real estate.................	Bil. dol.....	43	36	33	31	31	33	33	35	32
Policy loans................	Bil. dol.....	63	102	105	107	109	110	113	117	122
Other......................	Bil. dol.....	110	204	244	276	303	319	371	415	402
Interest earned on assets [5]......	Percent ...	8.89	7.05	5.38	5.03	4.80	4.90	5.35	5.71	5.70
Obligations and surplus funds [6]...	Bil. dol.....	1,408	3,182	3,380	3,888	4,253	4,482	4,823	5,092	4,648
Policy reserves.............	**Bil. dol....**	**1,197**	**2,712**	**2,507**	**2,895**	**3,160**	**3,360**	**3,608**	**3,791**	**3,471**
Annuities [7].................	Bil. dol.....	798	1,841	1,550	1,835	2,024	2,174	2,328	2,458	2,137
Group....................	Bil. dol.....	516	960	570	662	712	758	807	843	716
Individual................	Bil. dol.....	282	881	980	1,173	1,312	1,415	1,521	1,615	1,422
Supplementary contracts [8].....	Bil. dol.....	17	34	14	15	16	16	17	18	13
Life insurance..............	Bil. dol.....	349	742	833	921	988	1,029	1,110	1,148	1,134
Health insurance............	Bil. dol.....	33	96	111	123	134	141	153	166	186
Liabilities for deposit-type contracts [9]................	Bil. dol.....	18	21	364	405	445	456	487	517	454
Capital and surplus...........	Bil. dol.....	91	188	202	231	250	256	266	282	263

NA Not available. [1] Beginning 2000, includes life insurance companies that sell accident and health insurance. [2] Beginning 2001, excludes certain deposit-type funds from income due to codification. [3] Beginning with 2000, "surrender values" include annuity withdrawals of funds, which were not included in 1990. [4] Beginning 2001, excludes payments under deposit-type contracts. [5] Net rate. [6] Includes other obligations not shown separately. [7] Beginning 2001, excludes reserves for guaranteed interest contracts (GICs). [8] Through 2000, includes reserves for contracts with and without life contingencies; beginning 2001, includes only reserves for contracts with life contingencies. [9] Policyholder dividend accumulations for all years. Beginning 2001, also includes liabilities for guaranteed interest contracts, supplementary contracts without life contingencies, and premium and other deposits.
Source: American Council of Life Insurers, Washington, DC, *Life Insurers Fact Book*, annual (copyright).

Table 1221. Property and Casualty Insurance—Summary: 2000 to 2008

[In billions of dollars (305.1 represents $305,100,000,000). Minus sign (–) indicates loss]

Item	2000	2003	2004	2005	2006	2007	2008
Premiums, net written [1]	305.1	407.5	425.7	427.6	447.8	417.3	440.1
Automobile, private [2]	120.0	151.3	157.6	159.6	160.5	159.7	158.6
Automobile, commercial [2]	19.8	25.5	26.7	26.8	26.7	25.6	23.8
Homeowners' multiple peril	32.7	46.0	50.0	53.0	55.8	57.1	57.4
Commercial multiple peril	(NA)	27.4	29.1	29.7	31.9	31.3	30.1
Marine, inland and ocean	8.3	10.4	10.8	11.2	12.3	13.1	12.5
Workers' compensation	26.2	32.9	36.7	39.7	41.8	40.9	36.9
Medical malpractice	(NA)	8.8	9.1	9.7	10.4	10.0	9.5
Other liability [3]	(NA)	36.1	39.8	39.4	42.2	41.1	38.6
Reinsurance	(NA)	15.5	13.7	6.6	12.9	11.3	12.7
Losses and expenses	321.3	389.4	407.7	421.4	401.0	417.1	457.5
Underwriting gain/loss	−27.3	−3.0	6.0	−3.7	34.5	21.7	−19.3
Net investment income	42.0	38.6	40.0	49.7	52.3	55.1	51.2
Operating earnings after taxes	4.4	23.5	29.4	34.4	62.2	53.6	22.1

NA Not available. [1] Excludes state funds. Includes other lines of insurance not shown separately. [2] Includes premiums for automobile liability and physical damage. [3] Coverages protecting against legal liability resulting from negligence, carelessness, or failure to act.

Source: Insurance Information Institute, New York, NY, *The III Insurance Fact Book*, annual; and *Financial Services Fact Book*, annual (copyright). Data from ISO and Highline Data LLC. See also <http://www.iii.org>.

Table 1222. Automobile Insurance—Average Expenditures Per Insured Vehicle by State: 2000 and 2007

[In dollars. Average expenditure equals total premiums written divided by liability car-years. A car-year is equal to 365 days of insured coverage for a single vehicle. The average expenditures for automobile insurance in a state are affected by a number of factors, including the underlying rate structure, the coverages purchased, the deductibles and limits selected, the types of vehicles insured, and the distribution of driver characteristics. The NAIC does not rank state average expenditures and does not endorse any conclusions drawn from this data]

State	2000	2007	State	2000	2007	State	2000	2007	State	2000	2007
U.S.	690	795	ID	505	564	MO	612	658	PA	699	820
AL	594	684	IL	652	723	MT	530	666	RI	825	1,017
AK	770	923	IN	570	618	NE	533	554	SC	620	762
AZ	792	873	IA	479	518	NV	829	1,000	SD	482	534
AR	606	660	KS	540	569	NH	665	750	TN	592	649
CA	672	800	KY	616	720	NJ	977	1,104	TX	678	808
CO	755	738	LA	806	1,096	NM	674	730	UT	620	697
CT	871	964	ME	528	611	NY	939	1,047	VT	568	662
DE	849	1,012	MD	757	922	NC	564	591	VA	576	661
DC	996	1,140	MA	946	981	ND	477	512	WA	722	841
FL	781	1,040	MI	702	928	OH	579	628	WV	680	819
GA	674	782	MN	696	721	OK	603	646	WI	545	582
HI	702	837	MS	654	680	OR	625	723	WY	496	631

Source: National Association of Insurance Commissioners (NAIC), Kansas City, MO, Auto Insurance Database Report, annual (copyright). Reprinted with permission of the NAIC. Further reprint or distribution strictly prohibited without prior written permission of the NAIC.

Table 1223. Renters and Homeowners Insurance—Average Premiums by State: 2007

[In dollars. Average premium equals premiums divided by exposure per house-years. A house-year is equal to 365 days of insured coverage for a single dwelling and is the standard measurement for homeowners insurance. The NAIC does not rank state average expenditures and does not endorse any conclusions drawn from these data]

State	2007 Renters [1]	2007 Home-owners [2]	State	2007 Renters [1]	2007 Home-owners [2]	State	2007 Renters [1]	2007 Home-owners [2]
U.S.	182	822	KY	143	578	ND	112	771
AL	218	905	LA	248	1,400	OH	162	540
AK	175	861	ME	142	596	OK	223	1,054
AZ	200	634	MD	147	692	OR	161	496
AR	201	762	MA	223	1,023	PA	144	689
CA	231	925	MI	170	721	RI	182	950
CO	172	826	MN	138	800	SC	176	808
CT	196	929	MS	250	1,019	SD	113	618
DE	155	559	MO	154	726	TN	204	723
DC	190	1,089	MT	155	700	TX [3]	226	1,448
FL	202	1,534	NE	143	807	UT	138	505
GA	218	724	NV	201	695	VT	158	704
HI	209	850	NH	153	699	VA	145	683
ID	150	422	NJ	172	776	WA	170	506
IL	165	700	NM	185	667	WV	175	646
IN	169	647	NY	218	936	WI	122	491
IA	132	610	NC	133	674	WY	149	656
KS	168	904						

[1] Based on the HO-4 renters insurance policy for tenants. Includes broad named-peril coverage for the personal property of tenants. [2] Based on the HO-3 homeowner package policy for owner-occupied dwellings, 1–4 family units. Provides "all risks" coverage (except those specifically excluded in the policy) on buildings, broad named-peril coverage on personal property, and is the most common package written. [3] The Texas Insurance Commissioner promulgates residential policy forms which are similar but not identical to the standard forms.

Source: National Association of Insurance Commissioners (NAIC), Kansas City, MO, Dwelling Fire, Homeowners Owner-Occupied, and Homeowners Tenant and Condominium/Cooperative Unit Owners Insurance (copyright). Reprinted with permission of the NAIC. Further reprint or distribution strictly prohibited without prior written permission of the NAIC.

Table 1224. Real Estate and Rental and Leasing—Nonemployer Establishments and Receipts by Kind of Business: 2005 to 2007

[2,441.6 represents 2,441,600. Includes only firms subject to federal income tax. Nonemployers are businesses with no paid employees. Data originate chiefly from administrative records of the Internal Revenue Service; see Appendix III]

Kind of business	NAICS code [1]	Establishments (1,000)			Receipts (mil. dol.)		
		2005	2006	2007	2005	2006	2007
Real estate & rental & leasing, total	**53**	**2,441.6**	**2,420.9**	**2,327.1**	**207,688**	**193,105**	**183,264**
Real estate	531	2,357.3	2,338.3	2,243.5	201,075	186,400	176,526
Lessors of real estate	5311	869.2	804.1	780.0	117,430	105,927	102,825
Offices of real estate agents & brokers	5312	808.5	829.9	790.7	39,346	36,214	31,460
Activities related to real estate	5313	679.6	704.4	672.8	44,299	44,259	42,242
Rental & leasing services	532	82.8	81.1	81.8	6,465	6,564	6,583
Automotive equipment rental & leasing	5321	20.0	19.8	20.3	1,023	1,023	1,057
Consumer goods rental	5322	18.4	18.1	18.5	837	862	898
General rental centers	5323	3.8	3.9	3.9	375	358	348
Commercial/industrial equipment rental & leasing	5324	40.6	39.3	39.1	4,230	4,320	4,280
Lessors of other nonfinancial intangible assets	533	1.5	1.5	1.7	152	141	154

[1] Data are based on the 2002 North American Industry Classification System (NAICS); see text this section and Section 15.
Source: U.S. Census Bureau, "Nonemployer Statistics," June 2009, <http://www.census.gov/econ/nonemployer/index.html>.

Table 1225. Real Estate and Rental and Leasing—Establishments, Employees, and Payroll: 2006 and 2007

[(382.1 represents 382,100). Covers establishments with payroll. Employees are for the week including March 12. Most government employees are excluded. For statement on methodology, see Appendix III]

Kind of business	NAICS code [1]	Establishments (1,000)		Employees (1,000)		Payroll (bil. dol.)	
		2006	2007	2006	2007	2006	2007
Real estate & rental & leasing, total	**53**	**382.1**	**380.1**	**2,216.8**	**2,224.2**	**87.5**	**89.0**
Real estate	531	313.5	312.5	1,553.4	1,554.2	64.0	64.5
Lessors of real estate	5311	117.6	115.3	544.6	539.2	18.6	18.2
Offices of real estate agents & brokers	5312	114.0	111.0	377.3	367.1	18.6	17.8
Activities related to real estate	5313	81.8	86.2	631.5	647.9	26.8	28.6
Rental & leasing services	532	66.3	65.0	633.9	638.3	21.2	21.9
Automotive equipment rental & leasing	5321	13.6	13.5	184.5	199.9	6.3	6.6
Passenger car rental & leasing	53211	7.4	7.2	129.1	144.7	4.1	4.4
Truck, utility trailer & RV rental & leasing	53212	6.3	6.3	55.4	55.2	2.2	2.1
Consumer goods rental [2]	5322	33.3	31.3	253.6	237.1	5.4	5.2
Video tape & disc rental	53223	17.8	16.3	137.3	127.5	1.7	1.7
General rental centers	5323	5.6	5.4	35.9	35.5	1.2	1.2
Commercial/industrial equipment rental & leasing	5324	13.8	14.8	160.0	165.8	8.3	8.9
Lessors of other nonfinancial intangible assets	533	2.3	2.6	29.5	31.7	2.3	2.6

[1] North American Industry Classification System (NAICS), 2002; see text this section and Section 15. [2] Includes other kinds of business not shown separately.
Source: U.S. Census Bureau, "County Business Patterns," <http://www.census.gov/econ/cbp/>.

Table 1226. Rental and Leasing Services—Revenue by Kind of Business: 2003 to 2008

[In millions of dollars (96,387 represents $96,387,000). Covers taxable and tax-exempt employer firms. Estimates have been adjusted using the results of the 2002 Economic Census. Based on Service Annual Survey; see Appendix III]

Kind of business	NAICS code [1]	2003	2004	2005	2006	2007	2008
Rental & leasing services	**532**	**96,387**	**102,863**	**108,426**	**118,551**	**123,175**	**125,232**
Automotive equipment rental & leasing	5321	37,007	41,126	43,584	46,410	47,348	48,470
Passenger car rental & leasing	53211	23,007	24,793	25,925	27,649	28,596	29,677
Truck, utility trailer, & RV rental & leasing	53212	14,000	16,333	17,659	18,761	18,752	18,793
Consumer goods rental [2]	5322	21,923	23,412	22,777	23,617	24,646	24,271
Video tape & disc rental	53223	10,053	10,604	9,507	9,844	10,083	9,527
General rental centers	5323	3,611	3,710	3,362	3,666	3,908	3,858
Commercial/industrial equip. rental & leasing	5324	33,846	34,615	38,703	44,858	47,273	48,633

[1] Data for 2003 are based on the 1997 North American Industry Classification System (NAICS). Data 2004 through 2008 are based on 2002 NAICS; see text, this section and Section 15. [2] Includes other kinds of business not shown separately.
Source: U.S. Census Bureau, "Service Annual Survey: 2008," January 2010, <http://www.census.gov/services/index.html>.

Section 26
Arts, Recreation, and Travel

This section presents data on the arts, entertainment, and recreation economic sector of the economy, and personal recreational activities, the arts and humanities, and domestic and foreign travel.

Arts, Entertainment, and Recreation Industry—The U.S. Census Bureau surveys—*County Business Patterns, Economic Census, Nonemployer Statistics* and *Service Annual Survey,* provide data on the *Arts, Entertainment, and Recreation Sector.* The County Business Patterns annual data includes number of establishments, number of employees, first quarter and annual payrolls, and number of establishments by employment size class. The Economic Census, conducted every five years for the years ending '2' and '7,' provides information on the number of establishments, receipts, payroll, and paid employees for the United States and various geographic levels. Nonemployer statistics are an annual tabulation of economic data by industry for active businesses without paid employees that are subject to federal income tax. The Service Annual Survey provides estimates of operation revenue of taxable firms and revenues and expenses of firms exempt from federal taxes for industries in this sector of the economy. See Appendix III for more details.

Recreation and leisure activities— Data on the participation in various recreation and leisure time activities are based on several sample surveys. Data on the public's involvement with arts events and activities are published by the National Endowment for Arts (NEA). The NEA's Survey of Public Participation in the Arts remains the largest periodic study of arts participation in the United States. The most recent data are from the 2008 survey. Data on participation in

fishing, hunting, and other forms of wildlife associated recreation are published periodically by the U.S. Department of Interior, Fish and Wildlife Service. The most recent data are from the 2006 survey. Data on participation in various sports recreation activities are published by the National Sporting Goods Association. Mediamark, Inc. also conducts periodic surveys on sports and leisure activities, as well as other topics.

Parks and recreation— The Department of the Interior has responsibility for administering the national parks. The National Park Service publishes information on visits to national park areas in its annual report, *National Park Statistical Abstract. The National Parks:* Index (year) is an annual report which contains brief descriptions, with acreages and visits for each area administered by the service, plus certain "related" areas. This information can be found at: <http://www.nature .nps.gov/stats>. Statistics for state parks are compiled by the National Association of State Park Directors.

Travel—Statistics on arrivals and departures to the United States, cities and states visited by overseas travelers, and tourism sales and employment are reported by the International Trade Administration (ITA), Office of Travel & Tourism Industries (OTTI). Data on domestic travel and travel expenditures are published by the research department of the U.S. Travel Association. Other data on household transportation characteristics are in Section 23, Transportation.

Statistical reliability—For a discussion of statistical collection and estimation, sampling procedures, and measures of statistical reliability applicable to Census Bureau data, see Appendix III.

U.S. Census Bureau, Statistical Abstract of the United States: 2011

Table 1227. Arts, Entertainment, and Recreation Services—Estimated Revenue: 2003 to 2008

[In millions of dollars (149,360 represents $149,360,000,000). For taxable and tax-exempt employer firms. Except where indicated, estimates adjusted using the results of the 2002 Economic Census. Based on the Service Annual Survey, see Appendix III]

Industry	2002 NAICS Code [1]	2003	2004	2005	2006	2007	2008
Arts, entertainment, and recreation	71	**149,360**	**158,557**	**165,964**	**179,808**	**190,759**	**195,980**
Performing arts, spectator sports, and related industries	711	60,367	62,796	64,718	71,122	75,319	78,948
Spectator sports	7111	11,070	11,554	12,211	12,249	12,405	12,919
Performing arts companies	7112	22,445	23,659	24,471	26,948	29,277	31,302
Sports teams and clubs	711211	13,257	14,115	14,136	15,786	17,507	18,995
Racetracks	711212	6,582	7,022	7,358	7,957	8,273	8,444
Other spectator sports	711219	2,606	2,522	2,977	3,205	3,497	3,863
Promoters of performing arts, sports, and similar events	7113	12,872	13,571	14,342	17,069	18,302	18,749
Agents and managers for artists, athletes, entertainers and other public figures	7114	3,604	3,819	3,795	3,978	4,188	4,454
Independent artists, writers, and performers	7115	10,376	10,193	9,899	10,878	11,147	11,524
Museums, historical sites, and similar institutions	712	9,082	9,688	10,256	11,967	12,931	12,634
Amusement, gambling, and recreation industries	713	79,911	86,073	90,990	96,719	102,509	104,398
Amusement parks and arcades	7131	9,930	10,561	11,182	11,368	12,146	12,624
Amusement and theme parks	71311	8,737	9,344	9,882	9,963	10,746	11,141
Amusement arcades	71312	1,193	1,217	1,300	1,405	1,400	1,483
Gambling industries	7132	22,370	25,698	28,099	31,021	32,849	33,583
Casinos (except casino hotels)	71321	14,601	16,664	17,931	19,596	20,505	20,890
Other gambling industries	71329	7,769	9,034	10,168	11,425	12,344	12,693
Other amusement and recreation industries	7139	47,611	49,814	51,709	54,330	57,514	58,191
Golf courses and country clubs	71391	16,987	17,880	18,467	18,906	19,147	19,053
Skiing facilities	71392	1,839	1,980	2,054	2,239	2,399	2,559
Marinas	71393	3,382	3,393	3,637	3,992	4,267	3,949
Fitness and recreational sports centers	71394	16,130	16,839	17,620	18,473	20,054	20,949
Bowling centers	71395	3,293	3,505	3,427	3,347	3,738	3,672
All other amusement and recreation	71399	5,980	6,217	6,504	7,373	7,909	8,009

[1] Data for 2003 are based on the 1997 North American Industry Classification System. Data 2004 through 2008 are based on 2002 NAICS; see text, this section and Section 15.

Source: U.S. Census Bureau, Service Annual Survey: 2008, January 2010, <http://www.census.gov/services/index.html>.

Table 1228. Arts, Entertainment, and Recreation—Establishments, Revenue, Payroll, and Employees by Kind of Business: 2002 and 2007

[For establishments with payroll. (110,313 represents $110,313,000,000). These data are preliminary and are subject to change; they will be superseded by data released in later data files. Includes only establishments of firms with payroll. Definition of paid employees varies among NAICS sectors. Data are based on the 2002 and 2007 economic censuses which are subject to nonsampling error. For details on survey methodology, sampling and nonsampling errors, see Appendix III]

Kind of business	2002 NAICS code	Number of establishments		Revenue (mil. dol.)		Annual payroll (mil. dol.)		Paid employees (1,000)	
		2002	2007	2002	2007	2002	2007	2002	2007
Arts, entertainment, and recreation, total	71	**110,313**	**124,024**	**141,904**	**190,571**	**45,169**	**58,474**	**1,849**	**2,078**
Performing arts, spectator sports, and related industries [1]	711	37,735	43,791	58,286	77,696	21,231	27,784	423	442
Performing arts companies	7111	9,303	9,073	10,864	13,753	3,267	4,037	138	134
Spectator sports	7112	4,072	4,338	22,313	300,009	10,206	1,402	108	120
Promoters of performing arts, sports and similar events	7113	5,236	6,497	12,169	16,133	2,184	2,973	102	121
Agents and managers for artists, athletes, entertainers and others	7114	3,262	3,545	3,602	5,075	1,251	1,743	17	19
Museums, historical sites, and similar institutions [1]	712	6,663	7,120	8,608	13,043	2,935	3,653	123	130
Amusement, gambling, and recreation industries [1]	713	65,915	73,113	75,010	99,832	21,002	27,037	1,303	1,506
Amusement parks and arcades	7131	3,015	3,182	9,443	13,374	2,069	2,871	122	141
Gambling industries	7132	2,072	2,490	18,893	26,420	3,596	4,653	158	173
Other amusement and recreation services	7139	60,828	67,441	46,674	60,038	15,337	19,513	1,023	1,192

[1] Includes other industries, not shown separately.

Source: U.S. Census Bureau, 2007 Economic Census, Core Business Statistics, *Comparative Statistics 2007 and 2002, Arts, Entertainment and Recreation,* accessed January 2010, <http://www.census.gov/econ/census07/www/using_american_factfinder/index.html>.

Table 1229. Arts, Entertainment, and Recreation—Nonemployer Establishments and Receipts by Kind of Business (NAICS Basis): 2005 to 2007

[(972.5 represents 972,500). Includes only firms subject to federal income tax. Nonemployers are businesses with no paid employees]

Kind of business	2002 NAICS code [1]	Establishments (1,000)			Receipts (mil.dol.)		
		2005	2006	2007	2005	2006	2007
Arts, entertainment, and recreation	71	**972.5**	**1,001.8**	**1,119.6**	**23,704**	**24,782**	**27,357**
Performing arts, spectator sports, and related industries	711	828.8	855.7	967.4	17,741	18,733	20,841
Performing arts companies	7111	30.0	41.7	53.4	827	944	1,132
Spectator sports	7112	91.6	95.6	141.6	1,877	1,993	2,532
Promoters of performing arts, sports, and similar events	7113	35.5	37.8	39.8	1,434	1,475	1,584
Agents/managers for artists, athletes, and other public figures	7114	32.6	33.7	33.8	1,183	1,253	1,294
Independent artists, writers, and performers	7115	639.1	646.9	698.9	12,419	13,067	14,299
Museums, historical sites, and similar institutions	712	5.6	5.9	6.2	91	88	103
Amusement, gambling, and recreation industries	713	138.1	140.1	145.9	5,873	5,961	6,413
Amusement parks and arcades	7131	5.4	5.6	5.5	346	337	330
Gambling industries	7132	8.4	8.8	10.4	1,064	1,122	330
Other amusement and recreation services	7139	124.2	125.6	130.0	4,463	4,503	4,805

[1] Based on the 2002 North American Industry Classification System (NAICS); see text, Section 15.
Source: U.S. Census Bureau, Nonemployer Statistics, released June 2009, <http://www.census.gov/econ/nonemployer>.

Table 1230. Arts, Entertainment, and Recreation—Establishments, Employees, and Payroll by Kind of Business (NAICS Basis): 2006 to 2007

[(1,973.7 represents 1,973,700). Covers establishments with paid employees. Excludes self-employed individuals, employees government employees of private households, railroad employees, agricultural production employees and most government employees. For statement on methodology, see Appendix III. County Business Patterns excludes rail transportation (NAICS 482) and the National Postal Service (NAICS 491)]

Kind of business	2002 NAICO code [1]	Establishments		Employees (1,000)		Payroll (mil.dol)	
		2006	2007	2006	2007	2006	2007
Arts, entertainment, & recreation	71	**123,048**	**125,222**	**1,973.7**	**2,008.6**	**56,839**	**60,357**
Performing arts, spectator sports	711	12,430	11,260	424.9	430.1	26,636	28,932
Performing arts companies	7111	9,195	9,453	133.5	134.4	3,913	4,243
Theater companies & dinner theaters	71111	3,524	3,553	74.1	69.7	1,976	2,038
Dance companies	71112	620	703	9.3	9.5	225	250
Musical groups & artists	71113	4,522	4,612	43.3	43.3	1,470	1,584
Other performing arts companies	71119	529	585	6.8	12.0	243	371
Spectator sports	7112	4,564	4,631	120.3	126.1	13,298	14,591
Sports teams & clubs	711211	818	819	50.9	52.8	11,148	12,186
Racetracks	711212	741	733	48.3	51.2	1,220	1,000
Other spectator sports	711219	3,005	3,079	21.1	22.1	922	1,017
Promoters of performing arts, sports, and similar events	7113	5,779	6,367	107.1	112.4	2,665	2,992
Promoters of performing arts, sports, & similar events with facilities	71131	2,089	2,580	80.1	85.8	1,409	1,782
Promoters of performing arts, sports, & similar events without facilities	71132	3,690	3,787	27.0	26.6	1,256	1,210
Agents/managers for artists, athletes, and other public figures	7114	3,494	3,722	16.4	17.4	1,579	1,709
Independent artists, writers, & performers	7115	19,398	20,087	47.6	45.8	5,181	5,397
Museums, historical sites, & similar institutions	712	7,089	7,312	123.2	128.5	3,360	3,597
Museums	71211	4,787	4,920	80.7	83.7	2,235	2,404
Historical sites	71212	979	1,051	9.4	9.8	208	228
Zoos & botanical gardens	71213	611	595	26.5	28.5	742	784
Nature parks & other similar institutions	71219	712	746	6.6	6.6	174	180
Amusement, gambling, & recreation industries	713	73,529	73,650	1,425.6	1,444.0	26,843	27,828
Amusement parks & arcades	7131	2,927	3,097	136.4	128.4	2,662	2,755
Amusement & theme parks	71311	579	634	108.7	101.2	2,310	2,391
Amusement arcades	71312	2,348	2,463	27.6	27.1	352	364
Gambling industries	7132	2,600	2,729	196.0	205.3	5,540	5,851
Casinos (except casino hotels)	71321	468	488	133.6	136.9	3,861	4,099
Other gambling industries	71329	2,132	2,241	62.3	68.4	1,679	1,753
Other amusement & recreation services	7139	68,002	67,824	1,093.2	1,110.3	18,642	19,221
Golf courses & country clubs	71391	11,870	11,851	309.4	316.4	7,839	8,059
Skiing facilities	71392	381	402	75.3	75.7	624	651
Marinas	71393	4,025	4,085	28.3	28.8	894	945
Fitness & recreational sports centers	71394	32,432	31,453	507.9	514.5	6,478	6,617
Bowling centers	71395	4,615	4,571	81.3	80.5	1,000	997
All other amusement & recreation industries	71399	14,679	15,462	91.0	94.4	1,807	1,951

[1] Based on the 2002 North American Industry Classification System (NAICS); see text, this section and Section 15.
Source: U.S. Census Bureau, "County Business Patterns," released July 2009, <http://www.census.gov/econ/cbp/index.html>.

Arts, Recreation, and Travel **759**

Table 1231. Expenditures Per Consumer Unit for Entertainment and Reading: 1985 to 2008

[Data are annual averages. In dollars, except as indicated. Based on Consumer Expenditure Survey (CE); see text in Section 13 for description of survey. See also headnote, Table 685. For composition of regions, see map, inside front cover]

Year and characteristic	Entertainment and reading		Entertainment				Reading
	Total	Percent of total expenditures	Total	Fees and admissions	Audio and visual equipment and services	Other entertainment, supplies, and equipment services [1]	
1985.	1,311	5.6	1,170	320	371	479	141
1990.	1,575	5.6	1,422	371	454	597	153
1993.	1,792	5.8	1,626	414	590	621	166
1994.	1,732	5.5	1,567	439	533	595	165
1995.	1,775	5.5	1,612	433	542	637	163
1996.	1,993	5.9	1,834	459	561	814	159
1997.	1,977	5.7	1,813	471	577	766	164
1998.	1,907	5.4	1,746	449	535	762	161
1999.	2,050	5.5	1,891	459	608	824	159
2000.	2,009	5.3	1,863	515	622	727	146
2001.	2,094	5.3	1,953	526	660	767	141
2002.	2,218	5.5	2,079	542	692	845	139
2003.	2,187	5.4	2,060	494	730	835	127
2004.	2,348	5.4	2,218	528	788	903	130
2005.	2,514	5.4	2,388	588	888	912	126
2006.	2,493	5.2	2,376	606	906	863	117
2007.	2,816	5.7	2,698	658	987	1,053	118
2008, total	**2,951**	**5.8**	**2,835**	**616**	**1,036**	**1,183**	**116**
Age of reference person:							
Under 25 years old	1,656	5.6	1,608	271	681	656	48
25 to 34 years old	2,845	5.9	2,766	524	1,105	1,137	79
35 to 44 years old	3,705	6.3	3,603	823	1,168	1,613	102
45 to 54 years old	3,421	5.6	3,297	805	1,174	1,318	124
55 to 64 years old	3,193	5.8	3,036	643	1,113	1,280	157
65 to 74 years old	2,570	7.0	2,418	498	885	1,035	152
75 years old and over	1,481	3.6	1,349	268	628	453	132
Hispanic or Latino Origin of reference person:							
Hispanic	1,825	4.2	1,787	364	851	572	38
Non-Hispanic	3,097	6.0	2,971	648	1,060	1,262	126
Race of reference person:							
White, Asian, and all other races	3,148	6.0	3,022	672	1,056	1,294	126
Black	1,525	4.2	1,478	210	894	375	47
Region of residence:							
Northeast	3,101	5.6	2,960	724	1,090	1,145	141
Midwest	2,876	6.0	2,758	592	987	1,179	118
South	2,599	5.6	2,512	507	1,027	977	87
West	3,473	6.3	3,333	726	1,056	1,551	140
Size of consumer unit:							
One person	1,743	5.8	1,655	322	694	639	88
Two or more persons	3,443	5.9	3,315	736	1,176	1,404	128
Two persons	3,322	6.2	3,178	595	1,122	1,461	144
Three persons	3,193	5.4	3,070	720	1,206	1,143	123
Four persons	3,829	5.8	3,714	942	1,276	1,496	115
Five persons or more	3,710	5.6	3,612	949	1,177	1,486	98
Income before taxes: Quintiles of income:							
Lowest 20 percent	1,137	5.1	1,082	156	536	390	55
Second 20 percent	1,789	5.6	1,716	221	726	769	73
Third 20 percent	2,523	5.9	2,422	372	948	1,102	101
Fourth 20 percent	3,404	5.8	3,276	647	1,262	1,367	128
Highest 20 percent	5,898	6.1	5,673	1,681	1,707	2,286	225
Education:							
Less than a high school graduate	1,361	4.6	1,318	129	640	549	43
High school graduate	2,205	5.4	2,129	297	947	885	76
High school graduate with some college	2,800	5.9	2,700	525	1,005	1,169	100
Associate's degree	3,264	6.1	3,146	628	1,214	1,305	118
Bachelor's degree	4,216	6.4	4,048	1,054	1,246	1,749	168
Master's, professional, doctoral degree	4,788	6.0	4,530	1,477	1,340	1,713	258

[1] Other equipment and services include pets, toys, hobbies, and playground equipment; and other entertainment supplies, equipment, and services.

Source: U.S. Bureau of Labor Statistics, Consumer Expenditure Survey, "Consumer Expenditures in 2008," October 2009. See also <http://www.bls.gov/cex/home.htm#tables>.

Table 1232. Personal Consumption Expenditures for Recreation: 1990 to 2008

[In billions of dollars (314.7 represents $314,700,000,000), except percent. Represents market value of purchases of goods and services by individuals and nonprofit institutions. Table data have been revised, along with changes to "Type of products and services." These changes resulted from BEA's 13th comprehensive NIPA revision released in July 2009. For more on these changes and revisions, see <http://www.bea.gov/scb/pdf/2009/03%20March/0309_nipa_preview.pdf>]

Type of product or service	1990	2000	2004	2005	2006	2007	2008
Total recreation expenditures...............	**314.7**	**639.9**	**764.6**	**807.4**	**859.1**	**906.5**	**928.0**
Percent of total personal consumption [1]	8.2	9.4	9.2	9.2	9.2	9.2	9.2
Video and audio equipment, computers, and related services ...	81.1	184.4	224.8	239.4	256.1	269.8	276.2
Video and audio equipment..................	43.7	83.1	100.9	107.8	114.6	116.6	117.7
Information processing equipment	9.6	44.1	51.5	55.9	60.4	65.3	66.3
Services related to video and audio goods and computers......	27.8	57.2	72.4	75.7	81.1	87.9	92.2
Sports and recreational goods and related services...........	74.2	147.9	178.3	188.4	199.6	209.3	211.5
Sports and recreational vehicles.............	16.6	34.9	45.0	47.7	49.7	51.1	49.0
Other sporting and recreational goods........	55.4	108.7	128.1	135.2	144.2	152.1	156.9
Maintenance and repair of recreational vehicles and sports equipment..................	2.1	4.2	5.1	5.4	5.8	6.1	5.5
Membership clubs, sports centers, parks, theaters, and museums..................	49.7	91.9	106.5	110.6	117.8	125.1	128.3
Membership clubs and participant sports centers	14.3	26.4	29.4	30.5	31.9	33.3	33.9
Amusements parks, campgrounds, and related recreational services..................	19.2	31.1	33.1	34.9	37.4	40.2	41.7
Admissions to specified spectator amusements...........	14.4	30.6	38.5	39.2	42.1	44.5	45.6
Motion picture theaters..................	5.1	8.6	9.9	9.1	9.4	9.6	9.5
Live entertainment, excluding sports............	4.5	10.4	13.2	13.8	14.9	15.3	15.5
Spectator sports..................	4.8	11.6	15.5	16.3	17.8	19.5	20.5
Museums and libraries..................	1.9	3.8	5.5	5.9	6.4	7.0	7.2
Magazines, newspapers, books, and stationery	47.3	81.0	88.3	93.1	98.2	103.4	105.6
Gambling..................	23.7	67.6	89.8	95.6	103.9	109.6	113.7
Pets, pet products, and related services..............	18.8	39.7	49.8	53.1	56.9	61.6	65.1
Photographic goods and services..............	16.7	19.7	19.1	18.7	18.2	18.9	19.0
Package tours [2]..................	3.2	7.8	8.0	8.5	8.3	8.8	8.6

[1] See Table 676. [2] Consists of tour operators' and travel agents' margins. Purchases of travel and accommodations included in tours are accounted for separately in other personal consumption expenditures categories.

Source: U.S. Bureau of Economic Analysis, National Economic Accounts, *National Income and Product Account Tables, Table 2.5.5*, August 2009. See also <http://www.bea.gov/national/nipaweb/Index.asp>

Table 1233. Performing Arts—Selected Data: 1990 to 2008

[Sales, receipts, and expenditures in millions of dollars (282 represents $282,000,000). For season ending in year shown, except as indicated]

Item	1990	1995	2000	2002	2003	2004	2005	2006	2007	2008
Legitimate theater: [1]										
Broadway shows:										
New productions	40	33	37	37	36	39	39	39	35	36
Attendance (mil.)...............	8.0	9.0	11.4	11.0	11.4	11.6	11.5	12.0	12.3	12.3
Playing weeks [2,3]............	1,070	1,120	1,464	1,434	1,544	1,451	1,494	1,501	1,509	1,560
Gross ticket sales	282	406	603	643	721	771	769	862	939	938
Broadway road tours:[4]										
Attendance (mil.)	11.1	15.6	11.7	11.7	12.4	12.9	18.2	17.1	16.7	15.3
Playing weeks...............	944	1,242	888	863	877	1,060	1,389	1,377	1,400	1,138
Gross ticket sales.............	367	701	572	593	642	714	934	915	950	956
Nonprofit professional theatres: [5]										
Companies reporting [6]...........	185	215	262	1,146	1,274	1,477	1,490	1,893	1,910	1,919
Gross income	308	444	791	1,436	1,481	1,571	1,647	1,791	1,881	1,884
Earned income	188	281	466	761	787	856	845	923	962	955
Contributed income	119	163	325	675	694	715	802	868	919	929
Gross expenses................	306	445	708	1,405	1,476	1,464	1,530	1,667	1,742	1,860
Productions	2,265	2,646	3,241	10,000	13,000	11,000	12,000	14,000	17,000	15,000
Performances	46,131	56,608	66,123	157,000	170,000	169,000	169,000	172,000	197,000	202,000
Total attendance (mil.)...........	15.2	18.6	22.0	32.2	34.3	32.1	32.5	30.5	31.0	32.0
OPERA America professional member companies: [7]										
Number of companies reporting [8]..	98	88	98	86	91	95	93	94	97	85
Expenses [8]..................	321	435	637	684	692	678	742	752	872	826
Performances [9]..................	2,336	2,120	1,768	1,824.0	1,741	1,946	1,893	1,851	1,961	1,753
Total attendance (mil.) [9,10]........	7.5	4.1	6.2	4.9	5.8	5.1	5	5.3	5.3	5.1
Main season attendance (mil.) [9,11]..................	4.1	3.9	3.8	3.2	3.1	3.4	3.3	3.4	3.6	3.1
Symphony orchestras: [12]										
Concerts	18,931	29,328	33,154	37,118	38,182	37,263	37,196	36,731	37,169	(NA)
Attendance (mil.)................	24.7	30.9	31.7	30.3	27.8	27.7	26.5	29.1	28.8	(NA)
Gross revenue.................	378	536	734	764	781	827	812	945	1,052	(NA)
Operating expenses.............	622	859	1,126	1,312	1,315	1,483	1,513	1,603	1,808	(NA)
Support	258	351	521	580	576	639	626	713	721	(NA)

NA Not available. [1] Source: The Broadway League, New York, NY. For season ending in year shown. [2] All shows (new productions and holdovers from previous seasons). [3] Eight performances constitute one playing week. [4] North American Tours include U.S. and Canadian companies. [5] Source: Theatre Communications Group, New York, NY. For years ending on or prior to Aug. 31. [6] Beginning in 2002, nonprofit theatre data is based on survey responses and extrapolated data from IRS Form 990. [7] Source: OPERA America, New York, NY. For years ending on or prior to Aug 31. [8] U.S. companies. [9] Prior to 1993, and for 1999, U.S. and Canadian companies; 1993 to 1998 and 2000 to 2008, U.S. companies only. [10] Includes educational performances, outreach, etc. [11] For paid performances. [12] Source: League of American Orchestras, New York, NY. For years ending Aug. 31. Prior to 1995, represents 254 U.S. orchestras; beginning 1995, represents all U.S. orchestras, excluding college/university and youth orchestras. Also, beginning 1995, data based on 1,200 orchestras.

Source: Compiled from sources listed in footnotes. See also <http://www.livebroadway.com/>; <http://www.tcg.org/>; <http://www.operaamerica.org/>; and <http://www.americanorchestras.org/>.

Arts, Recreation, and Travel 761

Table 1234. Arts and Humanities—Selected Federal Aid Programs: 1990 to 2008

[In millions of dollars (170.8 represents $170,800,000), except as indicated. For fiscal year ending September 30]

Type of fund and program	1990	1995	2000	2003	2004	2005	2006	2007	2008
National Endowment for the Arts:									
Funds available [1]	170.8	152.1	85.2	101.0	105.5	108.8	112.8	111.7	129.3
Program appropriation [2]	152.3	138.1	79.6	95.2	99.3	99.5	100.7	100.3	119.6
Grants awarded (number) [3]	4,252	3,534	1,906	1,885	2,150	2,161	2,293	2,158	2,219
Funds obligated [4, 5]	157.6	147.9	83.5	99.3	102.6	104.4	107.0	106.5	125.5
National Endowment for the Humanities:									
Funds available [1]	140.6	152.3	102.6	111.6	127.1	119.8	121.5	122.3	128.6
Program appropriation	114.2	125.7	82.7	89.3	98.7	99.9	102.2	102.2	105.7
Matching funds [6]	26.3	25.7	15.1	16.0	15.9	15.9	15.2	15.2	14.3

[1] Includes other funds, not shown separately. Excludes administrative funds. [2] FY 1990 and FY 1995 include Regular Program Funds, Treasury Funds, Challenge Grant Funds, and Policy, Planning, and Research Funds. FY 2000 includes Regular Program Funds and Matching Grant Funds. [3] Excludes cooperative agreements and interagency agreements. [4] Includes obligations for new grants, supplemental awards on previous years' grants, cooperative agreements, and interagency agreements. [5] Beginning with 1997 data, the grantmaking structure changed from discipline-based categories to thematic ones. [6] Represents federal funds obligated only upon receipt or certification by endowment of matching nonfederal gifts.

Source: U.S. National Endowment for the Arts, *Annual Report*, and U.S. National Endowment for the Humanities, *Annual Report*. See also <http://arts.endow.gov/> and <http://www.neh.gov/>.

Table 1235. Total State Arts Agency Legislative Appropriations: 2009 to 2010

[In thousands of dollars (329,801 represents 329,801,000). For fiscal year ending September 30. The National Assembly of State Arts Agencies (NASAA) is the membership organization of the nations' state and jurisdictional arts agencies. Legislative appropriations include funds designated to the state arts agency by state legislatures. These include line items, which are not controlled by the agency but passed through to designated entities. State arts agencies also receive monies from other sources including other state funds, the federal government (primarily the National Endowment for the Arts), private funds, and legislative earmarks. Minus sign (–) indicates decrease in spending]

State	Legislative appropriations including line items 2009	2010	Percent change 2009 to 2010	State	Legislative appropriations including line items 2009	2010	Percent change 2009 to 2010	State	Legislative appropriations including line items 2009	2010	Percent change 2009 to 2010
U.S.	329,801	296,973	−10.0	KY	3,410	3,285	−3.7	OH	10,060	6,594	−34.4
AL	5,001	4,626	−7.5	LA	7,127	5,579	−21.7	OK	5,151	4,914	−4.6
AK	668	684	2.4	ME	694	723	4.0	OR	2,115	2,088	−1.3
AZ	1,454	956	−34.2	MD	14,183	13,312	−6.1	PA	15,615	11,992	−23.2
AR	1,597	2,121	32.8	MA	12,659	9,693	−23.4	RI	1,906	1,984	4.1
CA	4,286	4,300	0.3	MI	7,255	1,417	−80.5	SC	3,396	2,583	−23.9
CO	1,600	1,200	−25.0	MN	10,227	30,274	196.0	SD	644	669	3.9
CT	9,442	6,450	−31.7	MS	1,813	1,907	5.2	TN	8,084	8,383	3.7
DE	1,833	1,740	−5.1	MO	7,072	13,580	92.0	TX	3,898	7,745	98.7
DC	13,227	6,578	−50.3	MT	459	460	0.3	UT	3,555	2,911	−18.1
FL	7,160	2,500	−65.1	NE	1,480	1,489	0.6	VT	508	508	−
GA	3,951	2,595	−34.3	NV	1,719	1,102	−35.9	VA	5,234	4,421	−15.5
HI	6,596	6,160	−6.6	NH	807	603	−25.3	WA	2,448	1,876	−23.4
ID	898	788	−12.3	NJ	22,134	17,047	−23.0	WV	2,581	2,501	−3.1
IL	15,959	7,553	−52.7	NM	2,199	1,958	−11.0	WI	2,470	2,418	−2.1
IN	3,756	3,042	−19.0	NY	48,890	52,032	6.4	WY	1,254	1,144	−8.8
IA	1,217	1,024	−15.9	NC	9,767	8,678	−11.1				
KS	1,469	1,262	−14.1	ND	585	684	17.1				

– Represents zero.

Source: National Assembly of State Arts Agencies, "Legislative Appropriations Annual Survey," February 2010, <http://www.nasaa-arts.org/>.

Table 1236. Personal Participation in Various Arts or Creative Activities: 2008

[In percent, except as indicated (224.8 represents 224,800,000). For persons 18 years old and over. Represents participation at least once in the prior 12 months]

Item	Adult population (millions)	Classical music [1]	Painting [2]	Pottery	Sewing [3]	Photography	Creative writing	Purchased art [4]	Choir/chorale
Total	**224.8**	**3.1**	**9.0**	**6.0**	**13.1**	**14.7**	**6.9**	**28.7**	**5.2**
Sex:									
Male	108.5	3.0	7.1	4.5	2.3	13.3	6.2	29.6	3.9
Female	116.3	3.2	10.7	7.4	23.2	16.1	7.5	27.9	6.3
Race and ethnicity:									
White alone	154.5	3.5	9.4	6.9	15.5	16.1	7.0	29.6	4.9
African American alone	25.6	2.0	6.8	3.5	7.6	10.0	7.5	20.1	10.3
Other alone	14.3	4.7	11.9	6.1	10.2	16.2	8.2	16.5	5.5
Hispanic	30.4	1.1	7.4	3.6	7.1	10.9	5.3	30.6	2.2
Age:									
18 to 24 years old	28.9	5.9	14.7	6.4	9.0	17.8	11.3	37.2	6.1
25 to 34 years old	39.9	3.7	11.3	6.1	10.0	16.1	9.7	38.8	3.8
35 to 44 years old	41.8	3.0	9.9	7.5	11.4	18.6	6.2	27.1	4.3
45 to 54 years old	43.9	2.5	7.4	7.0	15.4	14.6	6.4	28.0	6.8
55 to 64 years old	33.3	2.4	6.8	5.4	15.7	13.0	4.4	25.6	5.3
65 to 74 years old	19.9	1.8	5.0	4.1	17.7	10.4	5.2	28.7	6.2
75 years old and older	17.1	1.4	4.4	2.1	15.4	5.5	3.1	14.2	3.6

[1] Of those who reported playing a musical instrument in the last 12 months. [2] Includes painting, drawing, sculpture, and printmaking. [3] Includes weaving, crocheting, quilting, needlepoint, and sewing. [4] Of those who reported owning original art.

Source: U.S. National Endowment for the Arts, "2008 Survey of Public Participation in the Arts," <http://www.nea.gov/pub/research/index.html>.

Table 1237. Attendance/Participation Rates for Various Arts Activities: 2008

[In percent, except as indicated (224.8 represents 224,800,000). For persons 18 years old and over. Represents attending, visiting, or reading at least once in the prior twelve months. Excludes elementary and high school performances]

Item	Adult population (million)	Jazz concert	Classical music concert	Musicals	Non-musical plays	Art museums/galleries	Craft/visual art festivals	Parks/historic buildings [1]	Read literature [2]
Total	**224.8**	**7.8**	**9.3**	**16.7**	**9.4**	**22.7**	**24.5**	**24.9**	**50.2**
Sex:									
Male	108.5	7.7	8.5	14.4	8.2	21.4	20.5	24.4	41.9
Female	116.3	7.9	10.0	18.9	10.6	24.0	28.3	25.4	58.0
Race and Ethnicity:									
White alone	154.5	8.8	11.3	20.0	11.4	26.0	29.3	29.5	55.7
African American alone	25.6	8.6	4.3	8.6	5.5	12.0	12.2	12.6	42.6
Other alone	14.3	4.0	8.8	13.4	6.1	23.4	17.0	20.0	43.9
Hispanic	30.4	3.9	3.8	8.1	4.3	14.5	13.7	14.0	31.9
Age:									
18 to 24 years old	28.9	7.3	6.9	14.5	8.2	22.9	17.8	21.9	51.7
25 to 34 years old	39.9	7.7	7.0	16.0	9.2	24.3	22.7	25.7	50.1
35 to 44 years old	41.8	7.2	8.9	18.2	8.9	25.7	27.2	26.8	50.8
45 to 54 years old	43.9	9.8	10.2	17.4	8.7	23.3	29.1	28.0	50.3
55 to 64 years old	33.3	9.7	11.6	19.5	12.3	24.3	28.9	27.6	53.1
65 to 74 years old	19.9	6.1	12.2	18.0	11.0	19.9	24.8	24.1	49.1
75 years old and older	17.1	4.0	9.7	10.0	7.4	10.5	12.7	11.2	42.3
Education:									
Grade school	11.2	1.5	1.8	1.7	0.7	3.8	4.9	3.8	18.5
Some high school	22.1	2.4	2.3	5.2	2.8	9.2	11.2	9.1	34.3
High school graduate	68.3	3.9	3.1	8.1	4.0	9.6	17.3	14.6	39.1
Some college	61.4	8.1	9.1	17.1	9.0	23.8	27.5	28.4	56.2
College graduate	41.3	13.7	16.7	30.1	17.5	40.6	35.8	39.4	66.6
Graduate school	20.5	17.4	27.1	37.9	24.3	52.2	41.6	48.1	71.2
Income: [3]									
Less than $10,000	11.6	4.3	4.0	6.6	4.2	9.4	10.7	10.3	38.6
$10,000 to $19,999	19.3	3.6	3.9	6.3	3.7	10.3	13.0	11.4	38.3
$20,000 to $29,999	23.4	4.1	4.4	7.7	4.1	11.9	15.5	13.9	41.7
$30,000 to $39,999	22.6	7.1	6.8	11.0	6.7	16.3	21.8	19.9	43.2
$40,000 to $49,999	18.8	8.9	8.7	15.4	7.4	20.2	24.7	23.2	51.9
$50,000 to $74,999	40.7	7.6	9.5	15.4	8.6	23.9	26.2	26.8	50.1
$75,000 to $99,999	27.2	8.7	11.7	21.8	13.4	31.3	33.8	32.6	59.1
$100,000 to $149,999	21.4	13.4	14.8	32.0	14.1	34.4	34.5	41.2	62.1
$150,000 and over	16.0	15.4	22.8	10.1	24.2	31.9	37.5	47.3	71.2

[1] Visiting historic parks or monuments or touring buildings or neighborhoods for the historic or design value.
[2] Literature is defined as poetry, novels, short stories, or plays. [3] Excludes results for respondents who did not report income

Source: U.S. National Endowment for the Arts, "2008 Survey of Public Participation in the Arts," <http://www.nea.gov/pub/>.

Table 1238. Attendance/Participation in Various Leisure Activities: 2008

[In percent, except as indicated (224.8 represents 224,800,000). See headnote, Table 1236]

Item	Adult population (mil.)	Attendance at— Movies	Attendance at— Sports events	Participation in— Exercise	Participation in— Playing sports	Participation in— Outdoor activities	Participation in— Gardening	Participation in— Volunteering/charity work	Participation in— Community activities
Total	**224.8**	**53.3**	**30.6**	**52.9**	**26.3**	**28.2**	**41.6**	**32.0**	**27.8**
Sex:									
Male	108.5	52.7	34.9	52.1	33.2	31.1	33.6	28.9	26.2
Female	116.3	54.0	26.6	53.6	20.0	25.4	48.9	34.9	29.3
Race and Ethnicity:									
White alone	154.5	55.7	34.0	57.4	29.2	16.9	47.2	35.8	31.8
African American alone	25.6	47.4	24.5	42.6	21.0	7.2	24.4	27.0	21.9
Other alone	14.3	49.3	21.8	48.6	23.5	26.1	40.1	25.7	22.7
Hispanic	30.4	48.1	22.1	40.7	17.9	17.3	28.0	20.1	14.7
Age:									
18 to 24 years old	28.9	74.2	37.4	57.4	42.0	34.8	15.1	27.2	19.4
25 to 34 years old	39.9	64.5	37.3	57.5	34.9	35.7	34.8	29.4	23.5
35 to 44 years old	41.8	59.5	36.7	59.5	32.0	34.3	43.9	37.6	33.2
45 to 54 years old	43.9	52.6	31.3	51.8	23.9	29.0	49.1	35.7	31.8
55 to 64 years old	33.3	46.2	25.9	51.8	17.1	22.4	52.4	33.4	29.7
65 to 74 years old	19.9	31.7	18.2	47.6	13.3	17.9	54.5	30.2	30.9
75 years old and over	17.1	18.9	10.3	30.0	6.4	6.3	41.0	23.2	21.5
Education:									
Grade school	11.2	15.9	6.6	21.1	6.7	8.2	30.3	11.4	8.4
Some high school	22.1	37.9	17.8	35.7	19.0	17.8	29.5	17.7	14.8
High school graduate	68.3	42.5	22.8	40.0	17.4	20.8	37.7	20.9	18.3
Some college	61.4	60.8	33.7	58.5	29.1	30.9	43.2	35.6	29.5
College graduate	41.3	68.8	44.9	70.8	38.9	39.8	49.0	48.1	42.6
Graduate school	20.5	71.6	44.2	77.1	40.0	42.3	53.3	51.5	48.0
Income: [1]									
Less than $10,000	11.6	32.3	14.9	35.6	15.9	14.6	25.3	16.0	15.0
$10,000 to $19,999	19.3	32.4	13.4	35.3	14.5	15.3	30.4	18.8	14.8
$20,000 to $29,999	23.4	38.2	21.1	40.4	14.9	18.3	35.4	19.6	18.1
$30,000 to $39,999	22.6	48.6	22.3	46.8	23.3	24.2	37.7	29.2	22.9
$40,000 to $49,999	18.8	54.0	28.7	54.9	26.5	28.7	44.9	31.5	25.9
$50,000 to $74,999	40.7	58.5	33.3	55.6	26.0	31.6	42.8	32.2	27.5
$75,000 or more	27.2	67.5	42.2	66.2	37.0	40.9	50.2	42.0	35.0
$100,000 to $149,999	21.4	71.4	46.8	73.3	39.1	39.7	54.0	49.6	47.2
$150,000 and over	16.0	76.7	53.1	73.2	46.0	43.9	50.9	49.0	43.9

[1] Excludes results for respondents who did not report income.
Source: U.S. National Endowment for the Arts, "2008 Survey of Public Participation in the Arts," <http://www.nea.gov/pub/>.

Arts, Recreation, and Travel 763

Table 1239. Adult Participation in Selected Leisure Activities by Frequency: 2009

[In thousands (16,135 represents 16,135,000), except percent. For fall 2009. Percent is based on total projected population of 225,887,000. Based on sample and subject to sampling error; see source]

Activity	Participated in the last 12 months [1] Number	Percent	Freqency of participation Two or more times a week Number	Percent	Once a week Number	Percent	Two to three times a month Number	Percent	Once a month Number	Percent
Adult education courses	16,135	7.1	2,889	1.3	2,281	1.0	835	0.4	918	0.4
Attend auto shows	18,908	8.4	129	0.1	338	0.2	610	0.3	909	0.4
Attend art galleries or shows	21,664	9.6	206	0.1	207	0.1	755	0.3	2,397	1.1
Attend classical music/opera performances	9,721	4.3	99	(Z)	57	(Z)	427	0.2	1,032	0.5
Attend country music performances . . .	12,534	5.6	116	0.1	122	0.1	230	0.1	471	0.2
Attend dance performances	10,673	4.7	86	(Z)	130	0.1	290	0.1	710	0.3
Attend horse races	6,836	3.0	111	0.1	187	0.1	266	0.1	398	0.2
Attend other music performances [2]	26,350	11.7	398	0.2	395	0.2	1,098	0.5	2,143	1.0
Attend rock music performances	25,919	11.5	175	0.1	247	0.1	930	0.4	1,741	0.8
Backgammon	4,391	1.9	476	0.2	310	0.1	588	0.3	406	0.2
Baking	50,905	26.1	10,575	4.7	8,901	3.9	13,141	5.8	9,268	4.1
Barbecuing	81,453	36.1	12,955	5.7	12,809	5.7	19,341	8.6	11,375	5.0
Billiards/pool	23,224	10.3	1,399	0.6	1,520	0.7	2,153	1.0	2,759	1.2
Bird watching	14,090	6.2	6,098	2.7	1,040	0.5	1,005	0.4	1,026	0.5
Board games	41,148	18.2	2,882	1.3	3,890	1.7	7,928	3.5	7,988	3.5
Book clubs	6,706	3.0	217	0.1	456	0.2	422	0.2	2,354	1.0
Chess	8,332	3.7	791	0.4	649	0.3	754	0.3	803	0.4
Concerts on radio	8,640	3.8	1,356	0.6	998	0.4	979	0.4	943	0.4
Cooking for fun	51,247	22.7	17,440	7.7	8,937	4.0	8,128	3.6	4,185	1.9
Crossword puzzles	32,676	14.5	12,773	5.7	3,849	1.7	3,912	1.7	2,604	1.2
Dance/go dancing	22,877	10.1	1,927	0.9	2,656	1.2	2,573	1.1	3,463	1.5
Dining out	116,074	51.4	21,862	9.7	25,939	11.5	28,531	12.6	14,558	6.4
Entertain friends or relatives at home . .	92,684	41.0	8,021	3.6	12,395	5.5	18,734	8.3	19,596	8.7
Fantasy sports league	7,820	3.5	1,969	0.9	1,724	0.8	380	0.2	495	0.2
Furniture refinishing	6,531	2.9	262	0.1	206	0.1	244	0.1	306	0.1
Go to bars/night clubs	45,635	20.2	3,423	1.5	5,450	2.4	8,186	3.6	7,144	3.2
Go to beach	56,671	25.1	2,867	1.3	2,621	1.2	5,544	2.5	5,956	2.6
Go to live theater	32,325	14.3	218	0.1	632	0.3	1,285	0.6	3,740	1.7
Go to museums	32,724	14.5	315	0.1	325	0.1	948	0.4	3,523	1.6
Home decoration and furnishing	24,058	10.7	752	0.3	1,342	0.6	2,248	1.0	3,901	1.7
Karaoke	9,274	4.1	301	0.1	758	0.3	714	0.3	1,299	0.6
Painting, drawing	13,861	6.1	2,103	0.9	1,606	0.7	1,695	0.8	1,885	0.8
Photo album/scrap book	18,392	8.1	1,347	0.6	1,156	0.5	1,839	0.8	3,365	1.5
Photography	26,268	11.6	4,075	1.8	3,236	1.4	5,568	2.5	4,178	1.9
Picnic	26,659	11.8	378	0.2	636	0.3	2,224	1.0	3,055	1.4
Play bingo	10,800	4.8	749	0.3	1,024	0.5	832	0.4	1,037	0.5
Play cards	48,249	21.4	5,680	2.5	5,488	2.4	6,838	3.0	6,978	3.1
Play musical instrument	17,863	7.9	6,321	2.8	2,240	1.0	1,913	0.9	1,042	0.5
Reading books	93,536	41.4	50,063	22.2	8,921	4.0	8,250	3.7	6,397	2.8
Reading comic books	5,624	2.5	1,028	0.5	504	0.2	649	0.3	605	0.3
Sodoku puzzles	26,250	11.6	8,719	3.9	3,292	1.5	3,330	1.5	2,704	1.2
Trivia games	14,136	6.3	2,447	1.1	1,360	0.6	1,708	0.8	1,311	0.6
Woodworking	12,001	5.3	1,909	0.9	1,344	0.6	1,633	0.7	1,373	0.6
Word games	23,596	10.5	7,998	3.5	3,188	1.4	2,715	1.2	1,796	0.8
Zoo attendance	30,685	13.6	143	0.1	283	0.1	630	0.3	1,765	0.8

Z represents less than 0.05. [1] Includes those participating less than once a month not shown separately. [2] Excluding country and rock.

Source: Mediamark Research & Intelligence, LLC, New York, NY, *Top-line Reports,* (copyright). See also <http://www.mediamark.com/>.

Table 1240. Household Pet Ownership: 2006

[Based on a sample survey of 47,000 households in 2006; For definition of mean, see source]

Item	Dogs	Cats	Birds	Horses
Total companion pet population [1]	72.1	81.7	11.2	7.3
Number of households owning pets	43.0	37.5	4.5	2.1
Percent of households owning companion pets [1]	37.2	32.4	3.9	1.8
Average number owned per household	1.7	2.2	2.5	3.5
PERCENT OF HOUSEHOLDS OWNING PETS				
Annual household income:				
Under $20,000	30.7	30.1	4.4	1.5
$20,000 to $34,999	37.3	33.6	4.2	1.7
$35,000 to $54,999	39.8	34.1	4.4	2.1
$55,000 to $84,999	42.8	35.5	3.7	1.9
$85,000 and over	42.1	33.3	3.7	2.3
Household size: [1]				
One person	21.9	24.7	2.1	0.8
Two persons	37.6	33.4	3.9	1.7
Three persons	47.5	39.1	5.1	2.3
Four persons	51.9	38.5	5.4	2.7
Five or more persons	54.3	40.0	6.6	3.6

[1] As of December 31, 2006.

Source: American Veterinary Medical Association, Schaumburg, IL, *U.S. Pet Ownership and Demographics Sourcebook, 2007,* (copyright). See also <http://www.avma.org/reference/marketstats/sourcebook.asp>.

Table 1241. Retail Sales and Household Participation in Lawn and Garden Activities: 2005 to 2009

[(35,208 represents $35,208,000,000). For calendar year. Subject to sampling variability; see source]

Activity	Retail sales (mil. dol.)					Percent households engaged in activity				
	2005	2006	2007	2008	2009	2005	2006	2007	2008	2009
Total...............	35,208	34,077	35,102	36,060	30,121	83	74	71	70	72
Lawn care.............	9,657	8,558	10,754	9,638	8,075	54	48	48	46	46
Indoor houseplants.......	1,464	1,156	988	1,177	1,081	42	35	31	31	30
Flower gardening.........	3,003	2,572	2,386	2,679	2,299	41	33	30	32	31
Insect control..........	1,869	1,746	2,103	1,734	1,567	30	26	25	25	22
Shrub care.............	1,109	840	913	746	623	31	25	23	22	21
Vegetable gardening......	1,154	1,164	1,421	1,402	1,762	25	22	22	23	27
Tree care..............	2,820	2,322	2,192	2,473	1,743	26	21	18	20	19
Landscaping...........	9,078	10,893	9,874	11,712	8,418	31	30	27	28	27
Flower bulbs..........	945	786	811	796	748	29	22	20	20	19
Fruit trees.............	507	640	477	538	575	13	11	10	10	11
Container gardening......	1,295	948	927	1,003	994	26	18	18	19	19
Raising transplants [1].....	237	257	320	220	241	11	9	7	8	9
Herb gardening..........	371	296	451	391	423	17	12	13	12	14
Growing berries.........	151	121	144	138	229	8	6	5	6	8
Ornamental gardening.....	678	493	561	424	445	12	7	6	6	6
Water gardening........	870	1,285	780	989	898	11	14	11	10	11

[1] Starting plants in advance of planting in ground.

Source: The National Gardening Association, Burlington, VT, *National Gardening Survey*, annual (copyright). See also <http://www.garden.org/>.

Table 1242. Selected Recreational Activities: 1990 to 2009

[21,000 represents 21,000,000]

Activity	Unit	1990	1995	2000	2004	2005	2006	2007	2008	2009
Golf facilities [1]...........	Number ...	12,846	14,074	15,489	16,057	16,052	15,990	15,970	15,979	15,979
Tennis players [2]...........	1,000.....	21,000	17,820	22,900	24,000	24,720	24,200	25,130	26,880	30,130
Tenpin bowling: [3]										
Establishments..........	Number ...	7,611	7,049	6,247	5,761	5,818	5,566	5,498	(NA)	(NA)
Membership, total [4].......	1,000.....	6,588	4,925	3,756	3,112	2,896	2,728	2,608	(NA)	(NA)
Skiing: [5]										
Skier visits [6].............	Million	50.0	52.7	52.2	57.1	56.9	58.9	60.1	57.1	59.7
Operating resorts.........	Number ...	591	520	503	494	492	478	481	473	471
Motion picture screens [7]....	1,000.....	24	28	37	37	39	39	40	40	(NA)
Receipts, box office.......	Mil. dol. ...	5,022	5,494	7,468	9,215	8,832	9,137	9,630	9,791	(NA)
Attendance..............	Million	1,189	1,263	1,385	1,484	1,378	1,395	1,400	1,364	(NA)
Boating: [8]										
People participating in recreational boating [9].....	Million	67.4	70.0	67.5	63.4	57.9	60.2	66.4	70.1	65.9
Retail expenditures on boating [10]..............	Mil. dol. ...	13,731	17,226	27,065	32,953	37,317	39,493	37,416	33,624	30,821
Recreational boats in use by boat type [11]...........	Million	16.0	15.4	16.8	17.4	17.7	16.8	16.9	16.9	16.7
Outboard..............	Million	(NA)	(NA)	8.3	8.4	8.5	8.3	8.3	8.3	8.2
Inboard...............	Million	(NA)	(NA)	1.0	1.1	1.1	1.1	1.1	1.1	1.1
Sterndrive.............	Million	(NA)	(NA)	1.6	1.7	1.7	1.6	1.7	1.7	1.5
Personal watercraft......	Million	(NA)	(NA)	1.2	1.3	1.2	1.2	1.2	1.3	1.3
Sailboat..............	Million	(NA)	(NA)	1.6	1.6	1.6	1.6	1.6	1.6	1.5
Other.................	Million	(NA)	(NA)	3.1	3.4	3.6	3.1	3.1	3.1	3.0

NA Not available. [1] Source: National Golf Foundation, Jupiter, FL. [2] Source: Tennis Industry Association, Hilton Head, SC. Players for persons 12 years old and over who played at least once. 2008 data are for players 6 years old and over who played at least once. [3] Source: United States Bowling Congress, Greendale, WI. [4] Membership totals are for U.S., Canada, and for U.S. military personnel worldwide. [5] Source: National Ski Areas Association, Kottke National End of Season Survey Report (copyright). [6] Represents one person visiting a ski area for all or any part of a day or night, and includes full- and half-day, night, complimentary, adult, child, season, and other types of tickets. Data are estimated and are for the season ending in the year shown. [7] Source: Motion Picture Association of America, Inc., Encino, CA. [8] Source: National Marine Manufacturers Association, Chicago, IL. (copyright). [9] People participating is now measured as adults 18 years and older. [10] Represents estimated expenditures for new and used boats, motors and engines, accessories, safety equipment, fuel, insurance, docking, maintenance, launching, storage, repairs, and other expenses. [11] 2009 data are estimated.

Source: Compiled from sources listed in footnotes.

Table 1243. College and Professional Football Summary: 1990 to 2009

[35,330 represents 35,330,000. For definition of median, see Guide to Tabular Presentation]

Sport	Unit	1990	1995	2000	2005	2006	2007	2008	2009
NCAA college: [1]									
Teams	Number . . .	533	565	606	615	615	619	628	630
Attendance	1,000	35,330	35,638	39,059	43,487	47,909	48,752	48,839	48,285
National Football League: [2]									
Teams	Number . . .	28	30	31	32	32	32	32	32
Attendance, total [3]	1,000	17,666	19,203	20,954	21,792	22,200	22,256	21,859	21,285
Regular season	1,000	13,960	15,044	16,387	17,012	17,341	17,345	17,057	16,651
Average per game	Number . . .	62,321	62,682	66,078	66,455	67,738	67,755	66,629	65,043
Postseason games [4]	1,000	848	(NA)	809	802	776	792	807	824
Players' salaries: [5]									
Average	$1,000	354	584	787	1,400	1,700	1,750	1,824	1,896
Median base salary	$1,000	275	301	441	569	722	772	788	790

NA Not available. [1] Source: National Collegiate Athletic Association, Indianapolis, IN, <http://www.ncaa.org/wps/portal> (copyright). [2] Source: National Football League, New York, NY, <http://www.nfl.com/>. [3] Preseason attendance data are not shown. [4] Includes Pro Bowl (a nonchampionship game) and Super Bowl. [5] Source: National Football League Players Association, Washington, DC., <http://www.nflpa.org/>.

Source: Compiled from sources listed in footnotes.

Table 1244. Selected Spectator Sports: 1990 to 2009

[55,512 represents 55,512,000]

Sport	Unit	1990	1995	2000	2004	2005	2006	2007	2008	2009
Baseball, major leagues: [1]										
Attendance	1,000	55,512	51,288	74,339	74,822	76,286	77,524	80,803	79,975	74,823
Regular season	1,000	54,824	50,469	72,748	73,023	74,926	76,043	79,503	78,588	73,368
National League	1,000	24,492	25,110	39,851	40,221	41,644	44,085	44,114	41,579	41,128
American League	1,000	30,332	25,359	32,898	32,802	33,282	34,503	35,390	34,464	32,239
Playoffs [2]	1,000	479	533	1,314	1,625	1,191	1,218	1,083	1,167	1,166
World Series	1,000	209	286	277	174	168	225	173	219	289
Players' salaries: [3]										
Average	$1,000	598	1,111	1,896	2,313	2,476	2,699	2,825	(NA)	(NA)
Basketball: [4, 5]										
NCAA—Men's college:										
Teams	Number . . .	767	868	932	981	983	984	982	1,017	1,017
Attendance	1,000	28,741	28,548	29,025	30,761	30,569	30,940	32,836	33,396	33,111
NCAA—Women's college:										
Teams	Number . . .	782	864	956	1,008	1,036	1,018	1,003	1,013	1,032
Attendance [6]	1000.	2,777	4,962	8,698	10,016	9,940	9,903	10,878	11,121	11,160
National hockey league:										
Regular season attendance. . .	1,000	12,580	9,234	18,800	20,356	([8])	20,854	20,862	21,236	21,475
Playoffs attendance	1,000	1,356	1,329	1,525	1,709	([8])	1,530	1,497	1,587	1,640
Professional rodeo: [9]										
Rodeos	Number . . .	754	739	688	671	662	649	592	609	560
Performances	Number . . .	2,159	2,217	2,081	1,982	1,940	1,884	1,733	1,861	1,656
Members	Number . . .	5,693	6,894	6,255	6,247	6,127	5,892	5,528	5,825	5,653
Permit-holders (rookies)	Number . . .	3,290	3,835	3,249	2,990	2,701	2,468	2,186	2,233	2,042
Total prize money.	Mil. dol.. . . .	18.2	24.5	32.3	35.5	36.6	36.2	40.5	39.1	38.0

[1] Source: Major League Baseball (previously, The National League of Professional Baseball Clubs), New York, NY, National League Green Book, and The American League of Professional Baseball Clubs, New York, NY, American League Red Book. [2] Beginning 1997, two rounds of playoffs were played. Prior years had one round. [3] Source: Major League Baseball Players Association, New York, NY. [4] Season ending in year shown. [5] Source: National Collegiate Athletic Association, Indianapolis, IN (copyright). [6] For women's attendance total, excludes double-headers with men's teams. [7] For season ending in year shown. Source: National Hockey League, Montreal, Quebec. [8] In September 2004, franchise owners locked out their players upon the expiration of the collective bargaining agreement. The entire season was cancelled in February 2005. [9] Source: Professional Rodeo Cowboys Association, Colorado Springs, CO., Official Professional Rodeo Media Guide, annual (copyright).

Source: Compiled from sources listed in footnotes.

Table 1245. Adult Attendance at Sports Events by Frequency: 2009

[In thousands (2,097 represents 2,097,000), except percent. For fall 2009. Percent is based on total projected population of 225,887,000. Based on survey and subject to sampling error; see source]

Event	Attend one or more times in a month		Attend less than once a month		Event	Attend one or more times in a month		Attend less than once a month	
	Number	Percent	Number	Percent		Number	Percent	Number	Percent
Auto racing—NASCAR	2,097	0.9	16,693	7.4	Weekend professional games . . .	4,715	2.1	18,721	8.3
Auto racing—Other	2,332	1.0	14,134	6.3	Golf	1,747	0.8	12,491	5.5
Baseball.	9,442	4.2	27,778	12.3	High school sports.	11,724	5.2	15,426	6.8
Basketball:					Horse racing:				
College games.	4,623	2.1	15,615	6.9	Flats, runners.	1,142	0.5	11,622	5.2
Professional games	3,990	1.8	17,893	7.9	Trotters/harness.	802	0.4	10,912	4.8
Bowling	1,878	0.8	11,478	5.1	Ice hockey	2,465	1.1	15,781	7.0
Boxing	1,199	0.5	11,124	4.9	Motorcycle racing	980	0.4	11,434	5.1
Equestrian events	471	0.2	11,111	4.9	Pro beach volleyball.	611	0.3	10,695	4.7
Figure skating	554	0.3	11,021	4.9	Pro bull riding [1]	716	0.3	11,488	5.1
Fishing tournaments	1,059	0.5	11,094	4.9	Rodeo [1]	1,312	0.6	12,107	5.4
Football:					Soccer	3,819	1.7	12,585	5.6
College games.	7,522	3.3	18,805	8.3	Tennis	1,101	0.5	11,396	5.0
Monday night professional					Truck and tractor pull mud racing. .	1,213	0.5	11,955	5.3
games	2,998	1.3	13,629	6.0	Wrestling—professional.	1,651	0.7	11,333	5.0

[1] Both pro bull riding and rodeo were measured as the combined "Rodeo/Bull riding."

Source: Mediamark Research & Intelligence. LLC, New York, NY, Top-line Reports (copyright). See <http://www.mediamark.com>.

U.S. Census Bureau, Statistical Abstract of the United States: 2011

Table 1246. Participation in NCAA Sports by Sex: 2008 to 2009

[For the academic year]

Sport	Males			Females		
	Teams	Athletes	Average squad	Teams	Athletes	Average squad
Total.................	8,465	244,267	(X)	9,560	182,503	(X)
Archery..................	(X)	(X)	(X)	1	12	12
Badminton................	(X)	(X)	(X)	2	19	9.5
Baseball.................	905	29,816	32.9	(X)	(X)	(X)
Basketball...............	1,030	16,911	16.4	1,054	15,381	14.6
Bowling..................	1	35	35	55	485	8.8
Cross country............	916	13,015	14.2	996	14,101	14.2
Equestrian [1,2].........	3	9	3.0	46	1,451	31.5
Fencing [2]..............	34	615	18.1	41	673	16.4
Field hockey.............	(X)	(X)	(X)	260	5,603	21.6
Football.................	633	64,879	102.5	(X)	(X)	(X)
Golf [2].................	792	8,299	10.5	543	4,308	7.9
Gymnastics...............	18	335	18.6	84	1,455	17.3
Ice hockey...............	139	4,101	29.5	84	1,976	23.5
Lacrosse.................	247	9,266	37.5	319	7,219	22.6
Rifle [2]................	30	220	7.3	35	172	4.9
Rowing...................	63	2,353	37.3	146	7,289	49.9
Rugby [1]................	1	63	63.0	5	184	36.8
Sailing [1]..............	25	520	20.8	(X)	(X)	(X)
Skiing [2]...............	38	505	13.3	41	502	12.2
Soccer...................	777	21,601	27.8	959	23,357	24.4
Softball.................	(X)	(X)	(X)	949	17,489	18.4
Squash [1]...............	(X)	(X)	(X)	28	381	13.6
Swimming/diving [2]......	393	8,868	22.6	510	11,626	22.8
Synchronized swimming [1]	(X)	(X)	(X)	8	109	13.6
Tennis...................	749	7,960	10.6	900	8,719	9.7
Track, indoor [2]........	593	21,258	35.8	661	21,054	31.9
Track, outdoor [2].......	701	24,418	34.8	758	22,955	30.3
Volleyball...............	83	1,319	15.9	1,015	14,827	14.6
Water polo...............	42	914	21.8	60	1,156	19.3
Wrestling................	224	6,522	29.1	(X)	(X)	(X)

X Not applicable. [1] Sport recognized by the NCAA but does not have an NCAA championship. [2] Co-ed championship sport.

Source: The National Collegiate Athletic Association (NCAA), Indianapolis, IN, *2008–09 Participation study* (copyright), <http://www.ncaa.org/wps/portal>.

Table 1247. Participation in High School Athletic Programs by Sex: 1980 to 2009

[Data based on number of state associations reporting and may underrepresent the number of schools with and participants in athletic programs]

Year	Participant [1]		Sex and sport	Most popular sports, 2008–2009 [2]	
	Males	Females		Schools	Participants
1980–81................	3,503,124	1,853,789	MALE		
1985–86................	3,344,275	1,807,121	Football (11-player).........	14,105	1,112,303
1987–88................	3,425,777	1,849,684	Track & field (outdoor).......	15,936	558,007
1988–89................	3,416,844	1,839,352	Basketball................	17,869	545,145
1989–90................	3,398,192	1,858,659	Baseball..................	15,699	473,184
1990–91................	3,406,355	1,892,316	Soccer....................	11,139	383,824
1991–92................	3,429,853	1,940,801	Wrestling.................	10,254	267,378
1992–93................	3,416,389	1,997,489	Cross country.............	13,647	231,452
1993–94................	3,472,967	2,130,315	Tennis....................	9,499	157,165
1994–95................	3,536,359	2,240,461	Golf......................	13,543	157,062
1995–96................	3,634,052	2,367,936	Swimming & diving.........	6,556	130,182
1996–97................	3,706,225	2,474,043			
1997–98................	3,763,120	2,570,333			
1998–99................	3,832,352	2,652,726	FEMALE		
1999–20................	3,861,749	2,675,874	Track & field (outdoor).......	15,864	457,732
2000–01................	3,921,069	2,784,154	Basketball................	17,582	444,809
2001–02................	3,960,517	2,806,998	Volleyball................	15,069	404,243
2002–03................	3,988,738	2,856,358	Softball (fast pitch).........	15,172	368,921
2003–04................	4,038,253	2,865,299	Soccer....................	10,548	344,534
2004–05................	4,110,319	2,908,390	Cross country.............	13,457	198,199
2005–06................	4,206,549	2,953,355	Tennis....................	9,693	177,593
2006–07................	4,321,103	3,021,807	Swimming & diving.........	6,902	158,878
2007–08................	4,372,115	3,057,266	Competitive spirit squads....	4,748	117,793
2008–09................	4,422,662	3,114,091	Golf......................	9,344	69,223

[1] A participant is counted in the number of sports participated in. [2] Ten most popular sports for each sex in terms of number of participants.

Source: National Federation of State High School Associations, Indianapolis, IN, *The 2008–2009 High School Athletics Participation Survey* (copyright), <http://www.nfhs.org/>.

Arts, Recreation, and Travel 767

Table 1248. Participation in Selected Sports Activities: 2008

[In thousands (267,586,000), except rank. Data are based on a questionnaire mailed to 10,000 households. The questionnaire asked the male and female heads of households and up to two other household members who were at least seven years of age to indicate their age, the sports in which they participated in 2008, and the number of days of participation in 2008. A participant is defined as an individual seven years of age or older who participates in a sport more than once a year. See source for methodology]

Activity	All persons Number	Sex		Age								Household income (dollars)						
		Male	Female	7–11 years	12–17 years	18–24 years	25–34 years	35–44 years	45–54 years	55–64 years	65 and over	Under 15,000	15,000– 24,999	25,000– 34,999	35,000– 49,999	50,000– 74,999	75,000– 99,999	100,000 and over
SERIES I SPORTS																		
Total	**267,586**	**130,281**	**137,304**	**19,439**	**25,116**	**29,348**	**37,808**	**40,807**	**43,821**	**32,985**	**38,261**	**25,974**	**25,236**	**27,414**	**35,463**	**57,246**	**38,092**	**58,162**
Number participated in—																		
Aerobic exercising [1]	36,177	10,519	25,657	1,458	2,324	4,330	8,814	6,727	6,439	3,230	2,854	2,030	2,792	2,872	3,875	7,904	5,691	11,014
Backpacking [2]	12,968	7,383	5,585	1,248	2,272	1,859	2,836	2,047	1,875	556	276	1,037	905	1,107	2,291	2,645	2,553	2,430
Baseball	15,166	12,338	2,828	4,004	3,264	2,045	2,208	1,487	992	647	519	1,245	993	882	2,142	3,747	2,358	3,802
Basketball	29,696	20,578	9,118	5,262	8,026	4,629	4,801	3,360	2,307	923	389	2,722	1,554	2,376	4,216	7,075	4,393	7,360
Bicycle riding [1]	44,707	25,294	19,413	8,976	9,076	3,794	5,366	6,858	5,870	3,006	1,761	2,830	2,689	2,908	4,837	10,978	7,068	13,396
Billiards	31,680	19,655	12,025	1,563	2,752	5,478	8,483	5,950	4,609	1,882	964	2,547	2,514	3,536	3,700	6,815	4,305	8,263
Bowling	49,522	24,691	24,831	6,482	7,706	7,995	9,602	8,400	5,413	2,166	1,758	3,457	2,747	4,575	6,238	11,099	8,600	12,806
Camping [3]	49,359	25,897	23,463	5,979	6,758	5,742	8,766	7,945	8,195	3,591	2,384	3,410	3,173	4,088	7,160	12,364	9,829	9,336
Exercise walking [1]	96,613	37,337	59277	3,839	5,826	8,948	14,958	16,433	19,539	13,622	13,448	8,136	8,520	8,579	12,353	21,453	13,824	23,750
Exercising with equipment [1]	62,982	29,688	33,295	1,246	4,364	8,812	12,830	11,549	10,818	6,802	6,561	3,314	4,166	5,567	7,418	13,856	9,898	18,763
Fishing (net)	42,161	28,440	13,722	4,126	4,659	4,396	7,304	7,564	7,054	4,193	2,865	3,480	3,514	4,627	6,472	9,936	6,399	7,733
Fishing—fresh water	37,798	25,347	12,452	3,847	4,452	4,156	6,783	6,756	5,984	3,523	2,297	3,325	3,022	4,376	5,989	8,893	5,637	6,556
Fishing—salt water	9,357	7,197	2,160	517	660	687	1,466	1,972	1,751	1,298	1,005	345	755	576	1,094	2,237	1,827	2,520
Football—tackle	10,477	9,391	1,086	1,939	3,569	2,047	1,372	617	378	228	328	1,133	623	909	1,401	2,760	1,611	2,040
Golf	25,620	19,927	5,692	1,379	1,468	2,420	5,104	4,708	4,621	3,240	2,679	514	968	2,077	2,418	5,280	4,788	9,575
Hiking	38,025	19,098	18,927	3,089	3,736	3,668	8,362	6,584	6,846	3,673	2,067	3,000	2,252	3,372	5,067	8,456	5,929	9,949
Running/jogging [1]	35,904	18,670	17,233	2,834	6,062	6,508	8,784	5,625	4,146	1,459	485	1,992	1,682	3,057	4,824	7,496	5,979	10,874
Soccer	15,492	9,015	6,477	5,050	4,234	1,701	2,271	1,161	787	201	86	1,420	652	1,103	2,022	3,245	2,392	4,677
Softball	12,843	6,613	6,230	1,805	2,442	1,869	3,065	1,763	1,077	649	172	1,334	572	1,311	1,630	2,914	1,942	3,139
Swimming [1]	63,507	30,152	33,354	10,010	10,522	6,769	9,956	9,426	8,527	4,496	3,799	3,685	3,899	4,449	7,983	15,079	9,993	18,419
Tennis	12,646	6,290	6,356	1,349	2,193	2,053	2,307	1,928	1,540	816	459	425	432	508	1,288	2,893	2,405	4,695
Volleyball	12,155	5,052	7,103	1,453	3,682	1,766	1,897	1,525	1,247	399	186	539	488	995	1,886	2,411	2,318	3,517
Weightlifting	37,504	24,015	13,488	370	4,191	6,240	9,848	6,973	5,842	2,574	1,465	1,515	2,470	3,243	4,631	7,896	6,345	11,403
Yoga	16,018	3,145	12,873	452	953	2,844	4,128	2,956	2,386	1,238	1,062	1,329	1,208	1,315	1,655	3,527	2,088	4,895

See footnotes at end of table.

Table 1248. Participation in Selected Sports Activities: 2008—Con.

[See headnote, page 768]

Activity	All persons Number	Sex Male	Sex Female	Age 7–11 years	12–17 years	18–24 years	25–34 years	35–44 years	45–54 years	55–64 years	65 and over	Household income (dollars) Under 15,000	15,000–24,999	25,000–34,999	35,000–49,999	50,000–74,999	75,000–99,999	100,000 and over
Total	267,586	130,281	137,304	19,439	25,116	29,348	37,808	40,807	43,821	32,985	38,261	26,489	23,657	26,916	38,998	57,859	35,525	58,141
Number participated in—																		
Boating-motor/power	27,816	15,401	12,415	2,360	3,318	3,349	5,060	4,001	4,797	2,688	2,243	913	1,486	1,570	3,663	6,432	4,355	9,397
Canoeing	10,344	5,843	4,501	1,066	1,257	1,635	1,885	1,768	1,524	731	479	268	361	887	1,447	2,608	1,707	3,065
Cheerleading	2,910	238	2,673	1,209	926	383	90	87	69	86	59	221	257	351	448	545	383	704
Hockey (ice)	1,911	1,396	515	207	391	337	322	315	214	39	87	97	136	43	247	253	442	694
Hunting with bow and arrow	6,173	5,542	631	341	446	740	1,033	1,631	1,127	479	376	278	395	766	1,152	1,195	969	1,418
Hunting with firearms	18,755	15,874	2,880	711	1,999	2,802	2,924	3,606	3,517	1,934	1,263	791	1,488	2,116	3,762	3,786	2,757	4,055
In-line roller skating	9,306	3,983	5,323	2,871	2,147	1,206	1,338	900	532	117	196	534	637	411	1,366	2,392	1,520	2,445
Mountain biking—off road	10,174	6,727	3,447	1,114	1,458	1,065	2,635	1,869	1,378	411	244	343	473	776	1,617	2,931	1,121	2,912
Muzzleloading	3,403	3,163	240	–	225	538	448	809	699	439	245	153	351	520	667	616	473	623
Paintball games	6,706	5,384	1,322	469	1,883	2,012	1,192	669	297	86	97	318	468	289	1,485	1,632	950	1,565
Scooter riding	10,130	5,707	4,423	4,470	2,523	819	659	611	501	302	244	769	319	546	1,186	2,850	1,414	3,045
Skateboarding	9,771	6,989	2,782	3,577	3,630	1,186	662	391	179	26	120	831	564	593	1,671	2,382	1,127	2,603
Skiing—alpine	6,514	4,059	2,455	850	1,177	1,019	1,006	1,069	1,048	161	184	200	13	300	547	1,149	1,060	3,245
Skiing—cross country	1,578	757	821	85	90	125	210	348	278	231	211	36	102	109	252	391	174	514
Snowboarding	5,854	4,210	1,645	1,166	1,559	1,321	985	463	162	54	144	323	243	42	807	2,010	310	2,120
Target shoot	20,268	15,456	4,811	365	2,050	3,354	4,847	2,976	3,662	1,833	1,180	907	1,534	1,942	3,392	4,851	2,460	5,180
Target shoot—airgun	4,955	3,919	1,036	715	1,091	515	844	640	628	215	308	367	269	665	1,165	1,035	308	1,146
Water skiing	5,592	3,099	2,494	454	969	933	1,260	844	718	244	169	149	184	189	436	1,290	1,153	2,192
Work out at club	39,349	17,767	21,581	433	2,477	6,824	9,107	6,914	6,278	3,624	3,693	1,118	1,679	2,454	4,218	10,301	6,291	13,288

SERIES II SPORTS

– Represents zero. [1] Participant engaged in activity at least six times in the year. [2] Includes wilderness camping. [3] Vacation/overnight.

Source: National Sporting Goods Association, Mt. Prospect, IL, Sports Participation in 2008: Series 1 and Series II, (copyright). See <http://www.nsga.org/i4a/pages/index.cfm?pageid=3479>.

U.S. Census Bureau, Statistical Abstract of the United States: 2011

Table 1249. Sporting Goods Sales by Product Category: 1990 to 2008, and Projection, 2009

[In millions of dollars (50,725 represents $50,725,000,000), except percent. Based on a sample survey of consumer purchases of 80,000 households, (100,000 beginning 2000), except recreational transport, which was provided by industry associations. Excludes Alaska and Hawaii. Minus sign (–) indicates decrease]

Selected product category	1990	2000	2003	2004	2005	2006	2007	2008	2009, proj.
Sales, all products	**50,725**	**74,442**	**79,779**	**85,811**	**88,434**	**90,472**	**91,423**	**79,632**	**72,055**
Annual percent change [1]	(NA)	4.6	2.6	7.6	3.1	2.3	1.1	–12.9	–9.5
Percent of retail sales	(NA)	2.5	2.4	2.5	2.4	2.3	2.3	2.0	1.8
Athletic and sport clothing	10,130	11,030	10,543	11,201	10,898	10,580	10,834	10,563	10,476
Athletic and sport footwear [2]	11,654	13,026	14,446	14,752	15,719	16,910	17,524	17,190	17,191
Aerobic shoes	611	292	222	237	261	262	280	260	257
Basketball shoes	918	786	890	877	878	964	892	718	726
Cross training shoes	679	1,528	1,407	1,327	1,437	1,516	1,584	1,626	1,640
Golf shoes	226	226	222	230	259	232	244	239	234
Gym shoes, sneakers	2,536	1,871	2,059	2,221	2,314	2,434	2,699	2,639	2,656
Jogging and running shoes	1,110	1,638	1,802	1,989	2,157	2,260	2,193	2,301	2,292
Tennis shoes	740	533	544	508	528	505	452	467	459
Walking shoes	2,950	3,317	3,468	3,496	3,673	4,091	4,197	4,204	4,164
Athletic and sport equipment [2]	14,439	21,608	22,394	23,328	23,735	24,497	25,061	24,883	24,638
Archery	265	259	320	332	372	396	396	394	383
Baseball and softball	217	319	340	352	372	388	401	396	387
Billiards and indoor games	192	516	625	622	572	574	531	426	395
Camping	1,072	1,354	1,487	1,531	1,447	1,526	1,453	1,460	1,431
Exercise	1,824	3,610	4,957	5,074	5,177	5,239	5,500	5,308	5,096
Fishing tackle	1,910	2,030	1,981	2,026	2,139	2,218	2,247	2,105	2,038
Golf	2,514	3,805	3,046	3,198	3,466	3,669	3,722	3,546	3,439
Hunting and firearms	2,202	2,274	2,654	3,175	3,563	3,732	3,942	4,584	4,938
Optics	438	729	847	859	887	1,014	1,019	1,024	1,034
Skin diving and scuba	294	355	338	351	358	369	376	373	363
Snow skiing [3]	475	495	462	452	643	501	531	494	479
Tennis	333	383	343	362	397	418	440	380	368
Recreational transport	14,502	28,779	32,397	36,531	38,082	38,485	38,003	26,996	19,750
Bicycles and supplies	2,423	5,131	4,736	4,898	5,343	5,161	5,393	5,285	4,968
Pleasure boats, motors, accessories	7,644	13,224	14,705	16,054	17,634	17,907	17,473	12,580	8,200
Recreational vehicles	4,113	9,529	12,058	14,753	14,366	14,732	14,505	8,587	6,011
Snowmobiles	322	894	898	826	739	685	632	544	571

NA Not available. [1] Represents change from immediate prior year. [2] Includes other products not shown separately. [3] Data through 2004 categorized as "Skiing Downhill."

Source: National Sporting Goods Association, Mt. Prospect, IL, *The Sporting Goods Market in 2009* and prior issues, (copyright). See <http://www.nsga.org/i4a/pages/index.cfm?pageid=3345>.

Table 1250. Consumer Purchases of Sporting Goods by Consumer Characteristics: 2008

[In percent. Based on sample survey of consumer purchases of 100,000 households. Excludes Alaska and Hawaii]

Characteristic	Total	Footwear					Equipment				
		Aerobic shoes	Fitness shoes	Gym shoes/ sneakers	Jogging/ running shoes	Walking shoes	Multi purpose home gyms	Rod/ reel combination	Golf club sets	Rifles	Soccer balls
Total	**100**	**100**	**100**	**100**	**100**	**100**	**100**	**100**	**100**	**100**	**100**
Age of user:											
Under 14 years old	18.8	6.4	12.7	42.1	7.6	6.3	–	10.5	7.6	3.5	53.6
14 to 17 years old	5.7	4.8	6.6	8.7	9.2	2.2	2.6	3.4	1.1	2.6	14.5
18 to 24 years old	9.8	6.6	6.6	5.2	7.2	3.4	1.1	2.9	3.8	7.1	5.6
25 to 34 years old	13.4	27.4	17.7	13.8	27.3	9.6	31.4	17.0	19.1	19.8	13.3
35 to 44 years old	14.3	18.7	15.7	11.2	20.3	13.4	18.5	24.7	9.3	17.1	8.7
45 to 64 years old	25.4	29.0	30.3	14.4	23.8	43.5	40.3	33.5	43.2	40.2	0.5
65 years old and over	12.6	7.1	10.4	4.6	4.6	21.6	3.9	7.1	15.9	9.7	–
Multiple ages	–	–	–	–	–	–	2.2	0.9	–	–	3.8
Sex of user:											
Male	49.3	17.8	36.7	56.6	47.0	37.0	58.0	82.3	80.6	90.3	68.9
Female	50.7	82.2	63.3	43.4	53.0	63.0	33.9	8.7	19.4	7.4	26.4
Household use	–	–	0.1	–	–	–	8.1	9.0	–	2.3	4.7
Annual household income:											
Under $15,000	11.3	7.5	8.0	6.0	2.7	7.7	–	7.4	0.5	11.9	2.6
$15,000 to $24,999	12.2	11.2	4.7	6.9	5.5	10.9	1.3	4.0	–	14.2	2.3
$25,000 to $34,999	12.7	11.9	12.2	13.1	7.6	9.2	9.6	15.4	2.8	12.3	8.9
$35,000 to $49,999	14.8	12.4	16.3	15.3	11.3	16.0	7.2	15.8	6.4	16.3	11.3
$50,000 to $74,999	18.2	16.3	13.9	21.0	21.0	20.5	20.0	24.8	22.1	20.1	18.9
$75,000 to $99,999	15.2	15.8	24.6	16.1	18.3	17.6	28.0	12.3	23.2	16.2	27.3
$100,000 and over	15.6	24.9	20.3	21.6	33.6	18.1	33.9	20.3	45.0	9.0	28.7
Education of household head:											
Less than high school	6.3	1.8	3.8	4.8	2.2	4.8	0.9	6.4	1.3	3.8	1.5
High school	22.7	11.4	18.9	21.3	13.4	22.9	10.0	24.2	8.3	26.6	11.6
Some college	36.1	35.3	29.9	37.8	27.1	37.4	30.4	45.1	23.8	39.5	29.8
College graduate	34.9	51.5	47.4	36.1	57.3	34.9	58.7	24.3	66.6	30.1	57.1

– Represents or rounds to zero.

Source: National Sporting Goods Association, Mt. Prospect, IL, *The Sporting Goods Market in 2009*, (copyright). See <http://www.nsga.org.public/pages/index.cfm?pageid=869\>.

Table 1251. National Park System—Summary: 1990 to 2008

[For year ending September 30, except as noted. (986 represents $986,000,000). Includes data for five areas in Puerto Rico and Virgin Islands, one area in American Samoa, and one area in Guam]

Item	1990	1995	2000	2004	2005	2006	2007	2008
Finances (mil. dol.): [1]								
Expenditures reported	986	1,445	1,833	2,371	2,451	2,463	2,412	2,614
Salaries and wages	459	633	799	956	984	998	1,005	1,066
Improvements, maintenance	160	234	299	332	361	389	381	428
Construction	109	192	215	354	381	300	280	303
Other	259	386	520	729	725	776	746	817
Funds available	1,506	2,225	3,316	4,087	4,218	4,242	4,266	4,537
Appropriations	1,053	1,325	1,881	2,388	2,425	2,450	2,484	2,636
Other [2]	453	900	1,435	1,699	1,793	1,792	1,782	1,901
Revenue from operations	79	106	234	264	286	308	346	404
Recreation visits (millions): [3]								
All areas	258.7	269.6	285.9	276.9	273.5	272.6	275.6	274.9
National parks [4]	57.7	64.8	66.1	63.8	63.5	60.4	62.3	61.2
National monuments	23.9	23.5	23.8	19.8	20.9	19.6	19.7	20.2
National historical, commemorative, archaeological [5]	57.5	56.9	72.2	77.0	74.9	73.6	75.1	76.2
National parkways	29.1	31.3	34.0	31.7	31.7	32.6	31.1	30.2
National recreation areas [4]	47.2	53.7	50.0	46.6	46.8	47.8	48.9	49.6
National seashores and lakeshores	23.3	22.5	22.5	21.3	21.7	19.6	19.9	19.3
National Capital Parks	7.5	5.5	5.4	4.7	4.3	6.2	4.9	5.1
Recreation overnight stays (millions)	17.6	16.8	15.4	13.7	13.5	13.2	13.8	13.7
In commercial lodgings	3.9	3.8	3.7	3.5	3.4	3.4	3.6	3.6
In Park Service campgrounds	7.9	7.1	5.9	5.4	5.2	5.0	5.1	5.0
In backcountry	1.7	2.2	1.9	1.7	1.7	1.7	1.7	1.8
Other	4.2	3.7	3.8	3.1	3.2	3.1	3.4	3.3
Land (1,000 acres): [6, 7]								
Total	76,362	77,355	78,153	79,023	79,048	78,810	78,845	78,859
Parks	46,089	49,307	49,785	49,892	49,910	49,912	49,911	49,916
Recreation areas	3,344	3,353	3,388	3,391	3,391	3,391	3,413	3,413
Other	26,929	24,695	24,980	25,740	25,747	25,507	25,521	25,530
Acquisition, net	21	27	186	12	17	16	23	7

[1] Financial data are those associated with the National Park System. Certain other functions of the National Park Service (principally the activities absorbed from the former Heritage Conservation and Recreation Service in 1981) are excluded. [2] Includes funds carried over from prior years. [3] For calendar year. Includes other areas, not shown separately. [4] For 1990, combined data for North Cascades National Park and two adjacent National Recreation Areas are included in National Parks total. [5] Includes military areas. [6] Federal land only, as of Dec. 31. Federal land acreages, in addition to National Park Service administered lands, also include lands within national park system area boundaries but under the administration of other agencies. Year-to-year changes in the federal lands figures includes changes in the acreages of these other lands and hence often differ from "net acquisition." [7] The decrease in the 2006 land total reflects corrected acreage by the Bureau of Land Management, and not by the National Park Service lands.

Source: U.S. National Park Service, National Park Statistical Abstract, annual and unpublished data. See also <http://www2.nature.nps.gov/stats/>.

Table 1252. State Parks and Recreation Areas by State: 2007

[For year ending June 30 (13,922 represents 13,922,000). Data are shown as reported by state park directors. In some states, park agency has forests, fish and wildlife areas, and/or other areas under its control. In other states, park agency is responsible for state parks only]

State	Acreage (1,000)	Visitors (1,000)[1]	Revenue Total ($1,000)	Revenue Percent of operating expenditures	State	Acreage (1,000)	Visitors (1,000)[1]	Revenue Total ($1,000)	Revenue Percent of operating expenditures
United States ...	13,922	747,964	935,005	40.1	Missouri	204	15,142	8,095	27.5
					Montana	55	5,333	4,952	55.3
Alabama	48	5,142	22,567	57.0	Nebraska	135	10,236	16,681	84.7
Alaska	3,361	4,977	2,791	35.2	Nevada	139	3,132	2,748	18.3
Arizona	64	2,348	9,639	38.9	New Hampshire	233	1,626	4,324	58.7
Arkansas	54	8,399	22,332	48.3	New Jersey	426	18,543	10,388	26.9
California	1,566	79,854	90,672	21.3	New Mexico	93	4,604	3,904	14.0
Colorado	420	11,834	25,811	66.9	New York	1,348	61,771	88,000	43.2
Connecticut	206	7,504	5,104	29.9	North Carolina	202	12,868	5,317	13.8
Delaware	26	5,022	12,397	53.6	North Dakota	18	879	1,585	47.0
Florida	700	20,737	42,779	54.8	Ohio	174	49,659	27,530	37.3
Georgia	86	10,351	35,272	56.2	Oklahoma	72	13,485	36,368	78.7
Hawaii	34	10,182	2,206	20.5	Oregon	99	42,605	17,187	36.1
Idaho	46	4,031	3,608	20.9	Pennsylvania	292	33,210	17,176	20.6
Illinois	486	45,159	6,804	11.9	Rhode Island	9	6,217	4,322	47.6
Indiana	179	18,043	41,379	78.1	South Carolina	84	7,050	21,116	77.9
Iowa	69	13,382	3,864	25.1	South Dakota	103	7,375	11,530	82.0
Kansas	33	6,875	5,998	57.1	Tennessee	174	32,264	37,770	44.6
Kentucky	49	7,082	54,983	61.1	Texas	602	7,142	38,172	43.8
Louisiana	43	1,679	7,669	24.6	Utah	151	4,554	10,694	34.3
Maine	100	2,124	3,027	34.4	Vermont	69	698	6,124	79.9
Maryland	133	11,330	16,694	49.4	Virginia	68	7,040	14,214	45.5
Massachusetts	341	31,635	11,299	14.6	Washington	117	41,590	17,881	25.7
Michigan	273	19,309	38,639	86.7	West Virginia	177	7,324	20,390	57.7
Minnesota	279	8,380	15,694	44.9	Wisconsin	139	14,516	17,011	80.4
Mississippi	24	1,212	8,926	63.0	Wyoming	122	2,511	1,371	19.0

[1] Includes overnight visitors.

Source: The National Association of State Park Directors, Raleigh, NC, 2007–2008 Annual Information Exchange, February 2009. See <http://www.naspd.org/>.

Table 1253. National Park Service (NPS) Visits and Acreage by State: 2009

[See headnote, Table 1254]

State	Recreation visits [1]	Gross area acres	Federal land			Nonfederal land	
			NPS fee acres [2]	NPS/OTFED less than fee acres [3]	Other federal fee acres [4]	Other public acres	Private acres
Total............	283,654,947	84,320,287	79,691,620	276,867	427,466	1,173,078	2,751,256
Alabama...........	790,752	22,737	16,715	202	–	3,295	2,525
Alaska............	2,278,488	54,654,052	52,636,434	27,959	8	188,256	1,801,395
Arizona...........	10,713,122	2,962,853	2,618,735	115	76,937	57,067	209,999
Arkansas..........	3,031,842	104,976	98,319	3,395	6	2,736	521
California..........	35,318,711	8,109,854	7,564,496	22,437	12,917	313,800	196,205
Colorado..........	5,443,039	673,589	609,880	6,859	42,451	862	13,537
Connecticut........	19,386	7,782	5,719	1,055	–	874	133
District of Columbia...	35,695,833	7,090	6,953	7	–	126	4
Florida............	9,495,437	2,638,354	2,436,859	1,330	45,839	129,192	25,135
Georgia...........	6,475,874	62,888	39,664	125	1,461	16,777	4,861
Hawaii............	4,312,818	369,122	357,772	1	22	11,228	98
Idaho.............	494,196	517,904	507,585	1,138	3,960	901	4,320
Illinois............	464,074	13	12	–	–	–	1
Indiana............	2,230,024	15,378	10,590	499	–	3,286	1,003
Iowa..............	241,063	2,713	2,708	–	–	5	1
Kansas............	101,906	11,636	461	269	–	39	10,866
Kentucky..........	1,828,340	95,415	94,395	137	–	831	52
Louisiana..........	443,314	24,107	17,531	–	–	2,476	4,101
Maine.............	2,227,698	90,282	66,919	11,120	22	10,646	1,575
Maryland..........	3,445,530	73,325	40,480	5,938	480	23,806	2,621
Massachusetts.......	9,772,738	57,954	32,946	973	40	21,915	2,080
Michigan...........	1,628,704	718,188	631,717	732	42	58,515	27,183
Minnesota..........	650,156	301,343	139,528	3,193	142	98,802	59,678
Mississippi.........	6,582,890	118,736	103,698	5,232	–	71	9,734
Missouri...........	3,933,043	83,475	54,382	9,262	–	14,070	5,760
Montana...........	4,195,484	1,274,374	1,214,184	1,233	6,137	1,464	51,355
Nebraska..........	273,444	45,735	5,650	494	981	386	38,223
Nevada............	5,836,491	778,512	774,751	–	2,508	81	1,172
New Hampshire......	34,558	21,894	8,391	1,556	5,772	162	6,013
New Jersey.........	5,828,477	99,206	35,362	140	3,208	59,000	1,497
New Mexico.........	1,659,574	391,029	376,528	5	2,524	3,365	8,607
New York...........	17,327,234	72,674	33,483	3,920	164	19,812	15,295
North Carolina......	18,198,530	406,159	363,042	12,272	20,782	3,289	6,774
North Dakota.......	631,459	72,579	71,250	256	151	56	867
Ohio..............	2,882,593	34,149	19,423	1,329	84	8,203	5,109
Oklahoma..........	1,249,011	10,241	10,008	9	189	8	27
Oregon............	891,783	199,095	192,020	1,404	4,975	183	513
Pennsylvania.......	8,885,894	137,660	49,927	2,590	387	19,627	65,130
Rhode Island.......	50,397	5	5	–	–	–	–
South Carolina......	1,504,680	32,618	31,125	61	5	51	1,376
South Dakota.......	4,134,663	297,417	141,313	122,328	–	79	33,697
Tennessee.........	8,061,847	384,752	356,476	1,679	9,629	3,614	13,353
Texas.............	6,938,238	1,244,635	1,199,425	85	1,013	5,079	39,033
Utah..............	8,755,401	2,117,043	2,097,106	833	1,142	12,803	5,160
Vermont...........	31,129	23,174	8,830	3,874	8,809	544	1,116
Virginia...........	22,953,894	363,640	304,105	6,843	24,914	7,002	20,776
Washington........	7,559,552	1,967,116	1,833,697	2,147	100,187	12,799	18,286
West Virginia.......	1,803,552	92,670	64,425	326	314	6,894	20,711
Wisconsin..........	452,365	133,754	61,744	11,484	802	47,624	12,102
Wyoming...........	5,895,719	2,396,390	2,344,852	21	48,462	1,380	1,675

– Represents zero. [1] See footnotes, Table 1254.

Source: U.S. National Park Service, Land Resource Board, and unpublished data. See also <http://www2.nature.nps.gov/stats/>.

Table 1254. National Park Service (NPS) Visits and Acreage by Type of Area: 2009

[Includes data for five areas in Puerto Rico and Virgin Islands, one area in American Samoa, and one area in Guam]

Type of area	Recreation visits [1]	Gross area acres	Federal land			Non-federal land	
			NPS fee acres [2]	NPS/OTFED less than fee acres [3]	Other federal fee acres [4]	Other public acres	Private acres
Total [5]	285,579,941	84,378,873	79,706,436	276,870	458,310	1,179,266	2,757,992
National historic sites......	9,975,007	33,980	21,204	783	51	922	11,020
National historical parks	28,432,210	182,300	130,460	3,556	360	28,716	19,207
National memorials........	30,559,258	10,638	9,428	8	138	63	1,000
National monuments.......	22,646,428	2,026,731	1,840,938	14,830	43,418	5,899	121,646
National parks............	62,950,968	52,095,017	50,393,545	148,822	49,270	497,192	1,006,188
National recreation areas ...	50,945,414	3,700,280	3,147,473	23,718	243,101	106,309	179,681
National seashores........	17,920,507	596,564	404,438	14,890	61,226	106,668	9,341
National parkways........	29,948,911	178,071	158,137	9,108	213	319	10,293

[1] Recreation visit represents the entry of a person onto lands or waters administered by the National Park Service (NPS) for recreational purposes excluding government personnel, through traffic (commuters), trades-persons, and persons residing within park boundaries. [2] Fee represents complete Federal ownership of all rights in the land. [3] Represents Federal ownership of some rights in the land. [4] NPS acreage lies under the jurisdiction of another federal agency (such as Bureau of Land Management). [5] Includes other "type of areas," not shown separately.

Source: U.S. National Park Service, Land Resource Board, and unpublished data. See also <http://www2.nature.nps.gov/stats/>.

Table 1255. Participants in Wildlife-Related Recreation Activities: 2006

[In thousands (33,916 represents 33,916,000). For persons 16 years old and over engaging in activity at least once in 2006. Based on survey and subject to sampling error; see source for details]

Participant	Number	Days of participation	Trips	Participant	Number	Days of participation
Total sportspersons [1] ..	**33,916**	**736,707**	**588,891**	Wildlife watchers [1]	71,132	(X)
Total anglers	29,952	516,781	403,492	Away from home [2]	22,977	352,070
Freshwater.	25,431	433,337	336,528	Observe wildlife	21,546	291,027
Excluding Great Lakes . .	25,035	419,942	323,265	Photograph wildlife	11,708	103,872
Great Lakes.	1,420	18,016	13,264	Feed wildlife.	7,084	77,329
Saltwater	7,717	85,663	66,963	Around the home [3]	67,756	(X)
Total hunters	12,510	219,925	185,399	Observe wildlife	44,467	(X)
Big game	10,682	164,061	115,255	Photograph wildlife	18,763	(X)
Small game	4,797	52,395	40,856	Feed wildlife.	55,512	(X)
Migratory birds.	2,293	19,770	16,390	Visit public parks	13,271	(X)
Other animals	1,128	15,205	12,898	Maintain plantings or natural areas	14,508	(X)

X Not applicable. [1] Detail does not add to total due to multiple responses and nonresponse. [2] Persons taking a trip of at least 1 mile from home for activity. [3] Activity within 1 mile of home.

Source: U.S. Fish and Wildlife Service, *2006 National Survey of Fishing, Hunting, and Wildlife Associated Recreation*, October 2007. See also <http://wsfrprograms.fws.gov/Subpages/NationalSurvey/nat_survey2006_final.pdf>.

Table 1256. Expenditures for Wildlife-Related Recreation Activities: 2006

[(42,011 represents $42,011,000,000). For persons 16 years old and over. Based on survey and subject to sampling error; see source for details]

Expenditure item	Fishing			Hunting			Wildlife watching		
	Expendi-tures (mil. dol.)	Spenders		Expendi-tures (mil. dol.)	Spenders		Expendi-tures (mil. dol.)	Spenders	
		Number (1,000)	Percent of anglers		Number (1,000)	Percent of hunters		Number (1,000)	Percent of watch-ers [2]
Total, all items [1]	**42,011**	**28,307**	**95**	**22,893**	**12,153**	**97**	**45,655**	**55,979**	**79**
Total trip-related [3].	17,879	26,318	88	6,679	10,828	87	12,976	10,113	05
Food and lodging.	6,303	22,572	75	2,791	9,567	76	7,516	16,415	71
Food	4,327	22,415	75	2,177	9,533	76	4,298	16,261	71
Lodging	1,975	5,304	18	614	1,599	13	3,218	6,624	29
Transportation	4,962	22,361	75	2,697	10,064	80	4,456	18,320	00
Public.	524	1,163	4	214	401	3	1,567	2,902	13
Private	4,438	21,979	73	2,483	9,982	80	2,889	17,447	76
Other trip costs	6,614	22,275	74	1,190	3,416	27	903	7,681	33
Total equipment and other expenditures.	24,133	25,355	85	16,215	11,745	94	32,780	52,178	73
Equipment [4]	5,332	19,082	64	5,366	9,287	74	9,870	49,040	69
Auxiliary equipment.	779	3,837	13	1,330	4,196	34	1,033	4,848	7
Special equipment [5].	12,646	1,818	6	4,035	505	4	12,271	1,914	3
Other expenditures [6]	5,376	20,000	09	5,483	10,632	85	9,606	19,070	27
Magazines, books	115	2,944	10	84	1,767	14	360	9,490	13
Licenses, stamps, tags, and permits	503	16,259	54	743	9,862	79	(X)	(X)	(X)

X Not applicable. [1] Total not adjusted for multiple responses or nonresponse. [2] Percent of wildlife-watching participants column is based on away-from-home participants for trip-related expenditures. For equipment and other expenditures the percent of wildlife-watching participants is based on total participants. [3] Information on trip-related expenditures for wildlife watching was collected for away-from-home participants only. Equipment and other expenditures for wildlife watching are based on information collected from both away-from-home and around-the-home participants. [4] Includes fishing, hunting, and wildlife-watching. [5] Special equipment includes boats, campers, cabins, trail bikes, etc. [6] Other expenditures not shown.

Source: U.S. Fish and Wildlife Service, *2006 National Survey of Fishing, Hunting, and Wildlife Associated Recreation*, October 2007. See <http://wsfrprograms.fws.gov/Subpages/NationalSurvey/nat_survey2006_final.pdf>.

Table 1257. Tribal Gaming Revenues: 2004 to 2009

[In millions (19,479 represents $19,479,000,000). For year ending September 30]

Region	2004		2005		2006		2007		2008		2009	
	Number of operations	Revenue	Number of operations	Revenue	Number of operations	Revenue	Number of operations	Revenue	Number of operations	Revenue	Number of operations	Revenue
Total [1]	375	19,479	392	22,579	394	24,889	391	26,143	405	26,739	419	26,482
Region I	45	1,602	49	1,829	46	2,080	46	2,264	47	2,376	49	2,376
Region II	54	5,822	57	6,993	56	7,675	58	7,796	59	7,363	62	6,970
Region III	45	2,160	48	2,529	45	2,719	46	2,874	46	2,774	47	2,600
Region IV	117	3,816	118	3,984	122	4,070	111	4,225	115	4,402	120	4,384
Region V	87	1,259	92	1,730	98	2,126	102	2,584	110	3,047	113	3,225
Region VI	27	4,821	28	5,514	27	6,219	28	6,400	28	6,776	28	6,783

[1] Portland (Region 1): Alaska, Idaho, Oregon, and Washington. Sacramento (Region 2): California, and Northern Nevada. Phoenix (Region 3): Arizona, Colorado, New Mexico, and Southern Nevada. St Paul (Region 4): Iowa, Michigan, Minnesota, Montana, North Dakota, Nebraska, South Dakota, Wisconsin, and Wyoming. Data for Montana not included for 2004. Oklahoma City (Region 5): Western Oklahoma, and Texas. Tulsa (Region 5): Kansas and Eastern Oklahoma. Washington (Region 6): Alabama, Connecticut, Florida, Louisiana, Mississippi, North Carolina, and New York.

Source: National Indian Gaming Commission, *Tribal Gaming Revenues*, annual. See also <http://www.nigc.gov>.

Arts, Recreation, and Travel **773**

Table 1258. Gaming Revenue by Industry: 2000 to 2009

[In millions of dollars (62,154 represents $62,154,000,000). Data shown are for gross revenue. Gross gambling revenue (GGR) is the amount wagered minus the winnings returned to players, a true measure of the economic value of gambling. GGR is the figure used to determine what an operation earns before taxes, salaries, and other expenses are paid]

Industry	2000	2003	2004	2005	2006	2007	2008	2009
Total [2]	62,154	73,036	78,589	84,433	90,931	[1] 92,272	[1,3] 92,157	[1,3] 89,262
Card rooms	949	979	989	1,025	1,104	[3] 1,180	[3] 1,282	[3] 1,232
Commercial casinos	26,455	[1] 28,669	[1] 30,595	[1] 31,775	[1] 34,113	[3] 34,407	[1,3] 33,031	[1,3] 31,379
Charitable games and bingo	2,466	2,331	2,336	[3] 2,338	[3] 2,237	[3] 2,220	[3] 2,131	[3] 2,067
Legal bookmaking	131	128	116	130	192	168	136	136
Lotteries	17,277	20,283	21,405	22,898	24,631	24,780	25,698	25,139
Parimutuel wagering	3,935	3,821	3,750	3,683	3,677	[3] 3,529	[3] 3,141	[3] 2,827

[1] Amount includes deepwater cruise ships, cruises-to-nowhere and noncasino devices. [2] Includes industry not shown separately. [3] Data are estimated.

Source: Christiansen Capital Advisors, LLC. Prepared for the American Gaming Association (AGA). Industry Information, Fact Sheets, *Gaming Revenue: Current-Year Data* (copyright), <http://www.americangaming.org/Industry/factsheets/index.cfm> and <www.cca-i.com>.

Table 1259. North America Cruise Industry in the United States: 2004 to 2008

[The North American passenger cruise industry is defined as those cruise lines that primarily market their cruises in North America. These cruise lines offer cruises with destinations throughout the globe. While most of these cruises originate in ports throughout North America, cruises also originate at ports in other continents]

Item	Unit	2004	2005	2006	2007	2008
Capacity Measures:						
Number of ships	Number	144	145	151	159	161
Lower berths [1]	Number	225,714	225,364	244,271	259,973	270,664
Passenger embarkations, global: [2]	**1,000**	**10,850**	**11,500**	**12,000**	**12,562**	**13,006**
United States	1,000	8,100	8,612	9,001	9,184	8,958
Florida	1,000	4,791	4,875	4,994	4,977	5,110
California	1,000	1,095	1,301	1,241	1,334	1,436
New York	1,000	547	382	512	537	524
Other U.S. ports	1,000	1,667	2,054	2,254	2,336	1,888
Canada	1,000	454	455	423	477	427
San Juan	1,000	450	581	555	534	521
Rest of world	1,000	1,846	1,852	2,021	2,367	3,100
United States expenditures of the North American cruise industry: [3,4]	**Bil. dol.**	**14.70**	**16.18**	**17.64**	**18.70**	**19.07**
U.S. purchases of the cruise lines	Bil. dol.	10.70	11.76	12.89	13.74	14.40
Passenger and crew	Bil. dol.	2.88	3.23	3.48	3.63	3.40
Wages & taxes paid by cruise lines	Bil. dol.	1.12	1.19	1.27	1.33	1.27

[1] Single beds. [2] Port of departure. [3] See details in the report for the sources of U.S. expenditures of the North American cruise industry. [4] Includes wages and salaries paid to U.S. employees of the cruise lines.

Source: Business Research & Economic Advisors (BREA), Exton, PA. The Contribution of the North American Cruise Industry to the U.S. Economy in 2008. Prepared for the Cruise Lines International Association, June 2009, <http://www.cruising.org>.

Table 1260. Top States and Cities Visited by Overseas Travelers: 2000 to 2009

[25,975 represents 25,975,000. Includes travelers for business and pleasure, international travelers in transit through the United States, and students. Excludes travel by international personnel and international businessmen employed in the United States. Starting with the 2006 data, the statistical policy for visitation estimates of international travelers to the United States has changed. For more information, go to <http://tinet.ita.doc.gov/outreachpages/2007_statistical_policy.html>. States and Cities are ranked by the latest overseas visitors data]

State and other area	Overseas visitors [1] (1,000)				City	Overseas visitors [1] (1,000)			
	2000	2005	2008	2009		2000	2005	2008	2009
Total overseas travelers [2,3]	**25,975**	**21,679**	**25,341**	**23,756**	New York City, NY	5,714	5,810	8,211	7,792
New York	5,922	6,092	8,413	8,006	Miami, FL	2,935	2,081	2,585	2,661
Florida	6,026	4,379	5,246	5,274	Los Angeles, CA	3,533	2,580	2,788	2,518
California	6,364	4,791	5,296	4,632	Orlando, FL	3,013	2,016	2,433	2,399
Nevada	2,364	1,821	2,103	1,900	San Francisco, CA	2,831	2,124	2,610	2,233
Hawaiian Islands	2,727	2,255	1,825	1,853	Las Vegas, NV	2,260	1,778	2,027	1,853
Massachusetts	1,429	867	1,267	1,259	Washington, DC (metro)	1,481	1,106	1,470	1,544
Illinois	1,377	1,149	1,419	1,164	Oahu/Honolulu, HI	2,234	1,821	1,495	1,497
Guam	1,325	1,127	1,191	1,140	Boston, MA	1,325	802	1,115	1,140
New Jersey	909	997	1,039	926	Chicago, IL	1,351	1,084	1,368	1,117
Texas	1,169	954	1,090	903	San Diego, CA	701	499	684	618
Pennsylvania	649	629	1,014	879	Philadelphia, PA	390	434	710	594
Georgia	805	650	634	689	Atlanta, GA	701	564	532	570
Arizona	883	564	710	665	Houston, TX	442	369	481	428
Virginia	364	282	329	380	Flagstaff, AZ [4]	(B)	(B)	431	428
Washington	468	369	456	380	Tampa/St. Petersburg, FL	519	455	380	404
Colorado	519	303	380	333	Seattle, WA	416	347	405	356
North Carolina	416	282	355	309	Anaheim-Santa Ana, CA	494	390	355	309
Ohio	390	369	304	309	Dallas-Plano-Irving, TX	494	347	380	285

[1] Excludes Canada and Mexico. [2] A person is counted in each area visited, but only once in the total. [3] Includes other states and cities, not shown separately. [4] Data include Flagstaff, Grand Canyon, and Sedona grouped together.

Source: U.S. Department of Commerce, International Trade Administration, Office of Travel and Tourism Industries, and the Bureau of Economic Analysis (BEA), May 2010, <http://www.tinet.ita.doc.gov/outreachpages/inbound.general_information.inbound_overview.html>.

Table 1261. Real Tourism Output: 2000 to 2008

[In millions of dollars (546,908 represents 546,908,000,000)]

Commodity	Direct output (current dollars)			Real output (chained 2000 dollars)		
	2000	2005	2008	2000	2005	2008
Total	546,908	660,004	767,043	546,908	590,822	603,487
Traveler accommodations	97,041	115,142	136,681	97,041	100,081	109,119
Food services and drinking places	83,683	110,599	128,573	83,683	96,194	100,108
Domestic passenger air transportation services	71,026	63,669	62,931	71,026	72,305	60,361
International passenger air transportation services	26,651	34,983	49,171	26,651	27,513	31,790
Passenger rail transportation services	1,145	1,225	1,587	1,145	1,239	1,377
Passenger water transportation services	5,526	8,658	10,016	5,526	10,665	12,554
Interurban bus transportation	1,537	1,917	1,919	1,537	1,613	1,403
Interurban charter bus transportation	966	864	811	966	740	633
Urban transit systems and other transportation services.	2,993	3,581	4,689	2,993	3,023	3,573
Taxi service	3,461	3,693	5,040	3,461	2,950	3,671
Scenic and sightseeing transportation services	2,316	2,490	2,794	2,316	2,130	2,184
Automotive rental................................	20,851	23,251	27,091	20,851	21,249	21,287
Other vehicle rental	525	643	815	525	552	660
Automotive repair services	11,014	11,277	12,306	11,014	9,761	9,360
Parking lots and garages..........................	1,315	2,045	2,011	1,315	1,652	1,424
Highway tolls	548	722	766	548	592	472
Travel arrangement and reservation services	30,735	36,287	39,605	30,735	36,074	37,785
Motion pictures and performing arts	9,466	12,304	12,909	9,466	10,021	9,692
Spectator sports	4,294	5,760	6,396	4,294	4,598	4,442
Participant sports................................	9,954	11,253	12,960	9,954	10,032	10,795
Gambling..	21,760	32,628	34,061	21,760	28,860	27,337
All other recreation and entertainment	13,620	16,239	18,900	13,620	14,123	15,179
Gasoline	38,430	57,474	79,670	38,430	37,885	37,001
Nondurable PCE [1] commodities other than gasoline.....	88,050	103,300	115,343	88,050	97,046	100,277

[1] Personal consumption expenditures.

Source: U.S. Bureau of Economic Analysis, "Industry Economic Accounts, U.S. Travel and Tourism Satellite Accounts for 2005–2008," <http://www.bea.gov/industry/>.

Table 1262. Domestic Travel Expenditures by State: 2008

[662,446 represents $662,446,000,000. Represents U.S. spending on domestic overnight trips and day trips of 50 miles or more, one way, away from home. Excludes spending by foreign visitors and by U.S. residents in U.S. territories and abroad]

State	Total (mil. dol.)	Percent distribu- tion	Rank	State	Total (mil. dol.)	Percent distribu- tion	Rank	State	Total (mil. dol.)	Percent distribu- tion	Rank
U.S. total ...	662,446	100.0	(X)	KS	5,596	0.8	38	ND	1,867	0.3	48
				KY	7,527	1.1	30	OH	15,796	2.4	12
AL	7,628	1.2	29	LA	9,326	1.4	24	OK	6,136	0.9	33
AK	1,000	0.5	47	ME	2,616	0.4	44	OR	7,747	1.2	28
AZ	12,688	1.9	17	MD	12,044	1.8	19	PA	19,766	3.0	7
AR	5,652	0.9	37	MA	13,540	2.0	15	RI	1,718	0.3	50
CA	83,015	12.5	1	MI	15,205	2.3	13	SC	9,870	1.5	22
CO	13,509	2.0	16	MN	10,353	1.6	21	SD	2,253	0.3	46
CT	9,053	1.4	26	MS	6,266	0.9	32	TN	14,024	2.1	14
DE	1,417	0.2	51	MO	12,144	1.8	18	TX	46,347	7.0	3
DC	5,660	0.9	36	MT	3,004	0.5	42	UT	5,669	0.9	35
FL	52,313	7.9	2	NE	3,934	0.6	39	VT	1,727	0.3	49
GA	19,026	2.9	9	NV	30,511	4.6	5	VA	19,220	2.9	8
HI	9,310	1.4	25	NH	3,401	0.5	40	WA	11,383	1.7	20
ID	3,363	0.5	41	NJ	18,433	2.8	10	WV	2,496	0.4	45
IL	28,385	4.3	6	NM	5,879	0.9	34	WI	9,379	1.4	23
IN	8,954	1.4	27	NY	39,467	6.0	4	WY	2,636	0.4	43
IA	6,407	1.0	31	NC	16,865	2.5	11				

X Not applicable.

Source: U.S. Travel Association, Washington, DC, *Impact of Travel on State Economies, 2008* (copyright). See also <http://www.ustravel.org/index.html>.

Arts, Recreation, and Travel 775

Table 1263. Travel Forecast Summary: 2007 to 2013

[In billions of dollars (13,254 represents $13,254,000,000,000)]

Measurement	Unit	2007	2008	2009 [1]	2010 [1]	2011 [2]	2012 [2]	2013 [2]
Real GDP	Billions	13,254	13,312	12,993	13,408	13,851	14,308	14,737
Unemployment rate	Percent	4.6	5.8	9.3	9.7	9.1	8.0	6.9
Consumer price index (CPI) [3]	Percent	207.3	215.2	214.5	219.0	223.4	229.6	235.9
Travel price index (TPI) [3]	Percent	244.0	257.7	241.5	249.9	260.8	272.1	281.0
Total travel expenditures in US	Billions	738.0	772.5	704.4	748.3	806.9	862.7	902.4
U.S. residents	Billions	641.3	662.4	610.2	647.9	697.1	740.2	771.7
International visitors [4]	Billions	96.7	110.1	94.2	100.4	109.8	122.5	130.7
Total international visitors to the United States	Millions	56.0	58.0	54.9	57.1	60.1	62.9	65.3
Total domestic person trips [5]	Millions	2,004.5	1,964.9	1,901.7	1,953.9	2,011.8	2,059.2	2,091.9

[1] Projected. [2] Forecast. [3] 1982 through 1984 = 100. [4] Excludes international visitors' spending on traveling to the U.S. on U.S. flag carriers, and other misc. transportation. [5] One person on one trip 50 miles or more, one way, away from home or including one or more nights away from home.

Source: U.S. Travel Association's Travel Forecast Model, Bureau of Labor Statistics, Department of Commerce, Bureau of Economic Analysis, Office of Travel and Tourism Industries. See <http://www.ustravel.org/index.html>.

Table 1264. Chain-Type Price Indexes for Direct Tourism Output: 2000 to 2009

[Index numbers, 2000=100. See headnote, Table 1265. For explanation of chain-type price indexes, see text, Section 13]

Tourism goods and services group	2000	2001	2002	2003	2004	2005	2006	2007	2008	2009
Traveler accommodations	100.0	102.0	101.2	102.8	108.7	114.8	119.1	124.8	125.0	116.6
Transportation	100.0	97.8	95.1	98.9	102.7	109.8	117.4	121.5	131.8	119.1
Passenger air transportation	100.0	95.8	90.3	93.2	92.2	96.6	102.8	104.6	114.8	104.2
All other transportation-related commodities	100.0	99.9	99.4	103.3	110.8	120.1	128.8	134.6	145.1	130.8
Food services and drinking places	100.0	103.2	106.0	108.2	111.5	115.0	118.6	122.9	128.4	132.9
Recreation, entertainment, and shopping	100.0	102.5	104.0	105.4	110.2	113.0	115.7	118.4	122.7	124.7
Recreation and entertainment	100.0	103.4	105.9	108.6	110.2	114.0	117.7	120.8	124.7	125.8
Shopping	100.0	101.8	102.6	103.1	104.9	106.5	108.4	110.7	115.1	117.5
All tourism goods and services	100.0	100.6	100.4	102.8	106.4	111.5	116.5	120.5	126.6	121.7

Source: U.S. Department of Commerce, Bureau of Economic Analysis, Office of Travel and Tourism Industries, United States Travel and Tourism Satellite Accounts (TTSAs), <http://www.bea.gov/bea/dn2/home/tourism.htm>.

Table 1265. Tourism Sales by Commodity Group and Tourism Employment by Industry Group: 2006 to 2009

[Sales in billions of dollars (710 represents $710,000,000,000). Employment in thousands (5,847 represents 5,847,000). Direct tourism-related sales comprise all output consumed directly by visitors (e.g., traveler accommodations, passenger air transportation, souvenirs). Direct tourism-related employment comprises all jobs where the workers are engaged in the production of direct tourism-related output (e.g., hotel staff, airline pilots, and souvenir sellers)]

Tourism commodity group	Direct tourism sales (bil. dol.)				Tourism industry group	Direct tourism employment (1,000)			
	2006	2007	2008	2009		2006	2007	2008	2009
All commodities [1]	**710**	**742**	**767**	**708**	**All industries**	**5,847**	**5,908**	**5,906**	**5,649**
Traveler accommodations	124	134	137	120	Traveler accommodations	1,363	1,376	1,376	1,297
Transportation	275	287	301	259	Transportation	1,117	1,131	1,130	1,056
Passenger air transportation	105	109	112	93	Air transportation services	447	452	454	428
All other transportation-related commodities	170	179	190	166	All other transportation-related industries	670	679	676	629
Food services and drinking places	118	123	128	129	Food and beverage services	1,908	1,940	1,944	1,899
					Recreation, entertainment, and shopping	1,199	1,198	1,195	1,151
Recreation, entertainment, and shopping	192	197	200	200	Recreation and entertainment	637	651	658	643
Recreation and entertainment	82	85	85	85	Shopping	562	547	536	508
Shopping	110	112	115	115	All other industries	260	264	262	246

[1] Commodities that are typically purchased by visitors from the producer: such as airline passenger fares, meals, or hotel services.

Source: U.S. Bureau of Economic Analysis, "Industry Economic Accounts, Satellite Industry Accounts, Travel and Tourism." See <http://www.bea.gov/bea/dn2/home/tourism.htm>.

Table 1266. International Travelers and Payments: 1990 to 2009

[(47,880 represents $47,880,000,000). For coverage, see Table 1267. Some traveler data revised since originally issued]

Year	Travel and passenger fare (mil. dol.)				U.S. net travel and passenger receipts (mil. dol)	U.S. travelers to international countries (1,000)	International travelers to the U.S. (1,000)
	Payments by U.S. travelers		Receipts from international visitors				
	Total [1]	Travel payments	Total [1]	Travel receipts			
1990..........	47,880	37,349	58,305	43,007	10,425	44,624	39,363
1995..........	59,579	44,916	82,304	63,395	22,725	51,285	43,491
2000..........	88,979	64,705	103,087	82,400	14,108	61,327	51,238
2003..........	78,436	57,447	80,250	64,359	1,814	56,250	41,218
2004..........	90,468	65,750	93,397	74,546	2,929	61,809	46,086
2005..........	95,119	68,970	102,769	81,799	7,650	63,503	49,206
2006..........	99,605	72,104	107,825	85,789	8,220	63,662	50,977
2007..........	104,768	76,331	122,542	96,896	17,774	64,024	55,979
2008..........	112,289	79,726	141,380	109,976	29,091	63,564	57,937
2009 [2]	99,210	73,230	120,341	93,917	21,131	61,419	54,958

[1] Includes passenger fares, not shown separately. [2] Preliminary estimates for the receipts payment figures, and U.S. travelers to international countries.

Source: U.S. Department of Commerce, International Trade Administration, Office of Travel and Tourism Industries, and the Bureau of Economic Analysis (BEA), June 2010, <http://www.tinet.ita.doc.gov>.

Table 1267. International Travel: 1990 to 2009

[In thousands (44,619 represents 44,619,000). U.S. travelers cover residents of the United States, its territories and possessions. International travelers to the U.S. include travelers for business and pleasure, excludes travel by international personnel and international businessmen employed in the United States. Some traveler data revised since originally issued]

Item and area	1990	1995	2000	2005	2006	2006	2007	2008	2009
U.S. travelers to international countries [1, 2]...	**44,619**	**51,285**	**61,327**	**63,503**	**63,642**	**63,662**	**64,024**	**63,564**	**61,419**
Canada..............................	12,252	13,005	15,188	14,391	13,835	13,855	13,371	12,504	11,667
Mexico..............................	16,377	19,221	19,285	20,325	19,659	19,659	19,425	20,271	19,452
Total overseas.......................	15,990	19,059	26,853	28,787	30,148	30,148	31,228	30,789	30,300
Europe...........................	8,840	9,590	13,373	11,976	12,029	12,029	12,304	11,238	10,635
International travelers to the U.S............	**39,363**	**43,491**	**51,238**	**49,206**	**50,980**	**51,063**	**55,979**	**57,937**	**54,949**
Canada..............................	17,263	14,663	14,667	14,862	15,995	15,992	17,760	18,910	17,964
Mexico..............................	7,041	8,189	10,606	12,666	10,017	10,017	14,327	13,686	13,229
Total overseas.......................	15,059	20,639	25,975	21,679	21,668	21,668	23,892	25,341	23,756
Europe...........................	6,659	8,793	11,597	10,313	10,136	10,136	11,406	12,783	11,550
Asia..............................	4,360	6,616	7,554	6,198	6,152	6,152	6,377	6,179	5,669
South America.....................	1,328	2,449	2,941	1,820	1,928	1,928	2,274	2,556	2,742
Caribbean.........................	1,137	1,044	1,331	1,135	1,198	1,198	1,317	1,201	1,206
Oceania..........................	662	588	731	737	756	756	834	852	872
Central America....................	412	509	822	696	694	694	786	776	758
Middle East.......................	365	454	702	527	553	553	620	681	666
Africa..............................	137	186	295	252	253	253	278	315	294

[1] A person is counted in each area visited but only once in the total. [2] 2009 U.S. outbound totals are preliminary estimates.

Source: U.S. Department of Commerce, International Trade Administration, Office of Travel and Tourism, June 2010, <http://www.tinet.ita.doc.gov>

Table 1268. Top 20 U.S. Gateways for Nonstop International Air Travel: 2007 and 2008

[160,846 represents 160,846,000. International passengers are residents of any country traveling nonstop to and from the United States on U.S. and foreign carriers. The data cover all passengers arriving and departing from U.S. airports on nonstop commercial international flights with 60 seats or more]

Gateway airport	2007 [1]	2008	Percent change 2007–2008	Gateway airport	2007 [1]	2008	Percent change 2007–2008
Total.....................	**160,846**	**160,379**	**-0.3**	Washington (Dulles), DC....	5,822	6,011	3.2
Total, top 20	**142,134**	**142,733**	**0.4**	Dallas-Ft. Worth, TX	5,031	4,938	-1.9
Top 20, percentage of total ...	**88.4**	**89.0**	**0.6**	Detroit, MI...............	3,830	3,800	-0.8
				Philadelphia, PA...........	3,611	3,724	3.1
New York (JFK), NY...........	21,460	22,029	2.7	Boston, MA.............	3,808	3,523	-7.5
Los Angeles, CA	16,869	16,164	-4.2	Honolulu, HI..............	3,858	3,414	-11.5
Miami, FL....................	15,586	15,999	2.7	Fort Lauderdale, FL........	2,883	3,073	6.6
Chicago (O'Hare), IL...........	11,539	11,106	-3.7	Seattle-Tacoma, WA	2,547	2,787	9.4
Newark, NJ	10,568	10,934	3.5	Orlando, FL	2,214	2,575	16.3
Atlanta, GA	8,911	9,232	3.6	Guam Island, GU..........	2,777	2,564	-7.7
San Francisco, CA.............	8,601	8,331	-3.1	Minneapolis-St. Paul, MN ...	2,515	2,560	1.8
Houston (G. Bush), TX..........	7,476	7,673	2.6	Charlotte, NC.............	2,110	2,297	8.9

[1] Data have been revised.

Source: U.S. Department of Transportation, Research and Innovative Technology Administration, Bureau of Transportation Statistics, Office of Airline Information, T-100 Segment data, September 2009, <http://www.bts.gov/publications>.

Arts, Recreation, and Travel 777

Table 1269. Selected U.S.-Canadian and U.S.-Mexican Border Land—Passenger Gateways: 2009

[(26,919 represents 26,919,000)]

Item and gateway	Entering the U.S. (1,000)	Item and gateway	Entering the U.S. (1,000)
All U.S.-Canadian land gateways [1]		**All U.S.-Mexican land gateways** [1]	
Personal vehicles	26,919	Personal vehicles	70,305
Personal vehicle passengers	53,509	Personal vehicle passengers	141,017
Buses	116	Buses	228
Bus passengers	2,503	Bus passengers	2,429
Train passengers	218	Train passengers	4
Pedestrians	380	Pedestrians	41,315
Selected top five gateways:		**Selected top five gateways:**	
Personal vehicles		Personal vehicles	
Buffalo-Niagara Falls, NY	5,292	El Paso, TX	13,355
Detroit, MI	4,082	San Ysidro, CA	10,529
Blaine, WA	2,843	Hidalgo, TX	6,178
Port Huron, MI	1,570	Brownsville, TX	5,513
Massena, NY	1,040	Laredo, TX	5,452
Personal vehicle passengers		Personal vehicle passengers	
Buffalo-Niagara Falls, NY	11,818	San Ysidro, CA	23,935
Detroit, MI	7,271	El Paso, TX	18,377
Blaine, WA	5,966	Laredo, TX	12,729
Port Huron, MI	3,320	Hidalgo, TX	12,074
Champlain-Rouses Point, NY	2,198	Brownsville, TX	11,157
Pedestrians		Pedestrians	
Buffalo-Niagara Falls, NY	245	El Paso, TX	7,638
Sumas, WA	27	San Ysidro, CA	6,188
Calais, ME	17	Nogales, AZ	4,090
Detroit, MI	17	Calexico, CA	4,038
International Falls, MN	15	Laredo, TX	3,905

[1] Data reflect all personal vehicles and buses, passengers, and pedestrians entering the U.S.-Canadian border and U.S.-Mexican border, regardless of nationality.

Source: U.S. Department of Transportation, Bureau of Transportation Statistics, based on data from the Department of Homeland Security, U.S. Customs and Border Protection, Office of Field Operations, Operations Management Reporting system. See also <http://www.transtats.bts.gov/BorderCrossing.aspx/>.

Table 1270. Foreign Visitors for Pleasure Admitted by Country of Citizenship: 2000 to 2008

[In thousands (30,511 represents 30,511,000). For years ending September 30. Represents non-U.S. citizens (also known as nonimmigrants) admitted to the country for a temporary period of time]

Country	2000 [1]	2005	2007	2008	Country	2000 [1]	2005	2007	2008
All countries [2]	**30,511**	**23,815**	**27,486**	**29,442**	Thailand	76	37	46	48
					Turkey	93	57	64	71
Europe [3]	11,806	10,016	10,703	12,558	United Arab Emirates	36	3	4	5
Austria	182	116	124	154	Africa [3]	327	212	228	253
Belgium	254	154	175	231	Egypt	44	19	24	27
Czech Republic	44	26	30	36	Nigeria	27	40	41	54
Denmark	150	153	191	236	South Africa	114	64	67	65
Finland	95	76	78	100	Oceania [3]	748	723	823	878
France	1,113	1,007	1,073	1,345	Australia	535	527	623	672
Germany	1,925	1,248	1,315	1,579	New Zealand	170	184	188	195
Greece	60	40	42	52	North America [3, 5]	6,501	5,546	8,071	7,867
Hungary	58	30	32	34	Canada	277	23	36	43
Iceland	27	34	44	49	Mexico	3,972	4,070	6,326	6,112
Ireland	325	398	501	585	Caribbean	1,404	876	1,081	1,049
Italy	626	636	700	884	Bahamas, The	24	257	334	302
Netherlands	559	483	515	638	Dominican Republic	195	189	228	207
Norway	144	117	143	184	Haiti	72	65	82	93
Poland	116	119	121	125	Jamaica	240	152	205	200
Portugal	86	81	98	114	Trinidad and Tobago	133	106	122	128
Russia	74	53	72	94	Central America	792	578	628	663
Spain	370	402	533	699	Costa Rica	172	109	122	138
Sweden	321	249	282	356	El Salvador	175	147	141	129
Switzerland	400	207	232	267	Guatemala	177	135	148	161
United Kingdom	4,671	4,232	4,211	4,568	Honduras	87	75	90	101
Asia [3]	7,853	5,688	5,745	5,693	Nicaragua	47	33	37	40
China [4]	656	221	278	319	Panama	106	64	72	77
India	253	247	379	421	South America [3]	2,867	1,498	1,856	2,114
Indonesia	62	42	45	45	Argentina	515	145	214	261
Israel	319	220	241	254	Bolivia	48	18	23	25
Japan	4,946	3,758	3,446	3,266	Brazil	706	385	491	600
Korea, South	606	528	625	600	Chile	194	82	98	106
Malaysia	64	32	34	37	Colombia	411	282	353	379
Pakistan	47	34	32	35	Ecuador	122	119	137	132
Philippines	163	144	156	170	Peru	190	142	135	148
Saudi Arabia	67	10	13	19	Uruguay	66	24	27	28
Singapore	131	57	64	77	Venezuela	570	270	348	404

[1] Due to the temporary expiration of the Visa Waiver Program from May through October 2000, data for business and pleasure not available separately for 2000 and 2001. [2] Total includes unknown visitors by country of citizenship. [3] Total includes other countries, not shown separately. [4] See Table 1331, footnote 4. [5] The majority of short-term admissions from Canada and Mexico are excluded.

Source: U.S. Dept. of Homeland Security, Office of Immigration Statistics, *2008 Yearbook of Immigration Statistics*. See also <http://www.dhs.gov/ximgtn/statistics/publications/yearbook.shtm>.

Section 27
Accommodation, Food Services, and Other Services

This section presents statistics relating to services other than those covered in the previous few sections (22 to 26) on wholesale and retail trade, transportation, communications, financial services, and recreation services. Data shown for services are classified by kind of business and cover sales or receipts, establishments, employees, payrolls, and other items.

The principal sources of these data are from the U.S. Census Bureau and include the *2007 Economic Census,* annual surveys, and the *County Business Patterns* program. These data are supplemented by data from several sources such as the National Restaurant Association on food and drink sales (Table 1282), the American Hotel & Lodging Association on lodging (Table 1281), and Magna Global on advertising (Table 1278).

Data on these services also appear in several other sections. For instance, labor force employment and earnings data appear in Section 12, Labor Force, Employment, and Earnings; gross domestic product of the industry (Table 669) appears in Section 13, Income, Expenditures, Poverty, and Wealth; and financial data (several tables) from the quarterly *Statistics of Income Bulletin,* published by the Internal Revenue Service, appear in Section 15, Business Enterprise.

Censuses—Limited coverage of the service industries started in 1933. Beginning with the 1967 census, legislation provides for a census of each area to be conducted every 5 years (for years ending in "2" and "7"). For more information on the most current census, see the Economic Census, *Guide to Economic Census,* found at <http://www.census.gov/econ/census/guide/index.html>. The industries covered in the censuses and surveys of business are defined in the *North American*

Industry Classification System (NAICS). For information on NAICS, see the Census Web site at <http://www.census.gov/epcd/www/naics.html>.

In general, the 2007 Economic Census has two final series of publications for these sectors: 1) subject series with reports such as product lines, and establishment and firm sizes and 2) geographic reports with individual reports for each state. For information on these series, see the Census Bureau Web site at <http://www.census.gov/econ/census07>.

Current surveys—The Service Annual Survey provides annual estimates of nationwide receipts for selected personal, business, leasing and repair, amusement and entertainment, social and health, and other professional service industries in the United States. For selected social, health, and other professional service industries, separate estimates are developed for receipts of taxable firms and revenue and expenses for firms and organizations exempt from federal income taxes. Several service sectors from this survey are covered in other sections of this publication. The estimates for tax exempt firms in these industries are derived from a sample of employer firms only. Estimates obtained from annual and monthly surveys are based on sample data and are not expected to agree exactly with results that would be obtained from a complete census of all establishments. Data include estimates for sampling units not reporting.

Statistical reliability—For a discussion of statistical collection and estimation, sampling procedures, and measures of statistical reliability applicable to Census Bureau data, see Appendix III.

U.S. Census Bureau, Statistical Abstract of the United States: 2011

Table 1271. Selected Service-Related Industries—Establishments, Sales, Payroll, and Employees by Kind of Business: 2007

[1,344,761 represents $1,344,761,000,000. Covers only establishments with payroll. For statement on methodology, see Appendix III]

Kind of business	2007 NAICS code [1]	Establish-ments, (number)	Sales or receipts (mil. dol.)	Annual payroll (mil. dol.)	Paid employ-ees [2] (1,000)
Professional, scientific, and technical services	54	**844,552**	**1,344,761**	**511,818**	**8,079**
Professional, scientific, and technical services	541	844,552	1,344,761	511,818	8,079
Management of companies and enterprises.	55	**51,069**	**112,895**	**255,147**	**2,779**
Administrative and support and waste management and remediation services	56	**389,073**	**636,657**	**293,803**	**10,196**
Administrative and support services	561	367,819	563,259	277,916	9,829
Waste management and remediation services.	562	21,521	75,740	16,872	386
Accommodation and food services.	72	**634,361**	**613,796**	**170,827**	**11,601**
Accommodation.	721	62,740	180,391	46,393	1,971
Food services and drinking places	722	571,621	433,405	124,434	9,630
Other services (except public administration)	81	**537,820**	**417,512**	**99,810**	**3,516**
Repair and maintenance	811	221,817	138,919	41,061	1,286
Personal and laundry services	812	208,130	83,207	26,710	1,330
Religious, grantmaking, civic, professional, and similar organizations.	813	106,503	197,874	33,133	882

[1] North American Industrial Classification System, 2007; see text, Section 15. [2] For employees on the payroll during the pay period including March 12.

Source: U.S. Census Bureau, 2007 Economic Census, "Economy-Wide Key Statistics," <http://factfinder.census.gov>, accessed August 2010.

Table 1272. Selected Service-Related Industries—Nonemployer Establishments and Receipts by Kind of Business: 2005 to 2007

[2,854 represents 2,854,000. Includes only firms subject to federal income tax. Nonemployers are businesses with no paid employees. Data originate chiefly from administrative records of the Internal Revenue Service; see Appendix III]

Kind of business	2002 NAICS code [1]	Establishments (1,000) 2005	2006	2007	Receipts (mil. dol.) 2005	2006	2007
Professional, scientific, and technical services	54	**2,854**	**2,904**	**3,029**	**118,575**	**124,237**	**130,386**
Professional, scientific, and technical services [2]	541	2,854	2,904	3,029	118,577	124,237	130,386
Legal services	5411	247	254	256	15,087	15,390	15,744
Accounting, tax preparation, bookeeping, and payroll services	5412	338	348	355	7,371	7,714	8,103
Architectural, engineering [3]	5413	231	238	232	10,807	11,308	11,420
Management, scientific and technical consulting	5416	580	536	642	24,232	25,653	29,011
Scientific research and development services	5417	28	31	35	987	1,086	1,196
Administrative and support and waste management and remediation services	56	**1,417**	**1,482**	**1,793**	**33,028**	**34,989**	**39,811**
Administrative and support services [2]	561	1,398	1,463	1,771	31,666	33,569	38,280
Office administrative services	5611	180	190	198	2,667	2,923	3,191
Business support services.	5614	185	193	224	5,274	5,521	5,969
Services to buildings and dwellings.	5617	816	850	1,047	16,548	17,702	20,625
Waste management and remediation services	562	19	19	21	1,364	1,421	1,531
Accommodation and food services.	72	**279**	**287**	**303**	**15,307**	**15,694**	**16,071**
Accommodation.	721	56	55	55	3,823	3,660	3,592
Food services and drinking places	722	223	232	249	11,483	12,034	12,479
Full-service restaurants.	7221	37	38	40	3,815	3,972	4,005
Limited-service eating places	7222	47	48	49	3,168	3,376	3,456
Special food services.	7223	115	122	133	2,917	3,085	3,352
Drinking places (alcoholic beverages).	7224	25	25	26	1,583	1,601	1,666
Other services (except public administration)	81	**2,873**	**2,931**	**2,965**	**74,025**	**77,986**	**80,653**
Repair and maintenance [2]	811	691	693	704	26,465	27,276	28,183
Automotive repair and maintenance	8111	289	289	305	13,706	13,987	14,634
Personal and household goods repair [4]	8114	302	303	297	8,397	8,765	8,853
Personal and laundry services	812	1,996	2,047	2,054	44,809	47,776	49,282
Personal care services	8121	827	870	911	17,707	19,266	20,661
Death care services.	8122	15	15	16	816	802	856
Drycleaning and laundry services	8123	36	35	35	1,884	1,966	2,004
Other personal services	8129	1,118	1,128	1,093	24,401	25,742	25,760
Religious, grantmaking, civic, professional, and similar organizations	813	186	190	206	2,752	2,933	3,189

[1] North American Industry Classification System, 2002; see text, Section 15. [2] Includes other kinds of business not shown separately. [3] Includes related services. [4] Includes maintenance.

Source: U.S. Census Bureau, "Nonemployer Statistics," August 2009, <http://www.census.gov/econ/nonemployer/index.html>.

Table 1273. Selected Service-Related Industries—Establishments, Employees, and Payroll by Industry: 2006 and 2007

[846 represents 846,000. Covers establishments with paid employees. Excludes self-employed individuals, employees of private households, railroad employees, agricultural production employees, and most government employees. For statement on methodology, see Appendix III]

Kind of business	2002 NAICS code [1]	Establishments (1,000)		Employees [2] (1,000)		Annual payroll (bil. dol.)	
		2006	2007	2006	2007	2006	2007
Professional, scientific, & technical services	**54**	**846**	**868**	**8,054**	**8,180**	**497.4**	**533.0**
Professional, scientific, & technical services	541	846	868	8,054	8,180	497.4	533.0
Legal services	5411	189	191	1,219	1,207	85.1	89.7
Offices of lawyers	54111	175	176	1,117	1,110	80.7	85.4
Accounting, tax preparation, bookkeeping, and payroll services	5412	121	123	1,357	1,357	53.2	55.9
Tax preparation services	541213	25	25	227	216	2.5	2.7
Architectural, engineering, & related services [3]	5413	115	117	1,391	1,435	91.3	98.6
Architectural services	54131	25	25	201	207	13.1	14.2
Engineering services	54133	57	58	933	961	66.3	71.4
Specialized design services [3]	5414	34	35	130	135	6.2	6.8
Graphic design services	54143	17	17	63	64	3.1	3.2
Computer systems design & related services [3]	5415	111	117	1,215	1,298	90.8	101.7
Custom computer programming services	541511	49	53	506	537	38.7	43.3
Computer systems design services	541512	47	49	487	540	35.8	41.5
Management, scientific, & technical consulting services [3]	5416	146	152	1,039	1,015	67.9	72.1
Management consulting services	54161	111	117	866	830	57.5	60.6
Environmental consulting services	54162	9	9	71	69	3.7	3.8
Scientific research & development services	5417	17	18	673	688	58.9	61.8
Research & development in the physical engineering & life sciences	54171	15	15	615	631	54.8	57.6
Advertising & related services [3]	5418	39	40	434	446	24.2	25.3
Advertising agencies	54181	14	14	167	173	12.2	12.5
Direct mail advertising	54186	3	3	73	73	3.0	3.0
Other professional, scientific, & tech services	5419	73	74	596	600	19.8	21.1
Veterinary services	54194	28	28	282	294	8.0	8.7
Management of companies and enterprises	**55**	**48**	**51**	**2,916**	**3,121**	**266.3**	**292.7**
Administrative and support and waste management and remediation services	**56**	**378**	**385**	**10,004**	**9,984**	**283.2**	**299.9**
Administrative & support services [3]	561	358	363	9,658	9,628	268.4	284.2
Employment services	5613	44	44	5,102	5,131	133.5	143.3
Temporary help services	56132	29	30	2,931	2,901	64.6	65.5
Business support services [3]	5614	36	36	779	766	22.2	22.0
Telephone call centers	56142	5	5	383	386	9.0	9.6
Collection agencies	56144	5	5	143	141	4.5	4.7
Credit bureaus	56145	1	1	22	25	1.6	1.8
Travel arrangement & reservation services	5615	23	22	254	244	10.7	12.5
Travel agencies	56151	17	16	129	123	5.3	6.5
Investigation & security services	5616	25	25	802	778	20.9	20.0
Investigation, guard, & armored car services	56161	15	15	680	658	15.7	15.1
Security systems services	56162	10	10	122	120	5.1	4.9
Services to buildings & dwellings	5617	176	180	1,707	1,723	38.0	40.4
Waste management & remediation services	562	20	21	345	355	14.9	15.7
Waste collection	5621	9	10	177	185	7.3	8.1
Waste treatment & disposal	5622	3	3	56	57	2.8	2.8
Remediation & other waste mgmt services	5629	8	9	112	113	4.8	4.8
Accommodation & food services	**72**	**612**	**632**	**11,381**	**11,565**	**167.2**	**176.3**
Accommodation	721	63	64	1,881	1,908	43.9	46.2
Traveler accommodation	7211	53	54	1,831	1,856	42.7	44.9
Hotels (except casino hotels) & motels	72111	48	49	1,436	1,454	30.6	32.4
RV (recreational vehicle) parks & recreational camps	7212	7	7	38	40	1.0	1.1
Rooming & boarding houses	7213	2	2	12	12	0.2	0.2
Food services & drinking places	722	550	569	9,501	9,657	123.3	130.2
Full-service restaurants	7221	214	219	4,519	4,580	62.9	67.1
Limited-service eating places	7222	256	267	4,074	4,137	45.3	47.9
Special food services	7223	33	35	546	576	10.7	10.6
Drinking places (alcoholic beverages)	7224	46	47	362	365	4.4	4.6
Other services (except public administration)	**81**	**736**	**744**	**5,459**	**5,520**	**133.6**	**140.7**
Repair & maintenance [3]	811	226	226	1,307	1,323	41.2	43.8
Automotive repair & maintenance	8111	164	166	888	893	24.6	25.6
Personal & household goods repair & maintenance	8114	23	23	98	95	2.7	2.8
Personal & laundry services [3]	812	210	213	1,358	1,380	27.6	28.3
Personal care services	8121	110	113	613	617	10.6	10.7
Death care services	8122	21	21	137	137	4.1	4.2
Drycleaning & laundry services	8123	42	41	374	374	8.1	8.3
Religious/grantmaking/civic/professional [4]	813	301	306	2,794	2,817	64.8	68.6
Religious organizations	8131	175	180	1,647	1,691	28.3	30.5
Grantmaking & giving services	8132	16	16	149	147	6.4	6.9
Social advocacy organizations	8133	14	15	123	129	4.2	4.7
Civic & social organizations	8134	31	30	328	330	5.2	5.4
Business/professional/labor/political [4]	8139	66	64	546	520	20.7	21.1
Labor unions [4]	81393	16	16	179	173	4.9	5.0

[1] North American Industry Classification System, 2002. See text, section 15. [2] Includes employees on the payroll for the pay period including March 12. [3] Includes other kinds of business not shown separately. [4] And similar organizations.
Source: U.S. Census Bureau, "County Business Patterns," July 2009, <http://www.census.gov/econ/cbp/index.html>.

Table 1274. Employed Persons—Sex, Race, and Hispanic or Latino Origin by Industry: 2009

[15,008 represents 15,008,000. Civilian noninstitutional population 16 years and older. Based on the Current Population Survey; see text, Sections 1 and 13, and Appendix III. For information on employees in other sectors, see Tables 615 and 631]

Industry	2007 NAICS code [1]	Total employed (1,000)	Percent of total			
			Female	Black [2]	Asian [2]	Hispanic or Latino [3]
Professional and business services	(X)	**15,008**	**41.7**	**8.9**	**5.7**	**13.9**
Professional and technical services	54	**9,159**	**43.8**	**5.9**	**8.0**	**7.2**
Legal services	5411	1,659	55.5	6.9	3.2	7.3
Accounting, tax preparation, bookkeeping, & payroll services	5412	1,014	62.7	6.2	6.6	9.6
Architectural, engineering, and related services	5413	1,493	26.3	4.0	5.7	7.9
Specialized design services	5414	350	60.7	4.8	6.8	5.1
Computer systems design & related services	5415	1,860	25.1	6.1	17.0	5.0
Management, scientific, and technical consulting services	5416	1,126	42.9	6.7	5.7	5.5
Scientific research & development services	5417	534	46.8	6.2	15.3	8.3
Advertising and related services	5418	498	47.3	6.4	3.2	9.5
Other professional, scientific, and technical services [4]	5419	353	53.6	7.3	5.6	8.8
Veterinary services	54194	271	81.5	3.0	1.6	8.1
Management, administrative, and waste services	55–56	**5,849**	**38.6**	**13.6**	**2.2**	**24.4**
Management of companies and enterprises	55	62	66.0	7.4	4.4	8.0
Employment services	5613	819	58.2	19.7	2.4	17.6
Business support services	5614	785	60.0	15.7	2.6	11.5
Travel arrangement & reservation services	5615	247	60.7	7.8	5.3	16.2
Investigations & security services	5616	782	23.2	24.1	1.5	14.7
Services to buildings and dwellings [5]	5617	1,297	52.5	12.0	2.5	33.9
Landscaping services	56173	1,180	7.5	5.2	1.1	38.9
Other administrative and support services	5611,2,9	242	43.3	9.3	4.6	17.7
Waste management and remediation services	562	434	14.3	13.5	1.5	20.5
Accommodation and food services	72	**9,717**	**53.1**	**11.0**	**6.7**	**21.7**
Accommodation	721	1,430	58.6	14.9	9.4	21.6
Traveler accommodation	7211	1,334	59.1	15.8	9.9	22.5
Recreational vehicle parks and camps, and rooming and board houses	7212,3	95	51.9	2.4	1.4	8.0
Food services and drinking places	722	8,288	52.2	10.3	6.2	21.8
Restaurants and other food services [6]	722	8,035	52.2	10.3	6.3	21.9
Drinking places, alcoholic beverages	7224	253	52.0	8.9	2.0	16.2
Other services	81	**6,935**	**52.1**	**9.7**	**5.7**	**17.5**
Other services (except private households)	81	6,152	47.2	10.0	6.0	14.9
Repair and maintenance	811	2,022	12.2	8.1	2.7	21.6
Automotive repair and maintenance [7]	8111	1,215	9.6	7.8	1.9	21.1
Car washes	811192	189	15.9	16.1	3.3	36.6
Electronic & precision equipment repair and maintenance	8112	174	15.4	6.5	5.8	13.3
Commercial and industrial machinery & equipment repair and maintenance	8113	260	8.5	6.7	1.2	20.9
Personal and household goods repair and maintenance [8]	8114	179	27.8	4.0	6.4	17.3
Footwear and leather goods repair	81143	5	(Z)	(Z)	(Z)	(Z)
Personal and laundry services	812	2,248	71.4	11.3	11.7	14.3
Barber shops	812111	94	21.5	29.6	3.0	18.0
Beauty salons	812112	987	89.3	11.0	5.3	12.1
Nail salons and other personal care services	812113,81219	393	77.6	3.8	36.9	7.2
Drycleaning & laundry services	8123	351	55.0	12.2	13.8	27.7
Funeral homes, cemeteries, and crematories	8122	121	33.5	9.9	0.4	11.3
Other personal services	8129	303	54.8	15.5	4.8	15.3
Membership associations and organizations	813	1,882	55.9	10.6	2.8	8.5
Religious organizations	8131	1,076	50.2	10.8	3.0	7.6
Civic, social, advocacy organizations, grantmaking & giving services	8132,3,4	584	66.7	11.9	2.2	10.9
Business, professional, political, and similar organizations [9]	8139	158	61.1	4.3	4.2	4.7
Labor unions	81393	64	40.8	11.3	0.9	12.6
Private households	814	783	90.6	7.1	3.5	37.8

X Not applicable. Z Base less than 50,000. [1] Based on the North American Industry Classification System, 2002; see Section 15. [2] The Current Population Survey (CPS) allows respondents to choose more than one race. Data represents persons who selected this race group only and exclude persons reporting more than one race. See also comments on race in the text for Section 1. [3] Persons of Hispanic or Latino ethnicity may be any race. [4] Excludes NAICS 54194 (veterinary services). [5] Excludes NAICS 56173 (landscaping services). [6] Excludes NAICS 7224 (drinking places, alcoholic beverages). [7] Excludes NAICS 811192 (car washes). [8] Excludes NAICS 81143 (footwear and leather goods repair). [9] Excludes NAICS 81393 (labor unions).

Source: U.S. Bureau of Labor Statistics, "Employment and Earnings Online," <http://www.bls.gov/opub/ee/home.htm> and <http://www.bls.gov/cps/home.htm>.

Table 1275. Selected Service-Related Industries—Establishments, Employees, and Annual Payroll by State: 2007

[8,180 represents 8,180,000. Covers establishments with paid employees. Excludes self-employed individuals, employees of private households, railroad employees, agricultural production employees, and most government employees. For statement on methodology, see Appendix III]

State	Professional, scientific, and technical services (NAICS 54) [1]			Administrative and support and waste management and remediation services (NAICS 56) [1]			Accommodation and food services (NAICS 72) [1]		
	Establish-ments	Employ-ees [2] (1,000)	Annual payroll (mil. dol.)	Establish-ments	Employ-ees [2] (1,000)	Annual payroll (mil. dol.)	Establish-ments	Employ-ees [2] (1,000)	Annual payroll (mil. dol.)
United States	867,556	8,180	532,997	384,501	9,984	299,933	632,489	11,565	176,344
Alabama	9,709	99	5,326	4,236	138	3,073	8,082	153	1,819
Alaska	1,880	14	825	1,074	23	1,019	2,017	25	539
Arizona	17,019	138	7,690	8,497	269	8,196	11,527	255	3,834
Arkansas	5,731	35	1,447	2,497	59	1,294	5,205	90	1,015
California	115,605	1,224	89,481	42,708	1,127	36,645	75,497	1,354	22,746
Colorado	23,364	176	11,408	8,217	194	6,571	12,125	230	3,573
Connecticut	10,233	103	7,329	5,342	89	3,142	7,871	133	2,538
Delaware	2,464	26	1,936	1,358	23	686	1,816	33	515
District of Columbia ...	4,745	91	9,299	952	34	1,285	2,146	52	1,280
Florida	70,459	459	25,555	32,836	1,350	42,423	34,887	749	12,014
Georgia	28,428	227	13,687	12,156	363	9,851	18,639	360	4,913
Hawaii	3,373	25	1,309	1,841	46	1,248	3,532	99	2,302
Idaho	4,341	33	1,549	2,196	39	875	3,495	56	681
Illinois.............	39,829	395	26,611	16,189	464	12,807	26,719	470	7,157
Indiana.............	13,248	104	5,127	7,238	174	4,729	12,912	254	3,233
Iowa..............	6,404	45	2,053	3,476	73	1,710	6,996	114	1,249
Kansas............	7,329	59	2,902	3,522	73	1,978	5,877	106	1,431
Kentucky	8,242	65	2,816	3,814	92	1,956	7,280	152	1,825
Louisiana	11,393	90	4,383	4,495	117	3,198	8,022	171	2,438
Maine.............	3,596	24	1,183	1,930	24	702	3,982	47	783
Maryland	19,896	246	17,154	8,040	178	5,694	10,680	192	3,037
Massachusetts.......	22,421	259	21,944	9,490	202	7,242	15,954	254	4,490
Michigan	23,005	260	17,159	12,196	311	9,881	19,627	335	4,199
Minnesota	17,087	141	8,775	7,095	150	4,551	11,291	220	3,059
Mississippi	4,866	34	1,468	2,295	50	1,076	4,811	115	1,757
Missouri...........	13,932	145	8,162	7,303	160	4,194	13,314	311	6,172
Montana...........	3,496	18	733	1,668	21	464	3,364	45	557
Nebraska..........	4,350	47	2,302	2,546	66	1,835	4,248	70	766
Nevada	8,157	61	3,407	4,184	108	2,888	5,615	319	8,919
New Hampshire......	4,122	31	1,767	2,145	36	1,442	3,497	56	858
New Jersey	31,948	310	22,380	13,427	293	9,269	19,345	287	5,342
New Mexico.........	4,923	45	2,605	1,955	46	1,122	4,122	81	1,083
New York	59,756	598	45,706	24,258	499	20,084	43,418	580	11,331
North Carolina.......	23,122	202	12,020	11,410	280	7,425	18,232	340	4,532
North Dakota........	1,512	12	503	890	13	304	1,852	31	345
Ohio..............	25,585	246	13,749	13,759	344	9,293	23,951	437	5,264
Oklahoma	9,302	71	3,227	4,315	98	2,439	6,918	129	1,457
Oregon............	11,697	81	4,350	5,371	93	2,530	10,357	152	2,246
Pennsylvania	30,417	320	20,303	14,525	296	8,388	26,815	420	5,645
Rhode Island	3,201	23	1,135	1,721	23	642	2,959	44	660
South Carolina.......	9,799	78	4,084	5,512	141	3,281	9,249	185	2,493
South Dakota.......	1,804	11	442	981	11	256	2,415	36	426
Tennessee	11,793	116	6,075	6,407	195	5,078	11,591	242	3,149
Texas.............	59,101	593	40,102	25,000	914	26,190	43,226	869	12,006
Utah..............	8,421	75	3,538	3,807	110	2,996	4,620	94	1,223
Vermont...........	2,206	17	695	1,031	8	195	1,940	30	430
Virginia...........	27,882	403	29,572	10,459	239	7,885	15,701	304	4,444
Washington	19,810	165	11,029	8,876	152	5,612	16,023	237	3,831
West Virginia	3,043	23	953	1,439	32	714	3,609	62	728
Wisconsin	11,567	101	5,338	6,829	138	3,425	14,401	226	2,584
Wyoming	1,943	9	402	897	8	210	1,758	26	427

[1] North American Industry Classification System, 2002. See text, section 15. [2] For employees on the payroll for the pay period including March 12.

Source: U.S. Census Bureau, "County Business Patterns," July 2009, <http://www.census.gov/econ/cbp/index.html>.

Table 1276. Professional, Scientific, and Technical Services— Estimated Revenue: 2000 to 2008

[In millions of dollars (803,527 represents $803,527,000,000). For taxable employer firms. Estimates have been adjusted to the results of the 2002 Economic Census. Based on the Service Annual Survey and administrative data; see Appendix III]

Kind of business	2002 NAICS code [1]	2000	2004	2005	2006	2007	2008
Professional, scientific, and technical services (except notaries) [2]	**54**	**803,527**	**966,437**	**1,052,382**	**1,137,393**	**1,247,415**	**1,319,755**
Legal services (except notaries)	5411	160,619	209,475	221,856	235,812	250,867	256,087
Offices of lawyers	54111	152,834	197,385	207,925	221,339	236,761	242,104
Other legal services	54119	7,785	12,090	13,931	14,473	14,106	13,983
Accounting, tax preparation, bookkeeping and payroll services	5412	79,361	92,884	101,042	109,161	122,112	128,439
Offices of certified public accountants	541211	45,773	50,679	54,508	57,744	63,239	65,847
Tax preparation services	541213	3,347	4,944	5,416	5,977	6,737	7,207
Payroll services	541214	21,394	25,359	27,942	31,162	36,140	38,110
Other accounting services	541219	8,847	11,902	13,176	14,278	15,996	17,275
Architectural, engineering, & related services [3]	5413	150,269	184,292	204,975	222,992	243,808	266,107
Architectural services	54131	25,021	28,609	31,668	34,721	40,139	40,900
Landscape architectural services	54132	(NA)	4,218	4,575	5,038	5,379	5,371
Engineering services	54133	111,929	132,814	148,349	161,097	172,753	193,352
Testing laboratories	54138	7,128	9,908	10,375	11,176	13,970	15,284
Other related services	54134,5,6,7	6,191	8,742	10,007	10,961	11,566	11,199
Specialized design services	5414	17,889	19,617	21,552	23,597	26,034	25,343
Interior design services	54141	6,798	8,061	8,838	10,065	11,365	10,773
Graphic design services	54143	8,962	8,528	9,217	9,597	9,872	9,977
All other design services	54142,9	(NA)	3,028	3,497	3,935	4,796	4,593
Computer systems design and services	5415	186,402	173,525	188,266	202,356	228,979	246,637
Custom computer programming services	541511	70,004	58,303	64,289	68,323	79,593	86,670
Computer systems design services	541512	82,763	77,042	84,995	91,983	101,540	105,908
Computer facilities management services	541513	21,816	23,422	22,748	23,934	26,661	30,949
Other computer-related services	541519	11,819	14,758	16,234	18,116	21,185	23,110
Management, scientific, and technical consulting services	5416	90,129	121,709	137,304	149,187	164,444	172,197
Management consulting services	54161	78,250	102,452	115,897	125,557	136,817	142,742
Environmental consulting services	54162	5,578	8,748	9,094	10,532	12,309	13,269
Other scientific and technical consulting services	54169	6,301	10,509	12,313	13,098	15,318	16,186
Scientific research and development services	5417	35,587	54,272	60,166	68,597	75,133	84,678
Research and development in physical, engineering and life sciences	54171	34,029	51,994	57,676	66,173	72,389	81,783
Research and development in social sciences and humanities	54172	1,558	2,278	2,490	2,424	2,744	2,895
Advertising and related services	5418	59,680	63,585	67,038	72,948	78,945	79,423
Advertising agencies	54181	21,584	24,551	25,482	27,976	30,824	32,078
Public relations agencies	54182	6,501	6,954	7,546	8,635	9,301	9,159
Media buying agencies	54183	1,036	1,405	1,478	1,704	1,709	1,841
Media representatives	54184	3,247	2,096	2,259	2,355	2,621	2,694
Display advertising	54185	4,752	5,440	6,181	6,611	7,373	7,369
Direct mail advertising	54186	10,351	11,570	12,190	12,371	12,255	11,677
All other advertising	54187,9	(NA)	11,568	11,902	13,296	14,862	14,605
Other professional, scientific, and technical services [4]	5419	23,591	47,080	50,186	52,744	57,093	60,846
Marketing research and public opinion polling	54191	11,683	11,851	12,293	13,072	13,812	14,463
Photographic services	54192	6,613	6,984	7,268	7,342	7,622	7,894
Photography studios, portrait	541921	4,642	5,031	5,262	5,272	5,613	5,715
Commercial photography	541922	1,971	1,953	2,006	2,070	2,009	2,179
Translation and interpretation services	54193	810	1,093	1,121	1,166	1,393	1,592
Veterinary services	54194	(NA)	19,144	20,595	22,368	24,553	25,788
All other professional, scientific, and technical services	54199	4,485	8,008	8,908	8,797	9,712	11,110

NA Not available. [1] Based on the North American Industry Classification System, 2002; see Section 15. [2] Prior to 2004, excludes NAICS 54132 (landscape architecture services) and NAICS 54194 (veterinary services). [3] Prior to 2004, excludes NAICS 54132 (landscape architecture services). [4] Prior to 2004, excludes NAICS 54194 (veterinary services).

U.S. Census Bureau, "Service Annual Survey 2008: Professional, Scientific, and Technical Sector Services," January 2010, <http://www.census.gov/econ/www/servmenu.html>.

Table 1277. Selected Service Industries—E-Commerce Revenue: 2007 and 2008

[128,425 represents $128,425,000,000). Includes data only for businesses with paid employees, except for accommodation and food services, which also includes businesses with and without paid employees. Except as noted, based on the Service Annual Survey]

Kind of business	2002 NAICS code [1]	E-commerce revenue (mil. dol.) 2007	E-commerce revenue (mil. dol.) 2008	E-commerce as percent of total revenue, 2008	E-commerce revenue, percent distribution, 2008
Selected service industries, total	(X)	**128,425**	**146,486**	**2.1**	**100.0**
Selected transportation and warehousing [2]	(X)	7,590	8,725	2.6	6.0
Truck transportation	484	7,420	8,524	3.6	5.8
Couriers and messengers	492	(S)	(S)	(S)	(S)
Warehousing and storage	493	(S)	(S)	(S)	(S)
Information	51	46,076	50,640	4.4	34.6
Publishing industries	511	19,334	20,505	6.8	14.0
Online information services	51811	(S)	(S)	(S)	(S)
Selected finance [3]	(X)	10,235	11,086	3.7	7.6
Securities and commodity contracts intermediation and brokerage	5231	9,898	10,593	6.7	7.2
Rental and leasing services	532	7,791	8,528	6.8	5.8
Selected professional, scientific, and technical services [4]	(X)	19,757	23,806	1.8	16.3
Computer systems design and related services	5415	4,388	5,344	2.2	3.6
Administrative and support and waste management and remediation services	56	12,425	14,117	2.3	9.6
Travel arrangements and reservation services	5615	7,215	7,528	23.0	5.1
Health care and social assistance services	62	1,042	1,222	0.1	0.8
Arts, entertainment, and recreation services	71	3,006	3,709	1.9	2.5
Accommodation and food services [5]	72	13,965	16,362	2.5	11.2
Selected other services [6]	(X)	6,538	8,291	2.1	5.7
Repair and maintenance	811	928	963	0.7	0.7
Religious, grantmaking, civic, professional, and similar organizations	813	4,028	5,418	3.3	3.7

X Not applicable. S Data do not meet publication standards. [1] North American Industry Classification System (NAICS), 2002; see text Section 15. [2] Excludes NAICS 481 (air transportation), 482 (rail transportation), 483 (water transportation), 485 (transit and ground passenger transportation), 486 (pipeline transportation), 487 (scenic and sightseeing transportation), 488 (support activities for transportation) and 491 (postal service). [3] Excludes NAICS 521 (monetary authorities-central bank), 522 (credit intermediation and related activities), 5232 (securities and commodity exchanges), NAICS 52391 (miscellaneous intermediation), 52399 (all other financial investment activities), 524 (insurance carriers and related activities) and 525 (funds and trusts). [4] Excludes NAICS 54112 (offices of notaries). [5] Based on 2008 Annual Retail Trade Survey. [6] Excludes NAICS 81311 (religious organizations), 81393 (labor and similar organizations), 81394 (political organizations) and 814 (private households).

Source: U.S. Census Bureau, "E-Stats," <http://www.census.gov/econ/estats/>.

Table 1278. Forecast Summary—Media Supplier Advertising Revenues: 2000 to 2009

[In millions of dollars (175,777 represents $175,777,000,000). See source for definitions of types of advertising]

Media supplier	2000	2003	2004	2005	2006	2007	2008	2009
Total supplier ad revenue	**175,777**	**174,355**	**186,366**	**194,463**	**203,079**	**204,527**	**193,730**	**163,610**
Total [1]	**173,811**	**174,012**	**184,382**	**194,190**	**200,876**	**204,200**	**191,335**	**163,129**
Direct	29,526	33,962	37,372	40,445	44,273	47,511	47,665	42,799
Direct mail	16,585	18,601	19,920	20,567	22,178	22,677	21,613	18,732
Direct online [2]	560	2,894	4,377	6,374	8,794	11,373	13,567	13,664
Directories [3]	12,382	12,467	13,075	13,503	13,301	13,461	12,485	10,403
National	53,494	52,018	55,632	59,230	61,897	64,578	63,241	56,982
National television [3,4]	25,574	29,049	31,457	33,236	33,718	34,836	35,136	33,700
Magazines [3]	19,025	17,112	17,961	19,351	20,373	20,975	19,533	15,609
National digital/online [5]	5,665	3,244	3,469	3,955	5,100	6,161	6,171	5,703
Network and satellite radio	1,065	1,118	1,175	1,161	1,178	1,226	1,220	1,100
National newspapers [3]	2,165	1,495	1,570	1,527	1,527	1,379	1,180	870
Local	90,791	88,032	91,377	94,515	94,706	92,111	80,429	63,348
Local newspapers [3]	46,506	43,444	45,133	45,880	45,074	40,830	33,559	23,951
Local TV [3,6]	18,389	19,385	19,845	21,089	20,781	21,790	19,538	16,872
Local radio [3]	18,819	18,570	18,932	19,018	19,031	18,476	16,536	13,203
Emerging outdoor	195	281	377	426	553	790	995	1,010
Other outdoor	5,040	5,224	5,457	5,875	6,252	6,493	5,997	4,891
Local digital/online [5]	1,843	1,129	1,633	2,227	3,015	3,732	3,804	3,421
Political [7]	1,180	343	1,280	273	1,553	327	1,795	482
Olympics [8]	785	–	704	–	650	–	600	–

– Represents zero. [1] Excludes political and olympic revenue. [2] Includes paid search, lead generation and Internet yellow pages. [3] Excludes Internet-based advertising revenues. [4] Includes English and Spanish-language network TV, national cable and national syndication. Excludes incremental olympic revenues. [5] Includes rich/online video, Internet classifieds, e-mail, digital display and mobile. [6] Includes local broadcast and local cable TV. Excludes local political advertising revenues. [7] Total political advertising revenue on local broadcast and local cable TV. [8] Incremental advertising revenue from olympics on network TV.

Source: MAGNAGLOBAL, New York, NY, (copyright), <http://www.magnaglobal.com>.

Table 1279. Administrative and Support and Waste Management and Remediation Services—Estimated Revenue: 2000 to 2008

[In millions of dollars (396,499 represents $396,499,000,000). For taxable and tax-exempt employer firms. Estimates have been adjusted to results of the 2002 Economic Census. Based on the Service Annual Survey and administrative data; see Appendix III]

Kind of business	2002 NAICS code [1]	2000	2004	2005	2006	2007	2008
Administrative and support and waste management and remediation services [2]	**56**	**396,499**	**484,288**	**526,968**	**561,823**	**591,537**	**606,616**
Administrative and support services [2]	561	345,302	425,645	463,913	493,366	520,786	532,692
Office administrative services	56111	26,288	38,014	43,112	45,665	48,501	51,410
Facilities support services	56121	13,211	12,520	14,028	15,655	17,215	19,279
Employment services	5613	144,242	145,717	159,043	170,919	177,937	179,387
Employment placement agencies	56131	4,985	6,513	6,772	7,184	7,695	8,099
Temporary help services	56132	79,622	77,660	85,077	90,236	93,821	92,377
Professional employer organizations	56133	59,635	61,544	67,194	73,499	76,421	78,911
Business support services	5614	41,203	48,166	50,823	54,140	55,160	55,289
Document preparation services	56141	1,920	2,483	2,631	2,835	2,934	2,833
Telephone call centers	56142	14,805	13,843	14,420	15,359	15,702	15,916
Telephone answering services	561421	2,135	1,783	1,923	1,877	2,174	2,256
Telemarketing bureaus	561422	12,670	12,060	12,497	13,482	13,528	13,660
Business service centers	56143	8,257	8,469	8,369	7,627	7,765	7,945
Private mail centers	561431	1,692	2,274	2,229	2,397	2,545	2,745
Other business service centers (including copy shops)	561439	6,565	6,195	6,140	5,230	5,220	5,200
Collection agencies	56144	7,300	10,860	11,479	11,600	12,113	11,773
Credit bureaus	56145	3,741	5,516	6,332	8,202	8,391	8,038
Other business support services	56149	5,180	6,995	7,592	8,517	8,255	8,784
Repossession services	561491	418	534	582	606	(S)	(S)
Court reporting and stenotype services	561492	1,250	1,792	1,847	2,023	2,048	2,000
All other business support services	561499	3,512	4,669	5,163	5,888	5,539	6,042
Travel arrangement and reservation services	5615	26,119	28,200	28,996	30,173	32,587	32,705
Travel agencies	56151	11,639	10,101	10,331	10,965	11,942	11,590
Tour operators	56152	3,564	3,515	3,614	3,574	3,944	3,990
Other travel arrangement and reservation services	56159	10,916	14,584	15,051	15,634	16,701	17,125
Convention and visitors bureaus	561591	1,020	1,256	1,313	1,408	1,600	1,712
All other travel arrangement and reservation services	561599	9,896	13,328	13,738	14,226	15,101	15,413
Investigation and security services	5616	27,594	33,723	37,100	37,592	39,972	41,991
Investigation, guard, and armored car services	56161	17,581	21,754	24,377	24,787	26,240	27,340
Investigation services	561611	2,350	3,345	3,668	3,539	4,052	3,970
Security guards and patrol services	561612	13,393	16,321	18,608	19,097	20,077	21,125
Armored car services	561613	1,838	2,088	2,101	2,151	2,111	2,245
Security systems services	56162	10,013	11,969	12,723	12,805	13,732	14,651
Security systems services (except locksmiths)	561621	8,683	10,488	11,083	10,961	11,787	12,702
Locksmiths	561622	1,330	1,481	1,640	1,844	1,945	1,949
Services to buildings and dwellings [2]	5617	35,790	85,991	93,493	100,452	109,037	111,455
Exterminating and pest control services	56171	5,723	7,673	8,144	8,535	8,783	9,017
Janitorial services	56172	24,593	30,288	31,743	32,781	36,501	38,537
Landscaping services	56173	(NA)	40,363	44,793	49,228	52,662	51,935
Carpet and upholstery cleaning services	56174	2,463	2,964	3,397	3,618	3,891	4,080
Other services to buildings and dwellings	56179	3,011	4,703	5,416	6,290	7,201	7,886
Other support services	5619	30,855	33,315	37,316	38,769	40,375	41,174
Packaging and labeling services	56191	4,432	5,591	6,658	7,236	7,925	8,293
Convention and trade show organizers	56192	8,410	9,517	10,727	11,408	11,334	12,087
All other support services	56199	18,013	18,207	19,931	20,125	21,116	20,794
Waste management and remediation services	562	51,197	58,643	63,055	68,456	70,751	73,924
Waste collection	5621	28,820	32,430	33,838	37,187	38,176	40,679
Solid waste collection	562111	27,032	30,436	31,781	34,818	35,588	37,870
Hazardous waste collection	562112	1,249	1,565	1,573	1,766	1,910	2,108
Other waste collection	562119	539	429	484	603	678	701
Waste treatment and disposal	5622	11,025	11,398	12,532	13,238	13,124	13,335
Hazardous waste treatment and disposal	562211	3,155	3,264	3,724	3,981	4,291	4,369
Solid waste landfill	562212	5,965	6,168	6,439	6,704	6,654	6,710
Solid waste combustors and incinerators	562213	1,261	1,303	1,587	1,672	1,286	1,314
Other nonhazardous waste treatment and disposal	562219	644	663	782	881	893	942
Remediation and other waste management services	5629	11,352	14,815	16,685	18,031	19,451	19,910
Remediation services	56291	6,750	8,834	10,206	11,115	11,363	11,501
Materials recovery facility	56292	1,593	2,633	2,742	2,811	3,505	3,917
All other waste management services	56299	3,009	3,348	3,737	4,105	4,583	4,492
Septic tank and related services	562991	2,197	2,132	2,372	2,563	2,732	2,753
All other miscellaneous waste management services	562998	812	1,216	1,365	1,542	1,851	1,739

NA Not available. S Data do not meet publication standards. [1] North American Industry Classification System, 2002; see text, Section 15. [2] Prior to 2004, excludes NAICS 56173 (landscaping services).

Source: U.S. Census Bureau, "Service Annual Survey 2008: Administrative and Support and Waste Management and Remediation Sector Services," January 2010, <http://www.census.gov/econ/www/servmenu.html>.

Table 1280. Estimated Accommodation and Food Services Sales by Kind of Business: 2000 to 2008

[In millions of dollars (443,642 represents $443,642,000,000). Estimates are based on data from the Annual Retail Trade Survey and administrative records and have been adjusted to the preliminary results of the 2007 Economic Census]

Kind of business	2002 NAICS code [1]	2000	2003	2004	2005	2006	2007	2008
Accommodation and food services, total	72	443,642	488,869	526,396	560,982	597,861	630,579	641,995
Accommodation	721	138,181	137,842	151,592	163,141	173,620	184,306	183,834
Traveler accommodation	7211	133,582	132,924	146,623	157,945	167,948	178,335	177,735
RV parks and recreational camps	7212	3,608	3,932	3,961	4,133	4,524	4,769	4,855
Rooming and boarding houses	7213	991	986	1,008	1,063	1,148	1,202	1,244
Food services and drinking places [2]	722	305,461	351,027	374,804	397,841	424,241	446,273	458,161
Full service restaurants	7221	134,204	156,013	165,779	174,720	186,642	196,211	197,618
Limited service eating places	7222	127,879	147,101	158,722	169,181	178,733	186,750	195,307
Drinking places	7224	15,415	17,363	17,703	18,163	19,486	20,109	20,466

[1] North American Industry Classification System, 2002; see text, Section 15. [2] Includes other kinds of business not shown separately.

Source: U.S. Census Bureau, "Annual Accommodation and Food Services—2008," <http://www.census.gov/retail/>.

Table 1281. Lodging Industry Summary: 1990 to 2008

Year	Average occupancy rate (percent)	Average room rate (dol.)	Room size of property	2008 Establishments	2008 Rooms (mil.)	Item	2008 Business traveler	2008 Leisure traveler
1990	63.3	57.96	Total	49,505	4.6	Typical night:		
1995	65.5	66.65				Made reservations		
2000	63.7	85.89	Percent:			(percent)	92	88
2004	61.3	86.24	Under 75 rooms	56.2	25.7	Amount paid (dol.)	$125.00	$112.00
2005	63.1	90.88	75–149 rooms	31.9	36.0	Length of stay (percent):		
2006	63.3	97.78	150–299 rooms	8.6	18.4	One night	35	41
2007	63.1	103.87	300–500 rooms	2.2	9.0	Two nights	26	31
2008	60.4	106.84	Over 500 rooms	1.1	10.9	Three or more	39	28

Source: American Hotel & Lodging Association, Washington, DC Lodging Industry Profile, annual (copyright). See also <http://www.ahla.com>.

Table 1282. Commercial and Noncommercial Groups—Food and Drink Establishments and Sales: 1990 to 2010

[In millions of dollars (238,149 represents $238,149,000,000). Excludes military. Data refer to sales to consumers of food and alcoholic beverages. Sales are estimated. For details, see source]

Type of group	Establishments, 2006	Sales (mil. dol.) 1990	1995	2000	2005	2008	2009	2010 [1]
Total	921,442	238,149	294,631	377,652	486,494	550,146	565,744	580,060
Commercial restaurant services [2,3]	720,628	211,606	265,910	345,345	445,078	521,294	517,315	530,352
Eating places [2]	458,527	155,552	198,293	259,743	329,598	385,818	380,476	388,511
Full-service restaurants	199,084	77,811	96,396	133,834	165,170	189,378	181,993	184,176
Limited-service restaurants [4]	201,269	[5] 69,798	[5] 92,901	107,147	136,903	157,670	160,036	164,836
Snack and nonalcoholic beverage bars	43,323	(⁵)	(⁵)	12,867	17,150	24,254	24,157	24,736
Bars and taverns [6]	48,856	9,533	9,948	12,412	15,002	18,292	18,475	18,844
Managed services [2]	20,693	14,149	18,186	24,841	32,030	38,257	39,296	40,869
Manufacturing and industrial plants	(NA)	3,856	4,814	6,223	6,570	7,258	6,686	6,653
Colleges and universities	(NA)	2,788	3,989	5,879	9,283	11,913	12,912	13,649
Lodging places	14,991	13,568	15,561	19,438	23,854	27,328	25,763	26,943
Retail hosts [2,7]	134,399	9,513	12,589	14,869	22,502	26,249	29,481	30,936
Department store restaurants	4,014	876	1,038	903	490	(NA)	(NA)	(NA)
Grocery store restaurants [7]	61,115	5,432	6,624	7,116	12,032	(NA)	(NA)	(NA)
Gasoline service stations	53,251	1,718	2,520	4,693	6,137	(NA)	(NA)	(NA)
Recreation and sports	36,080	2,871	3,866	4,772	11,397	13,171	12,212	12,518
Noncommercial restaurant services [2]	200,814	26,543	28,722	32,307	41,416	46,597	46,372	47,547
Employee restaurant services	3,261	1,864	1,364	986	548	463	417	426
Industrial, commercial organizations	975	1,603	1,129	717	260	(NA)	(NA)	(NA)
Educational restaurant services	105,070	7,671	9,059	9,977	11,007	11,728	12,180	12,227
Elementary and secondary schools	100,847	3,700	4,533	5,039	5,320	5,916	6,011	6,144
Hospitals	5,728	8,968	9,219	9,982	12,332	14,482	14,535	15,225
Miscellaneous	50,009	2,892	3,673	4,898	9,703	11,004	10,760	11,115
Clubs	26,689	1,993	2,278	3,164	7,555	(NA)	8,480	8,554

NA Not available. [1] Projection. [2] Includes other types of groups, not shown separately. [3] Data for establishments with payroll. [4] Fast-food restaurants. [5] Snack and nonalcoholic beverage bars included in limited service restaurants, prior to 1997. [6] For establishments serving food. [7] Includes a portion of delicatessen sales in grocery stores.

Source: National Restaurant Association, *Restaurant Numbers: 25 Year History, 1970–1995*, Washington, DC, 1998; *Restaurant Industry in Review*, annual; *National Restaurant Association 2010 Restaurant Industry Forecast*, December 2009, (copyright).

Accommodation, Food Services, and Other Services **787**

Table 1283. Other Services—Estimated Revenue for Employer Firms by Kind of Business: 2000 to 2008

[In millions of dollars (302,783 represents $302,783,000,000). For employer firms. Estimates have been adjusted to the results of the 2002 Economic Census. Based on the Service Annual Survey; see Appendix III]

Kind of business	2002 NAICS code [1]	2000	2006	2007	2008
Other services [2, 3]	**81**	**302,783**	**379,559**	**409,429**	**390,610**
Repair and maintenance [4]	811	112,719	133,932	137,944	137,404
Automotive repair and maintenance	8111	73,219	87,850	89,965	88,719
Automotive mechanical and electrical repair and maintenance	81111	37,879	45,148	46,728	45,909
General automotive repair	811111	30,988	38,293	39,893	39,441
Automotive body, paint, interior, and glass repair	81112	25,766	29,741	30,042	29,913
Automotive body, paint, and interior repair and maintenance	811121	22,018	26,016	26,582	26,190
Other automotive repair and maintenance	81119	9,574	12,961	13,195	12,897
Electronic and precision equipment repair and maintenance	8112	14,419	15,509	15,437	15,260
Commercial and industrial machinery and equipment (except automotive and electronic) repair and maintenance	8113	16,687	21,890	23,060	23,682
Personal and household goods repair and maintenance	8114	8,394	8,683	9,482	9,743
Home and garden equipment and appliance repair and maintenance	81141	3,866	3,347	3,909	4,021
Personal and laundry services [4]	812	(NA)	83,128	86,005	88,181
Personal care services	8121	18,264	26,738	28,545	29,776
Hair, nail, and skin care services	81211	15,553	20,851	21,880	22,488
Barber shops	812111	479	538	582	599
Beauty salons	812112	14,445	18,543	19,180	19,403
Nail salons	812113	629	1,770	2,118	2,486
Other personal care services	81219	2,711	5,887	6,665	7,288
Death care services	8122	13,707	15,304	14,813	14,933
Funeral homes and funeral services	81221	10,279	12,468	12,244	12,751
Cemeteries and crematories	81222	3,428	2,836	2,569	2,182
Drycleaning and laundry services	8123	19,950	22,278	22,591	22,454
Coin-operated laundries and drycleaners	81231	3,359	3,368	3,494	3,529
Drycleaning and laundry services (except coin-operated)	81232	7,846	8,547	8,881	9,035
Linen and uniform supply	81233	8,745	10,363	10,216	9,890
Pet care (except veterinary) services	81291	(NA)	2,215	2,383	2,544
Photofinishing	81292	3,809	2,219	2,200	2,165
Parking lots and garages	81293	6,389	7,537	7,406	7,749
All other personal services	81299	5,021	6,836	8,067	8,561
Religious, grantmaking, civic, professional, and similar organizations (except religious, labor, and political organizations) [5]	813	122,924	162,498	185,479	165,024
Grantmaking and giving services	8132	57,465	74,226	91,072	69,239
Social advocacy organizations	8133	10,852	15,340	16,895	17,669
Civic and social organizations	8134	13,703	18,507	19,419	19,292
Business, professional, and other organizations (except labor and political organizations)	8139	40,904	54,425	58,093	58,824

NA Not available. [1] Based on the North American Industry Classification System, 2002; see Section 15. [2] Except public administration, religious, labor, and political organizations, and private households. [3] Prior to 2004, excludes NAICS 81291 (Pet care services). [4] For taxable firms only. [5] For tax-exempt firms only.

Source: U.S. Census Bureau, "Service Annual Survey 2008: Other Sector Services," January 2010, <http://www.census.gov/econ/www/servmenu.html>.

Table 1284. National Nonprofit Associations—Number by Type: 1980 to 2009

[Data compiled during last few months of year previous to year shown and the beginning months of year shown]

Type	1980	1990	2000	2003	2004	2005	2006	2007 [1]	2008	2009
Total	**14,726**	**22,289**	**21,840**	**22,464**	**22,659**	**22,720**	**23,772**	**25,048**	**25,176**	**24,100**
Trade, business, commercial	3,118	3,918	3,880	3,818	3,812	3,789	3,942	4,072	4,003	3,840
Agriculture and environment	677	940	1,103	1,137	1,140	1,170	1,286	1,353	1,439	1,365
Legal, governmental, public admin., military	529	792	790	832	839	868	887	938	951	927
Scientific, engineering, technical	1,039	1,417	1,302	1,326	1,354	1,354	1,396	1,505	1,588	1,549
Educational	[2] 2,376	1,291	1,297	1,301	1,313	1,318	1,365	1,471	1,530	1,462
Cultural	([2])	1,886	1,786	1,749	1,735	1,733	1,782	1,881	1,896	1,761
Social welfare	994	1,705	1,829	1,941	1,972	2,072	2,218	2,307	2,582	2,531
Health, medical	1,413	2,227	2,495	2,808	2,921	2,982	3,089	3,383	3,552	3,460
Public affairs	1,068	2,249	1,776	1,836	1,881	1,854	1,938	1,951	1,842	1,769
Fraternal, nationality, ethnic	435	573	525	557	547	550	567	580	523	482
Religious	797	1,172	1,123	1,155	1,157	1,147	1,162	1,204	1,146	1,101
Veteran, hereditary, patriotic	208	462	835	802	803	774	790	774	645	602
Hobby, avocational	910	1,475	1,330	1,435	1,449	1,433	1,525	1,615	1,511	1,421
Athletic sports	504	840	717	760	755	762	863	960	1,008	972
Labor unions	235	253	232	211	213	208	209	227	212	195
Chambers of Commerce [3]	105	168	143	139	136	135	137	169	162	147
Greek and non-Greek letter societies	318	340	296	309	305	349	302	335	325	309
Fan clubs	(NA)	581	381	348	327	314	314	323	261	207

NA Not available. [1] The increase in the number of associations comes from the increase in newly discovered and established associations. [2] Data for cultural associations included with educational associations. [3] National and binational. Includes trade and tourism organizations.

Source: Gale, Cengage Learning, Farmington Hills, MI, compiled from *Encyclopedia of Associations*, annual (copyright).

Section 28
Foreign Commerce and Aid

This section presents data on the flow of goods, services, and capital between the United States and other countries; changes in official reserve assets of the United States; international investments; and foreign assistance programs.

The Bureau of Economic Analysis publishes current figures on U.S. international transactions and the U.S. international investment position in its monthly Survey of *Current Business. Statistics* for the foreign aid programs are presented by the Agency for International Development (AID) in its annual U.S. *Overseas Loans and Grants and Assistance from International Organizations.*

The principal source of merchandise import and export data is the U.S. Census Bureau. Current data are presented monthly in *U.S. International Trade in Goods and Services report Series* FT 900. The *Guide to Foreign Trade Statistics*, found on the Census Bureau Web site at <http://www.census.gov /foreign-trade/guide/index.html>, lists the Census Bureau's monthly and annual products and services in this field. In addition, the International Trade Administration and the Bureau of Economic Analysis present summary as well as selected commodity and country data for U.S. foreign trade on their Web sites: <http://ita.doc.gov/td/industry /otea/> and <http://www.bea.gov /international/index>, respectively. The merchandise trade data published by the Bureau of Economic Analysis in the *Survey of Current Business* and on the Web include balance of payments adjustments to the Census Bureau data. The U.S. Treasury Department's *Monthly Treasury Statement of Receipts and Outlays of the United States Government* contains information on import duties. The International Trade Commission, U.S. Department of Agriculture (agricultural products), U.S. Department of Energy (mineral fuels, like petroleum and coal), and the U.S. Geological Survey (minerals)

release various reports and specialized products on U.S. trade.

International accounts—
The international transactions tables (Tables 1285 to 1287) show, for given time periods, the transfer of goods, services, grants, and financial assets and liabilities between the United States and the rest of the world. The international investment position table (Table 1288) presents, for specific dates, the value of U.S. investments abroad and of foreign investments in the United States. The movement of foreign and U.S. capital as presented in the balance of payments is not the only factor affecting the total value of foreign investments. Among the other factors are changes in the valuation of assets or liabilities, including changes in prices of securities, defaults, expropriations, and write-offs.

Direct investment abroad means the ownership or control, directly or indirectly, by one person of 10 percent or more of the voting securities of an incorporated business enterprise or an equivalent interest in an unincorporated business enterprise. Direct investment position is the value of U.S. parents' claims on the equity of and receivables due from foreign affiliates, less foreign affiliates' receivables due from their U.S. parents. Income consists of parents' shares in the earnings of their affiliates plus net interest received by parents on intercompany accounts, less withholding taxes on dividends and interest.

Foreign aid—Foreign assistance is divided into three major categories— grants (military supplies and services and other grants), credits, and other assistance (through net accumulation of foreign currency claims from the sale of agricultural commodities). *Grants* are transfers for which no payment is expected (other than a limited percentage of the foreign currency "counterpart" funds generated by the grant), or which at most involve an obligation on the part

U.S. Census Bureau, Statistical Abstract of the United States: 2011

of the receiver to extend aid to the United States or other countries to achieve a common objective. *Credits* are loan disbursements or transfers under other agreements which give rise to specific obligations to repay, over a period of years, usually with interest. All known returns to the U.S. government stemming from grants and credits (reverse grants, returns of grants, and payments of principal) are taken into account in net grants and net credits, but no allowance is made for interest or commissions. *Other assistance* represents the transfer of U.S. farm products In exchange for foreign currencies (plus, since enactment of Public Law 87-128, currency claims from principal and interest collected on credits extended under the farm products program), less the government's disbursements of the currencies as grants, credits, or for purchases. The net acquisition of currencies represents net transfers of resources to foreign countries under the agricultural programs, in addition to those classified as grants or credits.

In 1952, economic, technical, and military aid programs were combined under the Mutual Security Act, which in turn was followed by the Foreign Assistance Act passed in 1961. Appropriations to provide military assistance were also made in the Department of Defense Appropriation Act (rather than the Foreign Assistance Appropriation Act) beginning in 1966 for certain countries in Southeast Asia and in other legislation concerning programs for specific countries (such as Israel). Figures on activity under the Foreign Assistance Act as reported in the *Foreign Grants and Credits* series differ from data published by AID or its immediate predecessors, due largely to differences in reporting, timing, and treatment of particular items.

Exports—The Census Bureau compiles export data primarily from Shipper's Export Declarations required to be filed with customs officials for shipments leaving the United States. They include U.S. exports under mutual security programs and exclude shipments to U.S. Armed Forces for their own use.

The value reported in the export statistics is generally equivalent to a free alongside ship (f.a.s.) value at the U.S. port of export, based on the transaction price, including inland freight, insurance, and other charges incurred in placing the merchandise alongside the carrier at the U.S. port of exportation. This value, as defined, excludes the cost of loading merchandise aboard the exporting carrier and also excludes freight, insurance, and any other charges or transportation and other costs beyond the U.S. port of exportation. The country of destination is defined as the country of ultimate destination or country where the merchandise is to be consumed, further processed, or manufactured, as known to the shipper at the time of exportation. When ultimate destination is not known, the shipment is statistically credited to the last country to which the shipper knows the merchandise will be shipped in the same form as exported.

Effective January 1990, the United States began substituting Canadian import statistics for U.S. exports to Canada. As a result of the data exchange between the United States and Canada, the United States has adopted the Canadian import exemption level for its export statistics based on shipments to Canada.

Data are estimated for shipments valued under $2,501 to all countries, except Canada, using factors based on the ratios of low-valued shipments to individual country totals.

Prior to 1989, exports were based on Schedule B, Statistical Classification of Domestic and Foreign Commodities Exported from the United States. Beginning in 1989, Schedule B classifications are based on the Harmonized System and coincide with the Standard International Trade Classification, Revision 3. This revision will affect the comparability of most export series beginning with the 1989 data for commodities.

Imports—The Census Bureau compiles import data from various customs forms required to be filed with customs officials. Data on import values are presented on two valuations bases in this section: The c.i.f. (cost, insurance, and freight) and the customs import value (as appraised by the U.S. Customs Service in accordance with legal requirements of the Tariff Act of 1930, as amended). This latter valuation, primarily used for collection of import duties, frequently does not reflect the actual transaction value. Country of origin is defined as country where the merchandise was grown, mined, or manufactured. If country of origin is unknown, country of shipment is reported.

Imports are classified either as "General imports" or "Imports for consumption." *General imports* are a combination of entries for immediate consumption, entries into customs bonded warehouses, and entries into U.S. Foreign Trade Zones, thus generally reflecting total arrivals of merchandise. *Imports for consumption* are a combination of entries for immediate consumption, withdrawals from warehouses for consumption, and entries of merchandise into U.S. customs territory from U.S. Foreign Trade Zones, thus generally reflecting the total of the commodities entered into U.S. consumption channels.

Beginning in 1989, import statistics are based on the Harmonized Tariff Schedule of the United States, which coincides with import Standard International Trade Classification, Revision 3. This revision will affect the comparability of most import series beginning with the 1989 data.

Area coverage—Except as noted, the geographic area covered by the export and import trade statistics is the United States Customs area (includes the 50 states, the District of Columbia, and Puerto Rico), the U.S. Virgin Islands (effective January 1981), and U.S. Foreign Trade Zones (effective July 1982). Data for selected tables and total values for 1980 have been revised to reflect the U.S. Virgin Islands' trade with foreign countries, where possible.

Statistical reliability—For a discussion of statistical collection and estimation, sampling procedures, and measures of statistical reliability applicable to Census Bureau data, see Appendix III.

U.S. Census Bureau, Statistical Abstract of the United States: 2011

Table 1285. U.S. International Transactions by Type of Transaction: 1990 to 2009

[In millions of dollars (706,975 represents $706,975,000,000). Minus sign (−) indicates debits]

Type of transaction [1]	1990	1995	2000	2002	2003	2004	2005	2006	2007	2008	2009
Exports of goods and services and income receipts	706,975	1,004,631	1,421,515	1,258,412	1,340,353	1,572,315	1,816,449	2,135,004	2,478,267	2,635,540	2,159,000
Exports of goods and services	535,233	794,387	1,070,597	977,470	1,019,897	1,158,576	1,281,186	1,452,783	1,648,665	1,839,012	1,570,797
Goods, balance of payments basis [2]	387,401	575,204	784,181	696,268	728,258	819,870	909,016	1,035,868	1,160,366	1,304,896	1,068,499
Services [3]	147,832	219,183	286,416	281,202	291,639	338,707	372,171	416,916	488,299	534,116	502,298
Transfers under U.S. military agency sales contracts [4]	9,932	14,643	6,088	4,656	5,916	8,878	12,164	15,678	17,216	14,936	17,096
Travel	43,007	63,395	82,400	66,605	64,359	74,546	81,799	85,789	96,896	109,976	93,917
Passenger fares	15,298	18,909	20,687	17,046	15,891	18,851	20,970	22,036	25,646	31,404	26,424
Other transportation	22,042	26,081	25,318	25,385	26,111	29,495	31,704	35,503	40,315	43,714	35,406
Royalties and license fees [5]	16,634	30,289	43,233	44,508	46,988	56,715	64,395	70,727	84,580	93,920	89,791
Other private services [5]	40,251	65,048	107,904	122,207	131,563	149,262	160,051	186,028	222,434	238,932	238,332
U.S. government miscellaneous services	668	818	786	795	810	959	1,087	1,155	1,212	1,234	1,333
Income receipts	171,742	210,244	350,918	280,942	320,456	413,739	535,263	682,221	829,602	796,528	588,203
Income receipts on U.S.-owned assets abroad	170,570	208,065	348,083	278,131	317,643	410,917	532,373	679,338	826,632	793,484	585,256
Direct investment receipts	65,973	95,260	151,839	145,590	186,417	250,606	294,538	324,816	370,712	403,225	346,073
Other private receipts	94,072	108,092	192,398	129,238	126,529	157,313	235,120	352,122	453,687	385,353	234,458
U.S. government receipts	10,525	4,713	3,846	3,303	4,697	2,998	2,715	2,400	2,233	4,906	4,724
Compensation of employees	1,172	2,179	2,835	2,811	2,813	2,822	2,890	2,883	2,971	3,044	2,947
Imports of goods and services and income payments	−759,290	−1,080,124	−1,779,241	−1,651,538	−1,789,227	−2,114,441	−2,458,268	−2,846,159	−3,080,813	−3,182,368	−2,412,489
Imports of goods and services	−616,097	−890,771	−1,449,377	−1,397,994	−1,514,080	−1,767,921	−1,995,362	−2,212,023	−2,350,763	−2,537,814	−1,945,705
Goods, balance of payments basis [2]	−498,438	−749,374	−1,230,413	−1,171,613	−1,269,802	−1,485,501	−1,692,817	−1,875,324	−1,983,558	−2,139,548	−1,575,443
Services [3]	−117,659	−141,397	−218,964	−226,381	−244,278	−282,420	−302,546	−336,700	−367,206	−398,266	−370,262
Direct defense expenditures	−17,531	−10,043	−12,698	−17,417	−22,978	−26,110	−27,676	−27,330	−27,917	−28,311	−30,474
Travel	−37,349	−44,916	−64,705	−58,715	−57,447	−65,750	−68,970	−72,104	−76,331	−79,726	−73,230
Passenger fares	−10,531	−14,663	−24,274	−19,969	−20,989	−24,718	−26,149	−27,501	−28,437	−32,563	−25,980
Other transportation	−24,966	−27,034	−36,712	−34,686	−40,174	−47,752	−52,475	−53,466	−53,513	−53,702	−41,586
Royalties and license fees [5]	−3,135	−6,919	−16,468	−19,353	−19,033	−23,266	−24,512	−23,518	−24,931	−25,781	−25,230
Other private services [5]	−22,229	−35,199	−61,223	−73,321	−80,526	−91,046	−98,684	−128,760	−151,894	−173,686	−168,892
U.S. government miscellaneous services	−1,919	−2,623	−2,883	−2,920	−3,131	−3,778	−3,979	−4,021	−4,184	−4,497	−4,871
Income payments	−143,192	−189,353	−329,864	−253,544	−275,147	−346,519	−462,905	−634,136	−730,049	−644,554	−466,783
Income payments on foreign-owned assets in the United States	−139,728	−183,090	−322,345	−245,164	−266,635	−337,556	−453,615	−624,646	−719,983	−634,190	−456,027
Direct investment payments	−3,450	−30,318	−56,910	−43,244	−73,750	−99,754	−121,333	−150,770	−129,134	−115,538	−94,010
Other private payments	−95,508	−97,149	−180,918	−127,012	−119,051	−155,266	−228,408	−338,897	−426,501	−352,053	−218,020
U.S. government payments	−40,770	−55,623	−84,517	−74,908	−73,834	−82,536	−103,874	−134,979	−164,348	−166,599	−143,997
Compensation of employees	−3,464	−6,263	−7,519	−8,380	−8,512	−8,963	−9,290	−9,490	−10,066	−10,364	−10,757
Unilateral current transfers, net	−26,654	−38,074	−58,645	−64,948	−71,794	−88,362	−105,772	−91,481	−115,548	−122,026	−124,943
U.S. government grants [4]	−10,359	−11,190	−16,714	−17,097	−22,173	−23,823	−33,647	−27,733	−34,437	−36,003	−41,638
U.S. government pensions and other transfers	−3,224	−3,451	−4,705	−5,125	−5,341	−6,264	−6,303	−6,508	−7,323	−8,390	−8,874
Private remittances and other transfers [6]	−13,070	−23,433	−37,226	−42,726	−44,280	−58,275	−65,822	−57,240	−73,788	−77,633	−74,431

See footnotes at end of table.

U.S. Census Bureau, Statistical Abstract of the United States: 2011

Table 1285. U.S. International Transactions by Type of Transaction: 1990 to 2009—Con.

[In millions of dollars (706,975 represents $706,975,000,000). Minus sign (−) indicates debits]

Type of transaction[1]	1990	1995	2000	2002	2003	2004	2005	2006	2007	2008	2009
Capital account transactions, net	−7,220	−222	−1	−141	−1,821	3,049	13,116	−1,788	384	6,010	−140
U.S.-owned assets abroad, excl. financial derivatives(increase/financial outflow (−))	−81,234	−352,264	−560,523	−294,646	−325,424	−1,000,870	−546,631	−1,285,729	−1,475,719	156,077	−140,465
U.S. official reserve assets	−2,158	−9,742	−290	−3,681	1,523	2,805	14,096	2,374	−122	−4,848	−52,256
Special drawing rights	−192	−808	−722	−475	601	−398	4,511	−223	−154	−106	−48,230
Reserve position in the International Monetary Fund	731	−2,466	2,308	−2,632	1,494	3,826	10,200	3,331	1,021	−3,473	−3,357
Foreign currencies	−2,697	−6,468	−1,876	−574	−572	−623	−615	−734	−989	−1,269	−669
U.S. government assets, other than official reserve assets	2,317	−384	−941	345	537	1,710	5,539	5,346	−22,273	−529,615	541,342
U.S. credits and other long-term assets	−8,410	−4,359	−5,182	−5,251	−7,279	−3,044	−2,255	−2,992	−2,475	−2,202	−4,069
Repayments on U.S. credits and other long-term assets[7]	10,856	4,125	4,265	5,701	7,981	4,716	5,603	8,329	4,104	2,354	2,133
U.S. foreign currency holdings and U.S. short-term assets	−130	−250	−24	−105	−165	38	2,191	9	−23,902	−529,766	543,278
U.S. private assets	−81,393	−341,538	−559,292	−291,310	−327,484	−1,005,385	−566,266	−1,293,449	−1,453,324	690,540	−629,552
Direct investment	−37,183	−98,750	−159,212	−154,460	−149,564	−316,223	−36,235	−244,922	−413,993	−351,141	−268,680
Foreign securities	−28,765	−122,394	−127,908	−48,568	−146,722	−170,549	−251,199	−365,129	−366,512	197,897	−208,213
U.S. claims on unaffiliated foreigners reported by U.S. nonbanking concerns	−27,824	−45,286	−138,790	−50,022	−18,184	−152,566	−71,207	−181,299	−23,089	421,153	124,428
U.S. claims reported by U.S. banks and securities brokers	12,379	−75,108	−133,382	−38,260	−13,014	−366,047	−207,625	−502,099	−649,730	422,631	−277,087
Foreign-owned assets in the United States, excluding financial derivatives (increase/financial inflow (+))	139,357	435,102	1,038,224	795,161	858,303	1,533,201	1,247,347	2,065,169	2,107,655	454,722	305,736
Foreign official assets in the United States	33,910	109,880	42,753	115,945	278,069	397,755	259,268	487,939	481,043	550,770	450,030
U.S. government securities	30,243	72,712	35,710	90,971	224,874	314,941	213,334	428,401	269,897	591,381	441,056
Other U.S. government liabilities	1,868	−105	−1,825	137	−723	−134	−421	2,816	5,436	8,912	57,971
U.S. liabilities reported by U.S. banks and securities brokers	3,385	34,008	5,746	21,221	48,643	69,245	26,260	22,365	109,019	−153,423	−70,851
Other foreign official assets	−1,586	3,255	3,127	3,616	5,275	13,703	20,095	34,357	96,691	103,900	21,854
Other foreign assets in the United States	105,447	325,222	995,466	679,216	580,234	1,135,446	988,079	1,577,230	1,626,612	−96,048	−144,294
Direct investment	48,494	57,776	321,274	84,372	63,750	145,966	112,638	243,151	271,210	328,334	134,707
U.S. Treasury securities	−2,534	91,544	−69,983	100,403	91,455	93,608	132,300	−58,229	66,845	161,411	22,781
U.S. securities other than U.S. Treasury securities	1,592	77,249	459,889	283,299	220,705	381,493	450,386	683,245	605,414	−166,490	59
U.S. currency	16,586	8,840	−3,357	18,861	10,591	13,301	8,447	2,227	−10,675	29,187	12,632
U.S. liabilities to unaffiliated foreigners reported by U.S. nonbanking concerns	45,133	59,637	170,672	95,871	96,526	165,872	69,572	244,793	182,355	−36,522	−1,460
U.S. liabilities reported by U.S. banks and securities brokers	−3,824	30,176	116,971	96,410	97,207	335,206	214,736	462,043	511,463	−411,968	−313,013
Financial derivatives, net	(NA)	(NA)	(NA)	(NA)	(NA)	(NA)	(NA)	29,710	6,222	−32,947	50,804
Statistical discrepancy	28,066	30,951	−61,329	−42,300	−10,391	95,107	33,758	−4,727	79,552	84,991	162,497
Balance on goods	−111,037	−174,170	−446,233	−475,345	−541,544	−665,631	−783,801	−839,456	−823,192	−834,652	−506,944
Balance on services	30,173	77,786	67,453	54,821	47,361	56,286	69,625	80,216	121,093	135,850	132,036
Balance on goods and services	−80,864	−96,384	−378,780	−420,524	−494,183	−609,345	−714,176	−759,240	−702,099	−698,802	−374,908
Balance on income	28,550	20,851	21,054	27,398	45,309	67,219	72,358	48,085	99,553	151,974	121,419
Unilateral current transfers, net	−26,654	−38,074	−58,645	−64,948	−71,794	−88,362	−105,772	−91,481	−115,548	−122,026	−124,943
Balance on current account	−78,968	−113,567	−416,371	−458,074	−520,668	−630,488	−747,590	−802,636	−718,094	−668,854	−378,432

NA Not available. [1] Credits, +: Exports of goods and services and income receipts; unlateral current transfers to the United States; capital account transactions receipts; financial inflows—increase in foreign-owned assets (U.S. liabilities) or decrease in U.S.-owned assets (U.S. claims). Debits, −: Imports of goods and services and income payments; unilateral current transfers to foreigners; capital account transactions payments; financial outflows—decrease in foreign-owned assets (U.S. liabilities) or increase in U.S.-owned assets (U.S. claims). [2] See Table 2 footnotes for explanations of the various balance of payments adjustments made to convert goods on a Census-basis to goods on a balance of payments basis. The adjustments are made to improve coverage, eliminate duplication and align the goods data with national and international accounting guidelines. [3] Includes some goods: Mainly military equipment and supplies in lines 5 and 22 that are commingled in the source data and cannot be separately identified. Beginning with statistics for 1999, line 5 excludes equipment and supplies exported under the U.S. Foreign Military Sales program that can be separately identified, and line 22 excludes petroleum purchases abroad by U.S. military agencies that can be separately identified. [4] Includes transfers of goods and services under U.S. military grant programs. [5] Beginning in 1982, these lines are presented on a gross basis. The definition of exports is revised to exclude U.S. parents' payments to foreign affiliates and to include U.S. affiliates' receipts from foreign parents. The definition of imports is revised to include U.S. parents' payments to foreign affiliates and to exclude U.S. affiliates' receipts from foreign parents. [6] Beginning in 1982, the "other transfers" component includes taxes paid by U.S. private residents to foreign governments and taxes paid by private nonresidents to the U.S. Government. [7] Includes sales of foreign obligations to foreigners.

Source: U.S. Bureau of Economic Analysis, *Survey of Current Business*, July 2010. See also <http://www.bea.gov/scb/index.htm>.

Figure 28.1
U.S. International Trade in Goods and Services: 2005 to 2009

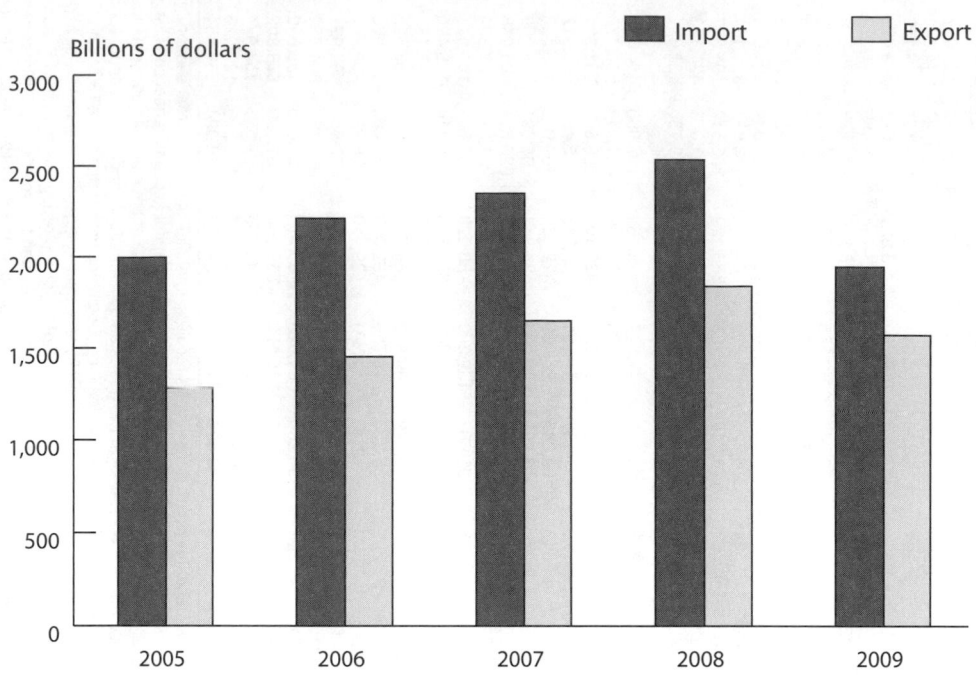

Source: Chart prepared by U.S. Census Bureau. For data, see Table 1299.

Figure 28.2
Top U.S. Trading Partners—Imports, Exports: 2009

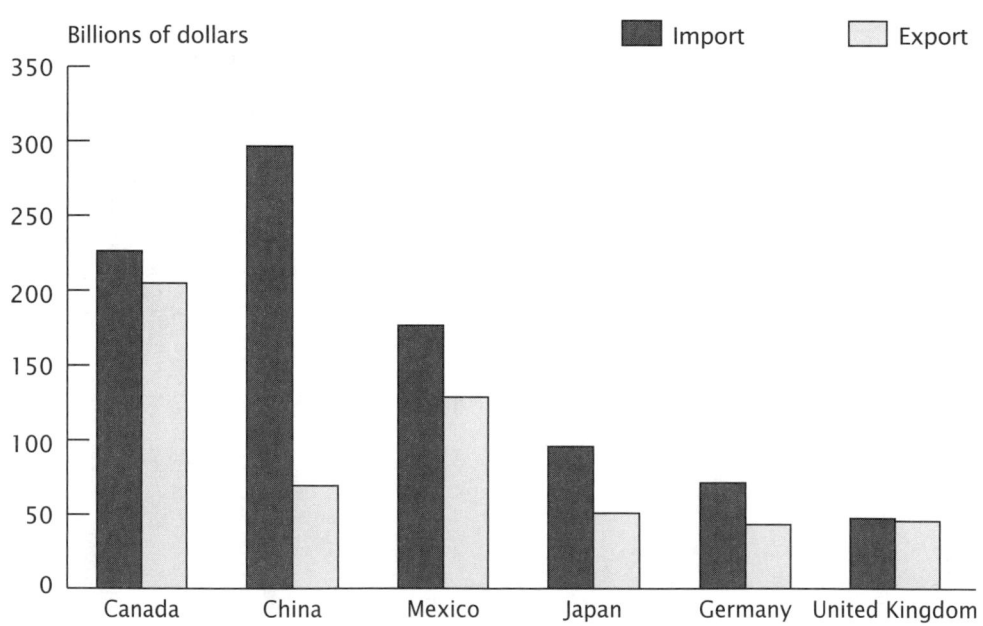

U.S. Census Bureau, Statistical Abstract of the United States: 2011

Table 1286. U.S. Balances on International Transactions by Area and Selected Country: 2008 and 2009

[In millions of dollars (–834,652 represents –$834,652,000,000). Minus sign (–) indicates debits]

Area or Country	2008, balance on— Goods [1]	Services	Income	Current account	2009, balance on— Goods [1]	Services	Income	Current account
All areas	**–834,652**	**135,850**	**151,974**	**–668,854**	**–506,944**	**132,036**	**121,419**	**–378,432**
Europe	–118,324	51,819	69,573	–5,302	–70,976	40,992	56,890	13,956
European Union	–98,473	44,968	66,583	8,073	–59,869	38,622	48,774	22,921
Euro Area [2]	–79,924	20,517	65,659	197	–50,181	22,021	59,615	26,457
Germany	–43,591	–6,089	9,229	–40,520	–28,096	–6,464	–3,041	–38,169
Italy	–20,910	1,437	4,225	–15,598	–14,286	590	4,630	–9,477
Netherlands	18,077	6,200	39,077	63,520	16,084	4,547	40,629	60,526
United Kingdom	–5,669	16,330	–1,495	10,872	–1,403	12,251	–9,543	2,632
Canada	–80,383	19,555	33,981	–28,596	–22,447	19,659	19,805	14,541
Latin America, other Western Hemisphere	–92,185	17,789	43,987	–63,874	–48,250	15,252	50,971	–9,077
Mexico	–68,341	8,352	–127	–73,946	–49,528	8,165	–847	–55,141
Venezuela	–38,926	4,141	1,335	–33,567	–18,811	4,209	2,927	–11,700
Asia and Pacific	–399,299	38,075	–40,239	–426,072	–311,648	47,007	–42,021	–335,175
Australia	11,572	5,861	10,253	27,049	11,512	6,569	8,361	26,019
China [3]	–267,831	5,580	–42,651	–307,736	–226,788	7,431	–41,551	–263,639
Hong Kong	15,627	–2,538	2,500	15,468	17,878	–902	1,908	18,710
India	–7,992	–2,268	1,699	–11,374	–4,793	–2,415	1,646	–8,536
Japan [4]	–75,439	16,642	–32,127	–91,478	–44,978	18,474	–23,393	–50,604
Korea, South	–12,561	4,326	828	–8,141	–10,185	4,321	1,213	–5,526
Singapore	11,513	5,396	13,318	30,167	6,235	5,546	6,247	17,974
Taiwan [3]	–10,689	–81	–2,976	–14,200	–9,301	1,566	–4,463	–12,667
Middle East	–59,224	2,930	–2,129	–71,581	–15,701	2,949	–3,172	–27,347
Africa	–85,238	3,783	7,117	–83,994	–37,922	3,545	5,325	–41,803
International and unallocated	(X)	1,899	39,685	10,564	(X)	2,633	33,622	6,473

X Not applicable. [1] Adjusted to balance of payments basis; excludes exports under U.S. military sales contracts and imports under direct defense expenditures. [2] See footnote 3, table 1353. [3] See footnote 4, Table 1331. [4] Includes Ryukyu Islands.

Source: U.S. Bureau of Economic Analysis, *Survey of Current Business*, July 2010. See also <http://www.bea.gov/scb/index.htm>.

Table 1287. Private International Service Transactions by Selected Type of Service and Selected Country: 2000 to 2009

[In millions of dollars (279,542 represents $279,542,000,000). For all transactions, see Table 1285]

Type of Service and country	Exports 2000	2005	2008	2009	Imports 2000	2005	2008	2009
Private services, total	279,542	358,919	517,946	483,869	203,383	270,891	365,459	334,917
TYPE OF SERVICE								
Travel	82,400	81,799	109,976	93,917	64,705	68,970	79,726	73,230
Passenger fares	20,687	20,970	31,404	26,424	24,274	26,149	32,563	25,980
Other transportation	25,318	31,704	43,714	35,406	36,712	52,475	53,702	41,586
Freight	12,547	15,952	22,153	17,247	27,388	43,559	42,046	29,341
Port services	12,771	15,752	21,561	18,159	9,324	8,916	11,656	12,245
Royalties and license fees	43,233	64,395	93,920	89,791	16,468	24,612	25,781	25,230
Other private services	107,904	160,051	238,932	238,332	61,223	98,684	173,686	168,892
By type: [1]								
Education	10,348	14,021	17,938	19,911	2,032	3,992	5,173	5,583
Financial services	(NA)	(NA)	60,798	55,446	(NA)	(NA)	20,154	16,454
Insurance services	3,631	7,566	13,538	14,651	11,284	28,710	56,107	55,233
AREA AND COUNTRY								
Europe	106,139	150,246	225,449	199,191	88,534	119,359	161,665	145,254
European Union	92,981	130,946	195,282	171,828	76,672	102,578	138,943	121,373
Euro Area	56,003	75,994	118,443	106,280	44,892	59,288	87,607	73,165
Belgium	2,590	3,185	4,255	3,839	1,997	2,105	3,266	3,304
Luxembourg	683	1,567	3,012	2,319	287	501	910	860
France	10,461	12,617	17,950	16,252	10,467	11,861	15,431	13,425
Germany	15,584	20,427	27,618	24,271	12,211	18,441	26,131	22,661
Italy	5,399	7,025	10,026	8,479	5,048	5,947	7,346	6,512
Netherlands	6,974	8,462	14,669	11,833	5,541	7,404	8,404	7,244
United Kingdom	31,660	44,682	61,093	51,042	27,856	34,201	43,814	38,101
Canada	24,443	32,409	44,657	42,005	17,835	21,895	24,799	22,020
Latin America, other Western Hemisphere	53,968	60,643	93,843	88,312	37,521	50,676	75,909	72,975
Mexico	14,243	20,149	23,737	21,827	10,757	13,999	15,237	13,517
Asia and Pacific	77,315	95,648	125,628	125,437	49,545	64,879	88,119	78,948
Australia	5,524	7,522	11,878	12,227	3,406	4,548	5,944	5,676
China [2]	5,009	8,394	15,046	15,661	3,166	6,154	9,445	8,204
India	2,532	5,068	10,153	9,940	1,882	4,958	12,462	12,377
Japan	32,809	40,492	41,858	40,869	16,361	20,379	23,733	20,773
Korea, South	6,921	9,563	12,874	12,618	4,584	5,865	7,253	6,441
Taiwan [2]	4,608	5,791	6,184	6,488	4,152	6,409	6,533	5,139
Middle East	6,719	8,837	15,597	15,769	3,310	5,117	7,893	8,625
Africa	4,896	6,098	9,840	10,372	2,690	3,888	5,925	6,831
South Africa	1,391	1,410	2,045	2,242	798	915	1,432	1,490
International organizations and unallocated	6,062	5,037	2,933	2,782	3,948	5,076	1,152	266

NA not available. [1] Royalties and license fees and "other private services" by detailed type of service include both affiliated and unaffiliated transactions. Additional historical estimates for royalties and license fees and "other private services" by detailed type that include only unaffiliated transactions are available in table 3b. [2] See footnote 4, Table 1331.

Source: U.S. Bureau of Economic Analysis, *Survey of Current Business*. See also <http://www.bea.gov/scb/index.htm>.

Table 1288. International Investment Position by Type of Investment: 2000 to 2009

[In billions of dollars (-1,337 represents -$1,337,000,000,000). Estimates for end of year; subject to considerable error due to nature of basic data. Unless otherwise specified, types below refer to current-cost method. For information on current-cost method and market value, see article cited in source]

Type of investment	2000	2004	2005	2006	2007	2008	2009, prel.
Net international investment position of the United States..	**−1,337**	**−2,253**	**−1,932**	**−2,192**	**−1,916**	**−3,494**	**−2,738**
Financial derivatives, net [1]	(X)	(X)	58	60	71	160	128
Net international investment position, excluding financial derivatives	−1,337	−2,253	−1,990	−2,251	−1,987	−3,654	−2,866
U.S.-owned assets abroad	**6,239**	**9,341**	**11,962**	**14,428**	**18,340**	**19,245**	**18,379**
Financial derivatives (gross positive fair value) [1]	(X)	(X)	1,190	1,239	2,559	6,127	3,512
U.S.-owned assets abroad, excluding financial derivatives...	6,239	9,341	10,772	13,189	15,781	13,117	14,867
U.S. official reserve assets	128	190	188	220	277	294	404
Gold [2]	72	114	134	165	218	227	284
Special drawing rights	11	14	8	9	9	9	58
Reserve position in the International Monetary Fund	15	20	8	5	4	8	11
Foreign currencies	31	42	38	41	45	49	50
U.S. government assets, other than official reserve assets...	85	83	78	72	94	624	83
U.S. credits and other long-term assets [3]	83	80	77	72	70	70	72
U.S. foreign currency holdings and U.S. short-term assets [4].	3	3	1	1	24	554	11
U.S. private assets	6,025	9,068	10,506	12,897	15,409	12,200	14,380
Direct investment at current cost	1,532	2,498	2,652	2,948	3,553	3,743	4,051
Foreign securities	2,426	3,545	4,329	5,604	6,835	3,986	5,471
Bonds	573	985	1,012	1,276	1,587	1,237	1,494
Corporate stocks	1,853	2,560	3,318	4,329	5,248	2,748	3,977
U.S. claims on unaffiliated foreigners reported by U.S. nonbanking concerns	837	794	1,018	1,184	1,174	795	794
U.S. claims reported by U.S. banks and securities brokers, not included elsewhere	1,232	2,231	2,507	3,160	3,847	3,676	4,064
Foreign-owned assets in the United States	**7,576**	**11,594**	**13,894**	**16,620**	**20,256**	**22,739**	**21,117**
Financial derivatives (gross negative fair value) [1]	(X)	(X)	1,132	1,179	2,488	5,968	3,384
Foreign-owned assets in the Unites States, excluding financial derivatives	7,576	11,594	12,762	15,441	17,768	16,771	17,733
Foreign official assets in the United States	1,037	2,020	2,313	2,833	3,412	3,940	4,374
U.S. government securities	756	1,510	1,725	2,167	2,540	3,264	3,592
U.S. Treasury securities	640	1,252	1,341	1,558	1,737	2,401	2,871
Other	116	258	385	609	803	864	721
Other U.S. government liabilities	26	24	23	26	32	41	99
U.S. liabilities reported by U.S. banks and securities brokers, not included elsewhere	153	270	297	297	406	253	187
Other foreign official assets	102	215	269	343	434	383	495
Other foreign assets	6,539	9,574	10,448	12,608	14,356	12,831	13,359
Direct investment at current cost	1,421	1,743	1,906	2,154	2,411	2,521	2,673
U.S. Treasury securities	382	562	644	568	640	851	826
U.S. securities other than U.S. Treasury securities	2,623	3,996	4,353	5,372	6,190	4,621	5,287
Corporate and other bonds	1,069	2,035	2,243	2,825	3,289	2,771	2,841
Corporate stocks	1,554	1,960	2,110	2,547	2,901	1,850	2,446
U.S. currency	205	272	280	283	272	301	314
U.S. liabilities to unaffiliated foreigners reported by U.S. nonbanking concerns	739	600	658	799	865	732	665
U.S. liabilities reported by U.S. banks and securities brokers, not included elsewhere	1,169	2,402	2,607	3,431	3,979	3,805	3,594
Memoranda:							
Direct investment abroad at market value	2,694	3,363	3,638	4,470	5,275	3,104	4,303
Direct investment in the United States at market value	2,783	2,717	2,818	3,293	3,597	2,553	3,121

X Not applicable. [1] A break in series in 2005 reflects the introduction of U.S. Department of the Treasury data on financial derivatives. [2] U.S. official gold stock is valued at market price. [3] Also includes paid-in capital subscriptions to international financial institutions and resources provided to foreigners under foreign assistance programs requiring repayment over several years. Excludes World War I debts that are not being serviced. [4] Beginning in 2007, includes foreign-currency-denominated assets obtained through temporary reciprocal currency arrangements between the Federal Reserve System and foreign central banks.

Source: U.S. Bureau of Economic Analysis, *Survey of Current Business*, July 2010. See also <http://www.bea.gov/scb.index.htm>.

Table 1289. U.S. Reserve Assets: 1990 to 2009

[In billions of dollars (83.3 represents $83,300,000,000). As of end of year, except as indicated]

Type	1990	2000	2003	2004	2005	2006	2007	2008	2009
Total	**83.3**	**67.6**	**85.9**	**86.8**	**65.1**	**65.9**	**70.6**	**77.6**	**130.8**
Gold stock	11.1	11.0	11.0	11.0	11.0	11.0	11.0	11.0	11.0
Special drawing rights	11.0	10.5	12.6	13.6	8.2	8.9	9.5	9.3	57.8
Foreign currencies	52.2	31.2	39.7	42.7	37.8	40.9	45.8	49.6	50.5
Reserve position in IMF [1]	9.1	14.8	22.5	19.5	8.0	5.0	4.2	7.7	11.4

[1] International Monetary Fund.

Source: U.S. Department of the Treasury, *Treasury Bulletin*, quarterly. See also <http://www.fms.treas.gov/bulletin/index.html>.

Table 1290. Foreign Direct Investment Position in the United States on a Historical-Cost Basis by Selected Country, 2000 to 2009, and by Industry, 2009

[In millions of dollars (1,256,867 represents $1,256,867,000,000). Foreign direct investment is defined as the ownership or control, directly or indirectly, by one foreign entity (as used here, "entity" is synonymous with "person" as the term is used in a broad legal sense including any individual, branch, partnership, association, trust, corporation, or government) of 10 percent or more of the voting interest of a U.S. business enterprise. Data are based on surveys of U.S. affiliates of foreign companies]

Country	2000	2005	2007	2008	2009			
					Total [1]	Manufacturing	Wholesale trade	Finance [2] and insurance
All countries	**1,256,867**	**1,634,121**	**2,055,176**	**2,165,748**	**2,319,585**	**790,568**	**328,430**	**293,204**
Canada	114,309	165,667	205,381	194,140	225,836	60,924	3,861	54,792
Europe [3]	887,014	1,154,048	1,478,383	1,555,208	1,685,279	609,358	171,114	243,460
Austria	3,007	2,425	2,696	2,947	2,868	1,386	701	-1
Belgium	14,787	10,024	24,479	23,066	38,541	19,211	6,810	1,449
Denmark	4,025	6,117	4,796	4,883	5,246	3,572	1,046	(Z)
Finland	8,875	5,938	4,729	7,341	7,628	4,343	2,258	-1
France	125,740	114,260	153,713	157,172	189,285	81,835	12,054	32,391
Germany	122,412	177,176	213,159	201,424	218,153	79,286	13,317	41,130
Ireland	25,523	17,465	26,943	26,146	32,610	18,593	-148	10,099
Italy	6,576	7,725	12,722	18,685	9,693	1,063	2,000	(D)
Luxembourg	58,930	79,680	120,945	118,283	127,768	50,394	3,387	8,075
Netherlands	138,894	156,602	189,469	199,137	237,959	82,822	27,116	50,627
Norway	2,665	9,810	7,644	8,873	7,260	-295	3,067	(Z)
Spain	5,068	7,472	27,705	39,142	43,901	4,102	89	3,215
Sweden	21,991	22,269	43,171	35,843	38,929	28,872	7,287	264
Switzerland	64,719	133,387	151,513	164,534	189,371	97,400	9,331	39,447
United Kingdom	277,613	371,350	424,046	454,328	453,875	106,217	82,053	53,156
Latin America and other Western Hemisphere [3]	53,691	57,175	49,828	46,130	27,864	9,548	13,912	-32,855
South and Central America [3]	13,384	22,507	15,390	16,539	17,733	3,049	6,436	210
Brazil	882	2,051	1,753	-294	-647	-2,820	(D)	(D)
Mexico	7,462	3,595	7,688	9,444	11,361	5,408	718	47
Panama	3,819	10,983	932	822	1,045	245	-90	194
Venezuela	792	5,292	4,181	4,567	4,850	44	(D)	3
Other Western Hemisphere [3]	40,307	34,668	34,438	29,591	10,131	6,499	7,476	-33,065
Bermuda	18,336	2,147	-2,676	4,116	-13,181	1,501	234	-24,053
Netherlands Antilles	3,807	5,531	5,428	5,752	7,354	96	(D)	-3
U.K. Islands, Caribbean	15,191	23,063	34,588	24,401	17,529	4,544	(D)	(D)
Other	1,719	3,277	-3,503	-4,745	-2,037	277	244	(D)
Africa	2,700	2,341	1,535	2,309	1,689	89	437	4
Middle East [3]	6,506	8,306	14,896	17,242	17,614	4,193	6,086	415
Israel	3,012	4,231	6,294	7,284	7,306	4,120	417	(D)
Saudi Arabia	(D)	(D)	(D)	(D)	(D)	8	(D)	2
Asia and Pacific [3]	192,647	246,585	305,154	350,718	361,303	106,456	133,021	27,389
Australia	18,775	36,392	37,514	40,626	45,663	6,958	211	2,961
Hong Kong	1,493	3,467	3,727	3,966	3,836	1,630	1,462	5
India	96	1,497	2,735	3,886	4,366	275	-49	(Z)
Japan	159,690	189,851	229,408	259,753	264,208	76,636	118,216	22,383
Korea, South	3,110	6,077	12,870	12,132	12,020	1,796	9,685	(D)
Singapore	5,087	3,338	11,716	23,074	22,893	(D)	200	(D)
Taiwan [4]	3,174	3,731	4,306	3,917	4,211	1,453	1,493	(D)

D Suppressed to avoid disclosure of data of individual companies. Z Less than $500,000. [1] Includes other industries not shown separately. [2] Excludes depository institutions [3] Includes other countries, not shown separately. [4] See footnote 4, Table 1331.

Source: U.S. Bureau of Economic Analysis, *Survey of Current Business,* July 2009, and previous issues. For most recent copy and previous issues, see <http://www.bea.gov/scb/index.htm>.

Table 1291. U.S. Majority-Owned Affiliates of Foreign Companies—Selected Financial and Operating Data by Industry of Affiliate: 2007

[In millions of dollars, except as indicated (12,012,130 represents $12,012,130,000,000). Preliminary. A majority-owned U.S. affiliate is a U.S. business enterprise in which a foreign entity (as used here, "entity" is synonymous with "person" as the term is used in a broad legal sense including any individual, branch, partnership, association, trust, corporation, or government) has a direct or indirect voting interest greater than 50 percent]

Industry	2002 NAICS Code	Total assets	Sales	Employment (1,000)	Employee compensation	Gross property, plant, and equipment	Merchandise exports	Merchandise imports
All industries	**(X)**	**12,012,130**	**3,277,167**	**5,519.5**	**403,606**	**1,283,009**	**215,554**	**533,430**
Manufacturing [1]	31–33	1,343,458	1,195,807	1,998.2	159,595	508,523	125,703	200,759
Petroleum and coal products	324	100,636	182,720	38.6	5,486	57,613	(D)	49,991
Chemicals	325	354,097	266,946	304.6	36,007	121,805	30,209	32,605
Computers and electronic products	334	82,071	56,362	134.6	10,227	22,502	13,476	14,310
Transportation equipment	336	245,112	247,001	408.3	29,112	84,720	34,228	59,134
Wholesale trade	42	613,345	895,917	620.3	51,019	258,978	80,214	316,993
Retail trade	44–45	69,024	144,431	534.5	18,255	43,620	673	6,300
Information	51	234,301	90,292	238.1	22,138	50,268	893	415
Finance and insurance	52, exc.	8,834,038	561,864	378.5	63,154	64,332	(D)	(D)
Real estate and rental and leasing	53	128,015	30,459	31.0	1,875	99,126	17	(D)
Professional, scientific, and technical services	54	111,933	71,646	234.1	21,672	14,121	532	491
Other industries	(X)	678,015	286,751	1,484.8	65,898	244,041	(D)	8,246

X Not applicable. D Suppressed to avoid disclosure of data of individual companies. [1] Includes industries not shown separately.

Source: U.S. Bureau of Economic Analysis, *Survey of Current Business,* November 2009, and *Foreign Direct Investment in the United States: Operations of U.S. Affiliates of Foreign Companies, Preliminary 2007 Estimates.* For more information: <http://www.bea.gov/international/di1fdiop.htm>.

Foreign Commerce and Aid 797

Table 1292. Foreign Direct Investment in the United States—Property, Plant, and Equipment and Employment of Majority-Owned U.S. Affiliates of Foreign Companies by State: 2002 and 2007

[Gross book value of property, plant, and equipment in millions of dollars (1,035,916 represents $1,035,916,000,000); employment in thousands (5,570.4 represents 5,570,400). A U.S. majority-owned affiliate is a U.S. business enterprise in which a foreign entity (as used here, "entity" is synonymous with "person" as the term is used in a broad legal sense including any individual, branch, partnership, association, trust, corporation, or government) has a direct or indirect voting interest greater than 50 percent.]

State and other area	Gross book value of property, plant, and equipment (mil. dol.)		Employment		
				2007	
	2002	2007	2002 (1,000)	Total (1,000)	Percentage of total employment in the state or area [1]
Total..................	1,035,916	1,283,009	5,570.4	5,519.5	4.7
Alabama	15,520	21,965	75.1	80.5	4.8
Alaska	30,052	34,336	12.6	11.7	4.8
Arizona	(D)	13,119	57.6	72.3	3.1
Arkansas..................	4,872	5,041	35.7	34.5	3.4
California..................	89,193	110,214	635.3	605.6	4.6
Colorado	13,026	(D)	77.7	81.2	4.0
Connecticut	(D)	13,615	(D)	99.0	6.6
Delaware	6,252	4,337	23.6	27.8	7.3
District of Columbia	5,135	5,489	17.5	16.0	3.3
Florida....................	28,993	33,647	258.3	245.8	3.4
Georgia	(D)	(D)	191.4	177.0	5.0
Hawaii	(D)	6,167	(D)	30.8	5.9
Idaho	2,131	2,035	12.5	13.7	2.4
Illinois....................	41,862	49,207	281.5	268.1	5.1
Indiana....................	27,991	(D)	133.3	144.1	5.5
Iowa......................	5,776	8,406	36.6	43.5	3.3
Kansas....................	5,238	8,011	34.9	52.8	4.6
Kentucky	24,091	28,272	88.4	90.0	5.7
Louisiana..................	26,993	30,701	50.5	52.4	3.3
Maine.....................	5,511	6,252	31.7	27.7	5.3
Maryland	(D)	13,538	(D)	106.1	4.9
Massachusetts..............	(D)	26,272	(D)	178.4	6.0
Michigan	(D)	22,681	(D)	150.4	4.1
Minnesota	9,805	16,276	88.1	94.3	3.9
Mississippi.................	5,097	10,962	25.8	24.5	2.6
Missouri...................	14,484	(D)	91.5	81.2	3.4
Montana...................	1,824	3,194	5.9	7.7	2.1
Nebraska..................	1,840	(D)	18.7	23.7	2.9
Nevada	(D)	9,681	25.9	34.3	2.9
New Hampshire..............	(D)	5,131	(D)	37.5	6.6
New Jersey	30,956	38,811	230.1	225.3	6.5
New Mexico................	(D)	4,054	13.0	16.1	2.4
New York	68,310	82,623	440.8	433.6	5.8
North Carolina..............	(D)	29,553	(D)	211.7	6.0
North Dakota...............	1,100	1,461	7.4	7.8	2.7
Ohio......................	32,124	42,938	214.2	229.5	4.8
Oklahoma	7,434	10,142	33.9	32.6	2.6
Oregon....................	(D)	10,142	51.3	44.3	2.9
Pennsylvania	(D)	37,822	(D)	261.5	5.0
Rhode Island...............	(D)	5,350	(D)	25.5	5.9
South Carolina..............	21,573	(D)	133.1	112.8	6.9
South Dakota...............	685	1,184	7.6	6.4	1.9
Tennessee.................	16,795	22,467	130.7	139.0	5.7
Texas.....................	88,116	119,255	353.0	418.5	4.7
Utah......................	10,612	6,413	32.3	36.6	3.4
Vermont...................	1,286	1,456	11.1	9.8	3.7
Virginia....................	(D)	(D)	142.2	157.0	5.0
Washington	(D)	22,400	84.7	90.1	3.6
West Virginia	7,388	6,605	22.7	21.1	3.5
Wisconsin	16,103	14,520	107.1	81.8	3.3
Wyoming	10,551	11,497	8.5	10.5	4.6
Puerto Rico	2,583	2,974	19.8	21.9	(NA)
Other U.S. areas	(D)	73,480	10.2	13.1	(NA)
Foreign	2,328	2,394	0.3	0.2	(NA)
Unspecified [2]	66,341	92,253	(NA)	(NA)	(NA)

D Suppressed to avoid the disclosure of data of individual companies. NA Not available. [1] The data on total employment in the state or area that is used to calculate the shares shown in this table are equal to employment in private industries less employment of private households. For consistency with the coverage of the private-industry employment data, U.S.-affiliate employment in Puerto Rico, in "other U.S. areas," and in "foreign" was excluded from the U.S.-affiliate employment total when the percentage shares were computed. 1. The data on total employment in the state or area that is used to calculate the shares shown in this table are equal to employment in private industries less employment of private households. For consistency with the coverage of the private-industry employment data, U.S.-affiliate employment in Puerto Rico, in "other U.S. areas," and in "foreign" was excluded from the U.S.-affiliate employment total when the percentage shares were computed. [2] Covers property, plant, and equipment not located in a particular state, including aircraft, railroad rolling stock, satellites, undersea cable, and trucks engaged in interstate transportation.

Source: U.S. Bureau of Economic Analysis, *Survey of Current Business*, November 2009, and *Foreign Direct Investment in the United States: Operations of U.S. Affiliates of Foreign Companies, Preliminary 2007 Estimates.* See also <http://www.bea.gov/international/di1fdiop.htm>.

Table 1293. U.S. Businesses Acquired or Established by Foreign Direct Investors—Investment Outlays by Industry of U.S. Business Enterprise and Country of Ultimate Beneficial Owner: 2000 to 2008

[In millions of dollars (335,629 represents $335,629,000,000). Foreign direct investment is the ownership or control directly or indirectly, by one foreign individual branch, partnership, association, trust, corporation, or government of 10 percent or more of the voting securities of a U.S. business enterprise or an equivalent interest in an unincorporated one. Data represent number and full cost of acquisitions of existing U.S. business enterprises, including business segments or operating units of existing U.S. business enterprises and establishments of new enterprises. Investments may be made by the foreign direct investor itself, or indirectly by an existing U.S. affiliate of the foreign direct investor. Covers investments in U.S. business enterprises with assets of over $1 million, or ownership of 200 acres of U.S. land]

Industry and country	2000	2003	2004	2005	2006	2007	2008, prel.
Total [1]	335,629	63,591	86,219	91,390	165,603	251,917	260,362
By type of investment:							
U.S. businesses acquired	322,703	50,212	72,738	73,997	148,604	223,616	242,799
U.S. businesses established	12,926	13,379	13,481	17,393	16,999	28,301	17,564
By type of investor:							
Foreign direct investors	105,151	27,866	34,184	40,304	44,129	88,337	47,078
U.S. affiliates	230,478	35,725	52,035	51,086	121,474	163,580	213,284
INDUSTRY [2]							
Manufacturing	143,285	10,750	18,251	34,036	56,330	118,370	141,079
Wholesale trade	8,561	1,086	(D)	3,489	8,273	5,631	3,977
Retail trade	1,672	941	3,073	1,262	1,295	6,867	2,775
Information	67,932	9,236	4,315	8,487	10,341	8,585	22,214
Depository institutions	2,636	4,864	(D)	7,973	7,547	12,307	15,996
Finance (except depository institutions) and insurance	44,420	23,511	26,234	5,529	33,776	27,497	29,584
Real estate and rental and leasing	4,526	2,817	6,335	8,756	12,441	17,852	3,796
Professional, scientific, and technical services	32,332	1,955	(D)	6,407	8,923	9,018	15,167
Other industries	30,264	8,429	10,121	15,453	26,677	45,790	25,775
COUNTRY [3]							
Canada	28,346	9,157	31,502	13,640	12,121	38,502	25,181
Europe [1]	249,167	39,024	43,815	56,416	106,732	132,454	157,853
France	26,149	2,955	6,415	5,608	18,140	14,307	16,565
Germany	18,452	8,830	4,788	7,239	20,514	15,831	12,823
Netherlands	47,686	1,077	461	2,609	4,769	8,357	12,545
Switzerland	22,789	649	6,505	2,332	12,401	6,501	9,041
United Kingdom	110,208	20,373	23,288	30,420	26,261	56,051	19,657
Latin America and other Western Hemisphere	15,400	1,607	2,629	5,042	(D)	(D)	18,259
South and Central America	5,334	182	1,382	980	2,273	(D)	3,551
Other Western Hemisphere	10,066	1,425	1,247	4,062	(D)	1,933	14,708
Africa	(D)	(D)	(D)	(D)	(D)	(D)	129
Middle East	947	1,738	1,010	5,061	11,766	21,002	12,263
Asia and Pacific [1]	40,282	11,469	6,015	10,924	15,759	34,408	44,863
Australia	(D)	9,032	3,850	4,713	5,650	12,983	10,522
Japan	26,044	1,544	1,027	4,245	8,350	7,928	28,041

D Suppressed to avoid disclosure of data of individual companies. NA Not available. [1] Includes other countries, not shown separately. [2] Based on 1997 North American Industry Classification System (NAICS). Beginning 2002, based on NAICS 2002; see text, Section 15. [3] For investments in which more than one investor participated, each investor and each investor's outlays are classified by country of each ultimate beneficial owner.

Source: U.S. Bureau of Economic Analysis, *Survey of Current Business*, June 2009. See also <http://www.bea.gov/bea/index.htm>.

Table 1294. U.S. Direct Investment Position Abroad, Capital Outflows, and Income by Industry of Foreign Affiliates: 2000 to 2009

[In millions of dollars (1,316,247 represents $1,316,247,000,000). See headnote, Table 1295]

Industry	Direct investment position on a historical-cost basis			Capitol outflows [inflows(−)]			Income [1]		
	2000	2008	2009	2000	2008	2009	2000	2008	2009
All industries, total [2]	1,316,247	3,219,725	3,508,142	142,627	330,491	248,074	133,692	382,575	325,467
Mining	72,111	153,442	171,106	2,174	27,293	22,259	13,164	40,940	27,542
Manufacturing [2]	343,899	484,596	541,080	43,002	33,955	47,707	42,230	60,895	44,624
Food	23,497	41,201	45,247	2,014	3,939	3,429	2,681	3,506	2,654
Chemicals	75,807	114,171	129,529	3,812	16,571	15,759	(D)	15,520	14,207
Primary and fabricated metals	21,644	20,078	23,186	1,233	2,445	611	1,536	1,788	735
Machinery	22,229	39,093	43,612	2,659	7,451	3,627	2,257	5,983	3,766
Computer and electronic products	59,909	65,530	65,598	17,303	4,687	182	8,860	10,213	6,416
Electrical equipment, appliances, and components	10,005	23,582	24,694	2,100	4,633	1,316	1,079	2,202	1,718
Transportation equipment	49,887	45,456	47,235	7,814	−11,614	804	4,107	1,420	−1,721
Wholesale trade	93,936	176,869	198,985	11,938	33,171	21,296	14,198	29,564	24,154
Information	52,345	135,037	149,826	16,531	13,635	11,700	−964	13,806	14,404
Depository institutions	40,152	70,205	91,768	−1,274	−3,395	17,755	2,191	−509	420
Finance and insurance	217,086	688,160	746,993	21,659	55,672	42,063	15,210	42,915	38,774
Professional, scientific, and technical services	32,868	74,691	77,474	5,441	10,253	6,545	3,548	6,732	6,743
Holding companies (nonbank)	(NA)	1,181,323	1,279,952	(NA)	133,959	99,246	(NA)	166,076	152,471

D Withheld to avoid disclosure of individual company data. NA Not available. [1] See footnote 2, Table 1293. [2] Prior to 2006, income is shown net of withholding taxes. For 2006, income is shown gross of withholding taxes. [3] Includes other industries, not shown separately.

Source: U.S. Bureau of Economic Analysis, *Survey of Current Business*, September 2009. For most recent copy and historical issues, see <http://www.bea.gov/scb/index.htm>.

Table 1295. U.S. Direct Investment Position Abroad on a Historical-Cost Basis by Selected Country: 2000 to 2009

[In millions of dollars (1,316,247 represents $1,316,247,000,000). U.S. investment abroad is the ownership or control by one U.S. person of 10 percent or more of the voting securities of an incorporated foreign business enterprise or an equivalent interest in an unincorporated foreign business enterprise. Negative position can occur when a U.S. parent company's liabilities to the foreign affiliate are greater than its equity in and loans to the foreign affiliate]

Country	2000	2003	2004	2005	2006	2007	2008	2009
All countries	**1,316,247**	**1,769,613**	**2,160,844**	**2,241,656**	**2,477,268**	**2,993,980**	**3,219,725**	**3,508,142**
Canada	132,472	187,953	214,931	231,836	205,134	250,642	239,170	259,792
Europe [1]	687,320	976,889	1,180,130	1,210,679	1,397,704	1,682,023	1,831,246	1,976,222
Austria	2,872	6,366	9,264	11,236	14,897	14,646	15,926	18,203
Belgium	17,973	27,415	41,840	49,306	51,862	62,491	65,028	69,773
Czech Republic	1,228	1,668	2,444	2,729	3,615	4,066	5,548	5,871
Denmark	5,270	5,597	6,815	6,914	5,849	8,950	10,278	9,318
Finland	1,342	1,677	2,208	1,950	2,107	2,202	2,072	2,094
France	42,628	51,229	63,359	60,526	63,008	74,179	81,753	85,801
Germany	55,508	72,262	79,467	100,473	93,620	100,601	108,217	116,832
Greece	795	1,431	1,899	1,884	1,804	2,179	2,139	2,028
Hungary	1,920	2,856	3,024	2,795	2,602	6,457	7,724	9,287
Ireland	35,903	60,604	72,907	55,173	86,372	117,708	146,672	165,924
Italy	23,484	23,092	25,184	24,528	25,435	28,216	28,679	31,470
Luxembourg	27,849	68,298	83,634	79,937	125,146	144,180	152,825	174,092
Netherlands	115,429	186,366	219,384	240,205	279,373	412,122	426,762	471,567
Norway	4,379	7,511	8,491	8,533	9,667	12,188	24,389	26,984
Poland	3,884	4,382	7,256	5,575	6,934	15,614	13,021	13,957
Portugal	2,664	2,402	1,915	2,138	2,832	2,991	2,969	2,461
Russia	1,147	2,511	6,088	9,363	11,371	15,029	20,628	21,328
Spain	21,236	41,119	48,409	50,197	49,356	61,093	50,809	50,644
Sweden	25,959	27,004	29,730	30,153	33,857	36,615	38,003	27,418
Switzerland	55,377	92,750	121,790	100,692	102,022	94,675	132,126	148,239
Turkey	1,826	2,213	2,682	2,563	3,141	5,584	5,721	6,268
United Kingdom	230,762	277,246	330,416	351,513	406,358	426,357	449,521	471,384
Latin America and other								
Western Hemisphere	266,576	297,222	351,709	379,582	418,429	556,160	591,363	678,956
South America [1]	84,220	66,256	68,685	73,311	80,477	104,732	100,442	125,949
Argentina	17,488	10,663	9,201	10,103	13,174	13,692	12,518	14,108
Brazil	36,717	29,553	29,485	30,882	33,504	48,807	44,532	56,692
Chile	10,052	9,021	10,804	11,127	10,927	16,337	16,412	22,608
Colombia	3,693	2,773	2,991	4,292	3,799	4,552	5,553	6,728
Ecuador	832	975	881	941	904	1,007	1,092	1,269
Peru	3,130	3,401	4,773	5,542	5,561	5,964	4,772	6,232
Venezuela	10,531	8,438	9,109	8,934	10,922	12,871	13,473	14,506
Central America [1]	73,841	64,647	73,214	82,496	91,811	102,472	104,128	113,793
Costa Rica	1,716	840	2,687	1,598	2,105	2,267	2,596	2,419
Honduras	399	272	755	821	864	626	787	844
Mexico	39,352	56,851	63,384	73,687	82,965	91,046	89,610	97,897
Panama	30,758	5,409	4,919	4,826	4,636	6,171	6,236	7,845
Other Western Hemisphere [1]	108,515	166,319	209,810	223,775	246,142	348,956	386,792	439,214
Bahamas, The	3,291	8,643	11,255	13,451	13,703	16,567	19,720	22,052
Barbados	2,141	984	3,249	3,881	4,831	2,136	2,873	3,650
Bermuda	60,114	84,508	100,856	113,222	133,480	211,708	213,863	245,671
Dominican Republic	1,143	816	1,028	815	789	712	714	1,006
Jamaica	2,483	3,406	3,551	1,018	940	801	958	707
Netherlands Antilles	3,579	2,926	4,712	5,607	3,924	6,483	13,493	17,667
Trinidad and Tobago	1,550	2,392	2,577	2,219	2,940	3,916	5,145	6,328
U.K. Islands, Caribbean	33,451	61,882	82,159	83,164	84,817	105,829	129,243	141,527
Africa [1]	11,891	19,835	20,356	22,756	28,158	32,607	37,221	44,805
Egypt	1,998	3,524	4,526	5,475	5,564	7,023	8,385	9,826
Nigeria	470	1,100	1,936	1,105	1,677	1,584	3,298	5,369
South Africa	3,562	3,580	3,913	3,969	3,980	5,240	4,919	5,922
Middle East [1]	10,863	16,885	18,963	21,115	24,206	28,448	31,886	37,012
Israel	3,735	7,020	6,171	7,978	9,168	9,487	9,729	10,013
Saudi Arabia	3,661	3,140	3,657	3,830	4,410	5,012	5,189	8,122
United Arab Emirates	683	1,934	2,962	2,285	2,670	2,967	3,424	3,993
Asia and Pacific [1]	207,125	270,830	374,754	375,689	403,637	444,101	488,839	511,355
Australia	34,838	48,447	(D)	75,669	67,632	84,331	94,451	106,370
China [2]	11,140	11,261	17,616	19,016	26,459	29,710	52,521	49,403
Hong Kong	27,447	36,426	32,735	36,415	39,636	40,720	40,014	50,459
India	2,379	4,868	7,658	7,162	9,746	14,622	16,571	18,610
Indonesia	8,904	(D)	(D)	8,603	9,484	14,978	16,284	16,005
Japan	57,091	57,794	71,005	81,175	84,428	85,224	101,918	103,643
Korea, South	8,968	13,063	17,747	19,760	27,299	23,558	22,361	26,953
Malaysia	7,910	7,057	8,909	11,097	11,185	12,140	12,295	13,486
New Zealand	4,271	3,859	4,620	5,191	5,933	5,527	4,802	5,816
Philippines	3,638	6,390	6,176	6,522	6,948	6,953	5,593	5,806
Singapore	24,133	51,053	61,076	76,390	81,879	93,529	86,048	76,862
Taiwan [2]	7,836	11,983	(D)	14,356	16,999	15,807	18,070	19,534
Thailand	5,824	6,886	7,499	10,352	10,642	10,284	9,309	10,209

D Suppressed to avoid disclosure of data of individual companies. [1] Includes other countries, not shown separately. [2] See footnote 2, Table 1331.

Source: U.S. Bureau of Economic Analysis, *Survey of Current Business*, July 2010, <http://www.bea.gov/international/index .htm#iip>.

Table 1296. U.S. Government Foreign Grants and Credits by Type and Country: 2000 to 2009

[In millions of dollars. (1,500 represents 1,500,000,000) See text, this section. Negative figures (-) occur when the total of grant returns, principal repayments, and/or foreign currencies disbursed by the U.S. Government exceeds new grants and new credits utilized and/or acquisitions of foreign currencies through new sales of farm products]

Country	2000	2003	2004	2005	2006	2007	2008	2009
Investment in financial institutions	1,500	1,434	1,994	1,263	2,024	1,651	1,385	1,676
Western Europe [1]	**429**	**706**	**348**	**345**	**98**	**231**	**262**	**342**
Ireland	–	44	50	–	30	–	34	7
Spain	–19	–19	–19	–19	–205	(Z)	(Z)	(Z)
Yugoslavia [2]	1	–	–	–	–	–	–	–
Bosnia and Hercegovina	52	47	66	72	49	46	29	35
Macedonia	50	58	42	67	30	2	34	30
Former Yugoslavia - Regional [2]	63	297	51	70	47	43	56	177
Other [3] and unspecified [4]	478	221	69	49	45	50	58	44
Eastern Europe [1]	**2,220**	**1,492**	**1,273**	**–70**	**257**	**1,062**	**1,877**	**1,502**
Albania	26	42	43	53	31	36	30	31
Romania	38	66	34	57	41	41	9	15
Newly independent states:								
Armenia	20	74	66	85	61	68	63	45
Azerbaijan	8	35	47	74	52	44	36	31
Belarus	1	(Z)	1	2	4	6	8	10
Georgia	36	66	113	169	75	87	352	124
Kazakhstan	42	50	56	69	40	43	44	43
Kyrgyzstan	15	35	39	60	50	26	38	42
Moldova	32	23	27	38	26	20	40	28
Russia	797	192	251	–681	–920	–41	403	332
Tajikistan	8	25	40	61	35	33	24	35
Turkmenistan	4	6	4	12	3	Z	–8	11
Ukraine	138	96	114	145	119	69	66	99
Uzbekistan	22	59	53	52	23	13	11	9
Former Soviet Union—Regional [4]	501	364	372	456	470	461	508	535
Other [3] and unspecified [4]	419	107	153	76	73	76	73
Near East and South Asia [1]	**3,304**	**2,268**	**3,704**	**5,487**	**4,748**	**9,938**	**9,045**	**11,778**
Afghanistan	5	555	1,382	2,304	3,808	7,541	6,124	8,557
Bangladesh	43	29	50	48	45	81	75	56
Egypt	3,091	2,055	2,689	2,827	149	1,761	1,802	1,734
Greece	–169	–287	–457	–114	–103	–74	–66	–74
India	–64	–150	–40	–70	61	46	28	32
Nepal	15	43	37	50	57	63	64	82
Pakistan	366	223	230	500	703	526	692	1,249
Turkey	–86	–322	–299	–228	–194	–296	–43	–25
UNRWA [4]	97	124	27	48	137	135	160	70
Other and unspecified [3]	21	14	79	54	47	117	150	71
Africa [1]	**1,058**	**3,909**	**2,460**	**2,100**	**1,042**	**3,523**	**4,580**	**6,022**
Algeria	–53	–123	–146	–173	–1,324	–19	–18	–8
Burundi	3	18	27	6	37	18	16	32
Congo (Kinshasa) [6]	9	1,078	229	135	131	94	1	12
Ethiopia	142	138	234	308	233	278	446	441
Ghana	40	50	67	53	54	55	55	67
Guinea	19	30	33	36	29	15	75	31
Kenya	44	58	82	91	186	178	282	391
Liberia	19	13	50	40	61	81	261	142
Madagascar	21	31	31	66	44	48	40	37
Malawi	45	42	54	46	61	68	81	94
Mali	50	50	45	55	52	43	42	69
Mozambique	119	107	105	64	92	106	144	178
Nigeria	–17	472	41	67	–178	123	200	213
Rwanda	26	36	35	47	55	71	93	110
Senegal	27	45	53	39	34	39	75	59
Somalia	7	10	16	7	33	40	168	108
South Africa	68	115	332	103	106	155	243	361
Sudan	17	41	120	130	390	363	529	514
Tanzania	15	49	66	62	75	104	117	188
Uganda	92	86	120	148	154	183	190	225
Zambia	44	52	56	90	89	105	157	151
Zimbabwe	23	23	31	27	32	69	141	153
Other and unspecified [4]	164	278	407	513	621	1,060	777	1,815
Far East and Pacific [1]	**544**	**712**	**–129**	**42**	**–106**	**141**	**611**	**594**
Cambodia	23	32	44	58	56	61	60	66
Hong Kong	–15	–23	–28	–28	–28	–28	–22	–16
Indonesia	270	821	–157	–8	–71	–18	–108	–52
Korea, South	–132	–137	–110	–43	–43	–40	182	–68
Malaysia	134	2	–45	–46	–45	–185	2	6
Philippines	20	–35	–15	–36	–28	46	131	127
Thailand	–102	–37	11	4	–67	(Z)	18	14
Pacific Islands, Trust Territory of the Pacific Island [7]	145	103	204	190	174	195	182	348
Other and unspecified [4]	19	22	40	47	39	182	200	215

See footnotes at end of table.

U.S. Census Bureau, Statistical Abstract of the United States: 2011

Table 1296. U.S. Government Foreign Grants and Credits by Type and Country: 2000 to 2009—Con.

[In millions of dollars. See headnote, page 801]

Country	2000	2003	2004	2005	2006	2007	2008	2009
Western Hemisphere [1]	1,621	1,658	1,986	2,164	1,537	1,409	2,023	4,173
Bolivia	136	212	217	159	142	155	135	141
Brazil	195	−78	−136	−93	−344	−181	−167	−84
Colombia	33	328	467	598	613	771	914	1,229
Ecuador	14	39	36	59	80	73	53	63
El Salvador	27	56	104	52	27	40	52	38
Guatemala	49	42	40	21	34	25	55	66
Haiti	63	64	83	118	154	164	192	232
Honduras	100	51	84	70	60	75	62	51
Mexico	−123	5	14	40	30	50	51	1,284
Nicaragua	53	41	28	36	53	71	57	46
Panama [8]	−13	5	14	7	11	6	9	7
Peru	87	93	167	127	71	−258	127	534
Other [9] and unspecified [4]	1,100	868	806	815	510	447	406	466
Other international organizations	2,837	3,207	2,485	4,201	3,770	4,843	5,324	7,883
Middle East	4,345	7,745	8,412	16,702	10,216	10,181	10,787	9,618
Iraq [10]	(z)	3,235	5,039	10,857	9,156	7,030	6,227	5,276
Israel	3,932	2,761	2,163	4,953	390	2,373	2,955	1,992
Jordan	317	1,420	800	582	462	417	632	686
Lebanon	22	24	30	37	45	146	252	250
Yemen	16	17	31	24	30	40	22	31
West Bank-Gaza Regional	64	195	171	179	128	152	473	811

− Represents zero. Z Less than $500,000. [1] Includes other countries, not shown separately. [2] In 1992, some successor countries assumed portions of outstanding credits of the former Yugoslavia (assignment of the remaining portions is pending). Subsequent negative totals reflect payments to the United States on these assumed credits which were greater than the extension of new credits and grants to these countries. [3] Includes European Atomic Energy Community, European Coal and Steel Community, European Payments Union, European Productivity Agency, North Atlantic Treaty Organization, and Organization for European Economic Cooperation. [4] In recent years, significant amounts of foreign assistance has been reported on a regional, inter-regional, and worldwide basis. Country totals in this table may understate actual assistance to many countries.
[5] United Nations Relief and Works Agency for Palestine refugees. [6] See footnote 5, table 1331. [7] Excludes transactions with Commonwealth of the Northern Mariana Islands after October 1986; includes transactions with Federated States of Micronesia, Republic of the Marshall Islands, and Republic of Palau. [8] Includes transfer of Panama Canal to the Republic of Panama on Dec. 1999. [9] Includes Andean Development Corporation, Caribbean Development Bank, Central American Bank for Economic Integration, Eastern Caribbean Central Bank, Inter-American Institute of Agricultural Science, Organizations of American States, and Pan American Health Organization. [10] Foreign assistance to Iraq in 1991–96 was direct humanitarian assistance to ethnic minorities of Northern Iraq after the conflict in the Persian Gulf. Foreign assistance to Iraq in 2003 thru 2009 includes Iraq Reconstruction and humanitarian assistance.

Source: U.S. Bureau of Economic Analysis, press releases, and unpublished data. See <http://www.bea.gov/scb/index.htm>.

Table 1297. U.S. Foreign Economic and Military Aid Programs: 1980 to 2008

[In millions of dollars (9,694 represents $9,694,000,000). For years ending September 30. Total aid programs are the sum of economic and military assistance. Major components in recent years include USAID, USDA, State Department and voluntary contributions to international financial institutions. Annual figures are in obligations]

Year and Region	Total foreign assistance	Military assistance	Economic assistance, by funding agency					
			Total	U.S. Agency for International Development	U.S. Department of Agriculture	State Department	Other U.S. agencies	Multilateral organizations
1980	9,694	2,122	7,572	4,062	1,437	459	137	1,478
1985	18,128	5,801	12,327	8,132	2,052	431	164	1,548
1990	16,015	4,971	11,044	6,964	1,643	590	377	1,469
1995	16,408	4,165	12,242	7,281	1,401	763	1,016	1,781
2000	18,208	4,876	13,331	5,907	2,567	2,486	1,262	1,110
2003	25,891	6,662	19,229	10,124	2,551	2,183	3,733	637
2004	33,614	6,144	27,469	11,330	2,150	4,018	7,087	2,885
2005	37,176	7,354	29,823	10,102	2,318	5,020	10,725	1,659
2006	39,394	12,288	27,106	9,618	2,033	5,347	8,615	1,492
2007	40,819	13,187	27,632	11,378	1,835	5,634	7,052	1,733
2008, total	**49,057**	**15,446**	**33,611**	**9,324**	**2,792**	**9,641**	**9,576**	**2,278**
Asia	12,026	6,423	5,603	2,700	462	985	1,382	75
Central Asia	2,479	47	2,432	411	13	98	1,910	
Eastern Europe	583	79	504	342	–	54	104	4
Latin America and Caribbean	2,694	76	2,618	760	171	970	683	34
Middle East and North Africa	13,956	8,382	5,574	2,614	47	848	2,065	–
Oceania	197	1	195	18	–	3	174	–
Sub-Saharan Africa	10,405	411	9,994	1,585	2,066	3,957	2,251	135
Western Europe	82	11	71	17	–	17	37	–
Canada	27		27	–	–	–	27	–
World, not specified	6,608	16	6,591	875	33	2,709	943	2,031

− Represents or rounds to zero.

Source: U.S. Agency for International Development (USAID), *U.S. Overseas Loans and Grants: Obligations and Loan Authorizations*, annual. See also <http://gbk.eads.usaidallnet.gov>.

Table 1298. U.S. Foreign Economic and Military Aid by Major Recipient Country: 2001 to 2008

[In millions of dollars (16,836 represents $16,836,000,000). For years ending September 30. Annual figures are in obligations]

Region/Country	2001	2005	2006	2007	2008 Total	2008 Economic aid	2008 Military aid
Total [1]	16,836	37,176	39,394	40,819	49,057	33,611	15,446
Afghanistan	106	2,252	3,739	5,812	8,892	2,880	6,012
Albania	55	43	54	35	46	43	3
Angola	88	67	52	50	58	58	–
Armenia	92	76	170	81	220	217	4
Azerbaijan	29	64	56	56	37	33	4
Bangladesh	162	84	82	93	171	170	1
Bolivia	203	162	224	181	128	128	–
Bosnia and Herzegovina	160	47	53	42	36	32	4
Bulgaria	60	44	39	27	26	18	8
Burundi	35	59	50	38	46	46	–
Cambodia	45	98	71	75	76	75	1
Chad	9	63	82	98	127	127	–
Colombia	264	824	1,348	497	888	834	54
Comoros	–	1	1	–	2	1	1
Congo (Kinshasa) [2]	99	121	171	150	255	249	6
Ecuador	65	87	76	66	52	51	–
Egypt	1,716	1,563	1,787	1,972	1,492	201	1,291
El Salvador	139	59	69	252	223	216	7
Eritrea	80	133	6	3	3	3	–
Ethiopia	212	693	322	473	1,009	1,007	1
Georgia	97	106	251	97	274	264	10
Ghana	70	72	94	433	230	229	1
Guatemala	80	96	106	84	111	111	–
Haiti	94	224	243	210	310	309	1
Honduras	52	271	89	63	74	72	2
India	222	214	177	161	148	146	1
Indonesia	195	588	269	236	208	194	14
Iraq	–	9,482	10,563	7,931	7,452	3,083	4,369
Israel	2,839	2,714	2,544	2,508	2,425	44	2,381
Jamaica	35	66	36	36	22	21	1
Jordan	272	683	562	535	833	532	301
Kazakhstan	47	66	110	104	112	109	2
Kenya	155	262	390	517	719	718	1
Kosovo	105	43		–	207	207	–
Liberia	54	148	152	257	220	133	88
Macedonia	64	48	45	35	32	28	3
Madagascar	50	89	55	67	119	119	–
Malawi	39	84	73	105	104	103	–
Mali	48	55	65	381	142	142	–
Marshall Islands	41	44	51	48	47	47	–
Mexico	55	102	185	89	95	95	–
Micronesia, Federated States of	82	94	100	100	80	80	–
Morocco	42	55	53	79	696	691	5
Mozambique	214	127	160	237	799	799	–
Namibia	16	50	64	91	129	129	–
Nepal	51	73	60	81	106	105	1
Nicaragua	67	96	164	58	145	143	2
Nigeria	98	151	187	340	485	483	2
Pakistan	188	758	957	975	963	605	358
Peru	216	191	338	165	159	159	–
Philippines	151	167	213	169	161	132	29
Poland	18	93	34	32	31	2	29
Romania	67	63	53	35	26	13	13
Russia	541	1,585	1,530	1,593	1,261	1,261	–
Rwanda	39	83	103	122	172	172	–
Senegal	41	48	65	71	78	77	1
Serbia and Montenegro [3]	205	90	5		–	–	–
South Africa	70	187	262	399	568	567	1
Sri Lanka	28	160	49	44	68	68	1
Sudan	96	1,043	908	1,180	1,196	997	199
Tajikistan	62	64	48	34	70	69	1
Tanzania	107	137	188	233	1,061	1,061	–
Turkey	7	54	23	30	21	12	10
Uganda	95	291	280	366	456	455	1
Ukraine	146	149	154	165	111	103	8
Uzbekistan	60	42	45	17	14	14	–
West Bank/Gaza [4]	240	350	274	165	575	575	–
Zambia	51	144	196	205	263	262	–
Zimbabwe	23	61	30	141	234	234	–

– Represents or rounds to zero. [1] Includes other countries, not shown separately. [2] See footnote 5, Table 1331.
[3] See footnote 4, Table 1374. [4] See footnote 7, Table 1331.

Source: U.S. Agency for International Development, *U.S. Overseas Loans and Grants: Obligations and Loan Authorizations*, annual. See also <http://gbk.eads.usaidallnet.gov>.

Table 1299. U.S. International Trade in Goods and Services: 2000 to 2009

[In millions of dollars (–379,780 represents –$379,780,000,000). Data presented on a balance of payments basis and will not agree with the following merchandise trade tables in this section]

Category	2000	2003	2004	2005	2006	2007	2008	2009
TRADE BALANCE								
Total................	**–378,780**	**–494,183**	**–609,345**	**–714,176**	**–759,240**	**–702,099**	**–698,802**	**–374,908**
Goods.................	–446,233	–541,544	–665,631	–783,801	–839,456	–823,192	–834,652	–506,944
Services...............	67,453	47,361	56,286	69,625	80,216	121,093	135,850	132,036
Travel...............	17,695	6,912	8,796	12,829	13,685	68,459	77,413	67,937
Passenger fares.........	–3,587	–5,098	–5,867	–5,179	–5,465	–13,198	–9,988	–6,180
Other transportation......	–11,622	–13,289	–17,204	–20,656	–19,093	59,649	68,140	64,561
Royalties, license fees.....	26,765	27,955	33,449	39,783	47,209	70,540	65,246	69,440
Other private services.....	47,384	51,799	59,010	62,233	60,550	–10,701	–13,375	–13,378
Other [1]...............	317	–11,981	–13,518	–10,536	–7,119	–2,972	–3,262	–3,538
U.S. govt misc. services....	–2,097	–2,321	–2,819	–2,892	–2,866	–2,972	–3,262	–3,538
EXPORTS								
Total................	**1,070,597**	**1,019,897**	**1,158,576**	**1,281,186**	**1,452,783**	**1,648,665**	**1,839,012**	**1,570,797**
Goods.................	784,181	728,258	819,870	909,016	1,035,868	1,160,366	1,304,896	1,068,499
Services...............	286,416	291,639	338,707	372,171	416,916	488,299	534,116	502,298
Travel...............	82,400	64,359	74,546	81,799	85,789	96,896	109,976	93,917
Passenger fares.........	20,687	15,891	18,851	20,970	22,036	25,646	31,404	26,424
Other transportation......	29,803	31,416	36,957	41,281	46,225	40,315	43,714	35,406
Royalties, license fees.....	43,233	46,988	56,715	64,395	70,727	84,580	93,920	89,791
Other private services.....	107,904	131,563	149,262	160,051	186,028	222,434	238,932	238,332
Other [1]...............	13,790	13,315	15,781	19,539	23,913	17,216	14,936	17,096
U.S. govt misc. services....	786	810	959	1,087	1,155	1,212	1,234	1,333
IMPORTS								
Total................	**1,449,377**	**1,514,080**	**1,767,921**	**1,995,362**	**2,212,023**	**2,350,763**	**2,537,814**	**1,945,705**
Goods.................	1,230,413	1,269,802	1,485,501	1,692,817	1,875,324	1,983,558	2,139,548	1,575,443
Services...............	218,964	244,278	282,420	302,546	336,700	367,206	398,266	370,262
Travel...............	64,705	57,447	65,750	68,970	72,104	76,331	79,726	73,230
Passenger fares.........	24,274	20,989	24,718	26,149	27,501	28,437	32,563	25,980
Other transportation......	41,425	44,705	54,161	61,937	65,318	53,513	53,702	41,586
Royalties, license fees.....	16,468	19,033	23,266	24,612	23,518	24,931	25,781	25,230
Other private services.....	60,520	79,764	90,252	97,818	125,478	151,894	173,686	168,892
Other [1]...............	13,473	25,296	29,299	30,075	31,032	27,917	28,311	30,474
U.S. govt misc. services....	2,883	3,131	3,778	3,979	4,021	4,184	4,497	4,871

[1] Represents transfers under U.S. military sales contracts for exports and direct defense expenditures for imports.

Source: U.S. Census Bureau, *U.S. International Trade in Goods and Services, Annual Revision for 2009*, Series FT-900(10-04), and previous reports. See also <http://www.census.gov/foreign-trade/Press-Release/2009pr/final_revisions/09final.pdf>.

Table 1300. U.S. International Trade in Goods by Related Parties: 2000 to 2009

[In millions of dollars (1,205,339 represents $1,205,339,000,000). "Related party trade" is trade by U.S. companies with their subsidiaries abroad as well as trade by U.S. subsidiaries of foreign companies with their parent companies. Based on the North American Industry Classification System (NAICS), 2002; see text, Section 15]

Country and commodity	2002 NAICS code	2000	2005	2007	2008	2009
IMPORTS FOR CONSUMPTION						
Total imports............................	(X)	1,205,339	1,662,380	1,942,863	2,090,483	1,549,163
Related party trade, total [1]................	**(X)**	**563,084**	**775,730**	**920,369**	**975,096**	**740,481**
Canada................................	(X)	100,689	127,719	146,906	156,666	107,315
Japan.................................	(X)	108,290	108,322	116,304	111,898	73,859
Mexico................................	(X)	89,068	99,709	120,551	111,979	100,935
China [2]...............................	(X)	18,061	62,716	82,404	89,339	84,829
Germany...............................	(X)	37,781	51,870	61,318	64,058	45,000
Transportation equipment.....................	336	161,150	188,445	207,668	189,984	132,812
Computer & electronic products...............	334	166,279	176,719	196,933	182,337	163,662
Chemicals..............................	325	45,452	84,459	109,734	137,095	118,149
Machinery, except electrical..................	333	39,918	56,804	61,272	62,192	42,216
Oil & gas...............................	211	13,241	48,725	69,394	104,091	61,700
EXPORTS						
Total exports...........................	(X)	780,418	803,992	1,162,708	1,300,136	1,056,932
Related party trade, domestic exports, total [1]...	**(X)**	**196,596**	**245,712**	**343,584**	**373,646**	**261,332**
Canada................................	(X)	64,133	76,331	88,396	89,928	71,478
Mexico................................	(X)	34,249	44,570	52,470	51,789	39,653
Japan.................................	(X)	20,313	17,427	17,486	18,825	15,038
Netherlands.............................	(X)	6,845	9,308	12,812	16,364	15,784
Germany...............................	(X)	6,751	9,250	16,185	18,275	11,902
Transportation equipment.....................	336	46,288	52,513	63,885	63,946	43,758
Chemicals..............................	325	26,376	48,121	58,343	61,497	54,655
Computer & electronic products...............	334	51,210	41,882	47,127	47,027	36,405
Machinery, except electrical..................	333	19,831	25,473	30,231	32,978	26,418
Electrical equipment, appliances & components....	335	7,575	9,888	12,205	11,806	8,624

X Not applicable. [1] Includes other countries and other commodities, not shown separately. [2] See footnote 4, Table 1331.

Source: U.S. Census Bureau, "Related Party Trade—2009." See also <http://www.census.gov/foreign-trade /Press-Release/2009pr/aip/related_party>.

Table 1301. U.S. Freight Gateways—Value of Shipments: 2008

[In billions of dollars, except as indicated (3,248.8 represents $3,248,800,000,000). For the top 50 gateways ranked by value of shipments. Excludes imports of less than $1,250, exports less than $2,500, and intransit shipments]

Port	Mode	Rank	Total trade	Exports	Imports	Exports as a percent of total
Total U.S. merchandise trade	**(X)**	**(X)**	**3,248.8**	**1,220.4**	**2,028.4**	**37.6**
Top 50 gateways	(X)	(X)	2,633.4	998.1	1,635.3	37.9
As a percent of total	(X)	(X)	81.1	81.8	80.6	(X)
Port of New York, NY and NJ.	Water	1	189.5	51.0	138.5	26.9
Port of Los Angeles, CA	Water	2	182.4	33.6	148.7	18.4
JFK International Airport, NY	Air	3	167.9	85.5	82.4	50.9
Port of Long Beach, CA.	Water	4	152.0	32.8	119.2	21.6
Port of Houston, TX.	Water	5	146.7	68.5	78.2	46.7
Port of Detroit, MI	Land	6	120.2	66.5	53.7	55.3
Port of Laredo, TX	Land	7	115.8	53.9	61.8	46.6
Chicago, IL.	Air	8	97.0	35.9	61.2	37.0
Port of Huron, MI	Land	9	81.2	35.2	46.0	43.4
Port of Buffalo-Niagara Falls, NY.	Land	10	80.8	40.3	40.5	49.9
Port of Los Angeles, CA	Air	11	78.3	41.3	37.0	52.7
Port of Charleston, SC.	Water	12	62.1	22.3	39.9	35.9
Port of Savannah, GA	Water	13	58.8	22.8	36.0	38.8
Port of Norfolk Harbor, VA	Water	14	56.3	26.5	29.9	47.0
San Francisco International Airport.	Air	15	52.8	26.6	26.2	50.4
Port of El Paso, TX	Land	16	48.2	20.2	28.0	41.8
Port of Baltimore, MD	Water	17	45.1	16.1	29.0	35.7
New Orleans, LA	Air	18	45.0	19.9	25.1	44.3
Port of New Orleans, LA	Water	19	41.7	20.2	21.4	48.6
Anchorage, AK	Air	20	41.4	10.2	31.2	24.6
Miami International Airport, FL	Air	21	40.0	29.2	10.8	73.0
Dallas-Forth Worth Airport, TX	Air	22	39.5	16.4	23.1	41.6
Port of Seattle, WA	Water	23	37.7	9.8	27.9	26.0
Port of Oakland, CA.	Water	24	37.7	12.8	24.9	33.9
Port of Morgan City, LA	Water	25	37.7	0.3	37.4	0.7
Port of Tacoma, WA.	Water	26	37.3	8.3	29.0	22.3
Atlanta, GA	Air	27	32.2	12.3	19.9	38.3
Port of Otay Mesa Station, CA.	Land	28	31.8	10.6	21.2	33.2
Cleveland, OH	Air	29	30.9	17.6	13.2	57.1
Port of Beaumont, TX	Water	30	29.9	5.2	24.7	17.2
Port of Corpus Christi, TX	Water	31	28.2	2.9	25.3	10.2
Port of Philadelphia, PA.	Water	32	25.1	3.7	21.4	14.6
Port of Champlain-Rouses Pt., NY	Land	33	23.6	9.4	14.2	39.9
Port of Jacksonville, FL	Water	34	23.4	2.7	20.7	11.7
Port of Port Everglades, FL	Water	35	23.1	12.5	10.6	54.3
Port of Jacksonville, FL	Water	36	22.9	11.2	11.8	48.7
Chicago, IL.	Land	37	22.7	–	22.7	–
Port of Gramery, LA.	Water	38	22.3	8.8	13.5	39.4
Port of Hidalgo, TX.	Land	39	22.1	9.9	12.3	44.5
Port of Miami, FL.	Water	40	21.6	10.5	11.1	10.7
San Juan, PR	Air	41	21.3	12.3	8.9	58.0
Port of Pembina, ND	Land	42	19.9	11.2	8.6	56.7
Port of Nogales, AZ.	Land	43	19.1	6.9	12.2	36.1
Port of Christiansted, VI.	Water	44	19.0	2.6	16.4	13.6
Port of General Edward Lawrence Logan International, MA.	Land	45	18.4	11.0	7.4	59.9
Washington Dulles Airport, ...	Air	46	17.5	5.6	11.9	32.1
Port of Portland, OR	Water	47	16.9	5.2	11.7	30.9
Portal, ND	Land	48	16.5	9.6	6.9	58.4
Port of Freeport, TX.	Water	49	16.2	2.3	13.9	14.1
Port of Sweetgrass, MT.	Land	50	15.8	7.9	8.0	49.6

– Represents zero. X Not applicable.

Source: U.S. Bureau of Transportation Statistics, *National Transportation Statistics*, annual. See <http://www.bts.gov /publications/national_transportation_statistics>.

Table 1302. U.S. Exports and Imports for Consumption of Merchandise by Customs District: 2000 to 2009

[In billions of dollars (780.0 represents $780,000,000,000). Exports are f.a.s. (free alongside ship) value all years; imports are on customs-value basis. These data may differ from those in Tables 1300, 1306, and 1307. For methodology, see Foreign Trade Statistics in Appendix III]

Customs district	Exports					Imports for consumption				
	2000	2005	2007	2008	2009	2000	2005	2007	2008	2009
Total [1]	780.0	901.1	1,148.2	1,287.4	1,056.0	1,205.6	1,673.5	1,957.0	2,103.6	1,559.6
Anchorage, AK	5.9	12.1	14.1	13.5	11.9	13.4	10.4	11.5	10.7	12.4
Baltimore, MD	6.2	9.0	14.4	16.5	11.2	18.6	29.6	30.3	31.3	21.0
Boston, MA	7.0	10.4	11.3	11.9	8.3	18.7	21.7	24.5	24.4	17.4
Buffalo, NY	38.2	35.0	41.4	43.5	35.7	38.4	42.6	45.1	46.0	31.6
Charleston, SC [2]	12.6	16.2	20.0	22.3	16.4	16.9	31.9	36.9	36.5	26.3
Chicago, IL	21.7	29.9	34.3	36.6	31.5	51.1	78.7	98.6	116.9	96.7
Cleveland, OH	22.7	20.8	22.3	23.8	21.4	36.5	49.0	61.3	70.4	55.8
Dallas/Fort Worth, TX	11.5	17.8	20.7	19.8	17.4	18.8	31.8	36.9	37.1	30.8
Detroit, MI	79.4	106.9	121.2	119.1	89.6	97.6	123.1	127.8	117.4	81.3
Duluth, MN	1.5	1.9	2.1	3.2	2.3	7.0	9.3	7.4	8.5	5.8
El Paso, TX	18.0	19.9	20.9	21.1	19.8	24.1	28.0	34.2	32.4	30.4
Great Falls, MT	5.0	9.8	14.8	18.0	15.3	14.3	27.1	30.1	34.9	21.7
Honolulu, HI	0.7	2.4	3.7	5.6	5.8	2.9	3.7	5.2	6.0	3.8
Houston/Galveston, TX	29.7	47.0	72.3	89.9	75.1	40.9	89.4	113.0	151.0	92.4
Laredo, TX	57.7	60.5	70.6	79.6	66.8	62.7	78.7	96.7	95.1	80.0
Los Angeles, CA	77.6	78.4	100.0	110.0	86.1	150.1	215.5	249.0	247.1	196.4
Miami, FL	31.0	34.1	45.5	54.9	49.5	23.3	31.8	33.6	35.4	29.6
Milwaukee, WI	0.1	0.1	0.2	0.2	0.1	1.5	1.3	1.5	1.1	0.7
Minneapolis, MN	1.4	2.3	3.3	2.3	2.0	4.3	6.9	13.1	16.6	11.4
Mobile, AL [2]	4.0	5.0	6.0	8.5	7.3	7.9	14.3	18.4	24.7	17.3
New Orleans, LA	35.9	32.6	52.1	65.6	57.0	54.0	97.8	123.7	151.3	94.2
New York, NY	79.5	90.9	123.7	143.7	110.9	145.6	176.7	200.0	209.5	155.6
Nogales, AZ	7.3	6.9	8.0	9.2	7.6	14.1	13.0	16.4	16.8	14.0
Norfolk, VA [2]	12.4	16.8	22.1	25.8	19.8	13.6	23.5	28.4	29.6	21.6
Ogdensburg, NY	12.4	13.3	15.4	16.5	13.5	23.7	28.2	30.9	33.0	23.9
Pembina, ND	8.7	13.6	18.0	22.0	16.9	11.0	12.8	15.1	17.4	12.5
Philadelphia, PA	6.0	10.2	14.3	19.4	13.1	28.3	47.8	60.4	73.3	49.2
Port Arthur, TX	1.2	2.1	3.1	5.3	4.9	10.9	20.9	25.1	32.4	20.1
Portland, ME	2.6	2.8	3.3	4.8	4.2	8.7	11.2	11.1	11.6	10.0
Portland, OR	7.2	6.3	9.9	14.3	10.3	12.5	14.2	18.2	16.9	11.0
Providence, RI	(Z)	0.1	0.2	0.3	0.2	1.3	4.4	4.5	5.7	4.0
San Diego, CA	12.7	15.0	16.0	16.6	14.0	22.2	28.4	38.2	37.4	30.4
San Francisco, CA	58.3	36.6	43.3	43.7	37.0	68.6	62.4	68.9	71.6	49.7
San Juan, PR	4.8	9.7	14.9	17.2	18.8	11.8	19.5	21.7	21.6	18.9
Savannah, GA	15.9	24.7	33.6	38.3	33.8	26.1	47.9	60.3	62.7	53.4
Seattle, WA	40.4	44.1	61.2	59.9	53.9	40.5	51.7	58.5	60.7	47.7
St. Albans, VT	4.5	4.3	3.7	3.8	2.9	9.4	12.6	11.0	10.2	7.6
St. Louis, MO	1.3	1.3	2.1	2.8	1.6	7.9	9.7	11.4	12.7	10.1
Tampa, FL	4.8	10.1	13.5	18.1	10.4	14.7	19.3	22.3	22.2	13.6
Virgin Islands, U.S.	0.3	0.5	0.8	2.7	1.2	4.8	9.1	11.0	16.6	9.2
Washington, DC	2.8	3.7	5.4	5.7	6.0	2.6	3.7	6.8	8.8	10.2
Wilmington, NC	2.5	2.2	2.8	3.2	4.0	10.6	15.4	16.9	15.3	12.9

Z Less than $50 million. [1] Totals shown for exports reflect the value of estimated parcel post and Special Category shipments, and adjustments for undocumented exports to Canada, which are not distributed by customs district. The value of bituminous coal exported through Norfolk, VA; Charleston, SC; and Mobile, AL is reflected in the total but not distributed by district. [2] Excludes exports of bituminous coal, which are included in "Total."

Source: U.S. Census Bureau, 2000–2004, U.S. Export History and U.S. Import History on compact disc; beginning 2005, U.S. Merchandise Trade: Selected Highlights, December issues, Series FT920. See also <http://www.census.gov/foreign-trade/Press-Release/ft920_index.html>.

Table 1303. Export and Import Unit Value Indexes—Selected Countries: 2005 to 2009

[Indexes in U.S. dollars, 2005 = 100. A unit value is an implicit price derived from value and quantity data]

Country	Export unit value					Import unit value				
	2005	2006	2007	2008	2009	2005	2006	2007	2008	2009
United States	**100.0**	**104.9**	**109.3**	**121.9**	**107.9**	**100.0**	**104.9**	**109.3**	**121.9**	**107.9**
Australia	100.0	102.7	109.5	119.8	111.3	100.0	102.7	109.5	119.8	111.3
Belgium	100.0	105.7	117.5	134.4	115.3	100.0	105.7	117.5	134.4	115.3
Canada	100.0	107.3	112.0	120.2	111.5	100.0	107.3	112.0	120.2	111.5
France	100.0	100.4	109.5	115.3	(NA)	100.0	102.0	112.4	120.1	(NA)
Germany	100.0	101.7	113.4	122.8	113.9	100.0	104.7	116.1	129.1	113.2
Greece	100.0	105.7	118.8	135.3	120.6	100.0	(NA)	(NA)	(NA)	(NA)
Ireland	100.0	99.3	104.4	109.0	105.6	100.0	103.8	112.8	122.3	115.8
Italy	100.0	106.1	121.6	137.5	129.0	100.0	110.5	124.1	144.8	124.7
Japan	100.0	97.7	98.6	105.6	104.3	100.0	108.0	114.5	142.1	117.4
Korea, South	100.0	100.6	103.8	107.8	90.4	100.0	107.7	114.0	136.8	104.2
Netherlands	100.0	104.2	115.3	129.0	112.0	100.0	104.6	116.2	130.0	114.1
Norway	100.0	120.1	131.7	164.8	120.3	100.0	104.9	119.4	129.3	115.1
Spain	100.0	105.7	118.2	128.9	113.9	100.0	107.7	111.5	122.4	109.5
Sweden	100.0	105.4	119.3	125.7	111.1	100.0	107.2	119.6	130.3	111.3
Switzerland	100.0	102.7	111.6	127.8	131.2	100.0	104.5	113.6	126.2	119.7
United Kingdom	100.0	103.7	113.8	119.4	103.7	100.0	104.7	115.1	119.7	104.4

NA Not available.

Source: International Monetary Fund, Washington, DC, International Financial Statistics, monthly, (copyright).

Table 1304. U.S. Exports of Goods by State of Origin: 2000 to 2009

[In millions of dollars (782,429 represents $782,429,000,000), except as indicated. Exports are on a f.a.s. (free along ship) value basis. Exports are based on origin of movement]

State and other area	2000	2008	2009 Total	Rank	State and other area	2000	2008	2009 Total	Rank
Total.............	782,429	1,287,442	1,056,043	(X)	Nebraska..........	2,511	5,412	4,873	35
					Nevada...........	1,482	6,121	5,672	33
United States......	372,726	1,222,545	487,147	(X)	New Hampshire.....	2,373	3,752	3,061	42
Alabama...........	7,317	15,879	12,355	25					
Alaska............	2,464	3,542	3,270	40	New Jersey........	18,638	35,643	27,244	11
Arizona...........	14,334	19,784	14,023	23	New Mexico........	2,391	2,783	1,270	46
Arkansas..........	2,599	5,776	5,267	34	New York.........	42,846	81,386	58,743	3
California..........	119,640	144,806	120,080	2	North Carolina......	17,946	25,091	21,793	15
Colorado..........	6,593	7,713	5,867	32	North Dakota......	626	2,772	2,193	44
Connecticut........	8,047	15,384	13,979	24	Ohio.............	26,322	45,628	34,104	7
Delaware..........	2,197	4,898	4,312	38	Oklahoma.........	3,072	5,077	4,415	37
District of Columbia...	1,003	1,196	1,091	47	Oregon...........	11,441	19,352	14,907	22
Florida............	26,543	54,238	46,888	5	Pennsylvania.......	18,792	34,649	28,381	10
					Rhode Island.......	1,186	1,974	1,496	45
Georgia...........	14,925	27,514	23,743	12					
Hawaii............	387	960	563	51	South Carolina......	8,565	19,853	16,488	19
Idaho.............	3,559	5,005	3,877	39	South Dakota......	679	1,654	1,011	49
Illinois............	31,438	53,677	41,626	6	Tennessee.........	11,592	23,238	20,484	16
Indiana...........	15,386	26,502	22,907	14	Texas............	103,866	192,222	162,995	1
Iowa.............	4,466	12,125	9,042	29	Utah.............	3,221	10,306	10,337	26
Kansas...........	5,145	12,514	8,917	30	Vermont..........	4,097	3,697	3,219	41
Kentucky..........	9,612	19,121	17,650	17	Virginia...........	11,698	18,942	15,052	21
Louisiana..........	16,814	41,908	32,616	9	Washington........	32,215	54,498	51,851	4
Maine............	1,779	3,016	2,231	43	West Virginia......	2,219	5,643	4,826	36
					Wisconsin.........	10,508	20,570	16,725	18
Maryland..........	4,593	11,383	9,225	28	Wyoming..........	503	1,081	926	50
Massachusetts.......	20,514	28,369	23,593	13					
Michigan..........	33,845	45,136	32,655	8	Puerto Rico.......	9,735	19,961	20,937	(X)
Minnesota..........	10,303	19,186	15,532	20	Virgin Islands.......	174	2,747	1,217	(X)
Mississippi.........	2,726	7,323	6,316	31	Other [1]...........	60,810	42,188	33,620	(X)
Missouri...........	6,497	12,852	9,522	27	Timing adjustments .	−346	(X)	(X)	(X)
Montana...........	541	1,395	1,053	48					

X Not applicable. [1] Includes unreported, not specified, special category, estimated shipments, and reexports.

Source: U.S. Census Bureau, *U.S. International Trades in Goods and Services*, December issues, Series FT-900, <http://www.census.gov/foreign-trade/Press-Release/2009pr/12/>.

Table 1305. U.S. Agricultural Exports by State: 2000 to 2009

[In millions of dollars (50,762 represents $50,762,000,000). For years ending September 30]

State	2000	2005	2007	2008	2009	State	2000	2005	2007	2008	2009
U.S.........	50,762	62,516	82,217	115,305	96,632						
AL..........	401	563	626	994	867	NE.........	2,816	2,821	4,063	5,930	4,826
AK..........	2	3	4	5	5	NV.........	39	44	45	60	72
AZ..........	391	412	496	746	626	NH.........	14	15	20	24	23
AR..........	1,210	1,713	2,123	3,200	2,616	NJ.........	150	193	244	334	311
CA..........	6,298	9,354	11,313	13,353	12,499	NM.........	82	143	271	383	262
CO..........	894	632	1,018	1,235	1,113	NY.........	515	626	836	1,163	928
CT..........	140	171	257	377	339	NC.........	1,525	1,802	2,068	3,107	2,879
DE..........	127	136	162	247	236	ND.........	1,475	1,705	2,545	3,949	3,186
FL..........	1,469	1,546	1,925	2,188	2,060	OH.........	1,348	1,579	2,202	2,840	2,671
GA..........	908	1,118	1,438	2,057	1,841	OK.........	534	761	890	1,632	982
HI..........	81	95	88	100	102	OR.........	749	912	1,194	1,551	1,340
ID..........	803	905	1,203	1,815	1,484	PA.........	989	1,151	1,516	1,941	1,732
IL..........	2,951	3,281	4,723	7,560	5,538	RI.........	7	11	13	15	16
IN..........	1,501	1,821	2,436	3,805	3,140	SC.........	333	344	390	663	550
IA..........	2,944	4,002	5,259	7,870	6,486	SD.........	1,094	1,236	1,864	3,054	2,327
KS..........	2,929	2,910	3,883	5,930	4,705	TN.........	561	817	785	1,365	1,202
KY..........	806	1,085	1,237	1,662	1,485	TX.........	2,877	3,626	5,210	6,042	4,747
LA..........	426	568	733	953	838	UT.........	246	249	334	462	374
ME..........	61	73	105	122	112	VT.........	14	75	119	155	130
MD..........	273	286	362	487	439	VA.........	490	513	548	825	718
MA..........	120	73	105	121	119	WA.........	1,595	1,942	2,665	3,174	2,968
MI..........	813	1,044	1,372	1,924	1,552	WV.........	36	40	49	70	67
MN..........	2,230	2,768	3,619	5,469	4,284	WI.........	1,283	1,512	2,090	3,014	2,238
MS..........	571	956	1,176	1,707	1,275	WY.........	48	51	62	114	104
MO..........	1,204	1,361	2,024	3,195	2,706						
MT..........	319	585	739	1,257	929	Unallocated ...	2,072	2,882	3,825	5,171	4,689

Source: U.S. Department of Agriculture, Economic Research Service, "State Export Data," <http://www.ers.usda.gov/data/stateexports/>.

Table 1306. U.S. Exports, Imports, and Merchandise Trade Balance by Country: 2005 to 2009

[In millions of dollars (901,082 represents $901,082,000,000). Includes silver ore and bullion. Country totals include exports of special category commodities, if any. Data include nonmonetary gold and include trade of Virgin Islands with foreign countries. For methodology, see Foreign Trade Statistics in Appendix III. Minus sign (–) denotes an excess of imports over exports]

Country	Exports, domestic and foreign					General imports					Merchandise trade balance				
	2005	2006	2007	2008	2009	2005	2006	2007	2008	2009	2005	2006	2007	2008	2009
Total [1]	901,082	1,025,967	1,148,199	1,287,442	1,056,043	1,673,455	1,853,938	1,956,962	2,103,641	1,559,625	-772,373	-827,971	-808,763	-816,199	-503,582
Afghanistan	262	417	495	482	1,509	67	45	74	85	116	195	372	421	397	1,392
Albania	19	28	34	40	48	37	24	10	12	15	-19	4	24	28	33
Algeria	1,106	1,102	1,652	1,243	1,108	10,446	15,456	17,816	19,355	10,718	-9,340	-14,354	-16,164	-18,112	-9,610
Angola	929	1,389	1,242	2,019	1,423	8,484	11,719	12,508	18,911	9,339	-7,555	-10,330	-11,266	-16,892	-7,916
Anguilla	32	43	93	81	53	4	4	5	4	6	28	39	88	77	47
Antigua and Barbuda	190	194	240	183	157	4	6	9	5	9	186	188	232	178	148
Argentina	4,122	4,776	5,856	7,536	5,569	4,584	3,979	4,487	5,822	3,890	-462	797	1,369	1,714	1,679
Armenia	65	80	111	151	77	46	46	33	43	78	19	34	78	109	–
Aruba	559	511	529	680	446	2,920	2,845	2,995	3,179	1,278	-2,361	-2,335	-2,466	-2,499	-833
Australia	15,589	17,546	19,178	22,219	19,599	7,342	8,204	8,615	10,589	8,012	8,246	9,342	10,563	11,630	11,588
Austria	2,544	2,961	3,110	2,649	2,537	6,103	8,304	10,669	8,457	6,379	-3,558	-5,343	-7,559	-5,808	-3,842
Azerbaijan	132	231	178	239	185	45	716	1,887	4,361	1,973	87	-485	-1,710	-4,122	-1,787
Bahamas, The	1,787	2,282	2,468	2,760	2,504	700	453	504	604	819	1,087	1,830	1,965	2,155	1,685
Bahrain	351	474	591	830	667	432	632	625	539	463	-81	-158	-33	291	204
Bangladesh	320	333	456	468	435	2,693	3,271	3,432	3,748	3,699	-2,373	-2,938	-2,976	-3,280	-3,264
Barbados	395	442	457	497	405	32	34	38	40	33	363	409	419	457	372
Belarus	35	75	102	134	137	345	539	1,033	1,070	574	-310	-465	-932	-935	-437
Belgium	18,691	21,340	25,259	28,903	21,608	13,023	14,405	15,281	17,308	13,826	5,668	6,935	9,977	11,595	7,782
Belize	218	239	234	353	253	98	147	105	154	100	119	92	129	199	153
Benin	72	115	289	846	397	1	1	5	31	–	72	115	284	815	397
Bermuda	490	634	660	822	807	87	16	24	140	13	403	618	636	682	794
Bolivia	219	215	278	389	431	293	362	363	511	504	-74	-147	-85	-122	-73
Bosnia and Herzegovina	18	52	20	34	21	70	26	25	25	25	-53	26	-5	9	-4
Botswana	67	27	54	62	93	178	252	187	219	132	-111	-225	-134	-157	-39
Brazil	15,372	18,887	24,172	32,299	26,095	24,436	26,367	25,644	30,453	20,070	-9,064	-7,480	-1,472	1,846	6,026
Brunei	50	48	140	112	100	563	550	405	114	42	-513	-502	-265	-3	59
Bulgaria	268	293	306	509	224	454	458	426	391	228	-186	-165	-120	119	-4
Cambodia	70	74	139	154	127	1,767	2,188	2,463	2,412	1,924	-1,697	-2,114	-2,325	-2,257	-1,797
Cameroon	117	120	133	125	154	158	273	297	614	250	-41	-153	-164	-489	-96
Canada	211,899	230,656	248,888	261,150	204,658	290,384	302,438	317,057	339,491	226,248	-78,486	-71,782	-68,169	-78,342	-21,590
Cayman Islands	681	632	640	746	643	53	15	21	14	14	627	617	619	732	630
Chad	54	61	66	63	63	1,498	1,918	2,145	3,334	1,984	-1,444	-1,857	-2,079	-3,272	-1,921
Chile	5,134	6,586	8,148	11,857	9,346	6,664	9,565	8,999	8,196	5,949	-1,531	-2,979	-851	3,661	3,396
China [2]	41,192	53,673	62,937	69,733	69,497	243,470	287,774	321,443	337,773	296,374	-202,278	-234,101	-258,506	-268,040	-226,877
Colombia	5,462	6,709	8,558	11,437	9,451	8,849	9,266	9,434	13,093	11,323	-3,387	-2,557	-876	-1,656	-1,872
Congo (Brazzaville) [3]	104	138	140	185	277	1,623	3,097	3,071	5,074	3,105	-1,519	-2,959	-2,931	-4,889	-2,828
Congo (Kinshasa) [3]	65	71	113	130	79	264	85	206	266	331	-199	-14	-94	-136	-251
Costa Rica	3,599	4,132	4,580	5,680	4,700	3,415	3,844	3,942	3,938	5,612	183	288	639	1,742	-912
Cote d'Ivoire	124	147	162	254	206	1,198	702	600	1,092	745	-1,074	-554	-439	-838	-539
Croatia	159	147	247	467	202	364	353	332	271	251	-206	-207	-85	196	-49
Cuba	369	340	447	712	533	–	–	–	–	–	369	340	447	711	533
Cyprus	84	199	169	217	179	31	51	17	14	53	54	147	152	204	126
Czech Republic	1,054	1,123	1,262	1,378	970	2,193	2,349	2,431	2,569	1,933	-1,139	-1,227	-1,168	-1,190	-964

See footnotes at end of table.

Table 1306. U.S. Exports, Imports, and Merchandise Trade Balance by Country: 2005 to 2009—Con.

[See head-note, page 808]

Country	Exports, domestic and foreign					General imports					Merchandise trade balance				
	2005	2006	2007	2008	2009	2005	2006	2007	2008	2009	2005	2006	2007	2008	2009
Denmark	1,918	2,268	2,890	2,711	2,056	5,144	5,540	6,064	6,446	5,511	-3,226	-3,272	-3,175	-3,735	-3,454
Djibouti	48	48	59	141	196	1	3	4	7	3	46	44	54	134	194
Dominica	62	68	84	105	77	3	3	2	2	3	58	65	82	103	74
Dominican Republic	4,719	5,351	6,084	6,594	5,269	4,604	4,532	4,216	3,978	3,329	115	818	1,868	2,617	1,939
Ecuador	1,964	2,727	2,936	3,450	3,338	5,759	7,094	6,135	9,048	5,273	-3,795	-4,367	-3,199	-5,598	-1,335
Egypt	3,159	4,029	5,259	6,002	5,253	2,091	2,396	2,377	2,370	2,058	1,068	1,633	2,883	3,632	3,195
El Salvador	1,854	2,152	2,313	2,462	2,019	1,989	1,857	2,044	2,228	1,822	-134	295	270	234	197
Equatorial Guinea	281	551	236	185	306	1,561	1,733	1,777	3,367	2,489	-1,280	-1,181	-1,541	-3,183	-2,184
Estonia	145	221	242	226	189	511	526	296	392	162	-366	-305	-54	-167	27
Ethiopia	456	137	167	302	267	62	81	88	152	113	394	56	79	149	154
Fiji	28	33	30	55	31	169	146	153	162	144	-141	-113	-123	-107	-113
Finland	2,254	2,648	3,133	3,761	1,362	4,342	4,974	5,266	5,903	3,985	-2,088	-2,326	-2,133	-2,142	-2,323
France	22,259	23,512	26,676	28,840	26,493	33,842	37,040	41,553	44,049	34,236	-11,583	-13,528	-14,877	-15,209	-7,743
French Guiana	27	33	31	18	17	-	1	-	-	-	27	33	31	18	17
French Polynesia	112	108	124	130	112	60	58	62	72	29	52	50	62	58	83
Gabon	99	135	478	284	71	2,816	1,361	2,182	2,279	1,231	-2,716	-1,226	-1,704	-1,995	-1,060
Georgia	214	264	364	586	264	194	105	212	208	70	20	158	153	379	294
Germany	34,184	41,159	49,420	54,505	43,506	84,751	89,082	94,164	97,497	71,498	-50,567	-47,923	-44,744	-42,991	-28,192
Ghana	337	289	416	608	716	158	192	199	222	135	179	97	218	386	581
Gibraltar	163	286	594	2,641	1,087	5	1	3	1	1	159	285	591	2,639	1,086
Greece	1,192	1,555	2,110	1,932	2,487	884	966	1,192	999	841	309	589	918	933	1,647
Grenada	82	74	83	84	59	6	4	8	7	6	77	70	75	77	53
Guadeloupe	55	65	139	384	206	2	3	5	7	2	52	62	134	377	204
Guatemala	2,835	3,511	4,065	4,718	3,875	3,137	3,102	3,026	3,463	3,148	-302	409	1,039	1,256	727
Guinea	94	65	74	101	95	75	94	99	106	67	19	-29	-26	-5	28
Guyana	177	179	188	289	260	120	125	123	146	173	57	54	65	143	87
Haiti	710	817	680	944	790	447	496	488	450	552	262	321	192	494	238
Honduras	3,254	3,687	4,461	4,846	3,568	3,749	3,717	3,912	4,041	3,319	-495	-30	549	805	48
Hong Kong	16,351	17,742	19,902	21,499	21,051	8,892	7,947	7,026	6,483	3,571	7,459	9,795	12,876	15,015	17,480
Hungary	1,023	1,188	1,292	1,431	1,233	2,561	2,584	2,828	3,103	2,223	-1,538	-1,397	-1,536	-1,672	-991
Iceland	512	366	630	470	350	269	228	206	241	179	243	138	424	229	170
India	7,919	9,674	14,969	17,682	16,441	18,804	21,831	24,073	25,704	21,166	-10,886	-12,157	-9,104	-8,022	-4,725
Indonesia	3,054	3,078	3,970	5,644	5,107	12,014	13,425	14,301	15,799	12,939	-8,960	-10,346	-10,332	-10,155	-7,832
Iran	96	86	145	683	280	174	157	173	104	65	-79	-71	-28	579	216
Iraq	1,374	1,491	1,560	2,070	1,772	9,054	11,546	11,396	22,080	9,263	-7,680	-10,055	-9,835	-20,010	-7,491
Ireland	8,447	7,621	7,777	7,611	7,465	28,733	28,526	30,445	31,346	28,101	-20,286	-20,904	-22,668	-23,736	-20,636
Israel	9,737	10,965	12,887	14,487	9,559	16,830	19,167	20,794	22,336	18,744	-7,093	-8,202	-7,907	-7,849	-9,185
Italy	11,524	12,546	14,150	15,461	12,258	31,009	32,655	35,028	36,135	26,430	-19,485	-20,109	-20,878	-20,674	-14,162
Jamaica	1,701	2,036	2,316	2,643	1,441	376	528	720	729	468	1,325	1,508	1,596	1,915	973
Japan	54,681	58,459	61,160	65,142	51,134	138,004	148,181	145,463	139,262	95,804	-83,323	-89,722	-84,304	-74,120	-44,669
Jordan	644	650	856	940	1,132	1,267	1,422	1,329	1,137	924	-623	-772	-473	-197	268
Kazakhstan	538	646	753	936	603	1,101	961	1,252	1,603	1,544	-563	-314	-499	-618	-940
Kenya	573	431	520	442	654	348	354	325	344	281	225	77	195	99	373
Korea, South	27,572	32,219	34,402	34,669	28,612	43,781	45,804	47,562	48,069	39,216	-16,210	-13,584	-13,161	-13,400	-10,604

See footnotes at end of table.

U.S. Census Bureau, Statistical Abstract of the United States: 2011

Table 1306. U.S. Exports, Imports, and Merchandise Trade Balance by Country: 2005 to 2009—Con.

[See headnote, page 808]

Country	Exports, domestic and foreign					General imports					Merchandise trade balance				
	2005	2006	2007	2008	2009	2005	2006	2007	2008	2009	2005	2006	2007	2008	2009
Kuwait	1,975	2,087	2,484	2,719	1,951	4,335	3,981	4,118	7,093	3,783	-2,360	-1,894	-1,634	-4,374	-1,831
Kyrgyzstan	31	71	49	44	57	5	4	2	2	6	27	67	47	42	51
Latvia	178	245	381	394	289	362	299	334	228	142	-185	-53	47	166	147
Lebanon	466	931	826	1,464	1,852	86	89	104	99	77	379	842	722	1,365	1,775
Lesotho	4	4	8	1	17	404	408	443	374	304	-400	-404	-436	-373	-288
Liberia	69	68	76	157	95	91	140	115	143	80	-22	-72	-39	13	14
Libya	84	384	511	721	666	1,590	2,472	3,385	4,191	1,919	-1,506	-2,088	-2,874	-3,458	-1,253
Liechtenstein	20	16	16	29	23	296	324	284	245	180	-276	-308	-268	-216	-156
Lithuania	390	567	720	831	399	634	570	456	750	590	-244	-3	265	81	-191
Luxembourg	711	581	926	988	1,292	389	534	526	536	443	323	47	399	452	849
Macau	102	200	226	307	209	1,249	1,230	1,095	915	237	-1,147	-1,030	-869	-609	-28
Macedonia	32	22	34	36	35	48	42	73	78	44	-17	-20	-39	-42	-9
Madagascar	28	45	32	71	106	324	281	338	324	253	-295	-236	-306	-254	-148
Malawi	28	46	51	45	40	116	59	59	65	63	-87	-14	-8	-20	-23
Malaysia	10,461	12,444	11,680	12,949	10,403	33,685	36,533	32,629	30,736	23,283	-23,224	-24,089	-20,948	-17,787	-12,879
Mali	32	43	32	31	37	4	8	9	5	4	29	35	22	26	33
Malta	194	163	207	253	208	283	371	329	279	219	-89	-208	-121	-25	-10
Martinique	35	32	194	289	263	22	41	7	8	5	13	-9	186	281	258
Mauritania	86	90	103	107	56	1	51	1	46	35	85	39	102	60	22
Mauritius	31	36	50	51	70	222	219	187	176	169	-191	-183	-138	-125	-99
Mexico	120,248	133,722	135,918	151,220	128,892	170,109	198,253	210,714	215,942	176,654	-49,861	-64,531	-74,796	-64,722	-47,762
Moldova	40	30	53	66	27	50	37	23	12	8	-10	-7	30	54	18
Monaco	17	33	43	63	18	37	32	21	21	39	-21	-2	21	40	21
Mongolia	22	23	26	57	41	144	114	83	53	15	-122	-91	-57	4	26
Montenegro	-	-	45	53	35	-	-	5	-	17	-	-	40	53	18
Morocco	481	838	1,294	1,436	1,630	446	521	610	879	468	35	317	684	557	1,162
Mozambique	63	64	115	213	190	12	16	5	17	39	51	49	110	197	151
Namibia	112	127	128	280	202	130	116	220	301	329	-17	11	-92	-21	-126
Nepal	25	17	29	29	31	111	99	90	85	55	-87	-83	-61	-56	-24
Netherlands	26,468	30,960	32,837	39,719	32,242	14,862	17,342	18,403	21,123	16,098	11,606	13,617	14,434	18,597	16,143
Netherlands Antilles	1,138	1,485	2,082	2,952	2,056	922	1,119	782	809	476	215	366	1,300	2,142	1,580
New Caledonia	38	44	58	89	78	27	51	79	50	27	11	-7	-22	39	51
New Zealand	2,592	2,806	2,718	2,534	2,159	3,155	3,116	3,113	3,171	2,558	-563	-310	-396	-637	-399
Nicaragua	625	752	890	1,094	715	1,181	1,526	1,604	1,704	1,612	-555	-774	-714	-609	-897
Niger	79	129	69	50	58	66	124	10	44	106	13	5	60	6	-48
Nigeria	1,620	2,233	2,778	4,102	3,687	24,239	27,863	32,770	38,068	19,128	-22,620	-25,630	-29,992	-33,966	-15,441
Norway	1,942	2,394	3,040	3,292	2,790	6,776	7,085	7,318	7,315	5,688	-4,834	-4,691	-4,277	-4,023	-2,898
Oman	571	829	1,059	1,382	1,126	555	909	1,041	852	907	16	-80	18	530	219
Pakistan	1,252	1,723	1,944	1,898	1,618	3,253	3,672	3,578	3,591	3,163	-2,002	-1,950	-1,634	-1,693	-1,545
Panama	2,162	2,660	3,669	4,887	4,293	327	379	365	379	302	1,835	2,281	3,304	4,508	3,991
Papua New Guinea	55	44	66	70	218	58	84	109	106	103	-3	-40	-43	-36	115
Paraguay	896	911	1,237	1,610	1,355	52	58	68	78	56	844	853	1,169	1,532	1,299
Peru	2,309	2,927	4,120	6,183	4,919	5,119	5,880	5,272	5,812	4,223	-2,810	-2,954	-1,152	371	696
Philippines	6,895	7,617	7,712	8,295	5,766	9,250	9,694	9,408	8,713	6,794	-2,355	-2,077	-1,696	-418	-1,028
Poland	1,268	1,961	3,123	4,131	2,302	1,949	2,253	2,226	2,587	2,038	-681	-292	897	1,544	263
Portugal	1,132	1,471	2,478	2,646	1,085	2,329	3,060	3,049	2,451	1,577	-1,197	-1,590	-571	195	-492
Qatar	987	1,279	2,524	2,716	2,713	448	262	477	484	506	539	1,017	2,046	2,232	2,207
Romania	609	554	677	1,048	672	1,208	1,119	1,054	1,107	752	-599	-565	-378	-58	-80

See footnotes at end of table.

Table 1306. U.S. Exports, Imports, and Merchandise Trade Balance by Country: 2005 to 2009—Con.

[See headnote, page 808]

Country	Exports, domestic and foreign					General imports					Merchandise trade balance				
	2005	2006	2007	2008	2009	2005	2006	2007	2008	2009	2005	2006	2007	2008	2009
Russia	3,962	4,700	7,283	9,335	5,332	15,307	19,828	19,314	26,783	18,200	-11,344	-15,128	-12,031	-17,448	-12,868
Saudi Arabia	6,805	7,640	10,396	12,484	10,792	27,193	31,689	35,626	54,747	22,053	-20,387	-24,049	-25,230	-42,263	-11,261
Senegal	141	97	150	137	176	4	21	19	18	7	138	76	132	119	169
Serbia	–	–	110	207	113	–	36	58	72	62	–	3	51	136	51
Sierra Leone	38	39	55	59	43	9	36	48	48	24	29	3	7	12	18
Singapore	20,466	23,826	25,619	27,854	22,232	15,110	17,768	18,394	15,885	15,705	5,356	6,057	7,225	11,969	6,527
Slovakia	150	422	503	548	210	961	1,405	1,505	1,301	628	-811	-983	-1,002	-754	-418
Slovenia	234	239	297	310	244	413	483	488	467	388	-179	-244	-192	-157	-144
South Africa	3,907	4,462	5,521	6,490	4,453	5,886	7,501	9,054	9,948	5,879	-1,979	-3,039	-3,533	-3,458	-1,426
Spain	6,839	7,401	9,766	12,190	8,717	8,615	9,778	10,498	11,094	7,857	-1,776	-2,377	-732	1,096	860
Sri Lanka	198	237	227	283	230	2,083	2,146	2,065	1,962	1,593	-1,885	-1,909	-1,838	-1,679	-1,363
St. Kitts and Nevis	94	127	111	124	108	50	50	54	54	48	44	77	57	70	60
St. Lucia	135	149	165	241	136	32	30	33	26	18	103	119	132	215	118
St. Vincent and the Grenadines	45	58	69	83	75	15	2	1	1	1	30	56	68	82	74
Sudan	108	77	79	143	78	14	6	7	5	10	95	71	72	138	69
Suriname	246	259	304	406	380	165	165	130	127	139	80	94	174	280	241
Swaziland	12	12	29	12	15	199	156	145	134	110	-187	-144	-116	-122	-95
Sweden	3,715	4,126	4,473	5,018	4,561	13,821	13,870	13,024	12,498	8,186	-10,106	-9,744	-8,551	-7,480	-3,625
Switzerland	10,718	14,375	17,039	22,024	17,504	13,000	14,230	14,760	17,782	16,053	-2,282	145	2,279	4,242	1,451
Syria	155	224	361	409	304	324	214	111	352	303	-169	11	251	57	1
Taiwan [2]	21,614	22,709	25,829	24,926	18,486	34,826	38,212	38,278	36,326	28,362	-13,211	-15,502	-12,449	-11,400	-9,877
Tajikistan	29	43	53	51	41	241	61	1	8	9	-212	-18	52	43	33
Tanzania	96	161	174	170	158	34	35	46	56	49	63	126	128	114	109
Thailand	7,257	7,915	8,336	9,067	6,918	19,890	22,466	22,755	23,538	19,082	-12,633	-14,551	-14,418	-14,472	-12,164
Togo	28	108	288	117	125	6	4	5	11	7	21	105	283	106	118
Trinidad and Tobago	1,417	1,615	1,780	2,250	1,988	7,891	8,362	8,790	9,030	5,180	-6,474	-6,748	-7,010	-6,780	-3,192
Tunisia	261	363	403	502	501	264	470	458	644	326	-3	-107	-55	-142	176
Turkey	4,239	5,291	6,499	9,959	7,095	5,182	5,359	4,601	4,642	3,662	-943	-68	1,898	5,317	3,433
Turkmenistan	215	113	127	60	294	135	76	219	140	93	80	37	-92	-80	201
Turks and Caicos Islands	238	366	396	434	248	9	12	13	10	11	228	354	383	424	237
Uganda	63	51	80	89	119	26	22	27	53	31	37	29	54	36	88
Ukraine	533	756	1,342	1,868	887	1,098	1,640	1,220	2,340	495	-565	-884	122	-472	392
United Arab Emirates	8,120	10,277	10,787	14,417	12,211	1,468	1,385	1,337	1,286	1,498	6,651	8,892	9,449	13,131	10,713
United Kingdom	38,568	45,410	49,981	53,599	45,704	51,033	53,513	56,858	58,587	47,480	-12,465	-8,103	-6,876	-4,988	-1,776
Uruguay	357	482	641	893	745	732	512	492	244	239	-376	-30	149	649	506
Uzbekistan	74	54	89	301	98	96	151	165	292	89	-22	-98	-76	8	8
Venezuela	6,421	9,002	10,201	12,610	9,315	33,978	37,134	39,910	51,424	28,059	-27,557	-28,131	-29,709	-38,814	-18,744
Vietnam	1,193	1,100	1,903	2,789	3,097	6,631	8,567	10,633	12,901	12,288	-5,438	-7,466	-8,730	-10,112	-9,191
Virgin Islands, British	125	215	176	310	233	34	26	43	11	6	91	189	133	299	227
Yemen	219	255	642	401	381	279	447	292	8	7	-60	-192	350	393	374
Zambia	29	52	69	79	57	22	29	48	52	8	7	23	21	27	49
Zimbabwe	46	48	105	93	85	61	104	72	112	22	-15	-56	33	-19	63

– Represents or rounds to zero. [1] Includes timing adjustment and unidentified countries, not shown separately. [2] See footnote 4, Table 1331. [3] See footnote 5, Table 1331.

Source: U.S. Census Bureau, *U.S. International Trade in Goods and Services*, December and annual revisions for 2009, Series FT-900 (10-04). See also <http://www.census.gov/foreign-trade/Press-Release/2009pr/final_revisions/>.

Table 1307. U.S. Exports and General Imports by Selected SITC Commodity Groups: 2000 to 2009

[In millions of dollars (781,918 represents $781,918,000,000). SITC = Standard International Trade Classification. For methodology, see Foreign Trade Statistics in Appendix III. N.e.s. = not elsewhere specified]

Selected commodity	Exports [1]				General imports [2]			
	2000	2007	2008	2009	2000	2007	2008	2009
Total.................	781,918	1,162,479	1,287,442	1,056,043	1,218,022	1,956,962	2,103,641	1,559,625
Agricultural commodities [3]....	51,296	89,921	115,248	98,423	39,186	72,067	80,662	71,849
Animal feeds..............	3,780	5,506	7,610	7,763	597	1,008	1,258	1,162
Cereal flour..............	1,310	2,839	2,870	2,957	1,753	3,774	4,268	4,161
Corn....................	4,695	10,095	13,931	9,146	160	257	350	283
Cotton, raw and linters........	1,893	4,589	4,812	3,365	28	14	12	1
Meat and preparations........	7,004	9,131	12,584	11,618	3,841	5,355	5,046	4,598
Soybeans.................	5,284	10,002	15,455	16,443	31	97	182	210
Vegetables and fruits.........	7,477	12,125	14,040	14,014	9,286	17,671	19,145	18,571
Wheat...................	3,374	8,328	11,294	5,380	229	501	1,080	698
Manufactured goods [3]........	625,894	868,297	912,382	743,321	1,012,855	1,479,971	1,490,383	1,185,889
ADP equipment, office machinery..............	46,595	29,914	28,639	21,282	92,133	101,602	96,526	91,098
Airplane parts..............	15,062	21,666	(X)	(X)	5,572	8,434	(X)	(X)
Airplanes.................	24,777	51,854	(X)	(X)	12,412	13,286	(X)	(X)
Alcoholic beverages, distilled...	424	984	80,206	1,007	2,946	5,521	5,478	5,011
Aluminum.................	3,780	5,806	1,049	4,291	6,949	13,947	13,429	8,679
Artwork/antiques............	1,387	4,335	6,204	4,605	5,864	8,740	7,513	5,031
Basketware, etc.............	3,309	6,995	5,409	8,068	4,840	10,810	12,196	11,530
Chemicals, cosmetics........	5,292	10,120	7,692	11,120	3,539	8,872	9,577	8,396
Chemicals, dyeing...........	4,089	5,807	11,534	5,546	2,667	3,115	3,073	2,424
Chemicals, fertilizers.........	2,249	3,339	6,238	3,475	1,684	4,981	8,377	4,156
Chemicals, inorganic.........	5,359	10,807	6,540	10,203	6,108	13,349	16,826	10,790
Chemicals, medicinal.........	12,893	32,755	12,846	41,809	14,685	53,798	59,212	60,002
Chemicals, n.e.s............	12,264	20,730	37,379	20,428	5,725	10,851	12,713	9,582
Chemicals, organic..........	17,990	33,869	25,287	27,779	28,578	42,178	47,802	42,183
Chemicals, plastics..........	19,519	37,129	34,256	33,078	10,647	18,248	18,912	13,694
Clothing..................	8,191	3,209	3,169	2,919	64,296	81,176	78,893	69,326
Copper...................	1,425	3,489	3,439	2,375	4,471	11,532	10,358	5,596
Cork, wood, lumber..........	4,320	4,412	4,241	3,495	8,227	8,282	5,704	3,574
Crude fertilizers............	1,724	2,009	2,428	1,765	1,401	1,854	2,966	1,682
Electrical machinery.........	89,917	81,452	82,049	63,964	108,747	113,613	112,623	91,683
Fish and preparations........	2,806	4,044	4,017	3,763	9,907	13,519	13,994	12,982
Footwear.................	663	578	673	620	14,842	19,408	19,545	17,523
Furniture and bedding........	4,744	5,123	5,170	4,023	18,923	33,853	31,371	24,588
Gem diamonds.............	1,289	5,305	5,943	2,156	12,068	18,937	19,744	12,736
General industrial machinery...	33,094	48,641	55,192	45,034	34,667	63,940	66,910	50,181
Glass....................	2,502	3,350	3,317	2,828	2,248	2,885	2,653	2,117
Gold, nonmonetary..........	5,898	13,344	18,714	13,898	2,657	4,670	6,120	8,810
Iron and steel mill products....	5,715	14,018	18,493	12,022	15,807	30,890	38,910	18,230
Jewelry..................	1,574	4,538	4,834	4,322	6,459	11,193	9,615	8,676
Lighting, plumbing..........	1,384	2,090	2,516	2,141	5,104	8,111	7,767	6,120
Metal manufactures, n.e.s.....	13,453	17,315	18,743	14,669	16,204	29,929	30,403	21,414
Metal ores; scrap...........	4,234	22,999	29,431	20,058	3,817	7,549	9,309	5,460
Metalworking machinery......	6,191	5,351	6,074	4,294	7,726	7,723	8,548	4,961
Nickel...................	401	1,379	1,567	931	1,425	4,903	3,430	1,665
Optical goods.............	3,246	3,210	2,860	2,773	4,019	4,698	5,090	4,513
Paper and paperboard........	10,640	13,480	14,668	12,891	15,185	17,913	18,073	14,463
Photographic equipment......	4,236	3,612	3,595	3,211	6,896	2,760	2,489	1,776
Plastic articles, n.e.s.........	7,607	9,427	9,511	8,224	8,034	15,348	15,793	13,743
Platinum.................	888	1,615	1,161	844	5,566	7,716	7,115	2,982
Power generating machinery...	32,743	49,933	33,658	28,056	33,773	50,191	48,187	36,181
Printed materials...........	4,776	6,190	6,355	5,601	3,680	5,548	5,372	4,231
Pulp and waste paper........	4,576	6,906	7,744	6,694	3,381	3,734	4,004	2,441
Records/magnetic media......	5,395	5,088	5,250	4,413	5,172	7,382	6,735	5,183
Rubber articles, n.e.s........	1,673	1,953	1,915	1,625	1,962	3,212	3,169	2,481
Rubber tires and tubes.......	2,379	3,517	3,981	3,641	4,785	9,380	9,705	8,136
Scientific instruments.........	30,984	42,315	42,588	38,105	22,007	35,604	37,275	31,975
Ships, boats..............	1,070	3,062	3,114	1,917	1,178	1,921	1,675	1,267
Specialized industrial machinery..............	30,959	48,357	51,928	36,956	22,711	35,761	35,574	24,235
Television, VCR, etc..........	27,921	24,735	24,379	19,992	70,468	129,796	133,187	119,392
Textile yarn, fabric..........	10,534	11,861	11,860	9,288	15,171	22,759	21,854	18,232
Toys/games/sporting goods....	3,609	5,039	4,697	4,170	20,011	31,807	32,617	27,918
Travel goods..............	351	436	463	449	4,430	7,625	7,986	6,444
Vehicles.................	57,421	95,187	98,871	65,288	161,544	210,431	190,799	127,863
Watches/clocks/parts........	348	392	416	356	3,481	4,454	4,340	3,065
Wood manufactures..........	1,842	2,125	2,270	1,725	7,228	10,390	8,446	6,230
Mineral fuel [3]	13,179	41,725	76,075	54,536	135,367	364,987	491,885	271,739
Coal....................	2,162	4,288	8,196	6,162	805	2,451	3,958	1,766
Crude oil.................	463	1,015	2,270	1,618	89,876	245,771	353,537	194,603
Petroleum preparations.......	5,746	26,522	51,384	36,351	25,673	74,108	87,103	52,584
Liquified propane/butane......	663	1,048	1,011	1,409	1,508	4,024	4,755	2,202
Natural gas...............	411	3,130	4,879	3,271	12,594	31,938	34,423	16,056
Mineral fuels, other mineral....	3,734	4,708	7,030	5,131	4,911	3,717	4,452	2,444
Reexports................	68,203	117,177	131,066	120,345	(X)	(X)	(X)	(X)

X Not applicable. [1] F.a.s. basis. Exports by commodity are only for domestic exports. [2] Customs value basis. [3] Includes other commodities, not shown separately.

Source: U.S. Census Bureau, *U.S. International Trade in Goods and Services*, Series FT 900, Final Reports, <http://www.census.gov/foreign-trade/Press-Release/2009pr/final_revisions/>.

812 Foreign Commerce and Aid

Table 1308. U.S. Total and Aerospace Foreign Trade: 1990 to 2009

[In millions of dollars (−101,718 represents −$101,718,000,000), except percent. Data are reported as exports of domestic merchandise, including Department of Defense shipments and undocumented exports to Canada, f.a.s. (free alongside ship) basis, and imports for consumption, customs value basis. Minus sign (−) indicates deficit]

Year	U.S. Merchandise Trade			Aerospace Trade						
						Exports				
								Civil		
	Trade balance[1]	Imports	Exports	Trade balance	Imports	Total	Percent of U.S. exports	Total	Transports	Total military
1990	−101,718	495,311	393,592	27,282	11,801	39,083	9.9	31,517	16,691	7,566
1993	−115,568	580,659	465,091	27,235	12,183	39,418	8.5	31,823	18,146	7,596
1994	−150,630	663,256	512,626	25,010	12,363	37,373	7.3	30,050	15,931	7,322
1995	−158,801	743,543	584,742	21,562	11,509	33,071	5.7	25,079	10,606	7,991
1996	−170,214	795,289	625,075	26,602	13,668	40,270	6.4	29,477	13,624	10,792
1997	−180,522	869,704	689,182	32,240	18,134	50,374	7.3	40,075	21,028	10,299
1998	−229,758	911,896	682,138	40,961	23,110	64,071	9.4	51,999	29,168	12,072
1999	−328,821	1,024,618	695,797	37,381	25,063	62,444	9.0	50,624	25,694	11,820
2000	−436,104	1,218,022	781,918	26,735	27,944	54,679	7.0	45,566	19,615	9,113
2001	−411,899	1,140,999	729,100	26,035	32,473	58,508	8.0	49,371	22,151	9,137
2002	−468,263	1,161,366	693,103	29,514	27,241	56,775	8.2	47,348	21,661	9,427
2003	−532,350	1,257,121	724,771	27,111	25,393	52,504	7.2	44,060	19,434	8,445
2004	−650,930	1,469,704	818,775	31,002	25,815	56,817	6.9	47,325	18,577	9,492
2005	−767,477	1,673,455	905,978	39,783	27,649	67,433	7.4	57,225	21,888	10,207
2006	−827,971	1,853,938	1,025,967	54,809	30,453	85,262	8.2	71,857	32,897	13,404
2007	−808,763	1,956,962	1,148,199	60,614	36,502	97,224	8.4	83,977	40,297	13,247
2008	−816,199	2,103,641	1,287,442	57,389	37,694	95,082	7.4	82,264	33,326	12,819
2009	−503,582	1,559,625	1,056,043	56,034	25,132	81,166	7.7	70,500	(NA)	10,666

NA Not available. [1] Exports minus imports.

Source: Aerospace Industries Association of America, Washington, DC, *Aerospace Facts and Figures*, annual, <http://www.aia-aerospace.org/resource-center/economics>.

Table 1309. U.S. High Technology Exports by Industry and Selected Major Country: 2000 to 2009

[In billions of dollars (222.5 represents $222,500,000,000)]

Selected industry	2000	2008	2009	Selected country	2000	2008	2009
Total exports	**222.5**	**218.8**	**187.7**	**Total exports**	**222.5**	**218.8**	**187.7**
Computers and office equipment	57.8	47.0	38.3	Canada	34.4	29.1	37.3
Consumer electronics	10.0	8.6	7.6	China [1]	4.6	15.0	28.1
Communications equipment	26.9	32.6	29.6	Japan	19.9	10.9	28.0
Electronic components	22.1	17.5	16.3	Korea, South	12.1	7.5	14.0
Semiconductors	60.0	50.2	43.6	Malaysia	7.8	8.3	9.0
Industrial electronics	30.5	38.7	28.3	Mexico	30.0	27.7	7.2
Electromedical equipment	8.1	18.3	20.2	Taiwan [1]	10.4	8.0	7.0
Photonics	7.1	5.9	3.9	European Union 27 [2]	51.5	46.9	7.0

[1] See footnote 4, Table 1331. [2] See footnote 5, Table 1377.

Source: AeA (formerly the American Electronics Association), *Cyberstates 2010*, annual (copyright), <http://www.aeanet.org>.

Table 1310. U.S. Exporting Companies Profile by Employment-Size Class: 2000 and 2008

[(668,310 represents $668,310,000,000). Based on data from export trade documents and the Business Register. For information on data limitations, see the Technical Documentation in the source]

Employment-size class	Number of exporters		Known export value [1] (mil. dol.)		Percent of—			
					Number of exporters		Known export value	
	2000	2008	2000	2008	2000	2008	2000	2008
All companies, total	**246,452**	**288,747**	**668,310**	**1,147,669**	**100.0**	**100.0**	**100.0**	**100**
No employees	74,772	101,765	47,024	93,146	30.3	35.2	7.0	8.1
1 to 19 employees	96,268	112,220	45,272	81,787	39.1	38.9	6.8	7.1
20 to 49 employees	31,362	32,784	21,262	46,555	12.7	11.4	3.2	4.1
50 to 99 employees	16,988	16,955	19,711	35,163	6.9	5.9	2.9	3.1
100 to 249 employees	13,685	13,023	32,192	62,201	5.6	4.5	4.8	5.4
250 to 499 employees	5,454	4,921	27,397	40,798	2.2	1.7	4.1	3.6
500 or more employees	7,923	7,079	475,453	788,019	3.2	2.5	71.1	68.7

[1] Known value is defined as the value of exports by known exporters, i.e., those export transactions that could be matched to specific companies. Export values are on f.a.s. or "free alongside ship basis."

Source: U.S. Census Bureau, *A Profile of U.S. Exporting Companies, 2000 and 2007–2008*, <http://www.census.gov/foreign-trade/Press-Release/edb/2008/edb-3a.pdf>.

Table 1311. Domestic Exports and Imports for Consumption of Merchandise by Selected NAICS Product Category: 2000 to 2009

[In millions of dollars (712,285 represents $712,285,000,000). Includes nonmonetary gold. For methodology, see Foreign Trade Statistics in Appendix III. NAICS = North American Industry Classification System; see text, Section 15]

Product category	2000	2005	2006	2007	2008	2009
Domestic exports, total	**712,285**	**798,997**	**917,997**	**1,031,022**	**1,156,376**	**935,698**
Agricultural, forestry, and fishery products	29,153	37,109	41,518	53,517	68,233	55,552
Agricultural products, total	23,596	30,683	34,768	46,436	61,073	49,069
Livestock and livestock products	1,255	1,118	1,285	1,362	1,520	1,409
Forestry products, not elsewhere specified	1,644	1,686	1,713	1,925	1,894	1,622
Fish, fresh or chilled, and other marine products	2,658	3,622	3,752	3,795	3,746	3,452
Mining, total	6,187	12,629	13,968	17,013	24,751	17,332
Oil and gas	1,706	4,547	4,225	5,689	8,706	6,570
Minerals and ores	4,481	8,082	9,743	11,324	16,045	10,762
Manufacturing, total	644,440	708,205	810,606	897,516	987,582	802,183
Food and kindred products	24,966	28,937	32,151	38,793	48,476	43,843
Beverages and tobacco products	5,568	3,423	3,850	4,193	4,793	4,373
Textiles and fabrics	7,010	8,483	8,523	8,251	8,213	6,434
Textile mill products	2,236	2,344	2,573	2,651	2,611	2,276
Apparel and accessories	8,104	4,075	3,792	3,133	3,055	2,812
Leather and allied products	2,322	2,300	2,451	2,355	2,266	1,876
Wood products	4,854	4,463	4,915	4,973	5,041	3,976
Paper products	15,539	16,640	18,032	19,738	21,713	19,175
Printed, publishing, & similar products	4,869	5,526	5,816	6,321	6,504	5,747
Petroleum and coal products	8,862	17,979	25,943	30,976	58,440	41,494
Chemicals	77,649	114,821	129,615	147,596	166,249	145,896
Plastics and rubber products	16,970	18,784	20,551	22,041	23,403	20,340
Nonmetallic mineral products	7,830	6,663	7,555	8,372	8,927	7,482
Primary metal products	20,126	27,455	37,120	44,623	54,713	38,173
Fabricated metal products	21,737	23,370	27,281	29,878	32,483	27,737
Machinery, except electrical	85,038	97,001	109,430	122,669	134,117	104,139
Computers and electronic products	161,449	122,744	133,788	135,429	134,757	106,782
Electrical equipment, appliances and components	25,401	26,457	31,177	33,422	34,548	26,498
Transportation equipment	121,701	144,985	169,382	190,474	192,296	154,120
Furniture and fixtures	2,882	2,844	3,162	3,511	3,999	3,525
Miscellaneous manufactured commodities	19,327	28,909	33,498	38,117	40,978	35,486
Special classification provisions	32,505	41,055	50,995	62,069	75,010	59,866
Waste & scrap	4,948	10,389	15,806	22,020	28,943	21,784
Used or second-hand merchandise	1,950	2,570	4,228	5,708	7,326	6,005
Goods returned or reimported	333	65	57	36	47	31
Special classification provision, not elsewhere specified	25,274	28,030	30,905	34,305	38,693	32,046
Imports for consumption, total	**1,205,339**	**1,664,497**	**1,843,976**	**1,946,341**	**2,093,578**	**1,551,063**
Agricultural, forestry, and fishery products	24,378	30,761	34,621	37,678	41,068	36,802
Agricultural products, total	11,771	15,818	17,333	19,677	22,477	21,508
Livestock and livestock products	3,085	3,277	4,105	4,691	4,435	3,600
Forestry products, not elsewhere specified	1,409	2,250	2,757	2,745	3,417	1,773
Fish, fresh or chilled, and other marine products	8,113	9,416	10,427	10,565	10,739	9,920
Mining, total	79,841	192,115	221,903	241,494	341,123	184,585
Oil and gas	76,166	185,621	214,130	233,384	329,397	177,929
Minerals and ores	3,675	6,494	7,772	8,110	11,726	6,655
Manufacturing, total	1,040,329	1,372,004	1,512,070	1,585,062	1,627,042	1,260,343
Food and kindred products	18,944	29,779	31,803	34,706	39,987	36,131
Beverages and tobacco products	8,350	12,849	14,616	15,937	15,877	14,454
Textiles and fabrics	7,042	7,450	7,364	7,451	6,943	5,283
Textile mill products	7,347	13,508	14,680	15,410	14,984	13,227
Apparel and accessories	62,928	74,478	77,007	78,947	76,182	66,818
Leather and allied products	21,463	26,559	28,467	29,400	29,479	25,548
Wood products	15,388	23,654	22,740	18,540	14,142	9,746
Paper products	19,080	22,094	23,467	23,472	24,014	18,514
Printed, publishing, & similar products	4,197	5,599	5,805	6,347	6,170	4,890
Petroleum and coal products	40,156	81,359	93,022	102,303	130,639	75,139
Chemicals	76,606	131,936	146,612	160,297	195,731	162,366
Plastics and rubber products	17,362	28,072	30,567	32,039	33,006	27,749
Nonmetallic mineral products	14,740	18,445	20,278	19,683	18,070	13,081
Primary metal products	43,833	64,666	88,622	88,928	99,327	55,412
Fabricated metal products	27,974	41,026	46,061	50,011	51,934	39,780
Machinery, except electrical	79,366	109,619	121,334	121,276	123,669	86,832
Computers and electronic products	250,694	269,921	295,214	312,769	300,391	265,557
Electrical equipment, appliances and components	39,567	55,179	62,269	67,115	67,758	55,519
Transportation equipment	213,110	251,386	269,391	277,450	254,296	180,256
Furniture and fixtures	15,607	25,096	27,027	27,674	26,321	21,566
Miscellaneous manufactured commodities	56,577	79,329	85,724	95,307	98,121	82,475
Special classification provisions	60,791	69,617	75,306	82,054	84,308	69,301
Waste & scrap	1,875	3,207	4,788	5,031	5,669	3,459
Used or second-hand merchandise	6,345	6,026	7,127	8,994	7,757	5,205
Goods returned or reimported	33,851	37,024	38,436	39,494	40,134	38,101
Special classification provision, not elsewhere specified	18,720	23,359	24,954	28,535	30,747	22,535

Source: U.S. Census Bureau, *U.S. International Trade in Goods and Services*, Series FT-900, December 2009, <http://www.census.gov/foreign-trade/Press-Release/2009pr/12/#exhibits>.

This section presents summary economic and social statistics for Puerto Rico, the U.S. Virgin Islands, Guam, American Samoa, and the Northern Mariana Islands. Primary sources are the decennial censuses of population and housing, County Business Patterns, and the Puerto Rico Community Survey conducted by the U.S. Census Bureau; the annual *Vital Statistics of the United States*, issued by the National Center for Health Statistics; and the annual *Income and Product* of the Puerto Rico Planning Board.

Jurisdiction—The United States gained jurisdiction over these areas as follows: the islands of *Puerto Rico* and *Guam*, surrendered by Spain to the United States in December 1898, were ceded to the United States by the Treaty of Paris, ratified in 1899. Puerto Rico became a commonwealth on July 25, 1952, thereby achieving a high degree of local autonomy under its own constitution. The *U.S. Virgin Islands*, comprising 50 islands and cays, was purchased by the United States from Denmark in 1917. *American Samoa*, a group of seven islands, was acquired by the United States in accordance with a convention among the United States, Great Britain, and Germany, ratified in 1900 (Swains Island was annexed in 1925). By an agreement approved by the Security Council and the United States, the Northern Mariana Islands, previously under Japanese mandate, was administered by the United States between 1947 and 1986 under the United Nations trusteeship system. The Northern Mariana Islands became a commonwealth in 1986.

Censuses—Because characteristics of Puerto Rico and the Island Areas differ, the presentation of census data for them is not uniform. The 1960 Census of Population covered all of the places listed above except the Northern Mariana Islands (their census was conducted in April 1958 by the Office of the High Commissioner), while the 1960 Census of Housing excluded American Samoa. The 1970, 1980, 1990, and 2000 Censuses of Population and Housing covered all five areas. Beginning in 1967, Congress authorized the economic censuses, to be taken at 5-year intervals, for years ending in "2" and "7." Prior economic censuses were conducted in Puerto Rico for 1949, 1954, 1958, and 1963 and in Guam and the U.S. Virgin Islands for 1958 and 1963. In 1967, the census of construction industries was added for the first time in Puerto Rico; in 1972, the U.S. Virgin Islands and Guam were covered; and in 1982, the economic census was taken for the first time for the Northern Mariana Islands.

Puerto Rico Community Survey—The Puerto Rico Community Survey (PRCS) began in 2005 and is a critical element in the Census Bureau's reengineered 2010 census plan. The American Community Survey is the equivalent of the PRCS for the United States (50 states and District of Columbia). The PRCS collects and produces population and housing information every year instead of every 10 years. About 36,000 households are surveyed each year from across every municipio in Puerto Rico.

Information in other sections—In addition to the statistics presented in this section, other data are included as integral parts of many tables showing distribution by states in various sections of the *Abstract*. See "Puerto Rico and the Island Areas" in the Index. For definition and explanation of terms used, see Sections 1, 2, 4, 17, 20, 21, and 22.

U.S. Census Bureau, Statistical Abstract of the United States: 2011

Selected Island Areas of the United States

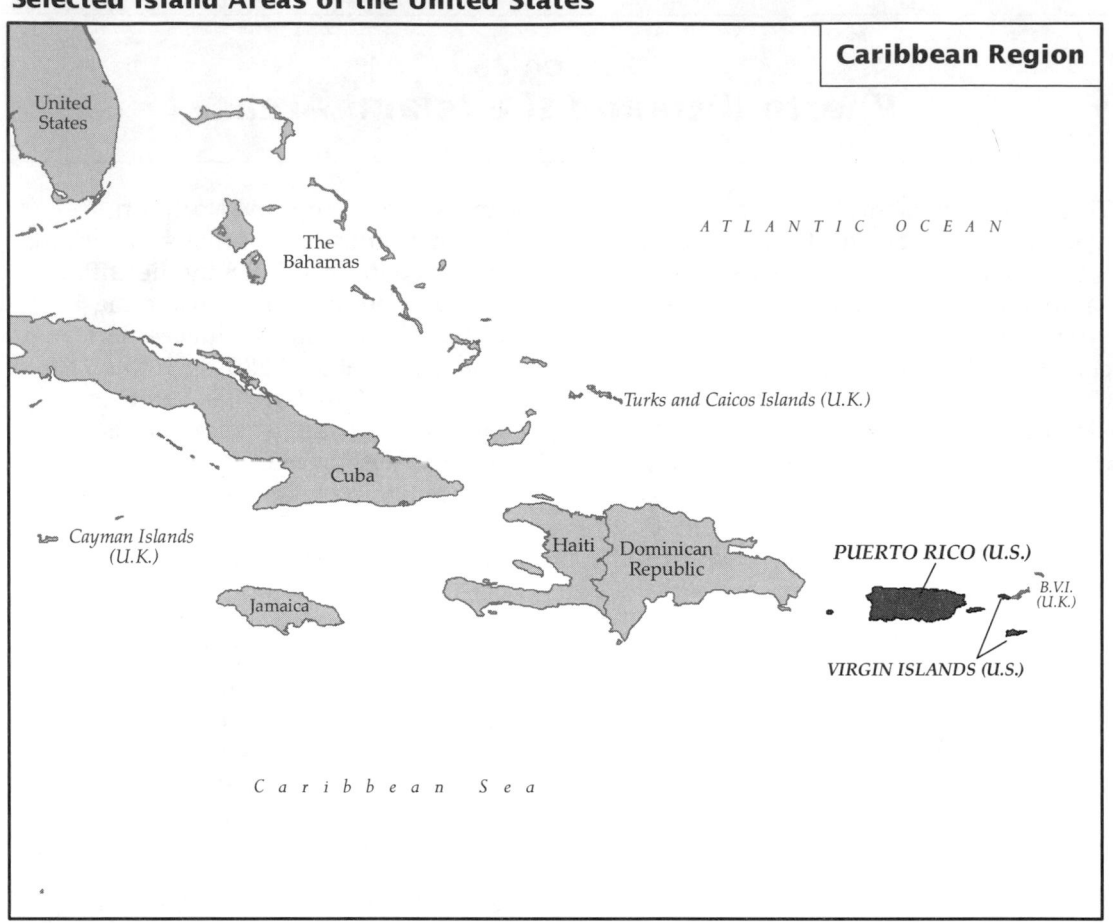

Caribbean Region

United States

The Bahamas

ATLANTIC OCEAN

Turks and Caicos Islands (U.K.)

Cuba

Cayman Islands (U.K.)

Haiti Dominican Republic **PUERTO RICO (U.S.)** *B.V.I. (U.K.)*

Jamaica

VIRGIN ISLANDS (U.S.)

C a r i b b e a n   S e a

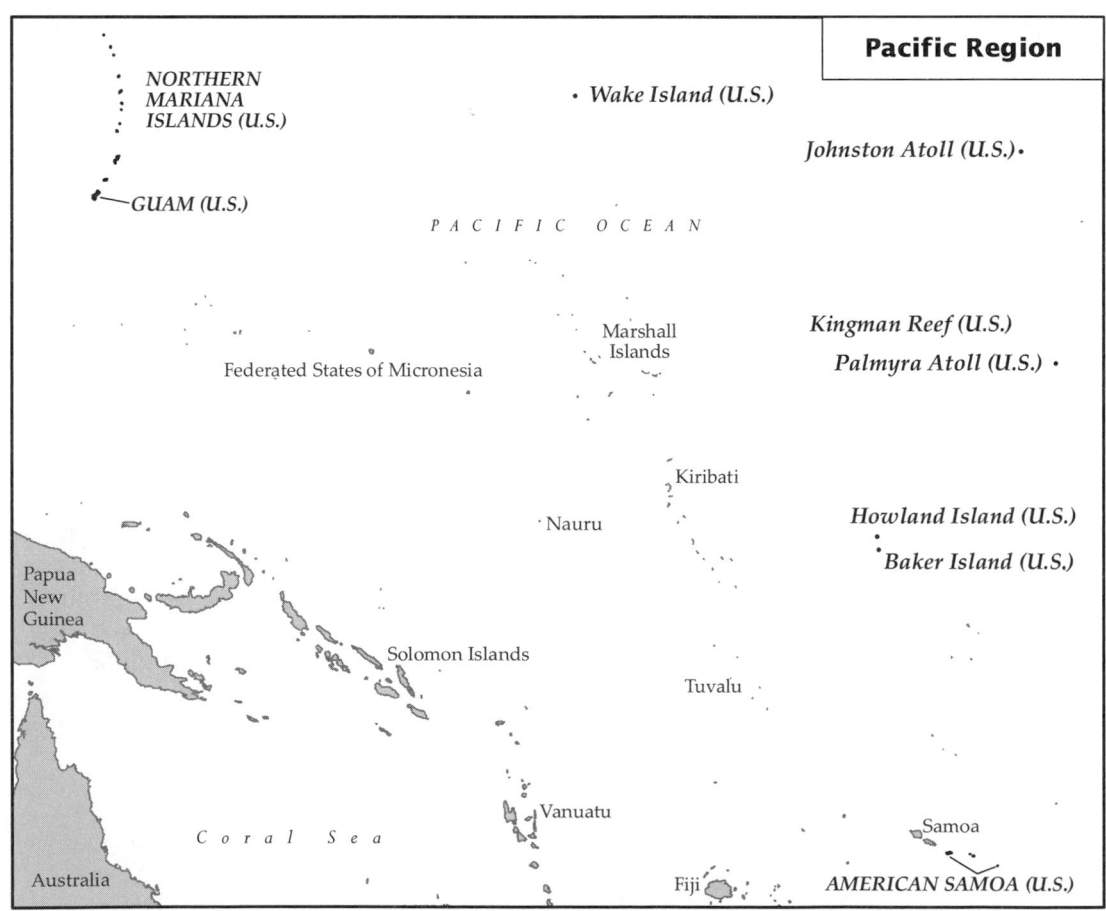

Pacific Region

NORTHERN MARIANA ISLANDS (U.S.)

• *Wake Island (U.S.)*

Johnston Atoll (U.S.) •

GUAM (U.S.)

PACIFIC   OCEAN

Kingman Reef (U.S.)

Marshall Islands

Palmyra Atoll (U.S.) •

Federated States of Micronesia

Kiribati

Nauru

Howland Island (U.S.)

Baker Island (U.S.)

Papua New Guinea

Solomon Islands

Tuvalu

C o r a l   S e a

Vanuatu

Samoa

Australia

Fiji **AMERICAN SAMOA (U.S.)**

U.S. Census Bureau, Statistical Abstract of the United States: 2011

Table 1312. Estimated Resident Population With Projections: 1990 to 2025

[In thousands (3,537 represents 3,537,000). Population as of July 1. Population data generally are de-facto figures for the present territory. Data for 1990 to 2000 are adjusted to the 2000 Census of Population for Puerto Rico only. See text, Section 30, for general comments regarding the data. For details of methodology, coverage, and reliability, see source]

Area	1990	2000	2005	2007	2008	2009	2010	Projected		
								2015	2020	2025
Puerto Rico	3,537	3,814	3,911	3,941	3,955	3,967	3,979	4,024	4,051	4,055
American Samoa.	47	58	62	64	65	66	66	71	75	79
Guam.	134	155	169	174	176	178	181	193	204	214
Virgin Islands.	104	109	110	110	110	110	110	109	108	107
Northern Mariana Islands	44	70	71	59	55	51	48	44	49	53

Source: U.S. Census Bureau, International Data Base, <http://www.census.gov/ipc/www/idb/>, accessed June 2010.

Table 1313. Vital Statistics—Specified Areas: 1990 to 2008

[Births, deaths, and infant deaths by place of residence. Rates for 1990 and 2000 based on population enumerated as of April 1; for other years, on population estimated as of July 1]

Area and year	Births		Deaths		Infant deaths	
	Number	Rate [1]	Number	Rate [1]	Number	Rate [2]
Puerto Rico:						
1990.	66,417	18.8	25,957	7.3	888	13.4
1995.	63,425	17.0	30,032	8.1	804	12.7
2000.	59,333	15.2	28,369	7.2	574	9.7
2005.	50,564	12.9	29,531	7.5	466	9.2
2006.	48,597	12.4	28,206	7.2	426	8.8
2007.	46,642	11.8	29,169	7.4	394	8.5
2008 [3]	45,622	11.5	(NA)	(NA)	(NA)	(NA)
Guam:						
1990.	3,839	28.6	520	3.9	31	8.1
1995.	4,180	29.0	592	4.1	38	9.4
2000.	3,766	24.4	648	4.2	22	5.8
2005.	3,187	18.9	677	4.0	34	10.7
2006.	3,391	19.8	679	4.0	45	13.3
2007.	3,483	20.1	778	4.5	36	10.3
2008 [3]	3,459	19.7	(NA)	(NA)	(NA)	(NA)
Virgin Islands:						
1990.	2,267	21.8	480	4.6	33	14.6
1995.	2,063	18.1	664	5.8	34	16.6
2000.	1,564	12.9	641	5.3	21	13.4
2005.	1,605	14.8	663	6.1	11	(R)
2006.	1,687	15.5	624	5.7	9	(B)
2007.	1,697	15.5	703	6.4	12	(B)
2008 [3]	(NA)	(NA)	(NA)	(NA)	(NA)	(NA)
American Samoa:						
2000.	1,731	26.4	219	3.3	11	(NA)
2005.	1,720	27.6	272	4.4	12	(B)
2007.	1,288	20.1	250	3.9	11	(B)
2008 [3]	1,332	20.5	(NA)	(NA)	(NA)	(NA)
Northern Marianas:						
2000.	1,431	19.9	136	1.9	11	(NA)
2005.	1,335	16.6	186	2.3	6	(B)
2007.	1,387	16.4	137	1.6	5	(B)
2008 [3]	1,266	22.9	(NA)	(NA)	(NA)	(NA)

NA Not available. B Base figure too small to meet statistical standards of reliability. [1] Per 1,000 population. [2] Rates are infant deaths (under 1 year) per 1,000 live births. [3] Data for 2008 are preliminary.

Source: U.S. National Center for Health Statistics, National Vital Statistics Reports (NVSR), *Births: Preliminary Data for 2008*, Vol. 58, No. 16, April 2010, and *Deaths: Final Data for 2007*, Vol. 58, No. 19, May 2010. See also <http://www.cdc.gov/nchs/nvss.htm>.

Table 1314. Public Elementary and Secondary Schools by Area: 2007

[For school year ending in year shown, unless otherwise indicated. (3,268,200 represents $3,268,200,000)]

Item	Puerto Rico	Guam	U.S. Virgin Islands	Northern Marianas	Item	Puerto Rico	Guam	U.S. Virgin Islands	Northern Marianas
Enrollment, fall.	526,565	(NA)	15,903	11,299	Teachers	40,826	(NA)	1,518	550
					Student support staff	3,703	(NA)	120	28
Elementary (kindergarten–grade 8)	372,514	(NA)	10,770	8,140	Other support services staff . . .	16,844	(NA)	728	94
Secondary (grades 9–12 and post graduates). . .	154,051	(NA)	5,133	3,159	Current expenditures [1]				
Staff, fall.	71,847	(NA)	3,137	1,111	($1,000)	3,268,200	219,881	157,446	55,048
School district staff	1,265	(NA)	122	81	Per pupil [2] (dol.)	6,006	(NA)	9,669	4,707
School staff	50,035	(NA)	2,167	908					

NA Not available. [1] Public elementary and secondary day schools. [2] Per pupil expenditures include current expenditures, capital expenditures, and interest on school debt and excludes "other current expenditures" such as community services, private school programs, adult education, and other programs not allocable to expenditures per pupil in public schools.

Source: U.S. National Center for Education Statistics, *Digest of Education Statistics*, annual. See also <http://nces.ed.gov/annuals>.

Puerto Rico and the Island Areas 817

Table 1315. Occupational Employment and Average Annual Wages in Guam, Puerto Rico, and Virgin Islands: 2009

[The Occupational Employment Survey (OES) program conducts a semiannual mail survey designed to produce estimates of employment and wages for specific occupations. For more details on the survey, see <http://www.bls.gov/oes/oes_emp .htm#scope>]

Selected occupation	SOC code [1]	Guam		Puerto Rico		Virgin Islands	
		Employ-ment	Average annual wages [2]	Employ-ment	Average annual wages [2]	Employ-ment	Average annual wages [2]
Total, all occupations [3, 4]	(X)	60,910	29,810	962,030	25,690	43,220	35,050
Management	11	4,920	54,900	34,490	66,140	2,040	75,440
Business and financial operations	13	2,090	44,980	43,390	35,090	1,810	48,040
Computer and mathematical	15	480	43,040	8,720	42,410	360	54,520
Architecture and engineering	17	870	50,440	13,280	50,030	320	66,100
Life, physical, and social science	19	360	46,440	9,580	42,200	250	46,610
Community and social services	21	690	33,740	17,480	26,280	570	44,550
Legal	23	250	69,030	4,760	58,290	470	81,700
Education, training, and library	25	4,080	(NA)	69,740	31,550	3,090	37,250
Arts, design, entertainment sports	27	580	29,020	7,300	29,860	310	37,580
Healthcare practitioner and technical	29	1,530	56,020	46,290	32,070	1,380	52,610
Healthcare support	31	680	22,750	14,030	17,620	590	24,190
Protective service	33	2,540	28,840	64,210	22,570	2,570	32,390
Food preparation and serving related	35	6,440	17,330	65,820	17,080	4,140	21,440
Buildings and grounds cleaning and maintenance . . .	37	3,290	18,120	43,070	17,350	2,840	21,920
Personal care and service	39	2,180	31,180	11,870	18,590	880	22,050
Sales and related occupations	41	5,040	19,940	103,260	20,830	4,560	25,930
Office and administrative support	43	10,870	26,260	185,710	22,720	7,940	29,860
Farming, fishing, and forestry	45	(NA)	(NA)	1,740	22,020	30	34,500
Construction and extraction	47	5,610	25,870	52,940	19,790	2,620	39,150
Installation, maintenance, and repair	49	3,460	28,360	34,500	26,460	2,220	40,240
Production	51	1,540	25,270	74,670	21,640	1,870	41,780
Transportation and material moving	53	3,380	23,120	55,160	19,650	2,370	27,990

NA Not available. X Not applicable. [1] Office of Management and Budget's Standard Occupational Classification (SOC) is used to define occupations. SOC categorizes workers into 1 of 801 detailed occupations and aggregates; the detailed occupations into 23 major occupational groups. [2] Annual wages have been calculated by multiplying the hourly mean wage by a "year-round, full-time" hours figure of 2,080 hours; for those occupations where there is not an hourly mean wage published, the annual wage has been directly calculated from the reported survey data. [3] Estimates for detailed occupations do not sum to the totals because the totals include occupations not shown separately. [4] Estimates do not include self-employed workers.

Source: U.S. Bureau of Labor Statistics, "Occupational Employment Statistics," <http://www.bls.gov/oes/data.htm>, accessed August 2010.

Table 1316. Prisoners in Custody of Correctional Authorities in U.S. Territories and Commonwealths: 2007 and 2008

[As of December 31. Minus sign (−) indicates decrease]

Jurisdiction	Total inmates			Sentenced to more than 1 year			Incar-ceration rate, 2008 [1]
	2007	2008	Percent change 2007–2008	2007	2008	Percent change 2007–2008	
Total [2]	14,678	13,576	−7.5	11,465	10,346	−9.8	237
American Samoa	236	132	−44.1	122	48	−60.7	74
Guam [2]	535	578	8.1	320	304	−5.0	173
Northern Mariana Islands	137	124	−9.5	78	78	0.0	141
Puerto Rico	13,215	12,130	−8.2	10,553	9,642	−8.6	244
U.S. Virgin Islands	555	612	10.3	392	274	−30.1	249

[1] The number of prisoners with a sentence of more than 1 year per 100,000 persons in the resident population. [2] Data for Guam 2008 are estimates.

Source: U.S. Bureau of Justice Statistics, *Prisoners in 2008*, NCJ 228417, December 2009. See also <http://bjs.ojp.usdoj.gov /index.cfm?ty=pbdetail&iid=1763>.

Table 1317. Federal Direct Payments: 2008

[In thousands of dollars (6,944,719 represents $6,944,719,000). For fiscal years ending September 30]

Selected program payment	Puerto Rico	Guam	Virgin Islands	American Samoa	Northern Mariana Islands
Direct payments to individuals for retirement and disability [1]	6,944,719	244,794	202,372	52,434	30,254
Social security:					
Retirement insurance	2,960,862	92,355	122,871	14,108	7,617
Survivors' insurance	1,278,912	41,239	30,993	13,931	5,590
Disability insurance	1,893,913	22,944	24,384	12,586	2,005
Federal retirement and disability:					
Civilian [2]	268,565	56,130	17,308	1,685	7,489
Military	21,381	8,217	1,772	1,808	899
Veterans benefits:					
Service-connected disability	308,938	19,765	2,999	7,045	957
Other benefit payments	181,969	3,311	694	1,082	120
Other	30,179	833	1,352	190	23

[1] Includes other payments, not shown separately. [2] Includes retirement and disability payments to former U.S. Postal Service employees.

Source: U.S. Census Bureau, Consolidated Federal Funds Reports, *Consolidated Federal Funds Report for Fiscal Year, 2008*, CFFR/08, July 2009. See also <http://www.census.gov/govs/cffr/>.

Table 1318. Selected Social, Demographic, and Housing Characteristics in Puerto Rico: 2008

[The Puerto Rico Community Survey universe includes the household population and the population living in institutions, college dormitories, and other group quarters. Based on a sample and subject to sampling variability; see text, this section and Appendix III]

Characteristic	Estimate	Percent	Characteristic	Estimate	Percent
Total..........................	3,954,037	100.0			
			Never married	576,668	34.6
SEX AND AGE			Now married, except separated............	599,969	36.0
Male..........................	1,895,974	48.0	Separated	63,707	3.8
Female........................	2,058,063	52.0	Widowed	180,810	10.9
			Divorced	244,140	14.7
Under 5 years	235,543	6.0			
5 to 9 years	261,299	6.6	HOUSEHOLDS		
10 to 14 years	307,304	7.8	Total households	1,186,497	100.0
15 to 19 years	300,416	7.6	Family households (families)	878,424	74.0
20 to 24 years	278,241	7.0	With own children under 18 years	360,833	30.4
25 to 34 years	546,407	13.8	Married-couple families	512,928	43.2
35 to 44 years	537,076	13.6	With own children under 18 years	190,678	16.1
45 to 54 years	504,368	12.8	Male householder, no wife present	70,751	6.0
55 to 59 years	224,249	5.7	With own children under 18 years	25,412	2.1
60 to 64 years	219,129	5.5	Female householder, no husband present . . .	294,745	24.8
65 to 74 years	304,461	7.7	With own children under 18 years	144,743	12.2
75 to 84 years	169,685	4.3	Nonfamily households	308,073	26.0
85 years and over	65,859	1.7	Householder living alone.................	275,806	23.2
			65 years and over	115,891	9.8
MARITAL STATUS					
Males 15 years and over	1,484,597	100.0	Average household size	3.29	(X)
Never married	634,711	42.8	Average family size	3.94	(X)
Now married, except separated.....	602,887	40.6			
Separated	44,249	3.0	DISABILITY STATUS OF THE CIVILIAN		
Widowed	43,362	2.9	NONINSTITUTIONALIZED POPULATION		
Divorced	159,388	10.7	Population 5 years and over	3,922,338	100.0
Females 15 years and over......	1,665,294	100.0	With a disability	844,736	21.5

X Not applicable.

Source: U.S. Census Bureau, 2008 Puerto Rico Community Survey, DP-2 PR, "Selected Social Characteristics Puerto Rico: 2008," <http://factfinder.census.gov/>, accessed November 2009.

Table 1319. Tenure by Household Type in Puerto Rico: 2008

[The Puerto Rico Community Survey universe includes the household population and the population living in institutions, college dormitories, and other group quarters. Based on a sample and subject to sampling variability; see text, this section and Appendix III]

Household Type	Owner occupied	Renter occupied	Household Type	Owner occupied	Renter occupied
Total households	859,531	326,966	Householder 15 to 34 years	17,557	47,419
Family households.................	654,102	224,322	Householder 35 to 64 years	107,858	65,263
Married-couple family	431,959	80,969	Householder 65 years and over...	49,342	7,306
Householder 15 to 34 years	36,089	26,112	Nonfamily households	205,429	102,644
Householder 35 to 64 years	277,832	46,041	Householder living alone..........	186,338	89,468
Householder 65 years and over......	118,038	8,816	Householder 15 to 34 years	10,534	12,531
Other family......................	222,143	143,353	Householder 35 to 64 years	87,588	49,262
Male householder, no wife present . . .	47,386	23,365	Householder 65 years and over...	88,216	27,675
Householder 15 to 34 years	6,409	9,167	Householder not living alone.......	19,091	13,176
Householder 35 to 64 years	27,302	11,639	Householder 15 to 34 years	2,553	6,273
Householder 65 years and over.....	13,675	2,559	Householder 35 to 64 years	11,977	5,884
Female householder, no husband			Householder 65 years and over...	4,561	1,019
present........................	174,757	119,988			

Source: U.S. Census Bureau, 2008 Puerto Rico Community Survey, B25011, "Tenure by Household Type and Age of Householder," <http://factfinder.census.gov/>, accessed November 2009.

U.S. Census Bureau, Statistical Abstract of the United States: 2011

Table 1320. Puerto Rico—Summary: 1990 to 2009

[3,512.4 represents 3,512,400]

Item	Unit	1990	2000	2004	2005	2006	2007	2008	2009
POPULATION									
Total [1]	1,000	3,512.4	3,808.0	3,886.7	3,903.5	3,919.9	3,934.6	3,947.7	3,960.7
Persons per family	Number	3.7	3.4	3.3	3.3	3.2	3.2	3.2	3.2
EDUCATION [2]									
Enrollment, total	1,000	953.0	971.5	(NA)	959.0	1,016.9	1,009.5	962.0	951.3
Public (except public colleges or universities)	1,000	651.2	612.3	584.9	575.9	563.5	548.1	526.5	503.7
College and university	1,000	156.0	175.5	207.1	208.0	209.5	225.4	225.4	235.6
Expenses	Mil. dol	1,686.4	4,254.1	5,230.5	5,902.4	6,353.4	6,588.5	6,814.5	7,240.9
As percent of GNP	Percent	7.8	10.3	10.3	11.0	11.2	11.1	11.1	11.5
Public	Mil. dol	1,054.2	3,160.4	3,641.2	4,274.6	4,533.9	4,811.9	5,026.3	5,395.6
Private	Mil. dol	644.2	1,093.7	1,589.3	1,627.8	1,819.5	1,776.6	1,788.2	1,845.3
LABOR FORCE [3]									
Total [4]	1,000	1,124	1,303	1,360	1,385	1,422	1,409	1,368	1,349
Employed [5]	1,000	963	1,159	1,206	1,238	1,256	1,263	1,218	1,168
Agriculture [6]	1,000	36	24	25	26	22	16	15	19
Manufacturing	1,000	168	159	136	138	136	135	129	112
Trade	1,000	185	239	253	261	271	260	257	244
Government	1,000	222	249	268	274	280	296	279	271
Unemployed	1,000	161	143	155	147	166	147	151	181
Unemployment rate [7]	Rate	14.0	11.0	11.4	10.6	11.7	10.4	11.0	13.4
Compensation of employees	Mil. dol	13,639	23,504	27,769	29,372	30,027	30,234	30,966	31,522
Average compensation	Dollar	14,854	20,280	23,026	23,725	23,907	23,938	25,424	26,988
Salary and wages	Mil. dol	13,639	23,504	24,016	25,393	25,844	26,102	26,777	27,243
INCOME [8]									
Personal income:									
Current dollars	Mil. dol	21,105	38,856	45,566	48,820	50,842	52,110	55,584	59,035
Constant (1954) dollars	Mil. dol	5,551	8,491	9,289	9,611	9,555	9,542	9,645	9,816
Disposable personal income:									
Current dollars	Mil. dol	19,914	36,239	42,476	45,488	47,333	48,752	52,467	56,099
Constant (1954) dollars	Mil. dol	5,238	7,919	8,659	8,955	8,896	8,927	9,104	9,328
Average family income:									
Current dollars	Dollar	22,232	34,693	38,688	41,273	41,505	42,381	45,055	47,697
Constant (1954) dollars	Dollar	5,847	7,581	7,887	8,125	7,800	7,761	7,818	7,931
BANKING [9]									
Assets	Mil. dol	27,902	58,813	94,427	109,292	112,658	109,320	110,558	106,960
TOURISM [8]									
Number of visitors	1,000	3,426	4,566	4,889	5,073	5,022	5,062	5,213	4,783
Visitor expenditures	Mil. dol	1,366	2,388	3,024	3,239	3,369	3,414	3,535	3,473
Average per visitor	Dollar	399	523	619	638	671	674	678	726
Net income from tourism	Mil. dol	383	615	735	771	806	(NA)	(NA)	(NA)

NA Not available. [1] 1990 and 2000 enumerated as of April 1; all other years estimated as of July 1. [2] Enrollment for the first school month. Expenses for school year ending in year shown. "Public" includes: Public Preschool, Public Elementary, Public Intermediate, Public High School, Public Post-High School, Public Technological, Public Adult Education, Public Vocational Education, and Public Special Education. "College and university" includes both public and private colleges and universities. [3] Annual average of monthly figures. For fiscal years. [4] For population 16 years old and over. [5] Includes other employment not shown separately. [6] Includes forestry and fisheries. [7] Percent unemployed of the labor force. [8] For fiscal years. [9] As of June 30. Does not include federal savings banks and international banking entities.

Source: Puerto Rico Planning Board, San Juan, PR, *Economic Report of the Governor*, annual. See also <http://www.gobierno.pr/gprportal/inicio>.

Table 1321. Puerto Rico—Economic Summary by Industry: 2007

[In thousands of dollars (16,849,370 represents $16,849,370,000). Covers establishments with payroll. Excludes self-employed individuals, employees of private households, railroad employees, agricultural production employees, and most government employees. For statement on methodology, see Appendix III]

Industry	2002 NAICS code [1]	Establishments	Employees [2]	Annual payroll (1,000)
Total, all industries [3]	(X)	**47,340**	**767,247**	**16,849,370**
Construction	23	2,911	58,455	1,000,163
Manufacturing	31–33	2,104	109,935	3,607,428
Wholesale trade	42	2,330	36,250	1,188,462
Retail trade	44–45	11,196	135,703	2,074,238
Transportation and warehousing	48–49	1,089	16,738	410,410
Information	51	532	22,459	819,292
Finance and insurance	52	2,159	40,004	1,491,822
Real estate and rental and leasing	53	1,753	15,109	307,023
Professional, scientific, and technical services	54	4,246	31,662	976,202
Management of companies and enterprises	55	99	5,423	215,439
Admin/support waste mgt/remediation services	56	1,783	74,893	1,096,021
Educational services	61	768	34,804	662,119
Health care and social assistance	62	6,993	78,522	1,537,840
Arts, entertainment, and recreation	71	445	4,035	66,184
Accommodation and food services	72	4,321	75,595	925,693

X Not applicable. [1] North American Industry Classification System, 2002. See text, Section 15. [2] Covers full- and part-time employees who are on the payroll in the pay period including March 12. [3] Includes other industries, not shown separately.

Source: U.S. Census Bureau, "County Business Patterns," July 2009, <http://www.census.gov/econ/cbp/index.html>.

Table 1322. Puerto Rico—Gross Product and Net Income: 1990 to 2009

[In millions of dollars (21,619 represents $21,619,000,000). For fiscal years ending June 30. Data for 2009 are preliminary. Minus sign (–) indicates decrease]

Item	1990	1995	2000	2005	2007	2008	2009
Gross product	**21,619**	**28,452**	**41,419**	**53,752**	**59,521**	**61,527**	**62,759**
Agriculture	434	318	407	499	430	613	633
Manufacturing	12,126	17,867	24,489	35,581	37,637	40,548	43,548
Contract construction and mining [1]	720	1,006	2,157	2,155	2,027	1,991	1,782
Transportation & other public services [2]	2,468	3,276	2,579	2,841	3,183	3,113	3,101
Trade	4,728	5,989	6,093	7,368	7,223	7,343	7,469
Finance, insurance, real estate	3,896	5,730	10,511	14,694	18,380	18,845	18,205
Services	3,015	4,724	9,987	11,520	10,940	11,710	11,715
Government	3,337	4,440	5,478	8,151	8,585	8,762	9,254
Commonwealth	2,884	3,793	4,601	7,032	7,281	7,350	7,728
Municipalities	453	647	877	1,118	1,304	1,412	1,526
Rest of the world	–8,985	–14,195	–20,283	–29,056	–28,884	–31,399	–32,949
Statistical discrepancy	*–121*	*–703*	*585*	*141*	*–464*	*–215*	*–538*
Net income	**17,941**	**23,653**	**32,610**	**43,484**	**48,132**	**49,057**	**49,924**
Agriculture	486	442	385	479	432	616	636
Manufacturing	11,277	16,685	22,627	33,427	35,223	37,929	40,693
Mining	26	30	34	42	44	44	38
Contract construction	679	903	1,764	1,718	1,711	1,674	1,476
Transportation & other public services [2]	1,778	2,360	1,961	2,075	2,488	2,403	2,326
Trade	3,420	4,108	4,995	6,043	6,016	6,074	6,076
Finance, insurance, and real estate	3,280	4,735	8,175	11,634	13,505	13,477	12,662
Services	2,643	4,146	7,475	8,972	9,011	9,476	9,711
Commonwealth government [3]	3,337	4,440	5,478	8,151	8,585	8,762	9,254
Rest of the world	–8,985	–14,195	–20,283	–29,056	–28,884	–31,399	–32,949

[1] Mining includes only quarries. [2] Includes warehousing and other public utilities. [3] Includes all other services not elsewhere classified.

Source: Puerto Rico Planning Board, San Juan, PR, *Economic Report of the Governor*, annual. See also <http://www.gobierno.pr/gprportal/inicio>.

Table 1323. Puerto Rico—Transfer Payments: 1990 to 2009

[In millions of dollars (4,871 represents $4,871,000,000). Data represent transfer payments between federal and state governments and other nonresidents. Data for 2009 are preliminary]

Item	1990	1995	2000	2005	2007	2008	2009
Total receipts	**4,871**	**6,236**	**8,659**	**10,551**	**12,025**	**13,925**	**14,989**
Federal government	4,649	5,912	7,966	9,673	10,842	12,797	13,715
Transfers to individuals [1]	4,577	5,838	7,868	9,547	10,707	12,602	13,499
Veterans benefits	349	440	491	491	492	609	821
Medicare	368	661	1,196	1,825	2,016	2,306	2,642
Old age, disability, survivors (social security)	2,055	2,912	3,863	5,118	5,787	6,134	6,300
Nutritional assistance	880	1,063	1,193	1,306	1,472	1,513	1,638
Industry subsidies	72	74	98	127	135	196	216
U.S. state governments	18	18	15	15	23	24	36
Other nonresidents	205	307	679	863	1,160	1,103	1,238
Total payments	**1,801**	**2,301**	**2,763**	**3,583**	**3,688**	**3,762**	**3,924**
Federal government	1,756	2,132	2,693	3,516	3,626	3,695	3,757
Transfers from individuals	817	1,052	1,326	1,792	1,882	1,924	1,974
Contribution to Medicare	97	162	191	303	380	392	441
Employee contribution for social security	720	888	1,133	1,483	1,495	1,526	1,528
Transfers from industries	16	49	51	74	99	103	101
Unemployment insurance	247	184	234	221	231	226	231
Employer contribution for social security	675	847	1,081	1,429	1,413	1,442	1,451
Other nonresidents [2]	45	164	70	67	62	67	167
Net balance	**3,070**	**3,935**	**5,897**	**6,968**	**8,337**	**10,163**	**11,065**
Federal government	2,893	3,780	5,273	6,157	7,217	9,103	9,958
U.S. state governments	16	13	10	10	20	21	32
Other nonresidents	162	143	614	801	1,101	1,040	1,075

[1] Includes other receipts and payments not shown separately. [2] Includes U.S. state governments.

Source: Puerto Rico Planning Board, San Juan, PR, *Economic Report of the Governor*, annual. See also <http://www.gobierno.pr/gprportal/inicio>.

Table 1324. Puerto Rico—Merchandise Imports and Exports: 1980 to 2009

[In millions of dollars (9,018 represents $9,018,000,000). Imports are imports for consumption; see text, Section 28]

Item	1980	1985	1990	1995	2000	2003	2004	2005	2006	2007	2008	2009
Imports	9,018	10,162	16,200	18,969	27,006	35,945	37,335	40,499	42,380	43,482	41,560	38,780
From U.S.	5,345	6,130	10,792	12,213	15,172	16,949	18,124	20,994	21,982	22,402	19,777	20,038
From other	3,673	4,032	5,408	6,756	11,834	18,996	19,211	19,505	20,398	21,080	21,783	18,742
Exports	6,576	11,087	20,402	23,573	43,191	55,814	54,997	56,836	59,219	62,401	63,658	59,594
To U.S.	5,643	9,873	17,915	20,986	38,335	46,880	45,311	47,121	47,452	47,507	46,439	40,779
To other	933	1,214	2,487	2,587	4,856	8,934	9,686	9,715	11,767	14,894	17,219	18,815

Source: U.S. Census Bureau, Foreign Commerce and Navigation, *U.S. Trade with Puerto Rico and U.S. Possessions*, FT 895, and unpublished data. See also <http://www.census.gov/foreign-trade/statistics/index.html>. Beginning 2009, USATradeOnLine, <http://www.usatradeonline.gov/>.

Puerto Rico and the Island Areas 821

Table 1325. Puerto Rico—Agricultural Summary: 2002 and 2007

[1 cuerda = .97 acre]

All farms	Unit	2002	2007	All farms	Unit	2002	2007
Farms	Number...	17,659	15,745	Tenants	Number...	1,636	2,425
Farm land	Cuerdas...	690,687	557,530	Farms by type of			
Average size of farm	Cuerdas...	39.1	35.4	organization:			
Approximate land area	Cuerdas...	2,254,365	2,254,365	Individual or family	Number...	15,843	13,958
Proportion in farms	Percent...	30.6	24.7	Partnership	Number...	162	49
Farms by size:				Corporation	Number...	595	575
Less than 10 cuerdas	Number...	7,943	7,502	Other	Number...	1,059	1,163
10 to 19 cuerdas	Number...	3,847	3,545	Farms by value of sales:			
20 to 49 cuerdas	Number...	3,228	2,680	Less than $1,000	Number...	3,977	4,442
50 to 99 cuerdas	Number...	1,282	865	$1,000 to $2,499	Number...	3,471	2,771
100 to 174 cuerdas	Number...	590	524	$2,500 to $4,499	Number...	3,044	2,428
175 to 259 cuerdas	Number...	281	207	$5,000 to $7,499	Number...	1,575	1,206
260 cuerdas or more	Number...	488	422	$7,500 to $9,999	Number...	1,087	882
Tenure of operator:				$10,000 to $19,999	Number...	1,781	1,497
Operators	Number...	17,659	15,745	$20,000 to $39,999	Number...	1,062	1,030
Full owners	Number...	13,693	11,402	$40,000 to $59,999	Number...	375	281
Part owners	Number...	2,330	1,918	$60,000 or more	Number...	1,287	1,208

Source: U.S. Department of Agriculture, National Agricultural Statistics Service, *2007 Census of Agriculture—Geographic Area Series Part 52, Puerto Rico*, Vol. 1, 2009. See also <http://www.agcensus.usda.gov/Publications/2007/Full_Report/index.asp>.

Table 1326. Puerto Rico—Farms and Market Value of Agricultural Products Sold: 2007

[515,686 represents $515,686,000]

Type of product	Number of farms	Market value ($1,000)	Average value per farm (dol.)	Type of product	Number of farms	Market value ($1,000)	Average value per farm (dol.)
Total	**15,745**	**515,686**	**32,752**	Horticultural specialties	524	44,576	85,068
Crops, including horticultural				Grasses and other crops	256	13,372	52,236
specialties	10,206	218,835	(NA)				
Coffee	5,678	41,824	7,366	Livestock, poultry, and their			
Pineapples	53	527	9,942	products	5,662	296,850	52,428
Plantains	3,756	44,875	11,947	Cattle and calves	3,568	33,005	9,250
Bananas	1,980	10,082	5,092	Poultry and poultry products	1,079	63,574	58,919
Grains	969	1,553	1,603	Dairy products	354	184,543	521,307
Root crops or tubers	1,691	6,683	3,952	Hogs and pigs	1,075	6,239	5,803
Fruits and coconuts	2,350	19,904	8,470	Aquaculture	40	833	20,818
Vegetables and melons [1]	1,007	35,440	35,194	Other	787	8,657	11,000

NA Not available. [1] Includes hydroponic crops.

Source: U.S. Department of Agriculture, National Agricultural Statistics Service, *2007 Census of Agriculture—Geographic Area Series Part 52, Puerto Rico*, Vol. 1, 2009. See also <http://www.agcensus.usda.gov/Publications/2007/Full_Report/index.asp>.

Table 1327. Guam, Virgin Islands, and Northern Mariana Islands—Economic Summary: 2007

[Sales and payroll in millions of dollars (6,244 represents $6,244,000,000). Based on the 2007 Economic Census; see Appendix III. Selected kinds of businesses displayed]

Selected kinds of business	Guam	Virgin Islands	Northern Mariana Islands	Selected kinds of business	Guam	Virgin Islands	Northern Mariana Islands
Total:				Paid employees [2]	2,394	797	872
Establishments [1]	3,143	2,583	1,191	Retail trade:			
Sales	6,244	19,479	1,284	Establishments	660	641	255
Annual payroll	1,101	1,085	246	Sales	1,618	1,397	272
Paid employees [2]	52,394	35,300	22,622	Annual payroll	150	146	29
Construction:				Paid employees [2]	8,219	6,773	2,770
Establishments	317	195	50	Professional, scientific, and			
Sales	579	352	31	technical services:			
Annual payroll	121	115	7	Establishments	227	257	87
Paid employees [2]	6,011	3,388	528	Sales	231	284	25
Manufacturing:				Annual payroll	77	60	9
Establishments	63	70	59	Paid employees [2]	2,217	1,370	404
Sales	167	(D)	190	Accommodation & Food			
Annual payroll	39	(D)	57	Services:			
Paid employees [2]	1,495	([3])	7,094	Establishments	429	255	140
Wholesale trade:				Sales	635	461	173
Establishments	191	58	72	Annual payroll	155	130	45
Sales	800	288	143	Paid employees [2]	11,477	6,146	4,772
Annual payroll	56	25	10				

D Withheld to avoid disclosing data for individual companies; data are included in higher level totals. [1] Includes other industries, not shown separately. [2] For pay period including March 12. [3] 1,000 to 2,499 employees.

Source: U.S. Census Bureau, 2007 Economic Census of the Island Areas, "General Statistics for Island Areas: 2007," <http://factfinder.census.gov/>, accessed August 2010.

This section presents statistics for the world as a whole and for many countries on a comparative basis with the United States. Data are shown for population, births and deaths, social and industrial indicators, finances, agriculture, communication, and military affairs.

Statistics of the individual nations may be found primarily in official national publications, generally in the form of yearbooks, issued by most of the nations at various intervals in their own national languages and expressed in their own or customary units of measure. (For a listing of selected publications, see Guide to Sources.) For handier reference, especially for international comparisons, the United Nations Statistics Division compiles data as submitted by member countries and issues a number of international summary publications, generally in English and French. Among these are the *Statistical Yearbook;* the *Demographic Yearbook; International Trade Statistics Yearbook; National Accounts Statistics: Main Aggregates* and *Detailed Tables; Population and Vital Statistics Reports, semi annually;* the *Monthly Bulletin of Statistics;* and *the Energy Statistics Yearbook.* Specialized agencies of the United Nations also issue international summary publications on agricultural, labor, health, and education statistics. Among these are the *Production Yearbook* and *Trade Yearbook* issued by the Food and Agriculture Organization, the *Yearbook of Labour Statistics* issued by the International Labour Office and *World Health Statistics* issued by the World Health Organization, and the *Statistical Yearbook* issued by the Educational, Scientific, and Cultural Organization.

The U.S. Census Bureau publishes estimates and projections of key demographic measures for countries and regions of the world in its International Data Base at <http://www.census.gov/ipc/www/idb/>.

The International Monetary Fund (IMF) and the Organization for Economic Cooperation and Development (OECD) also compile data on international statistics. The IMF publishes a series of reports relating to financial data. These include *International Financial Statistics, Direction of Trade,* and *Balance of Payments Yearbook,* published in English, French, and Spanish. The OECD publishes a vast number of statistical publications in various fields such as economics, health, and education. Among these are *OECD in Figures, Main Economic Indicators, Economic Outlook, National Accounts, Labour Force Statistics, OECD Health Data,* and *Education at a Glance.*

Statistical coverage, country names, and classifications—Problems of space and availability of data limit the number of countries and the extent of statistical coverage shown. The list of countries included and the spelling of country names are based almost entirely on the list of independent nations, dependencies, and areas of special sovereignty provided by the U.S. Department of State.

In the last quarter-century, several important changes took place in the status of the world's nations. In 1991, the Soviet Union broke up into 15 independent countries: Armenia, Azerbaijan, Belarus, Estonia, Georgia, Kazakhstan, Kyrgyzstan, Latvia, Lithuania, Moldova, Russia, Tajikistan, Turkmenistan, Ukraine, and Uzbekistan. In the South Pacific, the Marshall Islands, Micronesia, and Palau gained independence from the United States in 1991. Following the breakup of the Socialist Federal Republic of Yugoslavia in 1992, the United States recognized Bosnia and Herzegovina, Croatia, Slovenia, and Macedonia as independent countries.

The Treaty of Maastricht created the European Union (EU) in 1992 with 12 member countries. The EU is not a state intended to replace existing states, but it is more than just an international organization. Its member states have set up common institutions to which they

U.S. Census Bureau, Statistical Abstract of the United States: 2011

delegate some of their sovereignty so that decisions on specific matters of joint interest can be made democratically at a European level. This pooling of sovereignty is also called "European integration." The EU has grown in size with successive waves of accessions in 1995, 2004, and 2007. The 27 current members of the EU are: Austria, Belgium, Bulgaria, Cyprus, Czech Republic, Denmark, Estonia, Finland, France, Germany, Greece, Hungary, Ireland, Italy, Latvia, Lithuania, Luxembourg, Malta, the Netherlands, Poland, Portugal, Romania, Slovakia, Slovenia, Spain, Sweden, and the United Kingdom.

In 1992, the EU decided to establish an economic and monetary union (EMU), with the introduction of a single European currency managed by a European Central Bank. The single currency—the euro—became a reality on January 1, 2002, when euro notes and coins replaced national currencies in 12 of the then 15 countries of the European Union (Belgium, Germany, Greece, Spain, France, Ireland, Italy, Luxembourg, the Netherlands, Austria, Portugal, and Finland). Since then, 12 countries have become members of the EU, but Slovakia, Slovenia, Malta, and Cyprus have been the only new members of the EU to adopt the euro as the national currency.

On January 1, 1993, Czechoslovakia was succeeded by two independent countries: the Czech Republic and Slovakia. Eritrea announced its independence from Ethiopia in April 1993 and was subsequently recognized as an independent nation by the United States. In May of 2002, Timor-Leste won independence from Indonesia.

Serbia and Montenegro, both former republics of Yugoslavia, became independent of one another on May 31, 2006. This separation is seen in the population estimates tables (Tables 1331, 1357, and 1405), but some tables still show both countries as combined. On February 17, 2008, Kosovo declared its independence from Serbia, making it the world's newest independent state.

The population estimates and projections used in Tables 1328–1331, 1333, and 1338 were prepared by the Census Bureau. For each country, available data on population, by age and sex, fertility, mortality, and international migration were evaluated and, where necessary, adjusted for inconsistencies and errors in the data. In most instances, comprehensive projections were made by the cohort-component method, resulting in distributions of the population by age and sex and requiring an assessment of probable future trends of fertility, mortality, and international migration.

Economic associations— The Organization for European Economic Co–operation (OEEC), a regional grouping of Western European countries established in 1948 for the purpose of harmonizing national economic policies and conditions, was succeeded on September 30, 1961, by the Organization for Economic Cooperation and Development (OECD). The member nations of the OECD are Australia, Austria, Belgium, Canada, Chile, Czech Republic, Denmark, Finland, France, Germany, Greece, Hungary, Iceland, Ireland, Israel, Italy, Japan, Luxembourg, Mexico, the Netherlands, New Zealand, Norway, Poland, Portugal, Slovakia, Slovenia, South Korea, Spain, Sweden, Switzerland, Turkey, the United Kingdom, and the United States.

Quality and comparability of the data—The quality and comparability of the data presented here are affected by a number of factors:

(1) The year for which data are presented may not be the same for all subjects for a particular country or for a given subject for different countries, though the data shown are the most recent available. All such variations have been noted. The data shown are for calendar years except as otherwise specified.

(2) The bases, methods of estimating, methods of data collection, extent of coverage, precision of definition, scope of territory, and margins of error may vary for different items within a particular country, and for like items for different countries. Footnotes and headnotes to the tables give a few of the major time

U.S. Census Bureau, Statistical Abstract of the United States: 2011

periods and coverage qualifications attached to the figures; considerably more detail is presented in the source publications. Many of the measures shown are, at best, merely rough indicators of magnitude.

(3) Figures shown in this section for the United States may not always agree with figures shown in the preceding sections. Disagreements may be attributable to the use of differing original sources, a difference in the definition of geographic limits (the 50 states, conterminous United States only, or the United States including certain outlying areas and possessions), or to possible adjustments made in the United States' figures by other sources to make them more comparable with figures from other countries.

International comparisons of national accounts data—To compare national accounts data for different countries, it is necessary to convert each country's data into a common unit of currency, usually the U.S. dollar. The market exchange rates, which often are used in converting national currencies, do not necessarily reflect the relative purchasing power in the various countries. It is necessary that the goods and services produced in different countries be valued consistently if the differences observed are meant to reflect real differences in the volumes of goods and services produced. The use of purchasing power parities (see Tables 1347, 1348, and 1394) instead of exchange rates is intended to achieve this objective.

The method used to present the data shown in Table 1348 is to construct volume measures directly by revaluing the goods and services sold in different countries at a common set of international prices. By dividing the ratio of the gross domestic products of two countries expressed in their own national currencies by the corresponding ratio calculated at constant international prices, it is possible to derive the implied purchasing power parity (PPP) between the two currencies concerned. PPPs show how many units of currency are needed in one country to buy the same amount of goods and services

that one unit of currency will buy in the other country. For further information, see *National Accounts, Main Aggregates, Volume I*, issued annually by the Organisation for Economic Cooperation and Development, Paris, France.

International Standard Industrial Classification—The original version of the International Standard Industrial Classification of All Economic Activities (ISIC) was adopted in 1948. Wide use has been made both nationally and internationally in classifying data according to kind of economic activity in the fields of production, employment, national income, and other economic statistics. A number of countries have utilized the ISIC as the basis for devising their industrial classification scheme.

Substantial comparability has been attained between the industrial classifications of many other countries, including the United States and the ISIC by ensuring, as far as practicable, that the categories at detailed levels of classification in national schemes fit into only one category of the ISIC. The United Nations, the International Labour Organization, the Food and Agriculture Organization, and other international bodies use the ISIC in publishing and analyzing statistical data. Revisions of the ISIC were issued in 1958, 1968, 1989, 2002, and 2008.

International maps—A series of regional world maps is provided on pages 826–834. References are included in Table 1331 for easy location of individual countries on the maps. The Robinson map projection is used for this series of maps. A map projection is used to portray all or part of the round Earth on a flat surface, but this cannot be done without some distortion. For the Robinson projection, distortion is very low along the Equator and within 45 degrees of the center but is greatest near the poles. For additional information on map projections and maps, please contact the Earth Science Information Center, U.S. Geological Survey, 507 National Center, Reston, VA 22092.

U.S. Census Bureau, Statistical Abstract of the United States: 2011

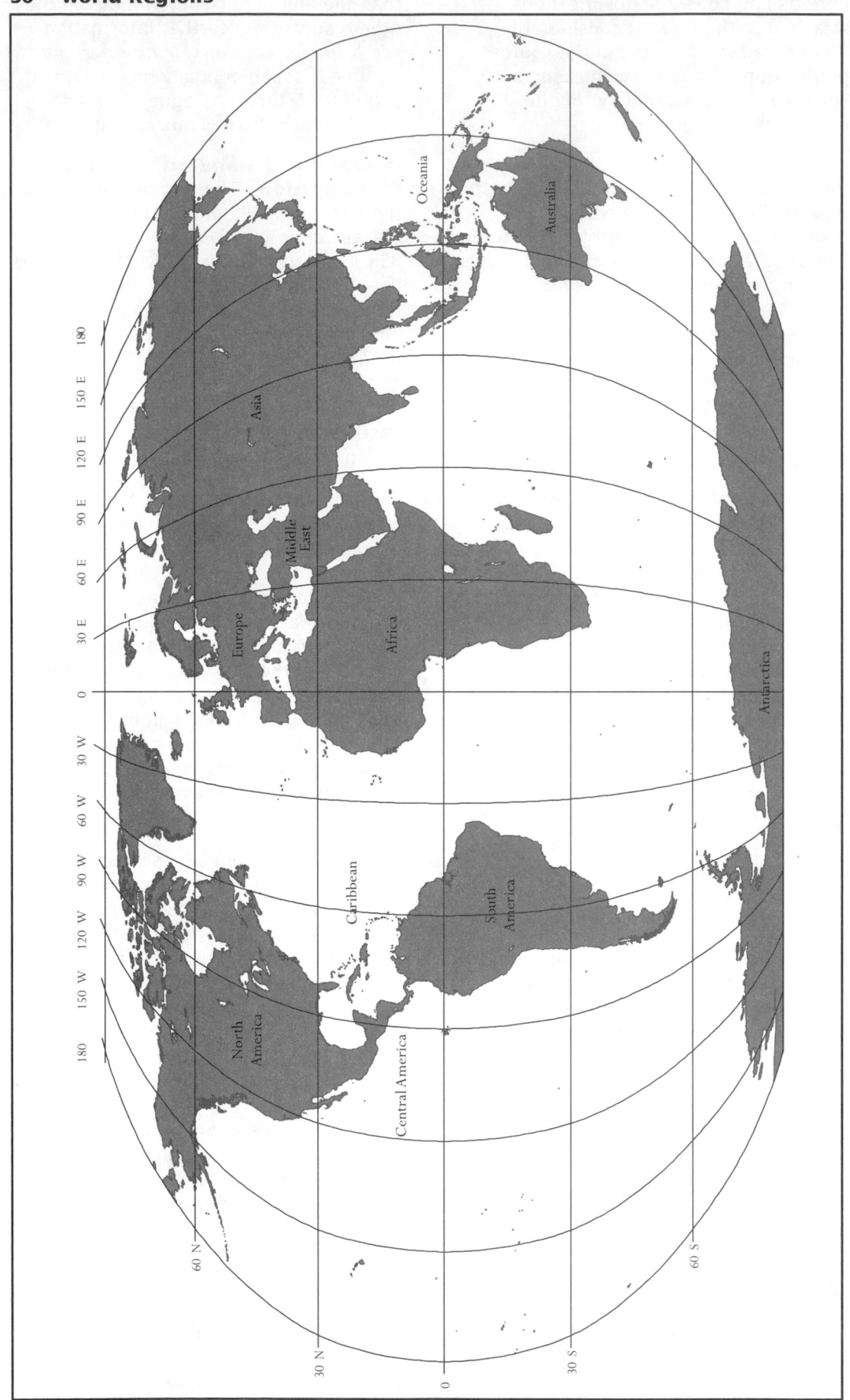

U.S. Census Bureau, Statistical Abstract of the United States: 2011

U.S. Census Bureau, Statistical Abstract of the United States: 2011

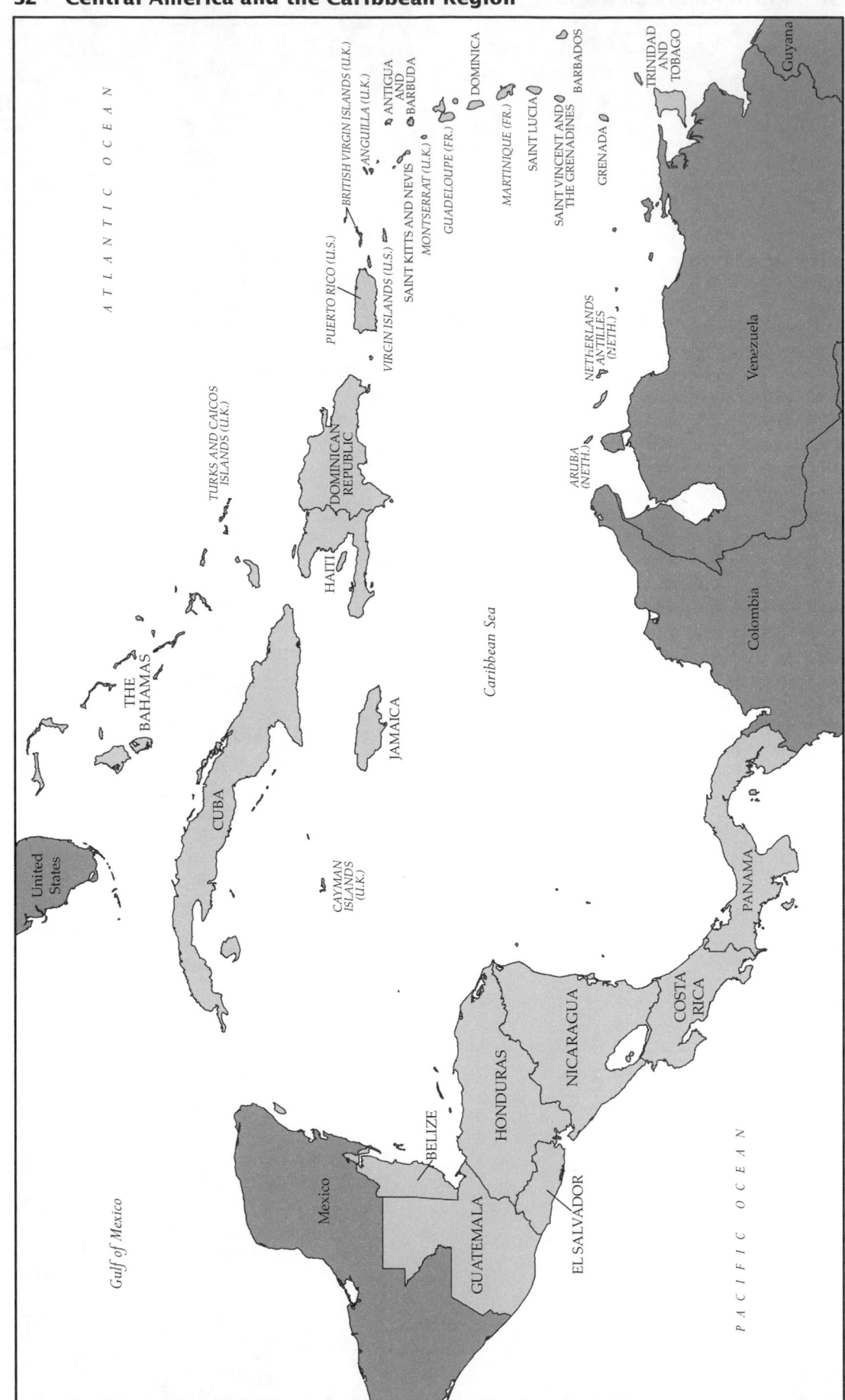

U.S. Census Bureau, Statistical Abstract of the United States: 2011

U.S. Census Bureau, Statistical Abstract of the United States: 2011

ICELAND

Norwegian Sea

FAROE ISLANDS (DEN)

SWEDEN

FINLAND

ATLANTIC OCEAN

SHETLAND ISLANDS (U.K.)

NORWAY

Baltic Sea

ESTONIA

Russia

North Sea

LATVIA

DENMARK

LITHUANIA

RUSSIA

NETHERLANDS

BELARUS

Celtic Sea

UNITED KINGDOM

IRELAND

GERMANY

POLAND

UKRAINE

Area Enlarged Below

BELGIUM

LUXEMBOURG

LIECHTENSTEIN

Black Sea

Bay of Biscay

FRANCE

SWITZERLAND

ITALY

ANDORRA

MONACO

PORTUGAL

SPAIN

CORSICA (FR)

Turkey

SARDINIA (IT)

Tyrrhenian Sea

Ionian Sea

BALEARIC ISLANDS (SP)

SICILY (IT)

GREECE

CRETE (GR)

Mediterranean Sea

Morocco

Algeria

Tunisia

MALTA

POLAND

UKRAINE

CZECH REPUBLIC

GERMANY

SLOVAKIA

MOLDOVA

AUSTRIA

HUNGARY

ROMANIA

Egypt

Libya

SLOVENIA

CROATIA

BOSNIA AND HERZEGOVINA

SERBIA

BULGARIA

SAN MARINO

Adriatic Sea

KOSOVO

Turkey

MONTENEGRO

MACEDONIA

Sudan

HOLY SEE

ITALY

ALBANIA

Chad

GREECE

Aegean Sea

U.S. Census Bureau, Statistical Abstract of the United States: 2011

U.S. Census Bureau, Statistical Abstract of the United States: 2011

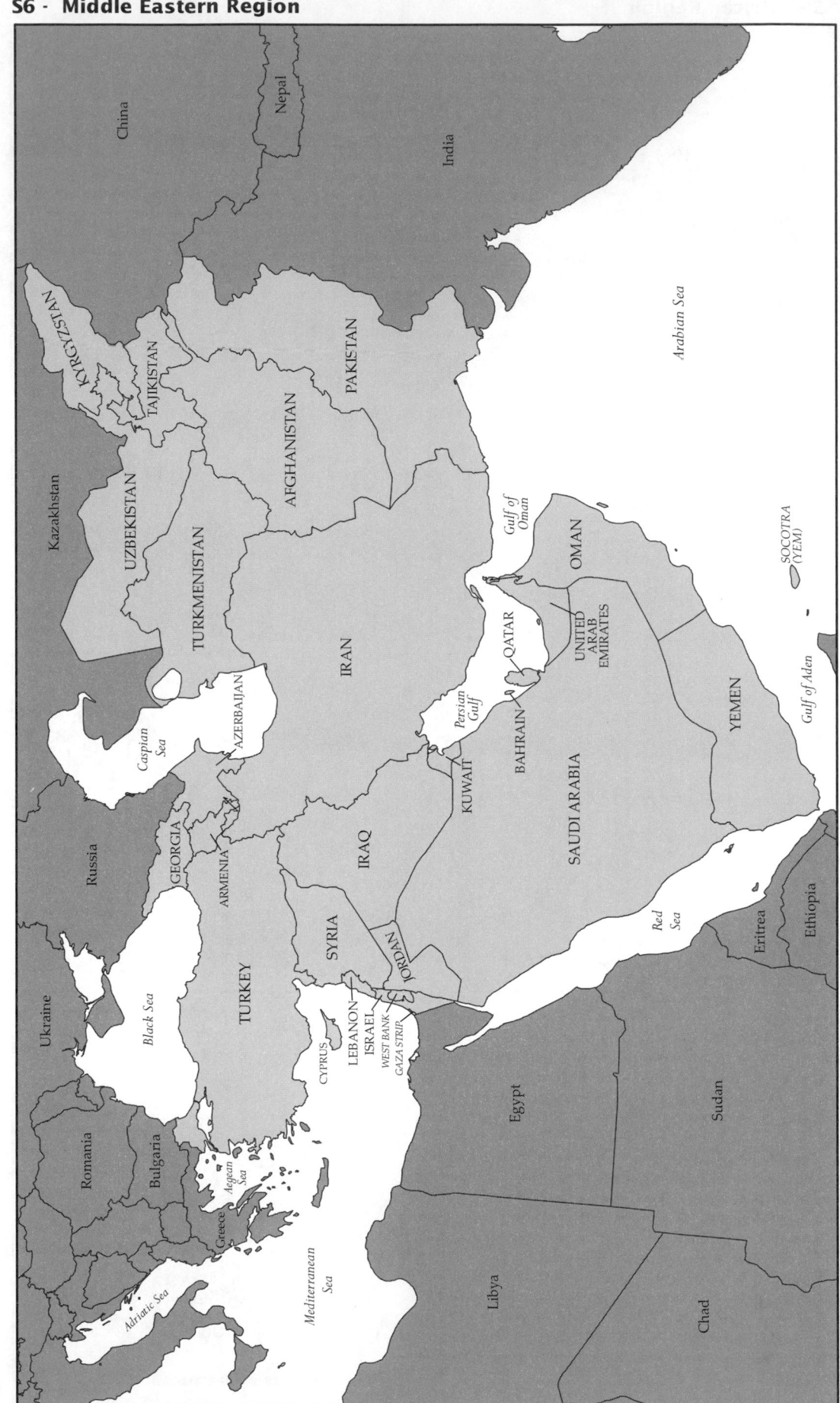

U.S. Census Bureau, Statistical Abstract of the United States: 2011

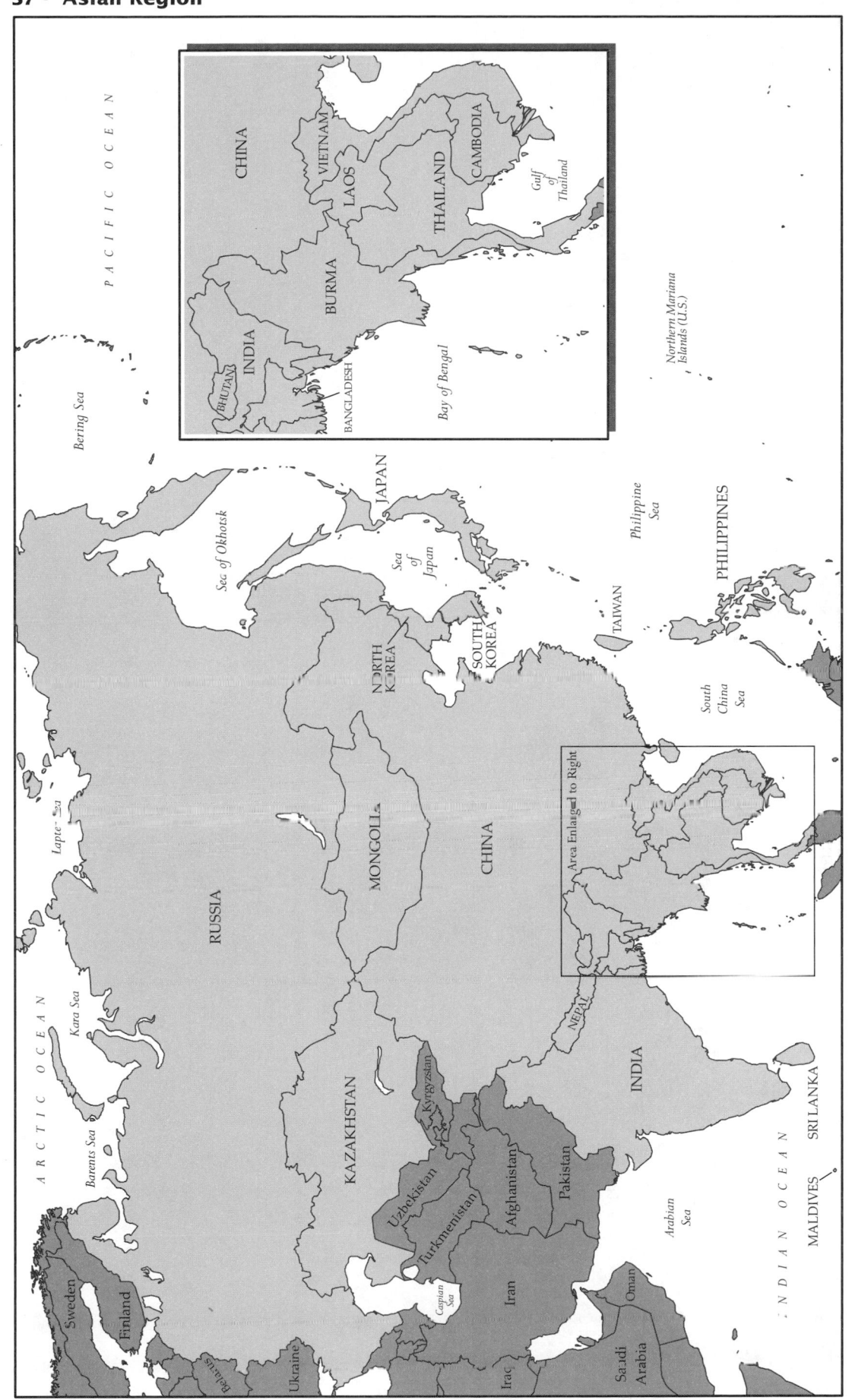

U.S. Census Bureau, Statistical Abstract of the United States: 2011

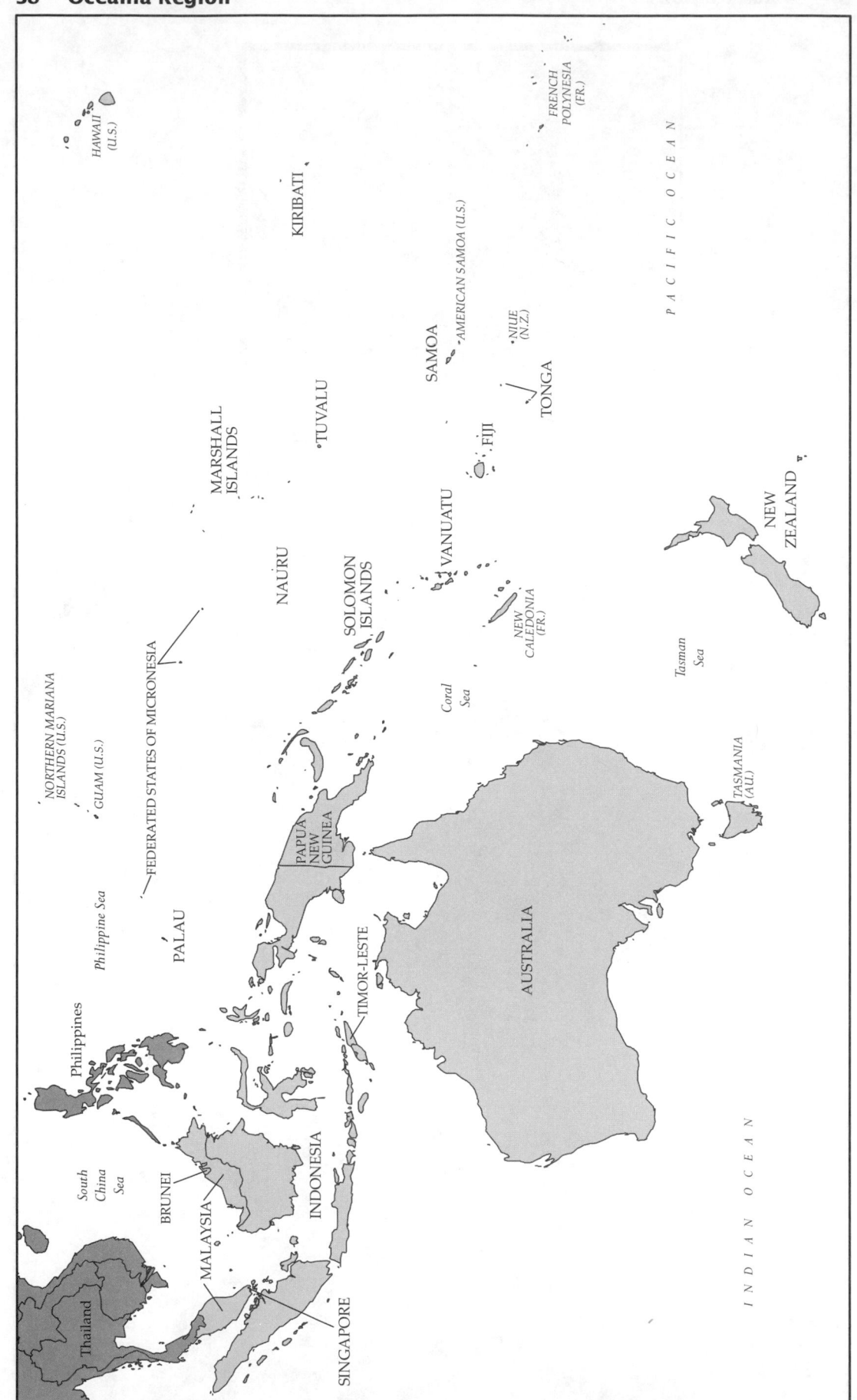

U.S. Census Bureau, Statistical Abstract of the United States: 2011

Table 1328. Total World Population: 1980 to 2050

[As of midyear (4,453 represents 4,453,000,000)]

Year	Population (mil.)	Average annual [1] Growth rate (percent)	Average annual [1] Population change (mil.)	Year	Population (mil.)	Average annual [1] Growth rate (percent)	Average annual [1] Population change (mil.)
1980.........	4,453	1.8	82.7	2015........	7,231	1.0	74.7
1985.........	4,858	1.7	83.7	2020........	7,597	0.9	70.8
1990.........	5,289	1.6	83.0	2025........	7,941	0.8	65.6
1995.........	5,700	1.4	80.1	2030........	8,259	0.7	60.4
2007.........	6,624	1.2	77.2	2035........	8,551	0.6	55.5
2008.........	6,701	1.1	76.2	2040........	8,820	0.6	50.8
2009.........	6,777	1.1	76.1	2045........	9,064	0.5	45.9
2010.........	6,853	1.1	76.1	2050........	9,284	(NA)	(NA)

NA Not available. [1] Represents change from year shown to immediate succeeding year.

Source: U.S. Census Bureau, International Data Base, <http://www.census.gov/ipc/www/idb/>, accessed June 2010.

Table 1329. Population by Continent: 1980 to 2050

[In millions, except percent (4,453 represents 4,453,000,000). As of midyear]

Year	World	Africa [1]	North America [1]	South America [1]	Asia	Europe [1]	Oceania
1980....................	4,453	479	371	242	2,644	695	23
1990....................	5,289	630	424	297	3,189	723	26
2000....................	6,089	803	486	348	3,691	730	30
2010....................	6,853	1,015	539	396	4,133	734	35
2020....................	7,597	1,261	595	440	4,531	731	39
2030....................	8,259	1,532	648	477	4,841	718	43
2040....................	8,820	1,827	695	504	5,049	698	46
2050....................	9,284	2,138	739	520	5,167	671	49
PERCENT DISTRIBUTION							
1980....................	100.0	10.7	8.3	5.4	59.4	15.6	0.5
2000....................	100.0	13.2	8.0	5.7	60.6	12.0	0.5
2050....................	100.0	23.0	8.0	5.6	55.7	7.2	0.5

[1] Estimates and projections for France include the four overseas departments of French Guiana, Guadeloupe, Martinique, and Reunion in the national total. These areas are included in the same regions as France (Europe). Saint Barthelemy and Saint Martin recently voted to become French overseas collectivities apart from Guadeloupe and are included in the totals for North America.

Source: U.S. Census Bureau, International Data Base, <http://www.census.gov/ipc/www/idb/>, accessed June 2010.

Table 1330. Population and Population Change by Development Status: 1950 to 2050

[(2,557 represents 2,557,000,000). As of midyear. Minus sign (−) indicates decrease. The "less developed" countries include all of Africa, all of Asia except Japan, the Transcaucasian and Central Asian republics of the New Independent States, all of Latin America and the Caribbean, and all of Oceania except Australia, New Zealand, and Hawaii. This category matches the "less developed country" classification employed by the United Nations]

Year	Number (mil.) World	Number (mil.) Less developed countries [1]	Number (mil.) More developed countries [1]	Percent of world Less developed countries [1]	Percent of world More developed countries [1]
POPULATION					
1950...............	2,557	1,749	807	68.4	31.6
1960...............	3,042	2,132	911	70.1	29.9
1970...............	3,713	2,709	1,004	73.0	27.0
1980...............	4,453	3,371	1,082	75.7	24.3
1990...............	5,289	4,145	1,144	78.4	21.6
2000...............	6,089	4,895	1,193	80.4	19.6
2010...............	6,853	5,622	1,231	82.0	18.0
2020...............	7,597	6,338	1,259	83.4	16.6
2030...............	8,259	6,984	1,275	84.6	15.4
2040...............	8,820	7,539	1,281	85.5	14.5
2050...............	9,284	8,005	1,279	86.2	13.8
POPULATION CHANGE					
1950–1960..........	486	382	104	78.7	21.3
1960–1970..........	670	578	93	86.2	13.8
1970–1980..........	740	662	78	89.4	10.6
1980–1990..........	836	774	62	92.5	7.5
1990–2000..........	800	751	49	93.8	6.2
2000–2010..........	764	727	38	95.1	4.9
2010–2020..........	744	716	28	96.2	3.8
2020–2030..........	662	646	16	97.6	2.4
2030–2040..........	561	555	6	99.0	1.0
2040–2050..........	464	466	−2	100.3	−0.3

[1] See footnote 1, Table 1329.

Source: U.S. Census Bureau, International Data Base, <http://www.census.gov/ipc/www/idb/>, accessed June 2010.

U.S. Census Bureau, Statistical Abstract of the United States: 2011

Table 1331. Population by Country or Area: 1990 to 2020

[5,288,828 represents 5,288,828,000. Covers countries or areas with populations of 5,000 or more in 2010. Population data generally are de facto figures for the present territory. Population estimates were derived from information available as of spring 2010. See text of this section for general comments concerning the data. For details of methodology, coverage, and reliability, see source. Minus sign (–) indicates decrease]

Country or area	Map refer- ence [1]	Mid-year population (1,000)				Popula- tion rank, 2010	Annual rate of growth,[2] 2010 to 2020 (percent)	Popula- tion per sq. mile, 2010	Area [3] (sq. mile)
		1990	2000	2010	2020, proj.				
World	S0	**5,288,828**	**6,088,684**	**6,853,019**	**7,597,239**	(X)	**1.0**	**134**	**50,972,239**
Afghanistan	S6	13,449	22,021	29,121	35,975	41	2.1	116	251,826
Albania	S4	3,245	3,158	2,987	3,075	135	0.3	282	10,578
Algeria	S5	25,089	30,429	34,586	38,594	35	1.1	38	919,591
Andorra	S4	53	65	85	86	199	0.1	468	181
Angola	S5	8,297	10,377	13,068	15,898	70	2.0	27	481,351
Antigua and Barbuda	S2	64	75	87	98	198	1.2	508	171
Argentina	S3	33,036	37,336	41,343	45,379	32	0.9	39	1,056,637
Armenia	S6	3,377	3,043	2,967	3,017	137	0.2	272	10,889
Australia	S8	16,956	19,053	21,516	23,939	54	1.1	7	2,966,138
Austria	G4	7,723	8,113	8,214	8,220	92	(Z)	258	31,832
Azerbaijan	S6	7,200	7,809	8,304	9,058	91	0.9	260	31,903
Bahamas, The	S2	245	283	310	338	177	0.8	80	3,865
Bahrain	S6	501	635	738	827	163	1.1	2,580	286
Bangladesh	S7	112,213	132,151	156,118	183,109	7	1.6	3,106	50,258
Barbados	S2	262	274	286	295	180	0.3	1,721	166
Belarus	S4	10,201	10,034	9,613	9,249	88	–0.4	123	78,340
Belgium	S4	9,969	10,264	10,423	10,465	79	(Z)	892	11,690
Belize	S2	191	248	315	380	176	1.9	36	8,805
Benin	S5	4,705	6,619	9,056	11,956	90	2.8	212	42,711
Bhutan	S7	615	606	700	782	164	1.1	47	14,824
Bolivia	S3	6,574	8,195	9,947	11,640	84	1.6	24	418,263
Bosnia and Herzegovina	S4	4,424	4,035	4,622	4,592	120	–0.1	234	19,763
Botswana	S5	1,265	1,680	2,029	2,312	144	1.3	9	218,815
Brazil	S3	151,170	176,320	201,103	222,608	5	1.0	62	3,266,183
Brunei	S8	253	325	395	464	175	1.6	194	2,033
Bulgaria	S4	8,894	7,818	7,149	6,569	98	–0.8	171	41,888
Burkina Faso	S5	8,361	11,588	16,242	21,978	61	3.0	154	105,714
Burma	S7	40,464	47,439	53,414	59,126	24	1.0	212	252,320
Burundi	S5	5,536	6,823	9,863	13,429	85	3.1	995	9,915
Cambodia	S7	9,368	12,351	14,454	16,927	66	1.6	212	68,152
Cameroon	S5	11,884	15,343	19,294	23,471	58	2.0	106	182,513
Canada	S1	27,791	31,100	33,760	36,387	36	0.7	10	3,511,006
Cape Verde	S5	340	430	509	583	169	1.4	327	1,557
Central African Republic	S5	3,085	3,980	4,845	5,991	116	2.1	20	240,534
Chad	S5	5,841	7,943	10,543	12,756	78	1.9	22	486,177
Chile	S3	13,129	15,156	16,746	18,058	60	0.8	58	287,186
China [4]	S7	1,148,364	1,263,638	1,330,141	1,384,545	1	0.4	360	3,694,942
Colombia	S3	33,147	38,910	44,205	49,085	29	1.0	103	428,225
Comoros	S5	429	579	773	1,001	160	2.6	896	863
Congo (Brazzaville) [5]	S5	2,266	3,104	4,126	5,444	126	2.8	31	131,853
Congo (Kinshasa) [5]	S5	39,047	51,849	70,916	95,605	19	3.0	81	875,308
Costa Rica	S2	3,023	3,883	4,516	5,098	122	1.2	229	19,714
Cote d'Ivoire	S5	12,491	16,885	21,059	25,504	57	1.9	172	122,781
Croatia	S4	4,508	4,411	4,487	4,427	123	–0.1	208	21,612
Cuba	S2	10,513	11,106	11,477	11,647	73	0.1	271	42,402
Cyprus	S6	745	920	1,103	1,267	157	1.4	309	3,568
Czech Republic	S4	10,310	10,270	10,202	10,013	81	–0.2	342	29,825
Denmark	S4	5,141	5,337	5,516	5,642	109	0.2	337	16,384
Djibouti	S5	499	669	741	922	162	2.2	83	8,950
Dominica	S2	70	71	73	74	201	0.2	251	290
Dominican Republic	S2	7,084	8,469	9,824	11,109	86	1.2	527	18,656
Ecuador	S3	10,318	12,446	14,791	16,905	65	1.3	138	106,888
Egypt	S5	54,907	65,159	80,472	96,260	16	1.8	209	384,344
El Salvador	S2	5,110	5,850	6,052	6,217	106	0.3	756	8,000
Equatorial Guinea	S5	371	491	651	836	166	2.5	60	10,830
Eritrea	S5	3,138	4,197	5,793	7,260	108	2.3	149	38,996
Estonia	S4	1,569	1,380	1,291	1,203	154	–0.7	79	16,366
Ethiopia	S5	48,397	64,165	88,013	120,420	14	3.1	228	386,100
Fiji	S8	740	805	876	936	158	0.7	124	7,056
Finland	S4	4,986	5,169	5,255	5,272	112	(Z)	45	117,303
France	S4	58,168	61,137	64,768	67,518	21	0.4	262	247,125
Gabon	S5	938	1,236	1,545	1,877	151	1.9	16	99,485
Gambia, The	S5	949	1,368	1,824	2,317	147	2.4	472	3,861
Georgia	S6	5,426	4,777	4,601	4,440	121	–0.4	171	26,911
Germany [6]	S4	79,380	82,188	82,283	81,422	15	–0.1	611	134,622
Ghana	S5	15,408	19,752	24,340	28,784	47	1.7	277	87,851
Greece	S4	10,130	10,559	10,750	10,742	75	(–Z)	213	50,443
Grenada	S2	94	102	108	113	191	0.5	812	133
Guatemala	S2	8,966	11,085	13,550	16,264	68	1.8	328	41,374
Guinea	S5	6,118	8,350	10,324	13,420	80	2.6	109	94,871
Guinea-Bissau	S5	996	1,279	1,565	1,893	150	1.9	144	10,857
Guyana	S3	772	786	748	754	161	0.1	10	76,003
Haiti	S2	6,798	8,413	9,649	10,693	87	1.0	907	10,641
Honduras	S2	4,794	6,359	7,989	9,465	93	1.7	185	43,201
Hungary	S4	10,372	10,147	9,992	9,772	83	–0.2	289	34,598
Iceland	S1	255	281	309	329	178	0.6	8	38,707
India	S7	838,159	1,006,300	1,173,108	1,326,093	2	1.2	1,022	1,147,951
Indonesia	S8	181,770	213,829	242,968	267,532	4	1.0	347	699,447
Iran	S6	58,100	68,632	76,923	86,543	18	1.2	130	591,349

See footnotes at end of table.

U.S. Census Bureau, Statistical Abstract of the United States: 2011

Table 1331. Population by Country or Area: 1990 to 2020—Con.
[See headnote, page 836]

Country or area	Map refer- ence [1]	Mid-year population (1,000)				Popula- tion rank, 2010	Annual rate of growth, [2] 2010 to 2020 (percent)	Popula- tion per sq. mile, 2010	Area [3] (sq. mile)
		1990	2000	2010	2020, proj.				
Iraq	S6	18,140	22,679	29,672	36,889	40	2.2	176	168,868
Ireland	S4	3,508	3,822	4,623	5,177	119	1.1	174	26,596
Israel	S6	4,478	6,115	7,354	8,479	96	1.4	880	8,356
Italy	S4	56,743	57,719	58,091	57,028	23	−0.2	512	113,568
Jamaica	S2	2,347	2,616	2,847	3,051	138	0.7	681	4,182
Japan	S7	123,537	126,729	126,804	121,633	10	−0.4	901	140,728
Jordan	S6	3,267	4,688	6,407	7,278	102	1.3	187	34,286
Kazakhstan	S7	16,398	15,032	15,460	15,977	63	0.3	15	1,042,355
Kenya	S5	23,354	30,508	40,047	48,319	33	1.9	182	219,745
Kiribati	S8	71	85	99	112	195	1.2	318	313
Korea, North	S7	20,019	21,263	22,757	23,433	50	0.3	490	46,490
Korea, South	S7	42,869	46,839	48,636	49,362	26	0.1	1,300	37,421
Kosovo	S4	1,862	1,700	1,815	1,933	148	0.6	432	4,203
Kuwait	S6	2,142	1,974	2,789	3,744	139	2.9	405	6,880
Kyrgyzstan	S6	4,382	4,851	5,509	6,314	110	1.4	74	74,054
Laos	S7	4,210	5,397	6,368	7,447	104	1.6	71	89,112
Latvia	S4	2,664	2,376	2,218	2,077	141	−0.7	92	24,034
Lebanon	S6	3,440	3,791	4,125	4,243	127	0.3	1,044	3,950
Lesotho	S5	1,703	1,916	1,920	1,969	146	0.3	164	11,720
Liberia	S5	2,139	2,601	3,685	4,727	129	2.5	99	37,189
Libya	S5	4,146	5,125	6,461	7,759	101	1.8	10	679,359
Liechtenstein	S4	29	32	35	37	211	0.5	567	62
Lithuania	S4	3,695	3,654	3,545	3,435	130	−0.3	146	24,201
Luxembourg	S4	383	439	498	556	170	1.1	498	998
Macedonia	S4	1,861	2,015	2,072	2,113	143	0.2	211	9,820
Madagascar	S5	11,633	15,742	21,282	28,374	56	2.9	95	224,533
Malawi	S5	9,546	11,802	15,448	20,204	64	2.7	425	36,324
Malaysia	S8	17,882	23,151	28,275	32,652	43	1.4	223	126,895
Maldives	S7	217	300	396	392	174	−0.1	3,439	115
Mali	S5	8,327	10,621	13,796	17,890	67	2.6	29	471,116
Malta	S4	359	390	407	419	173	0.3	3,334	122
Marshall Islands	S8	46	53	66	78	204	1.7	942	70
Mauritania	S5	1,925	2,501	3,205	4,005	100	2.2	8	397,954
Mauritius	S5	1,062	1,186	1,294	1,379	153	0.6	1,651	784
Mexico	S1	84,914	99,927	112,469	124,654	11	1.0	150	750,558
Micronesia, Federated States of	S8	109	108	107	102	192	−0.5	395	271
Moldova	S4	4,394	4,391	4,317	4,267	124	0.1	340	12,699
Monaco	S4	30	32	31	31	213	0.1	39,609	1
Mongolia	S7	2,218	2,664	3,087	3,535	134	1.4	5	599,828
Montenegro	S4	583	732	667	639	165	−0.4	128	5,194
Morocco	S5	24,000	28,113	31,627	34,956	38	1.0	184	172,317
Mozambique	S5	12,667	18,125	22,061	26,480	52	1.8	73	303,622
Namibia	S5	1,471	1,893	2,128	2,263	142	0.6	7	317,873
Nauru	S8	9	10	9	10	223	0.5	1,143	8
Nepal	S7	18,918	24,818	28,952	34,209	42	1.7	523	55,348
Netherlands	S4	14,952	15,908	16,783	17,330	60	0.0	1,285	13,080
New Zealand	S8	3,414	3,802	4,252	4,615	125	0.8	41	103,363
Nicaragua	S2	3,685	4,935	5,996	7,030	107	1.6	129	46,328
Niger	S5	7,842	10,951	15,878	22,749	62	3.6	32	489,073
Nigeria	S5	96,604	123,179	152,217	182,344	8	1.8	433	351,648
Norway	S4	4,242	4,492	4,676	4,836	118	0.3	40	117,483
Oman	S6	1,794	2,432	2,968	3,635	136	2.0	25	119,498
Pakistan	S6	118,816	152,429	184,405	213,719	6	1.5	620	297,635
Palau	S8	15	19	21	22	218	0.4	118	177
Panama	S2	2,393	2,900	3,411	3,894	132	1.3	119	28,703
Papua New Guinea	S8	3,683	4,813	6,065	7,259	105	1.8	35	174,849
Paraguay	S3	4,200	5,418	6,376	7,192	103	1.2	42	153,398
Peru	S3	21,600	26,087	29,907	33,230	39	1.1	61	494,207
Philippines	S7	65,088	81,222	99,900	119,329	12	1.8	868	115,124
Poland	S4	38,119	38,654	38,464	37,949	34	−0.1	327	117,473
Portugal	S4	9,923	10,336	10,736	10,842	76	0.1	304	35,317
Qatar	S6	446	627	841	905	159	0.7	188	4,473
Romania	S4	22,866	22,447	21,959	21,303	53	−0.3	247	88,761
Russia	S7	147,973	146,710	139,390	132,242	9	−0.5	22	6,323,451
Rwanda	S5	6,999	8,398	11,056	14,327	74	2.6	1,161	9,524
Saint Kitts and Nevis	S2	42	46	50	54	208	0.8	495	101
Saint Lucia	S2	138	153	161	166	188	0.3	688	234
Saint Vincent and the Grenadines	S2	107	108	104	101	194	−0.3	694	150
Samoa	S8	163	176	192	204	185	0.6	176	1,089
San Marino	S4	23	27	31	34	212	0.8	1,336	24
Sao Tome and Principe	S5	116	141	176	211	187	1.8	472	372
Saudi Arabia	S6	16,061	21,312	25,732	29,819	46	1.5	31	829,996
Senegal	S5	7,348	9,469	12,323	15,736	71	2.4	166	74,336
Serbia	S4	7,786	7,604	7,345	7,012	97	−0.5	246	29,913
Seychelles	S5	71	79	88	96	197	0.8	503	176
Sierra Leone	S5	4,228	3,809	5,246	6,625	113	2.3	190	27,653
Singapore	S8	3,047	4,037	4,701	5,015	117	0.6	17,723	265
Slovakia	S4	5,263	5,400	5,470	5,494	111	(Z)	295	18,573
Slovenia	S4	1,991	2,011	2,003	1,951	145	−0.3	257	7,780
Solomon Islands	S8	321	434	559	685	168	2.0	52	10,805
Somalia	S5	6,692	7,386	10,112	13,272	82	2.7	42	242,215

See footnotes at end of table.

U.S. Census Bureau, Statistical Abstract of the United States: 2011

Table 1331. Population by Country or Area: 1990 to 2020—Con.

[See headnote, page 836]

Country or area	Map refer- ence [1]	Mid-year population (1,000) 1990	2000	2010	2020, proj.	Popula- tion rank, 2010	Annual rate of growth, [2] 2010 to 2020 (percent)	Popula- tion per sq. mile, 2010	Area [3] (sq. mile)
South Africa	S5	38,476	45,064	49,109	48,530	25	−0.1	105	468,907
Spain	S4	39,351	40,589	46,506	50,016	27	0.7	241	192,656
Sri Lanka	S7	17,365	19,436	21,514	23,112	55	0.7	862	24,954
Sudan	S5	25,888	34,109	43,940	56,292	30	2.5	48	917,374
Suriname	S3	395	432	487	537	172	1.0	8	60,232
Swaziland	S5	882	1,144	1,354	1,513	152	1.1	204	6,642
Sweden	S4	8,601	8,924	9,074	9,245	89	0.2	57	158,430
Switzerland	S4	6,837	7,267	7,623	7,751	94	0.2	494	15,443
Syria	S6	12,500	16,471	22,198	24,744	51	1.1	313	70,900
Tajikistan	S6	5,272	6,230	7,487	8,874	95	1.7	137	54,637
Tanzania	S5	25,214	33,712	41,893	49,989	31	1.8	122	342,008
Thailand	S7	55,197	62,157	67,090	70,768	20	0.5	340	197,255
Timor-Leste	S8	746	847	1,155	1,389	156	1.8	201	5,743
Togo	S5	3,721	4,992	6,587	8,608	100	2.7	314	20,998
Tonga	S8	92	102	123	141	189	1.4	443	277
Trinidad and Tobago	S2	1,255	1,252	1,229	1,209	155	−0.2	621	1,980
Tunisia	S5	8,211	9,568	10,589	11,559	77	0.9	177	59,985
Turkey	S6	56,561	67,329	77,804	86,757	17	1.1	262	297,155
Turkmenistan	S6	3,658	4,385	4,941	5,529	115	1.1	27	181,440
Tuvalu	S8	9	10	10	11	222	0.8	1,043	10
Uganda	S5	17,456	23,956	33,399	47,691	37	3.6	439	76,100
Ukraine	S4	51,622	49,005	45,416	42,561	28	−0.6	203	223,679
United Arab Emirates	S6	1,826	3,219	4,976	6,495	114	2.7	154	32,278
United Kingdom	S4	57,411	59,140	62,348	65,761	22	0.5	667	93,409
United States	**S1**	**249,623**	**282,172**	**310,233**	**341,387**	**3**	**1.0**	**88**	**3,537,438**
Uruguay	S3	3,110	3,328	3,510	3,653	131	0.4	52	67,573
Uzbekistan	S6	20,530	25,042	27,866	30,565	44	0.9	170	164,247
Vanuatu	S8	154	190	222	251	184	1.2	47	4,706
Venezuela	S3	19,325	23,493	27,223	31,276	45	1.4	80	340,560
Vietnam	S7	67,258	79,178	89,571	98,721	13	1.0	748	119,718
Yemen	S6	12,416	17,407	23,495	29,727	48	2.4	115	203,849
Zambia	S5	7,858	10,345	13,460	18,065	69	2.9	47	287,026
Zimbabwe	S5	10,156	11,820	11,652	15,832	72	3.1	78	149,362
OTHER									
Taiwan [4]	S7	20,278	22,183	23,025	23,278	49	0.1	1,849	12,456
AREAS OF SPECIAL SOVEREIGNTY AND DEPENDENCIES									
American Samoa	S8	47	58	66	75	203	1.2	865	77
Anguilla	S1	8	11	15	18	220	2.0	420	35
Aruba	S1	63	90	105	119	193	1.3	1,505	69
Bermuda	S1	58	63	68	72	202	0.5	3,274	21
Cayman Islands	S1	26	38	50	62	207	2.1	493	102
Cook Islands	S8	18	16	11	9	221	−2.9	126	91
Faroe Islands	S4	47	46	49	52	209	0.5	91	538
French Polynesia	S8	202	249	291	329	179	1.2	197	1,478
Gaza Strip [7]	S6	646	1,130	1,604	2,121	149	2.8	11,542	139
Gibraltar	S4	29	27	29	30	215	0.2	11,506	3
Greenland	S1	56	57	58	58	206	(−Z)	(Z)	160,075
Guam	S8	134	155	181	204	186	1.2	861	210
Guernsey	S4	63	62	65	67	205	0.3	2,151	30
Hong Kong	S7	5,688	6,659	7,090	7,328	99	0.3	17,422	407
Isle of Man	S4	69	76	84	90	200	0.8	380	221
Jersey	S4	84	87	93	101	196	0.8	2,085	45
Macau	S7	352	432	568	614	167	0.8	52,163	11
Mayotte	S5	90	156	231	312	182	3.0	1,601	144
Montserrat	S2	11	4	5	5	227	0.5	130	39
Netherlands Antilles	S2	189	210	229	243	183	0.6	740	309
New Caledonia	S8	169	211	252	290	181	1.4	36	7,056
Northern Mariana Islands	S8	44	70	48	49	210	0.1	270	179
Puerto Rico	S2	3,537	3,814	3,979	4,051	128	0.2	1,162	3,425
Saint Barthelemy	S2	5	7	7	7	225	−0.4	913	8
Saint Helena	S5	7	7	8	8	224	0.2	64	119
Saint Martin	S2	30	28	30	33	214	0.7	1,439	21
Saint Pierre and Miquelon	S1	6	6	6	5	226	−1.1	64	93
Turks and Caicos Islands	S2	12	18	24	29	217	2.2	64	366
Virgin Islands	S2	104	109	110	108	190	−0.1	822	134
Virgin Islands, British	S2	16	20	25	29	216	1.5	428	58
Wallis and Futuna	S8	13	15	15	16	219	0.3	280	55
West Bank [7]	S6	1,253	1,980	2,515	3,058	140	2.0	1,155	2,178
Western Sahara	S5	217	336	492	652	171	2.8	5	102,703

X Not applicable. Z Less than 0.05 percent or less than one person per square mile. [1] See maps on pp. 826–834 for geographic locations. [2] Computed by the exponential method. For explanation of average annual percent change, see Guide to Tabular Presentation. [3] Source: Central Intelligence Agency, "CIA World Factbook," accessed August 2010. (Data converted from square kilometers to square miles). [4] With the establishment of diplomatic relations with China on January 1, 1979, the U.S. government recognized the People's Republic of China as the sole legal government of China and acknowledged the Chinese position that there is only one China and that Taiwan is part of China. [5] "Congo" is the official short-form name for both the Republic of Congo and the Democratic Republic of the Congo. To distinguish one from the other the U.S. Department of State adds the capital in parentheses. This practice is unofficial and provisional. [6] Data for 1990 are for former West Germany and East Germany combined. [7] The Gaza Strip and West Bank are Israeli occupied with interim status subject to Israeli/Palestinian negotiations. The final status is yet to be determined.

Source: Except as noted, U.S. Census Bureau, International Data Base, <http://www.census.gov/ipc/www/idb/>, accessed June 2010.

Table 1332. Foreign or Foreign-Born Population, Labor Force, and Net Migration in Selected OECD Countries: 2000 and 2007

[31,108 represents 31,108,000. In Australia and the United States, the data refer to people present in the country who are foreign born. In the European countries and Japan, they generally refer to foreigners and represent the nationalities of residents. Minus sign (−) indicates net loss]

| Country | Foreign population [1] | | | | Foreign labor force [2] | | | | Average net migration 1990–2007 [3] |
| | Number (1,000) | | Percent of total population | | Number (1,000) | | Percent of total population | | |
	2000	2007	2000	2007	2000	2007	2000	2007	(per 1,000 population)
United States	**31,108**	**41,100**	**11.0**	**13.6**	**18,029**	**24,778**	**12.9**	**16.3**	**4.0**
Australia.	4,412	5,254	23.0	25.0	2,373	2,827	24.7	25.8	5.7
Austria.	702	840	8.7	10.1	346	452	10.6	13.1	3.9
Belgium	862	971	8.4	9.1	388	449	8.6	9.5	3.2
Denmark	259	299	4.8	5.5	97	127	3.4	4.4	2.2
France	(NA)	(NA)	(NA)	(NA)	1,578	1,486	6.0	5.4	1.3
Germany	7,297	6,745	8.9	8.2	3,546	3,874	8.8	9.4	3.0
Italy [4]	1,380	3,433	2.4	5.8	838	1,638	3.9	6.6	3.8
Japan [5].	1,686	2,151	1.3	1.7	155	194	0.2	0.3	−0.1
Luxembourg.	165	206	37.3	43.2	153	222	58.0	66.6	9.8
Netherlands.	668	688	4.2	4.2	300	314	3.9	3.6	1.8
Spain [6]	1,371	5,221	3.4	11.6	455	1,981	2.5	9.0	7.0
Sweden	477	525	5.4	5.7	222	(NA)	5.0	(NA)	3.0
Switzerland [7]	1,384	1,571	19.3	20.8	717	876	20.1	21.3	4.3
United Kingdom [8].	2,342	3,824	4.0	6.5	1,107	2,035	4.0	7.2	0.7

NA Not available. [1] Data are from population registers of foreigners except for France, Greece, Mexico, and Poland (census), Ireland and the United Kingdom (Labour Force Survey), Portugal (residence permits), Australia (inter- and post-censal estimates), and the United States (Current Population Survey). [2] Includes unemployed except for Belgium, Greece, Norway, Luxembourg, Netherlands, and the United Kingdom. Germany, Luxembourg, and Netherlands include cross-border workers. Belgium and Italy include the self-employed. Data for Austria, Germany, and Luxembourg are from social security registers, and for Denmark, from the register of population. Data for Italy, Spain, and Switzerland are from residence or work permits. Figures for Japan and Netherlands are estimates. Data for other countries are from labor force surveys. [3] Or latest period available. [4] Children under 18 who are registered on their parents' permit are not counted. [5] Data are based on registered foreign nationals which include foreigners staying in Japan for more than 90 days. [6] Number of foreigners with a residence permit. Permits of short duration (less than 6 months) as well as students are excluded. [7] Number of foreigners with an annual residence permit or with a settlement permit (permanent permit). Seasonal and frontier workers are excluded. [8] Estimated from the annual labour force survey. Fluctuations from year to year may be due to sampling error.

Source: Organization for Economic Cooperation and Development (OECD), 2010, "International migration database", OECD International Migration Statistics database and "Population and vital statistics," Labour Force Statistics database (copyright), <http://dx.doi.org/10.1787/data-00287-en> and <http://dx.doi.org/10.1787/data-00342-en>, accessed May 2010.

Table 1333. Age Distribution by Country or Area: 2010 and 2020

[In percent. Covers countries with 13 million or more population in 2010]

| Country or area | 2010 | | 2020, proj. | | Country or area | 2010 | | 2020, proj. | |
	Under 15 years old	65 years old and over	Under 15 years old	65 years old and over		Under 15 years old	65 years old and over	Under 15 years old	65 years old and over
World	**26.5**	**7.8**	**24.6**	**9.6**	Madagascar	43.3	3.0	41.4	3.3
					Malawi	45.3	2.7	43.1	2.8
Afghanistan	42.9	2.4	38.2	2.7	Malaysia	29.9	4.8	26.8	6.9
Algeria	24.7	5.1	21.9	6.9	Mali	47.5	3.0	44.9	2.9
Angola	43.4	2.7	41.5	2.5	Mexico	28.7	6.4	25.0	8.3
Argentina	25.5	10.9	23.7	12.4	Morocco	28.2	6.0	24.9	7.5
Australia	18.4	13.7	17.6	17.0	Mozambique	44.1	2.9	42.1	3.1
Bangladesh	34.8	4.6	28.3	5.8	Nepal	35.6	4.3	27.6	5.1
Brazil	26.5	6.6	23.6	8.8	Netherlands	17.2	15.2	15.5	19.4
Burkina Faso	46.0	2.5	44.3	2.4	Niger	49.7	2.3	48.4	2.3
Burma	27.9	5.0	24.7	6.2	Nigeria	41.2	3.1	37.9	3.4
Cambodia	32.5	3.7	30.2	4.6	Pakistan	36.1	4.2	29.7	4.8
Cameroon	40.7	3.3	37.4	3.7	Peru	28.5	5.8	24.4	7.6
Canada	15.9	15.5	15.4	20.1	Philippines	34.9	4.2	31.6	5.4
Chile	22.7	9.3	19.9	12.4	Poland	14.8	13.5	14.6	18.6
China [1]	17.9	8.6	17.0	12.4	Romania	14.9	14.8	14.1	17.6
Colombia	27.2	6.0	23.3	8.4	Russia	15.0	13.3	16.3	16.0
Congo (Kinshasa) [2]	46.7	2.5	44.4	2.6	Saudi Arabia	30.1	2.9	25.0	3.8
Cote d'Ivoire	40.2	2.9	35.6	3.7	South Africa	28.6	5.5	26.9	7.4
Ecuador	30.6	6.3	25.8	8.1	Spain	15.0	16.9	15.0	18.5
Egypt	32.8	4.4	30.3	6.0	Sri Lanka	23.6	8.3	21.1	11.5
Ethiopia	46.2	2.7	45.4	2.7	Sudan	42.5	2.6	39.6	3.1
France	18.6	16.5	17.8	20.0	Syria	35.8	3.7	30.0	4.6
Germany	13.5	20.4	12.9	22.6	Taiwan [1]	16.2	10.8	12.9	15.5
Ghana	36.8	3.6	32.4	4.0	Tanzania	42.5	2.9	36.4	3.3
Guatemala	38.7	3.8	33.0	4.9	Thailand	20.1	8.9	17.9	12.3
India	30.1	5.3	26.3	6.7	Turkey	26.9	6.2	23.4	8.1
Indonesia	27.7	6.1	23.8	7.7	Uganda	50.0	2.1	49.5	1.9
Iran	24.4	5.0	23.3	6.1	Ukraine	13.7	15.5	14.5	17.8
Iraq	38.4	3.1	33.7	3.9	United Kingdom	17.4	16.3	17.6	18.5
Italy	13.4	20.3	12.0	23.1	**United States**	**20.1**	**13.0**	**20.0**	**16.1**
Japan	13.3	22.6	11.3	28.3	Uzbekistan	27.3	4.7	23.2	5.9
Kazakhstan	21.6	7.6	22.2	9.5	Venezuela	30.0	5.3	26.1	7.4
Kenya	42.3	2.7	36.4	3.3	Vietnam	25.6	5.5	22.6	0.9
Korea, North	20.9	9.6	19.6	10.6	Yemen	43.5	2.6	37.3	3.0
Korea, South	16.2	11.1	12.6	15.6	Zambia	46.7	2.5	46.2	2.5

[1] See footnote 4, Table 1331. [2] See footnote 5, Table 1331.

Source: U.S. Census Bureau, International Data Base, <http://www.census.gov/ipc/www/idb/>, accessed June 2010.

Table 1334. Births to Unmarried Women by Country: 1980 to 2008

[Percent of all live births]

Country	1980	1990	2000	2005	2006	2007	2008
United States	**18.4**	**28.0**	**33.2**	**36.9**	**38.5**	**39.7**	**40.6**
Canada	12.8	24.4	28.3	25.6	27.1	27.3	(NA)
Japan.	0.8	1.1	1.6	2.0	2.1	(NA)	(NA)
Denmark	33.2	46.4	44.6	45.7	46.4	46.1	46.2
France	11.4	30.1	43.6	48.4	50.5	51.7	52.6
Germany [1]	(X)	15.1	23.4	29.2	30.0	30.8	32.1
Ireland	5.9	14.6	31.5	31.8	32.7	(NA)	(NA)
Italy	4.3	6.5	9.7	15.2	16.2	17.7	(NA)
Netherlands	4.1	11.4	24.9	34.9	37.1	39.5	41.2
Spain	3.9	9.6	17.7	26.6	28.4	30.2	31.7
Sweden	39.7	47.0	55.3	55.4	55.5	54.8	54.7
United Kingdom	11.5	27.9	39.5	42.9	43.7	(NA)	(NA)

NA Not available. X Not applicable. [1] Data are for 1991 instead of 1990.
Source: U.S. Bureau of Labor Statistics, updated and revised from "Families and Work Transition in 12 Countries 1980–2001," *Monthly Labor Review*, September 2003, with national sources, some of which may be unpublished.

Table 1335. Marriage and Divorce Rates by Country: 1980 to 2008

[Per 1,000 population aged 15–64 years]

Country	Marriage rate				Divorce rate			
	1980	1990	2000	2008	1980	1990	2000	2008
United States [1]	**15.9**	**14.9**	**12.5**	**10.6**	**7.9**	**7.2**	**6.2**	**5.2**
Canada	11.5	10.0	7.5	6.4	3.7	4.2	3.4	(NA)
Japan.	9.8	8.4	9.2	(NA)	1.8	1.8	3.1	(NA)
Denmark	8.0	9.1	10.8	10.3	4.1	4.0	4.0	4.1
France	9.7	7.7	7.9	6.6	2.4	2.8	3.0	(NA)
Germany [2]	(X)	8.2	7.6	6.9	(X)	2.5	3.5	3.5
Ireland [3]	10.9	8.3	7.6	(NA)	(NA)	(NA)	1.0	(NA)
Italy	8.7	8.2	7.3	6.3	0.3	0.7	1.0	1.3
Netherlands	9.6	9.4	8.2	6.7	2.7	2.8	3.2	2.9
Spain	9.4	8.5	7.9	6.2	(NA)	0.9	1.4	3.5
Sweden	7.1	7.4	7.0	8.3	3.7	3.5	3.8	3.5
United Kingdom	11.6	10.0	8.0	(NA)	4.1	4.1	4.0	(NA)

NA Not available. X Not applicable. [1] Divorce rates exclude data for California, Georgia, Hawaii, Indiana, Louisiana, and Minnesota in 2008.
[2] Data are for 1991 instead of 1990. [3] Divorce not allowed by law prior to 1997.
Source: U.S. Bureau of Labor Statistics, updated and revised from "Families and Work in Transition in 12 Countries, 1980–2001," *Monthly Labor Review*, September 2003, with national sources, some of which may be unpublished.

Table 1336. Single-Parent Households: 1980 to 2009

[In thousands (6,061 represents 6,061,000), except for percent. For the United Kingdom in 1981, children are defined as those under 15 and those who are 15, 16, or 17 and attended school full-time; for later years, children are defined as those under 16 and those who are 16 or 17 and attend school full-time. For Ireland, children are defined as those under 15. For Denmark for 2009 and France, children are defined as those under 25. For Canada for 2001 onward and for Germany for 1995 onward, children are of all ages. For Germany in 1991 and all other countries, children are defined as those under 18 living at home, or away at school. Data are generally for the entire year, but in some instances they are only for a particular month within the year]

Country and year	Number (1,000)	Percent of all households with children	Country and year	Number (1,000)	Percent of all households with children
United States:			Germany:		
1980.	6,061	19.5	1991.	1,429	15.2
1990.	7,752	24.0	1995 [1]	2,496	18.8
2000.	9,357	27.0	2000 [1]	2,274	17.6
2008.	10,536	29.5	2008.	2,616	21.7
Canada:			Ireland: [2]		
1981.	437	12.7	1981.	30	7.2
1991.	572	16.2	1991.	44	10.7
2001 [1]	1,184	23.5	2002.	50	17.4
2006.	1,276	24.6	2006.	78	22.6
Japan:			Netherlands:		
1980.	796	4.9	1988.	179	9.6
1990.	934	6.5	2000.	240	13.0
2000.	996	8.3	2009 [1]	310	16.0
2005.	1,163	10.2	Sweden:		
Denmark: [2]			1985.	117	11.2
1980.	99	13.4	1995 [1]	189	17.4
1990.	117	17.8	2000.	233	21.4
2001.	120	18.4	2008.	200	18.7
2009 [1]	165	21.7	United Kingdom: [3]		
France:			1981.	1,010	13.9
1982.	887	10.2	1991.	1,344	19.4
1990.	1,175	13.2	2000.	1,434	20.7
1999.	1,494	17.4	2008.	1,750	25.0
2005 [1]	1,725	19.8			

[1] Break in series. [2] Data are from family-based, rather than household-based, statistics. [3] Great Britain only (excludes Northern Ireland).
Source: U.S. Bureau of Labor Statistics, updated and revised from "Families and Work in Transition in 12 Countries, 1980–2001," *Monthly Labor Review*, September 2003, with national sources, some of which may be unpublished.

Table 1337. Percent Distribution of Households by Type and Country: 1980 to 2009

[Data are generally for the entire year, but in some instances they are only for a particular month within the year]

Year	Total	Married-couple households [1] Total	With children [2]	Without children [2]	Single parent [2]	One person	Other [3]
United States:							
1980.............	100.0	60.8	30.9	29.9	7.5	22.7	9.0
1990.............	100.0	56.0	26.3	29.8	8.3	24.6	11.0
1995.............	100.0	54.4	25.5	28.9	9.1	25.0	11.5
2000.............	100.0	52.8	24.1	28.7	8.9	25.5	12.7
2008.............	100.0	50.0	21.6	28.4	9.0	27.5	13.5
Canada:							
1981.............	100.0	66.8	36.3	30.5	5.3	20.3	7.6
1991.............	100.0	62.8	29.6	33.2	5.7	22.9	8.6
2001 [4].........	100.0	58.5	33.4	25.2	10.2	25.7	5.5
2006.............	100.0	57.4	31.4	26.1	10.3	26.8	5.5
Japan:							
1980.............	100.0	68.4	42.9	25.6	2.2	19.8	9.5
1990.............	100.0	65.2	33.1	32.1	2.3	23.1	9.4
1995.............	100.0	62.8	27.4	35.4	2.0	25.6	9.6
2000.............	100.0	60.3	23.6	36.7	2.1	27.6	10.0
2005.............	100.0	57.6	20.8	36.8	2.4	29.5	10.5
Denmark: [5]							
1980.............	100.0	50.3	25.0	25.3	3.9	44.9	1.0
1990.............	100.0	45.6	19.5	26.1	4.2	49.6	0.6
1995.............	100.0	44.9	18.2	26.6	4.2	50.4	0.5
2001.............	100.0	45.7	18.5	27.2	4.2	49.6	0.6
2009 [4]..........	100.0	47.4	21.2	26.1	5.9	46.2	0.6
France:							
1982.............	100.0	67.5	39.8	27.7	4.5	24.6	3.4
1990.............	100.0	64.0	35.9	28.1	5.5	27.1	3.4
1999.............	100.0	59.3	29.9	29.4	6.3	31.0	3.4
2005 [4].........	100.0	56.4	27.2	29.2	6.7	32.8	4.1
Germany:							
1991.............	100.0	55.3	31.6	23.7	7.1	33.6	4.0
1995.............	100.0	53.3	29.2	24.0	6.8	34.9	5.1
2000 [4].........	100.0	56.8	28.0	28.8	6.0	36.1	1.2
2005.............	100.0	54.7	25.5	29.1	6.4	37.5	1.4
2008.............	100.0	52.6	23.6	29.0	6.5	39.4	1.5
Ireland:							
1901.............	100.0	(NA)	(NA)	(NA)	(NA)	16.9	(NA)
1991.............	100.0	61.6	47.9	13.7	10.6	20.2	7.6
1996.............	100.0	59.6	44.5	15.1	11.2	21.5	7.7
2002.............	100.0	59.2	41.4	17.7	11.7	21.6	7.6
2006.............	100.0	57.3	37.4	20.0	11.6	22.4	8.7
Netherlands:							
1988.............	100.0	64.7	37.3	27.4	5.4	28.7	1.2
1993.............	100.0	63.1	33.3	29.9	5.0	30.9	1.0
2000 [4].........	100.0	60.2	30.6	29.6	6.0	32.4	0.7
2005.............	100.0	58.5	29.4	29.1	6.3	34.5	0.7
2007.............	100.0	57.7	28.7	28.9	6.4	35.3	0.7
2009.............	100.0	57.0	28.1	28.9	6.5	35.8	0.7
Sweden:							
1985.............	100.0	54.8	23.8	31.0	3.2	36.1	5.9
1990.............	100.0	52.1	21.9	30.2	3.9	39.6	4.4
1995 [4].........	100.0	50.7	21.2	29.4	4.6	42.3	2.4
2000.............	100.0	45.8	19.1	26.7	5.3	46.5	2.3
2008.............	100.0	44.5	18.6	25.9	4.4	48.1	3.0
United Kingdom: [6]							
1981.............	100.0	65.0	31.0	34.0	5.0	22.0	8.0
1991.............	100.0	61.0	25.0	36.0	6.0	27.0	6.0
1994–95..........	100.0	58.0	25.0	33.0	7.0	27.0	8.0
2000.............	100.0	58.0	23.0	35.0	6.0	29.0	7.0
2008.............	100.0	56.0	21.0	35.0	7.0	30.0	7.0

NA Not available. [1] May include unmarried cohabiting couples. Such couples are explicitly included under married couples in Canada, Denmark, Ireland, France, the Netherlands, Sweden, and the United Kingdom. In Germany, cohabitants are grouped with married couples beginning in 2000. In other countries, some unmarried cohabitants are included as married couples, while some are classified under "other households." [2] Children are defined as unmarried children living at home according to the following age limits: under 18 years old in the United States, Canada (1981–96), Japan, Denmark (1980–2007), Sweden, and the United Kingdom, except that the United Kingdom includes 15-, 16-, and 17-year-olds in 1981 and 16- and 17-year-olds thereafter only if they are attending school full-time; under 25 years old in Denmark (2009 only) and France; and children of all ages in Canada (2001 onward), Germany, Ireland, and the Netherlands. [3] Includes both family and nonfamily households not elsewhere classified. These households comprise, for example, siblings residing together, other households composed of relatives, and households made up of roommates. Some unmarried cohabiting couples may also be included in the "other" group. See footnote 1. [4] Break in series. [5] From family-based statistics. However, one person living alone constitutes a family in Denmark. In this respect, the Danish data are closer to household statistics. [6] Great Britain only (excludes Northern Ireland).

Source: U.S. Bureau of Labor Statistics, updated and revised from "Families and Work in Transition in 12 Countries, 1980–2001," *Monthly Labor Review*, September 2003, with national sources, some of which may be unpublished.

U.S. Census Bureau, Statistical Abstract of the United States: 2011

Table 1338. Births, Deaths, and Life Expectancy by Country or Area: 2010 and 2020

[Covers countries with 13 million or more population in 2010]

Country or area	Crude birth rate [1] 2010	Crude birth rate [1] 2020, proj.	Crude death rate [2] 2010	Crude death rate [2] 2020, proj.	Expectation of life at birth (years) 2010	Expectation of life at birth (years) 2020, proj.	Infant mortality rate [3] 2010	Infant mortality rate [3] 2020, proj.	Total fertility rate per woman [4] 2010	Total fertility rate per woman [4] 2020, proj.
United States	**13.8**	**13.5**	**8.4**	**8.5**	**78.2**	**79.5**	**6.1**	**5.4**	**2.06**	**2.06**
Afghanistan	38.1	34.4	17.7	15.2	44.7	48.3	151.5	129.1	5.50	4.38
Algeria	16.7	14.9	4.7	5.0	74.3	76.5	26.8	18.7	1.76	1.70
Angola	43.3	39.1	23.7	20.5	38.5	41.4	178.1	156.0	6.05	5.16
Argentina	17.8	15.6	7.4	7.3	76.8	78.5	11.1	8.5	2.33	2.15
Australia	12.4	11.9	6.8	7.5	81.7	82.5	4.7	4.1	1.78	1.76
Bangladesh	23.4	19.5	5.8	5.6	69.4	72.4	52.5	36.8	2.65	2.24
Brazil	18.1	15.5	6.4	6.6	72.3	74.8	21.9	15.9	2.19	2.06
Burkina Faso	44.0	39.9	13.0	10.6	53.3	56.9	83.0	67.8	6.21	5.49
Burma	19.5	17.3	8.2	7.9	64.5	68.0	50.8	37.2	2.28	2.09
Cambodia	25.6	21.3	8.2	7.3	62.3	65.9	56.9	43.7	2.90	2.39
Cameroon	33.6	28.3	12.0	10.7	54.0	57.0	62.2	50.4	4.25	3.47
Canada	10.3	10.1	7.9	9.0	81.3	82.2	5.0	4.4	1.58	1.61
Chile	14.5	13.2	5.9	6.7	77.5	79.2	7.5	6.0	1.90	1.77
China [5]	12.2	11.0	6.9	8.3	74.5	76.0	16.5	12.6	1.54	1.58
Colombia	17.8	15.4	5.2	5.6	74.3	76.6	16.9	12.3	2.18	1.94
Congo (Kinshasa) [6]	42.3	37.7	11.4	9.4	54.7	58.1	79.4	61.8	6.11	5.16
Cote d'Ivoire	31.5	26.1	10.4	9.1	56.2	59.9	66.4	51.6	4.01	3.15
Ecuador	20.3	17.0	5.0	5.2	75.5	77.5	20.3	15.0	2.46	2.09
Egypt	25.0	20.8	4.9	4.8	72.4	74.9	26.2	17.9	3.01	2.67
Ethiopia	43.3	39.8	11.3	9.1	55.8	59.4	79.0	61.7	6.07	5.53
France	12.4	11.3	8.7	9.6	81.1	82.0	3.3	3.1	1.97	1.90
Germany	8.2	8.4	11.0	12.2	79.4	80.7	4.0	3.6	1.42	1.49
Ghana	28.1	22.7	8.9	7.3	60.6	65.3	49.9	38.1	3.57	2.75
Guatemala	27.4	22.7	5.0	4.6	70.6	73.4	26.9	19.2	3.36	2.57
India	21.3	18.2	7.5	7.3	66.5	69.7	49.1	35.4	2.65	2.35
Indonesia	18.5	15.6	6.3	6.6	71.1	73.7	28.9	20.4	2.28	2.04
Iran	18.5	16.2	5.9	6.0	69.8	72.4	43.5	33.6	1.89	1.81
Iraq	29.4	23.4	4.9	4.3	70.3	73.1	43.2	30.3	3.76	2.96
Italy	8.0	7.3	10.8	12.0	80.3	81.4	5.4	4.6	1.32	1.42
Japan	7.4	6.7	9.8	12.5	82.2	82.9	2.8	2.7	1.20	1.30
Kazakhstan	16.7	14.1	9.4	9.1	68.2	71.2	24.9	18.2	1.87	1.83
Kenya	35.1	20.8	9.3	7.9	58.8	61.8	53.5	42.4	4.38	2.57
Korea, North	14.6	13.1	10.6	11.2	64.1	67.6	50.2	38.0	1.94	1.82
Korea, South	8.7	8.2	6.2	7.6	78.8	81.1	4.2	3.6	1.22	1.29
Madagascar	37.9	33.8	8.0	6.4	63.3	66.8	52.8	40.2	5.09	4.44
Malawi	41.3	36.5	13.7	10.9	50.9	55.3	83.5	63.1	5.51	4.68
Malaysia	21.4	18.3	4.9	5.3	73.6	75.9	15.5	11.4	2.70	2.43
Mali	46.1	41.0	14.6	11.4	52.2	56.6	113.7	91.9	6.54	5.51
Mexico	19.4	17.0	4.8	5.3	76.3	78.1	17.8	13.2	2.31	2.14
Morocco	19.4	16.9	4.7	5.0	75.7	77.7	28.6	19.5	2.23	2.07
Mozambique	37.8	36.2	19.8	18.2	41.4	43.2	103.8	86.2	5.13	4.58
Nepal	22.4	19.7	6.9	6.4	65.8	69.2	46.0	33.2	2.53	2.11
Netherlands	10.3	10.3	8.8	9.6	79.6	80.8	4.7	4.1	1.66	1.67
Niger	51.1	46.7	14.5	11.3	53.0	57.0	114.5	92.9	7.68	6.79
Nigeria	36.1	30.6	16.3	14.1	47.2	50.5	93.0	78.7	4.82	3.92
Pakistan	25.3	20.7	7.1	6.2	65.6	69.0	65.3	47.2	3.28	2.42
Peru	19.0	16.3	6.1	6.3	71.0	73.7	27.7	20.2	2.32	2.00
Philippines	25.7	22.2	5.1	4.9	71.4	74.0	19.9	14.7	3.23	2.83
Poland	10.0	8.8	10.1	10.8	75.9	77.8	6.7	5.6	1.29	1.39
Romania	9.6	8.5	11.8	12.0	73.7	76.0	11.3	8.7	1.27	1.38
Russia	11.1	9.3	16.0	15.6	66.2	68.6	10.3	8.6	1.41	1.48
Saudi Arabia	19.4	17.8	3.3	3.4	73.9	76.1	16.7	12.0	2.35	2.04
South Africa	19.6	18.1	17.0	17.3	49.2	51.4	43.8	36.8	2.33	2.12
Spain	10.9	8.7	8.7	9.3	81.1	82.0	3.4	3.2	1.47	1.51
Sri Lanka	15.9	13.3	6.2	6.8	75.3	77.3	18.1	13.2	1.96	1.85
Sudan	36.6	31.2	11.7	6.9	54.2	64.4	72.4	38.9	4.93	4.04
Syria	24.4	19.7	3.7	3.7	74.5	76.6	16.1	11.7	3.02	2.34
Taiwan [5]	9.0	8.2	6.9	8.2	78.2	79.7	5.3	4.6	1.15	1.23
Tanzania	33.4	25.6	12.3	11.2	52.5	54.9	68.1	56.4	4.31	3.00
Thailand	13.0	11.7	6.5	7.5	75.0	77.1	16.7	12.3	1.65	1.68
Turkey	18.3	15.1	6.1	6.3	72.2	74.8	24.8	17.3	2.18	1.96
Uganda	47.6	45.4	11.9	10.3	53.0	55.2	63.7	51.7	6.73	6.31
Ukraine	9.6	8.5	15.7	15.4	68.5	70.7	8.7	7.3	1.27	1.35
United Kingdom	12.3	11.9	9.3	9.5	79.9	81.1	4.7	4.1	1.92	1.86
Uzbekistan	17.5	16.1	5.3	5.4	72.2	74.8	22.7	16.3	1.92	1.74
Venezuela	20.3	18.1	5.1	5.6	73.8	75.3	21.1	17.0	2.45	2.22
Vietnam	17.3	14.5	6.0	6.0	71.9	74.4	21.6	15.7	1.93	1.77
Yemen	34.4	25.6	7.2	5.7	63.4	66.9	56.8	41.9	4.81	3.20
Zambia	44.6	38.9	12.8	11.0	52.0	54.1	68.4	50.6	6.07	5.26

[1] Number of births during 1 year per 1,000 persons (based on midyear population). [2] Number of deaths during 1 year per 1,000 persons (based on midyear population). [3] Number of deaths of children under 1 year of age per 1,000 live births in a calendar year. [4] Average number of children that would be born if all women lived to the end of their childbearing years and, at each year of childbearing age, they experienced the birth rates occurring in the specified year. [5] See footnote 4, Table 1331. [6] See footnote 5, Table 1331.

Source: U.S. Census Bureau, International Data Base, <http://www.census.gov/ipc/www/idb/>, accessed June 2010.

Table 1339. Life Expectancy at Birth and at Age 65 by Sex—Selected Countries: 1990 and 2007

| Country | Life expectancy at birth (years) | | | | Life expectancy at age 65 (years) | | | |
| | Females | | Males | | Females | | Males | |
	1990	2007	1990	2007	1990	2007	1990	2007
United States [1]	**78.8**	**80.4**	**71.8**	**75.4**	**18.9**	**19.9**	**15.1**	**17.2**
Australia.	80.1	83.7	73.9	79.0	19.0	21.6	15.2	18.5
Austria.	78.8	82.9	72.2	77.3	17.8	20.8	14.3	17.4
Belgium	79.5	82.6	72.7	77.1	18.8	21.0	14.3	17.3
Canada	80.8	(NA)	74.4	(NA)	19.9	(NA)	15.7	(NA)
Czech Republic	75.5	80.2	67.6	73.8	15.3	18.5	11.7	15.1
Denmark	77.8	80.6	72.0	76.2	17.9	19.2	14.0	16.5
Finland.	79.0	83.1	71.0	76.0	17.8	21.3	13.8	17.0
France	80.9	84.4	72.8	77.5	19.8	(NA)	15.5	(NA)
Germany	78.5	82.7	72.0	77.4	17.7	20.7	14.0	17.4
Greece.	79.5	82.0	74.6	77.0	18.0	19.6	15.7	17.4
Hungary.	73.7	77.3	65.1	69.2	15.3	17.3	12.0	13.4
Iceland.	80.5	82.9	75.4	79.4	19.5	20.6	16.2	18.3
Ireland	77.7	82.1	72.1	77.4	17.0	20.1	13.3	17.1
Italy	80.4	(NA)	73.9	(NA)	18.9	(NA)	15.1	(NA)
Japan.	81.9	86.0	75.9	79.2	20.0	23.6	16.2	18.6
Korea, South	75.5	82.7	67.3	76.1	16.3	20.5	12.4	16.3
Mexico.	74.1	77.4	68.3	72.6	18.0	18.2	16.2	16.8
Netherlands.	80.1	82.3	73.8	78.0	18.9	20.5	14.4	17.0
New Zealand	78.4	82.2	72.5	78.2	18.3	20.7	14.6	18.1
Norway.	79.9	82.9	73.4	78.3	18.7	20.8	14.6	17.5
Poland	75.2	79.7	66.2	71.0	16.1	18.9	12.4	14.6
Portugal.	77.5	82.2	70.6	75.9	17.1	20.2	14.0	16.8
Slovakia.	75.4	78.1	66.6	70.5	15.7	17.1	12.2	13.4
Spain	80.6	84.3	73.4	77.8	19.3	22.0	15.5	17.8
Sweden	80.4	83.0	74.8	78.9	19.0	20.7	15.3	17.8
Switzerland	80.9	84.4	74.0	79.5	19.7	22.2	15.3	18.6
Turkey	68.3	75.6	63.8	71.1	13.9	15.8	12.4	13.9
United Kingdom.	78.5	(NA)	72.9	(NA)	17.9	(NA)	14.0	(NA)

NA Not available.

[1] Source of 2007 life expectancy data: U.S. National Center for Health Statistics, National Vital Statistics Reports, *Deaths: Final Data for 2007*, Vol. 58, No. 19, May 2010, and unpublished data.

Source: Except as noted, Organization for Economic Cooperation and Development (OECD), 2010, "OECD Health Data," OECD Health Statistics database (copyright), <http:dx.doi.org/10.1787/data-00350-en>, accessed May 2010.

Table 1340. People Infected With HIV and AIDS-Related Deaths by Region: 2001 and 2008

[In thousands (29,000 represents 29,000,000), except percent. Estimates are based on ranges, called 'plausibility bounds,' which reflect the certainty associated with each estimate and define the boundaries within which the actual numbers lie]

| Region | Adults and children living with HIV | | Adults and children newly infected with HIV | | Adult (15–49 yrs.) prevalence (percent) | | Adult and child deaths due to AIDS | |
	2001	2008	2001	2008	2001	2008	2001	2008
Total	**29,000**	**33,400**	**3,200**	**2,700**	**0.8**	**0.8**	**1,900**	**2,000**
Sub-Saharan Africa	19,700	22,100	2,000	1,900	5.8	5.2	1,400	1,400
North Africa and Middle East.	200	310	30	35	0.2	0.2	11	20
South and South-East Asia	4,000	3,800	310	280	0.3	0.3	260	270
East Asia	560	850	99	75	(Z)	(Z)	22	59
Oceania.	36	59	6	4	0.2	0.3	(Z)	2
Latin America.	1,600	2,000	150	170	0.5	0.6	66	77
Caribbean	220	240	21	20	1.1	1.0	20	12
Eastern Europe and Central Asia	900	1,500	280	110	0.5	0.7	26	87
Western and Central Europe.	660	850	40	30	0.2	0.3	8	13
North America	1,200	1,400	52	55	0.6	0.6	19	25

Z Less than 0.1 percent or 1,000 deaths.

Source: Joint United Nations Programme on HIV/AIDS (UNAIDS) and World Health Organization (WHO), *AIDS Epidemic Update: December 2009* (copyright). See also <http://www.unaids.org/en/KnowledgeCentre/HIVData/EpiUpdate/EpiUpdArchive/2009/default.asp>.

Table 1341. Percentage of the Adult Population Considered to Be Obese: 2007

[Obesity rates are defined as the percentage of the population with a Body Mass Index (BMI) over 30 kg/m2. The BMI is a single number that evaluates an individual's weight status in relation to height (weight/height[2], with weight in kilograms and height in meters). For Australia, the United Kingdom, and the United States, figures are based on health examinations, rather than self-reported information. Obesity estimates derived from health examinations are generally higher and more reliable than those coming from self-reports because they preclude any misreporting of people's height and weight. However, health examinations are only conducted regularly in a few countries. For more information on methods by country, see <http://www.irdes.fr/EspaceAnglais/home.html>]

Country	2007	Country	2007	Country	2007
United States	[1] **34.3**	France	[1] 10.5	Luxembourg.	20.0
Australia.	[2] 21.7	Germany	[4] 13.6	Mexico.	[1] 30.0
Austria.	[1] 12.4	Greece.	[1] 16.4	New Zealand	26.5
Belgium	[3] 12.7	Hungary.	[5] 18.8	Norway.	[4] 9.0
Canada	15.4	Ireland	15.0	Spain	[1] 14.9
Czech Republic	[4] 17.0	Italy	9.9	Sweden	10.2
Denmark	[4] 11.4	Japan.	[1] 3.4	Switzerland	8.1
Finland.	14.9	Korea, South	[4] 3.5	United Kingdom. . . .	24.0

[1] 2006 data. [2] 1999 data. [3] 2004 data. [4] 2005 data. [5] 2003 data.

Source: Except as noted, Organization for Economic Cooperation and Development (OECD), 2010, "OECD Health Data," OECD Health Statistics database (copyright), accessed May 2010. See also <http://www.oecd.org>.

International Statistics 843

Table 1342. Daily Tobacco Consumption by Country and Sex: 1990 and 2008

[Daily smokers as percent of population. Includes tobacco forms consumed by smoking only]

Country	Total 1990	Total 2008	Females 1990	Females 2008	Males 1990	Males 2008
United States	**25.5**	**[1] 15.4**	**22.8**	**[1] 13.7**	**28.4**	**[1] 17.1**
Australia	[2] 28.6	[1] 16.6	[2] 27.0	[1] 15.2	[2] 30.2	[1] 18.0
Canada	28.2	[1] 18.4	26.7	[1] 16.0	29.8	[1] 20.3
Denmark	44.5	[3] 25.0	42.0	[3] 23.0	47.0	[3] 26.0
Finland	25.9	[1] 20.6	20.0	[1] 16.6	32.4	[1] 25.8
France	30.0	[3] 25.0	20.0	[3] 21.0	38.0	[3] 30.0
Greece	38.5	39.7	26.0	33.5	51.0	46.3
Iceland	30.3	[1] 19.4	29.9	[1] 18.2	30.8	[1] 20.7
Ireland	30.0	[1] 29.0	29.0	[1] 27.0	31.0	[1] 31.0
Italy	27.8	22.4	17.8	16.4	37.8	28.9
Japan	37.4	25.7	14.3	12.9	60.5	39.5
Luxembourg	[4] 33.0	20.0	[4] 25.0	18.0	[4] 41.0	23.0
Netherlands	37.0	[1] 29.0	32.0	[1] 26.0	43.0	[1] 32.0
New Zealand	28.0	[1] 18.1	27.0	[1] 17.0	28.0	[1] 19.3
Norway	35.0	21.0	33.0	22.0	36.0	21.0
Poland	(NA)	[5] 26.3	(NA)	[5] 19.3	(NA)	[5] 33.9
Sweden	25.8	[3] 14.5	25.9	[3] 16.7	25.8	[3] 12.3
United Kingdom	30.0	[1] 21.0	30.0	[1] 20.0	31.0	[1] 22.0

NA Not available. [1] 2007 data. [2] 1989 data. [3] 2006 data. [4] 1987 data. [5] 2004 data.
Source: Organization for Economic Cooperation and Development (OECD), 2010, "OECD Health Data," OECD Health Statistics database (copyright), <http:dx.doi.org/10.1787/data-00350-en>, accessed May 2010.

Table 1343. Road Fatalities by Country: 1990 to 2008

[Per million inhabitants]

Country	1990	2000	2005	2007	2008	Country	1990	2000	2005	2007	2008
EU-27 [1]	(NA)	117	91	86	79	Italy	123	115	94	86	79
United States [2]	**188**	**149**	**147**	**136**	**123**	Japan	90	93	70	52	47
Australia	137	95	81	77	68	Korea, South	(NA)	218	132	127	121
Austria	179	122	94	83	81	Luxembourg	188	172	101	90	72
Belgium	199	143	104	100	100	Mexico	66	53	46	51	51
Canada	150	95	91	83	82	Netherlands	92	73	50	48	46
Chile	120	110	100	99	106	New Zealand	217	121	99	100	86
Czech Republic	125	145	126	118	103	Norway	79	76	49	49	53
Denmark [3]	123	93	61	74	74	Poland	192	163	143	147	143
Estonia	(NA)	169	126	146	98	Portugal	267	186	118	81	83
Finland	130	76	72	72	65	Russia	238	203	237	235	211
France [4]	182	129	88	75	69	Slovakia	137	120	111	122	112
Germany	126	91	65	60	55	Slovenia	259	157	129	145	105
Greece	171	193	150	141	138	Spain	179	143	89	85	68
Hungary	235	118	127	123	99	Sweden	90	67	49	51	43
Iceland	96	113	64	48	38	Switzerland	141	82	55	51	47
India	43	80	98	115	(NA)	Turkey	124	58	62	68	57
Ireland	139	110	84	77	63	United Kingdom	97	62	55	50	43
Israel [5]	92	73	63	53	56						

NA Not available. [1] See footnote 5, Table 1377. [2] As of July 1. [3] As of January 1. [4] Data on January 1 of the following year. [5] For technical reasons, this database uses Israel's official statistics which include data relating to the Golan Heights, East Jerusalem and Israeli settlements in the West Bank.
Source: Organization for Economic Cooperation and Development (OECD), 2010, "Road Fatalities," *OECD Factbook 2010: Economic, Environmental and Social Statistics*, OECD Publishing (copyright). See also <http://dx.doi.org/10.1787/factbook-2010-96-en>.

Table 1344. Suicide Rates by Sex and Country: 2006

[Per 100,000 persons. Data are for 2006 or latest available year]

Country	Total	Men	Women	Country	Total	Men	Women
OECD average	**11.1**	**17.6**	**5.2**	Italy	4.8	7.9	2.2
United States	**10.1**	**16.6**	**4.0**	Japan	19.1	28.1	10.4
Australia	9.8	15.7	4.1	Korea	21.5	32.0	13.2
Austria	12.6	21.0	5.1	Luxembourg	10.8	18.4	4.1
Belgium	18.4	28.0	9.8	Mexico	4.3	7.6	1.3
Canada	10.2	15.7	4.9	Netherlands	8.1	11.5	4.9
Czech Republic	11.4	19.7	3.8	New Zealand	12.2	18.8	6.0
Denmark	9.9	15.0	5.3	Norway	10.8	16.0	5.6
Finland	18.0	28.1	8.3	Poland	13.2	23.7	3.7
France	14.2	21.8	7.3	Portugal	8.7	14.6	3.8
Germany	9.1	14.5	4.3	Slovakia	10.9	20.0	2.9
Greece	2.9	4.8	1.0	Spain	6.3	10.0	2.9
Hungary	21.0	36.3	8.4	Sweden	11.3	15.4	7.4
Iceland	10.7	15.3	6.0	Switzerland	14.0	19.7	8.9
Ireland	8.9	13.7	4.0	United Kingdom	6.1	9.7	2.7

Source: Organization for Economic Cooperation and Development (OECD), 2010, "Suicides," *OECD Factbook 2010: Economic, Environmental and Social Statistics*, OECD Publishing (copyright). See also <http://dx.doi.org/10.1787/factbook-2010-90-en>.

Table 1345. Health Expenditures by Country: 1980 to 2007

[In percent. GDP = gross domestic product; for explanation, see text, Section 13]

Country	Total expenditures on health (percent of GDP)					Public expenditures on health (percent of total)				
	1980	1990	2000	2005	2007	1980	1990	2000	2005	2007
United States	**9.0**	**12.2**	**13.6**	**15.7**	**16.0**	**40.8**	**39.2**	**43.2**	**44.4**	**45.4**
Australia.	6.3	6.9	8.3	8.7	8.9	62.6	66.2	66.8	66.9	67.5
Austria	7.4	8.3	9.9	10.4	10.1	68.8	73.4	76.8	76.1	76.4
Belgium	6.3	7.2	8.6	10.3	10.2	(NA)	(NA)	(NA)	(NA)	(NA)
Canada	7.0	8.9	8.8	9.9	10.1	75.6	74.5	70.4	70.3	70.0
Czech Republic	(NA)	4.7	6.5	7.2	6.8	96.8	97.4	90.3	87.3	85.2
Denmark	8.9	8.3	8.3	9.5	9.8	87.8	82.7	82.4	83.7	84.5
Finland.	6.3	7.7	7.2	8.5	8.2	79.0	80.9	71.1	73.5	74.6
France	7.0	8.4	10.1	11.1	11.0	80.1	76.6	79.4	79.3	79.0
Germany [1]	8.4	8.3	10.3	10.7	10.4	78.7	76.2	79.7	77.0	76.9
Greece.	5.9	6.6	7.9	9.4	9.6	55.6	53.7	60.0	60.1	60.3
Hungary.	(NA)	(NA)	6.9	8.3	7.4	(NA)	(NA)	70.7	72.3	70.6
Iceland.	6.3	7.8	9.5	9.4	9.3	88.2	86.6	81.1	81.4	82.5
Ireland	8.3	6.1	6.3	7.3	7.6	82.0	71.7	73.5	77.5	80.7
Italy	(NA)	7.7	8.1	8.9	8.7	(NA)	79.5	72.5	76.2	76.5
Japan.	6.5	6.0	7.7	8.2	(NA)	71.3	77.6	81.3	82.7	(NA)
Korea, South	4.1	4.3	4.7	5.7	6.3	20.1	36.5	44.9	52.1	54.9
Luxembourg.	5.2	5.4	5.8	7.7	(NA)	92.8	93.1	89.3	90.2	(NA)
Mexico	(NA)	4.4	5.1	5.8	5.9	(NA)	40.4	46.6	45.5	45.2
Netherlands	7.4	8.0	8.0	9.8	9.8	69.4	67.1	63.1	(NA)	(NA)
New Zealand	5.9	6.9	7.7	8.8	9.0	88.0	82.4	78.0	76.9	78.9
Norway.	7.0	7.6	8.4	9.1	8.9	85.1	82.8	82.5	83.5	84.1
Poland	(NA)	4.8	5.5	6.2	6.4	(NA)	91.7	70.0	69.3	70.8
Portugal.	5.3	5.9	8.8	10.2	(NA)	64.3	65.5	72.5	71.8	(NA)
Slovakia	(NA)	(NA)	5.5	7.0	7.7	(NA)	(NA)	89.4	74.4	66.8
Spain	5.3	6.5	7.2	8.3	8.5	79.9	78.7	71.6	70.6	71.8
Sweden	8.9	8.2	8.2	9.2	9.1	92.5	89.9	84.9	81.6	81.7
Switzerland	7.3	8.2	10.2	11.2	10.8	(NA)	52.4	55.4	59.5	59.3
Turkey	2.4	2.7	4.9	5.7	(NA)	29.4	61.0	62.9	71.4	(NA)
United Kingdom	5.6	5.9	7.0	8.2	8.4	89.4	83.6	79.3	81.9	81.7

NA Not available. [1] Data prior to 1991 are for former West Germany.

Source: Organization for Economic Cooperation and Development (OECD), 2010, "OECD Health Data," OECD Health Statistics database (copyright), <http://dx.doi.org/10.1787/data-00350-en>, accessed May 2010.

Table 1346. Medical Doctors and Inpatient Care—Selected Countries: 2000 to 2007

Country	Medical doctors per 1,000 population			Acute inpatient care					
				Beds per 1,000 population			Average length of stay (days)		
	2000	2005	2006	2000	2005	2007	2000	2005	2007
United States	**2.3**	**2.4**	**2.4**	**2.9**	**2.7**	**[1] 2.7**	**5.8**	**5.6**	**5.5**
Australia.	2.5	2.8	2.8	3.6	3.5	[1] 3.5	6.1	6.0	[1] 5.9
Austria	3.1	3.5	3.7	6.3	6.1	6.1	6.7	5.9	5.7
Belgium	3.9	4.0	4.0	4.7	4.4	4.3	7.7	7.7	[1] 7.2
Canada	2.1	2.1	2.2	3.2	2.8	[1] 2.7	7.2	7.2	[1] 7.3
Czech Republic	3.4	3.6	3.6	5.7	5.3	5.2	8.7	8.0	7.7
Denmark	2.7	3.1	3.2	3.5	3.1	2.9	3.8	3.5	[2] 3.5
Finland.	2.7	2.9	3.0	4.0	3.9	3.7	5.0	4.8	4.6
France	3.3	3.4	3.4	4.1	3.7	3.6	5.6	5.4	5.3
Germany	3.3	3.4	3.5	6.4	5.9	5.7	9.2	8.1	7.8
Greece.	4.3	5.0	5.4	3.8	3.9	[1] 3.9	6.2	5.6	[2] 5.6
Hungary.	3.1	2.8	3.0	5.8	5.5	4.1	7.1	6.5	6.0
Iceland.	3.4	3.7	3.7	(NA)	(NA)	(NA)	6.1	5.4	5.4
Ireland	2.2	2.8	2.9	2.8	2.8	2.7	6.0	6.0	[1] 5.9
Italy	4.1	3.8	3.7	4.1	3.3	3.1	7.0	6.7	[1] 6.7
Japan.	1.9	[3] 2.0	2.1	9.6	8.2	8.2	24.8	19.8	19.0
Korea, South	1.3	1.6	1.7	5.2	6.6	7.1	11.0	[4] 10.6	[2] 10.6
Luxembourg.	2.2	2.4	2.7	(NA)	4.6	4.4	7.5	7.6	7.3
Mexico	1.6	1.8	1.9	1.0	1.0	1.0	4.0	4.0	[1] 3.9
Netherlands	3.2	3.7	3.8	3.5	3.1	3.0	9.0	7.2	6.3
New Zealand	2.2	2.1	2.3	(NA)	(NA)	(NA)	4.3	[3] 5.9	[2] 5.9
Norway.	2.9	3.7	3.8	3.1	3.0	2.9	6.0	5.2	5.0
Poland	2.2	2.1	2.2	5.2	4.7	4.6	8.9	6.5	5.9
Portugal.	3.1	3.4	3.4	3.2	3.0	2.8	7.7	7.1	6.8
Slovakia	3.1	[3] 3.1	[3] 3.1	5.8	5.0	4.9	8.5	7.3	7.0
Spain	3.2	3.8	3.6	2.8	2.5	[1] 2.5	7.1	6.7	[1] 6.6
Sweden	3.1	3.5	3.6	2.4	2.2	2.1	5.0	4.6	4.5
Switzerland	3.5	3.8	3.9	4.1	3.6	3.5	9.3	8.5	7.8
Turkey	1.3	1.5	1.4	2.2	2.5	2.7	5.4	[5] 5.2	4.4
United Kingdom	1.9	2.4	2.4	3.0	2.9	2.6	8.2	7.8	7.2

NA Not available. [1] 2006 data. [2] 2005 data. [3] 2004 data. [4] 2003 data. [5] 2002 data.

Source: Organization for Economic Cooperation and Development (OECD), 2010, "OECD Health Data", OECD Health Statistics database (copyright), <http://dx.doi.org/10.1787/data-00350-en>, accessed May 2010.

Table 1347. Gross National Income (GNI) by Country: 2000 and 2008

[49 represents $49,000,000,000. GNI measures the total domestic and foreign value added claimed by residents. GNI comprises GDP plus net receipts of primary income (compensation of employees and property income) from nonresident sources]

Country	Gross national income [1]				GNI on purchasing power parity basis [2]			
	Total (bil. dol.)		Per capita (dol.)		Total (bil. dol.)		Per capita (dol.)	
	2000	2008	2000	2008	2000	2008	2000	2008
Algeria.............	49	144	1,610	4,190	156	271	5,120	7,890
Argentina...........	276	287	7,460	7,190	327	558	8,850	14,000
Australia...........	397	862	20,710	40,240	511	798	26,690	37,250
Bangladesh.........	50	83	350	520	115	233	820	1,450
Belarus............	14	52	1,380	5,360	51	117	5,120	12,120
Belgium............	260	477	25,360	44,570	289	379	28,180	35,380
Brazil.............	674	1,401	3,870	7,300	1,186	1,934	6,810	10,080
Bulgaria...........	13	42	1,600	5,490	50	87	6,180	11,370
Burkina Faso........	3	7	250	480	9	18	810	1,160
Cambodia..........	4	9	280	640	11	27	860	1,870
Cameroon..........	10	22	620	1,150	24	41	1,520	2,170
Canada............	681	1,454	22,130	43,640	851	1,290	27,670	38,710
Chile..............	75	157	4,840	9,370	137	223	8,910	13,250
China [3]...........	1,169	3,888	930	2,940	2,939	7,967	2,330	6,010
Colombia...........	91	208	2,280	4,620	221	380	5,550	8,430
Congo (Kinshasa) [4]...	4	10	80	150	10	18	200	280
Cote d'Ivoire........	11	20	620	980	25	33	1,430	1,580
Czech Republic......	60	174	5,800	16,650	151	239	14,650	22,890
Ecuador............	16	50	1,340	3,690	54	105	4,430	7,780
Egypt..............	97	147	1,390	1,800	250	446	3,570	5,470
Ethiopia............	8	22	130	280	30	70	460	870
France.............	1,482	[5] 2,696	24,450	[5] 42,000	1,556	2,136	25,680	33,280
Germany...........	2,097	3,507	25,500	42,710	2,113	2,952	25,700	35,950
Ghana.............	6	15	330	630	18	31	900	1,320
Greece............	137	319	12,560	28,400	202	318	18,460	28,300
Guatemala..........	19	37	1,730	2,680	39	64	3,460	4,690
Hong Kong..........	177	219	26,570	31,420	177	307	26,520	44,000
Hungary............	48	129	4,660	12,810	120	183	11,740	18,210
India..............	458	1,187	450	1,040	1,527	3,342	1,500	2,930
Indonesia...........	119	427	580	1,880	451	818	2,200	3,600
Iran...............	107	(NA)	1,670	(NA)	434	(NA)	6,790	(NA)
Italy..............	1,190	2,122	20,890	35,460	1,447	1,843	25,400	30,800
Japan..............	4,392	4,869	34,620	38,130	3,292	4,494	25,950	35,190
Kazakhstan.........	19	97	1,260	6,160	66	152	4,450	9,720
Kenya..............	13	28	420	730	35	60	1,120	1,560
Korea, South........	466	1,046	9,910	21,530	805	1,353	17,130	27,840
Madagascar.........	4	8	250	420	12	20	790	1,050
Malawi.............	2	4	150	280	7	12	600	810
Malaysia...........	80	196	3,450	7,250	194	371	8,350	13,740
Mexico.............	501	1,062	5,110	9,990	878	1,525	8,960	14,340
Montenegro.........	(NA)	4	(NA)	6,660	4	8	5,940	13,420
Morocco............	38	81	1,310	2,520	73	134	2,510	4,190
Mozambique........	4	8	230	380	8	17	420	770
Nepal..............	5	12	220	400	20	32	800	1,120
Netherlands.........	423	811	26,580	49,340	478	668	30,040	40,620
Niger..............	2	5	170	330	6	10	500	680
Nigeria............	33	177	270	1,170	141	299	1,130	1,980
Pakistan...........	68	157	490	950	233	430	1,690	2,590
Peru..............	53	115	2,050	3,990	123	229	4,750	7,950
Philippines.........	80	170	1,030	1,890	189	353	2,430	3,900
Poland.............	177	447	4,590	11,730	403	637	10,470	16,710
Portugal...........	119	220	11,590	20,680	170	237	16,670	22,330
Romania...........	38	178	1,690	8,280	130	288	5,780	13,380
Russia.............	250	1,371	1,710	9,660	1,086	2,194	7,420	15,460
Saudi Arabia........	168	440	8,140	17,870	361	604	17,500	24,500
Senegal............	5	12	510	980	13	22	1,270	1,780
Serbia [6]...........	11	41	1,470	5,590	42	76	5,630	10,380
Singapore..........	93	168	22,960	34,760	132	232	32,870	47,970
South Africa........	134	283	3,050	5,820	285	477	6,470	9,790
Spain..............	621	1,455	15,420	31,930	851	1,404	21,140	30,830
Sri Lanka...........	16	36	880	1,780	50	90	2,660	4,460
Sudan.............	11	46	320	1,100	37	79	1,070	1,920
Sweden............	260	469	29,280	50,910	244	348	27,530	37,780
Switzerland.........	289	425	40,270	55,510	245	300	34,060	39,210
Syria..............	16	44	960	2,160	52	92	3,150	4,490
Tanzania...........	9	18	270	440	26	52	770	1,260
Thailand...........	122	247	1,960	3,670	302	523	4,850	7,770
Turkey.............	265	667	3,990	9,020	580	992	8,730	13,420
Uganda............	6	13	270	420	17	36	680	1,140
Ukraine............	34	149	700	3,210	156	334	3,170	7,210
United Kingdom......	1,526	2,827	25,910	46,040	1,533	2,225	26,020	36,240
United States	**9,708**	**14,574**	**34,410**	**47,930**	**9,931**	**14,227**	**35,190**	**46,790**
Uzbekistan..........	15	25	630	910	35	73	1,420	2,660
Venezuela..........	100	258	4,100	9,230	203	359	8,360	12,850
Vietnam............	30	77	390	890	108	232	1,390	2,700
Yemen.............	7	22	400	960	31	51	1,710	2,220
Zimbabwe..........	6	(NA)	460	(NA)	3	(NA)	210	(NA)

NA Not available. [1] Gross national income calculated using the World Bank Atlas method; for details, see source. [2] For explanation of Purchasing Power Parity, see headnote, Table 1348. [3] See footnote 4, Table 1331. [4] See footnote 5, Table 1331. [5] Includes the French overseas departments of French Guiana, Guadeloupe, Martinique, and Reunion. [6] See footnote 4, Table 1405.

Source: The World Bank, Washington, DC, *World Development Indicators*, annual (copyright). See also <http://data.worldbank.org\>, accessed July 2010.

U.S. Census Bureau, Statistical Abstract of the United States: 2011

Table 1348. Real GDP Per Capita and Per Employed Persons by Country: 1990 to 2008

[U.S. figures based on the System of National Income and Product Accounts (NIPA) from the Bureau of Economic Analysis. All other countries, based on the 1993 United Nations System of National Accounts. Per capita data based on total resident population. Real GDP Is a macroeconomic measure of the size of an economy adjusted for price changes and inflation. Employment data include people serving in the armed forces for some countries. Real dollars are calculated based on 2005 Purchasing Power Parities (PPPs). PPPs are currency conversion rates used to convert GDPs expressed in different currencies to a common value (U.S. dollars in this case). A PPP for a given country is the number of national currency units needed to buy the specific basket of goods and services that one dollar will buy in the United States. See text, this section]

Country	Real GDP per capita (2005 U.S. dollars)				Real GDP per employed person (2005 U.S. dollars)			
	1990	2000	2007	2008	1990	2000	2007	2008
United States	32,135	39,292	43,170	43,250	66,465	80,222	88,238	89,626
Canada	27,086	32,598	36,377	36,123	56,905	67,389	70,746	69,991
Australia.	24,033	30,019	34,119	34,254	51,623	63,606	68,328	68,198
Japan.	25,936	28,600	31,652	31,446	49,961	55,630	62,763	62,578
Korea, South	11,398	18,755	25,021	25,498	27,017	41,673	51,741	52,568
Austria	25,763	31,682	35,396	35,868	55,312	67,000	72,618	72,622
Belgium	25,168	30,233	33,446	33,616	64,820	75,757	81,419	80,976
Denmark	25,445	31,659	34,608	34,013	50,135	62,309	66,144	64,840
France	24,327	28,344	30,667	30,624	61,897	70,738	76,063	75,989
Germany [1]	25,847	30,559	33,184	33,663	54,160	64,163	68,644	68,547
Italy	23,775	27,717	28,789	28,245	59,643	68,829	67,875	66,959
Netherlands.	26,284	33,698	37,415	38,035	62,085	68,390	72,582	72,995
Norway.	32,118	43,642	48,991	49,416	66,166	84,499	90,905	90,074
Spain.	19,611	24,792	28,010	27,747	51,118	58,890	59,242	60,283
Sweden	24,648	28,976	34,086	33,744	45,868	59,776	69,002	68,219
United Kingdom.	23,745	29,641	34,209	34,356	50,280	63,258	71,130	71,121

[1] Prior to 1991, data are for the former West Germany.

Source: U.S. Bureau of Labor Statistics, "International Comparisons of GDP per Capita and per Employed Person, Seventeen Countries, 1960–2008," July 2009, <http://www.bls.gov/fls>.

Table 1349. Average Annual Percent Changes in International Economic Composite Indexes by Country: 1990 to 2009

[Change from previous year; derived from indexes with base 2000 = 100. The coincident index changes are for calendar years and the leading index changes are for years ending June 30 because they lead the coincident indexes by about 6 months, on average. The G-7 countries are United States, Canada, France, Germany, Italy, United Kingdom, and Japan. Minus sign (–) indicates decrease]

Country	Leading index						Coincident index					
	1990	2000	2005	2007	2008	2009	1990	2000	2005	2007	2008	2009
Total, 13 countries.	2.1	6.3	5.1	3.2	0.4	−10.8	4.5	5.0	2.1	3.2	−2.3	−12.5
12 countries, excluding U.S. . . .	3.8	7.7	5.5	4.3	0.8	6.9	6.0	5.1	1.7	4.0	−0.1	−11.2
G-7 countries.	2.0	6.00	5.0	3.0	–	−11.3	4.5	4.8	1.9	3.0	−2.6	−13.0
North America	−0.9	4.1	4.3	1.4	–	−16.3	−0.2	4.8	2.8	0.7	−5.2	−14.1
United States	−1.0	3.9	4.4	1.2	−0.3	−17.3	−0.1	4.4	2.6	0.3	−5.8	−14.4
Canada	−1.1	7.1	3.1	3.8	3.2	−4.8	−1.7	9.7	4.7	5.2	−0.3	−11.5
Four European countries.	1.8	4.4	4.1	3.9	1.1	−7.6	5.9	9.8	2.0	7.2	1.2	−9.7
France	1.5	1.5	6.4	2.4	−0.7	−7.6	5.7	14.4	2.1	6.4	−1.9	−14.1
Germany	4.5	6.2	4.4	6.2	1.6	−6.9	7.2	7.9	−0.5	8.6	5.0	−7.0
Italy	0.2	7.2	2.4	4.9	−2.0	−9.2	9.3	16.2	5.3	8.9	−2.1	−14.0
United Kingdom.	−0.3	2.5	2.4	0.9	5.3	−7.3	0.9	4.0	3.4	4.3	1.5	−4.7
Seven Pacific region countries	6.1	11.2	6.9	4.6	0.2	−6.5	8.1	1.2	1.2	2.4	−1.6	2.6
Australia.	−1.4	8.2	5.3	1.2	4.7	−7.8	−0.4	5.1	3.7	6.8	2.0	−1.8
Taiwan [1]	4.9	8.5	6.5	4.9	2.6	−0.8	5.1	4.9	4.8	3.1	−0.8	−7.0
Thailand.	12.1	9.5	5.5	3.8	6.7	−0.8	11.6	9.4	6.5	2.5	3.1	−1.8
Japan.	6.6	11.3	7.1	4.6	−1.4	−7.5	8.6	−0.5	0.3	1.6	−2.6	−15.1
Korea, South	6.5	15.9	7.3	7.7	10.0	−0.1	9.9	13.7	4.7	6.0	2.9	0.2
Malaysia	5.0	19.8	8.4	8.0	12.7	−3.8	9.1	11.1	3.1	3.3	0.4	−7.2
New Zealand	0.8	4.6	1.2	3.1	1.1	−1.5	−1.2	2.7	6.0	4.7	−1.6	−7.4

– Represents zero. [1] See footnote 4, Table 1331.

Source: Foundation for International Business and Economic Research, New York, NY, *International Economic Indicators*, monthly.

Table 1350. Sectoral Contributions to Gross Value Added: 1997 and 2007

[In percent. According to the 1993 System of National Accounts (SNA) and the International Standard Industrial Classification (ISIC), Revision 3 (1990). Value added is estimated at basic prices and includes financial intermediation services indirectly measured (FISIM). Value added represents an industry's contribution to national GDP and is calculated as the difference between production and intermediate inputs. Value added comprises labor costs, consumption of fixed capital, indirect taxes less subsidies, and net operating surplus and mixed income]

Country	Agriculture [1]		Industry				Services	
			Total		Manufacturing			
	1997	2007	1997	2007	1997	2007	1997	2007
United States [2]	1.7	1.3	25.5	21.8	[3]17.3	13.3	72.8	76.9
Australia.............	3.4	2.6	27.7	29.1	14.3	10.5	68.9	68.4
Austria.............	2.3	1.8	30.9	30.6	19.9	20.2	66.8	67.7
Belgium.............	1.6	0.8	28.4	23.9	20.2	16.4	70.1	75.3
Canada.............	2.5	[4]2.2	30.9	[4]31.7	18.0	[4]16.2	66.6	[4]66.1
Czech Republic.......	4.2	2.4	40.6	38.9	27.3	27.4	55.2	58.7
Denmark............	3.2	1.2	25.6	26.5	17.0	15.0	71.2	72.4
Finland.............	4.1	3.3	32.3	32.6	24.6	23.6	63.7	64.2
France.............	3.2	2.2	23.5	20.4	[5]16.1	12.3	73.3	77.4
Germany............	1.3	0.9	31.0	30.4	22.4	23.9	67.7	68.7
Greece.............	7.7	3.8	20.0	20.4	[6]11.1	10.3	72.2	75.9
Hungary............	7.4	4.0	31.8	29.7	[6]23.5	22.1	61.1	66.3
Iceland [2]............	9.8	[7]5.8	28.9	[7]23.7	16 4	[7]10.1	61.3	[7]70.5
Ireland.............	5.2	1.7	38.6	33.6	30.8	21.9	56.2	64.8
Italy...............	3.2	2.1	29.5	27.5	21.7	19.0	67.3	70.4
Japan [8].............	1.7	1.4	32.8	28.5	22.2	20.6	65.5	70.1
Korea.............	5.2	2.9	37.9	37.1	25.6	27.6	56.2	60.0
Luxembourg.........	0.8	0.4	20.9	15.6	13.1	8.5	78.2	84.0
Mexico.............	5.5	[9]3.3	35.2	[9]35.8	21.4	[9]18.9	59.2	[9]60.9
Netherlands.........	3.5	2.0	25.8	24.4	16.2	13.7	70.7	73.6
New Zealand [10]	6.8	[4]6.2	25.5	[4]24.6	16.9	[4]15.3	67.6	[4]69.2
Norway.............	2.4	1.4	37.1	42.7	12.3	10.4	60.4	55.9
Poland.............	6.6	4.3	33.4	31.8	19.8	18.9	60.0	63.8
Portugal............	4.6	2.5	29.1	24.5	18.9	[9]14.3	66.3	73.0
Slovakia............	5.3	3.6	35.2	39.3	23.0	24.7	59.5	57.2
Spain..............	5.0	2.9	29.3	29.8	19.0	15.2	65.7	67.4
Sweden............	2.5	1.4	29.1	28.3	21.7	20.0	68.4	70.3
Switzerland.........	1.8	1.2	28.5	28.0	20.1	20.3	69.8	70.8
Turkey	10.8	8.7	37.2	27.8	27.9	18.7	52.2	63.5
United Kingdom.......	1.4	0.7	29.9	23.0	20.3	12.7	68.7	76.3

[1] Includes forestry, fishing, and hunting. [2] Value added is estimated at factor cost. [3] 1998. [4] 2004. [5] 1999. [6] 2000. [7] 2005. [8] Value added is estimated approximately at market prices. [9] 2006. [10] Value added is estimated at producer's prices.

Source: Organization for Economic Cooperation and Development (OECD), 2009, *OECD in Figures 2009* (copyright) and 2010, "OECD Factbook Statistics 2009," OECD Factbook Statistics database (copyright); <http://dx.doi.org/10.1787/data-00377-en>, accessed May 2010.

Table 1351. Index of Industrial Production by Country: 1990 to 2009

[Annual averages of monthly data. Industrial production index measures output in the manufacturing, mining, electric, gas, and water utilities industries. Minus sign (–) indicates decrease]

Country	Index (2005 = 100)								Annual percent change				
	1990	1995	2000	2005	2006	2007	2008	2009	2000 to 2001	2005 to 2006	2006 to 2007	2007 to 2008	2008 to 2009
OECD, total........	73.2	78.7	95.1	100.0	103.8	106.9	105.0	92.5	–2.3	3.8	3.0	–1.8	–11.9
Australia...........	74.5	81.8	93.8	100.0	101.9	104.8	107.9	104.8	1.0	1.9	2.8	3.0	–2.8
Austria............	59.6	64.4	85.3	100.0	107.5	113.6	115.7	102.0	3.0	7.5	5.7	1.8	–11.9
Belgium [1].........	82.6	83.2	96.2	100.0	105.2	107.9	107.4	92.8	–1.0	5.2	2.6	–0.5	–13.6
Canada [2].........	68.3	77.7	98.9	100.0	99.2	98.9	93.7	83.1	–4.0	–0.8	–0.3	–5.3	–11.4
Czech Republic [1]....	89.9	67.9	74.9	100.0	108.3	119.8	117.7	101.8	10.0	8.3	10.6	–1.8	–13.5
Denmark...........	71.9	82.0	96.5	100.0	103.2	102.2	101.7	85.4	1.2	3.2	–0.9	–0.5	–16.0
Finland............	58.9	66.6	91.2	100.0	109.6	114.6	115.5	91.4	0.7	9.6	4.6	0.8	–20.9
France	89.0	88.8	100.2	100.0	100.8	102.0	99.9	87.8	0.9	0.8	1.2	–2.1	–12.1
Germany [3].........	85.7	82.5	93.9	100.0	106.2	113.5	113.8	93.5	0.4	6.2	6.9	0.2	–17.8
Greece............	83.7	82.1	100.6	100.0	100.6	102.6	100.9	91.9	–1.8	0.6	2.0	–1.7	–8.8
Hungary [1].........	51.9	45.6	76.0	100.0	109.9	118.5	118.5	97.7	3.5	9.9	7.9	–0.1	–17.6
Ireland	23.6	37.5	74.9	100.0	102.9	108.1	106.5	102.0	11.0	2.9	5.0	–1.5	–4.1
Italy	90.2	96.9	104.2	100.0	103.5	105.4	101.7	83.0	–1.2	3.5	1.8	–3.5	–18.4
Japan [1]...........	96.9	94.0	98.4	100.0	104.3	107.2	103.8	81.7	–6.3	4.3	2.8	–3.2	–21.3
Korea, South [1]......	31.7	47.9	74.3	100.0	108.4	115.9	119.9	118.9	0.6	8.4	6.9	3.4	–0.8
Luxembourg.........	66.5	68.1	83.7	100.0	102.1	101.9	96.3	80.5	3.1	2.1	–0.3	–5.5	–16.4
Mexico [4]..........	67.1	70.1	99.6	100.0	105.7	107.8	107.2	99.4	–3.5	5.7	2.0	–0.6	–7.3
Netherlands........	77.9	84.4	95.2	100.0	101.5	103.8	105.3	97.6	0.5	1.5	2.2	1.5	–7.4
New Zealand	72.8	83.2	87.8	100.0	96.3	97.7	96.9	89.4	–0.2	–3.7	1.5	–0.8	–7.7
Norway............	74.2	93.7	104.5	100.0	97.8	96.7	97.1	93.3	–0.7	–2.2	–1.2	0.5	–3.9
Poland............	47.3	53.6	76.8	100.0	112.0	122.5	125.8	121.0	0.9	12.0	9.3	2.7	–3.8
Portugal...........	93.3	90.7	107.1	100.0	103.1	103.0	98.8	90.6	3.1	3.1	(–Z)	–4.0	–8.3
Spain	79.1	82.0	97.8	100.0	103.9	106.0	98.4	82.8	–1.5	3.9	2.1	–7.3	–15.8
Sweden [5, 6]........	64.3	77.0	92.4	100.0	103.6	107.7	104.5	85.8	–0.5	3.6	4.0	–3.0	–17.9
Switzerland	78.3	81.4	99.0	100.0	107.7	118.1	119.6	110.2	–0.7	7.7	9.7	1.3	–7.9
Turkey	57.1	66.8	81.0	100.0	107.8	115.3	114.3	103.2	–8.7	7.8	6.9	–0.9	–9.6
United Kingdom.....	91.4	97.2	104.2	100.0	100.1	100.5	97.5	87.0	–1.4	0.1	0.4	–3.0	–10.8
United States	65.0	75.0	96.7	100.0	102.3	103.8	101.5	91.6	–3.4	2.3	1.5	–2.2	–9.8

Z Less than 0.05 percent. [1] Not adjusted for unequal number of working days in the month. [2] Gross domestic product in industry at factor cost and 1986 prices. [3] Data prior to 1991 are for former West Germany. [4] Including construction. [5] Mining and manufacturing. [6] Annual figures correspond to official annual figures and differ from the average of the monthly figures.

Source: Organization for Economic Cooperation and Development (OECD), 2010, "Production and sales," Main Economic Indicators database (copyright), <http://dx.doi.org/10.1787/data-00048-en>, accessed May 2010.

Table 1352. Selected Indexes of Manufacturing Activity by Country: 1990 to 2008

[2002 = 100. Data relate to employees (wage and salary earners) in Belgium, and to all employed persons (employees, self–employed workers, and unpaid family workers) in the other countries. Minus sign (–) indicates decrease. For explanation of average annual percent change, see Guide to Tabular Presentation]

Index	United States	Canada	Japan	Belgium	France	Germany[1]	Italy	Netherlands	Norway	Sweden	United Kingdom
Output per hour:											
1990	56.9	70.7	70.9	73.9	63.6	69.8	78.1	68.3	87.8	50.9	72.8
1995	68.3	83.3	83.4	86.0	75.2	80.6	94.2	82.1	88.1	66.6	82.1
2000	89.5	100.5	98.5	96.8	94.0	96.5	100.9	96.6	94.6	92.8	93.7
2005	115.1	105.0	121.7	111.0	112.3	113.5	100.8	113.9	119.1	127.1	115.5
2007	126.2	110.2	127.2	120.2	116.3	129.3	103.1	121.4	116.4	139.7	123.8
2008	127.8	107.3	127.0	120.8	115.4	129.2	99.6	119.7	117.2	134.6	124.2
Average annual percent change:											
1995–2000	5.6	3.8	3.4	2.4	4.6	3.7	1.4	3.3	1.4	6.8	2.7
2006–2007	4.7	2.7	3.5	4.4	1.2	5.0	0.5	2.7	-0.2	0.6	3.3
2007–2008	1.2	-2.6	-0.2	0.5	-0.8	-0.1	-3.4	-1.4	0.7	-3.7	0.3
Compensation per hour, national currency basis:[2]											
1990	62.1	68.3	77.4	69.0	64.2	59.7	61.3	61.9	58.5	59.9	60.6
1995	73.4	81.7	92.4	83.2	79.9	81.2	82.5	77.0	69.2	71.7	72.1
2000	91.3	94.2	98.0	92.0	91.8	94.7	94.1	90.9	89.0	90.6	90.6
2005	112.5	112.4	99.6	109.4	109.4	104.1	110.8	110.0	112.6	111.0	115.9
2007	119.6	119.9	98.3	119.3	116.8	110.3	115.5	116.7	125.2	119.7	125.7
2008	123.2	122.5	100.1	122.8	120.3	113.0	118.5	120.5	132.2	123.3	128.8
Average annual percent change:											
1995–2000	4.5	2.9	1.2	2.0	2.8	3.1	2.7	3.4	5.2	4.8	4.7
2006–2007	4.3	3.5	-0.2	5.3	2.7	1.7	2.2	3.2	4.8	4.8	3.3
2007–2008	3.0	2.1	1.8	3.0	3.0	2.5	2.6	3.3	5.6	3.0	2.5
Real hourly compensation:[3]											
1990	82.9	87.5	82.7	88.1	79.6	78.2	93.4	85.2	77.0	79.3	84.7
1995	86.0	93.5	92.3	94.1	88.0	89.4	98.1	92.2	80.9	78.5	85.2
2000	95.4	98.7	96.5	95.8	95.1	97.9	99.1	97.8	92.9	95.0	93.7
2005	103.6	105.0	100.2	102.6	102.7	99.8	103.6	104.7	107.7	107.9	106.3
2007	103.8	107.3	98.5	108.0	106.3	101.8	103.8	108.1	116.2	111.9	107.2
2008	102.9	107.0	99.0	106.4	106.5	101.7	103.1	108.9	118.3	109.0	105.7
Average annual percent change:											
1995–2000	2.1	1.1	0.9	0.4	1.6	1.8	0.2	1.2	2.8	3.9	1.9
2006–2007	1.5	1.2	-0.3	3.4	1.0	-0.5	0.3	1.6	4.0	2.8	-0.9
2007–2008	-0.9	-0.3	0.5	-1.5	0.2	-0.1	-0.7	0.7	1.8	-2.6	-1.4
Unit labor costs, national currency:[2]											
1990	109.3	96.7	109.2	93.3	101.0	85.5	78.6	90.5	66.6	117.7	83.3
1995	107.5	98.0	110.8	96.7	106.1	100.8	87.7	93.8	78.5	107.6	87.9
2000	102.1	93.7	99.5	95.1	97.6	98.1	93.2	94.1	94.1	97.6	96.7
2005	97.7	107.0	81.8	98.6	97.4	91.7	110.0	96.6	94.5	87.3	100.4
2007	94.8	108.9	77.3	99.3	100.4	85.3	112.1	96.2	107.5	85.6	101.5
2008	96.4	114.1	78.8	101.7	104.3	87.5	119.0	100.7	112.8	91.6	103.7
Average annual percent change:											
1995–2000	-1.0	-0.9	-2.1	-0.4	-1.7	-0.5	1.2	0.1	3.7	-1.9	1.9
2006–2007	-0.4	0.8	-3.6	0.8	1.5	-3.2	1.7	0.5	5.0	4.2	-0.1
2007–2008	1.7	4.8	2.0	2.4	3.8	2.7	6.2	4.7	4.9	6.9	2.2
Unit labor costs, U.S. dollar basis:[2,4]											
1990	109.3	130.1	94.3	119.2	128.7	109.4	134.3	115.9	85.0	193.1	98.9
1995	107.5	112.1	147.7	140.1	147.7	145.6	110.2	136.3	98.9	146.5	92.3
2000	102.1	99.1	115.6	92.8	95.3	95.8	91.0	91.9	85.2	103.5	97.6
2005	97.7	138.7	93.0	129.8	128.3	120.8	144.8	127.2	117.2	113.7	121.6
2007	94.8	159.3	82.2	144.0	145.6	123.7	162.5	130.5	146.6	123.3	135.2
2008	96.4	168.1	95.5	158.4	162.4	136.3	185.4	156.8	159.8	135.2	128.0
Average annual percent change:											
1995–2000	-1.0	-2.4	-4.8	-7.9	-8.4	-8.0	-3.7	-7.6	-2.9	-6.7	1.1
2006–2007	-0.4	6.5	-4.8	10.1	10.8	5.7	11.0	9.7	15.0	13.8	8.5
2007–2008	1.7	5.6	16.2	10.0	11.5	10.3	14.1	12.4	9.0	9.7	-5.3
Employment:											
1990	116.1	98.7	128.7	118.2	117.0	131.2	110.8	111.4	102.2	119.9	134.1
1995	113.3	91.7	120.1	105.9	103.0	106.1	100.6	102.5	104.1	100.3	116.7
2000	113.0	102.2	108.0	102.9	101.4	101.9	99.4	102.9	105.0	101.3	109.9
2005	93.5	98.5	94.9	94.0	92.3	94.4	99.1	91.4	92.6	91.7	86.8
2007	91.4	92.6	96.9	92.1	89.3	94.8	100.7	91.2	102.1	91.5	82.6
2008	88.2	90.2	95.2	91.8	87.9	96.3	99.5	91.7	104.7	91.0	80.2
Average annual percent change:											
1995–2000	–	2.2	-2.1	-0.6	-0.3	-0.8	-0.2	0.1	0.2	0.2	-1.2
2006–2007	-1.7	-3.4	0.5	-0.9	-1.4	1.2	0.7	0.4	5.0	0.6	-3.2
2007–2008	-3.4	-2.6	-1.8	-0.3	-1.5	1.6	-1.2	0.5	2.5	-0.5	-2.9
Aggregate hours:											
1990	116.5	97.2	139.6	117.9	128.2	135.3	113.0	112.7	104.1	110.2	130.4
1995	115.9	91.8	122.0	104.5	111.3	111.7	101.6	103.7	107.3	101.3	118.2
2000	115.1	102.7	109.0	104.0	105.4	104.0	100.5	103.6	107.1	103.8	110.6
2005	93.6	98.1	96.3	91.9	93.7	95.0	97.0	91.6	95.8	94.2	88.1
2007	92.6	92.2	98.8	89.5	90.8	94.9	100.0	91.7	106.2	94.6	84.0
2008	89.0	89.3	95.7	88.6	89.4	95.6	98.9	92.4	108.6	94.8	81.3
Average annual percent change:											
1995–2000	-0.1	2.3	-2.2	-0.1	-1.1	-1.4	-0.2	–	–	0.5	-1.3
2006–2007	-1.8	-3.5	0.2	-1.7	-0.5	1.0	1.5	0.5	5.5	1.8	-2.7
2007–2008	-3.9	-3.2	-3.2	-1.0	-1.5	0.7	-1.2	0.8	2.3	0.2	-3.1

– Represents or rounds to zero. [1] Data prior to 1991 are for the former West Germany. [2] In Canada, France, Sweden, and the United Kingdom, compensation adjusted for employment taxes and government subsidies to estimate the actual cost to employers. [3] Index of hourly compensation divided by the index of consumer prices to adjust for changes in purchasing power. [4] Indexes in national currency adjusted for changes in prevailing exchange rates.

Source: U.S. Bureau of Labor Statistics, *International Comparisons of Manufacturing Productivity and Unit Labor Cost Trends 2008, Supplementary Tables 1950–2008*, October 2009. See also <http://www.bls.gov/ilc>.

International Statistics 849

Table 1353. Indexes of Hourly Compensation Costs for All Employees in Manufacturing by Country: 2000 to 2007

[United States = 100. Compensation costs include pay for time worked, other direct pay (including holiday and vacation pay, bonuses, other direct payments, and the cost of pay in kind), employer expenditures for legally required insurance programs and contractual and private benefit plans, and for some countries, other labor taxes. Data adjusted for exchange rates. Area averages are trade-weighted to account for difference in countries' relative importance to U.S. trade in manufactured goods. The trade weights used to compute the average compensation cost measures for selected economic groups are based on the relative dollar value of U.S. trade in manufactured commodities (exports plus imports) with each country or area in 2007; see source for detail]

Area or country	2000	2004	2005	2006	2007	Area or country	2000	2004	2005	2006	2007
United States	100	100	100	100	100	Austria	100	123	124	128	141
Total [1]	66	75	76	79	85	Belgium	89	114	113	116	127
OECD [2]	70	81	82	85	91	Czech Republic	14	23	24	27	32
Europe	88	115	114	118	129	Denmark	98	130	132	137	156
Euro Area [3]	91	119	117	122	133	Finland	81	112	113	118	130
Eastern Europe [4]	13	21	23	24	29	France	88	109	108	112	123
East Asia [5]	34	34	37	40	43	Germany	119	152	147	154	166
Argentina	33	15	18	22	26	Hungary	14	26	27	28	34
Brazil	17	13	17	20	23	Ireland	66	98	99	103	117
Canada	76	84	90	98	104	Italy	67	93	93	96	105
Mexico	12	12	12	12	13	Netherlands	85	118	117	118	129
Australia	70	95	99	102	114	Norway	106	145	150	157	180
Israel	52	47	47	48	52	Poland	14	17	19	21	25
Japan	103	88	86	81	78	Portugal	22	31	31	31	34
Korea, South	38	42	48	55	60	Slovakia	11	18	20	22	28
New Zealand	38	52	56	54	63	Spain	50	69	69	72	80
Philippines	4	3	4	4	4	Sweden	89	113	110	114	127
Singapore	47	45	44	46	50	Switzerland	100	123	121	121	125
Taiwan [6]	30	25	26	27	27	United Kingdom	82	104	105	108	120

[1] Trade-weighted measure includes all 32 foreign economies. [2] Organization for Economic Cooperation and Development; see text, this section. [3] Euro area refers to European Union member countries that have adopted the Euro as the common currency as of January 1, 2009, (Austria, Belgium, Cyprus, Finland, France, Germany, Greece, Ireland, Italy, Luxembourg, Malta, Netherlands, Portugal, Slovakia, Slovenia, and Spain). [4] Czech Republic, Hungary, Poland, and Slovakia. [5] South Korea, the Philippines, Singapore, and Taiwan. [6] See footnote 4, Table 1331.

Source: U.S. Bureau of Labor Statistics, *International Comparisons of Hourly Compensation Costs in Manufacturing, 2007*, March 2009. See also <http://www.bls.gov/fls/>.

Table 1354. Annual Percent Change in Labor Productivity and Hours Worked by Country: 1995 to 2008

[Change for period shown. For Advanced, Other Advanced, and Eastern European countries, labor productivity growth refers to the growth in gross domestic product per hour worked. Data are derived from The Conference Board Total Economy Database, in association with the Groningen Growth and Development Centre at the University of Groningen, Netherlands. Growth for regional aggregates is based on the weighted sum of country labor productivity growth, with the weight calculated as the two-period average of country share in PPP adjusted nominal GDP, plus a reallocation term. Gross domestic product for each country is measured in constant 2009 U.S. dollars, using GDP deflator changes. Minus sign (–) indicates decrease]

Country	Labor productivity 1995 to 2000	Labor productivity 2000 to 2008	Total hours worked 1995 to 2000	Total hours worked 2000 to 2008	Country	Labor productivity 1995 to 2000	Labor productivity 2000 to 2008	Total hours worked 1995 to 2000	Total hours worked 2000 to 2008
Advanced Economies [1]	2.3	1.7	0.9	0.4	Cyprus	2.0	1.2	1.7	2.4
United States	2.3	2.0	1.9	0.1	Czech Republic	1.9	3.9	−0.4	0.3
Japan	2.1	1.8	−1.1	−0.5	Estonia	8.1	5.0	−1.7	1.3
European Union (EU-27, enlarged) [2]	2.1	1.6	0.8	0.5	Hungary	2.4	2.8	1.4	0.4
European Union					Latvia	5.8	6.0	−0.6	1.0
(EU-15, old) [3]	1.8	1.1	1.1	0.7	Lithuania	4.2	5.7	0.1	1.4
Austria	1.8	1.3	1.2	0.7	Malta	2.2	0.9	0.7	1.0
Belgium	2.1	0.6	0.7	1.2	Poland	5.4	4.0	−0.1	0.1
Denmark	1.1	0.3	1.8	1.0	Romania	−1.1	7.5	−0.1	−1.6
Finland	2.8	1.9	2.0	0.9	Slovakia	4.8	5.0	−1.5	0.9
France	2.1	1.2	0.7	0.4	Slovenia	4.8	3.3	−0.5	0.9
Germany	2.0	1.2	–	–	Other Advanced				
Greece	4.0	2.6	−0.6	1.2	Economies	3.2	2.2	0.7	0.9
Ireland	5.1	2.1	4.2	2.2	Australia	2.6	1.4	1.2	1.8
Italy	0.9	–	1.0	0.8	Canada	2.1	0.7	2.0	1.6
Luxembourg	2.6	1.0	3.4	2.7	Cyprus	2.0	1.2	1.7	2.4
Netherlands	1.7	1.5	2.3	0.5	Hong Kong	0.6	3.3	2.0	1.1
Portugal	1.4	1.0	2.6	−0.1	Iceland	2.3	2.8	2.5	1.2
Spain	0.2	1.0	3.8	2.1	Israel	(NA)	(NA)	(NA)	(NA)
Sweden	2.4	1.8	0.8	0.6	New Zealand	1.0	0.7	1.7	2.1
U.K.	2.6	1.8	0.8	0.5	Norway	2.3	1.1	1.4	1.2
European Union					Singapore	2.0	0.8	4.2	3.9
(EU-12, new) [4]	3.3	4.5	−0.3	0.1	South Korea	4.6	4.3	−0.4	–
Bulgaria	1.7	3.2	−2.5	2.2	Switzerland	1.6	0.9	0.4	1.0
					Taiwan [5]	5.1	2.8	0.5	0.4

– Represents zero. NA Not available. [1] "Advanced" includes the U.S., EU-15, Japan, and "Other Advanced." [2] Referring to all members of the European Union. See footnote 5, Table 1377 for list of EU-27 countries. [3] Referring to membership of the European Union until April 30, 2004. [4] Referring to new membership of the European Union as of May 1, 2004. [5] See footnote 4, Table 1331.

Source: The Conference Board, New York, NY, The Conference Board, Total Economy Database," January 2010, <http://www.conference-board.org/economics/database.cfm>. Reproduced with permission from The Conference Board, Inc., 2010, The Conference Board, Inc.

Table 1355. Annual Percent Changes in Consumer Prices by Country: 2000 to 2009

[Change from previous year. See text, this section, for general comments concerning the data. For additional qualifications of the data for individual countries, see source. Minus sign (–) indicates decrease]

Country	2000	2005	2007	2008	2009	Country	2000	2005	2007	2008	2009
United States	**3.4**	**3.4**	**2.9**	**3.8**	**–0.4**						
						Japan	–0.7	–0.3	0.1	1.4	–1.4
Argentina	–0.9	9.6	8.8	8.6	6.3	Kenya	10.0	10.3	9.8	26.2	9.2
Australia	4.5	2.7	2.3	4.4	1.8	Korea, South	2.3	2.8	2.5	4.7	2.8
Austria	2.4	2.3	2.2	3.2	0.5	Malaysia	1.5	3.0	2.0	5.4	0.6
Bangladesh	2.2	7.0	9.1	8.9	5.4	Mexico	9.5	4.0	4.0	5.1	5.3
Belgium	2.5	2.8	1.8	4.5	–0.1	Netherlands	2.3	1.7	1.6	2.5	1.2
Bolivia	4.6	5.4	8.7	14.0	3.3	Nigeria	6.9	17.9	5.4	11.6	12.4
Brazil	7.0	6.9	3.6	5.7	4.9	Norway	3.1	1.5	0.7	3.8	2.2
Canada	2.7	2.2	2.1	2.4	0.3	Pakistan	4.4	9.1	7.6	20.3	13.6
Chile	3.8	3.1	4.4	8.7	1.5	Peru	3.8	1.6	1.8	5.8	2.9
Colombia	9.2	5.0	5.5	7.0	4.2	Philippines	4.0	7.6	2.8	9.3	3.3
Ecuador	96.1	2.4	2.3	8.4	5.2	Portugal	2.8	2.3	2.8	2.6	–0.8
Egypt	2.7	4.9	9.3	18.3	11.8	Romania	45.7	9.0	4.8	7.8	5.6
France	1.7	1.7	1.5	2.8	0.1	Russia	20.8	12.7	9.0	14.1	11.7
Germany	1.5	1.6	2.3	2.6	0.3	South Africa	5.3	3.4	7.1	11.5	7.1
Ghana	25.2	15.1	10.7	16.5	19.3	Spain	3.4	3.4	2.8	4.1	–0.4
Greece	3.2	3.5	2.9	4.2	1.2	Sri Lanka	6.2	11.6	15.8	22.6	3.4
Guatemala	6.0	8.4	6.5	12.6	1.9	Sweden	1.0	0.5	2.2	3.4	–0.3
India	4.0	4.2	6.4	8.4	10.9	Switzerland	1.5	1.2	0.7	2.4	–0.5
Indonesia	3.7	10.5	6.3	10.1	4.6	Thailand	1.6	4.5	2.2	5.5	–0.8
Iran	14.5	13.4	17.2	25.5	13.5	Turkey	54.9	10.1	8.8	10.4	6.3
Israel	1.1	1.3	0.5	4.6	3.3	United Kingdom	2.9	2.8	4.3	4.0	–0.6
Italy	2.5	2.0	1.8	3.3	0.8	Venezuela	16.2	16.0	18.7	31.4	28.6

Source: International Monetary Fund, Washington, DC, *International Financial Statistics,* monthly (copyright).

Table 1356. Comparative Price Levels—Selected OECD Countries: 2010

[Purchasing power parities (PPPs) are the rates of currency conversion that eliminate the differences in price levels between countries. Comparative price levels are defined as the ratios of PPPs to exchange rates. The PPPs are given in national currency units per U.S. dollar. The table is to be read vertically. Each column shows the number of specified monetary units needed in each of the countries listed to buy the same representative basket of consumer goods and services. In each case the representative basket costs a hundred units in the country whose currency is specified. Example of data: An item that costs $1.00 in the United States would cost $1.41 (U.S. dollars) in Japan]

Country	United States (U.S. dollar)	Canada (Canadian dollar)	Mexico (Mexican peso)	Japan (Yen)	France (Euro)	Germany (Euro)	Italy (Euro)	United Kingdom (Pound)
United States	**100**	**84**	**147**	**71**	**81**	**85**	**83**	**100**
Australia [1]	137	115	202	98	112	117	114	138
Austria	118	99	174	84	96	100	98	119
Belgium	124	104	182	90	100	105	102	124
Canada	119	100	176	85	97	101	99	119
Czech Republic	82	69	121	59	67	70	68	82
Denmark	165	138	243	117	134	140	136	165
Finland	143	120	210	101	116	121	118	143
France	123	103	181	87	100	104	102	123
Germany	118	99	174	84	96	100	97	118
Greece	108	91	159	77	88	92	89	108
Hungary	81	68	119	57	66	68	67	81
Iceland	109	91	161	78	89	93	90	109
Ireland	139	117	205	99	113	118	115	139
Italy	121	101	178	86	98	103	100	121
Japan	141	118	207	100	114	119	116	141
Korea, South	80	67	118	57	65	68	66	80
Luxembourg	131	110	193	93	106	111	108	131
Mexico	68	57	100	48	55	58	56	68
Netherlands	120	100	176	85	97	102	99	120
New Zealand [1]	115	96	169	81	93	97	95	115
Norway	167	140	245	118	135	141	138	167
Poland	76	64	113	54	62	65	63	76
Portugal	97	82	144	69	79	83	80	97
Slovakia	86	72	127	61	70	73	71	86
Spain	107	90	158	76	87	91	88	107
Sweden	130	109	191	92	105	110	107	130
Switzerland	163	136	239	115	132	138	134	163
Turkey	86	72	127	61	70	73	71	86
United Kingdom	100	84	147	71	81	85	83	100

[1] Estimates based on quarterly consumer prices.

Source: Organization for Economic Cooperation and Development (OECD), 2010, "Purchasing Power Parities and Comparative Price Levels", *Main Economic Indicators,* May 2010 (copyright). See also <http://www.oecd.org/dataoecd/48/18/18598721.pdf>.

Table 1357. Indexes of Living Costs Abroad: 2010

[As of January 2010. Washington, DC=100. Indexes compare the costs in dollars of representative goods and services (excluding housing and education) purchased at the foreign location and the cost of comparable goods and services in the Washington, D.C. area. The indexes are computed for private American employees and exclude special advantages that may be available only to U.S. Government employees. The indexes are place-to-place comparisons at specific times and currency exchange rates. They cannot be used for measuring cost changes over time at a foreign location. Since the indexes reflect only the expenditure pattern and living costs of American families, they should not be used to compare living costs of Americans in the United States with the living costs of foreign nationals living in their own country]

Country/Territory	City	Survey date	Local index [1]	Country/Territory	City	Survey date	Local index [1]
Algeria	Algiers	2/16/2009	127	Kenya	Nairobi	12/4/2007	143
Angola	Luanda	5/21/2008	190	Korea	Seoul	12/4/2007	176
Argentina	Buenos Aires	3/8/2009	111	Kuwait	Kuwait City	11/18/2007	132
Armenia	Yerevan	1/30/2007	138	Laos	Vientiane	12/30/2005	107
Australia	Canberra	5/23/2008	139	Latvia	Riga	5/30/2007	139
Austria	Vienna	3/11/2008	186	Lebanon	Beirut	4/23/2008	123
Azerbaijan	Baku	2/1/2009	156	Liberia	Monrovia	8/14/2009	149
Bahamas	Nassau	6/24/2009	143	Lithuania	Vilnius	9/25/2008	131
Bahrain	Bahrain	8/26/2007	123	Luxembourg		10/25/2007	160
Bangladesh	Dhaka	3/6/2006	88	Macedonia	Skopje	4/23/2007	135
Belarus	Minsk	3/15/2007	136	Madagascar	Antananarivo	1/23/2008	128
Belgium	Brussels	5/12/2009	179	Malaysia	Kuala Lumpur	8/24/2008	121
Belize	Belmopan	4/6/2008	132	Mexico	Mexico City	3/6/2009	99
Bolivia	La Paz	7/1/2009	110	Moldova	Chisinau	5/1/2008	115
Bosnia-Herzegovina	Sarajevo	8/6/2009	126	Mongolia	Ulaanbaatar	1/16/2009	136
Botswana	Gaborone	6/16/2009	119	Morocco	Rabat	12/13/2008	133
Brazil	Rio de Janeiro	12/29/2008	133	Mozambique	Maputo	8/16/2009	141
Bulgaria	Sofia	4/17/2008	135	Namibia	Windhoek	4/20/2006	122
Burma	Rangoon	10/22/2008	142	Nepal	Kathmandu	6/22/2007	103
Burundi	Bujumbura	7/7/2009	135	Netherlands	The Hague	4/23/2009	152
Cambodia	Phnom Penh	2/8/2009	122	New Zealand	Wellington	10/15/2007	157
Cameroon	Yaounde	3/27/2006	154	Nicaragua	Managua	4/15/2008	113
Canada	Montreal	1/12/2007	134	Niger	Niamey	6/11/2009	127
Central African Republic	Bangui	8/13/2008	189	Nigeria	Abuja	11/12/2008	161
Chad	Ndjamena	8/26/2009	176	Norway	Oslo	1/26/2009	176
Chile	Santiago	3/31/2008	142	Oman	Muscat	5/19/2009	125
China [2]	Beijing	7/27/2007	130	Pakistan	Islamabad	12/10/2004	102
Colombia	Bogota	1/4/2008	109	Panama	Panama City	7/31/2008	119
Congo [3]	Kinshasa	7/16/2008	167	Paraguay	Asuncion	1/16/2008	114
Costa Rica	San Jose	8/5/2008	119	Peru	Lima	12/7/2007	124
Cote d'Ivoire	Abidjan	12/21/2008	129	Philippines	Manila	12/2/2008	91
Croatia	Zagreb	3/22/2007	141	Poland	Warsaw	9/17/2009	130
Cuba	Havana	2/13/2008	145	Portugal	Lisbon	2/28/2008	148
Cyprus	Nicosia	6/11/2009	163	Qatar	Doha	8/15/2007	129
Czech Republic	Prague	9/15/2005	130	Romania	Bucharest	11/25/2008	134
Denmark	Copenhagen	3/30/2009	190	Russia	Moscow	2/26/2009	154
Djibouti	Djibouti City	4/10/2004	161	Rwanda	Kigali	11/16/2008	136
Ecuador	Quito	8/10/2009	120	Saudi Arabia	Riyadh	5/6/2008	120
Egypt	Cairo	3/13/2006	96	Serbia	Belgrade	3/17/2009	99
El Salvador	San Salvador	2/8/2009	123	Sierra Leone	Freetown	6/15/2009	131
Estonia	Tallinn	4/16/2008	141	Singapore		4/19/2009	133
Ethiopia	Addis Ababa	3/8/2009	124	Slovakia	Bratislava	5/31/2007	132
Finland	Helsinki	4/14/2009	171	South Africa	Johannesburg	10/23/2008	135
France	Paris	4/19/2007	190	Spain	Madrid	3/15/2008	169
Gabon	Libreville	11/16/2008	157	Sri Lanka	Colombo	4/9/2008	98
Georgia	Tbilisi	4/14/2009	140	Sudan	Khartoum	11/14/2008	139
Germany	Berlin	3/12/2008	179	Sweden	Stockholm	4/30/2008	204
Ghana	Accra	5/12/2009	115	Switzerland	Geneva	5/21/2008	235
Greece	Athens	9/4/2008	171	Syria	Damascus	3/26/2008	96
Guatemala	Guatemala City	6/4/2009	106	Taiwan [2, 3]	Taipei	2/24/2009	145
Guinea	Conakry	10/29/2008	162	Tajikistan	Dushanbe	3/19/2008	100
Guyana	Georgetown	7/28/2009	150	Tanzania	Dar es Salaam	11/15/2007	133
Haiti	Port-au-Prince	9/29/2008	129	Thailand	Bangkok	2/26/2008	126
Honduras	Tegucigalpa	6/10/2007	84	Timor-Leste	Timor-Leste	7/11/2007	128
Hong Kong		6/7/2009	156	Turkey	Istanbul	4/29/2009	151
Hungary	Budapest	5/7/2008	163	Turkmenistan	Ashgabat	10/31/2007	105
Iceland	Reykjavik	3/2/2009	151	Uganda	Kampala	8/17/2008	132
India	New Delhi	11/20/2008	107	Ukraine	Kyiv	10/5/2008	131
Indonesia	Jakarta	6/17/2009	116	United Arab Emirates	Dubai	6/9/2009	117
Ireland	Dublin	1/31/2008	175	United Kingdom	London	4/16/2009	159
Israel	Tel Aviv	4/6/2008	163	Uruguay	Montevideo	2/18/2009	136
Italy	Rome	3/31/2009	183	Uzbekistan	Tashkent	4/7/2009	107
Jamaica	Kingston	6/24/2009	112	Venezuela	Caracas	9/3/2008	172
Japan	Okinawa	5/24/2002	141	Vietnam	Hanoi	5/5/2008	113
Jordan	Amman	4/14/2008	130	Yemen	Sanaa	4/25/2009	92
Kazakhstan	Astana	5/22/2008	148	Zambia	Lusaka	7/1/2009	130
				Zimbabwe	Harare	1/14/2008	243

[1] Also called the "local index," the living cost index measures living costs for private American citizens.
The local index is a comparison of prices at the foreign post and in Washington, D.C., with the price ratios weighted by the expenditure pattern of American employees living at the foreign post. It is, thereby, a measure of the cost of living for Americans at the foreign post compared with the cost of living in Washington, DC. This is the index most appropriate for use by business firms and other private organizations to establish cost-of-living allowances for their American employees stationed abroad. [2] See footnote 4, Table 1331. [3] There are no U.S. Government employees in Taiwan. The figures listed in this column represent a living cost comparison for American employees of the American Institute in Taiwan, who have some duty-free and other special benefits that may not be available to other Americans in Taiwan.

Source: U.S. Department of State, Bureau of Administration, "Indexes of Living Costs Abroad, Quarters Allowances, and Hardship Differentials," January 2010, <http://aoprals.state.gov/content.asp?content_id=186&menu_id=81>.

Table 1358. Percent of Household Final Consumption Expenditures Spent on Food, Alcohol, and Tobacco Consumed at Home by Selected Countries: 2008

Country/Territory	Food [1]	Alcoholic beverages and tobacco	Country/Territory	Food [1]	Alcoholic beverages and tobacco
United States	6.8	1.9	Latvia.	19.2	6.6
			Lithuania	22.9	6.6
Algeria.	43.8	2.0	Malaysia	14.2	1.3
Australia.	10.6	4.0	Mexico	24.1	2.5
Austria	11.1	3.3	Morocco.	40.3	1.3
Azerbaijan	48.5	2.4	Netherlands	11.4	2.9
Belarus	44.0	6.0	New Zealand	12.1	4.3
Belgium	13.1	3.8	Nigeria	40.1	2.5
Bolivia	28.4	2.2	Norway.	13.1	4.5
Brazil	24.6	2.0	Pakistan.	45.6	2.5
Bulgaria	19.0	3.7	Peru	29.1	2.0
Canada	9.1	3.9	Philippines	37.0	1.7
Chile	23.4	0.8	Poland	20.4	6.6
China [2].	33.9	2.9	Portugal	15.7	3.5
Colombia	27.7	4.7	Romania	34.2	5.0
Croatia.	26.1	3.3	Russia	29.1	2.7
Czech Republic	15.9	7.7	Saudi Arabia	23.7	1.3
Ecuador.	19.9	1.9	Singapore	8.1	2.4
Egypt	38.3	2.3	Slovakia.	17.2	4.8
Estonia.	15.3	8.0	Slovenia.	14.6	4.5
Finland.	12.1	5.0	South Africa.	20.1	4.6
France	13.4	3.1	Spain	13.4	3.1
Germany	11.4	3.6	Sweden	11.6	3.7
Hong Kong.	12.3	0.8	Switzerland	10.3	3.6
Hungary.	16.6	8.1	Taiwan [2]	24.1	2.1
Indonesia.	44.1	6.3	Thailand.	24.9	5.6
Ireland	7.5	5.4	Tunisia	35.8	1.0
Israel	17.8	1.6	Turkey	24.5	4.1
Italy	14.4	2.7	Turkmenistan	28.7	3.0
Japan.	14.4	3.2	Ukraine	42.2	6.4
Jordan	40.8	4.8	United Arab Emirates . . .	9.0	0.4
Kazakhstan	35.4	3.7	United Kingdom.	8.9	3.7
Korea, South	15.3	2.6	Venezuela	29.3	3.1
Kuwait	14.6	1.6	Vietnam	38.5	2.8

[1] Includes nonalcoholic beverages. [2] See footnote 4, Table 1331.

Source: U.S. Department of Agriculture, Economic Research Service; "Food, CPI, Prices and Expenditures: Food Expenditure Tables," July 2010, <http://www.ers.usda.gov/Briefing/CPIFoodAndExpenditures/Data/>.

Table 1359. Gross Public Debt, Expenditures, and Receipts by Country: 1990 to 2009

[Percent of nominal gross domestic product. Gross debt includes one-off revenues from the sale of the mobile telephone licenses. Expenditures and receipts refer to the general government sector, which is a consolidation of accounts for the central, state, and local governments plus social security. Expenditures, or total outlays, are defined as current outlays plus capital outlays. Receipts cover current receipts, but exclude capital receipts. Nontax receipts consist of property income (including dividends and other transfers from public enterprises), fees, charges, sales, fines, capital transfers received by the general government, etc. Minus sign (−) indicates deficit]

Country	Gross debt			Expenditures			Receipts		
	1990	2000	2009	1990	2000	2009	1990	2000	2009
United States [1]	−4.3	1.5	−11.2	37.2	33.9	41.5	32.9	35.4	30.3
Australia.	−2.0	0.9	−4.0	35.8	35.2	37.5	33.7	36.1	33.5
Austria	−2.5	−1.9	−4.3	51.5	52.2	52.7	49.0	50.3	48.4
Belgium	−6.8	−0.1	−5.7	52.3	49.2	54.0	45.5	49.1	48.2
Canada	−5.8	2.9	−4.8	48.8	41.1	43.6	43.0	44.1	38.8
Czech Republic	(X)	−3.7	−5.7	(X)	41.6	45.7	(X)	37.9	40.0
Denmark	−1.3	2.3	−2.5	55.9	53.3	57.7	54.6	55.5	55.3
Finland.	5.4	6.9	−2.3	47.9	48.3	56.2	53.3	55.2	53.9
France	−2.4	−1.5	−8.2	49.4	51.6	55.5	47.0	50.1	47.3
Germany	(X)	1.3	−3.2	(X)	45.1	47.7	(X)	46.4	44.5
Greece.	−14.0	−3.7	−12.7	44.9	46.7	51.3	30.8	43.0	38.7
Hungary.	(NA)	−3.0	−4.3	(NA)	46.9	51.5	(NA)	43.9	47.2
Iceland.	−3.3	1.7	−15.7	38.9	41.9	55.9	35.6	43.6	40.2
Ireland	−2.8	4.8	−12.2	42.8	31.3	45.0	40.0	36.1	32.8
Italy	−11.4	−0.9	−5.5	52.9	46.1	51.7	41.5	45.3	46.2
Japan [2].	2.0	−7.6	−7.4	31.6	39.0	41.6	33.6	31.4	34.2
Korea, South	3.1	5.4	−1.8	19.0	22.4	33.8	22.1	27.9	31.9
Netherlands	−5.3	2.0	−4.5	54.9	44.2	50.3	49.6	46.1	45.9
New Zealand	−4.5	1.9	−1.2	53.2	39.2	42.4	48.7	41.1	41.2
Norway.	2.2	15.4	9.6	53.3	42.3	44.4	55.5	57.7	54.0
Portugal	−6.1	−3.0	−6.7	40.5	43.1	51.6	34.5	40.2	44.9
Spain	−4.1	−1.0	−9.6	42.8	39.1	46.3	38.7	38.1	36.8
Sweden	3.4	3.7	−2.0	60.1	57.0	56.2	63.4	60.7	54.2
United Kingdom	−2.0	3.7	−12.6	41.5	36.6	52.1	39.4	40.3	39.5

NA Not available. X Not applicable. [1] Receipts exclude the operating surpluses of public enterprises, while expenditures include them [2] The 2000 expenditures include capital transfers to the Deposit Insurance Company. Receipts include deferred tax payments on postal savings accounts in 2000.

Source: Organization for Economic Cooperation and Development (OECD), OECD Economic Outlook, (copyright), Vol. 2009/2, OECD Publishing. See also <http://dx.doi.org/10.1787/eco_outlook-v2009-2-en>.

Table 1360. Percent Distribution of Tax Receipts by Country: 1990 to 2008

Country	Total [1]	Income and profits taxes [2]			Social security contributions			Taxes on goods and services [5]		
		Total [3]	Individual	Corporate	Total [4]	Employ-ees	Employ-ers	Total [3]	General consump-tion taxes [6]	Taxes on specific goods, services [7]
United States:										
1990.	100.0	46.0	37.1	8.9	25.1	11.0	12.9	17.4	8.0	7.0
2000.	100.0	50.7	41.9	8.7	23.2	10.4	11.6	16.1	7.6	6.3
2008.	100.0	46.8	37.9	8.9	24.5	10.8	12.4	17.0	7.8	6.2
Canada:										
1990.	100.0	48.6	40.8	7.0	12.1	4.4	7.6	25.8	14.1	10.3
2000.	100.0	50.1	36.8	12.2	13.6	5.5	7.8	24.2	14.2	8.6
2008.	100.0	49.5	37.3	10.7	14.5	5.8	8.3	23.4	13.2	8.5
France:										
1990.	100.0	16.1	10.7	5.3	44.1	13.2	27.2	28.4	18.8	8.7
2000.	100.0	24.9	18.0	6.9	36.0	8.9	24.8	25.7	16.9	8.2
2008.	100.0	24.1	17.4	6.8	37.2	9.2	25.3	24.5	16.8	6.9
Germany:										
1990	100.0	32.4	27.6	4.8	37.5	16.2	19.1	26.7	16.6	9.2
2000.	100.0	30.1	25.3	4.8	39.0	17.2	19.2	28.1	18.4	8.8
2008.	100.0	31.9	26.8	5.2	36.4	15.9	17.2	28.9	19.4	8.5
Italy:										
1990.	100.0	36.5	26.3	10.0	32.9	6.3	23.6	28.0	14.7	10.6
2000.	100.0	33.1	24.8	6.9	28.6	5.4	19.9	27.9	15.4	9.6
2008.	100.0	34.6	26.8	8.6	31.1	5.5	21.2	24.4	13.7	8.3
Japan:										
1990.	100.0	50.2	27.8	22.4	26.4	10.6	12.7	13.7	4.4	7.5
2000.	100.0	34.8	21.1	13.8	35.2	14.7	16.4	19.3	9.1	8.0
2008.	100.0	55.4	32.6	22.8	(NA)	(NA)	(NA)	29.1	14.5	11.2
United Kingdom:										
1990.	100.0	39.3	29.4	9.9	17.0	6.6	9.9	31.1	16.9	12.6
2000.	100.0	39.1	29.3	9.8	17.0	6.8	9.6	31.9	18.1	12.4
2008.	100.0	39.9	29.9	9.9	19.2	7.9	10.8	28.8	17.8	9.8

NA Not available. [1] Includes property taxes, employer payroll taxes other than social security contributions, and miscellaneous taxes, not shown separately. [2] Includes taxes on capital gains. [3] Includes other taxes, not shown separately. [4] Includes contributions of self-employed, not shown separately. [5] Taxes on the production, sales, transfer, leasing, and delivery of goods and services and rendering of services. [6] Primary value-added and sales taxes. [7] For example, excise taxes on alcohol, tobacco, and gasoline.

Source: Organization for Economic Cooperation and Development (OECD), 2010, "Comparative Tables," Taxing Wages database (copyright), <http://dx.doi.org/10.1787/data-00265-en>, accessed May 2010.

Table 1361. Household Tax Burden by Country: 2008

[Percent of gross wage earnings of the average production worker. The tax burden reflects income tax plus employee social security contributions less cash benefits. Minus sign (–) indicates tax credit]

Country	Single person without children	One earner family with two children	Country	Single person without children	One earner family with two children
United States	**22.4**	**5.2**	Japan.	20.1	13.8
Australia.	22.0	8.6	Korea, South	11.8	9.1
Austria.	32.7	18.1	Luxembourg.	26.4	0.9
Belgium	41.5	20.2	Mexico	5.3	5.3
Canada	22.8	8.8	Netherlands	31.8	22.6
Czech Republic	22.2	–6.5	New Zealand	18.4	0.6
Denmark	39.4	28.8	Norway.	29.3	21.8
Finland.	29.2	22.6	Poland	24.3	17.8
France	27.7	17.1	Portugal	22.3	8.7
Germany	41.3	20.8	Slovakia.	21.3	2.4
Greece.	25.1	25.4	Spain	19.7	12.0
Hungary.	38.2	25.3	Sweden	25.3	17.9
Iceland.	23.9	3.0	Switzerland	21.5	8.1
Ireland	20.9	2.2	Turkey	27.2	25.7
Italy	29.3	15.1	United Kingdom. . . .	25.3	18.5

Source: Organization for Economic Cooperation and Development (OECD), 2010, "Comparative Tables," Taxing Wages database (copyright), <http://dx.doi.org/10.1787/data-00265-en>, accessed May 2010.

Table 1362. Household Net Saving Rates by Country: 1995 to 2008

[As a percentage of household disposable income. Household savings are estimated by subtracting household consumption expenditure from household disposable income, plus the change in net equity of households in pension funds. Households include households plus nonprofit institutions serving households. Net saving rates are measured after deducting consumption of fixed capital (depreciation), with respect to assets used in enterprises operated by households, as well as owner-occupied dwellings. The household saving rate is calculated as the ratio of household savings to household disposable income (plus the change in net equity of households in pension funds). Minus sign (–) indicates an excess of expenditures over income]

Country	1995	2000	2002	2003	2004	2005	2006	2007	2008
United States	**5.7**	**3.0**	**3.7**	**3.8**	**3.4**	**1.5**	**2.5**	**1.7**	**2.7**
EU-27 [1]	(NA)	6.6	7.4	7.3	6.6	6.4	5.8	5.5	5.8
Australia [2]	6.4	2.2	–2.7	–3.2	–2.1	–0.2	0.8	(NA)	(NA)
Austria	11.8	9.2	8.0	9.2	9.4	9.7	10.9	11.4	12.0
Belgium	16.4	12.3	12.9	12.2	10.8	10.0	10.9	11.2	11.5
Canada	9.4	4.8	3.5	2.7	3.2	2.2	3.6	2.6	3.8
Chile	(NA)	6.5	6.8	6.4	7.2	7.1	7.7	7.7	(NA)
Czech Republic	10.0	3.3	3.0	2.4	0.5	3.2	4.8	6.3	5.8
Denmark	1.3	–1.9	4.1	4.1	0.7	–1.5	0.4	–1.0	–0.3
Finland	3.9	–0.1	0.6	1.4	2.5	0.7	–1.4	–1.2	–1.0
France	12.7	11.8	13.7	12.5	12.4	11.4	11.4	12.0	11.6
Germany	11.0	9.2	9.9	10.3	10.4	10.5	10.5	10.8	11.2
Greece	(NA)	–6.0	–8.0	–7.3	–7.2	–8.0	–7.3	(NA)	(NA)
Ireland	(NA)	(NA)	5.4	5.4	8.3	5.6	3.8	2.7	4.1
Italy	17.0	8.4	11.2	10.3	10.2	9.9	9.1	8.2	8.6
Japan	(NA)	8.9	5.1	3.9	3.6	3.8	3.6	3.8	(NA)
Korea, South	(NA)	9.3	0.4	5.2	9.2	7.2	5.2	2.9	2.8
Netherlands	14.0	6.7	8.4	7.5	7.3	6.3	6.0	8.1	6.8
Norway	4.8	4.3	8.2	8.9	7.2	10.1	0.1	–1.2	(NA)
Poland	14.6	10.3	8.3	7.8	8.0	7.1	6.8	7.4	(NA)
Russia	(NA)	(NA)	12.8	13.2	11.8	12.0	12.6	(NA)	(NA)
Slovakia	5.2	6.1	3.5	1.2	0.5	1.2	0.5	2.5	1.8
Slovenia	(NA)	7.0	9.9	7.6	9.2	11.1	11.2	10.5	(NA)
Spain	(NA)	5.9	5.6	6.0	4.9	4.7	4.2	3.6	6.1
Sweden	9.5	4.8	9.1	9.0	7.7	6.8	7.8	9.1	12.1
Switzerland	12.7	11.7	10.7	9.4	9.0	10.1	11.4	12.7	(NA)
United Kingdom	6.9	0.1	–0.1	0.4	–1.7	–1.3	–2.9	–4.3	–4.5

NA Not available. [1] See footnote 5, Table 1377 for list of EU-27 countries. [2] Data refer to fiscal year.

Source: Organization for Economic Cooperation and Development (OECD), 2010, *OECD Factbook 2010: Economic, Environmental and Social Statistics*, OECD Publishing (copyright). See also <http://www.oecd-ilibrary.org/content/serial/18147364>.

Table 1363. Insurance and Pensions by Country: 1997 to 2008

Country	Insurance						Pension, [1] 2008		
	Direct gross premiums (percent of GDP)		2007 premiums (millions of U.S. dollars)		Financial assets [2] (millions of U.S. dollars)		Financial assets (millions of U.S. dollars)	Contributions to pension funds (percent of GDP)	Benefits paid by pension funds (percent of GDP)
	1997	2007	Life	Non-life	1997	2007			
United States	**10.1**	**10.8**	**568,983**	**813,994**	**2,709,790**	**5,487,884**	**8,180,856**	**(NA)**	**(NA)**
Australia	8.4	6.4	41,482	25,479	161,211	250,035	902,539	13.5	2.9
Austria	5.3	5.3	9,697	14,064	(NA)	58,070	17,126	0.4	0.3
Belgium	5.7	9.3	30,382	12,655	(NA)	(NA)	[3] 18,152	[3] 0.2	[3] 0.2
Canada	4.1	7.8	62,573	73,496	140,826	478,300	813,991	1.5	1.8
Czech Republic	2.6	3.7	2,668	3,882	2,926	13,017	[3] 8,241	[3] 1.0	[3] 0.3
Denmark	6.3	9.1	18,641	9,822	107,874	(NA)	161,649	0.5	0.6
Finland	3.6	3.3	3,807	4,482	(NA)	61,543	160,678	10.7	9.1
France	9.3	11.4	187,155	125,817	646,258	1,975,928	[3] 27,397	(NA)	(NA)
Germany	6.5	6.7	117,244	163,163	705,704	1,320,298	171,990	0.3	0.1
Greece	1.5	2.2	3,461	3,685	3,351	(NA)	[3] 34	[3] (Z)	–
Iceland	2.6	2.9	47	537	(NA)	(NA)	18,882	7.9	3.8
Ireland	9.0	23.9	52,860	10,374	(NA)	206,033	[3] 118,633	(NA)	(NA)
Italy	4.0	6.7	91,109	56,132	156,926	638,901	[3] 68,686	[3] 0.4	[3] 0.2
Japan	7.9	7.5	270,356	81,052	1,823,927	2,838,015	[3] 874,426	(NA)	(NA)
Korea, South	11.7	11.8	79,382	40,387	116,457	349,512	27,790	0.3	0.4
Luxembourg	26.1	30.9	13,706	1,627	(NA)	(NA)	[3] 512	[3] 0.1	[3] 0.1
Mexico	1.3	1.7	7,711	9,991	(NA)	32,472	112,676	1.2	0.2
Netherlands	8.8	8.3	36,590	28,688	224,644	303,956	[3] 1,058,153	[3] 4.3	[3] 3.6
Norway	4.6	5.1	12,077	7,719	51,063	138,215	[3] 27,385	[3] 0.6	[3] 0.2
Poland	2.4	3.7	9,222	6,590	3,230	29,382	57,927	1.7	(NA)
Slovakia	2.3	3.1	1,154	1,170	(NA)	(NA)	4,510	(NA)	(NA)
Spain	4.8	5.2	31,967	46,451	(NA)	252,282	[3] 108,404	[3] 0.7	[3] 0.3
Sweden	5.3	6.4	15,451	15,604	162,735	319,092	[3] 39,452	(NA)	(NA)
Switzerland	11.6	9.8	23,927	21,577	(NA)	293,976	[3] 504,601	[3] 8.7	[3] 5.4
Turkey	1.0	1.3	1,024	7,385	1,650	3,470	12,682	0.6	(Z)
United Kingdom	11.8	19.2	423,783	133,419	1,126,341	(NA)	[3] 2,186,472	[3] 2.8	[3] 2.8

– Represents zero. NA Not available or not applicable. Z Less than 0.05 percent. [1] All types of plans are included (occupational and personal, mandatory and voluntary) covering both public and private sector workers. Further details can be found at <www.oecd.org/daf/pensions/gps>. [2] Investments by direct insurance companies. [3] 2007 data.

Source: Organization for Economic Cooperation and Development (OECD), 2009, *OECD in Figures 2009*, OECD Publishing (copyright). See also <http://www.sourceoecd.org/vl=11904758/cl=12/nw=1/rpsv/ij/oecdthemes/99980088/v2009n8/s1/p1l>.

U.S. Census Bureau, Statistical Abstract of the United States: 2011

Table 1364. Percent of Women in National Parliaments by Country: 2009

[Compiled on the basis of information provided by National Parliaments as of May 2009]

Country	Lower or single House Election year	Lower or single House Percent women	Upper House or Senate Election year	Upper House or Senate Percent women	Country	Lower or single House Election year	Lower or single House Percent women	Upper House or Senate Election year	Upper House or Senate Percent women
Afghanistan	2005	27.7	2005	21.6	Lebanon	2005	4.7	(X)	(X)
Albania	2005	7.1	(X)	(X)	Liberia	2005	12.5	2005	16.7
Algeria	2007	7.7	2006	2.9	Liechtenstein	2009	24.0	(X)	(X)
Angola	2008	37.3	(X)	(X)	Lithuania	2008	17.7	(X)	(X)
Argentina	2007	40.0	2007	38.9	Luxembourg	2004	23.3	(X)	(X)
Armenia	2007	8.4	(X)	(X)	Macedonia	2008	28.3	(X)	(X)
Australia	2007	26.7	2007	35.5	Malawi	2009	(NA)	(X)	(X)
Austria	2008	27.9	(¹)	24.6	Malaysia	2008	10.8	(¹)	28.8
Azerbaijan	2005	11.4	(X)	(X)	Mali	2007	10.2	(X)	(X)
Bahrain	2006	2.5	2006	25.0	Mauritania	2006	22.1	2007	16.1
Belarus	2008	31.8	2008	33.9	Mauritius	2005	17.1	(X)	(X)
Belgium	2007	35.3	2007	38.0	Mexico	2006	23.2	2006	18.0
Bolivia	2005	16.9	2005	3.7	Mongolia	2008	4.1	(X)	(X)
Bosnia and Herzegovina	2006	11.9	2007	13.3	Montenegro	2009	6.2	(X)	(X)
Botswana	2004	11.1	(X)	(X)	Morocco	2007	10.5	2006	1.1
Brazil	2006	9.0	2006	12.3	Mozambique	2004	34.8	(X)	(X)
Bulgaria	2005	21.7	(X)	(X)	Namibia	2004	26.9	2004	26.9
Burkina Faso	2007	15.3	(X)	(X)	Nepal	2008	33.2	(X)	(X)
Burundi	2005	30.5	2005	34.7	Netherlands	2006	41.3	2007	34.7
Cambodia	2008	16.3	2006	14.8	New Zealand	2008	33.6	(X)	(X)
Cameroon	2007	13.9	(X)	(X)	Nicaragua	2006	18.5	(X)	(X)
Canada	2008	22.1	(¹)	34.4	Nigeria	2007	7.0	2007	8.3
Cape Verde	2006	18.1	(X)	(X)	Norway	2005	36.1	(X)	(X)
Central African Republic	2005	10.5	(X)	(X)	Oman	2007	–	2007	20.0
Chad	2002	5.2	(X)	(X)	Pakistan	2008	22.5	2009	17.0
Chile	2005	15.0	2005	5.3	Panama	2009	8.5	(X)	(X)
China [2]	2008	21.3	(X)	(X)	Paraguay	2008	12.5	2008	15.6
Colombia	2006	8.4	2006	11.8	Peru	2006	27.5	(X)	(X)
Congo (Brazzaville) [3]	2007	7.3	2008	12.9	Philippines	2007	20.5	2007	17.4
Congo (Kinshasa) [3]	2006	8.4	2007	4.6	Poland	2007	20.2	2007	8.0
Cote d'Ivoire	2000	8.9	(X)	(X)	Portugal	2005	28.3	(X)	(X)
Croatia	2007	20.9	(X)	(X)	Qatar	2008	–	(X)	(X)
Cuba	2008	43.2	(X)	(X)	Romania	2008	11.4	2008	5.8
Czech Republic	2006	15.5	2008	17.3	Russia	2007	14.0	(¹)	4.7
Denmark	2007	38.0	(X)	(X)	Rwanda	2008	56.3	2003	34.6
Djibouti	2008	13.8	(X)	(X)	Saudi Arabia	2009	–	(X)	(X)
Ecuador	2009	(NA)	(X)	(X)	Senegal	2007	22.0	2007	40.0
Egypt	2005	1.8	2007	6.8	Serbia	2008	21.6	(X)	(X)
El Salvador	2009	19.0	(X)	(X)	Sierra Leone	2007	13.2	(X)	(X)
Ethiopia	2005	21.9	2005	18.8	Singapore	2006	24.5	(X)	(X)
Finland	2007	41.5	(X)	(X)	Slovakia	2006	19.3	(X)	(X)
France	2007	18.2	2008	21.9	Slovenia	2008	13.3	2007	2.5
Gabon	2009	16.7	2009	17.6	Somalia	2004	5.9	(X)	(X)
Gambia	2002	9.4	(X)	(X)	South Africa [4]	2009	43.5	2009	29.6
Georgia	2008	6.0	(X)	(X)	Spain	2008	36.3	2008	30.0
Germany	2005	32.2	(¹)	21.7	Sri Lanka	2004	5.8	(X)	(X)
Ghana	2004	7.9	(X)	(X)	Sudan	2005	18.1	2005	6.0
Greece	2007	14.7	(X)	(X)	Suriname	2005	25.5	(X)	(X)
Guatemala	2007	12.0	(X)	(X)	Swaziland	2008	13.8	2008	40.0
Guinea-Bissau	2008	10.0	(X)	(X)	Sweden	2006	47.0	(X)	(X)
Guyana	2006	30.0	(X)	(X)	Switzerland	2007	28.5	2007	21.7
Haiti	2006	4.1	2009	(NA)	Syria	2007	12.4	(X)	(X)
Honduras	2005	23.4	(X)	(X)	Tajikistan	2005	17.5	2005	23.5
Hungary	2006	11.1	(X)	(X)	Tanzania	2005	30.4	(X)	(X)
Iceland	2009	42.9	(X)	(X)	Thailand	2007	11.7	2008	16.0
India	2009	10.9	2008	9.5	Timor-Leste	2007	29.2	(X)	(X)
Indonesia	2009	16.6	(X)	(X)	Turkey	2007	9.1	(X)	(X)
Iran	2008	2.8	(X)	(X)	Turkmenistan	2008	16.8	(X)	(X)
Iraq	2005	25.5	(X)	(X)	Uganda	2006	30.7	(X)	(X)
Ireland	2007	13.3	2007	21.7	Ukraine	2007	8.2	(X)	(X)
Israel	2009	17.5	(X)	(X)	United Arab Emirates	2006	22.5	(X)	(X)
Italy	2008	21.3	2008	18.0	United Kingdom	2005	19.5	(¹)	19.7
Japan	2005	9.4	2007	18.2	**United States [5]**	**2008**	**16.8**	**2008**	**15.3**
Jordan	2007	6.4	2007	12.7	Uruguay	2004	12.1	2004	12.9
Kazakhstan	2007	15.9	2008	4.3	Uzbekistan	2004	17.5	2005	15.0
Kenya	2007	9.8	(X)	(X)	Vanuatu	2008	3.8	(X)	(X)
Korea, South	2008	13.7	(X)	(X)	Venezuela	2005	18.6	(X)	(X)
Kuwait	2008	7.7	(X)	(X)	Vietnam	2007	25.8	(X)	(X)
Kyrgyzstan	2007	25.6	(X)	(X)	Yemen	2003	0.3	2001	1.8
Laos	2006	25.2	(X)	(X)	Zambia	2006	15.2	(X)	(X)
Latvia	2006	20.0	(X)	(X)	Zimbabwe	2008	15.2	2008	24.7

– Represents zero. X Not applicable. [1] Term of the chamber is not fixed (i.e., renewals do not take place on the same date, but rather when individual mandates expire). [2] See footnote 4, Table 1331. [3] See footnote 5, Table 1331. [4] The Upper House figures on the distribution of seats do not include the 36 special rotating delegates appointed on an ad hoc basis, and all percentages given are therefore calculated on the basis of the 54 permanent seats. [5] Percent of all voting members of the House.

Source: Inter-Parliamentary Union, Geneva, Switzerland, "Women in National Parliaments," May 2009 (copyright), <http://www.ipu.org/wmn-e/classif.htm>.

Table 1365. Civilian Labor Force, Employment, and Unemployment by Country: 1990 to 2009

[125,840 represents 125,840,000. Data based on U.S. labor force definitions (see source) except that minimum age for population base varies as follows: United States, Canada, France, Sweden, and United Kingdom, 16 years; Australia, Japan, Netherlands, Germany, and Italy (beginning 1993), 15 years; and Italy (prior to 1993), 14 years]

Year	United States	Canada	Australia	Japan	France	Germany [1]	Italy	Netherlands	Sweden	United Kingdom
Civilian labor force (1,000):										
1990	125,840	14,047	8,440	62,990	24,070	29,412	22,670	6,767	4,597	28,766
2000	[2] 142,583	15,637	9,590	66,710	26,591	39,302	23,361	[2] 8,052	4,490	28,962
2005	149,320	17,108	10,529	65,386	27,616	[2] 40,760	24,179	8,459	[2] 4,693	30,137
2008	154,287	17,987	11,254	65,660	28,021	41,542	24,836	8,780	4,875	31,126
2009	154,142	18,098	11,448	65,362	28,331	41,545	24,710	8,846	4,888	31,274
Labor force participation rate: [3]										
1990	66.5	67.4	64.7	62.6	55.5	55.0	47.2	57.0	67.4	64.3
2000	67.1	66.0	64.4	61.7	57.6	56.7	48.1	[2] 63.4	63.7	62.8
2005	66.0	67.4	65.4	59.5	57.4	[2] 57.6	48.7	64.7	[2] 64.8	63.1
2008	66.0	67.9	66.6	59.5	57.1	58.5	49.0	66.2	65.3	63.5
2009	65.4	67.3	66.5	59.3	57.3	58.6	48.4	66.4	64.6	63.3
Civilian employment (1,000):										
1990	118,793	12,964	7,877	61,710	22,075	27,952	21,080	6,251	4,513	26,713
2000	[2] 136,891	14,681	8,989	63,790	24,326	36,236	20,973	[2] 7,813	4,230	27,375
2005	141,730	16,080	9,998	62,910	25,187	[2] 36,185	22,290	8,056	[2] 4,334	28,674
2008	145,362	17,025	10,777	63,250	25,951	38,406	23,144	8,537	4,581	29,346
2009	139,877	16,769	10,809	62,242	25,755	38,324	22,765	8,542	4,486	28,880
Employment-population ratio: [4]										
1990	62.8	62.2	60.4	61.3	50.9	52.3	43.9	52.7	66.1	59.8
2000	64.4	62.0	60.3	59.0	52.7	52.2	43.2	[2] 61.5	60.1	59.4
2005	62.7	63.4	62.1	57.3	52.3	[2] 51.2	44.9	61.6	[2] 59.9	60.0
2008	62.2	64.2	63.8	57.4	52.8	54.1	45.6	64.3	61.4	59.9
2009	59.3	62.3	62.8	56.4	52.1	54.0	44.6	64.1	59.3	58.5
Unemployment rate:										
1990	5.6	7.7	6.7	2.0	8.3	5.0	7.0	7.6	1.8	7.1
2000	4.0	6.1	6.3	4.4	8.5	7.8	10.2	[2] 3.0	5.8	5.5
2005	5.1	6.0	5.0	3.8	8.8	[2] 11.2	7.8	1.0	[2] 7.7	4.9
2008	5.8	5.3	4.2	3.7	7.4	7.5	6.8	2.8	6.0	5.7
2009	9.3	7.3	5.6	4.8	9.1	7.8	7.9	3.4	8.2	7.7
Under 25 years old	17.6	14.0	11.6	8.8	21.6	11.2	25.7	6.7	24.6	19.2
Teenagers [5]	24.3	18.6	16.6	0.1	20.7	11.3	40.4	8.3	35.0	26.7
20 to 24 years old	14.7	11.2	8.2	8.7	20.8	11.1	23.0	5.4	20.0	15.2
25 years old and over	7.9	6.2	4.2	4.4	7.6	7.3	6.5	2.8	5.9	5.6

[1] Unified Germany for 1991 onward. Prior to 1991, data relate to the former West Germany. [2] Break in series. Data not comparable with prior years. [3] Civilian labor force as a percent of the civilian working-age population. Germany and Japan include the institutionalized population as part of the working-age population. [4] Civilian employment as a percent of the civilian working-age population. Germany and Japan include the institutionalized population as part of the working-age population. [5] 16 to 19-year-olds in the United States, Canada, France, Sweden, and the United Kingdom; 15 to 19-year-olds in Australia, Japan, Germany, Italy, and the Netherlands.

Source: U.S. Bureau of Labor Statistics, *International Comparisons of Annual Labor Force Statistics, 10 Countries, 1960–2009*, June 2010. See also <http://www.bls.gov/fls/flscomparelf.htm>.

Table 1366. Unemployment Rates by Country: 2000 to 2009

[Annual averages. The standardized unemployment rates shown here are calculated as the number of unemployed persons as a percentage of the civilian labor force. The unemployed are persons of working age who, in the reference period, are without work, available for work, and have taken specific steps to find work]

Country	2000	2005	2008	2009	Country	2000	2005	2008	2009
OECD, total	**6.2**	**6.8**	**6.0**	**(NA)**					
Euro area [1]	8.5	9.0	7.6	(NA)	Ireland	4.3	4.3	6.0	11.7
					Italy	10.2	7.7	6.7	7.8
United States	**4.0**	**5.1**	**5.8**	**9.3**	Japan	4.7	4.4	4.0	5.1
Australia	6.3	5.0	4.2	5.6	Korea, South	4.4	3.7	3.2	3.7
Austria	3.5	5.1	3.8	4.8	Netherlands	(NA)	6.5	3.9	4.9
Belgium	7.0	8.4	7.0	7.9	New Zealand	6.2	3.8	4.2	6.1
Canada	6.8	6.8	6.1	8.3	Norway	3.5	4.6	2.6	3.2
Czech Republic	8.9	7.9	4.4	6.7	Poland	16.1	17.8	7.1	8.2
Denmark	4.6	5.0	3.4	6.0	Portugal	3.9	7.6	7.6	9.5
Finland	9.8	8.4	6.4	8.2	Spain	13.9	9.2	11.3	18.0
France	(NA)	8.9	7.4	9.1	Sweden	4.7	7.1	6.2	8.3
Germany	7.8	11.1	7.5	7.7	Switzerland	2.5	4.3	3.4	4.2
Hungary	6.4	7.2	7.8	10.0	United Kingdom	5.4	4.8	5.7	7.6

NA Not available. [1] See footnote 3, Table 1353.

Source: Organization for Economic Cooperation and Development (OECD), 2010, "Labour: Labour Force Statistics," Main Economic Indicators database (copyright), <http://dx.doi.org/10.1787/data-00046-en>, accessed May 2010.

U.S. Census Bureau, Statistical Abstract of the United States: 2011

Table 1367. Percent of Persons Not in Education or at Work: 2007

[Represents those persons not in education and either unemployed or not in the labor force]

Country	15 to 19 years old			20 to 24 years old		
	Total	Unemployed	Not in the labor force	Total	Unemployed	Not in the labor force
Australia.............	6.5	3.3	3.2	10.7	3.3	7.4
Belgium.............	5.2	2.2	3.0	15.4	8.5	6.9
Brazil..............	14.7	4.1	10.6	23.4	8.2	15.2
Canada	7.3	2.8	4.5	13.8	5.6	8.2
Czech Republic.......	2.9	1.8	1.1	11.0	4.6	6.4
Denmark	3.9	1.4	2.5	8.2	3.2	5.0
Finland.............	3.6	1.5	2.1	13.3	6.7	6.6
France	5.8	3.4	2.4	15.1	9.7	5.4
Germany	4.2	2.5	1.7	15.3	8.1	7.2
Greece..............	8.5	2.6	5.9	17.7	11.1	6.6
Hungary............	5.0	1.6	3.4	16.9	6.7	10.2
Israel	14.7	4.1	10.6	39.6	7.1	32.5
Italy	10.2	2.9	7.3	22.6	8.1	14.5
Mexico.............	23.2	2.7	20.5	(S)	(S)	(S)
Poland	2.5	1.0	1.5	18.3	10.2	8.1
Portugal.............	8.5	4.3	4.2	15.2	9.2	6.0
Spain..............	10.9	4.3	6.6	17.5	8.4	8.9
Sweden	5.5	2.2	3.3	13.1	6.9	6.2
Switzerland	8.2	1.7	6.5	10.4	5.2	5.2
United States	**6.3**	**2.0**	**4.3**	**16.3**	**5.3**	**11.0**

S Figure does not meet publication standards.

Source: Organization for Economic Cooperation and Development (OECD), 2009, *Education at a Glance 2009: OECD Indicators*, OECD Publishing (copyright). See also <http://dx.doi.org/10.1787/eag-2009-en>.

Table 1368. Female Labor Force Participation Rates by Country: 1980 to 2008

[In percent. Female labor force of all ages divided by female population 15–64 years old]

Country	1980	1990	2000	2008	Country	1980	1990	2000	2008
Australia..............	52.5	62.3	66.1	71.1	Korea, South	48.6	51.8	54.9	58.7
Austria...............	(NA)	(NA)	62.2	69.6	Luxembourg..........	(NA)	42.7	52.0	59.5
Belgium..............	(NA)	46.3	56.9	60.1	Mexico..............	(NA)	(NA)	42.2	47.5
Canada	58.0	69.0	71.0	75.8	Netherlands..........	36.3	53.1	65.6	73.2
Czech Republic	(X)	(X)	64.2	61.7	New Zealand	(NA)	63.9	68.3	74.2
Denmark	(NA)	78.6	76.3	78.1	Norway..............	64.2	72.6	77.5	78.9
Finland..............	70.2	73.9	72.3	74.6	Poland..............	(NA)	(NA)	61.1	57.7
France	56.0	57.6	61.9	65.5	Portugal.............	54.2	61.3	67.5	73.0
Germany [1]	52.8	56.1	63.7	70.6	Slovakia.............	(X)	(X)	63.3	61.6
Greece..............	(NA)	43.6	50.5	55.7	Spain	33.8	42.6	53.2	64.5
Hungary.............	(NA)	(NA)	52.9	55.4	Sweden	75.9	83.3	77.3	79.4
Iceland..............	(NA)	(NA)	85.7	85.4	Switzerland	(NA)	(NA)	73.3	78.5
Ireland	(NA)	43.3	56.2	63.8	Turkey	(NA)	36.7	29.0	27.4
Italy	39.2	44.6	46.8	52.1	United Kingdom.......	(NA)	68.2	69.8	71.5
Japan...............	54.9	60.4	63.8	67.3	**United States**	**61.5**	**69.7**	**72.7**	**72.1**

NA Not available. X Not applicable. [1] Prior to 1991, data are for former West Germany.

Source: Organization for Economic Cooperation and Development (OECD), 2010, "Labour Market Statistics: Labour Force Statistics by Sex and Age: Indicators," OECD Employment and Labour Market Statistics database (copyright), <http://dx.doi.org/10.1787/data-00310-en>, accessed May 2010.

Table 1369. Civilian Employment-Population Ratio: 1990 to 2009

[Civilian employment as a percent of the civilian working-age population. See headnote, Table 1365]

Country	Women					Men				
	1990	1995	2000	2008	2009	1990	1995	2000	2008	2009
United States [1]	**54.3**	**55.6**	**57.5**	**56.2**	**54.4**	**72.0**	**70.8**	**71.9**	**68.5**	**64.5**
Canada	54.1	52.7	56.0	59.8	58.8	70.6	66.1	68.2	68.8	66.0
Australia..............	49.5	50.5	52.5	57.1	56.8	71.4	68.2	68.4	70.6	69.0
Japan...............	48.0	47.7	46.4	45.9	45.7	75.4	75.0	72.5	69.6	68.0
France	41.5	43.4	45.9	47.5	47.2	61.4	57.9	60.1	58.8	57.6
Germany [1,2,3,4]	40.5	42.7	44.4	47.8	48.3	65.6	63.1	60.6	60.8	60.2
Italy [1]	29.2	29.1	31.6	35.3	34.7	60.0	56.2	55.8	56.9	55.4
Netherlands [1,3,4]	39.4	44.4	52.0	57.7	57.9	66.5	66.7	71.4	71.2	70.5
Sweden [4]	61.8	54.7	56.1	57.4	55.8	70.6	62.0	64.2	65.5	62.8
United Kingdom...........	50.3	49.8	52.5	53.7	53.1	70.0	64.7	66.9	66.4	64.2

[1] Break in series between 1990 and 1995. [2] Unified Germany for 1991 onward. Prior to 1991, data relate to the former West Germany. [3] Break in series between 1995 and 2000. [4] Break in series between 2000 and 2008.

Source: U.S. Bureau of Labor Statistics, *International Comparisons of Annual Labor Force Adjusted to U.S. Concepts, 10 Countries, 1970–2009*, June 2010. See also <http://www.bls.gov/fls/flscomparelf.htm>.

Table 1370. Civilian Employment by Industry and Country: 2000 and 2009

[136,891 represents 136,891,000. Civilian employment approximating U.S. concepts. See headnote, Table 1365]

Industry	United States [1,2]	Canada [1]	Australia	Japan	France	Germany [2]	Italy	Sweden [3]	United Kingdom
TOTAL EMPLOYMENT (1,000)									
2000, total	**136,891**	**14,681**	**8,989**	**63,790**	**24,326**	**36,236**	**20,973**	**4,230**	**27,375**
Agriculture, forestry, fishing [3]	2,464	481	442	3,070	904	952	1,120	122	419
Industry [4]	30,050	3,216	1,856	19,710	5,219	11,898	6,634	1,000	6,660
Manufacturing	19,644	2,247	1,083	13,180	4,087	8,647	4,944	762	4,617
Services [5]	104,377	10,984	6,691	41,010	18,203	23,386	13,219	3,108	20,296
2009, total	**139,877**	**16,769**	**10,809**	**62,242**	**25,755**	**38,324**	**22,765**	**4,486**	**28,880**
Agriculture, forestry, fishing [3]	2,103	383	360	2,480	(NA)	814	846	97	464
Industry [4]	24,611	3,198	2,150	15,880	(NA)	10,914	6,440	884	5,481
Manufacturing	14,202	1,789	1,005	10,710	(NA)	8,338	4,446	585	3,064
Services [5]	113,163	13,188	8,299	43,882	(NA)	26,596	15,479	3,505	22,935
PERCENT DISTRIBUTION [6]									
2000, total	**100.0**	**100.0**	**100.0**	**100.0**	**100.0**	**100.0**	**100.0**	**100.0**	**100.0**
Agriculture, forestry, fishing [3]	1.8	3.3	4.9	4.8	3.7	2.6	5.3	2.9	1.5
Industry [4]	22.0	21.9	20.6	30.9	21.5	32.8	31.6	23.6	24.3
Manufacturing	14.4	15.3	12.0	20.7	16.8	23.9	23.6	18.0	16.9
Services [5]	76.2	74.8	74.4	64.3	74.8	64.5	63.0	73.5	74.1
2009, total	**100.0**	**100.0**	**100.0**	**100.0**	**100.0**	**100.0**	**100.0**	**100.0**	**100.0**
Agriculture, forestry, fishing [3]	1.5	2.3	3.3	4.0	(NA)	2.1	3.7	2.2	1.6
Industry [4]	17.6	19.1	19.9	25.5	(NA)	28.5	28.3	19.7	19.0
Manufacturing	10.2	10.7	9.3	17.2	(NA)	21.8	19.5	13.0	10.6
Services [5]	80.9	78.6	76.8	70.5	(NA)	69.4	68.0	78.1	79.4

NA Not available. [1] Data for the United States and Canada are based on the 2002 North American Industry Classification System (NAICS). [2] Break in series between 2000 and 2009. [3] Includes hunting. [4] Includes manufacturing, mining, and construction. [5] Transportation, communication, public utilities, trade, finance, public administration, private household services, and miscellaneous services. [6] Civilian employment as a percent of the civilian working-age population.

Source: U.S. Bureau of Labor Statistics, *International Comparisons of Annual Labor Force Statistics, 10 Countries, 1960–2009*, June 2010. See also <http://www.bls.gov/fls/flscomparelf.htm>.

Table 1371. Educational Performance: 2006 and 2007

[Tertiary-type A includes education leading to a BA, Master's, or equivalent degree, and advanced research programs. Performance figures were gathered from the Program for International Student Assessment (PISA), an internationally standardized assessment jointly developed by participating countries, which takes place in 3-year cycles. To implement PISA, each of the participating countries selects a nationally representative sample of 15-year-olds, regardless of grade level. Tests are typically administered to between 4,500 and 10,000 students in each country]

Country	Student performance on the combined reading, scientific, and mathematical literacy scales, 2006			Educational attainment of adult population and current graduation rates, 2007 (percent)	
	Mean score on the combined reading literacy scale [1]	Mean score on the mathematical literacy scale [2]	Mean score on the scientific literacy scale [3]	Upper secondary or higher attainment (25 to 64 years old) [4]	Tertiary-type A attainment (25 to 64 years old)
Australia	513	520	527	68.2	33.7
Austria	490	505	511	80.1	17.6
Canada	527	527	534	86.6	48.3
Czech Republic	483	510	513	90.5	[5] 13.7
Finland	547	548	563	80.5	36.4
France	488	496	495	68.7	26.8
Germany	495	504	516	84.4	24.3
Greece	460	459	473	59.6	22.7
Italy	469	462	475	52.3	13.6
Japan	498	523	531	(NA)	41.0
Korea	556	547	522	77.9	34.6
Luxembourg	479	490	486	65.7	26.5
Mexico	410	406	410	33.3	15.9
Poland	508	495	498	86.3	[5] 18.7
Spain	461	480	488	50.7	29.0
Sweden	507	502	503	84.6	31.3
Switzerland	499	530	512	86.0	31.3
United Kingdom	495	495	515	68.3	31.8
United States	**(NA)**	**474**	**489**	**87.9**	**40.3**
OECD mean	492	498	500	70.1	27.5

NA Not available. [1] Reading literacy is understanding, using, and reflecting on written texts in order to achieve one's goals, to develop one's knowledge and potential, and to participate in society. [2] Mathematical literacy is an individual's capacity to identify and understand the role that mathematics plays in the world, to make well-founded judgements, and to use and engage with mathematics in ways that meet the needs of that individual's life. [3] Scientific literacy is the capacity to use scientific knowledge to identify questions and to draw evidence-based conclusions in order to understand and help make decisions about the natural world and the changes made to it through human activity. [4] Excluding ISCED 3C short programs. [5] Includes all types of tertiary level degrees.

Source: Organization for Economic Cooperation and Development (OECD), 2006, *PISA 2006: Science Competencies for Tomorrow's World*; 2009, *Education at a Glance 2009: OECD indicators*, OECD Publishing (copyright). See also <www.pisa.oecd.org> and <http://dx.doi.org/10.1787/eag-2009-en>, respectively.

Table 1372. World Supply and Utilization of Major Crops, Livestock, and Products: 1995 to 2009

[In millions of units (214.3 represents 214,300,000). For major crops, data ending in year shown. For meat and dairy, calendar year data, selected countries]

Commodity	1995	2000	2003	2004	2005	2006	2007	2008	2009 [1]
Wheat:									
Area (hectares)	214.3	215.4	214.5	209.6	217.3	219.3	212.2	218.0	225.0
Production (metric tons)	523.1	585.8	567.9	554.1	625.7	619.9	595.7	610.5	682.7
Exports (metric tons) [2]	101.5	113.4	105.7	108.7	111.7	116.6	111.6	117.2	142.9
Consumption (metric tons) [3]	545.0	585.1	604.4	588.7	607.4	622.7	615.6	617.0	639.8
Ending stocks (metric tons) [4]	160.2	208.5	166.6	132.0	150.2	147.5	127.6	121.1	164.0
Coarse grains:									
Area (hectares)	323.6	299.7	292.0	306.1	300.1	300.8	305.1	318.0	312.5
Production (metric tons)	869.7	877.7	874.6	915.6	1,014.8	978.8	986.2	1,077.9	1,101.6
Exports (metric tons) [2]	98.6	104.9	102.1	103.2	100.9	107.1	117.6	127.1	112.0
Consumption (metric tons) [3]	858.8	882.3	902.4	944.7	977.7	992.8	1,012.1	1,056.0	1,072.5
Ending stocks (metric tons) [4]	190.8	232.8	170.7	141.6	178.7	164.7	138.7	160.5	189.6
Rice, milled:									
Area (hectares)	147.4	155.3	146.4	148.9	151.3	153.3	154.1	155.1	156.6
Production (metric tons)	363.6	408.9	379.0	392.6	401.8	418.6	420.6	434.4	447.3
Exports (metric tons) [2]	20.7	22.8	28.7	27.4	28.3	29.7	31.5	31.2	28.6
Consumption (metric tons) [3]	365.2	399.7	408.8	414.7	409.5	416.0	421.7	428.5	434.9
Ending stocks (metric tons) [4]	118.3	143.5	103.2	81.1	73.4	76.0	75.1	81.0	93.3
Total grains: [5]									
Area (hectares)	685.3	670.4	652.9	664.7	668.7	673.4	671.5	691.1	694.1
Production (metric tons)	1,756.4	1,872.4	1,821.5	1,862.3	2,042.3	2,017.3	2,002.6	2,122.7	2,231.6
Exports (metric tons) [2]	220.8	241.1	236.5	239.3	240.8	253.4	260.7	275.6	283.5
Consumption (metric tons) [3]	1,769.0	1,867.2	1,915.6	1,948.1	1,994.7	2,031.4	2,049.4	2,101.5	2,147.2
Ending stocks (metric tons) [4]	469.3	584.9	440.5	354.6	402.3	388.1	341.4	362.6	446.9
Oilseeds:									
Crush (metric tons)	238.3	246.3	269.9	279.5	302.9	318.8	328.3	338.8	340.0
Production (metric tons)	299.5	304.3	331.7	335.9	381.5	391.5	404.2	391.8	395.1
Exports (metric tons)	47.5	59.2	69.7	66.8	74.4	75.8	83.4	92.5	94.0
Ending stocks (metric tons)	28.1	38.2	48.8	45.0	57.3	64.6	73.2	61.7	54.3
Meals: [6]									
Production (metric tons)	166.2	167.9	186.0	190.7	207.1	216.5	224.2	231.1	230.1
Exports (metric tons)	61.5	46.7	53.8	58.4	61.5	66.0	68.2	71.2	68.4
Oils: [7]									
Production (metric tons)	73.4	86.0	96.1	102.8	111.7	118.7	121.5	128.0	132.1
Exports (metric tons)	27.3	28.7	36.1	39.0	42.6	47.6	48.9	53.9	55.3
Cotton:									
Area (hectares)	32.2	32.3	30.8	32.3	35.7	34.7	34.7	32.9	30.7
Production (bales) [8]	85.9	87.9	91.0	96.8	121.5	116.7	122.0	119.9	107.5
Exports (bales) [8]	28.4	27.2	30.5	33.2	35.0	44.6	37.3	38.5	30.2
Consumption (bales) [8]	84.4	90.5	97.6	97.2	107.8	115.1	122.0	120.9	107.5
Ending stocks (bales) [8]	29.9	51.1	47.6	48.1	60.6	62.4	63.1	62.7	62.4
Beef and Pork:									
Production (metric tons)	124.2	138.8	144.9	147.5	150.7	153.6	152.9	156.6	157.0
Consumption (metric tons)	123.2	138.5	144.8	147.0	149.9	152.6	152.4	155.8	156.1
Exports (metric tons) [2]	7.6	9.0	10.7	11.4	12.3	12.7	12.7	13.6	12.6
Broilers and Turkeys:									
Production (metric tons)	43.6	57.9	63.1	64.7	68.1	69.3	73.4	76.7	76.8
Consumption (metric tons)	43.1	57.4	62.6	63.9	67.4	69.1	73.1	75.8	76.1
Exports (metric tons) [2]	5.0	5.3	6.5	6.6	7.4	7.1	8.0	9.1	8.7
Dairy:									
Milk production (metric tons)	(NA)	389.4	409.9	415.9	421.7	428.1	436.8	435.0	432.5

NA Not available. [1] Forecast for crops, preliminary for meat and dairy. [2] Excludes intra-EU (European Union) trade but includes intra-FSU (Former Soviet Union) trade. [3] Where stocks data are not available, consumption includes stock changes.
[4] Stocks data are based on differing marketing years and do not represent levels at a given date. Data not available for all countries.
[5] Wheat, coarse grains, and rice. [6] Includes the following types of meals: copra, cottonseed, fishmeal, palm kernel, rapeseed, sunflower, soybean, and peanut. [7] Includes the following types of oils: coconut, cottonseed, olive, palm, palm kernel, peanut, sunflower, rapeseed, and soybean. [8] 480-pound bales.

Source: U.S. Department of Agriculture, Economic Research Service, "Agricultural Outlook: Statistical Indicators," February 2010, <http://www.ers.usda.gov/publications/agoutlook/aotables/>.

Table 1373. World Crop Production Summary: 2008 to 2010

[In millions of metric tons, (683.2 represents 683,200,000), except as indicated]

Country	Wheat 2008–2009	Wheat 2009–2010, prel.	Coarse grains 2008–2009	Coarse grains 2009–2010, prel.	Rice (milled) 2008–2009	Rice (milled) 2009–2010, prel.	Oilseeds [1] 2008–2009	Oilseeds [1] 2009–2010, prel.	Cotton 2008–2009	Cotton 2009–2010, prel.
World	**683.2**	**680.0**	**1,109.7**	**1,103.7**	**448.0**	**440.6**	**397.2**	**440.0**	**107.5**	**102.9**
United States	**68.0**	**60.3**	**325.9**	**349.2**	**6.4**	**6.9**	**89.0**	**98.9**	**12.8**	**12.2**
Canada	28.6	26.5	27.2	22.4	(²)	(²)	16.1	15.4	(²)	(²)
Mexico	4.0	4.3	32.3	28.4	0.2	0.2	0.7	0.6	0.6	0.4
EU-27 [3]	151.0	138.9	161.6	151.4	1.6	2.0	27.2	29.8	1.2	1.0
Russia	63.7	61.7	40.7	31.8	0.5	0.6	8.8	8.0	(²)	(²)
Ukraine	25.9	20.9	26.2	24.1	0.1	0.1	10.7	9.5	(²)	(²)
China	112.5	114.5	172.7	161.4	134.3	137.0	58.1	57.5	36.7	32.5
India	78.6	80.7	39.6	34.4	99.2	87.5	33.4	31.7	22.6	23.5
Indonesia	(²)	(²)	8.7	8.3	38.3	38.8	9.1	9.4	–	–
Pakistan	21.0	24.0	3.6	3.6	6.7	6.5	5.0	5.3	9.0	9.9
Thailand	(²)	(²)	4.6	4.2	19.9	20.3	0.7	0.6	–	–
Argentina	10.1	9.6	19.1	28.3	0.9	0.9	36.0	57.4	0.6	0.8
Brazil	5.9	4.9	53.6	55.5	8.6	7.8	60.3	71.5	5.5	5.8
Australia	21.4	22.5	12.3	11.6	–	0.1	2.4	2.6	1.5	1.6
South Africa	2.1	1.9	13.1	14.5	(²)	(²)	1.5	1.2	–	–
Turkey	16.8	18.0	10.4	10.6	0.4	0.4	1.6	1.5	1.9	1.8
All others	73.6	91.3	158.2	164.1	131.0	131.4	36.3	39.9	15.0	13.4

– Represents zero. [1] Includes soybean, cottonseed, peanut (in shell), sunflower seed, rapeseed for individual countries. Copra and palm kernel are added to world totals. [2] Indicates no reported or insignificant production. [3] See footnote 5, Table 1377.

Source: U.S. Department of Agriculture, Foreign Agricultural Service, *World Agricultural Production*, June 2010. See also <http://www.fas.usda.gov/wap_arc.asp>.

Table 1374. Wheat, Rice, and Corn—Exports and Imports of Leading Countries: 2000 to 2009

[In thousands of metric tons (28,027 represents 28,027,000). Wheat data are for trade year beginning in July of year shown; rice data are for calendar year; corn data are for trade year beginning in October of year shown. Countries listed are the ten leading exporters or importers in 2009]

Leading exporters	Exports 2000	Exports 2005	Exports 2009 [1]	Leading importers	Imports 2000	Imports 2005	Imports 2009 [1]
WHEAT				**WHEAT**			
United States	**28,027**	**27,252**	**22,500**	Egypt	6,050	7,771	8,800
EU [2]	15,675	15,701	19,000	Brazil	7,453	5,823	6,500
Canada	17,351	15,633	18,500	EU [2]	3,536	6,758	6,500
Russia	696	10,514	18,000	Indonesia	4,069	4,981	5,500
Australia	16,682	15,211	14,500	Algeria	5,600	5,476	5,300
Ukraine	78	6,461	9,000	Japan	5,885	5,469	5,300
Kazakhstan	3,972	3,817	7,500	Iraq	3,200	4,996	4,000
Argentina	11,396	8,216	4,500	Korea, South	3,127	3,884	4,000
Turkey	1,601	3,208	2,600	Iran	6,245	1,105	3,500
Mexico	705	533	1,200	Nigeria	1,913	3,678	3,500
RICE				**RICE**			
Thailand	7,521	7,376	10,000	Philippines	1,410	1,622	3,000
Vietnam	3,528	4,705	5,750	Nigeria	1,250	1,650	1,800
Pakistan	2,429	3,664	3,800	Iran	765	1,500	1,700
United States	**2,590**	**3,661**	**3,198**	EU [2]	1,310	1,124	1,350
India	1,685	4,688	2,000	Iraq	959	1,306	1,100
China [3]	1,847	1,216	850	Malaysia	596	751	1,070
Burma	670	47	800	Saudi Arabia	992	1,357	1,049
Cambodia	–	350	800	South Africa	523	725	885
Uruguay	736	834	750	Cote d'Ivoire	496	775	860
Argentina	381	485	600	Brazil	663	750	800
CORN				**CORN**			
United States	**48,329**	**56,084**	**48,000**	Japan	16,340	16,617	16,300
Argentina	12,229	10,707	12,000	Mexico	6,017	6,787	9,500
Brazil	3,741	2,826	8,000	Korea, South	8,728	8,483	7,500
Ukraine	397	2,464	5,000	Taiwan [3]	4,924	4,533	4,600
South Africa	1,415	1,406	2,500	Egypt	5,268	4,397	4,200
Serbia	(X)	(X)	2,000	Colombia	1,857	3,151	3,300
EU [2]	585	449	1,500	Iran	1,265	2,300	2,900
India	92	497	1,500	Malaysia	2,588	2,517	2,800
Paraguay	386	1,314	1,000	EU [2]	3,689	2,634	2,500
Thailand	407	121	750	Algeria	1,500	2,061	2,100

– Represents or rounds to zero. X Not applicable. [1] Estimates. [2] European Union (EU) has been updated to EU-27 for 1999–2008, but 1995–98 remains EU-15 data. EU-15: Austria, Belgium, Denmark, Finland, France, Germany, Greece, Ireland, Italy, Luxembourg, Netherlands, Portugal, Spain, Sweden, and United Kingdom. EU-25 added: Poland, Czech Republic, Hungary, Slovakia, Slovenia, Latvia, Lithuania, Estonia, Cyprus, and Malta. EU-27 added: Romania, Bulgaria. [3] See footnote 4, Table 1331.

Source: U.S. Department of Agriculture, Economic Research Service, unpublished data from the PS&D (Production, Supply, and Distribution) database.

Table 1375. Fisheries—Commercial Catch by Country: 1990 to 2007

[In thousands of metric tons, live weight (97,852 represents 97,852,000). Catch of fish, crustaceans, mollusks. Includes aquaculture (the farming of aquatic organisms), but not marine mammals and aquatic plants]

Country	1990	2000	2005	2007	Country	1990	2000	2005	2007
World [1]	**97,852**	**130,957**	**142,691**	**140,393**	Russia	7,604	4,048	3,312	3,560
					Philippines	2,209	2,291	2,803	3,209
China [2]	31,136	41,568	49,469	46,079	Norway	1,754	3,191	3,055	3,209
India	3,800	5,609	6,653	7,308	Burma	743	1,169	2,217	2,840
Peru	6,874	10,665	9,415	7,250	Korea, South	2,843	2,118	2,076	2,464
Indonesia	3,022	4,909	5,893	6,330	Bangladesh	846	1,661	2,216	2,440
United States [3]	**5,871**	**5,174**	**5,385**	**5,294**	Malaysia	1,005	1,441	1,390	1,564
Japan	10,361	5,751	4,836	4,977	Mexico	1,383	1,369	1,438	1,496
Chile	5,195	4,692	5,027	4,636	Taiwan [2]	1,444	1,338	1,322	1,490
Vietnam	939	1,949	3,367	4,278	Iceland	1,508	1,986	1,673	1,404
Thailand	2,790	3,736	4,118	3,859	Canada	1,685	1,125	1,235	1,175

[1] Includes other countries not shown separately. [2] See footnote 4, Table 1331. [3] The weight of clams, oysters, scallops, and other mollusks includes the shell weight.

Source: U.S. National Oceanic and Atmospheric Administration, National Marine Fisheries Service, *Fisheries of the United States*, annual. Data from Food and Agriculture Organization of the United Nations, Rome, Italy.

Table 1376. Meat Production by Type and Country: 2008 and 2009

[In thousands of metric tons (58,105 represents 58,105,000). Carcass weight basis for beef, veal, and pork. Broiler (chicken, 16-week-old) weight based on ready-to-cook equivalent]

Country	Beef and veal [1] 2008	Beef and veal [1] 2009, prel.	Country	Pork 2008	Pork 2009, prel.	Country	Broiler meat [2] 2008	Broiler meat [2] 2009, prel.
World [3]	**58,105**	**57,017**	**World** [3]	**98,528**	**100,780**	**World** [3]	**71,482**	**71,760**
United States	**12,163**	**11,889**	China [4]	46,205	48,890	**United States**	**16,561**	**15,935**
Brazil	9,024	8,935	European Union [5]	22,596	22,060	China [4]	11,840	12,100
European Union [5]	8,090	7,970	**United States**	**10,599**	**10,439**	Brazil	11,033	11,023
China [4]	6,132	5,764	Brazil	3,015	3,130	European Union [5]	8,594	8,660
Argentina	3,150	3,400	Russia	2,060	2,200	Mexico	2,853	2,789
India	2,525	2,610	Vietnam	1,850	1,850	India	2,490	2,550
Australia	2,159	2,100	Canada	1,786	1,790	Russia	1,550	1,772
Mexico	1,667	1,700	Japan	1,249	1,310	Iran	1,450	1,525
Russia	1,315	1,285	Philippines	1,225	1,225	Argentina	1,430	1,500
Canada	1,288	1,245	Mexico	1,161	1,162	Japan	1,255	1,255
Pakistan	1,168	1,226	Korea, South	1,056	1,062	Thailand	1,170	1,200

[1] May include meat of other bovines. [2] Excludes chicken paws. [3] Includes other countries not shown separately. [4] See footnote 4, Table 1331. [5] See footnote 5, Table 1377.

Source: U.S. Department of Agriculture, Foreign Agricultural Service, *Livestock and Poultry: World Markets and Trade*, annual. See also <http://www.fas.usda.gov/currwmt.asp>.

Table 1377. Meat Consumption by Type and Country: 2008 to 2009

[In thousands of metric tons (57,452 represents (57,452,000). Carcass weight basis for beef, veal, and pork. Broiler (chicken, 16-week-old) weight based on ready-to-cook equivalent]

Country	Beef and veal [1] 2008	Beef and veal [1] 2009 [3]	Country	Pork 2008	Pork 2009 [3]	Country	Broiler [2] 2008	Broiler [2] 2009 [3]
World	**57,452**	**56,365**	**World**	**98,356**	**100,542**	**World**	**70,770**	**71,065**
United States	**12,452**	**12,268**	China [4]	46,413	48,732	**United States**	**13,428**	**12,933**
European Union [5]	8,352	8,317	European Union [5]	21,024	20,683	China [4]	11,954	12,210
Brazil	7,252	7,374	**United States**	**8,806**	**8,995**	European Union [5]	8,564	8,589
China [4]	6,080	5,746	Russia	3,112	3,044	Brazil	7,792	7,802
Argentina	2,732	2,749	Japan	2,486	2,467	Mexico	3,281	3,272
Russia	2,441	2,172	Brazil	2,390	2,423	Russia	2,695	2,700
India [6]	1,853	2,020	Vietnam	1,880	1,876	India	2,489	2,549
Mexico	2,033	1,971	Mexico	1,605	1,770	Japan	1,926	1,951
Pakistan	1,174	1,230	Korea, South	1,519	1,480	Iran	1,460	1,536
Japan	1,173	1,210	Philippines	1,270	1,283	South Africa	1,341	1,371
Canada	1,035	1,010	Taiwan [4]	945	968	Argentina	1,270	1,327
Other countries	10,875	10,298	Other countries	6,906	6,821	Other countries	14,570	14,825

[1] May include meat of other bovines. [2] Excludes chicken paws. [3] Preliminary data. [4] See footnote 4, Table 1331.
[5] European Union-27: Austria, Belgium, Bulgaria, Cyprus, Czech Republic, Denmark, Estonia, Finland, France, Germany, Greece, Hungary, Ireland, Italy, Latvia, Lithuania, Luxembourg, Malta, Netherlands, Poland, Portugal, Romania, Slovakia, Slovenia, Spain, Sweden, and United Kingdom. [6] Includes buffalo.

Source: U.S. Department of Agriculture, Foreign Agricultural Service, *Livestock and Poultry: World Markets and Trade*, annual. See also <http://www.fas.usda.gov/currwmt.asp>.

Table 1378. EU and U.S. Organic Land, Farm Sector, and Sales: 2007 and 2008

[EU numbers for land and farms include those certified organic and in-conversion; U.S. numbers include only certified organic farms and land. "Certified organic" means that agricultural products have been grown and processed according to USDA's national organic standards and certified by USDA-accredited state and private certification organizations. 1 hectare = 2.47 acres]

Country	2007			2008			
	Total organic land (hectares)	Organic farms (number)	Farmland under organic production (percent)	Total organic land (hectares)	Organic farms (number)	Farmland under organic production (percent)	Retail sales (million Euros) [1]
United States	1,736,825	11,352	(NA)	1,949,781	12,941	0.6	16,529
Austria	372,026	19,997	13.4	491,825	19,961	17.4	810
Belgium	32,628	821	2.4	35,721	901	2.6	305
Denmark	145,393	2,835	5.5	150,104	2,753	4.6	724
Finland.	148,760	4,406	6.5	150,374	3,991	6.6	74
France	557,133	11,978	1.9	580,956	13,298	2.1	2,591
Germany	865,336	18,703	5.1	907,786	19,813	5.4	5,850
Greece.	278,397	23,769	3.3	317,824	24,057	3.8	58
Ireland	41,122	1,134	1.0	44,751	1,220	1.1	104
Italy	1,150,253	45,231	9.1	1,002,414	44,371	7.9	1,970
Luxembourg.	3,380	81	2.6	3,535	85	2.7	41
Netherlands	47,019	1,374	2.5	50,434	1,402	2.6	537
Portugal	233,475	1,949	6.4	229,717	1,949	6.6	70
Spain	988,323	18,226	3.9	1,129,844	21,291	4.5	350
Sweden	248,104	3,028	8.0	336,439	3,686	10.8	623
United Kingdom.	660,200	5,506	4.2	737,631	5,383	4.6	2,494
EU-15 [2]	5,771,549	159,038	(NA)	6,169,355	164,161	(NA)	16,601

NA Not available. [1] U.S. dollars converted using average exchange rate for 2008, 0.78 euro per dollar. [2] European Union-15: Austria, Belgium, Denmark, Finland, France, Germany, Greece, Ireland, Italy, Luxembourg, Netherlands, Portugal, Spain, Sweden, and United Kingdom.

Source: U.S. Department of Agriculture, Economic Research Service, "Market-Led Versus Government-Facilitated Growth: Development of the U.S. and EU Organic Agricultural Sectors," August 2005, and unpublished data. See also <http://www.ers.usda.gov/Publications/WRS0505/>.

Table 1379. World Production of Major Mineral Commodities: 1990 to 2009

[5,347 represents 5,347,000,000]

Commodity	Unit	1990	2000	2008	2009, prel.	Leading producers, 2008
MINERAL FUELS						
Coal.	Mil. short tons	5,347	4,893	7,271	(NA)	China, [3] United States, India
Dry natural gas	Tril. cu. ft.	73.8	88.4	109.8	(NA)	Russia, United States, Canada
Natural gas plant liquids [1]	Mil. barrels [2]	1,694	2,359	2,908	2,946	United States, Saudi Arabia, Canada
Petroleum, crude	Mil. barrels [2]	22,079	25,001	26,883	26,370	Russia, Saudi Arabia, United States
NONMETALLIC MINERALS						
Cement, hydraulic	Mil. metric tons.	1,160	1,600	2,840	2,800	China, [3] India, United States
						Russia, Botswana,
Diamond, gem and industrial. . .	Mil. carats	111	(NA)	159	162	Congo (Kinshasa),[4] Australia
Nitrogen in ammonia	Mil. metric tons.	97.5	109.0	133.0	133.0	China, [3] India, Russia
						China, [3] United States, Morocco,
Phosphate rock, marketable . . .	Mil. metric tons. . . .	162	133	161	158	Western Sahara
Potash, marketable	Mil. metric tons.	28.0	25.3	35.0	25.0	Canada, Russia, Belarus
Salt	Mil. metric tons.	183	214	258	260	China, [3] United States, Germany
Sulfur, elemental basis	Mil. metric tons.	58.0	57.2	69.0	70.0	United States, Canada, China [3]
METALS						
Aluminum [5]	Mil. metric tons.	19.3	24.0	39.0	37.0	China, [3] Russia, Canada
Bauxite, gross weight	Mil. metric tons.	113	135	205	200	Australia, China, [3] Brazil
Chromite, gross weight . . .	1,000 metric tons. . .	13,200	14,400	23,800	23,000	South Africa, India, Kazakhstan
Copper, metal content [6]	1,000 metric tons. . .	8,950	13,200	15,400	15,800	Chile, United States, Peru
Gold, metal content	Metric tons.	2,180	2,550	2,260	2,350	China, [3] United States, Australia
Iron ore, gross weight [7]	Mil. metric tons.	983	1,060	2,220	2,300	China, [3] Brazil, Australia
Lead, metal content [6].	1,000 metric tons. . .	3,370	3,100	3,840	3,900	China, [3] Australia, United States
Nickel, metal content [6].	1,000 metric tons. . .	974	1,250	1,600	1,430	Russia, Canada, Australia
Tin, metal content [6]	1,000 metric tons. . .	220	238	299	307	China, [3] Indonesia, Peru

NA Not available. [1] Excludes China. [2] 42-gallon barrels. [3] See footnote 4, Table 1331. [4] See footnote 5, Table 1331. [5] Unalloyed ingot metal. [6] Mine output. [7] Includes iron ore concentrates and iron ore agglomerates.

Source: Mineral fuels, U.S. Energy Information Administration, International Energy Statistics database, <http://tonto.eia.doe.gov/cfapps/ipdbproject/IEDIndex3.cfm>, accessed July 2010; nonmetallic minerals and metals, 1990, U.S. Bureau of Mines, thereafter, U.S. Geological Survey, *Minerals Yearbook*; *Annual Reports*; and *Mineral Commodity Summaries*, 2009.

Table 1380. World Primary Energy Production by Region and Type: 1980 to 2007

[In quadrillion Btu (287.6 represents 287,600,000,000,000,000). Btu = British thermal unit. For Btu conversion factors, see source]

Region and type	1980	1990	1995	2000	2002	2003	2004	2005	2006	2007 [1]
World total [2]	**287.6**	**350.0**	**363.5**	**394.4**	**406.0**	**421.3**	**444.9**	**459.2**	**467.7**	**475.1**
North America	83.2	92.0	96.2	99.0	100.1	98.6	99.3	98.8	100.6	100.8
United States	**67.2**	**70.9**	**71.3**	**71.5**	**70.9**	**70.3**	**70.4**	**69.6**	**71.0**	**71.5**
Central and South America	12.1	16.7	21.1	26.0	25.3	25.7	27.0	28.2	29.0	29.3
Europe	40.3	47.0	49.0	50.7	51.1	50.4	50.3	48.7	47.4	46.2
Eurasia [3]	56.5	72.1	51.9	55.4	59.1	62.9	66.1	68.1	69.9	71.6
Middle East	42.3	41.0	48.3	57.5	54.2	57.6	62.1	65.2	65.3	64.5
Africa	17.4	21.6	24.1	27.8	28.0	30.2	32.0	34.6	35.2	36.2
Asia and Oceania	35.9	59.6	72.9	78.1	88.3	95.9	108.0	115.5	120.3	126.4
Petroleum	133.1	136.2	141.8	156.5	153.8	159.1	166.5	169.1	168.7	169.1
Dry natural gas	54.7	76.1	80.4	91.0	96.3	98.5	101.5	104.8	107.2	104.8
Coal	71.3	91.0	88.5	90.4	97.7	105.3	114.1	122.1	128.5	122.1
Hydroelectric power	17.9	22.4	25.3	26.8	26.5	26.8	27.9	29.0	29.7	29.0
Nuclear electric power	7.6	20.4	23.3	25.7	26.7	26.4	27.3	27.5	27.8	27.5
Geothermal, solar, wind, wood, and waste	0.5	1.7	2.2	3.0	3.4	3.7	4.0	4.3	4.7	4.3

[1] Preliminary. [2] Includes geothermal, solar, and wood and waste energy produced in the United States and not used for generating electricity, not shown separately by type. [3] Prior to 1992, data were for the former U.S.S.R. only.

Source: U.S. Energy Information Administration, International Energy Statistics database, <http://tonto.eia.doe.gov/cfapps/ipdbproject/IEDIndex3.cfm>, accessed January 2010.

Table 1381. World Primary Energy Consumption by Region and Type: 1980 to 2007

[In quadrillion Btu (283.2 represents 283,200,000,000,000,000). Btu = British thermal unit. For Btu conversion factors, see source]

Region and type	1980	1990	1995	2000	2002	2003	2004	2005	2006	2007 [1]
World total [2]	**283.3**	**347.7**	**365.0**	**396.6**	**410.1**	**425.3**	**448.4**	**462.0**	**472.0**	**483.6**
North America	91.6	100.7	108.8	118.3	117.2	118.2	120.7	121.7	121.2	122.9
United States	**78.1**	**84.7**	**91.2**	**99.0**	**97.9**	**98.2**	**100.4**	**100.5**	**99.9**	**101.6**
Central and South America	11.5	14.5	17.6	20.8	21.1	21.6	22.4	23.4	24.3	25.0
Europe	71.9	76.4	76.8	81.3	82.3	84.0	85.4	85.8	86.4	85.6
Eurasia [3]	46.7	61.0	42.2	40.4	41.3	43.1	44.5	45.3	45.9	46.5
Middle East	5.8	11.2	13.8	17.3	19.0	19.8	20.9	22.8	23.9	25.1
Africa	6.8	9.5	10.6	12.0	12.7	13.4	14.0	14.5	14.6	15.1
Asia and Oceania	49.0	74.4	95.1	106.4	116.5	125.3	140.5	148.4	155.8	163.5
Petroleum	131.0	136.4	142.6	155.4	157.9	161.1	166.7	169.9	171.7	169.9
Dry natural gas	53.8	75.3	81.2	91.0	95.7	99.1	103.3	107.0	108.0	107.0
Coal	70.0	89.2	88.5	93.6	98.2	106.7	115.6	121.7	127.5	121.7
Hydroelectric power	17.9	22.4	25.3	26.8	26.5	26.8	27.9	29.0	29.7	29.0
Nuclear electric power	7.6	20.4	23.3	25.7	26.7	26.4	27.3	27.5	27.8	27.5
Geothermal, solar, wind, wood, and waste	0.5	1.7	2.2	3.0	3.4	3.7	4.0	4.3	4.7	4.3

[1] Preliminary. [2] See footnote 2, Table 1380. [3] Prior to 1992, data were for the former U.S.S.R. only.

Source: U.S. Energy Information Administration, International Energy Statistics database, <http://tonto.eia.doe.gov/cfapps/ipdbproject/IEDIndex3.cfm>, accessed January 2010.

Table 1382. World Energy Consumption by Region and Energy Source, 1990 to 2006, and Projections, 2010 to 2025

[In quadrillion Btu (347.7 represents 347,700,000,000,000,000). Btu = British thermal units. For Btu conversion factors, see source. Energy totals include net imports of coal coke and electricity generated from biomass in the United States. Totals may not equal sum of components due to independent rounding. The electricity portion of the national consumption values consists of generation for domestic use plus an adjustment for electricity trade based on a fuel's share of total generation in the exporting country]

Region and energy source	1990	2005	2006	Projections			
				2010	2015	2020	2025
World, total	**347.7**	**462.1**	**472.4**	**508.3**	**551.5**	**595.7**	**637.3**
North America	84.7	100.5	100.0	99.9	102.9	105.4	109.1
United States	**11.0**	**14.2**	**14.0**	**14.6**	**15.6**	**16.5**	**17.4**
Western Europe	27.0	38.4	38.7	39.5	41.8	43.1	43.9
Industrialized Asia	18.7	22.7	22.8	21.9	22.9	23.4	23.2
Eastern Europe and former Soviet Union	67.3	50.6	50.7	54.0	57.6	60.3	62.0
Developing Asia	47.4	109.4	117.6	139.2	163.2	190.3	215.4
Middle East	11.2	22.7	23.8	27.7	30.3	32.2	34.6
Africa	9.5	14.5	14.5	16.2	17.7	19.1	20.6
Central and South America	14.5	23.4	24.2	28.3	30.3	32.5	35.2
Oil	136.4	169.4	136.4	181.1	194.4	206.1	216.9
Natural gas	75.2	107.4	75.2	120.3	134.4	146.9	155.8
Coal	89.2	122.5	89.2	140.2	157.8	171.7	186.7
Nuclear	20.4	27.5	20.4	28.8	31.4	34.5	37.7
Other	26.2	35.5	26.2	42.0	45.0	49.3	54.7

Source: U.S. Energy Information Administration, *International Energy Outlook 2009*, May 2009. See also <http://www.eia.doe.gov/oiaf/ieo/ieorefcase.html>.

Table 1383. Energy Consumption by Country: 2000 and 2007

[396.6 represents 396,600,000,000,000,000. See text of this section for general comments about the data. For data qualifications for countries and Btu conversion factors, see source]

Country	Total (quad. Btu) 2000	Total (quad. Btu) 2007	Per capita (mil. Btu) 2000	Per capita (mil. Btu) 2007	Country	Total (quad. Btu) 2000	Total (quad. Btu) 2007	Per capita (mil. Btu) 2000	Per capita (mil. Btu) 2007
World, total	**396.6**	**483.6**	**65.2**	**73.1**	Japan	22.4	22.5	177.0	176.4
United States	**99.0**	**101.6**	**350.8**	**337.1**	Korea, North	0.9	0.9	40.4	38.9
Algeria	1.2	1.6	40.7	48.2	Korea, South	7.8	9.6	167.4	199.9
Argentina	2.7	3.2	71.5	80.0	Kuwait	0.9	1.2	460.8	461.0
Australia	4.9	6.1	254.7	295.1	Libya	0.6	0.8	122.9	126.2
Austria	1.4	1.5	171.5	183.8	Malaysia	2.0	2.4	90.7	97.1
Bahrain	0.4	0.5	574.7	735.8	Mexico	6.3	7.6	63.3	69.8
Bangladesh	0.5	0.8	3.7	5.2	Morocco	0.4	0.6	15.9	18.4
Belarus	1.1	1.2	104.9	122.4	Netherlands	3.8	4.1	238.5	245.7
Belgium	2.7	2.7	266.3	262.5	New Zealand	0.8	0.9	223.1	214.5
Brazil	8.5	10.1	48.4	52.2	Nigeria	0.8	1.0	6.6	7.3
Bulgaria	0.9	0.8	111.0	113.0	Norway	2.0	1.9	436.2	414.4
Burma	0.2	0.3	3.5	5.4	Pakistan	1.9	2.5	12.6	14.7
Canada	13.0	13.8	416.4	417.6	Peru	0.5	0.7	20.3	22.9
Chile	1.0	1.2	67.6	70.8	Philippines	1.3	1.3	15.4	13.9
China [1]	36.4	77.8	28.6	58.9	Poland	3.6	3.9	93.8	101.5
Colombia	1.2	1.3	30.1	31.6	Portugal	1.1	1.1	103.6	103.0
Congo (Kinshasa) [2]	0.1	0.1	1.8	1.6	Romania	1.6	1.7	70.6	77.4
Cuba	0.5	0.4	41.2	31.2	Russia	27.2	30.4	185.5	214.7
Czech Republic	1.4	1.6	135.9	158.5	Saudi Arabia	4.9	7.4	209.7	266.9
Denmark	0.9	0.9	163.7	160.1	Serbia and Montenegro [3]	0.6	0.5	62.5	53.4
Ecuador	0.3	0.5	27.7	33.4	South Africa	4.6	5.4	101.9	111.4
Egypt	2.0	2.7	30.8	35.8	Spain	5.6	6.7	140.4	164.8
Finland	1.2	1.3	234.1	254.0	Sweden	2.3	2.3	254.2	249.3
France	10.8	11.2	177.4	175.9	Switzerland	1.3	1.3	178.1	165.8
Germany	14.3	14.2	173.5	171.9	Syria	0.8	0.8	47.5	38.8
Greece	1.3	1.5	126.7	136.9	Taiwan [1]	3.8	4.7	169.3	207.6
Hong Kong	0.8	1.1	121.0	161.7	Thailand	2.6	3.9	41.7	59.4
Hungary	1.0	1.1	101.3	112.0	Trinidad and Tobago	0.4	0.8	336.0	670.7
India	13.5	19.1	13.4	17.0	Tunisia	0.3	0.3	31.5	31.2
Indonesia	3.9	4.9	18.3	20.8	Turkey	3.2	4.3	47.0	57.8
Iran	5.0	7.9	79.2	121.0	Ukraine	5.8	6.3	117.1	136.0
Iraq	1.1	1.2	47.8	45.0	United Arab Emirates	1.9	2.8	579.7	633.6
Ireland	0.6	0.7	158.3	171.6	United Kingdom	9.7	9.5	163.3	155.7
Israel	0.8	0.9	132.7	124.8	Venezuela	2.8	3.4	117.9	129.5
Italy	7.6	8.0	132.2	137.0	Vietnam	0.7	1.3	9.3	15.4

[1] See footnote 4, Table 1331. [2] See footnote 5, Table 1331. [3] As of June 2006, Serbia and Montenegro are separate countries.
Source: U.S. Energy Information Administration, International Energy Statistics database, <http://tonto.eia.doe.gov/cfapps/ipdbproject/IEDIndex3.cfm>, accessed January 2010.

Table 1384. World Daily Crude Oil Production by Major Producing Country: 1980 to 2008

[In thousands of barrels per day (59,558 barrels represents 59,558,000 barrels)]

Country	1980	1990	1995	2000	2004	2005	2006	2007	2008
World, total [1]	**59,558**	**60,492**	**62,385**	**68,495**	**72,481**	**73,728**	**73,446**	**72,989**	**73,709**
United States	**8,597**	**7,355**	**6,560**	**5,822**	**5,419**	**5,178**	**5,102**	**5,064**	**4,950**
Algeria	1,106	1,175	1,202	1,254	1,677	1,797	1,814	1,834	1,825
Angola	150	475	646	746	1,052	1,250	1,413	1,744	1,981
Argentina	491	483	715	761	733	704	696	679	661
Australia	380	575	562	722	436	446	429	465	477
Brazil	182	631	695	1,269	1,477	1,634	1,723	1,748	1,812
Canada	1,435	1,553	1,805	1,977	2,398	2,369	2,525	2,616	2,596
China [2]	2,114	2,774	2,990	3,249	3,485	3,609	3,673	3,729	3,790
Colombia	126	440	585	691	529	526	531	531	588
Ecuador	204	285	392	395	528	532	536	511	505
Egypt	595	873	920	768	673	658	639	637	603
India	182	660	703	646	683	665	689	698	694
Indonesia	1,577	1,462	1,503	1,428	1,096	1,067	1,019	964	973
Iran	1,662	3,088	3,643	3,696	4,001	4,139	4,028	3,912	4,050
Iraq	2,514	2,040	560	2,571	2,011	1,878	1,996	2,086	2,375
Kazakhstan	(X)	(X)	414	718	1,203	1,288	1,313	1,360	1,345
Kuwait	1,656	1,175	2,057	2,079	2,376	2,529	2,535	2,464	2,586
Libya	1,787	1,375	1,390	1,410	1,515	1,633	1,681	1,702	1,736
Malaysia	283	619	682	690	755	631	613	588	609
Mexico	1,936	2,553	2,618	3,012	3,383	3,334	3,256	3,076	2,792
Nigeria	2,055	1,810	1,993	2,165	2,329	2,627	2,440	2,350	2,165
Norway	486	1,630	2,766	3,222	2,954	2,698	2,491	2,270	2,182
Oman	282	685	851	970	751	774	738	710	757
Qatar	472	406	442	737	783	835	850	851	924
Russia	(X)	(X)	5,995	6,479	8,805	9,043	9,247	9,437	9,357
Saudi Arabia	9,900	6,410	8,231	8,404	9,101	9,550	9,152	8,722	9,261
United Arab Emirates	1,709	2,117	2,233	2,368	2,478	2,535	2,636	2,603	2,681
United Kingdom	1,622	1,820	2,489	2,275	1,845	1,649	1,490	1,498	1,391
Venezuela	2,168	2,137	2,750	3,155	2,557	2,565	2,511	2,433	2,394
Yemen	–	193	345	438	404	400	375	319	298

– Represents zero. X Not applicable. [1] Includes countries not shown separately. [2] See footnote 4, Table 1331.
Source: U.S. Energy Information Administration, International Energy Statistics database, <http://tonto.eia.doe.gov/cfapps/ipdbproject/IEDIndex3.cfm>, accessed January 2010.

Table 1385. World Dry Natural Gas Production by Major Producing Country: 1980 to 2008

[In trillion cubic feet (53.37 represents 53,370,000,000,000)]

Country	Natural gas production								
	1980	1990	2000	2003	2004	2005	2006	2007	2008
World, total [1]	53.37	73.79	88.40	94.69	97.25	100.07	103.42	105.77	109.79
Russia	(X)	(X)	20.63	21.77	22.39	22.62	23.17	23.06	23.39
United States	19.40	17.81	19.18	19.10	18.59	18.05	18.50	19.09	20.38
Canada	2.76	3.85	6.47	6.45	6.48	6.56	6.55	6.34	6.04
Iran	0.25	0.84	2.13	2.86	2.96	3.56	3.84	3.95	4.11
Norway	0.92	0.98	1.87	2.70	2.95	3.07	3.09	3.17	3.50
Algeria	0.41	1.79	2.94	2.85	2.83	3.11	3.08	3.00	3.05
Netherlands	3.40	2.69	2.56	2.57	3.04	2.77	2.73	2.70	2.99
Saudi Arabia	0.33	1.08	1.76	2.12	2.32	2.52	2.59	2.63	2.84
Qatar	0.18	0.28	1.03	1.11	1.38	1.62	1.79	2.23	2.72
China [2]	0.51	0.51	0.96	1.21	1.44	1.76	2.07	2.45	2.69
Turkmenistan	(X)	(X)	1.64	2.09	2.07	2.22	2.23	2.43	2.49
Indonesia	0.65	1.60	2.24	2.19	2.03	2.00	2.20	2.42	2.47
United Kingdom	1.32	1.75	3.83	3.63	3.43	3.12	2.82	2.55	2.47
Uzbekistan	(X)	(X)	1.99	2.03	2.11	2.11	2.22	2.30	2.39
Malaysia	0.06	0.65	1.60	1.84	1.90	1.97	1.97	1.96	2.02
Mexico	0.90	0.90	1.31	1.40	1.46	1.52	1.74	1.85	1.84
United Arab Emirates	0.20	0.78	1.36	1.58	1.63	1.66	1.72	1.78	1.77
Egypt	0.03	0.29	0.65	1.06	1.15	1.50	1.60	1.64	1.71
Australia	0.31	0.72	1.16	1.27	1.31	1.44	1.51	1.56	1.60
Argentina	0.28	0.63	1.32	1.45	1.58	1.61	1.63	1.58	1.56
Trinidad and Tobago	0.08	0.18	0.49	0.87	0.99	1.07	1.29	1.38	1.39
Pakistan	0.29	0.48	0.86	0.89	0.97	1.09	1.28	1.30	1.32
Nigeria	0.04	0.13	0.44	0.72	0.77	0.79	1.01	1.15	1.16
India	0.05	0.40	0.79	0.96	1.00	1.06	1.09	1.11	1.14
Thailand	–	0.21	0.66	0.77	0.79	0.84	0.86	0.92	1.02
Oman	0.03	0.10	0.32	0.56	0.61	0.70	0.84	0.85	0.85
Venezuela	0.52	0.76	0.96	0.86	0.96	1.01	0.92	0.93	0.85
Ukraine	(X)	(X)	0.64	0.69	0.68	0.69	0.69	0.69	0.70
Germany	(X)	(X)	0.78	0.78	0.73	0.70	0.69	0.63	0.58
Kazakhstan	(X)	(X)	0.31	0.25	0.32	0.34	0.34	0.35	0.40

– Represents or rounds to zero. X Not applicable. [1] Includes countries not shown separately. [2] See footnote 4, Table 1331.
Source: U. S. Energy Information Administration, International Energy Statistics database, <http://tonto.eia.doe.gov/cfapps/ipdbproject/IEDIndex3.cfm>, accessed January 2010.

Table 1386. World Coal Production by Major Producing Country: 1980 to 2008

[In millions of short tons (4,181.9 represents 4,181,900,000)]

Country	1980	1990	2000	2003	2004	2005	2006	2007	2008
World, total [1]	4,181.9	5,346.7	4,893.5	5,666.9	6,222.8	6,542.2	6,769.4	7,046.9	7,271.4
China [2]	683.6	1,190.4	1,271.5	1,863.7	2,299.7	2,500.9	2,572.1	2,743.7	2,848.0
United States	829.7	1,029.1	1,073.6	1,071.8	1,112.1	1,131.5	1,162.7	1,146.6	1,171.5
India	125.8	247.6	370.0	420.5	446.7	473.3	500.2	528.2	568.3
Australia	115.2	225.5	338.1	376.6	388.2	404.9	405.0	429.2	438.5
Russia	(X)	(X)	264.9	283.3	285.4	300.8	313.7	318.6	356.2
Indonesia	0.6	11.6	84.5	133.2	157.2	188.2	249.7	291.9	313.2
South Africa	131.9	193.2	248.9	263.8	267.7	270.1	269.8	273.0	259.6
Germany	(X)	(X)	226.0	229.1	232.7	227.0	220.6	225.5	214.4
Poland	253.5	237.1	179.2	179.2	178.3	175.0	171.1	159.8	157.9
Kazakhstan	(X)	(X)	85.4	93.6	95.8	95.4	106.1	107.8	119.8
Colombia	4.5	22.6	42.0	55.1	59.2	65.1	72.3	77.1	86.7
Turkey	20.8	52.3	69.7	53.5	51.1	64.3	70.8	83.1	83.5
Canada	40.4	75.3	76.2	68.5	72.7	72.0	72.8	75.4	75.1
Greece	25.6	57.2	70.4	75.3	77.2	76.5	71.4	73.1	72.4
Czech Republic	(X)	(X)	71.8	70.4	68.1	68.4	69.3	69.0	66.3
Ukraine	(X)	(X)	68.8	70.8	65.7	66.5	68.0	65.0	65.7
Vietnam	5.7	5.1	12.8	18.4	28.1	35.7	42.9	46.9	44.0
Korea, North	48.6	51.0	32.8	33.3	35.0	38.2	38.7	33.4	41.3
Romania	38.8	42.1	32.3	36.4	35.0	34.3	38.5	39.4	38.3
Bulgaria	33.3	34.9	29.2	30.1	29.2	27.2	28.3	31.4	31.7
Thailand	1.6	13.7	19.5	20.8	22.1	23.0	21.0	20.1	19.9
United Kingdom	143.8	104.1	33.7	30.6	27.0	22.1	19.9	18.2	19.4
Estonia	(X)	(X)	12.9	16.4	15.4	16.1	15.5	18.2	17.8
Mexico	4.0	8.6	12.5	10.6	10.9	11.9	12.7	13.8	12.7
Spain	30.9	39.2	25.9	22.7	22.6	21.5	20.3	18.9	11.2
Mongolia	5.3	7.9	5.5	6.2	7.5	8.3	9.2	10.5	11.2
Bosnia and Herzegovina	(X)	(X)	8.2	9.8	9.8	10.1	11.2	11.7	10.5
Hungary	28.7	19.7	15.5	14.7	12.4	10.5	11.0	10.8	10.4
Venezuela	(Z)	2.4	8.7	7.3	7.4	7.9	8.1	8.4	9.7
Brazil	5.8	5.1	7.4	5.1	6.0	6.9	6.5	6.6	7.1

X Not applicable. Z Less than 50,000 short tons. [1] Includes countries not shown separately. [2] See footnote 4, Table 1331.
Source: U.S. Energy Information Administration, International Energy Statistics database, <http://tonto.eia.doe.gov/cfapps/ipdbproject/IEDIndex3.cfm>, accessed January 2010.

Table 1387. Net Electricity Generation by Type and Country: 2008

[18,778.7 represents 18,778,700,000,000. kWh = kilowatt hours]

Country	Total [1] (bil. kWh)	Thermal [2]	Hydro	Nuclear	Country	Total [1] (bil. kWh)	Thermal [2]	Hydro	Nuclear
		Percent distribution					Percent distribution		
World, total [3]	18,778.7	67.8	16.0	13.8	Indonesia.............	134.4	86.7	8.3	–
					Norway...............	134.3	0.6	98.7	–
United States	4,156.7	72.0	6.0	19.4	Egypt...............	118.4	86.4	13.0	–
China [4].........	3,040.5	83.5	14.1	2.1	Venezuela	113.3	26.7	73.3	–
Japan..........	1,058.1	67.2	6.9	23.7	Argentina............	109.5	65.1	27.6	6.1
Russia..........	958.0	66.1	18.3	15.4	Malaysia	103.2	93.8	6.2	–
India..........	761.7	80.1	16.1	2.1	Netherlands..........	97.2	86.8	0.1	4.1
Canada	620.7	25.2	58.8	14.3	Pakistan............	90.8	66.2	31.3	2.5
Germany	593.4	62.5	3.5	22.5	Czech Republic	82.7	66.1	2.5	30.1
France	535.7	9.9	10.8	78.0	Belgium	82.2	39.5	0.5	55.8
Brazil	437.5	8.6	84.6	2.8	Finland.............	77.2	40.1	18.2	28.8
Korea, South	401.5	65.1	0.9	33.8	Kazakhstan	72.4	88.8	11.2	–
United Kingdom...	368.6	78.4	1.4	16.2	United Arab Emirates ...	71.5	100.0	–	–
Italy	289.7	83.7	11.2	–	Vietnam.............	66.8	55.7	44.3	–
Spain..........	283.2	61.5	9.7	18.5	Switzerland	63.9	1.4	54.6	41.5
Mexico..........	243.6	80.8	11.1	4.1	Chile	60.6	57.9	37.2	–
South Africa.....	240.3	94.5	1.0	4.9	Greece.............	58.8	92.9	4.4	–
Australia.........	239.9	92.3	5.9	–	Austria.............	58.6	30.0	60.8	–
Taiwan [4]	225.0	79.4	1.9	17.1	Romania	58.3	60.8	27.0	12.1
Iran	192.6	90.7	9.2	–	Philippines..........	56.6	67.8	15.0	–
Ukraine	185.2	47.4	5.5	47.1	Paraguay	53.2	(Z)	100.0	–
Turkey	181.9	80.1	19.5	–	Colombia............	50.6	16.9	81.9	–
Saudi Arabia	179.1	100.0	–	–	Israel	50.4	100.0	(Z)	–
Poland..........	149.1	96.5	1.6	–	Uzbekistan..........	46.3	86.3	13.7	–
Sweden	143.9	2.4	45.5	44.2	Portugal............	44.5	64.2	22.5	–
Thailand.........	135.2	91.1	5.9	–	Bulgaria	40.2	59.2	7.1	34.0

– Represents zero. Z Less than 0.05 percent. [1] Includes thermal, hydro, nuclear, and geothermal, solar, wind, and wood and waste generation. [2] Electricity generated from coal, oil, and gas. [3] Includes countries not shown separately. [4] See footnote 4, Table 1331.

Source: U.S. Energy Information Administration, International Energy Statistics database, <http://tonto.eia.doe.gov/cfapps/ipdbproject/IEDIndex3.cfm>, accessed January 2010.

Table 1388. Commercial Nuclear Power Generation by Country: 1990 to 2009

[Generation for calendar years; other data as of December (1,743.9 represents 1,743,900,000,000). kWh = kilowatt-hours. kW = kilowatts]

Country	Reactors				Gross electricity generated (bil. kWh)				Gross capacity (1,000 kW)			
	1990	2000	2008	2009	1990	2000	2008	2009	1990	2000	2008	2009
Total	368	433	441	441	1,743.9	2,540.5	2,690.2	2,546.6	301,745	373,804	396,214	397,295
United States	112	104	104	104	606.4	789.1	842.4	833.6	105,998	103,129	106,977	107,023
Argentina.........	2	2	2	2	7.0	6.2	7.4	8.2	1,005	1,005	1,005	1,005
Armenia..........	(X)	1	1	1	(X)	(NA)	2.5	2.5	(X)	408	408	408
Belgium	7	7	7	7	42.7	48.2	45.8	47.2	5,740	5,995	6,101	6,207
Brazil	1	2	2	2	2.0	6.1	14.0	12.9	657	1,966	2,007	2,007
Bulgaria	(X)	6	2	2	(X)	(NA)	15.8	15.3	(X)	3,760	2,000	2,000
Canada	19	21	21	21	74.0	73.8	94.1	90.9	13,855	15,795	15,367	15,367
China [1]..........	(NA)	2	11	11	(NA)	14.7	(NA)	(NA)	(NA)	1,968	9,014	9,014
Czech Republic	(X)	4	6	6	(X)	13.6	26.5	27.1	(X)	1,760	3,834	3,876
Finland...........	4	4	4	4	18.9	22.5	22.9	23.5	2,400	2,760	2,800	2,800
France	58	57	58	58	314.1	395.7	438.6	410.0	58,862	62,920	65,880	65,880
Germany	22	19	17	17	147.2	169.7	148.7	134.9	23,973	22,234	21,497	21,497
Great Britain	42	33	19	19	68.8	83.6	(NA)	(NA)	15,274	15,272	12,540	12,540
Hungary	4	4	4	4	13.6	14.1	14.8	15.4	1,760	1,851	1,940	2,000
India.............	6	13	17	17	6.0	15.5	15.5	17.0	1,330	2,960	4,120	4,120
Italy	2	(NA)	(NA)	(NA)	–	(NA)	(NA)	(NA)	1,132	(NA)	(NA)	(NA)
Japan............	40	52	55	56	191.9	319.8	251.7	272.3	31,645	45,082	49,580	50,492
Korea, South	9	16	20	20	52.8	108.9	150.9	147.8	7,616	13,768	18,393	18,393
Lithuania	(X)	2	1	1	(X)	7.8	9.9	11.6	(X)	3,000	1,300	1,300
Mexico...........	1	2	2	2	2.1	8.2	9.8	10.5	675	1,350	1,364	1,364
Netherlands.......	2	1	1	1	3.4	3.9	4.2	4.2	540	480	515	515
Pakistan..........	1	1	2	2	0.4	0.4	1.9	2.9	137	137	462	462
Romania	(X)	1	2	2	(X)	5.5	11.2	11.7	(X)	706	1,412	1,412
Russia	(X)	29	31	31	(X)	128.9	162.3	163.3	(X)	21,266	23,266	23,242
Slovakia..........	(X)	6	5	4	(X)	16.5	16.7	(NA)	(X)	2,640	2,260	1,894
Slovenia..........	1	1	1	1	4.6	4.8	6.3	5.7	664	664	727	727
South Africa.......	2	2	2	2	8.9	13.6	13.3	12.1	1,930	1,930	1,930	1,930
Spain	10	9	8	8	54.3	62.2	59.0	52.9	7,984	7,808	7,735	7,735
Sweden	12	11	10	10	68.2	57.3	63.9	52.3	10,344	9,844	9,398	9,685
Switzerland	5	5	5	5	23.6	26.3	27.5	27.5	3,079	3,322	3,352	3,370
Taiwan [1].........	6	6	6	6	32.9	38.5	40.8	41.6	5,146	5,144	5,144	5,144
Ukraine	(X)	14	15	15	(X)	77.3	89.8	82.2	(X)	12,880	13,880	13,880

– Represents zero. NA Not available. X Not applicable. [1] See footnote 4, Table 1331.

Source: Platts Energy, A Division of The McGraw-Hill Companies Inc., New York, NY, *Nucleonics Week*, February issue (copyright).

U.S. Census Bureau, Statistical Abstract of the United States: 2011

Table 1389. Carbon Dioxide Emissions From Consumption of Fossil Fuels by Country: 1990 to 2008

[In million metric tons of carbon dioxide (21,677.3 represents 21,677,300,000). Includes carbon dioxide emissions from the consumption of petroleum, natural gas, coal, and the flaring of natural gas]

Region/Country	1990	1995	2000	2004	2005	2006	2007	2008
World, total [1]	**21,677.3**	**22,218.5**	**23,876.6**	**27,620.0**	**28,471.0**	**29,040.5**	**29,873.3**	**30,377.3**
United States	**5,037.1**	**5,325.9**	**5,863.8**	**5,965.3**	**5,988.1**	**5,908.5**	**6,003.3**	**5,832.8**
Australia	268.9	290.5	358.3	388.1	411.2	414.6	421.7	437.4
Brazil	237.7	289.4	344.8	356.2	370.5	383.5	397.1	428.2
Canada	471.7	509.9	574.8	612.9	625.1	599.6	588.8	573.5
China [2]	2,289.0	2,885.4	2,871.5	5,131.8	5,558.5	5,862.0	6,246.5	6,533.6
France	368.4	373.1	402.2	411.4	414.5	417.2	401.5	415.3
Germany	(X)	894.3	858.0	870.8	850.6	853.8	835.1	828.8
India	582.5	876.4	1,009.8	1,131.6	1,189.1	1,288.9	1,385.7	1,494.9
Indonesia	156.1	215.1	266.7	308.8	331.6	361.5	402.3	434.1
Iran	202.1	262.2	320.7	406.6	445.8	475.9	491.1	511.1
Italy	416.0	431.9	448.2	469.6	472.5	468.1	461.5	454.9
Japan	1,049.5	1,119.0	1,205.1	1,260.7	1,245.5	1,244.2	1,262.7	1,214.2
Korea, South	243.1	382.5	440.3	488.0	496.0	485.6	516.1	542.1
Mexico	302.3	321.6	383.3	386.0	414.3	431.9	453.7	444.6
Netherlands	212.0	223.5	251.5	270.3	272.3	276.3	281.0	261.0
Poland	336.5	310.6	294.7	294.3	289.6	301.4	297.6	298.7
Russia	(X)	1,607.1	1,560.4	1,643.5	1,635.5	1,679.6	1,649.3	1,729.4
Saudi Arabia	208.0	235.3	290.5	388.8	405.5	406.2	433.9	466.0
South Africa	300.4	350.3	390.2	445.9	436.1	448.2	463.9	451.1
Spain	224.9	244.1	318.3	370.7	383.7	376.8	382.8	358.7
Taiwan [2]	118.7	183.1	257.3	286.8	290.3	298.7	308.0	304.8
Thailand	84.1	145.4	162.0	225.9	242.2	237.7	248.0	254.2
Turkey	130.1	153.8	202.8	211.3	231.9	252.0	281.3	271.5
Ukraine	(X)	423.3	326.2	346.0	354.9	334.8	359.3	349.9
United Kingdom	604.4	561.8	561.7	584.8	584.5	587.1	564.3	571.8

X Not applicable. [1] Includes other countries not shown separately. [2] See footnote 4, Table 1331.

Source: U.S. Energy Information Administration, International Energy Statistics database, <http://tonto.eia.doe.gov/cfapps/ipdbproject/IEDIndex3.cfm>, accessed January 2010.

Table 1390. Average Temperatures and Precipitation—Selected International Cities

[In degrees Fahrenheit, except as noted. Data are generally based on a standard 30-year period; for details, see source. For data on U.S. cities, see Tables 387–394. Minus sign (–) indicates degrees below zero]

City	January Average high	January Average low	January Warmest	January Coldest	January Average precipitation (inches)	July Average high	July Average low	July Warmest	July Coldest	July Average precipitation (inches)
Amsterdam, Netherlands	41	34	57	3	3.1	69	55	90	39	2.9
Athens, Greece	55	44	70	28	1.9	89	73	108	61	0.2
Baghdad, Iraq	58	38	75	25	1.1	110	78	122	61	–
Bangkok, Thailand	89	71	95	54	0.4	90	78	99	72	6.2
Beijing, China	34	17	54	1	0.2	86	72	104	63	8.8
Berlin, Germany	35	26	58	–11	(NA)	73	56	95	41	(NA)
Bogota, Colombia	66	43	84	27	1.9	64	47	82	32	1.8
Brasilia, Brazil	81	64	95	54	(NA)	79	52	97	37	(NA)
Buenos Aires, Argentina	85	64	104	44	4.2	58	41	88	23	2.3
Cairo, Egypt	65	49	86	32	0.2	93	72	108	63	–
Frankfurt, Germany	38	30	56	–4	1.8	75	57	97	38	2.4
Geneva, Switzerland	39	29	57	–2	2.2	77	56	96	41	2.8
Hong Kong, China	67	58	79	43	1.1	89	81	97	70	14.3
Istanbul, Turkey	46	37	64	16	3.7	82	66	100	50	0.7
Jakarta, Indonesia	83	75	92	72	(NA)	88	74	92	67	(NA)
Karachi, Pakistan	76	55	93	39	0.3	89	83	109	68	3.5
Lagos, Nigeria	82	79	93	64	(NA)	79	76	88	70	(NA)
London, England	45	36	61	15	2.4	72	56	93	45	1.8
Madrid, Spain	51	32	68	14	1.8	90	61	104	46	0.4
Manila, Philippines	86	71	95	61	0.8	88	76	99	70	15.9
Mexico City, Mexico	70	45	86	26	0.3	74	56	86	37	5.1
Montreal, Canada	21	7	52	–31	2.8	79	61	93	43	3.4
Moscow, Russia	21	11	46	–33	1.4	71	55	95	41	3.2
Nairobi, Kenya	77	58	88	45	1.8	71	54	85	43	0.5
New Delhi, India	68	48	85	32	0.9	93	81	111	70	7.9
Paris, France	43	34	59	1	(NA)	75	58	95	41	(NA)
Rio De Janeiro, Brazil	91	74	109	64	5.3	81	64	102	52	1.8
Rome, Italy	55	39	64	19	3.2	83	66	100	55	0.6
Seoul, Korea	33	21	55	–1	(NA)	82	71	97	55	(NA)
Singapore, Singapore	85	73	100	66	9.4	86	76	99	70	5.9
Sydney, Australia	79	65	109	49	4.0	62	44	80	32	2.5
Tel Aviv, Israel	62	46	84	32	(NA)	87	69	100	50	(NA)
Tokyo, Japan	48	35	66	25	2.0	82	71	95	55	5.3
Toronto, Canada	28	15	59	–24	1.9	79	60	99	45	2.8

– Represents zero. NA Not available.

Source: U.S. National Oceanic and Atmospheric Administration, *Climates of the World*. See also <http://www.ncdc.noaa.gov/oa/oldpubs/>.

Table 1391. Key Global Telecom Indicators for the World Telecommunication Service Sector: 2005 to 2009

[In millions (1,259 represents 1,259,000,000), except as indicated]

Indicators	2005	2006	2007	2008	2009
NUMBER (Mil.)					
Fixed telephone lines [1]	1,259	1,280	1,272	1,251	1,219
Mobile cellular subscribers	2,217	2,755	3,357	4,037	4,673
Internet users	1,036	1,159	1,375	1,603	1,833
Fixed broadband subscriptions	216	283	352	415	479
Mobile broadband subscriptions	73	159	291	444	667
PER 100 INHABITANTS					
Fixed telephone lines [1]	19.3	19.4	19.0	18.5	17.8
Mobile cellular subscriptions	33.9	41.7	50.2	59.6	68.2
Internet users	15.9	17.5	20.5	23.7	26.8
Fixed broadband subscriptions	3.3	4.3	5.3	6.1	7.0
Mobile broadband subscriptions	1.1	2.4	4.2	6.6	9.7

[1] See footnote 1, Table 1392.

Source: International Telecommunication Union, Geneva Switzerland, 2009, <http://www.itu.int/ITU-D/ict/statistics/at_glance /KeyTelecom.html>. Reproduced with the kind permission of ITU.

Table 1392. Telephones, Cellular Phones, and Computers by Country: 2008

[Rates per 100 persons. For data qualifications for countries, see source]

Country	Telephone main lines [1]	Cellular phone sub-scribers	Personal comput-ers [2]	Country	Telephone main lines [1]	Cellular phone sub-scribers	Personal comput-ers [2]
Afghanistan	0.37	29.03	(NA)	Iran	33.83	58.65	(NA)
Australia	44.46	104.96	(NA)	Italy	35.65	151.57	(NA)
Azerbaijan	15.01	75.00	8.00	Japan	38.04	86.73	(NA)
Belize	10.35	53.23	(NA)	Korea, South	44.29	94.71	(NA)
Brazil	21.48	78.47	(NA)	Macedonia	22.39	122.56	(NA)
Bulgaria	28.84	138.30	11.01	Mali	0.64	27.07	(NA)
Cambodia	0.30	29.10	(NA)	Mexico	18.88	69.37	(NA)
Canada	54.87	66.42	(NA)	Morocco	9.46	72.19	5.70
China [3]	25.48	47.95	(NA)	Namibia	6.57	49.39	(NA)
Colombia	17.89	91.90	11.25	Pakistan	2.50	49.74	(NA)
Cuba	9.85	2.96	5.62	Portugal	38.50	139.64	18.16
Denmark	45.64	125.72	(NA)	Romania	24.39	114.54	(NA)
Dominican Republic	9.90	72.46	(NA)	Russia	31.75	141.11	(NA)
Egypt	14.54	50.62	3.92	Saudi Arabia	16.27	142.85	68.25
Estonia	37.14	188.20	25.50	Serbia	31.35	97.76	19.31
Ethiopia	1.11	2.42	(NA)	Singapore	40.24	138.15	(NA)
France	56.42	93.45	(NA)	Slovak Republic	20.33	102.23	58.15
Gambia	2.94	70.24	(NA)	Slovenia	50.11	101.97	(NA)
Georgia	14.35	63.97	(NA)	Spain	45.41	111.67	(NA)
Germany	62.12	128.27	(NA)	Sweden	57.83	118.33	(NA)
Greece	53.65	123.90	(NA)	Switzerland	64.02	117.97	97.60
Haiti	1.09	32.40	(NA)	Syria	17.12	33.24	(NA)
Honduras	11.28	84.86	2.49	Taiwan [3]	62.37	110.31	83.47
Hong Kong, China	58.72	165.85	69.25	Turkey	23.68	89.05	(NA)
Hungary	30.90	122.09	(NA)	United Kingdom	54.24	126.34	(NA)
India	3.21	29.36	(NA)	**United States**	**49.62**	**86.79**	**(NA)**
Indonesia	13.36	61.83	(NA)	Venezuela	22.82	97.49	(NA)

NA Not available. [1] A fixed telephone line (previously called main telephone line in operation) is an active line (those that have registered an activity in the past three months) connecting the subscriber's terminal equipment to the public switched telephone network (PSTN) and which has a dedicated port in the telephone exchange equipment. This term is synonymous with the terms main station or Direct Exchange Line (DEL) that are commonly used in telecommunication documents. It may not be the same as an access line or a subscriber. This should include the active number of analog fixed telephone lines, ISDN channels, fixed wireless (WLL), public payphones and VoIP subscriptions. Fixed telephone lines per 100 inhabitants is calculated by dividing the number of fixed telephone lines by the population and multiplying by 100. [2] In many countries mainframe computers are used extensively, and thousands of users can be connected to a single mainframe computer; thus the number of personal computers understates the total use of computers. [3] See footnote 4, Table 1331.

Source: International Telecommunications Union, Geneva, Switzerland, *World Telecommunication Indicators* (copyright). See also <http://www.itu.int/itu-d/icteye/Indicators/Indicators.aspx>. Reproduced with the kind permission of ITU.

Table 1393. Patents by Country: 2009

[Includes only U.S. patents granted to residents of areas outside of the United States and its territories. See also Table 772]

Country	Total [1]	Inventions	Designs	Country	Total [1]	Inventions	Designs
Total	**96,896**	**84,967**	**11,091**	Netherlands	1,558	1,288	102
				Australia	1,550	1,221	299
Japan	38,066	35,501	2,415	Switzerland	1,454	1,208	241
Germany	10,353	9,000	1,197	Israel	1,525	1,404	92
Korea, South	9,566	8,762	785	Sweden	1,231	1,014	207
Taiwan [2]	7,781	6,642	1,114	Finland	997	864	132
Canada	4,393	3,655	712	Belgium	707	594	92
United Kingdom	4,011	3,175	782	Austria	767	503	264
France	3,805	3,140	628	Denmark	537	390	125
Italy	1,837	1,346	485	Other countries	6,758	5,260	1,419

[1] Includes patents for botanical plants and reissues, not shown separately. [2] See footnote 4, Table 1331.
Source: U.S. Patent and Trademark Office, Technology Assessment and Forecast Database.

Table 1394. Research and Development (R&D) Expenditures by Country

[Figures are for 2007, except as noted, or latest year available. GDP = gross domestic product; for explanation, see text, Section 13]

Country	GERD: Percent of GDP	GERD financed by—Government	GERD financed by—Industry	GERD: Per capita at current U.S. dollars, PPPs [1]	Gov. budget approp. for R&D, 2008: Percent of GDP	Gov. budget approp.: Percent defense R&D	BERD: Percent of GERD	BERD financed by—Government	BERD financed by—Industry	BERD performed in—High-tech industries [2]	BERD performed in—Medium high-tech industries [3]	BERD performed in—Medium low-tech and low-tech industries [4]	BERD performed in—Service industries [4]	HERD: Percent of GERD	HERD: Percent of GDP
OECD, total	**2.29**	**28.56**	**63.79**	**748**	**0.78**	**32.9**	**69.6**	**6.7**	**90.1**	**40.9**	**27.9**	**8.9**	**20.3**	**16.8**	**0.4**
EU-15 [5]	1.90	33.36	55.60	635	0.74	13.1	64.3	7.0	82.9	37.3	34.6	9.5	16.5	21.6	0.4
EU-27 [6]	1.77	34.11	54.98	530	0.69	12.5	63.4	7.2	82.7	37.1	34.4	9.5	16.8	21.8	0.4
Australia [7]	2.01	38.37	57.23	716	0.46	7.7	57.3	4.4	93.3	9.1	10.2	14.1	40.5	25.7	0.5
Austria [7]	2.56	35.60	47.68	952	0.68	(Z)	70.4	9.6	66.4	30.2	28.2	12.6	28.0	24.1	0.6
Belgium	1.87	24.65	59.68	662	0.60	0.3	69.3	6.2	78.7	41.2	23.7	15.7	17.0	21.8	0.4
Brazil	1.02	57.88	39.38	92	0.53	1.2	47.9	0.8	99.2	(NA)	(NA)	(NA)	(NA)	(NA)	(NA)
Canada [7]	1.88	31.42	49.40	724	0.57	4.0	56.0	2.3	82.5	35.3	9.2	15.7	35.8	33.7	0.6
China [8,9]	1.49	24.62	70.37	77	(NA)	(NA)	72.3	4.8	91.9	(NA)	(NA)	(NA)	(NA)	8.5	0.1
Czech Republic	1.54	41.19	53.96	369	0.61	2.3	63.8	13.6	82.2	15.1	38.5	7.4	36.6	16.9	0.3
Denmark	2.55	27.58	59.53	917	0.85	0.6	64.9	2.4	86.0	39.9	17.7	7.5	33.5	27.5	0.7
Finland	3.47	24.05	68.20	1,206	0.97	2.8	72.3	3.5	90.9	57.9	14.4	11.5	14.0	18.7	0.7
France	2.08	38.42	52.44	680	0.75	27.7	63.2	11.2	80.2	41.9	32.6	11.9	9.5	19.2	0.4
Germany	2.54	27.76	68.07	874	0.79	6.0	69.9	4.5	92.0	30.9	52.3	6.8	9.4	16.3	0.4
Greece	0.57	46.82	31.06	163	0.30	0.5	26.9	5.6	85.7	21.9	13.7	17.1	44.9	50.4	0.3
Hungary	0.97	44.41	43.86	181	0.37	0.1	50.3	9.6	74.9	53.7	16.0	6.6	21.4	23.4	0.2
Iceland	2.75	38.80	50.35	980	0.92	—	54.6	5.4	83.2	25.0	6.9	5.7	59.7	25.1	0.7
India	0.71	80.81	16.11	13	(NA)	(NA)	19.8	(NA)	(NA)	(NA)	(NA)	(NA)	(NA)	4.9	(Z)
Ireland	1.31	30.13	59.26	591	0.55	—	66.8	3.9	86.5	48.1	9.0	9.8	32.9	26.4	0.3
Italy	1.13	48.32	40.42	334	0.63	1.2	48.8	7.9	81.8	32.3	30.4	8.0	26.3	30.3	0.4
Japan [7]	3.44	15.63	77.71	1,157	0.70	5.2	77.9	1.1	98.5	38.0	40.2	11.7	8.5	12.6	0.4
Korea	3.47	24.80	73.65	861	0.96	18.0	76.2	6.2	93.4	53.8	27.9	8.3	7.1	10.7	0.4
Luxembourg	1.63	16.61	79.72	1,300	0.39	—	83.8	5.2	91.7	(NA)	(NA)	(NA)	(NA)	3.0	0.1
Mexico	0.46	45.34	46.49	57	0.19	—	49.5	5.7	92.6	37.4	28.5	8.9	21.9	27.4	0.1
Netherlands	1.70	36.23	51.06	669	0.70	2.0	60.4	3.4	81.6	(NA)	(NA)	(NA)	(NA)	26.6	0.5
New Zealand	1.21	42.66	40.14	325	0.56	—	42.7	8.8	79.4	12.4	18.9	13.5	41.1	30.1	0.4
Norway	1.64	44.87	45.25	878	0.68	5.2	53.3	8.7	79.6	19.2	27.1	12.1	40.0	31.4	0.5
Poland	0.57	58.61	34.26	91	0.32	1.4	30.4	11.7	83.1	12.0	5.1	2.6	29.7	33.9	0.2
Portugal	1.18	55.20	36.27	269	1.01	—	51.5	4.2	91.4	(NA)	(NA)	(NA)	44.0	29.9	0.4
Russia	1.12	62.62	29.45	165	0.40	52.1	64.2	55.3	36.6	(NA)	(NA)	(NA)	72.0	6.3	0.1
Slovakia	0.46	53.92	35.60	92	0.26	4.4	39.6	10.3	73.5	22.6	31.4	16.2	47.4	25.0	0.1
South Africa	0.92	38.19	43.87	76	1.08	(NA)	58.3	16.2	68.3	43.7	22.2	7.9	36.4	19.3	0.2
Spain	1.27	42.49	47.07	401	0.81	13.1	55.9	14.4	79.0	(NA)	(NA)	(NA)	33.2	26.4	0.3
Sweden	3.60	24.43	63.86	1,320	0.72	12.4	73.8	4.3	85.0	(NA)	(NA)	14.9	15.3	21.3	0.8
Switzerland	2.90	22.71	69.73	1,003	(NA)	0.6	73.7	1.5	90.9	(NA)	(NA)	(NA)	(NA)	22.9	0.7
Turkey	0.71	47.07	48.45	92	0.67	(NA)	41.3	9.7	89.1	(NA)	(NA)	(NA)	25.8	48.2	0.3
United Kingdom [7,10,11]	1.79	29.33	47.19	640	(NA)	24.2	64.1	6.6	70.1	49.0	18.8	7.6	23.2	24.5	0.4
United States [7,10,11]	**2.68**	**27.73**	**66.44**	**1,221**	**1.00**	**56.6**	**71.9**	**9.2**	**90.8**	**46.9**	**16.3**	**6.5**	**29.6**	**13.3**	**0.4**

— Represents zero. NA Not available or not applicable. Z Less than 0.05 percent. [1] Purchasing power parities. See headnote, Table 1348. [2] Aerospace; office and computing equipment; pharmaceuticals; radio, TV, and communication equipment; medical; precision and optical instruments. [3] Motor vehicles; chemicals; electrical machinery; other transport; machinery and equipment. [4] Rubber and plastics; nonmetallic mineral products; shipbuilding; ferrous and nonferrous metals; metal products; petroleum; other manufacturing industries. [5] See footnote 2, Table 1378. [6] See footnote 5, Table 1377. [7] Government budget appropriations for R&D: federal government only. [8] See footnote 4, Table 1331. [9] Percent of GERD/BERD financed by government or industry: the sum of the breakdown does not add to the total. [10] GERD, BERD: Excluding most or all capital expenditures. [11] HERD: Excluding most or all capital expenditures.

Source: Organization for Economic Cooperation and Development (OECD), 2010, "Main Science and Technology Indicators," OECD Science, Technology and R&D Statistics database (copyright), <http://dx.doi.org/10.1787/data-00182-en>, accessed May 2010.

Table 1395. Dow Jones Global Index by Country and Industry: 2000 to 2009

[Index figures shown are as of December 31. 1991 = 100. Based on share prices denominated in U.S. dollars. Stocks in countries that impose significant restrictions on foreign ownership are included in the world index in the same proportion that shares are available to foreign investors]

Country and industry	2000	2005	2008	2009	Country and industry	2000	2005	2008	2009
World, total	**210.9**	**234.1**	**171.9**	**226.9**	Asia/Pacific	93.0	132.0	93.6	123.0
Americas	299.1	307.3	226.1	296.5	Australia	156.0	312.5	228.9	389.7
United States	**306.9**	**302.4**	**219.7**	**276.6**	Hong Kong	245.6	273.6	253.3	420.8
Canada	225.3	365.4	278.6	433.9	Indonesia	31.2	79.0	66.3	152.1
Mexico	132.2	360.1	334.6	495.9	Japan	88.3	113.5	77.6	80.6
Europe	241.2	264.8	198.7	264.2	Malaysia	88.5	119.5	127.3	186.9
Austria	86.2	335.5	160.6	253.9	New Zealand	96.7	227.3	124.7	173.9
Belgium	196.9	321.2	213.0	323.6	Singapore	135.2	176.3	154.1	266.3
Denmark	220.1	375.1	307.8	435.1	Thailand	27.2	76.7	56.6	97.2
Finland	1,537.8	948.5	732.9	843.1					
France	252.9	273.3	222.9	286.0	Basic materials	117.6	213.8	176.8	301.0
Germany	219.1	224.3	214.2	264.9	Consumer goods	183.8	241.9	207.1	272.2
Ireland	312.3	470.4	167.1	216.9	Consumer services	192.8	214.4	156.0	200.4
Italy	192.2	213.8	135.3	166.0	Oil and Gas	230.7	383.3	346.6	444.0
Netherlands	335.7	309.6	198.9	281.7	Financial	207.1	259.8	131.8	173.7
Norway	151.8	276.1	175.5	344.0	Healthcare	329.9	310.6	272.0	320.0
Spain	193.5	288.6	282.0	374.6	Industrial	167.1	192.4	141.4	188.4
Sweden	339.0	378.3	250.8	410.7	Technology	552.7	375.1	251.4	402.6
Switzerland	388.8	452.5	416.9	514.2	Telecommunications	273.3	201.6	199.8	219.5
United Kingdom	199.8	217.6	142.4	198.1	Utilities	156.0	176.9	188.0	198.3

Source: Dow Jones & Company, Inc., New York, NY, *Dow Jones Indexes*, (copyright).

Table 1396. Foreign Stock Market Activity—Morgan Stanley Capital International Indexes: 2000 to 2009

[Index figures shown are as of December 31. January 1, 1970 = 100, except as noted. Minus sign (–) indicates decrease. Based on share prices denominated in U.S. dollars. EM = Emerging Markets]

Index and country	Index			Percent change [1]		Index and country	Index			Percent change [1]	
	2000	2008	2009	2008	2009		2000	2008	2009	2008	2009
ALL COUNTRY (AC) INDEXES											
AC World index [2]	290.1	227.7	299.4	–43.5	31.5	Switzerland	2,695	2,900	3,564	–31.6	22.9
AC World index except USA [2]	103.6	176.7	242.0	47.1	37.4	United Kingdom	1,146	787.7	1,082	–50.6	37.3
AC Asia Pacific [2]	89.6	89.6	120.5	–43.2	34.5	Hong Kong	5,475	4,697	7,290	–52.9	55.2
AC Europe [2]	376.5	301.0	400.2	–49.3	32.9	Japan	2,552	2,108	2,202	–30.5	4.4
European Union [2]	361.5	276.8	365.4	–49.8	32.0	Singapore	2,081	2,125	3,556	–49.5	67.3
DEVELOPED MARKETS						**EMERGING MARKETS**					
						EM Far East Index [4]	127.9	209.8	348.9	–52.0	66.3
World index	1,221	920.2	1,168	–42.1	27.0	China [6,7]	22.6	40.8	64.8	–51.9	58.8
EAFE® index [3]	1,492	1,237	1,581	–45.1	27.7	India [6]	114.5	233.6	468.5	–65.1	100.5
Europe index	1,378	1,099	1,442	–48.2	31.2	Indonesia	77.8	287.5	634.6	–57.6	120.8
Pacific index	1,832	1,656	2,006	–37.9	21.1	Korea, South	78.7	193.1	327.1	–55.9	69.4
Far East index	2,583	2,150	2,374	–33.8	10.4	Malaysia	160.7	231.3	341.8	–43.4	47.8
						Pakistan [6]	44.6	46.1	82.0	–75.4	78.1
United States	**1,250**	**854.4**	**1,061**	**–38.6**	**24.2**	Philippines	146.7	167.9	269.0	–53.8	60.2
Canada	832.5	1,031	1,574	–46.6	52.7	Sri Lanka [6]	36.3	58.9	167.4	–62.1	184.2
						Taiwan [7]	191.7	150.8	264.2	–48.7	75.1
Australia	317.7	476.4	804.1	–52.3	68.8	Thailand	58.9	132.8	225.8	–50.3	70.0
New Zealand [4]	56.4	67.4	96.4	–56.2	43.0						
						EM Latin America	915.6	2,078	4,117	–52.8	98.1
Austria	708.3	1,016	1,406	–69.0	38.4	Argentina	1,233	1,304	2,101	–55.3	61.1
Belgium	1,222	696.5	1,074	–67.5	54.3	Brazil	763.2	1,638	3,625	–57.6	121.3
Denmark	2,201	3,130	4,233	–48.2	35.2	Chile	604.7	1,131	2,052	–37.3	81.4
Finland [4]	921.8	429.2	460.2	–56.4	7.2	Colombia [6]	42.1	447.9	790.5	–27.7	76.5
France	1,509	1,253	1,600	–44.9	27.6	Mexico	1,465	3,357	5,138	–44.0	53.1
Germany	1,436	1,330	1,613	–47.2	21.3	Peru [6]	125.0	719.3	1,218	–42.4	69.3
Greece [4]	475.8	341.2	418.3	–67.1	22.6	Venezuela [6]	106.1	(NA)	(NA)	(NA)	(NA)
Ireland [4]	308.4	120.4	132.4	–72.7	9.9						
Italy	447.2	312.8	383.5	–52.1	22.6	Czech Republic [8]	79.9	455.5	544.6	–45.1	19.6
Luxembourg [5]	491.9	(NA)	(NA)	(NA)	(NA)	Hungary [8]	233.6	427.1	742.7	–62.4	73.9
Netherlands	2,177	1,459	2,011	–50.1	37.9	Jordan	55.1	162.5	149.9	–35.8	–7.7
Norway	1,181	1,513	2,761	–65.2	82.5	Poland [6]	499.0	657.5	902.4	–56.2	37.3
Portugal [4]	127.8	108.5	146.8	–53.6	35.4	Russia [8]	155.2	397.0	795.3	–74.2	100.3
Spain	347.1	492.7	672.4	–43.0	36.5	South Africa [6]	157.6	305.1	468.0	–40.0	53.4
Sweden	4,240	3,276	5,247	–51.4	60.2	Turkey	247.7	275.0	528.1	–63.4	92.0

NA Not available. [1] Percent change during calendar year (e.g., December 31, 2008 through December 31, 2009). Adjusted for foreign exchange fluctuations relative to U.S. dollar. [2] January 1, 1988 = 100. [3] Europe, Australasia, Far East Index. Comprises all European and Far East countries listed under developed markets plus Australia and New Zealand. [4] January 1, 1988 = 100. [5] MSCI Luxembourg Index discontinued as of March 29, 2002. [6] January 1, 1993 = 100. [7] See footnote 4, Table 1331. [8] January 1, 1995 = 100.

Source: MSCI Barra, <http://www.mscibarra.com/about/indexdata_tou.jsp?/products/indices/stdindex/performance.jsp>, (copyright). The MSCI data contained herein is the property of MSCI Inc. (MSCI). MSCI, its affiliates and information providers make no warranties with respect to any such data. The MSCI data contained herein is used under license and may not be further used, distributed, or disseminated without the express written consent of MSCI.

Table 1397. Foreign Stock Market Indices: 1980 to 2009

[As of year end. The DAX-30 index is a total return index which includes dividends, whereas the other foreign indices are price indices which exclude dividends]

Year	London FTSE 100	Tokyo Nikkei 225	Hong Kong Hang Seng	Germany DAX-30	Paris CAC-40	Dow Jones Europe STOXX 50
1980.........	647	7,116	1,477	481	(X)	(X)
1985.........	1,413	13,113	1,752	1,366	(X)	(X)
1990.........	2,144	23,849	3,025	1,398	1,518	835
1995.........	3,689	19,868	10,073	2,254	1,872	1,538
1996.........	4,119	19,361	13,452	2,889	2,316	1,850
1997.........	5,136	15,259	10,723	4,250	2,999	2,634
1998.........	5,883	13,842	9,507	5,002	3,943	3,320
1999.........	6,930	18,934	16,962	6,958	5,958	4,742
2000.........	6,223	13,786	15,096	6,434	5,926	4,557
2001.........	5,217	10,543	11,397	5,160	4,625	3,707
2002.........	3,940	8,579	9,321	2,893	3,064	2,408
2003.........	4,477	10,677	12,576	3,965	3,558	2,660
2004.........	4,814	11,489	14,230	4,256	3,821	2,775
2005.........	5,619	16,111	14,876	5,408	4,715	3,349
2006.........	6,221	17,226	19,965	6,597	5,542	3,697
2007.........	6,457	15,308	27,813	8,067	5,614	3,684
2008.........	4,434	8,860	14,388	4,810	3,218	2,065
2009.........	5,413	10,546	21,873	5,957	3,936	2,579

X Not applicable.

Source: Global Financial Data, Los Angeles, CA, <http://www.globalfinancialdata.com>, unpublished data (copyright).

Table 1398. U.S. and Foreign Stock Markets—Market Capitalization and Value of Shares Traded: 2000 to 2009

[In billions of U.S. dollars (15,104.0 represents $15,104,000,000,000). Market capitalization is the market value of all domestic listed companies at the end of the year. The market value of a company is the share price times the number of shares outstanding. Value of shares traded is the annual total turnover of listed company shares]

Country	Market capitalization				Value of shares traded			
	2000	2005	2008	2009	2000	2005	2008	2009
United States	15,104.0	16,970.9	11,737.6	15,077.3	31,862.5	21,510.0	36,467.4	46,735.9
Argentina..........	166.1	61.5	52.3	48.9	6.0	16.4	13.4	2.7
Australia..........	372.8	804.1	675.6	1,258.5	226.3	616.1	1,013.9	761.8
Austria............	29.9	124.4	72.3	53.6	9.4	45.9	104.5	25.5
Belgium...........	182.5	288.5	167.4	261.4	38.0	125.7	211.3	127.8
Brazil.............	226.2	474.6	589.4	1,167.3	101.3	154.2	727.8	649.2
Canada...........	841.4	1,480.9	1,002.2	1,681.0	634.7	845.0	1,770.6	1,239.6
Chile	60.4	136.4	132.4	209.5	6.1	18.9	36.6	37.6
China [1]...........	581.0	780.8	2,793.6	5,007.6	721.5	586.3	5,470.5	8,956.2
Denmark	107.7	178.0	131.5	186.9	91.6	152.0	211.9	148.3
Egypt.............	28.7	79.7	85.9	90.0	11.1	25.4	69.6	52.8
Finland...........	293.6	209.5	154.4	91.0	206.6	273.5	390.4	91.2
France	1,446.6	1,758.7	1,492.3	1,972.0	1,083.3	1,526.1	3,257.7	1,365.8
Germany	1,270.2	1,221.3	1,108.0	1,297.6	1,069.1	1,763.2	3,093.8	1,288.9
Greece............	110.8	145.0	90.4	54.7	95.1	65.3	105.6	51.7
Hong Kong.........	623.4	1,055.0	468.6	2,291.6	377.9	460.1	1,626.1	1,489.6
India..............	148.1	553.1	645.5	1,179.2	509.8	433.9	1,049.7	1,088.9
Indonesia..........	26.8	81.4	98.8	178.2	14.3	41.9	110.7	115.3
Iran	34.0	38.7	49.0	63.3	5.0	8.2	15.4	17.1
Ireland	81.9	114.1	49.4	29.9	14.4	64.7	82.5	18.5
Israel	64.1	120.1	134.5	182.1	23.4	59.9	109.2	88.3
Italy	768.4	798.2	520.9	317.3	778.4	1,115.2	1,478.8	459.7
Japan.............	3,157.2	4,736.5	3,220.5	3,377.9	2,693.9	4,997.4	5,879.4	4,192.6
Korea, South	171.6	718.2	494.6	836.5	1,067.7	1,203.0	1,466.0	1,581.5
Luxembourg........	34.0	51.3	66.5	105.6	1.2	0.2	1.7	0.3
Malaysia	116.9	181.2	187.1	256.0	58.5	50.0	85.2	73.0
Mexico............	125.2	239.1	232.6	340.6	45.3	52.7	108.2	77.1
Morocco...........	10.9	27.2	65.7	62.9	1.1	4.1	21.9	0.3
Netherlands........	640.5	592.9	387.9	542.5	677.2	835.8	1,143.0	604.2
New Zealand	18.6	43.4	24.2	67.1	10.8	17.4	16.5	37.2
Norway............	65.0	191.0	125.9	227.2	60.1	194.8	367.6	247.8
Philippines.........	51.6	40.2	52.1	80.1	8.2	7.0	17.2	3.1
Poland	31.3	93.9	90.2	135.3	14.6	30.0	68.0	17.2
Portugal...........	60.7	67.0	68.7	98.6	54.4	41.6	82.6	45.8
Russia	38.9	548.6	1,321.8	861.4	20.3	159.3	562.2	1.9
Saudi Arabia	67.2	646.1	246.3	318.8	17.3	1,103.5	524.7	682.5
Singapore	152.8	316.7	180.0	310.8	91.5	119.8	270.9	252.3
Sweden	328.3	403.9	252.5	432.3	390.0	464.0	638.8	390.3
Switzerland	792.3	938.6	862.7	1,070.7	609.1	883.3	1,511.0	795.6
Taiwan [1]...........	247.6	516.0	380.9	695.9	983.5	716.5	944.0	1,066.1
Thailand...........	29.5	124.9	102.6	138.2	23.3	89.3	116.8	134.9
Turkey	69.7	161.5	117.9	225.7	179.2	201.3	239.7	243.5
United Kingdom......	2,580.0	3,058.2	1,852.0	2,796.4	1,835.3	4,167.0	6,484.3	3,402.5

[1] See footnote 4, Table 1331.

Source: Standard and Poor's, New York, NY, Standard & Poor's Global Stock Markets Factbook 2010 (copyright).

Table 1399. Foreign Exchange Rates: 2009

[Foreign currency units per U.S. dollar. Rates shown include market, official, principal, and secondary rates]

Country	Currency	2009	Country	Currency	2009
Afghanistan [1]	Afghanis	(NA)	Laos	Kip	8,556.56
Albania	Leks	93.93	Latvia	Lats	0.52
Algeria	Algerian dinars	72.57	Lebanon	Lebanese pounds	1,507.50
Antigua and Barbuda	E. Caribbean dollars	(NA)	Lesotho	Maloti	9.80
Argentina	Argentine pesos	3.76	Liberia	Liberian dollars	(NA)
Armenia	Drams	360.07	Libya [1]	Libyan dinars	1.26
Aruba	Aruban guilders	(NA)	Lithuania	Litai	2.53
Australia	Australian dollars	1.29	Luxembourg	Euro	0.73
Austria	Euro	0.73	Macedonia	Denars	45.13
Bahamas, The	Bahamian dollars	1.00	Madagascar	Malagasy ariary	1,966.97
Bahrain	Bahrain dinars	0.38	Malaysia	Ringgit	3.55
Bangladesh	Taka	69.05	Mali	CFA francs	481.35
Barbados	Barbadian dollars	(NA)	Malta	Euro	0.73
Belarus	Belarusian rubel	2,850.00	Mauritania	Ouguiyas	(NA)
Belgium	Euro	0.73	Mauritius	Mauritian rupees	32.62
Belize	Belizean dollars	2.00	Mexico	Mexican pesos	13.64
Benin	CFA francs	481.35	Moldova	Lei	11.11
Bolivia	Bolivianos	7.07	Mongolia	Togrogs	1,442.80
Botswana	Pula	7.46	Morocco	Dirhams	8.06
Brazil	Reals	2.03	Mozambique	Meticais	27.40
Bulgaria	Leva	1.44	Namibia	Namibia dollars	8.54
Burkina Faso	CFA francs	481.35	Nepal	Nepalese rupees	77.44
Burma [1]	Kyats	1,090.00	Netherlands	Euro	0.73
Cambodia	Riel	4,135.39	Netherlands Antilles	Guilders	(NA)
Cameroon	CFA francs	481.35	New Zealand	New Zealand dollars	1.62
Canada	Canadian dollars	1.15	Nicaragua	Cordobas	20.34
Central African Republic	CFA francs	481.35	Niger	CFA francs	481.35
Chad	CFA francs	481.35	Nigeria	Naira	150.48
Chile	Chilean pesos	569.37	Norway	Norwegian kroner	6.40
China [2]	Yuan	6.82	Oman	Rials omani	0.38
Colombia	Colombian pesos	1,990.00	Pakistan	Pakistan rupees	81.41
Comoros	Comorian francs	(NA)	Panama	Balboas	1.00
Congo (Brazzaville) [3]	CFA francs	483.21	Papua New Guinea	Kina	2.77
Costa Rica	Colones	580.01	Paraguay	Guaranies	4,967.00
Cote d'Ivoire	CFA francs	469.21	Peru	Nuevos soles	2.88
Croatia	Kunas	5.43	Philippines	Philippine pesos	47.80
Cyprus	Euro	0.73	Poland	Zlotych	3.10
Czech Republic	Koruny	19.37	Portugal	Euro	0.73
Denmark	Kroner	5.47	Qatar	Qatar riyals	3.64
Djibouti	Djibouti francs	(NA)	Romania	Lei	3.07
Dominica	E. Caribbean dollars	(NA)	Russia	Russian rubles	32.00
Dominican Republic	Dominican pesos	36.14	Rwanda	Rwanda francs	568.75
Ecuador	U.S. dollars	1.00	Saint Kitts and Nevis	E. Caribbean dollars	2.70
Egypt	Egyptian pounds	5.60	Saint Lucia	E. Caribbean dollars	2.70
El Salvador	U.S. dollars	1.00	Saint Vincent and the		
Equatorial Guinea	CFA francs	481.35	Grenadines	E. Caribbean dollars	2.70
Estonia	Krooni	11.48	Saudi Arabia	Saudi A. riyals	3.75
Ethiopia [1]	Birr	11.86	Senegal	CFA francs	481.35
Fiji	Fiji dollars	(NA)	Sierra Leone	Leones	(NA)
Finland	Euro	0.73	Singapore	Singapore dollar	1.45
France	Euro	0.73	Slovakia	Euro	0.73
Gabon	CFA francs	481.35	Slovenia	Euro	0.73
Georgia	Lari	1.70	South Africa	Rand	8.54
Germany	Euro	0.73	Spain	Euro	0.73
Greece	Euro	0.73	Sri Lanka	Sri Lanka rupees	115.00
Guatemala	Quetzales	8.16	Sudan	Sudanese dinars	2.34
Guyana	Guyana dollars	204.57	Suriname [1]	Suriname dollar	(NA)
Haiti	Gourdes	41.37	Swaziland	Emalangeni	10.50
Honduras	Lempiras	18.90	Sweden	Swedish kronor	7.82
Hong Kong	Hong Kong dollars	7.75	Switzerland	Swiss francs	1.11
Hungary	Forint	200.64	Syria	Syrian pounds	46.86
Iceland	Kronur	128.42	Tanzania	Tanzania shillings	1,317.50
India	Indian rupees	46.78	Thailand	Baht	34.32
Indonesia	Rupiah	10,399.20	Togo	CFA francs	483.21
Iran	Rials	9,900.00	Trinidad and Tobago	Tt dollars	6.30
Iraq	Dinars	1,170.00	Tunisia	Tunisian dinars	1.35
Ireland	Euro	0.72	Turkey	Liras	1.55
Israel	New sheqalim	3.93	Uganda	Uganda shillings	2,073.30
Italy	Euro	0.73	Ukraine	Hryvnias	7.79
Jamaica	Jamaica dollars	88.67	United Arab Emirates	Dirhams	3.67
Japan	Yen	94.50	United Kingdom	Pounds sterling	0.65
Jordan	Jordanian dinars	0.71	Uruguay	Uruguayan pesos	23.02
Kazakhstan	Tenge	147.84	Vanuatu	Vatu	97.93
Kenya	Kenya shillings	78.00	Venezuela	Bolivares	2.15
Korea, South	Won	1,296.88	Yemen	Yemeni rials	203.05
Kuwait	Kuwaiti dinars	0.28	Zambia	Zambian kwacha	5,237.40
Kyrgyzstan	Soms	43.07	Zimbabwe	Zimbabwe dollar	(NA)

NA Not available. [1] End-of-year values were used if annual averages were unavailable. Some values were estimated using partial year data. [2] See footnote 4, Table 1331. [3] See footnote 5, Table 1331.

Source: Central Intelligence Agency, *The World Factbook, 2010.* See also <https://www.cia.gov/library/publications/the-world-factbook/index.html/>, accessed August 2010.

Table 1400. Reserve Assets and International Transaction Balances by Country: 2000 to 2009

[In millions of U.S. dollars (43,442 represents $43,442,000,000). Assets include holdings of convertible foreign currencies, special drawing rights, and reserve position in International Monetary Fund and exclude gold holdings. Minus sign (–) indicates debits]

Country	Total reserve assets		2009		Current account balance			Merchandise trade balance		
	2000	2008	Total	Currency holdings [1]	2000	2008	2009	2000	2008	2009
United States	**43,442**	**43,244**	**76,366**	**32,226**	**–417,425**	**–706,066**	**–419,870**	**–452,061**	**–836,271**	**–512,693**
Algeria.........	9,229	92,999	95,070	93,910	(NA)	(NA)	(NA)	(NA)	(NA)	(NA)
Argentina........	19,301	29,121	29,402	27,379	–8,981	7,037	8,635	2,452	15,464	18,621
Australia.........	13,906	19,926	24,846	21,051	–14,763	–47,786	(NA)	–4,862	–4,915	(NA)
Austria..........	10,990	5,786	5,176	3,050	–1,339	13,444	8,731	–3,978	–576	–2,974
Bangladesh......	1,141	3,694	6,518	6,060	–306	1,032	(NA)	–1,654	–6,065	(NA)
Belgium [2]........	7,671	6,050	10,147	4,976	(NA)	–14,275	2,557	(NA)	–16,332	–828
Brazil...........	24,894	125,201	151,410	147,917	–24,225	–28,192	–24,335	–698	24,836	25,347
Burma..........	171	(NA)	(NA)	(NA)	–212	(NA)	(NA)	–504	(NA)	(NA)
Cameroon.......	163	2,004	2,345	2,188	–249	–510	(NA)	502	541	(NA)
Canada.........	24,639	28,422	34,597	27,175	19,622	27,281	–20,004	45,047	63,700	12,331
Chile	11,540	14,979	16,128	15,213	–898	–2,513	4,217	2,119	8,848	13,982
China [3].........	129,155	1,265,530	1,541,150	1,530,370	20,518	426,107	(NA)	34,474	360,682	(NA)
Colombia........	6,843	15,243	15,786	14,772	795	–6,883	–5,146	2,670	976	2,560
Congo (Brazzaville) [4]....	170	2,510	2,428	2,357	648	(NA)	(NA)	2,037	(NA)	(NA)
Cote d'Ivoire	513	1,463	2,084	1,810	–241	488	(NA)	1,486	3,330	(NA)
Denmark	11,596	26,272	47,389	45,455	2,262	7,549	12,824	6,641	–645	6,704
Ecuador.........	727	2,427	1,833	1,799	926	1,120	(NA)	1,399	1,371	(NA)
Egypt..........	10,068	20,916	20,574	19,741	–971	–1,415	–3,349	–8,321	–19,759	–16,818
Finland..........	6,122	4,531	6,194	4,722	10,526	8,206	3,444	13,684	10,210	4,973
France..........	28,428	21,826	29,747	17,688	22,307	–64,229	–59,118	–3,173	–86,883	–64,894
Germany........	43,664	28,006	38,225	23,556	–32,279	246,055	168,019	55,466	265,097	188,130
Ghana	178	(NA)	(NA)	(NA)	–387	–3,543	(NA)	–830	–4,999	(NA)
Greece..........	10,303	[5]223	992	127	–9,820	–51,313	–37,043	–20,239	–65,046	–42,826
Hungary.........	8,588	21,936	28,114	27,097	–4,004	–10,808	409	–2,913	–53	5,678
India...........	29,091	160,633	169,154	164,945	–4,601	–36,088	(NA)	–10,641	–95,808	(NA)
Indonesia........	21,876	32,200	40,546	38,638	7,992	126	10,582	25,042	22,916	35,197
Ireland	4,114	566	1,238	330	–516	–14,222	–6,499	25,010	34,712	45,349
Israel	17,869	27,601	38,663	37,693	–2,210	1,349	7,189	–3,857	–7,238	–240
Italy	19,623	24,079	29,196	22,020	–5,781	–78,144	–66,199	9,549	–1,046	3,259
Japan..........	272,392	655,317	652,065	635,939	119,660	156,634	142,194	116,716	38,131	43,632
Kenya..........	689	1,869	2,455	2,219	–199	–1,978	(NA)	–1,262	–5,649	(NA)
Korea, South	73,781	130,590	172,185	169,168	12,251	–5,777	42,668	16,954	5,669	56,128
Kuwait	5,436	11,110	12,928	11,232	14,672	64,742	(NA)	13,027	64,004	(NA)
Malaysia	21,744	59,177	60,874	59,237	8,488	38,914	(NA)	20,827	51,261	(NA)
Mexico..........	27,254	61,759	63,526	60,026	–18,766	–15,903	–5,252	–8,337	–17,261	–4,678
Morocco.........	3,702	14,351	14,542	13,985	–501	–5,659	(NA)	–3,235	–19,497	(NA)
Nepal..........	726	(NA)	(NA)	(NA)	–299	384	(NA)	–814	–2,533	(NA)
Netherlands......	7,401	7,451	11,549	5,644	7,264	42,571	42,819	17,800	57,067	47,848
Nigeria.........	7,607	34,411	(NA)	(NA)	7,427	39,357	(NA)	10,415	43,986	(NA)
Norway..........	21,181	33,079	31,166	29,163	25,079	88,341	53,531	25,908	87,628	55,312
Pakistan.........	1,162	4,671	7,220	6,339	–85	–15,663	(NA)	–1,157	–17,002	(NA)
Peru...........	6,427	19,653	20,420	19,774	–1,546	–4,180	(NA)	–403	3,090	(NA)
Philippines.......	10,047	21,550	24,739	23,923	–2,225	3,897	(NA)	–5,971	–12,885	(NA)
Poland	20,387	38,503	48,430	46,816	–10,343	–26,909	–7,207	–12,307	–25,972	–4,476
Portugal.........	6,838	850	1,566	518	–11,595	–29,298	–23,380	–14,532	–31,336	–23,936
Romania	1,896	23,936	26,899	25,999	–1,355	–23,719	–7,139	–1,684	–28,182	–9,434
Saudi Arabia	15,032	287,351	261,336	253,078	14,317	132,322	(NA)	49,777	212,027	(NA)
Singapore	61,532	113,092	119,796	118,649	10,719	27,181	(NA)	13,956	30,912	(NA)
South Africa......	4,669	19,856	22,477	20,688	–191	–20,084	–11,295	4,698	–4,448	534
Spain	23,784	8,059	11,613	8,156	–23,185	–156,432	–78,683	–37,087	–128,285	–62,725
Sri Lanka........	797	1,603	2,944	2,884	–1,044	–3,876	(NA)	–1,044	–4,470	(NA)
Sudan	106	908	698	572	–557	–1,314	(NA)	440	3,441	(NA)
Sweden	11,407	16,813	27,339	24,586	6,617	47,767	29,564	15,215	17,556	12,125
Switzerland	24,769	29,255	62,640	58,439	32,830	5,094	23,636	2,064	13,482	1,204
Thailand.........	24,573	70,547	86,422	85,220	9,313	1,698	20,284	11,701	17,870	32,731
Trinidad and Tobago.........	1,064	6,130	5,854	5,519	544	(NA)	(NA)	969	(NA)	(NA)
Turkey	17,260	45,725	45,209	44,127	–9,920	–41,946	–14,042	–22,057	–53,021	–24,856
United Kingdom...	29,759	28,793	35,532	24,256	–38,800	–39,904	–28,690	–49,850	–173,929	–127,624
Venezuela	10,046	21,489	13,844	11,282	11,853	37,392	8,561	16,664	45,656	19,153

NA Not available. [1] Holdings of convertible foreign currencies. [2] Balance of payments current account and trade balance data for 2000 are for Belgium-Luxembourg. Thereafter, data is for Belgium only. [3] See footnote 4, Table 1331. [4] See footnote 5, Table 1331. [5] Break in series. Data not comparable to earlier years.

Source: International Monetary Fund, Washington, DC, *International Financial Statistics*, monthly, (copyright).

Table 1401. International Tourism Arrivals, Expenditures, and Receipts—Leading Countries: 2000 to 2008

[Arrivals in thousands of nonresident tourists at national borders, except as noted (77,190 represents 77,190,000); expenditures and receipts in millions of dollars. Receipts are dollars spent by foreign tourists on travel inside the country shown. Expenditures are dollars visitors (same-day visitors and tourists) from a given country of origin spend on travel outside their country of residence. Excludes international transport receipts]

Country	Arrivals (1,000)					Expenditures (mil. dol.)				Receipts (mil. dol.)				
	2000	2005	2006	2007	2008, prel.	2000	2005	2007	2008, prel.	2000	2005	2006	2007	2008, prel.
France	77,190	74,988	77,916	80,853	79,218	17,715	30,458	36,743	43,346	30,641	43,942	46,512	54,209	56,274
United States	51,238	49,206	50,977	55,979	57,937	67,043	73,320	81,517	85,372	97,943	102,070	106,906	119,781	134,908
Spain	46,403	55,914	58,004	58,666	57,192	5,922	15,246	19,724	20,363	29,802	47,789	51,297	57,734	61,978
China [1]	31,229	46,809	49,913	54,720	53,049	13,114	21,759	29,786	36,157	16,231	29,296	33,949	37,233	40,843
Italy	41,181	36,513	41,058	43,654	42,734	15,685	22,370	27,329	30,839	27,493	35,319	38,257	42,660	46,232
United Kingdom [2]	25,209	29,970	32,713	32,778	31,888	38,262	59,532	71,519	69,792	21,769	30,573	34,796	38,698	36,424
Ukraine	6,431	17,631	18,936	23,122	25,449	470	2,805	3,569	4,023	394	3,125	3,485	4,597	5,768
Turkey	9,586	20,273	18,916	22,248	24,994	1,713	2,872	3,260	3,506	7,636	18,152	16,853	18,487	21,951
Germany [3]	18,983	21,500	23,569	24,421	24,884	52,824	74,189	83,156	91,692	18,611	29,121	32,888	36,101	40,019
Russia	21,169	22,201	22,486	22,909	23,676	8,848	17,314	22,133	24,890	3,429	5,870	7,628	9,607	11,944
Mexico	20,641	21,915	21,353	21,370	22,637	5,499	7,500	8,375	8,526	8,294	11,803	12,177	12,852	13,289
Malaysia	10,222	16,431	17,547	20,973	22,052	2,075	3,711	5,586	6,709	5,011	8,846	10,427	14,053	15,293
Austria [3]	17,982	19,952	20,269	20,773	21,935	6,232	9,316	10,561	11,432	9,899	16,243	16,510	18,559	21,630
Hong Kong	8,814	14,773	15,821	17,154	17,319	12,502	13,305	15,042	15,888	5,868	10,209	11,509	13,563	15,043
Canada	19,627	18,771	18,265	17,935	17,142	12,438	18,217	24,716	27,306	10,778	13,768	14,689	15,459	15,267
Greece	13,096	14,765	16,039	16,165	15,939	4,558	3,039	3,423	3,930	9,219	13,334	14,402	15,550	17,416
Saudi Arabia [4]	6,585	8,037	8,620	11,531	14,757	(NA)	9,287	20,171	15,129	(NA)	4,626	4,768	5,972	5,910
Thailand	9,579	11,567	13,822	14,464	14,584	2,772	3,800	5,143	5,215	7,483	9,577	13,393	16,667	17,646
Poland	17,400	15,200	15,670	14,975	12,960	3,315	5,548	7,753	9,596	5,677	6,274	7,239	10,599	11,771
Egypt	5,116	8,244	8,646	10,610	12,296	1,072	1,629	2,446	2,915	4,345	6,851	7,591	9,303	10,985
Macao [4]	5,197	9,014	10,683	12,942	10,605	(NA)	358	463	554	(NA)	7,759	9,449	13,076	16,758
Portugal	12,097	10,612	11,282	12,321	(NA)	2,228	3,050	3,937	4,328	5,243	7,676	8,416	10,175	10,980
Netherlands [3]	10,003	10,012	10,739	11,008	10,104	12,191	16,140	19,110	21,825	7,197	10,450	11,382	13,339	13,346
South Africa	5,872	7,369	8,396	9,091	9,592	2,085	3,373	3,927	4,291	2,677	7,335	7,876	8,443	7,638
Croatia [3]	5,831	8,467	8,659	9,307	9,415	568	754	985	1,109	2,758	7,370	7,990	9,233	11,267
Romania [2]	5,264	5,839	6,037	7,722	8,862	425	925	1,543	2,178	359	1,052	1,308	1,606	1,992
Hungary [2]	(NA)	9,979	9,259	8,638	8,608	1,651	2,382	2,949	4,037	3,733	4,120	4,254	4,739	6,033
Switzerland [5]	7,821	7,229	7,863	8,448	8,608	5,419	8,782	10,116	10,973	6,652	10,041	10,808	12,183	14,464
Japan	4,757	6,728	7,334	8,347	8,351	31,884	37,565	26,511	27,901	3,373	12,430	8,470	9,345	10,820
Ireland	6,646	7,333	8,001	8,332	8,026	2,525	6,074	8,656	10,425	2,615	4,782	5,369	6,074	6,342
Morocco	4,278	5,843	6,558	7,408	7,879	426	612	880	1,090	2,039	4,610	5,984	7,181	7,221
United Arab Emirates [5,6]	3,907	7,126	(NA)	(NA)	(NA)	3,019	6,186	11,273	13,288	1,063	3,218	4,972	6,072	7,162
Singapore	6,062	7,079	7,588	7,957	7,778	4,535	10,070	12,477	14,189	5,142	6,205	7,545	9,179	10,583
Belgium [3]	6,457	6,747	6,995	7,045	7,165	9,429	14,948	17,579	19,317	6,592	9,845	10,311	10,996	11,810
Tunisia	5,058	6,378	6,550	6,762	7,049	263	374	437	458	1,682	2,143	2,275	2,575	2,953
Korea, South [2]	5,322	6,023	6,155	6,448	6,891	7,132	15,406	20,890	17,125	6,834	5,806	5,788	5,797	9,078
Czech Republic [3]	4,773	6,336	6,435	6,680	6,649	1,276	2,405	3,647	4,587	2,973	4,676	5,541	6,637	7,719
Indonesia	5,064	5,002	4,871	5,506	6,234	3,197	3,584	4,904	5,397	4,975	4,522	4,448	5,346	7,377
Bulgaria	2,785	4,837	5,158	5,151	5,780	538	1,309	1,826	2,380	1,074	2,412	2,612	3,130	3,804
Australia [2]	4,931	5,499	5,532	5,644	5,586	6,387	11,253	14,853	18,729	9,289	16,868	17,854	22,415	25,062

NA Not available. [1] See footnote 4, Table 1331. [2] Arrivals are of nonresident visitors at national borders. [3] Arrivals are of nonresident tourists in all types of accommodation establishments. [4] Receipts include both travel and passenger transport. [5] Arrivals of nonresident tourists in hotels and similar establishments. [6] Expenditures and receipts include both travel and passenger transport.

Source: World Tourism Organization, Madrid, Spain, World Tourism Barometer, April 2010 (copyright).

International Statistics 875

Table 1402. Household Expenditure on Recreation and Culture as a Percentage of GDP: 1980 to 2007

[Household expenditure on recreation and culture includes purchases of audio-visual, photographic, and computer equipment; CDs and DVDs; musical instruments; camper vans; caravans; sports equipment; toys; domestic pets and related products; gardening tools and plants; newspapers; tickets to sporting matches, cinemas, and theatres; and spending on gambling (including lottery tickets) less any winnings. It excludes expenditures on restaurants, hotels, and travel and holiday homes but includes package holidays]

Country	1980	1990	2000	2001	2002	2003	2004	2005	2006	2007
United States	**4.5**	**5.4**	**6.4**	**6.4**	**6.4**	**6.4**	**6.4**	**6.3**	**6.4**	**6.5**
Australia	5.8	6.1	7.3	7.1	7.2	7.1	7.0	6.8	6.6	(NA)
Austria	5.0	6.5	7.0	7.1	6.9	6.9	6.8	6.7	6.5	(NA)
Belgium	(NA)	(NA)	5.2	5.2	4.8	4.8	4.7	4.7	4.6	4.7
Canada	4.4	5.1	5.7	5.7	5.8	5.7	5.6	5.5	5.5	5.4
Czech Republic	(NA)	(NA)	6.1	6.2	6.0	6.2	6.0	5.9	5.7	5.6
Denmark	4.8	4.9	5.2	5.1	5.1	5.3	5.5	5.5	5.6	5.6
Finland	5.2	5.4	5.4	5.3	5.3	5.5	5.5	5.6	5.8	5.7
France	4.8	4.8	5.1	5.1	5.2	5.2	5.2	5.2	5.2	5.1
Germany	(NA)	(NA)	5.6	5.6	5.4	5.3	5.3	5.2	5.2	5.1
Greece	(NA)	(NA)	5.1	5.8	5.8	5.4	5.5	5.6	6.6	6.3
Hungary	(NA)	(NA)	4.1	4.2	4.2	4.2	4.2	4.3	4.2	(NA)
Iceland	(NA)	6.1	7.1	6.9	6.8	6.7	6.5	6.4	6.1	(NA)
Ireland	(NA)	(NA)	3.4	3.5	3.2	3.1	3.2	3.2	3.1	3.1
Italy	4.1	4.4	4.5	4.4	4.3	4.2	4.3	4.1	4.1	4.0
Japan	(NA)	(NA)	6.1	6.2	6.2	6.2	6.2	6.0	6.1	(NA)
Korea	2.2	3.9	4.1	4.2	4.4	4.0	3.6	3.7	3.7	3.7
Luxembourg	(NA)	(NA)	3.6	3.8	3.9	3.5	3.5	3.2	2.9	2.8
Netherlands	5.9	5.6	5.5	5.4	5.3	5.1	5.0	4.8	4.8	4.8
Norway	(NA)	(NA)	5.2	5.3	5.5	5.6	5.5	5.1	(NA)	(NA)
Poland	(NA)	(NA)	5.6	4.9	4.8	5.0	5.0	4.7	4.5	(NA)
Portugal	(NA)	(NA)	4.2	4.1	4.1	4.1	4.2	4.3	4.5	(NA)
Slovakia	(NA)	(NA)	4.7	5.2	5.0	4.7	4.8	4.9	4.8	5.0
Spain	(NA)	(NA)	5.7	5.7	5.6	5.5	5.5	5.5	5.3	(NA)
Switzerland	(NA)	5.2	5.1	5.1	5.1	5.1	5.0	4.9	4.6	(NA)
Turkey	(NA)	(NA)	3.8	3.4	3.5	3.4	3.8	3.7	3.5	3.2

NA Not available.

Source: Organization for Economic Cooperation and Development (OECD), 2010, "OECD Factbook Statistics 2009," OECD Factbook Statistics database (copyright), <http://dx.doi.org/10.1787/data-00377-en>, accessed May 2010.

Table 1403. Development Assistance by Country: 2007 and 2008

[119,759 represents $119,759,000,000]

Country	Official development aid (ODA), 2008 [1]			2007	
	Million U.S. dollars	Percent of GNI [2]	Percent of total DAC[3] ODA	Multilateral aid (percent of ODA)	Grants by NGOs [4] (percent of GNI)
DAC [3] total	119,759	0.30	100.0	29.6	0.05
EU-15 [5]	70,168	0.42	58.6	37.6	0.02
United States	**26,008**	**0.18**	**21.7**	**13.2**	**0.09**
Australia	3,166	0.34	2.6	15.0	0.08
Austria	1,681	0.42	1.4	26.8	0.03
Belgium	2,381	0.47	2.0	36.5	0.07
Canada	4,725	0.32	3.9	22.7	0.10
Denmark	2,800	0.82	2.3	35.6	0.03
Finland	1,139	0.43	1.0	40.5	0.01
France	10,957	0.39	9.1	36.7	(NA)
Germany	13,910	0.38	11.6	35.3	0.04
Greece	693	0.20	0.6	50.2	–
Ireland	1,325	0.58	1.1	30.9	0.15
Italy	4,444	0.20	3.7	68.0	–
Japan	9,362	0.18	7.8	24.8	0.01
Luxembourg	409	0.92	0.3	32.5	0.02
Netherlands	6,993	0.80	5.8	25.4	0.04
New Zealand	346	0.30	0.3	22.7	0.04
Norway	3,967	0.88	3.3	22.7	(NA)
Portugal	614	0.27	0.5	42.6	–
Spain	6,686	0.43	5.6	35.0	(NA)
Sweden	4,730	0.98	3.9	32.4	0.02
Switzerland	2,016	0.41	1.7	25.0	0.11
United Kingdom	11,409	0.43	9.5	43.1	0.02

– Represents or rounds to zero. NA Not available. [1] Preliminary. [2] Gross national income. See headnote, Table 1347. [3] DAC: OECD Development Assistance Committee. [4] NGO: Non-governmental organizations. [5] See footnote 2, Table 1378.

Source: Organization for Economic Cooperation and Development (OECD), 2010, "ODA by donor," and "Official and private flows," OECD International Development Statistics database (copyright), <http://dx.doi.org/10.1787/data-0063-en>, accessed May 2010.

Table 1404. Net Flow of Financial Resources to Developing Countries and Multilateral Organizations: 1995 to 2008

[172,755 represents $172,755,000,000. Net flow covers loans, grants, and grant-like flows minus amortization on loans. Military flows are excluded. The Development Assistance Committee (DAC) determines those countries that are to be considered "developing." GNI = gross national income. For explanation of GNI, see headnote, Table 1347. Minus sign (–) indicates net inflow]

Country	Amount (mil. dol.)				Percent of GNI			
	1995	2000	2007	2008	1995	2000	2007	2008
All donors, total [1]	172,755	139,725	457,268	294,754	14.34	24.83	35.16	23.93
United States	46,984	25,252	129,862	14,084	0.65	0.25	0.93	0.10
Australia.	2,536	1,961	10,307	3,997	0.73	0.53	1.25	0.43
Austria	958	1,135	20,405	11,302	0.41	0.61	5.62	2.82
Belgium	−234	2,281	3,818	4,425	−0.09	1.00	0.83	0.89
Canada	5,724	6,483	17,161	24,069	1.04	0.95	1.22	1.63
Denmark	1,799	2,176	4,807	5,150	1.07	1.39	1.51	1.50
Finland.	604	1,087	2,149	−222	0.48	0.91	0.86	−0.08
France	12,477	5,557	43,126	40,641	0.81	0.41	1.66	1.44
Germany	21,197	12,331	36,739	33,395	0.87	0.66	1.10	0.91
Greece.	(NA)	229	3,391	1,166	(NA)	0.20	1.10	0.35
Ireland	247	740	5,840	6,101	0.46	0.93	2.70	2.71
Italy	2,800	10,846	4,422	5,581	0.26	1.01	0.21	0.25
Japan.	42,295	11,423	30,315	31,783	0.79	0.24	0.67	0.63
Luxembourg.	72	129	384	426	0.40	0.73	0.94	0.99
Netherlands	6,795	6,947	18,142	−14,022	1.71	1.85	2.35	−1.61
New Zealand	166	142	404	433	0.31	0.32	0.34	0.38
Norway.	1,670	1,437	6,371	3,963	1.15	0.87	1.62	0.88
Portugal	395	4,622	2,215	1,528	0.38	4.45	1.03	0.67
Spain	2,025	23,471	21,662	30,087	0.37	4.25	1.55	1.96
Sweden	2,224	3,952	6,911	5,896	1.00	1.76	1.49	1.22
Switzerland	1,118	1,765	13,281	12,923	0.35	0.68	3.02	2.82
United Kingdom.	13,382	10,230	46,107	41,878	1.19	0.72	1.66	1.57

NA Not available. [1] Includes other donors, not shown separately.

Source: Organization for Economic Cooperation and Development (OECD), 2010, "Official and private flows," OECD International Development Statistics database (copyright), <http://dx.doi.org/10.1787/data-00072-en>.

Table 1405. External Debt by Country: 1990 to 2008

[In billions of dollars (28.1 represents $28,100,000,000). Total external debt is debt owed to nonresidents repayable in foreign currency, goods, or services. Total external debt is the sum of public, publicly guaranteed, and private nonguaranteed long-term debt, use of IMF credit, and short-term debt. Short-term debt includes all debt having an original maturity of one year or less and interest in arrears on long-term debt]

Country	1990	2000	2007	2008	Country	1990	2000	2007	2008
Algeria	28.1	25.4	5.8	5.5	Montenegro	(NA)	(NA)	1.3	1.5
Angola	8.6	9.4	11.5	15.1	Morocco.	25.0	20.7	20.5	20.8
Argentina	62.2	140.9	127.7	128.3	Nepal	1.6	2.9	3.6	3.7
Bangladesh	12.5	15.7	21.9	23.6	Nigeria	33.4	31.4	8.7	11.2
Brazil	119.7	241.6	237.5	255.6	Pakistan.	20.7	32.8	40.7	49.3
Bulgaria	10.9	11.2	33.0	38.0	Panama	6.5	6.6	10.2	10.7
Cameroon	6.6	10.3	2.9	2.8	Peru	20.0	28.6	28.9	28.6
Chile	19.2	37.3	56.5	64.3	Philippines	30.6	58.3	65.9	64.9
China [1]	55.3	145.7	373.8	378.2	Poland	49.4	64.8	195.4	218.0
Colombia	17.2	33.9	44.0	46.9	Romania	1.1	11.2	84.0	104.9
Congo (Kinshasa) [2] . . .	10.3	11.7	12.4	12.2	Russia [3]	(NA)	160.0	368.1	402.5
Cote d'Ivoire	17.3	12.1	13.9	12.6	Serbia [4]	17.8	11.5	26.4	30.9
Ecuador	12.1	13.2	17.4	16.9	Sierra Leone	1.2	1.2	0.3	0.4
Egypt	33.0	29.0	32.8	32.6	South Africa.	(NA)	24.9	43.6	41.9
Ethiopia	8.6	5.5	2.6	2.9	Sri Lanka	5.9	9.2	14.0	15.2
Ghana	3.7	6.1	4.5	5.0	Sudan	14.8	16.0	19.1	19.6
Guatemala.	2.8	3.9	14.6	15.9	Tanzania	6.4	7.1	5.0	5.9
India.	85.7	100.2	205.0	230.6	Thailand.	28.1	79.7	61.7	64.8
Indonesia.	69.9	143.4	142.6	150.9	Tunisia	7.7	11.3	20.4	20.8
Iran	9.0	7.7	21.1	13.9	Turkey	49.4	116.7	249.2	277.3
Jamaica	4.8	4.7	10.1	10.0	Ukraine	(NA)	12.2	73.6	92.5
Jordan	8.3	7.4	8.4	6.6	Uruguay.	4.4	8.4	11.5	11.0
Kazakhstan	(NA)	12.4	96.3	107.6	Venezuela	33.2	42.3	45.8	50.2
Lebanon.	1.8	9.9	25.6	24.4	Vietnam	23.3	12.8	23.9	26.2
Malaysia	15.3	41.9	61.6	66.2	Zimbabwe	3.3	3.8	5.3	(NA)
Mexico	104.4	150.9	192.8	204.0					

NA Not available. [1] See footnote 4, Table 1331. [2] See footnote 5, Table 1331. [3] The debt of the former Soviet Union is included in Russia's data after 1990 on the assumption that 100 percent of all outstanding external debt as of December 1991 has become a liability of Russia. Beginning in 2000, the data for Russia has also been revised to include obligations to members of the former Council for Mutual Economic Assistance and other countries in the form of trade-related credits amounting to $15.4 billion as of the end of 1996. [4] In June 2006, Serbia and Montenegro became separate countries (formerly Yugoslavia). Data for 2000 are for Serbia and Montenegro. Starting 2006, data excludes Montenegro. External debt obligations—excluding IBRD, IMF, and short-term—of Bosnia and Herzegovina before 2000 are included under Serbia and Montenegro. Data from 2000 onwards are estimates and also reflect borrowing by the former Yugoslavia that are not yet allocated to the successor republics.

Source: The World Bank, Washington, DC, 2010 World Development Indicators (copyright). See also <http://data.worldbank.org/>.

U.S. Census Bureau, Statistical Abstract of the United States: 2011

Table 1406. Foreign Direct Investment Flows in OECD Countries: 2000 to 2008

[In billions of dollars (1,000.0 represents $1,000,000,000,000). Data are converted to U.S. dollars using the yearly average exchange rate]

Country	Inflows 2000	Inflows 2007	Inflows 2008 [1]	Inflows Cumulative 1990 to 2008	Outflows 2000	Outflows 2007	Outflows 2008 [1]	Outflows Cumulative 1990 to 2008
OECD, total [2]	1,000.0	1,099.4	537.7	8,134.8	888.8	1,267.7	1,013.0	9,383.6
United States	293.4	(NA)	(NA)	1,515.7	105.8	(NA)	(NA)	987.7
Australia	8.1	30.7	40.4	166.5	1.1	10.6	30.4	92.9
Austria	8.7	29.0	12.8	85.8	4.8	15.4	15.2	73.5
Belgium	(NA)	121.5	98.1	356.4	(NA)	102.3	108.8	340.0
Canada	64.8	2.8	3.0	252.8	39.7	4.6	0.2	266.6
Czech Republic	4.8	10.0	9.0	76.2	(Z)	1.3	1.2	4.4
Denmark	31.4	7.6	2.7	100.2	22.7	12.1	12.0	106.5
Finland	8.8	12.2	−6.8	67.5	23.4	6.6	1.1	89.4
France	42.6	97.0	90.2	758.9	169.3	149.3	166.4	1,232.6
Germany	195.7	49.4	18.7	624.1	44.3	146.4	135.2	1,228.4
Greece	(NA)	1.7	4.0	21.7	(NA)	4.0	1.1	9.5
Hungary	(NA)	41.1	49.0	119.7	(NA)	65.6	54.7	138.3
Iceland	0.1	8.6	−0.1	13.9	0.3	9.8	−8.0	10.6
Ireland	(NA)	18.8	−19.4	32.4	(NA)	16.8	9.6	72.1
Italy	13.3	39.6	15.4	224.8	10.7	91.0	40.1	328.7
Japan	27.0	(NA)	17.2	179.2	39.3	(NA)	75.8	540.3
Korea, South	5.7	−0.6	5.3	50.9	1.3	7.1	5.7	33.5
Luxembourg	(NA)	145.5	−5.7	567.4	(NA)	167.9	87.0	713.8
Mexico	17.2	(NA)	20.7	178.2	(NA)	(NA)	(NA)	1.7
Netherlands	61.1	127.1	−12.7	420.6	71.3	27.5	32.3	497.7
New Zealand	1.3	2.1	1.1	39.6	0.6	2.5	(Z)	8.7
Norway	5.1	6.0	(NA)	48.2	6.2	1.8	(NA)	64.2
Poland	9.3	20.7	14.2	127.9	(Z)	3.9	2.0	16.5
Portugal	6.4	3.4	2.6	56.4	3.7	4.0	1.1	35.2
Spain	39.2	66.5	63.0	438.9	38.2	121.3	58.7	535.2
Sweden	20.4	25.1	36.2	256.3	38.1	27.4	18.7	207.2
Switzerland	18.6	50.9	−1.3	173.1	34.6	32.9	34.3	347.8
Turkey	1.5	17.5	13.2	66.0	0.9	0.3	1.7	5.8
United Kingdom	113.5	162.3	63.6	1,092.7	232.4	234.6	127.8	1,393.6

NA Not available. Z Less than $50 million. [1] Preliminary. [2] Includes Slovakia, not shown separately.

Source: Organization for Economic Cooperation and Development (OECD), 2010, "Foreign Direct Investment: Flows by Partner Country," OECD International Direct Investment Statistics database (copyright); <http://dx.doi.org/10.1787/data-00335-en>, accessed May 2010.

Table 1407. Military Expenditures, 2009, and Manpower, 2010, by Country

[119,607 represents 119,607,000. Manpower covers males and females deemed fit for military service, ages 15–49]

Country	Expenditures (percent of GDP [1])	Manpower (1,000)	Country	Expenditures (percent of GDP [1])	Manpower (1,000)
United States	[2] 4.1	119,607	Ireland	[2] 0.9	1,713
Afghanistan	1.9	7,530	Israel	[3] 7.3	2,922
Algeria	[3] 3.3	16,989	Italy	[2] 1.8	21,546
Argentina	[2] 0.8	16,711	Japan	[3] 0.8	44,284
Australia	3.0	8,588	Kazakhstan	[7] 0.9	6,446
Austria	[2] 0.8	3,162	Korea, North	(NA)	8,651
Belgium	[2] 1.3	3,841	Korea, South	[3] 2.7	21,194
Bolivia	1.3	3,674	Lebanon	[2] 3.1	1,858
Brazil	1.7	83,080	Libya	[2] 3.9	2,927
Bulgaria	[2] 2.6	2,697	Malaysia	[2] 2.0	11,114
Burma	[2] 2.1	21,270	Mexico	[3] 0.5	48,295
Cambodia	[2] 3.0	5,587	Morocco	[8] 5.0	14,268
Canada	[2] 1.1	13,045	Netherlands	[2] 1.6	6,348
Chile	[3] 2.7	7,143	Nicaragua	[3] 0.6	2,693
China [4]	[3] 4.3	613,415	Nigeria	[3] 1.5	39,654
Colombia	[2] 3.4	18,722	Norway	[2] 1.9	1,753
Congo (Brazzaville) [5]	0.9	1,105	Pakistan	[6] 3.0	70,347
Cote d'Ivoire	[2] 1.5	6,313	Peru	[3] 1.5	12,546
Cuba	[3] 3.8	4,967	Philippines	[2] 0.9	40,680
Czech Republic	[6] 1.5	4,090	Poland	[2] 1.7	15,689
Denmark	[6] 1.3	2,015	Russia	[2] 3.9	47,921
Ecuador	0.9	5,988	Saudi Arabia	[2] 10.0	13,333
Egypt	[2] 3.4	34,676	South Africa	[3] 1.7	14,198
El Salvador	0.6	2,413	Spain	[2] 1.2	15,838
Ethiopia	1.2	23,911	Sudan	[2] 3.0	12,308
France	[2] 2.6	23,818	Sweden	[2] 1.5	3,359
Germany	[2] 1.5	30,288	Syria	[2] 5.9	9,735
Greece	[2] 4.3	4,083	Thailand	[2] 1.8	27,414
Hungary	[2] 1.8	3,808	Turkey	[2] 5.3	34,621
India	[3] 2.5	480,390	Ukraine	[2] 1.4	15,985
Indonesia	[2] 3.0	106,503	United Kingdom	[2] 2.4	23,718
Iran	[3] 2.5	35,157	Venezuela	[2] 1.2	11,480
Iraq	[3] 8.6	12,635	Vietnam	[2] 2.5	41,134

NA Not available. [1] GDP calculated on an exchange rate basis. [2] 2005 data. [3] 2006 data. [4] See footnote 4, Table 1331. [5] See footnote 5, Table 1331. [6] 2007 data. [7] 2002 data. [8] 2003 data.

Source: Central Intelligence Agency, The World Factbook, 2010. See also <https://www.cia.gov/library/publications/the-world-factbook/index.html>, May 2010.

Guide to Sources of Statistics, State Statistical Abstracts, and Foreign Statistical Abstracts

Alphabetically arranged, this guide contains references to important primary sources of statistical information for the United States and other countries. Secondary sources have been included if the information contained in them is presented in a particularly convenient form or if primary sources are not readily available. Nonrecurrent publications presenting compilations or estimates for years later than 2000, or types of data not available in regular series, are also included. Data are also available in press releases.

Valuable information may also be found in state reports, foreign statistical abstracts, which are included at the end of this appendix, and in reports for particular commodities, industries, or similar segments of our economic and social structures, many of which are not included here.

Publications listed under each subject are divided into two main groups: "U.S. Government" and "Nongovernment." The location of the publisher of each report is given except for federal agencies located in Washington, DC. Most federal publications may be purchased from the Superintendent of Documents, U.S. Government Printing Office, Washington, DC, tel. 202-512-1800, (Web site<http://bookstore.gpo.gov>). In some cases, federal publications may be obtained from the issuing agency.

Title	Frequency	Paper	Internet PDF	Internet Other formats
U.S. GOVERNMENT				
Administrative Office of the United States Courts <http://www.uscourts.gov>				
Calendar Year Reports on Authorized Wiretaps (state and federal)	Annual	X	X	X
Federal Court Management Statistics	Annual	X		X
Federal Judicial Caseload Statistics	Annual	X		
Judicial Business of the United States Courts	Annual	X	X	
Statistical Tables for the Federal Judiciary	Semiannual	X		X
Agency for International Development <http://www.usaid.gov>				
U.S. Overseas Loans and Grants: Obligations and Loan Authorizations	Annual		X	X
Army Corps of Engineers <http://www.usace.army.mil>				
Waterborne Commerce of the United States (in five parts)	Annual	X		X
Board of Governors of the Federal Reserve System <http://www.federalreserve.gov>				
Assets and Liabilities of Commercial Banks in the United States H.8	Weekly	X	X	X
Consumer Credit G.19	Monthly	X	X	X
Federal Reserve Bulletin	Annual	X	X	X
Foreign Exchange Rates H.10	Weekly			X
Flow of Funds Accounts of the United States Z.1	Quarterly	X	X	X
Industrial Production and Capacity Utilization G.17	Monthly	X	X	X
Money Stock and Debt Measures H.6	Weekly	X	X	X
Statistical Supplement to the Federal Reserve Bulletin	Monthly	X	X	X
Bureau of Economic Analysis <http://www.bea.gov>				
Survey of Current Business	Monthly	X	X	X
Bureau of Justice Statistics <http://www.ojp.usdoj.gov/bjs>				
American Indians and Crime: A BJS Statistical Profile, December 2004	Periodic	X	X	X
Background Checks for Firearm Transfers	Annual	X	X	X
Capital Punishment, 2006, December 2007	Annual		X	X
Carjacking, 1993–2002, July 2004	Periodic		X	X
Census of Publicly Funded Forensic Crime Laboratories, February 2005	Periodic	X	X	X
Census of State and Federal Correctional Facilities, 2000, August 2003	Periodic	X	X	X
Civil Rights Complaints in U.S. District Courts, July 2002	Periodic	X	X	X
Civil Trial Cases and Verdicts in Large Counties, 2001, April 2004	Periodic	X	X	X
Compendium of Federal Justice Statistics, 2004, December 2006	Annual	X	X	X
Contacts Between Police and Public: Findings from the 2005 National Survey, April 2007	Periodic	X	X	X

U.S. Census Bureau, Statistical Abstract of the United States: 2011

Title	Frequency	Paper	Internet PDF	Internet Other formats
Bureau of Justice Statistics—Con.				
Contract Trials and Verdicts in Large Counties, 2001, February 2005.	Periodic	X	X	X
Crime and the Nation's Households, 2005, April 2007	Annual	X	X	X
Crimes Against Persons Age 65 or Older, 1993–2002, January 2005	Periodic	X	X	X
Criminal Victimization in the United States, 2006, December 2007	Annual	X	X	X
Cross-National Studies in Crime and Justice, September 2004	Periodic	X	X	X
Defense Counsel in Criminal Cases, November 2000	Periodic	X	X	X
Education and Correctional Populations, January 2003	Periodic	X	X	X
Family Violence Statistics	Periodic	X	X	X
Federal Criminal Case Processing, 2002, January 2005	Periodic	X	X	X
Federal Law Enforcement Officers, 2004, August 2006	Biennial	X	X	X
Felony Defendants in Large Urban Counties, 2004, April 2008	Biennial		X	X
Felony Sentences in State Courts, 2004, July 2007	Biennial	X	X	X
Firearm Use by Offenders, November 2001	Periodic	X	X	X
Hepatitis Testing and Treatment in State Prisons, April 2004	Periodic	X	X	X
Hispanic Victims of Violent Crime, 1993–2000, April 2002	Periodic	X	X	X
HIV in Prisons 2006.	Annual		X	X
Homicide Trends in the United States	Annual	X	X	X
Identity Theft, 2005, November 2007	Periodic	X	X	X
Immigration Offenders in the Federal Criminal Justice System, August 2002.	Periodic	X	X	X
Incarcerated Parents and Their Children, August 2000.	Periodic	X	X	X
Indicators of School Crime and Safety	Annual	X	X	X
Intimate Partner Violence, 1993 to 2001, February 2003	Periodic	X	X	X
Jails in Indian Country, 2004, November 2006	Annual	X	X	X
Justice Expenditure and Employment Extract Series, 2005, August 2007	Annual			X
Juvenile Offenders and Victims.	Periodic	X	X	X
Juvenile Victimization and Offending, 1993–2003.	Periodic	X	X	X
Law Enforcement Management and Administrative Statistics 2000: Data for Individual State and Local Agencies with 100 or More Officers.	Periodic	X	X	X
Local Police Departments, 2003, May 2006	Periodic	X	X	X
Medical Malpractice Trials and Verdicts in Large Counties, April 2004	Periodic	X	X	X
Money Laundering Offenders, 1994–2001, July 2003.	Periodic	X	X	X
Prevalence of Imprisonment in the U.S. Population, 1974–2001, August 2003.	Periodic	X	X	X
Prison and Jail Inmates at Midyear, 2006, June 2007.	Annual	X	X	X
Prisoners in 2006, December 2007.	Annual	X	X	X
Probation and Parole in the United States.	Annual	X	X	X
Profile of Jail Inmates, 2002, July 2004.	Periodic	X	X	X
Prosecutors in State Courts, 2001, May 2002.	Biennial	X	X	X
Rape and Sexual Assault: Reporting to Police and Medical Attention, August 2002	Periodic	X	X	X
Reentry Trends in the United States Current Data Electronic	Periodic		X	X
Sheriff's Offices, 2003, April 2006.	Periodic	X	X	X
Sourcebook of Criminal Justice Statistics	Annual	X	X	X
State Court Prosecutors in Large Districts, December 2001.	Periodic	X	X	X
State Court Prosecutors in Small Districts, 2001, January 2003.	Periodic	X	X	X
State Court Sentencing of Convicted Felons, 2004, July 2007	Biennial		X	X
State Prison Expenditures, 2001, June 2004	Periodic	X	X	X
Summary of State Sex Offender Registries, 2001, March 2002	Periodic	X	X	X
Survey of DNA Crime Laboratories, 2001, January 2002	Periodic	X	X	X
Survey of State Criminal History Information Systems, September 2003.	Biennial	X	X	X
Survey of State Procedures Related to Firearm Sales, 2005, November 2006	Periodic	X	X	X
Tort Trials and Verdicts in Large Counties, November 2004	Periodic	X	X	X
Traffic Stop Data Collection Policies for State Police, 2004, June 2005	Periodic	X	X	X
Violent Victimization of College Students, 1995–2002, January 2005	Periodic	X	X	X
Weapon Use and Violent Crime, 1993–2001, September 2003	Periodic	X	X	X
Bureau of Labor Statistics <http://www.bls.gov>				
100 Years of U.S. Consumer Spending: Data for the Nation, New York City, and Boston, Report 991	Periodic	X	X	
College Enrollment and Work Activity of High School Graduates	Annual	X	X	
Comparative Labor Force Statistics, Ten Countries.	Semiannual	X	X	X
Compensation and Working Conditions	Quarterly		X	X
Consumer Expenditure Survey, Integrated Diary and Interview Survey data	Annual	X	X	X
Consumer Prices: Energy and Food	Monthly	X	X	X
Consumer Price Index (CPI) Detailed Report	Monthly		X	X
Employer Costs for Employee Compensation	Annual	X	X	X
Employment and Earnings	Monthly		X	X
Employment and Wages	Annual	X	X	X
Employment Characteristics of Families	Annual	X	X	X
Employment Cost Index.	Quarterly	X	X	X
Employment Cost Indexes and Levels.	Annual	X	X	X
The Employment Situation	Monthly	X	X	X
Geographic Profile of Employment and Unemployment	Annual	X	X	X
International Comparisons of Hourly Compensation Costs for Production Workers in Manufacturing.	Annual	X	X	X
International Comparisons of Manufacturing Productivity and Unit Labor Cost Trends .	Annual	X	X	X
Metropolitan Area Employment and Unemployment.	Monthly	X	X	X
Monthly Labor Review.	Monthly		X	X
National Compensation Survey.	Annual	X	X	X
Occupational Injuries and Illnesses in the United States by Industry	Annual	X	X	X
Occupational Projections and Training Data	Biennial	X	X	X
Producer Price Indexes Detailed Report.	Monthly		X	X
Productivity and Costs by Industry	Periodic	X	X	X
Selected Service-Providing and Mining Industries, 2005	Annual	X	X	X
Manufacturing, 2005.	Annual	X	X	X

880 Appendix I

Title	Frequency	Paper	Internet PDF	Internet Other formats

Title	Frequency	Paper	PDF	Other formats
Bureau of Labor Statistics—Con.				
Wholesale Trade, Retail Trade, and Food Services and Drinking Places, 2005	Annual	X	X	X
Real Earnings	Monthly	X	X	X
Regional and State Employment and Unemployment	Monthly	X	X	X
Relative Importance of Components in the Consumer Price Indexes	Annual	X	X	X
Union Members	Annual	X	X	X
U.S. Import and Export Price Indexes	Monthly	X	X	X
Usual Weekly Earnings of Wage and Salary Workers	Quarterly	X	X	X
Work Experience of the Population	Annual	X	X	X
Bureau of Land Management				
<http://www.blm.gov/wo/st/en.html>				
Public Land Statistics	Annual	X	X	
Census Bureau				
<http://www.census.gov>				
2007 Economic Census:				
Comparative Statistics	Quinquennial	X	X	X
Bridge Between North American Industry Classification System (NAICS) and				
Standard Industrial Classification (SIC)	Quinquennial	X	X	X
Business Expenses	Quinquennial	X	X	X
Industry/Geography	Quinquennial		X	X
2007 Economic Census, Company Statistics Series, Survey of Business Owners	Quinquennial	X	X	X
American Indian- and Alaska Native-Owned Firms	Quinquennial	X	X	X
Asian-Owned Firms	Quinquennial	X	X	X
Black-Owned Firms	Quinquennial	X	X	X
Hispanic-Owned Firms	Quinquennial	X	X	X
Native Hawaiian- and Other Pacific Islander-Owned Firms	Quinquennial	X	X	X
American Community Survey Annual Earnings and Poverty Report	Annual	X	X	
Annual Revision of Monthly Retail and Food Services: Sales and Inventories	Annual		X	
Annual Revision of Monthly Wholesale Distributors: Sales and Inventories	Annual		X	X
Census of Housing Decennial (2000, most recent)	Decennial	X	X	X
Census of Population Decennial (2000, most recent)	Decennial	X	X	X
County Business Patterns	Annual		X	X
Current Construction Reports:				
New Residential Construction and New Residential Sales	Annual		X	
Value of Construction Put in Place, C30	Monthly		X	
Residential Improvements and Repairs, C50	Monthly		X	
Current Housing Reports:				
Housing Vacancies, H111	Quarterly		X	X
Who Can Afford to Buy a House, H121	Occasional	X	X	X
Survey of Market Absorption of Apartments (SOMA)	Quarterly		X	X
Characteristics of Apartments Completed, H131	Annual	X	X	X
American Housing Survey for the United States, H150	Biennial	X	X	X
American Housing Survey for Selected Metropolitan Areas, H170	Biennial	X	X	X
Current Industrial Reports	Annual		X	
Current Population Reports (Series P20 and P23)	Annual	X	X	X
Consumer Income and Poverty, P60, and Household Economic Studies, P70	Periodic	X	X	
Alternative Poverty Estimates in the United States: 2003	Periodic	X	X	
Alternative Income Estimates in the United States: 2003	Periodic	X	X	
Income, Poverty, and Health Insurance Coverage In the United States, 2007	Annual	X	X	X
Economic Census of Outlying Areas	Quinquennial	X	X	
Global Population Profile: 2002 (Series WP)	Periodic	X	X	X
International Briefs (Series IB)	Annual	X	X	
International Data Base	Annual			X
International Population Reports (Series P95)	Annual	X	X	
Manufacturer's Shipments, Inventories, and Orders	Monthly		X	
Manufacturer's Shipments, Inventories, and Orders: 1992–2005	Annual		X	
New York City Housing and Vacancy Survey, 2005	Every 3 years		X	X
Nonemployer Statistics	Annual		X	X
Population Estimates and Projections	Annual			X
Quarterly Financial Report for Manufacturing, Mining, and Trade Corporations	Quarterly		X	X
Residential Finance Survey, 2001	Every 10 years	X	X	X
Service Annual Survey Report	Annual		X	
Survey of Plant Capacity Utilization (Current Industrial Reports MQ-C1)	Annual		X	
U.S. International Trade in Goods and Services: includes cumulative data	Annual		X	X
U.S. Trade with Puerto Rico and U.S. Possessions (FT 895)	Monthly		X	
Vehicle Inventory and Use Survey (discontinued)	Quinquennial	X	X	X
Centers for Disease Control and Prevention, Atlanta, Georgia				
<http://www.cdc.gov>				
CDC Injury Fact Book	Periodic	X	X	X
Morbidity and Mortality Weekly Report	Annual	X	X	X
Centers for Medicare and Medicaid Services (CMS)				
<http://www.cms.hhs.gov>				
CMS Statistics	Annual	X	X	
Data Compendium	Annual	X	X	
Health Care Financing Review. Medicare and Medicaid Statistical Supplement	Annual	X	X	
Health Care Financing Review	Quarterly	X	X	
Trustees Report	Annual	X	X	
Wallet Card	Annual	X	X	
Central Intelligence Agency				
<http://www.cia.gov>				
World Factbook	Annual	X	X	X
Coast Guard (See Department of Homeland Security)				

Title	Frequency	Paper	Internet PDF	Other formats
Comptroller of the Currency <http://www.occ.treas.gov>				
Quarterly Journal.	Quarterly		X	X
Office of the Clerk U.S. House of Representatives <http://clerk.house.gov>				
Statistics of the Presidential and Congressional Election	Biennial		X	X
Council of Economic Advisers <http://www.whitehouse.gov>				
Economic Indicators	Monthly	X	X	X
Economic Report of the President	Annual	X	X	
Department of Agriculture, Economic Research Service <http://www.ers.usda.gov>				
Agricultural Income and Finance (Situation and Outlook Report)	Annual	X	X	X
Amber Waves	Periodic	X	X	X
Cotton and Wool Yearbook	Annual			X
Dairy Yearbook	Annual			X
Foodgrains Yearbook.	Annual		X	
Food Spending in American Households	Annual	X	X	
Fruit and Tree Nut Yearbook.	Annual		X	X
Oil Crops Yearbook	Annual		X	X
Poultry Yearbook	Annual			X
Red Meat Yearbook	Annual			X
Rice Yearbook	Annual		X	X
Sugar and Sweeteners Yearbook	Periodic			X
Situation and Outlook Reports. Issued for agricultural exports, cotton and wool, dairy, feed, fruit and tree nuts, agricultural resources, livestock and poultry, oil crops, rice, aquaculture, sugar and sweeteners, tobacco, vegetables, wheat, and world agriculture	Periodic	X	X	
Vegetable and Melons Yearbook	Annual		X	X
World Agricultural Supply and Demand Estimates	Monthly	X	X	X
Department of Agriculture, Food and Nutrition Service <http://www.fns.usda.gov/fns/default.htm>				
Characteristics of Food Stamp Households	Annual	X	X	
Food and Consumer Service Programs	Monthly			X
Department of Agriculture, Foreign Agricultural Service <http://www.fas.usda.gov>				
Livestock and Poultry World Markets and Trade	Biannual	X	X	
Department of Agriculture, National Agricultural Statistics Service <http://www.nass.usda.gov>				
Agricultural Chemical Usage	Periodic	X	X	X
Agricultural Statistics.	Annual	X	X	
Catfish Production	Annual	X	X	X
Cattle.	Biennial	X	X	X
Census of Agriculture	Quinquennial	X	X	
Cherry Production	Annual	X	X	X
Chickens and Eggs	Annual	X	X	X
Citrus Fruits	Annual	X	X	X
Cranberries	Annual	X	X	X
Crop Production Reports.	Monthly	X	X	X
Crop Values Report	Annual	X	X	X
Dairy Products.	Annual	X	X	X
Farm Labor	Quarterly	X	X	X
Farms, Land in Farms, and Livestock Operations	Annual	X	X	X
Floriculture Crops	Annual	X	X	X
Agricultural Land Values and Cash Rents	Annual	X	X	X
Livestock Slaughter	Annual	X	X	X
Meat Animals: Production, Disposition, and Income	Annual	X	X	X
Milk Production	Annual	X	X	X
Noncitrus Fruits and Nuts	Biennial	X	X	X
Poultry: Production and Value Summary	Annual	X	X	X
Stock Reports. Stocks of grain, peanuts, potatoes, and rice	Periodic	X	X	X
Trout Production	Annual	X	X	X
Turkeys: Hatchery and Raised.	Annual	X	X	X
Usual Planting and Harvesting Dates	Periodic	X	X	X
Vegetable Reports.	Periodic	X	X	X
Weekly Weather and Crop Bulletin Report	Weekly	X	X	
Winter Wheat Seedlings	Monthly	X	X	X
Department of Agriculture, Natural Resources and Conservation Service <http://www.nrcs.usda.gov>				
National Resources Inventory	Periodic	X		X
Department of Defense <http://www.defenselink.mil/pubs>				
Foreign Military Sales and Military Assistance Facts	Annual			X
Personnel Statistics	Annual		X	
Department of Education <http://www.ed.gov/index.jhtml>				
Department of Education, Rehabilitation Services Administration				
Caseload Statistics of State Vocational Rehabilitation Agencies in Fiscal Year.	Annual	X	X	X

882 Appendix I

Title	Frequency	Paper	Internet PDF	Internet Other formats
Department of Health and Human Services <http://www.hhs.gov>				
Annual Report	Annual	X		
Department of Homeland Security <http://www.dhs.gov/index.shtm>				
Budget in Brief.	Annual	X	X	
Department of Homeland Security, Coast Guard <http://www.uscg.mil/default.asp>				
Fact File	Periodic	X	X	X
Department of Homeland Security, Office of Immigration Statistics <http://www.dhs.gov/ximgtn/statistics/>				
Yearbook of Immigration Statistics.	Annual	X	X	
Department of Housing and Urban Development <http://www.hud.gov>				
Survey of Mortgage Lending Activity.	Monthly	X		X
Department of Justice, Bureau of Alcohol, Tobacco Tax, Firearms and Explosives <http://www.atf.treas.gov>				
Alcohol and Tobacco Summary Statistics	Annual	X		
Tobacco Products Monthly Statistical Releases	Monthly	X		
Department of Labor <http://www.dol.gov>				
Annual Report of the Secretary.	Annual	X	X	X
Department of State <http://www.state.gov>				
United States Contribution to International Organizations.	Annual			X
Department of Transportation <http://www.dot.gov>				
Air Travel Consumer Report	Monthly	X	X	X
Airport Activity Statistics of Certified Route Air Carriers	Annual	X		X
Transportation Safety Information Report	Quarterly	X		X
U.S. International Air Travel Statistics	Quarterly	X	X	X
Wage Statistics of Class I Railroads in the United States	Annual	X	X	
Department of the Treasury, Bureau of Public Debt <http://www.publicdebt.treas.gov>				
Monthly Statement of the Public Debt of the United States.	Monthly	X	X	X
Department of the Treasury, Financial Management Services <http://www.fms.treas.gov>				
Active Foreign Credits of the United States Government	Quarterly	X		
Combined Statement of Receipts, Outlays, and Balances	Annual	X	X	X
Monthly Treasury Statement of Receipts and Outlays of the United States Government	Monthly	X	X	X
Treasury Bulletin	Quarterly	X	X	X
Financial Report of the United States Government.	Annual	X	X	
Department of Veterans Affairs <http://www.va.gov>				
Disability Compensation, Pension, and Death Pension Data	Annual			X
Government Life Insurance Programs for Veterans and Members of the Service	Annual			X
Selected Compensation and Pension Data by State of Residence	Annual			X
Veterans Affairs Annual Accountability Report	Annual	X	X	X
Drug Enforcement Administration <http://www.whitehousedrugpolicy.gov>				
Drug Abuse and Law Enforcement Statistics	Irregular	X	X	X
Employment and Training Administration <http://www.doleta.gov>				
Unemployment Insurance Claims	Weekly			X
Energy Information Administration <http://www.eia.doe.gov>				
Annual Energy Outlook	Annual	X	X	X
Annual Energy Review	Annual	X	X	X
Annual Coal Report.	Annual		X	X
Electric Power Annual	Annual		X	X
Electric Power Monthly	Monthly		X	X
Electric Sales, Revenue and Retail Price	Annual			X
Emissions of Greenhouse Gases in the U.S..	Annual		X	X
International Energy Annual	Annual			X
International Energy Outlook.	Annual	X	X	X
Monthly Energy Review	Monthly		X	X
Performance Profiles of Major Energy Producers	Annual		X	X
Petroleum Marketing Annual	Annual		X	X
Petroleum Marketing Monthly	Monthly		X	X
Petroleum Supply Annual Volume 1	Annual		X	X
Petroleum Supply Annual Volume 2 (Web Only)	Annual		X	X
Petroleum Supply Monthly.	Monthly		X	X
Quarterly Coal Report	Quarterly		X	X
Renewable Energy Annual	Annual		X	
Residential Energy Consumption Survey	Quadrennial		X	X
State Electricity Profiles.	Annual		X	X
State Energy Data Report	Annual		X	X

Appendix I 883

Title	Frequency	Paper	Internet PDF	Internet Other formats
Energy Information Administration—Con.				
State Energy Price and Expenditure Report	Annual		X	X
U.S. Crude Oil, Natural Gas, and Natural Gas Liquids Reserves	Annual		X	X
Weekly Coal Production	Weekly		X	X
Environmental Protection Agency				
<http://www.epa.gov/>				
Air Quality Data	Annual			X
Drinking Water Infrastructure Needs Survey	Periodic	X	X	
Needs Survey, Conveyance and Treatment of Municipal Wastewater Summaries of Technical Data	Biennial		X	
Toxics Release Inventory	Annual		X	X
National Water Quality Inventory: 2000 Report (EPA-841-T-01-001)	Biennial	X	X	
Export-Import Bank of the United States				
<http://www.exim.gov/>				
Annual Report	Annual	X	X	
Report to the U.S. Congress on Export Credit Competition and the Export-Import Bank of the United States	Annual	X	X	
Farm Credit Administration.				
<http://www.fca.gov/FCA-HomePage.htm>				
Annual Report on the Farm Credit System	Annual	X	X	
Federal Bureau of Investigation				
<http://www.fbi.gov/ucr/ucr.htm>				
Crime in the United States	Annual		X	X
Hate Crime Statistics	Annual		X	X
Law Enforcement Officers Killed and Assaulted	Annual		X	X
Federal Communications Commission				
<http://www.fcc.gov/>				
Annual Assessment of the Status of Competition in the Market for the Delivery of Video Programming	Annual	X	X	
Annual Report	Annual	X	X	
High-Speed Services for Internet Access	Annual	X	X	
Statistics of Communications Common Carriers	Annual	X	X	
Telecommunications Industry Revenue	Annual	X	X	
Trends in Telephone Service	Annual	X	X	
Trends in the International Telecommunications Industry	Annual	X	X	
Federal Deposit Insurance Corporation				
<http://www.fdic.gov/>				
Annual Report	Annual	X	X	X
FDIC Quarterly	Quarterly	X	X	X
Historical Statistics on Banking	Annual			X
Quarterly Banking Profile	Quarterly	X	X	X
Statistics on Banking	Quarterly			X
Summary of Deposits	Annual			X
Federal Highway Administration				
<http://www.fhwa.dot.gov>				
Highway Statistics	Annual	X	X	
Federal Railroad Administration				
<http://www.fra.dot.gov>				
<http://safetydata.fra.dot.gov/officeofsafety>				
Railroad Safety Statistics	Annual	X	X	X
Fish and Wildlife Service				
<http://www.fws.gov/>				
Federal Aid in Fish and Wildlife Restoration	Annual	X	X	
National Survey of Fishing, Hunting, and Wildlife Associated Recreation	Quinquennial	X	X	
Forest Service				
<http://www.fs.fed.us/>				
An Analysis of the Timber Situation in the United States 1996–2050	Periodic			X
Land Areas of the National Forest System	Annual	X		X
U.S. Timber Production, Trade, Consumption, and Price Statistics 2001	Biennial	X	X	
RPA Assessment Tables	Periodic			X
General Services Administration				
<http://www.gsa.gov/				
Federal Real Property Profile	Annual		X	X
Geological Survey				
<http://ask.usgs.gov>				
Estimated Use of Water in the United States in 2000	Quinquennial	X	X	X
Mineral Commodity Summaries	Annual	X	X	
Mineral Industry Surveys	Monthly		X	X
Minerals Yearbook	Annual	X	X	X
Internal Revenue Service				
<http://www.irs.gov>				
Corporation Income Tax Returns	Annual	X	X	X
Individual Income Tax Returns	Annual	X	X	X
IRS Data Book	Annual	X	X	X
Statistics of Income Bulletin	Quarterly	X	X	X
International Trade Administration, Office of Travel and Tourism Industries				
<http://www.tinet.ita.doc.gov>				

Title	Frequency	Paper	Internet PDF	Internet Other formats
International Trade Administration, Office of Travel and Tourism Industries—Con.				
U.S. Travel and Tourism Statistics	Annual	X		X
International Trade Commission				
<http://www.usitc.gov>				
Recent Trends in U.S. Services	Periodic	X	X	
Synthetic Organic Chemicals, U.S. Production and Sales	Annual	X	X	
Library of Congress				
<http://www.loc.gov/index.html>				
Annual Report	Annual	X	X	
Maritime Administration				
<http://www.marad.dot.gov>				
Annual Report	Annual	X	X	
Cargo-Carrying U.S. Flag Fleet by Area of Operation	Semiannual	X	X	X
Merchant Fleet Ocean-Going Vessels 1,000 Gross Tons and Over	Quarterly			X
Seafaring Wage Rates	Biennial	X	X	
Mine Safety and Health Administration				
<http://www.msha.gov>				
Informational Reports by Mining Industry: Coal; Metallic Minerals; Nonmetallic Minerals (except stone and coal); Stone, Sand, and Gravel	Annual			X
Mine Injuries and Worktime (Some preliminary data)	Quarterly	X		X
National Aeronautics and Space Administration				
<http://ifmp.nasa.gov>				
Annual Procurement Report	Annual	X	X	
National Center for Education Statistics				
<http://nces.ed.gov>				
Characteristics of the 100 Largest Public Elementary and Secondary School Districts in the United States	Annual	X	X	X
Characteristics of Private Schools in the United States, 2005–2006	Annual	X	X	X
College and University Library Survey	Triennial			X
Computer and Internet Use by Children and Adolescents	Biennial	X	X	
The Condition of Education	Annual	X	X	
Digest of Education Statistics	Annual	X	X	
Enrollment in Postsecondary Institutions, Graduation Rates, and Financial Statistics	Annual		X	
Indicators of School Crime and Safety	Annual	X	X	
National Education Statistics Quarterly (last edition 4th quarter 2005)	Quarterly			X
The Nation's Report Card: Mathematics Highlights 2007	Periodic	X	X	
The Nation's Report Card: Reading Highlights 2007	Periodic	X	X	
The Nation's Report Card: Science 2005	Periodic	X	X	
The Nation's Report Card: History 2006	Periodic	X	X	
The Nation's Report Card: Writing 2007	Periodic	X	X	
Projections of Education Statistics	Annual	X	X	X
School and Staffing Survey	Quadrennial			X
Characteristics of Schools, Districts, Teachers, Principals, and School Libraries in the United States	Annual	X	X	
Status and Trends in the Education of Racial and Ethnic Minorities	Irregular	X	X	
National Center for Health Statistics				
<http://www.cdc.gov/nchs/>				
Ambulatory Care Visits to Physician Offices, Hospital Outpatient Departments, and Emergency Departments	Annual	X	X	
Health: United States	Annual	X	X	
Health Characteristics of Adults 55 Years of Age and Over	Periodic	X	X	
Fertility, Family Planning, and Reproductive Health of U.S. Women: Data from the 2002 National Survey of Family Growth	Periodic		X	X
National Hospital Discharge Survey: Annual Summary	Annual		X	
National Vital Statistics Reports (NVRS)	Monthly		X	
Vital and Health Statistics:				
Series 10: Health Interview Survey Statistics	Annual	X	X	
Series 11: Health and Nutrition Examination Survey Statistics	Irregular	X	X	
Series 13: Data from National Health Care Survey	Irregular	X	X	
Series 14: Data on Health Resources: Manpower and Facilities	Irregular	X	X	
Series 20: Mortality Data	Irregular	X	X	
Series 21: Natality, Marriage, and Divorce Data	Irregular	X	X	
Series 23: Data from the National Survey of Family Growth	Irregular	X	X	
National Credit Union Administration				
<http://www.ncua.gov>				
Annual Report	Annual	X	X	
Yearend Statistics	Annual	X	X	
National Endowment for the Arts				
<http://www.nea.gov>				
National Endowment for the Arts, Annual Report	Annual			X
The Performing Arts in the GDP, 2002	Periodic	X	X	
Artist Labor Force by State, 2000	Periodic	X	X	
Artist Employment, 2000–2002	Periodic	X	X	
The Arts in the GDP	Periodic	X	X	
Demographic Characteristics of Art Attendance, 2002	Periodic	X	X	
2002 Survey of Public Participation in the Arts	Periodic	X	X	
National Endowment for the Humanities				
<http://www.neh.gov>				

Title	Frequency	Paper	Internet PDF	Internet Other formats
National Endowment for the Humanities—Con.				
Budget Request...	Annual	X		X
National Guard Bureau				
<http://www.ngb.army.mil/default.aspx>				
Annual Review of the Chief...............................	Annual	X	X	
National Highway Traffic Safety Administration				
<http://www.nhtsa.dot.gov>				
Traffic Safety Facts......................................	Annual	X	X	
National Oceanic and Atmospheric Administration				
<http://www.lib.noaa.gov>				
Climates of the World, HCS 6-4..........................	Monthly			X
Comparative Climatic Data...............................	Annual		X	X
Daily Normals of Temp, Precip, HDD, & CDD/Clim 84......	Periodic			X
Fisheries of the United States...........................	Annual	X	X	
General Summary of Tornadoes...........................	Annual			X
Hourly Precipitation Data. Monthly with annual summary; for each state ...	Monthly			X
Local Climatological Data. Monthly with annual summary; for major cities	Monthly			X
Monthly Climatic Data for the World......................	Monthly			X
Monthly Normals of Temp, Precip, HDD, & CDD/Clim 84 ..	Periodic		X	X
Our Living Oceans......................................	Periodic	X	X	
Storm Data...	Monthly			X
U.S. Climate Normals....................................	Daily	X	X	X
Weekly Weather and Crop Bulletin National summary	Weekly	X	X	
National Park Service				
<http://www.nps.gov/>				
Federal Recreation Fee Report...........................	Annual	X		
National Park Statistical Abstract........................	Annual	X	X	
National Science Foundation				
<http://www.nsf.gov>				
Academic Institutional Profiles...........................	Annual		X	X
Academic Research and Development Expenditures	Annual		X	X
Characteristics of Doctoral Scientists and Engineers in the United States	Biennial		X	X
Characteristics of Recent Science/Engineering Graduates...	Biennial		X	X
Federal Funds for Research and Development..............	Annual		X	X
Federal Research and Development Funding by Budget Function Report	Annual		X	X
Federal Science and Engineering Support to Universities, Colleges, and Nonprofit Institutions	Annual		X	X
Graduate Students and Postdoctorates in Science and Engineering	Annual		X	X
National Patterns of Research and Development Resources....	Annual		X	X
Research and Development in Industry	Annual		X	X
Science and Engineering Degrees	Annual		X	X
Science and Engineering Degrees, by Race/Ethnicity of Recipients................	Annual		X	X
Science and Engineering Doctorate Awards...............	Annual		X	X
Science and Engineering Indicators	Biennial	X	X	X
Science and Engineering State Profiles	Annual		X	X
Science Resources Statistics Info Briefs (various topics)	Frequent	X	X	X
Scientific and Engineering Research Facilities at Universities and Colleges	Biennial		X	X
Women, Minorities, and Persons with Disabilities in Science and Engineering	Biennial		X	X
National Transportation Safety Board				
<http://www.ntsb.gov>				
Annual Review of Aircraft Accident Data: U.S. Air Carrier Operations..............	Annual		X	
Annual Review of Aircraft Accident Data: US General Aviation...................	Annual		X	
Office of Juvenile Justice and Delinquency Prevention				
<http://ojjdp.ncjrs.org/>				
Highlights of the 2006 National Youth Gang Survey (FS-200805).................	Annual		X	X
Juvenile Arrests 2004 (Bulletin, NCJ 214563).............	Annual	X	X	X
Victims of Violent Juvenile Crime (Bulletin, NCJ 201628)	Periodic	X	X	X
Office of Management and Budget				
<http://www.whitehouse.gov/omb>				
The Budget of the United States Government..............	Annual	X	X	
Office of Personnel Management				
<http://www.opm.gov>				
Demographic Profile of the Federal Workforce	Biennial		X	X
Employment and Trends	Bimonthly		X	X
The Fact Book..	Annual		X	X
Statistical Abstract for the Federal Employee Benefit Programs	Annual			X
Work Years and Personnel Costs	Annual		X	X
Patent and Trademark Office				
<http://www.uspto.gov>				
Technology Assessment and Forecast Reports	Periodic	X	X	X
All Technologies (Utility Patents).........................	Annual	X	X	X
Patent Counts by Country/State and Year, Utility Patents Report	Annual	X	X	X
Patenting Trends in the United States	Annual	X		
Railroad Retirement Board, Chicago, Illinois				
<http://www.rrb.gov/default.asp>				
Annual Report..	Annual		X	
Quarterly Benefit Statistics..............................	Quarterly	X		X

886 Appendix I

Title	Frequency	Paper	Internet PDF	Internet Other formats
Securities and Exchange Commission <http://www.sec.gov/about.shtml>				
Select SEC and Market Data.	Annual		X	
Small Business Administration <http://www.sba.gov>				
Annual Report.	Annual	X		X
Quarterly Indicators.	Annual	X	X	X
Small Business and Micro Business Lending	Annual	X	X	X
State and Territory Small Business Profiles.	Annual	X	X	X
The Small Business Economy.	Annual	X	X	X
The State of Small Business	Annual	X	X	
Social Security Administration <http://www.ssa.gov>				
Annual Statistical Report on the Social Security Disability Insurance Program	Annual	X	X	X
Annual Statistical Supplement to the Social Security Bulletin.	Annual	X	X	X
Children Receiving Social Security Income (SSI)	Annual	X	X	X
Congressional Statistics	Annual	X	X	X
Fast Facts & Figures about Social Security.	Annual	X	X	X
Income of the Population 55 and over.	Biennially	X	X	X
OASDI Beneficiaries by State and County	Annual	X	X	X
Social Security Bulletin	Quarterly	X	X	X
SSI Annual Statistical Report	Annual	X	X	X
SSI Disabled Recipients Who Work.	Annual	X	X	X
SSI Recipients by State and County	Annual	X	X	X
State Assistance Programs for SSI Recipients	Annual	X	X	X
Substance Abuse and Mental Health Services Administration <http://www.samhsa.gov>				
National Survey on Drug Use and Health	Annual	X	X	X
National Survey on Substance Abuse Treatment Services (N-SSATS).	Annual	X	X	X
NONGOVERNMENT				
Aerospace Industries Association, Washington, DC <http://www.aia-aerospace.org>				
Aerospace Facts and Figures	Annual	X	X	X
Aerospace Industry Year-End Review and Forecast	Annual		X	
Commercial Helicopter Shipments	Annual		X	
Employment in the Aerospace Industry.	Quarterly		X	
Exports of Aerospace Products.	Quarterly		X	
Imports of Aerospace Products.	Quarterly		X	
Manufacturing Production, Capacity, and Utilization in Aerospace and Aircraft and parts.	Quarterly		X	
Orders, Shipments, Backlog and Inventories for Aircraft, Missiles, and Parts.	Quarterly		X	
Air Transport Association of America, Incorporated, Washington, DC <http://www.airlines.org>				
Air Transport Association, Annual Report	Annual		X	
The Alan Guttmacher Institute, New York, NY <http://www.guttmacher.org>				
Perspectives on Sexual and Reproductive Health.	Quarterly	X	X	X
American Bureau of Metal Statistics, Incorporated, Secaucus, NJ <http://www.abms.com>				
Non-Ferrous Metal Yearbook.	Annual	X		X
American Council of Life Insurers, Washington, DC <http://www.acli.com>				
Life Insurers Fact Book	Annual	X	X	
American Dental Association, Chicago, IL <http://www.ada.org>				
Dental Students' Register	Annual	X		
Distribution of Dentists in the United States by Region and State.	Triennial	X		
Survey of Dental Practice	Annual	X		
American Forest and Paper Association, Washington, DC <http://www.afandpa.org>				
Annual Statistical Summary of Recovered Paper Utilization.	Annual	X	X	
Statistics of Paper, Paperboard, and Wood Pulp.	Monthly	X	X	
American Gas Association, Washington, DC <http://www.aga.org>				
Gas Facts	Annual	X	X	
American Iron and Steel Institute, Washington, DC <http://www.steel.org/AM/Template.cfm?Section=Home>				
Annual Statistical Report.	Annual	X		
American Jewish Committee, New York, NY <http://www.ajc.org>				
American Jewish Year Book	Annual	X	X	
American Medical Association, Chicago, IL <http://www.ama-assn.org>				
Physician Characteristics and Distribution in the U.S.	Annual	X		
State Medical Licensure Statistics, and License Requirements	Annual	X		

U.S. Census Bureau, Statistical Abstract of the United States: 2011

Title	Frequency	Paper	Internet PDF	Internet Other formats
American Osteopathic Association, Chicago, IL <http://www.osteopathic.org/index.cfm>				
American Osteopathic Association Fact Sheet	Biennial	X	X	
American Petroleum Institute, Washington, DC <http://www.api.org>				
The Basic Petroleum Data Book (online subscription)	Annual	X		
Joint Association Survey on Drilling Costs (JA5)	Annual	X		
Petroleum Industry Environmental Report	Annual	X		X
Quarterly Well Completion Report (online subscription)	Quarterly	X	X	
American Public Transportation Association, Washington, DC <http://www.apta.com>				
Public Transportation Fact Book	Annual	X	X	
Association for Manufacturing Technology, McLean, VA <http://www.amtonline.org>				
Economic Handbook of the Machine Tool Industry 2003–2004. (Online version by subscription only.)	Annual		X	
Association of American Railroads, Washington, DC <http://www.aar.org>				
Analysis of Class I Railroads	Annual	X	X	X
Cars of Revenue Freight Loaded	Weekly		X	X
Freight Commodity Statistics, Class I Railroads in the United States	Annual	X	X	X
Yearbook of Railroad Facts	Annual	X	X	
Association of Racing Commissioners International, Incorporated, Lexington, KY <http://www.arci.com>				
Statistical Reports on Greyhound Racing in the United States	Annual	X		
Statistical Reports on Horse Racing in the United States	Annual	X		
Statistical Reports on Jai Alai in the United States	Annual	X		
Book Industry Study Group, Inc., New York, NY <http://www.bisg.org>				
Book Industry Trends	Annual	X		
Used-Book Sales	Periodic	X		
Boy Scouts of America, Irving, TX <http://www.scouting.org>				
Annual Report	Annual	X		X
The Bureau of National Affairs, Incorporated, Washington, DC <http://www.bna.com>				
Basic Patterns in Union Contracts	Annual	X		
BNA's Employment Outlook	Quarterly	X		
BNA's Job Absence and Turnover	Quarterly	X		
Directory of U.S. Labor Organizations	Annual	X		
National Labor Relations Board Election Statistics	Annual	X		
Union Membership and Earnings Data Book	Annual	X		
Source Book on Collective Bargaining	Annual	X		
Carl H. Pforzheimer and Company, New York, NY				
Comparative Oil Company Statistics Annual	Annual	X		
Chronicle of Higher Education, Incorporated, Washington, DC <http://chronicle.com>				
Almanac	Annual	X		X
College Board, New York, NY <http://www.collegeboard.com>				
2007 College-Bound Seniors Total Group Profile Report	Annual	X	X	
Commodity Research Bureau, Logical Systems, Incorporated, Chicago, IL <http://www.crbtrader.com>				
Commodity Year Book Update CD	Quarterly			
CRB Commodity Index Report	Weekly	X		
CRB Commodity Year Book	Annual	X		
CRB Futures Perspective	Weekly	X	X	
Electronic Futures Trend Analyzer	Daily			X
Final Markets-End-of-day Data	Daily			X
Futures Market Service	Weekly		X	
The Conference Board, New York, NY <http://www.conference-board.org>				
Business Cycle Indicators	Monthly	X	X	
Corporate Contributions	Annual	X	X	
Productivity, Employment, and Income in the World's Economies	Annual	X	X	
Congressional Quarterly (CQ) Press, Washington, DC <http://www.cqpress.com/gethome.asp>				
America Votes	Biennial	X		
Consumer Electronics Association (Electronic Industries Alliance), Arlington, VA <http://www.ce.org>				
Consumer Electronics Association (CEA) Sales and Forecasts	Semiannual	X	X	
The Council of State Governments, Lexington, KY <http://www.csg.org>				
The Book of the States	Annual	X	X	
State Administrative Officials Classified by Function	Annual	X		
State Elective Officials and the Legislatures	Annual	X		
State Legislative Leadership, Committees, and Staff	Annual	X		

U.S. Census Bureau, Statistical Abstract of the United States: 2011

Title	Frequency	Paper	Internet PDF	Internet Other formats
Credit Union National Association, Incorporated, Madison, WI <http://www.cuna.org>				
The Credit Union Ranking Report	Annual	X		
Credit Union Services Profile	Annual	X		
Operating Ratios and Spreads	Semiannual	X		
Dow Jones and Company, New York, NY <http://online.wjs.com/public/us?>				
Wall Street Journal	Daily	X		X
Edison Electric Institute, Washington, DC <http://www.eei.org>				
Statistical Yearbook of the Electric Power Industry	Annual	X	X	X
Editor and Publisher Company, New York, NY <http://www.editorandpublisher.com/eandp/index.jsp>				
Editor and Publisher	Monthly	X		
International Year Book	Annual	X		X
Market Guide	Annual	X		
Euromonitor International, London, England <http://www.euromonitor.com>				
Consumer Asia	Annual	X		
Consumer China	Annual	X		
Consumer Eastern Europe	Annual	X		
Consumer Europe	Annual	X		
Consumer International	Annual	X		
Consumer Latin America	Annual	X		
European Marketing Data and Statistics	Annual	X		
International Marketing Data and Statistics	Annual	X		
Latin America Marketing Data and Statistic	Annual	X		
World Consumer Expenditure Patterns	Annual	X		
World Consumer Income Patterns	Annual	X		
World Economic Factbook	Annual	X		
World Retail Data and Statistics	Annual	X		
Federal National Mortgage Association, Washington, DC <http://www.fanniemae.com>				
Annual Report	Annual	X	X	
Food and Agriculture Organization of the United Nations, Home, Italy <http://www.fao.org>				
Fertilizer Yearbook	Annual	X		
Production Yearbook	Annual	X		
Trade Yearbook	Annual	X		
Yearbook of Fishery Statistics	Annual	X		
Yearbook of Forest Products	Annual	X		
The Foundation Center, New York, NY <http://www.foundationcenter.org>				
Foundation Yearbook	Annual	X		
FC Stats	Annual			X
General Aviation Manufacturers Association, Washington, DC <http://www.gama.aero/home.php>				
Shipment Report	Quarterly	X		X
Statistical Databook	Annual	X	X	
Girl Scouts of the USA, New York, NY <http://www.girlscouts.org>				
Annual Report	Annual	X	X	
Giving USA Foundation, Indianapolis, IN <http://www.aafrc.org>				
Giving USA	Annual			X
Health Forum, an American Hospital Association Company, Chicago, IL <http://www.healthforum.com>				
Annual Report	Annual	X		
AHA Hospital Statistics	Annual	X		X
Independent Petroleum Association of America, Washington, DC <http://www.ipaa.org>				
Domestic Oil and Gas Trends	Monthly	X		
Oil and Natural Gas Production in Your State	Annual	X	X	X
U.S. Petroleum Statistics	Annual	X	X	X
Information Today, Incorporated, Medford, NJ <http://www.infotoday.com>				
American Library Directory	Annual	X		
Bowker Annual Library and Book Trade Almanac	Annual	X		
Institute for Criminal Justice Ethics, New York, NY <http://www.lib.jjay.cuny.edu/cje>				
Criminal Justice Ethics	Semiannual	X		
Insurance Information Institute, New York, NY <http://www.iii.org>				
The I.I.I. Insurance Fact Book	Annual	X	X	X
The Financial Services Fact Book (published jointly with the Financial Services Roundtable)	Annual	X		X

U.S. Census Bureau, Statistical Abstract of the United States: 2011

Title	Frequency	Paper	Internet PDF	Internet Other formats
Inter-American Development Bank, Washington, DC <http://www.iadb.org>				
Annual Report	Annual	X	X	
Economic and Social Progress in Latin America	Annual	X		
International Air Transport Association <http://www.iata.org/index.htm>				
World Air Transport Statistics	Annual	X	X	X
International City Management Association, Washington, DC <http://www.icma.org>				
Compensation: An Annual Report on Local Government Executive Salaries and Fringe Benefits	Annual			X
Municipal Year Book	Annual	X		
International Labour Organization, Geneva, Switzerland <http://www.ilo.org>				
Yearbook of Labour Statistics	Annual	X		X
International Monetary Fund, Washington, DC <http://www.imf.org>				
Annual Report	Annual	X	X	X
Balance of Payments Statistics	Monthly	X		
Direction of Trade Statistics	Monthly	X		
Government Finance Statistics Yearbook	Annual	X		
International Financial Statistics	Monthly	X		
International Telecommunication Union, Geneva Switzerland <http://www.itu.int/home/index.html>				
ITU Yearbook of Statistics	Annual	X		
World Telecommunication Indicators	Annual	X		
Investment Company Institute, Washington, DC <http://www.ici.org>				
Mutual Fund Fact Book	Annual	X	X	X
Jane's Information Group, Coulsdon, United Kingdon and Alexandria, VA <http://www.janes.com>				
Jane's Air-Launched Weapons	Monthly	X		X
Jane's All the World's Aircraft	Annual	X		X
Jane's Armour and Artillery	Annual	X		X
Jane's Avionics	Annual	X		X
Jane's Fighting Ships	Annual	X		X
Jane's Infantry Weapons	Annual	X		X
Jane's Merchant Ships	Annual	X		X
Jane's Military Communications	Annual	X		X
Jane's Military Logistics	Annual	X		X
Jane's Military Training Systems	Annual	X		X
Jane's NATO Handbook	Annual	X		X
Jane's Spaceflight Directory	Annual	X		X
Joint Center for Housing Studies, Cambridge, MA <http://www.jchs.harvard.edu>				
The State of the Nation's Housing	Annual	X	X	X
Joint Center for Political and Economic Studies, Washington, DC <http://www.jointcenter.org>				
Black Elected Officials: A Statistical Summary	Annual	X	X	
McGraw-Hill Construction Dodge, a Division of the McGraw-Hill Companies, New York, NY <http://www.construction.com> <http://www.dodge.construction.com/Analytics/>				
Dodge Construction Potential (online subscription)	Monthly	X	X	X
National Academy of Sciences, Washington, DC <http://www.pnas.org>				
Summary Report. Doctorate Recipients from United States' Universities	Annual	X		
National Academy of Social Insurance, Washington, DC <http://www.nasi.org>				
Workers Compensation, Benefits, Coverage, and Costs	Annual	X	X	
National Association of Home Builders, Washington, DC <http://www.nahb.org>				
Home Builders Forecast (online subscription)	Monthly			X
Housing Economics (online subscription)	Monthly			X
Housing Market Statistics (online subscription)	Monthly			X
National Association of Latino Elected and Appointed Officials, Washington, DC <http://www.naleo.org>				
National Directory of Latino Elected Officials	Annual		X	X
National Association of Realtors, Washington, DC <http://www.realtor.org>				
Economist's Commentary	Daily			X
Investment and Vacation Home Buyers Survey	Annual		X	
NAR Member Survey	Annual	X		
Profile of Home Buyer and Sellers	Annual	X		
Real Estate Insights	Monthly			
Research Update	Annual	X		

Title	Frequency	Paper	Internet PDF	Internet Other formats
National Association of State Budget Officers, Washington, DC <http://www.nasbo.org>				
State Expenditure Report	Annual	X	X	
Fiscal Survey of the States	Semiannual	X	X	
National Association of State Park Directors, Raleigh, NC <http://www.naspd.org>				
Annual Information Exchange	Annual		X	X
National Catholic Educational Association, Washington, DC <http://www.ncea.org>				
Catholic Schools in America	Annual		X	X
United States Catholic Elementary and Secondary Schools Staffing and Enrollment	Annual	X		X
U.S. Catholic Elementary Schools and their Finances	Biennial			
U.S. Catholic Secondary Schools and their Finances	Biennial	X		
National Council of Churches USA, New York, NY <http://www.ncccusa.org>				
Yearbook of American and Canadian Churches	Annual	X		X
National Education Association, Washington, DC <http://www.nea.org/index.html>				
Rankings of the States and Estimates of School Statistics	Annual	X	X	
Status of the American Public School Teacher, 2000–2001	Quinquennial	X	X	
National Fire Protection Association, Quincy, MA <http://www.nfpa.org>				
NFPA Journal	Bimonthly			X
National Golf Foundation, Jupiter, FL <http://www.ngf.org/cgi/home.asp>				
Golf Consumer Profile	Annual		X	
Golf Facilities in the U.S.	Annual	X	X	
National Marine Manufacturers Association, Chicago, IL <http://www.nmma.org>				
Boating (A Statistical Report on America's Top Family Sport)	Annual	X	X	X
U.S. Recreational Boat Registration Statistics	Annual	X	X	
National Restaurant Association, Washington, DC <http://www.restaurant.org>				
Hourly Wages for Food Service Occupations	Annual	X	X	
Quick-Service Restaurant Trends	Annual	X	X	
Restaurant Economic Trends (online subscriptions)	Monthly			X
Restaurant Industry Forecast	Annual	X	X	
Restaurant Industry in Review	Annual	X	X	
Restaurant Industry Operations Report	Annual	X	X	
Restaurant Industry Pocket Factbook	Annual			X
Restaurant Performance Index	Monthly	X		X
Restaurant Spending	Annual	X	X	
State of the Restaurant Industry Work Force	Annual	X	X	
Tableservice Restaurant Trends	Annual	X	X	
National Safety Council, Itasca, IL <http://www.nsc.org>				
Injury Facts	Annual	X		X
National Sporting Goods Association, Mount Prospect, IL <http://www.nsga.org>				
The Sporting Goods Market in 2009	Annual	X	X	
Sports Participation in 2009	Annual	X	X	
New York Stock Exchange, Inc., New York, NY <http://www.nyse.com>				
Fact Book (online subscription)	Annual	X	X	
The New York Times Almanac, 2008	Annual	X		
Organization for Economic Cooperation and Development, Paris, France <http://www.oecd.org>				
OECD-FAO Agricultural Outlook	Annual	X		X
Bank Profitability: Financial Statements of Banks, 1924–2003	Biannual	X		X
Central Government Debt: Statistical Yearbook, 1996–2005	Annual	X		X
Coal Information	Annual	X		X
CO2 Emissions From Fuel Combustion, 1971–2004	Annual	X		X
Communications Outlook	Biannual	X		X
DAC Journal	Quarterly	X	X	
Education at a Glance: OECD Indicators	Annual	X		X
Electricity Information	Annual	X		X
Energy Balances of Non-OECD Countries	Annual	X		X
Energy Balances of OECD Countries	Annual	X		X
Energy Prices and Taxes	Quarterly	X	X	
Energy Statistics of Non-OECD Countries	Annual	X	X	X
Energy Statistics of OECD Countries	Annual	X	X	X
Environmental Data Compendium	Annual	X		X
Environmental Outlook	Sporadic	X	X	
Financial Market Trends	Triennial	X	X	
Geographical Distribution of Financial Flows to Aid Recipients	Annual	X		
Historical Statistics, 1970–2000. 2001 Edition	Discontinued	X	X	X
Information Technology Outlook, 2002 Edition	Biennial	X	X	X
Insurance Statistics Yearbook	Annual	X	X	X
International Development Statistics	Annual			X

U.S. Census Bureau, Statistical Abstract of the United States: 2011

Title	Frequency	Paper	Internet PDF	Internet Other formats
Organization for Economic Cooperation and Development Paris, France—Con.				
Internal Migration Outlook	Annual	X	X	
International Trade by Commodity Statistics	Annual	X	X	
Iron and Steel Industry in 2002, 2004 Edition	Annual			
Labor Force Statistics	Annual	X	X	
Main Economic Indicators	Monthly	X	X	
Main Science and Technology Indicators, Vol. 2003	Biennial	X	X	
Measuring Globalisation: The Role of Multinationals in Organisation for Economic Cooperation and Development (OECD) Countries	One time			
Monthly Statistics of International Trade	Monthly	X	X	
National Accounts of OECD Countries	Annual	X	X	X
Natural Gas Information	Annual	X	X	X
Nuclear Energy Data	Annual	X		
OECD Economic Outlook	Biennial	X		X
OECD Economic Studies	Annual	X		X
OECD Economic Surveys	Annual	X		X
OECD Employment Outlook	Annual	X		X
OECD Factbook	Annual	X	X	X
OECD Health Data	Annual	X	X	X
OECD Science, Technology, and Industry Outlook	Biennial	X	X	X
OECD Territorial Reviews	Quarterly	X	X	
OECD in Figures	Bimonthly	X		X
Oil Information 2003 Edition	Annual	X	X	
Oil, Gas, Coal, and Electricity Quarterly Statistics	Quarterly	X	X	
Quarterly Labour Force Statistics (discontinued as of 4th quarter 2004)	Quarterly	X	X	
Quarterly National Accounts	Quarterly	X	X	
Research and Development Statistics	Annual	X	X	X
Revenue Statistics 1965–2005, 2006 Edition	Annual	X	X	
Review of Fisheries in OECD Member Countries	Annual	X	X	
Structural Statistics for Industry and Services	Annual	X	X	
Taxing Wages	Annual	X	X	
Trends in International Migration 2004 Edition	Annual	X	X	
Trends in the Transport Sector	Annual	X	X	
Uranium Resources Production and Demand, 2001	Biennial	X	X	
World Energy Outlook	Annual	X	X	
PennWell Corporation, Tulsa, OK <http://www.pennwell.com>				
Offshore (online subscription)	Monthly	X	X	
Oil and Gas Journal (online subscription)	Weekly	X	X	
Puerto Rico Planning Board, San Juan, PR <http://www.jp.gobierno.pr>				
Activity Index	Monthly	X		X
Balance of Payments Puerto Rico	Annual	X		
Economic Report to the Governor	Annual	X		
External Trade Statistics	Annual	X		X
Income and Product	Annual	X		
Projections	Annual	X		
Selected Statistics on Construction Industry	Annual	X		
Selected Statistics on Puerto Rico's External Trade	Annual	X		X
Statistical Appendix-Economic Report to the Governor	Annual	X		X
Radio Advertising Bureau, New York, NY <http://www.rab.com>				
Media Facts	Annual		X	
Radio Marketing Guide and Fact Book	Quarterly		X	
Reed Business Information, New York, NY <http://www.reedbusiness.com/index.html>				
Library Journal	Semimonthly	X		
Publishers Weekly	Weekly	X		X
School Library Journal	Monthly	X		X
Regional Airline Association, Washington, DC <http://www.raa.org>				
Statistical Report	Annual	X	X	
Securities Industry and Financial Markets Association, New York, NY <http://www.sifma.com>				
Foreign Activity Report	Quarterly	X		
Securities Industry Trends	Periodic	X		
Securities Industry Yearbook	Annual	X		X
Standard and Poor's Corporation, New York, NY <http://www.standardandpoors.com>				
Analysts' Handbook	Monthly	X		
Corporation Records	Daily	X		
Daily Stock Price Records	Quarterly	X		
Standard and Poor's Global Stock Market Factbook	Annual	X		
United Nations Statistics Division, New York, NY <http://unstats.un.org/unsd/default.htm>				
Compendium of Human Settlements Statistics (Series N)	Annual	X		
Demographic Yearbook (Series R)	Annual	X	X	X
Energy Balances and Electricity Profiles (Series W)	Annual	X	X	
Energy Statistics Yearbook (Series J)	Annual	X	X	
Industrial Statistics Yearbook: (Series P)	Annual	X		X

Title	Frequency	Paper	Internet PDF	Internet Other formats
United Nations Statistics Division, New York, NY—Con.				
Commodity Production Statistics	Annual	X		
International Trade Statistics Yearbook (Series G)	Annual	X		
Monthly Bulletin of Statistics (Series Q)	Monthly	X		
National Accounts Statistics (Series X)	Annual	X		X
Main Aggregates and Detailed Tables	Annual	X		
Analysis of Main Aggregates	Annual	X		
Population and Vital Statistics Report (Series A)	Quarterly	X		
Social Statistics and Indicators (Series K)	Occasional	X		X
The World's Women: Trends and Statistics	Quinquennial	X	X	X
Statistical Yearbook (Series; also available in CD-ROM, Series S/CD)	Annual	X		X
World Statistics Pocketbook (Series V)	Annual	X		
United Nations Conference on Trade and Development, Geneva, Switzerland <http://www.unctad.org>				
Development and Globalization: Facts and Figures	Annual	X	X	X
Handbook of Statistics	Annual	X	X	X
United States Telecom Association, Washington, DC <http://www.usta.org>				
Statistics of the Local Exchange Carriers	Annual		X	X
University of Michigan, Center for Political Studies, Institute for Social Research, Ann Arbor, MI <http://www.umich.edu>				
National Election Studies Cumulative Datafile	Biennial	X		X
Warren Communications News, Washington, DC <http://www.warren-news.com>				
Cable and Station Coverage Atlas	Annual			X
Television and Cable Factbook	Annual	X		X
World Almanac, New York, NY <http://www.worldalmanac.com>				
The World Almanac and Book of Facts	Annual	X		X
The World Bank Group, Washington, DC <http://www.worldbank.org>				
Atlas of Global Development	Annual	X	X	
Global Development Finance, 2008	Annual	X	X	
The Little Data Book, 2008	Annual	X	X	
World Development Indicators, 2008	Annual	X		X
World Health Organization, Geneva, Switzerland <http://www.who.int/en/>				
Air Epidemic Update	Annual	X	X	
World Health Statistics	Annual	X	X	
World Trade Organization <http://www.wto.org>				
International Trade Statistics	Annual	X	X	X

Guide to State Statistical Abstracts

This bibliography includes the most recent statistical abstracts for states published since 2000, plus those that will be issued in late 2010. For some states, a near equivalent has been listed in substitution for, or in addition to, a statistical abstract. All sources contain statistical tables on a variety of subjects for the state as a whole, its component parts, or both. Internet sites also contain statistical data.

Alabama

University of Alabama, Center for Business and Economic Research, Box 870221, Tuscaloosa, AL 35487-0221. 205-348-6191. Fax: 205-348-2951. Internet site <http://cber.cba.ua.edu/>.

Alabama Economic Outlook, 2010. Revised annually.

Alaska

Department of Commerce, Community, and Economic Development, 550 West 7th Avenue, Suite 1770, Anchorage, AK 99501. 907-269-8100. Fax 907-269-8125. Internet site <http://www.dced.state.ak.us/dca/misc_resources.htm>.

The Alaska Economic Performance Report, 2006. Online.

Arizona

University of Arizona, Economic and Business Research Center, Eller College of Management, 1130 East Helen Street, McClelland Hall, Rm. 103, P.O. Box 210108, Tucson, AZ 85721-0108. 520-621-2155. Fax: 520-621-2150. Internet site <http://www.ebr.eller.arizona.edu/>

Arizona Statistical Abstract, 2003.

Arizona's Economy. Quarterly Online, 2010. Online.

Arizona Economic Indicators Databook, 2009. Semiannual. Online.

Arkansas

University of Arkansas at Little Rock, Institute for Economic Advancement, Economic Research, 2801 South University Avenue, Little Rock, AR 72204-1099. 501-569-8519. Fax: 501-569-8538. Internet site <http://www.aiea.ualr.edu/default.html>

Arkansas State and County Economic Data, 2008.

Arkansas Personal Income Handbook, 2008.

Arkansas Statistical Abstract, 2008. Revised biennially.

California

Department of Finance, 915 L Street, Sacramento, CA 95814. 916-445-3878. Internet site <http://www.dof.ca.gov/default.asp>.

California Statistical Abstract, 2009. Annual. Online only.

Colorado

University of Colorado at Boulder, Government Publications Library, University Libraries, 184 UCB, 1720 Pleasant Street, Boulder, CO 80309-0184. 303-492-8705. Internet site <http://ucblibraries.colorado.edu/>.

Colorado by the Numbers. Online only.

Colorado Office of Economic Development and International Trade, 1625 Broadway, Suite 2700, Denver, CO 80202. 303-892-3840. Fax: 303-892-3848. Internet site <http://www.colorado.gov/cs/Satellite/OEDIT/1162927366334>.

Colorado Data Book, 2008-09. Online only.

Connecticut

Connecticut Department of Economic & Community Development, 505 Hudson Street, Hartford, CT 06106-7106. 860-270-8000. Internet site <http://www.ct.gov/ecd/site/default.asp>.

Connecticut Town Profiles, 2010.

Delaware

Delaware Economic Development Office, 99 Kings Highway, Dover, DE 19901-7305. 302-739-4271. Fax: 302-739-5749. Internet site <http://dedo.delaware.gov>.

Delaware Statistical Overview, 2008. Online only.

District of Columbia

Business Resource Center, John A. Wilson Building, 1350 Pennsylvania Avenue, NW, Washington, DC 20004. 202-727-1000. Internet site. <http://brc.dc.gov/resources/facts.asp>.

Market Facts and Statistics. Online only.

Florida

University of Florida, Bureau of Economic and Business Research, P.O. Box 117145, 221 Matherly Hall, Gainesville, FL 32611-7145. 352-392-0171, ext. 219. Fax: 352-392-4739. Internet site <http://www.bebr.ufl.edu>.

Florida Statistical Abstract, 2008. Annual. Also available on CD-ROM.

Florida County Perspective, 2009. One profile for each county. Annual. Also available on CD-ROM.

Florida County Rankings, 2009. Annual. Also available on CD-ROM.

Georgia

University of Georgia, Terry College of Business, Selig Center for Economic Growth, Athens, GA 30602-6254. 706-542-8100. Fax: 706-542-3835 Internet site <http://www.selig.uga.edu/>.

Georgia Statistical Abstract, 2008-09.

University of Georgia, Center for Agribusiness and Economic Development, 301 Lumpkin House, Athens, GA 30602-7509. 706-542-2434. Fax: 706-542-0770. Internet site <http://www.georgiastats.uga.edu/>.

The Georgia County Guide, 2010. Annual.

Hawaii

Hawaii State Department of Business, Economic Development & Tourism, Research and Economic Analysis Division, Statistics and Data Support Branch, P.O. Box 2359, Honolulu, HI 96804. 808-586-2423. Fax: 808-587-2790. Internet site <http://www.hawaii.gov/dbedt/>.

The State of Hawaii Data Book 2008. Annual. Periodically updated.

Idaho

State of Idaho Department of Labor, 317 West Main St., Boise, ID 83735. 208-332-3570. Fax: 208-334-6430. Internet site <http://labor.idaho.gov/dnn/default.aspx?alias=labor.idaho.gov/dnn/idl/>.

County Profiles Idaho. Online.

Idaho Community Profiles. Online.

Illinois

The Institute of Government and Public Affairs, University of Illinois, 1007 W. Nevada Street, Urbana, IL 61801, MC-037. 217-333-3340. Fax: 217-244-4817. Internet site <http://www.igpa.uiuc.edu/>.

Indiana

Indiana University, Kelley School of Business, Indiana Business Research Center, 100 South Avenue, Suite 240, Bloomington, IN 47404. 812-855-5507. Internet site <http://www.ibrc.indiana.edu/>.

STATS Indiana. Online only.

Iowa

Office of Social and Economic Trend Analysis, 303 East Hall, Ames, IA 50010-1070. 515-294-9903. Fax: 515-294-0592. Internet site <http://www.seta.iastate.edu/>.

State Library of Iowa, State Data Center, Ola Babcock Miller Building, 1112 East Grand, Des Moines, IA 50319-0233. 800-248-4483. Fax: 515-242-6543. Internet site <http://www.iowadatacenter.org>.

Kansas

University of Kansas, Policy Research Institute, 1541 Lilac Lane, 607 Blake Hall, Lawrence, KS 66045-3129. 785-864-3701. Fax: 785-864-3683. Internet site <http://www.ipsr.ku.edu/>.

Kansas Statistical Abstract, 2008. 43rd ed. Online only.

Kentucky

Kentucky Cabinet for Economic Development, Division of Research, 300 West Broadway, Frankfort, KY 40601. 800-626-2930. Fax: 502-564-3256. Internet site <http://www.thinkkentucky.com/>.

Kentucky Deskbook of Economic Statistics. Online only.

Louisiana

Louisiana State Census Data Center, Office of Electronic Services, 1201 N. Third Street, Suite. 7-210, Baton Rouge, LA, 70802. 225-219-7000. Fax: 225-219-4027. Internet site <http://www.louisiana.gov/explore/demographics_and_geography/>.

Maine

Maine State Planning Office, 38 State House Station, 184 State Street, Augusta, ME 04333-0038. 800-662-4545. Fax: 207-287-6077. Internet site <http://www.maine.gov/spo/>.

Maryland

RESI, Towson University, 8000 York Road, Towson, MD 21252-0001. 410-704-7374. Fax: 410-704-4115. Internet site <http://wwwnew.towson.edu/>.

Maryland Statistical Abstract, 2006.

Massachusetts

MassCHIP, Massachusetts Department of Public Health, 250 Washington Street, Boston, MA 02108-4619. 617-624-6000. Internet site <http://masschip.state.ma.us/>.

Instant Topics. Online only.

Michigan

Michigan Economic Development Corporation, 300 North Washington Square, Lansing, MI 48913. 1-888-784-7328. Internet site <http://www.michigan.org/medc/miinfo>.

Minnesota

Minnesota Department of Employment and Economic Development, 1st National Bank Building, 332 Minnesota Street Suite E200, Saint Paul, MN 55101-1351. 800-657-3858. Internet site <http://www.deed.state.mn.us/facts/index.htm>.

Compare Minnesota: Profiles of Minnesota's Economy & Population. Online only.

Minnesota State Demographic Center, 658 Cedar Street, Saint Paul, MN 55155. Room 300. 651-296-2557. Internet site <http://www.demography.state.mn.us/>.

Mississippi

Mississippi State University, College of Business and Industry, Office of Business Research and Services, P.O. Box 5288, Mississippi State, MS 39762. 662-325-2850. Fax: 662-325-2410. Internet site <http://www.cbi.msstate.edu/dept/bizserv/abstract/>

Mississippi Statistical Abstract, 2007. 40th ed. Also available on CD-ROM.

Missouri

University of Missouri-Columbia, Economic and Policy Analysis Research Center, 10 Professional Building, Columbia, MO 65211. 573-882-4805. Fax: 573-882-5563. Internet site <http://eparc.mirrouri.edu/>.

Missouri Statistical Data Archive. Online only.

Montana

Census and Economic Information Center, Montana Department of Commerce, 301 S. Park Ave., P.O. Box 200505, Helena, MT 59620-0505. 406-841-2740. Fax: 406-841-2731. Internet site <http://ceic.mt.gov/>.

Nebraska

Nebraska Department of Economic Development, P. O. Box 94666, 301 Centennial Mall South, Lincoln, NE 68509-4666. 800-426-6505. Fax: 402-471-3778. Internet site <http://info.neded.org/>.

Nevada

Department of Administration, Budget and Planning Division, 209 East Musser Street, Room 200, Carson City, NV 89701-4298. 775-684-0222. Fax: 775-684-0260. Internet site <http://www.budget.state.nv.us/>.

Nevada Statistical Abstract. Online only.

New Hampshire

New Hampshire Office of Energy and Planning, 4 Chenell Drive, Concord, NH 03301-8501. 603-271-2155. Fax: 603-271-2615. Internet site <http://www.nh.gov/oep/index.htm>.

New Jersey

New Jersey State Data Center, NJ Department of Labor and Workforce Development, 1 John Fitch Plaza, P.O. Box 110 Trenton, NJ 08625-0110. 609-984-2595. Fax: 609-984-6833. Internet site <http://www.state.nj.us/labor/lra/>.

Labor Market Information, 2007. Online only.

New Mexico

University of New Mexico, Bureau of Business and Economic Research, MSC06 3510, 1 University of New Mexico, Albuquerque, NM 87131-0001. 505-277-6626. Fax: 505-277-2773. Internet site <http://bber.unm.edu/>.

New Mexico Business, Current Economic Report Monthly.

FOR-UNM Bulletin. Quarterly.

New York

Nelson A. Rockefeller Institute of Government, 411 State Street, Albany, NY 12203-1003. 518-443-5522. Fax: 518-443-5788. Internet site <http://www.rockinst.org/>.

New York State Statistical Yearbook, 2008 33rd ed.

North Carolina

Office of State Budget and Management, 116 West Jones Street, Raleigh, NC 27603-8005. 919-807-4700. Fax: 919-733-0640. Internet site <http://www.osbm.state.nc.us/osbm/>.

How North Carolina Ranks, 2010. Online only.

North Dakota

University of North Dakota, Bureau of Business and Economic Research, P.O. Box 8098, Grand Forks, ND 58202-8098. 800-225-5863. Fax: 701-777-2019. Internet site <http://business.und.edu/>.

North Dakota Statistical Abstract. Online only.

Ohio

Office of Strategic Research, Ohio Department of Development, 77 South High Street, 27th Floor, Columbus, OH 43216-1001. 614-466-2116. Fax: 614-466-9697. Internet site <http://www.odod.state.oh.us/research>.

Research products and services. Updated continuously.

Ohio County Profiles, 2008.

Ohio County Indicators. Updated periodically.

Oklahoma

University of Oklahoma, Center for Economic and Management Research, Michael F. Price College of Business, 307 West Brooks, Suite 4, Norman OK 73019. 405-325-2931. Fax: 405-325-7688. Internet site <http://www.ou.edu/price/cemr.html/>.

Statistical Abstract of Oklahoma, 2005.

Oregon

Secretary of State, Archives Division, Archives Bldg., 800 Summer Street, NE, Salem, OR 97310. 503-373-0701. Fax: 503-373-0953. Internet site <http://www.sos.state.or.us/bbook>.

Oregon Blue Book. 2009–2010. Biennial.

Pennsylvania

Pennsylvania State Data Center, Institute of State and Regional Affairs, Penn State Harrisburg, 777 West Harrisburg Pike, Middletown, PA 17057-4898. 717-948-6336. Fax: 717-948-6754. Internet site <http://pasdc.hbg.psu.edu>.

Pennsylvania Statistical Abstract, 2009. Also Available on CD-Rom.

Rhode Island

Rhode Island Economic Development Corporation, 315 Iron Horse Way, Suite 101, Providence, RI 02908. 401-278-9100. Fax: 401-273-8270. Internet site <http://www.riedc.com/>.

RI Databank. Online only.

South Carolina

Budget and Control Board, Office of Research and Statistics, 1919 Blanding Street, Columbia 29201. 803-898-9960. Internet site <http://www.ors2.state.sc.us/abstract/index.asp>.

South Carolina Statistical Abstract, 2008. Also available on CD-Rom.

South Dakota

South Dakota State Data Center, Business Research Bureau, The University of South Dakota, 414 E. Clark Street, 132 Patterson Hall, Vermillion, SD 57069. 605-677-5708. Fax: 605-677-5427. Internet site <http://www.usd.edu/brbinfo/>.

2006 South Dakota Community Abstracts.

Tennessee

College of Business Administration, The University of Tennessee, Temple Court, Suite 100, 804 Volunteer Blvd., 716 Stokely Management Center, Knoxville, Tennessee 37996-4334. 865-974-5441. Fax: 865-974-3100. Internet site <http://cber.bus.utk.edu/Default.htm>.

Tennessee Statistical Abstract, 2003. Last printed edition. Biennial.

Texas

Dallas Morning News, Communications Center, P.O. Box 655237, Dallas, TX 75265-5237. 214-977-8262. Internet site <http://www.texasalmanac.com/>.

Texas Almanac, 2010-2011. 64th ed.

Texas State Data Center and Office of the State Demographer, Institute for Demographic and Socioeconomic Research (IDSER), 501 West Durango Blvd., University of Texas at San Antonio, San Antonio, TX 78207-4415. 210-458-6543. Fax: 210-458-6541. Internet site <http://txsdc.utsa.edu/>.

Utah

Governor's Office of Planning and Budget, Demographic & Economic Analysis, Suite 150, P.O. Box 132210, Salt Lake City, UT 84114-2210. 801-538-1027. Fax: 801-538-1547. Internet site <http://www.governor.utah.gov/dea>.

2010 Economic Report to the Governor. Annual.

Utah Data Guide Newsletter, 2010. Quarterly. Also available online.

Vermont

Department of Labor, Labor Market Information, P.O. Box 488, Montpelier, VT 05601-0488. 802-828-4202. Fax: 802-828-4050. Internet site <http://www.vtlmi.info/>.

Vermont Economic-Demographic Profile, 2009. Annual.

Virginia

Weldon Cooper Center for Public Service, P.O. Box 400206, Charlottesville, VA 22904-4206. 434-982-5522. Fax: 434-982-5524. Internet site <http://www.coopercenter.org/>.

Stat Chat. Online only.

Washington

Washington State Office of Financial Management, Forecasting Division, P.O. Box 43113, Olympia, WA 98504-3113. 360-902-0555. Internet site <http://www.ofm.wa.gov/>.

Washington State Data Book, 2009. Online only.

West Virginia

West Virginia University, College of Business and Economics, Bureau of Business and Economic Research, 1601 University Ave, P.O. Box 6025, Morgantown, WV 26506-6025. 304-293-4092. Fax: 304-293-5652. Internet site <http://www.be.wvu.edu/bber/index.htm>.

2009 West Virginia County Data Profiles. Also available on CD-Rom.

West Virginia Economic Outlook, 2009. Annual. Also available on CD-Rom.

Wisconsin

Wisconsin Legislative Reference Bureau, One East Main Street, Suite 200, Madison, WI 53701-2037. 608-266-3561. Internet site <http://www.legis.state.wi.us/lrb/pubs/bluebook.htm>.

2009-2010 Wisconsin Blue Book. Biennial.

Wyoming

Department of Administration and Information, Economic Analysis Division, 2800 Central Avenue, Suite 206, Cheyenne, WY 82002-0060. 307-777-7504. Fax: 307-632-1819. Internet site <http://eadiv.state.wy.us/>.

The Equality State Almanac, 2009.

Guide to Foreign Statistical Abstracts

This bibliography presents recent statistical abstracts for member nations of the Organization for Economic Cooperation and Development and Russia. All sources contain statistical tables on a variety of subjects for the individual countries. Many of the following publications provide text in English as well as in the national language(s). For further information on these publications, contact the named statistical agency which is responsible for editing the publication.

Australia
Australian Bureau of Statistics, Canberra. <http://www.abs.gov.au>.
Year Book Australia. Annual. 2008. With CD-ROM. (In English.)

Austria
Statistik Austria, 1110 Wien. <http://www.statistik.at/index.shtml>.
Statistisches Jahrbuch Osterreichs. Annual. 2010. With CD-ROM. (In German.) With English translations of table headings.

Belgium
L'Institut National de Statistique, Rue de Louvain; 44-1000 Bruxelles. <http://statbel.fgov.be/info/links_en.asp>.
Annuaire statistique de la Belgique. Annual. 1995. (In French.)

Canada
Statistics Canada, Ottawa, Ontario, KIA OT6. <http://www.statcan.ca/start.html>.
Canada Year book. 2010. (In English.)

Czech Republic
Czech Statistical Office, Na padesatem 81, Praha 10. <http://www.czso.cz/>.
Statisticka Rocenka Ceske Republiky 2009. With CD-ROM. (In English and Czech.)

Denmark
Danmarks Statistik, Sejrogade 11, 2100 Kobenhavn O. <http://www.dst.dk>.
Statistisk ARBOG. 2010. Annual. English version available only on internet and is free of charge at: <www.dst.dk/yearbook>. (Printed version - In Danish only.)

Finland
Statistics Finland, Helsinki. <http://www.stat.fi/comment>.
Statistical Yearbook of Finland, Annual. 2009. With CD-ROM. (In English, Finnish, and Swedish.)

France
Institut National de la Statistique et des Etudes Economiques, Paris 18, Bld. Adolphe Pinard, 75675 Paris (Cedex 14). <http://www.insee.fr/fr/home/home_page.asp>.
Annuaire Statistique de la France. Annual. 2003. (In French.) 2005 CD-ROM only.

Germany
Statistische Bundesamt, D-65180 Wiesbaden. <http://www.destatis.de>.
Statistisches Jahrbuch fur die Bundes-republic Deutschland. Annual. 2009. (In German.) *Statistisches Jahrbuch fur das Ausland.* 2006.
Statistisches Jahrbuch 2005 *Fur die Bundes-reublik Deutschland und fur das ausland* CD-ROM.

Greece
National Statistical Service of Greece, Athens. <http:// www.statistics.gr/>.
Concise Statistical Yearbook 2008. (In English and Greek.)
Statistical Yearbook of Greece. Annual. 2008. (In English and Greek.)

Hungary
Hungarian Central Statistical Office, 1024 Budapest. <http://www.ksh.hu>.
Statistical Yearbook of Hungary, 2008. With CD-ROM. (In English and Hungarian.)

Iceland
Hagstofa Islands/Statistics Iceland. <http://www.hagstofa.is/template41.asp?PageID=251>.
Statistical Yearbook of Iceland. 2009. (In English and Icelandic.)

Ireland
Central Statistics Office, Skehard Road, Cork. <http://www.cso.ie>.
Statistical Yearbook of Ireland. Annual. 2008. (In English.)

Italy
Istituto Nazionale Statistica. Via Cesare Balbo 16 Roma. <http://www.istat.it>.
Annuario Statistico Italiano. Annual. 2008. With CD-ROM. (In Italian.)

Japan

Statistics Bureau, Ministry of Internal Affairs and Communications, Statistical Research and Training Institute, Ministry of Internal Affairs and Communications, Japan. <http://www.stat.go.jp/english/data/index.htm>.

Japan Statistical Yearbook. Annual. 2010. (In English and Japanese.)

Korea, South

Statistics Korea, Daejeon Government, #920 Dunsan-dong Seo-gu, Daejeon, Korea 302 701. <http://www.nso.go.kr/>.

Korea Statistical Yearbook. Annual. 2009. (In Korean and English.)

Luxembourg

Statec Centre Administratif Pierre Werner, 13 rue Erasme, B.P. 304, L-2013, Luxembourg. <www.statec.lu/>.

Annuaire Statistique du Luxembourg. 2009. (In French.) (Alphabetical numbering system).

Mexico

Instituto Nacional de Estadistica Geografia e Informatica, Av. Heroe Nacozari Num. 2301 Sur Fracc. Jardines del Parque, CP 20270 Aguascalientes, Ags. <http://www.inegi.gob.mx/difusion/ingles/fiest.html>.

Anuario estadistico de los Estados Unidos Mexicanos. Annual. 1998. Also on disc. (In Spanish.) Agenda Estadistica 1999.

Netherlands

Statistics Netherlands, Henri Faasdreef 312, 2492 JP The Hague. <http://www.cbs.nl/en/>.

Statistical Yearbook 2009 of the Netherlands. (In English.)

Statistisch Jaarboek 2010.

New Zealand

Statistics, New Zealand, Wellington. <http://www.stats.govt.nz/>.

New Zealand Official Yearbook. Annual. 2006. (In English.)

Norway

Statistics Norway, Oslo/Kongsvinger. <http://www.ssb.no/en/>.

Statistical Yearbook. Annual. 2008. (In English.)

Poland

Central Statistical Office al. Niepodleglosci 208, 00-925 Warsaw. <http://www.stat.gov.pl/english/index.htm>.

Concise Statistical Yearbook of Poland. 2009 CD-ROM. (In Polish and English.)

Statistical Yearbook of the Republic of Poland 2007. CD-ROM only. (In Polish and English.)

Portugal

INE (Instituto Nacional de Estatistica.) Av. Antonio Jose de Almeida P-1000-043 Lisboa. <http://www.ine.pt/index_eng.htm>.

Anuario Estatistico de Portugal. 2001. (In Portuguese and English.)

Russia

State Committee of Statistics of Russia, Moscow. <http://www.gks.ru/eng/>.

Statistical Yearbook. 2009. (In Russian.)

Slovakia

Statistical Office of the Slovak Republic, Postovy Priecinok 2, 845 02 Bratislava 45. <http://www.statistics.sk/webdata/english/index2_a.htm>.

Statisticka Rocenka Slovenskej Republiky. 2009. (In English and Slovak.) With CD-ROM.

Spain

INE (Instituto Nacional de Estadistica); Paseo de la Castellana, 183, Madrid 16. <http://www.ine.es/welcoing.htm>.

Anuario Estadistico de Espana. 2010. CD-ROM only. (In Spanish.)

Sweden

Statistics Sweden, SE-104 51 Stockholm. <http://www.scb.se/indexeng.asp>.

Statistisk Arsbok for Sverige. Annual. 2009. (In English and Swedish.)

Switzerland

Bundesamt fur Statistik, Hallwylstrasse 15, CH-3003, Bern.

Statistisches Jahrbuch der Schweiz. Annual. 2010. With CD-ROM. (In French and German.)

Turkey

State Institute of Statistics, Prime Ministry, Necatibey Cad/Ankara. No. 114 06100.

Statistical Yearbook of Turkey. 2004. With CD-ROM. (In English and Turkish.)

Turkey in Statistics. 1999. (In English only.)

United Kingdom

The Stationary Office; P.O. Box 29, Norwich, NR3 1GN. <http://www.statistics.gov.uk/>.

Annual Abstract of Statistics. Annual. 2002. (In English.)

Metropolitan and Micropolitan Statistical Areas: Concepts, Components, and Population

The United States Office of Management and Budget (OMB) defines metropolitan and micropolitan statistical areas according to published standards that are applied to U.S. Census Bureau data. The general concept of a metropolitan or micropolitan statistical area is that of a core area containing a substantial population nucleus, together with adjacent communities having a high degree of economic and social integration with that core. Currently defined metropolitan and micropolitan statistical areas are based on application of 2000 standards (which appeared in the Federal Register on December 27, 2000) to 2000 decennial census data. Current metropolitan and micropolitan statistical area definitions were announced by OMB effective June 6, 2003, and subsequently updated as of December 2003, November 2004, December 2005, December 2006, November 2007, November 2008, and December 2009.

Standard definitions of metropolitan areas were first issued in 1949 by the then Bureau of the Budget (predecessor of OMB), under the designation "standard metropolitan area" (SMA). The term was changed to "standard metropolitan statistical area" (SMSA) in 1959 and to "metropolitan statistical area" (MSA) in 1983. The term "metropolitan area" (MA) was adopted in 1990 and referred collectively to metropolitan statistical areas (MSAs), consolidated metropolitan statistical areas (CMSAs), and primary metropolitan statistical areas (PMSAs). The term "core-based statistical area" (CBSA) became effective in 2000 and refers collectively to metropolitan and micropolitan statistical areas.

OMB has been responsible for the official metropolitan areas since they were first defined, except for the period 1977 to 1981, when they were the responsibility of the Office of Federal Statistical Policy and Standards, U.S. Department of Commerce. The standards for defining metropolitan areas were modified in 1958, 1971, 1975, 1980, 1990, and 2000.

Defining Metropolitan and Micropolitan Statistical Areas—

The 2000 standards provide that each CBSA must contain at least one urban area of 10,000 or more population. Each metropolitan statistical area must have at least one urbanized area of 50,000 or more inhabitants. Each micropolitan statistical area must have at least one urban cluster of at least 10,000 but less than 50,000 population.

Under the standards, the county (or counties) in which at least 50 percent of the population resides within urban areas of 10,000 or more population, or that contain at least 5,000 people residing within a single urban area of 10,000 or more population, is identified as a "central county" (counties). Additional "outlying counties" are included in the CBSA if they meet specified requirements of commuting to or from the central counties. Counties or equivalent entities form the geographic "building blocks" for metropolitan and micropolitan statistical areas throughout the United States and Puerto Rico.

If specified criteria are met, a metropolitan statistical area containing a single core with a population of 2.5 million or more may be subdivided to form smaller groupings of counties referred to as "metropolitan divisions."

As of December 2009, there are 366 metropolitan statistical areas and 576 micropolitan statistical areas in the United States. In addition, there are eight metropolitan statistical areas and five micropolitan statistical areas in Puerto Rico.

Principal Cities and Metropolitan and Micropolitan Statistical Area Titles—

The largest city in each metropolitan or micropolitan statistical area is designated a "principal city." Additional cities qualify if specified requirements are met concerning population size and employment. The title of each metropolitan or micropolitan statistical area consists of the names of up to three of its principal cities and the name of each state into which the metropolitan or micropolitan statistical area extends. Titles of metropolitan divisions also typically are based on principal city names, but in certain cases consist of county names.

Defining New England City and Town Areas—In view of the importance of cities and towns in New England, the 2000 standards also provide for a set of geographic areas that are defined using cities and towns in the six New England states. The New England city and town areas (NECTAs) are defined using the same criteria as metropolitan and micropolitan statistical areas and are identified as either metropolitan or micropolitan, based, respectively, on the presence of either an urbanized area of 50,000 or more population or an urban cluster of at least 10,000 but less than 50,000 population. If the specified criteria are met, a NECTA containing a single core with a population of at least 2.5 million may be subdivided to form smaller groupings of cities and towns referred to as New England city and town area divisions.

Changes in Definitions Over Time— Changes in the definitions of these statistical areas since the 1950 census have consisted chiefly of (1) the recognition of new areas as they reached the minimum required city or urbanized area population and (2) the addition of counties (or cities and towns in New England) to existing areas as new decennial census data showed them to qualify.

In some instances, formerly separate areas have been merged, components of an area have been transferred from one area to another, or components have been dropped from an area. The large majority of changes have taken place on the basis of decennial census data. However, Census Bureau data serve as the basis for intercensal updates in specified circumstances.

Because of these historical changes in geographic definitions, users must be cautious in comparing data for these statistical areas from different dates. For some purposes, comparisons of data for areas as defined at given dates may be appropriate; for other purposes, it may be preferable to maintain consistent area definitions. Historical metropolitan area definitions are available for 1999, 1993, 1990, 1983, 1981, 1973, 1970, 1963, 1960, and 1950.

Excluding Tables 20 through 24 in the Population section; Table 594 in the Labor Force section; Table 682 in the Income section, and the tables that follow in this appendix, the tables presenting data for metropolitan areas in this edition of the Statistical Abstract are based on the 1999 or earlier metropolitan area definitions. For a list of component counties according to the 1999 definition, see Appendix II in the 2002 edition of the Statistical Abstract or <http://www.census.gov /population/www/estimates /pastmetro.html>.

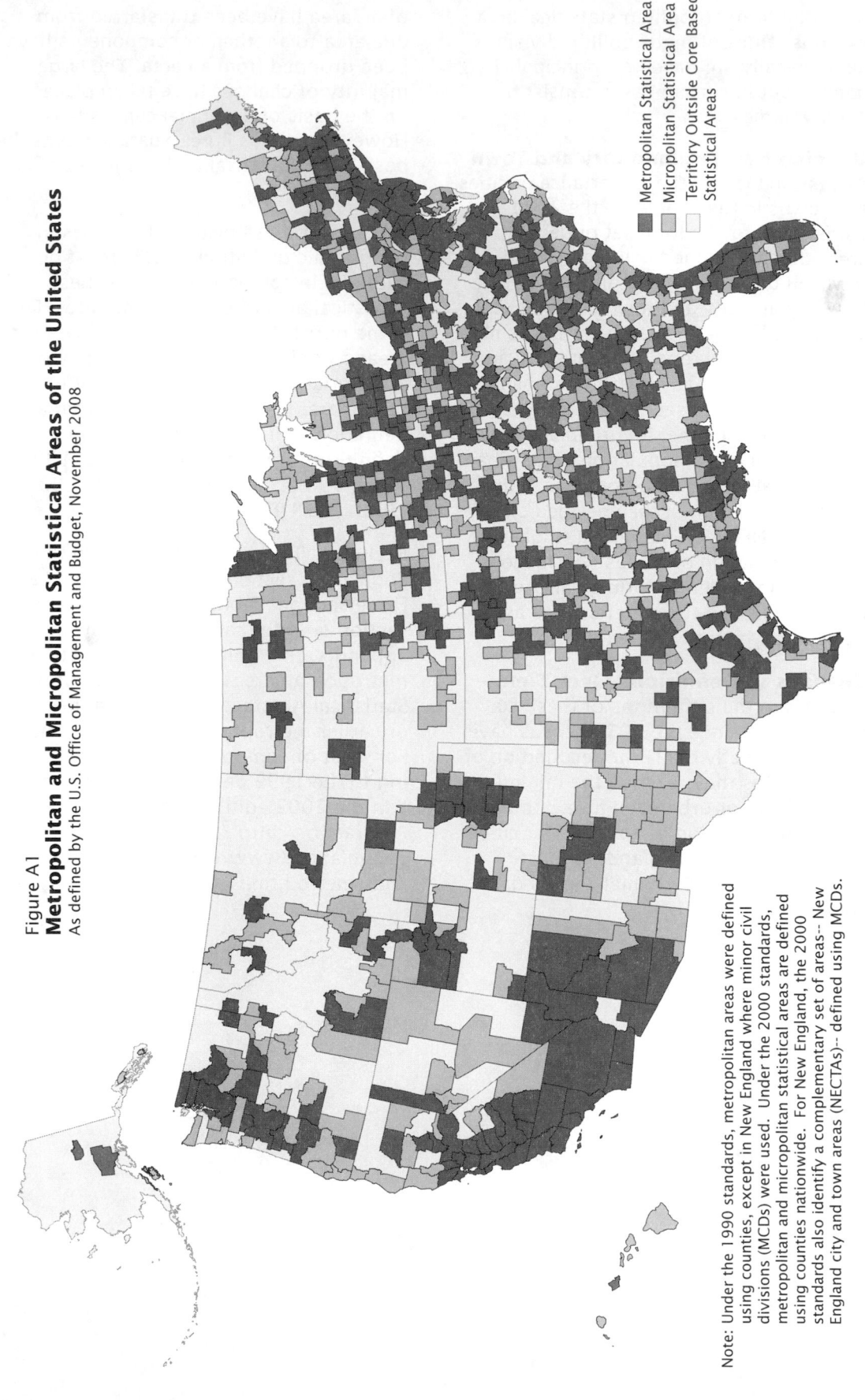

Figure A1

Metropolitan and Micropolitan Statistical Areas of the United States

As defined by the U.S. Office of Management and Budget, November 2008

Metropolitan Statistical Area
Micropolitan Statistical Area
Territory Outside Core Based
Statistical Areas

Note: Under the 1990 standards, metropolitan areas were defined using counties, except in New England where minor civil divisions (MCDs) were used. Under the 2000 standards, metropolitan and micropolitan statistical areas are defined using counties nationwide. For New England, the 2000 standards also identify a complementary set of areas-- New England city and town areas (NECTAs)-- defined using MCDs.

U.S. Census Bureau, Statistical Abstract of the United States: 2011

Figure A2
Metropolitan and Micropolitan New England City and Town Areas (NECTAs)
As defined by the U.S. Office of Management and Budget, November 2008

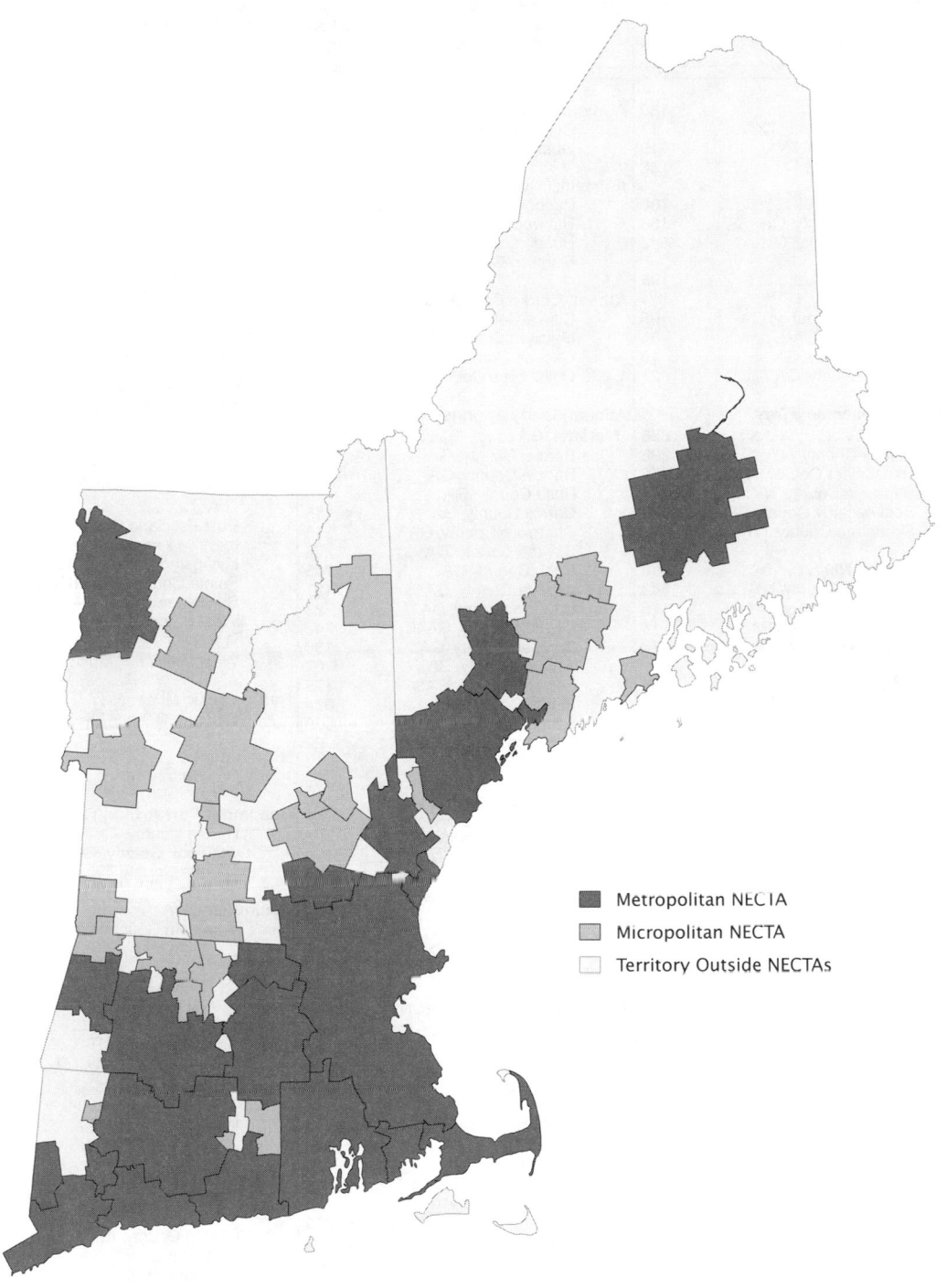

Metropolitan NECTA

Micropolitan NECTA

Territory Outside NECTAs

Note: Under the 2000 standards, metropolitan and micropolitan statistical areas are defined using
        counties nationwide. For New England, the 2000 standards also identify a complementary
        set of areas-- New England city and town areas (NECTAs) -- defined using MCDs.

U.S. Census Bureau, Statistical Abstract of the United States: 2011

Table A. Metropolitan Statistical Areas and Components—Population: 2009

[Population as of July 2009. (160 represents 160,000). Metropolitan statistical areas as defined by the U.S. Office of Management and Budget as of November 2008. All geographic boundaries for 2009 population estimates are defined as of January 1, 2009. All metropolitan areas are arranged alphabetically]

Metropolitan statistical area Metropolitan division Component county	Population, 2009 (1,000)	Metropolitan statistical area Metropolitan division Component county	Population, 2009 (1,000)	Metropolitan statistical area Metropolitan division Component county	Population, 2009 (1,000)
Abilene, TX	**160**	**Appleton, WI**	**222**	**Bakersfield, CA**	**807**
Callahan County, TX	13	Calumet County, WI	45	Kern County, CA	807
Jones County, TX	19	Outagamie County, WI	177		
Taylor County, TX	128			**Baltimore-Towson, MD**	**2,691**
		Asheville, NC	**413**	Anne Arundel County, MD	521
Akron, OH	**700**	Buncombe County, NC	231	Baltimore County, MD	790
Portage County, OH	158	Haywood County, NC	57	Carroll County, MD	170
Summit County, OH	542	Henderson County, NC	104	Harford County, MD	243
		Madison County, NC	20	Howard County, MD	282
Albany, GA	**165**			Queen Anne's County, MD	48
Baker County, GA	4	**Athens-Clarke County, GA**	**192**	Baltimore city, MD	637
Dougherty County, GA	96	Clarke County, GA	116		
Lee County, GA	34	Madison County, GA	28	**Bangor, ME**	**149**
Terrell County, GA	10	Oconee County, GA	33	Penobscot County, ME	149
Worth County, GA	21	Oglethorpe County, GA	14		
				Barnstable Town, MA	**221**
Albany-Schenectady-Troy,		**Atlanta-Sandy Springs-**		Barnstable County, MA	221
NY	**858**	**Marietta, GA**	**5,475**		
Albany County, NY	298	Barrow County, GA	72	**Baton Rouge, LA**	**787**
Rensselaer County, NY	156	Bartow County, GA	96	Ascension Parish, LA	105
Saratoga County, NY	220	Butts County, GA	24	East Baton Rouge Parish,	
Schenectady County, NY	152	Carroll County, GA	115	LA	435
Schoharie County, NY	32	Cherokee County, GA	215	East Feliciana Parish, LA	21
		Clayton County, GA	276	Iberville Parish, LA	33
Albuquerque, NM	**858**	Cobb County, GA	715	Livingston Parish, LA	123
Bernalillo County, NM	643	Coweta County, GA	127	Pointe Coupee Parish, LA	22
Sandoval County, NM	126	Dawson County, GA	23	St. Helena Parish, LA	11
Torrance County, NM	16	DeKalb County, GA	747	West Baton Rouge Parish,	
Valencia County, NM	73	Douglas County, GA	130	LA	23
		Fayette County, GA	107	West Feliciana Parish, LA	15
Alexandria, LA	**154**	Forsyth County, GA	175		
Grant Parish, LA	20	Fulton County, GA	1,034	**Battle Creek, MI**	**136**
Rapides Parish, LA	134	Gwinnett County, GA	808	Calhoun County, MI	136
		Haralson County, GA	29		
Allentown-Bethlehem-Easton,		Heard County, GA	12	**Bay City, MI**	**107**
PA-NJ	**816**	Henry County, GA	195	Bay County, MI	107
Warren County, NJ	110	Jasper County, GA	14		
Carbon County, PA	64	Lamar County, GA	18	**Beaumont-Port Arthur, TX**	**378**
Lehigh County, PA	344	Meriwether County, GA	23	Hardin County, TX	53
Northampton County, PA	299	Newton County, GA	100	Jefferson County, TX	243
		Paulding County, GA	137	Orange County, TX	82
Altoona, PA	**126**	Pickens County, GA	31		
Blair County, PA	126	Pike County, GA	18	**Bellingham, WA**	**200**
		Rockdale County, GA	85	Whatcom County, WA	200
Amarillo, TX	**246**	Spalding County, GA	65		
Armstrong County, TX	2	Walton County, GA	87	**Bend, OR**	**159**
Carson County, TX	6			Deschutes County, OR	159
Potter County, TX	122	**Atlantic City-Hammonton, NJ**	**272**		
Randall County, TX	116	Atlantic County, NJ	272	**Billings, MT**	**155**
				Carbon County, MT	10
Ames, IA	**87**	**Auburn-Opelika, AL**	**136**	Yellowstone County, MT	145
Story County, IA	87	Lee County, AL	136		
				Binghamton, NY	**245**
Anchorage, AK	**375**	**Augusta-Richmond County,**		Broome County, NY	195
Anchorage Municipality, AK	286	**GA-SC**	**539**	Tioga County, NY	50
Matanuska-Susitna		Burke County, GA	23		
Borough, AK	88	Columbia County, GA	113	**Birmingham-Hoover, AL**	**1,131**
		McDuffie County, GA	22	Bibb County, AL	22
Anderson, IN	**131**	Richmond County, GA	200	Blount County, AL	58
Madison County, IN	131	Aiken County, SC	156	Chilton County, AL	43
		Edgefield County, SC	26	Jefferson County, AL	665
Anderson, SC	**185**			St. Clair County, AL	82
Anderson County, SC	185	**Austin-Round Rock, TX**	**1,705**	Shelby County, AL	193
		Bastrop County, TX	75	Walker County, AL	69
Ann Arbor, MI	**348**	Caldwell County, TX	38		
Washtenaw County, MI	348	Hays County, TX	156	**Bismarck, ND**	**106**
		Travis County, TX	1,026	Burleigh County, ND	80
Anniston-Oxford, AL	**114**	Williamson County, TX	411	Morton County, ND	26
Calhoun County, AL	114				

U.S. Census Bureau, Statistical Abstract of the United States: 2011

Metropolitan statistical area Metropolitan division Component county	Popu- lation, **2009** (1,000)	Metropolitan statistical area Metropolitan division Component county	Popu- lation, **2009** (1,000)	Metropolitan statistical area Metropolitan division Component county	Popu- lation, **2009** (1,000)
Blacksburg-Christiansburg-		**Canton-Massillon, OH**	408	**Gary, IN**	704
Radford, VA	160	Carroll County, OH	29	Jasper County, IN	33
Giles County, VA	17	Stark County, OH	379	Lake County, IN	494
Montgomery County, VA	91			Newton County, IN	14
Pulaski County, VA	35	**Cape Coral-Fort Myers, FL**	587	Porter County, IN	164
Radford city, VA	16	Lee County, FL	587	**Lake County-Kenosha**	
				County, IL-WI	878
Bloomington, IN	186	**Cape Girardeau-Jackson,**		Lake County, IL	713
Greene County, IN	32	**MO-IL**	94	Kenosha County, WI	165
Monroe County, IN	131	Alexander County, IL	8		
Owen County, IN	22	Bollinger County, MO	12	**Chico, CA**	221
		Cape Girardeau County,		Butte County, CA	221
Bloomington-Normal, IL	168	MO	74		
McLean County, IL	168			**Cincinnati-Middletown,**	
		Carson City, NV	55	**OH-KY-IN**	2,172
Boise City-Nampa, ID	606	Carson City, NV	55	Dearborn County, IN	51
Ada County, ID	385			Franklin County, IN	23
Boise County, ID	7	**Casper, WY**	75	Ohio County, IN	6
Canyon County, ID	187	Natrona County, WY	75	Boone County, KY	119
Gem County, ID	16			Bracken County, KY	9
Owyhee County, ID	11	**Cedar Rapids, IA**	256	Campbell County, KY	88
		Benton County, IA	27	Gallatin County, KY	8
Boston-Cambridge-Quincy,		Jones County, IA	20	Grant County, KY	26
MA-NH	4,589	Linn County, IA	209	Kenton County, KY	159
Boston-Quincy, MA	1,918			Pendleton County, KY	15
Norfolk County, MA	666	**Champaign-Urbana, IL**	226	Brown County, OH	44
Plymouth County, MA	498	Champaign County, IL	196	Butler County, OH	363
Suffolk County, MA	754	Ford County, IL	14	Clermont County, OH	196
Cambridge-Newton-		Piatt County, IL	17	Hamilton County, OH	855
Framingham, MA	1,505			Warren County, OH	211
Middlesex County, MA	1,505	**Charleston, WV**	304		
Peabody, MA	743	Boone County, WV	25	**Clarksville, TN-KY**	269
Essex County, MA	743	Clay County, WV	10	Christian County, KY	81
Rockingham County-		Kanawha County, WV	192	Trigg County, KY	13
Strafford County, NH	423	Lincoln County, WV	22	Montgomery County, TN	161
Rockingham County, NH	299	Putnam County, WV	56	Stewart County, TN	13
Strafford County, NH	124				
		Charleston-North Charleston-		**Cleveland, TN**	113
Boulder, CO	303	**Summerville, SC**	659	Bradley County, TN	98
Boulder County, CO	303	Berkeley County, SC	173	Polk County, TN	16
		Charleston County, SC	355		
Bowling Green, KY	121	Dorchester County, SC	130	**Cleveland-Elyria-Mentor, OH**	2,091
Edmonson County, KY	12			Cuyahoga County, OH	1,276
Warren County, KY	109	**Charlotte-Gastonia-Concord,**		Geauga County, OH	99
		NC-SC	1,746	Lake County, OH	237
Bradenton-Sarasota-Venice, FL	688	Anson County, NC	25	Lorain County, OH	306
Manatee County, FL	318	Cabarrus County, NC	172	Medina County, OH	174
Sarasota County, FL	370	Gaston County, NC	209		
		Mecklenburg County, NC	914	**Coeur d'Alene, ID**	139
Bremerton-Silverdale, WA	241	Union County, NC	199	Kootenai County, ID	139
Kitsap County, WA	241	York County, SC	227		
				College Station-Bryan, TX	212
Bridgeport-Stamford-Norwalk,		**Charlottesville, VA**	197	Brazos County, TX	180
CT	901	Albemarle County, VA	95	Burleson County, TX	17
Fairfield County, CT	901	Fluvanna County, VA	26	Robertson County, TX	16
		Greene County, VA	18		
Brownsville-Harlingen, TX	396	Nelson County, VA	15	**Colorado Springs, CO**	626
Cameron County, TX	396	Charlottesville city, VA	42	El Paso County, CO	605
				Teller County, CO	22
Brunswick, GA	104	**Chattanooga, TN-GA**	524		
Brantley County, GA	16	Catoosa County, GA	64	**Columbia, MO**	166
Glynn County, GA	77	Dade County, GA	16	Boone County, MO	156
McIntosh County, GA	11	Walker County, GA	65	Howard County, MO	10
		Hamilton County, TN	337		
Buffalo-Niagara Falls, NY	1,124	Marion County, TN	28	**Columbia, SC**	745
Erie County, NY	909	Sequatchie County, TN	14	Calhoun County, SC	15
Niagara County, NY	215			Fairfield County, SC	23
		Cheyenne, WY	89	Kershaw County, SC	60
Burlington, NC	150	Laramie County, WY	89	Lexington County, SC	256
Alamance County, NC	150			Richland County, SC	372
		Chicago-Naperville-Joliet,		Saluda County, SC	19
Burlington-South Burlington,		**IL-IN-WI**	9,581		
VT	208	**Chicago-Naperville-Joliet, IL**	7,998	**Columbus, GA-AL**	293
Chittenden County, VT	152	Cook County, IL	5,287	Russell County, AL	51
Franklin County, VT	48	DeKalb County, IL	107	Chattahoochee County, GA	14
Grand Isle County, VT	8	DuPage County, IL	933	Harris County, GA	30
		Grundy County, IL	48	Marion County, GA	7
		Kane County, IL	512	Muscogee County, GA	190
		Kendall County, IL	105		
		McHenry County, IL	321		
		Will County, IL	685		

U.S. Census Bureau, Statistical Abstract of the United States: 2011

Metropolitan statistical area / Metropolitan division / Component county	Population, 2009 (1,000)
Columbus, IN	**76**
Bartholomew County, IN	76
Columbus, OH	**1,802**
Delaware County, OH	169
Fairfield County, OH	144
Franklin County, OH	1,150
Licking County, OH	158
Madison County, OH	43
Morrow County, OH	35
Pickaway County, OH	55
Union County, OH	49
Corpus Christi, TX	**416**
Aransas County, TX	25
Nueces County, TX	323
San Patricio County, TX	68
Corvallis, OR	**83**
Benton County, OR	83
Cumberland, MD-WV	**100**
Allegany County, MD	73
Mineral County, WV	27
Dallas-Fort Worth-Arlington, TX	**6,448**
Dallas-Plano-Irving, TX	**4,326**
Collin County, TX	792
Dallas County, TX	2,452
Delta County, TX	5
Denton County, TX	659
Ellis County, TX	152
Hunt County, TX	83
Kaufman County, TX	103
Rockwall County, TX	81
Fort Worth-Arlington, TX	**2,121**
Johnson County, TX	157
Parker County, TX	115
Tarrant County, TX	1,790
Wise County, TX	59
Dalton, GA	**134**
Murray County, GA	41
Whitfield County, GA	94
Danville, IL	**80**
Vermilion County, IL	80
Danville, VA	**106**
Pittsylvania County, VA	61
Danville city, VA	44
Davenport-Moline-Rock Island, IA-IL	**379**
Henry County, IL	49
Mercer County, IL	16
Rock Island County, IL	147
Scott County, IA	167
Dayton, OH	**835**
Greene County, OH	160
Miami County, OH	101
Montgomery County, OH	533
Preble County, OH	41
Decatur, AL	**151**
Lawrence County, AL	34
Morgan County, AL	117
Decatur, IL	**108**
Macon County, IL	108
Deltona-Daytona Beach-Ormond Beach, FL	**496**
Volusia County, FL	496

Metropolitan statistical area / Metropolitan division / Component county	Population, 2009 (1,000)
Denver-Aurora-Broomfield, CO	**2,552**
Adams County, CO	441
Arapahoe County, CO	565
Broomfield County, CO	56
Clear Creek County, CO	9
Denver County, CO	610
Douglas County, CO	288
Elbert County, CO	23
Gilpin County, CO	6
Jefferson County, CO	537
Park County, CO	17
Des Moines-West Des Moines, IA	**563**
Dallas County, IA	62
Guthrie County, IA	11
Madison County, IA	15
Polk County, IA	429
Warren County, IA	45
Detroit-Warren-Livonia, MI	**4,403**
Detroit-Livonia-Dearborn, MI	**1,926**
Wayne County, MI	1,926
Warren-Troy-Farmington Hills, MI	**2,478**
Lapeer County, MI	90
Livingston County, MI	183
Macomb County, MI	831
Oakland County, MI	1,206
St. Clair County, MI	168
Dothan, AL	**143**
Geneva County, AL	26
Henry County, AL	17
Houston County, AL	100
Dover, DE	**158**
Kent County, DE	158
Dubuque, IA	**93**
Dubuque County, IA	93
Duluth, MN-WI	**276**
Carlton County, MN	34
St. Louis County, MN	198
Douglas County, WI	44
Durham-Chapel Hill, NC	**501**
Chatham County, NC	65
Durham County, NC	270
Orange County, NC	129
Person County, NC	38
Eau Claire, WI	**160**
Chippewa County, WI	61
Eau Claire County, WI	99
El Centro, CA	**167**
Imperial County, CA	167
Elizabethtown, KY	**113**
Hardin County, KY	100
Larue County, KY	14
Elkhart-Goshen, IN	**201**
Elkhart County, IN	201
Elmira, NY	**88**
Chemung County, NY	88
El Paso, TX	**751**
El Paso County, TX	751
Erie, PA	**280**
Erie County, PA	280
Eugene-Springfield, OR	**351**
Lane County, OR	351

Metropolitan statistical area / Metropolitan division / Component county	Population, 2009 (1,000)
Evansville, IN-KY	**352**
Gibson County, IN	33
Posey County, IN	26
Vanderburgh County, IN	175
Warrick County, IN	59
Henderson County, KY	45
Webster County, KY	14
Fairbanks, AK	**99**
Fairbanks North Star Borough, AK	99
Fargo, ND-MN	**200**
Clay County, MN	57
Cass County, ND	143
Farmington, NM	**124**
San Juan County, NM	124
Fayetteville, NC	**360**
Cumberland County, NC	315
Hoke County, NC	45
Fayetteville-Springdale-Rogers, AR-MO	**465**
Benton County, AR	226
Madison County, AR	16
Washington County, AR	200
McDonald County, MO	23
Flagstaff, AZ	**130**
Coconino County, AZ	130
Flint, MI	**424**
Genesee County, MI	424
Florence, SC	**201**
Darlington County, SC	66
Florence County, SC	134
Florence-Muscle Shoals, AL	**144**
Colbert County, AL	55
Lauderdale County, AL	90
Fond du Lac, WI	**100**
Fond du Lac County, WI	100
Fort Collins-Loveland, CO	**298**
Larimer County, CO	298
Fort Smith, AR-OK	**293**
Crawford County, AR	60
Franklin County, AR	18
Sebastian County, AR	124
Le Flore County, OK	50
Sequoyah County, OK	41
Fort Walton Beach-Crestview-Destin, FL	**178**
Okaloosa County, FL	178
Fort Wayne, IN	**414**
Allen County, IN	354
Wells County, IN	28
Whitley County, IN	33
Fresno, CA	**915**
Fresno County, CA	915
Gadsden, AL	**104**
Etowah County, AL	104
Gainesville, FL	**261**
Alachua County, FL	244
Gilchrist County, FL	17
Gainesville, GA	**188**
Hall County, GA	188

U.S. Census Bureau, Statistical Abstract of the United States: 2011

Metropolitan statistical area Metropolitan division Component county	Popu- lation, **2009** (1,000)	Metropolitan statistical area Metropolitan division Component county	Popu- lation, **2009** (1,000)	Metropolitan statistical area Metropolitan division Component county	Popu- lation, **2009** (1,000)
Glens Falls, NY	129	**Hickory-Lenoir-Morganton,**		**Jackson, TN**	114
Warren County, NY	66	**NC**	365	Chester County, TN	16
Washington County, NY	63	Alexander County, NC	37	Madison County, TN	97
		Burke County, NC	90		
Goldsboro, NC	114	Caldwell County, NC	80	**Jacksonville, FL**	1,328
Wayne County, NC	114	Catawba County, NC	159	Baker County, FL	26
				Clay County, FL	187
Grand Forks, ND-MN	97	**Hinesville-Fort Stewart, GA**	74	Duval County, FL	857
Polk County, MN	31	Liberty County, GA	62	Nassau County, FL	71
Grand Forks County, ND	66	Long County, GA	12	St. Johns County, FL	187
Grand Junction, CO	146	**Holland-Grand Haven, MI**	262	**Jacksonville, NC**	173
Mesa County, CO	146	Ottawa County, MI	262	Onslow County, NC	173
Grand Rapids-Wyoming, MI	778	**Honolulu, HI**	908	**Janesville, WI**	160
Barry County, MI	58	Honolulu County, HI	908	Rock County, WI	160
Ionia County, MI	63				
Kent County, MI	608	**Hot Springs, AR**	98	**Jefferson City, MO**	147
Newaygo County, MI	49	Garland County, AR	98	Callaway County, MO	44
				Cole County, MO	75
Great Falls, MT	82	**Houma-Bayou Cane-**		Moniteau County, MO	15
Cascade County, MT	82	**Thibodaux, LA**	203	Osage County, MO	14
		Lafourche Parish, LA	94		
Greeley, CO	255	Terrebonne Parish, LA	109	**Johnson City, TN**	197
Weld County, CO	255			Carter County, TN	59
				Unicoi County, TN	18
Green Bay, WI	305	**Houston-Sugar Land-Baytown,**		Washington County, TN	121
Brown County, WI	247	**TX**	5,867		
Kewaunee County, WI	20	Austin County, TX	27	**Johnstown, PA**	144
Oconto County, WI	37	Brazoria County, TX	309	Cambria County, PA	144
		Chambers County, TX	31		
Greensboro-High Point, NC	715	Fort Bend County, TX	557	**Jonesboro, AR**	120
Guilford County, NC	480	Galveston County, TX	287	Craighead County, AR	95
Randolph County, NC	142	Harris County, TX	4,071	Poinsett County, AR	25
Rockingham County, NC	92	Liberty County, TX	76		
		Montgomery County, TX	448	**Joplin, MO**	174
Greenville, NC	180	San Jacinto County, TX	25	Jasper County, MO	118
Greene County, NC	21	Waller County, TX	37	Newton County, MO	56
Pitt County, NC	159				
		Huntington-Ashland,		**Kalamazoo-Portage, MI**	327
Greenville-Mauldin-Easley, SC	640	**WV-KY-OH**	286	Kalamazoo County, MI	248
Greenville County, SC	451	Boyd County, KY	49	Van Buren County, MI	78
Laurens County, SC	70	Greenup County, KY	38		
Pickens County, SC	118	Lawrence County, OH	63	**Kankakee-Bradley, IL**	113
		Cabell County, WV	95	Kankakee County, IL	113
Gulfport-Biloxi, MS	239	Wayne County, WV	41		
Hancock County, MS	41			**Kansas City, MO-KS**	2,068
Harrison County, MS	181	**Huntsville, AL**	406	Franklin County, KS	26
Stone County, MS	17	Limestone County, AL	79	Johnson County, KS	543
		Madison County, AL	328	Leavenworth County, KS	75
Hagerstown-Martinsburg,				Linn County, KS	9
MD-WV	266	**Idaho Falls, ID**	126	Miami County, KS	31
Washington County, MD	146	Bonneville County, ID	101	Wyandotte County, KS	155
Berkeley County, WV	104	Jefferson County, ID	25	Bates County, MO	17
Morgan County, WV	16			Caldwell County, MO	9
		Indianapolis-Carmel, IN	1,744	Cass County, MO	100
Hanford-Corcoran, CA	149	Boone County, IN	56	Clay County, MO	228
Kings County, CA	149	Brown County, IN	15	Clinton County, MO	21
		Hamilton County, IN	279	Jackson County, MO	706
Harrisburg-Carlisle, PA	537	Hancock County, IN	68	Lafayette County, MO	33
Cumberland County, PA	232	Hendricks County, IN	141	Platte County, MO	91
Dauphin County, PA	259	Johnson County, IN	142	Ray County, MO	23
Perry County, PA	46	Marion County, IN	891		
		Morgan County, IN	71	**Kennewick-Pasco-Richland,**	
Harrisonburg, VA	120	Putnam County, IN	37	**WA**	246
Rockingham County, VA	75	Shelby County, IN	45	Benton County, WA	168
Harrisonburg city, VA	45			Franklin County, WA	77
		Iowa City, IA	152		
Hartford-West Hartford-East		Johnson County, IA	131	**Killeen-Temple-Fort Hood,**	
Hartford, CT	1,196	Washington County, IA	21	**TX**	379
Hartford County, CT	880			Bell County, TX	286
Middlesex County, CT	166	**Ithaca, NY**	102	Coryell County, TX	73
Tolland County, CT	150	Tompkins County, NY	102	Lampasas County, TX	21
Hattiesburg, MS	143	**Jackson, MI**	160	**Kingsport-Bristol-Bristol,**	
Forrest County, MS	81	Jackson County, MI	160	**TN-VA**	306
Lamar County, MS	50			Hawkins County, TN	58
Perry County, MS	12	**Jackson, MS**	541	Sullivan County, TN	155
		Copiah County, MS	29	Scott County, VA	23
		Hinds County, MS	248	Washington County, VA	53
		Madison County, MS	93	Bristol city, VA	18
		Rankin County, MS	143		
		Simpson County, MS	28		

U.S. Census Bureau, Statistical Abstract of the United States: 2011

Metropolitan statistical area / Metropolitan division / Component county	Population, 2009 (1,000)
Kingston, NY	**181**
Ulster County, NY	181
Knoxville, TN	**699**
Anderson County, TN	75
Blount County, TN	123
Knox County, TN	436
Loudon County, TN	47
Union County, TN	19
Kokomo, IN	**99**
Howard County, IN	83
Tipton County, IN	16
La Crosse, WI-MN	**133**
Houston County, MN	19
La Crosse County, WI	114
Lafayette, IN	**196**
Benton County, IN	9
Carroll County, IN	20
Tippecanoe County, IN	168
Lafayette, LA	**263**
Lafayette Parish, LA	211
St. Martin Parish, LA	52
Lake Charles, LA	**194**
Calcasieu Parish, LA	188
Cameron Parish, LA	7
Lake Havasu City-Kingman, AZ	**195**
Mohave County, AZ	195
Lakeland-Winter Haven, FL	**583**
Polk County, FL	583
Lancaster, PA	**508**
Lancaster County, PA	508
Lansing-East Lansing, MI	**454**
Clinton County, MI	70
Eaton County, MI	106
Ingham County, MI	278
Laredo, TX	**241**
Webb County, TX	241
Las Cruces, NM	**206**
Doña Ana County, NM	206
Las Vegas-Paradise, NV	**1,903**
Clark County, NV	1,903
Lawrence, KS	**116**
Douglas County, KS	116
Lawton, OK	**113**
Comanche County, OK	113
Lebanon, PA	**131**
Lebanon County, PA	131
Lewiston, ID-WA	**61**
Nez Perce County, ID	39
Asotin County, WA	21
Lewiston-Auburn, ME	**107**
Androscoggin County, ME	107
Lexington-Fayette, KY	**471**
Bourbon County, KY	20
Clark County, KY	36
Fayette County, KY	297
Jessamine County, KY	48
Scott County, KY	46
Woodford County, KY	25
Lima, OH	**104**
Allen County, OH	104
Lincoln, NE	**298**
Lancaster County, NE	282
Seward County, NE	16
Little Rock-North Little Rock-Conway, AR	**685**
Faulkner County, AR	109
Grant County, AR	18
Lonoke County, AR	67
Perry County, AR	10
Pulaski County, AR	382
Saline County, AR	99
Logan, UT-ID	**128**
Franklin County, ID	13
Cache County, UT	115
Longview, TX	**207**
Gregg County, TX	120
Rusk County, TX	49
Upshur County, TX	38
Longview, WA	**102**
Cowlitz County, WA	102
Los Angeles-Long Beach-Santa Ana, CA	**12,875**
Los Angeles-Long Beach-Glendale, CA	**9,848**
Los Angeles County, CA	9,848
Santa Ana-Anaheim-Irvine, CA	**3,027**
Orange County, CA	3,027
Louisville/Jefferson County, KY-IN	**1,259**
Clark County, IN	109
Floyd County, IN	74
Harrison County, IN	38
Washington County, IN	28
Bullitt County, KY	76
Henry County, KY	16
Jefferson County, KY	722
Meade County, KY	27
Nelson County, KY	44
Oldham County, KY	58
Shelby County, KY	42
Spencer County, KY	18
Trimble County, KY	9
Lubbock, TX	**277**
Crosby County, TX	6
Lubbock County, TX	271
Lynchburg, VA	**247**
Amherst County, VA	32
Appomattox County, VA	15
Bedford County, VA	67
Campbell County, VA	53
Bedford city, VA	6
Lynchburg city, VA	74
Macon, GA	**232**
Bibb County, GA	156
Crawford County, GA	12
Jones County, GA	28
Monroe County, GA	25
Twiggs County, GA	10
Madera-Chowchilla, CA	**149**
Madera County, CA	149
Madison, WI	**570**
Columbia County, WI	55
Dane County, WI	491
Iowa County, WI	23
Manchester-Nashua, NH	**406**
Hillsborough County, NH	406
Manhattan, KS	**123**
Geary County, KS	32
Pottawatomie County, KS	20
Riley County, KS	71
Mankato-North Mankato, MN	**93**
Blue Earth County, MN	61
Nicollet County, MN	32
Mansfield, OH	**124**
Richland County, OH	124
McAllen-Edinburg-Mission, TX	**741**
Hidalgo County, TX	741
Medford, OR	**201**
Jackson County, OR	201
Memphis, TN-MS-AR	**1,305**
Crittenden County, AR	53
DeSoto County, MS	159
Marshall County, MS	37
Tate County, MS	27
Tunica County, MS	10
Fayette County, TN	39
Shelby County, TN	920
Tipton County, TN	59
Merced, CA	**245**
Merced County, CA	245
Miami-Fort Lauderdale-Pompano Beach, FL	**5,547**
Fort Lauderdale-Pompano Beach-Deerfield Beach, FL	**1,766**
Broward County, FL	1,766
Miami-Miami Beach-Kendall, FL	**2,501**
Miami-Dade County, FL	2,501
West Palm Beach-Boca Raton-Boynton Beach, FL	**1,280**
Palm Beach County, FL	1,280
Michigan City-La Porte, IN	**111**
LaPorte County, IN	111
Midland, TX	**132**
Midland County, TX	132
Milwaukee-Waukesha-West Allis, WI	**1,560**
Milwaukee County, WI	960
Ozaukee County, WI	86
Washington County, WI	131
Waukesha County, WI	383
Minneapolis-St. Paul-Bloomington, MN-WI	**3,270**
Anoka County, MN	332
Carver County, MN	92
Chisago County, MN	51
Dakota County, MN	397
Hennepin County, MN	1,156
Isanti County, MN	39
Ramsey County, MN	506
Scott County, MN	132
Sherburne County, MN	88
Washington County, MN	232
Wright County, MN	122
Pierce County, WI	40
St. Croix County, WI	83
Missoula, MT	**109**
Missoula County, MT	109
Mobile, AL	**412**
Mobile County, AL	412
Modesto, CA	**510**
Stanislaus County, CA	510

U.S. Census Bureau, Statistical Abstract of the United States: 2011

Metropolitan statistical area / Metropolitan division / Component county	Population, 2009 (1,000)
Monroe, LA	**174**
Ouachita Parish, LA	152
Union Parish, LA	23
Monroe, MI	**153**
Monroe County, MI	153
Montgomery, AL	**366**
Autauga County, AL	51
Elmore County, AL	79
Lowndes County, AL	12
Montgomery County, AL	224
Morgantown, WV	**120**
Monongalia County, WV	90
Preston County, WV	30
Morristown, TN	**138**
Grainger County, TN	23
Hamblen County, TN	63
Jefferson County, TN	52
Mount Vernon-Anacortes, WA	**120**
Skagit County, WA	120
Muncie, IN	**115**
Delaware County, IN	115
Muskegon-Norton Shores, MI	**174**
Muskegon County, MI	174
Myrtle Beach-North Myrtle Beach-Conway, SC	**264**
Horry County, SC	264
Napa, CA	**135**
Napa County, CA	135
Naples-Marco Island, FL	**319**
Collier County, FL	319
Nashville-Davidson— Murfreesboro—Franklin, TN	**1,582**
Cannon County, TN	14
Cheatham County, TN	40
Davidson County, TN	636
Dickson County, TN	48
Hickman County, TN	24
Macon County, TN	22
Robertson County, TN	67
Rutherford County, TN	257
Smith County, TN	19
Sumner County, TN	159
Trousdale County, TN	8
Williamson County, TN	177
Wilson County, TN	112
New Haven-Milford, CT	**848**
New Haven County, CT	848
New Orleans-Metairie-Kenner, LA	**1,190**
Jefferson Parish, LA	443
Orleans Parish, LA	355
Plaquemines Parish, LA	21
St. Bernard Parish, LA	41
St. Charles Parish, LA	52
St. John the Baptist Parish, LA	47
St. Tammany Parish, LA	231

Metropolitan statistical area / Metropolitan division / Component county	Population, 2009 (1,000)
New York-Northern New Jersey-Long Island, NY-NJ-PA	**19,070**
Edison-New Brunswick, NJ	**2,335**
Middlesex County, NJ	791
Monmouth County, NJ	644
Ocean County, NJ	574
Somerset County, NJ	327
Nassau-Suffolk, NY	**2,876**
Nassau County, NY	1,357
Suffolk County, NY	1,518
Newark-Union, NJ-PA	**2,126**
Essex County, NJ	770
Hunterdon County, NJ	130
Morris County, NJ	489
Sussex County, NJ	151
Union County, NJ	526
Pike County, PA	61
New York-White Plains-Wayne, NY-NJ	**11,732**
Bergen County, NJ	895
Hudson County, NJ	598
Passaic County, NJ	492
Bronx County, NY	1,397
Kings County, NY	2,567
New York County, NY	1,629
Putnam County, NY	99
Queens County, NY	2,307
Richmond County, NY	492
Rockland County, NY	300
Westchester County, NY	956
Niles-Benton Harbor, MI	**160**
Berrien County, MI	160
Norwich-New London, CT	**267**
New London County, CT	267
Ocala, FL	**329**
Marion County, FL	329
Ocean City, NJ	**96**
Cape May County, NJ	96
Odessa, TX	**135**
Ector County, TX	135
Ogden-Clearfield, UT	**542**
Davis County, UT	301
Morgan County, UT	9
Weber County, UT	232
Oklahoma City, OK	**1,227**
Canadian County, OK	110
Cleveland County, OK	245
Grady County, OK	52
Lincoln County, OK	32
Logan County, OK	39
McClain County, OK	33
Oklahoma County, OK	717
Olympia, WA	**251**
Thurston County, WA	251
Omaha-Council Bluffs, NE-IA	**850**
Harrison County, IA	15
Mills County, IA	15
Pottawattamie County, IA	90
Cass County, NE	25
Douglas County, NE	510
Sarpy County, NE	154
Saunders County, NE	20
Washington County, NE	20

Metropolitan statistical area / Metropolitan division / Component county	Population, 2009 (1,000)
Orlando-Kissimmee, FL	**2,082**
Lake County, FL	312
Orange County, FL	1,086
Osceola County, FL	271
Seminole County, FL	413
Oshkosh-Neenah, WI	**163**
Winnebago County, WI	163
Owensboro, KY	**114**
Daviess County, KY	95
Hancock County, KY	9
McLean County, KY	10
Oxnard-Thousand Oaks-Ventura, CA	**803**
Ventura County, CA	803
Palm Bay-Melbourne-Titusville, FL	**536**
Brevard County, FL	536
Palm Coast, FL	**92**
Flagler County, FL	92
Panama City-Lynn Haven-Panama City Beach, FL	**165**
Bay County, FL	165
Parkersburg-Marietta-Vienna, WV-OH	**161**
Washington County, OH	61
Pleasants County, WV	7
Wirt County, WV	6
Wood County, WV	87
Pascagoula, MS	**156**
George County, MS	23
Jackson County, MS	133
Pensacola-Ferry Pass-Brent, FL	**455**
Escambia County, FL	303
Santa Rosa County, FL	152
Peoria, IL	**376**
Marshall County, IL	13
Peoria County, IL	186
Stark County, IL	6
Tazewell County, IL	132
Woodford County, IL	39
Philadelphia-Camden-Wilmington, PA-NJ-DE-MD	**5,968**
Camden, NJ	**1,254**
Burlington County, NJ	446
Camden County, NJ	518
Gloucester County, NJ	290
Philadelphia, PA	**4,013**
Bucks County, PA	626
Chester County, PA	499
Delaware County, PA	558
Montgomery County, PA	782
Philadelphia County, PA	1,547
Wilmington, DE-MD-NJ	**702**
New Castle County, DE	535
Cecil County, MD	101
Salem County, NJ	66
Phoenix-Mesa-Scottsdale, AZ	**4,364**
Maricopa County, AZ	4,023
Pinal County, AZ	341

U.S. Census Bureau, Statistical Abstract of the United States: 2011

Metropolitan statistical area / Metropolitan division / Component county	Population, 2009 (1,000)
Pine Bluff, AR	**101**
Cleveland County, AR	8
Jefferson County, AR	79
Lincoln County, AR	14
Pittsburgh, PA	**2,355**
Allegheny County, PA	1,218
Armstrong County, PA	68
Beaver County, PA	172
Butler County, PA	185
Fayette County, PA	143
Washington County, PA	207
Westmoreland County, PA	362
Pittsfield, MA	**129**
Berkshire County, MA	129
Pocatello, ID	**90**
Bannock County, ID	83
Power County, ID	8
Portland-South Portland-Biddeford, ME	**517**
Cumberland County, ME	279
Sagadahoc County, ME	36
York County, ME	202
Portland-Vancouver-Beaverton, OR-WA	**2,242**
Clackamas County, OR	386
Columbia County, OR	50
Multnomah County, OR	727
Washington County, OR	537
Yamhill County, OR	99
Clark County, WA	432
Skamania County, WA	11
Port St. Lucie, FL	**406**
Martin County, FL	140
St. Lucie County, FL	267
Poughkeepsie-Newburgh-Middletown, NY	**677**
Dutchess County, NY	294
Orange County, NY	384
Prescott, AZ	**216**
Yavapai County, AZ	216
Providence-New Bedford-Fall River, RI-MA	**1,601**
Bristol County, MA	547
Bristol County, RI	50
Kent County, RI	169
Newport County, RI	80
Providence County, RI	628
Washington County, RI	127
Provo-Orem, UT	**556**
Juab County, UT	10
Utah County, UT	545
Pueblo, CO	**157**
Pueblo County, CO	157
Punta Gorda, FL	**157**
Charlotte County, FL	157
Racine, WI	**201**
Racine County, WI	201
Raleigh-Cary, NC	**1,126**
Franklin County, NC	60
Johnston County, NC	169
Wake County, NC	897
Rapid City, SD	**125**
Meade County, SD	24
Pennington County, SD	101
Reading, PA	**407**
Berks County, PA	407
Redding, CA	**181**
Shasta County, CA	181
Reno-Sparks, NV	**419**
Storey County, NV	4
Washoe County, NV	415
Richmond, VA	**1,238**
Amelia County, VA	13
Caroline County, VA	28
Charles City County, VA	7
Chesterfield County, VA	307
Cumberland County, VA	10
Dinwiddie County, VA	26
Goochland County, VA	21
Hanover County, VA	100
Henrico County, VA	296
King and Queen County, VA	7
King William County, VA	16
Louisa County, VA	33
New Kent County, VA	18
Powhatan County, VA	28
Prince George County, VA	37
Sussex County, VA	12
Colonial Heights city, VA	18
Hopewell city, VA	23
Petersburg city, VA	33
Richmond city, VA	204
Riverside-San Bernardino-Ontario, CA	**4,143**
Riverside County, CA	2,125
San Bernardino County, CA	2,018
Roanoke, VA	**300**
Botetourt County, VA	33
Craig County, VA	5
Franklin County, VA	52
Roanoke County, VA	91
Roanoke city, VA	94
Salem city, VA	25
Rochester, MN	**186**
Dodge County, MN	20
Olmsted County, MN	144
Wabasha County, MN	22
Rochester, NY	**1,036**
Livingston County, NY	63
Monroe County, NY	734
Ontario County, NY	106
Orleans County, NY	42
Wayne County, NY	91
Rockford, IL	**354**
Boone County, IL	54
Winnebago County, IL	300
Rocky Mount, NC	**147**
Edgecombe County, NC	52
Nash County, NC	95
Rome, GA	**96**
Floyd County, GA	96
Sacramento—Arden-Arcade—Roseville, CA	**2,127**
El Dorado County, CA	178
Placer County, CA	349
Sacramento County, CA	1,401
Yolo County, CA	199
Saginaw-Saginaw Township North, MI	**200**
Saginaw County, MI	200
St. Cloud, MN	**189**
Benton County, MN	40
Stearns County, MN	149
St. George, UT	**137**
Washington County, UT	137
St. Joseph, MO-KS	**127**
Doniphan County, KS	8
Andrew County, MO	17
Buchanan County, MO	90
DeKalb County, MO	12
St. Louis, MO-IL [1]	**2,829**
Bond County, IL	18
Calhoun County, IL	5
Clinton County, IL	36
Jersey County, IL	23
Macoupin County, IL	48
Madison County, IL	268
Monroe County, IL	33
St. Clair County, IL	264
Franklin County, MO	101
Jefferson County, MO	219
Lincoln County, MO	53
St. Charles County, MO	355
St. Louis County, MO	992
Warren County, MO	31
Washington County, MO	24
St. Louis city, MO	357
Salem, OR	**396**
Marion County, OR	318
Polk County, OR	78
Salinas, CA	**410**
Monterey County, CA	410
Salisbury, MD	**120**
Somerset County, MD	26
Wicomico County, MD	94
Salt Lake City, UT	**1,130**
Salt Lake County, UT	1,035
Summit County, UT	37
Tooele County, UT	58
San Angelo, TX	**110**
Irion County, TX	2
Tom Green County, TX	108
San Antonio, TX	**2,072**
Atascosa County, TX	45
Bandera County, TX	21
Bexar County, TX	1,651
Comal County, TX	115
Guadalupe County, TX	121
Kendall County, TX	34
Medina County, TX	45
Wilson County, TX	41
San Diego-Carlsbad-San Marcos, CA	**3,054**
San Diego County, CA	3,054

U.S. Census Bureau, Statistical Abstract of the United States: 2011

Metropolitan statistical area Metropolitan division Component county	Popu- lation, 2009 (1,000)	Metropolitan statistical area Metropolitan division Component county	Popu- lation, 2009 (1,000)	Metropolitan statistical area Metropolitan division Component county	Popu- lation, 2009 (1,000)
Sandusky, OH	77	**South Bend-Mishawaka,**		**Trenton-Ewing, NJ**	366
Erie County, OH	77	**IN-MI**	318	Mercer County, NJ	366
		St. Joseph County, IN	268		
San Francisco-Oakland-		Cass County, MI	50	**Tucson, AZ**	1,020
Fremont, CA	4,318			Pima County, AZ	1,020
Oakland-Fremont-Hayward,		**Spartanburg, SC**	287		
CA	2,533	Spartanburg County, SC	287	**Tulsa, OK**	929
Alameda County, CA	1,491			Creek County, OK	70
Contra Costa County, CA	1,041	**Spokane, WA**	469	Okmulgee County, OK	39
San Francisco-San Mateo-		Spokane County, WA	469	Osage County, OK	45
Redwood City, CA	1,785			Pawnee County, OK	16
Marin County, CA	251	**Springfield, IL**	208	Rogers County, OK	86
San Francisco County, CA	815	Menard County, IL	12	Tulsa County, OK	602
San Mateo County, CA	719	Sangamon County, IL	196	Wagoner County, OK	70
San Jose-Sunnyvale-Santa		**Springfield, MA**	699	**Tuscaloosa, AL**	211
Clara, CA	1,840	Franklin County, MA	72	Greene County, AL	9
San Benito County, CA	55	Hampden County, MA	471	Hale County, AL	18
Santa Clara County, CA	1,785	Hampshire County, MA	156	Tuscaloosa County, AL	184
San Luis Obispo-Paso Robles,		**Springfield, MO**	431	**Tyler, TX**	205
CA	267	Christian County, MO	77	Smith County, TX	205
San Luis Obispo County,		Dallas County, MO	17		
CA	267	Greene County, MO	270	**Utica-Rome, NY**	293
		Polk County, MO	31	Herkimer County, NY	62
Santa Barbara-Santa Maria-		Webster County, MO	37	Oneida County, NY	231
Goleta, CA	407				
Santa Barbara County, CA	407	**Springfield, OH**	140	**Valdosta, GA**	136
		Clark County, OH	140	Brooks County, GA	16
Santa Cruz-Watsonville, CA	256			Echols County, GA	4
Santa Cruz County, CA	256	**State College, PA**	146	Lanier County, GA	8
		Centre County, PA	146	Lowndes County, GA	107
Santa Fe, NM	148				
Santa Fe County, NM	148	**Stockton, CA**	675	**Vallejo-Fairfield, CA**	407
		San Joaquin County, CA	675	Solano County, CA	407
Santa Rosa-Petaluma, CA	472				
Sonoma County, CA	472	**Sumter, SC**	104	**Victoria, TX**	115
		Sumter County, SC	104	Calhoun County, TX	21
Savannah, GA	343			Goliad County, TX	7
Bryan County, GA	33	**Syracuse, NY**	646	Victoria County, TX	88
Chatham County, GA	257	Madison County, NY	70		
Effingham County, GA	54	Onondaga County, NY	455	**Vineland-Millville-Bridgeton,**	
		Oswego County, NY	121	**NJ**	158
Scranton—Wilkes-Barre, PA	549			Cumberland County, NJ	158
Lackawanna County, PA	209	**Tallahassee, FL**	360		
Luzerne County, PA	313	Gadsden County, FL	47	**Virginia Beach-Norfolk-**	
Wyoming County, PA	28	Jefferson County, FL	14	**Newport News, VA-NC**	1,674
		Leon County, FL	200	Currituck County, NC	24
Seattle-Tacoma-Bellevue, WA	3,408	Wakulla County, FL	33	Gloucester County, VA	39
Seattle-Bellevue-Everett, WA	2,611			Isle of Wight County, VA	36
King County, WA	1,916	**Tampa-St. Petersburg-**		James City County, VA	64
Snohomish County, WA	695	**Clearwater, FL**	2,747	Mathews County, VA	9
Tacoma, WA	797	Hernando County, FL	171	Surry County, VA	7
Pierce County, WA	797	Hillsborough County, FL	1,195	York County, VA	61
		Pasco County, FL	472	Chesapeake city, VA	222
Sebastian-Vero Beach, FL	135	Pinellas County, FL	909	Hampton city, VA	144
Indian River County, FL	135			Newport News city, VA	193
		Terre Haute, IN	170	Norfolk city, VA	233
Sheboygan, WI	115	Clay County, IN	27	Poquoson city, VA	12
Sheboygan County, WI	115	Sullivan County, IN	21	Portsmouth city, VA	99
		Vermillion County, IN	16	Suffolk city, VA	84
Sherman-Denison, TX	120	Vigo County, IN	106	Virginia Beach city, VA	434
Grayson County, TX	120			Williamsburg city, VA	13
		Texarkana, TX-Texarkana, AR	137		
Shreveport-Bossier City, LA	392	Miller County, AR	44	**Visalia-Porterville, CA**	430
Bossier Parish, LA	111	Bowie County, TX	94	Tulare County, CA	430
Caddo Parish, LA	254				
De Soto Parish, LA	26	**Toledo, OH**	672	**Waco, TX**	233
		Fulton County, OH	42	McLennan County, TX	233
Sioux City, IA-NE-SD	144	Lucas County, OH	463		
Woodbury County, IA	103	Ottawa County, OH	41	**Warner Robins, GA**	136
Dakota County, NE	21	Wood County, OH	125	Houston County, GA	136
Dixon County, NE	6				
Union County, SD	15	**Topeka, KS**	231	**Washington-Arlington-**	
		Jackson County, KS	13	**Alexandria, DC-VA-MD-WV**	5,476
Sioux Falls, SD	238	Jefferson County, KS	18	**Bethesda-Frederick-**	
Lincoln County, SD	41	Osage County, KS	16	**Rockville, MD**	1,200
McCook County, SD	6	Shawnee County, KS	176	Frederick County, MD	228
Minnehaha County, SD	183	Wabaunsee County, KS	7	Montgomery County, MD	972
Turner County, SD	8				

U.S. Census Bureau, Statistical Abstract of the United States: 2011

Metropolitan statistical area Metropolitan division Component county	Popu-lation, 2009 (1,000)	Metropolitan statistical area Metropolitan division Component county	Popu-lation, 2009 (1,000)	Metropolitan statistical area Metropolitan division Component county	Popu-lation, 2009 (1,000)
Washington-Arlington-Alexandria, DC-VA-MD-WV	**4,277**	**Weirton-Steubenville, WV-OH ..**	**121**	**Winchester, VA-WV**	**124**
District of Columbia, DC ..	600	Jefferson County, OH	68	Frederick County, VA	75
Calvert County, MD	89	Brooke County, WV	24	Winchester city, VA	26
Charles County, MD	142	Hancock County, WV.....	30	Hampshire County, WV ...	23
Prince George's County, MD................	835	**Wenatchee-East Wenatchee, WA.....................**	**110**	**Winston-Salem, NC**	**485**
Arlington County, VA	217	Chelan County, WA	72	Davie County, NC	41
Clarke County, VA	15	Douglas County, WA	38	Forsyth County, NC	360
Fairfax County, VA	1,038			Stokes County, NC	46
Fauquier County, VA	68	**Wheeling, WV-OH**	**145**	Yadkin County, NC.......	38
Loudoun County, VA	301	Belmont County, OH	68	**Worcester, MA**	**804**
Prince William County, VA .	379	Marshall County, WV	33	Worcester County, MA....	804
Spotsylvania County, VA ..	121	Ohio County, WV	44		
Stafford County, VA	124	**Wichita, KS**	**613**	**Yakima, WA.**	**239**
Warren County, VA.......	37	Butler County, KS	64	Yakima County, WA	239
Alexandria city, VA	150	Harvey County, KS	34	**York-Hanover, PA**	**429**
Fairfax city, VA	25	Sedgwick County, KS	491	York County, PA	429
Falls Church city, VA	12	Sumner County, KS......	23		
Fredericksburg city, VA ...	23			**Youngstown-Warren-Boardman, OH-PA**	**563**
Manassas city, VA	37	**Wichita Falls, TX.**	**147**	Mahoning County, OH....	237
Manassas Park city, VA ...	12	Archer County, TX	9	Trumbull County, OH	210
Jefferson County, WV	53	Clay County, TX.........	11	Mercer County, PA.......	116
		Wichita County, TX	128		
Waterloo-Cedar Falls, IA ..	**165**			**Yuba City, CA**	**166**
Black Hawk County, IA ...	129	**Williamsport, PA**	**117**	Sutter County, CA	93
Bremer County, IA	23	Lycoming County, PA.....	117	Yuba County, CA	73
Grundy County, IA	12				
		Wilmington, NC	**355**	**Yuma, AZ**	**197**
Wausau, WI.	**132**	Brunswick County, NC....	107	Yuma County, AZ........	197
Marathon County, WI.....	132	New Hanover County, NC .	195		
		Pender County, NC	52		

¹ The portion of Sullivan city in Crawford County, Missouri, is legally part of the St. Louis, MO-IL Metropolitan Statistical Area. The estimate shown here for the St. Louis, MO-IL Metropolitan Statistical Area does not include this area.

Source: U.S. Census Bureau, "CBSA-EST2009-alldata: Population Estimates and Estimated Components of Change for Metropolitan and Micropolitan Statistical Areas and Their Geographic Components: April 1, 2000 to July 1, 2009," <http://www.census.gov/popest/metro/files/2009/CBSA-EST2009-alldata.csv>.

Table B. Micropolitan Statistical Areas and Components—Population: 2009

[Population as of July 2009. (56 represents 56,000). Micropolitan statistical areas as defined by the U.S. Office of Management and Budget as of November 2008. All geographic boundaries for 2009 population estimates are defined as of January 1, 2009. All micropolitan areas are arranged alphabetically]

Micropolitan statistical area / Component county	Population, 2009 (1,000)	Micropolitan statistical area / Component county	Population, 2009 (1,000)	Micropolitan statistical area / Component county	Population, 2009 (1,000)
Abbeville, LA	56	**Ashland, OH**	55	**Bemidji, MN**	44
Vermilion Parish, LA	56	Ashland County, OH	55	Beltrami County, MN	44
Aberdeen, SD	39	**Ashtabula, OH**	101	**Bennettsville, SC**	29
Brown County, SD	35	Ashtabula County, OH	101	Marlboro County, SC	29
Edmunds County, SD	4	**Astoria, OR**	37	**Bennington, VT**	36
Aberdeen, WA	72	Clatsop County, OR	37	Bennington County, VT	36
Grays Harbor County, WA	72	**Atchison, KS**	16	**Berlin, NH-VT**	38
Ada, OK	37	Atchison County, KS	16	Coos County, NH	31
Pontotoc County, OK	37	**Athens, OH**	63	Essex County, VT	6
Adrian, MI	100	Athens County, OH	63	**Big Rapids, MI**	42
Lenawee County, MI	100	**Athens, TN**	53	Mecosta County, MI	42
Alamogordo, NM	63	McMinn County, TN	53	**Big Spring, TX**	33
Otero County, NM	63	**Athens, TX**	79	Howard County, TX	33
Albany-Lebanon, OR	117	Henderson County, TX	79	**Bishop, CA**	17
Linn County, OR	117	**Auburn, IN**	42	Inyo County, CA	17
Albemarle, NC	60	DeKalb County, IN	42	**Blackfoot, ID**	45
Stanly County, NC	60	**Auburn, NY**	80	Bingham County, ID	45
Albert Lea, MN	31	Cayuga County, NY	80	**Bloomsburg-Berwick, PA**	83
Freeborn County, MN	31	**Augusta-Waterville, ME**	121	Columbia County, PA	65
Albertville, AL	90	Kennebec County, ME	121	Montour County, PA	18
Marshall County, AL	90	**Austin, MN**	38	**Bluefield, WV-VA**	107
Alexander City, AL	52	Mower County, MN	38	Tazewell County, VA	45
Coosa County, AL	11	**Bainbridge, GA**	29	Mercer County, WV	62
Tallapoosa County, AL	41	Decatur County, GA	29	**Blytheville, AR**	47
Alexandria, MN	36	**Baraboo, WI**	59	Mississippi County, AR	47
Douglas County, MN	36	Sauk County, WI	59	**Bogalusa, LA**	46
Alice, TX	41	**Barre, VT**	59	Washington Parish, LA	46
Jim Wells County, TX	41	Washington County, VT	59	**Bonham, TX**	33
Allegan, MI	113	**Bartlesville, OK**	51	Fannin County, TX	33
Allegan County, MI	113	Washington County, OK	51	**Boone, IA**	26
Alma, MI	42	**Bastrop, LA**	28	Boone County, IA	26
Gratiot County, MI	42	Morehouse Parish, LA	28	**Boone, NC**	45
Alpena, MI	29	**Batavia, NY**	58	Watauga County, NC	45
Alpena County, MI	29	Genesee County, NY	58	**Borger, TX**	22
Altus, OK	25	**Batesville, AR**	35	Hutchinson County, TX	22
Jackson County, OK	25	Independence County, AR	35	**Bozeman, MT**	90
Americus, GA	36	**Bay City, TX**	37	Gallatin County, MT	90
Schley County, GA	4	Matagorda County, TX	37	**Bradford, PA**	43
Sumter County, GA	32	**Beatrice, NE**	23	McKean County, PA	43
Amsterdam, NY	49	Gage County, NE	23	**Brainerd, MN**	91
Montgomery County, NY	49	**Beaver Dam, WI**	87	Cass County, MN	29
Andrews, TX	14	Dodge County, WI	87	Crow Wing County, MN	63
Andrews County, TX	14	**Beckley, WV**	79	**Branson, MO**	79
Angola, IN	34	Raleigh County, WV	79	Stone County, MO	31
Steuben County, IN	34	**Bedford, IN**	46	Taney County, MO	48
Arcadia, FL	35	Lawrence County, IN	46	**Brenham, TX**	33
DeSoto County, FL	35	**Beeville, TX**	32	Washington County, TX	33
Ardmore, OK	57	Bee County, TX	32	**Brevard, NC**	30
Carter County, OK	48	**Bellefontaine, OH**	47	Transylvania County, NC	30
Love County, OK	9	Logan County, OH	47	**Brigham City, UT**	50
Arkadelphia, AR	24			Box Elder County, UT	50
Clark County, AR	24			**Brookhaven, MS**	35
				Lincoln County, MS	35

U.S. Census Bureau, Statistical Abstract of the United States: 2011

Micropolitan statistical area / Component county	Population, 2009 (1,000)	Micropolitan statistical area / Component county	Population, 2009 (1,000)	Micropolitan statistical area / Component county	Population, 2009 (1,000)
Brookings, OR	21	**Chester, SC**	32	**Coshocton, OH**	36
Curry County, OR	21	Chester County, SC	32	Coshocton County, OH	36
Brookings, SD	30	**Chillicothe, OH**	76	**Crawfordsville, IN**	38
Brookings County, SD	30	Ross County, OH	76	Montgomery County, IN	38
Brownsville, TN	19	**Claremont, NH**	43	**Crescent City, CA**	29
Haywood County, TN	19	Sullivan County, NH	43	Del Norte County, CA	29
Brownwood, TX	38	**Clarksburg, WV**	92	**Crossville, TN**	54
Brown County, TX	38	Doddridge County, WV	7	Cumberland County, TN	54
Bucyrus, OH	43	Harrison County, WV	69		
Crawford County, OH	43	Taylor County, WV	16	**Crowley, LA**	60
				Acadia Parish, LA	60
Burley, ID	41	**Clarksdale, MS**	27		
Cassia County, ID	22	Coahoma County, MS	27	**Cullman, AL**	82
Minidoka County, ID	19			Cullman County, AL	82
		Clearlake, CA	65		
Burlington, IA-IL	48	Lake County, CA	65	**Culpeper, VA**	47
Henderson County, IL	7			Culpeper County, VA	47
Des Moines County, IA	41	**Cleveland, MS**	37		
		Bolivar County, MS	37	**Danville, KY**	54
Butte-Silver Bow, MT	33			Boyle County, KY	29
Silver Bow County, MT	33	**Clewiston, FL**	40	Lincoln County, KY	25
		Hendry County, FL	40		
Cadillac, MI	46			**Daphne-Fairhope-Foley, AL**	180
Missaukee County, MI	15	**Clinton, IA**	49	Baldwin County, AL	180
Wexford County, MI	32	Clinton County, IA	49		
				Decatur, IN	34
Calhoun, GA	53	**Clovis, NM**	44	Adams County, IN	34
Gordon County, GA	53	Curry County, NM	44		
				Defiance, OH	38
Cambridge, MD	32	**Coffeyville, KS**	34	Defiance County, OH	38
Dorchester County, MD	32	Montgomery County, KS	34		
				Del Rio, TX	48
Cambridge, OH	40	**Coldwater, MI**	45	Val Verde County, TX	48
Guernsey County, OH	40	Branch County, MI	45		
				Deming, NM	27
Camden, AR	31	**Columbia, TN**	84	Luna County, NM	27
Calhoun County, AR	5	Maury County, TN	84		
Ouachita County, AR	25			**De Ridder, LA**	35
		Columbus, MS	60	Beauregard Parish, LA	35
Campbellsville, KY	24	Lowndes County, MS	60		
Taylor County, KY	24			**Dickinson, ND**	24
		Columbus, NE	33	Billings County, ND	1
Canon City, CO	48	Platte County, NE	33	Stark County, ND	23
Fremont County, CO	48				
		Concord, NH	149	**Dillon, SC**	31
Canton City, CO	37	Merrimack County, NH	149	Dillon County, SC	31
Fulton County, IL	37				
		Connersville, IN	24	**Dixon, IL**	35
Carbondale, IL	58	Fayette County, IN	24	Lee County, IL	35
Jackson County, IL	58				
		Cookeville, TN	104	**Dodge City, KS**	34
Carlsbad-Artesia, NM	53	Jackson County, TN	11	Ford County, KS	34
Eddy County, NM	53	Overton County, TN	21		
		Putnam County, TN	72	**Douglas, GA**	49
Cedar City, UT	45			Atkinson County, GA	8
Iron County, UT	45	**Coos Bay, OR**	63	Coffee County, GA	41
		Coos County, OR	63		
Cedartown, GA	42			**Dublin, GA**	58
Polk County, GA	42	**Corbin, KY**	39	Johnson County, GA	9
		Whitley County, KY	39	Laurens County, GA	48
Celina, OH	41				
Mercer County, OH	41	**Cordele, GA**	22	**DuBois, PA**	82
		Crisp County, GA	22	Clearfield County, PA	82
Central City, KY	31				
Muhlenberg County, KY	31	**Corinth, MS**	36	**Dumas, TX**	21
		Alcorn County, MS	36	Moore County, TX	21
Centralia, IL	39				
Marion County, IL	39	**Cornelia, GA**	44	**Duncan, OK**	43
		Habersham County, GA	44	Stephens County, OK	43
Centralia, WA	75				
Lewis County, WA	75	**Corning, NY**	97	**Dunn, NC**	116
		Steuben County, NY	97	Harnett County, NC	116
Chambersburg, PA	145				
Franklin County, PA	145	**Corsicana, TX**	49	**Durango, CO**	51
		Navarro County, TX	49	La Plata County, CO	51
Charleston-Mattoon, IL	63				
Coles County, IL	52	**Cortland, NY**	48	**Durant, OK**	41
Cumberland County, IL	11	Cortland County, NY	48	Bryan County, OK	41

914 Appendix II

Micropolitan statistical area Component county	Population, 2009 (1,000)	Micropolitan statistical area Component county	Population, 2009 (1,000)	Micropolitan statistical area Component county	Population, 2009 (1,000)
Dyersburg, TN	38	**Farmington, MO**	64	**Georgetown, SC**	61
Dyer County, TN	38	St. Francois County, MO	64	Georgetown County, SC	61
Eagle Pass, TX	53	**Fergus Falls, MN**	57	**Gettysburg, PA**	102
Maverick County, TX	53	Otter Tail County, MN	57	Adams County, PA	102
East Liverpool-Salem, OH	108	**Fernley, NV**	53	**Gillette, WY**	44
Columbiana County, OH	108	Lyon County, NV	53	Campbell County, WY	44
Easton, MD	36	**Findlay, OH**	75	**Glasgow, KY**	52
Talbot County, MD	36	Hancock County, OH	75	Barren County, KY	42
East Stroudsburg, PA	166	**Fitzgerald, GA**	28	Metcalfe County, KY	10
Monroe County, PA	166	Ben Hill County, GA	18	**Gloversville, NY**	55
Edwards, CO	62	Irwin County, GA	10	Fulton County, NY	55
Eagle County, CO	54	**Forest City, NC**	63	Granbury, TX	59
Lake County, CO	8	Rutherford County, NC	63	Hood County, TX	51
Effingham, IL	34	**Forrest City, AR**	26	Somervell County, TX	8
Effingham County, IL	34	St. Francis County, AR	26	**Grand Island, NE**	72
El Campo, TX	41	**Fort Dodge, IA**	38	Hall County, NE	57
Wharton County, TX	41	Webster County, IA	38	Howard County, NE	6
El Dorado, AR	43	**Fort Leonard Wood, MO**	46	Merrick County, NE	8
Union County, AR	43	Pulaski County, MO	46	**Grants, NM**	27
Elizabeth City, NC	64	**Fort Madison-Keokuk, IA-MO**	43	Cibola County, NM	27
Camden County, NC	10	Lee County, IA	35	**Grants Pass, OR**	81
Pasquotank County, NC	42	Clark County, MO	7	Josephine County, OR	81
Perquimans County, NC	13	**Fort Morgan, CO**	28	**Great Bend, KS**	27
Elk City, OK	21	Morgan County, CO	28	Barton County, KS	27
Beckham County, OK	21	**Fort Payne, AL**	69	**Greeneville, TN**	66
Elko, NV	50	DeKalb County, AL	69	Greene County, TN	66
Elko County, NV	48	**Fort Polk South, LA**	47	**Greensburg, IN**	25
Eureka County, NV	2	Vernon Parish, LA	47	Decatur County, IN	25
Ellensburg, WA	40	**Fort Valley, GA**	27	**Greenville, MS**	55
Kittitas County, WA	40	Peach County, GA	27	Washington County, MS	55
Emporia, KS	36	**Frankfort, IN**	34	**Greenville, OH**	52
Chase County, KS	3	Clinton County, IN	34	Darke County, OH	52
Lyon County, KS	34	**Frankfort, KY**	71	**Greenwood, MS**	45
Enid, OK	59	Anderson County, KY	22	Carroll County, MS	10
Garfield County, OK	59	Franklin County, KY	49	Leflore County, MS	35
Enterprise-Ozark, AL	97	**Fredericksburg, TX**	24	**Greenwood, SC**	70
Coffee County, AL	49	Gillespie County, TX	24	Greenwood County, SC	70
Dale County, AL	48	**Freeport, IL**	47	**Grenada, MS**	23
Escanaba, MI	37	Stephenson County, IL	47	Grenada County, MS	23
Delta County, MI	37	**Fremont, NE**	36	**Guymon, OK**	21
Espanola, NM	41	Dodge County, NE	36	Texas County, OK	21
Rio Arriba County, NM	41	**Fremont, OH**	60	**Hammond, LA**	119
Eufaula, AL-GA	32	Sandusky County, OH	60	Tangipahoa Parish, LA	119
Barbour County, AL	30	**Gaffney, SC**	55	**Hannibal, MO**	38
Quitman County, GA	3	Cherokee County, SC	55	Marion County, MO	28
Eureka-Arcata-Fortuna, CA	130	**Gainesville, TX**	39	Ralls County, MO	10
Humboldt County, CA	130	Cooke County, TX	39	**Harriman, TN**	54
Evanston, WY	21	**Galesburg, IL**	69	Roane County, TN	54
Uinta County, WY	21	Knox County, IL	52	**Harrisburg, IL**	26
Fairmont, MN	20	Warren County, IL	17	Saline County, IL	26
Martin County, MN	20	**Gallup, NM**	71	**Harrison, AR**	45
Fairmont, WV	57	McKinley County, NM	71	Boone County, AR	37
Marion County, WV	57	**Garden City, KS**	42	Newton County, AR	8
Fallon, NV	25	Finney County, KS	42	**Hastings, NE**	40
Churchill County, NV	25	**Gardnerville Ranchos, NV**	45	Adams County, NE	33
Faribault-Northfield, MN	63	Douglas County, NV	45	Clay County, NE	6
Rice County, MN	63			**Havre, MT**	17
				Hill County, MT	17

U.S. Census Bureau, Statistical Abstract of the United States: 2011

Micropolitan statistical area Component county	Popula- tion, 2009 (1,000)	Micropolitan statistical area Component county	Popula- tion, 2009 (1,000)	Micropolitan statistical area Component county	Popula- tion, 2009 (1,000)
Hays, KS	28	**Jacksonville, IL**	40	**La Follette, TN**	41
Ellis County, KS	28	Morgan County, IL	35	Campbell County, TN	41
		Scott County, IL	5		
Heber, UT	22			**La Grande, OR**	25
Wasatch County, UT	22	**Jacksonville, TX**	48	Union County, OR	25
		Cherokee County, TX	48		
Helena, MT	73			**LaGrange, GA**	65
Jefferson County, MT	11	**Jamestown, ND**	20	Troup County, GA	65
Lewis and Clark County, MT	62	Stutsman County, ND	20		
				Lake City, FL	69
Helena-West Helena, AR	21	**Jamestown-Dunkirk-Fredonia,**		Columbia County, FL	69
Phillips County, AR	21	**NY**	134		
		Chautauqua County, NY	134	**Lamesa, TX**	14
Henderson, NC	43			Dawson County, TX	14
Vance County, NC	43	**Jasper, IN**	54		
		Dubois County, IN	41	**Lancaster, SC**	78
Hereford, TX	18	Pike County, IN	12	Lancaster County, SC	78
Deaf Smith County, TX	18				
		Jennings, LA	31	**Laramie, WY**	34
Hilo, HI	178	Jefferson Davis Parish, LA	31	Albany County, WY	34
Hawaii County, HI	178				
		Jesup, GA	29	**Las Vegas, NM**	28
Hilton Head Island-Beaufort, SC	178	Wayne County, GA	29	San Miguel County, NM	28
Beaufort County, SC	155				
Jasper County, SC	23	**Juneau, AK**	31	**Laurel, MS**	86
		Juneau City and Borough, AK	31	Jasper County, MS	18
Hobbs, NM	60			Jones County, MS	68
Lea County, NM	60	**Kahului-Wailuku, HI**	145		
		Maui County, HI	145	**Laurinburg, NC**	36
Homosassa Springs, FL	140			Scotland County, NC	36
Citrus County, FL	140	**Kalispell, MT**	90		
		Flathead County, MT	90	**Lawrenceburg, TN**	41
Hood River, OR	22			Lawrence County, TN	41
Hood River County, OR	22	**Kapaa, HI**	65		
		Kauai County, HI	65	**Lebanon, MO**	35
Hope, AR	32			Laclede County, MO	35
Hempstead County, AR	23	**Kearney, NE**	52		
Nevada County, AR	9	Buffalo County, NE	46	**Lebanon, NH-VT**	172
		Kearney County, NE	6	Grafton County, NH	86
Houghton, MI	38			Orange County, VT	29
Houghton County, MI	35	**Keene, NH**	77	Windsor County, VT	57
Keweenaw County, MI	2	Cheshire County, NH	77		
				Levelland, TX	22
Hudson, NY	62	**Kendallville, IN**	48	Hockley County, TX	22
Columbia County, NY	62	Noble County, IN	48		
				Lewisburg, PA	44
Humboldt, TN	49	**Kennett, MO**	31	Union County, PA	44
Gibson County, TN	49	Dunklin County, MO	31		
				Lewisburg, TN	30
Huntingdon, PA	45	**Kerrville, TX**	48	Marshall County, TN	30
Huntingdon County, PA	45	Kerr County, TX	48		
				Lewistown, PA	46
Huntington, IN	38	**Ketchikan, AK**	13	Mifflin County, PA	46
Huntington County, IN	38	Ketchikan Gateway Borough,			
		AK	13	**Lexington, NE**	27
Huntsville, TX	64			Dawson County, NE	25
Walker County, TX	64	**Key West, FL**	73	Gosper County, NE	2
		Monroe County, FL	73		
Huron, SD	16			**Lexington Park, MD**	103
Beadle County, SD	16	**Kill Devil Hills, NC**	34	St. Mary's County, MD	103
		Dare County, NC	34		
Hutchinson, KS	63			**Liberal, KS**	23
Reno County, KS	63	**Kingsville, TX**	31	Seward County, KS	23
		Kenedy County, TX	(Z)		
Hutchinson, MN	37	Kleberg County, TX	31	**Lincoln, IL**	30
McLeod County, MN	37			Logan County, IL	30
		Kinston, NC	56		
Indiana, PA	87	Lenoir County, NC	56	**Lincolnton, NC**	76
Indiana County, PA	87			Lincoln County, NC	76
		Kirksville, MO	29		
Indianola, MS	30	Adair County, MO	25	**Lock Haven, PA**	37
Sunflower County, MS	30	Schuyler County, MO	4	Clinton County, PA	37
Iron Mountain, MI-WI	31	**Klamath Falls, OR**	66	**Logansport, IN**	39
Dickinson County, MI	27	Klamath County, OR	66	Cass County, IN	39
Florence County, WI	5				
		Kodiak, AK	13	**London, KY**	58
Jackson, WY-ID	30	Kodiak Island Borough, AK	13	Laurel County, KY	58
Teton County, ID	9				
Teton County, WY	21	**Laconia, NH**	61	**Los Alamos, NM**	18
		Belknap County, NH	61	Los Alamos County, NM	18

916 Appendix II

Micropolitan statistical area / Component county	Population, 2009 (1,000)
Lufkin, TX	84
Angelina County, TX	84
Lumberton, NC	130
Robeson County, NC	130
Macomb, IL	33
McDonough County, IL	33
Madison, IN	33
Jefferson County, IN	33
Madisonville, KY	46
Hopkins County, KY	46
Magnolia, AR	24
Columbia County, AR	24
Malone, NY	50
Franklin County, NY	50
Manitowoc, WI	81
Manitowoc County, WI	81
Marinette, WI-MI	66
Menominee County, MI	24
Marinette County, WI	42
Marion, IN	69
Grant County, IN	69
Marion, OH	66
Marion County, OH	66
Marion-Herrin, IL	65
Williamson County, IL	65
Marquette, MI	66
Marquette County, MI	66
Marshall, MN	25
Lyon County, MN	25
Marshall, MO	23
Saline County, MO	23
Marshall, TX	65
Harrison County, TX	65
Marshalltown, IA	39
Marshall County, IA	39
Marshfield-Wisconsin Rapids, WI	74
Wood County, WI	74
Martin, TN	33
Weakley County, TN	33
Martinsville, VA	70
Henry County, VA	55
Martinsville city, VA	15
Maryville, MO	22
Nodaway County, MO	22
Mason City, IA	51
Cerro Gordo County, IA	44
Worth County, IA	8
Mayfield, KY	38
Graves County, KY	38
Maysville, KY	31
Lewis County, KY	14
Mason County, KY	17
McAlester, OK	45
Pittsburg County, OK	45
McComb, MS	53
Amite County, MS	13
Pike County, MS	40

Micropolitan statistical area / Component county	Population, 2009 (1,000)
McMinnville, TN	40
Warren County, TN	40
McPherson, KS	29
McPherson County, KS	29
Meadville, PA	89
Crawford County, PA	89
Menomonie, WI	43
Dunn County, WI	43
Meridian, MS	106
Clarke County, MS	17
Kemper County, MS	10
Lauderdale County, MS	79
Merrill, WI	29
Lincoln County, WI	29
Mexico, MO	26
Audrain County, MO	26
Miami, OK	32
Ottawa County, OK	32
Middlesborough, KY	29
Bell County, KY	29
Midland, MI	83
Midland County, MI	83
Milledgeville, GA	56
Baldwin County, GA	46
Hancock County, GA	9
Minden, LA	41
Webster Parish, LA	41
Mineral Wells, TX	28
Palo Pinto County, TX	28
Minot, ND	64
McHenry County, ND	5
Renville County, ND	2
Ward County, ND	57
Mitchell, SD	22
Davison County, SD	19
Hanson County, SD	4
Moberly, MO	26
Randolph County, MO	26
Monroe, WI	36
Green County, WI	36
Montrose, CO	41
Montrose County, CO	41
Morehead City, NC	64
Carteret County, NC	64
Morgan City, LA	51
St. Mary Parish, LA	51
Moscow, ID	38
Latah County, ID	38
Moses Lake, WA	88
Grant County, WA	88
Moultrie, GA	46
Colquitt County, GA	46
Mountain Home, AR	42
Baxter County, AR	42
Mountain Home, ID	29
Elmore County, ID	29
Mount Airy, NC	72
Surry County, NC	72

Micropolitan statistical area / Component county	Population, 2009 (1,000)
Mount Pleasant, MI	67
Isabella County, MI	67
Mount Pleasant, TX	30
Titus County, TX	30
Mount Sterling, KY	44
Bath County, KY	12
Menifee County, KY	7
Montgomery County, KY	26
Mount Vernon, IL	48
Hamilton County, IL	8
Jefferson County, IL	40
Mount Vernon, OH	60
Knox County, OH	60
Murray, KY	36
Calloway County, KY	36
Muscatine, IA	54
Louisa County, IA	11
Muscatine County, IA	43
Muskogee, OK	71
Muskogee County, OK	71
Nacogdoches, TX	64
Nacogdoches County, TX	64
Natchez, MS-LA	50
Concordia Parish, LA	19
Adams County, MS	31
Natchitoches, LA	39
Natchitoches Parish, LA	39
New Bern, NC	121
Craven County, NC	99
Jones County, NC	10
Pamlico County, NC	12
Newberry, SC	39
Newberry County, SC	39
New Castle, IN	48
Henry County, IN	48
New Castle, PA	90
Lawrence County, PA	90
New Iberia, LA	75
Iberia Parish, LA	75
New Philadelphia-Dover, OH	91
Tuscarawas County, OH	91
Newport, TN	36
Cocke County, TN	36
Newton, IA	36
Jasper County, IA	36
New Ulm, MN	26
Brown County, MN	26
Nogales, AZ	44
Santa Cruz County, AZ	44
Norfolk, NE	48
Madison County, NE	35
Pierce County, NE	7
Stanton County, NE	6
North Platte, NE	37
Lincoln County, NE	36
Logan County, NE	1
McPherson County, NE	0
North Vernon, IN	28
Jennings County, IN	28

U.S. Census Bureau, Statistical Abstract of the United States: 2011

Micropolitan statistical area / Component county	Population, 2009 (1,000)	Micropolitan statistical area / Component county	Population, 2009 (1,000)	Micropolitan statistical area / Component county	Population, 2009 (1,000)
North Wilkesboro, NC	67	**Paris, TN**	32	**Pullman, WA**	43
Wilkes County, NC	67	Henry County, TN	32	Whitman County, WA	43
Norwalk, OH	60	**Paris, TX**	49	**Quincy, IL-MO**	77
Huron County, OH	60	Lamar County, TX	49	Adams County, IL	67
Oak Harbor, WA	81	**Parsons, KS**	22	Lewis County, MO	10
Island County, WA	81	Labette County, KS	22	**Raymondville, TX**	20
Oak Hill, WV	46	**Payson, AZ**	52	Willacy County, TX	20
Fayette County, WV	46	Gila County, AZ	52	**Red Bluff, CA**	61
Ocean Pines, MD	49	**Pecos, TX**	11	Tehama County, CA	61
Worcester County, MD	49	Reeves County, TX	11	**Red Wing, MN**	46
Ogdensburg-Massena, NY	110	**Pella, IA**	33	Goodhue County, MN	46
St. Lawrence County, NY	110	Marion County, IA	33	**Rexburg, ID**	51
Oil City, PA	54	**Pendleton-Hermiston, OR**	85	Fremont County, ID	13
Venango County, PA	54	Morrow County, OR	12	Madison County, ID	38
Okeechobee, FL	40	Umatilla County, OR	73	**Richmond, IN**	68
Okeechobee County, FL	40	**Peru, IN**	36	Wayne County, IN	68
Olean, NY	80	Miami County, IN	36	**Richmond-Berea, KY**	100
Cattaraugus County, NY	80	**Phoenix Lake-Cedar Ridge, CA**	55	Madison County, KY	83
Oneonta, NY	62	Tuolumne County, CA	55	Rockcastle County, KY	17
Otsego County, NY	62	**Picayune, MS**	58	**Rio Grande City-Roma, TX**	63
Ontario, OR-ID	54	Pearl River County, MS	58	Starr County, TX	63
Payette County, ID	23	**Pierre, SD**	20	**Riverton, WY**	39
Malheur County, OR	31	Hughes County, SD	17	Fremont County, WY	39
Opelousas-Eunice, LA	92	Stanley County, SD	3	**Roanoke Rapids, NC**	75
St. Landry Parish, LA	92	**Pierre Part, LA**	23	Halifax County, NC	55
Orangeburg, SC	90	Assumption Parish, LA	23	Northampton County, NC	20
Orangeburg County, SC	90	**Pittsburg, KS**	39	**Rochelle, IL**	55
Oskaloosa, IA	22	Crawford County, KS	39	Ogle County, IL	55
Mahaska County, IA	22	**Plainview, TX**	35	**Rockingham, NC**	46
Ottawa-Streator, IL	153	Hale County, TX	35	Richmond County, NC	46
Bureau County, IL	35	**Platteville, WI**	49	**Rockland, ME**	41
LaSalle County, IL	112	Grant County, WI	49	Knox County, ME	41
Putnam County, IL	6	**Plattsburgh, NY**	82	**Rock Springs, WY**	41
Ottumwa, IA	35	Clinton County, NY	82	Sweetwater County, WY	41
Wapello County, IA	35	**Plymouth, IN**	47	**Rolla, MO**	42
Owatonna, MN	37	Marshall County, IN	47	Phelps County, MO	42
Steele County, MN	37	**Point Pleasant, WV-OH**	56	**Roseburg, OR**	103
Owosso, MI	70	Gallia County, OH	31	Douglas County, OR	103
Shiawassee County, MI	70	Mason County, WV	26	**Roswell, NM**	64
Oxford, MS	44	**Ponca City, OK**	46	Chaves County, NM	64
Lafayette County, MS	44	Kay County, OK	46	**Ruidoso, NM**	21
Paducah, KY-IL	99	**Pontiac, IL**	38	Lincoln County, NM	21
Massac County, IL	15	Livingston County, IL	38	**Russellville, AR**	83
Ballard County, KY	8	**Poplar Bluff, MO**	41	Pope County, AR	60
Livingston County, KY	10	Butler County, MO	41	Yell County, AR	22
McCracken County, KY	66	**Portales, NM**	19	**Ruston, LA**	58
Pahrump, NV	44	Roosevelt County, NM	19	Jackson Parish, LA	15
Nye County, NV	44	**Port Angeles, WA**	71	Lincoln Parish, LA	43
Palatka, FL	73	Clallam County, WA	71	**Rutland, VT**	63
Putnam County, FL	73	**Portsmouth, OH**	76	Rutland County, VT	63
Palestine, TX	57	Scioto County, OH	76	**Safford, AZ**	45
Anderson County, TX	57	**Pottsville, PA**	147	Graham County, AZ	37
Pampa, TX	23	Schuylkill County, PA	147	Greenlee County, AZ	8
Gray County, TX	22	**Price, UT**	20	**St. Marys, GA**	48
Roberts County, TX	1	Carbon County, UT	20	Camden County, GA	48
Paragould, AR	41	**Prineville, OR**	23	**St. Marys, PA**	32
Greene County, AR	41	Crook County, OR	23	Elk County, PA	32

918 Appendix II

U.S. Census Bureau, Statistical Abstract of the United States: 2011

Micropolitan statistical area / Component county	Population, 2009 (1,000)	Micropolitan statistical area / Component county	Population, 2009 (1,000)	Micropolitan statistical area / Component county	Population, 2009 (1,000)
				Talladega County, AL	80
Salina, KS	60	**Silver City, NM**	30		
Ottawa County, KS	6	Grant County, NM	30	**Tallulah, LA**	11
Saline County, KS	54			Madison Parish, LA	11
		Silverthorne, CO	27		
Salisbury, NC	141	Summit County, CO	27	**Taos, NM**	32
Rowan County, NC	141			Taos County, NM	32
		Snyder, TX	16		
Sanford, NC	60	Scurry County, TX	16	**Taylorville, IL**	34
Lee County, NC	60			Christian County, IL	34
		Somerset, KY	61		
Sault Ste. Marie, MI	39	Pulaski County, KY	61	**The Dalles, OR**	24
Chippewa County, MI	39			Wasco County, OR	24
		Somerset, PA	77		
Sayre, PA	61	Somerset County, PA	77	**The Villages, FL**	78
Bradford County, PA	61			Sumter County, FL	78
		Southern Pines-Pinehurst, NC	87		
Scottsbluff, NE	38	Moore County, NC	87	**Thomaston, GA**	28
Banner County, NE	1			Upson County, GA	28
Scotts Bluff County, NE	37	**Spearfish, SD**	23		
		Lawrence County, SD	23	**Thomasville, GA**	46
Scottsboro, AL	53			Thomas County, GA	46
Jackson County, AL	53	**Spencer, IA**	17		
		Clay County, IA	17	**Thomasville-Lexington, NC**	159
Scottsburg, IN	24			Davidson County, NC	159
Scott County, IN	24	**Spirit Lake, IA**	17		
		Dickinson County, IA	17	**Tiffin, OH**	56
Seaford, DE	193			Seneca County, OH	56
Sussex County, DE	193	**Starkville, MS**	45		
		Oktibbeha County, MS	45	**Tifton, GA**	43
Searcy, AR	76			Tift County, GA	43
White County, AR	76	**Statesboro, GA**	69		
		Bulloch County, GA	69	**Toccoa, GA**	26
Sebring, FL	99			Stephens County, GA	26
Highlands County, FL	99	**Statesville-Mooresville, NC**	158		
		Iredell County, NC	158	**Torrington, CT**	189
Sedalia, MO	41			Litchfield County, CT	189
Pettis County, MO	41	**Staunton-Waynesboro, VA**	118		
		Augusta County, VA	72	**Traverse City, MI**	142
Selinsgrove, PA	39	Staunton city, VA	24	Benzie County, MI	17
Snyder County, PA	39	Waynesboro city, VA	22	Grand Traverse County, MI	86
				Kalkaska County, MI	17
Selma, AL	42	**Stephenville, TX**	36	Leelanau County, MI	22
Dallas County, AL	42	Erath County, TX	36		
				Troy, AL	30
Seneca, SC	72	**Sterling, CO**	21	Pike County, AL	30
Oconee County, SC	72	Logan County, CO	21		
				Truckee-Grass Valley, CA	98
Seneca Falls, NY	34	**Sterling, IL**	59	Nevada County, CA	98
Seneca County, NY	34	Whiteside County, IL	59		
				Tullahoma, TN	100
Sevierville, TN	86	**Stevens Point, WI**	69	Coffee County, TN	53
Sevier County, TN	86	Portage County, WI	69	Franklin County, TN	41
				Moore County, TN	6
Seymour, IN	42	**Stillwater, OK**	80		
Jackson County, IN	42	Payne County, OK	80	**Tupelo, MS**	134
				Itawamba County, MS	23
Shawnee, OK	70	**Storm Lake, IA**	20	Lee County, MS	82
Pottawatomie County, OK	70	Buena Vista County, IA	20	Pontotoc County, MS	29
Shelby, NC	99	**Sturgis, MI**	62	**Tuskegee, AL**	22
Cleveland County, NC	99	St. Joseph County, MI	62	Macon County, AL	22
Shelbyville, TN	46	**Sulphur Springs, TX**	35	**Twin Falls, ID**	97
Bedford County, TN	46	Hopkins County, TX	35	Jerome County, ID	21
				Twin Falls County, ID	75
Shelton, WA	58	**Summerville, GA**	27		
Mason County, WA	58	Chattooga County, GA	27	**Ukiah, CA**	86
				Mendocino County, CA	86
Sheridan, WY	29	**Sunbury, PA**	91		
Sheridan County, WY	29	Northumberland County, PA	91	**Union, SC**	27
				Union County, SC	27
Show Low, AZ	113	**Susanville, CA**	34		
Navajo County, AZ	113	Lassen County, CA	34	**Union City, TN-KY**	38
				Fulton County, KY	7
Sidney, OH	49	**Sweetwater, TX**	15	Obion County, TN	31
Shelby County, OH	49	Nolan County, TX	15		
				Urbana, OH	40
Sierra Vista-Douglas, AZ	130	**Tahlequah, OK**	46	Champaign County, OH	40
Cochise County, AZ	130	Cherokee County, OK	46		
				Uvalde, TX	27
Sikeston, MO	41	**Talladega-Sylacauga, AL**	80	Uvalde County, TX	27
Scott County, MO	41				
				Valley, AL	34

Appendix II 919

Micropolitan statistical area / Component county	Popula-tion, 2009 (1,000)	Micropolitan statistical area / Component county	Popula-tion, 2009 (1,000)	Micropolitan statistical area / Component county	Popula-tion, 2009 (1,000)
Chambers County, AL	34				
Van Wert, OH	28	**Warrensburg, MO**	53	**Willimantic, CT**	118
Van Wert County, OH	28	Johnson County, MO	53	Windham County, CT.	118
Vermillion, SD	13	**Warsaw, IN**	76	**Williston, ND**	20
Clay County, SD	13	Kosciusko County, IN.	76	Williams County, ND	20
Vernal, UT	32	**Washington, IN**	31	**Willmar, MN**	41
Uintah County, UT	32	Daviess County, IN	31	Kandiyohi County, MN.	41
Vernon, TX	14	**Washington, NC**	46	**Wilmington, OH**	43
Wilbarger County, TX.	14	Beaufort County, NC	46	Clinton County, OH	43
Vicksburg, MS	48	**Washington Court House, OH** .	28	**Wilson, NC**	78
Warren County, MS	48	Fayette County, OH	28	Wilson County, NC.	78
Vidalia, GA	37	**Watertown, SD**	32	**Winfield, KS**	34
Montgomery County, GA	9	Codington County, SD	26	Cowley County, KS	34
Toombs County, GA.	28	Hamlin County, SD	6	
Vincennes, IN	38	**Watertown-Fort Atkinson, WI** . .	81	**Winona, MN**	49
Knox County, IN.	38	Jefferson County, WI	81	Winona County, MN.	49
Wabash, IN	33	**Watertown-Fort Drum, NY**	119	**Woodward, OK**	20
Wabash County, IN	33	Jefferson County, NY.	119	Woodward County, OK	20
Wahpeton, ND-MN	22	**Wauchula, FL**	29	**Wooster, OH**	114
Wilkin County, MN	6	Hardee County, FL.	29	Wayne County, OH	114
Richland County, ND	16				
		Waycross, GA	54	**Worthington, MN**	21
Walla Walla, WA	59	Pierce County, GA	19	Nobles County, MN	21
Walla Walla County, WA	59	Ware County, GA.	36	**Yankton, SD**	22
Walterboro, SC	39	**West Plains, MO**	39	Yankton County, SD.	22
Colleton County, SC	39	Howell County, MO	39	**Yazoo City, MS**	28
				Yazoo County, MS	28
Wapakoneta, OH	47	**West Point, MS**	21	**Zanesville, OH**	85
Auglaize County, OH	47	Clay County, MS	21	Muskingum County, OH.	85
Warren, PA	41	**Whitewater, WI**	101	
Warren County, PA.	41	Walworth County, WI	101	

Z Less than 500.

Source: U.S. Census Bureau, "CBSA-EST2009-alldata: Population Estimates and Estimated Components of Change for Metropolitan and Micropolitan Statistical Areas and Their Geographic Components: April 1, 2000 to July 1, 2009," <http://www.census.gov/popest/metro/files/2009/CBSA-EST2009-alldata.csv>.

Limitations of the Data

Introduction– The data presented in this *Statistical Abstract* came from many sources. The sources include not only federal statistical bureaus and other organizations that collect and issue statistics as their principal activity, but also governmental administrative and regulatory agencies, private research bodies, trade associations, insurance companies, health associations, and private organizations such as the National Education Association and philanthropic foundations. Consequently, the data vary considerably as to reference periods, definitions of terms and, for ongoing series, the number and frequency of time periods for which data are available.

The statistics presented were obtained and tabulated by various means. Some statistics are based on complete enumerations or censuses while others are based on samples. Some information is extracted from records kept for administrative or regulatory purposes (school enrollment, hospital records, securities registration, financial accounts, social security records, income tax returns, etc.), while other information is obtained explicitly for statistical purposes through interviews or by mail. The estimation procedures used vary from highly sophisticated scientific techniques, to crude "informed guesses."

Each set of data relates to a group of individuals or units of interest referred to as the *target universe* or *target population,* or simply as the *universe* or *population.*

Prior to data collection the target universe should be clearly defined. For example, if data are to be collected for the universe of households in the United States, it is necessary to define a "household." The target universe may not be completely tractable. Cost and other considerations may restrict data collection to a *survey universe* based on some available list, such list may be inaccurate or out of date. This list is called a *survey frame* or *sampling frame.*

The data in many tables are based on data obtained for all population units, *a census,* or on data obtained for only a portion, or *sample*, of the population units. When the data presented are based on a sample, the sample is usually a scientifically selected *probability sample.* This is a sample selected from a list or sampling frame in such a way that every possible sample has a known chance of selection and usually each unit selected can be assigned a number, greater than zero and less than or equal to one, representing its likelihood or probability of selection.

For large-scale sample surveys, the probability sample of units is often selected as a multistage sample. The first stage of a multistage sample is the selection of a probability sample of large groups of population members, referred to as primary sampling units (PSUs). For example, in a national multistage household sample, PSUs are often counties or groups of counties. The second stage of a multistage sample is the selection, within each PSU selected at the first stage, of smaller groups of population units, referred to as secondary sampling units. In subsequent stages of selection, smaller and smaller nested groups are chosen until the ultimate sample of population units is obtained. To qualify a multistage sample as a probability sample, all stages of sampling must be carried out using probability sampling methods.

Prior to selection at each stage of a multistage (or a single stage) sample, a list of the sampling units or sampling frame for that stage must be obtained. For example, for the first stage of selection of a national household sample, a list of the counties and county groups that form the PSUs must be obtained. For the final stage of selection, lists of households, and sometimes persons within the households, have to be compiled in the field. For surveys of economic entities and for the economic censuses the U.S. Census Bureau generally uses a frame constructed from the Bureau's Business Register. The Business Register contains all establishments with payroll in the United States including small single establishment firms as well as large multi-establishment firms.

Wherever the quantities in a table refer to an entire universe, but are constructed from data collected in a sample survey, the table quantities are referred to as *sample estimates*. In constructing a sample estimate, an attempt is made to come as close as is feasible to the corresponding universe quantity that would be obtained from a complete census of the universe. Estimates based on a sample will, however, generally differ from the hypothetical census figures. Two classifications of errors are associated with estimates based on sample surveys:

(1) *sampling error*—the error arising from the use of a sample, rather than a census, to estimate population quantities and

(2) *nonsampling error*—those errors arising from nonsampling sources. As discussed below, the magnitude of the sampling error for an estimate can usually be estimated from the sample data. However, the magnitude of the nonsampling error for an estimate can rarely be estimated. Consequently, actual error in an estimate exceeds the error that can be estimated.

The particular sample used in a survey is only one of a large number of possible samples of the same size which could have been selected using the same sampling procedure. Estimates derived from the different samples would, in general, differ from each other. The *standard error* (SE) is a measure of the variation among the estimates derived from all possible samples. The standard error is the most commonly used measure of the sampling error of an estimate. Valid estimates of the standard errors of survey estimates can usually be calculated from the data collected in a probability sample. For convenience, the standard error is sometimes expressed as a percent of the estimate and is called the relative standard error or *coefficient of variation* (CV). For example, an estimate of 200 units with an esti-mated standard error of 10 units has an estimated CV of 5 percent.

A sample estimate and an estimate of its standard error or CV can be used to construct interval estimates that have a prescribed confidence that the interval includes the average of the estimates derived from all possible samples with a known probability. To illustrate, if all possible samples were selected under essentially the same general conditions, and using the same sample design, and if an estimate and its estimated standard error were calculated from each sample, then: 1) approximately 68 percent of the intervals from one standard error below the estimate to one standard error above the estimate would include the average estimate derived from all possible samples; 2) approximately 90 percent of the intervals from 1.6 standard errors below the estimate to 1.6 standard errors above the estimate would include the average estimate derived from all possible samples; and 3) approximately 95 percent of the intervals from two standard errors below the estimate to two standard errors above the estimate would include the average estimate derived from all possible samples.

Thus, for a particular sample, one can say with the appropriate level of confidence (e.g., 90 percent or 95 percent) that the average of all possible samples is included in the constructed interval. Example of a confidence interval: An estimate is 200 units with a standard error of 10 units. An approximately 90 percent confidence interval (plus or minus 1.6 standard errors) is from 184 to 216.

All surveys and censuses are subject to nonsampling errors. Nonsampling errors are of two kinds—*random* and *nonrandom*. Random nonsampling errors arise because of the varying interpretation of questions (by respondents or interviewers) and varying actions of coders, keyers, and other processors. Some randomness is also introduced when respondents must estimate. Nonrandom nonsampling errors result from total nonresponse (no usable data obtained for a sampled unit), partial or item nonresponse (only a portion of a response may be usable), inability or unwillingness on the part of respondents to provide correct information, difficulty interpreting questions, mistakes in recording or keying data, errors of collection or processing, and coverage problems (overcoverage and undercoverage of the target universe). Random nonresponse errors usually, but not always, result in an understatement of sampling errors and thus an overstatement of the precision of survey estimates. Estimating the magnitude of nonsampling errors would require special experiments or access to independent data and, consequently, the magnitudes are seldom available.

Nearly all types of nonsampling errors that affect surveys also occur in complete censuses. Since surveys can be conducted on a smaller scale than censuses, nonsampling errors can presumably be controlled more tightly. Relatively more funds and effort can perhaps be expended toward eliciting responses, detecting and correcting response error, and reducing processing errors. As a result, survey results can sometimes be more accurate than census results.

To compensate for suspected nonrandom errors, adjustments of the sample estimates are often made. For example, adjustments are frequently made for nonresponse, both total and partial. Adjustments made for either type of nonresponse are often referred to as *imputations*. Imputation for total nonresponse is usually made by substituting for the questionnaire responses of the nonrespondents the "average" questionnaire responses of the respondents. These imputations usually are made separately within various groups of sample members, formed by attempting to place respondents and nonrespondents together that have "similar" design or ancillary characteristics. Imputation for item nonresponse is usually made by substituting for a missing item the response to that item of a respondent having characteristics that are "similar" to those of the nonrespondent.

For an estimate calculated from a sample survey, the *total error* in the estimate is composed of the sampling error, which can usually be estimated from the sample, and the nonsampling error, which usually cannot be estimated from the sample. The total error present in a population

quantity obtained from a complete census is composed of only nonsampling errors. Ideally, estimates of the total error associated with data given in the *Statistical Abstract* tables should be given. However, due to the unavailability of estimates of nonsampling errors, only estimates of the levels of sampling errors, in terms of estimated standard errors or coefficients of variation, are available. To obtain estimates of the estimated standard errors from the sample of interest, obtain a copy of the referenced report which appears at the end of each table.

Source of Additional Material: The Federal Committee on Statistical Methodology (FCSM) is an interagency committee dedicated to improving the quality of federal statistics <http://www.fcsm.census.gov>.

Principal data bases—Beginning below are brief descriptions of 35 of the sample surveys and censuses that provide a substantial portion of the data contained in this *Abstract.*

U.S. DEPARTMENT OF AGRICULTURE, National Agriculture Statistics Service

Census of Agriculture

Universes, Frequency, and Types of Data: Complete count of U.S. farms and ranches conducted once every 5 years with data at the national, state, and county level. Data published on farm numbers and related items/ characteristics.

Type of Data Collection Operation: Complete census for number of farms; land in farms; farm income; agriculture products sold; farms by type of organization; total cropland; irrigated land; farm operator characteristics; livestock and poultry inventory and sales; and selected crops harvested. Market value of land, buildings, and products sold, total farm production expenses, machinery and equipment, and fertilizer and chemicals.

Data Collection and Imputation Procedures: Data collection is by mailing questionnaires to all farmers and

U.S. Census Bureau, Statistical Abstract of the United States: 2011

ranchers. Producers can return their forms by mail or online. Nonrespondents are contacted by telephone and correspondence follow-ups. Imputations were made for all nonresponse item/characteristics and coverage adjustments were made to account for missed farms and ranches. The response rate for the 2007 Census was 85.2 percent.

Estimates of Sampling Error: Weight adjustments were made to account for the undercoverage and whole-unit nonresponse of farms on the Census Mail List (CML). These were treated as sampling errors.

Other (nonsampling) Errors: Nonsampling errors are due to incompleteness of the census mailing list, duplications on the list, respondent reporting errors, errors in editing reported data, and in imputation for missing data. Evaluation studies are conducted to measure certain nonsampling errors such as list coverage and classification error. It is a reasonable assumption that the net effect of non measurable errors is zero (the positive errors cancel the negative errors).

Sources of Additional Material: U.S. Department of Agriculture (NASS), 2007 Census of Agriculture, Appendix A-1 Census of Agriculture Methodology, Appendix B-1 General Explanation and Census of Agriculture Report Form.

Basic Area Frame Sample

Universe, Frequency, and Types of Data: June agricultural survey collects data on planted acreage and livestock inventories on all land in the 48 contiguous states and Hawaii. The survey also serves to measure list incompleteness and is subsampled for multiple frame surveys.

Type of Data Collection Operation: Stratified probability sample of about 11,000 land area units of about 1 sq. mile (range from 0.1 sq. mile in cities to several sq. miles in open grazing areas). Sample includes 42,000 parcels of agricultural land. About 20 percent of the sample replaced annually.

Data Collection and Imputation Procedures: Data collection is by personal enumeration. Imputation is based on enumerator observation or data reported by respondents having similar agricultural characteristics.

Estimates of Sampling Error: Estimated CVs range from 1 percent to 2 percent for regional estimates to 3 percent to 6 percent for state estimates of major crop acres and livestock inventories.

Other (nonsampling) Errors: Minimized through rigid quality controls on the collection process and careful review of all reported data.

Sources of Additional Material: U.S. Department of Agriculture, National Agricultural Statistics Service, USDA's National Agricultural Statistics Service: The Fact Finders of Agriculture, March 2007.

Multiple Frame Surveys

Universe, Frequency, and Types of Data: Surveys of U.S. farm operators to obtain data on major livestock inventories, selected crop acreage and production, grain stocks, and farm labor characteristics, farm economic data, and chemical use data. Estimates are made quarterly, semi-annually, or annually depending on the data series.

Type of Data Collection Operation: Primary frame is obtained from general or special purpose lists, supplemented by a probability sample of land areas used to estimate for list incompleteness.

Data Collection and Imputation Procedures: Mail, telephone, or personal interviews used for initial data collection. Mail nonrespondent follow-up by phone and personal interviews. Imputation based on average of respondents.

Estimates of Sampling Error: Estimated CVs range from 1 percent to 2 percent at the U.S. level for crop and livestock data series and 3 to 5 percent for economic data. Regional CVs range from 3 to 6 percent, while state estimate CVs run 5 to 10 percent.

Other (nonsampling) Errors: In addition to above, replicated sampling procedures used to monitor effects of changes in survey procedures.

Sources of Additional Material: U.S. Department of Agriculture, National Agricultural Statistics Service), USDA's National Agricultural Statistics Service: The Fact Finders of Agriculture, March 2007.

Objective Yield Surveys

Universe, Frequency, and Types of Data: Monthly surveys during the growing season of corn, cotton, potatoes, soybeans, and winter wheat fields in top producing states for forecasting and estimating yield per acre.

Type of Data Collection Operation: Random location of plots in probability sample. Corn, cotton, and soybeans, are selected in June from Basic Area Frame Sample (see above). Winter wheat and potatoes are selected from March and June multiple frame surveys, respectively.

Data Collection and Imputation Procedures: Enumerators count and measure plant characteristics in sample fields. Production is measured from plots at harvest. Harvest loss is measured from post harvest gleanings

Estimates of Sampling Error: CVs for national estimates of production are about 2 to 3 percent.

Other (nonsampling) Errors: In addition to above, replicated sampling procedures are used to monitor effects of changes in survey procedures.

Sources of Additional Material: U.S. Department of Agriculture, National Agricultural Statistics Service), USDA's National Agricultural Statistics Service: The Fact Finders of Agriculture, March 2007.

U.S. BUREAU OF JUSTICE STATISTICS (BJS)

National Crime Victimization Survey

Universe, Frequency, and Types of Data: Monthly survey of individuals and households in the United States to obtain data on criminal victimization of those units for compilation of annual estimates.

Type of Data Collection Operation: National probability sample survey of about 40,000 interviewed households in 203 PSUs selected from a list of addresses from the 2000 census, supplemented by new construction permits and an area sample where permits are not required.

Data Collection and Imputation Procedures: Interviews are conducted every 6 months for 3 years for each household in the sample; 6,600 households are interviewed monthly. Personal interviews are used in the first interview; the intervening interviews are conducted by telephone whenever possible.

Estimates of Sampling Error: CVs for 2007 estimates are: 3.9 percent for personal crimes (includes all crimes of violence plus purse snatching crimes), 4.0 percent for crimes of violence; 13.2 percent for estimate of rape/ sexual assault counts; 9.2 percent for robbery counts; 4.3 percent for assault counts; 14.5 percent for purse snatching/pocket picking; 2.0 percent for property crimes; 4.0 percent for burglary counts; 2.0 percent for theft (of property); and 6.5 percent for motor vehicle theft counts.

Other (nonsampling) Errors: Respondent recall errors which may include reporting incidents for other than the reference period; interviewer coding and processing errors; and possible mistaken reporting or classifying of events. Adjustment is made for a household noninterview rate of about 8 percent and for a within-household noninterview rate of 14 percent.

Sources of Additional Material: U.S. Bureau of Justice Statistics, *Criminal Victimization in the United States,* annual.

U.S. BUREAU OF LABOR STATISTICS

Consumer Expenditure Survey (CE)

Universe, Frequency and Types of Data: Consists of two continuous components: a quarterly interview survey and a weekly diary or recordkeeping survey. They are nationwide surveys that collect data on consumer expenditures, income, characteristics, and assets and liabilities. Samples are national probability samples of households that are representative of the civilian noninstitutional population. The surveys have been ongoing since 1980.

Type of Data Collection Operation: The Interview Survey is a panel rotation survey. Each panel is interviewed for five quarters and then dropped from the survey. About 7,000 consumer units are interviewed each quarter. The Diary Survey sample is new each year and consists of about 7,000 consumer units. Data are collected on an ongoing basis in 91 areas of the country.

Data Collection and Imputation Procedures: For the Interview Survey, data are collected by personal interview with each consumer unit interviewed once per quarter for five consecutive quarters. Designed to collect information that respondents can recall for 3 months or longer, such as large or recurring expenditures. For the Diary Survey, respondents record all their expenditures in a self-reporting diary for two consecutive one-week periods. Designed to pick up items difficult to recall over a long period, such as detailed food expenditures. Missing or invalid attributes, expenditures, or incomes are imputed. Assets and liabilities are not imputed. The U.S. Census Bureau collects the data for the Bureau of Labor Statistics.

Estimates of Sampling Error: Standard error tables are available since 2000.

Other (nonsampling) Errors: Includes incorrect information given by respondents, data processing errors, interviewer errors, and so on. They occur regardless of whether data are collected from a sample or from the entire population.

Sources of Additional Material: Bureau of Labor Statistics, see Internet site <http://www.bls.gov/cex>.

Consumer Price Index (CPI)

Universe, Frequency, and Types of Data: A monthly survey of price changes of all types of consumer goods and services purchased by urban wage earners and clerical workers prior to 1978, and urban consumers thereafter. Both indexes continue to be published.

Type of Data Collection Operation: Prior to 1978, and since 1998, sample of various consumer items in 87 urban areas; from 1978–1997, in 85 PSUs, except from January 1987 through March 1988, when 91 areas were sampled.

Data Collection and Imputation Procedures: Prices of consumer items are obtained each month from about 25,500 retail outlets and from about 4,000 housing units in 87 areas. Prices of food, fuel, and a few other items are obtained monthly; prices of most other commodities and services are collected every month in the three largest geographic areas and every other month in others.

Estimates of Sampling Error: Estimates of standard errors are available.

Other (nonsampling) Errors: Errors result from inaccurate reporting, difficulties in defining concepts and their operational implementation, and introduction of product quality changes and new products.

Sources of Additional Material: U.S. Bureau of Labor Statistics, Internet site <http://www.bls.gov/cpi/home.htm> and BLS Handbook of Methods, Chapter 17, see Internet site http://www.bls.gov/opub/hom/pdf/homch17.pdf>.

Current Employment Statistics (CES) Program

Universe, Frequency, and Types of Data: Monthly survey drawn from a sampling frame of roughly 8.9 million unemployment insurance tax accounts in order to obtain data by industry on employment, hours, and earnings.

Type of Data Collection Operation: In 2009, the CES sample included about 140,000 businesses and government agencies, which represent approximately 410,000 individual worksites.

Data Collection and Imputation Procedures: Each month, the state agencies cooperating with BLS, as well as BLS Data Collection Centers, collect data through various automated collection modes and mail. BLS Washington staff prepares national estimates of employment, hours, and earnings while states use the data to develop state and area estimates.

Estimates of Sampling Errors: The relative standard error for total nonfarm employment is 0.1 percent. From April 2008 to March 2009, the cumulative net birth/death model added 779,000.

Other (nonsampling) Errors: Estimates of employment adjusted annually to reflect complete universe. Average adjustment is 0.3 percent over the last decade, with an absolute range from than 0.1 percent to 0.7 percent.

Sources of Additional Material: U.S. Bureau of Labor Statistics, Employment and Earnings, monthly, Explanatory Notes and Estimates of Errors, Tables 2-A through 2-F. See <http://www.bls.gov/web/cestntab.htm>.

National Compensation Survey (NCS)

Universe, Frequency, and Types of Data: NCS collects data from establishments of all employment-size classes in private industries as well as state and local governments. The survey stratifies its data by geographic area and industry. NCS collects data on work schedules, wages, salaries, and employer costs for employee benefits. For approximately 80 metropolitan areas and the nation, NCS produces information on workers' earnings and benefits in a variety of occupations at different work levels. NCS is also responsible for two quarterly releases: the Employment Cost Index (ECI), which measures percent changes in the cost of employment, and the Employer Costs for Employee Compensation (ECEC), which measures costs per hour worked for individual benefits. The survey provides data by industry sector, industry division, occupational group, bargaining status, metropolitan area status, census region, and census division. ECEC also provides data by establishment-size class.

Type of Data Collection Operation: Establishments are selected for the survey based on a probability-proportionate-to-employment technique. NCS replaces its sample on a continual basis. Private industry establishments are in the survey for approximately 5 years.

Data Collection and Imputation Procedures: A personal visit to the establishment is the initial source for collecting data. Communication via mail, fax, and telephone provide quarterly updates. Imputation is done for individual benefits.

Estimates of Sampling Error: NCS uses standard errors to evaluate published series. These standard errors are available at <http://www.bls.gov/ncs/ect/home.htm>.

Other (nonsampling) Errors: Nonsampling errors have a number of potential sources. The primary sources are (1) survey nonresponse and (2) data collection and processing errors. Nonsampling errors are not measured. The use of quality assurance programs reduces the potential for nonsampling errors. These programs include the use of reinterviews, interview observations, and the systematic professional review of reports. The programs also serve as a training device that provides feedback on errors for field economists (or data collectors). Quality assurance programs also provide information on sources of error. This information is used to improve procedures that result in fewer errors. NCS also conducts extensive training of field economists to maintain high standards in data collection.

Sources of Additional Material: Bureau of Labor Statistics, *BLS Handbook of methods,* Chapter 8 <http://www.bls .gov/opub/hom//pdf/homch8.pdf>.

Producer Price Index (PPI)

Universe, Frequency, and Types of Data: Monthly survey of producing companies to determine price changes of all commodities and services produced in the United States for sale in commercial transactions. Data on agriculture, forestry, fishing, manufacturing, mining, gas, electricity, construction, public utilities, wholesale trade, retail trade, transportation, healthcare, and other services.

Type of Data Collection Operation: Probability sample of approximately 30,000 establishments that result in about 120,000 price quotations per month.

Data Collection and Imputation Procedures: Data are collected by mail and facsimile. Missing prices are estimated by those received for similar products or services. Some prices are obtained from trade publications, organized exchanges, and government agencies. To calculate index, price changes are multiplied by their relative weights taken from the Census Bureau's 2002 shipment values from their Census of Industries.

Estimates of Sampling Error: Not applicable.

Other (nonsampling) Errors: Not available at present.

Sources of Additional Material: U.S. Bureau of Labor Statistics, *BLS Handbook of Methods,* Chapter 14, Bulletin 2490. U.S. Bureau of Labor Statistics Internet site <http://stats.bls.gov/ppi>.

BOARD OF GOVERNORS OF THE FEDERAL RESERVE SYSTEM

Survey of Consumer Finances

Universe, Frequency, and Types of Data: Periodic sample survey of families. In this survey a given household is divided into a primary economic unit and other economic units. The primary economic unit, which may be a single individual, is generally chosen as the person or couple who either holds the title to the home or is listed on the lease, along with all other people in the household who are financially interdependent with that person or couple. The primary economic unit is used as the reference family. The survey collects detailed data on the composition of family balance sheets, the terms of loans, and relationships with financial institutions. It also gathers information on the employment history and pension rights of the survey respondent and the spouse or partner of the respondent.

Type of Data Collection Operation: The survey employs a two-part strategy for sampling families. Some families are selected by standard multistage area probability sampling methods applied to all 50 states. The remaining families in the survey are selected using statistical records derived from tax returns, under the strict rules governing confidentiality and the rights of potential respondents to refuse participation.

Data Collection and Imputation Procedures: National Opinion Research Center (NORC) at the University of Chicago has collected data for the survey since 1992. Since 1995, the survey has used computer-assisted personal interviewing. Adjustments for nonresponse are made through multiple imputation of unanswered questions and through weighting adjustments based on data used in the sample design for families that refused participation.

Estimates of Sampling Error: Because of the complex design of the survey, the estimation of potential sampling errors is not straightforward. A replicate-based procedure is available.

Other (nonsampling) Errors: The survey aims to complete 4,500 interviews, with about two thirds of that number deriving from the area-probability sample. The response rate is typically about 70 percent for the area-probability sample and about 35 percent over all strata in the tax-data sample. Proper training and monitoring of interviewers, careful design of questionnaires, and systematic editing of the resulting data were used to control inaccurate survey responses.

Sources of Additional Material: Board of Governors of the Federal Reserve System, "Recent Changes in U.S. Family Finances: Evidence from the Survey of Consumer Finances," *Federal Reserve Bulletin,* 2009, <http://www.federalreserve.gov /Pubs/Bulletin>.

U.S. CENSUS BUREAU

2007 Economic Census

(Industry Series, Geographic Area Series and Subject Series Reports) (for NAICS sectors 21 to 81).

Universe, Frequency, and Types of Data: Conducted every 5 years to obtain data on number of establishments, number of employees, payroll, total sales/ receipts/revenue, and other industry-specific statistics. The universe is all establishments with paid employees excluding agriculture, forestry, fishing and hunting, and government. (Nonemployer Statistics, discussed separately, covers those establishments without paid employees.)

Type of Data Collection Operation: All large employer firms were surveyed (i.e., all employer firms above payroll-size cutoffs established to separate large from small employers) plus, in most sectors, a sample of the small employer firms.

Data Collection and Imputation Procedures: Mail questionnaires were used with both mail and telephone follow-ups for nonrespondents. Businesses also had the option to respond electronically. Data for nonrespondents and for small employer firms not mailed a questionnaire were obtained from administrative records of other federal agencies or imputed.

Estimates of Sampling Error: Not applicable for basic data such as sales, revenue, receipts, payroll, etc. for sectors other than Construction (NAICS 23). Estimates of sampling error for construction industries are included with the data as published on the Census Bureau web site. Other (nonsampling) errors: establishment response rates by NAICS sector in 2002 ranged from 80 percent to 89 percent. Nonsampling errors may occur during the collection, reporting, keying, and classification of the data.

Sources of Additional Material: U.S. Census Bureau, see <http://www.census.gov/econ /census07/www/methodology/>.

American Community Survey (ACS)

Universe, Frequency, and Types of Data: Nationwide survey to obtain annual data about demographic, social, economic, and housing characteristics of housing units and the people residing in them. It covers the household population and, beginning in 2006, also includes the group quarter population living in prisons, nursing homes and college dormitories, and other group quarters.

Type of Data Collection Operation: Housing unit address sampling is performed twice a year in both August and January. First-phase of sampling defines the universe for the second stage of sampling through two steps. First, all addresses that were eligible for the second-phase sampling within the past four years are excluded from eligibility. This ensures that no address is in sample more than once in any 5-year period. The second step is to select a 20 percent systematic sample of "new" units, i.e. those units that have never appeared on a previous Master Address File (MAF) extract. All new addresses are systematically assigned to either the current year or to one of four back-samples. This procedure maintains five equal partitions of the universe. The second phase sampling is done on the current year's partition and results in approximately 3,000,000 housing unit addresses in the U.S. and 36,000 in Puerto Rico (PR). Group quarter sampling is performed separately from the housing unit sampling. The sampling begins with separating the small (15 persons or fewer) and the large (more than 15 persons) group quarters. The target sampling rate for both groups is a 2.5% sample of the group quarters population. It results in approximately 200,000 group quarter residents being selected in the U.S., and an additional 1,000 in Puerto Rico.

Data Collection and Imputation Procedures: The American Community Survey is conducted every month on independent samples. Each housing unit in the independent monthly samples is mailed a pre-notice letter announcing the selection of the address to participate, a survey questionnaire package, and a reminder postcard. These sample units addresses receive a second (replacement) questionnaire package if the initial questionnaire has not been returned by mid-month. Sample addresses for which a questionnaire is not returned in the mail and a telephone number is available is forwarded to telephone centers is available, is forwarded to telephone centers for follow-up. Interviewers attempt to contact and interview these mail nonresponse cases by telephone. Sample addresses that are still unresponsive after two months of attempts are forwarded for a possible personal visit. Unresponsive addresses are subsampled at rates between 1 in 3 and 2 in 3. Those addresses selected through this process are assigned to Field Representatives (FRs), who visit the addresses, verify their existence, determine their occupancy status, and conduct interviews. Collection of group quarters data is conducted by FR's only. Their methods include completing the questionnaire while speaking to the resident in person or over the telephone, or leaving paper questionnaires for residents to complete for themselves and then pick them up later. This last option is used for data collection in federal prisons. If needed, a personal interview can be conducted with a proxy, such as a relative or guardian. After data collection is completed, any remaining incomplete or inconsistent information on the questionnaire are imputed during the final automated edit of the collected data.

Estimates of Sampling Error: The data in the ACS products are estimates and can vary from the actual values that would have been obtained by conducting a census of the entire population. The estimates from the chosen sample addresses can also vary from those that would have been obtained from a different set of addresses. This variation causes uncertainty, which can be measured using statistics such as standard error, margin of error, and confidence interval. All ACS estimates are accompanied by margin of errors to assist users.

Other (nonsampling) Errors: Nonsampling Error—In addition to sampling error, data users should realize that other types of errors may be introduced during any of the various complex operations used to select, collect and process survey data. An important goal of the ACS is to minimize the amount of nonsampling error introduced through coverage issues in the sample list, nonresponse from sample housing units, and transcribing or editing data. One way of accomplishing this is by finding additional sources of addresses, following up on nonrespondents and maintaining quality control systems.

Sources of Additional Material: U.S. Census Bureau, American Community Survey Web site available on Internet, <http://www.census.gov/acs/www/index.html> U.S. Census Bureau, American Community Survey Accuracy of the Data documents available on the Internet <http://www.census.gov/acs/www/data_documentation/documentation_main/>.

American Housing Survey

Universe, Frequency, and Types of Data: Conducted nationally in odd numbered years to obtain data on the approximately 124 million occupied or vacant housing units in the United States (group quarters are excluded). Data include characteristics of occupied housing units, vacant units, new housing and mobile home units, financial characteristics, recent mover households, housing and neighborhood quality indicators, and energy characteristics.

Type of Data Collection Operation: The national sample was a multistage probability sample with about 57,000 units eligible for interview in 2005. Sample units, selected within 394 PSUs, were surveyed over a 4-month period.

Data Collection and Imputation Procedures: For 2005, the survey was conducted by personal interviews. The interviewers obtained the information from the occupants or, if the unit was vacant, from informed persons such as landlords, rental agents, or knowledgeable neighbors.

Estimates of Sampling Error: For the national sample, illustrations of the Standard Error (SE) of the estimates are provided in the Appendix D of the 2005 report.

Other (nonsampling) Errors: Response rate was about 90 percent. Nonsampling errors may result from incorrect or incomplete responses, errors in coding and recording, and processing errors. Appendix D of the 2005 report has a complete discussion of the errors.

Sources of Additional Material: U.S. Census Bureau, *Current Housing Reports,* Series H-150 and H-170, *American Housing Survey see* <http://www.census.gov/hhes/www/ahs.html>.

Annual Survey of Government Employment and Payroll

Universe, Frequency, and Types of Data: The survey measures the number of state, local and federal civilian government employees and their gross payrolls for the pay period including March 12. The survey is conducted annually except in years ending in '2' and '7', when a census of all state

and local governments is done. The survey provides data on full-time and part-time employment, part-time hours worked, full-time equivalent employment, and payroll statistics by governmental function (elementary and secondary education, higher education, police protection, fire protection, financial administration, central staff services, judicial and legal, highways, public welfare, solid waste management, sewerage, parks and recreation, health, hospitals, water supply, electric power, gas supply, transit, natural resources, correction, libraries, air transportation, water transport and terminals, other education, state liquor stores, social insurance administration, and housing and community development).

Type of Data Collection Operations: The survey sample was taken from the 2002 Census of Governments and contains approximately 11,000 local government units. These units were sampled from a sampling frame that contained 83,767 local governments (county, city, township, special district, and school districts) in addition to 50 state governments and the District of Columbia. This frame was slightly different from the Annual Finance Survey sampling frame. Forty-two of the state governments provided data from central payroll records for all or most of their agencies/institutions. Data for agencies and institutions for the remaining state governments were obtained by mail canvass questionnaires. Local governments were also canvassed using a mail questionnaire. However, elementary and secondary school system data in Florida, North Dakota, and Washington were supplied by special arrangements with the state education agency in each of these states. All respondents receiving the mail questionnaire had the option of responding using the Employment Web site developed for reporting data. Approximately 26% of the state agency and local government respondents chose to respond on the Web.

Editing and Imputation Procedures: Editing is a process that ensures survey data are accurate, complete, and consistent. Efforts are made at all phases of collection, processing, and tabulation to minimize errors. Although some edits are built into the Internet data collection instrument and the data entry programs, the majority of the edits are performed after the case has been loaded into the Census Bureau's database. Edits consist primarily of two types: consistency and a ratio of the current years reported value to the prior year's value. The consistency edits check the logical relationships of data items reported on the form. For example, if a value exists for employees for a function then a value must exist for payroll also. If part-time employees and payroll are reported then part-time hours must be reported and vice versa. The current year/prior year edits compare data for the number of employees, the function reported for the employees, and the average salary between reporting years. If data fall outside of acceptable tolerance levels, the item is flagged for review. Some additional checks are made comparing data from the Annual Finance Survey to data reported on the Annual Survey of Government Employment and Payroll to verify that employees reported on the Annual Survey of Government Employment and Payroll at a particular function have a corresponding expenditure on the Finance Survey. For both types of edits, the edit results are reviewed by analysts and adjusted when needed. When the analyst is unable to resolve or accept the edit failure, contact is made with the respondent to verify or correct the reported data.

Imputation: Not all respondents answer every item on the questionnaire. There are also questionnaires that are not returned despite efforts to gain a response. Imputation is the process of filling in missing or invalid data with reasonable values in order to have a complete data set. For general purpose governments and for schools, the imputations were based on recent historical data from either a prior year annual survey or the most recent Census of Governments, if it was available. These data were adjusted by a growth rate that was determined by the growth of units that were similar (in size, geography, and type of government) to the nonrespondent. If there was no recent historical data available, the imputations were based on the data from a randomly selected donor that was similar to the nonrespondent. This donor's data were adjusted by dividing each data item by the population (or enrollment) of the donor and multiplying the result by the nonrespondent's population (or enrollment). For special districts, if prior year data are available, the data are brought forward with a national level growth rate applied. Otherwise, the data are imputed to be zero. In cases where good secondary data sources exist, the data from those sources were used.

Estimates of Sampling Error: For intercensal surveys, estimated coefficients of variation for all variables are given in tabulations on the Website. For U.S. and state-and-local government-level estimates of total full-time equivalents and total payroll, most relative standard errors are generally less than one percent, but vary considerably for detailed characteristics.

Other (nonsampling) Errors: Although every effort is made in all phases of collection, processing, and tabulation to minimize errors, the sample data are subject to nonsampling errors such as inability to obtain data for every variable from all units in the sample, inaccuracies in classification, response errors, misinterpretation of questions, mistakes in keying and coding, and coverage errors. These same errors may be evident in census collections and may affect the Census of Governments data used to adjust the sample during the estimation phase and used in the imputation process.

Sources of Additional material: <http://www.census.gov/govs/www /apes/index.html> and <http://www.census.gov/govs/www /apesstl06.html>.

Annual Survey of Government Finances

Universe, Frequency, and Types of Data:
The United States Census Bureau conducts an Annual Survey of Government Finances, as authorized by law under Title 13, United States Code, Section 182. Alternatively, every 5 years, in years ending in a '2' or '7', a Census of Governments, including a Finance portion, is conducted under Title 13, Section 161. The survey coverage includes all state and local governments in the United States. For both the Census and annual survey, the finance detail data is equivalent, encompassing the entire range of government finance activities—revenue, expenditure, debt, and assets.

Type of Data Collection Operations: The data collection phase for the annual survey made use of three methods to obtain data: mail canvass, internet collection, and central collection from State sources. In 28 states, all or part of the general purpose finance data for local governments was obtained from cooperative arrangements between the Census Bureau and a state government agency. These usually involved a data collection effort carried out to meet the needs of both agencies—the state agency for purposes of audit, oversight, or information, and the Census Bureau for statistical purposes. Data for the balance of local governments in this annual survey were obtained via mail questionnaires sent directly to county, municipal, township, special district, and school district governments. School district data were collected via cooperative arrangements with state education agencies. Data for state governments were compiled by analysts of the Census Bureau, usually with the cooperation and assistance of state officials. The data were compiled from state government audits, budgets, and other financial reports, either in printed or electronic format. The compilation generally involved recasting the state financial records into the classification categories used for reporting by the Census Bureau.

Data Collection and Imputation Procedures: Survey is conducted by mail with mail follow-ups of nonrespondents. Imputation for all nonresponse items is based on previous year reports or, for new governments, on data from similar donors.

Estimates of Sampling Error: The local government statistics in the intercensal survey years are developed from a sample survey. Therefore, the local totals, as well as aggregates of state and local government data, are considered estimated amounts subject to sampling error. State government finance data are not subject to sampling. Consequently, State-local aggregates shown here have a relative standard error less than or equal to the local government estimates they include. Estimates of major United States totals for local governments are subject to a computed sampling variability of less than one-half of 1 percent. State and local government totals are generally subject to sampling variability of less than 3 percent.

Other (nonsampling) Errors: The estimates are also subject to inaccuracies in classification, response, and processing. Efforts were made at all phases of collection, processing, and tabulation to minimize errors. However, the data are still subject to errors from imputations for missing data, errors from misreported data, errors from miscoding, and difficulties in identifying every unit that should be included in the report. Every effort was made to keep such errors to a minimum through care in examining, editing, and tabulating the data reported by government officials.

Sources of Additional Material:
<http://www.census.gov/govs/index.html> and <http://www.census.gov/govs/state/index.html>.

Annual Survey of Manufactures (ASM)

Universe, Frequency, and Types of Data:
The Annual Survey of Manufactures is conducted annually, except for years ending in '2' and '7' for all

manufacturing establishments having one or more paid employees. The purpose of the ASM is to provide key intercensal measures of manufacturing activity, products, and location for the public and private sectors. The ASM provides statistics on employment, payroll, worker hours, payroll supplements, cost of materials, value added by manufacturing, capital expenditures, inventories, and energy consumption. It also provides estimates of value of shipments for 1,800 classes of manufactured products.

Type of Data Collection Operation: The ASM includes approximately 50,000 establishments selected from the census universe of 346,000 manufacturing establishments. Approximately 24,000 large establishments are selected with certainty, and the remaining 26,000 other establishments are selected with probability proportional to a composite measure of establishment size. The survey is updated from two sources: Internal Revenue Service administrative records are used to include new single-unit manufacturers and the Company Organization Survey identifies new establishments of multiunit forms.

Data Collection and Imputation Procedures: Survey is conducted by mail with phone and mail follow-ups of nonrespondents. Imputation (for all nonresponse items) is based on previous year reports, or for new establishments in survey, on industry averages.

Estimates of Sampling Error: Estimated relative standard errors for number of employees, new expenditures, and for value added totals are given in annual publications. For U.S. level industry statistics, most estimated relative standard errors are 2 percent or less, but vary considerably for detailed characteristics.

Other (nonsampling) Errors: The unit response rate is about 85 percent. Nonsampling errors include those due to collection, reporting, and transcription errors, many of which are corrected through computer and clerical checks.

Sources of Additional Material: U.S. Census Bureau, *Annual Survey of Manufactures,* and Technical Paper 24.

Census of Population

Universe, Frequency, and Types of Data: Complete count of U.S. population conducted every 10 years since 1790. Data obtained on number and characteristics of people in the United States.

Type of Data Collection Operation: In the 1990, and 2000 censuses the 100 percent items included: age, date of birth, sex, race, Hispanic origin, and relationship to householder. In 1980, approximately 19 percent of the housing units were included in the sample; in 1990 and 2000, approximately 17 percent.

Data Collection and Imputation Procedures: In 1980, 1990, and 2000, mail questionnaires were used extensively with personal interviews in the remainder. Extensive telephone and personal follow-up for nonrespondents was done in the censuses. Imputations were made for missing characteristics.

Estimates of Sampling Error: Sampling errors for data are estimated for all items collected by sample and vary by characteristic and geographic area. The coefficients of variation (CVs) for national and state estimates are generally very small.

Other (nonsampling) Errors: Since 1950, evaluation programs have been conducted to provide information on the magnitude of some sources of nonsampling errors such as response bias and undercoverage in each census. Results from the evaluation program for the 1990 census indicated that the estimated net undercoverage amounted to about 1.5 percent of the total resident population. For Census 2000, the evaluation program indicated a net overcount of 0.5 percent of the resident population.

Sources of Additional Material: U.S. Census Bureau, The Coverage of Population in the 1980 Census, PHC80-E4; *Content Reinterview Study: Accuracy of Data for Selected Population and*

Housing Characteristics as Measured by Reinterview, PHC80-E2; *1980 Census of Population*, Vol. 1, (PC80-1), Appendixes B, C, and D. *Content Reinterview Survey: Accuracy of Data for Selected Population and Housing Characteristics as Measured by Reinterview*, 1990, CPH-E-1; Effectiveness of Quality Assurance, CPH-E-2; Programs to Improve Coverage in the 1990 Census, 1990, CPH-E-3. For Census 2000 evaluations, see <http://www.census.gov/pred/www>.

County Business Patterns

Universe, Frequency, and Types of Data: County Business Patterns is an annual tabulation of basic data items extracted from the Business Register, a file of all known single- and multi-location employer companies maintained and updated by the U.S. Census Bureau. Data include number of establishments, number of employees, first quarter and annual payrolls, and number of establishments by employment size class. Data are excluded for self-employed individuals, private households, railroad employees, agricultural production workers, and most government employees.

Type of Data Collection Operation: The annual Company Organization Survey provides individual establishment data for multilocation companies. Data for single establishment companies are obtained from various Census Bureau programs, such as the Annual Survey of Manufactures and Current Business Surveys, as well as from administrative records of the Internal Revenue Service, the Social Security Administration, and the Bureau of Labor Statistics.

Estimates of Sampling Error: Not applicable.

Other (nonsampling) Errors: The data are subject to nonsampling errors, such as inability to identify all cases in the universe; definition and classification difficulties; differences in interpretation of questions; errors in recording or coding the data obtained; and estimation of employers who reported too late to be included in the tabulations and for records with missing or misreported data.

Sources of Additional Materials: U. S. Census Bureau, County Business Patterns <http://www.census.gov/econ/cbp/index.html>

Current Population Survey (CPS)

Universe, Frequency, and Types of Data: Nationwide monthly sample designed primarily to produce national and state estimates of labor force characteristics of the civilian noninstitutionalized population 16 years of age and older.

Type of Data Collection Operation: Multistage probability sample that currently includes 72,000 households from 824 sample areas. Sample size increased in some states to improve data reliability for those areas on an annual average basis. A continual sample rotation system is used. Households are in sample 4 months, out for 8 months, and in for 4 more. Month-to-month overlap is 75 percent; year-to-year overlap is 50 percent.

Data Collection and Imputation Procedures: For first and fifth months that a household is in sample, personal interviews; other months, approximately 85 percent of the data collected by phone. Imputation is done for item nonresponse. Adjustment for total nonresponse is done by a predefined cluster of units, by state, metropolitan status and CBSA size; for item nonresponse imputation varies by subject matter.

Estimates of Sampling Error: The national total estimates of the civilian labor force and of employment have monthly CVs of about 0.2 percent and annual average CVs of about 0.1 percent. Unemployment is a much smaller characteristic and consequently has substantially larger CVs than the civilian labor force or employment. The national unemployment rate, the most important CPS statistic, has a monthly CV of about 2 percent and an annual average CV of about 1 percent. Assuming a 6 percent unemployment rate, states have annual average CVs of about 8 percent. The estimated CVs for family income and poverty rate for all persons in 2005 are 0.4 percent and 1.2 percent, respectively. CVs for subnational areas, such as states, tend to be larger and vary by area.

Other (nonsampling) Errors: Estimates of response bias on unemployment are available. Estimates of unemployment rate from reinterviews range from −2.4 percent to 1.0 percent of the basic CPS unemployment rate (over a 30-month span from January 2004 through June 2006). Eligible CPS households are approximately 82 percent of the assigned households, with a corresponding response rate of 92 percent.

Sources of Additional Material:
U.S. Census Bureau and Bureau of Labor Statistics, Current Population Survey: Design and Methodology, (Technical Paper 66), available on the Internet <http://www.census.gov/prod/2006pubs/tp-66.pdf> and the Bureau of Labor Statistics, <http://www.bls.gov/cps/> and the *BLS Handbook of Methods*, Chapter 1, available on the Internet at <http://www.bls.gov/opub/hom/homch1_a.htm>.

Foreign Trade—Export Statistics

Universe, Frequency, and Types of Data:
As of October 1, 2008, the Shipper's Export Declaration (SED) Form 7525-V became obsolete. Electronic Export Information (EEI) replaced the SED and all export information must be filed through the Automated Export System (AES) by either a United States Principal Party in Interest (USPPI) or an Authorized U.S. agent. The EEI filings are processed each month to obtain data on the movement of U.S. merchandise exports to foreign countries. Data obtained include value, quantity, and shipping weight of exports by commodity, country of destination, district of exportation, and mode of transportation.

Type of Data Collection Operation: USPPIs or Authorized U.S. Agents are required to submit EEI for exportation of merchandise valued over $2,500. Data for shipments valued under $2,501 are estimated, based on established percentages of individual country totals.

Data Collection and Imputation Procedures: The EEI filings are received on a daily basis from ports throughout the country and subjected to a monthly processing cycle. They are fully processed to the extent they reflect items valued over $2,500. Estimates for shipments valued at $2,500 or less are made, based on established percentages of individual country totals.

Estimates of Sampling Error:
Not applicable.

Other (nonsampling) Errors: The goods data are a complete enumeration of EEI reported in AES and are not subject to sampling errors; but they are subject to several types of nonsampling errors. Quality assurance procedures are performed at every stage of collection, processing and tabulation; however the data are still subject to several types of nonsampling errors. The most significant of these include reporting errors, undocumented shipments, timeliness, data capture errors, and errors in the estimation of low-valued transactions. The number of data errors and the overall data quality are expected to improve due to the elimination of paper SEDs and the mandatory filing of export data through the AES. Additional information on errors affecting export data can be found at <http://www.census.gov/foreign-trade/Press-release/current_press_release/explain.pdf>.

Sources of Additional Material: Effect of Mandatory Electronic Filing on Export data, <http://www.census.gov/foreign-trade/aip/mandatoryelectronicfiling.html\>, U.S. Census Bureau, FT 900 U.S. International Trade in Goods and Services, FT 925 (discounted after 1996), U.S. Merchandise Trade, FT 895 U.S. Trade with Puerto Rico and U.S. Possessions, FT 920 U.S. Merchandise trade: selected highlights, and Information Section on Goods and Services at <http://www.census.gov/ft900>.

Foreign Trade—Import Statistics

Universe, Frequency, and Types of Data:
The import entry documents collected by U.S. Customs and Border Protection are processed each month to obtain data on the movement of merchandise imported into the United States. Data obtained include value, quantity, and shipping weight by commodity, country of origin, district of entry, and mode of transportation.

Type of Data Collection Operation: Import entry documents, either paper or electronic, are required to be filed for the importation of goods into the United States valued over $2,000 or for articles which must be reported on formal entries. U.S. Bureau of Customs and Border Protection officials collect and transmit statistical copies of the documents to the Census Bureau on a flow basis for data compilation. Estimates for shipments valued under $2,001 and not reported on formal entries are based on estimated established percentages for individual country totals.

Data Collection and Imputation Procedures: Statistical copies of import entry documents, received on a daily basis from ports of entry throughout the country, are subjected to a monthly processing cycle. They are fully processed to the extent they reflect items valued at $2,001 and over or items which must be reported on formal entries.

Estimates of Sampling Error: Not applicable.

Other (nonsampling) Errors: The goods data are a complete enumeration of documents collected by the U.S. Customs and Border Protection and are not subject to sampling errors; but they are subject to several types of nonsampling errors. Quality assurance procedures are performed at every stage of collection, processing, and tabulation; however the data are still subject to several types of nonsampling errors. The most significant of these include reporting errors, undocumented shipments, timeliness, data capture errors, and errors in the estimation of low-valued transactions. Additional information on errors affecting import data can be found at <http://www.census.gov/foreign-trade/Press-Release/current_press_release/explain.pdf>.

Sources of Additional Material: U.S. Census Bureau, FT 900 U.S. International Trade in Goods and Services, FT 925 (discounted after 1996), U.S. Merchandise Trade, FT 895 U.S. Trade with Puerto Rico and U.S. Possessions, FT920 U.S. Merchandise Trade: selected highlights, and Information Section on Goods and Services at <http://www.census.gov/ft900>.

Monthly Retail Trade and Food Service Survey

Universe, Frequency, and Types of Data: Provides monthly estimates of retail and food service sales by kind of business and end of month inventories of retail stores.

Type of Data Collection Operation: Probability sample of all firms from a list frame. The list frame is the Bureau's Business Register updated quarterly for recent birth Employer Identification (EI) Numbers issued by the Internal Revenue Service and assigned a kind of business code by the Social Security Administration. The largest firms are included monthly; a sample of others is included every month also.

Data Collection and Imputation Procedures: Data are collected by mail questionnaire with telephone follow-ups and fax reminders for nonrespondents. Imputation is made for each nonresponse item and each item failing edit checks.

Estimates of Sampling Error: For the 2006 monthly surveys, CVs are about 0.4 percent for estimated total retail sales and 0.7 percent for estimated total retail inventories. Sampling errors are shown in monthly publications.

Other (nonsampling) Errors: Imputation rates are about 22 percent for monthly retail and food service sales, and 29 percent for monthly retail inventories.

U.S. Census Bureau, Statistical Abstract of the United States: 2011

Sources of Additional Material: U.S. Census Bureau, Current Business Reports, Annual Revision of Monthly Retail and Food Services: Sales and Inventories.

Monthly Survey of Construction

Universe, Frequency, and Types of Data: Survey conducted monthly of newly constructed housing units (excluding mobile homes). Data are collected on the start, completion, and sale of housing. (Annual figures are aggregates of monthly estimates.)

Type of Data Collection Operation: A multistage probability sample of approximately 900 of the 20,000 permit-issuing jurisdictions in the U.S. was selected. Each month in each of these permit offices, field representatives list and select a sample of permits for which to collect data. To obtain data in areas where building permits are not required, a multistage probability sample of 80 land areas (census tracts or subsections of census tracts) was selected. All roads in these areas are canvassed and data are collected on all new residential construction found. Sampled buildings are followed up until they are completed (and sold, if for sale).

Data Collection and Imputation Procedures: Data are obtained by telephone inquiry and/or field visit. Nonresponse/undercoverage adjustment factors are used to account for late reported data.

Estimates of Sampling Error: Estimated CV of 5 percent to 6 percent for estimates of national totals of units started, but may be higher than 20 percent for estimated totals of more detailed characteristics, such as housing units in multiunit structures.

Other (nonsampling) Errors: Response rate is over 90 percent for most items. Nonsampling errors are attributed to definitional problems, differences in interpretation of questions, incorrect reporting, inability to obtain information about all cases in the sample, and processing errors.

Sources of Additional Material: All data are available on the Internet at <http://www.census.gov/starts>, <http://www.census.gov/newhome-sales> or <http://www.census.gov/const/www/newresconstindex.html>.Further documentation of the survey is also available at those sites.

Nonemployer Statistics

Universe, Frequency, and Types of Data: Nonemployer statistics are an annual tabulation of economic data by industry for active businesses without paid employees that are subject to federal income tax. Data showing the number of firms and receipts by industry are available for the U.S., states, counties, and metropolitan areas. Most types of businesses covered by the Census Bureau's economic statistics programs are included in the nonemployer statistics. Tax-exempt and agricultural-production businesses are excluded from nonemployer statistics.

Type of Data Collection Operation: The universe of nonemployer firms is created annually as a byproduct of the Census Bureau's Business Register processing for employer establishments. If a business is active but without paid employees, then it becomes part of the potential nonemployer universe. Industry classification and receipts are available for each potential nonemployer business. These data are obtained primarily from the annual business income tax returns of the Internal Revenue Service (IRS). The potential nonemployer universe undergoes a series of complex processing, editing, and analytical review procedures at the Census Bureau to distinguish nonemployers from employers, and to correct and complete data items used in creating the data tables.

Estimates of Sampling Error: Not applicable.

Other (nonsampling) Errors:
The data are subject to nonsampling errors, such as industry misclassification as well as errors of response, keying, nonreporting, and coverage.

Sources of Additional Material:
U. S. Census Bureau, Nonemployer Statistics at <http://www.census.gov/epcd/nonemployer/index.html>.

Service Annual Survey

Universe, Frequency, and Types of Data:
The U.S. Census Bureau conducts the Service Annual Survey to provide nationwide estimates of revenues and expenses for selected service industries. Estimates are summarized by industry classification based on the 2002 North American Industry Classification System (NAICS). Selected service industries covered by the Service Annual Survey include all or part of the following NAICS sectors: Transportation and Warehousing (NAICS 48–49); Information (NAICS 51); Finance and Insurance (NAICS 52); Real Estate and Rental and Leasing (NAICS 53); Professional, Scientific, and Technical Services (NAICS 54); Administrative and Support and Waste Management and Remediation Services (NAICS 56); Health Care and Social Assistance (NAICS 62); Arts, Entertainment, and Recreation (NAICS 71); and Other Services, except Public Administration (NAICS 81). Data collected include total revenue, total expenses, detailed expenses, revenue from e-commerce transactions; and for selected industries, revenue from detailed service products, revenue from exported services, and inventories. For industries with a significant nonprofit component, separate estimates are developed for taxable firms and firms and organizations exempt from federal income taxes. Questionnaires are mailed in January and request annual data for the prior year. Estimates are published approximately 12 months after the initial survey mailing.

Type of Data Collection Operation:
The Service Annual Survey estimates are developed from a probability sample of employer firms and administrative records for nonemployers. Service Annual Survey questionnaires are mailed to a probability sample that is periodically reselected from a universe of firms located in the United States and having paid employees. The sample includes firms of all sizes and covers both taxable firms and firms exempt from federal income taxes. Updates to the sample are made on a quarterly basis to account for new businesses. Firms without paid employees, or nonemployers, are included in the estimates through imputation and/or administrative records data provided by other federal agencies. Links to additional information about confidentiality protection, sampling error, nonsampling error, sample design, definitions, and copies of the questionnaires may be found at <http://www.census.gov/services/index.html>.

Estimates of Sampling Error: Coefficients of variation (CVs) for the 2007 Service Annual Survey estimates range from 0.7 percent to 2.3 percent for total revenue estimates computed at the NAICS sector (2-digit NAICS code) level. The full 2007 Service Annual Survey results, including coefficients of variations (CVs), can be found at <http://www.census.gov/services/index.html>. Links to additional information regarding sampling error may be found at <http://www.census.gov/services/sas/cv.html>.

Other (Nonsampling) Errors: Data are imputed for unit nonresponse, item nonresponse, and for reported data that fails edits. The percent of imputed data for total revenue for the 2007 Service Annual Survey estimates range from 6.4 percent to 14.2 percent for total revenue estimates computed at the NAICS sector (2-digit NAICS code) level.

Sources of Additional Material:
U.S. Census Bureau, Current Business Reports, *Service Annual Survey*, Census Bureau Web site: <http://www.census.gov/services/index.html>.

U.S. DEPARTMENT OF EDUCATION
National Center for Education Statistics

Integrated Postsecondary Education Data Survey (IPEDS), Completions

Universe, Frequency, and Types of Data: Annual survey of all Title IV (federal financial aid) eligible postsecondary institutions to obtain data on earned degrees and other formal awards, conferred by field of study, level of degree, sex, and by racial/ethnic characteristics (every other year prior to 1989, then annually).

Type of Data Collection Operation: Complete census.

Data Collection and Imputation Procedures: Data are collected through a Web-based survey in the fall of every year. Missing data are imputed by using data of similar institutions.

Estimates of Sampling Error: Not applicable.

Other (nonsampling Errors): For 2005–06, the response rate for degree-granting institutions was 100.0 percent.

Sources of Additional Material: U.S. Department of Education, National Center for Education Statistics, *Postsecondary Institutions in the United States: Fall 2007 and Degrees and Other Awards Conferred: 2006–07 and 12-month enrollment, 2006–07.* See <http://www.nces.ed.gov/ipeds/>.

National Household Education Surveys (NHES) Program

Universe, Frequency, and Types of Data: The National Household Education Surveys Program is a system of telephone surveys of the noninstitutionalized civilian population of the United States. Surveys in NHES have varying universes of interest depending on the particular survey. Specific topics covered by each survey are at the NHES Web site <http://nces.ed.gov/nhes>. A list of the surveys fielded as part of NHES, each universe, and the years they were fielded is provided below.

1) Adult Education—Interviews were conducted with a representative sample of civilian, noninstitutionalized persons aged 16 and older who were not enrolled in grade 12 or below (1991, 1995, 1999, 2001, 2003, 2005).

2) After-School Programs and Activities—Interviews were conducted with parents of a representative sample of students in grades K through 8 (1999, 2001, 2005).

3) Civic Involvement—Interviews were conducted with representative samples of parents, youth, and adults (1996, 1999).

4) Early Childhood Program Participation—Interviews were conducted with parents of a representative sample of children from birth through grade 3, with the specific age groups varying by survey year (1991, 1995, 1999, 2001, 2005).

5) Household and Library Use—Interviews were conducted with a representative sample of U.S. households (1996).

6) Parent and Family Involvement in Education—Interviews were conducted with parents of a representative sample of children age three through grade 12 or in grades K through 12 depending on the survey year (1996, 1999, 2003, and 2007 forthcoming).

7) School Readiness—Interviews were conducted with parents of a representative sample of 3–7 year-old children (1993 and 1999) and of 3–5 year old children, not yet in kindergarten, 2007 forthcoming).

8) School Safety and Discipline—Interviews were conducted with a representative sample of students in grades 6–12, their parents, and the parents of a representative sample of students in grades 3–12 (1993).

Type of Data Collection Operation: NHES uses telephone interviews to collect data.

Data Collection and Imputation Procedures: Telephone numbers are selected using random digit dialing (RDD) techniques. Approximately 45,000 to 64,000 households are contacted in order to identify persons eligible for the surveys. Data are collected using computer-assisted telephone interviewing (CATI) procedures. Missing data are imputed using hot-deck imputation procedures.

Estimates of Sampling Error: Unweighted sample sizes range between 2,250 and 55,708. The average root design effects of the surveys in NHES range from 1.1 to 1.5, except for the Adult Education survey of 1991. In 1991, average root design effects for the Adult Education survey ranged from 2.3 to 4.5.

Other (nonsampling) Errors: Because of unit nonresponse and because the samples are drawn from households with telephone instead of all households, nonresponse and/or coverage bias may exist for some estimates. However, both sources of potential bias are adjusted for in the weighting process. Analyses of both potential sources of bias in the NHES collections have been studied and no significant bias has been detected.

Sources of Additional Material: Please see the NHES Web site at <http://nces.ed.gov/nhes>.

Schools and Staffing Survey (SASS)

Universe, Frequency and Types of Data: NCES designed the SASS survey system to emphasize teacher demand and shortage, teacher and administrator characteristics, school programs, and general conditions in schools. SASS also collects data on many other topics, including principals' and teachers' perceptions of school climate and problems in their schools; teacher compensation; district hiring practices and basic characteristics of the student population. The SASS has had four core components: the School Questionnaire, the Teacher Questionnaire, the Principal Questionnaire, and the School District Questionnaire. For the 2003–04 SASS, a sample of public charter schools is included in the sample as part of the public school questionnaire. Since 1987–88, the SASS is the largest, most extensive survey of K through 12 school districts, schools, teachers, and administrators in the U.S. Surveys have been conducted every 3 to 4 years depending on budgetary constraints. The SASS includes data from public, private, and Bureau of Indian Education (BIE) school sectors. Therefore, the SASS provides a multitude of opportunities for analysis and reporting on elementary and secondary educational issues.

Type of Data Collection Operation: The U.S. Census Bureau performs the data collection and begins by sending advance letters to the sampled Local Education Agencies (LEAs) and schools in August and September of collection years. Beginning in October, questionnaires are delivered by U.S. Census Bureau field representatives. The sampling frame for the public school sample is the most recent Common Core of Data (CCD) school file. CCD is a universe file that includes all elementary and secondary schools in the United States. Schools operated by the Department of Defense or those that offered only kindergarten or pre-kindergarten or adult education were excluded from the SASS sample. The list frame used for the private school sample is the most recent Private School Universe Survey (PSS) list, updated with association lists. An area frame supplement is based on the canvassing of private schools within specific geographical areas. A separate universe of schools funded by the Bureau of Indian Education (BIE) is drawn from the Program Education Directory maintained by the BIE. To avoid duplicates in the BIE files, BIE schools in the CCD school file are treated as public schools.

Estimates of Sampling Error: Sample errors can be calculated using replicate weights and Balanced Repeated Replication complex survey design methodology. Errors depend on cell sizes and range from less than 1 percent to over 5 percent (for reasonable cell sizes).

U.S. Census Bureau, Statistical Abstract of the United States: 2011

Other (nonsampling) Errors: Because of unit nonresponse, bias may exist in some sample cells. However, bias has been adjusted for in the weighting process. Analysis of bias has been studied and no significant bias has been detected.

Sources of Additional Material: Please see the SASS Web site at <http://nces.ed.gov/surveys/sass/>.

U.S. DEPARTMENT OF JUSTICE, FEDERAL BUREAU OF INVESTIGATION

Uniform Crime Reporting (UCR) Program

Universe, Frequency, and Types of Data: Monthly reports on the number of criminal offenses that become known to law enforcement agencies. Data are also collected on crimes cleared by arrest or exceptional means; age, sex, and race of arrestees and for victims and offenders for homicides, number of law enforcement employees, on fatal and nonfatal assaults against law enforcement officers, and on hate crimes reported.

Type of Data Collection Operation: Crime statistics are based on reports of crime data submitted either directly to the FBI by contributing law enforcement agencies or through cooperating state UCR Programs.

Data Collection and Imputation Procedures: States with UCR programs collect data directly from individual law enforcement agencies and forward reports, prepared in accordance with UCR standards, to the FBI. Accuracy and consistency edits are performed by the FBI.

Estimates of Sampling Error: Not applicable.

Other (nonsampling) Errors: During 2008, law enforcement agencies active in the UCR Program represented 94.9 percent of the total population. The coverage amounted to 96.0 percent of the United States population in Metropolitan Statistical Areas, 87.6 percent of the population in cities outside metropolitan areas, and 90.0 percent in nonmetropolitan counties.

Sources of Additional Material: U.S. Department of Justice, Federal Bureau of Investigation, *Crime in the United States,* annual, *Hate Crime Statistics,* annual, *Law Enforcement Officers Killed and Assaulted,* annual, <http://www.fbi.gov/ucr/ucr.htm>.

U.S. INTERNAL REVENUE SERVICE

Corporation Income Tax Returns

Universe, Frequency, and Types of Data: Annual study of unaudited corporation income tax returns, Forms 1120, 1120-A, 1120-F, 1120-L, 1120-PC, 1120-REIT, 1120-RIC, and 1120S, filed by corporations or businesses legally defined as corporations. Data provided on various financial characteristics by industry and size of total assets, and business receipts.

Type of Data Collection Operation: Stratified probability sample of approximately 115,000 returns for Tax Year 2007, allocated to sample classes which are based on type of return, size of total assets, size of net income or deficit, and selected business activity. Sampling rates for sample classes varied from 0.25 percent to 100 percent.

Data Collection and Imputation Procedures: Computer selection of sample of tax return records. Data adjusted during editing for incorrect, missing, or inconsistent entries to ensure consistency with other entries on return and to comply with statistical definitions.

Estimates of Sampling Error: Estimated CVs for Tax Year 2007: Coefficients of variation are published in the 2007 Statistics of Income Corporation Income Tax Returns, Table 1, by industry group. Sampling rates are contained in Section 3 of the same report.

Other (nonsampling) Errors: Nonsampling errors include coverage errors, processing errors, and response errors.

Sources of Additional Material:
U.S. Internal Revenue Service, *Statistics of Income, Corporation Income Tax Returns*, annual.

Individual Income Tax Returns

Universe, Frequency, and Types of Data: Annual study of unaudited individual income tax returns, Forms 1040, 1040A, and 1040EZ, filed by U.S. citizens and residents. Data provided on various financial characteristics by size of adjusted gross income, marital status, and by taxable and nontaxable returns. Data by state, based on the population of returns filed, also include returns from 1040NR, filed by nonresident aliens plus certain self employment tax returns.

Type of Data Collection Operation: Stratified probability sample of 336,226 returns for tax year 2007. The sample is classified into sample strata based on the larger of total income or total loss amounts, the size of business plus farm receipts, and other criteria such as the potential usefulness of the return for tax policy modeling. Sampling rates for sample strata varied from 0.10 percent to 100 percent.

Data Collection and Imputation Procedures: Computer selection of sample of tax return records. Data adjusted during editing for incorrect, missing, or inconsistent entries to ensure consistency with other entries on return.

Estimates of Sampling Error: Estimated CVs for tax year 2007: Adjusted gross income less deficit 0.08 percent; salaries and wages 0.16 percent; and tax exempt interest received 1.07 percent. (State data not subject to sampling error.)

Other (nonsampling) Errors: Processing errors and errors arising from the use of tolerance checks for the data.

Sources of Additional Material:
U.S. Internal Revenue Service, *Statistics of Income, Individual Income Tax Returns*, annual, (Publication 1304).

Partnership Income Tax Returns

Universe, Frequency, and Types of Data: Annual study of preaudited income tax returns of partnerships related to financial and tax-related activity during calendar years 2004 to 2007 and reported on Forms 1065 and 1065B to the IRS in calendar year 2008. Data are provided by industry, based on the NAICS industry coding used by IRS.

Type of Data Collection Operation: Stratified probability sample of approximately 40,000 partnership returns from a population of 3.3 million filed during calendar year 2008. The sample is classified based on combinations of industry code, gross receipts, net income or loss, and total assets. Sampling rates vary from 0.07 percent to 100 percent.

Data Collection and Imputation Procedures: The sample of tax return records are selected via computer after data are transcribed by IRS and placed on an administrative file. Data are manually adjusted during editing for incorrect, missing, or inconsistent entries to ensure consistency with other entries on return. Data not available due to regulations are handled with weighting adjustments.

Estimates of Sampling Error: Some of the estimated Coefficients of Variation (the estimated standard error of the total divided by the estimated total) for tax year 2007: For number of partnerships, 0.36 percent; business receipts, 2.63 percent; net income, 2.83 percent; and ordinary business income, 2.23 percent.

Other (nonsampling) Errors: The potential exists for coverage error due to unavailable returns; processing errors; and taxpayer reporting errors, since data are preaudit.

Sources of Additional Material:
U.S. Internal Revenue Service, *Statistics of Income, Partnership Returns* and *Statistics of Income Bulletin*, Vol. 28, No. 2 (Fall 2008).

Sole Proprietorship Income Tax Returns

Universe, Frequency, and Types of Data: Annual study of unaudited income tax returns of nonfarm sole proprietorships, Form 1040 with business schedules. Data provided on various financial characteristics by industry.

Type of Data Collection Operation: Stratified probability sample of 90,983 sole proprietorships for tax year 2006. The sample is classified based on presence or absence of certain business schedules; the larger of total income or loss; size of business plus farm receipts, and other criteria such as the potential usefulness of the return for tax policy modeling. Sampling rates vary from 0.1 percent to 100 percent.

Data Collection and Imputation Procedures: Computer selection of sample of tax return records. Data adjusted during editing for incorrect, missing, or inconsistent entries to ensure consistency with other entries on return.

Estimates of Sampling Error: Estimated CVs for tax year 2006 are available. For sole proprietorships, total business receipts, 0.53 percent; depreciation 1.21 percent.

Other (nonsampling) Errors: Processing errors and errors arising from the use of tolerance checks for the data.

Sources of Additional Material: U.S. Internal Revenue Service, *Statistics of Income, Sole Proprietorship Returns* (for years 1980 through 1983) and *Statistics of Income Bulletin,* Vol. 28, No. 2 (Fall 2008, as well as bulletins for earlier years).

U.S. NATIONAL CENTER FOR HEALTH STATISTICS (NCHS)

National Health Interview Survey (NHIS)

Universe, Frequency, and Types of Data: Continuous data collection covering the civilian noninstitutional population to obtain information on demographic characteristics, conditions, injuries, impairments, use of health services, health behaviors, and other health topics.

Type of Data Collection Operation: Multistage probability sample of 49,000 households (in 198 PSUs) from 1985 to 1994; 36–40,000 households (358 design PSUs or 449 effective PSUs when divided by state boundaries) from 1995 to 2005; an estimated completed 35,000 households (428 effective PSUs) beginning in 2006.

Data Collection and Imputation Procedures: Some missing data items (e.g., race, ethnicity) are imputed using a hot deck imputation value. Sequential regression models are used to create multiple imputation files for family income. Unit nonresponse is compensated for by an adjustment to the survey weights.

Estimates of Sampling Error: For 2008, medically attended injury episodes rates (crude) in the past 12 months by falling for: females 50.43 (4.30) and males 34.87 (3.73) per 1,000 population; for 2008, injury episodes rates (crude) during the past 12 months inside the home—27.90 (2.28) per 1,000 population.

Other (nonsampling) Errors: The response rate was 93.8 percent in 1996; in 2008, the total household response rate was 84.9 percent, with the final family response rate of 84.5 percent, and the final sample adult response rate of 62.6 percent. (Note: the NHIS questionnaire was redesigned in 1997, and a new sample design was instituted in 2006).

Sources of Additional Material: National Center for Health Statistics, Summary Health Statistics for the U.S. Population: National Health Interview Survey, 2008, Vital and Health Statistics, Series 10, No. 243; National Center for Health Statistics, Summary Health Statistics for U.S. Children: National Health Interview Survey, 2008, Vital and Health Statistics, Series 10, No. 244; National Center for Health Statistics, Summary Health Statistics for U.S. Adults: National Health Interview Survey, 2008, Vital and Health Statistics, Series 10, No. 242; U.S. National Center for

Health Statistics, Design and Estimation for the National Health Interview Survey, 1995–2004, Vital and Health Statistics, Series 2, No. 130.

National Survey of Family Growth (NSFG)

Universe, Frequency, and Types of Data: Periodic survey of men and women 15–44 years of age in the household population of the United States. Interviews were conducted in 2002 in person by trained female interviewers. Interview topics covered include births and pregnancies, marriage, divorce, and cohabitation, sexual activity, contraceptive use, and medical care. For men, data on father involvement with children were collected. The most sensitive data—on sexual behavior related to HIV and Sexually Transmitted Disease risk—were collected in a self-administered form in which the data are entered into a computer.

Type of Data Collection Operation: In the 2002 (Cycle 6) NSFG, the sample was a multistage area probability sample of men and women 15–44 years of age in the household population of the United States. Only one person 15–44 was selected from households with one or more persons 15–44. Data were collected and entered into laptop (notebook) computers. In the self-administered portion, the respondent entered his or her own answers into the computer. Sample included 12,571 interviews. The response rate was 79 percent. Hispanic and Black persons, as well as those 15–19 years of age, were sampled at higher rates than White adults. All percentages and other statistics shown for the NSFG are weighted to make national estimates. The weights adjust for the different rates of sampling for each group, and for nonresponse.

Data Collection and Imputation Procedures: When interviews are received, they are reviewed for consistency and quality, and analysis variables (recodes) are created. Missing data on these recodes were imputed using multiple regression techniques and checked again for consistency.

Variables indicating whether a value has been imputed ("imputation flags") are included on the data file.

Estimates of Sampling Error: Sampling error codes are included on the data file so that users can estimate sampling errors for their own analyses. Sampling error estimates for nine illustrative analyses are shown on the NSFG Web site at <http://www.cdc.gov/nchs/nsfg.htm>. Sampling error estimates are also shown in most NCHS reports.

Other (nonsampling) Errors: In any survey, errors can occur because the respondent (the person being interviewed) does not recall the specific fact or event being asked about. The NSFG questionnaire in 2002 was programmed to check the consistency of many variables during the interview, so that the interviewer and respondent had a chance to correct any inconsistent information. Further checking occurred after the interview and during recoding and imputation. Typically, less than 1 percent of cases need imputation because of missing data.

Sources of Additional Material: The following references can be found at <http://www.cdc.gov/nchs/nsfg.htm>. "National Survey of Family Growth, Cycle 6: Sample Design, Weighting, and Variance Estimation." *Vital and Health Statistics*, Series 2, Number 142, July 2006. "Plan and Operation of Cycle 6 of the National Survey of Family Growth." *Vital and Health Statistics*, Series 1, No. 42. August 2005. "Sexual Behavior and Selected Health Measures: Men and Women 15–44 Years of Age, United States, 2002." *Advance Data from Vital and Health Statistics*, No. 362, Sept 15, 2005.

National Vital Statistics System

Universe, Frequency, and Types of Data: Annual data on births and deaths in the United States.

Type of Data Collection Operation: Mortality data based on complete file of death records, except 1972, based on 50 percent sample. Natality statistics 1951–1971, based on 50 percent sample of birth certificates, except a 20 percent to 50 percent sample in 1967, received by NCHS.

Data Collection and Imputation Procedures: Reports based on records from registration offices of all states, District of Columbia, New York City, Puerto Rico, Virgin Islands, Guam, American Samoa, and Northern Marianas.

Estimates of Sampling Error: For recent years, there is no sampling for these files; the files are based on 100 percent of events registered.

Other (nonsampling) Errors: It is believed that more than 99 percent of the births and deaths occurring in this country are registered.

Sources of Additional Material: U.S. National Center for Health Statistics, *Vital Statistics of the United States,* Vol. I and Vol. II, annual, and the *National Vital Statistics Reports.* See the NCHS Web site at <http://www.cdc.gov/nchs/nvss.htm>.

National Highway Traffic Safety Administration (NHTSA)

Fatality Analysis Reporting System (FARS)

Universe, Frequency, and Types of Data: FARS is a census of all fatal motor vehicle traffic crashes that occur throughout the United States including the District of Columbia and Puerto Rico on roadways customarily open to the public. The crash must be reported to the state/jurisdiction and at least one directly related fatality must occur within thirty days of the crash.

Type of Data Collection Operation: One or more analysts, in each state, extract data from the official documents and enter the data into a standardized electronic database.

Data Collection and Imputation Procedures: Detailed data describing the characteristics of the fatal crash, the vehicles and persons involved are obtained from police crash reports, driver and vehicle registration records, autopsy reports, highway department, etc. Computerized edit checks monitor the accuracy and completeness of the data. The FARS incorporates a sophisticated mathematical multiple imputation procedure to develop a probability distribution of missing blood alcohol concentration (BAC) levels in the database for drivers, pedestrians, and cyclists.

Estimates of Sampling Error: Since this is census data, there are no sampling errors.

Other (nonsampling) Errors: FARS represents a census of all police-reported crashes and captures all data reported at the state level. FARS data undergo a rigorous quality control process to prevent inaccurate reporting. However, these data are highly dependent on the accuracy of the police accident reports. Errors or omissions within police accident reports may not be detected.

Sources of Additional Material: The FARS Coding and Validation Manual, ANSI D16.1 Manual on Classification of Motor Vehicle Traffic Accidents (Sixth Edition).

Appendix IV
Weights and Measures

For assistance on metric usage, call or write:

Elizabeth J. Gentry
National Institute of Standards and Technology (NIST)
Weights and Measures Division
100 Bureau Drive – Mail Stop 2600
Gaithersburg, MD 20899-2600

Telephone: 301-975-3690 or 4004   FAX: 301-975-8091

E-mail: TheSI@nist.gov

Internet site: <http://ts.nist.gov/WeightsAndMeasures/Metric/mpo_home.cfm>

[Conversions provided in table are approximate]

Symbol	When you know conventional	Multiply by	To find metric	Symbol
in	inches	2.54	centimeters	cm
ft	feet	30.48	centimeters	cm
yd	yards	0.91	meters	m
mi	miles	1.61	kilometers	km
in^2	square inches	6.45	square centimeters	cm^2
ft^2	square feet	0.09	square meters	m^2
yd^2	square yards	0.84	square meters	m^2
mi^2	square miles	2.59	square kilometers	km^2
	acre	0.41	hectare	ha
oz	ounces [1]	28.35	grams	g
lb	pounds [1]	0.45	kilograms	kg
oz (troy)	ounces [2]	31.10	grams	g
	short tons (2,000 lb)	0.91	metric tons	t
	long tons (2,240 lb)	1.02	metric tons	t
fl oz	fluid ounces	29.57	milliliters	mL
c	cups	0.24	liters	L
pt	pints	0.47	liters	L
qt	quarts	0.95	liters	L
gal	gallons	3.78	liters	L
ft^3	cubic feet	0.03	cubic meters	m^3
yd^3	cubic yards	0.76	cubic meters	m^3
°F	degrees Fahrenheit (subtract 32)	0.55	degrees Celsius	°C

Symbol	When you know metric	Multiply by	To find conventional	Symbol
cm	centimeters	0.39	inches	in
cm	centimeters	0.03	feet	ft
m	meters	1.09	yards	yd
km	kilometers	0.62	miles	mi
cm^2	square centimeters	0.15	square inches	in^2
m^2	square meters	10.76	square feet	ft^2
m^2	square meters	1.20	square yards	yd^2
km^2	square kilometers	0.39	square miles	mi^2
ha	hectares	2.47	acre	
g	grams	0.04	ounces [1]	oz
kg	kilograms	2.21	pounds [2]	lb
g	grams	0.04	ounces [2]	oz (troy)
t	metric tons	1.10	short tons (2,000 lb)	
t	metric tons	0.98	long tons (2,240 lb)	
mL	milliliters	0.03	fluid ounces	fl oz
L	liter	4.23	cups	c
L	liters	2.13	pints (liquid)	pt
L	liters	1.05	quarts (liquid)	qt
L	liters	0.26	gallons	gal
m^3	cubic meters	35.32	cubic feet	ft^3
m^3	cubic meters	1.32	cubic yards	yd^3
°C	degrees Celsius (after multiplying, add 32)	1.80	degrees Fahrenheit	°F

[1] For weighing ordinary commodities.   [2] For weighing precious metals, jewels, etc.

U.S. Census Bureau, Statistical Abstract of the United States: 2011

Appendix V
Tables Deleted From the
2010 Edition of the Statistical Abstract

U.S. Census Bureau, Statistical Abstract of the United States: 2011

NOTE: Index citations refer to **table** numbers, not page numbers.

U.S. Census Bureau, Statistical Abstract of the United States: 2011

NOTE: Index citations refer to **table** numbers, not page numbers.

NOTE: Index citations refer to **table** numbers, not page numbers.

U.S. Census Bureau, Statistical Abstract of the United States: 2011

NOTE: Index citations refer to **table** numbers, not page numbers.

U.S. Census Bureau, Statistical Abstract of the United States: 2011

B

NOTE: Index citations refer to **table** numbers, not page numbers.

NOTE: Index citations refer to **table** numbers, not page numbers.

NOTE: Index citations refer to **table** numbers, not page numbers.

U.S. Census Bureau, Statistical Abstract of the United States: 2011

NOTE: Index citations refer to **table** numbers, not page numbers.

U.S. Census Bureau, Statistical Abstract of the United States: 2011

NOTE: Index citations refer to **table** numbers, not page numbers.

U.S. Census Bureau, Statistical Abstract of the United States: 2011

NOTE: Index citations refer to **table** numbers, not page numbers.

U.S. Census Bureau, Statistical Abstract of the United States: 2011

NOTE: Index citations refer to **table** numbers, not page numbers.

NOTE: Index citations refer to **table** numbers, not page numbers.

NOTE: Index citations refer to **table** numbers, not page numbers.

U.S. Census Bureau, Statistical Abstract of the United States: 2011

NOTE: Index citations refer to **table** numbers, not page numbers.

U.S. Census Bureau, Statistical Abstract of the United States: 2011

NOTE: Index citations refer to **table** numbers, not page numbers.

U.S. Census Bureau, Statistical Abstract of the United States: 2011

NOTE: Index citations refer to **table** numbers, not page numbers.

NOTE: Index citations refer to **table** numbers, not page numbers.

Index 967

NOTE: Index citations refer to **table** numbers, not page numbers.

NOTE: Index citations refer to **table** numbers, not page numbers.

NOTE: Index citations refer to **table** numbers, not page numbers.

U.S. Census Bureau, Statistical Abstract of the United States: 2011

NOTE: Index citations refer to **table** numbers, not page numbers.

U.S. Census Bureau, Statistical Abstract of the United States: 2011

NOTE: Index citations refer to **table** numbers, not page numbers.

U.S. Census Bureau, Statistical Abstract of the United States: 2011

NOTE: Index citations refer to **table** numbers, not page numbers.

U.S. Census Bureau, Statistical Abstract of the United States: 2011

NOTE: Index citations refer to **table** numbers, not page numbers.

NOTE: Index citations refer to **table** numbers, not page numbers.

U.S. Census Bureau, Statistical Abstract of the United States: 2011

NOTE: Index citations refer to **table** numbers, not page numbers.

NOTE: Index citations refer to **table** numbers, not page numbers.

U.S. Census Bureau, Statistical Abstract of the United States: 2011

NOTE: Index citations refer to **table** numbers, not page numbers.

NOTE: Index citations refer to **table** numbers, not page numbers.

U.S. Census Bureau, Statistical Abstract of the United States: 2011

NOTE: Index citations refer to **table** numbers, not page numbers.

U.S. Census Bureau, Statistical Abstract of the United States: 2011

NOTE: Index citations refer to **table** numbers, not page numbers.

U.S. Census Bureau, Statistical Abstract of the United States: 2011

NOTE: Index citations refer to **table** numbers, not page numbers.

NOTE: Index citations refer to **table** numbers, not page numbers.

U.S. Census Bureau, Statistical Abstract of the United States: 2011

NOTE: Index citations refer to **table** numbers, not page numbers.

NOTE: Index citations refer to **table** numbers, not page numbers.

U.S. Census Bureau, Statistical Abstract of the United States: 2011

NOTE: Index citations refer to **table** numbers, not page numbers.

NOTE: Index citations refer to **table** numbers, not page numbers.

U.S. Census Bureau, Statistical Abstract of the United States: 2011

NOTE: Index citations refer to **table** numbers, not page numbers.

U.S. Census Bureau, Statistical Abstract of the United States: 2011

NOTE: Index citations refer to **table** numbers, not page numbers.

U.S. Census Bureau, Statistical Abstract of the United States: 2011

NOTE: Index citations refer to **table** numbers, not page numbers.

U.S. Census Bureau, Statistical Abstract of the United States: 2011

NOTE: Index citations refer to **table** numbers, not page numbers.

U.S. Census Bureau, Statistical Abstract of the United States: 2011

NOTE: Index citations refer to **table** numbers, not page numbers.

U.S. Census Bureau, Statistical Abstract of the United States: 2011

NOTE: Index citations refer to **table** numbers, not page numbers.

U.S. Census Bureau, Statistical Abstract of the United States: 2011

NOTE: Index citations refer to **table** numbers, not page numbers.

NOTE: Index citations refer to **table** numbers, not page numbers.

U.S. Census Bureau, Statistical Abstract of the United States: 2011

NOTE: Index citations refer to **table** numbers, not page numbers.

U.S. Census Bureau, Statistical Abstract of the United States: 2011

NOTE: Index citations refer to **table** numbers, not page numbers.

U.S. Census Bureau, Statistical Abstract of the United States: 2011

NOTE: Index citations refer to **table** numbers, not page numbers.

NOTE: Index citations refer to **table** numbers, not page numbers.

U.S. Census Bureau, Statistical Abstract of the United States: 2011

NOTE: Index citations refer to **table** numbers, not page numbers.

NOTE: Index citations refer to **table** numbers, not page numbers.

U.S. Census Bureau, Statistical Abstract of the United States: 2011

NOTE: Index citations refer to **table** numbers, not page numbers.

NOTE: Index citations refer to **table** numbers, not page numbers.

U.S. Census Bureau, Statistical Abstract of the United States: 2011

NOTE: Index citations refer to **table** numbers, not page numbers.

U.S. Census Bureau, Statistical Abstract of the United States: 2011

NOTE: Index citations refer to **table** numbers, not page numbers.

U.S. Census Bureau, Statistical Abstract of the United States: 2011

NOTE: Index citations refer to **table** numbers, not page numbers.

U.S. Census Bureau, Statistical Abstract of the United States: 2011

NOTE: Index citations refer to **table** numbers, not page numbers.

U.S. Census Bureau, Statistical Abstract of the United States: 2011

NOTE: Index citations refer to **table** numbers, not page numbers.

NOTE: Index citations refer to **table** numbers, not page numbers.

U.S. Census Bureau, Statistical Abstract of the United States: 2011

NOTE: Index citations refer to **table** numbers, not page numbers.